LONGMAN
LEXICON
OF
CONTEMPORARY
ENGLISH

Tom McArthur

Longman

Longman Group Limited,
Longman House, Burnt Mill, Harlow, Essex CM20 2JE, England
Associated Companies throughout the world

First published by Longman Group Limited 1981
Sixth impression 1986

ISBN 0 582 55636 8 (cased)
ISBN 0 582 55527 2 (limp)

Produced by Longman Group (FE) Ltd
Printed in Hong Kong

Acknowledgments

Over the eight years of its gestation, the *Lexicon* has been informed
by the advice and talent of many.

In the early days, when nobody was sure what such a book would be
like, I received invaluable encouragement, advice, and critical help
from Professor David Abercrombie, Louis Alexander, Professor
David Crystal, Professor Randolph Quirk, and D. K. Swan. From
start to finish, sympathetic management in the Longman
organization itself was essential, and this was amply provided by Tim
Rix, Charles McGregor, and Della Summers.

The *Lexicon* was put together in two corners of Great Britain:
Longniddry in Scotland, and Harlow in England. It survived the
experience, and this was due in great part to Paul Procter of the
Longman Lexicographic Unit and editor-in-chief of the *Longman
Dictionary of Contemporary English*, with whom it was always a
pleasure to work. In addition, I owe much to a whole phalanx of
definers, especially Jean Robinson; the Longman clerical staff,
especially Joyce Nairn; and, of course, to the illustrators, Tony
Baskeyfield, Richard Bonson, Malcolm Booker, Brian Lee, Hugh
Marshall, Julia Rout, and Clive Spong.

In Longniddry, Feri McArthur built up the Index and managed the
flow of material to and from Harlow, sharing the weight of
compilation while there was also a family to bring up. To her, as
always, my unbounded affection and admiration. Valerie Sinclair
and Ana-Maria Ballesteros also have my grateful thanks for the
typing of a never-ending manuscript.

Inevitably, in a project of this nature, an enormous amount of
editorial work had to be done. It fell to James Coakley, Janet Dalley,
Robert Scriven, and Adrian Stenton. The final high standard of
production is in great part a tribute to their patience and skill.

Contents

Preface

Lexicography has traditionally used the alphabet as its principal means of organizing information about words. Indeed, most of us think about wordbooks as 'dictionaries', and dictionaries as, necessarily, having an alphabetical order.

There has, however, been an alternative tradition, in which compilers have used groups of topics instead of the alphabet as their basis for organization. The alphabet, with all its virtues, places animals and zoos, uncles and aunts far apart in its scheme of things, whereas in the human mind such words go close together. The alphabetical dictionary has a logic, but it is not the logic of everyday life. In principle, one feels, words should be defined in the company they usually keep. Two famous moves in this direction have been the *Janua Linguarum Reserata* in 1631, the work of the Bohemian educator Comenius, and Roget's *Thesaurus*, first published by Longman in 1852. The *Longman Lexicon of Contemporary English* belongs in this tradition.

Comenius had a hundred chapters and a religious bias, while Roget used a scheme of universal concepts as a framework for his prodigious lists. The *Lexicon*, however, has only fourteen 'semantic fields' of a pragmatic, everyday nature, a simple system of letters and numbers for easy reference, and an index that helps make reference easier still. Its special feature as a reference tool for students of English is its detailed definitions. Synonyms, antonyms, hyponyms, and other related words are presented in linguistically appropriate ways without, however, demanding that the user be familiar with linguistic terminology. The definitions are, additionally, supplemented with style labels and examples of usage, tabular and pictorial material being added where needed.

We believe that no previous wordbook has ever provided such a compact description of the central vocabulary of the English language.

The *Lexicon* is not intended to be exhaustive. It describes some 15,000 items in, we believe, a clear and useful way. Within the limits necessary for a work of this size, it provides the core language for a range of topics as varied as grammar and war, travel and tools, mathematics, sport, laughter, life, and love.

Tom McArthur
August 1980

List of Sets

Set titles are shown in **bold type**, with major cross-references listed underneath

A   Life and Living Things

A1   Life and Living Things

C1	People
C20	Courting, Sex, and Marriage
C50	Death and Burial
I74	The Life Sciences
L200	Old, New, and Young
N1	Being, Becoming, and Happening

A30   Living Creatures Generally

B1	The Body Generally
E	Food, Drink, and Farming

A50   Animals/Mammals

C1	People
E31	Meat

A70   Birds

M19	Moving
E31	Meat

A90   Reptiles and Amphibians

A100   Fish and Other Water Creatures

L86	Areas of Water
E31	Meat
M19	Moving

A110   Insects and Similar Creatures

A120   Parts of Animals

E34	Cuts of Meat

A130   Kinds and Parts of Plants

E30	Food

A150   Plants Generally

B   The Body: its Functions and Welfare

B1   The Body Generally

C324	Souls, Spirits, and Ghosts
E30	Food
H1	Substances and Materials Generally
G1	Mind, Thought, and Reason

B10   The Body: Overall

A120	Parts of Animals
A130	Kinds and Parts of Plants

B20   The Head and the Face

F240	Actions of the Face Related to Feelings
G1	Thinking, Judging, and Remembering

B30   The Trunk, Arms, and Legs

E30	Food

B50   The Skin, the Complexion, and the Hair

A120	Parts of Animals
D170	Cleaning and Personal Care
L20	Light and Colour

B60   Fluids and Waste Products of the Body

D40	The Bathroom
D42	Plumbing and Pipes
H13	Rubbish and Waste

B80   Bodily States and Associated Activities

F1	Feeling and Behaviour Generally
F260	Senses and Sensations

B110   Bodily Conditions Relating to Health, Sickness, and Disability

F260	Senses and Sensations

B140   Diseases and Ailments

E80	Cigarettes and Drugs

B160   Medicine and General Medical Care

I170	Science and Technology

C   People and the Family

C1   People

A1	Life and Living Things
A50	Animals/Mammals
C212	Inheriting and Bequeathing
D60	Residence
D130	Clothes and Personal Belongings

C20   Courting, Sex, and Marriage

A1	Life and Living Things

C40   Friendship and Enmity

C270	Fighting, War, and Peace
F140	Admiration, Pride,,Contempt, and Abuse
F170	Kindness and Unkindness
F190	Honesty, Loyalty, Trickery, and Deceit

C50   Death and Burial

A1	Life and Living Things

How to use the Lexicon

The *Longman Lexicon of Contemporary English* is a completely new kind of vocabulary reference book. The *Lexicon* brings together words with related meanings and lists them in sets with definitions, examples, and illustrations so that you can see the similarities and differences between them. These sets may include words with the same meaning, or opposite meanings, or may list the names of the different parts of something.

FOR EXAMPLE:
In a dictionary you will find *funny* between *funnel* and *fur*.

In the *Lexicon* you will find **funny** with **entertaining, amusing, diverting, comic, humorous, jocular,** and **hilarious.**

In a dictionary you will find *root* between *rooster* and *rope*.

In the *Lexicon* you will find **root** with **stem, stalk, bulb, leaf, blade, needle, spine, trunk, bark, branch, limb, twig, twiglet,** and **stump.**

The definitions of these words are based on the *Longman Dictionary of Contemporary English*, and use its 2000-word defining vocabulary. This means that when you look up **funny** or **root** you can understand simply what it means and how it differs from the other words in the set. In this way the *Lexicon* can help you to increase your vocabulary quickly. It will help you to understand how, when, and where to use new words. It will also improve your understanding of words that you already know.

You can use the *Lexicon* in two ways. You can look for a single word in the alphabetical INDEX at the back of the book, or you can look for a subject in the LIST OF SETS.

Using the List of Sets

The LIST OF SETS shows the subjects included in the *Lexicon*. Each subject is given a reference letter from **A** to **N**. Within each subject you will find many sets of related words. So that:
A is **Life and living things.**
Within **A,**
A50 – A61 is **Animals and mammals**
A70 – A78 is **Birds**
A130 – A141 is **Parts of plants**

If you turn to set **A131** you will find the vocabulary you need to be able to read and write about plants and their parts, with definitions, examples, and illustrations.

Using the Index

The INDEX is an alphabetical listing of all the words in the *Lexicon*. It gives the pronunciation of the word, together with irregular tenses, plurals, etc, and the reference letter and number of the set of words that it is included in.

To find the word you want:
(i) look it up in the Index and note its reference(s)
(ii) use the references printed at the top of each page to find the set's place in the book
(iii) look through the set to find the word you want, then study it in relation to the other words in the set

FOR EXAMPLE:
If you want to know what an *atlas* is, you look up the word *atlas* in the Index:

atlas /ˈætləs/
n G165

This directs you to the set of words **G165: reference books.** Here you will find **atlas** with its definition and example:

atlas [C] a book of maps: *The teacher asked a pupil to give out the atlases.*

This set also contains **reference book, work of reference, dictionary, thesaurus, lexicon, encyclopedia, directory, catalogue, gazetteer,** and **album,** so that you have a list of the different types of reference book, and can see what kind of information each contains.

Words with several meanings

Some words have a wide range of meanings. The Index shows these.

FOR EXAMPLE:
If you hear the sentence,

John isn't coming today, he's feeling a bit funny.

and you are not sure of this use of *funny*, look up *funny* in the Index:

funny / ˈfʌni/
adj amusing K3
peculiar N68
unwell B111

This means that the word *funny* has three meanings, each shown at its own place in the

Lexicon with other words that are related to it. You choose the most likely use for the sentence that you heard, in this case *unwell*, and turn to set **B111**. Here the definition tells you what this use of *funny* means (slightly unwell), notes that it is an informal usage (by means of the label *infml*) and so more appropriate to spoken language, and gives an example which shows the use of *feel funny*. The rest of the entries in the set help to define *funny* more clearly by giving you some other words meaning unwell, and by showing how they differ from *funny* in meaning, by use, or grammar. (For an explanation of the grammatical codes see p.912.)

B111 *adjectives* : **showing poor bodily condition**

ill [F; (B)] not in good health; not well: *She's ill, so she can't come. Oh, I'm not ill enough to need a doctor. Oh God, I feel ill!*

unhealthy [Wa1;B] **1** not generally in good physical and mental condition; often ill; not strong: *They're unhealthy children, because they don't get good food and fresh air.* **2** not likely to give good health: *This place has a hot wet unhealthy climate.* **3** not good for the body or mind: *He has an unhealthy interest in murder and similar crimes.* **4** showing illness or poor health: *Her skin is an unhealthy greenish colour.*

unwell [F] ill, esp for a short time: *He was unwell yesterday, but he's fine again today.*

unfit [Wa2;B] in bad health: *He's pretty unfit; he needs medical treatment and a lot more exercise.*

sick [Wa1;B] **1** *esp AmE, ScotE* not well; ill: *She was sick for three months. He was off sick for a week and missed a lot of work.* **2** about to vomit: *I feel sick; it must be something I ate.* [⇒ B119 VOMIT]

sickly [Wa1;B] always or often ill: *What a sickly child she is; she's constantly catching colds.*

diseased [B] showing signs of, or damaged by, disease or infection: *The plant is diseased and will soon die.*

upset [Wa5;B] slightly ill: *The child has an upset stomach.*

bad *infml* **1** [F] unwell: *Oh God, I feel bad! He's been bad for a week; it's his back, you know.* **2** [B] weak or unsound: *He's been ill with a bad back for months. She's got a bad heart and can't climb stairs.*

poorly [F] *esp BrE infml* not (very) well: *Oh, I am feeling poorly. He's been very poorly lately; he might die.*

ailing [Wa5;B] *infml* unwell, esp over a period of time and not seriously: *The doctor was called out to attend to an ailing child. He's an old man now and has been ailing for a long time.*

run down [B] *not fml* not in good health; not well: *She's pretty run down; she needs a rest.*

morbid [Wa5;B] *med* concerned with disease; showing disease: *The doctor detected a morbid lung condition.*

dizzy [Wa1;B] feeling as if everything is turning round: *Gosh, I feel dizzy! She felt dizzy and fainted.* **-iness** [U] **-ily** [adv]

funny [B] *infml* **1** slightly unwell: *She always feels a bit funny if she looks down from a height.* **2** slightly mad: *He went rather funny (in the head) after the death of his only son.*

See also the Guide to the Lexicon on the next page.

Guide to the Lexicon

starting with the INDEX ——

set reference letter and number

funny / fʌni/

adj unwell B111
peculiar N68
amusing K3

set title ————

K3 *adjectives* : **entertaining and amusing** [B]

grammatical code here refers to every headword

headword ————

entertaining amusing and interesting: *That was an entertaining story.* **-ly** [adv]
amusing causing pleasant laughter or enjoyment: *That's an amusing story!* **-ly** [adv]
diverting *esp fml & pomp* amusing **-ly** [adv]
funny 1 *not fml* amusing; causing laughter: *I heard such a funny story this morning. He's a very funny man* (= can make people laugh with amusing stories). *I don't think that's at all funny* (= is a suitable cause for laughter). *It was the funniest thing out* (= the most amusing I've ever heard). 2 *infml* (used esp by or to children) pleasantly amusing; nice (esp in the phr **funny old**): *Look at that funny old dog!* 3 *infml* deceiving; using tricks; too clever: *'Don't try anything funny while my back's turned, or you'll be in trouble,' he said to his prisoner. Don't get funny with me.* **-ily** [adv] **-iness** [U]

definition

label shows use or context of headword

examples of use

different forms of headword

comic, comical amusing; funny, esp to watch, esp because silly, unusual, etc: *It was a rather comic business and we laughed, even though it wasn't supposed to be funny. That's very comical!* **-(al)ly** [adv Wa4]

ending that can be added to the headword to make a new word (humorously)

humorous funny; full of humour: *What a humorous girl she is!* **-ly** [adv]

cross-reference to a set of related words

jocular *esp fml* enjoying amusing people, making jokes [⇒ K87], etc: *He spoke in a jocular way.* **jocularity** [U] cheerfulness, esp in making jokes

numbers show different meanings of headword

hilarious 1 full of laughter: *The party got quite hilarious after they brought more wine.* 2 causing wild laughter: *We thought his mistake was the most hilarious thing we'd ever heard.* **-ly** [adv] **hilarity** [U] cheerfulness, expressed in laughter

related word

N68 *adjectives* : **strange and peculiar**

strange [Wa1] **1** [B] hard to accept or understand; surprising: *It's strange you've never met him. What a strange idea!* **2** [B] not known or experienced before: **...**
peculiar 1 [B] strange; unusual (esp in a troubling or displeasing way): *What a peculiar thing to say.* **...**
odd 1 [Wa1;B] strange; unusual: **...**
queer [Wa1;B] **1** *not fml* strange: **...**
funny [Wa1;B] *not fml* strange unexpected; hard to explain: *What can that funny noise be? It's a funny thing, but I put the book here five minutes ago and now I can't find it. He's a funny sort of person; I don't understand him at all.*
-nily [adv]: *Funnily enough, I knew what he meant although he didn't speak English.*
curious [B] strange and interesting: **...**

B111 *adjectives* : **showing poor bodily condition**

ill [F; (B)] not in good health; not well: *She's ill, so she can't come. Oh, I'm not ill enough to need a doctor. Oh God, I feel ill!*
unhealthy [Wa1;B] **1** not generally in good physical and mental condition; **...**
unwell [F] ill, esp for a short time: *He was unwell yesterday, but he's fine again today.*
unfit [Wa2;B] in bad health: **...**
funny [B] *infml* **1** slightly unwell: *She always feels a bit funny if she looks down from a height.* **2** slightly mad: *He went rather funny (in the head) after the death of his only son.*

K87 *nouns, etc* : **humour**

[ALSO ⇒ K2–3, 75]

humour *BrE*, **humor** *AmE* [U] **1** the quality of causing amusement: *It is a play with no humour in it.* **2** the ability to be amused: *She has a good sense of humour.*
joke 1 [C] anything said or done that causes laughter or amusement: *She told some very*

— part of speech

— British and American forms shown

— grammatical code here refers to this meaning only (see Grammar Table p.912)

A

Life and living things

Life and death

[ALSO ⇒ C50–59 DEATH AND BURIAL]

A1 *verbs* : **existing and causing to exist**

[ALSO ⇒ N1]

exist [Wv6;I0] to be real; be there in fact: *The world exists and we are part of it. The planet Earth has existed for millions of years. Fairies don't exist in real life, only in stories.* [⇒ L2 PLANET]

be [Wv6;I0] *fml & tech* to exist: *Whatever is, is right. The universe is, but we don't know why.* [⇒ L1 UNIVERSE]

create [T1] to cause to exist: *Many people say that God created the world.*

animate [T1] **1** to give life to **2** to make lively or exciting: *Laughter animated his face for a moment.* **3** to cause to become active; interest: *His excitement animated us all.* **animated** [B] **1** full of life or action; excited **2** moving as if possessing life: *animated pictures*

A2 *verbs* : **living and dying**

[ALSO ⇒ C51]

live [Wv6;I0] **1** to continue to be alive: *It isn't easy to live on poor food like that. The girl in the accident will live; she wasn't badly hurt. If he goes on driving like that, he won't live long.* (*fig*) *A writer's work lives beyond his death.* **2** *fml* to be alive: *The rich live, while the poor die.*

live on [v adv I0] to go on living: *He lived on for another 20 years, till he was 91.* (*fig*) *A writer's works live on after his death. Her memory lives on; we won't forget her.*

exist [I0 (*on*)] **1** to continue to live, esp with difficulty: *We can hardly exist on the money he gives us; it isn't enough. They don't have much food; they only just manage to exist.* **2** to live, but without satisfaction or happiness: *He exists from day to day, just eating and sleeping. Nothing exciting happens here; we just exist!*

die [I0] to cease living: *He died last week after a long illness. The crops were dying because of lack of rain.*

decay **1** [T1; I0] to (cause to) go through chemical changes that destroy or damage: *Meat decays quickly in warm weather.* **2** [I0] (*fig*) to fall to a lower or worse state; lose health, power, strength, activity, etc: *History seems to teach us that all nations decay in time.*

decompose [I0] (esp of bodies once alive) to decay: *The decomposing flesh of the dead animal began to smell.*

rot [I0] (esp of plants, meat, etc) to decay; go bad: *The meat began to rot. The ground was covered with/in rotting plants.* **rotten** [B] having rotted: *Throw away this meat; it's rotten. Don't eat rotten meat.*

survive **1** [I0] to continue to live, esp after coming close to death: *We survived although others died in the accident. He is the only man who survived after the explosion.* **2** [T1] to continue living after: *He survived the explosion, but no one else did. She survived her own daughter by ten years.*

A3 *adjectives* : **living and dead**

living [Wa5;B] **1** continuing to live: *Some of the plants are dead, but most of them are still living/alive.* **2** actually existing: *Is he a living person or just a character in a book?* **3** (*fig*) continuing in use: *French is a living language, but for most people Latin isn't.*

alive [F] **1** [Wa5] continuing to live: *His mother is dead, but his father is still alive/living. Only three men were left alive after the explosion.* **2** full of life; active: *Although old, he is very much alive.* **3** still in existence or operation; still remembered: *The argument was kept alive by the politicians. She died ten years ago, but she remains very much alive in his memory.*

live [Wa5;B] having life: *There is a dead fish among all the live ones.*

animate [B] **1** [Wa5] *precise & tech* (of plants and animals) alive; living: *animate beings* **in-**[neg]: *inanimate objects* **2** *loose* moving or able to move: *The clock was the only animate thing in the house.*

dead [Wa5,(1); B] **1** no longer alive: *The field was full of dead animals, killed by the storm. Can dead people come back to life?* (*fig*) *His love for her is dead; he doesn't care about her any more.* **2** not able to live: *The hillside was covered with dead material; there were only stones—no plants at all.* **3** (*fig*) not in use: *Most people consider Latin (to be) a dead language, but for some purposes it is still a living language.*

dying [Wa5;B] **1** about to die: *The dying man spoke his last words.* **2** ill with a disease which will lead to death: *She's a dying woman; she has an illness which cannot be cured.* (*fig*) *a dying industry*

A4 nouns : life and death

life 1 [U] the active force that is present in those forms of matter (animals and plants) that grow through feeding and produce new young forms of themselves, but is not present in other matter (stones, machines, objects, etc): *Life is a mystery; we do not know how it began or why it continues.* **2** [U] matter having this active force: *There is no life on the moon.* **3** [U] the state of being alive: *Life depends on food and air. Life is important to living creatures; they usually fight to stay alive.* **4** [U] the condition of existence, esp of a human being: *Life isn't all fun; it has its bad moments.* **5** [U] living things in general: *The valley was full of rich plant and animal life.* **6** [U] existence as a set of widely different experiences: *You'll never see life if you stay at home all the time. Go out into the world and see what life has to offer.* **7** [U] a way of living; social relations, etc: *Well, how do you find life in the city/city life?* **8** [C] the period between birth and death: *He is dead now, but what an interesting life he led! They spent the whole of their lives in that town.* **9** [C; U] a part of life given to a particular activity: *She spent most of her working life in that job. My social life is my business, not yours!* **10** [C] personal condition of being alive: *His life will be in danger if he stays here. We must try to save those people's lives; we can't let them die! No lives must be lost in this work.* **11** [C *usu sing*] (*fig*) the period for which a machine, organization, etc, will work or last: *These electric batteries have a long life; they are long-life batteries. During the whole life of this association we have had no legal problems.*

existence 1 [U] a state of existing: *His existence is not important to her any more. They know about the existence of this money and they plan to get it all. We were talking about the existence of life on other worlds.* **2** [C] life, esp without any special interest, pleasures, etc: *She leads a rather sad existence now that her husband is dead.*

creation [U] the act of creating or being created: *The creation of new life is an important reason for people getting married. Many people believe that the creation of the universe was the work of a god.* [⇒ L1 CREATION, UNIVERSE]

animation [U] actual life; activity and excitement; the appearance of such life: *She lacks animation; I think she is ill. He was full of animation at the party. The machines moved with such animation that they seemed to be alive.*

birth 1 [U] the act or time of being born, of coming into the world, esp out of the body of a female parent: *The birth of the child was an occasion of great joy in the family.* **2** [U] the act or fact of producing young: *She gave birth to a baby girl. The process of birth is usually painful.* **3** [C] the occasion of any person or animal being born: *There were four births in the hospital last night.* **4** [U] family origin: *For many people, being rich or poor is just an accident of birth. He claims to be of noble birth, but nobody believes him.* **5** [U] (*fig*) beginning, start, or origin: *It was a great meeting—the birth of a new political movement.*

nativity [C] *fml* birth, esp (*with cap*) that of Jesus Christ

death 1 [U;C] the end of life; the time or manner of dying: *He was happy till the day of his death. Car accidents have caused many deaths.* **2** [S] the cause or occasion of loss of life: *If you go out without a coat, you'll catch your death of cold.* (*fig*) *That defeat meant the death of all his hopes. Drinking whisky will be the death of him yet.* **3** [U] the state of being dead: *Enjoy your life; death lasts a long time. The old house was as still as death.* **4** [R] (*usu cap*) the destroyer of life, usu shown as a skeleton [⇒ B11]: *In that picture you can see Death leading a dance of dead people.* **a natural death** death from natural causes like illness or old age, not as the result of an accident, murder, etc: *She lived a long happy life and died a natural death.* **at death's door** about to die; in danger of dying: *He is very sick; he is at death's door, I'm afraid.*

mortality [U] **1** the state of being mortal (= having to die) **2** the number of deaths in an area, for a group, etc: *Infant mortality in that country is high* (= Many children there die young).

decay [U] **1** the decayed parts (esp of the teeth): *There's a lot of decay in his teeth.* **2** the action or state of decaying: *That university has fallen into decay in the last 100 years. The decay of ancient Rome took a long time.*

decomposition [U] decay (esp of bodies once alive): *Soil is improved by the steady decomposition of dead plants and animal bodies.*

rot [U] decay, esp caused by disease: *Rot has started in the wood.*

survival 1 [U] the fact or possibility of surviving: *His survival is still uncertain; he has been very badly hurt and may die.* **2** [C] something which survives, often unexpectedly, from an earlier time: *Crocodiles are survivals from the age of the dinosaurs.* [⇒ A91 CROCODILE, A93 DINOSAUR]

survivor [C] a person who has continued to live in spite of coming close to death: *Out of the hundreds of people concerned in the accident there were only a few survivors. She is 90 years old and the only survivor of her family.*

A5 verbs : giving birth

bear 1 [D1(*to*); T1] to give birth to: *His wife bore (him) three fine children.* **2** [T1; I∅] to produce (fruit or young): *The trees have borne a heavy crop of fruit this year. The young apple tree is bearing this year.*

produce [T1; I∅] to provide (fruit, young, etc): *Our trees produce excellent apples.*

lay [T1; I∅] (of birds, esp hens) to produce (eggs): *The hen laid an egg. The hens are laying well* (= laying a lot of eggs).

spawn 1 [T1; IØ] (esp of fishes and frogs) to lay (eggs) in large numbers together **2** [T1] *infml*, (*fig*) & *usu derog* to give birth to, esp in large numbers: *He spawned many strange ideas in his long life.* **spawning grounds** [P] areas in the sea where fish gather to spawn.

hatch [T1; IØ] to (cause to) come out of an egg: *The hen hatched all her eggs. The eggs all hatched successfully, and we now have plenty of young birds.*

A6 *adjectives* : **being born** [Wa5]

born 1 [F] brought into existence by or as if by birth: *The baby was born at 8 o'clock. The new political party was born at a small meeting . (fig) I feel as if I have been born again.* **2** [F7,9] being in a stated condition at or from birth: *He was born French, but grew up in Argentina. She was nobly born, a daughter of one of the highest families in the land.* (*old use*) *You cannot marry that low-born fellow!* **born and bred** having come into the world and grown up: *He was born and bred in Yorkshire. He was Yorkshire born and bred.*

newborn [A] just born: *They could hear the cry of a newborn child.*

unborn [A] not yet born: *If a pregnant woman smokes, she could harm her unborn child.*

A7 *adjectives* : **present from birth**

born 1 [A] having a quality from or as if from birth: *He is a born leader of men. She was a born artist.* **2** [F3] fated from or as if from birth: *She was born to succeed in life.*

inborn [A; (B)] present from birth; part of one's nature: *He has an inborn ability to do arithmetic. She has an inborn love of jokes.*

innate [B] (of qualities) which one was born with: *She says that language is an innate ability in human beings.* **-ly** [adv]

inherent [B] forming a natural part (of a set of qualities, a character, etc): *It is an inherent part of human nature to avoid pain. Sympathy is an inherent part of friendship.* **-ly** [adv]

natural [A; (B)] **1** belonging to someone by birth, not learned: *She has great natural charm. He seems to have a natural ability for this kind of work.* **2** also **natural born** not needing to be taught: *He is a natural (born) musician.* **-ly** [adv] **un-** [neg]

congenital [Wa5;B] (of diseases, etc) present from or before birth: *The child has congenital heart disease.* **-ly** [adv]

A8 *ordinary verbs* : **killing**

[ALSO ⇒ C239, N338]

kill 1 [T1; IØ] to cause (a person, plant, or animal) to die: *He killed the other man in a fight.* **2** [T1] (*fig*) to cause to finish or fail: *This*

medicine will kill the pain. That mistake has killed his chances. The suggested law was killed before it could be passed.*

slay [T1] *poet* to kill: *The king slew his enemy. The dragon was slain by St George.* [⇒ A93 DRAGON]

murder [T1; IØ] to kill unlawfully, esp on purpose: *He murdered his friend in order to get the gold. He has murdered once; he may murder again.* **murderer** [C] a person who murders someone **murderess** (*fem*)

assassinate [T1] to murder (a ruler, politician, etc) for political reasons or reward: *Several American presidents have been assassinated.* **assassination 1** [U] the act of assassinating **2** [C] an example or occasion of this **assassin** [C] a person who murders esp a ruler or politician for political reasons or reward

butcher [T1] **1** to kill and prepare (animals) for sale as food: *He has been butchering pigs all morning.* **2** to kill bloodily or unnecessarily: *The soldiers were butchered; they had no chance to fight.*

slaughter [T1] **1** to kill (animals) for food; butcher **2** *esp emot* to kill (esp many people) cruelly or wrongly; massacre: *Many people are needlessly slaughtered each year in road accidents.* **3** *infml* to defeat severely: *We were slaughtered, 9 points to 0.*

massacre [T1; IØ] to kill (a large number of esp defenceless people): *They massacred all the prisoners after the battle. They went through the land, burning and massacring.* (*fig*) *He made a powerful speech, massacring his opponents.*

A9 *euphemistic verbs* : **killing** [T1]

eliminate to kill: *The criminals eliminated their enemies.*

liquidate to kill: *These men are dangerous; they must be liquidated immediately!*

A10 *informal verbs* : **killing**

make/do away with [v adv prep T1] to kill or murder (someone or oneself) esp secretly: *She made away with her husband late one night. They did away with him during the night.*

do in [v adv T1] *sl* to kill: *If he says that again I'm really going to do him in! She did her husband in so as to get his money.*

bump off [v adv T1] *sl* to kill; murder: *He bumped off eight people before the police caught him. She just bumped him off one night.*

A11 *adjectives* : **killing and death**

deadly [Wa2] **1** [B] causing or likely to cause death: *Run! You are in deadly danger. The poison gas was deadly; it killed them all.* **2** [adv] suggesting death: *What's wrong with him?*

He's deadly pale. **3** [B; adv] (*fig*) like death in lack of interest: *What a deadly (dull) conversation!*

fatal [B] likely to cause, or which has caused, death: *She took a fatal dose of poison. There was a fatal accident last night; two people died when their car hit a wall. The wound proved fatal; he died next day.* **-ly** [adv]

lethal [B] able or certain to kill: *People are not permitted to carry lethal weapons here. She took a lethal amount of poison and died.* **-ly** [adv]

mortal [Wa5;B] **1** which must die; which cannot live forever: *All men are mortal.* **2** *esp poet or pomp* causing death: *He received a mortal wound in the battle.* **-ly** [adv]: *mortally wounded*

deathly 1 [B] suggesting death: *There was a deathly silence in the house.* **2** [adv] in a death-like way: *The body was deathly cold.*

A12 poetic & formal adjectives : without death [B]

[ALSO ⇒ L153, L180]

undying which will never die or end: *She expressed her undying gratitude to him for what he had done.*

immortal which will not die; which continues forever: *The Greeks told stories about the immortal gods. He says that Bach's music is immortal.* **immortality** [U] **1** the state of being immortal; a never-ending life: *No man expects immortality.* **2** endless fame: *the immortality of Shakespeare's poetry* **immortalize, -ise** [T1] to give endless life or fame to: *Dickens' father was immortalized for ever as Mr. Micawber in 'David Copperfield'.*

A13 nouns : killing

kill [C *usu sing*] **1** the act of killing, esp hunted birds or animals: *The kill took place near the trees.* **2** the bird(s) or animal(s) killed in hunting: *The lion didn't leave his kill until he had satisfied his hunger.* **(to be) in at the kill** (to be) actively present when something is killed or (*fig*) at the end of a struggle/competition, etc

killing [U] the action of killing people or animals: *The killing went on for hours until dead bodies lay everywhere.*

slaughter [U] **1** the killing of animals usu for food **2** the killing of one or more people in a bloody, cruel, or thoughtless way: *This slaughter of people in road accidents goes on year after year.*

carnage [U] *esp poet & emph* slaughter: *The carnage on that day was terrible.*

butchery [U] cruel and unnecessary killing, esp of human beings: *That wasn't war; it was simply butchery!*

massacre [C] the killing of large numbers, usu of people who cannot defend themselves properly, without caring about their death: *Those soldiers are responsible for several massacres of defenceless villagers.*

murder [C] the unlawful killing of a person, esp on purpose: *There were two murders in the city last night.*

A14 nouns & adjectives : sexual types

[⇒ A16 SEXUAL ACTIVITIES, C23 SOCIAL MEANINGS OF SEX]

sex 1 [U] the condition in most living things of being either male or female: *We are not sure just what determines the sex of a child.* **2** [C] grouping as either male or female: *Attraction between the sexes is quite usual. He was very interested in the opposite sex. The female sex is the more important sex in many species of spiders.* [⇒ A33 SPECIES, A112 SPIDER]

gender [U; C] *old use* sex; the division into male and female: *She's very interested in the male gender. It's a question of gender; if he was a girl, he would feel differently about it.*

sexual [B] of sex or the sexes: *Most people expect to get some kind of sexual satisfaction in life. Sexual intercourse is natural in animals.* **-ly** [adv] **sexuality** [U] sexual qualities

male 1 [Wa5;B] of the sex that does not give birth to young: *He has four male monkeys and only two females.* **2** [B] suitable to or typical of this sex: *He has a very male way of looking at life.* **3** [Wa5;B] (*fig*) (of a part of a machine) made to fit into a hollow part **4** [C] a male person or animal: *In some countries all healthy males must go into the army at a certain age. In most birds the male is bigger and brighter in colour than the female.*

masculine [B] of, or having the qualities suitable for, a man: *She says she likes his masculine appearance. Some women look more masculine than feminine.*

female 1 [Wa5;B] of the sex that gives birth to young: *The animal in the picture was a female elephant.* **2** [B] suitable to or typical of this sex, rather than the male sex: *The female form, with or without clothes, is often a subject in painting. This illness is a female problem; it doesn't happen to men.* **3** [Wa5;B] (*fig*) (of a part of a machine) having a hollow part into which another part fits **4** [C] a female person or animal: *In some religions females must sit in a separate place during worship. The female was sitting on the eggs, while the male bird brought food.*

feminine [B] of or having the qualities of a woman, esp those regarded by men as desirable in a woman: *She is a very feminine woman, and men find her very attractive.*

neuter 1 [Wa5;B] (of plants etc) without male or female parts **2** [Wa5;B] (of insects) sexually undeveloped; sterile [⇒ A17]: *Worker ants are physically neuter.* **3** [C] an animal which has had part of the sex organs removed: *An ox is a neuter.*

A15 *verbs* : **sexual action**

mate [I0; T1] to form (into) a couple, esp of animals, for sexual union and the production of young: *Birds mate in the spring. They mated a horse with a donkey and got a mule.*

copulate [I0] *fml* to have sexual intercourse: *The bull and the cow began to copulate. The bull copulated with three cows during the day.*

reproduce [I0] to produce young: *Most animals and plants reproduce easily. The rabbits reproduced in great numbers.* **reproduce oneself** to produce new young of one's own kind

breed [I0] **1** (of animals) to produce young: *Some animals will not breed when kept in cages.* **2** to produce (large numbers of) young: (*fig*) *Those people breed like rabbits.* [⇒ ALSO A36]

A16 *nouns* : **sexual activities** [U]
[⇒ C23 SOCIAL MEANINGS OF SEX]

sex 1 sexual activity and any subject related to it: *Some people think there is too much sex in modern films.* **2** sexual intercourse: *The doctor asked them how often they had sex each week.*

(sexual) intercourse the act of inserting the penis into the vagina [⇒ B40 PENIS, VAGINA]: *Sexual intercourse is a normal part of human and animal life. The doctor asked them how often they had intercourse each week.*

mating the act of coming together by animals for sexual activity: *Mating among birds usually happens in the spring.* **the mating season** the spring, when most animals mate

copulation the act of copulating

reproduction the process of reproducing life

coitus, coition *fml & tech* (human) sexual intercourse **coital** [Wa5;B] of or connected with coitus

breeding 1 the producing of young by animals, birds, fish, or plants: *Next month is the beginning of the breeding season.* **2** the business of keeping animals, birds, or fish for the purpose of obtaining new and better kinds, or young for sale: *He is interested in (the) breeding (of) new kinds of fish. Cattle-breeding is his business.*

puberty the time or stage of change in the human body from childhood to the state in which it is possible to produce children: *The sexual organs first become fully active at puberty.*

menstruation [U; (C)] a woman's monthly flow of blood from the womb **menstruate** [I0] to have blood flow in this way **menstrual** [Wa5;B] of, concerning, or like menstruation

menopause the time of life when and after which a woman is no longer able to have a child

A17 *adjectives* : **sex and reproduction** [B]
[⇒ E135 FARMING]

fertile 1 able to produce young or fruit: *The offspring* [⇒A20] *of a horse and a donkey is not itself fertile.* **2** producing many young, fruits, or seeds: *She is very fertile; she gets pregnant easily and has six children already. Some fish are very fertile; they lay hundreds of eggs.* **in-** [neg] **fertility** [U]

fecund *fml & rare* very fertile; very productive: *This is a fecund fruit tree.* (*fig*) *Books flowed from his fecund pen.* **fecundity** [U]

barren 1 not able to reproduce: *Atomic radiation can make women barren.* **2** bearing no fruit or seed: *The fruit trees were mostly barren and brought him little money.* **3** [(of)] (*fig*) useless; empty; producing no result: *It is pointless to continue such a barren argument. The scientist's hard work was barren of any result.* **barrenness** [U]

sterile [Wa5] *tech* not fertile; barren: *Working with unusual chemicals has made him sterile; he can't have any children. A mule is the sterile young of a horse and a donkey.* **sterility** [U]

impotent (of men) unable to perform the sex act: *He went to see his doctor because he had become impotent.* **impotence** [U]

pregnant [(*with*)] **1** [Wa5] (of a woman or female animal) having an unborn child or unborn young in the body: *She has been pregnant for 5 months. She is five months pregnant.* **2** (*fig*) full of important but unexpressed or hidden meaning: *His words were followed by a pregnant pause. The pause was pregnant with meaning.* **pregnancy** [U; C] the state of being pregnant; the time when pregnant: *She had an easy pregnancy the third time, but her first and second pregnancies were bad.*

A18 *verbs* : **sex and reproduction**

fertilize, -ise [T1] to make fertile: *The male sperm fertilizes the female ovum in the womb or uterus* [⇒ B40]. **fertilization** [U]

impregnate [T1] to make pregnant; fertilize: *The mating was successful and the female was impregnated first time.* **impregnation** [U]

germinate [I0; T1] to (cause to) start growing: *The seeds have begun to germinate. The sun's heat will help to germinate the seeds.* (*fig*) *He has an idea germinating.* **germination** [U]

conceive [I0; T1] (of a woman) to become pregnant (with): *She conceived (the child) last February.* **conception 1** [U] the action or process of conceiving or being conceived **2** [C] an example of this: *There have been many successful conceptions among the animals.*

sterilize, -ise [T1] to make sterile: *The doctor sterilized the woman after her fifth birth, so that she would not have any more children. This radiation can sterilize living creatures; they won't be able to reproduce.* [⇒ A15] *The nurse sterilized the medical instruments, so as to make them free of germs.* [⇒ A37] **sterilization** [U]

castrate [T1] *esp tech* to remove the sex organs of (a male animal or person): *These male cats have been castrated.* **castration 1** [U] the action of castrating or being castrated **2** [C] an example of this

emasculate [T1] *esp poet & fig* to remove the sex organs or reduce the male qualities of (a man): *Those people used to emasculate some of their male slaves.* (*fig*) *If I take these parts out of the story it'll be emasculated!* **emasculation** [U]

neuter [T1] to castrate or sterilize: *That cat has been neutered.*

A19 *nouns* : **early states of life**

embryo [C] **1** the young of any creature in its first state before birth or before coming out of an egg: *The human embryo passes through a number of stages before birth.* **2** (*fig*) the beginning stage: *I have just had the embryo of an idea.* **embryonic** [B] of or connected with an embryo

foetus *also esp AmE* **fetus** [C] a fully developed embryo in the womb or in an egg **foetal, fetal** [B] of or connected with a f(o)etus

cell [C] a very small unit of living matter, with a centre of activity (**nucleus**), which may form a simple creature or, in other creatures, is used in large numbers to form the substance and organs of the body: *Most living creatures consist of millions of specialized cells. Nerve cells, muscle cells, and blood cells are all important parts of living bodies.*

nucleus [C] the centre of activity of almost all cells of living matter

germ [C] **1** *Also* **germ cell** a small part of a cell of a living thing which can grow into a new plant, animal, etc: *Certain processes of preparing wheat can destroy the wheat germ, which is a valuable food.* **2** (*fig*) the beginning point: *I've just had the germ of an idea!*

seed 1 [C] the fertile [⇒ A17] part of a plant (or animal): *He planted the seeds at the right time and got an excellent crop of vegetables. I like raspberries* [⇒ A154], *but their seeds get between my teeth.* **2** [U] seeds collectively: *What seed do you use for your potatoes?*

spore [C] a sort of seed produced by some plants and some simple animals from which a new plant or animal can be produced, often after a period of time: *Some small one-celled animals can live through bad conditions by forming spores with hard surfaces, which become new animals when conditions get better.*

egg [C] **1** a rounded object containing the embryo of certain living creatures, esp birds, reptiles, and insects: *Birds' eggs have thin hard but easily broken shells. Most people enjoy eating the eggs of hens.* **2** the seed of life in a woman or female animal which joins with the male seed or sperm to make an embryo

yolk [C] the yellow part in an egg

white [C] the white or clear part of an egg

sperm 1 [C] *precise* the male germ or sex cell in animals and humans **2** [U] *loose* semen

semen [U] the liquid in a male human or animal which carries the sperm **seminal** [Wa5;B] of or concerning semen

ovum [C] the female germ or sex cell in animals and humans

spawn [U] **1** the eggs of fish, frogs, etc, laid together in a soft mass **2** *infml usu deprec* the young of any creature

A20 *nouns* : **young creatures generally**

[⇒ C3 CHILD]

young 1 [Wn3; C *usu pl*] a young living creature, esp an animal: *Most higher animals try to protect their young from danger. The young of a lion is called a cub.* **2** [P] young people considered as a group: *The young are better fed today in many countries than ever before.* **with young** *fml* (esp of animals) expecting to give birth

offspring [Wn3;C *usu pl*] *fml* the young of an animal; child: *The offspring of the cat are called kittens.*

progeny [Wn3;C *usu pl*] *fml, tech, & pomp* offspring

issue [GU] *old use and law* children (*esp in the phr* **to die without issue**): *He died without issue and left all his money to a home for cats.*

litter [GC] a group of young animals born at the same time to one mother, as of kittens (= young cats): *Our cat had a litter of four (kittens). The litter is healthy, every one. The litter are all healthy.*

Living creatures generally

A30 *nouns* : **living things**

(living) creature [C] a living thing, esp an animal: *Animals and plants are living creatures. The beach was covered with small creatures. What kind of creature is that? He saw a cat-like creature among the trees.*

being [C] a living creature, esp a person or with a personality: *Do other kinds of being live on other planets?* [⇒ C1 HUMAN BEING, L2 PLANET]

animal [C] a living thing, not a plant, having senses and able to move when it wants to: *Snakes, fish, and birds are all animals in the broadest sense of the word, but the word 'animal' is usually kept for creatures like cats, dogs, and horses.* [⇒ A50]

plant [C] **1** a living thing that has leaves and roots and grows usu in earth: *Vegetables, flowers, and trees are all plants. Treat that plant carefully; it isn't strong. All plants need water and light. He is studying the plant life of the area.* **2** esp such living things smaller than trees: *He has a lot of unusual plants in his garden and several fine old trees. She bought a cactus plant and put it in a pot. Tea is made from the leaves of the tea plant.* [⇒ A150]

organism [C] any form of life which is made up of parts which work together to keep life going; an individual animal or plant: *Good soil is full of small organisms.*

fauna [U] all the animals living wild in a particular place, or belonging to a particular age in history: *Fauna in ancient times included many animals not alive today.*

flora [U] all the plants of a particular place or time: *He studies the flora (and fauna) of Britain.*

wildlife [U] animals (and plants) which live and grow wild: *The wildlife of the area is diverse and fascinating. She is concerned with wildlife preservation.*

biped [C] *tech* a creature with two legs: *Human beings and birds are bipeds.*

quadruped [C] *tech* a creature with four legs: *Horses and dogs are quadrupeds.*

A31 nouns : emotive expressions for living things [C]

animal *genl* a living thing, not a plant or a human: *Some people consider themselves quite different from animals, but others consider human beings as no more than animals. Don't treat me like an animal—I'm a human being.* (*fig deprec*) *To him she is just an animal, not a person.*

beast 1 *usu apprec or deprec* a four-footed animal: *A large heavy beast was moving through the forest. What a splendid beast the elephant is! I can't stand dogs; get that beast away from me! The birds and the beasts of the forest were silent.* **2** cow or horse or other larger animal which is used by people: *He drove the beasts back to the cowshed. Water those beasts, then give them something to eat.* **3** a person, esp a man, behaving badly: *Don't make a beast of yourself; eat properly! That beast!—He is cruel to everybody. That boy is a horrible little beast—very badly behaved.* **bestial** [B] *usu deprec* like a beast esp in being cruel **-ly** [adv] **bestiality** [U] **1** the state of being bestial **2** the act of sexual intercourse [⇒ A16] with animals

brute 1 an animal, esp if large and regarded as dangerous: *That dog is a dangerous brute; it bites people.* (*fig*) *People here used to live the lives of brutes; there was little civilization.* **2** an unfortunate animal: *The fire spread to the doghouse and we couldn't save the poor brute.* **3** a rough, cruel, insensitive, or bad-mannered person, esp a man: *He is an unfeeling brute! A great brute of a man attacked her.* **brutal** [B] (cruel) like a brute **-ly** [adv] **brutality** [U]

A32 nouns : kinds of living creature

animal [C] *precise* a four-footed creature, usu a mammal and excluding reptiles, birds, etc: *Many people would call a horse an animal, but not a snake. The forest is full of birds and animals of all kinds.* [⇒ A50]

higher animal [C] a creature with a complex physical structure, esp a mammal: *Cats and monkeys are among the higher animals.*

lower animal [C] a creature with a fairly simple physical structure: *Insects, crabs, and reptiles are among the lower animals.*

mammal [C] an animal which feeds its young with milk from a breast [⇒ B31], udder [⇒ A128], or similar organ: *Cats, monkeys, and human beings are all mammals.* **mammalian** [Wa5;B] of or concerning mammals

beast of prey [C] an animal, usu larger, which hunts and eats other animals: *The lion is a beast of prey.*

rodent [C] an animal which has strong teeth which grow all the time: *Rabbits and rats are rodents.* [⇒ A60]

marsupial 1 [C] an animal the female of which carries the young in a pouch [⇒ H183] after birth **2** [Wa5;B] of or concerning such animals

bird [C] a creature with wings and feathers, the female of which lays eggs: *Birds were singing in the trees. The mother bird sat on the nest, while the father looked for food.* [⇒ A70]

bird of prey [C] a bird which hunts and eats other animals: *The eagle is a bird of prey.*

fowl [C] *old use & poet* a bird: *God made all the fowls of the air.* [⇒ A70]

wildfowl [P] birds living in natural conditions, esp if hunted and shot for food: *Wild ducks and geese are included in the term 'wildfowl'.*

waterfowl [Wn2;C *usu pl*] birds living in, on, or close to water, usu rivers and lakes [⇒ A73]

reptile [C] a creature with lungs whose blood changes temperature according to the temperature around it: *Snakes and crocodiles are reptiles.* [⇒ A90] **reptilian** [Wa5;B] of, like, or concerning reptiles

amphibian [C] an animal which is specially adapted to live both on land and in the water: *Frogs are typical amphibians.* [⇒ A94] **amphibious** [B] having these qualities: *An amphibious vehicle is useful both on land and in the water.*

fish [Wn2;C] **1** *precise* a creature which breathes in water by means of gills [⇒ A122] and whose blood changes temperature according to the temperature around it: *He found some dead fish beside the sea. The water was full of little fishes.* **2** *loose* any fairly large creature which lives in water: *A whale is a very big fish.* [⇒ A100]

shellfish [Wn3; C] any sea creature which typically has a hard shell of any kind: *Oysters are molluscs and crabs are crustaceans but generally they are called shellfish.* [⇒ A102–3]

crustacean [C] *tech* any shellfish which has a hard shell and jointed legs: *Crabs and lobsters are crustaceans.* [⇒ A102]

mollusc *esp BrE*, **mollusk** *AmE* any animal, usu small and without limbs, usu found in the sea or near water, with a soft body and usu a hard shell: *Oysters are molluscs and have shells but slugs are also technically molluscs although they do not have shells.* [⇒ A103]

insect [C] **1** *precise & tech* a small creature with no bones and a hard outer covering, six legs, and a body divided into three parts: *Ants and flies are insects. She was bitten by an insect in the garden.* **2** *loose* any very small animal of a similar kind: *She doesn't like ants, bees, spiders, and other insects like that.* [⇒ A110]

A33 *nouns* : **classes of living things** [C]

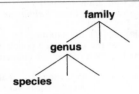

family a group of living things with a number of common characteristics and a common origin

genus a division of a family

species [Wn3] a group of plants or animals that are of the same kind, which are alike in all important ways, and which can breed together to produce young of the same kind; a division of a genus

A34 *nouns* : **breeds and strains of living things**

breed [C] a kind or class of animal or plant usu developed under the influence of man: *The Alsatian is a special breed of dog.*

strain [C] a breed or type of creature, esp plants, insects, and bacteria, usu developed or developing over a period of time: *He has developed a new strain of peas. These insects are a new strain which aren't affected by this poison.*

race [C] a breed or type of animal or plant, esp one useful to man for producing young of the same type

pedigree 1a [C; U] (a series of) people from whom or animals from which a person, family, or animal is descended: *These two families have fine pedigrees. This dog is of unknown pedigree.* **b** [U] *apprec* the ancient series of people from whom a person or family is descended: *She comes from a family of (high) pedigree.* **2** [C] a list or drawing showing the families from which a person or animal is descended: *Can you show me the dog's pedigree?* **3** [A] (of animals) descended from a long and recorded (and usu specially chosen) series of animals, and therefore of high quality: *He breeds pedigree cattle.*

A35 *nouns* : **kinds of living things as bred by mankind** [C]

thoroughbred an animal, esp a horse, which descends from parents of one particular type with particular qualities, often thought to be the best of a kind: *These horses are racing thoroughbreds.*

cross [(*between*)] an animal or plant which is a mixture of breeds or kinds: *The mule is a cross between the horse and the donkey.*

crossbreed an animal esp in agriculture which is produced by breeding two kinds of the same species of animal: *That sheep is a crossbreed of two different breeds.*

hybrid *fml* a cross: *The mule is a hybrid (animal).*

mongrel an animal, esp a dog, which is of no particular breed but whose parents come from different breeds: *Mongrels are often healthier than pure-bred animals.*

A36 *verbs* : **man breeding living things**

breed [T1] to keep (esp animals or fish) for the purpose of producing young, esp when the choice of parents is controlled: *They breed fine cattle on that farm. He breeds dogs as a hobby.*

interbreed [I0] to breed with one another: *Separate species do not normally interbreed.*

crossbreed [T1] to cause to interbreed: *Can you crossbreed these two kinds of sheep?* **crossbred** [Wa5;B] produced by crossing breeds

cross [T1 (*with*)] to produce a cross by mixing (breeds or varieties): *He crossed a horse with/ and a donkey and got a mule.*

hybridize, -ise *fml* **1** [T1] to cross; cause to interbreed: *He hybridized the roses and got a fine new variety. It is not easy to hybridize animals which do not normally interbreed.* **2** [I0] to interbreed **hybridization** [U]

tame [T1] to make (a wild, uncontrollable, or fierce animal) gentle or tame [⇒ F220], esp in order to live with man and be useful: *She tamed that horse herself. He tames lions; he's a lion-tamer.* (*fig*) *Man has tamed much of nature and made it work for him.*

domesticate 1 [T1] to make (a kind of animal or a particular animal) tame through breeding or training: *People first domesticated the dog thousands of years ago.* **2** [I0] to become tame in this way: *Some kinds of animals domesticate more easily than others.* **domestication** [U] the act or result of domesticating (an animal or animals): *The domestication of the dog took place thousands of years ago.* **domestic** [Wa5;B] (of animals) kept or used by or living with people: *Dogs and cats are domestic animals.*

A37 nouns : **very small living things**

bacteria [P] *tech* very small living things related to plants, some of which cause disease: *Bacteria exist in water, soil, air, plants, and the bodies of animals and people.*

virus [C] *tech* a living thing even smaller than bacteria which causes infectious diseases in the body: *Viruses reproduce only in living cells. He is suffering from a virus disease.*

microbe [C] *tech* a very small living creature which can only be seen through a microscope [⇨ H123], esp a kind of bacteria which causes disease: *Bacteria and viruses are microbes.*

germ [C] *infml* a microbe which causes disease: *I have a bad cold—Don't come too close or you'll get my germs! She's ill; she must have picked up a germ somewhere.*

bug [C] *infml* a germ; a virus infection: *She's ill; she must have picked up a bug somewhere. She's got the flu bug.* [⇨ B140 FLU]

A38 nouns : **living things which cause trouble**

pest [C] **1** a usu small animal or insect that harms or destroys food supplies: *Rats and mice are pests.* **2** [usu sing] *infml* an annoying person or thing: *That child is a real pest, continually asking questions.*

vermin [GU] **1** wild animals which are harmful to plants, animals, and birds in which humans are interested: *He said that foxes were vermin and should be killed, but she didn't agree.* **2** insects and similar creatures which live on the bodies of larger creatures: *Lice and fleas* [⇨ A110] *are vermin.* **3** *deprec* (*fig*) human beings who are considered harmful to society **verminous** [B] **1** having a lot of lice or fleas **2** [Wa5] caused by insects: *There are many verminous diseases.* **-ly** [adv]

A39 nouns : **living things which eat or are eaten**

predator [C] an animal which hunts other animals for food: *Lions and hawks are predators.*

predatory [B] **1** living by killing and eating other animals: *The cat is a predatory animal.* **2** concerned with or living (as if) by robbery and taking the property of others: *Their land was attacked by predatory tribes.* (*fig*) *This town is full of predatory hotel-keepers charging*

very high prices. **predation** [U] the actions of a predator

prey 1 [U] an animal that is hunted and eaten by another animal: *The lion seized its prey and ate it. Chickens on a farm often fall prey to foxes.* **2** [S] (*fig*) a person who is helpless and suffers (easily or often) from harm: *He trusts people too much; he's an easy prey and almost anyone can trick him out of money. Some people with disordered minds become a prey to all kinds of fears.*

scavenger [C] an animal which feeds on animals which it finds dead, esp when the flesh is decaying: *Jackals are scavengers.*

parasite [C] **1** a plant or animal that lives on or in another and gets its food from it: *This insect is a parasite that feeds on human blood.* **2** (*fig*) *deprec* a useless person who is supported by the wealth or efforts of others: *These people are just parasites on the State; they do no useful work.* **parasitic** [B] *deprec* (& often *fig*) of, concerning, or like a parasite: *She leads a parasitic life, doing no work herself but helped by everyone else.* **-ally** [Wa4; adv] **parasitism** [U] the state or way of behaving of parasites

A40 collective nouns : **groups of the same kind of living things** [GC]

colony *tech* a group of living creatures of the same kind living or growing closely together in a place: *There are several bird colonies on islands near here.*

herd 1 a group of land animals of one kind which live and feed together: *Herds of elephants were moving across the plain.* **2** a group of animals of one kind bred by a farmer: *That farm has one of the finest herds of cattle in the country.* **3** (*fig*) *usu deprec* people generally thought of as acting all alike, like animals: *She believes she is above the common herd* (= the ordinary people).

flock 1 a group of sheep, goats, or birds: *The shepherd* [⇨ E144] *brought his flock down from the hills. A flock/flight of birds flew overhead.* **2** (*fig*) *infml* (of people) a crowd: *A large flock of people crowded into the hall.*

flight a group of birds moving through the air: *A flight of starlings flew down towards the roof.*

shoal a large number of fish of one kind swimming in a group: *Shoals of herring can be found in that part of the sea.*

school a large number of fish or sea mammals [⇨ A32] swimming in a group: *A school of whales swam past the ship.*

pack 1 a number of dogs which are kept for hunting: *The pack chased the fox.* **2** a group of animals, usu like dogs, which hunt other animals: *Wolves hunt in packs. The wolf pack attacked the horse.* **3** (*fig*) *deprec* a gang: *He was cheated by a pack of thieves.*

troop a group of animals, esp monkeys and similar long-legged animals, esp when moving: *The troop of baboons crossed the plain.*

A41 nouns : places where creatures live and shelter [C]

nest 1 a shelter which is built by many kinds of birds, where the female lays her eggs: *There was a bird's nest high in the tree. Some birds build their nests on houses.* **2** the shelter built by some kinds of insects: *Wasps had built their nest in the old wall.*

lair the home or shelter of a wild animal, where it hides, rests, sleeps, etc: *The fox returned to its lair with its prey. (fig) The police tracked (= followed) the thieves to their lair.*

den the home or shelter of a (usu large) wild meat-eating animal: *The lion lay asleep in its den. (fig) That house is just a den of thieves; no one's money is safe there!*

burrow a shelter, esp for foxes, rabbits, etc, which consists of a hole or tunnel(s) under the ground

A42 nouns : places where creatures are kept by man [C]
[⇨ ALSO E140 STABLE, KENNEL, etc]

zoo also fml **zoological gardens** a place, usu large and like a park, where animals of all kinds are kept for people to see: *He likes going to the zoo in Edinburgh/to Edinburgh Zoo. Modern zoos are much better places than zoos used to be.*

aquarium 1 a glass container for fish and other water animals **2** a building (esp in a zoo) containing many of these

aviary a place where many birds are kept, esp in a zoo: *Let's go to the aviaries next, Daddy.*

apiary a place where people keep bees [⇨ A110] **apiarist** a person who keeps bees

A43 verbs & nouns : noises made by certain animals [I∅;C]

bleat 1 to make a noise like a sheep, goat, or calf: *The lamb was bleating for its mother.* **2** the sound made by a sheep, goat, or calf **3** (fig) a sound like this: *He heard the bleat of an old man's high shaky voice.*

neigh 1 to make the loud and long cry that a horse makes: *The horse neighed in fear.* **2** the loud and long cry of a horse: *The horse gave a neigh of fear.*

whinny also **snicker** or **whicker 1** to make the gentle sound which horses make: *The horse whinnied when its master appeared.* **2** the gentle sound which horses make: *He heard the whinny of a horse.*

snort 1 to make a noise by blowing air down the nose: *The horse snorted in fear.* **2** such a noise: *He heard a snort of anger from one of the men.*

grunt 1 to make a low noise like a pig: *The pigs were grunting happily as they ate. He grunted in reply; I couldn't understand what he said.* **2** such a noise: *I could hear the grunts of the pigs. He gave a grunt in reply.*

bark 1 to make the sharp loud sound a dog makes: *The dogs began to bark when the man climbed over the wall.* **2** such a sound: *The dog uttered a short sharp bark.*

miaow, meow also **mew 1** to make the crying sound a cat makes: *The kitten miaowed. Cats were mewing somewhere nearby.* **2** such a sound: *He heard the sudden miaow of a cat. The kitten let out a frightened mew.*

squeal 1 to make a high long noise like certain animals in pain or in fear: *The little pig squealed when the dog attacked it. The child squealed in fear.* **2** such a noise: *She gave a squeal of fear.*

hoot 1 to cry like an owl: *An owl hooted in a nearby tree.* **2** such a cry: *The hunter gave two hoots like an owl.*

quack 1 to make a noise like a duck **2** such a noise

Animals/mammals

A50 nouns : man and the monkey
[⇨ B10 THE BODY, C1–18 PEOPLE AND THE FAMILY]

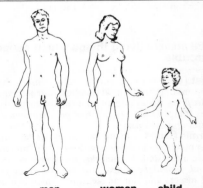

man   **woman**   **child**

man 1 [C] a (male) human being: *He could see some men and horses on the hillside.* **2** [R] the human race: *Man and the monkey have many things in common.*

monkey [C] a higher animal which is covered with hair: *Monkeys generally have long arms and can swing easily from tree to tree, but some kinds, like baboons, live mainly on the ground. Most kinds of monkeys are much smaller than men, and have tails.*

ape [C] any large kind of monkey without a tail: *Gorillas and chimpanzees are apes.*

anthropoid (ape) [C] any large manlike ape, esp the gorilla and chimpanzee

langur also **langur monkey** [C] an Asian long-tailed monkey

gorilla
(Africa)

baboon
(Africa)

tail

marmoset
(South America)

chimpanzee
infml abbrev **chimp**
(Africa)

gibbon
(Asia)

rhesus (monkey)
(Asia)

toe

orang utan
(Asia)

A51 *nouns* : the horse and similar animals [C]

[⇨K199 HORSE RIDING, K200 HORSE RACING]

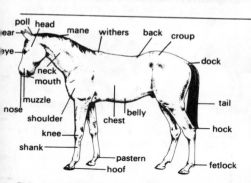

poll head
ear
eye
mane withers back croup
neck
mouth
muzzle
nose
shoulder
knee
shank
pastern
hoof
dock
tail
hock
belly
chest
fetlock

horse

Names for the horse according to age and sex		
age *sex*	*male*	*female*
full-grown	stallion	mare
young	colt	filly
very young newborn	foal	

Other varieties and breeds of horses and similar animals

pony a horse of a small breed, esp as used by children: *The children enjoyed riding (on) the ponies. They enjoyed the pony rides.*
gelding a stallion which has been castrated [⇨ A18]

mustang a small wild horse of the North American plains
stud 1 *esp AmE* a male horse kept for breeding **2** a number of horses or other animals kept for breeding

donkey *or* **ass**

mule

zebra

donkey, ass (*fig*) a foolish person: *Don't be such an ass—It's a silly thing to do! He's a bit of a donkey; he does silly things.*
jackass 1 a male ass **2** (*fig*) a foolish person

mule a cross between a horse and a donkey: *The cart was pulled by two mules.*
zebra a striped animal from Africa, related to the horse

A52 nouns : the cow and similar animals [C]

[⇒ E34 FOR THE PARTS OF THE COW AS MEAT]

Names for the cow according to age and sex		
age \ sex	female and general	male
full-grown	cow	bull
young	heifer	bullock
very young	calf pl calves	

horn

Guernsey cow **Spanish bull** **African cow**

udder

Other varieties of cows and similar animals

cattle [P] cows, etc, collectively: *The cattle were in the fields. On that farm they have a thousand head of cattle* (= a thousand cows, bulls, etc).

bullock 1 a young bull **2** a castrated [⇒ A18] bull

steer a young, usu castrated bull, esp if it is raised as food

ox 1 a fully-grown castrated bullock, esp when it is used to pull carts, etc **2** *old use* any domestic [⇒ A36] cow, bull, etc **3** any large cowlike animal

longhorn a cow or bull of a kind with long horns

shorthorn a cow or bull of a kind with short horns

buffalo (Africa) **water buffalo (Asia)** **North American bison**

buffalo [Wn1] **1** *precise* a large animal like the cow, usu found in Africa and Asia **2** *loose* the American bison

bison [Wn2] *precise* **1** the European wild ox **2** the North American wild ox

A53 nouns : the cat and similar animals [C]

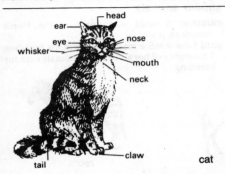
head
ear
eye
whisker
nose
mouth
neck
claw
tail
cat

Names for the cat according to age and sex		
age \ sex	male	female
full-grown	tomcat *infml* tom	tabby
young	kitten	

cat 1 a small domestic [⇒ A36] animal with fur: *Many families keep a cat, usually to kill mice, but often as a pet for the children.* **2** any animal of a group which includes the domestic cat and

the lion **3** (*fig*) *deprec* a woman who says unkind things about other women

puss *also* **kitty** (the name used for talking to or calling cats): *Here, puss, puss! Come on, puss, drink your milk! Here, kitty-kitty—where are you?*

pussy *infml* a cat: *That's a nice pussy (cat). What beautiful pussies!*

cub the young of the larger cats

Varieties of large nondomestic cats

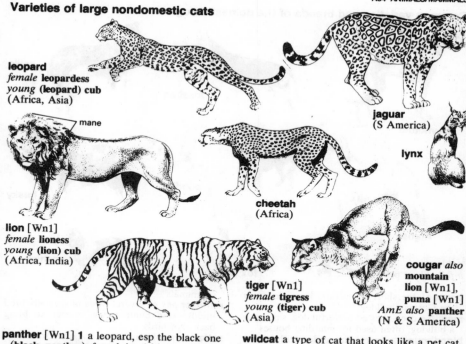

leopard
female **leopardess**
young **(leopard) cub**
(Africa, Asia)

mane

jaguar
(S America)

lynx

cheetah
(Africa)

lion [Wn1]
female **lioness**
young **(lion) cub**
(Africa, India)

tiger [Wn1]
female **tigress**
young **(tiger) cub**
(Asia)

cougar *also*
mountain
lion [Wn1],
puma [Wn1]
AmE also **panther**
(N & S America)

panther [Wn1] **1** a leopard, esp the black one (**black panther**) found in Africa and Asia **2** *AmE* cougar

wildcat a type of cat that looks like a pet cat, naturally wild and fierce, and lives in some parts of Europe

A54 nouns : the dog and similar animals [C]

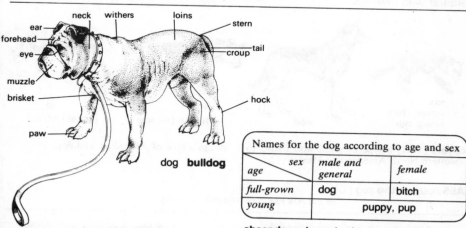

neck withers loins

ear
forehead
eye

muzzle
brisket

paw

stern

tail
croup

hock

dog **bulldog**

	sex	male and general	female
	Names for the dog according to age and sex		
age	*sex*	*male and general*	*female*
full-grown		**dog**	**bitch**
young		**puppy, pup**	

dog a domestic [⇒ A36] animal with a coat of hair, which is bred in many varieties: *Many families keep dogs, usually as a pet but also to guard their property.*

hound 1 [*often in comb*] a hunting dog: *foxhounds; deerhounds* **2** *deprec* a dog: *Get that offensive hound out of this house!* **follow the hounds/ride to hounds** to go fox-hunting

sheepdog a dog trained to drive sheep and keep them together

mongrel a dog of mixed breed [⇒ A35]

cur 1 a dog of no particular breed, esp a bad-tempered one **2** *deprec* a man of whom the speaker does not have a good opinion: *What a cur that man is!*

bitch 1 a female dog **2** *deprec* a woman: *Tell that bitch to leave me alone!*

Common varieties and breeds of the domestic dog

greyhound

Alsatian

collie

Afghan

chow

poodle

husky

pekinese
infml abbrev **peke**

fox terrier

spaniel

boxer a large, short-haired dog, descended from the German bulldog

mastiff a deep-chested powerful dog, similar to a bulldog, often used for guarding houses

bloodhound a large hunting dog with a very good sense of smell, used for tracking people or animals

retriever any of several types of specially bred middle-sized hunting dog, trained to bring back shot birds

setter a type of long-haired dog often trained to point out the position of animals for shooting

Similar wild animals

fox
female **vixen**
young **cub**

wolf

hyena (Africa)

jackal (Africa)

coyote [Wn1] a type of small wolf native to western North America and Mexico

dingo a type of Australian wild dog

A55 *nouns* : **the pig** [C]

[⇒ E34 FOR PARTS OF THE PIG AS MEAT]

snout

pig

tusk

boar

hog 1 *esp AmE* a pig **2** a castrated [⇒ A18] boar raised for food

swine [Wn3] **1** *esp old use & lit* a pig or pigs collectively **2** *derog* (*fig*) a person or people whom the speaker really does not like: *Tell that/those swine to get out of here!*

Names for the pig according to age and sex		
age \ sex	*male*	*female*
full-grown	boar	sow
young	piglet	

A56 *nouns* : **the sheep** [Wn3;C] **and the goat** [C]

[⇒ E34 FOR PARTS OF THE SHEEP AS MEAT]

ewe and **lamb**

Names for the sheep according to age and sex		
age \ sex	*female*	*male*
full-grown	ewe	ram
young	lamb	

horn

Names for the goat according to age and sex		
age \ sex	*male*	*female*
full-grown	billy (goat), he-goat	nanny (goat), she-goat
young	kid	

ram   **goat**

GRAMMATICAL NOTE All the nouns in the tables are [C]: *a ewe, ewes, the ewe; a billy, billies, the billy,* etc

A57 *nouns* : **deer** [Wn3] **and similar animals** [C]

[⇒ E32 FOR THE DEER AS FOOD]

Kinds of Deer

antler

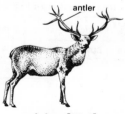

red deer [Wn3]

elk [Wn1]

reindeer [Wn3] a type of large deer with long branching horns that is used in the coldest parts of Europe for its milk, meat, and skin, and for pulling carriages (**sledges**) across the snow

caribou [Wn1] a type of North American reindeer

roe deer [Wn3] a kind of small European and Asian forest deer

fallow deer [Wn3] a small deer of Europe and Asia having a light brownish-yellow coat with, in the summer, white spots

elk [Wn1] *BrE* any of several types of deer of Europe and Asia of the largest kind, with very big flat antlers

moose [Wn3] a type of large deer, very similar to an elk, living in the northern parts of America

Similar animals

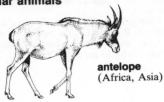

antelope
(Africa, Asia)

Names for deer and similar animals according to size, sex, and age			
age \ sex		*male*	*female*
full-grown { *larger kinds* *smaller kinds*		stag buck	hind doe
young		fawn	

gazelle one of many kinds of small soft-eyed graceful antelope common in Africa and southern Asia

springbok a kind of swift South African gazelle

GRAMMATICAL NOTE The above three nouns are [Wn1;C]: *an antelope; antelopes* or *antelope; the antelope,* etc

A58 *nouns* : **sea and amphibious|mammals** [C]

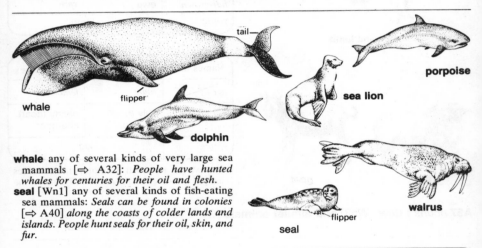

tail—

porpoise

flipper

sea lion

whale

dolphin

walrus

flipper

seal

whale any of several kinds of very large sea mammals [⇒ A32]: *People have hunted whales for centuries for their oil and flesh.*

seal [Wn1] any of several kinds of fish-eating sea mammals: *Seals can be found in colonies* [⇒ A40] *along the coasts of colder lands and islands. People hunt seals for their oil, skin, and fur.*

A59 *nouns* : **other large animals** [C]

Names for the elephant according to age and sex		
age \ sex	*male*	*female*
full-grown	bull (elephant)	cow (elephant)
young	calf	

African elephant [Wn1]

tusk

trunk—

toe—

Indian elephant [Wn1]

mammoth a large kind of elephant with long hair which lived on earth during the early stages of human development

mammoth

brown bear

teeth—

grizzly bear

polar bear

bear 1 [Wn1] any of various kinds of usu large and heavy animals with thick rough fur that usu eat fruit and insects as well as meat: *Many kinds of bears sleep through the winter.* **2** (fig) a rough, bad-tempered man: *She's nice but her husband's a bit of a bear.*

Names for the bear according to age and sex		
age \ sex	*male*	*female*
full-grown	(he-)bear	she-bear
young	(bear) cub	

dromedary
(Africa, W Asia)

Bactrian camel
(Asia)

head
eye

giraffe [Wn1]

porcupine

ant-eater

kangaroo [Wn1]

horn

hippopotamus [Wn1]
infml abbrev **hippo**

rhinoceros [Wn2]
infml abbrev **rhino**

A60 *nouns* : **rodents** [C]

rabbit

Names for the rabbit according to sex	
male	*female*
buck	doe

rabbit any of several kinds of small rodents [⇒ A32] living in holes in the ground (**burrows**) and having brownish-grey fur in the natural state but black, white, or bluish-grey in domestic [⇒ A36] varieties

bunny (rabbit) *infml* (used esp by or to children) a rabbit: *The child shouted that there were bunnies in the field.*

hare

hare [Wn1] a rodent larger than the rabbit, with long ears, strong back legs, and a divided upper lip: *Hares can run very fast.*

rat

rat a rodent which lives in old houses and beside rivers, etc: *People normally regard rats as dangerous to health.*

mouse

mouse any of several kinds of small rodents which live in houses and fields: *I'm sure there are mice in that old house.*

field mouse any of various kinds of usu small mice that live in the fields

vole any of several types of small thick-bodied short-tailed rodents which live in fields, woods, banks of rivers, etc: *a water vole; a bank vole*

gopher a small ratlike rodent of North and Central America which makes and lives in holes in the ground and has large spaces (**pouches**) inside its cheeks

shrew

squirrel

beaver

vole

A61 *nouns* : **other smaller animals** [C]

badger

hedgehog

stoat

ferret

weasel

mole

wing

bat

Birds

A70 *nouns* : **domestic fowl**

[⇒ E31 FOWLS AS FOOD]

hen

cock — comb

hen [C] any of several kinds of common domestic [⇒ A36] egg-laying bird: *The hen laid an egg.*
fowl [Wn2;C] a farmyard bird, esp a hen: *They keep fowls and sell the eggs.*
poultry [U] farmyard birds, such as hens, ducks, geese, etc: *He raises poultry of all kinds. He is a poultry farmer.*
chicken [C] a hen (or perhaps cock), esp when young but older than a chick; *esp AmE* (now common name for) the hen: *They keep chickens on that farm. He has a chicken farm.*
bantam [C] a small kind of hen

Names for fowls according to age and sex		
sex / *age*	*general and female*	*male*
full-grown	hen, chicken	cock, *AmE usu* rooster
younger		cockerel
young	chicken	
newborn	chick	

turkey

A71 *nouns* : **ducks and geese** [C]

duck

webbed feet

duck [Wn1] any of several wild and domestic kinds of common waterbird

Names for the duck according to age and sex		
age / *sex*	*female and general*	*male*
full-grown	duck	drake
young	duckling	

goose

goose any of several wild and domestic kinds of waterbird larger than a duck

Names for the goose according to age and sex		
age / *sex*	*female and general*	*male*
full-grown	goose	gander
young	gosling	

A72 *nouns* : **seabirds** [C]

(sea)**gull**

penguin

puffin

cormorant

seabird any bird which lives mainly or generally over, on, or near the sea

A73 *nouns* : **waterbirds** [C]

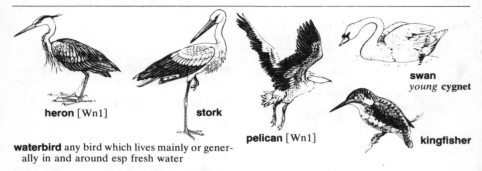

heron [Wn1]   **stork**   **pelican** [Wn1]

swan
young **cygnet**

kingfisher

waterbird any bird which lives mainly or generally in and around esp fresh water

A74 *nouns* : **common wild birds** [C]

finch   **wren**   **pigeon** [Wn1]

tail   head   eye   be

feather   wing   **blackbird**

claw

toe

sparrow   **swift**

thrush   **starling**   **swallow**

robin

magpie a type of noisy bird with black and white feathers, which often picks up and takes to its nest small bright objects

lark any of several small light brown birds with long pointed wings, esp the **skylark**

cuckoo a type of large grey European bird that lays its eggs in other birds' nests. It flies south for winter and has a call that sounds like its name

tit *also fml* **titmouse** any of several types of small European bird: *a blue tit; a great tit*

dove any of various types of pigeon; a soft-voiced bird often used as a sign for peace

A75 *nouns* : **common pet birds** [C]

budgerigar *also infml* **budgie**—a small bright-coloured bird of Australian origin often kept as a cage bird in British houses

canary a type of yellow finch kept as a cage bird esp for its singing

parrot

A76 *nouns* : **unusual birds** [C]

— crest

cockatoo

toucan

ostrich

peacock

kiwi a type of New Zealand bird that cannot fly, having very short wings, a long beak, strong legs, and grey hairlike feathers

A77 *nouns* : **birds which are hunted as game** [C]

pheasant [Wn2]

grouse [Wn3] any of several kinds of smallish fat birds with feathered feet, which are shot for food and sport
partridge [Wn1] any of various middle-sized birds with a round body and short tail, shot for sport and food
snipe [Wn2] any of several birds with very long thin beaks, that live on the ground in wet places and are often shot for sport

gamebird any bird which is hunted for food [⇒ ALSO E31]

A78 *nouns* : **birds of prey and scavengers** [C]

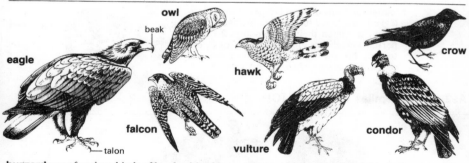

owl

beak

eagle

hawk

crow

falcon

vulture

condor

talon

buzzard any of various kinds of hawk with wide rounded wings
kite a large hawk with long narrow wings and a forked tail, that eats insects and small animals
carrion crow a type of large black crow that eats dead flesh and small animals

raven a large shiny black kind of crow, with a black beak and a deep unmusical voice, sometimes thought to be unlucky
rook a large black European crow which flies about in groups that build nests together in a **rookery**

Reptiles and amphibians

A90 *nouns* : **snakes** [C]

snake any of various types of long, legless, flesh-eating reptiles which crawl on the ground or move through trees: *Many snakes are poisonous, but others crush their prey to death.*

serpent *lit & fml* a snake: *The serpent persuaded Eve to eat the fruit.* **serpentine** [B] like a serpent, esp in having twists: *They drove along a serpentine road.*

boa constrictor   **viper**

cobra a type of African or Asian poisonous snake that can spread the skin of its neck to make itself look bigger and more dangerous

python any of several types of non-poisonous tropical snakes (**constrictors**) that kill small animals for food by winding round them and crushing them

rattlesnake *also esp AmE* **rattler** a poisonous American snake that makes a noise with its tail when it is angry

mamba a type of large very poisonous black or green African tree snake

adder a small poisonous snake found in northern Europe and northern Asia

A91 *nouns* : **lizards** [C]

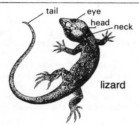

tail   eye
         head   neck

lizard

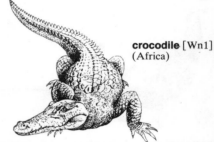

crocodile [Wn1] (Africa)

lizard any of various types of usu smaller reptiles with four short legs and a long tail: *A little brown lizard sat on the stone, without moving, watching an insect. Crocodiles and alligators are particularly large lizard-like reptiles.*

alligator [Wn1] a large fierce cold-blooded animal like the crocodile that lives on land and in lakes and rivers in the hot wet parts of America and China

chameleon 1 any of various types of small four-legged long-tailed lizards able to change their colour to match their surroundings **2** (*fig*) a person who changes his behaviour, ideas, etc, to suit his own purpose: *He's a political chameleon, always changing his views to win votes.*

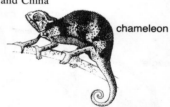

chameleon

A92 *nouns* : **reptiles with shells** [C]

tortoise   **turtle**

A93 *nouns* : **reptiles that do not exist** [C]

dragon

fang

brontosaurus (a dinosaur)

dragon a large creature in stories, usu like a flying snake or lizard: *In the story he kills a fire-breathing dragon and saves the beautiful princess.*

dinosaur any of several types of very large long-tailed reptiles that lived in very ancient times and no longer exist

A94 *nouns* : **amphibians**
[⇨ A32 DEFINITION]

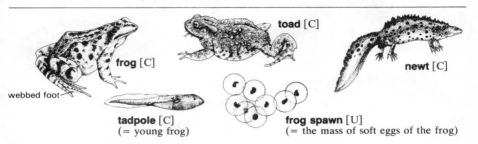

frog [C]

webbed foot

tadpole [C]
(= young frog)

toad [C]

newt [C]

frog spawn [U]
(= the mass of soft eggs of the frog)

Fish and other water creatures

A100 *nouns* : **common fish** [C]
[⇨ A32 DEFINITION]

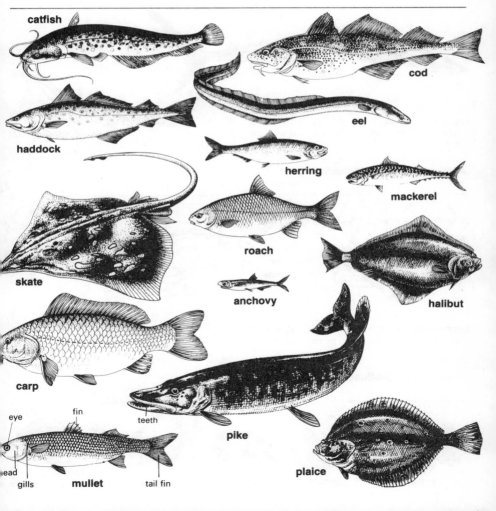

catfish

cod

eel

haddock

herring

mackerel

roach

skate

anchovy

halibut

carp

pike

fin

teeth

eye

ead

gills

mullet

tail fin

plaice

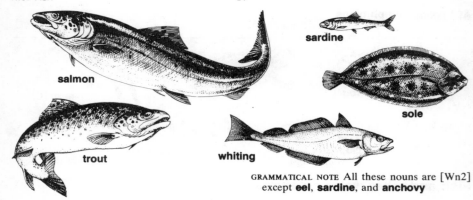

salmon

sardine

sole

trout

whiting

GRAMMATICAL NOTE All these nouns are [Wn2] except **eel**, **sardine**, and **anchovy**

A101 *nouns* : **larger and dangerous fish** [C]

shark

ray any of various types of large flat sea fish related to the shark that have a long pointed tail

dogfish [Wn2]

A102 *nouns* : **crustaceans** [C]
[⇨ A32 DEFINITION]

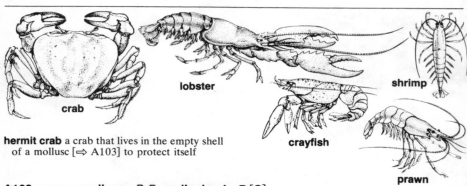

crab

lobster

shrimp

crayfish

hermit crab a crab that lives in the empty shell of a mollusc [⇨ A103] to protect itself

prawn

A103 *nouns* : **molluscs** *BrE,* **mollusks** *AmE* [C]
[⇨ A32 DEFINITION]

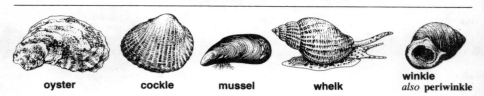

oyster

cockle

mussel

whelk

winkle
also periwinkle

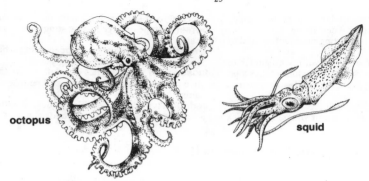

octopus

squid

A104 *nouns* : **other sea creatures**

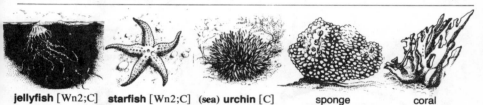

jellyfish [Wn2;C]   **starfish** [Wn2;C]   **(sea) urchin** [C]   sponge   coral

sponge 1 [C] a sea animal which stays in one place and grows a rubber-like skeleton that can take in water **2** [U; C] (a piece of) the material of this skeleton or of rubber or plastic like it: *Sponge rubber is useful for packing breakable things.*

coral [U] a very small sea animal which lives in one place, with a hard skeleton which combines into a solid mass with others of the same kind, and is often used for making jewellery

Insects and similar creatures

A110 *nouns* : **common insects** [C]
[⇨ A32 DEFINITION]

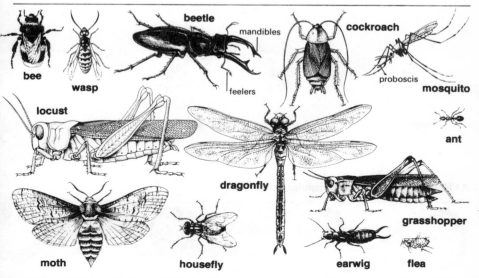

beetle

mandibles

cockroach

bee

wasp

feelers

proboscis

mosquito

locust

ant

dragonfly

grasshopper

moth   housefly   earwig   flea

bumblebee a type of large hairy bee which makes a loud noise when flying

hornet a type of large stinging insect related to the wasp

cricket a type of small brown insect similar to the grasshopper, the male of which makes loud short noises by rubbing its leathery wings together

cicada a type of tropical insect with a large wide head and large transparent wings. It makes a special loud shrill noise, esp in hot weather

horsefly a type of large fly that stings horses and cattle

greenfly [Wn2] a very small green insect which feeds on the juice from young plants

louse any of several types of small insects that live on the skin and in the hair of people and animals, esp when they are dirty

bedbug a type of wingless blood-sucking insects that lives in houses and esp beds

A111 *nouns* : **stages in the lives of insects** [C]

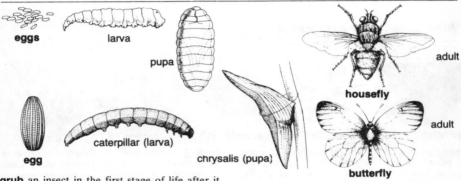

eggs   larva
            pupa
                                                adult
                                        housefly
egg
            caterpillar (larva)   adult
                    chrysalis (pupa)
                                        butterfly

grub an insect in the first stage of life after it comes out of the egg

larva *tech* a grub **larval** [Wa2; B]

caterpillar the grub of a butterfly or moth

chrysalis 1 the resting (**larval**) stage in an insect's life, between being a grub and flying as a moth, butterfly, etc **2** the case which covers it during this time

pupa *tech* a chrysalis

A112 *nouns* : **creatures similar to insects** [C]

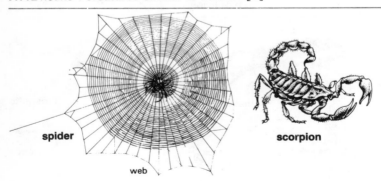

spider   scorpion
        web

A113 *nouns* : **worms and similar creatures** [C]

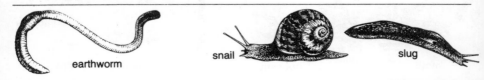

earthworm   snail   slug

worm a long thin creature with no backbone or limbs, like a round tube of flesh, esp the **earthworm** which lives in and moves through earth
snail a small animal with a soft body, no limbs, and a hard shell on its back and thin horns on its head

leech a small wormlike creature living in wet places that pricks the skin of animals and drinks their blood, formerly used to lower the blood pressure of sick people
slug a small animal with a soft body and no limbs which is often a pest [⇒ A38] in gardens

Parts of animals

[ALSO ⇒ B1, 10, 20 THE BODY]

A120 *nouns* : **parts around the head and neck** [C]

[⇒ pictures at A51, A53, A54, A59, A74]

head that part of a living creature's body which contains the eyes, ears, nose, and mouth – in animals at the front of the body, in man on top
neck that part of the body of many living crea-
tures which connects the head and the rest of the body, on which the head turns
eye the organ of sight, usu two in number
ear the organ of hearing, two in number

A121 *nouns* : **things growing from the head and face**

horn 1 [C] a hard pointed growth found in a pair on the top of the heads of deer, cattle, sheep, goats, etc: *Bulls have horns.* **2** [U] the material a horn is made of: *The handle of the knife is made of horn. The knife has a horn handle.* [⇒ pictures at A52, A56, A59]
antler [C] the branched horn of the stag, bull, elk, etc [⇒ picture at A57]
mane [C] **1** the mass of long hair on the neck of a horse, lion, etc **2** any similar mass of hair, esp on a human being [⇒ pictures at A51 and A53]

crest [C] **1** the feathers that stand up on the head of such birds as the lark and cockatoo [⇒ picture at A76] **2** the comb of any fowl
comb [C] the red fleshy crest on a fowl, esp a cock [⇒ picture at A70]
whisker [C] one of the long stiff hairs growing near the mouth of a cat, rat, etc [⇒ picture at A53]
feeler [C] the organ of certain creatures, esp insects, with which they test things by touch [⇒ pictures at A110]
antenna [C] *tech* a feeler

A122 *nouns* : **the mouth and related parts of different creatures** [C]

nose 1 the organ of smell and its general area above the mouth in the face of an animal [*also* ⇒ B25, pictures at A51, A53] **2** (*fig*) the pointed front of something: *the nose of an aeroplane*
mouth 1 the opening in the face through which an animal may take food into the body, and by which it makes sounds and may breathe [ALSO ⇒ B26] **2** (*fig*) any similar opening: *the mouth of a cave, river, etc*
snout 1 the nose, esp if large, of an animal **2** the nose, mouth, and jaws of some animals, such as the pig [⇒ picture at A55] **3** (*fig*) the pointed front of anything: *the snout of a submarine*
trunk the long nose of an elephant or similar animal: *The elephant lifted the piece of wood with its trunk.* [⇒ picture at A59]
muzzle 1 the nose and mouth of a dog or similar animal: *He caught hold of the dog by its muzzle.* [⇒ picture at A54] **2** an apparatus which covers the muzzle of a dog, to prevent it biting people
mask the face or head of a usu wild dog, cat, or similar animal: *He found himself looking into the terrible mask of a hungry tiger.*

beak 1 the hard horny upper and lower parts of a bird's mouth, esp if it is curved [⇒ pictures at A74, A78] **2** any similar part of any other creature's face such as a turtle **3** (*fig*) anything which looks like a beak: *He has a great beak of a nose.*
bill 1 a bird's beak, esp if it is straight **2** any similar part of any other creature's face
crop a baglike part of a bird's throat where food is stored and partly changed into simpler forms by the body's chemical action
mandible 1 the movable usu lower jaw [⇒ B21] of an animal or fish, or its jawbone **2** the upper or lower part of a bird's beak **3** one of the two biting or holding parts on insects and crabs [⇒ picture at A110]
proboscis 1 the long part of the mouth of such insects as the mosquito [⇒ picture at A110] **2** *tech* the trunk of the elephant **3** *humor* any nose
gill [*usu pl*] the organ with which a fish breathes, one on either side of the head [⇒ picture at A100]

A123 *nouns* : **the teeth of different creatures** [C]

[ALSO ⇒ B26]

tooth one of the small hard bony objects growing in the upper and lower jaws of most animals, which are used for biting and tearing food [⇒ pictures at A59]

fang 1 one of two teeth in a snake along which its poison passes **2** a long sharp tooth, esp of dogs and wolves: *The wolf showed its fangs in a vicious snarl.* [⇒ picture at A93]

tusk a very large long pointed tooth, usu one of a pair coming out from the closed mouth of certain animals: *The elephant had very large tusks.* [⇒ pictures at A55, A59]

A124 *nouns* : **the feet of different creatures** [C]

[ALSO ⇒ B44]

leg 1 a limb on which an animal walks and which supports its body: *Tigers have four legs but monkeys have only two.* **2** that part of this limb above the foot: *The cat hurt its foot but not its leg.*

foot the movable part at the end of the leg, on which an animal walks and stands: *A bird's foot is very different from a monkey's.*

toe one of two to five small parts on the end of the foot of many animals, which can usu bend at their joints: *Birds' feet have three toes while monkeys' feet have five.*

hoof the hard hornlike part of the foot of a horse, cow, deer, etc **cloven hoof** the divided hoof of the cow, goat, and sheep

paw the foot of such animals as the dog and cat, which is soft and has claws or nails

pad the soft fleshy underpart of a paw or similar kind of foot: *A cat's claws can move in and out of its pads.*

claw the pointed and usu curved nail on the feet of such animals as the cat and all birds [⇒ pictures at A53, A74]

talon a large curved claw esp of a beast or bird of prey: *The eagle held the lamb in its talons.* [⇒ picture at A78]

web skin joining the toes of waterbirds, bats, frogs, and some other water animals **web-footed/toed** [Wa5;B] having web feet/toes **webbed** [Wa5;B] having the toes joined by webs [⇒ pictures at A71, A94]

sucker an organ in some animals which allows them to rest on a surface or to hold on to something by sucking out the air between the sucker and the surface: *Some sea animals have suckers which help them hold on to other larger animals.*

A125 *nouns* : **special parts of different creatures** [C]

wing one of usu two organs by which a bird, bat, or insect flies: *If pigs had wings, they would fly.* [⇒ pictures at A61, A74]

tail the movable part extending from the backbone at the back or end of the body of many animals and birds: *She cut off the heads and tails of the fish. That bird has lost its tail (feathers).* [⇒ pictures at A50, A51, A58, A74, A91, A100]

brush the thick hairy tail of a fox

fin 1 one of those parts of a fish which can be moved to help it to swim **2** (*fig*) anything shaped or used like a fin: *an aeroplane's tail-fin* [⇒ picture at A100]

flipper the limb of some of the larger sea animals, which is flat for use in swimming [⇒ picture at A58]

A126 *nouns* : **the skin, hair, and related parts of different creatures**

[ALSO ⇒ B50–51, H88]

skin 1 [U] the smooth outer covering of the body of animals, in which hair may grow **2** [C] the whole skin with hair, fur, etc, which has been cut off an animal: *He collected a large number of animal skins.* **-skin** [*comb form*] the skin of that particular creature: *bearskin, sheepskin, crocodile skin,* etc

hide 1 [C] an animal's skin, etc, esp if it is thick or rough **2** [U; C] the material of such a hide when it is used for making things: *The bag was made of hide. The material is cowhide.*

pelt [C] **1** the skin of a dead animal **a** with the fur or hair still on it **b** with the fur or hair removed, ready to be prepared as leather **2** the fur or hair of a living animal: *The dog had a fine silky pelt.*

hair 1 [C] a fine threadlike growth from the skin of animals; a similar growth on certain plants **2** [U] such hairs collectively **hairy** [Wa1;B]

covered in hair: *Monkeys are hairy animals.*
shaggy [Wa1;B] having a lot of rough thick hair: *The field was full of shaggy cattle.*
bristle [C; U] stiff hair: *The boar* (= male pig) *has bristles along its back. Paint brushes are made of boar's bristle.*
fur 1 [U] thick hair which covers such animals as rabbits, bears, and cats: *That cat has beautiful fur.* **2** [C; U] an animal skin with fur on it: *He sold them some furs. What kind of fur is that? She bought a fur coat. What a lovely fox fur.*
furry [Wa1;B] like or covered with fur: *She likes small furry animals.*
fleece [C] **1** the whole covering of a sheep or similar animal: *That sheep has a very thick fleece.* **2** the whole skin cut from such an animal: *These are very fine fleeces. The rug is made from the fleece of a goat.* **fleecy** [Wa1;B] like or covered with a fleece: *These sheep are very fleecy. She bought a pair of gloves with a fleecy lining.*
wool [U; C] the soft hair of sheep and similar animals **woolly** [Wa1;B] like or covered with wool
feather [C] one of the many parts of the covering which grows on a bird's body, each of

which has a stiff rod-like piece in the middle, with soft hair-like material growing from it on each side [⇒ picture at A74] **feathered** [Wa5;B] covered with or having feathers: *Most birds are feathered creatures.* **feathery** [Wa5;B] like feathers: *Ferns* [⇒ A139] *are feathery plants.*
plumage [U] the mass of a bird's feathers: *Some birds have beautiful plumage.*
shell 1 [C] the hard outer covering of, or on the back of, some animals: *Shellfish are so named because of their shells. A tortoise has a shell covering its back.* **2** [U] the material a shell is made of
scale [C] one of the small thin, usu hard plates of material which cover the bodies of many fish and reptiles **scaly** [Wa1;B] like or covered with scales: *Crocodiles are scaly animals.*
spine *also* **prickle** [C] one of the many sharp needle-like parts of some animals: *Hedgehogs are covered with a mass of spines/prickles.*
quill [C] **1** a long sharp stiff spine: *Porcupines have a mass of quills on their backs.* **2** *also* **quill feather** a large wing or tail feather: *People wrote with quills before metal pen nibs were invented.*

A127 *nouns* : **marks on animals** [C]

spot one of any number of small, usu round marks on the skin of an animal, usu darker than the rest of the skin: *Leopards have spots.* **spotted** [B] covered with spots: *The jaguar is a large spotted cat.*

stripe a long narrow band, usu of a darker colour than the rest of the skin: *Tigers have stripes.* **striped** [B] covered with stripes: *The tiger is a large striped cat.*

A128 *nouns* : **parts of a female animal where milk can be got by the young** [C]

[ALSO ⇒ B31 BREAST]

udder the round bag on a cow, goat, or similar animal from which the milk comes: *The cow's udder was painfully full.* [⇒ picture at A52]
teat a nipple [⇒ B31] or the part which serves

the same purpose on a female animal: *He squeezed milk from the sheep's teats.*
dug the udder or teat of a female animal

Kinds and parts of plants

A130 *nouns* : **parts of plants**

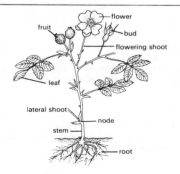
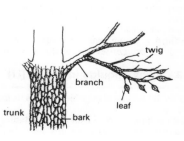

stem [C] **1** the part of a plant coming up from the roots **2** the part of a leaf, flower, or fruit that joins it to a main stalk or twig **-stemmed** [*comb form*] having a stem of a certain kind: *long-stemmed, thick-stemmed,* etc

stalk [C] **1** a stem, esp if large or long **2** a part of any plant which supports a flower or flowers but is not woody

bulb [C] a thick almost round base of a plant below the ground that sends roots downwards and leaves, etc, upwards: *Onions and lilies grow from bulbs.* **bulbous** [B] shaped like, having, or growing from such a bulb: *He has a bulbous nose.* **-ly** [adv] **-ness** [U]

root [C] the part of a plant which is normally under the soil and which draws water and minerals from it: *He pulled the plant up by its roots.*

leaf [C] a part of a plant, usu green and flat, which grows from the stem or branches of a plant: *In autumn the leaves fall from most trees.* **come into leaf** to grow leaves: *In spring the trees will come into leaf again.*

blade [C] a flat long narrow leaf, esp of grass and similar plants

needle [C] a very thin pointed leaf, esp of the pine tree [⇒ A156]: *The ground was covered in pine needles.*

spine *also* **prickle** [C] one of the many sharp needle-like parts of some plants: *Most cactuses* [⇒ A139] *have spines on them.*

trunk [C] the main stem of a tree

bark 1 [U] the tough outer covering of a tree **2** [T1] **a** to take the bark off: *The boys barked several trees badly.* **b** (*fig*) to take the skin off: *She barked her shins* [⇒ B43] *on the sharp metal.*

branch [C] **1** a large long growth from the trunk of a tree, which divides into further growths: *The great branches of the tree spread out over his head.*

limb [C] *esp lit & fml* a (large) branch of a tree

twig [C] a small branch

twiglet [C] a small twig

stump [C] **1** the short part of a tree left above the ground after it has been cut down, fallen over, etc **2** any short remaining part of something which used to be long: *the stump of a pencil; the stump of an arm*

A131 *nouns, etc* : **the flower on plants**

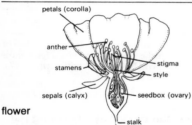

petals (corolla)

anther

stamens

stigma

style

sepals (calyx)

seedbox (ovary)

flower

stalk

flower [C] **1** that part of a plant, often beautiful, which produces seeds **2** (*fig*) the best part; the most perfect: *She was in the flower of her youth. The flower of the nation's young men died in that battle.* **in flower** having the flowers open: *The trees are in flower.*

petal [C] one of the leaf-like divisions of a flower: *The petals fell off one by one.*

bud 1 [C] a leaf, flower, or branch when it is just

beginning to grow **2** [C] a partly opened flower **3** [I∅] to begin to have buds: *The trees are budding; spring is here.* **in bud** having or sending out buds: *The trees are all in bud.*

bloom 1 [C] a flower, esp a large one; a flower grown esp to be looked at: *What beautiful blooms!* **2** [I∅] to be in flower or bear flowers: *The flowers are blooming.* **3** [I∅] (*fig*) to look well and beautiful: *Mary was blooming after her week in the country.* **in bloom** flowering: *The gardens are now in (full) bloom.*

blossom 1 [C] a flower, esp of a fruit tree: *The blossoms don't last long.* **2** [U] the mass of blossoms on a tree: *The apple blossom is beautiful this year.* **3** [I∅] to come into flower: *The trees have blossomed.* (*fig*) *His plans are blossoming beautifully.* **in blossom** blossoming: *The trees are all in blossom.*

seedbox [C] the part of a plant which is a container for seeds

A132 *nouns* : **new growth in plants** [C]

shoot a new growth from (a part of) a plant, esp a young stem and leaves, but also a branch on a tree: *Shoots started coming out on the rose bushes. There's a new shoot coming up; the plant isn't dead.*

seedling a young plant recently grown from seed: *He bought several seedlings; he doesn't*

like growing plants from seed himself.

sapling a young tree: *He planted saplings at the bottom of his garden.*

sprout a new growth from a plant, such as a bud or shoot

sucker a shoot growing out through the ground from the root or lower stem of a plant

A133 *nouns* : **liquids in plants** [U]

sap the liquid in a plant which carries its food to all parts

juice the liquid part of fruit and vegetables: *The oranges are full of juice this year.* [⇒ E61

DRINKS] **juicy** [Wa1; B] **1** having a lot of juice: *a juicy orange* **2** (*fig*) interesting: *some juicy information* **-iness** [U]

A134 *nouns etc* : **fruit and seed**

larger	fruit
smaller	berry
harder	nut
small & hard	seed

fruit [U; C] **1** the part of a plant in which the seed is developed: *Grapes are the fruit of the vine.* **2** the part of certain trees and bushes with the seed(s) surrounded by a fleshy substance, which can be eaten: *Apples are the fruit of the apple tree.* **3** the eatable produce of such plants generally: *She went to the shop and bought some fruit: apples, pears, and bananas. Various fruits can grow in this climate.* [⇒ A150] **4** [*usu pl*] (*fig*) good results: *It's time to enjoy the fruits of your success.* **fruity** [Wa1; B] *usu apprec* (tasting or smelling) like fruit: *The medicine had a fruity taste.*

berry [C] **1** a small soft fruit, esp one that can be eaten: *The birds ate the berries on the bushes.* [⇒ A154] **2** also **bean** the dry seed of some plants, such as coffee

nut [C] **1** a dry fruit with one or more seeds inside a hard covering: *He picked some nuts and berries off the trees.* **2** the seed inside, which is eaten: *The chocolate had nuts in it.* [⇒ A153]

seed [C] the part of a plant which is able to develop into a new plant: *He planted the seeds. The birds were eating all the seeds. He chewed the fruit, seeds and all. She likes eating melon seeds.*

grain [C] a seed of any cereal plant, esp as food: *He gave the beggar some grains of rice.* [⇒ A152 CEREALS]

cone [C] the fruit of a pine, fir, or other coniferous tree which has several partly separate pieces laid over each other, each containing a seed: [⇒ A135 CONIFERS, A156 PINE, FIR] *Fir cones open out in dry weather, letting the seeds out.*

pod 1 [C] a long narrow seed container of various plants, esp beans and peas: a *peapod* [⇒ picture at A151] **2** [I0 (*up*)] (of bean plants, peas, etc) to produce pods: *The beans are beginning to pod (up).*

stone [C] a single hard seed inside some fruits: *Cherries have stones in them.* [⇒ A150 CHERRY]

kernel [C] **1** the softer inside, usu eatable, part of a nut; the inside part of a fruit stone **2** (*fig*) the important or main part of something, often surrounded by unimportant or untrue matter: *He told a number of lies, but there was a kernel of truth in his story.*

cob [C] **1** also **corncob** the large hard central part of an ear of corn **2** a type of large nut, esp one from the hazel tree

shell [C] the hard covering of a nut, egg, or some seeds: *He cracked the shell of the nut with his teeth.*

husk [C] **1** the dry outer covering of some fruits and seeds, esp of grain **2** (*fig*) the useless outside part of anything

rind [C] the thick, usu rough, sometimes hard outer covering of certain fruits, esp of the melon and lemon [⇒ A150]

peel [U; C] the outer covering of those fruits and vegetables which people usu pull off before eating: *She removed the peel from the oranges. Put the orange and apple peel in the dustbin.*

peelings [P] thin lengths of skin peeled from fruit and vegetables: *The sink was full of potato peelings.*

skin [U; C] the outer covering of such fruits as the banana; the peel, rind, husk, etc, generally

A135 *nouns, etc* : **larger plants**

larger	tree
smaller	bush

tree [C] a plant which lives for many years, grows high, and has a trunk of wood and branches, with leaves, growing out from the top of the trunk: *Tall trees grew beside the house. Trees are of two kinds—deciduous and coniferous. Deciduous trees lose their leaves in autumn, but conifers are generally evergreen.* [⇒ A155–6]

conifer [C] any of various types of trees which bear cones [⇒ A134 CONE, A156]

evergreen 1 [C] a tree whose leaves or needles remain on the tree and stay green all the year round **2** [Wa5; B] (of conifers etc) always having leaves

deciduous tree [C] any of various types of trees which lose their leaves in autumn and grow new leaves in spring [⇒ A155]

bush [C *often in comb*] a plant smaller than a tree, with no trunk but a number of thinner woody stems growing up from near the ground: *The ground near the river was covered with thick bushes. There were thorn bushes on the hillside.* [⇒ A157]

shrub [C] a low bush with a number of woody stems: *He planted a number of flowering shrubs in the garden.*

A136 nouns, etc : general words for plants

flower-[C] a plant grown for the beauty of its flowers: *The flowers in his garden are always lovely at this time of year.* [⇒ A158] **flowery** [Wa2;B] **1** *infml* of, concerning, or like flowers: *She wore a flowery dress.* **2** (*fig*) *often deprec* using too many words: *His speeches are too flowery.* **floral** [Wa5;B] *tech* of, with, concerning, or like flowers: *What a beautiful floral arrangement!*

weed 1 [C] a wild plant growing where someone does not want it: *The garden was full of weeds.* **2** [T1] to take the weeds out of (a garden, the ground, etc): *She was busy weeding the garden.* **weed out** [v adv T1] (*esp fig*) to remove as if by taking out weeds: *They tried to weed out from the group everyone who disagreed with them.*

herb [C] any one of several kinds of low plant which die down at the end of the growing season, esp one whose leaves or seeds are used in medicine or in adding to the taste of food

herbal [Wa5;B] of or concerning herbs (and also medicinal) **-ly** [adv] **herbaceous** [Wa5;B] *tech* (of plants) having stems that are not woody

vegetable 1 [C] a plant that is grown for food, usu to be eaten with or as the main part of a meal and usu of a type which grows in or near the ground: *Get some vegetables from the garden—some potatoes, cabbages, and beans.* [⇒ A151] **2** [U] plant life: *Is the object animal, vegetable, or mineral?* **veg** [Wn3;C;U] *esp BrE infml abbrev* vegetables: *meat and two veg*

greens [P]**1** *esp BrE* green leafy vegetables: *Cabbages and lettuces* [⇒ A151] *are greens.* **2** *AmE* leaves and branches used for ornament, esp at Christmas

pulse 1 [U] the seeds of such plants as beans, peas, and lentils [⇒ A151] used as a food **2** [C *usu pl*] any plant from which these are obtained

A137 nouns : collective words for many plants together

vegetation [U] **1** plant life in general, usu when growing: *The hillside was covered in thick vegetation.* **2** all the plants in a particular place: *The vegetation of central Africa is mainly tropical.*

foliage [U] leaves in general, esp when growing: *That tree has thick foliage.*

greenery [U] green foliage; green plants, esp when used as ornaments

shrubbery 1 [U] shrubs collectively: *It's difficult to get into that part of the garden because of all that shrubbery.* **2** [C] a (part of a) garden planted with shrubs or bushes: *He was sitting on a seat in the shrubbery.*

undergrowth [U] bushes, tall plants, etc, smaller than the trees around them: *It was difficult to travel fast through the undergrowth.*

A138 nouns, etc : kinds of grasses and similar plants

grass

grass 1 [U] various kinds of common low-growing green plants whose blades and stems are eaten by sheep, cows, etc, on hills and in fields **2** [U] land covered by grass [⇒ D52 LAWN]: *Don't walk on the grass.* **3** [C] any of various green plants with tall straight stems and flat blades: *The children hid behind some tall grasses.* **4** [T1] to cover (land) with grass: *They grassed the whole area.*

turf 1 [U] (pieces of) earth thickly covered with (esp short) grass **2** [T1] to lay turf on; cover with turf

cereal [C *usu pl*] any kind of cultivated grass used for food; plants which are grown to produce grain: *They grow cereals on that farm. Maize and barley are cereal crops.* [⇒ A152]

straw 1 [C] a dry cut stalk of corn **2** [C] a tube like this for drinking with: *The child drank his milk through a straw.* **3** [U] dry cut stalks of corn: *Straw is used as bedding for animals like horses. They made a roof of straw for the house.*

bamboo [C; U] a tall plant of the grass family, found esp in tropical areas with hard hollow pointed stems, of which some parts can be eaten when young [⇒ H72]

cane 1 [C; U] the hard smooth hollow stem of certain plants (such as tall grasses) **2** [C] the stem of certain fruit-producing plants that grow straight from the root [⇒ H72]

reed [C] a tall grass-like plant that grows in wet places

A139 *nouns* : ferns, heather, and other special plants

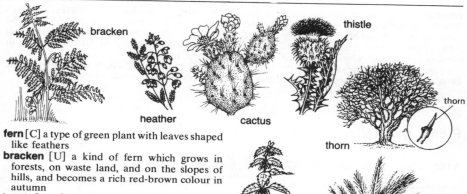

bracken

thistle

thorn

heather

cactus

thorn

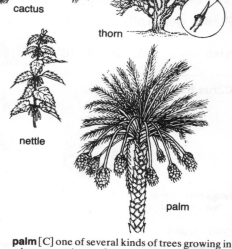

nettle

palm

fern [C] a type of green plant with leaves shaped like feathers

bracken [U] a kind of fern which grows in forests, on waste land, and on the slopes of hills, and becomes a rich red-brown colour in autumn

heath [C; U] any one of several kinds of low evergreen shrubs with small flowers [⇨ A135 EVERGREEN]

heather [U; C] a plant which grows on hills and has many small purple, pink, or white flowers: *The hillsides of Scotland are covered in heather.*

thistle [C; U] a type of plant with many sharp prickles or spines [⇨ A130]

nettle [C] a type of plant that stings when touched

thorn 1 [C; U] any kind of plant with sharp spines or prickles growing from it: *Be careful of that thorn bush.* 2 [C] such a sharp spine or prickle: *He got a thorn in his finger when he touched the plant.*

cactus [C] any of a number of desert plants protected by sharp prickles [⇨ A130] with thick fleshy stems and leaves

palm [C] one of several kinds of trees growing in hot countries and having the branches and leaves growing at the top: *Some palm trees produce dates, while others produce coconuts.*

A140 *nouns* : lichens, fungi, and similar plants

mushroom

toadstool

seaweed

lichen [U; C] a dry-looking greyish, greenish, or yellowish flat spreading plant that covers the surface of stones and trees

moss [U; C] any of several kinds of small green or yellow plants growing in thick masses on wet surfaces: *There were different mosses on the stones.*

fungus [U; C] a type of plant with no leaves, flower, or green colouring, which feeds on other plants or dead matter

mushroom [C] any one of several kinds of fast-growing fungus, some of which can be eaten

toadstool [C] any one of several kinds of fungus, some of which are poisonous

mould *BrE,* **mold** *AmE* [C; U] any of several kinds of woolly or furry fungus which grow on slightly wet surfaces such as leather, cheese, or objects left in warm wet places **mouldy** [Wa1]: *Bread goes mouldy if you leave it in the larder too long.*

mildew [U] a usu destructive growth of tiny fungi which forms on plants, leather, food, etc, in warm wet conditions

plankton [U] the forms of very small plant and animal life that live in the sea or in lakes, etc, just below the surface of the water

seaweed [U; C] any of various plants growing in or near the sea, usu dark green with long stems

A141 *nouns* : **climbing plants**

creeper [C; U] any of various plants which climb up surfaces (esp walls) or along the ground: *My foot got caught in a creeper and I fell. Virginia creeper grew on the wall.*

climber [C] a plant which climbs usu up and around other plants or sticks

liana *also* **liane** [C] a woody plant that climbs round trees, up walls, etc, in tropical countries

vine [C] **1** a climbing plant whose fruit is the grape **2** any plant with long thin stems that spread along the ground, like the melon, or climbs, like peas

ivy [U] an evergreen climbing plant with dark green shiny leaves [⇨ A135 EVERGREEN]

Plants generally

A150 *nouns* : **kinds of fruits** [C]
[⇨ A134 DEFINITION]

Citrus fruits

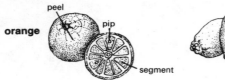

orange — peel, pip, segment

lemons

tangerine a small sweet orange with a loose skin that comes off easily

grapefruit [Wn2] a large round yellow fruit, with a thick skin like an orange but a more acid taste

Other fruits

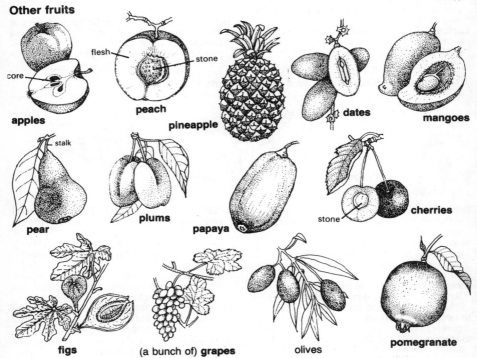

apples — core, flesh

peach — stone

pineapple

dates

mangoes

pear — stalk

plums

papaya

cherries — stone

figs

(a bunch of) grapes

olives

pomegranate

apricot a round soft pleasant-tasting but slightly sour fruit with a furry outside like a peach and a single large stone. It is orange or yellow and red

greengage a soft juicy greenish-yellow kind of plum

prune a type of dried fruit, esp a plum, usu gently boiled until soft and swollen before eating

currant a small dried grape, used esp in cooking

sultana a dried grape, larger and lighter in colour than a currant, used esp in cooking

raisin a large dark dried grape, usu with seeds in: *She baked a cake with sultanas, raisins, and currants in it.*

olive the fruit of the olive tree, used for its oil and as a food: *We cooked the vegetables in olive oil.*

A151 *nouns* : **kinds of vegetables**

[⇨ A136 DEFINITION]

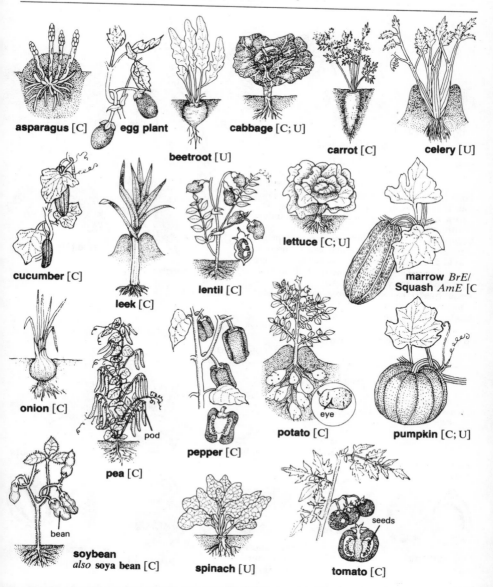

asparagus [C] **egg plant**

beetroot [U]

cabbage [C; U]

carrot [C]

celery [U]

cucumber [C]

leek [C]

lentil [C]

lettuce [C; U]

marrow *BrE*/ **Squash** *AmE* [C

onion [C]

pod

pea [C]

pepper [C]

eye

potato [C]

pumpkin [C; U]

bean

soybean *also* **soya bean** [C]

spinach [U]

seeds

tomato [C]

artichoke (globe artichoke) [C]

radish [C]

rhubarb [U]

turnip [C]

A152 nouns : kinds of cereal

[⇨ A138 DEFINITION]

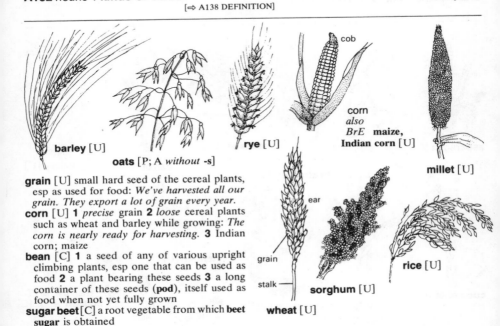

barley [U]

oats [P; A without -s]

rye [U]

cob

corn
also
BrE **maize,**
Indian corn [U]

millet [U]

ear

grain

stalk

wheat [U]

sorghum [U]

rice [U]

grain [U] small hard seed of the cereal plants, esp as used for food: *We've harvested all our grain. They export a lot of grain every year.*

corn [U] **1** *precise* grain **2** *loose* cereal plants such as wheat and barley while growing: *The corn is nearly ready for harvesting.* **3** Indian corn; maize

bean [C] **1** a seed of any of various upright climbing plants, esp one that can be used as food **2** a plant bearing these seeds **3** a long container of these seeds (**pod**), itself used as food when not yet fully grown

sugar beet [C] a root vegetable from which **beet sugar** is obtained

beet [C] **1** a sugar beet **2** *AmE* a beetroot

A153 nouns : kinds of nuts [C]

[⇨ A134 DEFINITION]

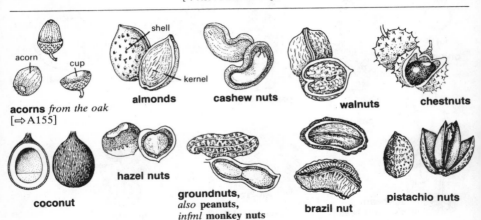

acorn

cup

acorns *from the oak*
[⇨A155]

shell

kernel

almonds

cashew nuts

walnuts

chestnuts

coconut

hazel nuts

groundnuts,
also **peanuts,**
infml **monkey nuts**

brazil nut

pistachio nuts

A154 nouns : **kinds of berries** [C]

[⇨ A134 DEFINITION]

blackberries
also **bramble**

cranberries

elderberries

strawberries

gooseberries

blackcurrants

raspberries

bilberry (the fruit of) a low North European bush growing on hillsides and in high woods
blueberry (the fruit of) any of several types of small North American bush like the bilberry
loganberry a type of red berry from a plant which is half blackberry and half raspberry

A155 nouns : **common kinds of deciduous trees** [C]

[⇨ A135 DEFINITION]

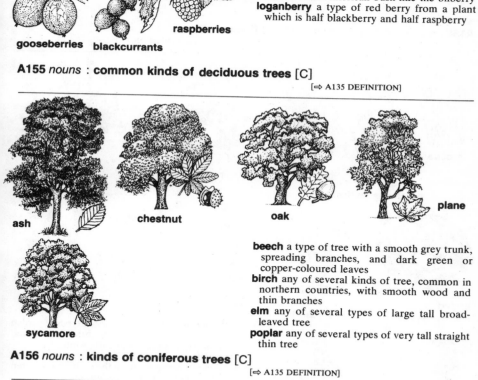

ash

chestnut

oak

plane

sycamore

beech a type of tree with a smooth grey trunk, spreading branches, and dark green or copper-coloured leaves
birch any of several kinds of tree, common in northern countries, with smooth wood and thin branches
elm any of several types of large tall broad-leaved tree
poplar any of several types of very tall straight thin tree

A156 nouns : **kinds of coniferous trees** [C]

[⇨ A135 DEFINITION]

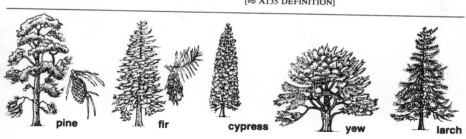

pine

fir

cypress

yew

larch

spruce any of about 40 kinds of ornamental and wood-producing trees found in colder northern countries and having short needle-shaped leaves that grow singly around the branches

redwood any of several types of tall coniferous trees that grow in California

A157 *nouns* : **some common kinds of smaller trees and bushes**

[⇨ A135 DEFINITION]

holly [U; C] a type of small tree with dark green shiny prickly leaves and red berries

hawthorn *also* **may** [C; U] a type of small tree with white or red flowers which often grows beside country roads, and has red berries in autumn

broom [U] a type of large bushy plant with yellow flowers that grows on sandy or waste land

gorse [U] a type of bush with prickles and bright yellow flowers, which grows wild

laurel [C; U] a type of small tree with smooth shiny leaves that do not fall in winter

bay [C; U] any of several trees like the laurel, whose leaves are sweet-smelling when crushed, and may be used in cooking

A158 *nouns* : **some common kinds of flowers** [C]

[⇨ A136 DEFINITION]

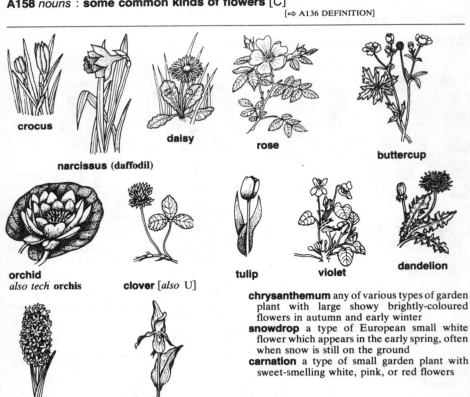

crocus

narcissus (daffodil)

daisy

rose

buttercup

orchid
also tech **orchis**

clover [*also* U]

tulip

violet

dandelion

hyacinth

lily

chrysanthemum any of various types of garden plant with large showy brightly-coloured flowers in autumn and early winter

snowdrop a type of European small white flower which appears in the early spring, often when snow is still on the ground

carnation a type of small garden plant with sweet-smelling white, pink, or red flowers

B

The body, its functions and welfare

The body generally

B1 nouns : the body itself

body [C] **1** the whole of a person or animal, esp as opposed to the soul or mind: *The body is the physical structure* [⇒ H116] *of any living thing. We know that the body exists but·we cannot prove that the soul exists.* [⇒ C324 SOUL, ⇒ G1 MIND] **2** this without the head or limbs: *He was wounded in the leg, not the body.* **3** (*fig*) a large number or amount : *a body of men/water/information* **4** (*fig*) an object: *The sun and moon are heavenly bodies.* [⇒ L2]

physique [C] the form and character of a human body: *That man has a powerful physique; look at his muscles. Her physique is excellent for her age.*

build [C; U] the way in which a body, esp of a man, is built; the shape and size, esp of the human body: *That young man has a very good build. We are both of the same build.*

constitution [C] the general condition of the body, esp a person's ability to keep off disease or tiredness: *He has a healthy constitution; he should live for many years yet.*

figure [C] the human form, esp in its general appearance and what it suggests: *That girl has a beautiful figure. He is a fine figure of a man. They saw some dark figures among the trees. She says she has lost her figure since having her second child* (= lost the shape which she liked best).

person [C; *of* U] a living human body or its outward appearance: *He put his person between the little girl and the mad dog. The dead man had no money on his person. She was small and neat of person.* **in person** bodily, physically: *I can't attend the meeting in person* (= myself, personally), *but I am sending someone to speak for me.*

B2 adjectives : the body itself [Wa5]

bodily **1** [A] of or in the (human) body: *They supply all our bodily needs. He was the victim of violent bodily assault.* **2** [adv] in a body; as a whole: *He lifted her bodily out of the car.*

physical [B] of or concerning the body: *He is a man of great physical strength. Food is one of our physical needs.* **non-** [neg] **-ly** [adv]

constitutional [B] of or concerning the human constitution **-ly** [adv]

organic [B] **1** of an organ or organs [⇒ B4] of the body: *The wound is in the flesh only; there is no organic damage.* **2** having bodily organs: *All organic creatures need oxygen in order to live.* **3** of, concerning, or obtained from living creatures: *Organic chemistry deals with the nature and products of animal and plant bodies.* **in-** [neg] **-ally** [adv]

B3 nouns : kinds of dead bodies

body [C] a dead person: *There was a body lying in the hall, the body of a middle-aged man. Bodies lay all over the battlefield.*

corpse [C] the dead body of a human being, usu stiff or dead for some time: *A corpse lay uncovered on the hospital table. The corpse of a child was found on the beach this morning.*

cadaver [C] a corpse, esp as used in medical experiments **cadaverous** [B] like a cadaver: *He had a thin, cadaverous face.*

carcass, carcase [C] **1** the dead body of an animal, esp one prepared for cutting up as meat: *Several sheep carcasses hung up in the butcher's shop.* **2** *deprec often humor* a human body: *Come on, move your carcass, you lazy devil!*

remains [P] *often fml* the decaying corpse or bones of a human being or animal: *His remains lie in a local churchyard. They found the remains of a man and some animals in that cave.*

carrion [U] dead and decaying flesh: *Birds such as crows eat carrion.*

B4 nouns : substances of the body

flesh [U] **1** the soft material which covers the bones of human beings and animals, including fat and muscle: *The lion had eaten the flesh off the dead animal's leg. He had a flesh wound; no organs were damaged.* **2** any similar material in parts of fruit, nuts, etc

meat [U] *infml often humor* flesh: *Poor man,*

40

he's very thin; there's hardly any meat on his bones. [⇒ E31 MEAT AS FOOD]

membrane [C] a thin covering or connection inside an animal, plant, etc: *There is a fine elastic membrane inside the shell of an egg.*

tissue [U; C] cells of the body in a mass, esp of one kind and soft: *The body is made up of various tissues such as muscle tissue and nerve tissue.*

bone 1 [C] one of the hard parts of the body, which protect the organs within, and round which are the flesh and skin: *He broke a bone in his leg.* **2** [U] the material from which these parts are made: *Some ornaments are made of bone.*

cartilage [U; C] a strong white tissue attached to the joints [⇒ B11]: *He damaged a cartilage in his knee.*

gristle [U] *not tech* cartilage

organ [C] a part of a living creature, esp an animal, that has a special purpose: *The heart is one of the body's most important organs.*

gland [C] one of the organs of the body which produce a liquid, either to be poured out of the body or into the bloodstream: *sex glands* **glandular** [Wa5;B] of or concerning glands

muscle [C; U] (any of the pieces of) material in the body which can tighten to produce movement, esp bending of the joints: *He has well-developed muscles and can lift heavy weights. The muscles in her right arm were badly damaged in a car crash, and she can't move it properly. He has a pain in the muscle of his upper arm.* **muscular** [B] **1** [Wa5] of or concerning muscles: *muscular tissue* **2** having big muscles: *a muscular man*

sinew 1 *also* **tendon** [C; U] a strong cord in the body connecting a muscle to a bone **2** [C usu pl; U] (*fig*) means of strength; part of a powerful framework: *the strong sinew(s) of our national defence* **sinewy** [B] of, concerning, or like a sinew

nerve [C] one of the threadlike pieces of material or bands of these in the body which carry messages to and from the brain so that sensations can be felt and movement made in each part of the body: *The brain is the nerve centre of the body.* **nervous** [Wa5;A] *tech* of or connected with the nerves: *the nervous system*

fat [C; U] (a kind of) oily white or yellow substance found in animal bodies: *He has too much fat on him; he needs to go on a diet* [⇒ E1]. *This meat has a lot of fat on it; I want leaner meat. Fat tissue helps to keep animals warm in cold climates.* **fatty** [B] of, concerning, or like fat

marrow [U] the soft fatty substance inside bones

limb [C] *esp lit & fml* a leg or arm of a human being or animal: *He lost a limb in the war.*

The body : overall

B10 *nouns* : male and female bodies

SEE FACING PAGE

B11 *nouns* : bone structures

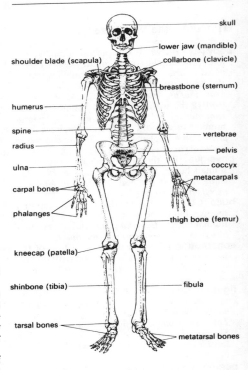

skeleton

skeleton [C] **1** the framework of all the bones in a human or animal body; the bones of a human or animal in the position which they had in life **2** a set of these bones, usu kept for medical purposes, forming a fleshless figure held together in the normal position they would take when inside the body **skeletal** [Wa5;B] of, concerning, or like a skeleton

skull [C] **1** the bony framework of a human or animal head: *They dug up the skull and some bones of a prehistoric man.* **2** the figure or outline of this framework: *A skull was painted on the wall.* **3** the bone which covers the brain at the top and back of the head: *He was struck a severe blow on the skull.*

death's head [C] skull (def 2): *The bottle was marked poison with a death's head on the label.*

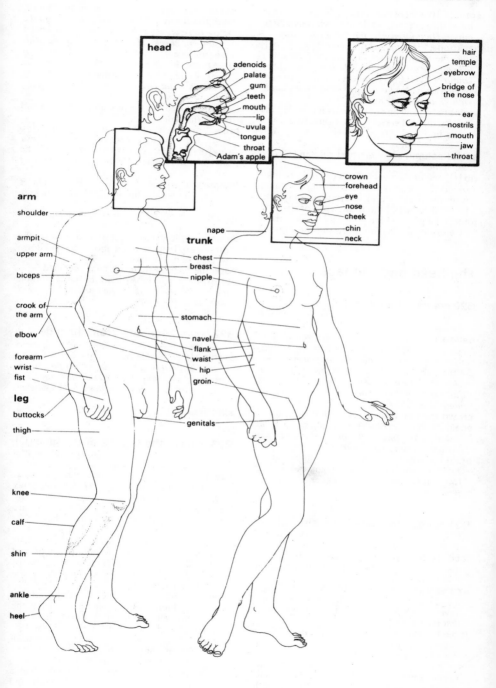

head

adenoids
palate
gum
teeth
mouth
lip
uvula
tongue
throat
Adam's apple

hair
temple
eyebrow
bridge of
the nose
ear
nostrils
mouth
jaw
throat

crown
forehead
eye
nose
cheek
chin
neck

nape

trunk

arm

shoulder

armpit
upper arm
biceps

crook of
the arm
elbow

forearm
wrist
fist

leg

buttocks
thigh

knee

calf

shin

ankle

heel

chest
breast
nipple

stomach

navel
flank
waist
hip
groin

genitals

spine [C] the set of bones down the centre of the back, through the middle of which runs a large nerve: *He injured his spine in a car crash.*

backbone 1 [C] *not fml* the spine **2** [*the* R (*of*)] (*fig*) the main support of a group, plan, etc: *I tell you, the small farmer is the backbone of this country!* **3** [U] (*fig*) firmness of mind; strength of character: *No backbone – that's the trouble with young people today!*

vertebra [C] any one of the parts into which the spine is divided **vertebrate** [C] a creature with a spine **in-** [neg] (*fig*): *Frogs are vertebrates; worms are invertebrates.*

spinal column *also* **vertebral column** [C] *tech* the spine

rib [C] one of the twelve pairs of bones running round the chest of a human being or animal from the backbone to where they join at the front **rib cage** [C] the framework of the ribs

joint [C] a place where bones join, usu capable of movement: *His joints are stiff; he's getting old.*

The head and the face

B20 *nouns* : **the head** [C]
[⇨ PICTURE AT B10]

head 1 the part of the body which contains the eyes, ears, nose, mouth, and brain: *He was injured in the head, not the body/arm/leg, etc.* **2** the part of the head above and behind the eyes: *My head aches.* **3** *infml* the mind or brain: *Can't you get it into your head that we lost the game?* [⇨ G1 MIND]

crown the rounded top of the human head

scalp the skin (and hair) of the top of the head, excluding the face: *Rub your scalp hard when you are washing your hair.*

brain the organ of the body in the upper part of the head which controls thought and feeling: *The brain is the centre of higher nervous activity.*

B21 *nouns* : **the face generally** [C]
[⇨ PICTURE AT B10]

face the front part of the head, with the eyes, nose, and mouth: *He had a surprised expression on his face.*

expression the way a person's face looks, esp at a particular time: *There was an expression of anger on his face. I knew by their expressions that they didn't believe his story.*

look 1 *infml* expression: *There was a look of anger on her face.* **2** a way of looking: *She gave him an angry look.*

jaw 1 one of the two bony parts of the face (upper and lower jaws) in which the teeth are set: *The boxer's jaw was hurt in the fight.* **2** the appearance of the lower jaw: *He said that a strong square jaw was a sign of firm character.*

chin the front part of the face below the mouth

cheek the fleshy part on each side of the face below the eye, esp in human beings: *He kissed her on the cheek. Her cheeks went red with embarrassment.*

cheekbone 1 the bone which lies under the cheek. **2** the line of this bone as seen shaping the cheek: *That girl has a lovely face with very high cheekbones.*

forehead the part of the face above the eyes and below the hair

brow 1 the forehead **2** [*usu pl*] an eyebrow [⇨ B24]: *His brows went up in surprise.* **3** [*usu sing*] (*fig*) the upper part of a slope on a hill; the edge of a steep place: *He went over the brow of the hill.*

temple [*usu pl*] one of the two rather flat places on each side of the forehead: *He is going grey at the temples.*

throat the front of the neck: *A beautiful necklace hung round her throat.*

Adam's apple the part that sticks forward in the throat, esp in men, which moves up and down when a person speaks

nape the back of the neck near the head

scruff [*the* S *of the neck*] *infml* the nape: *He took the boy by the scruff of the neck and dragged him out of the room.*

B22 *nouns* : **the face from the side**

profile 1 [C; U] a side view of someone's head or face: *She prefers to have her left profile photographed; she says that's her better side.* **2** a drawing of a profile: *He does profiles better than full face.*

side view [C] *infml* a profile

B23 *nouns* : **the organs of the face** [C]
[⇨ PICTURE AT B10]

eye the organ of sight, of which there are two at the front of the human head: *He hurt one of his eyes in a car crash.*

ear 1 the organ of hearing, of which there are two, one on each side of the human head: *The ear has two parts, the inner and outer ear. You needn't shout into my ear like that; I can hear you perfectly well.* **2** the outer part of that organ **3** [S9] (*fig*) sympathetic attention or notice: *John will arrange everything; he has the ear of the President.*

nose that part of the face above the mouth, which in human beings stands out from the face, through which air is drawn in to be breathed, and which is the organ of smell

nostril either of the two openings at the end of the nose, through which air is drawn

bridge the upper bony part of the nose

mouth the opening on the face through which a human being may take food into the body, and by which he or she makes sounds and may breathe

B24 *nouns & verbs* : **the eye in detail**

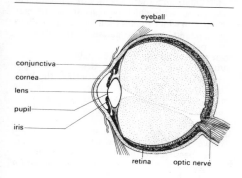

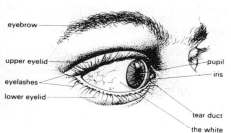

the eye

eyebrow [C] the line of hairs above each of the two human eyes: *He has very thick dark eyebrows; they make him look fierce.*

eyelid [C] one of the pieces of covering skin which can move down to close each eye: *Fish do not have eyelids and some creatures have more than one on each eye. He blinked his eyelids to clear his eyes.*

eyelash [C] one of the small hairs of which a number grow from the edge of each eyelid in humans and most hairy animals: *The eyelashes keep dust from the eyes. I have an eyelash in my eye; it's hurting my eye.*

eyeball [C] the whole of the eye, including the part inside the head, which forms a more or less round ball

pupil [C] the small black round opening which can grow larger or smaller in the middle of the coloured part of the eye, through which light passes

iris [C] the round coloured part of the eye which surrounds the pupil

white [C] the white part of the eye around the iris, which shows all the time in the human eye, but is usually hidden in animals: *The whites of his eyes were bloodshot from lack of sleep. The frightened horse showed the whites of its eyes.*

blink 1 [T1; I∅] to shut and open (the eyes) quickly, usu because of strong light, surprise, tears, etc: *She blinked (her eyes) in surprise.* **2** [I∅](*fig*) (of distant lights) to seem to be unsteady; seem to go rapidly on and off: *The ship's lights blinked at us across the water.* **3** [T1; I∅] *AmE* to wink **4** [C] an act of blinking: *The blink of an eye.*

wink 1 [T1; I∅] to shut and open (one eye) quickly, sometimes with quick slight movement of the head, to show friendliness, amusement, a shared secret, etc: *He winked his left eye. She winked at him and smiled.* **2** [C] an act of doing this: *He gave a friendly wink.*

B25 *nouns* : **kinds of noses** [C]

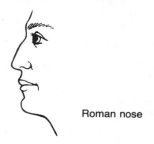

Roman nose

Roman nose a nose that curves out near the top at the bridge

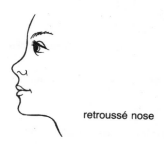

retroussé nose

retroussé nose a nose that is turned back at the lower end

snub nose

snub nose a nose that is short and flat with the end turned back

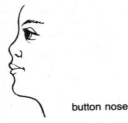

button nose

button nose a nose that is flat like a button

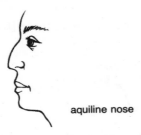

aquiline nose

aquiline nose a nose that is thin and curves gradually like the beak of an eagle [⇨ A78]

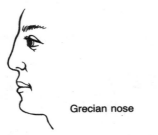

Grecian nose

Grecian nose a nose that comes down almost straight from the forehead

B26 *nouns* : **the mouth in detail** [C]
[⇨ PICTURE AT B10]

lip 1 one of the two edges of the mouth where the skin is delicate and reddish: *He kissed her on the lips.* **2** this area with the ordinary skin around it: *Hair grows on the top lip of many men.*

tooth one of the small hard bony objects growing in the upper and lower mouth, which are used for biting and tearing food: *One of my teeth hurts; I must go to the dentist soon.*

gum either of the two areas of firm pink flesh in which the teeth are fixed, at the top and bottom of the mouth: *The dentist said that the child had healthy gums.*

tongue the movable organ of taste, which moves food about in the mouth and onto the teeth and which human beings use in speech

palate the top part of the inside of the mouth **cleft palate** an unnatural crack or separation in the palate with which persons are sometimes born, and which makes their speech difficult to understand **hard/soft palate** the front/back of the palate

roof of the mouth *infml* the palate

uvula a small soft piece of flesh which hangs down from the top of the mouth at the back **uvular** [Wa5;B] **1** of, concerning, or like the uvula **2** (of sounds) produced by a movement of the uvula: *The /r/ sound in French is a uvular r.*

throat the passage from the back of the mouth down inside the neck, which divides to form other passages to the lungs and stomach: *The hot tea burnt his throat. She had a cold and a sore throat.* [⇨ B21]

gullet *also* **oesophagus** *tech* the passage for food from the mouth to the stomach

windpipe the passage for air from the nose and mouth to the lungs

larynx the hollow boxlike part at the upper end of the windpipe

vocal cords *also* **vocal chords** [P] either of the two pairs of folds in the larynx which produce the sound of the voice

pharynx the tube at the back of the mouth that leads from the back of the nose to the point where the gullet and the windpipe divide

tonsil [*usu pl*] one of the two small organs at the back of the throat which sometimes become diseased and have to be removed **tonsillitis** [U] disease of the tonsils

The trunk, arms, and legs

B30 *nouns* : **the main body** [C]
[ALSO ⇨ B1]

body the main part of a person or animal, without the head, arms, and legs: *He has spots on his body but not his face.*

trunk the main part of the body, apart from the head and limbs: *She has spots on her trunk but not her arms.*

torso the trunk, esp on a statue [⇨ I50]

chest the upper front part of the body which encloses the heart: *What a hairy chest he has! He hurt his chest muscles.*

B31 *nouns* : **the breast** [C]
[ALSO ⇨ A128]

breast 1 either of the two parts of a woman's body that produce milk, or the smaller parts on a man's body: *The baby was at its mother's breast.* **2** *lit* the upper front part of the body between the neck and the stomach: *The sleeper's breast was rising and falling.*

bosom 1 *genl* a woman's breasts: *That girl's got a big bosom. She held the child to her bosom.* (*esp lit*) *Her bosom heaved with violent emotion.* **2** *rarer* a breast (def 1): *Her bosoms were full of milk.*

bust 1 *euph* a woman's breasts and their general appearance: *She has a beautiful bust.* **2** a measurement round a woman's breasts and back: *Her bust measurement is 36 inches. She's 36 round the bust.* **3** the human head, shoulders, and chest, esp as shown in sculpture [⇒ I48]: *He collects busts of famous poets.*

tit, titty *sl* a breast

boobs [P] *sl* breasts

nipple one of two small areas of delicate skin which are reddish or brown and stand out from the breasts, through which a baby may suck milk from a woman

B32 *nouns* : **the back and shoulders**
[⇒ PICTURE AT B10]

back [C] the part of the body of a human or animal, down the middle of which the backbone runs

small of the back [*the* R] the base of the back, where it curves in

shoulder [C] **1** the joint at the top of the arm **2** the part of the body from the top of the arm to the neck or the top of the back: *The little boy sat on his father's shoulders. He carried the boys on/over his shoulders. His shoulders were bent by/with the weight of the boys.*

B33 *nouns* : **the buttocks** [C]
[⇒ PICTURE AT B10]

buttock 1 *usu pl, used for simple description* the part of the body on which a person sits **2** either side of this part of the body: *The doctor gave him an injection in the left buttock.*

bottom *infml* the buttocks: *He told the child to be quiet or she would get a smack on her bottom. Riding on a horse makes your bottom sore.*

behind *infml* the buttocks: *Get off your (lazy) behind and do some work!*

backside *infml & often humor* the buttocks: *Be careful or you'll fall on your backside.*

bum *esp BrE infml, often humor & with children* the buttocks: *Don't just sit on your bum doing nothing; come on! She has a nice little bum, hasn't she?*

butt *AmE sl* the buttocks

arse *BrE,* **ass** *AmE not polite* the buttocks: *He sits on his arse all day doing nothing.*

rump *esp of an animal or humor of a fat person* the buttocks: *He struck the horse on the rump.*

seat *also* **rear** *polite euph* the buttocks: *He hurt his seat/rear when he fell.*

hindquarters [P] *of animals & humor, euph of people* the buttocks: *There was blood on the dog's hindquarters.*

anus *med* the opening between the buttocks through which waste matter passes out **anal** [Wa5;B] of or concerning the anus **-ly** [adv]

rectum *med* the lower end of the intestine, of which the anus is the opening

B34 *nouns* : **the front of the body** [C]
[⇒ PICTURE AT B10]

waist 1 the narrow part of the human body just above the hips: *He put his arm round her waist. How much does she measure round the waist?* **2** (*fig*) the narrow middle part of any apparatus, such as a stringed musical instrument; the middle part of a ship

waistline the waist regarded as something to be measured; the distance round the waist: *I must watch my waistline; I'm getting fat!*

abdomen *tech & fml* the front of the body between the chest and thighs, containing the stomach and bowels, etc: *The doctor pressed his patient's abdomen with his fingers.* **abdominal** [Wa5;B] of or connected with the abdomen

belly 1 *infml, often less polite* the abdomen; the part of the human body between the chest and the legs, which contains the stomach: *What a big belly that man has! I have a pain in my belly.* **2** the underside and inside parts of esp such large animals as the horse and whale **3** (*fig*) a surface or object curved or round like this part of the body

navel the small sunken place in the middle of the stomach

belly button *infml* the navel

paunch the belly, esp if very large, round and fat: *That man got his great paunch by drinking a lot of beer.*

midriff 1 *infml* the part of the human body between the chest and the waist **2** *tech* the muscle that separates the chest from the lower part of the body

lap the front part of a seated person between the waist and the knees: *She sat with the cat sleeping in/on her lap.*

hip the fleshy part of one of the two sides of the human body above the legs: *Women have rounder hips than men. The man wore a gun on his hip.*

crotch *also* **crutch** the place where the top of the leg meets the front of the body: *He was accidentally kicked in the crotch/crutch.*

groin the hollow place where the stomach joins the tops of the legs; this region of the stomach

B35 nouns : the stomach and general area

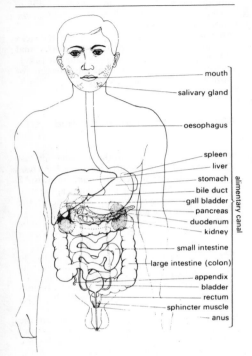

digestive and excretory system

stomach [C] **1** a baglike organ in the body where food is digested (= broken down for use by the body) after being eaten: *It takes time for the food in the stomach to be digested.* **2** *infml* abdomen: *The boy hit the other boy in the stomach.*

tummy [C] *infml* (*used esp by or to children*) stomach, abdomen: *The child has a pain in his tummy. He has tummy ache. She had some tummy trouble when she went to Africa.*

bowel [C] *fml tech* a long tube continuing down from the stomach and taking the waste matter out of the body

bowels [P] **1** *genl & infml* the mass of the bowel: *He had a pain in his bowels. Are her bowels working properly?* **2** (*fig*) the inner lower part of anything (esp in the phr **the bowels of the earth**)

innards [P] *infml* the stomach and bowels: *She's got something wrong with her innards and must go into hospital.*

insides [P] *infml* the general area of the stomach and bowels: *His insides hurt after that big meal.*

intestine [C] *med* the bowel **small/large intestine** the upper/lower parts of the bowel **intes-**

tines [P] *fml* the bowels **intestinal** [Wa5; B] of or connected with the bowel(s)

guts [P] *infml less polite* the bowels: *He's got a pain in the guts from eating too much.*

gut [C] **1** *esp AmE* the bowel **2** *infml* the belly: *That fellow's got a big gut.*

viscera [P] *tech* the internal organs of the body, esp the intestines: *The butcher cut out the sheep's viscera.* **visceral** [Wa5; B] of or connected with the viscera

entrails [P] *old use & lit* the viscera

appendix [C] a small worm-like part attached to the large intestine: *He had his appendix taken out.* **appendicitis** [U] a diseased condition of the appendix

B36 nouns, etc : the heart and the blood

[⇨ PICTURE AT B35]

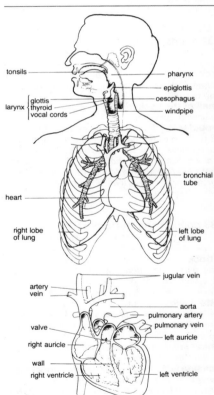

respiratory and circulatory system

heart [C] **1** the organ inside the chest which controls the flow of blood by pushing it through the blood vessels: *He was frightened and his heart began to beat faster.* **2** the same organ when thought of as the centre of feelings, esp of kind feelings: *My heart bled* (= I was very sorry) *for him. I felt sick at heart. He has a kind heart.* **3** something in a shape like this organ: *She sent him a birthday card with a heart on it.* **4** (*fig*) the centre of something: *Let's get to the heart of the matter.*

(heart)beat [C] the regular repeated stroke of the heart: *She put her hand on his chest and felt his heartbeat. Her heart missed a beat because of the shock.*

blood [U] the red liquid which flows round the body, bringing the materials which the cells need to continue living **bleed** [I∅; T1] to (cause to) lose blood from the body: *He was bleeding from a cut in his hand. Doctors used to bleed their patients to make them feel better.* (*fig*) *He bled them of all their money.*

bloodstream [(the) R;(C)] the blood as it flows through the heart and blood vessels: *infection of the bloodstream*

plasma [U] the colourless liquid part of the blood: *Blood consists of plasma and many other things carried in the plasma. The medical team carried a supply of plasma to help people in accidents.*

pulse [C *usu sing*] the regular beat of blood as it moves in the arteries, as felt for example at the wrist: *The doctor felt his patient's pulse. The patient's pulse was weak.*

blood vessel [C] a tube through which blood flows in the body

artery [C] one of the blood vessels that carry blood from the heart to the rest of the body **arterial** [Wa5;B] of, concerning, or like (what happens in) an artery or arteries: *Arterial blood is bright red.*

vein [C] one of the blood vessels which carry blood back to the heart **venous** [Wa5;B] of, concerning, or like the veins

circulation [U] the system by which blood moves around the body from and back to the heart: *He suffers from poor circulation. Her circulation is very good. He rubbed his legs to get the circulation going.* **circulatory** [⇨ M1] [Wa5;A] of or concerning circulation

B37 *nouns & verbs* : **the lungs and breathing**

[⇨ PICTURE AT B35]

lung [C] either of the two chest organs of breathing: *He filled his lungs with air.*

breathe [T1; I∅] to take air into and let it out of the lungs: *The injured man was breathing normally again. Breathe deeply – what wonderful fresh air! He breathed the fresh air with satisfaction. Don't breathe that gas; it's dangerous!*

breathe in [v adv I∅; T1] to take (air, gas, etc) into the lungs: *The doctor told his patient to breathe in. He breathed in some dangerous fumes.* [⇨ H84]

breathe out [v adv I∅; T1] to let (air, gas, etc) out of the lungs: *He held his breath for some time then slowly breathed out. She was breathing out whisky fumes over everybody.*

inhale [I∅; T1] *tech* to breathe in **inhalation 1** [U] the act of breathing in **2** [C] anything breathed in

exhale [I∅; T1] *tech* to breathe out **exhalation 1** [U] the act of breathing out **2** [C] anything breathed out

breath [C; U] air which is or has been taken into and/or let out of the lungs; the action of taking air in: *Take a deep breath; fill your lungs with air. He took several deep breaths. The swimmer held his breath underwater. That child has very bad breath* (= its breath smells bad). *I'm out of breath after running so hard.*

wind [U] **1** breath or breathing: *He couldn't get his wind* (= could not breathe properly, regularly) *after running so far.* **2** (the condition of having) air in the stomach, as when swallowed with food: *The baby has wind. You get wind when you eat too quickly.*

B38 *nouns* : **the kidneys and bladder** [C]

[⇨ PICTURE AT B35]

kidney one of the pair of human or animal organs in the lower back area, which separate waste liquid from the blood, ready to pass out of the body

bladder the bag of skin in which the waste liquid [⇨ B64 URINE] of the body collects

B39 *nouns* : **the liver and spleen** [C]

[⇨ PICTURE AT B35]

liver the large organ which cleans the blood

spleen the organ near the stomach which has an effect on certain cells in the blood

B40 *nouns, etc* : **the genitals and related organs**

genitals *also fml & tech* **genitalia** [P] the outer sexual organs **genital** [Wa5;A] of or concerning the sex organs

penis [C] the organ for sexual union and passing urine in men and some male animals

phallus [C] **1** an image of the penis, esp in some religious art as a sign of the power of man to produce children **2** *esp lit* the penis **phallic** [B] of or concerning the phallus

prick [C] *taboo sl* **1** the penis **2** a stupid person

cock [C] *taboo infml* the penis

testicle [C] either of the two male sex glands

testis [C] *tech* a testicle

scrotum [C] *tech* the bag of flesh holding the testicles of male animals

balls *taboo infml, also* **bollocks** *BrE* **1** [P] the testicles **2** [U] *often used as an interjection* nonsense

vulva [C] *tech* the opening to the vagina

vagina [C] *tech* the passage leading to the female sex organs   **vaginal** [Wa5; B] of or concerning the vagina

pudenda [P] *old use & euph* the outer sexual organs, esp of the female

cunt [C] *taboo* **1** the vagina or vulva **2** *sl* a woman or girl when regarded as a sexual object **3** *sl* a stupid or bad person

womb [C] the sex organ of a woman and female mammals where the young can develop

uterus [C] *med & tech* the womb   **uterine** [Wa5;B] of or concerning the womb **intra-uterine** [Wa5; B] inside the womb: *An intra-uterine device (IUD [⇨ B182]) can be used to prevent conception.*

pubic [Wa5;A] concerned with or in a position near the genitals **pubic hair** [U] hair around the genitals

B41 *nouns* : **the arm** [C]

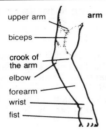

arm **1** either of the two upper limbs of a human being or monkey **2** that part of this limb above the hand: *He hurt his arm, but his hand is all right.*

wrist the joint between the hand and the lower part of the arm

B42 *nouns* : **the hand** [C]

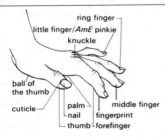

hand the movable part at the end of the arm, including the fingers

finger 1 any of the five movable parts with joints at the end of each hand **2** any of these other than the thumb   **fingerprint** a mark made by the finger when it is pressed on to a surface: *Detectives found the criminal by examining the fingerprints he had left on the safe.* **fingermark** the mark of a dirty finger on a wall, etc

thumb the short thick movable part of the inner side of each hand, which can be pressed against any of the fingers   **thumbprint** a mark made by the thumb when it is pressed on to a surface, esp when it is used as a signature by people who cannot write

fist the tightly closed hand, esp when it is used for fighting: *He held the coin in his closed fist. Put up your fists and fight!*

knuckle a finger joint

palm the soft inner surface of the hand between the base of the fingers and the wrist: *He had a small coin in the palm of his left hand.*

B43 *nouns* : **the leg** [C]

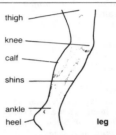

leg 1 either of two limbs on which a person walks and which supports the body **2** that part of this limb above the foot: *He had a leg injury, but his foot was all right.*

ankle 1 the joint between the foot and the leg **2** the thin part of the leg just above the foot

B44 *nouns* : **the foot** [C]

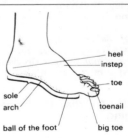

foot the movable part at the end of the leg on which a human being walks and stands

toe one of the five small jointed parts on the end of each foot

The skin, the complexion, and the hair

B50 *nouns* : **the skin**
[ALSO ⇨ A126 OF ANIMALS]

skin [U] the smooth outer covering of the body, in which hair may grow

pore [C] any of the many small openings in the skin through which sweat [⇒ B62] passes
porous [B] **1** *tech* having or full of pores: *porous skin* **2** allowing liquid to pass slowly through: *This clay pot is porous.*

wrinkle [C] a line in something which is folded or crushed, esp on the skin, esp when a person is old **wrinkled** [B] full of or covered with wrinkles

complexion [C] the natural appearance and colour of the skin, esp of the face: *That girl has a beautiful complexion. It's a pity he has such a spotty complexion.*

colour *BrE*, **color** *AmE* **1** [U] the amount of redness in the face of a white-skinned person: *She's very pale; there isn't much colour in her face. She doesn't have much colour.* **2** [C] the colour of the skin: *What colour is he—black or white?* **coloured** *BrE*, **colored** *AmE* [Wa5;B] belonging to a race that does not have a white skin: *He was a coloured man.*

pigment [U] *tech* the natural colouring matter in the skin and hair

B51 *nouns* : **hair on the head and face**
[⇒ A126 OF ANIMALS]

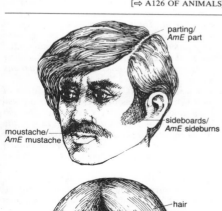

parting/
AmE part

moustache/
AmE mustache

sideboards/
AmE sideburns

hair

beard

hair 1 [C] a fine threadlike growth from the skin and (esp) on the head: *There was a long blond hair on his jacket. I can see a grey hair; you're getting old, Daddy!* **2** [U] such hairs collectively: *His hair is growing very long; it needs cutting.* **hairy** [Wa1;B] having a lot of hair: *What a hairy fellow he is!* **-haired** [*comb*

form] having hair of a certain kind: *red-haired, long-haired*

moustache *BrE*, **mustache** *AmE* [C] hair growing on the upper lip: *He grew a short/long moustache to make him look older.*

beard [C] **1** the hair of the lower part of the male face: *He grew a beard while he was on holiday.* **2** this hair as it appears when a man needs a shave: *My beard grows quickly; I need to shave twice a day.* **3** any similar growth on an animal or plant: *a billy-goat with a beard.* **bearded** [B] having or wearing a beard: *I don't remember his name, but he was a tall bearded man.*

sideboards *BrE*, **sideburns** *AmE* [P] hair on the upper part of the sides of the face

whiskers [P] hair growing on the sides of a man's face

stubble [U] a short stiff growth of beard; the hair of the male face when it needs to be shaved again: *He hasn't shaved for two days and the stubble on his chin looks terrible!*

bristles [P] stubble **bristly** [Wa2;B] having a lot of short stiff hairs: *He has a very bristly beard/moustache.*

dandruff [U] small white pieces of dead skin in the hair of the head

B52 *nouns, etc* : **styles of hair**
[⇒ PICTURE AT B51, D183–6 CARE OF THE HAIR]

parting *BrE*, **part** *AmE* [C] the line on the head where the hair is parted

plait

plait [C] a length of hair made by plaiting [⇒ I57]: *She wore her hair in long plaits down her back.*
braid [C] *esp AmE* a plait

pony tail

pony tail [C] a thick length of a woman's or girl's hair that is tied at the back of the head and hangs down the back of the neck rather like a horse's tail

pigtail

pigtail [C] a plait hanging down the back, esp of a young girl or if heavily greased [⇒ H10]: *Sailors used to wear their hair in a single pigtail. The little girl had two long pigtails.*

bun

bun [C] a thick knot into which long hair is twisted at the back or on top of the head: *She wore her hair in a bun.*

bob 1 [C] a way of cutting a woman or girl's hair so that it hangs short and loose above the shoulders: *She wears her hair in a bob.* **2** [Wv5; T1 *usu pass*] to cut (hair) in this way: *She had her hair bobbed.*

crop 1 [C] a way of cutting a person's hair very short all over **2** [Wv5;T1 *usu pass*] to cut (hair) in this way: *His hair was close cropped.*

B53 *adjectives & nouns, etc* : **colour of hair and skin**

black 1 [Wa1;B] (of hair) black or very dark brown: *Who is that girl with the black hair?* **2** [Wa1;B] (of skin) any of several shades of dark brown, usu depending on the view of the speaker: *Most Africans have black skins. Black is beautiful.* **3** [C] a black person: *There are more blacks in the city than whites.*

dark [Wa1;B] **1** (of hair) brunette **2** (of skin, depending on the view of the speaker) any of several shades of brown: *To people from Scandinavia Italians are dark, but to South Indians they are fair.*

brunette *also* **brunet** *esp AmE* **1** [C] a white person with brown or black hair and usu brown eyes: *He's going out with a lovely brunette.* **2** [Wa5; B] (of hair) brown, tending to black

swarthy [Wa1;B] *lit & derog* having a darker skin than most, and usu darker hair: *Who is that swarthy, dangerous-looking fellow?*

white 1 [Wa1;B] (of hair) having lost all colour, usu through age or sometimes shock: *The old woman had white hair.* **2** [Wa1;B] (of skin) pale; pinkish or very light brown: *In the city there are many white as well as black people.* **3** [C] a white person: *There are more whites in the city than blacks.*

fair [Wa1;B] with a pale skin and hair; light-coloured: *He has quite a fair complexion for someone from that part of the world. Who is that fair-haired girl?*

light [Wa1;B] (of skin and hair) not dark; having little pigment: *She is dark, but he has a very light complexion.* [⇒ B50]

blond 1 [Wa1;B] (of hair) light-coloured, usu yellowish **2** [C] a person, esp a male, with light-coloured skin and yellowish hair

blonde 1 blond (def 1) **2** [C] a woman with yellowish hair, a fair complexion and usu blue eyes: *He's going out with a beautiful blonde.*

grey *BrE*, **gray** *AmE* [Wa1;B] (of hair) dark and white mixed: *He is going grey at the temples.*

pale [Wa1;B] (of skin) white, esp if more so than expected: *You are looking pale—are you feeling all right? He is rather pale; a few weeks in the sun should help. The people in the north have paler complexions than the southerners.*

sallow [Wa1, 2;B] (of the skin) of an unhealthy yellow colour: *He looks very sallow after his illness.*

tan 1 *also* **suntan** [C] the brown condition of light skin which has been exposed to the sun for a time: *She got a lovely tan on her Spanish holiday. Put on some suntan lotion to stop the sun burning your skin.* **2** [I∅; T1] to get a tan or give a tan to: *He tans quickly. The sun tanned them brown.* **tanned** [B] having a tan: *He had a tanned complexion.*

sunburn [U] the condition of skin being darkened or burnt by the sun's rays **sunburnt** [B] tanned or burnt red by the sun: *His face was sunburnt from living so long in the open.*

weatherbeaten [B] (of faces) darkened and usu wrinkled [⇒ B50] by the sun, wind, and rain: *The sailor had a weatherbeaten face like old leather.*

freckle 1 [C] a small light-brown spot on the skin of fair people: *She gets freckles when she goes out in the sun too much.* **2** [I∅] to become covered with freckles: *Some people freckle very easily.* **freckled** [B] having freckles: *He has a freckled face.*

red [Wa1;B] (of hair) reddish-brown: *She has beautiful red hair. Red hair and freckles often go together.*

redhead [C] a person, esp a woman, with red hair: *He's going out with a beautiful redhead.* **-ed** [Wa5;B]

auburn [Wa5;B] (of hair) reddish-brown

ginger [Wa5;B] (of hair) orange-brown

bald [Wa1;B] **1** with little or no hair (on the

head): *The man had a shiny bald head. He's fairly young but he's going bald on top/at the sides.* **2** (*fig*) with little or no ornament: *He gave them a bald statement of the facts.* **-ness** [U] **-ly** [adv]

balding [Wa5;B] (of people) becoming bald: *He's balding at the temples.* [⇒ B21]

shaggy [Wa1;B] having rough thick untidy hair: *He has grown a long shaggy beard.* **-ily** [adv] **-iness** [U]

Fluids and waste products of the body

B60 *nouns* : **fluids generally** [U]

saliva *tech* the liquid produced in the mouth which helps in moving and breaking down food: *The appetizing smell made her mouth fill with saliva.* **salivary** [Wa5;B] of or concerning saliva

spit *infml* saliva, esp when outside the mouth: *The floor of the pub was covered in spit.*

spittle *infml & old use* spit: *She spat at him, but he did not wipe the spittle from his face.*

sputum *tech* **1** saliva **2** material like saliva produced by coughing

phlegm *tech* the thick liquid which forms in certain parts of the body esp the inner throat and in the nose: *He tried to clear the phlegm in his throat by coughing.*

mucus *tech* phlegm **mucous** [Wa5;B] of mucus: *mucous membranes*

snot *taboo sl* the sticky liquid which comes from the nose **snotty** [Wa1;B] covered in snot **snotty-nosed** [Wa2] **1** having snot coming out of the nose: *He doesn't enjoy the company of snotty-nosed children.* **2** *sl* acting as if important

bile the bitter brownish-yellow liquid which the liver produces to help in the digestion of food **bilious** [B] caused by too much bile: *He had a bilious headache.*

B61 *verbs* : **saliva, etc**

salivate [I∅] to produce saliva: *Pavlov managed to get dogs to salivate whenever a bell rang; the dogs expected food.* **salivation** [U]: *The sight of food caused salivation in Pavlov's dogs.*

spit [I∅; T1] to send (saliva, etc) out of the mouth: *He spat in his enemy's face. The old man spat the tobacco juice out in a long stream. She spat out the food as though it was poison.*

expectorate [I∅] *fml* to spit; let out phlegm by coughing **expectoration** [U]

dribble [I∅] to let saliva, etc, out slowly drop by drop, esp from the side of the mouth: *The baby was dribbling.*

water [I∅] (of the eyes or mouth) to fill with liquid: *The smoke made his eyes water. The smell of food started my mouth watering.*

B62 *nouns* : **sweat and tears**

sweat [U] liquid which comes out from the body through the pores [⇒ B50] of the skin to cool it, or because of fear: *Sweat formed on his brow as he worked.*

perspiration [U] *fml* **1** sweat: *His face was wet with perspiration.* **2** the action of sweating

lather [U;S] foaming [⇒ L90] sweat on a horse: *The horses were in a lather of sweat.*

tear *also* **teardrop** [C] a drop of liquid containing salt, which flows from the eye, esp during pain and sadness: *She burst into tears when she saw that he was hurt. Tears poured down the child's face.* [⇒ F155–6 CRYING]

B63 *verbs* : **relating to sweat**

sweat [I∅; T1] to (cause to) produce sweat: *He was sweating after working so hard. This heat will sweat all that beer out of you!*

perspire [I∅] *fml* to sweat: *Work until you perspire, then have a rest.*

B64 *nouns* : **urine** [U]

urine *tech* liquid containing waste material which flows from the body

piss *taboo* urine

water *euph* urine: *There seems to be blood in the patient's water, doctor.*

B65 *verbs & nouns* : **relating to urine**

urinate [I∅] *tech* to let the urine out of the body: *The patient has difficulty urinating, doctor.* **urination** [U]

piss *taboo* **1** [I∅] to urinate: *He was too drunk to piss straight.* **2** [T1] **a** to make wet by urinating: *He's pissed his trousers!* **b** to cause to come out of the body by urinating: *He began to piss blood.* **3** (*it* I∅) (*fig*) to rain heavily: *It's just pissing down.* **4** [S] act of urinating: *I must go and have a quick piss.*

pee *infml* **1** [I∅; T1] *esp with children* to urinate or make wet in this way: *He peed his trousers yesterday.* **2** [S] an act of urinating: *Excuse me; I must go and have a pee. He's just gone for a pee.*

wee-wee *also* **wee** *infml with small children* **1** [I∅] to urinate: *He needs to wee/wee-wee; come on, son.* **2** [C] an act of urinating: *Come on, darling, do a wee in your potty* (= pot).

pass water [I∅] *euph* to urinate: *Has the patient passed water today, nurse?*

B66 *nouns* : **excrement**

excrement [U] *tech* the waste matter which passes, usu in a solid state, out of the bowels: *The smell of excrement was everywhere; the place had no proper lavatories.*

excreta [P] *fml* waste products of the body: *Sweat, urine, and excrement are all excreta.*

faeces *BrE*, **feces** *AmE* [P] *tech & euph* excrement **f(a)ecal** [Wa5] of or concerning f(a)eces

crap *taboo* **1** [U] excrement **2** [S] act of passing excrement from the bowel **3** [U] (*fig*) rubbish: *Don't give us that load of crap; tell us the truth!*

turd [C] *taboo* **1** a ball or lump of excrement **2** *deprec sl* a stupid or undesirable person: *Tell that silly turd to go away!*

dung [U] the excrement of such animals as the horse and cow, esp when dropped in fields and used as manure [⇒ E136 MANURE]

stool [C] *med* excrement, esp in its solid state: *We must first examine the patient's stools. The patient had a stool test.*

shit *taboo* **1** [U] excrement **2** [S] the act of passing excrement from the bowel: *He hasn't had a good shit for days.* **3** [U] (*fig*) silly or useless things or talk: *What a load of shit he talks!* **4** [C] (*fig*) *deprec* a person whom the speaker does not like or respect: *I think he's a bit of a shit.*

B67 *verbs* : **relating to excrement**

excrete [T1] to discharge (waste matter) from the body: *Animals excrete sweat through the skin and faeces from the anus.* [⇒ B62 SWEAT, B33 ANUS] **excretion** [U] the act of excreting

defecate [I0] *med* to empty the bowels: *The patient is defecating regularly now.* **defecation** [U] the act of defecating

shit *taboo* **1** [I0] to defecate: *Hey, someone has shit in the corner of the room!* **2** [T1] to defecate in or on: *He shit his trousers (with fright).*

crap [I0] *taboo* to defecate: *He crapped all over his trousers.*

Bodily states and associated activities

B80 *adjectives* : **not sleeping**

waking [Wa5;A] not sleeping: *In a waking state he is very calm, but in his sleep he twists and turns all night.*

awake [F] not being asleep; having woken and knowing what is happening: *I was still awake at 3 a.m. last night. He's awake now; you can talk to him.* **wide awake** [B] not at all sleepy

wakeful [B] **1** awake and watchful: *The guards were wakeful all night in case of attack.* **2** not sleeping or able to sleep; sleepless: *She spent a wakeful night worrying about him.* **-ness** [U]

aware [F (*of*), F5,6a] knowing (what is happening): *The animals are fully aware of what is happening to them. He was suddenly aware of a movement in the darkness under the trees. I am aware of the need for secrecy, believe me. She was aware that he had changed his mind.* **-ness** [U] **un-** [*neg*]

conscious [F (*of*); F5] *often tech & fml* awake and aware: *The patient is (fully) conscious now, doctor. Is he conscious enough to answer questions? She was very conscious of his interest in everything she did.* **un-** [*neg*] **-ness** [U] **semi-conscious** [B] only partly conscious

alert [B] fully alive or awake; very watchful: *What an alert child he is! The guards were (fully) alert in case of danger.* **-ness** [U]

mindful [F *of*] *esp emot & fml* aware, conscious: *Please be mindful of what might happen. We are fully mindful of your difficulties and will try to help.* **un-** [*neg*] **-ness** [U]

B81 *adjectives* : **sleeping and wanting to sleep**

sleeping [Wa5;B] not awake: *He was careful not to disturb the sleeping children.*

asleep [Wa5;F] **1** sleeping: *He was (fast) asleep when I came home. Wake up! You look half asleep.* **2** (*fig*) not thinking: *Come on; are you asleep? You must solve this problem!* **3** (of an arm or leg that has been in one position too long) unable to feel; numb: *When he stood up he found that his right leg was asleep.*

sleepy [Wa1;B] **1** ready or inclined to fall asleep. **2** (*fig*) not thinking: *Come on; are you asleep? You must solve this problem!* **3** (of 3 giving the appearance of peaceful inactivity: *What a sleepy little town this is!* **-iness** [U] **-ily** [adv]

drowsy [Wa1;B] **1** pleasantly ready to fall asleep: *I feel drowsy after taking that medicine.* **2** making one pleasantly sleepy: *It was a pleasant warm drowsy summer afternoon.* **3** giving the appearance of pleasantly peaceful inactivity: *She lives in a drowsy little village on the river.* **-iness** [U] **-ily** [adv]

somnolent [B] *fml* sleepy; about to fall asleep: *He looks somnolent half the time.* **-nce** [U]

dozy [Wa1;B] *infml* **1** sleepy **2** a little slow in thinking: *He always looks dozy, but he's more alert than you think.* **-iness** [U] **-ily** [adv]

B82 *verbs* : **sleeping and waking**

sleep [I0] (of humans and animals) to enter or be in a state of natural unconsciousness [⇒ B80]: *He normally sleeps for 7 or 8 hours every night. She was really tired, and slept soundly till he woke her.*

go/get to sleep to enter the state of sleep: *I went to sleep about 11 last night. He got to sleep at midnight.*

fall asleep [I∅] to go or pass into the sleeping state: *The child fell asleep in her mother's arms.*

doze [I∅] to sleep lightly: *The old man sat dozing by the fire.*

doze off [v adv I∅] to fall into a light sleep: *He was tired and dozed off by the fire.*

drowse [I∅] to doze or be only half-awake: *He drowsed through the warm afternoon.*

nod [I∅] (to start) to fall asleep, esp when sitting, when the head drops down towards the chest: *The old man sat nodding beside the fire.*

nod off [v adv I∅] to fall asleep in this way: *Oh, what time is it?—I must have just nodded off.*

drop off [v adv I∅] *infml* to fall asleep: *Drink this and you'll soon drop off (to sleep). He dropped off quite naturally; he was pretty tired.*

dream [T1, 5a; I∅ (*of, about*)] to imagine (events, pictures, etc) while asleep: *Last night I dreamt (that) I was in China. Do you dream a lot? I dreamt about you last night.*

wake [I∅, T1] to stop sleeping: *He woke at 7 o'clock. She woke several times during the night. Please don't wake me till about 8. The child woke about 3 a.m. and woke her parents too.*

wake up [v adv I∅; T1] to stop sleeping: *Come on, everybody—wake up! He woke up suddenly in the middle of the night. Please don't wake up the baby.*

waken [I∅; T1] *fml* to (cause to) wake: *He wakened at 7 o'clock. Waken me about 7, please. That noise is enough to waken the dead! Something wakened me, but I don't know what.*

waken up [v adv I∅; T1] *fml* to become awake or cause to wake: *He wakened everyone up at 6 a.m.*

awake [I∅; T1] *fml* to wake: *Awake the men! He awoke at 6 a.m., wondering what was happening.*

awaken [T1; I∅] *fml & old use* to wake: *Please don't awaken the children yet.*

yawn [I∅] to open the mouth wide, esp when tired or not very interested: *She yawned widely. Stop yawning and go to bed if you're tired.* (*fig) The hole yawned open in front of them.*

retire [I∅] *fml, esp formerly* to go to bed: *'Mr and Mrs Browne have retired for the night', said the servant.*

B83 *nouns* : **the state of sleep**

sleep 1 [U] the state of being asleep: *Sleep is a necessity for all animals. People can't go on for long without sleep.* **2** [S] the time when sleeping: *Did you have a good sleep? A good night's sleep makes you feel great in the morning.*

doze [S] a light sleep: *He fell into a doze by the fire.*

stupor [S; U] a state of being nearly unconscious because of illness, tiredness, drugs, or shock [⇨ F127]: *He lay on the ground in a stupor.*

nap [C] a short, usu light sleep during the day-time: *I'll just have a nap, then I'll get the work done. She enjoys an afternoon nap.*

catnap [C] a very short light sleep: *He managed to have some catnaps although he was kept busy for most of the night.*

forty winks [P] *infml* a short sleep in the day-time: *He said he wanted to have forty winks before going back to work.*

yawn [C] an act of yawning: *His yawns suggested he was either tired or bored.*

B84 *verbs & nouns* : **relaxing**
[⇨ B89 ADJECTIVES]

relax [I∅] to become less anxious and tense [⇨ B88]: *Relax; have a drink and enjoy yourself. He's very tense; I wish he would relax. I want to sit back, relax, and do nothing.* **relaxation** [U] the process of relaxing; an activity which helps people relax

rest 1 [I∅] to be still and/or quiet; not to be active: *Let's rest; I'm a bit tired after all that work. They rested under a tree before continuing the journey.* **2** [U] the condition of resting: *Rest is good for you. The doctor said that the patient needed rest.* **3** [C] an occasion of resting: *I need a short rest; I'm tired. They took rests from work every 3 hours.*

unwind [I∅] *infml* to stop being tense; relax: *It's nice to unwind at the end of a busy day. A glass of sherry before dinner helps him (to) unwind.*

let oneself go *infml* to relax completely: *At the party she just let (herself) go and had a great time.*

B85 *nouns, etc* : **dreaming and hallucinating**

dream [C] **1** something seen or experienced while sleeping: *Dreams often seem very real. I can never remember my dreams. He says he can see the future in his dreams. She seems to live in a dream world.* **2** (*fig*) a hope or ambition which is like a dream: *He had dreams of building a house here.* [⇨ B82 *as verb*]

nightmare [C] **1** a frightening dream: *The child often has nightmares.* **2** (*fig*) a terrible experience, like a nightmare: *That time was a nightmare and I hope never to live through such an experience again. They live in nightmare conditions.*

daydream 1 [C] a dreamlike state while awake: *She is an imaginative child and gets lost in daydreams sometimes.* **2** [I∅] to have day-dreams: *Oh, stop daydreaming, and concentrate on your work!*

reverie [U; C] thoughts and daydreams: *She seemed to be in a state of reverie. I interrupted his reverie by asking for his help.*

trance [C] (*esp in the phr* **in a trance**) a state of mind like a dream, when a person does not notice things around him: *He stepped off the pavement in front of a bus as if he was in a* *trance. The medical hypnotist put his patient in a trance.*

daze [C] (*esp in the phr* **in a daze**) a confused state of mind: *He was in a daze after hitting his head against the low ceiling. Her mind was in a daze because of her excitement.* **dazed** [B] mentally confused: *He felt dazed after the bad news.*

hallucination [C] an occasion of seeing something which is not there: *He says he saw a ghost. – Well, people do have hallucinations sometimes.* **hallucinate** [I∅] *tech* to have hallucinations

mirage [C] something which looks real but is not, esp trees in a desert or 'water' on a hot dry road: *The desert travellers thought they saw a pool of water, but it was only a mirage.* (*fig*) *That political party's hopes of gaining power are just a mirage.*

B86 *verbs* : **hypnotizing people**

hypnotize, -ise [T1] to produce (in someone) a state like sleep in which they may be persuaded to do or think as the person in control suggests: *The doctor hypnotized his patient in an attempt to find out his deeper problems.* **hypnotist** [C] a person who can hypnotize others **hypnotism** [U] the technique(s) of hypnotizing **hypnosis** [U] the state of a hypnotized person **hypnotic** [B] **1** [Wa5] relating to hypnosis and hypnotism **2** (*fig*) very compelling: *That man has a hypnotic manner.* **-ally** [adv Wa4]

mesmerize [T1] **1** *esp old use* to hypnotize **2** to influence or surprise (someone) very much, esp to make speechless and unable to move: *The country girl stood by the roadside, mesmerized by the cars racing past.* **mesmerism** [U] the ability to mesmerize

B87 *nouns* : **tension and suspense**
[⇨ F90 WORRY AND ANXIETY]

tension [U; C] (a feeling of) nervous anxiety: *There was a terrible tension as they waited to hear who had been killed in the plane crash. She suffers a lot from physical tension. The tensions in the city are very noticeable and could lead to violence.*

strain 1 [U] a state of tension: *The doctor said that the woman was suffering from great mental and physical strain.* **2** [C; U] a fact or state which tests the power, esp of mind and body: *The additional work put a great strain on him. He has been working under a lot of strain for some months. These strains can cause tension.*

overwork [U] the result or effects of working too hard for too long: *He collapsed due to overwork.*

suspense [(*in*) U] uncertainty and anxiety which cause tension: *They waited in* (*great*) *suspense for the results of the election/test.*

Please don't keep us in suspense—tell us what happened!

B88 *adjectives* : **tense**
[⇨ F92 ANXIOUS]

tense [Wa2;B] having or showing nervous anxiety: *I was so tense the night before the examination that I couldn't understand what I was reading. She had a tense expression on her face, as though she was expecting trouble.*

tensed-up [B] *infml* very tense: *He's all tensed-up; he badly needs to relax.*

uneasy [Wa1;B] unpleasantly tense and uncertain: *I feel uneasy; I think something is going to happen soon. The people in the city were anxious and uneasy, expecting trouble.* **-iness** [U] **-ily** [adv] **unease** [U] *fml* uneasiness

strained [B] very tense and uneasy: *The soldiers had strained looks on their faces. Relations between the two families are now rather strained.*

ill at ease [F] not comfortable or able to relax: *The poor boy looked very ill at ease among all those strange adults.*

nervous [B] uncomfortably tense and uneasy: *Don't be nervous; nothing is going to go wrong. He was nervous before the concert, but he sang very well indeed. She was so nervous when the doorbell rang that she nearly jumped right out of her skin.* **-ness** [U] **-ly** [adv]

nervy [Wa1;B] *infml* suffering from nervous strain: *Don't be so nervy; I won't hurt you.*

jumpy [Wa1;B] *infml* nervous and tense: *Don't be so jumpy!—Nothing is going to happen to you.*

restless [B] never still; uneasy and tense: *He has been restless and unhappy ever since he lost his job. What a restless fellow he is—always travelling, never settling down.* **-ness** [U] **-ly** [adv]

unsettled [B] (*fig*) generally restless and uncertain: *He's been very unsettled since he came back from his Army service. The future looks a bit unsettled but we can hope for the best.*

highly-strung [B] very nervous by nature: *He's a highly-strung child; don't shout at him or he'll start crying.*

overwrought [B] tired, nervous, and tense because of too much work or excitement: *She's overwrought because of all the work and difficulties since her mother died. I'm feeling a bit overwrought.*

uptight [B] *sl* very tense: *Oh, don't get so uptight about things!*

B89 *adjectives* : **not tense** [B]

relaxed not tense: *He has a friendly, relaxed manner. This club has a nice relaxed atmosphere.*

restful causing rest: *She thought that the place was very pleasant and restful. Those delicate*

colours are very restful to/on the eye. **-ness** [U]
-ly [adv]

easy [Wa1] pleasantly relaxed and friendly: *He has a nice easy manner at parties.* **take it easy** *infml* to relax: *I told him to take it easy and not work so hard.* **take things easy** *infml* to relax generally: *The doctor told him to take things easy for a while.*

calm [Wa1] not upset: *She is calm now; she has stopped crying. The older man was calm, but the younger man was angry.* **-ly** [adv]

peaceful quiet; untroubled; not violent; showing little or no (sudden or strong) movement: *This is a nice peaceful place, full of peaceful people.* **-ly** [adv]

pacific *fml* peaceful; very calm and still: *The Pacific Ocean is so called because it was so calm and pacific when it was first seen by Europeans.*

soothing causing a person to be calm or to feel less pain or less tension: *This music is very soothing after a busy day.* **-ly** [adv]

B90 *verbs* : **relating to tension and doing too much**

tense [IØ; T1] to become or make (oneself) tense: *His muscles tensed as he tried to turn the wheel. He tensed (himself) to jump across the water.*

strain 1 [IØ, 3] to try too hard (to do something): *He strained to turn the wheel, but he couldn't. Don't strain so hard; you'll hurt yourself.* **2** [T1] to damage by straining or over-using: *He strained his heart lifting heavy weights. You'll strain your eyes working in that poor light.*

overdo [T1] to do too much, and harm oneself: *He overdid it at work and damaged his heart. The doctor told him not to overdo things.*

B91 *adjectives* : **strong** [B]

[ALSO ⇒ N233–8]

strong [Wa1] **1** having great power of body or mind: *He's a very strong man; he can tear a telephone book in two. I'm not strong enough to lift that weight.* **2** powerful; effective: *She has a very strong character/mind; she does what she wants to do, not what people tell her to do.* **-ly** [adv]

powerful full of physical (or mental or social) power; strong: *He has a powerful physique* [⇒ B1]. *She has a powerful position in local politics.* **-ly** [adv]

tough [Wa1] strong; not easily weakened: *He's a very tough man and he has survived two similar accidents.* **-ness** [U]

stalwart *apprec* (esp of a fighter) large and strong in body: *These soldiers are stalwart men.*

sturdy [Wa1] strong and firm in body: *He's a sturdy child and very healthy.* **-iness** [U] **-ily** [adv]

robust having or showing good health: *The*

whole family are pretty robust; they have very few colds and ailments. **-ness** [U] **-ly** [adv]

resilient (of people and living things) strong enough to recover from difficulty, disease, etc: *She's a resilient kind of person and will soon get over the shock/illness.* **-nce** [U] **-ly** [adv]

B92 *nouns* : **strength** [U]

strength the quality of being strong: *He can lift heavy weights; this shows his great strength. She has the strength to survive the illness.*

stamina the quality of having strength which lasts; power to do tiring things and to keep on doing them: *He won't be able to swim so far; he hasn't the stamina. His stamina is remarkable; the work he has done would kill a lesser man.*

staying power *infml* stamina: *He doesn't have the staying power to finish the work. He failed—the trouble with him is, he has no staying power.*

endurance the state or power of enduring [⇒ F9]; continuing strength: *The endurance of the soldiers was remarkable; they kept fighting for three weeks.*

B93 *adjectives* : **not strong** [B]

[ALSO ⇒ B134 OLD AGE]

weak [Wa1] not strong; having little power: *He is still weak after his illness. Children are much weaker than adults.*

feeble very weak: *He was strong once, but now he is old and feeble.*

frail weak and easily harmed: *She's such a frail old lady; she can hardly walk.*

B94 *nouns* : **relating to strength and life** [U]

energy the power to do things or to be active: *He's full of energy and works very hard. I just don't seem to have the energy to keep going, Doctor. This food will give you plenty of fresh energy.*

life *infml* the energy needed for life: *That child is full of life—always running about. She hasn't got much life in her, has she? Put some life into your work, please!*

vitality 1 the ability to stay alive or working in an effective way: *The fever has reduced her vitality. (fig) Some people doubt the vitality of the United Nations Organization.* **2** *apprec* gay forcefulness of character or manner: *What vitality those children have!*

B95 *adjectives* : **showing energy and life** [B]

energetic full of energy; done with or needing plenty of energy: *He is a very energetic boy,* *always playing active games. This is energetic work—I'm sweating already!* **-ally** [adv Wa4]

active energetic and always doing things or prepared to do them: *He is 70 years old and still very active (for his age).* **in-** [*neg*] **-ly** [adv]

lively [Wa1] full of life, in a gay and cheerful way: *She has a very pleasant lively manner. He was listening to some very lively dance music.* **-liness** [U]

B96 adjectives : not showing energy

lazy [Wa1;B] unwilling to be active or to work: *He's a lazy fellow; he doesn't like games or hard work. I feel lazy today; I'm just going to take things easy.* **-iness** [U] **-ily** [adv]

tired out [B] very tired: *I'm tired out; I should sleep well tonight.*

exhausted [B] completely tired; having no strength left: *The exhausted men fell in the road and slept where they lay. I feel really exhausted; I must rest.* **-ly** [adv]

weary [Wa1;B] *emot* tired, usu from something lasting a period of time: *He was weary after his long journey. Come on, sit down and rest your weary legs.* **-iness** [U] **-ily** [adv]

B97 adjectives : not showing energy
infml

done in [F] *infml* exhausted: *What a hard day it's been; I feel quite done in.*

worn out [F] *infml & emot* exhausted: *She's quite worn out from years of working too hard. I feel really worn out and yet I haven't been doing much; I think I'll go and see my doctor.*

played out [F] *sl* exhausted: *After the game I was really played out.*

shattered [F] *esp BrE infml* exhausted: *I always feel shattered after children's birthday parties. Let me sit down; I'm shattered.*

B98 verbs : losing energy

tire 1 [I∅] to become tired: *She tires easily nowadays; she isn't as strong as she was.* **2** [Wv4;T1 (*out*)] to make tired: *This work is pretty tiring; it tires me out. Don't tire the horses; we'll need them later.*

exhaust [T1] to tire completely; take all the energy from: *That game has exhausted me—I must have a rest now! She is physically exhausted from having too many children.*

weary [T1] *emot* to tire very much, usu over a period of time: *This work wearies me; I sometimes think I'll never finish it. His long speech wearied his audience.*

fatigue [T1] *emph* to tire very much; take the strength from: *What fatiguing work this is! The exercises fatigued her.*

B99 nouns : states of being tired [U]

tiredness the state of being tired: *Tiredness after work is perfectly normal.*

exhaustion the state of being exhausted; great tiredness: *He was in a state of exhaustion after his long climb.*

weariness *emot* tiredness: *A great weariness settled over him when he considered what must be done.*

fatigue *emph* great tiredness, esp over a long period: *She is suffering from fatigue; she has been working too hard for too long.*

B100 adjectives : having much fat [B]

fat [Wa1] (of people and their bodies) having too much fat; not thin: *There were two men there, one fat and the other thin. She's too fat; she should start slimming* [⇒ B103]. **-ness** [U]

stout [Wa1] rather fat and heavy: *The stout man had difficulty climbing the steep street; he stopped regularly to get his breath back.* **-ness** [U]

plump [Wa1] **1** pleasantly fat: *She isn't fat; she is just plump and I find her very attractive. The baby has nice plump cheeks.* **2** *euph* fat: *Well, he is rather plump, isn't he?* **-ness** [U]

tubby [Wa1] rather fat, esp in the stomach: *Do you know the man I mean?—He's the tubby chap who drinks a lot of beer.* **-iness** [U]

chubby [Wa1] (of people or animals) having a full round, usu pleasing form; slightly fat: *He's a fine chubby healthy baby. She has lovely round chubby cheeks.* **-iness** [U]

flabby [Wa1] having flesh that is too soft: *He isn't just fat, he's flabby! Maybe he should take more exercise.* **-iness** [U]

corpulent *derog* fat: *What a great corpulent fellow he is; he needs to slim down.* **-nce** [U]

obese very fat: *That old man is really obese; it can't be healthy.* **-sity** [U] *med* being very fat

overweight too heavy physically; too fat: *He was overweight so he went on a diet, and got his weight down quite a bit.*

rotund *often euph* round (because fat): *He's a pleasant, rotund little man; he always looks very well-fed.* **-ity** [U]

B101 adjectives : having little fat [B]

thin [Wa1] having little fat on the body: *There were two girls there, a thin one and a fat one. He's much thinner nowadays than he used to be; I think he's been ill.* **-ness** [U]

lean [Wa1] **1** *usu apprec* (of people, usu men, and of animals) thin, usu in a healthy way: *He has a lean handsome face. His body was lean and hard, like a leopard's.* **2** (*fig*) producing little or having little value: *1975 was a lean year for profits.* **-ness** [U]

slim [Wa1] **1** (of people) pleasantly thin; not fat: *She won't eat because she wants to be/stay slim. He has a fine slim muscular build.* **2** (*fig*) *infml* small: *He hopes to win the race but his chances are slim.* **-ness** [U]

slender [Wa2] **1** (esp of women and children) very thin in a pleasant way: *She has a beautiful slender body. What lovely long slender fingers you have.* **2** (*fig*) *infml* small: *He hopes to win the race but his chances are slender.* **-ness** [U]

slight [Wa1] **1** (of people) thin in build and also usu small: *The wind nearly lifted her slight body off the ground.* **2** (*fig*) small: *His chances of winning the race are slight.* **-ness** [U]

underweight not heavy enough physically: *She's underweight; I don't think she has been eating properly for some months.*

skinny [Wa1] *usu derog* very thin: *Who is that tall skinny fellow? He has a good build except for rather skinny arms.* **-iness** [U]

skin and bone [F] *infml* very thin, so that the shape of the bones shows under the skin: *The prisoners were just skin and bone, no more than walking skeletons.*

emaciated *fml* so thin that the shape of the bones shows under the skin: *His long period in prison left him emaciated. During the worst of the famine we saw many emaciated people.* **emaciation** [U]

B102 *verbs* : **becoming fatter**

put on weight to become physically heavier; to put on more flesh and fat: *She has put on (a lot of) weight since I last saw her; I think she likes her food. He's trying to avoid putting on weight.*

fatten 1 [I0] to become fat: *He has fattened a lot, especially in the face, since I saw him last.* **2** [T1] to make fat: *The farmer has fattened the cattle for market.*

fatten up [v adv T1] to make much fatter: *His wife has really fattened him up; he was quite skinny before he got married.*

fill out [v adv I0] *infml* to become fatter: *He has filled out a lot since he got married; it must be his wife's cooking.*

B103 *verbs* : **becoming thinner**

lose weight to become physically lighter; lose flesh and fat: *He has lost (a lot of) weight since his illness. She wishes she could lose weight as easily as her sister.*

diet [I0] to limit oneself to certain foods in smaller than usual amounts, usu in order to slim: *She's dieting in order to get her weight down. You are overweight; you'd better diet for a few weeks.* [⇒ E1 DIET AS A NOUN]

slim [Wv4; I0] to reduce one's weight, usu by taking exercise and/or eating less (of certain kinds) of food: *I'm slimming; I've got to get my weight down. You should slim; there are plenty of slimming exercises you could do.*

slim down [v adv I0; T1] to (cause to) slim a great deal; lose a lot of weight: *She has slimmed down a lot; she used to be very fat. Work-*

ing here will soon slim you down; it's hard work.

waste away [v adv I0] to become slowly thinner and thinner: *She has just wasted away (to nothing) since her husband died.*

B104 *adjectives* : **having a lot of flesh** [B]

full-bodied (esp of women) having plenty of flesh on the breasts, hips, and thighs: *She's certainly a full-bodied young woman.*

buxom (of women) healthy-looking, attractive, and full-bodied: *She's a fine buxom girl!*

bosomy also **busty** [Wa1] *infml* (of women) having a large bosom [⇒ B31]: *He likes big bosomy girls. She's a bit busty, isn't she?*

fleshy [Wa1] *deprec* having too much flesh; fat: *He's rather a fleshy fellow, isn't he!* **-iness** [U]

B105 *adjectives* : **heavily built** [B]

stocky [Wa1] (of people and animals) thick, short, and strong in body: *He is a stocky fellow. The cattle in these parts are stocky little animals.* **-iness** [U]

hefty [Wa1] *infml* big and strong: *He has several hefty fellows working for him.* **-iness** [U]

thickset short and broad in body: *The boxer was a thickset strong-looking man.*

dumpy [Wa1] *usu deprec* short and fat: *Several of the girls were, in his opinion, rather plain and dumpy.*

squat [Wa1] *often deprec* short and thick in body: *He is tall and he thinks that the local people are all squat and dumpy.*

B106 *adjectives* : **lightly built** [Wa1;B]

lanky (esp of a person) very thin and ungracefully tall or long: *Who is that lanky youth with the untidy hair?*

leggy *infml* having noticeably long thin legs: *He's interested in a leggy blonde at the moment. Young horses always look very leggy.*

bony having the shapes of bones showing under the skin: *He had a thin bony face and long bony fingers.*

Bodily conditions relating to health, sickness, and disability

B110 *adjectives* : **showing good bodily condition**

healthy [Wa1;B] **1** fit and well in body and mind: *Their children are well-fed, active, and healthy. She's much healthier now that she is* *living in the country.* **2** likely to give good health: *This place has a fine dry healthy climate.* **3** good for the body or mind; natural: *That book is not healthy reading for a child. He has a healthy interest in girls.* **-ily** [adv] **-iness** [U]

fit [Wa1;B] **1** strong and healthy in body: *He runs three miles every morning; that's why he's so fit.* **2** in good health; free from illness: *He's a lot fitter now than he used to be. She isn't a fit woman; she has some kind of stomach trouble.*

well [F] in good or returned health: *She was ill for a month but she's looking well again. How well the children look after their holiday!*

better 1 [Wa5;F] no longer ill: *Now that he's better he can play football again.* **2** [F9] less ill than before: *Are you feeling any better?*

sound [Wa1;B] (esp of parts of the body) healthy and strong: *Well, I've checked him and he's perfectly sound; he should live for years yet. Your lungs are sound; they are in a very sound condition.* **sound in wind and limb** very fit, esp of horses: *That horse is sound in wind and limb; he will serve you well.*

fine [Wa1;F] *infml* very good or well: *How are you feeling now?—Oh, I'm feeling fine, just fine.*

all right [Wa5;F] *infml* quite good or well: *How are you feeling now?—All right, thank you. His heart's all right; it's his lungs I'm worried about.*

okay, OK [Wa5;F] *infml* all right; satisfactory: *How is she feeling after the accident?—Oh, she was a bit shocked, but she's okay now.*

bracing [B] *emot* giving health and strength: *This sea air is very bracing, isn't it? This is a fine bracing climate to live in.*

healthful [B] *fml* likely to give good health: *This is a healthful place—fresh air and plenty of sunshine!*

salubrious [B] *fml & euph* healthful: *This climate is indeed salubrious, is it not?*

B111 *adjectives* : **showing poor bodily condition**

ill [F; (B)] not in good health; not well: *She's ill, so she can't come. Oh, I'm not ill enough to need a doctor. Oh God, I feel ill!*

unhealthy [Wa1;B] **1** not generally in good physical and mental condition; often ill; not strong: *They're unhealthy children, because they don't get good food and fresh air.* **2** not likely to give good health: *This place has a hot wet unhealthy climate.* **3** not good for the body or mind: *He has an unhealthy interest in murder and similar crimes.* **4** showing illness or poor health: *Her skin is an unhealthy greenish colour.*

unwell [F] ill, esp for a short time: *He was unwell yesterday, but he's fine again today.*

unfit [Wa2;B] in bad health: *He's pretty unfit; he*

needs medical treatment and a lot more exercise.

sick [Wa1;B] **1** *esp AmE, ScotE* not well; ill: *She was sick for three months. He was off sick for a week and missed a lot of work.* **2** about to vomit: *I feel sick; it must be something I ate.* [⇒ B119 VOMIT]

sickly [Wa1;B] always or often ill: *What a sickly child she is; she's constantly catching colds.*

diseased [B] showing signs of, or damaged by, disease or infection: *The plant is diseased and will soon die.*

upset [Wa5;B] slightly ill: *The child has an upset stomach.*

bad *infml* **1** [F] unwell: *Oh God, I feel bad! He's been bad for a week; it's his back, you know.* **2** [B] weak or unsound: *He's been ill with a bad back for months. She's got a bad heart and can't climb stairs.*

poorly [F] *esp BrE infml* not (very) well: *Oh, I am feeling poorly. He's been very poorly lately; he might die.*

ailing [Wa5;B] *infml* unwell, esp over a period of time and not seriously: *The doctor was called out to attend to an ailing child. He's an old man now and has been ailing for a long time.*

run down [B] *not fml* not in good health; not well: *She's pretty run down; she needs a rest.*

morbid [Wa5;B] *med* concerned with disease; showing disease: *The doctor detected a morbid lung condition.*

dizzy [Wa1;B] feeling as if everything is turning round: *Gosh, I feel dizzy! She felt dizzy and fainted.* **-iness** [U] **-ily** [adv]

funny [B] *infml* **1** slightly unwell: *She always feels a bit funny if she looks down from a height.* **2** slightly mad: *He went rather funny (in the head) after the death of his only son.*

B112 *nouns* : **relating to good bodily condition** [U]

health the condition of being healthy; a good natural condition of the body (and mind): *His physical and mental health are excellent. She has been in poor health for some years. His health is a matter of importance to me, Doctor. Badly-kept food can be a danger to public health.*

fitness the condition of being fit: *Physical fitness is a necessity of life. The doctor checked his general fitness.*

well-being the condition of general health and contentment: *Most doctors are interested in the health and the general well-being of their patients. After the meal he had a warm feeling of (bodily) well-being.*

welfare the condition of having good health and a satisfactory life: *He has worked for the welfare of his people for 30 years. She cares about the welfare of all the men and women who work for her.*

B113 nouns : relating to poor bodily condition

illness 1 [U] the state of being ill: *There has been a lot of illness in the family recently. Illness makes one weak. The degree of illness of patients in hospitals is not always obvious to the eye.* **2** [C] kind of illness; occasion of illness; disease: *He is recovering from a serious illness, some kind of liver trouble. Coughs, colds, and minor illnesses happen in every family. This hospital deals with infectious illnesses.*

ill health [U] *emot* the condition of being unhealthy; a general state of illness: *She has suffered from ill health for most of her life.*

disorder [C] **1** state of the body or mind when something is not working properly: *Mental disorders* (= disorders of the mind) *are common in big crowded cities.* **2** a small or short illness: *The doctor says it's just a stomach disorder—nothing serious.*

disease 1 [C] a more or less serious disorder of the body in animals or plants: *He is suffering from a rare tropical disease. This hospital deals particularly with infectious diseases.* **2** [U] disorders of this kind generally: *There is a lot of unnecessary disease in this town because of bad sanitation.*

sickness *emot & genl* **1** [U] illness; ill-health: *Is there a lot of sickness in that family? His absence was caused by sickness, not laziness.* **2** [C] *esp emot* an illness; disease: *She died of some strange tropical sickness.* (*fig*) *He suffers from a sickness of the spirit, not the body.*

upset [C] an illness of a short or minor nature: *The child had a tummy upset.*

ailment [C] an illness, esp one that is not serious: *She was complaining yesterday of some ailment or other. Colds and other ailments are common in winter.*

indisposition [C] *fml* an illness: *The prime minister retired to bed early because of a slight indisposition; it is nothing serious.*

disability [C] a state of the body when a part cannot be used normally, esp in the limbs and sense organs: *He walks with a limp; that is his only disability. Poor eyesight and flat feet are disabilities; you can't usually get into the police or army if you have them.*

breakdown also **nervous breakdown** [C] a loss of esp mental health through having too many troubles, too much to do, etc: *She had suffered a complete breakdown.*

handicap [C] **1** *esp emot* a disability: *Blindness is a great handicap.* **2** a quality or event which gives one a disadvantage: *Being small is a handicap in a crowd like this.* **handicapped** [B] having a handicap: *He is handicapped by deafness. She is physically handicapped* (= has a disability). *What can we do to help the handicapped?*

trouble [U] a disorder of a certain kind, usu over a period of time: *She has a lot of trouble with her stomach. He has heart trouble.*

problem [C] *genl* an illness or disorder: *Doctors deal with all sorts of physical and psychological problems. He has some kind of kidney problem that the doctors don't quite understand.*

condition 1 [S] state of health: *The patient is in a very grave condition; he may well die. Well, her condition is satisfactory; the operation was a success and she is out of danger.* **2** [C] *med* a specific usu unsatisfactory state of an organ: *The patient has a serious heart condition.*

B114 verbs : showing poor bodily condition

suffer from [v prep T1] to experience (an illness), esp over a long period of time: *He has suffered from heart disease for years.*

fall ill to become ill; to begin to suffer from an illness: *She fell ill last week and was taken to hospital; it's quite serious. He doesn't often fall ill and hasn't been off work for years.*

be taken ill to become ill suddenly: *He was taken ill last night and we called the doctor immediately.*

take ill *old use* to become ill: *He took ill of a fever and died shortly afterwards.*

sicken [I0] *old use* to fall ill: *The child sickened and died.*

sicken for [v prep T1] *infml* to begin to show signs of (a disease): *He seems to be sickening for something.*

B115 verbs & nouns : losing consciousness

[⇨ B80 CONSCIOUS]

faint 1 [I0 (*away*)] to lose consciousness: *He fainted from loss of blood. The great pain made him faint. When she heard the bad news, she fainted* (*clean away*). **2** [S] the act or condition of fainting: *She fell down in a faint.* **3** [F] inclined to faint: *She suddenly felt faint.*

pass out [v adv I0] *not fml* to become unconscious suddenly: *It was so hot that she passed out.*

flake out [v adv I0] *infml* to faint: *He flaked out because of the pain.*

B116 nouns : becoming ill suddenly [C]

attack the sudden coming on of a disease or illness: *She's in bed with an attack of flu. He's had several heart attacks, none of them severe. While he was eating he had an attack of coughing.*

fit 1 a very sudden and usu short attack: *He burst into a fit of coughing. She often has fainting fits.* **2** a sudden attack of apoplexy [⇨ B144], epilepsy [⇨ B146], hysteria [⇨ B149], etc: *An apoplectic fit can be very severe. He has epileptic fits and lies on the floor, his limbs moving violently.*

turn 1 *infml* an attack: *She has heart trouble, and had a bad turn on the way upstairs last night.* **2** *infml* a nervous shock: *The bad news gave her quite a turn.* **3** a development: *His condition took a turn for the worse yesterday; he may not recover.*

stroke a sudden attack of illness in the brain: *If someone has a stroke he usually loses feeling or the ability to move in parts of his body. He suffered a severe stroke and was paralysed* [⇒ B146] *down one side of his body.*

B117 *verbs & nouns* : **noises relating to bodily conditions**

[⇒ B37 BREATHING]

gasp 1 [I∅ (*for*)] to breathe quickly, esp with difficulty, making a sudden noise: *I came out of the water and gasped for breath.* **2** [T1 (*out*)] to say while breathing in this way: *He gasped out the message.* **3** [C] an act or sound of gasping: *When the news was announced there were gasps of surprise in the audience.*

pant 1 [I∅] to take short, quick breaths: *He was panting because he had run so fast. She could hear the sound of someone panting hard.* **2** [T1 (*out*)] to say while panting: *He panted (out) his message.* **3** [C] an act or sound of panting: *His breath came in painful pants and gasps.*

puff 1 [I∅] to breathe quickly, esp after running or exercise: *He was puffing and gasping after the run.* **2** [C] an act or sound of puffing: *He was breathing in puffs and pants.*

snort 1 [I∅] to force air violently through the nose: *He snorted to show his anger at the whole idea.* **2** [C] an act or sound of snorting: *He gave an impatient snort when he heard the plan.*

cough 1 [I∅ (*up*)] to send out air from the lungs violently and noisily: *He coughed in order to clear his throat (of phlegm).* [⇒ B61] *A sore throat can make you cough, and coughing makes the throat worse. He was coughing (up) blood.* **2** [C] an act or sound of coughing: *He heard a quiet cough and turned to see her standing there. The air was full of coughs and sneezes; everyone had a cold.*

sneeze 1 [I∅] to have air burst uncontrollably through the nose and mouth: *He began to sneeze into his handkerchief. She's sneezing all over the place; she has a bad cold and she's giving us all her germs.* [⇒ A37] **2** [C] an act or sound of sneezing: *He heard a loud sneeze coming from the bathroom.*

sniff 1 [I∅] to draw in air through the nose with a slight sound: *She sniffed to show her disapproval. They all had colds and were sniffing and sneezing.* **2** [T1] to draw in through the nose: *She sniffed the perfume of the flowers appreciatively.* [⇒ F278] **3** [T1; I∅(*at*)] to get the smell of (something) by sniffing: *The dog was sniffing (at) the clothing.* **4** [C] the act or sound of sniffing: *She gave a sniff to show her disap-*

proval. *The air was full of sniffs and sneezes. He took a sniff of the medicine and made an unhappy face. Get a sniff of that wonderful sea air!*

sniffle [I∅] to sniff, esp noisily and continuously, to clear liquid from the nose, esp when crying or because of a cold in the head: *Stop sniffling like that; it's irritating!*

hiccup *also* **hiccough 1** [I∅] to have a stopping of the breath with a sharp sound like a cough, usu in a series: *He began to hiccup after drinking too much.* **2** [C] an act or sound of hiccuping: *His hiccups could be heard across the room. She had a sudden attack of (the) hiccups. I had the hiccups at a party once and couldn't stop.*

burp 1 [I∅; T1] to send, or cause to send, wind from the stomach and through the throat: *He burped gently after eating. She was busy burping the baby after its feed.* **2** [C] an act or sound of burping: *The baby gave quite a loud burp.*

belch 1 [I∅] to send wind forcefully from the stomach and through the throat: *In some societies it is considered polite to belch after an enjoyable meal, but in others belching at any time is rude.* **2** [T1; I∅ (*out*)] (*fig*) to throw or come out with force or in large quantities: *The factory chimneys were belching (out) smoke. Smoke belched out from the volcano.* **3** [C] an act or sound of belching: *He gave a loud belch after the meal.* (*fig*) *A belch of smoke rose from the chimney.*

whistle 1 [I∅; T1] to make a high clear noise by forcing air through a small opening, such as the rounded lips: *He whistled (a tune) as he walked along. The air came whistling out of the hole. Wheezing produces a whistling sound from the lungs.* **2** [C] an act or sound of whistling: *He gave a low whistle to warn them he was coming.*

wheeze 1 [I∅] to breathe, usu with some difficulty, with a rough whistling sound coming from the lungs: *People with asthma often wheeze when they speak. He was wheezing and panting as he climbed the hill.* **2** [C] an act or sound of wheezing: *He has bronchitis and his coughs and wheezes sound terrible.* [⇒ B141 ASTHMA, BRONCHITIS]

sigh 1 [I∅] to take a deep breath that can be heard: *She sighed and looked sad. He sighed, shook his head, and refused to sign the paper. She sighed with relief when she heard the good news.* **2** [C] an act or sound of sighing: *He gave a (great) sigh (of relief) when he heard the good news. Her sighs made it clear she was unhappy.*

snore 1 [I∅] to breathe roughly and noisily while sleeping: *I'm afraid he snores. The sound of snoring came from the next room.* **2** [C] an act or sound of snoring: *His snores were loud and regular.*

fart *taboo* **1** [I∅] to send out wind from the bowel: *He farted in public.* **2** [C] an act or sound of farting: *He let out a loud fart.*

B118 *verbs* : **making breathing difficult**

[⇒ B37 BREATHING]

choke 1 [I∅] to be unable to breathe because of something in the windpipe [⇒ B26] or strong emotion: *He choked while he was eating. He choked to death on a fishbone. She nearly choked with anger at the news.* **2** [T1] to stop (someone's) breathing by pressing or blocking the windpipe: *He choked the girl (to death). He threatened to choke the life out of the man. Her voice was choked with sobs.* **3** [T1] to stop (someone's) breathing: *The smoke almost choked him. Choking fumes filled the house.*

stifle [Wv4;T1] to give (someone) the feeling that it is difficult to breathe: *This room is stuffy; I feel stifled in here. The heat was stifling so I went out for a breath of cool air. The smoke in the burning building almost stifled the firemen.*

suffocate 1 [I∅] to suffer or die because it is difficult or impossible to breathe: *He suffocated because there was no air left in the room.* **2** [T1] to kill by making breathing impossible: *He suffocated her with a cushion (over her mouth). The horses were suffocated by the smoke.* **suffocation** [U] the process of suffocating or being suffocated.

asphyxiate [T1 *usu pass*] *tech* to make ill or kill through lack of enough (clean) air to breathe: *The miners were asphyxiated by lack of oxygen/by poisonous gases.* **asphyxia** [U] a physical condition caused by lack of air in the lungs **asphyxiation** [U] the process of asphyxiating or being asphyxiated

strangle [T1] to kill (someone) by squeezing the throat; to prevent (someone's) breathing: *He strangled his wife when he found she had a lover. (fig) This tight collar is strangling me.* **strangulation** [U] the action or process of strangling or being strangled **strangler** [C] a person who strangles or has strangled other people

B119 *verbs* : **having food come back up from the stomach**

be sick [I∅] to have food come back up from the stomach and out of the mouth: *He was (violently) sick last night; it must have been something he ate.*

feel sick [I∅] feel the need to be, or possibility of being, sick: *Ugh, I feel sick. She felt really sick last night but seems to be okay now.*

vomit *fml & tech* **1** [I∅] to be sick: *He has been vomiting all night.* **2** [T1] to have (food) come back up. from the stomach and out of the mouth: *He vomited all his food.* **3** [U] food which has been partly changed by acids in the stomach, but passed back through the mouth because of illness instead of continuing through the body: *His bed was covered with vomit.*

bring up [v adv T1; (I∅)] *esp BrE* to be sick: *Ugh, I feel sick; I think I'm going to bring up (my food).*

puke [I∅] *infml* to be sick: *He had too much to drink and puked all over his clothes. Hell, this news is enough to make you puke!*

spew [I∅; T1 (*up*)] to be violently sick, sending food matter far out of the mouth: *The drunk man spewed all over the bar. He spewed up all his food.*

sick up [v adv T1] *BrE infml* to vomit (food): *He sicked up his dinner; I think he has caught a chill.*

throw up [v adv I∅] *infml* to vomit (food): *He threw up after drinking too much.*

retch [I∅] to make the sound and movements of vomiting but without bringing anything up from the stomach: *He's still retching, but there's nothing left in his stomach.*

gag [I∅] to retch or choke without being sick: *That horrible smell made me gag.*

B120 *nouns* : **states of being sick** [U]

[ALSO ⇒ B150]

sickness the feeling or condition of being sick or vomiting: *A feeling of sickness crept over him.*

seasickness	sickness caused by the movement of a(n)	boat
carsickness		car
airsickness		aeroplane

sick feeling *infml* a feeling of being about to vomit: *He had a sudden sick feeling in his stomach.*

nausea *emot & med* the condition of needing to or feeling likely to vomit: *Waves of nausea passed over her. The patient is suffering slight nausea but is otherwise fine.* **nauseate** [Wv4; T1] to cause to feel sick: *What a nauseating meal/idea/smell! That person really nauseates me; he's so dirty.* **nauseous** [B] causing nausea

B121 *nouns* : **feelings of pain**

pain 1 [U] suffering or great discomfort of the body or mind: *It's a serious wound and is causing (him) a great deal of pain. The boy was in pain after he broke his arm. His unkind behaviour caused his parents a great deal of pain.* **2** [C] a feeling of suffering or discomfort in a particular part of the body: *What could cause such severe stomach pains?* **3** [S] *sl* **a** a feeling of annoyance or displeasure: *You give me a pain!* **b** a person, thing or happening who or which makes one angry and tired, but is difficult to avoid; a nuisance: *She's a real pain. It really is a pain (in the neck) to have to go to that party.*

agony [U; C] very great pain or suffering of mind and body: *He lay in agony until the doctor arrived. The driver was in an agony of sorrow because he had knocked the girl down. He suffered agonies from his broken arm. She was in agonies of doubt over what to do.* **pile/put/turn on the agony** *infml* to say that one's sufferings, feelings, etc are stronger or greater than they are, esp for effect

suffering [U; C *usu pl*] pain over a period of time: *His wound caused him great suffering. She caused him great mental suffering by leaving him. She doesn't want to hear about the sufferings of others; her own suffering is bad enough.*

ache [C] a continuous dull pain, esp in the body: *She suffers from various aches and pains. The ache in her head was terrific and she couldn't think straight.*

twinge [C] a sudden sharp pain: *He sometimes experiences a twinge or two (of pain); nothing serious. Do you get any pains in your stomach?—Oh, just the odd/occasional twinge, nothing more.*

stab [C *of*] a short, very sharp pain: *He felt a sudden stab of pain in his chest.*

pang [C (*of*)] a sudden, sharp feeling which hurts in some way: *He felt the pangs of hunger. She felt a pang of remorse for having left him.*

sting [C] **1** a sharp organ used as a weapon by some animals, often poisonous: *That insect has a sting in its tail. Does a bee die when it loses its sting?* **2** a pain-producing substance contained in hairs on a plant's surface: *Some plants such as nettles have a sting.* **3** a sharp pain, wound or mark caused by a plant or animal **4** a strong pain, usu on the outer skin **5** an ability to cause pain or hurt feelings: *the sting of her tongue* (= her sharp, hurtful way of speaking)

B122 *verbs* : **feelings of pain**

hurt 1 [I∅; T1] to cause (a person or creature) to feel pain of any kind: *Does your arm still hurt (you)?—Yes, it hurts quite a lot.—No, it doesn't hurt at all now. Hey, don't hit me again—it hurt!* **2** [T1; I∅] to cause (someone) to suffer in the mind or feel offended: *What he said hurt (her) very much. Be careful what you say to him; he's easily hurt.*

ache 1 [I∅] to have or suffer a continuous pain, esp in the body: *I ache all over. My head aches.* **2** [I∅ (*for*), I3] to have a strong feeling of desire: *He aches to see her again.*

pain *usu fml or old use* **1** [T1] to cause to feel pain: *My foot isn't paining me now. It pains me to have to disobey you, but I must.* **2** [I∅] to give or have a sensation of pain: *My foot isn't paining now.*

sting 1 [T1] to cause sharp pain to: *The whip stung him. The rain is stinging my eyes.* (*fig*) *Her words stung him into anger.* **2** [T1] to prick with a sting: *An insect stung me.* **3** [I∅] to have a sting: *Some insects sting. This is a stinging plant*

and it's called a nettle. **4** [I∅] to feel a sharp pain: *My eyes are stinging from the rain.*

B123 *adjectives* : **feelings of pain**

painful [B] causing pain: *The wound was deep and painful. This news is painful to us all; I am very sorry to bring it to you.* **-ness** [U] **-ly** [adv]

painless [B] causing no pain: *The dentist's treatment was (quite) painless.* **-ness** [U] **-ly** [adv]

tender [Wa2;B] **1** hurting a little when touched; slightly painful: *Her skin was red and tender where he had beaten her. My throat is still tender after singing so much.* **2** easily hurt or damaged; quickly feeling pain: *Her skin is very tender, like a baby's.* (*fig*) *You touched me on a tender spot; that is a subject I don't enjoy discussing.* **-ness** [U] **-ly** [adv]

sore [Wa1;B] **1** painful when touched or used: *My leg feels sore. She has a sore throat and a cough. How is your sore foot today?* **2** (*fig*) very sad: *She has a sore heart over what he did to her.* **3** (*fig*) painful: *This is a sore subject with me; let's not discuss it.* **-ness** [U]

agonizing [B] very painful: *his toothache was agonizing and nearly drove him mad. This is an agonizing decision to make; I don't know what to do.* **-ly** [adv]

severe [Wa2;B] (of something bad, esp pain and illness, etc) strong in effect: *The pain of the wound was severe. She has suffered a very severe shock. He was weakened by a severe illness as a child.* **-ly** [adv] **severity** [U]

acute [B] **1** very severe and strong: *She was in acute pain.* **2** (of a disease) coming quickly to a dangerous condition: *He has acute appendicitis and must have an operation immediately. Acute diseases are short and severe, while chronic diseases are less severe and last a long time.* **-ness** [U] **-ly** [adv]

sharp [Wa1;B] sudden or severe: *He felt a sharp pain in his arm.* **-ness** [U] **-ly** [adv]

piercing [B] very sharp: *She felt a piercing pain in her side.* **-ly** [adv]

stabbing [Wa5;A] coming like a series of stabs from a knife: *He felt terrible stabbing pains in his chest.*

aching [Wa5;B] giving continuous pain: *His aching knee is giving him a lot of discomfort.* (*fig*) *His aching heart longed for her.* **achingly** [adv] (*fig*) affecting very strongly: *That picture is achingly beautiful.*

dull [Wa1;B] not sharply or clearly felt: *The pain in his arm was a continual dull ache. I have a dull sort of headache; I've taken two aspirins* [⇒ B173] *for it.* **-ness** [U] **dully** [adv]

throbbing [Wa5;A] coming again and again like a pulse [⇒ B36]: *He felt a dull throbbing pain in his head.*

chronic [Wa5;B] **1** (of a disease or condition) lasting a long time: *Chronic diseases are not necessarily fatal or especially painful. He has a* *chronic chest condition.* **2** habitual: *I'm afraid he's a chronic smoker. She's a chronic invalid now.* **3** *BrE sl* severe; intense: *Oh, the pain was something chronic, I tell you!* **-ally** [adv Wa4]

B124 *verbs* : **showing bodily disorders**

swell [I∅] to become larger than normal: *His face swelled when he had mumps. The toothache made one side of his mouth swell. Her leg has swollen badly.* **swollen** [B] of an increased size, often because of water or air within, which is not usually present: *His swollen arm is very painful.*

inflame [T1] cause to become red and swollen: *If you do that you will inflame the wound.* **inflamed** [B] (of a part of the body) red and swollen (after being hurt): *The cut looks badly inflamed. Inflamed tissue can be very painful.*

fester [Wv4;I∅] (of a cut or wound) to become infected and diseased: *His wounds were not treated and began to fester. These festering sores* [⇨ B127] *must be treated immediately.*

blister 1 [T1] to have blisters [⇨ B126] form on: *His hand is badly blistered because of the heat.* **2** [I∅] to form one or more blisters: *He wasn't used to hard physical work and his hands blistered easily.*

B125 *general nouns* : **showing bodily disorders**

swelling [U] the process of swelling: *In this disease swelling occurs in all the limbs.*

inflammation [U] swelling and soreness, which is often red and hot to the touch: *He is suffering from acute inflammation of the bowel.*

-itis [*suffix*] *med* inflammation of: *Arthritis is inflammation of the joints. Hepatitis is inflammation of the liver.*

B126 *particular nouns* : **showing minor bodily disorders** [C]

[ALSO ⇨ B148]

spot a small inflamed place on the skin: *This disease causes spots to appear on the face and arms.*

swelling a part of the body which has increased in size and usu stands out from the rest: *He has several unusual swellings on his arms and legs.*

pimple a small inflamed swelling on the skin: *The boy had a lot of pimples on his face. He gets a lot of pimples and boils.* **pimply** [Wa1,3;B] tending to get or covered with pimples

boil a painful swelling, larger than a pimple, under the skin: *The boy had a lot of boils on his face. She has a tendency to get boils on her neck.*

pock a spot on the skin caused by smallpox [⇨ B143]

wart 1 a small hard ugly swelling on the skin, esp on the face and hands: *He has warts all over his hands.* **2** a swelling of the same kind, esp on a tree

blister a thin watery swelling under the skin caused by rubbing, burning, etc: *His heavy shoes raised blisters on his feet.*

chilblain a painful swelling, esp on the hand or foot, caused by cold: *She gets chilblains (on her feet) every winter.*

bunion an inflamed swelling, esp on the large joint of the big toe: *If you wear tight shoes, you may get bunions.*

corn an area of hard skin on or under the foot, which is painful when pressed in: *He has a lot of corns on his feet.*

bump a swelling on the body made by knocking it against something, or something hitting it: *He got a nasty bump on his head when he fell.*

B127 *particular nouns, etc* : **showing major bodily disorders**

sore [C] a place on or in the body where the skin or flesh is damaged and which (usu) does not get better quickly: *His body is covered in terrible sores. She has bedsores from lying in one position too long.*

ulcer [C] an open sore on the inside or on the surface of the body which may bleed or produce poisonous matter: *He has a stomach ulcer. She suffers a lot from mouth ulcers.* **ulcerous** [B]

growth [C] *med* a lump produced by an unnatural and unhealthy increase in the number of cells in a part of the body

cancer [C; U] (a) diseased growth in the body: *He's got a cancer in his throat. He's got cancer of the throat.* **cancerous** [Wa5;B] like or producing cancer: *He had a cancerous growth on his face.*

tumour *BrE* **tumor** *AmE* [C] *med* a group of cells in the body which have divided and increased too quickly, causing swelling and illness: *He died of a brain tumour.*

cyst [C] a swollen place under the skin or inside the body, containing liquid: *The surgeon removed the cyst from her womb.*

pus [U] a thick yellowish-white liquid produced in an infected wound or poisoned part of the body

abscess [C] a swelling on or in the body where pus has gathered: *The dentist found an abscess in her tooth.*

gangrene 1 [U] (a disease which is) the decay of the flesh of part of the body because blood has stopped flowing there, usu after a wound: *The surgeon removed the soldier's leg because gangrene had set in* (= had started). **2** [I∅] to get gangrene: *The soldier's wound gangrened, and he died.*

B128 *particular nouns, etc* : **marks on the body after certain disorders** [C]

scab a piece of rough material which forms over a cut or wound and drops off when the skin has healed: *Don't pick at your scabs; let them heal.*

pockmark the mark left by a pock [⇒ B126]: *Her face has very few pockmarks, which is unusual for a smallpox* [⇒ B143] *victim.* **pockmarked** [B] covered with pockmarks

blemish a mark spoiling someone's beauty: *The only blemish on the baby's skin was a red mark on its neck.* (*fig*) *The court declared him not guilty, and he was freed without a blemish on his character.*

birthmark a mark on the body from the time of birth: *You can identify him by a small heart-shaped birthmark on his right arm.*

scar 1 a mark left on a part of the body, usu the skin, after damage from disease, wounding or a burn has been put right: *He will have a scar on his cheek for the rest of his life from that cut. The soldier was proud of his (battle) scars.* **2** [T1] to mark in such a way as to produce scars: *A sword cut scarred his face when he was a young man. His scarred hands showed that he had been burned.*

B129 *verbs & nouns* : **harming the body generally**

wound 1 [Wv5; T1] to damage the body of (someone): *He wounded his opponent in the arm with his knife. Wounded men lay on the carts.* **2** [C] a damaged place in the body, usu a hole or tear through the skin, esp done on purpose by a weapon, such as a gun: *He died of his wounds. The soldier had a terrible wound in his belly.* (*fig*) *His words to her caused a wound which took many years to heal.*

maim [T1] to wound so that some part of the body becomes useless: *He was badly maimed in the war.*

maul [T1] **1** (esp of animals) to wound by tearing the flesh: *The hunter was mauled by a lion and badly hurt. He got a mauling from a bear.* **2** to handle roughly or in an unpleasant way: *She said she wouldn't go out with him again because he kept mauling her while they were watching the film.*

injure [T1] to damage (esp a living creature) so that something does not function properly: *He was injured in a train crash. Dead and injured people lay everywhere after the bomb went off.* (*fig*) *You can injure people by unkind words.* **injury** [C; U] act or occasion of being injured: *His injuries in the car crash were terrible. She had injuries to her face and legs. Will he recover from his injuries? Wearing these clothes will protect you from possible injury.*

disfigure [T1] to spoil the appearance of (someone's) person and esp face: *The wound has permanently disfigured her face. His features were badly disfigured in a car crash.* **dis-** **figurement 1** [U] disfiguring or being disfigured: *The injury caused permanent disfigurement.* **2** [C] something that disfigures: *Her broken nose is unfortunately a disfigurement; it spoils her beauty.*

cripple 1 [Wv3;T1] to damage the legs or nerves (of a person) so that moving or walking is difficult or impossible: *The accident crippled him for life. She was crippled by/with arthritis.* [⇒ B145] **2** [C] a person who is crippled: *She has been a cripple since a childhood accident. Some of the beggars were cripples.* **crippling** [B] severe enough to cripple: *He felt a crippling pain in the left leg.* **-ly** [adv]

disable [T1 *usu pass*] to cause to be unable to use all or any one of the limbs: *The disabled soldiers were sent home. He was disabled by wounds in his legs.* **disablement** [U] the fact or state of being unable to use some or all of the limbs: *Since his disablement in the war he has had to use a wheelchair.*

B130 *verbs & nouns* : **harming the body by cutting**

cut 1 [T1] to make an opening or mark in the flesh with a sharp object: *He cut himself/his finger with a knife. She cut her hand on a piece of glass.* **2** [C] the result of cutting or being cut: *He had a deep cut in his hand and blood was dripping from it. Did you hurt yourself?—No, it's nothing; just a slight cut.*

bite 1 [T1] to cut into with the teeth: *The dog bit him. The lion bit a large piece of flesh out of the dead antelope. He bit her playfully on the ear.* **2** [C] an act of biting: *That's a bad bite—Was it a dog? Dog bites can be dangerous.* [⇒ E6]

nick 1 [C] a small cut like a V: *It's not a bad cut, just a nick.* **2** [T1] to make a cut or nick in: *He nicked himself/his face shaving.*

gash 1 [C] a long deep cut or wound: *Blood poured from the gash in his face.* **2** [T1] to make a gash or gashes in: *The drunk man gashed his face with a razor while trying to shave.*

slash 1 [C] a long thin cut or gash: *His body was covered with knife slashes.* **2** [T1] to make a slash or slashes in: *The man slashed her face with a knife.*

scratch 1 [T1] to make lines or small cuts and holes in the skin of: *The cat scratched his arm with its claws. She scratched his face with her fingernails.* **2** [C] the result of scratching or being scratched: *Are you hurt?—No, it's nothing; just a scratch. There was a scratch (mark) on his face.*

claw [I0 (*at*); T1 (*out*)] to cut, scratch, pull, etc with claws, nails, fingers, etc: *The cat clawed at the door to get in. He was badly clawed by a lion. 'I'll claw his eyes out!' she said angrily.*

stab 1 [T1] to cut deep into with the point of a knife, etc: *The robber stabbed his victim in the back. Help!—I've been stabbed!* **2** [C] the result or action of stabbing or being stabbed: *He* *received several stabs in the chest. This stab wound must be treated immediately.*

incision [C; U] *tech, esp med* a cut into something, done with a special tool for a special reason, esp a medical one: *He made an incision into the leather. An incision was made into the diseased organ.* **incisive** [B] (*only fig*) cutting deep into the heart of the matter: *an incisive argument* **-ly** [adv]

B131 *verbs & nouns* : harming the body by beating

beat [T1] to strike the body of (someone) severely again and again: *The men beat him unmercifully. He was beaten unconscious. They broke several of his ribs and one arm when they beat him.*

batter [T1] to beat very severely, often with something heavy: *He battered his wife almost to death. Battered babies often suffer damage for life. He battered the man's head in with a metal rod.*

blow [C] a hard stroke which hurts, makes unconscious, etc: *The blow to his head must have been made from behind. He tried to escape the blows which the men rained on him.*

bruise 1 [C] a damaged place on the skin (and flesh) from a blow or knock: *That's a bad bruise on his face—how did he get it? That child is always covered in bruises. He escaped from the accident with only minor cuts and bruises.* **2** [T1] to cause a bruise or bruises to: *He bruised his hand while boxing. Be careful not to bruise yourself climbing that wall.*

brain [T1] to kill or knock (someone) unconscious by striking on the head: *She brained him with a heavy stick.*

B132 *verbs & nouns* : breaking and straining parts of the body

break 1 [T1; I0] to separate into two or more pieces: *Be careful you don't break your leg jumping across there. His leg broke like a piece of dry wood.* **2** [C] the place where breaking has happened: *His leg will be all right—it's a clean break.*

fracture *med* **1** [I0; T1] to break: *His leg fractured in three places when he fell.* **2** [C] a break: *He has multiple fractures of the pelvis.* [⇒ B11 PELVIS; ⇒ J10 MULTIPLE]

sprain 1 [T1] to weaken (the muscle of) a part of the body, esp by violent activity: *She fell and sprained her ankle.* **2** [C] the result of spraining: *She twisted her ankle and got a bad sprain.*

strain [T1] to damage or weaken by pulling or twisting (a muscle, etc) too much: *He has strained his heart doing all that heavy work.* **2** [U] the result of straining: *He is suffering from heart strain.*

pull [T1] *infml* to strain: *He pulled a muscle exercising too hard.*

B133 *adjectives, etc* : being unable to do certain things

blind 1 [Wa1;B] unable to see: *She has been blind from birth. Cats are born blind but soon begin to see. He is blind in one eye.* **-ness** [U] **-ly** [adv] **2** [Wa1;F (*to*)] (*fig*) of poor judgement: *She is blind to the results of her stupid behaviour.* **3** [*the* P] blind people: *He wants to help the blind enjoy as full a life as possible.* **4** [T1] to make blind: *He was blinded in the war. The bright headlights of the approaching car (temporarily) blinded their driver.*

shortsighted [B] unable to see clearly things that are some distance away: *I'm afraid I'm rather shortsighted; come a little closer, please.* (*fig*) *He is being a bit shortsighted about this plan; he can't see how successful it will be.* **-ness** [U] **-ly** [adv]

longsighted [B] unable to see clearly things that are near: *He's very longsighted and needs glasses for close work.* **-ness** [U] **-ly** [adv]

deaf 1 [Wa1;B] unable to hear well or at all: *He's totally deaf; he can't hear a thing. She's partially deaf in her right ear.* **-ness** [U] **2** [*the* P] deaf people: *The deaf find social life difficult.* **3** [F (*to*)] (*fig*) unwilling to listen: *He was deaf to her request.* **stone deaf** [B] *infml* completely deaf **deafen** [T1] to make unable to hear: *The loud sounds deafened us.*

hard of hearing [F] *euph* (rather) deaf: *She's hard of hearing; speak a little louder.*

dumb 1 [Wa5;B] unable to speak clearly or at all: *The child seemed dumb because he was in fact deaf. People often talk about dogs and cats and so on as 'dumb animals' because they can't speak.* **2** [F] silent; not speaking: *He remained dumb when asked the questions again.* (*fig*) *She was struck dumb with horror at what she had seen.* **-ness** [U] **-ly** [adv]

mute 1 [Wa1;B] not speaking; silent: *He stood looking at her in mute astonishment.* **2** [Wa5; B] *old use* dumb: *He has been mute since infancy.* **3** [C] a person who is or has been made dumb: *The queen was served by mutes, men whose tongues had been removed. He's a deaf mute and cannot tell anyone their secrets.*

lame [Wa1;B] not able to walk properly: *He has been lame in one leg since the accident. The horse went lame because of an injury to the right foreleg.* **-ness** [U]

B134 *adjectives* : relating to inability through age [B]

[ALSO ⇒ B93 NOT STRONG]

decrepit made weak by old age or hard use: *He's pretty decrepit now; of course, he's 82. That decrepit old horse won't get you very far.* **-ude** [U]

infirm physically weak, esp through age: *He walked over with very infirm steps.* **-ity, -ness** [U]

senile *med* showing the weaknesses of old age: *He's senile; he sometimes forgets his own name.* **senility** [U]

B135 *verbs & nouns* : **communicating disease**

infect [T1 (*with*)] **1** [*often pass*] to put disease into a body: *They deliberately infected the animals with a disease in order to study the effects. She became infected with a rare disease. The spreading disease infected her eyes and she became blind.* **2** to spread into and make impure: *Waste gases infected the air and made it difficult to breathe.* **3** (*fig*) to make (someone else) have feelings of the same type: *His courage infected his friends, who had been discouraged before. She infected the whole class with her enthusiasm.*

infection **1** [U] the process or result of being infected: *If you don't clean this place there will be a great risk of infection spreading among the patients.* **2** [C] an infectious disease: *There is a chance at this time of year of catching various infections, none serious.*

pass on [v adv T1] to give (esp an infection) to someone else: *People pass infections on to each other in crowded buses and offices.*

contagion *med* **1** [U] the act of passing on disease by touching: *People get these diseases by simple contagion.* **2** [C] such a disease: *I'm afraid the contagion is spreading and we are powerless to stop it.*

contaminate [T1] to make impure by the addition of poisonous matter: *Don't eat this food; it may have been contaminated by that dirty water.*

contamination [U] the process or result of contaminating or being contaminated: *Contamination can result from dirty drinking water.*

contaminant [C] anything which serves to contaminate

pollute [T1] to make dirty or impure: *The river has been polluted by all kinds of industrial waste.* (*fig*) *These magazines can pollute a young person's mind!* [⇒ D181–2]

pollution [U; C] the process or result of polluting or being polluted: *River pollution is now contributing to the pollution of the seas. These various pollutions can cause human disease.*

pollutant [C] anything which pollutes

B136 *adjectives* : **communicating disease** [Wa2]

infectious [B] spread by or likely to cause infection: *These diseases are highly infectious. That child is infectious and must be isolated immediately. Burn these infectious clothes.* (*fig*) *Her enthusiasm was highly infectious.* **-ness** [U]

catching [F; (B)] *infml* infectious: *Many childhood illnesses are catching.* (*fig*) *She is very*

enthusiastic and I hope the others will find it catching.

contagious [B] which can spread by touching: *If a person has a contagious disease, he should be kept away from other people till he recovers.*

immune [Wa5;B (*to*)] unable to be harmed because of special powers in the person or animal: *These people are immune to TB.* **immunity** [U; C] the state or condition of being immune: *He has immunity from that disease.* [⇒ B174]

B137 *nouns* : **occurrences of disease**

outbreak [C] a sudden appearance or beginning of a dangerous disease: *The doctors there have just reported an outbreak of cholera/a cholera outbreak.*

epidemic [C] *esp med* many cases of the same disease spreading rapidly among many people in an area for a time: *We had an epidemic of influenza last winter. The flu epidemic was terrible last winter. The outbreak of flu became an epidemic.* (*fig*) *We have had an epidemic of engagements and marriages in the firm this year.*

plague **1** [U; C] a terrible infectious disease which spreads over large areas, attacking and killing many people: *Bubonic Plague or the Black Death was once a terrible disease in Asia and Europe. Plague victims* [⇒ B167] *were dying like flies. Plagues were once very common because people lived in unhealthy conditions.* **2** [C] any terrible disaster with the same kind of effects: *The farms were attacked by a plague of insects.* **3** [S] (*fig*) a person who makes life difficult for others: *What a plague that child is!* **be plagued with** to suffer from: *They have been plagued with bad luck in that family.*

pestilence [C; U] *fml* any kind of epidemic or terrible event: *The Black Death was one of the worst pestilences in human history. These insects are a pestilence; they must be destroyed.* **pestilential** [B] **1** of or like a pestilence; highly infectious **2** (*fig*) very annoying

Diseases and ailments

B140 *nouns* : **colds and fevers**

cold [C] an illness common in winter in which the nose and/or throat become(s) painful, blocked by mucus [⇒ B60], etc: *I've got a cold coming on. The children have all got colds. She has a slight cold. He has a bad cold in the head.*

influenza [U] a disease like a bad cold but more serious: *There is likely to be an influenza epidemic this winter. People used to die of influenza, but that is much less likely nowadays.*

flu [(*the*) U] *infml* influenza: *He's got (the) flu.*

catarrh [U] inflammation of the nose and throat, causing a flow of liquid: *Can I have another handkerchief—this catarrh is terrible. His nose is blocked up with catarrh.*

cough [C] the (medical) condition of coughing often: *Poor fellow, what a bad cough he's got. Winter is a time of coughs and colds.*

chill [C] an illness marked by coldness and a shaking of the body: *Put on warm clothes so that you don't catch a chill.*

fever [C; U] a (medical) condition associated with many illnesses in which the sufferer develops a high temperature: *She has a slight fever; she should go to bed immediately. Some fevers can be very dangerous.*

B141 nouns : disorders of the lungs and breathing [U]

pneumonia a serious illness with inflammation [⇒ B125] of one or both lungs: *His chill developed into pneumonia and he died three days later. Pneumonia causes difficulty in breathing.*

bronchitis inflammation of the tubes between the windpipe and the lungs   **bronchitic** [Wa5;B] suffering from or concerning bronchitis

tuberculosis a serious disease affecting many parts of the body but chiefly the lungs: *People living in cold damp places often get tuberculosis.* **TB** *abbrev* **tubercular, -ous** of, suffering from, or causing tuberculosis

consumption (the old name for) tuberculosis

asthma a disease or condition which at times makes breathing very difficult **asthmatic 1** [B] suffering from or concerning asthma **-ally** [adv Wa4] **2** [C] an asthmatic person

B142 adjectives : relating to fevers [B]

feverish 1 having or showing a (usu slight) fever: *Her skin felt feverish; in a feverish condition.* **2** [was] caused by a fever: *a feverish dream* **3** (*fig*) unnaturally fast: *feverish work* **-ly** [adv]

fevered having a fever: *He looked fevered and ill.*

febrile *med* of or caused by fever

flushed hot and pink with blood: *Her face looks flushed; she may have a slight fever.*

hot [Wa1] having a higher temperature than normal: *His forehead is hot; he may be developing a fever. He had a hot, flushed look.*

B143 nouns : infectious diseases

measles [(*the*) U] an infectious disease in which the sufferer has a fever and small red spots on his face and body: *The child caught (the) measles at school.*

German measles [U] an infectious disease in which red spots appear on the body, not

serious in children but serious in pregnant [⇒ A17] women, as the disease may harm the unborn baby

chickenpox [U] a disease caught esp by children that is marked by a slight fever and spots on the skin

whooping cough [U] a disease caught esp by children in which the sufferer coughs noisily

mumps [(*the*) U] an infectious disease, esp of children, with painful swellings in the neck

scarlet fever [U] an infectious disease, esp of children, marked by red spots and a red painful throat

yellow fever [U] an infectious and dangerous tropical disease which causes the skin to turn yellow: *He caught yellow fever in West Africa.*

diphtheria [U] a serious infectious disease of the throat

typhus [U] a serious disease marked by fever, great weakness, and purple spots on the body

typhoid (fever) [U] a form of typhus which attacks the stomach **paratyphoid** a disease of the stomach similar to typhoid but milder

smallpox [U] a serious infectious disease with spots on the face which leave permanent marks (**pockmarks**): *He had smallpox as a child and nearly died.*

cholera [U] a very serious infectious disease causing sickness, repeated emptying of the stomach and bowels, and often death: *Cholera outbreaks are still common in India.* [⇒ B147]

tetanus [U] a disease caused by infection in cuts and wounds in which the muscles become tight and hard: *He was given an injection against tetanus/an anti-tetanus injection.*

lockjaw [U] *infml* tetanus

bubonic plague [U] a plague carried mainly by rats, spreading quickly and marked by fever and swellings under the arms and in the lower stomach: *Many thousands of people died of bubonic plague in the Middle Ages.*

rabies [U] a disease which passes to man from animal bites, causing madness and inability to drink: *You can get rabies from the bite of a mad dog.* **rabid** [Wa5;B] suffering from rabies: *Rabid dogs must be shot.*

hydrophobia [U] *med & tech* rabies

leprosy [U] a disease which can be passed from one person to another and which slowly destroys the skin and the parts of the body underneath it **leper** [C] a person who has leprosy

B144 nouns, etc : disorders of the heart and blood

anaemia *BrE*, **anemia** *AmE* [U] the unhealthy condition of not having the proper number of red cells in the blood: *He has suffered from anaemia for years.* **anaemic** [B] having anaemia

blood pressure [U] the force with which the blood pushes through the arteries: *His blood pressure is normal. She is overweight and suffers from high blood pressure.*

blood clot [C] a thickened or half-solid mass or lump formed from the blood

thrombosis [U; C] *med* the condition of having a blood clot

hemorrhage *also* **haemorrhage** *BrE* **1** [U] any bleeding **2** [C] any escape of blood or bursting of a blood vessel: *He has had several hemorrhages during the night.* **3** [IØ] (of blood vessels) to burst: *He hemorrhaged badly and died before we could get help to him.*

apoplexy [U] **1** a hemorrhage of any tissue but esp in the brain: *He died of apoplexy.* **2** a sudden serious stopping of the workings of the body due to a hemorrhage **apoplectic 1** [Wa5; B] of or concerning apoplexy **2** [C] a person suffering from apoplexy

heart disease [U] any disease of the heart: *He suffers from chronic heart disease.*

heart failure [U] the failure of the heart to work properly: *Her father died of heart failure.* *(infml) Gosh, I nearly had heart failure when I heard the news!*

heart attack [C] a sudden failure in the working of the heart: *He has had two heart attacks and if he has another it could kill him.*

seizure [C] a sudden attack of illness, esp a heart attack

coronary thrombosis [U] a medical condition in which there is a blood clot in the blood vessel near the heart called the coronary artery **coronary** [C] *infml* such a thrombosis; a heart attack: *If you lift those heavy things you'll get a coronary!*

varicose veins [P] a condition of having veins [⇨ B36], usu in the legs, which are larger or more swollen than usual: *She suffers from varicose veins.*

phlebitis [U] an inflamed condition of the blood vessels

B145 *nouns* : disorders of the bones and teeth

rheumatism [U] any of various diseases causing pain and stiffness in the joints of the body: *He has suffered for years from rheumatism in the feet and hands. She's a martyr to rheumatism.*

rheumatics [U] *infml* rheumatism

rheumatic fever [U] a serious infectious disease, esp in children, with fever, swelling of the joints, and possible damage to the heart

lumbago [U] pain in the lower back: *He suffers from lumbago, and is often off work with it.*

backache [U; C] (a) pain in the (usu lower) back; lumbago

arthritis [U] a disease causing pain and swelling in the joints of the body **arthritic 1** [B] suffering from or concerning arthritis **2** [C] an arthritic person

rickets [U] a disease of children in which the bones are very soft and may lose their proper shape, due to lack of proper food

caries [U] decay of the bones

dental caries [U] tooth decay

toothache [U] pain in a tooth: *He had severe toothache and went to see his dentist.*

B146 *nouns* : disorders of the muscles and nerves

spasm [U; C] tightening and hardening of the muscles which cannot be controlled: *When she has an attack of her illness, her whole body goes into spasm. His body heaved in several violent spasms then lay still.*

cramp [U; C] sudden tightening of the muscles, as in the legs during or after violent exercise: *I got cramp while swimming, and had to shout for help. Some people get cramp at night and it can be very painful.*

paralysis [U] **1** a loss of feeling in and control of all or some of the muscles: *She had paralysis of the left arm and leg after her accident.* **2** (*fig*) a loss or lack of ability to move, act, think, etc: *Lazy people suffer from paralysis of the will. Without electricity the country would be in a state of paralysis.* **paralyse** *BrE*, **-yze** *AmE* [T1] to cause paralysis in: *Fear paralysed him. He is paralysed below the waist from polio.* **paralytic 1** [Wa5;B] of or concerning paralysis; unable to move **2** [C] a paralysed person

palsy [U] *old use* paralysis

poliomyelitis [U] an acute disease, most common in very young people, with inflammation of the nerves and paralysis **polio** [U] *abbrev*

epilepsy [U] a disorder of the nervous system which causes fits and unconsciousness **epileptic 1** [Wa5;B] suffering from or concerning epilepsy **2** [C] a person suffering from epilepsy

coma [C] a deep, unnatural state like sleep, usu caused by illness or an injury, esp to the brain: *The man lay in a coma.* **comatose** [B] being in a coma: *He has been comatose ever since the accident.*

B147 *nouns* : disorders of the bowel, bladder, genitals and anus

constipation [U] the condition of being unable to empty the bowel [⇨B35] frequently enough or effectively **constipated** [B] suffering from constipation

piles [P] the swelling of a vein [⇨ B36] or veins, esp at or near the anus [⇨ B33]

hemorrhoids *also* **haemorrhoids** *BrE* [P] *med* piles

diarrhoea *BrE*, **diarrhea** *AmE* [U] an illness in which the bowels [⇨ B35] are emptied too often, in too liquid a form: *He had a bad attack of diarrhoea, probably caused by something he ate.*

dysentery [U] a painful disease of the bowels that causes them to be emptied more often than usual and to produce blood and mucus [⇨ B60]: *Dysentery is a common complaint in countries where food is not hygienically prepared.* [⇨ B143]

cystitis [U] a condition in which water must be passed often from the body, often with pain and difficulty

incontinence [U] the condition of being unable to control the bowel or bladder [⇒ B38], so that waste matter is passed from the body when one does not wish it **incontinent** [B] suffering from incontinence: *The elderly patient was doubly incontinent* (= incontinent of both bladder and bowel).

bedwetting [U] incontinence of urine, esp in young children, in bed at night

venereal disease [U] any of several types of disease passed from one person to another during sexual intercourse [⇒ A16] **VD** *abbrev*

gonorrhea *also* **gonorrhoea** *BrE* [U] a venereal disease causing infection and burning feelings in the reproductive organs

syphilis [U] a serious venereal disease which can also be passed on from parent to child **syphilitic 1** [Wa5;B] having or related to syphilis **2** [C] a person suffering from syphilis

B148 *nouns, etc* : **disorders of the skin**

spot [C] a small area of swollen red skin on the body, often with poisonous matter inside: *He has a lot of spots on his arms and legs—is it a rash?* [⇒ B126]

rash [C] a set of spots on the face and/or body: *He has broken out in a rash. Children get various rashes in such illnesses as measles and chickenpox.*

shingles [U] a painful disease among adults in which a ring of red spots spreads round the body, esp the waist, due to the infection of certain nerves

acne [U] a condition common among adolescents in which there are many pimples [⇒ B126] on the face

itch 1 [C] a sore feeling which makes a person or animal want to rub the skin **2** (*fig*) a strong desire: *He has an itch for power.* **3** [*the* R] scabies **4** [IØ] to have an itch: *If your skin itches, (don't) scratch (it).*

scabies [U] a contagious skin disease caused by very small creatures which live under the skin: *Scabies causes a severe itch.*

B149 *nouns* : **mental and nervous problems**

allergy [C] *med* a condition of being highly sensitive to certain things such as food, animals, medicine, etc, often resulting in rashes or difficulty in breathing: *Hay fever is an allergy.* **allergic** [B (*to*)] *He's allergic to penicillin.*

hay fever [U] an allergic condition affecting the nose and throat, caused by dust from any of various plants: *She gets hay fever every year in early summer.*

neurosis [C] trouble of the mind caused by

disorders of the nervous system or a deep anxiety **neurotic 1** [B] suffering from a neurosis; easily made anxious, excited, etc **2** [C] a neurotic person **-ally** [adv Wa4]

hysteria [U] **1** a disturbance of the nervous system with outbursts of often uncontrollable emotion **2** senseless, uncontrolled excitement: *The young pop fans were in a state of hysteria when their star arrived.* **hysterical** [B] caused by or suffering from hysteria: *His hysterical laughter frightened her. The child became hysterical with fear.* **-ly** [adv Wa4] **hysterics** [P] attack(s) of hysteria: *She went into hysterics when she heard the terrible news.*

phobia [C] a strong, unnatural and usu unreasonable fear and dislike: *She has a phobia about water and won't learn to swim.* **claustrophobia** [U] the fear of being shut into a small space **claustrophobic** [B] of, concerning or causing claustrophobia

insomnia [U] *med & tech* inability to sleep

B150 *nouns* : **digestive disorders** [U]
[ALSO ⇒ B119–20]

indigestion pain in the stomach because of difficulty in dealing with (= **digesting**) food: *He often gets indigestion after eating too much.*

dyspepsia *med* indigestion **dyspeptic** [B] of, concerning, like or caused by dyspepsia **-ally** [adv Wa4]

heartburn *infml* indigestion

B151 *nouns* : **disorders of the head and balance**

headache [C] a pain in the upper part of the head: *God, I've got a splitting headache; it's terrible.*

migraine [U; C] a severe headache, usu only on one side of the head or face: *She gets regular attacks of migraine.*

vertigo [U] a disorder in which a person feels dizzy [⇒ B111]: *He gets vertigo if he looks down from a high place.*

B152 *nouns* : **disorders of the liver** [U]

jaundice a disease caused by a stopping of the flow of bile [⇒ B60], with a yellowing of the skin and the whites of the eyes

hepatitis *med* inflammation of the liver

B153 *nouns & verbs* : **poisoning**

poison 1 [U; C] a substance causing death or harm if swallowed or taken in by a living thing: *I need some poison to kill these rats. He put down weed poison in the garden. She gave her husband poison in his whisky.* (*fig*) *These ideas are a poison in our society and we must resist* *them.* **2** [T1] to give poison to or put poison on; infect: *He poisoned most of the rats. This river has been poisoned with industrial waste. She succeeded in poisoning her husband/by poisoning his whisky. (fig) He has poisoned your mind against me. These bad experiences have poisoned her life.* **poisoner** [C] a person using poison against others **poisonous** [B] **1** acting as poison or equipped with poison: *The house was full of poisonous fumes. Be careful; that snake is poisonous.* **2** causing great harm: *What a poisonous look!* **-ly** [adv]

intoxicate [T1 *usu pass*]; (I∅)] (of alcohol) to cause loss of control of actions and feelings in (a person): *The man drove his car while in an intoxicated state. (fig) He was intoxicated by the excitement in the city.* **intoxication** [U] the condition of being intoxicated; alcoholic poisoning: *The man drove while in a state of intoxication and crashed his car.* **intoxicant** [C; U] something, esp a liquid to drink, which intoxicates

venom [U] *esp tech or lit* liquid poison which certain snakes, insects and other creatures pass by biting and stinging **venomous** [B] full of or using venom: *venomous snakes*; *(fig) venomous words* **-ly** [adv] **-ness** [U]

antidote [C; U] medicine used against a poison or to stop a disease from having an effect: *Do you have an antidote to snakebite?*

antivenom [U; C] *med* a medicine used against snake venom

poisoning [U] the condition of being poisoned: *He died of poisoning.*

blood poisoning [U] the condition of having poisoned blood: *He got blood poisoning from cutting his hand on a dirty knife.*

food poisoning [U] the condition of being poisoned or made ill by eating food which has gone bad: *There were several cases of food poisoning from people eating tinned meat that had not been properly sealed.*

toxin [C; U] *tech* poison: *These substances are toxins.* **toxic** [B] *tech* poisonous: *These are toxic substances.*

Medicine and general medical care

B160 *verbs, etc* : **caring for people**

look after [v prep T1] to be responsible for and take care of: *Nurse, would you look after this patient, please? He has looked after his aged and ailing* [⇒ B111] *mother for years. Don't worry—I'll look after you.*

take care of [T1] **1** to help while ill: *Lie still in bed; we'll take care of you. She's good at taking care of people.* **2** to attend to: *You do that, and I'll take care of these other matters.*

care for [v prep T1] *fml* to look after: *He has cared for her throughout her long illness.*

tend [T1] to take care of very carefully: *She tended him day and night for a fortnight, until he began to recover. Tending an invalid can be very tiring.*

attend [T1 *usu pass*] to go to be with and care for (esp an ill person): *She is attended by Dr Smith. Who is attending the patients now?*

nurse 1 [T1] to tend; to look after as a nurse would: *She nursed him back to health.* **2** [I∅] to spend time as a nurse: *She's been nursing for a year now.*

neglect 1 [T1] to take no care of or pay no attention to: *She neglects her children badly.* **2** [T3] to fail to do: *He neglected to give them back the money.* **3** [U] the condition of being neglected: *The children live in a state of neglect.* **negligent** [B] not careful enough: *She's very negligent in her work; she's a negligent worker.* **-ly** [adv] **negligence** [U] the state of being negligent

B161 *verbs* : **examining and curing people**

[ALSO ⇒ B164, B178 FOR RELATED NOUNS]

examine [T1] to study, in order to make a **diagnosis** (= to decide the nature of a disease, etc): *The doctor examined his patient.*

diagnose [T1 (*as*)] *med & tech* to decide the nature of (a disease, etc) by studying the **symptoms** (= signs on the body or in the activities of the patient): *The doctor diagnosed her illness as anaemia* [⇒ B144].

treat [T1] to try to cure by medical means: *The doctors hope to treat his illness successfully. She is being treated with a new drug. Which doctor is treating her?*

cure [T1] **1** to bring back to good health: *The doctor hopes to cure her of the disease quite quickly. He's cured now; he should be back to normal health in a few weeks.* **2** to treat successfully: *The doctor cured the disease. We can cure some types of cancer.*

heal 1 [I∅] (of wounds, etc) to get better; return to normal: *The wound is healing nicely. The cut in her hand has healed completely, without leaving a scar.* **2** [T1] *emot* to cure: *He has healed her; she is her old healthy self again. This medicine will help heal the wound.*

dose [T1] to give a (heavy) dose esp of medicine: *He dosed himself with medicines to stop the cold from getting worse.*

set 1 [T1] to put (a broken limb or bone) in a fixed position with material round it which prevents movement and allows healing: *His leg was set at the hospital.* **2** [I∅] (of bones and limbs) to have the parts join firmly together again: *His leg has set beautifully.*

bandage [Wv5;T1 (*up*)] to put a bandage [⇒ B175] on: *The nurse bandaged (up) his wounds. He had a bandaged hand; he had burnt himself badly. He bandaged her arm as well as he could with a piece of cloth.*

dress [T1] to clean, bandage, etc (a wound or

injury): *Nurse, dress that man's wounded arm, please.*

B162 *verbs* : **reducing pain**

soothe [T1] **1** to reduce the pain of: *The cold water soothed the pain of the burn.* **2** to comfort: *She soothed the upset child.*

deaden [T1] to cause to lose force, feeling, etc: *The sedative deadened the pain.*

lessen [I0; T1] to become or make less: *The pain lessened during the night. The treatment lessened his discomfort considerably.*

alleviate [T1] *tech* to make (pain, suffering, anger, etc) less: *The medicine alleviates his pain but does not cure his illness.* **alleviation** [U]

ease 1 [I0] (as of pain) to become less: *The pain eased a little in the morning.* **2** [T1] to cause (pain) to become less: *The doctor helped to ease her pain before she died.*

assuage [T1] *lit & fml* to make (pain, suffering, desire, thirst, etc) less: *Nothing could assuage the pain.*

allay [T1] *fml* to make (pain, fear, anger, doubt, etc) less: *This medicine will allay the pain. Her friendly manner allayed his fears.*

B163 *verbs* : **getting better after illness**

recover [I0] to return to a usual state of health, strength, ability, etc: *He is very ill and unlikely to recover. She has recovered from her bad cold and can go out tomorrow.*

recuperate [I0] *tech* to recover after an illness or accident: *He was very seriously ill, and he is still recuperating (from the illness). She needs time to recuperate.*

get well/better [I0] *infml* to recover: *He's getting well again; don't worry. She's getting better every day and will soon be on her feet again. Get well soon, darling! I hope he gets better quickly.*

convalesce [I0] to spend time getting well after an illness: *He went to the mountains to convalesce in the pure air.* **convalescent** [B] in the process of convalescing

pull through [v adv] *infml* **1** [I0] to live on after a bad illness or accident: *Don't worry; he'll pull through.* **2** [T1] to help live on: *The doctors will pull him through.*

B164 *nouns* : **things which help people get better**

cure [C] a means of (possibly) bringing someone back to good health: *The cure isn't certain, but it often works very well. There is, I'm afraid, no (known) cure for this condition. He tried various cures, but none worked.*

remedy [C] *old use & more genl* a cure: *Is there any remedy for this disease/trouble? We have tried all the remedies, but none work(s).* **reme-**

dial [Wa5;B] for the purpose of curing, helping, improving, etc: *remedial care; remedial language lessons* **-ly** [adv]

treatment [C; U] way of treating or trying to cure anyone: *We are trying a new treatment for this disease. The treatment was a great success. She is still undergoing treatment for her condition.*

care [U] general treatment and nursing: *The patient is receiving intensive care at the moment; he is very ill. The standard of care in these hospitals is very high.*

aftercare [U] special treatment given after the main treatment for a disease or condition or after an operation: *Aftercare is very important in cases like these.*

attention [U] the act of attending someone, esp a person who is not well: *He will need a lot of care and attention if he is to get better.*

recovery [U; S] the process or result of recovering from an illness, etc: *Full recovery may not be possible, but we can expect a partial recovery. He damaged his eyes in the car crash and recovery of sight in one eye is not certain. She made a remarkable recovery from the illness.*

recuperation [U] the process of recuperating

convalescence [U] the process of convalescing

B165 *nouns* : **processes which help people get better**

healing [U] **1** the process of returning to health: *Healing is often slow in cases where the patient has lost a lot of blood.* **2** an activity which heals or tries to heal: *He is engaged in healing by means of a Chinese method using needles.*

therapy [U] *tech* treatment helping in a cure: *Exercise is the best therapy in this case.*

occupational therapy	treatment of illness of body or mind by useful activities
radiotherapy	treatment by controlled radiation
physiotherapy	treatment by heat, light, electricity, exercise, and other natural forces
psychotherapy	treatment of disorders of the mind by means of action on the mind itself, using psychology [⇒ G6] rather than drugs, operations etc

B166 *nouns* : **people who care and cure** [C]

doctor [*also* N] a person who has been trained in the use of medical science: *Send for a doctor,* quickly; there's been an accident! The doctor prescribed tablets for her blood condition. It takes at least six years to train a doctor. Thank you, Doctor.

physician 1 old use a doctor: He is physician to the Royal Family. The prince was attended by his personal physician. **2** tech a doctor who can practise medicine but not surgery

specialist a doctor who has made a special study of a particular branch of medicine: Her doctor sent her to see a heart specialist.

consultant 1 a doctor who can give special advice on certain medical difficulties in addition to that given by an ordinary doctor: Several famous consultants have given their opinions and they all agree. **2** esp BrE a senior hospital doctor

general practitioner a doctor who is not a specialist in any particular branch of medicine and treats illnesses, etc generally: General practitioners and specialists are complementary in the medical profession. **GP** abbrev

family doctor a general practitioner who is normally called in by a family for any of its medical problems: He has been a family doctor as well as a consultant, so he knows all the problems.

surgeon a doctor who practises surgery [⇒B168]: The surgeon took out his patient's appendix [⇒B35].

dentist a person who has been trained to look after people's teeth and gums: I must go to the dentist; I've got terrible toothache.

dental surgeon a dentist trained in surgery useful to dental care

veterinary surgeon BrE, **veterinarian** AmE a trained animal doctor **vet** abbrev

quack 1 a person dishonestly claiming to have special (esp medical) knowledge and practising a skill he does not have: I don't want to be treated by a quack; I want a proper doctor! **2** derog a doctor whom one dislikes or does not respect: Don't let that quack near me!

healer any person who can heal: She went to an old village healer to get a cure for backache.

faith healer a person healing or claiming to heal by means of religious faith

medical practitioner a person trained and skilled in any branch of medicine

nurse [also N] a person, usu a woman and often in a hospital, who helps doctors by caring for their patients in practical ways during ordinary daily activity and during operations: She has been a nurse for 20 years. She has passed her exams and is now a qualified nurse. Thank you, Nurse.

male nurse a man working as a nurse: Male nurses are particularly important in caring for men in mental hospitals.

sister [also N] (the title of) a nurse in charge of a hospital ward: Thank you, Sister; you have done a good job here.

matron [also N] (the title of) a woman in charge of a hospital who has control over the work of

all the nurses and those who work there, but not over doctors: The Matron is on her daily round of the wards. Thank you, Matron.

midwife a woman, usu a nurse, who has been trained to help other women in childbirth: The midwife delivered a healthy baby boy.

therapist a person trained in any kind of therapy

orderly an attendant in a hospital, usu a man and without special professional training: Can you get an orderly to take this patient out? He is a hospital orderly.

B167 nouns : people who need to be treated [C]

patient 1 a person receiving medical treatment from a doctor or in a hospital: All the patients in the doctor's waiting room looked ill. Nurse, please help this patient to undress. **2** one of the group of people who go to a particular doctor when they need medical treatment: Send a copy of this letter to all my patients.

outpatient a sick person who goes to a hospital for treatment while continuing to live at home: He has been attending the hospital as an outpatient for some months. She was asked to attend at the Outpatients' Department at 10 am.

case 1 an instance of a disease, injury, etc needing medical treatment: We have discovered three cases of smallpox [⇒B143] in the city. The woman is a bad case of arthritis [⇒B145]. **2** a medical or surgical patient: We have several new cases to handle tonight. He's a hospital case, I'm afraid. Nurse, move this case to another ward [⇒B180].

casualty a person hurt in an accident, war, etc: There were 20 serious casualties in the train crash. They treat 30 casualties a night in that hospital. The casualties in the battle on both sides were very heavy. (fig) He was a casualty of the last election; he lost his seat in Parliament. Your plan is the first casualty of the new economies, I'm afraid.

invalid a person made weak by illness: After that illness he was an invalid for the rest of his life. She has an old invalid mother to look after. **invalid chair** also **wheelchair** a wheeled chair for invalids to sit in

convalescent a person who is convalescing [⇒ B163]

sufferer a person who is suffering, or often suffers, from an illness: She has been a sufferer from arthritis for many years.

victim a person who suffers the results of illness, actions, or happenings which he did not cause: Several people fell ill, victims of food poisoning. The accident victims were taken to hospital. He was the victim of ill-treatment as a child. **fall victim to** to suffer because of (an illness or action): He fell victim to polio [⇒ B146]. She fell victim to a desire for new clothes, and soon had no money left.

B168 *nouns* : **kinds of medical work** [U]

medicine 1 the science and practice of treating and understanding disease and other bodily disorders: *He is studying medicine at the university.* **2** the part of that science which uses medicines but not the part which uses surgery in treating patients: *He is qualified in both medicine and surgery.*

surgery 1 the science and practice of treating injuries and diseases by operations on the body: *He has specialized in heart surgery.* **2** the activity of a surgeon: *Surgery will be necessary, Nurse; prepare the instruments, please. Major surgery was needed to save the crash victims' lives.*

dentistry the work of a dentist [⇒ B165]

veterinary science medicine for animals, esp domesticated [⇒ A36] species

nursing (the practice of) the skill of nursing sick people: *She won a prize for her nursing ability. Nursing is a career which has traditionally depended on women rather than men.*

midwifery (the practice of) the skill of helping at childbirth

first aid (the study and practice of) treatment to be given by an ordinary person to a person hurt in an accident, or suddenly taken ill: *He pulled the drowning man from the water and gave him first aid. He goes to first aid classes.*

B169 *nouns* : **medical studies** [U]

anatomy 1 the science or study of the bodies and body parts of animals: *He studied anatomy in medical school.* **2** the body or body parts of a person or animal: *These pictures are of the human anatomy.* **3** the cutting into pieces of a body or body part of a person or animal in order to study it **4** (*fig*) the way something works, as discovered by careful examination: *The book studies the anatomy of modern society.* **anatomist** [C] a person engaged in anatomy **anatomical** [B] of or concerning anatomy **-ly** [adv Wa4]

physiology 1 the science concerned with the study of how the bodies of living things, and their various parts, work: *Anatomy and physiology are generally studied together.* **2** the system by which any particular living thing keeps alive: *The textbook discusses the physiology of the horse.* **physiologist** [C] a person whose work is in physiology **physiological** [Wa5;B] of or concerning physiology **-ly** [adv Wa4]

pathology 1 the study of disease: *Pathology is a major branch of medicine.* **2** the special nature of (a disease): *The pathology of this illness is very unusual.* **pathologist** [C] a person whose work is in pathology **pathological** [B] of or concerning pathology **-ly** [adv Wa4]

gynaecology *BrE*, **gynecology** *AmE* the study of the workings of the female sex organs, esp in

child-bearing and diseases, and the practice of medical tests and treatments in such diseases **gyn(a)ecologist** [C] a person whose work is in gynaecology **gyn(a)ecological** [Wa5;B] of or concerning gynaecology **-ly** [adv Wa4]

obstetrics *tech* the branch of medicine concerned with the birth of children **obstetrician** [C] a person whose work is in obstetrics **obstetric(al)** [Wa5;B] of or concerning obstetrics **-(al)ly** [adv Wa4]

B170 *adjectives* : **relating to medical work and medicine** [Wa5;B]

medical 1 relating to the science and practice of medicine: *What is the patient's medical history? He is a very experienced medical practitioner. This is a medical matter best left to doctors to decide* **2** able to cure illness: *This chemical compound has important medical properties.* **-ly** [adv Wa4]

medicinal 1 used as medicine: *He says he drinks only for medicinal purposes, not as a pleasure. This food has great medicinal value.* **2** having the effect of curing, like medicine: *The waters of this town are highly medicinal.*

medicated treated with medicine: *She got the child some medicated sweets for his sore throat.*

clinical 1 relating to a clinic [⇒ B180] **2** concerned with or based on actual medical experience rather than theory or experiments: *We must run proper clinical tests on this drug. You will receive a full clinical examination.* **3** rather cold; appearing more interested in scientific than personal details: *He has a clinical manner when working, but is very friendly when off-duty.* **-ly** [adv Wa4]

surgical related to or useful in surgery: *He must have a surgical operation if he is to live. These are all surgical instruments and must be kept clean. The patient is in the surgical ward with the others who are undergoing surgery.* **-ly** [adv Wa4]

dental related to the teeth, their care or to dentistry: *We must protect our teeth against dental decay. She has an appointment at the dental hospital.*

veterinary connected with the medical care and treatment of animals (esp farm animals and pets)

curative for the purpose of or having the power to cure: *The air here is very pure and curative for people with lung disorders.*

therapeutic for the purpose of healing: *This medicine is given in carefully controlled therapeutic doses.* **-ally** [adv Wa4]

B171 *nouns* : **medicines and drugs**
[ALSO ⇒ E80–7 DRUGS]

medicine [C; U] any substance used for treating disease: *She has taken a lot of different* *medicines, but none have cured the disease. Take this medicine three times daily after meals.*

medication 1 [U] the act of giving medicine (to) **2** [C; U] a medical substance, esp a drug: *It is better to sleep naturally than to take any kind of medication.*

drug [C] **1** any substance used for medical purposes, either alone or in a mixture, which has an effect on the working of cells or organs: *Doctors prescribe drugs carefully; the misuse of drugs can be dangerous.* **2** a substance which helps to cause sleep or hallucinations [⇨ B85] (and is habit-forming): *Be careful you don't become addicted to drugs. Tobacco, alcohol, and hashish are habit-forming drugs.*

tonic 1 [C] a medicine intended to give the body more strength, esp when tired: *She is taking an iron tonic* (= one which contains iron) *to improve her blood.* **2** [C *usu sing*] (*fig*) anything which increases health and energy: *Sea or mountain air is the best tonic for a person who lives in a big city. She's a real tonic for me—so full of life!*

pick-me-up [C] *infml* something, esp a drink or a medicine, that makes a person feel stronger and more cheerful: *I need a pick-me-up; I feel depressed.*

B172 *nouns* : **pills and powders** [C]

pill a small ball, capsule or other hard form in which medicine can be taken: *He swallowed his pills. She's on a course of little pink pills; she says they're doing her a lot of good.*

tablet a hard flat rounded pill: *He has a bottle of aspirin in tablet form; I'll get it. Take two tablets three times a day after meals. Dissolve two tablets in water.*

lozenge a sweet-tasting tablet made to melt slowly in the mouth: *a cough lozenge*

capsule a tiny container for a dose of medicine: *The medicine is pink and comes in oval capsules.*

mixture [*also* U] a set of substances mixed together as a liquid medicine: *Shake the mixture well before use. Take two teaspoonfuls of the mixture morning and evening. He bought some cough mixture from the chemist.*

powder [*also* U] medicine in the form of a powder: *She took a headache powder dissolved in warm water.*

course *esp BrE* a planned series of pills, drugs or other treatment: *He is on a course of drugs and goes once a week to the clinic to get them.*

dose a measured amount (esp of liquid medicine) given or to be taken at one time: *He has just had his daily dose of medicine. There are only about two doses left in the bottle.* **dosage** [C *usu sing*] the giving of medicine in quantity; the quantity of a single dose: *What is the dosage?—Oh, two teaspoonfuls after each meal.*

B173 *nouns* : **various kinds of medicines and medical substances**

ointment [U; C] a thick substance, usu medicinal, containing oil or fat, to be rubbed on the skin

liniment [U; C] a liquid containing oil to be rubbed on the skin, esp to help soreness and stiffness of the joints

lotion [U; C] any kind of liquid, usu medicinal, for rubbing on the skin or hair or placing on the eyes: *This lotion will soothe those insect bites. He uses eye lotion because his eyes get tired easily.*

drops [P] medicinal liquid to be applied in single drops to the eye, ear, nose, etc: *The doctor gave him drops to put in his eyes, to cure the inflammation* [⇨ B125].

antiseptic [C; U] chemical substance able to prevent flesh, blood, etc from going bad, esp by killing germs [⇨ A37]: *Carbolic soap is a powerful antiseptic.*

antibiotic [C] a medical substance produced by living things and able to stop the growth of, or destroy, harmful bacteria [⇨ A37] that have entered the body: *The doctor put him on a course of antibiotics.*

penicillin [U] a widely-used antibiotic that stops germs from multiplying

analgesic [C] *med & tech* a drug which lessens pain

pain-killer [C] *not fml* an analgesic

aspirin 1 [U] a kind of medicine that lessens pain and fever: *Aspirin is a powerful pain-killer.* **2** [C] this medicine in the form of a tablet: *He took two aspirins for his headache.*

sedative [C] *tech* a medicine or drug which calms the nerves, reduces tension [⇨ B87] and/or helps a person to sleep: *The doctor prescribed a sedative to calm her down.* **sedation** [U] treatment with sedatives; the result of this treatment: *The patient is under* (*heavy*) *sedation.*

tranquillizer, iser [C] *tech & genl* a sedative: *She's on tranquillizers because of her nerves.*

laxative [C] a medicine which helps relieve constipation, causing the bowels [⇨ B35] to empty

smelling salts [P] a medical preparation for smelling in cases of feeling faint, headaches and nausea [⇨ B120]

B174 *verbs & nouns* : **relating to special treatment**

[ALSO ⇨ B143]

inject [D1 *with/into*; T1] to force (a liquid, drug, vaccine, etc) into (someone's bloodstream) usu by means of a hypodermic syringe [⇨ B176]: *The doctor injected penicillin into his patient's bloodstream. She injected the patient with penicillin.*

injection 1 [C] any instance of injecting a serum, vaccine, antibiotic, etc into a person: *He has* had his *anti-tetanus injection*. **2** [U] the act of injecting

immunize, ise [T1] to make (a person or an animal) safe against disease by putting certain substances into the body, usu by means of a hypodermic needle **-ization, -isation** [U] [⇒ B136]

serum [U; C] **1** a thin liquid taken from the blood **2** such a liquid containing matter which can cause disease but prepared in a special way for immunizing people

inoculate [T1 *often pass*] to introduce a weak form of a disease into (someone's body) to prevent the disease in later life: *Babies are usually inoculated against several diseases nowadays.* **inoculation** [U; C]

vaccine [C; U] a substance from the blood of a cow, used to protect persons from smallpox, etc by giving them a slight but not dangerous form of the disease: *Some vaccines are more effective than others. The supply of new vaccine arrived yesterday.* **vaccinate** [T1] to protect against smallpox, etc by injecting vaccine: *The children were all vaccinated against smallpox.* **vaccination** [U; C]

shot [C] *not fml* an injection: *The patient has received his various shots. You'll need several shots of penicillin.*

jab [C] *infml* an injection of any kind: *Have you had your smallpox jabs yet?*

jag [C] *ScotE infml* a jab

B175 nouns : **bandages, crutches, and similar medical aids**

[ALSO ⇒ B161]

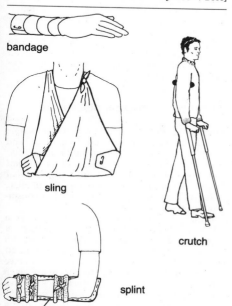

bandage

sling

crutch

splint

splint

bandage [C] a strip of cloth for binding round a wound or injury: *The soldier had a bandage round his head. It's time to change those bandages.*

dressing [C] anything such as bandages, ointments, etc, used for dressing wounds and sores, etc: *Put a dressing on that patient's wound.*

lint [U] soft material used for protecting wounds: *The nurse put some lint on the wound and then bandaged the patient's arm.*

sling [C] a piece of cloth tied at the shoulder and supporting a broken or damaged arm: *The man had his arm in a sling.*

splint [C] a piece of stiff material tied against a broken limb to keep it straight

crutch [C] a stick of wood, metal, or other material shaped to fit under the arm and rest on the floor, supporting the body: *He walked quite well with the help of a crutch.*

B176 nouns : **medical instruments**

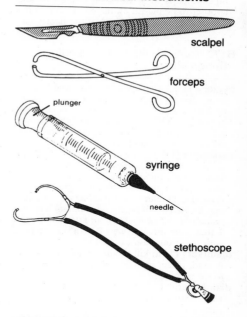

scalpel

forceps

plunger

syringe

needle

stethoscope

scalpel [C] a small knife used in surgery [⇒ B168]

forceps [P] an instrument like scissors which can be used by dentists for pulling out teeth, or by surgeons for taking hold of things

probe [C] a long thin metal instrument with a blunt end, used by doctors for learning about the depth and direction of a wound, etc

syringe [C] a sort of very thin pipe used in medicine and science into which liquid can be drawn and from which it can be pushed out

needle [C] a very thin hollow pointed tube (esp at the end of a hypodermic syringe) which is pushed into someone's skin to put a liquid (esp medicine) into the body

hypodermic needle/syringe [C] a needle/syringe for putting a liquid under the skin into the body

suture [C] **1** a type of thread used to stitch a wound together **2** a stitch made with this

(cat)gut [U] a strong thread of usu man-made materials used for sutures (and as strings for musical instruments and tennis rackets)

cotton wool *BrE*, **cotton** *AmE* [U] a soft mass of cotton which has not been spun into thread, esp used for cleaning parts of the body or putting medical liquids on to it

surgical spirit [U] alcohol used for cleaning wounds or skin (as in hospitals)

anaesthetic *BrE*, **anesthetic** *AmE* [C; U] a substance that makes one unable to feel pain, heat, etc, either in the whole body (**general anaesthetic**) or in a limited area (**local anaesthetic**)

stethoscope [C] a medical instrument with two pipelike parts to be fitted on to the ears and another to be placed on the chest, so that the doctor may hear the sound of the heartbeat

B177 nouns & verbs, etc : **keeping things clean**

hygiene [U] **1** the rules for clean and healthy living: *She studies hygiene as part of her domestic science course.* **2** cleanness; freedom from germs [⇒ A37]: *The hygiene of this kitchen isn't very good.* **hygienic** [B] free from germs **-ally** [adv Wa4] **un-** [neg]

sanitation [U] **1** general and public hygiene: *Good sanitation is necessary for everyone's health. Bad sanitation includes poor sewerage and dirty streets.* **2** the arrangements for removing human waste products from buildings by systems of pipes: *The sanitation here is rather old and badly-kept, isn't it?* **sanitary** [B] **1** free from dirt **in-** [neg] **2** [Wa5] concerned with the protection of health

disinfect [T1] to kill the infectious germs in (a wound, place, etc): *Has the room been disinfected yet?*

disinfectant [C; U] a chemical, usu in liquid form, which disinfects: *Use this disinfectant to clean the wound.*

sterilize, ise [T1] to make (medical instruments, etc) free from all very small, sometimes harmful, living things (germs and bacteria): *All the material and tools used in hospital operations are sterilized before use.* **sterilization, -isation** [U]

B178 nouns & verbs : **medical activities**

[ALSO ⇒ B161]

examination [C; U] (a period of) time spent looking at a patient in order to make a diagnosis of his or her condition: *He had a thorough examination; two doctors checked him over. We must give the patient a very thorough examination.*

diagnosis [C; U] the process or result of diagnosing: *The doctor's diagnosis was anaemia and he prescribed a course of treatment. Various diagnoses were made but no one was certain what was wrong with the patient.*

symptom [C] a sign in the body, usu of a change from normal, showing that a patient is ill or what illness he or she has: *These are the symptoms of smallpox, I'm afraid. All the symptoms point to cancer.* **symptomatic** [B (*of*)] serving as a symptom

medical [C] *not fml* a medical examination: *The children have all had their school medicals. It will soon be time for your next medical.*

checkup [C] *infml* a usu general medical examination: *He went to his doctor for his annual checkup. You look tired and ill; why don't you have a checkup?*

test 1 [C] a partial medical examination: *He had an eye test last week.* **2** [T1] to give such a test to: *The optician tested the child's eyes.* **3** [C *usu pl*] chemical checks helping in a diagnosis: *We have run a number of tests but are not yet sure what is wrong with him. They did a blood test and a urine test.*

operation [C] the cutting of the body in order to put something right or remove a diseased part: *The surgeon performed the operation with calm skill. He had a minor eye operation last year.* **operate** [I0 (*on*)] to perform a surgical operation: *The surgeon operated (on the patient) last night. We must operate immediately, Nurse.*

post-mortem [C] **1** *tech* a surgical examination of a person after death: *The post-mortem showed that he had died of liver poisoning.* **2** (*fig*) a discussion of past events in order to decide how good or bad they were: *Let's have a post-mortem on the course.* **PM** *abbrev*

autopsy [C] *med & tech* a post-mortem

B179 nouns : **medical places, etc**

hospital [C *BrE also* U] a place where people who are seriously ill or injured are treated and nursed: *The doctor decided that she must go to hospital; she needed treatment which could not be given to her at home or in his clinic. Hospital food isn't always very interesting.* **hospitalize, -ise** [T1] to send or admit (a person) to a hospital **-ization, -isation** [U]

infirmary [C] **1** *esp old use and in names* a hospital: *She works in the Royal Infirmary in Glasgow* **2** (in a school or other institution) a room used for people who are sick or injured

clinic [C] **1a** (part of) a hospital or similar place where medical advice and treatment are given **b** a group of people, esp doctors, who give medical treatment, or their place of work: *She attends the Clinic once a month. He has opened a private clinic in London. The doctors have* *their own clinic where poorer people are treated.* **2** an occasion in a hospital when medical students are taught: *Are you attending his clinic tomorrow?* **3** (*fig*) a class or group engaged in special work to help people: *He attends a speech clinic to get rid of his stammer.*

ward [C] a separate usu large room in a hospital, where several patients are kept in bed: *Which sister is in charge of this ward? Matron is in the children's ward at the moment. Hospital wards are usually very clean places.*

(operating) theatre [C] *BrE* the room where operations are performed in a hospital

casualty (ward, department) [R; C] the place in a hospital where people hurt in accidents are taken for treatment: *They rushed her to casualty but she was dead on arrival.*

outpatients (department) [C; R] the place in a hospital where people attend for medical examination and treatment without staying overnight: *You are wanted in Outpatients, Nurse.*

surgery *BrE* **1** [C] the place where one or more doctors see patients: *The doctor's surgery was crowded.* **2** [C; U] the time when this takes place: *Surgery is at 7 pm.*

consulting room [C] the room in a surgery where a doctor sees his patients

waiting room [C] the room in a surgery where patients wait to see a doctor

sickbay [C] a place for sick people, on a ship, in a boarding school, etc: *He's in sickbay at the moment, but should be on duty again next week.*

sickroom [C] the room in a house where a person is lying ill: *Try to keep the children away from the sickroom as much as possible.*

sickbed [C] the bed of a sick person

sick list [C] a list of persons who are sick: *The sick list at the factory is pretty long this week.* **on the sick list** in poor health: *Mrs Smith has been on the sick list for weeks.*

ambulance [C] a vehicle for carrying sick or injured people to hospital: *an ambulance driver*

stretcher [C] a frame, usu made of two poles and one large piece of strong cloth, for carrying someone who is ill or has been hurt: *They put her on a stretcher.* **stretcher bearer** [C] a person carrying a stretcher

B180 *nouns & verbs* : **relating to childbirth**

[ALSO ⇨ A3]

childbirth [U; C] the process or act of giving birth to a child: *Childbirth can be a painful but satisfying experience for a woman. She has had two difficult childbirths.*

labour *BrE*, **labor** *AmE* [U] the process immediately before the act of giving birth: *She has been in labour for 7 hours. Her labour pains began at 2 am.*

deliver [T1] **1** to help in the birth of: *The midwife had delivered the baby before the doctor arrived.* **2** [*usu pass*] to help to give birth: *She was delivered of a baby girl at 2 am.*

delivery [C; U] act or occasion of the birth of a child: *The delivery was fairly comfortable. The maternity hospital had four deliveries during the night.*

caesarean (section, birth, operation) [C] the delivery of a child by cutting the walls of the abdomen [⇨ B34] and uterus [⇨ B40]: *She has had two babies; both caesareans.*

premature [B] (of a baby or young animal) born or happening too soon: *The birth was premature. Premature babies are very delicate.* **-ly** [adv] **premature birth** [C] a birth that comes before its proper time

stillborn [Wa5;B] born dead: *She has given birth to two stillborn children.*

miscarriage [C] the act or occasion of producing stillborn young: *She fell downstairs when she was eight months pregnant and had a miscarriage.*

miscarry [I0] to have a miscarriage; to give birth too early: *I'm afraid she has miscarried because of the accident.*

abortion [C; U] the removal of a foetus [⇨A19] from the uterus esp during the first 28 weeks of pregnancy: *She had an abortion; she didn't want another child. Abortion is much more easily available nowadays, although there are still powerful religious pressures against it.* **abortionist** [C] *often deprec* a (usu skilled) person who brings about an abortion deliberately

abort **1** [I0; T1] to give birth too early to (a dead child): *The illness caused the woman to abort (her baby).* **2** [T1] to cause (a child) to be born too soon or to end a pregnancy too soon, so that the child cannot live: *The doctor had to abort the baby.*

B181 *nouns, etc* : **relating to birth control**

[ALSO ⇨ A14–19, B40]

birth control [U] (any method of) preventing unwanted pregnancy: *There are many forms of birth control available today.*

contraception [U] *tech* birth control; the act, practice or methods of preventing the producing of children: *Some doctors give advice on contraception. When they decided to have a child they stopped practising contraception.*

contraceptive **1** [C] a drug or any object or material used to prevent conception: *There are various contraceptives available today, some for men to use, some for women.* **2** [Wa5;B] relating to contraception: *There are several contraceptive devices on the market.*

the Pill [R] *infml* a contraceptive drug taken by women as a pill: *She's on the Pill; she doesn't want to have any more children.*

condom [C] a thin rubber covering for the penis to prevent semen entering the vagina: *The condom is a contraceptive (device).*

rubber sheath [C] *infml* a condom

sheath [C] *BrE* a condom

rubber [C] *AmE* a condom

French letter [C] *BrE sl* a condom

coil [C] a coil-like object fitted inside a woman to prevent her conceiving a child

loop [C] a piece of metal or plastic put inside a woman to prevent her conceiving a child

IUD (intra-uterine device) a loop or coil to prevent conception

cap *also* **Dutch cap, diaphragm** a round contraceptive device usu made of rubber fitted inside a woman during and for a period after having sex

C

People and the family

People

C1 *nouns* : **people generally**

person [C] **1** a human being considered as having a character of his or her own, or as being different from all others: *Would you call a week-old baby a person? You're just the person I wanted to see.* **2** *fml* (often in official writings) anyone in general; somebody unknown or not named: *No person may enter the hall without permission. Some person or other has torn my newspapers.* **3** *deprec* somebody not considered worthy of respect: *Who is that person who came to the party with her?* **4** a human being in one of the many parts or activities of his life: *He's a different person altogether when he is at the club. The party has a faithful supporter in the person of Jim Brown.*

sing	pl	difference
person	**people**	*generally*
	persons	*usu fml or law*

persons [P] *usu fml or law* more than one person: *The verdict was murder by a person or persons unknown.*

people [P] **1** persons in general; persons other than oneself: *Were there many people at the meeting? People don't like to be told that they are wrong.* **2** the persons belonging to a particular place, class, trade, etc: *People who live in the south of England speak in a different way from people in the north. I like theatre people. The local people don't like him.*

folk [P] *infml, esp ScotE & N EngE* people: *Some folk don't know when they are lucky. Can you help me, please? There were a lot of folk at the meeting.*

folks [P] *infml esp AmE* people: *Now, folks, let's sing a song. Ask the old folks if they would like to eat now.*

human [C] a member of the human race: *Humans will suffer as well as animals if the rains don't come.*

humanity [U] *fml* all humans: *The whole of humanity is interested in these matters, not just us.*

human being [C] a man, woman, or child, not an animal: *Treat them like human beings; at the moment they are living like pigs.*

C2 *nouns* : **man and woman**

[ALSO ⇨ A50]

age \ sex	male	female
older	man	woman
younger	child	
	boy	girl
newborn	baby	

man **1** [C] a fully-grown human male: *Ask the men to come in, but not the boys or the women.* **2** [C] a male person with the qualities expected of a man: *'Be brave, be a man,' he said to his son. This work will make a man of him.* **3** [N] (a word used to address a man, esp when excited, angry, etc): *Wake up, man; you can't sleep all day!* **4** [C] the right man: *He's my man for the job; he's the best there is. You want a good footballer? Well, he's the very man.* **manly** [Wa1;B] *apprec* like a man: *He's very manly.* **-liness** [U] **mannish** [B] *deprec* (of women) like a man: *That woman is a bit too mannish for me.* **-ness** [U] **manlike** [B] *neutral* like a man or human being: *Monkeys are manlike animals.* **manfully** [adv] bravely, in a manly way: *He did the work manfully.* **manhood** [U] the state of being or time when a man: *He reached manhood in a time of unemployment. He feels that his manhood is affected by her attitude to him.*

woman **1** [C] a fully-grown human female: *Ask the women to come in, but not the girls or the men.* **2** [C] a female person with the qualities expected of a woman: *He thinks she is quite a woman. What a woman she is!* **3** [N] (a word used to address a woman, esp when excited, angry, etc): *Wake up, woman, you can't sleep all day.* **4** [C] the right woman: *She's the woman for the job; she's the best there is.* **womanly** [B] *apprec* like a woman: *She's a very womanly woman, isn't she?* **-liness** [U] [⇨ A14 FEMININE] **womanish** [B] *deprec* (of men) like a woman: *That fellow is a bit womanish for my liking!* **-ness** [U] **womanlike** [B] *neutral* like a woman **womanhood** [U] the state of being or time when a woman: *She reached womanhood when men were still the leaders in her country.*

She feels that he questions her womanhood, and it makes her unhappy.

boy [C; N] a young male person: *When the child was born, the nurse said, 'It's a boy!' 'Come here, boy!' the man shouted. The boys were playing football. You have done well, my boy.* **boyish** [B] like or in the manner of a boy: *His behaviour is still rather boyish. He has a pleasant, boyish smile.* **-ness** [U] **-ly** [adv]

girl [C; N] a young female person: *When the child was born, the nurse said, 'It's a girl!' 'Come here, girl!' shouted the woman. The girls were playing in the garden. You have done well, my girl.* **girlish** [B] like a girl: *Her behaviour is still a bit girlish for a woman of 25.* **-ness** [U] **-ly** [adv]

C3 *nouns* : **parent and child**

[ALSO ⇒ A20 YOUNG CREATURES]

parent [C *usu pl*] **1** father or mother: *Either parent can attend the school meeting. One-parent families face many difficulties. Both parents can attend the meeting if they wish. They were told to do what their parents asked them to do.* (*fig*) *The Bible says that Adam and Eve were our first parents.* **2** [A; (C)] any living thing that produces another: *This is the parent tree from which all the others have come.* (*fig*) *Our club is the parent association of all the other clubs.* **parenthood** [U] the state or condition of being a parent: *He spoke about the need for planned parenthood in the modern world.* **parental** [Wa5;B] relating to parents; like a parent: *Parental duties aren't always pleasant.* **-ly** [adv]

guardian [C] a person who is responsible in law for the care of a child who is not that person's own child: *After her parents died he became her guardian. The form must be signed by the (child's) parent or guardian.* **guardianship** [U] the state or condition of being a guardian

child [C] **1** a young human being: *Several children, aged about five, were playing in the street.* **2** (*fig*) a person who behaves like a child: *Don't be such a child: you're 18 years old now! She is still a child in the ways of the world.* **childish** [B] *deprec* like a child: *Don't be so childish; you're 18 now, and should behave like a grown man!* **-ly** [*adv*] **-ness** [U] **childlike** [B] neutral or apprec like or having the (good) qualities of a child: *She followed him with childlike trust.*

bastard 1 [C] a child of unmarried parents: *Children of unmarried parents are not usually called bastards in general conversation, although 'bastard' is a word used in law.* **2** [C] taboo a person whom the speaker does not like: *Tell that bastard to leave me alone!* **3** [C] taboo a person who does bad things: *He is a dirty bastard, that man!* [also ⇒ C189, 190]

baby [C] **1** a very young child, esp one who has not yet learnt to speak: *She has a new baby: it was born last week. They have one child, a baby*

girl. **2** a young animal: *I like the baby monkeys.* **3** the youngest of a group: *She is the baby of the family/class.* **4** (*fig*) a smaller than usual object: *They bought a baby car.* **5** (*fig*) *deprec* a person behaving like a baby: *Oh, don't be such a baby; stop crying! What a crybaby she is; she's always crying.* **babyish** [B] *deprec* (behaving) like a baby: *Oh, don't be so babyish!* **-ly** [adv] **-ness** [U] **babylike** [B] *neutral* like a baby

twin [C] one of two children born of the same mother at the same time: *She had twins last week. He's my twin brother. She's his twin. One of the twins came to see us.* (*fig*) *The plane has twin engines* (= two engines exactly like each other). *It's a twin-engined plane.*

triplets, quadruplets, quintuplets [P] three, four, or five children born of the same mother at the same time: *She had triplets last week, all girls.* **quads** [P] *infml abbrev* quadruplets **quins** [P] *infml abbrev* quintuplets

ward [C] a young person who is in the care of a guardian or of a set of officials: *She has been his ward since her parents died. The child was made a ward of court* (= in the care of a court of law).

orphan [C] a child neither of whose parents is alive: *He is an orphan and has no one to look after him.* **orphanage** [C] a place where orphans stay and are looked after

C4 *nouns* : **kinds of men**

gentleman [C; (*pl*)N] *fml & polite* a man: *Ask those gentlemen if they would be so good as to come this way. Gentlemen, we are ready to begin. Ladies and gentlemen, thank you for your help.* [also ⇒ C157] **gent** *infml abbrev esp S EngE, esp working class* a gentleman; man: *That gent over there can help us. Come on, gents; time to leave.*

fellow [C] **1** *genl* a man or boy: *Ask those fellows over there to come and help us. Hey, you fellows, what are you doing?* **2** *deprec* a man considered not worthy of respect: *Tell that fellow what's-his-name to get out of here and not come back. Some fellow or other wants to see you.*

guy [C; (*pl*) N] *infml, esp AmE* a man; a person: *He's a nice guy; he'll help. Hey, you guys, come here a minute!*

chap *infml, esp BrE esp middle class* **1** [C; N] a man: *Ask that chap if he can help us. Come on, chaps, we mustn't be late. Can you help me, old chap? You chaps don't know this town, do you?* **2** [C] a man speaking of himself or men generally: *A chap doesn't always know what to do at times like that, does he?*

bloke [C] *infml, esp BrE, esp working class: He's a nice bloke; he'll help. There was a funny-looking bloke standing outside the shop.*

boy [C; (*pl*) N] *infml, esp AmE and usu apprec* a man of any age: *John Smith? Yes, he's a local boy. Tell the boys to be ready at 7 o'clock. She said that her husband was out with the boys.*

lad 1 [C; N] *infml, esp ScotE & N EngE and usu apprec* a boy or man, esp as a friendly form of address: *Ask those lads if they want a drink. Come on, lads, let's go.* 2 [C] *BrE infml* a rather bold or wild man, esp towards women: *He's quite a lad with the girls. Yes, he was a bit of a lad when he was younger.*

Mr [A] 1 (the title given to a man): *Ask Mr Smith to come in, please.* 2 (the title used in speaking to certain officials): *Mr President, we need your help.*

mister [N] (*sl* or used by children; a way of speaking to a man): *Hey, mister, what's the time?*

sir [N] (the polite form used in addressing a man, esp in shops, by children talking to male teachers, in writing letters, etc): *May I help you, Sir/sir? Please, sir, what does this word mean? Dear Sir . . .*

C5 *nouns* : **kinds of women**

lady [C; (*pl*)N] *fml & polite* a woman: *Ask those ladies if they would be so good as to come this way. Come this way, ladies, please. Ladies (and gentlemen), it is time to begin the meeting.*

girl [C; (*pl*)N] *infml, esp AmE and usu apprec* a woman of any age: *Jean Smith? Yes, she's a local girl. Ask the girls to come at 7 o'clock. He said that his wife was out with the girls.*

female [C] *deprec* a woman not worthy of respect: *Tell that female to stop annoying us.*

dame [C] *sl esp AmE* a woman: *Some of these dames are pretty good-looking. Get that dame out of here!*

broad [C] *AmE sl* a woman, esp if she has loose sexual morals: *She's a good-looking broad and knows all about life. He's only interested in broads.*

Madam [N] (a respectful form of address to a woman, esp if older and often used in shops, in letters, etc): *May I help you, Madam? Dear Madam . . .*

Mrs [A] the title given to a married woman: *Ask Mrs Smith to come in, please.*

missus, missis *sl esp BrE* 1 [N] (a way of speaking to an older woman): *Hey, missus, what's the time?* 2 [R9] one's wife: *The/My missus has gone out; she'll be back soon.*

miss [*usu cap*] 1 [A] (the title for a girl or an unmarried woman): *Ask Miss Smith to come in, please. (pl esp formerly) The Misses Smith are coming to the party.* 2 [N] (the title used by children to address a female teacher): *Please Miss, can I help you?* 3 [C] *apprec or deprec* (the title of) a young woman; a girl: *Miss France won the beauty competition; what a lovely girl she is! She's a troublesome little miss, that girl.*

C6 *nouns* : **young men**

youth 1 [C] a young man or older boy: *Some youths were standing near the bus stop. The police caught a youth trying to break into a shop. He showed little interest in music as a youth, but now he is very interested.* 2 [GU] young men and women considered as a group: *The youth of the country are ready to work hard. Youth today are very different from a hundred years ago.*

lad [C; N] *esp ScotE and N EngE & usu affec* a boy: *The lads were playing football. He's just a lad; he can't do a man's work yet.*

laddie [C; N] *infml esp ScotE* a boy: *He's a good laddie and works well at school. Come here, laddie!*

Master [A] *becoming rare* (the title used before a boy's name, esp in addressing letters): *Send the letter to 'Master John Smith'; he's eight years old.*

C7 *nouns* : **young women** [C]

virgin 1 a (young) woman who has not had sex: *She wasn't a virgin when she got married. She's 40 and still a virgin.* 2 a person who has not (yet) had sex: *A fine-looking boy like that won't be a virgin for long!* **virginal** [Wa5;B] (pure) like a virgin

maiden *old use & lit* a girl who is not married and is still a virgin: *The young maidens of the town watched from the windows as the men passed.*

maid *old use & lit* a girl or (young) woman who is not married: *Joan of Arc was called the Maid of Orleans.*

lass [*also* N] *esp ScotE, N EngE & older lit & usu affec* a girl or woman: *She's a fine lass. Come on, lass; you'll be feeling better soon.*

lassie [*also* N] *esp ScotE & N EngE* 1 a girl or young woman: *She's a fine-looking lassie.* 2 a young man's girl friend

bird *sl esp BrE* a young woman: *He's always after some bird or other.*

chick *sl esp AmE* a young woman: *I like the look of that chick.*

C8 *nouns* : **kinds of child** [C]

infant 1 a very young child: *Mothers with infants go into that part of the hospital. He enjoys playing with his infant son.* 2 a schoolchild aged 5–7: *She teaches in the infant school.* 3 *BrE law* a minor; person under 18 years of age **infancy** [U] the state of being or time when an infant: *He had a lot of illness during (his) infancy.*

toddler *infml* a baby who has learnt to walk unsteadily (**toddle**): *There were a lot of toddlers in the hall.*

tot *infml* a very small child

kid [*also* (*usu pl*) N] *infml* 1 a child: *The kids enjoyed the game very much. He's still just a kid; he has a lot to learn. Come on, kids; race* *you there!* **2** *esp AmE* a young person: *The store was full of college kids.*

youngster a child or young person, esp a boy: *Let the youngsters enjoy themselves; stop telling them what to do. When I was a youngster life wasn't as easy as it is now.*

brat *deprec* a bad-mannered child; a child whom one does not (at that moment) like: *Get that noisy brat out of here! She has three nasty little brats with no manners.*

C9 *nouns & adjectives* : **people according to age**

[ALSO ⇨ L206, 7]

adult [C; B] *often fml* (of) a fully-grown person, esp a person over an age stated by law, usu 18 or 21: *This film is for adults only. The adults stayed up, but the kids went to bed. He has a very adult manner although he's only 12.* **adulthood** [U] the state of being or time when an adult

grown-up [C; B] *not fml* (of) an adult: *He's a grown-up now; let him decide his own future. It is often said that grown-ups don't understand young people. She has a very grown-up manner for one so young.*

minor [C] a person under the age of being accepted as an adult in law, usu 18 or 21: *She is still a minor.*

adolescent [C; B] (of) a boy or a girl in the period between being a child and being a fully grown person: *Adolescents often have difficulties as they grow up.* **adolescence** [U] the state of being or time when an adolescent

teenager [C] a young person between 13 and 19 years old (**in one's teens**): *This is a party for teenagers, not adults.* **teenage** (d) [Wa5; A] of, for, or being a teenager: *teenage fashions; a teenage boy*

juvenile **1** [C] *fml* a young person: *There is a special court for juveniles who break the law.* **2** [B] *often deprec* suitable for or typical of young people: *This is a juvenile book; it really is silly.*

elder [C *usu pl*] a person of greater age: *He thinks youngsters should always follow the advice of their elders.*

C10 *nouns* : **kinds of people** [C]

individual a person or member of a group, esp when treated separately: *The rights of the individual are among the most important rights in a free society. I remember one individual particularly, an old lady. What a bad-tempered individual he is!*

character *infml* **1** *often deprec* a person: *Some character just walked up and stole her bag.* **2** a person with special or unusual qualities: *Oh, he's quite a character in the village; a very interesting man.*

figure an important person: *He's famous now—a figure of worldwide importance.*

personality a person who is well-known to the public or to people connected with some particular activity: *He is a well-known television personality. She is a much-admired personality in the sporting world.* **personage** *fml or pomp* a famous or important person: *Several noble personages belong to this club.*

member a person belonging to a group, club, etc: *He is one of our club/team members. She's a member of the swimming team.* [also ⇨ C75]

C11 *nouns* : **relating to the family**

family **1** [C] *precise* any group of people related by blood or marriage, esp a group of two adults and their children: *My family is very large. A family of five live in that flat. This is a family matter.* **2** [U] *loose* children: *There are many children in our house, but I have no family of my own.* **3** [C] all those people descended from a common ancestor [⇨ C17]: *Our family has lived in this house for hundreds of years.*

folks [P] *infml* (used with *my*, *your*, etc) a person's parents: *He's taking his girl friend home to meet his folks this weekend.*

household **1** [C] all the people living in a house, usu as part of a family over a long period of time: *He is the head of the household.* **2** [A] something kept and used in a house: *All our household belongings were lost in the fire.*

tribe [C] a usu large number of families of common origin which live together in an area, usu having the same language and customs: *North America once belonged to many different Red Indian tribes. The Basuto tribe in Africa can also be called the Basuto nation.* **tribal** [Wa5; B] relating or belonging to a tribe **-ly** [adv] **tribesman/woman** [C] a member of a tribe

clan **1** [C] a group of families, often inside a larger tribal or national group, all descendants of one person or having the same family name: *The tribe is divided into ten clans.* **2** (esp and originally in Scotland, esp in the Highlands) a group of families of common origin and loyalty to a chief: *Clan Campbell and the MacDonald clan are well-known Scottish clans.* **clannish** [B] *usu deprec* showing clan feeling; (of people) in the habit of supporting one another against outsiders: *The people in that place are very clannish; they stick together and are hard to get to know.* **-ness** [U] **-ly** [adv] **clansman/woman** [C] a member of a clan

descent [U9] the family, tribal, national, etc, origin of a person: *He is an American of Irish descent.*

lineage [U] *often fml* the line of descent from one person to another (in a family): *The lineage of their family goes back to ancient times.*

stock [U9] the type of people a person is descended from: *She is of Irish stock, I believe. He comes of good farming stock.*

C12 *nouns & adjectives* : **family relations**

relationship	*sex* male	female
parent	father	mother
child in relation to parents	son	daughter
child in relation to other children	brother	sister

father [C] the male parent: *His father is a shopkeeper. She doesn't get on well with her father.* **fatherly** [B] *usu apprec* like a (good) father: *He has a pleasant fatherly manner.* **fatherhood** [U] the state of being a father: *Fatherhood seems to suit him; he loves the baby.*

sire [C] **1** *old use* a father or male ancestor [⇒ C17] **2** the male parent of an animal: *These racehorses all have famous sires.*

mother [C] the female parent: *Her mother used to run a shop. He doesn't get on well with his mother.* **motherly** [B] *usu apprec* like a (good) mother: *She is a very motherly woman.* **motherhood** [U] the state of being a mother: *Motherhood seems to suit her; she looks happy.*

dam [C] **1** *old use* a mother or female ancestor **2** the female parent of an animal: *The dog's dam won many prizes.*

son 1 [C] a male child: *Mr and Mrs Brown have two sons. He was carrying his baby son.* (*fig*) *Robert Burns is one of Scotland's greatest sons.* **2** [N] *affec* (form of address to a boy or younger man): *Come on, son; let's go now.* **sonny** [N] (used in speaking to a young boy): *Better go home to your mother, sonny.*

daughter [C] **1** a female child: *Mr and Mrs Smith have three daughters. She had brought her teenage* [⇒ C9] *daughter with her.* (*fig*) *Joan of Arc was one of France's greatest daughters.* **2** (*fig*) something thought of as a daughter: *French is a daughter language of Latin.* **daughterly** [B] *usu apprec* like a (good) daughter: *She has a daughterly love for the old man.*

brother [C] a male relative with the same parents: *My older brother works in New York. His brothers are all younger than him/than he is.* (*fig*) *All the men in this association are brothers with the same aims. He is not accepted by his brother lawyers in town.* **brotherly** [B] *usu apprec* like a (good) brother: *He has a very brotherly manner towards the little boys.*

sister [C] a female relative with the same parents: *His older sister started a new job last week. She's prettier than both her sisters.* (*fig*) *French is a sister language of Spanish.* **sisterly** [B] *usu apprec* like a (good) sister: *She has a sisterly love for him.*

sibling [C] *tech* a brother or sister: *Siblings do not always like each other.*

paternal 1 [B] *sometimes deprec* of, like, or received from a father: *He has a very paternal attitude towards his students. His uncle gave him some paternal advice.* **2** [Wa5;A] on one's father's side of the family: *She is his paternal grandmother.* **paternity** [U] **1** fatherhood: *Paternity is a state which most men reach.* **2** origin on the father's side: *The paternity of the child is unknown.*

maternal 1 [B] of, like, or natural to a mother; (kind) like a mother: *She has a warm, maternal nature.* **2** [Wa5;A] on one's mother's side of the family: *He is her maternal grandfather.* **maternity 1** [U] motherhood: *Women are prepared by nature for maternity.* **2** [A] for the purposes of or relates to giving birth: *She is going to have the baby in a maternity hospital.*

fraternal [B] *fml* of, like, or suitable to a brother: *They sent their fraternal greetings to him, as a member of the same group.*

filial [B] *fml* in the manner of a (good) son or daughter: *It is your filial duty to obey your father.*

C13 *nouns* : **names for one's father and mother** [N; C]

father

dad	*infml also with any much older man*	*Come on, Dad! The dads and mums were invited to see their children's work at the school*
daddy	*infml esp by & to children*	*Help me, Daddy! 'Is your daddy at home, dear?' he asked the little girl.*
pa	*infml esp AmE & BrE working class*	*Come on, Pa; time to go.*
papa	*old use esp by & to children, esp upper class*	*Papa, may we leave the room, please? Ask your papa about it, darling.*
poppa	*infml esp AmE*	*Come on, Poppa; let's go now. My poppa says I should work hard at school.*
pop	*infml esp AmE also with any much older man*	*Come on, Pop; let's have a drink.*

mother

mum	infml BrE	Help me, Mum. The mums are usually more interested in these things than the dads.
mummy	infml BrE esp by & to children	Mummy, Mummy, look what I've got! Tell your mummy I'd like a word with her, please.
mom	infml AmE	Say, Mom, can I have something to eat?
mommy	infml AmE esp by and to children	Would you tell your mommy I'm here, please, dear?
ma	infml esp AmE & BrE working class (often used with any much older woman)	Anything to eat, Ma? Old Ma Harris was taken to hospital yesterday.
mam	infml N EngE & WelshE esp working class	Anything to eat, Mam?
mammy	infml esp ScotE & N EngE esp working class	Ask your mammy if I could have a word with her, please.
mama	old use esp by and to children, esp upper class	My mama cannot speak to you; she is engaged at the moment. You are looking well. Mama.
momma	infml esp AmE	His momma told him to go home.

C14 verbs : relating to having children [T1]

father (of a man) to cause the birth of (one's child): *He fathered two famous artists and a well-known politician.*

sire *fml* (esp of horses and pedigree animals) to be the father of: *He sired a famous son. The winner of the race was sired by the great horse Shamrock.* [⇒ A34 PEDIGREE]

mother to take care of, like a mother: *She has really mothered that child like one of her own. (deprec) Do you need me to mother you or can you stand on your own feet now?*

suckle [*also* I∅] to feed on milk at the breast or udder [⇒ A128]: *She suckled her children herself and never used a bottle. The young calf was suckling happily.*

breast-feed *also* **nurse** to suckle (a baby): *She breast-fed her children herself. Nursing mothers visit this hospital regularly.*

nurture *fml* to give care and food to: *They nurtured their children well. She is a gently nurtured child, with no knowledge of the world.*

bring up [v adv] to care for and educate in the family until fully grown: *She brought up three children without any help. He was brought up in London, in the East End.*

raise *esp AmE* to bring up: *He raised the children by himself; his wife died years ago. Where were you raised? She was raised in the country. He raised those goats from newborn kids.*

rear (esp of animals and birds) to care for until fully grown: *He reared those birds himself. It's difficult to know what is the best way to rear children.*

adopt to take (someone, esp a child) into one's family as a relation forever, and to take on the full responsibilities in law of a parent: *They had no children of their own, so they adopted a boy and a girl.* **adoption** [U; C] the act of adopting a child: *Adoption may be the answer for childless couples unable to have babies of their own.*

foster to care for (a child who is not one's own), usu for a short period: *They have fostered several youngsters* [⇒ C8] *who had no home to go to, till they got started in the world.*

C15 nouns : other family relations

age \ sex	male	female
first generation	uncle	aunt
next generation	nephew	niece

uncle [C; A; N] the brother of one's father or mother, the husband of one's aunt, or a man whose brother or sister has a child: *He is my uncle. I am an uncle now; my sister had a baby last night. Can I help you, Uncle (Charles)?*

aunt *also* (*infml*) **auntie, aunty** [C; A; N] the sister of one's father or mother, the wife of one's uncle, or a woman whose brother or sister has a child: *She is my aunt. I am an aunt now; my sister had a baby last night. Can I come, Aunt (Mary)?*

nephew [C] the son of one's brother or sister or of one's husband's or wife's brother or sister: *My nephew is staying with us at the moment.*

niece [C] the daughter of one's brother or sister or of one's husband's or wife's brother or sister: *Is that girl your niece?*

cousin *also* **first/full cousin** [C] the child of an uncle or aunt: *The boys are cousins.* **second cousin** a child of a first cousin

C16 *nouns* : relations generally

relation *also* **relative** [C] a member of one's family: *She's a very close relation of mine. She's my sister! I met one of my distant relatives last night.* **related** [Wa5;B] being relations by blood or marriage: *Yes, we're related; he is my cousin.*

kin [P] *esp old use* members of one's family: *He has no kin in America.* **kinsman/woman** [C] *old use* a relation **kin(s)folk** [P] *old use* relations, kin

next of kin [Wn3] *esp law* a person's closest relative: *His next of kin have been told of his death. Please write the names of your next of kin on the form.*

nearest and dearest [Wn3] *infml* close relations: *He's phoning his nearest and dearest.*

one's own flesh and blood *often emot* a member or members of one's own family, esp children: *You are my own flesh and blood, and yet we can't understand each other!*

C17 *nouns* : family in the past or future

ancestor, *rare fem* **ancestress** [C] a person, esp one living a long time ago, from whom one is descended: *His ancestors went there from Ireland.* **ancestral** [Wa5;A] belonging to or becoming from one's ancestors: *Our ancestral home is in this valley.* **ancestry** [U] the ancestors of a person's family considered as a group or continuous line: *What is his ancestry?*

forefather [C *usu pl*] *poet* an ancestor; a relative in the past: *One of his forefathers was an early settler in North America.*

forebears [P] *esp lit* ancestors: *His forebears came to Australia from Scotland.*

descendant [C] a person who is descended from other persons named, usu over a long period of time: *She is one of the last living descendants of the Incas. His descendants still live in the same village.*

generation [C] all the people who belong by age more or less to the same time: *Fathers and sons belong to different generations. Past generations did not have the same ideas as the younger generation today.*

heredity [U] the passing sexually of certain qualities from an earlier generation of a group of living things to the next generation: *Blue eyes and yellow hair are part of her Scandinavian heredity.* **hereditary** [Wa5;B] **1** passed through heredity: *Certain things in our lives are hereditary; others we learn. He had a hereditary*

disease. **2** passed from parent to child, esp by some kind of rule or law: *He is hereditary chief of the tribe.*

C18 *combining forms, etc* : relations, family and related words

grand- (used to show that a relationship is between a person and the parent of a parent or the child of a child): *The boy is his only grandson. She is a grandmother now. The boy's grandparents came to see him. Her grand-dad/grandad arrived last night. My grandma died recently.*

granny, *sometimes* **gran** [C; N] *infml* grand-mother

great- (used to show three or more stages of direct descent): *My great-grandfather on my father's side is still alive. Oh, she was his great-great-something-grandmother.*

-in-law (used to show relations by marriage): *He is my father-in-law* (= my wife's father). *My brother-in-law often visits us.* **in-laws** [P] the father and mother (and other relations) of a person by marriage: *My in-laws are staying with us just now.*

step- having the relation stated due only to the remarriage of one parent: *She is my step-mother; my own mother died when I was a child.*

half- [Wa5;A] having one but not both the same parents: *He is her half-brother by her father's first marriage.*

kid [Wa5;A] used *esp in AmE* to show that a brother or sister is younger: *Can my kid brother come with us?*

foster- (used for or in connection with a child brought up by people who are not its parents): *He is a foster-child. My foster-brother is as dear to me as though he was really my brother. She was very fond of her foster-parents.*

Courting, sex, and marriage

C20 *verbs & nouns* : courting and flirting

court 1 [T1] (of a man) to spend time with (a woman), esp in order to persuade (her) into marriage: *He courted her unsuccessfully for three years.* **2** [I0] (only with the **-ing** form) to have a relationship with someone one is likely to marry: *They're courting. She's courting, though she's only 17.* **courtship** [U] the business or time of courting: *Their courtship lasted a year.* **courting couple** [C] a (young) man and woman who are courting: *There was no one in the park except two or three courting couples.*

go out with [v adv prep T1] to go to cafés, cinemas, etc, with (a member of the opposite sex) usu as a start to, or part of, courting: *She's* *going out with a very nice young fellow. Will you go out with me sometime?*

date [IØ] *esp AmE infml* to go out courting with (someone): *She's been dating him for months but it's not serious yet. They've been dating (each other) for a long time.*

woo [T1; IØ] *old use* (of a man) to try to persuade (a woman) into love and marriage: *He wooed her unsuccessfully for three years but at last she accepted him. The prince went wooing.*

flirt [IØ (*with*)] to behave as if very attracted to someone, but with no serious intentions: *She says she doesn't like going to parties because her husband always flirts with every girl in the room. Young girls often flirt, but don't expect to be taken seriously.* (*fig*) *I have been flirting with the idea of going to Australia.* **flirtatious** [B] showing a desire to flirt: *She's rather a flirtatious girl. He gave her a flirtatious look.* **-ly** [adv] **-ness** [U]

C21 *nouns* : **persons courting and flirting, etc** [C]

boyfriend a male companion with whom a woman spends time and shares amusements: *She changes her boyfriends as often as she changes her hairstyle. Oh, he's been a boyfriend of hers for years; it's nothing very serious. He's her steady boyfriend.*

girlfriend a woman companion with whom a man spends time and shares amusements: *He's had a lot of girlfriends over the years, but never got married. Is your girlfriend? Do you go out with her a lot? She's his steady girlfriend.*

steady *infml* a regular boy/girlfriend: *She's his steady. Oh, he doesn't have a steady; you should see his address book.*

couple a man and a woman spending time together because they are courting: *They make a nice couple, don't they? Several courting couples sat on the grass.*

date *esp AmE infml* a person with whom one has a date: *Of course you can bring your date to the party.*

suitor *old use* a man trying to persuade a woman to marry him: *The princess had many suitors (for her hand) but accepted none of them.*

flirt a person, esp a girl, who generally flirts: *She's a terrible flirt; no man is safe. I think her husband is a bit of a flirt; he seems to like the girls.*

C22 *verbs & nouns* : **actions relating to courting and sex**

kiss 1 [T1] to touch with the lips as a sign of love or as a greeting: *He took her in his arms and kissed her. She kissed him on the lips.* (*fig*) *The wind kissed her hair.* **2** [D1; X9, esp *away*] to express, or put by means of a kiss: *He kissed his wife and children goodbye. She kissed away the boy's tears.* **3** [IØ] to kiss each other: *They*

kissed when they met. They kissed goodbye at the station. (*fig in games*) *The balls kissed* (= touched each other). **4** [C] the act of kissing: *His sudden kiss was unexpected. Her kisses were violent.*

hug [T1 (*to*)] **1** to put the arms tightly round, usu as a sign of affection: *When he met her again he hugged her tightly to him. Oh, you wonderful girl, I could hug you!* **2** [C] the act of hugging: *He gave his mother a big hug.*

embrace 1 [T1; IØ] *fml* to take (someone) in one's arms, usu as a sign of love: *He embraced his father warmly. She embraced him, but there was little love in the action. They embraced.* **2** [C] an act of embracing; a situation where two people are in each other's arms: *Her embrace was formal, not friendly. He found the lovers in a tight embrace.*

stroke 1 [T1] to pass the hand along, again and again: *She gently stroked his arm. He stroked her hair lovingly.* **2** [C] an act of stroking: *She felt the stroke of his hand on her hair.*

pat 1 [T1] to touch lightly, usu with the hand: *He patted the dog. She patted his cheek.* **2** [C] an act of patting: *He felt the pat of her hand on his cheek.*

caress 1 [C] a light, tender stroke, touch or kiss showing one's love for someone: *She enjoyed his caresses.* **2** [T1] to give a caress to (someone): *He caressed her lovingly.*

fondle [T1] to touch gently and lovingly and (usu) continuously for some time: *He fondled her breasts/ear/hair.*

cuddle 1 [T1] to take into the arms and hold lovingly: *She cuddled the child close. The girl cuddled her little sister.* **2** [C] act of cuddling or being cuddled: *Come on, darling, let's have a cuddle!*

snuggle [L9, esp *up*] to get or lie close to someone, for love, warmth, etc: *The child snuggled up to her father. They snuggled close together in bed; the night was cold.*

pet 1 [T1] to touch kindly with the hands, showing love: *She sat petting the little cat in her arms.* **2** [T1] to show special kindness and care for the comfort of: *I enjoy staying there; she always pets her guests.* **3** [T1; IØ] to kiss and touch in sexual play: *The policeman found them petting in the back of the car.*

neck [IØ] (of two people, usu young, concerned in a sexual relationship) to kiss, fondle, etc, each other: *They enjoy necking in the back seats of the cinema. He found them necking openly at the bus-stop.*

C23 *nouns* : **relating to sex**

[ALSO ⇒ A14–16]

sex [U] the bodily act between a man and a woman in which the penis [⇒B40] enters the vagina [⇒ B40] for purposes of pleasure and/or reproduction [⇒ A16], or all the associations of this act: *He has had sex with several girls. She said that all he seemed to want* *was sex. Sex interests most people. Sex relations are more than just the sex act itself.* [*also* ⇒ B40 PENIS, VAGINA, ETC]

(sexual) intercourse [U] the act of sex: *They have intercourse two or three times a week.*

orgasm [C] the high point of sexual excitement during intercourse: *She reaches her orgasm easily.*

heavy petting [U] sexual play up to but not including sexual intercourse: *People often discuss whether heavy petting is a morally safe thing for young people to do.*

love affair [C] a strongly emotional interest between two people, usu of opposite sexes, over a period of time, with or without sexual intercourse: *Their love affair was stormy, but lasted 30 years.*

affair [C] a sexual relationship, usu secret or not socially acceptable, between two people, at least one of whom is already married: *He had an affair with a married woman. The affair didn't last long and was rather unhappy.*

C24 verbs, etc : relating to sex

make love [IØ] **1** to have sex together: *They made love before going to sleep.* **2** *esp old use* to show sexual interest in: *He's been making love to her for years, but she shows little interest in him.* **3** [(*to*)] (usu of men) to have sex with: *He made love to her later that evening.*

go to bed with *also* **sleep with** *euph* to have sex with: *Did she go to bed with him? He has slept with her on several occasions.*

seduce [T1] to use charm and greater experience, etc to persuade (someone) into sexual intercourse: *He seduced the girl when he was 19 and she was about 16.* **seduction** [U] the act of seducing or being seduced

have [T1] *infml* to have sex with: *He's had her several times.*

have it off *sl, esp BrE* (usu of a man) to have sex: *He says he had it off with her last night, but I don't believe him.*

lay *sl* **1** [T1] (esp of a man) to have sex with: *He managed to lay her at last. He's laid quite a few in his time.* **2** [C] a woman considered by men for her part in the sexual act: *He says she was a good lay.*

make [T1] *sl, esp AmE* (esp of a man) to succeed in having sex with: *Have you made her yet?* **make it** *sl* to have sex: *Have you made it with her?*

score [IØ] *sl,* to have sex with someone: *Did you score last night?*

knock off [v adv T1] *sl, esp BrE* (of a man) to have sex with: *He says he knocked her off last night, but I don't believe it.*

knock up [v adv T1] *AmE sl* to make pregnant [⇒ A17]: *He knocked up his girlfriend and her family were angry.*

fuck [T1] *taboo* (esp of a man) to have sex with: *He has fucked a lot of birds* (= girls) *in his time.*

screw *taboo sl* **1** [T1] (esp of a man) to have sex

with: *He screws her every Friday.* **2** [IØ] to have sex: *They were screwing (away) all last night.*

sleep around [v adv IØ] to have sex with several partners one after another over a period of time: *She sleeps around quite a bit and has done for quite some time.*

C25 adjectives : relating to sex [B]

sexy [Wa1] very attractive sexually: *She says he's a very sexy man. What a sexy dress she wore last night; one of the sexiest I've seen.* **-ily** [adv] **-iness** [U]

seductive having the power to seduce [⇒ C24]; very attractive (sexually): *She gave him a seductive smile.* (fig) *I find these ideas very seductive.* **-ly** [adv]

erotic related to or causing sexual love and desire: *They sell a lot of erotic books and pictures in that shop. Her bedroom was full of highly erotic art.* **-ally** [adv] **-ness** [U] **eroticism** [U] interest in erotic things; erotic conditions

bawdy [Wa1] funny about sex: *He has a very bawdy sense of humour. No more bawdy jokes, please.* **-ily** [adv] **-iness** [U]

lecherous full of strong and usu nasty sexual desire: *Don't let that lecherous old man near me!* **-ly** [adv] **lechery** [U; C] great sexual desire (and activity) **lecher** [C] a lecherous man

raunchy [Wa1] *esp AmE* lecherous and bawdy: *What a raunchy book that is!*

randy *esp BrE*, **horny** *esp AmE* [Wa1] *infml* full of sexual desire: *He says he's feeling randy/horny tonight!*

C26 verbs, etc : activities associated with sex

masturbate [IØ; T1] to excite the sex organs (of) by handling, rubbing, etc: *When people can't get sex, they will often masturbate instead.* **masturbation** [U] the act of masturbating

fornicate [IØ] *deprec* to have sex (often) outside marriage: *Many religions are against people fornicating.* **fornication** [U] the act of fornicating

rape 1 [T1] (usu of a man) to have sex with (a woman) against her will: *He attacked and raped a young girl.* **2** [U; C] the act or crime of raping a woman: *He was found guilty of rape. There were more cases of rape than usual last year.*

ravish [T1] *lit* to rape: *The man ravished the girl.*

C27 verbs : marrying and living together

marry 1 [IØ (*into*); T1] to take (a person) in marriage: *He married late in life and his sister never married at all. They are just married; can't you tell? He asked her to marry him.* (fig) *She married money, you know* (= married a rich man). *He married into a rich family.* **2** [T1] (of a priest or an official, etc) to cause to be married: *He married them in his church. The official married them according to the law.* **3** [T1 *(off)*] to cause to marry: *She wants to marry her daughter (off) to a rich man.* **married to** [Wa5; F] having as a husband or wife: *He's married to a local girl.* *(fig) She's married to her work.*

wed [I0; T1] *old use & fml* to marry: *She never wed. He wed a local girl.* **wedded to** 1 [Wa5; A] having been lawfully married **2** [F] *(fig)* very interested in: *He's wedded to his work.*

propose [I0; T1 *(to)*] (usu of a man) to make an offer of (marriage) to someone: *He wants to propose to her. Has he proposed yet? If he doesn't propose soon, she will!* **proposal** [C *(of)*] an offer of marriage: *She turned down* (= did not accept) *his proposal.*

live with [v prep T1] to live in the same house as (someone), like a married person: *She's been living with an artist in Paris for a year or more. That couple? No, they're not married, but they live with each other all the same.*

live together [I0] to live as a married couple when not married: *They're not married but they've been living together for years now.*

co-habit [I0] *fml* to live together as though married although not married: *The couple are known to have been co-habiting for several years.* **co-habitation** [U] the activity of co-habiting

divorce [T1] to end a marriage with or between: *The court divorced them. She divorced her first husband in 1970.*

C28 *adjectives, etc* : **relating to marriage** [Wa5;B]

married 1 having a husband or wife: *Yes, he's a married man. Married people usually have a different view of life from single people. Who lives in the flat upstairs?—Oh, a young married couple. A newly-married couple live upstairs.* **2** [A] of the state of marriage: *Well, how are you enjoying married life?*

single not married; not having a husband or wife: *She's single; she never got married. He's a single man.* **singles** [P] *esp AmE* unmarried people: *This party is for singles, not married people.*

unmarried not married: *Is she single?—Yes, she's unmarried.*

engaged having agreed to marry: *My daughter is engaged (to be married). Edward and I have just got engaged.*

betrothed *fml & old use* engaged, esp from an early age, esp by arrangement

divorced no longer married: *He's divorced, after 15 years of marriage. Divorced people often get married again.*

separated married but not living together because of some disagreement: *They are separated, and the children live with her.*

Separated couples usually end up in the divorce court.

get (**married, engaged, divorced**, etc) *genl* to become (married, etc): *He got married last week. When did you get engaged? She got divorced last year. He got himself married at last, to a London girl.*

C29 *nouns, etc* : **engagement, marriage, and divorce**

engagement [C] an agreement to marry: *John and Mary announced their engagement. Edward has broken off his engagement* (= said he no longer wishes to marry the girl). *Most engagements lead to marriage. We held an engagement party for them.*

betrothal [C; U] *fml & old use* engagement

marriage [C; U] the social union of a man and woman by a ceremony recognized by the law; the state of being married: *The institution of marriage is age-old. Most women and men are interested in love and marriage and raising a family. Their marriage lasted two years and led to a particularly nasty divorce action. Church marriages are rather different from civil marriages.* **marital** [Wa5;B] of or concerning marriage: *Religions are usually concerned with the marital lives of believers.* **pre-marital** [Wa5;B] happening before marriage: *Most religions do not believe that pre-marital sex is right.*

matrimony [U] *fml* the state of marriage: *Matrimony is a serious and ancient institution. The priest united the couple* [⇒ C32] *in holy matrimony.* **matrimonial** [Wa5;B] of or concerning matrimony

wedlock [U] *old use & law* the condition of being married: *The child was born out of wedlock and is therefore a bastard* [⇒ C3]. *The priest joined them in (lawful) wedlock.*

wedding [C] a marriage ceremony or service: *How many people have you invited to the wedding? Mothers always cry at their daughters' weddings. The wedding day arrived at last.*

honeymoon 1 [C] the holiday taken by a newly-married man and woman: *They went to Majorca for/on their honeymoon. The hotel staff recognized the honeymoon couple immediately.* **2** [S] *(usu fig)* a pleasant beginning to anything: *The political honeymoon for the new government didn't last long.* **3** [I0] to have one's honeymoon: *They honeymooned in Majorca.*

divorce [U; C] a complete breaking up of a marriage by a court of law: *Is divorce allowed in that country? She obtained a divorce after years of unhappiness.*

C30 *nouns* : **relating to marriage**

monogamy [U] *tech* the custom or practice of having one wife at one time **monogamous**

[Wa5;B] relating to or practising monogamy: *These tribes are monogamous.*

bigamy [U] *tech (law)* the state of being married to two people, usu wives, at the same time: *Bigamy is considered a crime in many countries. He committed bigamy.* **bigamist** [C] a person who has committed bigamy **bigamous** [Wa5;B] relating to or practising bigamy: *She didn't know her marriage was bigamous.*

polygamy [U] *tech* the state of being married to two or more people, usu wives, at the same time: *Polygamy is not so common today as it once was.* **polygamous** [Wa5;B] relating to or practising polygamy: *Muslim society was once largely polygamous.*

harem [C] **1** the women's part of a Muslim household and the women in it **2** any (polygamous) group of women belonging in any way to one man: *The chief of the tribe had a harem of 50 wives.* (humor) *Oh, he has a harem of about ten adoring secretaries in his office!*

adultery [U] *tech* sexual activity between a married person and someone outside the marriage: *Adultery is considered wrong by many religions and is often given as a reason for divorce.* **adulterer** [C] a person, usu a husband, who has engaged in adultery **adulteress** [C] *esp emot* a woman who has committed adultery **adulterous** [Wa5;B] relating to or practising adultery

incest [U] sexual relationship between close relatives in a family, as between brother and sister **incestuous** [B] **1** (of people or relationships) including or doing acts of incest **2** *esp deprec* (of relationships) unusually close, esp in a way that does not include outsiders or that is thought to be unhealthy **-ness** [U] **-ly** [adv]

C31 *nouns* : **persons not married and just married**

bachelor [C] an unmarried man: *This club is for bachelors only.*

spinster [C] *old use & fml* an unmarried woman: *Who lives in the flat downstairs?— Oh, an elderly spinster.*

bachelor girl [C] an unmarried woman, usu younger, with a career of her own

old maid [C] **1** an old unmarried woman: *She never married and died an old maid.* **2** *deprec* a man or woman who is very careful and difficult to please: *Oh, stop being such an old maid!*

fiancé [C] a man to whom a woman is engaged: *Her fiancé lives in Liverpool.*

fiancée [C] a woman to whom a man is engaged: *His fiancée is from Hong Kong.*

betrothed [Wn3;C] *fml & old use* a fiancé or fiancée: *She met her betrothed for the first time last night.*

newlyweds [P] *infml* a man and woman recently married: *Ah, here come the newlyweds!*

happy couple/pair [*the* GC] *infml & often pomp* a man and woman just engaged or married: *Let us drink to the happy couple!*

C32 *nouns* : **persons who are or have been married** [C]

husband the man to whom a woman is married: *Her husband was killed in a car crash.*

wife the woman to whom a man is married: *My wife is coming on the trip with me. Their wives went with them.*

(married) couple a man and a woman who are married to each other; a husband and wife: *A young (married) couple live upstairs.*

spouse *fml* a husband or wife: *Your spouses will be notified of the change of plan.*

matron an older married woman, esp one of quiet, careful behaviour: *The matrons of the town did not like the new nightclub.*

widow a woman whose husband has died, and who has not married again: *She's a widow—a war widow actually. He left his widow a lot of money.* **widowhood** [U] state of being a widow

widower a man whose wife has died, and who has not married again: *He has been a widower for 10 years.*

divorcée a divorced person: *Is she married or single?— Well, she's a divorcée, actually.*

ex- [*prefix*] (used to show divorce): *She's his ex-wife. She meets her ex-husband from time to time.*

ex *infml* (someone's) divorced husband or wife: *She met her ex unexpectedly at a party.*

C33 *nouns* : **people at a wedding** [C]

bride a woman about to be married, or just married: *The bride was dressed in white. He kissed the bride.* **bridal** [Wa5;A] of or relating to brides and weddings

(bride)groom a man about to be married or just married: *The bride and (bride)groom both looked nervous.*

bridesmaid a girl or unmarried woman who attends a bride on the day of the marriage

matron of honour a married woman serving as a bridesmaid

best man the male companion of the bridegroom: *The best man usually keeps the wedding ring until the bridegroom puts it on the bride's finger.*

page (boy) a young boy who attends a bride on the day of the marriage

C34 *nouns & adjectives* : **relating to homosexuality, etc**

homosexual 1 [C] a person, esp a man, sexually attracted to members of the same sex: *He is a homosexual and goes to bars where he can meet other homosexuals.* **2** [Wa5;B] related to or possessing the qualities of homosexuals **homo** *sl abbrev* a homosexual **homosexuality** [U] the state or condition of being a homosexual

heterosexual 1 [C] a person sexually attracted to members of the opposite sex: *The majority* *of human beings are heterosexuals.* **2** [Wa5;B] related to sex between male and female: *heterosexual urges* **-ity** [U]

bisexual 1 [C] a person sexually attracted more or less equally to both sexes **2** [Wa5;B] related to or possessing the qualities of bisexuals or of both sexes **-ity** [U]

lesbian 1 [C] a woman sexually attracted to other women: *She's a lesbian; men don't interest her sexually.* **2** [Wa5;B] related to or possessing the qualities of lesbians   **lesbianism** [U] the state or condition of being a lesbian

queer *sl derog* **1** [C] a male homosexual: *An old queer lives in the flat downstairs.* **2** [Wa5;B] homosexual: *He's queer, you know.*

fag [C] *esp AmE sl* a male homosexual

poof *also* **poofter** [C] *BrE derog sl* **1** a male homosexual **2** *often also humor* a man whose behaviour or actions are weak, ineffective, or lacking in courage

pansy [C] *infml* **1** a male homosexual **2** a woman-like or girlish young man

dike *also* **dyke** [C] *sl* a lesbian

gay *infml* **1** [Wa5;B] homosexual: *They go to a gay club on Saturdays.* **2** [C] a homosexual: *Gays go to that bar. Many homosexuals prefer to be called 'gays'.*

bugger [C] **1** *derog* a homosexual **2** *sl* a silly or nasty person: *Tell that bugger to get out of here!* **buggery** [U] *tech* the act of anal [⇒ B33] intercourse   **bugger off** [v adv I0] *sl* to go away: *He just buggered off and left me with all the work to do. Bugger off!*

C35 *nouns* : **persons associated with love and sex** [C]

lover a person, usu a man, with whom someone has an affair: *Her husband didn't satisfy her, so she took a lover. They are homosexuals and have been lovers for years.*

mistress the woman with whom a man has a sexual relationship outside his marriage: *In some societies mistresses are more accepted than in others. His secretary was also his mistress. He set his mistress up in a house of her own.*

concubine a woman whom a man takes to live with him as a (or another) wife: *In some societies rich and powerful men have had several wives and many concubines.*

C36 *nouns & verbs* : **relating to persons who sell sex**

prostitute 1 [C] a woman who earns money by having sex with anyone who will pay for it: *When she couldn't meet (= pay) the bills she became a prostitute. Prostitutes can be found in most societies, given various degrees of social acceptance.* **2** [T1] to make into or use as a prostitute: *The old man prostituted his daughter and various other girls.* (*fig deprec*) *I am not*

going to prostitute my art so that men can make a lot of money!

male prostitute [C] a man who earns money by having sex with anyone who will pay him

prostitution [U] **1** the business of being a prostitute or of controlling prostitutes: *Prostitution is often said to be the world's oldest profession.* **2** *deprec* selling a talent, etc just for money: *Doing this work for that company is just prostitution.*

streetwalker [C] *usu derog* a prostitute who gets her business by waiting in a street

call girl [C] a prostitute who arranges on the telephone for men to meet her for sex

whore *emot* **1** [C] a prostitute or a woman thought to behave like one: *A lot of whores live in that part of the town. Well, that girl has always been a bit of a whore.* **2** [I0 (*away*)] to act as a whore: *She's been whoring away for years.* **3** [I0] to enjoy the company of whores: *He loves to go whoring and drinking when he gets some money.*

tart [C] *esp BrE sl derog* a whore: *These girls are just common tarts, nothing more.*

harlot [C] *esp old use, lit and emot* a whore: *That painted old harlot runs a brothel* [⇒ C38] *in the East End of London.*

tramp [C] *AmE infml* a prostitute

hooker [C] *AmE sl* a prostitute

courtesan [C] *esp formerly* a prostitute for men of high class or great wealth, whom she may choose for herself: *Some courtesans in history have had great political power.*

C37 *nouns, etc* : **persons connected with prostitution**

madam [C] *infml* a woman who runs a brothel [⇒ C38]: *Several madams have houses in this part of the town.*

pimp 1 [C] a man who controls or finds business for one or more prostitutes and gets in return a share in any earnings **2** [I0] to (try to) find business for a prostitute

procurer [C] *fml* a pimp

C38 *nouns* : **houses of prostitution** [C]

brothel a house of prostitutes, where sex can be bought

bordello *lit & euph* a brothel

bawdy house *also* **disorderly house** *old use* a brothel

house of ill fame/repute *old use & euph* a brothel: *The religious leader spoke out strongly against houses of ill repute.*

whorehouse *deprec* a brothel

red-light district the part of a city where brothels can be found: *A town's red-light district tends to be near the docks.* [⇒M160]

Friendship and Enmity

C40 nouns : **people who are friends** [C]

friend 1 a person who shares the same feelings of natural liking and understanding, the same interests, etc (but is not closely related): *Bill and Ben are friends. He's a friend, not a relation. They are sisters, but luckily they are also friends. Mary's an old friend of mine; we were at school together. He's no friend of mine. Must you quarrel all the time?— Can't you be friends? The children are good/bad friends* (=like/dislike each other very much). *Are you staying at a hotel?— No, we're staying with friends.* **2** a helper; supporter; adviser; person showing kindness and understanding: *That rich lady is a friend of the arts; she provides money for concerts. Our doctor's been a good friend to us; he's always helped us when we've needed him. He says he's no friend of the government. A girl's best friend is her mother. He didn't get the job on his own abilities; he had a friend in high places* (=someone in a position to influence others to help him). **3** someone who is not an enemy; a person from whom there is nothing to fear: *'Who goes there: friend or foe?' shouted the soldier on guard duty. The escaped prisoner met some men in the wood; he found himself among friends, for they didn't tell the police about him.* **4** *fig & fml* a useful quality, condition, or thing: *Bright light is the painter's best friend.* **5** [N] *neutral* a form of address to a man: *Look, friend, I have no wish to argue with you. What can I do for you, my friend?* **6** *usu derog and ironical* of a stranger noticed for some reason, usu amusement or displeasure: *Our friend with the loud voice is here again, I see. Our friend the postman is late again, it seems.*
friendship [U; C] the state or condition of being a friend: *Her friendship means a lot to me. Friendships don't always last for ever. He values their friendship highly. He struck up a friendship with one of the shopkeepers.*
acquaintance a person whom one knows, esp through work or business, but who may not be a friend: *Well, he's more (of) an acquaintance than a friend. He has a wide circle of acquaintances but few real friends.* **acquaintanceship** [U] state or condition of being an acquaintance
pal *infml* **1** a friend: *Oh, he's an old pal of mine; we used to play football together. They've been pals for years.* **2** [N] *esp AmE* (a friendly form of address to a man): *Say, pal, can you lend me a dollar?*
chum 1 a good friend, esp among young people: *They were boyhood chums and still see a lot of each other.* **2** [N] *sometimes deprec* (a form of address to a man): *Okay, chum, it's time for you to go.*
mate *esp BrE infml*, *esp working class* **1** a friend: *He's going to a dance on Saturday with (some*

of) his mates. **2** [N] *esp EngE* friendly form of address to a man: *Sorry, mate, can't help you; it's not my job.*
buddy *esp AmE infml* **1** a friend: *He is going there with (some of) his buddies. He's a buddy of mine.* **2** *also* **bud** [N] (a friendly form of address to a man): *Hey, bud(dy), you got a light?*

C41 nouns : **people who are not friends** [C]

enemy 1 a person who tries or wishes to harm or attack another, or to see that other persons suffer: *He is not my friend; he is an enemy. Most important people have their enemies. Try not to make an enemy of him* (=Don't do anything which will cause him to be your enemy). **2** [*the* R; A] the armed forces of a nation with whom one's country is at war: *The enemy began their attack. He was actively helping the enemy throughout the war. An enemy aeroplane attacked the ship.* **3** *fig & fml* anything that harms: *The greatest enemy of our civilization is material greed.* **enmity** [U] the active hatred of an enemy: *He feels great enmity towards you for what you did.*
foe *lit & fml* an enemy, esp in war: *They have been deadly foes for years. He attacked the foe* (=his military enemies). *What is he, friend or foe?*
opponent a person who takes the opposite side, esp in playing, fighting, or an argument: *The two opponents in the game were of almost equal skill. My opponents hope to see me defeated this time, but they will be surprised.*
antagonist a person who is opposed to another, esp actively; *fml* an opponent: *They have been fierce antagonists in this matter for years.* **antagonism** [U] the state or condition of being antagonists; enmity: *He feels great antagonism towards them.*

C42 nouns : **neighbours and partners** [C]

neighbour *BrE*, **neighbor** *AmE* **1** a person who lives near oneself or the speaker/writer, esp in a house in the same street: *They are near neighbours; they live only two houses apart. My nextdoor neighbour is a very helpful person. Our nearest neighbour lives five miles away.* **2** the object next to the one being discussed: *This is a good book but its neighbour on the left is even better.* **3** a country or group next to another or one another: *France and West Germany are neighbours.*
companion 1 a person who spends time with another, because he is a friend or by chance, such as when travelling: *They have been close companions since childhood. They were travelling companions on a trip to France.* (*fig*) *Her dog is her most faithful companion; it always*

keeps her company. **2** a person present with another: *Who is her companion?— I haven't seen him before.* **3** a person paid to be in the company of another: *She spent several years as companion to a rich old lady.* **companionship** [U] the state or condition of being a companion: *Their companionship dates back to their schooldays. Marriage is a matter of companionship as well as sex.* **company** [U] the presence of a friend, on a journey, etc: *I enjoyed his company on the train. She keeps company with* (= is friendly with, and goes out with) *several girls who work here. He isn't very good company when he has been working so hard. I met him on the ship and was sorry to part company with him* (= leave his company) *when we reached port.*

friend *euph* a person present with another: *Well, John, who's your friend?*

comrade *often emot* a person who works closely with one; a fellow worker who is treated as a friend: *Comrades, we must unite against injustice. He was a comrade of mine during the war. He says he won't turn against his old political comrades.* **comradeship** [U] the state or condition of being a comrade/comrades

colleague a fellow worker in any occupation or activity: *My colleague will call and see you next week. All his colleagues objected to the way he was treated.*

associate 1 a person connected with another, esp in work: *He is not a friend but a business associate. The thief and his associates were caught by the police. They are business associates.* **2** a person who is a member of a society but with only limited rights: *Both full members and associates/associate members may vote.*

partner 1 [(*in, with*)] a person who shares in the same activity: *She was a partner with her brother on a trip to Brazil. Those two men have been partners in crime for years. They have been partners for years in many undertakings. He is my business partner.* **2** one of two people dancing together, or playing together against two others, or married to each other: *Ladies and gentlemen, take your partners for a waltz. They are tennis/bridge partners. The partners to a marriage have many responsibilities.* **3** [N] *infml esp AmE* (a form of address to a friend): *Come on, partners, let's have a drink.*

mate 1 [*often in pl and in comb*] a fellow worker or companion: *His schoolmates waited for him. He went with his workmates to a pub.* **2** a helper to a skilled workman: *He's a builder's mate.*

ally 1 a person who helps and supports another: *He is one of your allies in this fight, isn't he?* **2** a country that is joined to another by political agreement, esp to provide support in war: *The two countries are military allies. The allies undertook a combined assault on the enemy positions.*

accomplice a person who helps another person esp to do wrong: *He was your accomplice in the crime, wasn't he? They have been accomplices in wrongdoing for years.*

confederate *sometimes deprec* a person, country, or state that joins or works together with others: *They were confederates in the bank robbery.*

C43 nouns : people who support others [C]

supporter a person giving support to another, in politics, arguments, etc: *He is a powerful man with many supporters in the city.*

henchman *often derog* a faithful supporter, usu a man, esp in politics, who obeys his leader without argument and may use violent or dishonest methods

minion *also* **lackey** *old use usu derog* a supporter or servant who slavishly does what his or her leader says

yes-man *infml derog* a slavish henchman: *Oh, don't be such a yes-man; you agree to everything he wants!*

side-kick *infml esp AmE* a faithful henchman

C44 verbs : being and becoming friends

be friends with to have a friendship with; to be a friend of: *She is friends with Susan.*

make friends (with) to form friendships (with): *He has a pleasant manner and makes friends easily. She doesn't know anyone in that town, but she'll soon make friends there. Have you made friends with your neighbours yet? Sam and Joe have just met, but they seem to have made friends* (= with each other) *already. They had an argument, but they've made friends again* (= have forgiven each other).

meet up with [v adv prep T1] *infml* to make friends with: *He has met up with some other youngsters of his own age.*

pal up (with) [v adv (prep) I∅; T1] *infml* to become very friendly (with): *He has palled up with Jim again, I'm glad to say. It's nice to see your children palling up like this. Did she manage to pal up with anyone at her new school?*

get acquainted (with) *infml* to become familiar (with), so as to make friends: *Well, he says he likes her and hopes to get acquainted. She got acquainted with him at a dance.*

get to know to become familiar (and friendly) with: *I've managed to get to know some nice people in this town. It can take a long time to get to know a new town and its people.*

befriend [T1] *usu fml* to act as a friend towards: *He befriended us when we had little money and nowhere to live.*

ally [Wv5;T1;I∅: (*with, to*)] to join, unite, or work together with as by political agreement or marriage: *The small country allied itself with the stronger power. Will the workers in the two factories ally against their employers?*

C45 *verbs & nouns* : **arguing and quarrelling**

[ALSO ⇒ F106–8]

argue [IØ (*with*)] to say that one disagrees, usu strongly: *They began to argue over which political party had the better record. Please don't let's argue/let's not argue. I'm tired of arguing with him; he never admits he's wrong. Don't argue (with me), my mind is made up; I won't change my decision.* **argument 1** [U] arguing generally: *I want no argument; I won't change my decision. Discussion is better than argument.* **2** [C] an occasion of arguing: *They keep getting into heated political arguments. I had an argument with him last night.* **argumentative** [B] *fml* tending to argue, usu strongly and often: *Some people are very argumentative just to be difficult.* **-ly** [adv] **-ness** [U]

quarrel 1 [C] a strong argument, disagreement, or show of dislike: *They had a bad quarrel last night. The quarrel between them looks like being serious. He had a noisy quarrel with a government official. I'm tired of their endless quarrels; I wish they could live together in peace.* **2** [S] a cause for argument, etc: *I have no quarrel with him or his opinions.* **3** [IØ (*with*)] to have a quarrel: *The two boys quarrelled over the same girl. Stop quarrelling, you people! What are you quarrelling about? He has quarrelled with his girlfriend and now he wants to quarrel with everyone else.* **quarrelsome** [B] tending to quarrel often: *He's a quarrelsome fellow; keep away from him.* **-ness** [U]

row 1 [C] a noisy and often violent quarrel, usu not lasting long: *Her father and mother often have rows, shouting at each other. Let's not have another row.* **2** [IØ] to have a row: *They're rowing again, I'm afraid. They row a lot, but I think they quite enjoy it.*

dispute 1 [C] a strong argument, disagreement, or quarrel: *There have been several disputes over who owns this land.* **2** the state or fact of disagreement (*esp in the phr* **in dispute (with)**): *The matter in dispute is the ownership of this land. Well, this is beyond dispute* (= without doubt) *the best house in the village. He has been in dispute with the government over this matter for years.* **3 a** [IØ] to argue, quarrel, or debate: *She is always disputing over something.* **b** [T1, 6a, b] to disagree with: *I dispute the result of the election; count the votes again. I don't dispute what you say; it is the way you say it which annoys me. They were disputing whether to lend him the money or not.* **disputatious** [B] *fml* tending to dispute (things) all the time **-ness** [U]

feud 1 [C] a state of strong dislike and enmity, often violent and continuing for some time, usu as a result of a quarrel between two people or families, etc: *This feud has gone on now for 30 years and killed six people. He has a personal feud with the government.* **2** [IØ] (*esp of two families*) to keep up a feud, the memory of a quarrel, etc often with violence: *The families have been feuding for 30 years.*

C46 *adjectives* : **relating to being friends**

friendly [Wa1] **1** [B] acting or ready to act as a friend: *He's not very friendly, is he? What a friendly little dog!* **2** [F] sharing the relationship of friends: *They quarrelled once, but are quite friendly now. Bill is very friendly with Ben.* **3** [F *to*] favouring/ready to accept (ideas): *The business company was friendly to change.* **4** [B] kind and generous; ready to help; supporting or protecting: *It would be a friendly thing to do. Visiting the old lady was a very friendly act. You're always sure of a friendly welcome at this hotel. The sick man was glad of a friendly arm to lean on.* (*fig*) *We found shelter from the rain under a friendly tree.* **5** [B] showing (possible) friendship: *She gave him a friendly smile.* **6** [B] politically co-operative: *A trade agreement has just been made with several friendly nations.* **7** [B] not causing or containing bad feeling: *They had a friendly argument over politics.* **8** [Wa5;B] (esp in sport) not serious: *The two teams played a friendly game last Saturday; the season's serious matches don't start till later.* **-liness** [U]

sociable [B] fond of people and often in the company of others: *He's a very sociable fellow, but his wife is much less sociable. Come on, try to be a bit more sociable, John; come and meet these people.* **-bly** [adv]

amiable [B] of a pleasant friendly nature; good-tempered: *I enjoy talking to that old man; he is very amiable. She has a nice amiable manner.* **-bly** [adv] **amity** [U] *often fml or pomp* friendship or friendliness: *The cat and the dog live together in surprising amity.*

amicable [B] as suitable between friends; peaceable and friendly: *We reached an amicable agreement over the ownership of the land; no quarrels.* **-bly** [adv] *The matter was settled amicably.*

affable [B] friendly; easy and polite to talk to; ready to be friends: *What an affable, amusing fellow he is! She sent him an affable reply to his letter.* **affability** [U] **-bly** [adv]

intimate [B] **1** close in relationship: *They have been intimate friends for years.* **2** [Wa5 (*with*)] concerned in a sexual relationship with someone/with each other: *They were intimate, not just friends. She was intimate with him, I believe.* **3** detailed: *He has an intimate knowledge of the town.* **-ly** [adv] *I know them both intimately; we used to work together.* **intimacy** [U;C] **on intimate terms 1** close in friendship **2** concerned in a sexual relationship **on terms of intimacy** *fml* on intimate terms

close [Wa1;B] with deep feelings and/or of great importance: *They have been close friends since childhood. They aren't married, but they have a pretty close relationship.* **-ness** [U]

pally [Wa1;B] *infml* friendly: *She used to be very pally with Joan. John and Bill are very pally.*

chummy [Wa1;B] *esp BrE infml, sometimes derog* friendly: *They aren't always so chummy, you know.*

matey [Wa1;B] *BrE infml, esp working class* friendly: *He's pretty matey with Bill. Why are you so matey all of a sudden?*

warm [Wa1;B] (*fig*) friendly in a pleasant way: *They gave us a very warm welcome. She looked at him with a warm smile on her face.* **-th** [U]

cordial [B]*fml* warm, sincere, and friendly: *May I express my cordial thanks for what you have done for this town? They gave us a very cordial reception* (= warm welcome). **-ly** [adv] *He greeted them cordially.* **-ity** [U]

C47 *adjectives* : **relating to not being friends** [B]

unfriendly [Wa1] not friendly: *He has a rather unfriendly manner. Why must you be so unfriendly towards him? He's only trying to help.* **-liness** [U]

unsociable not sociable; not fond of company: *She's been pretty unsociable since he went away.* **-bly** [adv]

hostile 1 very unfriendly (and therefore dangerous); showing dislike: *The local people are hostile to outsiders. She gave him a hostile look.* **2** [Wa5] belonging to or caused by an enemy: *You can expect hostile action soon. Hostile aircraft crossed into our air space several minutes ago.* **hostility** [U] the state or condition of being hostile: *His hostility to your plan is well-known.*

inimical *fml* hostile and harmful: *These actions are inimical to good relations between our two countries.*

antagonistic very much against something; hostile: *These people are antagonistic to change; they like things as they are.*

difficult (of people) unfriendly and always quarrelling; not easily pleased: *Don't be so difficult! She has always been a difficult child.*

reserved not liking to talk too much about oneself or to make one's feelings known: *She's rather a reserved girl; she doesn't make friends easily.*

distant also **remote** [Wa2] (*fig*) showing a lack of personal warmth or friendliness: *His manner was reserved and distant/remote, as though he had no intention of making friends.*

cool [Wa1] (*fig*) (esp of people) not particularly friendly: *She gave him a cool smile. He treated her in rather a cool way; it upset her because he had been so friendly before.*

cold [Wa1] (*fig*) (of people or their acts) very unfriendly: *His manner towards her became cold and distant. His smile was cold.*

aloof [*also* adv] (of a person) keeping at some distance from others and therefore (considered) unfriendly: *He has an aloof manner,* but when you get to know him he's very nice. He stood aloof from all the others.*

C48 *adjectives* : **lonely and alone**

lonely [Wa1;B] (unhappy because) having no friend, person, animal, etc near: *She feels rather lonely; she has no friends in the town. They live a lonely life in a lonely house in the hills. Aren't you lonely here?—No; I have the animals for company.* **-liness** [U]

alone 1 *also more emph* **all alone** [F; adv] without any other person or thing near: *She sat all alone on the hillside. He has been alone in the world since his wife died.* **2** [adv Wa5] and nothing more: *You can't live on bread alone.*

solitary [Wa5;A; (B)] having no other person or thing nearby; alone; single: *A solitary figure* (= person) *stood in the road. She leads a very solitary life.* **solitude** [U] the state of being solitary; loneliness: *The solitude of the place was complete; very few people ever went there. He likes solitude; he doesn't like big cities.*

lone [Wa5;B] having no others near (and liking things better that way): *A lone bird flew over.*

loner [C] a person who lives, works, etc alone: *He is a loner with almost no friends.*

lonesome [B] *esp AmE infml & emot* lonely: *She's a bit lonesome and far from home.*

Death and burial

[ALSO ⇒ A1–20]

C50 *verbs & nouns* : **relating to someone dying**

[ALSO ⇒ F84]

lose [T1] to suffer the death of: *She lost her husband and youngest son within weeks of each other.*

loss [U] state of having lost someone: *The loss of her son has aged her a lot.*

mourn [T1; I0] to feel and/or show grief at (someone's death): *She mourned her dead husband for months and could not be consoled. They are still mourning, although he died a year ago.* [⇒C55]

grieve [I0 (*for*)] to mourn greatly or constantly: *She just sits there, grieving for her lost children. Don't grieve; death comes to us all.*

grief [U; C] the state of grieving: *His grief at the death of his wife was terrible.*

bereave [T1] *fml* to leave sad and mourning because of a death: *He was bereaved (of his wife).*

bereavement [U; C] the state of being bereaved: *I was sorry to hear of your bereavement.*

C51 verbs : dying

[ALSO ⇒ A2 DIE]

pass on [v adv IØ] euph to die; (religious) to go to another life: Your father has passed on, my dear; he wouldn't want you to grieve.

pass away [v adv IØ] euph to die, usu peacefully: The old lady passed away in her sleep.

expire [IØ] fml, euph & lit to die: The elderly gentleman expired.

give up the ghost old use & lit to die: The king sighed and gave up the ghost.

kick the bucket BrE sl to die: The old fellow kicked the bucket and left his wife a fortune!

C52 adjectives, etc : relating to death and mourning

bereaved [Wa5;B] left (alone) after the death of someone dear: The bereaved woman sat alone in the church. Many people have been left bereaved by this terrible disaster.

widowed [Wa5;B] made a widow [⇒ C32]; left alone after the death of one's husband or wife: My widowed mother lives in London. He was widowed in an air crash.

orphaned [Wa5;B] made an orphan [⇒ C3]; left without a father and mother: Many children were orphaned by that plane crash.

late [Wa5;A] who has died recently: Her late husband was a keen gardener. The late Captain Jones was a member of the local golf club. **late lamented** [Wa5;A] old use & lit late: Her late lamented husband left her this house.

mortal [Wa5;A] which can die/decay [⇒ A2]: They buried his mortal remains (= his dead body) in the village churchyard.

deceased euph & fml 1 [Wa5;B] dead: The deceased man was apparently seen here just before the accident. 2 [Wn3;C] a dead person: The deceased had been killed in a road accident.

dear departed [Wn3;C] fml & religious & sometimes humor a dead person: Let us pray for the dear departed. Well, friends, let's drink to (the memory of) the dear departed!

C53 verbs : burying and cremating

bury [T1] to place (a dead body) in a hole in the ground and cover with earth, or in the sea: They buried their dead and moved on. He was buried at sea, having died of a fever. These people burn their dead; they don't bury them.

cremate [T1] to burn (a dead body) in a special ceremony: His father asked to be cremated when he died.

embalm [T1] to treat (a dead body) with special substances in order to prevent natural decay: The ancient Egyptians embalmed their dead. **-ment** [U]

mummify [T1] to preserve as a mummy [⇒ C54]: The ancient Egyptians mummified their kings and queens. **-fication** [U]

inter [T1] fml to bury: The body was interred without a ceremony.

disinter [T1] to take (a dead body) out of the grave: People do not disinter human remains (= a body) without good reasons.

exhume [T1] to disinter on a legal [⇒ C189] order: The body was exhumed and examined for signs of poison. **exhumation** [U]

dig up [v adv T1] infml to disinter; exhume

lie in state [IØ] (of the dead body esp of an important person) to lie in a church or similar place so that mourners [⇒ C55] can walk past, paying their last respects (= showing respect): The body of the king lay in state in the cathedral.

C54 nouns : burying and cremating

[ALSO ⇒ B3]

burial [C; U] an act or occasion of burying a dead body: The burial was done early in the morning, without a ceremony. **burial place** [C] the place where someone has been buried

cremation [C; U] the act or occasion (= ceremony) of cremating a dead body: The cremation was at 11 am; only the family and some close friends were invited. Cremations are as common as burials nowadays.

funeral 1 [C] a usu religious ceremony of burying or cremating a dead person: Many people attended the old lady's funeral. **2** [A] of or connected with the last ceremonies after death: Funeral customs vary with different religions. A funeral service was held at the graveside [⇒ C57].

mummy [C] a dead body preserved from decay by treatment with special substances: Pictures of mummies can be seen in most books about ancient Egypt.

ashes [P] the remains of a dead body after cremation [⇒ C53]: Her last request was that her ashes should be scattered on the sea.

C55 nouns : relating to funerals

[ALSO ⇒ F84]

undertaker [C] a person whose job is to arrange funerals

mortician [C] AmE an undertaker

funeral director [C] euph an undertaker

wreath [C] flowers and/or leaves twisted and woven together, usu in a circle, to be placed on a coffin [⇒ C56], grave, or memorial to the dead: He laid a wreath on the grave [⇒ C57] of the man who died in the fire.

hearse [C] a usu black carriage or car used for carrying a coffin at a funeral

(funeral) cortege [C] the line of attendants and mourners at a (large) funeral

pallbearer [C] a person who walks beside the coffin at a funeral

mourning [U] (the wearing of) certain clothes, usu black but in some societies white, as a sign of mourning [⇒ C50]: *She wore mourning for several months after her husband's death. They are still in mourning for their dead father.*

mourner [C] a person present at a funeral and personally mourning for the dead: *In some societies, professional mourners take part in the funeral services. The mourners were invited to pay their last respects* (= to show respect) *to the dead.*

C56 nouns : **coffins, etc** [C]

coffin the box in which a dead person is buried: *The coffin was gently lowered into the grave.*

casket *esp AmE euph* a coffin

pall a heavy cloth placed over a coffin at a funeral

shroud, *also* **winding sheet** the cloth or sheet which covers a dead body at burial

urn a vase [⇒ H170] used for holding the ashes of a cremated person

C57 nouns : **graves, etc** [C]

grave (the position of) the hole in the ground where a dead person is buried: *They slowly lowered him/his body into the grave. His grave is not known. The war graves stretched over whole fields.* **graveside** [*the* R] the ground beside a grave

last resting place *euph* a grave: *They carried him to his last resting place.*

tomb a grave, esp if large and with a hollowed-out shape like a cave: *They laid the king (to rest) in the great tomb. Ancient tombs have been found in this valley.*

sepulchre *BrE*, **sepulcher** *AmE fml, lit & old use* a tomb

mausoleum a large stone tomb, often a building, raised over a grave, esp that of a famous or important person

vault an underground room, usu large, for burying people, usu members of the same family, in: *He is buried in the family vault.*

C58 nouns : **places of burial and cremation** [C]

cemetery an area of ground, usu not belonging to a church, used only for the burial of dead people: *The cemetery is well cared for; most of her family are buried there.*

graveyard a piece of ground, often near a church, where dead people are buried

churchyard the area around a church and usu enclosed by a wall, in which graves are usu found

mortuary a place, as in a hospital, where dead bodies are kept before burial

morgue a place where dead people are kept,

esp when their names are not known and their relatives must be found: *The body of the man killed in the accident was taken to the city morgue.*

crematorium, *also esp AmE* **crematory** a building in which dead people are burnt, sometimes with a surrounding garden where the ashes can be buried

C59 nouns : **relating to graves and death**

gravestone [C] a stone put up over a grave, bearing the name, dates of birth and death, etc of a dead person

tombstone [C] a (large) gravestone

headstone [C] a gravestone at a position above the head of a buried person

memorial [C] an object, often a stone, esp with a message on it or a list of names, in memory of one or more persons or of an important event: *The war memorial listed 42 dead from that village alone.*

monument [C] a building, structure, etc that preserves, or is intended to preserve, the memory of a person or event

epitaph [C] words describing a dead person, written on his or her gravestone, tomb, or memorial

in memoriam *Lat* (often on gravestones and memorials) in memory of

RIP [*abbrev*] 'Rest in peace' or the Latin equivalent 'Requiescat in pace' (letters often written on gravestones)

obituary [C] a notice that someone has died; an account of someone's life, printed just after his or her death: *I saw his obituary in the paper. The obituary notices included a list of all the writer's works. His obituary was written before his death.*

Social organization in groups and places

C70 nouns : **people and populations**
[ALSO ⇒ C1–11]

people 1 [P] the persons belonging to a particular place, class, trade, etc: *People who live in the north of England speak in a different way from people in the south. Banking people have their own way of looking at life, very different from, say, theatre people.* **2** [C] a race or nation: *The peoples of South-East Asia have ancient cultures. The Chinese are a hard-working people.*

race [C] **1** any of several kinds of people with particular kinds of hair, skin, etc: *The Caucasian or 'white' race is very different in appearance from the Negroid or 'black' race. The various races are not sharply separated;*

they shade into each other; they are not separate
species [⇒ A33]. **2** a particular large group of
human beings regarded or regarding themselves as in some bodily or other way separate
from everyone else: *The Spanish and Por-*
tuguese races have produced great travellers.
John Beddoe wrote a book called 'The Races of
Britain'. These people regard themselves as a
race apart (= a separate race).

mankind *also lit* **human kind** [U] all the people
in the world: *The world wars have been bad for*
the whole of mankind.

human race [*the* R] mankind: *The human race*
is made up of many different peoples.

humanity [U] *esp fml & emot* human beings
generally; the human race: *All humanity will*
suffer if the nations do not unite.

nation [C] a particular large group of human
beings usu living in one area, organized in one
way, and speaking a common language: *The*
Sioux are a famous Red Indian nation. These
people do not live in a state of their own, but
they regard themselves as a nation. Nations and
states are not always the same thing.

folk [GC *usu sing*] *old use* a people or nation:
The Dutch are a Teutonic folk. [⇒ C71]

population [C] the number of people (or animals) living in a place, country, city, etc: *There*
has been a steady fall in the population of Scot-
land since 1945. The local cat population is
quite large. There is a population problem in
this part of the city. **populate** [T1] to put or have
people in; (of people) to move into: *This island*
was populated from across the sea. London is a
heavily populated city; some say that it is over-
populated (= has too many people). *The*
mountains of Scotland are now under-
populated (= have too few people).

C71 *nouns* : **the people**

people [*the* P] all the members of a state: *It is the*
will of the people, as shown in a fair election,
that there should be a change of government.
The people have accepted the changes in the
law.

(general) public [*the* GU] the whole of a place,
esp the ordinary people: *The law was intended*
for the good of the (general) public. He said that
the public no longer believes what politicians
say.

populace [*the* GU]*fml* the great mass of people
in the country; the ordinary people: *This*
information is not available to the general
populace/to the populace at large.

community [*the* GC] *sometimes fml* the people
in general, esp in a particular place: *He says*
that the new laws are for the good of the (whole)
community. It is their duty to serve the com-
munity, not to destroy it. Education is usually a
community service.

folk 1 [P] *emot* the ordinary people: *These songs*
still survive among the common folk/among
country folk. **2** [A *and in comb*] relating to the

traditions of a people: *She loves folk-music,*
folk-singing and folk-dancing. Many folk
beliefs are regarded by unsympathetic people
as pure superstition. **3** [P] *AmE* usu **folks**
people generally: *The folks here say that the*
weather was bad last year. Some folk don't like
him.

C72 *nouns* : **culture and civilization**
[U]

[ALSO ⇒ C150–7]

culture development in art and thought, common to a society and represented at various
levels in its members: *These are people of great*
culture. He is a man of little culture, I'm afraid;
culture means nothing to him.

society 1 *genl* the social organization of people,
with common customs, laws, etc: *Society is*
changing rapidly. British society is very differ-
ent from what it was a hundred years ago. **2** [*esp*
A] *apprec or deprec* the upper class of a society: *She is a well-known society hostess.* **high**
society the upper social class

civilization, -isation the fact of becoming or
state of being highly developed socially, with a
system of government, methods of education,
etc: *In 20 years they have reached the level of*
civilization it took our society a century to
reach.

C73 *nouns* : **cultures and civilizations**
[C]

culture the particular system of art, thought,
and customs of a society: *This tribe/people has*
a culture which has never been scientifically
studied. Many ancient cultures are only known
through archaeology [⇒ I77].

society a group of people with the same customs, laws, etc: *Many societies permit*
polygamy [⇒ C30], *although Western societies*
today do not.

civilization, -isation a society with its own particular social organization, writing system, etc:
The ancient Egyptian civilization existed for
several thousand years. Civilizations rise and
fall.

community a group of people living together
and/or having close common interests: *This is*
a community of fishing people and hill farmers.
Various local communities are objecting to the
high taxes. He is interested in most community
matters.

C74 *nouns* : **groups and parties**

group [GC] a number of persons, animals, etc
gathered together (for any purpose) or naturally associated with each other: *A group of*
men gathered outside the pub. He is a member

of a local political group. The people stood in groups watching.

band [GC] a group of people or higher animals, formed, usu under one leader, for a purpose, and often travelling, hunting, fighting, etc together: *He is the leader of a band of thieves. A band of wandering dancers came to the town. Bands of armed men came to the town.*

company 1 [GC] a group of people together for some purpose such as travelling: *The company of travellers moved slowly towards the city. A company of horsemen came riding along.* **2** [U] certain people together: *She keeps strange company. I won't mention it in present company; I'll tell you later. She's in good company; they're all nice people. Be careful you don't get into bad company in the big city.*

party [*often in comb*] **1** [GC] a group of people doing something or going somewhere together in an organized way: *He saw a party of school-children get(ting) off the bus. She is taking a school party to France this year. He organized a search party to find the missing climbers.* **2** [C] a gathering of people, usu by invitation, for food and amusement: *She likes giving/going to parties, because she enjoys meeting people. She wore a new party dress at the birthday party.*

faction [C] *often deprec* a group of people, esp inside a larger group, esp in politics, religion, government, etc which has special opinions, plans, ideas, etc: *He is the leader of an important faction in the local communist party.* **factional** [Wa5;B] of, concerning, or like a faction **-ly** [adv]

gang [GC] *often deprec* a group of people going together for bad and esp criminal purposes: *Those men are a gang of thieves and murderers. Some politicians have got together in a gang hoping to run the country. There was a gang fight last night* (= a fight between two gangs).

clique [C] *usu deprec* a group of people united by a certain interest who do not allow or want others to join them: *This town is run by a clique of criminals. She has her own little clique and they talk all the time about the other girls.*

coterie [C] *lit* a clique

set [GC9] *usu sing sometimes deprec* a group of people of a certain kind, considered unusual, special, or fashionable: *I'm flying about a lot these days; I must apply to join the jet set even if I'm not a millionaire. She doesn't belong to/in his set at all. He's mixing with a funny artistic set in London.*

C75 nouns : **societies, clubs** [*often cap*] **and parties**

society [C] a group of people who form an organization for certain activities, with certain rules, etc: *He is a member of the Royal Society for the Prevention of Cruelty to Animals (RSPCA). She decided to join the local dramatic society.*

association [C; A] a society or group of societies which bring(s) together people with a common interest or purpose: *The club is a member of the Football Association. They formed an association to help blind people. The village has its own community association to look after its interests. This is an association problem, not a public matter.*

institution [C] **1** a usu large society or organization, usu set up to do something for others: *a public institution to help the poor* **2** the building in which an institution does its work

club 1 [C; A] a society of people with a special interest, usu a sport or entertainment: *He is a keen member of the local boys' club. The village has its own football and cricket clubs. He is having a drink at the local working men's club. You must try to follow the club rules.* **2** [C] (in England) a set of men or women who can spend time, have meals, or hire a bedroom in a certain building; a private hotel: *They are members of the same London club.* **3** [C] the building in which a club meets: *He's dining at his club. Let's have a drink at the club.*

party 1 [C; A] an association of people having the same political aims, esp as formed to try to win elections or control states: *The two main British parties in the 1960s were the Conservative Party and the Labour Party. This is a party matter; it isn't a public matter.* **2** [U] support for such a party and its interests: *He always puts party before country/his personal life.*

union [C] an association of people who see themselves as uniting for a particular purpose: *Our club is a member of the Union of Boys' Clubs. The Rugby Union is different in its organization in Britain from the Rugby League. We must form a union to fight for our views.*

commune [C] **1** an organized group of people concerned with local interests, esp raising crops and animals and with machines, buildings, etc held in common: *Communes are common in some socialist countries.* **2** a group of people living together and sharing property and responsibilities

circle [C] a group of people associated in an informal way because of common interests: *She is associated with a local ladies' circle. He's happy to stay in his own circle, and afraid to make new friends. In artists' circles there are many new fashions. He has a large circle of friends.*

membership [GC] all the members [⇒ C10] of a society, club, union, etc: *We have a very large and active membership. The membership is/are unhappy with the present chairman. Where is the membership list?*

C76 nouns : **other larger groups of people** [GC]

body [*usu sing*] a (large) number of people (close) together: *A body of horsemen rode* *towards them. Those soldiers are a fine body of men. The angry crowd came forward in a body. The workers marched in a body towards the factory.*

crowd a large number of people together, usu without organization: *A crowd of excited people waited to see the film stars. The streets were full of crowds of people. I couldn't get to you because of the crowds. He goes around with a crowd of other young men.*

mob 1 a (large) noisy (and usu violent) crowd: *The policeman was attacked by an angry mob. Mobs of armed men were in the streets, looking for trouble.* **2** deprec a crowd whom the speaker does not like: *Get that mob of people out of my office!*

horde 1 often deprec a large crowd: *Hordes of tourists come here every summer to lie on the beach.* **2** a wandering tribe: *The Roman Empire was attacked by hordes from Central Asia.*

bunch infml a group with no clear organization: *A bunch of young fellows was waiting to meet him at the airport.*

C77 nouns : other smaller groups of people [GC]

pair 1 two people closely connected: *Achilles and Patroclus are a famous pair of friends. They were entertained by a pair of dancers.* **2** infml two people closely connected who cause annoyance or displeasure: *You're a fine pair coming as late as this! What a pair they are!*

couple a pair of people, usu male and female, who like being together: *Married couples are welcome in this club. What a lovely couple they make together! Couples took the floor for the last dance.*

trio a group of three people acting or working together: *Those boys are a very active trio!*

C78 nouns : country and state [C]
[⇨ ALSO C90]

country a large social organization, usu of one kind of people, in a particular part of the world: *He has visited many foreign countries. Italy is a great country with a long history. Britain is the mother country of several modern nations. Write down ten European countries and their capitals.*

land esp emot & lit a country: *This is my native land and I'll defend it with my life! People from distant lands came to see the beautiful church.*

nation a particular large group of people living in one country or the country belonging to such a group: *Spain and Portugal are the two nations which occupy the Iberian peninsula [⇨ L85]. Trade between nations is better than war. The British nation is a union of several older*

nations whose separate natures can still be seen.

state 1 [also the R often cap] the social and political organization of people in a country; the government of a country: *These industries are run by the State. They are state-controlled industries. Relations between independent states are not always cordial.* **2** one largely self-governing division of a federation [⇨ C91]: *There are fifty states in the United States of America (USA); state law and federal law [⇨ C93] are different things.*

nation-state a state which is also a nation: *Modern nation-states such as Britain and France are the product of a slow centralization of government in a capital city.*

C79 nouns : parts of countries [C]

region 1 a large division of a country: *The northern region of the country is mountainous. People from the regions often resent the political importance of the capital.* **2** a large division of land, sea, space, etc

province 1 a large administrative or political division of some countries and empires: *Canada is made up of provinces such as Alberta and British Columbia.* **2** (fig) infml a person's particular duty, business, or activity: *It's my province to look after the firm's mail.* **the provinces** [P] often deprec all the parts of a country outside its capital

district 1 a division of land for any reason, usu administrative or political: *The districts inside American states are called counties. She visits the English Lake District every year.* **2** a division of any place for any special purpose or work: *What postal district do you live in? This area is the district where I work; he works in another district, down by the river.*

county 1 a division of a country in the British Isles, Canada, and New Zealand, for official purposes such as education, police, etc: *He was employed by Warwickshire County Council as a teacher. The county boundary runs along this field. Many of the old counties in Britain were re-organized in the early 1970s and the names of many have changed.* **2** an administrative division of a state of the USA: *He lives in Clark County.*

shire [esp in comb] a British county: *She often goes to Yorkshire in England and to Stirlingshire in Scotland.*

department one of the large administrative divisions of countries such as France

commune the smallest administrative division in countries like France, Switzerland, Italy, etc, governed by a mayor [⇨ C101] and a council

country [the R; A] all land outside towns and cities: *She prefers the country to the town/prefers country life to town life.* **countryside** [(the) U] the land outside towns and cities, esp as seen: *What lovely countryside!*

C80 *nouns* : **towns and cities, etc**

general and smaller	town
larger	city
small	village
very small	hamlet

town 1 [C] a group of houses, buildings, etc where people live: *There are several little towns in this valley. London is a big town; it's usually called a city.* **2** [S] *affec* a city: *Dear old Glasgow/London town; it's nice to be back!* **townspeople** [P] the people in a town **townsfolk** [P] *infml* townspeople

city [C *often in names*] a (very) large town with a centre where business goes on and entertainments [⇒ K2] can be found: *New York is one of America's busiest cities. Mexico City is the capital of Mexico. The city police caught a lot of criminals last year.*

village 1 [C] a (small) group of houses: *It's quite a big village now with its own village school, but you couldn't call it a town. He walked down the village street to the village shop.* **2** [S *esp in names*] part of a city still regarded as a village: *She lives in Duddingston Village in Edinburgh. Tye Green Village is in the town of Harlow.* **villager** [C] a person living in a village

hamlet [C] a very small village; a few houses together: *He lives in a sleepy little hamlet beside the river.*

settlement [C] a place with some buildings where people have (fairly recently) started to live: *There are four settlements along the river. We hope to build a permanent settlement near the mines* (= a settlement which will become a town).

township [C] **1** a town (and the area around it) which has its own local government **2** a small town which serves as the business centre of an area **3** a settlement which is developing into a town

C81 : **parts of towns and cities** [C]

district a division of a town: *There are two main districts, the richer and the poorer parts. They visited the town's red-light district* (= the district where there are brothels [⇒ C38]).

ward a division of a town for administrative or political purposes: *The city is divided into six electoral wards for local elections.*

precinct *esp AmE* a ward

suburb an outer area of a city, where people live and less business is done: *He lives in a fashionable suburb of Athens.* **the suburbs** [P] the whole of such an area: *They live in the suburbs now; they sold their city-centre flat.* **suburban** [B] of, concerning, or like the suburbs **suburbia** [U] *sometimes deprec* the area of the suburbs and the ideas, etc of people living there

quarter a part of a city, often typical of certain people: *They live in the student quarter. The French quarter of the city has many good restaurants.*

colony 1 a number of people coming from the same place and sharing certain things like a language and customs, living in a country or in a district, esp of a city: *The American colony in Paris is quite big.* **2** the district or quarter occupied by such a group or a group of people with similar interests: *He likes visiting the German colony in Yorkville. The artists' colony is in the old part of the town.*

shanty town (a part of a city or) a town made up of poorly-built houses, not made of brick or stone, usu for poor people: *There are shanty-towns around many of the world's biggest and richest cities.*

slum [*often pl*] a house or district in a town or city where living conditions are dirty and unhealthy and where poor people live: *He grew up in the slums of New York/Glasgow/Marseilles. This house is a slum; it's very dirty!* **slummy** [Wa1;B] like a slum

ghetto 1 (formerly, in some countries) the Jewish quarter of a town **2** a section of a town where people live who are not accepted as social equals by the majority of its citizens

C82 *nouns* : **kinds of towns and cities** [C]

capital (city) 1 the city which serves as the centre of government in a country: *Paris is the capital (city) of France and one of Europe's finest capitals.* **2** a city considered the centre of anything: *Paris is the fashion capital of the world.*

metropolis *fml* a capital city: *He lives in the metropolis.*

centre *BrE*, **center** *AmE* an area of heavy population: *Liverpool is one of England's great urban* [⇒ C85] *centres. Bombay is a centre of Indian industry.*

county town the town which is the administrative [⇒ C100] centre of a county [⇒ C79]

market town the local town to which farmers, etc bring produce and goods to sell and where they buy other things which they need

borough 1 (as in England) a town with royal permission to have its own local government **2** (in certain states in the USA) a municipality smaller than a city

burgh *ScotE* a borough

municipality a town, city, or district with its own local government

C83 *nouns* : **people belonging to cities and countries, etc** [C]

citizen 1 a person who lives in a particular city or town, esp one who has certain voting or other rights in that place: *The citizens of Bristol* *swore to defend their historic rights.* **2** a person who belongs to a particular country by birth or naturalization (= being officially allowed to belong): *He is a citizen of the United Kingdom. They are all American citizens.* **3** a person who gives his or her loyalty to a particular country and who expects protection from it: *She's a British citizen but lives in India.* **citizenship** [U] the status of being a citizen of a country

national a person, esp someone abroad, who belongs to another usu stated country: *These people are all United States nationals living in France. Foreign nationals were asked to leave immediately.* **nationality** [C;U] status as a national: *What nationality is he? Many nationalities were present at the meeting. This problem is one of nationality, not religion.*

subject a person who owes loyalty to a certain country or royal ruler: *She is a United Kingdom subject, a subject of the Queen. The King addressed his subjects.*

ethnic *esp AmE* a member of an ethnic [⇒ C84] group, who is loyal to its customs, language, etc as well as to the customs and official language of the country to which he or she belongs

native 1 someone who was born (in a place): *He is a native of New York City but lives mostly in California.* **2** someone who lives in a place all the time or has lived there a long time: *Are you a native here, or just a visitor?* **3** someone who belongs to an earlier, original, or local people, esp *(derog and becoming rare)* the non-Europeans, living there: *The colonial government of the island treated the natives badly.* **4** a plant or animal living naturally (in a place): *The bear was once a native of Britain.*

local a person living in an area: *John? Oh, yes, he's a local. The locals don't like all these London people buying summer cottages here.*

provincial *often deprec* someone who lives in or comes from a province [⇒ C79] (and is therefore not thought as good as a person from the capital): *These provincials, they really do lack culture* [⇒ C72]! **provincialism** [U] the manner of a provincial; preference for a province or the provinces

foreigner *sometimes deprec* a person from another country: *He is a foreigner, but he seems nice enough. She doesn't trust foreigners and has never been abroad herself. To these people, anyone from over the hill is a foreigner.*

alien *fml & tech* a foreigner or foreign national: *Aliens are required to register with the police on arrival in this country.*

stranger someone not known or familiar, or not familiar with a place: *He saw a stranger come into the village. I'm a stranger here; can you direct me to the town hall?— Sorry, I can't; I'm a stranger here myself! She's no stranger to this place; she was educated here.*

C84 adjectives : relating to nations and races [B]

national [Wa5] of, belonging to, or related to a nation: *She is interested in her country's national dancing. National life has changed a lot since I was young. The national banks are closed on Monday. These people have been influenced for centuries by foreigners, but they have kept most of their national customs.* **-ly** [adv]

racial 1 [Wa5] related to a race: *He has the racial characteristics of the people in South East Asia.* **2** [Wa5] among races: *We hope for greater racial harmony here in future. Racial enmity* [⇒ C41] *can lead to terrible things sometimes.* **3** favouring one race against all others: *I'm afraid he's a bit racial at times.* **-ly** [adv] **racialism** *BrE*, **racism** *AmE* [U] *often deprec* beliefs, esp of a social and political kind, that depend on a difference in race, and esp the belief that one race is better than others **racialist** *BrE*, **racist** *AmE* [C] a person who believes in racialism

ethnic [Wa5] relating to a race or to the various human races: *Ethnic studies can be useful in understanding human nature. Many people in the United States are proud of their special ethnic origins.* **-ally** [adv]

native [Wa5] of or belonging to a place by birth, origin, etc: *She has a book of the native flowers of Britain. The red deer is native to the Scottish Highlands. The native architecture is very interesting here.*

local of or in a certain place, esp the place one lives in: *The local doctors are very good. In Harlow, Essex, the local restaurants are not very varied.*

foreign 1 [Wa5] in, from, concerning, etc another country (or place) than one's own: *He has never been to any foreign countries. The soldiers are at present on foreign service. He is the agent of a foreign power. They are bringing in a lot of foreign workers speaking foreign languages. She is a student of foreign affairs.* **2** [*(to)*] having no place (in); having no relation (to): *Travel by air is quite foreign to the old lady's experience. He's a very nice fellow and violence is foreign to his nature.* **3** [Wa5;A] coming or brought in from outside; not belonging; harmful: *The swelling in her finger seems to be caused by a foreign body* (= something small from outside) *in it.*

alien 1 [Wa5] *often emot* belonging to another country or race; foreign: *We don't want any more alien workers here!* **2** different in nature or character, esp so different as to be opposed: *Their ideas are quite alien to our way of thinking.*

stateless [Wa5] not being the citizen of any state: *They have a lot of stateless people living in this town.*

international 1 [Wa5] among or between nations and/or their peoples: *They went to an international meeting on the international law* *of the sea.* **-ly** [adv] **2** belonging to or interested in all peoples and not just one nation: *He is a very international person and has friends all over the world.* **-ly** [adv] **3** [C] a game played among or between nations: *He watched the football international on television.* **internationalism** [U] any idea that nations should work together or people from different nations should meet each other, become more friendly, etc **internationalist** [C] a person who believes in internationalism

cosmopolitan 1 of, from, or having the qualities of many different parts of the world: *He is very cosmopolitan in his ideas. Montreal is a cosmopolitan city.* **2** [C] a person who has no particular national preferences: *The people here are all cosmopolitans.* **cosmopolitanism** [U] the ideas, way of life, etc in a cosmopolitan place or of cosmopolitan people

C85 adjectives : relating to societies and cities

social [Wa5] **1** [B] of or concerning human society, its organization, or quality of life: *He is concerned about the social and political freedoms of the individual.* **2** [B] of, concerning, or spent in time or activities with friends: *She has a very full social life.* **3** [A] of or to do with conditions in society or with services provided by the government to improve conditions in society: *There is a real need for trained social workers in big cities.* **-ly** [adv]

communal [Wa5;B] relating to, of, or shared by a community [⇒ C73]: *This is a matter of great communal concern. We must have a communal approach to the problem, not just the feelings of a lot of different people.* **-ly** [adv]

public 1 [Wa5;B] relating to people in general: *It is a matter of great public interest. This lack of money is a public disgrace.* **2** [Wa5;B] for the use of everyone: *The city has a fine public library and public parks. There is a public path across the field; the farmer must let you use it.* **3** [B] in the sight or hearing of many people; not said privately: *He made a public statement of his intentions. This place is too public for a talk about personal matters; anyone might hear what we're saying.* **4** [B] known to all or to many: *The president of the state is a public figure. The news of the King's death was not made public for several days.* **5** [Wa5;A] connected or concerned with the affairs of the people, esp with government: *He wants a career in public life* (= to get a job in government or politics). *Some politicians never hold public office* (= an important government post). **-ly** [adv]

civil [Wa5;A] **1** relating to organized society: *We all have civil rights and civil duties. Civil disobedience is a refusal, for some political reason, to obey the law. Civil law deals with the rights of the citizen. Civil war is a war inside a state.* **2** relating to cities and civilized life: *Civil*

engineering includes things like dams, bridges, and roads. The civil service of a country looks after its general administration* [⇒ C100].

popular [Wa5;A] *fml* relating to the people: *A popular vote has shown that everyone wants a change of government. The loss of all this money is a matter of popular concern.*

urban [B] relating to a town or city: *Urban populations continue to increase while those in the countryside decrease. This is an urban problem, not a rural one.*

civic [B] relating to (the official buildings, ceremonies, meetings, etc) of a city: *The mayor* [⇒ C101] *gave the visitors a civic welcome. It is a matter of civic pride to keep the city clean.*

municipal [Wa5;B] of a town or city which has its own local government: *The municipal taxes are going up this year.*

metropolitan [Wa5;B] relating to the capital: *The metropolitan water board looks after water supplies in the capital. He is a member of the Metropolitan Police Force.*

rural [B] relating to the countryside; concerning country or village life: *These small rural communities do not have many of the things that you can find in big towns.*

regional [B] relating to a region [⇒ C79]: *The people are interested in regional rather than national problems at the moment. This shop sells regional geographies of the British Isles.*

provincial 1 [Wa5;A] relating to a province: *The country has ten provincial assemblies* [⇒ C103] *and a federal* [⇒ C93] *assembly in the capital. He went to the provincial capital.* **2** [B] *often deprec* not as cultured, imaginative, etc as people in the capital city: *She said that he had a very provincial way of looking at problems.*

Government

[ALSO ⇒ C78]

C90 nouns : republics and kingdoms [C]

republic a state governed by representatives and usu a president: *France has been a republic for many years, but was once a monarchy. Most of the world's countries are republics.*

kingdom 1 a country which has a king or queen, whether or not he or she directly governs it: *The United Kingdom consists in part of two separate older kingdoms, England and Scotland.* **2** (*fig*) an area over which a person has complete control: *The kitchen is a cook's kingdom.*

realm *esp lit & fml* a kingdom: *The king was greatly concerned about the safety of the realm.*

monarchy 1 a state which has a king or queen: *Denmark and Sweden are monarchies.* **2** [U]

the institution of having a monarch: *Monarchy is a very ancient institution.*
principality a country ruled by a prince: *Wales is a principality.*
sheikhdom the land ruled by a sheikh [⇒ C96]: *The sheikhdoms of the Gulf are rich in oil.*

C91 nouns : unions and federations [C]

union two or more states joined closely together: *Scotland and England came together as a union in 1707. The United States is a union of many states on a federal [⇒ C93] basis; it is a federal union.*
federation a group of two or more states united under one central government which decides foreign affairs, defence, etc and in which each state has its own government to decide its own affairs: *The United States is a federation.* **federate** [I0; T1] to come or bring together in a federation
confederacy *also* **confederation 1** a group of two or more states working together for certain common aims, each member keeping much of its independence: *The European Common Market is a loose confederacy rather than a federation.* **2** any group of people or parties working together in such a way

C92 nouns : empires and colonies [C]

empire [*also* U] a group of countries ruled by or from one of those countries: *The Roman Empire lasted for many centuries, but did not control as many lands as the British Empire did. The demands of empire are usually too great for a single nation, and so empires come to an end.*
colony 1 a country or area ruled from another usu distant, country and often settled by people from the ruling country: *Many modern nations are former European colonies. The ancient Greeks established colonies in many parts of the Western Mediterranean.* **2** a country ruled by another: *India was a British colony for many years.* **colonist** [C] a person who goes to live in, develop, etc a colony **colonize, -ise** [T1] to make (a place) into a colony: *The ancient Greeks colonized parts of southern Italy and France.* **colonization, -isation** [U] the act of colonizing a place
protectorate a country controlled or protected by a more powerful country that takes charge of its defence and foreign affairs: *The British Empire contained many colonies and protectorates.*
commonwealth 1 *mainly old use* a state; **2** a group of states which work together for their common good: *He is a citizen of the Commonwealth of Australia. When the British Empire broke up many of its states became members of the Commonwealth.*

C93 adjectives : relating to states and kinds of government [Wa5;B: often cap]

republican 1 relating to a republic: *Republican government is very different from imperial or monarchic government.* **2** favouring a republic: *That country is a monarchy, but many of its citizens are republican in their views. He has republican ideas, and doesn't like kings.*
monarchic(al) relating to or favouring a monarchy
federal relating to a federation: *The Federal Government of the USA is responsible for foreign policy and national defence.* **-ly** [adv]
confederate relating to a confederacy: *In the American Civil War the Confederate troops fought well but were defeated.*
imperial relating to an empire or its ruler: *Napoleon's imperial ideas changed the face of Europe. The Roman Emperor approached the steps with imperial dignity.*
colony 1 a country or area ruled from another, *government's colonial policy has changed. That country once had colonial aims. The people there are tired of colonial status.* **2** *esp AmE* in the style of the British colonies in North America: *This New England town has a lot of colonial buildings.*

C94 nouns : people relating to kinds of states and government [C]

[ALSO ⇒ C113]

republican a person who favours republican government: *He is a republican and does not like monarchies.*
monarchist a person who favours monarchic rule: *He has always been a monarchist.*
royalist a person who supports monarchism against any republican aims
unionist a person who supports a political union: *The Unionists in Scotland did not accept the aims of the Nationalists, who sought independence for the country.*
confederate a person who supports a confederacy: *The Unionists defeated the Confederates in the US Civil War.*
colonial *sometimes deprec* a person living in or coming from a colony, esp one who has helped develop it: *'The colonials think they are as important as the mother country,' the old man said angrily.*

C95 nouns : democracy and dictatorship

democracy 1 [U] 'government of the people, by the people, and for the people' (Abraham Lincoln) **2** [U] government by elected representatives of the people **3** [C] a country governed by its people or their representatives:

How can that country claim to be a democracy, when all the leaders of the opposition are in prison? **4** [U] social equality and the right to take part in decision-making: *How close have we in this country come to industrial democracy today? Great gaps between rich and poor are against real social democracy.* **democratic** [B] of, concerning, or like (a) democracy **-ally** [adv Wa4]

dictatorship 1 [U] the system or behaviour of a dictator [⇒C102] or single ruler or group with complete personal power: *We are tired of foreign dictatorship; we want self-determination. His dictatorship lasted 5 years.* **2** [C] a country run by a dictator: *There are many dictatorships in the world.*

autocracy *tech* **1** [U] rule by one person with unlimited power: *The citizens were tired of autocracy and wanted the return of free elections and freedom of speech.* **2** [C] a country, group, etc ruled in this way: *That country is an autocracy, ruled by one man.*

totalitarianism [U] a system in which a single person or party controls all thought and action: *Fascist Italy and Nazi Germany are examples of what totalitarianism can produce.*

police state [C] a usu totalitarian state which controls its citizens by using a large and powerful police force, army, etc

tyranny 1 [U] the use of too great, or cruel power to rule a country (or a person or group): *They said they would fight against tyranny, whether it was foreign or by their own leaders. These acts of tyranny must stop.* **2** [C] a government or system which uses tyranny: *The world has experienced many tyrannies.* **tyrannical** [B] of, concerning, or like (a) tyranny **-ly** [adv Wa4]

oligarchy [U;C] *tech* a government chosen from a small group of people by members of that small group

self-determination [U] the wish or right of a country or people to have self-government: *The United Nations has supported the demands for self-determination of many peoples.*

independence [U] complete political freedom from a colonial, imperial, or similar situation: *The Americans fought for their independence 200 years ago.*

self-government [U] the situation where a country or people controls itself without being controlled from outside

autonomy [U] *fml & tech* self-determination and self-government: *The local people regard themselves as a nation and are seeking autonomy.* **autonomous** [B] having autonomy; self-governing: *It is a fully autonomous country. Our group is autonomous.* **-ly** [adv]

C96 *nouns* : **kings and emperors**
[C *often cap*]

ruler the person ruling a country, usu personally: *One family has provided the rulers of* many western European countries for several centuries. *The Bourbons were once the rulers of France.*

king 1 [*also* A] (the title of) a male ruler: *This church is the burial place of many kings. He was king for only a short time, but ruled his kingdom well in that time. He was crowned king of France. King George III was king of both Scotland and England.* **2** (*fig & emot*) a man who has more importance, ability, or power than all or most others in the same group: *He is the king of the footballers! Her father was a king among men.* **3** (*fig*) the most important member of a group: *That tall tree is the king of the forest.* **kingship** [U] the condition of being a king

queen 1 [*also* A] (the title of) a female ruler or the wife of a king: *Her Majesty Queen Elizabeth II of England and I of Scotland. The king and queen are coming here next week.* **2** (*fig*) the leading female, often chosen in a competition: *She is a beauty queen; she was Miss Canada. She's queen of this village, or so she thinks.*

prince 1 [*also* A] (the title of) a son or other near male relative of a king or queen: *The young princes were riding in the park. Prince Charles is the eldest son of Queen Elizabeth.* **2** [*also* A] a ruler, usu of a small country or of a state protected by a bigger country: *Prince Rainier rules Monaco. In former times many parts of India were ruled by princes.* **3** a great ruler or leader: *King Louis XIV of France was a great prince. The Pope spoke to the princes of the Church.* **4** *lit or pomp* a very great successful or powerful man of some stated kind: *Shakespeare was a prince among poets/the prince of poets.*

(prince) consort the husband of a ruling queen: *Philip, the Duke of Edinburgh, is Queen Elizabeth's consort.*

princess [*also* A] (the title of) a daughter or other near female relation of a king or queen: *Princess Margaret is the sister of Queen Elizabeth. The young princesses were taken back to the palace.*

royal *usu infml* a member of a royal family: *Several Royals came to the function.*

crown [*the* R; A] the king or queen of a country; a monarchy: *The Crown owns this land. This is Crown land.*

regent (the title of) a person who rules in place of a king (or queen) when he or she is not able to rule because of absence, illness, or being too young: *The regent sought power for himself and not the young prince. The Regent John was an evil man.*

viceroy (the title of) a person acting on behalf of a king, usu in governing a colony: *The British used to govern India through a viceroy.* **vicereine** the wife of a viceroy **viceregal** [Wa5;B] of, concerning, or like a viceroy

emperor (the title of) the ruler of an empire: *Napoleon called himself Emperor of the French. George VI was King of Great Britain and Emperor of India. The Roman emperors were often cruel.*

empress (the title of) a female emperor or the wife of an emperor: *Victoria was the Queen-Empress of the British Empire. Louis Napoleon's empress was Eugenie.*

monarch *often fml* a king, queen, emperor, or empress; ruler: *The Monarch must give his royal permission before we can proceed.*

sovereign 1 *fml* a monarch: *The people fell silent as their sovereign began to speak.* **2** [Wa5;A] (of esp political power, freedom, etc) complete; not affected by any other person, group, etc: *That country is a sovereign state; we can't tell them what to do.* **sovereignty** [U] sovereign power: *The king had sovereignty over many lands.*

court 1 [*also at, to* U] the place where a king or queen lives: *He is at Court, attending the King.* **2** the officials of a king, queen, etc: *The whole Court knows what happened, but does the Queen know?*

sheikh [*also* A] **1** (the title of) an Arab chief or prince **2** a Muslim religious leader

C97 *adjectives* : **relating to kings** [B]

royal *often emot* relating to, suitable for, favoured by, or belonging to (the family of) a king or queen: *The royal palace was built on a hill. His Royal Highness will see you now. We are the royal bakers. They gave him a royal welcome* (= a welcome good enough for a king). **-ly** [adv]

regal *often fml* relating to or suitable for a monarch: *The gathering was a display of regal dignity and power.* **-ly** [adv]

kingly	[Wa2] *usu apprec* in relation to what a	king	should be
queenly		queen	like
princely		prince	

C98 *nouns* : **majesty and dynasties**

majesty [U] the appearance and/or quality of a king, queen, etc; greatness: *The people enjoyed the majesty of the occasion. He said that the message was an insult to the majesty of the king!* **Your, His, etc Majesty** [N] (the form used when speaking to or about a king, queen, etc)

royalty 1 [U] the condition of being royal: *The king considered the poor man's angry words (to be) an insult to his royalty.* **2** [GU] members of a royal family or families collectively: *Royalty often attends these shows. She takes a great interest in the doings of royalty.*

dynasty [C] a line of rulers belonging to one family: *The Bourbon dynasty ruled France for centuries. This ancient Egyptian tomb belongs to the 12th Dynasty.* **dynastic** [Wa5;B] of or concerning a dynasty

crown 1 [C] the usu highly ornamented band worn round the head of a king, queen, etc, as a sign of power **2** [*the* R *often cap*] (*fig*) the power of a king, queen, etc: *That land belongs to the Crown.* **3** [C] a mark like a crown, often put on the property of a king, queen, etc **4** [T1; X1] to put a crown on (a king, queen, etc): *They crowned him (King of France).*

coronation 1 [U] the act of crowning **2** [C] a ceremonial occasion of crowning

C99 *verbs* : **ruling and administering**

rule [I0; T1] to have and use the highest form of social power over (a country, people, etc), esp as a king or queen: *Long ago kings ruled with complete power, but nowadays most countries are governed by parliaments, assemblies, or councils. He ruled the country well.*

govern [I0; T1] to control the political affairs of (a country, etc and its people): *The Queen is said to rule Britain, but it is her prime minister who actually governs (the country).*

reign [Wv4;I0 (*over*)] to be king or queen: *The Queen of Great Britain reigns but does not govern. The king reigned over his people for 15 years. Queen Elizabeth was the reigning monarch* [⇒ C96] *at that time.*

administer [T1] **1** to control (esp the business or affairs of a country, group or person): *He administers this place directly, without outside help or influence.* **2** to put into operation; make work; organize; give: *The courts administer the law and also administer punishment to criminals.* **3** to give (the official form of a promise or religious service): *I administered the oath* [⇒ G110] *to him. The priest administered the last sacrament* [⇒ C335] *to the dying man.*

run [T1] *often infml* to be in control of and cause to work: *Who is running this country? The various ministers run their departments of state.*

preside over [v prep T1] *fml* to run or administer: *He presided over the affairs of the nation for 40 years.*

police [T1] to control very firmly, with or like a police force: *He policed those lawless places until men could feel safe again. Who will police the country if he takes his soldiers abroad?*

C100 *nouns* : **ruling and administering**

rule [U9] **1** (the possession of) the power to rule: *This country has been under foreign rule for centuries.* **2** the time or way of ruling: *They lived for years under the rule of a hard master. His rule lasted 20 years. They suffered under the empress's iron rule.*

reign [C] the time when a monarch rules: *His reign was not a peaceful one, and lasted only two years.*

regency [U] the condition of being or having a regent [⇒ C96]; the time when a regent rules a country: *During his regency life became very unpleasant for the enemies of the regent.*

government 1 [U] the act or situation of governing (a state): *The young prince was not suited to government and proved to be a bad king.* **2** [U] the form or method of governing: *The country has always had fair government/ suffered from bad government.* **3** [GC *often cap*] the people who rule (a state) collectively: *Governments come and go. A new government was formed/chosen. The government has/have decided the matter. This is a Government matter.* **governmental** [Wa5;B] of, concerning, or by a government

administration 1 [U] the control or direction of affairs, as of a country or business: *The administration of the country over the last few years has not been very good.* **2** [GC *often cap*] *esp AmE* the government: *Not much was done about this matter by the last administration.* **3** [U] the act of putting something into operation, esp by someone with the official power to do so: *The administration of the laws is the concern of the Ministry of Justice.* **4** [U] *fml* the act of giving the official form of a promise or a religious ceremony: *The administration of an oath* [⇒ G110] *by a public official is part of that ceremony.* **administrative** [Wa5;B] of or concerning (an) administration **-ly** [adv]

regime [C] *sometimes deprec* a particular type of government: *Things will change under the new regime. 'This evil regime cannot last forever!' he shouted. The men said that the new manager's methods were like the regime of a tyrant* [⇒ C102].

authority 1 [U] the ability, power, or right to control and command: *Although he has no official power, he is still a man of authority. Who is in authority here? A teacher must show his authority.* **2** [C *often pl*] a person or group with this power or right, esp in public affairs: *The government is the highest authority in the country. The authorities at the town hall are slow to deal with complaints. The health authorities are handling his case now.* **3** [U] power to influence: *I have some authority with the boy; I'll talk to him.* **4** [U9] right or official power, esp for some stated purpose: *What authority do you have for entering this house?* **5** [C *usu sing*] a paper giving this right: *Here is my authority.* **authoritative** [B] of, concerning, or having authority **-ly** [adv]

C101 *nouns* : **heads of state, high officials, etc** [C *often cap*]

head of state *genl* the official leader or ruler of a country, whether a president or monarch: *There were many heads of state at the king's funeral.*

head of government *genl* a prime minister or

executive president: *Ten heads of government attended the conference.*

prime minister [*also* N] (the title of) the head of the government or leading minister in certain countries: *Edward Heath and Harold Wilson were British prime ministers in the 1970s. The Prime Minister spoke to the nation on radio and television. May I ask you another question, (Mr) Prime Minister?* **PM** *abbrev*

premier *less common* a prime minister: *The premier considers the economic situation serious.* **premiership** [U] the time when a premier governs

president 1 [*also* A] the head of state or government in many modern states that do not have a king or queen: *The President of France is here on a state visit. President Lincoln was a US President in the 19th century. Some countries have executive presidents who run governments; others have presidents who are largely ceremonial.* **2** the head of some councils or government departments: *He is now President of the Board of Trade.* **presidential** [Wa5;B] of, concerning, or like a president or what is done for a president. **-ly** [adv] **presidency** [U] the time when a president governs: *That happened during Roosevelt's presidency.*

vice-president [*also* A] the assistant to a president: *If anything happens to a president (of the United States), the vice-president takes his place.*

minister a person in charge of a particular department of the government: *He is the Minister for Overseas Aid and she is Health Minister. Various Cabinet Ministers called at No 10 Downing Street (in London) during the morning. The Foreign Minister attended the talks.* **ministerial** [Wa5;B] of or concerning a minister: *He has full ministerial responsibility in this matter.*

secretary 1 a minister in the government in charge of one of certain departments: *That minister was Secretary of State for Foreign Affairs.* **2** the chief helper of a government minister in his department

governor 1 [*also* A] a person who governs a state or province [⇒ C79]: *Every US state has an elected governor.* **2** a person who controls one of certain types of organization: *He is the governor of a prison.* **3** a member of a governing body which controls a school, hospital, etc: *The school governors met for a special meeting.* **governorship** [C; U] the condition of being a governor

governor-general a person who represents Britain in many Commonwealth countries but has little or no power to govern

mayor the head of a town or city council

mayoress *fem* a female mayor or wife of a mayor

provost a mayor in Scotland

administrator a person who administers law and order (in a state, through a special service, etc): *He was one of our ablest administrators.*

This college has trained many of our country's administrators.

C102 *nouns* : **rulers with too much power** [C]

dictator a ruler or similar person with full personal power or a wish to have such power: *Mussolini was dictator of Italy. They don't want dictators in their country.* **dictatorial** [B] of, concerning, or like a dictator **-ly** [adv]

autocrat *tech* a dictator or similar person: *He ruled his family like an autocrat.* **autocratic** [B] of, concerning, or like an autocrat **-ally** [adv Wa4]

tyrant a cruel ruler: *He was an evil tyrant who harmed his people. 'Kill the tyrant!' they cried.*

oppressor a person, esp a ruler or enemy, who oppresses [⇒ C132] people: *The people fought back against their oppressors.*

bully a person who hurts or frightens someone weaker than himself or herself, esp for pleasure: *The school bully tried to frighten the new boy.*

C103 *nouns* : **parliaments and senates** [often cap]

parliament 1 [GC] a body of persons (**members of Parliament**) wholly or partly elected by the people of a country, to make laws **2** [R *usu cap*] the main law-making body in the United Kingdom, made up of the King or Queen, the Lords and the elected representatives of the people: *Parliament has passed a new law on divorce. Parliament meets in the Houses of Parliament.* **parliamentary** [Wa5;B] of, concerning, or like a parliament or what is done in a parliament

congress 1 [*(the)* R; GC] the elected law-making body of certain countries, esp the US **2** [GC] any large gathering for discussion of laws, rules, etc **congressman/woman** [C] a person serving in a congress, esp the US Congress **congressional** [Wa5;B] of, concerning, or like a congress, esp the US Congress

senate 1 [*the* R; GC] the upper house of a law-making body, as in the US **2** [GC] any similar political body   **senator** [C] a person serving in a senate   **senatorial** [Wa5;B] of, concerning, or like a senator

soviet [C] a political council elected by local working people in the USSR since 1917: *The soviets together elect the Supreme Soviet which runs the Soviet Union.*

legislature [GC] the body of people who have the power to make and change laws, esp in a country: *He is a member of the State Legislature.* **legislator** [C] a person who passes laws; a member of a legislature [⇒ C187]

assembly [GC] a body of representatives gathered for passing laws or discussing political, social, religious, etc matters: *A national assembly debated the new constitution* [⇒

C181]. **assemblyman** [C] a member of an assembly

council [GC] a group of people concerned with organizing (part of) the life of a town, a church, or any social group, esp in local government: *The Town Council meets regularly. You must write to the District Council about your problem.* **councillor** [C] a member of a council

committee [GC] a group of people, chosen usu from a large group, to organize that group or to decide certain things or to gain information for the group: *The club committee is re-elected next week. He is the chairman of the Parliamentary Committee on Housing.*

convention [C] a meeting or series of meetings of a body of people with a common interest, to talk about and/or decide certain matters: *A convention on world health was held in Geneva. The National Convention decided some important constitutional* [⇒ C181] *matters.*

junta [C] a government, esp a military one, that has come to power by armed force rather than by election

C104 *nouns* : **parts of governments** [GC *often in comb; often cap*]

cabinet (in various countries) the most important ministers of the government, who meet as a group to make decisions or to advise the head of the government: *There were two meetings of the British Cabinet that week. This is a Cabinet decision and the ministers have collective responsibility for it.*

department a part of a government or civil service: *The departments of state make effective the decisions of the government. He organized the Department so that there was less bureaucracy.*

ministry a department of state under a minister: *He took over the Ministry of Education. This is a Ministry matter.*

office one of certain departments of state, the civil service [⇒ C105], etc: *The British Foreign Office looks after external affairs while the Home Office takes care of internal matters. The General Post Office in Britain has a monopoly* [⇒ J138] *on the delivery of mail.*

secretariat the part of an organization, esp in government and international bodies, with a secretary [⇒ C101] as its head: *The party secretariat functions better now. The United Nations Secretariat is in New York.*

bureau *often fml* an esp government office, department, ministry, etc: *He works for the Employment Bureau. Where is the nearest Bureau of Information?*

C105 *nouns* : **administration**

civil service [GC; *the* R; A *often cap*] all the various departments (except the armed forces, law courts, or religious organizations) of a state which deal with the relationship between people and government and which are responsible for putting into practice laws and government decisions: *He works in the Civil Service. This is a Civil Service matter.*

bureaucracy *often deprec* **1** [C; U] the (official workings of the) civil service: *The politicians pass laws and the bureaucracy carries them out.* **2** [S] **a** government officers who are appointed rather than elected **b** a group of people like this. **bureaucratic** [B] *deprec* of, concerning, or esp like (the way of working of) a bureaucracy: *I don't like the bureaucratic way he does things; everything must be written down and talked about over and over again!* **-ally** [adv Wa4]

red tape [U] *usu deprec* bureaucracy; government which is too slow and formal: *With all this red tape and forms to fill in I can't get my proper work done!*

diplomacy [U] the management of a country's foreign interests by its representatives abroad: *His profession is diplomacy.* **diplomatic** [B] of, concerning, or like diplomacy **-ally** [adv Wa4]

diplomatic corps [GC] the whole group of foreign diplomats [⇒ C107] in a capital city

foreign service [GC; *the* R; A *often cap*] a division of the foreign office of a country that looks after diplomatic and consular [⇒ C107] work in other countries: *He works in the Foreign Service.*

protocol [U] the rules of behaviour between officials of different governments when meeting each other and working together

C106 nouns : **people in government service** [C]

civil servant a person employed in the civil service of a country

official a person who has a public office; civil servant: *The meeting was for officials only. An official of the local government called to see him.* **officialdom** [U] *sometimes deprec* all officials; bureaucracy

bureaucrat *often deprec* a civil servant or government official: *'These bureaucrats in the capital don't know what life is like here!' he said angrily.*

deputy [*often in comb*] an official who acts for another: *The Prime Minister is away and the Home Secretary is acting as his deputy/as Deputy Prime Minister. I'll send my deputy to see you.* **deputize, -ise** [I0; T1] to (cause to) act as a deputy: *He deputized us to act for him. I am deputizing for him.* **depute** [T1] to give (somebody) one's permission and authority to do all or a part of one's work for a time: *He couldn't come to the meeting so he deputed me.*

delegate a person acting for others, usu on official business, at a meeting or conference [⇒ G65], etc: *The delegates of the various governments sat down at the table.* **delegate 1** [T1

(*to*)] to give (part of one's power, rights, etc) for a certain time: *I have delegated my command to Captain Roberts.* **2** [T1; V3] to appoint as one's representative: *I have delegated Captain Roberts (to serve in my place).* **delegation 1** [U] the act of delegating **2** [GC] a group of delegates: *The delegation from the south has arrived, sir.*

C107 nouns : **people in a country's foreign service** [C]

diplomat a person who represents his government and country abroad and looks after its various political, economic, and social relations: *A number of foreign diplomats use this club.*

ambassador a diplomat of the highest rank representing his country in another country either for a special occasion or for a longer period: *The American Ambassador was invited to the gathering.* **ambassadress** [*fem*] *rare*

high commissioner a representative of one member of the Commonwealth in the country of another, having the rank of an ambassador

minister a diplomat of high rank (but usu below ambassador)

envoy 1 a special messenger from one government to another **2** an official in the foreign service of a country second in rank to an ambassador

consul a person, appointed by a government who lives in a city of a foreign country, and who protects and helps his countrymen who are living or working there **consular** [Wa5;B] of, concerning, or by a consul

vice-consul a diplomat of a rank below consul: *One of the vice-consuls from the Embassy will see you now.*

emissary *fml* an envoy, often carrying a secret or special message

representative a diplomat acting in the place of a government ruler, etc: *He is Her Majesty's representative in these parts. He spoke to the representatives of the US Government.*

attaché *Fr* a person, esp a diplomat, military officer, etc, who does special work at an embassy: *a military attaché; a press attaché*

C108 nouns : **groups in and places used by a foreign service**

embassy 1 [GC] a group of officials, usu led by an ambassador, who are sent by a government to do its business with the government of another country: *The Queen sent an embassy to Spain.* **2** [C *sometimes cap*] the official building where an ambassador and those with him work (and live) in a foreign country: *The American Embassy is a big building. He went to an embassy party.*

high commission [C *sometimes cap*] an embassy of one Commonwealth member the country of another: *The UK High Commission was surrounded by angry people.*

consulate 1 [C] the office or position of a consul: *He was given the consulate in Marseilles.* **2** [C] the official building where a consul and those who work with him can be found: *He called in at the British Consulate in Casablanca.*

legation 1 [GC] a group of officials working under a minister next in rank below an ambassador who represent their government and country in a foreign country **2** [C *often cap*] the offices of such a group **3** [C] the official home of the minister in charge of the group

mission [GC *often in comb*; *sometimes cap*] a group of persons acting for a special reason: *The British trade mission to China was well received.*

Politics and elections

C110 *nouns & adjectives* : **politics**

politics [U; P] the business, art, and/or science of government: *Local politics interest(s) him, but not national or international politics. He hopes for a career* [⇒ J210] *in politics. The politics of education can be very complex.*

politician [C] a person who takes part in politics: *There were several well-known politicians at the meeting.*

political [B] relating to the state, government, and/or public affairs: *They are worried about loss of political freedom. He hopes for a political career. These are political rather than social matters.* **non-** [*neg*] **-ly** [*adv* Wa4]

party politics [U; P] politics between or among two or more parties: *Some people regard party politics as a way of preventing dictatorship* [⇒ C95]; *others see it as a divisive* [⇒ N322] *evil.*

statesman [C] a politician in control of state affairs, esp a wise and careful one: *Attending the conference were some of the greatest statesmen of the time.* **statesmanlike** [B] *usu apprec* in the manner of a (wise) statesman: *That was a very statesmanlike decision.* **statesmanship** [U] *usu apprec* the ability of a wise statesman; great political ability: *He handled the conference with real statesmanship.*

ideology [C; U] a set of ideas, esp if typical of social systems, esp in politics: *Marxist ideology* **ideologue** [C] a person who follows a particular ideology   **ideological** [B] of, concerning, or like an ideology

C111 *nouns* : **political movements and parties** [U]

conservatism 1 (the principles of any party which favours) no change or very slow change, greater personal freedom, and less state control **2** a tendency or desire to keep things as they are or prefer things as they were

Labour *BrE*, **Labor** *AmE* the party, esp in Britain, which represents most socialists

socialism (the principles of any party which favours) state ownership of most important industries, services, and materials in a country and the social care of the people by the state

social democracy (the principles of any party which favours) considerable control by the state over the wealth and well-being of its citizens for the general good

communism (the principles of any party which favours) the sharing of all wealth, all property belonging to the state or to society as a whole, not to particular members

Marxism (the principles of any party which favours) the communist teachings and practices of Karl Marx

Leninism (the principles of any party which favours) the communist teachings of Vladimir Ilyich Lenin

Maoism (the principles of any party which favours) the communist teachings of Mao Tse Tung

liberalism 1 (the principles of any party which favours) reform [⇒ C131], free trade, and less centralized government **2** a tendency or desire to keep a society as free as possible

moderation a tendency or desire to avoid extremism

extremism a political view or tendency which favours strong, often violent, action to get what one wants, either on the right or the left [⇒ C112]

radicalism 1 (the principles of any party favouring) great social change in a short time **2** a tendency or desire for great change

reaction *often deprec* extreme conservatism: *He fears the forces of reaction.*

fascism 1 (the principles of any party which favours) extreme nationalism (and anticommunism) together with a strong central-government interest in industry and social organization generally **2** *usu derog* extreme conservatism; reaction

patriotism great love of and pride in one's country

nationalism 1 (too great) love of and pride in a country by its citizens: *Their nationalism was one cause of the war.* **2** a desire by a social or racial group to form an independent country or to become independent once again: *Scottish nationalism was a powerful force in British politics at that time.*

imperialism *often deprec* (the principles of any party or the aims of any country which favours) control over one or more countries by another country

colonialism *usu deprec* (the principles of any party or the aims of any country which favours) the developing of colonies [⇒ C92] of one country in other lands

capitalism the system in which capital [⇒ J113], business, and property are owned and looked after by private persons and groups, and not usu by the state

anarchism *also* **anarchy** (the principles of any party which, or the aims of any person who, favours) the destruction of all government

neo- [*comb form*] happening again, as in **neo-colonialism** (= an old colonial system developing again perhaps in a slightly different form)

ultra- [*prefix*] extreme, as in **ultra-rightwing** (= on the extreme right [⇒ C112] of a movement)

C112 *general adjectives & nouns* : relating to politics and political movements

left 1 [*the* GU *sometimes cap*] (the ideas and political position of) parties or groups such as socialists and communists: *The left demand(s) social equality. She is on the left of her party. She is well to the left on this subject. The party has had a swing to the left.* **2** [F] belonging to, connected with, or favouring the left in politics: *She votes left.*

left wing 1 [*the* GU] the group of members of a political party such as the socialists or communists, or a group favouring greater political changes than others favour: *The left wing of the party want to nationalize the steel industry.* **2** [F] belonging to or favouring the left **left-wing** [A]: *He has left-wing views on most subjects.* **leftwinger** [C] a left-wing person; socialist

right 1 [*the* GU *sometimes cap*] (the ideas or political position of) parties or groups such as conservatives and fascists: *The right want(s) things to stay pretty much as they are. He is on the right of his party, and well to the right on law and order.* **2** [F] belonging to, connected with, or favouring the right in politics

right wing 1 [*the* GU] the group of members of a political party such as the conservatives or fascists or a group favouring fewer political changes: *The party's right wing don't want any changes. People on the right wing of the party are very angry.* **2** [F] belonging to or favouring the right: *He is very right wing in matters of law and order.* **right-wing** [A] **rightwinger** [C] a right-wing person; conservative

centre *BrE*, **center** *AmE* [*the* GU *sometimes cap*] (the ideas and political position of) parties or groups who are neither left nor right; those who are moderate in politics **centrist 1** [B] relating to the centre; neither right nor left; moderate in politics **2** [C] a person who is in the political centre

moderate 1 [B] having no extreme views; against extremism in politics **2** [C] a person who is politically moderate

middle-of-the-road [B] *infml* centrist; moderate

pro- [*prefix*] in favour of: *He is pro-conservative in his views. She has always been pro-French and anti-American.*

anti- [*prefix*] against; not in favour of: *He is*

anti-British in many things. She is anti-fascist and pro-revolution.

C113 *adjectives & nouns* : relating to particular politics and political movements

conservative 1 [B] liking old ways; not liking change or too much change too quickly: *He is conservative by nature.* **2** [B *sometimes cap*] believing in conservatism: *He is a member of the British Conservative Party.* **3** [C *often cap*] (esp in Britain) a conservative person or politician; a believer in conservatism: *The Conservatives won/lost the last election.*

Tory 1 [C] *infml* a member of the Conservative Party, esp in Britain **2** [Wa5;B] relating to or favouring the Conservative party

reactionary *often deprec* **1** [C] a person against or preventing changes in a society: *These reactionaries can't stop change forever!* **2** [B] against social changes; favouring things as they are or were; very conservative: *He said that reactionary politicians could wreck social reform.*

socialist [*often cap*] **1** [C] a person favouring socialism: *He has been a socialist since childhood, when he saw his father struggling for workers' rights.* **2** [B] favouring or relating to socialism: 'These are socialist ideas,' he said. Socialist states are very common in the modern world.

Labour *BrE*, **Labor** *AmE* [Wa5;B] relating to the Labour Party, esp in Britain: *He has strong Labour ties* (= loyalties).

communist [*often cap*] **1** [C] a person believing in communism: *The communists want to bring an end to capitalism* [⇒ C111] *in that country.* **2** [B] favouring or relating to communism: *He considered the book a piece of Communist propaganda. Communist countries have a government-controlled Press.*

Marxist	(1) [C] a person believing in the teachings of	Marxism or Marx
Leninist	(2) [B] favouring or relating to	Leninism or Lenin
Maoist		Maoism or Mao Tse Tung

capitalist *often deprec or apprec* **1** [B] *also* **capitalistic** favouring capitalism **2** [C] **a** a person who favours capitalism **b** a businessman, esp one with a lot of money and conservative ideas

liberal 1 [B] favouring freedom in politics or religious matters; favouring wide possibilities of self-expression, trade, etc: *She has a very* *liberal view of things.* **2** [Wa5;B *sometimes cap*] favouring liberalism: *He always votes Liberal in the elections.* **3** [C *sometimes cap*] a liberal person or politician; a believer in liberalism: *The Liberals wanted greater electoral reform* [⇒ C131].

Whig 1 [C] *mainly old use & infml* a member of the Liberal Party **2** [Wa5;B] relating to or favouring that party

democrat [C] **1** a person believing in democracy **2** [*always cap*] a member of the Democratic Party in the USA

social democrat [C] a person believing in social democracy, esp a member of a social democratic party

radical 1 [B] concerned with making important (**radical** [⇒ N251]) changes in society: *He has radical views on these matters. His solutions are much more radical than ours.* **2** [B] believing in radicalism [⇒C111]: *The meeting was addressed by several radical speakers.* **3** [C] a radical person or politician: *The radicals demanded immediate reforms.*

anarchist 1 [C] a person who believes in anarchy or anarchism **2** [C] a person who tries or wishes to destroy all forms of government and control and not put anything in their place **3** [B] of or concerning anarchism

extremist 1 [C] a person who holds extreme political or other opinions (and favours extreme solutions to problems): *These extremists on both the left and the right could create a violent situation.* **2** [B] favouring extremism: *'Extremist ideas can only add to our problems,'* he said.

patriot [C] *usu apprec & emot* a person who loves and is willing to defend or die for his country   **patriotic** [B] having or expressing the qualities of a patriot: *They sang patriotic songs.* **-ally** [adv Wa4]

nationalist 1 [C] a person who wants political independence for his social or racial group or nationality: *He is an enthusiastic Scottish nationalist.* **2** [C] *often deprec* a person who has great or too much love of and pride in his or her country. **3** *also* **nationalistic** [B] favouring or relating to nationalism: *There is a strong nationalist party/movement in Wales.*

imperialist *often deprec* **1** [C] a person who favours an empire: *He accused the Americans of being imperialists in Latin America.* **2** *also* **imperialistic** [B] relating to imperialism: *That country once had great imperialist(ic) dreams.*

colonialist *often deprec* **1** [C] a person who favours colonialism: *He said that the men were colonialists exploiting the country for the benefit of their own foreign interests.* **2** [B] favouring or relating to colonialism: *He has a lot of old-fashioned colonialist ideas.*

fascist *often deprec* **1** [C] a person favouring fascism, supporting reaction, and willing to be violent and to punish socialists, communists, etc: *He is a fascist and won't work with socialists.* **2** [B] relating to or favouring fascism: *He says these ideas are fascist and reactionary.*

Nazi *now derog* [C] **1** a member of the German Nazi (=National Socialist) Party **2** a fascist

totalitarian 1 [Wa5;B] (of a political system or state) controlled by a single person and/or party, who may not be opposed **2** [Wa5;B] relating to or favouring totalitarianism [⇒ C95] **3** [C] a person with totalitarian views

C114 *nouns* : **statements of political policy** [C]

policy (a statement of) the plan of action of a political party, etc: *It is our policy to have most of the industries in this country under local ownership. The Government's economic policies were not a success. This is a policy matter/decision.*

mandate 1 the right and power given to a government or any body of people chosen to represent others, to act according to the wishes of those who voted for it: *The country has given a clear mandate to its leaders to continue the reforms* [⇒ C131]. **2** a command to act in a certain way, given by a higher to a lower official: *In the past the law could be changed by the king's mandate.*

manifesto a written statement making public the intentions, opinions, etc of a ruler or group of people, esp of a political party: *Have you read the party manifesto?*

C115 *verbs* : **nominating, voting, and electing**

nominate [T1] to put (someone) forward for election to a position: *She nominated him for the committee of the club.* **nomination 1** [U] the act of nominating **2** [C] an example, occasion, or result of this; a person nominated: *How many nominations are there?*

vote 1 [I0; (T1)] to show in a formal way which person, action, etc one wishes to choose, as by raising the hand or marking a piece of paper: *I didn't vote in/at the last election. Who did you vote for? I voted against him at the meeting. She voted Liberal.* **2** [X9] to put into or out of power according to a count of such actions: *They voted him in* (=into power) *with an increased majority* [⇒ C117]. *The government was voted out* (=out of office).

outvote [T1] to give more votes to someone else than to the person in question: *He was outvoted in the meeting; ten voted against him and only two in favour.*

elect [T1] to choose (somebody) by voting: *They elected him (as) their local member of parliament. The people will elect our party, not yours.*

poll [T1] to receive (a certain number of votes) in an election: *John Smith polled 30% of the votes. He polled 15,000 votes.*

campaign [I/0 (*for*)] to lead, take part in, or go on a campaign: *Jean is campaigning for equal* *rights for women.* **campaigner** [C] a person who campaigns politically

canvass *also* **canvas** [I∅;T1] **1** to go through an area or to people to ask for (political support or orders for one's goods) or to find out (people's opinions): *I'm canvassing tonight. The politicians were trying to canvass votes here last week. The milkman's always canvassing for new orders.*

ballot [I∅ *(on)*] to take a vote (by ballot) [⇒ C117]: *They've balloted for the new chairman, but nobody knows the result yet.*

electioneer [I∅] *sometimes deprec* to canvass, make speeches, etc for oneself or someone else in an election: *Don't start electioneering here, please.*

enfranchise [T1] to give the right to vote to: *Women were only enfranchised recently in that country.* **dis-** [T1] to take away the right to vote from (somebody)

C116 *verbs* : **being a candidate or in office**

stand [I∅ *(for)*] *BrE* to be or become a candidate [⇒ C119] for an office or position: *He stood for Parliament. Are you standing against him in the election? There are three people standing (in next week's election).*

run [I∅ *(for)*] *AmE* to be or become a candidate for an office or position: *He is running for Congress/for President. There are three people running in the next election.*

represent [T1] to be the Member of Parliament, Congressman, etc for: *The answer to this question is very important to the people he represents.*

C117 *nouns* : **voting and electing**

vote 1 [S] the power to vote: *Have you used your vote? Women got the vote in Britain early in the 20th century* **2** [C] an act of voting: *He got my vote. They cast* (= made) *their votes in the morning. Have you recorded your vote yet? The votes were counted and the winning candidate was announced.* **3** [*the* U] the full number of votes (for any party) in an election: *The Conservative vote was less this time than last. The popular vote was for reform.* **voter** [C] a person who votes

franchise [*the* U] the right to vote at elections: *These people all have the franchise.*

election 1 [U] the choice of someone or a party by voting: *The method of choosing the government is by election.* **2** [C] an occasion for electing (people and/or parties): *The election was last week. When will the election results be known?* **general election** [C *often cap*] the time when elections for a parliament are held throughout a country **electoral** [Wa5;B] of or concerning an election or elections **elector** [C] a person who elects someone else

poll 1 [C *usu sing*] voting at an election: *There has been a light/heavy poll this time. We are anxiously awaiting the results of the poll.* **2** [C *usu pl*] a place where voting takes place: *The people are going to the polls in great numbers.* **polling day** [C] the day chosen for a poll **polling station** [C] the place where people go to vote **polling booth** [C] the closed area in a polling station where a person votes secretly

campaign [C] a set of planned activities before an election, to help someone to be elected: *The presidential campaign begins about a year before the actual election. He is our campaign organizer.*

ballot 1 [C] a piece of paper or a ticket which is used in secret voting: *Have you all got your ballots/your ballot papers? You should put your ballot papers in this ballot box.* **2** [C;*by* U] an occasion of voting: *The election was done by secret ballot. Let's take a ballot and see who wins.*

referendum [C] a direct vote by all the people who can vote on a matter of (national) importance: *Britain held a referendum on whether or not to stay in the European Common Market.*

plebiscite [C] *fml & tech* a national referendum esp to choose between rulers

majority [C] the number of votes by which a person wins in an election: *He won by a majority of 300.*

C118 *nouns* : **electoral areas**

constituency [C] **1** a parliamentary or other division whose people are represented by one elected member of parliament, etc **2** the people in a constituency: *The MP is supporting the new law although his constituency is against it.* **constituent** [C] a person who has the right to vote in a constituency; a person in a constituency

electorate [(*the*) GC] all the people who can vote in an election: *The electorate are not fools; they will recognize just arguments. Very few of the electorate failed to vote.*

electoral roll/register [C] the list of the names of people who can vote in an election

C119 *nouns* : **candidates and representatives** [C]

candidate a person who wants, or who is wanted by others, to be chosen for a position, esp in an election: *He was the strongest candidate for the position. She always supports her party's candidate.* **candidacy** [U] the state, condition, occasion, etc of being a candidate: *Do you support his candidacy?*

representative a person representing others, in Parliament, Congress, etc: *He is the people's representative and must be heard. Their elected representatives speak for them.*

nominee a person suggested by name for an office or position: *He is our nominee for the job.*

agent a person who acts for another, esp one who looks after or represents a candidate in an election campaign: *His local agent helped him win the election.*

Member (of Parliament) *esp in Britain, Ireland, etc* a representative of the people, elected to Parliament: *Who is you local Member?* **MP** *abbrev*: *All our MPs were present.*

Political tension and trouble

C130 *verbs* : **reforming and protesting**

reform [T1] to make or become better by taking away or putting right what is wrong or not good enough: *We must reform these unjust laws. The government needs to be reformed/needs reforming.* **reformer** [C] a person who wants and works for reform

crusade [I0 (*against, for*)] to take part in a crusade: *She crusaded for women's rights.* **crusader** [C] a person who crusades

oppose [T1] to set oneself or fight against: *I intend to oppose his plan. They oppose the government's new policies.*

resist [T1; I0] to use force against (a force or change): *She says she will resist their attempts to take the child away. We must resist with force! The conservatives intend to resist the reforms.*

protest 1 [I0] to express disagreement, feelings of injustice, annoyance, etc: *The students protested because of bad food in their hostel. We must protest against injustice!* **2** [T1] *AmE* to make a protest against: *They stood in the street, protesting the war.* **protester** [C] a person who protests

demonstrate [I0] to arrange or take part in a public show of strong feeling or opinion, often with marching, big signs, etc: *The students demonstrated in favour of better teaching. The people were demonstrating against the government.* **demonstrator** [C] a person who demonstrates

agitate [I0 (*for*)] to ask strongly for something, esp by protesting and demonstrating: *The workers are agitating for better conditions and more money.* **agitator** [C] *often deprec* a person who agitates: *The government doesn't like political agitators.*

C131 *nouns* : **reforming and protesting**

reform [U; C] social action or a social action which does or should improve conditions, remove unfairness, etc in a society: *The 1830s were a time of great social reform in Britain. The new law brought in several reforms.*

reformation [U] the act of reforming or state of being reformed: *The full reformation of these laws is necessary.*

crusade [C (*against, for*)] **1** any struggle or movement for the defence or advancement of an idea, principle, etc: *a crusade against crime*; *a crusade for women's rights* **2** [*usu cap*] any of the Christian wars to win back the Holy Land from the Muslims in the 11th, 12th, and 13th centuries

opposition 1 [U] the state of being opposed: *They have been in opposition (to our policies) for years.* **2** [U] active resistance: *Many people are in natural opposition to change. The soldiers met with strong local opposition.* **3** [(*the*) GU] **a** those who oppose: *The opposition are angry.* **b** [*usu cap*] the party not in power at the moment: *The leader of the Opposition stood up to speak.*

resistance 1 [U] the fact of resisting, or ability to resist: *Many people have a natural resistance to change.* **2** [*the* U] people who resist an invader or a government: *The local resistance leader killed several soldiers.*

protest 1 [U] unwillingness, dissatisfaction, and opposition, etc as shown or expressed in some manner: *His silence is a form of protest against his imprisonment. He spoke out in protest against the increasing costs. The shops closed in protest against the new taxes.* **2** [C] a (written or official) complaint or an expression of dissatisfaction, disagreement, opposition, etc: *They all signed the protest and it was sent to their local member of parliament. No one listened to their protests.* **under protest** unwillingly and with a feeling of injustice: *It's unfair to increase my rent and I am paying under protest.*

demonstration [C] a public show of strong feeling or opinion, often with marching, big signs, etc: *They held several demonstrations against the war.* **demo** *infml abbrev*: *Where shall we hold the demo?*

agitation [U] public argument, action, unrest, etc for or against political or social change: *Their agitation for higher pay moved from argument to taking possession of the firm's offices.*

riot [C] violent actions, noisy behaviour, etc by a number of people together, esp in a public place: *There was a riot last night in the city; two people were killed. The riot police were called in to stop the riot.* [⇒ C134]

sedition [U] behaviour which may or does cause action against the government or people in power: *Publishing the article was regarded as sedition. The newspaper editor was arrested for sedition.* **seditious** [B] of, concerning, or like sedition. **-ly** [adv]

C132 *verbs* : **limiting people's freedom** [T1]

keep down [v adv] to stop from opposing or resisting: *The king has kept these provinces* *down for years and is hated by most of the people.*

hold down [v adv] to keep down very firmly: *Your job is to hold the province down; there must be no more rebellions!*

oppress to rule in a very hard way, by allowing very little freedom: *The king oppressed his people with terrible taxes and punishments.* **oppression** [U; C] the act of oppressing or being oppressed **oppressive** [B] causing or for the purpose of oppressing **-ly** [adv] [⇒ C102]

repress to rule by holding back from (natural feelings, actions, etc): *The king has repressed his people for years. All freedom has been actively repressed.* **repression** [U; C] **repressive** [B] causing or for the purpose of repressing **-ly** [adv]

suppress to rule in a very hard way, by taking away the right to act: *They live in a police state* [⇒ C95] *which has suppressed all free speech. The people there are cruelly suppressed.* **suppression** [U; C]

put down [v adv] to suppress: *The rebellion was ruthlessly put down by the armed forces.*

C133 *verbs* : **defeating anyone, esp governments** [T1]

[ALSO ⇒ C280–3]

defeat to cause to stop ruling: *'We must defeat this evil regime!'* [⇒ C100] *he shouted. The government was defeated in the election.*

bring down [v adv] *emot* to defeat: *The government has been brought down by popular anger.*

overthrow defeat and remove from power, often with force: *The rebels have overthrown the government.*

usurp to take (power or position) for oneself, esp unlawfully: *He usurped his brother's throne* (=took his brother's place as king). *That party intend to usurp power illegally.* **usurpation** [U] the act or result of usurping **usurper** [C] a person who usurps power

subvert to (seek to) overthrow by secret action: *He intends to subvert lawful government in this country.*

take over [v adv *also* IØ] to take control (of): *They took over the government of the country from the defeated dictator. The rebels took over last night.* **takeover** [C] an act of taking over

C134 *verbs* : **moving against those in power** [IØ]

rebel to act violently against those who have power, or against the unfair use of power: *They have rebelled against the government and must be punished. Don't rebel; be patient and work for better times.* **rebellious** [B] inclined to rebel **-ness** [U] **-ly** [adv]

rise *emot* to rebel: *The people have at last risen against their oppressive rulers.*

revolt to act violently against those in power so as to take power from them: *The army revolted against the bad government.*

mutiny to take part in a mutiny: *The sailors mutinied against their cruel captain. He urged the soldiers to mutiny.* **mutinous** [B] **1** about to or ready to mutiny, or guilty of having mutinied: *mutinous soldiers* **2** showing signs of mutiny: *a mutinous look on one's face* **-ly** [adv]

riot to take part in a riot [⇒ C131]: *The people rioted against the great rises in the price of food.* **riotous** [B] disorderly; wild: *riotous behaviour* **-ly** [adv] **-ness** [U]

C135 *nouns* : **moving against those in power**

rebellion 1 [C] (an example of) the act of rebelling against a government or those in power: *There have been several armed rebellions lately.* **2** [U] the act or state of rebelling: *The people are in open rebellion against the king.*

revolt [C; (*in*) U] (an example of) the act or state of revolting: *There have been two armed revolts in three years. The people were in revolt against the king.*

insurrection [C; U] *fml* the act or occasion of rising against the people who have power: *There was an armed insurrection against the government of the province. 'Insurrection must be stopped,' he said.*

insurgency [U] *fml* a state of insurrection

coup (d'etat) [C] a sudden action against the government, to force it to be changed: *The coup took place at dawn.*

rising [C] *lit & emot* the occasion of moving against the rulers; a small rebellion

uprising [C] *emot* a rising or rebellion: *The uprising was put down without mercy. There have been many uprisings against the emperor.*

mutiny [C; U] **1** (an example of) the act of taking power from the person in charge, esp from a captain on a ship or an officer in an army: *The sailors were all found guilty of mutiny. A mutiny took place in the army camp.* **2** a state of feelings or set of actions against someone's power: *She sat in silent mutiny because of what her mother had said. He started his own private mutiny against his school teachers.*

revolution [C; U] (a time of) great social change, esp the changing of a ruler or a political system by force: *After a revolution things can never be the same again. Nothing less than revolution will satisfy them.*

subversion [U] the act or an act of subverting: *His behaviour is plainly subversion; he will cause his fellow soldiers to mutiny if we let him continue! 'Subversion and conspiracy will not succeed; the government will not be defeated in this way.' he said.* **subversive** [B] of, concerning, like, or for the purpose of subversion: *subversive acts* **-ly** [adv] **-ness** [U]

overthrow [(*the*) *usu sing*] removal from official power, esp by force; an act of overthrowing

C136 nouns & adjectives : **persons moving against those in power** [C]

rebel a person who habitually rebels or has rebelled: *The soldiers were ordered to capture or kill all the rebels. The rebel leaders were executed. He is something of a rebel and will not behave like the others.*

insurgent [*also* Wa5;B] *fml* (a person who is) ready to fight against the people who have power: *The soldiers killed the insurgents.*

mutineer a person who is taking part or has taken part in a mutiny: *The captain of the ship hanged three of the mutineers.*

revolutionary 1 a person who favours and tries to bring about a revolution: *They are revolutionaries who hope to bring down the government.* **2** [Wa2;B] favouring or taking part in a revolution: *These are revolutionary ideas! His revolutionary acts caused his death.*

terrorist a person who tries to enforce [⇒ C185] his political demands by doing or threatening acts of violence: *The terrorists blew up a railway bridge. terrorist acts*

partisan 1 a member of an armed group that fights in secret against an enemy that has conquered its country: *Armed partisans attacked the army post.* **2** a strong, esp unreasoning, supporter of a party, group, plan, etc: *He is a partisan of extreme nationalism. What partisan ideas!*

guerrilla, guerilla a person who actively and violently works against an invader [⇒ C275] or a government: *The guerrillas attacked iso-lated army posts. Guerrilla activity increased in the hills.*

freedom fighter *often euph* a guerrilla, terrorist, or partisan who claims or is claimed to be fighting for a people's freedom

subversive a person engaged in subversion: *The police were looking for subversives.*

C137 verbs : **plotting and spying**

plot [I∅;T1] to make secret plans (for): *He is plotting against the government/plotting to overthrow the government. They are plotting treason [⇒ C138].*

conspire [I∅, 3] to plot together: *They are con-spiring to overthrow the government. They conspired (together) against us.*

betray [T1] **1** to be disloyal or unfaithful to: *He betrayed his country to the enemy.* **2** to give away or make known: *He betrayed the news to their enemies.*

collaborate [I∅ (*with*)] to help the army, etc of an enemy country which has entered one's own: *He was killed because he collaborated with the enemy.*

hatch [T1 (*up*)] to think of and develop (plots, etc): *They are hatching a plan to destroy the government. What new plots are you hatching up now?*

spy [I∅ (*on*)] to watch secretly; to seek to get

information secretly: *She spies on all her neighbours. He has been spying for the enemy!*

C138 nouns : **plotting and spying**

plot [C] a secret plan, usu to change a govern-ment or other social system: *It's a plot to over-throw lawful government! The plot was dis-covered and the ringleaders put in jail.*

conspiracy 1 [U] the act of conspiring: *Conspi-racy can sometimes be a crime.* **2** [C] a plan made by conspiring or a group which con-spires: *The conspiracies of the government's enemies were uncovered. There is a strange conspiracy of silence to prevent the truth (from) being made known.*

betrayal [U; C] the act or an act of betraying or being betrayed: *The betrayal of Jesus by Judas led to his arrest. She's tired of his constant betrayals.*

spying [U] the activities of a spy: *The penalty for spying is often death.*

espionage [U] *fml* spying: *He was found guilty of espionage and shot. Industrial espionage happens a lot; one company tries to steal the ideas of others.*

sabotage [U] destructive acts, esp in war, done by one person or a small group against an enemy, sometimes within the enemy's own country, to prevent their fighting effectively: *The guerrillas committed various acts of sabot-age against government buildings.*

treason [U] betrayal of one's country, by help-ing its enemies or by violence against those in power: *This is an act of treason; the leaders must be arrested immediately.* **high treason** *fml* treason against a king or a country

C139 nouns : **persons plotting and spying** [C]

plotter a person who starts or takes part in a plot

conspirator a person taking part in a conspi-racy; *fml* a plotter **conspiratorial** [B] of or like conspiracies and conspirators

spy a person who is employed to find out the political secrets of one country and pass them on to an enemy country: *They are enemy spies; arrest them! He likes reading spy stories.*

ringleader *emot & deprec* the leader in a secret group, plot or any activity considered subver-sive

saboteur a person who performs acts of sabot-age: *Saboteurs blew up the dam.*

traitor a person who betrays anything, esp his country by giving away secrets: *He was a traitor to his country and was executed for the crime of high treason.* **traitorous** [B] of or like a traitor: *What a traitorous act!*

collaborator a person who collaborates with an invader [⇒ C275]

quisling *emot & derog* a collaborator

Social classifications and situations

C150 *nouns* : **social position**

position [C; U] a person's place in relation to others: *What position does he hold in the company? The child's position was 14th in a class of 32. These people have a rather low position in society. People of high position often visit that house. A man in his position in society should be careful what he does. Position and money are all that matter to him.*

rank 1 [U] high social position: *He is a person of rank; be careful how you speak to him.* **2** [C] degree of value, ability, importance, etc: *He will become a soldier of the highest rank.* [⇒ C297–300]

status [U; C] (high) position in a social group: *He has a job with a rather low status. The presence of a great tennis player gave status to the club's events. This change will not affect your status in the company.* **status symbol** [C] an object which serves to show the high status of its owner: *An expensive car is a status symbol.*

station [C] *fml & old use* a social position: *He has fallen to a much lower station in life than he used to have.*

standing [U; S] *genl* status: *His standing in this town is high. He is a person of some standing in this town.*

class 1 [U] the fact that there are different social groups of various ranks: *Questions of class divide the nation. Politics often relate to class.* **2** [C] a social group of a certain rank: *The various classes of society do not always get on well together. He said that class differences in that country are not as obvious as in this one.*

caste 1 [C] a social division of society based on differences of wealth, rank, rights, profession, or job, esp one of the social classes of Hinduism: *He belonged to the lowest caste and could not therefore eat with the others.* **2** [U] social position: *Caste is the most important thing in her life.* **lose caste** to come down in social rank; lose people's respect

C151 *nouns* : **breeding and repute**

breeding [U] social condition, usu of being superior socially, due to a person's birth, upbringing, or to both of these: *The old duchess* [⇒ C158] *insisted that a person's breeding always showed; she said that a man of breeding* (= high social background) *always knew how to behave. What bad/good breeding she shows/has!*

class [U] *infml* social or personal excellence: *That girl's got class; she's wonderful. People of class use that hotel.* **classy** [Wa1;B] *infml* hav-

ing class: *She was wearing a classy outfit at the party. Where did you get that classy tie?*

reputation [C] general opinion about the qualities of a person: *He has an excellent reputation as a doctor. She has gained quite a reputation (for herself) as a cook.*

repute [U] *often fml* good or bad reputation: *He is a doctor of great repute. I know him by repute, not personally. She is a person of low repute here.*

name [C] **1** [usu sing] a reputation; recognition by others: *He has a good name in the business; you can trust him. She made quite a name for herself/made her name* (= became famous) *as a painter. The school has a name for good science teaching.* **2** *infml* a person (esp in the phrs **big name**, **famous name**, etc): *There were several (big) names* (= famous people) *at the party.*

C152 *nouns* : **classes in societies** [(the) GC]

ruling class all the members of the families of those who rule any society or country: *She belongs to the ruling class and has considerable political power.*

upper class a small social class whose members belong to a few old families, are very rich and own a great deal of land: *The upper class in Britain is not as politically powerful as it once was. He spoke with an upper-class accent.*

middle class the (usu large) social class whose members belong to professions or run businesses: *The middle class in Britain increased rapidly after the Industrial Revolution. He has typical middle-class views on private property and hard work; he believes in both.*

working class the large social class to which people belong who work with their hands: *Many of the students in that college come from the working class. She comes from a respectable working-class home.*

lower class *often deprec* a social class generally regarded as being of the lowest rank: *He obviously belongs to the lower classes, my dear! 'Must you bring your lower-class friends home with you, John?' his mother asked.*

C153 *nouns* : **levels in societies** [ALSO ⇒ C72]

establishment [*the* GU; A *often cap*] *esp BrE*, *often derog* the powerful organizations and people who (are said to) control public life and support the established order of society: *The new play attacks the Establishment. The Establishment are against these new ideas. He doesn't like her Establishment ideas.*

élite [GC] *sometimes deprec* the most important people in a social group: *He is a member of the élite, and believes he is a natural leader. Social élites generally wish to keep power to them-*

selves. He belongs to the scientific élite of his country.

aristocracy [*(the)* GC] **1** members of the upper class, esp people from noble families and with titles of rank: *She belongs to the landed aristocracy.* **2** (*fig*) the finest members of any group or class in any activity

nobility [*(the)* GU] people of the upper class, who have titles, land, etc: *The nobility usually resist social change, because it generally reduces their power and wealth.*

gentry [*(the)* GU] people socially just below the nobility: *He belongs to the local landed gentry. The gentry don't like him because he's a bit of a radical* [⇒ C113].

bourgeoisie [*(the)* GU] *sometimes deprec* (esp in socialism) the middle or capitalist class

proletariat [*(the)* GU] (esp in socialism) the mass of wage-earners, esp those working with their hands   **proletarian 1** [Wa5;B] relating to the proletariat **2** [C] a member of the proletariat

masses [*the* P] the lowest social classes of society: *He spent his time trying to improve the living conditions of the masses.*

C154 *nouns & adjectives* : **persons of the same social level**

equal [C] a person who is the same as another, esp socially, mentally [⇒ G7], physically [⇒ B2], etc: *They are equals in these matters. She is not his social equal and he can't marry her.*

peer [C] an equal in age, rank, quality, or worth, etc: *Older boys and girls form groups of their peers/form peer groups. These people are peers in all except name.*

egalitarian, *also less common*   **equalitarian 1** [C] a person who believes that all people are essentially equal: *He is an egalitarian in social matters.* **2** [B] relating to any idea or set of ideas which take all people as equals **egalitarianism, equalitarianism** [U] the system of all people being equal; any situation where such principles are used

C155 *adjectives, etc* : **relating to levels in societies**

noble [A;(B)] *esp old use* belonging to the upper class: *He is a young man of noble family/birth.*

titled [B] having a social title [⇒ G233] and therefore belonging to the upper class: *She is a member of the titled aristocracy.*

common: [Wa5;B]*esp old use* not noble: *He is a common fellow of no breeding* [⇒ C151].

betters [P] those people whom the speaker regards as higher socially than the person spoken to/about: *You must not speak so rudely to your betters! He shows no respect towards his betters.*

C156 *adjectives & nouns* : **(relating to) persons of higher or lower social position**

superior 1 [Wa5;B] higher in social or other rank: *They occupy a very superior position in local society.* **2** [C] a person of higher social or other rank: *Tell him to address his superiors more politely. I'll speak to your superior about this careless work! I must pass this report to my superior.*

inferior 1 [Wa5;B] lower in social or other rank: *These people occupy an inferior position in local society.* **2** [C] *sometimes deprec* a person of lower social or other rank: *He's their inferior socially. Don't be afraid of making your inferiors work harder. They regarded their servants as their inferiors in every way.*

subordinate 1 [Wa5;B] of a lower rank or position: *He has a very subordinate position in the company. She is subordinate to her husband in every way.* **2** [C] a person who is of lower rank in a job: *He treats his subordinates well, but expects them to work hard.*

C157 *nouns* : **persons and ranks in societies**

noble [C] *esp old use* a person who has a title passed down to him in his family: *The king was surrounded by his nobles.*

nobleman/noblewoman [C] *old use* a man/woman of noble birth: *The king summoned the local noblemen to the castle.*

peer [C] (in Britain) **1** a member of any one of five ranks of noblemen (baron, viscount, earl, marquis, and duke) **2** any person who has the right to sit in the House of Lords (= the upper house in Parliament)   **peer of the realm** a peer who received his rank from a king or queen through his parents, and who passes it to his eldest son when he dies   **life peer** a peer who holds his rank only during his own lifetime and cannot pass it to his eldest son

peeress [C] a woman peer

peerage 1 [U;C] the whole group of peers **2** [C] the rank of a peer

aristocrat [C] a person of noble family and/or with the ideas and inclinations of the nobility **aristocratic** [B] of or like an aristocrat or the aristocracy [⇒ C153]: *He has a very aristocratic manner.* **-ally** [adv Wa4]

gentleman [C] **1** *old use* a man of a higher social position but not of a noble family, esp one who serves a king or nobles **2** (*formerly*) a man who had money and did not need to work **3** a man who behaves well towards others and who can be trusted to keep his promises and always act honourably **4** [*also (pl)* N] *polite* a man: *A gentleman called to see you. Ladies and gentlemen, let us begin.*

lady [C; (*pl*) N]*polite* a woman, esp a woman of higher social position or of good manners and

education: *She's a real lady. Ask the ladies to come in. There's a lady to see you, sir.*
commoner [C] a person who is not noble: *There are stories of nobles marrying commoners, but these are unusual; the two groups normally did not intermarry.*

C158 *nouns, etc* : **ranks and titles of the British aristocracy, etc**

Ranks according to sex and position

position \ sex	male	female
highest	duke	duchess
	marquis,	
	marquess	marchioness
	earl	countess
	viscount	viscountess
	baron	baroness
	baronet	lady
lowest	knight	lady

duke [C; A] (the title of) a prince: *Prince Charles is also the Duke of Cornwall. Duke William of Normandy invaded England.* **ducal** [Wa5;B] relating or belonging to a duke or duchess
count [C; A] (a title for) a nobleman in Europe **countess** [C; A] (the title of) the wife of an earl or count, or a woman of the same rank
baron [C] **1** [*also* A] (a nobleman with) the lowest rank in the House of Lords **2** [*also* A; N] (the title of) certain European noblemen: *Come, Baron, we must talk.* **3** *esp AmE* a very important and powerful businessman: *He is a newspaper baron. The cattle barons held a meeting.* **baroness** [C; A] (the title of) the wife of a baron, or a woman of the same rank
baronet [C] (a man who has) a rank below that of a baron and above that of a knight, but is not a peer: *Sir George is a local baronet; his title is hereditary* [⇒ C17] *and he wasn't personally knighted.*
knight 1 [C] (formerly) a noble soldier on horseback, usu serving a ruler: *The knights charged the enemy.* **2** [C] a man who has been given a certain title of honour by a king or queen of Great Britain, with a rank below the rank of lord: *George Smith was made a knight for his service to his country and thereafter was known as Sir George (Smith).* **3** [T1] to make into a knight: *The king knighted George Smith.* **knighthood** [U; C] the status of being a knight
lord [C] **1** a peer [⇒ C157]: *The king summoned his lords.* **2** any nobleman with power: *Several great local lords attended the hunt.* **3** [*also* A; *my* N *often cap*] the title of a lord, king, bishop, etc: *There is good news, my Lord. Lord George came to see Lady Jane.*
lady [C; A; *my* N *often cap*] a title of a marchioness, countess, baroness; the wife of a baronet

or a knight: *Lady Mountbatten visited the hospital. Sir George and Lady Smith were among the guests.*
Sir [A] the title of a knight or baronet: *Sir George is a knight, not a baronet.*
squire [C] **1** (formerly) a young man attending a knight until he himself became a knight **2** (in England) the chief landowner, often titled (=having a title), in a country parish: *Sir George is the squire hereabouts.*

C159 *nouns* : **persons in social positions** [C]

toff *sl esp BrE* a person of social importance, esp well-dressed: *Some toffs gave him the money; he didn't steal it!*
snob *deprec* a person who thinks it important to be of a high social class and dislikes (and does not want to know) those of a lower class and their ways: *I'm afraid she is a bit of a snob. Those people are all snobs.* **-bery** [U] **snobbish** [B] like a snob: *Don't be snobbish about people.* **-ness** [U] **-ly** [adv]
upstart *deprec* a person who has risen suddenly or unexpectedly to a high position and who is felt to be taking advantage of the power he has gained
social climber *often deprec* a person who wants to join a higher social class and tries to do this by friendship with people from this class

C160 *nouns* : **leaders and bosses** [C]

leader 1 a person who guides or leads a group, movement, etc: *The miners' leaders talked together and came to a decision.* **2** a person or thing that leads or is in advance of others. *That paper is the national leader for political news.*
head (*fig*) a leader: *He is the head of the group. The conference is for heads of government.*
lord (formerly) a ruler; a man in charge of land and the people who work on it: *He was a great lord and has four castles. The lord of the manor* [⇒ D5] *ordered his men to kill any peasant* [⇒ C169] *hunting on his land.*
lady a woman in a position of command or control: *She's the lady of the house. The lady of the manor sent for him.*
chief a leader; ruler; person with highest rank; head of a party, organization, tribe, etc: *Everyone obeyed the chief of the clan* [⇒C11] *obeyed the clan chief. Crazy Horse was war chief of the Sioux nation. The chief of police/The police chief spoke to his men.* **-in-chief** [*comb form*] having the highest rank: *In World War Two General Eisenhower was commander-in-chief of the armed forces.*
chieftain the leader of a (smaller) tribe or other such group **chieftaincy, chieftainship** [U] the condition or status of being a chief or chieftain
master 1 a man in control of or owning people, animals, things: *After hard fighting the defen-*

ders were still masters of the city. Only its master can ride that horse. **2** a man who is the head of a house, etc: *Send for the master; there are strangers coming!* **3** (esp formerly) a man employing workers or servants (*often in the phr* **masters and men**): *He is master of 1,000 workers.* **be one's own master** be independent **mastery** [U] the position or power of a master

mistress a woman who is in the position of a master: *Better ask the mistress's permission before going. She is mistress of the whole house. The servants obeyed their mistress in everything.*

boss *often infml* (esp in places of work) a leader, employer: *He's the boss here; better ask his permission. Where's your/the boss, Bill? She's the boss in that family, not her husband.* **bossy** [Wa1;B] *infml deprec* like a boss; inclined to give too many orders **-ily** [adv] **-iness** [U]

C161 *nouns* : **servants and menials** [C]

servant a person who works for another, esp in the other's house or in personal service: *That family have always had plenty of servants. I'll get a servant to see you to your car.*

servitor *old use or fml* a servant: *An old servitor opened the door.*

domestic (servant) a servant in a house: *Don't let the domestics know that he has left.*

attendant 1 a person who goes with and serves or looks after another: *The king came with many attendants.* **2** a person employed to look after and help visitors to a public place: *The museum attendants were very helpful.*

retainer (esp formerly) a servant, esp one who has always worked for a particular person or family: *He called his faithful retainer and asked him to bring in the money.*

manservant *fml* a male servant: *A manservant answered the door.*

maidservant *fml* a female servant, usu of another woman: *Her maidservant attended to her needs.*

man *infml* a male servant: *My man will look after my clothes.*

woman *infml* a female servant or helper: *She has a woman who cleans for her twice a week.*

girl *infml* a (young) female servant: *The girl washes up.*

menial *often deprec* a servant, esp in a house, esp one who must do all the hardest work

C162 *nouns* : **specific kinds of servants** [C]

butler the head manservant in a large family house, in charge of valuables, wine, etc: *Ring for the butler. James, the butler, announced the guests.*

steward 1 the man, esp a servant, who controls supplies of food in a large house **2** an official

who does this for a club, college, etc **3** one of a number of men who arrange and control a public meeting **4** *also ScotE* **factor** a man who is employed to look after a house and lands, such as a large farm

valet a gentleman's personal manservant who looks after his clothes, etc

gentleman's gentleman *euph* a valet

footman a manservant in special dress who opens the door of a carriage, car, etc and waits at table, etc

groom 1 *old use* a manservant **2** a man employed to look after horses: *The grooms were busy rubbing the horses down.*

chauffeur a person employed to drive someone's car

chauffeuse a female chauffeur

lackey 1 *old use* a manservant, esp one whose clothing showed by its colour and shape who his master was **2** *derog* a person who behaves like a servant by obeying others without question

nanny (esp formerly in rich families in Britain) a woman employed to take care of children: *Some rich American parents like to have a British nanny for their children.*

(house)maid a woman servant in a house: *Ring for the maid to take these things away.*

chambermaid a maid, or woman in a hotel, who looks after bedrooms

C163 *nouns* : **slaves** [C]

slave a servant who is owned by a master: *Many ancient empires, such as Rome and Babylon, had large populations of slaves/large slave populations. The American Civil War began over the question of whether men should keep other men as slaves.* **slavish** [B] *deprec* like a slave **-ly** [adv] **-ness** [U]

serf a slave, esp formerly when men worked on the land for a lord: *The great lord was the master of thousands of serfs.*

chattel *usu derog* (esp formerly) a slave: *I am your wife but I'm not your chattel!*

bondsman, bond(s)woman, bond(s)maid a slave who belongs to his or her master because of a written paper (**bond**) which gives possession

C164 *nouns* : **service and slavery** [U]

(domestic) service the work which servants do in a house: *Fifty years ago there were few jobs for women, and most of these were in (domestic) service.*

slavery 1 the condition of being a slave: *The local people were reduced to slavery* (= made into slaves) *by their enemies.* **2** the institution of having slaves: *The American Civil War was fought over slavery in the Southern States. Slavery has been abolished in most parts of the world.* **3** hard work like that of a slave: *Her* *life after her marriage was slavery to a cruel husband.*

servitude *fml* slavery

servility the manner of a slave; obedience which is too great   **servile** [B] *deprec* like a slave

bondage 1 slavery **2** a state like this from which one cannot escape: *The local miners lived in bondage; none could leave the mines. Her father's selfishness kept her in bondage until she married.*

C165 verbs, nouns, etc **freeing slaves**

free [T1] **1** to let out of bondage, slavery, etc: *The slaves were freed.* **2** [Wa1;B, B3] not held or kept in one place or condition, or a prison, etc but able to go anywhere or most places and do most of the things one wants to do, without being stopped: *The men were free; they were free to go where they wanted. A free nation will usually fight to stay free.*

freedom [U] the state of being free: *Their mistress gave the slaves their freedom.*

set free [T1] to cause to become free (from slavery, etc): *The black slaves on the West Indian plantations were at last set free.*

liberate [T1] to make free (from some kind of bondage, tyranny, etc): *These guerrillas believe they can liberate the people of this country. Many women want to be liberated from the power of men.*

liberation [U] the act of liberating or being liberated: *He was present at the allied liberation of Paris.*

liberty [U] freedom from a master or too powerful a government or from foreign rule: *The people have lost their liberty.*

emancipate [T1] *tech* to set free by legal means; to give more freedom to: *This Act will emancipate thousands of slaves.*

emancipation [U] the situation of emancipating or being emancipated: *He worked for the greater emancipation of women.*

release *often fml* **1** [T1] to free or set free: *He released the captured men.* **2** [S;U] act of freeing or being freed: *His release took place last Friday.* [⇒ C211]

C166 adjectives & nouns : **relating to the values of society**

respectable [B] showing or having character and standards acceptable to society: *They are very respectable people indeed. This is a respectable house and you will not shame it!* **-bly** [adv] **-bility** [U]

conventional [B] living according to convention [⇒ C182], following the usual ways, not new or unusual ways of doing things: *She is rather conventional in her daily life.* **un-** [neg] **-ly** [adv]

orthodox [B] **1** generally accepted, wanted, used, thought, etc **2** having esp religious ideas

that are generally accepted in a place, country, group, etc **un-** [neg] **orthodoxy** [U] the state of being orthodox

conformist 1 [B] following only socially acceptable and established ways and standards: *She is pretty conformist in most things.* **2** [C] a person who is conformist: *These people are all conformists; they won't change anything.* **non-** [neg]

bourgeois 1 [B] of, related to, or typical of the middle class **2** [B] *deprec* having or showing more interest in possessions and good manners than in ideas and feelings: *She has some very bourgeois attitudes.* **3** [C] a member of the middle class **4** [C] *deprec* a bourgeois person

C167 adjectives : **relating to social values and attitudes** [B]

polite [Wa2] **1** having good manners: *What a polite child; he always says 'please' and 'thank you'.* **im-** [neg] **-ly** [adv] **-ness** [U] **2** *pomp* belonging (or pretending to belong) to a higher and therefore more desirable social rank: *She is not welcome in polite society.*

civil [Wa2] **1** (of others) as polite as one would wish: *He was very civil to us when we went to see him. It was civil of you to help me yesterday. He wasn't very civil to her when they met.* **2** just polite enough to be acceptable, though not friendly: *Try to be civil to her, even if you don't like her. Keep a civil tongue in your head!* (=stop speaking rudely) **-ly** [adv] **civility** [U] the state or manner of being civil **in-** [neg]

well-mannered having good manners; polite: *He's a well-mannered child.*

courteous very polite, kind, etc: *What a courteous man he is!* **dis-** [neg] **-ly** [adv] **courtesy** [U; C] polite and kind behaviour: *He showed us great courtesy; we were glad of his many courtesies.* (*fml*) *Please do us the courtesy of trying* (=be polite enough to try) *to understand our difficulties.* **dis-** [neg]

sophisticated *sometimes deprec* with highly developed (or over-civilized), not simple, social behaviour: *I feel rather gauche* [⇒ C168] *among all these sophisticated people. She is a person with very sophisticated ideas about sex and drugs.*

refined having or showing delicacy of feeling, a certain kind of education, etc: *What a refined speaker he is! Oh stop trying to be so refined and snobbish!* [⇒ C159]

well-bred *usu apprec* (thought to be) well-behaved and polite, probably as the result of being well brought up: *She's very well-bred and is never rude to anyone.*

high-class *infml* belonging to the upper class: *She's a high-class girl; she won't marry you!*

posh *sl esp BrE* belonging to or similar in manner to the upper class: *That bloke* [⇒ C4] *had a posh accent, didn't he? She's very posh now that she's got some money. Wow, what a posh car!*

cultivated *usu apprec* with good education and manners: *He has a very cultivated mind.*

cultured having a (high) degree of culture: *What a cultured girl she is; she loves music and painting.*

delicate refined, careful, and precise [⇒ N212]: *She expressed her opinion in a very delicate way, so as to offend no one.* **-ly** [adv] **-cacy** [U] the state of being delicate

C168 *adjectives* : **showing social attitudes** [B]

common [Wa1] **1** ordinary: *The common man isn't usually interested in such matters.* **2** *usu deprec* typical of the bad qualities or behaviour of uneducated people who have no feeling for art, beauty, good manners, etc: *The way she speaks is so common! His way of dressing—how common it is!* **-ness** [U]

vulgar 1 having or showing lack of education, delicacy of feeling, etc: *What vulgar people they are!* **2** relating to sex, the sex organs, and the body's waste products in a very or too direct a way: *I wish he'd stop telling all these vulgar jokes to my mother!* **-ly** [adv] **vulgarity 1** [U] the condition of being vulgar **2** [C] a vulgar act

coarse [Wa1] socially rough and undesirable: *What coarse behaviour! He spent the evening getting very drunk and telling coarse jokes.* **-ly** [adv] **-ness** [U]

ill-mannered, *also* **bad-mannered** having bad manners; impolite: *What ill-mannered people they are!*

indelicate *euph* coarse; vulgar: *I'm afraid he used rather indelicate language to describe her.* **-ly** [adv]

rude [Wa1] not at all polite; wishing or serving to insult: *What rude language he uses! It's rude to say you don't like her food, when she took so much trouble preparing it. Don't be rude!* **-ly** [adv] **-ness** [U]

low-bred not respectable; rude; coming from the lowest social classes: *He is a low-bred fellow, don't speak to him.*

low-class *deprec* belonging to the lower classes and therefore socially unsatisfactory: *What low-class people he has for friends!*

ill-bred showing that a person has been badly brought up: *That was a very ill-bred remark, young man.*

gauche [Wa2] socially awkward: *He's rather gauche; he hasn't found his feet socially yet.* **-ness** [U]

uncouth coarse, awkward, and uncultured: *What an uncouth fellow he is!— He never seems to say or do anything right.* **-ly** [adv] **-ness** [U]

boorish uncouth; behaving like a boor [⇒ C169]: *He is a very boorish fellow.* **-ly** [adv] **-ness** [U]

C169 *nouns* : **persons considered of low social standing** [C]

ruffian a rough, bad, perhaps violent man: *He was attacked in the street by several ruffians.*

boor a coarse, bad-mannered person: *They are boors; they have no manners whatever.*

lout a rough, bad-mannered, awkward man: *He is a lout and doesn't understand these things.*

hooligan a noisy, rough person who causes trouble by fighting, breaking things, etc

ragamuffin *esp old use* a dirty young child in torn clothes

savage an uncivilized and undeveloped person, esp one who is fierce and violent: *The savages who lived on that island used to eat people.*

barbarian an uncivilized or uncultured person: *Those people are barbarians; they have destroyed that beautiful building.*

philistine a person who does not understand (and actively dislikes) art, music, and beautiful things, and is proud or content to remain in this condition: *As far as good music is concerned he's a philistine.*

peasant 1 (now used only or mainly of underdeveloped countries or esp historically) a person who works on the land, esp one who owns and lives on a small piece of land: *The local lords often treated the peasants badly. She was wearing colourful peasant dress.* **2** *derog* a person without education or manners: *Don't worry about what these peasants think.* **peasantry** [GU] the peasants of a place

yokel *humor or derog* a simple or foolish person living in the country: *You don't expect these (country) yokels to understand, do you?*

C170 *nouns* : **persons with no fixed home** [C]

vagrant 1 a person who leads a wandering life, usually without a job and often begging for food, shelter, etc **2** *law* anyone (such as a drunken person) who is found by the police wandering about without any lawful means of support: *The policeman arrested three vagrants.* **vagrancy** [U] the offence of being a vagrant

vagabond a person who lives an irregular or wandering life, esp one who is thought to be lazy or worthless: *The townspeople threatened to put vagabonds in jail.*

tramp *often derog* a person who lives a wandering life, with no home or job

hobo *also* **bum** *esp AmE* a tramp

beggar a person who does not or cannot work to get money, food, etc but asks people to give them to him or her: *The city streets were full of noisy beggars.* **2** *infml, sometimes affec or deprec* person; animal: *Poor beggar, he has a lot of troubles. That dog's a friendly little beggar, isn't he?*

dropout a person who turns away from (**drops**

out of) society: *The old house was a home for dropouts taking drugs.*

hippie, hippy *sl* a dropout, usu young, who wears unusual clothes and adopts unusual living habits to show his attitudes to conventional [⇒ C166] people

nomad 1 a member of a tribe which travels about, esp to find grass for its animals to eat: *The nomads of central Asia have travelled from place to place with their animals for thousands of years.* **2** a person who habitually wanders: *He walked across Europe for three months, but in the end he got tired of being a nomad.* **nomadic** [B] of or like a nomad **-ally** [adv Wa4]

gipsy, gypsy 1 [*sometimes cap*] a person belonging to a tribe of people whose families can be found travelling in many parts of Europe: *The Gipsies came originally from India. He likes gipsy music.* **2** a person behaving or looking like one of these; a nomad (def **2**)

C171 *adjectives* : **relating to formality and dignity** [B]

formal keeping to the rules and conventions [⇒ C182] of behaviour: *He paid a formal call on the American ambassador, in return for the ambassador's formal visit earlier in the year. This ceremony is purely formal; it has no practical value. I'll write you a formal reply to your suggestions later, but will give you my ideas informally now.* **-ly** [adv] **formality 1** [U] the condition of being formal **2** [C] any formal act or requirement

stiff [Wa1] formal and tense [⇒ B88]: *He gave a stiff little bow. Her manner was stiff and artificial throughout the ceremony.* **-ly** [adv] **-ness** [U]

dignified calm, serious, and showing social importance: *He walks in a very dignified way, like a king. You look very dignified in that uniform.* **dignity** [U] the state or condition of being dignified: *He is a man of great dignity.*

stately grand and dignified (and therefore slow in movement): *The duke lives in one of the stately homes of England. The great ship continued its stately progress into the harbour. She has a very stately manner.* **-liness** [U]

pompous so formal and/or dignified as to be (a little) silly; showing too much self-importance: *He was very pompous at the meeting, wasn't he? She behaves in a very pompous way on these occasions.* **-ly** [adv] **-ness** [U], **pomposity** [U] the condition of being pompous: *The old man's pomposity annoyed us all.*

majestic having the style of a king, etc: *What a majestic place the palace is!* **-ally** [adv Wa4]

C172 *adjectives* : **relating to informality** [B]

informal not formal; without ceremony; belonging to more relaxed social situations: *What*

dress should we wear at the party—formal or informal? He likes to keep these meetings informal and friendly. In informal situations people often use different words from those used in more formal situations. **-ly** [adv] **informality** [U] the state of being informal

casual very informal and relaxed: *He prefers casual clothes; he doesn't like getting all dressed up. Her manner was casual; she didn't seem to think the matter important.* **-ly** [adv] **-ness** [U]

offhand so casual as to be impolite: *His reply was rather offhand; he obviously didn't think seriously about it. Don't be so offhand and impolite to these people.* **-edly** [adv] **-edness** [U]

Law and order generally

C180 *nouns* : **rules and laws**

rule [C] a principle or order which guides behaviour, says how things are to be done, etc (and is expected to be obeyed for any reason): *These are the rules of the game; if you play it any other way it's a different game. Please keep to the club rules.*

regulation [C] an esp official rule or order: *The regulations are quite clear; you cannot enter the building without permission. I am tired of all these rules and regulations telling me what I must and must not do!*

law 1 [C] a rule that is supported by the power of government and that governs the behaviour of members of society: *I haven't broken any law, have I?* **2** [U; *the* R] the whole body of such rules in a country: *The law forbids stealing. English law is different from Scots law. It's against the law to do that.* **3** [U] the condition of society when such a body of rules is generally respected and obeyed: *Law and order break(s) down when too many people are discontented.* **4** [U] the whole body of these rules and the way in which they work: *He is studying law.* **5** [U *sometimes cap*] the body of people who have studied these rules and whose job it is to see that they are put into effect properly: *You'll get into trouble with the law if you do that.* **6** [U] the operation of these rules in court, as in punishing criminals and deciding claims: *It is a question of law, not a question of fact.* **7** [U] the body of these rules concerned with a particular subject: *He's interested in business law.* **8** [C] a generally accepted rule of behaviour; a convention: *It's a social law that people don't stand too close to each other when talking.* **9** [C] a rule of action in a sport, art, business, etc **10** [C] a statement expressing what has been seen always to happen in certain conditions: *Boyle's law is a scientific principle.* **11** [*the* GU *sometimes cap*] *infml* the police or a policeman: *The law was/were there in force.*

statute [C] *fml* an established law or rule, esp a written law made by a law-making body such as Parliament: *Their statutes cover most matters of importance to them.*

decree [C] an order given by a ruler or a government and having the force of a law: *The new government decrees forbid demonstrations* [⇒ C131] *and demand hard work from the people.*

ordinance [C] *fml* a law or decree: *The emergency ordinances require people to be off the streets by midnight.*

by(e)law [C] a law or regulation made by an authority such as a town council, a railway company, etc: *The local bylaws about dogs state that they must be locked up at night.*

standing orders [P] rules and regulations (usu in an army, police force, etc) which remain in force until officially changed: *Standing orders in the camp forbid smoking in these buildings.*

C181 nouns : bills and acts

bill [C] the form or draft (= first written form) of a new law going before a legislature [⇒ C187]: *The Members of Parliament voted on the new bill.*

act [C] a law made by a legislature: *The bill is now an act and part of the law of the land. The Reform Act of 1832 was very important in British history.*

constitution [C] the laws and principles according to which a state is governed: *Great Britain has an unwritten constitution, while the United States, like most other countries, has a written constitution.* **constitutional** [Wa5;B] of or concerning a constitution **un-** [*neg*] **-ly** [adv]

code [C] **1** an official body of laws: *The legal code clearly indicates the penalties for such behaviour. Have you studied the Highway Code?—You need to know it to pass your driving test.* **2** a set of often unwritten conventions by which people work or live: *The police force has its own special code of conduct.*

jurisprudence [U] *fml* the science or knowledge of law

jurisdiction [U] **1** the power held by an official or an official body, esp in a court of law: *That official has no jurisdiction outside the city.* **2** the right to use such power: *The prisoner refused to accept the jurisdiction of the court.* **3** the limits of this right (*esp in the phrs* **within/outside someone's jurisdiction**): *The minister cannot help you in a case that lies outside his jurisdiction.*

C182 nouns : conventions, orders, and precedents

convention [C;U] a general agreement, not talked about much, to do something in a certain way: *It used to be (the) convention for women to wear hats in church. Many old conventions have been replaced by new ones.*

order [C;*by* U] any spoken or written statement which must be obeyed: *You have your orders; carry them out. The work was done by order of the king.*

ruling [C] a decision by a judge, chairman, etc, which is accepted by everyone concerned: *The judge gave his ruling on the matter.*

precedent [C] an earlier happening, ruling, order, or law which can be taken as an example or rule for what comes later: *There is no precedent in law for this kind of thing. This action will establish a bad precedent for others. What he has done is without precedent.* **unprecedented** [Wa5;B] having no precedent: *This action is quite unprecedented.*

custom **1** [U] things as they are usually done in a society: *Custom affects people strongly; most of us don't like going against custom.* **2** [C] any action which is usu done in a society or by a person: *Shaking hands when people meet is much more the custom in France than in Britain. It is her custom to go there once a month. He is interested in old local customs.* **3** [U] the habit of going to a particular shop to buy things: *You'll lose a lot of custom if you raise the prices so much.*

institution [C] *fml* a custom, habit, etc which has been in existence for a long time: *Marriage is an institution in most societies.* (*fig & humor*) *That old man has been coming here so long that he's become a local institution!*

usage **1** [U] the way in which a thing is done, esp socially; custom: *It isn't the usage here to do that; local usage is different.* **2** [U] the way of using words, language, etc: *Usage changes as time passes.* **3** [C] a way in which words, etc are used: *Many English usages are difficult for foreigners to understand.*

principle **1** [C, C5] a general truth or belief that is used as a base for reasoning or action or for the development of further ideas: *the principle of freedom of speech; One of the principles of this book is that explanations should be in simple language. Reasoning from the false principle that the earth was flat, people formerly thought there was a danger of falling off its edge.* **2** [C, C5] **a** a law of nature as scientifically discovered and stated: *the principle of Archimedes* **b** such a law as governing the making or working of a machine, apparatus, etc: *A bicycle and a motorbike are built on the same principle though the force that moves them is different.* **3** [C, C5] a rule used by a person as a guide for action; habit based on some fixed belief: *It's a principle of mine not to eat between meals. She acts on the principle that it's pleasanter to make others wait than to be early and wait for them.* **4** [U] strong belief in and practice of honourable behaviour: *My father was a man of principle who would never do anything dishonest or unfair.*

standard [C] a principle or condition, often in judging, measuring, etc, by which various things can be judged: *The standard of length in France is the metre. Sweden has a high standard of living. What standards does he have in life; is* *he honest? Those houses are badly built; they are well below standard/below the necessary standard.* **substandard** [Wa5;B] below the necessary standard: *He builds substandard houses; don't buy one.*

criterion [C] a standard by which one can judge something: *By what criteria do you judge a good cook?*

C183 *verbs* : **ruling and ordering**

rule [T5; L9] to give (as) a decision: *The chairman ruled on the matter, and his decision was accepted. He ruled that the money be returned to the woman.*

decree [T1, 5] to state in or by means of a decree: *The king decreed the use of the army. He decreed that there would be no further taxes on salt.*

order [T1, 5] to state as an order: *He ordered the men's imprisonment. He ordered that the men be put in prison.*

C184 *verbs* : **making laws**

enact [T1 *often pass*] to make (something) into a law: *This new law was enacted last year.* **enactment 1** [U] the act of enacting **2** [C] something enacted; a law

legislate [I∅] to make a law or laws: *We must legislate against these practices. Parliament legislates for the nation.*

pass [T1] to make (a law): *The legislature passed the Reform Bill and it is now the Reform Act. New laws have been passed to protect our citizens.*

dispense [T1] to provide: *The judges dispensed the law impartially, favouring no one.* **dispensation 1** [U] the act of dispensing: *The proper dispensation of the law is important.* **2** [C] an example or result of this **3** [C] a special statement of permission to do something which is normally not allowed

repeal [T1] to put a official end to a law: *The legislature repealed the unpopular Rent Act.*

annul [T1] to make no longer legal or legitimate [⇒ C189]: *Her marriage has been annulled. This unjust law must be annulled.* **annulment 1** [U] the act of annulling something: *She is hoping for the annulment of her marriage.* **2** [C] an example or result of this: *She got an annulment (of her marriage).*

C185 *verbs* : **keeping the law** [T1]

keep to make sure that (law and order, etc) continue: *The police are employed to keep law and order. The policeman advised the man to keep the peace and to go home quietly.*

maintain *also* **uphold** *fml* to keep: *It is a policeman's job to maintain law and order. He has upheld the law in these parts for many years.*

maintenance [U] the action of maintaining esp the law

enforce *emph* to keep by using force if necessary: *The police exist to enforce the law.* **enforcement** [U] the act or intention of enforcing esp the law: *The police are a law-enforcement organization.*

C186 *verbs* : **not keeping the law** [T1]

break not to keep (a law, etc); to go actively against: *If you do this, you will be breaking the law. He broke the speed limit by driving his car at 80 mph.*

contravene *fml & tech* to go against; break: *The policeman told the hotel-keeper that he had contravened the fire regulations for small hotels by locking the doors.* **contravention** [U; C] the act or an act of contravening

commit *tech* to do (something wrong): *He was arrested for committing several crimes. She has committed murder and must be punished.*

C187 *nouns* : **justice and law-making**

justice [U] **1** the quality of being right and fair, esp in law: *The king was famous for his justice.* **2** the law and its administration [⇒C100] **3** the action or power of the law: *The police brought the criminals to justice.* **injustice 1** [U] lack of justice **2** [C] any instance of such a lack of justice: *'These injustices must end!' he cried.*

law-making [U] the business of making or passing laws: *Parliament is a body engaged in law-making/a law-making body.*

legislation [U] *fml* **1** law-making: *Parliament is normally engaged in legislation and debating.* **2** the laws made: *This new legislation will help the poor.* **legislative** [Wa5;B] for the purpose of making laws

legislature 1 [C] a law-making body: *Parliament is the British legislature and Congress is the US legislature.* **2** [U] *fml & tech rare* law-making: *Has there been any recent legislature on this matter?* [⇒ C103]

C188 *nouns* : **order and disorder in societies**

order [U] a condition of the least possible social trouble; a state of controlled planning, behaviour, etc: *The news could disturb the whole social order. Their behaviour is contrary to good military order and discipline.*

law and order [U; P] a condition of good government and social order: *Criminals operate against the forces of law and order.*

martial law [U] government under special laws by the army, esp when there has been fighting against the usual government: *The governor of the province declared (a state of) martial law. The province was under martial law for a month.*

disorder [U] a condition of social trouble and lack of organization: *The riots led to greater national disorder.*

anarchy [U] absence of government, control, or order; lawlessness and social and political disorder: *The country is in a state of increasing anarchy.* **anarchical** [B] of, concerning, or like anarchy

chaos [U] complete disorder: *The country slowly sank into chaos. The administration is in a state of chaos because of strikes.* **chaotic** [B] of, concerning, or like chaos **-ally** [adv Wa4]

civil war [U; C] a war or state of war between opposing groups of people in the same country: *Civil war is a terrible thing. That country has had many civil wars.*

civil strife [U] trouble in a country which comes close to or includes civil war

C189 adjectives : relating to the law

legal [Wa5;B] **1** allowed or made by law: *Is it legal for boys of that age to drink alcohol?* (= alcoholic drinks) **2** of, concerning, or using the law: *All his legal business is handled by a New York law firm.* **-ly** [adv] **-ity** [U] **legalize, -ise** [T1] to make legal: *Abortion* [⇒B181] *has been legalized in many countries.*

lawful [Wa5;B] **1** *often emot* allowed by law: *I don't know if it's lawful for you to be in this place.* **2** *tech* recognized by law: *Is their marriage lawful? This building is a place of lawful assembly. He was going about his lawful business when it happened.* **-ly** [adv] **-ness** [U]

legitimate [B] **1** allowed by law: *Their actions were perfectly legitimate, and the police cannot stop them.* **2** [Wa5] born to a mother who is married: *He has three legitimate children and two bastards* [⇒ C3]. **-acy** [U]

licit [Wa5;B] *rare & fml* legal; permitted

forensic [Wa5;A] relating to or used in courts of law: *He is an expert in forensic medicine.*

judicial [B] **1** [Wa5] relating to or done by a court of law, a judge, etc: *This is a judicial and not a medical matter: you need a lawyer, not a doctor. Judicial proceedings in courts of law are often slow.* **2** having the qualities of a judge: *He has a very judicial approach to such matters.* **-ly** [adv]

juridical [Wa5;B] *fml & tech* of or related to the law or to judges

official [B] being done because of or having some special legal authority, esp from or in a government, organization, etc: *The chief minister made an official visit to the town. She received an official letter from the committee.* **un-** [neg] **-ly** [adv]

C190 adjectives : against the law

illegal [Wa5;B] clearly against the law: *These are illegal acts and will lead to your arrest.* **-ly** [adv] **-ity** [U]

illegitimate [B] **1** against the law: *Seizing his ship was an illegitimate act.* **2** not allowed by the rules: *It's illegitimate to use force in a situation like this.* **3** [Wa5] born to a mother who is not married: *The child is illegitimate and we don't know who the father is.* [⇒ C3 BASTARD]

illicit [Wa5;B] not acceptable in law or convention [⇒ C182]: *He engaged in an illicit love affair.*

unlawful [B] *esp emot & tech* against the law: *He was arrested for the unlawful possession of firearms.* **-ly** [adv] **-ness** [U]

lawless [B] **1** (of a country or place) not governed by laws; not obeying the (or any) law(s): *Your life isn't safe on those lawless mountain roads.* **2** uncontrolled: *He is a wild, lawless fellow; be careful not to anger him.* **-ly** [adv] **-ness** [U]

disorderly [B] **1** (esp of people) behaving badly, esp in public: *The football crowds were very disorderly.* **2** (of things and persons) untidy: *What a disorderly room; she must be pretty disorderly herself!*

C191 adjectives : required by law, etc [Wa5;B]

statutory (to be done) according to a statute or law: *The government have a statutory obligation to collect taxes.*

obligatory which must be done; necessary under the law: *Is it obligatory to have a safety belt in a car?* **-rily** [adv] [⇒ F63 OBLIGATION]

compulsory which must be done for any reason: *You must go; it's compulsory and you'll be fined if you don't.* **-rily** [adv]

mandatory **1** which must be done or must be so: *It's mandatory to pay these debts within a certain period of time.* **2** containing or carrying a command

enforceable that can be enforced (esp by law): *I'm afraid these laws aren't enforceable; we just don't have enough inspectors/policemen to do it.*

binding which must be done or kept to because of an earlier agreement: *These clauses of the contract were legally binding the moment you signed the paper.*

voluntary **1** (of a person or his actions) acting or done willingly, without payment and/or without (the doer) being forced: *She's a voluntary worker at the hospital. She does voluntary work looking after old people. His offer was entirely voluntary; nobody pushed him. He made a voluntary statement to the police, admitting his guilt.* **2** [A] controlled or supported by people who give their money, services, etc of their own free will: *Many social services are still provided by voluntary societies.* **-ly** [adv]

C192 verbs : letting and allowing

let [V2; T1] to allow (to do or happen): *Let him*

go. Let me see it. Don't let her leave. The police let them have the book.

allow 1 [T1, 4; V3] *often fml* to let (somebody) do something or let (something) be done: *They do not allow smoking in this place/you to smoke in this place. You are allowed into the room. I have spent more (money) than I was allowed. We must allow him to be a member of our team.* **2** [T1; V3] to make possible; provide: *This plan allows 20 minutes for lunch. Your gift allows me to buy a car.* **3** [D1; T1] to give (esp money or time): *My father allows me some money for books. I can allow you 10% off the price if you pay now. The bank allows 5% on money kept with them.*

permit 1 [T1; V3] *usu fml* to allow: *I cannot permit such cruelty. I have too much to do to permit my going on holiday. (polite) Permit me to inform you that you are wrong.* **2** [I0] to make it possible for a stated thing to happen: *I will come in June if my health permits. Weather permitting (= if the weather is good enough), we'll come and see you.* **3** [X9] to allow to be or to come, etc: *She won't permit dogs in the house.*

license, *also sometimes* **licence** [T1] to allow officially: *They have licensed the restaurant for the sale of alcoholic drinks. Is this shop licensed (for the sale of firearms)?*

authorize, -ise 1 [T1; V3] to give power to: *I authorized him to act for me while I was away.* **2** [T1] to permit by some special power: *I authorized the payment of this bill.*

grant [D1; T1] to agree to give, allow, authorize, etc: *The governor granted the prisoner one request. He has been granted his freedom on condition he leaves the country. She was granted a widow's pension when her husband was accidentally killed. They granted permission to build the house.*

sanction [T1] *fml* to permit: *They officially sanctioned the work.*

warrant [Wv6; T1] to give someone a reason for doing or thinking (a stated thing); have a right to do (a stated thing): *Your plan certainly warrants careful attention. His position in the government does not warrant these actions; they are against the law.*

C193 *verbs* : **not letting or allowing**

refuse [T1,3; D1; I0] to say or show that one will not (accept, do, or give): *We asked him but he refused to go. She refused. He refused me the book. The government have refused (them) permission to build here.*

deny [D1; T1] to refuse to grant: *His request for help was denied. The government has denied the local authorities' requests for more money.*

revoke [T1] to take away or back (any special freedom, permission, etc): *His licence to trade here has been revoked by the local officials; he must stop trading immediately.*

C194 *nouns* : **licences and permits**

licence *BrE*, **license** *AmE* **1** [C, C3] an official paper, card, etc, showing that permission has been given to do something, usu in return for a fixed payment: *Can I see your driving licence, please? He has a licence for his gun/dog.* **2** [C, C3] permission given, esp officially, to do something: *He has a licence from the government to trade in these parts.* **3** [U, U3] freedom of action, speech, thought, etc: *We do not have as much licence to say these things in our country as in yours.* **4** [U] *deprec* misuse of freedom, esp in causing harm or damage; uncontrolled behaviour: *His actions weren't moderate; they were acts of licence.*

permit [C, C3] an official written statement giving one the right to do something: *You can't enter the military camp without a permit. Who issued the permits for entering the camp? The motorists show their parking permits on the windscreens of their cars.*

permission [U, U3] the act of permitting or being permitted: *Do you have permission to visit him in hospital? He went there without our permission. With your permission I'll leave now.*

authority [U, U3] right given to someone to do something: *He has the authority to put them in prison. By whose authority have you come here? He did it on his own authority; no one told him to. They had the authority of the Government behind them.*

authorization, -isation 1 [U, U3] the right or official power to do something: *I have the owner's authorization to use the house.* **2** [C, C3] a paper giving this right: *Show me your official authorizations, please.*

sanction [U] permission by someone in authority to do something: *The work was done with/without official sanction.*

pass [C] a piece of paper with printing, which shows that one is permitted to do a certain thing (such as travel on a railway, leave an army camp for a short time, etc) esp without paying: *Show me your pass, please. He entered the camp without a proper pass.*

passport [C] **1** a small official book, obtained from a government by one of its citizens, to be shown when entering or coming back from a foreign country, etc **2** [(to)] (*fig*) something (a quality, connection, name, etc) that permits a person easily to do or get something else: *He thought that money was a passport to happiness.*

visa [C] a stamp or signed note in a passport or a paper, which shows that a person is free to enter and/or leave a place, usu a foreign country: *You need a visa to go to that country. He has an entry permit/visa.*

warrant 1 [C (*for*), C3] a written legal permit to do something: *He has a warrant to search the house. Does he have a search warrant? The police have a warrant for his arrest [⇒ C226]. The governor of the prison made out the death* *warrants for the condemned* [⇒ G106] *men.* **2** [U *(for),* U3] authority or right: *What warrant do you have for these actions? You have no warrant for saying those things.*

charter [C] a written or printed statement made, esp formerly, by some authority which gives someone a particular power, right, etc: *The town's charter goes back to the time of King James and it gives the town a number of special rights.* **chartered** [Wa5;A;(B)] having a charter, licence, etc: *He is a chartered accountant* (= he can officially work as an accountant).

C195 *verbs* : **forbidding and banning things**

forbid 1 [V3] to order (esp someone) not to do something: *I forbade him to go.* **2** [T1, 4] to refuse to allow: *I forbid this marriage! Entry is forbidden to unauthorized people.*

prohibit [T1] *fml & official* to forbid: *Smoking is prohibited in these buildings.*

ban [T1] to make unlawful; to order not to be done, used, etc: *The government has banned demonstrations. Those books should be banned. The play was banned by the censor* [⇒ C196].

outlaw [T1] **1** *esp formerly* to declare to be an outlaw [⇒ C228]: *They outlawed him because of his crimes.* **2** to declare unlawful: *Drugs like opium* [⇒ E87] *have been outlawed except for medical purposes.*

censor [T1] (of books, films, etc) to prevent being seen or to cut out parts which are not considered suitable: *His book has been censored; it is impossible to get copies of it. 'These films full of sex and violence should be properly censored,' he said.*

ostracize, -ise [T1] to refuse to have social dealings with: *He was ostracized by the people in the town.*

shun [T1, 4] *emot* to avoid seeing, having, etc: *She shunned him when she heard what terrible things he had done. He shuns meat; he only eats vegetables and fruit.*

C196 *nouns, etc* : **banning things**

prohibition 1 [U] the act of prohibiting: *The prohibition of smoking in these places has improved people's health considerably. Prohibition was a period in US history when alcohol was prohibited.* **2** [C] an act or order prohibiting anything: *She's tired of his various prohibitions on what she can do and where she can go.*

ban [C] an order which bans: *There's a ban on books like that. The government has lifted the ban on buying and selling gold.*

ostracism [U] the situation of ostracizing or being ostracized: *Social ostracism can be a terrible thing.*

taboo [C;B] (something) which is forbidden by religious belief, law, etc: *Among Hindus there is a taboo against killing cows. Killing cows is taboo/is a taboo act among the Hindus.*

censor [C] an official with the authority to examine and censor books, letters, films, etc: *The board of film censors studied the film carefully and ordered several cuts.*

censorship [U] the position, duties, etc of a censor; the act of censoring: *Censorship is generally a difficult thing to do well.*

C197 *nouns & verbs* : **blockades and sanctions**

blockade 1 [C] the act of surrounding a town, area, etc to stop people or food etc moving in or out: *The enemy blockade caused much suffering in the city.* **2** [T1] to surround in this way: *The enemy ships blockaded the harbour.*

boycott 1 [T1] to join in an agreement not to work with, talk to, do business with, etc (a person, group, or country): *They boycotted the other country's goods.* **2** [C] an act of boycotting: *They have placed a boycott on our goods.*

embargo [C] an official order which forbids trade etc with people, a country, etc: *There is an embargo on trade with that country.*

sanctions [P] actions taken against one country by others as punishment, usu including not doing business with that country

Courts of law and legal work

C200 *nouns* : **in the courtroom**

court (of law) *also* **law court** [C; prep U] a place where (criminal) cases are heard: *You will be fairly tried in a court of law. The law courts are situated near the city centre. The prisoner is in court now.*

courtroom [C] a room in which a (criminal) case is being heard: *The judge entered the courtroom.*

tribunal [C] **1** a special court of law, esp in an army, etc: *A military tribunal sentenced the terrorists to death.* **2** a court with specially appointed people as judges with powers to deal with particular matters: *The tenant* [⇒ D64] *took her case to the rents tribunal so that a fair rent would be fixed for the flat.*

bench [*the* R] **1** the area where a judge sits **2** (*fig*) judges generally

bar [*the* R] a railing or barrier in a law court, between the part where the legal business is done and the part where people can watch and listen   **prisoner at the bar** the accused [⇒ C207] person   **to be tried at the bar** to be tried in an open court, not secretly

dock [*the* R] the closed area in a criminal court where the prisoner is kept

C201 nouns : **lawyers, etc** [C]

lawyer a person whose business it is to advise people about laws and to represent them in court: *I want to speak to my lawyer before I sign these papers.*

solicitor (esp in England) a lawyer who advises his customers on matters of law, appears in the lower courts, and prepares written agreements and cases for the higher courts

attorney *esp AmE* a lawyer **power of attorney** the power to act for another person, esp in matters of law and business, given by means of an official warrant [⇒ C194] (**letter of attorney**)

barrister (esp in England) a lawyer who has the right of speaking and arguing in the higher courts of law **2** [*the* GU, *cap*] **a** (in Britain) (the members of) the profession of barrister **b** (in the USA) (the members of) the profession of lawyer **be called to the bar** to become a barrister/lawyer

advocate 1 a person, esp a lawyer, who speaks in defence of or in favour of another person **2** (in Scotland) a barrister **3** [(*of*)] a person who speaks for or supports an idea, way of life, etc: *He is an advocate of cold baths in the morning.*

counsel [GU] one or more lawyers acting for someone in a court of law: *He asked counsel for the defence to explain the point.*

jurist a person, usu a lawyer, with a thorough knowledge of law: *They consulted a leading jurist on the matter.*

notary (public) an official who has the authority to act as an official witness to the signing of papers, etc

C202 nouns : **judges and juries** [C]

judge 1 a public official who has the power to decide questions brought before a court of law: *He is a judge of the High Court/a High Court judge.* **2** a person who has the right to make a decision, esp in a competition: *He has often been a judge in these flower shows.* **3** a person who has the knowledge and experience to give valuable opinions: *I'm no judge of music, but I know what I like.*

magistrate an official who has the power to judge cases in the lowest courts of law, esp a police court: *The boy comes up before the magistrate next week.*

justice of the peace *tech* a magistrate: *He spoke to several justices of the peace.* **JP** *abbrev*

justice 1 *AmE* a judge (of a law court) **2** a judge of high rank, in a Supreme Court: *The Lord Chief Justice will give his decision shortly.* **3** (used as a part of the title of a judge of a law court): *Mr Justice Smith has been made Chief Justice.*

squire (the title of) a local justice of the peace or judge in a country district or small town in the USA

sheriff 1 an official who is in charge of justice in a county in the USA **2** the chief judge of a district in Scotland **3** (in England, formerly) a judge appointed by the king in each county

jury [GC] **1** a group of usu 12 people chosen to decide questions of fact in a court of law, and who have solemnly promised to give an honest opinion: *Members of the jury, you must now give your verdict* [⇒ C204]. **2** a group of people chosen to judge a competition of any kind, and pick the winner: *He was on the TV jury which picked the winning girls.* (*fig*) *He faced the jury of public opinion.* **juror, juryman** a member of a jury **jury box** the enclosed place where the jury sit during a law case

C203 verbs : **taking someone to court**

sue [I0; T1] to bring a claim in law against, esp for an amount of money: *If you do that, I'll sue (you).*

go to law [I0] to begin a case in law on a matter that concerns one: *Please don't go to law over this business; it isn't worth it.*

take .. to court *infml* to sue: *She took them to court to get her money back.*

litigate [I0] *fml & tech* to go to law; to make a claim in a court of law **litigant** [C] a person engaged in a lawsuit

charge [T1, 5] to declare officially and openly that one thinks (someone) has broken the law or done something wrong: *The police are going to charge him with murder.*

accuse [Wv5; T1 (*of*)] to charge (someone) with doing wrong or breaking the law; blame: *The police accused him (of murder). He was accused of running away when the enemy attacked. The angry man gave her an accusing look. The accused man stood up.*

C204 nouns : **lawsuits and pleas**

lawsuit [C] a non-criminal [⇒ C228] case in a court of law

(legal/court) action [C] a process of law in a court of law

(legal) proceedings [P] legal action: *He has taken legal proceedings against her and is suing for divorce.*

litigation [U] *fml & tech* action in law, as in making and defending claims in court

case [C] a matter which a judge or other person in a court of law decides on: *This is one of the most interesting cases in legal history. The lawyer put the case simply. This is a case of murder/a murder case.*

charge [C] a statement that a person has done wrong (esp as made by the police or in a court of law): *What is the charge?—The charge is dangerous driving.*

accusation [C] an act of accusing or being accused: *What is his accusation? She made several accusations against me.*

writ [C] an official paper given in law to tell someone to do or not to do a particular thing

(court) injunction [C, C3] an esp written order, stronger than a writ, from a court of law, demanding that something will or will not be done: *I'll get an injunction to stop you doing that!*

interdict (in Scotland) an injunction

plea [C] a legal statement made by or for a person charged in a court of law: *The prisoner's plea was 'not guilty'.*

verdict [C] **1** the official decision made by a jury in a court of law, declared to the judge at the end of a trial: *Ladies and gentlemen of the jury, what is your verdict – guilty or not guilty?* (*fig infml*) *The general verdict was that her party was most enjoyable.*

C205 *nouns & verbs* : **trials and hearings**

trial [C] an examination of a person or a point of law in a court: *His trial is fixed for the 19th of the month. The book describes a number of famous murder trials.*

court-martial 1 [C; *by* U] the trial of a person in the armed forces for a military offence: *There have been several court-martials this year. He was tried by court-martial and found guilty.* **2** [T1] to put through a court-martial: *The officer was court-martialled for deserting* [⇒ C282] *his men in the battle.*

hearing [C] an occasion or chance to be heard, esp in pleading [⇒ C206] a case: *Please give him a fair hearing! The judicial* [⇒ C189] *hearings will be held in public.*

bail [U] money left with a court of law so that a prisoner may be set free until his trial: *He stood bail of £1,000 for his friend. The prisoner was released on bail.* **bail out** [v adv T1] to pay the bail of (someone held by the police): *We need £100 to bail her out.*

C206 *verbs* : **relating to lawsuits**

try [T1 *often pass*] to examine in law (a person or case): *He was tried for murder. The case was tried in London. We can't try this man; he is mentally unfit to plead.*

hear [T1] *tech* to listen to (something, esp a case or evidence) as part of a trial, hearing, etc: *The court heard the evidence for the accused. Which judge is to hear the case?*

plead *tech* **1** [T1] (of lawyers) to present (someone's case) to a court of law: *He needs a good lawyer to plead his case.* **2** [I0; T1] to put forward (as) a plea: *We must plead insanity; otherwise he will be convicted and executed. 'How do you plead?' the judge asked.— 'Not guilty, my Lord/your Honour.'* **3** [I0] to address a court of law as an advocate: *He will plead for the defence.* **plead guilty/not guilty** to admit/deny that one is guilty

defend [T1; I0] to act as a lawyer for (the person who has been charged) in court: *The barrister defended him in court. Who is defending in this case?*

prosecute 1 [T1; I0] to bring a criminal charge against (someone) in a court of law: *He was prosecuted for stealing.* **2** [I0] (of a lawyer) to represent in court the person who is bringing the criminal charge against someone: *Who is prosecuting in this case?*

C207 *verbs & nouns* : **relating to courts of law**

appeal 1 [I0] to call on a higher court to change the decision of a lower court: *I will appeal against his being found guilty. She intends to appeal (to a higher court).* **2** [C] an act of appealing: *His appeal will be heard next month. She lost her appeal, and had to pay the fine.*

prosecution 1 [U] an action of prosecuting or state of being prosecuted by law: *If you break into that building you will risk prosecution.* **2** [C] an example of this: *A number of prosecutions have been started against this man but he always gets off.* **3** [(*the*) GU] the person or group who are concerned with bringing a criminal charge against someone in a court: *A famous lawyer is appearing for the prosecution. She is a witness for the prosecution/a prosecution witness.*

defence *BrE*, **defense** *AmE* **1** [U] the legal argument used to defend someone or something in a court of law: *The defence was weak and the prosecution easily destroyed it.* **2** [(*the*) GU] the person or group who are concerned in defending a criminal charge in a court: *A famous lawyer is appearing for the defence. She is a witness for the defence/a defence witness.*

plaintiff [C] a person who brings a charge against somebody in court

defendant [C] a person against whom a legal action is brought: *The defendant was found guilty.*

accused [Wa5; *the* + GU] a person charged with a crime, etc: *The judge asked the accused to stand up. Several of the accused were found guilty.*

witness [C] **1** a person who is present when something happens: *She was a witness of the accident. There were no witnesses, I'm afraid.* **2** a person who tells in a court of law what he saw, etc happening: *The judge asked the witness to speak louder.*

C208 *nouns* : **evidence and behaviour in court**

evidence [U] anything which helps to prove something in a court of law: *The evidence strongly suggests that he was involved in the crime.*

testimony [U;C] a statement, esp in court, telling what happened in a situation, etc: *The witness's testimony sounded convincing; we believed it/him.*

perjury 1 [U] the act of telling lies on purpose, esp in a court of law: *A person found guilty of perjury might be sent to prison.* **2** [C] a lie told on purpose, esp in a court of law **perjure oneself** to commit perjury: *Don't perjure yourself for his sake.*

contempt (of court) [U] the offence of behaving badly in words or actions in a court of law, esp by disobeying an order: *He was found guilty of contempt of court, because he shouted repeatedly at the judge.*

C209 *adjectives* : **responsible, guilty, and innocent**

responsible 1 [F (*for*, *to*)] being in control of or causing anything so as to be blamed if things do not go well afterwards: *He is the captain of the ship and is responsible for (the safety of) everyone on board. I am not responsible for her behaviour! You will be held fully responsible for anything that happens.* **2** [B] showing a willingness to be given trust or authority: *She is a responsible adult and can be given the job. The child is very responsible for his age and looks after his sister well.* **-bly** [adv] *She behaves very responsibly.* **responsibility 1** [U] the state of being responsible: *You must accept full responsibility if anything happens to the child. She has no sense of responsibility; don't ask her to help.* **2** [C] something one is responsible for: *Keeping the house clean is one of his responsibilities.* **ir-** [*neg*] **-bility** [U]

guilty 1 [Wa1;B] responsible for a crime: *He was found guilty and charged. The defendant pleaded 'not guilty.' 'They are guilty men and must be punished,' he said.* **2** [Wa1;A] showing that one is guilty: *The man had a guilty look on his face when they found him in the room.* **-ily** [adv] **guilt** [U] the condition of being guilty: *His guilt was obvious to everybody.* **guiltless** [Wa5;B] *emot & lit* not guilty; innocent

innocent [B] **1** [Wa5] (of people) not responsible for a crime: *He was charged with murder but they found him innocent (of the charge). 'He is an innocent man!' she cried.* **2** (of things) not causing harm: *It was just innocent fun; they meant no harm.* **-ly** [adv] **-nce** [U]

answerable [Wa5;F (*for*, *to*)] having to explain or defend one's actions: *I cannot do as I like; I am answerable to the government for any decision I make. If you do this I won't be answerable for the results.*

liable [Wa5;F] **1** [(*for*)] responsible, esp in law, for paying for something: *He declared that he was not liable for his wife's debts.* **2** [*to*] likely to get: *Thieves are liable to imprisonment if caught. People who walk on the grass here are liable to a fine of £5.* **liability 1** [U] the state of being liable: *It's our liability if the car is dam-*

aged; *we must pay. He has no liability in the matter; the liability is hers.* **2** [C] a person or thing that causes trouble: *These big cars are a real liability; they cost too much to run. In this kind of work he would be a liability; we don't want him.*

accountable [Wa5;F (*for*, *to*)] with the duty of having to give an explanation: *If anything happens to the boy I will hold you accountable. He is accountable in law for what happens here. I'm not accountable to you for my actions.* **-bility** [U]

culpable [B] *fml* deserving blame: *He is guilty of culpable homicide, and will be tried by a court of law.* **-bly** [adv] **-bility** [U]

blameworthy [B] deserving blame: *His blameworthy behaviour led to his appearance in court.* **un-** [*neg*] **-iness** [U]

C210 *verbs* : **punishing and fining** [T1]
[ALSO C250–63]

punish to cause (someone) to suffer for (a crime, misdeed [⇒ C227], or fault): *His father punished him for stealing. Dangerous driving should be punished in some way.*

convict [(*of*)] to find (a person) guilty in court: *He was convicted of dangerous driving. If the court convicts him, he could get five years in prison.*

sentence [(*to*) *often pass*] to give a punishment to: *He was tried and sentenced. They sentenced him to three years' imprisonment. In those days people could be sentenced to death for stealing a sheep.*

fine [*also* D1 *often pass*] to take (money) from (someone) as a punishment: *They fined him heavily for the offence. He was fined £200.*

C211 *verbs* : **not punishing**

let off [v adv T1] to excuse (someone) from punishment, duty, etc: *I'll let you off with a warning this time, but next time you will be punished.*

get off [v adv I0] to escape being punished: *He got off with a warning that he would be severely punished if he did it again.*

release [T1] to allow to go; set free: *The king released all his political prisoners. She was released from jail after serving only two years of a four-year sentence.* [⇒ C165]

acquit [T1] *tech* to let off or release: *The prisoner was acquitted because of lack of evidence against him. The jury returned a verdict of 'not guilty' and the prisoner was acquitted.* **acquittal** [U;C] the act or result of acquitting or being acquitted: *There have been several acquittals lately; there wasn't enough evidence to convict them.*

discharge [T1 (*from*)] to allow (a person) to go: *The judge discharged the prisoner. The aircraft discharged its passengers. I was discharged* *from the army at the end of the war.* **discharge** [U; C] the act, occasion, or result of discharging or being discharged

pardon [T1] to forgive completely: *He has been pardoned and set free. The king pardoned the rebels, but warned them not to give him trouble again.*

clear [T1] to show that (someone) is not guilty: *The lawyer cleared him of the charge of murder. He's been cleared and can't be tried again for the same offence.*

drop [T1] *infml* to give up (a case in law, etc); not continue with: *The lawyer decided to drop the case. Proceedings against him have been dropped through lack of evidence.*

exonerate [T1] to remove all blame from: *After an enquiry, he was exonerated from all blame.*

C212 *verbs* : **inheriting and bequeathing**

inherit 1 [T1] to receive (a property, a title, etc) left by someone who has died: *He inherited a lot of money from his uncle.* **2** [I0] to be the one who receives what is left, or to take possession of what one has a right to: *John inherits and his three sisters get nothing. He inherits when he's 21.* **3** [T1] to receive (qualities of mind or body) from one's parents, etc: *He inherited his good looks from his mother.*

leave [D1 (*to*); T1] to give through a will after the death of the giver: *She left him the house and £5,000. She left everything to a home for cats.*

bequeath [T1] *fml & tech* to leave: *She bequeathed everything to him.*

hand down *also* **pass on** [v adv T1] to pass from one generation [⇨ C17] to the next: *These customs have been handed down from father to son for centuries. She has passed on her love of music to her children. These things have been handed down through seven generations.*

entitle [V3; D1 *to usu pass*] to give someone the right to something, although he or she may not have or get that thing: *He is entitled to get the land; it was his father's. She was fully entitled to the money, but she never got it. This ticket entitles you to enter the sports ground, but it does not entitle you to a seat.*

C213 *nouns* : **inheriting and bequeathing**

inheritance 1 [U] the act of inheriting **2** [C] a property, title, or quality of mind and body received by inheritance: *The lawyer told him to claim his inheritance as soon as possible.*

will [C] the wishes of a person in regard to sharing his property among other people after his death, esp in an official written form: *The lawyer read out the old man's will.* **last will and testament** [C] *fml* a will

legacy [C] **1** money or personal possessions that pass to someone on the death of the owner according to his will: *He received a small legacy in his father's will.* **2** something passed on or left behind by someone else: *This house is her legacy from earlier generations.*

bequest 1 [U] the act of bequeathing **2** [C] something bequeathed: *He left several bequests to his servants and to favourite charities.*

(family) heirloom [C] something handed down in a family for several generations: *These paintings are old family heirlooms.*

entitlement 1 [U] the state of being entitled to something **2** [C] something to which one is entitled: *The money is one of your entitlements.*

C214 *nouns* : **persons inheriting and bequeathing** [C]

benefactor a person doing good to others, esp by leaving money, property, etc in a will

beneficiary a person who receives something in a will: *All the benificiaries (of the will) gathered in the solicitor's office.*

heir [(*to*)] a person legally receiving property, money, a title, etc when another person dies: *He is my son and heir. He left little to his heirs. He fell heir (= became the heir) to a great fortune. The prince is heir to the throne* (= will become the king).

heiress a female heir, esp a woman who is heir to a fortune: *The criminals kidnapped [⇨ C232] a wealthy heiress.*

legatee a person to whom a legacy has been left

inheritor a person who inherits something

C215 *nouns, etc* : **mortgages and covenants**

mortgage 1 [C] an agreement to lend money in which a piece of property is to pass to the lender if the money is not properly paid back: *He must get a mortgage on his house in order to keep his business going.* **2** [C] an agreement to lend money, esp to help someone buy a house, in which the house will belong to the lender if the money is not properly paid back: *I can't get a mortgage, so I can't buy the house.* **3** [C] the money lent on a mortgage: *Mortgages are available for these new houses. He has a big mortgage repayment every month.* **4** [T1] to get a mortgage on: *I'll have to mortgage the house in order to keep my business going.*

conveyancing [U] the job of preparing official papers in law for changes of ownership of property

covenant [C] an agreement in writing, esp to pay money regularly to a society for those who need it

The police, security services, crime, and criminals

C220 nouns : the police

police [GU] the group of people, mainly in uniform, who are paid to look after law and order in a city, county, region, state, etc: *The New York police are world famous. Send for the police quickly; someone has taken the money! This is a police matter; I'll phone them.*

police force [C] a police organization: *The Metropolitan Police Force looks after law and order in London. Most police forces throughout the world work together on important cases.*

policeman [C] a man who is a member of a police force, of any rank but esp of the lowest

policewoman [C] a woman who is a member of a police force, of any rank but esp of the lowest

(police) constable [C; A] *esp BrE* (the title of) a policeman of the lowest rank: *Constable Smith was sent to the house to get some information. Several constables were injured in the riot.*

patrolman [C; A] *esp AmE* (the title of) the lowest rank of policeman; a policeman who regularly patrols a particular district: *Patrolman O'Hara saw the crime take place.*

police officer [C] *often fml* a policeman of any rank: *Who are you?— I am a police officer, Madam.*

officer [N; C; A] a policeman, esp when spoken to; the title of a police officer in some forces: *Excuse me, officer; I need your help. Officer Smith will help you, ma'am.*

Higher ranks and titles common to many police forces	
(police) sergeant (police) inspector	*lower*
superintendent (of police) commissioner (of police)	*higher*

C221 nouns : informal names for policemen [C]

cop *esp AmE* a policeman: *Call the cops!*

copper *esp BrE* a policeman: *A copper in uniform was standing at the corner.*

bobby *esp BrE* a police constable: *Tourists seem to like London bobbies.*

C222 nouns : persons connected with or similar to policemen [C]

sheriff [*also* N; A] (the title of) the officer who enforces the law in a county in the USA: *Sheriff Smith was a well-known local lawman.*

marshal [*also* N; A] (in the USA) **1** (the title of) an official who carries out the judgements given in a court of law; a person who has the duties of a sheriff: *A US marshal is coming to take the prisoners away. Marshal Smith attended the court session.* **2** a chief officer of a police or fire-fighting force

lawman *esp AmE* any officer of the law; policeman, sheriff, etc: *Wyatt Earp was a famous lawman.*

detective a person, usu a police officer, who investigates [⇒ N360] crime: *Police detectives were searching the house for clues as to the murderer's identity.*

private investigator/detective a person who is paid privately to do work similar to that of the police and who usu has a licence [⇒ C194] to do so

private eye *infml esp AmE* a private investigator

plain clothes policeman/detective, etc a policeman/detective, etc who does not wear a uniform on duty

C223 nouns : guards and wardens [C]

guard a person, usu paid, whose duty it is to protect a person, group, or place: *The guards shot two of the robbers. A bank guard was hurt when the bank was held up. The officer posted soldiers as guards at every door of the building. The soldiers were on guard duty. The prison guards stopped the men from escaping.*

guardian *usu fml* a guard or protector: *The priest is the guardian of their ancient customs.*

warden 1 a person, usu paid, who looks after a place (and people): *She is the warden of an old people's home. He was an air-raid warden in London during the war. The school appoints some of the pupils as fire wardens.* **2** an official who helps to see that certain laws are obeyed: *He is a local traffic warden; he makes sure people don't park their cars in the wrong places. The game wardens in that reserve protect the animals well.*

watchman a guard, esp of a building or area with buildings on it: *The company employs watchmen on a 24-hour basis. The night-watchman was found sleeping while on duty.*

custodian *fml* a person who guards, esp a public place, custom, etc: *The custodians of the museum have decided to close this part of the museum because there were too many thefts. (fig) He doesn't like us to see that kind of film; he thinks he is the custodian of our morals.*

keeper 1 a person who guards or protects: *The keepers in the Zoo look after the animals very well. I'm not her keeper; she's old enough to look after herself.* **2** [*in comb*] a person who is in charge of or who has special duties in relation to the stated thing: *The shopkeeper closed his shop. The doorkeeper was told not let any strangers in.*

bodyguard a person whose duty it is to keep someone else safe: *The President is constantly* *attended by armed bodyguards. His personal bodyguard checks all his visitors for guns.*

caretaker 1 a person employed to look after a house or land, etc when the owner is absent: *He has appointed a caretaker to look after the estate. (fig) We have a caretaker government till the elections next month.* **2** *esp EngE* a person employed to look after a school or other usu large public building and to be responsible for small repairs, cleaning, etc

janitor *esp AmE and ScotE* a caretaker (def **2**)

sentry a soldier or other person guarding a place: *The captain posted sentries round the camp. The criminals posted sentries to keep watch for the police.*

sentinel *fml & old* a sentry: *No one will pass our sentinels; they are too watchful.*

warder a guard, esp in a prison

C224 nouns : relating to the police and guards

(police) station *also esp AmE* **(police) headquarters** [C; R] the building(s) where the police have their central organization in any district: *I must ask you to come to the (police) station with me. Get back to headquarters and collect the photographs.*

(police) precinct [C] *AmE* an area esp of a city where a local police group operates; the police headquarters in that area

squad [GC] a small group of policemen working together; a police organization with particular work to do: *Send a squad to deal with the riot. The Drugs Squad are working on the problem now.* [⇒ E80 DRUG]

patrol [GC; on U] a group of policemen, soldiers, etc which moves through an area for any reason: *Send some two-man patrols to protect the area. One of their foot patrols was attacked. He is on patrol tonight.*

beat [C] the area where a policeman regularly works and patrols: *The constable was on his beat. This isn't my beat; it's his.*

patrol/squad car [C] a car used by the police for patrolling roads

Black Maria *also* **patrol/police wagon** *AmE* [C] an enclosed vehicle in which the police take prisoners from place to place

C225 verbs : guarding and protecting [T1]

guard to keep danger away from; to put guards on or act as a guard, esp to keep safe or to prevent from escaping: *Guard these men and see that nothing happens to them. He guarded the valuable jewels. The men guarded their prisoners well.*

protect to keep safe against attack, etc: *The soldiers were there to protect the people and their property. She has always protected her children against the real world. This coat will protect you from the cold.*

patrol [*also* I∅] to go at regular times round (a district, building, etc) to see that there is no trouble, that no one is trying to get in or out or do anything unlawfully, etc: *How many policemen are patrolling tonight? The coast is regularly patrolled to catch smugglers* [⇒ C231].

cordon off [v adv] to guard an area so that no one can enter or leave it, esp with policemen or soldiers around it: *The building has been completely cordoned off.*

C226 verbs & nouns : arresting and cautioning

arrest 1 [T1] to seize in the name of the law and usu put in prison: *The policeman arrested the thief. Arrest that man!* **2** [C] an occasion when someone is arrested: *The police have made two arrests in connection with the murder. An arrest is expected soon.*

apprehend [T1] *fml* to arrest: *He did not stop when told to do so and I therefore apprehended him, sir. The criminals have all been apprehended.*

pinch [T1] *esp BrE infml* to arrest: *She's been pinched twice for shoplifting* [⇒ C230].

pick up [v adv T1] *infml* (of the police) to take to the police station and perhaps arrest: *The police picked him up last night for questioning.*

caution *tech* **1** [T1] to speak a warning to (a person who has done something wrong or broken the law) that a repetition will be more severely punished, or that what he says will be used as evidence [⇒ C208] of guilt in court: *The policeman cautioned the angry driver.* **2** [C] an example of this: *He got off with a caution; the policeman told him not to do it again.*

book [T1 *often pass*] *esp BrE infml* (of the police) to record a formal charge against: *He got booked for driving too fast. Book him for driving too fast.*

C227 nouns : crimes and offences

crime 1 [C] an act which is against the law: *These crimes will be punished. Theft is a crime.* **2** [U] unlawful action: *Crime doesn't pay. The police fight (against) crime.*

petty crime [U; C] crime or a crime which is of a minor kind: *He isn't a dangerous criminal; he lives off petty crime(s).*

offence *BrE,* **offense** *AmE* [C] *tech & emot* a crime or wrong thing done: *It is an offence to drive a car while under the influence of alcohol. Murder was once a capital offence* (= Murderers were once killed). *Your offences are not serious: I forgive you.* **offend** [I∅ (*against*)] *often tech* to do wrong, esp by breaking the law: *'People who offend against the law must be punished,'* he said.

misdemeanour *BrE,* **misdemeanor** *AmE* [C] **1** a bad or improper act that is not very serious: *I can forgive his various misdemeanours; they harm no one but himself.* **2** *tech* a crime that is less serious than, for example, murder or theft: *Misdemeanours like traffic offences are punishable with a fine.*

villainy *often emot* **1** [U] wicked or criminal behaviour: *Your villainy will not go unpunished!* **2** [C *usu pl*] an act of this kind: *History records his many villainies.*

delinquency [U] *often fml & euph* crime: *He led a life of delinquency.*

law-breaking [U] the action of breaking the law: *By entering the house without the owner's permission you are in fact guilty of law-breaking.*

wrongdoing: [U] *esp emot* bad behaviour which is morally or legally wrong: *You are guilty of wrongdoing and must be punished, young man.*

misdeed [C] *often euph* a crime or act of wrongdoing: *Young man, your misdeeds are becoming well known locally!*

breach [C; U: *of*] an act of breaking, not obeying, or not fulfilling a law, agreement, custom, etc: *Your action is a breach of our agreement. He is in breach of (his) contract if he does that. These actions are a breach of military regulations and must be punished. He was punished for various breaches of discipline.*

C228 nouns & adjectives : **relating to persons committing crimes**

criminal 1 [C] a person who engages in crime, usu as an occupation: *These criminals must be punished for their crimes. He is a hardened criminal and prison won't change him.* **2** [B] relating to crime: *His criminal behaviour is well-known. It's criminal to do a thing like that!* **-ly** [adv] *This is a hospital for the criminally insane.* [⇨ G52]

offender [C] **1** a person who offends, esp by breaking a law: *'They are offenders against the laws of God!' he cried.* **2** *euph* a criminal: *The building is an institution for young offenders.*

crook [C] *infml* a criminal: *This club is a meeting place for all kinds of crooks. He's a crook; he'll cheat you out of your money.*

villain [C] **1** *esp lit* a person who does evil things: *That wicked villain wants to kidnap* [⇨ C232] *the princess!* **2** *esp BrE* a criminal: *'We'll bring the villains to justice, Madam,' said the policeman.* **villainous** [B] in the manner of or like a villain: *What villainous behaviour!* **-ly** [adv]

culprit [C] a person who should be blamed for a crime, bad happening, etc: *He's the culprit; arrest him, not me! We'll catch the culprits, never fear.*

outlaw [C] a criminal, esp formerly one who was not protected by law and/or who was forced to live outside normal society: *Robin Hood led a*

band of outlaws who lived in Sherwood Forest.

wrongdoer [C] *esp euph or emot* a person who commits or has committed one or more crimes. *We must try to make these poor wrongdoers see the error of their ways. The wrongdoers will be punished!*

delinquent 1 [C] a (young) wrongdoer: *This court deals with juvenile* [⇨ C9] *delinquents.* **2** [B] not having obeyed the law or done one's duty: *He has been delinquent in paying his debts. The delinquent children come from broken homes.* **3** [Wa5;B] (of debts, etc) not having been paid (in time)

law-breaker [C] a person who breaks the law in any way: *Criminals are law-breakers, but all law-breakers are not necessarily criminals.*

C229 nouns : **criminals, usually in gangs** [C]

gangster a criminal who is a member of a gang of criminals: *The gangsters attacked and killed most of the members of the other gang. He likes gangster films* (=films about gangsters).

mobster *esp AmE infml* a gangster

hoodlum *esp AmE sl* a gangster

thug a violent man who commits violent crimes: *She was attacked by two young thugs who stole her handbag.* **thuggery** [U] the action of a thug

vandal a person who intentionally damages or destroys beautiful or useful things belonging to others, makes beautiful places ugly, etc: *The walls had been covered with paint by young vandals.* **vandalize, -ise** [T1] to destroy or damage for no good reason: *The youths vandalized the empty house for fun.* [⇨ C237]

C230 nouns : **acts of stealing**

theft 1 [U] the act of taking someone else's property; stealing: *Petty theft* (= theft of small things) *is increasing among out-of-work youths.* **2** [C] an example of this: *These thefts have been going on for a long time.*

robbery 1 [U] theft, esp if it is done violently: *She was arrested for armed robbery.* **2** [C] an example of this: *He took part in an unsuccessful bank robbery. The robberies were done without killing anyone.*

larceny [U; C] *tech* stealing or an act of stealing: *He was convicted of larceny and sent to jail. Her crimes are just petty larceny* (= minor thefts), *but his amount to grand larceny* (= major thefts).

burglary 1 [U] the crime of entering a building, esp a home, by force, in order to steal: *He engaged in burglary as a night-time activity while during the day he was a clerk.* **2** [C] an example of this: *We have had three burglaries in this neighbourhood in one week.*

housebreaking [U; C] *less fml* burglary

breaking and entering [U] *tech* burglary: *He was charged with breaking and entering.*

break-in [C] *infml* a burglary: *There were several break-ins last night.*

shoplifting [U] the act or crime of taking goods from a shop without paying for them: *She was caught and fined for shoplifting.*

mugging 1 [U] the act of one or more persons attacking and robbing another **2** [C] an example of this: *There were two muggings last night in the park.*

hijacking 1 [U] an act of hijacking [⇒ C232] anything: *Hijacking for political reasons has become common throughout the world.* **2** *also esp AmE* **hijack** [C] an example of this: *The firm has suffered several hijackings of its lorries and their loads. There was a hijack here last month.*

piracy [U] robbery by a pirate [⇒ C231]: *Their crime was piracy on the high seas, and they were hanged.*

smuggling [U] the act or crime of bringing goods into one country from another, esp by sea, without paying the necessary tax: *There used to be a lot of smuggling along this coast.*

C231 nouns : kinds of thief [C]

thief a person who steals or has stolen: *That city is full of thieves, many of them just children. A thief stole his watch.*

robber a person who robs or has robbed: *The robbers stopped the train and stole the gold.*

burglar a person who breaks into houses, shops, etc, to steal things esp at night   **burglar alarm** an apparatus that makes a loud warning noise when a thief breaks into a building

housebreaker *less fml* a burglar, esp during the day

shoplifter a person who shoplifts

pickpocket a person who steals things from people's pockets, esp in a crowd

mugger a person who mugs or has mugged one or more people

pirate (esp formerly) **a** a person who sails the seas stopping and robbing ships **b** a ship used by pirates

hijacker a person who hijacks [⇒ C232]

smuggler a person who habitually smuggles [⇒ C232] goods

bandit a person, usu an outlaw, who lives by robbing others, usu in lonely places: *The bandits came down from the hills and attacked the camp. Armed bandits raided the little town.*

banditry [U] the activity of a bandit or bandits

C232 verbs : robbing and stealing

rob [T1 (*of*)] to take something unlawfully from (its owner): *The bandits robbed us of all our money. Robin Hood robbed the rich to give to the poor. Please don't rob us! The bank has been robbed.*

steal [T1; I∅ (*from*)] to take, usu, unlawfully (what belongs to someone else): *He stole her money. Robin Hood stole from the rich to give to the poor. Help, my money has been stolen!* USAGE Generally one steals things. One robs people (of things): *I've been robbed; someone has stolen all my money.*

thieve [Wv4; I∅] *rare* to steal (things) or rob (people): *Those thieving villains stole all his money. She begs and thieves for a living.*

pinch [T1] *esp BrE infml* to steal: *Hey, someone's pinched my money!* (*fig*) *Don't pinch my girl while I'm out of town.*

pilfer [T1; I∅] to steal something small in small amounts, or a lot of small things from (a place): *He was caught pilfering in the department store. He began his life of crime by pilfering (from) his fellow pupils' school lockers.*   **pilferer** [C] a person who pilfers   **pilferage** [U] **1** loss through pilfering **2** the act of pilfering

rustle [T1] *esp AmE* to steal (cattle or horses): *He used to take part in cattle rustling. No one dares rustle his stock; he has too many guards.*   **rustler** [C] a person who rustles: *a cattle rustler*

lift [T1] *infml* to steal, rustle, etc: *Hey, someone has lifted my wallet! The bandits lifted 20 head of cattle from* (= 20 cows, etc) *his ranch.*

burgle *BrE*, **burglarize** *AmE* [T1] to steal from (a building, home, etc): *The house was burgled. We've been burgled!*

break in [v adv I∅] to enter a house, etc by force, against the law: *Someone broke in (to our house) last night.*

break into [v prep T1] to enter by force: *The house was broken into last night.*

pirate [T1] **1** to steal as a pirate would: *The sailors pirated the cargo.* **2** [Wv5] to make and sell (a book, newly-invented article, etc) without permission or payment, when the right to do so belongs to someone else: *This is a pirated edition of his book.*

smuggle [T1; I∅] to bring (goods, etc) into one country from another without paying the necessary tax: *They smuggled gold into, and opium out of, the country. His business is to smuggle people out of the country.*

kidnap [T1] to take (someone) away unlawfully in order to demand money or something else for their safe return: *They kidnapped the rich man's son.* **kidnapper** *BrE*, **kidnaper** *AmE* [C] a person who kidnaps people or has kidnapped someone

abduct [T1] *usu fml* to kidnap; to take away unlawfully, usu by force: *He abducted the heiress in order to get money for her safe return. The police think the missing woman has been abducted.* **abductor** [C] a person who abducts someone   **abduction** [U; C] an act or instance of abducting or being abducted

carry off [v adv T1] *infml* to abduct; kidnap: *The bandits carried their women prisoners off into the hills.*

hijack [T1] to take control of (a vehicle) by force of arms, formerly for the purpose of stealing, now more often for other (such as political) aims: *The terrorists hijacked an airliner at gunpoint* (= by pointing guns at the crew).

hold up [v adv T1] to stop (a vehicle) or go into (a place) in order to rob it: *Some criminals held up the local bank.* **holdup** [C] an act of holding something up: *This is a holdup; don't move!*

C233 *nouns* : **deceiving and stealing**

fraud 1 [U] deceiving behaviour for the purpose of gain, which may be punishable by law: *The judge found the man guilty of fraud.* **2** [C] an example of this: *His plan for getting money is one of the cleverest frauds in recent years.* **fraudulent** [B] for the purposes of or related to a fraud **-ly** [adv]

embezzlement [U] the use of money placed in one's care in a wrong, usu unlawful, way for one's own purposes: *He was convicted of embezzlement.*

racket [C] a fraud or trick, esp in business, so as to make money dishonestly; a criminal business or undertaking: *This racket is making him a lot of money at other people's expense. He has worked various rackets, including drugs and prostitution.*

swindle [C] a racket in which a person or group of persons is cheated out of money: *This promise of shares in a gold-mine is just a swindle; there is no such mine!*

extortion [U] the action of extorting [⇒ C234] usu money, from people: *The charge was extortion with threats.*

blackmail [U] the obtaining of money or what one wants, usu unlawfully, by threatening to make known unpleasant facts about a person or group: *Pay me or I'll tell them what really happened!— That's blackmail! Never give in to blackmail.*

confidence trick [C] the action of a criminal who makes someone or some people trust him enough to give him money: *This promise of quick profits is just a confidence trick.* **con** *infml* abbrev a confidence trick: *It's a con; don't believe him!*

black market [(*the*) C] the unlawful buying and selling of goods, foreign money, etc, where such trade is controlled, esp during or after a war: *They bought butter on the black market/ they bought black-market butter.*

C234 *verbs* : **deceiving and stealing**
[ALSO ⇒ F203]

deceive [T1] to cause (someone) to accept as true or sound something that is false or unsound: *I trust him because I know he would never deceive me. Do my eyes deceive me, or is that an elephant pulling that carriage? Don't deceive yourself into thinking that bad plan is a good one. We were deceived by him; he was really a thief.* **deceit** [U] activity or action which deceives: *His deceit is disgusting; he took everybody in! I'm tired of your lies and deceit.* **deception** [U;C] deceit; an action which

deceives: *Her deceptions have made us all mistrust her.* **deceptive** [B] caused by deceit or intended to deceive **-ly** [adv]

cheat 1 [T1 (*of, out of*)] to take from (someone) unfairly, dishonestly, or deceitfully: *The rich lord cheated the poor old woman (out) of her land.* **2** [I0] to act dishonestly or deceitfully to win an advantage, esp in a game: *He always cheats at cards. Don't play with her; she cheats.* **3** [T1] (*fig*) to avoid or escape as if by deception: *The swimmers cheated death in spite of the storm.*

trick [T1 (*into*)] to make (someone) believe what is not true, usu in order to get something: *She tricked him into giving her the money. Don't try to trick me!* **trickery** [U] the activity of someone who likes to trick people **tricky** [Wa1;B] *infml* clever at tricking people: *Watch that fellow; he's tricky!*

take in [v adv T1 *usu pass*] *infml* to trick or deceive: *Don't be taken in by his nice smile; he'll cheat you. She took them all in with her sad story.*

defraud [T1] to deceive so as to get or keep something wrongly and usu unlawfully: *She defrauded her brother (out) of his share of the land.*

swindle [T1] to cheat (someone), esp unlawfully: *Don't try to swindle me with your clever schemes. He swindled her out of £2,000.*

embezzle [T1] to use (money placed by others in one's care) for one's own purposes, usu unlawfully: *He embezzled £15,000 before they caught him.*

extort [T1 (*from*)] to obtain by threats, usu unlawfully: *He extorted money from her by blackmail and threats.*

con [T1 (*into*)] **1** *infml* to cheat or trick: *These advertisements con you into thinking their products the best.* **2** to perform a confidence trick on: *He was conned, and lost all his money.*

blackmail [T1] to obtain money and/or what one wants from (someone) by using blackmail: *Don't think you can blackmail me (into doing what you want); I'll report you to the police.*

C235 *nouns* : **people who and things which cheat** [C]

deceiver *esp emot & lit* a person who deceives people: *What a lying little deceiver she is.*

cheat 1 a person who cheats; a dishonest person: *Don't play with him; he's a cheat.* **2** *infml* an example of cheating; a dishonest, deceitful trick: *That's a cheat!*

fraud *derog* **1** a person who pretends or claims to be what he or she is not: *She's just a fraud; she isn't a doctor at all.* **2** a thing which does not do what it is supposed or claimed to do: *His scheme is a fraud, to make him rich at your expense.*

swindler a person who swindles someone else: *There are plenty of swindlers around, waiting to take people's money by promising them more.*

confidence trickster a person who habitually performs confidence tricks on people

conman *infml* a confidence trickster: *Don't listen to him; he's just a conman!*

racketeer a person who makes money by dishonest business methods, usu in an organized racket: *The city used to be full of gangsters and racketeers.*

embezzler a person who embezzles or has embezzled money

extortionist a person who extorts or has extorted anything, esp money, from anyone

blackmailer a person who blackmails or has blackmailed anyone

black marketeer a person who sells goods on the black market

C236 *verbs & nouns* : **defaming**

defame [T1] to (try to) damage the good name of (a person), usu by unfair means: *He has been defaming us for years but luckily few believe his lies.* **defamation** [U] the act of defaming or being defamed: *I'll sue you for defamation of character if you go on telling these lies.* **defamatory** [B] for the purpose of defaming: *He must stop making these defamatory statements.*

slander 1 [T1] to defame (someone) in speech: *Stop slandering us; no one believes your lies anyway!* **2** [C] a spoken statement about someone that unfairly damages his or her good name: *These slanders must stop* **3** [U] the making of such statements: *This is pure slander and I'll sue* [⇒ C203] *him for slander if he doesn't apologize.* **slanderous** [B] of, concerning, like, or likely to cause slander: *She is saying a lot of slanderous things about him.* **-ly** [adv] **-ness** [U]

libel 1 [T1] to defame (someone) in writing or print: *He seems to enjoy libelling me.* **2** [C] a printed or written statement, picture, etc about someone that unfairly damages his or her good name: *These libels are quite ridiculous.* **3** [U] the printing etc of such a statement, etc: *This statement is libel; I'll sue him for libel if he prints it.* **4** [C] *infml* an unfair or untrue remark: *It's a libel; it isn't true!* **libellous** [B] of, concerning, like, or likely to cause libel: *What you have written is libellous.* **-ly** [adv] **-ness** [U]

C237 *nouns* : **violent or dangerous crimes** [U]

assault [*also* C] a sudden violent unlawful attack with blows against another person, or the threat of such an attack: *The man was charged with assault.* **assault and battery** [U] *tech* an assault which includes actual blows: *He was found guilty of assault and battery.*

fire-raising deliberately and usu unlawfully setting fire to property in order to cause destruction: *These men are quite capable of fire-raising.* **fire-raiser** [C] a person who takes part in fire-raising

arson the criminal act of fire-raising: *He committed arson by burning down two buildings.* **arsonist** [C] *tech* a fire-raiser

vandalism intentional, needless, and usu widespread damage and destruction, esp of public property: *Vandalism can cost the country millions of pounds annually.*

looting *tech* the action of looting [⇒ C238]: *The police arrested many people for looting during the riots.*

C238 *nouns & verbs* : **stolen goods and stealing goods**

stolen goods [P] any goods which have been stolen: *He was charged with receiving stolen goods.*

loot 1 [U] goods, esp valuable objects, taken away unlawfully, as by soldiers after defeating an enemy, or by thieves: *The bandits divided their loot. Where did the thieves keep the loot?* **2** [T1] to take loot (from): *The soldiers looted and burnt the village.*

plunder *esp lit* **1** [U] goods seized by soldiers, etc, usu by force; stolen goods: *The conquering army filled many carts with their plunder. The thieves hid the plunder in a cave.* **2** [T1] to seize (goods) unlawfully or by force from (people or a place), esp in time of war or disorder: *The soldiers plundered the helpless villagers. Crowds were busy plundering the shops. The soldiers were forbidden to plunder.* **3** [U] the act of plundering: *Those lawless men lived by plunder.*

spoils [P] *esp lit* goods taken unlawfully or by force, as in time of war or by thieves: *The soldiers expected the spoils of victory to be divided up among them. Well, where are the spoils?*

booty [U] *esp lit or old use* loot; plunder

C239 *nouns* : **murder and suicide**
[ALSO ⇒ A8, 10]

murder 1 [U] the crime of killing a person unlawfully: *He is guilty of murder. She loves reading murder stories.* **2** [C] an occasion of murder: *The police are investigating two local murders.* **murderer** *fem* **murderess** [C] a person who commits or has committed murder [⇒ F110 MURDEROUS]

manslaughter [U] the crime of killing a person unlawfully but not intentionally: *The man was found guilty of manslaughter; the charge of wilful murder was dropped.*

homicide [U; C] *tech* murder or a murder: *She is guilty of homicide. The Homicide Squad* [⇒ C224] *will look into this murder.* **homicidal** [Wa5; B] relating to or likely to commit homicide **-ly** [adv]

suicide 1 [U] the act of killing oneself, usu seen as unlawful: *She committed suicide while her mind was disturbed.* **attempted suicide 2** [C] an example of this: *The police are investigating* [⇒ N360] *several murders that have been made to look like suicides.* **3** [C] a person who commits or tries to commit suicide **suicidal 1** [B] relating to or likely to commit suicide: *He was feeling suicidal.* **-ly** [adv] **2** dangerous to oneself: *It is suicidal to drive that broken-down old car!*

Prison and punishment

C250 *nouns* : **prisons and cells** [C]

prison [*also* U] a set of buildings in which people who have done wrong are kept locked up; a place where a person is shut up against his or her will: *He has been sent to prison for three years. Several men have escaped from a local prison.*

jail [*also* U] *also* **gaol** *BrE* a public prison: *Lock him up in jail. The town jails are full of arrested people.*

penitentiary *also infml abbrev* **pen** *AmE* a prison

lockup *infml* a prison or jail: *They put the drunken men in the lockup for the night.*

dungeon a dark prison underground, usu in a castle: *Throw the prisoners into the dungeons!*

cell a small room in a prison: *They put all the prisoners in one cell.* **condemned cell** the cell in which a person condemned to death is kept

bonds [P] *esp lit* ropes, chains, etc; (*fig*) imprisonment: *They kept him in bonds for a year. The prisoner broke his bonds and got away.*

C251 *verbs* : **imprisoning and confining** [T1]

imprison to put in a prison or to keep in a place or state from which one cannot get out: *They imprisoned him for seven years.* (*fig*) *I'm imprisoned in this terrible life; there's no escape.*

jail, *also* **gaol** *BrE* to put in jail: *The sheriff jailed him on a charge of theft.*

lock up [v adv] *not fml* to put (someone) in prison or a hospital for mad people: *The police locked him up for his own safety. He should be locked up; he's dangerous.*

put away [v adv] *infml* to lock up: *They put him away; he was quite mad.*

detain 1 to keep (a person) from leaving during a certain time: *The police have detained two men for questioning at the police station.* **2** *tech* to keep in custody [⇒ C252]: *He has been detained indefinitely.* **3** to delay: *I am sorry to*

detain you, but I have one more question to ask. This matter isn't very important and shouldn't detain us very long.

intern to put in prison, or limit the freedom of movement of (someone considered dangerous), esp in wartime or for political reasons: *Several hundred people were interned in case some of them were enemy agents.*

confine [(*to*)] to keep in a small space or within narrow limits: *The child was confined to his room. His illness confines him to a chair. The madman was confined in case he attacked anyone.* **-ment** [U (*to*)]

C252 *nouns* : **imprisoning and confining** [U]

imprisonment the condition of being (put) in prison: *His sentence was imprisonment for five years. His period of imprisonment was up; he was set free. Imprisonment for a length of time can have strange effects on people.*

prison confinement in a prison: *She's in prison for theft.*

jail, *also* **gaol** *BrE* confinement in a jail: *He's in jail for assault and battery* [⇒ C237].

captivity the state of being a captive [⇒ C253]: *His captivity ended last night. Many animals breed better when they are free than they do when in captivity.*

confinement the condition of being confined in or to a place; *euph* imprisonment: *He is finding his confinement rather boring; he hates being confined to the house/to (his) bed. The prisoners are all safely under confinement.* **solitary confinement** being imprisoned completely alone, esp as a punishment in prison or in the army

house arrest confinement to one's home: *He has been under house arrest for two years; the government won't imprison him but they won't let him have freedom of movement either.*

custody 1 *tech* imprisonment under guard: *The prisoner is in custody, awaiting trial.* **2** a protected condition: *His money is in safe custody in the bank/in their hands.* **3** *tech* legal care: *When her parents died she was placed in the custody of her aunt.*

detention 1 the condition of being detained (usu by force) against a person's wishes: *The men have all been placed in detention/are all under detention until we can decide who is to blame.* **2** the act of detaining: *The detention of these men will cause trouble; they are foreign nationals.*

internment the act of interning or the period of time during which a person is imprisoned: *The internment of political prisoners without trial is quite common.*

guard 1 the condition of being guarded: *He was sent for trial under (armed) guard.* **2** a condition of being alert and watchful (*esp in the phr* **on guard**): *Be on (your) guard against surprise attacks.*

C253 *nouns* : **prisoners** [C]

prisoner a person who has been put in a prison: *Bring the prisoners here for questioning. The prisoners were allowed out of jail for exercise once a day.*

captive a person taken prisoner, esp in war: *The captives were all killed.*

convict *tech* a person being kept in prison: *The convicts were locked in their cells.* **ex-convict** a person who was a convict at a time in the past

jailbird *sl* a convict

detainee a person under detention

internee a person who is interned

cellmate a prisoner who shares a cell with another: *They were cellmates in prison for two years.*

C254 *nouns* : **warders and jailers** [C]

guard a person (usu paid) to guard prisoners, convicts, etc

warder a guard, esp in a prison: *Two prison warders guarded the men.*

jailer, *also* **gaoler** *BrE* a person in charge of or working in a jail: *The jailer carried a big bunch of keys.*

governor a person in charge of a prison: *The (prison) governor arranged the prisoner's parole* [⇒ C262].

C255 *verbs* : **punishing and deterring** [T1]

[ALSO ⇒ C210, 11]

punish to cause to suffer bodily, by imprisonment, etc for some crime or act which is not acceptable: *We shall punish him if he disobeys. The criminals will be punished for their crimes.*

deter to make less willing to do (something): *Many people believe that the threat of punishment deters possible criminals. If we stop him, we may deter others from doing the same thing.*

chasten 1 to make (a person who has done wrong) behave correctly by punishment: *5 years in prison had not chastened him.* **2** [Wv4, 5] to make (someone or someone's behaviour) improve: *He had been chastened by various experiences in life but especially by the death of his wife. Life has had a chastening influence on him.*

chastise *fml* **1** to punish severely: *The father chastised his wicked son with a whip.* **2** to blame severely: *Parliament intends to chastise the slowness of the government in making a new prices and incomes agreement with the unions.*

persecute 1 to punish unfairly, esp by treating cruelly; cause to suffer (esp for religious or political beliefs): *The Romans persecuted the early Christians, often causing them to be eaten by lions. He has an illness of the mind in which he thinks that everyone is persecuting him.* **2** to

trouble continually; annoy: *She is persecuting her husband with complaints.*

victimize, -ise *esp emot* to make (someone) a victim [⇒ B167]; persecute (someone): *Stop victimizing these men just because they tell the truth!* **victimization, -isation** [U] the act of victimizing

C256 *nouns* : **punishments and deterrents**

punishment 1 [U] the act of punishing; the condition of being punished: *The punishment he suffered was terrible.* **2** [C] an act of usu lawful punishing: *What is the punishment for this crime? There are various punishments.*

corporal punishment [U] bodily punishment of a person: *Corporal punishment can include beating a criminal.* **capital punishment** [U] punishment by death: *Capital punishment can be by hanging or shooting.* **capital** [Wa5;B] punishable by death: *Murder used to be a capital offence in Britain.*

penalty 1 [U] punishment for breaking a law, rule, or agreement in law (*often in the phr* **pay the penalty**): *If you break the law you must pay the penalty/must be ready to suffer the full penalty. If they do this, it will be under penalty of death.* **2** [C] something (such as a number of years in prison or an amount of money to be paid) that is ordered as a punishment: *Fishing in this river is forbidden—penalty £10. Some people think that the penalties suffered by criminals are too light.* **3** [C] suffering or loss that is the result of one's unwise action or of one's condition or state: *One of the penalties of fame is that people point at you in the street. He had indigestion; he was paying the penalty for eating too much.* **penal** [B] **1** [Wa5] of, concerning, or for the purpose of punishment in law: *The penal code* (=laws concerning punishment) *must be changed.* **2** severe as if in punishment: *These taxes aren't just high; they are penal!* **penal servitude** [U] punishment by being sent to prison and made to do specially hard work: *The murderer was sentenced to penal servitude for eight years/for life.*

hard labour *BrE*, **hard labor** *AmE* [U] a prison sentence with very hard work: *He was sentenced to five years' hard labour.*

life (imprisonment) [U] the punishment of being put in prison for the rest of a person's life or for a very long but unfixed time: *The sentence was life imprisonment. He was given life.*

deterrent [C] anything, esp a punishment, which serves to deter: *Many people believe that capital punishment is a deterrent to murder.*

chastisement [C;U] *fml* (a) severe punishment: *The people suffered badly under the enemy's chastisements. Chastisement is often not the best way to improve someone's character.*

fine [C] a sum of money taken from someone as a punishment, esp by a court of law: *The fine* *for what he did was £20. Has she paid the fines yet?*

persecution 1 [U] the act of persecuting: *Persecution of a religious group usually fails to destroy it.* **2** [U] the state of being persecuted: *The defeated nation live in persecution.* **3** [C] a case or example of this: *This race has suffered terrible persecutions.*

sentence [C] the punishment given to someone for some crime, esp by a judge in a court of law: *He received a ten-year prison sentence for his crimes. She faces* (= may receive) *a sentence of ten years' imprisonment.*

C257 verbs & nouns : punishing by beating, etc

beat [T1] to strike repeatedly with a whip, stick, etc: *Beat him hard; he deserves to be punished. The man was beaten to death with heavy sticks. He gave the man a beating.*

thrash [T1] to beat severely: *The man thrashed his enemy. They thrashed him until he could not stand.*

whip 1 [C] a piece of rope, leather, etc, often with a stick as a handle, used for beating persons, animals, etc: *He struck her with a whip. She used her whip to make the horse go faster.* **2** [T1; IØ] to strike or beat with a whip: *She whipped the horse to make it go faster. 'That man deserves to be whipped/deserves a whipping!' he said.*

flog [T1] to whip or beat severely: *Flog him! The sailor was flogged for not doing as he was told.*

lash 1 [C] an esp long thin whip: *She struck him with her lash.* **2** [C] a blow from a whip: *They gave the prisoner twenty lashes.* **3** [T1] to strike or beat with a lash: *He lashed the horse to get it to go faster. The sailor was lashed for not doing as he was told.* **4** [IØ] to move with great force: *The waves lashed against the rocks/ship.* **5** [IØ out (at)] to attack someone forcefully: *He lashed out (at them) with his feet.* **6** [X9] to tie (someone) tightly: *They lashed him to a tree.*

birch [T1] to strike with a birch (= one or more sticks cut from a birch [⇒ A155] tree): *The boy was birched for stealing.*

cane [T1] to beat with a cane [⇒ H42]: *The teacher caned the boy.*

C258 verbs : punishing by killing [T1]

execute to kill according to law or any custom, plan, etc: *They executed murderers in those days. He was executed for treason* [⇒ C138]. **execution** [U; C] the act or an act of executing: *The sentence was death by execution. They carried out the execution at dawn.*

hang to execute by hanging (by the neck): *In those days a man could be hanged by the neck until dead. 'Hang him!' the people cried.* **hanging** [U; C] the action or an act of hanging someone: *Hanging was abolished some years*

ago in this country. The hangings took place in prison.

behead to execute by cutting off the head: *The executioner beheaded the prisoner with an axe.*

guillotine to behead by guillotine [⇒ C260]: *The men were guillotined.*

chop off [v adv] to cut off in one or several sharp blows: *The axeman chopped off Mary Queen of Scots' head.*

decapitate *fml* to behead: *The prisoners were all decapitated.* **decapitation** [U] the act of decapitating

crucify to kill by nailing or tying to a cross and leaving to die

crucifixion 1 [C; U] (an example of) the act of crucifying **2 a** [*the* R *usu cap*] the death of Christ on the Cross **b** [C] a picture or figure of this

C259 nouns : people punishing by killing [C]

executioner a person who executes criminals condemned [⇒ L156] to death: *The public executioner hanged the criminal.*

hangman an executioner who hangs condemned prisoners on a gallows [⇒ C260]

axeman an executioner who uses an axe to cut off the heads of condemned prisoners

C260 nouns : ways of punishing by killing

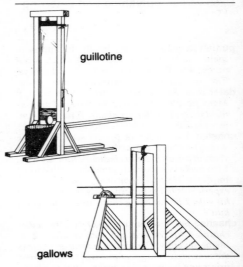

guillotine

gallows

gallows [Wn3; C; P] a wooden framework from which criminals are hanged: *He paid (the price) for his crime on the gallows.*

scaffold 1 [C] a platform (as of a gallows) **2** [*the* R] the gallows: *He died on the scaffold. You'll go to the scaffold if you kill her!*

guillotine [C; *the* R] a framework with a blade which can rise and fall, used esp in France, to behead condemned [⇨ L156] persons: *She went to the guillotine in the French Revolution.*

(execution) block [C; *the* R] the wooden block on which a person's head rests when being beheaded: *He went to the block for his crimes.*

(electric) chair [C; *the* R] an electrified chair used in some states of the US for the execution of condemned criminals: *He went to the (electric) chair for a crime he didn't commit.*

gas chamber [C; *the* R] a room which can be filled with poisonous gas, used for executing people: *He died in the gas chamber.*

firing squad [C] a group of armed men, usu soldiers, who are used to shoot condemned persons: *He died before a firing squad.*

C261 *verbs & nouns* : **punishing by sending away**

banish [T1] **1** to send away, usu out of the country, as a punishment: *He was banished for political reasons.* **2** (*fig*) to stop thinking about: *You can banish from your mind any idea of a holiday; we're not going anywhere.* **banishment** [U] the state of being banished

exile 1 [T1] to send into banishment: *They exiled Napoleon to the island of St Helena.* **2** [U] the state of exile: *The Scots lord was living in exile in France.* **3** [C] an exiled person; a person far from home: *These exiles cannot return to their native land, as they fear execution.*

extradite [T1] to send (someone who may be guilty of a crime and who has escaped to another country) back for trial: *He was extradited from France to Britain to stand trial for murder.* **extradition** [U; C] the act or an act of extraditing: *The minister signed the extradition (order).*

deport [T1] to send (an unwanted person) out of a country: *They deported him after he wrote a critical newspaper article about their government.* **deportation** [U; C] the act or an act of deporting or being deported: *The minister signed the deportation order.*

evict [T1] to take (a person) away (from a house or land) by law or by force: *The landlord had the legal right to evict his tenants* [⇨ D64], *by force if necessary.* **eviction** [U; C] the act or an act of evicting or being evicted

C262 *nouns* : **remission, pardon, and parole**

remission [U; C] (an act of) reduction in full or in part of a prison sentence: *He got three years' remission (of sentence) for good behaviour. There cannot be any remission for him; his crimes were too grave.*

pardon [C; U] (an act of) forgiveness, esp in legal remission of a sentence: *He was released from prison with a full pardon. Does he expect pardon for his offences?*

amnesty [C] a general pardon, esp for offences against the state, in which prisoners may be released: *The new governor declared a total amnesty for political offenders.*

parole [U] **1** the letting out of a person from prison, on condition that the person behaves well (esp in the phr **on parole**) **a** before the end of the period of imprisonment **b** for a particular time within that period: *He was let out of prison for a week on parole, to see his sick wife. The parole board decides when a prisoner may be let out.* **2** this letting out, or the length of time it lasts: *He was out on six weeks' parole. Her parole will soon be over.* **break (one's) parole** to fail to return to prison after being out on parole

probation [U] the legal system in which (esp young) offenders [⇨ C228] are not put in prison if they do not do anything against the law for a certain length of time: *He's on three years' probation. Her probation officer (= a social worker who advises people on probation) warned her to keep away from her criminal friends.*

C263 *verbs* : **relating to punishment** [T1]

serve *tech* to live through: *The prisoner served his sentence and was released.*

parole [*usu pass*] to set free on parole: *He was paroled last week.*

commute [(*to*)] to reduce (a punishment in law) in severity: *His death sentence was commuted to life imprisonment.*

remit to shorten: *His sentence was remitted by three years for good behaviour.*

pardon to release from a charge or a sentence: *He was publicly pardoned for his crimes.*

Warfare, defence, and the army

Fighting, war, and peace

C270 *nouns* : **war and peace**

war [U] **1** armed force used by two or more countries or groups against each other: *War is terrible. They are afraid that war will break out soon. Few people nowadays welcome war. The two countries are at war. He declared war on his enemies. They went to war against us. Waging war for any length of time is costly.* **2** a struggle between opposing forces or for a particular purpose: *The class war in Britain has been long and bitter. We must wage war against disease.*
wartime [U] the time when a war is happening: *Wartime conditions are usually hard.*
warfare [U] making war; the condition of (being at) war: *He has experience of this kind of warfare.* *(fig) He's used to political warfare.*
peace [U] **1** a time or condition when there is no war or violence: *The peace was too short; war broke out again. They signed a peace treaty at the end of the war. The two countries have been at peace for years.* **2** a state of freedom from disorder in a country, with the citizens living according to the law: *The people kept the peace. There were no breaches of the peace last night.* **peacetime** [U] a time when a nation is not at war: *These things don't happen in peacetime.*
fighting [U] continuing armed violence or quarrelling: *The fighting went on for eight days. When did the fighting stop?*
conflict [U] a condition of war; violent quarrelling: *We expect conflict over these matters; neither country is going to back down. The area is in a state of armed conflict.*
combat [U] fighting, usu between individuals or small numbers: *Have you been in combat yet? Combat conditions were terrible. He is an expert in unarmed combat.*
action [U] fighting generally: *That regiment has often seen action. The Royal Scots went into action behind their pipers.*
hostilities [P] acts of war: *Hostilities began last week.*
fight [U] ability or capacity to go on fighting: *There is no fight left in the men; they are exhausted.*
battle [U] *lit* **1** willingness to fight: *The light of battle was in his eyes.* **2** fighting: *He enjoys books about battle and sudden death. The soldiers went into battle* (= went forward to fight).

confrontation [U] the act of facing, confronting, being ready to fight, argue, etc: *Confrontation between states can start wars.*

C271 *nouns* : **wars and battles** [C]

war an occasion or period of war: *There have been wars since the human race began its history. They hope to avoid another war. The First World War began in 1914.*
conflict an occasion of conflict: *These minor conflicts do not add up to open war. You can expect a conflict of opinion between those two men.*
clash **1** [(*between*)] a fight; battle: *A border clash between the two armies started the war.* **2** an example of opposition or disagreement: *a clash of colours; clash of interests* **3** a loud confused noise: *The soldiers were woken by the clash of weapons.*
fight an occasion or period of violent action: *The two men got into a fight last night. Fights broke out in the bar. It was a long hard fight between the two nations.*
battle **1** a fight, usu between (large) armies, navies, etc in a particular place: *The battle began at dawn. In the past there were many battles between the English and the Scots.* **2** *(fig)* struggle, effort: *It's quite a battle to get money to pay the rent.*
struggle *esp emot* a violent or long fight; a struggling [⇒ C274] action: *She tried to escape but her struggles were useless. Help us in our struggle to free our country from the enemy.*
confrontation a time when people face each other in anger, argument, or readiness for trouble: *This confrontation between the two groups could lead to killing.*
duel a fight, esp between two people according to certain rules, esp formerly with swords or guns: *The two men fought a duel over the woman. The battle in the air was made up of duels between the many planes.*

C272 *nouns* : **fronts and fields**

front [C; *the* R *sometimes cap*] in war, the line along which fighting takes place together with the part behind it concerned with supplies: *The* *reserves were sent up to the front. The war is being waged successfully on all fronts. The Minister of War visited the soldiers at the Front. The enemy attacked on a wide front. The front collapsed* (=was destroyed) *and the enemy forces poured through.*

front line [C; *the* R] **1** the line of soldiers, defences, etc at the front: *These men are going straight to the front line.* **2** (*fig*) the most advanced or responsible position: *These doctors are in the front line in the fight against disease.* **front-line** [Wa5;A]: *These are front-line troops.*

line [C; *the* R; A] (esp formerly) the line of battle taken up by an army: *These are regiments* [⇒ C292] *of the line and will not run when the enemy attack. The enemy broke through our line.*

lines [P] **1** the line along which an army is organized: *He was taken prisoner behind the enemy lines.* **2** an army camp: *Tell the men not to leave the lines tonight.*

battlefield [C] a particular place where a battle is or has been fought: *This peaceful-looking place was one of the worst battlefields of the First World War.*

battleground [C] a place where battles (often) happen: *The borderland was a battleground for centuries.*

field [*the* R] the place where a battle, war, or campaign takes place or was fought: *He died on the field of battle. The old soldier said that life in the field was different from peacetime soldiering.*

C273 adjectives : relating to war [B]

[ALSO ⇒ F220, 221]

warlike 1 ready for or threatening war: *The two states began to behave in a very warlike manner.* **2** liking or skilled in war: *The Scots in the past were a warlike nation.*

belligerent at war; having or showing anger and readiness to fight: *I don't like your belligerent manner, Jones.* **-ly** [adv]

bellicose *fml* warlike: *He is rather a bellicose person.*

martial of or concerning war; ready to fight: *He spoke about the martial spirit of his soldiers.*

military of, for, by, or connected with soldiers, armies, or war fought by armies

militant having or expressing a readiness to fight or use force; taking an active part in war, a fight, or a struggle: *That country is militant in making its claims. A few militant members of the crowd began throwing stones at the police. His speech was extremely militant.* **-ly** [adv] **militancy** [U] the state or condition of being militant

embattled 1 surrounded by enemies: *The soldiers in the embattled town soon lost heart* (=became discouraged). **2** (*fig*) (of a person) continually troubled by annoying or harmful influences **3** (of castles, forts, etc) having a wall

round the roof with openings to shoot through **4** (of armies, etc, esp formerly) arranged for battle

combative ready or liking to fight: *He has a rather combative manner.*

C274 verbs : fighting and warring

wage [T1] to begin and continue (a struggle of some kind): *They have been waging war against us for years. He waged the campaign* [⇒ C285] *well.*

break out [v adv I∅] to begin: *War broke out in 1939.*

fight 1 [I∅; T1] to use (armed) forces (against); to struggle (against): *He fought (the enemy) well. We shall fight this injustice.* **2** [I∅; T1] to resist by using force: *If you attack, we'll fight (back).* **3** [I∅] to struggle together: *The two men were fighting in the street. The armies fought until they were exhausted.*

combat [T1] *often fml* to resist by fighting: *We shall combat these assaults with every weapon we have.* (*fig*) *Doctors have been trying to combat this disease for years.*

battle [I∅] *esp emot* to fight hard: *He battled to victory against many enemies.*

struggle [I∅, 3] *esp emot* to fight violently, esp to escape: *She struggled to get away from him. They have struggled for years to free their country from the enemy.*

war [I∅] *esp lit & emot* to fight, usu over a longer period: *We shall war against injustice till we have a better world. These tribes have been warring for centuries.*

duel [I∅] to fight a duel [⇒ C271]: *The famous swordsman enjoyed duelling.* **duellist** *BrE*, **duelist** *AmE* [C] a person who fights (in) a duel

C275 verbs : attacking and ambushing

[ALSO ⇒ N335]

attack [I∅; T1] to move or act violently against (a person, enemy, place, etc): *The soldiers attacked. They attacked the castle. The politician attacked his opponents in his speech.*

assault [T1] **1** *esp old use & lit* to attack: *The soldiers assaulted the castle.* **2** to attack personally: *Get a policeman!—that man is assaulting those women!*

invade [T1] **1** to attack so as to take control of (a country, city, etc): *The enemy armies invaded the country at two points.* **2** to enter in large numbers: *Holiday-makers invade this place during the summer months.* **3** (*fig*) to enter into and spoil: *I don't want to invade your private life unnecessarily.*

overrun [T1] *esp emot* to invade completely: *The enemy overran the country in one short week* (=in only a week). *The defences were overrun and the soldiers were killed.*

occupy [T1] to take (land, a country, etc) by force: *The army occupied the forts which the* enemy had left. The invading army occupied the capital city. The partisans began to attack the occupying forces wherever possible. **occupation** [U *sometimes cap*] the act or an act or time of occupying or being occupied

engage [T1] to meet and fight: *Our men engaged the enemy at dawn.*

besiege [T1] to attack (a place) by surrounding with soldiers, so that no one can get in or out: *The king began to besiege the castle/walled city.*

invest [T1] *old use & lit* to besiege: *The army invested the city.*

breach [T1] to break through; to make a hole or breach in (esp a wall): *The soldiers breached the walls and poured into the city.*

storm [T1] to attack with great force, numbers, speed, etc, usu successfully: *The soldiers stormed and took the castle.*

raid [T1; I0] to make a raid [⇒ C276] (on); to attack for a short time or quickly, usu with a smaller number of soldiers, criminals, etc: *They raided the enemy positions almost daily. The thieves raided the shop and stole a lot of money.* **raider** [C] a person who raids any place

thrust [I0] to attack suddenly and forcefully: *The army thrust (forward) towards the enemy headquarters.*

drive [I0 (*on, forward*)] to thrust again and again, further and further: *The army drove on towards the enemy capital.*

push [L9, esp *on, forward*] to attack steadily: *Our men are pushing forward on all fronts against weakening enemy resistance.*

ambush [T1] to attack unexpectedly from secret positions: *The company was ambushed in the hills and wiped out to a man* (= every man was killed). *They plan to ambush our troops.*

C276 nouns : attacking and ambushing

attack [C] an action, usu military, against a person, group, place, etc: *The attack was timed for dawn. The enemy attacks failed. Many men died in the attack.* (*fig*) *The politican began an attack on his opponents' policies.*

assault [C] a strong attack: *The assault failed. After several fierce assaults the soldiers took the town.*

offensive [C; *the* U] *tech* an attack: *When did the enemy offensive begin? We go on the offensive soon* (= We attack soon).

invasion [C; U] an occasion of invading or being invaded: *The enemy invasions were fiercely resisted. Invasion is a common occurrence in human history.*

engagement [C] *often tech* a battle: *Although it was only a short engagement, a lot of men were killed or wounded.*

siege [U; C] an attack on a place by keeping an army round it and stopping anyone or anything from getting in or out: *The siege of the castle lasted for six months. The city is in a state of siege.*

action [C] an occasion of fighting or military action: *The action did not last long and no one was killed. The war consisted largely of limited actions.*

skirmish [C] a brief usu unimportant and unplanned fight: *The front between the armies was quiet except for occasional skirmishes. He was killed in a local skirmish.*

thrust [C] a strong attack (intended) to go deep behind enemy lines: *The thrust was successful and reached the enemy headquarters* [⇒ J227].

push [S] a large and steady attack: *The big push began last night.*

raid [C] a sudden, secret, or unexpected attack, usu by a small group: *The enemy began armed raids across the border. In an air raid last night enemy aircraft bombed the city. The tribesmen carried off many animals in their cattle raids/ their raids on our cattle.*

foray [C] *esp lit & emot* a raid: *They made a foray into enemy territory. These vicious forays against our men must be stopped!*

ambush [C; U] (the placing of soldiers, etc for) a surprise attack, usu in difficult country: *The bandit chief planned the ambush carefully. The soldiers lay in ambush.*

bombardment [C] (an) attack firing big guns: *He could hear the sound of a navy bombardment. The bombardments lasted a week.*

C277 verbs : facing, defending, and retreating

face [T1] to go, turn, or look towards or to stand looking at (a person, group, etc that is a danger, enemy, etc): *Bravely he faced his enemies. She did a terrible thing and now she can't face him any more.* (*fig*) *The men faced great dangers fearlessly.* **face up to** [v adv prep T1] *emph* to face; accept (something unpleasant): *Come on; face up to your troubles.* **face the music** *infml* to accept one's punishment or trouble one has helped to cause: *She's afraid to face the music.*

confront 1 [T1] *esp fml* to face or face up to: *He confronted his enemies bravely.* **2** [T1 *with*] to bring face to face: *She confronted him with the facts about his crimes.*

defend [T1] to fight for (a place, people, idea, etc): *He defended the castle against its attackers. Defend yourselves!—The enemy are coming. I'll defend these opinions against anyone. She tries to defend her children against all outside criticism.*

fight back [v adv I0] (of people, animals, etc) to defend themselves: *The defenders fought back bravely. If they attack, we'll fight back with everything we have.*

resist [I0; T1] *fml* to fight back (against): *Attack and we'll resist. The city was besieged for months but the citizens resisted every attack.*

drive back, *also* **drive off** [v adv T1] *esp emot* to force by fighting to go back or away: *They drove back the invaders. He drove them off.*

repel [T1] *often tech* to drive back or off: *The sailors repelled the men trying to board our ship. The enemy was repelled with heavy losses.*

repulse [T1] *fml* to drive back; repel: *The citizens of the besieged town repulsed the enemy.*

dislodge [T1] to force (soldiers, etc) from a position by attacking: *They dislodged the enemy from their positions on the hill.*

reinforce [T1] **1** to send extra troops to: *He used his last reserves [⇒ C293] to reinforce the defenders of the town.* **2** to strengthen: *The walls were reinforced with concrete.* **reinforcement** [U] the act of reinforcing

retreat [IØ] (of armies, etc) to go back because unable to go forward: *The enemy retreated under heavy attack.*

C278 nouns : defending and retreating

defence *BrE*, **defense** *AmE* **1** [U] the act or action of defending: *The defence of this town is of great strategic [⇒ C285] importance. There was no defence against the enemy/the disease. Attack is the best form of defence.* **2** [C *usu pl*] something used or prepared for defence: *The town's defences were very weak. What defences do you have?* **defensive** [B] **1** that defends; that is for defence: *defensive weapons* **5** *sometimes deprec* (for someone's behaviour or language) always seeming to be expecting attack: *Why is he so defensive about his wife's work?* **on the defensive** prepared for an expected attack **-ly** [adv] **-ness** [U]

position [C] a place to be defended, attacked, etc: *Where are the enemy's main positions? The position was attacked and overrun yesterday. The soldiers took up defensive positions and waited.*

resistance 1 [U] the act or action of resisting: *Their resistance of/against the invading forces was heroic [⇒ F129]. Surrender! [⇒ C282] Resistance is useless.* **2** [S; U] an act of resisting: *They put up a brave resistance (against the enemy) but were defeated in the end.* **3** [(the)] GU *sometimes cap*) the movement(s) in a country which resist an occupying power: *The invaders executed several leading members of the local Resistance. The resistance movement could not be stamped out [⇒ N338].*

retreat 1 [U] the act or action of retreating: *The enemy is in (full-scale) retreat!* **2** [C] an act of retreating: *There will be no more retreats; we stand and fight in this place!*

C279 verbs : bombing and shelling [T1]

[ALSO c H242, 246]

bomb to drop bombs on: *The enemy aircraft bombed the city.*

bombard to keep attacking heavily (as if) with big guns: *The warships bombarded the port. The speaker was bombarded with questions.*

shell to fire shells at: *The big ships shelled the harbour. The soldiers were ordered to shell the town.* **shellfire** [U] the firing of shells

strafe to attack with heavy gunfire from a low-flying aircraft: *The diving plane strafed the ship.*

rake to fire (with guns) at, from end to end: *The enemy guns raked our defences.*

C280 verbs : winning and defeating

[ALSO ⇒ C133, K107]

win [IØ; T1] to be successful in (a war, game, etc): *We have won! We won the war. He fought to win, not just to survive [⇒ A2].* **winner** [C] a person who wins

defeat [T1] **1** to win an (esp military) victory over (a person, group, army, nation, etc): *Our men have defeated him. Hitler was defeated in 1945. Our men were heavily defeated in the battle.* **2** to cause to fail: *It was a lack of men and equipment that defeated him, not the enemy.*

rout [T1] *emph* to defeat completely: *He routed the enemy in a decisive battle.*

vanquish [T1] *esp lit & old use* to defeat: *He has vanquished all his foes.*

triumph [IØ (*over*)] *esp emot* to win completely and gloriously: *He has triumphed at last over all his enemies/problems.*

conquer [T1; IØ] to defeat completely (esp a country, people, etc): *The Romans conquered all the lands and peoples around them. You may conquer a place, but you cannot necessarily conquer people's minds. They attacked and conquered.* **conqueror** [C] a person who conquers

overcome [T1; IØ] *esp emot* to conquer: *We will overcome our enemies even if it takes a thousand years! She overcame all her difficulties by working hard. 'We shall/will overcome!' he cried.*

master [T1] **1** to gain control over: *The horse tried to run away, but he succeeded in mastering it.* **2** to gain as a skill: *He never mastered the art of public speaking. I am too old to master a new language.*

C281 verbs & nouns : capturing and liberating

capture 1 [T1] to get by fighting: *The soldiers captured the hill from the enemy. Many enemy soldiers were captured in the battle.* **2** [U] the action of capturing or being captured: *His capture ended the war.*

take [T1] *esp emot* to capture: *After heavy fighting our men took all the enemy positions.*

'I shall take the city or die in the attempt!' he cried.

appropriate [T1] to take for oneself, esp by force, stealing, etc: *The government appropriated his land.* **appropriation 1** [U] the act of appropriating **2** [C] an example of this **3** [C] something, esp money, taken, kept, or set aside for a particular purpose

seize [T1] to capture or take quickly or very forcefully: *Enemy troops seized the city in a sudden night attack.* **seizure** [U] the action of seizing or being seized: *His seizure of the city started a war.*

annex [T1] to take control over or seize (esp land): *He annexed the little country by force.* **annexation 1** [U] the act or result of annexing or being annexed **2** [C] an example of this

commandeer [T1] (esp of soldiers, etc) to seize (buildings, animals, food, money, etc) for military purposes: *The army arrived in the town and commandeered almost everything.*

liberate [T1] to set free from a conqueror: *The Allied Forces liberated Paris.* **liberation** [U] the action of liberating or being liberated

relieve [T1] **1** to stop the siege [⇨ C276] of (a place): *An army was sent to relieve (the troops besieged in) the city.* **2** to take over duty from: *I'll relieve you at 2 a.m.* **relief** [U] the act of relieving or being relieved: *The relief of the city took place too late to save his life.*

C282 *verbs* : **losing and giving up**
[ALSO ⇨ K107]

lose [I0; T1] to fail in (a war, battle, etc); not win: *The enemy lost; we have won. Their army lost the battle and this caused them to lose the war.* **loser** [C] a person who loses

surrender 1 [I0] to stop fighting and allow soldiers, police, etc to take one as a prisoner: *The general told his men that they would never surrender. 'I surrender—don't shoot!'* **2** [T1] to hand over: *He surrendered his weapons to the enemy officer.*

yield [I0; T1:(to)] *esp emot & lit* to surrender: *We shall never yield! They are not the kind of people to yield to threats. He yielded the castle to his enemies.*

give in [v adv I0] *esp emot* to admit defeat; surrender: *Well, do you give in or must we go on fighting?*

give up [v adv] *esp emot* **1** [I0] to admit defeat and stop resisting: *The soldiers gave up one by one. Why don't you accept your defeat and give up?* **2** [T1] to surrender; hand over: *He gave himself up to the police. Give up your weapons and surrender.*

desert [I0; T1] (of soldiers) to leave (an army, post, etc) illegally: *He deserted (his post) and was shot.* **deserter** [C] a person who deserts or has deserted **desertion** [U;C] the act or an act of deserting: *He was shot for desertion. There have been many desertions from the army.*

C283 *nouns* : **victory, defeat, and surrender**

victory 1 [U] the condition of winning or state of having won: *We must fight on; victory is in sight.* **2** [C] an occasion of winning: *His victory over his enemies will go down in history. We have not always had victories; there have also been times of defeat.* **victor** [C] a person who has won a victory; (*fml*) a winner **victorious** [B] experiencing victory **-ly** [adv]

triumph 1 [U] complete victory: *Triumph showed on the faces of the victors.* **2** [C] an occasion of great victory: *Winning this battle is the general's greatest triumph. The team has had many sporting triumphs.* **triumphant** [B] showing triumph **-ly** [adv]

conquest [U;C] the process, time, or result of conquering or being conquered: *The Norman Conquest of England began in 1066. This sad situation is the result of foreign conquest. The king's conquests were considered a great national glory.*

defeat 1 [U] the act of defeating: *The defeat of the army was terrible news.* **2** [U] the act or state of being defeated: *Their defeat was total.* **3** [C] a case of being defeated: *In twelve games this year our team had only two defeats.*

loss 1 [U] the condition or fact of losing (something or someone): *The loss of their seaport was a great problem for the army. They suffered the loss of one of their great cities.* **2** [C usu sing] an occasion of losing (something or someone): *He has had a considerable loss of blood from the wound. Another loss like this one and we'll lose the whole war.*

losses [P] persons, usu soldiers, killed in a war or battle: *Losses on both sides were heavy. They suffered heavy/great losses in the last war.*

casualty [C] a person who is wounded (or killed) in a war, battle, accident, etc: *The army suffered heavy casualties in the attack. He is a casualty of the last war; he lost the sight of one eye.*

rout [C] *emph* a complete defeat: *Many men died in the rout.*

surrender [U] the act of surrendering: *Surrender is unthinkable; we fight here until we die. The enemy's unconditional surrender was accepted by our highest-ranking general.*

setback [C] a difficulty which causes someone to fail, lose, etc esp for a short time: *The advancing soldiers received an unexpected setback when they attacked the city and failed to take it.*

C284 *nouns* : **stopping fighting**

disengagement [U;C] the action of separating or being separated, esp of two armies, etc: *The disengagement was slow and many soldiers were killed before all the fighting ended. He approves of the disengagement of the Church from national politics.*

ceasefire [C] the act of stopping fighting for a long or short period: *The ceasefire was ordered for the 11th hour of the 11th day. The general said that there would be no ceasefire and no mercy.*

truce [C; U] an agreement during a war or a battle to stop fighting (for a time)

armistice [C] *fml* a truce: *The Armistice was signed in late 1918 and the Great War came to an end.*

peace treaty [C] a treaty [⇒ G110] or common agreement at the end of a war: *Many nations signed the Peace Treaty.*

C285 *nouns, etc* : **planning and action in war**

strategy 1 [U] the art of planning and moving forces, etc, esp in war, politics, etc: *The general's understanding of strategy was responsible for his many victories.* **2** [C] an example of this: *None of his strategies worked. Let's try a different strategy.* **strategic** [Wa5;B] relating to strategy; important in someone's strategy: *The men were moved from the base for strategic reasons. This bridge is of great strategic importance to the enemy and must be destroyed.* **-ally** [adv Wa4] **strategist** [C] a person practising or good at strategy

tactics [GU] the art of using or moving forces, etc esp in war, politics, etc or in a battle, particular situation, etc: *They moved the troops back in a sudden change of tactics.* **tactical** [Wa5;B] relating to tactics: *The general had great tactical ability but was less able in wider matters of strategy.* **-ly** [adv] **tactician** [C] a person engaged in or good at tactics

operations [P] movements of troops, ships, etc in war, during manoeuvres, etc: *His plan of operations was classically simple. The operations went ahead smoothly.* **ops** *tech abbrev* operations

manoeuvres *BrE*, **maneuvers** *AmE* [P] planned movements of troops, ships, etc as training for war: *The soldiers were all out on manoeuvres.*

campaign 1 [C; *on* U] a connected set of military actions with a particular purpose: *Napoleon's Spanish campaign and the campaign to take Moscow were both failures. He was on campaign for a year. The spring campaign went well.* **2** [I∅] to wage or go on a campaign: *He campaigned in India for five years. When will you start campaigning again?* **campaigner** [C] a person who campaigns, esp a soldier who has been on many campaigns (*esp in the phr* **an old campaigner**)

The armed forces

C290 *nouns, etc* : **armed forces**

(armed) forces [P] the military forces of a country, usu the army, navy, and air force

(armed) services [P *often cap*] the armed forces, esp during peace time: *He joined the Services as a boy and left an old man.*

army 1 [(*the*) GC *often cap*] the military forces of a country, esp those trained to fight on land: *He had joined the Army to become a soldier. He became an army officer.* **2** [C] a large body of people armed and trained for war **3** [C] any large group, esp one that is ordered: *An army of workers built the dam. He saw an army of ants approaching.*

troops [P] soldiers organized or operating collectively: *The dancers went to entertain the troops. The general withdrew his frontline [⇒ C272] troops for a rest and sent up his reserve [⇒ C293] troops to replace them. The city was full of troops.*

paratroops [P] a number of paratroopers [⇒ C295] trained to fight together: *They saw enemy paratroops dropping from aircraft.*

garrison 1 [C] the soldiers, etc in a fort, town, etc to guard it: *The garrison of the fort defended it bravely.* **2** [T1] to put a garrison in: *We must garrison all these forts and outposts properly.* **garrison town** [C] a town where troops are permanently stationed

navy [(*the*) GC *often cap*] the organization, including the ships, people, buildings, etc which makes up the power of a country for war at sea: *Britain has always had a large navy, called the Royal Navy. The Navy want(s) more money for ships this year.*

air force [(*the*) GC *often cap*] that part of the military organization of a country that is concerned with attack and defence from the air: *The US Air Force and the Royal Air Force were working together.*

marines [(*the*) P] the soldiers who serve in a ship of the navy

C291 *adjectives* : **relating to armed forces** [Wa5;B]

[ALSO ⇒ 273]

military 1 of, for, by, or connected with soldiers, armies, or war by armies: *In some countries every healthy young man must do a year's military service* (= be a soldier for a year) *when he comes of military age* (= is old enough). *When the old general died he was given a military funeral. It was decided not to defend the town, which was of little military value. They engaged the enemy in combined military and naval operations. His bearing was very military* (= he looked and acted like a soldier). *He was treated in a military hospital. He comes from an old military family* (= his father, grandfather, etc were soldiers). **2** [*the* GU] soldiers collectively; the army: *As the police were no longer able to keep order in the city, the military were called in to help them.* **militarily** [adv]

naval of, relating, or belonging to a navy or ships of war: *He took part in a great naval battle.*

civilian being of or belonging to any person or

organization which is not military: *The country has a military, not a civilian government.*

C292 *nouns* : **special parts of armies** [GC]

[ALSO ⇨ C305]

section *esp BrE*, **squad** *esp AmE* a small group of men in an army, usu a corporal and eight or ten men

platoon a group of soldiers fighting on foot, usu of about 30 men, and part of a company

troop a group of esp soldiers mounted on horses or in armoured vehicles, two or more making up a squadron

company one of the groups of men in an army, usu about 120, three or four of which make up a battalion

squadron a group of cavalry or armoured vehicles, three or four of which make up a regiment

battery a group of large guns (**artillery**) and the soldiers who use them, several of which make up a regiment

battalion in modern warfare, a fighting unit of about 600 infantrymen

regiment 1 a large military group usu commanded by a colonel; an important unit of cavalry, armour, artillery, engineers, etc: *He commanded a tank regiment in the war.* **2** a military organization, usu drawn from one area of a country, which sends battalions of infantrymen to serve in an army: *He belongs to the 1st Battalion of the Royal Border Regiment. The Black Watch are a famous Scottish regiment of infantry. The English County regiments have changed a lot in recent years. When the war broke out he joined his local regiment.* **regimental** [Wa5;B] relating or belonging to a regiment **-ly** [adv]

brigade a part of an army division, usu consisting of three battalions

division a large military or naval group, esp one able to fight on its own without needing additional support or supplies, and often in an army consisting of two or more brigades or about 20,000 men: *The men of the Highland Division held the bridge against all enemy attacks.*

corps [Wn3] **1** a large trained group in an army: *He was posted to command the 3rd Infantry Corps.* **2** a group in the army with special duties and responsibilities: *He joined the Intelligence Corps. The job of the Corps of Signals is to keep communications going.*

C293 *nouns* : **other parts and kinds of armies**

legion [C] **1** (in ancient Rome) a division of the army containing between 3,000 and 6,000 foot soldiers: *The Ninth Legion disappeared without trace in Scotland.* **2** a group of present or former soldiers or other servicemen: *He's a*

member of the British Legion. He fought in the French Foreign Legion in North Africa.* **3** (*fig*) a large group of people: *She has a legion of admiring boy-friends.*

commando [C] *BrE* a group of soldiers trained for certain kinds of surprise attacks: *He served in a Royal Marine Commando during the war.*

force [C] any organized military group: *The government sent a small force to protect the people. A force of armed men attacked the village.*

assault force *also* **task force** [C] a military force trained for a special assault [⇨ C276] or dangerous job: *Task Force 'Victor' attacked last night. An enemy assault force landed in small boats on the coast.*

expeditionary force [C] a military force sent on a special campaign [⇨ C285]: *He was with the British Expeditionary Force in France in the Second World War.*

column [C] a usu large and long line of soldiers, vehicles, ships, etc esp when moving: *A French column was marching towards the city.*

contingent [C] a group (of soldiers, ships, etc) esp put together to give special help: *Two contingents of newly-trained men arrived in the camp.*

detachment [C; *on* U] a group of esp soldiers separated from a larger group and sent on special duty: *The detachment arrived at its camp. The soldiers are on detachment at the moment.*

host [GC] *esp formerly* a large number, esp of armed men: *The enemy host approached. They killed a host of enemy soldiers.*

war-party [GC] a group of men, usu belonging to a less developed society, and gathered for war: *A war-party of Sioux Indians attacked the US fort.*

levy [C] the soldiers collected in a levy [⇨ C304]: *He commanded one of the local levies.*

reserve [C *usu pl*; U] forces kept in reserve: *The general did not want to commit* (= send into battle) *his reserves until the decisive moment. He held two battalions in reserve.*

reinforcements [P] forces brought to help those already fighting: *Send for reinforcements!*

flank 1 [C] the side, esp of an army, animal, etc: *The enemy attacked our left flank. They attacked on both flanks.* **2** [Wv4;T1] to attack (an army, etc) on one or both flanks: *They flanked us. They did a flanking attack.* **3** [T1 *usu pass*] to be at one side of: *The general was flanked by his chief officers.*

C294 *nouns* : **parts of navies, etc** [C]

fleet a number of ships, esp warships in a navy: *A fleet of enemy warships was approaching the coast. There are a hundred vessels in their submarine fleet. The admiral* [⇨ C298] *of the fleet arrived. The US First Fleet is in the area, on manoeuvres* [⇨ C285].

flotilla a (small) group of small warships: *Several flotillas of ships are sailing in the area.*

squadron 1 a number of warships: *A squadron of five ships sailed last night.* **2** a number of military aircraft: *The squadron of fighter planes passed overhead. He is a pilot in 294 Squadron.*

armada a large fleet esp of armed ships: *The Spanish Armada sailed against England in 1588.*

C295 *nouns* : **servicemen** [C]

serviceman a member of the armed forces of a country: *Servicemen stationed locally use this pub a lot.* **ex-serviceman** [C] a person who was at one time in the armed forces: *He joined his local ex-serviceman's club.*

soldier 1 a man, usu in uniform, trained to fight, esp for his country, on land: *Squads of soldiers patrolled [⇒ C225] the streets. He has been a soldier for most of his life.* **2** also **private (soldier)** a person of the lowest rank in an army. **soldierly** [B] having or showing the good qualities of a soldier **-liness** [U]

sailor also **seaman** a man who belongs in a navy: *There were a number of soldiers and sailors in the bar.*

airman a man in an air force, esp one not above the rank of a non-commissioned officer **airwoman** [*fem*]

marine a soldier who serves on a ship of the navy

paratrooper a soldier trained to drop from an aircraft using a parachute **para** *BrE infml abbrev*

commando a soldier in a commando force [⇒ C293]: *He was a commando during the war.*

C296 *nouns* : **military ranks generally**
[ALSO ⇒ J215, 6]

rank [U; C] the position of a person (in an army, navy, etc): *By 25 he had reached the rank of captain. What is your rank? He stated his name, rank, and number.*

ranks 1 [*the* P] the ordinary soldiers of an army: *He rose from the ranks to become a general. The sergeant was reduced to the ranks* (= made an ordinary soldier) *for refusing to obey an order.* **2** [P9] (*fig*) *pomp* (the) class or group (of): *He joined the ranks of the unemployed.*

rank and file [(*the*) GU] **1** the ordinary soldiers of an army collectively **2** (*fig*) the ordinary members of an organization

other ranks [P] common soldiers, usu below the rank of sergeant

men [P] *infml* **1** soldiers not including their officers: *Give the men their orders, Sergeant.* **2** soldiers generally: *The men don't like what's happening, Sir.* **enlisted men** [P] soldiers collectively

commission [C] (an official paper stating) the authority to act as an officer of the higher level in an army, navy, or air force: *He held a commission in the army. He resigned his commission.*

warrant [C] (an official paper stating) the authority to act as an officer of the lower level in an army, navy, or air force

C297 *nouns* : **particular ranks in the Army**

BRITISH ARMY	US ARMY
Field-Marshal	General of the Army
General	General
Lieutenant-General	Lieutenant General
Major-General	Major General
Brigadier	Brigadier General
Colonel	Colonel
Lieutenant-Colonel	Lieutenant Colonel
Major	Major
Captain	Captain
Lieutenant	1st Lieutenant
2nd Lieutenant	2nd Lieutenant
	Chief Warrant Officer
Warrant Officer 1st Class	Warrant Officer
Warrant Officer 2nd Class	
Staff Sergeant	Sergeant Major
	Specialist 9
Sergeant	1st Sergeant
	Master Sergeant
	Specialist 8
	Sergeant First Class
	Specialist 7
	Staff Sergeant
	Specialist 6
	Sergeant
	Specialist 5
Corporal	Corporal
	Specialist 4
Lance Corporal	Private 1st Class
Private	Private

C298 *nouns* : **particular ranks in the Navy**

ROYAL NAVY	US NAVY
Admiral of the Fleet	Fleet Admiral
Admiral	Admiral
Vice-Admiral	Vice Admiral
Rear-Admiral	Rear Admiral
Commodore	Commodore
Captain	Captain
Commander	Commander
Lieutenant-Commander	Lieutenant Commander

Lieutenant	Lieutenant
Sub-Lieutenant	Lieutenant Junior Grade
Acting Sub-Lieutenant	Ensign
	Chief Warrant Officer
Fleet Chief Petty Officer	Warrant Officer
	Master Chief Petty Officer
	Senior Chief Petty Officer
Chief Petty Officer	Chief Petty Officer
Petty Officer	Petty Officer 1st Class
	Petty Officer 2nd Class
Leading Seaman	Petty Officer 3rd Class
Able Seaman	Seaman
Ordinary Seaman	Seaman Apprentice
Junior Seaman	Seaman Recruit

C299 nouns : particular ranks in the Air Force

RAF	USAF
Marshal of the Royal Air Force	General of the Airforce
Air Chief Marshal	General
Air Marshal	Lieutenant General
Air Vice Marshal	Major General
Air Commodore	Brigadier General
Group Captain	Colonel
Wing Commander	Lieutenant Colonel
Squadron Leader	Major
Flight Lieutenant	Captain
Flying Officer	First Lieutenant
Pilot Officer	Second Lieutenant
	Chief Warrant Officer
Warrant Officer	Chief Master Sergeant
	Senior Master Sergeant
Flight Sergeant	Master Sergeant
Chief Technician	Technical Sergeant
Sergeant	Staff Sergeant
Corporal	Airman First Class
Junior Technician	—
Senior Aircraftman	Airman Second Class
Leading Aircraftman	Airman Third Class
Aircraftman	Airman Basic

C300 nouns : kinds of officers [C]

officer also **commissioned officer** *fml* a person in a position of command in the armed forces and (usu) with a commission: *The colonel summoned his officers. The men were led by a junior officer. Only senior serving officers were allowed to attend* (*the meeting*).

commanding officer the officer with general authority in a (usu larger) unit: *He asked to see his commanding officer.* **CO** *abbrev*

officer in command the officer commanding a (usu smaller) unit: *Who is the officer in command here?* **OC** *abbrev*

second in command the officer next to the officer in command

commandant a usu military officer in charge of a fort, prison, etc: *The word 'commandant' is not used much in the British or US armed forces.*

orderly officer *esp BrE*, **officer of the day** *also* **duty officer** *esp AmE* the officer on general duty for a period of 24 hours and responsible for emergencies, guards, etc during that period

noncommissioned officer an officer of the lower level in an army, etc, esp a sergeant or corporal: *No army can function properly without good noncommissioned officers.* **NCO** *abbrev* **non-com** *rare abbrev*

ensign 1 (in Britain before 1871) (the title of) an army officer of the lowest rank who carried the flag **2** (the title of) a US Navy officer of the lowest rank

lieutenant 1 [⇨ C297, 8 RANK LISTS] **2** (*fig*) a person who is chief helper to another: *Ask Miss Smith; she is my lieutenant in these matters.* **lieutenancy** [U] the condition of being a lieutenant in the army or navy

captain 1 [⇨ C297, 8 RANK LISTS] **2** (the title of) a person commanding a ship, plane, etc: *The captain brought the ship safely into harbour. Ask Captain Smith if I can speak to him.* **3** (*fig*) a leader: *He is one of the great captains of industry.* **captaincy** [U] the condition of being a captain in the army or navy

midshipman (the title of) a boy or youth who is being trained to become a naval officer

warrant officer 1 (in Britain) (a man who holds) the highest noncommissioned rank in the army, air force, or marines **2** (in the USA) (a man who holds) the highest noncommissioned rank in the army, air force, marines, or navy **WO** *abbrev*

petty officer (the title of) a noncommissioned officer of high rank in the navy

general staff [(*the*) GC *often cap*] the officers in an army who work for the commanding officers and help to plan military actions

C301 nouns : various names for soldiers, etc [C]

warrior 1 a man, usu in a less developed society, who is habitually ready for war or to fight for his chief, tribe, etc: *The chief called his warriors.* **2** *infml* a person who has military experience, inclinations, interests, etc: *The old warrior has seen many campaigns* [⇨ C285]. *He's quite a warrior, always getting into fights with people.*

fighting man *esp emot* a soldier, esp one in the army for a long time: *'Our country has a great tradition of proud fighting men!' he cried.*

man-at-arms (esp formerly) a soldier, esp in armour (and often riding a horse): *The king's own men-at-arms guarded the castle.*

mercenary a soldier who fights for the country, etc which pays him: *Many European mercenaries have fought in African wars.*

legionary a member of a military legion [⇒ C293] of any kind: *The Roman legionaries were tough, disciplined soldiers.*

legionnaire (the title of) a soldier esp in the French Foreign Legion

combatant a person who fights or is fighting: *Only combatants were allowed near the front line* [⇒ C272].

noncombatant a person who does not fight or is not fighting

belligerent a person actively engaged in a war, rebellion, etc: *All belligerents will be shot on sight.* [*also* ⇒C273]

hostile any person regarded as belonging to or fighting for an enemy force: *A party of hostiles was seen in the hills.*

militant a militant [⇒ C273] person: *These student disorders may have been started by a few militants.*

civilian a person who is not a member of the armed forces: *The officer told all civilians to leave the area. Several innocent civilians were killed by the bombs.*

partisan a member of a group fighting against an enemy occupying their country: *The partisans blew up a number of bridges which were important to the invaders of their country.*

C302 *nouns* : **kinds of soldiers according to kinds of service** [C]

regular a soldier who is a member of an army by choice over a period of time: *The army consisted of both regulars and conscripts.*

irregular a soldier or armed person who fights in a war, campaign, etc only part of the time or for short times, or who has been recruited [⇒ C304] in some unusual way: *The officers led local irregulars against the enemy.*

volunteer a soldier who has joined the army or offered his services for a particular job without being forced: *He joined the local regiment of volunteers.*

conscript a man who has been taken into the armed services whether he wishes it or not, usu as part of a national plan: *The conscripts boarded the train to the camp where they would be trained.*

territorial a person, usu a man, who receives part-time training for the armed forces of a country: *Several local territorials were killed in the manoeuvres* [⇒ C285].

reservist a person who can be called on at any time to serve in the armed forces: *He was a regular for three years and a reservist for five.*

recruit a person who has joined an organization, esp an army, as a conscript or a regular: *The sergeant was told to train the recruits.*

rookie *sl* a recruit (to the armed forces, police, etc)

veteran a person with long or special experience, esp in an army: *The new recruits were impressed by the stories which the veterans told them.*

C303 *adjectives* : **relating to soldiers and length of service**

élite *also* **crack** [Wa5;A] highly-trained and able: *The general sent his élite soldiers to lead the attack. They wasted their crack regiments defending the capital while the war went on elsewhere.*

veteran [Wa5;A] having long or special experience: *The general placed his veteran troops in the most difficult positions.*

raw *also* **green** [Wa1;B] *infml* not experienced; untrained: *You can't send raw recruits like these into battle! The new soldiers looked very green to the veterans.*

C304 *verbs, etc* : **gathering armies and joining the army**

gather [T1] to choose and bring together, or order to come together: *The king gathered his forces near the border. They are gathering an army to attack us.*

recruit 1 [I0] to go looking for new members, soldiers, etc: *The sergeant went recruiting.* **2** [Wv4;T1] to persuade, get, etc to join (an army, club, etc): *The sergeant recruited ten men for his regiment. The recruiting teams have done well this year.* **recruitment** [U] the activity of recruiting or being recruited

enlist 1 [I0 (*in*)] to enter (a branch of) the armed forces: *He has enlisted in his local regiment.* **2** [T1] take into (a branch of) the armed forces: *They enlisted him into the Corps of Signals.* **enlistment** [U] the activity of enlisting or being enlisted **enlisted men** [P] soldiers generally

sign on [v adv I0] to join (a branch of) the armed forces by signing a paper: *He signed on for nine years in the army.*

conscript [T1] to take (a person) into the armed services whether he wishes it or not, usu as part of a national plan: *The government conscripted all healthy 18-year-old men.* **conscription** [U] the activity of conscripting or being conscripted

draft *esp AmE* **1** [T1 (*into*)] to conscript: *All the men were drafted (into the army).* **2** [*the* U; A] conscription: *The draft was ended in the United States in 1972.* **3** [U] a group of people chosen by conscription: *That year's draft was the largest ever.*

mobilize, -ise [T1 *often pass*] to gather (men, equipment, etc) for service or use, usu in war: *The army has been mobilized.* **mobilization, -isation** [U] the action of mobilizing or being mobilized

levy 1 [T1] to gather (men to join an army), often by force: *They levied recruits among the local people.* **2** [C] the occasion or result of this: *The levy produced 4000 men.* [*also* ⇒ C293]

call up [v adv T1 *usu pass*] to order (esp a young man) to join the armed forces: *He was called up in 1941.* **call-up** [C] the act, occasion, result, etc of calling someone up: *His call-up was in 1941. There was a general call-up of all men who were 18 years old before September that year. He got his call-up papers.*

C305 nouns : kinds of soldiers collectively

infantry [(*the*) GU] soldiers who usu fight on foot, usu in battalions or regiments [⇒ C292] and whose main purpose is to win ground: *The general ordered the infantry to attack. He is an infantry officer.*

cavalry 1 [(*the*) GU] soldiers who fight on horseback: *The cavalry galloped past. He was a cavalry officer.* **2** [U] **a** *esp AmE* light, fast armoured vehicles used to protect larger, slower forces **b** *esp BrE* armour

armour *BrE*, **armor** *AmE* [U] military vehicles with armour, such as armoured cars and esp tanks: *The general attacked with all his armour.*

artillery 1 [U] large guns, esp those that are attached to wheels or fixed in one place, as on a ship or in a fort: *The artillery bombarded the town.* **2** [(*the*) GU] the part of the army trained to use such weapons: *He was a Royal Artillery Officer.*

ordnance [U] **1** big guns on wheels: *Bring up the ordnance now.* **2** military supplies, such as weapons, ammunition [⇒ C309], and vehicles used in fighting

fighting arms [P] those parts of an army which meet the enemy in combat: *The infantry and armour are the main fighting arms of a modern army.*

support arms [P] *also* **support** [U] those parts of an army which provide support, supplies, etc for the fighting arms: *Good support arms are vital in war.*

C306 nouns : kinds of soldiers as individuals [C]

infantryman a soldier who is in the infantry: *They need all the trained infantrymen they can get.*

foot soldier *esp old use* an infantryman

cavalryman a soldier who fights on horseback

trooper 1 a cavalryman or a soldier in an armoured regiment **2** [*also* A] *BrE* (the title of) a soldier of the lowest rank in the armoured regiments: *Send Trooper Jones in, Sergeant.* **3** *AmE* one of several kinds of police officer in a car or on horseback

guardsman 1 a soldier serving in a royal or

other force guarding a king, etc **2** [*often cap*] *BrE* a soldier or officer of the Guards (= the regiments which once guarded the king or queen)

artilleryman a soldier in the artillery

gunner [*also* A] *esp BrE* (the title of) a soldier (of lowest rank) in the artillery: *He was in the Gunners during the war. Send Gunner Jones in, Sergeant.*

engineer a soldier who is responsible for digging and building, etc

sapper [*also* A] *BrE* **1** an army engineer **2** (the title of) the lowest rank of soldier among army engineers: *Send Sapper Jones in, Sergeant.*

pioneer one of a special group of soldiers who go forward to prepare the way for an army's advance, by clearing roads, building bridges, etc

signaller *BrE*, **signaler** *AmE* a man in the army or navy whose job it is to send signals (as messages)

military policeman [*often cap*] a member of the military police of any army **MP** *abbrev*

orderly a soldier who attends an officer or performs duties for a commanding officer

batman *BrE* (in the armed services) an officer's personal servant

C307 nouns : kinds of soldiers, esp formerly [C]

grenadier 1 a soldier, formerly one who threw grenades [⇒ H246] **2** [*also* A] (the title of) a soldier of the lowest rank in the Grenadier Guards regiment: *Send Grenadier Smith in, Sergeant.*

fusilier [*also* A] (the title of) a soldier (of the lowest rank) in any of several British regiments who in former times were armed with a special type of light gun, but who now carry modern rifles [⇒ H238]: *Send Fusilier Smith in, Sergeant. He fought with the Lancashire Fusiliers.*

musketeer (formerly) a foot soldier who fought with a musket [⇒ H238]

bombardier 1 a man on a military aircraft who drops the bombs **2** [*also* A] *BrE* (the title of) a member of the artillery with a rank equal to corporal [⇒ C297]: *Bombardier Smith, come here!*

cavalier *old use* a horseman, knight or gentleman who supports a royalist [⇒ C94] cause

hussar a soldier in part of a European cavalry, who carried light arms

dragoon a soldier in part of a European cavalry, who carried heavy arms

C308 verbs : arming and disarming [T1]

arm 1 to give weapons to: *These countries are being armed for war. Arm the men, Sergeant.* **2** [I0] to get weapons: *The men are arming for* war. **3** to make ready to fire, etc: *Arm the warhead* [⇒ H251].

disarm 1 to take weapons away from: *The police disarmed the gunman. The soldiers were disarmed as they surrendered* [⇒ C282]. **2** to make unable to fire, etc: *Disarm the warhead.*

disarmament [U] the state of being disarmed or the act of disarming people, a nation, etc, fully or partly: *The two governments are having talks about disarmament/disarmament talks.*

C309 *nouns* : **weapons generally**
[ALSO ⇒ H230]

weaponry [U] weapons collectively

arms [P] weapons: *The sergeant handed out arms and ammunition to the men.*

armament [U] *also* **armaments** [P] military forces and equipment; weapons, esp large guns, ships, tanks, aircraft, etc: *The two nations have the necessary armaments for war. He is trying to build up their armament industry.*

ammunition [U] bullets, explosive materials, etc for war: *The soldiers ran out of ammunition and had to surrender. Get me some more ammunition for this rifle.* **ammo** *abbrev*

munitions [P] military supplies, esp guns, shells, ammunition, etc: *The enemy left a munitions dump near here. He worked in a munitions factory.*

C310 *verbs* : **military activities**
[ALSO ⇒ M22]

parade 1 [T1; I∅] to gather together in ceremonial order, to be looked at, to march, etc: *The soldiers parade at 10 o'clock. The officer paraded his men at 10 o'clock.* **2** [T1] *(fig)* to walk about (in order to show): *She paraded the room in her new dress. She paraded herself in her new dress.*

salute [T1; I∅] (esp in the armed forces) to show respect (for) or mark a meeting (with) by raising the hand or a weapon or by firing a gun: *The soldiers saluted their captain and he saluted back. The fleet saluted its new admiral.*

muster [T1] to bring (soldiers, etc) together, esp for review, inspection, etc or as an army: *The captain told the sergeant to muster the men. The king is mustering an army.*

inspect [T1] to look at (soldiers, etc) in order to examine the state of their uniforms, weapons, etc: *Sergeant, I'll inspect the men now.*

review [T1] to inspect very formally, esp of large numbers of men, ships, etc: *The general reviewed the troops.*

drill [T1] **1** (esp of soldiers, etc) to instruct and exercise by repeating certain movements: *The sergeant drilled the recruits on the square* [⇒ C312]. **2** [I∅] to exercise in this way: *The soldiers drilled on the square.* **3** [T1] to instruct and exercise by any kind of repeating: *The*

language teacher drilled the students in pronunciation.

march past [v prep T1] to march in military style before an officer, etc, as part of a review, celebration, etc: *The soldiers marched past the saluting base.*

C311 *nouns* : **military activities**

parade 1 [U] (esp of soldiers, etc) a gathering together in ceremonial order, for the purpose of being officially looked at, or for a march: *The soldiers are all on parade.* **2** [C] an example of this: *The parade began at the army camp. I like watching parades. A parade of players took place before the football match. (fig) A parade of witnesses appeared in court.* (BrE) *The police held an identification parade so that she could pick out the man who attacked her.* **muster parade** [C] *BrE* a parade, esp in the morning in an army camp, where all the soldiers, etc stand together to be inspected, given duties for the day, etc: *Muster parade is at 0800 hrs.* **inspection parade** [C] *BrE* a parade only for the purpose of inspecting soldiers, etc

salute [C] an act of saluting, either by hand or moving a weapon into a formal position, or by firing one or more guns: *The captain returned his men's salutes. The ships gave the president a 21-gun salute.*

inspection [U; C] the act or an act or occasion of inspection or being inspected: *The inspection was to be at 0800 hrs, and the men were to be in their best uniforms.*

review [C] an occasion when (usu large numbers of) troops, etc are ceremonially reviewed by an officer of high rank, a member of a royal family, a person of importance in government, etc: *The review was held last week.*

march-past [C] an occasion of troops marching past a particular point (= a saluting base), usu as part of a review: *The march-past was accompanied by the band of Her Majesty's Royal Marines.*

drill 1 [U] the training of soldiers, etc by or in making and repeating certain movements, esp in marching: *The recruits have drill on the square every day. It's a drill period now.* **2** [U; C] the act or an act of training and instructing in a subject, esp by means of repeating and following exact instructions: *The class was doing English pronunciation drills.*

C312 *nouns* : **military places** [C]
[ALSO ⇒ D68 BARRACKS]

(barrack) square a parade ground in an army barracks; an area, usu square, for drilling soldiers: *Tell the men that it's drill on the square in 10 minutes' time!*

parade ground [*also* A] a large, flat area, usu in an army barracks, where troops can parade;

fml a barrack square: *The parade ground was full of marching men. The sergeant-major shouted in his best parade-ground voice.*

saluting base *BrE* a platform on a parade ground, at a review, etc where an officer of high rank or other person is saluted and in turn salutes the troops, etc

Religion and beliefs

C320 *nouns* : **religion and theology** [U]

belief the condition, esp religious, of believing: *Belief in some kind of god or gods is common in most human societies.*

religion belief in a god or gods, esp the belief that he, she, or they made the world and control it and give(s) men life after death: *Religion has been a powerful force in human affairs.*

faith strong belief in something: *His faith (in God) is unshakable. Keep your faith, brother, and all will be well. He has great faith in you; don't disappoint him.*

theology the study of religion, or of a particular religion: *He is a student of theology.* **theological** [Wa5;B] of, concerning, or like theology: *theological arguments* **-ally** [adv Wa4] **theologian** [C] a person who studies theology

mysticism [U] the theory or practice of gaining a knowledge of real truth (and union with God) by prayer and meditation [⇒ C333]

fanaticism *often deprec* intense belief, usu causing a person to see everything else only as it relates to that belief: *She saw the light of fanaticism in his eyes. Their fanaticism makes it impossible to argue with them.*

fellowship friendly coming and being together, esp among people of the same religion: *The minister urged greater Christian fellowship among the believers. We have a fellowship meeting every Sunday evening.*

C321 *nouns* : **religions and beliefs** [C]

religion a particular system of belief and the worship, behaviour, etc associated with it: *There are many religions. The Christian and Jewish religions are historically related.*
coreligionist a person belonging to the same religion as oneself

faith *often emot* a religion: *He is a member of our faith. Do not deny* [⇒ G127] *the faith of your fathers! We welcome people of other faiths here.*

denomination a particular religious body with special beliefs different from those of others with the same general religious faith: *Among Christians there are many denominations. What denomination is he?* **denominational** [Wa5;B] of or concerning a denomination

sect a smaller group of people with special beliefs within a larger religious group: *There are many religious sects in this city.*

cult (the group of people believing in) a particular system of religious worship, with special customs and ceremonies: *He belongs to a strange cult that worships trees.*

belief 1 the feeling, esp religious, that something is true or that something really exists: *He has a firm belief in God. It's my belief that she is right.* **2** something believed; an idea which is considered true, often one which is part of a system of ideas: *These people have very unusual religious beliefs.*

creed a stated set of religious beliefs: *He learned the Creed by heart, from 'I believe in one God' to 'life everlasting, Amen'. All colours and creeds are welcome here* (= we don't exclude anyone because of colour or religion).

C322 *nouns* : **gods**

god [C] **1** a being, seen or unseen, worshipped as having power over (some part of) nature and control over (some part of) human affairs; an image of such a being: *Mankind seems always to have believed in gods/to have had its gods. In Hinduism Hanuman is a god in the form of a monkey. In some societies certain human beings are considered (to be) gods. Cupid was the Roman god of love. The ancient Greek gods lived on Mount Olympus.* **2** (*fig*) a greatly admired or powerful person or thing: *To these people he is a god. Don't make money your god/Don't make a god of money. He thinks he's a little god because he has some authority.* **goddess** [*fem*] *Venus was the goddess of love in ancient Rome. There are many goddesses in India.*

demigod [C] **1** (in ancient times) someone greater than a man but less than a god **2** a person who is, is believed to be, or believes himself to be more like a god than a man **demigoddess** [*fem*]

deity 1 [U] the rank or nature of a god: *Among these people his deity is unquestioned; he is a god.* **2** [C] a god or goddess: *He was reading about the deities of ancient Egypt.* **3** [C] a person considered and treated as good, interesting, and/or powerful in the highest degree: *These film stars are her deities.*

divinity [C] *fml* a god: *He makes pictures of the divinities of Hinduism.*

idol [C] **1** an image worshipped as a god **2** (*fig*) someone or something admired or loved too much: *He's her idol; she worships him.* **idolize** [T1] to treat as an idol: *He idolizes his father.* **idolatry** [U] **1** the worship of idols **2** (*fig*) too great admiration **idolater** [C] a worshipper of idols; (*fig*) great admirer **idolatrous** [B] **1** worshipping idols **2** like idolatry

C323 *nouns* : **angels, spirits, and devils** [C]

angel 1 a messenger and servant of God, usu

represented as a person with large wings and dressed in white clothes **2** *also* **guardian angel** a spirit who watches and guards a person **3** a person, esp a woman, who is very kind, good, beautiful, etc: *She's an angel; she's so helpful.* **angelic** [B] of, concerning, or like angels or an angel **-ally** [adv Wa4]

archangel (the title of) an angel with the highest rank: *The Archangel Gabriel came to him in a dream.*

spirit a supernatural [⇨ C355] being, often thought of as lower and less powerful than a god: *Good and evil spirits seem to be common in the beliefs of ancient societies. She says she can talk to spirits.*

evil spirit a supernatural being who wants or tries to harm people: *The tribesmen are afraid of evil spirits which seek to steal their souls* [⇨ C324].

devil 1 an evil spirit: *She is possessed of a devil* (= She has an evil spirit inside her). **2** an evil person: *That devil will do everything he can to injure you.* **3** *infml* a high-spirited person, usu a man, who is ready for adventure: *He's a devil with the ladies. Be a devil and have another drink. What a devil of a fellow he is!* **4** [*the* R] (used to give force to various expressions of displeasure): *What the devil happened? Who the devil is he? Where the devil has she gone? This is the devil of a problem. It's a devil of a job getting him to help. I'm coming!— The devil you will* (= No, you won't)*!* **devilish** [B] evil; of, concerning, or like devils or a devil **-ly** [adv] **diabolical** [B] devilish **-ly** [adv Wa4] [*also* ⇨ C326]

demon 1 an evil spirit: *They believe that demons live in this cave.* **2** something or someone considered as being like an evil spirit: *The demon hatred has been with them a long time. That child is a little demon!* **3** *infml* a person of unusual force, activity, or energy: *He's a demon for work. Ah, here comes the demon driver!* **demonic** [B] of, concerning, or like demons or a demon **-ally** [adv Wa4]

fiend 1 a particularly evil spirit **2** a particularly nasty and cruel person: *He is a fiend; he loves hurting people.* **fiendish** [B] of, concerning, or like fiends or a fiend **-ly** [adv]

imp 1 a little devil **2** (*fig*) a child: *What is that young imp doing now?* **impish** [B] like an imp **-ly** [adv] **-ness** [U]

C324 nouns : souls, spirits, and ghosts [C]

soul the non-material part of a person, believed in many religions to exist forever: *Christians believe that the (human) soul never dies. Do animals have souls?*

spirit the soul, esp if thought of as separate from the body: *She said she saw the spirits of dead people. Can the spirits (of the dead) communicate with us? The priests say that the human spirit lives on when the body dies.*

ghost the spirit, esp if seen or heard, of a dead person: *He says he saw the ghost of his father. Do you believe in ghosts? He enjoys a good ghost story.* **ghostly** [Wa2;B] like a ghost: *He saw a ghostly figure among the trees.*

phantom the shadowy likeness of a dead person that seems to appear on earth; a ghost: *The phantom passed through the wall. Phantom horsemen rode by in the night.*

shade *lit & old use* a ghost

spook *infml* a ghost

apparition (something like) a ghost, esp as it appears to the eye: *Several strange apparitions appeared in the doorway.*

spectre *BrE*, **specter** *AmE esp lit* a ghost or apparition

C325 nouns : heaven and hell

heaven 1 [R] the place where God or the gods live; the place of complete happiness where the souls of good people go after death **2** [U; C] *infml* great happiness: *I was in heaven when I heard the good news! This house is a little heaven.* **3** *also* **heavens** [R] *euph* (in exclamations of surprise) God: *Heaven forbid (that this should happen)! Thank Heaven you came! Good Heavens, what did you do?* **heavenly** [Wa2;B] of, concerning, or like heaven: *What a heavenly place!*

paradise 1 [R *usu cap*] heaven **2** [R *usu cap*] the Garden of Eden: *Adam and Eve were expelled from Paradise.* **3** [S] a place of perfect happiness: *The quiet village was a paradise far from the noisy city.* **4** [S9] *infml* a favourite place in which there is everything one wants: *These forests are a hunter's paradise.*

hell 1 [R] (esp in the Christian religion) a place where the souls of the wicked are said to be punished after death: *The priest said they would go to hell for their sins* [⇨ C341]. **2** [U; C] a place or state or great suffering: *His life has been a hell since his wife came back to him.* **3** (a swearword used in anger or to strengthen an expression): *I won't, you say?— By hell I will! What the hell is going on here? What the hell's that thing on your head—a hat? That's a hell of a good story! Go to hell— Leave me alone! Like hell I will!* (= I won't) **hellish** [B] like or belonging to hell; terrible **-ly** [adv]

inferno 1 [*the* R *sometimes cap*] *esp lit* hell: *She said she had suffered the pains of the Inferno during the last few years.* **2** [C] (*fig*) a burning place: *The blazing building was an inferno; no one could get in or out.* **infernal** [B] [Wa5] like or belonging to hell **2** terrible **-ly** [adv]

purgatory 1 [R *sometimes cap*] (esp in Roman Catholic teaching) a condition or place in which the soul of a dead person must remain and be made pure by suffering for wrongdoing on earth until it is fit to enter Heaven **2** [U] *often humor* any place, state, or time of great (but not lasting) suffering: *His years in the army were pure purgatory. Angela has a* *sharp voice; it's purgatory to be in the same room with her.*

limbo 1 [R *sometimes cap*] (esp in Roman Catholic teaching) a condition or place, neither heaven nor hell, where the souls of those who have not done evil may go even though they were not Christians during their life: *Children who died before they could be baptized* [⇒ C334] *and those who lived before Christ are said to wait in limbo until Christ comes again.* **2** [U; (S)] a state or place where nothing happens, where changes are impossible: *I'm in limbo, waiting to see if I've been accepted for the new job. The town is just a limbo of old factories and out-of-date ideas.*

C326 nouns : God, Christ, etc [R]

God 1 the one great spirit or power, usu thought of as having a personality, usu expressed as male, in religions such as Christianity, Judaism, and Islam: *They prayed to God for His guidance. Only God knows where they are now.* **2** (in expressions showing emotion, whether or not God as such is intended): *Oh God, I don't know what to do! Thank God, you're safe! Dear God, what are you doing now? I wish to God you would go away! For God's sake stop doing that!*

Supreme Being [*the*] *fml* God

Deity [*the*] *fml* God

Allah (the Islamic name for) God

Christ *also* **Jesus (Christ) 1** the man who established Christianity, considered by Christians to be the son of God and to be still alive in heaven where he forms one of the persons of the Trinity, and considered in Islam as a major prophet [⇒ C343] **2** (in usu powerful expressions of emotion, taboo for some people): *Christ, what are you doing? I wish to Christ you'd told me about it! In the name of Christ why did you do it? Oh Christ, I was scared! Jesus (Christ), what's happening?*

Lord 1 [*the; also* A] a god, but esp the Christian God or Christ: *Thank the Lord! The Lord God helped us. 'Lord Krishna will help,' said the Hindu.* **2** (in expressions of emotion, not as strong as **God** or **Christ**): *Good Lord! Lord help you!*

Virgin (Mary) [*the*] (in the Christian religion) the mother of Christ

Holy Ghost *also* **Holy Spirit** [*the*] (in the Christian religion) God in the form of a spirit

(Holy) Trinity [*the*] (in the Christian religion) the three forms of God the Father, the Son (Christ) and God the Holy Ghost or Spirit **trinitarian** [Wa5;B *often cap*] of or concerning the Trinity

Devil [*the*] **1** the most powerful evil spirit; the enemy of God in such religions as Christianity: *The Devil and his fiends in hell are described in the first book of Milton's 'Paradise Lost'.* **2** (in expressions of emotion, surprise, etc): *Where*

the Devil have you been? What in the name of the Devil does she want now?

Satan (a name for) the Devil: *He gave his soul to Satan in return for earthly power.* **satanic** [B *often cap*] (wicked) like Satan: *dark satanic practices*

C327 nouns : major religions [R]

[ALSO ⇒ J44 CROSS & CRESCENT]

Christianity 1 the religion based on the life and teachings of Christ and the belief that he (is The Son of God who) came to save the world: *Christianity teaches that Christ will come again in the future to judge the world.* **2** [U] the condition or fact of being a follower of any of the various branches of this religion: *I have never doubted his Christianity, although he isn't very kind to some people.*

Christendom *esp formerly* all Christian people in general; the Christian countries of the world: *The Church wanted all Christendom to join in a holy war against its enemies.*

Islam the religion taught by Mohammed in Arabia in the 6th & 7th centuries AD: *The followers of Islam do not usually eat pork or drink alcohol.*

Mohammed the founder of Islam **Muhammad** (preferred spelling for academic, etc works on Islam) **Mahomet** *now rare* (older European form of Mohammed)

Judaism the religion and culture of the Jews: *Judaism has several features in common with Christianity and Islam, including belief in one God, and is older than both.*

Hinduism the Hindu religion and its customs, mainly in India, such as its social caste [⇒ C150] system, general belief in reincarnation [⇒ C342] and many deities [⇒ C322]

Buddhism the religion and/or philosophy [⇒ G6] taught by Gautama the Buddha in about the 6th century BC in India: *The removal of desire is a central element of Buddhism.*

Shinto(ism) the traditional religion of Japan, including the worship of deities [⇒ C322] and ancestors [⇒ C17]

Confucianism the beliefs and practice(s) of those who follow Confucius [⇒ C328], esp in China in former times

C328 adjectives : relating to the major religions [B]

Christian 1 [Wa5] of or relating to Christ, Christianity, or Christians: *Her Christian faith is well-known. 'I don't like the way Christian ideas work in practice,' said the angry politician. He tries to lead a Christian life.* **2** following the example of Christ; having qualities such as kindness, generosity, etc: *He behaved in a (very) Christian way to all people, even his enemies. What a truly Christian thing to do!*

Islamic *also* **Muslim** *also* **Moslem** [Wa5] of or

relating to Islam: *He studies Islamic law. Muslim law traditionally allows a man four wives, although today in practice this is becoming less common.*

Jewish [Wa5] of or relating to the Jews or Judaism: *He is interested in the Jewish religion.*

Hebrew [Wa5] of or relating to the Hebrews, the Hebrew language, or Jews, Judaism, etc

Hindu [Wa5] relating to Hindus or Hinduism

Buddhist [Wa5] of or relating to Buddhism: *There is a Buddhist shrine [⇨ C351] near the village.*

Shinto [Wa5] of or relating to Shintoism: *They visited the Shinto temple [⇨ C351].*

Confucian [Wa5] relating to the ideas of Confucius or Kung Fu Tse, who lived in China in the 5th and 6th centuries BC and taught standards of behaviour such as being loyal to one's ruler, father, husband, etc

C329 *nouns* : **persons belonging to the major religions** [C]

Christian a person who believes in any of the various branches of Christianity; a person who lives a good Christian life and who is always willing to help others: *The early Christians were not well treated in ancient Rome.*

Muslim *also* **Moslem** a person accepting Islam: *Moslems and Christians have not always lived in peace together.*

Jew a person who is considered by religious belief or by blood to belong to a religion or race, once living only in the land of Israel **Jewry** [R] the whole Jewish community

Hindu a person accepting Hinduism: *Modern India is not a religious state, but the majority of its people are Hindus.*

Buddhist a person accepting Buddhism

C330 *nouns & adjectives* : **kinds of Christianity**

(Roman) Catholic [C; Wa5;B] (a member) of or belonging to the Roman Catholic Church: *The Catholic Church has very many members throughout the world. The priest wanted to send Catholic children to Catholic schools. The priest said that the man was a good Catholic/that the girl was from a good Catholic family.* **RC** *abbrev* **-ism** [U] the beliefs and religious system of Roman Catholics

Protestant [C; Wa5;B] (a member) of any of several branches of Christianity that separated from the Roman Catholic Church in the 16th century **-ism** [U] the beliefs and religious system of Protestants

Orthodox Church [*the* R] any of several Christian churches with members esp in Eastern Europe and the Near East **Orthodox** [Wa5;B] relating to any Orthodox church

Anglican [C; Wa5;B] (a member) of the Angl-ican Church, esp the Church of England **-ism** [U] the beliefs and religious system of Angl-icans

Episcopalian [C; Wa5;B] **1** (a person accepting a church) having bishops [⇨ C347] **2** Anglican **-ism** [U] the beliefs and religious system of Episcopalians

Presbyterian [C; Wa5;B] (a member) of a Protestant church governed by a body of official people all of equal rank, as in Scotland **-ism** [U] the beliefs and religious system of Presbyterians

Lutheran 1 [C; Wa5;B] (a member) of the Protestant church founded by Martin Luther in 16th-century Germany **2** [Wa5;B] relating to Luther, his ideas, writings, etc **-ism** [U] the beliefs and religious system of Lutherans

Methodist [C; Wa5;B] (a member) of a Christian group which follows the teachings of John Wesley **Methodism** [U] the beliefs and religious system of Methodists

Baptist [C; Wa5;B] (a member) of a denomination [⇨ C321] which believes that baptism [⇨ C335] should be only for people old enough to understand its meaning and that they should be immersed (= placed) fully in water

C331 *nouns, etc* : **persons believing or not believing in religion** [C]

believer [(*in*)] **1** a person who has religious faith: *Believers in Christianity should try to live together in peace.* **2** a person who believes (in) something or someone: *He is a great believer in fresh air as a cure for illness.*

unbeliever *often deprec* a person who has no faith (in something, esp a religion)

nonbeliever a person who has no special reason, wish, or need to believe (in something, esp a religion)

infidel *usu deprec* someone who does not follow the speaker's religion; an unbeliever (used esp in former times by Muslims and Christians of each other): *Kill the infidels!*

adherent [(*of*)] a person who favours and supports a particular idea, opinion, or political party: *The people there are mainly adherents of Islam.*

devotee [(*of*)] a person who devotes him/herself to religion; a very religious person (usu of a stated kind): *The temple was full of devotees. He is a devotee of the Hindu goddess Kali.*

convert [(*to*)] a person who has been converted [⇨ C340] to anything, esp a religion: *She is a recent convert to Roman Catholicism.*

pilgrim a person who travels to a sacred place, special shrine [⇨ C351], etc as an act of religious devotion, penance [⇨ C341], to be healed, etc: *Many Catholics go as pilgrims to Lourdes in France. The Hindu pilgrims were travelling to Benares.* **pilgrimage** [U; C] the act or an act of going on a journey as a pilgrim

fanatic *often deprec* a person who engages in fanaticism [⇨ C320] or who has a very strong religious belief: *He is a religious fanatic.* **fanatical** [B] like a fanatic: *He's a fanatical supporter of his local football team.* **-ly** [adv Wa4]

heretic a person who supports or is guilty of heresy [⇒ C336]: *The heretics were condemned to death.*

agnostic 1 a person who says that he does not know whether there is a God or not, or which religion, etc is true: *He was born a Christian but he is now an agnostic. In these matters I am an agnostic. He is a political agnostic.* **2** [B] claiming not to know: *I am agnostic in religious matters.* **-ally** [adv Wa4] **-ism** [U] the ideas, etc of agnostics

atheist a person who denies the existence of God or any gods **atheism** [U] the ideas, etc of atheists **atheistic** [B] of or concerning an atheist or atheism **-ally** [adv Wa4]

evangelist 1 a preacher [⇒C344] of the Gospel [⇒ C337], esp one who travels and holds meetings wherever he can for whoever will listen **2** any of the writers of the Gospels **evangelism** [U] the beliefs, etc of evangelists **evangelical** [Wa5;B] of or concerning evangelists or evangelism **-ly** [adv Wa4]

proselyte a person who has been persuaded to join a religious, political, etc, group different from the one to which he previously belonged **proselytism** [U] any effort to persuade anyone to join a religion, etc

apostle 1 a follower of a great man or woman, esp one who is sent to spread his or her teachings, **2** [*usu cap*] any of the original twelve followers of Jesus Christ **apostolic** [Wa5;B] **1** of or like an apostle or the Apostles **2** (esp in Roman Catholicism) coming from the time of the Apostles, esp the Apostle Peter

C332 *verbs* : **believing and worshipping**

believe in [v prep T1] **1** to have faith or trust in: *Christians believe in Jesus. She firmly believes in nature cures for all illnesses.* **2** to consider (something) to be true; consider (something or someone) to exist: *Do you believe in everything the Bible* [⇒ C337] *says? Christians and Muslims both believe in God.*

worship [T1; I∅] to give praise and admiration to (esp God) in prayer, singing, etc: *'Let us worship God,' said the priest. Many Hindus worship more than one god. Don't talk while they are worshipping.* (*fig*) *She worships her husband.* **worshipper** *BrE*, **worshiper** *AmE* [C] a person who worships (a god, etc)

revere [T1] to give great respect and admiration to: *The people revere their priest.* **reverence** [U] **1** the act of revering: *He showed great reverence for/towards the pictures of the god.* **2** the state of revering **reverent** [B] showing reverence: *He went up to the church door in a very reverent manner.* **ir-** [*neg*] **-ly** [adv]

venerate [T1] to revere or worship greatly: *The priests venerate the shrine* [⇒ C351] *as the*

holiest in their religion. **veneration** [U] the act of venerating

adore [T1] to show great, esp religious, love to: *The peasant girl adored the statue of the Virgin Mary.* **adoration** [U] the act of adoring

C333 *verbs* : **praying and meditating**

pray [I∅ (*for*)] to (try to) communicate ideas, feelings, needs, wishes, etc to God or a god: *The people knelt to pray. Let us pray. She prayed for God's help. We can only wait and hope and pray. The farmers are praying for rain. He prayed to God for help.*

preach 1 [T1; I∅] to speak publicly about (a religion, etc): *He preached the Gospel* [⇒ C337] *to the unbelievers. What will he be preaching about on Sunday? The priest preached against evil.* **2** [I∅ (*to*)] *deprec* to give moral advice (to): *The teacher began preaching to the pupils about good behaviour. Don't start preaching (to me)!* **3** [T1] (*fig*) to urge; teach: *Their leaders are preaching war as a solution to their problem.*

chant [I∅; T1] **1** [I∅] to sing with little change of voice level: *The priest began to chant.* **2** [T1; I∅] to repeat (words) continuously in time: *The crowd chanted 'Down with the government!' When the football crowd is chanting you can hear them a mile away.*

meditate [I∅] to fix and keep the attention on one matter, having cleared the mind of other thought, esp for religious reasons or to gain peace of mind: *She says she has learnt to meditate by using Hindu techniques. Well, meditate and you may find an answer to your problems.* **meditation** [U] the activity of meditating

C334 *verbs* : **blessing, baptizing, etc** [T1]

bless 1a (of God) to look with favour on: (*May God) Bless you, and may you have all you could wish for!* **b** to ask God's favour for: *The priest blessed the ship before it left port.* **2** to make holy, esp for religious use: *The priest blessed the bread and wine.* **3** to praise or call holy: *Bless the name of the Lord!*

consecrate to make holy or give to God's use esp in a special ceremony: *The bishop consecrated them to the service of God* **consecration** [U] the act of consecrating a place or person

desecrate *esp emot* to destroy the holiness of (a place, etc): *The unbelievers have desecrated the greatest shrine* [⇒ C351] *of our faith by keeping their horses there!* **desecration** [U; C] the act or action of desecrating a place, religion, etc

profane to treat (a holy place, thing, etc) without proper respect: *Your behaviour profanes this temple! Do not profane the name of God in this way!*

solemnize to perform the ceremony of: *The priest solemnized their marriage.*

initiate [*often pass*] to introduce to (someone) some secret or mysterious knowledge; to introduce (someone) into a society, group, etc esp with special ceremony: *He has been initiated into the brotherhood* [⇒ C346]. *Who will initiate her in the mysteries of the faith?*

baptize, -ise 1 to perform the ceremony of baptism [⇒ C335] on: *They baptized him into the faith last week.* **2** [X1] to admit as a member of a given church by baptism: *He was baptized a Roman Catholic.* **3** [X1] to give (someone) a name at baptism: *He was baptized John Jones, but he's changed his name since.*

christen 1 to make (someone) a member of a Christian church by baptizing: *He was christened last Sunday.* **2** [X1] to give (someone) a name by baptizing: *They christened the baby John.* **3** [X1] (*fig*) to name (esp a ship) at an official ceremony: *We asked the Queen to christen the ship. The ship was christened Queen Mary.*

circumcise to cut off the skin (**foreskin**) at the end of the sex organ of (a man) or part of the sex organ (**clitoris**) of (a woman): *Muslims circumcise their young boys according to the laws of their religion. There are still one or two African tribes who circumcise their women, but it is against the law in most countries.* **circumcision** [U; C] the act of circumcising, esp as part of a Jewish or Muslim religious service

ordain [*often pass*] to make (someone) a priest, minister, etc: *He was ordained in 1960.* **ordination** [U; C] the act or ceremony of ordaining or being ordained

C335 nouns : praying, blessing, baptizing, etc

prayer 1 [U; C] the act or an act of praying: *Prayer is usually an important part of a religion. She said her prayers before going to bed. Let us offer up a prayer to God. Where is my prayer book?* **2** [U; C *usu pl*] a service or form of worship: *Are you coming to prayer? Morning Prayers are at seven. When is the prayer meeting?* **3** [C] the form of words used in prayer: *You must learn the Lord's* [⇒ C326] *Prayer.*

amen [interj] (a word used at the end of a prayer, esp by Christians and Jews, meaning 'May it be so').

worship [U] the activity of worshipping: *In the evening they all join in worship/in the worship of God. What form of worship do they have in that religion?*

service [C *often in comb*] a (usu Christian) form of religious worship following a certain pattern of prayers, songs, etc: *The church service is at 10.30 am every Sunday. We are holding an evening service tomorrow. The funeral service was brief.*

sermon [C] **1** a religious talk, usu Christian and given as part of a church service: *The priest's sermon was on love and fellowship.* **2** (*fig*) *deprec* advice that is not asked for: *Please*

don't give me a sermon on how to lead my life!

chant [C; U] **1** an often repeated tune, often with many words sung on one note, in which the time is largely controlled by the words, esp in religious services: *Can you hear the chant of the priests? I enjoy listening to monastic* [⇒ C351] *chants.* **2** words continuously repeated in time: *The chant of the crowd was 'Equal rights for all'.*

hymn [C] a religious song, usu to praise God, a god, or gods: *The people stood up to sing a hymn. Let us sing Hymn 42 in the hymn book. The priests sang hymns to their gods.*

psalm [C] a sacred song, esp those in the Bible [⇒ C337]

blessing [C] **1** an act of asking or receiving God's favour, help, or protection: *The blessing of the Lord be upon you all. Don't expect any blessings to fall from heaven.* **2** (*fig*) *infml* approval; encouragement: *The government has given its blessing to the new plan, and will provide the necessary money.* **3** a gift from God; something one is glad of: *It's a blessing to have her here to help us. Count your blessings: you're luckier than you think. What a blessing this fine weather is!* **a blessing in disguise** something not very pleasant, which however is really a good thing after all: *The storm was a blessing in disguise because it kept us at home when you telephoned.*

ceremony [C; U] a special action or set of actions done, esp by a priest, official, etc at a particular time, in a particular place, for a particular purpose, etc, usu formal and often religious: *The wedding ceremony was simple but beautiful.* **ceremonial 1** [Wa5;B] of, concerning, or like a ceremony or ceremonies; formal, as in a ceremony: *She was wearing ceremonial dress.* **-ly** [adv] **2** [U; C] ceremonial acts: *The religious service was full of ancient ceremonial(s).* **ceremonious** [B] **1** liking or interested in (what happens in) ceremonies: *Some religions are more ceremonious than others.* **2** very or unnecessarily polite, formal, etc **un-** [neg] **-ly** [adv]: *She left quickly and unceremoniously.*

rite [C *usu pl*] a form of behaviour with a fixed pattern, usu for a religious purpose: *They performed the funeral rites for the dead.*

ritual 1 [C; U] one or more ceremonies or customary acts which are often repeated in the same form: *Buddhist ritual is very different from Christian church services. She went through the ritual of preparing the meal.* **2** [Wa5;A] of, concerning, or like ritual: *The women began a ritual dance.* **-ly** [adv]

devotions [P] *fml & old use* prayers, meditation, etc: *The priest was interrupted at his devotions.*

litany [C] a form of prayer, esp in the Christian churches, in which the priest calls out and the people reply, always in the same words

liturgy [C; U] **1** a form of worship in the Christian churches using prayers, songs, etc according to fixed patterns in religious services **2** [*the* R *sometimes cap*] the written form of these services

sacrifice [C;U] the act of giving something (precious) to another person or to God or the gods: *In past times many peoples made human sacrifices to their gods. We must make a fitting sacrifice to show our faith.* (*fig*) *She made a lot of sacrifices in order to give her children a good start in life.* **sacrificial** [B] of or being (a) sacrifice: *a sacrificial lamb* **-ly** [adv]

sacrament 1 [C] any of several religious ceremonies in the Christian churches said to give strength to the soul: *The Roman Catholics have seven sacraments, including the marriage service, but Protestants have only baptism and communion.* **2** [*the* R *often cap*] communion **Blessed Sacrament** [*the* R] the bread eaten in the Eucharist, and sometimes also the wine which is drunk

communion, *also sometimes* **Holy Communion** [R *sometimes cap*] the service, esp in Protestant churches, in which bread and wine are taken as a sign of Christ's body and blood

mass 1 [C; R *often cap*] an esp Roman Catholic church service in memory and honour of Christ's last supper: *They go to Mass every Sunday.* **2** [C] the music for such a service: *He has written a new mass.*

Eucharist [*the* R] *fml* Holy Communion; the mass

baptism 1 [U] a Christian religious ceremony in which a person is touched by or placed in water to make him or her pure and show that he or she has been accepted as a member of a church **2** [U] a ceremony in any other religion in which water is used to make people pure **3** [C] an example of these ceremonies: *There haven't been many baptisms in the village church this year.* **baptismal** [Wa5;B] of or concerning baptism: *His baptismal name was John.*

C336 nouns : holy writings and teachings

scripture [U; C *usu pl: sometimes cap*] the holy writings of a religion, esp the Bible: *He read to them from Scripture. She is well acquainted with Hindu scriptures.* **scriptural** [Wa5;B] of, concerning, or like scripture **-ly** [adv]

holy writ [U *often cap*] scriptures; sacred writing or law: *What he says is not according to Holy Writ.*

canon [C] **1** a religious, usu Christian law: *The canons of the Church forbid this.* **2** a set of generally accepted scriptures: *The Buddhist Canon was laid down long ago.* **3** *fml* a general social principle: *Your actions violate every civilized canon!* **canonical** [B] according to the canons; (religiously) authorized **-ly** [adv Wa4]

doctrine [C; U] a principle, esp religious, or the whole body of principles in a branch of knowledge or system of belief: *Christian and Muslim doctrines are very different. Political doctrines*

change with political fashions. His ideas are against established doctrine. **doctrinal** [Wa5;B] concerning or according to doctrine **-ly** [adv]

dogma [C;U] a belief or system of beliefs, usu religious, political, etc to be accepted as true without question: *'These dogmas are old-fashioned,' he said.* **dogmatic** [B] of, concerning, like, or having the nature of dogma **-ally** [adv Wa4] **dogmatize, -ise** [T1;I0] to express as dogma

teachings [P] the things which are taught, esp by a religious leader: *Mahatma Gandhi's teachings are about peace among the different religions.*

heresy [U;C] (a) belief or opinion that is against what is generally accepted, esp in religion: *It is heresy to say or believe that! He was burnt at the stake* (= while tied to a wooden post) *for heresy/for many heresies.* **heretical** [B] of, concerning, like, or having the nature of heresy **-ly** [adv Wa4]

sacrilege [U] the act of using something holy for purposes which are not holy: *It is sacrilege to use this church as a military base! You have committed sacrilege by entering the forbidden shrine!* [⇒ C351] **sacrilegious** [B] showing no respect for what is holy: *It is a sacrilegious act, wearing shoes inside a mosque.* **-ly** [adv]

C337 nouns : major holy books

Bible [C; *the* R] **1** (a copy of) the holy book of the Christians, consisting of the **Old Testament** and the **New Testament 2** (a copy of) the holy book of the Jews, corresponding to the Old Testament **bible** (*usu fig*) (a copy of) a book of great importance: *That dictionary is his bible for studying English.* **biblical** [B *sometimes cap*] of, like, or about the Bible: *He wrote in a biblical style. These things happened in Biblical times.*

gospel 1 [*often cap*] **a** [*the* R] the life and teachings of Jesus Christ in the first four books of the New Testament of the Bible: *He taught them the Gospel.* **b** any of these four books: *These words are from the Gospels/from the Gospel of St John/the Gospel according to* (*St*) *John.* **2** [S] (*fig*) a thing that may be or can be believed completely: *He teaches a gospel of health and love.* **gospel truth** [*the* R] *infml* something which is completely true: *It's the gospel truth; believe me!*

Koran, *less common* **Quran** [C; *the* R] the holy book of the Muslims **Koranic, Quranic** [Wa5;B] of, like, or about the Koran

Vedas [*the* P] the (four) principal scriptures of the Hindus **Vedic** [Wa5;B] of, like, or about the Vedas

C338 adjectives : relating particularly to religion [B]

religious 1 [Wa5] of or concerning religion: *He*

enjoys religious music and books on religious subjects. **2** having a great interest in or desire for religion: *She is very religious by nature.* **ir-** [*neg*] **-ly** [*adv*]

spiritual of or concerning the soul or spirit, not the mind or body; very much influenced by religion: *She leads a very spiritual life. He felt a spiritual sympathy with the local religion.* **-ly** [*adv*] **spirituality** [U] the state or condition of being spiritual

ecclesiastical [Wa5] of or concerning the or any Christian church: *He knows a lot about ecclesiastical history.* **-ly** [*adv* Wa4]

devotional of, about, or used in devotions: *She thinks that Hindu devotional literature is wonderful.*

sectarian of, or like the way of, a religious sect [⇒ C321]: *Let us try to forget sectarian differences.* **-ism** [U]

ecumenical of or concerning the whole Christian religion or the universal Church: *The ecumenical movement seeks to bring the many Christian denominations* [⇒ C321] *closer together.* **-ly** [*adv* Wa4] **ecumenism** [U] the ecumenical movement; an ecumenical way of treating religious matters

holy [Wa1] (in the service) of God or religion: *He reads the Holy Bible every night. The Koran is the holy book of the Muslims. She is a true saint* [⇒ C343] *and leads a very holy life.* **holiness** [U] the state of being holy

sacred *often fml* connected with or made for God; holy: *The Koran is the sacred book of Islam. Jerusalem is sacred to all Christians, Jews, and Muslims.* **-ness** [U]

godly [Wa1] *fml & sometimes pomp* deeply religious: *He was a godly man and led a godly life.* **un-** [*neg*] **-liness** [U]

divine 1 [Wa5] of, from or like God or a god or gods; relating to religion: *Charles I believed in the divine right of kings to rule their lands. Divine Service is at 11 o'clock.* **2** *infml* excellent; wonderful: *Oh, the music was just divine!* **-ly** [*adv*] **divinity** [U] the state of being divine

heavenly [Wa5] belonging to heaven; God: *'Our Heavenly Father will look after us,' the priest said.*

celestial [Wa5] **1** of or belonging to the sky or heaven: *The sun, the stars, and the moon are celestial bodies.* **2** heavenly; having the qualities of a god: *Her beauty was celestial. In former times China was called the Celestial Empire.*

C339 *adjectives & nouns* : **relating generally to religion**

lay [Wa5] **1** [A; (B)] of, relating to, or performed by people who are not in official positions within a religion: *He is a lay preacher* [⇒ C344]. **2** [A] not trained in or having knowledge of a particular profession or branch of learning such as law or medicine: *To the lay*

mind these things are very technical and mysterious.

secular [B] **1** of or concerning the ways of the world, not the (spiritual) values of religion: *He is no longer a priest; he leads a secular life. Most states are secular but some have a religious basis.* **2** [Wa5] of the power of the state, not the church: *In some countries there are both religious and secular courts of law.*

profane [B] **1** not sacred; worldly: *He reads both sacred and profane literature.* **2** having or showing lack of respect for God or religion: *That man uses very profane language.* **profanity** [U; C] the state or condition of being profane; anything profane **profanities** [P] foul language

worldly [Wa1; B] *sometimes deprec* not spiritual; material: *He is more interested in worldly glory than in salvation* [⇒ C341]. *These worldly people have no time for religion.* **-liness** [U]

earthly [Wa5; B] belonging to the world and not heaven, God, etc: *He seeks no earthly reward; his reward will come in heaven.*

pagan [B; C] (a person who is) not part of a major world religion, esp not Christianity: *They tried to convert the pagan people of the islands to Christianity.* **-ism** [U]

heathen [B; C; *the* P] *usu deprec* (a) pagan: *He became a missionary* [⇒ C344], *to teach Christianity to the heathen. These people are heathens; they have no proper religion or culture. What heathen ideas!* **-ism** [U]

C340 *verbs* : **converting people**

convert [T1 (*from, to*)] to cause to accept new religious beliefs, esp those of Christianity: *He was converted to Christianity from paganism. He converted them to Buddhism.*

evangelize, -ise 1 [I0] to (try to) spread (belief in) one's religion, esp Christianity **2** [T1] to teach (and convert): *He went out to evangelize the heathen.*

proselytize, -ise [I0] to try to persuade people to adopt one's own beliefs, religion, etc: *He is always proselytizing for his religion.*

save [T1] (in the Christian religion) to free (someone) from evil; to redeem from evil: *He has spent his life saving souls for Jesus. Are you saved, brother? 'Christ died to save us all!' the priest cried.*

redeem [T1 (*from*)] to buy or gain freedom for (a person), esp (in the Christian religion) freedom from evil: *his belief will redeem him from sin* [⇒ C341]. **redemption** [U] **1** the action of redeeming **2** the state of being redeemed

repent [I0; T1] to be sorry for (evil things one has done): *'Do you truly repent, my son?' asked the priest. He repented his sins* [⇒ C341] **repentant** [B] showing or feeling repentance **un-** [*neg*]

C341 nouns : salvation, sin, and penance

salvation [U] the act or state of being saved, esp (in the Christian religion) from sin: *His work was the salvation of souls. Pray for their salvation.*

grace [U] (in the Christian religion) **1** the mercy of God: *By the grace of God/By God's grace the ship came safely home.* **2** the state of the soul when freed from evil: *His experience changed his life and he believed he had been brought to grace. The man died in a state of grace, attended by a priest.*

sin 1 [U] (esp in the Christian religion) wrong-doing; action against moral rules (thought to have been) established by God: *'Sin and wickedness fill the world,' said the priest.* **2** [C] an example of this: *It is a sin to tell a lie. He is guilty of the sin of adultery* [⇒ C30]. *'God will punish them for their sins!' he said.*

original sin [U] (esp in Roman Catholic teaching) mankind's first disobedience of God, which is said to mark everyone from birth

penitence [U] the quality or state of repenting: *The thief expressed penitence for all his past actions.* **penitent 1** [B] showing or feeling penitence **2** [C] a penitent person

repentance [U] the act of repenting or feeling of having repented one's sins: *'Come to repentance!' cried the priest.*

penance 1 [U] punishment of oneself done freely to show that one is sorry for having done wrong: *She is doing penance for her sins.* **2** [U; C] punishment ordered esp by a Roman Catholic priest by which forgiveness of sin can be obtained **3** [C] *not fml* something that one must do but greatly dislikes: *Some people enjoy speaking in public, but for others it is a penance.* **do penance for** *humor* to suffer for (something foolish that one has done): *You'll have to do penance tomorrow for all the wine you've drunk tonight.*

C342 verbs : raising from the dead, making holy, etc

resurrect [T1 *often pass*] to bring (the dead, old ideas, etc) back to life or use: *Christ was resurrected from the dead. I wish you wouldn't resurrect these old problems all the time.* **resurrection 1** [U; C] the act or an act of resurrecting **2** [*the* R *usu cap*] in the Christian religion **a** the rising of Jesus from the grave or the anniversary of this **b** the rising of all the dead, esp for judgement on the Last Day

deify [T1] to make into a god: *The local villagers deified the old holy man and said he was God on earth.* (*fig*) *He has sort of deified his mother; in his eyes she can do no wrong.* **deification** [U] the process of deifying or being deified

canonize, -ise [T1] (esp in the Roman Catholic Church) to make into a saint [⇒ C343] **canon-**

ization, -isation [U] the act of canonizing or being canonized

sanctify [T1] to make holy: *'Many saints have lived here and sanctified the stones by their presence,' said the priest. God's grace, they said, would sanctify the believers against sin and the works of Satan.* **sanctification** [U] the act of sanctifying or state of being sanctified

incarnate [T1 *usu pass*] to put (God, a spirit, idea, etc) into bodily form: *According to the Christian religion, God was incarnated in Jesus Christ.* **incarnation 1** [U; C] the act or an act of incarnating: *She is the incarnation of all good things. The local Hindus call him an incarnation of the god Krishna.* **2** [*the* R *usu cap*] (in Christianity) the coming of God to earth in the body of Jesus Christ

reincarnate [T1 *usu pass*] to cause to become again a living creature with a body, after death, esp according to religious beliefs such as Hinduism **reincarnation 1** [U; C] the act or an act of being reincarnated: *Some Buddhists believe in the reincarnation of people as animals.* **2** [C] the creature, person, etc that results: *He believes he must not kill any animal, because it may be a reincarnation of a human being.*

transmigrate [I0] (of souls) to pass at death to the body of a new person (or animal) according to religious beliefs such as Hinduism **transmigration** [U] the process of transmigrating

C343 nouns, etc : religious persons [C]

holy man a man who gives his life completely to religion, esp when giving up normal life, clothes, eating habits, etc: *India is a land which venerates* [⇒ C332] *its holy men.*

saint [*also* A *often cap*] a person of a holy and admired way of life, esp one given the title of saint in the Roman Catholic Church after death: *Saint Teresa lived in Avila. He is one of the living saints of Hinduism.* **sainthood** [U] the condition of being a saint **saintly** [Wa2;B] like a saint; having the qualities of a saint **-liness** [U]

messiah [*often cap*] a new leader in a (new) religion, esp one whom prophets have spoken about and esp [*cap*] Christ in the Christian religion or the man still expected by the Jews: *Our Messiah will come. He is the new messiah of the poor and oppressed.* **messianic** [Wa5;B] of, concerning, or like a messiah

saviour *BrE*, **savior** *AmE* [*sometimes cap*] a person who saves others, esp [*cap*] Christ in the Christian religion, who is said to save people from sin [⇒ C341]: *The priest told them to have faith in their Saviour, Christ the Lord. She regards him as her saviour; he helped her in a time of great trouble.*

prophet 1 (esp in the Christian, Jewish, and Muslim religions) a person who believes that he is directed by God to make known and explain (God's will) or to lead or teach a (new) religion: *Muslims accept Christ as a prophet but regard the Prophet Mohammed as more important.* **2** a thinker, poet, etc who introduces and teaches some new idea which (he thinks or someone thinks) will make people's lives better: *The poet Shelley was a prophet of social reform.* **3** a person who foretells [⇒ L158] or claims to foretell the future: *Farmers or sailors are usually good weather prophets.*

seer *fml & old use* a prophet (*esp* def **3**)

medium a person who is said to be able to talk to the dead and give their messages to the living

mystic a person who practises mysticism [⇒ C320], who has or claims to have secret or higher spiritual knowledge ·

martyr 1 a person who is killed or caused to suffer greatly, esp for his or her religious or political beliefs: *the ancient Christian martyrs; a martyr to science* **2** [T1] to kill or cause to suffer as a martyr: *He was martyred by his religious enemies.* **3** [C] (*fig*) a sufferer, usu from an illness: *He is a martyr to sore throats.*

martyrdom [U] death or suffering as a martyr

C344 nouns : priests and ministers of religion [C]

priest a man specially trained, esp in some Christian churches and esp in the Roman Catholic Church, for various religious duties such as performing certain holy ceremonies and services, doing good works, etc: *She asked to see a priest. The priest celebrated mass* [⇒ C335]. *Roman Catholic priests are not free to marry. Hindu priests are called 'brahmins'.*

priesthood 1 [(*the*) U] the office, position, or rank of a priest: *He entered the priesthood* (= became a priest) *last year.* **2** [GU] the whole body of priests, usu of a particular religion or country: *The Dutch priesthood is different from the Italian priesthood.* **priestly** [Wa5;B] of or like a priest: *He has his priestly duties to perform.* **priest-ridden** [B] *deprec* (of a ruler or nation) too much under the control of a priest or priests

priestess (in some religions but not Christianity, Islam, or Judaism) a woman trained to perform special religious acts, esp in a temple [⇒ C351], to give advice to people, etc: *She was a priestess of the goddess Kali.*

minister a person who has been officially approved to look after the spiritual needs of a Protestant [⇒ C330] community: *The local minister takes the service every Sunday.*

ministry 1 [*the* R] the office, profession, or work of a minister **2** [*the* GU] the whole body of ministers

preacher a person who preaches [⇒ C333] esp a form of Christianity: *The preacher told them to give up their evil ways and ask for God's forgiveness.* **lay preacher** a person who is not a priest or minister but preaches for a denomination [⇒ C321] of Christianity

clergyman a priest or minister of a Christian church **clergy** [*the* GU] priests or ministers collectively

cleric *esp fml* a clergyman **clerical** [Wa5;B] relating to or like a clergyman or the clergy

churchman *fml & old use* a (usu senior) clergyman

ecclesiastic *fml* a clergyman

chaplain a priest or minister looking after a chapel [⇒ C350], or in the armed forces: *He served as an army chaplain for some years.*

padre a priest or minister in the armed forces; chaplain: *Ask the padre to see him.* **2** [*also* N] any Christian priest, esp when addressed: *Would you help me, Padre?*

pastor [*also* A] (the title of) a Christian priest or minister in charge of a church and its members, esp a priest of a Church other than the Catholic Church or the Church of England: *Pastor Smith was waiting at the church door.* **pastoral** [Wa5;B] concerning a pastor or his religious work

vicar a priest in charge of a church and the spiritual [⇒ C338] needs of a community in the Church of England: *The local vicar took the Sunday service.*

elder an official of some Christian churches, esp an elected member of the governing body of a Presbyterian church

missionary a person who works, esp in a country not his or her own, to persuade people to accept his or her religion, as a Christian does in a non-Christian country: *Many churches used to send missionaries to China.*

C345 nouns : monks and nuns

monk [C] a member of a male religious group united in giving their lives to God or a religious purpose and living in a monastery [⇒ C351] together where they follow a set of rules, own nothing as individuals and do not marry: *The monks were praying in the chapel* [⇒ C350]. **monkish** [B] *often deprec* like a monk

nun [C] a member of a female religious group united in giving their lives to God or a religious purpose and living in a convent [⇒ C351] together where they follow a set of rules, own nothing as individuals and do not marry

friar [C; A] (the title of) a man belonging to any of several Catholic Christian groups similar to monks, esp formerly leading a wandering life as preachers [⇒ C344]: *Two Dominican friars came along the road. Friar John waited at the church door.*

hermit [C] **1** *esp formerly* a holy man who lived alone, thinking and praying: *A hermit used to live in that cave.* **2** a person who avoids other people: *He's a bit of a hermit; he likes to be left alone.* **hermitage** [C] the place where a hermit lives or has lived

religious [Wn3;C] a person who has given his or her life to the service of God; a monk or nun

ascetic [C; B] (of or like) a person who does not

allow himself or herself bodily pleasures (and may gladly suffer bodily pain), esp for religious reasons **-ally** [adv Wa4] **asceticism** [U] the way of life, ideas, etc of ascetics

C346 nouns : titles of priests and other religious persons

Reverend [N; A] (a title of respect for) a clergyman, etc: *Reverend Jones has moved to a new church. When will the new church be finished, Reverend? Will the nuns accept the changes, Reverend Mother?* **Rev** also **Revd** abbre: *Revd T. R. Jones, 3 New Road.*

Father [A; C; N] (a title of respect for) a priest or a monk, esp in the Roman Catholic Church: *Father Brown is our local priest. One of the Fathers met us at the monastery* [⇒ C351] *gates.*

Mother [A; C; N] (a title of respect for) a nun who is in charge of other nuns in a convent [⇒ C351]: *Mother Teresa will see you now. May I speak to you alone, Mother?* **Mother Superior** (the title of) the nun in charge of a convent

brother [C; A *often cap*] (a title for) a male member of a religious group, esp a monk: *The Brothers live a simple life. Can I help, Brother John?* **brotherhood 1** [GC] a group of men, usu monks, leading a religious life, usu together in one place **2** [U] the condition of being spiritual brothers: *He believes in the brotherhood of all peoples.*

brethren [P; N] (often in formal or solemn address) the members of a religious group (male and female) or the members of an association or profession: *Dearly beloved brethren, we are gathered here to remember our departed friend* (= our friend who has just died). *His medical brethren disagree with him.*

sister [C; A; N *often cap*] (a title for) a nun: *Can I help, Sister?* **sisterhood** [GC] a group of women, usu nuns, leading a religious life, usu together in one place

C347 nouns : persons and titles in various Christian churches [C]

pope [*often cap*] (the title of) the head of the Roman Catholic Church: *The Pope appeared before the people. Most popes have been Italians. Pope John received his visitors.* **papal** [Wa5;B *often cap*] of the Pope or the Papacy **papacy 1** [*the* R *sometimes cap*] the power and office of the Pope **2** [C] the time during which a particular Pope holds office: *This happened during the papacy of Pope John.* **3** [U *often cap*] the system of having a Pope at the head of the (Roman Catholic) Church **popery** [U] *derog* the teachings and forms of worship of the Roman Catholic Church **popish** [B] *derog* Roman Catholic

patriarch 1 [*usu cap*] any of several chief bishops of the Eastern Churches: *The Patriarch of Jerusalem was present.* **2** [*usu cap*] a bishop of the Roman Catholic Church ranking just below the Pope **3** *apprec* an old and much respected man **patriarchal** [Wa5;B] of, concerning, or like a patriarch

cardinal [*also* A] (the title of) a priest with one of the highest ranks in the Roman Catholic Church, who is a member of the Sacred College which elects the Pope

bishop [*also* A; N] (the title of) a priest of high rank in several Christian churches **episcopal** [Wa5;B] **1** *fml* of or concerning bishops: *The bishop wore his episcopal ring on his finger.* **2** (of a Church) governed by bishops: *The Church of England is an episcopal church.*

archbishop [*also* A] (in many Christian churches) (the title of) the highest or a very high rank of priest

canon [*also* A] (the title of) a Christian priest with special duties in connection with a cathedral [⇒ C350]

abbot a monk who is in charge of an abbey [⇒ C350]

abbess a nun who is in charge of a convent [⇒ C351]

prior 1 a monk who is the head of a priory [⇒ C350] **2** the monk next in rank below an abbot

prioress a nun who is the head of a priory

deacon an officer of various Christian churches, below a priest or minister

deaconess a female deacon

C348 nouns : districts and groups in churches

parish 1 [C] a district in the care of a single priest or minister and served by one church: *The priest had a large parish of poor people in his care. He was looking for the parish church. The parish register records all the marriages performed in this church.* **2** [*the* GC] the people living in a parish: *The parish don't want this new kind of service.* **parishioner** [C] a person living in a particular parish, esp one who regularly attends the parish church **parochial** [B] **1** [Wa5] relating, belonging, or limited to a parish **2** (*fig*) not having a wide view of things or experience of the world: *He has very parochial ideas.*

see [C] the district under the government of a bishop or archbishop

diocese [C] *fml & tech* a see **diocesan** [Wa5;B] of or concerning a diocese or see

bishopric [C] **1** the position, rank, or office of a bishop **2** the see or diocese of a bishop

synod [C] a meeting about church affairs to decide important matters for a whole group of churches: *The Synod of Whitby was held in 664 AD* (*when the churches of the British Isles were reorganized*).

congregation [GC] a group of people who worship regularly in a particular church or the group present there at one particular time: *We* have a large active congregation in this parish. *The congregation stood up to sing.*

flock [GC] (*fig*) a congregation: *The priest tried to care for all the members of his flock.*

Church [*often cap*] an organization of Christian believers as **1** [*the* R] all the Christian believers in the world **2** [*the* R] the members of the various branches of Christianity: *She lived and died a member of the (true) Church.* **3** [C] the body of Christians in a town or area: *Paul went to address the Church at Rome.* **Established Church** [C] a form of Christianity officially supported by the state

Kirk [*the* R *usu cap*] ScotE the Church, esp the Church of Scotland

C349 nouns : parts of a church building [C]

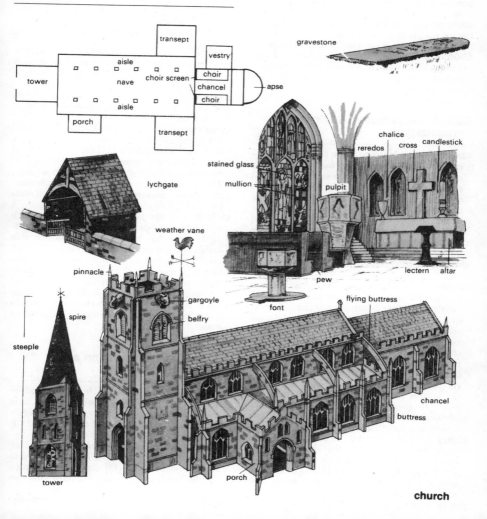

church

altar 1 a table or raised level surface on which offerings are made to God or a god **2** the table, esp in a church on which the bread and wine are blessed in a Communion [⇒C335] service

pulpit the (usu small) raised structure in a church from which a clergyman [⇒ C344] addresses the congregation [⇒ C348]

nave the long central part of a church where people sit to worship, usu between two aisles

aisle a passage, usu one of two, leading through the length of a church and divided from the nave by a row of pillars [⇒ D26]

choir 1 [GC] a group of people who sing together esp during religious services **2** that part of a church building where such a group of people sit: *The procession of priests moved through the choir to the altar.*

pew a long seat with a back to it, for people to sit on in a church

steeple a pointed tower which is part of a church

belfry 1 a tower for a bell, as in a church **2** the part of this tower on which the bell hangs

churchyard an open space around and belonging to a church and in which dead members of that church can usu be buried [*also* ⇒ C58 GRAVEYARD]

C350 *nouns* : **church buildings and organizations**

church 1 [C] a building made for public Christian worship: *Most churches have towers, bells, and windows made from stained* (= coloured) *glass. I hope they don't make that old church into a garage.* **2** [*the* R] the profession of the clergy [⇒C344]: *When he was 30 he joined the church and became a priest.* **3** [U *often cap*] religious power (as against state power): *Do you agree with the separation of church and state/Church and State?*

kirk [C] *ScotE* a church: *That's a beautiful old kirk.*

chapel 1 [C] a place, such as a small church, a room in a hospital, prison, etc, but not a parish church, used for Christian worship **2** [C] a part of a large church with its own altar and used esp for private prayer and small religious services **3** [C] (esp in England and Wales) a church or place of worship of Nonconformists (= those who do not belong to the established church or the Roman Catholic Church) **4** [C] (in Scotland) a Roman Catholic church **5** [U] the way of worshipping God in such a place: *He goes to chapel every Sunday night.*

cathedral [C] the chief church of a diocese [⇒ C348], usu large and ornamented

abbey 1 [C] (esp formerly) a building in which Christian monks or nuns live shut away from others; a Christian monastery or convent [⇒ C351] **2** [*the* GU] the group of people living in such a building **3** [C] a church or house that was once such a building

priory [C *often cap*] a Christian religious house

where monks or nuns live, but smaller and less important than an abbey

C351 *nouns* : **other places of worship** [C]

[ALSO ⇒ C327–9]

temple a place of worship, esp other than Christian: *The Hindus worship in temples.*

shrine 1 a holy place, in a church, temple, or outdoors, such as a small building by the roadside: *The pilgrims* [⇒ C331] *stopped at the wayside shrine to pray. Lourdes is an important Catholic shrine.* **2** a set of holy objects; the remains of a holy person, body, etc, kept together after his or her death

sanctuary 1 a holy place, esp an inner part of a church, where one cannot enter unless given the special right to do so **2** a place of protection, often formerly a religious building, where no harm can be done **3** [U] protection, as in such a place

mosque a building in which Muslims worship

minaret a tall tower, one or more of which form part of a mosque, from which Muslims are called to pray

pagoda a Buddhist temple built of several floors or levels, often with an ornamented roof at each level

monastery a building in which monks [⇒C345] live together: *There are Buddhist monasteries in Nepal.* **monasticism** [U] the way of life of monks and nuns **monastic** [Wa5;B] of or concerning monks, monasteries, or monasticism: *They lead an almost monastic life in that house.*

convent *also* **nunnery** a building in which nuns [⇒ C345] live together

cloister 1 [C *usu pl*] a covered passage which surrounds an open square garden or courtyard, which has open archways on one side facing into the garden or courtyard and which usu forms part of a church, monastery, or convent **2** [C *usu sing*; *the* R] a place of religious peace and quiet; convent; monastery: *The religious girl dreamed of life in the cloister.* **cloistered** [B] shut away from the world in or as if in a monastery: *He led a cloistered life as a young man.*

C352 *nouns* : **superstition and mythology**

superstition [U] belief which is not based on reason or fact but on association of ideas, as in magic: *Superstition still has a powerful hold on many minds. Believing that the number 13 is unlucky is typical of superstition.*

mythology 1 [U;C] a system of beliefs contained in myths [⇒ C353]: *He is interested in Greek mythology.* **2** [U] the study of myths: *'Mythology is an important but often forgotten part of psychology'* [⇒ I76], *he said.*

myth [U] old stories which are not (strictly)

historical; imagination and nothing else: *These stories are pure myth; those things never happened. 'This is all myth; I don't believe a word of it!' he said.*

folklore [U] the study (and collection) of old stories belonging to a tribe, people, etc: *This story is found in the folklore of many countries.*

folklorist [C] a person who studies folklore

C353 nouns : **superstitions and legends**

superstition [C] a belief which is not based on reason: *There is a superstition that if you step on a worm it will rain. These people believe in all sorts of old superstitions; for them seeing a black cat means good luck, but the number 13 means bad luck.*

myth [C] an ancient story, usu containing religious or magical ideas which may (try to) explain natural or historical events: *He enjoys reading the Greek myths, especially the stories of Odysseus.* **-ical** [B] of, concerning, or like a myth: *Dragons [⇒ A93] are mythical beasts.*

legend 1 [C] an old story about great deeds and people of ancient times, having a slight possible base in truth: *There is a legend that a princess died here. Celtic legends contain many ideas which seem strange today.* **2** [U] the kind of tradition that legends belong to: *According to legend, a princess died here.* **legendary** [B] of, concerning, or like a legend: *A legendary princess died here. His ability in football has become legendary.*

fable [C] **1** a story, esp about animals, that is meant to teach people a lesson about how to behave: *Aesop's Fables were written in ancient Greece.* **2** a story which is not accepted as true: *Stop telling us your fables; tell the truth.* **fabled** [Wa5;B] *esp lit & poet* famous in stories: *He is a great footballer.—Yes; I've come to see his fabled footwork* (= the movement of his feet, when playing football) *that people talk so much about.*

fairy tale *also* **fairy story** [C] **1** a story about fairies [⇒ C357], etc: *The children love listening to fairy tales. This is an old Romanian fairy tale.* **2** a story which is hard to believe, esp one intended to deceive: *Stop making up these fairy tales; no one believes you. That's a great fairy story—Where did you get it?* **fairy-tale** [A] of or suitable to a fairy tale; unreal; magical: *The shop had a fairytale atmosphere; the children loved it.*

folktale [C] a popular story passed on in speech from an earlier time or in a simple society: *They have published a book of Indian folktales.*

C354 nouns : **magic**

magic [U] **1** the system of trying to control events, nature, etc by calling on spirits, secret forces, etc: *They claim to use magic to change the weather, bring rain, and so on.* **2** *tech* the system of thought which imagines that objects cause effects: *The people who believe in magic think that pricking the figure of a man will wound the man himself.* **3** the art employed by a theatrical performer who produces unexpected objects and results by tricks **4** strange influence or power; a charming and mysterious quality: *She seemed to know my feelings by magic. The magic of that evening still affects me.*

black magic [U] magic believed to be done with the help of evil spirits or the Devil

white magic [U] magic believed to be done with the help of God, angels, good fairies [⇒ C357], etc

occult [*the* R *sometimes cap*] *fml* magic, black magic, mysticism, etc: *He has studied the Occult for many years.*

witchcraft [U] the practice of magic, esp that of a witch or wizard [⇒ C356], in order to make things happen: *She was burned alive for practising witchcraft. What witchcraft is this?—Are you trying to tell me that the dead can live again?*

sorcery [U; C *usu pl*] acts of magic, esp to make things happen to people and things: *This is sorcery and must be punished by the true Church! The wizard's [⇒ C356] sorceries made everyone fear him. The work of the scientists seemed like sorcery to the simple people.*

voodoo [U] a type of religion, esp in Haiti and other parts of the West Indies, whose practices are like black magic: *Voodoo practices include attempts to kill at a distance by magic.*

spell [C] **1** a condition caused by magical power: *The witch put a spell on the young girl, turning her into a fish.* **2** (*fig*) a strong attractive power: *The children fell under the spell of his wonderful storytelling.* **cast a spell (on)** put a spell (on): *The witch cast a spell (on the young girl).*

C355 adjectives : **relating to magic and supernatural things** [B]

magic 1 [Wa5] relating to magic: *He used magic power to bring rain. Can you do magic tricks?* **2** mysterious, like magic: *What a magic influence he has on her!*

magical *sometimes deprec* generally relating to magic of any kind: *Her sudden disappearance seemed magical. Stop all this magical nonsense and be sensible.*

mystic having or claiming a hidden spiritual meaning, nature, or power: *The cult has various mystic ceremonies. He was reading the mystic works of Roumi. This story comes from the Mystic East.*

mystical *sometimes deprec* generally relating to mystic things, mystics, and mysticism: *His writings are full of mystical nonsense!*

occult secret; hidden from ordinary people; magical and mysterious: *He claimed that the secrets of occult power were known to him.*

supernatural beyond what is considered

natural or explained by known physical laws: *He seemed to have supernatural strength and power. Angels and demons are supernatural beings.* **-ly** [adv] **supernatural** [*the* R *often cap*] all and any happenings which are or appear to be supernatural **-ly** [adv]

superstitious feeling, showing, or believing in superstitions of any kind: *What a superstitious person he is; he won't sleep in Room 13!* **-ly** [adv]

C356 *nouns* : **persons concerned with magic** [C]

magician 1 (in stories) a person who can make strange things happen by magic: *The old magician turned him into a mouse.* **2** a person who does magic tricks: *They have a professional magician on the show tonight.*

witch a woman who has, or is believed to have, magic powers, esp who can cast spells on people: *The wicked witch cast her spells. She's a witch; she has a strange power over people.*

warlock *esp old use* a male witch: *On that night witches and warlocks came to dance among the standing stones.*

wizard (esp in stories) a man who has magic powers, esp to cast spells: *The wise old wizard helped them to defeat the evil witch.* **wizardry** [U] the actions, etc of a wizard; great skill

sorcerer a wizard or magician

sorceress a female wizard; a witch

medicine man a man believed to have magical powers: *The Red Indian tribes of North America valued their medicine men greatly.*

witchdoctor a man in an undeveloped society, who is believed to have magical powers: *The African tribal witchdoctor began to make spells.*

C357 *nouns* : **various supernatural beings** [C]

fairy a usu small imaginary figure with magical powers and shaped like a human, often female

elf a type of small fairy which is said to play tricks on people

goblin a usu unkind or evil spirit which plays tricks on people

gnome 1 (in fairy stories) a little (old) man who lives under the ground and guards stores of gold **2** a stone figure representing this: *a garden gnome*

nymph one of the beautiful young girls believed, esp by the ancient Greeks, to live in trees, rivers, etc and to guard them

ogre 1 (in fairy stories) a frightening creature like a very large man **2** (*fig*) a frightening person **ogress** [*fem*]

satyr 1 (in Greek myth) one of a group of man-like creatures with legs and a tail like a goat, famous for their sexual powers and desires **2** a man with great sexual desires

centaur a being in Greek mythology whose lower parts are like a horse and upper parts are like a man

D

Buildings, houses, the home, clothes, belongings, and personal care

Architecture and kinds of houses and buildings

D1 *verbs* : **building things**

[ALSO ⇨ I3]

build [D1 (*for*); T1] to make by putting together parts, materials, etc, esp so as to rise above the ground: *They built the house themselves. Can you build me a house/build a house for me? He built the hut out of wood.* (*fig*) *The manager of the firm hopes to build the business into something big.* **build in** [v adv T1] **1** [*usu pass*] to make a fixed part of (usu) a room: *These cupboards are built in. They are built-in cupboards.* **2** [*pass*] (*fig*) to cause to be a part of something which cannot be separated from it: *The difficulties here seem to be built in.* **build into** [v prep D1 *usu pass*] **1** to fix to (something) so as to make a part of it: *The cupboards are built into the walls.* **2** to cause to be a part of: *The difficulties are built into the work.* **build on** [v adv T1 *often pass*] to make as an addition to a building: *This part of the hospital was built on later.* **build up** [v adv T1 *usu pass*] to cover with buildings: *The area has been built up a lot since I lived here. It has become a built-up area.*

construct [T1] *more fml* to build, esp part after part as a system: *They wanted to build a new bridge and he has to construct it for them.* (*fig*) *He tried to construct a theory to fit the facts, but he did not know enough about what had happened.*

erect [T1] *fml* to build, esp from the ground upwards: *They erected the new building in six months. He plans to erect a memorial* [⇨ C59] *to his father.*

put up [v adv T1] **1** *infml* to build: *The firm are putting up a new block of flats.* **2** to raise; to fix in position: *Put the tent up here.*

synthesize, -ise [T1] **1** to put (things) together to make a whole **2** to make (something) by synthesis: *Scientists synthesize many natural materials now.* **synthetic 1** [Wa5;B] of, concerning, like, or the result of synthesis **2** [C] something made this way: *This cloth is a synthetic.* **-ally** [adv Wa4]

D2 *nouns* : **building things**

[ALSO ⇨ I4]

building [U] (the business, art, etc, of) making buildings, houses, etc: *He works in the building trade.* **builder** [C] **1** a person who builds (esp houses): *He's a local builder.* **2** [*in comb*] something that brings into being or develops: *Hard work is a great character builder.* **building society** [C] (in Britain) an association into which people put money. This money is then lent to those who want to buy or build houses: *He put his savings* (= the money he had saved) *in a building society. Building societies lend people's savings to other people in the form of mortgages* [⇨ C215]. *They got a mortgage from a building society and bought a house.*

construction [U] action or way of constructing or being constructed: *The Minister discussed the construction of new roads. The railway is under construction at the moment. This house is of excellent construction. The workmen were all in the construction camp.* **constructor** [C] a person who constructs things

architecture [U] **1** the art and science of building, including the planning and making of buildings, etc: *He's a student of architecture.* **2** the style or manner of building, esp as belonging to a particular country or period of history: *He is interested in the architecture of ancient Greece.* **architectural** [Wa5;B] of or concerning buildings, esp their style: *That factory is well built but has little architectural value.* **-ly** [adv Wa4] **architect** [C] **1** a person who plans new buildings and sees that they are built properly **2** (*fig*) a person who plans and makes anything: *He was the architect of the new law.*

synthesis 1 [U] the putting together of several parts or things in order to make a whole **2** [C] an example or result of this: *His work is a synthesis of several ideas.*

D3 *nouns* : **things built and lived in, etc** [C]

building something built, in which people can live or work: *The city has many fine buildings. He works in that new building near the river.* **building site** the place where a new building is being put up: *He is a labourer on a building site.*

edifice 1 *fml or pomp* a large fine building, such as a palace or a church: *The UN building in New York is an imposing edifice.* **2** (*fig*) a framework of hopes, doubts, or other feelings: *Her edifice of hopes fell to pieces when she failed the examination.*

house 1 a building for people to live in: *That's a nice little house. They have built some new houses in the village.* **2** the people in a house: *The whole house was woken up by the noise.* **3** [usu in comb] a building for animals or goods: *He opened the door of the henhouse/ the henhouse door. Put the supplies in the storehouse.*
housing [U] houses generally: *He is Minister for Housing in the new government. They discussed the country's poor housing/the country's special housing problems.* **household** [A] relating to a house or the people in it: *The household expenses are getting bigger. They bought some new household equipment.* **housewife** [C] a married woman who looks after the house in which she and her family live **housekeeper** [C] a woman who is paid to look after a house, esp for a group or for a man who is not married **housework** [U] work done in a house, esp cooking, cleaning, etc

modern caravan

gypsy caravan

caravan 1 a covered horse-drawn cart in which people such as gipsies [⇨ C170] live or travel **2** *also* (*esp AmE*) **trailer** a vehicle which can be pulled by a car, which contains apparatus for cooking and sleeping and in which people live, usu for holidays: *He bought a three-berth caravan* (= a caravan in which three people can sleep). *Many people use that caravan site* (= a place for putting caravans) *while on holiday.*
caravanning [U] using caravans for holidays, etc **caravanner** a person using a caravan

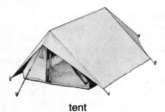

tent

tent a shelter of skins or cloth (esp canvas) [⇨H87] supported by one or more poles or a frame and usu held in position by ropes tied to the ground: *The soldiers were living in tents. They go camping every summer in a family-sized tent.*

D4 *nouns* : **smaller houses** [C]

cottage a small house, esp in the country: *She lives in a cottage by the sea. The villagers were told to leave their cottages.* **cottager** a person living in a cottage
hut a small building, often made of wood: *The people lived in mud huts. The workmen put up a hut where they could have their food.*
shack a hut, usu not carefully made
hovel *deprec* a small dirty house or hut: *What a hovel he lives in!*
shanty a very roughly made hut, usu in a town: *The workers live in shanties outside the factory.* **shantytown** (a part of) a town made up of shanties, where poor people live
cabin a small roughly built, usu wooden house: *One of our greatest presidents was born in a log cabin.*
chalet 1 a usu wooden house with a steeply sloping roof, esp common in Switzerland **2** a small hut used by shepherds [⇨ E144] in the Alps during the summer

D5 *nouns* : **larger houses** [C]

palace 1 a large grand house **a** where a ruling king or queen officially lives **b** where a bishop [⇨ C347] lives: *The Party leaders were received at the Palace by the Queen. They met in the palace gardens.* **2** any large and splendid house: *The nobles of Florence built themselves great palaces. The Soviet Palace of Culture is in Moscow.* (*fig*) *Her home is a palace compared with our poor little house.* **3** a large, often showy, building used for public amusement, dancing, etc: *They went to the local fun palace.* **palatial** [B] of or like a palace, esp in size **-ly** [adv]
mansion (house) a large house, usu belonging to a wealthy person: *The millionaire's mansion was on the hill.*
country house (esp in Britain) a large house in the country belonging to one family, with land around it: *Their country house has been in the family for five generations.*
manor house (in England esp formerly) a large house with land around it **manor** (formerly) a large area of land owned by one family
lodge 1 a country house used as a place from which to hunt or shoot animals **2** a smaller house near a country house, esp one at the entrance to the grounds **3** a room for a person who is responsible for seeing who enters a building, as in a block of flats or a college
villa a country house with a large garden, esp as in Italy, Spain or France, or as built by the ancient Romans

D6 *nouns* : **modern kinds of houses**

detached house a house which is not connected in any way with another house

semidetached house *also* (*BrE infml*) **semi** a house which is one of two built together: *She lives in a semidetached house in Surbiton. They have a nice suburban* [⇨ C81] *semi, just outside Manchester.*

villa (in Britain) a detached or semidetached house, esp in the outer parts of a town

terraced house one house which is part of a line of joined houses

bungalow a type of house which is all on one floor

chalet 1 a small house with a sloping roof **2** a hut in a holiday camp

D7 *nouns* : **flats and annexes** [C]

flat *BrE*, **apartment** *AmE* a set of rooms, esp on one floor, including a kitchen and bathroom, usu one of many such sets in a building or block: *They divided the big house into flats. The people in the top flat are friends of mine.*

apartment *esp BrE* **1** [*usu pl*] a room, esp a large or splendid one, or one used by a particular person or group: *'The Royal or State Apartments are only for special hotel guests', he said.* **2** a large and expensive flat

penthouse an expensive set of rooms on the top floor of a large building

bed-sitter *also* **bed-sitting room, bed-sit** (*infml*) *BrE* a single room used for both living and sleeping in

annexe a building joined or added to a larger one: *The Smiths live in the annexe. The doctors were working in the hospital annexe.*

D8 *nouns* : **blocks and skyscrapers** [C]

block 1 a large building divided into separate parts, esp flats and offices: *She lives in a block of flats in London. The new office block will be finished soon.* **2** *esp AmE* (the distance along one of the sides of) the area or building surrounded by four streets in a town: *He lives two blocks along from here.*

tenement (house) a large building divided into flats, esp in the poorer areas of a city: *Although he was born in a Glasgow tenement, he is now very rich.*

skyscraper *esp AmE* a very tall building: *New York is famous for its skyscrapers, such as the Empire State Building.*

D9 *nouns* : **castles and parts of castles** [C]

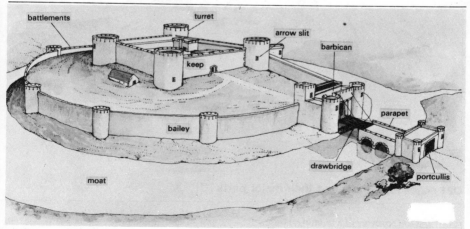

castle a large strongly-built building or set of buildings made in former times to be defended against attack: *There is an old castle near the town. Have you visited Edinburgh Castle?*

tower a tall, narrow building, sometimes (part of) a castle: *The castle had four towers. He was a prisoner in the Tower of London.*

keep a great tower of a castle

moat a long, deep ditch that in former times was dug for defence round a castle, fort, etc, and was usually filled with water: *The castle had a moat but there was no longer any water in it.*

D10 *nouns* : **forts and other defended buildings** [C]

fort 1 a strongly-made building used for defence at some important place **2** [A *usu cap as part of a name*] (a town containing) a fixed army camp: *In former times the British army kept lots of soldiers at Fort William in Scotland.*

fortification [*usu pl*] towers, walls, gun positions, etc, set up as a means of defence: *The fortifications of the town were very good.*

fortress a large fort; a place strengthened for defence: *The fortress was built on a hill. His house was (like) a fortress and could be defended against an army.*

citadel 1 (esp formerly) a strong, heavily-armed fort usu commanding a city, built to be a last place of safety and defence in times of war: **2** any very heavily-armed and strongly-defended place **3** *tech* (on a warship) a heavily-armed part protected by strong armour

blockhouse a small strong building used as a shelter (as from enemy fire) or for watching dangerous explosions

stronghold 1 any fort, citadel, etc **2** (*fig*) any place where certain ideas, beliefs, etc, are strong: *That town is a stronghold of the Conservative Party.*

Parts of houses

D20 *nouns* : **houses and their major parts** [C]

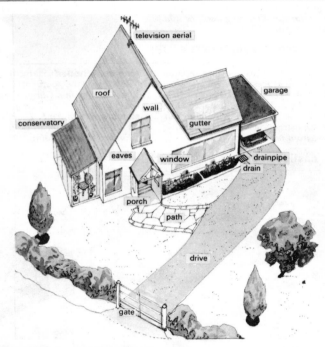

D21 *nouns etc* : **roofs and their major parts** [C]

roof 1 the top covering of a building, house, etc: *The roofs of the local houses are red. The roof of the car was hot in the sun.* **2** [T1] to put a roof on: *They roofed the house with wood.*

chimney a hollow passage often rising above the roof of a building which allows smoke and gases to pass from a fire or other very hot substance: *In the industrial towns factory chimneys poured smoke into the air.* **chimney**

pot a short pipe made of hardened clay or metal sometimes fixed to the top of a chimney, esp in a house

tile 1 a thin shaped piece of baked clay used for covering roof, walls, floors, etc **2** an object like this made from plastic, metal, etc **tiled** [Wa5;B] covered with tiles: *The house has a tiled roof.*

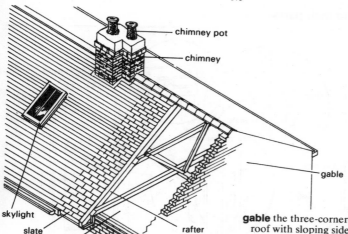

gable the three-cornered surface at the end of a roof with sloping sides and a pointed top: *Old Edinburgh houses have high gables.*

ceiling 1 the inner surface of the top of a room: *There was a lamp hanging from the ceiling.* **2** (*fig*) an upper limit

dome 1 a rounded top on a building or room: *The dome of St Paul's Cathedral is well known in London.* **2** (*fig*) something of this shape: *He looked up at the blue dome of the sky.*

slate 1 [U] heavy rock formed from mud by pressure and easily split into flat, thin pieces **2** [C] a small piece of this or other material used for laying in rows to cover a roof: *One of the slates on the roof is loose.* **3** [T1; IØ] to cover (a roof) with slates: *He is good at slating (roofs).*

D22 *nouns* : **kinds of walls** [C]

wall 1 an upright dividing surface (esp of stone or brick) intended for defence or safety, or for enclosing something: *In some parts of Britain fields are surrounded by stone walls. The city wall had stood successfully against three attacks.* **2** the side of a building or a room: *Hang the picture on that wall. They painted the wall white.* **3** (*fig*) an upright mass of anything: *The wall of the cliff/The cliff wall was difficult to climb. A wall of fire stood between them and safety.* **4** (*fig*) something that separates or opposes: *The inquirers were met with a wall of silence. The protesters formed a living wall against the police.* **wall in** [v adv T1] to surround with walls: *He walled in the garden.* **wall up** [v adv T1] to close up with a wall: *He walled up the door.* **walled** [Wa5;B] having a wall or

walls: *Carcassonne is an old walled town in France.*

partition something that divides, esp a thin wall inside a house: *There is only a wooden partition between the beds.*

panel a separate usu four-sided division of the surface of a door, wall, etc, which is different in some way from the surface round it: *The door had a glass panel in it, to let some light in. He broke one of the wooden panels in the wall.*

rampart [*usu pl*] a wide bank of earth built esp formerly to protect a fort or city: *Soldiers stood on the ramparts, waiting for the enemy attack.*

dike, dyke 1 a thick bank or wall built to control water and prevent flooding **2** a narrow passage dug to carry water away **3** *ScotE* a wall, esp around a field

D23 *nouns* : **windows and their major parts** [C]

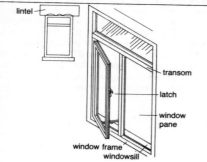

window a space in a wall, esp in a house, to let in light and air, esp of glass, which can be opened: *He looked out (of) the window to see if she was coming.*

pane a single sheet of glass for use in a frame, esp of a window

pelmet a narrow piece of wood or cloth above a window that hides the pole on which curtains hang

fanlight a small window above a door

D24 *nouns* : **doors and their parts**

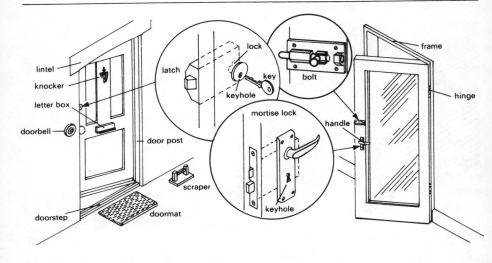

door 1 [C] a movable upright flat surface that opens and closes the entrance to a building, room, or piece of furniture: *He knocked on the door. She closed/opened the door.* (*fig*) *Good luck is often the door to success. This agreement opens the door to advances in every field.* **2** [C] also **doorway** the space taken by a door: *She came in through the door. You can't get a piano in there; the doorway isn't wide enough.* **3** [C] (*fig*) house or building: *My sister lives only two doors away/She lives just next door to us. The taxi will take you from door to door. He sells books from door to door; he's a door-to-door salesman. That terrible crime is next door to murder!* (= is almost murder) **front/back door** [C] the door at the front/back of a house **outdoors** [adv Wa5] outside a house, etc: *The children like playing outdoors.* **outdoor** [Wa5; A] outside a house, etc: *They like outdoor games.* **out-of-doors** [adv Wa5] *fml* outside **indoors** [adv Wa5] inside a house, etc: *He stayed indoors.* **indoor** [Wa5;A] happening inside a house: *She enjoys indoor games.* **within doors** [adv Wa5] *fml* indoors **answer the door** *infml* to go to the door to see who is there **show someone the door** to make it clear that someone is not welcome and should leave **show someone to the door** to go politely to the door with someone who is leaving

gate [C] **1** a movable upright frame, often with bars across, which closes an opening in a fence, wall, etc: *The farmer closed the gate behind him as he left the field.* [⇒ picture at D20] **2** one of a pair of large frames used to control water

levels or which close the road over a railway line

portal [C *often pl*] *fml* a (very grand) door or entrance to a building

porch [C] a roofed entrance built onto a house or church

access 1 [C] a means of entering: *The only access to that building is along the track. Access roads were built to the new houses* **2** [U] (*fig*) means or right of using, reaching, or entering: *Students need easy access to books. Only high officials have access to the Minister.*

way in [C] any passage, door, etc, which lets someone into a place, building, etc: *This is the way in—come on!*

way out [C] any passage, door, etc, which lets someone out of a place, building, etc: *Where's the way out of this place?*

entrance [C] *sometimes fml & genl* a door, gate, or other opening by which one enters: *The car stopped at the entrance to the railway station. The police were waiting at all entrances and exits.*

entry [C] *fml & less common* entrance: *Which way is the entry? The sign said 'No entry'.*

-way [*comb form*] used for the space where a door or gate is placed or where a road, etc, goes: *The man stood in the doorway. The roadway was covered with broken glass.*

exit [C] a way out, esp from a theatre (and often written over a door): *The exit doors are open at the end of the performance. Take the first exit off the motorway.*

D25 *nouns* : **ground, floors, and foundations**

ground [U] the surface of the earth: *The branch of the tree fell to the ground. Her long skirt touched the ground. The ground on which the house was built is sandy.*

floor 1 [C] the part of a room, house, etc, on which one walks: *The floors of the house were dirty.* **2** anything like this: *The floor of the car was clean.* **flooring** [U] material for making or covering floors

foundations [P] **1** the solid stonework, brickwork, etc, first set in holes dug in the earth, to support the walls of a building: *The explosion shook the building to its foundations* (= caused it to shake dangerously). *The workmen are laying the foundations of the new hospital.* **2** (*fig*) the base; that by which things are supported: *He laid the foundations of his success by study and hard work.*

D26 *nouns* : **pillars, columns, and beams**

[⇨ H39–42]

pillar [C] **1** a large tall upright, usu round post made usu of stone **a** used as an (ornamental) support for a roof **b** standing alone, as in a square, in memory of some person or event: *The roof of the building was supported by pillars, not walls.* **2** (*fig*) anything tall and upright that looks like this: *A pillar of smoke rose from the fire.*

column [C] **1** a large pillar: *The church had some very fine columns.* **2** (*fig*) anything like a pillar in shape or use: *He saw a column of smoke rising over the houses.*

arch [C] a curved top sometimes with a central point resting on two supports, as under a bridge or above a door: *The building was built on arches. The roof was in the shape of an arch.* **archway** a passage [⇨ D29] under an arch, esp in a doorway **arched** [B] having an arch or arches or such a shape

beam [C] any large long heavy piece of wood, usu squared, esp one of the main pieces used to support a building or to go from one side of a ship to the other: *The roof was made stronger by using several great beams.*

rafter [C] one of the sloping beams which support a roof

piles [P] heavy wooden, metal, or concrete [⇨ H66] beams hammered upright into the ground as a support for a building, bridge, etc

D27 *nouns* : **parts of larger houses and buildings** [C]

portico a grand entrance to a building, consisting of a roof supported by one or two rows of pillars

colonnade a row of pillars with equal spaces between, usu supporting a roof or row of arches **colonnaded** [Wa5;B] having colonnades: *The colonnaded temples of ancient Greece are famous.*

arcade a covered passage, esp one with an arched roof or with a row of shops on one or both sides

wing one side of a very large house, building, etc: *The bedrooms are in the west wing. They are adding a new wing to the hospital.*

tower a tall narrow part of a large building, rising well above the other parts: *The house has two towers. Her bedroom is in the tower.*

D28 *nouns* : **levels in buildings** [C]

[ALSO ⇨ D43]

level a position of height in a city, building, etc: *Their office is below street level. The building is built on two levels.* **split-level** [Wa5;A] built on two levels: *He has a split-level house.*

floor a level in a building: *His office is on the 8th floor.*

ground floor the part of a building, often the lowest, at ground level: *The lift went down to the ground floor. He has a ground-floor office.*

first floor 1 *BrE* the first floor above ground level **2** *AmE* the ground floor

storey *BrE*, **story** *AmE* a floor or level in a building: *There are three storeys/stories including the ground floor. It is a three-storey house.*

landing 1 the level space or passage at the top of a set of stairs from which one enters rooms **2** a level space between two sets of stairs

basement the lowest level of a building, usu wholly or partly underground

platform 1 a raised floor of boards for speakers, performers, etc: *The election result was given out from a platform outside the town hall. This singer always gets nervous on the concert platform.* **2** the speakers seated on this: *Please address your remarks to the platform.*

D29 *nouns* : **passages and halls** [C]

passage(way) a usu long narrow connecting way, esp inside a building: *She was standing in the passage(way); she did not know which door to open.*

corridor 1 a long passage in a building, train, etc, with doors and rooms on one or both sides: *He walked along the corridor to Room 41.* **2** (*fig*) a very narrow area of land, esp of a country with foreign land on both sides **3** (*fig*) a narrow area of space in the air along which aeroplanes are allowed to fly

hall the wide passage just inside the entrance of a house from which the rooms open: *The visitors waited in the hall until he was ready to meet them.*

lobby a hall or corridor, not a room, which leads from the entrance to the rooms inside a building: *He was waiting for her in the hotel lobby.*

vestibule *often fml* a wide passage or small room just inside the outer door of a (public) building through which all the other rooms are reached; an entrance hall: *I can't deal with Mr McGregor in my office just now; ask him to wait in the vestibule.*

foyer an entrance hall to a theatre or hotel, where people gather and talk: *Meet me in the foyer at 7.30.*

cloakroom *AmE usu* **checkroom**, a room, as in a theatre, where hats, coats, bags, etc, may be left for a short time, usu under guard: *He asked the cloakroom attendant for his coat.*

D30 *nouns* : **stairs and lifts** [C]

[ALSO ⇒ H117]

stairs [*usu pl with sing meaning*] a number of fixed steps one above the other, on which one can go up or down in a building, from one level to another: *She went up/down the stairs to her room.* **stair** [*sing*] one of these steps: *She stood waiting on the top stair.* **staircase/way** a set of (usu large) stairs considered as a whole: *What a fine staircase that is.* (*fig*) *This job is your stairway to success.* **downstairs, upstairs** [A; adv:Wa5] at or towards the bottom or top of a staircase: *He went upstairs. She lives in the downstairs flat.*

flight (of stairs) a set of stairs: *A flight of stairs led down into the room below. He ran up two flights and walked the rest.*

escalator a moving staircase, consisting of an endless chain of steps moving continuously up or down: *Take the escalator to the third floor of the store.*

lift (*AmE* **elevator**) a machine that takes people up or down to another floor inside a building: *He took the lift/elevator to the 9th floor.*

ladder an apparatus made esp of two long pieces of wood, metal, or rope, joined together by many short pieces (**rungs**) up which one climbs: *He put the ladder against the side of the house.* **stepladder** a ladder with flat pieces (steps) for the feet, having a support so that it can stand alone: *He put the stepladder in the middle of the room.*

fire escape a set of usu metal stairs leading down outside a building to the ground, by which people could escape in case of fire

ramp a slope, esp a passage, that connects two places at different levels: *They walked up a ramp onto the second floor of the building.*

chute a sloped passage along or down which something may be passed or dropped: *Put the waste down the chute, please. The boxes go down a chute from the second to the first floor.*

D31 *nouns, etc* : **fences, rails, and low walls** [C]

fence 1 something made of wood or metal and usu put up in order to divide two pieces of land or to stop animals or people from moving easily from one place to another: *He put a high fence round his field.* **2** [T1] to put a fence round: *He has fenced his fields.* **fence off** [v adv T1] to separate (from something else) by means of a fence: *He has fenced off his fields.*

rail a long narrow piece of wood or metal, or a number of such pieces, used at the side of stairs or along balconies, etc, to keep people from falling, passing, etc: *He held the rail as he climbed higher.*

railing 1 [*often pl*] a fence, esp a set of rails to protect people or keep them in or out: *The dog could not get through the railing.* **2** any of the pieces in such a fence: *The dog got its head stuck between the railings.*

ban(n)ister [*often pl*] a row of upright pieces of wood or metal with a bar along the top guarding the outer edge of stairs: *He looked over the banister to see what was happening below.*

balustrade 1 a row of upright pieces of stone or wood with a bar along the top, guarding the outer edge of stairs or steps or of any place from which people might fall **2** *fml* a type of railing

parapet 1 a low wall at the edge of a roof, bridge, etc: *Don't lean over the parapet or you'll fall in the river.* **2** a protective wall of earth or stone

D32 nouns : **verandahs and balconies** [C]

veranda(h), *also* **piazza, porch** *AmE* an addition to a house, built out from any of the walls, having a floor and a roof (usu supported by pillars) but no outside wall

balcony a place for people to stand or sit on, built out from the upper part of wall of a house or other building, and usu enclosed with a railing: *They stood on the balconies, looking down at the people below.*

terrace 1 a flat level area cut from a slope, esp it one of a number rising one behind and above the other: *In China hill farmers grow rice on terraces.* **2 a** an area next to a house, used as an outdoor living area **b** a flat roof used as an outdoor living area

D33 nouns : **kinds of room generally** [C]

room 1 [C *often in comb*] a division of a building, with its own walls, floor, and ceiling [⇒ D34]: *I want a double room* (= for two people) *with a view. The house had many rooms, including ten bedrooms and five bathrooms.* **2** [P *often cap*] the people in one such division: *Ask Room 5 if they want coffee.*

chamber *often fml* **1** a room: *He waited in an outer chamber of the great house.* **2** a bedroom:

'My lady is in her (bed)chamber,' said the servant.

hall 1 [*often in comb*] a large room in which meetings, dances, etc, can be held: *They met at a dance at the local hall.* **2** (in a college, university, etc) a room where all the members eat together **3** *also* **hall of residence** a building where members live together: *The students all live in halls of residence.*

D34 nouns : **the inside of a room**

living room

D35 nouns : **spaces set in walls** [C]

alcove 1 a small space in the form of a small room added to another room for a bed, chair, books, etc **2** a space like this, such as for a seat in a wall

recess 1 a space in the wall of a room for shelves, cupboards, etc **2** [*often pl*] (*fig*) a secret inner part of a place, that is hard to reach: *The animal waited in the darkest recesses of the cave.*

niche 1 a hollow place in a wall, usu made to hold an ornament, books, etc **2** (*fig*) a suitable place, job, position, etc: *He's found a niche for himself in that firm.*

cubicle 1 a very small enclosed division of a larger room, such as for dressing or undressing at a swimming pool **2** a small room

hatch an opening in a wall, esp so that food can be passed from a kitchen to the room where people eat

D36 nouns : **the fireplace** [C]
[⇨ PICTURE AT D34]

fireplace the place in the wall of a room where a fire is usu lit: *The room had a very large fireplace.*

fireside the position by the fire(place), often representing the pleasures of home life: *She sat by the fireside. That is the fireside chair he likes best. The comfort of his own fireside made him wish to go home instead of to the meeting.*

chimney a hollow passage rising above a fireplace which allows smoke to pass from a fire

flue a pipe or tube up which smoke or heat passes, usu to a chimney

hearth 1 the area around the fire in one's home, esp the floor of the fireplace: *A burning log fell into the hearth. We sat around the hearth together.* **2** (*fig*) the home: *He likes to stay close to the family hearth.*

grate the bars and frame which hold the coal, etc, in a fireplace

poker a thin metal bar used to poke a fire in order to make it burn better

tongs [P] an instrument consisting of two moveable arms joined at one end, used for holding or lifting various objects: *Pick up a lump of coal with the tongs.*

coalscuttle a bucket in which coal is carried and from which it can be poured

D37 nouns : **rooms in houses** [C]

living room the main room in a house where people can do things together, (usu) apart from eating: *Come and sit in the living room and watch television.*

lounge a comfortable room for sitting in, as in a house, hotel, or inn: *Come into the lounge; let's talk there.*

sitting room *esp BrE* **1** a living room **2** a lounge in a hotel: *They were in the sitting room watching television.*

parlour *BrE*, **parlor** *AmE* **1** *now rare* a room in a private house used by the family for receiving guests, reading and other amusements: *What Grandmother called the parlour we now call the living room or sitting room.* **2** [C9] *esp AmE in comb* a shop furnished like a room, for some kind of personal service or for selling a particular type of article: *Many women attend a beauty parlour to have their faces, hair, nails, etc, treated: Where's the ice-cream parlour/the local funeral* [⇨ C54] *parlour?*

front room *esp formerly* the room at the front of a house, esp for guests; a living room or parlour

reception room (esp used by people selling houses) a living or dining room; any room that is not a kitchen, bedroom, or bathroom

salon 1 a spacious living room, esp in a French house **2** (typically in France in the 18th century) a regularly-held fashionable gathering, esp of writers, artists, etc, at the home of a well-known person **3** a stylish or fashionable business: *She runs a beauty salon/a shoe salon.*

study a room, esp in a large house, school, etc, where a person can study books, etc: *Come and see me in my study in half an hour.*

studio 1 a room where (esp) an artist, photographer, etc, can work **2** a room or place where films or recordings are made, information, etc, is sent out by radio, television, etc: *He is at the studios, recording.*

library a room, usu in a large house, school, etc, which contains many books: *He was reading in the library.*

workroom a room where a person can do work, usu of a particular kind: *an artist's workroom*

bedroom 1 a room for sleeping in: *The house has two bedrooms. That's a two-bedroom(ed) house. We need a new bedroom carpet.* **2** such a room used for sex: *That film has a lot of bedroom scenes.*

dining room a room where meals are served or taken: *Let's eat in the kitchen; the dining room's too cold. We had breakfast in the hotel dining room.*

D38 *nouns* : **the kitchen and similar rooms** [C]

kitchen and kitchen equipment

kitchen a room used for cooking: *They sometimes take their meals in the kitchen.*

kitchenette a very small kitchen, or a separate part of a larger room which is the part used for cooking

scullery *becoming rare* a room next to the kitchen, esp in large or older houses, for cleaning and keeping dishes and cooking pots, and for other rough cleaning jobs

larder a storeroom or cupboard for food in a house

pantry 1 a small room with shelves where food is kept; a larder **2** a room in a big house, hotel, ship, etc **a** where glasses, dishes spoons, etc, used for eating are kept **b** where cold food is prepared

galley the kitchen on a ship

D39 *nouns* : **the kitchen sink** [C]

sink a basin for washing (in *BrE* esp a large one in a kitchen) fixed to a wall and usu with pipes to supply and carry away water: *Put the dirty dishes in the sink; we'll wash them later.*

sink unit a sink in a kitchen together with draining board and cupboards underneath: *She's*

pleased with her new sink unit; it makes washing dishes much easier.

draining board a sloping board on which dishes are placed after washing, to allow them to dry

dishcloth a cloth for washing dishes

dishwasher a machine or person that washes dishes

D40 *nouns* : **the bathroom** [C]

[ALSO ⇨ D172–3]

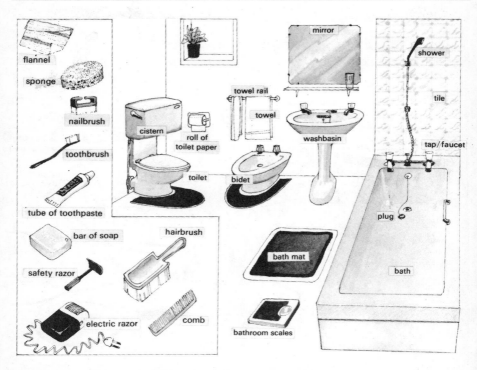

bathroom a room with a bath in it, usu also containing a lavatory, wash basin, etc: *He spends a long time in the bathroom every morning.*

bath 1 *also* **bathtub** a large, usu fixed, container in which a person can sit in order to wash the body and nowadays usu with its own hot and cold water brought and taken away in pipes **2** any similar large container for washing anything

shower an apparatus which provides showers with controls for water and usu built as an enclosure in a bathroom, above a bath, etc: *We have a bathtub but no shower in our house. He turned the shower on/off.*

wash basin a large basin for water, for washing the hands and face

bidet a kind of small low bath for sitting across, to wash the genitals [⇨ B10], etc

medicine cabinet/chest a small cupboard where medicines are kept, esp in the home, esp in the bathroom

towel 1 [C] a piece of cloth or paper used for drying someone or something that is wet: *Can I have a clean towel, please?* **2** [T1 (*down*)] to dry (esp oneself) with a towel: *He towelled himself down.* **towelling** *BrE*, **toweling** *AmE* a type of soft cloth used for making towels

D41 *nouns* : **the lavatory** [C]

lavatory 1 a large seatlike bowl fixed to the floor and connected to a pipe (= drain) used for getting rid of the body's waste matter **2** a room containing this **3** a small building containing a number of lavatories

toilet *also* **bathroom** *euph* a lavatory: *I must go to the toilet/bathroom.*

water closet a lavatory which is emptied by a flow of water from the pipes

WC *abbrev* a water closet

bog *BrE sl* a lavatory

loo *BrE* **john** *AmE infml* a lavatory

(public) convenience *fml & euph* a public lavatory

restroom *esp AmE* a public lavatory

urinal 1 a container for urine [⇨ B64] **2** a public lavatory for men

D42 *nouns, etc* : **plumbing and pipes**
[ALSO ⇒ H41]

plumbing [U] **1** all the pipes, containers for water, etc, in a building: *There's something wrong with the plumbing in that house.* **2** the work of a plumber **plumber** [C] a person, usu a man, who looks after the plumbing of buildings and fits pipes in houses

tap *BrE*, **faucet** *AmE* [C] any apparatus for controlling the flow of liquid or gas from a pipe, barrel, etc

stopcock [C] a tap which controls the flow of water, usu in pipes

plug [C] a small, usu round piece of rubber, wood, metal, etc, used to close a hole, esp a pipe: *She pulled the plug out of the bath and the dirty water flowed away.*

tank [C] a large container for storing liquid or gas

cistern [C] a container with a pipe leading in and out, used in a garden for storing rain water or in a house as part of the plumbing, for holding water

flush 1 [S9] a flow of water for washing out a toilet bowl: *This toilet has a strong flush.* **2** [S (*of*)] a sudden flow (of liquid, esp water): *The flush of water took all the dirt away.* **3** [T1] to make clean by such a flow: *He flushed the toilet.* **4** [T1 *out*] to remove by flushing: *They flushed out the dirty water.*

pipe [C *often in comb*] a tube used for carrying liquids away, often underground and in houses: *The pipes in this house are all new. The waterpipe has a hole in it.*

waste pipe [C] a pipe for carrying away liquids that one wants to get rid of

drain [C] a pipe, tube, sewer, etc, which serves to take waste liquids, etc, away from buildings: *The drains are blocked.* **drainage** [U] drains generally; the action or process of draining liquid from any place

drainpipe [C] a pipe for drainage, esp of water and waste from inside buildings

sewer [C] a man-made passage or large pipe under the ground for carrying away water and waste material, esp in a city, to a body of natural water or for chemical treatment (**sewage disposal**), sometimes by turning the waste onto an area of ground (**sewage farm**)

sewage [U] the waste material and water carried in sewers: *Before chemical treatment sewage is called raw sewage.*

sewerage [U] the (system of) removing and dealing with waste material and water through sewers: *This town has modern sewerage.*

(water) main [C] a large pipe carrying a supply of water; the chief pipe supplying water or gas; the chief sewer pipe taking waste, water, etc, out from a building

D43 *nouns* : **other rooms in a house, esp at the top or in the basement** [C]
[ALSO ⇒ D28]

cellar 1 an underground room, usu used for storing goods **2** a person's store of wine: *He keeps a very good cellar.*

attic a room or area, usu small, immediately below the roof of a house: *He lived in the attic of an old house in London; he had very little money at that time.*

garret *esp formerly* an attic, esp if very small

loft 1 a room under the roof of a building; an attic **2** a room over a stable, where dried grass (= **hay**) is kept

spare room *also* **guest room** a (bed)room which is not in use but is kept for use: *He can sleep in the spare room tonight.*

storeroom a room where goods are kept till needed: *The boxes are in the storeroom at the back of the shop.*

Areas around and near houses

D50 *nouns* : **yards and gardens** [C]

yard 1 an enclosed or partly enclosed area next to a building or group of buildings: *Leave your car in the yard; it'll be safe there.* **2** [*usu in comb*] an area enclosed for a special purpose, activity, or business: *shipyard, coalyard* **3** *esp AmE* the general area, sometimes including a garden, round or beside a house

court (esp formerly) an open area inside a large building or surrounded by buildings: *The courts of Oxford colleges are pleasant places in summer.*

courtyard *genl* an open place without a roof in or near a large building, in a castle, etc: *He stood in the courtyard, looking up at the windows.*

backyard 1 *BrE* a yard behind a house, covered with smooth stones **2** *also* **yard** *AmE* a yard behind a house, usu covered with grass

backcourt *ScotE* a backyard, covered in stones and/or grass

close 1 (in England) **a** the grounds [⇒ D51] round a large church, school, etc, usu with its buildings, etc **b** a narrow passage between such buildings **2** (in Scotland) the entrance to flats in a tenement [⇒ D8]

garden 1 (*AmE* **yard**) a piece of land, often near a house, on which flowers and vegetables may be grown: *Our neighbours' apple tree grows over our garden.* **2** [*often pl*] a public place with flowers, grass, paths, and seats

D51 *nouns* : **estates and parks**

estate [C] **1** a (large) piece of land in the country, usu with one large house on it and one owner: *Sir John Smith lives most of the year on* his country estate. **2** *BrE* a piece of land in which buildings (of a stated type) have all been built together in a planned way: *An industrial estate has factories on it and a housing estate has houses on it.*

park 1 [C] *BrE* a large enclosed stretch of land with grass, trees, etc, round a large country house **2** [C] a large, usu grassy, enclosed piece of land, or public gardens, in a town, used by the public for pleasure or rest

grounds [P] land surrounding a large building such as a country house or hospital, usu made into gardens and enclosed by a wall or fence: *The house stands in its own grounds. The grounds of the hospital were laid out as gardens and walks.*

D52 nouns : **lawns and patios** [C]

lawn a stretch of (usu flat) ground, esp next to a house, covered with closely-cut grass

patio 1 an open space between a house and garden, with a stone floor, used for sitting on in fine weather **2** an inner roofless courtyard of a Spanish or Spanish-American house

D53 nouns, etc : **places to park cars, etc**

garage 1 [C] a building in which motor vehicles can be kept: *The bus is on its last journey before it goes back to the garage for the night. He put his car in the garage and locked the garage door. Their garage is part of their house.* **2** [T1] to put in a garage: *He garaged the car for the night. Where do they garage their vehicles?*

carport [C] a shelter, having only a roof and one or two sides, often built against the side of a house, and in which a car is kept

car park [C] *esp BrE* **1** an open place where cars and other vehicles may be left, sometimes for a small payment **2** an enclosed place beneath the ground or in a building used for this purpose: *There is a multi-storey car park* (= a car park built on many levels) *in the town. The car park is on the third floor of the building.*

park [I0; T1] to put or leave (a vehicle, esp a car) in a particular place for a certain length of time: *Can I park here/Is this a parking place? No, you can't park (your car) here, but you can park at/by the side of the road.*

parking lot [C] *esp AmE* a (usu public) car park

drive [C] a road for vehicles, esp through a public park or the grounds of a building or to a private house: *A car was parked in the hospital drive.*

driveway [C] *esp AmE* a short private road leading from the street to a house, garage, or car park; a drive

D54 nouns : **sheds and outbuildings** [C]

shed [*often in comb*] a lightly-built (partly)

enclosed building, usu for storing things: *He keeps his old things in the shed.*

garden shed a shed built in or near a garden and used esp for storing things which are needed in the garden

potting shed a shed in or near a garden where plants can be put in pots

greenhouse a building with a glass roof and sides and usu some form of heating, in which plants can be grown which need warmth, light, and freedom from winds

glasshouse a building for growing plants where sunlight and warmth are directed in by the glass walls and roof

hothouse a warm building where flowers and delicate plants can grow

outbuilding a smaller building forming part of a group with a larger main building

outhouse 1 *BrE* an outbuilding, esp if smaller **2** *AmE* an enclosed outside lavatory [⇒ D41]

Residence

D60 verbs : **living and lodging**

live [L9] to have one's home: *Where do you live? He lives at No 5, Long Street. I used to live in London, but now I live in Edinburgh.*

dwell [L9] *fml & old use* to live: *He dwelt for a time in France, then went on to Italy.*

reside [L9] *fml* to have one's home (at, in a place): *They usually reside abroad. She resides at No 8, Mount Square. Where do you reside?*

stay [L9] **1** to be living for a short time: *He is staying at a local hotel/staying with friends.* **2** *ScotE* to live: *Where do you stay? He stays in London most of the year.*

lodge 1 [L9] to stay, usu for a short time and paying rent: *I'm lodging in the town. He is lodging at a friend's house/with friends.* **2** [I0] to live in lodgings: *Do you have a flat or do you lodge?*

board [T1; I0] to (cause to) get meals and usu lodging for payment: *She arranged to board some students from the university. I'm boarding with a friend/at a friend's house.* **board out** [v adv T1; I0] to (cause to) get food (and usu live) regularly away from home: *The children were boarded out with friends while their parents were abroad.*

put up [v adv L9] *infml* to stay: *He puts up at a friend's house when he comes here.*

occupy [T1] to be in (a place) during a particular period of time: *He occupied a room here for two years.*

inhabit [T1] *fml & tech* to live in: *What animals/people inhabit those islands? His people have inhabited these mountains for hundreds of years.* **inhabitable** [B] able to be lived in: *Are those islands inhabitable?* **un-** [*neg*]

D61 *verbs* : **accommodating people**

accommodate [T1] *often fml* to provide with a room in which to live or stay: *I can accommodate you for a few nights. The new hotel will accommodate 500 guests.*

put up [v adv T1] *infml* to accommodate: *Oh, we'll manage to put you up somewhere for the night.*

house [T1] **1** to provide with a place to live for a short or long time: *All the children must be housed and fed.* **2** to (provide space to) store: *We can house all your old furniture upstairs.*

lodge [T1] to give or find (someone) a home for a time, sometimes for payment: *We're going to lodge our son with a foreign family.*

settle [T1] to cause (someone) to live in a place, esp after moving (that person) from another place: *They moved the local people and settled them in another place. They were settled in Australia, although they did not want to go there.* **settled** [B] **1** not moving about: *The place is a desert with no settled population.* **2** [Wa5] (of a place) having people living in homes: *The settled areas of Australia are mainly on the coast.* **3** fixed; unlikely to change: *He has settled habits. This is a matter of settled principles of law; we know what to do.*

D62 *verbs* : **camping and settling**

camp [IØ (*out*)] to set up or live in a camp [⇒ D68]: *The hunters camped near the top of the mountain. We go camping every summer. The two boys camped out last night* (= slept out in a tent). **camping** [U] the activity of living in a tent or in tents: *They went camping last summer.*

encamp [IØ] to set up a (usu large) camp: *The army encamped along the river.*

settle [L9] to come or go to live in a place; to (decide to) live in a place after travelling for a long time: *The family settled in New Zealand. He finally settled in Canada and got married.*

settle down [v adv IØ] **1** to establish a home and live a quiet life: *I hate all this travel; I want to get married and settle down.* **2** to become used to a way of life, job, etc: *I'm sure the child will soon settle down in his new school.*

settle in [v adv IØ; T1] to (help or cause to) move comfortably into or get used to a new home, job, etc: *I haven't yet settled in/got settled in in my new job; I still get lost in the office building.* **settle into** [v prep T1] to get used to (new surroundings, a new job etc): *They settled into a new house/office.*

squat [IØ] to settle on land or in a house which no one lives in, without the permission of the owner or any legal right to do so: *They had no home so they decided to squat in an empty house.*

D63 *nouns* : **persons residing, lodging, and settling** [C]

resident someone who lives (in a place) and is not just a visitor: *This hotel serves meals to residents only.*

dweller *fml & lit* one who lives in a place: *The dwellers in the forest did not like visitors.*

occupant someone who is in a particular place, esp a house, room, etc, at a particular time: *Who are the occupants of that flat?*

occupier the person who occupies or lives in a house, flat, room, etc: *He is the occupier but not the owner of the flat.*

lodger a person who pays rent to stay in somebody's house: *The Smiths have two lodgers.*

boarder 1 a person who pays to live and receive meals at another person's house; lodger: *Mrs Brown takes in boarders for a living.* **2** a school child who lives at the school: *Most of the boys are boarders.*

settler one who settles, esp one of a (new) population, esp in a place with few people: *His family were 19th century settlers in Western Canada.*

pioneer 1 one of the first settlers in a new or unknown land, who is later followed by others: *The pioneers cleared the waste land and began to make farms; a pioneer town.* **2** a person who does something first and so prepares the way for others: *a pioneer of operations on the human heart; a pioneer plan*

squatter a person who lives on empty land or in an empty house without permission: *He asked the police to get the squatters off his land.*

inhabitant *esp tech* a person who lives in a place, esp as one of a group which has been there a very long time: *The inhabitants of the island are friendly. Have you met any of the local inhabitants?*

D64 *nouns* : **persons owning and occupying houses** [C]

owner the person who owns something, esp a house, flat, etc: *The tenants asked the owner for permission to paint the house.*

owner-occupier a person who owns the house or flat in which he or she lives

landlord 1 a person from whom someone rents all or part of a building, land, etc: *His landlord is a local farmer.* **2** a person who owns or is in charge of an inn, hotel, etc: *Landlord, more beer, please!*

landlady a woman who keeps lodgers: *Mrs Smith is his landlady.*

tenant a person who pays rent for the use of a room, building, land, etc: *Do you own your house or are you a tenant?* **tenancy 1** [U] occupation of a place as a tenant **2** [C] the use of a house, etc, as a tenant: *His tenancy was for three years and no longer.*

D65 nouns, etc : home

home [C] **1** the house where one lives: *My home isn't very big, but it's comfortable.* **2** the place where one was born or habitually lives: *His home is in London. Glasgow is her home town.* *(fig) This college is a home of learning.* **3** the house and family one belongs to: *He worked hard to make his home a happy place. A good home life is very important.* **4** a place where a living thing can be found living and/or growing wild, esp in large numbers: *The wild rose has its home along country roads. India is the home of elephants and tigers.* **5** a place for the care of a group of people or animals of the same kind, who do not live with a family: *She works in a children's home/an old people's home. She left her money to a home for cats.* **at home 1** in the house or family **2** ready to receive visitors: *If the telephone rings, say I'm not at home (to visitors).* **be/feel at home** to be comfortable: *He doesn't feel at home with people like that.* **make oneself at home** *(often imper)* to behave freely, sit where one likes, smoke, etc, as if at home: *Come in and make yourself at home.* **leave home** to go away from one's family to live independently for the first time, esp after an argument: *She has left home and says she won't go back.* **homely** [Wa2;B] liking things as they are at home; pleasant like one's home: *The house had a homely look about it.*

residence [C] *fml* the place where one lives; a house, esp a large grand one: *Lord Jones is at his country residence.* *'This desirable town residence for sale' (advertisement).* *(humor) How nice of you to visit me at my humble residence!* **in residence** actually living in a place, esp **1** (of an official) in his official house **2** (of students) at a university: *The students are not in residence during the holidays.* **resident** [Wa5;B] living (and working) in a place: *That big hotel has a resident doctor.*

domicile 1 [C] *fml* one's home; the place where one lives **2** [C] *law* the place where for official purposes one is considered to live, whether or not one really spends much time there **3** [Wv5;X9] to establish in or provide with a domicile: *He travels about a lot but he is domiciled in London.*

dwelling [C] *fml* a house; a place where someone lives: *The poor people's dwellings were cold and unhealthy.*

dwelling-place [C] *fml* a place where someone dwells; a domicile

habitat [C] the place in which an animal, plant, etc, lives or can usu be found: *The natural habitat of these animals is in the mountains. Different habitats have different kinds of animal living in them.*

habitation 1 [U] the act of living in a place: *The moon is not suitable for human habitation.* **2** [C] *fml & pomp* a house, home, etc: *Where are the people's habitations?*

domesticity [U] the state of being in or like a home; life in or with a family: *He prefers domesticity to travelling. The room had an air of domesticity.* **domestic** [B] **1** [Wa2] of, concerning, or like the home: *They sell all the usual domestic equipment in that shop. Their domestic life isn't very happy.* **2** [Wa5] concerning one's own country: *That nation does not like other governments taking too great an interest in its domestic affairs.*

D66 nouns : accommodation and board

[ALSO ⇒ M79]

accommodation [U] **1** a place to live; a room, flat, house, hotel, etc: *What sort of accommodation can you get in this city?* **2** *esp AmE* a room and food, as in a hotel: *They provide good accommodation.*

occupancy [U] the condition or right of actually living in a building or on a piece of land: *When do you get the occupancy of your new house?*

premises [P] *usu fml* a building, house, etc, and the land that belongs with it: *Get off these premises now or I'll send for the police! Most of these buildings are business premises.*

lodging [S; U] a place to stay: *He tried to find a lodging for the night.*

lodgings [P] **1** the room(s) one pays rent for in a private house: *My lodgings are only two rooms.* **2** a house where rooms are rented out: *He was staying in lodgings.*

board [U] (the cost of) meals: *He pays £20 a week for full board* (= all meals).

board and lodging [U; P] the provision of meals and a bed for payment: *She pays £30 a week board and lodging.*

digs [P] *BrE infml* lodgings, esp for students: *Are you in college* (= lodging in rooms at the college) *or in digs?*

D67 nouns, etc : shelter

shelter 1 [C] something that covers or protects, usu in the form of a building, etc: *They looked for a shelter from the bad weather/the bombs. They waited for the bus at the bus shelter.* **2** [U] cover; protection: *Please, can you give us shelter for the night?* **3 a** [T1] to give shelter to (a person, animal, etc): *The old house didn't shelter them well from the bad weather. They sheltered him from his enemies.* **b** [L9] to get shelter: *Where can we shelter from the weather?*

refuge *esp poet & lit* [C; U] (a place that provides) protection or shelter from danger: *They spent the night at a mountain refuge for climbers. Where can we find refuge from the storm?*

D68 nouns : camps

[⇒ C80 TOWNS AND SETTLEMENTS]

camp 1 [C; U] a place where people live in tents

[⇒ D3] or huts [⇒ D4] for a short time, usu nowadays for pleasure or in an army:*When we were on holiday we stayed in a camp. The climbers had a camp near the top of the mountain. We were all in camp by 6 o'clock. The hunters spent the night at a Red Indian camp.* **2** [C *usu in comb*] a place where people live, often unwillingly: *The political prisoners were sent to a labour camp. The men in the prison camp had to work hard.* **3** [GC] a group of people or organization with the same ideas: *The workers were divided into two camps.* **camper** [C] **1** a person who lives in a camp **2** *AmE* a motor vehicle big enough to live, cook, and sleep in when on holiday

encampment [C] a large camp, esp military; a place where soldiers camp [⇒ D62]: *There was a wire fence round the encampment.*

barracks [Wn3; C; P] **1** a building or group of buildings in which (esp) soldiers live: *He must be back in barracks by 9 o'clock tonight.* [⇒ C312] **2** (*fig*) a big bare plain, usu ugly building: *You can't expect us to live in a great barracks like that!*

Belonging and owning, getting and giving

D80 *verbs, etc* : **belonging**

belong to [Wv6; v prep T1] to be owned by: *This book belongs to him; it's his. Who does that car belong to?*

belong [Wv6] **1** [L9] to be suited to, advantageous, or fitting: *A telephone belongs in every home. A man with his ability belongs in teaching.* **2** [I∅] to be in the right place: *That subject belongs with the sciences. After years of living here I feel that I belong.*

be [L7] (*esp with possessive pron*) to belong to: *That book is his* (= That book belongs to him). *The car is mine/my car.*

of [prep] **1** (used to show ownership or connection): *He is the father of the child. Who is the owner of this book?* **2** (used to show that something or someone characteristically has something): *She is a woman of great beauty.* **3** (used to show that someone or something is part of a larger group): *For most of the people there is not enough food. One member of our group left.* **4** (used to express measurement): *a kilogram of sugar; four pounds of butter* **5** (used with a possessive noun or pronoun to express one of a number of persons or things): *She is a friend of his/of Bill's.* (*emph*) *That son of his is causing a lot of trouble!* **6** (used to show distance or separation of one thing from another): *The house is within a kilometre of the shops. They travelled to the west of the mountains.* **7** (used to show a cause or reason): *They died of hunger.* **8** (used to express an object relationship after certain verbs and nouns): *I'm tired of sitting here. His love of animals is well known.* **9** (used to express a subject rela-

tionship): *The love of some dogs for their owners is easily seen.* **10** (used to show that something is made from or contains something else): *a book made of paper; a box of chocolates* **11** (used with *it* to show what one thinks about someone's action): *It was nice of him to help us. It was wrong of you to do that!*

D81 *verbs* : **having and owning** [T1]

have [Wv6; *not pass*] **1** *infml* to keep, use, etc, as one's own: *He has two cars. Do you have any money?* (*fig*) *She has blue eyes. He doesn't have a very friendly manner. Do you have a good opinion of him?* **2** to contain as part: *This coat has no pockets* (= There are no pockets in this coat).

have got [Wv6] *esp BrE genl infml* to have, esp of a particular thing on a present occasion: *Have you got any money?—Sorry, I haven't got any money.*

possess [Wv6] **1** *fml* to have (esp as belonging to one): *He possesses two cars. He never possessed much money, but he has always had good health.* **2** (of a feeling or idea) to influence (someone) so completely as to control or direct actions: *Fear possessed him and prevented him from moving. She was possessed by a single desire. What(ever) possessed you to act so strangely?* (= caused you . . .) **3** [*usu pass + of*] (of an evil spirit or the devil) to enter into and become master of (someone): *'She was possessed of a devil,' said the priest.* **4** [*of*] *old use or pomp* to cause (oneself) to be the owner: *For the purpose of study you should possess yourself of a dictionary.* **possession** **1** [U] the condition of possessing: *He has possession of the house and can tell them to leave.* **2** [C] something possessed: *This is a valuable possession; guard it carefully.* **possessive** wanting very much to have or to keep things: *She is a rather possessive mother; she likes to keep her children near her.* **-ly** [adv] **-ness** [U] **possessor** [C] a person who possesses something; (*fml*) owner

own [Wv6] to have or possess (something), esp by lawful right: *Who owns this house/dog? He owns a lot of land in this part of the country.* **owner** [C] a person who owns something **ownership** [U] the condition of owning or being an owner

keep **1** to own and have the use of: *He keeps two horses and a car.* **2** to have for some time or for more time: *Please keep this book for me till I come back. He was in trouble at first but he managed to keep his job. These old clothes are not worth keeping.* **3** to have without the need of returning: *You can keep the book; I don't need it. Here's more money than you need to buy the dress; keep the change.* **4** to own and make money from: *They keep a shop/a small hotel.* **5** to own and take care of in order to use or make money from: *He keeps sheep.* **6** (*fig*) to know without telling: *Can you keep a secret? She kept the news to herself.*

D82 *nouns* : **belonging and owning**

belongings [P] things that belong to a person: *Are these your belongings? Please take all your belongings out of this room and put them upstairs.*

things [P] *infml* belongings: *Where can I put my things?—Oh, put them with my things in the bedroom.*

possessions [P] things a person possesses: *These books are her most precious possessions.*

property 1 [U] that which is owned (and has some value); possession(s): *That box is my property, and you can't take it without my permission. The police found some stolen property, and returned it to its rightful owners. Jane considers Tom to be her own property.* **2** [U] land, buildings, or both together, esp as owned by someone: *What's his business?—Oh, he's in property. Property in the city centre is expensive.* **3** [C] a building, piece of land, or both together, esp as owned by someone: *He has several properties for sale or to let.* **4** [U] ownership according to the law: *The idea of private property is found in most societies, but public property is a more modern thing.* **propertied** [Wa5;B] owning a lot of property: *Big landowners are often called the propertied classes.* **common property** [U] **1** an article that is shared or used by all: *That book is common property.* **2** (*fig*) something that is known to everyone: *Anything that happens here is soon common property.* **proprietor** [C] a person owning something as property: *Who is the proprietor of this shop?*

D83 *verbs* : **getting and earning**

get *genl & infml* **1** [T1] to be given, sent, etc; to experience; to have as a natural fact: *I got a letter today. He got a blow on the head and needed medical attention. The room doesn't get much light because the windows are so small.* **2** [D1 (*for*); T1] to go for, buy, or be given in some particular way; to take, etc: *We'll get the shopping tomorrow. I'll get (you) some money before the bank closes.*

receive [T1] *often fml* to get: *I received a letter today. He received a blow on the head and needed medical attention. The room doesn't receive much light through this window.* **reception** [U] the act of receiving or being received: *His reception of the money/news was surprising; I expected him to be happy about it, but he wasn't.*

obtain [D1 (*for*); T1] *often fml* to get, esp by making some effort: *I haven't been able to obtain that record anywhere; can you obtain it for me?*

gain [T1] to get or obtain (something useful, necessary, wanted, etc), esp over a length of time and as an addition to what one has/what is there, etc: *I'm new in the job but I'm already gaining experience. Eat well if you want to gain*

strength after your illness.

acquire [T1] *often fml* **1** to get for oneself by one's own work, skill, action, etc: *He acquired a knowledge of the language by careful study.* **2** to gain or come to possess: *With the money he had won he was able to acquire some property.* **acquisition 1** [U] the action of acquiring: *His main interest is the acquisition of property.* **2** [C] something acquired: *This house is one of his latest acquisitions.*

come by [v prep T1] *infml & sometimes deprec* to gain or obtain: *How did he come by so much money? Did he steal it? He came by the house in some mysterious way.*

merit [T1] to deserve, esp because of one's good qualities, hard work, etc: *He merits more money for his work. This book merits careful study.*

earn 1 [T1 (*by*)] to get (money, etc) by working: *He earns £4,000 a year (by writing stories).* **2** [T1 (*by*)] to get (something that one deserves) because of one's qualities: *Alexander earned the title of 'the Great' by his victories in war.* **3** [D1] to cause (someone) to get or be worthy of: *His victories earned him the title of 'the Great'*

procure 1 [D1 (*for*); T1] *fml* to obtain, esp by effort or careful attention: *Can you procure that rare old book for me? The lawyer is working hard to procure the boy's freedom from prison.* **2** [T1 (*for*); I0] to provide (a woman) for someone else's sexual satisfaction: *It's against the law here to procure.* **procurement** [U] the act of procuring

deserve [Wv6; T1] to be worthy of getting: *He deserved the job but he didn't get it. She deserves a holiday; she has worked very hard. Give the money to the most deserving person* (= to the person who deserves it most). **deservedly** [adv] by deserving; justly: *He was deservedly the winner.* **un-** [*neg*] **deserts** [P] what one deserves, usu because of bad actions: *The criminal got his (just) deserts when he was put in prison.*

D84 *verbs, etc* : **taking and choosing**

take [T1] **1** to put out one's hand and get (something): *Take a cake, please. Please take one of the books.* **2** (*fig*) to have; make (a stated action): *Take a look at that beautiful girl! He took a deep breath.*

pick 1 [T1] to choose, esp by taking, pointing, etc: *I don't know which of the three dresses to pick; I like them all.* **2** [D1 (*for*); T1; I0] to pull or break off part of (a plant) by the stem; gather: *Have I picked enough beans for dinner? He picked her a rose. They've gone (fruit) picking today.* **pick and choose** to choose very carefully, considering each choice for a long time: *I'll take any work that is offered to me; I can't afford to pick and choose.* **pick a winner** *infml* to make a very good choice: *She picked a winner when she chose John as her husband.* **pick 1** [S] choice (*often in the phr* **take**

your pick): *Which of the books is your pick? Which one do you want?—Take your pick.* **2** [*the* S *of*] the best (of many): *These apples are the pick of the crop.*

choose 1 [D1 (*for*); T1, 4, 6a,b; V3; X (*to be*) 1; I∅ (*between, from*)] to show (what one wants) by taking; take from a greater number: *She chose a book from among those on the table. Have you chosen a hat yet? If you had to choose between staying here alone or going with me, what would you choose? The people chose John Smith to go to the President and tell her of their demands. I've just chosen a new car for my wife. Will you help me choose myself a new coat? Who did you choose to be/as your new member of parliament? There are ten to choose from and I don't know which to choose.* **2** [T3; 5c, 6a,b; I∅] to decide by choosing: *He chose not to go home until later. He chose that we should stay. Who is going to choose what to do? Will you choose, please?* **choice 1** [U; C] the act of choosing or being chosen: *Choice is difficult; I don't know which/what to choose. Their choices were made yesterday.* **2** [C] something or someone chosen: *Which of these is your choice? Their choices weren't very good, in my opinion. He is my choice.* **3** [S] a variety from which to choose: *There was a big choice of shops in the small town.* **4** [Wa1;B] well-chosen; worth choosing; very good: *This is a choice selection of fruits.* **choosy** [Wa1;B] *infml* careful in choosing anything: *Don't be so choosy—pick one!*

select [T1; V3] to choose as best, most suitable, etc, from a group: *He selected a pair of socks to match his suit. Which of them did you select for the job?* **select** [B] chosen or choosing from a larger group (and therefore limited): *This is a very select group of workers/a very select school.* **selection 1** [U] the act of selecting or being selected: *She spent an hour in the shop over the selection of a new dress.* **2** [C] something that is selected: *The performance included some musical selections.* **3** [C *usu sing*] a collection of things of a kind, as of goods for sale: *The shop has a fine selection of cheeses.* **selective** [B] **1** careful in choosing: *With 30 people wanting the job, the employer could be selective in his choice.* **2** [Wa5] acting with, or concerning, only certain items; not general: *The government placed selective controls on goods brought into the country for sale. This tax is selective in its effects.* **selector** [C] a person or instrument that selects

D85 *verbs* : **picking and lifting**

pick 1 [T1 (*from*)] to take up or remove, usu with the fingers or a pointed instrument, esp separately or bit by bit: *The little birds were picking the grain. Let me pick that hair from your dress. He picked the meat from the bone.* **2** [T1] to remove unwanted things from, esp with a finger or a pointed instrument: *He*

always picks his teeth after eating. Don't pick your nose. **3** [T1 (*in*)] to make with or as with a pointed instrument (*usu in the phr* **pick a hole/-holes in**): *The birds were picking holes in the tree for their nests.* **4** [T1] to pull apart: *As this skirt fits badly I shall pick it to pieces and remake it.*

lift 1 [T1 (*up*)] to raise from one level and hold or move to another level: *Lift (up) the stone. The baby was lifted onto the bed.* **2** [I∅] (of movable parts) to move or go upwards or outwards: *The top of this box won't lift.* **3** [T1 (*up*)] to raise or move upwards or to an upright position: *The dog lifted (up) its ears.* **4** [I∅] (esp of clouds, mist, etc) to move upwards, thin out, or disappear: *The clouds lifted.* **5** [T1] to bring to an end; remove: *The unpopular tax was soon lifted.* **6** [T1] (in some games) to cause (a ball) to rise, often unintentionally **7** [T1] *infml* to steal (esp small articles): *I'm afraid he has been lifting things again.* **8** [T1] to take and use (other people's ideas, writings, etc) as one's own without stating that one has done so: *He lifted that idea from her book.* **9** [T1] *tech* to dig up (root crops, or plants), esp carefully **10** [T1 (*up*)] to make (the voice) loud, as in singing

pluck 1 [D1 (*for*); T1] to pick (a flower, fruit, or leaf): *He plucked her a rose. He plucked a rose for her.* **2** [T1 (*out*)] to pull (esp something unwanted) sharply (from); pick: *She tried to pluck out some of her grey hairs. He plucked a feather from the bird's wing. She plucked the chicken* (= pulled out its feathers before cooking it).

D86 *verbs* : **taking and putting back** [v adv T1]

take back to take (something which was one's own or someone's at an earlier time): *I'll take the money back to them. He gave me the book last week but now he wants to take it back.* (*fig*) *It's too late to take back all the terrible things you said.*

get back [*also* D1] *genl* to obtain in any way (something which was one's own or someone's at an earlier time): *I don't know how he got the money back, but he has got it back. Get it back for me and quickly! Get the books back to her immediately.*

bring back [*also* D1] to bring (something which was one's own or someone's or which happened at an earlier time): *He has brought all the money back to us. She wants to bring back all the old customs.*

put back to put (something in a place where it was at an earlier time): *Put the money back, please. He put back all the books on their proper shelves. He put (the hands of) the clock back an hour as they crossed the border.*

fetch back [*also* D1] *infml & genl* to bring, get, or take back: *Fetch back those books, please, from the other shop. When you're out, fetch me back a newspaper.*

send back 1 to direct, post, etc (something to a place where it was at an earlier time): *He sent the money back by post.* **2** [*also D1*] to send (something, a message, etc) to a place where someone wants it, esp to a place where the speaker has been: *She sent (us) back a message that everyone was well and happy.*

D87 *verbs & nouns* : restoring, returning, and regaining

restore [T1] *usu fml* **1** [(*to*)] to give back: *He restored the stolen property. Our lost child has been restored to us.* **2** to bring back into use; introduce again: *They restored the old customs. Call in the army to restore law and order.* **3** [(*to*); *usu pass*] to bring back to a proper state, esp of health: *I feel quite restored (to health) after my holiday.* **4** [(*to*)] to put back into a former position: *They restored him (to his old job).* **5** to put (old buildings, furniture, or works of art) back into the original state: *They restored an old oil painting/a ruined temple.* **restoration** [U; C] the act of restoring or being restored; an example or result of this

replace [T1] to put (something) back in the right place: *He replaced the book on the shelf.* **replaceable** [B] that can be replaced **ir-** [*neg*] **-bly** [*adv*] **replacement** [U; C] the act of replacing or being replaced; an example or result of this

return 1 [T1 (*to*)] to give or send back: *Don't forget to return my keys! We returned the empty bottles (to the shop).* **2** [I∅ (*from, to*)] to come or go back: *He returned home. She returned to London. What time does your husband return (from work)?* **3** [T1] to answer (used with the actual words spoken): *'Yes, if you like!' she returned, smiling.* **4** [T1] to bring in as a profit: *These shares return a good rate of interest.* **5** [T1] to state officially (an amount of money), esp in answer to a demand: *He returned his earnings as £7,000 on the tax declaration. Don't forget to return the details of what you spend.* **return a favour** to do a kind action in return for another **return thanks** *fml* to say that one is grateful, as in a speech or a prayer **return** [U; C] the act of returning or being returned; an example or result of this: *On his return he went to see her.*

retrieve 1 [T1 (*from*)] to get back; find and bring back: *He retrieved the gloves I left in the train. This dog can retrieve sticks thrown into the water.* (*fig*) *He retrieved the poor girl from moral ruin.* **2** [T1] to put right; make up for (a mistake, loss, defeat, etc): *He retrieved the defeat by winning the next game.* **3** [I∅; T1] (of a dog) to bring back (shot birds): *That's a dog that retrieves well.* **retrieve one's fortunes** to get money again after losing it by back luck: *When he lost his job he tried to retrieve his fortunes by robbing a bank.* **retrievable** [B] able to be retrieved **ir-** [*neg*] **-bly** [*adv*] **retrieval** [U] the act of retrieving or being retrieved: *Retrieval of information is important in the modern world.*

recover 1 [T1] to get back (something lost or taken away): *The police recovered the stolen jewellery. When he recovered consciousness after the accident he asked, 'Where am I?' She's beginning to recover her strength after her fever.* **2** [I∅ (*from*)] to return to a usual state of health, strength, ability, etc: *He is very ill and unlikely to recover. He has recovered from his bad cold and can go out tomorrow.* (*fig*) *Has the country recovered yet from the effects of the war?* **recover oneself** to get back into a proper state or position: *He almost fell, but succeeded in recovering himself. She soon recovered herself and stopped crying.* **recovery** [U; C] the act of recovering or being recovered; an example or result of this: *The recovery of the stolen jewellery made her happy. His recovery from the illness was slow but steady.*

regain [T1] **1** to get or win back (something): *He regained his health quickly.* **2** to get back to; reach again (a place): *The swimmer soon regained the shore.* **regain one's footing/balance** to get back on one's feet after slipping or beginning to fall

D88 *verbs & nouns* : changing and replacing

change [I∅; T1] to become or make different; to have (one thing) in the place of (another): *She has changed; she is very different from the girl I once knew. He has changed his job; he has a different job now. Can you change this book?—I want a different one.* **2** [U; C] the act of changing or being changed; an example or result of this: *It's a nice change to find him so friendly. There have been a lot of changes in the world since 1900. Change happens all the time; nothing stays the same for long.*

substitute 1 [T1 (*for*)] to put (something or someone) in place of another: *We substituted red balls for blue, to see if the baby would notice. They don't like potatoes, so we substituted rice.* **2** [I∅ (*for*)] to be used instead of: *Water must substitute (for wine) until we can get some more wine. He substituted for (= took the place of) the worker who was ill.* **substitution** [U; C] the act of substituting or being substituted; an example or result of this **substitute** [C] something or someone that substitutes for something or someone else: *Water isn't a proper substitute for wine.*

replace [T1] to take the place of: *George has replaced Edward as captain of the team.* **replacement** [U; C] the act of replacing or being replaced; an example or result of this; someone who replaces someone else

stead [U] *fml & old use* place (*in the phr* **in someone's stead**): *He went there in her stead* (= to take her place). **instead** [adv Wa5] taking the place of, or as a change from, something or someone else: *I couldn't go, so he went instead. Don't do that; do this instead.* **instead of** [prep] taking the place of, or as a change from (something or someone else): *Instead of helping her, he helped her enemies. She went instead of him.*

D89 *verbs* : **getting rid of things** [T1]

[ALSO ⇒ H15]

get rid of to cause (something or someone) to go away, to be taken away, etc: *We must get rid of all these books; we don't need them any more. Please get rid of those animals; they are dirty.*

rid of [v prep D1] *esp fml & emph* to make (a place, etc) free from: *He rid the town of rats.*

dispose of [v prep] *sometimes fml* to get rid of; finish with: *Dispose of these old newspapers. She disposed of all their unwanted property. (fig) I can dispose of his argument easily.*

dispense with [v prep] *often fml* **1** to do without: *We shall have to dispense with the car; we can't afford it.* **2** to make unnecessary: *This new office machine will dispense with the need for a secretary.*

throw away [v adv T1] *infml* to get rid of (something), esp without being interested in what happens (to it): *Throw away these papers; we don't need them any more. I'm afraid the papers have been thrown away.*

throw out [v adv T1] to get rid of, esp from a place: *He threw the old clothes out. Throw him out (of here) and tell him not to come back!*

take away [v adv T1] to get rid of, by carrying or leading away from a place: *Take these papers away; I'm finished with them.*

take out [v adv T1] to get rid of, by carrying, leading, lifting, cutting, etc (something or someone) out (of a place, book, etc): *Take him out (of here); I don't want to see him again. I don't like this sentence; take it out (of the paragraph).*

put away [v adv T1] to put (something) in some place so as not to be seen, etc: *Put your books away, children; we have finished today's work.*

put out [v adv T1] to put (something) outside a place: *Put the cat out for the night; I don't like it in the house at night. They put him out of his home because they needed it for someone else.*

get away/out [v adv T1] *genl & infml* to take or put (something or someone) away/out: *Get this thing away from me! Get him out of here! They got the man out (of the house).*

cast off [v adv T1] *esp old use, lit & emot* to throw away; take off forcefully: *He cast off his clothes and jumped into the water. (fig) You can't just cast her off like an old coat!*

D90 *verbs* : **abandoning and removing things** [T1]

abandon 1 to leave completely, never to return: *The sailors abandoned the burning ship. Don't abandon me here!* **2** to leave (a relation or friend) in a thoughtless or cruel way: *He abandoned his wife and went away with all their money.* **3** to give up, esp without finishing, often to do something else: *The search was*

abandoned when night fell even though the child had not been found. The plan was abandoned because of the cost/in favour of another plan. **4** to give (oneself) up completely to a feeling, desire, etc: *He abandoned himself to grief.*

jettison *often tech* to get rid of: *They jettisoned lots of heavy equipment to make the ship lighter. (fig) He will jettison anything and anybody if that helps his plans.*

remove 1 [T1 *(from)*] to take away (from a place); take off: *He removed his hat. You must remove your shoes in a mosque. They removed the child from the class.* **2** [T1 *(from)*] to get rid of; clean off: *Please remove the mud from your shoes. He tried to remove her fears by telling her what would happen.* **3** [T1 *(from)*] *fml* to dismiss: *That officer must be removed (from his position).* **4** [I0 *(from, to)*] to go to live or work in another place: *Our office has removed (from London to Harlow)/(to Harlow from London).*

D91 *nouns* : **disposing of and removing things**

disposal [U9] **1** the act or action of getting rid of: *His business is waste disposal. She arranged the disposal of their unwanted property by sale.* **2** the power or right to use freely (*esp in the phr* **at someone's disposal**): *I put my car at his disposal. My car was completely at his disposal.*

removal [C; U] (an) act of removing: *The removal of the children made her angry. Removals are unpleasant, but it will be nice when we get into the new house.*

abandonment [U] the act or result of abandoning: *Their abandonment of the plan upset her.*

riddance [S; U] *infml* (a) clearing away of something unwanted (*esp in the phr* **Good riddance!**): *They've gone at last—good riddance (= I'm glad they've gone)!*

D92 *verbs* : **giving up** [T1]

[ALSO ⇒ C282]

give up [v adv; *also* T4] to stop having or doing; abandon [⇒ D90] one's use or charge of: *The doctor told him to give up sugar and smoking. I've given up the idea; it won't work. Don't give up hope. He gave himself up to the police.*

surrender to allow to pass to others; (*fml*) abandon; give up: *They surrendered the city to the enemy. You must surrender yourself to the police. He surrendered control of the company.*

yield *fml esp formerly* to give up control of; surrender: *They yielded (up) the city to the enemy. We were forced to yield the city.*

D93 *verbs* : **keeping things** [T1]

keep to have as one's own and not (plan to) give away: *I'll give you that book but I'm keeping* this one. *He keeps his things all to himself. Oh, keep your money; I don't want it!* (*fig*) *She can keep her love if it's so important to her; I don't need it.*

keep back [v adv] to keep (usu some of something) in one's possession: *I kept a few pounds back and gave him the rest of the money.*

withhold 1 to keep (something) back or away on purpose: *He withheld the money until he was sure they would use it properly. I think she is withholding information from the police.* **2** *fml* to say that one refuses; not give: *I withhold my agreement.*

retain 1 to keep possession of; avoid losing: *He retained all his hair until he was 90.* **2** to hold in place: *They built a wall to retain the water of the lake.*

hang/hold onto [v prep] *infml* **1** to (try to) keep: *We should hang onto the house and sell it later when the prices are higher. Hold onto the money; you may need it.* **2** (*fig*) to find support or help in: *The old lady had only her religion to hang onto when her family had gone.*

store 1 to keep ready for use when needed: *Store the food in that room.* **2** to put or keep in a safe place: *He stored his furniture here when he went to America.*

D94 verbs : **keeping things going** [T1]

keep [*also* X7] to take care of and provide with necessary goods and/or services, etc: *He keeps his sister and her children; her husband abandoned* [⇒ D90] *them all. He needs more money to keep his family. He keeps that car in good condition. It isn't easy to keep a car free of rust* [⇒ H69].

keep up [v adv] to keep (something) in good condition: *How do you keep up this big house?*

maintain *often fml* **1** to keep in good condition or in operation: *The Government maintain the roads and schools.* **2** to look after, feed, clothe, etc: *He has a wife and three children to maintain.* **3** to continue to keep, usu unchanged: *The two countries have maintained friendly relations for many years.*

D95 nouns : **keeping things going** [U]

keep the cost of feeding and sheltering, etc, someone: *You must pay for your keep. She contributes £5 a week towards her keep.*

upkeep the act and/or cost of keeping (something, usu a house, etc) in good condition: *The upkeep of this house is expensive.*

retention the act of retaining or being retained: *They hope for the retention of the old laws.*

maintenance 1 the act of maintaining: *The maintenance of the house costs a lot.* **2** the money given to wives or children by a husband who does not live with them   **maintenance order** [C] an order made by a court of law that a person, esp a man, should maintain others, esp his wife and children

supply [C; U *often in comb*] something which is or can be supplied [⇒ D100], usu regularly in known amounts: *We have a good supply of water here. The water supply here is good. The army needs bigger supplies of food. Food is in short supply* (= Food cannot easily be obtained).

store 1 [C *usu sing*] a supply (of something) to keep ready for use when needed: *He always keeps a good store of food in case he can't get to the shops.* **2** [(*the*) C] a place where such goods are kept: *Put the bottles in the store.* **storage** [U] **1** the act of storing **2** a place for storing goods: *He put all his furniture in storage when he went to America. What storage space do you have here?*

D96 verbs : **holding things** [T1]

hold 1 to keep with a part of the body, esp the hands: *He held the flowers while she cut some more. She's holding the baby (in her arms).* **2** [X9] to put or keep (a part of the body) in a certain position: *They held their hands up. The dog held its tail between its legs. Hold (yourself) still. Hold your hand out.* **3** to keep back or control: *They held their breath in fear.* **4** to keep in control or in one's possession: *The city is held by the enemy.* **5** [Wv6] to possess (money, land, or a position): *He holds a half-share in the business. They hold the right to hunt on this land. She holds the office of chairman.* **6** [*also* X7] (*fig*) to keep (in an interested state of mind): *His speech held them silent/held their attention. We held ourselves in readiness for bad news.* **7** [*often pass*] (of objects) to keep or support in position: *The car holds the road well. Her hair was held back by a piece of string. The roof was held up by pillars.* **8** [*often pass*] to make (something) happen: *We were holding a meeting. The meeting was held last night.*

take to get in one's hands, etc: *He took the book which she gave him, and looked at it. Take this and keep it carefully. He took my hand and shook it.* (*fig*) *They took control of the business from the others. He took a walk in the park.*

seize 1 to take hold of quickly, eagerly, or strongly: *He seized my hand, shook it, and said how glad he was to see me.* **2** to take possession of **a** by force: *The enemy army seized the fort.* **b** by official order: *The unlawful weapons found in the house were seized by the police.* **3** [*often pass* (*with*)] to attack or take control of (someone's body or mind): *He was seized with sudden chest pains. The desire to be a singer had seized her.* **seize (up)on** [v prep] to take and use eagerly: *She had always wanted to go to Greece so she seized on the offer of a free trip.*

grip 1 to hold tightly: *She gripped his hand in fear. He gripped the nail and pulled it out.* (*fig*) *Fear gripped my heart.* **2** to attract and hold (one's attention): *The strange stories gripped* the hearers. *The pictures gripped my imagination.*

grasp 1 to hold firmly; take a firm hold of, with the hands: *He grasped the door handle and pulled, but the door wouldn't open. She grasped the knife and threatened to kill him.* **2** *(fig)* to succeed in understanding: *Did you grasp the main points of the speech?* **3** *(fig)* to be eager to take: *Grasp this opportunity while you can!*

grab to seize with a sudden rough movement, esp for a selfish reason: *She grabbed the money. He grabbed the seat nearest the fire. He grabbed the apple and ran off (with it). (fig) He eagerly grabbed the chance to go to Paris.* **grab at** [v prep] to try to grab: *He grabbed at the chance of going.*

snatch 1 to take quickly and violently: *The thief snatched the woman's bag.* **2** to take quickly while there is a chance: *He snatched a few hours' (peace to have a) sleep.* **snatch at** [v prep] to try to snatch: *He snatched at the book but I did not let him get it.*

clutch to hold tightly: *The mother clutched her baby in her arms.* **clutch at** [v prep] to try to clutch: *He clutched at the branch but he could not reach it.*

D97 nouns : holding things

hold 1 [U] the act of holding: *Don't lose hold of him.* **2** [C] something which can be held, esp in climbing: *Can you find a hold for your hands/a handhold? He got a foothold on the cliff.* **3** [C] the forceful closing of a hand: *He's got a strong hold/grip.* **4** [C] *(fig)* control; influence: *What hold does he have over/on her?* **hold of** *emph* (used with verbs of holding): *He took hold of the box and wouldn't let go. Where can I get hold of a doctor? She grasped hold of his arm. Grab hold of that rail and hang on tight!*

grip 1 [C] a very tight strong hold: *The policeman didn't let go his grip on the thief. The dentist took a firm grip on the tooth and pulled it out.* **2** [S] *(fig)* control; power: *He kept a firm grip on his children. Don't get into the grip of money-lenders. Keep a grip on yourself (= Don't lose control/act hastily)!* **3** [S] *(fig)* the power of understanding or doing: *I seem to be losing my grip. He has a good grip of several European languages.* **4** [C] a handle or part of an apparatus that can be gripped or that grips

grasp [S9] **1** a firm hold: *He kept her hand in his grasp.* **2** the position from which one can take something: *The books lay just beyond his grasp/reach, so he got up and went over to them.* **3** *(fig)* power; control: *She is in the grasp of a wicked man.* **4** *(fig)* understanding: *This problem is beyond my grasp. You must get a grasp of the rules of the game.* **5** *(fig)* Success is within his grasp at last! (= He at last has the chance to succeed).

grab [C] a sudden attempt to seize something: *He took a grab at the money. The company*

made a grab at the property; they bought it immediately.

clutch 1 [C *usu sing*] the act of clutching; a tight hold: *His clutch was not tight enough and he fell from the tree.* **2** [S] the fingers or hands in the act of clutching **clutches** [P] *(fig)* control; power; possession: *Once he was in the clutches of the enemy he would never escape.*

seizure [U] *fml* the act or result of seizing: *The court ordered the seizure of all his property.*

D98 verbs, etc : taking and catching things [T1]

take to get control of by force: *Our soldiers took the castle yesterday. They took the fort and burned it. The army took the city and held it.*

capture 1 to take control of (something) by force from an enemy; win; gain: *The enemy never captured this city.* **2** to take (a person or animal) prisoner: *They managed to capture an elephant. He was captured while trying to get out of the country. (fig) Her beauty captured him.* **3** *(fig)* to preserve (something or someone) in an unchanging form, on film, in words, etc: *He captured his daughter's first smile on film. In his book he tried to capture the beauty of Venice.* **capture 1** [U] the act of taking or being taken by force: *The capture of the enemy capital was going to be difficult. The capture of our general was a serious loss/blow.* **2** [C] something that has been taken, caught, or won by force: *Nelson's captures included a 120-gun warship.*

seize to take by force, esp suddenly, violently, or unlawfully: *The soldiers seized the house and turned it into their headquarters. The soldiers seized control of the radio station. One of the political parties seized power in the capital city.*

catch 1 to stop and hold (something or someone): *He caught the ball. She helped to catch the thief.* **2** *infml* to get; take: *He caught the last train to London. (fig) He caught a cold and wasn't able to work.* **3** to cause to look, etc: *The beautiful picture caught my eye/attention.*

trap to capture or seize by a trick or in a place where escape is not possible: *The thief was trapped by the police in an old house. (fig) They are trying to trap me with their questions, but I won't tell them what they want to know.*

corner to capture or trap (as if) in a corner: *He cornered the animal and put a rope round its neck. We have him cornered; he can't escape. You won't corner me so easily!*

collar *infml* to take hold of someone (as if) by the collar: *The policeman collared the thief.* **2** *sl* to get hold of someone, esp forcefully: *I'll try to collar him tonight and talk to him about it.*

pocket 1 to put into one's pocket: *He picked up the pencil and pocketed it.* **2** to take (money or something small) for one's own use, esp dishonestly: *Someone has pocketed my cigarettes! He spent some of the money as we asked, but he pocketed most of it.*

D99 *verbs, etc* : **letting people have things**

let . . . have *genl & often infml* to pass (to another): *Let him have the book. I'll let you have the money if you agree to work harder.*

give 1 [D1 (*to*)] to pass into someone's hands or care; let have: *Give me the baby/Give the baby to me. He gave me full control while he was away. Can you give me a job?* **2** [*also* T1; I∅] to pass (things) to another person as a present: *He gave you the money and you wasted it. He gives freely (to the poor).* **3** (*fig*) to cause; have an effect on: *I hope my son hasn't given you a lot of trouble. This work has given me a headache.*

donate [T1; I∅ (*to*)] to make a gift (of), esp for a good purpose: *He donated land to the city for a park. My husband donates to that group every year.*

offer 1 [D1 (*to*); T1: (*for*)] to hold out (to a person) for acceptance or refusal: *She offered me £10,000 for that book.* **2** [T3; I∅] to express willingness (to do something): *He offered to go.*

tender [D1 (*to*); T1] *esp fml & tech* to offer; give to be accepted: *He tendered them his deepest thanks.*

hold out [v adv T1] *usu infml & fig* to offer: *I don't hold out much hope that these troubles will get better.*

extend [T1] *fml* to offer; give: *I wish to extend a warm welcome to our visitors.*

present 1 [D1 *to/with*; T1] *fml* to give (something), esp at a ceremonial occasion: *He presented the prizes at the school sports day. I'm happy to present you with this cheque for £1,000.* **2** [X9] to offer or bring to someone's notice directly; put forward for consideration or acceptance: *This report ought to be presented in greater detail and in clearer language.* **3** [T1] *fml & polite* to offer: *I would like to present my apologies for being late for the last meeting.* **presentation 1** [U] the act of presenting **2** [C] an example of this; something presented

contribute 1 [T1; I∅: (*to*)] to join with others in giving or supplying (money, help, etc): *I couldn't contribute money to the collection for the poor so I gave clothes instead. Although he has plenty of money he never contributes to anybody's leaving present at work.* **2** [I∅ (*to*)] to be one of the causes: *Plenty of fresh air contributes to good health. Too much alcoholic drink will contribute to your ruin.*

volunteer 1 [I∅, 3] to (offer or agree to) do something by one's own choosing, not through force: *When the war began, he volunteered (to be a soldier). He couldn't go, so she volunteered to go instead.* **2** [I∅, 3] to offer, esp without being asked: *He volunteered his services/ to do the work.* **3** [C] a person who volunteers

D100 *verbs* : **giving and administering**

give 1 [D1 (*to*); T1] to let (someone) have (something), esp as wanted or planned: *Cows give milk. That book has given me several ideas.* **2** [D1] to allow to have: *Give him enough time to get home before you telephone. Give me a chance to do the job. Were you given a choice or did you have to do it?* **3** [D1 (*to*)] (*fig*) to be the cause of someone's illness: *Moving the furniture always gives me a pain in the back. Cows can give sickness to humans.* **4** [D1 (*to*); T1] (*fig*) to keep; set aside (time, thought, strength, etc): *She gives all her time to her family. Give your work more attention.* **5** [D1 (*to*)] to allow (part of the body) to be used: *He gave her his arm to support her as she walked. She gave her body to him* (= She had sex with him). *He gave his body to the hospital before he died.* **6** [D1 (*to*)] to supply with; administer to: *The mayor and the city council gave the great man the freedom of their city. They gave him a medal for bravery. The doctor gave him medicine to take twice a day.*

hand [D1 (*to*)] to pass (something) to (someone), esp by hand: *Hand me that book, please.*

hand over [v adv T1] to give, esp from the control of one person or group to another: *The army handed over their prisoners to the police. Hand over the money, now!*

supply [T1] **1** [(*to*)] to give (something) to someone, usu regularly, as in business: *In Britain milk is supplied to each house in bottles.* **2** [(with)] to give things to (a person) for use: *The firm who used to supply us have closed their business.*

provide 1 [T1; D1 *with/for*] to supply (something needed or useful): *That hotel provides good meals. Can your shop provide tents for 20 campers? The shop provided the campers with tents.* **2** [T5] to make a special arrangement: *The law provides that valuable ancient buildings must be protected by the government.* **make provision for** *fml* to provide

equip [T1] to give (someone) what is needed for working, fighting, climbing, etc: *Equip the men with the best clothes and tools. The soldiers were very well/badly equipped. Nature has equipped cats with very good weapons.*

lay on [v adv T1] to supply or provide: *When will the gas be laid on to our new home? A large meal was laid on for us.*

administer [T1] *esp fml & tech* to give as medicine, punishment, etc: *The doctor administered the drug carefully. The headmaster of this school administers any punishment.*

devote to [v prep D1] to give fully or completely to: *He devoted his life to religion. Please devote more time to your work. That newspaper devotes itself to/is devoted to making money and little else.* **devotion** [U (*to*)] **1** the act of devoting oneself, etc, to something **2** the state of being devoted to something: *His devotion to work is well-known.*

D101 *verbs* : **conferring and rewarding**

confer [T1 (*on*)] *fml* to give, esp something special: *They conferred the freedom of the city on him. They conferred on him the freedom of the city. Who confers the awards?*

accord [D1 (*to*)] *fml* to give with friendly feelings: *They accorded him a warm welcome/their warmest thanks.*

award [D1 (*to*); T1] *fml* **1** to give, esp as the result of an official decision: *He was awarded the prize for being the fastest runner. They awarded him a medal.* **2** to give by a decision in a court of law: *The judge awarded a large sum of money to those hurt in the explosion.*

honour *BrE*, **honor** *AmE* [T1] **1** to show respect for (someone), esp by doing something, usu in a ceremony: *The people honoured him by making him their president.* **2** to keep (an agreement), esp by making a payment, as in giving money: *Please honour our arrangement by exchanging the damaged goods. You must have enough money to honour your cheques before writing them.* **3** to show or feel respect for (someone): *The Bible tells Christians to honour their fathers and mothers. I'm honoured that you should notice me.*

reward [T1 (*for, with*)] to make a gift to (someone who has done something good, helpful, etc): *They rewarded him (for his great help) with a gift of money. I would like to reward you in some way but I don't know how.*

D102 *nouns* : **presents and honours**

present [C] something given freely: *I got this pen as a present from my uncle. I've got a little present for you. The children opened their Christmas presents. I'll make you a present of the book since you like it so much.*

gift 1 [C] a present: *These things would make nice Christmas gifts.* **2** [S] *old use* the power of giving: *The house and job are in his gift* (= He can appoint whom he wants to them).

donation [C] a present or gift, esp of money, for a good purpose: *Have you made any donations to the church this year?*

contribution 1 [C (*of*)] something given by someone as one among many: *His contributions of money are always generous. No contribution is too small. Can I make a contribution of work rather than money?* **2** [U] the act of contributing: *Payment is by contribution.*

offer [C] something held out, given, etc, for someone's acceptance or refusal: *Her offer for the book was £10,000. How many offers have you had for the house? Make me an offer (for the house).*

award [C] **1** something given as the result of an official decision; a prize or medal [⇒ K110]: *He won the award for best student of the year.* **2** a decision, or that which is given by a decision, in a court of law: *The award was £100,000.*

reward [C] something (to be) given to someone for what he or she has done: *He got a reward (of £50) for helping them. There is a special reward offered by the police, to anyone who helps them find that man.*

honour *BrE*, **honor** *AmE* **1** [C] something which shows people's respect: *It is an honour to be asked to come here and speak to you all. He received many honours from many cities, colleges, and societies.* **2** [U] a high standard of character; reputation: *They said they would fight to save the honour of their country. He said that he did not steal the book and that his personal honour had been attacked.* **honorary** [Wa5] **1** (of an office, university degree, etc) held as an honour only **2** [A] (of the holder of an office) serving without pay as an honour: *He is the Honorary President of the club.*

D103 *nouns* : **keepsakes and souvenirs** [C]

keepsake a gift made to someone who, by keeping it, can remember the person who gave it: *She gave me the ring as a keepsake.*

souvenir [(*of*)] something, esp bought or received as a gift, that reminds one of a place, person, etc: *This picture is a souvenir of (my trip to) Morocco.*

remembrance [(*of*)] something which reminds one of a person, place, etc: *He keeps these books as a remembrance of his father.*

D104 *verbs* : **distributing and sharing things** [T1]

distribute to give, send, share, etc, by passing on to others: *He distributed the food to the hungry people. These books are distributed free* (= costing nothing). *Goods from the factory were distributed to the shops and sold.* **distribution 1** [U] the act of distributing **2** [C] an example or occasion of this **distributional** [Wa5;B] of or concerning distribution **distributor** [C] a person who distributes things, esp goods in business

give out [v adv] *not fml* to distribute, esp personally: *The teacher gave out the books to the class.*

hand out [v adv] to distribute, esp by hand: *The teacher handed the books out.* **handout** [C] anything handed out, esp costing nothing

share 1 [*also* I∅: (*with/among/between*)] to use, pay, have, take part in, etc, (with others) or among a group: *We haven't enough books for everyone; some of you will have to share. Everyone in the house shares the bathroom. I have to share the bathroom with the rest of the family. Would you like to share the cost of a taxi with me?* **2** [*out, among/between*)] to divide and give out in shares: *At his death his property was shared (out) between his children.* **3** [*also* I∅: (*with*)] to give a share (of) to one or more others: *Children should be taught to share. Please share your newspaper with me.*

4 [(with)] to tell others about: *I'd like to share with you something that happened last week.* **5** [(with)] to be among those who have (esp an opinion or idea): *I'm sorry; I can't share your faith that everything will be all right.*

share out [v adv] to distribute equally: *He shared out the food. They shared the food out among the poor/among themselves.* **share-out** [S] *not fml* an act of sharing something out: *Let's have a share-out of the money.*

allocate 1 to divide and give as shares: *We must allocate the money carefully.* **2** [*also* D1 (*to*)] to give as a share: *We allocated the society some money.* **3** [*also* D1 (*to*)] to set apart for somebody or some purpose: *That space has already been allocated.* **allocation 1** [U] the act of allocating; the giving of shares or places: *The allocation of rooms will take place after lunch.* **2** [C] an example of this; a share, as of money or space

allot to give, distribute, allocate, esp offically: *He allotted this work to me, not you.* **allotment 1** [U] the act of allotting **2** [C] something allotted

D105 *nouns* : **shares** [C]

share the part belonging or due to, or done by, a person: *If you want a share in/of the pay, you'll have to do your fair share of the work. I had no share in this trick—I had nothing to do with it. The government must take a large share of the blame for the failure of the plan.* **go shares** *BrE* to divide the cost, ownership, profit, etc, among two or more people: *I went shares with two others in hiring a car for the day.*

D106 *nouns, etc* : **stages and phases** [C]

stage a particular point or period in a development, activity, journey, etc: *The little boy was at the stage of asking questions all the time. What stage have you reached in your work? They travelled to the city in/by stages* (= stopping at places on the way).

step a stage, esp something done in order to make something else happen: *What is the next step in your plan?* **take steps to** to do something in order to: *They took steps to change the law. They took the first necessary steps to change the law.*

phase 1 one of the changing states or stages through which a thing, person, or group passes: *The first phase of the plan will be completed by 1985. The child is going through a difficult phase at the moment.* **2** [T1 *usu pass*] to arrange in phases: *The work was carefully phased.*

D107 *nouns, etc* : **range and scope**

range 1 [C; U] the amount, distance, etc, within which something can happen or be done: *They used a wide range of building materials. What* are the ranges of prices here? The range of the gun (= the distance over which it can fire) is two miles. I don't know what they were saying; they were just outside hearing range. **2** [L9] to move or happen over a distance, within certain limits, etc: *The prices range from very low to very high.* **3** [X9] to put in order or line: *He ranged the children from the tallest to the shortest.* **4** [T1; I0 (*over*)] to move freely (across): *The animals ranged the whole valley for food. The animals ranged widely over the land.* **5** [L9 *from . . . to*] to stretch: *His land ranges from here to the river 50 miles away.*

scope [U] the range or limits within which someone can do something or in which something can be done: *There's no scope for improvement here; the work is very good. There's plenty of scope for young people here. This job is quite beyond his scope* (= He can't possibly do it). *The scope of his new idea is very great; it covers many things which couldn't be done before.*

D108 *verbs & nouns* : **service and amenity**
[ALSO ⇒ I28, N139]

do . . . for [v prep D1] to do (something) in order to help (someone): *'What can I do for you, sir?' the shop assistant asked.*

serve [T1] **1** to do something for (someone); work for: *He has served us well. The shop assistant served the customer badly.* **2** to present: *Shall I serve dinner now?* **3** to be a servant to: *He served their family (well) for 30 years.*

service 1 [C; *of* U] something done by one person for another: *Thank you for your services, Doctor. (fml) May I be of service to you, sir* (= May I serve you)? **dis-** [*neg*] **2** [C] something provided regularly, esp by a company, government, etc, for people: *The train service in that country is very good/bad.* **3** the way in which one is served: *I don't like the service in that hotel.*

facility [C *usu pl*] something, esp a service or equipment, that makes life easier, pleasanter, etc: *This university has very good sports facilities. What facilities do you have for learning English?*

amenity 1 [C *often pl*] a thing or condition in a town, hotel, place, etc, that one can enjoy and which makes life pleasant: *The amenities of the town include a swimming pool, a library, public gardens, and some beautiful parks.* **2** [U9] *rare* pleasantness: *The amenity of the weather allowed us to eat in the garden.*

Furniture and household fittings

D110 *nouns* : **furniture and fittings**

furniture [U] all large or quite large movable articles that are placed in a house, room, or other area, in order to make it usable, comfortable, or pleasant as a space for living in: *Tables, chairs, and beds are all furniture. This old French table is a valuable piece/bit of furniture. That shop sells garden/bedroom furniture. He owns a furniture shop.*

furnishings [P] articles of furniture or other articles fixed in a room: *Baths, curtains, and carpets are all furnishings.* **soft furnishings** [P] such furnishings as carpets [⇨ D118], bedding [⇨ D115], etc

fittings [P] any furniture or articles which must be fitted to other furniture, larger articles, rooms, vehicles, etc: *Are all the fittings in place?*

suite [C (*of*); *esp in comb*] a set of pieces of furniture: *She wants a new suite for the living room. That's a nice suite of furniture. He bought her a three piece suite* (= two armchairs and a couch).

D111 *verbs, etc* : **furnishing and decorating** [T1]

furnish [*often pass*] to put furniture in (a room, building, etc); supply with furniture: *The new hotel's finished but not yet furnished.*

fit out [v adv] *often infml* to furnish fully: *The new house will be fitted out long before you move in.*

fit up [v adv] *often infml* to furnish, esp by putting fittings, etc, in their proper place: *The house is fitted up with everything you will need.*

decorate 1 to furnish with something ornamental, esp for a special occasion: *They decorated the house with pictures and plants. The streets were decorated with flags.* **2** [*also* I∅] to paint or put a surface covering on the walls or outside of (a house): *After the house is built, how much will it cost to decorate (it)?* **3** to be or serve as an ornament to: *Those pictures decorate the walls very well.* **4** to give (someone) an official mark of honour, such as a medal [⇨ K110]: *The soldiers were decorated for bravery.* **decoration 1** [U] the act of decorating or being decorated: *The decoration of this house will cost a lot of money.* **2** [C] an example or result of this: *These pictures make very good decorations. The soldier had a lot of decorations for bravery.*

ornament to (try to) make (something) beautiful by adding special things as decorations: *He ornamented the wall with many small drawings.* **ornament 1** [C; *for* U] something that decorates or ornaments: *The room was full of pictures and other beautiful ornaments.* **2** [S] (*fig*) a person who is useful, beautiful, etc: *He is an ornament to our society.* (*deprec*) *He's just an ornament; he can't do anything useful.* **ornamentation 1** [U] the act or result of ornamenting **2** [C] an example of this

adorn *esp lit* to (try to) make more beautiful by decorating, ornamenting, etc: *They adorned him with flowers. She was adorned with jewels.* **adornment 1** [U] the act or result of adorning

2 [C] an example of this; something which adorns a person or thing; a decoration or ornament

renovate to decorate, furnish, etc, for a second time; redecorate; make (an old house, etc) look new: *This place needs renovating/to be renovated. They renovated the old building.* **renovation 1** [U] the act of renovating or being renovated: *Renovation costs money.* **2** [C] an example or result of this: *These renovations make the old building look quite new.*

do up [v adv] *infml* to decorate: *They did up the house beautifully.*

beautify to make beautiful: *They have beautified the town by improving the public gardens and parks.* **beautification** [U] the act of beautifying

D112 *nouns* : **kinds of table** [C]
[⇨ PICTURE AT D34]

table 1 a piece of furniture with a flat top supported by one or more upright legs: *Do you think six people can sit round this table? When we arrived at the restaurant we asked for a table for two in a corner. This is a table made (mainly) of glass; it is a glass table.* **2** such a piece of furniture specially made for the playing of various games: *a billiard table, card table, etc* **3** [S] the food served at a meal: *This restaurant keeps a good table* (= provides food of high quality). **4** [GC] (*fig*) the people sitting at a table: *John's clever stories kept the whole table amused.*

kitchen table	a table (meant to be) used	in a kitchen
dining room table		in a dining room
dressing table		in a bedroom for dressing oneself (esp for women)
coffee table		in a livingroom, for serving coffee

desk

bureau

desk a table, often with drawers, at which one reads, writes, or does business: *He was sitting at his desk writing, when I came in.*

bureau 1 a type of desk, usu with drawers and a top for writing, etc, which can be closed by lifting it upwards on hinges [⇨ H134] **2** a large writing table with a wooden cover which slides over the top to close it

D113 *nouns, etc* : **kinds of chairs and seats**

[⇨ PICTURE AT D34]

bench

stool

rocking chair

armchair

chair [C] a piece of furniture on which a person may sit which has typically a back, seat, usu four legs, and sometimes arms

seat 1 [C] a piece of furniture, part of a vehicle, etc, on which one sits or can sit **2** [C] the part of a chair, etc, on which one sits: *The seat of the chair is broken.* **3** [C] *often euph* the part of the body on which one sits [*also* ⇨ B33]: *He has hurt his seat.* **4** [C] a place, esp a chair, where someone usu sits or expects to sit: *Hey, that's my seat!* **5** [T1 *often pass*] to put in a seat; provide seats for: *Seat the people here, please. We can't seat all these people. Friends, please be seated.*

seating [U] provision of furnishing for seats: *He is in charge of seating/of the seating arrangements at the large dinner. Do we have enough seating for everyone?*

throne [C] **1** an official and usu highly ornamented chair of a king, queen, etc **2** (*fig*) the king or queen on that throne

bench [C] a long seat for two or more people: *They sat on a bench in the park/on a park bench.*

stool [C] **1** a seat without a supporting part for the back or arms: *They sat on three-legged stools.* **2** *also* **footstool** a small stool for putting one's feet on, esp when sitting in a chair: *Put your feet on this (foot)stool.*

D114 *nouns* : **couches and divans** [C]

couch a long chair looking like or sometimes used as a bed or for lying down: *She was sitting/lying on the couch.*

sofa a long comfortable seat like a couch, with cushions, a back, and arms: *Let's sit on the sofa.*

settee a long seat for more than one person, esp a small sofa

settle a long wooden seat with a high solid back, and a bottom part which is a chest having the seat for its lid

divan 1 a long soft seat on a wooden base, usu without a back or arms, placed against a wall **2** *also* **divan bed** the same used for sleeping

D115 *nouns & verbs* : **beds and parts of beds**

bed [C; U] an article of furniture to sleep on: *The room had two beds in it. We can give you a comfortable bed for the night. Get out of (your) bed! It's time for bed/It's bedtime.*

bedstead [C] the main wooden or metal framework of a bed

mattress [C] a large bag of solid movable material, usu wool, hair, feathers, rubber, or metal springs, on which one sleeps, which is placed in a bed frame: *These mattresses aren't dry; we can't sleep on them.*

blanket [C] **1** a thick covering, usu of wool, used mainly for covering someone in bed: *I need another blanket on my bed; it's cold at night. He put a blanket round the dog.* **2** (*fig*) anything like this: *There was a blanket of snow on the ground.* **3** [T1] (*fig*) to cover like a blanket: *Snow blanketed the ground.*

quilt *also* **eiderdown** [C] a warm covering made from a large bag of thin cloth filled with something warm and soft, esp feathers, with stitching to keep the filling in place

(bed)sheet [C] a thin covering, often of linen, used mainly on beds, one on the mattress and the other beneath the blankets: *It's time to change the sheets on these beds.*

bedspread, bedcover [C] an ornamental cloth spread over a bed

bedding [U] **1** blankets, sheets, bedspreads, etc **2** material on which a person or animal can sleep: *This straw should make good bedding for the animals.*

bedclothes [P] blankets and sheets: *He slept badly last night and pulled all the bedclothes off his wife.*

bedside [C *usu sing*] the side of a bed: *He has been called to the bedside of his dying father.*

pillow 1 [C] a cloth bag longer than it is wide, filled with soft materials, used to support the head in bed **2** [C] any object used in this way **3** [X9;T1] to rest (esp one's head) on or as if on a pillow: *She pillowed his head on a folded coat. She sat on the floor and her legs pillowed the child's head.*

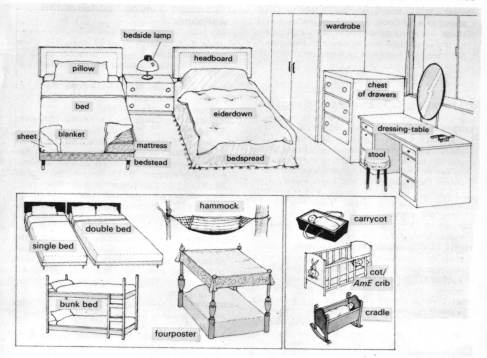

pillowcase *also* pillow slip [C] a washable bag-like cloth covering a pillow

bolster [C] a long pillow which goes across the head of the bed under the pillow(s)

D116 *nouns* : **kinds of bed** [C]

[⇒ PICTURE AT D115]

double bed a bed big enough for two people

single bed a bed for one person

twin bed one of two single beds of the same kind close to each other

cradle 1 a small bed for a baby, usu able to be rocked (= moved) from side to side, or backwards and forwards 2 (*fig*) a place where something begins: *The Middle East is the cradle of civilization.*

cot *BrE* crib *AmE* a bed for a child, usu with bars on the sides to keep the child from falling out

carrycot *esp BrE* a small boxlike container, usu having two handles, for carrying a baby

bunk 1 a narrow bed, fixed to a wall like a shelf, as in a ship or a train 2 one of two or more narrow beds fixed or built one above the other *also* bunk bed

camp bed *BrE* cot *AmE* a narrow bed, often made of cloth stretched on a frame, for use in tents, etc

hammock a piece of canvas or net which can be hung up by the ends to form a bed

D117 *nouns* : **cupboards and lockers** [C]

[⇒ PICTURES AT D115]

cupboard a piece of furniture or a place built into a wall, closed by a door and used for storing things: *Is there any food in the cupboard?*

wardrobe a cupboard, large box, or small room, with a door, in which one hangs up clothes: *Put your clothes in the wardrobe.*

chest of drawers a piece of furniture, about half the height of a wardrobe and consisting of one drawer above the other, used for storing clothes

bureau *AmE* a chest of drawers for bedroom use

sideboard a piece of dining room furniture like a long table with a cupboard below to hold dishes, glasses, etc

cabinet 1 a fine piece of usu wooden furniture, often with glass doors, used for storing or showing things 2 a container like this for a television, record player, etc 3 *also* filing cabinet a piece of metal or wooden office furniture used for storing esp written material

dresser 1 *esp BrE* a piece of furniture for holding dishes and other articles used in eating, having open shelves above and cupboards below: *That's a beautiful Welsh dresser.* 2 *AmE* a chest of drawers used esp for clothing, often with a mirror on top

locker a small cupboard or a box fixed to a wall, which can be locked, used in places where there are many people who need a place for their own clothes, belongings, etc: *The school-boys keep their things in lockers near their beds.*

D118 *nouns, etc* : **carpets and rugs**

carpet 1 [U] heavy woven, often woollen, material for covering floors or stairs **2** [C] a shaped piece of this material, usu fitted to the size of a particular room: *We need a new carpet for our bedroom.* **3** [C] (*fig*) any covering which covers the ground like this: *There was a carpet of leaves/flowers in the garden.* **4** [T1] to cover with or as if with a carpet: *It will cost a lot to carpet the stairs.*

carpeting [U] heavy woven, often woollen, material used for making carpets

rug [C] **1** a usu smaller or thicker carpet: *Animal skins are often used as rugs. The cat slept on a rug near the fire* (= **hearthrug**). **2** a thick blanket [⇒ D115] esp for keeping someone's legs warm

mat [C *esp in comb*] a flat covering, esp one like a small rug on a floor or plate on a table, for protecting a surface against dirt, heat, etc: *He sat on a mat on the floor. Put the doormat just outside the door. Do we need tablemats under the plates?*

D119 *nouns & verbs* : **cushions and upholstery**

cushion 1 [C] a small bag of cloth usu filled with soft material and used on chairs, etc, to make them more comfortable **2** [T1] to protect or make less sharp or hard (as if) with a cushion: *His hat helped to cushion the blow to his head when he was attacked.* (*fig*) *The new child allowances will help to cushion poor families from inflation* (= higher living costs).

padding [U] material such as hair, cloth, etc, used to fill furniture, clothes, etc: *The padding in this armchair isn't very good.* **padded** [B] having padding: *These are specially padded chairs.*

pad 1 [C] something soft, like a cushion, filled with or made of soft material and used for comfort, protection, etc: *The arms of these chairs have pads on them.* **2** [T1] to put pads or padding on: *They padded the chairs.*

upholstery 1 [U] the materials used to fit chairs and other pieces of furniture with softer parts, such as springs, cloth, leather, etc; the work of fitting chairs, etc, in this way: *The upholstery of the chairs is very old but very good. He is in the upholstery business.* **upholster** [T1] to fit (chairs, etc) in this way **upholsterer** [C] a person who does this

D120 *nouns & verbs* : **curtains and wallpaper**

curtain 1 [C] a large piece of cloth, esp when hung from above, over a window inside a room: *What nice curtains there are in this room!* **2** [C] (*fig*) anything like this: *A curtain of smoke hung over the burning town.* **3** [T1] to put a curtain or curtains in or on: *Have you curtained the bedrooms yet?*

drapes [P] *AmE* curtains: *She has nice drapes in her house.*

drapery 1 [U] *AmE* heavy cloth used as curtains **2** [U; C] cloth or a garment arranged in folds: *The photograph was taken against a background of drapery.* **3** [U] the arrangement of cloth in folds: *Can you arrange the drapery of the cloth in our windows?*

hangings [P] curtains and other materials hanging over the walls, windows, doors, etc, of a house

wallpaper 1 [U] ornamental paper to cover the walls of a room: *I like the wallpaper in your room.* **2** [T1] *also* (*infml*) **paper** to put wallpaper on (a wall, etc): *He is wallpapering his living room. They are papering their whole house again.*

canopy [C] a covering, often held up by poles and usu made of cloth or sometimes wood over a bed, doorway, large chair, etc

awning [C] a piece of strong cloth over or in front of a door, window, etc, to protect it from the sun, rain, etc

Clothes and personal belongings

D130 *nouns* : **clothes generally**

clothes [P] things to wear on the body, such as trousers, shirts, etc: *She's gone to buy some new clothes.* **clothier** [C] a person who makes or sells clothes or cloth **clothes peg** *BrE* **clothespin** *AmE* a small forked instrument made of one or two small pieces of wood or plastic, used for holding wet washed clothes on a rope (= **clothesline**) for drying

clothing [U] *often fml & tech* clothes generally: *She spends half her income on clothing.*

garment [C] (the name used, esp by the makers, for) an article of clothing: *A new garment should be washed carefully. Keep the receipt in case you should wish to exchange this garment.*

dress 1 [U] clothing, esp outer clothing: *In this old play, the actors wear the dress of 100 years ago.* **2** [U9] clothing worn on special occasions or by special types of people: *They wore evening dress. The captain wore his full dress uniform.* **3** [A] **a** (of clothing) suitable for a formal occasion: *He wore a dress suit.* **b** requiring or permitting formal dress: *The evening is a dress affair.* **dress material** [U] material used for making dresses, clothes, etc

wear [U *in comb*] things to wear; clothes as in: **rainwear** (= clothes to keep off the rain); **underwear** (= underclothes).

attire [U] *fml* dress; clothes: *He was wearing formal evening attire.* **attired** [Wa5;F9] dressed: *He was attired in black.*

apparel 1 [U] *lit & old use* clothes, esp of a fine or special sort: *He was dressed in golden apparel.* **2** [U9] *esp AmE* clothes; clothing: *They sell ready-to-wear ladies apparel.*

garb [U] *lit & humor* clothing of a particular style, esp which shows one's type of work or is unusual: *He went to change his clothes and came back in the garb of a priest. A stranger appeared in red and yellow garb.* **garbed** [Wa5;F9] dressed: *He was garbed in red and yellow.*

lining [C *usu sing*] a piece or layer of material inside some other material, but esp one kind of cloth inside another as part of a garment: *The coat had a warm lining.* **line** [T1 *usu pass*] to put a lining in: *The coat was lined with fur. She wore a fur-lined coat.*

rags [P] old torn clothes: *The beggar wore rags.*

castoffs *also* **hand-me-downs** [P] clothes which someone no longer wants: *He wore his older brother's castoffs/hand-me-downs.*

D131 nouns, etc : **uniforms and outfits**

uniform [C; (*in*) U] a certain type of clothing which all members of a group wear, esp in the army, a school, or the police: *They all wear uniform at school. The nurses have a new uniform. Policemen and postmen wear dark blue uniforms in Britain. He was in uniform for three years* (= in the armed forces).

tunic [C] **1** a loose-fitting short-sleeved [⇒ D161] or sleeveless outer garment reaching to the knees, worn by both sexes among the ancient Romans or Greeks **2** a specially-shaped short coat worn by policemen, soldiers, etc, as part of a uniform **3** a loose armless dress, esp as worn by girls as part of a school uniform **4** a garment like this worn by women for sport, exercise, dancing, etc

costume 1 [U] the clothes or style of dress typical of a certain period, country, rank, or profession, esp as worn on the stage by an actor or actress **2** [C] a suit or dress of this sort: *The actors were in Victorian policemen's costumes.*

outfit 1 [C] all the things, esp clothes, needed for a particular purpose: *She bought a new outfit to wear at work.* **2** [T1 (*with*)] to provide with an outfit, esp of clothes: *They were outfitted for their new school/job.*

strip [C] *BrE* the special clothing worn by players in a team, esp with different colours, esp in football

D132 nouns : **appearance**

appearance [U] how someone or something appears to the eye, esp clothes and the way someone wears them: *He was a man of neat and tidy appearance.*

getup [S] *infml* set of clothes, esp their general appearance: *That's a funny getup you're wearing.*

turnout [C] the manner or style in which a person is dressed: *That's a smart turnout! His turnout is always good.*

D133 verbs : **wearing clothes** [T1]

wear [*also* X7] to have (esp clothes) on the body: *He's wearing a new coat. She never wears a hat. He wore a short beard/wore his beard short. She wears her hair up.*

have on [v adv Wv6] to be wearing: *He had a beautiful new suit on. They took a picture of the baby when he had nothing on.*

put on [v adv] to cover part of the body with (something, esp clothing); wear or place on the body: *She put her hat and coat on. He put on his glasses to read the letter. Mary puts on too much face powder.*

get on [v adv] to put on, usu quickly: *Get your clothes on; hurry up!*

take off [v adv] to remove (something, esp clothing) from part of the body: *She took off her hat and coat. He took off his glasses when he had read the letter. Mary, you've put on too much face powder; take it off!*

get off [v adv] to take off, usu quickly: *They told him to get his clothes off.*

don *old use or pomp* to put on (clothing and hats): *He donned his hat and coat.* (*fig*) *She donned a look of innocence.*

doff *old use or pomp* to take off: *He doffed his hat to the ladies.*

sport to wear or show publicly, esp so as to show off: *She came in today sporting a fur coat.*

D134 verbs : **clothing people**

clothe [T1] to provide clothes for: *He has to work hard to feed and clothe his large family. It's hard to clothe my young son; he's growing all the time.* (*fig*) *Mist clothed the hills.*

dress 1 [T1;I∅] to put clothes on (oneself or someone else): *I'll be ready in a minute; I'm dressing. Please dress the baby, George. What's the best way to dress for the journey?* **2** [T1;I∅] to provide (oneself or someone else) with clothes: *She dresses well on very little money. He's very well-dressed.* **3** [T1] to make or choose clothes for: *They dress their children well.* **4** [I∅] to put on special correct clothes for a special occasion, the evening, etc: *Do they expect us to dress for dinner here? How do you dress on these occasions?* **5** [L9] to wear clothes: *She often dresses in black.* **dressing** [U] the act or action of a person who dresses: *She's very fast at dressing.* **dresser** [C9] a person who dresses, esp in a stated way: *She's a fashionable/careless dresser.*

D135 verbs : **undressing and stripping**

undress 1 [I∅] to take one's clothes off: *She undressed and went to bed. Please help him to undress; he can't do it himself.* **2** [T1] to take (someone's) clothes off: *She undressed the child and put him to bed.*

disrobe [I∅] *esp old use, fml, or pomp* to take one's clothes off: *The queen disrobed.*

bare [T1] to take esp clothing off (part of one's body): *He bared his head as the dead body was carried past.*

strip [I∅ (*off*)] to (cause to) take one's clothes off: *He stripped and went for a swim. Strip off, men! The dancing girl began to strip.*

D136 adjectives : **wearing clothes**

clothed [F] having one's clothes on: *He was out of bed and (fully) clothed by 6 a.m.* **un-** [neg]

dressed [F] having one's clothes on, esp in a way suitable to an occasion: *Are you dressed yet? He was properly dressed for the party.* **un-** [neg]

clad [F9] *esp lit* covered or clothed: *He was clad in armour. The old lady was clad in a fur coat.* (fig) *The mountains were clad in mist.*

D137 adjectives, etc : **not wearing clothes**

naked [Wa5;B] **1** (of [a part of]) a person's body) not covered by clothes: *He was completely naked. She dipped her naked arm in the hot water.* **2** (fig) not having the usual covering: *He took all the pictures down and look sadly at the naked walls.* **3** (fig) not hidden: *He told them the naked facts.* **-ly** [adv] **-ness** [U]

nude 1 [Wa5;B] *often more fml* naked: *Nude figures were bathing in the pool.* **2** [Wa5;A] of, for, by, etc, people not wearing clothes: *They held a nude party. He likes nude swimming.* **3** [C] a (usu female) person not wearing any clothes, esp one appearing in a photograph or a piece of art **4** [C] a piece of art showing a person, usu a woman, without clothes **5** [U] the state of being nude: *He stood there in the nude.* **nudity** [U] the state of being nude

bare [Wa1] **1** [B] uncovered: *His head was bare. The children ran about quite bare. The fields were bare* (= had no plants in them). **2** [F *of*] without; empty: *The fields were bare of trees. The room was bare of furniture.* **3** [A] not more than: *He killed the man with his bare hands.* **4** [T1] to take off a covering from: *He bared his head* (= took off his hat). **barefoot** [B; adv] without shoes or other covering for the feet: *The barefoot children of the poor stood watching the rich people. The boy went barefoot.* **bareheaded** [B; adv] with the head uncovered; without a hat: *Women are now permitted to go to church bareheaded.* **barelegged** [B; adv] with nothing on the legs; not wearing stockings

buff [*the* U] *esp BrE infml* the condition of being naked: *He stripped to the buff.*

D138 nouns, etc : **fashion**

fashion 1 [C; U] the way of dressing or behaving that is considered the best at a certain time: *There's a fashion for painting your nails green. Fashions have changed since I was a girl. Wide trousers are the latest fashion. It's not the fashion to send children away to school now. We must keep up with fashion/follow (the) fashion.* **2** [U] changing custom, esp in (women's) clothing: *She studies the history of fashion.* **come into/be in fashion** to (start to) be considered the best and most modern: *Long hair is very much in fashion.* **go/be out of fashion** to stop being/no longer be considered the best and most modern **set a fashion** to be an example to others by doing something new **(someone) of fashion** *old use* someone of the upper class of society and therefore well-dressed: *The restaurant was crowded with women of fashion.*

style [U; C] (a) particular, usu good way of dressing, etc: *He dresses with/in great style. I like the style of her new dress. The styles of these coats are good/bad.*

mode [*the* R] the style of dressing, esp by women, or of doing something favoured by most people at a certain moment: *Very long skirts are the present mode. Giving people greater freedom is all the mode in that country.*

model [C] **1** a person, esp a young woman, employed to wear articles of clothing, and to show them to possible buyers, in a shop, by means of being photographed, walking, standing, etc **2** an article of (esp women's) clothing worn by a model or shown in a shop, and described as the only one, or one of a very few, of its kind

mannequin [C] **1** *esp old use* a model **2** a figure of a body used for showing clothes in a shop window

D139 nouns : **suits and dresses, etc** [C]

suit a set of outer clothes which match, usu including a short coat (= **jacket** [⇒ D142]) with trousers or skirt: *He bought himself a new suit. She's wearing a blue suit today.*

dress a woman's or girl's outer garment that covers the body from shoulder to knee or below: *That's a nice dress. She wore her blue dress; she prefers it to her other dresses. She had on a full-length evening dress.*

frock *not fml* a woman's or girl's dress

robe [C] **1** a long flowing indoor garment for informal occasions: *She was dressed in a Middle-Eastern robe.* **2** [often pl] such a garment when worn for official or ceremonial

suits

occasions: *The judge wore black robes.* **3** *esp
AmE* a warm covering for the lower body, often
made of fur, used when sitting out of doors
gown [C] **1** *esp fml* a woman's dress, esp if long
2 a long loose coat worn esp formerly over
ordinary clothes by judges, university and
other teachers, students, etc

D140 *nouns* : **trousers and tights**

trousers   jeans   shorts

trousers [P] *esp BrE* an outer garment divided
into two parts, each fitting a leg, worn from the
waist down esp by men and boys: *I'd like a new
pair of trousers. She wore trousers.*
slacks [P] **1** *esp AmE* trousers, esp of a loose-
fitting kind and not part of a suit **2** *esp BrE*
trousers as worn by women
pants [P] **1** *AmE* trousers **2** *esp BrE infml* trousers **3** *esp. BrE* trousers worn by women
shorts *also fml* **short trousers** [P] trousers
with short legs, usu stopping above or at the knee:
The runners wore shorts.
jeans *also* **blue jeans** [P] trousers made of a
strong, usu blue, cotton cloth worn for work
and informally by men, women, and children

tights [P] a very close-fitting garment covering
the legs and body worn by dancers, etc
pair [C (*of*)] any of various garments, etc, made
from two like parts joined: *He put on a different pair of jeans.*

D141 *nouns* : **skirts and kilts** [C]

skirt   kilt

skirt 1 a woman's outer garment that fits around
the waist and hangs down with one lower edge
all round **2** a part of a coat or dress that hangs
below the waist **3** (*fig*) anything like these, esp
on a machine
kilt 1 a short skirt worn by men, esp pleated [⇒
D162] as in Scotland and usu worn as part of
Highland dress or a military uniform **2** a similar skirt worn by women or children

D142 *nouns* : **coats and jackets** [C]

coat 1 an outer garment with long sleeves, often
fastened at the front with buttons, and usu
worn for warmth or protection: *She was wearing a fur coat.* **2** *esp AmE* a jacket; the top half
of a suit [⇒ D139]
jacket a short coat with sleeves [⇒ D161], often
the top half of a suit: *He wore a brown jacket
and grey trousers.* [⇒ picture at D139]
anorak a short coat which has a protective hood
[⇒ D146] for the head and which keeps out
wind and rain
waistcoat *BrE* **vest** *AmE* a men's close-fitting
garment without sleeves that reaches to the
waist and is worn under the jacket of a 3-piece
suit [⇒ picture at D139]
jerkin a short usu sleeveless coat often made of
leather, usu worn by men

D143 *nouns* : **overcoats and cloaks** [C]

overcoat a long warm coat worn over other
clothes by men and women when going out,
esp in cold weather
raincoat a coat worn to keep the rain off
fur coat a coat made of fur [⇒ A126, H88]
duffel coat a loose coat made of a type of thick
woollen cloth (= **duffel**), usu fastened with
long tubelike buttons (= **toggles**) and often

having a hood [⇨ D146] joined to the neck

cape a long loose outer garment fastened at the neck and hanging from the shoulders: *A cape gives good protection in wet weather.*

cloak 1 a loose, usu sleeveless outer garment **2** (*fig*) something which covers, hides, or keeps secret: *Her friendly behaviour was a cloak for her real intentions.*

shawl a piece of usu soft heavy cloth, either square or long and narrow, for wearing over a woman's head or shoulders

D144 nouns : **jerseys, pullovers, etc** [C]

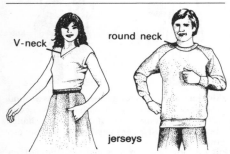

V-neck

round neck

jerseys

jersey close-fitting, usu knitted wollen garment, with sleeves, for the upper part of the body: *She always wears a jersey in cold weather.*

pullover a usu woollen garment for the top half of the body, that has no fastenings and is pulled on over the head and drawn down over the body

slipover a light pullover

sweater a jersey or jacket, usu of wool, worn for warmth or by someone who has been playing or working hard, usu after this activity: *She put on her sweater after running. He wore a sweater because the night was cold. He wore a polo-necked sweater* (= one with a thick rolled collar).

jumper 1 *BrE* a sweater for women **2** *AmE* a sleeveless [⇨ D161] dress worn over a blouse [⇨ D145]

cardigan a knitted woollen short coat with sleeves but usu without a collar and usu fastened at the front with buttons or a belt: *She put on a cardigan over her dress before going out.*

D145 nouns : **shirts and blouses** [C]

shirt a piece of clothing for the upper part of the body, usu of light cloth with a collar and sleeves (covering the arms), typically worn by a man inside a coat **shirtfront** the part of a shirt covering the chest, esp the stiff front of a formal white shirt **shirtsleeve** [Wa5;A] being without, or showing no need for, coats, as because of hot weather or informality: *They had a shirtsleeve meeting to talk about their*

problems. **in one's shirtsleeves** wearing nothing over one's shirt: *On such a hot day the men in the office were working in their shirtsleeves.* **shirttail** the front or back part of a shirt below the wearer's waist **shirtwaister**, *AmE usu* **shirtwaist** a woman's garment (a dress or blouse) in the style of a man's shirt

blouse 1 a usu loose garment for women, reaching from the neck to about the waist **2** the upper part of a soldier's or airman's uniform, usu with outside pockets

D146 nouns : **headgear, etc**

headgear [U] clothing for the head

hat [C] a covering for the head which is placed on top of, not around the head, and partly covers both sides

cap [C] a type of soft flat tight-fitting head covering worn by men and boys

beret [C] a round, usu woollen cap with a tight headband and a soft full flat top, esp as worn by Frenchmen, Spaniards, and soldiers

headscarf [C] a scarf [⇨ D151] worn over the head: *The women all put on headscarves before going into the church.*

bonnet [C] **1** a round head covering tied under the chin and often with a piece in front that shields the face, worn by babies and in former times by women **2** a soft flat cap worn by men, esp soldiers, in Scotland

hood [C] **1** a loose covering for the whole of the head and neck except the face, usu fastened on at the back, as to a coat, so that it can be pushed back when not needed **2** a covering for the head of a hunting bird **3** anything like these **hooded** [Wa5;B] wearing or having a hood; hidden by a covering

helmet [C] a hard covering like a hat, to protect the head: *Soldiers often wear helmets when fighting, and so do people riding on motorcycles.* **helmeted** [Wa5;B] wearing a helmet

veil 1 [C] a covering of fine cloth or net for all or part of the head or face, worn esp by women often for reasons of fashion or religion: *In some countries, Muslim women wear veils in public.* **2** [S (*of*)] (*fig*) something which covers or hides something else: *a veil of secrecy* **draw a veil over something** to avoid speaking about or describing something unpleasant: *Let's draw a veil over what happened to the unfortunate prisoners.* **take the veil** (of a woman) to become a nun [⇨ C345] **under the veil of** under the (deceiving) appearance of: *Many evil deeds have been done under the veil of religion or love of one's country.*

turban [C] **1** (esp in the Middle East, India, etc) a covering for a man's head consisting of a long length of cloth wound tightly round the head **2** a woman's hat looking like this **turbaned** [Wa5;B] wearing a turban

umbrella [C] a light frame covered with cloth, plastic, etc, that can be opened or shut and is held on a stick over the head as a way of keeping off rain, snow, strong sunlight, etc

D147 nouns : underclothes generally

underclothes [P] *also* **underclothing** [U], **underwear** [U] the clothes worn next to the skin, under dresses, suits, and trousers
undies [P] *infml* underclothes esp for women
undergarment [C] *sometimes euph* an article of underwear

D148 nouns : men's underclothes

underpants [P] a man's or child's undergarment worn below the waist and which usu does not cover (much of) the upper part of the leg
pants [P] *BrE* underpants
briefs [P] very short close-fitting underpants, esp as worn by men
singlet [C] *esp BrE* a man's sleeveless garment worn as an undershirt or as an outer shirt esp when playing some sports
vest *BrE* **undershirt** *AmE* [C] a short undergarment, usu without coverings for the arms, worn on the upper part of the body next to the skin

D149 nouns : women's underclothes, etc

panties [P] **1** an undergarment worn below the waist and which does not cover the upper part of the leg, worn by women and girls **2** *infml* pants worn by children
knickers [P] women's underpants
tights [P] a very close-fitting garment covering the legs and lower parts of the body, as worn by girls and women
corset [C] a very tight-fitting undergarment worn, esp by women, to give shape to the waist and hips [⇨ B34]
girdle [C] **1** an undergarment for women, meant to hold the flesh firm; a sort of light corset **2** a cord tied round the waist **3** (*fig*) anything which goes round anything else in this way
brassiere [C] a close-fitting undergarment worn to support the breasts
bra [C] *infml & genl* a brassiere: *They sell bras in that shop. What size of bra does she wear?*
petticoat [C] a type of skirt worn as an undergarment
slip [C] an undergarment like a short dress not covering the arms or neck
shift [C] **1** *old use* a slip **2** a loose-fitting straight simple dress

D150 nouns : night clothes

nightdress [C] a loose dress made to be worn by a woman in bed
nightie [C] *infml* a nightdress: *She bought herself a new nightie.*
pyjamas *esp BrE*, **pajamas** *esp AmE* [P] **1** a soft loose-fitting pair of trousers and short coat made to be worn in bed, esp by a man **2** loose

cotton or silk trousers tied round the waist, worn by Muslim men and women
dressing gown *BrE* **(bath)robe** *AmE* [C] a garment rather like a long loose coat, worn after rising from bed and before putting on outer clothes, or when resting during the day
bathrobe [C] a loose robe usu made of a material that takes in water easily and worn before and after bathing, esp by men

D151 nouns : neckwear

neckwear [U] *tech* (used in shops) clothing, esp ties, worn around the neck: *Our neckwear is famous, sir.* [⇨ picture at D139]
tie, *also* **necktie** *AmE* [C] a band of coloured cloth worn round the neck, usu inside a shirt collar and tied in a knot at the front
bow tie [C] a short band of coloured cloth worn round the neck and fastened at the front with a knot in the shape of a bow
scarf [C] a piece of cloth, usu (for men) long and narrow or (for women) square, for wearing around the neck, head, or shoulders for warmth or ornament
muffler [C] *esp old use* a thick scarf
neckerchief [C] a square of cloth which is folded and worn round the neck
cravat [C] a small scarf or piece of cloth, tied round the neck with the ends worn inside a shirt with its neck open

D152 nouns, etc : buttons, zips, etc

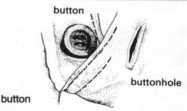

button

buttonhole

button

button [C] **1** a small, usu round or flat object that is fixed to parts of garments and usu passed through an opening (= **buttonhole**) in another part of the garment to act as a fastener **2** a part, object, or piece of apparatus like a button
buckle [C] a device, usu of metal, for fastening a belt

zip

zip *also* **zip fastener, zipper** *AmE* [C] a fastener made of sets of metal or plastic teeth and a sliding piece that joins the edges of an opening in material by drawing the teeth together

stud [C] a kind of button that can be taken out or put in, in one piece or more, usu to fasten a collar to a shirt or fasten the front of a shirt

press-stud [C] a stud, usu fixed in position in a garment, with two parts that can be pressed together, to close a dress, shirt, etc

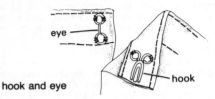

hook and eye

hook and eye [C] a kind of fastening for dresses, etc, where small hooks can be fitted into small holes (= **eyes**)

cufflink [C usu pl] a fastening for the cuff [⇒ D161] of a shirt

belt [C] a band worn round the waist: *She wore a new leather belt. He needs a belt to hold up his trousers.* [⇒ pictures at D140]

braces *BrE* **suspenders** *AmE* [P] elastic cloth bands worn over the shoulders to hold up men's trousers

D153 *verbs* : **buttons, zips, etc**

button [I∅; T1: (*up*)] to close or fasten with buttons: *He buttoned (up) his shirt. This shirt doesn't button (up) very easily.* **un-** [*neg*]

buckle [T1; I∅] to fasten with a buckle: *Buckle your belt. This belt doesn't buckle properly.* **-un** [*neg*]

zip [X7] to put into the stated condition with a zip: *He zipped the bag open/shut.* **-un** [*neg*]

zip up [v adv T1] to fasten (a person into something) with a zip: *Will you zip me up, please? She zipped her dress up.*

do up [v adv T1] *genl* to button, fasten, or zip up: *She asked him to do her (dress) up at the back.* **undo** [*neg*]

belt 1 [X9, esp *on*] to fasten (something onto something else) with a belt: *He belted on his gun.* **2** [T1 (*up*)] to fasten (something) with a belt: *He belted (up) his raincoat.*

robe [Wv5; I∅; T1: (*in*)] to dress (oneself or another) in robes [⇒ D139]; put on a robe: *The king and queen were robed in red.*

cloak [Wv5; I∅; T1] to dress (oneself or another) in a cloak [⇒ D143] *He was cloaked and ready to go.* (*fig*) *The hills were cloaked in low cloud. The history of the family is cloaked in mystery.*

D154 *nouns* : **handbags and wallets, etc** [C]

handbag a small bag for a woman to carry her money and personal things in

purse 1 a small flattish leather or plastic bag used esp by women for carrying money: *She*

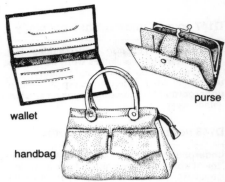

purse

wallet

handbag

carried her purse in her handbag. **2** *AmE* a woman's handbag (for carrying a purse, handkerchief, money, etc)

wallet 1 a small flat leather case which can usu be folded, for holding papers and paper money, usu carried by a man in his coat or back trouser pocket **2** a long leather case for official papers **3** *old use* a bag for food, clothes, etc, carried by travellers, etc

billfold *AmE* a man's wallet

handkerchief a piece of cloth for drying the nose, eyes, etc

hankie *infml* a handkerchief

accessory [*usu pl*] something added to what is usu worn, esp by a woman, such as shoes, hat, handbag, etc: *She wore a black suit with white matching accessories.*

D155 *nouns* : **gloves** [C]

glove a garment which covers the hand, with separate parts for the thumb and fingers: *Woollen gloves are warm in winter. He bought a new pair of gloves.*

gauntlet 1 a long glove covering the wrist, which protects the hand, esp in certain sports **2** a glove covered with metal, used formerly as armour by soldiers

mitten also **mitt** a glove with one part only for the fingers and another part for the thumb: *It is difficult to handle money when wearing mittens.*

D156 *nouns* : **footwear**

footwear [U] *tech* shoes and boots: *A shopkeeper would say he sold footwear; we would say he sold shoes. You need good footwear for wet weather.*

shoe [C] an outer covering for the human foot, usu of leather and having a hard base (= **sole**) and a support (= **heel**) under the heel of the foot: *Put on/Take off your shoes. This shoe doesn't fit well. He bought a new pair of shoes.*

shoehorn [C] a curved piece of horn, metal, plastic, etc, for putting inside the back of a shoe when slipping it on, to help the heel go in easily

boot [C] a covering of leather or rubber for the foot and some part of the leg, usu heavier than a shoe, and with a part for supporting the ankle

tie his (shoe) laces. **2** [T1 (*up*)] to draw together or fasten with a lace **3** [T1 (*up*)] to pass (a lace, string, etc) through holes in (something)

heel the back part of a shoe, sock, etc, which covers the heel, esp the raised part of a shoe underneath the foot: *There's a hole in the heel of my stocking.*

toe the front part of a shoe, sock, etc: *There's a hole in the toe of my sock.*

upper the top part of a shoe above the heel and sole

D158 *nouns* : **stockings**

stocking [C] a garment for the foot and leg which is shaped to fit closely, esp one made of very thin material such as nylon and worn by women **in one's stocking(ed) feet** wearing stockings or socks, but no shoes

sock [C] a covering of soft material, such as wool or nylon, for the foot and usu part of the lower leg, usu worn inside a shoe: *Knee socks* (= coming up to the knee)

tights [P] an almost transparent close-fitting garment, usu made of nylon, covering the part of the body below the waist and the legs and feet, as worn by women and girls

hose [P] **1** *tech* stockings or socks; **2** tight-fitting leg coverings worn by men in former times

hosiery 1 [U] stockings, underwear, etc **2** [C] *now rare* the shop where these are sold

suspender [C *usu pl*] *BrE* a band and/or fastener used to keep up a stocking or sock

D159 *nouns* : **jewellery and ornaments, etc**

jewellery *BrE*, **jewelry** *AmE* [U] ornaments, esp containing jewels [⇒ H65] or stones like jewels and usu worn on the body, clothes, etc: *She likes buying jewellery.*

brooch [C] an ornamental pin worn on women's clothes

necklace [C] a string of jewels, etc, on a chain of gold, silver, etc, worn around the neck as an ornament, esp by a woman

necklet [C] a short necklace

bracelet [C] a band or ring, usu of metal, worn round the wrist or arm as an ornament

bangle [C] a metal band worn round the arm or ankle as an ornament

ring [C *often in comb*] a ring of metal, worn esp on a finger but also in the ear and nose: *She wore a gold wedding ring on the third finger of her left hand.* **earring** [C] an ornament worn on the ear

hairpin [C] a pin made of a piece of wire bent into a U-shape to hold the hair in position

D160 *nouns* : **aprons, smocks, etc**

apron [C] a simple garment worn over the front part of one's clothes to keep them clean while doing something dirty, or esp when cooking

wellington (boot), *also esp BrE infml* **wellie** [C *usu pl*] a boot of rubber which keeps water from the feet and lower part of the legs

clog a kind of shoe **a** with a thick, usu wooden bottom (= **sole**) **b** completely made from one piece of wood

sandal [C] a light shoe made of a flat bottom with bands, esp of leather, to hold it on the foot

slipper, *also* (*fml*) **carpet slipper** [C] a light shoe with tops (= **uppers**) made from soft material and usu worn indoors

high heels [P] women's shoes with high heels: *She was wearing high heels.*

pair [C9] two shoes, socks, etc, one for each foot: *Can I have a new pair of slippers, please? He bought a pair of rubber boots.*

D157 *nouns, etc* : **parts of footwear** [C]
[⇒ PICTURE AT D156]

lace 1 *also* **shoelace**, **bootlace** a thin string or cord that is pulled through holes in shoes, etc, to draw their edges together: *He bent down to*

smock [C] a light loose coatlike garment for putting on over one's clothing while working

tracksuit [C] a loose-fitting suit of warm material worn by sportsmen when training but not when playing, racing, etc

dungarees [P] high loose trousers often fastened over the shoulders and worn esp by men workers over other clothes

overalls [P] trousers or work clothes made of heavy cotton cloth, usu blue

boiler suit [C] a garment made in one piece, worn for dirty work

D161 *nouns, etc* : **parts of clothing**

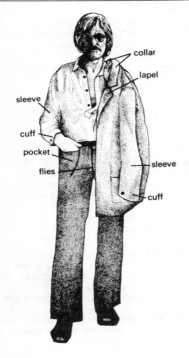

collar
lapel
sleeve
cuff
pocket
flies
sleeve
cuff

sleeve [C] a part of a garment for covering (part of) an arm: *The dress had long/short sleeves; it was a short-sleeved/long-sleeved dress.*

cuff [C] the end of a sleeve: *The cuffs of his shirt are dirty. His shirt cuffs are dirty.*

collar [C] a part of a garment, etc, that fits round the neck: *He turned up the collar of his coat to keep his neck warm.*

neckband [C] a part of a shirt, etc, that goes round the neck

lapel [C] the part of the front of a coat or jacket that is folded back below the neck on each side towards the shoulders

hem 1 [C] the edge of a piece of cloth when turned under and sewn down, esp the lower edge of a skirt or dress **2** [T1] to put a hem on: *The curtains haven't been hemmed yet.*

flies [P] *esp BrE* the front opening of a pair of trousers, with a band of cloth on one side to cover the zip or buttons: *Your flies are undone* (= open).

fly [C; A] flies: *Your fly's undone. A fly button.*

pocket [C] a small bag added to or forming part of an article of clothing, etc, for carrying things in: *He put his hands in the pockets of his trousers. The money was in his left-hand trouser pocket.*

D162 *nouns* : **special shapes in clothing** [C]

[ALSO ⇒ D176]

fold 1 a mark made by folding, esp clothes **2** the part at which an article of clothing folds

pleat a flat narrow fold sewn into an article of clothing **pleated** [Wa5;B] arranged in or having pleats: *She wore a pleated dress.*

crease 1 a line made on cloth, paper, etc, by crushing, folding, or pressing: *You've got a crease in your dress where you've been sitting. The crease in the back of your shirt shows you've not pressed it properly.* **2** a straight thin line down the front and back of each leg in a pair of trousers: *Boys who don't have creases in their trousers look untidy. Give me your trousers and I'll press a crease in them.*

D163 *nouns, etc* : **tailors and cobblers**

tailor 1 [C] (the shop of) a person who makes outer garments to order, esp for men **2** [I∅; T1] to make (an outer garment) by cutting, esp fitting closely to the person's measurements and sewing cloth: *Mr Jones tailors for the king. That's a nicely-tailored suit.* **3** [X9] (*fig*) to prepare for a special purpose: *We can tailor our insurance to your special needs.*

clothier *esp formerly* a person who deals in clothes and cloth

jeweller *BrE*, **jeweler** *AmE* (the shop of) a person who deals in jewels, watches, etc

cobbler [C] (the shop of) a person whose work it is to mend shoes, boots, etc

Cleaning and personal care

D170 *verbs* : **washing and cleaning**

[ALSO ⇒ D179]

wash 1 [T1 (*down, off, out*); (I∅)] to clean with or as if with liquid: *He was washing his clothes/car/dog/hands. She washed herself carefully with soap and water. He washed the car down. She washed the soap off. He washed the room out. You wash (the dishes) and I'll dry.* **2** [I∅ (*with*)] to clean oneself or a part of one's body with liquid: *She washed (with soap and water) before dinner.* **3** [L9; (I∅)] to bear cleaning with liquid without damage: *These clothes don't wash easily.* **4** [I∅ (*with*) nonassertive] *infml* to be easy to believe: *That story just* *won't wash (with me).* **5** [I∅ (*against, over*); T1] to flow over or against (something) continually: *The waves washed (against/over) the shore.* **6** [X9, esp *away, off*] to cause to be removed as stated, with or as if with liquid: *I washed the dirt off (my hands). The waves washed away the swimmer.* **7** [T1; I∅ (*for*)] to pour water over (esp small stones) in search of precious metal: *We kept washing (the mud) (for gold) but found nothing.*

clean 1 [T1; I∅] to (cause to) become clean: *Please clean the windows as I can hardly see out. Metal ornaments clean easily.* **2** [T1] to cut out the bowels and inside parts of the body from (birds and animals that are to be eaten): *I have to clean the chicken before I can cook it.*
cleaner [C] a person whose work it is to clean a place [⇒ also D178]

cleanse 1 [T1] to make (usu a cut, wound, etc) clean or pure; to clean fully: *The nurse cleansed the wound before stitching it.* **2** [D1 *from/of*; T1 (*of*)] (*fig*) to remove (something bad, an illness, etc) from (a person) by or as if by cleaning: *'Please cleanse me of my sin!' he asked the priest. My soul has been cleansed (of sin).*

scrub 1 [I∅; T1; X7] to clean by hard rubbing, as with a stiff brush: *She said that a wife does nothing but cooking and scrubbing all day. He scrubbed the floor clean. I scrubbed the shirt to remove the spot.* **2** [X9, esp *out*] to remove in this way: *She scrubbed the spot out. Scrub the dirt off the floor.*

scour 1 [T1 (*down, out*)] to clean (a surface) by very hard rubbing with a rough material: *He scoured the walls down with a stiff brush. She scoured out the dirty pan.* **2** [X9, esp *from, off, out*] to remove (dirt, oil, etc) in this way: *He scoured the dirt off the floor.* **3** [T1 (*out*)] (of a stream of water) to form by wearing or washing away: *Water had scoured out a channel in the soft sand.*

rinse 1 [T1 (*out*)] to wash (esp clothes) in clean water so as to take away soap, dirt, etc: *I'll just rinse (out) these shirts. Rinse your mouth (out). Please rinse (out) my cup.* **2** [X9, esp *out (of)*] to wash (soap, dirt, etc) out (of something) with clean water: *Rinse the soap out of these shirts. She rinsed out the sea water from her bathing-suit.*

dry [T1; I∅: (*up, out*)] to become or make (something) dry, esp after washing, cleaning, etc: *You wash the dishes and I'll dry them. You wash and I'll dry. The clothes have dried. Has the fire dried (out) the clothes yet?*

shampoo [T1] to wash (esp the head and hair) with soap: *She shampooed her hair last night.*

sponge [T1] to clean with a sponge [⇒ D178] *He sponged the blood off his skin. Don't wash this garment; just sponge it.*

wipe 1 [T1 (*on*)] to pass a cloth or other material against (something) to remove dirt, liquid, etc: *He wiped his nose (on a handkerchief). Wipe down the walls with a cloth. He wiped the sink out. Wipe your feet (on the mat) when you come*

in. **2** [X9 (*up*)] to remove by wiping: *He wiped away her tears. Wipe up the water on the table.*

D171 nouns : **washing and cleaning** [S]

wash 1 the act or action or an example of washing or being washed: *Go upstairs and have a wash. Give the car a good wash.* **2** the flow, sound, or act of a mass of water (such as a wave): *I heard the wash of the waves.*
clean an act of cleaning dirt, esp from the surface of something: *She gives the room a good clean every day.*
scrub an act of scrubbing: *Give that dirt/floor a good scrub.*
scour an act of scouring: *Give the inside of the oven a scour.*
rinse an act of rinsing: *Give these wet cloths/ clothes a rinse.*
dry an act of drying: *Give these plates a dry. The wet clothes were put out for a dry in the sun.*
shampoo an act of shampooing: *She gave her hair a good shampoo last night.*
brush an act of brushing: *I'll just give my coat/ hair a quick brush.*
wipe an act of wiping: *Give the table a wipe with a wet cloth.*

D172 nouns : **baths and showers**
[ALSO ⇒ D40]

bath [C] **1** an act of washing one's whole body at one time: *He had (BrE)/took (AmE) a bath.* **2** the water for a bath: *He got into a cold/hot bath.* (*fig*) *He had a steam bath. I had a lovely bath of sunshine.* **3** the quality or state of being covered with a liquid: *He was in a bath of sweat* [⇒ B62]. **baths** [P] a building with one or more rooms used for bathing or swimming: *He goes to the public baths every week.*
bathe [C usu sing] BrE infml the act of going into a body of water or a swimming pool to bathe or swim: *Let's go for a bathe.*
bathing [U] the act or practice of going into water to bathe or swim: *Mixed bathing (by men and women) is allowed in this pool. The bathing in this part of the lake is considered dangerous.*
shave [C usu sing] an act or result of shaving: *He looks much better after having a shave and a haircut.*
shower [C] a washing of the body by standing under an opening where water comes out in many small streams: *She took/had a shower after playing tennis.*
wash and brush up [C usu sing] esp BrE a usu quick act of washing, esp one's hands and face and brushing one's hair and clothes, esp after a journey: *Come on, there's time for a wash and brush up.*
ablution [C usu pl] fml or humor the act of washing oneself: *She performed her ablutions, then went to bed.*

D173 verbs : bathing and showering

bath *BrE* **1** [IØ] to have a bath; wash one's body completely: *He can't see you now; he's bathing.* **2** [T1] to give a bath to: *He's bathing the baby.*

bathe **1** [IØ] *esp BrE* to go into a body of water or swimming pool for pleasure, to swim, for reasons of health, etc: *I like to bathe in the sea. Don't bathe too soon after eating.* **2** [T1] to pour water or other liquid over; place in water or other liquid, usu for medical purposes: *Bathe your twisted ankle twice a day in warm water.* **3** [T1] *euph* to flow along the edge of: *The Mediterranean bathes the sunny shores of Italy.* **4** [IØ] *esp AmE fml* to bath **5** [X9 *often pass*] to spread over with light, water, etc: *The room was bathed in light. Her eyes were bathed with/in tears.* **bathing costume** *BrE* **bathing suit** *esp AmE* the type of clothing worn by women for bathing or swimming   **swimsuit** *genl* a bathing costume

shower [IØ] to take a shower: *He showered and put on some clean clothes.*

shave **1** [T1 (*off*); IØ] to cut off (hair or beard) close to the skin with a razor: *Most men shave every morning. He has decided to shave off his beard.* **2** [T1; L9] to cut all the hair from (a part of the body): *She shaves her legs and under her arms.* **-shaven** [*comb form*] shaved: *He has a clean-shaven face* (= with no beard).

D174 nouns : places and things relating to cleaning clothes, etc

laundry **1** [C] a place or business where clothes, sheets, etc, are washed (and ironed) **2** [U] clothes, sheets, etc, needing to be washed or that have just been washed (and ironed): *Bring in the laundry, please.*

laund(e)rette *also esp AmE* **laundromat** [C] a place where the public may wash their clothes in machines that work when coins are put in them

wash *also* **washing** [U] things to be washed, or being washed; laundry: *Have you done the wash yet? Hang out the washing to dry.* **in the wash** being washed: *Your best shirt is in the wash; it isn't dry yet.*

(dry) cleaner's [(the) C] a place where clothes, material, etc, can be taken to be (dry-)cleaned for money: *If I take my suit to the cleaner's today it should be ready by Saturday.*

shoeshine [C] an occasion of having one's shoes shined, esp by a person working at this in the street, a hotel, etc: *Shoeshine, sir?*

D175 verbs , etc : special actions in cleaning clothes, etc

launder **1** [T1] to wash (and iron) (clothes, sheets, etc) **2** [IØ] (of clothes, sheets, etc) to be able to be washed (and ironed)

dry-clean [T1 *usu pass*] to clean (clothes, material, etc) with chemicals without using water: *I always have my suit dry-cleaned as it's not supposed to be washed.*

iron **1** [IØ] (of clothes) to become smooth by the action of an iron [⇒ D178]: *You wouldn't expect this pair of socks to iron well.* **2** [T1; IØ] to cause (clothes) to become smooth by using an iron: *Your shirt is already ironed. I've been (doing the) ironing all day.*

press [T1; X7; L9] to (cause (cloth or clothes) to) receive and keep smoothness or a sharp fold (**crease**) by means of pressure with a hot iron: *She washed and dried the shirt and then pressed it with an electric iron. This dress presses easily.* **2** [S] *infml* an act of pressing: *Give these trousers a press with an iron.*

polish **1** [T1, (*up*); X7; L9, esp *up*; (IØ)] to make or become smooth and bright by continual rubbing: *Polish your shoes with a brush. Silver polishes easily. She polished up the silver buttons. The buttons didn't polish up well. Polish it clean.* **2** [S] an act of polishing: *He gave his shoes a quick polish.* [⇒ H92, 95]

shine **1** [T1] *not fml* to polish: *Shine your shoes before going out. He shined their shoes for them.* **2** [S] an act of shining: *Give your shoes a shine; they need it.* **3** [S] The result of shining something: *What a beautiful shine on those shoes.*

brush **1** [T1] to clean or smooth with a brush: *She brushed her teeth/hair/coat.* **2** [S] an act of brushing: *Give your clothes a good brush before you go out.*

comb **1** [T1 (*out*)] to pass a comb [⇒ D178] through (esp the hair, wool, etc): *She combed her hair. He combed the wool out. He combed the pieces of dirt out of the wool.* **2** [S] an act of combing: *He gave his hair a comb.*

D176 verbs : folding and creasing
[⇒ ALSO D162]

fold (T1; IØ) to (cause to) bend so that one part is on or against another: *She folded the clothes carefully. This cloth doesn't fold well.*

crumple [IØ; T1: (*up*)] to (cause to) become full of irregular folds by pressing, crushing, etc: *This cloth isn't suitable for making clothes; it crumples up too easily. Take care not to crumple your dress by packing it carelessly.*

crease **1** [Wv5; T1] to make a line or lines appear on (a garment, paper, cloth, etc) by folding, crushing, or pressing: *Don't sit for too long or you'll crease your new dress. She wanted to wear her black dress but it was too creased.* **2** [Wv5; T1] to make a thin straight line appear down the back and front of each leg of (a pair of trousers): *Don't put those trousers on until I've creased them.* **3** [IØ] to become creased: *This new material won't crease.*

D177 *verbs* : **cleaning and getting ready**

clean out [v adv T1] **1** to make (esp a room, box, drawer, etc) clean and tidy: *The servants cleaned out the bedrooms.* **2** (*fig*) *infml* to take all the money, etc, from (someone) by stealing or winning: *I got cleaned out playing cards. The thieves cleaned out the store.* **cleanout** [C *usu sing*] *infml* an act of cleaning out: *Give the house a good cleanout.*

clean up [v adv] **1** [I0; T1] to clean (a place) fully: *Clean up this broken glass on the floor. It's your turn to clean (the bedroom) up.* **2** [T1] (*fig*) *infml* to gain (money) as profit: *He cleaned up a fortune playing cards.* **cleanup** [C *usu sing*] *infml* an act of cleaning up: *Let's have a good cleanup today.*

tidy [I0; T1: (*up, out*)] to make neat: *Tidy up your room before going out. It took me all morning to tidy up in the kitchen. She tidied the room out while he was away.*

dust [T1; I0] **1** to remove dust from (something), esp when cleaning: *She dusted the table.* **2** [(*with*)] to put dust, etc, on something: *He dusted the surface of the table with chalk dust. The cook dusted the cake with flour.*

get ready 1 [T1] to make (someone or something) ready, clean, etc: *He got the children ready to go out.* **2** [I0] to make oneself ready: *Are you getting ready to go out?—Yes, I'm putting my dress on.*

refresh [T1] to make fresh, new, strong, etc, again: *He refreshed himself with a glass of cold water, then went back to work. Let me refresh your memory with some facts.* **refreshment** [U] the act of refreshing

freshen up [v adv] **1** [T1; I0] to cause (oneself) to feel more comfortable by washing: *I must just go and freshen (myself) up before tea.* **2** [T1] to cause (someone) to feel more comfortable by washing: *That bath has freshened me up.* **3** [T1] to make newer and more attractive: *He's freshened up the house with a new coat of paint.*

smarten up [v adv T1; I0] to (cause (oneself) to) become clean, good-looking, neat, etc: *He smartened himself up before his guests arrived. Smarten (yourself) up—you look really untidy!*

spruce up [v adv T1] to smarten (someone or something) up a lot: *He spruced himself up for the party. Let's spruce up the house with some paint.*

do up [v adv T1] *not fml* to get (someone) ready; make (someone) more beautiful, etc: *She has done herself up for the party.*

do out [v adv T1] *esp BrE infml* to clean thoroughly: *She did the room out while he was away.*

D178 *nouns* : **things for cleaning with, etc**

[ALSO ⇒ H156]

cleaner [C] a machine, apparatus, or substance used in cleaning

cleanser [C; U] a substance, such as a chemical liquid or powder, used for making cleaning easier and more effective

scourer [C] a tool, esp a small ball of plastic wire or net, for cleaning cooking pots and pans

shaver [C] a tool for shaving, esp an electric-powered instrument held in the hand for shaving hair off the face and body

iron

iron [C] a piece of equipment heated either by electricity or directly and used for making clothing and cloth smooth esp after washing

brush [C *often in comb*] an instrument for cleaning, smoothing, or painting, made of sticks, stiff hair, nylon, etc: **clothesbrush**; **toothbrush**; **paintbrush**

hairbrush [C] a brush used for pulling through the hair to get out dirt and make the hair smooth

scrubbing brush [C] a stiff brush for heavy cleaning jobs (like scrubbing floors)

comb [C] a flat piece of plastic, rubber, metal, etc, with many separate parts (=**teeth**), usu held in the hand and used to arrange the hair smoothly: *Have you got a comb? This comb has a lot of teeth missing.*

sponge [C] a soft material full of holes, used for cleaning things: *Sponges fill with water when you use them. He washed himself with soap, a sponge, and hot water.*

D179 *adjectives, etc* : **clean, tidy, and pure**

[⇒ ALSO B177]

clean [Wa1; B] **1** free from dirt, unwanted matter, disease, etc: *The water is clean. He had clean hands.* **2** not yet worn or used; fresh: *She was wearing clean clothes.* **3** (*fig*) morally pure; free from guilt: *He leads a clean life and tells clean jokes. He is a clean fighter.* **4** (*fig*) well-formed: *That aeroplane has a clean shape.* **5** [adv] so as to be clean; in a clean way: *Wash the cups clean. Play the game clean.*

cleanly [Wa1; B] personally clean and neat; careful to keep clean: *Cats are one of the clean-*

liest animals there are. **-liness** [U]: *Your son's state of cleanliness is very good.*

tidy [Wa1;B] having everything well arranged and in its right place: *What a nice tidy room she has!* **un-** [*neg*] **-ily** [adv] **-iness** [U]

neat [Wa1;B] **1** in good order; arranged well; showing care in appearance; tidy: *She has neat hair. He keeps the office neat.* **2** liking order and good arrangement; orderly: *Cats are neat animals. She has a neat mind.* **-ly** [adv] **-ness** [U]

orderly [Wa2;B] liking everything kept or done in the proper place, at the proper time, etc: *He has an orderly approach to life. The room looked neat and orderly.* **dis-** [*neg*] **-liness** [U]

smart [Wa1;B] **1** neat and pleasing in appearance or clothes: *You're looking very smart in that new suit. He has a very smart-looking new car.* **2** used by, concerning, etc, very fashionable people: *They go to very smart restaurants.* **-ly** [adv] **-ness** [U]

fashionable [B] smart and wearing the latest fashion [⇒ D138] in clothes: *She looked very fashionable yesterday, didn't she?* **un-** [*neg*] **-bly** [adv] *She was very fashionably dressed.*

trim [Wa1;B *but of persons usu* F] (looking) neat and tidy: *She looked very trim in her new dress. He wears a trim little beard.* **-ly** [adv] **-ness** [U]

spruce [Wa2;B] tidy and clean, esp in appearance; smart; trim: *A banker in his spruce coat and hat was walking along the street.* **-ly** [adv] *He was very sprucely dressed.* **-ness** [U]

well-turned-out [Wa2;F;(B)] *not fml* well dressed: *They were all looking very well-turned-out at the wedding.*

spick-and-span [B] *infml* clean and bright; like new: *She keeps her home spick-and-span.*

spotless [B] completely clean: *The room was spotless.* **-ly** [adv]: *What a spotlessly clean room!* **-ness** [U]

immaculate [Wa5;B] **1** clean and unspoilt: *She was wearing immaculate white shoes.* **2** pure; unmarked; without fault: *His immaculate behaviour made him welcome everywhere.* **-ly** [adv] **-ness** [U]

stainless [B] **1** spotless: *He lived a life of stainless purity.* **2** of a kind not easily broken down chemically, esp rusted [⇒ H29] by air and water: *Stainless steel contains 12% or more of the metal chromium. She bought a set of stainless (steel) knives and forks.*

pure [Wa1;B] **1** clean; free from dirt, dust, bacteria [⇒ A37], or any harmful matter: *This is pure drinking water. The air here is very pure and healthy.* **2** (clean because) not mixed with any other substance: *The box is made of pure silver. Is this garment made of pure wool?* **-ly** [adv]: *Is this garment made purely of wool?* **-ness** [U]

D180 *adjectives* : **not clean**

dirty [Wa1;B] **1** not clean: *He has dirty hands. This is a very dirty town, dirtier than the other one. My dress is getting dirty and needs wash-*

ing. **2** causing people or things to become unclean: *Repairing cars is a dirty job.* **3** (*fig*) (of thoughts or words) concerned with sex in a unpleasant way: *They sat up drinking and telling dirty stories.* **4** *infml* (of the weather) rough and unpleasant: *The fishermen won't go out on such a dirty night.*

soiled [B] slightly dirty, esp on the surface: *These clothes are soiled; get them cleaned.*

filthy [Wa1;B] **1** very dirty; covered with filth: *Take those filthy boots off!* **2** (*esp fig*) showing or containing filth: *What a filthy mind you've got! Stop telling those filthy stories.* **-ily** [adv] **iness** [U]

foul 1 [Wa1;B] very dirty; unclean; impure; evil-smelling or evil-tasting: *The air in this room is foul; open the window! What a foul-tasting medicine. He has foul breath!* **2** [Wa5;A] (of a pipe, chimney, etc) blocked with dirt or waste matter, so that liquid, smoke, etc, cannot pass freely **3** [Wa1;B] (of weather) rough; stormy: *It's a foul night tonight; its pouring with rain.* **4** [Wa1;B] (*fig*) *deprec* evil; cruel; wicked; shameful: *Murder is a foul deed. She has a foul temper; that's why she has so few friends.* **5** [Wa1;B] (*fig*) *deprec* (of language) full of curses and swear words **6** [Wa1;B] (*fig*) *infml* very bad; disagreeable; unpleasant: *I've had a foul morning; everything's gone wrong. That was a foul meal to offer anybody.*

sordid [B] **1** very dirty or poor: *sordid living conditions.* **2** marked by unpleasantness and bad qualities: *He told them a sordid story of dishonesty.* **-ly** [adv] **-ness** [U]

squalid [B] **1** very dirty and uncared for; filthy: *They live in squalid conditions.* **2** having, expressing, or about low moral standards; sordid: *What a squalid story of sex and violence!* **-ly** [adv]

D181 *verbs* : **making things dirty**

dirty [T1] to make dirty: *Please try not to dirty the house. They dirtied the floor when they came in from the wet garden.*

soil [T1; I0] to make or become dirty, esp slightly or on the surface: *His shirt collar was badly soiled and would never be white again. These papers won't soil when handled carefully.* (*fig*) *I wouldn't soil my hands by accepting money from a person like him.*

foul [T1] to make very dirty: *The cats fouled the room with their urine* [⇒ B64].

mark [T1] to make or leave marks on: *He marked the floor with his boots.*

stain [T1] to discolour [⇒ L28] in a way that is lasting or not easy to change: *His teeth are stained with years of smoking.*

pollute [T1] to make (air, water, soil, etc) dangerously impure or unhealthy for use: *Their drinking water is polluted; oil has got into the well.* **2** (*fig*) *deprec* to destroy the purity of (the mind): *She thinks that books about sex* *pollute the minds of children.* **3** to make (esp a holy place) ceremonially unclean [⇨ B135]

defile [T1 *often pass*] to make unclean or impure: *Their evil words defiled the holy place.*

mess [X9, esp *up*; L9, esp *about*] *not fml* to make a mess (of): *Who messed up my papers? Stop messing about with my work!*

D182 *nouns* : **dirt and pollution**

[ALSO ⇨ H64]

dirt [U] unclean material on a floor, furniture, etc: *How did that dirt get on my clean kitchen floor?*

filth [U] very unclean material: *There's filth all over my clean kitchen floor!* (*fig*) *Don't read that book; it's filth.*

muck [U] *infml* dirt: *I've got muck on my shoes.*

mark [C] a small cut, stain, etc, on a surface which should be smooth: *He has made marks on the table with that knife!*

spot [C] a small area of dirt or some substance on a surface which should be clean: *There are (dirty) spots on the (clean) cloth.*

stain [C] a stained place; a large spot: *There are stains on the cloth; I think they are bloodstains* (= stains of blood). (*fig*) *He has many dark stains on his character; he has led a bad life.*

pollution [U] **1** the action of polluting: *The pollution of rivers kills fish.* **2** the state of being polluted: *The pollution of our sea shores is very serious.* **3** things that pollute: *The pollution in the sea is very bad.*

pollutant [C; U] a substance or thing that pollutes: *Smoke from factory chimneys is a pollutant.*

defilement 1 [U] the act of defiling **2** [C] an example of this; something that defiles

mess [U] a dirty, untidy state: *What a mess the house is in! Who made this mess? The dog has made a mess on the floor.*

D183 *nouns, etc* : **care for the hair**

[ALSO ⇨ B51–3]

haircut [C] the occasion of having the hair cut, or the style it is cut in, esp for men: *They've both got the same haircut. He needs a haircut.*

hairdo [C] the occasion of a woman having her hair shaped, and the appearance that results: *I don't like her new hairdo.*

shampoo [C] **1** a usu liquid soaplike product used for shampooing: *She uses a creamy shampoo for dry hair.* **2** an act of shampooing: *She had a shampoo and set at the hairdresser's.*

rinse 1 [C9; U9] (a) liquid for colouring the hair: *She bought a (bottle of) blue rinse.* **2** [C] the act or result of using this on the hair: *She had a blue rinse.*

crop 1 [S] hair cut very short: *With a crop like that you look as if you've just come out of the army!* **2** [T1; X7] to cut (a person's hair or a horse's tail) short: *The barber cropped his hair (short).*

D184 *nouns* : **relating to the hair** [C]

wig an arrangement of false hair to make a covering for the head, to hide one's real hair or lack of hair: *The actress wore a black wig over her fair hair. Judges in Britain wear wigs in court.*

hairpiece a piece of false hair used to make a person's own hair seem thicker

toupee a small wig or hairpiece specially shaped to fit exactly over a place on a man's head where the hair no longer grows

hairnet a net which stretches over the hair to keep it in place

D185 *nouns & verbs* : **cosmetics and special body care**

cosmetic [C *usu pl*] a preparation such as a face-cream, body-powder, etc, intended to make the skin or hair more beautiful: *This chemist keeps a large range of cosmetics. Mother has a special cosmetic(s) bag for keeping her cosmetics in.*

make-up [U; C *usu sing*] powder and paint, etc, used on the face, or the appearance produced by the use of this: *Too much make-up looks unnatural. She changed her make-up. He was wearing make-up in the play to make him look like an old man.*

make up [v adv T1; I0] to use make-up on (the face of) (someone or oneself) so as to alter or improve the appearance: *She makes herself up/makes up her face in 10 minutes in the morning. You have 10 minutes to make up. In the play he is made up as an old man.*

massage 1 [U] the system of treating the body by pressing and moving the hands (or feet) on it to take away pain or stiffness from the muscles and joints **2** [C] an example of this **3** [T1] to give a massage to (someone or a part of the body): *She massaged his neck.*

manicure 1 [U; C] (a) treatment for the hands and esp the fingernails, including cutting, cleaning, etc **2** [T1] to give a manicure to (the hands): *She had newly manicured hands/nails.*

D186 *nouns* : **persons looking after hair, skin, clothes, etc** [C]

barber a person (usu a man) who cuts men's hair and shaves them: *He went to the barber/barber's for a haircut.*

hairdresser someone who shapes the hair into a style, by cutting, setting, etc, or (usu of women's hair) changes its colour: *She fixed a time to see her hairdresser.*

hair stylist *euph & pomp* a hairdresser

beautician a person who gives beauty treatment (as to skin and hair and nails) **beauty parlour** a place where women are given beauty treatments

masseur *Fr* a person who massages others

masseuse *Fr* a female masseur

manicurist a person who manicures nails

laundress a woman whose work it is to wash and iron clothes

washerwoman *esp formerly & often deprec* a woman who washes clothes

E

Food, drink, and farming

Food generally

E1 *nouns* : **food and diet**
[⇒ E142 ANIMAL FOODS IN FARMING]

food [U; C] anything to be eaten or that can be eaten (and/or drunk); solid substances generally that can be eaten; anything nourishing [⇒ E5]: *Food and drink are necessary to keep us alive. The food's good at this restaurant. They sell quite a wide choice of foods at this shop. Milk is a good food. We've no food of any kind in the house.*

foodstuff [U; C] *tech* any substance used as food, esp in large amounts before cooking, etc: *Where do they store the foodstuff? The price of foodstuffs is going up.*

fare [U] food, esp as provided (in large quantities) at a meal, party, in hotels, etc: *The fare here is simple but good. What splendid fare she provided at the party.*

sustenance *fml & pomp* [U] **1** food (and drink) when seen as sustaining life (= keeping people, etc, alive) **2** the qualities of food (and drink) which keep people, etc, alive

eats [P] *infml* things to eat: *Have you brought the eats?*

eatables [P] *usu infml* things that can be eaten: *All the eatables are in the basket.*

provisions [P] substances provided as food: *Have we enough provisions for the journey/the winter?*

diet **1** [U; C] the sort of food and drink usually taken (by a person or a group): *Proper diet and exercise are both important for health. The Irish used to live on a diet largely of potatoes.* **2** [C usu sing] a limited list of food and drink that one is allowed, esp by a doctor: *The doctor ordered him a diet without sugar. He's on a diet in order to reduce his weight. The doctor put him on a diet. She went on a diet to try to slim* (= in order not to become fat, or to lose weight).

staple [C; A] a chief food or product of a country, people, etc: *Rice is the staple* (*diet*) *in southern India.*

grub [U] *esp BrE infml* food: *Is the grub ready yet?*

bulk [U] rough food often eaten to help the movement of the bowels: *There isn't enough bulk in the food you eat.*

roughage [U] coarse matter which does not feed, but which helps the bowels to work; bulk: *Potato skins provide valuable roughage.*

E2 *nouns* : **drinks**
[ALSO ⇒ E60]

drink [U; C] liquid that can be drunk; an amount of liquid in a glass, etc, to be drunk: *Food and drink will be served soon. Can I have a drink (of water), please? Bring the drinks over to this table.*

beverage [C] *fml* a drink, esp if not water: *He always has an alcoholic beverage at this time. The shop sells several kinds of hot beverage.*

potion [C] *esp lit* a single drink of a liquid mixture, intended as a medicine, poison, or a charm: *The doctor gave her a sleeping potion. The witch* [⇒ C356] *prepared a love potion.*

brew [C usu sing] (the quality of) a drink made by brewing [⇒ E101]: *That's a good brew of tea. I don't like these brews she makes. The brew is ready now.*

E3 *general verbs* : **eating and drinking**

eat **1** [T1; I∅] to take in through the mouth and swallow (solid food or soup): *Eat your dinner! John eats too quickly. He ate an apple. Eat/Drink your soup while it is still hot.* (*fig*) *That big house just eats money. You look so nice I could eat you!* **2** [I∅] to have a meal: *What time do we eat? Have you eaten yet?* **eat one's head off** (of people and esp of animals) to eat large and expensive quantities of food **eat someone out of house and home** (of people) to eat a lot of food that someone else must pay for **eater** [C] a person who eats in a stated way, esp in the phr **a big eater** a person who habitually eats a lot

feed **1** [T1] to cause to eat and drink: *Have you fed the baby/cows yet?* **2** [I∅] *infml or humor* to take food; eat and drink: *Have you people fed yet?—Yes, we fed an hour ago.* **feed on** [v prep T1] to live by eating: *Foxes feed on small animals.*

drink [T1; I∅] to take in through the mouth and swallow (liquid food, liquids, soup, etc): *He was so thirsty he nearly drank the whole bottle of milk. They were drinking beer when I last saw them. Drink this medicine.* (*fig*) *My car just drinks petrol; it's costing me too much to run.*

drinker [C] a person who drinks, esp alcohol, in a stated way, esp in the phr **a heavy drinker** a person who drinks a lot of alcohol

eat/drink up [v adv] **1** [I0] to eat/drink more of anything or (more) quickly, in order to finish: *Eat up; we must leave soon. Come on, drink up now; we're late. Hurry! Eat your food up!* **2** to eat/drink all of or the rest of: *The child ate up all her food nicely. Drink up your milk!* (*fig*) *This car just drinks up petrol. He just sat there, eating her up with his eyes.*

imbibe [T1] *fml* to drink: *The doctor said that the patient had imbibed too much alcohol.*

drain [T1] to drink all of: *He drained his glass and asked for more beer.*

take [T1] to introduce into the body through the mouth; eat or drink: *She took the medicine the doctor had given her. Take a deep drink of this; it'll help you feel better. He took a bite out of the apple. Take a sip* [⇒ E8] *of this wine.*

have [T1] to eat, drink, or take into the body: *We were having breakfast when he arrived. Have another drink! He has three cigarettes every morning. When do you usually have your lunch? He had a piece of the cake. Have a drink from this glass.*

E4 *informal verbs* : **eating and drinking**

get down [v adv T1] to swallow, usu unwillingly: *She got the food down somehow, although she felt sick.*

go down [v adv I0] to be swallowed; pass down to the stomach: *Well, that meal went down very nicely. A mouthful of food went down the wrong way* (= into the windpipe, the passage through which one breathes).

keep down [v adv T1] to keep in the stomach after swallowing: *I was sick last week: I just couldn't keep anything down.*

dig in *also* **tuck in** [v adv I0] to start eating: *Okay friends, dig/tuck in and enjoy yourselves!*

put away *also* **tuck away** [v adv T1] to eat: *Well, he certainly tucks away a lot of food!*

peck at [v prep T1] to eat in small amounts, usu without much interest: *She didn't feel hungry and just pecked at her food.*

finish off [v adv T1] to eat until nothing is left: *The boys finished off the ice cream at great speed.*

polish off [v adv T1] to finish off: *They polished off all the food.*

toss off [v adv T1] to swallow (a liquid) quickly: *He tossed off his drink and walked out.*

knock back [v adv T1] to drink quickly, usu in a single movement: *He knocked back two double whiskies in quick succession.*

scoff [T1] *sometimes deprec* to eat eagerly and fast: *He scoffed all the food and left none for us.*

E5 *formal & technical verbs & nouns* : **eating and drinking**

consume [T1] to eat or drink; take into the body: *They consumed a lot of food and drink at that party.* **consumption** [U] the action or result of consuming: *The consumption of food has gone up.*

nourish [Wv4;T1] to cause to stay alive or grow by giving food, water, etc; keep alive and healthy (with food); give food to: *This is nourishing soup. These foods will nourish you as well as anything. That's a well-nourished baby. The rain nourished the grass.* (*fig*) *His speech nourished our hopes that the government would act soon. She nourished a strong dislike for him.* **nourishment** [U] **1** something that nourishes; food: *The man refused all nourishment although the doctor had told him to eat.* **2** the act of nourishing or condition of being nourished

nutrition [U] **1** the action of getting or giving nourishment **2** the science of food values **nutritious** [B] nourishing; helping to nourish **nutriment** [U;C] nourishing food **malnutrition** [U] poor insufficient nourishment

digest [T1] **1** to change (food, etc) in the stomach and bowels, so as to be used to nourish the body: *Food and drink are digested in the stomach.* **2** (*fig*) to think about and (try to) understand, deal with, etc: *We are still digesting the information; we haven't decided what to do. He needed time to digest the bad news.* **digestion** [U] the action or result of digesting; ability to digest food: *Some kinds of food actively help in digestion. The proper digestion of food is a matter which interests doctors.* **digestive** [Wa5;B] relating to or helping digestion: *It is important to have a healthy digestive system. The digestive processes* [⇒ I22] *begin in the mouth.* **indigestion** [U] illness or pain caused by the stomach being unable to digest food: *He suffers very badly from indigestion.*

assimilate [T1] **1** to take (food) into the body after eating; digest: *Babies can only assimilate milk.* **2** [I0] (of food) to be taken into the body; be digested: *Some fats do not assimilate easily.* **assimilation** [U]

subsist on [v prep T1] to stay alive by eating: *The people in that country subsist (mainly) on rice and beans.* **subsistence** [U] the condition of subsisting on any kind of food.

absorb [T1] **1** to take (esp a liquid) in, esp through many small holes: *This kind of material absorbs water easily. Plants absorb sunlight.* **2** (*fig*) to study and learn (something, esp information) well: *She absorbed everything in the book.* **3** [*usu pass* (*in*)] (*fig*) to get the full interest of (someone): *The lesson absorbed everyone. They were absorbed in their work.* **absorbent** [B] able to absorb: *This material is highly absorbent.* **absorption** [U] **1** the action of absorbing **2** [(*in*)] (*fig*) great interest

E6 *verbs, nouns, etc* : **biting and chewing**

bite 1 [I0; T1] to cut, crush, or seize (something) with the teeth: *Does that dog bite? That child* *just bit me on the hand. He bit (into) the cake and began to chew. The little boy bit into the big cake. (fig) This new tax is going to bite (deeply) into my income. Bite a piece off and tell me whether you like it or not. She bit off a piece of cheese and chewed it slowly.* **2** [X9] to cause to exist in this way: *The dog has bitten a hole in my trousers.* **3** [IØ; T1] (of snakes, insects, etc) to prick the skin (of) and draw blood: *A snake will not bite you if you leave it alone.* **4** [IØ] (of fish) to accept food on a fisherman's hook: *I've sat here for hours but the fish are not biting today. (fig) I hoped she would be interested in my plan, but she didn't bite.* **5** [C] an act of biting: *The dog gave its owner's hand a playful bite. He took a bite out of the apple.* **6** [C] a wound made by biting: *Her face was covered in insect bites. He was taken to the hospital to be treated for snakebite.* **7** [C] a piece bitten off: *I found there was a large bite taken out of the apple.* **8** [S] *infml* something to eat: *He's hungry because he hasn't had a bite (to eat) all day.* [⇒ B130 WOUND, CUT, BITE]

chew 1 [IØ; T1] to move and crush (something) in the mouth with the teeth: *Always chew (your food) well before swallowing.* **2** [C] an act of chewing: *He had a few chews but found the meat too tough to eat.* **chew up** [v adv T1] to chew fully; reduce to pieces by chewing: *The dog chewed up the meat and the puppy (= young dog) chewed up the slippers.*

masticate [IØ; T1] *tech & fml* to chew: *Food should always be masticated thoroughly.* **mastication** [U] the action of masticating

crop [T1; X7] (of an animal) to bite off and eat the tops of (grass, plants, etc): *The sheep cropped the grass short.*

gnaw [IØ (at); T1] to bite steadily and continuously, esp rubbing with the teeth: *The dog gnawed (at) the bone. She gnawed her fingernails with anxiety. (fig) Hunger gnawed at them.*

nibble 1 [IØ (at); T1] to bite gently, with small movements of the mouth: *The boy was nibbling (at) a biscuit. The rabbit nibbled the leaves.* **2** [C] an act of nibbling: *He had a nibble at the cake.*

munch [T1 (up); IØ] to chew with strong movements of the mouth: *The cattle munched (up) their food. The child was munching (the sweets) happily.*

away [adv] **1** continuously; steadily: *He munched away at his food. The rats nibbled away at the woodwork. The animal gnawed away at the tree.* **2** to an end; to nothing: *The woodwork has been chewed away by rats.*

E7 *verbs & nouns* : **swallowing and gobbling**

swallow 1 [T1; IØ] to cause to or let (something) go down the throat: *He tried to swallow, but his throat was too dry. She swallowed her medicine with the help of some water.* **2** [T1] *deprec* to eat

without chewing: *He just swallows his food; he's always in a hurry.* **3** [C] an act of swallowing: *He had a few swallows of tea and then hurried out.*

bolt [T1 (down)] to eat or swallow very or too quickly: *He bolted his food and hurried out. That child just bolts his food down.*

gobble [T1 (up)] to eat (greedily [⇒ F180]), noisily, and quickly: *They gobbled all the food (up) before I could get any.*

guzzle [T1; IØ] **1** to drink greedily, noisily, and quickly **2** *BrE* to eat in this way: *She doesn't like watching him guzzle/guzzling his food. She guzzles a lot of food, doesn't she?*

wolf [T1 (down)] to eat quickly and greedily, like a wolf (= a large wild dog): *He just wolfs his food (down); you'd think we didn't feed him enough.*

gorge [T1] to fill (oneself) with food: *He gorged himself on cakes.*

E8 *verbs & nouns* : **sucking and licking**

suck 1 [T1] to draw (liquid, gas, etc) from something into the mouth, through closed or tightened lips: *He was sucking his drink through a straw. He sucked in air, then went under the water again. The elephant sucked up all the water with its trunk* [⇒ A122]. **2** [T1] to hold (something) in the mouth, while drawing liquid from it: *The boy had a sweet in his mouth and was sucking it (hard).* **3** [C] *esp infml* an act of sucking: *'Have a suck of my orange!' the child said.*

sip 1 [T1] to drink (something) a little at a time: *She sipped her drink slowly, to make it last/ because it was hot.* **2** [C] an act of sipping or an amount sipped: *He had a few sips of the strange drink. Take a sip of my drink and see if you like it.*

lick 1 [T1] **a** to pass the tongue over **b** to consume by doing this: *The child licked the ice cream. The dog licked up the salt.* **2** [C] an act of licking: *He had a lick at the ice cream.*

lap up [v adv T1] to lift up with the tongue: *The cat lapped up the milk. (fig) She just laps up (= enjoys) praise.*

E9 *verbs* : **feeding and watering** [T1]

feed to give food to; nourish [⇒ E5]: *It's time to feed the baby/the chickens. Does she feed her husband properly? She was in the park, feeding the birds. What do you feed the cat on? We'll have to feed you up after your illness. (fig) Good books feed the mind. He fed them a lot of false information.*

water to take or give water to: *It's time to water the horses. He was in the garden watering the plants.*

E10 *verbs & nouns* : **not taking or having food or drink**

diet [I0;] to (cause to) live on a diet [⇒ E1]: *He's always dieting, but he's still too fat.*

fast 1 [I0] to refuse or avoid food, esp for a religious reason: *Muslims have to fast between sunrise and sunset during the month of Ramadan.* **2** [C] an act or occasion of fasting: *The religious leader went on a fast to influence his followers.*

starve [I0; T1] **1** to (cause to) die from lack of food: *Those animals will starve (to death) if someone doesn't get food to them soon.* **2** to (cause to) have no food over a long period: *He starved himself to try to lose weight.*

hunger [I0 *(for)*] *lit* to feel hunger: *They hungered and thirsted.* (*fig*) *He hungered for a chance to prove his abilities.*

thirst [I0 *(for)*] *lit* to feel thirst: *They thirsted in the desert.* (*fig*) *He thirsts for knowledge.*

E11 *nouns* : **hunger and thirst**

hunger 1 [U] the wish or need for food: *They felt weak with hunger.* **2** [U] lack of food: *There is hunger in many parts of the world.* **3** [S] (*fig*) any strong wish: *His hunger for excitement got him into a lot of trouble.*

famine [C; U] (a case of) very serious shortage of food: *Many people died during the famine. India has experienced many famines. It was a time of famine and hardship.*

starvation [U] the condition of starving; lack of food over a long period: *The poor people in that land often suffer from starvation. He died of starvation. Those people live in starvation conditions.*

appetite [U; C] **1** a desire or wish, esp for food: *Don't eat anything that will spoil your appetite for dinner.* (*fig*) *He had no appetite for hard work.* **2** a desire to satisfy any bodily want: *His sexual appetites were great.* **whet one's appetite for** to make eager to enjoy or have more of: *That story whetted our appetite for more details.*

thirst 1 [U] the wish or need for something to drink: *Thirst in a hot climate can be a terrible experience.* **2** [C] a wish or need for something to drink: *I have a terrific thirst. Their thirsts were only satisfied by a long cool beer each.*

drought [C] a long period of dry weather when there is not enough water: *The crops and cattle died during last year's drought.* (*fig*) *This place suffers from a musical drought.*

E12 *adjectives* : **hungry and thirsty** [B]

hungry [Wa1] **1** feeling or showing hunger: *I'm hungry after my long walk. He had a hungry look on his face. If you don't eat this food you can go hungry* (= remain without food). (*fig*) *We're hungry for news about our brother.*

2 causing hunger: *This is hungry work.* **-rily** [adv]

ravenous very hungry: *After all that work you must be ravenous.* **-ly** [adv]

starving *also* **famished** *infml* very hungry: *I'm starving! What's for dinner? You must be famished; come in and eat something.*

thirsty [Wa1] **1** feeling or showing thirst: *I'm thirsty after running so far.* **2** causing thirst: *This is thirsty work.* **-tily** [adv]

parched *infml* very thirsty: *I'm parched; I need a long cool drink.*

dry [Wa1] *infml* very thirsty; parched

E13 *nouns* : **kinds of meals**

meal [C] **1** an amount of food eaten at one time: *She cooks a hot meal in the evenings. When did you last have a good meal?* **2** the occasion of eating a meal: *The family have their meals together.* **a square meal** a meal which satisfies: *When did you last have a square meal?*

repast [C] *fml* a meal: *That was an excellent repast.*

snack [C] a light informal meal: *We only have time for a quick snack.*

refreshments [P] light snacks usu sold or given out in a public place: *Refreshments are usually served after the meeting. The sign at the station said 'refreshments'.*

feast [C] a large meal with plenty to eat and drink; a very large, splendid, and sometimes barbaric [⇒ C169] meal: *What a feast she provided! Most of the chiefs came to the great feast.*

banquet [C] **1** a rich feast: *Everything you cook for me is a banquet, darling!* **2** a dinner for many people in honour of a special person or occasion, esp one at which speeches are made

buffet [C] **1** (a place, esp a long table or sideboard [⇒ D117] where one can get) food, usu cold, to be eaten standing up or sitting down somewhere else: *They ate a buffet lunch.* **2** a bar for lunch, refreshments, etc, in a railway station, etc

spread [C] *infml* a table, etc, spread with plenty of food and drink: *What a spread she provided; it was terrific.*

picnic [C] **1** a pleasure trip in which (cold) food is taken to be eaten somewhere in the country or by the sea: *They went on/for a picnic with their friends. They ate a picnic lunch. The food's in the picnic basket.* **2** the meal itself: *That was a good picnic!* **3** [*usu sing*] (*fig*) *infml* something especially easy or pleasant to do: *It's no picnic having to look after small children all day.*

barbecue [C] a meal, usu outdoors, where meat is cooked over an open fire: *Let's have a barbecue on the beach.* [also ⇒ E100]

dinner 1 [C; U] the main meal of the day, eaten either at midday or in the evening: *I'm busy cooking (the) dinner. It's dinner-time/time for dinner. I've cooked you a nice hot dinner. Dinner's ready! What are we having for dinner?*

They ordered two hot dinners. John and Mary are giving a dinner party. **2** [C] a formal occasion in the evening when this meal is eaten: *The firm are having an important dinner on Tuesday and I must be there. He's been to quite a lot of public dinners lately.*

E14 *nouns* : **times for meals in Britain**

among the English middle class, and the upper class generally	among the English working class, and in Scotland generally	time (approximately)
breakfast		in the morning, on getting out of bed
lunch *fml* luncheon	dinner	12 noon (1200 hrs) – 2 pm (1400 hrs)
(afternoon) tea	a cup of tea	4 pm (1600 hrs) – 5 pm (1700 hrs)
	(high) tea	5 pm (1700 hrs) – 6 pm (1800 hrs), a cooked meal, but less than dinner
dinner, supper		7 pm (1900 hrs) – 8.30 pm (2030 hrs), a large cooked meal, usu the main meal of the day
	supper	9 pm (2100 hrs) – 10 pm (2200 hrs), a small meal before going to bed

E15 *verbs* : **having a meal**

breakfast [IØ] to have breakfast: *They breakfasted early/late/at.7*
lunch [IØ] to have lunch: *He usually lunches at a little restaurant round the corner. She lunches out* (= out of the office, college, etc) *but the*

other girl *lunches in* (= in the office, college, etc).
dine [IØ] *often fml* to have dinner: *They dined at eight with the Smiths. She dined in, but he dined out* (*of college*). **diner** [C] **1** a person who is dining in a place **2** esp one beside a road: *We ate at Fred's Diner in Blackett Street.*
banquet 1 [IØ] to take part in a banquet [⇒ E13]: *They banqueted until the early hours of the morning.* **2** [T1] to arrange or have a banquet for (someone): *They banqueted her royally when she became director of the company.*
picnic [IØ] to go on or have a picnic: *We're picnicking tomorrow. They picnicked under the trees.* **picnicker** [C] a person on a picnic
feast [IØ (*on*)] to eat a lot of food: *They feasted on chicken and rice.*
serve [T1] **1** to give food to (people eating): *This is a buffet lunch; please serve yourselves.* **2** to put (food) on the table, on plates, etc: *She served the whole meal herself.*
dish out [v adv T1 (*to*)] *infml* to serve (food) to a number of people: *She dished out plenty of food to everybody.*
dish up [v adv T1] *infml* to serve (food) into dishes, ready to be eaten: *Dish up the food while it is still hot.*

E16 *nouns* : **parts of meals** [C]

dish (an amount of) cooked food of one kind: *Baked apples are his favourite dish. I like Italian dishes. What was the main dish/course?*
portion a quantity of food for one person as served in a restaurant, etc: *He was hungry and ordered two portions of fish.*
helping *not fml* a portion of food: *I'd like a second helping, please. The helpings are generous in that restaurant.*
seconds [P] *infml* second helpings
serving 1 a portion or helping **2** *also* **sitting** (at large gatherings) a first or second opportunity to be served food: *Those who missed the first serving/sitting ate later, at the second serving/sitting.*
course a part or stage of a meal, often served formally and often described according to the main food provided (as in the **fish course, meat course,** but usu not in the sweet, coffee, etc): *The number of courses in a meal varies according to the formality and the size of the meal. It was a four-course meal.*
ration the amount, esp of food, given to one person or animal at one time: *This is the prisoner's ration for today. The soldiers' rations arrived.*
menu 1 the list of dishes, etc, available in a restaurant, hotel, etc: *What is today's menu?* **2** the card, paper, or booklet in which the menu is printed or written: *Pass me a menu, please. The new menus have just been printed.*

E17 *nouns* : **courses in meals**

aperitif [C] *Fr* a small alcoholic drink served to increase the appetite [⇒ E11] before a meal: *Would you care for an aperitif?*

hors d'oeuvre [C *usu pl*] *Fr* one of several types of tasty food offered in small quantities at the beginning of a meal: *The hors d'oeuvres were excellent.*

appetizer, -iser *also infml* **starter** [C] a small serving of juice, fruit, seafood, etc, at the beginning of a meal to make people want to eat: *This is just an appetizer; don't eat too much.*

soup [U;C] the usu first course in a (formal) dinner or meal [⇒ E38]

fish [U] the fish course in a formal meal, usu served after the soup and before the entrée

main course [C] the chief course, usu a hot meat dish, in a (formal) dinner or meal

entrée [C] *Fr* the main course of a meal, usually the third course in a formal dinner, generally a hot meat dish

dessert [C;U] sweet food served towards the end of a meal

sweet [U;C] *BrE* a sweet dish, usu a pudding [⇒ E51] or made with fruit, usu served after the main course in a meal

pudding [U;C] *also* **pud** *BrE infml* dessert

afters [P] *BrE infml* the part of a meal that comes after the main dish, usu something sweet: *What's for afters?—Chocolate cake.*

cheese and biscuits [GU] a selection of cheeses and biscuits [⇒ E44], esp served at the end of a formal dinner

delicacy [C] something pleasing to eat that is (considered) rare or expensive: *That food is a great delicacy here.*

savoury *BrE*, **savory** *AmE* [C] something pleasant to eat but with a salty rather than a sweet taste; last course in a formal meal

coffee [U] the last stage of most present-day European and American dinner parties, where coffee is taken either at the table or in the living room

leftovers [P] food remaining uneaten after a meal, esp when served at a later meal

E18 *nouns, etc* : **cutlery**

cutlery [U] knives, forks, and spoons used when eating

fork [C] an instrument for holding food or carrying it to the mouth, having a handle at one end and two or more points at the other

knife [C] a blade fixed in a handle, used for cutting

spoon [C *often in comb*] an instrument with a small bowl and a handle used for taking food, liquid, etc esp to the mouth when eating

spoonful [C] the amount that can be taken in a spoon: *He put two spoonfuls of sugar in his tea.*

teaspoon [C] a small spoon used when taking tea **teaspoonful** [C] the amount that can be taken in a teaspoon

tablespoon [C] a larger spoon used esp for soup, etc **tablespoonful** [C] the amount that can be taken in a tablespoon: *Take a tablespoonful of the medicine before meals.*

ladle 1 [C] a large deep spoon with a long handle, used for serving liquids **2** [T1] to serve by using a ladle: *He ladled the soup into her plate.*

Food

E30 **A general note on vegetables, etc**
[⇒ A134 FRUIT, BERRIES, NUTS, GRAIN, SEEDS]
[⇒ A136 VEGETABLES]

The same word is used for vegetables when growing and when being cooked or eaten, but some words are usu [U] and others [C], and some are both, depending on how they are cooked and served, as in the following lists:

always [U]	[C]; *in cooking or as food* [U]	[C *usu pl*]
asparagus	aubergine *BrE*/	bean
celery	egg plant *AmE*	brussels
spinach	beetroot [Wn2]	sprout
	cabbage	carrot
	cauliflower	leek
	cucumber	lentil
	lettuce	mushroom
	marrow *BrE*/	pea
	squash *AmE*	radish
	onion	
	potato	
	tomato	
	turnip	

Note: All these words can be [A]: *Would you like asparagus soup, onion soup, or lentil soup?*

Examples: Have some more asparagus. We've got lots of cabbages in the garden, but we don't like boiled cabbage very much. Carrots are very cheap—it's good for you to eat carrots.

vegetarian [C; Wa5;B] (of) a person who does not eat meat: *They like eating in that vegetarian restaurant although they aren't vegetarians themselves.* **vegetarianism** [U] the ideas, way of life, etc, of a vegetarian

E31 *nouns* : **meat, etc**

meat [U;C] the flesh [⇒ B4] of animals, apart from fish and birds, which is eaten: *This meat is tough; it's hard to eat. The butcher sells different kinds of meat/different meats. Two meat pies* [⇒ E46]*, please. Some people are meat-eaters; others are vegetarians.*

fowl [U] the flesh of birds as food: *Roast* [⇒ E100] *fowl was served at the dinner.*

poultry [U] birds kept as a source of food, such as chickens and geese: *They eat a lot of poultry.*

fish [U] the parts of fish that can be eaten: *They had fish for tea.*

kipper [C] a salted herring (= a kind of sea fish) either smoked or dried so that it will not go bad

egg 1 [U] the parts inside the shell of an egg, esp of a hen, esp when eaten: *The child got egg on his face while eating. Is there egg in this pudding?* **2** [C] an egg, esp of a hen, esp as for eating: *Can I have bacon and two fried eggs, please? She had a boiled egg for breakfast.*

game [U] (the meat of) any animal living wild or hunted for its meat: *This is very good game soup.*

E32 *nouns* : **kinds of meat** [U]
[⇒ A52–7 ANIMALS]

beef 1 the meat of farm cattle: *They had a meal of boiled beef and potatoes.* **2** any form of cattle, esp an ox, when fattened to produce meat: *He raises beef on his farm.*

pork fresh meat from pigs: *It's roast* [⇒ E100] *pork for dinner. Can I have a pork pie* [⇒ E46], *please?*

ham meat from a pig's leg, esp if salted, or smoked: *She likes boiled ham.*

bacon salted or smoked meat from the back and sides of a pig: *He likes bacon and eggs. A kilo of bacon please.*

gammon *BrE* the lower end of a side of bacon

mutton the meat of the sheep: *She got some mutton from the butcher. Two mutton chops* [⇒ E33], *please.*

lamb the meat of a young sheep: *Roast lamb is one of his favourite dishes/meals.*

veal the meat of a calf (= young cow)

venison the meat of the deer: *Venison is considered a delicacy by many.*

NOTE 1 For most other animals, birds, and fish the same word is used for both the meat [U] and the creature [C]: **chicken,** from a chicken; **salmon,** from a salmon; **rabbit,** from a rabbit, etc

NOTE 2 The organs of an animal's body when prepared as a food generally keep the same name [U]: **liver,** from the liver; **heart,** from the heart; **chicken liver,** from a chicken's liver, etc

E33 *nouns* : **ways of cutting meat for cooking**

cut [C] a piece of meat got by cutting it from the dead animal: *He sold her several nice cuts of beef.*

joint [C] any part of an animal body, as cut up by a butcher for cooking: *That's a nice joint of beef.*

slice [C] a thin piece cut from the body of an edible [⇒ E108] animal: *Two slices of veal, please.*

cutlet [C] a slice of meat, fish, etc (for one person)

steak 1 [C; U] a (usu large) thick cut of meat or fish: *He enjoys a good (beef) steak. What's for dinner?—Cod steaks* (= steaks of cod, a large sea fish). **2** [U] *BrE* chopped meat prepared by stewing [⇒ E100], etc: *A kilo of your best stewing steak, please.*

chop [C] a small thick piece of meat, usu containing a bone, for one person to eat: *We're having lamb chops for dinner.*

fillet [C; U] **1** a piece of meat without bones **2** the flesh of a fish with the bones removed

side [C] a large piece cut from the side of an edible animal: *He bought a whole side of pork.*

flitch [C] a side of bacon

rasher [C] a slice of bacon or ham to be fried or grilled [⇒ E100]

leg [C; U] the leg of a fleshy animal as food: *That's a nice leg of lamb.*

E34 *nouns* : **cuts of meat** [C; U]

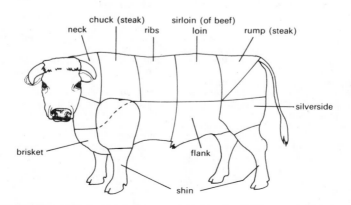

of beef

neck   chuck (steak)   ribs   sirloin (of beef)   loin   rump (steak)

silverside

brisket   flank   shin

of mutton/lamb

of pork

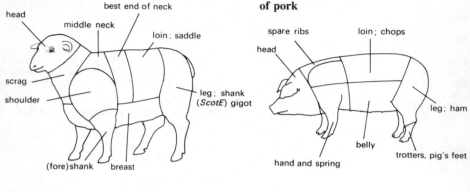

parts of poultry

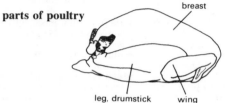

E35 nouns : offal and other meats

offal [U] *esp BrE* parts of an animal (the heart, liver, kidneys, brains, etc) which are sometimes not considered as good as the flesh for food

tripe [U] the lining or walls of the stomach of a bullock [⇒ A52] used as food

giblets [P] the inner parts of poultry (neck, heart, liver, etc, usu used for soup and stock [⇒ E39]

tongue [U] the tongue of an animal, usu a cow or sheep, prepared as food

oxtail [U; C] the tail of a cow or ox, used esp for stews and soups

E36 nouns : ways of presenting meat as food

[ALSO ⇒ E100]

stew [U; C] stewed [⇒ E100] meat of any kind: *She's good at making tasty stews. What's for lunch?—Beef stew.*

mince *BrE*, **ground beef** *AmE* [U] minced [⇒ E103] meat, used for stews, etc: *Mince and potatoes is a popular dish in Scotland.*

roast [C *usu sing*] meat when it is to be, or has been, roasted: *We're having a roast for dinner tonight.*

curry [U; C] a type of food in and from India made to taste hot with spices [⇒ E49]: *Curry can have meat or vegetables or both in it. He enjoys South Indian curries. That's a nice chicken curry.*

E37 nouns : sausages and similar foods

sausage 1 [C] pork [⇒ E32] or other meat, minced [⇒ E103] and packed tightly into tubes (**skins**) usu made from the gut [⇒ B35] of an animal, sometimes fried [⇒ E100] and eaten hot, sometimes cut up and eaten cold: *He likes German sausages. She ate a meal of sausages and potatoes.* **2** [U] *also* **sausage meat** the kind of minced meat, seasoning [⇒ E49], etc, usu put in tubes of this kind

sausage roll [C] a cooked roll of pastry with sausage meat inside

rissole [C] minced meat made into a cake or ball, fried [⇒ E100] in fat

frankfurter [C] a sausage of minced pork, lightly smoked and usu about 20 cm in length

hamburger *also* **beefburger** [C] a cake of minced beef [⇒ E32], fried or grilled and sometimes served with fried onions and eaten in a bread roll

hot dog [C] *esp AmE* a frankfurter sausage boiled and put in a soft bread roll and served hot

haggis [U; C] *esp ScotE* a seasoned [⇒ E105] mixture of liver, heart, etc, mixed with oatmeal [⇒ E43] and cooked in a bag made from the stomach of a sheep

pudding [U9; C9] **1** *also* **pud** *infml BrE* an unsweetened dish of a mixture of flour, fat, etc, either covering or enclosing meat and boiled with it: *I love steak and kidney pud(ding).* **2** a type of sausage filled with meat cut small: *She likes black pudding.*

stuffing [U] any mixture (such as sausage meat, minced pork, herbs [⇒ A136], rice, bread-crumbs, and vegetables) chopped [⇒ E33] or minced and seasoned, with which meat, poul-try, or game [⇒ E31] is filled (**stuffed**)

E38 nouns : soups

soup [U; C] **1** a liquid food, usu served before solid food, made by cooking meat and/or vege-tables in water, etc, and usu named according to the main things in it: *He likes chicken soup but my favourite is mushroom soup. Her mother's tomato soups are delicious.* **2** (*fig*) anything thick and full of various things, like soup

broth [U; C] a thick soup, usu made with bones, with vegetables, flour, etc, added to thicken it: *That's a nice beef broth.*

consommé [U; C] *Fr* a clear soup, often obtained from bones

cream [U *of*] a strong thick soup: *She likes cream of chicken soup.*

E39 nouns : juices and gravies [U; C]

juice the liquid in meats

gravy 1 the juice which comes out of meats when cooked, usu flavoured with stock and thickened with flour, usu served with or added to a meat dish **2** any similar (meat) juice

stock the juice of boiled bones, etc, used in making soup and gravy and often kept spe-cially for this purpose

sauce a (sweet or salty) liquid served with or on food

E40 nouns : fats and oils [U]

fat the fat of animals used for cooking: *She fried* [⇒ E100] *the potatoes in deep fat.* **fatty** [Wa1;B] of or like fat; containing a lot of fat **-tiness** [U]

lard the fat of the pig made pure by melting, used in cooking

suet hard fat used for cooking

oil [*often in comb*] any of several types of fatty liquids (from animals, plants, or under the ground) used for cooking: *She always cooks in corn oil.* **oily** [Wa1;B] of or like oil; containing a lot of oil **-iness** [U]

dripping fat and juices which come from meat during cooking

ghee, ghi butter in liquid form, as used in India for cooking

grease animal fat when soft after being melted: *You never get the grease off the plates if you don't wash them properly.* **greasy** [Wa1;B] of or like grease; containing a lot of grease **-sily** [adv] **-siness** [U]

E41 nouns : milk and milk products, etc

milk [U] **1** a white liquid produced by human or animal females for the feeding of their young, and (of certain animals such as the cow or goat) drunk by human beings or made into other foods: *Drink your milk. That's a nice milk pudding.* **2** a whitish liquid or juice obtained from certain plants and trees, such as **coconut milk**

cream 1 [U] that part of milk which contains the most fat and which rises to the top when milk is left to stand **2** [*the* R] (*fig*) the best of any-thing: *Those children are the cream of the school.*

butter [U] **1** fat, usu yellow, made from milk, spread on bread, used in cooking, etc **2** [U9] a substance like butter made from something else: *He likes peanut* [⇒ A153] *butter.*

margarine, *also esp BrE infml* **marge** [U] a food like butter but made esp from vegetable oils: *He doesn't eat butter and only has mar-garine on his bread.*

cheese [U; C] a solid food made from sour milk and made in both hard and soft forms: *There are many kinds of cheese and French and Italian cheeses are famous.*

yoghurt, yogurt, yoghourt [U] milk that has turned thick and slightly acid through the action of certain bacteria [⇒ A37], often eaten with fruit

curds [P] a thick soft near-liquid food formed from sour milk **curdle** [IØ] (of liquids, esp milk) to separate when sour to form a thick substance (**curds**) on top and thin liquid (**whey**) underneath

skimmed milk *also* **skim milk** [U] milk from which the cream has been removed

buttermilk [U] the liquid that remains after butter is made from milk

E42 verbs : relating to milk

milk 1 [T1; IØ] to take the milk from (a cow, goat, or other animal): *On modern farms cows are no longer milked by hand. The farmer sang as he milked.* **2** [T1] (*fig*) to get money, know-ledge of a secret, etc, from (someone or something) by clever or dishonest means: *He milked his rich aunt until she hadn't a penny left.*

butter [T1] to spread with or as if with butter: *She buttered some bread for the children.*

cream [Wv5; T1] to beat (some food, such as potatoes) until creamy

pasteurize, -ise [Wv5; T1] to heat (esp milk) in a certain way in order to destroy bacteria: *pasteurized milk.*

homogenize, -ise [Wv5; T1] to make (parts of a whole) become evenly spread: *homogenized milk* (= where there is no cream, because the fat is broken up all through the liquid)

E43 *nouns* : **flour and dough** [U; (C)]
[ALSO ⇒ A134, 152 GRAIN]

flour powder made from grain, esp wheat, and used for baking bread, cakes, etc

meal coarse flour

oatmeal meal made from oats [⇒ A152]

dough flour mixed with water and ready for baking

yeast a type of very small plant life (**fungus**) that is used to make bread light and soft and to produce alcohol in beer and wine

leaven 1 a yeast acting on dough to make it rise **2** a mass of dough and leaven kept to produce similar effects in new dough **3** (*fig*) anything that acts in any other thing to produce a change **leavened** [Wa5;B] treated with leaven **un-** [*neg*]

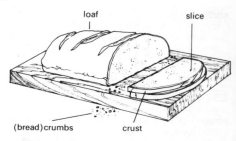
loaf   slice

(bread)crumbs   crust

crust [C; U] the harder top or outer part of a loaf

slice [C] a wide flat piece cut from a loaf

(bread)crumbs [P] small pieces of bread, esp as used in cooking, to cover meatballs, fish, etc, for cooking in hot fat

E44 *nouns* : **bread and cakes**

bread [U *often in comb*] a common food made of baked flour, either leavened [⇒ E43] or not: *He put butter and jam on his bread. I prefer brown bread to white bread.*

roll *also* **bread roll** [C] a small amount of leavened dough baked in a ball: *She ordered a dozen rolls.*

cake 1 [C; U *often in comb*] a shaped piece of baked dough, esp leavened and usu sweetened and soft and one of many kinds: *She served them tea and cakes. Have some fruitcake. Have another rice cake.* **2** [C] any baked piece of dough of any kind **3** [C] a flattened mass of material formed by pressing or drying and not necessarily for eating: *a cake of soap*

biscuit [C] **1** *BrE* any of many types of flat dry unleavened cakes, sweetened or unsweetened and baked hard, as sold in tins or packets **2** *AmE* a scone

bun [C] **1** a small round soft sweet cake, made of leavened dough: *He had some tea and buns.* **2** *esp AmE* a bread roll (as for hamburgers [⇒ E37])

cookie [C] **1** *esp AmE* a biscuit **2** *ScotE* a bun

pancake [C] a thin soft flat cake made of flour, milk, eggs, etc, cooked in an open pan and usu eaten hot

scone [C] *BrE* a soft cake of flour, fat, and egg: *She gave them tea and hot buttered scones.*

oatcake *also* **bannock** *ScotE & N EngE* a thin hard dry flat cake of unleavened oatmeal or barley meal [⇒ E43]

toast [U] bread in slices which have been toasted: *Have some more toast.*

E45 *nouns* : **a loaf of bread and its parts**

loaf [C] a mass of bread baked as a separate amount and sold or eaten separately: *Two loaves and a pint of milk, please.*

E46 *nouns* : **pastry and pastries**

pastry 1 [U] a firm mixture made of flour, fat, and liquid, eaten when baked, used esp to enclose other foods: *Her pastry is always lovely and light.* **2** [C] an article of food (esp a small sweet cake) made wholly or partly of this: *That baker sells a lot of different pastries.* **3** [U] these articles in general

paste [U; C] a mixture of flour, fat, and a small amount of liquid, for making pastry

pie [C; U] an often round pastry case filled with meat or fruit, baked usu in a deep dish (**pie dish**): *He ate a meat pie and an apple pie. Have some more pie.*

tart [C] a circle of pastry baked in an open rather flat dish, and covered with fruit or jam [⇒ E47]: *She made some jam tarts for tea.*

batter [U] a mixture of flour, eggs, milk, etc, for cooking in hot fat, esp covering other food: *The fish was fried in batter.*

fritter [C] a thin piece of fruit, meat, or vegetable, covered with batter and cooked in hot fat: *He likes apple fritters.*

wafer [C] flour, sugar, etc, cooked in the form of a very thin flat cake: *The ice cream was shaped like a ball and had a wafer in it.*

noodle [C] a usu long piece of a paste made from flour, water, and eggs: *The noodles are boiled until soft and eaten in soups, with meat, etc.*

E47 *nouns* : **jams and spreads**

jam [U; C] fruit boiled in sugar until it can be spread on bread: *Have some more bread and jam. That's nice strawberry jam.*

marmalade [U; C] a type of jam made from oranges or other citrus fruit (⇒ A150)

jelly [U; C] fruit (or other) juice boiled with sugar until soft, clear, and fairly solid, used for eating on bread or with meat, etc: *Jelly is clear and has no solid pieces of fruit in it; jam is cloudy and can contain pieces of fruit.*

honey [U] the sweet sticky soft material produced by bees, which is usu eaten on bread

paste [U; C] a food made by crushing solid foods into a smooth soft mass, used for spreading on bread: *He put fish paste on his sandwiches. What kind of meat paste is this?*

spread [U; C] a food made soft enough to spread on bread: *Have some cheese spread; it's very nice. This salmon* (= a large kind of fish) *spread is excellent.*

E48 nouns : forms of potatoes as food

mashed potatoes [P] *also* **mash** *esp EngE* [U] potatoes mashed (= crushed) into a soft mass: *He likes mashed potatoes with his stew. She made them sausages and mash.*

chip *BrE*, **French fry, French fried potato** *AmE* [C *usu pl*] a piece of cut-up potato cooked in hot deep fat: *He had fish and chips for his tea.*

crisp *BrE*, **chip** *AmE* [C] a thin slice of potato cooked in hot fat until hard: *He bought a packet of (potato) crisps/chips.*

E49 nouns : condiments

condiment [C] *fml* a substance such as salt or pepper used at the table

salt [U] salt kept on the table or in the kitchen for use in or on food: *Pass the salt, please. There's too much salt in this soup.* **salty** [Wa1;B] of or like salt; having the taste of salt **-iness** [U] **saltcellar** [C] a container for salt on a table, usu with one or more holes in the top

pepper [U] **1** a hot-tasting, greyish, black, or pale yellowish powder made from the crushed seeds of certain plants (**black pepper; white pepper**) used to make food more tasty **2** a similar powder made from certain other plants, such as **paprika** **peppery** [Wa2;B] of or like pepper; having the taste of pepper **pepper pot** *also* **pepperbox** *AmE* a container with small holes in the top, used for shaking pepper onto food

mustard [U; C] a yellow or brown powder made from the seeds of the mustard plant, mixed with water or vinegar and used as seasoning: *He likes English mustard but she prefers French mustards.*

vinegar [U] a kind of weak acid made from wine, cider [⇒ E67], beer, etc, and used to preserve or flavour food: *He sprinkled* [⇒ M59] *vinegar on his fish and chips.* **vinegary** [Wa2;B] of or like vinegar; having the taste of vinegar

cruet [C] **1** a metal stand or holder for containers of salt, pepper, mustard, vinegar, etc **2** any of these containers placed on the table

seasoning [U; C] a substance or substances that improve the taste of food: *There is a lot of seasoning in this soup.*

spice 1 [C; U] a substance, usu a powder, made from dried vegetables, used to improve the taste of food: *Ginger is a spice.* **2** [U] (*fig*) excitement; greater interest: *Adventure adds spice to life.* **spiced** [B] treated with spices **spicy** [Wa1;B] of or like spice; tasting of spice **-iness** [U]

pickle [U] *also* **pickles** [P] vegetables, fruit, etc, which have been pickled [⇒ E107] and are served as a condiment: *Have some lemon pickle.*

(tomato) ketchup *also* **catsup** [U] a thick red sour liquid used to give a pleasant taste to food, prepared from tomatoes

E50 nouns : salads and sandwiches, etc

salad [U; C] any dish made up (mainly) of raw vegetables and served alone with or without cold meat, or with cheese: *Pass the salad. That's a nice cheese salad* (cheese served with salad).

salad dressing [U] a liquid mixture such as mayonnaise added to salad to improve the taste

mayonnaise 1 [U] a thick yellowish liquid with eggs, oil, vinegar, etc, in it, which may be poured over cold foods **2** [U9] a dish which contains solid food in a liquid of this type: *He likes egg mayonnaise.*

French dressing [U] a liquid made of oil and vinegar, used for putting on salads

sandwich [C] usu two slices of bread with some kind of food spread over one slice and then covered by the other, eaten in a light meal or on a picnic, etc: *He had some chicken sandwiches in his bag.*

roll [C9] a small loaf for one person, cut and filled with the stated food: *He had some cheese rolls in his bag.*

E51 nouns : puddings, jellies, and ices

pudding [C; U] a usu solid sweet dish based on pastry, grain, bread, etc, with fat and (dried) fruit or other substances added to it. It is then baked, boiled, or steamed, and served hot: *We had an apple pudding for dessert. She loves rice pudding. Mum makes wonderful puddings!*

mincemeat [U] a mixture of dried fruit, dried orange skin, and other things, all cut into very small pieces, that is used as a sweet food to put inside pastry **mince pie** [C] a kind of small pie containing mincemeat

jelly [U; C] **1** *AmE usu* (*tdmk*) **jello** a sweet soft food substance that shakes when moved, made with gelatin [⇒ H9] **2** other substances that are not sweet

ice cream [U; C] a sweet mixture which is frozen and eaten cold: *Let's buy some ice cream. Two ice creams, please—one strawberry ice cream and one chocolate ice cream.*

ice [C] an ice cream: *These ices are very nice.*

ice-lolly *AmE usu* **popsicle** *tdmk* [C] a piece

of ice on a stick, which tastes of fruit, etc: *The children were licking ice-lollies.*

vanilla [U] a substance from a plant of the same name, that is used to give a special pleasant taste to food such as ice cream and puddings: *vanilla ice cream*

E52 *nouns* : forms of sugar

sugar [U; C] a sweet substance, usu a powder, obtained from the juice of certain plants (**sugar cane, sugar beet, sorghum,** and the **maple tree**) and used to sweeten foods and to ferment [⇒ E70] alcoholic drinks: *He put two spoonfuls of sugar in his tea.* **sugary** [Wa2;B] **1** of or like sugar **2** (*fig*) *deprec* too sweet **-iness** [U]

syrup [U; C] any thick sweet liquid made from sugar, fruit, etc **syrupy** [Wa2;B] of or like syrup; *fig deprec* too sweet

treacle *BrE*, **molasses** *AmE* [U] a thick dark syrup obtained when making sugar **treacly** [Wa1;B] of or like treacle

icing [U] a thick paste of sugar used for putting on cakes

icing sugar [U] the loose powdery sugar used in making icing

E53 *nouns* : sweets and candies

sweet [C] *esp EngE* something sweet, usu made of sugar, to eat or to suck: *The child had a big bag of sweets. May I have a sweet?*

candy 1 [C; U] *esp AmE* (a shaped piece of) various types of boiled sugar sweets or chocolates **2** [U] a very sweet soft sugary food: *He eats too much candy; it'll make him sick.*

confectionery [U] sweets and candies generally: *The shop sells newspapers, tobacco, and confectionery.*

sweetmeat [C] *old use* a sweet

sweetie [C] *BrE* (*used esp by or to children*) & *ScotE* a sweet

chocolate 1 [U] a solid sweet brown substance made from the crushed seeds of a tropical American tree (**cacao**), eaten as a sweet: *Have another piece of chocolate.* **2** [C] a small sweet made by covering a centre, such as a nut, with this substance: *Never eat chocolates before dinner.* **3** [U] a sweet brown powder made by crushing this substance, used for giving a special taste to sweet foods and drinks [⇒ ALSO E62 COCOA]

(chewing) gum [U] a gum [⇒ H9], usu sweetened, etc, made to be kept in the mouth and chewed [⇒ E6] steadily but not swallowed

toffee, also **taffy** *AmE* [U; C] a sweet made from sugar or molasses to be chewed: *Have some toffee. These are nice toffees.*

lollipop also **lolly** *infml BrE* [C] a hard toffee or similar sweet on a stick: *The child put out his tongue and licked his lollipop.*

caramel 1 [U; B] (of, concerning, or like) a sweet substance made from sugar which has been slightly burnt **2** [C] a piece of this substance eaten as a sweet: *Have some caramels.*

Drinks

E60 *nouns* : kinds of drink generally
[ALSO ⇒ E2]

drink [U; C] a liquid suitable for swallowing

draught *AmE usu* **draft,** [C] **1** an act of swallowing liquid or the amount of liquid swallowed at one time, usu large: *He drank the glass of water in one draught.* **2** *lit* a liquid for drinking, esp a medicine: *He took a sleeping draught.* **on draught** (of liquids) drawn from a large container such as a barrel **draught beer** [U] beer on draught

hot/cold drink [C] a drink which is served or taken hot/cold

alcoholic drink/beverage [C] a drink/beverage with alcohol in it

strong drink [U] alcoholic drinks generally

non-alcoholic drink [C] a drink without alcohol in it

soft drink [C] a non-alcoholic drink: *They are only allowed to sell/provide soft drinks at school dances.*

E61 *nouns* : cold non-alcoholic drinks

(fruit) juice [U; C; *often in comb*] the juice of a fruit taken as a drink: *Have some more (orange) juice.*

lemonade [U; C] **1** *BrE* a drink made from sugar, water, and lemon [⇒ A150] flavouring, with added gas **2** *AmE* a drink from fresh lemons, sugar, and water **3** *BrE* lemon squash

pop [U; C] a usu sweet drink with added gas

soda (water) [U; C] **1** water which contains carbon dioxide [⇒ H74], often drunk mixed with whisky [⇒ E65]: *Two whisky and sodas, please.* **2** *esp AmE* pop

tonic (water) [U; C] water which contains a substance (**quinine**) and carbon dioxide, usu taken in cocktails [⇒ E66], or with gin [⇒ E65]: *Two gin and tonics, please.*

squash [U; C] *BrE* a drink made from sweetened fruit juice which is mixed with water before serving

mineral water 1 [U; C *usu pl*] water that comes from a natural spring and contains minerals, often drunk for health reasons: *Visitors to this town drink its mineral water.* **2** [U; C] *BrE* a drink containing gas, often sweetened and given a particular taste (as of oranges), mostly sold in bottles

cola [U; C] a drink made with the juice of the cola nut

Coca cola [U;C] *tdmk* a cola drink containing carbon dioxide
coke [U;C] *infml* Coca cola
ginger ale/beer [U;C] a gassy drink made with ginger

E62 *nouns* : **warm non-alcoholic drinks**

tea 1 [U] a drink, usu served hot, made from the leaves of the tea bush: *She likes her tea with milk and sugar in it. Is that Indian or China tea?* **2** [C] tea in a cup: *Two teas, please.*
coffee 1 [U] a drink served hot, made from the dried bean of the coffee tree: *He likes his coffee without milk. They sell all kinds of coffee in that shop. Would you like your coffee black* (= without milk) *or white* (= with milk), *Sir?* **2** [C] coffee in a cup: *Two coffees, please.*
cocoa *also* **hot/drinking chocolate 1** [U] chocolate powder which can be mixed with hot milk (and water) to make a hot drink: *Two cups of chocolate, please.* **2** [C] (a cupful of) a drink made from these substances: *I had a coffee and she had a chocolate.*

E63 *nouns, etc* : **alcoholic drinks generally**

alcohol [U] **1** the pure colourless liquid present in (and responsible for) drinks that can make a person drunk, such as wine, beer, and spirits **2** the drinks containing this **alcoholic 1** [B] containing alcohol **2** [B] of, concerning, or caused by alcohol **3** [C] a person who cannot break the habit of drinking alcoholic drinks too much, esp one whose health is damaged because of this **4** [B] of or like an alcoholic **alcoholism** [U] the habit or illness of an alcoholic
drink 1 [U] alcoholic drinks generally: *He took to drink when his business failed.* **2** [C] an alcoholic drink: *Can I buy you a drink?*
booze *sl* **1** [U] alcoholic drink **2** [I0] to drink alcohol, esp too much alcohol: *He spends every night boozing with his friends.*
liquor [U] **1** *BrE fml or tech* alcoholic drink **2** *AmE* strong alcoholic drink, such as whisky
tot [C] a small measure of drink, esp of an alcoholic drink, esp of whisky, etc

E64 *nouns* : **spirits generally**

spirits [P] strong alcoholic drink, esp such distilled [⇒ E70] drinks as whisky, brandy, and gin
liqueur [U;C] *Fr* an alcoholic drink made by mixing (esp) brandy with sugar and other substances to give it a special taste

E65 *nouns* : **particular spirits, etc**

whisky 1 [U;C] a strong alcoholic drink made from malted grain such as barley [⇒ A152] and containing 43–50% alcohol **2** [C] an amount of whisky drunk in one glass: *Two whiskies, please.*
whiskey [U;C] whisky esp from Ireland or the USA
Scotch [U;C] *EngE & AmE* any type of whisky made in Scotland: *Have some Scotch. Two Scotches, please.*
bourbon [U;C] a type of American whiskey, usu made from maize [⇒ A152]
rye [U;C] a type of American whiskey, usu made from rye [⇒ A152]
mash [U;C] grain placed for a long time in hot water in making whisky
malt 1 [U] grain left in water and allowed to grow a little as part of the preparation of whisky **2** [C] a whisky made wholly from this **malted** [B] (of grain) made into or becoming malt
brandy [U;C] a strong alcoholic drink made usu from the juice of grapes [⇒ A150] but also from apples or other stated fruit: *This is excellent brandy. She poured him some plum brandy. Have another brandy.*
rum [U;C] a strong alcoholic drink made from molasses [⇒ E52]
gin [U;C] a colourless alcoholic drink made from grain
martini [C] a cocktail [⇒ E67] made by mixing gin, vermouth [⇒ E68], and bitters: *Two dry martinis, please.*
vodka [U;C] a type of strong, colourless, and almost tasteless alcoholic drink first made in (and very popular in) Russia and Poland
bitters [U;P] a liquid, usu alcoholic, in which bitter herbs [⇒ A136] have been placed for a long time and used in giving other drinks a special taste

E66 *nouns* : **kinds of beer**

beer 1 [U] a bitter alcoholic drink made from grain: *He was so thirsty he drank a whole pint of beer down.* **2** [C] a separate drink or container of this: *He had several beers before lunch.*
ale [U;C] any of various types of strong beer, esp one that is pale in colour
stout [U;C] *esp BrE* a dark sweet ale with a strong malt [⇒ E65] taste
lager 1 [U] a light kind of beer **2** [C] a drink, glass, or bottle of this: *Two lagers, please.*
mild [U] *esp BrE* dark beer or ale which is less bitter than usual: *A pint of mild, please.*
bitter [U] *esp BrE* beer that is more bitter than usual: *A half* (*pint*) *of bitter, please.*
shandy [U;C] (a drink of) beer with lemonade or ginger beer in it: *She prefers shandy to ordinary beer. Two shandies, please.*

E67 nouns : other alcoholic drinks

wine [U; C] an alcoholic drink made from grapes [⇒ A150]: *He likes wine with his evening meal. These Spanish wines are excellent. Which would you prefer—red wine or white?*

cider 1 [U] *also esp AmE* **hard cider** an alcoholic drink made from the juice of apples **2** [U] *also esp AmE* **soft cider** juice pressed from apples and used as a drink or for making vinegar [⇒ E49] **3** [C] a drink, glass, or bottle of either of these: *I'd like two ciders and a beer, please.* **cider press** [C] a machine in which apples are pressed to produce juice

mead [U] an alcoholic drink made from honey [⇒ E47] and water, drunk esp formerly by the Celts and in England

cocktail [C] any of various mixed alcoholic drinks, usu cooled and sometimes sweetened and often served at parties: *Mix me a cocktail, please.*

E68 nouns : kinds of wine [U; C]

claret (any of various kinds of) red table wine, esp from the south-west of France: *This is one of the finest clarets I've ever tasted.*

sherry (any of various kinds of) pale or dark brown wine, esp from Spain: *That's a nice sherry. Two dry sherries, please.*

hock (any of various kinds of) German white wine

champagne (any of various kinds of) white wine with carbon dioxide [⇒ H74] in it, esp from Champagne in France

vermouth white wine with the taste of herbs [⇒ A136], often taken in cocktails

port (any of various kinds of) usu sweet red or white wine from Portugal

E69 adjectives & nouns : relating to alcoholic drinks

strong [Wa1;B] (of alcoholic drinks) containing a lot of alcohol

sweet [Wa1;B] (of wine) tasting of sugar

dry [Wa1;B] (of wine) not sweet or sugary

red 1 [Wa5;B] (of wine) made from dark grapes **2** [U; C] wine of this kind: *This is a fine red; try it.*

white 1 [Wa5;B] (of wine) made from light-coloured grapes and yellowish in colour **2** [U; C] wine of this kind: *She prefers white to red. This white is very good with chicken.*

rosé *Fr* **1** [Wa5;B] (of wine) made from dark grapes without the skins; pink in colour **2** [U; C] a pinkish wine

vintage 1 [C] (the wine from) the grapes of a particular year: *This wine is the 1969 vintage.* **2** [Wa5; A] of high quality; dating from a good year: *This is vintage wine.* (fig) *He bought a vintage car.*

E70 verbs : making alcoholic drinks

ferment [T1; I0] to break the sugar in (a substance) down into alcohol and carbon dioxide [⇒ H74], etc, using yeast [⇒ E43]: *The beer was fermenting.* **fermentation** [U] the process or result of fermenting

distil [T1; I0] to reduce the water content of (alcoholic liquids) so as to obtain a higher amount of alcohol, by heating the alcohol until it boils and becomes vapour [⇒ L45], then catching and cooling the vapour back to a liquid **distillation** [U; C] the process or result of distilling

fortify [Wv5; T1] (of wine) to make stronger by adding alcohol: *Sherry is a fortified wine.*

E71 nouns, verbs, & adjectives : relating to drinking

drink to [v prep T1] to wish (someone or something) good health, success, happiness, etc

toast 1 [C] any drink, usu wine, drunk on a special occasion, esp a marriage or a formal dinner: *Friends, I give you a toast—to our president!* **2** [T1] to drink to (anyone or anything) in this way: *They toasted the health of the newly-married couple.*

propose [T1] *fml* to ask a social gathering to drink to someone, while raising a glass of wine which is afterwards drunk (usu in the phr **propose a toast/propose someone's health**): *'I have the honour of proposing the health of all the ladies present,' he said.*

round [C] all the drinks for a group bought by one person in turn: *He bought a round of drinks. It's my round this time; what'll you have?*

E72 adjectives, etc : drunk and sober

drunk 1 [Wa1;F] under the influence of alcohol, so as to be unable to think or behave normally: *He had too much wine and became drunk.* **2** [C] *deprec* a very drunk person: *Several drunks lay on the floor.* **drunkard** [C] *deprec* a person who is often drunk

drunken [A] drunk: *He lay on the floor in a drunken sleep. A drunken man was walking unsteadily along the street.* **-ly** [adv] **-ness** [U]

intoxicated [B] *fml* having taken alcoholic drink; *euph* drunk: *'He's a bit intoxicated, but he isn't drunk,' she said.* **intoxication** [U] the state of being intoxicated; (euph) drunkenness

sober [Wa2;B] not drunk; not having taken any alcoholic drink or having recovered from its effects: *He's perfectly sober; he can drive the car.* **sober up** [v adv I0; T1] to (cause to) become sober (again): *He sobered up quickly when he heard the bad news. Sober him up; he needs to drive the car.*

Cigarettes and drugs

E80 *nouns & verbs* : **drugs and stimulants**

[ALSO ⇨ B171 MEDICINES AND DRUGS]

drug 1 [C] a habit-forming substance: *Tobacco and alcohol can be dangerous drugs.* **2** [T1] to add drugs to, esp so as to produce unconsciousness: *They drugged his drink.* **3** [T1 *often pass*] to influence with drugs; give drugs to, esp so as to produce unconsciousness: *He lay in a drugged sleep.*

narcotic 1 [C *often pl*] a drug which in small amounts causes sleep or takes away pain, and in large amounts is harmful and habit-forming: *The use of narcotics is controlled by narcotics laws. He was sent to prison on a narcotics charge* (= he was charged with an offence concerning selling or using these drugs). **2** [Wa5;B] taking away pain or (esp) causing sleep: *He took a narcotic drink.* (*fig*) *The effects of the dull speech were narcotic.* **3** [Wa5;B] of or related to narcotics: *This is a narcotic substance.*

stimulant [C] a drug or drink which stimulates (= excites and increases feelings, thoughts, etc): *Alcoholic drink is generally considered a stimulant.*

dope *infml* **1** [U] a narcotic drug, taken to improve the performance of people or animals, to produce unconsciousness, or because of a pleasant effect on the body or mind **2** [T1 (*up*)] to give dope to, or put dope in: *After the race, they found that someone had doped the winning horse.*

hard drug [C] *not fml* a drug which is likely to cause addiction, and is dangerous to health: *Heroin* [⇨ E87] *is a hard drug.*

soft drug [C] *not fml* a drug which is slightly habit-forming, but not especially addictive or dangerous: *Cannabis* [⇨ E86] *is usually considered to be a soft drug.*

E81 *nouns, etc* : **drug addicts**

addict [C] a person who is unable to free him/herself from a harmful habit, esp of taking drugs: *He is a drug addict.* **be addicted to** to need or be in the habit of having: *He is addicted to opium* [⇨ E87]. (*fig*) *She's addicted to reading detective stories.* **addiction 1** [U] the state of being addicted **2** [C] an example of this: *Does he have any other addictions besides smoking?* **addictive** [B] causing addiction, habit-forming: *These drugs are addictive.*

junkie [C] *sl* a drug addict, esp one who takes heroin [⇨E87]

E82 *nouns* : **relating to tobacco**

tobacco 1 [U] a type of plant grown for its leaves, used chiefly in smoking **2** [U] the leaves of this plant, specially prepared for use in cigarettes, pipes, chewing, etc **3** [C] a particular type of this: *This is a mixture of the best tobacco. It is one of the world's finest tobaccos.*

mixture [C;U] loose tobacco as mixed for smoking in a pipe: *This is a good mixture.*

nicotine [U] a chemical which is poisonous alone and which gives tobacco its taste and effect

tar [U;C] a substance formed by chemical change when tobacco is smoked: *This kind of tobacco has a high tar content* (= has a lot of tar in it).

E83 *nouns* : **relating to cigarettes, pipes, etc** [C]

cigarette finely-cut tobacco rolled in a thin tube of thin paper, for smoking: *He used to smoke cigarettes, but he has stopped.*

fag *sl esp BrE* a cigarette: *Can I have a fag, please?*

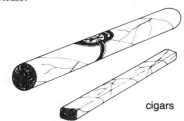

cigars

cigar a tight roll of uncut tobacco leaves, for smoking and usu pointed at one or both ends: *He smoked Havana cigars* (= cigars from Havana).

cheroot a usu small cigar which is not pointed at either end

pipe 1 a small tube with a bowl-like container at one end, used for smoking tobacco **2** *also* **fill, pipeful** the amount of tobacco the bowl of this will hold: *Let me try a pipe of that tobacco of yours. Have a fill of my tobacco.* **3** [*usu sing*] the smoking of a pipeful of tobacco: *He sat down before the fire and enjoyed a pipe.*

smoke *infml* the act or occasion of smoking tobacco; the cigarette, cigar, etc, smoked: *'I must have a smoke,'* he said.

E84 *nouns* : **parts of pipes** [C]

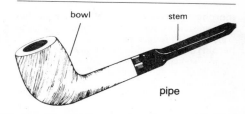

bowl   stem

pipe

E85 *nouns* : **parts of cigarettes**

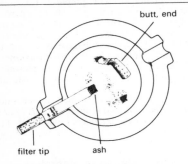

butt, end

filter tip   ash

(cigarette) butt/end [C] the last unsmoked part of a cigarette

fag end [C] *infml esp BrE* a cigarette butt

filter tip [C] **1** a filter [⇒ H153] on the end of a cigarette which cleans some harmful substances from the smoke **2** a cigarette made in this way: *She only smokes filter tips.*

ash [U] the soft grey powder that falls from a burning cigarette, cigar, etc

ashtray [C] a small dish for the ash of cigarettes, etc

E86 *nouns* : **cannabis** [U]

cannabis the drug produced from the cannabis or Indian hemp plant, sometimes smoked in cigarettes to give a feeling of pleasure

hemp 1 any one of a family of plants which are used to make strong rope and a rough cloth and some of which produce cannabis **2** the drug itself: *He smokes hemp.*

marijuana the common form of cannabis, not usually powerful in its effect: *Marijuana is the dried flowers, stems, and leaves of the cannabis plant.*

hashish *also sl* **hash** a drug made from cannabis, usu powerful in its effect

pot *also* **grass, dope** *sl* cannabis

E87 *nouns* : **opium**

opium [U] a sleep-producing drug made from the seeds of a particular plant (**the white poppy**): *He learned to smoke opium in the Far East.*

opiate [C] a sleep-producing drug made from opium

morphine *also old use* **morphia** [U] a white bitter substance obtained from opium and used in medicine to reduce pain

heroin [U] a drug made from morphine, used to make someone feel less pain and which one can become dependent on: *These people are heroin addicts* [⇒ E81].

junk [U] *sl esp AmE* a narcotic drug, esp heroin

E88 *verbs* : **smoking**

smoke [I0; T1] to draw in the smoke of (a cigarette, pipe, etc) through the mouth and then let it out again: *He started smoking at the age of 10. Do you smoke this kind of cigarette?—No; I don't smoke at all; I gave it up* (= stopped). *He smokes a pipe.* **smoker** [C *often in comb*] a person who smokes: *He is a pipe-smoker.* **non-** [*neg*] *This room is for non-smokers.*

light up [v adv] **1** [T1] (of cigarettes, pipes, etc) to cause to begin burning: *Having found a match, he lit up his pipe.* **2** [I0] *infml* to begin to smoke a cigarette or pipe: *Having filled his pipe, he lit up.*

put/stub out [v adv T1] to stop (a cigarette, etc) burning by pressing down the end

The preparation and quality of food

E100 *verbs* : **cooking**

cook 1 [I0; D1 (*for*); T1] to prepare (food) by using heat: *She went to the kitchen to cook some food. Don't stop cooking just because I've come in. Shall I cook you some food? Shall I cook some food for you?* **2** [I0] (of food) to change by cooking: *This meat cooks easily.*

cooking using hot liquids

fry 1 [I0; D1 (*for*); T1] to (cause to) be cooked in hot fat or oil: *Shall I fry the fish for dinner? The eggs were frying in the pan. He had fried rice for his evening meal. Shall I fry you an egg? Shall I fry an egg for you?* **2** [I0] to be changed by frying: *This kind of food doesn't fry well.* **3** [I0] *infml* to have the skin burnt (by the sun): *We shall all fry if we stay out long in this hot sun.* **deep fry** [T1; I0] to fry in a deep container of hot fat or oil

boil 1 [I0; D1 (*for*); T1] to cook (food) in water at 100°C: *Boil the potatoes for 20 minutes. The potatoes have been boiling for 20 minutes. Shall I boil you an egg? Shall I boil an egg for you?* **2** [I0] (of food, etc) to continue in water at this heat: *The potatoes are boiling.* **3** [Wv5;X7] to cause to reach the stated condition by cooking in water: *Please boil my egg hard. He likes soft-boiled eggs.*

stew [T1; I0] to cook in liquid in a covered container over a long(er) period: *You'll have to stew that meat well; it's pretty tough. The meat was stewing. This meat doesn't stew well.*

braise [Wv5; T1] to cook food slowly in fat and a little liquid in a closed container: *She braised the mutton.*

simmer [T1; I0] to cook in water which is at or just below boiling heat: *Simmer the meat for ten minutes more. The soup was simmering.*

poach [Wv5;T1] to cook (eggs, etc) by simmering: *He likes a poached egg for breakfast.*
scramble [Wv5;T1] to cook (eggs) by beating then heating in a saucepan with butter and milk: *He ate some scrambled eggs.*
curry [Wv5;T1] to stew with hot spices [⇨ E49]: *He curried the meat. I love curried chicken and rice.*
steam [Wv5;T1] to cook (food) in steam: *She wanted to steam the fish.*

cooking using dry heat

bake [I0; D1 (*for*); T1] to cook (food) by using direct heat in an oven [⇨ H120]: *She bakes her own bread. Do you bake? That baked fish was very good. I'll bake a cake tomorrow. I'll bake you a cake/bake a cake for you.*
roast [T1; I0] to cook (food) **a** by using heat in or from a fire **b** by baking uncovered in an oven **c** by burning until dry, under direct heat **d** by cooking on hot coals: *He was roasting a piece of meat over the fire. We can roast the chicken in the oven. The meat must be properly roasted.*
grill 1 [T1; (X7)] to cook under or over direct heat: *The meat has been grilled (dry). I can grill the meat while you set the table.* (fig) *He is grilling himself under a hot sun.*
baste [T1] to cook by adding fat or oil while roasting or grilling: *I'll baste this meat, I think.*
barbecue [T1] to roast or grill **a** on a framework over an open fire, usu outdoors **b** on a long thin piece of metal which is slowly turned over direct heat **c** in an oven, often basting with a hot sauce [⇨ E39]

E101 *verbs* : **making things for eating and drinking**

make [T1] to prepare or get ready: *Make a pot of tea, please. I've just made some fresh coffee.*
brew 1 [T1] to make (beer): *This kind of beer is brewed not once but twice.* **2** [T1] to mix (tea or coffee) with hot water and prepare for drinking: *Let's brew some tea.* **3** [I0] (of tea or coffee) to become ready for drinking after being mixed with hot water: *The tea is brewing.* [ALSO ⇨ E2]
percolate *also infml* **perk 1** [T1] to prepare (coffee) by passing hot water through ground coffee beans **2** [I0] (of coffee) to be made in this way: *The coffee is percolating* **percolation** [U] the action or result of percolating **percolator** [C] a kind of apparatus in which boiling water percolates through something, esp coffee

E102 *verbs* : **preparing animals, etc, for cooking** [T1]

skin (usu of animals) to remove the skin from: *He skinned the rabbit.*

shell to remove the shell from: *She shelled the hard-boiled eggs.*
pluck to remove the feathers from: *They plucked the chickens.*
bone to remove the bones from: *They boned the chickens.*
peel (usu of certain vegetables) to remove the peel or skin of: *He peeled the potatoes. Peeling onions makes you cry.*

E103 *verbs* : **preparing food for eating** [Wv5;T1]

[ALSO ⇨ N320 CUTTING AND CARVING]

chop [(*up*)] to cut into small pieces: *Chop up the onions, please.*
mince to cut or shred into very small pieces: *She minced the meat.*
mash to beat or crush into a soft mixture: *She mashed the potatoes.*
shred to reduce to many small strips or pieces by pulling, grating, tearing, etc: *She shredded the vegetables.*
grate 1 to shred (something) into very small pieces by rubbing against a rough surface **2** to rub very small bits off (something): *He grated the carrots* [⇨ A151].
whip to beat (eggs, cream, etc) with a fork, etc, in order to make stiff or make smooth
beat to mix (things) together with a circular movement, using (esp) a spoon
cream to soften (butter, fats, etc) usu by adding sugar and beating and pressing with a spoon until soft and creamy
ice to cover (a cake) with a mixture of a special sugar (**icing sugar**) and liquid
knead to make (dough [⇨ E43] etc) into a soft mass by working steadily with the fingers

E104 *verbs* : **actions in cooking and preparing food** [T1]

turn to change the position of (food in a pan, while cooking) so that what is on top goes underneath: *Turn my egg, please; I like my eggs turned.*
stir to move around and mix (esp something mainly liquid) esp with a spoon: *Stir the soup please.*
brown to make the surface (of any food) brown by cooking quickly in hot fat or oil or at a high temperature in an oven [⇨ H120]
stuff to fill (esp a bird) tightly with special foods (**stuffing**) in order to add to the taste and help keep the original shape: *She stuffed the chicken.*
spread [D1 *with/on*] to cover (bread, etc) thinly with (butter, etc): *He spread butter on his bread. He spread his bread with butter.*
butter to spread with butter: *He buttered his bread.*
steep to place (vegetables, etc) wholly in water, usu for some time

E105 *verbs* : **adding tastes to food** [T1]

---

flavour *BrE*, **flavor** *AmE* [(*with*)] to improve the taste of (food) by adding something else, esp sugar, salt, herbs [⇨ A136], etc: *She flavoured the soup with lemon juice.*

spice [Wv5] to put spices [⇨ E49] in or on: *The soup is highly spiced. He likes spiced food.*

season to improve or change the taste of (food) by adding (esp) salt, spices, or herbs: *The meat is well seasoned with salt.*

salt [Wv5] to put salt on or in: *He likes his food well salted. She was eating salted nuts.*

pepper to put pepper on or in: *He likes his food well peppered.*

garnish [(*with*)] to serve (meat, etc) with small extras, such as small vegetables, pieces of vegetable, etc

E106 *verbs* : **preserving and freezing food** [T1]

---

preserve to prepare (food) for being kept for a long time by some special treatment: *Mother always preserves fruit in bottles.*

smoke [Wv5] to dry and preserve (meat, fish, etc) by hanging in the rising smoke of wood fires: *She likes smoked fish.*

salt [Wv5] to preserve by treating with salt, usu by rubbing it on: *This salted meat will keep for months.*

cure to preserve (meat, etc) by smoking, salting, or drying: *The meat of pigs is called pork except when it is cured; then it is called ham or bacon.*

pickle [Wv5] to preserve food in pickle [⇨ E107] or vinegar [⇨ E49]: *She pickled the onions.*

freeze to reduce to a low or freezing temperature: *If you freeze the meat it will keep for a long time. The meat was frozen.*

refrigerate *tech* to freeze: *Meat is packed and refrigerated in that factory.*

quick/deep-freeze [Wv5] to freeze quickly for keeping over a long time: *They sell deep-frozen meat. If you quick-freeze this meat it will keep for a long time.*

E107 *nouns* : **relating to pickling and preserving** [C *usu pl; U*]

---

pickle 1 a type of liquid, such as vinegar [⇨ E49] or salt water, used to preserve meat or (esp) vegetables **2** a (piece or pieces of) vegetable preserved in this: *These vegetables make good pickles. Would you like some pickle with your cheese?*

preserve 1 a substance made from fruit boiled in sugar, used esp for spreading on bread **2** *older use* jam [⇨ E47]: *Would you like some apple preserve?*

E108 *adjectives* : **able or not able to be eaten**

---

eatable [B] in a fit condition to be eaten; worth eating: *This food is terribly old—it isn't eatable.* **un-** [*neg*]

edible [B] able to be eaten; suitable to eat: *This kind of fruit is not edible for humans—it's poisonous.* **in-** [*neg*]

drinkable [B] able to be drunk; worth drinking: *Is this water drinkable? This wine is terrible; it isn't drinkable.* **un-** [*neg*]

digestible [B] able to be digested [⇨ E5]: *Some foods are more readily digestible than others.* **in-** [*neg*]

fresh 1 [Wa1;B] in good natural condition because not long gathered, caught, produced, etc; not spoilt in taste, appearance, etc, by being kept too long: *You can buy fresh fruit and vegetables in the market. This fish smells; I don't think it's quite fresh. Neither meat nor butter will keep fresh (for) long in hot weather.* **2** [Wa5;A; (F)] (of water) not salt; drinkable **3** [Wa5;A] (of food) not preserved by salting, tinning, bottling, freezing, or other means: *Tinned fruit never has quite the same taste as fresh fruit. Fresh butter has no salt added to it.* **4** [Wa5;A;F *from*] newly prepared; newly cooked: *Let me make you a fresh pot of tea. This bread is fresh from the oven* [⇨ H120] (= is newly baked). **-ly** [adv] **-ness** [U]

stale [Wa1;B] **1** not fresh; kept too long or used too much: *This bread is a bit stale. The air in this room is stale; open a window.* (*fig*) *He is always telling stale old jokes that everybody has heard.* **2** (of persons) not in the best condition for something, esp by doing too much: *I'm getting stale; I think I need a holiday.*

mouldy *BrE*, **moldy** *AmE* [Wa1; B] covered in mould [⇨ A140], and therefore not good to eat: *I'm not having any of that mouldy cheese. This bread is mouldy.*

E109 *adjectives* : **qualities of food** [B]

---

raw [Wa5] (of food) not cooked: *He eats raw vegetables. He eats his vegetables raw.*

cooked ready to be eaten after being cooked: *Do you want your eggs raw or cooked?*

uncooked raw or not yet cooked

tough [Wa1] difficult to chew [⇨ E6]: *This meat is tough; the animal must have been old.* **-ness** [U]

tender [Wa1] easy to chew: *What lovely tender meat!* **-ness** [U]

E110 *adjectives* : **good qualities of food** [B]

---

wholesome (of food) good for the body: *She always gives her children good wholesome meals.* **-ly** [adv]

appetizing, -sing causing desire, esp for food (**appetite**): *What an appetizing smell!* **-ly** [adv]

delicious pleasing to the body's senses, esp of taste or smell: *What delicious food! What's that delicious smell?* **-ly** [adv]

mouth-watering (of food) that makes one want to eat; good to eat **-ly** [adv]

luscious 1 having a very pleasant taste or smell; sweet: *He enjoyed the luscious fruit/wine.* **2** juicy, ripe, and healthy: *Luscious red apples were hanging on the trees.* **3** (*fig*) very attractive; beautiful: *What a luscious girl!* **-ly** [adv] **-ness** [U]

succulent 1 *apprec* juicy: *The fruit/meat was very succulent.* **2** [Wa5] *tech* (of a plant) thick and fleshy **-nce** [U]

tasty [Wa1] **1** (esp of food) having a pleasant taste; pleasing to the taste: *That was a tasty meal.* **2** (*fig*) *infml* (esp of news) interesting: *She gave us a tasty piece of news about our neighbours.* **-ily** [adv] **-iness** [U]

E111 *adjectives* : **bad qualities of food** [B]

tasteless having no taste and therefore not enjoyable: *This soup is tasteless.*

insipid lacking a strong effect, esp a taste: *The food in that hotel is pretty insipid.*

rotten 1 decayed; gone bad: *These apples are completely rotten.* **2** tasting or smelling like this; bad: *What a rotten smell! This food is rotten!* (*fig*) *What rotten luck!*

rancid (of butter, fat, etc) bad to taste or smell **-ness** [U]

rank [Wa1] *esp emot & deprec* bad to taste or smell; completely bad: *rank tobacco;* (*fig*) *rank dishonesty* **-ly** [adv] **-ness** [U]

E112 *adjectives* : **hot and spicy** [B]

hot [Wa1] tasting of hot spices [⇒ E49], pepper, etc: *Indian food is usually rather hot. What a hot curry that was!* **-ness** [U]

pungent having a strong sharp taste or smell: *He likes pungent food like curry.*

peppery containing or tasting of pepper: *This soup is too peppery for my taste.*

spicy [Wa1] containing or tasting of (esp hot) spice: *She likes spicy foods.*

E113 *nouns* : **relating to recipes** [C]

recipe a set of instructions for cooking something: *Follow the recipe carefully.* (*fig*) *His ideas are a recipe for failure/success.*

ingredient a substance used in cooking or preparing food: *What ingredients do you need for this cake besides flour and sugar?*

cookery book *BrE*, **cookbook** *AmE* a book of recipes, etc

Places and people associated with food and drink

E120 *nouns* : **places where people can eat** [C]

[ALSO ⇒ E15 DINER]

restaurant *Fr* a place where food is sold and eaten: *They ate in a little local restaurant/in the hotel restaurant.*

eating-house *fml & pomp* a restaurant

eating-place *genl* a restaurant, cafe, etc

café *Fr* a small restaurant where light meals and (in Britain only non-alcoholic) drinks are served: *He went into a local café for a cup of tea.*

cafeteria a restaurant where customers serve themselves, often in a factory, college, etc: *The workers have their own cafeteria.*

canteen a place in a factory, office, military camp, etc, where food is sold and eaten

refectory (in schools, colleges, etc) a large hall in which meals are served: *They eat most days in the college refectory.*

snack bar a bar or small cafe where people can have light meals (**snacks**) and drinks (in Britain usu only non-alcoholic drinks), esp when sitting or standing at or near the bar where the food is served

E121 *nouns* : **places where people can drink** [C]

pub (esp in Britain) a building or part of a building, not a club or hotel, containing usu two or more rooms where alcohol may be bought and drunk during fixed hours [⇒ ALSO M79 INN]

public house *fml* a pub

bar 1 (a room with) a counter [⇒ J190] where alcoholic drinks are sold: *They went to the bar for a drink. Is there a bar in this hotel?* **2** (a room with) a counter where food and drinks are served: *He went into a coffee bar. He eats in a local snack bar* [⇒ E120].

public bar *BrE* a room in an inn, hotel, pub, etc, that is open to the public generally and where people go mainly for drinking beer, etc

saloon bar *also* **lounge bar** *BrE* a room in an inn, hotel, etc, that is usu quite formally ornamented and where people go when they want to drink in pleasanter surroundings than the public bar

tavern *esp formerly* a place, inn, etc, where beer, etc, is sold

saloon 1 a large public drinking place esp in an American wild west town **2** *BrE* a saloon bar

E122 *nouns* : **persons and shops selling tobacco and alcoholic drinks** [C]

tobacconist a person who or shop which sells tobacco, cigarettes, etc: *He buys his cigarettes at a tobacconist's down the street.*

liquor store *esp AmE* a shop that sells alcoholic drinks in bottles

off-licence *BrE* a shop or part of a pub, hotel, etc, where alcoholic drinks can be bought and taken away

licensed premises [*also* P] a place, esp a hotel or inn, which is officially permitted to sell alcoholic drinks

E123 *nouns* : **persons making and serving food** [C]

cook a person who cooks, esp in a hotel or restaurant

chef *Fr* a male cook, esp a chief cook, in a hotel or larger restaurant

waiter a person who serves food in a restaurant

waitress a female waiter

E124 *nouns* : **persons making and serving drinks** [C]

brewer a person who makes (**brews**) beer **brewery** a place where beer is made

distiller a person who distils [⇨ E70] strong alcoholic drink such as whisky **distillery** a place where distilling is done, esp of whisky

publican *esp BrE* a person who (owns and) looks after a pub

saloon-keeper *esp AmE* a person who owns or looks after a saloon

barman a man who sells drinks in a bar, pub, etc

barmaid a woman who serves drinks in a bar, pub, etc

bartender a barman or barmaid

Farming

E130 *nouns* : **farming generally** [U]
[ALSO ⇨ E144]

farming the practice or business of operating or working on a farm **farmland** land that is good for farming

agriculture *tech* the art or practice of farming, esp of growing crops **agricultural** [B] of or concerning agriculture **-ly** [adv]

agronomy *tech* the scientific study of soil and the growing of crops **agronomic(al)** [B] of or concerning agronomy

husbandry *fml & tech* farming, esp of a special kind: *animal husbandry*

horticulture *tech* the science and practice of growing fruit, flowers, and vegetables **horticultural** [B] of or concerning horticulture **-ly** [adv]

market gardening the practice or business of growing vegetables and fruit for sale

E131 *nouns* : **farms and ranches** [C]

farm an area of land, together with its buildings, concerned with the growing of crops and/or the raising of animals: *They own a farm. The farm has a lot of fields. He has a sheep farm in Australia.*

market garden a large area for growing vegetables and fruit for sale

plantation a large piece of land, esp in hot countries, on which crops such as tea, cotton, sugar, and rubber are grown: *They own a coffee plantation.*

estate *fml* a plantation: *They own several tea estates.*

ranch 1 [C] (in the western US and Canada) a very large farm where cattle, horses, or sheep are produced **2** [C9] *AmE* any farm that produces one (stated) thing: *He owns a fruit/ chicken ranch.*

smallholding *BrE* an area of land for growing crops, raising animals, etc, but smaller than a farm: *He started on a smallholding; now he farms five hundred acres.*

E132 *nouns* : **fields and orchards** [C]
[ALSO ⇨ E142 PASTURE]

field [*often in comb*] a stretch of land on a farm, etc, marked off in some way or surrounded by a fence or wall, and used for animals or crops: *There were fields of corn/cornfields near the house. The field was full of sheep.*

kitchen garden a garden where fruit and vegetables are grown, usu for eating at home rather than for sale

patch [*often in comb*] a small area of ground esp for growing vegetables: *He was working in his potato patch.*

allotment (in Britain) a small piece of land rented out, esp by a town council, to people who will grow vegetables on it

orchard a field of fruit trees: *They own apple orchards in Kent.*

vineyard a piece of land planted with vines [⇨ A141] for wine production

E133 *nouns, etc* : **crops and harvests**

crop 1 [C] a plant or plant product such as grain, fruit, or vegetables grown or produced by a farmer: *Wheat is a widely grown crop in Britain.* **2** [C] the amount of such a product produced and gathered in a single season or place: *We've had the biggest wheat crop ever this year because of the hot summer.* **3** [S9] (*fig*) a group or quantity appearing at any one time: *The minister's speech caused a crop of questions in Parliament.* **4** [L9] to bear a crop: *The potatoes and beans have cropped well this year, but the wheat badly.*

crops [P] *genl* all the kinds of plants growing (in one season or place): *The farmers are worried* about the effect the dry weather will have on their crops.

produce [U] things which are produced esp on farms; plants, milk, eggs, etc: *Local produce costs less than foreign produce.*

harvest [C] **1** the act or occasion of gathering the crops: *They all helped in the harvest. The weather was good for the harvest.* **2** the (amount of) crops gathered: *There was a good harvest that year.* **3** (*fig*) the results of work done: *All his letter-writing produced a harvest of interested people.*

yield [C] that which is produced or the amount that is produced, as of fruit, crops, etc: *The trees gave a high yield this year.*

E134 *nouns* : **livestock** [GU]

(live)stock animals kept on a farm: *That farmer looks after his livestock well. He needs a lot of food to feed his stock.*

fatstock livestock fattened for selling as food

E135 *adjectives, etc* : **relating to fertility** [B]

[ALSO ⇒ A17]

fertile (of land) which produces or can produce good crops in large numbers: *fertile soil* **fertility** [U] the condition of being fertile: *The fertility of the fields here is well known.* **-in** [neg]

productive able to produce well: *All the farms here are highly productive.* **productivity** [U] the (measured) ability to grow things or the (calculated) rate of making goods: *The employers are considering ways to increase the productivity of the factory.*

rich [Wa1] fertile; productive: *This farm has very rich land.*

arable 1 (of land) suitable or used for growing crops: *This is the finest arable land in the country.* **2** [U] land that is used for growing crops: *I have three fields of arable and twenty cows.*

pastoral 1 (of land) grassy; suitable for feeding sheep and cattle **2** *esp lit* concerning simple peaceful country life, esp as lived by shepherds [⇒ E144]: *A pastoral scene of cows drinking from a stream.*

agrarian of land, esp farmland, or its ownership: *Agrarian laws deal with the use and ownership of farmland.*

fruitful *esp lit* (of earth, trees, etc) rich; yielding good crops

fallow [Wa5] **1** (of land) dug or ploughed [⇒ E137] but left unplanted to improve its quality: *They left the land fallow for a year.* **2** [U] fallow land **lie fallow** stay unplanted: *They let the land lie fallow for a year.*

barren 1 (of land) having poor soil that cannot produce a good crop **2** (of animals, trees, plants etc) unable to produce young life; bearing no fruit or seed **-ness** [U]

bare [Wa1 (*of*)] uncovered by any (particular) plants: *The fields were bare (of any plants).*

arid 1 (of land or a country) having so little rain that it is very dry and unproductive **2** (*fig*) not leading to any really new discovery: *These are arid scientific studies concerned only with dry facts.* **3** (*fig*) uninteresting; dull

E136 *nouns, etc* : **dung and fertilizer**

[⇒B66 EXCREMENT]

dung [U] the waste material of animals which is put on the land to make it more fertile: *He put horse dung around the roots of the rose bushes.*

manure 1 [U] *fml & tech* dung **2** [T1] to put manure on: *The farmer manured his fields.*

fertilizer, -iser [C; U] (any type of) chemical or natural substance that is put on the land to make crops grow better: *He bought a bag of chemical fertilizer. Crushed bones make one of the best fertilizers.*

muck [U] *infml* manure

E137 *verbs* : **farming**

farm [I∅; T1] to use (land) for growing crops, raising animals, etc: *His friend farms in Wales. They should farm the land instead of letting it lie waste/fallow.*

cultivate [T1] **1** [Wv5] to prepare (land) for the growing of crops: *New farming methods are allowing us to cultivate much land previously thought unproductive.* **2** to plant, grow, and care for (a crop) by preparing the soil, providing water, etc: *Rice can only be cultivated in hot countries with plenty of rain.* **3** (*fig*) to improve or develop by careful attention, training, or study: *He has cultivated a love of art. He's trying to cultivate his mind by reading widely.* **4** (*fig*) to seek the friendship or good will of (a person): *He always tries to cultivate people who are useful to him professionally.* **cultivation** [U] the act of cultivating: *The farmer wants to bring new land under cultivation. The cultivation of cotton has declined in recent years.* (*fig*) *Cultivation of the mind can bring much pleasure. By his cultivation of important people John advanced himself socially.* **cultivator** [C] **1** a person who cultivates **2** a tool or machine for loosening the earth around plants, destroying unwanted plants, etc **cultivable** [B] that can be cultivated

grow [T1; I∅] to (cause or allow to) grow: *He grows vegetables. What crops do you grow here? This is all locally-grown produce. Plants can't grow without water.*

garden [I∅] to work in a garden, making plants grow: *He spends his time gardening and reading.*

sow [I∅; T1] **1** to plant or throw (seeds) on (a piece of ground): *The farmer sowed the field with corn. He sowed several rows of peas in the* *garden.* **2** (*fig*) to give, put in, or cause to produce future results: *'Whatever a man sows, that he will also reap'* (*The Bible*).

plant 1 [T1; I∅] to put (plants or seeds) in the ground to grow: *Plant flowers about 6 inches apart. April is the time to plant.* **2** [T1] to supply (a place) with seeds or growing plants: *We're planting a small garden. The hillside was planted with trees.* **3** [X9] (*fig*) to put (an idea, belief, etc) in the mind: *His evil talk planted the seeds of hatred in their hearts.* **4** [X9] to fix or place firmly or with force: *He planted himself in a chair by the fire.*

seed 1 [T1] to sow with seeds [⇒ A136]; throw seeds on: *The farmer seeded his fields.* **2** [I∅] to produce seeds: *The plants have all seeded.* **3** [T1] to take seeds from: *This kind of fruit is best seeded before eating.*

plough 1 [T1; I∅] to break up or turn over (land) with a plough [⇒ E139]: *Farmers plough (their fields) in autumn or spring. The ground was ploughed up and planted with corn.* (*fig*) *The ship ploughed the sea.* **2** [I∅] (of land) to be fit to plough: *Frozen soil won't plough.*

E138 *verbs* : **gathering the harvest**

reap [I∅; T1] to cut and gather (a crop of grain): *The farmer reaped the corn. The men were all out reaping.* (*fig*) *He reaped a big profit on his work.*

thresh *also less common* **thrash** [I∅; T1] to separate (grain) from the rest of the plant by beating it: *The farmers used to thresh the grain by hand, but now machines thresh it. Have they started threshing yet?* **threshing floor** [C] the floor or ground where grain is threshed

bale [I∅; T1] to make (plants) into bales [⇒ E143]: *The farmworkers baled the dried grass.*

bind [T1] to tie: *The farm-workers bound the corn into sheaves* [⇒ E143].

harvest [T1; I∅] to gather or reap (a crop): *Have you harvested (your crops) yet?*

E139 *nouns* : **large-scale farming equipment** [C]

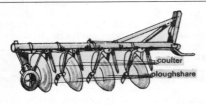

plough

plough *BrE*, **plow** *AmE* **1** a farming tool with a heavy cutting blade drawn by a vehicle or animal(s): *Ploughs break up and turn over the*

earth in fields. **2** [often in comb] any tool or machine, such as a **snowplough** that looks or works like this **to be under the plough** (of land) to be used for farming

ploughshare *BrE*, **plowshare** *AmE* the heavy cutting blade of a plough

tractor a motor vehicle used esp in farming to pull machinery, esp across fields: *The farmer fixed the plough behind his tractor. Tractors or horses can be used to pull a plough.*

baler a farming machine that gathers crops like wheat into a large tightly tied mass (**bale**)

binder a farming machine that binds crops

harvester 1 a machine which cuts grain and gathers it in **2** a person who is harvesting crops

combine harvester a machine which harvests grain, separates it from the stems, and cleans it

E140 *nouns & verbs* : **farm buildings** [C]

farm(house) the main house on a farm

farmyard the (main) yard of a farm

outhouse *also* **outbuilding** a building on a farm away from the main farmhouse

barn 1 a farm building for storing crops and food for animals **2** *esp AmE* a farm building for crops, food for animals, and the animals themselves **3** (*fig*) a big bare plain building: *You'd never get me to live in a great barn like that!*

barnyard the yard around, near, or among barns, often (esp formerly) where hens are kept

kennel 1 a usu small house for a dog **2** [T1] to keep or put in a kennel

kennels *BrE* [P], **kennel** *AmE* [C] a place where small animals are looked after while their owners are away

pigsty *also* **sty 1** an enclosure with a small building in it where pigs are kept **2** (*fig*) *derog* a very dirty house or room

pigpen *AmE* a pigsty

hen house the (usu wooden) hut in which hens sleep

battery a line of small boxes in which hens are kept and specially treated so that they will grow fast and lay eggs often

pen 1 [often in comb] a small piece of land enclosed by a fence or wall, used esp for keeping animals in, as in **sheep pen 2** [T1] to shut (animals) in a pen: *We don't pen our sheep here.*

stall [C] a place, esp as part of a large stable in which a horse, cow, etc, can be kept

(bee)hive 1 a place where bees live: *Where do you keep your hives?* **2** [GC] the group of bees who live together: *When bees swarm it means the whole hive is flying together.* **3** (*fig*) a crowded busy place: *This place is a real beehive; what a hive of industry!*

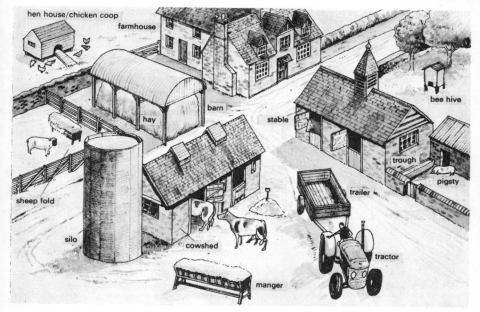

E141 *nouns & verbs* : **food for animals**
[ALSO ⇒ E1–12 FOOD GENERALLY]

---

hay [U] grass which has been cut and dried, esp for cattle food: *We had a good crop* [⇒ E133] *of hay this year.* **haystack** [C] a carefully made pile of hay esp in a field

silage [U] *tech* green food for cattle, esp when stored in a special building or hole kept for such a purpose (**silo**)

fodder [U] *tech* rough food for cattle or horses, gathered from the fields and stored

forage [U] *genl* food supplies for horses and cattle

feed 1 [U] food for animals: *He bought a bag of hen feed. How much does this kind of feed cost?* 2 [C] food or a meal taken by an animal or baby: *How many feeds a day does a camel get?*

graze 1 [T1; IØ] (of animals) to feed on grass: *The cattle are grazing (in the field).* 2 [X9] to cause animals to feed on grass: *They graze the cattle in that field.* 3 [T1] to use (land) for grazing: *The farmer said he would graze the bottom field.*

grazing [U] land on which animals can graze

pasture 1 [U] **a** growing grass, considered or used as food for cattle **b** land where this is grown and where cattle feed on it: *Cattle are moved to hilly pasture during the summer.* 2 [C] a piece of land where this is grown: *He loved the rolling pastures of Southern England.* 3 [T1] (of people) **a** to put (farm animals) in a pasture **b** to feed (farm animals) on pasture: *This is the best grass for pasturing one's cattle.* 4 [T1; L1] (of cattle, sheep, etc) to feed on (an area of growing grass), esp in a pasture: *This field has been well pastured by the cattle. Goats can pasture on mountain slopes.* 5 [T1] to use (land) as pasture: *It is now possible to pasture waste land.*

pasturage [U] 1 growing grass for feeding cattle, horses, etc 2 the right to use land for feeding one's cattle, horses, etc 3 *also* **pasture-land** (natural) grassland suitable for feeding cattle on

---

E142 *nouns* : **parts of fields, things in farms and fields, etc**

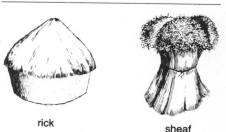

rick   sheaf

---

stubble [U] the short ends of corn stems left standing in fields after the grain has been cut

clod [C] a lump or mass of earth, clay, etc, esp in a field

sheaf [C] a number of corn stems tied together, usu before the corn is threshed [⇒ E138]

bale [C] a large tightly tied mass of corn, or of

dried grass (**hay**), esp as cut and gathered by machine

rick [C] a large pile of straw or hay shaped like a little house, that stands in the open air until it is needed

stack [C] a very large pile, esp of bales of straw or hay, usu shaped like a box

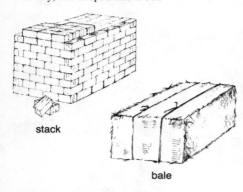

stack

bale

ditch [C] a long narrow passage dug in the ground to allow water to flow away

hedge [C] a row of bushes or small trees, esp when cut level at the top, which divides a field or garden from another **hedgerow** [C] a long hedge along the side of a field, road, etc

furrow [C] a long narrow track cut by a plough [⇒ E139] in farming land

rut [C] a long deep cut between raised edges, esp in the earth: *The country roads were muddy and full of ruts left by farm carts.* **rutted** [B] having ruts

E143 *nouns* : **people generally connected with farming** [C]

[ALSO ⇒ E130–31]

farmer a person whose work is farming, or who owns a farm

husbandman *old use & lit* a farmer

farm worker *also* **farm labourer** *BrE*/**laborer** *AmE* a man who works on a farm for a farmer

farmhand *infml* a farm worker

rancher a person who owns a ranch

agriculturalist a person who works in agriculture

agronomist a person who practises agronomy

horticulturist a person who works in horticulture

market gardener a person who owns or works in a market garden

stockbreeder *also* **cattle-breeder** a farmer who breeds cattle

shepherd a person who looks after sheep, esp in hilly places

sheepman a person, esp a farmer or farmworker, who keeps or looks after sheep

cattleman a person, esp a farmer, who keeps or looks after cattle

herdsman *also* **stockman** a farm worker employed by a farmer to look after stock (= animals)

cowboy *AmE* a man who looks after cattle on a ranch

ploughman *also* (*formerly*) **ploughboy** a man whose work on a farm is to plough [⇒ E137] fields

gardener a person who looks after a garden or gardens, esp for pay

smallholder a person who has a smallholding

F

Feelings, emotions, attitudes, and sensations

Feeling and behaviour generally

F1 *verbs* : **relating to feeling**

[ALSO ⇒ F260–2]

feel 1 [T1] to get knowledge of by touching: *Just feel the quality of the cloth.* **2** [Wv6;T1] to experience the touch or movement of: *I can feel a pin sticking into me.* **3** [L7] to experience (a condition); be consciously: *I felt really cold/ ill last night. She feels tired and wants to rest.* **4** [T5a] (*fig*) to think or consider: *He says he feels that he has not been well treated. I feel (that) you don't understand the problem.*

sense [T1,5] to feel esp through the senses, often without clear reasons: *The dog sensed danger. He sensed that she didn't like him.*

experience [T1] *often fml* to feel, have, or know: *He experienced a lot of difficulties doing that work. In that place she experienced real fear for the first time in her life.*

enjoy [T1] to have or feel (something good): *He has always enjoyed good health.*

suffer from [v prep T1] to have or feel (something bad): *She has always suffered from ill health. She has suffered (a lot) from various illnesses.*

suffer [T1] *often fml* to experience (something bad): *He suffered the loss of a leg during the war.*

F2 *nouns* : **relating to feeling**

feeling 1 [U] the ability to feel: *After the accident he had no feeling in his legs.* **2** [C] *genl* something which a person feels inside him/her-self; an emotion, or idea: *I have a feeling he doesn't like me. What are her feelings towards him? Try not to hurt his feelings again* (= to, upset him, his pride, etc). **3** [C *usu sing*] something which a person, animal, etc feels through the senses: *When that thing touched me it was a very strange feeling.*

sensation *often fml* **1** [U] the power of feeling in the body: *The doctor said that the patient had no sensation in his legs.* **2** [C] a bodily feeling: *She felt a sensation of heat against her face.*

emotion 1 [C] any one of the strong feelings that a person can have inside: *Love, hatred, and grief are emotions. His speech had an effect on our emotions rather than on our reason.* **2** [U] strength of feeling; an excited state of the feel-ings: *He described the accident in a voice shaking with emotion.*

sentiment 1 [C] *fml* a feeling; emotion: *He is not interested in such sentiments as pity and love.* **2** [U] human sympathy: *They consider senti-ment in business a waste of time.*

mood 1 [C] a state of the emotions at a particu-lar time: *When she came home she found him in a bad mood. Her moods change quickly; one minute she's happy, the next minute she's sad.* **2** [C] a state of feeling in which a person is bad tempered, violently angry, or displeased, etc: *Don't ask him to help when he's in one of his moods. She's in a mood and won't speak to me.* **3** [(*the*) S] the right state of mind (for a particu-lar activity, thing, etc): *I can't write any letters today; I'm not in the mood. She was tired and in no mood for dancing. Do you feel in the mood for some music?*

instinct 1 [U;C] the inborn force in animals and people which causes certain patterns of behaviour, such as nest building in birds, which are not based on learning or thinking: *Most animals have an instinct to protect their young.* **2** [C *often pl*] natural feeling(s) (in human beings); the ways of behaviour which one would follow before thinking: *Trust your instincts in this matter. Some instinct made him turn round at that moment.*

morale [U] an attitude in a person or group of people towards difficulties, work, etc: *The morale of the soldiers was high/low* (= good/poor).

F3 *nouns* : **attitudes and similar feelings**

attitude [C] **1** manner of feeling and behaving: *He has a happy attitude to life. I dislike her unfriendly attitude.* **2** judgment; opinion: *What is your attitude to this idea/in this matter?*

temper [C] a particular state or condition of the mind, with regard to anger: *She is in a bad temper because she missed the bus and had to walk to work. He's in a very good temper today; what happened?* [*also* ⇒ F103]

temperament [C] a person's character as shown by his attitudes, behaviour, feelings, interests, etc: *She has a happy, friendly temperament. He doesn't have the temperament for office work.*

disposition [C; U] one's feelings, general way of behaving, etc: *She has a friendly disposition. What one does when one isn't working is a matter of personal disposition.*

inclination [U; C *often pl*] what one likes; liking: *She always follows her own inclinations. I have no inclination to do that kind of work.*

impulse [C; U] a sudden wish to do something: *She almost gave way to a wild impulse to dance in the street. I telephoned her on impulse. He usually follows his impulses and does what he wants.*

urge [C] a strong desire: *I was angry and felt an urge to hit him. Sexual urges are perfectly natural.*

bias [C] a tendency of mind, feelings, etc: *Her scientific bias showed itself in early childhood; she was interested in everything scientific.*

F4 *adjectives* : **relating to feeling** [B]

emotional 1 (of people) having feelings which are strong or easily moved: *Women are often said to be more emotional than men.* **2** (of words, music, literature, etc) showing or able to cause strong feeling; emotive: *She sang an emotional song about love and death.* **3** [Wa5] relating to the emotions: *He continues to have emotional difficulties.* **un-** [*neg*] **-ly** [adv]

emotive which causes or may cause emotion: *'Home' is a much more emotive word than 'house'.* **-ly** [adv]

affecting causing deep feeling: *Meeting her again was a very affecting experience.*

moving causing deep feeling; affecting: *It was a deeply moving ceremony.*

sentimental having or showing a lot of, or too much, sentiment or emotion: *She's very sentimental about animals. They like singing warm, sentimental songs.* **-ly** [adv] **-ity** [U]

moody [Wa1] **1** having moods that change often and quickly: *She's a moody child, sad one minute, happy the next.* **2** bad-tempered, angry, displeased, or unhappy, esp when such feelings or the reasons for them are not expressed: *He became rather moody while waiting for the results of the exam.* **-ily** [adv] **-iness** [U]

impulsive likely to act suddenly without thinking about the results, suitability, etc of one's acts: *Children can be very impulsive sometimes. Her impulsive behaviour worries me.* **-ly** [adv] **-ness** [U]

instinctive [Wa5] resulting (as if) from instinct: *The way in which he did the work was almost instinctive.* **-ly** [adv] **-ness** [U]

F5 *verbs* : **wanting things**

want [T3, 1] to have or feel a need, real or imagined, to do or to get: *He wanted to eat. I want to talk to you. He wants very much to go there. I want that book, not the other one.*

wish 1 [T5a] to want (what is at present impossible): *I wish we had more money.* **2** [X7, 9] *emph* to want (something) to be: *We wished the long journey over, but it wasn't. They wished her anywhere but in their house.* **3** [D1] to hope that (someone) is or has (something), esp expressed as a greeting: *I wish you well/a merry Christmas.* **4** [I0 (*for*)] to want and try to cause a particular thing, esp when it can only come by magic: *Go to the well and wish for what you want most of all.* **5** [T3, V3] *polite & fml* to want: *Do you wish to eat alone, sir? Does he wish us to come back later?*

feel like [v prep T1, 4] *infml* to want: *I feel like an apple. Do you feel like going for a walk?*

like [T1, 3] (*used with* **should, would**) *infml* to want: *I would/I'd like another cake. Would you like a new bicycle? Would you like to go there?*

care for [v prep T1] (*esp in polite questions*) to want; like: *Would you care for another cake? I don't much care for people like him.*

fancy [T1] *infml* to wish for; have a liking for: *Do you fancy that car?—It's nice, isn't it?*

will [T1, 5; V3] to use the powers of one's mind to make or intend: *He willed that she would succeed. He willed her to succeed. The priest said that she died because God willed it. He willed himself to keep working, although he was very tired.*

F6 *verbs* : **wanting things very much**

desire 1 [T1, 3, 5] *fml* to wish or want very much: *She desires only your happiness. I desire to be happy. The Queen desires that you (should) come at once. She desires you to come at once. Give your guests whatever they desire.* **2** [T1] to want to have sex with: *Antony desired Cleopatra.* **desirable** [B] worth having, doing, or desiring: *These good ideas have had several desirable results. For this job it is desirable to know French.*

long [I0 (*for*), I3] to wish or want very much (something which one cannot have, esp at that time): *She longs to go back to her home town. He longs for her to come back to him.*

crave 1 [T1; I0 (*for*)] to desire (and keep desiring): *The unhappy children craved their parents' love. He gave up drinking, but you can see he still craves (for) a drink.* **2** [T1] *fml & pomp* to ask strongly but very politely for: *I crave your forgiveness, Sir.*

covet [T1] to desire very much (esp something that belongs to someone else): *He covets my land, but he won't get it! He really covets the prize for best swimmer.* **covetous** [B (*of*)] *esp lit* wanting something very much: *He looked at the money with covetous eyes.* (*esp fml & lit*) *He is covetous of her money.* **-ly** [adv]

lust after *also* **lust for** [v prep T1] to desire very strongly, esp in a sexual way; covet greatly: *He* *lusted after the girl, but could not have her. Those men lust (only) for gold.*

miss [T1, 4] to feel sorry or unhappy at the absence or loss of (someone or something): *The old man told his children that they'd miss him when he was dead. He missed the sunshine when he returned to England after four years in a hot country. Now she's poor, and misses having servants to do all the work in the house.*

hope [I0 (*for*); T3, 5a, b] to wish or expect (that something will happen): *I hope (that) he'll come. She hopes to go. Will he do it?—I hope so./I hope not. He hoped for peace but caused a war.*

despair [I0 (*of*)] to lose hope: *Don't despair; something good will happen soon. She sometimes despaired of her son; he never seemed to do anything right. He gave a despairing cry and died.*

resign [V3] to prepare (esp oneself) without complaining: *He resigned himself to losing all the money.* **resignation** [U] the condition of having resigned oneself to something

give up [v adv I0] *not fml* to despair and resign oneself to something: *I give up; I can't do this job.*

[⇒ D81]

lack 1 to be without; not have: *We lacked food.* **2** to have less than enough of: *She lacks the strength to do the work.*

need to want, esp for some necessary or useful purpose: *He says he needs the book now for his work. I need her and can't live without her.*

require *fml* to need: *We require more money; arrange it with the bank. Do you require any further assistance* (= help), *sir? He is required at once in the Manager's office.*

want 1 [*also* T4] to need, usu badly: *This house wants painting/a good coat of paint. This work wants doing now!* **2** [T3] *not fml* ought: *You know, you want to see a doctor about that cough. You're tired; you don't want to work so hard. This work wants to be done carefully.* **3** *often fml* to lack; not have enough of: *His reply wanted politeness.* **4** *often fml* to suffer from the lack of: *Many people still want food and shelter.* **5** [*often pass*] to need (the presence of): *The servants won't be wanted this afternoon. Don't go where you are not wanted. Your country wants you.* **6** [Wv5] (esp of the police) to hunt or look for in order to catch: *The police want him for questioning. He is wanted for murder; he's a wanted man.* **7** now rare to lack (for completion): *What time is it?—Oh, it wants 3 minutes to 12.* **8** [I0] to lack enough food, clothing, shelter, etc: *I'll see that she never wants again.* **want in/out** *ScotE & AmE* to desire to come/go: *The cat wants in and the dog wants out. I want out of this agreement.*

can/could use *also* **can/could do with** *infml* would like to have; want; need: *Boy, I'm thirsty; I could use a cold beer right now! Can you use some extra money? You bet I can! That little girl could do with a bath; she's very dirty.*

lack [U (*of*)] the condition of not having (something necessary): *The plants died through/for lack of water.*

want 1 [U (*of*)] *fml* lack or absence (*often in the phrs* **for/from want of**): *The plants died for/from want of water. I'll take this one for want of a better. She felt the want of a good friend.* **2** [U] severe lack of the things necessary to life: *Want can make your life hopeless. It's terrible to live in want. 'War on want' is a movement to lessen world hunger.* **in want of** *esp formerly* in need of: *Are you in want of money? This house is in want of repair.*

need 1 [U (*of, for*)] the condition of lacking or wanting (something necessary or useful): *He sensed her need for help. There's no need for a new law. They are in great need of help.* **2** [U] the state of not having enough food or money: *Illness and need brought about his early death.* **3** [C *usu pl*] *often fml* something necessary to have: *He always looks after the needs of others and forgets himself.*

wish 1 [C, C3] a feeling of wanting, esp what at present is impossible: *He has a wish to visit India. It's her wish to be left alone.* **2** [C] an attempt esp by magic to make something happen: *She made a wish. The old woman gave him three wishes.* **3** [C] *usu fml* what is wished for: *That is my wish; please do it.*

will 1 [C; U, U3] the power or intention to make things happen: *He has the will to live; he'll recover. She has a very strong will; she'll do what she wants, not what we want.* **2** [U9] what is wished or intended (by the stated person): *Her death is God's will. It is the will of the King.* **3** [U; S] the power to control one's mind and body: *He did it by force of will/by* **will power.** **4** [U; C] the power in the mind to choose one's actions: *Free will makes us able to choose our way of life.* **at will** as one wishes **of one's own free will** according to one's own wishes and no one else's

requirement [C] *esp fml* anything needed: *What are your requirements, sir?*

desire 1 [C, C3, 5c] *often fml* a strong wish: *He was filled with a desire to see her again. She has a great desire to succeed/for success. He has many unsatisfied desires. It is my desire that you go.* **2** [C9] something desired: *What is your greatest desire?* **3** [C (*for*)] a strong wish for sex: *Antony's desire for Cleopatra caused his death.*

craving [C (*for*) *usu sing*] a very strong continuing desire: *He has a craving for sweets; he never stops wanting them.*

lust [U; C] a very strong desire, esp in sex: *He felt a great lust for the girl, but could not have her. These people have a terrible lust for gold.*

'Among all the lusts of the flesh (= the body), *sex is strongest,'* said the priest.

hope [U; C] the wish or feeling that something (good) could, will, or may happen: *Don't give up/lose hope. She has no hope of success/succeeding. There is now little hope that he is still alive. They have great hopes of winning. She had a look of hope in her eyes.* **hopeful** [B] having, giving, or feeling hope: *I'm hopeful about the examination results. She had a hopeful look on her face.* **-ly** [adv]: *He waited hopefully. Are you coming?*—*Hopefully* (= I hope so). **-ness** [U] **hopeless** [B] **1** having or giving no hope: *The news is hopeless; we are losing the war. She had a hopeless look on her face.* **2** bad at doing things: *He's hopeless; he can't do anything right.* **-ly** [adv]: *He got the papers hopelessly mixed up.* **-ness** [U]

despair [U] loss of hope: *Her face showed her complete despair.* **despairing** [A] showing or causing despair: *He gave a despairing cry as he read the bad news.*

desperation [U] the state of being without hope: *He kicked at the locked door in desperation.* **desperate** [B] **1** having lost all hope; willing to do anything to get what one wants: *He was desperate; his family had no food.* **2** violent and dangerous: *Desperate men often do desperate things.* **3** very difficult and dangerous: *This is a desperate job; I don't like doing it.*

optimism [U] the attitude of hoping for or expecting something good to happen: *She is full of optimism about her new job; she thinks it will be really good.* **optimistic** [B] showing or having optimism: *He is optimistic about getting a better job.* **-ally** [adv Wa4] **optimist** [C] an optimistic person

pessimism [U] the attitude of expecting only bad things to happen: *She is full of pessimism about her new job; She thinks it won't be any good.* **pessimistic** [B] showing or having pessimism: *He is pessimistic about passing the examination; he thinks he'll fail.* **-ally** [adv Wa4] **pessimist** [C] a pessimistic person

F9 *verbs* : **bearing and enduring**

bear [T1, 3, 4] to accept, experience, or suffer: *He bore the pain well.* (*fig*) *I can't bear that dull friend of yours. She can't bear sleeping in a cold bed. She can't bear to see him in pain/seeing him in pain.* **bearable** [B] that can be borne or suffered: *The pain was just bearable* **un-** [neg] **-bly** [adv]

stand [T1, 3, 4] (*often neg*) *infml* to bear: *He says he can't stand the pain any longer. I don't know how you can stand her; she is such a fool.*

stand for [v prep T1] *infml* to bear; accept: *Why do you stand for his bad behaviour?*

take [T1] *infml* to bear; accept: *You shouldn't take that bad behaviour from those children. She took his cruel treatment for years without complaining. I just can't take it any more; I'm leaving you!*

tolerate [T1] *esp fml* to bear or endure; accept: *I can't tolerate this noise any longer! She tolerated his bad behaviour patiently, hoping he would begin to behave better.* [*also* ⇒ F175]

endure [T1, 3, 4] (*often neg*) *emph & fml* to bear (pain, suffering, etc): *Be quiet! I can't endure that noise a moment longer. She could never endure being/to be treated unkindly.*

suffer [T1] *esp lit* to endure: *She has suffered him/his behaviour in silence for years.*

put up with [v adv prep T1] *often infml* to suffer (someone or something) without complaining: *I can't put up with your bad behaviour any longer; I'm leaving. That poor woman has a lot to put up with* (= has many troubles to bear).

stomach [T1] (*often neg*) **1** to eat without dislike or illness: *I cannot stomach heavy food.* **2** (*fig*) to accept or bear, without displeasure: *I can't stomach his jokes.*

F10 *verbs* : **behaving**

behave 1 [L9] to do things, live, etc, usu in a stated way: *She behaved with great courage when her husband died. He behaved badly to*(*wards*) *his mother.* **2** [T1; I0] to do things, go about, meet people, talk, etc in a socially acceptable or polite way: *You must learn how to behave in company. Behave* (*yourself*)*! They have very well-behaved children.* **misbehave** [I0] to behave badly: *The children were misbehaving again.*

act 1 [L9] to behave as stated: *He acted bravely when the house was on fire.* **2** [L1] to behave like: *Oh, stop acting the fool!* **3** [I0] *deprec* to behave as if performing on the stage: *I can't take her seriously; she always seems to be acting.*

go on [v adv I0] *esp BrE infml* to behave: *He was going on in a very strange way at the party.*

conform [I0] (*to, with*)] to behave in the same way (as others): *You must conform to the rules of the group. His ideas don't conform with ours. She refuses to conform.* **conformity** [U] *fml* the condition of conforming: *Conformity to society's customs is not always acceptable to young people.*

treat [X9] **1** to behave towards or use (someone or something) in a particular, usu stated, way: *She treated him badly. Please treat the matter seriously. How did he treat you; did he treat you well?* **2** to deal with, discuss, etc: *He treats the subject very interestingly in his new book. The book treats that subject very interestingly.*

patronize, -ise [Wv4; T1] **1** to treat (someone) in a friendly way while showing that one thinks oneself more important, clever, etc: *Stop patronizing me! She's a very patronizing kind of person.*

F11 *nouns* : **behaving**

behaviour *BrE*, **behavior** *AmE* [U] way of

behaving: *The boy's behaviour was disgraceful. He was on his best behaviour at the party.*
misbehaviour [U] bad behaviour
action [C] a way of doing something: *I can tell by his actions that he is unhappy.*
doings [P] *infml* things which have been or are being done: *Tell me about all his doings in Wales.*
conduct [U] **1** a person's way of behaving: *The children's conduct at the meeting was very good/bad.* **2** the way of directing or organizing something: *The Government's conduct of the war led to heavy losses.*
manners [P] ways of behaving towards or with others: *That child has no manners. What good manners he has.*
treatment 1 [U *of*] behaviour towards someone or something: *His treatment of the girl was very bad.* **2** [U; C: *of*] a way of dealing with something: *His treatment of the subject in his book is very interesting.*
carriage [U] a person's way of walking, of holding himself or herself while moving: *Her carriage is excellent.*
deportment [U] a person's way of behaving, esp on formal occasions: *The girl was given lessons in deportment.*
poise [U] the way of holding esp the head; an esp calm way of behaving: *She showed great poise during that difficult time.*
bearing [U; S] a way of acting, walking, or behaving: *He has a military bearing; he must have been a soldier once.*

F12 *nouns* : **prejudice and favouritism**

prejudice 1 [U] unfair (and often unfavourable) feeling or opinion not based on reason or enough knowledge, and sometimes resulting from fear or distrust of ideas different from one's own: *A judge must be free from prejudice. They have a law against racial prejudice* (= prejudice against members of other races). **2** [C] an example of this: *They have a prejudice against lending money, because they are afraid they won't get it back. He has a prejudice in favour of anything modern. She has always lived in a small village and her mind is full of prejudices against strangers.* **prejudiced** [B] feeling or showing prejudice; unfair: *This newspaper supports one political party and gives rather prejudiced reports on government action.* **un-** [*neg*] **prejudicial** [B] *fml* harmful: *Smoking is prejudicial to health.* **-ly** [adv]
bias [C; U] a tendency to be in favour of or against something or someone without knowing enough to be able to judge fairly; a prejudice: *He has a bias towards/against Scottish products.*
aversion [U; S: (*to*)] (a) hate or dislike of a person, group of people, thing, or things, etc often without clear reason: *She has an aversion to cats.*
favouritism [U] unfair preference for one person or group over another: *'I can tell you there is no favouritism in this school,' the teacher said.*

F13 *verbs* : **prejudice** [T1]

prejudice 1 to cause (someone or someone's mind) to have a prejudice; influence: *His pleasant voice prejudiced me in his favour.* **2** to weaken or harm (someone's case, expectations, etc): *Ill health has prejudiced his chances of success.*
bias to cause to form settled favourable or unfavourable opinions, usu without enough information to judge fully; to cause to prefer; to prejudice: *Her background biased/biassed him in her favour.* **biased/biassed** [B] having a bias **un-** [*neg*]

F14 *adjectives* : **objective and impartial** [B]

objective not affected by one's own feelings, prejudices, hopes, ideas, etc: *He wrote an objective account of what happened. He tried to be objective about it, but his own interests were too strong.* **-ly** [adv] **objectivity** [U] the state of being objective
impartial fair to both sides in an argument, law case, etc, because objective; unbiassed: *A judge should be impartial and should study every matter objectively.* **-ly** [adv] **impartiality** [U] the state of being impartial
disinterested willing to judge or act fairly because not influenced by personal advantage: *He was not a disinterested advisor; he hoped to make money from the deal.*

Liking and not liking

F20 *verbs* : **liking and loving**

like 1 [T1, 4] to be interested in, enjoy the presence of, want to know and do things with, etc; enjoy: *He likes her. She seems to like him. I like being with him.* **2** [T1, 3, 4] to be happy to have or do: *I like ice cream. Do you like swimming? I like it* (= life) *here. I'd like to go there with you.* [also ⇒ F140]
fancy [T1, 4] *usu infml* to like and (usu) to want: *'That girl's pretty,' he said. 'I quite fancy her.' She said she fancied a swim. I quite fancy going there.*
love [T1, 3, 4] to like very much: *He loves her. I love this kind of food. She loves being with him. He used to love her, but now he seems to hate her. They love swimming. I'd love to go there with you.* **lover** [C] *often in comb* a person who loves: *He is a lover of music/a music-lover.*
adore 1 [T1] to love deeply (and respect highly): *She adores her father. I adore you!* **2** [T1, 4]

infml to like very much: *She adores the cinema/going to the cinema.*

care for [v prep T1] to like or love: *He told her he cared for her greatly.*

cherish [T1] to like, love, enjoy, and value, etc, over a long time: *She cherished his memory for years, although she never saw him again. I shall always cherish your friendship.*

F21 *verbs* : **liking and loving** *informal*

be fond of [T1,4] to like: *He's very fond of her. I'm fond of Chinese food/going there.*

be attached to [T1] to be fond of, esp over a long time: *She's very attached to her parents.*

be keen on [T1,4] to like a lot: *He's really keen on her. Are you keen on swimming?*

take to [v prep T1] to begin to like: *She took to the children immediately, and they took to her.*

F22 *nouns* : **liking and loving**

liking [S] what one likes; a feeling of liking: *This house is (very much) to my liking. He has a liking for hot food. The children seem to have taken a liking to him.* **likes and dislikes** [P] things that one likes and does not like: *What are his likes and dislikes in food?*

fancy [S] a liking formed without the help of reason (*often in the phr* **take a fancy to**): *I have taken (quite) a fancy to that hat. This idea has really caught his fancy.*

love 1 [U *(of, for)*] great liking; strong emotional [⇒ F4] interest: *His love (for her) was obvious to everyone. Is she in love with him? I have a great love of/for Indian food. A mother's love for her child is very strong.* **2** [C] an example of this: *She is a person of sudden loves and hates.* **3** [C] the object of one's love: *Music was one of the great loves of his life. She's one of his old loves.* **4** [N] (a friendly term of address): *Hello, love!*

fondness 1 [U *(for)*] the condition of being fond of someone or something: *Her fondness for children was well known.* **2** [S] *esp pomp* a liking: *She has an unfortunate fondness for chocolates and puts on weight accordingly.*

attachment [C *usu sing*] *often fml & euph* a feeling of liking, fondness, affection, etc, esp over a longer time: *She formed an attachment for him over the years. I feel a certain attachment for her; I've known her a long time.*

affection [U] gentle, lasting love, as of a parent for a child; fondness: *Her affection for them was clear in the way she spoke.*

care [U] interested or concerned affection: *Her care for his well-being showed in her worried expression.*

devotion [U *(to)*] great fondness (for): *His devotion to his friends is well-known.*

adoration [U *(for)*] deep love and respect: *They feel a great adoration for him.*

desire 1 [U] strong love and need, esp sexual:

His desire for her was great. **2** [C] a strong love or need: *She kept her sexual desires under control.*

passion [U; C] great emotion [⇒ F2] and love, often sexual: *She had a passion for chocolates. His passion for her made him unhappy, because she did not love him in return.*

F23 *adjectives* : **liking and loving**

loving [B] showing, expressing, or having love (for someone): *She is very loving towards the children.* **-ly** [adv]

affectionate [B] showing gentle love: *He received an affectionate letter from his sister.* **-ly** [adv]

fond [Wa1] **1** [F *of*] feeling a liking or love for: *He's very fond of his sister/of chocolates. He's fonder of his sister than his brother.* **2** [A] *deprec* over-loving: *Her anxiety is typical of the fond mother who is afraid to lose her son.* **-ly** [adv]

devoted 1 [B *(to)*] loving and loyal; caring a great deal: *She's a devoted wife and mother. He is very devoted to his family and his work.* **2** [F *to*] spending a great deal of time and/or effort (on); fond (of): *He's devoted to music/to helping others.* **-ly** [adv]

adoring [A] showing or having great love: *She looked at him with adoring eyes.* **-ly** [adv]

passionate [B] having or showing passion; showing great love, desire, strong feelings, etc: *Casanova is said to have been a passionate lover. His letters to her were very passionate.* **-ly** [adv]

partial 1 [F *to*] *esp infml* having a liking for: *I think she's quite partial to him. I'm partial to a bit of cheese; can I have some more, please?* **2** [B] *often deprec* liking one (person, group, etc) better than another: *Stop being so partial; we know you like them better than us.* **-ly** [adv] **partiality** [U] the state of being partial; unfairness **im-** [neg]

F24 *adjectives & nouns* : **able to be liked, loved, etc**

lik(e)able [B] easy to like; deserving, causing, or worthy of love; attractive and pleasant: *He is a very likeable person.* **-bly** [adv]

lov(e)able [B] easy to love: *That dog is very lovable. What a lovable person she is!* **un-** [neg] **-bly** [adv]

desirable [B] **1** causing desire, esp sexual desire: *She's a very beautiful and desirable woman.* **2** *often fml* wanted as the best thing: *It isn't really desirable to have him working here.* **un-** [neg] **-bly** [adv]

adorable [B] **1** worthy of being loved deeply: *She's an adorable girl.* **2** *infml* lovely or attractive: *Her face is perfectly adorable.* **-bly** [adv]

much-loved [Wa1;B] greatly loved: *We were sorry to hear of your father's death; he was a much-loved man.*

dear 1 [B (*to*)] loved very much: *His daughter is very dear to him. His money is dearer to him than his wife.* **2** [C; N] a loved person, esp when spoken to: *Come, my dear. She's a dear; I like her a lot.* **3** [C] a helpful person: *Be a dear and make a cup of tea. Make a cup of tea, there's a dear!* **4** [A] (used in writing letters): *Dear Sir . . .; Dear Mr Smith . . .* **5** [interj] (used in expressing surprise, worry, etc): *Oh dear, what shall I do? Dear, dear, that's bad!*

darling *esp emot & emph* **1** [B] loved very much; easy to love: *She's a darling girl! What a darling little dog!* **2** [C; N] a loved person: *Come on, darling; let's go. The children were good today, the darlings!* **3** [C] a very helpful person: *Be a darling and make a cup of tea!*

beloved 1 [A; (F)] *esp lit & old use* greatly loved: *Her beloved father died yesterday.* **2** [A; (F)] *deprec ironical* loved too much: *Can't you put your beloved books in another place?* **3** [Wn3;C;N] *old use, lit, pomp & humor* a loved one: *Come, beloved! He has been talking on the phone to his beloved for hours!*

popular [B] **1** favoured by many people: *She sang a popular song. Beards were popular among young men at that time.* **2** generally admired by great numbers of people: *He's a good politician but he isn't popular.* **3** well liked, esp by people one meets in daily life: *He is popular with girls; he's so amusing.* **4** general; common; widespread: *That is quite a popular belief. 'Mary' is a very popular name for a girl.* **popularity** [U] the quality of being well liked, favoured, or admired: *This game once had great popularity. The politician was eager for popularity.*

F25 *verbs, etc* : **attracting and interesting** [T1]

[ALSO ⇨ F224, K10]

attract 1 to cause to like, admire, or notice: *He was attracted by her beauty.* **2** to draw towards one: *He attracted large numbers of followers.* **3** to draw by unseen forces: *The moon attracts the earth's seas towards it/her.*

draw to attract: *The play is drawing big crowds. You know, I feel very drawn to that girl.*

appeal to [v prep] to be attractive to: *She appeals to him very much. This new job really appeals to me.*

interest to cause (someone) to give attention; attract: *Music interests her more than painting. I think he interests her.*

concern 1 [Wv6] to be important, interesting, etc to: *This matter concerns you all; listen carefully. How does her business concern you?* **2** [U] the condition of being important, interesting, etc: *This matter is no concern of mine. This is a matter of some concern to us all.*

suit 1 to please or be satisfactory to (someone): *Will it suit you if we eat now? The change of plan did not suit him at all.* **2** (of clothes, col-

ours, etc) to look pleasing, attractive, etc on (someone): *Blue suits her* (= She looks good in clothes with the colour blue). *That new dress suits you very well.*

become [Wv6] *often fml* (of clothes, colours, etc) to suit (someone): *That blue dress really becomes you.* (*fml*) *It does not become you to use insulting words like that!*

F26 *verbs* : **attracting and interesting very much** [Wv4;T1]

fascinate to interest very much, so that one must continue to look, visit, do, etc: *This story fascinates me; I must go on reading it. I'm fascinated by old houses; I must look round this one. The way she dressed fascinated him.*

enthrall to fascinate completely: *He's enthralled by that book. What an enthralling story!*

enchant to fascinate and (usu) delight, esp in a way or situation which is like magic: *She was enchanted by the beautiful old house and its lovely gardens. What an enchanting dress you are wearing!*

charm to please and fascinate: *She charmed all the young men; they wouldn't leave her alone.*

captivate to charm, excite, and attract (esp someone): *Venice's beauty completely captivated the old man and he went to live there.*

F27 *verbs* : **tempting and enticing**

[⇨ G87 PERSUADE]

tempt 1 [T1] to (try to) make (someone) do something wrong or improper: *Have some more to eat—No, please; don't tempt me! He tempted his friends into stealing the money.* **2** [V3] to cause (someone) to want to do or wish for something: *I was greatly tempted to telephone her, but I didn't. Can I tempt you to have another drink?*

entice [X9] to tempt greatly; to persuade (someone) with great success, esp to do something wrong or improper: *He enticed her to his room. They enticed him into doing what they wanted, although he knew he shouldn't. Can I entice you into having another drink?*

F28 *nouns* : **attracting, fascinating, and enticing**

attraction 1 [U] the act of attracting: *The attraction of the city's bright lights was difficult to resist. Work has little attraction for him.* **2** [C] something which attracts: *Her greatest attraction for him is her voice. The city's bright lights and theatres are great attractions.*

appeal [S; U] a tendency to attract: *His ideas have a certain appeal, I must admit.*

interest [U] a quality which attracts attention: *This is a matter of great interest to us.*

fascination 1 [U] the ability to fascinate or the condition of being fascinated: *He has a great fascination for women; they find him very attractive. He sat there in a state of fascination, listening to everything the great man said.* **2** [C] something which fascinates: *She has many fascinations for him* (= She fascinates him in many ways).

charm 1 [U] the quality of attraction, fascination, and pleasure: *These girls have great charm. He felt the charm of the house and garden.* **2** [C] something which charms: *Her many charms are well known; she is a beautiful girl.*

enchantment [U; C] a delightful influence or feeling of fascination: *The beauty of the scene filled him with enchantment.*

temptation 1 [U] the act of tempting or being tempted: *'Temptation is always with us; we always want to do things that we shouldn't do,' said the priest.* **2** [C] something which tempts: *All that money on the table is a temptation to someone to steal it. There are many temptations in life.*

enticement 1 [U] the quality of being enticing: *The idea of living on a sunny island has great enticement for him.* **2** [C] something which entices: *They offered him various enticements to change his job.* **3** [U] *tech* the act of enticing, esp of enticing a young person away for sexual reasons: *He was sent to prison for enticement.*

F29 *adjectives* : **attracting and interesting** [B]

attractive having the power to attract: *She is an attractive woman; most men think so. I find his ideas very attractive; I like them.* **un-** [*neg*] **-ly** [adv]

appealing 1 able to move the feelings: *She looked at him with appealing eyes.* **2** attractive or interesting: *There is something very appealing about happy children.* **un-** [*neg*] **-ly** [adv]

becoming (esp of clothes, colours, etc) pretty, attractive, and suitable: *That hat looks very/most becoming (on you).* **un-** [*neg*]

interesting which takes (and keeps) someone's attention or attracts a person: *That's an interesting idea; I must think about it.* **un-** [*neg*] **-ly** [adv]

fascinating which interests very much: *He told us a fascinating story about Africa; he's a fascinating speaker.* **-ly** [adv]

enchanting fascinating and delightful: *What an enchanting evening/dress/child!* **-ly** [adv]

tempting causing someone to be tempted; that will tempt people: *The food looked very tempting.* **-ly** [adv]

enticing causing someone to be enticed; very attractive: *That is an enticing idea, but we must consider it carefully first. She looked enticing in her new dress.* **-ly** [adv]

F30 *verbs* : **preferring** [T1]

like better/more *infml* to like (one thing) more than another: *I like Mary's dress, but I like Jane's dress better/more.*

prefer [*also* T3, 4, 5c; V3] *fml* to choose (one thing or action) rather than another; to like better: *I like Mary's dress, but I prefer Jane's. Would you like meat or fish?—I'd prefer meat, please. She prefers dogs to cats. May I wash the dishes?—I'd prefer you to dry them/prefer it if you dried them. He prefers swimming to riding as a sport. May I come with you?—I should prefer to go alone.*

favour *BrE*, **favor** *AmE* [T1] to choose or support for some special reason: *He favours the team in blue, but I favour the greens. She seems to favour his ideas over all the others.*

F31 *nouns* : **preferring**

preference [C; U] **1** a liking (for one thing rather than another): *He has a preference for fruit over vegetables. Would you like tea or coffee?—I have no special preference(s). I'd choose the small car in preference to* (= rather than) *the big one, if I were you.* **2** choice; that which is liked better or best: *Tea or coffee— which is your preference? In planning the meals she always considers her husband's preferences.*

favour *BrE*, **favor** *AmE* [U] special love, position, or support: *He is in favour with his mother at the moment, and his brother is out of favour.* (*old use*) *The nobles hoped to gain the King's favour for their plan.* **disfavour** *BrE*, **disfavor** *AmE* [U] *fml* **1** dislike; disapproval: *Mary looks on/regards/views him with great disfavour.* **2** the state of being disliked: *John seems to be in/have fallen into disfavour (with Mary). How have I incurred* (= caused) *your disfavour?*

favourite *BrE*, **favorite** *AmE* [C] something or someone liked most: *Her second son is her favourite. This sweet is my favourite; what's yours?*

priority 1 [U] the special right or need to be done, seen, heard, etc before others: *This matter is top priority* (= very important). *This is a priority matter; we must give it priority over all other business.* **2** [C] an example of this; something to which priority is given: *What are your priorities in this matter?*

F32 *verbs* : **disliking and hating** [T1, 4]

dislike not to like; think to be unpleasant: *She dislikes big cities/wearing stockings/being spoken to like that. I don't actually dislike her but we're not really friends. He got himself much disliked because of his bad manners.*

hate [*also* T3; V3; I0] to dislike very much: *I hate such cruelty. He hates his little sister* *because she breaks all his toys. I hate everything to be changed when I'm away. He has learnt to hate.*

detest to hate with very strong feeling: *I detest people who tell lies.*

loathe (esp of living things) to detest, with a feeling of disgust [⇨ F36] *She loathes insects. 'I loathe you!' she shouted angrily.*

abhor (esp of ideas and actions) to detest and want to keep away from: *He abhors cruelty in any form.*

cannot stand to hate; be unable to bear [⇨ F9]: *'I cannot stand spoilt children!' she said.*

F33 *nouns* : **disliking and hating**

dislike [C; U] (a) feeling of not liking (something or someone): *I have a dislike of/for cats. She took a sudden dislike to him. She spoke to him with great dislike.*

hate [U; C] a strong feeling of dislike: *The man's hate showed on his face.*

hatred [U; C] a state or feeling of hating; hate: *She is full of hatred for the driver who killed her child. Old hatreds keep these families apart.*

animosity **1** [U (*against, towards, between*)] powerful and often active hatred: *I have/feel no animosity towards her. There is a lot of animosity between them.* **2** [C *usu pl*] an example of this: *I have no time for animosities.*

odium [U] *fml* widespread hatred: *He earned the odium of all his friends because of what he did.*

detestation [U] the condition of detesting; great hatred: *He feels detestation for things like that.*

abhorrence *also* **loathing** [U] great hatred and disgust [⇨ F36]: *He holds cruelty to children in abhorrence. She feels only loathing for the man who left her and her children.*

F34 *adjectives* : **hating** [B]

hateful very unpleasant in manner or to experience: *You're always hateful to me and nice to everybody else. It's hateful to be left at home alone.* **-ly** [adv] **-ness** [U]

odious *esp fml & pomp* hateful: *What an odious fellow he is!*

detestable fit to be detested: *This is a detestable job; I hate it.* **-bly** [adv]

loathsome hateful and disgusting: [⇨ F37] *'What loathsome creatures these insects are!' she said.* **-ness** [U]

abhorrent hateful and disgusting; completely against what one likes or wants (to do): *Cruelty is abhorrent to her.*

F35 *verbs* : **disgusting and repelling** [T1]

disgust to cause a feeling of sick dislike in : *His ideas disgust me; they are terrible.*

put off [v adv] to cause dislike in; discourage: *If you do things like that, you'll put everybody off.*

repel to cause to turn or go away in strong dislike: *His manner and way of life repel me.*

alienate [(*from*)] to turn away the friendship of (someone); cause to feel or become an enemy or unfriendly; cause to feel that one does not belong: *His cold manner alienated her. She became alienated from him. He feels alienated; he isn't happy in his work.*

F36 *nouns* : **disgusting and repelling** [U]

disgust the strong feeling of often sick dislike caused by an unpleasant sight, sound, or smell, or bad behaviour: *The food at the hotel filled him with disgust. He left in disgust at their cruelty to their animals.*

repulsion the state of being or feeling repelled by something or someone

revulsion a very strong feeling of repulsion

alienation [U] **1** the separation from or loss of friendship of another person **2** a sense of not belonging to or being part of one's surroundings

F37 *adjectives* : **disgusting and repelling** [B]

disgusting causing disgust: *What a disgusting smell!—Is it coming from the drains? I find his ideas on sex quite disgusting.* **-ly** [adv]

revolting causing great disgust: *What revolting colours they have used to paint the room! This is a revolting book; it is full of obscene* [⇨ F60] *pictures.* **-ly** [adv]

repellent causing a person or thing to turn or go away: *I find his manner generally repellent.*

repulsive very repellent and nasty: *What a repulsive person he is; I don't want to meet him again.* **-ly** [adv] **-ness** [U]

off-putting *infml* unfriendly; not warm or welcoming: *I found his manner a bit off-putting; he didn't try to make us feel at home.*

F38 *adjectives* : **not good to look at** [B]

ugly [Wa1] not attractive to look at: *What an ugly dog! He had an ugly, dangerous look on his face. That house isn't beautiful; it's ugly; it's the ugliest house I've ever seen!*

hideous having a terrible effect on the senses, esp shocking to the eyes: *The man had a hideous face. What is that hideous noise? He suffered a hideous fate when taken by the enemy.* **-ly** [adv] **-ness** [U]

ghastly [Wa2] **1** (of a person) very pale and ill-looking: *He looked ghastly.* **2** very frightening or ugly: *What a ghastly place that house is!* **-iness** [U]

plain [Wa1] *euph* (esp of women) not pretty or good-looking; ugly: *I'm afraid she's rather a plain girl.* **-ness** [U]

homely [Wa1] *AmE* (of people) not good-looking: *She's a homely girl but she's kind-hearted.* **-liness** [U]

unsightly *often euph* ugly; not pleasant to look at: *He had an unsightly mark on his face.* **-liness** [U]

F39 adjectives : **good to look at** [B]

good-looking (of people) pleasant to look at: *He's a good-looking man, isn't he? She's a good-looking girl too. They make a good-looking pair/couple* [⇒ C77].

beautiful 1 (usu of women, places, and things) very good-looking or worth looking at: *What a beautiful girl she is, with such beautiful long hair. This is one of the most beautiful houses in the town.* 2 *infml* very good: *That was a beautiful game of tennis.*

lovely [Wa1] 1 pleasingly beautiful: *That's a lovely dress, isn't it? What a lovely smile she has. It's a really lovely day for a picnic.* 2 *infml* very good: *It's lovely to see you again! A present for me; how lovely!* **-liness** [U]

pretty [Wa1] 1 (esp of a woman, a child, or a small thing) pleasing or nice to look at, listen to, etc; charming but not beautiful or grand: *She looks much prettier with long hair than with short hair. She has quite a pretty singing voice. What a pretty little garden.* 2 *deprec* (of a boy) charming and graceful in a girlish way 3 *apprec* causing admiration for neatness, cleverness, or skill: *That was a pretty shot—well played! He writes with a pretty turn of phrase* (= expresses himself well). 4 *derog ironical* not nice; displeasing: *It's a pretty state of affairs when I come home from work and she hasn't even cooked my dinner.*

attractive (usu of females, now increasingly of males) having good looks; pretty: *She's an attractive girl and he's an attractive man.* **un-** [*neg*] **-ness** [U] **-ly** [adv]

comely [Wa1] *old use & lit* beautiful: *She was a most comely young woman.*

handsome [Wa2] 1 (esp of men) good-looking; of attractive appearance: *He's a handsome lad, the handsomest/most handsome in town.* 2 (esp of women) attractive but looking grand rather than delicate or pretty: *What a handsome girl she is and what a fine character she has.*

striking (of persons) interesting to look at (but not necessarily beautiful): *What a striking face she has.* **-ly** [adv] *He is strikingly handsome.*

presentable fit to be shown, heard, etc in public; fit to be seen (and judged): *She's a very presentable young woman. I have nothing presentable to wear. Make yourself presentable; our guests will be here soon.* **-bly** [adv]

shapely [Wa1] (esp of women) having a pleasing or beautiful shape: *She's a shapely young woman and suits that low-cut dress.* **-liness** [U]

fair [Wa1] *often lit* (of women) beautiful to look at: *She was young and fair and he loved her.*

elegant beautiful in appearance, in moving, etc; well-made; fashionable: *She wore an elegant dress and walked in a very elegant way.* **in-** [*neg*] **-ly** [adv]

picturesque 1 beautiful, charming, or interesting enough to be made into a picture: *the picturesque ruins of the old castle* 2 (of people, their manner, dress, etc) rather strange and unusual: *He was a picturesque figure with his long beard and strange clothes.* 3 (of language) unusually clear, strong, and descriptive

---

F40 nouns : **good or not good to look at**

beauty 1 [U] the condition of being beautiful: *This is a city of great beauty. Her beauty filled him with desire.* 2 [C] a beautiful woman: *That girl will be a beauty when she grows up. What beauties these girls are!* 3 [C] a beautiful thing, animal, etc: *This diamond is a real beauty. Where did you get those horses?—They are beauties!*

elegance [U] the condition of being elegant: *She is well known for her elegance.*

grace [U] 1 beauty of movement: *She moves with great grace.* 2 pleasant manners: *He thanked them with grace.* **graceful** [B] showing grace: *She's a very graceful girl.* **-ly** [adv]

ugliness [U] the state of being ugly: *The ugliness of the old house depressed her.*

Good and evil

F50 adjectives & adverbs : **relating to the right qualities**

good 1 [B] having the right qualities: *This is a good book but that one is better. These arguments are all good, and that one is the best of all. She's a good friend of mine.* 2 [B] favourable: *It's a good day for a drive. The weather's good. He has a good chance of getting the job.* 3 [B] enjoyable: *That was a good story. They had a good time at the party.* 4 [B] morally right; in accordance with religious standards: *He led a good life.* 5 [B] (esp of children) well-behaved: *Please be good when your uncle comes.* 6 [B] suitable for its purpose: *He gave some good advice. That's a good idea.* 7 [A] (in exclamations): *Good heavens! Good God!* 8 [A] (in greetings): *Good morning, John.*

well [adv] 1 in the right manner; satisfactorily: *They spent their money well and were pleased with what they had bought.* 2 with kindness or favour: *They speak well of him in the school.* 3 [Wa5] justly or suitably: *I couldn't very well refuse when she asked me to go.* 4 to a high standard: *She paints well.* **5** closely as a person: *I know her well.*

nice [Wa1;B] **1** good; kind; well done or well made: *It's nice to see you. It's hard to be nice to someone you don't like. That was a nice shot you played. She did a nice piece of work for our company.* **2** pleasant, pleasing: *It's a nice day today, isn't it?* (=with good weather)? *This soup tastes very nice. How nice to see you again!* **3** *becoming rare & sometimes deprec* having or showing (too) high standards morally or socially: *Nice girls don't do things like that. This couldn't happen in nice society.* **4** *derog ironical & infml* bad, wrong: *You're a nice friend; you won't even lend me £5! Lend you £5?—That's a nice state of affairs!* **-ly** [adv]

fair [Wa1;B] *esp lit* (esp of weather conditions) good: *They had fair weather for their voyage.*

pleasant [Wa2;B] **1** pleasing to the senses, feelings, or mind; enjoyable: *We had a very pleasant time at their house last night. What a pleasant taste the food has. It was a pleasant surprise to see her again.* **2** (esp of people) likeable, friendly: *She seems a pleasant (sort of) person. Make an effort to be pleasant at the party, please. She had a very pleasant smile.* **3** (of weather) fine; favourable: *It's quite pleasant today although there is a cold wind.* **un-** [neg] **-ly** [adv] **-ness** [U]

fine [Wa1;B] **1** good in quality, contents, ideas, etc: *This is a fine book; you'll enjoy it.* **2** (of weather) not raining, etc; sunny, etc; very good: *It's a fine day. What fine weather!* **3** good morally, in nature, etc: *He's a fine man; he'll help us.* **4** (of things) well-made: *What a fine piece of work that painting is!* **5** [adv] *AmE & ScotE* very well: *I like him fine.*

congenial [B] pleasant and suitable: *She is a congenial person to work with. This is a congenial place to live in.* **un-** [neg] **-ly** [adv]

F51 *adjectives* : **relating to the right qualities** [Wa5;B] *infml*

great very enjoyable, good, etc: *What a great idea! It's great to see you again.*

grand very pleasant, delightful: *That was a grand party, wasn't it?*

swell *esp AmE* great; grand: *What a swell idea! It was swell to see you all again.*

super *esp BrE* great; grand: *What a super party! It was super of you to help.*

smashing *esp BrE* great; grand: *It would be smashing to see her again. What a smashing dress!*

F52 *adjectives* : **relating to the right qualities** [B]

excellent very good; of high quality: *She enjoys excellent health. What excellent work he has done! She will make him an excellent wife.* **-ly** [adv] **-ence** [U]

splendid very good; worth admiring: *What a splendid idea! It was splendid of him to help you. They live in a splendid house in the country.* **-ly** [adv]

superb really grand; very splendid; of the finest quality: *What a superb cook she is! His work is quite superb.* **-ly** [adv]

superior good or better in quality than other persons or things of the same kind: *This is a superior car, sir; drive it and you will see why. She is a very superior kind of girl.*

capital *esp formerly* very good: *That's a capital plan; let's do it! What a capital idea!*

superlative [Wa5] better than all others: *work of superlative quality*

supreme [Wa5] highest in quality, position, power, etc: *It was the supreme moment in his life. Rome was supreme/the supreme power in the Mediterranean world for many years.* **-ly** [adv]: *He did the work supremely well* **supremacy** [U] the state of being supreme, esp in power over others: *The supremacy of Rome lasted many years.*

de luxe *Fr* especially good and intended for the wealthy: *The de luxe model costs a lot more than the standard one.*

prime [Wa5] **1** *apprec* (usu of meat, esp beef) of the very best quality or kind: *This meat is very dear.—Yes, but it's a prime joint; it's in prime condition.* **2** first in time, rank, or importance: *This is a matter of prime importance. He is the Prime Minister of the country.*

choice [Wa1] (esp of food) worthy of being chosen; of high quality: *The shop was selling very choice apples. Give me a pound of the choicest meat, please. Those look very choice apples.* (fig ironical) *She swore at him but he used even choicer phrases* (=even stronger and more offensive) *in reply.*

select chosen very carefully and therefore (thought to be) the best or very good; accepting only (those who are thought to be) the best or very good: *These are select apples. He belongs to a very select club.*

classic [Wa5] **1** [A] very good, esp because of a kind that has for a long time been considered good, special, etc: *This is a really classic French wine.* **2** very true or suitable: *This is a classic example of how Roman houses were built/of how not to teach a language.* **3** *also* **classical** very good because simple: *She wore a dress with classic lines/of classical simplicity.*

F53 *adjectives* : **relating to the right qualities** *emot*

wonderful unusually good: *What wonderful news! It's wonderful to see you again.* **-ly** [adv]

marvellous wonderful, esp because surprising: *It's absolutely marvellous to be here again! What marvellous weather for the time of year!* **-ly** [adv]

magnificent great, grand, generous, etc: *The queen was wearing a magnificent dress. He gave* them a magnificent gift woxth hundreds of pounds. **-ly** [adv] **-ence** [U]

glorious 1 very beautiful; splendid: *The trees are all glorious colours in autumn.* **2** *infml* very enjoyable: *This is a glorious joke!* **3** *now less common* having or worthy of great honour and fame: *He performed glorious deeds in battle.* **-ly** [adv]

stupendous very good, and causing great satisfaction or surprise: *What a stupendous thing to do!* **-ly** [adv]

fabulous 1 nearly unbelievable: *She inherited a fabulous sum of money.* **2** *infml* very good or pleasant; excellent: *We had a fabulous holiday in Spain.* **-ly** [adv]

sensational very good, and causing strong feeling, excitement, etc: *The news was really sensational; it has set everyone talking. What a sensational dress she was wearing!* **-ly** [adv]

F54 adjectives : **more or less good** [B]

decent *infml* rather good: *You can get quite a decent meal in that restaurant without spending too much money.* **-ly** [adv]

fair [Wa1] quite good, large, fine, etc: *The profit was fair but not as big as they had hoped. His exam results were not wonderful, but they were fair. How did he do in the exam?—Fair.*

satisfactory good enough for the purpose but not really good, or what one wanted: *Your son's work is satisfactory, but he could do better.* **un-** [neg] **-ily** [adv]

average [Wa5] of the usual or ordinary kind or quality: *There was nothing special about the meal; it was average. His exam results were just average.* **-ly** [adv]

adequate 1 enough for the purpose: *We took adequate food for a short camping holiday.* **2** having the necessary ability or qualities: *I hope he will prove adequate to the job.* **3** only just good enough: *The performance was adequate but hardly exciting.* **in-** [neg] **-ly** [adv] **-ness, -quacy** [U]

passable [Wa5] just good enough to pass (a test, standard): *The food in that restaurant is passable, nothing more.* **-bly** [adv]

mediocre of not very good or bad quality or ability, but usu not good enough: *The hotel was comfortable but the food was mediocre. He is a rather mediocre poet.* **-crity** [U] **-ly** [adv]

middling [Wa5] *infml* average: *Was the food good?—Middling; it was nothing special* (= not particularly good). [also ⇒ N88]

F55 nouns : **relating to the right qualities**

good 1 [U] that which is right and useful in accordance with religious beliefs or moral standards: *By behaving well you can be an influence for good. He does a lot of good for the town by giving money to build new schools.*

There's good in her, in spite of her bad behaviour. **2** [U] that which causes gain or improvement: *He works for the good of his family. You must live in a dry country for the good of your health. You must take this medicine for your own good. I'd lend him the money if I thought it would do (him) any good.* **3** [the P] good people generally; the people who do what is right: *Christians believe that the good go to heaven when they die.*

virtue 1 [U] *esp formerly* goodness, nobleness, and worth of character as shown in right behaviour: *You can trust him; he's a man of great virtue.* **2** [C] any good quality of character or behaviour: *Among his virtues are courage and truthfulness.* **3** [U] good advantage: *There's no virtue in waiting here for him any longer; he clearly isn't coming. There is some virtue in doing this, but not much.*

honour *BrE,* **honor** *AmE* [U] *esp formerly* personal virtue: *The knight said he would fight to save his honour.*

F56 adjectives : **(esp of people) having the right qualities** [B]

virtuous 1 *apprec* having virtue: *She is a virtuous woman.* **2** *deprec* (too) satisfied with one's own good behaviour and expressing this in one's manner towards those who (may) have done wrong: *Oh, stop being so damned virtuous; you aren't perfect, either!* **-ly** [adv]

noble [Wa2, 3] **1** of high quality, esp morally; deserving praise; worthy; unselfish: *His attempt to save the poor people's homes was truly noble. What a noble woman she is; she works all the time to help others.* **ig-** [neg] **-bly** [adv] **2** admirable in appearance; grand: *It is a building of noble proportions* [⇒ J40]. **nobility** [U]

worthy [Wa1] **1** *often pomp or humor & ironical* deserving praise: *He is indeed a worthy man and has led a good life. I'm afraid our worthy friends won't help us.* **2** [(of)] deserving something stated: *This man is worthy of praise; he has done well.* **un-** [neg] **-ily** [adv] **-iness** [U]

conscientious taking care to work well: *She is a conscientious student; she always tries hard.* **-ly** [adv] **-ness** [U]

selfless caring for and thinking (only) of others, not oneself; completely unselfish and therefore noble: *What a selfless person she is, always helping other people!* **-ly** [adv] **-ness** [U]

F57 adjectives & adverbs : **relating to the wrong qualities** [B]

bad not good; not what someone or something should be, morally, socially, religiously, etc: *What bad weather! She's a bad child; she won't do what we want her to do. This apple is bad; I won't eat it. I've got a really bad headache, much worse than last week; it feels like the worst* *(headache) I've ever had. Don't try to read in this bad light.* **-ly** [U] **-ness** [U]

ill [adv Wa5 *often in comb*] **1** unfavourably: *to think/speak ill of someone* **2** hardly; scarcely; not enough: *I can ill afford the time. The child looked ill-fed.* **3** badly, cruelly, or unpleasantly: *The child was ill-treated.*

nasty [Wa1] **1** morally bad or improper: *This is a nasty book; the work of a nasty mind.* **2** very ugly or unpleasant to see, taste, smell, etc: *It's nasty to drink from a dirty cup. Fish tastes nasty if it isn't fresh. What nasty foggy weather!* **3** harmful; painful: *There was a nasty accident here yesterday and two people were killed. He got a nasty cut on the head in a fight. Our hotel bill came as a nasty shock.* **-ily** [adv] **-iness** [U]

foul [Wa1] (esp of weather, character, etc) very bad: *He has a foul temper* [⇒ F103] *when he doesn't get what he wants. This weather is really foul; it has been raining heavily all week.* **-ly** [adv] **-ness** [U]

rotten [Wa2] *infml & emot* bad: *It was rotten of you to tell him what I said about him. What rotten weather! The book was rotten; I didn't like it at all.* **-ness** [U]

selfish concerned with or directed towards one's own advantage without care for others: *She is a selfish person, and everything she does is for selfish reasons.* **-ly** [adv] **-ness** [U]

base [Wa1] *esp lit & old use* bad, esp because doing things, or done, for selfish, dishonest, etc reasons: *It was a base action to take her money!*

offensive 1 causing annoyance or anger or offence [⇒ F149]: *What an offensive thing to say! She is a very offensive person sometimes.* **in-** [*neg*] **2** unpleasant: *What's that offensive smell?* **-ly** [adv] **-ness** [U]

F58 *adjectives* : **relating to the wrong qualities** [B]

evil [Wa2] very bad, esp in thought or behaviour; wicked or harmful: *He is an evil man with evil ideas, and leads an evil life.* **-lly** [adv]

wicked [Wa1] very bad; evil: *What a wicked man he is!* **-ly** [adv] **-ness** [U]

devilish evil; like a devil [⇒ C323]: *Stop playing such devilish tricks on people!* **-ly** [adv]

diabolical *fml & pomp* devilish; evil: *He had a diabolical plan to kill his family.* **-lly** [adv Wa4]

sinful 1 evil; guilty of, or being, sin [⇒ F62, C341]: *'What a sinful city that is!' the priest said. He has led a sinful life, harming many people.* **2** *infml* shameful; seriously wrong or bad: *What a sinful waste of money!* **-lly** [adv] **-ness** [U]

abysmal *usu deprec* (of work, qualities, etc) very bad; very much worse than usual: *He is an abysmal failure at his work. She showed abysmal ignorance* (= lack of knowledge) *last night!* **-lly** [adv]

F59 *adjectives* : **behaving badly** [B]

wicked [Wa1] **1** *infml esp old use* behaving badly: *You wicked child—go to bed at once!* **2** suggesting ideas, actions, etc which could be exciting (but perhaps immoral): *She gave him a wicked smile and left the room. You're looking wicked—what are you planning?* **-ly** [adv] **-ness** [U]

naughty [Wa1] **1** (usu of a child) bad in behaviour; not obeying a parent, teacher, set of rules, etc: *You naughty boy; its naughty to pull you sister's hair. It was naughty of Father to stay out so late.* **2** *euph* (esp in newspapers) morally, esp sexually, improper: *He wrote an amusing and naughty book.* **-ily** [adv]

mischievous 1 *deprec* causing harm, often with intention: *Someone is spreading mischievous stories about the minister's private life* (= is saying that it is bad). **2** having or showing a liking for playfulness, esp of a rather troublesome kind: *One expects healthy children to be mischievous at times. The little girl had a mischievous expression on her face.* **-ly** [adv] **-ness** [U]

F60 *adjectives* : **not good in particular ways**

sinister [B] intending, threatening, or leading to evil: *He had a sinister look on his face. She has a sinister plan to get control of the company.*

ulterior [Wa5;A; (B)] *infml* hidden or kept secret, esp because bad: *He has an ulterior motive* (= reason or intention) *for wanting to see her; he is going to ask for money.*

obscene [B] **1** (esp of ideas, books, etc, usu about sex) nasty and dirty: *What an obscene mind he has! She doesn't read obscene books, she says.* **2** very bad indeed: *I think his behaviour is quite obscene.* **-ly** [adv]

depraved [B] having (developed) a bad character: *That young man has become thoroughly depraved; he drinks too much and has forgotten what truth and honesty are.*

F61 *infml adjectives* : **not good** [B]

awful very bad: *What awful weather!* **-ly** [adv] *How awfully unkind!*

terrible very bad indeed: *What terrible weather! Don't read that book; it's terrible.* **-bly** [adv] *He behaved terribly.*

diabolical *often humor* very bad: *We went to see the new play last night; it was really diabolical.* **-lly** [adv Wa4]

dreadful very bad, unpleasant, or shocking: *What is that dreadful smell! His exam results are dreadful.* **-lly** [adv]

horrible very unpleasant or ugly: *What a horrible picture she's painted!* **-bly** [adv]

ghastly [Wa2] very bad: *We had a ghastly time at that party.*

appalling of very bad quality: *Mary is an appalling cook.* **-ly** [adv]

frightful very bad; horrible:• *What frightful weather!* **-lly** [adv] [*also* ⇨ F124]

F62 *nouns* : **relating to wrong qualities**

evil [U; C] great wickedness or misfortune: *He warned his son to beware of evil/of the evils of the big city.*

sin 1 [U] evil as understood in a religion: *These people say that the city is a place full of sin and you must leave it.* 2 [C] an evil act, esp as understood in a religion: *In some religions it is a sin to eat the meat of pigs and drink alcohol. 'His sins could affect his children's lives,' said the priest.* [*also* ⇨ C341]

mischief 1 [U] bad, but not seriously bad, behaviour or actions, as of children, probably causing trouble and possibly damage or harm: *If his mother leaves him alone for five minutes, the little boy gets into mischief. Give him a toy to play with; that'll keep him out of mischief. She knew the children were up to some mischief* (= doing or planning something wrong) *and she found them in the garden digging up the flowers. Go to bed; you've done enough mischief (for) today.* 2 [U] troublesome playfulness or an expression, such as a smile or a look, of a desire to behave in this way: *She gave her father a smile that was full of mischief, and he wondered what trick she planned to play on him.* 3 [C] *infml* a person, esp a child, who is often troublesomely playful: *Before long, the baby will be as big a mischief as his three-year-old brother.* 4 [U] damage, harm, or hurt done by a person, animal, or thing; wrong-doing: *The monkey did a lot of mischief before it was caught and put back in its cage; it broke a number of things. He's sorry for having told lies, but the mischief* (= the harm caused by his lies) *has been done and can't be undone.* **do someone/oneself a mischief** *usu humor* to hurt someone/oneself: *If you try to lift a heavy weight like that you'll do yourself a mischief.* **to make mischief (between people)** to speak so as to cause trouble, disagreement, quarrels, unfriendly feelings, etc (between people): *That old woman has an evil tongue and is always making mischief between her son and his wife.*

vice 1 [U] wickedness of character: *He's a wild boy but there's no vice in him.* 2 [C] a serious fault of character; a bad habit: *His laziness is his greatest vice. His vices are smoking and drinking too much.* 3 [U; C] evil living: *There's a lot of vice in big cities.*

obscenity 1 [U] the quality of being obscene: *He was upset by the obscenity of the film and did not think that young people should see it.* 2 [C] an obscene act, practice, or habit: *'These obscenities should not be allowed; they must be stopped!' he said. For some people, wearing no clothes in public is an obscenity.*

depravity 1 [U] the quality or state of being depraved: *His depravity led him into crime.* 2 [C] a depraved act, practice, or habit: *The depravities of the evil king made him hateful to all good men.*

F63 *nouns* : **rules of behaviour**

morality [U] the rightness (or not) of behaviour, of an action, etc: *I am worried about the morality of what he is doing.* **im-** [*neg*]

morals [P] rules of behaviour; behaviour itself, esp in matters of sex: *A society's morals change slowly as time passes. She thinks his morals aren't very good.*

ethics 1 [P] moral rules: *What ought I to do? —It's a question of ethics.* 2 [U] the study of morality: *He was reading a book on ethics.*

conscience [C; U] an inner sense that knows the difference between right and wrong, judges one's actions according to moral laws and makes one feel guilty, good, evil, etc: *My conscience is clear. There is nothing troubling my conscience. She has a guilty conscience.* **have no conscience** to be unable to tell the difference between right and wrong: *Jean's got no conscience; she'd steal anything from anybody.* **in all conscience** without offending one's conscience: *I couldn't do such a wicked thing in all conscience.* **matter of conscience** a question which only one's conscience can decide: *I can't advise you on such a question; it's a matter of conscience.* **on one's conscience** causing one to feel guilty: *How can you sleep with such a thing on your conscience?*

scruple [C *usu pl with sing meaning*] a feeling of doubt about whether one is doing right or not: *He has no scruples; he'll do anything for money.* **scrupulous** very careful, esp in not doing anything wrong: *She is a scrupulous worker.* **un-** [*neg*] **-ly** [adv] **-ness** [U]

duty [C; U] what one must do either because of one's job or because one thinks it right: *When duty calls I must obey. She has a strong sense of duty. Do your duty. It's my duty to help you. He paid a duty visit* (= because of conscience) *to his mother.* **dutiful** [B] showing a strong sense of duty: *He was always a very dutiful son/worker.* **-lly** [adv] **-ness** [U]

obligation [C; U] *usu fml* duty; what one must do: *You have an obligation to help us; we have helped you in the past. I am under an obligation to help him* (= I must help him). *You have no obligation to buy* (= You don't need to buy). *He did it from a sense of obligation* (= He felt he ought to do it and so he did it). [*also* ⇨ C191]

F64 *nouns* : **right and wrong**

right 1 [U] what is right or morally good: *The child is old enough to know the difference between right and wrong.* 2 [S; U; (*of, to,* 3)] (a) morally just or lawful claim: *She has a right.*

has no right/has less right than I have (to say that). He has the right to do it. The law gave him the right of cutting wood in the forest. **by right of** because of (something that gives a just claim): She is British by right of marriage. **in one's own right** because of a personal claim that does not depend on anyone else: Elizabeth II is queen of England in her own right. **be in the right** to have justice on one's side; not to deserve blame: I must find out which of them was in the right.

wrong 1 [U] what is not right; standards according to which some things are bad: He knows right from wrong well enough. **2** [C] esp lit any bad action, esp one which causes pain: The wrongs he has done will not be forgotten. **in the wrong** deserving blame **two wrongs don't make a right** you ought not to harm someone as punishment for harming you

F65 adjectives : right and wrong

right [B (in); F3] just; morally good: This is the right thing to do. I'll try to do whatever is right. It's not right, but wrong, to tell lies. I was right in selling/right to sell the farm. It seemed only right to give her something. **-ness** [U]

wrong [B (in); F3] morally bad; evil: Telling lies is wrong—it's wrong to tell lies. **-ness** [U]

moral 1 [Wa5;A] concerning character, behaviour, or actions, considered or judged as being good or evil, right or wrong: Commercial matters must be judged by moral as well as business standards. **2** [Wa5;A] based on the idea of what is right (compared with what is lawful): He refused to join the army, saying that no one had a moral right to kill others. She is a woman of great moral courage. His judgment was based on the law of the land and not on moral law. **3** [B] apprec good (in character, behaviour, etc): He didn't lead a very moral life. **im-** [neg] What an immoral thing to suggest! **4** [Wa5;A] able to understand the difference between right and wrong, good and evil: Is a baby born with a moral sense? Animals are not moral beings in the way in which humans appear to be. **5** [B] teaching, showing, or intended to show that which is good or right in human behaviour: The film was not just amusing; it gave a valuable moral lesson as well.

ethical [B] morally right or good: I shouldn't do that; it isn't ethical. **-lly** [adv Wa4]

F66 adjectives & combining forms : relating to quality

high-, top- very good: This is a high-quality book. They are all top-grade students.

low- not at all good: This is a low-quality film. They ate in a low-class restaurant.

class type or quality: He only sells high-class materials in his shop. This is a third-class film; it isn't very good. These people say that they are

treated like second-class citizens [⇒ C83] in their own country.

-grade (esp of substances) type or quality: This is a high-grade coal; it's very good. He sold us some low-grade building materials.

-rate level or quality: What a first-rate book that is! He is a second-rate actor, not the best.

Happiness and sadness

F70 adjectives : feeling pleasure

happy [Wa1] **1** [B] (of people) feeling pleasure and contentment: I'm so happy to be back home. She's a happy girl; she enjoys life. He's happiest when he's working. **2** [B] (of relationships) giving pleasure to the people concerned: They are a happy family, and seldom quarrel. **3** [A] (of events) fortunate: By a happy chance I met him again yesterday. **4** [A] (of behaviour, thoughts, etc) suitable: That wasn't a very happy remark. **5** [F3] pleased; not finding it difficult (to): I'll be happy to meet him when I am free. **6** [A] (of wishes) joyful: Happy New Year! A happy birthday, darling! **-ily** [adv]

glad [Wa1] **1** [F, F3, 5a] esp emot happy: I was glad to see her again. I'd be glad to help him if he asked. **2** [A] esp formerly showing happiness: She gave a glad cry when she saw him. **-ly** [adv] **-ness** [U]

pleased [B] feeling or showing happiness or satisfaction: I always feel pleased when I've finished a piece of work. I'm very pleased you've come. She had a pleased look on her face. I'm pleased with his work. **be pleased to (do something) 1** polite to be very willing to; be glad to: Thank you for your invitation, which we shall be pleased to accept. **2** fml (of a ruler) to decide (as a favour) to: The Queen is pleased to appoint our firm as personal shoemakers. **pleased with oneself** esp ironical (too) satisfied with what one has done: He's feeling rather pleased with himself after his successful results in the examinations.

cheerful [B] happy and bright: She had a cheerful smile on her face. He gave me a cheerful wave. Try to be a bit more cheerful; your life hasn't ended. **-lly** [adv] **-ness** [U]

F71 adjectives : feeling particular pleasure [B]

carefree 1 apprec free from anxiety; happy; without sorrow or fear: On a day like this I feel quite carefree. Her mind was full of carefree thoughts. **2** deprec irresponsible: He's carefree with his money. His carefree nature makes life difficult for his wife.

joyful full of joy; very happy: She looks really joyful at being a grandmother. This is a joyful occasion; let's all be happy. **-lly** [adv]

merry [Wa1] **1** happy (esp in entertainment): *The men were having a merry time, drinking and singing.* **2** *infml* rather drunk: *He was a bit merry after all that wine.* **-ily** [adv] **-iment** [U]

gay [Wa1] **1** cheerful; merry; happy: *He could hear gay, laughing voices.* **2** bright and attractive, so that one feels happy: *They sang a gay marching song. The fields were gay with flowers. This is the gayest place in town. They decorated the kitchen in gay colours.* **3** not serious; only concerned with pleasure: *She exists only for the gay life.* [*also* ⇒ C34] **gaily** [adv] **gaiety** [U]

festive merry, particularly at parties and special occasions (**festivities**): *Come on, it's Christmas! Join in the festive spirit!* **the festive season** Christmas and the New Year

jolly 1 [Wa1] merry: *He seems a very jolly old man. That was a jolly party; I enjoyed it.* **2** [adv Wa5] *infml esp middle class* very: *What a jolly kind thing to do! I say, he's a jolly nice chap, isn't he?*

F72 adjectives : **feeling great pleasure** [B]

delighted very pleased: *The delighted looks on the children's faces showed their pleasure. He was delighted at the news. I shall be only too delighted to come.* **-ly** [adv]

overjoyed *emot* very pleased; really delighted: *She was overjoyed to see him.*

F73 adjectives : **satisfied and happy**

satisfied [B] having (got) what one needs or wants: *He had a satisfied expression on his face. Most of the people were completely satisfied with the result.* **un-** [neg] not satisfied **dis-** [neg] *deprec* seldom satisfied; hard to satisfy

content [F] pleased and satisfied: *She's very content with what she has. I am content to leave the decision to you.*

contented [B] relaxed, happy, and satisfied: *He had a contented smile on his face.* **dis-** [neg]

F74 nouns : **pleasure**

pleasure 1 [U] the state or feeling of happiness or satisfaction resulting from an experience that one likes: *He listened with pleasure to the beautiful music. It gives me no pleasure to have to tell you this. Pleasure is the opposite of pain.* **2** [U] the enjoyment of the body, food, comfort, etc: *He'll soon tire of this life of pleasure and start working again. She lives only for pleasure.* **3** [C] a cause of happiness, enjoyment, or satisfaction: *It's been a pleasure to talk to you. His work was his only pleasure. Some people have few pleasures in life.* **4** [the S] *polite* enjoyment gained by doing or having (something or some activity): *May I have the pleasure*

of the next dance? May we have the pleasure o your company at dinner? **5** [S] *polite* somethin; that is not inconvenient and that one is please to do: *Thank you for helping me—Not at all My pleasure/It was a pleasure.* **take (great, n etc) pleasure in** *often fml* to get enjoyment o satisfaction (of a stated kind) from: *She take: pleasure in helping others. I take little pleasur in such things. They took no pleasure in doin it.*

happiness [U] the state of being happy: *I am concerned for her happiness; I want her to b happy.*

joy 1 [U] great happiness: *Her face showed he joy. He was filled with joy when he heard th good news.* **2** [U] something that shows joy: saw joy in her face.* **3** [C] a person or thing tha causes joy: *These are just the joys and sorrow. of life. My children are a great joy to me.* **for jo** because of (feeling) joy: *She jumped for jo when the news came.*

joyfulness [U] the state of being joyful

delight 1 [U] great pleasure or satisfaction; joy *I read his book with real delight.* **2** [C] someon or something that gives great pleasure: *You new daughter/book is a real delight. She wa: enjoying the delights of London's night life* **take delight in** to get great pleasure from (something), often while annoying others: *H takes (great) delight in singing when I want t read quietly.*

cheer [U] *esp old use & lit* happiness: *Be of good cheer, friends.*

treat [C *usu sing*] **1** something unusual whicl gives pleasure: *The visit to the country was real treat for the children.* **2** an act of buyin; something for someone else to enjoy: *It's m treat; what would you like?*

kick [C] **1** *infml* a strong feeling of pleasure: *H gets a (real) kick out of playing that game. Sh does it for kicks.* **2** a strong effect: *That drin has a real kick (in it).*

F75 nouns : **satisfaction and wellbeing**

satisfaction 1 [U] the state of being satisfie His satisfaction at/with the result was obvious **dis-** [neg] **2** [C] something which satisfies: *Liv ing here is one of the great satisfactions of he life.*

content [U] the state of being content: *They liv here in peace and content.* **dis-** [neg]

contentment [U] the state of being contented *His contentment with life was very obvious* **dis-** [neg]

enjoyment 1 [U] the state of enjoying: *Hi enjoyment of the party was clear to everybody* **2** [U] pleasure from enjoying something: *Thi good wine should add to your enjoyment (of th meal).* **3** [C] something one enjoys: *Playin; golf is one of his few enjoyments in life.*

wellbeing [U] personal and bodily (happines and) comfort, esp good health: *His walk in th sunshine gave him a sense of general wellbeing*

The nurses are concerned with the wellbeing of all the children in their care. [*also* ⇒ B112]

appeasement [U] **1** the act of appeasing [⇒ F76] **2** the esp political idea that peace, satisfaction, etc can be obtained by giving an enemy what he or she demands

F76 verbs, etc : relating to pleasure

enjoy 1 [T1, 4] to get happiness from (things or experiences): *She enjoyed her dinner. I enjoyed listening to the music.* **2** [T1] to have or use (something good): *He has always enjoyed* (= had) *very good health.* **enjoy oneself** to be happy; experience pleasure: *Did you enjoy yourself at the party? He enjoyed himself dancing.*

please 1 [T1; I0] to make (someone) happy; to give satisfaction (to): *He's very hard/easy to please. The girl in the shop was eager to please (everybody). He bought it to please his wife. We're very pleased with our new car.* **2** [interj] (used in asking politely for things): *Could I come, please?* (*emph*) *Please could I come?* (*more emph*) *Could I please come?*

gladden [T1] *esp formerly* to make glad: *The news gladdened their hearts.*

delight [T1; I0] to (cause to) feel great satisfaction, enjoyment, or joy: *This book is certain to delight (everyone). He delighted the audience with his performance. 'That girl delights me,' he said.* **delight in** [v prep T1, 4] to take great pleasure in, often while annoying others: *He delights in this kind of work. These people seem to delight in being nasty.*

cheer [T1] *fml & sometimes pomp* to make (someone) happy: *Your visit has cheered us all. We are all cheered to learn that his work was a success.*

cheer up [v adv T1; I0] *infml* to become or make cheerful: *Come on, cheer up!—Life hasn't ended. He's very unhappy; try to cheer him up.*

satisfy [Wv4;T1] to supply a need or desire of (someone): *Did the service in the shop satisfy you? Were you satisfied with the service? That was a very satisfying meal.*

appease [T1 *usu pass*] to satisfy or make (someone) calm by meeting demands or by giving or doing something: *The angry man wasn't appeased when they said they were sorry. His hunger was appeased by a large meal.*

F77 verbs : showing pleasure

rejoice [I0 (*at, over*), 3, 5] *fml & lit* to feel or show great joy: *She rejoiced at/over our good news. I rejoice (to hear) that you are coming home. 'Rejoice with me; for I have found my sheep which was lost'* (*the Bible*). **rejoice someone's heart/the heart of someone** to make someone feel glad: *The victory rejoiced the heart of the whole nation.*

give thanks [I0 (*to, for*)] to express one's thanks, usu to God: *Friends, let us give thanks (to God) for what happened.* **thanksgiving 1** [C; U] an expression of thanks, esp to God; **2** *also* **Thanksgiving Day** [R *cap*] an official day in the year for thanksgiving, usu the fourth Thursday in November in the US

thank 1 [T1 (*for*)] to express one's gratefulness to (someone); give thanks to (someone): *The old lady thanked me for helping her across the road. Did you thank Mrs Brown for your present?* **2** [X9, esp *for*; V3] (*used when requesting something forcefully or widely*) to be pleased with (someone) for something: *I'll thank you for that book. I'll thank you to be quiet while I'm speaking.* **have (oneself) to thank** *ironical* to be responsible for something (oneself): *You've only got yourself to thank for the accident. John's got himself to thank for being late so let's go without him.* **have (someone) to thank** to place blame or responsibility rightly on (someone): *You've got John to thank for your cold. He caught it first and passed it on to everyone.* **thank God/goodness/heaven** (an expression of great thankfulness): *Your son's alive.—Thank God!*

F78 adjectives : grateful and relieved

grateful [B (*for*)] feeling or showing thanks to another person: *He gave a grateful smile. I'm really grateful to you for your help.* **-lly** [adv] **-ness** [U]

thankful [B (*for*)] very glad and grateful, esp to God or the gods, etc: *I'm thankful he's safe after that terrible accident. Doctor we're thankful you came when you did.* **-lly** [adv] **-ness** [U]

relieved [F] (of a person) given relief: *Your mother will be very relieved (to hear) that you are safe.*

beholden [F (*to*)] *often fml & lit, esp formerly* owing thanks: *She has no wish to be beholden to him for anything. Thank you; I am greatly beholden to you for your help.*

F79 nouns : gratitude and relief

gratitude [U] the state or feeling of being grateful; kind feeling towards someone who has been kind: *She showed her gratitude (to us) by inviting us to dinner.*

thanks [P] words expressing gratitude: *Kneel down and give thanks to God. Thanks should also be given to Mrs Brown for her kind help. She returned the borrowed book with thanks.* **thanks to** because of: *Thanks to her hard work we collected £100 towards the cost of repairing the church roof. It was thanks to your stupidity that we lost the game!*

relief 1 [S; U] (a) feeling of comfort at the end of anxiety, fear, or pain: *The medicine will give/bring some/a little relief. It is a drug for the relief of pain. It was a great relief to me when I heard* he was safe. **2** [U] help for people in trouble: *We sent relief* (=food, clothes, etc) *to the people who lost their homes in the flood.*

F80 *adjectives* : **feeling little or no pleasure**

unhappy [Wa1;B] not happy or satisfied: *His plan made her very unhappy. I'm unhappy about the new house; it isn't what I expected.* **-ily** [adv] **-iness** [U]

sad [Wa1;B] **1** not happy: *His death has made us all very sad. It's sad to think he won't be working here any more.* **2** causing unhappiness or sorrow: *We heard the sad news of your father's death.* **-ly** [adv] **-ness** [U]

poor [Wa5;A] unlucky (and unhappy): *Poor John, life isn't easy for him.*

miserable [B] **1** very unhappy: *She's miserable because he left without saying goodbye.* **2** *infml* very unsatisfactory: *What miserable weather today! He paid her a miserable weekly wage.* **-bly** [adv]

wretched [B] **1** very miserable: *Can't we help the wretched woman in some way?* **2** [A] *deprec* disliked and annoying: *Please tell that wretched man to go and bother someone else!* **3** [A] miserable, esp in living conditions: *They live in a wretched little house with no electricity or running water.*

pitiable [B] **1** worthy of pity: *The wounded soldiers were lying on the ground in a pitiable condition.* **2** *derog* worthless: *As an actress she's pitiable; it was a pitiable performance.* **-bly** [adv]

pitiful [B] **1** causing or deserving pity: *She made a pitiful attempt to get out of bed but she was too weak and sick to do so.* **2** *deprec* not good or deserving respect: *She cooked the food too long and the dinner was pitiful.* **-lly** [adv]

sorry [Wa1;A] *emot* pitiful: *The wet campers were a sorry sight. She's in a sorry state now; no money and no one to help her.*

touching [B] affecting the emotions: *That was a very touching story he told about the boy who loved his dog.* **-ly** [adv] [*also* ⇒ F4 MOVING]

pathetic [B] **1** (making one feel) very sad: *What a pathetic story! She had a pathetic look on her face; she looked really pathetic.* **2** *deprec* worthless; hopelessly unsuccessful: *What a pathetic little person you are! She made pathetic attempts to learn French.* **-ally** [adv Wa4]

F81 *adjectives* : **feeling depression and discontent**

depressed [B] sad; low in spirits: *I feel really depressed today, nothing went right.*

fed up [F] *infml* depressed (and feeling unable to do what one wants to do): *I'm fed up with this job! She went home looking pretty fed up.*

bored [F] not interested in anything and therefore not happy: *He was bored in London; he*

had no friends and no money and couldn't find anything to do.

discontented [B] (typical of a person) dissatisfied and restlessly unhappy: *She has a discontented look, as if she never enjoys life. He's very discontented with his wages.* **-ly** [adv]

low [Wa1;F] *infml* depressed; fed up etc: *I'm feeling a bit low today because she's gone.*

browned off [B] *BrE infml* fed up and dissatisfied

blue [Wa1;F] *infml* (of people) sad and without (much) hope: *I'm feeling rather blue today.*

bleak [Wa1;B] (of conditions) sad and without (much) hope: *His future looks bleak.* **-ly** [adv] **-ness** [U]

F82 *nouns* : **relating to little or no pleasure**

misery 1 [U] great unhappiness: *Life was pure misery last month; the children were ill and I had almost no money.* **2** [C] something or someone causing this: *Colds and coughs are among the miseries of a British winter. Oh, don't be such a misery!*

depression [U;C] a feeling of sadness and hopelessness: *His depression came to an end when she kissed him. She often has depressions.*

pity 1 [U] sensitiveness to and sorrow for the suffering or unhappiness of others: *I felt no pity for him; he was a murderer. Don't help me out of pity, please; help me because you want to.* **2** [S] a sad, unfortunate, or inconvenient state of affairs: *It's a pity it's too cold to go swimming today. What a pity you won't be back before I leave! Usually we wouldn't mind her staying away, but the pity of it is that there were some good friends of hers here.* **for pity's sake** *emph* please: *For pity's sake, help me!*

sin *also* **shame** [S] *infml* pity: *It's a sin/shame that he has to leave so soon!*

sorrow 1 [U] sadness: *His death caused us great sorrow.* **2** [C] something causing sadness: *His death was a sorrow to us all. Losing her job is just one of the many sorrows in her life.*

grief 1 [U] great sorrow or feelings of suffering, esp at the death of a loved person: *She went nearly mad with grief after the child died. The dog died of grief when its master did not return.* **2** [C] a cause of sorrow or anxiety: *His wild behaviour was a grief to his mother.*

pathos [U] the quality in something, esp a story, that makes one feel sad, full of pity, etc: *There was great pathos in the story.*

F83 *nouns* : **sadness about something that has happened**

regret [U (*at*)] unhappiness at the loss of something, or because something has or has not happened: *They said goodbye with great regret. We heard with regret that you had failed the examination. He felt regret at her absence.*

(much/greatly) to one's regret one is sorry to say: *Much to my regret, I must leave you now.*

remorse [U (*for*)] sorrow for having done wrong: *He felt/He was filled with remorse for his evil deed.* **without remorse** without mercy or sorrow

F84 *verbs* : **pitying and mourning**
[ALSO ⇨ C55]

pity [T1] **1** to feel pity for: *Everyone who has heard about his troubles pities him.* **2** *deprec* to consider to be pitiable; have a low opinion of: *I pity you if you can't do something like this.*

grieve 1 [I0] to suffer from grief [⇨ F82] and sadness, esp over a loss: *She is still grieving for her dead husband.* **2** [T1] to cause grief to; to make very unhappy: *It grieves me to see him so ill. The loss of our chairman has grieved all the members of the commitee.*

sadden [T1] to make sad: *The terrible story of how they lost their house saddened him.*

depress [Wv4,5;T1] to sadden or discourage: *The bad news depressed her spirits. I feel really depressed! What depressing news!* **-ingly** [adv]

mourn 1 [I0] to feel sadness or grief, esp for the death of someone; be sorrowful: *The old woman still mourns her lost son who died in the war 30 years ago.* **2** [T1] to grieve for (the death, loss, etc of someone): *The whole nation mourned the death of the president.* **in mourning 1** dressed (completely) in mourning [⇨ C55] **2** showing or feeling (strong or deep) mourning

sorrow [Wv4;I0 (*over, at, for*)] *esp lit* to feel or express sorrow; grieve: *a sorrowing heart; the sorrowing relatives*

F85 *verbs* : **regretting and deploring**

regret [T1, 4, 5a] to feel regret [⇨ F83] for: *She regrets what happened/that she did not come. He never regretted doing it. Try not to regret it too much.*

be/feel sorry [I0 (*about, for*); T5a] to regret, esp wishing that it was possible to do or to have done something different: *Can you come? —No, I'm sorry I can't. I'm sorry that I can't come. I'm really sorry about this; it shouldn't have happened. I feel really sorry about this; I wish it hadn't happened. He felt sorry for her because she had had such a sad life.*

deplore [T1] to be very sorry about (and consider wrong): *One must deplore such (bad) behaviour. The closing of this post office will be deplored; many people use it.*

rue [T1] *esp poet & emot* to be sorry for: *'He'll rue the day he came here!' she said angrily.*

F86 *adjectives* : **showing unhappiness** [B]

sorrowful causing or full of sorrow [⇨ F82]:

The old man's funeral was a sorrowful event; everyone had really loved him. **-lly** [adv]

mournful sad, as if mourning [⇨ F84]: *You look pretty mournful—what's wrong?* **-lly** [adv]

regretful feeling regret [⇨ F83]: *He was sorry to leave, when he saw their regretful faces. Don't feel regretful; you were not to blame.* **-lly** [adv] **-ness** [U]

rueful [B] showing that one is sorry about something: *He had a rueful look on his face.* **-lly** [adv] **-ness** [U]

remorseful feeling remorse [⇨ F83]: *He looked very remorseful when he learned what he had done, and said he was sorry.* **-lly** [adv] **-ness** [U]

heartbroken *also* **brokenhearted** *emot* (of a person) full of sorrow: *She was heartbroken when he left her. Her death left him brokenhearted.*

grief-stricken *emot* grieving [⇨ F84] greatly: *His family were grief-stricken at his death.*

F87 *verbs* : **caring and worrying** [I0 (*about*)]

care [*also* T6a] to be strongly interested (in) and anxious (about): *She really cares what happens to you. Don't you care any more (about what happens)?*

be concerned to care or be anxious: *I'm rather concerned about his future.*

worry to be anxious, esp over a period of time: *Worrying about your health can make you ill. Don't worry; he'll come home soon.*

F88 *verbs* : **upsetting and agitating** [T1]

upset [Wv4] to make unhappy: *She upset him by what she said. This news is very upsetting; I feel really upset about it. Don't upset yourself; these problems aren't really serious.*

worry 1 [Wv4] to make anxious or uncomfortable: *Her late hours* (=coming home late) *worry her mother. The bad smell doesn't worry him at all.* **2** (esp of a dog) to chase and bite (an animal): *The dog was worrying the sheep.* **worry at** [v prep] to keep trying to overcome or persuade: *He was worrying at the problem all night.*

disturb [Wv4; *often pass*] *often fml* to cause (a person) to become anxious; to upset: *His ideas disturbed her very much. I was disturbed to hear that you are thinking of leaving your job. This news is disturbing.* **-ingly** [adv]

dismay to make (someone) worried; to fill with dismay [⇨ F90]: *Don't let this accident dismay you.*

distress [Wv4] to make (someone) unhappy and worried; to cause distress [⇨ F90] to: *Your dishonest actions have distressed us greatly. It distresses me that she has left home like this.* **-ingly** [adv]

agitate to cause anxiety to; trouble or worry, esp so as to cause some bodily sign of this: *I hope* *the bad news will not agitate him too much. The news agitated him; he kept walking up and down.*

disquiet [Wv4] *usu fml* to make anxious: *The bad news disquieted us.*

confuse 1 [Wv4] to cause (someone) to be uncertain, unable to think clearly, etc: *All the people talking at the same time confused the child.* **2** [(*with*)] to fail to tell the difference between: *I'm sorry; I confused you with another person.* **confusion** [U] **1** the act of confusing (def **1**) **2** confused conditions: *In the confusion I lost her.*

confound 1 to cause great surprise or confusion to; disturb greatly: *His new ideas completely confounded them.* **2** *emot* (as a way of showing anger, etc): *Confound it, why did she do that? Confound you, you are wasting my time!* **confounded** [Wa5;A] *not fml* very annoying: *Tell that confounded man to go away and mind his own confounded business!*

F89 *verbs* : **causing to be upset**

bother 1 [T1] to cause to be nervous; annoy or trouble, esp in small ways: *I'm busy; don't bother me just now. His phoning me all the time bothers me a lot.* **2** [T1] (*in polite expressions*) to cause inconvenience to: *I'm sorry to bother you, but can you tell me the time?* **3** [I0, 3] to cause inconvenience to oneself; trouble oneself: *Shall I go?—Oh, don't bother (to (do it)). Don't bother about (helping) him.* **bother oneself about, be bothered with/to** to trouble oneself because of/to do: *Don't bother yourself about me; I'm doing quite well. I can't be bothered with him; he can't be bothered to say hello!*

trouble [Wv3] **1** [T1] to cause worry, discomfort, etc to (someone): *What's troubling you—money problems? I'm rather troubled by the way he is behaving. Her teeth are troubling her; she has toothache.* **2** [T1] to cause inconvenience to; bother: *Please don't trouble yourself; I'll do it for you.* (polite) *Could I trouble you a moment, please? I need your advice.* **3** [I0, 3] to take trouble; make an effort: *Why did she trouble (to do it) when I could have done it for her easily?*

F90 *nouns* : **anxiety, worry, and dismay**

[ALSO ⇒ F120]

anxiety 1 [U] fear, esp as caused by uncertainty about something: *Not knowing whether or not she would die caused us great anxiety.* **2** [C] an example of this: *After listening to his advice she had no more anxieties.* **3** [U, U3; C, C3] *infml* a strong wish to do something; eagerness: *The child has a great anxiety to please you.*

worry 1 [U] the feeling of anxiety: *Worry can make you ill.* **2** [C] a person or thing that makes one worried: *It's a worry to me having to leave the children alone in the house. Money is only one of our worries* (= there are others).

concern [U] **1** care; anxiety: *He felt real concern for the children's safety. It is my concern for/about your future that makes me ask all these questions.* **2** special interest or problem: *That child's health is no concern of mine. This is our concern, not theirs. What concern is it of yours what happens to her?*

distress 1 [S] something that causes suffering of the mind: *The girl's leaving home was a great distress to her family.* **2** [U] the state of suffering caused by lack of money or of the necessary things of life: *Someone must help these poor people in their (great) distress.* **3** [U] a state of danger or great difficulty: *If the storm continues on the mountain, the climbers will be in distress by morning. The sailors sent out a distress signal.* **4** [U] great suffering of the mind or body; pain or great discomfort

anguish [U] very great worry, suffering, and pain, esp of the mind: *She was in anguish over her missing child.*

agitation [U] the condition of being agitated [⇒ F92]: *Her agitation increased as the hours passed and there was no news of her child.*

dismay [U] a strong feeling of unhappiness, fear, and hopelessness: *They listened in/with dismay to the news. The news filled/struck them with dismay. To my dismay I found I had lost my money.*

F91 *nouns* : **troubles and upsets**

trouble 1 [C; U] difficulty, worry, or discomfort: *His son is a great trouble to him, always getting into trouble with the police. Was it difficult to get that job?—No, no trouble at all. Her teeth are giving her trouble again; she needs to see a dentist. They have had a lot of money troubles lately.* **2** [C; U] special care: *She took a lot of trouble preparing that meal; I hope you thanked her. Thanks for all your trouble in helping me. He went to the trouble of finding out when our train was leaving.* **3** [U] social disturbance: *There was some trouble in the hotel last night; a fight in the bar, I think.* **troublesome** [B] causing trouble: *Being short of money is a bit troublesome but we'll do what we can.*

bother 1 [U] trouble; inconvenience or anxiety usu caused by small matters and lasting a short time: *We had a lot of bother finding our way to his house.* **2** [C *usu sing*] something or someone that causes this: *I don't want to be a bother to you, but could I possibly use your telephone?* **bothersome** [B] causing bother: *bothersome people/demands*

nuisance [C] **1** an action or state of affairs which causes trouble, offence or unpleasantness: *What a nuisance! I've forgotten my* money. *Playing the radio too loud in a flat can be a nuisance to one's neighbours.* **2** a person or animal that annoys or causes trouble: *Don't make a nuisance of yourself; sit down and be quiet!*

problem [C] something which causes difficulties, trouble, etc: *I've got a problem; can I talk to you about it? They have family problems. Life is full of problems.*

upset [C] something which disturbs, annoys, or troubles, usu slightly: *I hope these upsets don't make you unhappy.*

F92 *adjectives* : **anxious and agitated** [B]

anxious 1 feeling anxiety; troubled; fearful: *He was anxious about the possibility of losing all his money. He was anxious for the safety of his family.* **2** causing anxiety or worry: *The period of his illness was an anxious one for us all. We had an anxious time/wait until the doctor said the child was safe.* **3** [*also* F3] *infml* having a strong wish to do something; eager: *He was anxious to please his guests.* **-ly** [adv]

worried anxious: *She had a worried look on her face. He's obviously very worried about something.* **-ly** [adv]

concerned feeling concern: *I'm really concerned about her health. He doesn't look very concerned, but he's very concerned indeed. I was talking to various rather concerned people, and they want to find a solution to the problem.*

upset unhappy and anxious: *She's really upset about losing the money. You look upset—what's happened?*

nervous 1 worried and excited: *Don't be nervous (about it); the doctor will help you.* **2** [Wa5] of or resulting from this kind of condition: *He made a nervous movement of the hands. She gave a nervous smile.* **3** (of a person) easily excited and worried: *He's too nervous a person to talk in front of a large group of people.* **-ly** [adv] **-ness** [U]

nervy [Wa1] *BrE sl* nervous; anxious: *He was looking very nervy.*

disturbed upset or not in one's usual condition: *His mind is disturbed; he needs care and freedom from worry.*

dismayed filled with dismay: *He looked round at their dismayed faces; they had not expected the disappointing news. We were dismayed to hear what had happened.*

distressed filled with distress: *Their distressed expressions told me everything; they did not need to speak.*

anguished feeling or expressing very great distress, suffering, or pain, esp of the mind: *He heard her anguished cries.*

agitated anxious, troubled, or worried so as to show some bodily sign of this: *She was so agitated that she could not sit still.*

disquieted *fml* made anxious: *His mother is*

disquieted that she has received no letters from him for four months.

Anger, violence, stress, calm, and quietness

F100 *verbs* : **annoying and displeasing** [T1]

annoy to cause (someone) trouble; to make rather angry, esp by certain repeated acts: *These flies are annoying me. I was annoyed by what those men did.*

irritate 1 to make (someone) angry or excited in an unpleasant way: *That noise irritates me/my nerves.* **2** to make (something) painful and sore: *Rough material irritates the skin.*

vex 1 to irritate (someone); cause to feel angry: *The boy's bad behaviour vexed his mother.* **2** [*often pass*] to irritate (someone) continually; to keep in discomfort: *Travellers in the desert are often vexed by flies. She's vexed by many cares.*

displease to cause (someone) to be annoyed, angry, etc: *Her behaviour displeased him.*

provoke to make (a person or animal) angry or bad-tempered: *I try to be patient with the child, but he provokes me with his noise.*

nettle *esp emot* to annoy or anger (someone): *Her words really nettled me!*

F101 *verbs* : **trying and teasing**

try [T1] to make (someone) annoyed, tired, etc (*esp in the phr* **try someone's patience**): *That child really tries me; he's very badly-behaved. That child really tries my patience. That child would try the patience of a saint* (= a very good person indeed).

tease [T1; I0] to make fun of (a person or animal) playfully or unkindly: *At school the other children always teased me because I was fat. The wicked girl teased the dog by pulling its tail. It's wrong to tease a person because he can't speak properly. Stop teasing!*

pester [T1 (*for, with*); I0] to annoy (someone) continually, esp with demands: *The beggars pestered the travellers for money. We were pestered by flies. Stop pestering (me)!*

badger [T1 (*for, with*)] to tease, worry, annoy, etc (someone) esp again and again with questions, requests, small actions, etc: *Stop badgering me with your questions! He badgered his mother till she did what he wanted.*

muck/mess about/around [I0] *not fml* to behave in a silly way for fun: *Stop mucking about and listen to what I'm saying.*

bug [T1] *esp AmE sl* to annoy; upset: *What's bugging you tonight?*

F102 *verbs* : **annoying and displeasing greatly** [T1]

anger to make (someone) angry: *Her cruel words angered him.*

enrage to make (someone) very angry: *Her behaviour enraged him. It enrages me that you should say that. She was enraged at/by his words. The enraged lion attacked him.*

infuriate to make (someone) wildly angry: *Her behaviour really infuriated me.*

madden to make (someone) wild or angry: *The horse was maddened by the pain and kicked its owner. It maddens me when I see her making the room untidy.*

incense *fml* to anger: *This kind of wastefulness incenses her. He was very incensed when he heard about their change of plan.*

F103 *nouns* : **anger and annoyance**

anger [U] a fierce feeling of displeasure, usu leading to a desire to punish the person or to harm the thing causing it: *The cruelty he saw filled him with anger.*

temper [C] an angry, impatient, or bad state of mind: *He's in a temper today, so keep away from him.* [also ⇒ F3] **fly into a temper** to become angry quickly and suddenly: *She flew into a temper when I asked her where she had been.* **keep one's temper** to stay calm: *Whatever she says to annoy you, try and keep your temper.* **lose one's temper** to become angry: *He behaved so stupidly that I lost my temper with him.* **out of temper** *fml* angry: *The boss is out of temper with him today.*

huff [S] a state of bad temper when offended (*esp in the phr* **go into a huff**): *She's gone into a huff because my brother didn't remember her name. Don't go off in a huff; we didn't mean we wanted you to leave.*

annoyance 1 [U] the state of being annoyed: *His annoyance showed on his face.* **2** [U] the act of annoying: *Stop all this annoyance!* **3** [C] something which annoys: *Those noisy cats are a great annoyance late at night.*

provocation 1 [U;C] the act of provoking or state of being provoked: *He was found guilty of provocation and causing a fight.* **2** [U] the reason for provoking or being provoked: *After giving us such provocation, is he surprised we are angry?* **3** [C] something that tests one's powers of self-control: *There are many provocations in teaching a class of badly-behaved children.*

displeasure [U] dislike, disapproval, and anger: *He showed his displeasure by leaving the room.*

vexation 1 [U] the feeling or state of being vexed [⇒ F100]; displeasure: *She cried with vexation when the wind blew her hat into the river.* **2** [C] something that causes this feeling: *He enjoyed the work in spite of its many vexations.*

irritation 1 [U] the feeling of being irritated [⇒ F100] **2** [C] something which irritates

fury [U;C] great, usu wild, anger: *He's in a fury about not being picked to play for the football team. She attacked him with/in fury. His sudden furies terrified her.*

rage [U;C] great, often uncontrolled, anger: *His rage when he heard the news was frightening. Don't get in a rage; calm down.*

F104 *adjectives* : **angry and annoyed**

angry [Wa1;B] filled with anger: *She'll be angry if you go there. I was angry because I missed that film.* **-ily** [adv]

cross [Wa1;F;(A)] angry: *She's feeling very cross because you didn't come. Please don't be cross with me; I'm sorry I didn't come.*

annoyed [B] a little angry; made angry by certain repeated acts: *I'm annoyed because he kept asking me silly questions. She had an annoyed look on her face.*

peeved [B (*at*)] *infml* annoyed: *She's peeved at/with him because he didn't help her.*

peevish [B] *infml* easily annoyed: *Oh, don't be so peevish; I was only joking!* **-ly** [adv] **-ness** [U]

huffy [Wa1;B] in a huff: *Oh, don't be so huffy!* **-ily** [adv] **-iness** [U]

irate [B] *fml* angry: *We were chased out of the field by an irate farmer.* **-ly** [adv]

nasty [Wa1;B] angry or threatening: *He has a nasty temper; be careful. She turned nasty* (=started to threaten me) *when I didn't give her the money.* **-ily** [adv] **-iness** [U]

furious [B] **1** angry, usu in an uncontrolled way: *He'll be furious with us if we're late. He'll be furious at being kept waiting. It makes me furious when people don't listen, and then ask silly questions.* **2** powerful and suggesting anger: *He struck his enemy a furious blow. There was a furious knocking at the door. Last night the storm was furious.* **3** (*fig*) wild; uncontrolled: *He has a furious temper. She drove the car at a furious speed.* **-ly** [adv]

wild [Wa1;F] *infml* angry: *She'll be wild at you if you don't get home before midnight.*

mad [Wa1;F] *infml* very annoyed: *Don't be mad at me, please; I won't do it again. He was mad with her because she took the money.*

infuriated [B] full of fury: *He looked really infuriated when he saw how much the work cost.*

enraged [B] full of rage: *He looked enraged when he heard the news.*

incensed [B] *fml* very angry: *Several incensed readers telephoned the newspaper editor about the front-page story.*

livid [B] *often infml* very angry: *Dad's livid because you got home so late last night! He was livid with anger.*

irritated [B] rather angry: having been irritated [⇒ F100]

F105 *adjectives* : **annoying and maddening** [B]

annoying causing annoyance or slight anger: *This really is annoying; now I won't be able to go to town.* **-ly** [adv]

irritating making a person get angry easily: *He's a very irritating person. This is irritating; it means I can't go until later.* **-ly** [adv]

provocative causing or intended to cause anger: *His speech was provocative and caused a lot of angry comment.* **-ly** [adv]

vexatious displeasing; troublesome; causing vexation: *After a lot of vexatious delays the building of the house was begun.* **-ly** [adv]

trying making a person annoyed, tired, etc: *What a trying child he is; he's very badly behaved! I've had a trying day; nothing went well.*

infuriating causing fury: *He can be quite infuriating sometimes because he's so selfish.* **-ly** [adv]

maddening 1 *infml* very annoying: *He's got a maddening way of pretending to be interested, but afterwards you find he wasn't listening at all.* **2** causing much pain or worry: *The pain was maddening and she couldn't sleep.* **-ly** [adv]

F106 *verbs* : **quarrelling and disputing**
[ALSO ⇒ C45]

quarrel [IØ] to have a (strong) argument: *The two brothers quarrelled. I don't want to quarrel with you.*

squabble [IØ] *emot* to quarrel, esp over something unimportant: *The children were squabbling over who would play with the toy soldiers first.*

argue [IØ] to disagree in, or fight with, words; quarrel: *Do what you are told and don't argue (with me). They were arguing about who lost the ball.*

bicker [IØ] to quarrel, esp about small matters: *Those two children are always bickering (with each other) about all sorts of things. Stop bickering!*

row [IØ (with)] *infml* to quarrel, often noisily or violently: *They're rowing again. She always breaks dishes after rowing with her husband.*

fall out [v adv IØ (with)] *infml* to quarrel: *I'm afraid she has fallen out with him; they fell out last week over some stupid little thing or other.*

disagree [IØ (with)] **1** (of people) to have different opinions; to quarrel slightly: *Bill and I often disagree but we are good friends. I disagreed with him about/over/as to what we ought to do.* **2** (of statements, reports, etc) to be unlike: *These two reports of the accident disagree. This newspaper report disagrees with the account on the radio.*

dispute 1 [T1, 6a,b; IØ] to argue (about), esp angrily and for some time: *They disputed for hours (about) where to go.* **2** [T1] to disagree about; doubt: *The honesty of his intentions was*

never disputed. **3** [T1] to struggle against, esp in defence: *Our soldiers disputed the advance of the enemy.* **4** [T1] to struggle over or about, esp in defence: *The defending army/the two armies disputed every inch of ground.*

conflict [IØ (with)] to be in disagreement: *The two ideas conflict; they can't be brought together.*

clash [IØ (with)] **1** to come into opposition: *Every time they meet they clash. The enemy armies clashed near the border. Those colours she's wearing clash* (= don't match). **2** (of events) to be at the same time on the same date and therefore cause difficulty: *Her wedding clashed with my examination so I couldn't go.*

F107 *nouns* : **quarrelling and disputing**

disagreement 1 [C; U] the fact or a case of disagreeing; *polite* a quarrel: *There has been serious disagreement between the political parties over this question. Bill and I have had a few disagreements lately.* **2** [U] (of statements, reports, etc) unlikeness: *There is some disagreement between these two statements.*

argument [C] a disagreement, esp one that is noisy; quarrel: *The argument made her cry.*

quarrel 1 [C] an argument, etc: *He had a quarrel with his best friend. Their sudden quarrels are well known, but basically they are a loving family. This quarrel between the two families has gone on for years.* **2** [S] a cause for or point of disagreement: *I have no quarrel with his opinions.* **pick a quarrel with (someone)** to make an argument happen: *I certainly don't want to pick a quarrel with anyone. He deliberately tried to pick a quarrel with me; he planned to do it.*

squabble [C] *emot* a quarrel, esp over something unimportant: *It's just a squabble; they'll be friends again soon.*

row [C] a noisy quarrel, sometimes with violent actions: *He's always having rows with his wife.* **kick up/make a row** *sl* to cause trouble, esp by complaining loudly or angrily

dispute [C; U] *fml* an argument or quarrel: *They had a long dispute about where to eat. This international dispute should have been settled long ago. His position of leadership in the country is beyond dispute. Without dispute that is the best plan. The matter in/under dispute is difficult to decide. The workers at the factory are in dispute with the management.*

F108 *adjectives* : **quarrelling and disputing** [B]

quarrelsome (of a person) likely to quarrel; often quarrelling: *She's a very quarrelsome girl.* **-ly** [adv] **-ness** [U]

argumentative (of a person) likely to argue:

*Oh, don't be so argumentative all the time;
agree for once!* **-ly** [adv] **-ness** [U]

disputatious tending to argue or dispute: *He is
rather a disputatious sort of person.* **-ly** [adv]
-ness [U]

irascible *euph & fml* easily made angry: *Yes,
I'm afraid he is a little irascible sometimes; he's
getting old, you know.* **-bly** [adv] **-ibility** [U]

touchy [Wa1 *(about)*] *infml* easily made angry:
*She's a little touchy about losing the money;
don't talk to her about it.* **-ily** [adv] **-iness** [U]

F109 nouns : aggression and violence

aggression 1 [U] the starting of a quarrel, fight,
or war, esp without just cause: *The army's
move was an act of aggression against their
eastern neighbours.* **2** [C] an attacking action
made without just cause: *Their aggressions will
provoke* [⇒ F100] *a war.* **aggressor** [C] a person or country that begins a quarrel, fight, war,
etc

violence [U] **1** very great force in action: *She
was frightened by the violence of her father's
anger.* **2** rough treatment; the use of (bodily)
force on or against others, esp unlawfully: *He
said that too much violence was shown on television.*

cruelty 1 [U] the state or quality of being cruel
[⇒ F110]: *Cruelty to animals is usually
unnecessary. The king's cruelty to his family is
well known.* **2** [C] a cruel act, expression, or
other example of this: *She suffered many cruel-
ties in her short life.*

fierceness [U] the condition of being fierce:
*She was surprised by the fierceness of his attack
on her father.*

ferocity [U] *fml* the condition of being ferocious: *He was surprised by the cat's ferocity in
defending her young.*

savagery [U; C *usu pl*] the condition of being
savage: *The savagery of the attack on the old
man horrified the local people. Their savageries
are well-known; they are terrible people who
kill very easily.*

F110 adjectives, etc : aggression and violence [B]

aggressive 1 *deprec* always ready to quarrel or
attack; threatening: *He is an aggressive person
and likely to start a fight. Nobody likes his
aggressive behaviour.* **2** *apprec* not afraid of
opposition: *If you want to be a successful businessman, you must be aggressive and not worry
about other people's feelings. His aggressive
selling methods made him rich.* **-ly** [adv]

violent 1 (of a person) uncontrollably fierce
(and dangerous) in action: *He gets very violent
when he is drunk.* **2** acting with or using great
damaging force: *That night there was a violent
storm.* **3** powerful beyond what is needed:
They had a violent argument. **4** produced by or

being the effect of damaging force: *He died a
violent death.* **5** (of feelings) unusually strong
or difficult to control: *The boy had a violent
pain in his stomach after eating too much fruit.
She was in a violent temper and began to throw
things about.* **-ly** [adv]

offensive [Wa5] for the purpose of attacking:
He carried an offensive weapon **-ly** [adv]

cruel [Wa1] **1** liking to cause pain or suffering;
taking pleasure in the pain of another; unkind;
merciless: *The cruel master beat his slaves mercilessly with a whip. Any man who enjoys
watching his dogs kill a rabbit must be cruel. It
was cruel of you to hit him just for breaking a
cup.* **2** painful; causing suffering: *a cruel
punishment/disease/remark; a cruel wind* **-lly**
[adv] **-ness** [U]

fierce [Wa1] **1** angry, violent, and cruel: *A fierce
dog guarded the house. He made a fierce
speech, urging them to fight. How fierce you
look when you're angry.* **2** (*fig*) (of feelings,
heat, etc) very great: *He felt fierce anger. The
heat was fierce.* **-ly** [adv] **-ness** [U]

ferocious very fierce: *The ferocious lion
attacked him. The punishment was ferocious.
Fig) The heat is ferocious today.* **-ly** [adv]
-ness [U]

savage 1 forcefully cruel or violent; uncontrollably fierce: *He was attacked by a savage dog.
The newspaper's attack was savage.* **2** (typical)
of an uncivilized place or people: *The scenery
was savage. Their customs were once very
savage.* **-ly** [adv]

barbarous savage and cruel, like a barbarian
[⇒ C169]: *What a barbarous thing to do! These
people are known for their barbarous
ways/behaviour.* **-ly** [adv] **barbarity** [U;C]

barbarian like a barbarian in manner and therefore cruel, savage, etc because not knowing
any better: *They lead a barbarian life.*

barbaric 1 like a barbarian in art, ideas, clothing, etc: *The people wore all sorts of barbaric
ornaments.* **2** *esp lit* savage and cruel; barbarous: *What a barbaric act!* **-ally** [adv Wa4]

murderous dangerous; suggesting murder: *She
gave him a murderous look.* **-ly** [adv]

wild 1 [Wa5] (of an animal) free; not kept by
people; not tame [⇒ F220]: *You can't keep a
wild animal in a house.* **2** [Wa5] (of a plant)
growing naturally; not grown by people:
Some wild flowers were growing in the garden.
3 [Wa1] (of people and places, etc) not civilized, cultivated, etc: *They live in a wild mountain area east of here.* **4** [Wa1] (of feelings,
expressions, etc) not controlled: *He had a wild
look in his eyes. She was wild with anger.* **-ly**
[adv]: *She looked around wildly for help.* **5**
[adv Wa5] in a wild way: *The flowers grow wild
in the hills. When he was a child he ran wild.*
-ness [U]

Fear and courage

F120 *nouns* : **fear and panic**

[ALSO ⇒ F90]

fear 1 [U] a feeling caused by the possibility of danger to oneself or others who are important: *His fear showed on his face. She stood there, shaking with fear. She felt fear for her child's safety. Fear caused him to be sick.* **2** [C] a feeling of this kind, usu for a particular reason: *His fears are unnecessary; we won't hurt him. She has a fear of high places.* **3** [U] chance; danger: *There is no fear of her coming here; she is in London. There isn't much fear of him losing the money.*

fright 1 [U] fear coming in a sudden sharp attack: *Fright gave the old lady heart failure. The child was shaking with fright. I nearly died of fright at the sight of the escaped lion. The horse took fright* (= became frightened) *at the sound of the explosion.* **2** [C] an experience that causes sudden fear; shock: *She's had two nasty frights during the last month. You gave me a fright by knocking so loudly on the door. I got the fright of my life* (= the biggest fright I've ever had) *when the machine burst into flames.* **3** [S] (*fig*) *infml* a person who or thing that looks silly, unattractive, or shocking: *She looks a fright in that old black dress.*

scare *not fml* **1** [S] a sudden feeling of fear: *What a scare you gave me, appearing suddenly in the dark!* **2** [C] a usu mistaken or unreasonable public fear: *War was avoided, but only after several bad war scares.* **3** [A] something intended to cause fear: *These are just scare stories; don't read them.* **scaremonger** [C] a person who spreads reports intended to cause a public scare

dread 1 [U;S] a great fear, esp of some harm to come: *She suffers from* (*a*) *great dread of heights.* **2** [C *usu sing*] the cause of great fear: *Illness is the great dread of his life.*

terror 1 [U] very great fear: *The people ran from the enemy in terror. That government rules by terror and has successfully crushed all opposition.* **2** [C] someone or something that causes such fear: *The criminal was the terror of the neighbourhood.* **3** [C] *infml* an annoying person: *Your son's a real terror! Can't you control him any better?*

alarm 1 [U] sudden fear and anxiety as caused by the possibility of danger: *After hearing the gunshots we were all in a state of alarm.* **2** [C] a warning of danger, as by ringing a bell or shouting: *I gave/raised the alarm as soon as I saw what was happening. There were several alarms during the night but no actual attacks.* **2** [C] any apparatus, such as a bell, noise, or flag by which a warning is given: *The electric alarm told everyone of the danger.*

siren [C] an instrument that makes a loud noise to give warning esp of danger, esp on ships,

moving vehicles, etc: *The ship sounded its siren. He heard a police siren, then saw the police car passing.*

panic [C; U] a (state of) sudden uncontrollable and quickly spreading fear: *He got into a panic about his examination. There is the strong likelihood of panic if a fire starts in the building.*

apprehension [U; C *usu pl*] anxiety, esp about the future; *fml* fear: *She felt apprehension for the safety of her son. Her apprehensions about an accident weren't fulfilled.*

F121 *verbs* : **fear and dread**

fear [Wv6;T1, 3, 4, 5a,b, 6a] to be afraid of: *She fears him; I don't know why. He fears to tell her what happened. He fears telling her what happened. She fears that he won't come back. I fear what he will do.*

fear for [v prep Wv6;T1] to be afraid for: *I feared for his safety in that place.*

be frightened [Wv6;IØ (*of*)] to feel (a certain amount of) fear: *Is she frightened of insects? Don't be frightened; I won't hurt you.*

dread [Wv5;T1 3, 4, 5, 6] to fear greatly: *I dread him/to see him/seeing him/that he will come/what he will say. At last the dreaded examination came.*

be scared [Wv6;IØ (*of*)] *not fml* to feel fear: *She is scared of the dark. Don't be scared, it's only a spider!*

F122 *verbs* : **frighten and panic**

frighten 1 [Wv4;T1] to fill with fear: *The little girl was frightened by the big dog. He had a frightening dream last night.* **2** [X9, esp *off*, *away*] to influence or drive by fear: *The little boy ran into the garden and frightened the birds away. He frightened off his attacker.*

scare *not fml* **1** [T1] to cause sudden fear to (someone); to frighten: *Don't let the noise scare you; it's only the wind.* **2** [IØ] to become fearful: *He is a man who doesn't scare easily.* **3** [X9, esp *off*, *away*] to drive, cause to go, or become, etc by or as if by fear: *He got a gun and scared off the thief. The high price is scaring away possible buyers. That noise scared the life out of me! He was scared into wearing a seat belt in his car.*

terrify [Wv5;T1] to fill with terror or fear: *Heights terrify me. The thought of flying terrified him so much that he decided to go by boat. The woman looked terrified.*

petrify [Wv5; T1] to put into a state of shock or fear so that the power of thought and action is lost: *The thought of the examination petrified him and he couldn't do any work.*

terrorize, -ise [Wv5;T1] to fill (someone) with terror by threats or acts of violence: *The terrorized people lived in fear of their lives* (= thought they might be killed).

alarm [T1] **1** to excite with sudden fear and anxiety: *The sound of guns alarmed us.* **2** to make conscious of danger: *The sight of the policemen alarmed the thief.*

panic 1 [I0] to feel panic; to feel sudden uncontrollable fear: *The crowd panicked at the sound of the guns. She panicked when she could not find her ticket.* **2** [T1] to cause to feel panic: *The thunder panicked the horse.* **3** [T1] *AmE sl* to cause to be very amused: *His funny stories panicked everybody.*

F123 *adjectives* : **frightening and alarming** [B]

frightening causing fear: *What a frightening thing to happen! It's frightening to think that so many people are attacked in the streets in that city.* **-ly** [adv]

scary [Wa1] *not fml* causing or marked by fear: *She walked along a dark scary street. That was the scariest story I've ever heard.*

fearful very frightening: *The book was full of pictures of fearful monsters.* **-lly** [adv]

terrifying very frightening; causing terror: *It was a terrifying thing to happen.* **-ly** [adv]

alarming causing alarm: *The alarming news came late at night and made it impossible for him to sleep.* **-ly** [adv]

blood-curdling *also* **spine-chilling** causing a feeling of fear to run through the whole body: *They heard blood-curdling cries from the hunters. That's a spine-chilling story; don't read it late at night.* **-ly** [adv]

F124 *adjectives* : **awful and frightful** [B]

awful terrible; frightening; shocking: *The pain was awful. What awful news! It was an awful accident; twelve people were killed.*

terrible full of or causing terror: *The terrible animal opened its great mouth.* **-bly** [adv]

horrible causing horror [⇒ F127]: *There was a horrible accident here last night; three people died.* **-bly** [adv]

dreadful causing great fear or anxiety; terrible: *I've just heard the dreadful news of his death.* **-lly** [adv]

frightful terrible; shocking: *There was a frightful car crash near the town centre and many people were killed or injured.* **-lly** [adv]

F125 *adjectives* : **afraid and apprehensive**

afraid 1 [F (*of*) F3, 5a] full of fear: *Don't be afraid of these dogs. She was afraid to excite him in case he became dangerous. She was afraid that it would bite him.* **2** [F (*of*), F3, 5a] worried or anxious about possible results: *Don't be afraid of asking for help. He was weak and she*

was afraid (that) he could not do the job. He was afraid to go into the house and meet his father. **3** [F5a,b] *polite* sorry for something that has happened or is likely to happen: *I am afraid that I can't come tomorrow. Can you help me?—I'm afraid not.*

frightened [B (*at, of*); F3, 5] **1** put into or being in a state of fear: *The frightened horse ran away from the fire. He was frightened at the thought of his coming examination. She was frightened to look down from the top of the tall building. The little girl was frightened that her mother wouldn't come back.* **2** [F *of*, F3] habitually afraid: *Some people are frightened of thunder, others of snakes.*

scared [B (*of*); F3, 5, 7] *not fml* frightened: *She saw a scared child with a scared expression on his face. Why won't you come; are you scared? What are you scared of? I'm scared to fly/of flying in an aeroplane.*

scary [Wa1;B] *not fml* easily scared; afraid: *Don't be so scary; we're quite safe.*

fearful [B] in a state of fear: *She is fearful in case something happens to him.* **-ly** [adv]

terrified [B] very frightened: *Terrified people ran out of the burning building.*

alarmed [B] feeling alarm: *She had an alarmed look on her face. Don't be alarmed; there is no danger.*

panicky [B] *esp infml* beginning to feel or feeling panic: *Don't get panicky; sit quiet.*

nervous [B (*of*)] *BrE* slightly afraid: *He's nervous of going too near the wild animals.* **-ly** [adv] **-ness** [U]

apprehensive [B] fearful, esp about the future; worried; anxious: *He had an apprehensive look on his face. She was apprehensive of being killed in that place. They were apprehensive for their son's safety.* **-ly** [adv]

timid [Wa2;B] not brave [⇒ F129]; nervous in character: *Don't be so timid; no one will hurt you.* **-ly** [U] **-ity, -ness** [U]

shy [Wa1] **1** [B] not bold; nervous in the company of others; not putting oneself forward: *She's shy with strangers but amusing with friends.* **2** [B] expressing this quality: *a shy smile* **3** [F *of*] having doubts or distrust: *I'm shy of saying too much on this delicate subject.* **4** [B] (of animals) unwilling to come near people **-ly** [adv] **-ness** [U]

petrified [B] so stiff with shock or fear that the power of thought or action is lost: *She stood there petrified while the huge animal came nearer.*

F126 *verbs* : **shock and horrify** [T1]

shock [*also* I0] to cause usu unpleasant or angry surprise to (someone): *I was shocked by his sudden illness/his rudeness/his wild ideas. It shocked me to see how my neighbours treated their children. His examination failure shocked him into studying harder. It's a bad book, written only to shock.*

appal to shock deeply; fill with fear, hatred, terror, etc: *These terrible things appal me. He was appalled at the loss of life in the war.*

horrify to fill with horror; to shock in a horrible way: *The film had a murder scene which horrified everyone.*

F127 *nouns* : **shock and horror**

shock 1 [U] the state or strong feeling caused by something unexpected and usu very unpleasant: *The bad news left us all speechless from shock. The opposition expressed anger and shock at the government's decision.* **2** [C] something causing this; an unpleasant piece of news: *It came as a shock* (= it was a shock) *to learn of his death.* **3** [U; (C)] (a) violent force, as from a hard blow, crash, explosion, etc: *The shock of the explosion was felt far away.* (*fig*) *The people felt the shock of rapid social change.* **4** [U] *med* the weakened state of the body with less activity of the heart, lungs, etc, usu following damage to the body: *He was taken to hospital suffering from shock. She was in a state of shock after the accident.* **shocker** [C] *not fml* a person or thing that shocks as being improper, wild, immoral, etc **shockproof** [B] (esp of a watch) not easily damaged by being dropped, hit, shaken, etc

horror 1 [U] a feeling of great shock, fear, and dislike: *We were filled with horror at the terrible news. She cried out in horror when she saw the man killed. To my horror I found that the baby had fallen to the ground.* **2** [C] anything that causes this: *The horrors of war drove her mad.* **3** [C] *not fml* an unpleasant person: *The little horror never stops playing tricks on his mother.* **have a horror of** to hate and fear: *She has a horror of snakes.*

F128 *adjectives* : **shocking and horrific** [B]

shocking 1 causing shock; very improper, wrong, or sad: *That was a shocking accident. She finds his ideas quite shocking.* **2** *not fml* bad but not evil: *What a shocking waste of time!* **-ly** [adv] *His behaviour was shockingly rude.*

appalling very frightening; shocking; terrible: *What an appalling thing to happen; I can't believe anything as bad as that could happen!* **-ly** [adv]

horrifying causing horror: *The newspaper had a horrifying story of how the children died.* **-ly** [adv]

horrific able or meant to cause horror, shock, etc: *The film showed the most horrific murder scenes.* **-ally** [adv Wa4]

horrendous *emph* really terrible; very frightening: *This situation is horrendous; many people may be killed.* **-ly** [adv]

horrid making someone feel dislike; horrible: *This is a horrid house; I don't want to stay here. Don't be horrid to your younger brothers!* **-ly** [adv]

F129 *adjectives* : **feeling or showing no fear** [B]

brave [Wa1] not feeling or showing fear: *He is a brave man; I think he was afraid but he still did it. How brave she is; she goes into that dangerous place every day!* **-ly** [adv] **-ness** [U]

courageous *esp lit, fml & pomp* showing courage; brave: *What a courageous man he is/thing to do! It was courageous of her to go into the burning building to save the child.* **-ly** [adv]

spirited showing that one is not afraid; full of spirit: *She gave him a spirited answer and said she was not frightened of him.* **-ly** [adv]

intrepid (of people or their acts) showing no fear: *The intrepid adventurers went on into the tropical forest.* **-ly** [adv]

heroic showing the qualities of a hero [⇒F133]; needing or showing bravery: *He is a heroic man. Saving the child's life was a heroic act.* **-ally** [adv Wa4]

fearless having no fear: *He seemed quite fearless when he faced the dangerous animal.* **-ly** [adv] **-ness** [U]

gutsy [Wa1] *infml esp AmE* brave

daring 1 *apprec or deprec* very brave: *He's a daring man. That was a daring thing to do! The men took part in a daring crime.* **2** unusual or new in a brave way: *That is a daring plan!* **3** shocking: *We went to see a very daring film.* **-ly** [adv]

bold [Wa1] (of a person or his behaviour) daring; courageous; adventurous: *Taking the fort from the enemy was a very bold action.* **-ly** [adv] **-ness** [U]

valiant (of a person or act) very brave, esp in war: *The soldiers never forgot his valiant deeds in battle.* **-ly** [adv]

valorous *lit & pomp* brave

gallant *esp lit* **1** courageous: *These gallant soldiers will protect you.* **2** beautiful, esp in a warlike way: *The warship made a gallant sight as it sailed away.* **-ly** [adv]

nervy [Wa1] *AmE* boldly rude; having nerve [⇒F132]

F130 *adjectives* : **relating to being brave and also foolish** [B]

audacious brave, often to a degree that is considered foolish: *That was a very audacious act; luckily he succeeded.* **-ly** [adv]

forward 1 *deprec* (esp of a young person) sure of oneself, esp in an unpleasant way; too bold, often in sexual matters: *She's too forward for* *me to like her.* **2** *less common* ready and eager: *He's always forward with help.*

foolhardy too bold; taking or needing useless or unwise risks: *It's a foolhardy act to start out on a long mountain climb without taking food or warm clothing. A foolhardy general may lose many battles and cause the death of many of his soldiers. He was foolhardy to try when he knew he'd fail.* **-diness** [U]

reckless [(*of*)] (of a person or his behaviour) too hasty; not caring about danger: *He is quite reckless of danger/of what may happen. His reckless driving will cause an accident one day.*

rash [Wa1] (of a person or his behaviour) foolishly bold; not thinking enough of the results: *He always makes/takes rash decisions. The rash young soldier got himself killed.* **in a rash moment** without thinking enough of the results: *I promised in a rash moment to buy the children a pet monkey.*

brash [Wa1] hasty and too bold, esp from lack of experience: *He behaves in a brash way.* **-ly** [adv] **-ness** [U]

callous (often recklessly) unkind; without feelings for the suffering of other people: *He's very callous; he never thinks of my troubles. He was callous to do such a terrible thing; it was a callous action.* **-ly** [adv] **-ness** [U]

F131 *adjectives* : **having or showing fear** [B]

cowardly typical of a coward [⇨ F133]; not at all brave: *Don't act in such a cowardly way! His cowardly behaviour caused their deaths.* **-liness** [U]

spineless *emot* cowardly; unable or unwilling to do anything (brave): *What a spineless person/thing to say!* **-ly** [adv] **-ness** [U]

F132 *nouns* : **bravery and guts** [U]

bravery the state of being brave: *His bravery was seen by everyone when he saved the child from the burning building.*

courage *esp lit, fml & pomp* bravery: *He showed great courage in saving the child from death in the burning building.*

daring **1** bravery: *He is a man of great daring.* **2** bold newness in ideas: *This is a plan of great daring.* **3** ability to shock: *It's a sex film of great daring.*

spirit *esp lit & old use* courage and energy: *The soldiers were full of spirit before the battle. He showed spirit in the fight.*

audacity boldness; bravery: *I admired the audacity with which she told the great man what she thought of his book. What audacity!*

valour *BrE,* **valor** *AmE esp lit* great bravery, esp in war: *The soldier's valour saved the whole army.*

guts [*also* P] *infml* bravery: *He showed terrific guts in saving their lives.*

nerve [*also* S] *infml* boldness, esp if very cool and showing disrespect: *It took real nerve to blow up that train. He lost his nerve and couldn't finish the work. This work is a test of your nerve.*

bravado *often deprec* the (often unnecessary) showing of courage or boldness: *He did it out of bravado, to show you he was brave.*

F133 *nouns* : **persons who are or are not brave** [C]

hero a person remembered for bravery, strength, or goodness, esp when admired for an act of courage under difficult conditions: *Achilles and Heracles were ancient Greek heroes. He was quite a hero in the war.*

heroine [*fem*] hero

daredevil [*also* A] a person who is very brave but not properly careful: *That daredevil is going to jump into the water from a great height! What a daredevil thing to do!*

coward a person who is unable to face danger, pain, or difficulty because of lack of courage; a person who shows fear in a shameful way: *Don't be such a coward! You coward—you ran away!*

F134 *nouns* : **heroism and cowardice** [U]

heroism **1** the quality of being a hero: *You don't often find soldiers with as much heroism as he has.* **2** great courage: *It was an act of heroism to stop the train like that.*

cowardice lack of courage: *His cowardice in the battle caused their deaths.*

F135 *verbs* : **daring and risking**

dare **1** [Wv2, 6; I∅, 2] to be brave (or rude) enough to: *I dare not/daren't go there. Dare you ask him? I don't know whether he dare try. He dare not/daren't come. How dare you say such a thing? That is as much as I dare spend on it.* **2** [Wv6; T2, 3] to be brave (or rude) enough (to): *He does not/doesn't dare (to) answer. Don't (you) dare (to) touch it! He would never dare (to) come. I wonder how he dared (to) say that.* **3** [T1] to be brave enough to deal with: *He dared the anger of her family.* **4** [T1] to be brave enough to try (esp something new): *The actress dared a new way of playing that famous character.* **5** [V3; (T1)] to say that (someone) is not brave enough (to do something): *I dared him to jump. I dared him (to), but he didn't.* **6** [C] an act of daring; an action performed in response to such an act

brave out [v adv T1] to face (trouble, blame, etc) bravely (*esp in the phr* **brave it out**): *I don't want to see her after what I said last time, but I suppose I'll have to brave it out.*

risk 1 [T1] to place in danger: *You will risk your health if you do that. He risked his own life to save mine.* **2** [T1, 4] to take the chance of: *You risk failure if you do that. He risks losing his money at cards. He risked his parents' anger by marrying her.*

venture [L9; I3] to take a chance and go, do, etc: *He did not dare (to) venture into the forest by night. (fml) May I venture to suggest a change of plan?*

F136 verbs & nouns, etc : boasting

boast 1 [I0 (*about*)] *usu deprec* to speak too much of how brave, good, clever, etc one is, one's family are, etc: *Stop boasting so much! He was boasting about how he won the race.* **2** [T5] *usu deprec* to say too proudly: *He boasted that he was the bravest man in the army. She boasted that she would win.* **3** [Wv6;T1] *not deprec* to be proud of having: *The town boasts four swimming pools.* **4** [C] what someone says when boasting: *His boast was that he could always win. It is the town's proud boast that . . .* **boastful** [B] boasting a lot or too much **-ly** [adv] **-ness** [U]

brag [I0] *esp emot & deprec* to boast: *Oh, stop bragging about your great success!* **braggart** [C] one who brags

crow [I0] **1** to make the loud high cry of a cock (= a fully grown male chicken): *At 5 o'clock each morning I'm woken by the cock crowing.* **2** [(*about*)] (*fig*) *infml & deprec* to speak proudly: *I wish he would stop crowing about his examination results!* **crow over** [v prep T1] to delight in (the defeat or misfortune of someone): *The spiteful boy crowed over his enemy's failure.*

F137 adjectives : firm, determined, and obstinate, etc [B]

firm [Wa1] strong and definite in mind, ideas, intentions, etc; not ready to change easily: *He's firm in his plan to go abroad.* **-ly** [adv]: *She believes firmly in her religion.* **-ness** [U]

determined [*also* F3] **1** (of persons) having made a strong, definite, etc decision to do, get, or be something: *She is determined to come.* **2** having the kind of nature to get what one wants: *She is a very determined girl; determined to do well in life.* **-ly** [adv] **determination** [U] the state of being determined: *She worked with great determination but did not succeed.*

strong-minded having a strong mind, opinions, etc; (*emph, emot & apprec*) determined: *She's a strong-minded girl.* **-ly** [adv] **-ness** [U]

resolute *esp lit* determined; firm in one's decisions: *He is a resolute person; he won't give up* (= stop doing what he is doing) *easily.* **ir-** [neg] **-ly** [adv] **-ness** [U] **resolution** [U] firmness, esp in deciding what to do

obstinate not easily changed from one's plans,

opinions, etc; refusing to obey, agree, etc: *She's an obstinate child; if she doesn't want to eat, she won't and that's that.* **-ly** [adv] **obstinacy** [U] the state of being obstinate

stubborn [Wa2] fixed in ideas, opinions, etc; hard to move, change, etc; not willing to co-operate [⇒ I103]: *He's a stubborn man; he won't change his mind. These nails are stubborn; they won't come out.* **-ly** [adv]: *He fought stubbornly to win.* **-ness** [U]

pig-headed *emph, emot & deprec* obstinate; stubborn: *I've talked to him, but he's too pig-headed to listen.* **-ly** [adv] **-ness** [U]

Admiration, pride, contempt, and abuse

F140 verbs : admiring and honouring

admire [T1] **1** to regard with pleasure and respect; have a good opinion of: *I admire her for her bravery.* **2** to look at with pleasure: *I sat down to admire the view.* **admirer** [C] a person who admires someone, esp a man who is attracted to a particular woman: *She has always had lots of admirers.*

respect [T1] **1** to feel respect for (esp a person or qualities): *I deeply respect him/his courage. No girl who respects herself would go out dressed like that!* **2** to show respect for: *I promise to respect your wishes.*

look up to [v adv prep Wv6;T1] *infml* to admire and respect: *She looks up to him professionally but not in other ways. She's the kind of person you can look up to.*

honour *BrE*, **honor** *AmE* [T1] to respect (someone) greatly: *We honour him; he is a great man who helped us all.* [*also* ⇒ D101]

impress 1 [T1] to make (someone) admire greatly (the person or thing mentioned): *His ideas impressed me. I was very impressed by/at/with her performance.* **2** [D1 *on/with*; T5 *on*] to make the importance of (something) clear to (someone): *My father impressed on me the value of hard work. She impressed (it) on me that I must come home early. He impressed me with the value of hard work.*

F141 nouns : admiring and honouring

admiration 1 [U] a feeling of pleasure and respect: *She was filled with admiration for his courage. His courage filled her with admiration.* **2** [*the* S *of*] person or thing that causes such feelings: *He was the admiration of his friends.*

respect 1 [S; U: (*for*)] admiration: *She showed respect for her parents' wishes. He is held in the greatest respect by the whole village. I have a* *great respect for his ability.* **2** [U (*for, to*)] attention (to); care (for): *Do you have no respect for the speed limit? A dictionary should pay respect to its readers' needs.* **without respect** paying no respect to; without considering: *Everybody can come to this school, without respect to social class, race, or sex.*

honour *BrE*, **honor** *AmE* [U] great respect, often publicly expressed: *We hold him in great honour. He won honour for what he did to help us all.* [*also* ⇒ D102] **honours** [P] marks of respect, such as titles given in Britain to people on the Queen's birthday and at New Year **do the honours** to act as the host, by offering drink, etc: *Who's going to do the honours tonight?*

glory 1 [U] great honour, praise, etc: *He fought for glory, not money. They worked for the greater glory of God.* **2** [C] something beautiful or deserving praise, admiration, etc: *'Remember our past national glories!' he cried.* **glory in** [v prep T1, 4] *often deprec* to enjoy very much and be proud of: *He glories in fighting/his ability at football.* **glorious** [B] full of glory: *He said that the battle was a glorious victory.* **-ly** [adv] **glorify** [T1] to make glorious: *Never glorify war. She glorifies everything her husband does.* **glorification** [U] the act of glorifying: *The church was built for the greater glorification of God.*

splendour *BrE*, **splendor** *AmE* [U] *fml & poet* glory: *The splendour of the sunset delighted them. The splendour of ancient Rome existed beside much evil and unhappiness.*

pomp [U] a great formal show, esp as part of a ceremony: *There was a lot of pomp and splendour when the two kings met.*

F142 *adjectives* : **admiring and honouring** [B]

admirable worthy of admiration; very good: *This is an admirable plan; I like it very much. Saving the girl's life was an admirable thing to do.* **-bly** [adv]

honourable *BrE*, **honorable** *AmE* worthy of honour or respect; showing good character: *This is the honourable plan of honourable people.* **-bly** [adv]

impressive giving one a feeling of size or importance; causing one to be impressed: *It is a very impressive building. What an impressive person she is!* **-ly** [adv] **-ness** [U]

promising likely to do well or be good in future: *She is a very promising student indeed.*

noble [Wa1] admirable and fine: *What a noble character he has! It was noble of you to try to help him.* **ig-** [neg] **-bly** [adv] **-bility** [U]

proud [Wa1] **1** *apprec* having the quality of self-respect and showing this in one's standard of behaviour: *They are poor but they are proud; they won't accept help from anyone. She was too proud to show her grief in public.* **2** [(*of*); *also* F3, 5] having or expressing a proper

personal feeling of satisfaction and pleasure in something connected with oneself: *He is very proud of his new car. Our football team is proud that it has won all its matches this season. I'm proud to tell you that my son has just won first prize in the race.* **3** splendid, noble, grand; glorious: *Rome is a proud Italian city. It was a proud moment in her life when she became mayor.* **-ly** [adv]

respectful showing respect: *They were very respectful towards the great man.* **dis-** [neg] **-lly** [adv]

appreciative 1 showing thanks, one's respect, etc: *Try to be more appreciative when people give you help.* **2** showing a high opinion of someone: *His appreciative words pleased them all.* **un-** [neg] **-ly** [adv] **-ness** [U]

humble [Wa2,3] **1** (of people) low in rank or position: *His parents were humble country people.* **2** (of positions) unimportant; not held in high regard by society: *He is a man of humble birth but great ability.* **3** having a low opinion of oneself and a high opinion of others: *What a humble, hard-working person he is!* **-bly** [adv Wa3] **-ness** [U] **humility** [U] *esp fml* the condition of being humble

lowly [Wa1] *esp lit & emot* very humble: *His parents were lowly country people.* **-liness** [U]

F143 *adjectives* : **proud and superior** [B] *deprec*

[ALSO ⇒ C159]

proud [Wa1] having too high an opinion of oneself or a false idea of one's importance: *He's too proud to be seen in public with his poorly-dressed mother.*

conceited having or showing too much pride: *She became very conceited after she passed those examinations.* **-ly** [adv] **-ness** [U]

vain [Wa1] full of self-admiration; thinking too highly of one's appearance, abilities, etc: *Too much praise can make a man vain.*

superior thinking oneself higher or better than others: *Oh, stop being so superior about people's clothes, just because you can buy whatever you want!*

arrogant proud and self-important in a rude way that shows disrespect for other people: *He was an arrogant official with arrogant manners.* **-ly** [adv]

F144 *nouns* : **pride, conceit, and snobbery**

pride 1 [U] *deprec* too high an opinion of oneself because of one's rank, wealth, abilities, etc: *He was so full of pride that he didn't know that people usually laughed at him.* **2** [U] *apprec* reasonable self respect; a proper high opinion of oneself: *She wanted to ask him to stay, but her pride would not let her. If you offer him money, it will hurt his pride.* **3** [U; S] a feeling of satisfaction, delight, and pleasure in what one can do or has done, or in someone or something connected with one: *He takes a pride in his work. They spoke with pride of their pretty daughter.* **4** [*the* S *of*] the most valued thing or person: *This fine picture is the pride of our collection.*

vanity [U] the quality or state of being too proud of oneself or one's importance, abilities, etc: *You'll only make his vanity worse if you tell him how clever he is. She's always looking at herself in the mirror—what vanity!*

conceit **1** [U] *deprec* too high an opinion of one's own abilities, value, etc; too much pride: *That girl is full of conceit. I dislike conceit, especially in a young person.* **2** [C] *tech* a humorous or clever thought or expression: *Her poetry is full of little conceits.*

disdain [U] lack of respect; the feeling that someone or something is low and worthless: *The soldiers treated their prisoners with disdain. She looked at him with cold disdain.*

contempt [U] **1** the feeling that someone or something is of a lower rank and undesirable: *Some employers have contempt for their workers. I feel nothing but contempt for such dishonest behaviour!* **2** total disregard or disrespect: *I treat those fools with the contempt they deserve.* **3** the condition of being thought of low rank and undesirable: *'People who smoke and drink to much should be held in contempt,' she said.*

arrogance [U] pride and self-importance shown in a way that is rude and disrespectful to others: *Although what he said was reasonable his arrogance angered everyone.*

snobbery [U] the state or quality of being a snob, too interested in social position, wealth, etc: *Her snobbery made her stop seeing her old friends when she became rich.*

F145 *verbs* : **despising and being proud** [T1]

despise to regard as worthless, low, bad, etc; to dislike very angrily: *The soldiers despised those enemies who refused to fight. He began to despise himself for the way he had treated his friends.*

look down on [v adv prep] *infml* to despise, esp socially: *She looks down on people who are not rich.*

disdain [Wv6] to treat with a lack of respect, interest, etc: *He disdains them and won't talk to them. She disdains work; she never does any.*

humble to make (someone or oneself) humble or in a lower position: *He humbled his enemies publicly. It humbled his pride to admit his mistakes. 'You must humble yourself before God,' said the priest.*

pride oneself on [*also* V4b] to take a proper pride in: *She prides herself on her teaching, and she is very good indeed.*

F146 *adjectives* : **despising and being proud** [B]

disdainful showing disdain: *She gave him a disdainful smile. He is very disdainful/towards stupid people.* **-lly** [adv]

contemptuous showing contempt: *He spoke in a very contemptuous way about them. There was a contemptuous smile on his face.* **-ly** [adv]

F147 *adjectives* : **despised and held in contempt** [Wa3;B]

despicable that should be or deserves to be despised: *It is (quite) despicable of you to leave your wife and family without any money.* **-bly** [adv]

contemptible that should be shown or deserves contempt: *What a contemptible thing to do/say!* **-bly** [adv]

F148 *verbs* : **insulting people** [T1]

insult to say or do something to offend: *They insulted him and he can't forgive them or forget it. He was insulted when they insisted on paying for him.*

offend [*also* IØ] to insult and annoy (a person) by doing or saying something: *You offended her by saying that she only bought the cheapest clothes. Please don't be offended; I didn't mean to offend (you). He was offended when they didn't ask him to go with them.*

abuse to say unkind, cruel, or rude things to (someone) or about (somebody or something): *She abuses her ex-husband mercilessly.*

disparage [Wv4] to speak without respect of/for; make (someone or something) sound of little value or importance: *She's always disparaging the successes of others; is she jealous? In spite of your disparaging remarks I think she sings beautifully.*

decry to speak ill of; say bad things about (something powerful or dangerous to the public): *He decried the harmful influence of television.*

run down [v adv] *not fml* to say bad things about: *Stop running him down; he's not as bad as that!*

do down [v adv] *BrE infml* to say bad things about (someone, esp someone who is not present): *They praise him to his face, but do him down behind his back.*

cheek [(up)] *BrE infml* to behave, speak, etc boldly, rudely, or disrespectfully to(wards) (someone): *Don't cheek (up) your teacher!*

snub [*often pass*] to rudely pay no attention to: *He was snubbed by his former friends, because of what he did.*

F149 *nouns* : **insulting people**

insult **1** [U] speech or action which insults: *I*

don't like insult; I prefer politeness. **2** [C] an example of this: *To offer him so little money is an insult.*

offence *BrE*, **offense** *AmE* [U] *esp fml* the state of being insulted, offended: *I hope I didn't cause you any offence; I certainly meant no offence.*

abuse [U] unkind, cruel, or rude words: *He greeted us with a stream of abuse.*

disparagement [U] the act of disparaging someone or something: *He has met a lot of disparagement in his work, but he is not worried by it.*

snub [C] an act of snubbing: *He had to suffer the snubs of his former friends.*

F150 adjectives : insulting people [B]

insulting causing insult: *What an insulting thing to say! They spoke in a very insulting way.* **-ly** [adv]

abusive using or containing unkind, cruel, or rude words: *His language was very abusive when he spoke to her.* **-ly** [adv]

disparaging showing that one considers someone or something of little value or importance: *He made some disparaging remarks about her singing, but I think she's good.* **-ly** [adv]

pejorative [B] *fml* (of a word, phrase, etc) that suggests that someone or something is bad or worthless; insulting: *The words he used were clearly pejorative; he suggested that their leader was a fool.* **-ly** [adv]

depreciatory serving to lessen the value of someone or something; pejorative: *Stop making depreciatory remarks about him.*

derogatory strongly depreciative; showing that someone has a low opinion of someone else: *His remarks were very derogatory; I felt insulted.*

F151 verbs : disgracing, shaming, and embarrassing [T1]

disgrace 1 to be a disgrace to: *He disgraced himself/us all last night by drinking too much.* **2** [*usu pass*] to put (a public person) out of favour/position in disgrace: *The dishonest minister was publicly disgraced.*

shame 1 to bring dishonour to; disgrace: *He shamed his family by being sent to prison.* **2** to cause to feel shame: *It shames me to say it, but I told a lie.* **3** to appear very much better than: *Their good work shames all the others.* **4** [*into* or *out of*] to force or urge (to do something) by causing feelings of shame: *I tried to shame her into voting in the elections but she has no sense of duty.* **ashamed 1** [F (*of*) F3, 5a] feeling shame, guilt, or sorrow (because of something done): *You should be ashamed (of yourself/ your behaviour)! You should be ashamed to tell such lies. He was ashamed that he had lied. He was ashamed of asking/having asked such a*

simple question. I'm ashamed that he found me doing it. **2** [F3] unwilling through fear of feeling shame or being laughed at: *He was ashamed to ask such a simple question.* **-ly** [adv]

embarrass [Wv4] to cause to feel ashamed or socially uncomfortable: *She was embarrassed when they asked her age. I don't like making speeches in public; it is so embarrassing. He embarrassed her by telling dirty jokes.*

show up [v adv] *esp BrE* to make (someone) feel shame: *When we go to dinner parties my husband always shows me up with the rude jokes he tells.*

humiliate to cause (someone) to feel humble [⇒ F142] in a bad way; or to lose the respect of others: *His remarks humiliated me; I felt really small and silly.*

stigmatize, -ise [T1] to mark (a person) out by a sign of shame; tell or show that (someone) is shameful: *They stigmatized their opponent as a liar.*

F152 nouns : disgracing, shaming, and embarrassing

disgrace 1 [U] loss of honour and respect: *His actions brought disgrace on his family. Being poor is no disgrace. The child is in disgrace because he behaved badly at dinner.* **2** [S (*to*)] a cause of loss of respect: *Bad doctors like that are a disgrace to our hospitals.*

shame 1 [U] the painful feeling of the guilt, wrongness, inability, or failure of oneself or a close friend, relative, etc: *He felt no shame for all the bad things he had done. Her face reddened with shame when she heard of her mistake.* **2** [U] disgrace of this kind: *His bad behaviour brings shame on us all!* **3** [S] something that deserves blame: *It's a shame, the way they waste money.*

embarrassment 1 [U] the act of embarrassing; the state of being embarrassed: *They asked me to sing to them, much to my embarrassment.* **2** [C] a person or thing that embarrasses: *That nasty child is an embarrassment to his parents.*

humiliation 1 [U] the act of humiliating or being humiliated **2** [C] an example of this: *She has had many humiliations in her life but she has never accepted them.*

stigma [C] a sign of shame; a feeling of being ashamed: *There is a sort of stigma about having to ask for money; the stigma of being different from other people.*

F153 adjectives : disgracing, shaming, and embarrassing [B]

disgraceful bringing disgrace: *What a disgraceful thing to do/way to behave!* **-lly**

shameful deserving blame; causing the feeling or condition of shame: *What a shameful thing to do/say! It's shameful the way they waste money!* **-lly** [adv]

shamefaced showing shame or unsureness about oneself: *He made his excuses in a shamefaced way.* **-ly** [adv]
humiliating causing someone to feel humiliated: *The way they spoke to her was most humiliating for her.* **-ly** [adv]
embarrassing causing someone to feel ashamed or socially uncomfortable: *I made an embarrassing mistake; I called him by the wrong name.* **-ly** [adv]

F154 *adjectives* : **having no shame** [B]

shameless 1 (of a person) unable to feel shame: *'She is an immodest and shameless young woman!' he said.* **2** done without shame; indecent: *His behaviour was a shameless insult to us all.* **-ly** [adv] **-ness** [U]
bold [Wa1] *deprec* (of a person, esp a woman or her behaviour) without shame: *She's a bold girl, isn't she?* **-ly** [adv] **-ness** [U]
brazen *emot* shameless: *They are quite brazen about their evil behaviour; they don't hide it.* **-ly** [adv] **-ness** [U]

F155 *adjectives* : **rude and cheeky** [B]

rude [Wa1] (of a person or his behaviour) not at all polite: *It's rude to say you don't like the food, when she spent so long preparing it. Don't make such rude remarks. Don't be so rude to your father.* **-ly** [adv]
impudent very rude in speech or act: *What an impudent remark/thing to say! He is a very impudent child.* **-ly** [adv]
impertinent rude; not at all respectful: *What an impertinent remark/child!* **-ly** [adv]
insolent (of people and their acts) showing rudeness; insulting: *What insolent behaviour! The man's manner was very insolent.* **-ly** [adv]
brash [Wa1] rudely disrespectful and proud: *Oh, don't be so brash towards these people!* **-ly** [adv] **-ness** [U]
cheeky [Wa1] *infml* rude; not respectful: *I don't like cheeky little girls who are rude to older people.* **-ily** [adv] *The child behaved very cheekily.* **-iness** [U]
fresh [Wa1] *AmE* cheeky: *Don't be so fresh!*
audacious daringly impolite or disrespectful, as to someone of high rank: *What an audacious thing to do!* **-ly** [adv]

F156 *nouns* : **rudeness and cheek** [U]

rudeness the state or condition of being rude: *I don't want to see him again; his rudeness last time was unforgivable.*
impudence the state or condition of being impudent: *The child's impudence surprised us.*
impertinence the state or condition of being impertinent: *What impertinence!*
insolence the state or condition of being insol-

ent: *'His insolence must be punished!' the king said.*
disrespect lack of respect, esp by being rude: *Those children showed great disrespect to their parents.*
audacity daring rudeness or disrespect: *I was surprised at her audacity in wearing such a dress!*
cheek *infml* bold, disrespectful, rude behaviour: *No more of your cheek or else I'll hit you!*
freshness *AmE* cheek
nerve [*also* S] *deprec* boldness, esp if it is rude and disrespectful: *He's very untidy and he has the nerve to tell me my shoes need cleaning! The nerve of him! What a nerve!*

F157 *verbs* : **disappointing people** [T1]

disappoint 1 to fail to fulfil the hopes of (a person): *I'm sorry to disappoint you, but I can't come after all. He was disappointed to learn that you couldn't come. Please don't be too disappointed if I can't do it.* **2** to defeat (a plan, hope, etc): *I'm sorry to disappoint your hopes.* **disappointing** [B] causing one to be unhappy at not seeing hopes come true: *What disappointing news! Your examination marks are rather disappointing; I hoped you would do better.* **-ly** [adv] *The day of the garden party was disappointingly cold and wet.*
let down [v adv] *not fml* to cause (someone) to be disappointed esp in one's loyalty; to fail to keep a promise to: *I'm sorry I let you down yesterday; I won't do it again. She let us all down by not coming.*

F158 *nouns* : **disappointing people**

disappointment 1 [U] the state of being disappointed: *He left the station in great disappointment, for she wasn't on the train.* **2** [C] someone or something disappointing: *Our son has been a disappointment to us. He suffered various disappointments in his attempts to get work.* **to someone's disappointment** which makes someone feel disappointed: *She learnt, to her disappointment, that they hadn't invited her.*
letdown [C] *not fml* a disappointment: *It was a real letdown; she didn't come although she had promised.*

Kindness and unkindness

F170 *adjectives, etc* : **showing helpful interest** [B]

kind [Wa1 (*of*)] helpful; (that shows one is) interested in the happiness or feelings of others: *She is a kind person. That was a kind* *thing to do. What a kind thought! Be kind to animals. Would you be kind enough to do it? Would you be so kind as to do it? It was very kind of you to do it.* **-ly** [adv] **-ness 1** [U] the quality of being kind **2** [C] a kind action

kindly 1 [Wa2] pleasant; friendly: *She gave him a kindly smile. He is the kindliest/most kindly person I have ever met. She spoke in a kindly way.* **2** [adv] [Wa1] in a kind manner: *She spoke kindly to him.* **not take kindly to** not accept easily or willingly: *He didn't take kindly to his new responsibilities.*

kind-hearted [Wa2] having or showing a kind heart (**nature**): *He's the very kindest-hearted person I know.* **-ly** [adv]

beneficent *esp fml* kind: *He behaved in a very beneficent way towards them.* **-ly** [adv] **beneficence** [U] the state of being beneficent; kindness

benevolent kind and liking to help other people: *The old man felt benevolent towards the poor children and gave them some money.* **-ly** [adv] **benevolence** [U] the state of being benevolent; kindness to other people

benign 1 (of people) kind and friendly: *He met them with a benign smile.* **2** (of weather) pleasant; not too hot or too cold **3** *tech* (of diseases) not very harmful **-ly** [adv]

good [Wa5 (*to, of*)] kind and helpful: *She's always been very good to me. It's good of you to help. Would you please be good enough to close the door? They hadn't a good word for her* (= They talked unkindly about her).

humane showing human kindness and the qualities of a civilized person: *His way of looking after the animals is very humane.* **-ly** [adv]

human 1 showing the feelings, esp those of kindness, which human beings have: *He seems quite human when you know him.* **2** of or concerning man: *the human voice* **-ly** [adv]

considerate [(*of*)] thoughtful of the rights and feelings of others; helpful: *What a very considerate young man he is! It was considerof you to come and meet me.* **-ly** [adv] **-ness** [U]

thoughtful [(*of*)] paying attention to the wishes, feelings, etc of other people; taking other people into account: *It was thoughtful of you to meet me here. He is a very thoughtful kind of person.* **-lly** [adv]

helpful [(*of*)] willing to help; useful: *She's a helpful girl. It was a helpful thing to do. It was helpful of you to do that.* **-lly** [adv]

beneficial having a helpful or good effect: *This holiday has been really beneficial; I've enjoyed it very much.* **-lly** [adv]

well-disposed showing kindness: *He is well-disposed towards most people. She's a very well-disposed person.*

obedient doing what one is told to do; obeying [⇒ G115] one's parents, teachers, officers, etc, esp without arguing: *She is a very obedient child. The dog is well-trained and obedient to its master's orders.* **-ly** [adv] **obedience** [U] the

condition of being obedient: *Obedience to orders is important in an army.*

F171 *adjectives* : **tender and gentle** [B]

tender [Wa1] gentle and loving; kind: *She has a tender way with people. She gave her child a tender look. What a tender heart he has!* **-ly** [adv] **-ness** [U]

tender-hearted *esp emot* easily moved to love, pity, or sorrow: *She's very tender hearted about those poor people.* **-ness** [U]

gentle [Wa1, 3] **1** kind and ready to help others: *She is a very gentle person, who never loses her temper.* **2** not violent; soft in movement: *There was a gentle wind among the trees. They climbed up a gentle slope.* **-tly** [adv Wa3] **-ness** [U]

F172 *adjectives* : **sympathetic and understanding** [B]

sympathetic [(*to*)] of, feeling, or showing sympathy: *She was sympathetic to my aims. It's no use just being sympathetic; help me!* **-ally** [adv Wa4]

warm-hearted having or showing warm and friendly feelings **-ly** [adv] **-ness** [U]

tolerant showing or practising friendly feelings: *He is a Muslim/Catholic but is very tolerant towards those who have different religious opinions. What a tolerant woman she is!* **in-** [neg] **-ly** [adv]

understanding kind, because able to understand: *She was very helpful and understanding about what happened. Try to be a little more understanding!*

F173 *adjectives* : **humanitarian and charitable** [B]

humanitarian concerned with trying to improve life for human beings by giving them better conditions to live in and by changing laws, esp those which punish too severely

generous showing readiness to give money, help, kindness, etc: *She's not very generous with the food; she gives you small amounts. You are far too generous with your money.* **-ly** [adv]

liberal generous, esp in giving or being given quickly and easily or in large amounts: *He is very liberal with his money. She gave us liberal helpings of food.* **-lly** [adv]

magnanimous having or showing unusually generous qualities towards others: *A country should be magnanimous towards its defeated enemies.* **-ly** [adv]

charitable showing kindness and charity [⇒ F175]: *Be charitable; try to help them.* **-bly** [adv Wa3]

F174 *adjectives* : **merciful and clement**
[B]

merciful 1 [*(to)*] showing mercy; willing to be kind, to forget bad things done, or to forgive people for bad things done, instead of punishing them, etc: *The king was merciful and did not kill his enemies. The merciful king saved him from death.* **2** by the kindness of God, fortune, etc: *He had a merciful death and did not suffer too much pain.* **-ly** [adv Wa4] **-ness** [U]

lenient 1 merciful in judgment; gentle: *Be lenient with her, please; she's only a child.* **2** allowing less than the highest standards of work, behaviour, etc: *You are too lenient with these children; you must make them work harder.* **-ly** [adv]

clement *often fml & pomp* (esp of weather, conditions) pleasant; kind; gentle: *The weather is much more clement today, I think. He wore a clement smile on his face.*

F175 *nouns* : **showing helpful interest**

kindness 1 [U] the quality of being kind **2** [C] a kind action: *They have shown me many kindnesses in the past. Please have the kindness to answer this letter quickly.* (BrE) *Please do me the kindness to answer this letter quickly.*

goodwill [U] kind feelings towards or between people and/or willingness to act to increase the good fortune of these others: *Owing to the goodwill of the people of this town we have collected enough money to educate these children.*

humaneness [U] the quality of being humane

humanity [U] the quality of being human and/or humane

considerateness [U] the quality of being considerate

consideration [U *(for)*] thoughtful attention to the wishes and feelings of others: *He never shows any consideration for his mother's feelings. Have you no consideration for others, you nasty boy?*

sympathy [U] **1** the ability to share the feelings of another: *I have no sympathy for him or for what he has done.* **2** (the expression of) pity **sympathies** [P] **1** feelings of support: *His sympathies are/lie with our enemies.* **2** a message of comfort in grief: *He sent them his sympathies on the death of their father.*

tolerance [U] the ability or willingness to let other people do what they want, say and think what they like, etc: *He is a man of great tolerance.* **in-** [*neg*]

toleration [U; S] the ability to tolerate [⇒F9] or accept what one does not really like: *He has some toleration of/for people like that now, but he finds it difficult to work with them.*

charity 1 [U] kindness; the feeling of generosity: *Charity made her give food to the old woman.* **2** [U] Christian love for God and man:

The Bible says that 'of faith, hope, and charity, the greatest of all is charity'. **3** [U] help to the poor: *She was always very generous in her charity. I don't want to live on charity for ever.* **4** [C] a society or organization that gives help to the poor: *There are many charities in Britain which send help to hungry people abroad.* **5** [U] sympathy and kindness shown when judging others: *She was only set free because of the judge's charity.* **charity begins at home** one's first duty is to one's family; after that, to others

mercy 1 [U *(to, towards)*] the quality of being merciful; willingness to forgive and not punish: *He showed mercy to* (wards) *his enemies and let them live.* **2** [U; C *usu pl with sing meaning*] kindness or pity towards those who suffer or are weak: *God's mercy has/mercies have no limits.* **at the mercy of** powerless against: *Without a gun he was at their mercy. They were lost at sea, at the mercy of wind and weather.*

leniency [U] the quality of being lenient

clemency 1 [U] mercy, esp when used to make a punishment less severe: *The prisoner asked for clemency.* **2** (esp of the weather) gentleness

generosity 1 [U] the quality of being generous **2** [C] a generous act

liberality [U] generosity with things or ideas

condolence [C *often pl* (*on*); U] (an expression of) sympathy for someone who has experienced sadness, sorrow, misfortune, etc: *Please accept my condolences on your mother's death.*

solace 1 [U] comfort in grief or anxiety; lessening of trouble in mind: *She looked for solace in hard work.* **2** [C] something that provides this: *Hard work was a great solace to her in her grief.*

consolation 1 [U] comfort during a time of sadness or disappointment: *She got many letters of consolation when her mother died. Your remarks are no consolation at all!* **2** [C] a person or thing that consoles: *Your presence was a consolation to me at such a sad time.*

F176 *verbs* : **showing helpful interest**

consider [T1, 5, 6a] to take (someone's difficulties, etc) into account: *We must always consider people's feelings.*

sympathize, -ise [I∅ (*with*)] to feel or show sympathy: *I know you feel angry and I sympathize, but what can we do? She was crying and he was sympathizing with her.*

feel for [v prep T1] *not fml* to sympathize with: *I really felt for her when she lost her child in that accident.*

understand [T1; I∅] *genl* to consider (someone's difficulties) and to sympathize: *I think he understands what you feel. Please try to understand!*

console [T1 (*with*)] to give comfort or sympathy to (someone) in times of disappointment or sadness: *She tried to console the murdered man's wife. After fire destroyed my home, I consoled myself with the thought that it might have been worse. That thought consoled me.*

solace [T1] *esp lit* to give solace to or for: *Hard work helped to solace her grief.*

F177 *adjectives* : **not helpful or friendly** [B]

nasty [Wa1] not helpful, friendly, kind, pleasant, etc: *What a nasty man he is! If he is nasty to me, I'll be even nastier to him!* **-tily** [adv] **-tiness** [U]

mean [Wa1] *AmE* bad-tempered; liking to hurt: *That's a mean dog; be careful it doesn't bite you.* **-ness** [U]

sour [Wa1] having or expressing a bad temper; unsmiling: *What a sour-faced old man! Why are you (looking) so sour?* **-ness** [U]

spiteful acting out of spite; cruel in a small mean way: *It was spiteful of him to tear up your letter.* **-lly** [adv]

malicious showing a wish or intention to hurt: *She was malicious towards them; she did everything she could to make life difficult for them.* **-ly** [adv] **-ness** [U]

aggrieved 1 *fml* showing or suffering from a personal offence, hurt feelings, etc: *I felt very aggrieved after our quarrel.* **2** *law* having suffered a wrong: *The aggrieved person had had his leg broken.*

F178 *nouns* : **not helpful or friendly** [U]

spite unreasonable dislike for and desire to annoy another person, esp in some small way: *I'm sure he did that just out of/from spite. It was spite and nothing else!*

malice the wish, desire, or intention to hurt one or more others: *There is no malice in him; he didn't intend to cause you trouble.*

F179 *adjectives* : **showing no kindness or pity** [B]

merciless showing no kindness, mercy, or willingness to help or save anyone: *The enemy were merciless in their attack on the town; they killed everyone.* (*fig*) *What merciless weather!* **-ly** [adv] **-ness** [adv]

pitiless 1 showing no pity; merciless: *He was a pitiless king who made all his subjects suffer.* **2** unbearably severe: *The north wind was pitiless. They studied the plan in the cold pitiless light of reason.* **-ly** [adv] **-ness** [U]

ruthless showing or having no kindness, pity, etc at all: *He is completely ruthless and will stop at nothing to get what he wants.* **-ly** [adv] **-ness** [U]

remorseless showing no remorse [⇒ F83]: *She was quite remorseless in hurting him.* **-ly** [adv] **-ness** [U]

heartless showing no kindness or pity: *It was heartless to leave the little dog to die of hunger.* **-ly** [adv] **-ness** [U]

F180 *adjectives* : **unhelpful and greedy** [B]

mean [Wa1] **1** ungenerous; unwilling to share or help: *He's too mean (with his money) to buy us a meal.* **2** unkind; unpleasant in behaviour: *Let me go out; don't be so mean to me. I felt mean for not letting him go out.* **-ness** [U]

miserly mean like a miser: *He is very miserly with his money/the food he gives us.* **-liness** [U]

mercenary *usu deprec* doing something only for money, gain, or greed: *She is a very mercenary kind of person. Don't be so mercenary; do something for nothing for once in your life.*

grasping *emot* mean, esp with money: *They are very grasping people; they take all they can get and ask for more.*

selfish wanting or keeping as much as possible for oneself: *Oh, don't be so selfish with your money! She is one of the most selfish people I've met.* **un-** [neg] **-ly** [adv] **-ness** [U]

greedy [Wa1] **1** *usu derog* full of greed for anything, esp food, money, etc: *The greedy little boy ate all the food. Don't put your greedy hands on that cake/money!* **2** [for] needing something badly: *The roots of the plant were greedy for water. He was greedy for love.* **-dily** [adv] **-iness** [U]

avaricious *fml* having too great an eagerness and desire, esp for wealth; greedy: *He is a very avaricious man; he takes but seldom gives.* **-ly** [adv] **-ness** [U]

F181 *nouns* : **greed**

greed [U (for)] a strong desire to obtain a lot or more than what is right, esp of food, money, or power: *He had a greed for gold.*

avarice [U] *fml* greed: *What unbelievable avarice; he wants all the money!*

miser [C] a person who loves money for its own sake and spends as little as possible; a mean person: *Don't be a miser; lend me £5.*

F182 *adjectives* : **jealous, resentful, and vengeful** [B]

jealous [(of)] **1** wanting to keep what one has; possessive [⇒ D81]: *He is jealous of his wife's love.* **2** wanting to get what someone else has: *He is jealous of their success and wealth.* **3** shocked and angry at not being liked as much as someone else: *He was jealous when he discovered she loved someone else.* **-ly** [adv] *The dog jealously guarded its bone.*

envious [(of)] feeling or showing envy; wanting what someone else has: *She was envious of her sister's beauty. He looked at my new car with envious eyes.* **-ly** [adv] *'Aren't you lucky!' said Mary enviously.*

resentful [(about)] feeling angry or bitter at someone: *He is resentful at being called a fool. She felt very resentful because he left her. He* gave her a resentful look. Don't be so resentful! **-lly** [adv] **-ness** [U]

vengeful (of an action or feeling) based on a fierce desire or wish to harm another for what has been done to oneself: His mind was full of vengeful plans. **-lly** [adv]

sullen 1 silently showing dislike; silently resentful; not cheerful or interested: He worked in a sullen way. She had a sullen look on her face. **2** (fig) dark and unpleasant: The sky was sullen. **-ly** [adv] **-ness** [U]

F183 nouns : jealousy, resentment, and revenge [U]

jealousy 1 jealous feeling; the state of being jealous **2** [C] anything done or said that shows jealousy: His many little jealousies harmed their marriage.

envy 1 a feeling of wishing that one had someone else's qualities, possessions, etc: His good luck filled them with envy. The boy's new bicycle was an object of envy to all his friends. She felt envy at her friend's good luck. **2** [the S of] a thing one wishes to own or a person one wishes to be like: Their beautiful garden is the envy of their neighbours. She's so pretty, she's the envy of the other girls.

resentment the feeling of resenting (what one thinks is) bad treatment: She feels some resentment against him/at what he did/because of what he did/for what he did. I don't bear you any resentment now.

vengeance great harm or damage done to another person because of what he or she had earlier done to oneself or one's family, etc: He killed them in an act of vengeance. We shall take vengeance on them for these crimes!

revenge usu unlawful action to punish someone who has or may have done wrong to oneself, one's family, friends, etc: I must get revenge for this! She took (her) revenge on him for what he did to her. She did it in revenge for what he had done.

F184 verbs : jealousy and resentment

envy [D1; T1] to feel envy for or of: I don't envy you your journey in this bad weather. Religion teaches us not to envy other people. The girls all envied Mary's beautiful legs. **-ingly** [adv]

resent [T1, 4] to feel angry or bitter at: He resented being called a fool. I (strongly/bitterly) resent your remarks.

F185 verbs : getting one's revenge

avenge [T1] **1** to get satisfaction (**revenge** or **vengeance**) for (a wrong) by punishing the wrongdoer: He avenged his father's death by burning the village. He avenged the death on the village. **2** to punish someone for a wrong done

to (oneself or somebody else): I shall avenge my brother; the man who killed him shall die. They avenged themselves on their enemies.

pay back [v adv T1 (for)] not fml to make (someone) suffer in return for something he or she did: I'll pay you back for this! He paid them back for what they did to his family.

get one's own back not fml to take one's revenge, esp in some small way: I'll get my own back for what she did!

get even [I0] not fml to be avenged; to get one's own back: I'll get even if it takes (me) a hundred years!

Honesty, loyalty, trickery, and deceit

F190 adjectives : honest and truthful

honest [B] **1** (of people) not likely to lie or cheat: He's an honest man; he won't tell you lies. **2** (of actions, appearance, etc) showing such qualities: That man has an honest face. **3** direct; not hiding facts: This is my honest opinion. It's the honest truth; believe me! **-ly** [adv]

trustworthy [B] fit to be trusted; (emot) honest: He's completely trustworthy; he won't cheat you. **un-** [neg] **-thily** [adv]

reliable [B] fit to be relied on [⇒ F201]: He's a reliable man; if he says he will do the job, he'll do it. **un-** [neg] **-bly** [adv Wa3]

straight [F] infml honest: Be straight with me and I'll play straight with you.

upright [B] emot reliable; honest: He's a very upright sort of man; completely trustworthy and very religious. **-ness** [U]

truthful [B] always or usu telling the truth; honest in what one says, writes, etc: She's a truthful girl; she won't tell you lies. **un-** [neg] **-lly** [adv] **-ness** [U]

F191 adjectives : not honest and truthful [B]

dishonest (of a person or behaviour) not honest: She's a very dishonest girl; don't trust her. It's dishonest to tell people you are doing something and then to do something different. **-ly** [adv] He's behaved very dishonestly.

crooked usu infml dishonest, usu in a criminal way: I don't like his business activities; they are thoroughly crooked.

deceitful emot dishonest, esp in telling lies: Stop being so deceitful; tell the truth! **-lly** [adv] **-ness** [U]

F192 adjectives : frank and straightforward [B]

frank [Wa1] free and direct in speech; open in

manner; plain and honest; truthful: *He had a frank, friendly look. If you want my frank opinion, I don't think the plan will succeed. Will you be quite frank with me about this matter* (= tell me the truth, without trying to hide anything)?

open 1 not hiding anything; honest: *Let's be open with each other.* **2** not hidden: *There was open hatred between the two men.*

aboveboard without any trick or attempt to deceive; honourable: *His part in the affair was quite (open and) aboveboard. He was honest and aboveboard with us.*

sincere [Wa2] (of a person, feelings, or behaviour) free from deceit, pretence, or falseness; real, true, or honest: *He had a sincere admiration of his opponent's qualities. She was not completely sincere in what she said. You have my sincerest/most sincere sympathy, dear friend.* **-ly** [adv] **-ness** *also* **sincerity** [U]

genuine very sincere: *He is genuine in his desire to help. He has a genuine desire to help.* **-ly** [adv] **-ness** [U]

forthcoming *infml* ready to be helpful, friendly, and honest: *He was quite forthcoming about what happened; he told us everything.*

forthright direct in manner and speech; expressing one's thoughts and fee feelings plainly: *His forthright behaviour shows that he's honest, but he seems rude to some people.* **-ness** [U]

straightforward 1 honest; without hidden meanings: *He gave us a straightforward answer.* **2** expressed or understood in a direct way, without difficulties: *It's a straightforward matter.* **-ly** [adv] **-ness** [U]

candid open, direct, and honest **-ly** [adv] **candour** [U]

F193 *adjectives* : **not frank and straightforward** [B]

insincere not sincere: *He made some insincere remarks about being happy to see them.* **-ly** [adv] **-ity** [U]

furtive quiet, secret, and/or not direct, as expressing guilty feelings; trying to escape notice **-ly** [adv] **-ness** [U]

stealthy [Wa1] moving or acting in a way which suggests a wish to be secret or not to be seen; furtive: *A stealthy figure moved among the trees.* **-thily** [adv] **-thiness** [U]

secretive fond of keeping secrets [⇨ F207]; choosing to hide one's doings or plans: *She's very secretive about where she got all this money; I wonder if she got it honestly.* **-ly** [adv]

F194 *adjectives* : **direct and blunt** [B]

direct (of people and behaviour) honest and easily understood: *He gave me a direct answer to my question. She's always very direct and open in her manner, so I know what she's thinking.* **in-** [neg] **-ly** [adv] **-ness** [U]

overt not secret; open to all; public: *It was an overt act of friendliness/war.* **-ly** [adv] *They were overtly unfriendly.*

explicit (of statements, rules, etc) clear and fully expressed: *He gave us explicit instructions. He said to go home; he was quite explicit about it.* **-ly** [adv] **-ness** [U]

blunt [Wa1] **1** (of a person) speaking roughly and plainly; telling what one thinks or what is true without trying to be polite, kind, or careful: *I'll be blunt about this, I don't like you.* **2** (of speech) rough; plain; honest: *He told her the sad truth in a few blunt words.* **-ly** [adv] **-ness** [U]

F195 *adjectives* : **not direct and blunt** [B]

implicit 1 [(*in*)] (of a statement, rule, etc) meant though not plainly expressed: *This is an implicit threat. There was a threat implicit in the way he looked. His leaving us is implicit in the way he has written this report.* **2** [A; (B)] unquestioning and complete: *You have my implicit trust.* **-ly** [adv] **-ness** [U]

implied expressed indirectly: *It's implied in his report that he will leave us soon.*

hidden *esp emot* not open: *He has hidden reasons for doing these things.*

secret kept hidden or known only to a few: *The plans must remain secret. They met at a secret meeting* **-ly** [adv] *It was done secretly.* **secrecy** [U]: *It was done in secrecy.*

covert [Wa5] *esp lit* secret; hidden; not shown openly: *The two lovers exchanged covert expressions of their love. He has covert reasons for what he is doing; I don't know what they are.* **-ly** [adv]

concealed *esp fml* not open; hidden: *She has a concealed dislike for all of them. She has a well/badly-concealed dislike for them.* **un-** [neg]

confidential 1 spoken or written in secret; to be kept secret: *This information is confidential.* **2** [Wa5] trusted with private or secret matters: *He is her confidential secretary.* **3** showing full trust, special or secret knowledge, etc: *She gave him a confidential look.* **-ly** [adv]: *Confidentially, I don't like him.*

F196 *adjectives* : **innocent and trusting** [B]

innocent knowing little about life; having little or no experience; easily deceived: *She is a very innocent kind of person.* **-ly** [adv] **-cence** [U]

naive, naïve 1 having or showing no experience (as of social rules or behaviour), esp because one is young: *The young boy was laughed at for his naive remarks.* **2** believing what anyone says or what is most favourable: *It's naive (of you) to believe he'll do what he says.* **3** *tech* having almost no knowledge or experience of a particular subject: *We need naive people*

(= who have not studied the subject before) *to take this test.* **-ly** [adv] **naivety** [U]

artless not trying to deceive or influence others; simple, almost foolish; natural: *She seemed to be just an artless child, but she wasn't.* **-ly** [adv] **-ness** [U]

trusting *emot* ready to trust others: *She had a trusting look in her eyes.* **-ly** [adv]

trustful *genl* ready to trust others: *Try to be a bit more trustful.* **-lly** [adv] **-ness** [U]

F197 adjectives : cunning and sneaky [B]

cunning *often deprec* showing or having cleverness in deceiving: *He's as cunning as a fox. That's a cunning idea/trick!* **-ly** [adv]

tricky [Wa1] *not fml* always playing tricks [⇨ F207], esp to deceive people: *What a tricky girl she is!* **-ily** [adv] **-iness** [U]

crafty [Wa1] *esp emot* very cunning: *Be careful or that crafty old man will take all your money.* **-ily** [adv] **-iness** [U]

sly [Wa1] **1** clever in deceiving; dishonestly tricky; crafty: *That was a sly trick to play.* **2** playfully amusing: *He played a sly joke on her.* **on the sly** secretly (as of something done dishonestly or unlawfully) *He's been married for years, but he still sees other women on the sly.* **-ly** [adv] **-ness** [U]

artful **1** cleverly deceitful; tricky; cunning: *He's very artful and usually succeeds in getting what he wants.* **2** skilfully put together; cleverly considered: *That artful arrangement of pieces of wood was made to catch mice.* **-lly** [adv] **-ness** [U]

sneaky [Wa1] *infml* cunning and tricky: *She's the sneakiest person I've ever met; she'd deceive herself if she could!* **-ily** [adv] **-iness** [U]

F198 adjectives : respectable and decent [B]

respectable *not always apprec* showing or having character and standards acceptable to society: *How dare you talk to a respectable woman like that? It's not respectable to be drunk in the street. Put on a clean shirt and (try to) look respectable.* **-bly** [adv Wa3] **-bleness** [U]

decent respectable; good and suitable: *They are decent people living decent lives. Put on a decent shirt and try to look decent.* **in-** [neg] **-ly** [adv] **-ness** [U]

law-abiding keeping the law: *She is a respectable, law-abiding person.*

F199 adjectives : loyal and constant

loyal true to one's friends, group, country, etc: *He has always been a loyal friend to me. She is loyal to her friends.* **-lly** [adv] **dis-** [neg]: *He has never been disloyal to his friends.* **-lly** [adv]

faithful **1** full of or showing loyalty: *He is a faithful friend. He remained faithful to his friend.*

constant *lit* loyal: *He was very constant during all our difficulties.*

F200 nouns : honesty, faith, and allegiance [U]

honesty the quality of being honest: *His honesty is well known; he won't deceive you.* **dis-** [neg]

trust **1** firm belief in the honesty, goodness, dependability, justice, power, etc of someone or something; faith: *I don't place any trust in his promises. Put all your trust in God. My husband trusts me and I don't intend to break that trust.* **2** solemn responsibility: *He holds a position of trust in society.* **3** [S] *fml* a solemn responsibility given to someone: *This is a trust that we lay on you; we know that you will do your best.* **4** the condition of being given to someone for care, protection, etc: *I left my pets in trust with a neighbour while I went on holiday.* **5** care; keeping: *After my parents' death I was put in my grandmother's trust.* **take on trust** to accept without proof or close examination: *You'll have to take what I said on trust.* **distrust** *also* **mistrust** lack of trust: *He keeps his money at home because he has a great, mistrust of banks.*

trustworthiness the quality of being trustworthy; *emot* honesty: *His trustworthiness is not in doubt.*

faith **1** strong trust and belief: *He will not steal my money; I have faith in him.* **2** the condition of being sincere; loyalty: *He acted in good faith. She acted in bad faith and hoped to cheat them.*

reliance *esp emot/lit* trust: *I place complete reliance on his judgment.* **reliant** [F (*on*)] showing reliance on someone or something; dependent: *We are completely reliant on him/his help.*

reliability ability to be trusted or relied on: *He's a good man for the job; I can speak for his reliability.* **un-** [neg]

integrity complete honesty and goodness: *He is a man of the greatest integrity; he would not steal your money.*

loyalty the quality of being loyal: *His loyalty to his friends was never in doubt.* **dis-** [neg]

constancy *emot* faithfulness; loyalty: *She loved her husband for his constancy to her.*

allegiance *esp emot* loyalty, faith and dutiful support to a king, country, idea, etc: *That political party no longer deserves our allegiance.*

F201 verbs : trusting and relying on people

trust **1** [Wv4;T1;D3] to believe in the honesty and dependability of (someone or something);

have faith in: *You shouldn't trust him; he's dishonest. Trust my judgment! You can't trust him to do anything right. You don't trust your daughters to stay out so late, do you? You're far too trusting. It was stupid of you to let that man into the house even if he did say he was a policeman.* **2** [T1; D3] to depend on: *You can't trust the trains (to run on time).* **3** [T1] to allow (someone) to have money or goods and to pay for them at a later date: *Can you trust me for a packet of cigarettes until Friday?* **4** [I0; T5a] *fml* to hope: *Everything went all right, I trust. I trust you enjoyed yourself?*

rely on/upon [v prep] **1** [T1, 4; V4a] to depend on (something or something happening): *You can't rely on the weather here. I think I can come, but don't rely on it. Don't rely on going to India* (= perhaps you won't go). *Don't rely on me/my going to India* (= perhaps I won't go). **2** [T1; V3] to trust (someone, or someone to do something): *You may rely on me (to help you).*
USAGE Some people think *rely on his coming* is better English than *rely on him coming*; but in *rely on him to come* one can use only *him*.

depend on upon [v prep] **1** [T1; V3, 4a] to trust; get help or support from: *I depend on you to do it. He doesn't work but depends on his father (giving him money).* **2** [T1, 6a *no pass*] to be affected by: *Our success will depend on hard work/on how hard we work.*

depend [Wv6; I0] to depend on (def **2**) certain things: *Will he succeed?—That depends!* **dependent** [B (*on*)] *esp fml* that depends on: *She is dependent on him; she needs him.* **dependence** [U] the state of depending, being dependent **in-** [*neg*] **dependable** [B] able to be trusted or depended on: *He is a very dependable person; you can rely on him.* **dependability** [U] the state of being dependable **dependant, dependent** [C] someone who depends on another, esp for food, clothes, etc, esp as a child: *His wife and children are his dependants.*

F202 nouns : decency and respectability [U]

decency the quality of being decent: *Please have the decency to move your coat from that chair! She's a good woman; her decency is well known.* **in-** [*neg*]
respectability the state or condition of being respectable: *Her respectability is well known.*

F203 verbs : lying, cheating, and betraying

[ALSO ⇒ C234]

lie [I0] to not tell the truth: *She lied. She lied to me. She lied about what happened. She's a lying kind of a person.* **liar** [C] a person who lies: *They are all liars; don't believe a word they tell you.*

cheat *esp emot* **1** [T1 ((*out*) *of*)] to take from (someone) unfairly, dishonestly, or deceitfully: *He cheated the old woman ((out) of her money) by making her sign a paper she didn't understand.* **2** [I0 (*at*)] to act dishonestly or deceitfully to win an advantage, esp in a game: *Don't play cards with him; he always cheats. I always cheat at cards, it's the only way I can win.* **3** [T1] *lit* to avoid or escape as if by deception: *The swimmers cheated death in spite of the storm.* **4** [I0 (*on*)] *infml* to be sexually unfaithful, esp to one's husband or wife: *They've been married for only 6 months and already she's started cheating (on him)!*

deceive [T1 (*in* or *into*); I0] *esp fml* to cause (someone) to accept as true or good what is false or bad: *I trust him because I know he would never deceive me. Do my eyes deceive me, or is that really an elephant pulling a carriage? Don't deceive yourself into thinking that bad plan is really good.*

fool [T1] to deceive: *You can't fool me—I know you're not really ill.*

trick [T1 (*into*)] to cheat or deceive by a trick or tricks: *She tricked me! She tricked him into giving her all his money.*

fox [T1] *infml* **1** to deceive cleverly: *He foxed us and got away with all the money.* **2** *usu pass* to cause not to understand: *I'm really foxed by what's happening!*

take in [v adv T1] *infml* to cheat; deceive: *Their mother was taken in by the businessman's offers to help her and stupidly gave him most of her money. Don't be taken in by what he says; it isn't true. He successfully took us all in!*

kid [T1; I0] *infml* to deceive or pretend, esp in a playful manner: *He's not really hurt; he's only kidding. Stop trying to kid me; I know you're not telling the truth. You're kidding!* (= The things that you are saying are hard to believe). *He's coming tomorrow; no kidding.*

do [T1] *BrE sl* to cheat; deceive: *He has done us all! I've been done; he's taken all the money!*

pass off [v adv T1] *not fml* to present falsely; pretend that (someone or something) is different and better: *He tried to pass himself off as a doctor. She passed the fake money off as real money.*

mislead [T1] to cause (someone) to think or act wrongly or mistakenly; to guide wrongly (sometimes with the intention to deceive): *Her appearance misled him; he thought she was young, but she wasn't. The traveller was misled by the old and incorrect map he was using, and lost his way. Don't let his friendly words mislead you into trusting him.*

pretend [T1, 3, 5a; I0] to say, claim, or appear falsely in order to mislead: *He pretended to like us, but he didn't. She pretends that she likes them, so that she can get their help. He pretended illness and didn't go. He doesn't like her; he's only pretending. She pretended to be surprised, but she wasn't really.* **pretender** [C] **1** one who pretends **2** (esp formerly) one who claims to be the king of a country, etc

277

betray 1 [T1] to be disloyal or unfaithful to: *I thought he was too good to betray his friends. She betrayed her country to the enemy.* **2** [T1] to give away or make known (esp a secret): *He betrayed the news to all his friends.* **3** [T1, 5; (V3)] to be a sign of (something one would like to hide): *Her red face betrayed her nervousness/betrayed (the fact) that she was nervous.*

sell out [v adv T1; I0] *not fml* to be disloyal or unfaithful to (one's purposes or friends), esp for money: *He is a good writer who sold out (his artistic standards) and now just writes for money.*

F204 *nouns* : lying, cheating, and betraying

lie [C] an act of lying, of not telling the truth: *He tells lies. What a lie he told her! It's all lies; don't believe him.*

falsehood 1 [C] *usu fml* an untrue statement, for the purpose of cheating; (*euph*) a lie: *His story was full of falsehoods.* **2** [U] *esp poet* the condition of being false **3** [U] willingness to cheat and betray: *His heart is full of falsehood.*

disloyalty 1 [U] the state of not being loyal **2** [C *usu pl*] a disloyal act: *We have not forgotten his many disloyalties to his country.*

deceit *also* **deception** [C; U] (an) activity or action which deceives: *His deceit is shameful. I'm tired of all your lies and deception(s).*

treachery 1 [U] disloyalty; deceit; falseness, esp to a friend, king, etc: *His treachery in joining the enemy made everyone hate him.* **2** [C] a disloyal action

treason [U] (the crime of) disloyalty to one's country, esp by helping its enemies or by violent opposition to those in power: *Joining the enemy was an act of treason; he will be hanged if we catch him.*

cunning [U] cleverness, esp in deceiving: *The fox showed its cunning by swimming down the stream so that the hunting dogs wouldn't be able to smell it.*

perfidy *fml & esp lit* **1** [U] *also* **perfidiousness** disloyalty; treachery: *It is an act of perfidy to sell one's country's secrets to the enemy.* **2** [C *usu pl*] an example of this: *All your little perfidies have not gone unnoticed.*

betrayal 1 [U] the act of betraying **2** [C] an example of this: *The story of the betrayal of Jesus by Judas is in the Bible.*

sellout [C] *not fml* an act of disloyalty or unfaithfulness to one's purposes or friends; betrayal: *'It's a sellout!' he said in anger.*

pretence *BrE*, **pretense** *AmE* **1** [U] the act of pretending: *No more pretence, please; tell the truth.* **2** [C] (an esp false) claim: *Don't listen to his pretences; he is lying.*

pretension *fml & pomp* **1** [C (*to*)] a pretence; claim: *I have no pretensions to being an artist.* **2** [U] pretence: *Stop all this pretension.*

imposture [U] the pretence of being another person: *His imposture was discovered; he was not Dr Smith at all.*

impostor [C] a person who pretends to be someone else; a cheat: *He's an impostor; he isn't a famous doctor.*

stealth [(*by*) U] a quiet and secret way of doing something: *He did it by stealth. She showed great stealth in her business activities; he knew nothing about them.*

F205 *adjectives* : not honest and loyal [B]

dishonest not honest: *He is a very dishonest man; don't trust him. He got his money in dishonest ways.* **-ly** [adv] *He got his money dishonestly.*

deceitful *emot* dishonest: *She has been very deceitful about everything she's done!* **-lly** [adv] **-ness** [U]

misleading causing someone to be misled: *He gave us a very misleading description of the house.* **-ly** [adv]

disloyal not loyal: *He was disloyal to his employers; his action was completely disloyal.* **-lly** [adv]

treacherous 1 very disloyal and deceitful: *The president swore to punish his minister's treacherous actions.* **2** very dangerous: *Treacherous currents make swimming in this part of the river dangerous.* **-ly** [adv]

perfidious *fml & esp lit* disloyal; treacherous: *His perfidious actions in selling our country's secrets have not been forgotten.* **-ly** [adv]

F206 *verbs* : plotting and trapping

plot [I0; T1, 3, 6a,b] to plan together secretly: *They're plotting against him. They're plotting to kill him. She plotted his murder/plotted how to murder him.*

conspire 1 [I0, 3: (*with, together*)] *esp fml* to plot something unlawful or bad: *The criminals conspired to rob a bank.* **2** [I3] (*fig*) (of events) to combine: *Events conspired to produce great difficulties for us all.*

trap [T1] to catch or keep (a person or animal) in or by a trap; to catch by plotting and planning: *He trapped her; she couldn't get away. Help; I'm trapped! They trapped the animals and killed them.*

snare [T1] **1** to catch (as if) in an animal trap, esp cleverly: *He was snared in their arguments.* **2** to get by skilful actions: *She snared a good job.*

F207 *nouns* : secrets, plotting, tricking, and trapping

plot [C] a secret plan to do something usu against a person, needing combined action by several people: *The police discovered a plot to kill the minister.*

conspiracy 1 [C] a secret plan to do something unlawful: *The police discovered the generals' conspiracy to seize control of the government.* **2** [U] the act of secretly planning to do something unlawful: *He was hanged for conspiracy in 1845.*

secret [C] something that is secret [⇒ F195], not known or usu told to others; a hidden reason, cause, etc: *Can you keep a secret? Let me tell you a secret. This is a secret plan; don't tell anyone. What is the secret of her power over children?*

trick [C] **1** something done to deceive or cheat someone: *He got the money by a trick!* **2** something done to someone to make him or her look stupid and so give amusement to others: *The children loved playing tricks on their teachers. What a nasty trick to play!* **trickery** [U] the use of tricks to deceive or cheat

subterfuge *esp fml* **1** [C] a trick or dishonest way of doing something or succeeding in something: *He won by a subterfuge.* **2** [U] the attempt to gain one's aims secretly: *Must you always use subterfuge?*

ploy [C] *sometimes deprec* an idea or action, esp one used in order to gain some advantage: *Her usual ploy is to pretend to be ill, so that people will take pity on her.*

device [C] a plan, esp for a purpose which is not wholly good: *He'll use any device to get what he wants.*

stratagem [C] *esp fml* a trick to deceive someone: *What stratagem did he use to get past the enemy?*

trap [C] **1** a trick by which one catches people, animals, etc: *The soldiers fell into the enemy's trap and were killed. Be careful; it may be a trap.* **2** [*often in comb*] an apparatus with which one can catch esp animals: *The mouse was caught in the trap/the mousetrap.*

snare [C] **1** a trap for catching an animal, esp an apparatus with a rope which catches the animal's foot **2** [*often pl with sing meaning*] *esp lit* something in which one may be caught; a course which leads to being trapped: *the snares of evil*

artifice 1 [C] a skilful trick, esp one intended to deceive: *She used a little artifice to get what she wanted.* **2** [U] inventive skill in deceiving: *She used artifice to get what she wanted.* **3** [C] a clever arrangement or thing: *The use of mirrors in a room is an artifice to make the room look larger.*

F208 *verbs & nouns* : **hiding and disguising**

hide 1 [T1] to put or keep out of sight; make or keep secret: *I hid the broken plate behind the table. You're hiding some important facts. Don't hide your feelings; say what you think.* **2** [I0] to place oneself or be placed so as to be

unseen: *I'll hide behind the door.* (*fig*) *Where's that book hiding?* **in hiding** hiding oneself: *The criminals were in hiding from the police. He has been in hiding for months.*

conceal [Wv5;T1 (*from*),4] *esp fml* to hide; to keep from being seen or known: *It is wrong for a man to conceal things from his wife. Trees concealed the entrance to the park. There is a concealed entrance here. He concealed having been there.*

concealment [U] **1** the act of concealing: *Concealment of stolen property is a crime punishable by imprisonment.* **2** the state or condition of being concealed: *The criminals stayed in concealment until the police had passed.*

disguise 1 [T1 (*as*)] to change the usual appearance, etc of (someone, one's face, something, etc) so as to hide the true nature: *She disguised herself as a man, but couldn't disguise her voice. The door in the wall was disguised as a bookcase.* **2** [T1] to hide (the real state of things): *He disguised his fear by looking angry. There is no disguising the fact that business is bad.* **3** [C] something that is worn or used to hide the true nature of a person or thing: *The thief wore a false beard as a disguise. Nobody saw through his disguise.* **in disguise** disguised: *He came in disguise.*

mask 1 [C] a covering for the eyes, face, or head: *The thief wore a mask, so I couldn't see his face.* **2** [Wv5;T1] to cover with a mask: *The money was taken by two masked thieves.* **3** [T1] (*fig*) to cover or hide: *He masked his feelings well.*

F209 *verbs* : **hiding and moving secretly**

lurk [I0] **1** to wait in hiding, esp for an evil purpose: *The murderer lurked behind a tree.* **2** to move quietly as if having done wrong and not wanting to be seen **3** to exist unseen: *Danger lurks in that quiet river.*

haunt [T1] **1** (of a spirit) to visit, appearing in a strange form: *That house is haunted. A headless man haunts the castle.* **2** [*usu pass*] to be always in the thoughts of (someone): *She's haunted by her memories/fear. I was haunted by his last words to me.* **3** *esp lit* to visit a place regularly: *Sea birds haunt the shore.*

prowl 1 [I0] (esp of an animal looking for food, or of a thief) to move about in a quiet way trying not to be seen or heard: *Cats like to prowl at night. I woke in the middle of the night and heard someone prowling about the garden.* **2** [L9] *infml* to wander about looking and examining: *She likes to prowl round the shops.* **3** [T1] to move silently and secretly through (a place): *He prowls the streets after dark.* **on the prowl** prowling: *He saw a lion on the prowl.*

steal [L9] to move quietly so as not to be seen or heard: *She tried to steal through the gate without being seen. He stole past the other man into the house.*

F210 *verbs* : **uncovering and revealing**

uncover [T1] to find out (something unknown or kept secret): *The police have uncovered a plan to steal £1,000,000.*

expose [T1] **1** to uncover so as to leave without protection: *She exposed her skin to the sun. The soldiers were warned to remain hidden and not to expose themselves. (fig) Her youth and beauty will expose her to many dangers. The house is in an exposed position on top of a high hill.* **2** to make known (a secretly guilty person or action): *I threatened to expose him/the plan (to the police).* **3** to place in view: *They exposed the goods for sale in the market.* **4** tech to uncover (a film) to the light, when taking a photograph: *This film has already been exposed.* **expose (oneself or another) to** to make (oneself or another) suffer: *His fatness exposes him to a lot of joking at the office.* **expose oneself** to show one's sexual parts on purpose in the hope of making people feel excited

reveal 1 [T1] to allow to be seen: *a dress that reveals part of her stomach; The curtains opened, to reveal a darkened stage.* **2** [T1, 5: (*as*); X (*to be*) 1, 7] (*not used with actual spoken words*) to make known (to be): *She revealed the secret. She suddenly revealed (the fact) that she was not married. These letters reveal him as/reveal him to be an honest man.*

Relaxation, excitement, interest, and surprise

F220 *adjectives, etc* : **quiet, calm, and peaceful** [B]

quiet [Wa1] **1** free from (unwanted) activity; at rest: *We lead a quiet life in this village. The sea seems quieter now. The trains are quiet in the afternoon.* **2** not making oneself/itself noticed by activity: *The children's quiet behaviour was unusual.* **-ly** [adv] **-ness** [U]

calm [Wa1] **1** free from excitement; quiet and untroubled: *Even after her husband died she was calm. Although the enemy was only five miles away, the city was calm.* **2** (of weather) not windy: *After the storm it was calm.* **3** (of water) not rough; smooth: *The sea was calm.* **-ly** [adv] **-ness** [U]

peaceful 1 quiet; untroubled: *How peaceful it is in the country now. She had a peaceful death.* **2** loving peace: *All peaceful nations will disapprove of that country's warlike actions.* **-lly** [adv] **-ness** [U]

patient having or showing willingness to wait, do things, help, etc, esp calmly, even though one might really want to do something else: *That teacher is very patient with the slower children.* **im-** [*neg*] **-ly** [adv]

leisurely 1 calm in movement; not hurrying: *He*

did the work in a leisurely way. **2** [adv] *infml* calmly and slowly: *He went leisurely about his business.*

tame [Wa1] (of an animal) not wild [⇒ F110]; used to people; not dangerous: *Are those horses tame? He keeps a tame lion.* **-ly** [adv] **-ness** [U]

F221 *adjectives* : **calm in special ways** [B]

pacific *lit, euph & pomp* peaceful: '*What a beautifully pacific place this is!*' *he said. The people are pacific here; we never have any trouble.*

tranquil calm, quiet, and peaceful; free from anxiety, worry, etc: *She leads a tranquil life in the country, in a tranquil little village.* **-lly** [adv]

serene completely calm and peaceful; without trouble, sudden activity, or change: *It was a serene summer night. She had a serene trust in God.* **-ly** [adv] **serenity** [U]

relaxed calm and peaceful in body or mind: *He was relaxed in his chair, and spoke in a relaxed way to his friends.*

equable 1 (of a person) of even temper; not easily annoyed: *I like working with him; he is so calm and equable.* **2** (of temperature, character, etc) without great changes **-bly** [adv]

even-tempered calm and never becoming angry: *He is the most even-tempered man I know.*

comfortable 1 giving comfort, esp to the body: *This is a comfortable chair. The room was at a comfortable temperature.* **2** having or providing comfort: *He has a comfortable job.* **3** [F] free from (too much) pain, grief, anxiety, etc: *The doctor said that mother was comfortable after her operation.* **4** [A] simple and undemanding: *His life has settled into a comfortable pattern that never changes.* **-ably** [adv]: *They live comfortably on his income.*

snug [Wa1] **1** giving or enjoying warmth, comfort, peace, protection, etc; cosy: *a snug little room with the fire going; sitting snug by the fire; a snug harbour* **2** (as of clothes) fitting closely, or sometimes too tightly: *a comfortable snug-fitting coat.* **-ly** [adv]: *I don't like a coat to fit too snugly.* **-ness** [U]

F222 *nouns* : **quiet, calm, and peace**

quiet [U] the state of being quiet; quietness (*often in the phr* **peace and quiet**): *The quiet of the night was disturbed by singing. All he wants in life is peace and quiet.* **on the quiet** without telling anyone; secretly: *She did it on the quiet.*

quietness [U] the state of being quiet: *The quietness of the children worried their mother.*

calm [U; S] **1** a time of peace and quiet; absence of excitement or worry **2 a** an absence of wind or rough weather: *The air didn't move; it was* *the calm before the storm.* **b** (of water) a period of stillness: *There was a calm on the sea.*

peace [U] **1** calmness; quietness: *He sat on the bank, enjoying the peace of the lake. Please let me do my work in peace. The place had an air of peace and quiet.* **2** freedom from anxiety or troubling thoughts: *This news is bad for my peace of mind.*

tranquillity *BrE*, **tranquility** *AmE* [U] the state of being tranquil

serenity [U] the state of being serene: *Her serenity relaxes other people.*

patience [U] **1** the ability **a** to wait for something calmly for a long time: *You need to have patience if you want to get served in this shop.* **b** to control oneself when angered, esp at foolishness or slowness: *If you don't stop making that noise I'm going to lose my patience.* **2** the power of bearing pain or other unpleasant things without complaining: *His patience during his long illness was remarkable.* **3** (the power of showing) care and close attention to work that is difficult or tiring: *I wouldn't have the patience to sit mending watches all day.*

ease [U] the state of being comfortable and without worry or anxiety: *She's rich and leads a life of ease. Let me put you at your ease; we are all here as your friends, not to make life difficult for you. She sat at ease by the fire with a drink.*

relaxation 1 [U] the act of relaxing; the condition of being relaxed: *Relaxation in a hot bath after work can be very pleasant.* **2** [C; U] something done to make one relaxed: *He plays the piano for (a bit of) relaxation; it's one of his few relaxations.*

comfort 1 [U] the state of being free from anxiety, pain, or suffering and of having all one's bodily wants satisfied; complete contentment: *For comfort indoors the temperature should be set at 70°. He's lived all his life in great comfort.* **2** [U] strengthening help, kindness, sympathy, etc, given to a person who is suffering, grieving, or unhappy: *The priest spoke a few words of comfort to the dying man. The child ran to his mother for comfort.* **3** [C] a person or thing that gives strength or hope or that makes grief or pain easier for an unhappy person: *My husband was a great comfort to me when I was ill.*

F223 *verbs* : **relaxing and calming**

relax 1 [Wv5;IØ;T1] **a** (of people) to become less active and stop worrying: *Sit down and relax! He was lying in the sun looking very relaxed and happy.* **b** to make (someone) do this: *The music will help to relax you.* **2** [IØ;T1] to make or become more stiff or tight: *His muscles relaxed. He relaxed his hold on the wheel.* **3** [T1] to make (effort or control) less severe: *You must not relax your efforts for a moment.*

calm [T1;IØ] to make or become calm: *The mother calmed her child. Calm yourself! The fisherman calmed the water by pouring oil on to it. She calmed after a while.*

calm down [v adv] **1** [IØ] (of a living being or something active) to become calm: *The excited girl quickly calmed down. At last the wild wind calmed down.* **2** [T1] to make (a living being) calm: *I'll go and calm your brother/the animals down.*

cool down [v adv] *not fml* **1** [IØ] (of an angry or excited person) to become calmer and less excited: *She didn't cool down for hours after that argument.* **2** [T1] to cause (an angry or excited person) to become calmer or less excited: *I tried to cool her down but she was still very angry when she left.*

unwind [IØ] *infml* to relax, usu slowly: *It's nice to unwind in the evening after a hard day's work.*

quieten [IØ; T1 (*down*)] to (cause to) become quiet: *They were shouting at first but they quietened (down) after a while. She quietened her behaviour. I quietened her worries.*

quiet [T1] *esp AmE* to quieten: *Quiet the children, please.*

ease 1 [T1] to make more comfortable: *I eased her mind by telling her that the children were safe.* **2** [T1] to take away (pain or worry): *I gave him some medicine to ease the pain.* **3** [T1 (*of*)] to free (someone) from pain or worry: *I eased him (of his difficulty) by telling him what to do.* **4** [T1] to make looser: *My new coat is too tight and must be eased under the arms.* **5** [IØ (*off*)] to become less troublesome or difficult: *The relationship between these two countries has eased. The wind has eased off.* **6** [X9] to cause (something) to move as stated, esp slowly and gently by using skill and care (*note the phr* **ease something open**): *The drawer in my desk was stuck fast, but I eased it open with a knife. I eased the heavy load off my shoulders and sat down for a rest.*

comfort [T1] to give comfort to (an unhappy, ill, or anxious person or animal): *I tried to comfort her after her mother's death.*

F224 *verbs* : **interesting and exciting** [T1]

[ALSO ⇒ F25, K10]

interest to cause (someone) to be, want to see, do, think about, have, etc: *That book interests me; I must get/read it. These things have interested him for years and he has learnt a lot about them.*

excite 1 to cause (someone) to lose calmness and to have strong feelings, often pleasant: *The story excited the little boy very much. Don't excite yourself!* **2** [*also* V3] to cause (someone to do something or something to happen) by raising strong feelings: *The army's cruelty excited a rising of the people/excited the people to rise against him.* **3** to make (an organ of the body, one's interest, etc) active: *Strong coffee excites your nerves. The beggar's story excited my pity.*

thrill [Wv4; *also* L9] to (cause to) feel a thrill or thrills: *Our hearts thrilled to the news. She thril-*

led at the thought of meeting the queen. It was a thrilling story of violence and murder. The match was so exciting that it thrilled everyone.

exhilarate [usu pass] emph to make (someone) happy and excited: I was exhilarated by/at her visit.

stimulate [Wv4] **1** to increase in activity: Exercise is stimulating. Cold air stimulates the blood. **2** to excite (the body): Some plants are stimulated by light. We found the talk very stimulating. **3** to encourage: He was stimulated into new efforts. The first success stimulated even more new discoveries. **stimulation** [U] **stimulus** [C] something which is the cause of activity: Light is a stimulus to growth in plants. Success can be a stimulus to one's efforts.

F225 adjectives : interesting and exciting [B]

interesting causing interest: That's an interesting book. What a very interesting idea. **un-** [neg] **-ly** [adv]

absorbing taking all one's attention; very interesting: The play was so absorbing we didn't notice how late it was. **-ly** [adv]

engrossing (esp of books) very interesting: That's an engrossing story. **-ly** [adv]

exciting causing strong, usu pleasant feelings: That was a very exciting story. He finds her exciting/an exciting person. **un-** [neg] **-ly** [adv]

thrilling causing one to feel thrilled: What a thrilling story/thing to happen! **-ly** [adv]

sensational often deprec **1** causing excited interest: There was a sensational murder here last year. I haven't been doing anything sensational; just working. **2** (esp of writing, news, etc) intended to cause quick excitement or **-lly** [adv] shock: He doesn't like sensational newspapers.

exhilarating causing one to feel exhilarated: This weather is wonderful, and very exhilarating. **-ly** [adv]

breathtaking 1 very exciting: The race was quite breathtaking **2** very unusual: She had a breathtaking beauty. It was an act of breathtaking stupidity. **-ly** [adv] She was breathtakingly beautiful.

F226 adjectives : interested and excited

interested 1 [B] concerned; having or showing an interest: I was interested in your remark. He had an interested look on his face. **2** [A] personally concerned; on whom there will be an effect; who cannot make a judgment from the outside: He is the interested person in this matter. All the interested parties (= people) came to the meeting. **-ly** [adv]

excited [B] full of strong, pleasant feelings; not calm: The excited children were opening their Christmas presents. I'm very excited about the party tomorrow. **un-** [neg] **-ly** [adv]

frantic [B] very excited, worried, etc, esp so that one moves too much, cannot think or behave properly, etc: She was in a frantic state when the child didn't come home at the right time. **-ally** [adv Wa4]: He tried frantically to telephone her, but couldn't get through.

thrilled [B] very excited: I'm thrilled to see you! She had a thrilled expression on her face when she met him.

exhilarated [B] emph very excited and happy: He felt exhilarated when he heard the good news.

frenzied [B] being in a state of great excitement, fear, etc and unable to think, act, etc properly: There was a frenzied look on her face. **-ly** [adv]

keen [Wa1] **1** [(BrE) B, F3; (AmE) A] (of a person) having a strong active interest in something; eager or anxious to do something: He's a keen student of politics. (BrE) He's keen to pass the examination. (BrE) Her father wants her to go to university, but she's not keen. **2** [B] (of a game or struggle of any kind) done with eagerness or activity on both sides: There was keen competition for the job. **3** [B] (of the mind, feelings, the five senses, etc) good, strong, quick at understanding, deeply felt, etc: She has a keen mind. He had a keen desire to win. She has keen eyesight. **4** [F on] esp BrE infml having a strong liking for or a strong active interest in something or someone; eager or anxious to do something: She's keen on music. I'm keen on passing this examination. She's keen on him. **-ly** [adv] **-ness** [U]

eager [B; F3, 5c] full of interest or desire; keen: He listened to the story with eager attention. He is eager for success. I'm not so eager to get a new car now; the prices have gone up. (fml) The committee is eager that all the workers should come on time. **-ly** [adv] **-ness** [U]

enthusiastic [B] full of enthusiasm [⇒ F228] and eager interest: She is enthusiastic about going to France. The most enthusiastic students were also the most successful. **-ally** [adv Wa4]

zealous [B (for, in); F3] fml & pomp eager: He is zealous for fame/in doing his duty/to do his duty. **-ly** [adv] **-ness** [U]

ardent [B] esp lit, emph & pomp strongly felt; strongly active; eager; fierce: It is our ardent hope that the war will end soon. He is an ardent supporter of the party. **-ly** [adv]

avid [B (for)] esp fml & lit eager; keen: She is an avid reader. He is avid for praise. He is avid in his desire to please us. **-ly** [adv]

desirous [F of, F5] fml, pomp & old use feeling or having a desire: She has always been desirous of fame/of being famous. The president is strongly desirous that you should attend the meeting.

F227 adjectives : wanting to know, learn etc

curious 1 [F3] eager to know or learn: The children were curious to know more about life *abroad. A good student should always be curious to learn.* **2** [B; F3] too eager to know or learn, esp about what does not concern one; having or showing too much interest in other people's affairs. *He was so curious to know what was in the letter that he opened it, even though it was addressed to his father. The only disadvantage of living in this street is the curious neighbours.* **in-** [*neg*] **-ly** [adv]: *Curiously (enough), he seemed to know that already.*

inquiring [B] which shows an interest in knowing about things; asking for information: *He has an inquiring mind.* **-ly** [adv]: *She looked at him inquiringly.*

inquisitive [B] (of people and their acts) of a type which tries to find out (too many) details about things and people: *Don't be inquisitive about her private life, she doesn't like it if you ask too many questions.* **-ly** [adv] **-ness** [U]

nosy, *sometimes* **nosey** *infml & usu deprec* [Wa1;B] showing too much interest in other people's affairs: *What does he say in the letter?—Don't be so nosy!* **-sily** [adv] **-siness** [U]

F228 *nouns* : **interest and excitement**

interest 1 [U; S: (*in*)] the condition of being interested, wanting to know, see, learn, do, etc: *He shows (a) great interest in this subject.* **2** [C] an example of this: *What are your interests in life? This has always been one of her many interests.*

excitement 1 [U] the condition of being excited: *He has a weak heart and should avoid all excitement.* **2** [C] an exciting event: *Life will seem very quiet after the excitements of our holiday.*

sensation [C] **1** (a cause of) a state of excited interest: *The new discovery was/caused a great sensation everywhere.* **2** excitement: *He enjoyed the new sensation of flying in an aeroplane.*

thrill [C] a sudden very strong feeling of joy, fear, excitement, pleasure, etc, that seems to flow round the body like a wave: *It gave me quite a thrill to meet the president. He enjoys the thrill of hunting.*

exhilaration [U] the state of being exhilarated, very excited and happy: *Her exhilaration showed on her face.*

frenzy [U; S (*of*)] a state of great feeling, esp of excitement or fear, etc, so that one cannot think, act, etc properly: *She was in a frenzy (of excitement) when she heard the news.*

keenness [U] the state of being keen: *His keenness for swimming is well-known.*

eagerness [U] the state of being eager: *Her eyes showed her eagerness.*

enthusiasm [C; U; (*for, about*)] a strong feeling of interest (and admiration): *I am full of enthusiasm for this book. I don't feel much enthusiasm about that book. Among his many enthusiasms is a great fondness for Eastern music.* **enthusiast** [C] a person who is habitu-

ally full of enthusiasm (about something): *He's a chess enthusiast. They are enthusiasts for/ about cycling.*

zeal [U] *fml* eagerness; keenness: *He shows great zeal for knowledge.*

avidity [U] *esp fml & lit* great desire; eagerness; keenness

ardour *BrE,* **ardor** *AmE* [U; (C)] *esp lit, emph & pomp* a strong burning feeling, due to something pleasing; excitement; eagerness: *In the ardour of love he said he would do anything for her. His political ardour led him into many arguments.*

F229 *nouns* : **curiosity**

curiosity [U, U3; S, S3] the desire to know or learn: *The boy burned with (a) curiosity to know what was in the letter addressed to his mother. Curiosity caused the girl to open the door, even though it was clearly marked 'private'.*

inquisitiveness [U] the state of being inquisitive: *Her inquisitiveness made people dislike her; she was always asking questions about what they were doing.*

F230 *verbs & nouns* : **boring and frustrating**

bore 1 [Wv4;T1;I∅] to make (someone) tired or uninterested, esp by continual dull talk: *The teacher bored his students. The lesson was boring, and the students were bored (by it).* **2** [C] a person who causes others to lose interest in him or her, esp by continual dull talk: *He really is a bore.* **3** [S] *esp BrE infml* something which is rather unpleasant: *It's a bore having to go out again on a cold night like this.*

frustrate [T1] **1** [Wv4] to cause (someone) to have feelings of annoyed disappointment: *This is really frustrating! I feel frustrated; I can't go after all!* **2** to prevent the fulfilment of or defeat (someone or someone's effort, hopes, etc): *The bad weather frustrated all our hopes of going out. In his attempts to escape the prisoner was frustrated by a guard.*

F231 *adjectives* : **boring and frustrating** [B]

boring causing one to be bored: *What a boring film/book! The talk was very long, dull, and boring.* **-ly** [adv]

frustrating causing one to feel frustrated: *It's a frustrating experience going to catch a plane/ train and then finding it has been held up* (= made late). **-ly** [adv]

tiresome boring and annoying; causing one to feel bored and tired: *What a tiresome man he is/day it has been!* **-ly** [adv] **-ness** [U]

tedious tiring and boring: *What a tedious lecture!* **-ly** [adv]

monotonous boring, because always the same: *The teacher's lessons/the school dinners were monotonous.* **-ly** [adv]

apathetic without feeling or interest; lacking the desire to do anything: *He is apathetic about the job; it doesn't interest him.* **-ally** [adv Wa4]

F232 *nouns* : **boring and frustrating**

boredom [U] the condition of being bored: *He nearly died of boredom; he had nothing to do. She suffers from boredom because she has nothing to do.*

frustration 1 [U] the condition of being frustrated: *Frustration can make people ill.* **2** [C] something that frustrates: *All these frustrations are making him ill.*

tedium [U] the condition or instance of being tedious

monotony [U] the condition of being monotonous: *The monotony of her existence made her want to break away* (= go and do something new).

apathy [U] lack or feeling of interest in something or everything; lack of desire or ability to act in any way: *He was sunk in apathy after his failure.*

F233 *adjectives* : **excitable and tense** [B]

excitable (of a person or animal) easily excited: *These dogs are very excitable.* **-bly** [adv Wv3] **-bility** [U]

tense [Wa1] not calm or relaxed: *The city seems tense tonight, as if something is going to happen. She is tense because of tomorrow's examinations.* **-ly** [adv] **-ness** [U]

F234 *adjectives* : **sensitive and hysterical** [B]

sensitive 1 (too) quick to show or feel the effect of a force or the presence of something: *She is sensitive to cold/pain. He has sensitive skin. This is light-sensitive photographic paper.* **2** (of an apparatus) measuring exactly: *This is a sensitive pair of scales.* **3** showing delicate feelings or judgment: *He made a sensitive study of the racial problem.* **4** *sometimes deprec* (of a person) easily hurt in the feelings, esp of self-respect: *She is a sensitive child who shouldn't be scolded too severely. She was sensitive about being tall and walked with her head bent down. Don't be so sensitive! I meant no harm in what I said.* **in-** [neg] **-ly** [adv] **sensitivity** also **sensitiveness, sensibility** [U] the quality, state, or degree of being sensitive **in-** [neg] **sensitize, -ise** [Wv5;T1] to make sensitive: *This is sensitized photographic film.*

highly-strung (of persons, animals) very tense by nature; easily excited: *He is a highly-strung child; please don't upset him.*

overwrought too nervous and excited: *She is overwrought after all these exciting happenings.*

worked up *not fml* very excited; showing strong feelings, esp when worried (*esp in the phr* **get worked up**): *That child gets worked up very easily, and starts crying.*

hysterical 1 (of people) in a state of hysteria: *The shock of the accident made her hysterical.* **2** (of feelings) expressed wildly, in an uncontrolled manner: *He gave way to sudden hysterical anger.* **-ally** [adv Wa4]

F235 *nouns* : **tension and hysteria**
[ALSO ⇒ B87]

tension 1 [U] the state or condition of being tense: *There was a lot of tension in the room/air last night, at the meeting. Tension made her ill.* **2** [C] an example of this: *Tensions can make people ill.*

stress *esp emot* **1** [U] tension and what it does to people: *Stress made her ill. She has been under a lot of stress lately.* **2** [C] an example of this: *The stresses and strains of work made him ill.*

suspense [U] a state of uncertain expectation (*often in the phr* **keep someone in suspense**): *We waited for the decision and the suspense was terrible. He wouldn't tell them, but kept them in suspense all day.*

hysteria [U] **1** a condition of nervous excitement in which the person laughs and cries uncontrollably **2** wild excitement: *The people were in a state of hysteria.*

hysterics [P] attacks of hysteria: *She went into hysterics when she heard what had happened.*

F236 *nouns* : **surprise and astonishment**

surprise 1 [U] the feeling caused by an unexpected thing happening: *Her surprise showed on her face.* **2** [C] an unexpected event: *I don't like surprises. What a nice/nasty surprise! She gave a surprise party.* **3** [(by) U; A] the act of coming on (someone, often an enemy) unprepared: *They took the animals by surprise. Their visit took us by surprise. The soldiers made a surprise attack on the town.*

wonder 1 [U] a feeling of strangeness, surprise, etc, usu combined with admiration and the wish to find out about the thing which excites this feeling: *She was filled with wonder at what she saw.* **2** [C] a wonderful act or a producer of such an act: *We saw many wonders in that place. He is a wonder, the way he arranges everything all alone.* **3** [C] a wonderfully-made object: *The Temple of Diana was one of the Seven Wonders of the World in ancient times.* **it's a wonder (that)** it's surprising (that): *It's a* *wonder that you remembered me after all these years!*

astonishment [U] great surprise; wonder: *His astonishment at finding us there was very clear. To my astonishment he was there before us.*

amazement [U] great surprise; wonder: *To my amazement I came first in the competition. She was filled with amazement at the story. I listened in complete amazement.*

F237 *verbs* : **surprising and astonishing** [Wv5;T1]

surprise 1 to cause surprise to: *The taste surprised him; it was not as he'd imagined it. He was surprised to see the change in her. She had a surprised look on her face.* **2** to shock or cause to disbelieve: *Your behaviour surprises me. I'm surprised at you!* **3** to come on or attack when someone or something is unprepared: *They surprised us with a visit. The soldiers surprised their enemies.* **-singly** [adv]

astonish [*often pass*] to produce surprise or wonder in (someone): *We were astonished to hear what had happened. It astonishes me to hear that. He gave her an astonished look.* **-ingly** [adv]

startle to cause to jump or be quickly surprised; give an unexpected slight shock to: *You startled me; I didn't hear you come in! It was startling to see how much older he looked.* **-lingly** [adv] *She was a startlingly beautiful girl.*

astound [*often pass*] to surprise and shock: *He was astounded when he heard he had won the prize.* **-ingly** [adv]

amaze to fill with great surprise; cause wonder in: *Your knowledge amazes me. I was amazed by/at your performance. It amazed me to hear that you were leaving.* **-zingly** [adv]

stun to surprise or shock into helplessness: *He was stunned by the unfairness of their judgment.* **stunningly** [adv]

take aback [v adv *often pass*] to surprise and confuse (someone): *The news of the election defeat took the government aback. The old lady was quite taken aback by the priest's rudeness.*

flabbergast [*usu pass* (*at* or *by*)] *infml* to surprise very much: *She was quite flabbergasted at such a bold suggestion.*

dumbfound to make unable to speak, because of wonder, surprise, or lack of understanding: *The strange news completely dumbfounded us.*

F238 *verbs* : **puzzling and wondering**

puzzle [I∅ (*over*); T1] to (cause to) think hard, perhaps not being able to find an answer, explanation, etc: *Her story puzzles me; I find it hard to believe/understand. I'm puzzled by what she said. He has been puzzling over her story for weeks.* **puzzlement** [U] the state of being puzzled

mystify [T1] to cause (someone) to be puzzled:

His strange behaviour mystifies me. **mystification** [U] the state of being mystified

wonder 1 [T6a,b; (I∅)] to ask oneself: *He wondered why she did that. 'Why did she do that?' he wondered.* **2** [I∅; T6a,b] to feel interested, curious, etc: *She was wondering about him and how he got all that money.* **3** [T5a; I∅ (*at*)] to be surprised: *I don't wonder at their happiness; I'd be happy too if I was them. Do you seriously wonder that she didn't help him?* **4** [T6a] (in asking politely): *I wonder whether I could come?*

F239 *nouns* : **puzzling and wondering**

puzzle [C] **1** something that is difficult to understand: *His strange behaviour is a complete puzzle to me.* **2** something which tests the mind and is done as an amusement: *The children like doing puzzles. I bought them a puzzle book.*

mystery 1 [C] something that puzzles, is difficult or impossible to explain, understand, etc: *The whole matter is a complete mystery to me. There are many mysteries in life. He enjoys reading mystery stories.* **2** [U] the condition of being strange, difficult to explain, understand, etc: *There was a look of mystery about her.* **mysterious** [B] strange; difficult to explain or understand: *His death was very mysterious. A mysterious stranger came to the town.* **-ly** [adv]

enigma [C] *fml or lit* **1** a puzzle or mystery **2** a statement that is meant to be difficult to understand **enigmatic** [B] strange and difficult to understand **-ally** [adv Wa4]

marvel [C] something very surprising, interesting and unusual, esp that one does not see often or expect to happen, or finds difficult to understand: *Television is one of the marvels of modern life. The way he spoke in seven languages one after the other was a marvel to everybody.* **marvellous** [B] *esp lit* of or like a marvel: *The story was full of marvellous happenings.* **-ly** [adv]

miracle [C] a happening which cannot (easily) be explained naturally and is thought to be caused by a god or special power: *Many people believe that Jesus Christ performed miracles, such as bringing the dead back to life. The doctor used a new miracle drug to save the man's life.* **miraculous** [B] of, concerning, or like a miracle; strange and wonderful: *The way he climbed the mountain was quite miraculous; no one else could have done it that way.* **-ly** [adv]

wonder 1 [C] something or someone that causes surprise, interest, admiration, etc: *She does everything well; what a wonder she is!* **2** [U] a feeling of surprise, interest, admiration, etc: *They looked at the thing in the sky with wonder; they had never seen anything so strange before.* **(it's) no wonder** it is no surprise that: *No wonder you can't sleep when you eat so much before going to bed.*

prodigy [C] someone or something that is very

unusual or clever and causes puzzlement, wonder, etc: *A child who can play the piano at the age of four is a prodigy.*

Actions of the face related to feelings

F240 *nouns* : **smiling and laughing** [C]

smile an expression of the face with the mouth turned up at the ends and the eyes bright, that usu expresses amusement, happiness, approval, or sometimes bitter feelings: *She has a beautiful smile. He put on an unpleasant fixed smile. The new father wore a proud smile.* **all smiles** very happy-looking: *The winner was all smiles as he heard the results of the voting.*

grin a smile which shows the teeth; a smile which seems almost to be laughing, esp a very wide smile, which may sometimes also be an expression of suffering: *He didn't understand; he just stood there with a silly grin on his face.*

leer an unpleasant smile or sideways look expressing cruel enjoyment, rudeness, or thoughts of sex

laugh 1 the act or sound of laughing **2** an expression of amusement, happiness, careless disrespect, etc through laughing **3** *infml* something done for a joke or amusement: *He just did it for a laugh; he meant no harm.*

guffaw a laugh which is loud and perhaps rude

giggle a form of laughing which is repeated in an uncontrollable manner, esp by young girls: *The girls went into a fit of (the) giggles; they had the giggles for some time after that.* **do something for a giggle** *infml BrE* to do something for a joke, not for serious reasons

chuckle a quiet laugh: *He gave a chuckle as he read her letter.*

F241 *verbs* : **smiling and laughing**

smile 1 [I∅; (T1)] to have or make (a smile): *She smiled at me; how wonderful! It's rare to see him smile. He smiled his most welcoming smile.* **2** [L9] to have a feeling which a smile expresses; consider something slightly funny or silly: *He smiled to think what a fool he'd been.* **3** [I∅ (on)] (*fig*) to act or look favourably: *The weather smiled on us; it was a fine day.* **4** [T1] to express with a smile: *She smiled a greeting.* **smilingly** [adv]

grin [I∅] to make a grin: *They grinned with pleasure when I gave them the sweets. He grinned from ear to ear at the good news. You don't like the news?—Well, you must just grin and bear it* (= suffer it without complaint).

leer [I∅] to look with a leer **-ingly** [adv]

laugh 1 [I∅] to express amusement, happiness, careless disrespect, etc by making explosive

sounds with the voice, usu while smiling: *Stop laughing (at me)!* **2** [L9] to experience the feeling for which this is the expression: *He laughed silently to himself.* **3** [X9] to bring, put, drive, etc with laughing: *They laughed her out of her anxiety.* **4** [X7] to cause (oneself) to become by laughing: *He laughed himself sick.* **5** [T1] to express with a laugh: *She laughed her disrespect.* **-ingly** [adv] **laughter** [U] *genl* laughing: *He heard the sound of laughter.*

guffaw [I∅] to laugh loudly and perhaps rudely

giggle 1 [I∅] to make giggles: *She thought it was funny and giggled uncontrollably.* **2** [T1] to express with giggles: *She giggled her amusement.*

chuckle [I∅] to laugh quietly to oneself: *I could hear him chuckling to himself as he read that funny article.*

F242 *verbs* : **frowning and scowling**

frown 1 [I∅] to draw the hair-covered parts above the eyes (**the eyebrows**) together in anger or effort, to show disapproval, or to protect the eyes against strong light, causing lines to appear on the forehead: *She frowned when the sun got in her eyes. 'The boys are late,' he said, frowning anxiously at the clock. The teacher frowned at the noisy class.* **2** [T1] to express by doing this: *The teacher frowned his disapproval at the noisy class.* **3** [I∅] (*fig*) (of a thing) to have a dangerous or frightening appearance when seen from below: *The mountains frowned down on the plains.*

scowl 1 [I∅ (*at*)] to make an angry or threatening expression; to frown angrily: *The teacher scowled at his noisy class. What a scowling face you have!* **2** [T1] to express in this way: *He scowled his displeasure.*

grimace [I∅] to make an expression of pain, annoyance, etc which makes the face look unnaturally twisted: *He grimaced when he tasted the coffee without sugar in it. She grimaced at the sight of all the work.*

snarl 1 [I∅] (of an animal) to make a low angry sound while showing the teeth **2** [I∅; T1] (of a person) to speak or say in' an angry, bad-tempered way: *'Get out of here!' he snarled.*

F243 *nouns* : **frowning and scowling** [C]

frown an act of frowning: *She had a frown on her face because the sun was very strong/because she was angry.*

scowl an angry, threatening expression; an angry frown: *He had a scowl on his face as he faced his enemy.*

grimace an act of grimacing: *She made a grimace at the mention of all the work.*

snarl an act of snarling: *He answered with a snarl. He could hear the snarls of animals.*

F244 *verbs* : **mocking and sneering**

mock 1 [Wv4;T1;I0 (*at*)] to laugh at (someone or something) when it is wrong to do so; speak or act with regard to (someone or something) as if one is not serious, esp when one should be: *The Roman soldiers mocked Christ by calling him king. He had no religious beliefs, and he went to church only to mock. The pupil did his best, and the teacher was wrong to mock at his efforts, however bad they were. What made him angry wasn't losing the game but the mocking laughter of the man who'd beaten him.* **2** [T1] to copy (something) in such a way that the person or thing copied is laughed at: *He made all the other boys laugh by mocking the way the teacher spoke and walked.* **3** [T1] *fml* to cause (the efforts, skill, strength, etc of other people) to be useless or have no effect, success, etc: *For five years that small country has mocked the strength of the powerful nation with which it is at war.* **-ingly** [adv] **make mock of** *fml, lit & pomp* to mock: *Don't make mock of him!*

ridicule [T1] to laugh unkindly at; make unkind fun of: *They all ridiculed the idea.*

caricature [T1] to ridicule (someone) by **a** acting like him or her in a way intended to amuse: *He made his friends laugh by caricaturing their teacher.* **b** making a drawing which makes that person seem more odd, noticeable, or amusing than he or she really is

scoff [I0 (*at*)] to speak or act disrespectfully; to laugh at or ridicule: *She came to the meeting to scoff but stayed to learn. As a young man he scoffed at religion.* **-ingly** [adv]

jeer 1 [T1 (*at*)] to laugh rudely at: *The crowd jeered (at) the prisoners.* **2** [I0] to laugh rudely: *As the prisoners passed, the crowd jeered.* **-ingly** [adv]

sneer [I0] **1** to express proud dislike by a kind of usu one-sided smile **2** [(*at*)] to act proudly; treat something as if unworthy of serious notice: *That is a piece of work not to be sneered at. She sneers at all opinions but her own.*

F245 *nouns* : **mocking and sneering**

mockery 1 [U] the act or action of laughing at something that should not be laughed at or of treating something serious as if it is not: *He finished his speech, in spite of the noisy mockery of his listeners.* **2** [C *usu sing*] a person or thing that is foolish, shameful and/or worthy of being laughed at: *The teacher is so foolish, and does his work so badly, that he's (become) a mockery to the whole school.* **3** [S] something untrue or pretended, that is unworthy of any respect or serious consideration: *The medical examination was a mockery; the doctor hardly looked at the child.* **4** [C *often pl*] an act of mocking **hold someone or something up to mockery** to cause or attempt to cause someone or something to appear foolish: *This book*

holds many of our present-day politicians up to mockery. **make a mockery of 1** to cause to be done without useful result: *His failure made a mockery of the teacher's great efforts to help him.* **2** to prove to be untrue or pretended: *His evil life makes a mockery of his claims to be a holy man.*

ridicule [U] unkind laughter; the condition of being made fun of: *His behaviour deserves ridicule rather than blame.* **hold someone up to ridicule** to invite people to laugh unkindly at someone: *It's not fair to hold me up to ridicule because I can't spell!* **lay oneself open to ridicule** to do things that will make people laugh at one

ridiculous [B] silly; deserving ridicule: *She looks ridiculous in those tight trousers. It would be (quite) ridiculous to spend all their money.* **-ly** [adv]

scoff 1 [C *usu pl*] a scoffing remark: *He didn't enjoy listening to the scoffs of the crowd.* **2** [S] an object of scoffing: *His ideas were the scoff of the scientific world.*

jeer [C] a jeering remark or noise: *He has known praise and hatred, and has gone from cheers to jeers.*

sneer [C] a sneering expression of the face, way of speaking, or remark: *He greeted the idea with a sneer.*

F246 *nouns* : **groans and growls** [C]

groan 1 a rather loud sound of suffering, worry, or disapproval which is made in a deep voice: *There were loud groans when they heard the bad news.* **2** a sound caused by the movement of wood or metal parts: *The old chair gave a groan when the woman sat down in it.*

moan 1 a low sound of pain, grief, or suffering: *From time to time, during the night, there was a moan (of pain) from the sick man. Her tears and moans were pitiful, as she sat holding her dead baby in her hands.* **2** (*fig*) sounds that give the idea of sadness or suffering: *The moan of the wind in the trees made her feel afraid.*

howl a long loud cry, as in pain, anger, etc, esp that made by such animals as wolves and dogs

growl a deep rough sound in the throat to show anger or a warning: *He answered her with a growl (of anger). (fig) They heard the growl of distant guns/thunder.*

F247 *verbs* : **groaning and growling**

groan 1 [I0] to make a groan: *The old man who had been in the accident lay groaning beside the road. The floorboards groaned as he crossed the room. (fig) The table groaned with food.* **2** [T1 (*out*)] to say in a low voice which seems about to groan: *He groaned out the story of how his friends had been killed.* **3** [I0] (*fig*) to suffer: *The people groaned under the heavy taxes. My heart groaned at the thought of the work.*

moan 1 [I0] to make a moan or moans: *The sick child moaned a little, and then fell asleep. The wind moaned round the house all night; it wasn't a cheerful sound.* **2** [T1 (*out*)] to express with moans: *The prisoner moaned* (*out*) *a prayer for help.* **3** [I0] *derog* to complain; to speak in a complaining voice: *Stop moaning; you really have nothing to complain about. He's always moaning about the unjust way in which he thinks he's been treated.*

howl 1 [I0] to make howls: *The dogs howled all night. The wind howled in the trees. We howled with laughter.* **2** [T1 (*out*)] to say or express with a howl: *He howled* (*out*) *my name.* **3** to weep loudly

growl 1 [I0] (usu of animals) to make a growl: *The dog growled at the postman.* **2** [I0] (of things) to make a sound like this: *The guns were growling in the distance.* **3** [T1 (*out*)] to express in a voice which seems to growl: *When he came late, he growled* (*out*) *an excuse.*

F248 *verbs, etc* : **crying and weeping**

cry 1 [I0; (T1)] to produce tears from the eyes with or without sounds expressing grief, sorrow, sadness, etc: *She cried with sadness when she heard news of her friend's death. The little girl was crying because she was lost. When she knew her baby was safe the mother cried for joy. Paul was crying for some more cake* (= because he wanted some more cake). *On the day of mother's death my father cried real tears for the first time in his life.* **2** [I0 (*out*)] to make loud sounds expressing fear, sadness, or some other feeling: *The baby cried from hunger. He cried out in pain.*

burst into tears to start crying: *She burst into tears when she heard the bad news.*

in tears crying: *She was in tears because of what happened.*

weep 1 [T1; I0] *esp fml & lit* to cry: *He lost control of his feelings and began to weep.* (*fig*) *she wept bitter tears.* **2** [X7, 9] to put (oneself) into a certain state by weeping: *She wept herself silly* (= into an over-excited state). **3** [I0] to lose liquid: *His wound began to weep.*

sob 1 [I0] to breathe while weeping in sudden short bursts making a sound in the throat: *A little girl was sitting and sobbing in the corner.* **2** [T1 (*out*)] to say or tell by weeping: *'It can't be true!' he sobbed. He sobbed out the whole sad story.* **3** [X9] to bring by weeping: *She sobbed herself to sleep.* **4** [C] an uncontrolled short breath while weeping; a sound of sobbing: *Hearing her sobs, he asked what the matter was.*

F249 *adjectives, etc* : **crying and weeping** [B]

tearful crying: *A tearful young girl stood in the doorway.* **-lly** [adv]: *She told him tearfully what had happened.*

weepy [Wa1] *infml* **1** tending to cry, or crying often: *She isn't very well and is feeling weepy.* **2** (of a story, film, etc) as if intended to make one sad **-pily** [adv] **-piness** [U]

Senses and sensations

F260 *verbs* : **touching, feeling, and sensing**

touch 1 [I0; T1] to be not separated (from): *Stand so that your shoulders are touching. The branches hung down and touched the water.* **2** [I0; T1] to feel with a part of the body, esp the hands or fingers: *Don't touch! Visitors are requested not to touch the paintings.* **3** [T1] to strike lightly or quietly with the hand, finger, etc; press with slight force: *You only need to touch the bell for it to ring.* **4** [T1] to handle or have: *Don't touch anything until the police come. He swore he'd never touch a drink again.* **5** [T1] to eat or drink a little of: *You haven't touched your food; I hope you're not ill.* **6** [T1 usu neg] (*fig*) to compare with; be equal to: *Your work will never touch her standard.* **7** [T1] (esp of a ship) to reach (esp land): *We touched land after three months at sea.* **8** [Wv4; T1] (*fig*) to cause (someone or his heart) to feel pity, sympathy, etc: *His sad story so touched my heart that I really wept.* **9** [X9 usu pass] to mark slightly with colour: *She wore a blue dress touched with red.*

feel [T1] to touch, handle, etc, esp with the fingers, esp for a purpose: *She felt the cloth to see how soft it was. The dog felt the substance with its nose.*

finger [T1] to touch with the fingers: *She fingered the cloth to see what it was like.*

paw [T1] **1** to touch, esp with a paw or the hand in the shape of a paw **2** *deprec* to touch too much: *'Stop pawing me!' she told him.*

tap [T1; I0 (*on*)] to touch quickly and lightly: *He tapped me on the shoulder. She tapped on the door.*

sense [T1] to be aware of through the senses, esp by touching: *She sensed his anger although he was not looking at her. It is possible to sense heat through your clothes.*

handle [T1] to touch or feel with the hands: *'Please do not handle the goods,' said the shopkeeper.*

F261 *nouns* : **touching and sensing**
[ALSO ⇒ F1]

touch 1 [U] that sense by which a material object is felt and by which it is known to be hard, smooth, rough, etc **2** [C] the effect caused by touching something; way something feels: *the silky touch of soft smooth cloth* **3** [C] an act of touching: *She felt the touch of his* *hand.* **4** [C] a way of touching: *He has a light touch.* **5** [S] (*fig*) a slight attack, as of an illness: *She has a touch of cold/fever.* **6** [C] a slight stroke or blow: *It was just a touch, nothing more.* **7** [C] an addition or detail that improves or completes something; slight added effort in finishing any piece of work: *That was a nice touch! I'm just putting the finishing touches to* (= adding the last details to) *the cake.* **8** [S9] a special ability to do something needing skill, esp artistic work: *Your recent work's been bad. I hope you're not losing your touch.* **9** [C] a person's particular way of doing things: *The wording of this letter bears her touch but is not written in her handwriting.* **10** [C] (*fig*) a slight amount of some quality or substance: *This soup could do with a touch more salt. She spoke with a touch of disrespect in her voice.* **in/out of touch (with) 1** regularly/not regularly exchanging news and information: *Are you still in touch with your parents? Please write; it would be nice to keep in touch.* **2** having/not having information about something: *I would like to go back to teaching but I'm out of touch with my subject now.* **lose touch** to stop exchanging news and information: *If we write regularly we won't lose touch.* **to the touch** when felt: *It's cold to the touch.* **touch and go 1** a delicate state of affairs; uncertain: *It was touch and go whether we'd win or not.* **2** a narrow escape: *I was very lucky. It was touch and go.*

contact 1 [U] the condition of meeting, touching, or coming together with: *body contact* **2** [U] relationship; connection: *The tribe had no contact with the outside world for centuries. Have you been in contact with your sister recently? That poor madman has lost all contact with reality.* **3** [C] *infml* a social, professional, or business connection; a person one knows in a position to be of help to one: *Her contacts in the government warned her that she ought to leave the country.* **make contact** to get in touch, esp after much effort: *Our generals have made contact with the enemy.*

tap [C] (the sound of) a quick light touch: *I felt a tap on the shoulder. There was a tap on the door.*

senses 1 [(*the*) P] the five natural powers (sight, hearing, feeling, tasting, and smelling) which give a person or animal information about the outside world: *Food and wine are pleasures of the senses.* **2** [B] one's powers of (reasonable) thinking: *Are you mad? Have you taken leave of/lost your senses? Are you out of your senses? Perhaps losing his job will bring this lazy boy to his senses. She felt faint in the hot room, but the fresh air made her come to her senses again.* **sensational** [Wa5;B] *tech* of or relating to the senses

F262 *adjectives* : **touching and sensing** [B]

sensory [Wa5] of, from, or concerning the bod-

ily senses and their use: *Sensory information is carried to the brain by sensory nerves.*

sensual 1 *lit & usu deprec* interested in, related to, or giving pleasure to one's own body, such as by sex, food, and drink: *He enjoys sensual things.* **2** [Wa5] of or seen, felt, etc by the senses **-lly** [adv] **-ity** [U]

sensuous *lit* being, of, concerning, causing, interested in, etc feelings, esp of pleasure, by the senses: *The cat stretched itself with sensuous pleasure.* **-ly** [adv] **-ness** [U]

tactile [Wa5] that can be felt by touch; experienced by touch: *It was a tactile sensation.*

contiguous [Wa5 (*to, with*)] *tech & fml* **1** touching; next (to); having a common border: *England is the only country contiguous to/with Wales.* **2** next or near in time or order: *Were these events contiguous?* **-ly** [adv]

tangible [Wa5] **1** that can be felt by touch **2** clear and certain; real; not imaginary: *There are no tangible reasons for thinking him guilty.* **-in** [*neg*] **-bly** [adv Wa3] **-bility** [U]

palpable [Wa2] that can be touched or felt; easily and clearly known by the senses or the mind: *He told us a palpable lie. The silence in the house was almost palpable.* **-im** [*neg*] **-bly** [adv Wa3]

numb [Wa1] not able to feel anything (or to move): *He felt numb with cold/fear.* **-ly** [adv]: *She listened numbly to the bad news.* **-ness** [U]

audible *tech* able to be heard: *The sounds were clearly audible.* **in-** [*neg*] **-bility** [U]

auditory [Wa5] *tech* of, by, or for hearing: *She had auditory difficulties for which an ear operation was necessary. The animal had damaged auditory apparatus.*

F263 *verbs* : **seeing and looking**

see 1 [Wv6;I0] to use the eyes; have or use the power of sight: *See! Here comes the train. It was so dark he could hardly see (to do his work). He doesn't see very well in his right eye. She claims to see into the future* (= know what is to happen). **2** [Wv6;T1, 5a,6a; V2,3 (*fml & only pass*), 4, 8] to look at; get sight of; notice, examine, or recognize by looking: *I looked for her but I couldn't see her in the crowd. I saw the train come/coming into the station. Can you see what's going on over there? Let me see your ticket, please.* (*fml*) *The prisoner was seen to take the money. I could see (that) my friend needed my help. I saw the whole accident with my own eyes. I saw the man knocked down and the driver driving away.* **3** [Wv6;I0;T1, 5a,b, 6a] to understand or recognize: *Do you see what I mean?—Yes, now I see. I see in the paper (that) the government lost a vote in Parliament. Try to see the matter my way. When seen in the light of your arguments, the question is simple.* **4** [I0; T6a, b] to (try to) find out or determine: *Will you see if you can repair my car? I'll see what I can do/see what the trouble is. I'm not sure if I can lend you that much money; I'll have* *to see.* **5** [Wv6;T5a] to make sure; take care: *See that you're ready at 8 o'clock. I promise to see that the job is done on time.* **6** [Wv6;T1, 4; V4, 8] *not fml* to form a picture in the mind of; imagine: *I can't see (myself) lending her money; can you see her ever paying it back? I can see a great future for you in music. Can you see him bent over a desk studying? I admit it's hard to see.* **7** [Wv6;T1, 4; *usu neg*] *not fml* to be in favour of: *I put my opinion to the chairman but he couldn't see it.* **8** [Wv6;T1] *lit* to be an occasion of (an event or course in history): *The 5th century saw the end of the Roman Empire in the West.* **9** [Wv6;T1] to have experience of: *You and I have seen some good times together. This old house has seen better days; now it's in bad repair.* (*infml*) *I don't know her age for sure, but she'll never see 40 again* (=she's older than 40). *I thought I'd never see the day when such a thing could happen.* **10** [T1] to visit, call upon, or meet with: *The doctor can't see you yet; he's seeing someone else at the moment. Mrs Johnson, may I see you a moment, please?* **11** [X9] to go with: *Someone ought to see the old lady safely home. Please see this troublesome fellow out of the office and tell him not to come back.* **let me see** (used for expressing a pause for thought): *Do you recognize this music? Let me see . . . Yes, now I do.* **see here** *usu pomp* (used to express warning or disapproval): *See here, boys, you mustn't ever do that again.* **seeing is believing** *infml* **1** I'll believe it when I see it, and not before. **2** Now I've seen it, so I believe it. **see something in someone** *infml* to like or be fond of someone: *I wonder why she fell in love with him; I'll never know what she sees in him.* **see nothing/little/a lot of someone** *infml* to see or be in company with a person never/seldom/often, etc: *Where's John? I've seen nothing of him all week. They're good friends and see a lot of one another.* **you see** *not fml* (used with rather weak meaning in explanations): *Why are you so late?—Well, you see, the bus broke down.* **see things** *not fml* to think that one sees something that is not there: *I must be seeing things! I can't believe the neighbours have got a new car!* **so I see** what you say is already clear or easy to see: *I'm afraid I'm a bit late.—So I see.*

sight [T1] to see, esp for the first time: *The men in the boat sighted land. She finally sighted her husband on the other side of the crowded room. Several rare birds have been sighted in this area.*

spot [T1] **1** to see (someone or something) quickly or suddenly, esp as one among many, or in a place where things are difficult to see: *She spotted him immediately among the people in the railway station, because he was wearing his yellow hat.* **2** to guess or choose: *Can you spot the winner of the next race?*

look 1 [I0 (*at*)] to give attention to in seeing: *He went to look at the baby. We looked at him running. You could see it if you'd only look.* **2** [L (*to be*) 1, 7] to seem from how someone or something is seen: *You look ill. He looked*

tired. Things are looking better now; they are looking up. Judging by her letter, she looks to be the best person for this job. You look good in that dress. **3** [T1] to express with the eyes: *She said nothing but she looked all interest.* **4** [L9] to turn the eyes and see in a certain direction: *Look round the corner/over the wall.*

regard [T1] *fml* to look at: *She regarded him thoughtfully.*

face [T1; L9] **1** to look towards (a particular direction) because one's face and body are turned that way: *They faced east. He faced towards the rising sun.* **2** (of a building, etc) to have the front built so as to be towards (a particular direction): *The house faces south/the sea.*

watch 1 [T1; V2, 4; I0] to look at (some activity, amusement, or event) usu while sitting or standing: *Do you often watch television? They watched the games while sitting under the trees.* **2** [T1] to keep one's eyes fixed on (someone or something): *She watched the train till it disappeared from sight.* **3** [T1, 3] to look for; to expect and wait (for): *She watched her chance/her moment to cross the street.* **4** [T1, 5] to take care of, be careful with, or pay attention to: *I'll watch the baby while you are away. You'd better watch Smith; I think he's a thief. Watch that the milk doesn't boil over.* **5** [T1, 6a, b; V2, 4] to attend carefully to (someone or someone's action): *Watch him jump/doing it. Watch how to do this. Watch what I do, then do the same.* **watcher** [C] a person who watches

scan [T1] **1** to look at quickly without careful reading: *He scanned the pages of the book to see what it was about.* **2** to look at or examine fully or closely, esp in search: *She scanned the doctor's face for a sign of hope. They scanned the sky for enemy aeroplanes.*

observe 1 [T1; V4] to see and notice; watch carefully: *She has observed the stars all her life. They were observed entering the bank at 8.32.* **2** [T1] to act in accordance with law or custom: *Does everyone observe the speed limits in your country?* **observer** [C] a person who observes **observation 1** [U] the act of observing **2** [C] an example of this: *He made his observations of the animals from the top of a tree.*

view 1 [T1] *esp tech* to examine; look at thoroughly: *Several possible buyers are coming to view the house.* **2** [X9] to consider, regard, or think about: *He viewed his son's lawless behaviour as an attack on himself.* **3** [T1; I0] to watch (esp television): *What are you viewing tonight?* **viewer** [C] a person who views (esp television)

notice [Wv6;I0;T1, 5a, b, 6a, b; V2, 4] to pay attention (to) with the eyes, other senses, or mind: *She was wearing a new dress, but he didn't even notice (it). Did you notice me leave/leaving the house? It's good to notice that the price has gone down. Yes, so I've noticed.*

note 1 [T1, 5, 6a, b] to pay attention to and remember: *Please note that this bill must be paid within 10 days.* **2** [T1, 5, 6a] to recognize;

observe: *You may have noted that my address has changed.* **3** [T1, 5, 6a] to call attention to; make known; show: *In her speech she first noted the importance of the occasion. The newspapers failed to note what happened next.*

witness 1 [T1] to be a witness [⇨ C207] of; (*esp lit*) to see: *He witnessed the accident himself; he saw it all.* **2** [L9] to serve as a witness: *Several people witnessed against her.* **3** [I0; T1] to show by one's signature [⇨ G141] that the proper person has signed (his name, a paper, etc): *I'll sign and you witness, please. Will you witness my signature, please?*

glimpse [T1] to have a passing view of: *I glimpsed her among the crowd, then she disappeared from sight.*

glance 1 [L9] to give a rapid look: *He glanced at his watch. I glanced round the room before I left. She glanced down the list of names. She glanced through the library book. He glanced over the report.* (*fig*) *In his book he only glances at the difficulties of the new government before passing on to the history of the country.* **2** [I0] (of bright surfaces) to flash as light falls on it/them: *The glasses glanced in the firelight.*

sightsee [I0] to go about, as on holiday, visiting places of interest (*esp in the phr* **go sightseeing**)

sightseer [C] a person who goes sightseeing

eye [T1 (*up and down*)] *sometimes deprec* to look at someone, esp carefully or for a long time, esp for a reason: *He eyed the man thoughtfully. She eyed him up and down and asked him what he wanted. Stop eyeing me like that!*

peer [L9] to look very carefully or searchingly, esp as if not able to see well: *She peered through the mist, trying to find the right path. He peered at me over the top of his glasses.*

stare [I0 (*at*)] to look, esp for a long time at (something or someone), esp with very wide-open eyes: *She stared at him in surprise. He was staring out to sea. She looked at him with strange staring eyes.*

gaze [I0 (*at*)] to look, esp for a long time over esp a wide distance, esp with great interest, etc: *He gazed at her beauty. The children were gazing at the toys.*

gape [I0 (*at*)] to look at (something or someone) with one's mouth open: *He gaped at her in surprise. Don't just stand there gaping: do something!*

behold [T1] *old use, lit, fml & pomp* to see: *Behold, the King comes! He beheld a terrible sight.* (*humor*) *Lo and behold, she came in through the window!*

F264 nouns : seeing and noticing

sight 1 [U] *also* **eyesight** the sense of seeing; the power of the eye: *He had his sight tested by a doctor. She has good sight for a woman of 80.* **2** [U; S] the seeing of something: *The crowd waited for a sight of the Queen passing by. The house is hidden from sight behind some trees.*

He felt faint at the sight of blood. **at first sight** at the first time of seeing or considering: *They fell in love when they first met; it was love at first sight. At first sight the difficulty looks greater than it really is.* **at/on sight** as soon as seen or presented; without delay: *The guard had orders to shoot on sight* (= without finding out who was there). *I can't sing this hard music at sight; I'll need practice.* **in sight 1** in view: *The car remained in sight until it turned the corner.* **2** within a little of being reached; near: *Peace was in sight at last after 2 years of war.* **in the sight of** *lit* in the judgment or opinion of: *'Do those things that are pleasing in his sight'* (*The Bible*); *punishable in the sight of the law* **know someone by sight** to recognize someone without knowing him personally or without knowing his name **lose sight of 1** to cease to see: *He lost sight of his friend in the crowd.* **2** to cease to get news about; lose touch with: *She lost sight of her school friends over the years.* **3** to forget; fail to consider: *In the heat of the argument we mustn't lose sight of our main purpose.* **out of sight 1** out of the range of being seen: *Stay out of sight; she mustn't see us.* **2** *infml* very high, great, etc: *The chairman said that labour costs had gone out of sight in the past year.* **3** *sl* very good; wonderful: *A party? That would be out of sight! I'd love it.* **sight unseen** without a chance for seeing or examining: *You can't expect anyone to buy a car sight unseen.*

vision [U] **1** (the) ability to see: *I've had my eyes tested and the report says that my vision is perfect. The windows of the car gave the driver good vision all round.* **2** (*fig*) *apprec* power of imaginative thought and expression; wisdom in understanding the true meaning of facts, esp with regard to the future: *The new director worked hard but he lacked vision. We need a man of vision as our president.*

notice 1 [U] attention: *His writings brought him into public notice. Local events are beneath the notice of the largest newspapers. Don't take any notice* (= pay any attention) *to what he says. Take particular notice of* (= pay close attention to) *the road signs.* **2** [C] a usu short written statement of information or directions to the public: *He sold the car by putting a notice in the newspaper. The notice on the wall says 'No smoking'.* **3** [C *often pl*] a statement of opinion, as in a newspaper, about a new book, play, etc: *The new play got mixed notices* (= some good, some bad) *after its first night.* **4** [U] a warning or information about something that will happen: (*fml*) *These rules are subject to* (= may) *change without notice. Can you be ready at 10 minutes' notice/at short notice?* (= if I tell you only 10 minutes/a short time before). **b** formal warning of the end of living or working in a place: *The company gave notice to 10 workers/gave 10 workers their notice. I gave the company/the owner of the flat my notice* (= said I planned to leave). *They wanted three weeks' notice before I left.* **sit up and take notice** *infml* to (be made to) pay attention or show respect: *My new*

book will make the world sit up and take notice!
until further notice *fml* from now until another
change might be made: *This office will close at
5 o'clock from May 1 until further notice.*

F265 *nouns* : **looking and scanning, etc**

look [C] *usu infml* **1** an act of looking: *Take a
look at this. He had a good look at the picture.*
2 the way someone or something seems when
seen; appearance: *I like the look of him. I like
his looks.*

sight 1 [C] something that is seen: *What a beautiful sight those roses make! She saw the familiar
sight of the postman going along the street.*
2 [U] presence in one's view; the range of what
can be seen: *She's too careful with her children,
never letting them out of her sight. The boat was
within sight of land. The train came in (to) sight.
Get out of my sight and don't come back!*

sighting [C] act of seeing or sighting: *There
have been several sightings of enemy ships/
those rare birds.*

scan [S] an act of scanning, esp a searching look:
*They did a quick scan of the area, looking for
the enemy.*

view 1 [U] ability (esp of the person or thing
stated) to see or be seen from a particular
place; sight: *My view of the stage was blocked
by the big hat of the woman sitting in front of
me. The car turned the corner and was lost to
our view/passed out of view* (= could not be
seen any more). *The valley was hidden from
view in the mist. When we reached the top of the
mountain, we came in view of* (= were able to
see) *a wide plain below. A wide plain came into
view* (= was able to be seen). *He fell off his
horse in full view of his friends* (= seen by all
and himself able to see all of them). *There was
no shelter within view* (= that could be seen)
anywhere. **2** [C *(of)*] **a** something seen from a
particular place, esp a stretch of pleasant country: *One splendid mountain view followed
another during our journey. There's no view
from my bedroom window except of some factory chimneys.* **b** a picture or photograph of a
piece of scenery, a building, etc: *This artist has
painted many views of the rocky west coast.* **3** [S
(of)] a special chance to see or examine someone or something: *Have you ever had a close
view of the princess? If we stand at this window,
we'll get a better view (of the procession).* **4** [C
(of) usu sing] *(fig)* a general consideration of a
matter in all its details: *We need a fresh view of
the whole affair before we decide. The lawyer
hasn't yet formed a clear view of the case.* **5** [C
(about, on)] *(fig)* a personal opinion, belief,
idea, etc about something: *In my view, he's a
fool. He has strong views about the evils of
playing cards. What are your views on university education?*

glimpse [C] **1** a quick look at or incomplete
view of *(esp in the phr* **get/catch a glimpse**): *I*
only caught a glimpse of the parcel, so I can't
guess what was inside it.* **2** *(fig)* a moment of
understanding: *When I saw how worried he
was I had a glimpse of his true feelings.*

glance [C] **1** a rapid look: *One glance at his face
told me he was ill. He took a glance outside at
the weather.* **2** a rapid movement of the eyes:
*He gave her an admiring glance. He saw what
was happening at a glance.*

F266 *nouns* : **sights and visions** [C]

sight 1 [*often pl*] something special, unusual, etc
that is seen: *What a fine sight these mountains
are! The tourists went to see the sights of
London. They had a tour of the main sights.* **2**
[S] *deprec* something which looks very bad or
laughable: *What a sight you are, with paint all
over your clothes! This room looks a sight; it's
very untidy.*

spectacle 1 a grand public show or scene: *He is
a film producer who makes spectacles based on
the Bible.* **2** *deprec* a silly sight; an object of
laughing or disrespect: *She made a spectacle of
herself! I never thought I'd see the spectacle of a
minister standing on his head.* **spectacular** [B]
causing people to look or pay attention; making a spectacle; very great, exciting, etc: *It
is a spectacular film about ancient Rome.
His success in sport was spectacular.* **-ly**
[adv]

vision 1 something that is without bodily reality,
seen (as) in a dream, when in a sleeplike state,
or as a religious experience: *She saw/had a
vision in which God seemed to appear before
her.* **2** a picture seen in the mind; an imaginative idea, esp as a fulfilment of a desire: *He has
a clear vision of the future for his children. The
student had visions of getting a degree with first
class honours.* **3** *lit & apprec* something seen,
esp unexpectedly: *The clouds opened and they
had a sudden vision of the mountains.*

stare a long look with (esp) wide-open eyes: *He
did not like the stares of the people as he passed
them.*

gaze [*usu sing*] a long interested look: *Under his
gaze she turned red/dropped her eyes.*

gape a look while one's mouth is open

F267 *adjectives* : **relating to sight** [Wa5;B]

[ALSO ⇒ B133]

ocular 1 *tech* of the eyes **2** *becoming rare* that
can be seen: *He demanded ocular proof.*

optical of or about the sense of sight **-ly** [adv
Wa4]

ophthalmic *med* of the study and treatment of
the eyes **-ally** [adv Wa4]

visual 1 gained by seeing: *He has no visual
knowledge of the place.* **2** connected with or
having an effect on the sense of sight: *The*

visual arts include painting and dancing, as opposed to music. **3** *tech* concerned with the power of sight: *This animal's visual organs are different from ours.* **4** (esp of the directing of aircraft) performed without the help of radio, calculating instruments, etc: *The pilot made a visual landing.* **-ly** [adv]

sighted (of a person) able to see; not blind: *Sighted people find it difficult to understand the needs and feelings of blind people.* **-sighted** [*comb form*] showing or having the stated kind of ability to see: *He is very weak-sighted/ near-sighted/short-sighted*

sightless *esp lit & emot* unable to see; blind: *He turned his sightless eyes towards her.*

F268 *adjectives* : **relating to seeing and being seen** [B]

visible that can be seen: *The aircraft got smaller and smaller in the distance until it was no longer visible to the people on the ground.* **in-** [*neg*] **-bly** [adv Wa3] **-bility** [U]

noticeable that can be noticed; worth noticing: *There was a noticeable change in the weather.* **-bly** [adv Wa3]

conspicuous noticeable; attracting attention; easily seen: *She's always conspicuous because of her fashionable clothes. He was conspicuous for his bravery. That was a very conspicuous mistake. They made themselves conspicuous by wearing strange clothing. You were conspicuous by your absence yesterday.* **in-** [*neg*] **-ly** [adv]

prominent **1** noticeable or most easily seen: *Our house is the most prominent one in the street; it's painted red.* **2** standing or stretching far out (beyond a surface): *Her appearance is spoilt by her prominent teeth.* **3** (*fig*) of great ability, fame, importance, etc: *She is a prominent actress. He is a prominent politician in that city.* **-ly** [adv] **prominence** [U] the state of being prominent

apparent **1** [(*to*)] easily seen or understood; plain: *Her anxiety was apparent to everyone.* **2** according to appearances; not necessarily true or real; seeming: *Their apparent grief soon turned to laughter.* **-ly** [adv]

clear [Wa1] easily seen or allowing one to see easily: *The print on the page is large, clear, and easy to read. It's a lovely clear day today.* (*fig*) *It is quite clear to me that he won't help us.* **un-** [*neg*] **-ly** [adv] **-ness** [U]

graphic very clear; easily imagined, understood, etc: *He gave a graphic word picture of what happened.* **-ally** [adv Wa4]

evident plain, esp to the senses: *It's evident (that) he can't do it.* **-ly** [adv]

obvious easy to see or understand; clear; which must be recognized: *The best way to go was obvious to everybody except him. It's obvious that a boy isn't strong enough to lift an elephant.* **-ly** [adv]

F269 *adjectives* : **watchful and wary** [B]

watchful careful to notice things: *Let's remain watchful for any sign of trouble/danger/enemy activity.* **-ly** [adv] **-ness** [U]

vigilant continually watchful or on guard; always prepared for possible danger: *The police should be vigilant in the fight against crime.* **-ly** [adv] **vigilance** [U] the condition of being vigilant; (*fml*) watchfulness

observant noticing things quickly: *What an observant child he is!*

alert **1** watchful and ready to meet danger: *They are alert soldiers; they'll stay alert in case the enemy approaches.* **2** *apprec* quick to see and act: *She's an alert child, very observant.* **-ly** [adv] **-ness** [U] **on the alert** very watchful: *He was on the alert for any strange noises.*

cautious careful; paying no attention; having or showing caution [⇒ G39]: *She is cautious of/about telling secrets. You should be very cautious when crossing the road. Don't be too cautious over this work; let us have your opinion.* **-ly** [adv] **-ness** [U]

wary [Wa1] *emot* careful; looking out for danger: *He had a wary look in his eyes.* **warily** [adv] **wariness** [U]

F270 *adjectives* : **transparent and clear** [B]

transparent **1** allowing light to pass through so that objects behind can be clearly seen: *Most glass is transparent.* **2** fine enough to be seen through: *Her silk dress was almost transparent.* **3** (*fig*) clear; easily understood: *He has a transparent style of writing.* **4** about which there is no doubt; certain: *He is a man of transparent honesty. That was a transparent lie!* **-ly** [adv] **transparency** **1** [U] the state of being transparent **2** [C] *also* **slide** a picture, photograph, etc that has been put on transparent material esp so that it can be shown on a screen [⇒ K59], etc

clear [Wa1] easy to see through; transparent: *What a lovely clear sky. The water here is very clear; I can see the bottom of the lake. He looked through the clear green glass.* **un-** [*neg*] **-ly** [adv] **clarity** [U] **-ness** [U]

translucent not transparent but clear enough to allow light to pass through: *The translucent glass in their bathroom window allowed light to come in without letting people see.*

diaphanous (esp of cloth) so fine and thin that it can be seen through: *She wore a diaphanous silk skirt.*

see-through *not fml* that can be seen through, allowing what is inside to be (partly) seen: *She wore a sexy see-through dress.*

F271 adjectives : **opaque and dense**
[B]

opaque 1 not allowing light to pass through: *The glass in the door was opaque.* 2 (*fig*) hard to understand: *His words were quite opaque.* **-ly** [adv] **-ness** *also* **opacity** [U]
dense [Wa1] difficult to see through: *The mist was dense.*

F272 verbs : **hearing and listening**

hear 1 [Wv6;T1; V2,4; I∅] to receive and understand (sounds) by using the ears: *I can't hear very well. I heard him say so. I can hear someone knocking.* 2 [Wv6;T1, 5a,b] to be told or informed: *I heard that he was ill.* 3 [T1, 6a] to listen with attention (to), esp to a case in court: *The judge heard the case.*
listen [I∅ (*to*)] to give attention in hearing: *Are you listening or are you just pretending? Listen to the music, don't make a noise.* **don't listen to someone:** Don't believe or do what someone says
sound 1 [Wv6; L1,7,9] to have the effect of being; seem when heard: *Your idea sounds (like) a good one. Does this sentence sound right? It sounds as if the government don't know what to do. The minister sounds unsure of himself.* 2 [I∅] to make a sound; produce an effect that can be heard: *His advice seemed to keep sounding in my ears. The bell sounded at 8 o'clock for dinner.* 3 [T1] to cause (as a musical instrument) to make a sound: *A bell is sounded at 8 o'clock. Sound your horn to warn the other driver.* 4 [T1] to signal by making sounds: *Sound the 'all clear' after an air attack.* (*fig*) *Let me sound a note of warning to you.* 5 [T1 *usu pass*] to express as a sound; pronounce: *The s in island is not sounded.*

F273 nouns : **hearing and listening**

hearing 1 [U] the sense by which one hears sound: *Her hearing is getting worse.* 2 [U] the distance at which one can hear: *Don't talk about it in his hearing.* 3 [U;C] the act or experience of listening: *At first hearing I didn't like the music.* 4 [C] a chance to be heard explaining one's position (*esp in the phr* **gain/ get a hearing**): *It's a good idea, so try to get a hearing with the people in charge.* 5 [C] *law, etc* trial of a case by a judge: *I was not present at the hearing. At the official hearing both sides presented their cases well.* **hearing aid** [C] a small electric machine fitted near the ear which makes sounds seem louder
earshot [U] (*esp in the phrs* **within/out of earshot**) (within/beyond) the distance up to which a sound can be heard: *If you want to talk about Mary, let's make sure she's not within earshot.*
listen [S] *infml* an act of listening: *Have a listen to this.*

sound 1 [U] what can be heard: *She could hear the sound of cars passing outside. Sound travels fast, but light travels faster. Sound waves take a certain time to travel.* 2 [C] an example of this: *She heard a sound outside. The sounds of the night came through the window.* 3 [S9] (*fig*) idea: *I don't like the sound of that; I don't agree.*
noise 1 [U;C] (an) unwanted or unpleasant sound: *Try not to make any noise when you go into the bedroom. She enjoyed the holiday, away from city noises.* 2 [U] confused, meaningless, and continuing sound, esp **a** the sound heard in any public place: *There's so much noise in this restaurant I can hardly hear you talking.* **b** *also* **static** unwanted sound which keeps sounds on radio, telephones, etc from being heard clearly 3 [C] an unmusical sound that is difficult to describe or strange: *What's wrong with my car? The engine is making funny noises. She heard a noise like a train.*
din [S] *deprec* a loud, continuous, confused, and unpleasant noise: *The children are making a terrible din in the school hall.* **kick up a din** *infml* to make a noise of this kind: *Stop kicking up such a din!*
racket [S] *deprec* a loud noise: *Stop making such a racket upstairs!*
percussion [U] *tech* 1 the striking of two usu hard things together 2 the noise produced in this way

F274 adjectives : **loud and noisy**
[Wa1;B]

loud being or producing great strength of sound; not quiet: *What loud music! Can you make the radio louder please?* 2 (*fig*) attracting attention by being unpleasantly noisy or colourful: *What a loud tie he is wearing!* **-ly** [adv] **-ness** [U] **aloud** *also* **out loud** [adv Wa5] so as to be (easily) heard: *He read the letter aloud to us. He read it out loud to us.* (*emph*) *They shouted aloud/out loud with joy!*
noisy *usu deprec* making or marked by a lot of noise: *What a noisy car! It's very noisy in this office.* **-sily** [adv] **-siness** [U]

F275 adjectives : **not loud and noisy**
[B]

quiet [Wa1] with little noise: *She played some quiet music on the record-player. He has rather a quiet voice.* **-ly** [adv]: *He spoke quietly.* **-ness** [U]
noiseless without any noise: *He crossed the dark room with noiseless footsteps.* **-ly** [adv] **-ness** [U]
silent 1 free from noise; quiet: *The night was dark and silent.* 2 not speaking; not using spoken expression: *They were silent; no one spoke. Her lips moved in silent prayer/reading.* 3 making no statement; expressing no opinion, decision, etc: *The law is silent on this difficult*

point. **4** [Wa5] *tech* (of a letter in a word) not having a sound; not pronounced: *The* w *in* '*wreck*' *is silent; it is a silent* w. **5** [Wa5] being or concerning films with no sound: *It was a silent film.* **-ly** [adv] **silence** [U; C] the state of being silent; an occasion when people, etc are silent: *the silence of the night; a moment of complete silence*

reticent (of a person) not saying much, esp where one could say a lot: *Don't be reticent; tell us. She was reticent about her past life.* **reticence** [U] the state of being reticent

taciturn (of a person) saying very little; silent by nature: *a taciturn manner* **taciturnity** [U] the state of being taciturn

tacit [Wa5] accepted or understood without one having to say anything or without saying anything: *I think he had your tacit agreement to do it, even if you did not agree officially.* **-ly** [adv]

laconic saying something in the fewest possible words **-ally** [adv Wa4]

F276 *verbs & nouns, etc* : **special sounds**

rattle 1 [IØ] to make a number of short sharp sounds, usu together: *The stones in the box rattled when he shook it.* **2** [T1] to cause to do this: *He rattled the (stones in the) box.* **3** [C] such a noise: *I could hear the rattle of the stones in the box.* **4** [C] anything that rattles, esp a child's toy: *He shook the rattle.*

bang 1 [IØ] to make a sharp loud noise or noises: *The door banged. There's someone banging about upstairs.* **2** [C] a sudden loud noise: *The door shut with a bang.*

bump 1 [IØ] to make a sudden dull noise: *Something bumped in the night.* **2** [C] a sudden dull noise: *She fell down with a bump.*

crash 1 [IØ] to make a sudden loud noise: *The drums crashed. The lightning flashed and the thunder crashed.* **2** [T1; IØ] to (cause to) fall or strike the ground noisily and violently: *The teacher crashed her book down on the desk to show how angry she was. The tree crashed to the ground.* **3** [C] a sudden loud noise as made by a violent blow, fall, break, etc: *He heard the crash of thunder.*

roar 1 [Wv4; IØ] to make a very loud noise: *The lion/the football crowd/the engine roared. The roaring wind shook the trees.* **2** [L9] to move while making this noise: *The cars roared along.* **3** [T1, 5 (*out*)] to express in this way: *They roared their answer. 'Put it down!' he roared.* **4** [IØ] *infml* to laugh long and loudly: *Mother will roar when she hears this!* **5** [C] a deep loud continuing sound: *the roar of an angry lion/of a football crowd/of an aircraft engine/of the wind and waves* **6** [C *of*] a deep loud sound of the stated kind: *roars of laughter* **set the room/the table in a roar** to make everyone in the room/at the table laugh loudly

thud 1 [C] a dull sound, as caused by a heavy object striking something soft: *The dead man*

fell to the floor with a thud. He landed with a thud on the grass.* **2** [Wv4; L9] to make a thud by beating, striking, landing, falling, etc: *We jumped from the branch and thudded onto the grass. He heard a thudding noise.*

thump 1 [Wv4; IØ] to produce a repeated dull sound by beating, striking, falling, walking heavily, etc: *The old man thumped noisily along the passage. My heart thumped with excitement. We could hear a thumping noise coming from the car engine.* (*fig*) *I've got a thumping headache.* **2** [T1; L9] to strike with a heavy blow: *I'll thump you if you annoy me any more. The brick thumped against the tree. The teacher thumped the desk angrily.* **3** [C] the dull sound produced by this **4** [C] a heavy blow: *I'll give you a thump if you continue to annoy me.*

ring 1 [IØ (*out*); T1] to (cause to) give a sound like a bell: *The church bells rang (out). The telephone was ringing. Ring the doorbell.* **2** [C] an act of ringing: *Give the doorbell a ring. She heard several rings on the doorbell.*

peal 1 [IØ (*out*)] (esp of bells) to ring out or sound loudly (and continually): *Listen to the church bells pealing. His loud voice pealed out.* **2** [T1] to cause (bells) to ring out **3** [S] the sound of the loud ringing of bells: *the peal of the bells from many churches* **4** [C] a musical pattern made by the ringing of a number of bells one after another: *People form bell ringers' associations to ring peals for their own pleasure.* **5** [C] (*fig*) a loud long sound or number of sounds one after another: *a peal of thunder; peals of laughter*

toll 1 [IØ; T1] (of esp large bells) to sound slowly and deeply: *The great bells tolled (his death). They heard the bells tolling sadly.* **2** [S] such a sound: *They heard the toll of the bells.*

pop 1 [C] a sound like that of a slight explosion: *As he opened the bottle of wine there was a loud pop.* **2** [adv] with a small explosive sound (*esp in the phr* **go pop**): *When he opened the bottle it went pop.* **3** [IØ] to make a sound like a pop **4** [L9] to move suddenly, esp with a popping sound: *The top popped out of the bottle.* **5** [T1] *infml* to put quickly and lightly: *She popped a sweet into her mouth.*

F277 *verbs* : **smelling and stinking**

smell [Wv6] **1** [IØ] to use the nose; have or use the sense of the nose: *Here, smell; what do you think this liquid is? That old dog can hardly smell any longer.* **2** [T1, 4, 5, 6a; V4] to notice, examine, discover, or recognize by this sense: *I can smell smoke/cooking. I could smell that the milk wasn't fresh. He can always smell when rain is coming. Can you smell something burning?* **3** [T1, 4, 5; V4] (*fig*) to notice, come to know of, recognize, etc, by some natural unexplained ability: *He is a writer who can always smell a good idea. I could smell (someone) cheating. I could smell that I was no longer welcome.* **4** [L7, 9, *esp of, like*] to have an effect on the nose; have a particular smell: *It was a sweet-smelling flower. This book smells old. The room smelt of beer and tobacco. It smelt as if something was on fire.* **5** [IØ (*of*)] to have an offensive effect on the nose; have an unpleasant smell; stink: *The meat had been left out for days and had started to smell.*

sniff 1 [IØ (*at*)] to draw air into the nose with a sound, esp in short repeated actions: *The cat sniffed at the food before deciding to eat it.* **2** [T1] to do this to discover a smell in or on: *The dogs were sniffing the ground. He sniffed the air for gas but couldn't smell any.* **3** [T1] (*fig*) to say in a proud complaining way: *'I expected something rather nicer,' she sniffed.*

scent 1 [T1] (esp of animals) to smell, esp to tell the presence of (someone or something) by smelling: *The dogs scented the fox.* **2** [T1, 5] (*fig*) to get a feeling or belief of the presence or fact (of): *She scented danger/scented that all was not well.* **3** [Wv5; T1 (*with*) *usu pass*] to fill with a scent: *The air was scented with spring flowers. She had a scented handkerchief.*

stink [IØ] to smell very unpleasant: *He stinks; does he never wash?* (*fig*) *Your whole plan stinks; I don't like it at all!* **stink the place out** to stink very much: *That animal stinks the place out; get rid of it!*

F278 *nouns* : **smelling and stinking**

smell 1 [U] the power of using the nose; the sense that can discover the presence of gases in the air: *These dogs track by smell alone. She has a sharp sense of smell.* **2** [C] a quality that has an effect on the nose; something that excites this sense: *Some flowers have stronger smells than others. What a smell! What's burning?* **3** [C *usu sing*] an act of smelling something: *Have a smell of this wine; does it seem all right?*

odour *BrE*, **odor** *AmE fml* smell (defs **1** & **2**)

scent 1 [C] a smell, esp **a** as left by an animal and followed by hunting dogs, etc: *The dogs followed the fox's scent as far as the river; then they lost the scent.* **b** a particular, usu pleasant smell: *The scent of roses was strong in the garden.* **2** [S] (*fig*) *not fml* a way of discovery: *The scientist thought he was on the scent of a cure for heart disease, although others thought he was following a false scent.* **3** [S] (of animals) the power of smelling: *The dog has a good scent.* **4** [U; C] *esp BrE* perfume: *It's that cheap scent she uses.*

perfume [U; C] **1** a sweet or pleasant smell, as of flowers **2** a sweet-smelling liquid, often made from flowers, for use on the body

fragrance 1 [U] *apprec* the quality of being fragrant: *The fragrance of the air was wonderful.* **2** [C] a (sweet or pleasant) smell: *This soap is made in several fragrances.*

aroma [C] **1** a strong usu pleasant smell: *The aroma of hot coffee came out of the shop.* **2** (*fig*) an appearance, feeling, or sensation con-

sidered typical of some quality: *There was an aroma of wealth in the room.*

pong *infml BrE* **1** [C] an unpleasant smell: *Oh, what a pong!* **2** [IØ] to have or make a pong

stink also **stench** [C] *emph* a very unpleasant smell: *What's that awful stink? He smelled the stench of dead bodies.* (*fig*) *That place has the stink of evil.*

sniff [C] an act or sound of sniffing: *Take a sniff of this chemical; what is it?*

F279 *adjectives* : **smelling and stinking** [B]

fragrant *apprec* having a sweet or pleasant smell (esp of flowers): *The air in the garden was warm and fragrant.*

perfumed [Wa5] having a sweet smell; covered with perfume: *The room was perfumed with the scent of flowers.*

scented [Wa5] having a pleasant smell; covered with scent: *The room was scented with the perfume of flowers.*

sweet-smelling [Wa2] having a very pleasant smell: *The garden was full of sweet-smelling flowers.*

aromatic having a strong pleasant smell: *Aromatic herbs* (=plants) *are often used in cooking.* **-ally** [adv Wa4]

acrid 1 (of smell or taste) bitter; sour **2** (*fig*) bitter in manner; bad-tempered: *What an acrid speech that was!*

smelly [Wa1] having a bad smell: *That place is dirty and smelly! Burn these smelly old clothes.*

evil-smelling [Wa2] having a very bad smell: *What an evil-smelling liquid; what is it?*

stinking *deprec* **1** very evil-smelling: *He had stinking breath.* **2** (*fig*) very bad: *Take your stinking ideas out of here!*

F280 *verbs* : **tasting things**

taste 1 [T1] to test (food or drink) by taking a little into the mouth: *I always taste the wine before allowing the waiter to fill my glass. I've never tasted meat but I know I wouldn't like it.* **2** [T1] to tell the taste of (something): *I've got a cold so I can't taste what I'm eating. I can't taste the pepper in this soup; you've not put enough in.* **3** [T1] to eat or drink: *The prisoner had not tasted food in the three days since he'd escaped.* **4** [L7, 9, esp *of*] to have a particular taste: *These oranges taste nice. This meat's been cooked for too long and doesn't taste of anything. This soup tastes of chicken but I thought you said it was vegetable.* **5** [T1] (*fig*) to experience: *Once people have tasted freedom they're unwilling to become slaves again.*

flavour *BrE*, **flavor** *AmE* [T1 (*with*)] to give flavour [⇒ F281] to: *She flavoured the cake with chocolate.*

savour *BrE*, **savor** *AmE* [T1] to enjoy, as by tasting, slowly and purposefully: *He drank the* *wine slowly, savouring every drop. She savoured the pleasures of country life in the summer.* **savour of** [v prep T1] to have a (slight) quality of, as in a taste, smell, etc: *He disliked any law that savoured of more government control.*

F281 nouns : tasting things

taste 1 [C; U] one of the special senses, by which a person or animal knows one food from another by its sweetness, bitterness, saltiness, etc: *I've got a cold so my taste's quite gone.* **2** [C; U] the sensation produced when food or drink is put in the mouth and that makes it different from other foods or drinks, by its saltiness, sweetness, bitterness, etc: *Sugar has a sweet taste. This cake has no/very little taste. This fish has an odd taste; it tastes like cheese.* **3** [C (*of*) usu sing] a small quantity of food or drink: *I had a taste of soup to see if it was nice.* **4** [U] (*fig*) the ability to enjoy and judge beauty, style, art, music, etc; ability to choose and use the best manners, behaviour, fashions, etc: *His speech offended many people present and was in very bad taste. You need good taste before you can enjoy this music. She has excellent taste in dress.* **5** [C; U; (*for, in*)] (*fig*) a personal liking for something: *He has a taste for music. She has expensive tastes in clothes. Popular music is not to everyone's taste.* **6** [C (*of*) usu sing] (*fig*) an experience: *Once you've had a taste of life in our country you won't want to return home. It was the prisoners' first taste of freedom.*

flavour *BrE,* **flavor** *AmE* **1** [C] a taste; quality that only the tongue can experience: *It had a strong flavour of cheese. Choose from six popular flavours!* (*fig*) *It is a story with an unpleasant flavour.* **2** [U] the quality of tasting good or pleasantly strong: *This bread hasn't much flavour/has plenty of flavour.*

savour *BrE,* **savor** *AmE* [S; U] **1** taste or smell: *The meat had cooked too long and lost its savour.* (*fig*) *I could hear a savour of distrust in his voice.* **2** (*fig*) (power to excite) interest: *She used to say that argument adds savour to conversation, but now argument has lost its savour for him.*

F282 adjectives : tasting things [B]
[ALSO ⇒ E110]

tasty [Wa1] *esp infml* having a good taste; enjoyable to eat: *That was a tasty meal.* **-tily** [adv] **-tiness** [U]

savoury *BrE,* **savory** *AmE* [Wa2] **1** pleasant or attractive in taste: *There was a savoury smell coming from the kitchen.* **2** *not fml* morally attractive or good: *That isn't a very savoury book he's reading.* **un-** [*neg*]: *unsavoury ideas*

flavoured *BrE,* **flavored** *AmE* having been flavoured; having a flavour: *He was drinking some flavoured water/water flavoured with fruit juice.*

delicious very tasty; savoury; good to taste or eat: *What a delicious meal!* **-ly** [adv]

bland [Wa1] (of food) not hurting the stomach and without much taste: *The doctor says that the sick woman must have only bland food. This soup is too bland for me.*

insipid *deprec* not having much or any taste: *The food in that hotel is rather insipid.*

flat *deprec* (esp of a drink) having lost its taste: *The beer is a bit flat.*

F283 adjectives : kinds of taste [B]

sweet [Wa1] tasting like or of sugar: *She takes a lot of sugar in her tea; it would be too sweet for me. It tastes very sweet.*

bitter [Wa1] **1** having a peculiar sharp biting taste, like beer or black coffee without sugar: *Beer has a bitter taste. Beer tastes bitter.* **2** (*fig*) (of cold winds, etc) very sharp **3** (*fig*) causing pain or grief: *His failure was a bitter blow.* **-ly** [adv] **-ness** [U]

sour [Wa1] **1** having a peculiar sharp taste like acid: *Lemons have a sour taste. Lemons taste sour.* **2** (*fig*) unfriendly and unhappy: *She really looks sour this morning.*

acid 1 having a sour taste like that of unripe fruit or vinegar [⇒ E49] **2** (*fig*) bad-tempered; angry in speech: *Her acid remarks made him angry.* **-ly** [adv] **acidity** [U] the condition of being acid

salt [Wa5] *tech & fml* tasting like or of salt: *This liquid tastes salt/has a salt taste.*

salty [Wa1] *infml* **1** tasting like or of salt: *It has a salty taste.* **2** *fig* interesting: *He tells very salty stories.*

hot [Wa1] tasting of pepper [⇒ E49]; causing a burning taste in the mouth: *This food is too hot for me; it's very spicy.*

pungent 1 having a strong sharp stinging taste or smell, that may or may not seem unpleasant: *The old man smokes a rather pungent kind of tobacco.* **2** (*fig*) (of speech or writing) producing a sharp, direct effect that awakens interest or expresses an unfavourable opinion: *He made some pungent remarks about my lateness.* **-ly** [adv]

savoury [Wa5] *BrE* (of a dish, of food) having the taste of meat, cheese, vegetables, etc without sugar

G

Thought and communication, language and grammar

Thinking, judging, and remembering

G1 nouns : mind, thought, and reason

[ALSO ⇒ B20]

mind 1 [C; (U)] the part of a person which thinks: *We don't know exactly what goes on in the mind, or the exact relationship of mind and brain.* **2** [C] the ability to think: *She has a good mind for this kind of work.* **3** [C *usu pl*] a very clever person: *Some of the best minds in the country are working there.* **-minded** [*comb form*] **1** having the kind of mind described: *evil-minded; strong-minded* **2** having a mind that is interested in or sees the value of the thing stated: *safety-minded people*

mentality [U; C] a person's way of thinking: *He has just the right mentality for this work. I can't understand mentalities like hers.*

brain 1 [C] the organ in the head with which a person thinks, which controls the actions of animals, etc **2** [C; U] the mind: *She has a good brain; I wish she would use it.* **3** [C] *infml* a person with a good mind: *Some of the best brains in the country are working there.* **-brained** [*comb form*] having a brain or brains as stated: *These are large-brained animals. My silly bird-brained secretary can't spell!*

thought 1 [U] the act of thinking: *He sat there, deep in thought. She seemed lost in thought. The power of thought can change the world.* **2** [C; U] something that is thought; a product of thinking; idea, opinion, etc: *Let me have your thoughts on the subject. You must give up all thought of going there.* **3** [U9] the particular way of thinking of a social class, person, period, country, etc: *Ancient Indian thought interests me.* **4** [U] serious consideration: *Give his offer plenty of thought before you accept it.* **5** [U (*of*)] intention: *I had no thought of annoying you. The enemy's thought was to defeat us quickly.* **6** [C; U: (*for*)] (an example of) attention; regard: *With no thought for her own safety she jumped into the river to save the drowning child. The teacher's only thought was for the pupils.*

reason 1 [U] the power to think, understand, and form opinions: *People are different from animals because they possess reason.* **2** [U] a sound mind that is not mad (*esp in such phrs as* **lose one's reason**) **3** [U] good sense: *There's a lot of reason in his advice. Why don't you listen to reason? He'll do anything within reason to help you.*

rationality [U] *fml* the power of reason **ir-** [*neg*]

cognition [U] *fml & tech* the state of thinking, knowing, and being aware; the act of thinking generally

intellect 1 [U] the power of reasoning, esp on difficult matters: *She is a woman of great intellect.* **2** [C] a person who has great ability of this kind: *They are among the greatest intellects in the country.*

think [S (*about*)] *infml* an act of thinking, esp about a difficulty or question; occasion or need for thinking: *I'll have to have a think about this before I give you an answer. If you think I'm going to lend you a pound you've another think coming!* (=you'll have to think of someone else to ask, because I certainly won't lend you a pound)

G2 verbs : thinking and reasoning

think 1 [I∅ (*about*); T1] to use the power of reason; make judgments; use the mind to form opinions; have (a thought): *Do you still think in English when you're speaking French? If animals can think, what do you think they think about? She sat there, thinking great thoughts.* **2** [T5a, b; X1, 7] to believe; consider: *I think she's wrong, don't you? He thinks himself a great poet. Do you think it will rain?—Yes, I think so! I thought he was going to die.* **3** [T6a, b] (*used after* **cannot** *and* **could not**) to imagine; understand: *I can't think why you did it! You can't think how nasty she is to me!* **4** [T6a, b] (*used in questions*) to believe: *Who do you think murdered the old lady? How do you think the robbers got in?* **5** [T6a] to reason about; bring to mind: *Think how big and varied the world is.* **6** [I∅; T6a, b] to consider carefully: *I'll have to think deeply before I give you an answer. Think before you accept his offer! The criminal was thinking what to do next when the police arrived.* **7** [T5a, b, (*fml*) 3] to have as a half-formed intention or plan: *We thought to return early. We thought we'd go swimming tomorrow. I thought to catch a bus home but it* *was so nice I decided to walk.* **8** [T6a, b] (*used after* **cannot** *and* **could not** *and in infin after* **try**, **want**, etc) to remember: *I can't think what his name is. I'm trying to think what his address is/how to get there.* **9** [T5a; L9] to expect: *Little did he think the police would be waiting for him. We didn't think we'd be this late. I thought as much* (used when one has heard some news, to mean 'that's just what I expected'). **10** [T1] to have as the centre of one's thoughts: *He thinks business all day.* **11** [L9] *not fml* to direct the mind in a particular way: *You must try/learn to think big!* **I don't think** *sl ironical* (used esp when bitterly or nastily attacking someone, to mean) I certainly do not think so: *You're clever, I don't think!* **to think aloud** to speak one's thoughts as they come **think twice** to think very carefully about something: *Think twice before accepting this offer.*

reason 1 [I0] to use one's reason: *She can reason very clearly.* **2** [T5] to argue (that); give an opinion based on reason (that): *I reasoned that since she had not answered my letter she must be angry with me.* **3** [T1 *into* or *out of*] to persuade: *Try to reason him out of that idea/into going away quickly.*

rationalize, -ise [I0; T1] to find reasons for (one's own unreasonable behaviour or opinions): *Stop rationalising! That's not the real reason for what you did.*

G3 *verbs* : **solving things and working things out**

solve [T1] to find a way of doing (something which seemed difficult to do); come to an answer, explanation, or way of dealing with (something): *I can't solve this problem; it's too difficult for me. This is still an unsolved question* (= no one has solved it). **solution** [C; U] an act or way of finding an answer to a difficult problem: *This sheet of practice questions is provided with solutions. It's a difficulty that hardly admits solution.*

think out *also esp AmE* **think through** [v adv T1] to consider in detail with care; reach a decision about (something) after much careful thought: *Thank you for your suggestion, but I must think this whole matter out for myself.*

reason out [v adv T1b] to find an answer to (something) by thinking of all the possible arguments: *Let's reason the matter out.*

work out [v adv] **1** [T1, 6a, b] to solve; get the correct answer to; find by performing all the right actions: *I can't work this sum out. He worked out all the answers correctly. I can't work out where we are on this map.* **2** [I0] to have an answer which can be calculated: *The sum won't work out/doesn't work out (properly).*

G4 *verbs* : **considering and meditating**

consider [T1; I0] to think slowly and fully: *I*

need time to consider this matter. Consider carefully before you decide.

reflect [I0; T5] to consider very carefully: *After reflecting for a while (on the matter), we decided not to go. She reflected that life was full of difficulties.*

speculate [I0; T5] to think (about a matter) in a way that is not serious or without facts that would lead to a firm result: *Let's speculate on the chances of rain/about the date of the next election.*

ponder [T1, 6; I0] to spend time in considering (a fact, difficulty, etc): *When I asked advice, she pondered (the matter) and then told me not to go. He pondered over/about those strange events. The prisoner pondered how to escape.*

deliberate [T1, 6a, b; I0] *often fml* to consider (important and difficult questions) carefully, often in formal meeting(s), with other people: *The judges are deliberating (the question). They deliberated (upon/about) what to do next.*

muse [I0 (*on*)] *often lit & pomp* to think deeply (about something), esp not noticing what is happening at the time: *He sat in a chair, musing (on life).*

meditate 1 [I0 (*on, upon*)] to think seriously or deeply: *He meditated for two days before giving his answer.* **2** [I0] to fix and keep the attention on one matter, having cleared the mind of thoughts, esp for religious reasons or to gain peace of mind [⇒ C333] **3** [T1] to plan and consider carefully: *They are meditating a change in the office arrangements.*

contemplate 1 [T1] to look at (something or someone) quietly and solemnly, usu while thinking: *The art student stood contemplating the famous painting.* **2** [T1, 4, 6; I0] to think deeply about; consider with continued attention: *The doctor contemplated the difficult operation he had to perform. I hope your mother isn't contemplating coming to stay with us! I lay in bed contemplating what to do next. She often sits in church and contemplates.* **3** [T1] to expect: *The police contemplated various kinds of trouble after the football match.*

entertain [T1] *often fml* to be ready and willing to think about (ideas, doubts, suggestions, etc): *He refused to entertain for a moment the thought that his son was a thief. I am prepared to entertain your suggestion.*

G5 *nouns* : **considering and meditating**

consideration *often fml* **1** [U] careful thought; thoughtful attention: *We shall give your request careful consideration. I've sent them my book for (their) consideration. The matter is still being given consideration by the minister of foreign affairs. Taking everything into consideration, we must refuse your request.* **2** [C] a fact to be considered when making a decision: *Time is an important consideration. A number of considerations have led me to refuse your request.*

reflection 1 [U] deep and careful thought: *On reflection, he agreed to do it. I am sorry that I spoke quickly and without reflection.* 2 [C] an example or result of this; a thought: *He told us his reflections on Indian politics.*

speculation [U; C] (an example of) reasoning, not seriously or without all the facts: *There is nothing in what he says; it's pure speculation.* **speculative** [B] 1 of or being speculation 2 based on reason alone and not facts about the world **-ly** [adv]

deliberation *fml* 1 [U] the fact of deliberating, of thinking slowly and deeply. 2 [U; C] careful consideration; thorough examination of a matter: *After much deliberation we found that nothing could be done. Our deliberations were useless.* 3 [U] the quality of being slow, careful, or unhurried in thought, speech, or movement: *The old man rose from his chair with great deliberation and left the room.* **deliberate** [B] 1 carefully considered; thoroughly planned: *The government is taking deliberate action to lower prices.* 2 intentional [⇒ G17]; on purpose: *That shooting was not accidental, but a deliberate attempt to kill him!* 3 (of speech, thought, or movement) slow; careful; unhurried: *The old man rose from his chair in a deliberate way and left the room.* **-ly** [adv] **-ness** [U]

meditation 1 [U] the act, state, or time of meditating 2 [U] the practice of deep, usu religious thought [⇒ C333] 3 [C *often pl*] an example of deep thought on a subject in a piece of speech or writing: *She enjoyed reading his meditations.*

contemplation [U (*of*)] the act of thinking deeply and quietly; deep thought: *Each morning the priest spent an hour in quiet contemplation. She seemed lost in contemplation (of the future).*

G6 *nouns* : **reasoning and logic**

reasoning [U] the use of one's reason: *He shows great power(s) of reasoning. Your reasoning in the matter was quite correct.*

logic [U] 1 the science of reasoning by formal methods: *He wants to study logic.* 2 a way of reasoning: *I don't understand his logic at all.* 3 *infml* reasonable thinking: *There's no logic in spending money on useless things. I don't see the logic in that/of doing that.*

philosophy 1 [U] the study of the nature and the meaning of existence, reality, knowledge, goodness, etc: *She is a student of philosophy and logic.* 2 [C] a special system of thought having this as its base: *He was studying the philosophy of Aristotle.* 3 [C] a rule or set of rules for living one's life, esp based on one's beliefs and experiences: *Eat, drink, and be merry; that's his philosophy.* 4 [U] calmness and quiet courage, esp in spite of difficulty or unhappiness: *He accepted his misfortune with philosophy and never complained.* **philosopher**

[C] a person who studies philosophy or uses it in life

psychology [U] 1 the study or science of the mind and the way it works, and of behaviour as an expression of the mind: *She is a student of psychology.* 2 a branch of this study that deals with a particular group or division of human activity: *His main interest is criminal/educational psychology.* 3 *infml* the mind and patterns of behaviour of a particular person or group; a person's character: *I can't understand that man's psychology.* 4 *infml* cleverness in understanding people: *You must use psychology if you want to get his help.* **psychologist** [C] a person skilled in psychology

G7 *adjectives, etc* : **reasoning and logic** [B]

mental [Wa5] of or concerning the mind: *Mental illness is often harder to cure than bodily illness. His mental abilities are very good.* **-ly** [adv]

intellectual 1 of or concerning the intellect, mind, higher thought, etc: *Philosophy is an intellectual exercise. She isn't interested in intellectual things.* 2 having, showing, or needing great mental ability: *intellectual work* **-ly** [adv] 3 [C] a person who is intellectual: '*Philosophy interests intellectuals, but not ordinary people,*' he said.

rational 1 (of people) having the power of reason: *A rational man wouldn't do things like that.* 2 (of ideas and behaviour) according to reason: *Is there any rational explanation of what happened? That wasn't a very rational thing to do.* **ir-** [*neg*] **-ly** [adv]

logical 1 according to the rules of logic or reason: *The logical result of such behaviour is punishment.* 2 having or showing good reasoning: *Try to be logical about your plans.* **il-** [*neg*] **-ly** [adv Wa4]

abstract 1 concerned with an idea or ideas in the mind rather than actual things, events, etc: *Good people exist, but the idea of 'goodness' is abstract. He is good at abstract thinking.* 2 difficult to understand because concerned with ideas rather than actual things: *These abstract matters make no sense to me; give me concrete* [⇒ N13] *everyday things to deal with.* 3 (of kinds of art) not showing actual pictures but rather shapes, colours, patterns, etc: *He is an abstract painter.* **in the abstract** as an idea: *He considered the matter in the abstract first, before dealing with it in real life.*

conceptual of or concerning a concept or concepts [⇒ G9]; relating to ideas in the mind: *There is a conceptual difference between 'good' and 'true'; they are not the same thing. His conceptual ability is good; he can think well in the abstract.* **-ly** [adv]

philosophical 1 of, concerning, or like philosophy: *That was a good philosophical argument.* 2 calm and thoughtful about things, esp in spite of difficulty or unhappiness: *He was very philosophical about losing the money.* **-ly** [adv Wa4]

psychological of, concerning, or like psychology: *They made a psychological study of his behaviour. Try to be psychological; if you know how he'll behave you'll be able to stop him doing it.* **-ly** [adv Wa4]

cognitive [Wa5] of, about, or needing cognition [⇒ G1] or reasoned thought: *Cognitive psychology tries to study how people think.* **-ly** [adv]

coherent (esp of thought, speech, ideas, etc) being naturally or reasonably connected: *He isn't a very coherent thinker, is he?* **in-** [neg] **-ly** [adv]

G8 *verbs* : **considering, supposing, and conceiving**

〈 [ALSO ⇒ I 43]

consider [T1, 4, 5, 6a, b; X (*to be*) 1, 7] to think or suppose: *I consider him (to be) a fool. She considered (that) it (was) time to go.*

regard [T1; X9, esp *as*] *not fml* to consider: *She regards him as a fool.*

look on *also* **think of** [X9] *not fml* to regard: *She looks on/thinks of him as a fool.*

assume [T1, 5a, b; X (*to be*) 1, 7] to take as a fact or as true without proof: *I assumed that he was there. I assumed him (to be) able to read. He was there, or so I assumed. Assuming it rains tomorrow, what shall we do?*

suppose 1 [T5a, b; V3] to take as likely; consider as true: *If we suppose that man is an animal/suppose man to have descended from animals, then we can learn something useful from animal behaviour. I suppose he's gone home. He must be dead, then.—Yes I suppose so.* **2** [T5a, b; V3 *often pass*; X1, 7, 9] *often fml* to believe: *I suppose that's true. I supposed him to be a workman, but he was in fact a thief. He was commonly supposed (to be) foolish. I supposed him in the office. Where's the house? It's supposed to be here.* **3** [V3 *pass*] **a** to expect, because of duty, responsibility, or other condition: *Everyone is supposed to wear a seat belt in the car.* **b** [neg] to allow: *You're not supposed to smoke in here.*

guess 1 [I0; T1, 5a, b] to consider, judge, or state (something) without being sure: *He didn't know the answer to the question, so he guessed (it). He guessed correctly/wrongly. I guessed (that) he would do it.* **2** [T5a, b *not pass*] *infml, esp AmE* to suppose: *Is he coming?—I guess so. He says he won't do it and I guess he means it.*

reckon 1 [X (*to be*) 1, 7; X9 esp *among, as*] to consider; regard: *He is reckoned (to be) a great actor. She was reckoned (to be) very beautiful. I reckon him as a friend/among my friends.* **2** [T5a, b] *infml* to guess; suppose; calculate (a number) without counting exactly: *I reckon*

(that) he'll come soon. How much do you reckon (that) she cares?

imagine 1 [T5a, b, 6a, b] to suppose; have an idea about, esp mistakenly: *I can't imagine what she means. He imagines that people don't like him.* **2** [T1, 4; V4] to form a picture or idea of in the mind: *I can imagine the scene clearly in my mind.*

fancy 1 [T1, 4] to form a picture of; imagine: *Fancy working every day! Fancy her saying such rude things! Fancy that!* **2** [T5a] to believe without being certain; think: *I fancy I have met you before.*

conceive *also* [v prep] **conceive of** [T1, 4] to think of; imagine: *In ancient times people conceived (of) the world as flat. When did scientists first conceive of space travel? It's difficult to conceive of travelling to the moon. How did he ever conceive such an idea?*

G9 *nouns* : **assuming and conceiving**

[ALSO ⇒ I 45]

assumption [C, C5] something that is taken as a fact or as true without proof: *Our assumption that we would win was wrong.*

supposition 1 [U, U5] the act of supposing or guessing: *We must work on the supposition that he borrowed the money, not that he stole it.* **2** [C] an idea which is the result of this: *My supposition is that he took the money, meaning to pay it back later. Suppositions will not explain the reasons.*

guess [C] an opinion, judgment, etc that one is not sure about: *He made a guess as to how many people were there. His guess was 200. At a guess I'd say 200 people. I'll give you three guesses.*

imagination 1 [U; C] the ability to imagine: *She has great visual imagination; she can see things easily in her mind. What imaginations these children have!* **2** [U] the working of one's mind, in forming a picture or idea, esp mistakenly: *The difficulties are all in your imagination.*

fancy 1 [U] imagination, esp in a free and undirected form: *His mind went where fancy took it.* **2** [U] the power of creating decorative images, esp in poetry **3** [C] an image, opinion, or idea imagined and not based on fact: *I think he will come but it's only a fancy of mine. Is someone knocking at the door or is it a fancy?*

idea [C] **1** a picture in the mind: *I've got a good idea of what he wants.* **2** a plan: *I have an idea for a new book.* **3** an opinion: *He'll have his own ideas about that.* **4** a guess; a feeling of probability: *I have an idea that she likes him better than anyone else.* **5** [*also* C5a] understanding: *You have no idea how worried I was! She doesn't have any idea how to do the job.* **6** a suggestion or sudden thought: *What a good idea! Don't start putting ideas into his head; he has enough work to do at the moment.*

concept [C (*of*), C5] *often tech & fml* an idea, thought, or understanding: *I disagree with your* *concept that all history is the history of the struggle between social classes.*

conception [U, U5, (6b); C: (*of*)] (a) general understanding; idea: *Different people have different conceptions of what he means. Having studied history we can have some/a conception of what life was like in the past. The conception that the earth is flat developed in ancient times. I have no conception (of) why you left home.*

afterthought [C] **1** an idea that comes later: *Have you had any afterthoughts about it?* **2** something added later: *Surprisingly, the best part of the book was an afterthought, added just before it was printed.*

impression [C] **1** the image or idea that a person or thing gives to someone's mind: *She made a good/bad impression on his mother. First impressions of people can be wrong. We wanted to make a big impression on her family.* **2** a feeling about the nature of something: *I had an impression of a large animal but it all happened so quickly that I'm not sure what kind of beast it was. I got the impression that they had just had an argument. My impression was that he was uncertain about the plan.*

notion 1 [C, C5, 6a, b] an idea, belief, or opinion (in someone's mind); conception: *I don't believe in the notion of a perfectly just man. I haven't the faintest notion what you are talking about.* **2** [C, C3, 5] a desire or liking, esp an unreal or sudden one: *His head is full of silly notions. I've a notion to go to a film tonight.*
notional [B] coming from notions, ideas, thoughts, etc and not necessarily from experience **-ly** [adv]

intuition 1 [U] the power to know without reasoning how something happens/will happen; the (feeling of) understanding which results **2** *also infml* **hunch** [C] an example of intuition or the piece of knowledge that results: *I have an intuition/a hunch that he'll come tomorrow.* **intuitive** [B] **1** having intuition: *an intuitive person* **2** understood or got by intuition: *intuitive knowledge* **-ly** [adv]

insight 1 [U] the power of using one's mind to understand something, without help from outside information: *It is insight, not knowledge or experience that helps her to understand other people's difficulties.* **2** [C] an example of this or the understanding which results: *I had an unexpected insight into the child's feelings last night. These new scientific insights are very useful.*

opinion 1 [C] that which a person thinks about something: *His opinions are usually based on facts. In my opinion you're wrong.* **2** [U] that which people in general think about something: *(Public) opinion has changed in favour of that group.* **3** [C] professional judgment or advice: *You should get a second opinion* (=from another doctor) *before you decide to have an operation.* **be of the opinion that . . .** to think or believe that **have a good/bad/high/low opinion of** to think well/badly of **opinionated**

[B] *derog* very sure of the rightness of one's opinion

mind [C *usu sing*] one's opinion; what a person thinks, believes, plans, etc (*esp in the phrs* **change one's mind, be in two minds, make up one's mind, be of the same mind**): *I've changed my mind on what do. She's in two minds on what to do/She can't make up her mind on what to do* (= She can't decide what to do). *You and I are just not of the same mind in this matter* (= We do not agree).

regard [U;S] *often fml* a good opinion (of someone or something): *I hold his ideas in high/low regard. She has a special regard for him.*

point of view [C] a way of considering or judging a thing, person, event, etc: *We need someone with a fresh point of view to suggest changes. You can study this matter from several points of view. From my point of view no changes should be made.*

viewpoint *also* **standpoint** [C] *more emph* point of view: *People all look at things from different viewpoints. From his standpoint this seems (to be) a good idea.*

hypothesis [C] an idea which is thought likely to explain the facts about something: *His new hypothesis gives a possible reason for the changes in the weather.* **hypothetical** [B] of, concerning, or like a hypothesis: *Your suggestions are purely hypothetical; there is no way of showing that they are true or false.* **-ly** [adv Wa4]

theory 1 [C; S 5] a statement or group of statements established by reasoned argument based on known facts, intended to explain a particular fact or event; explanation which has not yet been fully proved but which appears to be reasonable: *According to Darwin's theories man and apes are descended from the same ancient animal. Do you agree with the wave theory of light?* **2** [U] the part of a science or art that deals with general principles and methods as opposed to practice; rules or principles for the study of a subject: *The government plans seem good in theory but I doubt if they'll work in practice. He was studying Maoist political theory.* **3** [C] an opinion based on limited information or knowledge: *He has a theory about the girl's murder but I think he's wrong.* **theoretical** [Wa2;B] of, concerning, or like a theory: *This work is still theoretical; we haven't tested anything yet.* **-ly** [adv Wa4] *Theoretically* (= in theory) *you're right, but things may not work like that in fact.*

G10 *verbs* : **deducing and concluding** [T1]

deduce 1 *precise* to decide from general principles in relation to a particular thing, fact or event: *From the fact that Socrates is a man and the principle that all men are mortal* (= will die), *we can deduce that Socrates was mortal.*

2 *loose* to infer: *What do you deduce from what she said?*

induce to decide (general principles) from known facts

infer to draw the meaning (from something): *I infer from your letter that you don't want to see us.*

conclude to decide after thinking, deducing, inducing, inferring, etc: *The judge concluded that the prisoner was guilty.*

draw to make or get by reasoning: *He drew a useful comparison between the two languages. What conclusion can you draw from all this information?*

gather to understand (from something said or done): *I gather she's ill and that's why she hasn't come. I didn't gather much from the confused story she told me. I gather that you mean you don't like it.*

G11 *nouns* : **deducing and concluding**

deduction 1 [U; C] the act or action of deducing: *Deduction is important in mathematics.* **2** [C] that which is deduced: *All her deductions were correct. The deduction that he was guilty worried them.*

induction 1 [U] inducing or being induced **2** [C] a way of reasoning, using known facts to produce general laws

inference 1 [U] the act of inferring: *I know this by inference, not from anything he actually said.* **2** [C] the meaning which one draws from something done, said: *He never arrives on time and my inference is that he feels the meetings are useless.*

conclusion [C] a judgment or decision based on deduction, induction, inference, etc: *Do you think the judge can arrive at a satisfactory conclusion with such limited information? What conclusions did you come to/draw/reach?*

G12 *verbs* : **judging, analysing, and criticizing**

[ALSO ⇒ K111]

judge 1 [T1, 5, 6b; X (*to be*) 1, 7; I∅] to form or give an opinion about (someone or something): *A man should be judged by what he does, not what he says. She can judge people very well. I judge it (to be) the bigger of the two. How can I judge? I don't know the facts.* **2** [C] one who judges: *Is he a good judge of (people's) character?* [⇒ C202, K194]

assess [T1] to judge the quality or worth of: *He can quickly assess a person's character.* **assessor** [C] one who assesses

weigh up [v adv T1, 6a] *not fml* to (try to) understand; form an opinion about: *I can't weigh him up. She tried to weigh up what he meant. He weighed up all possibilities and chose the simplest solution.*

evaluate [T1] *fml* to judge or calculate the value or amount of (something): *I can't evaluate his ability without more information.*

appraise [T1] *oftentech* to judge the worth, quality or condition of; work out the value of: *They all appraised the house carefully before offering to buy it.*

review [T1] to consider and judge; to go over again in the mind (events or a situation): *He reviewed the events of the past week and decided what to do next.*

see [X9] *infml* to judge; consider: *I see him as rather a foolish man.*

call [X1, 7] *infml* to consider: *I call him a fool. I don't call Russian a hard language. That's what I call dishonest.*

interpret [T1; X1 *as*] to understand the likely meaning of (something): *She interpreted his silence as anger. I'm not sure how to interpret their behaviour.* **2** [T 1] to show the (possible) meaning of (something), esp in art, theatre, etc: *He interprets Shakespeare in a very modern way.*

analyse *also* **analyze** *AmE* [T1] to examine carefully in order to find out about: *We must analyse our present system before we try to improve it.*

criticize, ise [T1; (I∅)] **1** to make judgments about the good and bad points of (someone or something): *Would you like to read and criticize my new book? In his latest article our reporter criticizes the way in which the war is being handled.* **2** to find fault with (someone or something); judge severely: *Although he praised my work in general the minister criticized my methods in this particular matter. Before you start criticizing you should make sure you have no faults yourself.* **critic** [C] **1** a person who is good at forming and expressing judgments **2** a person who (regularly) finds fault with someone or something: *She is one of his strongest critics. She is her own severest critic.*

arbitrate 1 [T1; I∅ (*between*)] to judge (an argument), esp at the request of both sides: *We must get someone to arbitrate (this difficulty). Someone must arbitrate between them.* **2** [T1; I∅] to settle (an argument, etc) by together choosing a person to make a decision: *I think we should arbitrate. We should arbitrate industrial disagreements.* **arbitrator** [C] a person chosen by both sides of an argument to examine the facts and make a decision to settle the argument **arbiter** [C] a person or group that has complete control or great influence over actions, decisions, etc: *He is the arbiter here on how people dress.*

G13 *nouns* : **judging, analysing, and criticizing**

judg(e)ment 1 [C] an opinion: *I want you to form a judgment of his ability. In my judgment, he can do the job.* **2** [U] the ability to judge correctly: *He has good/weak judgment. She* *makes too many errors* (= mistakes) *of judgment.*

assessment 1 [U] the act of assessing, forming opinions **2** [C] a judgment or opinion: *What is your assessment of this state of affairs?*

evaluation 1 [U] the act of evaluating **2** [C] an example or result of this; a careful judgment: *What is your latest evaluation of the situation in that country?*

appraisal 1 [U] the act of working out the value, quality, or condition of something **2** [C] a statement of value, quality, or condition

review [C] an act of reviewing: *After a careful review of what had happened, he decided to change his plans.*

interpretation 1 [U] the act of interpreting **2** [C] a meaning understood from what happens in a play, etc; a meaning of something that a performer shows in music, etc **interpretative** [Wa5;B] of or concerning interpretation.

analysis 1 [U] the act of analysing something; careful study or examination: *This matter needs careful analysis.* **2** [C] an examination of something together with thoughts and judgments about it: *Write an analysis of the murderer's character.* **analyst** [C] a person who makes an analysis, esp of chemical materials: *He is a chemical analyst.* **analytical** also more tech **analytic** [B] of, concerning, or like analysis or an analysis: *He has a fine analytical mind. An analytic study of the matter could help us a lot.* **-(al)ly** [adv Wn4]

criticism 1 [U] the act of forming and expressing judgments about the good or bad qualities of anything, esp artistic work **2** [U] unfavourable judgment; disapproval; the act of finding fault: *The military government intends to stop unfavourable criticism by controlling newspapers and broadcasting. If you don't like criticism, you won't like politics.* **3** [C] an article, report, etc giving opinions about the good or bad qualities of something: *He has written several criticisms of that play.* **4** [C] an unfavourable opinion or remark: *Your criticism seems to have offended him. That was an unfair criticism.* **critical** [Wa2;B] **1** of, concerning, or like criticism: *He wrote a critical study of the poem. He was critical, but helpful at the same time.* **un-** [neg] **2** making unfavourable remarks: *Try not to be so critical of people/about what she wears.* **-ly** [adv Wa4]

critique 1 [U] the art or practice of criticism **2** [C] an article or book criticizing artistic or other work or a person: *Marx's critique of Hegel is well known.*

arbitration [U] the settlement of an argument by the decision of a person or group chosen by both sides: *The government wanted all industrial arguments settled by arbitration.* **go to arbitration 1** (of a business, group of workers, etc) to give or choose to give an argument to a person chosen by both sides: *The two firms were willing to go to arbitration.* **2** (of an argument) to be given to a person chosen by both

sides: *Since no agreement could be reached the matter went to arbitration.*

G14 *verbs & nouns* : **believing and accepting**

believe 1 [T1, 6a] to consider to be true or honest: *I believe you/what you say. Believe me, it really happened!* **2** [T5a, b; V3; X1, 7] to hold as an opinion; suppose: *I believe he has come. He has come, I believe. Has he come?— I believe so. I believe he did it.* (old use & lit) *I believe him to have done it. I believe him (to be) honest.*

belief 1 [U] the activity of believing: *Belief in God is important to many people.* **2** [C] something which is believed: *A belief in God is important to many people. He has many strange beliefs.*

credit [T1, 5, 6a; V4] *emph* to believe: *Do you really credit the government's statement? I can hardly credit that a man in his position would do such a foolish thing! I can't credit her doing such a stupid thing.* **credence** [U] *often fml* acceptance as true; belief: *The newspapers are giving no credence to the government's latest statements.* **credo** [C] a statement of beliefs and principles. [⇒ C321 CREED]

credit with [v prep D1; V4b] to believe (someone or something) to have: *People credit the holy man's bones with great power. Please credit me with some sense.*

accept [Wv5;T1] to believe: *I can't accept what he says.* **-ance** [U]

attribute to 1 [v prep D1, 6a; V4] to believe to be the result of: *He attributes his success to hard work/to how hard he has always worked/to working hard.* **2** [D1 *usu pass*] to consider (something) to have been written by (someone): *This tune is usually attributed to Bach.* **attribution** [C; U] the act of attributing: *The attribution of the play to that poet was shown to be wrong.*

ascribe to [v prep D1 *often pass*] *esp fml* to attribute to: *He ascribes his success to hard work. No one is sure who wrote the play, but it is usually ascribed to her.* **ascription** [C; U] the act of ascribing: *The ascription of their failure to lack of money is not honest.*

G15 *adjectives* : **believing** [B]

believable that can be believed: *Is what he says believable or not?* **un-** [neg] **-bly** [adv Wa3]

credible deserving or worthy of belief or trust: *This is a credible news report. After this latest affair he hardly seems credible as a politician.* **-bly** [adv Wa3] **-bility** [U]

credulous too willing to believe, esp without certain proof: *These people are pretty credulous; they'll believe almost anything you tell them.* **in-** [neg] **-ly** [adv] **-ness** [U] **credulity** [U] the state of being credulous **in-** [neg]

gullible easily tricked, esp into a false belief: *He is very gullible; he gave money to a strange man who said he lost £5 in the street.* **-bly** [adv Wa3] **-bility** [U]

farfetched *not fml* difficult to 'believe: *What a farfetched story! His story was pretty farfetched; nobody believed it.*

G16 *verbs* : **expecting, anticipating, and planning**

expect 1 [T3, 5a, b] to think (that something will happen): *I expect (that) he'll pass the examination. He expects to fail the examination. Will she come soon?— I expect so.* **2** [T1] to think that (someone or something esp good) will come (*used often in the continuous tense*): *I'm expecting a letter. I expect him home after 6.* **3** [T1] to believe, hope, and think that one will receive (something considered as one's right): *He expects obedience from his children.* **4** [V3] to believe, hope, and think that (someone will do something): *The officer expected his men to fight well in the coming battle.* **5** [Wv6;T5a,b] *infml* to suppose; think (that something is true): *Who broke that cup?—Oh, I expect it was the cat. Is he coming?—I expect so.* **to be expected** usual; that one feels sure will happen: *She was 90 years old, so her death was only to be expected.* **expectant** [B] waiting or expecting: *There was an expectant silence as everyone waited for his news.* **-ly** [adv]: *They waited expectantly.*

anticipate 1 [T1, 4] *often fml* to expect: *We are not anticipating trouble when the factory opens again. We anticipate (meeting) a lot of opposition to our new plan.* **2** [T1] to do something before (someone else): *We anticipated our competitors by getting our book in the shops first.* **3** [T1, 5, 6a] to see (what will happen) and act as necessary, often to stop someone else doing something: *We anticipated that the enemy would try to cross the river and so seized the bridge. We anticipated where they would cross.* **4** [T1] to prevent (someone) doing something by acting first: *They have anticipated us and seized the bridge.* **5** [T1] to provide for the possibility of (something) happening: *We anticipated their visit by buying plenty of food.* **6** [T1] to make use of, deal with, or consider before the right or proper time: *Do not anticipate your earnings by spending a lot of money.* **7** [T1, 5, 6a; I0] to speak or write (something) before the proper time: *If I told you what is going to happen in the story, I would be anticipating. I won't anticipate the story.*

look forward to [v adv prep T1, 4] to expect to feel pleasure in (something about to happen): *I'm looking forward to my dinner. I'm not looking forward to seeing her again.*

bargain for *also esp AmE* **bargain on** [v prep T1; V3, 4] *not fml* to take into account; consider: *I had not bargained for such heavy rain,*

and I got very wet without a coat. I hadn't bargained for John coming/to come, and his arrival surprised me.

intend 1 [T3, 5c; V3] to have it in mind to do: *I've made a mistake, though I didn't intend to. Yes, we intend to go. (fml) We intend that they should go.* **2** [X9. *esp for, as; V3 usu pass*] to be kept, meant, etc, for: *That chair was intended for you, but she took it. It was intended as a joke. It was intended to be cooked slowly.*

mean [T3, 5c; V3; X9] *not fml* to intend: *I've made a mistake, though I didn't mean to. Yes we mean to go. That chair was really meant for you, not her. It was meant to be cooked slowly.*

plan [T1 (*out*), 3; I0/(*for, on, ahead*)] to prepare in advance (for something); to prepare (something); for use etc at a later time: *We've been planning this visit for months. It's all planned (out). She never plans ahead, she just does things suddenly. I'd planned on doing some work this afternoon.* **planner** [C] a person who plans (something)

G17 *nouns* : **expecting, anticipating, and planning**

expectation 1 [U] *often fml & pomp* the act of expecting: *Will he pass the exam?—That's my expectation, yes. She lives in expectation of his letter. It's our expectation that you will do well.* **2** [C] an example of this: *I hope he will live up to (= be equal to) her expectation (of him).*

expectancy [U] the state of expecting: *There was a look of expectancy on their faces when he came in. She waited in expectancy.*

anticipation [U] the act of anticipating: *We waited at the station in anticipation of her arrival. Our anticipation of our competitors meant greater sales for our book.*

plan [C] **1** a (carefully considered way of preparing (something or for something) in advance: *The police have a plan to catch the thief. If you have no plans for tomorrow night perhaps you'd like to come out with me?* **2** any arrangement of parts in a group or system: *They had a seating plan for their guests at dinner. This shop sells plans of the streets of the city. Everything went according to plan (= happened as planned).*

intention [U;C] (an act or result of) intending, planning, hoping, expecting, etc to do something: *It wasn't my intention to make you angry. I had no intention of doing that. She has very good intentions but her plans don't always work.* **-al** [B] intended **-ally** [adv] **un-** [*neg*]

G18 *nouns* : **reasons and motives**

[ALSO ⇒ G 105, N 152]

reason 1 [C (*for*), C3, 5, 6a *why*; U3] the cause of an event; the explanation or excuse for an action: *The reason for the flood was all that heavy rain. I have many reasons to fear him. The reason that/the reason why he died was lack* of medical care. There is/We have reason to believe that he was murdered. **2** [C (for), C3, 5] what makes one decide on an action; the cause of an intention: What is your reason for wanting to enter the country? **by reason of** fml because of: He escaped punishment by reason of his youth. **with reason** (of something said or believed) rightly: He thinks, with reason, that I don't like him.

USAGE Some people think that The reason for my absence was because I was ill is bad English. It may be better to say: The reason for my absence was that I was ill.

motive [C] a cause of, or reason for, an action; that which urges a person to act in a certain way: In case of murder, the police question the people who might have a motive. The love of money is the only motive that drives him to work so hard. We understood the motive behind his actions. What were his real motives for giving the money to the hospital? **motivate** [Wv5;T1] to cause a person to do something by giving him or her a motive for doing it: What motivates him to work so hard?—He's motivated by the need for more money. **motivation 1** [U] the act of motivating **2** [C] an example of this **motivational** [B] of, concerning, or for the purpose of motivating **-ly** [adv]

grounds [P] a reason (esp in the phr **on (the) grounds**): We have good grounds for thinking that he stole the money. What were the grounds for his leaving? He left on grounds of ill-health/on the grounds that he was ill.

basis [C (of, for)] the main or most important part, idea, fact, motive, etc: What is the basis of his argument? On what basis do you suggest spending more money? There is no basis for his opinion that the earth is flat.

excuse [C; U: (for)] the reason, whether true or untrue, given when asking to be forgiven for wrong behaviour: Have you any excuse to offer for coming so late? Stop making excuses! That's no excuse. Don't be late again without (good) excuse.

cause 1 [U] reason: Don't complain without cause. There's no cause for you to leave; I still love you. There is more cause for you to stay than to go. Is there sufficient cause for you to sell this house? **2** [C] a reason: What were the causes of the First World War?

incentive 1 [U; C: (to)] the reason which urges greater activity: His interest gave me (an) incentive and I worked twice as hard. War gives (an) incentive to trade. **2** [U usu neg] the urge and ability to get things done: He's got no incentive/little incentive.

G19 verbs : remembering and reminding

remember 1 [T1 (as), 4, 5, 6; V3] to keep in memory; call back into the mind: I shall always remember that terrible day. Certainly I posted your letter; I remember posting it. I can't

remember where she lives/what happened then. Do you remember me/my asking you that same question? I remember him, as (= when he was) a child, playing the piano beautifully. I remember that she wore a green hat. **2** [I∅; T3] to take care not to forget: Don't forget to post my letter; please remember!—Yes, (I promise) I'll remember to post your letter. **3** [T1] to give a present to: Please, remember the taxi-driver! She always remembers me at Christmas. **remember someone to** infml to send someone's greetings to (someone one knows but does not actually love): Please remember me to your mother. He asked to be remembered to you.

USAGE Note the difference between remember posting the letter (**1**) and remember to post the letter (**2**). In the first case the letter is already posted, while in the second case it has not been posted yet.

recall [T1, 4, 5, 6a, b] to remember: I can't recall his face/seeing him/that he came/where he lives/how to do it.

recollect [Wv6;T1, 4, 6a, b] to remember (something past): Do you recollect her name/meeting her/where she lives/how to get there? As far as I (can) recollect, her name is Juliet.

bring back [v adv T1] not fml to cause to return to the memory: The Beatles singing 'Yesterday' certainly brings that year back/brings back memories (for me).

bring to mind also **call to mind** esp emph to remember: I remember the name but I just can't bring/call him to mind.

remind [T1; D5; V3] **1** to tell (someone) to remember (a fact, or to do something): I must write to mother; will you remind me? Remind me to write to mother. She reminded me that I hadn't written to mother. 'You haven't written to mother,' she reminded me. **2** (of a thing or event) to make (someone) remember (a fact, or to do something): The sight of the clock reminded me that I was late/reminded me to leave at once. What a big elephant! That reminds me; have you been to India again? **remind of** [v prep D1] to make (someone) remember (someone or something) by seeming the same: This hotel reminds me of the one we stayed in last year.

G20 verbs : not remembering

forget 1 [T1, 3, 4, 5a, 6a, b; I∅] to fail to remember or keep in the memory: I'm sorry; I've forgotten your name. Don't forget to bring the cases. I'll never forget finding that rare old coin in my garden. I'm sorry; I was forgetting (that) you don't like beans. I forget who it was that said it. I forget where to go. What's her name?—I forget. **2** [T1] to fail to remember to bring, buy, etc (something): Don't forget the cases. I've got the meat and potatoes, but I'm afraid I forgot the bread. **3** [T1; I∅] to stop thinking about; put out of one's mind: They *agreed to forget their disagreements and be friends again. I'm sorry I broke your teapot.—Forget it. You should forgive and forget.* **4** [T1] to fail to give attention to; treat with inattention: *He forgot his old friends when he became rich. 'Don't forget me,' the little boy said, as his mother was giving out jelly to the other children.* **forget oneself 1** to lose one's temper or self control, or act in a way that makes one look silly: *The little girl annoyed him so much that he forgot himself and hit her. He so far forgot himself as to leave the table before everyone had finished eating.* **2** to act in an unselfish way **not forgetting** also including; and also: *This song has been requested for Bill, Maggie, and little Teresa, not forgetting Fido the dog.*

overlook [T1] to fail to see, notice, or remember: *I'm afraid I overlooked your name; I'll add it to the list immediately.*

leave out [v adv T1 (*of*)] not to put in; to forget to put in: *He left out several words by mistake. Don't leave me out of the group going to the dance!*

miss [T1 (*out*)] *infml & genl* to leave out: *Do these ones and miss those others; we'll do them another time. Don't miss me out; I want to come too!*

omit *esp fml* **1** [T1] to leave out: *The teacher omitted the exercises on page 21 of the book.* **2** [T3] *BrE* not to do: *He omitted to tell us when to go.* **omission 1** [U] the act of omitting **2** [C] an example or result of this; something omitted: *There are several important omissions in his letter to us.*

G21 *nouns* : **memory and reminders**

memory 1 [C; U] an ability to remember events and experience: *Memory is a quality which is not highly developed in most animals.* **2** [C (*of*)] an example of remembering: *One of my earliest memories is of this house. I have a clear memory of his face.* **3** [(*the*) S9] the time during which things happened which can be remembered: *There have been two wars within the memory of my grandfather.* **4** [C] the opinion held of someone after his death: *We must praise his memory.* **commit something to memory** to learn and remember on purpose **in memory of** as a way of remembering or being reminded of: *in memory of his death* **within living memory** in the time which can be remembered by people now alive **to the best of my memory/my remembrance/my recollection** as well as I can remember; if I remember right: *To the best of my memory, she came on Thursday.*

remembrance 1 [C; U: (*of*)] *often fml* (a) memory; the state or act of remembering: *Christians eat bread and drink wine in remembrance of Jesus. I have many happy remembrances of our days together.* **2** [C (*of*)] something kept or given to remind one: *He gave me his photograph as a remembrance (of him).*

mind [U] *not usu fml* memory: *Please try to keep in mind what he wants. Out of sight, out of mind* (proverb: = If you can no longer see something, you forget it).

recall [U] the power to remember something learned or experienced: *He has total recall; he never forgets anything.*

recollection 1 [U] the act or power of recollecting or remembering anything: *I find recollection difficult; it all happened a long time ago.* **2** [C] an example of this: *His recollections of his childhood are very interesting.* **to the best of my recollection** if I remember right: *To the best of my recollection that happened in 1959.*

reminder [C] something which causes one to remember something else; an action of causing someone to remember: *I saw his book; it was a reminder that I must phone him today. Please give me a reminder this afternoon to phone him. He hasn't paid his bill; send him a reminder.*

G22 *adjectives* : **forgetful**

forgetful [B] (of persons) likely to forget: *He's getting old and a bit forgetful.*

oblivious [F (*of*)] (of persons) not remembering, noticing, seeing, hearing, etc: *He worked on, completely oblivious of everything/of the passage of time.*

G23 *nouns* : **forgetfulness** [U]

forgetfulness the state of forgetting or being likely to forget: *His forgetfulness is well known; better tell him again.*

oblivion 1 the state of having forgotten; unconsciousness: *He was tired and sank quickly into oblivion.* **2** the state of being forgotten: *Oblivion is the fate of most writers.*

G24 *nouns* : **fame and distinction**

fame [U] the condition of being well-known to many people, esp for a particular reason: *His fame as a film actor made his family very proud of him. All she thinks about is fame and money.*

renown [U] *fml & lit* fame: *He is a scientist of great renown.*

distinction [U] fame, esp for being better than most others at a particular thing: *He served with distinction in the army. She is a person of considerable scientific distinction.*

celebrity 1 [U] the state of being famous; fame: *Many famous people find that celebrity is sometimes inconvenient.* **2** [C] a famous person: *Who's the most well-known celebrity in London?*

G25 *adjectives, etc* : **well-known, famous, and noteworthy** [B]

well-known [Wa2;(*for*)] known to many people: *She is well-known for her work with children. He is a well-known writer.*

famous [(*for*)] *usu apprec* well-known: *He is famous for his work with animals. She is a famous singer.* **famously** [adv] very well: *How did you enjoy your visit to Italy?—Very much; I got on famously there.* **infamous** [B] *deprec* famous for bad reasons: *What an infamous man Hitler was!* **-ly** [adv]

celebrated *often pomp* well-known; famous: *Venice is celebrated for its beautiful buildings. Meet the celebrated author tonight!*

distinguished (appearing) important, or famous for doing something very well: *Her father is a distinguished doctor. Who is that man, the one who looks so distinguished?*

outstanding 1 very important, famous, etc: *He is one of the most outstanding artists of our time.* **2** very good, clever, etc: *This is outstanding work; she is an outstanding student.* **3** easily seen, remembered, etc: *That meeting was an outstanding moment in the history of our country.* **-ly** [adv]

noted (of a person) famous: *He is one of our most noted scientists.*

notable (of a happening) worth noticing, remembering, seeing, etc: *That was a notable meeting.* **-bly** [adv Wa3]

noteworthy worth noticing: *His book on animals is really noteworthy; you should read it.*

recognized, -ised famous as an important person or thing, esp in a particular way: *He is a recognised authority on that subject.*

Knowing and learning

G30 *verbs* : **knowing and being conscious**

know [Wv6] **1** [T1, 5a, (b); I∅] to have in the mind: *I know (that) that is true. I knew all about it. You can be sure he knows (it) by now. This has been known for a long time.* **2** [T6] to have learnt: *I know how to swim/where to go/how that should be done.* **3** [V3] to accept the fact that (someone or something is): *I know him to be a fool.* **4** [V3, *BrE* 2] to have seen, heard, etc: *I've known him to run/(BrE) run faster than that.* **5** [T1] to have experienced: *He has known both grief and happiness.* **6** [T1] to have met and spoken to (someone) several times: *I've known him for years.* **7** [T1] to be able to recognize: *He knows good wine when he tastes it.* **8** [I∅] to agree: *He's very ill.—Yes, I know.* **there's no knowing** it's not possible to know: *There's no knowing what he will do next.*

be aware [T1 *of*; T5] *often fml & pomp* to know: *Are you aware of the difficulty/that there is a difficulty?*

be conscious of [T1] *often fml & pomp* to know well: *He is conscious of what he must do. Are you conscious of all the trouble you are causing us?*

recognize, -ise 1 [T1] to remember the name, nature, etc of (someone or something), esp when seeing, hearing, etc: *Do you recognize him?—Yes; I do. Can you recognize her from this picture? He recognized his old friend without difficulty, although they hadn't met for years. I could hardly recognize her; she has changed so much!* **2** [T1, 5] to accept (something) as true: *You must surely recognize the danger in/of what you are doing? He now recognizes that he was wrong.* **3** [T1 *often pass*] to accept (someone or something) officially: *His work has at last been recognized by his fellow scientists* (=other scientists). *Our government doesn't recognize the government of that country.*

G31 *verbs* : **understanding and realizing**

understand 1 [T1; I∅] to know or get the meaning of: *Do you understand (this word)? 'I can't understand modern literature', he said.* **2** [T1, 6a] to know or feel closely the nature of (a person, feelings, etc): *I can't understand him when he behaves so badly. I understand how you feel. Who can understand the way another person's mind works? Nobody understands me.* **3** [T5a, b] *often fml or polite* to learn; have found out (a fact): *I understand you're coming to work for us. I'm coming to work for you.—So I understood. I understood she was married, but I find I was misinformed* (=they gave me wrong information). **4** [T1 (*by*), 5a; V3: *often pass*] to take or judge (as the meaning): *What do you understand by the order to move on; where do they want us to go? By 'children' it's understood (that) they mean 14-year-olds. 'Children' is understood to mean 14-year-olds. We understood them to mean that they would wait for us.* **5** [T1 *often pass*] to add (esp a word) in the mind for completion: *When I say 'come and help', the object 'me' is supposed to be understood.* **make oneself understood** to make one's meaning clear to others, esp in speech **understand one another/each other** to know what is wished, esp to agree: *Now we understand one another, we can make the right changes.* **give someone to understand** *fml* to cause someone to judge or believe: *He gave me to understand that he would be there by 3; can I have misunderstood?*

comprehend [T1, I∅] *usu fml* to understand: *The child read the story but did not (fully) comprehend its meaning. The ability to comprehend written information is very important in the modern world. He reads but he doesn't comprehend.*

realize, -ise [T1, 5a, 6a] to understand and believe or accept (a fact): *He didn't realize his* *mistake. Do you realize it's Saturday? We realize what a good book this is!*

perceive [T1, 5, 6a, b] *esp tech & fml* to become aware of (something) through any of the senses; see, understand, etc: *He was only able to perceive light and colour; he could not see properly. Do you perceive what I mean?*

grasp [T1, 6a, b] *esp emot & emph* to understand: *I didn't quite grasp what she meant. Did you grasp the full meaning of what he said?*

appreciate [T1] **1** to understand fully: *I don't think you appreciate the dangers of this job. Do you appreciate .the difference between good wine and excellent wine?* **2** to understand the high worth of: *His abilities were not appreciated in that school.* **3** to understand and enjoy the good qualities of: *A sensitive mouth is necessary to appreciate good wine.*

fathom [T1, 6a, b] to understand (something that is specially difficult, mysterious, etc): *Can you fathom his plan? I just can't fathom her/ what she wants to do.*

follow [T1; I0] to understand (something, esp someone's spoken or written ideas) as one listens or reads: *Can you follow him/his line of thought? Sorry, I just can't follow/I'm just not following.*

see [T1, 6a, b; I0] *infml* to understand: *Do you see what I mean?—Yes, I see. He saw the point of what they were doing. I'm afraid I just can't see why.*

get [T1, 6a, b] *infml & genl* to understand: *Do you get what I mean?—Yes, I get it. He didn't get the point of what they were doing. I'm afraid I just don't get it* (= understand).

dawn on [v prep T1] to become clear to (someone): *It dawned on me at last that he had been telling me lies.*

G32 *verbs* : **learning**

learn 1 [I0; T1, 3, 6b] to gain knowledge (of) or skill (in): *The child is learning quickly. I'm trying to learn French. She is learning to be a dancer. He is learning how to play the drums.* **2** [T1] to fix in the memory; memorize: *You should learn this list of words by tomorrow.* **3** [T1, 5a, b, 6a, b; I0 (*of* or *about*)] to become informed (of): *Haven't you learnt the truth? His mother learnt in the newspapers of her son's success.* **learn one's lesson** to suffer so much from doing something that one will not do it again

acquire [T1] to learn, esp through a plan, over a long time, etc: *She acquired her (knowledge of) French while living in Paris.*

get [T1] *infml & genl* to learn, acquire: *Where did she get that very good knowledge of French?*

gain [T1] *often fml* to learn, acquire (esp something worth knowing): *When she was in France she gained an excellent knowledge of French. He gained all this information from books, not from direct experience.*

pick up [v adv T1] *infml* to learn, usu without hard work: *She picks up foreign languages easily. He picked up a knowledge of these things when he was in the East.*

memorize, -ise [T1, 6a, b] to learn and remember, on purpose: *He memorized the poem/what to do.*

study 1 [T1; I0] to look at, read, or listen to (something) in order to learn: *He is busy studying French. She studied hard for her examinations.* **2** [T1] to examine carefully: *She studied the book/his face with interest. This organization studies social matters.*

G33 *verbs* : **teaching and training**

[ALSO ⇒ I 130, ETC]

teach [D1 (*to*), 5, 6a, b; T1, 4; V3, 4; I0] to give knowledge or skill of, or training or lessons in (a particular subject, how to do something, etc) to (someone): *I teach boys history and my wife teaches girls French. You can't teach an old dog new tricks. John teaches politics to university students. I would rather teach older than younger children. The priest taught the people that they should love their neighbours as themselves. The teacher taught the children why they should love their country. The children should be taught how to read and write. He wants to be taught (to play) cricket. The Bible teaches that we should all love each other. My husband teaches at a local school/(AmE) teaches school locally.*

instruct 1 [T1, 5b; D5b, 6a, b] to give knowledge or information to: *They instructed me in the best way of doing the job. I'll instruct him whether (he needs) to come today or tomorrow.* **2** [V3] to give orders to: *I instructed him to come to work earlier.* **3** [D5, 5b; V3; T1] *law* to advise

educate [T1] to teach, esp to train in the mind or character generally: *She educated her younger daughter at home. He was educated at the local school.*

train 1 [T1; V3; D6 *esp how*] to give teaching or practice, esp in an art, profession, or skill; instruct: *He was trained for the priesthood at a college in Rome. At school they should train young children (how) to be good citizens.* **2** [I0; T3] to be taught or given practice, esp in an art, profession, or skill: *He trained to be a doctor but decided to become a priest instead.* **3** [I0; T1 (*for*)] to make ready for a test of skill: *Every morning he spends two hours training for the race. Who trains Manchester City football team?*

coach 1 [T1] to train or teach (a person or a group of people), esp for a special purpose, examination, sport, etc; to give instruction or advice to (a person or a group of people): *He coached the football team well. She coaches people for English examination. She coaches people in English.* **2** [I0] to act or be employed in coaching people: *He coaches at our school.*

tutor 1 [T1; (IØ) (*in*)] to act as a private teacher to: *He tutored the boy in French.* **2** [T1] to train in obedience: *You really must tutor that horse. Try to tutor your feelings and you won't lose your temper so easily.*

discipline [T1] **1** to train and control firmly: *You must learn to discipline yourself.* **2** to punish in order to train: *She never disciplines her children and they are uncontrollable.* **disciplinary** [Wa5;B] *fml* for the purpose of disciplining: *The teacher took no disciplinary action against the badly-behaved boys and so they behaved even worse.* **disciplinarian** [C] a person who believes in disciplining children, soldiers, etc firmly: *That teacher is a real disciplinarian.*

school [T1 (*in*)] *esp lit* to teach, train, or discipline (someone): *They schooled him well. She schooled him in crime. He was schooled by life itself.*

civilize, ise [Wv5;T1] to teach certain kinds of arts, sciences, government, etc to (people who do not have such things): *The Romans helped to civilize many European peoples long ago.*

G34 *nouns* : **knowing and realizing**

knowledge [U] **1** understanding; the condition of knowing: *He has little knowledge of the facts.* **2** learning; that which is known: *Knowledge is power. She hasn't much/any knowledge of French.* **3** familiarity with; information about: *My knowledge of Mr Smith is not great. He has a good knowledge of London/Latin.* **bring to (someone's) knowledge** to cause (someone) to know: *The matter was never brought to the knowledge of the minister.* **come to (someone's) knowledge** to become known to/by someone: *The matter never came to the knowledge of the minister.* **to the best of one's knowledge (and belief)** so far as one knows: *I am not quite sure, but to the best of my knowledge his story is true.* **to one's knowledge** so far as one knows: *He isn't there to my knowledge.* **without someone's knowledge** although someone didn't know: *He left home without his wife's knowledge.*

consciousness [U] the state of being conscious and knowing what is happening; understanding: *The man lost consciousness when he fell and hit his head on a stone. He wants people to have a greater consciousness of what life is all about.*

awareness [U] the state of being aware, of being fully conscious: : *The animal knew what was happening; its awareness showed in its eyes.*

cognizance [U] *fml & tech* awareness; (proper) knowledge and understanding: *This story is beyond the cognizance of younger children.* **take cognizance of** to take notice of, take into consideration: *The judge has taken cognizance of the new facts in your case.*

comprehension 1 [U] *fml* the act of understanding **2** [U] the ability of the mind to under-

stand: *I'm happy about your son's comprehension of written information; it is good.* **3** [C; U] (in schools) an exercise to test and improve a pupil's ability to understand language: *Comprehension is a good way of learning. She sets her students a comprehension every week.*

realization, -isation [U;S] (an experience of) understanding and believing: *He now has a full realization of what happened. The realization of his guilt came to him at last.*

perception *esp tech & fml* **1** [U] the act of perceiving; the ability to perceive: *His perception is very good.* **2** [C] something perceived; thought: *What are your perceptions of the matter?*

grasp [S; U] *esp emot & emph* understanding: *She has a good grasp of the subject. He has no grasp of the subject at all.*

appreciation 1 [U] judgement, as of the quality, worth, or facts of something: *The teacher's appreciation of his pupil's chances of passing the examination was correct.* **2** [U] the understanding of the good qualities or worth of something: *Their appreciation of the performance was expressed in loud cheers.* **3** [C] a written account of the worth of something: *The pupil wrote an appreciation of the play he had just seen.*

recognition [U] the act of recognizing or being recognized [⇒ G30]: *She showed no signs of recognition; she didn't seem to know us. He received money in recognition of his services. Recognition of that government by ours is not likely.*

G35 *nouns* : **learning and teaching**
[ALSO ⇒ I 130, ETC]

learning [U] deep and wide knowledge gained through reading and study: *This school has produced many men and women of great learning. Edinburgh University is a centre of learning.*

teaching 1 [U] the act, occupation, etc of teaching people, esp children: *He has been in teaching for 20 years. People in the teaching profession* (= the business of teaching) *are usually interested in what their students do in later life.* **2** [C *often pl*; U] that which is taught, esp the moral, political, or religious beliefs taught by a person of historical importance: *They try to follow Christ's teaching(s).*

instruction 1 [U] the act of instructing; teaching: *He's not yet trained, but still under instruction.* **2** [C *often pl*] an order (to a person or machine); advice or order to do something

tuition [U] the act of teaching, esp one person, esp privately: *He does a lot of (private) tuition. The tuition fees* (= the money to be paid for being taught) *are quite high at that college.*

education 1 [U;C *usu sing*] teaching or the training of mind and character: *All governments spend money on education. She has had a good education.* **2** [U] a field of knowledge dealing with how to teach effectively: *He trained to be a teacher at a college of education.*

training [U] the action or business of making people ready or getting ready for some occupation, skill, etc: *He is in training now for the big* (= most important) *race. Training times are shown on the wall.*

coaching [U] the teaching or training of a person or a group of people, esp for a special purpose, examination, sport, etc: *His coaching (of the team) was very good. She needs coaching (in that subject).*

civilization, -isation [U] the act of civilizing, esp over a period of time: *The civilization of the northern European peoples at the time of the Romans took hundreds of years.*

G36 *adjectives* : **knowing and learning** [B]

well-informed *genl* knowing many things: *He is a very well-informed person in this matter; ask him to help you. She spoke in a well-informed way about it.*

knowledgeable (of a person) having a good deal of knowledge; well-informed: *He's very knowledgeable about wines.* **-bly** [adv Wa3]: *He speaks very knowledgeably about wines.*

aware 1 [F (*of*), F5] having knowledge or consciousness: *Are you aware of the difficulty/that there is a difficulty?* **2** [B9] having knowledge or consciousness of the stated type: *She is very politically/artistically aware. He is a politically aware kind of person.* **3** [B] having or showing understanding of oneself, one's surroundings and other people: *It's nice to be with such an aware person.* **-ness** [U] [⇒ G30]

cognizant [F *of*] *fml & tech* aware: *The judge said he was not cognizant of the case.*

learned 1 having much knowledge as a result of study and reading: *He's a learned man.* **2** of, for, or concerning advanced study: *She wrote a learned book on butterflies.* **-ly** [adv]

knowing (showing that one is) well-informed or provided with the necessary information: *She gave him a knowing look/smile.* **-ly** [adv] *She smiled knowingly.*

educated [*often in comb*] having been educated: *An educated person should not behave as he does. She's a well-educated girl. Many self-educated people are very well-informed. He has an educated ear for music.*

trained having been trained; having had the proper training for a subject, job, etc: *He is a trained teacher. He is trained for the job. They are well-trained people.*

polished having had the necessary additional training, or experience which makes one specially good at something: *She is a very polished performer. He gave a polished performance.*

G37 *adjectives* : **good at learning and doing** [B]

clever [Wa1] **1** quick at learning and understanding; having a quick, effective, and able mind: *He's a clever boy; he'll do well in life.* **2** skilful, exp at using the hands or body: *She's a clever worker.* **3** being the result of a quick able mind; showing ability and skill: *That's a clever idea.* **-ly** [adv] **-ness** [U]

intelligent having or showing good mental powers: *All human beings are much more intelligent than animals.* **un-** [*neg*] **-ly** [adv]

brainy [Wa1] *infml* clever: *What a brainy fellow he is!* **-ily** [adv] **-iness** [U]

smart [Wa1] *infml* sometimes *deprec* clever and quick: *That child is smart; he'll do well in life. Oh yes, you think you're smart, but you aren't! Don't try to be smarter than your friends all the time.*

bright [Wa1] (of a person who is) clever; quick at learning: *She's a bright child. That's a bright idea.* **-ly** [adv] **-ness** [U]

acute (of the mind or the senses) able to note small differences, as for meaning or sound; working very well; sharp: *With his acute mind he was able to find an answer quickly.* **-ly** [adv]

apt [Wa2; (*at*)] clever and quick to learn and understand: *He is an apt student, very apt at understanding difficult ideas.* **-ness** [U]

subtle [Wa1] **1** very clever in noticing and understanding **2** clever in arrangement: *That's a subtle plan.* **3** delicate, hardly noticeable, and esp pleasant: *It is a subtle taste. There are subtle differences between the two things.*

ingenious 1 (of people) clever at making or inventing things **2** (of things) cleverly made; original **-ly** [adv]

clear-sighted [Wa2] having a sharp mind; clever: *A clear-sighted politician would have avoided such difficulties.*

astute clever and able to see quickly something that is to one's advantage: *He is a very astute lawyer.* **-ly** [adv] **-ness** [U]

shrewd [Wa1] **1** clever in judgement, esp of what is to one's own advantage: *He is a shrewd buyer who gets good value for money. She is a shrewd lawyer who knows all the tricks.* **2** well reasoned and likely to be right: *That was a shrewd guess!* **-ly** [adv] **-ness** [U]

brilliant very clever: *He is one of our most brilliant minds/mathematicians.* **-ly** [adv]: *She did the work brilliantly.*

G38 *adjectives* : **showing good sense** [B]

wise [Wa1] having or showing good sense, cleverness, the ability to understand what happens and decide on the right action: *She made a wise decision; she went away.* **un-** [*neg*] **-ly** [adv]

judicious having or showing good judgment; wise, esp in deciding things: *He made a judicious choice.* **in-** [*neg*] **-ly** [adv]

prudent sensible [⇨ N229] and wise; careful to consider one's advantage, esp by considering possible difficulties, unpleasantness, etc: *It's prudent to wear a thick coat when the weather is cold. She's a prudent girl; she plans everything carefully. Don't make a quick decision; be prudent.* **im-** [*neg*] **-ly** [adv]

cautious careful; taking great care: *Cautious people don't take chances.* **in-** [*neg*] **-ly** [adv]

thoughtful thinking very carefully before doing anything and therefore wise and helpful: *He always behaves in a thoughtful way.* **-ly** [adv] **ness** [U]

ill-advised, well-advised [⇨ G121 ADVISE]

G39 *nouns* : **intelligence and wisdom**

intelligence [U] (good) ability to learn and understand: *There is no doubt about his high intelligence. He took an intelligence test and did very well.*

brains [U] *infml* the ability to think: *He's got a lot of brains. Brains is more than just education.*

subtlety 1 [U] the quality of being subtle: *the subtlety of his argument* **2** [C *often pl*] a subtle idea, thought, or detail: *These subtleties are too difficult for me.*

ingenuity [U] skill and cleverness in making or arranging things: *She showed great ingenuity in getting a meal ready so quickly.*

genius 1 [U] great ability, esp in producing works of art: *There's genius in the way this is painted/written.* **2** [S] (sometimes unpleasant in effect) a special ability: *She has a genius for finding mistakes in my work.* **3** [C] a person of great/special ability: *He's no genius but he writes well. These men were all geniuses.*

brilliance [U] great intelligence: *Her brilliance at mathematics is well-known. He showed brilliance in doing the work so quickly and so well.*

wisdom [U] the quality of being wise: *You showed wisdom in doing what you did. People often gain wisdom with age.*

sense [U] *often infml* wisdom: *She showed a lot of sense when she said that. There's no sense in going out; it's raining.*

prudence [U] sense and wisdom; care to consider one's advantage, esp by considering possible difficulties, unpleasantness, etc: *His prudence with money is one of the best things about him.*

caution [U] carefulness; the act of paying attention or of taking great care: *Lack of caution causes many road accidents.*

tact [U] careful or wise behaviour which shows or suggests that one understands the feelings of another person: *She didn't want to go, but he used a lot of tact to get her to go.* **tactful** [B] having or showing tact: *Be tactful with her; don't say anything to annoy her.* **-ly** [adv] **-ness**

[U] **tactless** [B] having or showing no tact: *Don't be so tactless with her.* **-ly** [adv] **-ness** [U]

diplomacy [U] tact, esp used in order to stop arguments, make people agree, etc **diplomatic** [B] having or showing diplomacy: *He was very diplomatic when he asked her to help.* **-ally** [adv Wa4]

G40 *adjectives* : **able to be understood** [B]

understandable that can be understood: *His anger is understandable; I would be angry if I was/were him!*

comprehensible *usu fml* that can be (easily) understood: *One often finds a writer's book more comprehensible if one knows about his life and the time when he was alive.* **in-** [*neg*] **-ibly** [adv Wa3] **-ibility** [U]

intelligible able to be understood: *She doesn't speak intelligible English.* **un-** [*neg*]**-bly** [adv Wa3]

perceptive of, concerning, or having perceptions: *He is a very perceptive person and asks very perceptive questions.* **-ly** [adv]

perceptible able to be perceived: *There has been no perceptible change in temperature.* **im-** [*neg*] **-ibility** [U] **-bly** [adv Wa3]

clear [Wa1] **1** (of ideas, sounds, writing, people, etc) easily understood, heard, seen, read, etc: *He writes very clear articles on politics. Is what I have said clear to you?* **2** (esp of the mind or a person) thinking without difficulty; understanding well: *He is a clear thinker. His mind was clear even though he was very ill.* **3** certain: *She seems very clear about her plans.* **-ly** [adv] **-ness** [U]

coherent (esp of thought, speech, ideas, etc) easily understood because well connected: *His speech wasn't at all coherent; at first, I couldn't follow/understand it.* **in-** [*neg*] **-ly** [adv]

lucid very easy to understand: *She writes in a lucid, pleasant way.* **-ly** [adv] **-ness** [U]

G41 *nouns* : **understanding** [U]

understanding [*also* S] ability to understand, esp in a helpful way: *Try to show some understanding (of her difficulties) (towards her). He has a good understanding of French/of her difficulties. He listened with understanding to what he said.*

comprehension *fml* ability to comprehend or understand: *I am not worried about his comprehension of our difficulties, but I am worried about his understanding. Comprehension of a foreign language is not always easy.*

clarity *sometimes fml* clearness in thinking, writing, etc: *The clarity of his thought surprised them. She writes with great clarity.*

coherence 1 clearness in thinking, speaking, etc: *There wasn't much coherence in what he* *said.* **2** natural or reasonable connection, esp in thoughts or words: *Is there any coherence in his arguments?* **in-** [*neg*]

lucidity clearness in being understood: *She spoke with great lucidity on the subject.*

G42 *adjectives* : **showing ability** [B]

good [(*at*)] having the ability to do something: *He's quite a good driver/writer/singer. She's good at her job, but he's better. She's good with her hands/with children.* **well** [adv]: *He works very well at that job.*

clever [Wa1] good, esp with the hands or body: *He's clever at doing this/clever with his hands.* **-ly** [adv] **-ness** [U]

able 1 [F3] having the power, skill, knowledge, time, etc necessary to do something: *As I had plenty of money, I was* (*better/more*) *able to help her.* **2** [Wa1] clever; skilled: *He's an abler actor than I thought. She's old but still able.* **ably** [adv]: *She did it all very ably.*

competent 1 having the ability or skill to do what is needed: *He isn't a very competent driver.* **2** very satisfactory: *Does he have a competent knowledge of languages? She did a competent job.* **3** [F, F3] *esp law* having the power to deal with something: *This court is not competent to deal with the case.* **in-** [*neg*] **-ly** [adv]

capable 1 [(*of*)] having the ability or the power to do: *She's capable of any crime. Let's see what you're capable of.* **2** [F *of*] ready for; open to: *That's capable of being misunderstood. Your position is capable of improvement.* **3** able; clever: *He's a capable doctor. She's very capable but not very friendly. My son's capable in history but not in English.* **in-** [*neg*] **-bly** [adv Wa3]

skilful *BrE*, **skillful** *AmE* having or showing skill: *He is a skilful lawyer and uses skilful arguments.*

skilled having or needing skill: *He is a skilled artist.*

talented having or showing talent [⇒ G43]: *What a talented young man he is! She is very talented.*

gifted *esp apprec* having one or more special abilities; talented: *She's a gifted artist.*

proficient *often fml & tech* thoroughly skilled; well practised in an art, science, skill, or branch of study: *Her voice isn't of the finest quality, but she is a proficient singer. He is proficient at most games.* **-ly** [adv]

practised *usu apprec* being skilled through long practice, experience, work, etc: *He is a very practised writer; he knows exactly what he is doing.*

accomplished 1 skilled, clever; good at something but not professional: *She's an accomplished singer.* **2** *polite becoming rare* skilled in ladylike arts: *She's a very accomplished young woman.*

G43 *nouns* : **ability and talent**

ability [U; C *often pl*] (esp of the mind) the power, knowledge, etc needed (to do something): *She is a person of great ability. He should use his abilities to help others. Her mental ability* (= ability to use her mind) *is very great.*

skill [U; C] (a use of) practical knowledge and power; ability to do something (well): *She is a writer of great skill. He shows great dancing skill. This is a test of your skill with numbers. You must learn the skill of flying a plane. Reading and writing are two different skills.*

aptitude [U; C (*for, in*)] natural ability or skill, esp in learning: *He showed great aptitude for/in painting. She shows an aptitude for writing. The students had to take an aptitude test.*

competence [U] **1** ability to do what is needed; skill: *He drives with competence. She lacks the necessary competence for learning languages.* **2** *tech* (of courts of law) the ability to act: *This case is beyond the competence of this court.*

know-how [U] *infml* practical ability or skill; knowing how to do things: *He's good but he lacks the necessary know-how for this job.*

capacity [U] ability, power: *He has a big capacity for enjoying himself/for work. Her capacity for remembering things is interesting. This book is beyond my son's capacity at the moment.*

capability [U; C] ability; practical power: *He has the capability to do the job. She thinks nothing is beyond her capabilities.*

proficiency [U] *often fml & tech* the state or the quality of being proficient, very able: *Proficiency in several foreign languages is needed for work as a traveller's guide. She shows great proficiency at that work.*

talent 1 [C; U (*for*)] (a) special natural or learnt ability or skill, esp of a high quality: *She has a talent for drawing. musical/artistic talent* **2** [U] people of such ability: *There was a lack of local talent so the acting club hired an actor from London to take the main part.*

gift [C] a natural ability to do something: *She has the gift of speaking well. He has a gift for music.*

flair [S; U] (a) great natural ability: *He has a flair for this kind of work. She shows flair in everything he does.*

accomplishment [C] *polite becoming rare* a skill: *Riding is one of his many accomplishments.*

facility 1 [U; S] ability to do or perform something easily: *His facility with languages is amazing. She has a great facility in languages.* **2** [U] the quality of being able to be done or performed easily: *The facility of this piece of music makes it a pleasure to play.*

ease [U] the ability to do something without noticing difficulty: *He did the difficult work with* (*great*) *ease.*

resource [U] ability to do and think things: *He showed a lot of resource in helping us.* **resource-**

ful [B] able to get (esp difficult) things done: *She is a very resourceful woman.* **-ly** [adv]

G44 *adjectives* : **not showing knowledge** [B]

ignorant 1 *precise* lacking knowledge: *She's rather ignorant about these things.* **2** *infml & loose* rude; impolite: *Oh, don't be so ignorant; help the people put on their coats!* **-ly** [adv]

uninformed *often euph* not knowing much or anything: *We are very uninformed in these matters; please tell us what to do.*

untutored never having been taught: *Sometimes untutored people can have great natural skill.*

ill-taught *deprec* badly taught, esp in the opinion of the speaker: *These ill-taught people think they know everything!*

G45 *adjectives* : **not showing ability** [B]

slow [Wa1] *often euph* not very clever: *He is a little slow at school, I know.*

stupid [Wa2;F] lacking in power of mind, either by nature or through the influence of something which makes the mind unclear: *I think he was born stupid. I'm sorry, I don't understand: I must be stupid. Forgive me for being stupid, but why are you doing this? He was still stupid with sleep. They had been made stupid by drink.*

awkward (of a person or animal) not good at moving or doing things easily and smoothly: *He's an awkward child; he's always falling down or knocking things over. I'm rather awkward with tools; you do the job.* **-ly** [adv] **-ness** [U]

thick [Wa1] *esp BrE infml deprec* stupid; very slow at learning or understanding: *Try not to be so thick. He is pretty thick, isn't he?*

dumb [Wa1] *esp AmE infml deprec* thick

backward 1 behind in development **2** *sometimes euph* not clever: *He's a rather backward child.*

retarded *tech* backward, esp because of some difficulty of mind or body, or some personal problem: *This is a school for retarded children.*

G46 *adjectives, etc* : **not clever or reasonable**

foolish [B] *usu deprec* **1** unwise; without good sense: *It would be a foolish thing to spend money on something you can't afford. Only a foolish person would do this!* **2** showing lack of thought; stupid; laughable: *There were a lot of foolish answers given to the third examination question.* **-ly** [adv]

silly 1 [Wa1;B] having or showing little judgment; foolish; not serious; not sensible [⇨ N 229]: *Ask a silly question and get a silly answer. It's silly to go out in the rain if you don't have to. The book's title sounded silly but it was really a serious study. Don't be silly!* **2** [Wa1;B] *becoming rare* weak-minded: *The poor old man is getting rather silly. She's a silly young girl who doesn't know her own mind.* **3** [Wa5;F] *infml* senseless (*in such phr as* **knock/bore someone silly**) **4** [C;N] (an inoffensive word for) a silly person: *No, silly, I didn't mean that! What sillies you are!* **-iness** [U]

idiotic [B] *emph* very foolish; like an idiot [⇨ G48]: *What a really idiotic thing to do!* **-ally** [adv Wa4]

stupid [Wa2;B;N] silly or foolish, either generally or in a certain action: *He's rather a stupid person and it was stupid of him to do that. What stupid behaviour; what a stupid thing to do! Don't pick up that hot plate, stupid!* **-ly** [adv]

clownish [B] foolish on purpose; of or like a clown [⇨ G48]: *He's being clownish again, trying to make people laugh.* **-ly** [adv]

daft [Wa1;B] *infml, esp BrE* silly; wild; foolish: *What a daft person he is and what a thing to do!* **-ly** [adv] **-ness** [U]

absurd [B] **1** against reason or common sense; clearly false or foolish: *That was an absurd statement. Even sensible men do absurd things sometimes.* **2** funny because clearly false or impossible: *What an absurd idea!* **-ly** [adv] **-ity, -ness** [U]

scatterbrained [B] foolish; not (the result of) thinking carefully: *My scatterbrained wife never remembers her keys when she goes out. What a scatterbrained idea!* **scatterbrain** [C] *infml* a likeable but careless, forgetful, or unthinking person

absent-minded [B] so concerned with one's thoughts as not to notice what is happening, what one is doing, etc (and therefore doing silly things): *Try not to be so absent-minded; you've forgotten everything!* **-ly** [adv] **-ness** [U]

brainless [B] *esp infml & emot* foolish; silly; stupid **-ly** [adv] **-ness** [U]

mindless [B] *esp emot* stupid, esp in doing bad things **-ly** [adv] **-ness** [U]

G47 *nouns* : **lacking knowledge or wisdom**

ignorance [U] lack of knowledge: *Ignorance of the law is no excuse if you break the law.*

stupidity 1 [U] the condition of being stupid: *I don't know if he did it through ignorance or just plain stupidity.* **2** [C] an example of this: *These stupidities must stop; they are costing too much money.*

foolishness 1 [U] the condition of being foolish: *It's just plain foolishness to do that!* **2** [C] an example of this: *Her various foolishnesses when she was young have now been forgotten.*

idiocy 1 [U] the condition of being an idiot [⇨ G48]; *emph* great foolishness: *What idiocy is* *this?* **2** [C] an example of this: *His action yesterday was just another of his many idiocies.*

absurdity 1 [U] the state of being absurd **2** [C] an example of this; an absurd act, thing, or statement: *Life is full of absurdities.*

G48 nouns : persons lacking good sense [C; (you) N]

fool 1 *derog* a person whom one considers to be silly; person lacking in judgment or good sense: *What fool has put the wet paintbrushes on my chair? What a fool I was to think that she really loved me! Don't do that, you fool!* **2** (in former times) a manservant at the court of a king or noble, whose duty was to amuse his master **make a fool of oneself** to behave unwisely and lose people's respect: *He lost his temper in public last night and made a fool of himself in front of everybody. I hear the old doctor has made a fool of himself with a young girl he was treating* (= has formed or tried to form a sexual relationship with her). **make a fool of someone** to trick someone; make someone seem stupid: *The stranger made a fool of the trusting old lady and went off with a lot of her money.* **no fool/nobody's fool** a person who cannot be tricked: *He tried to sell me that old car but I'm nobody's fool; I could see it hadn't got an engine.* **play the fool** to act in a foolish manner: *Schoolmasters don't like boys to play the fool during the lessons.* **more fool you** (**him, them,** etc) I think you were (he was, etc) a fool to do, accept, expect, etc that: *He picked up a strange cat and it bit him. More fool him; he should have known it would do that!*

idiot 1 [*also* A] *old use* a person of very weak mind who cannot behave or think in the ordinary way: *He is the village idiot. They have an idiot child.* **2** *usu derog* a foolish, stupid person: *Idiot! You've dropped the books!*

dolt *derog* a slow-thinking foolish person

oaf a stupid, ungraceful person esp male: *What oafs those men are!* **oafish** [B] like an oaf **-ly** [adv] **-ness** [U]

ass *infml* a stupid/foolish person: *Don't be such an ass!*

clot *infml, esp BrE* a silly person: *What a clot he is!*

nitwit *also* **halfwit** *infml* a silly, foolish person

moron 1 *derog* a very foolish person **2** *tech* a person born with a weakness of mind, whose powers of understanding remain at the level of those of a child between the age of 8 and 12 **moronic** [B] of, connected with, or like a moron; like the behaviour, ideas, etc of a moron; stupid: *That was a pretty moronic thing to do!* **-ally** [adv Wa4]

buffoon a rough and noisy fool: *He was playing the buffoon at the party.*

clown 1 a performer, esp in the circus, who dresses funnily, tries to make people laugh by his jokes, or acts stupidly **2** someone who

behaves like this: *Oh, stop being such a clown!* **clownish** *deprec* like a clown: *Stop that clownish behaviour!* **-ly** [adv] **-ness** [U]

nut *sl & deprec* a foolish or mad person: *He's a complete nut!*

crank *infml & deprec* a person with fixed, strange, or foolish ideas, esp on one particular thing: *I'm afraid he's a bit of a crank on such matters as food and health.* **cranky** [Wa1;B] like a crank **-iness** [U]

mug *also* **sucker** *infml* a fool, esp one who is easily deceived, esp into buying things of poor quality

G49 verbs : without good sense

fool 1 [I0 (*about, around*)] to behave like a fool: *Stop fooling (about)!* **2** [T1] to trick (someone); to make (someone) feel a fool: *He fooled me completely.*

clown [I0 (*about, around*)] to behave like a clown; act stupidly or foolishly, esp on purpose: *Stop clowning (about)! He started clowning/to clown so as to make the children laugh.*

G50 adjectives : relating to a normal mind [B]

normal not mad or unusual in the mind in any way: *These children are quite normal; there is nothing wrong with them in mind or in body.* **-ly** [adv]: *She wasn't behaving normally at all.* **ab-** [neg]: *He began acting in an abnormal way. She was behaving abnormally.*

balanced having a steady, normal mind, character, nature, etc: *He is a very balanced kind of person. Balanced people don't do mad things like that. He's very well-balanced.*

sane [Wa1] **1** *esp tech* healthy in mind; not mad: *He is quite sane; there is no need to treat him like a mad person.* **2** produced by good reasonable thinking; sensible: *They have made some very sane suggestions for changes in the law.* **in-** [neg] **-ly** [adv] **-ness** [U]

G51 nouns : relating to a normal mind [U]

sanity *esp tech* the state of being sane, not mad; the condition which one considers reasonable: *His sanity is not in doubt; he is as sane as you or I. The sanity of their suggestions suggests that we can work well with them.* **in-** [neg]

normality the state of being a normal person: *She has returned to normality after a severe mental illness.* **ab-** [neg]

balance the normal steady state (of one's mind): *He killed her while the balance of his mind was disturbed.*

G52 *adjectives* : **not normal in the mind**

mad [Wa1] **1** [B (*with*)] showing that one suffers from a disease of the brain or disorder of the mind (*often in the phrs* **go mad**): *She went mad after the death of her son. There's a mad look in his eye.* (*fig*) *She is mad with grief.* **2** [B] *also tech* **rabid** (of a dog) suffering from a disease which causes wild behaviour **3** [B] very foolish and careless of danger: *You mad girl, to go out with no coat on such a cold day!* **4** [F (*about, for*)] filled with strong feeling, interest, etc: *He's mad about football. I'm mad about you. They're mad for new clothes* (= are always buying them). **drive someone mad** to worry someone enough to make him go mad: *You're driving me mad with the noise you're making!* **like mad** *infml* very hard/fast/loud, etc: *He shouted like mad but they were too far away to hear. They ran like mad to catch the moving bus.*

crazy [Wa1] *infml* **1** [B] mad; ill in the mind: *You're crazy to go out in this weather. The criminal went crazy.* **2** [B] impractical, foolish: *That's the craziest idea I've ever heard!* **3** [F] wildly excited: *I'm really crazy about her.* **-zily** [adv] **-ziness** [U]

crazed [Wa5;B] dangerously mad: *He's crazed; he'll kill somebody if we don't stop him! She had a crazed look on her face.*

insane [B] *esp tech* (of people and their acts) mad: *He was put in a home for insane people. What an insane thing to do!* **-ly** [adv]

deranged [B] put in a state of disorder, esp in relation to the mind: *The poor woman's mind has been deranged for many years. She is deranged.*

unbalanced [B] not in a normal state of mind: *She's been behaving in a pretty unbalanced way for some months now. I don't think he's actually unbalanced, but he should see a doctor.*

lunatic [B] *esp emot* completely mad: *That's a lunatic idea!*

raving [B] (up to the point of) talking wildly; *emot* mad: *He's a raving madman. He's raving (mad).*

berserk [B] mad and showing violent anger (*esp in the phrs* **go berserk**): *On hearing the news he went berserk (with anger) and broke several pieces of furniture. He looked berserk with anger.*

nuts [F] *infml* (slightly) mad: *He's been nuts for a long time.*

nutty [Wa1;B] *BrE infml* slightly mad: *What a nutty idea!*

off one's head *infml* quite mad: *He went off his head years ago. You're off your head if you think that!*

off one's rocker *infml* off one's head

out of one's mind *not fml* (completely) mad: *You're out of your mind if you think that!*

morbid [B] (of a person or the mind) unhealthy; not normal; having an unhealthy desire or need to think about death, illness, etc: *He has a*

morbid fear of death. **morbidity** [U] the state of being morbid

G53 *nouns* : **not normal in the mind**

madness [U] the state or condition of being mad, all the time or at any time: *Madness is often caused by what happens to a person. It's (an act of) madness to do a thing like that!*

insanity [U] *esp tech* the state of being mad or insane: *His insanity caused him to do some terrible things. It is sheer* (= complete) *insanity to do that!*

lunacy [U] *esp emot* (complete) madness, esp in particular ideas, acts, etc: *What lunacy! That idea is pure/sheer lunacy! He was near lunacy when he did/said that.*

mania **1** [U] disorder of the mind of a very forceful kind, dangerous to others **2** [C (*for*)] *not fml* a desire so strong that it seems mad: *She has a mania for (driving) fast cars.* **3** [U9] *not fml*, *tech in comb* a strong unreasonable desire or keenness: *He's got car mania. She suffers from kleptomania* (= a desire to steal things)/*megalomania* (= a desire for great power and importance).

G54 *nouns* : **persons who are not normal in the mind** [C; (*you*) N]

madman a male person who is mad: *That madman killed two people.* (*fig*) *He drives like a madman; I'm sure he'll have an accident one day.*

lunatic **1** *esp emot* a madman: *He drives like a complete lunatic; he'll kill himself or someone else one of these days.* **2** *formerly* a person who is mad and needs care: *They put him in an asylum* (= special home) *for lunatics.*

maniac **1** a person (thought to be) suffering from mania of some kind: *I'm sure he's a sex maniac.* **2** *esp emot* a mad person; a wild, thoughtless person: *He drives like a maniac; I'm sure he'll kill somebody one day. She was killed by a maniac.*

imbecile **1** a person of weak mind **2** *derog* a fool or stupid person: *What an imbecile, going out without a coat in weather like that! Imbecile—I told you to take some money!*

crackpot *infml & emot* a mad person: *He is really a crackpot; he has some very strange ideas. What a crackpot idea!*

Communicating, mainly by speaking and talking

G60 *verbs* : **saying, speaking, and telling**

say **1** [T1] to pronounce (a sound, word, etc): *What did you say?—I said, 'You're standing on* *my toe!' You must learn to say 'please', young man!* **2** [T1, 5a, b, 6a, b; *(in questions, with words like* **no**, **not**, *etc and in subordinate clauses)* 1Ø] to express (a thought, intention, opinion, question, etc) in words: *Don't believe anything he says. He said (that) I was standing on his toe. Will it rain?—I should say so/not. Will your party win the election?—I'd rather not say/Who can say?/It's not for me to say! In this letter he says where to meet him, but does not say when. It says in this book that most of the earth is covered by water.* **3** [same as **2**] *not fml* to show: *What time does your watch say? She was smiling but her eyes said she was unhappy.* **4** [T1, 5 a *imper*] *not fml* to suppose: *(Let's) say your plan fails: then what do we do? Would you take an offer of, say, £100 for your car? Can you come to dinner, say, 7.30?* **5** [Wv6;T3] *not fml* to direct or instruct someone: *She says to meet her at the station. It says on the bottle to take a spoonful every four hours.* **it goes without saying** *not fml* of course, clearly: *It goes without saying that your plans depend on the weather.* **I say** *BrE infml* **1** (a rather weak expression of surprise, interest, anger, sorrow, etc): *My husband is ill today—Oh, I say! I'm sorry to hear that.* **2** (used to call someone's attention): *I say, isn't it getting late? I say, I've just had a wonderful idea!* **I wouldn't say no** *BrE infml* yes please; I'd like it/some: *Have another drink?—Well, I wouldn't say no.* **say** *AmE infml* (used to express surprise or a sudden idea): *Say, haven't I seen you somewhere before? Say, now I remember!* **say for oneself/something** to offer as an excuse or as something in favour or defence: *You're late again: What have you got to say for yourself? She is a stupid person with nothing to say for herself. It is a bad idea with very little to be said for it.* **say what you like** *not fml* even though you may not agree: *Say what you like, (but) I think British weather is nice.* **that is to say** *(abbrev* **i.e.**) in other words; expressed another (more exact) way: *Working as hard as before, that is to say not very hard.* **they say** *not fml* people say; it's usually thought: *They say that falling in love is wonderful.* **what do you say?** *infml* you'll agree, won't you?: *Let's go into business together: what do you say? What do you say we go into business? What do you say to going into business together?* **you don't say (so)!** *infml* (an expression of slight surprise) **you said it!** *AmE infml* you're right; I agree: *Let's go home—You said it! I'm tired.*

speak 1 [1Ø] to say things; express thoughts aloud; use the voice: *Don't speak with your mouth full of food. He was speaking to a friend when I came along. 'Can I speak, please?' he asked the chairman of the meeting.* **2** [1Ø] to express thoughts, ideas, etc in some other way: *The book speaks of the writer's childhood. Actions speak louder than words. Everything at the meeting spoke of careful planning.* **3** [1Ø] to make a speech: *I've invited her to speak at/to our club on any subject she likes. I hope she'll*

speak (for) about 20 minutes and then answer questions. **4** [T1] to be able to talk in (a language): *We need someone who can speak French. No English is spoken there. She is from a Spanish-speaking country.* **5** [T1] *often emph* to express or say: *Speak the truth! He was hardly able to speak a word.* **6** [1Ø *(to)*] to be feeling friendly enough to speak: *After their fight they're not speaking (to each other).* **on speaking terms 1** willing to talk and be polite to another, esp after a quarrel: *She and her mother are not on speaking terms after last night* **2** good enough friends to exchange greetings **so to speak** as one might say: *He was up to his neck, so to speak, in debt.* **speak one's mind** to express one's thoughts directly: *I'm angry and I want a chance to speak my mind to the director.* **speak volumes** it means a lot: *She only said 'perhaps', but that spoke volumes.*

tell 1 [D1 *(to)*, 5a, b; T1 *(of)*] to make (something) known in words to (someone); express in words; speak: *Did you tell Aunt Joan the news about Paul? If you tell your secret to Jessie you might as well tell the whole town. John told us he'd seen you in town. I can't tell you how pleased I am to be here tonight. Can you tell me what time the party starts? Good children always tell the truth. I always tell my daughter a story before she goes to sleep. Don't tell me you've missed the train* (= I'm worried by the fact that you seem to have missed the train). *I'm right, I tell you!* (= you can be certain that I'm right) **2** [T1; V3; D5a, b] to warn; advise: *I told you mother would beat you if she heard you swearing. I told you that man was evil but you wouldn't listen to me. I told you to expect trouble, and now look what's happened!* **3** [D6a, b; X9] to show; to make known: *This light tells you if the machine is on or off. Will you tell me how to do it?* **4** [Wv6;T1, 6a, b] to find out; know: *It's impossible to tell who'll win the next election. How do you tell which handle to turn when the light goes out?* **5** [V3; D6a, b; X9] to order; direct: *Children should do as they're told. I told you to get here early, so why are you late? Don't try to tell me whether I can or not!* **6** [Wv6;T5a, 6a *(whether, if)*, b *(whether)*; X9, esp *from, apart;* 1Ø] to recognize; know: *It was so dark I couldn't tell it was you. It's difficult to tell Jean from Joan; they look so alike. I can't tell if it's him or not. Which team will win?—Who can tell?* **7** [1Ø] to be noticeable; have an effect: *Her nervousness began to tell as soon as she entered the room.* **8** [1Ø] to speak someone's secret to someone else: *If I let you know my secret will you promise not to tell?* **all told** altogether; when all have been taken into account: *There were over 500 visitors all told.* **tell the time** to read the time from a clock or watch **there is/was/will be no telling** it is/was/will be impossible to know: *There's no telling what will happen if she meets him while she's in this temper.* **you can never tell** *also* **you never can tell** one can never be sure about something because one can easily be deceived without knowing it **you're telling me** *infml* (a strong way of saying) I know this already

relate [T1 (*to*)] *fml* to tell (esp a story): *He related (to us) the story of his escape from the enemy. Strange to relate, I once shot a lion.*

recount [T1] *esp lit* to tell or relate: *He recounted the story to us as fully as possible.*

name [X1] to give a name to (someone or something), esp in a speech but also in writing: *They named the boat 'The Electra'. The boy was named John.*

call 1 [X1, 7, 9] to say that (someone) is (something): *She called him fat. Call me what you like.* **2** [X1, 7] to consider: *I call him a fool. I don't call Russian a hard language. That's what I call dishonest.* **3** [X1] to name: *We'll call the baby Jean. Let's call the new town Harlow.*

G61 *verbs* : **pronouncing and reciting**

[ALSO ⇒ G231]

pronounce [T1; X1; L9] to make the sound of (a language, a letter, a word, etc) (in a particular way): *She pronounces Spanish very well. In the word 'knew' the 'k' is not pronounced; the word is pronounced without the 'k'. In 'chemical' the 'ch' is pronounced /k/. Try to pronounce (the word/sound) clearly.*

recite 1 [T1; I0 (*from*)] to say (something), esp from memory or as a list: *He recited (from) the Bible to them.* **2** [T1] *emph & usu deprec* to say strongly, esp as a list: *As usual he began to recite all his complaints to us.*

utter [T1] to make (any sound) with the mouth; *esp emot & emph* speak or say: *The first sound a child utters is usually 'ma'. He didn't utter a word but you could see that he was very angry.*

G62 *verbs etc*: **talking, not talking, and interrupting**

talk 1 [I0] to use human words; have the power of speech; make words; speak: *Human beings can talk; animals can't.* **2** [I0] to make words, thoughts, ideas, etc known by means of speech: *I'm talking seriously now! When I'm talking to your father I expect you to be quiet. There's an important matter I want to talk about with you.* **3** [I0] to copy human speech: *Have you taught your bird to talk?* **4** [I0] to express thoughts as if by speech: *People who cannot speak or hear can talk by using signs.* **5** [T1] to speak about: *Let's not talk business now. We talked music all night.* **6** [T1] to express in words: *Talk sense!* **7** [T1] *less common* to be able to speak (a language): *Do you talk French?* **8** [I0] to give information, usu unwillingly: *Have you persuaded the prisoners to talk yet?* **9** [I0] to speak about other people's actions and private lives: *Don't do anything foolish; you know how people talk. I hope you've not been talking about me again.* **talk big**

infml to speak with too much pride in oneself or one's actions; make oneself or one's actions seem more important than they are

converse [I0 (*on/about* and/or *with*)] *often fml* to talk informally: *After a year of studying at university I feel able to converse with anyone about anything.*

confer [I0 (*together*, *with*)] *esp fml & pomp* to talk: *We must confer soon. They conferred (together) on the matter. They conferred with us about it.*

chat [I0 (*away*)] *infml* to talk in a friendly, familiar, informal manner: *The two friends sat in a corner and chatted (away) to each other about life in general. I like to chat with her now and then.*

chat up [v adv T1] (esp of men) to make friends by talking to (esp a woman): *He's always trying to chat up the girls.*

fall silent [v adv I0] *esp lit* to stop talking: *When he walked into the room they all fell silent.*

shut up [v adv] **1** [I0] *esp infml* to stop talking: *They all shut up when he walked into the room. Shut up, will you!* **2** [T1] to cause to stop speaking: *Shut these men up, please! The bad news shut them up very quickly.*

clam up [v adv I0] *infml* to become suddenly and fully silent: *She clammed up whenever I mentioned her husband.*

interrupt [T1; I0] to stop (someone speaking, etc) by speaking oneself or doing something noisy, etc: *Please don't interrupt (me) while I'm talking/speaking. They keep interrupting! Their noise interrupted what we were doing.* **interruption** [U; C] the act of interrupting or being interrupted; an example of this: *All the interruptions made him forget what he wanted to say.*

in [adv] (used in verbs of interrupting such as:)

break in [v adv I0] *infml* to interrupt: *Excuse me breaking in, but I have some news for you. She broke in with some ideas of her own. He broke in on our conversation.*

butt in [v adv I0] *sl often deprec* to interrupt, usu by speaking: *I wish you wouldn't keep butting in to/on our conversation.*

burst in [v adv I0] *infml*, *emot & emph* to interrupt suddenly or strongly: *She burst in (on our conversation) with some very bad news.*

chip in [v adv I0 (*with*)] *infml sometimes deprec* to enter a conversation suddenly with an opinion: *We were talking sensibly until he chipped in with his foolish idea. She chipped in that it was time to go home.*

chime in [v adv I0 (*with*); T5] *infml* to interrupt or join in a conversation by expressing (an opinion): *He's always ready to chime in with his opinion. She chimed in that it was time to go home.*

into [prep] (used in verbs of interrupting such as:)

break into [v prep T1] *infml* to interrupt: *She broke into our conversation and asked us to help her.*

butt into [v prep T1] *sl often deprec* to interrupt: *Stop butting into our conversations!*

G63 *verbs* : **communicating and informing**

[ALSO ⇒ G190]

communicate *fml* **1** [T1] to make (news, opinions, feelings, etc) known: *I don't think that politician communicates his thoughts very clearly.* **2** [I0] to share or exchange opinions, news, information, etc: *Has the Minister of Foreign Affairs communicated with the Americans yet? I can't communicate with them; the radio doesn't work.* **3** [T1] to pass on (a disease, heat, movement, etc): *This one person communicated the disease to the whole town.* **4** [I0 *(with)*] to join: *Our bedroom communicates with the bathroom.*

contact [T1] to write, telephone, go and talk to, etc (someone): *Contact me when you arrive.*

inform [T1 *(of, about)*; D5a] *often fml* to tell; to give information to: *He informed us (that) he was coming.*

let ... know *infml* to pass information to (someone): *I'll let you know about it as soon as I can. He didn't let us know when to come. Don't forget to let me know soon!*

notify [D1 *to/of*, D5; T1] to tell (someone), esp formally: *She notified us of the meeting. Why weren't we notified in time? He notified the accident to the police. He notified the police of the accident.* **notification 1** [U] the act of notifying **2** [C] an example of this, esp a piece of paper giving notification

confide [I0 *(in)*; X9] to tell someone (something) as a secret: *Can I confide in you? She confided the matter to me.*

advise [T1; D5, 5b, 6a] *fml* to inform; give notice to: *I have advised her that we are coming. Would you please advise us as to your plans? Will you advise us (of) when the bags should arrive.*

brief [T1 *(on)*] to tell (someone, esp a lawyer) the necessary information: *He briefed his lawyer on what to do. You must brief me; I don't know what happened.*

G64 *verbs* : **speaking and lecturing**

speak to [v prep T1] **1** to talk, esp formally, to (a group of people): *He is speaking to our club next week about his books.* **2** to talk to (someone) about something unsatisfactory that he or she has done: *All right, I'll speak to him about it.*

address *fml* **1** [T1] to speak to: *He addressed the meeting last night.* **2** [X9] to direct (one's speech or writing) to a person or group: *Please address your remarks to the chairman. He addressed himself to the meeting on the subject of employment.* **3** [T1 *(as)*] to speak or write to (someone): *Don't address me as 'Officer'.*

lecture 1 [I0] to give a lecture [⇒ G65]: *He lectured on biology last night. What's he lecturing on tomorrow?* **2** [I0] to work in a college, university, etc as a lecturer [⇒ I134]: *She lec-*tures at Glasgow University. **3** [T1] to talk solemnly and at length to: *She lectured us on coming home late every night.*

speechify [I0] *infml often deprec* to make a speech or speeches, esp in a (too) proud, fine-sounding way: *I'm only a simple man and no good at speechifying.*

speak up [v adv I0] speak more loudly: *Speak up, please; I can't hear you.*

speak out [v adv I0] to speak boldly, freely, and plainly: *He was afraid to speak out in case he should lose his job. She spoke out against their real enemies.*

G65 *nouns* : **talk and conversation**

talk 1 [C] something which one says, or has prepared to say, to a group of people: *He gave us a very interesting talk on India. I heard his talk on the radio last night.* **2** [C] an occasion of talking, usu seriously: *The two governments had/held talks about their common troubles. I'll have a talk to him about his bad behaviour. She had a talk with him about his plans.* **3** [U] *often deprec* anything that someone says: *Every time I see him it's just talk, talk, talk!* **4** [*the* R9, esp *of*] any subject of conversation: *Her sudden marriage is the talk of the street.* **5** [U *often in comb*] a particular way of speech or conversation: *baby talk* (= the way babies talk, or the way adults talk to babies); *shop talk* (= talk about business) **6** [U] empty or meaningless speech: *His threats were just talk; don't worry. My husband's all talk and no action; he has plenty of ideas but never puts them into practice.*

conversation [C; U] (an) informal talk in which people exchange news, feelings, and thoughts: *Mrs Smith spends a lot of time in conversation with her neighbour. I had a long conversation with Paul this morning; he's very nice to talk to informally.*

conference [C] a meeting to talk about some matter of work, government, etc: *He is attending a scientific conference at Leeds University.* **in conference** having a meeting: *Mr Smith can't see you at the moment; he is in conference.*

banter [U] light, joking talk: *The actress exchanged banter with reporters.*

chat *infml* **1** [C] a friendly, informal conversation: *I had a long chat with him about his garden when I last saw him.* **2** [U] the act of chatting: *We need less chat and more work if we're to finish today.*

speech [C] **1** an act of speaking formally to a group of listeners: *He gave/made a speech there last week. We keep records of all their speeches.* **2** the words so spoken: *The minister's speech was sent to the newspapers in advance.* **3** a usu long set of lines for an actor to say in a play: *He learned the speech very carefully.*

address [C] *fml* a speech, esp one that has been formally prepared and made to a group of people gathered specially to listen: *His address lasted an hour.*

lecture [C] **1** a speech spoken or read before a group of people, esp as a method of teaching at universities, etc. **2** *sometimes deprec* a long solemn warning: *He gave me a lecture on driving carefully. Here comes another of his lectures on how to behave.*

recitation 1 [U] the act of reciting [⇒ G61] **2** [C] an example of this **3** [C] anything, esp a poem, when recited or used for reciting: *Say your recitation. He bought a book of recitations.*

word 1 [C *often pl*] *infml* a short speech or conversation: *Can I have a word with you (about him)? I had a few words with her on the subject.* **2** [S] the shortest (type of) statement: *In a word, no. I don't believe a word of what he said. Don't say a word to anyone.*

utterance 1 [U] the act of uttering [⇒ G61] sounds: *Animals have the power of utterance, but not of speech.* **2** [C] *deprec* anything spoken; word: *Don't listen to his utterances; they have little value.*

G66 nouns : monologue and dialogue

monologue, *also* **monolog** *AmE*[C] **1** a spoken part in a play where one person speaks at length **2** a poem or other piece of writing intended to be spoken on a stage by one person **3** *infml* a rather long speech by one person that prevents others taking part in the conversation.

dialogue *also* **dialog** *AmE* [C; U] **1** (a) written conversation in a book or a play: *She can write dictionaries but she can't write good dialogue. Turn to the page with the dialogue between Smith and Brown.* **2** (a) conversation which examines differences of opinion, as between leaders: *At last there can be (a) meaningful dialogue between our two governments.*

G67 adjectives : talking a lot, too much, or well [B]

talkative *infml* tending to talk a lot: *She's a very talkative girl.* **-ly** [adv] **-ness** [U]

chatty [Wa1] *infml* **1** fond of talking: *She's a chatty sort of girl.* **2** having the style and manner of informal conversation: *She wrote them a chatty letter.* **-tily** [adv] **-tiness** [U]

garrulous habitually talking too much, esp about unimportant things **-ly** [adv] **-ness** [U]

loquacious *usu fml, emph, or pomp* liking to talk a great deal: *Yes, he is rather loquacious, isn't he?* **-ly** [adv] **loquacity** [U] the quality of being loquacious

eloquent 1 talking well, so as to persuade, interest, etc: *What an eloquent speaker he is!* **2** persuading in this way: *His eloquent words produced the effect he wanted and people gave money to help him.* **-ly** [adv] **eloquence** [U]

G68 verbs : talking in various ways

whisper 1 [T1; I0] to speak with normal lip and tongue movements and noisy breath, but not with the usual movements in the throat which produce the voice, so that only a person nearby can hear: *Stop whispering in the corner; say whatever it is out loud. She whispered a few words weakly before she fell unconscious.* **2** [I0] (*fig*) (usu of the wind) to make a soft sound: *The wind whispering in the roof.* **3** [X9 (*about*) *often pass*] to tell (a secret) widely: *His adventures have been whispered through the village/ whispered about/whispered everywhere.*

chatter [I0] **1** (of people) to talk rapidly and at length, usu about something unimportant: *Two people annoyed everyone by chattering right through the film. I wish you'd stop chattering on about things you don't understand.* **2** (of certain animals and birds) to make quick speech-like sounds: *The monkeys were chattering (away) in the trees.* **3** (of the teeth) to knock together through cold or fear: *Her teeth were chattering with the cold.* **4** (*fig*) (of machines) to make a noise of this kind: *Machine guns chattered in the distance.*

natter [I0 (*away, on*)] *BrE infml* to talk continuously about unimportant things; chatter: *They nattered (away) all afternoon and never did any work. They kept nattering (on) about silly things.*

babble 1 [I0] to talk foolishly or in a way that is hard to understand: *During his fever he babbled without stopping.* **2** [T1] to express by babbling: *She babbled her thanks in a great hurry.* **3** [T1 (*out*)] to repeat foolishly; tell (secrets): *He babbled the secrets (out) to his friends.* **4** [I0 (*away*)] to make continuous sounds, like a baby learning to speak: *The baby babbled (away) for hours.* **5** [Wv4; I0] to make continuous sounds, like a stream running gently over rounded stones: *The water babbled past/along.*

blab [I0; T1 (*out*)] *sl* to tell (a secret), usu foolishly: *Here come the police; someone must have blabbed. He blabbed out everything they wanted to know.*

mumble [T1, 5; I0] to speak (words) unclearly: *What did you say? Stop mumbling! The old woman mumbled a prayer.*

mutter [T1, 5; I0] to speak (usu angry or complaining words) in a low voice, not easily heard: *He muttered a threat. She kept (on) muttering to herself.*

G69 nouns : talking in various ways

whisper 1 [C] whispered words **2** [C *usu sing*] (*fig*) a soft, windy sound: *the whisper of the wind in the roof* **3** [U] the type of sounds made by the throat when whispering

chatter [U] **1** rapid informal unimportant conversation: *I dislike chatter when I'm trying to work.* **2** a rapid knocking sound made by teeth, machines, etc; the rapid speech-like sounds made by certain animals and birds: *The chatter of typewriters could be heard outside the room.*

natter [S] *BrE infml* an informal conversation, esp about unimportant things

babble 1 [U] childish, disordered, or foolish talk: *Stop that babble at once!* **2** [S] a confused sound of many people talking at once: *A babble of voices came from the room.* **3** [U] speech that is hard to understand because of its speed and pronunciation **4** [U; S] a sound like that of water running gently over rounded stones

mumble [S] the sound of mumbling: *All I could hear through the door was a mumble of voices.*

mutter [S] the sound of muttering: *the mutter of angry voices*

G70 *verbs* : **remarking and expressing**

remark 1 [T5a] to say (not in answer to anything): *He remarked that it was getting late. 'It's getting late,' he remarked.* **2** [T1, 5] *fml & old use* to notice: *I remarked her absence of hair/that she had no hair.*

comment [I0; T5a] to make a remark; give an opinion: *The king refused to comment on the election results. She commented that it was time to go home.*

observe [T5a] *often fml* to make a remark; to say: *He observed (to her) that the meal was excellent.*

express [T1, 6a] to show (a feeling, opinion, or fact) in words or in some other way: *She expressed her thanks. The prices are expressed in both dollars and pounds. I can't express how grateful I am. She tried to express her opinion/feelings, but couldn't.*

air [T1] *often deprec* to express (opinions, etc): *He began to air his ideas about crime and punishment. She airs her views on sex to anyone who'll listen.*

word also **phrase** [X9] to express or put into words: *How would you like me to word this invitation? I don't like the way this note is phrased.*

put [X9] *infml & genl* to express or word: *I'm not sure how to put my plan to you. Let's put it like this: I want to help you.*

compliment [T1 (*on*)] to praise someone with a compliment: *He complimented her on her new dress.* **complimentary** [B] **1** expressing praise, etc **un-** [*neg*] **2** given free, out of kindness, for business reasons, etc: *complimentary tickets for the theatre*

G71 *nouns* : **remarking and expressing**

remark 1 [C (*about, on*)] a spoken or written opinion: *Don't make/pass rude remarks about her appearance.* **2** [U] *fml* notice: *Her absence of hair could hardly escape remark/was worthy of remark.*

comment [C; U] (an) opinion, explanation, or judgment written or spoken about an event, book, person, state of affairs, etc: *What comments have you on/about my son's behaviour? I read your comments on his new book but disagree with them. Her behaviour at the dance caused a lot of comment. Do you buy your newspaper for its political comment? There's no comment I can make on this matter. No comment* (= I don't want to say anything about it).

observation [C] a remark, often descriptive: *His clever observations (about people's behaviour) at the party made them laugh.*

expression 1 [C; U] (an act of) expressing: *They greeted him with many expressions of pleasure. A government should permit the free expression of political opinion. He's not educated enough to give expression to all his thoughts.* **2** [U] the quality of showing or performing with feeling: *She has a beautiful voice, but doesn't sing with much expression.*

compliment [C] an expression of praise, admiration, respect, etc: *You did well! — Thanks for the compliment. He's always paying her compliments; he thinks she's wonderful.*

aside [C] **1** a remark in a low voice not intended to be heard by everyone present **2** a remark or story told during a speech but which has no part in the speech: *His speech was uninteresting but he made many amusing asides.* **3** words spoken by an actor to those watching the play and not intended to be heard by the other characters

G72 *verbs* : **stating and affirming**

state 1 [T1, 5, 6a, b] *often fml* to say, express, or put into words, esp formally: *State your name and address. This book states the case for women's rights very clearly. I'd like to state that I have never seen this woman before.* **2** [Wv5; T1] to set in advance; fix; specify [⇒ N63]: *Theatre tickets must be used on the stated date.*

attest *fml & rare* **1** [T1, 5, 6a] to declare solemnly: *I attested the facts. I attested what I had seen.* **2** [T1] to be or give proof of: *His success attests his ability.* **3** [T1] to show to be true by signing as proof that one was present: *I attested the agreement that the two businessmen made with each other.* **4** [T1] to make (somebody) promise to tell the truth, as in court **attest to** [v prep T1] *fml* to be or give proof of: *His success attests to his ability.*

declare 1 [T1; X1, 7] to make known publicly or officially, according to rules, custom, etc: *Our government has tonight declared war on Ruritania. Jones was declared the winner of the fight. The young prince declared himself king before anyone could stop him. I declare Alvin B. Schiff elected!* **2** [T1, 5a; X (*to be*) 1, 7; L9] to state or show (one's view) with great force so that there is no doubt about the meaning:

He declared his position. He declared (that) he was right. He declared himself (to be) a member of the party. They declared for/against the plan. (lit) His actions declared him (to be) an honest man.· **3** [T1] to make a full statement of (property for which money may be owed to the government): He declared his new Swiss watch when he returned to Britain and had to pay £5. Have you anything to declare? **declare oneself** to state clearly one's point of view or intentions **declarable** [Wa5;B] that should/ must be declared: Have you any declarable goods?

assert 1 [T1, 5; X (to be) 1, 7] to state or declare forcefully: She asserted her ideas loudly and clearly. He asserted that he was not guilty. She asserted her belief that he was not guilty. **2** [T1] to make a claim to; defend in words: He angrily asserted his rights. **3** [T1] to show, esp forcefully, the existence of: He asserted his control by making them stop talking.

affirm 1 [T1, 5] to declare (usu again or in answer to a question): He affirmed his love for her. He affirmed that he was telling the truth. **2** [I0] to promise to tell the truth in a court of law, but without mentioning God or the Bible in the promise: He said the Bible meant nothing to him and that he chose to affirm rather than to swear.

pronounce [T5; X (to be) 1, 7] **1** to declare as one's opinion after consideration: Everyone pronounced the dinner to be very good. He pronounced himself too tired to go any further. The doctor pronounced the man dead. **2** fml to state or declare officially or with ceremony: At the end of the marriage ceremony the priest said, 'I now pronounce you man and wife.'

proclaim [T1, 5; X (to be) 1, 7] fml to make (esp. something of national importance) known publicly; declare officially: The ringing bells proclaimed the end of the war. Peace was proclaimed.

G73 nouns : stating and affirming

statement 1 [C] often fml something that is stated; a written or spoken declaration esp of a formal kind: Do you believe the witness's statement? The penalty for making false statements to the tax officer can be severe. This writer makes a lot of foolish statements; he doesn't know his subject well at all. The minister is under pressure to make an official statement. **2** [U] expression in words: The details of the agreement need more exact statement.

declaration 1 [U] the act of declaring: The declaration of the winner of the election took place last night. **2** [C] an example of this: His words were (like) a declaration of war. There were many declarations against the war.

assertion 1 [U] the act of asserting **2** [C] a forceful statement or claim: He repeated his assertions that he was not guilty. **assertive** [B] marked by or making assertions: You couldn't

fail to notice that assertive young man. **-ly** [adv] **-ness** [U]

affirmation 1 [U] the act of affirming **2** [C] something affirmed, esp a solemn declaration in a court of law to tell the truth: He made an affirmation that what he said was the truth.

pronouncement [C] an official statement: They waited for the government to make its pronouncement on housing.

attestation 1 [U] the act of attesting **2** [C] a declaration or statement that the maker promises to be true

ultimatum [C] a statement of conditions to be met, esp under threat of force, as when one nation threatens war unless another agrees (often in the phr **give one's ultimatum, give someone an ultimatum**): Their ultimatum threatened war.

G74 verbs : claiming and announcing

claim 1 [T1; I0] to ask for or demand (a title, property, money, etc which one does not yet possess) as the rightful owner or as one's right: The King of France claimed the Spanish crown as his by right. Did you claim on the insurance after your car accident? **2** [T1] to call for; deserve; need: This difficult document claimed all our attention for several weeks. **3** [T1] to take (a title, property, money, etc) as the rightful owner: Passengers should claim their property as soon as they leave the plane. Lost property which is not claimed in three months is sold. **4** [T3, 5a] to declare to be true, esp in the face of doubt, disagreement, opposition, etc: He claims to own that car but I don't believe him/it.

allege [T1, 5, 5b] fml to state or declare without proof or before finding proof: The newspaper alleges that the man was murdered but they have given no proof. So they allege, but have they any proof? **allegedly** [adv Wa5] according to statements made without proof: Allegedly he killed his wife.

aver [T1, 5] fml to state forcefully; declare: He averred that he had never seen her before.

announce 1 [T1, 5] to make known publicly: The government announced that they would pay their debts. They announced the date of their wedding in the newspaper. **2** [T1] to state in a loud voice (the name of a person, etc on arrival, etc, as of people at·a party or aircraft at an airport): Will you announce Mr and Mrs Smith, please? British Airways announce the departure of their Flight 123 to Edinburgh. **3** [T1] to read (news) or introduce (a person or act) on the radio, television, stage, etc **4** [T1, 5] (fig) to make clearly known: The bright flowers and warm winds announced that spring had come.

intimate [T1, 5b] fml to make known, esp indirectly; suggest: He intimated a wish to go by saying that it was late. He intimated that he wanted to go.

G75 nouns : claiming and announcing

claim [C] **1** a demand for something as one's by right: *The government would not even consider his claim for money.* **2** a right to something: *The prince had a claim to the Russian crown.* **3** a statement of something as fact: *The government's claim that war was necessary was mistaken.* **4** something claimed, esp an area of land **5** a sum of money claimed, esp from an insurance company: *Did you get that claim you asked for?*

allegation 1 [U] the act of alleging: *Allegations against other people won't help him now.* **2** [C] *fml* a statement that charges someone with doing something bad or criminal but which is not supported by proof: *Can you provide proof to support these allegations? He made allegations of cruelty unsupported by proof.*

announcement 1 [U] the act of announcing or being announced: *The announcement of the names of the winners in the competition will take place tomorrow.* **2** [C] an example of this; something announced: *He heard several announcements about what would happen, both on radio and television.* (*fig*) *The bright flowers were an announcement that spring had come.*

intimation *fml* **1** [U] the act of intimating **2** [C] an example of this, esp when written: *We received no (written) intimation of his intentions.*

G76 verbs : repeating [T1]

say . . . again [*also* T5] to say for a second or third etc time: *Let me say (once) again that I think we can help you. He kept saying it again and again.*

repeat [*also* T5] *esp fml* to say (something) again, for a second or further time: *He repeated his question.*

reiterate *fml & pomp* to repeat: *Please be good enough to reiterate your point.* **reiteration** [U] the action of reiterating

restate to state (something) again, either as before or in a slightly different (and better) way: *He restated his position more clearly/strongly.*

re-phrase to say (something) again in a different or better way: *Re-phrase the question, please.*

re-express to express (something) again, usu in a different (and better) way: *I think you should re-express that point.*

G77 verbs : insisting and emphasizing

insist 1 [T5a; I∅] to declare firmly (when opposed): *He insisted that she was wrong. Please, I must insist!* **2** [T5c; I∅ (*on*)] to order (something to happen): *She insisted on him* going. *You must come; I insist (on it). I insist that you come.*

demand [T1, 3, 5c; (I∅)] to claim as if by right; to ask or ask for and not take 'No' for an answer: *I demand my rights/my money! I demanded his name/a clear answer. The letter demands £10,000 for your daughter's life. I demand to know the truth! I demand that he (should) go there at once! 'What is the meaning of this?' he demanded. I'm not just asking; I'm demanding.*

stress [T1] to give a sense of importance to (a certain matter): *He stressed the need for careful spending if they were not to find themselves without money.*

emphasize, -ise [T1] to place emphasis (on); stress: *The band emphasized the beats in the music to show that it was a marching tune. The teacher emphasized the importance of care in crossing the road.*

underline [T1] **1** to mark (one or more words) by drawing a line underneath esp to show importance or to give force: *The example sentences in this book were first underlined by hand to tell the printer to print them in italics.* **2** (*fig*) to give force to (an idea, feeling, etc) which has been expressed or shown): *His refusal to go underlined his dislike of the place.*

rub in [v adv T1] (*esp in the phr* **rub it in**) *infml often deprec* to emphasize or keep repeating something: *All right, I understand, but I don't like it; don't rub it in!/stop rubbing it in!*

point up [v adv T1] to add to, show the qualities of, or make clearer: *The writer has pointed up his story with an effective use of local scenery.*

highlight [T1] to pick out or take (something) as an important point; to throw attention on to: *His sister's refusal highlighted his offer to help.*

G78 nouns : insisting and emphasizing

insistence [U] the act of insisting: *His insistence on seeing her annoyed us all.*

demand [C] an act of demanding a claim: *The workers' demand for higher wages seems reasonable.* (*fig*) *This work makes great demands on my time. The demand for change has a lot of popular support.*

stress [U] a sense of special importance (*esp in the phr* **lay stress on**): *The speaker laid stress on the importance of the new laws to women and children.*

emphasis [C; U (*upon, on*)] special force given to certain words, ideas, or details, in speaking, writing, drawing, etc, to show that they are particularly important: *That textbook places/lays/puts a special emphasis on grammar. 'Surely you're not coming?' he said, with great emphasis on 'you'* (= he said the word slowly, loudly, and clearly).

G79 verbs : overstating and understating

exaggerate [Wv5; I0; T1] to say or believe more than the truth or what is necessary (about); to make (something) seem larger, better, etc than in reality: *We mustn't exaggerate the danger. She has an exaggerated idea of her own beauty* (= She thinks she is more beautiful than she is). *He always exaggerates; don't believe everything he says.* **-dly** [adv]: *He is exaggeratedly proud of his position.*

overstate [T1] to state more strongly than is usual or acceptable, etc, making things appear better, worse, or more important than they really are (*esp in the phr* **overstate one's case**): *People won't believe you if you overstate your case.*

pile on [v adv T1] (*esp in the phr* **pile it on**) *infml* to exaggerate or overstate: *He tells great stories about life when he was young, but I think he piles it on a bit, don't you?*

understate [T1] to state less strongly than is usual or acceptable, etc, making things appear better, worse, or less important than they really are: *Don't understate what you've done; tell us the facts.*

G80 nouns : overstating and understating

exaggeration 1 [U] the act of exaggerating, of saying or believing more than the truth or what is necessary: *To say she is the most beautiful girl in the country is just exaggeration.* **2** [C] an example of this: *It's an exaggeration to say she is the most beautiful girl in the country.*

overstatement [U; C] the act of overstating: *Be careful; the overstatement of your case could harm your position.*

understatement [U; C] the act of understating: *British humour often contains understatement(s).*

G81 verbs : explaining and describing

[ALSO ⇨ I 43]

explain [I0; T1, 5a, 6a, b] to give the meaning of (something); to make (something) clear, by speaking or writing: *I don't understand this; please explain. The lawyer explained the new law (to us). He explained how to use the telephone. Explain what this word means. She explained that she was a foreigner.* **explain oneself** to make one's meaning clear: *I don't understand what you're talking about; would you explain yourself a little?* [⇨ N 227]

account for [v prep T1, 4, 6a] to explain or give a reason for: *He could not account for his foolish mistake. It is difficult to account for the absence of policemen at the meeting.*

describe 1 [T1, 6a, b] to give a picture in words of: *He described the man/place/event. Try to describe exactly what happened before the accident.* **2** [T1] *tech* to draw the shape of: *He described a circle within a square.* **3** [T1] (*fig*) to move in the shape of: *The falling star described a long curve in the sky.* **descriptive** [B] **1** [Wa5] that describes: *descriptive writing* **2** that describes well: *It's the most descriptive writing I have ever read. Your words are very descriptive; I understand exactly.* **-ly** [adv] **-ness** [U]

define [T1] **1** to explain the exact meaning of (a word, phrase, etc): *This book defines many words. Can you define 'life' for me?* **2** to make (something) clear and see to understand: *He defined the matter very well.* **definitive** [B] **1** serving to define or as a means of defining **2** the best, most useful, etc of a usu stated kind: *He wrote the definitive book on the subject.* **-ly** [adv]

put across also **put over** [v adv T1] to cause to be understood; explain: *He puts it across very well, he almost convinces me.*

G82 nouns : explaining and describing

explanation 1 [U] the act of explaining, giving meanings, or making (something) clear: *Explanation isn't always easy.* **2** [C] an example of this: *Can you give us an explanation of what you did? His explanation of the new law was very interesting.*

description 1 [U] the act of giving a picture in words: *Description isn't always simple.* **2** [C] an example of this: *He gave us a description of the man/place/event.*

account [C] a written or spoken report; a description, explanation, or story: *She gave them an account of what happened in her own words. Their two accounts are very different.*

definition 1 [U] the act of defining **2** [U] the clearness of something, esp when seen, drawn, or heard: *The drawing lacks definition.* **3** [C] an example of defining; an explanation of the meaning of (something): *This book is full of definitions.*

G83 verbs : discussing and debating

talk about [v prep T1, 6] to talk (with someone) on a particular matter: *Let's talk about the job/ what to do/where to go.*

discuss [T1, 6a, b] to talk about (something with someone) from several points of view: *She refuses to discuss the matter with him. The women were discussing hats. We discussed what to do and where to go.*

argue 1 [I0; T1, 5] to present reasons for or against (something), esp clearly and in proper order: *He argues well. They argued the case for hours. He argued that she should not go.* **2** [I0 (*against*; *about/over* and/or *with*)] to reason strongly in defence of one's opinions and in opposition to those of others: *He's always* ready to argue (*about politics*) (*with me*). *He argued* (*with her*) (*over the new plan*). *He's always arguing against me/my ideas.* **3** [T5, 5b] to give reasons to prove or try to prove: *The scientist argued that his discovery had changed the course of history. So he argued, but I don't believe him/it.* **4** [T1 *into* or *out of*] to persuade by showing reasons for or against, often with strong feeling: *She argued him into/out of his decision.* **arguable 1** [B] able to be supported with reasons: *It is arguable that the criminal is a necessary member of society.* **2** [B] doubtful in some degree: *That their decision was the best one is arguable.* **in-** [neg] **-bly** [adv Wa3]

debate 1 [I0; T1] to argue about (something) usu in an effort to persuade other people: *We debated until the bar closed. I debated* (*upon/about*) *the question* (*with Mary*). *I debated with Mary* (*upon/about the question*). **2** [T1] to consider in one's own mind the arguments for and against (something): *I debated the idea in my mind until I fell asleep.* **debatable** [B] **1** able to be debated: *The matter is debatable; let us meet again next week.* **2** doubtful in some degree: *That their decision was the best one is debatable.* **-bly** [adv Wa3]

have it out *infml* to discuss something fully and openly: *Look, let's talk about it; we must have it out, then we'll feel better.*

G84 *nouns* : **discussing and debating**

discussion 1 [U] the act of discussing: *They find discussion* (*of the subject*) *difficult.* **2** [C] an example of this: *Let's have a discussion about it/on the matter. These radio discussions aren't very interesting.*

argument 1 [C] a reason given to support or disprove something: *There are many arguments against smoking.* **2** [U] the use of reason to persuade someone: *We should try to settle this problem by argument, not by fighting.*

debate 1 [C] a usu public meeting or situation in which a question is talked over by at least two people or groups, each expressing a different point of view: *There will be a long debate in Parliament before the new law is passed. The national debate on how the country should be run became boring.* **2** [U] formal public argument: *The use of prisons has become a matter of debate.*

G85 *verbs* : **convincing and reassuring**

convince [T1 (*of*); V3; D5] to cause (someone) to believe or feel certain; to persuade (someone): *It took many hours to convince John of his wife's guilt. We convinced Anne to go by train rather than plane. It's going to be hard to convince my wife that we can't afford a new car.*

assure [D5a; T1 (*of*)] to try to cause (someone) to believe or trust in something; to promise; to

try to persuade: *I assure you that this medicine cannot harm you. He assured us of his ability to work.*

reassure [T1 (*about, of*); D5] to comfort and make (someone who is anxious or uncertain) free from fear or uncertainty: *Let me reassure you that all is going well.* **-ringly** [adv]

G86 *nouns* : **convincing and reassuring**

conviction [C; U] (a) very firm and sincere belief: *I always try to act in accordance with my convictions. I speak in the full conviction that our cause is just. From the way she spoke you could tell she was speaking from conviction.* **carry conviction** to be likely to cause belief; be likely to persuade: *If your arguments carry conviction many people will support you.* **open to conviction** ready to listen to a person's opinions and be persuaded by them if they seem right: *I've never supported your political party but I'm open to conviction.*

assurance 1 [U] *also* **self-assurance** strong belief in one's own ability and powers: *The businessman had great assurance and people trusted him quickly. The teacher lacked assurance in front of his class.* **2** [C (*of*), C5 *often pl with same meaning*] a trustworthy statement; promise: *He gave me his assurance that he would come. In spite of all his assurances, he did not come.*

reassurance 1 [U] the act of reassuring **2** [C *often pl with same meaning*] an example of this: *She won't believe it in spite of all our reassurances.*

G87 *verbs* : **persuading and coaxing**
[ALSO ⇒F 27]

persuade 1 [T1 (*of*); D5a] to cause to feel certain: *She was not persuaded of the truth of his statement. I can't persuade myself that this is the right thing to do.* **2** [T1; V3] to cause ((not) to do something) by reasoning, arguing, begging, etc: *Try to persuade him to let us go with him. Nothing would persuade him. None of us could persuade him out of his stupid plans.* (*fig*) *He persuaded the piece of wood into the little crack* (= made it go into it gradually). **persuasion** [U; C] (an) act of persuading: *She tried persuasion to get him to do it.* **persuasive** [B] for the purpose of, or able to, persuade: *She can be very persuasive when she wants to.* **-ly** [adv]

dissuade [T1 (*from*)] to persuade not to do something: *Can't I dissuade you* (*from doing these silly things*)? *Nothing would dissuade her; she went.* **dissuasion** [U] the act of dissuading

coax 1 [T1] to persuade (someone) by gentle kindness or patience: *I coaxed him into taking me to the theatre. She coaxed me out of my depression. He coaxed her to take her medicine.*

2 [X9] to obtain by gently persuading: *I coaxed a kiss from the little girl.*

get round [v prep T1] *infml* to persuade (someone) to accept one's own way of thinking: *Father doesn't want to let us go, but I know I can get round him.*

brainwash [T1 (*into*)] *infml & derog* to cause (someone) to change beliefs by means which are not limited to reason or force: *After several months in prison with very little sleep and talking only to the enemy he was brainwashed into joining them.* (*fig*) *Don't let all those television advertisements brainwash you into buying that soap.* **brainwashing 1** [U] the act or action of brainwashing **2** [C] an example of this: *He received a brainwashing from them.*

indoctrinate [T1 (*with*)] *usu deprec* to put ideas into (someone's mind); *tech* to brainwash: *They have those beliefs because they have been indoctrinated since childhood.* **-tion** [U]

G88 *verbs* : **suggesting and implying**

[ALSO ⇒ G119]

suggest 1 [T1, 4, 5a, c, 6a, b] to say or write (an idea to be considered): *I suggest bringing/(that) we bring the meeting to an end.* **2** [T1] to cause to come to the mind: *The sight of the birds suggested a new idea for flying machines.* **3** [T1] to bring (itself) to the mind: *An idea suggested itself.* **suggestive** [B (*of*)] causing someone to think or believe something, often about sex: *He said something highly suggestive about the girl's behaviour. Her actions were suggestive of fear.* **-ly** [adv]

propose [Wv5] **1** [T1, 4, 5c] to suggest; put forward for consideration: *I propose a short rest before we continue the work. I propose that we have half an hour's rest.* **2** [T1, 3, 4; (I∅)] to form (as) (a plan or intention); intend: *I propose to go to London tomorrow.*

put forward [v adv T1] *not fml* to propose: *He put forward a plan for the committee to consider.*

put . . . to [v prep D1, 5] *infml* to suggest to: *Let me put my plan to you. I put it to you that you can't win the game!*

hint [I∅; T1, 5a] to suggest indirectly: *She hinted (to him) that she was dissatisfied with his work. She hinted (to him) her dissatisfaction with his work.* **hint at** [v prep T1] to suggest indirectly: *He hinted at her foolishness. She hinted at the possibility of more money.*

imply [T1, 5a, b] to suggest without expressing in words: *Her refusal to answer implies her guilt. His manner implies that he would like to come with us.*

get at [v prep T1] (*usu in questions*) *not fml* to imply; hint at: *I don't understand; just what are you getting at?*

insinuate [T1, 5a] *fml usu deprec* to imply; hint: *I don't know exactly what you are insinuating but I don't like it. He seemed to insinuate that you got the money unlawfully.*

entail [T1] to make necessary as a means or result of getting something else: *He needs a bigger house and this will entail getting more money.* **entailment** [U] the condition of entailing or being entailed

G89 *nouns* : **suggesting and implying**

suggestion 1 [U] the act of suggesting: *Force won't work; try suggestion and persuasion.* **2** [C] something suggested: *We could change our plans and leave early; but that's only a suggestion.* **3** [S (*of*)] a slight sign: *Her face held a suggestion of anger.* **4** [U] a way of causing an idea to be accepted by the mind by indirect connection with other ideas: *Advertisers use suggestion to sell goods when they show babies and beautiful girls using their products.*

proposal 1 [U] the act of proposing: *Everyone stood politely during the proposal of the president's health. The proposal of a short rest period met (with) everyone's approval. The proposal that we should rest for a while was a good one.* **2** [C *often pl*] a plan or suggestion offered: *He made proposals for a new system of street lighting. There were several proposals that we should rest more frequently.*

proposition 1 [C] an unproved statement in which an opinion or judgment is expressed: *It is a reasonable proposition that new rules on the speed of cars should be made, but it is an arguable proposition that all drivers will obey them.* **2** [C] a suggestion, (business) offer, arrangement, or settlement (*often in the phr* **make someone a proposition**): *The firm has made me a proposition; it wants me to act as its adviser on trading possibilities in Europe.* **3** [S9] *infml* a person who or thing that must be dealt with, considered with regard to the difficulty or chance of success, etc: *Getting over these snow-covered mountains isn't a practical proposition* (= is not a matter that is possible) *in winter. Be careful in dealing with him; he's a nasty proposition, who always gains the advantage by some clever trick.* **4** [C] (*esp in the phr* **make someone a proposition**) *euph* a suggested offer to have sex with someone, esp with a woman

hint [C] **1** a small or indirect suggestion: *I know it's a secret, but can't you give me a hint (of what it is)?* **2** a small suggestion: *I kept looking at my watch, but she couldn't take the hint (that I wanted to leave). You don't have to ask me to leave; I can take a hint.* **3** (*fig*) a small sign: *There's a hint of summer in the air, although it's only May.* **4** [*often pl*] useful advice: *His hints helped me a lot in my work.*

innuendo 1 [C] *often deprec* a hint: *She is always making little innuendoes about how rich her family are.* **2** [U] *lit* the use of hints and implications: *The poem is full of political innuendo.*

implication 1 [U] the act of implying; indirect suggestion: *We can get his meaning by implication, not directly.* **2** [C] an example of this;

something, esp a possibility or difficulty, that one learns indirectly: *What are the implications of his decision? The implication that I was refusing unnecessarily made me angry.*

insinuation [U;C] act of insinuating: *I don't like his insinuations that I got the money unlawfully!*

G90 *verbs, etc* : **mentioning and quoting**

mention 1 [T1, 5] to tell someone about (something) in a few words, spoken or written: *He mentioned their interest in flowers. He never mentioned that he's already been there.* **2** [T1] to say the name of: *He mentioned a useful book. She never mentions the son she lost. Soon after going abroad with the army he was mentioned in despatches* (= honoured for bravery). **not to mention (something/the fact that)** and in addition there's . . . : *They have three dogs to find a home for, not to mention that cat and the bird.* **Don't mention it** *polite* There's no need for thanks; I'm glad to help: *Thanks very much.—Don't mention it.*

refer to [v prep] **1** [T1] to mention; speak about: *Don't refer to that lady as a cow!* **2** [T1] to look at for information: *If you don't know what this word means, refer to the dictionary.* **3** [T1] to concern; be directed towards: *The new law does not refer to land used for farming.* **4** [D1 (*back*)] to send (someone or something) to (usu someone else) for decision or action: *The shop referred the complaint (back) to the makers of the article.*

raise [T1] *often fml* to mention or refer to: *Can I raise this matter with you now/at our next meeting?*

allude to [v prep T1] *fml* to speak of (someone or something) indirectly: *She did not say Mr Smith's name, but it was clear she was alluding to him. What are you alluding to?*

bring up [v adv T1] to raise, introduce, or mention (a subject): *I'm sorry to bring this matter up again, but I must have an answer soon. She says she will bring it up at the next meeting.*

quote 1 [T1; I0] to repeat in speech or writing another (supposedly powerful) person's words: *He quotes (from) the Bible to support his own wishes. Don't quote me on that! Oh, stop quoting!* **2** [T1] to mention in order to add power to one's own point of view: *I quote Bill, who always holds parties in the afternoon. He quoted the case of the man whose wife went with him to Alaska.* **3** [D1 (*to*); T1] to give (a price): *I can quote you a price lower than anyone else's. The value of the pound was quoted regularly.*

cite [T1] **1** to mention (a passage written or spoken by someone else or the person who wrote or spoke such a passage): *It's no use citing the Bible to someone who doesn't believe in it.* **2** [*usu pass*] to make a formal statement

that (someone) is worthy of praise: *The soldier was cited by the king for his bravery.*

according to [prep] (*used esp in quoting*) following the words of: *According to her he is a fool. According to the Bible, Adam and Eve lived in the Garden of Eden. If you go according to the map you'll find the street easily.*

G91 *nouns* : **mentioning and quoting**

mention 1 [U] the act of mentioning: *He made no mention of his wishes.* **2** [C *usu sing*] a short remark: *I thought he would talk about the importance of rest after an operation, but he never gave it a mention.* **3** [C *usu sing*] *not fml* a naming of someone, esp for honour: *He was given a mention in the list of helpers.*

reference [C; U (*to*)] **1** (a case of) mentioning: *Did you hear all those nasty references to me that Janet kept making?* **2** (a case of) looking at for information: *Keep this dictionary on your desk for easy reference.* **in/with reference to** in connection with

quotation 1 [U] the act of quoting: *Some speakers do a lot of quotation from books.* **2** [C] an act of quoting: *His speeches are full of quotations.* **3** [C] something quoted: *Can you get me some good quotations from that writer? What's the latest quotation on the pound?*

allusion [U; C (*to*)] the act of speaking of something indirectly, or something spoken or written of indirectly, esp while speaking or writing about something else: *His allusions to our failures were unnecessary.*

citation 1 [U] the act of citing: '*Such citation of the Bible proves nothing,*' *he said.* **2** [C] a short passage taken from something written or spoken by someone else: *People who write dictionaries sometimes use citations to show the meaning of words.* **3** [C] a formal statement of a person's qualities, esp bravery in battle: *He got a presidential citation for his bravery in the war.*

G92 *verbs* : **asking and inquiring**

ask 1 [T1, 6a, b; D1, 6a, b; I0] to call on (a person) for an answer (to); request (information) from someone: *Ask him! I asked who he was/where to go. Ask him his name. He asked her a question.* (*fml*) *He asked a question of her. He asked about his health. Did you ask* (*him*) *a question?* **2** [T1, 3, 5c; V3; I0 (*for*)] to make a request for or to: *She asked his advice/him for advice. They asked to go for a walk. I asked that I (should) be allowed to see her. She asked him to wake her at 6 o'clock. She asked for his advice. She asked to be woken at 6 o'clock. She asked (for permission) to go. Don't ask (me) for money! Has anyone asked for me at the office?* **3** [T1 (*for, of*)] to demand (something, such as a price); expect: *He is* *asking a lot of money (for his house). The job asks a great deal (of me).*

inquire 1 [T1] *fml* to ask: *I inquired his reason for coming.* **2** [T6a, b] to ask: *I inquired what he wanted/whether he would come.* **3** [IØ] to ask for information: *I'll inquire about the trains. I don't know the times; I must inquire.*

enquire [T1, 6a, b; IØ] *fml* to inquire: *May I enquire how much money you can provide?*

ask after *infml*, also **inquire/enquire after** *fml* [v prep T1 *pass rare*] to inquire about the health or well-being of (someone): *My mother asked/was asking after you.—Oh, how kind of her! They were enquiring after your health.*

G93 nouns : replying and answering

reply [U; C (*to*)] speaking, writing, etc in return: *I asked him, but he made no reply. What did you say in reply to his suggestion? We received several replies in answer to our advertisement.*

answer [C] **1** a spoken or written reply, as to a question, request, letter, or polite greeting: *Although I wrote a month ago I've had no answer yet. I said good morning to him but he gave no answer.* **2** a reply in the form of action: *Her answer was a smile. In answer to her shouts people ran to help (her).* **3** a reply to an argument or charge **4** something, at first unknown, which is discovered as a result esp of thinking, using figures, etc: *I gave her all the necessary figures and she found the answer quickly. The answers are all given at the end of the book. The answer (to the sum) was 179.* **5** a piece of (usu written) work to show knowledge or ability, as in an examination: *The teacher asked the pupils to hand in their answers/the answer sheets.*

response *often fml* **1** [C (*to*)] an answer: *He made/gave no response (to my question). There have been several responses (to our advertisement).* **2** [C; U (*to*)] (an) action done in answer: *There has been very little response to our call for help.* **in response to** as an answer to: *He opened the door in response to a knock.* '*In response to your inquiry . . .*' (in a business letter)

G94 verbs : replying and answering

reply [IØ (*to*); T5a] to give a reply to (something): *I asked him where to go but he didn't reply. 'Of course not,' she replied. She replied that she was not amused. Have you replied to his letter?*

answer 1 [T1; IØ] to give an answer (to); reply (to): *You didn't answer his question. Why didn't you answer? Answer any three questions. I will answer her (letter) today.* **2** [IØ (with)] to do something as a reply (to): *I answered his question with a smile.* **3** [T1; IØ] to attend or act in reply to (a sign, such as a telephone ringing, a knock on the door, or a whistle): *I telephoned*

this afternoon but nobody answered (the telephone). **4** [IØ (*to*); T1] to act or move in reply (to); obey: *The dog answers to his name. The car answered (to) his lightest touch.* **5** [IØ; T1] to be satisfactory (for): *This tool will answer (for) (our needs) very well.* **6** [IØ; T1] (*fig*) to be as described in: *He answers (to) the description.* **7** [T1] (*fig*) to satisfy: *The government just didn't answer our hopes.* **8** [T1; IØ] to reply to (a charge or argument): *Well it's time for you to answer (the charge).*

respond *often fml* **1** [IØ (*to*); T5a] to answer: *I offered him a drink but he didn't respond (to my offer). 'I can't marry you,' she responded sadly.* **2** [IØ (by, to, with)] to act in answer: *He responded (to my suggestion) with a laugh/by laughing.*

G95 nouns : questioning and doubting

question [C] **1** a sentence or phrase which asks for information: *I asked you a question and you didn't reply. No more questions, please; the speaker is tired.* **2** a doubt: *There is no question of his coming. There was some question as to his honesty.* **out of the question** impossible: *Can you go?—No, it's out of the question.*

query [C] a question or a doubt: *Have you any queries about what to do next?*

inquiry also **enquiry** [C] an act or occasion of inquiring: *He has been making inquiries into what you were doing here last month. The inquiry showed that he had taken all the money for himself.*

dispute [U] strong argument; great doubt: *There is no dispute about what happened; we all saw it.*

doubt 1 [C; U, 5, 6a (*whether, if, about*)] (a feeling of) uncertainty of belief or opinion: *He was troubled by religious doubt/doubts. There is some doubt (as to) whether/(about) whether he will come on time. There's no doubt that he'll come.* **2** [C; U (*about*)] (a feeling of) mistrust: *He says he can cure me, but I still have my doubts (about him/it).* **3** [U] a tendency not to believe or accept: *His continual doubt makes it hard for him to act.* **in doubt** in a condition of uncertainty: *The result is still in doubt. I'm still in doubt about it.* **without doubt** also **no doubt** it is certain: *John will come on time, without doubt. No doubt he'll come.*

suspicion 1 [U] **a** the act of suspecting or state of being suspected: *He is under suspicion of theft. There is some suspicion about his actions.* **b** lack of trust or willingness to accept: *She always treated us with suspicion. The dog smelled the meat with suspicion.* **2** [C] **a** a feeling of suspecting: *I have a suspicion that he's right.* **b** a belief about someone's guilt: *The police have not found the thief but they have their suspicions.* **3** [S (*of*)] a slight amount (of something seen, heard, tasted, etc): *There was a suspicion of tears in her eyes./a suspicion of summer in the air.*

328

scepticism *BrE*, **skepticism** *AmE* [U] a doubting state or habit of mind; dislike of believing without being certain; doubt: *He has a healthy scepticism about what is said in advertisements. Her scepticism showed on her face when she heard the story.* **sceptic** *BrE*, **skeptic** *AmE* [C] a person who is (habitually) unwilling to believe a claim or promise: *He is a sceptic about politicians' promises.* **sceptical** *BrE*, **skeptical** *AmE* [B (*of, about*)] of, concerning, or like a sceptic: *His employer looked sceptical when he said he'd been ill the day before. I'm sceptical of/ about the team's chances of winning.* **-ly** [adv Wa4]

cynicism [U] a state of mind in which a person thinks that others always have bad or strongly personal reasons for doing things, even when they seem to be good, kind, and unselfish; doubt about people's good, etc acts: *His cynicism is well-known.* **cynic** [C] a person showing cynicism: *Oh don't be such a cynic!* **cynical** [B] of, concerning, or like cynicism or a cynic: *He gave a cynical smile when the rich girl said she planned to help the poor.* **-ly** [adv Wa4]

G96 *verbs* : **questioning and doubting**

question·[T1, 6a] *genl* to raise doubt about: *I question whether I could have arrived in time. She never questioned his honesty.*

query [T1] to question or raise a doubt about, sometimes by marking (?) on a piece of writing: *I'd like to query several points that you made in your talk.*

dispute 1 [T1] to disagree about; call into question; doubt: *The honesty of his intentions was never disputed.* **2** [T1, 6a, b; I0] to argue about (something), esp angrily and for some time: *They disputed for hours (about) where to go.*

doubt 1 [T1, 5a, 6a (*whether, if*)] to be uncertain (about): *I doubt the truth of it. I doubt whether it's true. I don't doubt that John will come on time.* **2** [T1, 6a (*whether, if*)] to mistrust: *I doubt his honesty. I doubt if he's honest. He says he can cure me, but I still doubt him.* **3** [T5a] to consider unlikely: *I doubt that John will come on time. I doubt he'll come now.*

suspect 1 [T1, 5a] to believe to exist or be true; think likely: *We suspected trouble. We suspected that he was lost, even before we were told.* **2** [T1 (*of*); V3] to believe to be guilty: *They suspect him of murder. They suspected him to be the murderer.* **3** [T1] to be doubtful about the truth or value of: *I suspect his motives* (= real reasons for what he does). **4** [T5a, b] *infml* to suppose or guess: *I suspect you may be right. I suspect that's true.* **suspect** [C] a person who is suspected of doing something: *The police have several suspects. She was a murder suspect* (= They thought she might have murdered or killed someone).

G97 *verbs* : **contradicting and refuting**

contradict 1 [T1; I0] to declare (a person, opinion, something written or spoken) to be wrong or untruthful: *How dare you contradict me! 'Young children should never contradict what their parents say,' she said angrily. Don't contradict!* **2** [T1] (of a statement, action, fact, etc) to be opposite in nature or character to (a statement, action, fact, etc): *The various reports contradict each other. Your actions contradict your declared moral principles.*

refute [T1] *usu fml & tech* to prove **a** (someone) to be mistaken: *I refuted him easily.* **b** (a statement) to be untrue: *I refuted his claim that the world was flat.*

G98 *nouns* : **contradicting and refuting**

contradiction 1 [U] **a** the act of contradicting: *His father punishes contradiction severely.* **b** the state of being contradicted: *Contradiction makes my teacher angry.* **2** [U] direct opposition between things compared; disagreement (*often in the phr* **in contradiction**): *There is no contradiction between my behaviour and my principles; they are not in contradiction.* **3** [C] a statement, action, or fact that contradicts another or itself: *There are many contradictions in industrial society. It is a contradiction to say you support the government but would not vote for it in an election.* **contradictory** [Wa5;B] of, concerning, or like a contradiction; serving to contradict: *His two statements are contradictory.*

paradox 1 [C] a statement which seems to be foolish or impossible, but which has some truth in it: *'More haste, less speed' is a paradox.* **2** [C] an improbable combination of opposing qualities, ideas, etc: *It is a paradox that in such a rich country there should be so many poor people.* **3** [C] a statement, idea, or fact that is opposite to what is generally believed to be true: *The idea that the earth is round, not flat, was described in ancient times as a paradox.* **4** [U] the use of such statements in speaking or writing: *a writer who is very fond of paradox* **paradoxical** [B] of, connected with, or like a paradox **-ly** [adv Wa4]

refutation [C; U] (a) proof that something is untrue

G99 *verbs* : **questioning and interrogating**

question [T1] to ask (someone) a question or questions: *Can I question you on that point? The questioning went on for hours.*

cross-examine *also* **cross-question** [T1] to keep asking (someone) questions: *The police are cross-examining him about where he was when*

329

the murder took place. Stop cross-questioning me!

interrogate [T1] to question for a special purpose, esp at length: *He was interrogated for several hours by the police.* **interrogation** [U;C] the action of interrogating or being interrogated

G100 *verbs* : **asking, requesting, and begging**

ask for [v prep T1] **1** to show that one wants (something) by asking to have or get it: *He asked for the book.* **2** (*esp in tenses using the -ing form*) to behave so as to cause (something bad): *If you climb that mountain in this bad weather you're asking for trouble. When he got into trouble I said, 'You asked for it!'*

request [T1, 5c (*of*); V3] *esp fml* to ask for (something) politely (not used with the actual words spoken): *May I request your attention? I requested (of him) that he (should) leave. I requested them to stop making such a noise.*

appeal [I0 (*to, for*)] to ask strongly for help, support, money, etc: *The speaker appealed to his hearers for silence/help/money. The government is appealing to everyone to save water. The police appealed for anyone with information to come forward and help them. We appealed to be allowed to leave. I don't like appealing, but I need help.*

appeal to [v prep T1] to look to for support, help, etc: *I am appealing to you; please help me!*

beg **1** [T1;I0] to ask humbly for (food, money, or other necessary things): *He lives by begging. He begged (for) money (from people) in the streets.* **2** [T1, 5c; V3;I0, 3] *often fml* to ask humbly (something not material): *May I beg a favour (of you)? He begged me not to leave. He begged and begged until I agreed to do it. She begged (her mother's) forgiveness.* **3** [T3] *fml* to allow oneself: *I beg to point out that your facts are not correct.*

beseech [T1;V3] *fml & lit* to ask eagerly and anxiously: *He besought a favour of the judge. I beseech you to help. Help me, I beseech you! She gave him a beseeching look.* **-ingly** [adv] *She looked beseechingly at him.*

plead **1** [I0] to make continual and deeply felt requests: *She wept and pleaded until he agreed to do as she wished. He pleaded for more time to pay.* **2** [T1] to give as an excuse for an action: *I'm sorry I didn't answer your letter; I can only plead forgetfulness.* **3** [T1] to speak or argue in support of: *He was pleading the cause of the unemployed. Which lawyer is pleading this case in court?*

implore [T1;V3] *esp emph* to ask (someone) in a begging manner (for something or to do something): *I implored him to help me. I implored his help, but he didn't do anything.*

apply [I0 (*for*)] to request (something) esp officially and in writing: *I will apply for the job*

tomorrow. You must apply to the minister for permission.

petition **1** [T1 (*for*);V3] to make a (written) petition to: *They are petitioning their employers for better working conditions. They petitioned the government to reconsider its decision.* **2** [I0 (*for*), 3] to ask or beg some official body: *The people petitioned to be allowed to return to their island.* **petitioner** [C] **1** a person who makes or signs a petition **2** *law* a person asking for the ending of his or her marriage

solicit [T1] to beg or appeal for (something); try strongly to get: *He solicits money from everyone he meets. She tried to solicit his advice.*

G101 *nouns* : **requesting**

request [C] *esp fml* a polite demand: *She made a request for help. Her repeated requests that I should play with her annoyed me.* **at someone's request** because someone asked: *I bought it at your request/at the request of my father.* **by request (of)** because asked for (by): *The band are playing by request of the Queen.* **in (great) request** *also* **much in request** popular; being asked for by many people: *These yellow socks have been much in request lately.* **on request** when asked for: *The band will play on request.*

appeal [U;C] (a) strong request for help, support, money, etc: *His appeal for forgiveness went unanswered. The appeals for money with which to build the new hall were very successful. There was a look of appeal in her eyes.*

plea **1** [C (*for*)] *fml* an eager or serious request: *She wouldn't listen to his plea for forgiveness.* **2** [(*the*) S] an excuse given for doing or not doing something: *He refused the invitation to dinner on the plea of being too busy.*

application **1** [U] the act of requesting, esp officially and in writing: *Tickets may be bought on application to/at the theatre.* **2** [C] such a request: *I wrote five applications for jobs but got nothing.*

petition [C] **1** (a piece or pieces of paper containing) a (respectful) request or demand made to a government or other body, usu signed by many people: *We signed the petition that asked the council for better street lights.* **2** a proper official letter to a court of law, asking for consideration of one's case **3** a solemn prayer to God

G102 *verbs* : **complaining and objecting**

complain **1** [I0;T5a] to express (in) annoyance, pain, unhappiness, dissatisfaction, grief, etc; speak or say in an unhappy, annoyed, dissatisfied way: *She is always complaining about something. Stop complaining and eat your dinner!* **2** [I0] to make a usu formal report about someone or something one considers annoying, wrong, etc: *Our next-door neighbour said he'd complain (about us) (to the police) (if we made any more noise)*.

grumble [I0;T5a] to complain, usu in a low unhappy voice: *Oh, stop grumbling! 'They want me to do all the work here,' he grumbled.*

moan *also infml* **grouse** [I0;T5a] *deprec* to complain; speak or say in a complaining voice: *Stop moaning; you really have nothing to complain about. He's always grousing about the unjust way in which he thinks he is being treated.*

gripe [I0] *infml* to complain, esp continuously

beef [I0 (*about*)] *sl* to complain: *Stop beefing about your troubles!*

bitch [I0 (*about*)] *sl* to complain; speak nastily: *Stop bitching (about him)*.

object [I0 (*to*)] to be against someone or something: *Do you object to smoking? They objected (against him) that his language was bad. I objected because of his bad language at the party. What are you objecting about now?*

G103 *nouns* : **complaining and objecting**

complaint [C;U (*against*)] (an) expression of annoyance, pain, unhappiness, dissatisfaction, grief, etc in speech or in writing: *Do you have any complaints against us? Please read our complaints. If persuasion [⇒ G87] doesn't work, try complaint. He took his complaints to his lawyer.*

moan *also infml* **grouse** usu deprec [C] a complaint, expressed in a voice that has a suffering or discontented sound: *She's never satisfied; she always has some moan/grouse or another.*

gripe [C] *infml* a complaint or moan: *What gripes have you got today?*

objection [C;U (*to, against*)] an act or expression of objecting: *Do you have any objection to/against what we are doing?—No, no objection.*

G104 *verbs* : **apologizing and forgiving**

apologize, -ise [I0 (*to, for*)] to express sorrow, as for a fault or causing pain: *I apologized (to her) for stepping on her foot. I apologized at once.*

forgive 1 [D1;T1 (*for*);I0] to say or feel that one is no longer angry about or wishing to give punishment to (someone) for (something): *'Forgive me', she said; 'forgive the wrongs I've done you.' He forgave her the wrongs she had done him. I'll never forgive you for what you said to me last night. It's best to forgive and forget.* **2** [D1] to say that (someone) need not repay (something): *I lent you that £2.50 a month ago; I'll forgive you the 50p, but I want the £2 back.*

excuse 1 [T1, 4] to forgive (someone) for (a small fault): *Please excuse my bad handwriting/my opening your letter by mistake/me for opening your letter by mistake.* **2** [T1 *usu neg*] to make (bad behaviour) seem less bad: *Nothing will excuse his cruelty to his children.* **3** [T1 (*from*); (*also BrE*) D1 *usu pass*] to free (someone) from a duty: *Can I be excused from football practice today? (BrE) Can I be excused football practice today?*

excuse oneself 1 to offer an excuse **2** to ask permission to be absent: *He excused himself from the party.* **excuse me** forgive me; I'm sorry: *Excuse me; can you tell me the time? He said 'excuse me' when he stepped on my foot.*

pardon [T1;D1 (*for*)] to forgive; excuse: *Please pardon my carelessness. I hope you will pardon me for disagreeing with you. We must pardon him his little faults.*

let off [v adv T1] *infml* to excuse, forgive, or allow to go free or unpunished: *All right, I'll let you off this time, but never again! The judge let the man off with a warning not to cause trouble again.*

G105 *nouns* : **apologizing and forgiving**

[ALSO ⇒ G18 REASON, EXCUSE, ETC]

apology [C] **1** a statement expressing sorrow for a fault, causing trouble or pain, etc: *I must offer her an apology for not going to her party. I must make an apology to her. Please accept my apologies.* **2** a very poor example of something: *This bit of burnt potato is no more than an apology for a meal.* **apologetic** [B] **1** expressing sorrow for some fault or wrong: *He wrote her an apologetic letter.* **2** (of a person's manner) as if unwilling to cause trouble: *He asked in an apologetic voice if we would mind getting out of his way.*

forgiveness [U] **1** the act of forgiving or the state of being forgiven: *'Ask for God's forgiveness for what you have done, my son,' said the priest. Her forgiveness (of his bad behaviour) made him happy again.* **2** willingness to forgive

pardon [U;C (*for*)] **a** forgiveness: *He prayed for God's pardon for his evil deeds.* **b** an act or example of forgiveness **2** [C] *tech* **a** an action of a court or ruler forgiving a person for an unlawful act or forgiving the act **b** (a paper giving) a freedom from punishment for an unlawful act **I beg your pardon** *also* **pardon me** *polite* **1** please excuse me for having accidentally touched/pushed you **2** please get out of my way as I wish to pass **3** *also infml* **beg pardon, pardon** I did not hear/understand what you said and would like you to repeat it **4** I'm afraid I disagree with what you have just said: *I beg your pardon, but you are wrong.* **5** (*said in a firm unfriendly voice*) I'm afraid I think that what you have just said is not true/proper

G106 *verbs* : blaming and accusing

blame [D1 *on/for*; T1 (*for*)] to consider (someone) responsible for (something bad): *They blamed the failure on George. They blamed George (for the failure).*

accuse [Wv4, 5; T1 (*of*)] to charge (someone) with doing wrong or breaking the law; blame: *The police accused him (of murder). He was accused of running away. The angry man gave her an accusing look. The judge asked the accused man to stand up.*

condemn 1 [T1 (*as*)] to express strong disapproval of (someone or some action): *Most people are willing to condemn violence of any sort (as evil).* **2** [T1 (*for*)] to judge (a person) guilty: *He was imprisoned and condemned in a day. The court condemned her for her crime.* **3** [Wv5;X9; V3] to state the punishment for (a guilty person), esp a punishment of death or long imprisonment: *The prisoner was condemned to death. The court condemned her to spend all her days in prison. The condemned man spent his last hours praying. A condemned man is a man condemned to death.* **4** [X9; V3] to force (someone) into an unhappy state of affairs: *His bad leg condemned him to a wheelchair. She was condemned to live a life of unhappiness because of her husband's actions.* **5** [Wv5;T1 (*as*)] to declare (something) officially unfit for use: *Although this house is condemned (as unfit), an old lady still lives here. The council ought to have condemned these houses long ago.* **6** [T1] to show the guilt of (a person): *His evil face condemned him.*

denounce [T1] *usu fml* **1** to speak or write against (someone or something): *They denounced him (to the police) as a criminal.* **2** to declare publicly and officially the end of (an agreement, esp one between nations): *They denounced the treaty.*

G107 *nouns* : blaming and accusing

blame [U] **1** responsibility for something bad: *We decided on whom the blame lay. The judge laid/put the blame (for the accident) on them. She was ready to take/bear the blame for what had happened.* **2** bad opinion: *You will bring the blame of others (up)on yourself if you fail in this.*

accusation 1 [U] the act of accusing or of being accused **2** [C] a charge of doing wrong: *The accusation was that he had murdered a man.*

condemnation 1 [U (*of*)] the act of condemning **2** [C (*of*)] an example of the act of condemning: *The priest made a bitter condemnation of violence.* **3** [C *usu sing*] a cause or reason for being condemned: *His evil face was his condemnation.*

denunciation [U;C] *usu fml* (an) act of denouncing (someone or something): *I won't listen to these denunciations!*

G108 *verbs* : acknowledging, confessing, and conceding

acknowledge 1 [T1, 4, 5] to agree to the truth of; recognize the fact or existence (of): *I acknowledge the truth of your statement. We will make them acknowledge defeat. They acknowledged that they were defeated. They acknowledged having been defeated.* **2** [T1 (*as*); X (*to be*) 1, 7] to recognize, accept, or admit (as): *He was acknowledged (to be) the best player. He was acknowledged as their leader. They acknowledged themselves (to be/have been) defeated.* **3** [T1] to show that one is grateful for, as by giving or saying something: *His long service with the company was acknowledged with a present.* **4** [T1] to state that one has received (something): *We must acknowledge his letter.* **5** [T1] to show recognition of, as by smiling or waving: *He walked right past me without even acknowledging me/my existence.*

admit [T1, 4, 5a; I0 (*to*); V3] to state or agree to the truth of (usu something bad); to confess: *The thief admitted his crime. He admitted to the murder. She admitted stealing. I admit that it was difficult. They admitted him to be mad.*

confess 1 [T1, 4, 5a, 6a; I0 (*to*)] to admit (a fault, crime, or something wrong): *The prisoner has confessed her crime. I confessed to hating the king. She confessed she'd eaten all the cakes. Did he confess what he did last night? You must confess to all your crimes!* **2** [X (*to be*) 1, 7] to declare (oneself) to be: *The minister confessed himself guilty/to be a thief.* **3** [T1, 4, 5a, 6a; I0 (*to*)] *tech* to make (one's faults) known to a priest or God: *He confessed his desire for sex. Won't you confess and be at peace with God?* **4** [T1] *tech* (of a priest) to hear the confession of (a person): *The priest confessed 90 people on Saturday morning.* **must/have to confess** to admit: *I must confess I hate this work.*

accept 1 [T1; I0] to take or receive (something offered or given), esp willingly; receive with favour: *I cannot accept your gift. He asked her to marry him and she accepted (him).* **2** [Wv5; T1, (*fml*) 5] to believe; admit; agree to: *I accept your reasons for being late. She accepts that we must do the work this way.*

adopt [T1] to accept or take (something) and use it for some purpose: *He adopted our plan/suggestion. The local people have adopted new customs from abroad.*

concede 1 [T1, 5; I0; D1 (*to*)] to admit as true, just, or proper, often unwillingly (*often in the phr* **concede defeat**): *The government conceded defeat as soon as the election results were known. I'm willing to concede that a larger car would have cost more but I still think we should have bought one. I concede (you) that point, but I still think you're wrong generally. Does he still refuse to concede, even after he's been given all the facts?* **2** [D1 (*to*); T1] to give as a right; allow; yield: *After the First World War Germany conceded (to) her neighbours much val-*

uable territory (= land). *How much territory did France concede after her defeat in 1815? The leading player conceded 10 points to me at the start of the game, but, even so, he beat me!* **3** [IØ] to admit defeat: *I conceded when I saw I had lost. 'I concede,' he said, and the match was over.*

G109 *nouns* : acknowledging, confessing, and conceding

acknowledg(e)ment *often fml* **1** [U] the act of acknowledging (*often in the phr* **in acknowledgement of**): *He was given a present in acknowledgement of his work for the business.* **2** [C] something given, done, or said as a way of thanking: *Please accept this payment as an acknowledgement of your work for our business.* **3** [C] a statement, letter, etc saying that something has been received: *He sent us an acknowledgement of our request.*

admission 1 [U] the act of admitting: *By her own admission she committed the crime.* **2** [C] an example of this: *He made an admission of guilt.*

confession 1 [U] the act of confessing **2** [C] an example of this: *He made a confession of murder.*

acceptance 1 [U] the act of accepting or being accepted **2** [C] an example of this: *How many acceptances have we received?* **3** [U] favour; approval: *The suggestion met with everyone's acceptance.* **4** [C] (in business) an agreement to pay

adoption [U; C] the act of adopting: *His adoption of our suggestion pleased us. He suggested an adoption of their plan in part but not completely.*

concession 1 [U] the act of conceding **2** [C] an example of this: *We can make no concessions to people who use force. This low price is a special concession to people who work with us a lot.*

G110 *nouns* : promising and guaranteeing

promise 1 [C] a statement, which someone else has a right to believe or depend on, that one will or will not do something, give something, etc: *If you make a promise you must keep it. She broke her promise to me* (= She did not keep her promise). *She gave me a promise to help. She gave me her promise* (*that*) *she would help.* **2** [U; S] expectation or hope (esp of success or of something good or deserved): *The news of the war brings little promise* (*of peace*). *The sky contained a promise of rain.* **3** [U] *apprec* signs or reasons for such expectation or hope: *The boy is showing great promise as a footballer.*

pledge [C] **1** a solemn promise or agreement: *They made a pledge to work for the freedom of*

their country. **2** something given or received as a sign of faithful love or friendship: *Take this ring as a pledge of our friendship.*

oath 1 [C; prep U] *usu fml* a solemn promise: *He swore an oath in the name of God. He took an oath to tell the truth. You are under/on oath to tell the truth.* **2** [(the) S] the form of words used in making an oath: *He wrote out the oath.*

word [S] a promise (*esp in the phr* **to give/break one's word**): *He gave his word that he would help. She often breaks her word; don't trust her.*

undertaking [C] *often fml* a promise: *Will you give me an undertaking not to see him again/that you won't see him again?*

guarantee [C] **1** an agreement to be responsible for someone's fulfilling a promise, esp paying a debt: *I give you my guarantee* (*that*) *he'll pay.* **2** a formal written declaration of good quality by the maker of an article which makes an agreement to repay or replace it if it is found imperfect within a period of time: *He got a 3-year guarantee with the watch.* **3** something of value given to someone to keep until the owner has fulfilled a promise (esp) to pay: *He gave the bank the papers which proved he owned the land as a guarantee that he would repay the loan.* **4** *infml* something that happens which makes something else certain: *Good habits are a guarantee of good health.* **guarantor** [C] a person who gives a guarantee

warranty [C] a written or printed guarantee: *Can you give me a warranty to cover the next few months of use of this car?*

treaty 1 [C] a (usu formal) agreement between countries in which certain promises, guarantees, etc are exchanged: *The treaty nations have agreed on these matters. They all signed the peace treaty.* **2** [(by) U] *esp tech* an agreement between persons: *The house was sold by private treaty.*

commitment [C] a promise, etc to which one has committed oneself (= which one has agreed to do): *He has a lot of commitments and cannot take on* (= accept) *any more.*

G111 *verbs* : promising and guaranteeing

promise 1 [T1, 3, 5a; V3; D1, 5a; IØ] to make a promise to do or give (something) or that (something) will be done: *Do you promise secrecy? I promise to return your car in good condition. She promised him never to lie to him again. They promised that the work would all be finished by next week. She isn't coming tonight—But she promised! I can't give you the book; I've promised it to her.* **2** [T1; D1, 5a] *infml* to say that (something) is certain; to warn (someone) of (something): *He promised his son a beating if he disobeyed him.* **3** [T1, 3; L9] to cause to expect or hope for (something); give promise (of): *That clear sky promises good weather. It promises to be a fine day. He promises well as an actor.* **promising** [B] having or showing promise: *That girl is a very promising singer.* **-ly** [adv]

pledge *esp lit & emot* **1** [T3, 5] to make a solemn promise or agreement: *He pledged never to come back until he found her. They have pledged that they will always remain faithful.* **2** [T1] to give (one's word, etc) at the risk of losing one's honour: *I pledged my word (of honour) that I would never again get into debt.* **3** [T1; V3] to bind (someone) with a solemn promise: *He was pledged to secrecy. They pledged themselves never to tell the secret.* **4** [T1] *fml* to express a wish for (the health, success, etc of) by or before taking alcoholic drink: *Everyone at the table stood up and pledged the success of the new company.*

swear *fml* **1** [T3, 5a] to promise formally: *He swore to obey. He swore by his honour/on his father's grave that he would be loyal. He swore he would win.* **2** [T1 (*to*); I0] to (cause to) take an oath, as in court: *They swore him to silence. The witnesses must swear before speaking.* **3** [T1 (*on*)] **a** to take (an oath): *He swore an oath to obey the King.* **b** to declare the truth of by oath: *He swore his evidence.*

undertake [T3, 5] *often fml* to promise or agree: *He undertook to improve the working arrangements.*

guarantee **1** [Wv5;T1; X7] to give a promise of quality, payment, or fulfilment about (something or someone): *They guarantee the watch for three years. They give you guaranteed service or your money back.* **2** [T1, 3, 5; D1] to promise (that something will certainly be so): *We can't guarantee your safety if you go alone. I guarantee that you'll enjoy yourself.*

warrant **1** [X (*to be*) 7; (T1), 5a] to guarantee: *The grower warrants these plants (to be) free from disease.* **2** [T5a; D5a] *infml* to declare as if certain: *I'll warrant (you) (that) he's back there drinking again.*

commit [T1] *fml* **1** to promise (oneself, one's property, etc): *He has committed himself to the work; he must now do it.* **2** *tech* to send: *The prisoner has been committed for trial. They have committed him to a mental hospital; he is not right in the head.*

vouch for [v prep T1] to say that (someone or something) is good, correct, acceptable, etc: *I can vouch for him; he will work well.*

G112 *verbs* : **swearing and cursing**

swear [I0 (*at*)] to use bad language: *Stop swearing in front of the children. The drunk man stood there, angrily swearing and cursing. Don't swear at me!*

curse [T1] *emph* to swear at: *The rider cursed his unwilling horse. I'm so angry I could curse the day I met you!* **2** [I0] to swear: *The drunken sailors cursed and swore at passing soldiers.*

damn [T1] to curse at: *It's as likely that he'll damn me as (that he'll) say 'Hello'.*

G113 *nouns* : **oaths and curses**

bad/foul language [U] words, usu related to sex, bodily waste and religion, used to express strong feelings, amusement, etc and not usu considered polite: *'Don't use bad language in front of the children!' she said.*

oath [C] an expression of strong feeling using religious or sexual words improperly

curse [C] a word or words used in swearing; a word or words expressing anger, hate, etc: *Listen to his curses; I don't think he likes us!*

swearing [U] the act of using bad language

damn **1** [C] the word 'damn' as a curse: *His speech is full of 'damns' and worse curses.* **2** [S] *infml* even a small unimportant amount: *I don't care/give a damn what he does. His promise isn't worth a damn.* **3** *also* **(God)damned** [Wa5;A] *sl* (used for giving force to an expression, good or bad): *He's a damn fool! It's damn foolish to do that. He ran damn fast. That's damn nice of you!* **4** [interj] *sl* (an expression of strong anger or disappointment): *Damn!* **damn all** nothing: *He's the most ungenerous person I know; you'll get damn all out of him.* **Well, I'll be damned** *infml* (a strong way of saying): *I'm very surprised.* **(God) Damn it/you/silly fool**, etc *sl* a strong way of expressing anger, meaning: *May God damn it/you/that silly fool*, etc **I'll be damned if I will** *infml* (a strong way of saying) I won't

blasphemy **1** [U] disrespectful or bad language about God or holy things: *They charged him with blasphemy (against religion).* **2** [C] an example of this: *Their conversation was full of blasphemies.*

G114 *verbs & nouns* : **cursing and damning**

curse **1** [T1] to call down God's anger, evil, misfortune, etc, upon (someone): *The priest cursed the hunters for daring to stand on holy ground. The terrorized villagers cursed their violent lord.* **2** [C (*on*)] a word or sentence asking God, heaven, a spirit, etc, to bring down evil or harm on someone or something: *The tribal chief pronounced a curse on all white men.* **3** [C (*on*)] the evil or harm called down in this way: *There is a curse on our tribe; our animals die and our crops don't grow. Our tribe is under a curse.* **4** [C] a cause of misfortune, evil, etc: *Foxes can be a curse to farmers. Inequality is the curse of modern society.* **cursed with** to suffer misfortune or great harm because of (someone or something): *My mother is cursed with blindness and difficulty in hearing. We're cursed with bad luck.*

damn [T1] **1** (esp of God) to send to punishment without end after death: *You will be damned to hell for this!* **2** to declare to be very wrong or bad: *The play was bad and the newspapers all damned it.* **3** to ruin or be the ruin of: *With this* latest foolish action he had damned himself in everyone's opinion.

blaspheme [I∅ (*against*); T1] to speak without respect of or use bad language at (esp God or religious matters): *What a terrible person. He can hardly speak without blaspheming* (*against God*). **blasphemous** [B] **1** tending to blaspheme **2** (of words, pictures, etc) presenting God or holy things as bad or foolish **3** (of people) having the habit of speaking against God or things considered holy

G115 *verbs* : **ordering and commanding**

order 1 [T5c, (b); V3] tell (someone) what to do, that (something) must be done, etc: *The officer ordered that the men* (*should*) *fire the guns/that the guns* (*should*) *be fired. He ordered the men to fire the guns. He ordered the guns to be fired.* **2** [T1] to say that (something) should be done or made: *Order an attack! The government has ordered an inquiry into the state of all private schools.* **3** [X9] to tell (someone or something) to go (to the stated place): *If you make any more noise I shall order you out of the hall.* **4** [D1 (*for*); T1)] (of a doctor) to advise (something) as necessary: *The doctor ordered her a month's rest in bed.* **5** [D1 (*for*); T1; I∅] to ask for (something) to be brought, made, etc, in return for payment: *He ordered himself three new suits. Don't forget to order a taxi. Please order some fish for me. I've ordered dinner at the restaurant for 8 o'clock. 'Have you ordered yet, sir?' asked the waiter.*

tell [V3; D6a, b; X9] *genl* to order: *Tell him to go now. Please do as you are told. I told you to get here early, so why didn't you? Don't try and tell me whether I can or I can't!*

say [T3] *not fml* to direct someone: *She says to meet her at the station. It says on the bottle to take a spoonful every 4 hours.*

instruct [T1; V3] *often fml* to order: *I instructed him to come to work earlier. Instruct him in what he must do.*

direct [T1, 5c] *fml* to order: *He directed his men to do it. She directed that it be done at once.*

command 1 [T1, 5b, c; V3; I∅] *esp fml* to direct (a person or people), with the right to be obeyed: *The general commanded his men to attack the city. Our leader is not fit to command. She commanded that it be done at once. Who commands here?* **2** [T1] to deserve and get: *His abilities command our respect.* **3** [T1] to be in a position to use or get; have at one's service: *The employers command a great amount of wealth but we have nothing. He can command a high salary.* **4** [T1] to be in a position to control (a city, area, etc): *This fort commands the whole valley.* **commander** [C] a person, esp in a military force, who commands others

boss [T1 (*about*); (I∅)] *infml & deprec* to order people to do things, esp too much or when one

has no right to do so: *He is always bossing me about and I don't like it!* **bossy** [Wa1; B] *deprec* liking to give orders to other people: *Stop being bossy!* **- sily** [adv] **-siness** [U]

dictate [I∅ (*to*)] *usu deprec* to order: *Stop dictating to me! He likes dictating to people, but nobody obeys him.*

obey 1 [I∅; T1] to do what one is told to do: *He told them what to do and they obeyed.* **2** [T1] to follow the order of (someone): *Soldiers must obey their officers.*

G116 *nouns* : **ordering and commanding**

order [C; *by* U] an official message telling what to do: *These are your orders; now do the work. It's an order; do it! A soldier who doesn't obey/follow his orders will be in serious trouble. His orders are that you must be home by 10 o'clock* (= He ordered this). *My orders are to let no one into the building* (= I have been so ordered). *Give the order now! This road is closed by order of the chief of police.* **orders are orders** *infml* orders must be obeyed **under orders** having received orders: *He is under orders to go to London.*

instruction [C *usu pl*; A] *often fml* an order (to a person or a machine): *You have your instructions; now do the work. Read the instruction book.*

directions [P] orders; information about what to do: *Please follow his directions. The directions on the bottle tell you when to take the medicine.*

directive [C] *fml* an official order: *The government directives must be obeyed/followed.*

command 1 [C] *esp fml* an order: *All his commands were obeyed.* **2** [U] control: *The army is under the King's direct command. You need experience before you get command of an army.* **3** [S; U] the ability of control and use: *He has* (*a*) *good command of spoken French.* **at someone's command** ready to obey someone: *I'm at your command.*

commandment [C *often cap*] an esp religious or divine command: *Moses is said to have received the Ten Commandments from God.*

dictation [U] *usu deprec* the act of dictating: *I'm not going to work to his dictation!* **dictates** [P] *usu deprec* orders: *I'm not going to obey the dictates of a man like him!*

G117 *verbs* : **calling and inviting**

call [T1] **1** to (try to) cause to come by speaking loudly or officially: *Mother is calling me. He called me over/down* (*from the tree*)/*in* (*from outdoors*). *The minister called the union leaders to a meeting. The King called Parliament* (*together*). **2** to cause to happen by making an official declaration: *The King called an election. The minister called a meeting.* **3** to waken (someone): *She called me early today. When shall I call you, sir?*

call in [v adv T1] **1** to ask to attend: *Call the doctor in; the child is ill.* **2** to request the return of: *The makers have called in some cars with dangerous faults. I'm going to call in the money.*

recall [T1] **1** to call (someone) back: *The government recalled the general after he lost the battle.* **2** to take back: *The car factory has recalled all the cars made in January, because there is something wrong with them.*

summon [T1 (*to*); V3 *often pass*] *fml* to give an official order (to do, come, etc): *He was summoned (in)to the presence of the Queen. She summoned a servant. He summoned his soldiers to fight.*

invite [T1] **1** to ask (someone) to a social occasion: *We invited all our relatives. Why don't you invite me in (to the house)? I've been invited out* (= to a home or place outside one's home)/*out to dinner.* **2** to ask for, esp politely: *Questions were invited after the meeting.*

ask [T1; V3] *not fml* to invite: *I have asked some friends* (*for dinner*)*. I have asked them to come* (*for dinner*)/(*for/to tea*)*. She asked him to her house. I asked her in/up/down for a drink. I asked her* (*to come*) *out* (*for the evening*)*.*

G118 *nouns* : **calling and inviting**

call [C] a command to move, come, or do something: *The minister waited for a call to the palace. The call came at 6 o'clock and they went immediately. In the war many people answered the call of duty. He felt a call* (*from God*) *to become a priest.*

recall [S; U] the act of recalling or being recalled: *The general's recall surprised us. The recall of the cars made in January caused us a lot of trouble.* **beyond recall** *esp lit* not/no longer able to be recalled: *They are gone, beyond recall.*

summons [C] an order to appear, esp in court, often written: *He received a summons. They served a summons on him* (*to appear in court*)*.*

invitation **1** [U] the act of inviting or being invited: *The meeting is by invitation only; you can't just go in.* **2** [C] an example of this: *We have been getting lots of invitations to parties lately.* (*fig*) *His words were an invitation to do exactly what they wanted.* **3** [C] a written note inviting someone to something: *Can I see the invitation, please?*

G119 *verbs* : **recommending and supporting**

[ALSO ⇒ G88]

recommend **1** [D1 (*to*); T1 (*as, for*)] to speak to (someone) in favour of; praise (as being good for a purpose): *Can you recommend me a good dictionary? Can you recommend a good dictionary* (*to me*)*? They recommended him for the job/as a good lawyer.* **2** [T4, 5c; V3] to

advise or suggest: *I recommend buying this book/you to buy this book/that everyone* (*should*) *buy this book.* **3** [T1 (*to*)] (of a quality) to make attractive: *This hotel has nothing to recommend it* (*to travellers*) *except cheapness.*

commend [T1 (*to*)] *fml* **1** to present as being worthy of praise, notice, etc; speak favourably of: *I can commend this man's work to you. Our shop has always been very highly commended. Your behaviour doesn't commend you to me.* (*fig*) *Your behaviour doesn't commend itself to me.* **2** to put (someone or something, esp oneself) into the care or charge of someone else: *The dying man commended his soul/himself to God.*

advocate [T1, 4] *emph* to speak in favour of (esp an idea or plan): *I do not advocate building larger factories.*

sponsor [T1] to speak in favour of (esp a person or plan): *Who is sponsoring this young man? He sponsored the plan at the meeting.*

support [T1] **1** to be in favour of: *The results support my original idea. I support his plan.* **2** to approve of and encourage: *She supports the new political party. I will support him if he suggests change.*

back [T1] *infml* to recommend; sponsor; support: *I'll back him for the job! He was backed by many important people.*

be (all) for *infml* to support strongly; be strongly in favour of: *I'm all for that! She is all for telling him what to do.*

G120 *nouns* : **recommending and supporting**

recommendation **1** [U; C] (an) act of recommending: *He came to us with very high recommendations.* **2** [C] a quality that recommends: *Her two great recommendations are youth and beauty.*

commendation **1** [U; C] (an) act of commending **2** [C] a special honour: *He got a commendation for bravery in the war.*

advocacy [U9] the act or action of supporting an idea, way of life, person, etc: *She objected to his advocacy of large schools; she preferred small ones.*

sponsorship [U] the condition of sponsoring, taking responsibility for someone or something: *He is under our sponsorship; we recommend him.*

support [U] willingness, ability or action to support someone; encouragement and help: *You have my support in this/in what you plan to do. The results give/lend support to my original idea.*

backing [U] material or moral support or help: *I'll give you my backing when you put your plan to the group. The plan has plenty of backing, and will probably succeed.*

reference [C] **1** a piece of written information about someone's character, ability, etc, esp when he is looking for employment: *His references show that he's just the man we want! We will lend you the money if you get a banker's reference* (= a note from the bank to say that there is money in your account). **2** *BrE also* **referee** a person who provides such information: *Ask Dr Smith if he will act as one of your references.*

testimonial [C] **1** a formal written statement of a person's character, ability, willingness to work, etc **2** something given or done as an expression of respect, praise, thanks, etc: *He was given a gold watch as a testimonial after 50 years with the company.*

credentials [P] written proofs of a person's position, trustworthiness, etc: *Never let a stranger into your house until you have seen his credentials.*

G121 *verbs* : **advising and consulting**

advise [T1, 4, 5b, c; I∅; D5, 5b, 6a, b; V3] to tell (somebody) what one thinks should be done; give (advice): *I advise waiting till the proper time. I will do as/what you advise. I advised her that she should wait. I advised her to wait. I advised her where to stay. So I advised (him).* **advisable** [F] that is advised or thought the best to do; sensible; wise: *It is advisable to leave now/that you leave now.* **advisedly** [adv] after careful thought; purposely: *I'm sure he did it advisedly.* **adviser**, *also* **advisor** *AmE* [C] a person who gives advice, esp one who is often asked for advice, as by a government or business **advisory** [Wa5;B] **1** having the power or duty to advise **2** containing advice rather than orders: *Our report is only advisory because we have no power to act.* **ill-advised** [B] unwise: *You'd be ill-advised to go there.* **well-advised** [Wa2;B] wise: *You'd be well-advised to stay at home today.*

counsel [T1, 4; V3] *fml* to advise: *I have waited months for news and now you counsel patience! The soldier counselled against travelling at night. I would counsel you not to marry too young.*

consult [T1] to go to (a person, book, etc) for information, advice, an opinion, etc: *Have you consulted your doctor about your illness? I regularly consult a dictionary.*

look up [T1] **1** [v adv] to find and study (something in a book): *Look up his number in the telephone directory* (= book of telephone numbers). *She looked the word up in a dictionary.* **2** [v prep] *infml* to consult: *Did you look up a dictionary for the meaning of that word?*

G122 *nouns* : **advising and consulting**

advice [U] opinion given by one person to another on how that other should behave or act: *I asked the doctor for his advice. On his advice I am staying in bed.*

counsel [U] *often fml* advice: *The King refused to listen to his ministers' counsel and declared war. He kept his own counsel in the matter* (= He gave and took no advice).

consultation 1 [C; U (*with*) *often pl with sing meaning*] (an example of) the act of consulting (*often in the phr* **in consultation** (**with**)): *The minister of foreign affairs today had consultations with the president of France. Mr Smith is in consultation with his advisors at present. Please call back later.* **2** [C] a meeting held to exchange opinions and ideas: *The employers held a consultation to decide whether to increase their workers' wages.*

G123 *verbs* : **warning and threatening**

warn 1 [Wv4;I∅;T1,5a;D5a;V3] to tell (of something bad that may happen, or of how to prevent something bad): *I warned him of the danger. She warned them against us. He warned her not to go. I warned her that it would happen. A red warning light flashed.* **2** [T1] to give knowledge (often officially) of some future need or action: *If you warn the police when you go away on holiday they will watch your house.*

warn off [v adv T1] to try to cause to stay away from (a place, etc) by warning: *They warned him off, but he kept going back to the dangerous river.*

admonish [T1] *fml* to warn, usu gently, esp of possible punishment: *Her mother admonished her for being careless.*

alert [T1] to warn (esp people who are ready to do something): *He alerted us to our danger. Alert the army; the enemy are attacking! The police alerted all road users about the need to go carefully.*

threaten 1 [Wv4, 5;T1 (*with*)] to express a threat against: *Don't threaten me! I was threatened with a beating unless I obeyed.* **2** [Wv4, 5; T1, 3] to express (a threat) against someone: *The killer threatened to murder me if I didn't obey. Father is threatening a beating if I don't obey.* **3** [Wv4;T1] to give warning of (something bad): *The black clouds threatened rain. There was a threatening silence.* **4** [Wv4;T1] to be a threat against: *Immoral behaviour threatens our way of life.* **-ingly** [adv]

beware [Wv6;I∅ (*of*); T6, esp *what*] (*used in giving or reporting orders*) to be careful: *It's getting closer; beware! Beware of the dog. Beware (of) what you do with this dangerous substance. He told us to beware.*

G124 *nouns* : **warning and threatening**

warning 1 [U; C (*of*)] the act of warning or the state of being warned: *They attacked without warning/without giving a warning.* **2** [C (*of*)] something that warns: *Let that be a warning to you. Take that for a warning of what may hap-*

pen. His life should be a warning to us all. **3** [C
(of)] a person who is an example of what not to
do: *He's a warning to us all of what happens to
people who drink too much.*

alert [C] a warning of danger, etc, esp for people
who can do or must know something: *There
has been a general alert; the enemy seem to be
about to attack. Sound the alert!*

threat 1 [C; *under* U *(of)*] an expression of an
intention to hurt, punish, cause pain, etc, esp if
one's instructions are not obeyed: *I obeyed his
order but only under threat of punishment. We
did not take their threats seriously.* **2** [C *(to)* usu
sing] a person, thing, or idea regarded as a
possible danger: *While the killer goes free he is
a threat to everyone in the town.* **3** [C9, esp *of*,
usu sing] *(fig)* a sign or warning of coming
danger: *The clouds brought a threat of rain.*

premonition [C *(of)*] a feeling that something
(esp something unpleasant) is going to happen
or will be found to have happened: *He had a
strong premonition that his son had been killed
in battle.*

forewarning [C *(of)*] *poet & emot* a premonition

admonition *also* **admonishment** [C; U] a usu
gentle warning, esp of possible punishment:
*She got an admonition for being careless.
Admonishment isn't necessary; he is sorry for
what he did.*

G125 *verbs* : **accepting, agreeing, and approving**

accept [Wv5;T1, *(fml)* 5] to take as satisfactory,
possible, etc: *I accept your plan. She fully
accepts his account of how the accident happened.*

agree 1 [Wv5;I0 *(to)*] to accept an idea, opinion,
etc, esp after unwillingness or argument; to
approve: *They finally agreed to the plan. We
met at the agreed place. My idea was agreed to.*
2 [I0 *(with, on)*;I3, 5] to have or share the
same opinion, feeling, or purpose: *She agreed
with me. We agreed on the plan. We agreed to
leave soon. They agreed that they should ask
him. We agreed on a price for the car.* **3** [I0] to
be happy together; to get on well together:
*They will never agree. They agree together all
the time.* **4** [T1] *esp BrE* to accept (an idea,
opinion, etc) esp after unwillingness or argument: *The workers have agreed the government's plan. The government's plan was
agreed.*

agree with [v prep T1 *no pass*] to be in accordance with: *Your story agrees with his in everything except small details.*

concur 1 [I0 *(with)*] to agree: *I concurred with
him in his belief that sex before marriage is
wrong. Our opinions on this matter concur.*
2 [I0, 3] to happen at the same time: *Everything concurred to produce the desired effect.
Happiness and love do not always concur.*

consent [I0 *(to)*, I3] to agree; give permission:

*She tried to persuade her father but he refused to
consent. He consented to help the old lady. Did
the king consent to your plan? He would never
consent to his daughter travelling abroad alone.*

assent [I0 *(to)*] *fml* to agree to a suggestion,
idea, etc: *I won't assent to her plan. Why don't
you assent? I assented to listen to her.*

acquiesce [I0 *(in)*] *fml* to agree, often unwillingly, without raising an argument; accept
quietly: *He acquiesced in the plans his parents
had made for him.* **acquiescent** [B] ready to
agree without argument: *They are acquiescent
people.*

confirm 1 [T1, 5a, 6a] to support; make certain;
give proof (of): *Please confirm your telephone
message in writing. The King confirmed that the
election would be on June 20th. Can you confirm where you were yesterday?* **2** [T1] to give
approval to (a person, agreement, position,
etc); agree to: *The King confirmed him as
minister of foreign affairs. When do you think
the President will confirm you in office?*

endorse [T1] **1** to express approval or support
of (opinions, actions, etc): *I fully endorse your
opnions on this subject.* **2** to write, esp one's
name, on the back of (esp a cheque): *The bank
clerk asked her to endorse the cheque and then
paid her the money.*

approve [T1] to agree officially to: *The minister
approved the building plans.* **approve of** [v prep
T1, 4; V4] to consider good, right, true, etc: *I
don't approve of wasting time.*

applaud [T1] *fml & emph* to agree strongly with
(a person, idea, etc): *They applauded the new
plan to save water.*

G126 *nouns* : **accepting, agreeing, and approving**

acceptance 1 [U] the act of accepting: *Your
acceptance of the plan is expected.* **2** [C] an
example of this, esp in the form of letters: *We
have had 100 acceptances from all over the
world.*

agreement 1 [U] the state of having the same
opinion, feeling, or purpose; thinking in the
same way: *We are in agreement with their decision. There is very little agreement about what
to do.* **2** [C] an arrangement or promise of
action, as made between people, groups, businesses, or countries: *You have broken our
agreement by not doing the work you promised.
The two countries signed an agreement to
respect each other's rights.*

concurrence 1 [C] an agreement of opinion:
*The concurrence of all three judges was that the
man was guilty.* **2** [C] an example of actions,
events, etc, happening at the same time: *This is
an interesting concurrence of events.* **3** [U] the
act of concurring

consent [U] agreement; permission: *Governments should rule only with the consent of the
governed. Her parents refused their consent to
her marriage.* **age of consent** the age at which

one may lawfully marry or have sex **with one consent** with complete agreement

assent [C; U] *esp fml* agreement: *Once we have his assent we can start.* **with one assent** with the expressed agreement of all **by common assent** by general, often unspoken, agreement

acquiescence [U] quiet or unwilling agreement

confirmation 1 [U] the act of confirming: *We have had government confirmation of the plans.* **2** [U; C] (a) proof; something that confirms: *Your news was confirmation for my beliefs.*

endorsement [U; C] the act or action of endorsing: *The committee's decision has not yet received the chairman's endorsement.*

approval 1 [U] the act of approving **2** [U; (C)] official permission

G127 *verbs* : **rejecting, refusing, and denying**

reject [T1] not to accept, esp for use: *They have rejected his plan. Don't reject this idea straightaway; think about it.*

disagree [I∅] **1** (of people) to have different opinions; quarrel slightly: *Bill and I often disagree but we're good friends. I disagree with him about/as to/on what we ought to do.* **2** (of statements, reports, etc) to be unlike: *These two reports of the accident disagree.*

dissent [I∅] to disagree; refuse to agree: *I dissent altogether (from such an unwise idea).*

refuse [I∅; T1, 3; D1] not to accept or do or give: *He asked her to marry him but she refused (to marry him). She refused his offer. She refused him even a kiss.*

turn down [v adv T1] *infml* to reject or refuse: *She turned him down; she won't marry him. They turned down his plan; they won't use it.*

pass up [v adv T1] *infml* not to accept, do, have, etc: *He passed up a good chance to go to France with the local football team and he's sorry now.*

decline [T1, 3; I∅] to refuse, usu politely; be unwilling: *We asked them to come to our party, but they declined (the invitation). The minister declined to make a statement to the newspapers.*

deny 1 [T1, 4, 5; V3] to declare untrue; refuse to accept (as true, as a fact): *Can you deny the truth of his statement? He denied it to be the case/that it was the case. He denied telling me/that he had told me.* **2** [T1] to disclaim connection with: *Don't tell me he has denied his country and his principles!*

G128 *nouns* : **rejecting, refusing, and denying**

rejection [C; U] (a case of) rejecting or being rejected: *She had a feeling of rejection; no one wanted her. I've had so many rejections I've stopped trying to help him.*

reject [C] something rejected for use, sale, etc:

The factory sells some of its better rejects cheaply, but throws most of the rejects away.

disagreement 1 [C; U] the fact or a case of disagreeing: *There has been serious disagreement between the two political parties over this question. Bill and I have been having a few disagreements lately.* **2** [U] (of statements, reports, etc) unlikeness; disagreeing: *There is some disagreement between these two statements.* **in disagreement** in the state of disagreeing: *I am in total disagreement with you as to the value of your plan. The two sets of figures are in disagreement.*

dissent [U] disagreement; difference of opinion: *When I asked for agreement there was no dissent.*

refusal [C; U] (a case of) refusing: *My offer met with a cold refusal. Refusal was impossible; I had to do what they asked.* **(the) first refusal** (the) right of deciding whether to buy something before it is offered to other people: *If you sell your house will you let me have (the) first refusal?*

denial 1 [U] the act of denial **2** [C] an example of this: *No one accepted his angry denials.*

G129 *verbs* : **shouting and screaming**
[ALSO ⇒ F247]

shout 1 [I∅] to use one's voice loudly: *Why are those people shouting? He shouted with joy.* **2** [T1 (*out*)] to tell by shouting: *He shouted a warning. She shouted out the news.*

call 1 [T1; I∅ (*out*)] to shout, speak, or say in a loud clear voice: *He called for help. They called for an hour but no one heard them. The fisherman called (out) to the men on the shore. Are they still calling?* **2** [T1] to speak (a list): *He called the numbers. Please call out the names of all the people.* **3** [I∅; T1] **a** (of an animal) to make the usual cry to (another animal): *The birds were calling (each other).* **b** to signal to (someone or something) with typical sounds: *The drums were calling.* **c** to attract: *The sea is calling him.*

exclaim [T1; I∅] to say something suddenly and loudly: *She exclaimed that she wouldn't do it. 'I won't do it!' she exclaimed.*

cry [I∅ (*for*); T1 (*out*)] to call loudly; shout: *The trapped woman cried out for help. 'Run! Run!' cried the citizens as enemy soldiers entered the city.*

cheer 1 [I∅] to shout, esp because of happiness, special interest, etc: *The people cheered when their leader arrived. 'We won the game!' he shouted, and we all cheered.* **2** [T1] to do this for (someone or sometimes something): *They cheered him as he went to fight. The people cheered the passing car, hoping that it would win the race.*

scream 1 [I∅] to cry out loudly on a high note, as in fear, pain, great excitement or anger, or sometimes laughter: *She screamed (with terror) when she saw the man with a gun. They* screamed for help/screamed with laughter at the good joke. (*fig*) *The wind screamed down the chimney. The birds screamed at the approaching cat.* **2** [T1, 5 (*out*)] to say or express in this way: '*Help!' she screamed. He screamed that he was dying. He screamed (out) a warning not to touch the electric wire.* **3** [T1, 5 (*out*); (I∅)] (*fig*) to draw attention, as by such a cry (to): *The newspapers screamed (out) the news in large letters.* **4** [I∅ (*about*)] to complain loudly or excitedly: *He was screaming about the loss of their powers under the new law.* **5** [I3 (*out*)] *also* **scream for** [T1] to demand; to be in great need (of): *The whole political system screams (out) for change. Haven't you finished the report? The chairman is screaming to have it.*

shriek 1 [I∅; T1] to cry out on a very high note, as in terror or pain: '*Leave me alone!' she shrieked. They were all shrieking with laughter.* (*fig*) *He could hear the shrieking of the terrible wind.*

screech [I∅; T1] **1** *esp emot* to scream on a very high, unpleasant note: '*Stop it!' she screeched. Birds were screeching in the trees.* **2 a** (of machines, esp tyres and brakes) to make a noise like this: *The car screeched to a halt/stop.* **b** to cause (brakes) to make a noise like this: *The driver screeched to a stop.*

bellow 1 [I∅] to make the loud deep hollow sound typical of a bull **2** [T1, 5; I∅ (*with*), (*out*)] to shout (something) in a deep voice: *He bellowed (out) with excitement/pain. He bellowed (out) his orders. He bellowed (out) that he was hurt.*

yell 1 [I∅ (*at*)] to make a loud cry or shout, as of fear or excitement: *Don't yell at me like that!* **2** [T1 (*out, at*)] to say or shout loudly: *He yelled (out) orders at everyone.*

squeal [I∅] to make a long very high sound or cry: *He heard the squealing tyres/pigs. The children squealed with delight.*

G130 *nouns, etc* : **shouting and screaming** [C]

[ALSO ⇒ F246]

shout an act of shouting: *I can hear shouts; who is it? He gave a loud shout to warn them.*

cry an act of crying out: *He could hear the cries of a man in pain/of animals. She gave a loud cry of fear.*

exclamation 1 an act of exclaiming: *He gave a loud and angry exclamation.* **2** a word such as 'oh' that is used when exclaiming

call 1 a shout or cry, usu with a purpose: *They heard a call for help.* **2** the special cry of an animal: *The call of this bird is very loud.* **3** an instrument which makes a sound like the cry of, and which attracts, a bird or animal: *When hunting ducks he always uses a call.*

cheer an act of cheering: *They gave a great cheer. Three cheers for the winner!*

hurray *also* **hurrah** [*also* interj] a shout of joy,

welcome, happiness, etc: '*Hurray!' they cried.* (*lit*) *They gave a loud hurray/hurrah.*

scream 1 a sudden loud high cry expressing anger, pain, fear, or sometimes laughter: *Her loud screams could be heard for miles.* (*fig*) *I heard the scream of the circular saw* [⇒ H142] *as it cut the log.* **2** [S] *esp BrE sl* a very funny person, thing, joke, etc: *She thought it was a scream when I fell off my chair, but I failed to see the joke.*

shriek a wild high cry (as of pain or terror): *They heard her shrieks and came running to help.*

screech a very high unpleasant sound (as) of screeching: *The forest seemed full of monkeys' screeches. A screech of brakes made us look to see what had happened in the street.*

bellow an act of bellowing: *His bellows were very loud.*

yell 1 a loud cry, as of fear or excitement **2** *AmE* a cheer or cry of fixed words or sounds, esp one shouted to encourage a school team

squeal a long very high cry or noise: *I could hear squeals of delight from the children. There was a squeal of tyres turning the corner at high speed.*

G131 *verbs* : **difficulties in speech**

stutter [I∅; T1] to speak with difficulty in producing sounds, esp habitually holding back the first consonant: '*C-come and h-h-help me,' he stuttered.* **-ingly** [adv] **stutterer** [C] a person who stutters

stammer 1 [I∅] to speak with pauses and repeated sounds, either habitually or because of excitement, fear, etc **2** [T1 (*out*)] to say while doing this: *He stammered his thanks.* **-ingly** [adv] **stammerer** [C] a person who stammers

lisp [I∅; T1 (*out*)] to speak or say with /s/ sounds which are not clear, esp when the tongue is placed on the teeth, making the /s/ seem like /θ/

G132 *nouns* : **difficulties in speech** [C usu sing]

stutter the fault of stuttering in speech: *He spoke with a stutter.*

stammer the fault of stammering in speech: *She speaks with/has a stammer.*

lisp the fault in speech of lisping: *She speaks with a lisp.*

Communicating, mainly by reading and writing, printing and publishing, radio and television

G140 *verbs, etc* : **reading things**

read 1 [I∅; T1] (*often with* **can**) to understand (language in print or writing): *The child can* read/is reading quite well now. He reads well for a six-year-old. I like reading in bed. He read the book last week. **2** [Wv6;T1] to understand (something printed or written): He can read music. She read the map. I can read French but I can't speak it. (fig) I can read your thoughts (from your face). **3** [D1 (to); L9, esp to; T1 (aloud)] to say (printed or written words) esp to give pleasure to others: She read the children a story. The teacher read the poem aloud to the class. **4** [I0; T1, 5, 6b] to get (the stated information) from (print or writing): They read about the murder. They read the account of the murder in the paper. They read that the murderer had been caught. She read how to make pastry. **5** [L9] (of something written) to influence people (in the stated way): Her letters always read well/always read as if she copied them from books. **6** [T1] BrE to study (a subject at university level): John's reading history/law at Oxford. **7** [L1, 9] (of written words) to be or mean when said: The name reads 'Benson' not 'Fenton'. The two copies read the same/differently. **8** [T1] (of measuring instruments) to show: The thermometer reads 33 degrees. **9** [T1] fml (to a person, with **please**) understand the stated printed or written words to mean: For £50 please read £15. Please read £50 as £15. £50 was read (as) £15. **10** [S] esp BrE infml an act or period of reading: Can I have a read of your paper? **11** [S9] esp BrE infml something (of the stated kind) to be read: It's not great literature but it's a very good read. **read oneself/someone to sleep** to make oneself/someone go to sleep by reading **reader** [C] **1** a person who reads or is reading **2** a book which helps a person (esp a child) to learn to read

browse 1 [I0] to read here and there in books: He was browsing through the bookcase when I came in. **2** [S] a period of time spent in browsing: While you were out I had a good browse through your books.

skim [T1; I0 (through, over)] to read quickly to get the main ideas: Skimming (through a book) can sometimes be useful. He skimmed the pages for what he wanted.

scan [T1; (I0)] to look over the whole of (something, esp a book, newspaper, etc), esp quickly to get the main ideas: She scanned the book for his name, but couldn't find it.

read aloud/out loud to read and speak what is read at the same time: He read the letter aloud/out loud. Read out loud, please!

G141 verbs, etc : **writing and typing**

write 1 [T1; I0] to make (marks that represent letters or words) by using a tool held in the hands, esp (in modern times) with a pen or pencil on paper: Many people still can't read or write. Write the word. **2** [T1] to express and record in this way: He wrote his name. She is writing her report now. **3** [T1; I0] to be a writer

(of books, plays, etc): He writes for the stage. Charlotte Brontë wrote 'Jane Eyre'. **write out** [v adv T1] **1** to write in full: He wrote out the report. **2** to write (something formal): She wrote out a cheque/receipt.

scribble 1 [I0; T1] to write (meaningless marks): The child can't write but she loves to scribble with a pencil. **2** [T1] to write carelessly or in a hurry (usu something that is hard to read): Let me scribble a note to the milkman before we go. There was a scribbled signature at the bottom of the letter but I couldn't make it out.

scrawl [T1] to write in a careless, irregular, awkward, or unskilful way, usu covering more space than necessary: He scrawled his signature at the bottom of the letter. There was a name scrawled on the wall.

print [T1; I0] to write (something) using the square, unjoined letters used in books: Most children learn to print before they learn proper handwriting. Please print the address clearly in capital letters. [⇒ G173]

compose [T1; I0] to write (music, poetry, etc): This musician has composed a lovely piece of music.

inscribe [T1 often pass] **1** to write by marking into a surface: His name was inscribed on the metal plate beside the door. **2** to write (a name) in a book, esp when giving it as a present or on a special occasion

transcribe [T1; I0] fml to put (something) into a written form: Have you transcribed his speech yet?

pen [T1] pomp to write, esp with a pen: He penned a letter to his friend.

pencil [T1] to draw, write, or mark with a pencil: Please pencil (your note) at the side of the page.

type [T1 (out); I0] to print on paper by using a typewriter [⇒ G152]: She typed (out) the letter carefully. It's easy to learn to type.

jot [T1 (down)] to write quickly, esp without preparation: He jotted (down) some notes for the talk he was going to give. **jotting** [C usu pl] a rough note: Here are a few jottings I've made for the talk tonight.

note [T1] to write as a note; to write in a short form: He noted the points on a piece of paper.

sign [T1; I0] to write (one's name) on a piece of paper, etc: Sign here, please. He signed his name at the bottom of the page. **signature** [C] the special way one writes one's name, esp for letters, official papers, etc: Put your signature here here, please.

autograph 1 [T1] to sign (a letter, statement, book, etc) with one's own name to show that one is the writer: Will you autograph your new book for me? **2** [C] a person's own writing done by hand, esp his signature written in this way: May I have your autograph, sir?

annotate [Wv5;T1] to add short notes to (a book) to explain certain parts: An annotated edition of the book is a copy with notes. **annotation 1** [U] the writing of notes **2** [C] a written note, esp on the pages of a printed book

spell 1 [D1; T1 (*with*)] to name in order (the letters) of (esp a word): *My name is spelled S.M.Y.T.H. Do you spell judgement with an e?* **2** [T1 *no pass*] (of letters in order) to form (a word): *B.O.O.K spells 'book'.* **3** [I∅] to form words (correctly) from letters: *You must learn to spell. The children can't spell well.* **4** [T1] (*fig*) to add up to (a result); mean: *His disapproval spells defeat for our plan.* **spell out 1** to write or say (a word) letter by letter **2** (*fig*) to explain in the plainest or most understandable way: *He spelt out the government's plans in a speech.* **spelling 1** [U] the action or proper way of forming words from letters: *Her spelling has improved. I'm no good at spelling.* **2** [C] an ordered set of letters forming a word: *a word for which British and American spellings are different* **speller** [C] **1** a person who spells or can spell: *The child is a good speller.* **2** a book which helps in teaching spelling

G142 *verbs* : composing and editing
[ALSO ⇨ G162]

compose [T1; I∅] to put (ideas) into writing: *I'm trying to compose a letter; please don't make so much noise.*

edit [T1; I∅] to prepare (the writings of some other person) to go into a newspaper, book, etc: *He edited her article, making as few changes as possible. Stop editing now, please.*

draft [T1] to make a draft of: *He drafted a speech. The new laws were drafted last year.*

rewrite [T1] to write (something) again in a different and more suitable way, esp to make (it) better: *I don't like this; rewrite it. He rewrote the article carefully.*

reword [T1] to write or say in different words, esp better or more suitably: *Reword this; as it is, our readers won't like it.*

rework *also* **reshape** [T1] to write or develop (one's material, ideas, etc) in a second, better form: *If you rework this a bit, it'll be a lot better.*

re-do [T1] *genl* to rewrite, reword, or rework (something)

write up [v adv T1] **1** to write (again) in a complete and useful form: *I'll write up my notes and let you have a copy.* **2** to write a report on (goods, a play, etc), esp giving a good judgement: *He wrote the play up in the local newspaper.*

G143 *verbs* : writing things down
[v adv T1]

write down 1 to record in writing (esp what has been said): *Write your idea down while it is clear in your mind. She wrote down what he said.* **2** [X1] (*fig*) to describe as: *They wrote him down as a lazy worker.*

scribble down to write down in a scribble [⇨ G145], carelessly or (too) quickly: *She scribbled the name down on a piece of paper.*

jot down to write down quickly in a short form: *He jotted some points down for the talk he was to give that evening.*

note down to write down, usu carefully and esp in the form of notes: *He noted down what he had to do next day on a piece of paper.*

take down *genl* to write down, esp as asked: *She took down the various points and then prepared a written report of what had been said.*

put down *genl* to write down: *Let me put down your telephone number before I forget it. Put your plan down on paper, please.*

get down *very genl & infml* to write down in some way: *Get your ideas down on paper and let me have them as soon as possible!*

set down to write down clearly: *He set his ideas down on paper and sent them to us.*

mark down to put down on paper as marks of some particular kind: *He marked the results of the games down (on paper).*

G144 *verbs* : removing written things
[T1]

rub out [v adv] *not fml* to remove (something, esp a pencil mark) from paper, etc: *He rubbed out what he had written. The teacher rubbed out what he had written on the blackboard.*

erase *often fml* to rub out: *He erased his mistakes with a rubber.* (*fig*) *She tried to erase the memory from her mind. He erased the recording from the tape* [⇨ K50].

delete to take, rub, strike, or cut out (something written or printed): *If you delete 50 words, we can put the whole story on one page. Delete his name from the list of members.* **deletion 1** [U] the act of deleting; the state of being deleted **2** [C] something deleted: *The page contained several deletions.*

G145 *nouns* : reading and writing

reading 1 [U] the activity of reading: *Reading is an important part of work in a school.* **2** [C] something (to be) read: *He prepared some readings from the books he liked best.*

writing 1 [U] the activity of writing: *Writing is his life.* **2** [C; U] written work: *That's a good piece of writing. His writings are now famous.* **3** [U] handwriting: *I can't read the doctor's writing.*

handwriting [U] **1** writing done by hand **2** the style or appearance of such writing by a particular person: *She has very neat handwriting.*

calligraphy [U] (the act of producing) beautiful writing by hand: *Calligraphy was once the most important subject in Chinese schools.*

scribble 1 [C *often pl with sing meaning*] a meaningless mark written on paper: *The child made scribbles on the wall.* **2** [S] a way of writing which is careless and hard to read: *His writing is nothing but a scribble.* **3** [C] an unimportant note written in a hurry: *She wrote a scribble to the milkman before she left.*

scrawl 1 [C *usu sing*] something written awkwardly or fast and carelessly: *Her postcard was just a scrawl saying she was having a good time.* **2** [S] an awkward or irregular way of writing: *This letter must be from Frank; I recognize his scrawl. The words were written in a scrawl across the page.*

printing [U] letters printed by hand: *The address on the box was in printing, not in handwriting.*

print [U] letters, words, or language in printed [⇒ G173] form: *I can't read the small print on this page without my glasses.*

script [U] (a way of) writing done by hand, esp as in English with the letters of words joined: *He covered the page with his neat script.*

black and white [U] *infml* writing or print: *It's all down here* (= on this paper) *in black and white.*

shorthand [U] a way of writing (esp spoken language) down quickly by using special signs: *She uses Pitman's shorthand. He is a shorthand typist* [⇒ J233].

longhand [U] ordinary handwriting, esp when compared with shorthand or typing: *He took her words down in longhand.*

screed [C] *not fml* a long and usu dull speech or piece of writing: *This report is too much of a screed; try to make it shorter.*

G146 *adjectives* : **written and readable** [B]

written [Wa5] having been written: *Send me a written report of what happens.*

handwritten [Wa5] written by hand rather than printed: *It was a handwritten letter, not typed.*

typewritten *also* **typed** [Wa5] written by means of a typewriter: *Send me a typewritten/typed report of what happens.*

readable 1 that can be read (easily): *His handwriting isn't readable.* **2** worth reading; interesting: *What a very readable book!* **un-** [*neg*] **-bly** [*adv* Wa3]: *He writes very readably.*

legible (of handwriting or print) that can be read, esp easily: *This sheet is hardly legible.* **il-** [*neg*] **-bly** [*adv* Wa3] **-ibility** [U]

literate 1 (of people) able to read and write: *These people are all literate. India has had a literate civilization for thousands of years.* **2** relating to (the good qualities of) reading and writing: *This is very literate work indeed.* **il-** [*neg*] *usu deprec* **non-** [*neg*] *genl & neutral*

G147 *nouns* : **alphabets and scripts**

alphabet [C] the set of letters used in writing any language, esp when arranged in order: *The English language uses the Roman alphabet in its own special way.* **alphabetic(al)** [B] of, belonging to, or in the order of the/an alphabet: *In a dictionary the words are arranged in alphabetical order.* **-(al)ly** [*adv* Wa4] **alphabetize, -ise** [T1] to put (words) into alphabetic order

script [C9; U9] the set of letters used in writing a language; an alphabet: *The work is printed in Arabic script. Persian and Arabic used to be written in two different scripts.*

cipher, cypher [C; U] a form of secret writing in which letters of the alphabet are changed with other letters, signs, and numbers so as to be unreadable except to someone who understands the secret: *The letter was in cipher.*

decipher [T1] to translate, from a cipher into ordinary language: *Can you decipher the message/what the letter says?*

code [C; *in* U] **1** a system of secret words, letters, numbers, etc, used instead of ordinary writing to keep messages secret: *The message was in code, so I couldn't read/understand it.* **2** a system of signals used instead of letters and numbers in a message that is to be broadcast, telegraphed, etc **3** a system of numbers by which such things as books can be organized, as in a library **code** [T1] **1** *also* **encode** to translate (words, etc) into a code: *Code the message so that the enemy won't understand it. They encoded the message.* **2** to give a special code (esp a number) to: *You haven't coded these books yet; how can I put them in order?* **decode** [T1] to translate (words, etc) out of a code: *Decode this message quickly; we must know what it means!* **crack a code** to find out how a code works: *They haven't managed to crack the enemy's latest code.*

inscription [C] something inscribed [⇒ G141] such as **a** a piece of writing marked into the surface of stone or something hard, such as a coin **b** a piece of handwriting at the beginning of a book saying who gave the book to whom and giving the date, year, etc

transcription 1 [U] the act of transcribing [⇒ G 141] **2** [C] something transcribed, esp the way someone speaks a language, gives a speech, etc: *They made a transcription of his speech.* **3** [C] *tech* a way of writing or printing the sounds of a language: *Many dictionaries use special phonetic* [⇒ G238] *transcriptions of English words.*

G148 *nouns, etc* : **letters**

letter [C] one of the signs of an alphabet, that represents a speech sound **lettering** [U] **1** the act of writing, drawing, etc letters or words **2** the letters or words written or drawn, esp with regard to their style

character [C] **1** (in writing systems which do not use letters) a sign used for representing a word: *Chinese has no alphabet and is written in characters.* **2** a written or printed mark (as a letter or figure) having a recognized meaning: *I wish this book were written in bigger characters; these are so difficult to read.*

capital (letter) [C] a large letter such as A, B and C in alphabets such as the Roman alphabet: *Please write/print in capitals.* **block capitals/letters** [P] capitals: *Please write your name in block letters.*

lower case [U] the ordinary letters of an alphabet such as the Roman alphabet: *The sentence was printed in lower case.*

lower-case letter [C] an ordinary letter such as a, b and c

small letter [C] *infml* a lower-case letter

initial 1 [C] *also* **initial letter** a large letter at the beginning of a name, esp when used alone to represent a person's first name(s) and last name: *The second initial is for my middle name.* **2** [T1] to sign one's name on a piece of writing by writing one's initials, usu to show that one has read it or approves of it, etc: *He initialled each page.*

G149 *nouns & adjectives* : **letters and print**

roman [Wa5;B;U] (of or connected with) a type of writing or printing where the letters are upright as in this piece of printing

cursive [Wa5;B;U] (of or connected with) a type of writing or printing where the letters are joined together

italic [Wa5;B; C *often pl*; U] (of or concerning) a type of writing or printing where the letters are narrower, slope to the right and have hooks on the ends: *She writes italic. This example is printed in italics.* **italicize, -ise** [T1; I∅] to put (writing, printing, etc) into italics

Gothic [Wa5;B;U] (of) a type of printing with thick, pointed letters

printable [B] **1** fit to be printed; suitable for reading by anyone: *In his bad temper he used language that was hardly printable.* **un-** [*neg*] **2** that can be printed or printed from: *This fine 300-year-old block is still printable.*

publishable [B] able to be published; worth publishing: *That material isn't publishable in its present form.* **un-** [*neg*]

G150 *nouns* : **punctuating and spacing**

punctuation [U] the way in which written or printed material is divided into sentences, phrases, etc, by means of marks so that understanding is made easier **punctuate** [T1; I∅] to arrange (printing, writing, etc) with the most suitable marks: *He doesn't punctuate (his work) properly; he always uses commas where he should have used full stops.*

layout [U;C] the way in which printed matter is set out on paper: *I like the layout of that book.*

spacing [U] the way in which distance between letters and lines of letters is arranged on a printed page or page with writing, etc on it

white space [U] *tech* the unused area of paper on a printed page

G151 *nouns, etc* : **punctuation marks**

punctuation mark [C] any mark used in punctuation

period *esp AmE* **1** [C] a sign (.) marking the end of a sentence or a shortened form of a word **2** [adv] (used at the end of a sentence, expressing strong feeling) and that is all I am going to say on the subject; and that is what I have firmly decided: *I'm not going to do it, period.*

full stop [C] *esp BrE* a period: *Put full stops at the end of your sentences.*

point [C] a period: *Put points after your sentences.*

dot [C] *infml* a full stop or point

comma [C] the mark (,) for showing a short pause

colon [C] the mark (:) for directing the reader from one part of a piece of writing to another

semicolon [C] the mark (;) for showing longer pauses, connecting two sentences that are closely related, or separating members of lists

exclamation mark/point [C] the mark (!) which is written after the actual words of an exclamation: *'I'm hungry!' she exclaimed.* (Compare: *She exclaimed that she was hungry*).

question mark [C] the mark (?) which is written after the actual words of a question: *Are you coming?* (Compare: *She asked if I was coming*).

apostrophe [C] the sign (') used in writing **a** to show that one or more letters or figures have been left out of a word or figure (as in *Don't*, *I'm* and *'47* for *do not*, *I am* and *1947*) **b** before or after *s* to show possession (as in *lady's hat*, *ladies' hats*, *children's hats*) **c** before *s* to show the plural of letters and figures (as in *There are 2 f's in off* and *Your 8's look like S's*)

asterisk 1 [C] a star-like mark (*) used **a** to call attention to a note at the bottom of a page **b** to mark that certain letters are missing from a word **c** to show that a word, phrase, sound, etc is wrong or may never have existed (as in the example '*In English we say 3 boys not *3 boy*'). **2** [T1] to mark with an asterisk: *Asterisk those words.*

hyphen [C] a short written or printed line (-) which can join words, parts of words, or syllables **hyphenate** [T1] to join with a hyphen

dash [C] the mark (—) which can separate parts of sentences very clearly from each other

slash (mark) [C] the mark (/) used usu to show 'or', to show fractions, etc: *man/woman* (= man or woman)

oblique [C] a slash (/)

solidus [C] a slash (/)

swung dash [C] the mark (~) used in certain dictionaries, etc to replace a word instead of printing it again

tilde [C] a swung dash, esp as used in Spanish to

indicate the sound /nj/ and in Portuguese to mark a nasal pronunciation

circumflex [C] a mark (ˆ) put over a letter (as *être* in French)ˆ to show that it has a special sound

acute (accent) [C] the mark (´) above the vowel in such French words as *émigré*

grave (accent) [C] the mark (`) above the vowel in such French words as *mère*

bracket 1 [C *usu pl*] either of various pairs of signs such as ( ), and [ ] used in writing and printing to separate something from the rest of a sentence, equation, etc: *Put these words in round brackets and those words in square brackets. He put brackets round the words, to show that they were his own opinion and not part of the story.* **2** [T1] to put between brackets: *He bracketed the words.*

parenthesis [C] **1** either of a pair of round brackets used esp to separate one part of a piece of writing or printing from the rest: *Put that phrase in parentheses.* **2** a group of words separated in this way or by commas or dashes **parenthetical** [B] (as if) being in parentheses: *The phrase was parenthetical.* **-ly** [adv Wa4]

G152 *nouns* : **tools for writing with**

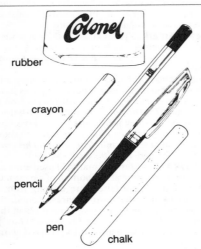

rubber

crayon

pencil

pen

chalk

pen 1 [C] an instrument used for writing in ink [⇒ H93] **2** [*the* R] (*fig*) (the art of) writing: *He hoped to live by the pen. 'The pen is mightier (= stronger) than the sword'* (saying).

pencil 1 [C] a narrow pointed usu wooden instrument containing a thin stick of a black substance (**graphite**) or coloured material, used for writing or drawing **2** [U] the writing material in a pencil: *Should I sign this paper in pencil or ink?*

crayon [c] a stick of coloured wax or chalk used for writing or drawing, esp on paper

chalk [U; C] (a piece of) white or coloured soft

rock used for writing or drawing: *Pass me the/ some chalk, please. The teacher wrote with a stick of chalk on the blackboard. These are very good chalks.*

typewriter

typewriter [C] a machine that prints letters by means of keys which when struck by the fingers press onto paper through an inked ribbon

rubber [C] *esp BrE* a piece of the substance rubber (made from the juice of a tropical tree) used for removing pencil marks from paper

eraser [C] *fml or AmE* an object, esp a rubber, for removing writing

G153 *nouns* : **things to write on**

paper [U] material, esp made from wood, which is prepared in sheets of various sizes, is usu white and used for writing, drawing, etc on: *Can I have some more paper, please?*

writing paper [U] paper for writing letters on, usu smooth and of quite good quality and cut into various standard sizes

notepaper [U] paper suitable for writing letters and notes

letterhead 1 [C] the name and address of a person or business printed at the top of their writing paper **2** [U] writing paper with the letterhead printed on it

sheet [C] a flat thin piece of paper, usu cut square or nearly square and used esp for writing or typing on or in books, newspapers, etc for printing on: *Write on a fresh (= new) sheet of paper.*

card [C] a small sheet of stiff(ened) paper, usu with information on it or to be used for information, and having various uses: *He wrote the words on cards and arranged them alphabetically as a card index* [⇒ G163]. *Show me your union/club/membership card, please.*

page [C] **1** one side of a sheet of paper in a book, newspaper, etc, usu numbered: *There is a picture of a ship on page 44. This newspaper has 24 pages.* **2** the whole sheet (on both sides): *Someone has torn a page out of this book.* **3** (*fig*) *lit* something which could be written in a book: *These years will be remembered as some of the finest pages in our country's history.*

stationery [U] writing materials, esp sheets of paper: *We must buy some more stationery. Do you know any stationery shops near here?*

papyrus 1 [U] a grass-like water plant formerly common in Egypt, used in ancient times esp for making paper **2** [U] a type of paper made from this plant **3** [C] a piece of ancient writing on this paper

parchment 1 [U] (esp formerly) writing material made from the skin of a sheep, goat, etc **2** [U] paper that looks like parchment **3** [C] a piece of this: *He wrote everything down on a parchment.*

G154 *nouns & verbs* : **papers, documents, and records**

paper [C *usu pl*] a special piece of paper with something typed, printed, or written on it, often for official purposes: *Can I see your papers, please? Does he have any papers to show who he is?*

document 1 [C] a paper, small book, etc that gives information, proof, or support of something else: *Let me see all the official documents concerning the sale of this land* **2** [T1] to prove or give examples of (something), esp in or by showing documents: *He documented the whole case very well.* **documentary** [Wa5;B] of, concerning, or like a document or documents: *We need documentary proof of this.*

record 1 [C] a written, typed, or printed paper or set of papers, etc that describes or gives the facts about someone or something, esp about past actions, events, etc: *His record at school/His school record was good. Keep a record of everything you do; we may need it later. The official records are kept in that building.* **2** [T1] to put something down in writing as a record: *She recorded everything that was said at the meeting.*

register 1 [C] a list, record, book, etc esp kept for official purposes: *The government keeps a register of all births, marriages, and deaths. The teacher has the class's attendance register, showing which students were in school on a particular day. Sign your name in the hotel register. A cash register is a machine used in shops to record how much money is taken each day.* **2** [IØ;T1] to (cause to) write in a register, list, etc: *He registered for the night at a local hotel. The child's birth was registered locally. Are you registered as a voter/registered to vote?* **3** [T1] to record or show: *The instrument called a thermometer registers heat. The thermometer registered 35 degrees.* (*fig*) *Her face registered anger and surprise.* **4** [IØ] *infml* to be understood: *The bad news didn't register* (*with me*) *for several minutes.* **registration** [*often in comb*] **1** [U] the act of registering or being registered: *The registration of births is done locally, not at a national centre.* **2** [C] an example of this: *How many registrations have you had today?* **registrar** [C] a person, esp an official, who makes and keeps a register: *marriage registrar* **registry** [C] an office, etc where a register of any kind is kept **registry office** [C] an office where people can be married without a religious ceremony

G155 *nouns, etc* : **letters and notes** [C]
[ALSO ⇒ G190–193]

letter a written or printed message sent usu in an envelope: *She wrote some letters last night; one was a business letter and the others were personal.* **air letter 1** any letter that is sent by air **2** a sheet of very thin paper on which a letter can be written and which is then folded and stuck to itself and sent off without an envelope

epistle *fml or humor* a letter, esp a long and important one: *This solemn 10-page epistle is from my Aunt Martha.*

note 1 a short letter: *She sent me a note to say everything was fine.* **2** a short piece of writing, esp made while listening, talking, etc: *He made a note to telephone her. Can I look at the notes I took at the meeting?*

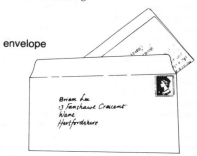

envelope

Brian Lee
13 Fanshawe Crescent
Ware
Hertfordshire

envelope a paper covering for a letter: *He put the letter in an envelope.*

label 1 a piece of paper or other material fixed to something, on which is written what it is, where it is to go, who owns it, etc: *The label on the bottle said that it contained oil.* **2** [T1;X1, 7] **a** to fix or tie a label on: *The doctor labelled the bottle Poison/Poisonous.* **b** (*fig*) to put into a kind or class; describe as: *His enemies labelled the boy a thief.*

G156 *nouns* : **notebooks** [C]

notebook a book in which notes are or may be written: *I kept a notebook on my trip abroad* (= recorded my experiences in a book). *He bought a notebook to use in class.*

pad a usu thick set of sheets of paper one on top of the other and fixed together at one end in some way, used for writing

notepad a pad for taking notes

exercise book a book of sheets of paper, esp as used in schools for written exercises

jotter 1 a notepad **2** *ScotE* a school exercise book: *The teacher told her pupils to open their jotters.*

folder a piece of cardboard folded or made into an envelope for holding loose papers: *He had all his notes in a red folder.*

file 1 something for holding letters, papers, etc, usu a folder **2** a collection of papers usu in files giving information about someone or something: *The police keep files on these people.*

G157 *nouns* : **stories and reports** [C]

story 1 an account of events, real or imagined: *He likes telling the children stories.* **2** *infml* (*used by and to children*) a lie (*esp in the phr* **to tell stories**) **3** the plot of (= what happens in) a book, film, play, etc: *The film is a love story.* **4** (material for) an article in a newspaper, magazine, etc: *He said the fight was unpleasant, but it made a good story. This event will be a good story for the paper.* **the same old story** the usual excuse or difficulty

tale 1 *esp poet* a story of imaginary events: *He told them a tale about good fairies. She was reading tales of adventure.* **2** a report of events: *On returning from the war he told us tales of fear and sadness.* **3** a lie; false story: *'Tell me why you're late and don't tell me a tale,' shouted the angry teacher. The wicked little girl was always telling her mother tales.* **4** a piece of news, esp when false or intended to hurt: *It was nasty of you to go round telling tales you know weren't true. People who tell tales aren't worth knowing.*

anecdote a short, interesting or amusing story about a particular person or event **anecdotal** [B] of, containing, telling, or full of anecdotes

yarn *often infml, sometimes deprec* a story, esp one told by someone returning from an adventure or long travels and not necessarily true (*often in the phr* **spin a yarn**)

account a written or spoken story, report, or description: *Give us an account of what happened.*

description a statement, account, or story that describes: *He wrote a fine description of the place and what happened there.*

version 1 a person's account of an event as compared with that of another: *I believe the driver's version of the accident/of what happened. The newspapers gave very different versions of what took place.* **2** a translation or adaptation of a play, book, etc: *I like the French version better than the English one. The King James Version of the Bible appeared in 1611. Did you read the short or full version of the book?*

report 1 an account or description of events, experiences, etc: *He read some newspaper reports of the accident/the company's report for the year. She wrote an official report on the danger of smoking.* **2** [*also* U] (a piece of) talk that spreads without official support: *According to report/There is a report that there will soon be a change of government.* **of good/evil report** *fml* said to be good/evil: *a man of evil report*

write-up *usu not fml* a written report, esp one giving a good judgment, as of goods or a play: *The concert got a good write-up in the local newspaper.*

G158 *nouns* : **essays and papers** [C]

essay a piece of writing, not poetry or a story, usu short and on one subject: *There was a prize for the best essay on Shakespeare.*

composition a piece of writing; an essay, story, or description, esp an exercise done for educational purposes: *The teacher told them to write a composition.*

dissertation *esp tech* a long piece of writing, esp as done after studying a subject for some time: *He wrote a dissertation on deep sea fish.*

thesis *esp tech* **1** a long written argument, description, etc esp as prepared for a university degree: *He wrote his thesis for the degree of Ph.D in three years.* **2** [*usu sing*] an argument: *His thesis is that the world's temperatures are changing.*

paper *usu tech* something written on a matter of interest to certain people, usu to be read at a special meeting: *He read his latest paper to a conference of doctors in Edinburgh.*

G159 *nouns* : **articles and headlines** [C]

article 1 a complete piece of writing in a newspaper, magazine, etc: *That newspaper usually has good articles on politics. Have you read the article on new industries?* **2** a complete or separate part in a written law agreement: *I have written 12 articles into our agreement.*

feature a special article in a newspaper: *He writes features for The Times; he's one of their feature writers.*

piece [*usu sing*] *infml* a short written statement in a newspaper, magazine, etc: *Did you see the piece in the paper about Mrs Smith's accident? Can you do a piece on local politics for our paper?*

sketch a short informal piece of writing: *He wrote some travel sketches for a magazine.*

column an article by a particular writer that regularly appears in a newspaper or magazine: *I always read his column in the Guardian.*

editorial, *also* **leader, leading article** *BrE* the article in a newspaper that gives the paper's opinion about a particular subject or group of subjects

headline 1 the heading printed above a story in a newspaper: *The headline read 'SEVEN DEAD IN CRASH'.* **2** the titles shown on large notices where newspapers are sold **3** [*usu pl*] one of the main points of the news as read on radio or television: *Here are the news headlines.*

G160 *nouns* : **reading matter**

reading matter [U] material which people can read: *What kind of reading matter do you like best?*

material [U] written or recorded information,

ideas, etc that can be used in a book, newspaper, etc: *This material isn't much good.*

copy [U] *esp tech* written material ready to be printed: *She sent us some really good copy today.*

print [U] letters, words, or language in newspapers, books, etc: *She likes to see her name in print.*

printed word [*the* R] what is stated in a newspaper, book, etc: *Many people have a strong belief in the printed word; they think it must be true.*

G161 *nouns, etc:* **summaries**

summary [C] a short account of a piece of writing, a meeting, radio talk, lecture, etc which gives the most important facts: *He made a summary of the report/of what had been done.*
summarize, -ise [T1] to make a summary of: *He summarized the book in 10 pages.* **sum up** [v adv] **1** [T1; I∅] to give the main points of (a meeting, etc) esp at the end: *When the discussion ended, the chairman of the meeting summed up.* **2** [T1] to form an opinion about (someone): *He is good at summing people up.*
digest [C] a summary, esp of a piece of writing: *He sent her a digest of the report.*
synopsis [C] *fml* a digest: *I read his synopsis of the paper, but not the paper* [⇒ G158] *itself.*
abstract [C] *tech* a summary or summarizing statement of a book, thesis [⇒ G158], etc esp if printed at the beginning of the book
breakdown [C] a simple explanation esp showing the size, etc of each part: *I'd like a breakdown of these figures, please.*
roundup [C] a gathering together of the main parts of a discussion into one account, last discussion, etc: *Here is a roundup of today's news.*
abridg(e)ment 1 [U] the act of making (something, esp a story or a book) shorter **2** [C] something, such as a story, book, or play, that has been made shorter: *This is an abridgment for radio in five parts.* **abridge** [T1] **1** [Wv5] to make (something written or spoken) shorter by using fewer words; cut short: *'Ulysses' has been abridged for radio. Many schools use abridged versions of Shakespeare.* **2** *lit* to make (a meeting, period of time, etc) shorter
abbreviation 1 [U] the act of making something (usu a word) shorter **2** [C] a shortened form, esp of a word **abbreviate** [T1] to make (a story, speech, visit, word, etc) shorter: *In this book, the word 'adjective' is abbreviated to 'adj'.* [⇒ G274]
précis *also* **precis 1** [*C usu sing*] a shortened form of a speech or piece of writing, giving only the main points **2** [T1] to make a précis of: *Will you précis this report?*
brief 1 a summary of the main facts about a case, etc, esp for a lawyer before he or she speaks in court: *Have you read the brief?* **2** *tech* a piece of work, esp given to a lawyer: *I have a brief for*

you. **3** [*usu sing*] *not fml* a particular job to be done at a particular time: *Your brief is to find out all about his plans.*

G162 *nouns* : **books and manuscripts** [C]

book 1 a collection of sheets of paper fastened together as a thing to be read, or to be written in: *He bought some new books.* **2** one of the main divisions or parts of a larger written work (as of a long poem or the Bible): *I'm reading Book Two at the moment.* **3** any collection of things fastened together in a similar way: *Can I have a book of stamps/tickets?* **4** written material considered as the contents of a (possible) book: *He wrote a book once, but it wasn't published.*
title *esp tech* a book: *One publisher* [⇒ G174, 176] *asked the other how many titles he had published that year.*
manuscript 1 *also abbrev* **MS** the first or only copy of a book or piece of writing, esp in handwriting: *We could hardly read his manuscript because of his handwriting.* **2** a handwritten book of the time before printing was invented
scroll 1 a long straight piece of animal skin, papyrus [⇒ G153], or (rarely) paper, often rolled around handles at both ends and used esp in ancient times for books, records, and other formal writings **2** an ornament or shape with a curve like this (as often at the top of a pillar, at the end of the arm of a chair, etc)
typescript a copy of a book or piece of writing in the typewritten form, esp before it is printed: *He sent the typescript to his publisher.*
script a written or (esp) typed form of speech, play, or broadcast to be spoken: *Where's my script?* **scripted** [Wa5;B] (esp of a speech or broadcast) having, or read from, a script: *The show wasn't scripted, so no one knew what might be said in it.* **un-** [*neg*]
draft the (first) rough written form of anything, esp a speech or article; a rough plan: *I've made a first draft of my speech for Friday, but it still needs a lot of work. This is his draft plan for the new law.*
textbook a book which gives information about a subject, esp for use in schools, etc: *He was reading a science textbook.*
manual *also infml* **handbook** a textbook intended to be useful esp when working directly with something: *She was reading a gardening manual/a handbook on gardening.*
diary 1 a book in which a person writes what has happened during the day, what he or she thinks about people, etc: *They have kept diaries since they were children.* **2** a record of daily happenings, meetings, etc: *Put the date in your diary so that you don't forget.* **diarist** *esp fml & lit* a person who writes a diary: *Samuel Pepys was a famous 17th-century diarist.*
log 1 a daily written record of a ship's speed,

distance sailed in a day, position, etc: *The information was entered in the ship's log.* **2** any written record of such a kind, of daily events, etc: *He kept a log of everything that happened.* **3** [T1] to write (something) in a log: *He logged the time as 2200 hrs.* **logbook** a book used as a log

G163 *nouns, etc* : **books and their parts**

book

binding [C] the cover of a book: *The binding of this book is broken.* **bound** [Wa5;B *often in comb*] (of a book) fastened with covers: *It's a Bible bound in leather. That's rather a fine old leatherbound Bible.*

blurb [C] *infml* a short description by the publisher of the contents of a book, printed on its paper cover or in advertisements: *Who will write the blurb for this dictionary?*

introduction [C] **1** a written explanation at the beginning of a book **2** a book which gives one a knowledge of the most important things, training, etc before going on to advanced studies

preface 1 [C] an introduction to a book or speech: *He wrote a preface to his book, explaining why he had written it.* **2** [C] (*fig*) *infml* an action that is intended to introduce something else more important: *She says she has nothing to wear at the party.—Hmm, that's probably a preface to asking for a new dress.* **3** [T1] to be an introduction to or come before (something more important): *Tell us about the arguments that prefaced the fight at the meeting.*

foreword [C] a preface, esp in which someone who knows the writer and his work says something about them: *What does it say in his foreword to the story/play?*

prologue *also* **prolog** *AmE* [C] **1** an introduction to a play, long poem, etc: *She was reading the Prologue to Chaucer's 'Canterbury Tales'.* **2** (*fig*) an act or event that leads up to, introduces, or causes another more important

event: *Their marriage was the prologue to a life of happiness.*

contents [P] what is contained in the printed pages of a book, etc: *Look at the list of the contents/the contents list in the book.*

chapter [C] **1** one of the main divisions of a book or long article, usu having a number or title: *Chapter 5 is the best in the book.* **2** (*fig*) a special period in history, someone's life, etc: *Was the period of the Empire the finest chapter in British history? There was a chapter in his life when everything seemed to go wrong.*

instalment [C] one part of a book, play, television programme, etc, which appears in regular parts until the story is completed: *He listened to the second instalment last night.*

epilogue *also* **epilog** *AmE* [C] a part of a story, play, or poem, etc that is added after the end, usu to give (a little) more information.

appendix [C] a part at the end of a book, report, etc giving additional information: *The writer describes the house in Appendix C.*

bibliography 1 [C] a list of all writings used in the preparation of a book or article, etc, usu appearing at the end **2** [C] a list of writings which share some quality: *They made a bibliography of all the works published by Longman in the past 250 years.* **3** [U] the history or description of books or writing **bibliographical** [Wa5;B] of, concerning, or like (what is done in) a bibliography

index 1 [C] an alphabetical list at the back of a book, of names, subjects, etc mentioned in it and the pages where they can be found: *This lexicon has a large index.* **2** [C] anything like this: *He keeps an index of his works on cards (= a card index).* **3** [T1] to make an index for: *Can you index this book?* **indexer** [C] a person making an index or indexes

cross-reference [C] a note directing the reader from one place in a book to another place in the same book: *In this book cross-references are shown with an arrow (⇨).* **cross-refer** *also* **cross-index** [T1; I0 (*from, to*)] to direct (the reader) from one place in a book to another place in the same book: *In this book arrows are used to cross-refer from one word to another.*

G164 *nouns* : **kinds of printed books, etc**

hardback 1 [C] a book with a strong cover or binding **2** [U] the form of such a book (*often in the phr* **in hardback**): *Is this book available in hardback?—Yes, there is a hardback edition* [⇨ G180].

paperback 1 [C] a book bound with a thin cardboard cover: *That shop sells only paperbacks.* **2** [U] the form of such a book (*often in the phr* **in paperback**): *Is this book available in paperback?—Yes, there is a paperback edition.*

volume 1 [C] **a** one of a set of books of the same kind or together forming a whole: *We have a set of Dickens' works in 24 volumes.* **b** one of a set of connected reports, magazines, papers, etc, of the same kind put together in book form, often yearly: *Can I see the 1970 volume of the magazine?* **2** *fml* a book, esp a large one: *They published a thin volume of his poetry. The library was full of fine old volumes.*

tome [C] *old use & humor* a very large book: *What's that tome you're reading?*

pamphlet [C] a small book with paper covers, printed on sheets of paper that are not bound together, which deals usu with some matter of public interest

booklet [C] a small book, usu with a paper cover; a pamphlet

leaflet [C] a small sheet, often folded, of printed matter, usu given free to the public

brochure [C] a booklet, esp one giving instructions or details of a service offered for money: *She picked up a holiday brochure/an advertising brochure.*

circular [C] a printed paper or notice or advertisement intended to be given to a large number of people to read: *Did you see that circular from the government telling us about their attack on prices?* **circularize, -ise** [T1] to send circulars to (a group of people): *We must circularize the whole town if we want to win the next election.*

G165 *nouns, etc* : **reference books**

reference book [C] a book that provides a large amount of information, usu of a particular kind: *Dictionaries and encyclopedias are reference books.*

work of reference [C] *fml* a reference book

dictionary [C] a book that gives a list of words in ABC (= alphabetical) order, with their meanings and pronunciations: *He looked up the word in his dictionary. He bought a French–English dictionary. Can I buy a dictionary of place names here?*

thesaurus [C] a book containing lists of words put together in groups according to likenesses in their meanings but not usu in ABC order or given definitions: *Roget's Thesaurus is a well-known reference book.*

lexicon [C] *esp fml* a dictionary or similar book dealing with words: *He bought a Greek–English lexicon. This book is called 'The Lexicon of Contemporary English' because it gives a lot of information about English words and is a combination of dictionary and thesaurus.* [⇒ G234]

encyclopedia, -paed- *also old use* **cyclopaedia** [C] a book or a set of books dealing with every branch of knowledge, or with one particular branch, in ABC order: *A dictionary explains words and an encyclopedia explains facts.*

directory [C] a book or list of names, facts, etc, usu arranged in ABC order: *The telephone directory gives people's names, addresses, and telephone numbers.*

catalogue, *also* **catalog** *AmE* **1** [C] a list of

places, names, goods, etc, usu in book form, with information about them put in a special order so that they can be found easily: *Can I have a catalogue of goods for sale, please? This book wasn't in the library catalogue, but I found it on the shelves.* **2** [T1] to make a catalogue of (a list of goods, places, names, etc): *Can you catalogue the furniture you sell and send me a copy?* **3** [T1] to enter (a book, place, name, etc) into a catalogue.

atlas [C] a book of maps: *The teacher asked a pupil to give out the atlases.*

gazetteer [C] a list of names of places, printed as a dictionary, or as a list at the end of an atlas

album [C] a book in which photographs, stamps, etc can be kept: *He has four albums full of stamps. Can I look at your photograph album?*

G166 *nouns* : **literature and verse**

literature 1 [U] **a** written works which are of artistic value: *English literature is world famous.* **b** these books as a subject for study **2** [U] written works which are not scientific: *He prefers literature to science.* **3** [U9] a set of works written in a certain country or at a certain time, esp as a subject for study: *He studies 19th century American literature.* **4** [C9; U9] a set of works on a particular subject: *There is a large body of scientific literature which no one person can read. There is a developing literature of social work.* **5** [U] *infml* printed material, esp giving information: *The postman put a pile of literature through the door, but it was all advertisements.*

prose [U] written language in its usual form (as different from poetry): *Newspapers are written in prose. He isn't a poet; he's a prose writer. She writes a very clear simple prose.*

poetry 1 [U] the art of the poet: *Poetry is a difficult art.* **2** [U] poems in general: *She bought a book of poetry/a poetry book. I like Dryden's poetry.* **3** [U] *(fig)* a quality of beauty, grace, and deep feeling: *This dancer has poetry in her movements.*

verse [U] writing arranged in regular lines, with a pattern of repeated beats (as in music) and (usu) words of matching sound at the end of some lines; language in the form of poetry: *Not all verse is great poetry. It was a book of prose and verse. He made a verse translation of the 'Aeneid'.*

rhyme *also old use & poet* **rime** [U] (the use of) words or lines of poetry or verse that end with the same sound

blank verse [U] verse without rhyme: *Much of Shakespeare's writing is in blank verse.*

G167 *nouns, etc* : **novels, poems, and fiction**

novel 1 [C] a long written story, usu in prose and printed as a book, dealing with invented people and events: *'War and Peace' is a great Russian novel.* **2** [*the* R] the art of writing novels; novels generally: *He studies the novel in the 19th century.*

novelette [C] a short novel; a long short story, often of a light kind

short story 1 [C] a story in written form, too short to be a novel or novelette, usu one of a number in a book: *He writes short stories.* **2** [*the* R] the art of writing short stories; short stories generally

poem [C] a piece of writing, arranged in patterns of lines and sounds, expressing in imaginative language some deep thought, feeling, or human experience

anthology [C] a collection of poems or of other writings, often on the same subject, chosen from different books or writers, usu considered the best or very good examples of their kind **anthologist** [C] a person who makes or has made an anthology

classic [C] a work of literature, esp if written long ago or in a special way which is considered very good: *Most of Shakespeare's plays are now classics of the theatre/theatre classics.* **the classics** [P] the literature of ancient Greece and Rome **classical** [B] **1** *often cap* of, concerning, or like the literature, ideas, etc of ancient Greece and Rome **2** *of music* serious: *Beethoven wrote classical music.* **-ly** [adv Wa4]

history [C] a (written) account of (any part of) history: *He wrote a short history of the last war.*

chronicle *esp lit* **1** [C] a story of usu real events over a period of time, written or told in the order in which they happened **2** [T1] to write about (something) as a chronicle: *He chronicled the events carefully.* **chronicler** [C] a person writing or keeping a chronicle

biography 1 [C] a written story of a person's life: *Boswell's famous biography of Dr Johnson is still widely read.* **2** [U] this branch of literature: *I like poetry better than biography.* **biographer** [C] the writer of one or more biographies **biographic(al)** [Wa5;B] of biography **-(al)ly** [adv Wa4]

autobiography 1 [C] a book written by oneself about one's own life **2** [U] such books or the writing of such books **autobiographic(al)** [B] of or concerning the facts of one's own life, esp as written in a book

memoirs [P] a written account of a person's life, esp as he or she remembers it in old age: *The general retired from the army and wrote his memoirs.*

fiction [U] stories, novels, etc that are about things which have not happened but come from the imagination of writers **fictional** [Wa5;B] of, concerning, or like fiction **-ly** [adv] [⇨N12]

nonfiction [U] literature other than poetry, plays [⇨K76], stories, and novels: *Most libraries divide books into Fiction and Nonfiction.*

G168 *nouns* : **serials and bestsellers** [C]

serial 1 a written or broadcast story appearing in parts at fixed times: *'The Archers' is a British radio serial that has been heard every day for many years. His new book will appear in serial form in a magazine.* **2** *tech* (used in libraries) (a book, magazine, etc printed as one of) a continuing set with a single name and numbered 1, 2, 3, etc

series a group of books printed by one company in the same style and often under a single name: *They produced a series of books on animals of the world.*

bestseller something, esp a book, whose sales are among the highest of its class: *His latest book is a bestseller.*

G169 *nouns, etc* : **verses and rhymes**

verse [C] **1** a set of lines of poetry which forms one part of a poem, and usu has a pattern that is repeated in the other parts: *Today I learned three verses of a poem at school.* **2** a set of such lines forming the words to which the tune of a song is sung **3** *tech* a line of poetry: *In this poem, each verse has five beats.*

stanza [C] a group of lines in a repeating pattern forming a division of a poem; *fml* a verse of poetry: *The poem has four stanzas.*

canto [C] one of the main divisions of a long poem: *Read Canto 5 of the poem.*

rhyme *also old use & poet* **rime 1** [C] *not fml* a verse or verses, esp for children: *Learn this rhyme.* **2** [C] a word or line that ends with the same sound as another. **3** [IØ] to be like this: *'Day' and 'say' rhyme (with each other). The lines don't rhyme.* **4** [T1] to put together (two words that end with the same sound, or a word with another that does this): *You can rhyme 'duty' with 'beauty', but you can't rhyme 'box' and 'sacks'.*

G170 *nouns* : **kinds of poems** [C]

nursery rhyme a short usu well-known song or poem for small children

couplet a pair of lines of writing, one following the other, that are of equal length and end in the same sound

limerick a type of short, usu humorous poem with five lines

lyric a poem, usu short and full of feeling, usu intended for singing

sonnet a 14-line poem with any of several fixed formal patterns of rhyme [⇒ G166, 169]

ballad 1 a short story told in the form of a poem **2** a simple song **3** a popular love song: *Bing Crosby sang some of the most popular ballads of the 1930s and 40s.*

epic a long poem (or book, film, etc) telling the

story of the deeds of gods, great men, or the early history of a nation: *The 'Ramayana' is an epic of ancient India, and the 'Odyssey' is an epic of ancient Greece.* (*fig*) *His book about his travels in the desert is an epic. He produced a cinema epic with thousands of actors.*

ode a type of usu long poem

elegy a type of poem or song written to show sorrow for the dead or for something lost: *He wrote an elegy on the death of his friend. Gray's 'Elegy in a Country Churchyard' is one of the most famous poems in the English language.*

G171 *adjectives* : **relating to literature and poetry** [B]

literary 1 [Wa5] of or concerning literature 2 producing literature; being a writer: *He is a literary man.* 3 studying literature: *He is a literary man.* 4 (of words) of or suitable to the written language, not the language of conversation

poetic 1 [Wa5] of, like, or connected with poets or poetry: *What fine poetic style/language! Shakespeare's plays are written in poetic form.* 2 *apprec* beautiful and imaginative; expressing great feeling: *The dancer moved with poetic grace.* **-ally** [adv Wa4]

poetical 1 poetic 2 [Wa5] written in the form of poems: *He has the complete poetical works of Wordsworth.* **-ly** [adv]

lyrical *also old use* **lyric** 1 [Wa5] of or related to lyrics; of or intended for singing 2 expressing strong personal feelings, of the kind written about in lyrics 3 very happy: *She was quite lyrical about her new house.* **-ly** [adv Wa4]

epic [Wa5] (of stories, events, etc) full of brave actions and excitement, like an epic: *This is the tale of an epic fight of a small ship against six larger enemy ships.*

G172 *nouns* : **persons who write** [C]

writer a person who writes for a job or who has written a particular thing: *He is a writer, but can't make enough money to live from his books. The writer of this article has some strange ideas.*

scriptwriter a writer of plays or other material to be spoken on radio or television or in a film

scribe 1 a person employed to copy things in writing, esp in times before the invention of printing: *This is a beautiful manuscript, the work of a skilful scribe.* 2 *humor* a writer

scribbler *derog & humor* a writer

author 1 the writer of a book, newspaper article, play, poem, etc 2 the person who begins or thinks of anything, esp an idea or play **-ess** [*fem*]

novelist a person who writes a novel or novels

poet 1 a person who writes (good) poems **-ess** [*fem*] 2 (*fig*) *apprec* an artist, musician, etc who

shows great feeling and imagination in his or her work

bard *lit & poet* a poet: *Shakespeare is sometimes called the Bard of Avon.*

composer a person who writes music: *Beethoven is one of the greatest composers who ever lived.* [⇒K39]

editor a person who edits [⇒ G142], esp a newspaper or books: *He is the sports editor of The Times. The author did not like the way his editor changed things in the book.*

G173 *verbs* : **printing and copying**

print 1 [T1] to press (a mark) onto a soft surface: *The mark of a man's shoe is clearly printed in this mud.* 2 [T1; I0] to press letters or pictures onto (paper) by using inked shapes: *This machine can print 60 sheets/pages a minute. Why has the machine stopped printing?* 3 [T1] to press (letters or pictures) onto paper by using inked shapes: *The bottom line on this page hasn't been properly printed.* 4 [T1; I0] to make (a book, magazine, etc) by means of pressing letters or pictures onto paper: *This firm prints a lot of educational books. Our company doesn't print any longer; it only sells books.* 5 [T1] to cause (something) to appear in or be produced as a book, newspaper, etc: *Are you going to have your poems printed? All today's newspapers print the minister's speech in full.* 6 [I0] to produce a copy by printing: *This metal plate is too worn to print.* 7 [T1] to make or copy (a photograph) on paper sensitive to light, from a specially treated sheet of photographic film 8 [L9] to be produced as a copy by printing: *The photograph didn't print well.* 9 [Wv5 (*with*);T1] to ornament (cloth or wallpaper) with a coloured pattern pressed or rubbed on the surface [⇒ G141]

compose [T1] *tech* to form (words, sentences, pages, etc) ready for printing

set [T1 (*up*)] to arrange ((in) metal letters) for printing: *Today most books are set (up) by machine.*

copy [D1 (*for*); T1] to make a written, printed, photographed, etc copy of (something): *Please copy this letter for me/copy me this letter. He copied the letter by hand.*

bind [T1] to put a cover on (a book): *Who bound those books?* **binder** *also* **bookbinder** [C] a person whose work it is to bind books, etc

G174 *verbs* : **publishing**

publish 1 [T1; I0] (of a kind of business firm) to choose, arrange, have printed, and offer for sale to the public some kind of written work in the form of a book, magazine, newspaper, etc, or records, etc, *This firm publishes educational books. Many newspapers are published daily. The firm prints and publishes music.* 2 [T1] to sell the works of (a writer) in this way: *This* *firm has published many well-known writers.* **3** [T1;I∅] (of a writer) to have (one's work) printed and put on sale: *She has only been writing for 18 months but already she has published a book. I've finished the work but I'm not going to publish till I find a good publisher.* **4** [T1;I∅] (of a newspaper or magazine) to print (something written): *It's a good story, but we can't publish (it); too many people would be offended.* **5** [T1 *often pass*] to make known generally; give public notice of: *The death of the ruler was kept secret; the news wasn't published for several days.*

bring out [v adv T1] to publish; produce: *They are bringing out a new book on that subject.*

put out [v adv T1] *sometimes deprec* to publish; produce, esp in large numbers: *He puts out a lot of books every year. They put out some very strange books.*

get out [v adv T1] *loose* to publish; produce: *He got the book out very quickly.*

issue [T1] to bring out (esp something printed) for the notice of the public: *The government have issued a number of booklets explaining their plans. He issued a general invitation. They plan to issue a new stamp soon.*

G175 *nouns* : **printing and publishing** [U]

printing 1 the act or action of printing: *Who does the printing for this office? There are a few mistakes in the printing.* **2** the art of printing: *The invention of printing made it possible for many people to be educated.*

binding the act or action of binding

publishing the business or profession of publishing books, newspapers, records, etc

G176 *nouns* : **persons who print and publish, etc** [C]

printer 1 a person employed in the trade of printing **2** an owner of a printing business

typesetter a person who arranges or sets metal letters for printing

compositor a person who arranges words, news, pages, etc for printing

typographer a person who plans the appearance of printed work

publisher a person whose business is to publish [⇒ G174] books, newspapers, etc, or to make and sell records or music

bookseller a person whose business it is to sell books (in a shop): *He is one of the biggest booksellers in the country.*

librarian a person who is in charge of or helps to run a library

G177 *nouns* : **businesses, etc relating to books, etc**

press 1 [C *usu cap*] a business for printing or

publishing books, magazines, etc: *Edinburgh University Press published his book.* **2** [C] a printing press: *Stop the presses! Some late news has come in.* **3** [(the) U] printing: *Can you have your report ready for the press by next week? The book is in (the) press now; it will shortly be published.*

printing press [C] a machine that prints books, newspapers, etc

printer [C] a machine for making copies, esp one for making photographs

bookshop *also* **bookseller** [C] a shop that sells books: *You can get this book at your local bookshop/at any good bookseller/bookseller's.*

bookstall [C] a table or small shop open at the front, where books, magazines, etc are shown for sale, esp on railway stations

library [C] **1** a building or part of a building which contains books that may be borrowed by the public (**public library**) or by members of a special group: *Is that a library book or is it your own?* **2** a collection of books: *He has built up quite a library over the years.* **3** a room or other place where books are kept and may be looked at, usually with tables at which to study: *He was in the library, not the living room.* **4** a series of books looking alike, usu on related subjects

G178 *nouns* : **elements in printing**

typography [U] **1** the work of preparing and setting matter for printing **2** the arrangement, style, and appearance of printed matter **typographic(al)** [Wa5;B] of, related to, or caused by typography **-(al)ly** [adv Wa4]

type 1 [U] raised letters of metal or wood used with ink for printing **2** [C] any one of these **3** [U] printed words

fount *also esp AmE* **font** [C] a set of letters (type) of one size, used by a printer

typeface [C] the size and style of the letters used in printing: *How many different typefaces are used in this book?*

artwork [U] the matter in a book, etc which has been prepared by an artist

graphics [P] the (way of producing) the style of a book, page, etc

G179 *nouns* : **authorship and copyright**

authorship [U] **1** the identity of the author [⇒ G172] of a book, play, poem, etc: *The book's authorship is not known. Authorship is sometimes hard to prove.*

copyright [C;U] the right in law to be the only producer, seller, or broadcaster of a book, play, film, record, etc, for a fixed period of time: *Have you kept the copyright to your books or did you sell them to a firm?*

rights [P] permission to copy and use a piece of work, esp a book, in various usu stated ways:

How much did he get for (selling) the film rights on his new book?

royalty [C] **1** part of the price of a book, etc paid to the writer on each copy sold: *Royalties are also paid to the writer of a play or piece of music, when it is performed. He receives royalties/a royalty of 5% on his book.* **2** a share of the profits, as of an oil well or a mine or a new machine, paid in this way to an owner or inventor

G180 *nouns* : **publications and editions**

publication 1 [C] something published such as a book, magazine, or article: *This part of the shop contains only scientific publications.* **2** [U] the act or action of offering books etc for sale to the public

edition [C] **1** one printing of a book, newspaper, magazine, etc: *It's an edition of 20,000 this time.* **2** the form in which a book is printed: *We are preparing a new edition (of that book) with many changes.*

issue [C] something, esp printed, brought out in a new form: *Have you seen the latest issue of that magazine? There's a new issue of Christmas stamps every year.*

copy [C] one of the total of magazines, books, newspapers, etc printed at one time, on one day, etc: *Can I get a copy of that book here? Buy me two copies of today's local newspaper.*

impression [C] a number of copies of a book published at one time: *This is the third impression of that book in one year.*

printing [C] an act of printing; a number of copies of a book; impression: *This is the third printing of the book.*

imprint [C] the name of a publisher, etc at the beginning of a book

Communication and information

G190 *verbs* : **communicating and keeping in touch** ·

[ALSO ⇒ G155 LETTERS]

communicate [I0 (*with*, *together*)] *fml* to share or exchange opinions, news, information, etc: *Has the Minister of Foreign Affairs communicated with the American President yet?*

write [D1; T1; I0] to produce and send (a letter) to (someone): *He writes her a letter every day. He writes to her every day (BrE)/He writes her every day (esp AmE). I wish he would write more often. Write soon, please!*

correspond [I0] to exchange letters regularly: *Janet and Bob corresponded for many years before they met.* **correspondent** [C] a person

with whom another person exchanges letters regularly

get in touch (with) *infml* to communicate (with (someone)) by any, often stated, means: *Can you get in touch with him soon by letter/telephone/radio? How can we get in touch?*

keep in touch (with) *infml* to continue to communicate (with (someone)) by any, often stated, means: *We keep in touch (with each other) by letter.*

G191 *nouns* : **communication, post, and mail**

communication 1 [U] the act or action of communicating: *All communication with France was stopped when the enemy gained control of the sea. Radio and television are important means of communication.* **2** [U] the exchange of information, news, ideas, or opinions: *We must improve communication between workers and employers. Speech and writing are man's most important methods of communication.* **3** [C] *usu fml* something communicated: *We have received communications from many people about this.*

post *esp BrE* **1** [U] the official system for carrying letters, parcels, etc from the sender to the receiver: *He sent the parcel by post. My letter to him was a week in the post* (= was not delivered for a week). **2** [S] a single official collection or delivery of letters, parcels, etc by this means: *Has the morning post arrived? Have I missed the (last) post?* **3** [U] *also* **mail** letters, parcels, etc: *Has any post come for us this morning?* **4** [S9] all the letters, parcels, etc dealt with by the postal services: *There's always a very large post at Christmas. The post at Christmas is always very large.* **5** [*the* R] an official place, box, etc where stamped letters are left for sending: *I've just taken her birthday card to the post.* **by return of post** by the next post **postal** [Wa5;A] of, concerning, or used by the service which carries letters, etc from one place to another: *the postal service* **postage** [U] the amount of money to be paid when posting anything: *What is the postage on this letter to France?*

mail *esp AmE* **1** [U9] the postal system organized by a government: *Airmail is much quicker than sea mail.* **2** [U] letters and anything else sent or received by post, esp those travelling or arriving together: *He collects his mail from the post office.*

correspondence [U] **1** the exchange of information, news, etc by letter: *I was in correspondence with her for many years but then she moved and I lost her address.* **2** the letters exchanged between people: *The library bought all Queen Victoria's correspondence with her daughters.*

address [C] **1** the number of the building, name of the street and town, etc where a person works or (esp) lives: *Shall I give you my home* *address or my business address?* **2** such information written down, as on an envelope or parcel: *I can't read the address on this letter.*

printed matter/papers [U/P] printed articles (such as official advertisements) that can be sent by post at a special cheap rate

G192 *verbs* : **post and mail**

post *BrE* **1** [T1 (*off*)] to take or put (a letter, parcel, etc) to a post office or into a collection box for sending: *I must post (off) all my Christmas cards this week. Please post this letter for me as I'm too busy to go out.* **2** [D1] to send by post: *Did you post me the book?* **to keep someone posted (about)** to continue to give someone all the latest news about something: *I want to know how she's getting on after her illness, so keep me posted.*

mail [D1 (*to*); T1] *AmE* to post: *He mailed the letters.*

remit [D1 (*to*); T1] to send (esp money) esp by post: *He remitted the money to her. He remitted her the money.* **remittance 1** [U] the sending of money **2** [C] the amount of money sent: *He has stopped the monthly remittances.*

address [T1] to write on (an envelope, parcel, etc) the address of a person, firm, etc: *He addressed all the letters himself.*

label 1 [T1] to put a label [⇨ G155] on: *He labelled the box and sent it.* **2** [X1, 7, 9] (*fig*) to call or describe: *She labelled him (as) a thief.*

send [D1; T1; V3, 4] *genl & infml* to cause (a letter, etc) to go or be taken (somewhere): *I sent all the mail yesterday.*

dispatch, despatch [T1] *fml* to send (letters, messengers, etc): *Despatch someone at once with the news!*

register [Wv5;T1] to send (a letter, etc) by registered post, a service in which the person receiving the letter, etc must sign to show that he or she has done so: *You pay more if you register the letter/send the letter registered. It's a registered letter; sign here, please.*

deliver [T1] to hand over (letters, etc) to the person(s) to whom they are addressed: *The postman delivers the mail every morning.*

G193 *nouns* : **relating to the post and mail**

post office 1 [C *often cap*] a building, office, shop, etc which deals with the post, telephones, and other government business for a particular area **2** [*the* GC] the organization which deals with post

letterbox [C] *esp BrE* **1** a box in which letters can be placed (**posted, mailed**) for collecting by the Post Office and sending on **2** the opening in the door of a house through which a postman, etc can drop letters, etc, often with a small box fixed to it inside the door

pillar-box [C] (esp in Britain) a round hollow iron box about 5 feet high standing in the street, with a hole in it for people to post letters: *In Britain, pillar-boxes are painted red.*

postbox [C] **1** an official metal box, often set into a wall, into which letters are put for sending by post **2** *BrE* a pillar-box

mailbox [C] *esp AmE* **1** an iron box in a public place for posting letters in **2** a place where one's mail is left near the house; a letterbox separate from the door

postman [C] *esp BrE* a man employed to collect and deliver letters, parcels, etc

mailman [C] *esp AmE* a postman

postbag [C] *BrE* the bag carried by a postman

mailbag [C] **1** a bag made of strong cloth for carrying mail in trains, ships, etc **2** *AmE* a mailman's bag

G194 *nouns & verbs* : **information and news**

information [U] (something which gives) knowledge: *That's a bit of useful information; I must remember it.*

data [GU] *often tech* information; necessary facts: *The data are/is all ready for examination.*

particulars [P] the necessary information esp about a person: *Can you give me his particulars: name, address, colour of hair and so on?*

news [U] **1** what is reported, esp about a recent event or events; new information: *We received news of the election results. She heard the bad news on the radio. Our latest news of (= about) our son was a letter a month ago. This is an important piece of news.* **2** [*the*] any of the regular reports of recent events broadcast on radio and television: *She listened to the 7 o'clock news on radio.* **newsy** [Wa1;B] *infml* filled with news of a not very serious kind: *She wrote him a newsy letter.* **newsworthy** [B] important and interesting enough to be reported as news **-thiness** [U] **news agency** [C] a company or organization supplying news and information to newspapers, radio, and television

bulletin [C] **1** a short public usu official notice: *Here is the latest bulletin on the King's health.* **2** a short news report intended to be made public without delay: *He read the news bulletins.*

rumour *BrE*, **rumor** *AmE* **1** [U] what people are telling each other: *Don't listen to rumour. Rumour has it (= I have heard) that you are leaving us; is it true?* **2** [C] a story that people are telling each other, that may or may not be true: *Never listen to rumours. It's just an idle rumour (= a rumour with no truth in it). I've heard rumours that you are leaving us; is it true?* **3** [T1 *usu pass*] to pass as a rumour: *It is rumoured that you are leaving us; is it true?*

gossip 1 [U] talk about the details of other people's actions and private lives, which may not be correct: *It's just gossip; don't believe it.* **2** [U] writing in newspapers, magazines, etc about the lives of well-known people (*esp in the phr* **gossip column** [⇨ G159]) **3** [C] a person who likes telling gossip: *She's an old gossip; don't believe anything she tells you.* **4** [I∅] to talk or write gossip: *She enjoys gossipping.*

talk [U] *infml often deprec* gossip; anything that people say: *Don't believe what they say; it's just talk.*

chat *also* **chitchat** [U] *infml* gossip: *Don't believe a word of it; it's just (chit) chat.*

G195 nouns : messages

message [C] **1** a spoken or written piece of information passed from one person to another: *They brought her a message to return home at once/that she should return home at once.* **2** the important or central idea: *What is the message of this book?* **3** teachings of moral or social value: *Christ brought the message that God loved the world.* **get the message** *sl* to understand what is wanted or meant

word [U] *infml* a message or news: *Send us word of what you do. We have had no word from him for weeks. Word came through at last (that he was well).*

communication [C] something communicated; *fml* a message: *This communication is secret, so no one but you must see it.*

dispatch, despatch *usu fml* **1** [U] the action of sending: *After the dispatch of the messenger we waited.* **2** [C] a message carried by a government official, or sent to a newspaper by one of its writers: *He sent/carried a dispatch from Rome to London.* **3** [U] speed and effectiveness: *He did the job with great dispatch.*

G196 nouns. : signals and signs

signal [C] **1** a sound or action intended to warn, command, or give a message: *A red lamp is often used as a danger signal. American Indians sometimes used to send smoke signals. She made a signal with her arm for a left turn. When I look at my watch, it's a signal (for us) to leave.* **2** [usu sing] an action which causes something else to happen: *His scolding was a signal for the girl to start crying.* **3** a sound, image, or message sent by waves, as in radio or television: *We live too far from the city to get a strong television signal.*

sign [C] **1** a standard mark; something which is seen and represents a known meaning: *Crowns, stars, stripes, etc are signs of military rank. The number −5 begins with the sign −, the minus sign. Written music uses lots of signs, like ♭ and ♯.* **2** a motion of the body intended to express a meaning; signal: *Don't ring the bell yet; wait until I give the sign. She put her finger to her lips as a sign to be quiet.* **3** a board or other notice giving information, warning, directions, etc: *Pay attention to the traffic/road signs. Can't you read that sign? It says 'No*

smoking'. *You'll have no trouble driving to the office; just follow the signs to Harlow. He's got a job as a sign painter.* **4** (*fig*) something that shows a quality or the presence or coming of something else: *All the signs are that business will get better. Swollen ankles can be a sign of heart disease. There was no sign of rain, not a cloud in the sky. Your work shows signs of improvement.* **a sign of the times** something that is typical of the way things are just now: *Nearly empty churches on Sunday are a sign of the times.*

token [C (*of*)] **1** an outward sign; something that represents some fact, event, feeling, etc; a small part representing something greater: *All the family wore black as a token of their grief. We gave the Queen flowers as a token of our admiration and love. He made a token payment (of £5). The workers went on a token strike.* **2** something that serves as a reminder: *My husband gave me a ring as a token of our first meeting.*

symbol [C] **1** a sign, shape, or object which represents a person, idea, value, etc: *In the picture the tree is the symbol of life and the snake the symbol of evil.* **2** a letter or figure which expresses a sound, number, or chemical substance: *'H_2O' is the symbol for water.* **symbolic** [B] of, concerning, having, like, or serving as a symbol: *His act was purely symbolic. She likes symbolic art.* **-ally** [adv Wa4] **symbolize, -ise** [T1] **1** to be a symbol of: *The picture symbolizes peace.* **2** to have, make, etc a symbol for: *How can we symbolize our feelings?* **symbolization, -isation 1** [U] the act or result of symbolizing **2** [C] an example of this **symbolism** [U] the use of symbols esp in art to represent ideas

gesture 1 [C] a movement, usu of the hands, to express a certain meaning: *He made an angry gesture.* **2** [U] such movements in general: *English people do not use as much gesture as Italians.* **3** [C] an action which is done to show one's feelings, either friendly or unfriendly: *We went to the party as a gesture of friendliness, although we did not feel very sociable at the time.*

G197 verbs : signals and signs

signal 1 [I∅ (*to, for*)] to give a signal: *The general signalled to his officers for the attack to begin. She was signalling wildly, waving her arms.* **2** [V3 (*to*); D5 (*to*); T1, 3, 5] to express, warn, or tell by a signal or signals: *The policeman signalled (to) the traffic to move forward slowly. The thief signalled (his friend) that the police were coming. The whistle signalled the start of the race.* **3** [T1] to be a sign of: *The defeat of 1066 signalled the end of Saxon rule in England.*

sign [V3 (*to, for*); L9] to make a motion as a sign to (someone); signal: *The policeman signed (to/for) me to stop.*

gesture [L9] to make a gesture: *He gestured towards the children who were already asleep as he described the tiring journey.*

gesticulate [I0] to make movements of the hands and body to express something, esp while speaking **gesticulation 1** [U] the act of gesticulating **2** [C] an example of this: *We didn't understand the man's shouts and gesticulations.*

G198 nouns : persons taking messages, signalling, etc [C]

messenger a person who takes a message to someone from someone

signaller *BrE*, **signaler** *AmE* a person who sends (and receives) signals

courier 1 a person who carries a special, official, or urgent message **2** *old use* a messenger **3** a person who goes with a group of travellers and arranges things (hotels, etc) for them

herald 1 (formerly) a person who carried messages from a ruler and gave important news to the people **2** (*fig*) a sign of something about to come, happen, etc: *A red sky is a herald of good weather.*

runner a person, esp in an army, who runs with messages from one person or place to another

G199 verbs : meaning

mean [Wv6] **1** [T1, 5a, 6a] to represent (a meaning): *What does this French word mean? The red light means 'Go'. The sign means that cars cannot enter. It doesn't mean what you thought* (*it meant*). **2** [T1, 3, 5a; V3; D1] to intend (to say); have in mind as or for a purpose: *She said Tuesday, but she meant Wednesday. I mean to go tomorrow. He means that he wants your help. We didn't mean you to go out alone. We meant it as a present for you. Although he seems angry with his son, he means him nothing but good/means* (*him*) *no harm. He is very angry and he means trouble* (= his purpose is to cause trouble). **3** [T1, 6a] to be determined about/to act on: *I mean what I say. I said I would change things, and I meant it.* **4** [T1 (*for*), 3 *usu pass*] to intend (to be) because of abilities, fate, etc: *He is not meant for a soldier and will always be unhappy in the army. His parents meant him for a priest. He believes he is meant to be a great man.* **5** [T1, 4, 5a] to be a sign of: *The dark clouds mean rain. That expression means that he's angry. His expression means trouble. Missing the train means waiting for an hour* (= one will have to wait one hour). **6** [T1 (*to*)] to be of importance: *Does success in examinations really mean anything when considering ability for a job? It doesn't mean a thing to her that we are all waiting because she's late. I thought he was my friend, but all his expressions of interest meant nothing.* **mean business** *not fml* to intend seriously to act **mean mischief** to have evil

intentions **mean well** to do or say what is intended to help, but often doesn't **mean well by someone** to intend to do what is best for someone **be meant to** *esp BrE* to have to; to be supposed to: *You're meant to take your shoes off when you enter a Hindu temple.*

signify 1 [T1, 5] *often fml* to be a sign of; represent; mean: *What does this strange mark signify? A fever usually signifies a disorder in the body.* **2** [T1; I0] to make known (esp an opinion) by an action: *Will those in favour of the suggestion please signify* (*their agreement*) *by raising their hands?*

G200 nouns, etc : meaning, sense and nonsense

[ALSO ⇒ G237]

meaning [U; C] **1** the idea which one must (try to) understand: *This sentence has no meaning. This sentence has two different meanings.* **2** a sense of importance: *He says that his life has lost its meaning since his wife died.*

significance [U; S] *often fml* meaning; value; importance: *This is an industry of great significance to the country. It is a familiar story but with a new significance. Don't read significance into* (= try to find it in) *every careless remark I make.*

sense 1 [U] *esp emot* meaning: *There's no sense in what he says!* **2** [C] a meaning, esp one of several: *This word has at least three senses in which it can be used.* **3** [U] good thinking: *He showed some sense at last, and didn't leave his job.* **4** [U] something that is not foolish: *Talk sense!*

nonsense 1 [U; (*BrE*) S] speech or writing with no meaning: *She left out three words when she copied the sentence and the result was* (*a*) *nonsense.* **2** [U] speech, writing, thinking, etc, that goes against good sense: *A lot of the government's new ideas are nonsense. I can't go out dressed like this. – Nonsense!/What nonsense! You look fine.* **3** [U] foolish behaviour: *Stop that nonsense, children! Behave yourselves. The teacher would stand no nonsense from the children.* **4** [U] humorous and fanciful poetry usu telling a meaningless story: *I like Edward Lear's wonderful nonsense* (*poetry*). **make nonsense of**, *also* **make a nonsense of** *BrE* to spoil or make of no effect: *Your foolish anger made nonsense of our plans for peace with the enemy.*

waffle *BrE infml* **1** [U] nonsense expressed in words that sound good: *Don't talk such waffle, man!* **2** [Wv3; I0 (*on*)] to talk nonsense expressed in words that sounded good: *I asked him a question but he just went on waffling.*

G201 nouns : newspapers and magazines

newspaper 1 [C] a paper printed and sold to the

public usu daily or weekly, with news, notices, advertisements, etc: *He sells newspapers at the bus station.* **2** [C] a company which produces one or more of these papers: *One of our oldest national newspapers went out of business because of low sales.* **3** [U] the kind of paper on which these are printed, esp after printing: *Wrap the food in some newspaper.*

paper [C] *infml* a newspaper: *What's in today's paper?*

news sheet [C] a small newspaper, usu of one or two pages

newsletter [C] a small newspaper sent to a particular group of people

bulletin [C] a printed news sheet, esp one produced by an association or group

newsprint [U] a cheap kind of paper used mostly for newspapers, esp before printing: *Newsprint is not as cheap as it used to be.*

magazine *also infml abbrev* **mag** [C] a sort of book made of large folded sheets of paper with no hard cover, which contains writing, photographs, and advertisements, usu on a special subject or for a certain group of people, and which is printed and sold every week or month: *All the women's magazines have stories and articles on the same sort of subjects.*

periodical [C] a magazine that appears at regular times, such as monthly or weekly (but not daily): *This periodical is obtainable on the last day of every month.*

journal [C] *fml esp old use & tech* a periodical: *I read about it in a scientific journal.*

G202 *nouns* : **kinds of newspapers, etc according to frequency of appearance** [C]

daily a newspaper appearing once a day: *What's in the dailies?*

weekly a newspaper or magazine appearing once a week: *The weeklies are full of stories about the new president.*

monthly a magazine appearing once a month

annual a book produced once each year having the same title but containing different stories, pictures, etc

G203 *nouns* : **journalism and the press**

journalism [U] the work or profession of producing, esp writing for, newspapers and other news media [⇒ G208]: *He has gone from newspaper journalism to TV journalism.*

journalistic [B] of, concerning, or like journalism and journalists: *He writes in a journalistic way.*

press [(*the*) GU] (*sometimes cap*) newspaper writers in general: *The minister invited the press to a meeting to explain his actions. The Press think this is a good story.*

G204 *nouns* : **journalists and correspondents** [C]

journalist a person whose profession is journalism

newspaperman *infml & loose* a person, esp a man, working for a newspaper; a journalist: *There were a lot of newspapermen at the party.*
newspaperwoman *rare* [*fem*]

reporter a journalist whose work is to report news, esp by going to a place to see what is happening and talking to people: *A local reporter covered* [⇒ G206] *the story.*

correspondent someone hired by a newspaper, television, radio station, etc, to report (local) news from a distant area: *The London newspaper's war correspondent was sent to Asia.*

columnist a person who writes a regular article for a newspaper or magazine [⇒G159]

G205 *nouns* : **people selling newspapers** [C]

newsagent *BrE* a person in charge of a shop selling newspapers and magazines: *You can get this paper at your local newsagent/at the newsagent's.*

news dealer *AmE* a newsagent

newsvendor a person who sells newspapers, esp in the street

news stand a table, often outdoors inside a shelter, from which newspapers and sometimes magazines and books are sold: *The papers are now on the news stand; I'll get one.*

newsboy a boy or man who sells or delivers newspapers

G206 *verbs* : **reporting news, etc**

report 1 [T1; I∅ (*on*)] to make a report [⇒ G157] (of): *Who reported the meeting? She reported on what had happened.* **2** [T1] to give information, usu unpleasant, about (someone or something) to an authority: *Be careful or I'll report you/your behaviour to the authorities!*

cover [T1] to report the details of (an event, particular state of affairs, etc) as for a newspaper: *I want our best reporter to cover the political trials.*

write up [v adv T1] *not fml* to write a report on (something), esp giving a good judgement, as of goods or a play: *He wrote up the play. Write it up tonight and let me have it tomorrow.*

G207 *verbs* : **advertising and publicizing**

advertise 1 [T1, 5; I∅] to make (something for sale, services offered, rooms to let, etc) known to the public, as in a newspaper or on film or television: *They advertised (that they had) a house for sale.* **2** [I∅ (*for*)] to ask (for someone or something) by placing an advertisement in a newspaper, shop window, etc: *We should advertise for someone to look after the garden. How can we find a good used car?—You should advertise (for one)*.

post 1 [T1 (*up*)] to make public or show by sticking, nailing, etc to a wall, board, post, etc: *The names of the members of the team will be posted (up) today. A description of the escaped criminal is posted on the door.* **2** [T1] to cover (a wall, board, etc) with public notices **3** [T1; X7 *usu pass*] to make known (as being), by putting up a notice: *The ship was posted missing.*

publicize [T1] to bring to public notice; get publicity for: *We must publicize the meeting widely.*

broadcast [T1] to make widely known: *She broadcast the news to all her friends.* [⇒ G217]

announce 1 [T1, 6a, b] to tell people about (something) esp publicly: *He announced their plan last night. She announced what she was planning to do.* **2** [T1; I∅] to read (news) or introduce (a person or act) on the radio, television, etc: *Who announces the news on BBC television? He announces on the radio.*

present [T1] **1** to announce (something, news, etc) in a particular usu stated way: *She presented her plan well. How do you propose to present this new product (to the public)?* **2** to show or cause to be shown, esp on radio, television, in a theatre, etc: *Let me present that great singer, the one and only Miranda Smith! She presents herself well on television.*

G208 *nouns* : **communications and the media**

communications [P] the various ways of travelling, moving goods and people, and sending information between two places or in an area; roads, railways, radio, telephone, television, etc: *Moscow has excellent communications with all parts of the Soviet Union. Some countries have better communications than others.*

medium [C] a method of giving information; a form of art in which ideas, etc can be expressed: *He writes stories but the theatre is his favourite medium. Television is a medium for giving information and opinions, for amusing people and for teaching them foreign languages and other subjects.*

(news) media [(*the*) P; (GU)] the organizations which make news public, esp newspapers, radio, and television: *The (news) media have been reporting all sorts of strange things lately.*

mass media [P] the media when seen as making possible communication with very large numbers of people

broadcasting [U] the action or business of sending out sound (or images) by means of radio or television [⇒ G217]

coverage [U] the time and space given by television, a newspaper, etc to report a particular piece of news or an event; the way in which a particular piece of news or an event is reported: *I liked the radio coverage of the election better than the television coverage.*

circulation [S9; A] the average number of copies of a newspaper, magazine, book, etc sold or read over a certain period: *This magazine has a circulation of over 400,000. What are that newspaper's circulation figures?*

publicity [U] **1** the state of being generally or widely known; public attention: *The film actress's marriage got a lot of publicity.* **2** the business of bringing someone or something to (favourable) public notice, esp for purposes of gain: *A soap-making firm has appointed him to be in charge of its publicity.* **3** ways used for doing this: *The concert was a good one, but because of poor publicity very few people came.*

public relations, *infml abbrev* **PR 1** [P] the relations between an organization and the general public, which must be kept friendly in various ways: *If we plant flowers in front of the factory it will be good (for) public relations.* **2** [U] the work of keeping these relations friendly: *Public relations is big business, today. He is a public relations man for that company.*

advertising [U] the business which concerns itself with making known to the public what is for sale and encouraging them to buy, esp by means of pictures in magazines, notices in newspapers, and messages on television: *He works in advertising.*

G209 *nouns* : **persons publicizing and advertising, etc** [C]

[ALSO ⇒ K83]

publicist a person whose business is to bring something to the attention of the public, esp products for sale

press agent a person in charge of keeping an actor, musician, theatre, etc, in favourable public notice by supplying photographs, interesting facts, details of coming performances, etc to newspapers, etc

public relations officer, *infml abbrev* **PRO** a person employed by a firm, government, etc to keep the public informed about its affairs, so that the public can have favourable feelings towards it

advertiser a person or business that advertises, as in a newspaper or on television

sponsor a person or business that gives money to a radio or television programme, a performance in a theatre, etc usu in return for publicity and the right to advertise goods

G210 *nouns* : **radio**

[ALSO ⇒ K58]

radio 1 [U] (the method of) sending or receiving sounds through the air by means of electrical waves: *He talked to them by radio.* **2** [C] *also*

radio set an apparatus to (send and) receive sounds in this way: *That shop sells radios.* **3** [U] the radio broadcasting industry: *She got a job in radio.* **4 on the radio a** (of a sound) broadcast: *I heard it on the radio.* **b** (of a person) broadcasting: *John was on the radio again today.*

wavelength [C] (esp in broadcasting) a radio signal sent out on radio waves that are a particular distance apart: *What wavelength is Radio 2 on?*

(wave) band [C] a set of esp radio waves of similar lengths: *Radio 2 is the programme on the medium waveband.*

channel [C] a particular band of radio waves used for broadcasting television; the shows, information, news, advertisements, etc broadcast from a particular television station: *Which channel is the film on? I don't like this; switch to another channel.*

short wave [U] broadcasting on radio waves of short length: *You need a good short-wave radio to pick up Radio Tehran in Britain.*

medium wave [U] broadcasting on radio waves of medium length: *Is Radio 2 on medium wave or long wave?*

long wave [U] broadcasting on radio waves of longer length

beam [C] a set of radio waves sent out in a narrow line in one direction only, often to guide aircraft

station [C] a place or building from which broadcasting takes place: *He has a job at the local radio station. This is Station XYZ calling you!*

G211 *nouns* : **television**

television 1 [U] the method of broadcasting still and moving pictures and sound over a distance by means of electrical waves moving through the air: *Television was invented in the early 20th century.* **2** [U] the news, plays, advertisements, pictures, etc broadcast in this way: *Watching television is how most people spend their spare time. I'd rather watch television than listen to the radio. They saw what happened on the television news.* **3** [C] *also* **television set** a boxlike apparatus for receiving pictures and sound: *We bought our first television in 1953.* **4** [U] the industry of making and broadcasting plays, films, etc on television: *She works in television as a journalist.* **on (the) television a** broadcast by television: *What's on television tonight? The match was on the television last night; did you see it?* **b** broadcasting by television: *The King spoke to the people on television.*

TV [U; C] *infml abbrev* television: *What's on TV tonight? That's a nice TV set.*

telly [U; C] *esp BrE infml* television; a television set

box [*the* R] *esp BrE infml* television: *What's on the box tonight?*

G212 *nouns, etc* : **broadcasts and newscasts**

broadcast 1 [C] a single radio (or television) presentation: *He gave a number of broadcasts.* **2** [B] made public by means of radio (or television)

programme *BrE*, **program** *AmE* [C] a complete show or performance, esp on radio or television: *What is your favourite radio/television programme?*

announcement [C] a statement, often on radio or television or in a newspaper, saying what has happened or will happen: *The government will make an announcement on the matter next week.*

newscast [C] a radio or television broadcast of news

G213 *nouns* : **broadcasters and newscasters** [C]

broadcaster a person who broadcasts on radio or television, esp regularly or professionally

announcer a person who reads news or introduces people, acts, etc, esp on radio or television

newscaster, *also* **newsreader** *BrE* a person who broadcasts news on radio and television

G214 *nouns* : **films and the cinema**
[ALSO ⇨ K59, 70]

cinema *esp BrE* **1** [*the* R] the art of making moving pictures: *The cinema is a very exciting art form, as can be seen from the many interesting new films which have recently been produced.* **2** [*the* R] the moving-picture industry: *He has worked in the cinema all his life.* **3** [*the* R] a showing of a moving picture: *Let's go to the cinema tonight.* **4** [C] a building or theatre in which moving pictures are shown: *He owns two cinemas.* **cine-** [*comb form*] *esp BrE* of, for, or related to moving pictures or the film industry: *Cinecameras use cinefilms.* **cinematography** [U] the art or science of moving-picture photography

picture 1 [C *usu sing*] what is seen at the cinema or on a television set: *Can you get the picture on the television a little clearer? You can't get a good picture on this set. The film broke and we waited impatiently for the picture to come back.* **2** [C] a cinema picture: *I saw a good picture last night.*

film [C] a moving picture: *I saw a good film last night, at the local cinema/on television.*

movie [C] *infml & AmE* a cinema film **movies** [*the* P] *AmE* the cinema (defs **1**, **2**, **3**): *Let's go to the movies this afternoon.*

newsreel [C] a short cinema film of news

documentary [C] a presentation of facts through art, esp on the radio or television or in the cinema: *We saw a documentary about*

Yorkshire coal miners. He makes documentary films.

advertisement 1 [C] a notice of something for sale, services offered, a job position to be filled, room to let, etc, as in a newspaper, painted on a wall, or made as a film: *She put an advertisement in the local newspaper.* **2** [U] the action of advertising

advert [C] *infml esp BrE* an advertisement: *I'm going to put some adverts in the paper.*

ad [C] *very infml* an advertisement: *She saw the ad and went to see if she could get the job.*

commercial [C] an advertisement on television or radio: *He made a cup of coffee while the commercials were on.*

G215 nouns : telephones and telegraph

telephone 1 [U] a method of sending sounds, esp speech, over long distances by electrical means: *The captain could speak to officials on the shore by radio telephone. If a matter of international importance arises the governments of our two countries can exchange information and opinions by telephone.* **2** [C] the apparatus that receives or sends sounds, esp speech, in this way: *If the telephone rings can you answer it? Your mother was on the telephone earlier* (= she rang up earlier). *Can you telephone her back this evening?* **telephonist** [C] a person who sends and receives telephone calls, esp for others **(telephone) operator** [C; N] *genl* a telephonist: *Operator, can you get me this number, please?*

phone [C; U] *infml & genl* a telephone: *The phone is ringing. He told me the news by phone on/over the phone. My phone bill* (= the money I must pay for using the phone) *is big this month.*

telegraph 1 [U] a method of sending messages along wire by electric signals: *He sent the message by telegraph.* **2** [C] the apparatus that receives or sends messages in this way **telegraphic 1** [Wa5;B] of, concerning, like, having, or using a telegraph or telegraphy **2** [B] short, as in a telegram **-ally** [adv Wa4]: *She sent the message telegraphically. He always speaks rather telegraphically.*

telegraphy [U] the art, etc of sending messages by telegraph **telegraphist** [C] a person skilled in telegraphy

teleprinter *BrE,* **teletypewriter** *AmE* an apparatus with a keyboard (= a set of buttons with letters on them) for sending and receiving printed messages telegraphically

telecommunications [P] the various means of sending information between two places or in an area by telegraphy, telephone, etc

G216 nouns : telegrams and cables
[C; *by* U]

telegram 1 a message sent by telegraph: *I sent him the news of grandmother's death by tele-*

gram/an international telegram. **2** [C] a piece of paper on which this message is delivered

cable *infml* a telegram: *I got a cable from my sister in Ireland saying that she'd arrive tomorrow.*   ▮

cablegram *fml* a cable, telegram

wire *infml esp AmE* a telegram: *I got a wire from home this morning.*

telex 1 a telegraphic method of passing printed messages from one place to another by teleprinter: *Telex is an international service provided by the post offices of various countries.* **2** a message received or sent in this way: *A telex has just arrived from Hong Kong.*

G217 verbs : communicating by radio, etc

radio [I∅; T1] to send (a message) through the air by radio: *The ship radioed for help. She radioed her congratulations.*

broadcast 1 [T1] to send out or give as a radio (or television) presentation: *The BBC will broadcast the news at 10 o'clock.* **2** [I∅] to send out one or more radio (or television) presentations: *The BBC broadcasts every day.* **3** [I∅] to speak or perform on radio (or perhaps television): *He's broadcasting very often these days.* [⇒ G207]

transmit 1 [T1; I∅] to send out (electric signals, messages, news, etc) by telegraphic wire or radio; broadcast: *Our local radio station only transmits from 4 o'clock in the afternoon to 10 o'clock in the evening.* **2** [T1] to carry (force, power, etc) from one part of a machine to another: *How is power transmitted from the engine to the wheels of the car?* **3** [T1] to send or pass from one person, place, or thing to another: *to transmit a disease/infection/message* **4** [Wv6;T1] to allow to travel through or along itself: *Glass transmits light but not sound.* **transmission 1** [U] the act of transmitting **2** [C] an example or occasion of this; something transmitted, esp by radio **transmitter** [C] a radio which transmits messages

send out [v adv T1] *infml* to transmit: *The radio continued to send out signals.*

beam [T1 *usu pass*] (of the radio) to send out in a certain direction: *The radio news was beamed to West Africa.*

receive [T1] (of a radio or television set) to turn (radio waves sent by someone) into sound or pictures: *Hullo; are you receiving me?—Yes, receiving you loud and clear.*

pick up [v adv T1] *infml* to receive: *We picked up signals for help on the radio.*

get [T1] *infml & genl* to receive or pick up: *Can you get Tokyo* (= transmissions from Tokyo) *on that (radio) set?*

tune in [v adv] **1** [T1 (*to*)] to move the controls of (a radio, etc) so as to get the transmission correctly: *Is that radio properly tuned in?* **2** [I∅ (*to*)] *infml* to listen (to a radio station): *Tune in to London tomorrow night at 7.*

televise 1 [T1] to broadcast by television: *The royal funeral will be televised so that people throughout the world can see it as it happens.* **2** [L9] to be broadcast by television: *This play was written specially for television and should televise well.*

telephone 1 [D1 (*to*); T3; V3; I0] to speak (a message) to (someone) by telephone: *I telephoned your aunt the sad news of father's death. Did you telephone Bob? Please telephone work and tell them I'm ill and am staying in bed today. I telephoned mother to come as soon as she could. John's just telephoned through to say he'll be late home tonight. Are you going to telephone or shall I? If you don't want to go to the shops today you can telephone your order and they'll deliver it.* **2** [D1 (*to*); T1] to send (something) to (someone) by telephone: *If the post office is closed you can telephone a telegram. We telephoned her a telegram on her wedding day.* **3** [L9; T1] to (try to) reach (a place or person) by telephone: *I've been telephoning all morning but I've not been able to speak to the minister. You can't telephone Glasgow directly from here, you have to go through the operator.*

phone [T1 (*up*); D1, 5a; I0 (*up*), 3] *infml & genl* to telephone: *I phoned him (up) last night. She phoned to say she couldn't come. I'll phone you the news.*

dial [I0; T1] to make a telephone call; call (a number, person, or place) on a telephone: *How do I dial Paris? To get the police, dial 999. Put in the money before dialling (your number).*

ring [v adv T1; I0 (*up*)] *infml esp BrE* to telephone: *I'll ring him (up) when I get home. Ring her up now, please. Someone rang up about the job.*

call up [v adv T1; I0 *not pass*] *infml esp AmE* to telephone: *I'll call you up later today.*

telegraph [D1 (*to*), 5a; T1, 5a; V3; I0] to send (someone) (something) by telegraph: *We telegraphed her the bad news. Did you telegraph that father had died? They telegraphed us to go as soon as possible. Should I write or telegraph?*

cable [D1 (*to*), 5a; T1, 5a; V3; I0] to send (someone) (something) by telegraph: *I cabled (him) some money. He cabled her (to come). He cabled (us) that he was coming. I'll cable right away.*

wire [D1 (*to*), 5; T1] *infml esp AmE* to cable: *He wired me he was coming.*

telex [D1 (*to*), 5a; T1, 5a; V3; I0] to send (a message, information, news, etc) to (a person, place, firm, etc) by telex: *Telex Australia that prices are to be increased 10%.*

G218 nouns : interference and static

interference [U] the noises and shapes which spoil the working of electrical apparatus, esp when a radio station is difficult to listen to because of the effect of another one near to its wavelength [⇒ G210]

static [U] noises heard on a radio because of electricity in the air

atmospherics [P] *tech* static

Language

G230 nouns : language, speech, and dialect

language 1 [U] the system of human expression by means of words, sentences [⇒ G235], etc **2** [C] a particular system of words, etc as used by a people or nation: *He is learning two foreign languages.* **3** [C; U] any system of signs, movements, etc, used to express meanings or feelings: *The actions of the cat were clearly part of his language of anger.* **4** [U] a particular style or manner of expression: *She liked the poet's beautiful language.* **5** [U] the words and phrases of a particular group, science, profession, etc: *The paper was written in very scientific language.* **6** [U] words and phrases that are impolite or shocking (*esp in the phrs* **bad language**, **strong language**)

tongue [C] *lit & pomp* a language: *The men spoke in a foreign tongue.*

speech [U] **1** the act or power of speaking; spoken language: *He tried to put his thoughts into speech. Speech was impossible with so much noise around.* **2** the way of speaking of a person or group: *He is studying American speech. By your speech I can tell you are from Liverpool.*

voice 1 [U] the sounds expressed by human beings in speaking and singing: *The human voice can express every possible kind of feeling.* **2** [U] the ability of a person to produce such sound(s): *I have no voice today; I've lost my voice as a result of a bad cold.* **3** [U; C] (the quality or force of) such sound as particular to a certain person or creature: *She lowered her voice as she told me the secret; she spoke in a low voice. When you spoke over the telephone I didn't recognize your voice. She has a very pleasant voice. We could hear the children's voices in the garden. Her voice broke* (=became unsteady) *as she told us the sad news. The boy's voice is breaking* (=becoming like a man's). **4** [U] (*fig*) (the expressing of) an opinion; the right to express an opinion: *The crowd was large, but they were all of one voice. I can't help you get this job, as I have little voice in the decision of the directors.* **5** [C] **a** ability as a singer: *He's got a good voice; he sings well.* **b** a singer performing with others in a particular piece of music: *This song is arranged for (singing by) three voices.* **6** [C] (*fig*) an expression of something which is like the human voice either in sound or because it expresses human feelings, ideas, qualities, etc: *She listened to the*

low, sad voice of the sea. He was angry at first but in the end the voice of reason won, and he recognized that the suggestion was fair and just.
7 [U] tech the sound produced when a speaker makes his breath act on his vocal cords [⇨ B26] as it passes through them **vocal** [B] **1** [Wa5] of, concerning, or like the voice; using the voice: vocal language **2** talking very much or a lot: a very vocal kind of person

dialect [C; U] a variety of a language, spoken in one part of a country, which is different in some words, grammar, or pronunciation from other forms of the same language: He speaks the Yorkshire dialect of English. This is a poem written in Scottish dialect. **dialectal** [Wa5;B] of, concerning, or like dialect **-ly** [adv]

accent [C; (U)] a particular way of speaking, usu connected with a country, area, or class: He speaks with a German accent. There are many accents in the English-speaking world. She studies different types of accent.

slang [U] language that is not usu acceptable in serious speech or writing, including words, expressions, etc regarded as very informal or not polite and those used among particular groups of people (marked sl in this book): There are lots of slang words for money, like 'bread' and 'dough'. He likes to use army/schoolboy slang. Slang often goes in and out of fashion quickly. **slangy** [Wa1;B] **1** being or like slang: That's a rather slangy word. **2** using esp rude and impolite slang: That's an unworthy and slangy attack.

jargon [U; C] often derog language that is hard to understand, esp because it is full of special words known only to members of a certain group: He spoke in a meaningless jargon. The jargon of scientists isn't easy to understand. The explanations in a dictionary must be kept as free of jargon as possible.

baby talk [U] **1** the speechlike sounds that babies make in the early stages of learning language **2** the things that fully grown people say to babies intended to be like baby talk

G231 verbs : **pronouncing and articulating**

pronounce [T1; X1; I0] to make the sound of (a language, a letter, a word, etc) (in a particular way): She pronounces French very well. Don't pronounce the 'k' in 'know'. Pronounce the 'ch' in 'chemical' as 'k'. She must learn to pronounce more clearly. [⇨ G61] **mispronounce** [T1; I0] to pronounce (something) badly or wrongly

enunciate [T1; I0] fml to pronounce or say (words, etc) very clearly and carefully: The teacher told him to enunciate (his words) fully.

articulate 1 [T1; I0] fml & tech to speak: He articulated each word carefully. **2** [T1] to express clearly and effectively: He articulated his anger.

stress 1 [T1] to pronounce (a word or a part of a

word) with added force or on a different musical note, or both: Stress the word 'pronounce' on the second syllable [⇨ G273]. He stressed the word 'danger'. **2** [T1, 5, 6] to give added importance to: He stressed the need for more money. She stressed that she wasn't going to help.

emphasize, -ise [T1, 5, 6] fml to stress: Emphasize the second syllable of 'pronounce'. He emphasized the need for more money. She emphasized what we expected her to emphasize.

accent [T1] rare to stress

accentuate [T1] **1** to pronounce with great force: He accentuated everything he said. **2** (fig) to give more importance to; direct one's attention to: The dark frame accentuates the brightness of the picture.

voice [T1] **1** to express in words, esp forcefully: He voiced his opposition to the plan. The chairman voiced the feeling of the meeting when he demanded more pay. **2** [Wv5] tech to produce (a sound) with a movement of the vocal chords as well as with the breath: /d/ and /g/ are voiced sounds but /t/ and /k/ are not.

collocate [I0 (with)] tech (of words) to go together or with another word in a way which sounds natural: 'Strong' collocates with 'coffee' but 'powerful' does not. The words 'strong' and 'coffee' collocate.

G232 nouns : **pronouncing and articulating**

pronunciation 1 [U] the way in which (a particular) language is pronounced: He knows very little about English pronunciation; he needs pronunciation training. **2** [U; S] a particular person's way of pronouncing a language or the words of a language: His pronunciation of English is very strange. **3** [C] the way in which a word is usually pronounced: There are two acceptable pronunciations of the word 'either'.

enunciation [U] the action of enunciating: The enunciation of his words was almost too perfect.

articulation [U] **1** the production of speech sounds: Her articulation is very good. **2** the expression of thoughts and feelings, esp in words: The articulation of one's real feelings is not always easy.

elocution [U] the art of good, clear speaking in public, with proper attention to the control of the voice and the making of the sounds: That young actor needs lessons in elocution/elocution lessons.

diction [U] **1** the way in which a person pronounces words: Actors need training in diction. **2** the choice of words and phrases **poetic diction** the use of special words and phrases in poetry which are not used in other ways of writing or speaking

stress [U; C] importance given to a word or part or a word by saying it with more force or on a different musical note or both: The stress in the word *'pronounce'* is on the second syllable [⇨ G273].

emphasis [U;C] **1** *fml* stress: *Where is the emphasis in the word 'pronounce'? He put the emphasis on the wrong syllable/word.* **2** mark of great importance: *In his work the emphasis is on how to make money.* **emphatic** [B] **1** expressed with emphasis: *He answered the question with an emphatic 'No'.* **2** (of ideas, beliefs, etc) strongly held: *It is my emphatic opinion that . . .* **3** (of events) perfectly certain and noticeable: *It was an emphatic success for him.* **-ally** [adv Wa4]

accent [C] **1** stress: *The accent in the word 'important' is on the second syllable.* **2** the mark used, esp above a word or part of a word, in writing or printing, to show what kind of sound is needed when it is spoken: *The grave and acute accents in French can be seen in set G151.*

accentuation [U] the action of accentuating: *He gave the important words special accentuation.*

collocation [U;C] the act of collocating: *The collocation of 'strong' and 'coffee' is acceptable, but 'powerful' and 'coffee' is not.* [⇨ G235]

G233 *nouns, etc* : **words and names**

word [C] **1** one or more sounds which can be spoken (together) to represent an idea, object, action, etc: *How do you pronounce the word 'either'? Tell me what happened in your words. She only said one word, but it was enough; I understood her perfectly.* **2** the written representation of this: *Can you read this word? What does this word here mean? How do you pronounce these words?* **3** the shortest (type of) statement: *In a word, no. I don't believe a word of what he said. Don't say a word to anyone.*

term [C] a word or expression with a special meaning, or used in a particular activity, job, profession, etc: *What is the scientific term for this? He knows all the medical terms; I don't.*

name **1** [C; *by* U] the word(s) that someone or something is called or known by: *Her name is Mary (Wilson). Does that cat have a name? The doctor had a metal name plate on his door. He spoke about her by name.* **2** [C] a (usu offensive) title for someone arising from his character: *He will always have the name of a thief in this town.* **surname** a person's family name: *His surname is McGregor.* **forename** *also* **Christian name** *fml* a person's first name

title **1** [C] a word or name, such as 'Mr', 'Lord', 'Doctor', 'General', 'Lady', etc, given to a person to be used before his name as a sign of rank, profession, etc **2** [C] a name given to a book, painting, play, etc: *The title of this play is 'Othello'.* **3** [S; U (*to*)] *tech* the lawful right to ownership or possession: *The prince has no title to the crown. Has Britain any title to this island?*

form of address: [C] *usu fml* the correct title or expression of politeness to be used to someone in speech or writing: *What is the correct form of address to the Prince of Wales?*

alias **1** [C] a name other than the usual or officially recognized name used by a person (esp a criminal) on certain occasions; a false name: *He used the alias of Edward when trying to get money from the old lady.* **2** [adv] (esp of a criminal) also known as; also called: *The police said the thief's name was John Smith alias Jim Jones.*

part of speech [C] any of the classes in grammar into which words are divided according to their use: *'Noun', 'verb', and 'adjective' are parts of speech.*

G234 *nouns* : **vocabulary and terminology**

vocabulary **1** [C; U] all the words known to a particular person: *Our baby is only just starting to talk; he has a vocabulary of about ten words. His Spanish vocabulary is getting bigger all the time.* **2** [U; C] the special set of words used in a particular kind of work, business, etc: *I find it difficult to understand the vocabulary of the law courts.* **3** [C] a list of words, usu in alphabetical order and with explanations of their meanings, less complete than a dictionary: *You'll find the English meaning of this French word in the vocabulary at the back of the book.*

lexis [U;C] *tech esp BrE* all the words in a particular language, or that a person knows, or that belong to a particular subject, etc: *This book is about the lexis of English/English lexis.*

lexicon [C *usu sing*] *tech esp AmE* lexis: *This book is about the lexicon of the English language/about the English lexicon.*

terminology **1** [U;C] (a system of) specialized words and expressions used in a particular science, profession, activity, etc: *Each profession has its own terminology. I don't understand scientific terminology.* **2** [U] the science that studies this **terminological** [Wa5;B] of or connected with terminology **-ly** [adv Wa4]

usage [C; U] **1** one or more standards practised by users, esp in using a language: *modern English usage(s)* **2** customs of behaviour: *Meals based on rice are not in common usage in England.*

nomenclature *usu fml* **1** [U;C] a system of naming things: *He is learning the nomenclature of chemical compounds. Words in scientific nomenclature are usually called 'tech' in this book.* **2** [U] a set of names or acts of naming: *The nomenclature of towns in Britain is interesting.*

coinage **1** [U] (of words) the act of inventing: *Coinage of new words goes on all the time.* **2** [C] a word or phrase recently invented: *That's an interesting coinage.*

neologism *tech* **1** [U] the making of new words: *Neologism is a natural part of language.* **2** [C] a new word or use of a word: *That's a neologism, isn't it?*

G235 *nouns* : **expressions, phrases, and sentences** [C]

expression a word or group of words: *The book contains most of the common expression in English. 'Shut up' is a rude expression for some people, but not for others. What was the expression he used to show his anger; was it 'blowing his top'?*

statement something stated, in one or more words: *His statement of what happened was written down. The statement 'I blew my top' means 'I became very angry'.*

phrase 1 a *loose* a small group of words **b** *precise tech* a group of words without a verb that shows tense or person [⇒ G261], esp as forming part of a sentence: *'Walking along the road' and 'a packet of cigarettes' are phrases.* **2** a short expression, esp one that is clever and very suited to what is meant: *His speech contained many fine phrases.* **phrasal** [Wa5;B] of, concerning, or like a phrase **-ly** [adv]

sentence a group of words that forms a statement, command, exclamation, or question, usu contains a subject and a verb, and (in writing) begins with a capital letter and ends with one of the marks (.!?). The following are all sentences: *'Sing the song again.' 'Birds sing.' 'How well he sings!' 'Who sang at the concert last night?'*

period *esp formerly* a complete sentence, esp one that is a combination of several smaller sentences **periodic** [Wa5;B] relating to a period or to periods

clause a group of words containing a subject and verb, forming part of a sentence, and often doing the work of a noun, adjective, or adverb

idiom 1 a phrase which means something different from the meanings of its separate words: *'To be hard up' is an English idiom meaning 'to lack money'.* **2** the way of expression typical of a person or a people in their use of language: *The French and the English idioms have very different characters. Each writer has his own idiom, some more difficult to understand than others.* **idiomatic** [B] of, concerning, or like an idiom or idioms: *She speaks good idiomatic Spanish. That phrase is idiomatic.* **-ally** [adv Wa4]

figure of speech an expression which is not necessarily true or possible but which is used to give force to or help to explain something: *'He fought like a lion' and 'he was a lion in the fight' are figures of speech.*

collocation an arrangement of words which sounds natural: *'Strong coffee' is an English collocation but 'powerful coffee' is not.*

colloquialism an expression used in, or suitable for, ordinary familiar or informal conversation

cliché *usu deprec* an unchanging idea or expression used so commonly that it has lost much of its expressive force: *His speech was full of tired political clichés.* (fig) *She says her life is just a cliché.*

G236 *nouns* : **sayings, proverbs, and axioms** [C]

saying a well-known (usu wise) statement: *As the saying goes, there's no smoke without fire* (= if people think something, usu bad, is happening, it probably is).

proverb a short, well-known saying that expresses a simple truth in popular language: *'Let sleeping dogs lie' is a proverb that means 'Do not disturb things unnecessarily'.* **proverbial** [B] of, concerning, or like a proverb **-ly** [adv]

adage an old wise phrase; proverb

maxim a rule for good and sensible behaviour, esp when expressed in a short, well-known saying: *One of her maxims was 'Early to bed and early to rise, makes a man healthy, wealthy, and wise.'*

dictum 1 a formal statement of opinion, made (as if) with full knowledge; a wise saying: *'You have nothing to lose but your chains' was a dictum of Karl Marx, talking to the workers of the world.* **2** *law* an opinion expressed by a judge in court

motto a short sentence or phrase, usu suggesting a way to behave and used by a school, college, and formerly by families: *The school motto is 'Never Give Up'.*

axiom a statement, esp one that is short, that is generally accepted as true and does not need to be proved **axiomatic** [Wa5;2] **1** *tech* of, like, or containing one or more axioms **2** not needing to be proved: *It is axiomatic that hard work is the way to success.* **-ally** [adv Wa4]

G237 *nouns* : **grammar, sound, and meaning**

[ALSO ⇒ G200]

grammar 1 [U] the study and practice of the rules by which words change their forms and are combined into sentences **2** [C] a book which teaches these rules; a grammar book: *This is the best Italian grammar I've seen.* **grammarian** [C] a person who studies grammar

syntax [U] the rules of grammar which are used for ordering and relating words to one another in a sentence

phonetics 1 [U] the study and science of speech sounds **2** [P] *infml* the speech sounds of a particular language: *Although I can read Russian, I can't manage its phonetics well enough to speak it.* **phonetician** [C] a person who studies phonetics

phonology [U] **1** the study of speech sounds, esp the history of their changes in a particular language and the laws governing these **2** the system of speech sounds in a particular language at a particular time in history: *Old English phonology* **phonologist** [C] a person who studies phonology

meaning [U;C] the idea which is intended to be understood in any kind of language: *What is the meaning of this French word? Some words change their meanings over the years. Ogden & Richards wrote a book called 'The Meaning of Meaning'.*

sense [C] **1** an intended meaning: *The sense of the sentence was hard to understand. The sense of Mary's letter is that she would like to visit us, although she doesn't say so directly.* **2** any of several (different kinds) of meanings: *In what sense do you mean 'bad'—'wicked' or 'of low quality'? He used the word 'man' in its broadest sense, including both men and women.* **3** any of the parts of a definition of a word separated as in this book by the numbers **1**, **2**, etc

semantics [U] **1** the study of meanings of words and other parts of language **2** the general study of signs and what they stand for **semanticist** [C] a person who studies semantics

style [C;U] a type of choice or way of using words, esp which marks out the speaker or writer as different from others: *The letter is written in a formal style. The work is in the style of the 18th century. That writer's style is difficult to copy.*

rhetoric [U] **1** the art of using words to persuade people **2** *sometimes deprec* language that is fine to hear or read but that does not mean much

linguistics [U] the study of language in general and of particular languages, of the patterns of their grammar, sounds, etc, their history, origins, and use **linguist** [C] **1** a person who studies linguistics **2** a person who has a (good) knowledge of foreign languages

philology [U] the science of the nature and growth of words, language, or a particular language **philologist** [C] a person who studies philology

etymology 1 [U] the scientific study of the origins, history, and changing meanings of words **2** [C] (an account of) the history of a particular word: *Just look up the etymologies of these words for me.* **etymologist** [C] a person who studies etymology

G238 *adjectives* : **grammar, sound, and meaning** [B]

grammatical 1 [Wa5] concerning grammar: *This book is partly a grammatical work.* **2** according to the rules of grammar: *That is not a grammatical sentence.* **un-** [*neg*] **-ly** [adv Wa4]

syntactic(al) [Wa5] of or by the rules of syntax **-(al)ly** [adv Wa4]

phonetic [Wa5] **1** of or concerning the sounds of human speech: *a phonetic study of this rare language* **2** (of a system of writing down speech sounds (**transcription**)) having the possibility of using more than one sign for each phoneme, depending on its actual sound quality: *In a phonetic representation of English, two differ-*

ent sorts of 'l' would have to be shown, even though 'l' is only one phoneme [⇒G273 PHONEMIC]. **3** (of a language) with all the words spelled very much as they sound: *The difference in the pronunciation of 'rough' and 'though' shows that English spelling is not phonetic.* **-ally** [adv Wa4]

phonological [Wa5] of or by the rules of phonology **-ly** [adv Wa4]

colloquial (of words, phrases, expressions, style, etc) of, suitable for, or related to ordinary, informal, or familiar conversation; not formal or used a lot in formal writing **-ly** [adv]

semantic [Wa5] of or related to meaning in language **-ally** [adv Wa4]

stylistic [Wa5] of or concerning style, esp in writing or art: *A stylistic change will not improve the subject matter. Could I ask a stylistic question?* **-ally** [adv Wa4]

rhetorical *sometimes deprec* concerned with rhetoric (and nothing more) **-ly** [adv Wa4]

linguistic [Wa5] **1** concerning one or more languages: *He has great linguistic knowledge.* **2** concerning words and patterns of words: *What is the linguistic analysis of this sentence? Linguistic development/change interests him.* **-ally** [adv Wa4]

lexical [Wa5] of or concerning words **-ly** [adv Wa4]

philological [Wa5] of or concerning philology **-ly** [adv Wa4]

etymological [Wa5] of or concerning etymology **-ly** [adv Wa4]

G239 *adjectives, etc* : **relating to speech and hearing**

verbal [Wa5;B] **1** spoken, not written: *He gave a verbal description of the place. We'll accept a verbal report.* **2** connected with words and their use: *He has great verbal skill as a speaker and as a writer.* **3** that produces the exact words of something: *That child has a good verbal memory; she can repeat things exactly even when she doesn't understand them.* **4** concerned with the actual words in which something is expressed, and not with the real meaning: *There's only a verbal difference between 'late in the afternoon' and 'early in the evening'.* **-ly** [adv]

oral [Wa5;B] spoken, not written: *She had/took an oral examination in English/an English oral examination.* **-ly** [adv]: *Please answer orally.*

aural [Wa5;B] (esp of language) of or received through hearing **-ly** [adv]

-lingual [*comb form*] relating to language and languages, as in: **bilingual 1** [Wa5;B] of, containing, or expressed in two languages: *He bought a bilingual French–English dictionary.* **2** [Wa5;B] able to speak a second language (almost) as well as one's first language **3** [C] a bilingual person: *They are all bilinguals.*

-glot [*comb form*] *esp tech* relating to language and languages, as in: **monoglot** [Wa5;B] of or

· having only one language: *There are few purely monoglot countries in the world.* **polyglot** [Wa5;B] of or having many languages: *Singapore is a polyglot city.*

G240 *adjectives* : **relating to ability to speak** [B]

fluent 1 (of a person) speaking in an easy, smooth manner: *He is fluent in five languages.* **2** (of speech, writing, etc) expressed readily and without pause: *She speaks fluent but not very correct English.* **-ly** [adv]

articulate 1 expressing or able to use sounds or to express thoughts and feelings clearly, esp in words: *He is an articulate person. That is a very articulate magazine.* **2** (of speech) having clear separate sounds or words **in-** [*neg*] **-ly** [adv] **-ness** [U]

coherent (of speech) well connected and spoken: *She has a very coherent way of talking about things.* **in-** [*neg*] **-ly** [adv]

clear [Wa1] (of speech, writing, etc) easy to understand; understood; well-expressed: *I hope what I have said is (quite) clear (to you). He spoke in a clear, strong voice.* **un-** [*neg*] **-ly** [adv] **-ness** [U]

lucid (of speech, writing, etc) very easy to understand; speaking very easily: *Her way of speaking is nice and lucid; I can follow her very well.* **-ly** [adv]

G241 *nouns* : **relating to the ability to speak** [U]

fluency the state or quality of being fluent; the ability to speak in an easy, smooth manner; ready continuous expression: *I am not sure about her fluency in Spanish.*

articulacy the state or quality of being articulate; the ability to use sounds or to express thoughts and feelings clearly: *Articulacy among children is an important matter in schools.* **in-** [*neg*]

coherence the state of being coherent, well-connected, and well-expressed: *The coherence of his speech and arguments makes him a welcome speaker.* **in-** [*neg*]

clarity the state of being clear, well understood; the state of expressing things well: *The clarity of her voice and ideas was a great help in understanding a difficult subject.*

lucidity the state of being lucid; ease and clearness of expression

G242 *nouns* : **contexts, texts, and passages**

context [C; U] **1** the setting of a word, phrase, etc among the surrounding words, phrases, etc, often used for helping to explain the meaning of the word, phrase, etc: *In some contexts*

'mad' means 'foolish' in some 'angry' and in others 'insane'. You should be able to tell the meaning of this word from the/its context.* **2** the general conditions in which an event, action, etc takes place: *In the context of late 19th-century Italy it was difficult to be both a practising Christian and a politician.* **contextual** [Wa5;B] of or concerning a context or contexts **-ly** [adv]

setting [C *usu sing*] **1** the time and place where the action of a book, film, etc is shown as happening: *Our story has its setting in ancient Rome.* **2** a set of surroundings: *These mountains form a beautiful setting for a holiday trip.*

discourse 1 [U] general speech or writing: *In everyday discourse that particular word is hardly ever used.* **2** [U] *fml* serious conversation: *The judges had solemn discourse together.* **3** [C (*on, about*)] a serious speech or piece of writing: *The priest delivered a long discourse on the evils of money.*

text 1 [C; U] the main body of writing in a book; words in a book written by the writer as opposed to notes, pictures, etc: *Children won't like this book because there is too much text and too few pictures.* **2** [C; U] the original words of a speech, article, etc: *What the politician really meant will not be clear until we examine the text of his speech.* **3** [C9] any of the various forms in which a book, article, etc exists; copy: *Certain mistakes were made when the Latin text was copied from the Greek. Who has the original text of 'War and Peace'?* **4** [C] a sentence from the Bible to be read and talked about by a priest in church **textual** [Wa5;B] of, concerning or about a text **-ly** [adv]

passage [C] a part of a text: *Read the passage on page 22, please.*

paragraph [C] a division of a written or printed piece made up of one or more sentences, of which the first word is usu set a little inwards to the right of a new line

G243 *nouns* : **subjects and topics** [C]

subject 1 something being considered, as in conversation: *Don't change the subject; answer the question. He wrote to me on the subject of changing his job.* **2** a branch of knowledge studied as in a system of education: *She takes three subjects in her examination. His subject is history/chemistry.* **3** a cause: *His strange clothes were the subject of great amusement/a subject for amusement.* **4** the main area of interest treated in a work, esp written: *a book on the subject of love. The teacher said 'Children, take as your subject "My Holiday".'* **5** a certain occasion, object, etc, represented in art: *The subject of the painting is the Battle of Waterloo.* **6** a person or animal chosen to experience something or to be studied in an experiment: *The subject of their cruelty was a small bird. She gave the test to the seven subjects.*

topic a subject for conversation, talk, writing, etc: *Politics or religion are always interesting topics of conversation.*

theme 1 the subject of a talk, book, etc: *What is your theme tonight?* **2** a tune repeated again and again in a piece of music: **thematic** [Wa5;B] *tech* of, concerning, or like a theme **-ally** [adv Wa4]

matter a subject to which one gives attention: *Can we discuss this matter now, please? It is a matter of great concern to me.*

question 1 a matter for discussion: *It's a question of finding more time and we must talk about it now.* **2** [*also* U] a (reason for) doubt: *There is no question of his coming* (= he is definitely not coming). *There was some question as to his honesty.*

issue an esp urgent matter for discussion: *This is an important issue; we must discuss it now. The issue is whether we give them the money or not; nothing else matters. What are the latest issues in politics in your country?*

aspect 1 [*of*] a part of a difficulty, question, subject, etc that is, can, may, or should be particularly discussed: *There is another interesting aspect of this matter which needs thinking about.* **2** *esp lit* appearance: *The house's aspect was dark and unattractive. His aspect was frightening.*

angle a way of looking at a subject or writing about it: *Try seeing things from my angle for a change; it may make you think again. He didn't know what angle to write the story from.*

slant a way of presenting, talking or writing about a subject: *She didn't know whether to give her article a political slant or not. She gave a religious slant to the article.*

affair [*often pl*] *usu fml & pomp* something which one must do, study, etc; matter or question: *This is my affair, not theirs. He has many affairs to look after. The Minister for Foreign Affairs is abroad at the moment.*

business [*usu sing*] *not fml* an affair, concern, or interest: *It is no business of yours what I do. This is his business, not ours; stop asking him all these questions. It was a strange business; we still do not know exactly why he did it.*

G244 *nouns* : **common figures of speech** [C; U]

simile (the use of) an expression making a comparison in the imagination between two things, using the words *like* or *as*: *'As white as snow' is a simile.*

metaphor (the use of) a phrase which describes one thing by stating another thing with which it can be compared (as in *the roses in her cheeks*) without using the words 'as' or 'like': *She said he was a fox, planning everything so carefully; and the metaphor was very suitable.*

allegory (the style of) a story, poem, painting, etc in which the characters and actions represent good and bad qualities

metonymy (the use of) a phrase which describes one thing by referring to something which is near to it or part of it: *Writing is often called 'the pen'; that is metonymy.*

synecdoche (the use of) a phrase which describes one thing by referring to only a part of it: *Synecdoche is often called 'the part for the whole', as in a 'worker' being called a 'hand'.*

onomatopoeia the formation or use of words that are like natural sounds, as when the word 'cuckoo' is used to name the bird that makes that sound

G245 *nouns* : **other figures of speech and ways of expressing oneself**
[ALSO ⇨ G98 CONTRADICTION, PARADOX]

irony [U; C] **1** a way of speaking which expresses by its manner the opposite of what the words say: *The irony in his words was unmistakable.* **2** the sort of event or result which is just the opposite of what one would hope for or meant to happen, or the state when this happens: *The irony lay in the fact that he was there all the time, although I didn't see him.*

sarcasm [U] speaking or writing which tries to hurt someone's feelings, esp by expressions which clearly mean the opposite to what is felt: *'Thank you for bringing back my bicycle so quickly; you've only had it six months,' he said with heavy sarcasm.*

satire [C; U] (a work of) literature, theatre, speaking, etc intended to show the foolishness or evil of some establishment or practice in an amusing way: *Swift was a master of satire. 'Gulliver's Travels' was a satire on British politics in Swift's time.*

litotes [U] a way of expressing a thought by its opposite, esp with 'not': *It's not at all bad'* (= it's good) *and 'He was no small help to us'* (= he helped us a lot) *are examples of litotes.*

circumlocution *fml* **1** [U] the use of a large number of unnecessary words to express an idea needing fewer words, esp when trying to avoid directly answering a difficult question **2** [C] an example of this

apostrophe [U; C] (in a speech or piece of writing) words addressed to a person who is usu absent or to an idea or quality as if it were a person

personification [U; C] representing something (a part of nature, an animal, etc) as a person: *'The sky smiled' is an example of personification.*

alliteration [U; (C)] the appearance of the same sound or sounds at the beginning of two or more words that are next or close to each other (as in *round the rocks runs the river*)

G246 *adjectives* : **relating to figures of speech and expressions** [B]

literal 1 following the usual meaning of the

words without any additional meanings: *The literal meaning of the word 'cat' is an animal, not a girl.* **2** not imaginative: *He has a literal approach to his subject.* **3** exact: *Can I have a literal version of the conversation?* **4** giving one word for each word (as in a foreign language): *A literal translation is not always the closest to the original meaning.* **-ly** [adv]

figurative (of words) used in some way other than in the ordinary sense, to make a word picture or comparison: *'A sweet tongue' is a figurative expression but 'sweet coffee' is not.* **-ly** [adv]

metaphoric(al) 1 using or concerning the use of metaphor: *It is a metaphorical poem.* **2** not meant to be understood in the ordinary meaning of the words: *It was a metaphorical phrase; we didn't really mean that he has green fingers, but that he is good at gardening.* **-(al)ly** [adv Wa4]

allegorical of, concerning, or having the quality of an allegory **-ly** [adv Wa4]

metonymic of, concerning, or having the quality of metonymy **-ally** [adv Wa4]

onomatopoeic, onomatopoetic of, concerning, or having the quality of onomatopoeia **-ally** [adv Wa4]

ironic(al) of, concerning, or like irony: *This is a very ironical thing to happen. It was ironic that she left just when he needed her most, but was always there when he didn't want her. He gave her an ironical smile.* **-(al)ly** [adv Wa4]

sarcastic using or marked by sarcasm: *Must you always be so sarcastic when I ask you anything? 'How clever you are!' he said in his sarcastic way.* **-ally** [adv Wa4]

satirical fond of, being, using, etc satire: *Jonathan Swift's 'Gulliver's Travels' is a satirical book.* **-ly** [adv Wa4]

alliterative being, having, or using alliteration: *Alliterative phrases are easily remembered.* **-ly** [adv]

G247 *verbs* : **relating to figures of speech and expressions**

allegorize, -ise [T1; (I∅)] to present or describe (something) as an allegory [⇒ G244]: *John Bunyan allegorized the Christian life as a difficult journey in his allegory 'A Pilgrim's Progress'.*

satirize, -ise [T1] to write or speak using satire against (someone or something): *In his new play he satirizes the government.*

apostrophize, -ise [T1; I∅] to make an apostrophe [⇒ G245] to (someone or something): *The poet apostrophized (the moon).*

personify [T1] **1** (of something in nature, an animal, etc) to represent a person **2** (of a person) to represent a quality: *He personifies goodness itself* (= He is a very good person). *He is goodness personified.*

alliterate [I∅; T1] to (cause to) have the same sound or sounds at the beginning of two or more words: *The phrase 'running river' alliterates. Why not alliterate the words?*

G248 *nouns* : **words and meanings** [C]

synonym a word with the same or nearly the same meaning as another word in the same language: *'Sad' and 'unhappy' are synonyms.* **synonymous** [Wa5;B (*with*)] having the same or nearly the same meaning (as): *Being a soldier is synonymous with being a brave man, in his opinion.* **-ly** [adv] **synonymy** [U] the condition of words being synonymous

antonym a word opposite in meaning to another word: *'Pain' is the antonym of 'pleasure'.* **antonymous** [Wa5;B] having an opposite or nearly opposite meaning: *The words 'pain' and 'pleasure' are antonymous.* **-ly** [adv] **antonymy** [U] the condition of words being antonymous

homonym a word which has both the same sound and spelling as another, though different in meaning: *'Bear' meaning the animal and 'bear' meaning to carry are homonyms.* **homonymous** [Wa5;B] having the nature of homonyms. **-ly** [adv] **homonymy** [U] the condition of being homonymous

homophone a homonym in sound only: *For some speakers of English in England the words 'sure' and 'shore' are homophones.* **homophonous** [Wa5;B] having the nature of a homophone

homograph a homonym in writing only: *'Wind' is a homograph with two pronunciations and meanings, one a noun and the other a verb.* **homographous** [Wa5;B] having the nature of a homograph

G249 *verbs & nouns* : **translating and interpreting**

translate 1 [T1; I∅] to turn (speech or writing) from one language into another: *This book was first translated into English in the 15th century. He earns money by translating.* **2** [I∅] to be turned from one language into another: *These poems do not translate into English well.* **3** [T1] to explain; make clear: *How would you translate his silence?* **4** [T1] *fml* to bear or change from one place, state, or form to another **translation 1** [U] the act of translating **2** [*in* U] having been translated: *I've only read Tolstoy in translation.* **3** [C] an example of translating; a result of being translated: *This is a very good translation of Tolstoy.* **translator** [C] a person who translates from one language to another, esp as a profession

interpret 1 [T1; I∅] to put (a language) into the words of another language usu by speech: *Who will interpret for you at the meeting?* **2** [X9, esp as] to understand the likely meaning of (something): *How can I interpret this behaviour? I interpret his silence as dislike.* **interpreting** [U]: *Who will do the interpreting at the meeting?*

interpreter [C] a person who interprets, esp one who says in another language the words of a speech that is being, or has just been, given

Grammar

G260 *nouns* : **the four major parts of speech** [C]

noun a word that is the name of a person, place, thing, quality, action, etc, that can be used as the subject or object of a verb: *'John', 'woman' and 'earth' are nouns.* **nominal** [Wa5;B] of, related to, or used as a noun: *Some suffixes like* ness *and* -ation *are nominal endings.* **-ly** [adv]

adjective a word which describes the thing for which a noun stands (such as the word 'black' in the sentence *'She wore a black hat'*). **adjectival** [Wa5;B] having the nature of or doing the work of an adjective **-ly** [adv] **predicative adjective** an adjective that usu or always comes after a verb: *In the sentence 'The child is asleep' the last word is a predicative adjective.*

verb a word or phrase that tells what someone or something is, does, or experiences: *In 'She is tired' and 'He wrote a letter', the words 'is' and 'wrote' are verbs.* **verbal** [Wa5;B] of, coming from, or connected with a verb or verbs: *The word 'guide' is not only a noun; it also has a verbal use.* **-ly** [adv]

adverb a word which describes or adds to the meaning of a verb, adjective, another adverb, or a sentence, and which answers such questions as *how*? *when*? or *where*? (as in 'He ran *slowly*'. 'It was *very* beautiful'. 'Come *tomorrow*'. 'Come *here*'. '*Generally* (speaking), things are getting better'.) **adverbial** [Wa5;B;C] (something) like, used as, or having qualities typical of an adverb: *an adverbial phrase* **-ly** [adv]

G261 *nouns* : **aspects of the four major parts of speech**

number [U;C] variation in the form of words, esp (in English) nouns and verbs, depending on whether one or more than one thing is talked about: *The word 'horses' is plural in number* [⇒ G262].

gender 1 [U] the grouping of nouns and pronouns according to sex (masculine, feminine or neuter) or according to form [⇒ I6] and syntax 2 [C] one of these classes: *What gender is the word for 'stone' in Spanish?* [⇒ G263]

person 1 [U] the grouping of pronouns into classes 2 [C] one of these classes: *'I' is the first person singular in English.* [⇒ G264]

tense 1 [U] the form of a verb that shows time or aspect 2 [C] one such form: *How do you form the present tense in Japanese?* [⇒ G265]

voice [C *usu sing*] the form of the verb which shows whether the subject of a sentence acts or is acted upon: *I am writing this sentence in the active (voice). This sentence is written in the passive (voice).* [⇒G266]

mood [U;C] the form of a verb, showing whether things are considered certain, possible, etc or whether something is a statement, an order, etc [⇒ G267]

aspect [U;C] the form a verb takes to mark the difference in time, as between a continuing form (as in *'is singing'*) and a completed action (as in *'sang'*): *Aspect is quite important in English grammar.* **aspectual** [Wa5;B] of or concerning aspect: *There is an aspectual difference between 'singing' and 'sang'.* **-ly** [adv]

degrees of comparison [P] 1 the three forms of an adjective or adverb (such as *nice—nicer—nicest* or *good—better—best*) 2 the three phrases containing an adjective or adverb such that the relations among them are like the relations among 'nice—nicer—nicest': *The degrees of comparison of 'interestingly' are 'interestingly—more interestingly—most interestingly'* [⇒ G268].

G262 *nouns & adjectives* : **one or more than one** [Wa5;B;C]

[ALSO ⇒J8]

singular (a form of word) that expresses one and no more: *'Dog' is singular and 'dogs' plural.*

plural (a form of word) that expresses more than one: *'Dogs' is a plural noun; it is the plural of 'dog'.*

dual (in some languages such as Greek) (a form of word) that expresses two

G263 *nouns & adjectives* : **masculine, feminine, or neuter**

masculine 1 [Wa5;B] (in many languages) in or related to a gender of words that is male alone or is not feminine or neuter: *In Spanish the word for 'wine' is masculine.* 2 [C *usu sing*] **a** a masculine word or word form **b** the class of such words and forms: *Put this Latin adjective into the masculine.*

feminine 1 [Wa5;B] (in many languages) in or related to a gender of words that is female alone or is not masculine or neuter: *In Spanish the word for 'stone' is feminine.* 2 [C *usu sing*] **a** a feminine word or word form **b** the class of such words and forms: *Put this Latin adjective into the feminine.*

neuter 1 [Wa5;B] (in many languages) in or related to a gender of words not male or female or not masculine or feminine 2 [C *usu sing*] **a** a neuter word or word form **b** the class of such words and forms: *Does Hebrew have a neuter? Put this Latin adjective into the neuter.*

G264 nouns : I, you, or some other person [the R]

first person the person who is speaking: *In English 'I' and 'we' are singular and plural pronouns in the first person. I don't like putting these remarks in the first person; I'll use 'one' instead of 'I'.*

second person the person who is being spoken to: *'Thou' is the old form of the second person singular in English. 'You' is now both the singular and the plural of the second person.*

third person the person who is being spoken about: *'He' is the masculine singular of the third person in English. She usually writes her stories in the third person, but her latest book is in the first person.*

G265 nouns : the tenses of the verb [the R]

(simple) present (tense) that tense which usu deals with time now or at the time of a story but which in English often means all times generally: *In the sentence 'He comes here every week' the verb is in the present (tense) and means that he always or usually does this.*

(simple) past (tense) that tense which usu deals with time past and completed actions: *In the sentence 'He came here last week' the verb shows that he did something which is not happening now.*

(simple) future (tense) that tense which usu deals with time to come and in English uses 'will/shall': *In the sentence 'He will come here next week' the 'will' shows that he is expected or plans to do something.*

present continuous/progressive (tense) that tense which usu deals with continuing time now or at the time of a story but also often in English describes the future: *The sentence 'He is coming now' means that he is at this moment doing something, but in the sentence 'He is coming next week' the same tense describes a future action.*

present perfect (tense) that tense which usu deals with time from the past to the present moment or the time of a story: *The sentence 'He has worked here for years' means that in the past he worked here and is still working here.*

present perfect continuous/progressive (tense) that tense which usu deals with continuing time from a point in the past to the present moment or the time of a story: *The sentence 'He has been working on this since last Thursday' means that he began last Thursday, did not stop, and is still doing the work now.*

past continuous/progressive (tense) that tense which usu deals with time continuing in the past but in English is also used to show plans in the past: *In the sentence 'He was coming when I saw him' the verb 'was coming' shows that he continued to do something, but in the sentence 'He was coming, but he isn't coming now' means that he planned to come but changed his plan later.*

past perfect (tense) that tense which usu deals with time from the earlier past to another point in the past: *The sentence 'He had worked there for years' means that until a certain time in the past he worked there, but no longer.*

past perfect continuous/progressive (tense) that tense which usu deals with continuing time from the earlier past to another point in the past: *The sentence 'He had been working there for years, then suddenly left' means that he worked there continuously until a particular time.*

future continuous/progressive (tense) that tense which usu deals with continuing time in the future: *In the sentence 'He will be working here next week' the person is described as continuing to work for some time during the next week.*

future perfect (tense) that tense which usu suggests time completed at a certain point in the future: *The sentence 'He will have finished with the work by 6 o'clock' means that the person is expected to have finished the work at 6 o'clock (a future time).*

future perfect continuous/progressive (tense) that tense which usu suggests continuing time up to a point in the future: *In the sentence 'At 6 o'clock she will have been waiting more than two hours' the person is seen as waiting in the future for at least two hours.*

definite/emphatic tense that tense which uses the helping verb 'do' to emphasize a point: *The sentence 'He goes there every week' has no special emphasis, but 'He does go there every week' emphasizes his action.* [⇒ G77 EMPHASIZE; G78 EMPHASIS]

G266 adjectives & nouns : the voices of the verb [Wa5;B; C]

active (of a verb or sentence) having as the subject the person or thing doing the action (as in *'The boy kicked the ball'*): *The sentence is in the active (voice).*

passive (of a verb or sentence) having a subject that is acted on by the verb rather than that performs the action (as in *'The ball was kicked by the boy'*): *The sentence is in the passive (voice).*

G267 nouns & adjectives : words describing uses of words

infinitive [C] the part of the verb that can be used after other verbs and with 'to' before it: *'To go' is an infinitive. 'Must' takes the infinitive without 'to' (I must go) but 'ought' takes the infinitive with 'to' (I ought to go).*

indicative *also* **declarative** [Wa5;B] a verb form (= mood [⇒ G261]) which states that something happens, happened, will happen, etc:

'He goes' and 'he went' are both indicative uses of the verb.

affirmative [B; C] *often fml* (a word) declaring 'yes': *The answer was a strong affirmative. The answer was in the affirmative. It was an affirmative answer.*

negative [B; C] *often fml* (a word) declaring 'no': *The answer was a strong negative. The answer was in the negative. It was a negative answer.*

imperative [Wa5; B; C] (a mood) which gives an order: *'Go!' is the imperative of the verb 'to go'.*

interrogative [Wa5; B; C] (a mood) which asks questions: *Are you coming?'* is interrogative, while *'You are coming'* is indicative or declarative.

conditional [Wa5; B; C] (a mood in certain languages, or a clause) expressing a condition, esp in English starting with 'if' or 'unless'

subjunctive [Wa5; B; C] (a mood in certain languages) often expressing doubt, wishes, a dependent verb, etc

attributive 1 [Wa5; B] (of an adjective, noun, or phrase) describing and coming before a noun, as 'green' in 'a green hat' **2** [C] an adjective, noun or phrase that is attributive

predicative [Wa5; B] (of an adjective or phrase) describing a noun but coming in the predicate [⇨ G269] of a sentence or clause: *'Sleeping' is attributive in the phrase 'a sleeping child, but 'asleep' is predicative in the sentence 'the child is asleep'.* [⇨ G260]

demonstrative [Wa5; B; C] (of) a word, esp a pronoun, that points to someone or something: *'This' is a demonstrative pronoun.*

G268 *adjectives & nouns* : **the degrees of adjectives and adverbs** [Wa5; B; C]

positive (of or related to) the simple form that expresses no comparison: *'Good' is the positive form of the adjective, while 'better' and 'best' are not.*

comparative (of or related to) the form of adjectives or adverbs expressing an increase in quality, quantity, or degree: *'Bigger is the comparative (form) of 'big' and 'more beautiful' is the comparative of 'beautiful'.*

superlative (of or related to) the form of adjectives or adverbs expressing the most in quality, quantity, or degree: *'Biggest' is the superlative (form) of 'big' and 'most beautiful' is the superlative of 'beautiful'.*

G269 *nouns* : **subject, object, and predicate, etc**

subject [C] a set of one or more words saying who or what performed an action or exists in a state (as in the first nouns and pronouns in these sentences: *John did it. I saw him do it. He loves her.*)

object [C] a set of one or more words saying with whom or with what a preposition [⇨ G272] is most directly associated (= **object** of a preposition), who is concerned in the results of an action (= **indirect object** of a verb), or to whom or to what something has been done (= **direct object** of a verb) (as shown, in that order, as follows): *In Rome John gave Mary a book.*)

predicate [C] the part of a sentence which makes a statement about the subject: *In 'Fishes swim' and 'She is an artist', 'swim' and 'is an artist' are predicates.*

antecedent [C] the word, phrase, or sentence that comes before a pronoun, etc and is represented by that pronoun, etc: *What is the antecedent of 'him' in line 10?*

apposition [U; (C)] a state of affairs in grammar in which one (simple) sentence contains two or more main phrases that describe the same person or thing and are used in the same way (*often in the phr* **in apposition (to)**): *In the sentence 'The rich man, a banker, was a criminal.', the phrase 'the rich man' and the phrase 'a banker' are in apposition (to each other).*

G270 *adjectives & nouns* : **kinds of noun** [C]

countable noun a noun that can have a plural form and be counted: *We can say 'a book', 'two books', 'three books', etc, so 'book' is a countable noun.*

uncountable noun *also* **mass noun** a noun that cannot, at least in certain uses, have a plural form and is regarded as a quantity or mass: *'Bread' in the sentence 'Have some more bread' is an uncountable noun. In the sentence 'This is good wine; have some more', the noun 'wine' is uncountable, but in the sentence 'These are good wines', meaning different kinds of wines, the noun 'wine' is countable.*

abstract noun a noun which is the name of a quality or state, such as 'beauty', 'strength' and 'hopelessness'

collective noun a noun singular in form but naming a collection of people, animals, or things, as a group: *'Flock' is a collective noun for a group of birds.*

proper noun a name used for a single particular thing or person and spelt with a capital letter: *'James' and 'Edinburgh' are proper nouns.*

common noun a noun that does not begin with a capital letter

verbal noun a noun which describes an action or experience and has the same form as a present participle [⇨ G271]: *'Building' is a verbal noun in 'the building of the house' but not in 'The bank was a tall building'.*

gerund 1 the English form of the verb ending in **-ing**, when used as a noun; verbal noun **2** (in Latin) a form of the verb used as a noun

G271 *nouns* : **forms of the verb; kinds of verbs** [C]

participle (in English grammar) either of the two forms of a verb (= **past participle** or **present participle**) which may be used in compound forms of the verb or as adjectives: *The present participle always ends in -ing. In the sentence 'I am running' the form 'running' is a present participle. It is also a participle in the phrase 'the running men'. The past participle ends in -ed in regular verbs, but may be different in irregular verbs. The past participle of 'walk' is 'walked' but of 'drive' is 'driven'.* **participial** [Wa5;B] of, concerning, containing, or like a participle: *In the phrase 'running water' the word 'running' is a participial adjective.*

transitive verb a verb that takes a direct object [⇨ G269]: *In the sentence 'I saw him' the verb saw is transitive because it has a direct object, 'him'.*

intransitive verb a verb that has no direct object: *In the sentence 'I was eating' the verb 'was eating' is intransitive because it has no direct object.*

auxiliary verb *also* **helping verb** a verb that goes with another verb to show person, tense, voice, aspect, etc (such as *am, did* and *have* in *'I am running, I did climb, they have heard')*

regular verb (in English grammar) a verb that has its three forms for the present, the past, and the past participle formed in the usual way **ir-** [*neg*]

modal verb/auxiliary any such verb forms as *will, would, may, might, etc*

phrasal verb a group of words acting as a verb and usu consisting of a verb with an adverbial or prepositional particle [⇨ G272]: *'Get up' and 'get by' are phrasal verbs.*

prepositional verb *also* **fused phrasal verb** a phrasal verb formed from a verb and a preposition, as in the sentence *'I came across* (= met) *an old friend last week'.*

G272 *nouns* : **minor parts of speech** [C]

determiner a word that limits the meaning of a noun and comes before adjectives that describe the same noun: *In the phrase 'his new car', the word 'his' is a determiner.*

article either 'the' (**definite article**) or 'a, an' (**indefinite article**), two special kinds of determiner in English

particle any of several kinds of usu short words, esp adverbs such as 'up' and 'down', prepositions, and conjunctions

preposition a word placed before a noun or pronoun to show its connection with another word: *In 'a house made of wood' and 'a man like my brother' the words 'of' and 'like' are*

prepositions. **prepositional** [Wa5;B] as or having the nature of a preposition: *In 'He fell down' the word 'down' is an adverb, but in 'He fell down the stairs' there is a prepositional use of 'down'.* **prepositional phrase 1** a group of words that acts as a preposition: *'Because of' and 'on top of' are prepositional phrases.* **2** a phrase consisting of a preposition and the noun following it: *'In bed' and 'on top' are prepositional phrases.*

conjunction a word such as 'but' or 'and' that connects parts of sentences, phrases, etc

pronoun a word that is used in place of a noun or a noun phrase: *Instead of saying 'the man came' you can use a pronoun and say 'he came'.* **personal pronoun** a word standing for a noun and used for showing the speaker, the one spoken to, or the one spoken of [⇨ G264]: *'I', 'you' and 'they' are personal pronouns.* **demonstrative (pronoun)** a pronoun that points out the one meant and makes clear that it is different from others of the same class. *'This—that—these—those' can be demonstrative pronouns.* **relative pronoun** a pronoun that relates or connects clauses, such as 'that' in 'this is the book that I want'.

intensifier a word which makes an adjective stronger in feeling: *'Very' is an intensifier, as in 'very good'.*

exclamation the word(s) expressing a sudden strong feeling: *'Good heavens!' is an exclamation.*

interjection a word which expresses a sudden remark: *'Oh!' is an interjection.*

G273 *nouns* : **elements of sound in language** [C]

syllable a word or part of a word which contains a vowel sound or a consonant acting as a vowel: *There are two syllables in the word 'button'.* **syllabic** [Wa5;B] of, concerning, having, or like a syllable or syllables **-ally** [adv Wa4] **monosyllabic** [Wa5;B] **1** (of words) having only one syllable **2** (of persons) speaking only in words of one syllable (**monosyllables**) **-ally** [adv Wa4] **polysyllabic** [Wa5; B] **1** (of words) having many syllables **2** (of persons) speaking mainly in words with many syllables **-ally** [adv Wa4]

consonant 1 a speech sound made by partly or completely stopping the flow of air as it goes through the mouth **2** a letter representing a consonant **consonantal** [Wa5; B] *tech* **-ly** [adv]

vowel 1 any one of the human speech sounds in which the breath is let out without any stop or any closing of the air passage in the mouth or throat and that can be heard: *The sounds /i/ and /e/ are vowels.* **2** a letter used for representing any of these: *The vowels in the roman alphabet as used in English are a, e, i, o and u, and sometimes y.* **vocalic** [Wa5;B] *tech* of, concerning, or like a vowel or vowels: *vocalic speech sounds* **-ally** [adv]

monophthong a single vowel sound produced with the organs of speech remaining in the same position

diphthong 1 a compound vowel sound made by moving the tongue from one vowel position to another: *The vowel sound in 'my' is a diphthong* **2** *also* **digraph** two letters that represent one sound, esp when written or printed close together

segment *tech* a small part of the flow of natural speech, usu a vowel or consonant sound, when separated from the rest

phone *tech* a single sound made in speaking

phoneme *tech* the smallest part or unit of speech that can be used to make a (part of a) word sound different from another that is the same in every other way: *In English, the 'b' in 'big' and the 'p' in 'pig' are two different phonemes.* **phonemic** [Wa5;B] **1** (of a system of writing down speech sounds (= transcription)) using only one sign for each phoneme [⇒ G238 PHONETIC] **2** of or connected with phonemes **3** (of speech sounds) that are (different) phonemes: *In English, 'p' and 'b' are phonemic.* **-ally** [adv Wa4] **phonemics** [U] the study and description of the phonemic systems of languages

G274 nouns : elements, etc of word-formation and word-use [C]

base the main, usu meaningful, part of a word on which other parts or other words are formed: *'Walk' is the base of 'walks'. The word 'directorship' is formed on the verb base 'direct' and has two suffixes.*

root 1 *loose* a base **2** *precise* the part of a word, often no longer having a meaning, on which it was formed long ago: *In the words 'direct' and 'receive' the parts 'rect' and 'ceive' are roots.*

affix a group of letters or sounds added to the beginning or end of a word or base to change its meaning or its use (as in *un*tie, *mis*understood, kind*ness*, quick*ly*)

prefix an affix that is placed at the beginning of a word or base: *'Re-' meaning 'again' is a prefix in 're-fill/refill'.*

suffix an affix that is placed at the end of the word: *In the word 'directorship', '-or' and '-ship' are suffixes.*

infix an affix that is placed inside a base form

complex word a word that is made up of a base or root and one or more affixes: *'Directorship' is a complex word.*

compound (word) a combination of two or more words that together form a new word with its own meaning: *'Everybody' is a compound of 'every' and 'body', and 'teapot' is a compound of 'tea' and 'pot'.*

combining form *also* **compound(ing) element** a form that combines with a word or part of a word to make a new word, but is not usu considered to be an affix: *The combining form 'Russo-' combines with 'American' to make the* compound word 'Russo-American'. Some people regard '-able' as a suffix; others consider it to be the combining form of the adjective 'able'.

abbreviation a shortened form of a word, often one used in writing (such as *Mr*) [⇒ G161]

acronym a word made up from the first letters of the name of something, esp an organization (such as *NATO* from *North Atlantic Treaty Organization*)

archaism a word or phrase no longer in general use **archaic** [B] of or concerning an archaism **-ally** [adv Wa4]

General grammatical words

G280 personal pronouns

Person	Gender	Subject		Object	
		sing	*pl*	*sing*	*pl*
1st	–	I	we	me	us
2nd	–	you			
3rd	*masculine*	he		him	
	feminine	she	they	her	them
	neuter	it		it	
	impersonal	one	–	one	–

G281 possessive pronouns & adjectives

Person	Gender	Adjectival		Predicative	
		sing	*pl*	*sing*	*pl*
1st	–	my	our	mine	ours
2nd	–	your		yours	
3rd	*masculine*	his		his	
	feminine	her	their	hers	theirs
	neuter	its		its	
	impersonal	one's	–	one's	–

own 1 *usu emph* (*after possessive pronoun*) belonging to or concerning a particular person; not concerning other people: *This is my own book, not theirs. This book is his own, not hers. Mind your own business* (= Don't try to find out about things which do not concern you). **2** by or for oneself: *She makes her own*

clothes. Cook your own food; I won't cook for you!

personal 1 [Wa5] concerning, belonging to, or for the use of a particular person; private: _That is father's personal chair. The letter was marked 'personal'._ **2** [Wa5] done or made directly by a particular person, not by a representative: _The minister made a personal visit to the scene of the fighting._ **3** [Wa5] of the body or appearance: _Personal cleanliness is important for health._ _(fml) She is a woman of great personal beauty._ **4 a** (of things said) directed against (the appearance or character of) a particular person; rude: _making personal remarks about the size of his stomach_ **b** (of people) (in the habit of) directing personal remarks; rude: _You should try to argue without becoming personal._ **5** [Wa5] _tech_ concerning all possessions of a person except land **personally** [adv] **1** [Wa5] directly and not through somebody acting for one: _He is personally in charge of all the arrangements._ **2** [Wa5] speaking for oneself only; as far as oneself is concerned: _She said she didn't like it, but personally I thought it was very good._ **3** [Wa5] as a person; not considered for any qualities that are not personal: _Personally she may be very charming, but will she be a good secretary?_ **4** in a private way: _May I speak to you personally about this difficult matter?_ **5** as directed against oneself in a personal way: _You must not take my remarks about your plan personally._

subjective [B] **1** existing only in someone's mind: _subjective ideas, not scientific facts_ **2** giving the thoughts, ideas, etc of one person, not facts: _a subjective book_ **-ly** [adv] **subjectivity** [U] the state of being subjective

private 1 [Wa5;A] _often fml & emph_ personal; one's own; not shared with others: _This piano is my private property; leave it alone. It's wrong to read other people's private letters without permission._ **2** [Wa5;B] not intended for everyone, but for a particular person or chosen group; not public: _A well-known singer is giving a private performance at the party in our house tomorrow. You mustn't go in there; the door is marked 'Private'._ **3** [Wa5;A;(B)] independent; not connected with government, public service, etc: _Treatment in government hospitals is free; but if you go to a private hospital you must pay._ **4** [Wa5;A;(B)] unofficial; not connected with one's business, work, rank, etc, or with one's public life: _The minister has gone on a private visit to America to see his sister. He's such a busy doctor that he has hardly any time for his private life. He has retired into private life_ (= has ceased to be a public official). **5** [Wa5;A] without rank or official position: _Private citizens aren't allowed to attend some of the meetings of the town council._ **6** [B] quiet; hidden from view; sheltered: _Is there some private corner in the club, where we can sit and talk by ourselves?_ **7** [B] (of a person) (liking to be) away from the society of others: _Please go away; I wish to be private._

She's a very private person. **8** [B] secret; not generally (made) known or intended to be talked about: _Don't repeat what I've told you to anyone; it's private. Only his wife shares in his private thoughts._ **-ly** [adv]: _May I talk to you privately?_ **privacy** [U] **1** the state of being away from the presence, notice, or activities of others: _Most people like privacy when they're dressing or undressing. There's not much privacy in this building; you can hear what a person in the next room is saying quite clearly. He worked in the privacy of his own room._ **2** secrecy; avoidance of public notice: _The greatest privacy is desirable over this unfortunate affair._

G282 reflexive pronouns

Person	Gender	Singular	Plural
1st	–	**myself**	**ourselves**
2nd	–	**yourself**	**yourselves**
3rd	_masculine_	**himself**	
	feminine	**herself**	**themselves**
	neuter	**itself**	
	impersonal	**oneself**	–

self 1 [U] one's own private interests, wishes, hopes, etc: _He did it without any thought of self_ (= without thinking of himself). **2** [C9 _usu sing_] a person's character: _He has changed from his former self_ (= from what he was like before). **self-** [_comb form_] **1** concerning oneself: _She is very self-centred_ (= She thinks only about herself). **2** done by or for oneself: _He is self-educated/a self-educated man._ **3** working by oneself, itself, etc: _The car has a self-starter_ (= a device that allows it to start itself).

G283 _pronouns & adverbs_ : **some-, any-, every-** and **no-**

someone _also_ **somebody 1** a person, esp one who is not known or whom it is not necessary to name: _Ask someone in the other room to go. Somebody told me you were coming; they said you were coming next week._ **2** _infml_ an important person: _He is somebody in this town_ (= he is important here).

something a thing, esp one which is not known or which it is not necessary to name: _Can I have something to eat?_

somewhere [Wa5] to or at a place, esp one which is not known or which it is not necessary to name: _She lives somewhere near here._

somehow [Wa5] in some way, esp one which is not known or which it is not necessary to name: *He did the work somehow; I don't know how. Somehow he managed to do it.*

anyone *also* **anybody** a person, but no particular person: *Ask anyone you like; they will all tell you the same thing. I don't know anybody in that town. She's not just anybody; she's an important woman.*

anything a thing, but it is not known or not important which thing: *Is there anything I can do to help? She didn't say anything.* (*emph*) *She didn't say a single thing.*

anywhere [Wa5] a place, but it is not known or not important which place: *Put the box down anywhere.*

anyhow [Wa5] *usu infml* in any way one wishes: *Do the work anyhow, as long as it is done.*

everyone *also* **everybody** each person; all the people (in a place, group, etc): *She told everyone to come and they all said they would come. Is everybody here now?*

everything each thing; all things: *I did everything myself. She left everything to him/for him to do.*

everywhere [Wa5] each place; all places: *There was trouble everywhere in the city.*

no one *also* **nobody** no person: *There's nobody in the house except me. Don't tell anyone;* (*emph*) *tell no one. I saw nobody at all, not a single person.*

nothing no thing: *I saw nothing interesting in the house. She had nothing to do all day* (*long*).

nowhere [Wa5] no place: *He had nowhere to go.*

G284 relative pronouns, etc

who [pron] **1** (*in asking questions, referring to a person or persons, usu as subject of a sentence*) which person: *Who is he? Who told you that?* **2** (*in indirect speech*) which person: *He told me who did it.* **3** *also* (*infml*) **that** (used to help to describe a person or persons): *This is the man who/that did the work.* **whom** [pron] *esp fml & old use* (the form of **who** when it is the direct or indirect object of a sentence): *Whom did you talk to? To whom did you give the book? This is the man to whom he spoke.* **whose** [pron] of what person: *Whose book is this? The men whose names were called left the room.* **whoever** [pron] **1** any person who: *Whoever told you that is a fool.* **2** no matter who: *I'll find the person who did this, whoever he is!*

USAGE Although **whom** is accepted by most people as more grammatically correct than **who** as an object and after a preposition, in modern informal English **who** is commoner: (*fml*) *Whom did you see?* (*infml*) *Who did you see?* (*fml*) *With whom are you going?* (*infml*) *Who are you going with?*

what **1** [pron] (asking for a particular description or example of a type of thing): *What is his job? What's the time?* **2** [pron] (used for having words said again, when not heard, or when the hearer is surprised): *What did you say? I got up*

at half-past four.—What? **3** [pron] (asking about a purpose or use): *What is money without health? What's this for?* **4** [pron] that one or the (small) amount: *I gave her what I had.* **5** [adv Wa5] in what way; to what degree: *What do you care about it?* **6** [Wa5;A] (*asking about the type of a particular thing or for a particular example*) which: *What fool told you that? What time will you come?* **7** [Wa5;A] how surprisingly good/bad, etc: *What a face he made when he took the medicine! What lovely weather!* **8** [Wa5;A] those (ones) or the few/little: *What money I have is yours.* **whatever** **1** [pron] anything at all: *She does whatever he asks her to do.* **2** [pron] anything (else) like that: *Do it and whatever else needs doing.* **3** [pron] no matter what: *Whatever happens now, I'll never forget you.* **4** [pron] (*used to show surprise*) what: *Whatever will he do next?* **5** [Wa5;F] (*placed after a noun with* **any** *or* **no** *before it*) at all: *Have you any interest whatever in the work?*

which **1** [pron] what person or thing? **2** [pron] *also* the one(s) that: *He lives in the house which/that is opposite ours. That is the house* (*which*) *I built. This is the house* (*which/that*) *I went into/into which I went.* **3** [Wa5;A] what (person or thing) of two or more: *Which house do you live in?* **whichever** **1** [pron] any one that: *Have whichever you want. Have two, whichever you want.* **2** [pron] no matter which: *Whichever you want is yours.* **3** [Wa5;A] any (ones) that: *Take whichever seat you like.* **4** [Wa5;A] no matter which: *It has the same result, whichever way you do it.*

where **1** [adv Wa5] at/to what place, position, etc: *Where can he be? Where will all this trouble lead* (= What result will it have)? **2** [conj] at/to what place, position, etc. *I know where he is. There's no present where there's no money.* **3** [conj] at/to which (place): *the house where we used to live* **4** [conj] at which (point)/in which (position): *He has reached the point where a change is needed.* **5** [conj] at/to any places at all: *Go where you like.* **6** [conj] there where/to where: *Keep him where you can see him. Take him where it's quiet.* **wherever** **1** [adv Wa5] (used to show surprise, etc) where: *Wherever did you get that idea?* **2** [adv Wa5] anywhere at all; any such place: *at home, at school, or wherever* **3** [conj] at/to all places/any place: *Wherever you go, I go too.* **4** [conj] at/to any place at all: *Go wherever you like.* **whither** [adv Wa5] **1** *old use* to where: *Whither is he going?* **2** *rare* to which place: *They go whither they will* (= wherever they want). **whence** [adv Wa5] **1** *old use* from where: *Whence came he?* (= Where did he come from?) **2** *rare* from which place; from where: *They returned to the land* (*from*) *whence they came.* **3** *rare* to the place from which: *They returned whence they came.*

why **1** [adv Wa5] for what reason: *Why did he go there again? I don't know why he went. Why not come with me? That is* (*the reason*) *why I* *am not coming.* **2** [interj] (*used to express surprise, etc*) well: *Why, it's you!*

how [adv Wa5; conj] **1** in what way: *How did she do it? Tell me how she did it.* **2** to what degree: *How hot is it? How many were there? Ask him how hot it was.* **3** in what condition: *How is he now; is he feeling better?* **4** for what reason; why: *How is it (that) she can't come?* **5** what is your opinion about: *How do you find life in the country?* **6** *emph*: *How wonderful to see you!*

however 1 [adv Wa5] *also more fml* **howsoever** to what degree: *However cold it is, she always goes swimming.* **2** [conj] in whatever way: *In one's own home one can act however one wishes.*

when [⇒ L259]

that [conj] *not fml* **1** who or which: *It's Jean that makes the decisions here. Did you see the letter that came today? He's the greatest man that ever lived!* **2** whom or which: *He's not the man (that) he was! That's the man (that) I was talking about.* **3** in, on, for, or at which: *the day (that) she arrived; the speed (that) she drives at* **4** (used to introduce some further information): *(The fact) that you don't like her has nothing to do with it. There is no proof that he killed her.* **5** *lit* (expressing desire, etc): *Oh, that I could fly!*

USAGE (1) When the word before **that** is not the subject of the following clause, **that** is usu left out. (2) **that** is often used instead of **who**, but with **any**, **only** and superlatives, **that** is commoner: *Any person that has the money can join the group. He's the only man that can do it. She's the prettiest girl that I've ever seen.*

G285 determiners and demonstratives, etc

the [det] **1** (showing that something or someone has already been spoken or written about): *That is the man I saw yesterday. Is that the book/girl you told me about?* **2** (showing that something or someone is already known to the speaker, hearer, etc): *Put the books on the table. Is this the book you want?—Yes; that's the book.* **3** (used with things, places, people, etc because they are well-known): *I must go to the bank and get some money. The roads are full of cars today.* **4** (showing that something or someone is the only one of its kind: *The sun went down.* **5** (showing that the speaker or writer means one particular thing): *What is the name of that book? He sailed across the Atlantic Ocean in a little boat. The Nile is a river in Africa.* **6** (used for particular sets of things, esp the parts of the body, houses, machines, instruments, etc): *the head; the back of the car; the side of the house; playing the piano* **7** (*esp with adj*) all those of a stated kind: *She helps the old and the poor.* **8** (showing a species (= a special kind of animal, plant, etc)): *The cat is an animal and the rose is a flower* (= Cats are animals and roses are flowers). **9** (showing the relation between one thing and another): *This*

car does 30 miles to the gallon (= a measurement of petrol). **10** (*with compar*) by a stated amount: *The more she has, the more she wants. The bigger the house is, the better he likes it.* **11** (with superl): *This is the oldest house in the town.*

this 1 [det] being the one of two or more people or things that is here, nearer in place, time, thought, etc: *You look in this box (here), and I'll look in that box (there). Take these books to his room, please. Where is this place you want to go to? He is very busy these days* (= nowadays). *This time last year he was in China.* **2** [det] being the one or amount stated, shown or understood: *I saw Mrs Jones this morning* (= before midday today). *Have you heard this story? Who's this John Smith everybody is talking about?* **3** [det] *infml* (esp in telling stories) a certain: *Then this man came up to me and said . . . There were these two men, John and Bill, and . . .* **4** [pron] one of two or more people, things, kinds, or ideas that is nearer in place, time, thought, etc: *This is your book/my sister Jane. Take this, not that. Are these what you want? Who is this? — This is John Smith speaking.* **5** [pron] a thing, idea, etc, that is understood, stated, going to be stated, etc: *Who told you this? Wait till you've heard this! What's this? This is what you must do . . .* **6** [pron] (not used with people) the one or kind here: *Please take this (box).* (Compare: *Please take this child.*) **7** [adv Wa5] *infml* so; this degree: *She's never been out this late before* (= as late as this before). *Cut off about this much thread* (= as much thread as this). **like this** in such a way; in the way shown **What's all this?** What is the trouble, matter,etc, here?

that 1 [det] being the one of two or more people or things that is there, further away in place, time, thought, etc: *You look in that box (there), and I'll look in this one (here). Take those books to his room, please. In those days* (= at that time; then) *he was very busy, but not now.* **2** [det] being the one or amount stated, shown, or understood: *Have you really eaten all that chocolate we bought yesterday? Who's that man she was talking to?* **3** [pron] one of two or more people, things, kinds, or ideas that is further in place, time, thought, etc: *That is your book/his sister Jane. Take that, not this. Are those what she wants? Who is that? — That is John Smith.* **4** [pron] a thing, idea, etc, that is understood, stated, etc: *Who told you that? I'd never heard that before. Who's that? — It's me. That is what you should do.* **5** [pron] (not used with people) **a** the one or kind there: *Please take that (box).* (Compare: *Please take that child.*) *Just look at that!* **b** the one or kind: *The best coal is that from Newcastle. Have you any more apples? — What, have you finished all those I gave you?* **6** [adv Wa5] *infml* so; to such a degree: *I like him but not (all) that much.* **7** [conj] often more *fml* (used for introducing various kinds of clause): *It is true (that) he's French. I'll make certain (that)* *he comes. I believe (that) you want to leave. He was so rude (that) she refused to speak to him. Bring it closer so (that) I can see it better. I'll give you it on condition (that) you don't break it. The reason was (that) he was afraid.* **after that** after what had happened; then **and all that** and so on: *He used to take drugs and all that when he was younger.* **at that** additionally; besides; as well: *It's an idea, and a good one at that!* **like that** in such a way: *Do they always dance like that in France?* **that is (to say)** in other words; more correctly **that's that** that is the end of the matter; that settles the matter **with that,** *also* **at that** when he had done that; then: *he kissed her and with that he left.*

G286 conjunctions & adverbs : and, etc

and [conj] **1** (*used to show connection or addition, esp of words of the same type or sentences of the same importance*) as well as; together with; with; also; besides: *He started to shout and sing. The boy and girl went for a walk. He was cold and hungry.* **2** (used to express result or explanation): *Water the seeds and they will grow. Work hard and you might pass the examination* (= If you work hard, you might pass). *She was sick and took some medicine* (compare: *She took some medicine and was sick*). **3** (used to join repeated words and suggest continuing time, action, state, etc): *We ran and ran. We waited for hours and hours. It came nearer and nearer.* **4** (*after* **come, go, try,** etc) to: *Come and have tea with me. You'll go and see her.*

then [adv Wa5] **1** (and) the next thing: *He left and then he came back. He wrote some letters; then he dug the garden; then he cleaned the car.* **2** if that is so: *He's hungry.—Then he should eat something.* **3** in addition: *I was there; then there were my mother and father and my brother.*

than [conj] (used after the compar of an adj or adv): *He is bigger than she is/than her. They work more quickly than we do/than us.*

USAGE In modern English *'He is bigger than her'* is commoner than *'He is bigger than she'*, which is generally considered formal, pompous, or old-fashioned.

so 1 [conj] with the result or purpose that: *I had broken my glasses, so I couldn't see what was happening. I've packed you a little food so you won't get hungry.* **2** [conj] therefore: *I had a headache, so I went to bed.* **3** [conj] (*used at the beginning of a sentence*) **a** (with weak meaning): *So here we are again.* **b** (to express discovery): *So now I see what's happening!* **c** what if?; What does it matter that?: *So, I made a mistake; what are you going to do about it?* **4** [Wa5;F] in agreement with the facts; true: *Some things just aren't so. If what you say is really so, I'll have to change my mind.* **5** [F] (used in place of an adjective already stated): *Of all the careless people no one is more so than Bill. He's clever—probably too much so for his*

own good. **just so** *not fml* **1** as long as; if only: *Just so he gets his three meals a day he doesn't care what happens.* **2** arranged exactly and tidily: *If everything is not just so, he'll be angry.*

thus [adv Wa5] *esp fml & formerly* in this way; because of this: *Do it thus. We have plenty of money and workers; thus we can hope to do more next year.*

therefore [adv Wa5] for that reason: *He had gone; she therefore gave the money to me.*

accordingly [adv Wa5] *usu fml* therefore, esp by agreement: *He was asked to go, and accordingly he left at once.*

consequently [adv Wa5] *usu fml* because of this; as a result of this; therefore: *They cannot do the work; consequently, we must find another company.* **in consequence** *very fml* consequently

hence [adv Wa5] *fml* consequently: *This work will cost over £1 million, which is more than we can afford; hence, we cannot do it at this time.*

furthermore [adv Wa5] *fml & emph* additionally: *They cannot do it, and furthermore no one else appears to want to do it either.*

G287 conjunctions & adverbs, etc : but, etc

but [conj] (used to make a contrasting statement): *She is rich but he is poor. He is poor but (he is) honest. She is rich but he is not. He wanted to go, but she didn't.* **all but** very nearly: *The work is all but finished.* **but for** without: *She would have died but for him* (= He saved her life; without his help she would have died). **nothing but** only; nothing other than: *That child causes nothing but trouble.*

although [conj] (*used at the beginning of a clause*) but: *Although I don't want to (come), I'll come/I'll come, although I don't want to (come)* (= I don't want to come, but I'll come).

though [conj] *infml* **1** (*used at the end of a clause*) but: *He is poor; he is honest though. I've never eaten this kind of food before; I like it though.* **2** although: *I'll go, though I don't want to. Though it's expensive, I'll buy it.*

even if/though [conj] *emph* although: *I want him to go even if he doesn't (want to go)!*

in spite of [prep] in opposition to: *In spite of the fact that they are poor, they are honest/In spite of being poor, they are honest* (= They are poor but they are honest).

despite [prep] *fml* in spite of: *Despite being poor, they are honest. We'll go, despite the rain* (= We'll go, even if it is raining).

however [conj] *fml* but: *He is poor; however he is honest/He is, however, honest/He is honest, however. I have never eaten this kind of food before; I like it, however. I have no wish to go; however, I shall go.*

nevertheless [conj; adv Wa5] *often emph* however: *He is poor; nevertheless he is honest/he is, nevertheless, honest/He is honest, nevertheless.*

nonetheless [adv Wa5] **1** no less (than others):

He is nonetheless honest for being poor.
2 nevertheless: *You may tell me not to come, but I'll come nonetheless!*
even so [adv Wa5] however; although that is true: *He is poor but even so he is honest. He does not want me to go, but even so I'm going! Her book has many faults; even so, it is worth reading.*
still [adv Wa5] *often emot* **1** even so: *We knew he was unlikely to win, but it's still unfair that he didn't get a higher mark.* **2** however: *It's a very unpleasant affair; still, we can't change it. He's poor; still, he's honest!*

G288 *conjunctions* : if, etc

if 1 (showing a condition): *(future) If he goes, I'll go with him. (past) If he had gone, I would have gone with him. (possibility) If he were to go, I would go with him/If he went, I would go with him.* **2** *(for politeness)* please: *If you (would be so good as to) give me the money, I'll buy the books* (= Please give me the money and I'll buy the books). **3** *(for general statements)* when(ever): *If the shops are closed, you can't buy anything.* **4** (with negative, showing surprise): *Well, if it isn't my old friend Bill!* **5** although: *He's friendly, if a little too talkative* (= although he talks too much). **as if 1** *also* **as though** in a way that suggests: *She talks as if/though she knows all about everything. He isn't careful; it's as if he doesn't want to do well.* **2** *infml* but not: *She hasn't asked you to her party.—As if I cared!* (= But I don't care) **if only** (showing a strong wish): *If only he had helped us, we wouldn't be in these difficulties now!—Ah yes; if only!* **only if** (showing a special condition): *I'll come only if you really need me.*
whether [conj] **1** if ... (or not): *He asked me whether she was coming (or not). He wondered whether to come (or not). It was uncertain whether he would come (or not). The decision whether to see her (or not) was mine alone. I worry about whether I hurt her feelings.* **2 a** no matter if ... (or) ... : *I shall go, whether you come with me or stay at home.* **b** (no one knows) if it can be ... (or) ... *(esp in the phrs* **whether by accident or design** (= through luck or on purpose)): *Whether by accident or design they met. Whether through choice or obedience I don't know but he certainly did all the work very well.*
unless [conj] if ... not: *I won't go unless you go too* (= If you do not go, I won't go). *Unless he's a fool, he will do it* (= He will do it, if he is not a fool).
supposing *also* **assuming (that)** *(in proposing possibilities)* if: *Supposing he wants to come, what will you do? Assuming that he wants to get to London today, he must leave now.*
on condition (that) *(in stating conditions clearly)* if: *I'll come on condition that the work is done immediately.*

G289 *conjunctions & prepositions, etc* : giving reasons

because [conj] for the reason that: *I did it because she asked me to (do it). Because she asked me to do it, I did it. Why did you go?—Because I wanted to. Just because he says nothing, it doesn't mean he's happy.*
USAGE After '*the reason is*', a clause beginning with **that** is preferred: *The reason (why) we're going is that my mother is ill* (= We're going because my mother is ill).
since [conj] *(in giving a reason as a result of some thing)* because: *Since you ask, I will tell you why. I'll tell you why, since you ask. Since you're tired, I'll do the work.*
as [conj] *(esp in giving a reason when it is obvious or thought to be obvious)* because: *As it's sunny, I'll go for a walk. As she didn't come, we left without her.*
because of [prep] by reason of: *Because of her kindness to them the children like her very much* (= The children like her very much because she is kind to them). *Because of his long illness, he cannot work very hard now.*
on account of [prep] *sometimes more fml* because of: *On account of the rise in prices, we must also charge more. He couldn't come, on account of being busy.*
due to [prep] directly caused by: *The trouble was all due to his bad behaviour. She can't come due to illness. Due to bad weather, all the buses were late.*
owing to [prep] (at the beginning of phrases) due to: *She can't come, owing to illness. Owing to bad weather, all the buses were late.*
through [prep] *emph* because of; due to: *It all happened through his carelessness!*
from [prep] as a result of: *He died from drinking too much for too long.*
sake [C] **1 for the sake of** *also* **for someone's/something's sake a** for the good or advantage of: *If you won't do it for your own sake* (= to help yourself), *then do it for my sake* (= to please me). *For both our sakes, please do as I ask.* **b** for the purpose of: *Please listen: I'm not talking just for talking's sake or for the sake of hearing myself! Just for argument's sake, let's suppose ...* **2 for God's/Christ's/goodness/ pity('s) sake** *infml* (used to give force to an urgent request or sometimes an expression of annoyance): *For goodness sake, stop arguing! What do you want from me, for God's sake?*

G290 intensifiers, etc

certainly [adv] without doubt: *The team will certainly lose if he doesn't play. Can I come? —Certainly (you can).*
definitely [adv] without any possible doubt: *The team will definitely lose if he doesn't play. Can I come?—You definitely must/Definitely!*
of course *usu emph* [adv Wa5] **1** certainly: *Can I come?—Of course (you can). Of course he's*

the best man for the job! **2** naturally: *I told them, of course, that I could not do it. He came too, of course.*

indeed [adv Wa5] *usu fml & emph, esp formerly* (*said in answer to a speaker who has suggested the answer*) certainly: *Were you pleased? —Indeed I was (pleased)! Lovely weather, isn't it?—It is indeed (lovely weather).*

G291 interjections, etc : **greetings and farewells**

hello, *also* **hallo,** **hullo** *BrE infml* **1** (used for greeting): *Hello, everybody! He didn't say hullo to me.* **2** (showing surprise): *Hallo, what's this?* **3** (in answering the telephone): *Hello, 441 2894.*

hi *also* **hi there** *infml, esp AmE* hello: *Hi, everybody!*

how do you do *fml* hello: *My name is John Smith; how do you do?—How do you do? I'm David Green.*

goodbye **1** (used for leaving people): *Goodbye, everybody! She said goodbye to them.* **2** [C] an act or occasion of saying goodbye: *When all the goodbyes had been said, she felt very sad.* **'bye** *infml* goodbye: *'Bye, everybody!*

farewell *lit & old use* **1** goodbye: *Farewell, my friends; it is time to depart.* **2** [C] an act or occasion of saying farewell: *They said their farewells.*

cheerio *BrE infml* goodbye: *Cheerio, everybody! He said cheerio and left.*

cheers *esp BrE infml* **1** cheerio **2** (said before starting an esp alcoholic drink with friends): *Cheers!* **3** thank you: *'That's just what I want. Cheers! she said when I gave her the present.*

G292 adverbs **yes and no**

yes (used to show agreement, willingness, etc): *Are you going?—Yes/Yes, I am. She said yes.*

yes-man [C] *deprec infml* a person who always agrees with his employer, superior, etc

aye *esp ScotE, N EngE & formerly* yes: *Can he do it?—Aye, he can.* **aye-aye** (used on ships when obeying orders): *Move those boxes! —Aye-aye, sir!*

uh-huh *infml* yes: *Are you going?—Uh-huh.*

no (used to show disagreement, unwillingness, etc): *Are you going?—No/No, I'm not. She said no.*

nay *esp N EngE & formerly* no

G293 interjections in general

ah 1 (used to show surprise, interest, etc): *Ah, so that's what he wants!* **2** (used when speaking slowly and thinking as one speaks): *I think that—ah—he should tell them to—ah—come here.* **ah-hah** *emph* ah (*def* 1): *Ah-hah, now I understand what he wants!*

ahem (usual spelling for a sound made when clearing the throat, disagreeing, giving a quiet warning, etc): *Ahem, excuse me, please.*

bah (used to show anger about, dislike for, etc something said, etc): *Bah! What a fool he is!*

eh (used to show surprise, doubt, or to ask for agreement): *What do you think about it, eh?*

oh (used to show surprise, fear, etc): *I'm going too.—Oh, are you? He's coming.—Oh, no!*

ouch *also* **ow** (used to express sudden pain): *Ouch, that hurt! Ow, don't do that!*

phew (used to show strong feeling, surprise, dislike, etc): *Phew, it's hot, isn't it?*

ugh (used to suggest disgust): *Ugh, what a horrible thing to do!*

H

Substances, materials, objects, and equipment

Substances and materials generally

H1 nouns : substances and materials

substance 1 [C] what things are formed out of: *What kind of substance is that?—It's a kind of wood. Solid substances are different from liquid substances.* **2** [U] (*fig*) strength, importance, wealth, etc: *He likes a drink with substance in it. He is a man of substance.* **3** (*fig*) truth: *There is no substance in what he says about her.*

material [U; C] any substance, usu solid, from which something is or may be made: *Rubber is a widely-used material. When building materials cost more the price of houses increases.*

matter [U] the material which makes up the world and everything in space which can be seen or touched

stuff [U] *infml & genl* usu solid substance; material: *What kind of stuff is that?—It's like paper. This isn't good stuff to work with. Can I have more of that stuff over there, please?*

resources [P] **1** materials, etc which a person, country, etc has, esp in a natural state: *Scotland has great (natural) resources—oil, water, trees, coal, and so on.* **2** wealth; possessions: *What resources does he have?*

H2 nouns : nature and composition

nature [U; C] the qualities which make something or someone different from others: *What is the nature of the new chemical? The natures of these chemicals are very different (from each other).*

composition [U] the way in which something is formed: *He was studying the composition of the local rock. What is the composition of your team?*

H3 adjectives : simple, compound, and complex [B]

simple [Wa1, 3] (of a single whole) consisting of only one or a few parts: *This is a simple substance; it is not made out of other substances simpler than itself.* **-ply** [adv] **-plicity, -pleness** [U]

complex [Wa5] (of a single whole) consisting of many closely related or connected parts: *This is a complex substance; it is made up of many simple substances. There is a complex network of roads connecting Glasgow and Edinburgh.* **-xity, -xness** [U]

compound [Wa5] (of a single whole) consisting of two or more separable parts, substances, etc: *This is a compound substance; it is made up of at least two substances simpler than itself.*

composite [Wa5] (of something whole) made up of several parts, each of which is complete in itself: *The material is a composite substance formed of several other materials, each of which is itself complex.* **-ness** [U]

H4 nouns & adjectives : elements and constituents [C]

element any of more than 100 simple substances that consist of atoms of only one kind and that, alone or in combination, make up all substances: *Both hydrogen and oxygen are elements of water, which is formed when they combine, and so water is not itself an element.*

constituent [*also* Wa5;A] (being) one of the parts that make up a whole: *What are the constituents of this material?* What are its constituent materials?

component [*also* Wa5;A] *esp tech* (being) any of the parts that make up a whole (esp of a machine or system): *Have you got all the components you need to make the machine? The component pieces were all provided.*

base [C] a substance which can combine with an acid [⇒ H73] to form a salt

ingredient (esp of food) one of the parts of a mixture: *What ingredients do you use? There are several ingredients in this plan.*

factor one of the forces, conditions, influences, etc that act with others to cause a result: *The speed of their work is a factor we must not forget.*

feature an important, or special, etc, part of anything: *One of the features of the new car is its safety. Which features in the new car interest you most?*

item one thing among a set or on a list: *Number*

the items from 1 to 10. Which item do we take first? That book is a costly item. **itemize**, **-ise** [T1] to express (a set of things) one by one as items: *Please itemize everything you bought.*

detail [*also* U] a small part, component, fact, item, etc of something larger: *He worked well and took care of all the details. When we should go, what we should take with us, what we could eat, and so on. Some of the details in the picture were not as well painted as others. There is a lot of detail in that picture. The detail in the film was good. He told us what happened in detail* (= *fully*). *Don't go into detail(s); just tell me the main points.* **detail** [T1] to describe fully: *He detailed everything that happened.*

H5 *nouns* : **atoms and molecules** [C]

atom 1 the smallest piece of an element that still has the same qualities and can combine with other elements to form molecules: *Two hydrogen atoms combine with one atom of oxygen to produce a water molecule.* **2** *infml* a very small bit: *There's not an atom of truth in that statement.*

nucleus the central part of an atom

molecule the smallest part of any substance that can be separated from the substance without losing its own chemical form and qualities

particle a piece of matter smaller than, and part of, an atom

electron a particle with a negative charge of electricity, going round the nucleus of an atom [⇨ H201–2]

H6 *nouns* : **chemicals and minerals** [C]

chemical any substance used or produced by chemistry; any of the substances classed as elements or the compounds formed from them: *Oxygen is the chemical most necessary to human life. What chemicals do you need to make that kind of gas? He works in a chemical factory.*

mineral any of various esp solid substances that are formed naturally in the earth (such as stone, coal, salt, oil, etc), esp as obtained from the ground for man's use: *Some countries are richer in minerals than others. The mineral resources* [⇨ HI] *of that country are very great.*

compound something consisting of a combination of two or more parts, substances, etc, esp a chemical substance consisting of at least two different elements combined in such a way that it usu has properties different from those of the elements from which it is made

composite something consisting of several parts, each of which is complete in itself: *These rocks are mineral composites.*

amalgam 1 *fml* a mixture or combination **2** [*also* U] *tech* a mixture of metals [⇨ H67, 68] one of

which is mercury: *Fill the tooth with amalgam, not gold.*

H7 *nouns, etc* : **solids, liquids, and gases**

solid [C] a substance that cannot easily change its shape and at lower temperatures does not usu flow: *Metals are solids, but when heated to a high temperature become liquids.*

liquid [C; U] a substance that flows more or less easily: *Water and oil are both liquids.*

fluid [C; U] **1** a liquid, esp when it flows **2** any substance that flows, esp easily

gas 1 [U; C] a substance like air, which is not solid or liquid: *There are several kinds of gas in air. Air contains various gases.* **2** [U] a substance of this type which is burnt in the home to supply heat for warmth and cooking and (formerly) for light: *Streets in Britain used to be lit by gas.*

bubble 1 [C] a thin ball of liquid containing air: *The child was enjoying himself making and bursting soap bubbles. Bubbles rose on the surface of the boiling liquid.* **2** [IØ (*up*)] to send up bubbles: *The hot liquid began to bubble (up).*

H8 *adjectives* : **relating to materials, etc, generally** [B]

material [Wa5] **1** of or concerning matter or substance: *Is the material world opposed to the world of the mind and spirit? The storm did a great deal of material damage* (= to buildings and such). **2** of the body rather than the mind or soul: *She was too poor to satisfy her children's material needs* (= food, clothing, etc).

elemental [Wa5] **1** of or concerning natural forces, such as wind, rain, etc **2** simple in form, like an element

mineral [Wa5] of, connected with, containing, or having the nature of minerals; belonging to the class of minerals: *Salt is a mineral substance. Many African countries have great mineral wealth.*

chemical [Wa5] of, connected with, used in, or made by chemistry: *A chemical change takes place in paper when it burns.*

molecular [Wa5] *tech* of, connected with, or produced by a molecule [⇨ H5]

atomic [Wa5] **1** of or concerning an atom or atoms **2** working on or moving by atomic power: *This is an atomic ship.* **3** possessing atom bombs: *The USA and the USSR are atomic powers.*

nuclear [Wa5] **1** of, concerning, or being a nucleus [⇨ H5] **2** of, concerning, or using the nucleus of an atom, atomic energy, or the atom bomb: *They built a nuclear power station. She is afraid of nuclear war. He is a nuclear scientist.*

solid [Wa2] **1** (of substances) not changing form easily at lower temperatures; not liquid or gaseous: *Wood is a solid substance.* **2** of the same material throughout; not hollow: *The wall was made of solid wood.* **3** (*fig*) *infml* without a break: *He waited for them for two solid hours but they didn't come.* **4** (*fig*) dependable or sensible: *He is a very solid businessman. That is a good solid piece of work.* **solidity** [U] the quality or state of being firm, not hollow, well made, dependable or in agreement: *I don't think much of the solidity of this report/this wall.* **solidify** [T1; IØ] to (cause to) become solid, hard, or firm: *Cold should solidify the mixture. Opinion on the question had begun to solidify.* **solidification** [U] the act of solidifying

liquid (of substances) flowing or moving easily; not solid or gaseous: *Water is a liquid substance.* **liquefy** [T1;IØ] to (cause to) become liquid *liquefaction* [U]

fluid 1 having the quality of flowing, like liquids, air, gas, etc; not solid **2** (*fig*) unsettled; not fixed: *We have only just begun to plan the work and our ideas on the subject are still fluid.* **-ity** [U]

viscous (of liquids) thick or sticky; not flowing easily **-ness** [U] **viscosity** [U] *tech*

gaseous of or like gas

gassy [Wa1] full of (a) gas: *I like natural fruit juice, but not gassy drinks.*

H9 *nouns* : **oil, jelly, and glue** [U; C]

oil any of several types of fatty liquid (from animals, plants, or under the ground), some used for making machines run easily, and others for cooking and burning, etc: *He put oil on all the moving parts of the machine, to make them turn more smoothly. There are many oils in use today.*

grease 1 any thick substance like oil: *Put some grease on the wheels, so they don't make that noise when they move. He puts grease on his hair* (= to make it shiny). **2** animal fat when soft after having been melted: *Candles are made out of grease. There was a lot of grease on the plates.*

paste any soft wet mixture of powder and liquid that is easily shaped or spread: *This is where they mix the paste for toothpaste.*

jelly any clear, almost soft substance which shakes or yields when touched: *She likes eating cakes and jellies. He shook like a jelly; he was very frightened.*

gelatin(e) a substance, used esp in cooking, which has no colour or taste and is obtained from bones, etc, which melts in hot water and becomes jelly when cold

gum 1 any of several kinds of sticky substance obtained from the stems of some trees and bushes **2** a sticky substance used for sticking things together

glue a sticky substance which is obtained from animal bones or fish and is used for joining things together

H10 *verbs* : **oiling, greasing, and gluing**

oil [T1] **1** to put oil on or in to make parts work or run more easily: *He oiled the machine.* **2** to rub oil on or into: *She oiled the table to preserve the wood.*

grease [T1] to put grease on: *Grease the tin with butter before baking the cake. The swimmers greased their bodies to keep warm in the cold water.*

lubricate [T1] to make (a machine, etc) work better by putting oil or grease on moving parts: *The car needs lubricating.* **lubrication** [U] the act of lubricating: *Regular lubrication keeps a car in good running condition.* **lubricant** [C; U] an oil used in lubricating; any substance that lubricates

paste [X9] to stick or fasten with paste: *Please paste these sheets of paper together.*

gum [X9] to stick (something somewhere) with gum: *The actor gummed on a false beard. She gummed the picture into her book. Gum the envelope down properly before posting it.*

glue [T1] to join with glue: *He glued the pieces of wood together.*

H11 *verbs* : **sticking and adhering**

stick 1 [IØ (*to, together*)] (of one thing) to become fixed (to another thing) with glue [⇒ H9] or any substance like it: *The paper stuck to the wall. The paper is sticking; it won't come off. The papers stick together.* **2** [X9] to cause to become fixed like this: *Stick the papers to the wall. Stick the stamp on the letter.*

adhere [IØ] *esp fml* to stick firmly: *This surface will adhere to that one; it adheres well.*

cohere [IØ] **1** to stick together; be united: *The party must cohere if it's to win the next election.* **2** [Wv6] to be reasonably and naturally connected, esp in thought: *Do his religious and political beliefs cohere?* **cohesion** [U] **1** the act or state of sticking together tightly: *The social and political cohesion of this country is the result of history. We need more moral cohesion if we're to defeat the enemy.* **2** (in science) the force which holds parts of a substance or body together **cohesive 1** producing cohesion: *Cohesive forces in society* **2** *tech* tending to cohere: *Is water cohesive by nature or not?* **-ly** [adv] **-ness** [U]

H12 *adjectives, etc* : **relating to oil, grease, glue, etc** [B]

oily [Wa1] of, concerning, like, or covered in oil: *The water looked oily. His hands were oily after working on the engine of his car.* (*fig*) *The man had an oily manner/smile, and so I didn't trust him.* **-liness** [U]

oleaginous [Wa5] *fml* oily; like oil: *The liquid was oleaginous.*

gelatinous [Wa5] of, concerning, or like gelatin: *He used a gelatinous material.*

greasy [Wa1] **1** covered with or containing grease: *I don't like greasy food or washing greasy plates. He has rather greasy hair.* **2** slippery: *The roads are greasy after the rain.* **-sily** [Adv] **-siness** [U]

sticky [Wa1] **1** tending to stick to something: *This paper is sticky; is there glue on it?* **2** (*fig*) difficult: *This is a sticky matter.*

gluey [Wa1] **1** sticky like glue **2** covered with glue

adhesive 1 [Wa5] able to stick or cause sticking **2** [C] an adhesive substance, such as a sticky liquid (**glue**) [⇨ H66]

H13 *nouns* : **rubbish and waste** [U]

rubbish 1 things which have been, will be, or should be thrown away; anything useless: *Get rid of that rubbish. Put the rubbish in the rubbish bin* (= a special box, etc, for rubbish before it is taken away). **2** (*fig*) *deprec* stupid and useless ideas, words, etc: *What rubbish; I don't believe it! She talks rubbish all the time.*

garbage *esp AmE* **1** waste material; rubbish: *The street is covered with old cans and other kinds of garbage.* **2** (*fig*) *deprec* rubbish: *He's talking a load of garbage; you can see how he doesn't know anything about the subject.*

refuse things which have been used and have been, can be, or will be thrown away: *When is your refuse collected? People collect the refuse twice a week here.*

waste [*also* C *often pl*] used, damaged, or unwanted matter: *A lot of poisonous waste comes/wastes come from that chemical factory. Waste from the body passes out from the bowels.*

scrap material which cannot be used for its original purpose but which may have some value: *Sell that car for scrap/for its scrap value* (= as metal to be used again). *He did his writing on scrap paper first.*

trash *esp emot* rubbish; something which is considered of low quality, value, etc: *Put the trash in that box. 'That book is just trash,' she said.*

litter [*also* S9] useless things, esp when thrown away, lying where they should not be, etc: *The streets used to be nice and clean but now they're full of litter/now they are a litter of broken bottles and bits of paper.*

lumber *esp BrE* useless or unwanted articles, such as furniture, stored away somewhere

junk *infml* **1** useless things; things no longer wanted: *What will you pay him for all this old junk?* **2** *deprec* material of poor quality: *His latest book is junk.*

salvage useful or valuable property saved from being destroyed: *They held a sale of salvage from the wrecked ship. The children saved old metal milk bottle tops as salvage.*

H14 *nouns* : **sediment and debris** [U]

sediment [*also* S] *esp tech* solid material that settles to the bottom of a liquid: *There was (a) brown sediment in the bottom of the cup.* [⇨ H63]

sludge 1 thick sediment or mud **2** *tech* the product of the treatment of sewage [⇨ D42] **3** dirty waste oil in an engine

residue [*also* S] what is left of anything after some of it, usu the more important part, has been taken away: *There was a residue of liquid at the bottom of the bottle.* **residual** [Wa5;B] being a residue: *After the heavy rains residual water took a long time to go away.* **-ly** [adv]

rubble broken stones, bricks, pieces of walls, etc: *After the war many cities were full of rubble/of the rubble of buildings.*

debris *Fr* **1** the remains of something broken to pieces or destroyed; ruins: *After the bombing there was a lot of debris everywhere.* **2** *esp tech* heaps of pieces of rock

detritus *tech* **1** heavier matter which sinks or falls down to the bottom, as from sewage when it is being treated chemically **2** substances rubbed away from rock by the wind or by water, such as sand

effluent [*also* C] *esp tech* a stream of usu dirty water flowing from a factory, sewage system, waste pipes, etc: *Industrial effluent often causes a problem to people's health.*

H15 *verbs* : **getting rid of and scrapping things** [T1]

[ALSO ⇨ D89]

get rid of to put, take, or send away (something or someone that one no longer wants): *Please get rid of all these old papers.*

dispose of [v prep] *genl* to get rid of (something or someone), esp officially: *They dispose of the city's waste in the sea.*

discard to put away (something one does not need): *He discarded his clothes and jumped into the water. You can't just discard people like old clothes!*

scrap *esp emph* **1** to get rid of as no longer useful or wanted; discard: *The weather was bad so they scrapped the plan to go camping.* **2** to make into scrap: *They scrapped all battleships built before 1942.*

junk *infml & emph* to get rid of as worthless: *Let's junk this old plan and think of a new one.*

dismantle *tech* to take (esp a machine) to pieces: *He dismantled one engine and used its parts to mend the other engines.*

cast to let fall or allow to come off, esp as part of a natural action: *The snake cast its skin. The horse cast a shoe.*

moult *BrE*, **molt** *AmE* [I0; (T1)] (of animals and birds) to lose hair, feathers, etc, at certain times so that new hair, feathers, etc, can grow

shed 1 to cast or moult: *The snake shed its skin. The dog is shedding hair everywhere. The trees* *are shedding their leaves.* **2** to give out: *That lamp sheds a good light.*

H16 *verbs* : **covering and littering** [T1]

cover 1 to be or lie on the surface of; spread over (something): *Dust covered all the furniture. The road was covered with sand. Cats are covered with fur. He is covered in spots; I think he's ill.* **2** to place or spread something upon, over, or in front of (something) in order to protect, hide, etc: *The noise was so loud that she covered her ears with her hands. Mother covered the table with a cloth. He covered over the letter with a book so that she couldn't see it.*
litter to cover or make untidy with litter [⇒ H13]: *Old paper littered the room. Stop littering the place with those old papers!*

H17 *verbs* : **including and containing** [T1]

[ALSO ⇒ D81]

include 1 to have as a part or member; containing in addition to other parts or members: *The price includes postal charges. When I say two hours, that includes time for eating. There were six people, including three women. All of us went including me/me included.* **2** to put in with something else: *I included eggs on the list of things to buy.*
cover to include, esp in planning, discussion, etc: *We covered everything at the last meeting; we don't need another meeting. Can we cover all the points before three o'clock?*
count *usu not fml* to include: *There are five people here, (not) counting me.* **count in** [v adv] to include in a group: *Count me in; I'm coming too!* **count out** [v adv] not to include in a group: *Count me out; I'm not doing it!*
contain to have within itself: *This bottle contains two glasses of beer. This book contains important information. How much does this packet contain? Orange juice contains things which help keep you healthy.* **content** [U] what is contained in something, esp the main ideas, facts, etc in a book, article, etc: *The content of the book is very good but I don't like the pictures.* **contents** [P] the things contained in something: *The police were interested in the contents of the murdered woman's bag/stomach. Look at the contents page of the book.*
hold [Wv6] to be able to contain: *How much water does the pan hold? The car can hold four adults.* (*fig*) *Life holds many surprises.*
have in [Wv6] *not fml* **1** [v prep D1] (of a container) to keep within (itself): *What does the box have in it?* **2** [v adv] *also* **have got in** to keep a supply of (something): *Does she have enough sugar in* (= in the house, shop, etc)?
involve to cause (someone) to be included in or troubled by something: *Don't involve me in your fights, please.* **involvement 1** [U] the con-

dition of being involved **2** [C] something which involves one: *No more involvements, please; I have enough to do.*
implicate 1 [*usu pass*] to involve, esp in something bad: *I didn't want to get implicated.* To show that (someone else) is also to blame: *The prisoners implicated two other people in the crime.* **2 implication** [U] the condition of being implicated

H18 *verbs* : **excluding** [T1]

exclude 1 to keep out (from somewhere): *The meeting was secret and everyone except the committee members was excluded. They excluded children from (joining) the club.* **2** not to cover among the rest: *You're all guilty; I can exclude no one from blame. There were 30 people in the hotel, excluding the hotel workers.* **3** to shut out from the mind (a reason or possibility): *We can exclude the possibility that he did it.*
except to exclude (someone or something) from something, esp for a particular reason: *I except him from my complaint; he worked well, although the others didn't.*
keep out [v adv] to prevent (something or someone) from entering: *This notice should keep unwelcome visitors out. The notice read: 'Keep out!' These windows are very good; they keep the cold air out and the warm air in.*

H19 *nouns* : **including and excluding**

inclusion 1 [U] the act of including or state of being included: *With the inclusion of a few more words, the list will be complete.* **2** [C] something that is included: *We ought to have that as an inclusion in the dictionary.*
exclusion [U (*from*)] the act of excluding: *His exclusion from the tennis club hurt him very much.* **to the exclusion of** so as to leave out (all other members of a group): *He studied history at the university, to the exclusion of all other subjects.*

H20 *adjectives, etc* : **relating to including and excluding** [B]

inclusive 1 [B] containing or including everything (or many things): *£10 is an inclusive charge; there is no more to pay.* **2** [Wa5;E] including all the numbers or dates: *He will be here Wednesday to Friday inclusive.* **3** [Wa5;E (*of*)] (of a price or charge) including other costs that are often paid separately: *The rent is £20 inclusive of heat. The rent is £20 inclusive (of everything).* **-ly** [adv]
all-inclusive [Wa5] including everything: *They had an all-inclusive tour of Hong Kong. The rent is all-inclusive.*
comprehensive including much or all of some-

thing: *The teacher gave a comprehensive description of the subject.* **-ly** [adv] **-ness** [U]

exclusive 1 [Wa5;A] not shared with others: *This bathroom is for the President's exclusive use. He gave the newspaper an exclusive story. He bought the exclusive rights* (= for example, to make a film from a book). **2** [B] **a** that excludes unsuitable people and charges a lot of money: *an exclusive school/club/hotel/shop.* **b** (of a person) not willing to make friends **3** [C] a newspaper story at first given to or printed by only one newspaper **4** [C9] a product on sale only in the stated shop: *It is a G and W exclusive.*

except [prep] not including: *Everyone came except her. Except for her, everyone came. He is quite happy, except that she isn't here with him.*

but [prep] except: *Everybody went but me.*

H21 *verbs* : **being made up of things** [Wv6;T1]

be made (up)/(out) of *usu not fml* to have as the parts or material: *What is that made of?— It is made of wood. Water molecules* [⇨ H5] *are made up (out) of two atoms of hydrogen* [⇨ H74] *and one atom of oxygen* [⇨ H74]. *The population of the city is made up equally of Indians and Chinese.*

consist of [v prep T1] *often fml* to be made up of: *The United Kingdom consists of Great Britain and Northern Ireland. Dinner consisted of bread and cheese.*

comprise [T1] *usu fml* to consist of; include; be made up of: *The United Kingdom comprises England, Wales, Scotland and Northern Ireland.*

be composed of *genl & sometimes fml* to be made up of: *The United Kingdom is composed of four countries which united at various times in history. What is this material composed of?*

H22 *verbs* : **making up something** [Wv6;T1]

make up [v adv] to be or form by some fact, law, etc: *Indians and Chinese make up the largest part of the city's population.*

comprise *loose* to make up; form: *The population of the United States is comprised of people from many different parts of the world. Fifteen separate republics comprise the Soviet Union.*

constitute *fml & precise* to make up; form: *Seven days constitute a week. Fifteen separate republics constitute the Soviet Union.*

H23 *verbs* : **putting things in other things** [T1]

put in [v adv] to move, place, etc (something) inside another thing: *Take that box and put all the books in. Put in as many as you can.*

get in [v adv] **1** *genl, infml & emph* to (manage to) put in: *The box was pretty full but we managed to get the books in.* **2** to collect or buy a supply of: *The farmers are getting the crops in. We should get some wine in for the party.*

insert [T1 (*in(to)*)] *often fml* to put (something) inside something else: *He inserted a key in the lock. Insert the word you left out. After we inserted the advertisement (in the newspaper) several people came to buy the car.* **insertion 1** [U] the act or action of inserting **2** [C] something inserted, esp an advertisement in a newspaper

H24 *verbs* : **taking things out of other things** [T1]

take out [v adv] to move, lift, carry, etc, (something) out of something else: *This box is full of books; please take them all out.*

get out [v adv] *genl, infml & emph* **1** to (manage to) take out: *This box is full of books; get them all out now, please. Get those people out (of here)!* **2** to produce: *We'll get the goods out by next month.*

have out [v adv] *loose* to take or get out, esp when ordered, planned, etc: *Can you have these people out (of the houses) next week?*

remove *esp fml* to take out: *He removed the books from the box. Please remove everything from the house.*

extract *esp fml & tech* to take (directly) out, esp by force, with care, etc: *The dentist extracted two of her teeth. Can you extract the necessary information from these reports by this time next week? He carefully extracted the paper from the pile.*

abstract *tech* to remove, esp by separation (of one thing) from others: *Salt can be abstracted from sea water.*

H25 *verbs & nouns* : **surrounding and enveloping** [T1]

surround to (move in order to) be on all sides of: *A wall surrounds the house and garden. The house and garden are surrounded by trees. The police surrounded the house.*

encircle to surround, esp in a circling movement: *The attacking army encircled the camp.* **encirclement** [U] the act or result of encircling

circle to put a circle round: *He circled the numbers on the page.*

wrap to put round or cover by putting round, esp using cloth or paper: *She wrapped her coat round the child, to keep him warm. She wrapped the child in her warm coat. The bread comes wrapped in paper. Wrap up these books in brown paper, please.* **wrapper** [C] a piece of paper used to wrap, esp a book **wrapping** [U; (C)] any material put round things, esp for posting

envelop to wrap up or cover completely: *The*

building was soon enveloped in flames. The clouds enveloped the mountain. Why must we envelop this subject in mystery? **envelopment** [U] the act of enveloping

frame 1 to surround with a solid protecting edge; put a border round: *I'm having this picture framed, so that I can hang it on the wall. The copier framed each page with a beautiful pattern drawn with a fine pen.* **2** to act as a setting or background to: *A large hat framed the girl's pretty face.* **3** (*fig*) to give shape to (words, sentences, ideas, etc); express: *Unless a law is very carefully framed, someone will find a way to avoid obeying it. An examiner must frame his questions clearly.* **4** (*fig*) to build; make: *Forts were framed for defence against land or sea forces, but are useless against an air attack.*

enclose 1 to put a wall, etc round: *He enclosed the land and made it into two farms.* **2** to put (something) inside something else, esp additional papers in a letter: *I enclose two tickets along with this letter.* **enclosure 1** [U] the act of enclosing **2** [C] a place surrounded by a wall, etc **3** [C] something put in an envelope, sent with a letter, etc

muffle [(*up*)] to wrap up very fully so as to keep warmth or sound from getting out: *The children were well muffled up against the cold. Their voices sounded muffled.*

H26 *verbs, etc* : **gathering and collecting**

gather 1 [T1;I∅ (*round*)]to (cause to) come together: *Gather round and I'll tell you a story. A crowd gathered to see what had happened. There's a storm gathering. He gathered all his courage before going in. His speech gathered a large crowd.* **2** [T1] to obtain (information or qualities) bit by bit: *He travels about the world gathering facts about little-known countries. As we came onto the open road we gathered speed.* **3** [T1 (*in*)] to collect or pick (flowers, crops, several objects, etc): *Gather your toys up. The farmers are gathering in the corn.* **4** [Wv5;T1] to draw into small folds usu by making small stitches with a long thread, then pulling the thread up so that the material is pushed together: *a gathered skirt* (= at the waist). **gathering 1** [C] a (usu large) group of people gathered together for any purpose **2** [S] an act of gathering: *His work is a kind of gathering together of all the information on the subject.*

collect 1 [T1;I∅] to (cause to) gather together: *Collect the books and put them in a pile on my desk. A crowd of people collected to cheer the new King. I collected £50 for homeless people in London.* **2** [T1] to gather (objects) as a sport or hobby, for study, etc: *John collects foreign coins. Paul collects stamps and shells.* **3** [T1] to call for and take away (someone or something): *I called at the station to collect my grandmother. I've just been to John's to collect*

the table I bought from him. **4** [T1] to regain [⇒ D87] control of (oneself, one's thoughts, senses, etc): *Once she'd collected herself she behaved as though nothing had happened. I tried to collect my thoughts but was too excited.* **5** [T1;I∅] to obtain payment of (money): *The government could save money by improving the way it collects taxes. I haven't paid yet; when are you going to collect?* **collection 1** [U] the act of collecting **2** [C] the emptying of a postbox by a postman: *What time's the next collection? There are six collections a day from this postbox.* **3** [C] a group of objects collected as a hobby, for study, etc: *Janet has a very good collection of foreign coins.* **4** [C] a sum of money collected, esp at a religious service: *What does the church do with the money it gets from collections?* **5** [C] the gathering of such money: *When the time came for the collection the priest asked the people to be generous.* **6** [C usu sing] a pile of material, paper, dust, dirt, etc, often unwanted and unplanned: *There was a collection of dust in the corner. The car broke down because of a collection of dirt in its engine.* **collective** [Wa5;B] **1** formed by collection; considered as a whole: *We must turn our collective mistakes to our advantage.* **2** of or related to a number of people or groups of people considered or acting as one: *It is the collective opinion of the governments of Western Europe that peace is always better than war.* **3** shared by all members of a group: *collective ownership.* **-ly** [adv]: *We must work for peace collectively.* **collective** [GC] **1** a group; a body of people considered as a whole: *The workers' collective won't like the new industrial plan.* **2** a business or firm owned and controlled by the people who work in it **collector 1** [C] a person employed to collect taxes, tickets, debts, etc: *a tax-collector.* **2** a person who collects stamps, coins, furniture, etc, for pleasure or interest: *a stamp-collector.*

assemble 1 [T1;I∅] *often fml* to (cause to) come, move, put, gather, etc, together: *The people assembled in the city centre. Assemble the men here.* **2** [T1] to make by putting parts together: *They assembled the little car without anyone else's help.* **assembly 1** [U] the act of assembling **2** [C] anything, group, etc, assembled

mass [Wv5;T1;I∅] to gather together in large numbers: *Crowds massed along the road where the Queen would pass. Massed bands played music in the park. Dark clouds massed and we expected rain.*

amass [T1] to gather or collect (money, goods, power, etc) in great amounts: *He amassed a fortune in gold before he died.*

congregate [I∅] to come together: *The people congregated in the centre of the town.* **congregation 1** [U] the act of congregating **2** [C] any group which congregates, esp for religious purposes regularly

convene [T1;I∅] to (cause to) come together for a meeting: *The King convened his parlia-*

ment. The meeting will be convened next week. When do we convene? **convener, convenor** [C] a person who convenes a meeting, group, etc, esp regularly

round up [v adv T1] *not fml* to collect together from various places: *Round up the men; we have work to do. He was busy rounding up his cattle.* **roundup** [C] an act or occasion of rounding up: *a roundup of the cattle; a cattle round-up*

herd [T1; L9] to gather or move in a herd [⇒ A40] esp forcefully: *They herded the animals towards the river. The soldiers herded their prisoners into an old building.*

pool [T1] to put (esp money, possessions, equipment, etc) together so that all the people who do this can get a result: *They pooled their resources* (= everything they had) *and began working together.*

Objects generally

H30 *nouns* : **things and objects** [C]

thing *genl & usu not fml* **1** whatever has a shape and can be seen, touched, etc: *What's that black thing lying over there? Get all these things off the table, please!* **2** whatever can be felt, thought, etc: *I've just thought of another thing that he didn't talk about! Fear is a terrible thing.* **3** [(*the*) S] a particular act, kind of behaviour, idea, difficulty, etc: *The best/worst thing she ever did was to buy that house! The thing to do now is have something to eat. The thing is* (= the difficulty is) *I don't know where to go. Living in the country is a good thing to do.*

object **1** *esp fml & tech* a thing, esp as seen, touched, etc: *What's that black object lying over there?* **2** [*of*] something or someone that produces interest or an emotional effect: *She is his latest object of interest. The old buildings are objects of wonder among the local people.*

article a particular or separate thing or object, esp one of a group: *I am wearing several articles of clothing.*

H31 *nouns* : **pieces of things** [C]

piece **1** a part (of anything solid) which is separated, broken, or marked off from a larger or whole body: *He owns a piece of land near here. She tore off a small piece of paper. Would you like a piece of cake? Yes, a small piece, please.* **2** A single object that is an example of a kind or class, or that forms part of a set: *Can I have another piece of paper, please? This is a nice piece of furniture. The coffee set has 14 pieces.* **3** one of many parts made to be fitted together: *I bought this table in pieces, but one piece is missing.* **4** [*usu sing or in comb*] one

object or person forming part of a set: *They play in an eighty-piece band.* **5** a usual size or weight in which something is made or sold: *This kind of board is sold only in pieces 1 metre by 1.5.* **6** [C9 *usu sing*] a small amount: *That's a good piece of news. Let me give you a piece of advice.* **7** [C9 *usu sing*] an example of something made or done, esp of a stated quality: *This watch is a fine piece of work.* **in one piece** *infml* **1** (of a thing) undamaged: *Fortunately the cup I dropped is still in one piece.* **2** (of a person) unharmed, esp after an accident **piece by piece** one by one; one part at a time: *He made it carefully, piece by piece.*

lump a piece of matter, etc, without a definitive shape: *He picked up a lump of earth. He had a lump on his head where someone had hit him. The wet sugar was full of lumps.*

chunk **1** a short, thick piece or lump that is bigger than pieces into which something is usually cut: *When I asked for some more meat, she gave me a really big chunk.* **2** a fairly large amount: *Having spent a large chunk of his life in prison for political crimes he had no reason to support the government.*

slice a thin, flat piece cut from something: *Have another slice of meat/bread. She cut the bread in thin/thick slices.*

shred **1** [*often pl*] a small, narrow piece torn or roughly cut off: *He tore the letter to shreds in his anger.* **2** [S] *esp emot* a small piece or bit: *There is not a shred of truth in his statement!* **in shreds** badly torn; ruined by tearing

H32 *nouns* : **parts of things** [C]

part **1** something which is smaller than a whole a larger object, etc: *The house has two parts, one newer than the other. He lives in the older part of the house.* **2** a piece into which something is divided: *The story was told in four parts. A penny is a hundredth part of a pound* **partial** [Wa5;B] of, for, or concerning a part **-ly** [adv]

section a part of a larger object, place, group etc, that is (regarded as) more or less separate *The bookcase comes apart into sections. He lives in the richest section of the city. She plays in the brass section of the band. Signals control each section of railway track. This is the section of the organization that deals with record-keeping.* **sectional** [Wa5;B] of, for, or concerning a section **-ly** [adv]

compartment [C] one of several parts of a structure, esp a seating area in a railway carriage *Your seat is in Compartment 4, sir. He put the book in the glove compartment of the car* (= the little area where passengers can keep gloves, books, etc).

segment **1** any of the parts into which something may be cut or divided: *The runner went fastest in the middle segment of the course* **2** any of the natural equal parts of some fruits such as an orange: *They ate a dish of orange* *segments.* **segmental** [Wa5;B] of or concerning a segment of something

fraction (esp in mathematics, etc) a part into which something is or can be divided; a small part of a whole: *This work can be done at a fraction of the present cost if we take more care* [*also* ⇒ J3]. **fractional** [Wa5;B] of or concerning a fraction **-ly** [adv]

fragment a small piece that is broken off a larger piece or whole: *When the bomb went off, fragments flew in all directions. Only a fragment of the ancient book remains now.* **fragmentary** [Wa5;B] of or concerning a fragment

layer something that lies or is placed, spread, etc between or on top of something else; a thickness of material: *The cake had a layer of chocolate in it. How many layers of clothing are you wearing?*

stratum a layer of rock or earth: *The earth's surface is made up of rock strata.*

seam a layer of one kind of mineral, esp coal, between masses of other rocks

H33 *nouns, etc* : **small pieces or parts of things** [C (*of*)]

bit *usu infml* a piece or quantity of something, esp if small: *He ate every bit of food on the table. That's a nice bit of wood. She made her notes on a bit of paper.* **to bits** to small pieces: *The bridge was blown to bits by the explosion.*

grain 1 one piece from a substance which is made up of small, hard pieces: *Grains of sand had got into his shoes.* **2** (*fig*) the smallest possible bit or amount: *It is a false statement with a few grains of truth in it. If you had a grain of common sense you'd put your coat on before going out in the rain.*

particle 1 a piece (of something that is made up of very small pieces): *Dust particles floated in the sunlight.* **2** a very small, or the smallest, quantity (of something): *Particles of food were left on the plate.* (*fig*) *There isn't a particle of truth in what he said.*

scrap a small piece, esp if not very important or greatly needed: *Have you a scrap of paper I could write on? Any scraps of news/food? I only heard some scraps of their conversation.*

chip 1 a small piece knocked or cut off wood, glass, stone, etc: *Some wood chips were lying on the floor.* **2** the place where such a piece has been knocked or cut off: *There's a chip on this cup.* **3** [T1] to knock or cut such a piece from: *Someone has chipped this cup.*

pinch a small amount, esp that can be taken between finger and thumb: *Can you put a pinch of salt in the soup?*

drop 1 a very small rounded amount of liquid usu coming from above or lying on a surface: *Drops of rain* (= **raindrops**) *began to fall. She put two drops of red liquid in the warm water.* **2** *usu infml* a small amount: *Can I have a drop more wine/a drop more to drink, please?*

pellet a small rounded mass of any soft material made by or as if by rubbing something between the fingers: *The little boy threw a mud pellet at the window.*

flake 1 a small light piece of something: *flakes of pastry/snow.* **2** [I0 (*off*)] to come off in flakes: *The paint on the wall is flaking (off).* **flaky** [Wa1;B] full of flakes: *flaky pastry.*

H34 *nouns* : **larger or special masses of things** [C (*of*)]

mass 1 a usu large quantity of matter in one place: *The ship cut its way slowly through a mass of/masses of ice.* **2** a large number (of things or persons): *His story is a mass of lies. The garden was a mass of flowers. She ate masses of ice cream. Masses of people waited to see him.*

pile 1 a mass of things, one (piece or object) on top of the other, esp if tidy: *Put the books in a pile in the corner.* **2** *infml* a lot: *He has piles of money.*

mound 1 a pile of earth or a small hill, esp if made by a person, animal, etc **2** a large pile of anything

heap 1 a mass of things, one on top of the other, esp if not tidy: *The books lay in a heap on the floor.* **2** *infml* a lot: *She's had a heap of trouble. We have heaps of time to get there.*

bunch 1 a number of things (usu small and of the same kind) fastened, held, or growing together at one point: *He bought her a bunch of flowers.* **2** *infml* often humor or deprec a group: *They're a nice bunch of youngsters. He isn't much good, and he's the best of the bunch!*

cluster a number of things of the same kind growing or being close together in a group: *Stars in the sky can often be seen in clusters.*

stack a large heap or pile made neatly and carefully: *a stack of wood/books/hay* [⇒ E142, 3].

H35 *verbs* : **making masses of things**

pile 1 [X9, esp *up*] to put (one thing) on top of another, to form a pile: *He piled the books (up) in a corner. He piled the books on top of each other.* **2** [T1; L9, esp *in, out*] to move in a mass or in masses: *Right, the cars are here; pile everything in and then pile in! They piled out (of the cars). The earth slowly piled up.*

heap 1 [D1 *on/with*; X9, esp *up*] to put in a heap; form or become a heap: *He heaped the plate with food. He heaped food on the plate.* **2** [X9; L9, esp *up*] to collect or gain in large amounts: *The earth slowly heaped up.*

lump together [v adv T1] (*esp fig*) to put together in a large amount: *They lumped all the people together without considering their different needs.*

bank up [v adv I0; T1] to (cause to) become a large heap or bank: *The clouds were banking up over the hills. Bank up the fire, please* (= Put more coal, wood, etc on it to burn more slowly).

stack [T1 (*up*)] to put in a stack: *He stacked the books against the wall.*

H36 *nouns* : **the main parts of things** [(*the*) S (*of*)]

bulk the main or greater part: *The bulk of the work has now been done.*

gist the general meaning, esp of a long statement; the main points (as of an argument): *I haven't time to read this report; can you give me the gist of it?*

essence the central part of something: '*Freedom of speech is the essence of our way of life*', said the politician.

H37 *nouns* : **shares and portions** [C]
[ALSO ⇨ D103–4]

share a part of something, esp when (to be) given to a particular person: *What is my share of the money? We all take equal shares.*

portion *often fml* a share of something that is divided among two or more people: *We each got equal portions of fish. A portion of the blame must be borne by the driver.*

H38 *nouns* : **solid shapes, esp of stone and metal** [C]

block 1 a solid mass or piece of wood, stone, etc: *The floor was made of blocks of wood.* **2** a quantity of things considered as a single whole: *a block of seats in the theatre; a block of shares in a business*

brick 1 [*also* U] (a hard piece of) baked clay used for building: *He used yellow bricks for the walls. It's a red-brick house. The colour is brick-red. The house is made of brick.* **2** anything like this **brickwork** [U] any piece of building work in which bricks are used; bricks used together in the form of a wall or ornament **brick up** [v adv T1] to close (something, esp a door, window, etc) with a wall of bricks: *They bricked up the entrance to the dangerous old mine.*

bar 1 a piece of solid material that is longer than it is wide: *The iron was shaped into bars. Can I have a bar of soap/chocolate? The gold bars weighed a lot.* **2** a length of wood or stiff metal across a door, gate, or window to keep it firmly closed

ingot a lump of metal in a regular shape, often brick-shaped: *gold ingots*

bolt a usu rounded metal bar, esp one that slides across to fasten a door or window

H39 *nouns, etc* : **solid shapes, esp of wood** [C]
[ALSO ⇨ D26]

beam [⇨ D26] a large heavy piece of wood, usu squared, esp one of the main pieces used to support a building or to go from one side of a wooden ship to the other: *Great beams held up the roof.*

board 1 a long thin flat piece of cut wood: *He cut the wood into boards.* **2** [*often in comb*] a flat surface with patterns, used for playing a (stated) game on: *I want to play chess* [⇨ K136] *but I can't find the board. I'm looking for the chessboard.* **3** [*often in comb*] a flat piece of hard material used for putting a (stated) food on: *Put the bread on the* (*bread*)*board for cutting.* **4** *also* **notice board** a flat piece of hard material fastened to a wall in a public place to pin notices on: *Put this notice up on the board.* **board up** [v adv T1] to close up (esp a door, window, etc) with boards: *They boarded up all the windows when they left the house.*

-board [*comb form*] **1** material of the stated type formed as a thin flat sheet: *It was a box made of cardboard. The room had a hardboard floor.* **2** a board used for the stated purpose: *He pulled up the floorboards.*

plank a long usu heavy piece of board, 5 to 15 cm thick and at least 18 cm wide

sleeper *BrE,* **tie** *AmE* one of the large heavy pieces usu of wood that is used to support railway lines

bat a special piece of wood, etc used esp for hitting a ball in such games as baseball and cricket: *She hit the ball with her bat. He bought a new cricket bat.*

H40 *nouns* : **solid shapes, esp for supporting things** [C]
[ALSO ⇨ D26]

rafter one of the sloping beams that serves or helps to support a roof: *He was up among the rafters of the house, looking for birds' nests.*

prop 1 something firm placed to hold something very heavy that is pressing down or out: *The coal miners used wooden props to hold up the roof of the tunnel.* **2** (*fig*) a person on whom someone or something depends for support, strength, courage, etc: *Some people say that the government needs the army as its prop.*

strut a piece of wood or metal that is placed at an angle to support something: *Struts were used to hold the wall in position.*

girder a strong beam, usu of iron or steel, which supports the smaller beams in a floor or roof or forms the base of one part of a bridge

support *genl* any of these when considered as supporting or holding something else up or in position: *We need supports to keep the wall from falling down.*

H41 *nouns, etc* : **pipes and tubes** [C]

[ALSO ⇒ D42]

pipe [*often in comb*] a long, hollow rounded object suitable for carrying liquid or gas, often underground: *The workmen have dug up the road and are laying water pipes.*

tube a usu thin pipe of metal, glass, rubber, etc used esp for carrying or holding liquid

roll something looking like a tube: *He had a big roll of paper in his hand. Two rolls of cloth, please.* [⇒ H47]

hose 1 a piece of pipe which can be moved and bent to direct water onto fires, a garden, etc **2** [T1 (*down*)] to use a hose, esp for washing (something): *hosing the car down; to hose the yard out; to hose the garden*

cylinder 1 a long round hollow or solid body. **2** an object or container shaped like this, esp a metal tube

duct 1 any kind of pipe in the ground for carrying liquid or other substances, or electric power lines **2** a pipe for carrying air into, out of, or inside a building, ship, etc **3** a pipelike part in plants which carries water, air, etc **4** a pipelike part of the body which carries liquid, esp from glands: *tear ducts*

H42 *nouns* : **poles and shafts** [C]

[ALSO ⇒ D26]

pole [*often in comb*] a long straight rounded object, usu of wood or metal, usu quite thin, used as a support, to guide a flat-bottomed boat, to join two animals to a cart or carriage, etc: *The hut was made of poles covered with grass mats. There was a flag at the top of the pole* (= a **flagpole**).

stick 1 a usu thin piece of wood: *He picked up sticks to make a fire.* **2** such a thing used to help a person walk: *The man had a bad leg and walked with a stick/and used a walking stick.*

rod 1 a long thin pole or bar of any stiff material such as wood, metal, or plastic **2** a stick used for beating people

post 1 [*often in comb*] a strong thick upright pole or bar made of wood, metal etc that is fixed into the ground or some other base, esp to support or mark something: *The fence was made of wire and metal posts.* **2** [*usu in comb*] a main support: *a bedpost; a four-poster bed; a doorpost*

stake a length of wood with a point at one end, that can be driven into something, esp the ground

spit a thin pointed rod for sticking meat onto and turning for cooking over a fire

spar a pole to which the sails of certain kinds of ship can be fixed; a pole fixed across a mast

mast a high, usu large pole **a** on a ship to which ropes, sails, etc, are fixed **b** *also* **flagpole** on which a flag can be hung **c** (usu of metal and very high) by means of which radio and television signals can be sent

shaft 1 the long thin, usu wooden part of a weapon such as an arrow or spear: *He made the shafts of the arrows as straight as possible.* **2** one of usu two poles by which a horse, etc, is tied so as to pull a cart, etc: *The horse stood between the shafts of the carriage.* **3** the main part of a pillar **4** a bar which turns or around which a belt or wheel turns to pass power through a machine **5** the long handle of certain tools, such as an axe, golf club, etc: *He broke the shaft of his axe.*

haft *tech* the pole which is used as the handle of an axe or of some long-handled weapons

crook a long stick or tool with a bent or curved end: *The shepherd* [⇒ E144] *carried a crook.*

staff 1 a large long stick used when walking, climbing, etc, or as a weapon held in both hands **2** a smaller stick used as a sign of a person's position or authority [⇒ C100]

pointer 1 a long stick used to point with **2** a hand on a clock, etc, serving to show the time, a number, etc **3** [(to)] (*fig*) something that suggests something else: *His words were a pointer to his feelings.*

cane a thin stick made from a piece of cane [⇒ H72] used esp to beat people or to help a person in walking: *The teacher was holding a cane.*

wand a thin stick carried in the hand, esp used for magic, tricks, etc: *The magician waved his wand, and a rabbit appeared.*

H43 *nouns* : **plates and sheets** [C]

plate [*often in comb*] a flat thin, usu large piece of metal, glass, etc, for use in building, in parts of machinery, as a protection, etc: *When the engine exploded, the ship's steel plates burst apart.*

sheet a very thin plate: *He broke two sheets of glass and bent one of the metal sheets.*

pane a sheet, esp of glass in a window, etc: *He broke a pane of glass/a window pane.*

slab a large thick piece or sheet, esp of stone: *The floor of the old building was made of great slabs of stone.*

H44 *nouns, etc* : **bands and tapes**

band [C] **1** a thin flat narrow piece of material, esp for fastening things together, or for putting round something to strengthen it: *The large wooden box had iron bands round it. He kept the cards together with a rubber band.* **2** [*often in comb*] a thin flat narrow piece of material forming part of an article of clothing: *neckband, waistband.* **3** a line of a different colour or pattern that stands out against the background on which it is painted or fixed: *There were bands of white round the black box.*

tape 1 [U] narrow material used for tying parcels, etc: *Use some sticky tape.* **2** [C] a piece of this or something like it

ribbon 1 [C; U] (a piece of) silk or other cloth woven in a long narrow band and used for tying things, for ornament, etc: *He bought her a box of chocolates with (a) red ribbon. She used a black typewriter* [⇨ G152] *ribbon. He wore the ribbon of the Victoria Cross on his chest.* **2** [C] a long irregular narrow band: *The old torn curtains were hanging in ribbons.* (*fig*) *There was a ribbon of mist along the river bank.*

belt [C] a usu large long piece of leather, rubber, or other such material in the form of a band, used esp to drive a machine or for carrying materials

strap 1 [C] a long piece of leather, cloth, or metal, usu with a purpose such as tying or holding: *The boxes were tied with straps.* **2** [T1 (*up, in*)] to fasten with a strap: *The driver of the vehicle was strapped in.*

strip [C] a long narrow piece of cloth, metal, wood, land, etc; a line of paint, etc: *He tore the cloth into strips. He made the strip of land near the house into a garden.*

H45 *nouns* : **strings and fibres**

[ALSO ⇨ H86]

string 1 [C; U] a long thin line, esp if made or woven out of wool, cotton, etc: *He bought a ball of string.* **2** [C; U] anything like this, esp used for tying things up: *nylon string. The books were tied together with string.* **3** [C] a thin piece of material, often one of several, stretched across musical instruments to give sound: *guitar strings* **4** [C (*of*)] a set (of things) connected together: *a string of pearls* [⇨ H65]. **5** [C (*of*)] (*fig*) a set (of words, actions, etc) following each other closely: *a string of cries/ prayers*

cord [C; U] a thick string, esp for tying things: *He tied the parcel with a (piece of) cord.*

thread 1 [C; U] (a length of) very fine material made by spinning cotton, wool, silk, etc, used in sewing or weaving **2** [C9] (*fig*) anything fine or thin like this: *A thread of light passed through the crack.* **3** [C] (*fig*) a line of reasoning connecting the parts of an argument or story: *He lost the thread of his argument.* **4** [C] a raised line that winds around the outside of a screw or the inside of a nut [⇨ H148], a bolt, etc

strand [C (*of*)] a single piece or thread (of a material made up of many threads, wires, etc): *Many strands are twisted together to form a rope.*

fibre *BrE*, **fiber** *AmE* **1** [C] one of the thin threadlike parts that form many animal and plant growths such as wool, wood, or muscle: *Some plant fibres are woven into cloth.* **2** [U] a mass of these, used for making cloth, rope, etc: *cotton fibre is widely used.* **3** [C] a (type of) thread made chemically to serve the same purposes in weaving: *Nylon is a man-made fibre.* **4**

[U9] (*fig*) (of mind or morals) **a** quality: *He is a man of coarse fibre.* **b** strength: *He lacks moral fibre.* **fibrous** [B] of, concerning, or like fibre

filament [C] a very thin thread: *The threads of a spider's web* [⇨ A112] *are more suitably called filaments, because they are so thin.*

wire [C; U] (a piece of) thin metal like a thread: *The fence was made with wire; it was a wire fence. Electricity is carried along wires.*

H46 *nouns* : **ropes, cables, and chains**

rope [C; U] (a) thick strong line or cord, made by twisting thinner cords together: *People climbing high mountains tie themselves together with ropes.*

cable [C; U] a kind of thick rope (esp nowadays) made out of metal wires twisted together: *The bridge was supported by pillars and steel cables.*

hawser [C] a thick rope or steel cable, as used on a ship

chain [C; U] a number of metal ring-like objects (= **links**) joined together and usu used like a rope: *The dog was tied to the wall by/with a chain.*

stay [C] a rope or wire, usu one of a set, that keeps a pole, etc, in position

line [C; U] *genl* any string, wire, rope, etc: *She put the wet clothes on the line to dry. Throw me a line!*

H47 *nouns* : **round quantities of cloth, etc** [C]

roll a quantity of cloth, etc, rolled into a tube shape: *He bought two rolls of cloth. The carpet came in a large roll.*

bolt (of cloth) a roll, esp as it comes from the factory: *They bought a bolt of cotton.*

H48 *nouns* : **rounded objects** [C]

ball 1 a a round object, esp as used in play: *He threw me the ball.* **b** anything of like shape: *The Earth is a ball.* **2** a round mass: *He held a ball of clay in his hand. The child threw a snowball at me.* **3** a rounded part of the body: *the ball of the foot; an eyeball*

globe 1 an object in the shape of a ball **2** such an object on which a map of the earth or sky, etc, is painted, and which may be turned on its base **globular** [B] having the shape of a globe **global** [Wa5;B] **1** *rare* like a globe **2** *common* belonging to or found in the whole world; worldwide: *He has global business interests.*

sphere 1 *esp fml & tech* a ball or globe, esp if

perfectly round: *The Earth is not quite a sphere.* **2** (*fig*) an area of knowledge, interest, etc: *Politics isn't his sphere. The USA and USSR have different spheres of influence in the world.* **spherical** [B] of, concerning, or like a sphere **-ly** [adv Wa4]

bulb the rounded ball-like end, esp of glass instruments such as a thermometer

H49 *nouns* : **rings, hooks, and pegs** [C]

[ALSO ⇒ H128]

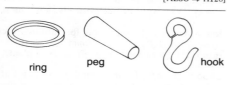

ring   peg   hook

ring 1 a circular band (esp of the stated substance or for the stated purpose): *A key ring is for carrying keys on. He likes to smoke a cigarette and blow smoke rings.* **2** a circle worn on the finger often **a** made of the stated metal: *five gold rings.* **b** ornamented with the stated precious stone: *a diamond ring.* **c** worn to show the stated fact: *She wears a wedding ring to show that she is married.* **3** a circular line, mark, or arrangement: *Count the rings of the tree when it is cut across. The children were dancing in a ring.*

hoop a circular band of wood or metal, esp round a barrel: *The barrel had several iron hoops round it, to hold it together. The dog jumped through the hoop that its master held up. The child was playing with a hoop.*

hook a curved piece of metal, plastic, etc, for catching something or hanging things on: *Hang your coat on the hook.*

peg 1 a rather short piece of wood, metal, etc, usu thinner at one end than at the other, esp **a** used to stick through a hole to hold (esp wooden) surfaces together **b** fixed to a wall for hanging coats and hats on: *a hat peg* **c** *also* **tent peg** hammered into the ground and used to hold the ropes supporting a tent **d** hammered into the ground to mark the limits of a piece of land **e** placed in the hole in the side of a barrel **2** *also* **pin** a wooden screw used to tighten or loosen the strings of certain musical instruments

Specific substances and materials

H60 *nouns* : **rock and stone**

rock 1 [U] the solid mineral material which forms the greatest part of the earth: *They cut a passage through (the) solid rock. That's an*

interesting *rock formation.* **2** [C *often cap*] a large mass of stone standing up above the level of its surroundings: *Edinburgh Castle stands on the Castle Rock.* **3** [C] a large piece of stone: *There was danger from falling rocks.* **4** [C] *AmE* a stone: *Don't throw rocks at people.* **as firm/steady/solid as a rock 1** perfectly firm and hard; unlikely to move **2** (of people) trustworthy; sound

stone 1 [U *often in comb*] (a type of) rock: *The walls were built of stone/sandstone/limestone and wood. They were stone walls. The stonework of the house was very good.* **2** [C] a piece of this, esp if small: *He threw a stone into the water. Stones flew out from under the wheels of the moving cart.*

boulder [C] a large stone or a mass of rock which is rounded and shows signs of wear

pebble [C] a small roundish smooth stone found esp on the seashore or on a riverbed

lava [U] rock in a very hot liquid state flowing from an exploding mountain (= **volcano**)

pumice [U] lava when it has become cool and turned into a grey solid with many small air holes

H61 *technical adjectives* : **kinds of rock** [Wa5;B]

igneous (of rocks) formed from lava

sedimentary (of rocks) made of sediment [⇒ H63]

metamorphic (of rocks) formed by changes caused by the heat, pressure, etc, on earlier kinds of rock

H62 *nouns, etc* : **kinds of rock, etc** [U]

granite a hard type of grey igneous rock, used for building and making roads

basalt a type of dark greenish-black igneous rock

flint [*also* C] a very hard smooth kind of stone: *If you strike two pieces of flint/two flints together, you usually get a spark* [⇒ H75]. *Men long ago used flint axes with wooden handles.*

limestone a type of rock from which lime is obtained

sandstone a rock made of sand fixed in a natural cement

marble a hard sort of limestone used (when cut and polished) for building, art, gravestones, etc, and usu showing an irregular pattern of lines: *The statue* [⇒ I 50] *of the King was of the finest marble.*

crystal a hard mineral substance which has a regular shape and looks like glass **crystalline** [Wa5;B] of or like crystal

quartz a hard mineral substance appearing in many forms including some precious stones

chalk 1 a type of soft white limestone formed in ancient times from the shells of very small sea animals, used for making lime and various writing materials: *The white cliffs of Dover are made of chalk.* **2** this material in white or coloured pieces used for writing or drawing: *Pass me the chalk, please. The teacher wrote with a stick/piece of chalk. Do you need some more chalk?*

lime *also* **quicklime 1** a white substance obtained by burning limestone, used in making cement **2** the substance made by adding water to this

clay heavy firm earth, soft when wet, becoming hard when baked at a high temperature, from which bricks, pots, etc, are made **clayey** [Wa2;B] of or like clay

gravel 1 a mixture of small stones with sand, used esp on the surface of roads or paths **2** [Wv5;T1] to cover with gravel: *They have a gravelled path leading to the house.*

grit small pieces of a hard material, usu stone: *Grit is spread on roads to make them less slippery in icy weather. She got some grit in her eye when she leaned out of the window of the train.*

H63 *nouns, etc* : **soil and earth**

soil [U;C] the (usu soft) material found generally on top of rock, in which plants can grow: *That farm has a very rich soil. The soil in these parts (of the country) is sandy. Some soils are more suitable for farming than others. Soil conditions here are good.*

earth [U] *genl* soil: *He filled the pot with earth and planted a rose in it. The hut had an earth floor.*

sand [U] loose material of very small fine grains, found in broad masses along seacoasts and in deserts, and used for making cement and glass and for rubbing away roughness **sandy** [Wa1;B] of, like or covered with sand: *sandy soil* **-iness** [U]

dust [U] very small pieces of dry earth, etc, like powder: *The air was full of dust after the cars passed. The teacher's hands had chalk dust on them.* **dusty** [Wa1;B] of, like, or covered with dust: *The dusty road made the travellers dusty too.* **-ily** [adv] **-iness** [U]

powder 1 [U;C] anything that has been made into or like dust: *They broke the stones up into a white powder. She put on some face powder.* **2** [T1] to put powder on: *She powdered her face.*

mud [U] **1** earth with water in it: *The roads were covered with mud after the heavy rain. There is mud at the bottom of most rivers.* **2** [esp A] earth which was wet but is now dry: *The hut had a mud floor. They lived in mud huts.* **muddy** [Wa1;B] of, like, or covered with mud: *The muddy road made the travellers muddier than ever.*

sediment [U] *fml* mud [⇒ H14] **sedimentary** [Wa5;B] of, concerning, or like sediment [⇒ H61]

silt [U] loose sand, mud, soil, etc, carried in running water and then dropped (at the entrance to a harbour, bend in a river, etc): *The fields were covered with silt after the flood.* **silt**

up [v adv I∅; T1] to fill with silt: *The old harbour silted up long ago; it's now all silted up.*

slime [U] **1** soft, partly liquid mud, often with small greenish plant life in it, esp regarded as ugly, bad-smelling, etc **2** thick liquid produced by the skin of various fish and snails [⇒ A113] **slimy** [Wa1;B] **1** like, being, or covered with slime; unpleasantly slippery **2** *fig* very unpleasant and offensive: *That was a slimy thing to do!* **-iness** [U]

ooze 1 [U] thick soft mud, esp at the bottom of a river **2** [L9] (of liquids) to move slowly, esp through a small hole or holes: *Water oozed out.* **oozy** [Wa1;B] of or like ooze **-ily** [adv] **-iness** [U]

loam [U;C] rich soil, good for farming, etc **loamy** [Wa1;B] of or like loam

humus [U] a rich soil made of decayed plants, leaves, etc

deposit [C (*of*)] **1** a thick kind of substance at the bottom of containers full of liquid, of rivers, lakes, etc: *There was a thick deposit of mud at the bottom of the river.* **2** a (usu thick) line or large amount of a substance in the earth, in rock, etc: *They found large deposits of gold/oil in the area.*

alluvium [U;C] *tech* soil put down in a place by the movement of rivers, floods, etc: *Crops grow well in the alluvium of wide valley floors.* **alluvial** [Wa5;B] being, concerning, or made of alluvium: *Alluvial soils usually grow the best crops.*

H64 *nouns, etc* : **dirt and grime**
[ALSO ⇒ D182]

dirt [U] **1** soil; loose earth: *The children were outside, playing happily in the dirt.* **2** unclean matter, esp in the wrong place: *Wash the dirt off the floor. I've got a lot of dirt on my shoes.* **3** (*fig*) nasty talk or writing about sex: *That was a good story but it had a lot of dirt in it.* **4** (*fig*) *infml* nasty talk about people: *She enjoys hearing a bit of dirt about her neighbours.*

muck [U] *infml* dirt: *Get that muck off my clean floor!*

grime [U] a surface of thick black dirt: *His face and hands were covered in grime.*

smudge 1 [C] a dirty mark of any kind: *There were smudges of dirt/ink on the paper.* **2** [T1] to put smudges on: *He smudged the paper with ink.*

smut 1 [U] dirt, esp from burning coal, etc **2** [C] a black mark made by a piece of dirt **3** [U] (*fig*) nasty talk or writing, esp about sex **smutty** [Wa1;B] of, like, or covered with smut **-ily** [adv] **-iness** [U]

H65 *nouns, etc* : **precious stones**

(precious) stone [C] a rare and valuable kind of mineral: *Diamonds are precious stones. He sells other stones as well as diamonds.*

diamond 1 [C; U] a very hard valuable precious stone, usu colourless, which is used for cutting things and also in jewellery: *He bought her a diamond ring. Cut the glass with a piece of diamond.* **2** [C] an ornament set with one or more of these stones: *Shall I wear my diamonds tonight?*

ruby 1 [C] a bright red precious stone **2** [U;Wa5;B] the colour of this stone: *The glass was a ruby colour. It was ruby red.*

sapphire 1 [C] a kind of transparent precious stone of a bright blue colour: *He gave her a gold ring with three sapphires in it.* **2** [U;Wa5;B] the colour of this stone: *The glass was a sapphire colour. It was sapphire blue.*

emerald 1 [C] a bright green precious stone **2** [U;Wa5;B] the colour of this stone: *She wore a bright emerald dress. The dress was emerald green.*

opal [C; U] a precious stone which looks like milky water with colours in it

jade 1 [U] a precious, usu green stone from which ornaments and jewellery are made **2** [U;Wa5;B] the colour of this stone: *The dress was a jade colour. It was jade green.*

amber 1 [U] a yellowish brown hard clear substance used for jewels, ornaments, etc **2** [U;Wa5;B] the colour of this substance: *She wore an amber dress. The dress was amber yellow.*

jet 1 [U] a hard black material that can be made to shine brightly, used to make ornaments **2** [adv Wa5] like the colour of this material: *She wore a jet black dress.*

topaz 1 [U] a transparent yellowish mineral **2** [C] a piece of this, specially cut and polished, considered a precious stone

pearl 1 [C] a hard round small silvery-white mass formed inside the shell of shellfish, esp oysters [⇨ A103], highly valued as a jewel: *She had a string of pearls round her neck.* **2** [C] a man-made copy of this **3** [c] something which has the shape or colour of a pearl: *In the early morning each blade of grass seems to have a pearl of dew [⇨ L45] on it.* **4** [C] something or esp someone very precious: *As a cook, she is a real pearl.* **(mother of) pearl** [U] a hard shiny substance found on the inside of certain shells, esp oysters **pearly** [Wa1;B] like or ornamented with pearls or pearl: *The dress was a pearly grey. She had pearly teeth.* **pearl diver** [C] a person who swims underwater at sea, looking for shells containing pearls

agate [U; C] a hard stone with bands of various colours, used in jewellery

jewel [C] **1** a precious stone **2** an ornament for wearing that contains one or more jewels: *She keeps her jewels in a safe place.* **3** a precious stone in the machinery of a watch, to make it run smoothly: *Our best watches contain 21 jewels, sir.* **4** (*fig*) a person or thing considered of great value: *He has a jewel of a wife.* [*also* ⇨ D159 JEWELLERY]

H66 *nouns & verbs* : **concrete and similar materials**

concrete 1 [U] a building material made by mixing sand, very small stones, cement, and water **2** [T1; I∅] to cover (a path, a wall, etc) with concrete: *The workman is still busy concreting the road. I think I'll concrete in the morning and paint in the afternoon.*

cement 1 [U] a grey powder, made from a burned mixture of lime and clay, which becomes hard like stone after having been mixed with water and allowed to dry **2** [U] any of the various types of thick sticky hard-drying chemical liquids (= **adhesives** [⇨ H12]) used for filling holes, as in the teeth, or for joining things together: *He made a toy plane using pieces of plastic and cement.* **3** [T1] to join together or make firm (as if) by cement: *Cement these bricks together, please.* (*fig*) *The government hopes to cement their friendship with the other local states.* **4** [T1 (*over*)] to cover with cement: *Cement over these cracks today, please. We've decided to cement (over) our garden as we don't like flowers.*

plaster 1 [U] a pastelike mixture of lime, water, sand, etc, which hardens when dry and is used on walls, etc, to give a smooth surface **2** [T1] to put wet plaster on; cover with plaster: *These rough places on the wall should be plastered (over).*

mortar [U] a mixture of lime, sand, and water used in building to hold bricks, stones, etc, together: *bricks and mortar*

H67 *nouns, etc* : **metal generally**

metal [C; U] any (usu solid, usu shiny) mineral substance of a group which can all be shaped by pressure and used for passing an electric current, and which share other qualities: *The object is made of metal. Copper and silver are both metals.* **metallic** [Wa5;B] of, concerning, or like metal **precious metal** [U; C] a rare and valuable metal often used in ornaments, such as gold and silver **base metal** [C] a metal which is not valuable when compared with gold or silver: *Platinum is not a base metal, but iron is. Men once tried to change base metals into gold.*

alloy 1 [C] a metal made by mixing two or more different metals: *Brass is an alloy of copper and zinc.* **2** [T1] to mix (one metal) with another

ore [U; C] rock, earth, etc, from which metal can be obtained

lode [C] a quantity of ore in a rock

seam [C] a narrow band of one kind of mineral, esp coal, between masses of rock

plate [U] common metal with a thin covering of esp gold or silver: *He has a lot of gold and silver plate.*

H68 nouns : particular metals [U]

aluminium *BrE*, **aluminum** *AmE* a silver-white metal that is a simple substance or element [⇒H4] (sign **Al**), light in weight and easily shaped

brass a very hard bright yellow metal, a mixture of copper and zinc

bronze 1 an alloy mainly of copper and tin **2** [C] a work of art made of bronze: *He has many fine bronzes in his collection.* **3** the colour of bronze

copper 1 a soft reddish metal that is an element (sign **Cu**), easily shaped, and allowing heat and electricity to pass through it easily **2** a reddish-brown colour

gold 1 a valuable soft yellow metal that is an element (sign **Au**), used for making coins, jewellery, etc: *He wore a gold watch. Gold is found in rocks and streams.* **2** gold coins or objects generally: *People used to pay in gold. The Indian girl wore gold ornaments on her arms.* **3** the colour of gold: *The sun shone on the gold of her hair. That's a nice gold paint.*

iron 1 a hard silver-white metal that is an element (sign **Fe**), the most useful metal used for making tools: *Iron is a common metal. This is an iron bar.* **2** the same metal, found in natural foods (eggs, vegetables), which is used in the formation of blood

lead a soft greyish-blue metal that is an element (sign **Pb**), easily melted and used to cover roofs, for water pipes etc

mercury *also esp formerly* **quicksilver** a heavy silver-white metal that is an element (sign **Hg**) and is liquid at normal temperatures

nickel a hard silver-white metal that is an element (sign **Ni**), and is used in the production of other metals

platinum a soft valuable greyish-white metal that is an element (sign **Pt**), used in jewellery and, mixed with other metals, for industrial purposes: *He gave her a platinum ring.*

plutonium a man-made metal that is an element (sign **Pu**), used esp in producing nuclear power

radium a rare shiny white metal that is an element (sign **Ra**), used in the treatment of certain diseases: *He had radium treatment.*

silver 1 a valuable whitish metal that is an element (sign **Ag**), used for making coins, ornaments, etc: *He wore a silver watch.* **2** silver dishes or other objects: *Clean the silver, please.* **3** silver coins **4** the colour of silver: *The dress was silver and blue.*

steel iron in a hard strong form containing some carbon [⇒ H73] and sometimes other metals, and used in building materials, cutting tools, machines, etc: *The knife had a steel blade. He works in the steel industry.* (*fig*) *He is a man of steel* (= very strong).

tin a soft whitish metal that is an element (sign **Sn**), easily shaped and used to cover (**plate**) metal objects with a protective shiny surface

uranium a heavy white metal that is an element (sign **U**), and is used in the production of atomic power

zinc a bluish-white metal that is an element (sign **Zn**), used in the production of other metals, and to plate metal objects with a protective surface

H69 nouns & verbs : rust and verdigris

rust 1 [U] a reddish-brown coating that forms on iron and some other metals when attacked by water and air **2** [U *usu in comb*] the colour of this: *She wore a rust-coloured dress.* **3** [I∅; T1] to (cause to) become (covered with) rust: *The metal will rust if it is left in this wet place. The weather rusted the metal.*

oxide [C; U] *tech* a chemical substance in which something else is combined with oxygen: *Rust is iron oxide.* **oxidize, -ise** [I∅; T1] to (cause to) become an oxide; *tech* to (cause to) combine with oxygen **-ization, -isation** [U]

verdigris [U] a greenish-blue substance which forms a thin covering on articles of copper or brass as a result of age or of being left unpolished in wet conditions

tarnish 1 [U] dullness; loss of polish **2** [Wv5;T1; I∅] to (cause to) become dull, discoloured, or less bright: *Clean the tarnished brass.* (*fig*) *His honour is tarnished.*

H70 nouns : wood

wood [U; C] the material of which the trunks and branches of trees are made, which is cut and dried in various forms for making material for burning, for making paper or furniture, etc

timber 1 [U] wood for building **2** [U] growing trees, esp considered as a supply of wood for building **3** [C] a wooden beam

lumber [C] *AmE* wood that has been prepared for use, as by being cut into boards **lumberjack** [C] a man who cuts down trees for wood **lumberman** [C] a man whose business is the cutting down of trees and the selling of wood

log [C] a thick piece of wood from a tree: *He cut the tree into logs.*

pulp [U] wood and other vegetable material (such as cotton cloth) softened and broken up by chemicals or other means and used for making paper

rubber [U] a substance, made from the juice of a tropical tree, which keeps out water and springs back into position when stretched: *Motor tyres are made of rubber. The child was playing with a rubber ball.*

H71 nouns : kinds of wood generally [U]

hardwood strong heavy wood from trees like oak, used to make good furniture

softwood wood from evergreen [⇒ A135]

trees (such as pine and fir) that is cheap and easy to cut

plywood a stiff material made of several thin sheets of wood stuck together to form a strong board

hardboard 1 a sort of light wood made out of pieces of wood pressed together **2** a sort of board made out of fine pieces of wood pressed into sheets and used in work where a light wood is needed

chipboard a type of board made from waste pieces of wood, used as a building material

H72 *nouns* : **well-known kinds of wood** [U]

[ALSO ⇒ A115]

oak the hard wood from the oak tree [⇒ A155], often used for making furniture

walnut the wood of the walnut tree, of great value for making furniture [⇒ A153]

pine(-wood) the white or yellowish soft wood of the pine tree [⇒ A156], used for making furniture

mahogany the dark reddish hard wood from the mahogany tree, used for making good furniture

teak a very hard yellow wood from the teak tree, which grows in India, Burma, and Malaysia, used for making furniture, ships, etc

cane lengths of the hard smooth hollow stem of certain tall grasses, used as a material for making furniture [⇒ A138]

bamboo lengths of the hard hollow stems of the bamboo plant, used to make furniture, etc [⇒ A138]

H73 *nouns, etc* : **basic substances**

water [U] **1** the most common liquid, without colour, taste, or smell, which falls from the sky as rain, forms rivers, lakes, and seas, and is drunk by people and animals: *The prisoner was given only bread and water.* **2** a supply of this liquid, esp piped: *He threatened to turn off the water.* **3** a body of this liquid (*esp in the phr* **by/on the water**): *He has a house by the water. Let's go on the water this afternoon. Help! He's fallen in the water!* **4** a liquid like or containing this liquid: *Waiter, take back this water that you call soup!* **5** a liquid like or containing this liquid, produced by some parts of the body **6** the movement of people or goods by river or sea rather than by land (*often in the phr* **by water**): *Let's go by water this time.* **7** the level of the sea (or some rivers) at a particular time, tide [⇒ L89]: *high/low water.* **8** the stated degree of completeness or excellence (*esp in the phr* **of the first water**): *She is a scientist/chief of the first water.*

acid 1 [U;C] *precise* a chemical substance containing a particular gas (hydrogen) which may be replaced by a metal to form another type of substance (**a salt**) **2** [U] *loose* something with a sour taste, such as lemon juice **acidity** [U] the state of being or having acid, esp more than usual

alkali [U;C] any of various substances that form chemical salts when combined · with acids **alkaline** [B] of, containing, or like an alkali; having the qualities of an alkali or alkalis **alkalinity** [U] the state of being alkaline, of having alkaline qualities

salt 1 [U] *genl* a very common colourless or white solid substance (**sodium chloride, NaCl**) found in the earth and in sea water and with many uses including preserving food and improving its taste: *He worked in a salt mine. The vegetables need more salt.* **2** [C] *precise & tech* any of a class of chemical substances including this, which may be formed by the combining of an acid and a metal

alcohol 1 [U] *genl* the pure colourless liquid present in (and responsible for) drinks that can make one drunk, such as wine, beer, etc **2** [C] *precise & tech* any of a class of chemical substances of which the alcohol in wine is one

carbon 1 [U] a simple substance (element, sign **C**) found in a pure form as diamonds, graphite, etc, or impure as coal, petrol, etc **2** [C] a stick of this burnt to produce light in some kind of lamp

graphite [U] *also not tech* **lead** the kind of carbon used in pencils

soda [U] the name given to various substances used for washing, baking, etc

sodium [U] a soft silver-white metal (element, sign **Na**), found in salt, soda, etc

starch 1 [U;C] a white substance which is the main kind of foodstuff in bread, potatoes, etc: *There is too much starch in his diet* (= He eats too much starch). **2** [U] this substance mixed with water and used to make clothes stiff **3** [T1] to put starch in: *He starched his shirt.* **starchy** [Wa1;B] **1** of, containing, or like starch: *starchy food* **2** (*fig*) *infml* stiff; formal: *He is a very starchy kind of person.* **-ily** [adv] **-ness** [U]

arsenic [U] **1** a grey substance (element, sign **As**) used esp in making glass, dyes, etc **2** a white compound [⇒ H6] of this, which is a poison

sulphur *BrE*, **sulfur** *AmE* [U] a yellow substance (element, sign **S**) that burns with a blue flame and has a strong smell **sulphurous** *BrE*, **sulfurous** *AmE* [Wa5;B] of, containing, or like sulphur: *sulphurous smoke; a sulphurous smell*

H74 *nouns* : **kinds of gas** [U]

oxygen a gas that is a substance or element [⇒ H4] (sign **O**), forms about 20% of the air, is without colour, taste, or smell, is found in nearly everything and is necessary to all plants and animals and for the process of burning

nitrogen a gas that is an element (sign **N**), without colour or smell, that forms most of the earth's air and that is found in all living things

hydrogen a gas that is an element (sign **H**), without colour or smell, and that burns very easily

helium a gas that is an element (sign **He**), that will not burn, used in airships and some lights

carbon dioxide the gas (sign CO_2) produced when animals breathe out or when carbon is burned in air

carbon monoxide a poisonous gas (sign **CO**) produced when carbon (esp petrol) burns in a small amount of air: *She started the car in the closed garage and died of carbon monoxide poisoning.*

ammonia a strong gas with a sharp smell, used in explosives, in machines (**refrigerators**) to keep things cold, in chemicals (**fertilizers**) to help plants grow, etc

methane a natural gas which is formed from decaying matter and burns easily, sometimes causing explosions in mines

marsh gas *infml* methane

butane a natural gas used for cooking, heating, and lighting

H75 *nouns* : **fire and burning**
[ALSO ⇨ H120]

fire 1 [U] the condition of burning; flames and great heat: *She's afraid of fire.* **2** [C] a heap of burning fuel lit on purpose for cooking, warmth, etc: *They sat round the fire. He lit the kitchen fire.* **3** [U] destruction by fire: *He was insured against fire. There was a danger of fire in the old wooden house.* **4** [C] a case of destruction by fire: *He lost his life in a forest fire.* **5** [U] (*fig*) strong feeling and excitement: *The boy is full of fire and courage.* **blow (up) a fire** to make a fire burn more strongly by blowing air on it   **fire and sword** burning and killing in war   **lay a fire** to put the paper and sticks ready for lighting   **make a fire** to put the paper and sticks ready and then light them   **make up a fire** to add more fuel to a fire   **on fire** (of something not really meant to burn) burning: *The house is on fire!*

combustion [U] **1** the act of catching fire and burning **2** *tech* the chemical activity, usu in the presence of oxygen, that produces light and heat

flame [C; U] (a tongue of) red or yellow burning gas: *The dry sticks burst into flame(s).* **in flames** (of something not meant to burn) burning: *The whole city was in flames.*

blaze [C *usu sing*] **1** the sudden sharp shooting up of a flame; a very bright fire: *The fire burned slowly at first, but soon burst into a blaze.* **2** a brightly shining light or bright colour: *The whole building was a blaze of light. The flowers made a blaze of red.* **3** a big destructive fire: *The dry grass was on fire, and we tried to put out the blaze.* **4** (*fig*) a sudden explosion of feeling: *In a blaze of anger he shouted at them.*

spark [C] **1** a small bit of burning material thrown out by a fire or by the striking together of two hard objects **2** a light-producing passage of electricity through a space **3** (*fig*) a direct cause of an event regarded as a fire or explosion: *The spark that set off the war was the murder of the prince.* **4** (*fig*) a very small but important bit: *He doesn't have a spark of cleverness.*

flare 1 [S] a short strong blaze of fire or light: *There was a sudden flare as she lit the gas.* **2** [C] (something that provides) a bright light out of doors, as in a street market or as a signal at an airfield: *It's misty; go and turn on the flares.*

burn [C] **1** *tech* a (usu short) period of burning and using power **2** a hurt place, effect, or sensation produced by burning: *She had burns on her hand. He felt the burn of the medicine on the cut in his arm.*

brand [C] a mark made on cattle, etc, by burning, usu to show who owns them: *Whose brand is on that cow?*

scorch [C] a scorched place; a mark made by burning on a surface: *There were several scorches on the tablecloth that had been drying too near the fire.*

H76 *verbs* : **fire and burning**

catch fire [I∅] to start burning: *Don't let your dress catch fire!*

burn 1 [I∅] to be on fire: *The house is burning; help!* (*fig*) *He's burning (with fever).* **2** [Wv6; I∅] to be able to be on fire: *Paper burns easily.* **3** [I∅ (*away*)] contain a fire: *The had a little heater burning (away) in the corner.* **4** [I∅] to give off light; shine: *a light burning in the window.* **5** [Wv4; I∅] to produce or experience an unpleasant hot feeling: *That medicine burns so! The burning sands hurt her feet.* **6** [I∅ (*with*), 3] (*usu in* -**ing** *form*) (*fig*) to experience a very strong feeling: *He was burning with anger/desire. She's burning to tell us what happened.* **7** [L9; X9] to force or make (a way) be or as if by force or great heat: *Her words burned (their way) into his heart.* **8** [I∅; L7] to change for the worse or be destroyed by fire or heat: *The potatoes have burnt (black) and we cannot eat them.* (*fig*) *She burns easily in the sun* (= her skin burns). **9** [T1] to destroy by fire: *He burned all his old papers.* **10** [T1] use for power, heating, or lighting: *The ship burned coal. The lamp burns oil.* **11** [X9] to change by fire or heat: *They are burning clay to make bricks. The papers were burnt to ashes.* **12** [X9] to produce by fire: *He burned a hole in his shirt. She burnt her name into the wood.* **13** [T1] to hurt or damage by fire or heat: *She burnt her hand on the hot metal.* **14** [T1] to kill by fire: *Joan of Arc was burnt (at the stake).*

brand 1 [T1] to burn a mark onto: *They branded the cattle with the farmer's own mark.* **2** [X1, *(fig)* to give (a name) to: *He was branded (as) a liar and a cheat.* **branding iron** [C] a piece of iron used for burning brands onto the skin of animals, etc

flame [Wv4;I0 *(up)*] to burn in flames: *The fire flamed (up) dangerously when he put oil on it.*

blaze [Wv4] **1** [I0] to (begin to) burn with a bright flame: *A wood fire was blazing (away), but there was no other light in the room. The fire blazed (up) suddenly when oil was poured on it.* *(fig) Her eyes were blazing with anger.* **2** [I0] to show very bright colour; shine brightly or warmly: *Masses of flowers were blazing in all parts of the garden. Lights blazed in every part of the house.*

spark 1 [Wv4;I0] to throw out sparks **2** [I0] to produce a spark **3** [T1 *(off)*] to lead to; be the cause of: *What sparked off the quarrel?* **4** [X9] to lead into action: *He sparked his team to victory.*

flare [I0 *(up)*] to blaze or flame strongly: *The lights flared.*

rage [I0] to burn very strongly: *The fire raged (through the forest) for days before rain put it out.*

smoke [I0] to give out smoke [⇒ H84]: *The fire was smoking badly.*

scorch 1 [T1; I0] to burn on the outside so as to change in colour, taste, or feeling but not burn up: *She scorched the shirt with an iron that was too hot. The meat was black and scorched on the outside but still raw inside. (fig) The drink was cold but strong and it seemed to scorch my throat. (fig) He scorched the pages of the book with his angry writing.* **2** [T1] to dry up and take the life out of (plants) with a strong dry heat: *fields scorched by the hot summer sun.*

H77 *verbs* : **setting fire, etc to things**

set fire to [T1] *genl* to cause to burn, often by mistake, carelessly, with bad intentions, etc: *She set fire to the papers and watched them burn. Who or what set fire to the house?*

light [T1] to cause (some particular thing) to burn, usu for a purpose: *Light the fire please. He lit the gas lamp.*

kindle 1 [T1; I0] to (cause to) start to burn or *(fig)* become a fiery red colour: *We tried to kindle the wood but it was wet and wouldn't kindle easily. The evening sun kindled the western sky.* **2** [T1;I0] *(fig)* **a** to cause (a feeling) to start: *His actions kindled hatred in the hearts of the people.* **b** (of a feeling) to start: *Her desire for him kindled with every word.* **3** [I0 *(with)*] to show a feeling: *When she saw him her eyes kindled (with desire).*

ignite [I0; T1] *often tech* to set fire to or catch fire: *The dry wood ignited. He ignited the wood with a match.*

feed [T1] to keep adding fuel to (a fire, etc) so that it will continue burning: *She fed the flames with pieces of wood. (fig) His words fed their hopes.*

fuel 1 [I0] to take in fuel: *Aircraft sometimes fuel in midair.* **2** [T1] to provide with fuel: *That car is being fuelled ready to try to beat the speed record.*

power [T1 *usu pass*] to supply power to (esp a machine): *Our grass-cutting machine is powered by electricity.*

coal 1 [T1] to supply (a ship, engine, etc) with coal **2** [I0] (of ships, engines, etc) to take a supply of coal: *Ships only call at this port to coal.*

H78 *verbs* : **putting fires out**

put out [v adv T1] to make (something) stop burning: *She put the light/fire out and went to bed.*

extinguish [T1] *fml* to put out (a light, fire, etc): *Smoking is forbidden; please extinguish your cigarettes. (fig) Nothing could extinguish his faith in human nature.*

quench [T1] to take away the heat of flames, steel, desire, etc, by water or other methods: *He quenched his thirst with a long drink of cold water.*

douse [T1] to put out (a fire, etc) by pouring water on it: *Douse those flames!*

go out [v adv I0] *infml & genl* to be extinguished: *The light/fire went out.*

H79 *adjectives, etc* : **relating to burning** [B]

combustible 1 [Wa3] able (easily) to burn: *These materials are highly combustible.* **2** [C] a substance that can catch fire and burn easily: *The workers demanded more pay for handling the dangerous combustibles.*

flammable [Wa3] easily set on fire: *These chemicals are highly flammable.* 'Flammable' is now the preferred word to describe chemicals and other things that burn easily. **non-flammable** [neg]

inflammable [Wa3] *becoming rare* easily set on fire: *These chemicals are highly inflammable.* The word 'inflammable' is not used so much now because 'in-' suggests 'not' and mistakes have happened because people did not understand the word.

fiery [Wa1] **1** like or of fire: *There was a fiery light in the sky.* **2** *(fig)* easily made angry: *He has a fiery temper.* **-iness** [U]

H80 *nouns* : **fuel and power**

fuel 1 [U] material that is used for producing heat or power by burning: *Wood, coal, oil, and gas are different kinds of fuel. The farmer cut up the old tree for his winter fuel (= to burn in his house). That car engine uses a lot of fuel.* **2** [U] material that can be used to produce atomic power **3** [C] a type of these: *Petrol is no* *longer a cheap fuel.* **4** [U] (*fig*) something that increases anger or any other strong active feeling: *The workers weren't satisfied with their wages, and when they were asked to work longer hours, it added fuel to the flames* (= made them more angry).

power [U] **1** force that may be used for doing work, driving a machine, or producing electricity: *People used to depend on wind power or water power, but now other forms of power are used. The damaged ship was able to reach port under her own power. This empire is losing power.* **2** the degree of this produced by something: *What is the power of this engine?*

energy [U] the power which does work and drives machines: *The energy of the sun seems never to get less.*

H81 *nouns* : **coal, etc, as a fuel**

coal [U] a black or dark-brown mineral which is dug (**mined**) from the earth, which can be burned to give heat, and from which gas, coal tar, and many other products can be made: *We must produce more coal for our industries. He worked in a coalmine.* ⌐ ·*likes a coal fire better than an electric fire.*

charcoal [U] (pieces of) the black substance made by burning wood in a closed container with little air, burnt in fires to give heat or used in sticks for drawing with: *In former times charcoal was used for melting iron because it was hotter and purer than coal.*

coke [U] the solid substance that remains after gas has been removed from coal by heating and which is burnt to give great heat, esp when making steel

peat **1** [U] partly decayed vegetable matter which takes the place of ordinary soil in a certain area (**peat bog**), and is used for burning instead of coal or for making plants grow better **2** [C] a piece of this cut out to be used for making fires

H82 *nouns* : **oil, etc, as a fuel**

oil [U;C] any of several kinds of fatty liquid (from animals, plants, or, esp, under the ground) used for lighting and heating: *Many kinds of oil are used today, to make machines move or to provide heat and light. The price of heating oil has gone up again.*

coal gas [U] gas used esp for lighting and heating, produced by burning coal

natural gas [U] gas which is taken from under the earth (or under the bottom of the sea) and mainly used for burning to cook and heat

petroleum [U] a mineral oil obtained from below the surface of the earth, used to produce petrol, paraffin, and various chemical substances

petrol [U] a liquid obtained esp from petroleum, used esp to produce power in the engines of cars, aircraft, etc: *We can fill up with petrol at the next petrol station.*

gasoline, -ene *AmE* petrol

gas **1** natural gas or coal gas **2** *AmE infml* gasoline

diesel (oil) **1** [U] a heavy fuel oil **2** [C] any machine, esp a vehicle, that runs on diesel fuel

paraffin [U] **1** *also* **paraffin oil** an oil made from petroleum, coal, etc, burnt for heat and in lamps for light **2** *also* **paraffin wax** a waxy substance got from petroleum, coal, etc used esp in making candles

kerosene [U] *AmE* paraffin (def **1**)

benzine [U] a kind of petrol

benzene [U] a colourless liquid, obtained from coal, that burns easily and changes fats from solid to liquid form when mixed with them

turpentine *also* **turps** *infml abbrev* [U] a kind of oil used esp for mixing paints

H83 *nouns* : **electricity as a fuel** [U]

electricity **1** the power which is produced by rubbing (**friction**) or by chemical means (a **battery**) or by a machine called a **generator**, and which gives us heat, light, and sound and drives machines **2** electric current: *They turned off the electricity in the house when they went away for their holiday.*

hydroelectricity electricity produced by the power of falling water

power electric power: *These are all power tools, you need to plug them into a power source.*

H84 *nouns* : **the results of burning**

smoke [U] a cloud of gases, etc, which can be seen, smelled, etc, as it rises from anything that is burning: *The smoke from the fire rose into the air. The room was full of smoke.* **smoky** [Wa1;B] **1** giving off smoke **2** full of smoke: *don't like the smoky air in that room.* **-ily** [adv] **-iness** [U] **smokeless** [B] **1** burning without smoke **2** free from smoke **-ly** [adv] **-ness** [U]

fumes [P] strong-smelling and often dangerous smoke, gases, etc: *That factory gives off a lot of nasty fumes.*

ash [U] the soft grey powder that remains after something has been burnt: *Clean the ash from the fireplace. The cigarette ash fell on the floor* **ashen** [B] **1** like ash in colour **2** consisting of ash

ashes [P] *genl* ash: *The house was burnt to ashes. Clean the ashes from the fireplace.*

coal [C] a flaming, burning, or already burnt piece of coal or wood: *A coal fell from the fire and burned the mat.*

ember [C *usu pl*] a red-hot piece of wood or coal, esp in a fire that is no longer burning with flames: *He warmed his hands over the dying embers.*

cinder [C] a small piece of partly burned wood

coal, etc, that is not yet ash and that can be burned but without producing flames

cinders [P] ashes: *Before making the fire remember to empty out yesterday's cinders.*

clinker [C; U] (a lump of) the partly-burnt matter left after coal or other minerals have been burned

H85 *nouns* : **cloth and textiles**

[ALSO ⇒ D130 CLOTHES]

cloth 1 [U; C] material made from wool, hair, cotton, etc, by weaving, and used for making garments, coverings, etc: *I need a lot of cloth if I'm going to make a new dress. They produce cloths of various kinds in this factory.* **2** [C *often in comb*] a piece of this used for a special purpose: *She cleaned the table with a cloth. She put a clean tablecloth on the table. He dried the dishes with a dishcloth.*

material [U; C] cotton or other woven cloth from which clothes may be made: *That's a nice material. This is good dress material* (= material for making dresses out of).

fabric 1 [C; U] cloth made by threads woven together in any of various ways: *They sell good cotton fabrics here.* **2** [U] (*fig*) the framework, base, or system: *The whole fabric of society was changed by the war.*

stuff [U; C] *infml & genl* cloth; material: *What kind of stuff is her coat made of? These are rather unusual stuffs.*

textiles [P] *genl & tech* cloths, fabrics, etc, esp as made in factories **textile** [Wa5;A] of or concerning textiles: *This is a textile factory/mill.*

H86 *nouns* : **threads and yarn**

[ALSO ⇒ H45, I 57–58]

thread [U; C] very fine cord made by spinning cotton, wool, silk, etc, and used in sewing and weaving

yarn [U] a long continuous thread, as of wool or cotton, used in making cloth, carpets, etc

braid 1 *also* **plait** [C] a narrow piece of material made by twisting several pieces together like a rope **2** [U] material of this kind put along the edges of clothing, esp as a decoration: *His coat was covered in gold braid.*

H87 *nouns* : **kinds of cloth** [U; C]

cotton 1 a type of plant grown in warm areas for the soft white hair that surrounds its seeds **2** the soft white hair of this plant used for making thread, cloth, cotton wool [⇒B176], etc **3** thread or cloth made from this

wool 1 the soft thick type of hair which sheep and some goats have: *Some sheep's wool was left on the fence.* **2** material made up from this or something like it in the form of a long string: *As she knitted* [⇒ I 57] *she kept the ball of wool*

beside her. **3** material from sheep's wool woven into cloth: *She wore a wool suit.*

worsted a fine wool cloth

poplin a strong shiny cotton cloth used esp for making shirts and suits

linen 1 a type of cloth made from the plant **flax**: *He wore a suit made of linen/a linen suit.* **2** clothes and cloths made of linen: *He changed his linen* (= linen underclothes). *Get clean bedlinen* (= linen bedsheets).

silk fine thread which is produced by a kind of insect (**silkworm**) and made into thread for sewing and into smooth soft cloth: *Her silk dress must have cost a lot of money.* **silken** [Wa5;B] *lit* soft or smooth like silk **silky** [Wa1;B] *not fml* of or like silk

satin a kind of very fine smooth cloth mainly of silk, which is shiny on the front and dull on the back **satiny** [Wa5;B] of or like satin, esp in a pleasant way

velvet a type of fine, closely woven cloth made up of silk and also of nylon, cotton, etc, having a soft thick raised surface of short cut threads on one side only: *She wore a dress of blue velvet.*

lace a netlike ornamental cloth made of fine thread: *She had handmade lace curtains.*

canvas strong, rough cloth used for tents, sails, bags, etc

jute a substance used for making strong and rough cloth, from either of two plants grown esp in East India and Bangladesh

tweed a type of coarse woollen cloth woven from threads of different colours, esp in Scotland **tweeds** [P] tweed clothes: *She was dressed in tweeds.*

felt a kind of hard cloth made from wool pressed flat: *He wore a felt hat.*

H88 *nouns, etc* : **kinds of skin**

[ALSO ⇒ A126]

leather [U] animal skin that has been treated (**tanned**) to preserve it, used for making shoes, bags, etc: *She wore a leather coat.* **leatherette** [U] a cheap material made to look like leather **leathery** [Wa2;B] like leather; hard and stiff

skin 1 [C; U *often in comb*] the natural outer covering of an animal, esp when used as leather, fur, etc: *Many skins are needed to make a fur coat. She wore a coat made of sheepskin; it was a sheepskin coat.* **2** [T1] to remove the skin from: *He skinned the deer.*

hide [C; U] (an) animal skin, esp when removed to be used for leather: *The bag was made of hide. He sold hides.*

suede [U] soft leather or goatskin with a rough surface

fur 1 [U] the soft thick fine hair that covers the body of some types of animal, such as bears, rabbits, cats, etc **2** [C] a hair-covered skin of certain special types of animal, such as foxes, rabbits, beavers [⇒ A60], etc, which has been or will be treated and used for clothing: *The*

402

*Canadian fur trader had a fine load of furs to
sell after his hunting trip.* **3** [C] a garment made
of one or more of these: *She was wearing a
silver fox fur across her shoulders. She wore a
fur coat.*

H89 *nouns* : **plastic and elastic** [U; C]

plastic any of various light man-made materials
produced chemically from oil or coal, that can
be made into different shapes when soft and
keep their shape when hard: *Nylon is a form of
plastic. Which of these coloured plastics do you
prefer?*
nylon a strong elastic material made from coal,
water, and air and made into cloths, cords, and
plastics
vinyl (any of several types of) firm bendable
plastic used instead of leather, rubber, wood,
etc: *He bought a new vinyl floor covering.*
elastic [*also* B] (material) which springs back
into its natural shape after it is stretched, such
as rubber [⇒ H70]: *This toy plane will fly if
you wind up the elastic that drives it. Put an
elastic band round your banknotes.*

H90 *nouns* : **kinds of paper**

paper 1 [U] material made into thin sheets from
wood, cloths, etc which is used for writing and
printing on, covering parcels, putting on walls,
etc: *Can I have some (more) paper? Wrap the
parcel in brown paper.* **2** [C] a piece of this: *The
papers lay on the floor.*
card 1 [U] stiffened paper: *You should use card
for this job, and cut it into pieces if necessary.*
2 [C] a small piece of stiffened paper, usu with
information printed on it and having various
uses: *The invitations were printed on cards.*
cardboard 1 [U] a thick stiff paperlike, usu
brownish material used for making boxes, the
backs of books, etc: *It was a cardboard box*
2 [A] (*fig*) something stiff, unreal, or unnatural:
Her new book is full of cardboard characters.

H91 *nouns* : **soaps and solvents** [U; C]

soap a product made from fat and alkali [⇒
H73], for use with water to clean the body or
other things: *She bought a bar/cake of soap.*
soapy [Wa1;B] of or like soap **-iness** [U]
soap powder soap in powder form: *Many kinds
of soap powder/Many soap powders are sold,
especially for use in washing machines.*
bleach a substance used to make something
(esp clothes) whiter or cleaner: *She used a
strong bleach to clean the bathroom.*
detergent a chemical product used for cleaning
esp clothing and dishes rather than the human
body: *Our new washday detergent washes our
clothes whiter than ever before.*

disinfectant a substance used for cleaning and
for killing harmful bacteria [⇒ A37] (**disinfect-
ing**): *The hospital smelled of disinfectant. This
is a special disinfectant soap.*
solvent a liquid able to break down dirt, and
used to clean metals, etc: *Alcohol and petrol
are useful solvents for spots that will not come
off in water.*

H92 *nouns* : **polish and lacquer**
[ALSO ⇒ H95, D175]

polish 1 [U; C] any liquid, powder, paste, etc,
used in polishing a surface: *What kind of
metal/shoe polish do you use? She uses a wax
polish on her furniture.* **2** [S9] a smooth shiny
surface produced by rubbing: *If you put hot
plates on this table they'll spoil its polish. What
a high polish* (= a very shiny surface) *you have
on your furniture!* **3** [U] (*fig*) *apprec* fine quality or perfection (of manners, education,
writing, etc); *She plays the piano with great
polish.*
varnish 1 [U; C] (any of several types of) liquid
made by mixing various substances with oil
which, when brushed onto articles made esp of
wood and allowed to dry, gives a clear hard
bright surface: *Varnish is usually put onto oil
paintings to protect the colours.* **2** [S] the shiny
appearance produced by using this substance:
Hot plates may spoil the varnish on a table.
lacquer [U; C] any one of several transparent,
sometimes coloured, substances used to form a
hard shiny surface on metal or wood, or to
make hair stay in place
wax [U; C] a solid material made of fats or oils,
greasy [⇒ H12] when melted by heat and used
for rubbing on surfaces, making candles [⇒
H119], etc
resin 1 [U; C] a sticky substance that comes out
of certain trees and is often used for making
varnish **2** a similar substance made from
plastic **resinous** [B] of, concerning, or like
resin

H93 *nouns* : **paint and dye**
[ALSO ⇒ I 46]

paint [U; C] **1** liquid colouring matter which can
be put or spread on a surface to make it a
certain colour: *Where are those tins of green
paint? The warning sign on the door said 'wet
paint'.*
coat [C] a covering, esp of paint, varnish, etc,
spread over the surface: *Give that wall another
coat of paint.*
dye [U; C] a vegetable or chemical substance,
usu liquid, used in colour things, esp by dipping: *Have you a bright blue dye in the shop?*
ink [U; C] coloured liquid, usu used for writing:
*Can I have some red ink? They use various inks
in this kind of printing.*

H94 *nouns* : **tar and pitch**

tar [U] a black substance, thick and sticky when hot and hard when cold, used for making roads, preserving wood, etc

tarmac *also fml* **tarmacadam 1** [U] a mixture of tar and crushed or very small stones used for making the surface of roads **2** [C] an area covered in tarmac, esp one used for landing aircraft on (a **runway**)

asphalt [U] a black sticky material that is firm when it hardens, used for the surface of roads: *They have good asphalt roads here.*

pitch [U] any of various black substances that are melted into a sticky material used for making hard protective coverings or for putting in cracks, esp in wooden ships, to stop water coming through

H95 *verbs* : **polishing, painting, and dyeing**

[ALSO ⇒ D175]

polish 1 [T1 (*up*); X7; L9, esp *up*] to make or become smooth and shiny by continual rubbing: *Polish your shoes with a brush. Silver polishes easily with this special cloth. He polished up the old copper coins. The coins didn't polish up very well.* **2** [Wv5;T1] (*fig*) to make (a speech, piece of writing, artistic performance, etc) as good as possible: *The writer spends a lot of time polishing his work. The piano player gave a very polished performance. What a very polished person she is; she's very good socially.*

varnish [T1] to cover with varnish: *He varnished the wooden table.*

lacquer [T1] to cover with lacquer: *She lacquered the table. She has lacquered hair.*

wax [T1] to treat with wax [⇒ H92]: *He waxed the car then polished it.*

paint [T1] to cover with paint: *He painted the walls. He painted the boat blue and white.*
painter [C] a person who paints things, esp as an occupation

coat [T1 (*with*)] to cover with a coat (as of paint): *The wall had been thickly coated with paint.*

dye [T1; X7; L7] to give a colour to by using dye: *She dyed the wool (blue).*

ink [T1 (*in, over*)] to cover with ink: *He inked in the darker parts of the picture.*

bleach [T1; (I∅)] to (cause to) become white or whiter, esp by using bleach [⇒ H91] or through the light of the sun: *They bleached the clothes. There were only a few dry bones left, bleached by the sun.*

tar [T1] to cover with tar: *The road was tarred yesterday.*

asphalt [T1] to cover (esp a road) with asphalt: *They asphalted the roads.*

tan [I∅; T1] **1** to make (an animal's skin) into leather: *Tanning is an important industry in that town. He tanned the skins.* **2** [*also* X7] to

(cause to) become brown: *His skin tans easily. The sun tanned her brown.* **tanner** [C] a person who tans skins **tannery** [C] a place where the tanning of skins is done

Equipment, machines, and instruments

H110 *nouns* : **equipment and apparatus**

equipment [U] **1** the things needed to do something: *We need modern office equipment. The climbers had all the necessary equipment for mountain climbing.* **2** the act of equipping: *The complete equipment of the new hospital will take a year.*

apparatus [U; C *usu sing*] **1** a set of instruments, machines, etc, that work together for a particular purpose: *This electric heating apparatus is very clean.* **2** a set of instruments, machines, tools, materials, etc, needed for a particular purpose: *The television men set up their apparatus ready to film.* **3** a group of parts that work together, esp inside the body: *The breathing apparatus includes the nose, throat, and lungs.* **4** an organization or system made up of many parts: *The political apparatus set up by the government is used to settle industrial troubles.*

gear [U] a set of things collected together, often equipment, esp when used for a particular purpose *Did you bring all your gear with you?*

kit [U] (a box for) a set of articles, esp tools, needed for a certain kind of work or for a particular purpose: *There is a shoe-cleaning kit in the cupboard. Where's my tool kit?*

stuff [U] *infml & genl* equipment, etc: *Bring all your stuff in here. Have you got the necessary stuff for the job?*

things [P] *infml & genl* equipment, etc, esp when carried with one: *Where can I put my things? I need to get the right things for the job.*

tackle 1 [U] equipment needed for a game or certain kinds of work: *fishing tackle. He had all his tackle with him.* **2** [C] a set of ropes and wheels, etc, for lifting heavy things or moving the sails of a ship

rig [C *often in comb*] equipment put together for a special purpose: *an oilrig*

paraphernalia [U] *esp pomp & ironical* the equipment, tools, etc, which a person has or which are (thought to be) needed for a job: *Do you really need all this paraphernalia to do a simple job like that? He has brought his paraphernalia with him.*

H111 *nouns* : **tools and utensils** [C]

tool 1 any instrument or apparatus such as an axe, hammer, spade, etc, held in the hands for doing special jobs **2** (*fig*) anything necessary for doing one's job: *Words are his tools. We must give the government the necessary tools for winning the war.* **3** (*fig*) a person unfairly or dishonestly used by another for his own purposes: *The king was the tool of the military government.*

implement *fml* a tool: *What implements did they use?—They used stone implements.*

artifact, artefact anything made by man, esp if useful: *wood and metal artifacts*

instrument 1 an object used to help in work: *Have we got all the medical instruments?* **2** *also* **musical instrument** an object which is played to give musical sounds **3** someone or something which seems to be used by an outside force to cause something to happen: *He didn't mean to do it; he was just an instrument of fate.*

utensil *fml or tech* **1** an object for use in a particular way, esp a tool: *He bought all the utensils for gardening.* **2** any tool, container, etc, used in the house, esp for cooking: *He washed the kitchen utensils.*

H112 nouns : machines and appliances [C]

machine 1 a man-made instrument or apparatus which uses power (such as electricity) to perform work: *That's a nice sewing machine. The factory machines are very noisy. That machine needs to be repaired.* **2** (*fig*) a person or group of persons which is like a machine: *The army turned him from a clever boy into a machine. The party machine is ready for the election.*

appliance an apparatus, instrument, or tool for a particular purpose, often one that is fitted to a larger machine: *Different appliances can be screwed onto this machine to crush coffee beans, prepare cake mixture, etc. She has all the modern kitchen appliances. They sell electrical appliances for the home.*

device an instrument, esp one that is cleverly thought out or made for a special purpose: *He invented a neat little device for sharpening pencils.*

gadget *infml* a small machine or useful apparatus: *What is that gadget used for?*

contraption *usu infml & deprec* a machine or device, esp if it looks unusual: *What on earth is that contraption? Get that dangerous contraption out of here before it hurts somebody!*

robot 1 a machine that can work (in some ways) like a person: *The plane has a robot pilot.* **2** (*fig*) a person who acts like a machine

automaton an automatic [⇒ I 73] machine that can behave like a person: *They work like automatons in that factory.*

spares [P] extra parts of machines, usu kept to take the place of parts which have been damaged, used too much, etc: *Do you keep spares for this kind of car?*

H113 nouns : machinery, engines, and motors, etc

machinery [U] **1** machines in general: *A lot of new machinery has been put into the factory.* **2** the working parts of an apparatus: *Something is wrong with the machinery of this clock; it isn't working.* **3** (*fig*) a system or organization by which action is controlled: *The machinery of the law works slowly.*

engine [C] any piece of machinery with moving parts which changes energy [⇒ H80] from steam, electricity, oil, etc, into movement: *That car engine is a good one. The car has engine trouble.*

motor 1 [C] a machine, esp small, that changes power, esp electrical power, into movement: *This grass-cutting machine is driven by an electric motor. He sells motor oils* (= oil for motors). **2** [A] driven by an engine: *No motor vehicle is allowed by law to use the roads if its condition makes it unsafe to drive. a motor vessel; a motor scooter; a motor mower* **3** [A] of, for, or concerning vehicles driven by an engine, esp those used on roads: *the motor industry. Motor insurance costs more if a car is used in a big city. motor sports; motor racing; a motor magazine*

mechanism [C *usu sing*] **1** the arrangement by which a machine works or is made: *I can't understand the mechanism of this machine.* **2** a small machine: *That's an interesting mechanism; how does it work?*

works [P] the moving parts (of a machine): *The clock has stopped; something must have got into the works.*

workings [P] the way in which something, esp a machine, works: *I shall never understand the workings of an engine.*

clockwork [U] **1** the machinery that works a clock **2** any machinery like this, that can usu be wound with a key, and that is esp used in toys: *The children played happily with their clockwork toys.*

bearing [C] a part of a machine on which a moving part rests, in which it can move **ball bearing** [C] **1** *less common* a part of a machine that turns on small metal balls **2** *more common* one of these balls: *What size ball bearings do you use?*

H114 nouns, etc : turbines, generators, and pumps, etc

turbine [C] a kind of engine which works by the force of gas or water turning a wheel **turbo-** [*comb form*] relating to a turbine: *a turbo-generator*

generator [C] a machine which makes (= **generates**), usu electricity: *The building has two electricity generators.*

dynamo [C] a machine (esp small) which turns some other kind of power into electricity:

There is a dynamo on my bicycle. (*fig*) *He is a real dynamo; he never stops working.*

pile [C] a type of apparatus that produces electricity or atomic power

reactor [C] an atomic pile

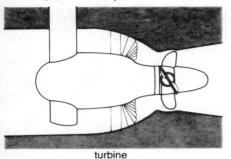

turbine

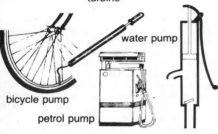

water pump

bicycle pump

petrol pump

pump 1 [C] a machine, usu with a tube and a handle, for forcing liquid, air, or gas into or out of something: *At the farm there was an old-fashioned pump for drawing water from a well. The heart is a kind of natural pump that moves the blood around the body. He used a bicycle pump to fill the tyres with air. The garage has four petrol pumps.* **2** [T1; L9] to move by means of a pump: *They pumped the water out of the ship.* **3** [IØ] to work a pump: *Stop pumping now.*

piston [C] a round metal plate or a short solid pipe-shaped piece of metal that fits into a tube (**cylinder**) in which it is moved up and down by pressure or explosion, used in engines, pumps, etc, to give movement to other parts of a machine by means of a connecting rod (**piston rod**)

fan 1 [C] an object used in the hand or electrically to cause the movement of air, usu in order to make a person or place less hot: *She waved* (= moved backwards and forwards) *her fan in front of her face. The fans set in the windows began to turn and draw fresh air into the room.* **2** [T1] to cool, etc, with a fan, or anything used in the same way: *She felt hot and fanned herself with a newspaper.*

H115 *nouns* : **meters and gauges, etc** [C]

meter a machine which measures the amount

used: *He read the amount of gas used on the meter. He read the gas meter. The parking meter allows two hours' parking for 20p.*

gauge an instrument for measuring size, amount, etc, such as the width of wire, the amount of rain, etc: *The rain gauge shows that 2 cm of rain fell here yesterday.*

dial 1 the front or face of any of various instruments such as a clock: *A dial shows the measurements of time, speed, pressure, etc, by means of a pointer and figures.* **2** the plate on the front of a radio set, with a pointer and names or numbers, which is used to find a particular radio station **3** the wheel on a telephone with holes for the fingers, which is moved round when one makes a telephone call.

clock *not fml* a dial, esp on a vehicle, esp for showing the speed or number of kilometres/miles travelled

scale 1 a set of marks, esp numbers, on an instrument at exactly fixed distances apart, as for measuring: *The distance is measured on a metric scale* (= one using metres, not feet). *This slide rule* (= special ruler for calculating, used by engineers, etc) *has six scales.* **2** a piece of wood, plastic, etc, with such marks on the edge **3** a set of numbers or standards for measuring or comparing: *The workers here are all on the same pay scale.*

indicator a needle or pointer on a machine showing the measure of some quality, or a substance which shows what is happening in a chemical mixture

panel a board on which controls or instruments of various kinds are fastened: *He could not understand the aeroplane's control panel.*

dashboard the long board in the front of a motor vehicle into which the instruments are set

switch 1 a movable apparatus for stopping an electric current from flowing, esp one which is moved up or down with the hand **2** a movable apparatus for causing a train to turn onto another railway line

switchboard 1 a board containing a number of switches **2** the arrangement of telephone wires, or the people who work on it, on a central board for connections

knob a switch in the form of a round lump: *He turned the knobs on the radio set. How do you turn the sound down on this machine?—Try the second knob on the left.*

H116 *nouns* : **frames and structures**

frame [C] **1** the set of main supports over and around which something is stretched or built: *In some parts of the world small boats are made of skins stretched over a wooden frame.* **2** the hard solid parts which are fitted together to make something: *This old bed has an iron frame.* **3** (the form or shape of) a human or animal body: *a man with a powerful frame. Such hardships are more than the human frame* *can bear.* **4** a firm border or case into which something is fitted or set, or which holds something in place: *In a silver frame on the table there was a photograph of his son. I can't close the door; it doesn't fit properly into its frame. The frame of her glasses needs mending; one of the pieces of glass* (**lenses**) *might fall out.*

framework [C] **1** a supporting structure: *In modern times most ships have a metal framework; formerly they were made of wood.* **2** (*fig*) a plan or system: *He gave a talk about the framework of modern government.*

network [C] **1** a large system of lines, tubes, wires, etc, that cross or meet one another: *Britain has a large railway network. The plant had a network of roots.* **2** (*fig*) a group or system whose members are connected in some way: *He has a network of business and personal friends in many cities.*

structure 1 [U] the way in which parts are formed into a whole: *He studied the structure of the brain/the cell structure of the body.* **2** [C] something formed of many parts, esp a building: *That building is a tall structure.* **structural** [Wa5;B] of, concerning, or having a structure: *The building has a structural fault.* **-ly** [adv] *The building is not structurally sound* (= strong).

scaffolding [U] poles and boards (to be) built into a system, usu to support people working on the outside of buildings

body [C] the main part or structure of a vehicle, place, etc: *The car's body was covered in rust* [⇒ H69]. *The body of the hall was filled with people.*

hull [C] the main body of a ship

chassis [C] **1** the framework on which the body and working parts of a vehicle, radio, etc, are fastened or built **2** the frame and working parts of a car, radio, etc, as opposed to its body **3** the landing apparatus of a plane

rack [C] a frame on which things can be kept: *A rack for tools is a tool rack and for luggage* (= cases, etc) *in a train is a luggage rack. He put the cases on the roof rack of the car.*

H117 *nouns* : **cranes and elevators** [C]
[ALSO ⇒ D30]

crane a machine for lifting and moving heavy objects by means of a very strong rope or wire fastened to a movable arm

pulley an apparatus consisting of a wheel over which a rope or chain can be moved, used for lifting heavy things

hoist an apparatus for lifting heavy goods

elevator 1 *AmE,* **lift** *BrE* a machine that takes people up or down to another floor inside a building: *Go up in the elevator. Take the elevator to the 6th floor.* **2** a machine consisting of a moving belt with buckets, used for raising grain and liquid, unloading ships, etc **3** a storehouse for grain **4** one of two movable parts in the tail of an aeroplane which make it able to climb and descend

H118 *nouns* : **clocks and watches** [C]
[⇒ pictures at L229]

clock an instrument for measuring and showing time, usu by means of two or three hands moving around a numbered face (= **dial**) to mark the hour, minute, and sometimes second: *The clock in the church tower struck nine. He makes clocks; he is a clockmaker.*

watch a small clock that is worn on the wrist (a **wristwatch**) or carried in a pocket (a **pocket watch**): *My watch is slow/fast/correct. He makes watches; he is a watchmaker.*

timepiece *fml & old use* a clock

chronometer a very exact clock or other instrument for measuring time, esp as used for scientific purposes

H119 *nouns* : **lamps and torches** [C]
[ALSO ⇒ L20 LIGHT]

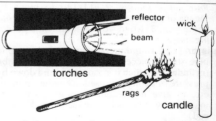

torches

candle

lamp [*often in comb*] **1** any of various types of apparatus for giving light, as from oil, gas, or electricity **2** any of various types of electrical apparatus used to produce health-giving forms of heat: *a sunlamp*

lantern 1 a container, usu of glass and metal, that encloses and protects the flame of a light **2** the top of a building or tower (such as a lighthouse) with windows on all sides

light [*often in comb*] anything which gives light, esp a lamp, lantern, small fire, etc: *He lit a light. The room had a small electric light beside the bed. Turn off all the lights. Most traffic lights are red, yellow and green.*

torch 1 *AmE usu* **flashlight** a small electric

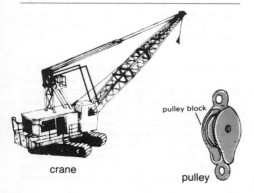

pulley block

crane

pulley

light carried in the hand to give light: *The policemen shone their torches into our faces.* **2** a mass of burning material tied to a stick and carried by hand to give light: *Light the torches!* (*fig*) *The dry forest went up like a torch* (= burned very fiercely). *The torch of knowledge/learning is burning brightly.*

beacon a usu large light, lantern, etc, used esp in one particular place to give warning of danger, esp to ships: *The beacon on the shore warned the ship to keep away. They lit a beacon on the hill-top.*

flare something that provides a bright light out of doors, esp in an airfield or street market, etc: *The ship is sinking; send up some flares!*

candle a usu round stick of wax which gives light when it burns

wick 1 a piece of twisted thread in a candle which burns as the wax melts **2** a tubelike piece of material in an oil lamp which draws up oil while burning

-light [*comb form*] light of a stated kind: *He read the book by lamplight/candlelight. She searched by torchlight for the lost money. Sunlight and moonlight are part of nature.*

H120 *nouns* : **fires and burners** [C]
[ALSO ⇒ H75–79]

fire a gas or electrical apparatus for warming a room, with the flames or red-hot wires able to be seen

furnace 1 a large enclosed fire used for producing hot water or steam: *Furnaces are used for heating buildings by means of pipes, or for driving steam engines. This room's like a furnace* (= it's much too hot). **2** an apparatus in a factory, in which metals and other substances are heated to very high temperatures in an enclosed space **2**

heater a machine for heating the air, or water, such as those which burn gas, oil, or electricity to produce heat

stove an apparatus for cooking or heating which works by burning coal, oil, gas, etc, or by electricity: *We have a gas stove and an oil stove.*

oven any of several types of enclosed boxlike spaces used for cooking, baking clay, etc **like an oven** uncomfortably hot: *It's like an oven in here; open the window.*

cooker an apparatus on which food can be cooked: *Do you have a gas cooker or an electric cooker in your kitchen?*

burner a thing that burns, esp the part of a heater, cooker, etc, that provides flames **-burner** [*comb form*] **1** having burners of a stated number or type: *It's a two-burner heater.* **2** an apparatus burning material of a stated type of power, heat, or light: *He bought an oil-burner.*

radiator 1 an apparatus consisting of pipes with steam or hot water passing through them, used for heating buildings **2** an electric heater for the same purpose

match a very small thin piece of wood with a

substance at one end which can be set on fire easily: *He lit a match. He lit a cigarette with a match.* **box of matches** [C] a small box full of such matches **matchbox** [C] a box for matches, esp if empty

lighter an instrument that gives a light in order to set something else on fire: *a cigarette lighter*

H121 *nouns* : **fireworks**

fireworks [P] **1** bright explosive lights used esp for entertainment: *The children enjoyed watching the fireworks.* **2** the tubes, etc, which are lit to produce fireworks: *He bought some fireworks.* **3** a show of fireworks, esp at a special ceremony **4** (*fig*) a show of anger: *I told you there'd be fireworks if you annoyed the teacher by talking in class.*

pyrotechnics 1 [U] the art or practice of making fireworks for entertainment or as signals for ships, aircraft, soldiers, etc **2** [P] *fml or tech* a public show of fireworks for entertainment **3** [P] (*fig*) a (too) splendid show of skill in words, music, etc: *We admired the pianist's pyrotechnics, but we felt that he didn't express the real meaning of the music.*

rocket [C] a stick attached to a tube-shaped case packed with gunpowder, that is shot high into the air and lets out stars of coloured flame; a kind of firework: *We'll let off some rockets on your birthday.*

H122 *nouns* : **magnets and compasses, etc** [C]

magnet 1 an object, esp a piece of iron, which can draw other objects, esp iron, towards it, either naturally or because of an electric current being passed through it: *The (centre of the) earth is a natural magnet. One can pick up pins with a magnet.* **2** (*fig*) a person or thing which draws or attracts (people): *High wages may act as a magnet to encourage people to work in the mines.* [⇒ H200–201]

compass 1 an instrument for showing direction, usu consisting of a freely-moving magnetic needle which always moves to point to the north: *A good sailor is never lost as long as he has a map and compass.* **2** any of several other instruments used for this purpose [*also* ⇒ L12]

needle the long thin pointed piece of metal in a dial [⇒ H115], esp of a compass: *The needle pointed north.*

H123 *nouns* : **lenses and glasses**

lens [C] **1** a piece of transparent glass or other material, curved on one or both sides, which makes a beam of light passing through it bend, spread out, become narrower, change direction, etc, used in glasses for the eyes, cameras, microscopes, etc: *Spectacles have two lenses, one for each eye.* **2** such an instrument made of natural animal material behind the black opening (**pupil**) in the front of the eye

glass [C] an object made of or containing glass, shaped esp to make things seem larger: *He looked at the insect through a magnifying glass* (= a glass that magnifies or makes things seem larger).

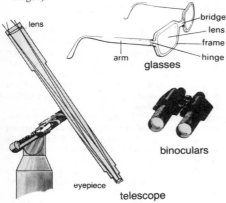

glasses

binoculars

telescope
eyepiece
lens

prism [C] a block, esp of glass, with three or more sides, that breaks up white light into the different colours of the spectrum [⇒ L27] **prismatic** [Wa5;B] of or like a prism **-ally** [adv Wa4]

glasses [P] an arrangement of two lenses in a frame which holds them over the eyes to help a person with imperfect eyesight to see clearly: *He wore (a pair of) glasses.*

spectacles [P] *fml* glasses: *He wore a (a pair of) spectacles.*

specs [P] *infml* glasses

telescope [C] a tubelike scientific instrument with lenses used for seeing distant objects by making them appear nearer and larger **telescopic** [Wa5;B] of, concerning, like, or with a telescope **-ally** [Adv Wa4]: *He examined the star telescopically.*

binoculars [P] a pair of short telescopes for both eyes, used to see distant objects: *Binoculars are used for sports and the theatre. He watched the bird through (a pair of) binoculars.*

microscope [C] an instrument with lenses through which one can look at very small things because it makes them appear much larger than they are: *He saw very small living things under/through the microscope.* **microscopic** [Wa2;B] small, as seen or needing to be seen through a microscopic **-ally** [adv Wa4]

H124 *nouns* : **bells and gongs** [C]

bell 1 a rounded, hollow metal vessel, which makes a ringing sound when struck **2** something with the form of a typical bell, hollow and

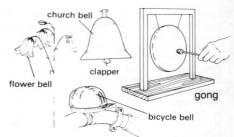

church bell

clapper

flower bell

gong

bicycle bell

widening towards the open end: *The bell of the flower was beautiful.*

clapper the hammerlike object hung inside a bell which strikes the bell to make it ring

gong a round piece of metal hanging from a frame, which when struck with a stick gives a deep ringing sound, as used in Eastern music or to call people to meals

H125 *nouns* : **scales and balances**

scale 1 [C *often plural with sing meaning*] *also* **pair of scales** [C] a pair of pans for weighing an object by comparing it with a known weight **2** any weighing machine: *I weighed myself on the scales in the bathroom/on the bathroom scales.*

balance 1 [C] an instrument for weighing things by seeing whether the amounts in two hanging pans are equal **2** *also* **counterweight** a weight or influence on one side which equals a weight or influence on the other: *The slow and steady Mr Smith is a balance to the clever but irresponsible Mr Jones.*

weight [C] a piece of metal of one of several standard weights, which can be balanced against any substance to measure an equal weight of that substance

H126 *nouns, etc* : **pins and clips** [C]
[ALSO ⇒ H49]

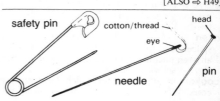

safety pin

cotton/thread

head

eye

pin

needle

pin 1 a short thin stiff piece of metal that looks like a small nail used for fastening together pieces of cloth, paper, etc **2** a quite short thin piece of metal, pointed at one end and with an ornament at the other, used esp as a form of jewellery **3** a short piece of wood or metal used as a support, to fasten things together, etc

clip a small, variously-shaped plastic or usu metal object for holding things tightly together or in place: *She keeps her hair in place with clips. Fasten those sheets of paper together with a clip, please.*

paper clip a small piece of curved wire used for holding sheets of paper together

staple 1 a small bit of thin wire with two square corners, which is driven into sheets of light material (esp paper) and usu bent over to hold them together **2** [Wv3;T1 (*together, to*)] to fasten with a staple: *She stapled the papers together. She stapled the small paper to the page.* **stapler** [C] a small machine used for stapling **3** a U-shaped short strong wire with pointed ends for driving with a hammer, as for holding a wire in place

safety pin a wire pin with a cover at one end and bent around so that its point can be held inside the cover

needle 1 a long thin pointed piece of metal with a hole (the **eye**) at one end, used esp for sewing **2** a similar piece of metal used as a pointer in a dial [⇨ H115]

H127 *nouns* : **stamps and seals** [C]
[ALSO ⇨ G191 POST]

stamp 1 *also fml* **postage stamp** a small usu four-sided piece of paper sold by post offices in various values for sticking on a piece of mail to be sent: *A 10-pence stamp, please. I collect foreign stamps; I keep most of them in a stamp album* [⇨ G165]. *Rare old ones have to be bought from stamp dealers.* **2** a piece of paper like this for sticking on certain official papers to show that tax (**stamp duty**) has been paid **3** *also fml* **trading stamp** a piece of paper like this given by a shop to a buyer at a fixed rate (such as one for each 2½ pence spent), for sticking in a book and later exchanging for goods or money: *Does this shop give stamps?—Yes, we give treble stamps* (= at three times the usual rate). **4** an instrument or tool for pressing or printing onto a surface: *He used a rubber stamp to put his name and address on the paper.* **5** a mark or pattern made by this: *The stamp in this library book says it must be returned tomorrow.* **6** an act of stamping, as with the foot: *The horse gave a stamp of impatience.* **7** [*usu sing*] (*fig*) a sign typical of something: *His remarks bear the stamp of truth.* **8** [*usu sing*] (*fig*) a lasting result; effect: *The events left their stamp on his mind.* **9** (*fig*) a kind; sort: *I don't like books of that stamp. Your ideas are of a quite different stamp.*

seal 1 an official, often round pattern belonging to, and being the sign of, a government, university, company, or, esp formerly, a powerful person **2** a piece of wax or soft metal into which such a pattern is pressed and which is fixed to some formal and official writings **3** such a pattern pressed into writing on paper to make it official **4** a circle of coloured paper with or without such a pattern, attached to something written, usu for the same purpose **5** a metal tool with such a pattern for pressing it into paper or hot metal or wax **6** a small piece of paper or wax which is fixed across an opening

as of an envelope or packet and which must be broken in order to open it

H128 *verbs* : **stamping or sealing** [T1]

stamp 1 to put a stamp on: *Stamp these letters, please.* **2** to print, etc, with a stamp: *The machine stamped his name and address on the papers.*

frank 1 [*also* Wv4] to print a sign on (a letter) to show that the charge for posting has been paid: *Business companies that send out many letters daily save time by using a franking machine.* **2** *tech* to make a special mark on (an official letter or packet) showing that no charge has to be paid for posting

seal 1 to complete with an official seal: *The letters have been signed and sealed.* **2** to close: *The letters have been signed and sealed.*

cancel to mark a stamp, letter, etc, to show that it has been used and to make sure that it cannot be used again: *Cancel the stamps properly.*

H129 *nouns* : **tickets and coupons** [C]

ticket 1 [C; *by* U] a printed piece of paper or card given to a person to show that he has paid for a service such as a journey on a bus, entrance into a cinema, etc: *He lost his bus/train/cinema ticket. No tickets are given on this bus. Entrance to the theatre is by ticket only.* **2** [C] a piece of card or paper fastened to, and giving information such as price, size, qualities, etc, about, an object for sale in a shop **3** a printed notice of an offence against the driving laws: *a parking ticket*

coupon 1 a ticket that shows the right of the holder to receive some payment, service, etc: *In some packets of cigarettes you get coupons which can be saved and exchanged for goods.* **2** a printed form on which goods can be ordered, an enquiry made, or a competition entered: *I forgot to post my football coupon.*

H130 *nouns* : **flags and slogans** [C]

flag a square or similar piece of cloth, usu with a design on it and fastened by one edge to a pole (**flagpole** or **flagstaff**) or to a rope: *Flags are used as the sign of a country or for signalling. The ship flew* (= had on its pole) *the national flag of Norway. The flags were hanging at half-mast* (= lower than the top of the pole) *as a sign of sorrow.*

banner 1 *lit* a flag: *May the banner of our country wave proudly forever!* **2** a long piece of cloth on which a sign is painted, usu carried between two poles: *Their banners all said 'We want work'.*

standard *lit* a flag: *Carry our country's standard proudly!*

placard a large printed or written notice or advertisement, put up in a public place or sometimes carried about: *The marching workers carried placards which said 'We want work'.*

poster a placard in a public place, esp advertising something: *His face is on all the posters.*

bill a written or printed notice, placard, or poster, often small enough to be given by hand (a **handbill**)

slogan a short phrase expressing a usu political or advertising message: *During the war the slogan 'Dig for Victory' sent people out to grow their own vegetables. The workers carried placards with the slogan 'We want work' on them. He wrote slogans on the wall.*

badge something worn to show that a person is a member of an organization, does certain work, has a certain rank, etc: *What badges of rank does an army captain wear?*

crest a special ornamental picture used as a personal or family mark on letters, envelopes, one's plates, etc **crested** [Wa5;B] having a crest: *The prince always writes on crested writing paper.*

emblem a drawing, sign, crest, badge, etc, which represents an organization, group, nation, etc: *The emblem of Scotland is a lion.*

H131 *nouns & verbs* : **locks and keys**
[ALSO ⇒ D24]

lock 1 [C] an apparatus for closing and fastening something by means of a key **2** [C] something which stops a wheel moving **3** [U] (in a machine) the state of being stopped or blocked: *in the lock position* **under lock and key** safely hidden and fastened in

padlock 1 [C] a lock that can be put on and taken off, having a movable metal ring that can be passed through a U-shaped bar and fixed by a key in the lock: *He fastened the chain to a ring in the post, by means of a padlock.* **2** [T1] to fasten, lock, or join by means of a padlock: *The iron gate in the fence is padlocked at night. He padlocked the two sides of the cupboard door together.*

combination lock [C] a kind of lock with a device (a **dial**) showing numbers or letters: *In a combination lock the numbers or letters are moved until the right set shows on the dial and the lock opens.* **combination** the right set of numbers for opening such a lock

key [C] **1** an instrument, usu made of metal, for locking or unlocking (a door), winding (a clock), tightening or loosening (a spring), or starting and stopping (a car engine) **2** (*fig*) something that explains, answers, or helps you to understand: *The key to the grammar exercises is at the back of the book. Her very unhappy childhood is the key to the way she behaves now.*

latch [C] **1** a simple fastening for a door, gate, window, etc, worked by dropping a bar into a U-shaped space **2** a spring lock for a house

door that can be opened from the outside with a key **off the latch** not fully closed; slightly opened **on the latch** fastened only with the latch; not locked

latchkey [C] a key for opening a lock on an outside door of a house or flat

keyhole [C] a hole for the key in a lock, a clock, etc

H132 *nouns* : **moving parts of doors, etc** [C]
[ALSO ⇒ D24]

handle a part of an object which is specially made for holding it, esp as used to open a door

knob a round handle or control button: *He opened the door by turning the (door)knob. The radio has its on–off knob on the right.*

hinge 1 one of the usu metal parts which join two objects together and allow the first to swing around the second: *The door swung easily on its hinges.* **2** (*fig*) the point on which something else depends: *The home is the hinge on which the family turns.* **hinged** [Wa5;B] fitted with a hinge or hinges: *The cupboard door is hinged on the right, so it opens on the left.*

panel a separate, usu four-sided division of the surface of a door, wall, etc, which is different in some way from the surface around it, usu by being higher or lower: *The door had a glass panel in it.*

H133 *nouns* : **refrigerators and freezers** [C]
[ALSO ⇒ D38]

refrigerator a large box or room in which food or drink can be kept for a while at a low temperature: *There's some beer in the refrigerator.*

fridge *esp BrE infml* a refrigerator

icebox 1 a box where food is cooled with ice **2** *AmE not fml* a refrigerator

freezer 1 *also* **deep freeze** a type of large refrigerator in which supplies of food can be stored at a very low temperature for a long time **2** *also* **freezing compartment** an enclosed part of a refrigerator in which there is a specially low temperature for making small ice blocks, storing frozen foods, etc

H134 *nouns* : **washing machines** [C]
[ALSO ⇒ D174]

washing machine *also* **washer** a machine for washing clothes

mangle a machine used esp formerly for pressing the water out of clothes which have just been washed so as to dry and smooth them

Tools

H140 *nouns* : **kinds of knives, etc** [C]

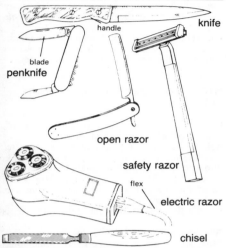

knife

handle

blade
penknife

open razor

safety razor

flex

electric razor

chisel

knife a blade fixed in a handle and used for cutting as a tool or weapon: *He cut up the meat with a knife. The men carried knives to protect themselves.*

penknife a small knife with usu two folding blades, usu carried in the pocket

pocket knife a knife with a blade that folds into the handle, and is carried in the pocket

sheath knife a knife with a fixed (not folding) blade, for carrying in a **sheath** (= a cover for the blade alone)

dagger a short pointed knife used as a weapon: *He struck out with his dagger and killed two men.* **at daggers drawn (with someone)** about to fight (with someone) **look daggers at someone** to look very angrily at someone

chisel a metal tool with a sharp cutting edge at the end of a blade, used for cutting into or shaping a solid material (such as wood, stone, etc)

razor a sharp instrument for removing hair from the skin, sometimes electric

H141 *nouns* : **scissors, etc** [P]

scissors two sharp blades having handles with holes for the fingers at one end, fastened at the centre so that they open in the shape of the letter X and cut when they close: *The scissors are sharp. Have you got a pair of scissors?*

shears 1 large scissors **2** any of various heavier cutting tools which work like scissors: *He bought (a pair of) garden shears.*

cutters an instrument for cutting

clippers *also* [C] **clipper** a tool or instrument, usu like scissors, used for clipping (= cutting

quickly), esp the nails and hair: *The clippers are on the table. Is the clipper in the cupboard?*

pliers a type of small tool made of two crossed pieces of metal with long flat jaws at one end, used to hold small things or to bend and cut wire: *Where are my pliers? He bought a new pair of pliers.*

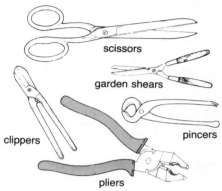

scissors

garden shears

clippers

pincers

pliers

pincers 1 a tool for holding things tight: *He held the hot metal with a pair of pincers.* **2** the claws of crabs, lobsters, etc [⇒ A102]

pair [C *of*] the two parts of these tools, as in: *a pair of scissors/pliers*

H142 *nouns & verbs* : **kinds of saw, etc**

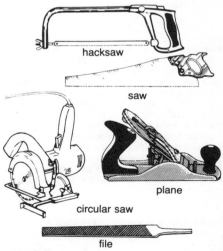

hacksaw

saw

plane

circular saw

file

saw 1 [C] a hand- or power-driven tool for cutting hard materials, having a thin flat blade with a row of v-shaped teeth on the edge: *He cut through the wood with a saw* **2** [I0; T1 (*through, up*)] to cut with a saw: *He sawed the wood. He sawed right through the piece of wood. He sawed the wood in half* (= into two equal pieces). *Saw up that wood; we need it for burning.*

hacksaw [C] a saw that has a blade which can be changed, esp one used for cutting metal

circular saw [C] a machine which can cut out wood very quickly by means of the sharp teeth on its power-driven round metal blade

plane 1 [C] a tool with a blade that takes very thin pieces off wooden surfaces to make them smooth **2** [T1 (*down*); X7] to smooth with a plane: *She planed the wood smooth.*

file 1 [C] a tool with a rough surface, used for smoothing hard materials **2** [T1; (I∅)] to smooth (a surface, material, etc) with a file: *He filed the metal bar.* **file away** [v adv T1] to remove by filing: *He filed away the rough bits from the bar.*

lathe [C] a machine that turns a piece of wood or metal round and round against a sharp tool that gives it shape

H143 *nouns* : **kinds of axe** [C]

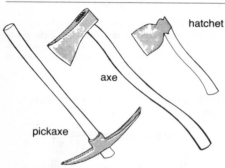

hatchet

axe

pickaxe

axe *AmE usu* **ax** a tool with a heavy metal blade on the end of a long handle, used to cut down trees or split logs

pickaxe *AmE usu* **-ax** a large tool with a wooden handle fitted into a curved iron bar with one sharp point and one flat edge, used for breaking up roads, rock, etc

pick 1 *infml* a pickaxe **2** [*usu in comb*] a sharp pointed, usu small instrument: *The climbers used icepicks. He got the pieces of food out of his teeth with a toothpick.*

hatchet a small axe with a short handle

chopper a small axe, used esp for chopping wood or meat

H144 *nouns & verbs* : **hammers**

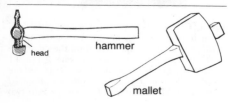

head

hammer

mallet

hammer 1 [C] a tool with a heavy head for driving nails into wood, or for striking things to break them or move them **2** [C] anything made to hit something else, as in a piano or part of a gun **3** [T1] to strike with a hammer: *Hammer the nails in. Hammer the top down.* **4** [I∅ (*away at*)] to hit repeatedly: *I hammered away at his head.*

mallet [C] **1** a small wooden hammer **2** a hammer with a wooden head **3** a hammer with a long handle, esp as used in certain games

H145 *nouns* : **parts of knives, tools, etc** [C]

blade the flat cutting part of a knife, sword, razor, or other cutting tool or weapon

point a sharp end, esp of a knife, weapon, etc: *She cut her hand on the sharp point of the knife.*

edge the thin sharp cutting side of a blade, tool, etc: *Please sharpen the edge of the axe.*

head the top part of a tool such as an axe, hammer, etc

handle the part by which a knife, tool, etc, is held

hilt the handle of a knife or sword

haft the handle of an axe or of some long-handled weapons

shaft 1 the long handle of a hammer, axe, golf club, or tool like that **2** a long or thin piece of wood forming the body of a spear, arrow, or weapon like these

H146 *nouns* : **kinds of drill** [C]

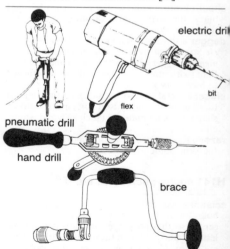

electric drill

bit

flex

pneumatic drill

hand drill

brace

drill a tool or machine for making holes

electric drill a drill worked by electricity

pneumatic drill a drill worked by air pressure

bit the part of a drill that makes a hole

brace a tool which holds a bit used for making holes in wood

H147 *nouns & verbs* : **various other tools for making holes**

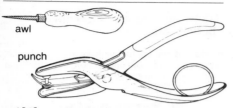

awl

punch

awl [C] a small pointed tool, often with a broad handle, for making holes in leather

punch 1 [C] a steel tool for cutting holes in, or pressing a pattern onto, paper, leather, metal, etc **2** [C] a tool for hammering the heads of nails below a surface **3** [T1] to make (a hole) in (something) with a punch: *He punched a hole in the paper. She punched my ticket before letting me into the theatre.*

H148 *nouns and verbs* : **nails, etc**

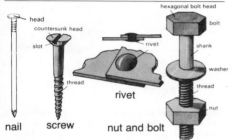

head
countersunk head
slot
thread
nail   screw
hexagonal bolt head
bolt
rivet
shank
washer
thread
nut
rivet
nut and bolt

nail 1 [C] a thin piece of metal with a point at one end for hammering into a piece of wood, usu to fasten the wood to something else **2** [T1 (*up*)] to fix with nails: *He nailed the wood to the door. He nailed up the door so that it would not open.*

spike 1 a long pointed piece of metal with an outward or upward point: *spikes along the top of a fence.* **2** any of several pieces of metal fixed in the bottom of shoes for holding the ground, esp in sports **3** a very large nail or pin for fastening **spiky** [Wa1;B] having sharp points: *spiky leaves.*

screw 1 [C] a usu metal pin having a head, usu with a cut (**slot**) straight across it, often a point at the other end, and a continuous raised edge (**thread**) going around and around it, so that when twisted and pressed, usu with a **screwdriver**, into a material it holds the material firmly and can fasten the material to something else **2** [C] an act of turning one of these; turn: *He gave it another screw to tighten it.* **3** [X9] to fix with a screw or screws: *He screwed the piece of wood into place. Screw it up tight!*
screwnail [C] a long screw
washer [C] a ring of metal, leather, or rubber, often as fitted on a screw, etc to help make it

tight or to stop a liquid from passing through a hole

nut a small, usu four- or six-sided piece of metal with a threaded hole through it for screwing onto a bolt

bolt 1 [C] a screw with no point, which fastens onto a nut to hold things together **2** [T1 (*together*)] to fix with bolts: *The pieces of metal were bolted together.*

rivet 1 [C] a metal bolt like a nail used to fasten sheets of metal together **2** [T1] to fasten with rivets: *The sheets were badly riveted together.*

H149 *nouns* : **screwdrivers, spanners, and other tools** [C]

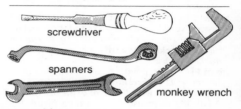

screwdriver

spanners

monkey wrench

screwdriver a tool with a narrow blade at one end which fits into the cut (**slot**) in the heads of screws for turning them into and out of their places

spanner *BrE*, **wrench** *AmE* a tool for holding a nut and turning it

monkey wrench a tool that, by turning a screw, can be used for holding or turning things of different widths

vice *AmE usu* **vise** an apparatus that holds a piece of wood, etc, very firmly between two parts that are moved close together for this purpose by turning a screw

H150 *nouns, etc* : **wheels and levers**

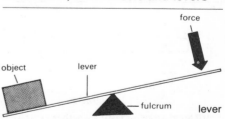

force

object   lever

fulcrum   lever

lever 1 [C] a bar or other strong tool used for lifting or moving something heavy or stiff. One end is placed under or against the object, the other end is pushed down with force, and the bar turns on a fixed point **2** [C] any mechanical instrument working in the same way **3** [C] (*fig*) something which may be used to influence others **4** [X9] to move with a lever: *He levered the big stones into another position.*

fulcrum [C] the point on which a lever turns or is supported in lifting or moving something

crowbar [C] an iron bar with a bent V-shaped

end put under heavy objects and pressed to raise them off the ground

wheel 1 [C] a circular object which turns round on a rod in its centre, on which vehicles can move, with which things can be turned, moved, etc: *Cars run on wheels. Turn the wheel slowly.* **2** [T1] to push or pull something which has a wheel or wheels: *He was wheeling his bicycle; he wasn't riding it.* **3** [X9] to carry in or on a vehicle with wheels: *The boxes were wheeled away.* **4** [I0; T1] to (cause to) move round like a wheel: *The soldiers wheeled right. Birds were wheeling in the sky.* **wheeled** [Wa5;B] having wheels: *a wheeled vehicle. a three-wheeled car.* **-wheeler** [*comb form*] (of a vehicle) having a stated number of wheels: *The car is a three-wheeler.*

track [C] a rolling band of metal, etc, usu one of two, on vehicles such as tanks and tractors, laid down for the wheels to run on: *Tanks run on tracks.* **tracked** [Wa5;B] having tracks: *a tracked vehicle.*

pivot 1 [C] a bar, point, etc, on which something balances: *The wheel turned on a wooden pivot.* (*fig*) *His ideas were the pivot of the discussion.* **2** [I0; T1] to (cause to) turn on a pivot: *The wheel pivoted. He pivoted the wheel.*

swivel 1 [C] a ring, hook, or pivot that is fixed to something else in a way that lets them both turn round easily; a pivot **2** [I0; T1] to (cause to) turn on a swivel; to pivot: *He swivelled the chair.*

H151 *nouns* : **tools for levels and angles** [C]

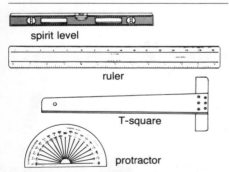

spirit level

ruler

T-square

protractor

spirit level a tool for testing whether a surface is level, made of a bar containing a short glass tube of liquid with a bubble which is in the centre if the surface is level

ruler *also esp tech* **rule** a straight piece of wood, metal, plastic, etc, used for measuring, drawing straight lines, etc: *Use a ruler if you want your lines to be straight.*

protractor an instrument, shaped like half a circle, for measuring angles on a flat surface

T-square a large ruler shaped like a letter T, used esp in drawing parallel lines

sextant an instrument used esp at sea to find out the height of the sun, a star, etc, so as to get an angle and then find out one's position

H152 *nouns* : **tools for opening bottles, etc** [C]

bottle opener any tool which can open a bottle

tin opener *BrE*, **can opener** *AmE* any tool that will open the top of a tin

corkscrew

corkscrew an apparatus of twisted metal with a metal, plastic or wood handle, used for drawing corks out of bottles

H153 *nouns* : **funnels and sieves** [C]

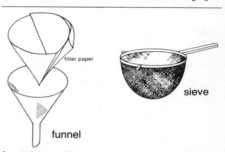

filter paper

sieve

funnel

funnel a tubelike vessel that is large and round at the top and small at the bottom, used in pouring liquids or powders into a small hole: *He used a funnel to fill the bottle with oil.*

filter an apparatus containing paper, sand, etc, through which liquids can be passed so as to make them clear: *We need a new oil filter.* **2** a (coloured) glass that reduces the quantity or changes the quality of the light admitted into a camera, telescope [⇒ H123], etc

sieve a tool of wire netting on a frame, or of a solid sheet with holes, used for separating large and small solids, or solid things from liquid **sift** [T1] to put through a sieve: *sift flour.* (*fig*) *Sift all the information carefully.*

H154 *nouns* : **tools for digging, cutting, etc** [C]

shovel 1 a long-handled tool with a broad, usu square or rounded blade for lifting and moving loose material **2** a part like this on a digging or earth-moving machine **3** such a machine itself **4** *also* **shovelful** the amount of material carried in any of these: *He lifted a shovelful of earth.*

spade 1 a tool like a shovel for digging earth, with a broad metal blade for pushing with the foot into the ground **2** *also* **spadeful** the amount (of earth, etc) that can be moved or carried by this

and see if I can find it. Rake over/through the pile of old letters. **4** [T1 (*with*)] to examine or shoot in a continuous sweeping movement along the whole length of: *The police raked the hillside with powerful glasses* (**binoculars**) *but did not see the escaped prisoner.*

hoe 1 [IØ] to use a hoe **2** [T1] to remove or break with a hoe

fork [T1] to lift, carry, move, etc, with a fork: *He watched the farmer forking the dried grass. I shall have to fork over the soil in the garden* (= turn it over with a fork).

mow [T1; IØ] to cut (grass, corn, etc), or cut that which grows in (a field or other area), with a mower or a scythe: *He mows the grass in the garden every Saturday afternoon. After the fields were mown, the grass was left to dry in the sun. If the weather's fine tomorrow, the farmer intends to mow.*

scythe [T1; IØ] to cut or mow with a scythe: *He scythed the long grass.*

H156 *nouns* : **cleaning tools** [C]

[ALSO ⇒ D178]

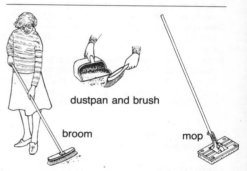

dustpan and brush

broom

mop

brush 1 [*often in comb*] an instrument for cleaning, smoothing, or painting, made of sticks, stiff hair, nylon, etc: *a clothesbrush; a toothbrush; a hairbrush; a paintbrush* **2** an act of using a brush: *I've just given my coat a* (*quick*) *brush.*

broom a large sweeping brush, usu with a long handle

mop 1 a tool for washing floors, made up of a long stick with a number of threads of rope or thick string or some soft material fastened to one end **2** a tool for washing dishes, made up of a short stick with a number of threads of thick string fastened to one end **3** [(*of*) *usu sing*] (*fig*) *infml* a thick mass (of hair), standing up from the head, and looking as if it is not brushed

H157 *verbs* : **using cleaning tools**

[ALSO ⇒ D175, 178]

brush 1 [T1] to clean or smooth with a brush: *She brushed her coat/the floor/her teeth/her*

---

rake 1 a gardening tool consisting of a row of teeth at the end of a long handle, used for making the soil level, gathering esp dead leaves, etc **2** the same kind of tool on wheels, pulled by a horse or by a machine **3** the same kind of tool used to draw together the money on the table during a game of chance

hoe a long-handled garden tool used for breaking up the soil and removing wild plants

fork a farm or gardening tool for breaking up the soil, lifting dried grass, etc, having a wooden handle with two or more metal points (**prongs** or **tines**) at one end

mower a machine for mowing, esp one for cutting grass in gardens (a **lawnmower**) having blades that turn round as it moves

sickle a small hand tool with a curved blade used for cutting grass, etc

scythe a large hand tool with a curved blade, used for cutting grass, etc

H155 *verbs* : **using tools for digging, cutting, etc**

[ALSO ⇒ I 114]

---

shovel 1 [T1; IØ] to take up, make, or work with a shovel: *He got a job shovelling snow. He shovelled a path through the snow.* **2** [X9] to move roughly as with a shovel: *He shovelled the papers into his desk.*

rake 1 [IØ; T1; X7] to make (a place) level with a rake: *He raked the garden paths. You rake and I'll dig.* **2** [T1 (*together, up*)] to collect (as if) with a rake: *Rake up the dead leaves. Rake the money together.* **3** [L9 esp *about, around, among, over, through*] to search carefully (as if) by turning over and stirring up a mass: *I'll rake about/around/among/through my papers* *hair.* **2** [X9, esp *away*,*off*] to remove with or as if with a brush: *He brushed the snow away. He brushed away the fly (with his hand).* **3** [X7,9] to put into a stated condition with or as if with a brush: *She brushed her teeth clean. He brushed his hair flat. She brushed the piece of paper off the table.*

mop [T1 (*up*)] to clean or move with a mop: *He mopped up the water on the floor.*

sweep [T1 (*up*)] to clean with a brush, broom, etc: *Please sweep the floor.*

H158 *nouns, etc* : **metal-working and its tools, etc**

anvil [C] a shaped iron block on which metals are hammered to the shape wanted

bellows [Wn3;C; P] **1** *also* [C] **a pair of bellows** an instrument used for blowing air into a fire to make it burn quickly **2** an instrument like this used for supplying a musical instrument with air

smithy *also* **forge** [C] the workshop of a blacksmith

blacksmith *also infml* **smith** [C] a man who works with iron, esp in making shoes for horses

smith [C esp *in comb*] a person who works with metal: *a coppersmith*, *goldsmith*, *silversmith*, etc

shoe 1 [C] *also* **horseshoe** an iron bar bent in the shape of the letter U which is nailed to the hoof of a horse by a blacksmith, etc: *The horse has cast* (= lost) *a shoe.* **2** [T1] to put such a shoe on a horse's hoof: *He shoed the horse.*

H159 *adjectives & verbs* : **sharp and not sharp**

sharp [Wa1;B] (of knives, tools, etc) able to cut easily: *Be careful; the (blade of the) knife is very sharp. The knife has a very sharp edge.*
sharpen [T1] to make sharp: *He sharpened the knife.* **sharpener** [C] a tool or person that sharpens knives, tools, etc: *He used a pencil sharpener to sharpen his pencil.*

blunt 1 [Wa1;B] not sharp; not able to cut easily: *The knife is blunt; please sharpen it.* **2** [T1] to make blunt; to cause to be unable to cut easily: *Be careful; don't blunt the knife.* (*fig*) *Her bad behaviour blunted his interest in her.*

Containers

H170 *nouns* : **containers, vessels, and bottles** [C]

container anything such as a box, bottle, etc used for holding something

vessel a usu round container such as a glass, pot, cup, bottle, etc, used esp for holding liquids: *Man first made drinking vessels out of baked clay.*

bottle 1 a container, typically of glass or plastic, with a rather narrow neck or mouth and usu no handle **2** a bag made of skin, for holding liquid **3** *also* **bottleful** the quantity held by a bottle: *He drank three bottles of wine.*

jar 1 a vessel like a bottle with a short neck and wide mouth, which may be of glass, stone, clay, etc **2** the contents of a jar: *We need several jars of that stuff to cook this special dish.*

flask 1 a narrow-necked bottle, esp for wine or oil, often covered, esp in Italy, with twisted plant stems (**wicker**): *He bought a flask of Italian wine.* **2** a flat bottle for carrying alcohol in a pocket, etc: *Flasks are often made of metal covered with leather.* **3** the amount of liquid which a flask contains [⇒ I79]

thermos (flask) *also* **vacuum flask 1** a bottle having two walls between which an empty space (**vacuum**) is kept, used for keeping liquids either hot or cold **2** the amount of liquid that it contains

vase a container, usu shaped like a deep pot, with a rather narrow opening at the top and made of glass or baked clay, used either to put flowers in or as an ornament

urn a large vase with handles in which **a** esp the ashes of a burnt dead body are kept **b** liquids are kept [⇒ H173]

H171 *nouns* : **jugs, etc** [C]

jug 1 *BrE* a pot for liquids, with a handle and a lip for pouring: *She put a jug of milk on the table.* **2** *also* **jugful** the amount a jug will hold: *He drank a jug of milk.* **3** a pot for liquids with a narrow opening at the top that can usu be closed with a cork

pitcher 1 *BrE* a large jug **2** *AmE* a jug of any size

flagon 1 a large container for liquids, usu with a lid, a handle, and a lip or spout for pouring **2** a large bottle in which esp wine is sold, containing about twice as much as an ordinary bottle **3** the amount of liquid which a flagon contains

H172 *nouns* : **cups, plates, and bowls**

cup 1 [C] a small round container, usu with a handle, from which liquids are drunk, esp hot liquids such as tea or coffee **2** [C] this container with the liquid in it: *If you're making a pot of tea I'd love a cup. He ordered two cups of tea and only one of coffee.* **3** [C] *also* **cupful** the amount held by one cup: *He drank two cups of coffee and left. Add one cup of flour to half a cup of milk and mix.* **4** [C] (*fig*) a shallow round object: *He drew the cup of the flower.* **5** [C] a specially shaped ornamental vessel, usu made of gold or silver, given as a prize to the winner of a competition: *Which team do you think will win the cup this year? My daughter won those cups for dancing.* **6** [U9; C9] a specially prepared drink of wine or another alcoholic drink: *cider* [⇨E67] *cup.* **7**[C9] (*fig*) that which comes to a person in life; experience: *When her child died her cup of sorrow seemed complete.*

mug [C] **1** a drinking vessel with a flat bottom, straight sides and a handle, not usu with a saucer: *She came in with three mugs of coffee.* **2** *also* **mugful** the contents of this: *He drank a mug of coffee.*

glass [C] **1** a drinking vessel, esp made of glass, or plastic, often with a stem: *He bought some wine glasses.* **2** *also* **glassful** the amount held by one glass: *Have a glass of wine.*

tumbler [C] **1** a large, flat-bottomed drinking glass with no handle or stem **2** *also* **tumblerful** the amount held by a tumbler

tankard [C] a large drinking cup or mug, usu with a handle and lid, esp for drinking beer

goblet [C] a drinking vessel, usu of glass or metal, with a base and stem but no handles and esp used for wine

dish [C] **1** a large flat, often round or egg-shaped vessel from which food is put onto people's plates: *Somebody has broken this dish.* **2** the amount that can go on a dish: *Bring another dish of rice, please.* **3** any object shaped like a dish

plate 1 [C] a flat, usu round dish with a slightly raised edge from which food is eaten or served: *She bought a set of dinner plates.* **2** [U] metal articles, usu made of gold or silver as used at meals or in services in church: *All the church plate has been locked up. This old silver pot is a beautiful piece of plate.*

saucer [C] **1** a small plate with edges curving up, made for setting a cup on: (*fig*) *Her eyes opened as wide as saucers in surprise.* **2** *also* **saucerful** the amount held by a saucer: *Give the cat a saucer of milk.*

bowl 1 [C] a deep round container for holding liquids, flowers, sugar, etc: *She broke the sugar bowl.* **2** [C] *also* **bowlful** the amount held by a bowl: *There are two bowls of sugar left.* **3** [S] (*fig*) a drinking vessel representing merrymaking: *As the bowl passes, let's drink to the lasses* (= girls). **4** [C] anything in the shape of a bowl: *The bowl of a pipe* (*for smoking*) *is usually rounded.*

tureen [C] a large deep dish with a lid, from which soup is served at table

crockery [U] cups, plates, pots, etc, esp made from baked earth (**earthenware**)

H173 *nouns* : **containers relating to making drinks** [C]

teapot a container in which tea is made and served

coffeepot a container in which coffee is made and served

urn a very large metal container in which large quantities of tea or coffee may be heated and kept

H174 *nouns* : **pots and pans**

pot [C *often in comb*] any of several kinds of round vessel in baked clay, metal, glass, etc, with or without a handle, cover, etc, made to contain liquids or solids, esp for cooking: *She put the pot on the cooker. She opened a fresh pot of paint. She put the plant in another pot. That's a nice teapot. The woman put the cooking pot on the fire.*

kettle [C] a usu metal pot with a lid, a handle, and a **spout** (= a narrow curved mouth for pouring), used mainly for boiling or heating water: *Put the kettle on* (= start heating the kettle); *I'd like a cup of tea.*

pan [C] **1** any of various kinds of container, usu with one long handle, used esp in cooking, often wide, not very deep, made of metal, and often without a cover: *Usually cooking pots have two small handles but pans have one long handle.* **2** the bowl of a water closet [⇨ D41] **3** either of the two dishes on a small weighing machine [⇨ H127]

saucepan [C] a deep usu round metal cooking pot with a lid and a handle

pots and pans [P] kitchen utensils [⇨ H111] generally

H175 *nouns* : **barrels and drums** [C]

barrel 1 a wooden or metal container with usu curved sides and flat top and bottom **2** *also* **barrelful** the amount of liquid, etc, held in a barrel

cask 1 a usu wooden barrel-shaped container for holding and storing liquids **2** the amount of liquid held in a cask: *You get 50 bottles of wine from one cask.*

keg a small barrel

vat a very large barrel or container for holding liquids such as beer, whisky, dye, etc, esp when they are being made

butt a large barrel for holding liquids: *The rain water falls and is collected in rain butts beside the house.*

drum a large container for liquids in the shape of a drum: *They rolled the oil drum down the hill.*

H176 *nouns* : **buckets** [C]

bucket

bucket 1 a type of container for liquids **2** *also* **bucketful** the amount of liquid, etc, held in a bucket

pail 1 a usu round open vessel of metal or wood, with handles, used for carrying liquids; a large bucket **2** *also* **pailful** the amount (of liquid) held in a pail: *How many pails of water will we need to fill this bath?*

tub 1 a large round, usu wooden vessel for packing, storing, washing, etc **2** *infml* the container in which one takes a bath **3** *also* **tubful** the amount of liquid, etc held, in a tub

bin a large container, usu with a lid, for liquids, water, etc

dustbin *BrE*, **trashcan**, **garbage can** *AmE* [C] a container for putting rubbish in

H177 *nouns* : **baskets**

basket

basket [C] **1** a usu light container which is made of bent sticks or other such material used for carrying things: *Put everything in my shopping basket, please.* **2** *also* **basketful** the amount of anything held in a basket: *Several baskets of fruit were eaten at the party.*

pannier [C] a basket, esp **a** either of a pair carried by a horse or donkey or on a bicycle **b** one used to carry a load on a person's back

wicker(work) [U] (an example of) the art of weaving twigs, etc, together to make baskets, etc: *He made a wicker basket. She is good at wickerwork.*

H178 *nouns* : **boxes, cases, and cages** [C]

box 1 [*often in comb*] a container for solids, usu with stiff sides and often with a lid: *He picked up the wooden/metal box. The new shoes were in the shoe box.* **2** *also* **boxful** the contents of a box

case 1 a large box in which goods can be stored or moved: *He opened the packing case.* **2** the amount such a box holds: *He drank a case of beer?—No wonder he was drunk!* **3** a box or container for holding and protecting something: *Her watch came in a small case to stop it getting broken.*

casket a small, usu ornamental box for holding jewels, letters, and other small valuables

chest a large wooden box for storing things, usu kept on the floor of a room

trunk a large chest; a large box for carrying or sending clothes, etc, from place to place

crate *also* **packing case** a large strong roughly made wooden box in which heavy articles are packed to be stored or sent elsewhere

container *tech* a very large, usu metal box in which goods are packed to make lifting them onto or off ships, trains, etc, easy

cage 1 a boxlike framework of wires or bars in which animals or birds may be kept or carried:

The door of the bird cage was open and the bird had gone. **2** an enclosure which has the form or purpose of such a framework **3** a framework in which men and apparatus are raised to or lowered from the surface of a mine

drawer a container like a box which slides in and out of pieces of furniture such as tables, cupboards, etc: *The cupboard had two drawers at the side for smaller pieces of clothing.*

sheath 1 a closefitting case for a knife or sword blade or the sharp part of a tool **2** a part of a plant, animal organ, or machine that acts as a covering like this

H179 *nouns* : **kinds of smaller cases for travelling** [C]

[ALSO ⇒ H184–185]

suitcase a flat case, usu with stiff sides, for carrying clothes and possessions, esp when travelling

briefcase a flat, usu soft leather case for carrying papers or books, which opens at the top

attaché case a thin hard case with a handle for carrying papers

H180 *nouns* : **tins and tubes** [C]

tin *esp BrE* a usu small round metal container without air, with a top that can be opened with a special tool (a **tin opener**), used for preserving various kinds of soup, etc until wanted: *He opened a tin of soup.*

can 1 *esp AmE* a tin: *He opened a can of soup* **2** a usu round metal container with an open top or removable lid and sometimes with handles used for holding milk, coffee, waste, ashes, etc

tin can a tin or can, esp when empty and no longer wanted: *The dirty street was full of old papers and tin cans.*

screw top

tube of toothpaste

tube a small container made of soft metal with a top that screws [⇒ H148] on: *She bought a tube of toothpaste/glue.*

H181 *nouns* : **packages and capsules** [C]

package 1 an amount or a number of things packed together: *He carried a large package of books under his arm.* **2** the container of these things: *The package got torn on the way to the station. Postal packages cost a lot to send nowadays.*

packet a small package; a number of small things tied or put together into a small box, case, or bag: *Sugar is sold in large and small* *packets. She bought a packet of envelopes at the shop.*

pack *AmE* a packet: *He bought a pack of cigarettes.*

carton a box made from stiff paper (**cardboard**) used for holding goods

capsule 1 a very small, usu rounded case **2** a small case for a measured amount of medicine, to be swallowed **3** *tech* the seed container for a plant

H182 *nouns* : **parcels and bundles** [C]

parcel *also esp AmE* **package** a thing or things wrapped in paper and tied or fastened in some other way for easy carrying, posting, etc: *I'm just going to take this parcel to the post office. A parcel has just come, addressed to you.*

bundle a number of articles fastened or held together, usu across the middle: *She was carrying a bundle of clothes.*

sheaf 1 a handful or more of long or thin things laid or tied together: *The speaker had a sheaf of notes on the desk in front of him.* **2** an armful of grain plants tied together, esp to stand up in a field to dry after gathering

bale a quantity of cloth, grass, paper, etc, tied together, esp to be carried by ship, rail, road, etc: *How many bales of cloth do you need?*

H183 *nouns* : **bags and purses** [C]
[ALSO ⇒ D154]

bag a container made of soft material such as cloth, paper, or leather, opening at the top: *Put the books in this plastic/paper bag.*

sack 1 a large bag, usu of strong cloth or leather, used for storing or moving flour, fruit, grain, etc **2** *also* **sackful** the amount held in one of these **3** *esp AmE* a bag of strong, usu brown paper with a flat bottom, such as large food shops give to people for carrying away the food they have bought: *She filled her grocery sack.*

pouch 1 a small soft bag, often of leather **2** a baglike fold of skin inside each cheek in certain animals, in which they carry and store food **3** a kind of pocket of skin in the lower part of the body in which certain animals (**marsupials** ⇒ A32) carry their young

carrier bag *BrE* a cheap, usu plastic bag for carrying goods away from a shop

H184 *nouns* : **packs and kitbags** [C]

pack a number of things wrapped or tied together, or put in a case, esp for carrying on the back by a person or animal: *In former times, goods were usually carried in packs on the backs of animals. The climber carried some food in a pack on his back.*

knapsack a bag of strong cloth or leather, used for holding necessary articles and carried on the back by soldiers, travellers, etc

rucksack a bag carried on the back or shoulders when walking, esp to hold necessary food and clothing, esp with a metal frame

haversack a usu smaller rucksack, esp without a metal frame

holdall a large simply-made bag of strong cloth, usu with two handles, for carrying clothes, etc: *He put everything in a holdall and left.*

satchel a small bag of strong cloth or leather, usu with a band for carrying over the shoulder: *He carried his books in a school satchel.*

kitbag a long narrow bag used by soldiers, sailors, etc, for carrying their kit, esp carried on one shoulder, with strings to pull it closed at the top

duffel bag a round, usu long bag made of heavy cloth, for carrying clothes and other belongings on a journey, with strings to pull it closed at the top

H185 *nouns* : **luggage and kit** [U]
[ALSO ⇒ H179]

luggage *esp BrE* all the bags and other containers with which a person travels

baggage 1 *esp AmE* luggage **2** tents, beds, etc esp of an army, which they take with them

kit *esp BrE* (the clothes and other) articles needed and carried by a soldier, sailor, etc, or carried by a traveller: *Don't lose any of your kit.*

H186 *nouns* : **covers, lids, and corks** [C]

cover something placed on top of another thing, esp a container, food, etc, to cover it

lid the piece that covers the open top of a vessel, box, or other container and that lifts up or can be removed

cap a protective covering which is placed over the top of a container: *Put the cap back on the bottle.*

top a lid or cap for the top of a container, esp a bottle

cork 1 a round piece of cork fixed into the neck of a bottle to close it tightly **2** an object like this made from rubber or plastic

stopper an object, esp a cork, that fits into the neck of a bottle and stops esp a liquid getting out

H187 *verbs* : **putting things in containers, etc** [Wv5;T1]

bottle 1 to put into one or more bottles: *They bottle the wine themselves.* **2** to preserve in bottles, as by heating: *She makes her own bottled fruit.*

cork to close (the neck of a bottle or other object) tightly with a cork

pot to put (a young plant) in a pot filled with earth

box to put in one or more boxes: *The oranges were boxed and sent off quickly.*

crate to put in a crate: *The fruit was crated and sent off.*

case to enclose or cover with a case: *Have you cased all the paintings?*

tin *BrE*, **can** *AmE* to preserve (food) by putting in a closed metal container without air: *She eats a lot of tinned meat.*

cage to put into a cage: *She doesn't like seeing caged birds.*

package 1 [(*up*)] to make into or tie up as a package: *Would you please package these bags so that they can be more easily carried? She packaged up the old clothes and put them in the cupboard.* **2** to place (food, etc) in a special package before selling to the public: *Most food shops sell packaged foods now.*

parcel [(*up*)] to make into a parcel: *Ask the shopkeeper to parcel (up) these goods for you.*

bundle [(*together*)] to put or make into a bundle: *She bundled her clothes together and put some string around them.*

pack 1 [*also* D1; I∅] to put (things, esp one's belongings) into cases, boxes, etc, for travelling or storing: *Let's pack some food and go out for the day. He ate a packed lunch. You can pack some of your clothes in my case if you like. She packed her husband some eggs for his dinner. We leave tomorrow but I haven't begun to pack yet!* **2** [X9; L9] to fit, crush, or push into a space: *If you pack those things down we can get a little more in the box. The railwaymen were packing the people into the train like animals. The moment the door was opened, people began to pack into the hall. The speaker spoke to a packed hall.* **3** [X9; I∅] to settle or be driven closely together or into a mass: *The wind packed the snow against the side of the house. The sea is very dangerous when the ice begins to pack in this way.* **4** [L9] to be suitable for easy putting into cases, boxes, etc: *These bottles pack easily, but the others do not, because of their shape.* **5** to prepare and put (food) into tins or other containers for preserving or selling in shops: *They intend to build a factory here for packing the fruit that grows locally.* **6** to cover, fill, or surround closely with a protective material: *These pipes should be packed, to prevent them from leaking. Pack some paper round the dishes in the box so that they will not break.*

cover to place or spread something over (something), esp a parcel or to make a parcel: *He covered the books with paper. Have you anything to cover these things with?*

sheathe 1 to put into a sheath: *He sheathed his sword.* **2** [(*with, in*)] to enclose in a protective outer cover

Electricity and electrical equipment

H200 *nouns* : **electricity, etc** [U]

electricity 1 the power that is produced by rubbing (**friction**) or by chemical means (a **battery**) or by a machine called a **generator** and which gives heat, light, and sound and drives machines **2** electric current: *They turned off the electricity in the house when they left.*

electronics 1 the branch of science that deals with the behaviour of electrons [⇒ H5] **2** the branch of industry that manufactures such products as radio, television, and recording apparatus, whose operation depends on the behaviour of electrons: *The electronics industry is growing very fast. He is in electronics.*

magnetism 1 the science dealing with the qualities of a magnet [⇒ H122] **2** the quality of strong magnetic attraction **3** (*fig*) strong personal charm; the power to attract people, etc: *She has great personal magnetism.*

H201 *adjectives* : **relating to electricity, etc** [Wa5;B]

electric *precise & tech* **1** (of machines) producing electricity: *They have an electric generator* [⇒ H114] *which uses oil and makes all the electricity for the farm.* **2** worked by electricity: *We have an electric clock and an electric fire. She uses an electric iron to press her clothes.* **3** being electricity: *The wire carries an electric current/charge.* (*fig*) *His exciting speech had an electric effect upon all the listeners.*

electrical *genl* concerned with electricity: *An electrical engineer works with many sorts of electrical apparatus.*

electronic 1 connected with electrons [⇒ H5] **2** connected with any apparatus that works by electronics **3** (of music) produced by means of electronics

magnetic having the qualities of a magnet [⇒ H122]: *The iron has lost its magnetic force.* (*fig*) *He has a very magnetic personality; he attracts almost everybody he meets.*

H202 *nouns* : **flow, current, and charges** [C; U]

flow the movement of electricity, esp along a wire

current the (rate of) flow of electricity past a fixed point, measured in amp(ere)s [⇒ H207] **direct current** (*abbrev* **DC**) electric current that flows in one direction only **alternating current** (*abbrev* **AC**) electric current which flows in one direction then in the opposite direction and so on at regular short intervals of time

input an electrical current put in (to any machine, system, etc)

output electric current coming out (of any machine, system, etc)

charge (a quantity of) electricity put into a battery [⇨ H208] or other electrical apparatus: *The charge was too great for the fine wire, which melted as a result.*

discharge electricity which is discharged [⇨ H203]: *There was a sudden discharge (of electricity), but no one was hurt.*

H203 *verbs* : **relating to electricity**

flow [I∅] (of electricity) to move in one direction, esp along a wire

charge [Wv5 (*with*);T1;I∅] to (cause to) take in the correct amount of electricity: *He charged the battery (with electricity). Does the battery [⇨ H209] charge easily?*

discharge 1 [I∅] (of an electrical apparatus) to send out (electricity) **2** [T1] to remove electricity from (an electrical apparatus)

conduct [T1;I∅] to act as the path for (electricity, heat, etc): *Copper conducts electricity well. Plastic doesn't conduct.* **conductor** [C] a substance or object that conducts electricity, heat, sound etc: *Iron is a good conductor of electricity and heat.*

generate [Wv4;T1] to produce (electricity or heat): *Two surfaces rubbing together generate heat. Our electricity comes from a new generating station* **generation** [U] the act of generating electricity, etc

H204 *nouns* : **technical terms in electricity** [U]

conduction the passage of electricity along a wire

conductance the ability of a conductor to carry electricity

resistance the power of a substance to resist (= to stop) an electric current passing through it: *Copper has less resistance to electricity than lead.* [*also* ⇨ H207 VOLT] **resistor** [C] a piece of wire or other material used for increasing electrical resistance

inductance the causing of movement electrically by a change in the current

induction the production of electricity in one object by another which already has electrical or magnetic power

capacitance the ability of a nonconductor to store electricity

H205 *nouns, etc* : **electrical poles, etc** [C]

earth *BrE* **ground** *AmE* **1** [(*the*) C *usu sing*] the wire which connects a piece of electrical apparatus to the ground **2** [T1] to connect (a

piece of electrical apparatus) to the ground: *The radio ought to be properly earthed.*

pole 1 either of the points at the ends of a magnet [⇨ H122] where its power of pulling iron towards itself is greatest **2** either of the two points at which wires may be fixed onto a battery [⇨ H208] in order to use that electricity

anode *tech* the part of an electrical instrument, such as a battery, which collects electrons [⇨ H5], often a rod or wire, shown as (+)

positive pole 1 an anode **2** the end of a magnet which naturally turns towards the earth

cathode *tech* the part of an electrical instrument, such as a battery, from which electrons leave, often a rod or wire, shown as (−)

negative pole 1 a cathode **2** the end of a magnet which naturally turns away from the earth

H206 *adjectives* : **positive, negative, and live** [Wa5;B]

positive (of or in electricity) of the type that is produced by rubbing glass with silk, caused by a lack of electrons [⇨ H5] and has the sign (+)

negative (of or in electricity) of the type caused by more than enough electrons and has the sign (−)

live carrying an electric current: *Don't touch that wire; it's live.*

H207 *nouns* : **standard units of electricity** [C]

amp the standard measure of the quantity of electricity that is flowing past a point: *From the main electricity system in a house which might have a current of 30 amps, you could run smaller systems of 2 amps, 5 amps, 15 amps, etc.*

ampere *fml* an amp **amperage** [U] the strength of an electric current measured in amps, as in an electricity system or as used by an electrical instrument

volt (a standard measure of electrical force used in causing a flow along wires, equal to) the amount needed to produce one amp of electrical current where the resistance [⇨ H204] of the conductor [⇨ H203] is one ohm **voltage** [U] electrical force measured in volts

ohm a measure of electrical resistance

watt a measure of electrical power: *A kilowatt is a thousand watts. He used a 30-watt bulb* **wattage** [U] electrical power in watts: *This electrical apparatus has a wattage of 3 kilowatts.*

H208 *nouns* : **wires, circuits, and fuses, etc**

[ALSO ⇨ N323]

wire [C; U] a long thread of metal used for carrying electricity: *Make sure the wires are not touching each other. Usually wires are covered with plastic so that people won't get a shock from them.*

wiring [U] the arrangement or quality of the wired electrical system in a building: *This old wiring must be changed soon; it is dangerous.*

lead [C] an electric wire for taking power from the supply point to an instrument, etc

circuit [C] the complete path of an electric current: *A break in the circuit had caused the lights to go out.*

printed circuit [C] a set of connections between points in an electrical apparatus made by means of putting onto a surface a continuous line of a substance that will carry electricity

load [C] the power of an electricity supply; how much electricity the wiring of a machine, place, etc, can carry

shock [C; U] the sudden violent effect of electricity passing through the body: *The wire is covered with plastic to prevent shock. You'll get a bad shock if you touch the bare wire.*

fuse 1 [C] a (small container with a) short piece of wire placed in an electric apparatus or in an electric system, which melts if too much electric power passes through it, and thus breaks the connection and prevents fires or other damage: *A fuse has blown (= been destroyed by melting), causing the lights to fail.*
2 [S] *infml* a failure of electric power, due to the melting of one of these: *The lights at the end of the house have gone out; has there been a fuse somewhere?*

fuse box [C] a box that contains a set of fuses for the electrical system in a house, vehicle, etc

fuse wire [U] special thin, easily-melted wire used for making fuses

cell [C] an apparatus for producing electricity by chemical action

battery [C] a piece of apparatus for producing electricity, consisting of a group of connected electric cells

transformer [C] an apparatus that changes the voltage [⇒ H207] of an alternating electric current [⇒ H202]

H209 *verbs* : **wires and fuses, etc**
[ALSO ⇒ N323 INSULATE]

wire [T1 *usu pass*] to put electric wires in: *The house was wired years ago. The hall is now wired for electricity/sound.*

overload [T1] to cause to produce or use too much electricity: *Don't overload the electrical system by using too many machines at once.*

shock [T1 *usu pass*] to give an electric shock to: *She got shocked when she touched the bare wire.*

fuse [T1; I0] to (cause to) stop working owing to the failure of a fuse: *If you connect all these apparatuses to the electricity supply at one place, you'll fuse all the lights. All the lights have fused; the whole place is in darkness.*

H210 *nouns* : **switches, plugs, and sockets** [C]

switch a small apparatus for turning electric current on and off: *Where are the switches in this room on this machine?*

plug a small plastic object with two or three metal pins, the pins being pushed into a power point to obtain power for a movable apparatus

socket *also* **(power)point** the part that forms a holder into which a plug can fit so that electricity can pass: *Put the plug in the socket. How many power points are there in this room?*

adapter, -or a plug that makes it possible to use more than one piece of electrical equipment at one time from one electrical supply point

overload [*usu sing*] the fact or amount of overloading: *An overload of 30% can be bad for the electrical system.*

H211 *verbs* : **switches and plugs**

switch on/off [v adv T1; I0] to put (an electrical apparatus) on/off: *Switch (the radio) on, please. He switched off because he didn't like the television programme.*

plug in [v adv T1; I0] to put the plug (of an electrical apparatus) in a socket: *Plug in now. Is the radio plugged in?*

H212 *nouns* : **coils, valves, and transistors** [C]

coil an electrical apparatus made by winding wire into a continuous circular shape, used for carrying an electric current

valve *also* **vacuum tube** *BrE,* **tube** *AmE* a closed glass tube with no air used for controlling a flow of electricity

transistor 1 *precise* a small solid electrical apparatus, esp used in radios, televisions, etc, for controlling the flow of an electrical current
2 *loose also* **transistor radio** a radio that has these instead of valves

H213 *nouns* : **electric lights** [C]

light an electric lamp: *Switch on the light, please. The lights were out; there had been a fuse* [⇒ H208].

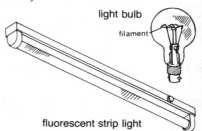

light bulb

filament

fluorescent strip light

fluorescent light a light which shines because of electricity which is passed through a tube covered with fluorescent material (= material which gives out a white light)

bulb the glass part of an electric lamp that gives out light: *We'll have to change the bulb; it has gone* (= it has stopped giving light).

filament the thin metal thread in an electric light, bulb, etc

H214 *nouns* : **fittings for electric lights** [C]

shade [*often in comb*] something that keeps out light or its full brightness: *Put a lampshade over the lamp.*

stand [*often in comb*] a support for an electric light: *He knocked over the new lampstand.*

bracket a piece of metal or wood put in a wall to support something, esp a lamp

Weapons

H230 *nouns* : **weapons and armaments generally**

[ALSO ⇒ C308–309]

weapon [C] a tool for harming and killing in attack or defence: *He picked up a stone as a weapon to defend himself. Swords and spears have long been weapons of war. Both the USA and the USSR have nuclear weapons.*

arms [P] *genl* weapons: *They picked up their arms as they went out to fight. Nuclear arms cause more damage than any other weapon.* **bear arms** to serve as a soldier **lay down arms** to stop fighting and yield; surrender **take up arms** to get ready to fight with weapons **under arms** (of soldiers) having weapons; armed: *The country kept 50,000 men under arms at all times.* **up in arms 1** having weapons and being ready to show disobedience to a government or other force **2** (*fig*) *infml* extremely angry and ready to argue, quarrel, or fight: *The women are up in arms over/about their low rate of pay.*

firearms [P] *genl* guns [⇒ H237]: *What firearms do the soldiers have?*

small arms [P] *genl* guns that can be carried by a person

armament 1 [C *often pl*] **a** the arms and other fighting material of an army, navy, etc **b** the weapons and defensive armour on a warship, aircraft, etc **c** the total armed forces of a country **2** [U] the act of arming a country in preparation for war

ammunition [U] bullets, bombs, explosives, etc, esp if fired from a weapon: *The soldiers said that they needed more ammunition; they would soon run out of* (= have no more) *ammunition and be unable to fight.* (*fig*) *The mistakes of the ministers provided perfect ammunition for their political enemies.*

ammo [U] *infml abbrev* ammunition

arsenal [C] **1** a government building where weapons and explosives are made or stored: *The men attacked the arsenal in order to get weapons.* **2** (*fig*) any large quantity of weapons: *The criminals had a small arsenal of guns in the house.*

magazine [C] a place where guns, ammunition, etc, are kept, esp on a ship

H231 *nouns* : **kinds of swords** [C]

[ALSO ⇒ H140, H145]

bayonet

sword

sword a weapon like a long knife, having a long blade and a handle: *There are a great many different kinds of swords. They fought with a sword and shield* [⇒ H232]. *He drew his sword* (*from its scabbard*) *and attacked. He hurt his sword-arm* (= the arm with which he carried his sword).

rapier a very light thin two-edged sword with a sharp point used for pushing (**thrusting**) into the body

sabre *BrE*, **saber** *AmE* a heavy military sword with a curved blade

claymore a large two-edged sword used formerly esp in the Scottish Highlands

cutlass a short sword with a slightly curved blade

bayonet a long knife fixed to the end of a rifle

scabbard the case (**sheath**) for a sword: *He drew his sword from its scabbard.*

H232 *nouns* : **spears, etc** [C]

[ALSO ⇒ H145]

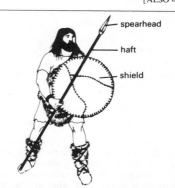

spearhead

haft

shield

spear a pole with a sharp point at one end used, esp formerly for throwing as a weapon: *The men carried spears.*

shield 1 a broad piece of metal, wood or leather carried by soldiers, etc, esp in past times as a protection from arrows, blows, etc: *The men had spears and shields.* (*fig*) '*The Lord is our shield*' (*The Bible*). *The police carried shields.* **2** a protective cover, esp a plate on a machine to protect the person running it from moving parts

javelin 1 a light spear for throwing, now used mostly in sport **2** [*the* R] the sport of throwing the javelin

lance 1 a long spearlike weapon used by horsemen **2** a spear used to catch fish

pike a type of long-handled spear formerly used by soldiers fighting on foot

H233 nouns : sticks and clubs [C]

stick a (usu) thin piece or rod of wood used as a weapon, tool, support, etc: *He beat the man with a stick.*

club a heavy wooden stick, thicker at one end than the other, suitable for use as a weapon

cudgel a short thick heavy club

nightstick *AmE* a short thick stick often carried by policemen in the USA

truncheon *esp BrE* a short stick carried as a weapon by policemen

baton 1 a truncheon **2** a short stick showing that the person who carries it has some special office or rank **3** a short thin stick used by a leader of music (**conductor**) to show the beat of the music **4** a hollow tube passed by one member of a team of runners to the next runner **5** a hollow metal rod, usu with a ball at one end, used for show by the leader of a public ceremonial march (**parade**)

H234 nouns : bows and arrows [C]

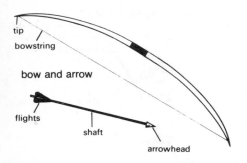

bow and arrow

bow a piece of wood held in a curve by a tight string and used for shooting arrows

arrow 1 a thin straight stick with a point at one end and usu feathers at the other that is shot in fighting or sport from a bow **2** a sign like an arrow, such as →, ⇨, used to show direction or the position of something

arrowhead a pointed piece of stone or metal attached to the front end of an arrow

H235 verbs : using swords, spears, etc [T1]

knife to drive a knife into: *The man knifed his enemy.*

bayonet to drive a bayonet [⇨ H231] into: *The soldiers bayoneted him.*

spear to drive a spear into; catch with a spear: *The soldier speared him. He speared some fish.*

impale to catch on a spear, etc: *He impaled the fish.*

club to beat or strike with a club: *He clubbed his wife to death.*

H236 nouns : slings and catapults [C]

sling a length of cord with a piece of leather in the middle, held at the ends and swung, for throwing stones with force: *David killed Goliath with a stone from his sling. He killed Goliath with a slingstone.*

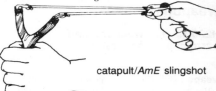

catapult/*AmE* slingshot

catapult 1 a machine for throwing heavy stones, balls, etc, into the air, in former times used as a weapon for breaking defensive walls **2** *BrE* a small Y-shaped stick with a rubber band fastened between the forks, used by children to shoot small stones at objects **3** a powerful apparatus for helping planes take off from a ship, etc

slingshot *AmE* a catapult (*def* **2**)

H237 nouns : guns and handguns [C]

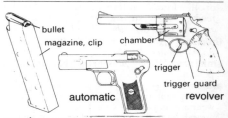

automatic   revolver

gun 1 a weapon from which bullets or larger metal objects are fired through a barrel: *He fired the gun at them.* **2** *BrE* (in hunting parties) a person carrying a gun: *There were ten guns in the party.* **3** a tool which forces out and spreads a substance by pressure

handgun any small gun held in one hand while firing, not raised against the shoulder

pistol a type of handgun

revolver a type of pistol containing several shots each in a part of the barrel (**chamber**) that turns round (**revolves**) after each shot is fired, so that one need not reload every time

automatic a weapon, esp a pistol, etc, which can fire many bullets quickly, one after another

H238 *nouns* : **rifles and shotguns**

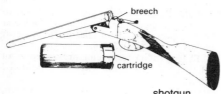

shotgun

rifle [C] a type of esp military gun fired from the shoulder, with a long barrel specially shaped (**rifled**) inside to make the bullet go in a straight line [⇒ picture at H240]

musket [C] an early type of gun

shotgun [C] a gun fired from the shoulder, which is smooth inside its one or usu two barrels, and shoots a quantity of small metal balls (**shot**) together for a short distance

-bore [*comb form*] a measurement of the width of the hollow inside a gunbarrel: *He had a 12-bore shotgun. These are all small-bore guns.*

H239 *nouns* : **cannons and field guns**

cannon [Wn2;C] a big gun fixed to the ground. or onto a usu two-wheeled carriage: *The general decided to use cannon against the enemy. In this castle are cannons from the 15th century.*

mortar [C] a type of heavy gun with a short barrel, firing an explosive that rises to a great height and then falls

machinegun [C] a quick-firing gun, often supported on legs, which fires continuously as long as the trigger is pulled

field gun [C] a light gun with wheels

antiaircraft gun [C] a gun directed against enemy aircraft

battery 1 [GC] a number of big guns, together with the men and officers who serve them; a set of guns mounted in a warship or in a fort **2** [C] (*fig*) a number of things of the same kind with which a person must deal: *He faced a battery of newspaper cameras/of questions.*

H240 *nouns* : **parts of guns** [C]

barrel a tubelike part of a gun that serves as a container along which bullets, shells, etc, can travel

clip a container in or fastened to a gun from which bullets and explosives can be rapidly passed into the gun for firing through the barrel

breech the part of a gun into which the bullet, etc, is put, esp in larger guns

chamber an enclosed space in a, esp smaller gun, to hold bullets: *Put the bullets in the firing chamber.*

H241 *nouns* : **words relating to guns** [C]

holster a usu leather holder for a pistol (small gun), esp one that hangs on a belt around the waist

sling a band of strong material on a rifle used for carrying it, etc

belt 1 [*often in comb*] a band worn around the waist and often used to support small guns, etc: *gunbelt; swordbelt* **2** a band of material on which bullets are fed into the breech of an automatic gun

bandoleer, -lier a belt that goes over a person's shoulder, and is used for carrying bullets

gun carriage a wheeled support for moving a gun

H242 *nouns* : **shot and bullets**

shot [U] very small balls of the metal lead, (to be) fired from a gun and used esp in hunting small animals

bullet [C] **1** a type of shot fired from a, usu smaller kind of gun, usu long and with a rounded end **2** something that looks like a bullet

lead [U] *sl* bullets

pellet [C] a small ball of metal made to be fired from a gun, esp a shotgun [⇒ H238]

buckshot [U] coarse lead shot used esp for hunting

cartridge [C] a usu metal or paper tube containing explosive and a bullet for use in a gun, or enough explosive to set off an explosion

round [C] a bullet, esp when (about to be) fired: *How many rounds have you fired/got left?*

slug [C] *sl* a bullet

shell [C] **1** an explosive (to be) shot from a large gun: *Shells burst all around them.* **2** *esp AmE* a bullet, esp the case holding the part to be fired from a weapon

ball [C] a round bullet or shell, now no longer used

cannonball [C] a heavy iron ball fired from a cannon

H243 nouns : **shots and volleys** [C]

shot 1 (the noise of) one firing of a gun: *He heard several shots.* **2** *not fml* a bullet, esp when about to be fired: *How many shots have you got left?* **3** the occasion of firing: *That was a good shot! His first shot missed.*

shoot an occasion for shooting (of animals, in competition, military training, etc): *They went on a weekend shoot.*

volley 1 a number of shots fired at the same time by soldiers, police, etc: *At the enemy's first volley many of our soldiers were wounded.* **2** a like attack but with named weapons: *The monkeys in the trees aimed volleys of fruit at us.* **3** a number of blows given, words spoken, etc, quickly and with force: *The angry man directed a volley of curses at them.*

fusillade a rapid continuous firing of shots: *As the soldiers marched forward, they were met by a fusillade from the fort.*

burst 1 a sudden, usu short firing of a number of bullets **2** the explosion of a shell

salvo 1 a firing of several guns at once, in a ceremony or battle **2** (*fig*) a sudden noisy burst, as of cheers, shouts, etc

ricochet 1 a sudden jumping change in the direction of a moving object such as a bullet or stone when it hits a surface at an angle **2** a blow from an object to which this has happened: *He was wounded by a ricochet, not by a direct hit.*

H244 adjectives & nouns : **conditions of ammunition** [Wa5;B]

live (of ammunition, etc) having power which can be used in an explosion: *This is live ammunition* [⇨ H230]; *handle it very carefully.*

spent already used; no longer for use: *Spent cartridges* [⇨ H242] *lay all around them. Their ammunition was all spent.*

dud 1 *infml* not able to fire **2** [C] a bullet, shell, etc that does not fire when expected to do so

H245 verbs : **shooting and firing**
[ALSO ⇨ K206]

shoot 1 [T1 (*off*);L9] to let fly with force (a bullet, arrow, etc): *This gun shoots (off) six bullets/shoots very well. I shot an arrow at the spot on the wall.* **2** [T1;I∅ (*at*)] to fire (a weapon): *I'm coming out with my hands up: don't shoot! Can you shoot a bow and arrow? He shot at a bird, but missed. With his bad eyes he can't shoot straight. If the police see the dangerous murderer, they'll shoot to kill.* **3** [T1] to hit, wound, or kill with something, as from a gun: *He shot the bird. He was shot three times in the arm. During the war he was found guilty of*

selling secrets and was shot (= killed by shooting). **4** [X7, 9] to cause to go or be by hitting with something from a gun: *Part of his foot was shot away* (= off) *in battle. She shot him dead.* **5** [D1;X9] (*fig*) to send forth as from a gun: *She shot him a distrustful look. It was a meeting where everyone shot questions at the chairman. The postman shot a letter under the door.*

fire 1 [I∅;T1 (*at*)] **a** (of a person or a gun) to shoot off (bullets): *He's firing at us! Can't you hear the guns firing?* **b** (of a person) to shoot off bullets from (a gun): *She fired her gun at them.* **2** [T1 (*at*)] (of a person, gun, or bow) to shoot off (bullets or arrows): *They fired poisoned arrows at us.*

aim [I∅;T1] to point or direct (a gun, weapon, blow, etc) at someone or something, usu in order to shoot, strike, hurt, etc: *The gun was aimed at him. Aim! Fire! He aimed a blow at her, but missed.* **aim at** [v prep T1, 4] (*fig*) to make an effort towards: *The factory must aim at increased production/at increasing production. She is aiming at being a writer.*

discharge [T1] *usu fml* to fire or shoot (a gun, arrow, etc): *They discharged their arrows into the air/at the enemy.*

plug: [T1] *sl* to shoot (someone) with a gun: *They plugged him.*

shell [T1] to fire shells [⇨ H242] at: *The enemy lines were softened up by shelling them before the attack.*

volley 1 [I∅] (of guns) to be fired all together: *When the guns volleyed the noise was frightening.* **2** [L9] (of shots fired or objects thrown) to come flying together through the air: *A mass of broken rocks volleyed down the mountainside.*

H246 nouns : **bombs and similar devices** [C]

bomb a hollow metal container filled with explosive or with other chemicals of a stated type or effect: *They planted* (= put) *a bomb in a post office. They dropped an atomic bomb on the city. He threw a smoke bomb. A time bomb explodes some time after it is placed in position. That country has the bomb* (= atomic weapons) *now.*

grenade 1 a small bomb which can be thrown by hand or fired from a gun **2** a small round container with a chemical substance inside, esp one for putting out fires

mine a metal case containing explosives **a** that is placed just below the ground and is exploded electrically or when stepped on or passed over **b** that is placed on or below the surface of the sea and is exploded when touched by a ship or electrically when a ship passes over it

minefield 1 an area of land where people have hidden mines **2** (*fig*) a difficult situation

charge the amount of explosive to be fired at one time or placed in a bullet, bomb, etc

depth charge a bomb that is dropped in the sea, to explode at a certain depth

booby trap a hidden bomb which explodes when some harmless-looking object is touched

torpedo a long metal container filled with explosives and sent through the water, esp to destroy ships: *They fired two torpedoes at the ship.*

H247 *verbs* : **using bombs and similar devices** [T1]

bomb [*also* IØ] to attack with bombs, esp by dropping them: *The aeroplanes bombed the enemy city.*

mine to put mines in (a place): *The whole field was mined. They mined the entrance to the river.*

booby-trap to fix a booby trap in (a place): *The room was booby-trapped.*

torpedo to hit (a ship) with a torpedo: *They torpedoed and sank 10 ships.*

H248 *nouns* : **armour and tanks, etc**

armour *BrE*, **armor** *AmE* [U] **1** the strong defensive metal covering on fighting vehicles, ships, and aircraft **2** the vehicles with such covers, rather than soldiers on foot or un-protected vehicles **3** the strong defensive metal or leather covering as worn in former times by (noble) fighting men (**knights**) and their horses

armoured car [C] a military vehicle protected with light armour and usu with a powerful gun, such as a **machinegun**

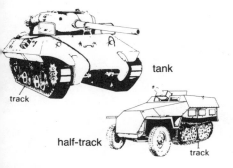

tank

track

half-track

track

half-track [C] a vehicle, esp a military one, with wheels at the front but with a track [⇨ H150] running over two or more back wheels on each side

tank [C] an enclosed heavily armoured vehicle that moves on two endless metal belts (**tracks**)

jeep [C] a type of small, esp military car suitable for travelling over rough ground and sometimes used to carry a machine gun

H249 *nouns* : **ships of war** [C; *by* U]

warship a naval ship for war, esp one armed with guns

battleship the largest kind of warship, usu with the biggest guns and heaviest armour

cruiser a fast warship

destroyer a small fast warship often used against submarines

frigate a type of small fast-moving armed naval ship, used for accompanying and protecting other ships

sloop *also* **cutter** a small armed ship

submarine *infml abbrev* **sub** a warship that can travel under water, and fires torpedoes [⇨ H246]

minesweeper a ship that sweeps the sea, etc, for mines (=searches the water and clears it of mines)

H250 *nouns* : **military aircraft** [C]

bomber an aircraft that carries and drops bombs

fighter an aircraft that carries guns and is used to attack or defend bombers, attack other fighters, etc

H251 *nouns* : **missiles** [C]

missile 1 an explosive weapon which can fly under its own power and which can be aimed at a distant object: *Powerful nations now possess missiles which, if used in war, could destroy whole cities.* **2** *fml often pomp* an object or a weapon thrown by hand or shot from a gun or other instrument: *The angry crowd at the football match threw bottles and other missiles at the players. A spear in the hands of a skilful thrower can be a dangerous missile.*

guided missile a weapon which can be directed to the place it will bomb by electrical means during its flight

projectile an object or weapon that is shot forward, esp from a gun or that shoots itself forward, esp if large: *Bullets and rockets are both forms of projectile.*

rocket 1 a tubelike machine driven by burning gases and carrying its own oxygen, and used as a form of power for aircraft engines and for space travel **2** a bomb or missile that is driven in this way

warhead the explosive front end of a bomb or, esp, a guided missile

H252 *nouns* : **persons using guns, bombs, etc**

marksman [C] a person who can hit the right mark easily, usu with a gun

shot [C9] a person who shoots with the stated degree of skill: *He is a poor shot (with a gun) but a good shot with a bow.*

sniper [C] a person, esp a soldier who is a marksman, who shoots (at an enemy, etc) from a place where he cannot be seen: *There was a sniper in the trees and he killed two of our men*. **snipe** [I0 (*at*)] to shoot (at an enemy) in this way: *Someone began sniping (at us) from the trees*. (*fig*) *She is always sniping at him, telling him he can't do things well*.

bomber [C] a person who puts bombs into buildings and other places, in order to kill people, cause damage, etc

I

Arts and crafts, sciences and technology, industry and education

Making things

I1 *verbs* : **making and producing** [T1]

[ALSO ⇒ N150]

make 1 [*also* D1 (*for*)] to cause (something) to be; form (something) by means of work or action: *She made a cake. Make yourself a cup of tea. Cheese is made from milk.* **2** to earn, gain, or win (money or success): *He made a lot (of money) in his job. She makes a (good) living from her shop. I hope you make a success of your work/life.*

manufacture 1 to make (something) by means of machinery, esp in large quantities: *Many countries sell manufactured goods abroad. The firm manufactures electrical apparatus.* **2** (*fig*) to invent (an untrue story, reason, etc): *He had no good reason for being late, but he manufactured one.*

produce 1 to make or manufacture: *That company produces cars.* **2** to cause to appear: *Birds produce eggs. Those fields usually produce wheat.*

fabricate 1 to make, esp by putting parts together: *The house will be specially fabricated from these parts.* **2** (*fig*) to make in order to deceive: *The story was fabricated; it was completely untrue.*

forge to make esp from heated metal in a forge [⇒ H158]: *A blacksmith forges horseshoes out of iron.*

coin to make (esp a word or phrase): *He has coined several new technical words which are now widely used. Who first coined the word 'radio'?*

secrete (esp of an animal or plant organ) to produce (a usu liquid substance): *That tree secretes a sticky substance called resin.* **secretion 1** [U] the production of some usu liquid material by part of a plant or animal **2** [C] such a product: *a sticky secretion in the branches of the diseased tree*

I2 *nouns* : **making and producing**

make [C] a kind of manufacture, style, etc: *That's not a very good make of car. That car, what make is it? He sells cars of various makes.*

manufacture 1 [C *usu pl*] that which is manufactured: *They sell their various manufactures locally.* **2** [U] the method of doing this: *It is a car of American manufacture.* **3** [U] the act of manufacturing: *He is interested in the manufacture of cars.*

product [C] **1** something (useful) produced by growth or from the ground, or made in a factory: *Nylon is a man-made product.* **2** something that is produced as a result of thought, will, planning, etc: *Poems are the product of a poet's imagination. Criminals are sometimes the product of bad homes.*

brand [C] (the name of) a kind of manufactured product: *Which brands of coffee do you sell? This is a new brand; is it good?*

production [U] **1** the action of producing or making products: *This used to be an important town for the production of cloth by hand. The costs of production have increased.* **2** the amount produced by this means: *Production has increased in the last few weeks.*

fabrication 1 [U] the act of fabrication **2** [C] something fabricated, esp to deceive: *His story is a complete fabrication; what he said isn't true.*

output [U] the amount of things produced, work done, etc: *The factory's output is very high/low.*

I3 *verbs* : **building and constructing**

[ALSO ⇒ D1–3]

build [D1 (*for*); T1: (*out of*); IØ] to make (one or more things) by putting pieces together: *He built the house himself. The house is built out of stone. What does he do?— He builds (houses). She built him a model ship out of wood.* **2** [T1 (*up*)] to bring into being or develop: *Reading builds the mind. This good food will build you up* (= make you strong).

construct [T1] *esp fml* to build, esp according to a plan: *How exactly will you construct a boat like that?*

erect [T1] *fml* **1** to build or establish (a solid thing which was not there before): *She erected a stone at the head of her husband's grave. This hospital was erected by Queen Charlotte.* **2** to fix or place in an upright position (a solid thing which was lying flat): *They erected their tents near the river.*

assemble [T1] to put (something) together out of various pieces or parts: *He assembled the boat himself, from parts which his friend made.*

put together [v adv T1] *often infml* to form;

make a group or single thing out of: *He put the machine together himself.*

put up [v adv T1] *infml* to raise, erect: *They put up the tents near the river.*

knock up [v adv T1] *BrE infml* to build, put together: *He knocked up the house in less than a year.*

I4 *nouns* : **building and constructing**

[ALSO ⇒ D1–3]

building [U] the art or business of making objects such as houses: *He is in the building trade.*

construction 1 [U] the act or manner of constructing: *There are two new hotels near here under construction. A chair is an object of simple construction.* **2** [U] the business or work of building; the building industry: *My husband works in the construction industry. Wages in construction are very good.* **3** [C] something constructed, esp a building: *This new bank seems a very strange construction.*

erection 1 [U] the act or fact of building something: *The erection of the new hospital so near the main road was a mistake.* **2** [C] *sometimes deprec* a building: *The new college building is a most peculiar erection.*

assembly [U] the action of assembling: *This factory is only for the assembly of cars from parts made in other factories.*

I5 *verbs* : **shaping and modelling**

shape 1 [D1 *from/into*; V3] to make in a particular way: *The bird shaped its nest from mud and sticks. The bird shaped mud and sticks into a nest.* **2** [T1] *(fig)* to influence the form of: *He is a powerful person who can shape events.*

form 1 [I0] to be made or shaped; appear; develop: *Steam forms when water boils. A plan began to form in his mind.* **2** [L1] to take the shape of: *The school buildings formed a hollow square, with a playground in the middle.* **3** [X9] to make (something solid): *People in far northern countries sometimes form small houses out of blocks of ice.* **4** [T1] to develop as a result of thought, effort, experience, or training: *School helps to form a child's character. They formed a friendship. Children should form good habits.* **5** [T1] to make according to rule: *He can't form a correct sentence in English. The past tense of 'look' is formed by adding -ed.* **6** [T1] to make up; gather together; arrange: *Let's form a club. The new chief minister is forming his government mainly from younger men.* **7** [L1] to be; be the substance of: *Flour, eggs, fat, and sugar form the main contents of a cake.* **8** [T1; L9] to (cause to) stand or move in (a certain order): *The men formed a chain to pass the goods from the carts to the boats. The teacher formed her class into 5 rows. The soldiers formed into a line.*

fashion [Wv5;X9] to shape or make (something into or out of something else) usually with one's hands or with only a few tools: *He fashioned a hat out of leaves. He fashioned some leaves into a hat. It was a little hut fashioned from cake and sweets.*

mould *BrE*, **mold** *AmE* [T1] **1** to shape or form (something solid): *He moulded the figure in clay. She moulded the pieces of soft bread into balls.* **2** *(fig)* to shape or form (character, behaviour, etc): *His character has been moulded more by his experiences in life than by the education he got at school.*

model [T1] to shape (something usu solid) out of something soft: *He modelled her head in clay.* **model oneself (up)on someone** to try to be like another person [also ⇒ I48]

I6 *nouns* : **shapes and models**

shape 1 [C; (U)] the outline or form of something that is seen: *Houses come (= are built) in all shapes and sizes. She made the cake in the shape of a heart. We saw a shape through the mist but we couldn't see who it was.* **2** [U] *(fig)* the organization or form in which something is expressed, run, thought, etc: *What shape will future society have?* **3** [U9] condition: *Our garden is in good shape after the rain.* **4** [S] a way of appearing; form: *He was ready to meet danger in any shape. He had some good luck in the shape of an offer of a job.* **-less** [B] **-lessly** [adv] **-lessness** [U]

form 1 [C; U] shape; appearance; body; figure; image: *She has a tall graceful form. In the early morning light we could just see the dark forms of the mountains. Churches are often built in the form of a cross. When water freezes it takes the form of ice. In the beginning the earth was without form.* **2** [C *(of)*] a general plan or arrangement; system; kind or sort; way something shows or expresses itself: *Different countries have different forms of government. A picture book is a suitable form of gift for a young child. This disease takes the form of high fever and sickness for several days. She dislikes this form of exercise.* **3** [U] the way in which a work of art is put together: *Some writers are masters of form, but the contents of their books aren't interesting.* **4** [U; C] a) way in which a word may be written or spoken as a result of variations in spelling or pronunciation, according to some rule: *There are two forms of the past of 'to dream': 'dreamed' and 'dreamt'. They are different in form but not in meaning.*

pattern [C] **1** a regularly repeated arrangement (esp of lines, shapes, or colours on a surface, with ornamental effect, or of sounds, words, etc): *The cloth has a pattern of red and white squares. Meals here follow a set pattern.* **2** the way in which something happens or develops: *The illness is not following its usual pattern.* **3** a small piece of cloth that shows what a large piece (of normal size) will look like **4** a shape used as a guide for making something, esp **a** a piece of paper used to judge the shape of a part of a garment **b** a piece of wood used to set the shape of metal parts of machinery, made by a man (**patternmaker**) in a special room (**pattern shop**) in a factory **5** [(*of*) *usu sing*] a person or thing that is an excellent example to copy: *This company is a pattern of what a good company should be.*

mould *BrE*, **mold** *AmE* **1** [C] a hollow vessel of metal, stone, glass, etc, having a particular shape into which melted metal or some soft substance is poured so that when the substance becomes cool or hard it takes this shape **2** [C *usu sing*; U] *esp lit* (a person's) character, nature, etc, considered as having been shaped by family, education, experience, etc: *He's made in his father's mould* (= He is very much like his father).

model 1 [C (*of*)] a small representation or copy (of something): *On this table you can see a model of the new theatre that's going to be built in this town. The little boy enjoys making models.* **2** [C (*of*) *usu sing*] *BrE* a person or thing exactly, or almost exactly like another, but not always of the same size: *She's a perfect model of her aunt.* **3** [C (*of*)] *apprec* a person or thing that can serve as a perfect example or pattern, worthy to be followed or copied: *This young man is a model of all that a good army officer should be. This pupil's written work is a model of care and neatness.*

motif [C] a main pattern in art, music, etc, esp one that is found, heard, etc, again and again in the same or slightly different form

I7 *verbs* : **inventing and designing**

invent [T1; I0] to make for the first time (esp a new or original thing or idea): *Alexander Graham Bell invented the telephone in 1876.* **inventive** [B] having the ability to invent: *That child has an inventive mind.* **-ly** [adv] **-ness** [U]

think up [v adv T1] *infml* to invent: *How did you manage to think that idea up? It's just something he thought up in his bath.*

formulate [T1] **1** to invent and prepare (a plan, suggestion, etc): *The government are formulating some new plans for decreasing unemployment.* **2** to express in a short clear form: *He's a man of many ideas, but most of them are useless, because he can never formulate them well enough for others to understand them.* **formulation 1** [U] the act or result of formulating **2** [C] an example of this; something formulated; (*tech*) an idea or plan

design 1 [T1; I0] to make a drawing or pattern of (something); draw the plans for (something): *She designs dresses for a famous shop. She designs for a famous shop.* **2** [X9; V3: *often pass*] to develop for a certain purpose or use: *This book is designed for use in colleges. The weekend party was designed to bring the two leaders together.* **3** [T1] to imagine and plan out in the mind: *He designed the perfect crime.*

pioneer 1 [T1] to begin or help in the early development of: *Our grandfathers pioneered this country. He pioneered the use of this new drug.* **2** [I0] to act as a pioneer [⇒ D63]: *As a young man he pioneered in America.*

I8 *nouns* : **inventing and designing**

invention 1 [U] the act of invention or being invented: *He is responsible for the invention of the atomic bomb.* **2** [U] cleverness, esp at making or thinking of things: *He has great powers of invention.* **3** [C] something invented: *Radio is a great invention. His inventions have made him famous.*

design [C] **1** a drawing or pattern showing how something is to be made: *This design for the new building looks good on paper, but will it work?* **2** a plan in the mind

style [C] the way in which something is made, shaped, etc: *I like the style of that dress. We have shoes in many styles; which style do you like?*

I9 *verbs* : **copying and forging**

copy 1 [T1 (*for*)] to make something which is exactly like (another usu stated thing): *Please copy this letter twice for me.* **2** [T1] to follow (someone or something) as a standard or pattern: *She always copies the way I dress; what I wear today she wears tomorrow.* **3** [T1; I0: (*from, off*)] *deprec* to cheat by writing or doing (exactly the same thing) as someone else: *You copied this work off him! I know because you've made exactly the same mistakes. If I find you copying again, I'll punish you.*

imitate [T1] **1** to copy the behaviour or way of doing things of (a person): *He imitates the way his father does things.* **2** *usu infml* to appear like (something else): *It's plastic, made to imitate leather.*

reproduce [T1; I0] to (cause to) produce a copy (of); cause to be seen or heard again: *I wonder if this photograph will reproduce? He reproduced the painting by photography. That recording doesn't reproduce his voice very well. They can reproduce the sound of thunder in the theatre.*

pattern 1 [X9, esp *after*, *on*, *upon*] to make according to a pattern; copy exactly: *This village in Wales is patterned on one in Italy. He patterned himself upon a man he admired.* **2** [T1 (*with*)] to make an ornamental pattern on: *The sun patterned the grass with light and shade.*

recreate [T1] to make (something) (as if) for a second time: *He has managed to recreate the old way of building houses here. The film tries to recreate life in ancient Greece.*

fake 1 [T1] to make or change (something, such

as a work of art or an account) so that it appears to be better, more valuable, etc, than it really is: *I thought the painting was old, but it had been faked. She faked the facts a little in order to get the job.* **2** [T1; I∅] *infml* to pretend: *She faked illness so that she wouldn't need to go out. I thought he was telling the truth, but he was faking.*

falsify [T1] **1** to make false as by changing something: *falsify the receipts/facts* **2** to state or represent falsely **falsification** [U; C] (an) act of falsifying

forge [Wv5; T1; I∅] to make a copy of (something) in order to deceive: *He got the money dishonestly, by forging his brother's signature on a cheque. He was sent to prison for forging.*

I10 *nouns* : **copying and forging**

[ALSO ⇒ I45 PICTURES, PAINTINGS, DRAWINGS]

copy [C] a thing made to be exactly like another: *He asked his secretary to make him four copies of the letter. It is a copy of a famous painting.*

imitation 1 [U] the act of imitating or being imitated **2** [C] a copy of something or of someone or of someone's behaviour, etc: *This material is an imitation of leather.*

reproduction 1 [U] copying: *The quality of reproduction isn't very good on this recording.* **2** [C] a copy, esp of a work of art, less exact than a replica: *a cheap reproduction of a great painting*

replica [C] a close copy, esp of a painting or other work of art, often made by the same artist

facsimile [C] an exact copy as of a picture or piece of writing

fake [C] a thing or person that is not what he or it looks like: *The painting looked old but it was a recent fake. I thought he was a priest but he was a fake and robbed me.*

forgery 1 [U] the act of forging something: *He was sent to prison for forgery.* **2** [C] an example of this; something forged: *Those pound notes are forgeries.*

sham [S] something false pretending to be the real thing; a piece of deceit: *The agreement was a sham; neither side intended to keep to it.*

I11 *adjectives* : **natural and real** [B]

natural not caused, made, or controlled by people: *This country has great natural mineral wealth. The furniture is all finished in natural colours.* **un-** [neg] **-ly** [adv] **-ness** [U]

real actually existing; true not false: *Is your ring brass or real gold? What was the real reason for your absence? The real amount was only £50.* **-ly** [adv] **-ness** [U]

genuine 1 (of an object) real; really what it seems to be: *This picture has proved to be genuine and not a copy.* **2** (of feelings) real, not pretended: *He seems to have a genuine interest in helping the children.* **-ly** [adv] **-ness** [U]

authentic known to have been made, painted, written, etc, by the person who is claimed to have done it: *This is an authentic painting of Rembrandt's.* **in-** [neg] **-ally** [adv Wa4] **authenticate** [T1 *usu pass*] to prove (something) to be authentic: *Now that this painting has been authenticated as Rembrandt's, it's worth ten times as much as I paid for it.* **authentication** [U] **authenticity** [U9] the quality of being true or of being made, painted, written, etc, by the person claimed: *The painting's authenticity is not in doubt; it is a real Rembrandt.*

I12 *adjectives* : **not natural** [B]

artificial 1 made by man; not natural: *There were some artificial flowers on the table.* **2** made to take the place of a natural product, esp a clothing material: *The dress was of artificial silk.* **3** lacking true feelings; insincere; unreal: *She welcomed him with an artificial smile.* **-ly** [adv] **-ity** [U]

synthetic [Wa5] *tech* artificial, esp of cloth: *This is a synthetic cloth; it isn't real wool.* **-ally** [adv Wa4]

imitation [Wa5] being a copy of something better: *This is imitation leather. This material is imitation; it isn't natural leather and it isn't as good.*

man-made [Wa5] **1** produced by the work of man; not found in nature: *This lake is man-made; there used to be a valley here until they changed the course of the river.* **2** (of materials) not made from natural substances, like wool or cotton but from combinations of chemicals; synthetic: *Nylon is a man-made fibre.*

contrived *often deprec* not natural: *His writing is very contrived; his characters never speak in a natural way.*

acquired [Wa5] having been specially or carefully learnt and therefore not natural: *His way of speaking is acquired; he didn't speak like that when we were at school. Beer is an acquired taste; it takes time to begin to enjoy it.*

I13 *adjectives* : **not real** [B]

false 1 not real: *He has false teeth. The diamonds she wears are false.* **2** made or changed so as to deceive: *The false weights made the goods appear heavier than they were.* **-sity, -ness** [U]

fake [Wa5] *not fml* made and intended to deceive: *He gave them fake money; the money was all fake.*

bogus *not fml & usu derog* false: *His whole story is bogus; don't believe it.*

sham [Wa5] *not fml* false but made to look or seem real: *This is a sham agreement; neither side intends to keep to it.*

I14 *verbs* : **destroying and demolishing**

[ALSO ⇒ N338]

destroy 1[T1; IØ] to tear down or apart; put an end to the existence or effectiveness of (something): *The enemy destroyed the city. The storm has destroyed my crops.* (*fig*) *He destroyed all her hopes.* **2** [T1] to kill (esp animals in homes, farms, or zoos [⇒ A42]): *The dog is mad and ought to be destroyed.*

demolish [T1] to destroy, pull or tear down: *They've demolished that old building and put up a new one.* (*fig*) *We've demolished all his arguments and he has nothing more to say.*

dismantle 1 [T1] to take (a machine or article) to pieces: *They dismantled the engine.* **2** [IØ] (of a machine or article) to be able to be taken to pieces: *The engine will dismantle easily.* **3** [T1] to take away the machines, furniture, etc, from (a building or ship): *They dismantled the factory.*

take apart [v adv T1] to take (something) to pieces: *He took the machine apart, then put it together again.*

pull down [v adv T1] *genl & not fml* to break in pieces and destroy (something built): *Half the houses in the street are being pulled down to make room for the new post office.*

tear down [v adv T1] *esp emot* to pull down violently: *Half the houses in the street have been torn down to make room for an ugly new building!*

break up [v adv] **1** [T1] to break (something) completely into pieces: *His business is breaking up old cars. He broke up the wooden boxes and put the pieces on the fire.* **2** [IØ] to come to an end, usu in a bad way: *Their marriage has broken up.*

I15 *nouns* : **destroying and demolishing**

destruction [U] **1** the act of destroying or state of being destroyed: *The destruction of the forest by fire was a terrible thing. The army left the enemy town in a state of complete destruction.* **2** that which destroys: *Pride was her destruction for it caused the loss of all her friends.*

demolition 1 [U] the action of demolishing: *They ordered the demolition of the old building.* **2** [C] a case of this: *There were several demolitions in our street.*

breakup [C (*of*)] the destruction or end by destruction (of something): *The breakup of their marriage after 15 years was sad.*

I16 *verbs* : **changing, adapting, and transforming**

[ALSO ⇒ I20]

change 1 [Wv5;T1; IØ] to (cause to) become different: *In autumn the leaves change from green to brown. You've changed such a lot since I last saw you. You'll never persuade me to change my feelings for him. He's been a changed man since his wife died.* **2** [T1 (*for*)] to give, take, or put something in place of (something else), usu of the same kind: *It's time you changed the oil in your car. Her new dress didn't fit so she took it back to the shop and changed it (for another).* **3** [IØ (*into, out of*); T1] to put (different clothes) on oneself: *I'm just going to change into something more comfortable. Why does it take you so long to change your clothes? The members of the team were in the changing room after the match.* **4** [T1] to put (fresh clothes or coverings) on a baby, child, bed, etc: *I change the sheets once a week.* **5** [T1] to put fresh clothes or coverings on (a baby, child, bed, etc): *How often do you change your bed?* **6** [T1] to exchange (two things): *Change places with me, please; I'd like to sit next to the window. She's just changed jobs. He changes sides in arguments!* **7** [IØ (*from, to*); T1] to leave and enter (different vehicles) in order to continue or complete a journey: *(All) change here (for London)! I had to change from a train to a bus for part of the journey.* **change hands** to go from the ownership of one person to another: *My car had only changed hands twice before I bought it.* **change one's mind** to come to have a new opinion: *I used to dislike him very much but now I've changed my mind and quite like him.*

alter [T1; IØ] to (cause to) be or become different; to change from one state to another: *I altered my plans, and went to France last month instead of this month. He has altered a lot since last I saw him; he looks much older now. Can you alter this dress for me, to make it longer/ shorter?*

adapt [T1; IØ] to change so as to be or make suitable for new needs, different conditions, etc: *He adapted an old car engine to drive his boat. We adapted ourselves to the hot weather. This book was adapted for foreign students by making the language simpler. Some people adapt easily to living in new places; some don't.*

assimilate 1 [T1; IØ] to (allow to) change so as to become part of (a different group, country, race, etc): *America has assimilated people from all over the world. Some foreigners assimilate easily (in)to our way of life.* **2** [T1] to take as one's own; use properly: *The factory quickly assimilated the new discoveries. He remembered the facts well, but had not really assimilated them.* **assimilate to** [v prep D1 *usu pass*] to make like: *The laws of the defeated country were assimilated to those of the stronger country. They assimilated the new laws to the old ones.*

adjust [T1; IØ: (*to*)] to change slightly, esp in order to make suitable for a particular job or new conditions: *He hasn't adjusted to his new job/life yet. I must adjust my watch; it's a little slow/fast. She adjusted herself (to the heat of the country) very quickly.*

vary 1 [IØ (*in*)] to be different; have qualities that are not the same as each other: *Opinions on this matter vary. Houses vary in size. This student never varies; his work is always very good.* **2** [Wv4;T1;IØ (*from*)] to (cause to) become different; change (continually): *The price of goods often varies according to how much people want them. Her health varies from good to rather weak. Old people don't like to vary their habits. During the last 10 years he's grown fruit in his garden with varying success; sometimes he's had large crops and sometimes none.*

turn 1 [T1] to change the nature of: *Success turned him from a kind gentle person into a nasty greedy employer. The fairy turned the girl's old clothes into a beautiful dress.* **2** [X7;L1,7] to (cause to) become: *In autumn the leaves turn brown. This heat will turn the grass brown. He is a Christian turned Buddhist.*

transform [T1] to change completely in form, appearance, or nature: *The magician transformed the man into a rabbit. A steam engine transforms heat into power. My life won't be transformed by winning all this money.*

transmute [T1] to change from one form, nature, substance, etc, into another: *The magician claimed he could transmute iron into gold.*

permute [T1] *esp math* to rearrange in a different order: *You can permute the numbers in any way you like, but the result will be the same.*

mutate [IØ;(T1)] *tech* (of living things) to (cause to) change in nature: *Many kinds of living things have mutated over millions of years into new forms of life.*

revert to [v prep] **1** [T1,4] to go back to (a former condition or habit): *He's stopped taking drugs now, but he may revert to taking them again.* **2** [T1] to talk about again; go back to (a former subject of discussion): *Reverting to your earlier remark about camels, do you think . . .?* **3** [T1] *law* (of property) to go back to (an owner): *When he dies his land will revert to the state.* **revert to type** to go back to the original state: *Mary tried to become an actress but she soon reverted to type and became a farmer like her father.*

switch [T1;IØ (*from/to;around*)] *infml* to change, esp suddenly: *He is always switching jobs/switching from one job to another. Stop switching around and keep to one job.*

I17 nouns : changing, varying, transforming, etc

change 1 [U] the condition in which something is changing or has changed: *Change is part of life.* **2** [C] an example of this: *There have been many changes in that city since I was last there.*

alteration 1 [U] the act of altering, of making or becoming different: *My shirt needs alteration.* **2** [C] a change; something changed: *The alterations to your shirt will take a long time.*

adaptation 1 [U] the act of adapting, or changing in some particular way: *This book needs some adaptation.* **2** [C] any example of this; a particular change: *Can you make a few adaptations in the book?*

assimilation [U] **1** the act of assimilating or being assimilated **2** *tech* the changing of a speech sound because of the influence of another speech sound next to it

adjustment 1 [U] the act of adjusting, or changing slightly: *The machine needs adjustment.* **2** [C] an example of this; a slight change: *He is making some adjustments to his plan.*

variation 1 [U] the action of varying: *Changing weather conditions are usually the result of variation in air pressure.* **2** [C] an example or degree of this: *If you go to a number of different shops you'll often find great variations in price for the same articles.* **3** [C] one of a set of repetitions [⇒ N127] of part of a simple piece of music, sometimes written by someone else, each with certain different ornamental changes or developments made to it: *Elgar wrote a piece of music called the Enigma Variations.* **4** [C; U] (an example of) change from what is usual in the form of a group of kind of living things, such as animals

version [C (*of*)] **1** one person's account of an event, as compared with that of another person: *According to the driver's version of it, the accident wasn't his fault. The two newspapers gave different versions of what happened.* **2 a** a translation: *The play was in German, but I'd read an English version so I was able to understand most of the action.* **b** [*usu cap*] an official translation of (part of) the Bible: *The King James Version of the Bible first appeared in 1611.* **3** a written or musical work that exists in more than one form: *Did you read the whole book or only the short version?* **4** a slightly different form, copy, or variation of an article: *This dress is a cheaper version of the one we saw in the shop. The new version of this kind of car has a more powerful engine.* **5** a performer's particular way of understanding and expressing some famous piece of music, character in a play, etc: *This singer's version of the song showed great tenderness of feeling but lacked the necessary force.*

transformation 1 [U] the act of transforming or being transformed **2** [C] an example of this: *What a transformation that dress makes! She looks very pretty now.*

transform [C] *tech, esp math* the result of a transformation: *ACB is a transform of ABC.*

transmutation 1 [U] the act of transmuting or being transmuted **2** [C] an example or result of this

permutation *esp math* **1** [U] the act of permuting or being permuted; re-arrangement in a different order **2** [C] an example or result of this; a complete change: *The six possible permutations of ABC are ABC, ACB, BCA, BAC, CAB, and CBA.*

mutation *tech* **1** [U] the action of change in the

cells of a living thing producing a new quality in the material or parts of the body, sometimes causing illness **2** [C] an example of this: *Pet animals often have fur of a colour not found in the wild, caused by a mutation.* **3** [C] a type of animal or plant caused by a mutation: *If a black rose really exists, it must be a mutation.*

mutant *often deprec* [C] a living thing which has been produced by a mutation

switch [C *usu sing*] *infml* an esp sudden act of changing: *He made a quick switch from an unfriendly to a friendly manner when he saw that they could help him.*

I18 *verbs* : **putting things right**

[ALSO ⇒ N215]

put . . . right [v adv T1b] **1** to make (something) right (again): *Let's put things right and start again.* **2 put . . . right/straight** [(*on*)] to correct (someone who is misinformed): *Let me put you straight (on this).* **3** to mend (something): *Can you put it right for me?*

set . . . right [v adv T1b] to make or put (something) right, esp in the right position: *He set the clock right and it began to work again.*

rectify [T1] *fml* to put right: *Please rectify these mistakes.* **rectification** [U] the act of rectifying

correct [T1] to make right: *Correct my spelling if it's wrong.*

I19 *verbs* : **repairing and mending**

repair 1 [I∅; T1] **a** to make (something worn or broken) able to work or be used again: *repair a broken watch/a road/old shoes* **b** (of something broken or worn) to be able to be mended: *This shirt is so old it won't repair.* **2** [T1] *fml* to make up for; put right (a wrong, mistake, etc): *How can I repair the wrong I have done to her?* **reparable, repairable** [Wa5;B] able to be repaired: *That broken chair is not repairable.* **ir-** [*neg*] **-bly** [adv] **repairer** [C] a person who repairs something: *My father was a watch repairer.*

mend 1 [T1] to repair (something with) a hole, break, fault, etc: *They've mended the door and it shuts properly now. I must take my shoes to be mended.* **2** [T1; I∅] to sew (something) so as to repair it: *I'll mend that shirt. I've been mending all night.*

fix [T1] to mend; repair: *I must get the radio fixed.*

sort [T1] *ScotE* to mend; repair: *I'll sort this bicycle for you. He had his old shoes sorted last week.*

darn [T1; I∅] to repair (a hole in cloth or a garment with a hole in it) by passing threads through and across (by needle-weaving): *Please darn my sock/the hole in my sock. She darns well.*

patch [T1] **1** to cover (a hole) with a patch [⇒ I21]: *He patched the hole in the tent.* **2** to put a patch on a hole, worn place, etc in (esp some

part of a garment): *The elbows of your coat have worn thin, so I must patch them.* **3** (of a material) to serve as a patch for: *This piece of material is just right to patch the roof.*

I20 *verbs* : **adjusting and overhauling**

adjust [T1] **1** to change slightly, esp in order to make more suitable for a particular job or new conditions: *I must adjust my watch; it's slow. You can adjust the car seats to the length of your legs.* **2** to put into order; put in place; set right: *Your coat collar needs adjusting.*

tinker [I∅ (*with*)] *often deprec* **1** to try to repair, usu in an unsatisfactory way: *Don't tinker with the engine; see someone who knows what to do.* **2** to go on adjusting, esp in small ways: *He tinkered with the engine until he was satisfied. She enjoys tinkering with engines.*

convert [Wv5;T1; I∅] to (cause to) change into another form, substance, or state, or from one use or purpose to another: *Coal can be converted to gas by burning. I believe they're going to convert this castle into flats. He lives in a converted church. I can't imagine this house converting into a shop very well.*

overhaul [T1] to examine thoroughly and perhaps repair if necessary: *He overhauled the car.*

I21 *nouns* : **putting things right**

correction 1 [U] the act of correcting: *Most teachers spend their evening on/in the correction of their pupils' work.* **2** [C] a change that corrects something; an improvement: *Teachers usually make corrections in red ink.* **3** [U] *euph* punishment: *The prisoner was sent to a labour camp for correction.*

repair [C *often pl*] an act or result of repairing: *Are the repairs to the house finished yet? I must get these repairs done.*

mend [C] a part mended after breaking or wearing: *That's a good mend; it doesn't show* (= people can't see it).

darn [C] a part darned: *His socks were old and full of darns.*

patch [C] **1 a** (usu small) piece of material used to cover a hole or a damaged place: *The boy's trousers need a patch on the knee.* **2** an (often irregularly shaped) part of a surface or space that is different (esp in colour) from the surface or space round it: *There were wet patches on the wall. The girls' dresses made patches of bright colour in the streets.* **patchy** [Wa1;B] **1** having a number of, or made up of, patches: *The sun has faded the curtains and their colour is now patchy.* **2** (of certain types of weather) appearing in patches: *The mist was patchy.* **3** usu deprec **a** incomplete: *His knowledge of science is patchy.* **b** partly good but partly (and chiefly) bad: *The concert was patchy.* **-chily** [adv] **-chiness** [U]

adjustment 1 [U (*to*)] the‚ act of adjusting: *Adjustment to a new job/country is not always easy.* **2** [C (*to*)] an example of this: *She made some adjustments to the dress. We must accept one or two adjustments to the way things are done here.*

conversion 1 [U] the act of converting: *Conversion of your heating system from coal to gas will be costly.* **2** [C] an example of this; a change from one use or purpose to another: *That firm specializes in house conversions.*

overhaul [C] an act of overhauling: *He gave the car a good/complete overhaul.*

I22 *verbs* : **preparing and processing**

prepare 1 [T1 (*for*); V3] to put (something) in a condition ready for use or for a purpose: *Please prepare the table for dinner* (= put a cloth, dishes, etc, on it). *If you want to plant seeds you have to prepare the ground first. The nurse is preparing the child to go to the hospital* (= getting together its clothes and other articles). **2** [D1 (*for*); T1] to put together or make by treating in some special way (such as by mixing or heating substances): *This special medicine must be freshly prepared each time. Mother is preparing a meal for us/us a meal.* **3** [T1 (*for*), 3) to get or make ready by collecting supplies, making necessary arrangements, planning, studying, etc: *Who prepared these building plans? Have you prepared an answer to this letter? He's preparing his speech for the meeting tomorrow. They are busy preparing to go on holiday.* **4** [T1 (*for*), 3; V3] to accustom (someone or someone's mind) to some (new) idea, event, or condition: *We've tried to prepare the child, but I don't think he'll understand why his father is leaving. Prepare yourself for a shock. Prepare to meet your fate. He prepared himself to accept defeat.* **5** [T1 (*for*); V3] to make (someone) fit for something by special training: *This college prepares boys for the army.* **preparatory** [Wa5;A] *usu fml* done in order to get ready for something: *Before he began his talk he gave a preparatory explanation about the exact meaning of the subject.* **preparatory to** (*usu with* **-ing** *form*) *fml* before; as a preparation for: *I have a few letters to write preparatory to beginning the day's work.* **preparedness** [U] (the state of) being ready for something, esp war: *They are in a state of full preparedness (for war).*

prepare for [v prep T1] **1** to get ready for: *Will you help me prepare for the party? The army was preparing for battle.* **2** to accustom one's mind to: *We must prepare for the worst.*

get ... ready [T1] *infml* to prepare: *Let's get the equipment ready for use.*

process [T1 *often pass*] to prepare and examine in detail: *The plans are now being processed.*

I23 *verbs* : **mixing and blending**

mix 1 [T1 (*up*); I0: (*with*)] to (cause (different substances, things, etc) to) be combined so as to form a whole, of which the parts no longer have a separate shape, appearance, etc, or cannot easily be separated one from another: *You can't mix oil and water. You can't mix oil with water. Oil and water don't mix. Oil doesn't mix with water. She put the flour, eggs, etc, into a bowl and mixed them together; she mixed them up well. The artist mixed blue with yellow paint to produce the green colour he wanted. I warned him that he'd be sick if he mixed his drinks* (= drank beer, wine, etc, at the same time). **2** [D1 (*for*); T1] to prepare (such a combination of different substances): *His wife mixed him a hot drink of milk, sugar, and chocolate.* **3** [I0 (*with*)] (*fig*) (of a person) to be, be put or enjoy being in the company of others: *He's such a friendly person that he mixes well in any company. She's a strange lonely child; she doesn't mix with the other children.*

blend 1 [T1; I0] *sometimes tech* to (cause to) mix: *Some kinds of tobacco do not blend well with each other. Blend the sugar, flour, and eggs (together) before baking the cake.* **2** [I0] to become combined into a single whole: *The houses seem to blend into the countryside. The countryside and the houses seem to blend (into each other).* **3** [T1] *esp tech* to produce (tea, coffee, whisky, etc) out of a mixture of several varieties: *They blend coffee just as I like it.*

compound [T1] **1** to mix (things) together to make something new or different **2** to add to or increase: *His second crime just compounds the first.*

merge [I0; T1] to (cause to) become part of something else, or parts of something larger; to blend: *The two businesses merged. They merged the two companies. He merged with the darkness as he walked away into the night.* **merger** [C] a union of two or more businesses

I24 *nouns* : **preparing and mixing, etc**

preparation 1 [U; S] the act or action of preparing: *Who's in charge of the preparation of the room for the concert? She was late and only had time for a hurried preparation of dinner.* **2** [U] the state or course of being prepared: *He had too little preparation for the examination, so he failed. Plans for selling the new product are now in preparation.* **3** [C *usu pl*] an arrangement (for a future event): *She is making preparations for her marriage.* **4** [C] *esp tech* something that is made ready for use by mixing a number of (chemical) substances: *The firm is selling a new preparation for cleaning metal.*

mixture 1 [U] the act of mixing: *The mixture of people in the city has made it very international.* **2** [C;U] the result of mixing; things mixed

437

together, esp liquids: *His art is a mixture of many styles. The doctor gave her a mixture to help her painful throat.*

mix 1 [U;C] a combination of different substances, prepared to be ready, or nearly ready, for (the stated) use: *She's too lazy to make cakes by mixing all the separate substances; she always buys cake mix from the shops.* **2** [S (*of*)] a group of different things, people,etc; mixture: *There was rather a strange mix of people at the party; doctors, postmen, lawyers, farmers, etc.*

blend [C] a product of blending: *We've been selling a great deal of this blend of coffee.* (*fig*) *His manner was a blend of friendliness and respect.*

I25 *verbs* : **developing things** [T1]

develop 1 to study or think out fully, or present fully: *I'd like to develop this idea a little more. The company is developing several new products.* **2** to bring out the economic possibilities of (esp land or natural substances): *We must develop all the natural resources of our country, its minerals and its farming.*

work up [v adv] to develop steadily: *He worked the firm up from nothing.*

I26 *verbs* : **using things** [T1]

use 1 to do things with: *He uses a pen to write with; he doesn't use a typewriter* [⇒ G152]. *What do you use that machine for? They use the buses a lot; they don't have a car.* **2** [*usu pass* (*up*)] to finish: *All the paper has been used* (*up*). **abuse** to use (something, usu not an object) wrongly or badly, esp in a way different from what was intended: *He abuses his power here; he has no right to tell people what to think. She abuses her health with all these late-night parties. We let him come here any time he wanted, but he abused the privilege by bringing more and more friends with him, so he is no longer allowed to come.* **misuse** not to use (something) properly: *He misused the money; it belongs to his club but he used it for himself.*

make use of to use in a general way; use well · *Can you make use of these machines? She makes (good) use of her free time; she's learning French.*

utilize, -ise *fml* to make (good or full) use of: *You should utilize your abilities as fully as possible. He utilizes his free time in improving his swimming.*

apply to bring or put to use: *Scientific discoveries are often applied to industrial production methods.*

employ *fml* **1** to use: *The police had to employ force to break up the crowd. This bird employs its beak as a weapon.* **2** to use (one's time): *She employs all her free time in sewing.*

exploit 1 to use or develop (a thing) fully to get profit or results: *The company exploited the oil under the sea. We must exploit what we have to the best of our ability.* **2** *deprec* to use (esp a person) unfairly for one's own profit: *He exploited the poor by making them work for low pay.*

deploy to spread out, use, or arrange for action, esp for military action: *We must deploy all our soldiers correctly in order to win the battle. They deployed all their skill to succeed in their new business.*

waste to use more of (something) than is needed; use improperly: *Stop wasting water; turn the tap off. He wasted his money on cheap clothes. Don't waste your time listening to his silly ideas.* **wastage** [U; S] wasting or that which is wasted: *Think of the wastage represented by all those people who don't finish their university courses! There was a wastage of 25% of all the goods produced.* **wasteful** [B] tending to waste or marked by waste: *wasteful habits* **-ly** [adv] **-ness** [U]

I27 *nouns* : **developing and using things**

development 1 [U] the act of developing or being developed: *The development of new products is important to the company.* **2** [C] an example of this; something new which is happening: *These developments are very interesting. What are the latest developments in science?*

use 1 [U] the act of using: *Their use of the house as a shop surprised me.* **2** [C; U] an example of this: *What uses does this machine have? He put the car to good use; he used it a lot.* **abuse** [U; C: (*of*)] (a) bad or wrong use of (something): *He is well known for his abuse of the law. There have been a number of abuses of the law here. He was arrested by the police for drug abuse* (= the wrong use, unlawful sale, etc, of drugs [⇒ E80]). **misuse** [U; C; (*of*)](a) use which is not proper: *He lost his job because of his misuse of money which belonged to the company.*

usage [U] the way in which a thing is used; (*fml*) use: *This book has had a lot of hard usage* (= has been used a lot).

utilization, -isation [U] *fml* the act of utilizing

application 1 [U] putting (something) to use (in relation to something else): *The application of new scientific discoveries to industrial production usually makes jobs easier.* **2** [C] an example of this: *These new applications interest me.*

employment [U] the act of employing: *The employment of force by the police seemed to be necessary.*

exploitation [U] the act of exploiting; the state of being exploited: *The company's exploitation of the oil under the sea is important to the whole country. The exploitation of the poor (by the rich) must stop.*

deployment [U] the act or way of deploying; the state of being deployed: *The general's bad deployment of his army was the mistake which lost them the war.*

I28 *verbs* : **functioning and serving**

function [I∅] (esp of a thing) to be in action; work: *The machine won't function properly unless you oil it well. A person dies when his brain ceases to function.*

serve 1 [T1] to be good enough for the use of (someone): *This stone will serve me for/as a hammer.* **2** [I∅; T1; I3] to be good enough or satisfying for a purpose: *Our room had to serve as/for both bedroom and living room. I haven't got a hammer, but this stone should serve (my purpose).*

do [Wv6; I∅ (*for*)] *infml* to serve or function, esp if there is nothing better: *This piece of wood will do; it will serve the purpose very well. If you can't get leather, then plastic will do.*

I29 *nouns* : **function and purpose**

function [C] the way in which someone or something is used, works, etc: *It's his function at these meetings to tell us what the government is doing. What function does the machine have?*

purpose 1 [C] an intention or plan; reason for an action: *Did you come to London for the purpose of seeing your family, or for business purposes? The purpose of his life seems to be to enjoy himself. It was a play with a purpose, intended to express the writer's political beliefs, not just to be amusing.* **2** [C] use; effect; result: *Don't waste your money; put it to some good purpose.* **3** [U] steady determination in following an aim; willpower: *It's no use deciding to become a doctor if you lack purpose in setting yourself to the necessary studies; you must have a sense of purpose.* **answer/fulfil/serve one's/the purpose(s)** to be or do all that is needed: *I haven't got a pen here, but a pencil will answer the same purpose.* **on purpose 1** intentionally; not by accident: *I'm sorry I stepped on your toe; it was an accident.—It wasn't! You did it on purpose.* **2** with a particular stated intention: *I came here on purpose to see you.* **to little/ no/some/much/good purpose** with little/no/some/ much/good result or effect: *You acted to good purpose when you bought that car; it was both good and cheap.* **to the purpose** useful; connected with what is being considered or what is needed: *His remarks about gardening were hardly to the purpose in an argument about farming.*

ambition 1 [U; C] strong desire for success, power, riches, etc: *That politician is full of ambition. One of his ambitions is to become a minister.* **2** [C] that which is desired in this way: *That big house on the hill is his ambition.* **ambitious 1** [B; F3] having a strong desire for suc-

cess, power, riches, etc: *He is an ambitious man. He is ambitious to succeed in politics.* **2** [B] showing or demanding a strong desire for success, great effort, great skill, etc: *It's an ambitious attempt; I hope it succeeds.* **-ly** [adv] **-ness** [U]

aim [C] the desired result of one's efforts; purpose; intention; ambition: *What is your aim in working so hard? He told me about his aims in life.*

Arts and crafts

I40 *nouns* : **art**

art [U] **1** the making or expressing of what is beautiful, interesting, or true, esp in a manner that can be seen, as in a painting: *Children's art can be very expressive. He doesn't like modern art.* **2** things produced in this way (*esp in the phr* **work of art**): *We studied the art of the early Japanese. Those paintings are very fine works of art.* **3** fine skill in making or doing or expressing something: *The art of painting well is not easily learnt. The story was told with great art. He is good at the art of making friends.*

art form [C] any way in which art can be expressed: *Which art form do you prefer—painting or music?*

fine arts [(*the*) P *often cap*] *fml* the arts generally (painting, music, sculpture, [⇨ I49] etc)

I41 *nouns* : **arts and crafts**

art [C] a skilful method of doing something, esp something difficult: *There is an art to making bread. Writing well is a real art.*

craft 1 [U *esp in comb*] skill or ability, esp in work done with the hands or in the arts: *The actor's stagecraft is good.* **2** [C] a job or trade needing such skill: *The jeweller's craft needs great care.*

handicraft [C] a skill needing careful use of the hands, such as sewing, weaving, etc

I42 *nouns* : **ways, means, techniques, and processes**

way [C] **1** how a thing is (to be) done, seen, said, held, used, etc: *Do it this way. Hold it that way. I know a better way of doing it. He likes the old ways of doing things.* **2** habit: *He has a nasty way of telling lies about people.* **by the way** (used in adding something new in a conversation) in addition: *Oh, by the way, have you seen John lately?* **in a way** to some degree: *In a way he is right about what happened.* **in a bad way** not in a good state: *He was in a bad way after the car accident.* **one way or another** somehow: *We'll do it one way or another; don't worry.*

get/have one's (own) way do what one wants to do: *That child gets his own way too often.*

means [S; P] way of doing something, esp a set of actions with certain tools, materials, etc: *What means did he use to do the work? They got into the house by means of an open window. They did it by some unknown means.* **by all means** emph certainly: *By all means come! Can I do it?—Yes; by all means.* **by fair means or foul** in any way possible, honestly or not: *He plans to win by fair means or foul.* **by no means** emph & fml not at all: *Is he good at that work? —By no means. I am by no means happy about his work.*

manner 1 [C usu sing] sometimes fml the way in which anything is done or happens: *He was walking in a rather unnatural manner.* **2** [S] a personal way of acting or behaving towards other people: *I don't like to talk to him; he has a very rude/unpleasant manner.* **3** [C9 usu sing] a way or style of writing, printing, building, etc, which is typical of one or more persons, or a country or of a time in history **4** [S of] old use kind or sort of person or thing (only in the phr **what manner of?**): *What manner of son can treat his mother so badly?*

method 1 [C] esp tech a particular way of doing things: *Do you know any new methods of teaching a language?* **2** [U] systematic planning, organization, etc: *They lack method; they never plan anything properly. There is method in everything she does.* **methodical** [B] showing or liking method; planned; systematic: *They are very methodical workers.* **-ly** [adv Wa4]

medium [C usu sing] **1** esp tech the means by which something can be done, passed from one person, place, etc, to another, etc: *Money is the commonest medium by which people can exchange goods.* **2** a method of giving information; a form of art in which work can be expressed: *He writes stories, but the theatre is his favourite medium. His best work was in the medium of oil paints. Television is a medium for giving information and opinions, for amusing people and for teaching them foreign languages and other subjects.* **3** a substance in which objects or living things exist or through which a force travels; the surroundings in which one lives: *A fish in water is in its natural medium. Sound travels through the medium of air.*

fashion [S] esp lit a way of doing something: *He does his work in a very careless fashion.*

mode 1 [C (of)] often fml a way or manner of thinking, behaving, speaking, writing, living, etc: *He suddenly became wealthy, which changed his whole mode of life. Do you know the correct mode of address when speaking to a princess?* **2** [C] tech a way, arrangement, or condition in which something is done or happens: *It is a fever which will return from time to time, if it follows its usual mode.*

technique 1 [C] **a** the manner in which a subject is treated by a writer, artist, etc; a method of artistic expression used in writing, music, art,

etc: *Your story is interesting but you must improve your writing technique if you want your book to be a success.* **b** a method or manner of play in sport: *The cricketer's perfect technique kept him out of trouble.* **2** [U] skill in art or some specialized activity

style [U; C] **1** the way of expressing oneself, one's ideas, etc, esp in art: *He is a writer with great style/an excellent style. Her style of painting is like Dali's.* **2** the form which art took at a usu stated time in history: *The house is in the Gothic style.*

handiwork [U] **1** work requiring the skilful use of the hands **2** sometimes deprec action, usu showing some sign of the person who has done it: *The criminals' handiwork was clear at the scene of the crime.*

process 1 [C] a particular system or treatment of materials, used esp in producing goods: *Cotton goes through several processes when being made into cloth.* **2** [C] a continued set of actions performed intentionally in order to reach some result: *Producing a dictionary is a slow process. The process of learning to read takes a long time.* **3** [C] any continued set of natural actions connected with (the continuation, development, and change of) life or matter, over which man has little control: *Heat will hasten the process of decay in foods. Coal was formed out of dead forests by chemical processes.* **4** [U] course; time during which something is still being done (esp in the phr **in (the) process of**): *The firm is now in the process of moving the machines to a new factory.*

formula [C] a fixed way, technique, or style, etc, of doing something: *They still work to the same formula that their father used.*

I43 verbs : **painting and drawing**
[ALSO ⇒ G8, G81]

paint 1 [T1; I0] to make (a picture or pictures of) (somebody or something) using paint: *Who painted this picture? He has a splendid strong face and I would very much like to paint him. She paints well; she may become an artist.* **2** [T1] (fig) to describe in clear well-chosen words, with lifelike effect (often in the phr **paint a picture**): *His letters paint a wonderful picture of his life in Burma.*

draw [T1; I0] to make (something) with a pencil or pen: *He drew a picture of his daughter.* (fig) *Shakespeare draws his characters well.*

sketch 1 [I0] to make rough, not detailed pictures: *This is a place where artists come to sketch.* **2** [T1] to make a rough picture of: *She sketched the scene (quickly).* **3** [T1 (in, out)] to describe roughly with few details: *They sketched in/out the main points of their plan.*

trace 1 [T1 (out)] to draw the course or shape of: *Trace out your journey on the map.* **2** [I0; T1] to copy by drawing on transparent paper the lines on (a drawing, map, etc) placed underneath: *He was busy tracing. Trace this map for* *me, please.* **3** [T1] to write slowly or with difficulty: *He traced his name slowly at the bottom of the page.*

depict [T1] **1** to represent by a picture: *This painting depicts the Battle of Agincourt.* **2** to describe: *The book attempts to depict life in a distant country. That song depicts the love of Margarethe for Faust.*

illustrate [T1] **1** to add pictures to (something written): *The book is well illustrated.* **2** to show the meaning of by giving related examples: *The speech he gave illustrates his ideas very clearly.*

picture [T1] **1** to paint or draw: *The artist has pictured him as a young man in riding clothes.* **2** to imagine: *Try to picture the scene. I can't quite picture myself as a father. Picture to yourself what will happen if you do that.* **3** to describe: *Let me try to picture the ceremony for you.*

outline [T1] to make an outline of: *He outlined the drawing in/with black ink. She outlined the main points of her talk.*

silhouette [T1] to cause to look like a silhouette: *a house silhouetted against the sky.*

I44 *nouns* : **painting and drawing** [U]

painting the art or practice of painting pictures: *She wants to study painting in Paris.*

drawing the art of drawing with lines made with a pen, pencil, etc: *She is good at drawing. He took drawing lessons.*

sketching the act of making rough pictures, usu before proper drawing, painting, etc

illustration the act or art of illustrating: *He has been working on the illustration of a book about animals. Illustration by example is better than explanations in words.*

I45 *nouns* : **pictures, paintings, and drawings**
[ALSO ⇨ G9, I10, N186]

picture 1 [C] a painting or drawing: *Draw a picture of that tree. The walls of the room were covered with pictures.* **2** [C] a photograph: *I was going to take some pictures, but I forgot my camera.* **3** [C usu sing] a representation of somebody or something made by painting, drawing, or photography: *Will you let me paint/take your picture?* (= a picture of you). **4** [S] *(fig)* a person who or thing that is beautiful to look at: *This garden is a picture in the summer.* **5** [(the) S] *(fig)* **a** the perfect example (of something that has no form): *That baby is the picture of health.* **b** the exact likeness or copy: *She's the picture of her mother.* **6** [C usu sing] *(fig)* an image in the mind, esp an exact one produced by a skilful description: *I've no clear picture (in my mind) of what happened. This book gives a good picture of life in England 200 years ago.*

image [C] **1** a picture, esp in the mind: *An image*

of a country garden came into my mind. **2** *old use* likeness; form: *God made man in His own image.* **3** a very similar copy: *He's the (very) image of his father.* **4** an object made to represent a god or person to be worshipped: *They worshipped God in the image of a bull.* **5** *lit* phrases suggesting something by means of a poetic form: *The phrase 'She is as beautiful as a rose' suggests the image of a rose representing the freshness of a young girl.* **6** one's appearance to other people, esp according to the amount of one's good qualities: *The government has a very bad image because it continues with plans that nobody likes.* **7** *tech* a picture formed of an object in front of a mirror or lens such as the picture formed on the film inside a camera, or one's reflection [⇨ L23] in an ordinary mirror **imagery** [U] images generally, or the use of them

painting [C] a picture made by painting: *I shall buy those paintings from the artist who painted them.*

drawing [C] a picture made by drawing: *He did a lifelike drawing of a cat.*

diagram [C] a drawing showing the important parts of something, esp in order to explain how it works, what it is, etc: *He drew a diagram of the main streets of Edinburgh, to help her get from one place to another.*

graph [C] a diagram showing by a line or lines the connection between two quantities: *The graph showed the increase in trade between the years 1960 and 1980.*

sketch [C] **1** a rough drawing without many details: *She looked at Rembrandt's sketches for his paintings. She made/drew a sketch to show the builder what she wanted done.* **2** a short description in words: *The speaker amused us with a sketch of city life in the 1890s. He made sketches for the scenes of a new play.*

illustration [C] a picture to go with the words of a book, speaker, etc: *He used photographs as illustrations for his talk.*

outline [C (*of*)] **1** the shape (of something): *He saw the outline of her face against a lighted window.* **2** a line or flat figure with the same shape as something else: *an outline map of Europe* **3** the main ideas or facts (of something): *an outline of history*

silhouette [C] **1** a picture in solid black (of someone or something) **2** anything seen as black against a light

fresco 1 [C] a picture painted in water colour on a surface of a fresh wet mixture of lime, water, sand, etc (**plaster**): *There's a beautiful fresco on the wall of that church.* **2** [U] the art of painting frescoes

tapestry [U; C] woven cloth hanging on a wall or walls, with pictures or designs of coloured wools or silks: *Those tapestries are beautiful, aren't they?*

cartoon [C] a humorous drawing, often dealing with something of interest in the news in an amusing way: *I buy that paper because I like the cartoons in it.*

caricature 1 [C] a representation of a person in art or literature made so that parts of his or her character appear more noticeable, odd, or amusing than they really are: *Newspapers often contain caricatures of well-known politicians.* **2** [C] an amusing representation by one person of another's character, voice, manners, etc **3** [U] the art of doing this: *He is more skilled at caricature than he is at acting.*

foreground [S] the part of a place, picture, etc, that is near the front, nearest to the person looking at it, etc: *Who are these people in the foreground of the photograph?* (*fig*) *He is now in the foreground of British politics.*

background 1 [S] the part of a place, picture, etc, that is at the back or in the distance: *Who is that man in the background of the picture?* **2** [C] the main colour on which other colours are placed, usu in a pattern: *The pattern is green and blue against a white background/a background of white.* **3** [C; U] (*fig*) information about where a person was born, who his parents were, where he went to school, has worked, etc: *Do you know anything about the man's background?* **4** [(*to*)] (*fig*) things that happened in the earlier part of a story, play, film, etc, esp in a series (= set) of such things: *What was the background to the story/murder?*

I46 *nouns* : **paints and colours**

[ALSO ⇒ H93, L27–39]

paint [U] liquid colouring matter which can be put or spread on a surface to make it a certain colour: *Where are those tins of green paint?*

paints [P] a usu complete set of small tubes or cakes of paint of different colours, usu in a box, as used by an artist: *She bought a new set of oil paints.*

watercolour *BrE*, **-color** *AmE* **1** [U] paint which is mixed with water **2** [C] a picture painted with this

oils *also* **oil colours** *BrE*, **oil colors** *AmE* [P] paints (esp for pictures) containing oil **in oils** using oils: *She paints very well in oils.*

charcoal 1 [U] (pieces of) the black substance made by burning wood in a closed container with little air, burnt in fires to give heat or used in sticks for drawing with: *Give me the charcoal, please; I'm going to draw a picture.* **2** [C] *also* **charcoal drawing** a picture made by drawing on paper with this material: *That's a beautiful charcoal you did of my wife.*

I47 *nouns* : **materials, etc, used in painting**

palette [C] a board with a curved edge and a hole through it, for holding with the thumb, on which an artist mixes his colours **2** the colours used by a particular artist or for a particular picture: *The artist has been using a new palette lately, mostly of blues and greens.*

palette knife [C] a thin bendable knife with a rounded end, used esp by an artist to mix colours, and sometimes to spread paint on a picture.

brush [C] an instrument for painting, smoothing, etc, in art

canvas [C] **1** a piece of canvas (strong rough cloth) used for an oil painting **2** a completed oil painting

easel [C] a wooden frame to hold a picture while it is being painted or to hold a blackboard

cartridge paper [U] strong thick whitish paper used for drawing on in pencil and ink

sketch pad/book [C] a number of sheets of paper fastened together, for making rough drawings

I48 *nouns* : **sculpture and modelling**

sculpture 1 [U] the art of shaping solid figures (as of people or things) out of stone, wood, clay, metal, etc: *They studied sculpture as a class in art school.* **2** [U; C] (a piece of) work produced by this art: *Which do you like better, Michelangelo's sculpture, or his paintings? There's some interesting sculpture in this church; a fine sculpture in the east end and some very good sculptures on the west door too.*

sculptural [Wa5;B] of, concerning, or looking like sculpture

modelling *BrE*, **modeling** *AmE* [U] the making of solid shapes in soft substances, esp clay [also ⇒ I5]

I49 *verbs* : **sculpture and engraving**

sculpture 1 [T1] to make a figure of (a person or thing) in sculpture: *The king was sculptured by the artist over a period of several weeks.* **2** [I0] to make works of sculpture: *She has all the tools for sculpturing in wood and clay.* **3** [Wv5;T1 *usu pass*] to make or shape as in sculpture: *The car body has a sculptured appearance.* (*fig*) *The water had sculptured rocks into strange shapes.*

sculpt [T1; I0] *fml* to sculpture

engrave [D1 *with/on*; T1] **1** to cut (words, pictures, etc) on (wood, stone, or metal): *He engraved her name on the box. The box was engraved with her name.* (*fig*) *The terrible memory was engraved in his mind.* **2** to prepare (special plates of metal) in this way for printing

I50 *nouns* : **statues and models** [C]

statue a usu large likeness, esp of a person or animal, made in some solid material (such as stone, metal, or plastic)

statuette a very small statue for putting on a table or shelf

figurine a small ornamental human figure made of baked clay or cut stone

relief a drawing, etc, that is raised above the surface on which it is set

piece 1 something whole and complete by an artist: *This piece (of music) should be played with great feeling. He has written a new piece for the theatre* (= a new play). **2** a short amount that is part of this: *Have you practised your piece (of music) for the examination?* **3** [*usu sing*] an example of something made or done, esp of a stated quality: *This watch is a fine piece of work.*

model a person or thing which an artist draws: *She sometimes works as an artist's model. What model did he use?*

I51 *nouns* : **artists and craftsmen** [C]

artist 1 a person who practises or works in one of the fine arts, esp painting: *Paris is famous for its artists.* **2** a person who shows inventive skill in his work: *He is no ordinary thief; he's an artist.* **3** a performer in an entertainment, such as an actor or singer: *Are all the artists ready?*

craftsman a highly skilled worker: *This jewellery is made by the finest craftsmen.*

stylist 1 a person with a good style of writing, drawing, etc **2** [C9] a person who is concerned with styles of appearance: *a hair stylist*

painter an artist who paints pictures

sculptor an artist who makes works of sculpture

master [*often attrib*] a person, usu a man, of great skill in art or work with the hands: *He is a master craftsman. The painting was the work of a master/done by a master hand.*

I52 *adjectives* : **relating to arts and crafts** [B]

artistic 1 [Wa5] of, concerning, or typical of art or artists: *He is interested in artistic matters.* **2** *apprec* made or arranged with inventive skill and imagination; beautiful: *Her playing was a very artistic performance of that piece of work.* **3** liking what is well done in art: *She has artistic feeling.*

arty [Wa1] *often deprec* making a show of being interested in art: *What an arty person she is!*

arty-crafty *usu deprec* of, using, or making handmade objects or clothes, esp to a degree that appears foolish: *That arty-crafty family make all their own clothes and look rather odd in them.*

craftsmanlike *apprec* (of work, works of art, books, etc) having or showing the qualities of work one expects from a good craftsman: *That's a craftsmanlike job!*

workmanlike *apprec* having or showing the qualities of a good workman: *He is very workmanlike in his treatment of the subject. She has a workmanlike approach to the matter.*

imaginative 1 (of people) good at inventing imaginary things or artistic forms, or at producing new ideas: *She is an imaginative and artistic child.* **2** (of things) informed by use of the imagination: *imaginative writing.* **-ly** [adv]

I53 *adjectives* : **relating to techniques and styles** [B]

technical [Wa5] relating to the ways in which art, crafts, etc, are done: *He has great technical skill.* **-ly** [adv Wa4]

stylistic [Wa5] *usu fml* relating to style: *He is a writer of great stylistic ability.* **-ally** [adv Wa4]

stylish *usu apprec* showing good style: *He is a very stylish dresser* (= he dresses in a stylish way). *That's a stylish way of doing things!* **-ly** [adv]

pictorial [Wa5] having or expressed in pictures: *There were a lot of road signs giving pictorial warnings of possible dangers.* **-ly** [adv]

illustrative 1 for the purpose of illustration [⇒ I43, 44] serving to illustrate (something, esp a book, idea, etc): *This book contains many illustrative sentences.* **2** [Wa5] able to illustrate: *He is a good illustrative artist.* **-ly** [adv]

I54 *nouns* : **artistry and craftsmanship** [U]

artistry inventive imagination and ability; artistic skill: *He showed great artistry in his work.*

craftsmanship the skill of a craftsman; great skill, esp with the hands

I55 *nouns* : **pottery**

pottery 1 [U] the work of a potter: *Pottery is an ancient art. She goes to a pottery class.* **2** [U] pots made out of baked clay: *Modern pottery is usually ornamental.* **3** [C] a potter's workroom or factory **potter** [C] a person who makes pots, dishes, etc, out of baked clay, esp by hand

ceramics 1 [U] the art or practice of making bricks, pots, etc, by shaping bits of clay and baking until hard: *She spent many happy hours studying ceramics.* **2** [P] articles produced in this way: *He keeps all his ceramics in the kitchen.* **ceramic** [Wa5;B] of, like, or connected with ceramics

I56 *nouns* : **materials, etc, used in pottery**

(potter's) wheel [C] a round flat plate which goes round with a circular motion and on which wet clay is placed to be shaped into a pot

kiln [C] a box-shaped heating apparatus for baking pots, bricks, or lime and also used for drying wood

potter's wheel

clay [U; (C)] a type of soft heavy earth which is used for pottery and in making plates, cups, etc

I57 *verbs* : **weaving, sewing, and knitting**

[ALSO ⇒ H85–7 CLOTH]

weave 1 [I∅] to form threads into material by drawing one thread at a time under and over a set of longer threads held out on a loom [⇒ I58] from one side to the other **2** [T1] to make by doing this: *to weave a mat* **3** [X9] to twist or wind: *He wove branches together to form a roof.* **4** [T1] to form by twisting: *to weave a nest out of wood and feathers* **5** [X9, esp *into*] to introduce: *He weaves his own ideas into the official speeches.* **6** [T1] to produce (a story), esp from a suggestion **7** [T1] to make (a plan), esp cleverly **weaver** [C] a person who weaves **get weaving** *infml* to start working hard at something

spin 1 [I∅; T1] to make (thread) by twisting (cotton, wool, etc): *She was spinning thread/ wool into thread.* **2** [T1] (of certain living things) to produce (thread, esp in a mass or net called a **web**): *The spider spun its web.* [⇒ picture at A112]

sew 1 [T1; I∅] to fix together or fasten (cloth, leather, paper, etc) by stitches made with thread; make or mend (esp pieces of clothing) with needle and thread: *Would you sew on this button/sew this button onto my shirt? He was sewing a new coat.* **2** [X9] to enclose in this way: *He sewed a £5 note inside/into his coat pocket.*

stitch [T1; I∅] to sew; put stitches on, to fasten together for ornamental effect

knit 1 [D1 (*for*); T1; I∅] to make (things to wear) by netting threads very closely together with long needles: *She is knitting her husband a pair of socks/a pair of socks for her husband.* **2** [T1; L9] *tech* (often used in giving instructions) to use the simplest stitch in this activity (for a time): *Knit to the last 10 stitches, then turn the*

needles and knit back. **knitter** [C] a person who knits **knitting** [U] **1** the activity of knitting **2** what is being knitted: *She kept her knitting in a bag.*

embroider 1 [I∅; T1] to do ornamental needle-work on (cloth): *Her mother taught her to embroider. She bought a dress embroidered with flowers in green silk thread. She embroi-dered a pattern on a cloth.* **2** [T1] (*fig*) to improve (a story) by adding ornamental details from the imagination **embroidery** [U] **1** the activity of embroidering **2** what is being embroidered

crochet [I∅] to do fancy work with a needle having at one end a small hook (**crochet-hook**), making new stitches by drawing thread through other stitches

plait [T1] to twist three or more pieces (of material, hair, etc) together to make a plait (= a ropelike length): *He plaited the thin pieces of gold. She plaited her hair.*

braid [Wv5; T1] **1** esp *AmE* to plait **2** to put braid [⇒ H86] on: *He wore a gold-braided coat.*

I58 *nouns* : **machines, etc, used in weaving, etc**

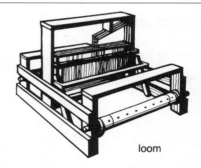

loom

loom [C] a frame or machine on which thread is made into cloth

warp [*the* S] the threads running along the length of cloth

woof *also* **weft** [*the* S] the threads in cloth which are woven across using the warp as a base

spindle [C] **1** a round pointed pin used for twist-ing the thread in spinning **2** a machine part around which something turns **3** any of various machine parts that are thin rods

bobbin [C] a small roller on which thread is wound, as in a sewing machine

reel [C] **1** a round object on which a length of wire, cinema film, fishing line, recording tape, etc, can be wound **2** *AmE* **spool** a usu small wooden or plastic one of these on which sew-ing thread is sold **3** the amount that any of those will hold: *Use up a whole reel of sewing cotton.*

stitch [C] **1** a movement of a needle and thread into cloth at one point and out at another in sewing: *She put a stitch in the coat.* **2** a turn of the wool round the needle in knitting: *She dropped* (= lost) *a stitch.* **3** the piece of thread or wool seen in place after the completion of such a movement: *That's a short stitch/a loose stitch.* **4** a particular style of sewing or knitting and the effect which it gives: *feather·stitch in sewing; the basic stitch in knitting*

seam [C] **1** a line of stitches joining two pieces of cloth, leather, etc, at or near their edges: *My trousers are coming apart at the seams. Sew the seam straight.* **2** the crack, line, or raised mark where two edges meet: *He made a good job of sticking the sheets of paper together; the seams hardly showed.*

I59 *nouns* : **galleries and museums** [C]

(art) gallery a place where (esp) works of art are shown to the public

museum a building where objects are kept and (usu) shown to the public because of their scientific, historic, and artistic interest: *She took the children to the British Museum in London.*

Science and technology

I70 *nouns* : **science, etc**

science 1 [U] (the study of) knowledge which can be made into a system and which usu depends on seeing and testing facts and stating general laws: *It was one of the great discoveries in science. Science cannot answer all our questions.* **2** [C; U] a branch of such knowledge, esp **a** anything which may be studied exactly: *Driving a car is an art, not a science.* **b** any of the branches usu studied at universities, such as physics [⇨ 175], biology [⇨ 174], chemistry [⇨ 175], engineering, and sometimes mathematics (**the sciences**): *She was studying a science subject. Government support for the sciences is quite good.* **have something down to a science** to have a complete exact knowledge of something, esp a skill: *He seems to have writing popular books down to a science* (= He writes one successful book after another).

technology [U; C] (the science of) the practical uses of the discoveries of science, esp in industry and in making machines: *Modern life depends on good technology. How good is the technology of these machines?*

engineering [U] **1** the science or profession of an engineer: *He studied electrical engineering at the university.* **2** the act or result of engineering: *He admired the engineering of the new· railway.*

I71 *adjectives* : **relating to kinds of science** [A]

pure (of a science or a branch of any study) considered only for its own nature as a skill or exercise of the mind, separate from any use that might be made of it

applied (esp of a science) put to a practical use

practical (esp of a science) related to actual experience or need

theoretical belonging to theory (= the general laws and principles of science or a science) **-ly** [adv Wa4]

natural (of science) related to biology [⇨ I74]

physical (of science) related to chemistry and physics [⇨ 175]

social (of science) relating to people's general lives and natures, as in sociology, anthropology, psychology [⇨ 176], linguistics [⇨ G237]

medical (of science) relating to medicine

I72 *nouns* : **persons concerned with science, technology, etc** [C]

scientist 1 a person who carries out new work in a science, esp physics, chemistry, or biology: *Many scientists are now studying moon rocks. She is a social scientist* (= one who works in social science) **2** *infml BrE* a person studying a science at a university: *Are you a scientist?—No, I'm reading/studying/doing history.*

technologist a specialist in technology

technocrat a person skilled in technology and using his skills for a purpose, esp in industry, etc, **technocracy** [U; C] the organization and control of industry, etc, by technocrats; a country where industry, government, etc, is controlled in this way **technocratic** [B] relating to technocrats or technocracy **-ally** [adv Wa4]

engineer 1 a person who understands the making of machines, roads, bridges, harbours, etc: *He is an electrical engineer. She is a civil engineer.* **2** a skilled person who controls an engine or engines, esp on a ship: *He is the chief engineer of the ship.* **3** a person who works with machines in a factory: *He is a member of the Engineers' Union.*

technician 1 a highly skilled scientific or industrial worker **2** a specialist in the practical details of a subject

mechanic a person who is skilled in using, repairing, etc, machinery: *The driver in the car race called his mechanic to find out what was wrong. The takeoff of the plane was delayed while the mechanics worked on the engines.*

draftsman a person who does technical drawings, for engineering, building, etc

draughtsman 1 a person (esp a man) who draws well: *Ingres was one of the greatest draughtsmen in the history of French painting.* **2** *esp BrE* draftsman

artisan a skilled workman, esp in industry

machinist 1 a person who makes machines **2** a

person who uses a machine at work, esp for sewing

I73 adjectives : relating to science, technology, etc [B]

scientific 1 [Wa5] of, being, or concerning science or its principles or rules: *The microscope is a scientific instrument. She had a scientific education and learned chemistry at the age of thirteen. That is a fine piece of scientific writing. The scientific spirit has an interest in exactness.* **2** needing or showing exact knowledge, skill, or use of a system: *He wrote a book on scientific baby care. They were scientific in their search, looking in all the possible places in an orderly way.* **-ally** [adv Wa4]

technological [Wa5] of or related to technology: *The development of the steam engine was the greatest technological advance of the 19th century.* **-ly** [adv Wa4]

technical 1 [Wa5] having special knowledge, esp of an industrial or scientific subject: *He joined the Association for Scientific and Technical Workers.* **2** of or related to a particular and esp a practical or scientific subject; concerning those subjects taught to provide skills for the hand rather than for the mind: *It is a technical college. He has had a good technical training. I had a more technical education than my husband.* **3** [Wa5] according to an unreasonably fixed acceptance of the rules: *The result was a technical defeat for the government but otherwise of limited importance.* **4** belonging to a particular art, science, profession, etc: *He has great technical skills. She uses technical language that the ordinary man cannot understand. This book is too technical for me.* **-ly** [adv Wa4]

mechanical 1 [Wa5] of, connected with, moved, worked, or produced by machinery **2** (*fig*) (of persons or their acts) as if moved by machinery; by habit, not will: *He was asked the same questions so many times that the answer became mechanical.* **-ly** [adv Wa4]: *The work is done mechanically.*

manual [Wa5] done with the hands: *manual work* **-ly** [adv]: *He did the work manually, not mechanically.*

automatic 1 (of a machine, system, etc) working by itself without needing a person to do anything: *The movements are completely automatic; you only need to start and stop the machines.* **2** done without thought, planning, etc: *Breathing is automatic; you do it without thinking.* **-ally** [adv Wa4]: *Everything in the factory works automatically.*

I74 nouns : the life sciences
[ALSO ⇨ A1 LIFE AND LIVING THINGS]

life sciences [*the* P] all the sciences which relate to living things

biology [U] **1** the scientific study of living things: *He studied biology at school.* **2** the scientific laws of the life of a certain type of living thing: *The biology of bacteria* [⇨ A37] *can be quite hard to understand.* **biological** [Wa5;B] of or connected with biology **-ly** [adv Wa4] **biologist** [C] a scientist who studies biology

zoology [U] the scientific study of animals: *She studied zoology at school.* **zoological** [Wa5;B] of or connected with zoology **-ly** [adv Wa4] **zoologist** [C] a scientist who studies zoology

botany [U] the scientific study of plants: *They studied botany at school.* **botanical** [Wa5;B] **1** of or connected with plants or botany: *That city has a beautiful botanical garden.* **2** obtained from plants: *These are all botanical drugs.* **-ly** [adv Wa4] **botanist** [C] a scientist who studies botany

anatomy [U] the scientific study of the nature of living bodies, esp by cutting into them [also ⇨ B169] **anatomical** [B] of or connected with anatomy **-ly** [adv Wa4] **anatomist** [C] a person skilled in anatomy

physiology [U] **1** the scientific study of how the bodies of living things and their various parts work **2** the system by which any particular living thing keeps alive: *The pictures showed the physiology of the horse.* **physiological** [Wa5;B] of or connected with physiology **-ly** [adv Wa4] **physiologist** [C] a person skilled in physiology

I75 nouns : the physical sciences

physical sciences [*the* P] all the sciences which relate to the nature of matter, force, structure, etc

physics [U] the science concerned with the study of matter and natural forces (such as light, heat, movement, etc): *He specializes in the physics of light. She has a degree in physics. They took a physics examination.* **physicist** [C] a scientist who specializes in physics

mechanics [U] **1** the science of the action of forces on objects **2** the science of making machines

chemistry [U] **1** the science which studies the substances (**elements**) which make up the earth, universe, and living things, how these substances combine with each other and how they behave under different conditions: *She is studying chemistry at university. I think more chemistry should be taught in our schools.* **2** the chemical make-up and behaviour of a substance: *Do you know much about the chemistry of life? He's trying to learn more about the chemistry of lead.* **chemical** [B] of or connected with chemistry **-ly** [adv Wa4] **chemist** [C] **1** a scientist who specializes in chemistry **2** *BrE* a pharmacist (*def* 2)

pharmacy 1 [U] the making and/or giving out of medicine: *She is a student of pharmacy.* **2** [C] a (part of a) shop where medicines are given out or sold **pharmacist 1** *AmE also* **druggist** [C] a person skilled in the making of medicine **2** *also*

BrE **chemist,** *AmE* **druggist** [C] a person who owns or runs a shop where (esp) medicines are sold **pharmaceutical** [Wa5;B] of or connected with pharmacy

pharmacology [U] the scientific study of medicines and drugs **pharmacological** [Wa5;B] of or connected with pharmacology **-ly** [adv] **parmacologist** [C] a scientist who specializes in pharmacology

geology [U] the scientific study of the materials (rocks, soil, etc) which make up the earth and their changes in the history of the world **geological** [Wa5;B] of or connected with geology **-ly** [adv Wa4] **geologist** [C] a scientist who specializes in geology

meteorology [U] the study of weather conditions and the activities and changes around the earth (esp in the air) that cause such conditions **meteorological** [Wa5;B] of or connected with meteorology **-ly** [adv Wa4] **meteorologist** [C] a person who specializes in meteorology

I76 *nouns* : **the social sciences**

social sciences [*the* P] all the sciences which relate to people's lives and natures

sociology [U] the scientific study of societies and human behaviour in groups **sociological** [Wa5;B] of or connected with sociology **-ly** [adv Wa4] **sociologist** [C] a scientist who specializes in sociology

anthropology [U] the scientific study of the nature of man, including the development of his body, mind, and society **anthropological** [Wa5;B] of or connected with anthropology **-ly** [adv Wa4] **anthropologist** [C] a scientist who specializes in anthropology

psychology 1 [U] the study or science of the mind and the way it works, and of behaviour as an expression of the mind: *She studies psychology. He was reading a psychology book.* **2** [U9] a branch of this: *His main interest is criminal/educational psychology.* [also ⇒ G6] **psychological** [Wa5;B] of or connected with psychology **-ly** [adv Wa4] **psychologist** [C] **1** a person who has studied or is skilled in psychology **2** *infml* a person who understands people's characters and what influences their behaviour: *You need to be a psychologist to be able to sell goods to people who don't really want to buy them.*

psychiatry [U] the study and treatment of diseases of the mind **psychiatric** [Wa5;B] of, concerning, or by psychiatry: *A person who suddenly begins to steal may be in need of psychiatric treatment.* **psychiatrist** [C] a doctor trained in psychiatry

criminology [U] the scientific study of crime and criminals **criminologist** [C] a person who specializes in criminology

penology [U] the study of matters concerned with the punishment of criminals and the operation of prisons **penologist** [C] a person who specializes in penology

I77 *nouns* : **the historical sciences**

archaeology *also esp AmE* **-cheo-** [U] the study of buried remains of ancient times, such as houses, tools, and weapons **archaeological** [Wa5;B] of or connected with archaeology **-ly** [adv Wa4] **archaeologist** [C] a person skilled in archaeology

pal(a)eontology [U] the science that deals with life on earth in earlier times, esp millions of years ago **paleontological** [Wa5;B] of or connected with paleontology **-ly** [adv Wa4] **paleontologist** [C] a scientist who specializes in paleontology

I78 *nouns* : **the laboratory, etc** [C]

laboratory a building or room in which a scientist works, with apparatus for the examination and testing of materials

lab *infml* laboratory

workshop a room or place as in a factory or business where heavy repairs and jobs on machines are done: *I'll have to send the broken sewing machines away to the workshop. I'll just go through to the workshop to see if the shoes have been mended yet.*

I79 *nouns* : **equipment used in laboratories** [C]

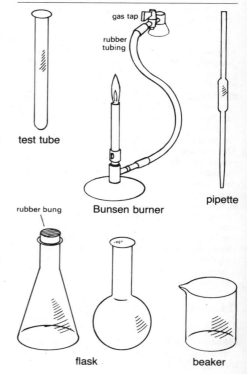

test tube

gas tap

rubber tubing

Bunsen burner

pipette

rubber bung

flask

beaker

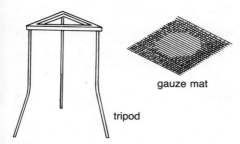

gauze mat

tripod

test tube a glass tube, closed at one end, in which liquids are tested in chemistry, etc
Bunsen burner a burner used in science in which gas is mixed with air before burning
retort a bottle with a long narrow bent neck, used for heating chemicals
pipette a thin glass tube used in chemistry into which small amounts of liquid can be sucked and taken from one place to another
flask a type of bottle used in laboratories [also ⇒ H170]

I80 *nouns* : **experiments and tests**
[ALSO ⇒ N361 FINDING & DISCOVERING]

experiment [C; U] (a) trial made in order to learn something or prove the truth of an idea, esp in science: *He developed the theory over ten years and proved it by experiment. They made/ carried out/performed an experiment. Much of our knowledge is based on experiments.*
test [C] **1** an examination, esp of substances, often done in laboratories to find out if they behave in certain ways: *The tests show that the medicine is safe and can cure people.* **2** a short medical examination: *He was given an eye test. She's gone to hospital for tests on her heart.* **3** a practical examination: *The government is carrying out tests to see if there is enough coal for mining here. Before buying the car he went for a test drive. They are making atom bomb tests.* **4** something used as a standard when judging or examining something else: *Employers will use this settlement as a test in dealing with future wage claims.* **5** a number of questions, jobs, etc, set to measure someone's skill, cleverness, or knowledge of a particular subject; a short examination: *They had a history test. We have a test at the end of each month and an examination once a year. You can't drive by yourself until you've passed your driving test.*
put something to the test to find out the qualities of something by using it in certain conditions
trial [C; U] a test or tests done usu over a long period of time: *The trials show that the medicine is safe for most people.* **trial and error** a way of getting the best results by learning from one's mistakes: *He learnt how to cook by trial and error.*
try [C] *infml* a test: *Let's give it a try!*

I81 *verbs* : **experimenting and testing**
[ALSO ⇒ N360 INVESTIGATING & EXAMINING]

experiment [I0] to make an experiment: *The engineers experimented with new materials. Some scientists experiment on animals. If we don't experiment, we won't learn.* **experimental** [B] for the purposes of experimenting: *This work is at the moment purely experimental.* **-ly** [adv Wa4] **experimentation** [U] *sometimes deprec* the act of experimenting: *Stop all this experimentation and do some useful work!*
test [T1] to do a test on (something or someone): *Have they tested the new medicine fully? Test the students before you begin the course.*
try [T1] to use (something or someone) in order to learn whether it, he, or she is what one wants or needs: *Have you tried the new medicine yet? He tried it and liked it.*
try out [v adv T1] to try fully: *Try out the new medicine for a year and we'll see how well it works.*

I82 *nouns* : **agents, catalysts, etc** [C]

agent a thing that works to produce a result: *Rain and sun are agents which help plants to grow.*
catalyst a substance which, without itself changing, causes chemical change in other substances
precipitate a solid substance that has been separated from a liquid by chemical action
solution a mixture made by putting a solid or gas into a liquid

Industry and work

I100 *nouns* : **industry and processing**
[ALSO ⇒ I1–2]

industry 1 [U] (the work of) factories and large organizations generally: *The country is supported by industry.* **2** [U] the private owners and shareholders of such factories and organizations: *Does industry agree with the government?* **3** [C9, (C)] a particular sort of work, usu employing lots of people and using machinery and/or modern methods: *He works in the clothing industry. The tourist trade has become a real industry.* **industrial** [B] of industry and the people who work in it: *This is an industrial area. They are all industrial workers here.* **-ly** [adv] **industrialist** [C] a person who owns a factory, etc: *There are a lot of big (=important) industrialists in the hotel at the moment.* **industrialize, -ise** [Wv5;T1] to build up the industries of (esp a country, place): *Glasgow was heavily industrialized in the nineteenth century.* **industrialization, -isation** [U] the act of industrializing

heavy industry [U] industries such as the coal and steel industries, the making of large machines, ships, etc

light industry [U] industries which make smaller machines, products, etc

service industry [C] any of the industries which move things and people from place to place, do certain services (such as providing food, entertainment, protection), etc

manufacturing [U] *genl* the business of making (manufacturing) things: *Manufacturing is an important part of industry generally. He is in one of the manufacturing industries.*

processing [U] the act, esp in an industry, of passing materials through a process [⇒ I142] to produce a finished object, product, etc

I101 *nouns* : **work**

work [U] **1** activity which uses effort, esp with a special purpose, not for amusement: *It takes a lot of work to build a house.* **2** (the nature or place of) a job or occupation: *His work is in medicine, as a doctor. She goes to work at 9. What time do you get home from work? I eat at work.* **3** what one is doing, esp for payment: *I hear you've changed jobs; is the work difficult at the new place? I'm taking some work home to do this evening. Don't stay inside today sewing; bring your work out into the garden.* **4** what is produced by work, esp of the hands: *This mat is my own work* (= I made it).

labour *BrE*, **labor** *AmE* **1** [U] work, esp if hard or heavy: *It needs/takes a lot of labour to build a road.* **2** [U] people doing such work: *Industry often has difficulties getting labour/has labour difficulties.* **3** [C] *old use & pomp* a piece of hard work: *His labours are now at an end, and he can rest.*

industry [U] *often fml & pomp* hard work: *They earned the money through their own industry.*

diligence [U] *usu fml* the ability to work hard; careful hard work

chore [C] **1** a small bit of regular work, quickly and easily done; daily necessary job, esp in a house or on a farm: *Each morning she would get up, do the chores, then go next door for a talk with her neighbour.* **2** a piece of uninteresting, difficult, or disliked work: *It's such a chore to do the shopping every day.*

effort 1 [U; S] strength, force, etc, that must be used (in an attempt) to do something; hard work: *It is really an effort to do this work. We need more effort if we want to win. What an effort it was to get the work done!* **2** [C] *often deprec* an attempt to do something: *He did the work, but the result was a poor effort.* **effortless** [B] (usu of something that is difficult to do) easy: *I couldn't lift the box, but it looked effortless when he lifted it.* **-ly** [adv] **-ness** [U]

assiduity *fml & pomp* **1** [U] careful continual attention: *He did the work with admirable assiduity.* **2** [C] an example of this

I102 *verbs* : **working**

work 1 [I0] to do something which uses effort, esp as employment: *He works in a factory. She's working on a new book.* **2** [T1] to make (a person) work: *They work us too hard in this office.* **3** [T1] to run (a place of work): *They have worked this coalmine for years.*

labour *BrE*, **labor** *AmE* **1** [I0; I3] *often fml & pomp* to work, esp hard: *They laboured to complete the job.* **2** [I0] (of the engine of a motor vehicle) to be working with difficulty at too low a speed: *The labouring engine could not take the car up the hill very quickly.*

slave [I0 (*away*)] *not fml* to work like a slave; work hard with little rest: *He slaved away all weekend digging in the garden.*

I103 *verbs* : **machines, etc, working**
[ALSO ⇒ N123]

work 1 [I0] (of a machine, moving part, plan, etc) to be active in the proper way, without failing: *Does this light work? The machine works on electricity. The clock hasn't been working since the electricity was off. Your idea won't work in practice.* **2** [T1] to make a machine work: *Stand there and work the machine. The machine is worked by hand/electricity.*

go [I0] *not fml* (of a machine or its parts that move, turn, etc) to work: *The car won't go. The wheel went round* (= turned). *The car went off down the road.*

run [I0; T1] to (cause to) work: *The car engine was running* (*well/badly*). *He runs the machines himself; no one helps him.*

operate *often tech* **1** [T1; I0] to (cause to) work: *He operates a machine/a factory. The new machines operate day and night.* **2** [L9; I3] to produce effects: *The new law doesn't operate in our favour; it operates to destroy our advantage.* **3** [L9] to be in action: *The army is operating over a large area. That business operates in several countries.* **operation 1** [U] (a state of) working; the way a thing works: *The operation of a big new machine can be hard to learn. It's not in operation.* **2** [U] a state in which effects can be produced: *When does the law come into operation?* **3** [C often pl] a thing (to be) done; an activity: *Let's begin our operations now. This is a difficult operation.* **operational 1** [A] of or about operations: *Operational costs are high.* **2** [F; (B)] (of things) in operation; ready for use: *The new machines are not yet operational.* **-ly** [adv] **operative 1** [F; (B)] (of plans, laws, etc) in operation; producing effects: *The law is now operative.* **2** [A] most important (*esp in the phr* **operative word(s)**) **-ly** [adv]

co-operate, cooperate [I0 (*with*)] to work together for some purpose: *All the people co-operated happily to get the work finished. I wish she would co-operate more fully with us.* **co-operation, coop-** [U] the act of co-operating: *Can we have your full co-operation in this matter?* **co-operative, coop- 1** [B] willing to co-operate: *She isn't a very co-operative person.* **un-** [*neg*] **-ly** [adv] **2** [C] a business which is owned by the people who work in it

I104 *adjectives* : **relating to work** [B]

laborious 1 requiring great effort: *This is very laborious work.* **2** showing signs of being done with difficulty: *He has a laborious style of writing.* **-ly** [adv]
hard-working working hard: *She is a hardworking girl.*
industrious *often fml & pomp* hard-working: *What industrious people they are!* **-ly** [adv]
demanding that needs a lot of attention or effort: *A new baby and a new job can both be very demanding.*
strenuous 1 taking great effort; needing a lot of work: *It's been a strenuous day! I don't like this job; it's too strenuous.* **2** showing great activity: *She is a strenuous supporter of women's rights.* **-ly** [adv]
diligent (of people and behaviour) hardworking; showing steady effort: *He's a diligent worker and deserves more pay. He made a diligent attempt to learn Russian.* **-ly** [adv]
painstaking 1 careful and thorough: *Producing a dictionary is painstaking work.* **2** hardworking and thorough: *He is not very clever but he is painstaking; he works hard.* **-ly** [adv]
menial (usu of work) unimportant, uninteresting, and not very pleasant: *He did not like doing the menial work in the house.* **-ly** [adv]
assiduous *fml & pomp* having or showing careful and continual attention: *They are assiduous workers. He was assiduous in visiting me in hospital.* **-ly** [adv]

I105 *adjectives* : **busy**

busy [Wa1;B] **1** working: *He is busy now and cannot see you. He is busy writing. She's busy with some important work.* **2** full of work or activity: *I've had a busy day. This is a busier place than that one.* **3** *esp AmE* (of telephones) in use; engaged: *I'm sorry the (telephone) line is busy.* **-ily** [adv]
active [B] **1** doing things or always ready to do things; able or ready to take action: *Although he is over seventy he is still active. He has an active brain. He leads an active life.* **2** able to produce a particular effect or act in a particular way: *Be careful! That dangerous chemical is still active!* **-ly** [adv]
engaged [F (*on*)] *esp fml* busy; working: *He is engaged at the moment; he will be able to see you later. She's engaged on some important matter.*
occupied [F (*with*)] *esp fml* busy; working: *He is fully occupied with some special work at the moment; he will be able to see you tomorrow.*

Are you occupied just now or can I come and talk to you?

I106 *adjectives* : **not busy** [B]

idle [Wa1,3] **1 a** not working: *Men are left idle when machines break down.* **b** (of time) not used for doing anything: *Idle hours flew by.* **2** lazy: *An idle worker is a waste of money.* **3** of no use; not producing anything good: *I knew what would happen, but it was idle to warn them; they wouldn't listen.* **idly** [adv] **-ness** [U]
vacant 1 empty; not filled with anything: *There is a vacant piece of land near the house; we can build there.* **2** (of a house, room, or seat) not being used or lived in: *The house has been vacant for several months.* **3** (of a position in employment) not at present filled: *I'm looking for work; are there any positions vacant in your firm? The part of a newspaper in which jobs are advertised is often called 'situations vacant'.*

I107 *verbs* : **relating to being busy or not**

busy [T1 (*with*)] to make or keep (esp oneself) busy: *To forget his troubles, he busied himself with answering letters.*
idle [Wv3;I0;T1 (*away*)] to waste (time) doing nothing: *Please stop idling and do something! He just idles his time away doing nothing.*

I108 *nouns* : **factories and mills**

factory [C] a building or group of buildings where goods are made, esp in great quantities by machines: *That city is full of factories. The factory workers go home at 5.*
complex [C] a number of factories, etc: *There is a big chemical complex near the city.*
plant [C; U] machinery, buildings, etc, used for some special, often stated purpose: *There is a big chemical plant near the city. We need new plant; the old machinery isn't good enough any more.*
works [Wn3;C *often in comb*] a factory: *He has a job at the local (steel)works. The Works Manager spoke to the men.*
mill [C *often in comb*] a building or factory in which work with a (stated) material is done: *Cotton cloth is made in a cotton mill. Paper is made in a paper mill. She works at the local mill.*

I109 *nouns* : **kinds of factories and mills, etc**

waterworks [P] buildings, pipes, and supplies of water forming a public water system
water mill [C] a mill whose power is gained from moving water

windmill [C] a mill whose power is gained by causing the wind to turn special moving parts

flourmill [C] (a building containing) a machine for crushing corn or grain into flour **miller** [C] a person making flour from grain in a mill, esp formerly

paper mill [C] a building where paper is made

gasworks [Wn3;C] a place where gas for use in the home is made from coal

power station [C] a large building in which electricity is made

refinery [C] a building and apparatus for refining (= making pure) metals, oils, sugar, etc: *He works in the local (sugar) refinery.*

distillery [C] a place or business firm where whisky, etc, is distilled (= made)

brewery [C] a place where beer is brewed (= made)

I110 *nouns* : **industrial workshops, etc**

shop [C] a place where things are made or repaired: *He works in the body shop in a car factory.*

workshop [C] a usu large room, esp in a factory where heavy work on or with machines is done: *He went into the workshop to see if the work had been done yet. Workshop conditions are often noisy and dirty.*

repair shop [C] a place where repairs [⇒ I21] are done: *Take the radio to the radio repair shop; they'll fix it for you. He went to the shoe repair shop to get his shoes.*

shop floor [*the* R; A] *not fml* the place regarded as where ordinary workers (not those who direct them, the **management**) do their work; the general work area in a factory: *What's the feeling on the shop floor about the rise in pay? There was a shop-floor quarrel between the two unions.*

I111 *nouns* : **assembly lines, etc** [C]
[ALSO ⇒ H140 TOOLS]

assembly line an arrangement of workers and machines in which each person has a particular job and the work is passed, often on a moving band (**a conveyor belt**), directly from one worker to the next until the product is complete

conveyer belt an endless moving belt that carries objects from one place to another

automation [U] any system of producing goods in a factory, etc, by the use of machines with the smallest possible number of persons operating them **automated** [B] working by automation: *We have a fully automated system now.*

I112 *nouns* : **workers** [C]

worker 1 a person or animal that works **2** a hard worker: *She's a real worker; she gets twice as*

much done as anybody else. **2** *also* **working man** a person who works with his hands rather than his mind; a working-class man

blue-collar worker *esp AmE* a worker who does hard or dirty work with his hands and has to wear special clothes for it: *Blue-collar workers have formed blue-collar unions.*

white-collar worker a person who does not work with his or her hands; an office worker, indoor worker, etc: *White-collar workers have jobs where they don't get dirty.*

manual worker a person who works with his or her hands

skilled worker a person who has learnt a special skill and uses that skill in his or her work

unskilled worker a person doing simple kinds of work that need no special skill

workman 1 a man who works with his hands, esp in a particular skill or trade: *The workman fixed the water system.* **2** [C9] a man who is skilled to a stated degree, esp in work with the hands: *He is a clever workman. A bad workman always blames his tools.*

work force [GC] the people who work in factories and industry generally, considered as a body: *The work force of this country consists of millions of people.*

labourer *BrE,* **laborer** *AmE* a worker whose job needs strength rather than skill

operator 1 a person who works a machine, apparatus, etc: *We have many skilled operators here.* **2** [C9] *infml & often derog* a person whose operations (in business, love, etc) are successful but perhaps unfair: *He is a clever/smooth operator; be careful of him.*

operative *esp fml* a worker or operator: *Send one of our best operatives.*

hand 1 [*now usu in comb*] a workman: *More hands are needed for the building work. He is a farmhand* (= He works on a farm). **2** one of the sailors on a ship: *Get one of the hands to do the work. All hands on deck!* (a call for all sailors to come up to deal with some trouble). **3** [C9] *usu infml* a performer: *He's a good hand at making cakes. She's an old hand* (= a very experienced person) *at this game.*

factory hand a person working in a factory at a simple job

shift [C] **1** a group of workers who take turns with one or more other groups: *The men are working in shifts to repair the railway line.* **2** the period of time worked by such a group: *a working day divided into three 8-hour shifts* **day/ night shift** [C] the shift working during the day/at night: *He's on the night shift now.*

I113 *nouns* : **mines and excavations**

mine 1 [C *often in comb*] a deep hole or network of holes under the ground from which coal, gold, tin, and other mineral substances are dug: *This is a tin mine. Many men were buried when there was an accident at the mine.* **2** [S (*of*)] (*fig*) a person from whom or thing from which one can obtain a great deal (of something, esp information or knowledge): *The old man has lived in the village all his life and he's a mine of information about its history.*

pit [C] **1** [*usu in comb*] a deep hole dug in the ground to get materials out: *There's an old chalkpit near here.* **2** [*often pl*] a coal mine **3** [*often pl*] the workers, machinery, etc, connected with a coal mine

colliery [C] a coal mine and the buildings, machinery, etc, connected with it

quarry [C] a place from which stone, sand, etc, are dug out of the ground

workings [P] the parts of a mine that have been dug out: *These workings aren't used any more.*

diggings [P] the place or places where (esp) miners dig for a particular purpose: *Work has stopped at the diggings.*

dig [C *usu sing*] **1** an ancient place, town, or building being uncovered and studied by archaeologists (= students of ancient times) **2** the digging up of a place like this: *go on a dig*

dugout [C] a rough usu covered shelter made by digging a hole, esp by soldiers

excavation 1 [C] a place where a hole or holes, usu large, have been dug in the earth: *He's working at the excavation. They made several excavations to find what they wanted.* **2** [U] the act of excavating

shaft [C *esp in comb*] a long narrow passage going usu in an up and down or sloping direction in the ground, a building, etc, esp in a mine

tunnel [C *often in comb*] an underground or underwater passage, esp for a road or railway or in a mine, through a hill or under a river, town, etc

I114 *verbs* : **digging and mining** [IØ; T1]

dig 1 to turn over (earth) with the hands, tools, etc; make (a hole) in (the ground): *The dog was digging in the garden. The men dug a hole/dug deep into the ground. The man was digging for gold.* **2** [T1 (*up, out*)] to get by digging: *The man was digging potatoes. They dug up an old metal box. He dug the stones out.*

dig in [v adv] to dig holes for (oneself): *The soldiers dug in/dug themselves in for the night.*

digger [C] **1** a person digging **2** any tool or machine used for digging

excavate to make (a hole) or uncover (something) by digging; (*fml*) to dig: *They excavated a large hole/the remains of an old Roman house. They were still excavating when I left.*
excavator [C] a machine used for digging

mine to dig in (a place) for (esp metals and coal): *The men were busy mining. They mined the whole area for coal.*

burrow [(*into*)] to dig (a hole like a tunnel), in earth, etc, as such animals as rabbits do: *The rabbits burrowed into the ground. The animals burrowed holes in the ground. The miners burrowed (their way) into the side of the hill.*

tunnel to make a tunnel through a place: *The miners tunnelled (their way) through the mountain. They have been tunnelling for weeks and found nothing.*

bore 1 to make round holes in something, esp by using a tool that turns round and round: *He bored a hole in the piece of wood. Can you bore through this wood?* **2** to do this while mining, etc: *The miners bored a tunnel under the mountain/sea.*

drill 1 to make a hole with a drill [⇒ H146]: *He drilled two holes in the wood. He drilled through the wall.* **2** [IØ (*down*)] to do this esp while mining, looking for oil, etc: *They are drilling for oil in the North Sea and in some places have drilled down a very long way.*

prospect [(*for*)] to examine (land, an area, etc) in order to find something, esp gold, silver, oil, etc: *He's been prospecting in these hills for years, prospecting for gold. The government is prospecting the sea bed for natural gas.* **prospector** [C] a person who prospects

I115 *nouns* : **persons working in mines, etc** [C]

miner [*often in comb*] a worker in a mine: *Those men are diamond miners.*

collier 1 a person employed to cut coal in a mine **2** a ship for carrying coal

quarryman a worker in a quarry

I116 *nouns* : **work with wood, metal, etc**

carpenter [C] a person who is skilled at making and repairing wooden objects **carpentry** [U] **1** the art or work of a carpenter **2** the objects made by a carpenter

joiner [C] a carpenter who makes doors, doorframes, windowframes, etc, inside a building **joinery** [U] **1** the art, skill, or trade of a joiner; woodwork in building **2** work done by a joiner: *In this house the joinery is very good.*

woodwork [U] **1** the skill of making wooden objects, esp chairs, tables, etc **2** *infml* carpentry **3** the objects produced **4** *not fml* the parts of a house that are made of wood: *There's a mouse behind the woodwork.* **5** the study and practice (esp as a school subject) of making wooden objects

turner [C] a person who shapes wood or metal on a lathe [⇒ H142]

fitter [C] someone whose work is either **a** putting together machines or electrical parts, or **b** cutting out and fitting clothes

plumber [C] a man whose job is to fit and repair waste pipes, bathroom articles, etc

metalworker [C] a person who makes things with or out of metal **metalwork** [U] **1** objects shaped in metal **2** the study and practice (esp as a school subject) of making metal objects

I117 *nouns* : **persons in charge of workers** [C]

[ALSO ⇒ C160]

foreman *fem* **forewoman** a skilled and experienced workman who is put in charge of other workers

charge-hand the leader of a group of workmen

master 1 *fem* **mistress** *old use* a man who employs workmen or servants **2** [A] a skilled workman with his own business: *He is a master builder.*

boss 1 [*also* N] *infml* a master, employer, or person having control over others: *He asked the boss for more money. Have you got a match, boss?* **2** *AmE usu derog* a political party chief

supervisor a person who keeps watch over work and workers as the person in charge
supervise [I0; T1] to work as a supervisor over (someone)

overseer a person who keeps watch over work, (esp formerly as done by slaves): *The overseer made them work very hard.*

Education

I130 *nouns* : **places for small children** [C; U]

playgroup *also* **playschool** a kind of informal school for very young children in which they learn to play with other children and learn other things mainly through play

nursery school a school for young children of two to five years of age in which they learn mainly by playing

kindergarten a playgroup, playschool, etc

I131 *nouns* : **kinds of school**

school 1 [C] a place of education for children: *Many new schools have been built by the government. They are children of school age* (= old enough to attend school). *What school do you go to? During the school holidays they went to France.* (*fig*) *He learned everything in the school of experience.* **2** [U] (*without* the) **a** attendance or study at such a place; a course of learning at such a place: *He began school at the age of five. She always found school difficult.* **b** one day's course at such a place: *School begins at 8.30. He walks home after school.* **3** [GC] (*fig*) the body of students (and teachers) at such a place: *She is a teacher liked by the whole school.*

state school [C] a school that is run by the state

comprehensive school [C] *BrE* a state school for children over the age of 11 of both sexes, all abilities, and from every kind of family in an area

public school [C; U] **1** (in England) a mainly upper class school for older pupils where education is paid for usu by parents and the pupils live as well as study **2** (esp in Scotland and US) a free local school supported by taxes

private school [C] a school owned and directed by a person or group not supported by government money, where education must be paid for

independent school [C] a private school

preparatory school [C] **1** (esp in Britain) a private school for pupils up to the age of 13 or 14, where they are made ready to attend a higher school, almost always a public school (*def* **1**) **2** (in the US) a private school that makes pupils ready for college

prep school [C] *infml* a preparatory school

primary school [C; U] the school that a child attends from the age of 5 to the age of 11

secondary school [C; U] the school that a child attends after primary school, usu at the age 11 or 12 until 16 to 18 years old

high school [C; U] *esp AmE* a secondary school, esp for children over the age of 14

grammar school [C; U] **1** (in England) a school (usu) for children over the age of 11, where they study languages, science, etc, for examinations which may lead to higher education **2** (in the US) a primary school

academy [C] (in Scotland, esp in names) a secondary school that prepares pupils for higher education

secondary modern school [C] (in England formerly) a secondary school which does not prepare students for a university or further study

single-sex school [C] a school where only boys or girls are taught

coeducational school [C] a school where boys and girls are taught together **coeducation** [U] the system of educating boys and girls together in the same buildings and classes

I132 *nouns* : **places and things in schools** [C]

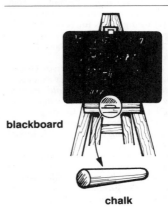

blackboard

chalk

classroom a room in a school, college, etc, in which a class meets for a lesson: *We have to move to another classroom for the next lesson. Classroom conditions in that school are not good.*

playground 1 a piece of ground kept for children to play on or in, esp at a school. **2** (*fig*) an area favoured for amusement: *The south of France is the playground of the rich.*

staff room a comfortable room in a school for the use of teachers: *What is staff-room opinion on this matter* (= What do the teachers think about it)?

I133 *nouns* : **college and university, etc**

college 1 [C; U] a school for higher and professional education, often connected to a university: *My son went to a teacher training college. I went to business college when I was 28. When did you leave college?* **2** [C; U] (in the United States) a school of higher learning giving a bachelor's degree **3** [C] (in Britain) a body of teachers and students forming a separate part of certain universities: *Oxford University is divided into colleges.* **4** [C; U] (in Britain) any of certain large private schools **5** [C] the building or buildings used by any of these educational establishments: *The college is just over the road from the station.* **6** [C9] *tech* a body of people with a common profession, purpose, duties or rights: *She is a member of the Royal College of Nurses.*

university 1 [C *often in comb*; *often cap*] a place of education at the highest level, where degrees are given: *Several new universities have been built. He studied at Edinburgh University/the University of Edinburgh.* **2** [C; U] one of these places when attended for a course of study: *Has she studied at university/been to university?* **3** [*the* GU] the members of this place, students and teachers: *The whole university is against the changes.*

polytechnic [C] a place of education for people who have left school, providing training in many arts and (esp) trades connected with skills and machines

academy [C] a school or college for training in a special art or skill: *Sandhurst in England and West Point in the US are military academies. She attends an academy of music.*

school 1 [C; U] an establishment for teaching a particular subject, skill, etc: *He worked all day and studied at night school in the evenings.* **2** [C] (esp in universities) a department or place where a certain subject is taught: *medical school; the School of Law; London School of Economics.* **3** [C; U] *AmE* a college or university: *She went to graduate* [⇒ I144] *school in Los Angeles.* **4** [C] a group of people with the same methods, opinions, etc: *There is a new school of thought about this.*

higher education [U;(C)] education at a university or college

higher education *also esp AmE* **adult education** [U] education after leaving school, but not at a university

I134 *nouns* : **teachers, etc** [C]

teacher [*also* A] a person who teaches, esp as a profession: *My husband's a history teacher in a local school. He is a member of the University Teachers' Association. It is a good teacher-training course.*

master 1 *esp BrE fml* a man who teaches in a school, esp a private school in England: *The children liked their French master* (= teacher of French). **2** [C9] a man who teaches subjects not usu taught in school; a tutor: *He is her riding master/dancing master.* **schoolmaster** a master in a school

mistress *esp BrE fml* a female teacher in a school: *All the girls like their new English mistress* (= teacher of English). **schoolmistress** a mistress in a school

lecturer 1 a person who gives lectures [⇒ G65], esp at a university or college **2** a person who holds the lowest teaching rank at a British university or college **lectureship** the position of a lecturer at a British university or college

professor 1 [*also* A; N] *BrE* (the title of) a teacher of the highest rank in a university department: *My new history professor is Professor Ward. She is Professor of History at my university. Good-bye, Professor (Ward).* **2** [A;N;(C)] *AmE* a teacher at a university or college: *Professor Smith has just started teaching here.* **3** [A; N; C9] (a title taken by those who teach or claim various skills (often to add an undeserved importance to the position)): *Madame Chores, professor of dancing, gives lessons daily.* **professorial** [Wa5;B] *fml* of or like a professor **-ly** [adv]

dean (in some universities) a person in charge of a division of study or in charge of students and their behaviour

academic a person who teaches at a university: *Many academics, including several well-known professors, were at the meeting.*

instructor a person who teaches one an activity: *My driving instructor is very helpful.* **instructress** [*fem*] *rare*

tutor 1 a private or special teacher: *He is her tutor in French. Who is their dancing tutor?* **2** *BrE* a university lecturer who looks after the studies of a group of students

trainer a person who trains sportsmen, horses, etc, esp in sports and racing

coach 1 a person hired privately to train a pupil or student for an examination: *He is her English coach.* **2** a person who trains sportsmen for games, competitions, etc: *He is the local football coach.*

I135 *nouns* : **head teachers, etc** [C]

head teacher the teacher in charge of a school
headmaster the male teacher in charge of a school
headmistress the female teacher in charge of a school
head *infml abbrev* a headmaster or mistress
principal the head of some universities, colleges, and schools
director a person who directs an (educational) organization

I136 *nouns, etc* : **pupils and students, etc** [C]

schoolboy/girl/child a boy, girl, or child who goes to school
pupil *esp BrE* a person, esp a child, who is being taught: *The school is large enough for about 500 pupils. Miss Smith takes private pupils in singing and piano-playing.*
student 1 a person who is studying at a place of education: *She is a High School student.* **2** *BrE* a person studying at a university of college **3** *AmE* a person studying at a school or college **4** [*of*] a person with a stated interest: *He is a student of human nature.*
scholar 1 the holder of a scholarship **2** *old use & fml* a child at school **scholarship** [C] an amount of money given to a student to help him or her to continue studying **scholastic** [Wa5;B] *esp fml & pomp* relating to schools, education, etc: *The child's scholastic abilities are not being given a chance to develop.* **-ally** [adv Wa4]
trainee a person who is being trained: *She is a trainee reporter.*
apprentice 1 a person bound by an agreement to serve, for a number of years and usu for low wages, a person skilled in a trade, in order to learn that person's skill **2** [T1] to make or send as an apprentice: *We apprenticed our son to an electrician. He apprenticed himself to an electrician.* **apprenticeship 1** [U] the condition of being an apprentice **2** [U; C] the time or period this lasts **3** [C] an example of such a condition: *Several apprenticeships could not be filled.*
cadet a person studying to become an officer in one of the armed forces or the police: *He is a police cadet.* **cadetship** [U; C] the condition of being a cadet; an example of this
disciple 1 a follower of any great teacher (esp religious): *Martin Luther King considered himself a disciple of Gandhi.* **2** [*often cap*] one of the twelve first followers of Christ
beginner a person who begins something, esp a person without experience; a learner in the first stages of learning: *It's the first time she has played; she's just/only a beginner.*
novice a person without any training or experience in a skill or subject: *He is a novice swimmer* (= a novice at swimming).

I137 *nouns* : **classes and seminars**

class 1 [GC] a group of pupils or students taught together: *Our class is the biggest in the school. How many students are there in your history class at college? How much class work must be done?* **2** [GC] *esp AmE* a number of students in a school or university doing the same course in the same year **3** [C] the occasion when such a group is taught: *I must go or I'll be late for my English class.*
lesson [C] **1** something to be learnt or taught, esp in a school, etc, esp in a class: *Did you enjoy that lesson? Afternoon lessons start at 2 o'clock. The teacher was working on his lesson plans.* **2** (*fig*) an experience or event seen as teaching something: *He learned many lessons in life while working there. The child has learnt her lesson and won't go near fire again.*
lecture [C] an occasion on which one must lecture or listen to someone lecturing: *I must go now or I'll be late for my lecture. She has a lecture at ten.*
tutorial 1 [C] *esp BrE* an occasion on which students meet a tutor: *I've a tutorial at 10.* **2** [A] of or relating to a tutor or tutorials
seminar [C] a small class of (advanced) students at a university, etc, meeting to study some subject with a teacher
course [C] a set of lessons on one subject: *What courses are you taking? A French course and a course in history.*
homework [U] work which a student is expected to do at home, not in school, etc
prep [U] *infml BrE* **1** homework **2** *also fml* **preparation** (at schools in which the pupils go home only in holiday periods) **a** studying and getting ready for lessons: *We have two hours' prep every evening.* **b** the time during which this is done

I138 *nouns* : **terms and sessions** [C]

term any one of usu three periods into which a year at a school, college, or university is divided, as in Britain
semester either of the two periods into which a year at a university is divided, esp in the US
session *AmE & ScotE* one of the parts of the year when teaching is given at a university; a term or semester

I139 *nouns* : **educational subjects, etc**

subject [C] something which is spoken, written about, looked at, or studied, etc: *What subject shall we discuss today? His main subject at university is the French language/is economics.* **subject matter** [U] whatever is being studied, etc, at a particular time, in a particular book, etc
topic [C] a subject, esp when it is being discussed, written, or spoken about, etc: *My main*

topic today is the history of the English language.

discipline [C] *usu fml* a branch of learning studied at a university: *You're no good at history, so you'd better choose one of the other disciplines.*

field [C] *genl* a branch of knowledge or activity: *What field does he work in? She is a lawyer famous in her own field/in the field of criminal law. That matter is outside my field* (= not my special subject).

study *often fml* **1** [U] the act of studying one or more subjects: *He spent the afternoon in study.* **2** [U; C *often pl*] a subject studied: *You must give time to your studies. The schoolchildren find nature study very interesting.* **3** [C] an exercise, esp piece of writing, on a particular subject: *He made a study of Shakespeare's plays.*

I140 *nouns, etc* : **educational exercises, etc**

exercise [C] a question to be answered by a pupil for practice: *The teacher told them to begin Exercise 14.*

project [C] (a plan for) work or activity of any kind, esp in a classroom or course: *The boys were given a project building a little house in a tree; they carried out their project in a few days. This student is doing a special project concerned with local government.*

drill **1** [U; C] training or instruction in a subject, esp by means of repeating and following exact orders: *This is a good drill for learning how to use French verbs.* **2** [T1; I∅] to instruct or exercise by repeating: *Let's drill them in English grammar.*

I141 *nouns* : **educational qualifications** [C; A]

certificate a sheet of paper (**document**) on which is written or printed a statement, usu made by a person officially given power to make it, that a certain fact or facts are true: *When they passed the examination, the students got their certificates. The doctor signed the death certificate.*

diploma an official paper showing that a person has successfully finished a course of study or passed an examination: *He holds/has been awarded* (= given) *a diploma in social studies.*

degree a title given by a university: *She has the degrees of BA, MA, and PhD.*

doctorate the degree, title, or rank of a doctor, esp a non-medical one: *He got his doctorate in 1977. Where did she do her doctorate?*

I142 *nouns* : **kinds of degrees** [C]

bachelor's (degree) the first degree in most universities in Arts, Sciences, Education, etc

master's (degree) the second degree given in most universities in Arts, Sciences, Education, etc

doctor's (degree) the highest degree given in universities in any subject

I143 *nouns* : **particular names for kinds of degrees**

NOTE These abbreviations may be written with or without full stops.

BA	Bachelor of Arts
BSc	Science
BEd	Education
BPhil	Philosophy
BLitt	Letters
MA	Master of Arts
MSc	Science
MEd	Education
MPhil	Philosophy
MLitt	Letters
MD	Doctor of Medicine
MB	Bachelor of Medicine
ChB	Surgery
PhD, DPhil	Doctor of Philosophy

I144 *nouns* : **students at universities, etc** [C; A]

undergraduate **1** a university student who has not yet taken his or her first degree **2** relating to undergraduates or their work

graduate **1 a** *BrE* a person who has completed a university degree course **b** *AmE* a person who has completed a course at a college, school, etc. **2** relating to graduates

postgraduate *also* esp *AmE* **graduate** (a person doing studies that are) done at a university after one has received a first degree: *He's taking a postgraduate course in teacher training.*

I145 *verbs & nouns* : **students leaving universities, etc, successfully**

graduate **1** [I∅] to obtain a degree at a university **2** [I∅] *AmE* to complete an educational course **3** [T1] to declare that (someone) has completed such a course and passed the examinations

graduation **1** [U] the act of graduating **2** [C] a ceremony at which one receives proof of having gained a university degree

qualify [I∅ (*as*), 3; V3] to (cause to) gain a certain level of knowledge or a qualification: *Being the son of a member of parliament doesn't qualify him to talk about politics. He qualified as a doctor of medicine this year.*

qualification **1** [U] the act of qualifying **2** [C] **a** an example or result of this **b** the training which leads to this **c** the papers, etc, which show this: *He is a doctor with the very best* *qualifications. What qualification does he have in this subject?*

I146 nouns : **special rewards in education**

prize [C; A] a reward, usu a book, given to a student at school or college for specially good work: *He has won the history prize.*

award [C] something that is given as a result of an official decision, esp a prize

distinction [C] a special mark of honour: *These are the highest distinctions that have ever been given in that subject. He gained a first-class certificate* [⇒ I141] *of distinction in French.*

honours *BrE*, **honors** *AmE* [P *often cap*] **1a** a specialized kind of first degree at a British university **b** a level gained in examinations for this degree: *He graduated with honours (in History/Science, etc). She had a First/Second Class Honours degree.* **2** a mark of high quality in an American university degree

I147 nouns : **experts and scholars** [C]

expert a person having some special knowledge, skill, experience, etc, esp one who is qualified by special training and employed to do certain things because of this: *That doctor is one of the country's leading experts on the human brain.* **expertise** [U] the ability of an expert: *She showed great expertise in doing the difficult work.*

master a person, usu a man, of great skill, knowledge, and experience: *What a master of the subject he is!* **masterly** [B] in the manner of a master: *His argument against the new law was masterly.*

scholar *usu apprec* a person who has great knowledge of a certain usu academic subject, such as literature, history, etc (and an ability to pass it on to others): *He is one of the country's leading scholars. She is a language scholar of some note/standing* (= an admired expert in one or more languages). **scholarly** [B] *apprec* of or like a scholar: *His work shows great scholarly care.* **scholarship** [U] the work of a scholar: *His scholarship is not good; he makes many false statements.* **scholastic** [B] *esp fml* relating to scholars and their work: *His scholastic ability is not of the highest* (= is not very good). **-ally** [adv Wa4]

authority [(*on*)] a person who is known to be an expert (on something): *She is one of the world's leading authorities on fish.*

consultant a person to whom people go for advice: *He is a consultant on business in South America. She is an art consultant for a big publishing company.* **consultancy 1** [U] the business of being a consultant **2** [C] the money paid by esp a business company to an expert whom they can then ask for special advice when they want it

specialist a person who has special interests or skills in a limited field of work or study: *a government specialist in foreign affairs* **specialize, -ise** [IØ (*in*)] to study (some particular thing) so much as to become an expert in it: *He specialized in tropical diseases.* **specialization 1** [U] the act of specializing **2** [C] an example or result of this **speciality** *also* **specialty** [C] *infml* something one specializes in

I148 adjectives : **relating to education** [B]

[ALSO ⇒ G32–36 LEARNING AND TEACHING]

educational relating to education; serving to educate or teach or to help someone learn: *This work has great educational value.* **-ly** [adv] **educationist** *also* **educationalist, educator** [C] a person who does educational work

educative *fml* educational **-ly** [adv]

educable *usu tech* able to be educated, taught, etc: *He thinks that some children are less educable than others.* **in-** [*neg*]

instructional *fml* relating to instructing or being instructed

instructive serving to instruct; educational: *What I saw was very instructive; I learned a lot.* **un-** [*neg*] **-ly** [adv]

academic 1 of or like schools, colleges, academies, etc (and therefore placing importance on thought, ideas, etc, rather than practical work): *She wants her child to have an academic education and to go to university. She thinks that the quality of academic life is not as good as it once was. The child is better at practical rather than academic work.* **non-** [*neg*] *neutral* **un-** [*neg*] *deprec* **2** *sometimes deprec* very theoretical and therefore of little or no practical use: *This idea is only of academic interest to us; let us decide what we actually do next!* **3** no longer of practical importance: *Last week these matters were important, but this latest news makes them academic.* **-ally** [adv Wa4]

J

Numbers, measurement, money, and commerce

Numbers and quantities

J1 nouns : kinds of numbers [C]

number 1 a member of the system used in counting and measuring: *Let x be a number from 1 to 10.* **2** a written form for one of those: *The page numbers are in the right-hand corners of the book.* **3** any such from 0 to 9: *This machine is able to print numbers as well as letters.* **4** [also in U] quantity or amount: *The number of chairs in the room is 10. The members of the club are four hundred in number.* **5** [A] (*before a number, usu written No./no.*) (having) the stated size, place in order, etc: *My room is Number Four/No. 4. We live at No. 17* (= our house has the number 17). **any number of** *infml & usu emph* a large quantity of; many: *I've told you any number of times to keep the door shut!* **by number** in a way that uses numbers: *He knows all the rooms in the building by number; he'll tell you who is in room 106.*

cardinal number one of the numbers 1, 2, 3, etc [⇨ J4]

ordinal number one of the numbers first (1st), second (2nd), third (3rd), etc, giving the order of any thing or things [⇨ J5]

distributive number a number that states how many times or occasions something happens: *'Once' and 'twice' are distributive numbers* [⇨ J10].

prime number a number that can be divided exactly only by itself and the number one: *Twenty-three/23 is a prime number.*

odd number one of the numbers 1, 3, 5, 7, etc

even number one of the numbers 2, 4, 6, 8, etc

serial number a particular number given to one of a large group: *A soldier's name, rank, and serial number are all that he may tell an enemy. What were the serial numbers of the stolen banknotes?*

whole number a number which is not or does not contain a fraction [⇨ J3]

J2 nouns : special terms for numbers, etc [C]

numeral any of the system of signs used for representing a number or numbers

digit *tech, also* **figure** any of the numbers from 0 to 9: *The number 1977 contains 4 digits/figures. He has a five-figure income* (= He makes at least £10,000 a year). **digital** [Wa5;B] relating to calculation with digits

unit 1 the smallest whole number; the number one **2** any fixed amount used in measuring, etc: *In most countries the unit of length is the metre.*

integer *tech* a whole number **integral** [Wa5;B] **1** of, concerning, or like an integer **2** necessary to make something whole: *His work is an integral part of what we do.* **-ly** [adv]

multiple a number which contains a smaller number an exact number of times: $3 \times 4 = 12$, so 12 is a multiple of 3.

factor a whole number that can be multiplied by another to form a given number: *2, 3, 4, and 6 are all factors of 12.*

logarithm, *infml abbrev* **log** a number which represents a value (**power** [⇨ J38]) of another number and which can be used for additions instead of multiplying the original number **logarithmic** [Wa5;B] **1** of or containing logarithms **2** increasing by multiplication **-ally** [adv Wa4]

base a number, such as 10, which is the starting point for a logarithmic or other number system

J3 nouns : fractions of numbers [C]

fraction 1 *math* a division or part of a whole number: $\frac{1}{3}$, $\frac{3}{8}$ and 0.392 are fractions. **2** *genl* a very small piece or amount: *She's careful with her money, and spends only a fraction of her earnings.*

decimal (fraction) a number like .5, .06, .375, etc **-ly** [adv]: *Counting decimally is easy to do.* **decimal point** the dot at the left of a decimal

vulgar fraction a fraction expressed by a number above and a number below a line (rather than as a decimal): $\frac{3}{4}$ and $\frac{107}{8}$ are vulgar fractions.

percentage 1 [C] an amount given as part of a whole which is 100: *Give me the answer as a percentage.* **2** [U] proportion: *What percentage of the people want change?* **per cent** (*sign* %) for each hundred: *twenty per cent* (20%) = *twenty in a hundred*

J4 *nouns* : **the cardinal numbers**

1	one	17	seventeen
2	two	18	eighteen
3	three	19	nineteen
4	four	20	twenty
5	five	21	twenty-one
6	six	22	twenty-two
7	seven	23	twenty-three
8	eight	30	thirty
9	nine	38	thirty-eight
10	ten	40	forty
11	eleven	50	fifty
12	twelve	60	sixty
13	thirteen	70	seventy
14	fourteen	80	eighty
15	fifteen	90	ninety
16	sixteen	100	a/one hundred

1,000 or **1 000** a/one thousand
10,000 or **10 000** ten thousand
100,000 or **100 000** a/one hundred thousand
1,000,000 or **1 000 000** a/one million

J5 *adjectives & nouns* : **the ordinal numbers**

1st	first	17th	seventeenth
2nd	second	18th	eighteenth
3rd	third	19th	nineteenth
4th	fourth	20th	twentieth
5th	fifth	21st	twenty-first
6th	sixth	22nd	twenty-second
7th	seventh	23rd	twenty-third
8th	eighth	30th	thirtieth
9th	ninth	38th	thirty-eighth
10th	tenth	40th	fortieth
11th	eleventh	50th	fiftieth
12th	twelfth	60th	sixtieth
13th	thirteenth	70th	seventieth
14th	fourteenth	80th	eightieth
15th	fifteenth	90th	ninetieth
16th	sixteenth	100th	a/one hundredth

1,000th a/one thousandth
10,000th ten thousandth
100,000th a/one hundred thousandth
1,000,000th a/one millionth

J6 *adjectives & nouns* : **first and second**

first 1 [*the* GU] **1st**; the first person or thing or group of people or things (to do or be something): *He was the first who was there/ the first to be there. They were the first who were there/ the first to be there. He was one of the first to collect Picasso paintings. He was among the first (people) who collected them.* **2** [C] *infml* a first thing or act of its kind; something never done before: *The college scored a first by being the first to give degrees to women.* **at first** at the beginning: *At first I didn't like him but now I do.* **first and last** always and most importantly:

Although he served in government he was first and last a great soldier.
second 1 [*the* GU] **2nd 2** [C] a person who helps another (**a principal**), esp someone who is fighting another person **3** [C *usu pl*] an article of imperfect quality for sale at a lower price: *If you want to buy dishes cheaply, you ought to get factory seconds.*

J7 *adjectives* : **primary, etc** [Wa5;B]

primary first or earliest in order, time, or importance: *Primary rocks are in the lowest level below the earth's surface. The primary cause of his failure is laziness.* **-ily** [adv]: *I'm primarily interested in this, not that.*
secondary 1 of second or less than first, rank, value, importance, etc: *In addition to the main question, there are various secondary matters to talk about. In this job, speed is secondary in importance to carefulness.* **2** later than, developing from, taken from, etc, something earlier or original: *He has a secondary infection brought on by a cold.*
tertiary of third rank, value, importance, etc: *Tertiary education* (= at a college, university, etc) *comes after primary and secondary education. Tertiary rocks are much nearer the surface than primary and secondary rocks.*
quaternary *rare* of the fourth rank, etc

J8 *adjectives* : **singular, etc** [Wa5;B]
[ALSO ⇨ G262]

singular 1 of a word or form representing exactly one **2** *esp old use* very unusual: *Some singular events led up to the murder.* **-ly** [adv]
dual 1 consisting of two parts or having two parts like each other; double **2** having a double character or nature
plural of a word or form representing more than one; consisting of many parts

J9 *adjectives & suffixes* : **-fold**

-fold by the stated number of times *His money has increased fourfold in five years. There has been a tenfold increase in club members.*
manifold [Wa5;B] many in number or kind: *His interests are manifold. He has manifold interests.*

J10 *adverbs & nouns* : **once, etc**

once one time; on one occasion: *I've done it once; I won't do it again. He comes to see us once a week/year. They didn't even once offer to help! Once is enough; never again. She did it just the once* (= that one time) *and never again.*
twice two times; on two occasions: *I've done it twice; I won't do it again. He comes to see us*

twice a week/month. Listen now; I won't say it twice/a second time!

thrice *old use* three times; on three occasions

times [P9] the stated number of times or occasions: *He came three/four/many times. I told you three times over. How many times must I tell you things? Do you know your ten times table* (= how to multiply by ten)?

J11 *adjectives & adverbs, etc* : **single, double, etc** [Wa5]

single 1 [A] being (the) only one: *The letter was written on a single sheet of paper. A single tree gave shade from the sun. His single aim was to make money. Not a single one of her neighbours gave her any help. Can you give me one single reason why I should do as you ask?* **2** [B] having only one part, quality, etc; not double or multiple: *For a strong sewing job use double, not single, thread. A single flower has only one set of petals* [⇒ A131]. **3** [A] separate; considered by itself: *Food is our most important single need. There's no need to write down every single word I say.* **singly** [adv] separately; by itself or themselves; one by one: *Some guests came singly, others in groups. These glasses aren't sold singly: you have to buy a set of six.*

only [A] **1** having no others **a** in the same group: *This is my only example. They were the only people in the room. She is the only person who wants the job.* **b** of the same quality; the best: *Long skirts were the only thing to wear in those days. She is the only person for the job.* **an only child/daughter/son** one having no brothers or sisters/sisters/brothers

alone [F; adv] without others: *He alone went there. She works alone.*

sole [A] *often emph* **1** single; one and only: *He was the sole member of the group to go.* **2** kept to only one person, group, etc: *We have the sole right to sell these books.* **-ly** [adv] alone, only: *I did it solely for him.*

solo [B; adv] being one person alone; without any other person: *He is a solo performer. He flew the plane solo.*

double 1 [B] having twice (the amount, size, or quality): *He got a double share of food. His share was double.* **2** [A] having or made up of two parts that are alike: *The room had double doors. He put a double lock on the door.* **3** [F] folded once: *Is this cloth just 18 centimetres wide or is it double?* **4** [A] made for two people, animals, etc: *They bought a double bed. He asked for a double room in the hotel.* **5** [A] having two different qualities, uses or ways in which to be considered: *This machine serves a double purpose.* **6** [U] something that is twice another in size, strength, speed, and quantity or value: *He paid her double what she offered to pay.* **7** [adv] twice (the amount, size or quality): *10 is double 5. They gave us double the amount we asked for. His weight is double what*

it was ten years ago. **8** [adv] two together; in groups of two or in pairs: *Mary and Jane can sleep double tonight and you can have one of their beds. I've drunk too much; I'm seeing double.* **doubly** [adv] by two times as much: *'I'm doubly happy today because my son has come home and we are moving to a better house,' she said.*

triple [B] **1** three times repeated: *He played a triple beat on the drum.* **2** having or made up of three parts

treble [adv] three times as big, as much, or as many as; multiplied by three: *He earns treble my wages.*

quadruple [B] **1** four times as big or as many as something mentioned or usual **2** having or made up of four parts

quintuple [B] **1** five times as big or as many as something mentioned or usual **2** having or made up of five parts

n-tuple [B] *n* times (= as many times as one chooses) as big or as many as something mentioned or usual

multiple [B] having or made up of many parts, types, etc

J12 *verbs* : **doubling, etc** [T1; I0]

double 1 to make, be, or become twice as great or as many: *I must double the amount, or it won't be enough. Sales doubled in five years.* **2** to cause to fold or bend sharply or tightly over: *Double the cover and put it over the child.*

triple 1 to make or become three times as great or as many: *He tripled his income last year.* **2** to multiply (a number or amount) by three.

treble *less common* to triple

quadruple to multiply by four

quintuple to multiply by five

J13 *adjectives* : **binary and ternary** [Wa5;B]

binary 1 consisting of two things or parts; double in form: *A binary star is a double star, consisting of two stars turning round each other.* **2** using the number 2 as a base: *A binary system of numbers is used in many computers* [⇒ J34].

ternary 1 consisting of three things or parts; triple in form **2** third in position or rank **3** using the number 3 as a base

J14 *adjectives & nouns* : **part and whole**

[ALSO ⇒ N252]

half [C] one of two equal parts; ½ of something: *He gave me half (of) his apple. Have half an apple; it's all I can give you. He cut the apple in halves. Half (of) the money is his.*

quarter *also less common* **fourth** [C] a fourth

part; ¼ of something: *A quarter of the money is his. He cut the apple in(to)* quarters.

three-quarters [P] three out of four parts; ¾ of something: *Three-quarters of the people went home. He got three-quarters of the money.*

third [C] a third part; ⅓ of something: *He got one third/a third of the money. One-third part is his.*

whole [S] the sum of the parts of something: *The two halves make a whole. The whole is often in some way more than the sum of its parts.*

sum [C *usu sing (of)*] the full amount obtained by adding numbers together: *What is the sum of 10, 9 and 8? The sum (of 10, 9 and 8) is 27.*

total [C] *esp fml & tech* sum; whole: *If you add 10, 9 and 8 the total is 27. Check your totals: I think two of them are wrong.*

J15 *verbs* : **making parts** [T1]

halve 1 to divide into halves: *Let's halve the work between the two of us.* **2** to reduce to half: *They halved our lunch hour.*

quarter to divide into four parts: *He quartered the body of the pig.*

J16 *nouns* : **pairs and other sets**

[ALSO ⇒ J40 SET]

pair 1 [C9] something made up of two parts that are alike and which are joined and used together: *a pair of trousers, a pair of scissors* **2** [C9] **a** two things that are alike or of the same kind and are usu used together: *a pair of shoes, a beautiful pair of legs* **b** two playing cards of the same value but of different kinds (**suits**): *a pair of kings* **3** [C] **a** two people closely connected: *a pair of dancers; a pair of friends* **b** a couple of people **c** *sl* two people closely connected who cause annoyance or displeasure: *You're a fine pair coming as late as this! What a pair you are!* **4** [C] two animals (male and female) that stay together for a certain length of time or for life

couple [C] **1** two things related in some way but not necessarily matched or part of a set; two things of the same kind: *I found a couple of socks in the bedroom but they don't make a pair.* **2** a man and a woman together, esp a husband and wife: *Bob and Jean make a lovely couple. Would all the married couples come this way please?* **3** *infml* a few; several; a small number: *I'll just have a couple of drinks and then I'll come home. Let's go to Paris for a couple of days.*

dozen [C; A] a group of 12: *Can I have a dozen eggs please? He bought several dozen eggs. I'll take a dozen (of them).* **by the dozen** in groups of 12: *He buys them by the dozen; it's cheaper.* **in dozens** in groups of 12: *Eggs are usually sold in dozens and half-dozens.* **dozens (and dozens) of** *infml* lots (and lots) (of): *I've been there dozens of times.— How many?— Oh, 30 times at least.* **doz** [abbrev]

half a dozen *also* (**a**) **half dozen** six; a set of six: *Can I have a half a dozen eggs, please? Can I have a half dozen, please?*

score [C; *often in comb*] (a group of) 20: *three-score or three score* (= 60); *fourscore or four score* (= 80) **scores (and scores) (of)** large numbers (of); numbers (of) which are larger than dozens but smaller than hundreds: *Scores of people, perhaps 80 or more, attended the meeting.*

gross [Wn3:C] 144; twelve dozen: *He bought a gross of pencils.*

J17 *verbs* : **pairing and coupling**

pair [T1; I∅; (*up, off*)] **1** to (cause to) form into one or more pairs: *The cupboard filled with shoes fell over and it took half an hour to pair (up) the shoes. Birds often pair for life. Will everyone pair off and we will start the dance?* (*infml*) *For the tennis match, Smith and Jones paired off.* **2** to make or join with somebody to make a pair: *These two members of Parliament often pair (with each other) in the voting.*

couple [Wv3; T1] to join (two or more things or sets of things) together; connect: *The scientist coupled the two electric systems together so that power could pass from one to the other. The train will be ready to leave when all the carriages have been coupled.*

J18 *nouns & pronouns* : **nothing and nought**

nothing 1 [pron] not any thing; no thing: *There's nothing in this box; it's empty. Nothing ever happens in this town. If you have nothing to do, come with me. This hotel leaves nothing to be desired* (= it has everything). *There's nothing unusual about my leaving the office early* (= I do it often). **2** [C] *genl* the number 0: *He wrote several nothings after the 5.*

nil [R] **1** *tech* nothing: *The new machine reduced labour costs to almost nil. The office sent in a nil return to head office* (= they sent head office a letter or form saying that nothing was needed, nothing had been done, etc). **2** *BrE esp in sport* a total of no points, marks, etc: *In the match they won by four points to nil. It was a four-nil victory.* (usu written or printed 4–0).

zero 1 [C] *tech* the name of the sign 0 and the number it stands for **2 a** the point between + and − on a scale; **b** on the centigrade scale, the temperature at which water freezes: *It was five below zero last night.* **3** [U] (often written or printed **0**) nothing; no size or quantity: *Our population has reached zero growth* (= is not growing any more).

cipher, cypher [C] **1** *rare* the figure 0; zero **2** (*fig*) *deprec* a person of no importance: *He's a cipher; forget him.*

o [C; U] *infml* the figure 0; zero: *His telephone number is 041—220—6060* (= spoken as, o-four-one, two-two-o, six-o-six-o). *He was born in 1906* (=often said as, nineteen-o-six).

nought *BrE*, **naught** *AmE* [C; U] *esp old use or math* the figure 0; zero: *0.6 is usually read as 'nought point six', and .06 is usually read as 'point nought six'.*

J19 *adverbs, determiners, etc* : **not, no, and none**

not [adv] **1** (used with verbs for changing a word or expression to one with the opposite meaning): *'Thou shalt not kill' (the Bible). I will not do it! I won't do it. I've not seen him this week/I haven't seen him this week. If you did not/didn't like it, you were wrong not to say so. Not saying anything was a bad idea.* **2** (used with other words for changing a word or expression to one with an opposite meaning): *Not everyone likes that book* (= Some people don't like it). *It's a cat, not a dog. The question is not easy to answer. Do you want a job?—Not me* (= I don't, but others may)*! Not all his work was successful* (= Some was unsuccessful). *Not all his work could save him* (= All his work, taken together, could not save him). **3** (with the indefinite article showing that something did not or will not happen or be done): *Not a single soldier was killed..How much did this cost?— Not a penny* (= nothing)*!* **4** (used in place of a whole expression, often after verbs marked [5b]): *Will he be here or not? Will it rain today?— I hope not* (= I hope it won't rain). *Have you got £5 to lend me?—I'm afraid not. Drop that gun. If not, you'll be sorry.* **5** *esp pomp* (used with negative words, esp those beginning with **un-** and words meaning small, slow, etc, to give force to the opposite meaning): *He is a not unwelcome guest here* (= He is very welcome here). *She is not slow to complain, and not without reason. He drank not a little* (= drank a lot) *of the wine. He had many enemies, but found he was not without friends as well.* **not at all** an answer to polite praise or thanks: *Thank you very much for all the trouble you took.— Not at all; I was glad to.* **not . . . but** to show one choice instead of another: *Shakespeare was not a musician but a writer. Othello said he loved not wisely but too well.* **not only . . . but also** to show a second choice in addition to a first one: *Shakespeare was not only a writer but also an actor.* **not but what** although: *He's never walked that far, not but what he could do it if he tried.* **not that** *not fml* I don't mean that; although . . . not: *Not that it matters, but how did you spend the money I gave you? Who were you with last night, not that I care, of course?* **not to say** *not fml* and almost; perhaps even: *He sounded impolite, not to say rude. It would be foolish, not to say mad, to sell your car now.*

no 1 [determiner] not a; not one; not any: *I've no money/no idea what to do. There's no sugar*

in the bowl/no telephone in our house. There are no buses in this part of town. You can't lie to me; I'm no fool! **2** [determiner] in formal commands, warnings, road signs, etc, expressing what is not allowed: *No smoking. No parking here. No bicycles against this wall, by order.* **3** [determiner] *infml* very little; hardly any: *We're almost home; we'll be there in no time* (= very soon). *It's no distance at all to the school; only a short walk.* **4** [adv] (used before numbers and 'other', meaning not): *No two people are the same* (= Everybody is different). *No other man would do these things* (= He is the only man who would do them). **5** [adv] (with comparative adjectives) not any: *It is no bigger now than it was last year. She could do no more* (= There wasn't any more she could do). **6** [determiner] (meaning the opposite): *He is no friend of ours* (= He is an enemy). **7** [C usu sing] an answer or decision of no: *He got a clear no to his request for more money.* **8** [C usu pl] a vote or voter against a question to be decided: *The noes won and the idea was dropped* (= not accepted).

none [pron] **1** not any; no amount or part: *Have you got any books?— No, I haven't got any; none at all.— No, none whatever.— None. She had none of her mother's beauty. None of your foolishness, please* (= Stop being foolish)*!* **2** not any, not one (usu of a group of more than two): *None of my friends ever come(s) to see me. None of the telephones is/are working. If you need a repairman, there's none better than my brother.* **3** *usu lit* not any such thing or person: *Once I had a lover, but now I have none.* **none but** *often lit* not any thing or person except: *None but the best is good enough for her. None but a strong man could have lifted it.* **have none of** to take no part in; not allow; not accept: *I'll have none of your stupid ideas! He was offered a job but he said he would have none of it, because they were breaking the law.* **none other (than)** used for expressing surprise, no one else (but): *It's none other than my old friend Bill! Can it really be Bill?— None other!* **none the** (before a comparative word) not; in no way: *He spent two weeks in hospital, but he's none the better for it. You'll be none the worse for a holiday* (= You should have a holiday). **none the wiser** not knowing about or not discovering a fact, secret, trick, etc: *If we take only one piece of cake, mother will be none the wiser.* **none too** (before an adj or adv) not very or not at all: *The service in this restaurant is none too fast. He gave a none-too-believable excuse for being late.*

Mathematics

J30 *nouns* : **kinds of mathematics**

mathematics [U] the study or science of numbers: *He was always good at mathematics; it is* his best subject. **maths** BrE, **math** AmE infml abbrev mathematics **mathematical**[B] **1** [Wa5] of or concerning mathematics **2** (of numbers, reasoning, etc) exactly correct **-cally**[adv Wa4] **mathematician** [C] a person who studies and knows about mathematics

arithmetic [U] **1** the science and techniques of using numbers **2** the adding, subtracting, multiplying, and dividing of numbers; calculation by numbers **arithmetical** sometimes **arithmetic** [Wa5;B] of or concerning numbers **-cally** [adv Wa4]: We found the answer arithmetically.

sums [P] not fml arithmetic: The boy was doing his sums.

algebra [U] a branch of mathematics in which signs and letters are used instead of numbers: We learn in algebra that if 2x = 6 then x = 3. **algebraic** [Wa5;B] of or concerning algebra **-cally** [adv Wa4]

statistics 1 [U] a branch of mathematics which presents facts, measurements, information, etc, in the form of numbers **2** [P] such facts, measurements, information, etc, in the form of numbers **statistical** [Wa5;B] of or concerning statistics **-cally** [adv Wa4] **statistician** [C] a person who studies and uses statistics

geometry [U] the study in mathematics of the angles and shapes formed by the relationships of lines, surfaces, and solids in space **geometric(al)** [Wa5;B] of or concerning geometry **-c(al)ly** [adv]

trigonometry [U] the branch of mathematics that deals with the relationship between the sides and angles of triangles (= three-sided figures) **trig** infml abbrev **trigonometric(al)** [Wa5;B] of, concerning, or like trigonometry **-c(al)ly** [adv Wa4]

logarithms [P] the techniques of using logarithms [⇒ J3]: Are you good at logarithms? **logarithmic** [Wa5;B] of or connected with logarithms **-cally** [adv Wa4] **logs** [P] infml abbrev logarithms

calculus [U] a way of making calculations about quantities which are continually changing, such as the speed of a falling stone or the slope of a curved line

J31 verbs, etc : counting and numbering

count 1 [I∅] to say or name the numbers in order, one by one or by groups: The child counted up to 100. He's only three (years old) but he can already count to 20. Don't talk to me; I'm counting. **2** [Wv6;T1] to say or name the numbers in regular order up to and including (a particular point): Count 20 and then come and find me. **3** [T1, 6] to say or name one by one in order to find the whole number in a collection: Count the apples in this box. Count how many people there are in this room. Have the votes been counted? **4** [T1] to total; add up: Remember to count your change before leaving

the shop. **5** [T1] to include: There were five people there, counting me.

add 1 [T1 (to, together, up); I∅] to join (numbers, amounts, etc) so as to find the total: If you add 5 and/to 3 you get 8. We added the numbers together/up and got 8. My young daughter has already learnt to add. **2** [T1 (to)] to put together with something else so as to increase the number, size, importance, etc: The fire is going out; add some wood. He added some wood to increase the fire. He added wood to the fire. The general added 10,000 men to his army. I should like to add a few words to what my friend has just said.

total [T1] **1** to add, esp together: Please total these numbers. **2** add up to: We have sales totalling over £1 million.

tot up [v adv T1] infml to add (up): Just tot up these numbers for me, please. All the numbers were totted up.

reckon [T1 (up)] to calculate; to add up (an amount, cost, etc): My pay is reckoned from the first of the month. Can you reckon up these figures for me?

number 1 [Wv6;L1,9] to reach as a total; be . . . in number: The books in the library number 5,065/in the thousands. **5** [X9;L9] to include or be included; count: He is numbered among the best writers in the USA. I'm glad to number him with my friends and not my enemies. **3** [Wv4,5;T1;X1,9 often pass] to give a number to: Number the question (from) 1 to 10. What numbering system shall we use? There are two pages numbered 16 in this book; that's a mistake. **4** [T1] poet to find the number of; count: Who can number the stars?

tally [T1; I∅] to (cause to) agree or be equal: Your figures and mine don't tally; we'd better add them up again. Your figures don't tally with mine. (fig) We must tally our stories exactly if they are to believe us.

up [adv] emph fully: Add these numbers (up). Count up to a hundred. She reckoned up the cost of the holiday.

J32 verbs : subtracting numbers
[ALSO ⇒ J109 DEDUCT, TAKE OFF]

subtract [T1 (from)] to take (a part or amount) from something larger: Subtract 10 and add 2; what is your result? He subtracted 10 from 30 and got 20. Please subtract a quarter of the money for your own use.

take away [v adv T1] not fml to subtract: Take away 10 and add 2; what do you get? He took 10 away from 30 and got 20.

take . . . from [v prep] not fml to subtract from: Take 10 from 30 and you get 20.

J33 verbs : multiplying and dividing

multiply 1 [T1 (by, together)] to increase by the

same amount a certain number of times: *If you multiply 2 by 3 you get 6. 2 multiplied by 3 is 6. Multiply the numbers (together).* **2** [T1: I∅] (*fig*) to increase: *Doing this will multiply your chances of success.*

square [T1 *usu pass*] to multiply (a number) by itself: *Square the numbers. What is 6 squared (6²)?*

divide [D1 *by/into*; T1; I∅] to find out how many times (one number) contains or is contained in (another number) as shown in the following expressions: *Divide 15 by 3; 15 divided by 3 is 5. Divide 3 by 15; 3 divided by 15 is ⅕. Divide 3 into 15; 3 divides into 15 5 times. Now you know how to divide.* **divisible** [Wa5;B (*by*)] able to be divided **in-** [*neg*] **-bly** [adv Wa3] **-bility** [U]

J34 *verbs, etc* : **calculating and computing**

[ALSO ⇨ J143 VALUING, ETC]

---

calculate **1** [Wv4;T1,5a,6a] to work out or find out (something) by using numbers: *Have you calculated the result? I calculated that we would arrive at 6.00 p.m. The scientist could not calculate when the spaceship would reach the moon. The new calculating instrument is very simple but quick to use.* **2** [T1, 5a, 6a, b; I∅] to work out by using one's judgment; estimate: *Did she calculate the cost? Yes, she calculated that it would cost £100. I'll calculate what it will cost. Have you finished calculating yet?* **3** [Wv5;T1,5a,6a,b] to plan; intend: *That was a calculated threat; she meant to annoy you.* **calculator** [C] a machine which makes calculations easier and faster

figure [I∅] *infml becoming rare* to do sums: *She learnt to read and write and figure.*

compute [T1; I∅] to calculate (a result, answer, sum, etc): *The scientists correctly computed the speed of the spaceship as being 30,000 miles an hour. Doctor Smith is busy computing at the moment but should be finished soon.* **computer** [C] a machine which can perform a large number of calculations very quickly and correctly according to a system of calculation given to it

program *also less common BrE* **programme** **1** [T1] to give a set of ordered instructions to (a machine, esp a computer): *They programmed the computer to give them each name and number together.* **2** [C] such a set of ordered instructions: *Which computer programs are they using?*

J35 *nouns* : **sums, calculations, and problems**

---

addition **1** [U] the act or result of adding or being added: *The addition of 5 and 3/of 5 to 3 gives you 8. My young daughter is quite good at addition. The addition of more wood to the fire*

made it brighter and warmer. **2** [C] an example of this; something added to something else: *Have you had any additions to your family?— No; three children are quite enough!* **additive** **1** [Wa5;B] formed by or using addition **2** [C] something that is added to something else, esp to change or improve the quality

subtraction **1** [U] the act or result of subtracting or being subtracted: *The subtraction of 2 from 10 gives you 8.* **2** [C] an example of this; something subtracted from something else

multiplication **1** [U] the act or result of multiplying or being multiplied: *The multiplication of 7 by 3 gives you 21. You can get the answer by simple multiplication.* **2** [C] an example of this: *There has been a great multiplication of rabbits/in the number of rabbits here lately.* **multiplication tables** [P] lists which young children can repeat to learn what number results when a stated number is multiplied by a number from 1 to 12

division [U] the act or result of dividing or being divided: *The division of 15 by 5 gives you 3.*

sum [C] *not fml* an exercise in arithmetic, esp in adding: *He didn't get that sum right, but the other sums are all right.*

equation [C] a statement that two quantities are equal: *x + 2y = 7 is an equation.*

calculation **1** [U] the art of calculating: *Calculation of the cost is necessary before spending public money.* **2** [C] (the result of) an act of calculating: *Her calculation was correct but his was wrong. Do the calculations now, please.*

computation **1** [U] the act or result of computing: *The scientists' computation of the speed of light is 186,000 miles per second.* **2** [C] an example of this: *His computations are not correct.*

theorem [C] *tech* (in the science of numbers) a statement that can be shown to be true by reasoning

problem [C] a question (esp connected with numbers, facts, etc) for consideration or for which an answer is needed: *An electrical apparatus called a computer can be used for finding the answer to difficult problems quickly. The little boy can already do simple problems in addition and subtraction.*

formula [C] **1** a set of mathematical or scientific signs (such as H_2O or r^2) that expresses a particular state or set of relations **2** a set of words, ideas, etc, used for any purpose: *What formula should we use for describing this work?*

J36 *general verbs* : **calculating and totalling** [Wv6]

---

make **1** [X1, (7)] *usu not fml* to calculate (and get as a result): *He added up the figures and made it 105, not 103.* **2** [T1] to add up to; come to (an amount) as a result: *2 and 2 make 4.*

get [T1] *infml* to reach (a total [⇨ J14] of): *He added up the figures and got a different total from me; I got 105, not 103.*

amount to [v prep Wv6;L1] **t**o be equal to, esp as a total: *The three sums together amount to a lot of money.* (*fig*) *His words amount to a refusal, though he did not actually refuse.*

come to [v prep T1] *usu not fml* to amount to: *The bill came to £40.*

J37 *nouns, adjectives, etc* : **plus and minus**

plus 1 [C] *also* **plus sign** *math* a sign (+) showing that two or more numbers are to be added together or that a number is greater than zero **2** [C] (*fig*) *infml* a welcome or favourable addition: *We knew she was clever but it's quite a plus that she's beautiful as well.* **3** [conj] with the addition of: *3 plus 6 is 9. The cost is a pound plus 45 pence for postage.* **4** [prep] *infml* and also: *This work needs experience plus care.* **5** [Wa5;A] *math* greater than zero: *3 is a plus quantity.* **6** [Wa5;B] electrically positive [⇒ H205] **7** [A] (*fig infml* additional and welcome (often in the phr **a plus factor**) **8** [Wa5;E] **a** (esp of age) and above (a stated number): *All the children here are 12 plus* (= are 12 or more years old). **b** (of a mark given for work done) and slightly more (than a stated mark): *B plus is a better mark than B.* **9** [Wa5;E] (*fig*) *infml* (of a quality) with something else: *She's got beauty plus.*

and [conj] *infml* plus: *2 and 2 are/make 4.*

minus 1 [C] *also* **minus sign** *math* a sign (−) used for showing that the stated number is less than zero: *−15* **b** that the second number is to be taken away from the first: *17 − 5 leaves 12.* **2** [C] a quantity that is less than zero: *He calculated his gains and losses of money and the result was a minus.* **3** [Wa5;A] (of a number or quantity) less than zero: *It is a minus temperature.* **4** [prep] made less by (the stated figure or quantity): *17 minus five leaves 12.* **5** [prep] being the stated number of degrees below the freezing point of water: *The temperature was minus 10 degrees.* **6** [prep] *infml* without: *He won the fight but when it ended he was minus two front teeth.*

from [prep] (in subtraction) out of: *If you subtract 10 from 15, 5 remains. 2 from 10 is 8.*

J38 *nouns, etc* : **roots, cubes, squares, and powers**

root [C *usu sing*] a number that when multiplied by itself a usu stated number of times gives another stated number: *2 is the 4th root of 16.*

square 1 [C *usu sing*] the number made by multiplying a number by itself once: *16 is the square of 4. The square of 3 is 9.* **2** [Wv5;T1] to multiply (a number) by itself once: *3 squared* (3^2) *is 9.*

square root [C *usu sing*] the number which when multiplied by itself once equals the given number: *3 is the square root of 9.*

cube 1 [C *usu sing*] the number made by multiplying a number by itself twice: *The cube of 3 is 27.* **2** [Wv5;T1] to multiply (a number) by itself twice: *3 cubed* (3^3) *is 27.*

cube root [C *usu sing*] the number which when multiplied by itself twice equals the given number: *If 3 is the cube root of 27* ($\sqrt[3]{27}$), *then* $3 \times 3 \times 3 = 27.$

power [C *usu sing*] **1** the number of times that an amount is to be multiplied by itself: *The amount 2 to the power of 3 is written 2^3, and means $2 \times 2 \times 2$.* **2** the result of this multiplying: *The 3rd power of 2 is 8.*

index *also* **exponent** *math* a number which shows how many times to multiply a number by itself (as *4* in x^4, $2^4 = 16$)

point [C] **1** *also* **decimal point** a symbol (.) used to separate a whole number from any following decimals: *Two point five is written 2.5.* **2** a measure of increase or decrease in cost, value, etc, according to some accepted standard: *The price of corn has fallen a few points this week.*

J39 *nouns & adjectives* : **averages**

average 1 [C] the amount found by adding together several quantities and then dividing by the number of quantities: *The average of 3, 8, and 10 is 7.* **2** [C; *above, below, on* U] a level or standard regarded as usual or ordinary: *He is above average in his work. The rain this month was below average. On average we receive 5 letters each/a day.* **3** [Wa5;A] found by making an average: *What is the average rainfall for July?* **4** [Wa5;B] of the usual or ordinary kind: *There was nothing special about it; it was only average.* **average out** [v adv I∅] to come to an average or ordinary level or standard, esp after being higher or lower: *The good things and bad things in life average out in the end, don't they? His mail averages out at 20 letters a day.*

mean 1 [C] an average amount, figure, or value: *The mean of 7, 9, and 14 is found by adding them together and dividing by 3.* **2** [C] a state or way of behaviour or course of action which is not too strong or weak, too much or little, but in between (*esp in the phr* **the golden mean**) **3** [Wa5;A] average: *The mean yearly rainfall is 20 inches.*

median *tech* **1** [C] a line passing from a point of a 3-sided figure (triangle) to the centre of the opposite side **2** [Wa5;A] in or passing through the middle

norm 1 [C] a usual or expected number, amount, pattern of action in behaviour, etc: *The national norm on this examination is 70 out of 100.* **2** [C *often pl*] a standard of proper behaviour or principle of right and wrong; rule: *In these times no religious group can force others to follow its own social norms.* **normal 1** [B] usual, average: *Normal working hours here are from 9 to 5.* **2** [Wa5;B] *tech* at right angles **3** [C] a line at right angles to something **-ly** [adv]

medium 1 [S] *usu not fml* middle point, way, or position (*esp in the phr* a **happy medium**): *He prefers a happy medium in life, neither too exciting nor too dull.* **2** [Wa5;B] taking a middle position; average: *She is a girl of medium height/ability.*

J40 *nouns* : **proportions, ratios, series, and sets**

proportion 1 [U] the correct relationship between the size, position, and shape of the different parts of a whole, esp as producing a beautiful effect: *The drawings of young children usually lack proportion; they make arms and legs look like sticks.* **2** [U (*of*)] compared relationship between two things in regard to size, amount, force, importance, etc: *The proportion of men to women in the population has changed so that there are now fewer women and more men.* **3** [C (*of*)] a part or share (as measured in amount and compared with the whole): *What proportion of your wages do you spend on rent?—About a quarter.* **4** [U] *math* equalness of relationship between two sets of numbers (*often in the phr* **in proportion**): *The statement 'as 6 is to 4, so is 24 to 16' is a statement of proportion. 4/2 = 10/5, so 4/2 and 10/5 are in proportion.* **in proportion to 1** according to; at the rate of: *Are you paid in proportion to the number of hours you work?* **2** As compared with (what is expected) in size, amount, etc: *Her legs are quite long in proportion to the rest of her body.* **in/out of proportion** (not) according to real importance; (not) sensibly: *When one is angry one often does not see things in proportion; the wrongs done to one seem much worse than they are.* **in the proportion of** in the measure of: *The paint should be mixed in the proportion of one part of paint to 2 parts of water.* **out of (all) proportion to** (much) too great as compared with: *The price of this article is out of all proportion to its value.* **sense of proportion** ability to judge what matters and what does not, without being influenced by personal feeling: *We shouldn't quarrel over such unimportant matters; let's keep our/a sense of proportion. In punishing the prisoner so heavily the general seemed to have lost all sense of proportion.* **proportional** *also more fml* **proportionate** [B] **1** in proper proportion; of, concerning, or like proper proportions **2** corresponding in amount or degree: *payment proportional to the work done* **-ly** [adv]

ratio [C] a figure showing the number of times one quantity contains another: *The ratio of 10 to 5 is 2 to 1.*

constant [C] **1** *loose* a fixed quantity; something that does not or cannot vary **2** *precise* (a number representing) a quantity that remains unchanged throughout given conditions

variable [C] **1** *loose* something that may or does vary according to conditions **2** *precise* (a sign that represents) a quantity that may take on any given value or set of values

function [C (*of*)] **1** *loose* a quality or fact which depends on and varies with another: *The size of the crop is a function of the quality of the soil and the amount of rainfall.* **2** *precise* a value which varies as another value varies: *In x = 5y, x is a function of y.*

parameter [C] **1** *loose* a variable (*def* **1**) **2** *precise* a quantity or quality that is constant in the case being considered but varies in different cases **parametric** [Wa5;B] of, concerning, or like a parameter or parameters **-cally** [adv Wa4]

series [Wn3] **1** [C] *math* the sum of the members of a group of things which follow each other: *All the numbers $1 + x + x^2 + x^3 + \ldots$ make up a series.* **2** [C] a group of things of the same kind or related in some way, coming one after another or in order: *A television series is a series of shows on television. A whole series of misfortunes happened to him.*

set [C] **1** *math* a formal object which is a collection of members with a shared characteristic: *9 is a member of the set of all numbers greater than 8. The set $\{x, y\}$ has two members.* **2** a group of naturally connected things; a group forming a whole: *He had two sets of gardening tools.*

group [C] **1** *math* a set (*def* **1**) together with an operation for combining any two of its elements (by addition, etc) to make a new element of the set **2** any number of things, persons, etc that is considered as being together for any reason

complement [C] **1** *precise* either of two parts or numbers necessary to complete anything **2** *loose* anything that completes a group, set, number, etc

unit [C] **1** a single thing or a person, group, piece of work, etc, that can be treated as a single thing: *He works in the third unit, in that building. We shall study Book 3, Unit 4 today.* **2** a piece of equipment that is of several parts but which has one purpose: *a kitchen unit* **3** a single thing used in a system for measuring, etc: *The metre is a unit for measuring length.*

J41 *nouns* : **points, lines, planes, and angles, etc** [C]

[⇨ M200 SURFACE, ETC]

point *geom* an imaginary spot or place that has position but no size

line *tech* a mark on a surface, having length but no breadth or thickness: *A straight line is the shortest distance between two points. Draw a line AB such that* (= so that) *it passes through the centre of a circle C.* **linear** [Wa5;B] of or in lines: *linear measure*

row a neat line (of things, people, etc) side by side: *a row of houses/of cups on a shelf; the* *front rows at the theatre; children standing hand in hand in a row* (= side by side, not one behind the other)

plane 1 any completely flat surface **2** *geom* a surface such that a straight line joining any two points lies only on that surface **3** (*fig*) level; standard: *Let's keep the conversation on a friendly plane.*

base the line or surface on which a figure stands or can stand: *In the triangle ABC, BC is the base. In the rectangle ABCD, let CD be the base.*

angle 1 the space between two lines or surfaces that meet or cross each other, measured in degrees that represent the amount of a circle that can fit into that space **2** a corner, as of a building or piece of furniture **3** (*fig*) *infml* point of view: *If you look at the accident from another angle you will see how funny it all was.* **at an angle** not upright; sloping **angular** [B] **1** having an angle or angles, corner or corners, esp acute [⇒ J43] angles **2** (of a person, face, etc) thin and with the bones showing **angularity** [U] the condition of being angular

degree a unit of measurement of angles: *This is an angle of ninety degrees* (written *90°*); *it is a right angle.*

section the figure formed by the points where a solid body is cut by a flat surface

J42 *adjectives & nouns* : **lines and positions**

[ALSO ⇒ N302–4]

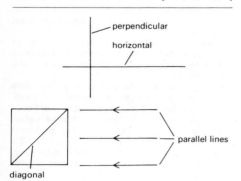

horizontal

perpendicular

parallel lines

diagonal

horizontal [Wa5;B] (of a line, surface, etc) parallel or considered parallel to the ground or the horizon [⇒ L113]; flat; level: *In a perfect square the lines at bottom and top are horizontal and parallel.*

perpendicular 1 [Wa5;B (*to*)] (of a line, surface, etc) at an angle of 90 degrees to a line or surface: *In a perfect square, the lines at the side are perpendicular to the line at the bottom.* **2** [B] exactly upright; not leaning to one side or the other: *This wall isn't perpendicular; it might fall down.* **3** [(*the*) U] a perpendicular position: *The fence is out of (the) perpendicular; it leans inwards.* **4** [C] a perpendicular line

oblique 1 [Wa5;B] (of an angle) more or less than 90° **2** [Wa5;B] in a sideways direction; sloping: *The line was oblique; it was an oblique line.* **-ly** [adv] **-ness** [U]

diagonal [C; Wa5;B] **1** (in the direction of) a straight line joining two opposite corners of a square, or other 4-sided flat figure: *The two diagonals of a square cross in the centre. Draw a diagonal line to divide the square into two.* **2** (any straight line) which runs in a sloping direction: *The cloth had a diagonal pattern.* **-ly** [adv]: *Cut the cloth diagonally.*

parallel 1 [Wa5;B] (of two or more lines or rows) running side by side but never getting nearer to or further away from each other: *In America, streets are often parallel.* **2** [Wa5;B (*to, with*)] (of one line or row) running side by side with (another line or lines) but never getting nearer to or further away: *The parallel road (to this one) is five miles away.* **3** [Wa5;B (*to*)] (*fig*) comparable: *My findings in this matter are parallel to yours.* **4** [C (*to, with*)] a parallel line or line of things, or surface (*often in the phr* **on a parallel with**): *The flat roof of a building is on a parallel with the floor.* **5** [C (*to, with*)] (*fig*) a comparable person or thing (*often in the phr* **without a parallel**): *As a musician he has no parallel today; he is the greatest.* **6** [C] (*fig*) a comparison that shows a likeness: *One can draw many parallels between these two plays of Shakespeare.*

J43 *adjectives, etc* : **relating to angles** [Wa5;B]

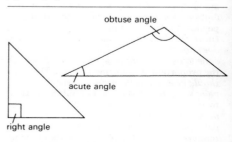

obtuse angle

acute angle

right angle

acute (of an angle) being less than 90 degrees; narrow **acute angle** [C] an angle of between 0° and 90°

obtuse (of an angle) being greater than 90 degrees; wide **obtuse angle** [C] an angle between 90° and 180°

right (of an angle) being 90 degrees **right angle** [C] an angle of 90 degrees, as at any of the four corners of a square **right-angled** having a right angle or right angles

J44 *nouns & adjectives* : **geometrical shapes** [C]

triangle 1 a flat figure with three straight sides and three angles **2** any three cornered or three-sided figure, object or piece: *a triangle of land*

rectangle a figure with four straight sides forming four right angles

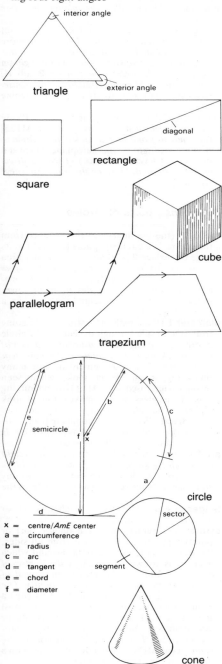

triangle

square

rectangle

cube

parallelogram

trapezium

circle

semicircle

sector

segment

x = centre/*AmE* center
a = circumference
b = radius
c = arc
d = tangent
e = chord
f = diameter

cone

quadrilateral [C] a figure with four sides

square a figure with four equal sides and four right angles

oblong a figure with four straight sides, forming four right angles, which is longer than it is wide

cube a solid object with six square sides

parallelogram a flat four-sided figure with opposite sides equal and parallel

rhombus a figure with four equal straight sides and unequal angles

trapezium *BrE tech* a four-sided figure in which only one pair of sides are parallel

circle 1 a flat round area enclosed by a curved line that is along its whole length equally distant from a fixed point **2** the curved line enclosing this area **3** anything having the general shape of this line; a ring : *The house lay in a circle of trees.*

disc *BrE*, **disk** *AmE* **1** something round and flat **2** a ball-shaped surface that looks flat: *the disc of the full moon*

loop 1 a shape produced by a curve crossing itself: *When writing the letters 'l' and 'h' most people use loops.* **2** part of a piece of string, wire, etc, formed into such a shape: *He tied the thread in a loop.* **3** a movement made, esp by an aeroplane when it flies first upwards then upsidedown then downwards, following a path like a loop **4** a part of a road, railway line, tape, etc, which leaves and then joins the main path again in the shape of a loop

cone 1 a solid object with a round base and a point at the top **2** any hollow or solid object shaped like this: *Many children would rather eat ice cream from cones than from dishes.*

cross 1 an upright post with a shorter bar crossing it near the top, on which people were nailed by their hands and feet and left to die **2** any of various symbolic representations of this, used for ornament, in art, etc: *Latin cross; St. George's cross; Maltese cross* **3** *also* **crucifix** a small silver or gold object shaped like this, worn round the neck on a chain as an ornament or sign of Christian faith **4** a sign shaped like a cross, made with the hand on one's chest as a religious act in church, before saying one's prayers, etc **5** [*often cap*] the shape of a cross as the symbol of the Christian faith or religion: *Lift high the Cross and announce the love of Christ in the world!* **6** [*the* R *often cap*] Christ's death as the act that saved the world: *'It is by the Cross that we were set free from death,' said the priest. Christ willingly accepted the Cross because he loved us so much.* **7** an example of sorrow or suffering as a test of one's patience or goodness: *Everyone has his own cross to bear in this life. That poor woman's got a heavy cross to bear.* **8** a cross built in a public place or at the end of a grave to remind people of the dead: *After the war the people of the town built a cross out of respect for the soldiers from the town who died fighting the enemy.* **9** a figure or mark formed by one straight line crossing another, as X, often used as a sign of where something is or that something is incorrect or by people who can't write, as a signature: *A cross marks our house on the map. The teacher put a red cross to show that my answer was wrong. If you can't write make your cross.*

crescent 1 the curved shape of the moon during its first and last quarters, when it forms less than half a circle **2** [*often cap*] this shape as a symbol of the faith and religion of Muslims: *The Cross and the Crescent.*

J45 *adjectives, etc* : **geometrical shapes** [B]

round shaped like a ball, circle, etc: *The area was perfectly round. The child had a round face. The Earth isn't completely round; it is slightly flattened at the poles* (= at the top and bottom).

rounded more or less round: *The local bread is not square; it is rounded. The bread has a rounded shape.*

circular in the shape of a circle; like a circle: *The house looks circular, but it isn't a complete circle.*

square [Wa5] **1** in the shape of or like a square; having four straight sides at right angles to each other: *Use a square box, not an oblong one.* **2** relating to the square, esp for measurement: *a square metre* **-ly** [adv] (*fig*) firmly: *He put his hat squarely on his head.*

oblong in the shape of or like an oblong; *infml* rectangular: *An oblong box is longer than it is wide.*

rectangular in the shape of or like a rectangle

cubic [Wa5] **1** in the shape of or like a cube **2** relating to the cube, esp for measurement: *cubic centimetres*

triangular [Wa5] in the shape of or like a triangle

isosceles [Wa5] (of a triangle) having two equal sides

scalene [Wa5] (of a triangle) having no two equal sides

conical [Wa5] in the shape of or like a cone: *The man wore a conical hat.* **-ly** [adv Wa4]

curved having a rounded bending shape: *He drew a curved line. The surface of the earth is curved, not flat.* **curvature** *tech* **1** [U] the condition of being curved: *curvature of the spine* (= backbone) **2** [C] an example of this

convex curving outwards; having the same shape as the outer part of a circle

concave curving inwards; having the same shape as the inner part of a circle

hollow 1 having an empty space inside: *The mountain is so full of caves that it is almost hollow. This ball is solid but that one is hollow.* **2** sounding as if coming from an empty space inside something: *The earth under them sounded hollow.* (*fig*) *He gave a hollow laugh.* **3** (*fig*) unreal; false: *His promises are hollow.* **-ly** [adv] **-ness** [U]

circuitous going a long way round instead of taking the quickest or straightest way: *He has*

some very circuitous ways of doing things. **-ly** [adv]

roundabout *infml* circuitous: *That's a roundabout way to go if you want to get home quickly.*

due [adv H] directly: *The planes flew due east.*

straight [Wa1;B; adv] **1** not in a curve; not turning: *Draw a straight line. The line was more or less straight. That line is straighter than this one. Go straight down the street. Go straight on to the end of the street, then turn left.* **2** [adv H] without delay: *She went straight into the house.* **straighten** [I0;T1] to (cause to) become straight

direct [Wa2;B] not turning or stopping: *Please tell me the most direct way/route* [⇒ M125] *from here to London. She took a direct flight to Rome* (= a flight in the aeroplane which did not land at any other place). *'I want a direct answer', she said. 'Tell me the truth.'* **in-** [*neg*] **-ly** [adv]

J46 *nouns* : **parts of circles** [C]

radius 1 (the line marking) the distance from the centre of a circle or sphere [⇒ H48] to its edge or surface **2** [C9] *not fml* a circular area measured from its centre point: *He lives somewhere within a two-mile radius of the town/ within a radius of two miles from the town.* **radial** [Wa5;B] of, connected with, or like a radius **-ly** [adv]

diameter 1 (the length of) a straight line going from side to side through the centre of a circle or other curved figure: *Measure the diameter of this circle. What is the diameter of the main stem of this tree?* **2** a measurement of how many times bigger an object looks when seen through a microscope [⇒ H123] or magnifying glass (= a glass which makes things look bigger): *This glass magnifies 20 diameters.* **diametrical** [Wa5;B] of, connected with, or like a diameter **-ly** [adv Wa4]: (*fig*) *He is diametrically opposed to the plan.*

arc 1 part of a curved line or circle: *The weight on the string swung through an arc of 110°.* **2** the curved path that the sun, moon, or any star appears to move along when seen from the earth

tangent a straight line which touches a circle or a curve at one point only

centre *BrE*, **center** *AmE* **1** a middle part or point; a point equally distant from all sides; the exact middle esp the point around which a circle is drawn: *Point A is the centre of the circle. Although London is the capital of Britain it is not at the centre of the country. The centre of the earth is very hot.* **2** [C9] (*fig*) a point, area, person, or thing that is most important in relation to an interest, activity, or condition: *She likes to be the centre of attraction all the time. Hull is Britain's biggest fishing centre.* **central** [Wa5;B] of or connected with a centre; in the centre **-ly** [adv]

segment 1 the area inside a circle between its edge and a straight line across it **2** the part of a line between two points on the line

circumference 1 the length round the outside of a circle or a round object: *The teacher asked the children to calculate the circumference of the circle. The earth's circumference is nearly 25,000 miles.* **2** the line round the outside edge of a figure or object

periphery [*usu sing*] **1** a line or area enclosing something; outside edge: *The factory was built on the periphery of the town.* **2** the part of a social or political group which is not near the centre of power, and is therefore of comparatively slight importance: *He is only on the periphery, so he can't have much influence.*
peripheral 1 of or connected with a periphery **2** of comparatively slight importance; not central: *matters of peripheral interest* **-ly** [adv].

perimeter 1 the border round any closed flat figure or special area of ground, esp a camp or airfield: *The perimeter of the airfield is protected by guard-dogs and a perimeter fence.* **2** the length of this: *What is the perimeter of this square?*

J47 common mathematical symbols

+	plus/and
−	minus/take away
±	plus or minus; approximately
=	equals/is equal to
≠	is not equal to; does not equal
≏	is approximately equal to
≡	is equivalent to/identical with
<	is less than
≮	is not less than
>	is greater/more than
≯	is not greater/more than
⊂	is included in; is a subset of
∈	is an element of (a set)
⊃	includes
→, ⇒, ⊃	implies
×	times/(is)multiplied by (as in $4 \times 2 = 8$); (for sizes) by (as in $22' \times 44'$)
÷	(is) divided by
%	per cent
3:9	three to nine
2:6::3:9	proportion: two is to six as three is to nine
∝	varies as; is proportional to
√	square root
∛	cube root
x^2	x squared
x^3	x cubed
x^4	x to the power of four; x to the fourth
π	pi
∠	angle
°	degree (geometry; temperature)
′	foot (as in $28'$); minute (of time; in geometry)
″	inch (as in $28'\ 11''$); second (of time; in geometry)
‖	is parallel to

J48 using and saying numbers in special combinations

1 Large numbers

It is common nowadays in *Br, US* and many other countries to use a space to separate thousands, but various conventions exist:

General
23 456 768

Br/US
23,456,768

Continental Europe etc
23.456.768

When saying such large numbers, always remember in *BrE* to put *and* after any hundred:

234   two hundred *and* thirty-four
2,345   two thousand, three hundred *and* forty-five
2,901   two thousand, nine hundred *and* one
35,897 thirty-five thousand, eight hundred *and* ninety-seven
987, 234 nine hundred *and* eighty-seven thousand, two hundred *and* thirty-four

2 Computer numbers

These are now common for business accounts and cheques, and are said in pairs, with double numbers as follows:
45673289 four-five six-seven three-two eight-nine
45663277 four-five double-six (six-six) three-two double-seven (seven-seven)

3 Telephoning

When telephoning or giving a telephone number:
(1) use only single numbers up to nine
(2) pronounce 0 as o/nought/zero
(3) give the same number as either 'double' or simply repeated: 22 double-two two-two examples:
3476 three-four seven-six
336 3562 three-three-six three-five six-two
999 (*Br* emergency number) nine-nine-nine
031-667-4567 o-three-one six-six-seven/ double-six seven four-five six-seven

4 For body measurements (See also Weights and Measures ⇒ J66)

Height (Traditional)	I am five foot eight (inches) (tall).
(Metric)	She is one metre sixty-four (centimetres).
Weight (Traditional)	*Br:* He is eleven stones five pounds.
	US: She is a hundred and twenty-six pounds.
(Metric)	He is seventy-nine kilos/kilograms.
Round the Body (for Women)	
(Traditional)	She is 36–24–36. (in.)
(Metric)	She is 91–61–91. (cent.)

5 Vulgar fractions

½ or 1/2 a half; one half [pl] halves; [T1] to halve

¼ or 1/4 a quarter; one quarter[T1] to quarter

⅓ or 1/3 a third; one third

¾ or 3/4 three-quarters

⅔ or 2/3 two-thirds

⅕ or 1/5 a fifth; one fifth

⅘ or 4/5 four-fifths

29¾   twenty-nine and three-quarters

6 Decimal fractions

.5 or 0.5 point five or (more accurately) nought point five

.75 or 0.75 point seven five or nought point seven five

23.33   twenty-three point three three

NOTE (1) In most European countries a comma is used for the Br/US decimal point. Thus, 23.33 is 23,33 in France.

(2) A point is also used for currency, but is not pronounced:

£2.50 two pound(s) fifty (pence)

$5.30 five dollars thirty; five dollars and thirty cents

Measurement

J60 *verbs* : **measuring and quantifying**

measure 1 [I0; T1] to find the size, length, amount, degree, etc (of a thing, place, person etc): *He measured her height with a ruler. The police measured the speed at which the car was travelling.* **2** [L1, 9] to be of (a certain size): *He measures more round the waist than he used to. The box measures 5 feet by 3 (about 1½ × 1 metre).* **3** [X9, esp *against*] to see if the size of (something) is right by comparing: *I measured the coat against her and found it was too long. We measured the curtains against the window and luckily they fitted.*

weigh 1 [T1] to find the weight of, esp by a machine: *He weighed himself and found that he was half a kilo heavier.* **2** [L1, 9] to have (a certain weight): *It weighed 6 pounds. I weigh less/more than I used to.* **3** [X9] (*fig*) to consider carefully: *He weighed the idea in his mind.*

quantify [T1] *fml* to measure (an amount or quantity): *Can you quantify the work done?*

J61 *nouns* : **measures and quantities**

[ALSO ⇒ N80 SIZE AND QUANTITY]

measure 1 [U] a system for calculating amount, size, weight, etc: *An ounce in liquid measure is different from an ounce in dry measure.* **2** [C] an amount in such a system: *An hour is a measure of time.* **3** [C9] an instrument or apparatus used

for calculating amount, weight, etc, esp a stick or container: *This glass is a litre measure. The tailor used a tape measure to get the man's measurements.*

measurement 1 [U] the act of measuring: *They use a different system of measurement from us.* **2** [C *esp pl*] a length, height, etc, found by measuring places, people, etc: *What are the measurements of the room/her measurements?*

mensuration [U] *math* **1** *fml* the act of measuring **2** the study and practice of measuring length, area, and volume [⇒ J65]

dimension 1 [C] a measurement esp of height, width, length, and/or thickness/depth **2** [C9 *pl*] size: *What are the dimensions of the room?* (*fig*) *The dimensions of the job are quite big; it will take a lot of work.* **3** [U] *fml* the quality of size: *Matter has dimension.*

J62 *adjectives etc* : **relating to kinds of measuring** [Wa5]

metric [B] concerning the system of measurement based on the metre and the kilogram **-ally** [adv Wa4]

cubic [B] being a measurement of the space that would fit into a cube with edges of the stated length: *The box has a volume of 10 cubic inches/feet/centimetres/metres, etc.*

imperial [A *often cap*] British standard (measures): *There are three feet in every imperial yard.*

avoirdupois [U; E] the system of weights used, esp formerly in Britain, the standard measures being the ounce, pound, and ton: *It weighs 6 ounces avoirdupois.*

troy (weight) [U; E *sometimes cap*] a British system of measuring the weight of gold, silver, and jewels: *3 pounds troy weight*

J63 *adjectives, etc* : **relating to measurement** [E]

[ALSO ⇒ N305–8]

long [Wa1; B] covering a distance: *How long is that piece of wood? It's three feet/metres long. It's a 3-foot long piece. It's a 3-metre long piece of wood.*

wide [Wa1; B] large from side to side or edge to edge: *This skirt is too wide. How wide is the road? The road is 24 feet/8 metres wide. It's an 8-metre wide road.*

broad [Wa1; B] (esp of solid things) wide; measuring a good deal from side to side or between limits: *How broad is the road? The road is 24 feet/8 metres broad.*

across [adv Wa5] from one side to the other (of): *How wide is the stream? The stream is 6 feet across.*

high [Wa1; B] (not usu of people) reaching some distance above ground, esp a large distance: *How high is the wall? The wall is 4 feet high. It is a 4-foot high wall.*

tall [Wa1;B] (of persons) having the stated height: *How tall is she? The child is four feet tall. What a tall man!*
deep [Wa1;B] **1** going far downward: *This is a deep well; it is 80 feet deep. It's an 80-foot deep well.* **2** going well inward from an outward surface: *He had a deep wound in his chest; it was several centimetres deep.* **3** going well back from a front surface: *This is a deep cupboard. It is 30 inches deep.*
thick [Wa1;B] (esp of materials) from one side to the other: *How thick is this piece of wood/this wall? It is three metres thick/three feet thick. It's a 3-metre thick wall.*

J64 *nouns* : **relating to measurement**

length 1 [U] the measurement from one end to the other or of the longest side of something **2** [S9] the distance of something stated: *We walked the length of the street.* **3** [C] the measure from one end to the other of a horse, boat, etc, used in stating distances: *The horse won by three lengths.* **4** [C (*of*)] a piece of something, esp of a certain length or for a particular purpose: *He cut me a length of string/a 5-inch length of rope.* **5** [(*the*) C] the amount of time from the beginning to the present or to the end: *The length of the holiday was 15 days.* **6** [U] the quality or condition of being long: *A book is not judged only on its length.* **7** [C] the amount of spoken, written, or printed words: *The student complained about the length of the examination paper.* **at length 1** after a long time; at last **2** for a long time; in many words **3** in great detail; thoroughly
width 1 [U] size from side to side: *What is its width?* **2** [U] the state of being wide: *We can't get it through the door because of its width.* **3** [C] a wide piece of material, esp as it was woven: *Half a width would do but they won't cut it lengthways. Two widths, please.*
breadth 1 [U;C] the distance from side to side; width: *What is the breadth of this road? The breadth is 60 feet. It is 60 feet in breadth. These roads are of different breadths.* **2** [U] (*fig*) the quality of taking everything or many things into consideration; range (as of knowledge, experience, etc): *The great breadth of Dr Smith's learning made his book the standard work on the subject.* **3** [U] (*fig*) the ability to consider other people's opinions even if different from one's own: *She is a woman of great breadth of mind/opinions.*
-ways [*comb form*] with the stated side nearest the viewer: *Look at this piece of wood lengthways/breadthways/sideways.*
height 1 [U] the quality or degree of being high or tall: *What's the height of this wall? His height makes him stand out in a crowd.* **2** [C *often pl*] a high position or place: *We looked down from a great height/the mountain heights to see the whole town below us.* **3** [(*the*) C] (*fig*) the main point; the highest degree: *Most people take*

their holidays in the height of (the) summer. It's the height of madness to sail at the height of the storm.
depth [U;C *usu sing*] the state of being deep: *What is the depth of this lake? It has a depth of 30 feet.* (*fig*) *The depth of her feelings surprised him.* **out of/beyond one's depth 1** in water that is deeper than one's height **2** beyond one's ability to understand: *I'm out of my depth when it comes to natural sciences.* **in depth 1** stretching out for some distance: *These defensive walls are built in depth.* **2** going beneath the surface appearance of things, esp if done with great thoroughness: *He made a study in depth of the poems/an in-depth study of the poems.*

J65 *nouns* : **area, etc**

[ALSO ⇒ N80 SIZE, ETC]

area 1 [C;U] the size of a surface measured by multiplying the length by the width: *The area of a room that is 10 feet by 15 feet is 150 square feet.* **2** [C] a particular space or surface: *You haven't cleaned the area under the table.* **3** [C] a part or division of the world, esp the one around one's home: *There aren't many wild birds in this area. This farming area produces good vegetables. I sell things in the area north of the big city. I am the area salesman for that part of the country.* **4** [C] (*fig*) a range, as of ideas, work, or activity; a subject or specialist field: *There have been many developments in the area of language teaching.*
mass [U] (in science) the amount of matter in a body, measured by the power used in changing its movement
volume [U] **1** size or quantity thought of as measurement of the space inside or filled by something: *The volume of this container is 100,000 cubic metres. The volume of water in the pan decreased when he boiled it.* **2** (degree of) fullness or loudness of sound: *He likes to listen to music with the radio turned on at full volume. The television is too loud; turn the volume down.*
weight 1 [U] the heaviness of anything, esp as measured by a certain system: *She never eats and is losing weight.* **2** [U] *tech* the force with which any body is drawn towards the centre of the earth: *The weight of an object is related to the force of gravity*, [⇒L9], *which is fixed, and to its mass.* **3** [C] a piece of metal of one of several standard weights which can be balanced against any substance to measure an equal weight of that substance: *This is a one-pound weight.* **4** [C] a heavy object used for holding something down: *We spread the map on the ground, putting stones as weights on each corner.* **5** [U] a system of standard measures of weight **6** [U] (*fig*) value or importance: *This is an idea which bears weight with us.* **7** [C] (something with) a large amount of weight: *It's not sensible to lift weights after an operation.*

8 [C] (*fig*) (something giving) a sense of worry or anxiety: *The loss of the money is a weight on my mind.* **weighted** [B] having a weight on; having had a heavy material added: *Fishing nets are weighted.*

capacity [C; U9] the amount that something can hold or produce: *The seating capacity of the theatre is 500. The capacity of the tank is 20 gallons/litres.*

liquid measure [U] **1** the system of units used in measuring the capacity of liquids **2** *tech* the cubic contents or volume, esp of liquid; the system by which this is measured

J66 weights and measures

Traditional British and American	Metric Equivalent
Length/Distance	
1 inch (in)	2.54 cm
12 inches = 1 foot (ft)	30.48 cm
3 feet = 1 yard (yd)	0.91 m
220 yards = 1 furlong	201.17 m
old use & tech	
1760 yards = 1 mile (ml)	1.61 m
8 furlongs	
Square Measure/Area	
1 square inch (sq in)	6.45 sq cm
1 square mile (sq ml)	2.59 sq km
100 sq ml	roughly 260 sq km
1 acre/4840 sq yd (for land measurement)	0.45 hectares
Weight/Mass	
1 ounce (oz)	28.35 grams
16 ounces = 1 pound (lb)	0.45 kg
14 pounds = 1 stone (st)	6.35 kg
8 stones = 1 hundredweight (cwt)	50.80 kg
20 cwt/2240 lb = 1 ton	1016 kg
Special US Weights	
100 pounds = 1 (short) hundredweight	45.36 kg
2000 pounds = 1 (short) ton	907.18 kg
20 (short) cwt	
Liquid Measure/Capacity (Br)	
1 gill	0.14 litres
4 gills = 1 pint (pt)	0.57 litres
2 pints = 1 quart (qt)	1.14 litres
8 pt/4 qt = 1 gallon (gal)	4.54 litres
Liquid Measure/Capacity (US)	
1 US liquid gill	0.118 litres
4 gills = 1 US liquid pint	0.473 litres
2 pints = 1 US liquid quart	0.946 litres
4 quarts = 1 US gallon	3.785 litres

J67 weights and measures : the metric system

Notes

1 The Latin compounding elements **deci-** (ten), **centi-** (hundred), and **milli-** (thousand) are used for fractions of a metric unit: one tenth, one hundredth, and one thousandth respectively.

2 The Greek compounding elements **deca-** (ten), **hecto-** (hundred), and **kilo-** (thousand) are used for multiplications of a metric unit; ten times, a hundred times, and a thousand times respectively. **Mega-** stands for a million times.

Metric Tables	Traditional Equivalent
Length/Distance	
1 centimetre (cm)	0.39 inches/ of an inch
100 cm = 1 metre (m)	39.37 inches
1000 metres = 1 kilometre (*BrE*) km kilometer (*AmE*)	0.62 of a mile/ 0.62 miles
Square Measure/Area	
1 square centimetre (sq cm)	0.155 square inches
1 square metre (sq cm)	1.196 square yards
1 hectare (for land measurement (ha)	2.47 acres
100 hectares	247 acres
Weight/Mass	
1 gram(me) (g/gm)	0.035 ounces
1 kilogram (kg)	2.205 pounds
1 tonne/metric ton (MT/t)	2204.6 pounds
1000 kilograms	0.984 of a ton/ tons (*Br*), 1.1 (*US*)
Liquid Measure/Capacity	
1 litre (1)	1.75 pints (*Br*), 1.057 quarts (*US*)
1 hectolitre = 100 litres	21.99 gallons (*Br*), 26.4 (*US*)

USAGE In writing abbreviations of weights and measures, many people add an 's' for plurals: **ozs, lbs, cms,** etc, for **oz, lb, cm.** In US spelling all -**tre** forms are -**ter: meter, liter,** etc. For measurement of volume, **cubic** is generally used in both systems: **cubic inches, cubic centimetres,** etc.

J68 *nouns* : **miles, knots, and acres**

mile [C] **1** (a measure of length or distance equal to) 1609 metres or 1760 yards: *A fast walker can walk 4 miles an hour. He has a 20-mile drive/a 10 miles' drive each day to and from his work. They walked for miles* (= a very long way) *without seeing a house.* **2** [*usu pl*] (*fig*) *infml* a very long way; a great deal: *He was miles out in his calculations* (= they were completely wrong). *This book is miles too difficult for a boy of his age. There's no one within miles of him/within a mile of him as a cricketer* (= he is the best one).

nautical mile [C] $\frac{1}{60}$ of a degree or 1,853 metres (= 6,080 feet), the measure of distance (and speed) used at sea

knot [C] a measure of the speed of a ship: *That ship can do 20 knots* (= is able to sail at 20 nautical miles an hour). *The ship was going at a good rate of knots* (= going fast).

fathom [C] a unit of measurement of the depth of water (= 6 feet; 1.8 metres): *The sunken ship lay at a depth of 20 fathoms/lay 20 fathoms deep.*

mileage [U] **1** the distance that is travelled or measured in miles: *How much mileage has that car done? His annual mileage is 10,000 miles* (= he drives 10,000 miles in a year). (*fig*) *You won't get much mileage out of him* (= He won't help you much). **2** *also* **mileage allowance** money paid for travelling on business at so much a mile: *When I use my car on business I get paid mileage; 10p a mile.*

acre [C] a measure of land; 4840 square yards or about 4047 square metres: *A full-sized football field measures a little more than 2 acres.*

Money

J80 *nouns, etc* : **money and finance**

money [U] **1** pieces of metal made into coins, or paper notes with their value printed on them, given and taken in buying and selling: *He doesn't usually carry much money on him* (= in his pockets). **2** wealth: *Money doesn't always bring happiness. He made his money* (= became rich) *buying and selling land for house building. He lost all his money when his business company failed.* **in the money** *infml* in a position where one can gain a great deal of wealth: *If this old picture of ours really is by a famous artist, we're in the money.* **one's money's worth** full value for the money one has spent: *We enjoyed the film so much that we felt we'd got our money's worth.* **pay good money (for something)** *infml* to pay a high price (for something): *Look after that watch your father gave you; he paid good money for it.* **put money into** to lend money to people starting or controlling (a business), in the hope of getting good interest

cash [U] **1** money in coins and notes, rather than cheques: *I've no cash on me, can I pay you tomorrow?* **2** *infml* money in any form: *If I had more cash I'd go round the world.* **cash down** payment made for goods in the form of notes and coins before the goods leave the shop.

currency [C; U] the particular type of money in use in a country: *The German currency is one of the strongest currencies in the world. How much currency may one take out of the country? How much foreign currency do you take with you when you go abroad?*

fund 1 [C] a supply or sum of money set apart for a special purpose: *Part of the school sports fund will be used for improving the condition of the football field.* **2** [C *usu sing*] (*fig*) a store or supply (of non-material things) ready for use as needed: *When explaining a new point to a class, it helps a teacher to have a fund of good examples to make his meaning clear.* **3** [T1 *usu pass*] to provide money for (an activity, organization, etc): *The scientists' search for a cure for this disease is being funded by the government.*

funds [P] money in one's possession, ready for use: *Our company's losses are being repaid out of government funds. I'm in funds just now* (= have plenty of money to spend). *By the end of the week I usually get a bit short of funds* (= without much money).

finance [U] money, esp of a government or large business: *Do you have enough finance for this job?*

finances [P] *genl* money as it is used: *What state are his finances in? The country's finances are not good.*

kitty [S] a sum of money collected by a group of people and used for an agreed purpose (esp in card games, taken by the winner): *How much money is left in the kitty?*

J81 *nouns* : **coins and change**

coin 1 [C] a piece of metal, usu flat and round, made by a government for use as money: *We don't use gold coins any more. In Britain we use a coin for 50 pence, not a note.* **2** [U] such pieces collectively: *He paid me in coin.*

coinage [U] **1** the act of making coins: *Only the government has the right of coinage today.* **2** metal coins collectively; currency: *What sort of coinage do they use in France?* **3** the coins made by coining

token [C] **1** a piece of metal used instead of coins for a particular purpose: *The council gives old people free tokens with which they can pay for journeys on buses.* **2** a receipt, usu fixed to a greetings card, which one can exchange for the stated thing in a shop: *My aunt sent me a record token for my birthday. He gave her a gift token*

(= that one can exchange for anything in a particular shop).

note *esp BrE*, **bill** *esp AmE* [C] a piece of paper money: *He gave her a pound note/a ten-pound note. Have you change for a dollar bill? How much of the money is in notes and how much in coin/ cash?*

banknote [C] a piece of paper money printed for the national bank of a country for public use

denomination [C] a standard of quantity, size, measurement, or esp value: *The banknotes were in denominations of five, ten, and twenty pounds.*

change [U] **1** coins of low value: *Have you got any change in your pockets? How much have you got in change?* **2** money in low value coins or notes exchanged for a coin or note of higher value: *Can you give me change for £5?* **3** the money returned when the amount given is more than the cost of the goods being bought: *If it cost 25 pence and you gave her a pound you should get 75 pence change. You've given me too much change by mistake!*

small change [U] coins, esp of low value: *I don't have any small change, only notes.*

J82 nouns : cheques and credits

cheque *BrE*, **check** *AmE* **1** [C; *by* U] a written order to a bank, usu made on a specially printed sheet of paper supplied by the bank, to pay a certain sum of money from one's bank account to another person: *I'd like to pay by cheque, please, rather than in cash.* **2** [C] a small printed sheet of paper supplied to a customer by a bank, on which such an order can be written: *Can you please let me have 30 cheques?* **crossed cheque** *esp BrE* [C] a cheque which must be put into a bank account before being paid   **cheque book** *BrE*, **check-** *AmE* [C] a book of new cheques supplied by a bank to a person who keeps money in the bank.

draft [C; *by* U] a written order for money to be paid by a bank, esp from one bank to another: *They made a draft on the Glasgow branch of the bank for £50 for Mr Smith. He got money from Paris to Rome by draft.*

order [C *often in comb*] a written or printed paper which allows the holder something, such as to be paid money, to see a house that is for sale, etc: *I have an order on the Bank of Scotland/an order to see the house.*

postal order *BrE* [C] an official paper of a certain value that one person can buy from a post office and send to another person, who can then take it to any post office and get the amount of money the first person paid for it

money order [C] **1** *BrE* an official paper, like a postal order but higher in value **2** *AmE* a postal order

J83 nouns : British money

Old British currency
(£ s d = pounds, shillings, and pence)

4 farthings	= 1 penny (1d)
12 pennies/pence	= 1 shilling (1/–)
20 shillings	= 1 pound (£1)
21 shillings	= 1 guinea (1gn)

New British decimal currency
(£ p = pounds and pence)

1 penny (p)	
100 pence	= 1 pound (£1 or £1.00)

halfpenny *also* **ha'penny** [C] **1** *also infml* **half p** (in Great Britain after 1971) a very small copper and tin (**bronze**) coin, two of which make a (new) penny; ½p **2** (in Great Britain before 1971) a bronze coin, two of which made a penny

penny 1 [C] *also* **new penny**, *infml* **p** (in Great Britain after 1971) a small bronze coin, 100 of which make a pound **2** [C] (in Great Britain before 1971) a bronze coin, 12 of which made a shilling; 1d **3** [S] a small amount of money: *The journey won't cost you a penny if you come in my car.*

NOTE In Great Britain, the USA, and Canada, the pl **pennies** is used when speaking or writing of the coins themselves, not as an amount of money: *He had a number of coins in his pocket, but no pennies.* The pl **pence** or **p** is used when speaking or writing about an amount of money: *It will only cost a few pence,* and esp when combined with a number, to name a particular amount of money that is more than 1 penny: *six pence; 10p* -**penny** [*comb form*] costing (the stated number of) pence: *a four-penny stamp*

sixpence [C] (in Great Britain until 1971) a coin worth six old pennies; 6d: *Have you got any sixpences to put in this machine?*

shilling [C] **1** (in Great Britain until 1971) a coin equal to 12 pence and 1/20 of £1: *£1 6s 3d = £1/6/3 = 1 pound six shillings and 3 pence.* **2** a coin worth this amount, now 5 decimal pence; *infml* a 5p coin

florin [C] (in Great Britain until 1971) a coin worth two shillings (= 10 pence)

crown [C] *formerly* a coin of value, esp a British coin worth 5 shillings or a quarter of a pound

half crown, half a crown [C] (in Great Britain until 1971) a coin worth two shillings and six-pence

pound 1 [C] the standard of money in several countries: *He bought Egyptian pounds.* **2** [*the* R] *also* **sterling** [U] the British money system **3** [*the* R] the value at any particular time of the British pound at international money exchange rate: *The pound rose yesterday* (= gained in value).

sovereign (in Great Britain formerly) a gold coin worth one pound but now having much greater value esp to collectors, etc, although not used as money

J84 *informal nouns* : **British money** [C]

copper a coin of low value made of the metals copper and tin; a penny
tanner a sixpence
bob [Wn3] a former coin, the shilling (= 5p): *It'll cost you four bob.*
quid [Wn3] a pound (in money)
fiver £5 or a 5-pound note
tenner £10 or a 10-pound note

J85 *nouns* : **North American money** [C]

US currency
  1 cent (1¢)
  5 cents = 1 nickel
  10 cents = 1 dime
  25 cents = 1 quarter
100 cents = 1 dollar ($1 or $1.00)
cent .01 of any of certain money standards, such as the dollar: *That will cost you 50 cents. Have you got a 5-cent coin?*
penny (in the US and Canada) (a coin worth) a cent
dollar 1 [*usu sing*] any of various standards of money, as used in the US, Canada, Australia, New Zealand, Hong Kong, etc. It is worth 100 cents and its sign is $: *What is the (American) dollar worth today?* **2** a piece of paper, a coin, etc, of this value: *He had a silver dollar.*

J86 *informal nouns* : **North American money** [C]

bit 12½ cents (*esp in the phr* **two bits**) (= 25 cents or a quarter): *I wouldn't give him two bits for that old book!*
buck a dollar: *How much does it cost?—Twenty bucks.*
greenback a dollar bill
grand [Wn3] 1,000 dollars

J87 *nouns* : **some other currencies** [C]

mark	(West) Germany
franc	France, Switzerland, Belgium, and many countries that formerly belonged to France
yen [Wn3]	Japan
peseta	Spain
lira	Italy
guilder, florin	the Netherlands

J88 *verbs* : **changing and converting money** [T1]

change (of a person or organization) to give and receive (one kind of money for another): *Can I*
change my British money for French money here? Where can we change our money?
exchange *more fml* (of a person or organization) to give and receive (something in return for something else): *Where can I exchange my dollars for pounds?*
convert *fml & tech* to change (money): *He converted all his dollars into yen.*

J89 *nouns* : **exchange rates, etc**

exchange rate *also* **rate of exchange** [C] the value of the money of one country compared to that of another country: *What is the exchange rate of the pound today?*
foreign exchange [U] money which a country, organization, or person has which belongs to countries other than his own: *How much foreign exchange do you have? Many countries are short of* (= don't have much) *foreign exchange.*
hard currency [U; C] **1** money based on gold, usu the US dollar **2** a currency which is based on a successful economy: *The Swiss franc is (a) hard currency.*

J90 *verbs* : **gaining and losing value**

appreciate [I0] to increase in value: *Houses in this area have all appreciated (in value) since the new road was built.*
depreciate [I0] to fall in value: *The value of houses seldom depreciates.*
gain *also* **rise** [I0] to become more in value: *The pound gained/rose against the dollar yesterday.*
lose *also* **fall 1** [T1] to fail to keep (part of a value): *The pound lost one cent against the dollar today.* **2** [I0] to become less in value: *The pound lost/fell against the dollar yesterday.*

J91 *nouns* : **gaining and losing value**

appreciation [U; S] a rise in value, esp of land or possessions: *There has been an appreciation in property values of 50% in 3 years.*
depreciation [U; S] a fall in value, esp of land or possessions: *The depreciation in the value of a car is greatest in its first year.*
gain *also* **rise** an increase in value: *There has been a gain/rise of 2 cents in the value of the pound against the dollar.*
loss *also* **fall** [C] a decrease in value: *There has been a loss/fall of 2 cents in the value of the pound against the dollar.*

J92 *verbs* : **inflation, etc**

inflate [T1 *usu pass*] to cause (a country's money) to increase in amount and therefore decrease in value: *The currency is inflated and is losing value.*

deflate [T1; I0] to reduce the supply of money (of) or lower the level of prices (of): *We must deflate (the economy) without producing unemployment.*

reflate [T1; I0] to increase the supply of money in (a money system) to a normal or desirable level

float 1 [T1] to allow the exchange value of (a country's money) to vary freely from day to day: *By floating the pound the British Government hoped to improve Britain's trading position.* **2** [I0] (of a country's money) to vary freely in exchange value from day to day: *The pound floated (up/down).*

devalue [T1; I0] to make the value of (money) less: *We had to devalue (our money) last year.*

revalue [T1] **1** to make (the value of money) more, esp in relation to gold: *The US Government revalued the dollar.* **2** to find or say again the value of: *They revalued their possessions for insurance purposes.*

J93 *nouns* : **inflation, etc** [U]

inflation the rise in prices thought to be caused by increases in the cost of production (**cost–push inflation**) or an increase in the money supply (**demand–pull inflation**) **inflationary** [B] of or likely to cause inflation

deflation a decrease in the amount of money (esp money to be lent) which is meant to produce lower prices

reflation the official practice of increasing the amount of money to a desirable level in relation to the amount of goods, in order to improve industrial activity

devaluation an official reduction in the exchange value of money by a lowering of its price in relation to the money of other countries or (esp in the past) in gold

depression *also* **recession** [C; U] a period of lowered business activity and high unemployment: *Many people still remember the great depression of the 1930s. We have suffered a mild recession in trade, but things are better now.*

Banking, wealth, and investment

J100 *verbs* : **lending and borrowing**

lend 1 [D1 (*to*); T1] to give (someone) the possession or use of (something, such as money or a car) for a limited time: *Could you lend me your car?* **2** [D1 (*to*); T1] to supply (someone) with (something) on condition that it or something like it will be returned later: *As the shops are shut I'll lend you some bread.* **3** [D1 (*to*); T1] to give out (money) for profit, esp as a business **4** [T1] (*fig*) to add or give: *The many*

flags lent colour to the streets. The presence of the King lent importance to the occasion. I lent the old woman my arm as she couldn't walk easily.

loan [D1 (*to*)] *esp AmE* to give someone the use of; to lend: *He loaned me the money. I loaned it to him.*

borrow 1 [T1; I0] to take or receive (something) for a certain time and with intention to return: *He borrowed (£5) from a friend. I'll borrow a book from a library.* **2** [T1] *euph* to take without permission: *Somebody seems to have borrowed my watch when I wasn't looking.* **3** [T1; I0] (*fig*) to take or copy (esp ideas, words, etc): *English has borrowed (words) from many languages.*

owe 1 [D1 (*to*); T1] to have to pay: *He owes (me) (£20) (for my work).* **2** [T1 (*to*); (D1)] to have to give: *We owe loyalty to our country.* **3** [D1 (*to*)] to feel grateful (to) for: *We owe our parents a lot.* **owe to** [v prep D1] to admit as the cause, discoverer, or point of origin of: *She owes her wealth to hard work and good luck. We owe that important new discovery to Einstein. We owe it to Marconi and Bell that we can now talk to people on the other side of the world.*

pay back [v adv D1 (*to*); T1] to return (esp borrowed money) to (someone): *I'll lend you £5 if you'll pay me back tomorrow. Don't lend anything to him; he never pays it back.*

repay [D1 (*to*); T1] *esp fml & tech* to pay back: *When can you repay the money I lent you?* (*fig*) *I can never repay you for all the things you have done for me. He repaid her love with hate.*

finance [T1] to provide & supply money for (something or someone doing something): *Who is financing this new business?*

J101 *adjectives, etc* : **lending and borrowing** [Wa5]

due 1 [F] *fml* owed or owing as a debt or right: *A great deal of money is due to you. Our grateful thanks are due to you.* **2** [A] *fml* proper; suitable; enough: *He drove with due care and attention.* **3** [prep] *esp AmE* owed or owing as a debt or right to: *A great deal of money is due you.*

overdue [B] **1** left unpaid too long: *This bill is (long) overdue. You must pay these overdue bills.* **2** [*also* E] later than expected: *The train is 15 minutes overdue.*

outstanding [B] still to be done or paid: *There are a number of outstanding bills (to be paid). These bills have been outstanding for some months.*

J102 *nouns* : **lending and borrowing**
[ALSO ⇒ J148, 150]

loan [C] **1** something which is lent: *The book is a loan, not a gift.* **2** an amount of money lent: *He* *got a £1,000 loan from the bank.* **3** the act of lending: *He got the loan of a book from a friend.* **on loan** being borrowed, as a book is from a library: *These books are on loan.*

repayment 1 [U] the act of repaying: *Repayment of the loan must be made soon.* **2** [C] an example of this: *Can I pay you back in several repayments?*

debt 1 [C; U] something owed to someone else: *He owed a debt of £10.* (*fig*) *I owe you a debt of gratitude* (= must be thankful) *for your help.* **2** [U] the state of owing; the duty of repaying that which is owed (*often in phrs like* **in debt; out of debt**): *He was in debt when he was poor but has been out of debt since he got rich. I am in debt to you for £10/your help.* **run into debt** to begin to owe money

due [C] something owing to someone or which someone deserves: *Have you paid your dues yet* (= what you must pay)? (*fig*) *Give him his due; he worked hard* (= Accept that he worked hard).

arrears [P] **1** money that is owed and should have been paid: *Your arrears for rent add up to a large sum.* **2** work that is still waiting to be done **in arrears 1** in the state of owing money, esp for something that should be paid regularly: *I am in arrears with my rent.* **2** (esp of money) being owed: *My rent is in arrears.*

overdraft [C] a payment to a person by a bank of more than that person has in the bank: *We've given her an overdraft of £100.*

credit [U] **1** a system of buying goods or services when they are wanted and paying for them later: *If you have difficulties getting the money for something you want now, you can always buy it on credit.* **2** time given in the future for payment of goods bought at the present time: *He gave us a year's credit but no more.*

deposit [C usu sing] a part payment of money, which is made so that the seller will not sell the goods to anyone else: *You must pay a deposit to the hotel if you want them to keep a room free for you. The deposit on the car was £500.*

J103 *nouns* : **persons lending money** [C]

lender a person lending (money, etc) to another person

moneylender *sometimes deprec* a person who lends money and charges interest on it, usu at a high rate

banker a person who owns or controls or shares in the control of a bank, and lends money to other persons, to organizations, etc

financier someone who controls or lends large sums of money [also ⇒ J80]

debtor a person who owes money

creditor a person or firm to whom money is owed

J104 *nouns* : **banks, etc** [C]

bank 1 a place in which money is kept and paid out on demand and where related activities go on **2** [C9] (*fig*) a place where something is held ready for use, esp organic products of human origin for medical use: *Hospital blood banks have saved many lives.* **3** (a person who keeps) a supply of money or pieces for payment or use in a game of chance **bankbook** *also* **passbook** a book given by a bank and kept by a person as a record of money put in and taken out of the bank **bank draft** *also* **banker's draft, bank bill** an order by one bank to another (esp a foreign bank) to pay a certain sum of money to someone

giro (in Britain) a system of banking in which a central organization runs the accounts, which are held at different branches, esp that used by the Post Office (**National Giro**)

exchange [C9 *often cap*] a place where business men and traders meet to buy and sell (goods of the stated type): *They sell corn at the Corn Exchange and shares in companies at the Stock Exchange.*

safe a box or cupboard with thick metal sides and a lock, sometimes built as part of a wall, used for protecting valuable things from theft and fire: *Put the money in the safe.*

strongbox a box made for keeping money and other things of value: *Put the money in the strongbox.*

strongroom a room esp in a bank, like a large safe, for keeping money

vault [*often pl*] an underground strongroom, esp for keeping money, esp in a bank

treasury 1 a place where money and other valuable things are kept **2** [*the* GU] a department of government that collects and pays out government money

J105 *nouns* : **accounts in banks, etc** [C]

account 1 a sum of money which may be added to and taken from, placed in a bank, etc; an arrangement with a bank etc for putting in and taking out money: *She has an account with us/a bank account. My account is empty.* **2** a statement of money owed: *I haven't paid last month's account from the shop. Will you add the cost to my account as I haven't any money with me?* (*fig*) *I have an account to settle with you for calling me a thief!* **3** a record or statement of money received and paid out, as by a bank or business, esp for a particular period or at a particular date: *The bank sends me an account/statement each month. The accounts show we have spent more than we received.*

current account *BrE,* **checking account** *AmE* a bank account which usu does not earn interest and from which money can be taken out at any time by cheque

deposit account *BrE* a bank account which

earns interest and from which money can be taken out at any time

savings account 1 *BrE* a bank account which earns interest and from which money can be taken out only if advance notice is given **2** *AmE* a deposit account

credit account *BrE*, **charge account** *AmE* an account with a shop which allows one to take goods at once and pay for them in the future/later: *He has a credit account with/at Harrod's.*

expense account the record of money spent on travel, hotels, etc, in the course of one's work, which will be paid by one's employer: *I'll charge the meal to my expense account.*

statement *also fml* **statement of account** a list showing amounts of money paid, received, owing, etc, and their total, esp in a bank account, etc: *I get a statement from my bank every month.*

J106 *verbs* : banking and saving

bank 1 [T1] to put or keep (money) in a bank: *It's better to bank your money than to keep it at home.* **2** [L9] to keep one's money (esp in the stated bank): *Where do you bank? I bank with The Royal Bank.*

deposit [T1] **1** to place in a bank or strongbox: *He's deposited quite a lot of money recently.* **2** to pay (part of a sum due) as a sign that the rest will be paid later: *I was asked to deposit £10 on a £60 suit and pay the rest in a month's time.*

save 1 [I∅] to keep and add to an amount of money for later use: *Children should learn to save. We're saving (up) for a new car.* **2** [D1; T1] to keep and not spend or use, as for a special purpose or for use later: *It'll save me 50p if I buy the large-size box. He saved his strength for an effort in the last minute of the race. It will save time if we drive the car instead of walking.*

save up [v adv T1; I∅] to save (money) esp for a purpose: *I'm saving up (my money/£5 a week) to buy her a present. He's saving up for a holiday.*

put away/by [v adv T1] *not fml* to save (esp money) for later use: *He has a good sum of money put away (in the bank) for his old age. Put it away for later.*

put aside [v adv T1] to save (esp part of a sum of money) for a special use: *Put aside £5 a week for your holiday.*

J107 *verbs* : paying in and investing money

pay in [v adv T1; (I∅)] to put (money) in a bank, special account, etc: *He paid the money in yesterday. Have you paid in yet?*

pay [X9, esp *into*] to put (a form of money) (into a bank, an account, etc) for safe-keeping: *He paid the cheque into his wife's account.*

invest [T1; I∅] to put (money) in a business where it will gain interest: *He invested £100. You should invest instead of wasting your money. Invest your money in/with the bank.*

speculate [I∅ (*in*)] to invest, buy, or sell goods, shares [⇒ J114], etc, in the hope of making a profit quickly: *He likes speculating in property.* **speculation** [U; C] the act or result of speculating **speculator** [C] a person who speculates

J108 *verbs* : drawing out and cashing money

draw 1 [X9; (T1)] to take (money) from a bank or other such place: *He drew some money from his account. He drew a lot of money out.* **2** [T1] (of money, business shares, etc) to earn: *His money is drawing interest in the bank.* **3** [T1] to prepare (esp a cheque) properly: *He drew a cheque on his New York bank.*

withdraw [T1] to take away or back (esp money in a bank): *He withdrew £50 from his bank account.*

take out [v adv T1] *not fml* to withdraw: *How much money did she take out of her account last week?*

cash [D1 (*for*); T1] to exchange (a cheque or other order to pay) for cash: *Cash me this, please. Can you cash this postal order for that old lady, please? Where can I get this cashed?*

encash [T1] *fml, pomp & old use* to cash: *He encashed the cheques.*

overdraw [T1] to be paid by a bank more money than one has in the bank: *Last week he overdrew by £5,000.*

J109 *verbs* : crediting and debiting [T1]

[ALSO ⇒ J152]

credit [(*with*)] **1** to enter in the right-hand or credit side of (an account): *Credit Mr Smith/Mr Smith's account with £10.* **2** to note that (a person) has received a sum of money: *Today we credited him with £100.*

debit 1 to enter in the left-hand or debit side of (an account): *Debit £10 against Mr Smith/Mr Smith's account.* **2** note that (a person) has had a sum of money taken out of his account: *Debit Mr Smith/Mr Smith's account with £10.*

deduct to take (an amount, a part) from a total: *Please deduct £1 a week from his wages until he has repaid all he owes us.* [also ⇒ J32]

take off [v adv] *infml* to deduct: *Take £5 off until he has paid back the loan.*

J110 *nouns* : credit and debit

credit 1 [U] (the amount of) money in a person's account, as at a bank **2** [U] the quality of being likely to repay debts and be honest with money: *His credit is good; you can trust him.*

3 [C] a record (in a book of accounts) of money received   **credit side** [C] the right-hand side of an account book on which credits are listed

debit [C] a record (in a book of accounts) of money spent or owed   **debit side** [C] the left-hand side of an account book on which debits are listed

J111 *nouns* : **persons working in a bank** [C]

teller *esp AmE* a person employed to receive and pay out money in a bank

clerk a person employed in a bank, office, shop, etc, to keep records, accounts, etc, and to do written work

cashier a person in charge of money receipts and payments in a bank, hotel, shop, etc

J112 *nouns* : **interest on money** [U]

interest 1 the money paid by a business, bank, etc, to someone who has lent an amount of money for their use **2** the same money when paid to the business by someone who has borrowed an amount of money

simple interest interest calculated on an original sum of money without first adding in the interest already earned

compound interest interest calculated on the original sum of money lent or borrowed and on all the unpaid interest already earned

J113 *nouns* : **savings and capital**

savings [P] money saved esp as in a bank: *Our savings aren't big enough yet to buy a good car.*

capital 1 [U] wealth, esp when used to produce more wealth; the machines, buildings, and goods used in a business: *'We must understand the difference between* **fixed capital** (= machinery, factories) *and* **circulating capital** (= half-finished goods),' *said the teacher.* **2** [S; U] (a sum of) money used for starting a business: *This business was started with a capital of £10,000. To be really successful, we need more capital than we've got.* **3** [S; U] *infml* (a sum of) money: *He saved every week and after 20 years had a capital of £10,000. My friend has enough capital to buy a house.*

investment [U] the act of investing [⇒ J107]

stock [U; C *often in comb*] money invested in a business, the work of a government, etc: *He bought a lot of government stock. He buys and sells stocks and shares.*

J114 *nouns* : **investments, shares, and securities**

investment [C] something, esp money, invested [⇒ J107], or in which one invests: *His investments in that business have done well. These shares are a good investment.* (*fig*) *Some people*

say children are a good investment against loneliness when one is old.

share 1 [C] any of the equal parts into which the ownership of a company may be divided: *He owns 50 shares in the business. They paid a dividend of 50p per share.* **2** [A] *BrE* of or concerning shares: *Share prices rose in heavy trading.* **3** [C; U] the part belonging or due to, or done by, a person: *If you want a share in/of the pay, you'll have to do your fair share of the work. The government must take a large share of the blame for the failure of the plan.*

premium [C] **1** an additional payment, esp to a worker, made as a reward for special efforts: *We're paying each salesman a £20 premium for each of last year's cars he sells, because we want to get rid of them.* **2** an additional charge made for something: *There's a premium of $10 for a seat on this special fast train.* **at a premium 1** (of a business share) at a rate above the usual value: *Our business is so successful this year that shares in it are now selling at a premium.* **2** rare or difficult to obtain and therefore worth more than usual: *During the holiday months of July and August hotel rooms are at a premium.*

put a premium on to cause (a quality or action) to be an advantage: *Work paid according to the amount done puts a premium on speed and not on quality.* [also ⇒ J159]

bond [C *often cap*] a paper in which a government or an industrial firm promises to pay back with interest money that has been lent (invested): *He bought 7½% National Savings Bonds. In Britain people can buy Premium Bonds from the Post Office.*

dividend [C] **1** the part of the money made by a business which is shared among those who have shares in it (**shareholders**) **2** the amount which each shareholder receives   **pay dividends** produce an advantage; be useful (in the future): *Learning French has paid dividends; I have a much better job now.*

security 1 [U] property of value promised to a lender in case repayment is not made or other conditions are not met: *He offered his house as security for the loan.* **2** [C *usu pl*] a paper, esp a bond or piece of stock, giving the owner the right to some property: *He trades in government securities.*

asset [C] **1** [*usu pl*] something such as a house or furniture, that has value and that may be sold to pay a debt: *What assets does he have?— None; no assets at all.* **2** (*fig*) a valuable quality or skill: *Intelligence was her main asset.*

stake [C] any great interest or share in something, esp if money, etc, is involved: *What stake does he have in the business?— He has a 20% stake. She has a big stake in everything he does.* [also ⇒ K122]

J115 *nouns* : **funds and trusts**

fund [C] a supply of money set apart for such purposes as investing [⇒ J107]: *This fund is* used to invest in new businesses in the United States. *The company has a pension fund* (= a fund for pensions, money to be used when a person is too old to work) *for all its employees.*

trust 1 [C] a group of people holding and controlling money or property for the advantage of others **2** [C] a property or sum of money held and controlled by someone or a group of people for the advantage of someone else: *The money isn't mine; it's a trust I'm holding for my youngest brother.* **3** [U] the act of holding and controlling property or money for the advantage of someone else: *The money will be held in trust for you until you're 21.*

unit trust *BrE*, **mutual fund** *AmE* [C] a company formed to control investments of many different types

J116 *adjectives* : **having money, etc**

rich [Wa1;B] **1** (of people) possessing a lot of money or property: *She is one of the richest women in the world.* **2** [(*in*)] possessing a lot (of the stated thing): *This fish is rich in oil. The city is rich in ancient buildings.* **3** (of possessions) costly, valuable, and beautiful: *What rich furniture!* **4** [*the* P] rich people: *The rich are not always generous to the poor.* **-ly** [adv] **-ness** [U]

wealthy 1 [Wa1;B] (of a person) rich: *He's a very wealthy man.* **2** [*the* P] wealthy people

prosperous [B] doing well in business, life, etc; wealthy: *The little town looked very prosperous. He is a prosperous local businessman.* **-ly** [adv]

well-off [Wa2;B] *infml* (of a person) rich: *He's pretty well-off for money, but they are even better-off. They are very well-off people.*

in credit having money in the bank, enough or more than enough to pay for what one buys, does, etc: *I'm in credit at the moment.* (*fig*) *He's very much in credit* (*with her*) *at the moment* (= She likes him).

solvent [B] able to pay for what one buys, does, etc; not in debt [⇒ J120]: *She's quite solvent; she can buy a new car.* **solvency** [U] the condition of being solvent

comfortable [B] fairly rich; not poor: *We're comfortable, but can't afford to buy some of the things we would like.* **-ably** [adv Wa3]: *They live comfortably on his income.* **comfortably off** fairly rich: *They're comfortably off; they can afford a new car every year.*

affluent [B] having plenty of money or other possessions; wealthy: *An affluent society is one in which a lot of its members have plenty of money and are keen on having possessions.* **affluence** [U] the condition of being affluent

J117 *nouns* : **having money, etc**

riches [P] things that make one rich, esp money, property, etc: *All his riches are no good to him*

if he is so ill. (*fig*) *The riches of English poetry are well-known.*

wealth *esp emot* **1** [U] (a large amount of) money and possessions: *His great wealth has not changed him. He is a man of wealth.* **2** [S (*of*)] a large number: *He provided us with a wealth of examples.*

prosperity [U] the condition of being prosperous; wealth: *His present prosperity is due to working hard in the past.*

fortune [C] wealth; a great amount of money, possessions, etc: *Some men have made great fortunes by developing oilfields. The jewels that the rich woman was wearing last night must be worth a fortune. He came into a fortune when his rich aunt died.* (*fig*) *Her face is her fortune* (= her (good) looks mean that she can earn a lot of money). **a small fortune** *infml* a lot of money: *Those jewels must have cost a small fortune.*

luxury 1 [U] great ease and comfort, as provided without worry about the cost: *He lived in luxury. They led a life of luxury. They lived in a luxury flat.* **2** [C] something that is not necessary and not often had or done but which is very pleasant: *This fruit is a real luxury at this time of year. Sleeping in a warm bed was a luxury for the poor man.*

treasure 1 [U;C] a collection of valuable things, metals, money, jewels, etc: *They say that there is buried treasure on this island.* **2** [C] something one values very much: *His books are his greatest treasure(s).* **3** [C] *infml* a person of great value or importance: *She's a real treasure.*

windfall [C] **1** a piece of fruit blown down off a tree: *These apples are windfalls, but they're good.* **2** (*fig*) an unexpected lucky gift or prize, esp money: *She had a windfall of £500 from a distant relative.*

J118 *adjectives* : **having little or no money** [B]

poor [Wa1] **1** having very little money and therefore a low standard of living: *He was too poor to buy shoes for his family. This is a poor neighbourhood, where many people cannot get work.* **2** less than is needed or expected; small in size or quantity: *We had a poor crop of beans this year. This product is in poor supply* (= We can't get it easily). **3** [*the* P] poor people: *He always helped the poor.*

badly-off [Wa2] *infml* poor: *He's rather badly-off at the moment, but many people are much worse-off.*

impoverished having become poor: *Many impoverished workers moved from the country to the cities to get work after the terrible storms.* (*fig*) *The land here used to be rich but it has been used too much and is impoverished now.*

short [Wa1; (*of*)] *infml* lacking enough (money): *I'm short of money this week; can you* *lend me some? — Sorry, I'm rather short myself.*

broke [F] *sl* completely without money: *He/His firm is broke.*

tight [Wa1] (of money) not easy to get: *Money is tight at the moment; I'm afraid the bank can't lend you any just now.*

penniless [Wa5] having no money: *Paying his son's debts left him almost penniless.*

needy [Wa1] needing more money; poor: *He tried to help the needier people in the town.*

penurious *fml & pomp* poor; needy: *He is in a most penurious condition at the moment.*

J119 verbs : losing money [T1]

impoverish 1 to make poor: *The family was impoverished by taxes.* **2** to make poor in quality: *The land has been impoverished by continuous growth of crops.*

beggar *esp emot* to impoverish: *If we follow his plan, it will beggar us completely!*

bankrupt to make bankrupt [⇨ J120] or very poor: *If you go on spending all my money on clothes, you'll bankrupt me!*

J120 adjectives, etc : in debt

in debt owing money: *He is in debt; he owes more than £1,000/a thousand pounds. He is in debt to the sum/tune of £1,000.* (*fig*) *I am in debt to you for all the things you have done for me; I shall always be in your debt.*

indebted [B] *old use or fig* in debt: *He is indebted to the sum/tune of £10,000.* (*fig fml*) *I am greatly indebted to you for your help.*

insolvent [B] **1** not having money or being able to pay what one owes **2** *infml* having finished one's money, esp wages **insolvency** [U] the condition of being insolvent

bankrupt 1 [Wa5;B] **a** unable to pay one's debts: *The company went bankrupt because it couldn't sell its products.* **b** (*fig*) *derog* lacking in some usu good quality: *The nation grew so rich and lazy that it became spiritually bankrupt.* **c** *derog* no longer able to produce anything good: *Theirs was a bankrupt civilization.* **d** [(*of*)] *derog* completely without (good things): *They seem to be bankrupt of all kind feelings.* **2** [C] **a** a person who is unable to pay his debts: *A court of law declared him a bankrupt.* **b** *derog* a person who is lacking in some (usu good) quality: *He is a moral bankrupt, who will do anything for money.*

J121 nouns : having little or no money

poverty 1 [U] the state of being very poor: *Poverty prevented the boy from continuing his education. There is a great deal of poverty in this part of the country.* **2** [U;S; (*of*)] *fml & deprec* (a) lack: *His later stories are not interesting because of their poverty of imagination.*

impoverishment [U] the state of being impoverished [⇨ J119]

penury [U] *esp fml & emph* the state of being very poor; poverty: *After the death of her husband she lived in penury.*

bankruptcy 1 [U] the quality or state of being bankrupt: *Hard times in the business world reduced his firm to bankruptcy.* **2** [C] an example of this: *There were many bankruptcies in the business world because it was hard to sell anything that year.* **3** [U] *derog* complete failure or inability to produce anything good: *The bankruptcy of the government's plans became clear when prices rose sharply.*

beggary [U] *esp emot & emph* the state of being very poor: *He was reduced to beggary by several business failures.*

J122 nouns : what people earn and spend

[ALSO ⇨ J219]

income [U;C] money which a person receives regularly: *What is his yearly income? Their incomes are greater than ours. She has less income now than she once had.*

outlay [C *usu sing*; (U); (*on, for*)] money spent for a purpose: *There has been a large government outlay on science in the last few years.*

expenditure [S; U; (*of, on*)] spending or using up (something, esp money): *We had an expenditure of £10,000 last year. The expenditure of time and effort was worth it; the plan was a success.*

J123 nouns : budgets and economies

[ALSO ⇨ J221]

budget [C] **1** a plan of how to spend money: *It's a family/business/weekly budget.* **2** a plan of how much money to take in (as by taxation) and how to spend it: *The government budget never gets smaller.* **3** the quantity of money stated in either type of plan: *They have a budget of £10,000.* **budgetary** [B] of, concerning, or for the purpose of (making) a budget: *There have been some budgetary difficulties.*

upkeep [U (*of*)] **1** the act of keeping something repaired and in order: *He spent time on the upkeep of his house.* **2** the cost of this: *The upkeep of the house is too much for me to pay.*

maintenance [U] *fml* upkeep: *The maintenance of the house is more than I can pay for.*

economy [C;U] (an example of) the careful use of money, time, strength, etc: *He practised economy all his life and died a rich man. It's an economy to buy good shoes because they last longer.*

thrift [U] *esp emot* careful control of money, possessions, etc: *Her thrift with her money allowed them to have a really good holiday.* **thrifty** [Wa1;B] using thrift; *esp emot* economical: *Try to be thriftier and make your money last longer.* **-ily** [adv] **-iness** [U]

cutback [C] *esp infml, emot & emph* an economy: *The government cutbacks are intended to save us all money.*

J124 nouns : deficits and shortfalls [C]

deficit 1 the amount by which money that goes out is more than money that comes in: *I'm afraid our business has a deficit of £3,000.* **2** a loss in business operations: *Our company has had a large deficit this year.* **3** an amount which is too small in quantity or too low in quality: *There has been a deficit in/of rain this year.* **4** (the amount of) a disadvantage: *Our team won in spite of a deficit of several runs at the beginning of the match.*

shortfall an amount which is lacking from the amount needed, expected, or hoped for: *We hoped to make £1,000 but after our bad luck there'll be a shortfall of at least £200.*

J125 verbs : budgeting [T1]

budget [IØ] to plan private or public spending with a certain amount of money: *He saved a lot of money by careful budgeting. Let's budget for next year.*

maintain [T1] to do all the necessary things to keep (something, esp property) in good condition: *How do you manage to maintain such a big house?*

keep up [v adv T1] *not fml* to maintain: *It's difficult to keep up big old houses like these.*

J126 adjectives, etc : budget, economy, etc

budget [Wa5;A] *euph* cheap (and therefore suitable in budgeting): *Enjoy our budget prices now!*

economy [Wa5;A] *euph* **1** cheap, low: *Enjoy our new economy prices!* **2** big (and therefore good value for money): *Buy the special economy size!*

economical [B] *genl* using money, time, materials, etc carefully; not wasteful: *A small car is more economical to drive than a big one, because it uses less petrol. Try to be more economical with your money!* **-ly** [adv Wa4]: *They live very economically.* [also ⇒ J198]

economic *esp tech* using money, time, materials, etc, carefully: *Small cars are more economic than large cars.* **-ally** [adv Wa4]

J127 verbs : economizing

economize, -ise [IØ (*on*)] to stop spending money unnecessarily or as much as before: *We*

must economize on food if we are going to live on the money we have. She tried to economize, but couldn't.*

cut down *also* **cut back** [v adv T1a, 4; IØ (*on*)] to reduce the quantity or amount (of); (*infml*) economize (on): *We must cut down on our spending/the amount of material we use. The unions strongly oppose any plans to cut back (on) industrial production.*

Commerce

J130 verbs : selling and buying

sell 1 [D1 (*to*); T1; X7; IØ] to give up (property) to another for money or other value: *He sold his house/car/business/books. I sold my brother my car for £500. I sold my car to my brother for £500. Some dishonest voters sold their votes to whoever paid most. I'd like to buy your house if you're willing to sell. He is a businessman who buys things cheap and sells them dear.* **2** [T1] to help or cause (something) to be bought: *Bad news sells newspapers. That name on the cover is enough to sell the book.* **3** [T1; IØ] to offer (goods) for sale: *My job is selling insurance. Do you sell cigarettes in this shop? The club's shop doesn't sell to non-members.* **4** [IØ] to be bought; find a buyer or buyers: *This newspaper sells for/at 10p. The tickets cost too much and sold badly/wouldn't sell. These fashions sell fast in the shops.*

retail [IØ; T1] *tech* to sell or be sold in shops, etc: *This book retails at £5. We retail this book at £5.*

realize, -ise [T1] *fml & tech* **1** *less common* to sell: *He realized the house.* **2** *more common* to get (money) by selling: *He realized a profit.* **3** *more common* (of something sold) to bring (money): *The house realized a profit.* **4** (*fig*) to carry out; make real (a hope or purpose): *She realized her hope of becoming an actress.*

market [T1] to place (goods) for sale in a market [⇒ J182] or generally: *They are not good at marketing their goods. We have been marketing this product very successfully for 10 years now.* **marketable** [B] able to be marketed

buy 1 [D1 (*for*); T1; X7; IØ] to obtain (something) by giving money (or something else of value): *He bought me a book from/off them for £5. He bought that car new/cheap. When prices are low, he buys.* **2** [T1] to obtain in exchange for something, often something of great value: *They bought peace with their freedom.* **3** [T1] to be exchangeable for: *Money buys less than it used to.*

purchase 1 [T1; (D1)] *fml or tech* to buy: *They've just purchased a new house in the country for £25,000.* **2** [T1 *often pass*] (*fig*) *fml* to gain (something) at the cost of effort, suffering or loss of something valued: *The victory was dearly purchased; it was purchased with the lives of many men who died in battle.*

483 J134 COMMERCE

acquire [T1] *esp fml & euph* to buy: *He acquired the house very cheaply.*

get [T1] *infml* to buy: *He got the house for a song* (= very cheaply).

pawn [T1] to get money by leaving (something of value, such as clothes, jewellery, etc) for return to one only when the money is paid back: *He pawned his watch for £10.* **pawnshop** [C] a shop where one can pawn things **pawnbroker** [C] a person who lends money in a pawnshop

treat [T1 (*to*)] to buy something for (someone) esp as a friendly act: *He treated the children to ice creams.* [*also* ⇒ F74]

patronize, -ise [T1] to buy things regularly from: *He always patronizes those shops.*

J131 *verbs, etc* : **costing and spending**

cost 1 [L1; D1] to have (an amount of money) as a price: *These eggs cost 5 pence each. It will cost you £50 to fly to Paris. This coat only cost me £25 at the local shop; it cost her £35 in London. The best goods usually cost most.* **2** [D1 *no pass*] to cause (a person) (loss or disadvantage): *Your crime will cost you your life. Your thoughtlessness has cost your poor mother many sleepless nights.* **3** [T1 *no pass*] *sl esp BrE* to be costly for someone: *It will cost you to go by train, so why not go by bus?*

worth [prep] (*esp after* be) **1** of the value of: *It's worth much more than I paid for it.* **2** having possessions amounting to: *He's worth £1,000,000.* **3** deserving: *You're not worth helping. It isn't worth waiting for him. The food's not worth eating. Don't lock the door; it isn't worth the trouble.*

fetch [T1] *not fml* to sell at; cost someone: *How much will the house fetch if you sell it? That painting would fetch quite a lot if you sold it now.*

spend 1 [T1 (*on, for*); I0] to give out (esp money) in payment: *He will spend £3,000 for/on a new car. She spent 10p on chocolate. There must be cuts in government spending. You spent this much just buying clothes?* **2** [T1 (*in*)] (*fig*) to pass or use (time): *He spent a pleasant hour (in) talking with friends. They will spend three years in prison. He's spent much of his life writing that book.* **3** [T1] (*fig*) *esp fml or lit* to wear out or use completely: *The storm soon spent itself/its force.*

J132 *verbs* : **affording and paying**

afford 1 [T1 (*usu with* **can, could, able to**)] to be able to buy: *At least we can/are able to afford a house!* **2** [T1, 3 (*usu with* **can, could, able to**)] to be able (to do, spend, give, bear, etc) without serious loss or damage: *Can you afford £45,000 for a house? Can you afford to lend me some money? I can't afford three weeks away*

from work. A man in your position can't afford to say that.

pay 1 [D1 (*to*); T1 (*for*); V3; I0 (*for*); I3] to give (money) for goods bought, work done, etc: *I paid (five pounds) for that book/to have my radio mended. I'll pay you five pounds for it. I don't mind paying to have my door painted. I'm afraid I can't pay (you) (anything) (for it). He paid them (£5) to take it away. He paid to see the show.* **2** [T1] to settle (a bill, debt, etc): *He is very slow at paying his bills.* **3** [T1; I0] to be profitable; be worth the trouble or cost (to somebody): *It doesn't pay (you) to argue with him. We must make this farm/business pay.* **4** [Wv5;L9] (of work, something done, etc) to bring or give one money or something of value in return: *This job/firm doesn't pay well. It's a badly-paid job.*

defray [T1] *fml* to pay for: *We shall defray your costs in travelling to New York.*

give [D1 (*to*); T1] *not fml* to pay in exchange: *She gave him a pound for his help. What price did you give?*

part with [v prep T1] *infml* to pay: *£200 is a lot (of money) to part with for that chair. How much did you part with to get that chair?*

J133 *verbs* : **pricing and charging**

price 1 [X7,9 *often pass*] to fix the amount of money to be paid for (something for sale): *The clothes in this shop are priced high.* **2** [T1 *usu pass*] to mark (goods in a shop) with what people must pay (for them): *These dresses have only just arrived in the shop and haven't yet been priced.*

charge [T1] **1** to ask a usu stated amount of money to be paid for (something for sale): *He charged £20 for doing it. They charged us too much. What do you charge for this?* **2** [(*to*)] to make a note that goods which are sent, given, etc, are to be paid for later by (someone): *I'll take the books now; charge me, please/charge them to me, please.*

J134 *nouns* : **sales, purchases, and bargains**

[ALSO ⇒ J183]

sale [C] **1** an act of selling; an agreement exchanging something for money: *The sale of my house hasn't been easy but now Mr Smith is interested and I hope I'll make the sale today. They had only four sales all day in the little shop.* **2** a special offering of goods in a shop at lower prices than usual: *I got this hat cheap at a sale. The regular price is £3, and the sale price is £1.50.* **3** [*often pl with sing meaning*] the total amount sold of something offered to be sold: *We're hoping for a large sale/large sales of our new product.* **for sale** offered to be sold, esp by a private owner: *The sign on that house says 'For Sale'; shall we find out the price? Is your* *house for sale?* **on sale 1** offered to be sold, esp in a shop: *The evening newspapers go on sale in the afternoon. Will the new product be on sale as early as next month?* **2** AmE at or in a sale: *I got this hat on sale; it was very cheap.*

realization, -isation [U9] *fml* the act of selling (esp property) or of getting (money from selling esp property): *The realization of the house brought him a lot of money.*

purchase 1 [C *often pl*] **a** an act of buying; a thing bought: *She made several purchases in the dress shop.* **b** an article that has just been bought: *The children helped to carry their mother's purchases from the shops.* **2** [U9; A] *fml* buying: *He gave his son some money for the purchase of books. What was the purchase price?*

buy [C] *usu infml* **1** an act of buying **2** something of value at a low price; bargain: *It's a real buy at that price!*

acquisition [C] *usu fml* something acquired [⇒ J130] or bought: *What new acquisitions do you have?*

bargain [C] **1** something that can be or has been bought for less than its real value: *These good shoes are a real bargain at such a low price. I can offer it to you at a bargain price.* **2** an agreement, esp one to do something in return for something else: *He made a bargain with his wife—'You cook and I'll wash up!'* **a good/bad bargain** one that favours/does not favour the person who is being spoken about

luxury [C] something that is not necessary and not often bought: *Shall I get some new chairs?— No, that's a luxury we can't afford at the moment. Buying a new hat now and again is one of the few luxuries left in her life.*

J135 *nouns* : **price and value**

price 1 [C] an amount of money for which a thing is offered, sold, or bought: *What price did you pay for the house? What is the price of this suit? Eggs are selling at a high price. For this week only we're selling two mats for the price of one. Show me the price list.* **2** [S] (*fig*) that which one must lose or suffer in order to do or get something one wants: *Loss of health is too high a price to pay for taking dangerous drugs.* **at a price** at a high price: *Can I get any good oranges in the town?—Yes, at a price; they're rather dear at the moment.*

value 1 [C; U] the worth of something in money or as compared with other goods for which it might be changed: *The value of the British pound is less than it was 100 years ago. Will the value of houses and land continue to increase? I paid him £50 for the painting but its real value must be about £500. Jewels are articles of value; they are articles of great value. These old ornaments are of little value. You can't judge everything in life by its money value.* **2** [U9] worth compared with the amount paid (*often in the phr* **value for money**): *If your coat wore out in*

less than a year it certainly wasn't good value; it was poor value for money. You always get value for money at that shop (= the goods are always worth the price charged). **3** [U] the (degree of) usefulness of something, esp in comparison with other things: *You'll find this instrument of great value in making certain kinds of measurement. Smoking has little value except in helping to calm the nerves. Certain types of plant are of value for making drugs.* **4** [C *usu pl*] a standard or idea which most people have about the worth of good qualities: *One way of judging a society is to consider its values* (= the worth which its people think that justice, kindness, freedom, etc, have). **5** [C] the exact meaning or effect of a word: *It's often not easy to decide the exact value which a poet intended to give to a particular word.* **6** [C] the length of a musical note: *Give this last note its full value as it's written in the music; don't cut it short.* **7** [C *usu sing*] *math* the quantity expressed by a letter of the alphabet or other sign: *Let x have the value of 25.*

cost 1 [C *often pl with sing meaning*] the price of making or producing something: *Their prices are high because production costs are very great. We must reduce labour costs if we are to make a profit this year.* **2** [S] the amount paid or asked for goods or a service; price: *If you buy more than 10 books we will reduce the cost of each book by 10%.* **3** [S; U] (*fig*) something needed, given, or lost, to obtain something: *The cost in human lives and suffering of the Second World War was very great indeed. We could make a direct attack on the fort but the cost in soldiers would be too great. He saved his daughters from the fire at the cost of his own life.*

expense [S; U] *fml* cost, esp of money but also time and effort: *I won't do it; it's too great an expense/the expense is too great.* **at great/ little/ almost no expense** costing a lot of/little/ almost no money: *She furnished the house at great expense.* **at someone's expense 1** with someone paying the cost: *He was travelling at the Government's expense. He had his book printed at his own expense.* **2** (esp of a joke or trick) against someone, so as to make him seem silly: *He tried to be clever at my expense.* **at the expense of** causing the loss of: *He finished the job at the expense of his health.* **spare no expense** try hard without considering cost: *Spare no expense to make the party a success.* **go to/put someone to the expense of** to pay for/make someone else pay for: *I don't want to put him to the expense of buying me dinner.*

worth [U] value: *After his unkindness I know the true worth of his friendship* (= It is worthless, has no value). **-worth** [*comb form*] a certain amount of the stated value: *Will you change this pound note for a poundsworth of pennies? He bought two pennyworth of sweets.*

charge [C] the price asked or paid for an article or service: *The charges here are too high; let's go elsewhere. The charge for a front row seat is £5.*

payment 1 [U] the act of paying: *I gave £10 in payment for the goods I bought.* **2** [C] an amount of money (to be) paid: *He paid 7 monthly payments of £15 each.* **3** [U; (S)] (*fig*) something done, said or given in return for something done or as a result of one's action: *He's very angry with me, and that's my payment for trying to help him!*

fare [C] **1** the price charged to transport a person, as on a bus, train or taxi: *Fares, please? What's the train/bus fare to Birmingham?* **2** a paying passenger, esp in a taxi: *He had no fares all morning.*

J136 *verbs* : **trading and bartering**

exchange [T1; (I∅)] to give (one thing) for (another): *They exchanged machines for (payment in) food.*

trade 1 [I∅] to carry on trade: *He made his money by trading in corn. The ships were trading between Spain and Italy.* **2** [T1 (*for*)] to buy, sell, or exchange (a product, goods, etc): *The early settlers traded copper for corn.* **3** [I∅ (*at, with*)] *AmE* to shop regularly

barter [T1; I∅] to exchange (goods) for goods without using money: *They bartered farm products (with each other). They bartered farm products for machinery. I prefer bartering to buying and selling. They bartered for food.*

traffic in [v prep T1 (*with*)] *often deprec* to carry on trade, esp of an unlawful or improper kind, in (a particular type of goods): *The criminals made large profits by trafficking in stolen goods.*

export [T1; I∅] to send (goods) out of a country for sale: *We export most of the cars we make. They sell to the home market* (= trade within the country), *but they don't export. We must export to live.* **exporter** [C] a person who exports goods: *He is an exporter of paper; he is a paper exporter.*

import [T1; I∅] to bring in (goods) from abroad/outside: *Britain imports meat (from abroad). We must import to live.* **importer** [C] a person who imports goods: *She is an importer of wine; she's a wine importer.*

J137 *nouns, etc* : **trading and bartering**

exchange [U; C] the act of giving (one thing) for (another); any example of this: *Trade by (the) exchange of goods without using money is quite common. What exchanges of goods have you been making?*

trade 1 [U] the business of buying, selling, or exchanging goods within a country or between countries: *Trade between our two countries increases yearly. International trade is important to us all. They made a trade agreement between the two countries.* **2** [*the* R9; A] a particular business or industry: *They work in*

the cotton trade/tourist trade. *I can't tell you how to make ice cream because it's a trade secret.* **3** [*the* GU] the people who work in a particular business or industry: *This talk is only likely to be of interest to the trade.* **4** [C; by U] a job, esp one needing special skill with the hands: *He's a printer by trade. How long did it take you to learn your trade?* **5** [S9] amount of business: *On the corner a girl was doing a good trade in flowers.*

barter [U] the exchange of goods for goods rather than goods for money: *Business was done by barter before money was invented.*

traffic [U] *often deprec* trade, esp of an unlawful or improper kind, in a particular type of goods: *Illegal traffic in drugs is quite common.*

export 1 [U] (the business of) exporting: *He is in the export trade. The export of gold is forbidden. This firm produces goods chiefly for export.* **2** [C often pl] anything that is exported: *Wool is one of the chief exports of Australia.* **invisible exports** [P] money brought into a country in other ways than by the sale of goods: *Teaching English to foreigners is one of Britain's invisible exports.*

import [C often pl] something brought into a country from abroad: *Imports of food are getting more expensive.*

contract 1 [C] a formal esp business agreement between two persons, groups, or companies, etc: *He signed the contract. We have a new contract to build houses in Glasgow.* **2** [I∅; T3] to make an agreement: *They contracted to build the new houses.* **contractual** [Wa5;B] of, concerning, or like a contract: *We have a contractual agreement with him.* **-ly** [adv] **contractor** [C] a person who works for contracts: *The contractor built the house very well.*

deal [C] an arrangement in business: *The deal pleased both businessmen. Well, is it a deal? —Yes; it's a deal. He has been busy with several new deals.*

transaction [C] *fml* a piece of business done or to be done; a deal: *Are all your business transactions complete?*

J138 *nouns* : **commerce and business**

commerce [U] the buying and selling of goods, esp between different countries; trade: *Our country has grown rich because of its commerce with other nations.* **commercial** [B] **1** of, concerning, or like commerce: *commercial work* **2** [Wa5] receiving support from commerce: *commercial radio* **3** [Wa5] used in commerce: *commercial vehicles* **4** *often deprec* doing things only for money, etc: *a commercial mind* **non-** [*neg*] **-ly** [adv]

business 1 [C; U] one's work or employment: *What I do is no business of yours. Other people's quarrels are a lawyer's business. I'm here on business, not for pleasure.* **2** [U] trade and the getting of money: *How's business? Business is good. They've done (some) busi-*

ness together. It's a pleasure to do business with you. After leaving college she went into business. **businesslike** [B] *usu apprec* using the best methods, ideas, etc, of business; effective: *He does his work in a very businesslike way.*

banking [U] the business of banks [⇒ J104] and bankers, esp in lending money and helping with investments [⇒ J114], etc: *He's quite important in banking/in the banking world.*

intercourse [U] the movement of goods, messages, ideas, etc, between groups, places, countries, etc: *The people in this town have little intercourse with outsiders.*

cartel [C] **1** an association between those who make or provide goods for sale or use in which they all agree to sell at the same prices and to produce only a certain amount of goods **2** an agreement of this kind

monopoly 1 [C (*of*)] a right or power of one person or one group and no other, to provide a service, trade in anything, produce something, etc: *A foreign company has been given the monopoly to produce oil, if any is found in this area; no others may produce it.* **2** [S *of*] possession of, or control over, something which is not shared by another or others: *There are two hotels in this small seaside town, but one has almost a monopoly of the summer trade; the other has very few visitors. He seems to think he has a monopoly of brains* (= that he alone is clever). *A university education shouldn't be the monopoly of those whose parents are rich.* **3** [C] something of which one person or one group has complete unshared control: *The postal services weren't always a government monopoly; in the past they were sometimes provided by private companies. If these two great industrial companies combine, they'll form a monopoly; there's no other company to do the work.* **monopolize, -ise** [T1] to treat as a monopoly: *He monopolizes her; no one else can talk to her while he is here.*

J139 *nouns* : **persons in trade and business** [C]

businessman 1 a person in business, esp as the director of a business firm **2** a person who would be successful in business, who knows how to get and save money: *That teacher's a good businessman.* **businesswoman** [*fem*]

trader a person who buys and sells goods, esp in foreign countries

tradesman 1 a person who buys and sells goods, esp a shopkeeper **2** a person who calls on private houses to deliver goods: *The tradesmen's entrance is at the back of the house.*

merchant *becoming rare* a person who buys and sells goods, esp in large amounts in foreign countries: *He's a wine merchant by trade.*

entrepreneur a person who makes the plans for a business or a piece of work and helps to start it up

J140 *nouns* : **persons selling things** [C]

salesman a person whose job is to sell a company's goods to businesses, homes, etc **saleswoman** [*fem*]

(sales) representative *esp fml* a person acting in place of one or more others in selling goods, etc: *Send a representative of Longman to the exhibition.*

rep *infml* a salesman or sales representative

(commercial) traveller *BrE*, **traveling salesman** *AmE* a person who travels from place to place trying to get orders for his firm's goods

J141 *nouns* : **the economy and economics**

economy 1 [*the* R] the economic [⇒ J126] life of a country; the workings of a country's money; industry and trade: *The oil that we have found will improve the state of the economy.* **2** [C] any one of a number of economic systems: *This country has an industrial economy. The economies of the USA and USSR are very different.*

economics 1 [U] the science of the way in which industry and trade produce and use wealth: *He has a university degree in economics. Economics is an interesting subject.* **2** [P] the principles of profit and the production of wealth: *The economics of national growth are of the greatest importance to all modern governments. From the point of view of economics it may be better to buy a house than to rent one.*

J142 *nouns* : **enterprises and undertakings**

enterprise 1 [U9] the way of organizing and carrying on business (*esp in the phrs* **private enterprise, free enterprise**): *Some people believe in private enterprise, while others believe in government ownership of industry. Too much government control is said to discourage the growth of free enterprise.* **2** [C] a plan to do something, esp to do something daring or difficult: *The greatest of his enterprises was to sail round the world alone in a small boat.*

venture [C] an attempt; a course of action (esp in business) of which the result is uncertain and there is risk of loss or failure as well as chance of gain or success: *Her only venture as a writer ended in failure; no one would print her book. He became rich by buying shares in several business ventures which were thought to be risky.*

undertaking [C] **1** work which one decides to do: *Selling books is one of his latest undertaking.* **2** work which one promises or must do: *I made an undertaking to go, and I will go.*

J143 verbs : valuing and estimating

[ALSO ⇒ J34 CALCULATING, ETC]

value 1 [T1] to calculate the value, price, or worth of: *If you want to sell your collection of stamps you should begin by having it valued. He valued the house and its contents at £22,000.* **2** [Wv5;T1] to consider (someone or something) to be of great worth: *Young people don't always value the advice given them by their parents. I've always valued your friendship very highly. He is a valued friend.*

evaluate [T1] to calculate the value or degree of: *I can't evaluate his ability.*

assess [T1] to calculate the value of (property) or the amount of (income) for tax purposes: *They are assessing his house. They assessed it at £15,000.*

estimate 1 [T1, 5a] to calculate (something which can be added or measured); form an opinion as to the degree of (something): *I estimate her age at 35. It's impossible to estimate his abilities yet. The driver estimated that the journey would take four hours.* **2** [I0] to calculate the cost of doing a job; offer to do a job for a certain price: *I asked building firms to estimate for the repairs to the roof.* **overestimate** [T1;I0] to estimate too highly **underestimate** to estimate too low

cost [T1] to calculate the price to be charged for (a job, someone's time, etc): *The job was costed by the builder at about £150.*

price [T1 *pass rare*] *infml* to ask the price of: *Before buying the coat, why not price it in a number of shops, as the prices vary for the same coat.*

prize [Wv5;T1] to value highly: *She prizes his friendship. Those books are among his most prized possessions.*

treasure [Wv5;T1] *esp emot* to value greatly: *She treasures those books because they were his.*

rate 1 [T1] to measure or value: *She rated him highly. How do you rate the team's chance of winning?* **2** [L7,9] to be valued: *She rates highly with me.* **overrate** [T1] to rate too highly: *He overrates himself.* **underrate** [T1] to rate too low: *She is very much underrated.*

J144 nouns : valuing and estimating

valuation 1 [U] the action of calculating how much money something is worth: *I spend most of my time at the office in the valuation of land.* **2** [C] a value or price decided upon: *I was offered a piece of land at the reasonable valuation of £1,500. I asked three different people how much they thought my painting was worth, and they gave me three different valuations.* **3** [C] the opinion or idea one has of someone's worth in regard to ability or character: *It's unwise to take people at their own valuation, as this is often quite different from the truth. Now*

that you're becoming so successful, we must put a higher valuation on your work.

evaluation 1 [U] the act of evaluating **2** [C] an example or result of this: *Can I have your evaluation of the matter as soon as possible?*

assessment 1 [U] the act of assessing **2** [C] an example or result of this; the value or amount at which something is calculated: *How did you make these assessments?*

estimate 1 [C] a calculation of something which can be added or measured, or of the degree or quality of something: *My estimate of her character was wrong. I can't form an exact estimate of the time it will take. On what figures do you base your estimate that it will cost £487,983?* **2** [C *often pl*] an offer to do a job for a certain price: *We got two or three estimates before having the roof repaired, and accepted the lowest.* **at a rough estimate** not speaking exactly: *The room is 20 feet long at a rough estimate.*

estimation 1 [U] the act of estimating **2** [C] *rare* an example of this; an estimate **3** [U] opinion: *In my estimation, it's a good house. He has gone down in our estimation* (= We do not think so highly of him as we once did).

J145 verbs : bargaining and haggling

bargain 1 [I0] to talk about the conditions of a sale, agreement, or contract: *We bargained with her about the price.* **2** [T5, (5c)] to get an agreement that: *The trade union bargained that its members should have another week's holiday.*

haggle [I0 (*over/about*)] to argue over something, esp over fixing a price: *Stop haggling and pay what he asks! He haggled over the price.*

negotiate 1 [I0] to talk with another person or group in order to settle a question or disagreement; try to come to an agreement: *The government has had to negotiate with the opposition party on/over the new law. The trade union is negotiating with the owners to get a better contract. Why fight when you can negotiate?* **2** [T1] to produce (an agreement) or settle (a piece of business) in this way: *The trade union negotiated a new contract with the owner. The two countries negotiated a trade agreement* (*with each other*). **3** [T1] *tech* to get or give money for (an order to pay money such as a cheque): *I'm sorry; our bank doesn't negotiate foreign cheques.* **negotiation 1** [U] the act of negotiating **2** [C *often pl*] an example or occasion of this: *The negotiations between the two groups were successful.* **negotiable** [B] able to be negotiated, paid, done, etc **-bly** [adv Wa3]

fix [T1 *often pass*] to agree or arrange (the price, etc, of something): *They fixed the prices for the coming year. The price is fixed at £50. The price is fixed; no haggling, please.*

settle for [v prep T1 *no pass*] to accept or agree to (something less than the best, or than hoped for): *I want £500 for my car and I won't settle for less. I could never settle for such a quiet life; I want excitement.*

J146 *verbs* : **settling a business matter** [T1]

clinch *not fml* to settle (a business matter) firmly (*esp in the phr* **clinch a deal**): *The two businessmen clinched the deal quickly.*

bring off [v adv] *not fml* to succeed in (something difficult esp in business): *He managed to bring off a difficult job/deal.*

pull off [v adv] *not fml* to succeed in (a difficult attempt, esp in business): *The deal looked impossible but she pulled it off.*

J147 *verbs* : **hiring, renting, and letting**

hire [T1] to get the use of (esp a car, boat, suit of clothes) for a special occasion on payment of a sum of money: *He hired a car for a week.*

rent **1** [T1 (*from*)] to pay money for the use of (esp a room, building, television set, or piece of land): *He rented a room from Mrs Jones.* **2** [D1 (*to*); T1] to allow to be used in return for money: *Mrs Jones rented him a room/rented a room to him.* **3** [L9, esp *at*] (of a building, land, etc) to bring in rent: *This house rents at £150 a month.* **4** [T1] *esp AmE* to hire

let [T1 (*to, out*)] to give the use of (a room, a building, land, etc) in return for regular payments: *We're hoping to let this field (to a farmer). This room is let (out) to a student.*

rent out [v adv; T1] to let (out)

sublet [T1; IØ] (of a person who rents property from its owner) to rent (part of the property) to someone else: *He rents the house and sublets a room to a friend.*

lease [D1 (to); T1(*out*)] to give or take the use of (land or buildings) on a lease: *He leased (me) the house for two years. I leased the house for two years.*

charter [T1] to hire a plane, bus, etc, for a special purpose: *The members of the group chartered a plane to take them to Greece.*

J148 *nouns* : **hiring, renting, and letting**

[ALSO ⇒ J102]

hire [U] **1** the act of hiring or state of being hired: *Boats for hire! He paid for the hire of a room.* **2** payment for this: *He works for hire.*

hire purchase *BrE*, **the instalment plan** *AmE* [U] a system of payment for goods by which one pays small sums of money regularly after receiving the goods (usually paying more than the original price)

easy terms *also* (**credit**) **terms** *infml* hire purchase

rent [C; U] **1** (a stated sum of) money paid regularly for the use of a room, building, television set, or piece of land: *Do you own your house or do you pay rent? He let the house at a rent of £30.00 a week.* **2** *esp AmE* money paid in this way for the use of a car, boat, suit of clothes, etc **free of rent** (of a room, building, or piece of land) used without payment: *They live in the flat free of rent.*

rental [C] *fml* a sum of money fixed to be paid as rent: *The house is let at a rental of £130 per month. They pay the television rental weekly.*

let [C *usu sing*] **1** an act of renting a house or flat to (or from) someone **2** a house or flat that is (to be) rented **3** *infml* a person who rents, or is willing to rent, a house or flat from one: *They can't find a let for their flat.*

lease [C *usu sing; on* U] **1** a written agreement, made according to law, by which the use of a building or piece of land is given (**let**) by its owner to somebody for a certain time in return for a regular payment (**rent**): *The house is on lease.* **2** the length of time such an agreement is to last: *He got the house on a 10-year lease.*

charter [C] an act or occasion of chartering: *How many charters do we have? They went on a charter flight to Athens.* **on charter** chartered: *The plane is on charter to Southern Airways.*

J149 *phrases & adjectives* : **hiring and selling**

for hire (of persons, machines, etc) ready for use if hired [⇒ J147]: *These cars are for hire. He is for hire; he'll work for you if you pay him.*

to let (of houses, flats, etc) ready for using, living in, etc, if rented: *The house is to let. The sign beside the house said 'To Let'.*

vacant [B] **1** [Wa5] empty; not filled with anything: *He owns that vacant piece of land.* **2** [Wa5] (of a house, room or seat) not being used or lived in: *The house has been vacant for several months, so you might be able to buy it.* **3** [B] (*fig*) **a** (of the mind) not thinking; empty **b** showing lack of active or serious thought: *She has a vacant look.* **c** foolish; senseless: *The man gave a vacant laugh.* **-ly** [adv]

for sale (of houses, cars, etc) ready to be sold: *The house is for sale. The sign beside the house said 'For Sale'.*

J150 *nouns* : **payments and instalments** [C]

[ALSO ⇒ J102]

payment an amount of money to be paid as part of the price of something: *He paid seven monthly payments of £15 each.*

down payment a part of the full price paid at the time of buying or delivery, with the rest to be paid later

part-payment a part of the full price paid weekly, monthly, etc, or in some agreed way, often by giving something instead of money: *He gave them his old car in part-payment for the new one.*

instalment one payment of a set which, in time, will complete a full payment: *He bought the furniture by instalments. He bought it on an instalment plan.*

J151 *nouns* : **bills and invoices** [C]

bill a list of things bought and the money owed or paid for them: *He hasn't paid his electricity bill.*

invoice a bill for goods received

receipt a written statement that one has received something, esp money, a letter, etc: *Ask the shop for a receipt when you pay the bill She made out* (= wrote) *the receipt in his name.*

voucher 1 a kind of ticket that may be used instead of money for a particular purpose: *He gave me some travel vouchers. Some firms give their workers vouchers with which they can get a meal in certain restaurants.* **2** *BrE* a kind of ticket that gives a buyer the right to receive certain goods free or at a lower price during a limited time **3** *law* a receipt or official declaration, written or printed, given to prove that accounts are correct or that money has already been paid

stamp a piece of paper to be fixed on something or a mark made with ink on paper, to show that something has been done, paid for, bought, sold, given, etc: *There's no stamp here, so you must pay now.* [also ⇒ H129]

coupon a ticket that shows the right of the holder to receive some payment, service, etc; voucher: *In every packet of cigarettes you get coupons which can be saved and exchanged for goods. In Bulgaria guests at hotels are given coupons which they can exchange for food in any restaurant. I have a coupon for 10 pence off that packet of soap.*

152 *verbs* : **bills and invoices**
[ALSO ⇒ J109]

bill [T1] to send a bill to: *I can't pay now; please bill me (for it) later.*

invoice [T1] **1** to make an invoice for (goods): *Invoice these boxes before they go out, please.* **2** to send an invoice to (someone): *We'll invoice you for these goods next month.*

charge [I0; T1; D1 (*for*)] to ask in payment by preparing or sending a bill; to prepare a bill for or send a bill to (someone): *He ordered the goods; charge him for them. If we send the goods to you, then we must charge (you) postage* (= the cost of posting).

J153 *verbs* : **handling and dealing in things** [T1]

handle to use (goods) in business, esp for sale: *We don't handle that sort of book.*

deal in [v prep *usu not pass*] to buy and sell; trade in: *This shop deals in woollen goods.*

keep 1 to own and make money from: *They keep a shop/a small hotel.* **2** to offer regularly for sale: *That shop keeps everything you will need.*

have to keep (in one's shop, store, etc): *Do you have this book here? Sorry, we don't have that book in stock* (= as part of what we have).

stock to keep a supply of: *Do you stock these books/goods?—No, we don't stock them here.* **stock up** [v adv I0 (*on, with*)] to get and keep a supply: *Better stock up on coffee; there will be a shortage soon.*

J154 *verbs* : **ordering things** [T1]

order to send to a factory, etc, for (something, esp to sell in one's shop, etc): *Can you order these goods for me?—Yes, I'll order them now.*

get in [v adv] *not fml* to collect, order, or buy a supply of: *We should get in some more wine; we have very little left.*

J155 *verbs & phrases* : **not having things in stock**

be ... out of [v adv prep; T1] *not fml* not to have: *We're (clean) out of milk!*

run out [v adv I0; T1 (*of*)] to have no more; to become short: *Time is running out. We're running out of time. The car ran out of petrol.*

sell out [v adv Wv5; T1;I0: (*of*)] to sell all (of something): *The shop sold out all their shirts. We are sold out; we have no more. All sold out!*

out of stock having none of something for sale in one's shop, store, etc: *Sorry, we're out of stock; all sold out.*

J156 *nouns* : **orders and consignments**

order [C] **1** [(*for*)] an act of ordering [⇒ J154]; asking someone to supply goods: *It's an order for 100 bottles of whisky a month. Can you fill my order* (= supply the goods I have asked for)? **2** the goods supplied in accordance with such a request: *Please come and collect your order.* **on order** having been ordered: *The goods are on order; they will be here soon.*

consignment 1 [U] the act of consigning (= sending or giving) **2** [C (*of*)] a number of goods consigned (= sent) together: *a consignment of books* **on consignment** sent to a person or shop that pays only for what is sold and returns what is unsold: *We only have a small shop in a small village so we usually only order goods on consignment.*

load [C] **1** an amount being carried, or to be carried, esp heavy: *A load of furniture has just come.* (*fig*) *Her grief is a heavy load to bear.* **2** [*in comb*] the amount which a certain vehicle can carry: *a carload/busload* **3** *tech* the work done by a moving part such as a motor or engine

burden [C] *often emot* something heavy to carry: *He put down his burden and rested for a moment.* (*fig*) *She has many burdens, including a sick husband and very little money.*

J157 *nouns, etc* : **goods and merchandise**

goods [P] **1** possessions which can be moved, not houses, land, etc **2** *BrE* heavy articles which can be carried by road, rail, etc: *A goods train passed.* **3** articles for sale: *There's a large variety of (leather) goods in the shops.*

merchandise [U] *fml* things for sale; goods to be traded: *There is a notice in the shop saying 'Please do not handle the merchandise'.*

stock [U; C] the goods in a shop, house, store, factory, etc: *Our stock of food won't last much longer. Buy now while stocks last. What do you have in stock?*

cargo [U; C] (one load of) the goods or freight carried by a ship, plane, or vehicle: *We sailed to Newcastle with a cargo of coal. We can't take any more cargo; we're full already.*

freight 1 [U] (money paid for) the carrying of goods by some means of transport: *This aircraft company deals with freight only; it has no passenger service. The freight must be added to the cost of the goods: that's why the prices are higher.* **2** [U] *esp AmE* the goods carried in this way: *This freight must be carefully handled when loading.* **3** [T1] to send (something) as freight **4** [T1] to load (esp a ship) with goods: *The boat is freighted with coal.*

carriage [U] the act or cost of carrying or moving goods from one place to another, esp by road, rail, or air: *The books arrived carriage paid, so we didn't have to pay any more for them.*

J158 *verbs* : **insuring things** [T1]

insure to protect (oneself or someone) esp against loss (of money, life, goods, etc) by insurance: *My house is insured against fire. The goods were insured*

assure *esp BrE* to insure, esp against death, esp one's own

cover to provide insurance for: *This insurance policy covers fire and theft, but does not cover war. Are you fully covered or do you need more insurance?*

J159 *nouns* : **insurance**
[ALSO ⇒ N366 PROTECTION]

insurance 1 [U] agreement to pay money, esp when someone cannot earn it because of misfortune (such as illness, death, or accident) in return for which this person pays small amounts regularly: *life insurance; car insurance* **2** [U] the large sum of money given by an insurance company or one of the payments made to them **3** [U; C] protection (against something): *I have one lock but I bought another as an additional insurance against theft.*

assurance [U] *esp BrE* insurance on something that is certain, such as one's death: *He works for a life assurance company.*

premium [C] a sum of money paid (regularly) to an insurance company to protect oneself against some risk of loss or damage: *They're charging me a higher premium this year for my car and house insurance.* [also ⇒ J114]

(insurance) policy [C] (a written statement of the details of) an agreement with an insurance company

cover [U] insurance: *Have you got enough cover in case of fire or accidents? This insurance policy provides full cover.*

J160 *nouns, etc* : **taxes and duties**

tax 1 [C; U] (a sum of) money paid in accordance with the law to the government according to income, property, goods bought, etc: *The government plans to increase taxes by 5% over the next year. If the tax on tobacco were increased fewer people would smoke cigarettes. How much income tax do you pay?— Half of my wages go in tax.* **2** [S *on*] (*fig*) a heavy demand; a demanding duty: *To travel a long way would be too much of a tax on my father's strength.* **taxation** [U] the act or result of taxing or being taxed; money taken as taxes: *The rate of taxation in that country is high/low.*

customs 1 [P] taxes paid on certain goods coming into a country **2** [(*the*) R *often cap*] the government department which collects such taxes; the place in a port, airport, etc, where officials (**Customs officers**) collect customs

duty [C *often pl with sing meaning;* U] any of various types of tax: *Customs duties are paid on goods entering the country, death duties on property when the owners die, and stamp duty when one sells a house.*

excise [(*the*) S] the government tax on certain goods produced and used inside a country: *We must pay the excise on cigarettes.*

levy [C] **1** an official demand for a tax **2** the collection of such a tax, etc **3** the money, etc collected **capital levy** a share taken by the state of the wealth owned by all the people in a country, group, etc

rate [C *usu pl*] *BrE* a local tax paid or payment made by owners of buildings: *The rates hav*

491   J164 COMMERCE

gone up this year. The water rate is the payment
in Britain for water when it is supplied to houses
and factories and so on.

toll 1 [C] a tax paid for the right to use a road,
harbour, etc **2** [C9 usu sing] (fig) the quantity
of things, esp lives, lost or destroyed in an
accident, war, etc: The war took a heavy toll in
dead and wounded. The holiday death toll on
the roads is very bad.

revenue [U; C usu pl] tech money coming in, esp
to a government from taxes

in bond (of goods) kept in a warehouse [⇒
M160] until tax is paid

J161 verbs : **taxing and levying**

tax 1 [T1] to charge a tax on: After it's been taxed
my income is very small. Tobacco and
alcoholic drinks are taxed heavily in Britain.
'Tax the rich!' he cried. Profits should be taxed
at a higher rate than at present. **2** [Wv4;T1] to
make heavy demands on; tire: Such a long
journey would be too taxing for my old uncle.
You're taxing my patience by asking such
stupid questions. **taxable** [Wa5;B] able to be
taxed: This money is not taxable.

rate [X7,9 usu pass] BrE to fix a rate on (a
building): My house is rated rather high/at
£500. **rateable, ratable** [Wa5;A] BrE (of a
building or its value) on which rates are
charged: What is the rateable value of this
shop?

levy [T1] to demand and collect officially: The
government plans to levy a higher tax on
tobacco.

J162 verbs & nouns : **bribing and tipping**

bribe 1 [T1; V3] to influence unfairly (esp
someone in a position of trust) by favours or
gifts: He bribed the policeman (to let him go
free/into letting him go free). (fig) The child was
bribed with a piece of cake to go to bed quietly.
2 [X9] to get or make in this way: He bribed his
way onto the committee. He bribed himself onto
the committee. **3** [C] something offered or
given in bribing: The official was charged with
taking bribes from people who wanted favours
in return.

bribery [U] the act of bribing (people): He used
bribery to get what he wanted.

graft [U] infml the gaining of advantage for oneself, esp in business, by secret influence, bribery, etc

tip [C] a usu small gift of money for a service, to
keep someone happy, etc: He gave the waiter a
tip when he paid for the meal.

gratuity [C] **1** a gift of money for a service done;
(fml) tip **2** esp BrE a gift of money to a worker
or a member of the armed forces when he or
she leaves that employment

J163 nouns, etc : **rates, commissions, and discounts**

rate [C9] a charge or payment fixed according to
a standard scale: Night telephone rates are
cheaper than day rates. Increase the rate of
pay for these workers. What is the rate for the
job?

commission [C; U] (an amount of) money, usu
related to the value of goods sold, paid to a
salesman, etc, for his services: He gets 10%
commission on everything he sells; if he sells
goods worth £100 his commission is £10.

discount [C; U] reduction made in the cost
when buying goods in a shop: The shop gave
me a 10% discount. **at a discount 1** below the
usual price: I was able to buy this coat at a
small discount. **2** (fig) not valued or wanted:
Honesty seems to be at rather a discount
today.

deduction [C] anything, esp money, that is
deducted or taken away: Several deductions
were made from her wages every week, for tax
and other purposes.

off [adv Wa5] taken from a price, esp as a discount: He got 10% off when he bought the car.
Can I have anything off if I pay the whole
amount now?

J164 nouns, adjectives & adverbs : **wholesale and retail**

wholesale 1 [U] the business of selling goods in
large quantities, esp to shopkeepers **2** [Wa5;B;
adv] (of or concerned in selling) in large
quantities or at the lower prices fixed for
such sales: He has a wholesale business. They sell
machines to the public wholesale. **3** [Wa5;B;
adv] in too large or unlimited numbers: There
was a wholesale rush from the burning cinema.

retail 1 [U] the sale of goods in shops to customers for their own use and not for selling again
2 [Wa5;B; adv] (of or concerned in) this
kind of selling: What is the retail price of
those goods? Can you buy these goods retail
here?

net(t) [Wa5] **1** [A] (of an amount) when nothing
further is to be subtracted: net profit (= after
tax, rent, etc, are paid); net weight (= of an
object without its packet) **2** [A] when everything has been considered (esp in the phr **net
result**) final: The net result of the tax was to
make the rich even richer. **3** [B; E] (of a price)
not allowed to be made lower: All prices in
this shop are net. The price of the book is £3
net; no bookshop will sell it for less. **4** [A]
a net amount, price, etc: The bill says 'net
30 days' (= it must be paid in full within a
month).

gross 1 [Wa5;A] total: The gross weight of the
box of chocolates is more than the weight of the
chocolates alone. **2** [U] the whole; the greater
part **in gross** BrE, **in the gross** AmE in large
amounts; wholesale

J165 nouns : **takings and turnovers**

takings [P] receipts of money, esp by a shop: *We must advertise more if we want to increase our takings.*

take [C *usu sing*] *infml* takings: *What's today's take?*

turnover [S9, esp *of*] the amount of business done in a particular period: *Their annual turnover is £250,000* (= They do £250,000 worth of business in a year).

profit [C; U] the money, etc, gained by a business or a piece of business: *The profit this year was £1 million. What are the profits like on this business? He made a profit of £1,000 on that sale. There's very little profit in selling land at present.*

profit margin [C] the amount which one makes on something one sells over the cost of producing it: *We need a profit margin of 20% in order to keep our business going.*

loss [C] **1** a failure to make a profit: *He made a loss on those shoes. Their losses this year were high/heavy; they made no profit at all.* **2** the amount by which the cost of an article is greater than the selling price: *The shop made a loss of £2 on those shoes.*

Shopping and general expenses

J180 nouns : **shops and stores** [C]

shop [*often in comb*] a room or building where goods are regularly kept and sold: *I bought it at the local village shop. The shops in town close at 5.30. The sweet shop is near the bookshop.*

corner shop *not fml* a (usu small) shop at the corner of two local streets: *You can get some milk at the corner shop.*

store 1 *esp BrE* a large shop: *He bought it in one of the big London stores.* **2** *esp AmE* a shop: *Get what you need at the local store.*

general store a shop which sells most things that people need for everyday life

department store a large shop divided into departments, in each of which a different type of goods is sold

self-service *not fml* a usu larger shop where one serves oneself with food and goods and pays as one leaves

supermarket a large shop selling mainly food where one serves oneself

hypermarket a large supermarket

J181 nouns : **special small shops, etc** [C]

stall [*often in comb*] *esp BrE* a table or small open-fronted shop in a public place: *She sold fruit at a market stall. He bought a newspaper at the station bookstall.*

booth 1 (at a market) a covered moveable shop **2** (at a fair) a tent or small building where goods are sold or games are played **3** an enclosed place big enough for one person at a time: *a telephone booth; a voting booth; a listening booth in a record shop* **4** an enclosed place for one person selling something: *a ticket booth* **5** an enclosed place in a restaurant, esp one with a table between two long seats

kiosk 1 a small open hut, such as one used for selling newspapers **2** *BrE fml* a public telephone box, indoors or outdoors

boutique 1 a small shop (usu for women) selling up-to-date clothes and other personal articles of the newest kind **2** a department of this kind within a large department store

J182 nouns : **markets and shopping centres**

market 1 [C] a building, square, or open place where people meet to buy and sell goods, esp food or sometimes animals: *It is cheaper to buy vegetables from the market than from a shop. He bought some animals at the local cattle market. They waited in the market square.* **2** [C] the gathering of people to buy and sell on certain days at a market: *There's no market this week.* **3** [C9] a district, country, or countries, where there is a demand for goods: *They sell to foreign markets/the home market. They have a world market.* **4** [U; C (*for*)] demand for goods: *There's no market for such goods.* (*fig*) *He can't find a market for his skills.* **5** [C] (the state of) trade in certain goods, esp the rate of buying and selling: *We'll lose money by selling on a falling market.* (= when prices are falling). *There's great activity in the tea market.* **on the market** (of goods) for sale: *The house will come/be put on the market soon. This is the best car on the market.* **in the market for** ready to buy: *He's in the market for a good house.* **market place** [C] the place, usu a town square or open area, where a market can be held: *She met him in the market place.*

mart [C *sometimes in comb*] a market; a place of trade, esp a busy one

bazaar [C] **1** (in Eastern countries) a market-place or a group of shops **2** (in English-speaking countries) a sale to get money for some good purpose: *They held a church/hospital bazaar.*

shopping centre [C] a group of shops of different kinds, usu outside the centre of a town and planned and built as a whole

(shopping) arcade [C] a covered passage, esp one with an arched roof and with a row of shops on one or both sides: *Burlington Arcade is a famous shopping place in London.*

(shopping) precinct [C] a part of a town planned for, or limited to, shopping: *They have opened the new shopping precinct.*

J183 *nouns* : **sales and auctions** [C]

sale 1 a selling of items to whoever offers the highest price: *He got all his furniture at a sale. She was buying animals at the local cattle sales.* **2** a special offering of goods in a shop at lower prices than usual: *I got this hat cheap at a sale. The regular price is £5, but the sale price was £3.*
auction [C; *by* U] a public sale of goods to the person who offers the most money: *He went to a furniture auction. I shall sell my house by auction.*

J184 *nouns* : **bids and tenders** [C]

bid 1 an offer to pay a certain price at a sale, esp at an auction: *He made a bid of £5 for that old book. Who will make the highest bid for the book?* **2** an offer to do some work at a certain price: *Bids for building the bridge were invited from British and American firms. Who will make the lowest bid for the job?* **3** a chance or turn to make such a declaration: *It's your bid now, Mr Jones.* **4** an attempt or effort to get, win, or attract: *They made a bid for our favour by making promises. The criminal made a bid for freedom by trying to run away.*
tender a statement of the price one would charge for providing goods or services or for doing a job; (*tech*) a bid: *The government is inviting tenders for building a new oil pipeline from Scotland to London.*

J185 *nouns* : **shopping**

shopping 1 [U] the act of shopping: *Shopping can be a tiring business.* **2** [U] what one buys when shopping: *She had two big bags full of (her) shopping. Where's my shopping; I'm sure I left it here.*
window shopping [U] looking at the goods shown in (several) shop windows: *We didn't have any money, so we went window shopping.* **window shopper** [C] a person who goes window shopping
bargain hunting [U] hunting (= shopping) for bargains: *Let's go to the shops in Green Street: they're usually good for bargain hunting.* **bargain-hunter** [C] a person who goes or is good at bargain hunting.

J186 *nouns* : **shopping**

shopping day [C] a day when shops are open for business/when shopping can be done: *Is Tuesday a full shopping day in this town?*
shopping list [C] a set of names of things to buy in a shop or shops: *I must remember to put 'salt' on my shopping list.*
shopping bag/basket [C] a bag or basket used for carrying things when shopping

J187 *nouns* : **persons shopping** [C]

shopper a person who is buying or will buy things in shops: *The streets were full of shoppers.*
customer 1 a person who buys goods or services from a shop or trader, esp regularly: *The new shop across the road has taken away some of my best customers. You'll lose customers if your prices keep rising.* **2** [C9] *sl* a person one has to deal with; fellow: *He is an odd customer, isn't he?*
client 1 a person who **a** pays a professional person, esp a lawyer, for help and advice **b** gets help or advice from any of the government's social services **2** *fml* a customer: *We try to give our clients complete satisfaction.* **clientele** [GU] the customers of a business, shop, professional man, etc: *My clientele has always favoured quality rather than quantity. Do your clientele like the new fashions?*

J188 *nouns* : **persons owning shops, etc** [C]

shopkeeper a person usu the owner, in charge of a small shop
-keeper [*comb form*] a person who owns or runs the place stated: *He is a local hotel-keeper.*
dealer a person in a usu stated type of business: *He is a used-car dealer.*
stockist a person who keeps certain goods for sale: *He is our stockist in your town.*

J189 *nouns* : **persons serving in shops, etc** [C]

(shop) assistant *BrE*, **(sales) clerk** *AmE* a person who serves buyers in a shop
salesman a usu skilled shop assistant **saleswoman** [fem]
salesgirl a usu young female shop assistant
saleslady *fml* a female shop assistant

J190 *nouns* : **things in shops, etc** [C]

counter a narrow table or flat surface on which goods are shown or at which customers in a shop, bank, etc are served: *If you want to buy bread you must go to the food counter at the other end of the shop.*
shelf 1 a flat, usu long and narrow board fixed against a wall or in a frame, for placing things on: *He fixed a 5-foot shelf for books on the wall.* **2** a group of things filling one of these
trolley *esp BrE* a container on wheels in large shops and supermarkets [⇒ J180] which one uses to serve oneself, and move goods to where one can pay for them before leaving
cart *esp AmE* a trolley
cash-register a business machine, esp used in shops for calculating and recording the amount of each sale and the money received, and sometimes for giving change

494

cash-desk (in a shop) the desk where payments are made

checkout a cash desk in a self-service store

J191 nouns : special parts of shops

shop front the front, including the door(s), windows(s), and name, of a shop: *The street was full of brightly-painted shop fronts.*

store front 1 *BrE* the front of a large shop **2** *AmE* a shop front

shop window the window of a shop: *He stood looking in the shop window, wishing he had some money.*

J192 nouns : particular shopkeepers and shops, especially those selling food [C]

grocer a shopkeeper who sells dry and preserved foods, like flour, coffee, sugar, rice, and other things for the home, such as matches and soap: *He got coffee at the grocer's (shop).* **grocery** [A; (C)] a grocer's business or shop: *There's a big new grocery store opening in the High Street soon.* **groceries** [P] things sold by a grocer

greengrocer *esp BrE* a shopkeeper who sells vegetables and fruit: *She bought her vegetables at the local greengrocer's (shop).*

delicatessen a shop that sells special, usu foreign foods, esp those which are ready to eat when sold: *You can get Italian food at the delicatessen.*

butcher a person who (kills and) sells animals for food: *She bought some meat at the butcher's (shop).*

fishmonger *esp BrE* a person who owns, runs, or works in a shop which sells fish: *Go to the fishmonger's and get some fish.*

baker 1 a person who bakes bread and cakes, esp professionally **2** a person who keeps a shop for selling bread and cakes, etc: *He got bread at the baker's (shop).* **bakery** a place where the baking of bread, cakes, etc is done: *Go to the bakery for more bread; we've sold all we have. He's in the bakery business.*

dairy 1 a shop where milk, butter, cheese, and sometimes eggs and other food products are sold **2** (on a farm) a place where milk is kept and butter and cheese are made **3** a farm where milk, butter, and cheese (**dairy products**) are produced

sweet shop *BrE*, **candy store** *AmE* a shop selling sweets

tuck shop *BrE* a shop esp near or in a school, where children can buy sweets, etc

tobacconist a person who owns, runs, or works in a shop that sells mainly tobacco and cigarettes: *He got his cigarettes at a local tobacconist's (shop).*

pharmacist *BrE* usu **chemist**, *AmE* also **druggist** a person who owns or runs a shop (**phar-**

macy *fml*, **chemist's shop** *BrE*, **drugstore** *AmE*) where esp medicines are sold

drugstore *AmE* a pharmacy, esp one which sells not only medicine, beauty products, film, etc, but also simple meals

J193 nouns : particular shopkeepers and shops selling clothing, etc [C]

tailor 1 a person who makes outer garments, esp for men: *He has a good tailor.* **2** a person who owns, runs, or works in a shop which sells clothes, esp for men

draper *BrE* a person, esp a shopkeeper, who sells women's clothes, cloth, curtains, etc: *She bought some cloth at the draper's (shop).*

hosier a shopkeeper who sells socks and men's underclothes

haberdasher 1 *BrE* a shopkeeper who sells pins, sewing thread, and other small things used in dressmaking **2** *AmE* a shopkeeper who sells men's hats, gloves, etc

J194 nouns : shops, etc, selling books, newspapers, etc [C]

bookshop esp *BrE*, **bookstore** esp *AmE* a shop that sells books

bookseller a person who sells books or runs a bookshop

stationer a shopkeeper who sells writing paper, pens, office materials, etc (= **stationery**)

newsagent a person in charge of a shop selling newspapers and magazines: *You can get that paper at your local newsagent's (shop).*

newsstall/newsstand a kiosk [⇨ J181] for selling newspapers

J195 nouns : other kinds of shopkeepers and shops

florist [C] a person who keeps a shop for selling flowers

dry goods also **soft goods** [P] articles of clothing, soft furnishings, etc, esp as sold in a shop

ironmonger *BrE*, **hardware store** *AmE* [C] a shopkeeper who sells metal goods: *He got his tools at a local ironmonger's (shop).* **ironmongery** also **hardware** [U] the kind of metal goods sold by an ironmonger

J196 adjectives : costing a lot of money [B]

dear [Wa1] *esp BrE* costing a lot or too much: *It's too dear; I can't afford it.*

high [Wa1] *not fml* not cheap; costing more than one expects or wants to pay: *These prices are rather high, aren't they? That country has a high cost of living.*

expensive *often fml* costing a lot of money: *He's just bought a very expensive new car. Diamonds come (= are) expensive.* **-ly** [adv] *The girl was expensively dressed.*

costly [Wa2] **1** having a high price; expensive: *He bought her a lot of costly jewels.* **2** (*fig*) gained or won at a great loss: *That was the costliest war in our history.*

pricy, pricey [Wa1;F;(B)] *infml esp BrE* dear in price: *These new cars are a bit pricey. That shop is too pricy for me; I can't afford to buy there.* **-cily** [adv] **-ciness** [U]

steep [Wa1] *infml* expensive: *Their prices are pretty steep; I can't buy anything in that shop.*

J197 *formal adjectives* : **costing too much** [B]

exorbitant *derog* (of costs, demands, etc) much greater than is reasonable: *That hotel charges exorbitant prices. He makes exorbitant demands on my time.* **-ly** [adv]: *She charges exorbitantly for her services.*

prohibitive (of a price) too high to be afforded

extortionate (of a demand, price, etc) very high; much too high: *I complained about the extortionate charges at the hotel.* **-ly** [adv] [⇒ C233 EXTORTION]

J198 *adjectives, etc* : **not costing a lot of money**

cheap [Wa1] **1** [B] **a** low in price; costing little: *Fresh vegetables are very cheap in the summer.* **b** worth more than the cost; good value for money: *Bread is cheap in this shop; it costs twice as much across the street.* **c** *BrE* reduced in price for a quick sale: *Buy now; the goods are going cheap.* **2** [B] charging low prices: *This is the cheapest restaurant in town.* **3** [B] (*fig*) needing little effort: *The army won a cheap victory over the enemy, who had few guns and soldiers.* **4** [F] worth little; of or considered of little value: *100 years ago life was a lot cheaper than it is today.* **5** [B] *esp AmE* careful with money; tight: *He's the cheapest man in town.* **6** [adv] in a cheap way: *I wish she wouldn't act so cheap.* **-ly** [adv] **-ness** [U] **on the cheap** *infml* cheaply; without paying the full cost: *She got some new trousers on the cheap down at the market. The government must learn that it can't provide good education on the cheap.*

free [Wa5;B adv] costing nothing: *You can get free books here. How much did it cost?— Nothing; it was free.*

for nothing *not fml* for no money; free: *I got this bicycle for nothing; a friend just gave it to me.*

low [Wa1;B] *not fml* not expensive; costing less than one expects or is ready to pay: *These prices are surprisingly low, aren't they? That country has a lower cost of living than this one.*

inexpensive [B] not expensive; low in price: *He*

bought her an inexpensive present. **-ly** [adv] *She was well, but inexpensively dressed.*

economical [B] not wasteful; using money, time, etc carefully: *She is an economical housekeeper and feeds her family carefully.* **un-** [neg] **-ly** [adv Wa3]

a bargain costing less than one would expect or be willing to pay: *I got the book for £1; it was a (real) bargain. What a bargain!*

J199 *adjectives* : **worth a lot of money, etc** [B]

valuable 1 worth a lot of money: *Your collection of pictures must be very valuable now that prices have increased so much.* **2** having great usefulness or value: *He gave the company years of valuable service. You'll find this little tool very valuable for cutting out small shapes. This new book will, we hope, be valuable to students of English.*

precious 1 of great value and beauty: *Gold is a precious metal.* **2** of great value and not to be wasted: *His time is precious; why do you want to see him?* **3** greatly loved or valued as being dear to one: *Your friendship is precious to me.* **4** [adv] *infml & ironical* very: *Her advice was of precious little use to me!*

superior 1 of high quality: *This is superior wool.* **2** (of people and things) good or better in quality or value: *He thinks he's superior to us because his father's an important man.* **-ity** [U]

priceless 1 of very great value; of worth too great to be described or calculated: *Only a very rich man could afford to buy these priceless paintings. Good health is priceless.* **2** *infml* very funny or laughably foolish: *You look priceless in those trousers! They're much too tight.* **-ness** [U]

invaluable (of a person, thing, or quality) too valuable for its worth to be measured: *These men are invaluable to me; they work very well. Your invaluable help saved my business.*

J200 *adjectives* : **not of good quality** [B]

cheap [Wa1] **1** of poor quality: *Her shoes looked cheap.* **2** in low or unpleasant taste: *I don't like his cheap humour.* **-ly** [adv] **-ness** [U]

poor [Wa1] **1** less than is needed or expected; small in size or quantity: *We had a poor crop of beans this year. This product is in poor supply* (= we can't get it easily). **2** *derog* much below the usual standard; low in quality: *Don't buy that coat; the cloth is of poor quality. The weather has been very poor this summer; we've had little sun.* **3** (of the body or its parts and their working) weak; not good: *He's still in poor health after his illness. Grandfather has poor eyesight.* **4** *derog* (of a person or his behaviour) not noble or generous (*esp in the phrs* **poor loser/sport**): *He gets angry when he* loses a game; he's a poor loser. **5** *usu derog* not respected, because of lack of ability or character: *The poor fool has got himself into debt again.* **6** [Wa5;A] *usu polite or humor & ironical* of little worth; not good enough for others; humble: *In my poor opinion you're making a great mistake.*

shoddy [Wa1] made or done cheaply and badly, usu to look like something better: *It is shoddy workmanship that won't bear close examination. They put the shoddiest goods on sale right next to the valuable articles.* **-dily** [adv] **-diness** [U]

tawdry [Wa1] cheaply showy; lacking taste: *She has a lot of tawdry jewellery.* **-riness** [U]

inferior [Wa5] (of people and things) not (or less) good in quality or value: *These goods are of inferior quality. His work is inferior to hers.* **inferiority** [U] the state of being inferior: *The inferiority of these goods to the others is easy to see.*

worthless 1 of no value: *It was a worthless action. The old type of £5 notes are worthless now.* **2** (of a person) of bad character: *He is a worthless member of society.* **-ness** [U]

valueless having no value: *This jewellery is valueless; it is made of glass and ordinary metals.* **-ness** [U]

Business, work, and employment

J210 *nouns* : work, jobs, trades, and professions

work [U] **1** activity which uses effort, esp with a special purpose, not for amusement: *It takes a lot of work to build a house.* **2** (the nature or place of) a job or occupation: *My work is in medicine/as a doctor. I go to work at 9. What time do you get home from work? I eat at work.* **3** what one is working on: *I hear you've changed jobs; is the work difficult at the new place? I'm taking some work home to do this evening. Don't stay inside to do your sewing; bring your work out with you.* **4** what is produced by work, esp of the hands: *This mat is my own work* (= I made it). *She sold her work to a local shop.* **at work (on)** doing something, esp work: *Danger; men at work (on this road).* **go/set to work (on)** to start doing **in work/out of work** having a job/unemployed

job [C] **1** a piece of work that has been or must be done: *Do a better job next time. He gets paid by the job.* **2** something hard to do: *It was a (real) job to talk with all that noise. You'll have a hard job doing that.* **3** regular paid employment: *He has a good job in a bank. Job safety is important.* **4** *infml* an example of a certain type: *That new car of yours is a beautiful job.*

This job is a bit bigger and more colourful than the one over there. **5** *sl* a dishonest or harmful piece of work, esp robbery or a beating: *He's in prison for a job he pulled* (= did) *in Liverpool. John's been in hospital since Paul did that job on him.* **on the job** (of people or, sometimes, machines) at work; working; busy **a job of work** *BrE infml* a piece of work, usu well done: *You can be sure my brother will do a job of work for the money you pay him.* **out of a job** unemployed: *You'll be out of a job if you keep coming late.* **a good/bad job** *BrE infml* good/bad: *That restaurant is not cheap, so it's a good job you've brought plenty of money. He's gone, and a good job too!* **make the best of a bad job** to do as much or as well as possible in unfavourable conditions **just the job** exactly the thing wanted or needed: *Thanks for that tool; it was just the job.*

task [C] a piece of (esp difficult) work which must be done: *It's a difficult task but I think you can do it. Our first task here is to build a wall.*

occupation [C] **1** a job; employment: *What is your father's occupation?* **2** *becoming rare* way of spending time: *Her favourite weekend occupation is reading.* **occupational** [Wa5;B] of or about an occupation **-ly** [adv]

living [C] **1** the earnings with which one buys necessities: *You can make a (good) living in industry.* **2** wages; income: *I make £100 a week on what I sell and that's my living.* **3** a trade or profession: *Teaching is his living.*

livelihood [C] the way by which one earns enough to pay for what is necessary: *He will lose his livelihood if the factory closes.*

career [C] **1** a job or profession for which one is trained and which one intends to follow for the whole of one's life: *He made the Church his career. Teaching is a satisfying career.* **2** (a part of) the general course of a person's working life: *Have you ever studied Gladstone's career as a politician? Churchill's career proves he was a great man.*

profession 1 [C;*by* U] a form of employment, esp one that is respected in society as honourable and is possible only for an educated person and after training in some special branch of knowledge (such as law, medicine, and the Church): *In the last century there was a great social difference between business(men) and the professions. He is a lawyer by profession. She intends to make teaching her profession.* **2** [*the* GU] the whole body of people in a particular profession: *The teaching profession claim(s) to be badly paid. Most people in the profession say so.* **professional 1** [Wa5;A] working in a profession: *Doctors are professional men.* **2** [C;A] *apprec* a person who makes his or her living by doing certain work: *He is a professional at it; he is very good. She is a professional singer.* **3** [B] *apprec* (well) done by or as if by a professional: *That is a very professional piece of work.* **un-** [neg] **-ly** [adv]: *She sings professionally. He did the job very professionally.*

trade [C; *by* U] an occupation, esp one needing special skill with hands: *He is a printer by trade. How long did it take to learn your trade?*

mission [C] a journey, esp to another country or place and often military, to do some particular work for which one has been sent: *The soldiers' mission was to destroy the bridge. He went abroad on a mission for the government.*

J211 *verbs* : **employing and appointing people**

employ [T1] **1** to use (a person) as a paid worker: *The firm employs about 100 men.* **2** to take on or appoint (a person) as a paid worker: *We're employing three new secretaries next Monday.* **3** *fml* to keep (oneself or another) busy: *She was employed in watering the garden.* **4** *fml* to spend (time): *She employs all her free time in sewing.* **employment** [(*in*) U] the act of employing; the condition of being employed: *He is badly in need of employment. They are considering the employment of 1,000 workers. He has been in our employment/in employment here for 10 years.*

hire [T1] to employ (someone) for a time for payment: *They hired some men to help with the work.*

engage [T1 (*as*)] to arrange to employ (someone): *He has engaged a new secretary. He engaged Mary as a secretary.* **engagement** [U] the act of engaging: *They have begun the engagement of new workers.*

take on [v adv T1] *not fml* to hire: *They decided to take on a servant to help with the house.*

appoint 1 [T1; X1; (V3)] to put in or choose for a position, job (or purpose); make into an officer (of a business, club, etc): *We must appoint a new teacher soon. They appointed him to catch all the rats in Hamelin.* **2** [T1] to set up; make by choosing: *We must appoint a committee.* **3** [T1] *fml* to arrange, settle; fix; decide: *We should appoint a time for the next meeting. Let's appoint a day to have lunch together.* **appointment 1** [U] the act of appointing: *He is considering the appointment of a new manager.* **2** [C] a special job or position in a business, school, etc: *The new appointments have all been filled* (= people have been given the new jobs).

recruit 1 [T1] to get as a new member: *Let's recruit some new people for the job/members for the club.* **2** [T1] to form (a group) with new members: *They are recruiting a new army/political party.* **3** [IØ] to find recruits [⇒ C302] **recruitment** [U] the act of recruiting

staff [T1 (*with*) *usu pass*] to supply with workers; provide the workers for: *It is a well-staffed office. The hospital is staffed with 20 doctors.*

fill [T1 *often pass*] to put someone in a (job, etc): *The position has been filled. We have filled two of the places, but not the third.*

J212 *verbs* : **dismissing and retiring people**

[ALSO ⇒ J219 PENSION OFF]

dismiss [T1 (*from*) *often pass*] **1** *fml* to send (someone) away (as from employment): *If you're late again you'll be dismissed (from your job).* **2** to allow to go: *The teacher dismissed the class 10 minutes early.*

discharge [T1 (*from*)] to dismiss (a person) from a job: *Anyone caught stealing will be discharged (from the firm).* **discharge** [C; U] the act or result of discharging: *He got his discharge/discharge papers from the Army.*

disband 1 [IØ] (of a group) to break up and separate: *The club has disbanded.* **2** [T1] to break up and separate (a group): *They disbanded the army.*

sack [T1 *often pass*] BrE *infml* to dismiss (someone) from work: *If he is late again, sack him. 200 men have been sacked at the factory.* **get the sack** to be sacked: *He got the sack (from his job) last week.*

fire [T1 *often pass*] *infml & emph* to dismiss (someone) from work: *You're no good; you're fired! He fired them last week.*

lay off [v adv/prep] **1** [T1; D1] to stop employing (a worker), esp for a period in which there is little work: *They laid us off (work) for three months.* **2** [T1, 4a; IØ] *infml* to stop: *Lay off work for a few months. Lay off, will you! Lay off hitting me!* **lay-off** [C] **1** (by a business) laying a worker or workers off **2** the period of time when this happens

retire [T1] to cause to leave a job, usu because of age: *They retired him early.* [also ⇒ J214]

J213 *verbs* : **joining and enlisting**

join [T1; IØ] to become a member (of): *He joined the Army/the club. Has he joined or not?*

join up [v adv IØ] to offer oneself, esp for military service: *He joined up in 1970.*

enlist [IØ; T1] to (cause to) enter the armed forces: *He enlisted when he was 18. He enlisted in the Army as a private (soldier). We must enlist more men.*

sign on [v adv IØ; T1] to (cause to) join (a work force); enlist: *He signed on as a sailor. The factory signed on ten new workers.*

J214 *verbs* : **leaving and retiring from jobs**

leave [T1; IØ] to go away (from); to stop doing work at (a place, job, etc): *I'm leaving this job; I don't like it. He didn't like the work, so he left.*

quit 1 [T1, 4; IØ] *infml often emph & emot* to stop doing something and leave: *I've quit my job. I've quit working there. I'd had enough, so I quit.* **2** [T1] *old use* to leave

give up [v adv T1, 4] *usu not fml* to stop having

or doing: *She has given up her job at the bank. He has given up smoking.*

resign [I0 (*from*); T1] *often fml* to give up (a job or position): *He resigned from the committee/post/job. If he resigns, who will get the job?* **resignation 1** [U] the act or result of resigning **2** [C] a written statement that one intends to resign: *He handed in his resignation.* **3** [C] an example of resigning: *There have been two resignations this week.*

vacate [T1] to give up (something, such as a job or position): *He vacated his job/post at the bank.* **vacation** [U] *fml* the act of vacating

retire [I0] to stop working for ever, usu because of age: *My father retired at the age of 60.* **retirement** [C; U] a case or the act of retiring: *His employer gave him a gold watch on his retirement. We've had two retirements here this year.*

J215 *verbs* : **promoting and transferring people**

[ALSO ⇒ C297 ARMY RANKS, ETC]

promote 1 [T1; *esp BrE* X1] to advance (someone) in position or rank: *The young army officer was promoted (to the rank of) captain. The owner's son was promoted over the heads of others* (= was given a higher position instead of others who had a better claim). **2** [T1] to help actively in forming or arranging (a business, concert, play, etc): *Who is promoting this boxing match? The three brothers are promoting a company to make aircraft.* **3** [T1] to bring (goods) to public notice in order to increase (sales): *The company are promoting their new sort of toothbrush on television. How can we promote the sales of this product?* **4** [T1] (*fig*) to support; help in the growth of: *Milk promotes health.* **promotion 1** [U] the act or result of promoting or being promoted **2** [C] an example of this

upgrade [T1] to raise in rank, position, or importance: *They upgraded him/his job so that they could raise his pay.*

transfer [T1] to move (someone) from one job or place of work to another: *They transferred him from New York to a new post in Washington. I've been transferred; I'm leaving for my new post next week.* **transfer** [C; U] (an example of) the act of transferring: *He wants a transfer to another job.*

assign [D1 (*to*); V3] to appoint to a job or duty; name: *She assigned him to wash the plates. I assigned you (to) the job; do it.* **assignment 1** [U] *rare* the act of assigning **2** [C] *common* a job which one is given or to which one is sent: *I shall soon be leaving on an assignment in India. The policeman's assignment was to discover the murderer.*

second [T1 *usu pass*] *BrE fml* to move (someone) from usual duties to a special duty, usu for a limited time: *If Mr Adams is ill much longer, someone will have to be seconded from another*

department to do his work. **secondment 1** [U] the act of seconding: *He is on secondment to/in Hong Kong.* **2** [C] an example, occasion, or result of this

delegate 1 [T1] to give (part of one's power, rights, etc) to another for a certain time: *I have delegated my command to Captain Roberts.* **2** [T1; V3] to appoint as one's representative: *I have delegated Captain Roberts (to serve in my place).*

J216 *verbs* : **demoting people**

demote [T1] to lower (someone) in position or rank: *He demoted the army officers (to a lower rank). Because he did not work well, he was demoted.* **demotion 1** [U] the act or result of demoting or being demoted **2** [C] an example of this

downgrade [T1] to lower in rank, position or importance: *They downgraded him/his job so that they could lower his pay.*

reduce [T1 *often pass*] to demote: *He has been reduced in rank for failing to do his work properly.* **reduced to the ranks** (of officers in armies) demoted to being an ordinary soldier, usu for doing something very bad

strip [D1 (*of*)] *infml & emot* to take away (esp a high ra(someone): *He has been stripped of his rank; he is just an ordinary soldier now.*

J217 *adjectives* : **relating to having jobs** [Wa5;B]

vacant (of a position in employment) not at present filled: *I'm looking for work; are there any positions vacant in your firm? The part of a newspaper in which jobs are advertised is often called 'Situations Vacant'.* **vacancy 1** [U] the condition of being vacant **2** [C] an example of this: *Are there any vacancies in your factory?*

redundant *esp BrE* (of a worker or group of workers) not needed; more than necessary: *These workers are now redundant.* **-ly** [adv] **redundancy** [U; C] the condition of being redundant; an example of this: *How many redundancies have there been in this factory?*

J218 *verbs* : **earning and profiting**

earn 1 [T1] to get (money) by working: *He earns £5,000 a year.* **2** [D1 (*for*); T1] to (cause to) get (something that one deserves) because of one's qualities: *His victories in the war earned him the title of 'Great'.*

gain 1 [T1] to obtain (something useful, necessary, wanted, etc): *I'm new in the job but I'm already gaining experience. Eat well if you want to gain strength after your illness.* **2** [T1; I0] to make (a profit or increase in amount): *I gained £3 by selling it for more than I paid for it. The* baby gains (half a pound) every week; he's getting bigger all the time.

make [T1] *infml* to earn: *How much do you make in/at your job? Secretaries make quite a lot here, but not in that other place.*

get [T1] *infml & genl* to earn: *How much does he get a week?*

profit 1 [I0] *fml* to gain: *You'll profit if you listen to him. They profited by putting their money in his business.* **2** [T1; D1] *fml or old use* (of a thing) to be of service, use, or advantage to (someone or something): *What can it profit (you) to tell him this? It will profit you nothing.*

bring in [v adv T1; D1] *not fml* to produce as profit or earnings: *The sale brought (us) in over £200. The boys are bringing in £40 a week.*

J219 *nouns* : **earnings and income**

[ALSO ⇨ J122, J135]

earnings [P] **1** money which is earned by working **2** money made by a company

pay [U] money received for work, esp in the Armed Forces: *He gets his pay on Fridays. There was less money in his pay packet* (= the envelope in which he gets his pay) *this week than last week.* **in the pay of** *esp deprec* employed by: *He is in the pay of the enemy.*

wages [P] a payment usu of money for labour or services (usu according to contract) calculated by the hour, day, week, or amount produced, and usu received daily or weekly: *What are your weekly wages? Wages are high in this country.*

wage [S; A] wages: *There is a high wage level in this industry. There was less money in his wage packet* (= the envelope in which he gets his wages) *this week than last week. What is your weekly wage? He gets a weekly wage of £60.* **a living wage** an amount of pay large enough to buy the food, clothing, etc, needed for living: *We have a right to a living wage.*

salary [C; U] fixed regular pay each month, three months, year, or sometimes each week, for a job, esp (rather than wages) as for workers of higher skill and rank: *The company pays good salaries. How much salary does the job pay?*

fee [C] a sum of money paid for professional services to a doctor, lawyer, private school, etc: *He paid the child's school fees. You can use the library for a small fee. Did the doctor charge you a fee?*

honorarium [C] *fml* money offered for professional services, for which by custom the person does not ask to be paid

retainer [C] a fee paid to someone so that he is ready to do some work for one at any time: *His annual retainer* (=fee for one year) *is £1,000.*

profit 1 [C; U] money gain; money gained by a business or a piece of business: *He sold his*

house at a profit (= sold it for more than it had cost him). *He made a profit of £1,000 on that sale. There's very little profit in selling land at present.* **2** [U] *fml* advantage gained from some action: *It would be to your profit to take her wise advice.*

income [U; C] money which one receives regularly for one's daily spending, usu payment for one's work, or interest from investments [⇨ J114]: *He receives income from investments. He has a very low/small income.*

stipend [C] money paid for professional work, esp to a priest

pension [C] an amount of money paid regularly (esp by a government or a company) to someone who can no longer earn (enough or any) money be working, esp because of old age or illness **pensioner** [C] a person receiving a pension **pensionable** [Wa5; B] (of work, etc) providing a pension **pension off** [v adv T1] to dismiss from work with a pension

J220 *nouns* : **expenses and allowances**

expenses [P] the money used or needed for a purpose: *If you want to go to Paris I'll pay your expenses. He managed to earn enough to cover his expenses. His employer pays all his travelling expenses. He has monthly expenses of about £50 and his company pays him these expenses (back). If you do this work you must travel a bit, but you get your expenses (paid).*

allowance [C] **1** something, esp money, provided regularly: *He received a yearly allowance of money from his father. She gets an allowance of £5,000 a year.* **2** money provided for a special purpose: *Many people in well-paid jobs are given travelling allowances. Workers now demand allowances to make sure their pay increases as quickly as the cost of living.* **3** money taken off (the cost of) something, usu for a special reason: *If you pay cash now I will give you an allowance of 10% off the price. In Britain people get allowances on tax for their children and don't pay any tax on that amount of money earned.*

grant [C] money given by the state, usu for educational purposes, as to a university or (esp) to support a student during his studies: *You can get a grant to improve your house. When prices rise, students find it difficult to live on a grant.*

subsidy [C] money paid, esp by the government or an organization, to make prices lower, make it cheaper to produce goods, etc: *The government provided a subsidy on bread. We must give the farmers a subsidy.* **subsidize, -ise** [T1] to give a subsidy to; provide a subsidy for: *The government subsidizes a lot of housing in Scotland.*

rise *BrE*, **raise** *AmE* [C] an increase in wages: *We all got a £6-a-week rise last month. I've had two rises this year.*

J221 *nouns* : **stoppages and cuts**
[ALSO ⇒ J123]

stoppage [U; C] the act of preventing something from being given, esp money: *Stoppage of pay is no longer a lawful punishment in a firm.*

reduction [C] the amount by which payment or the price of something is reduced (= made less): *He has had a reduction in pay. There have been reductions in the price of food.*

cut [C] *not fml* a reduction; an act of economizing [⇒ J127]: *We must make cuts; we are spending too much. They have had cuts in their wages* [⇒ J219].

J222 *nouns* : **accounts and book-keeping**

account [C *often pl*] a record or statement of money received and paid out, as by a bank or business, esp for a particular period or at a particular date: *The bank sends me an account each month. The accounts show we have spent more than we received.*

accountancy [U] the work or job of keeping accounts

bookkeeping [U] the act of keeping the accounts of money of a business company, a public office, etc

ledger [C] an account book recording the gains and money spent of a business, bank, etc

books [P] all the ledgers, etc, of a business: *He wants to see the books.*

J223 *nouns* : **staff and personnel**

staff 1 [GC] the group of workers who carry on a job or do the work of an organization: *The school's teaching staff is/are excellent. He has a staff of 15. The company has a staff newspaper. We need hotel space for the minister and his staff at the meeting.* **2** [P] *BrE* members of such a group: *She is in charge of about 20 staff. There have been several complaints by staff about working conditions. Office staff wanted—good pay.*

personnel 1 [GC] (all) the people employed by a company, the armed forces, etc: *A lot of army personnel live in the town. I would like to see the person in charge of personnel.* **2** [U] the department in a company that deals with (the complaints and difficulties of the) personnel: *She works in personnel.*

work force [GC] the people working in a place: *The factory has a work force of more than a thousand.*

crew [GC] **1 a** all the people working on a ship, plane, etc **b** all the people working on a ship, plane, etc, except the officers: *The crew annoyed at the captain's decision to visit the port. (fig) We went rowing today; my wife was the captain and I was the crew.* **2** a group of people working together: *He sent for the train track repair crew. They are the stage crew for the new play.* **3** *infml* a gathering of people: *We were a happy crew that day!*

team [GC] a group of people who work, play, or act together: *He is in the school cricket team. The company is led by an able team of skilled politicians.*

complement [C] the full number of people working in a place, on a ship, etc: *What is the ship's complement?*

J224 *adjectives, etc* : **permanent and temporary**

permanent [B] staying or intended to stay (with a company, etc) for a long time or for ever: *He is one of our permanent employees/members of staff.* **-ly** [adv]

temporary [B] staying or intended to stay (with a company, etc) for only a limited time: *Many students find temporary jobs during their summer holidays.* **-rily** [adv]

full-time [Wa5; A; adv] (working or giving work) regularly; the proper number of hours or days in an employment, course of study, etc: *She's a full-time student at the university. He is in full-time employment. He used to work full-time, but now he does only 4 days a week.*

part-time [Wa5; A; adv] (working or giving work) for only a part of the regular working time: *She is a part-time nurse. He has a part-time job. He only works part-time.*

J225 *nouns* : **businesses and firms**

business [C] a particular money-earning activity or place, such as a shop: *How's the business? He sold his business to me. He has several local businesses.*

company 1 [GC] a group of people combined together for business or trade: *The local bus company is very good. Which companies do they own? If the company refuses to pay you more, then find another job.* **2** [U] the members of such a group whose names do not appear in the official name: *John Greene and Company* (*abbrev* **& Co**) **3** [GC] an organization of musical performers, actors, etc: *The theatre company make/makes a tour of the country every summer.*

firm [GC] a business company: *Don't do other work in the firm's time, please. He owns a building firm.*

enterprise [C] an organization, esp a business firm: *They are one of the largest enterprises of the kind in the country.*

corporation [GC] a body of people permitted by law to act as a single person, esp for purposes of business, with rights and duties separate from those of its members: *The company's name is The British Steel Corporation. John works for a large American chemical cor-*

poration. **corporate** [Wa5;B] of, concerning, or like what is done in a group: *The big company has a corporate way of doing most things and it is much the same whether in Hong Kong or Hamburg.* **-ly** [adv]: *They are corporately responsible for everything that happens.*

conglomerate [C] a large business firm that controls the production of goods of very different kinds

office 1 [C] a place where business is done **2** [C] a place where a service is provided: *a ticket office* **3** [C] a place where written work is done in connection with a business: *office work* **4** [C9 *usu cap*] a government department: *the Foreign Office* **5** [C] employment and special duties: *the office of president*

agency [C] **1** a business that makes its money esp by bringing people into touch with others or the products of others: *The travel agency arranged for me to take a holiday planned by one of the biggest holiday firms. I got this job in the factory through an employment agency.* **2** the office or place of business of a person who represents a business: *The large firm has agencies throughout the world.*

line [C *often in comb*] a business that helps people or goods to move by road, railway, ships, air, etc: *He runs an airline. That shipping line is very well-known.*

J226 *adjectives* : **public and private** [Wa5]

public [B] of a business company that offers shares in itself for sale to the public on the Stock Exchange [⇨ J104]

private [B] (of a business) belonging to one or more people; not belonging to the state

nationalized, -ised [B] (of a business) bought or controlled by the state: *In Britain steel and coal are nationalized industries.* **nationalize, -ise** (of governments) to take (businesses, property, etc) from persons, groups, etc, and keep it by the state in the name of all the people of that state: *Britain nationalized its coal and steel industries.* **nationalization, -isation** [U] the act of nationalizing

state [A] belonging to the state: *The Steel Corporation is a state industry.*

J227 *nouns* : **headquarters, branches, and departments** [C]

headquarters [Wn3] the office or place where the people work who control a large organization such as the police or army or a private firm: *I've just had a message from headquarters. Our headquarters staff* [⇨ J223] *is not very large.* **HQ** *abbrev* headquarters

main office the office of greatest importance or size in a firm, etc

branch a division of a business: *The bank has branches in many cities.*

branch office the office of a branch: *Do you have a branch office there?*

department any of the important divisions or branches of a business, government, school or college, etc: *He is in the History Department of the University. She works in the children's clothing department of a large store.*

subsidiary any part which is less important, esp of a company

base a place from which one goes to and to which one returns when working over a large area, esp where one keeps supplies, etc: *He has his base in Manchester. Our base for sales in Scotland is Glasgow. The army has/have a large base near here. The air base was closed and there are no more planes here now. The climbers' base camp was high on the mountain.*

depot a building or place where goods, vehicles, etc, are kept for an organization, group, army, etc: *Where is the bus depot in this city?*

J228 *nouns* : **employers and executives** [C]

[ALSO ⇨ C160]

employer a person who employs others: *Mr Jones is my employer.*

boss [*also* N] *infml* an employer; person having control over others: *He asked the boss for more money.* (*fig*) *Have you got a match, boss?*

manager 1 [*fem*] **manageress** a person who controls a business: *The bank manager refused to lend him any more money. She took the faulty goods back to the shop and asked to see the manageress.* **2** a person who makes arrangements, esp for the use of money to live on: *She must be a very good manager to feed her children so well on so little money.*

executive a person concerned with making and carrying out decisions, esp in business: *He is a young (business) executive. He has an important job as an executive of the firm.*

steward a person, esp a man, who manages or helps to manage esp meetings, dances, etc

J229 *nouns* : **employees and members of staff** [C]

employee [C (*of*)] a person who is employed: *They are Government employees/employees of the Government.*

member of staff *esp BrE* a person working on the staff [⇨ J223] of a company, school, organization, etc

staffer *esp AmE infml* a member of staff

J230 *nouns* : **partners and shareholders** [C]

partner 1 [(*with, in*)] a person who shares (in the same activity): *They were partners in the job.* **2** [(*in*)] any of the owners of a business, who shares the profits and losses, esp equally: *There are three partners in this firm of lawyers.*

shareholder a person who holds shares [⇒ J114] in a business, company, etc: *There will be a meeting of shareholders/a shareholders' meeting next month.*

J231 *nouns* : **boards of directors, etc**

board [GC *often cap*] a committee or association, as of company directors or government officials, organized for a special responsibility: *He has joined/been elected to the board of a new company. Mary is the workers' representative on the Board. The President of the Board of Trade is a Minister in the British Government. The Board is not agreed on this matter. He is one of our Board members.*

chairman [C; A] a person **a** in charge of a meeting: *She's one of our best and most experienced chairmen. Permission to speak, (Mister/ Madam) Chairman!* (= May I speak please?) **b** who directs the work of a committee, department, etc: *He was elected (the) chairman of the education committee. He was reading the thoughts of Chairman Mao.*

governor [C] **1** a person who controls one of certain types of organizations: *He is the governor of the prison/the Bank of England.* **2** a member of a governing body who control a school, hospital, art gallery, etc: *The governors are meeting to decide if the name of the school is to be changed.*

director [C] **1** a person who directs an organization **2** a member of the board of directors who run a company

J232 *nouns* : **persons organizing business companies, etc** [C]

accountant a person whose job is to keep and examine the money accounts of businesses or people

treasurer the person who looks after the money of a club, society, organization, etc

secretary 1 a person with the job of preparing letters, keeping records, arranging meetings, etc for another: *He got a job as private secretary to the company chairman.* **2** an officer of an organization who keeps records, writes official letters, etc: *She was elected as secretary of the club.*

personal secretary the secretary who works most closely to an executive [⇒ J228], chairman [⇒ J231], etc: *He is Personal Secretary to the Prime Minister. My personal secretary will give you a time to see me about it.*

private secretary *fml & older use* a personal secretary

personal assistant a person who helps an executive, chairman, etc in various ways **PA** *abbrev*

J233 *nouns* : **typing personnel** [C]

typist 1 a person skilled at using a typewriter [⇒ G152] **2** a secretary employed mainly for typing letters, etc

shorthand typist a typist who also uses shorthand   **shorthand** [U] a system of rapid writing using signs or shorter forms for letters, words, phrases, etc: *She made shorthand notes.*

stenographer *esp AmE & BrE old use* a shorthand typist **stenography** [U] shorthand **steno** *abbrev* stenographer

audio-typist a typist who types spoken information, lectures, etc, esp from a dictating [⇒ J236] machine

typing pool a group of typists who type letters in a large office

J234 *nouns* : **other office personnel** [C]

clerk 1 a person employed in an office, shop, etc, to keep records, accounts, etc, and to do written work **2** an official in charge of the records of a court, town council, etc   **clerical** [Wa5;B] of, concerning, or like the work of a clerk or work done in an office: *We need more clerical help. She doesn't like doing clerical work.*

receptionist a person who receives people arriving in an office, a hotel, etc

filing clerk a clerk who looks after the filing system [⇒ J235] in a firm, etc

office boy a boy employed to do some of the less important clerical work in an office

J235 *nouns, etc* : **office equipment**

file [C] **1** any of various arrangements of drawers, shelves, or cases, usu fitted with wires or metal rods, for storing papers in an office **2** [(*on*)] a collection of papers on one subject, stored in this way: *Here's our file on the Middle East. She read her own personal file* (= the one that someone else kept to record her activities, judge her behaviour, etc). **keep/have a file on** to collect/store information about   **on file 1** stored in a file: *Put these papers on file.* **2** recorded in this way: *We have it on file that he's been married before.*

filing system [C] a way of keeping files so that they can be found (easily) when needed

filing cabinet [C] a cupboard, usu of metal, in which special boxes are fitted to hold files

folder [C] a folded piece of stiff cardboard used for holding loose papers & files

tray [C] a shallow object of wood, metal or plastic with a flat bottom and raised edges, placed on a desk to hold papers, letters, etc: *Each morning her secretary puts the letters in her tray.*

in-tray [C] the tray for letters, papers, etc, which have come in to be considered

out-tray [C] the tray for letters, papers, etc, which have been considered and which must go out, be posted, filed, etc
pending [Wa5; F; (B); U] (matters) waiting to be decided: *Put those papers in Mr Smith's pending file. Put it in pending, please.*

J236 *verbs* : **office activities**

file [T1] to put (papers or letters) in a file: *Please file this letter (away).*
dictate [I0; T1 (*to*)] to say (words) for someone else, esp a secretary [⇨ J232], to write down: *She dictates all her letters.* **dictation** [U] the act of dictating; anything that is dictated
copy [T1] to make a copy of: *These letters should be copied to heads of departments, please.*

J237 *nouns* : **trade unions, etc** [C]

union *also BrE* **trade union**, *AmE* **labor union**, *becoming rare* **trades union** an organization of workers to represent their interests and deal collectively with employers
shop steward a trade union officer who is elected by the members of his union in a particular place of work to represent them
closed shop a factory or other establishment in which the employer hires only people who are members of a particular trade union, usu by agreement with the union concerned

J238 *nouns* : **industrial action** [C]

industrial action [*also* U] any action by workers to show that they are not happy about their pay or working conditions: *The union leader said that they would take industrial action if they did not get more pay.*
(industrial) dispute a disagreement between workers and employers in a factory, business, etc
strike a time when no work is done because of disagreement as over working conditions (*often in the phr* **on strike**): *The men are all on strike. The country has had a lot of strikes lately. The union said it would take strike action. The strike leader met their employers.*
stoppage an act of stopping work, as in a strike: *There has been another stoppage at the factory.*
work-to-rule *esp BrE* a form of working which slows down activity, because attention is paid to every point in the rules, even when unnecessary
go-slow *BrE,* **slow-down (strike)** *AmE* the action of refusing to put more than the least

effort into work, as a form of industrial action: *The workers are on a go-slow today.*
picket 1 a man placed, esp by a trade union, at the entrance to a factory, shop, etc, to prevent anyone (esp other workers) from going in until a quarrel with the employers is over **2** *infml* a picket line
picket line a line of pickets: *He did not cross the picket line.*

J239 *verbs* : **industrial action**

strike [Wv4; I0 (*for*)] (of workers) to stop working because of disagreement: *They struck for better working conditions. The striking workers did not accept the offer made by their employers.*
picket [T1] to surround with or as pickets in order to stop work or activity: *The men picketed the factory/picketed all the people who wanted to go inside to work.*

J240 *nouns, etc* : **time off work**

holiday [C; U; A] a time of rest from work, a day (often originally of religious importance) or longer: *We've been given two days more holiday. We're taking a three-week holiday this summer.* **on holiday/on one's holidays** having a holiday, esp over a period of time   **half-holiday** *also* **half-day** half a day which is free from work, school, etc: *It's my half-day today. They have a half-holiday from school.*
vacation [C; U; A] **1** *esp BrE* one of the periods of holiday when universities (or law courts) are closed **2** *esp AmE* any period of holiday: *Bob and his family are on vacation; they've gone to Hawaii.*
leave 1 [C; (*on*) U] a period of time during which a person is allowed to be away from work or duty: *He gets leave twice a year. She is on leave at the moment. She is on six weeks' paid leave.* **2** [U] *fml* being permitted (to do something): *He gave us leave to do it.*
furlough [C; U] absence from duty, usu for a length of time, esp as permitted to government officers, soldiers, and others outside their own country; holiday: *He's on nine months' furlough. He's home on furlough.*
break [C] **1** a pause for rest; period of time between activities: *There was a break in the concert. Let's have a coffee break/a tea break.* **2** a change from the usual pattern or custom: *You need a break from this job. There has been a break in the bad weather.*
off [adv] (used after a stated time) free from work; not working: *He has a day off today. Did you get the morning off? She had two weeks off because she was ill.*

K

Entertainment, sports, and games

Entertainment generally

K1 *verbs* : **entertaining and amusing**

entertain 1 [I∅; T1] to give a party (for); to provide food and drink in one's house (for): *We're too busy to entertain much nowadays. He does most of his entertaining in restaurants. We're entertaining a few friends for drinks.* **2** [I∅; T1] to amuse and interest: *A teacher should entertain as well as teach. He entertained the children while his wife was busy in the kitchen.*

amuse [T1] **1** to satisfy or excite the sense of humour of; cause laughter in: *Your story/behaviour amuses me. I am amused to find you here. It amuses me that you knew my plans. It amuses me to find you here. He had an amused expression on his face.* **2** to cause to spend time in a pleasant or playful manner: *The new toys amused the child for hours. The children amused themselves by playing games while their parents talked.*

divert [T1] to amuse esp for a length of time: *He can always invent a new game to divert the children.*

play 1 [I∅] (esp of the young) to do things that pass the time pleasantly, esp including running and jumping; have fun: *Can he come out to play? The children are playing in the garden. The cat was playing with a piece of string.* **2** [T1] (of a child) to amuse oneself at (a game): *The children were playing ball with each other.* **3** [L1; T4] (of a child) to amuse oneself by pretending to be or do (something): *Let's play doctors and nurses.* **4** [D1 (*on*); T1] to plan and perform for one's own amusement or gain: *They played a joke on me. He played her a mean trick by taking all the money.* **5** [L9] to (seem to) move quickly, lightly, irregularly, or continuously: *A smile played about her lips. Lightning played across the sky as the storm began.*

celebrate [I∅; T1] to do something, esp have a party, to show that one is happy (about some event, special thing, day, etc): *He has passed the examination; we must celebrate! They celebrated his success by opening a bottle of wine. When the war ended, everyone celebrated (the victory).*

K2 *nouns* : **entertaining and amusing**
[ALSO ⇨ K70, 87]

entertainment [U] **1** the act of entertaining:

He and his wife spend a lot of money on entertainment. He gets an entertainment allowance for the entertainment of foreign businessmen. **2** amusement: *Old Uncle John is getting married again, greatly to the entertainment of his family.*

amusement 1 [U] the state of being amused; enjoyment: *To everybody's amusement the actor fell off the stage. I listened in/with amusement.* **2** [U] the act of amusing: *The amusement of the child took a lot of our time.* **3** [C] something that causes one's time to pass in an enjoyable way: *Big cities have theatres, films, football matches, and many other amusements.*

fun *not fml* [U] **1** playfulness: *The little dog's full of fun.* **2** [U] amusement; enjoyment; pleasure: *Children get a great deal of fun out of dressing in other people's clothes. You're sure to have some fun at the party tonight. There's no fun in spending the evening doing nothing. Have fun* (= enjoy yourself)! *What fun* (= how enjoyable)! **3** [U] a cause of enjoyment or pleasure: *He's good fun; we all enjoy being with him. Swimming in the sea is great fun on holiday. The play at the theatre was very poor fun; we hardly laughed at all.* **4** [U] amusement caused by laughing at someone else: *They had some fun with us yesterday; they told us our house was on fire, and we ran all the way home, to find it was just a trick. No one takes him seriously any more; he's become just a figure of fun.* **5** [A] *apprec, esp AmE* providing pleasure, amusement, or enjoyment: *It was a fun party and he is a fun person.* **for fun** also **for the fun of it, for the fun of the thing** for pleasure; without serious purpose: *He's learning French for fun.* **fun and games** playful tricks; high-spirited behaviour of a group **in fun** in playfulness; without serious or harmful intention: *I'm sorry I hid your book; I only did it in fun, I didn't mean to cause trouble. It was all in fun.* **make fun of** also **poke fun at** to laugh or cause others to laugh rather unkindly at: *It's cruel to make fun of an old person who can't hear properly. People poke fun at her because she wears such strange hats.*

diversion [C] *sometimes fml* something that diverts or amuses: *London offers lots of diversions for every type of person.*

play 1 [U] activity for amusement only, esp as performed by the young: *The young lambs were at play in the field. Children often copy in play the actions of their parents.* **2** [S] light quick, not lasting movement: *The play of sunshine and shadow among the trees was pleasant to look at.*

party [C] (the activities, entertainment, etc of) a group of people who have been invited to a house, hotel, etc for some kind of entertainment, celebration, etc: *Are you coming to the party? I enjoyed that party at John's (house). What a lovely birthday party she had! What party games did they play?*

celebration 1 [U] the act of celebrating **2** [C] an example of this: *Let's have a celebration/a celebration party; he has passed his examination!*

reception [C] *fml* a large formal party: *They gave/held a reception for him. The wedding reception was very enjoyable.*

function [C] *fml* **1** a public ceremony: *The minister has to attend all kinds of official functions, such as welcoming foreign guests of the government and opening new schools and hospitals.* **2** a large or important gathering of people for pleasure or on some special occasion: *You look as if you're dressed for some function or other. – Yes; I'm going to a friend's wedding.*

social [C] a planned informal friendly gathering of members of a group or (esp) church; a party: *There's a social and dance on Saturday night.*

get-together [C] *infml* a party when people come together, esp from many different places: *That was a great family get-together; we mustn't wait so long before the next one.*

carnival 1 [C;U] a public occasion for many people to enjoy themselves with feasting, dancing, drinking, and often processions and shows: *carnival time in Rio de Janeiro* **2** [C] a period of such activities: *the winter carnival*

K3 *adjectives* : **entertaining and amusing** [B]

entertaining amusing and interesting: *That was an entertaining story.* **-ly** [adv]

amusing causing pleasant laughter or enjoyment: *That's an amusing story!* **-ly** [adv]

diverting *esp fml & pomp* amusing **-ly** [adv]

funny 1 *not fml* amusing; causing laughter: *I heard such a funny story this morning. He's a very funny man* (= can make people laugh with amusing stories). *I don't think that's at all funny* (= is a suitable cause for laughter). *It was the funniest thing out* (= the most amusing I've ever heard). **2** *infml* (used esp by or to children) pleasantly amusing; nice (esp in the phr **funny old**): *Look at that funny old dog!* **3** *infml* deceiving; using tricks; too clever: *'Don't try anything funny while my back's turned, or you'll be in trouble,' he said to his prisoner. Don't get funny with me.* **-ily** [adv] **-iness** [U]

comic, comical amusing; funny, esp to watch, esp because silly, unusual, etc: *It was a rather comic business and we laughed, even though it wasn't supposed to be funny. That very comical!* **-(al)ly** [adv Wa4]

humorous funny; full of humour: *What a humorous girl she is!* **-ly** [adv]

jocular *esp fml* enjoying amusing people, making jokes [⇒ K87], etc: *He spoke in a jocular way.* **jocularity** [U] cheerfulness, esp in making jokes

hilarious 1 full of laughter: *The party got quite hilarious after they brought more wine.* **2** causing wild laughter: *We thought his mistake was the most hilarious thing we'd ever heard.* **-ly** [adv] **hilarity** [U] cheerfulness, expressed in laughter

K4 *nouns* : **sport and recreation**

sport 1 [C; U] an outdoor or indoor game or activity carried on by rules and calling for bodily effort and skill: *Do you really think cricket is an exciting sport? They are famous men in the world of sport.* (*humor*) *I think drinking is his favourite sport.* **2** [U] active amusement, play: *It's great sport, swimming in the sea.* **3** [U] joking fun: *The older girls were making sport of her. I'm sorry; I only meant what I said in sport.* **4** [C] a person of a kind who accepts defeat or a joke good-temperedly, or in the stated way: *You've been a real sport to laugh at the trick we played on you. I won't play with him again; he's a poor sport and gets angry when he loses.*

recreation [C; U] (any form of) amusement or way of spending free time: *Tennis is a popular recreation here. I am too busy for recreation. His only recreations are drinking beer and working in the garden. What are the recreation facilities* (= the places, equipment, etc, for recreation) *like here?*

leisure [U] time when one is free from employment or duties of any kind; free time: *A gentleman of leisure is so rich that he doesn't need to work. In his leisure hours he collects stamps. I have very little leisure time in this job.* **at leisure 1** not working or busy; free **2** without hurry **at one's leisure** at a convenient free time; when one pleases

relaxation 1 [U9] the act of relaxing or condition of being relaxed **2** [C; U] (something done for) rest and amusement: *He plays the piano for a bit of relaxation. It's one of his favourite relaxations.*

K5 *adjectives* : **sport and recreation**

sporting 1 [B] offering the kind of fair risk that is usual in a game: *He has a sporting chance of winning. It's very sporting of you to do that.* **2** [Wa5;A] of, concerning, or fond of field sports like hunting or horse racing: *He was a painter of sporting scenes.* **-ly** [adv]

sportive [B] *esp lit* being or fond of sport; playful **-ly** [adv] **-ness** [U]

sporty [Wa1;B] *not fml* **1** looking or acting as one who likes sport: *He's a sporty kind of person and wears sporty clothes.* **2** good-looking in a bright informal way: *sporty new trousers*

relaxed [B] not active, tense, or worried: *He was lying in the sun looking very relaxed and happy.*

recreational [Wa5;B] (of an activity) providing recreation: *This town has very good recreational facilities.*

K6 *nouns* : **games and hobbies**

game [C] **1** a form of play or sport or one instance or type of this: *Football is a game which doesn't interest/interests me very much. They saw three football games/games of football in two days. Let's have a game of cards.* **2** part of a set of games, when a match is divided into several parts, as in tennis: *He must win two more games to win.* **3** a set of things, usu a board and round pieces of wood or plastic (**counters**) which are used in play according to rules **4** a trick or secret plan: *What's your little game there? I don't know what game he is playing, but I'll soon find out.* **two can play at that game** I can behave just as deceitfully, etc, as you, if you go on doing so **the game's up** your/our plan has been found out and can succeed no further **give the game away** to let a secret plan be known **off one's game** below the usual level of one's performance in a game **make game of (someone)** to laugh at; make fun of **have the game in one's hands** to be in control and sure to win

pastime [C] something done to pass one's time in a pleasant way; recreation: *Do you consider gardening to be work or a pastime?*

hobby [C] an activity which one enjoys doing in one's free time: *Gardening is one of his hobbies.*

pursuit [C] any activity to which one gives one's time, as work or, esp for pleasure: *One of the boy's favourite pursuits is stamp collecting. Gardening is an outdoor pursuit.*

interest 1 [U; C] a readiness to give attention: *I have no interest in politics. He's showing an interest in music.* **2** [U] a quality of causing attention to be given: *There's no interest in going to a concert when you don't understand music.* **3** [C] an activity, subject, etc, which one gives time and attention to: *Eating seems to be his only interest in life.*

activity [C *often pl*] something that is done or is being done, esp for interest or education: *He has many activities that take up his time when he's not working.*

repertoire [C] a set of things a person or group knows, can perform, etc: *She has a very good repertoire of songs. What do you have in your repertoire?*

K7 *nouns* : **passions and crazes** [C]

passion *infml* a strong liking: *He has a passion for fishing.*

craze a very popular fashion, usu for a short time: *This new toy is the latest craze in America. The modern craze for Chinese art is catching on (= becoming popular) everywhere.*

K8 *nouns* : **enthusiasm and passion**

enthusiasm [C; U] a strong feeling of interest and admiration: *I am full of enthusiasm for this book. I don't feel much enthusiasm about that book. Among his many enthusiasms is a great fondness for Eastern music.*

gusto [U] eager enjoyment (in doing or having something): *He started painting with great gusto.*

zest 1 [S9; U] (a feeling of) being eager and excited: *He entered into the work with zest/with a zest which surprised us all.* **2** [S; U] (a quality of) being pleasant and exciting: *The danger of being caught gave/added (a) zest to the affair.*

zeal [U] eagerness; keenness: *He shows great zeal for knowledge.*

passion [U] strong feeling, esp enthusiasm: *He worked with passion on his new painting.*

K9 *adjectives* : **enthusiasm and passion**

keen [Wa1] **1** [*BrE* B; F3; *AmE* A] (of a person) having a strong active interest in something; eager or anxious to do something: *He is a keen student of politics. (BrE) He is keen to pass the examination. (BrE) Her father wants her to go to university but she is not keen.* **2** [B] (of a game or struggle of any kind) done with eagerness and activity on both sides: *It was a keen football match/struggle for power. Competition for the job was keen.* **-ness** [U]

enthusiastic [B] showing enthusiasm: *He is a very enthusiastic footballer.* **-ally** [adv Wa4]

zestful [B] showing zest; being eager and excited: *He has a zestful approach to life.* **-ly** [adv]

zealous [B] eager; keen: *He is zealous for fame/in doing his duty/to succeed.* **-ly** [adv] **-ness** [U]

passionate [B] very eager; strong: *She has a passionate interest in sports.* **-ly** [adv] *He is passionately interested in cricket.*

rapt [Wa5;B (*in*)] (typical of a person) giving the whole mind (to): *He was rapt in thought/in admiration/in his book. We listened with rapt attention.*

K10 *verbs* : **interesting and thrilling**
[ALSO ⇒ F25, F224]

interest [T1] to cause (someone) to want to do, see, have, etc, something: *That game interests him very much and he wants to become good at it.*

absorb [T1 *usu pass*] to take up all the attention, acts, interest, etc, of: *I was absorbed in the book and didn't hear you call.*

excite [Wv4;T1] to cause (someone) to have strong feelings, often pleasant: *The game excited him very much. What an exciting game!*

K11 *nouns* : **audiences and spectators**

audience [GC] the people listening to or watching a performance, speech, television programme, etc: *The audience was/were very excited by the show. He sang to an audience of 20,000.*

spectator [C] a person watching, esp a game: *The spectators enjoyed the football match.* **spectate** [IØ] to watch a sport, game, etc: *He was spectating at last Saturday's big game.*

K12 *verbs & nouns* : **praising and applauding**

praise 1 [T1 (*for*)] to speak favourably and with admiration of: *Everyone praised the actor's performance; they all said it was very good. The father praised the children for their cleverness.* **2** [T1] *fml or lit* to offer thanks and honour to (God), esp in song in a church service: *Praise God for His goodness.* **3** [U (*of*)] expression of admiration: *I only did my duty and that is no cause for praise. She wrote a book in praise of country life. The new film received high praise from everyone. Such courage is beyond praise* (= so splendid that words cannot express it). **4** [U] *fml or lit* glory; worship: *Praise be to God. Let us give praise to God.* **praises** [P] **1** words that praise someone or something: *He is loud in his praises of his new car.* **2** *fml or lit* words that praise God (esp in song): *Let us sing the praises of the Lord.* **sing one's own praises** *often derog* to praise oneself **sing the praises of** to praise very eagerly: *She's always singing the praises of some new medicine.* **praiseworthy** [Wa2;B] deserving praise (esp even though not successful): *The distance was too great for him to swim, but he made a praiseworthy attempt and got three-quarters of the way.* **-ily** [adv] **-iness** [U]

merit [U;C] ability, esp as it deserves praise: *There is a lot of merit in his work. Her greatest merit is her honesty.* **meritorious** [B] *esp fml & pomp* showing merit: *They praised him for his meritorious acts.* **-ly** [adv]

applaud [T1;IØ] to praise (a play, actor, performer, etc) esp by clapping: *They applauded her performance. The audience applauded loudly.* **applause** [U] the act or acts of applauding; loud praise for a performance or performer, esp by clapping or cheering: *The applause was great.*

clap 1 [S] noise made by striking the hands together: *The people gave him a clap because he sang well.* **2** [IØ;T1] to make such a noise with (the hands): *They clapped hard; they had enjoyed the singing. We heard the sound of (people) clapping. Clap your hands, children!* **3** [T1] to praise by doing this: *The people clapped him/his singing.*

congratulate [T1] to tell (someone) that one is happy, pleased, etc because he or she has been successful or lucky in some way: *Let me be the first to congratulate you! They congratulated him on his success.* **congratulation** [U; C *usu pl*] the act of congratulation: *Don't waste time on self-congratulation* (= on congratulating yourself)*; there is still work to do. He sent her his congratulations. Congratulations!* (*fml*) *May I express my congratulations on your success?*

Music and related activities

K20 *nouns* : **music, dance, and song**

music [U] **1** the arrangement of sounds into pleasant patterns: *Men have been making music for thousands of years.* (*fig*) *Her voice was music to my ears.* **2** an example of such an arrangement: *This music is Beethoven's 5th.* **3** the art of doing this: *She studies music. She is a music student.*

dancing [U] the actions of people dancing [⇒ K26,32]: *Are you interested in dancing? She goes to dancing classes every week.*

dance [(*the*) U] *fml* the art of dancing: *She is a student of the dance.*

choreography [U] the art of dancing or of arranging dances for the stage **choreographic(al)** [Wa5;B] of, concerning, or like choreography **choreographer** a person who plans, arranges, and directs dances for the stage

singing 1 [U] the art of the singer: *She studies singing. He has a poor singing voice.* **2** [U;C] the act or sound of voices in song: *The ceremony ended with the singing of 'God save the Queen'.* **3** [U] (*fig*) singing noise: *She listened to the singing of the wind in the chimney.*

song 1 [U] the act or art of singing: *She burst into song. He is interested in Scottish song and poetry.* **2** [U;C] the music-like sound of a bird or birds: *He has made a study of birdsong. That bird has a loud song.*

K21 *nouns* : **ballet and opera**

ballet 1 [C] a dance in which a story is told without speech or singing **2** [C] the music for such a dance: *Tchaikovsky and Stravinsky each wrote several famous ballets.* **3** [(*the*) U] the act of doing such dances: *She studied (the) ballet for 6 years.* **4** [GC] *also* **corps de ballet** a group of ballet dancers who work together: *The Royal Ballet gave an excellent performance.*

opera 1 [C] a musical play in which many or all of the words are sung **2** [(*the*) U] such musical plays as a form of art, a business, etc: *She enjoys the opera.* **operatic** [*usu* Wa5;B] of, concerning, or like opera: *She was once a great operatic singer.*

light opera *also* **operetta** [U; C] (the art of making, etc) a musical play in which many of the words are spoken, usu with a happy ending

K22 nouns : **songs and tunes**

song [C] **1** a usu short piece of music with words for singing: *Do you know this song?— Yes, it's a Scots love song. He bought a book of 16th-century English songs.* **2** a poem suitable or prepared for singing to music

tune [C] a number of musical notes, one after the other, that produce a pleasing pattern of sound; an arrangement of musical sounds: *He played a popular tune. Do you know the tune to this song?* **in/out of tune 1** at/not at the correct musical level (**pitch**): *The piano is out of tune. Try to sing in tune.* **2** (*fig*) in/not in agreement: *Your ideas and mine are completely out of tune. His ideas were in tune with the period in which he lived.*

signature tune [C] a short piece of music, used in broadcasting to begin and end a particular show or as the special mark of a radio station

melody 1 [C] a song or tune **2** [C] the part which forms a clearly recognizable tune in a larger arrangement of notes: *At this point the melody returns.* **3** [U] the arrangement of music in a pleasant way **melodic** [Wa5;B] *esp tech* of, concerning, or like a melody **-ally** [adv Wa4] **melodious** [B] *esp genl* of or producing a melody; pleasant to listen to: *a melodious voice* **-ly** [adv]

number [C] a short piece of music, usu a short part of a longer performance: *They played several numbers from the film. For my next number, I will sing . . .*

composition [C] a piece of music, esp when considered as something composed (= made): *This is one of his latest compositions; do you like it?*

arrangement 1 [U] the changing of a piece of music, as for different instruments: *He's working on the arrangement of an old piece of music for the piano.* **2** [C] the result of this: *It is an arrangement by the pianist himself.*

K23 nouns, etc : **words and choruses**

words [P] the words which are used with a piece of music: *I know the tune, but I don't know the words.*

lyrics [P] the words of a song, esp a modern popular song: *It's a nice tune; who wrote the lyrics?*

chorus 1 [GC] a group of people who sing together: *The chorus were very good, weren't they?* **2** [C] a piece of music written to be sung by such a group **3** [GC] a group of dancers, singers, or actors who play a supporting part in a film or show: *The chorus was too big for such a show.* **4** [C] a piece of music played or sung after each group of lines (= **verse**) of a song: *I do like the chorus of this song; let's sing it again.* **5** [C] something said by many people at one time: *The minister's speech was met with a chorus of shouts.* **6** [C] *tech* **a** (in ancient Greek plays) a group of actors who explain or give opinions on the action of the play **b** (in

Elizabethan plays) a person who makes a speech before, after, or during the play explaining or giving opinions on the action of the play **7** [I0; T1] to sing or speak at the same time: *The crowd could be heard chorusing on the other side of town. The papers all chorused the praises of the president.* [⇒ K43] **in chorus** all together: *The people shouted in chorus 'Long live the King!'.* **chorus girl** [C] a young woman who sings or dances in a chorus **choral** [Wa5;B] of, relating to, or sung by a choir or chorus: *a choral group; a choral society; a choral dance*

libretto [C] the set of words for a musical play, such as an opera [⇒ K21]

K24 nouns : **rhythm and beat**

rhythm 1 [U] the quality, of sounds or movements in speech, dancing, music, etc of happening at regular periods of time: *He plays the piano well but he needs to improve his rhythm. Every language has its own natural rhythm.* **2** [C] a particular pattern of this kind: *She likes the exciting rhythms of African drum music.* **rhythmic(al)** [B] of, concerning, or like a rhythm **-ally** [adv Wa4]

beat 1 [C] a regular sound produced by or as if by repeated beating: *I heard the beat of the drum/of my heart/of marching feet.* **2** [*the* R] time in music or poetry: *Every member of the orchestra must follow the beat very closely.*

time [U] *tech* the rate of speed of a piece of music: *You beat time and I'll play.*

tempo [C] **1** *tech* the speed at which music is (to be) played **2** the rate or pattern of movement, work, or activity: *The busy tempo of city life gets less busy at night.*

K25 nouns, etc : **tone and pitch**

tone 1 [C] any sound considered with regard to its quality, highness or lowness, strength, etc **2** [U] the quality or character of a particular instrument or singing voice as regards the sound it provides **3** [C] *also esp AmE* **step** *tech* a difference in the highness of a musical note equal to that between two notes which are two notes apart on a piano: *a tone between B and C sharp* **4** [C *often sing*] a particular quality of the voice as expressive of some feeling, meaning, etc; manner of expression: *He spoke in a tone of command.*

pitch 1 [C] the degree of highness or lowness of a musical note or speaking voice: *How can one change the pitch of this musical instrument?* **2** [S9] (*fig*) degree; level: *The children were at a high pitch of excitement before the holiday.* **3** [X7,9] to set the degree of highness or lowness of (a sound, music, etc): *Can you pitch the song a little lower? It's pitched too high for most of our voices.*

harmony [U] notes of music combined together in a pleasant-sounding way **harmonize** [T1; I0] to add another set of notes to (something which is played or sung), either in writing music or when performing: *The singers began to harmonize (the new song).*

K26 nouns : kinds of dances

dance [C] **1** an act or example of dancing [⇨ K32]: *She did a little dance.* **2** (the name of) a set of movements performed to music, usu including leg movements: *The waltz is a beautiful dance.* **3** a social meeting or party for dancing: *Let's give/have a dance tomorrow. Let's go to a dance.* **4** a piece of music for dancing: *The band played a slow dance.*

waltz 1 [C; *the* R] a social dance for a man and a woman, from Vienna, made up of 6 steps in 3/4 time: *I like dancing the waltz.* **2** [C] music for this dance: *They're playing a waltz by Strauss.* **3** [IØ] to dance a waltz **4** [X9] to cause to dance in this way, or to move quickly, in or into the stated condition: *He waltzed her over to the band.* **5** [L9] *infml* to move or advance easily, successfully, or showily: *We can't just waltz up to a complete stranger and introduce ourselves.*

jig [C] **1** (music for) a quick gay dance **2** a quick short movement, esp up and down

reel [C] (the music for) a lively Scottish or Irish dance: *They were dancing reels in the kitchen.*

tap dancing [U] stage dancing in which musical time is beaten on the floor by the feet of the dancer

jive 1 [U] (dancing performed to) a type of popular music with a strong regular beat **2** [C] a dance performed to this music

rock'n'roll [U] a kind of popular modern dance music played on electrical instruments: *Rock'n'roll has a strong beat and goes on repeating the same few simple phrases.*

rock [U] *abbrev* rock'n'roll: *She likes rock music.*

K27 nouns : music on paper

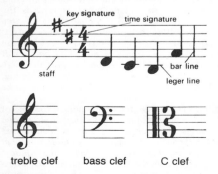

staff

treble clef   bass clef   C clef

music [U] a written or printed set of notes: *Give me my music and I'll play for you. Have you got the music for this song?*

score [C] **1** a written copy of a piece of music, esp for a large group of performers: *a full score*

(= showing all the parts in separate lines on the page); *a vocal score* (= showing only the singers' parts) **2** a long piece or group of pieces of music for a film or play: *There were some good songs in that film. Who wrote the score?*

staff *also* **stave** [C] a set of level lines, now five in number, with four spaces between them, on which music is written

bar [C] (downward lines that mark off) a few notes of music considered to form a group: *The new musical idea begins at the 50th bar. He played the opening bars of a well-known song.*

clef [C] a special sign put at the beginning of a line (**staff**) of written music to show the height (**pitch**) at which the notes should be played

K28 nouns : kinds of musical notes etc according to length [C]

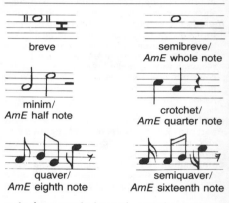

breve   semibreve/ AmE whole note

minim/ AmE half note   crotchet/ AmE quarter note

quaver/ AmE eighth note   semiquaver/ AmE sixteenth note

note 1 a a musical sound, usu of a particular length and pitch **b** a written sign for any of these sounds **2** [C9 *usu sing*, esp *of*] (*fig*) **a** a quality of voice: *There was a note of anger in what he said.* **b** any quality: *There was a careless note/note of carelessness in the way she acted.*

chord [C] **1** a group of three or more musical notes sounded at the same time **2** one of the strings of a stringed musical instrument

K29 nouns : musical scales

scale [C] a set of musical notes in upward or downward order and at fixed separations (different for major and minor scales): *She was playing scales on the piano. He played in the scale of A* (= with A for its base).

sol-fa [U] the system which represents each note of a musical scale by one of seven short words, esp for singing

octave [C] **1** a space of eight degrees between musical notes **2** a musical note eight degrees away from another: *a note and its octave* **3** a musical note and the note eight degrees away, played together **4** a musical note and the note eight degrees away, played together with the six other notes in between

K30 nouns & adjectives : musical keys

key [C] a set of musical notes with a certain starting or base note (**the key note**): *He played it in the key of C. The song was in too high a key for the singer.* (*fig*) *The book is not very exciting; it is written in a very low key from beginning to end.*

major key [C] in a key relating to a major scale, having two full tones between the key note and third note

minor key [C] in a key relating to a minor third (= an interval of three half tones)

major [Wa5;E] being in the stated major key: *He played in F major.*

minor [Wa5;E] being in the stated minor key: *The symphony was in F minor.*

K31 nouns : kinds of musical note according to raising or lowering

sharp 1 [C] a note higher by a half tone than a named note; the next black note to the right of a white note on the piano **2** [C] the sign [♯] as used before a note to raise it by this amount **3** [Wa5;E] (of a note in music) raised by a half tone: *Sing C sharp.*

flat 1 [C] a note lower by a half tone than a named note **2** [C] the sign [♭] as used before a note to lower it by this amount **3** [Wa5;E] (of a note in music) lowered by a half tone: *Sing C flat.*

natural [C] (in music) **1** a note which is not raised or lowered (by a sharp or a flat); a white note on the piano: *It was a piece of music played only on the naturals.* **2** *also* **natural sign** the sign [♮] showing that a note is not raised or lowered: *Should there be a natural sign in front of this G?* **3** [Wa5;E] (of a note in music) not raised or lowered (not sharp or flat); changed back from being raised or lowered: *Don't sing C sharp; sing C natural!*

K32 verbs, etc : playing, singing, dancing, and performing

play 1 [I∅] (of a musical instrument or apparatus) to produce sound: *This old piano won't play. The radio was playing too loudly.* **2** [T1;I∅] to perform on (a musical instrument): *He plays the piano. At the concert he sang and she played.* **3** [D1 (*for, to*); T1 (*on*)] to perform (a piece of music): *They're playing a march. Play us something happy! He played it on the piano. Play it for me. He played it to her.* **4** [D1 (*for, to*); T1 (*on*)] to perform the music of (a particular writer of music): *She plays Mozart well. Play some more Mozart for/to us. She was playing Mozart on the piano.* **5** [D1 (*for, to*); T1 (*on*)] to reproduce (sounds, esp music) on an apparatus: *She plays her radio all day long. Play us your favourite record. I'll play you my favourite song if I can find the record.*

sing 1 [D1; T1; I∅] to produce (music, musical sounds, songs, etc) with the voice: *Birds sing loudest in the morning. I like to sing, although I don't sing well. My sister can't sing a note* (= can't sing at all). *Sing your father a song Mary; sing one of your new songs to/for him. The words are new but they're sung to an old tune.* **2** [X9] to cause to go by this means: *She sang her baby to sleep. Sing your troubles away!* **3** [I∅] (*fig*) to make or be filled with a ringing sound: *An enemy bullet sang past my ear. My ears are still singing from the loud noise.* **4** [Wv4;I∅] (*fig*) (of speech or writing) to sound fine and pleasant: *a fine writer with a singing style* **5** [I∅; T1] *lit* to speak, tell, or praise in poetry: *Poets sang the king's praises; they sang of his brave deeds.*

whistle 1 [I∅] to make the sound of a whistle, esp with the mouth, as music or as a signal to draw attention: *He whistled as he worked. The train whistled. The wind whistled in the trees.* **2** [T1] to produce music by whistling: *He whistled 'Scotland the Brave'.* **3** [L9] to move with a whistling noise: *The wind whistled round them. The bomb whistled down.* **4** [C] the high sound made by passing air or steam through the mouth or a small tube-shaped area, esp in an instrument

dance 1 [I∅ (*to*)] to move to music: *She loves to dance to fast music.* **2** [T1] to move to the music of (a type of dance): *She danced the waltz* [⇨ K26] *with me.* **3** [X9] to cause to dance: *She danced her little daughter round the room.* **4** [X9; T1] to express or bring into a certain state by dancing: *She danced her thanks. She danced her way into the hearts of all who saw her.* **5** [I∅] (*fig*) to move quickly up and down, or about: *The waves danced in the sunlight.*

perform 1 [T1; I∅] to give a presentation of (a piece of music, a play, a part in a play, tricks, etc) esp before the public: *He will be performing on the horn/at the piano. What play will be performed tonight? He performs Hamlet better than anyone else. The magician performed his tricks. The actors refuse to perform.* **2** [T1] to direct or go through the form and actions of (a ceremony): *Our priest will perform the marriage ceremony.*

accompany [T1] to make supporting music for: *He accompanied her singing on the piano. Who is the person accompanying him on the piano?*

tune 1 [T1] to change the sound of an instrument to the correct musical level: *The musicians were tuning their instruments.* **2** [L9; X9; esp *in*] to (cause to) receive a particular broadcast esp on radio: *Stay tuned to this station. Tune in again tomorrow at the same time.*

K33 verbs : composing music, etc [T1; I∅]

compose to write (music, poetry, etc): *This musician has composed a lovely piece of music. He plays in a band at present but hopes to spend more time on composing in the future.*

arrange to change (a piece of music) as for different instruments: *I have arranged this old piece of music for playing at our concert.*

adapt to change (a piece of music, etc) as for different places, purposes, etc: *He adapted the local music for use in opera* [⇒ K21].

K34 *nouns, etc* : **concerts and performances**

concert [C] a musical performance given by a number of singers or musicians or both **in concert 1** playing or singing at a concert: *Tonight you can see the Rolling Stones in concert.* **2** (*fig*) working together; in agreement: *The various governments decided to act in concert over this matter.*

performance [C (*of*)] the action or an act of performing a piece of music, a (character in a) play, tricks, etc esp before the public: *What a fine performance of Schubert! His piano performance was very good. His performance of/as Othello was very good. There are two performances of the play on Wednesdays.*

recital [C (*of*)] a performance of esp music by one person or a small number of persons: *Have you been to any of his recitals?*

premiere 1 [C] the first performance of a film, play, etc **2** [T1 *usu pass*] to give a premiere of: *The film was premiered in London.*

preview 1 [C (*of*)] a private performance of a film, play, etc before it is shown to the general public **2** [T1] to give a preview of: *They previewed the film in London.*

K35 *nouns* : **kinds of musical performance**

concerto [C] a piece of music for one or more solo instruments and an orchestra: *Beethoven wrote five piano concertos.* [⇒ K37, 38]

sonata [C] a piece of music for one or two instruments, made up of usu three or four short parts of varying speeds played in order

symphony [C] a musical work for a large group of instruments in an orchestra, usu having four parts (**movements**) **symphonic** [Wa5;B] of, concerning, or like a symphony

overture [C] **1** a musical introduction to a large musical piece, esp an opera [⇒ K21]: *I like the overture to Mozart's 'Don Giovanni'.* **2** a shortish musical piece meant to be played by itself at the beginning of a concert: *She likes Elgar's concert overture 'In the South'.*

arrangement 1 [U] the arranging of a piece of music **2** [C] an example or the result of this: *That's a nice arrangement; I've never heard it before.*

accompaniment [C; U] music played on a musical instrument to support singing or another instrument: *The piano accompaniment was good.*

K36 *nouns* : **kinds of music** [U]

classical music music put together and arranged with serious artistic intentions and having an attraction that lasts over a long period of time: *People who don't like classical music often don't understand it. Bach and Beethoven wrote classical music.*

light music music which one can enjoy without listening to seriously

dance music music played for dancing

folk music the music that is typical of a people: *He likes Scots and Irish folk music.*

pop (music) modern music which is very popular with large numbers of people: *She likes pop.*

jazz (music) a kind of music first played by black musicians in the southern US

rock (music) music played for dances like rock'n'roll [⇒ K26]

K37 *nouns* : **kinds of groups of musicians** [GC]

orchestra a large group of people who play together, esp on stringed instruments (and usu also other sorts of instrument) **orchestral** [Wa5;B] of, concerning, for, or like an orchestra: *Wagner wrote great orchestral music.*

band a group of musicians, usu not including players of stringed instruments, with a leader, esp a group that plays 'popular' rather than 'serious' music

group a usu small number of players of popular music, sometimes with a singer: *The Beatles were perhaps the most well-known group of the 1960s.*

danceband a band which plays esp for dancing

brass band a band consisting mostly of brass (musical) instruments

pipe band a band consisting of pipes and drums, esp as in Scotland

ensemble 1 a small group of musicians who regularly play together: *The Mozart Ensemble will be performing here next week.* **2** [C] a piece of music such as a quartet [⇒ K38], written for a small number of players: *They played an ensemble for wind instruments.*

K38 *nouns* : **solos, etc**

solo 1 [C] a (part of) a piece of music (to be) played or sung by one person: *She played a solo. He wrote a piano solo.* **2** [C] a job or performance, esp an aircraft flight, done by one person alone **3** [Wa5; B; adv] without a companion: *He flew solo for the first time* (= made his first solo flight). **4** [Wa5;B] of, for, or played or heard as, a musical solo: *She has a fine solo voice. This phrase is to be played solo by the piano. The band played so loud I couldn't hear the solo part clearly.*

duet [C] a piece of music for two performers

trio 1 [GC] a group of three singers or musicians **2** [C] a piece of music written for a group of three singers or musicians **3** [GC] any group of three people or things

quartet 1 [GC] a group of four people playing instruments or singing together **2** [C] a piece of music for such a group **3** [GC] any group of four

K39 *nouns* : **persons performing, playing music, singing, etc** [C]

performer a person who performs a piece of music, in a play, etc

musician a person who plays music on an instrument, esp professionally

singer a person who sings, usu professionally: *The singer at that club is very good.*

dancer a person who dances, usu professionally: *The dancers performed well.*

dancing girl a girl, esp in the East, who dances to entertain esp men

artist a professional singer, actor, dancer, etc

artiste *tech or pomp* an artist

vocalist a singer of popular songs, esp one who sings with a band

instrumentalist a person who plays a musical instrument, esp in a group of people who make music, and in which one or more of whom sing

accompanist a person who plays a musical accompaniment [⇒ K35]

composer a person who makes (**composes**) music

K40 *nouns & adjectives* : **kinds of (esp female) singer**

soprano [C;U] **1** (a woman or child with, or a musical part for) a singing voice in the highest usual range **2** an instrument with the same range of notes as this **3** [Wa5;B] of, for, concerning, or having the range or part of a soprano: *She has a good soprano voice.*

contralto, *also* **alto 1** [C;U] (a woman with or a musical part for a woman with) a low singing voice, between soprano and tenor **2** [Wa5;B] of, for, concerning, or having this range or part

K41 *nouns & adjectives* : **kinds of (esp male) singer**

tenor 1 [C] (a man with) the highest male singing voice in general use: *There's a fine tenor.* **2** [C] an instrument with the same range of notes as this **3** [Wa5;B] of, for, concerning, or having the range or part of a tenor: *He has a high tenor voice.*

alto 1 [C;U] *also* **counter tenor** (a man with or a musical part for a man with) a high singing voice, between soprano and tenor **2** an instrument with the same range of notes as this **3** [Wa5;B] of, for, concerning, or having the range or part of an alto

baritone 1 [C;U] (a man with) the male singing voice lower than tenor and higher than bass: *There's a fine baritone!* **2** [Wa5;B] of, for, concerning, or having the range or part of a baritone

bass 1 [C;U] (a man with) the lowest male singing voice: *He is a fine bass. He sings bass. The bass was wonderful in the opera last night.* **2** [Wa5;B] (of a male singing voice or musical instrument) deep or low in sound: *He has a fine bass voice. He plays the bass drum.*

K42 *nouns* : **positions in groups of musicians**

conductor [C] the person who directs the playing of an orchestra, usu by regular movements of the hands

lead [*the* R; A] the player who leads the others

leader [C] **1** the chief musician or singer in a group, orchestra, choir, etc **2** *AmE* a conductor

first [A] the first musician of a particular kind: *She plays first violin.*

second [A] the second musician of a particular kind

K43 *nouns* : **choirs and choruses**

choir [GC] **1** a group of people who sing together, esp during religious services **2** any musical group or band

chorus [GC] a group of people who sing together: *She sings in the chorus* [⇒ K23].

K44 *nouns* : **general kinds of musical instrument**

(musical) instrument [C] an object which is played to give musical sounds

wind instrument [C] any musical instrument played by blowing air through it

woodwind [(*the*) GU] the set of instruments in an orchestra which are usu made of wood and are played by blowing

reed instrument [C] a wind instrument in which the sound is produced by the movement of a reed

brass instrument [C] a musical instrument that is made of brass and which is played by blowing

brass [(*the*) GU] the set of brass instruments in an orchestra

stringed instrument [C] a musical instrument with one or more strings

strings [P] the set of stringed instruments in an orchestra

percussion instrument [C] a musical instrument which is played by being struck

percussion [GU] *also* **percussion section** [C] the set of percussion instruments in an orchestra

key [C] any one of the parts of a musical instrument or other machine that is pressed down to produce the desired sound or other result: *the keys of a piano*

K45 *nouns* : **wind instruments** [C]

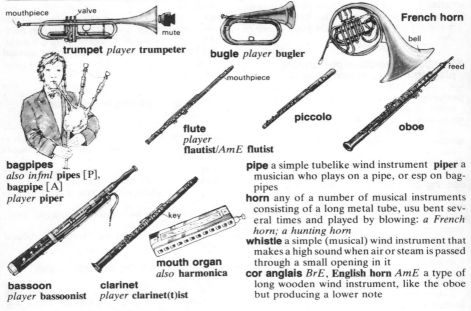

trumpet *player* **trumpeter**

bugle *player* **bugler**

French horn

piccolo

flute
player
flautist/*AmE* **flutist**

oboe

bagpipes
also infml **pipes** [P],
bagpipe [A]
player **piper**

bassoon
player **bassoonist**

clarinet
player **clarinet(t)ist**

mouth organ
also **harmonica**

pipe a simple tubelike wind instrument **piper** a musician who plays on a pipe, or esp on bagpipes

horn any of a number of musical instruments consisting of a long metal tube, usu bent several times and played by blowing: *a French horn; a hunting horn*

whistle a simple (musical) wind instrument that makes a high sound when air or steam is passed through a small opening in it

cor anglais *BrE*, **English horn** *AmE* a type of long wooden wind instrument, like the oboe but producing a lower note

K46 *nouns* : **string instruments** [C]

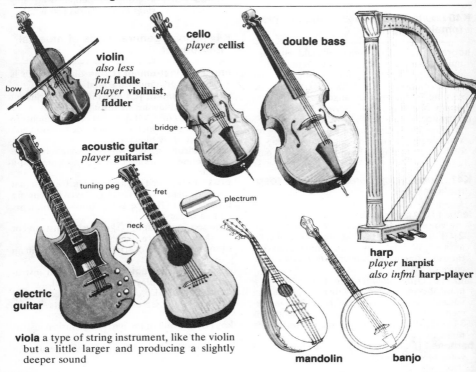

violin
also less fml **fiddle**
player **violinist**, **fiddler**

bow

cello
player **cellist**

double bass

bridge

acoustic guitar
player **guitarist**

tuning peg   fret

neck

plectrum

electric guitar

harp
player **harpist**
also infml **harp-player**

viola a type of string instrument, like the violin but a little larger and producing a slightly deeper sound

mandolin

banjo

K47 *nouns, etc* : **percussion instruments**

modern
drum
kit

triangle [C]

kettle drum

drum 1 [C] a musical instrument consisting of a skin or skinlike surface stretched tight over one or both sides of a hollow circular frame, and struck with hand or stick **2** [S] a sound like that of such an instrument: *I could hear the drum of the rain against my window.* **3** [C] (*fig*) something that looks like such an instrument, esp a part of a machine, a large container for liquids, or a hollow frame on which to wind string, rope, or wire: *an oil drum* **4** [IØ] to make sounds on a drum: *The men began drumming.* **5** [IØ; T1] to move (something, esp one's fingers) on a surface, so as to make a sound like this: *He angrily drummed his fingers on the table.* **drummer** [C] a person who plays a drum or drums

cymbals (**cymbal**) [C]

timpani [GU] a set of 2, 3, or 4 kettledrums played by one musician

gong [C] a round piece of metal hanging from a frame, which when struck with a stick gives a deep ringing sound, as used in Eastern music [⇒ picture at H124]

K48 *nouns* : **pianos and similar instruments** [C]

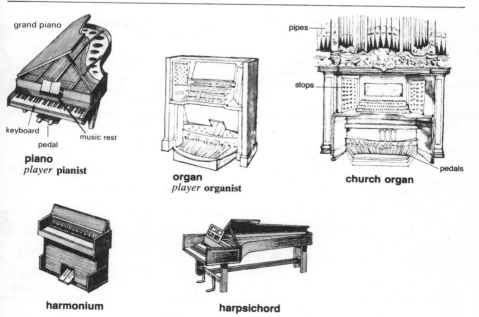

piano
player **pianist**

organ
player **organist**

church organ

harmonium

harpsichord

Recording sound, listening to the radio, etc

[ALSO ⇒ G210, 217]

K50 *nouns* : **records and tapes**

record [C] a circular piece of plastic on which sound is stored in the form of a long narrow line (**groove**) which has been cut in it: *Put on some records of dance music. She bought the latest hit record* (= very popular record).
disc *BrE*, **disk** *AmE* [C] a record
tape [C; U] (a length of) narrow plastic material covered with a special magnetic [⇒ H201] substance on which sound can be recorded
recording [C] anything which is recorded on tape, discs, etc: *Play me his latest recording. Let's make a recording of their music.*
tape recording [C] a length of tape on which a performance, a piece of music, speech, etc has been taped/recorded
cassette [C] a container holding magnetic tape which can be fitted into a tape recorder, or film which can be fitted into a camera
track [C] the part of a record or tape on which sound is recorded

K51 *verbs* : **records and tapes**

record [I∅; T1] to preserve (sound) so that it can be heard again: *The machine is recording now. I prefer live to recorded performances. That singer has recorded several songs.*
tape [T1; I∅] *also* **tape-record** to record (sound) on tape by using a tape recorder: *She taped the politician's speech so that her father could listen to it later. He's upstairs taping; don't make too much noise or else his machine will record it.*
play back [v adv T1] to play (a recording) at once after it is made, so that one can study it carefully: *Play it back, please; I want to hear how it sounds.* **playback** *also* **replay** [C] a recording which is played back in this way

K52 *nouns, etc* : **technical terms in recording, etc**

speed [C] the rate of movement of a record or tape: *He played the record at the wrong speed and it sounded very strange.*
volume [U] (the degree of) fullness or loudness of sound: *He likes to listen to music with the radio turned on at full volume, and all the neighbours are complaining of the noise. The television is too loud; turn the volume down. She has a voice that lacks volume.*
revolution [C] (of machines) one complete circular movement on a central point, as of a wheel: *The speed was 100 revolutions per minute.*
rev 1 [C] *tech abbrev* revolution: *The speed was 100 revs a minute.* **2** [T1; I∅; (*up*)] **a** to cause (an engine, etc) to move faster, at a faster rate

of revs: *He revved up* (*his motorcycle*). **b** (of an engine, etc) to do this

K53 *verbs* : **increasing and decreasing sound** [T1]

amplify to increase the strength of (something, esp sound coming through electrical instruments): *They amplified the music.* **amplification** [U] **1** the act of amplifying **2** the amount by which something is amplified
reduce (of volume) to make less: *Reduce the sound a bit, please.*

K54 *adjectives, etc* : **hi-fi and stereo**

high-fidelity [Wa5;B] (of tape-recorders, record-players, etc) able to give out sound which represents very closely the details of the original sound before recording: *It's a high-fidelity recording.*
hi-fi [Wa5;A;(C)] *abbrev* high fidelity (apparatus): *He has bought some new hi-fi equipment.*
stereo 1 [C] *also* **stereo set** a record player or tape recorder which gives out sound from two places by means of two loudspeakers **2** *fml* **stereophonic** [Wa5;B] which gives out, or is given out as, sound coming from two different places: *This is a stereo recording/record player.*
mono 1 [C] a record player or tape recorder which gives out sound from one place only **2** *fml* **monophonic** [Wa5;B] which gives out, or is given out as, sound coming from one place: *This is a mono recording.*

K55 *nouns etc* : **amplifiers and microphones** [C]

amplifier an instrument, as used in radios and record players, that makes electrical current or power stronger
(loud)speaker that part of a radio or record player that turns electrical energy into sound
relay an electrical arrangement or apparatus that receives sounds and passes them on over a further distance
tannoy a loudspeaker or public address system
intercom a system by which one can talk through a machine to people in a nearby place, often to several people at once, as used by someone to call a secretary to his or her office from an outer room
microphone an instrument for receiving sound waves and changing them into electrical waves, used in recording or carrying sound (as in radio, telephones, etc) or in making sounds louder
mike *infml* a microphone
bug *infml* **1** a small hidden microphone for listening secretly to what people say **2** [T1] to put such a thing in a place: *The room has been bugged.*

K56 nouns : equipment for recording and playing sounds [C]

record player an instrument which can turn the information stored in the narrow line (**groove**) of a record back into the original sounds, music, etc by letting a needle travel along it
gramophone *esp BrE* a record player, esp in older forms
phonograph *esp AmE* a gramophone
tape recorder an instrument which can record sound on and play sound back from tape
cassette recorder a kind of tape recorder, the tapes for which are contained in cassettes [⇒ K50]

K57 nouns : parts of such equipment

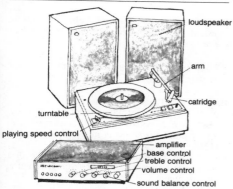

loudspeaker
arm
catridge
turntable
playing speed control
amplifier
base control
treble control
volume control
sound balance control

stereo equipment

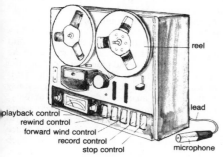

reel
lead
playback control
rewind control
forward wind control
record control
stop control
microphone

tape recorder

K58 nouns : radios, etc

[ALSO ⇒ G210–13]

radio 1 [U] (the method of) sending or receiving sounds through the air by means of electrical waves: *He talked to them by radio.* **2** [C] *also* **radio set** an apparatus to receive sounds broadcast in this way: *Let's buy a new radio.* **3** [U] the radio broadcasting industry: *He got a job in radio.* **4 on the radio a** (of a sound) broadcast: *I heard it on the radio.* **b** (of a person) broadcasting: *John was on the radio again today.*
transistor radio [C] a radio set which works by means of transistors [⇒ H212]
wireless (set) [C] *old use* a radio (set)

K59 nouns & verbs : photography and cameras

[ALSO ⇒ G214]

photograph 1 [C] a picture made by light passing through a curved piece of glass (**a lens**) onto a specially prepared surface (**a film**): *He took some photographs of the family.* **2** [T1] to take a photograph of: *He photographed the whole family.* **photo** [C] *infml abbrev* a photograph **photography** [U] the art, business, etc of taking photographs **photographic(al)** [Wa5;B] of, concerning, or like photography or photographs **photographer** [C] a person who takes photographs, esp for money
snap *infml* **1** [T1] to take a quick photograph of (someone or something): *He snapped the child as she ran towards him.* **2** [C] *also* **snapshot** a photograph: *Would you like to see our holiday snaps?*
camera [C] an apparatus of various sizes used for taking photographs: *He has two cameras. Some cameras take only one picture at a time; others can take a continuous set of pictures, to make a film. The camera crew* (= the people using a very large camera) *began to film* (= take pictures of) *the actors. Television cameras are different from cinecameras.* **cameraman** [C] a man whose work it is to take films with large cameras, esp for the cinema or television
film 1 [U; (C)] (a roll of) the smooth, flat material on which photographic pictures are made, esp for the cinema: *He had no film in his camera. She bought some special fast film for her new camera.* **2** [C] a continuous roll or reel of film, esp as shown in a cinema or on television: *He put the film in the projector.* **3** [T1] to take a film of (something): *They filmed the whole game.*
screen 1 [C] the flat smooth surface on which a film is shown (**projected**): *He put up the screen in the corner of the room. Cinemas have very large, wide screens.* **2** [C] the part of a television set on which the picture appears **3** [A; the R] the cinema or film business: *She's a great star of stage and screen/a great screen star.* **4** [T1] to show or put on a screen: *When will the new film be screened?*
project [T1] to send out (a film, light, etc) onto a screen, etc: *The film was projected onto a white wall, not a screen, but the picture was still nice and clear.* **projection** [U] the act of projecting (a film) **projector** [C] the machine which sends out the pictures of a film onto a screen, etc **projectionist** [C] the person who works the projector

darkroom [C] the room without ordinary day-light in which photographic film is developed

develop [T1] to treat (a film, etc) with chemicals so as to make a picture appear: *Has he developed the photos yet?* **developer** [C; U] the substance used in developing films

negative [C] a kind of film having light where dark should be and dark where light should be, from which positive prints can be made

print 1 [T1] to make (a photograph) on paper from a negative film **2** [C] such a photograph: *These are good prints.*

enlarge [T1] to make a large print of (a picture) from a negative film **enlarger** [C] the machine which makes prints of varying size from nega-tive film **enlargement** [C] an enlarged photo-graph

Drama, the theatre, and show business

K70 *nouns* : entertainment and show business

[ALSO ⇨ G214, K1, 2]

entertainment [C; U] (a) public amusement: *A cinema is a place of entertainment. There are very few evening entertainments in Little Titter-ing.*

show business [U] the business of performing; the job of people who work in television, films, the theatre, etc

show biz [*(in)* U] *infml* show business

films [P] *also* **cinema** [*(the)* R] (the business of making or showing) moving pictures

screen [*(the)* R] films or television: *She is one of the greatest screen performers.*

stage [*(the)* R] the business of performing in the theatre: *She has done this on the stage as well as on television. He is a star of stage, screen, and radio. It was his greatest stage performance.*

K71 *nouns* : theatre and drama

[ALSO ⇨ K75]

theatre *BrE*, **theater** *AmE* **1** [*(the)* U] the work or activity of people who write or act in plays: *He is interested in the modern Russian theatre. Some books, though very interesting to read, do not make good theatre.* **2** [C9] *(fig)* a scene of important military events: *He was reading about the Pacific theatre of World War II. Poland has often been a theatre of war.*

repertory [U] the practice of giving several plays, with the same company of actors and in the same theatre, one after the other on differ-ent days: *He got a job in repertory. This is a repertory theatre/company.*

rep [U] *infml* repertory (theatre)

acting [U] the art of representing a character, esp on a stage or for a film

drama 1 [C] a serious work of literature intended for theatrical presentation: *He is*

writing a new drama. **2** [*(the)* U] plays: *What do you think of modern American drama? Which do you like better—music or (the) drama?* **3** [U9] *(fig)* a group of events concerning forces in opposition to each other: *The drama of international politics interests her.*

melodrama 1 [C; U] a (type of) play which is too exciting to be believable, with sudden changes and events which are meant to have a strong effect **2** [C] *(fig)* any very exciting event which causes strong feeling or interest: *The argument between the neighbours provided a little melodrama in the street.*

(amateur) theatricals [P] stage performances, esp as done by amateurs

dramatics [U; (P)] **1** the study or practice of theatrical arts such as acting **2** *often deprec* dramatic [⇨ K77] behaviour or expression: *No more dramatics, please, Johnny; just give us the facts.*

play-acting [U] pretending; behaving with an unreal show of feeling: *It's just play-acting; don't believe him.*

K72 *nouns* : theatres, cinemas, nightclubs, etc [C]

theatre *BrE*, **theater** *AmE* a special building or place for the performance of plays

cinema *BrE*, **movie theater** *AmE* a special build-ing or place for showing moving pictures [⇨ G214]

music hall a special building or place with a stage where performances of singing, dancing, etc are given

nightclub a restaurant open late at night where people may drink, dance, and see a show

circus [*often cap*] **1** a group of performers who travel from place to place with their act, earn-ing money by performing for the public: *The circus is in town.* **2** a public performance by such a group, with various acts of skill and daring by people and animals: *Let's go to the circus.* **3** a tent-covered place with seats for the public round a ring in the middle, in which this performance takes place **4** *(fig)* deprec a noisy badly behaved meeting or other such activity: *The party meeting was a real circus which any civilized politician should have avoided.* **5** (in Ancient Rome) a round or four-sided space surrounded by seats for the public in which sports, races, etc, took place

funfair *also* **fair** *BrE*, **amusement park** *also* **car-nival** *AmE* a noisy brightly lit show which, for small charges, offers big machines to ride, competitions to enter, games of skill to attempt, etc, esp one that moves from town to town

K73 *nouns* : shows and performances [C]

show 1 *not fml* a performance, esp in a theatre or nightclub or on radio or television: *What* *television shows do you usually watch? Let's go out and see a show, or perhaps a film.* **2** a public showing; a collection of things for looking at: *Let's go to the car show. She put on a one-woman show of her paintings.*

act one of a number of short events performed for a theatre, circus, etc: *When can she do her act? The next act will be a snake charmer!*

turn *not fml* an act, esp one among a number coming after each other: *The snake charmer was one of the best turns in the show.*

performance an occasion of performing anything: *They give two full performances every day. That was one of her best performances! The first performance of the play takes place next month.*

stunt *infml* an act or action done in order to get attention, for special effect, because it is dangerous, etc: *He used to do circus stunts.*

routine a set of steps learnt and practised by a dancer for public performance: *She does a good little dance routine.*

curtain call the appearance of actors and actresses at the end of a performance to be applauded: *They liked her so much, she had three curtain calls!*

K74 *nouns* : **kinds of cabaret, etc**

cabaret 1 [U; C] a performance of music and dancing while guests in a restaurant have a meal **2** [C] a restaurant that presents such performances

floor show [C] *infml* a cabaret performance

variety, *also* **vaudeville** *AmE* [U] a kind of theatre or television show in which a number of amusing short performances are given (such as singing, music, dancing, acts of skill, telling jokes, etc): *He works in variety as a singer. She's a variety actress. His vaudeville act is singing and telling jokes.*

striptease [U; C] (an) entertainment, esp in cabaret, where a woman takes off her clothes slowly, usu while dancing to music

K75 *nouns* : **kinds of drama**

[ALSO ⇒ K71, 77]

tragedy 1 [C] a serious play that ends sadly: *'Hamlet' is one of Shakespeare's best known tragedies.* **2** [U] such plays considered collectively: *a writer of tragedy* **3** [U] the branch of the theatre dealing with such plays **4** [C; U] a terrible, unhappy, or unfortunate event: *Their holiday ended in tragedy when their hotel caught fire. The accident was a terrible tragedy; they all died.*

comedy 1 [C] a funny play, film, or other work in which the story and characters are amusing and which ends happily: *This play is the funniest comedy I've seen in a long time.* **2** [U] the branch of the theatre or film industry intended to amuse people with such plays or films: *The actor liked working in comedy because he loved*

to make people laugh. **3** [C; U] an event, activity, or type of behaviour in real life that is funny or amusing: *It was a comedy to watch Father painting the wall.* **4** [U] the amusing quality of a play, film, person, etc: *I like Shakespeare's comedy even in his serious plays.*

tragicomedy [C; U] (a) mixture of tragedy and comedy

farce 1 [C] a light humorous play full of ridiculous situations **2** [U] the branch of theatrical writing concerned with this type of play **3** [C] an occasion or series of events that is a ridiculous and empty show: *The discussions were a farce since the minister had already made the decision.*

slapstick [U] humorous acting that depends on fast violent action and simple jokes

burlesque [C; (U)] acting, speech, or writing in which a serious thing is made to seem foolish or a foolish thing treated solemnly so as to make people laugh

mime 1 [C; U] an act or the action of using actions to show meaning, as for amusement, when one cannot speak a language, etc: *The children were doing some mimes from the story they'd just read, and asking us to guess what each one meant. I couldn't speak Chinese, but I showed in mime that I wanted a drink.* **2** [C] (in ancient Greece and Rome) a type of simple theatrical play in which the actors made fun of real people and real events

charade [C] an act or position which is easily seen to be false or foolish: *Now we have the charade of a socialist government favouring bigger profits for private industry.* **charades** [U] a game in which words are acted by players, often part (= **syllable**) by part, until guessed by other players: *Let's play charades; it's my favourite game.*

K76 *nouns* : **plays and sketches**

play [C] **1** a piece of writing to be performed, esp in a theatre: *He has written a new play.* **2** a performance of this: *We've been to several plays this month.* **3** a printed copy of this: *She bought the plays of Shakespeare.*

sketch [C] a short informal play: *The performance included some funny sketches.*

revue 1 [C] a light theatrical show with songs and dances but no story, which usually contains jokes about the events and fashions of the moment **2** [U] this kind of show: *She's been appearing/performing a lot in revue lately.*

K77 *adjectives* : **relating to the theatre and drama** [B]

[ALSO ⇒ K71, 75]

theatrical 1 [Wa5] of, related to, or for the theatre: *theatrical performances; a theatrical company* **2** (of behaviour, manner, a person, etc) showy; not natural **-ly** [adv Wa4]

520

dramatic 1 [Wa5] of or related to the drama (def 2): *He enjoys the dramatic arts.* **2** (*fig*) exciting: *the dramatic events of international politics* **3** catching and holding the imagination by unusual appearance or effects: *She plays a very dramatic woman with flashing eyes and a long black dress.* **-ally** [adv Wa4]

melodramatic exciting in effect, often too much so to be thought real: *That's a very melodramatic statement; you know you wouldn't really do that! The neighbours started throwing things at one another and when the police arrived a very melodramatic scene met their eyes.* **-ally** [adv Wa4]

histrionic 1 [Wa5] concerning the theatre or acting **2** done or performed in a theatrical way; not showing real feelings but pretended ones: *In spite of his histrionic demands, he won't mind if we decide to change the plan.* **-ally** [adv Wa4]

comic of, relating to, or like comedy: *He does a comic act in the music hall.* **-ally** [adv Wa4]

tragic 1 of, relating to, or like tragedy: *He enjoys tragic plays like 'Hamlet'.* **2** very sad: *Her death in the car accident was tragic; she was only 18. I have only just heard the tragic news.* **-ally** [adv Wa4]

farcical like a farce; ridiculously funny: *He tried to be serious, but the evening was quite farcical.* **-ly** [adv Wa4]

K78 *nouns* : **production and rehearsal**

production [C] a play, film, etc, esp as it is being produced (= written, made, prepared, filmed, etc)

rehearsal 1 [C; U] the act or an occasion of rehearsing: *This play will need a lot of rehearsal(s). The play is in rehearsal now. We'll meet after rehearsal.* **2** [U] the action of rehearsing or something rehearsed: *The rehearsal of the parts will take all evening.*

dress rehearsal [C] the last rehearsal of a play before its first official public performance: *In a dress rehearsal, the actors wear the special clothes needed for the play, rather than ordinary clothes.*

audition [C] a test performance required of a singer, actor, etc, by the people from whom he or she hopes to get employment

K79 *verbs* : **playing and rehearsing**

play 1 [T1; L9] (of an actor or theatre group) to perform: *He played Othello. Othello was played by Olivier. Olivier is playing in 'Othello' at the National Theatre. You should not play the trial scene too slowly. Last night they played before the president.* **2** [T1 *no pass*] (of an actor or theatre group) to perform in (a certain town, theatre, etc): *Next week we're playing New York.*

act 1 [T1; I∅] to represent (a part), esp on the stage: *Olivier is acting (in) 'Othello' tonight. Is he acting tonight?* **2** [L1] *deprec* to play the part of, as in a play: *He is always acting the experienced man who has seen everything.*

star 1 [I∅] to appear as a star [⇒ K82]: *She starred with him in two films.* **2** [T1] to have as a star: *It's a film starring Sophia Loren.*

produce [T1] to prepare (plays, etc) for public performance at the theatre or on television or the radio: *Who produced that play?*

direct [T1; I∅] to control and be in charge of (the way a play, film, etc, is done): *Who directed that new Italian film?*

stage [T1] to put (a play, etc) on a stage [⇒ K70, 91], etc: *They first staged the play in Birmingham, then took it to London.*

rehearse 1 [I∅; T1] **a** to learn and practise (something) for later performance: *They rehearsed the play. The actors were rehearsing in the tent.* **b** to cause (someone) to do this: *She rehearsed the musicians.* **2** [T1] to tell fully (events or a story): *He rehearsed (the story of) all his sufferings in prison.*

perform 1 [I∅; T1] to act in (a play, etc): *He performed well as Othello. He performed (the part of) Othello well.* **2** [I∅] to act, sing, play music, etc, before other people: *Who is performing next? They performed every day for a month.*

prompt [T1; I∅] to give (an actor, etc) the next word to be said: *He forgot his lines several times and needed prompting. Would you prompt for us please?*

cue in [v adv T1b] to give (someone) a sign to be ready to do something: *The director will cue you in when it's your turn to sing.*

audition 1 [T1; I∅] to cause (someone) to give an audition: *We're auditioning (them) for parts in the play tomorrow.* **2** [I∅] to give an audition: *I'm auditioning for a part in the play tomorrow, and I hope I get it!*

cast [T1 (*as*)] to give (an actor) a part in a play: *He has been cast as Othello.*

typecast [Wv5; T1 (*as*)] to cast (an actor) as the same kind of character [⇒ K84] all the time: *He has played a policeman so often he has become typecast.*

K80 *nouns* : **parts of plays, etc** [C]

act (in a play) a main division: *They all die in the last act (of the play).*

scene 1 (in a play) any of the divisions, often within an act, during which there is no change of place: *It happens in Hamlet, act 3, scene 1.* **2** (in a film, broadcast, etc) a single piece of action in one place: *In the first scene he kills his wife.* **3** the background for (part of) the action of a play; set: *He is a scene-painter. The scene is the English court in 1685. This is a play with few scene changes.*

climax (in a play, book, film, etc) the most interesting and important part, usu near the end

anticlimax *often humor* a sudden change from something noble, serious, exciting, etc, to something foolish, unimportant, or uninteresting, esp in a play, book, etc

denouement *Fr* the end of a story when everything comes out right or is explained

finale the last scene of an opera [⇒ K20] or division of a long formal piece of music

K81 *nouns* : **scripts and cues**

script [C] the written form of a play: *I need a script; I want to learn my part.*

part [C] the words and actions of an actor in a play; a written copy of these: *I've left my part on the stage.*

lines [P] *infml* the part or words a particular actor has to learn: *Have you learnt your lines yet?*

scenario [C] **1** a written description of the action to take place in a film, play, etc: *The scenarios are very well done.* **2** (*fig*) a description of a possible course of action or events: *He presented a fearful scenario of atomic war.*

prompt [C] words spoken to remind an actor of his next words when he has forgotten: *The people sitting in the front row of the theatre could hear the prompts quite clearly.*

cue 1 (esp in a play) a word, phrase, or action serving as a signal for the next person to speak or act: *The actor missed his cue and came onto the stage late.* **2** (*fig*) an example of how to behave, what to do, etc; a guiding standard **take one's cue from** *infml* to use the practice of (another person) as a standard for one's own actions: *Take your cue from here and work harder.*

K82 *nouns* : **actors, etc** [C]

actor a person who acts in plays, etc, usu professionally

actress a female actor

player *esp old use* an actor

performer a person who performs in a play, etc

star [C] a famous actor, actress, singer, etc: *She was one of the stars in that film.* **stardom** [U] the condition of being a star: *He reached stardom years ago.* **film star** [C] a star in cinema films: *He's the son of a famous film star.* **superstar** [C] a particularly great or famous star **starlet** [C] an actress who is not yet a star but hopes to be

understudy an actor or actress learning an important part in a play so as to be able to take the place of the actor who plays that part if necessary: *The leading man is ill; call his understudy!*

stand-in 1 a person who takes the part of an actor at certain important or dangerous moments in films **2** a person who takes the place or job of another for a time

stunt man a person who does dangerous acts in a film so that the actor does not have to take risks **stunt woman** [*fem*]

tragedian an actor who acts (only or often) tragedies [⇒ K75]

ham (actor) a person, esp an actor, who acts unnaturally, wildly, etc

leading man the main actor in a play

leading lady the main actress in a play

K83 *nouns* : **playwrights, etc** [C]
[ALSO ⇒ G209]

playwright a writer of plays

dramatist a writer of plays, esp serious ones

script writer a writer of plays or other material to be spoken on radio or television or in a film

producer 1 a person who prepares a play for public performance at the theatre or on television or radio **2** a person who is in general control of, and provides the money for, making a cinema film but who does not direct the actors

director a person who directs a play or film, instructing the actors, cameraman, etc

patron [(*of*)] **1** a person or group that supports and gives money to a person, a group of people, or some worthy purpose: *The writer's patron died, so he had to give up writing.* **2** a person (esp one of importance) who takes an interest in and allows his or her name to be used in connection with some group: *The Queen is the patron of many societies.*

backer *usu not fml* a person who provides money to help in the making of a play, film, etc

critic a person who esp professionally goes to plays, watches films, etc, and writes his or her opinion of them in a newspaper, magazine, etc

reviewer a critic who writes reviews, esp of plays and books, in newspapers, magazines, etc

K84 *nouns* : **role and cast**

role, *also* **rôle** [C] the part taken by someone in life or in any activity; esp the part of some particular actor in a play: *Olivier played the role of Hamlet. She tried to fulfil her role as a mother.*

part [C] a character acted by an actor in a play; a role

character [C] a person in a play, story, etc: *Hamlet and Othello are two of Shakespeare's greatest characters. He is a character actor* (= he acts certain kinds of characters).

cast [GC] a set of actors in a play: *Who are the cast? The film has a cast of thousands.*

dramatis personae 1 [P] the characters (or actors) in a play: *The dramatis personae include Tom Lovewell, Old Sir Giles Tradewell, and Lady Wishfort.* **2** [(*the*) C *usu sing*] a list of these characters (or actors): *The dramatis personae appears on a board outside the theatre.*

troupe [GC] a company, esp of actors, dancers,

singers, members of a circus [⇨ K72], etc
trouper [C] a member of a troupe
hero [C] the most important male part in a play, story, etc
heroine [C] the most important female part in a play, story, etc
villain [C] (in old plays, films, and stories) a man who is the (or a) main bad character: *The villain carried off the pure young girl and tied her to the railway line.* **the villain of the piece** *infml often humor* the person or thing to be blamed; the one that has caused all the trouble on some occasion: *After listening to many different accounts of how the accident happened, I think the villain of the piece was the car driver.*

K85 *nouns, etc* : **impresarios and comperes** [C]

impresario the business manager of a theatre company, or of a single famous performer
maestro a great or famous performer, musician, teacher, etc
compere *esp BrE* a person who introduces the various acts in a stage or television show
master of ceremonies *esp AmE* a compere
MC *infml abbrev* a master of ceremonies
ringmaster the man whose job is directing performances in the circus ring

K86 *nouns* : **comedians and clowns** [C]

comedian 1 an actor who tells jokes or does amusing things to make people laugh, or acts in funny plays or films **2** *infml* a person who amuses others or tries to be amusing
comic *infml* a comedian: *He's quite a comic, isn't he?*
clown 1 a performer, esp in the circus, who dresses funnily and tries to make people laugh by his jokes, tricks, or actions **2** *deprec* a person who continually tells jokes or acts stupidly

K87 *nouns, etc* : **humour**

[ALSO ⇨ K2–3, 75]

humour *BrE,* **humor** *AmE* [U] **1** the quality of causing amusement: *It is a play with no humour in it.* **2** the ability to be amused: *She has a good sense of humour.*
joke 1 [C] anything said or done that causes laughter or amusement: *She told some very funny jokes.* **2** [C] a person, thing, or event that is laughed at and not taken seriously: *That old car of his is a joke; it can hardly go at all.* **3** [I0] to say things that cause laughter or amusement: *He was laughing and joking with them. Don't be upset; I was only joking.* **make a joke** to tell a joke **have a joke with someone** to share a joke with someone **I don't see the joke** I don't understand what is funny **play a joke on someone** to do something to make other people laugh at someone **the joke's on (someone)**

someone else has had the last laugh **he can't take a joke** he isn't amused when someone plays a joke on him **no joke** *infml* a serious or difficult matter: *War is no joke. It was no joke carrying those heavy bags.* **be/go beyond a joke** to be/become too serious or unpleasant to laugh at: *Some of his remarks were so nasty that they went beyond a joke.*
gag [C] *infml* a joke or funny story
punch line [C *usu sing*] the last few words of a joke or story that give meaning to the whole and cause amusement or surprise: *He's not very good at telling jokes; he always forgets the punch line.*

K88 *nouns* : **acrobats and similar performers** [C]

acrobat a person skilled in walking on ropes or swinging between ropes high in the air, balancing, walking on hands, etc, as an entertainment, esp at a circus **acrobatic** [B] of or like an acrobat or acrobats: *They give a fine acrobatic performance/a performance of acrobatic skill.* **-ally** [adv Wa4]
juggler a person skilled in juggling (= keeping several objects in the air at the same time by throwing them up quickly and catching them again)
ventriloquist a person who practises **ventriloquism** (= the art of speaking or singing with little or no movement of the lips or jaws, in such a way that the sound appears to come from somewhere else) usu in the theatre to amuse the public

K89 *nouns* : **places in the circus**

[ALSO ⇨ K72]

big top [*the* R] the large tent in which the performances in a circus are given
ring [C] the closed-in central space where things are shown or performances take place, as in a circus
trapeze [C] a level bar which can swing on two ropes and is used by acrobats in circuses, etc
sideshow [C] **1** a separate show at a fair or circus, typically with strange people (a sword swallower, bearded lady, etc) on view **2** (*fig*) a usu amusing activity beside a more serious main one

K90 *nouns* : **puppets** [C]

puppet 1 a wooden or cloth figure of a person or animal that is made to move by someone pulling wires or strings fixed to it **2** *also* **glove puppet** a cloth figure of a person or animal with a hollow inside into which the hand is put to move the figure **3** [C9; A] (*fig*) *often deprec* a person or group that is controlled and directed by the will of someone else: *The chief director has no power in this firm; he's only a puppet of the family that owns the firm. They are just a puppet government; they have no real power.*

puppeteer a person who performs with puppets
marionette *Fr* a puppet (def 1)
puppet show a performance by a puppeteer

K91 *nouns, etc* : **the stage, etc, in a theatre**

stage [C] the raised area in a theatre, hall, etc, where actors, singers, etc, perform: *He stood alone on the stage.* [⇒ K70]
set [C] **1** something built and provided with furniture, scenery, etc, to represent the scene of the action of a play **2** a place (of this kind or in natural surroundings) where a film is acted: *Everyone must be on the set ready to begin filming at 10 o'clock.*
scenery [U] the set of painted backgrounds and other articles used on a theatre stage
backcloth *also* **backdrop** [C] **1** a painted cloth hung across the back of a stage **2** (*fig*) things happening behind or around someone's action, etc: *The stormy political events of the 1930s formed a backdrop to the story of their love.*
upstage [adv] at or towards the back of the stage
downstage [adv] at or towards the front of the stage
backstage [Wa5] **1** [adv] behind the stage in a theatre, esp in(to) the dressing rooms of the actors: *He took me backstage after the performance.* **2** [adv] (*fig*) in secret: *That's what they say, but who knows what really goes on backstage?* **3** [B] of or about the private lives of theatre people: *She wrote 'Backstage Wife', the story of the wife of a famous actor loved by thousands of women.*
dressing room [C] a room behind the stage in a theatre where an actor can get ready for his or her performance, wash and change afterwards, etc
wings [P] (either of) the sides of a stage, where an actor is hidden from view
curtain [C] a sheet of heavy material drawn or lowered across the front of the stage in a theatre: *As the curtain rises a dead body is seen on the stage. Slowly everyone leaves the stage and the curtain falls.*
footlights [P] **1** a row of lights along the front of the floor of a stage at the theatre, to show up the actors **2** (*fig*) acting in the theatre: *She's always longed for the footlights* (= wanted to become an actress).
spotlight 1 [C] (a bright round area of light made by) a lamp with a movable narrow beam: *The spotlight followed the performer around the stage.* **2** [*the* R] (*fig*) public attention: *She was in the political spotlight this week. He wants a quiet life out of the spotlight.*
orchestra pit [C] the space in the front of a theatre where musicians sit and play during a (musical) play
trap(door) [C] a small door, covering an opening in the floor or a roof, but esp on a stage

K92 *nouns* : **other parts of a theatre**

box office *also* **ticket office** [C] the place just inside the entrance to a theatre, etc, where people can buy tickets for a performance
foyer [C] the hall at the entrance to a theatre, hotel, etc
aisle [C] the way between the seats in a theatre, church, etc
row [C] a neat line of seats for people side by side: *Our tickets are for row F at the theatre.*
stalls [(*the*) P] *BrE*, **orchestra** [(*the*) C] *AmE* **1** the seats in a theatre, cinema, etc, on the ground floor and usu nearer the stage: *We have seats in the front/back stalls.* **2** the people sitting there
pit [(*the*) C] **1** the seats at the back of the ground floor of the theatre **2** the people sitting there
balcony [(*the*) C] **1** the part of a theatre, cinema, etc, where people can sit above the ground floor **2** the people sitting there
circle [(*the*) C] **1** one of the upper parts in a theatre, cinema, etc, in which the seats are arranged in part of a circle across the building **2** the people sitting there
gallery [(*the*) C] **1** the highest upper floor in a theatre **2** the people who sit in the seats in the gallery, which are the cheapest in the house
gods [*the* + GU] *infml* the gallery
box [C] a small room or enclosed space in a theatre, at either side, from which a small group of people can watch a play

Sports and games generally

K100 *nouns* : **athletics and gymnastics**

athletics [U] the practice of bodily exercises and of sports demanding strength and speed, such as running and jumping
sports [P; A *often cap*] a meeting for athletics: *Are you going to the School Sports? He did well on Sports Day last year.*
games 1 [U] a school subject, including the playing of team games and other forms of bodily exercise **2** [P *usu cap*] an occasion or occasions when people take part in athletics, etc: *The Olympic Games were held in Montreal in 1976.*
gymnastics [U] the art of training the body by means of certain exercises, esp in a gymnasium [⇒ K140]
exercise [U; C] movements of the body, games, etc, which are done esp to make one strong, healthy, etc: *He does his morning exercises before he has breakfast. Are these exercises good for you? You need more exercise; why don't you buy a bicycle?*
keep fit [U; A] actions which are meant to keep one healthy and strong (**fit**): *He does a lot of keep fit/keep fit exercises. She goes to a keep fit class one evening a week.*

K101 *verbs* : **running, jumping, etc**

[ALSO ⇒ M19]

run 1 [I∅] to move on one's legs at a speed faster than walking: *The children ran to meet her.* **2** [T1] to cover (a distance) in this way: *He ran a mile in four minutes.* **3** [T1; I∅] to take part in (athletics, a race, etc) in this way: *They ran races in the park. He ran against them in the race.* **4** [T1] to cause (an animal) to take part in a race: *We won't run this horse in any races this season.* **5** [T1] to cause (a race) to happen: *The bicycle race will be run in Holland next year.*

jump 1 [I∅] to go esp up in the air by pushing off the ground with the feet: *He jumped up onto the wall. She jumped six feet.* **2** [T1] to pass over by jumping: *The horse jumped the wall. You can jump six feet easily.* **3** [I∅] (*fig*) to rise or move suddenly: *Prices jumped last week. Her heart jumped with fear.*

ride 1 [T1; I∅ (*on*)] to travel along, controlling and sitting on (a horse, bicycle, or motorcycle): *Can you ride a bicycle? I'll ride (on) your horse and you ride mine.* **2** [I∅] to travel along controlling and sitting on a horse, for exercise and pleasure: *Teach the children to ride. We're going (horse-) riding on Saturday.* **3** [L9] to go (somewhere) controlling and sitting on (esp) a horse: *We rode across the fields. He got on his bicycle and rode slowly down the road.* **4** [T1] to go along, across, or all over (a place) on a horse: *He rides the borders/the ranges.* **5** [L9] (of a vehicle) to travel over a surface in the stated manner: *This car rides smoothly.* **6** [L1] *tech* (of a professional rider in races (**jockey**)) to weigh when ready for racing: *George rides 115 pounds.* **7** [L7] (of a racetrack) to be (in a stated condition) for horse-racing: *The course will ride very hard in this weather.*

race 1 [I∅; T1] to run a race (against): *She's a very good swimmer and often races. I'll race you to the end of the road.* **2** [I∅] (of two or more people, vehicles, etc) to run a race against each other: *Let's race!* **3** [I∅, 3; X9] to (cause to) go (somewhere) very fast: *He came racing across the road. They raced to find a ladder. We raced the sick woman to hospital.* (*fig*) *The holidays raced by. Her heart was racing (with fear).* **4** [T1] to cause (an animal or vehicle) to run a race: *My horse has hurt his foot so I can't race him.* [also ⇒ K201]

swim 1 [I∅] to move through water by moving limbs and/or tail: *Some snakes can swim.* **2** [T1] to cross or complete (a distance) by swimming: *She swam the 100 metres (race) faster than anybody else.* [also ⇒ K204]

shoot 1 [T1; L9] to let fly with force (as a bullet, arrow, etc) **2** [T1; I∅; (*at*)] to fire (a weapon): *He shot at a bird, but missed. With his bad eyes he can't shoot straight.* **3** [L9] to go fast or suddenly: *Blood shot out of the wound. He shot past me in his fast car.* **4** [T1; I∅] to kick, throw, etc, a ball aimed to make (a point) in a game: *He shot three goals in the last half of the match. He was in a good position to shoot.* **5** [Wv4; L9]

(of pain) to move fast along a nerve: *Pain shot through his arm. It wasn't an ache but a shooting pain.* **6** [T1; I∅] to make a photograph or film (of): *This film was shot in California. The camera is set up for shooting.* **7** [T1] to play (a game of, esp billiards, craps, pool, marbles): *Let's shoot some/a game of pool.* **8** [T1] to pass quickly by or along: *He saw a car shooting traffic lights. The boat was shooting the rapids.*

K102 *nouns* : **games and competitions**

game [C] an occasion for playing a sport; a part of a set of such occasions: *He watches every game that the team plays. He won the first two games but lost the third.*

match [C] a game or sport event where teams or people compete: *He went to the football match.*

competition 1 [U] the act of competing (*often in the phr* **in competition with**): *He was in competition with ten others, so he did well to win the race.* **2** [C] a test of strength, skill, ability, etc: *My wife won first prize in a cooking competition yesterday. He took part in a beer-drinking competition.* **3** [U] the struggles to gain (an) advantage, profit, or success, from another or others: *Competition between Britain and Germany helped to cause the First World War. There was keen competition between the various teams fighting for first place. Is competition good or bad for industry/education?* **4** [(*the*) GU] the person or people against whom one competes: *The players nervously wondered what sort of competition there'd be at the match. We may not be perfect, but at least we're better than the competition.*

contest [C] **1** a competition, esp one judged by a group of specially chosen judges: *Who's judging this contest? The Games were a contest between the best sportsmen in the country.* **2** a struggle or fight in which two or more people compete for victory: *It was a contest of skill. A contest developed for the position of minister of foreign affairs.*

tournament [C] **1** a number of contests of skill between players, the winner of one contest playing the winner of another, until the most skilful is found: *The tennis tournament was a great success.* **2** *formerly* a contest of courage and skill between noble soldiers on horses (**knights**) fighting with weapons which usu have the sharp edges covered

challenge 1 [C] an invitation to compete in a fight or competition: *The prince accepted his enemy's challenge to fight.* **2** [U] the quality of demanding competitive action, interest, or thought: *The universe is full of challenge.* **3** [C] (*fig*) something with this quality: *The universe is a great challenge to men. To build a bridge in a day was a real challenge.*

championship 1 [C *often pl with sing meaning*] a competition held to find the champion [⇒ K106]: *Fifty men took part in the championship; but only one was successful. She won the*

1980 championships, just as we'd expected.
2 [C] the position, title, rank, etc, of being champion: *I don't think this new fighter can take the championship from him.* **3** [U] the act of championing: *Her championship of women's rights is well known.*

K103 *nouns, etc* : **rounds, laps, heats, and bouts** [C]

round (in sport) one stage, period, or game, as **a** (in golf) a complete game including all the holes **b** (in boxing) one of the periods of fighting in a match, separated by short rests: *They fought a match of 20 rounds. He was knocked out in the second round/in round 2.* **c** (in professional football) one of several sets of matches, of which all the winners will play against each other until one team is victorious: *They lost the first round of the Football Cup.*
lap 1 (in racing, swimming, etc) a trip once round the track or over the distance: *He is two laps ahead of the next man.* **2** one part or division of a planned action or development **3** (in racing, swimming, etc) **a** [T1] to be the distance of at least once round the track ahead of (a competitor) **b** [L9] to race completely round the track
heat a part of a race or competition whose winners compete against other winners until there is a small enough number to run the last part (**final heat**)
bout 1 a boxing match: *Who will win the next bout?* **2** a short period of activity: *He works in bouts of fierce activity followed by periods of rest.*

K104 *verbs* : **playing, exercising, and scoring**

[ALSO ⇨ K120, 121]

play 1 [I∅; T1] to (cause to) take part in a game: *He played (for us) last Saturday. We'll play him again next Saturday.* **2** [L1, 7; I∅ (as, at)] to have (a particular position and duty in a team): *Smith will play fullback* [⇨ K191]. *Smith will play as our third fast bowler* [⇨ K196].
exercise [I∅; T1] to (cause to) take exercise or do exercises [⇨ K100]: *He was exercising in the garden. You don't exercise enough. You should exercise yourself more. He exercises his muscles* [⇨ B4] *every day by lifting heavy things. Can you exercise the horses for me, please?*
score 1 [I∅; T1] to gain (one or more points, goals, etc) in a sport, game or competition: *He scored three points/times in the last half of the game. He scored a century (= 100 runs) in cricket. In this game points are scored in different ways.* **2** [L9; T1] to win (a total of points) in an examination: *He scored high (= scored well) in the test. He scored 80 out of 100. A right answer to this question scores 5 points.*

3 [I∅; T1] to gain or win (a success, victory, prize, etc): *The bomb scored a hit on the railway bridge. This writer has scored again with another popular book.* **4** [L9; X9; (off, against, over)] to make (a clever and successful point), esp in an argument against someone: *I hate conversations where people try to score (points) off each other.*
eliminate [T1 *(from)*] to remove (from a game, etc): *There were events to eliminate the weaker competitors before the main sports.*

K105 *verbs* : **competing**

compete [I∅, 3] to try to win something in competition with someone else: *He competed for a place in the team. Although there were only four horses competing, it was an exciting race. Before the First World War Britain and Germany competed to build ships. Various European countries competed with/against each other for trade in Africa in the 19th century.*
enter [I∅] to put one's name in a list in order to take part in (a sport, etc): *He has entered for the race.*
challenge 1 [T1 *(to)*; V3] to call (someone) to compete against one, esp in a fight, match, etc: *I challenged him to a game of cards. The enemy leader is going to challenge our king to fight.* **2** [T1] to demand official proof of the name and aims of (someone): *The soldier challenged the stranger as soon as she appeared.* **3** [T1] to question the lawfulness or rightness of (someone or something): *She challenged the justice of the new law.* **4** [T1; V3] to call (a person or thing) to competitive effort; test the abilities of (a person or thing): *This difficulty challenges my mind to find an answer. I don't like to study something unless it really challenges me.* **5** [T1; V3] to ask or demand as of right: *The soldier challenged the stranger to say who she was. (lit) This event challenges an explanation.*
contest [T1; (I∅)] **1** to compete (for); fight (for): *How many people are contesting this seat on the town council?* **2** to question the truth or rightness of (something): *The prince's enemies bitterly contested his claim to the crown. I intend to contest the judge's decision in another court.*

K106 *nouns, etc* : **people in sports, etc** [C]

sportsman 1 a man who is keen on, or good at, sport **sportswoman** [*fem*] **2** a man who is willing to take a chance: *He said he would do it; he's a real sportsman!*
player a person who plays in a game, often professionally: *There are eleven players in each team in a football match. The players played well.*
athlete a person who is skilled in bodily exercises and who competes in games that need

strength and speed, such as running and jumping **athletic** [B] **1** [Wa5] of or concerning athletes or athletics **2** (of people) strong in body, with plenty of muscle and speed **-ally** [adv Wa4]

gymnast a person who trains and is skilled in certain bodily exercises **gymnastic** [Wa5; B] concerned with bodily exercise and training **-ally** [adv Wa4]

contestant someone competing in a contest: *There were 50 contestants from all parts of the country in the competition.*

competitor a person, team, business organization, firm, etc, competing with another or others: *There were 10 competitors hoping to increase their trade in China.*

challenger a person who challenges another: *He is one of the new challengers in the Games, and could do well.*

champion 1 a person or animal unbeaten in competitions of courage, strength, or skill: *I think the champion will win; he's never lost a fight yet. Our team will be the champions this year. She became world champion at the age of 26.* **2** a person or animal that shows signs of being better than others: *This dog's only young but already you can tell he's a champion.* **3** a person who fights for, supports strongly, or defends a cause, movement, person, etc: *He was always a champion of the rights of the ordinary citizen; that's why they loved him.* **4** [T1] to fight for, support strongly, or defend (a cause, movement, person, etc): *Bob always champions the workers' cause because he believes in social justice.* **champ** *infml abbrev* a champion: *He's the local boxing champ.*

rival a person who tries to get something one wants oneself or to do things better: *He is one of my rivals in the competition. He is interested in her and looks on/considers me as a rival/his rival.* **rivalry** [U; C] the state of being rivals; strong competition: *There is a lot of rivalry between the two teams.*

K107 *verbs* : **winning and losing, etc**

[ALSO ⇒ C280–82]

win 1 [T1; I∅] to be the best or first in (a contest): *He won the race. Who won?* **2** [T1] **a** to gain (esp a prize): *He won a prize/cup/shield/a hundred pounds.* **b** to gain (the stated place) in a contest: *He won first place in the competition.* **3** [D1 (*for*); T1] to gain by effort or ability: *I can't win his friendship, though I've tried. By her hard work she won a place for herself on the school team.*

beat [T1] (esp in sports, games) to do better than (another): *He beat her at tennis. She beat him (in) running to the end of the road.* (*fig*) *This problem beats me.*

lose [T1; I∅] not to win: *He lost the race. Did he win or lose?*

defeat [T1] to beat; win a victory over (a person or group): *Our team defeated theirs.*

stump [T1 *often pass*] to be too difficult for: *I don't know the answer to that question; I'm stumped.*

tie [I∅] to be equal to an opponent or his or her result in a competition: *He/They tied for second place in the game.*

draw [Wv5; T1; I∅] to end (a game etc) without either side winning: *They drew (the game) 5 points to 5 (= 5 all). We've had several drawn matches this year.*

result in [v prep T1; V4a] to have as a result; cause: *The game resulted in a win for our side.*

K108 *nouns* : **winning and losing**

win [C] *not fml* a success: *How many wins did he have?*

victory 1 [U (*in, over*)] the act of winning or state of having won (in sport, war, or in any kind of struggle): *The football team hoped for victory.* **2** [C (*in, over*)] a success in a fight, struggle, etc: *He had a narrow victory in the competition; he won by only a few points. The football team won some great victories. This army has won/gained many victories.*

triumph [U; C] *esp emot, fml & pomp* (a) great victory

defeat [C; U] the condition or an occasion of losing: *It's defeat; we've lost. How many defeats have they had this year?*

tie [C] an equality of results, in scores, etc: *The match ended in a tie, so we still don't know who's the winner of the competition. The result is a tie.*

draw [C] an occasion when two teams, persons, etc, end a game without either side winning; such a game: *The game was a draw. It's a draw!*

result [C *usu pl*] the announcement of a person's success or failure or of a match won or lost: *He heard the football result on the radio. How did you get on in the competition and when will you know your results?*

K109 *nouns* : **winners and losers** [C]

winner a person who wins, esp in a game, sport, or competition: *The winners all received prizes.*

victor a winner in a race, game, competition, or other kind of struggle: *The crowd cheered as the victor in the 400 metres received his prize.*

loser a person who loses, esp in a game, sport, or competition: *The losers said they would win next year. He's a good/bad loser (= He doesn't mind/doesn't like losing).*

runner-up a person who comes second (or sometimes third) in a contest: *Who were the runners-up?*

prize-winner a person who wins a prize

K110 *nouns* : **prizes** [C]

[ALSO ⇒ D102, I146]

prize 1 something of value given to someone who is successful in a game, race, competition, game of chance, etc, or for some action that is admired: *Her beautiful roses gained first prize at the flower show. He finished only a yard behind the winner of the race but he had to be content with second prize.* **2** [A] something that has gained a prize in a show or competition: *He owns a lot of prize cattle. This is a prize rose.*

cup 1 a prize in the form of a (large) cup with handles: *He won a cup at the Games. Our team hopes to win the Cup this year.* **2** [usu cap] a game or games in which such a cup is given to the winner(s): *Their team played in the World Cup. Our team were Cup Finalists last year but didn't win the Cup.* **cup-tie** a match, esp in football, which is part of a set of matches in which the winner gets a cup

trophy 1 a prize given for winning a race, competition, or test of skill: *He has several cups and other trophies.* **2** something taken after much effort, esp in hunting, war, etc: *He put the lion's head on the wall as a trophy.*

award something given as the result of an official decision, esp a prize

medal a round piece of metal, esp given to someone for winning in sport or fighting bravely in war **medallist** *BrE*, **medalist** *AmE* a person who wins a medal **gold medal** a medal of gold, given to the winner of an important contest **silver medal** a medal of silver, given to the second in an important contest **bronze medal** a medal of bronze, given to the third in an important contest

K111 *nouns & verbs* : **judging**

[ALSO ⇒ G12]

judge 1 [C] a person who decides who or what is better in a sport, contest, etc: *There were three judges and they agreed on the winner.* **2** [I∅; T1] to act as a judge (for): *Who is judging (the contest)?*

adjudicator [C] *fml & tech* a judge, esp in competitions **adjudicate** [I∅; T1] *fml & tech* to judge **adjudication** [U] judging, esp at sports, in acting, etc

referee 1 [C] a judge in charge of a team game such as football **2** [I∅; T1] to act as referee (for): *John refereed (the football match).* **ref** [*infml abbrev*].

umpire 1 [C] the judge in some games and sports, such as cricket and swimming **2** [I∅; T1] to act as an umpire (for): *Who umpired (the match)?*

linesman [C] an official who stays near the lines marking the side of the playing area in such games as football, and decides which team has gone outside the limits, done something wrong, etc

K112 *nouns* : **teams** [GC]

team 1 a group of people who work, play, or act together: *He's in the school team. Which is the best football team in Britain? The government is led by an able team of skilled politicians.* **2** two or more animals pulling the same vehicle: *The carriage was drawn by a team of four white horses.*

side *usu not fml* a team: *They have a good side this year; perhaps they'll win. Which side do you support?*

K113 *nouns* : **singles and doubles** [Wn3;C]

singles a match, esp of tennis, with one player against one: *Who will win the women's singles? Let's play singles.*

doubles a match, esp of tennis, played between two pairs of players: *Who'll win the men's/women's doubles at Wimbledon this year?*

mixed doubles a match, esp of tennis, in which a man and a woman play against another man and woman: *Who'll win the mixed doubles at Wimbledon this year?*

K114 *nouns & adjectives* : **amateur and professional**

amateur 1 [C] a person who plays in sports, performs in plays, paints pictures, etc, for enjoyment and without being paid for it: *He is an amateur footballer. The professionals would not play against amateurs.* **2** [C] a person without experience or skill in sport, art, etc: *She's still an amateur at it.* **3** [B] *also* **amateurish** *often deprec* not as good as a professional: *His work is pretty amateur. He made an amateurish attempt to build a cupboard.* **-ishly** [adv]

am *infml abbrev* amateur (in sport)

professional 1 [C] a person who plays in sports, performs in plays, paints pictures, writes books, etc, for money: *I play a lot but I'm not good enough to be a professional. Some professionals are not as good as some amateurs.* **2** [C] (esp in golf and cricket) a person employed by a private club to play for it and to teach his sporting skill to its members **3** [B] *apprec* having the ability (expected) of a professional: *He is a very professional player.* **un-** [*neg*] **-ly** [adv]: *He plays professionally.*

pro *infml abbrev* professional (in sport)

K115 *nouns* : **fans and supporters** [C]

fan a very keen follower, esp of a sport, art, team, or person: *He is a fan of yours. The football fans enjoyed the game. The actor has a big fan club* (= a lot of fans).

supporter 1 a fan: *The team's supporters travelled a long way to see them play. He joined the* *local team's supporters' club.* **2** a person who supports another, a party, etc: *He is one of the movement's greatest supporters.*

K116 *adjectives* : **indoor and outdoor** [Wa5;A]

indoor which is done, used, etc, inside a building: *They have an indoor swimming pool. He likes most indoor games.*

outdoor which is done, used, etc, outside a building: *Outdoor swimming pools are often cold in this country. He likes watching most outdoor games.*

K117 *nouns* : **fields, pitches, etc** [C]

field *genl* a piece of land marked off in some way for sports, a game, etc: *We can't use the field today; it's too wet. Where is the local football/athletics* [⇒ K100] *field?*

pitch a special field or area on which certain games are played: *The football players ran out on to the pitch. Is it a good cricket pitch?*

court an area specially prepared and marked for various ball games, such as tennis: *The tennis courts are near here.*

ground a piece of land used for a particular purpose, often games and sports: *Where is the local football ground?*

track an area in which people, animals, vehicles, etc, can race

ring 1 the closed-in central place where certain sports take place **2** the square area, esp with ropes round it, in which people box, wrestle, etc

rink 1 a specially prepared surface of ice, for skating **2** any hard material for a similar sport: *I'll meet you at the rink.*

playing field a large area of ground for playing such games as football and cricket

K118 *nouns* : **stadiums, arenas, etc**

stadium [C] a large (usu unroofed) building with rows of seats surrounding a sports field

terracing [U] *also* **terraces** [P] the parts of a stadium where people can stand to watch a game

(grand)stand [C] the set of seats arranged one row above the other, esp in a stadium, and usu covered by a roof from which people may watch a match or sport

amphitheatre *BrE,* **-theater** *AmE* [C] a usu roofless building with rows of seats on a slope that completely surrounds and rises above a central usu circular area, esp one built in ancient Rome and used for competitions and theatrical performances

arena [C] **1** the middle part of a Roman amphitheatre for public sports and fights **2** a scene or place of activity, esp of competition or fighting: *The small country became the arena of*

war between the two big powers. **3** an enclosed area used for sports, public shows, amusements, etc: *Where's the new sports arena?*

K119 *nouns* : **clubs and leagues** [GC often cap]

club a society of people who join together for a certain purpose, esp sport or amusement: *He is a member of our football club.*

association a society of people joined together for a particular sport: *Let's form an association to help people who want to play this game. Association Football is very popular.*

league a group of sports clubs or players that play matches amongst themselves: *Let's start a league of football teams in this area. Is this game a league match?*

K120 *verbs & nouns* : **hitting and missing**
[ALSO ⇒ K104]

hit 1 [T1] to strike with something: *He hit the ball with a bat. Hit it hard!* **2** [C] a blow or stroke: *That was a good hit; it saved the game. The ball made a hit on the moving object. He scored two hits.*

miss 1 [T1, 4, 6a (*what*); I∅] to fail to hit, catch, find, meet, touch, hear, see, etc (something or someone): *The falling rock just missed my head. The fielder missed an important catch, and the cricket match was lost. He arrived too late and missed the train. She went to the station to meet her husband but missed* (= failed to meet) *him in the crowd. Please be quiet; I don't want to miss a word of the news on the radio. We arrived late at the theatre, and missed* (= failed to see and hear) *the first act of the play. Unless I miss my guess* (= if I'm guessing wrongly)*, that's old Frank over there. I don't want to miss seeing that singer on television tonight. There was such a noise that I missed what you were saying to me. The boy threw a stone at the window, but fortunately he missed.* **2** [C] a failure to hit, catch, hold, etc, that which is aimed at: *The hunter's first shot was a miss, but his second killed the lion. The fielder* [⇒ K196] *dropped an easy catch; it was a bad miss.*

knock up [v adv T1] *infml* to add (something) to a cricket score [⇒ K121]: *The cricket team needs to knock up 45 more runs before tea.*

K121 *nouns* : **points, runs, and goals** [C]
[ALSO ⇒ K104]

point a unit of gaining (**scoring**) in games, sports, and other competitions, etc: *He won by 10 points.*

goal 1 (in games like football) the two posts between which the ball must pass **2** the point gained (**scored**) when the ball is caused to do this

run (in games like cricket and baseball) the point scored by running between certain positions after hitting the ball

score [C] the number of points, goals, etc, won in a game: *The score was 2—1 for our team. What's the score so far?*

K122 *nouns & verbs* : **betting and gambling**

bet 1 [C] an agreement to risk money on the result of an uncertain event: *Let's make a bet on the next election. He placed a bet (with a bookmaker). She won/lost on the bet.* **2** [C] a sum of money so risked: *He placed a £5 bet.* **3** [D1; T1; 5a; I∅ (*on*)] to risk (money) on the result of an uncertain event: *He doesn't drink but he bets (on horses). I bet (him) (£5) that they'd win the election, and they did.*

wager *fml* **1** [C] a bet **2** [D1, 5a; T1 (*on*), 5a] to bet: *I'll wager (£5) he'll win the game.*

gamble 1 [C] a risky matter or act: *The operation may not succeed; it's a gamble whether he lives or dies.* **2** [I∅ (*at*)] **a** to play cards or other games for money: *He gambles at cards.* **b** to risk one's money in business: *He's gambling in a new company.* **3** [I∅ (*on*)] to take the risk that something will go well, or as one wishes, after doing something that depends on it: *We haven't eaten; we were gambling on the fact that they would be having dinner when we arrived and would invite us.* **gamble away** [v adv T1] to waste (money) by playing cards or other games for money **gambling den/house** a place where people gamble at cards and/or games

gaming [U] *esp old use* gambling generally: *He spent a lot of his time in gaming.*

lottery [C] an arrangement in which people buy numbered tickets, and prizes, usu of money, are given to those who hold numbers that are drawn by lot (= chosen by chance from among all the numbers)

pools, *also fml* **football pools** [*the* P;A] *esp BrE* an arrangement by which people risk small amounts of money on the results of certain football matches, and those who guess the results correctly (or nearly correctly) win large shares of the combined money: *He won a fortune on the pools. Have you ever had a pools win?*

stake 1 [C] money used in gambling or in guessing the result of a race, etc: *Who will hold the stakes till the race is over?* **2** [T1 (*on*)] to offer as a stake: *He staked £20 on that horse winning the race. I'd stake my life on his honesty!* **3** [T1] to make (a claim, etc): *He staked his claim to a gold mine in the hills.* [also ⇒ J114]

K123 *nouns, etc* : **gambling terms**

odds [P] the probability that something will or will not happen: *The odds are 10 to 1 that her horse will not win the race.* **give/lay odds** to

offer (someone) a bet at the stated odds: *I'll lay you (odds of) 3 to 1.* (= Give me £1, and I will give you £3 if you win.) **take odds** to accept such a bet **long odds** odds that are strongly against (for example, 100 to 1) **short odds** odds that are not strongly against (for example, 2 to 1)

evens chances that are the same for and against (as when one risks £2 on a horse to win £2)

against likely that something will not happen: *The odds are 10 to 1 against him winning. She made a bet at 2 to 1 against.* (= She risked £2 on a horse to win £4)

on likely that something will happen: *She made a bet at 2 to 1 on.* (= She risked £2 on a horse to win £1)

odds-on [Wa5; B] very likely to happen, win, etc (*esp in the phr* **odds-on favourite**): *The odds-on favourite came last in the race, to everyone's surprise. It's odds-on that he won't come.*

favourite *BrE*, **favorite** *AmE* [*the* + C] (in horse-racing, etc) the horse or competitor in each race that is expected to win

K124 *nouns* : **gamblers and bookmakers** [C]

gambler a person who gambles, usu at games of chance

punter *BrE infml* a person who risks money, esp on the result of a horse race: *The punters were happy when the horse won, but not the bookies.*

bookmaker a person who takes money in bets, risked on the results of competition, esp horse races

bookie *infml* a bookmaker

turf accountant *euph & fml* a bookmaker

Indoor games

K130 *nouns, etc* : **playing cards**

(playing) cards [P] the usu 52 pieces of flat stiff paper marked in various ways and used in various games: *Have you got the cards?*

pack [C] a complete set of cards used in playing a game: *We can't play if there is a card missing from the pack.*

deck [C] *esp AmE* a pack (of cards)

hand [C] a number of playing cards held by one person in a game: *This is a good hand! I've had nothing but bad hands all night.*

deal 1 [C] the act or right of giving out cards to players in a card game: *It's your deal this time. Who has the deal now? The next two deals will be interesting.* **2** [D1 (*to*); T1 (*out*); I∅] to give out (cards) to (players) in a game: *Who deals next?*

suit [C] one of four sets of playing cards

card table [C] a special table, usu small and with a green cloth top, at which people play card games

K131 *nouns* : the suits and names of playing cards [C]

heart   club

spade   diamond

heart [*usu pl*] a playing card with one or more hearts printed in red: *He played the Queen of Hearts.*

club [*usu pl*] a playing card with one or more clubs printed in black: *She held the King of Clubs.*

diamond [*usu pl*] a playing card with one or more diamonds printed in red: *He held up the 4 of diamonds. I've only one diamond left in my hand, the Jack.*

spade [*usu pl*] a playing card with one or more spades printed in black: *The Ace of Spades is said to represent Death.*

queen   king

jack   ace

ace a playing card that has a single mark or spot and which usu has the highest or lowest value in a game

king any of the four playing cards with a picture of a king: *He held the King of Clubs.*

queen any of the four playing cards with a picture of a queen: *He played the Queen of Hearts.*

jack *also* **knave** any of the four cards with a picture of a man and a rank between the queen and the ten

joker

joker an extra playing card, which in some games may have any value

court card *also* **face card** a playing card which is a king, queen, or jack

trump any card of a suit chosen to be of higher rank than the other three suits during a game

K132 *nouns* : **card games** [U]

poker a type of card game usu played for money: *They were playing poker. The poker game was exciting.*

whist a card game for two pairs of players, in which points are made by winning **tricks** (= a round of one card from each player, which the card of most value wins)

bridge a card game for four players developed from the game of whist and usu played as **contract bridge** or sometimes **auction bridge**

rummy *also* **gin-rummy** *also esp AmE* **gin** any of several simple card games for two or more players, in which each player tries to put together groups of three or more cards of the same rank or suit

canasta a card game like rummy using two packs of cards, in which players get special points for a group of seven cards of the same rank

snap (in Britain) a type of card game in which players lay down cards one after the other and try to be the first to notice when two like cards are laid down together

K133 *nouns & verbs* : **dice and dicing**

dice

dice 1 [Wn3;C] *BrE* a small 6–sided block of wood, bone, plastic, etc, with 1–6 spots on each side, used in games of chance: *Throw the dice. He had a pair of dice. A dice/One of the dice has rolled under the table.* **2** [P] *AmE* two or more of these **3** [U] any game of chance which is played with these: *He was playing dice.* **4** [I∅ (*for, with*)] to play dice (with someone, for money, possessions, etc): *He spent his time drinking and dicing. They were dicing for drinks. I diced with him for who should pay the bill.* **5** [X9 *no pass,* esp *into, out of*] to put, bring, etc, into or out of a state or the possession of something by playing dice: *He diced himself out of a large fortune.*

die *esp AmE* a dice

USAGE The singular form **die** is not used now in *BrE* except in the old saying *The die is cast* (= The decision has been made and cannot now be changed).

throw 1 [T1; I∅] to let (dice, etc) go through the air and fall on a table, etc: *He threw a six and a four. He threw, and lost.* **2** [C] an act of throwing: *Your throw now. If he loses the next throw, he loses everything.*

cast *fml* **1** [T1] to throw (dice, etc): *He cast the dice.* **2** [C] an act of throwing

K134 *nouns* : **relating to gambling**

casino [C] a building used for social activities, esp playing games for money

croupier [C] a person who collects the money lost and pays out the money won at a table where games are played for money

roulette [U] a game of chance in which a small ball is spun round a moving wheel and falls into a hole marked with a number

baccarat [U] a game of cards played by a banker (= a person who keeps the money) and two or more punters [⇨ K124] who bet against him

chemin de fer [U] a fast form of baccarat

pontoon *BrE, also* **blackjack**, *also AmE* **twenty-one** a card game usu played for money, in which players try to make a winning combination of cards worth 21 points

K135 *nouns* : **games in the home, etc** [U]

snakes and ladders [U] a board game with a counter for each player, in which the counter moves from square to square, the winner being the counter which reaches the last square (**home**) first: *In snakes and ladders it's good if you go up a ladder because that takes you nearer home, but bad if you have to go down a snake, because then you are nearly back where you started.*

ludo a children's game played with little flat objects (**counters**) on a board

Scrabble *tdmk* a game in which players make points by putting rows of separate letters on the squares of a board to form words

Monopoly *tdmk* a game in which the winner obtains all the pretended money, property, etc

K136 *nouns* : **board games**

chess [U *often in comb*] a game for two players each of whom start with 16 pieces (**chessmen**) which can be moved according to fixed rules across a chessboard in an attempt to trap (**checkmate**) the opponent's king

draughts *BrE,* **checkers** *AmE* [U] a game for two players, each with 12 round pieces on a board of 64 squares

backgammon [U] a game for two players, using round wooden pieces and dice [⇨ K133]

board [C *often in comb*] a flat surface with patterns, used for playing a (stated) game on: *I want to play chess but I can't find the board. Where's the chessboard?*

K137 *nouns* : **pieces and counters** [C]

piece one of a set of small round objects or figures used in playing certain board games, esp chess

counter a piece, esp when round and flat, esp in draughts or children's board games but not in chess

man [*often in comb*] *not fml* **1** a counter used in draughts **2** a piece used in chess, esp a pawn: *Move your man. These are beautiful chessmen; are they wood?*

K138 *nouns* : **pieces in chess** [C]

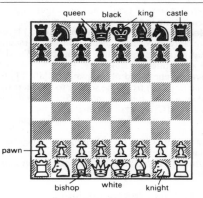

chessboard and pieces

king the most important piece, that moves only one square at a time in any direction and must be kept safe from attack

queen the most powerful piece in the game of chess, that moves any number of squares in straight lines or corner to corner

bishop a piece, usu with a hat like a bishop [⇨ C347], that moves any distance from corner to corner on squares of one colour

knight a piece, usu with a horse's head, that moves one square forward and two to the side or two squares forward and one to the side

castle *also* **rook** a piece that can move any distance in a straight line but not from corner to corner

pawn 1 any of the eight smallest and least valuable of a player's pieces **2** (*fig*) an unimportant person used by somebody else for his own advantage: *They were only pawns in the big political battle.*

K139 *nouns & verbs* : **some words used in chess**

gambit [C] **1** an opening move in which a piece is risked so as to gain advantage later **2** (*fig*) an action which is used to produce a future effect, esp as part of a trick or a clever plan: *He made his opening gambit by taking the chairman's seat.*

opening [C] an act of starting a game, esp chess

attack [C;U] a player's way of attacking, esp the other person's king

defence *BrE*, **defense** *AmE* [C;U] a player's way of defending, esp his king

check 1 [(*in*)] the position of a player's king when it is directly attacked: *Your king is in check.* **2** [T1] to put (the other player's king) in this position: *She checked his king.* **3** [interj] (said when doing this): *Check!*

checkmate 1 [C;U] the position of a king when under direct attack from an opponent's pieces from which escape is impossible: *The game ended with a checkmate. It was checkmate.* **2** [T1 *often pass*] to be put in this position: *He's checkmated.* (*fig*) *Their plans were checkmated.* **3** [interj] (said when putting the opponent's king in this position): *Checkmate!*

stalemate [C] the position from which a player can only move into check, and which means that neither player wins **stalemated** [Wa5;B] in a condition of stalemate

move (in chess and other games) **1** [I∅;T1] to take (a piece) from one square to another: *He takes a long time to move. She moved her queen.* **2** [C] an act of moving: *Your move now. That was a good/bad move. He will win in two moves.*

take [T1] to win (a piece belonging to the other player): *She took his queen.*

capture [T1] *fml* to take: *His queen was captured in the tenth move.*

K140 *nouns* : **the gymnasium**

gymnasium [C] a hall with bars on all or some of the walls (**wall bars**), ropes, and other equipment for bodily exercises, jumping, climbing, etc: *We have exercises in the school gymnasium. Our gymnasium equipment is very good.*

gym [C] *infml abbrev* a gymnasium: *Let's play in the gym/the gym hall.*

(parallel) bars [P] a pair of bars on four posts, parallel to each other, used for exercising the body

horse [C] an apparatus used for exercising the body by jumping over it, on it, etc

mat [C] a covering for part of a floor, esp in a gymnasium, in which a person can do exercises, people can wrestle [⇒ K143], etc

trampoline [C] an apparatus consisting of a sheet of material tightly stretched and held to a metal frame by strong springs, on which acrobats [⇒ K88] and gymnasts [⇒ K146] jump up and down to perform exercises

springboard [C] **1** a strong bendable board for jumping off to give height to a jump **2** [(*to*)] (*fig*) a starting point where power is built up: *He hopes to make this job a springboard to higher office.*

K141 *nouns* : **billiards and snooker**

billiards [U] a game played on a cloth-covered table with balls pushed with long sticks (**cues**) against each other or into 6 small net bags (**pockets**) at the corners and sides: *Billiards is his favourite game.* **billiard** [A] billiards: *He has his own billiard table.*

snooker [U] a game like billiards with 15 red and 6 (numbered) balls of other colours: *He likes playing snooker. Is there a snooker table here?*

pool [U] any of various American games that are like billiards, played usu with 16 (numbered) balls on a table that has 6 pockets: *Are you ready to shoot* (= play) *pool?*

poolroom [C] a (usu public) room in the US, where pool and games of chance are played for money

table [C9] a piece of furniture like a table specially made for playing a stated game: *billiard table; card table*

cue [C] a long straight wooden rod, slightly thicker at one end than the other, used for pushing the ball in billiards, snooker, etc

pocket 1 [C] any of the 6 small net bags round a billiard table, into which the ball is knocked: *He hit the black* (*ball*) *into the top pocket.* **2** [T1] to put in a pocket: *He pocketed the black.*

pot [T1] *BrE* (in billiards, etc) to hit (a ball) into one of the pockets: *He potted the black.*

white/red/black, etc [*the* R] (in billards, etc) the white/red/black, etc, ball: *He potted the white.*

K142 *nouns* : **other indoor games** [U]

table tennis a game played on a special large hard table by two people (**singles**) or two pairs (**doubles**) who use small bats to knock a very small light hollow plastic ball to each other across a net

ping pong *infml* table tennis

badminton a game played in an indoor court with rackets [⇒ K197] smaller than in tennis and with a ball-like object with feathers (**a shuttlecock**) across a high narrow net

squash *also fml* **squash rackets** a game played in a four-walled indoor court by two or four people with rackets smaller than in tennis and a small dark rubber ball, hitting the ball off a front wall

netball a game (usu played by women) in which a ball is thrown so as to fall through a net fastened to a ring at the top of a post, often played in a gymnasium

basketball a game played by two teams of five players each, who try to throw a large light ball into a net fixed on a ring ten feet above the ground

volleyball a game in which a large ball is struck by hand backwards and forwards across a net without being allowed to touch the ground

ice hockey a fast game like field hockey [⇨ K190] played on ice in a large indoor hall by two teams of six players each, wearing skates [⇨ K205] and carrying sticks with which to hit a flat round rubber object (**a puck**)

K143 *verbs & nouns* : **boxing and wrestling**

corner

ropes

boxing gloves

referee

boxer

ringside seats

boxing ring

box 1 [I∅ (*with, together*)] to fight by hitting with the closed hands (**fists**), esp when wearing large soft gloves (**boxing gloves**) and standing or moving in a square area with ropes round it (**a boxing ring**): *He boxes well. I haven't boxed for years. He hasn't boxed with that man before. They were boxing (together).* **2** [T1] to hit hard (*esp in the phr* **to box someone's ears**): *Get out of here or I'll box your ears for you!*

boxing [U] the sport or art of fighting with the fists: *He is good at boxing. There's a boxing match tonight.*

boxer [C] a man who boxes: *The two boxers climbed into the (boxing) ring.*

wrestle [I∅ (*with, together*)] to fight by holding and throwing the body: *He wrestles well. I haven't wrestled for years. He hasn't wrestled with that man before. They were wrestling (together) on the ground. She wrestled with her attacker. (fig) He was wrestling with a number of difficulties.*

wrestling [U] the sport or art of fighting by holding and throwing the body: *He's good at wrestling. There's a wrestling match tonight.*

wrestler [C] a man who wrestles: *He is one of the best wrestlers in the country.*

all-in-wrestling [U] a kind of wrestling in which the wrestlers are allowed to hit as well as to hold

judo [U] a kind of wrestling that began in Japan: *He is good at judo. She is a member of a judo club.*

K144 *nouns & verbs* : **boxing and wrestling terms, etc**

punch 1 [T1; I∅] to strike (someone or something) hard with the closed hand (**fist**): *He punched the man in the chest/on the jaw.* **2** [C (*in, on*)] a quick strong blow with the fist: *I'd like to give that fellow a punch in the face/on the nose. Both fighters have strong punches* (= both boxers punch hard). **3** [U] (*fig*) *apprec* forcefulness; effective power: *He's a successful businessman who has a lot of punch. That statement lacks punch; you should rewrite it.* **pull one's punches** to punch less hard than one should: *The boxer was pulling his punches.* (*fig*) *He doesn't pull his punches; he always says exactly what he thinks, even if it hurts people.* **roll with the punch** *not fml* to move back or sideways so as to soften the effect of a blow **beat someone to the punch 1** to hit someone hard before he can hit you **2** to take action, speak, etc, before someone else can do so **punch-drunk** [B] **1** showing unsteadiness, an inability to think clearly and other signs of brain damage from repeated blows to the head **2** (*fig*) confused

jab 1 [I∅; T1] to punch straight, hard, and quickly: *He jabbed the other boxer in the side.* **2** [C] a quick straight blow, usu from a short distance: *The two fighters aimed jabs at one another.*

sock *infml* **1** [T1] to punch: *Sock him! He socked him on the jaw.* **2** [C] a punch: *He gave him a hard sock on the chin.*

right [C] a punch with the right hand

left [C] a punch with the left hand

uppercut [C] a punch which comes quickly up from below

hook [C] a short curving punch with the arm bent: *He gave him a hard right hook* (= a hook with the right hand).

knock out [v adv T1] to punch (someone) unconscious (with one blow): *He knocked the other man out.* **2** to make (someone) unconscious: *The heavy piece of wood fell on his head and knocked him out.*

knockout [C] the act or result of knocking someone out: *It's a knockout: he's won! He won by a knockout.*

count [C] the act of counting up to ten, after which a boxer, if he is still lying down, has lost the match: *He was out for the count* (= unable to get up: knocked out). *He got up on a count of 8.*

points [(*on*) P] the score of successes in a match:

He won on points (= He did not knock the other boxer out, but he was thought to be the better fighter).

hold [C] a way of holding someone, esp in wrestling, so that it is difficult to move or the person must move in a particular direction: *He couldn't break* (= get out of) *the other man's hold. Have you learnt this hold yet?*

throw [C] a way or occasion of throwing someone in wrestling: *Have you learnt any new judo throws? That was a good throw!*

Children's games and toys

K170 *nouns & verbs* : **games and playing**

game [(of)] something, esp done by two or more children, to pass the time: *Let's play a game of dressing-up/play a dressing-up game!*

play 1 [IØ (with)] to do things that pass the time pleasantly, esp including running and jumping; have fun: *Can he come out to play (with me)? The children were playing in the garden. The cat was playing with a bit of string. The children were playing together at dressing-up.* **2** [T1] to amuse oneself by doing (the stated thing): *Let's play ball. They were playing games in the garden. Can we play dressing-up, Mummy?* **3** [L1; T4] to amuse oneself by pretending to be or do (the stated thing): *Let's play doctors and nurses!* **4** [(at) U] activity for amusement only: *Children often copy the actions of their parents in play. The young lambs were at play in the field.*

playtime [U] any time when a child is free to play: *It's playtime at the school now.*

playpen [C] a small enclosure like a cage in which a very young child can be left to play safely

playground [C] an area usu round or near a school or in a public place where children can play, often with swings, chutes, etc: *The children were running about in the playground.* (*fig*) *Monte Carlo is the playground of the rich.*

playroom *also esp old use* **nursery** [C] a place, room, etc, which children can use for playing, etc: *The children are all in the nursery.*

antics [P] strange or unusual actions, esp with odd, amusing, or foolish movements of the body, esp of or with children: *The children laughed at his antics.*

K171 *nouns, etc* : **things in children's playgrounds** [C]

swing a seat on ropes or chains, hanging from a bar, on which a person, esp a child, can swing or be pushed back and forward

chute a sloped passage down which a person, usu a child, can slide

slide *not fml* a chute

roundabout *BrE also* **merry-go-round** *also AmE* **carousel** a machine in a playground or amusement park on which children can ride round and round, often sitting on wooden animals, etc

seesaw 1 [C] a board balanced in the middle on some other object, so that persons, esp children, can sit at each end so that when one end goes up, the other goes down **2** [U] children's play on such a board: *She had an hour playing seesaw.* **3** [C] (*fig*) a movement backwards and forwards as in a game, battle, etc, where now one side and now the other is winning **4** [IØ] to play seesaw **5** [IØ] (*fig*) to move backwards and forwards, up and down, or between opposites or opponents: *Victory in the battle seesawed for hours between the two armies.*

K172 *nouns, etc* : **toys and dolls** [C]

toy an object for children to play with: *Tidy up all your toys and put them in the toy box. The toy soldier was broken. The little boy stood looking in the window of the toyshop/the toyshop window.* **toy with** [v prep T1] **1** to play with (something) purposelessly: *While he was talking to us he toyed with his pencil.* **2** to consider (an idea) not very seriously: *She's toying with (the idea of) going to London, but I don't think she'll go.*

plaything *not used by children* something that (esp) a child plays with; toy: *The shop sold various children's playthings.* (*fig*) *'I'm not your plaything,' she told him angrily.*

doll 1 a small figure of a person, esp of a baby, esp for a child to play with: *She put her dolls in the doll's house* (= a special small house for children to play with). **2** (*fig*) *infml* a pretty young girl

dolly *infml* a doll: *Where's my dolly, Mummy?*

golliwog *also* **golly** a kind of doll made of soft material dressed like a little man, with a black face with big white eyes and black hair standing out round his head

teddy bear *also infml* **teddy** a toy bear filled with soft material: *Teddy doesn't want to go to bed, Mummy. The little boy had a lot of teddies.*

balloon a bag made of rubber or other material which becomes large and rounded when air or a gas is blown into it: *The children had lots of balloons at their party. Don't burst my balloon!*

pet 1 [C] an animal kept by a person in the home as a companion: *He was a pet dog. He keeps a monkey as a pet.* **2** [C; A] a person (esp a child) or thing specially favoured above others: *She is the teacher's pet. Politicians are my pet hate.* **3** [C usu sing; N] a person who is specially loved or lovable: *Mary is a pet and everyone loves her. Come here, pet.* **4** [T1] to touch (esp an animal kindly with the hands): *She petted the dog.*

K173 *nouns* : **some things children like doing** [U]

---

dressing-up wearing someone else's clothes for fun or pretence: *My younger daughter likes dressing-up games. Let's play dressing-up; I'll be a nurse and you can be a soldier.*

hide-and-seek a game in which someone hides and the other person or persons go looking for him or her: *They played hide-and-seek among the trees.*

make-believe a state of pretending; things which are pretended: *It was all make-believe: none of it was true. He lives in a world of make-believe/in a make-believe world, if he thinks he can succeed without working hard.* **make believe** [T1;5] to pretend: *The children made believe they were princes and princesses.*

let's-pretend a game of pretending (to be or to do something): *The children were playing let's-pretend. They had a game of let's-pretend, in which he was the king.*

K174 *nouns* : **nursery rhymes and fairy stories** [C]

---

nursery rhyme a short, usu well-known song or poem for small children to learn, say, and sing

fairy story *also* **fairy tale 1** a story about fairies and other small magical people **2** a story or account that is hard or impossible to believe, esp one intended to deceive: *Oh, go and tell your fairy stories to somebody else!* **fairy-tale** [A] having the qualities, esp beautiful or strange, of a fairy story: *What a fairy-tale castle!*

bedtime story a story told to a child at the time of going to bed, esp to help him or her fall asleep: *Come on; it's time for your bedtime story.*

K175 *nouns* : **some games children like**

[ALSO ⇒ K135]

---

marbles [U] a children's game in which small hard glass balls are rolled along the ground or thrown towards each other

conkers [U] (esp in Britain) a children's game in which one person swings a conker (= (*infml*) a **chestnut**, the nut of a particular kind of large tree) which has been fastened to a piece of string, in an attempt to break the opponent's conker

jigsaw puzzle [C] a picture stuck onto wood and cut up into many small irregular pieces that can be fitted together for amusement, in order to make the original picture again

puzzle [C] any kind of game in which a person must think hard in order to get the answer, do something, or find something: *She gave him a book of puzzles to keep him amused.*

riddle [C] a game with words in which one must try to understand the meaning of the words, which do not usu appear to make sense: *She asked him the riddle, 'What goes on four legs in the morning, two legs in the middle of the day, and three legs in the evening?'. The answer was a person, who is a baby and then a grown-up and then an old man or woman with a stick to help in walking.* (*fig*) *Don't talk in riddles: tell me exactly what you want!*

Outdoor games

K190 *nouns* : **ball games**

---

ball game [C] *esp AmE* any game played with a ball, but esp baseball: *Are you going to the ball game?*

(association) football [U *often cap*] *BrE* a game in which the ball is moved mainly with the feet but also with the head, played by two teams of eleven players each on a large field [⇒ K191,2]

soccer [U] *BrE* (Association) football: *He likes watching soccer (matches) on television.*

rugby (football) [U *sometimes cap*] a kind of football played esp in Britain with an egg-shaped ball by two teams of either 13 men (**Rugby League**), or 15 men (**Rugby Union**) [⇒ K193,4]

rugger [U] *esp BrE infml* rugby

American football *BrE*, **football** *AmE* [U] a kind of football, played esp in the US, with an egg-shaped ball and two teams of eleven players each [⇒ K195]

baseball 1 [U] a game played with a bat and ball between two teams of nine players each on a large field in which there are four **bases** which a player must touch in order to score a run: *Baseball is the national game of the US.* **2** [C] the ball used in this game [⇒ K194]

rounders [U] a British ball game like baseball, usu played by children, in which a player hits the ball and then runs round the edge of a square area

(field) hockey [U] a game played with sticks and a ball on a field by two teams of eleven players each

cricket [U] a game popular in such countries as England, Australia, India, Pakistan, and the West Indies, played with a ball and a bat by two teams of eleven players each [⇒ K196]

(lawn) tennis [U] a game for two people (**singles**) or two pairs of people (**doubles**) who use rackets (= a kind of bat) to hit a small soft ball back and forwards across a low net dividing a level specially marked court [⇒ K197]

lacrosse [U] a game played on a field by two teams, each player having a long stick (**crosse**), with a net at the end to throw, catch, and carry the small hard ball

croquet [U] a game played on grass in which

players knock wooden balls through a number of small metal arches (**hoops**) with a long-handled wooden hammer (**mallet**)

golf [U] a game played by two or four persons with sticks (**clubs**) and small hard balls, each player trying to get his ball into a set of 9 or 18 holes in the smallest number of tries: *You have to walk a long way in a game of golf, as there is quite a long distance between each hole.*

bowls [U] a game played by rolling heavy esp wooden balls (**bowls**) across a grassy area (**bowling green**): *Let's have a game of bowls.*

K191 *nouns* : **association football**

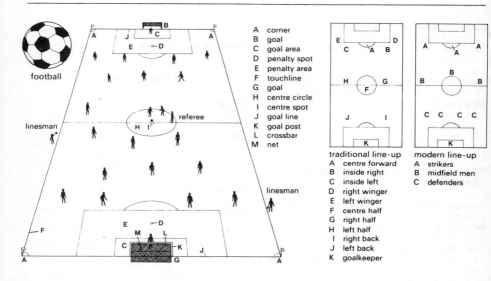

A corner
B goal
C goal area
D penalty spot
E penalty area
F touchline
G goal
H centre circle
I centre spot
J goal line
K goal post
L crossbar
M net

football
linesman
referee
linesman

traditional line-up
A centre forward
B inside right
C inside left
D right winger
E left winger
F centre half
G right half
H left half
I right back
J left back
K goalkeeper

modern line-up
A strikers
B midfield men
C defenders

K192 *nouns, etc* : **soccer terms**

pitch [C] the playing field for soccer

football *also esp infml* **bladder** the large round ball used in soccer

kick off [v adv I∅] to start a game of football: *They kicked off five minutes late.*

kickoff [C] the first kick, at the start of each half of a game of football: *The kickoff is at 3 o'clock today.*

(full) time [U] the end of the game, after 90 minutes' play

half time [U] the halfway point in a game, after which the teams change ends of the field

foul [C] a fault in games like football, usu by handling the ball or causing harm to a player in the other team

free kick [C] a kick allowed a team because of a foul by a player in the other team

penalty (kick) [C] a free kick allowed at the other team's goal

offside 1 [B; E] (of a player, esp in football) in a position in which play is not allowed, esp by receiving a forward-moving pass in the half of the field belonging to the other team when there are fewer than two players of the other team between oneself and the goal line **2** [Wa5; A] of or about such a position: *the offside rule*

wing [C] (in games such as football) the left or right side of the field, near the sidelines

winger [C] a player on either wing

corner (kick) [C] a kick from a corner of the field towards the goal, by a member of the team attacking that goal, allowed when the ball has been kicked over the goal line by one of the defending players

pass 1 [I∅ (*to*); T1] to pass (the ball) with the foot or head from one player to another in the same team: *He isn't good at passing; he likes to keep the ball to himself. He passed to Smith. Pass the ball to Smith!* **2** [C] an occasion of passing in this way: *That was a good pass!*

shoot [I∅] to kick the ball hard at the goal of the other team: *He shot and scored. Shoot!*

shot [C] the act or occasion of shooting: *That was a good shot! He tried for a goal but his shot went wide* (= missed the goal by quite a distance).

head [T1] to strike (the ball) with the head: *He headed the ball into the goal.*

header [C] an act or occasion of heading: *His header missed* (*the goal*).

shy [C] **1** an act of shying (= throwing the ball with both hands over the head) back into play from beyond the sideline **2** an occasion when such an action is necessary: *The ball went over the touchline and it was a shy for the other team.*

K193 *nouns* : **rugby football**

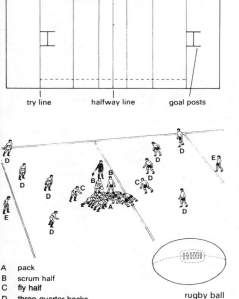

try line   halfway line   goal posts

A   pack
B   scrum half
C   fly half
D   three-quarter backs
E   fullback

rugby ball

scrum [C] **1** a group formed at certain times in the game by the eight forwards (= front players) of both teams pushing against each other with heads down and shoulders together, to try to get the ball, which is on the ground between the two sides **2** *infml* a disorderly crowd

wing [C] a forward whose place is on one or other side of the centre

point [C] the unit of scoring in rugby

try [C] the act of touching the ball down in the goal area of the other team, to score four points

goal [C] a kick which sends the ball over the crossbar of the goal, to score three points

K194 *nouns* : **American football** [C]

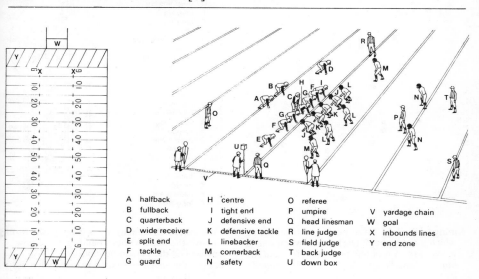

A halfback	H centre	O referee
B fullback	I tight end	P umpire
C quarterback	J defensive end	Q head linesman
D wide receiver	K defensive tackle	R line judge
E split end	L linebacker	S field judge
F tackle	M cornerback	T back judge
G guard	N safety	U down box

V   yardage chain
W   goal
X   inbounds lines
Y   end zone

K195 *nouns* : **baseball** [C]

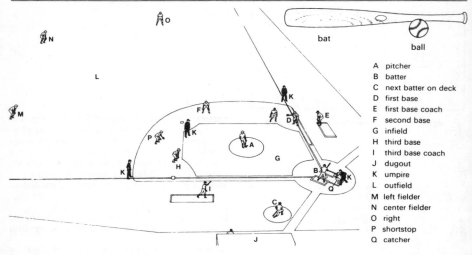

bat

ball

A pitcher
B batter
C next batter on deck
D first base
E first base coach
F second base
G infield
H third base
I third base coach
J dugout
K umpire
L outfield
M left fielder
N center fielder
O right
P shortstop
Q catcher

diamond 1 the field on which baseball is played **2** *also* **infield** the square in a baseball field which has the four bases as its corners
batter [C] a baseball player who bats (= hits the ball with his bat)

pitcher [C] a baseball player who pitches (= throws the ball towards the batter)
catcher [C] a baseball player who waits behind the batter to catch the ball

K196 *nouns, etc* : **cricket**

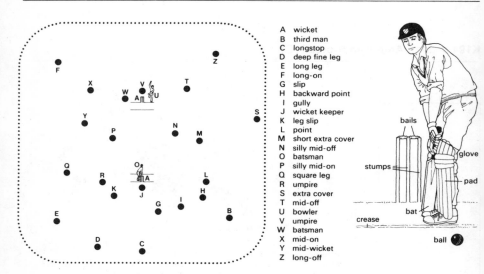

A wicket
B third man
C longstop
D deep fine leg
E long leg
F long-on
G slip
H backward point
I gully
J wicket keeper
K leg slip
L point
M short extra cover
N silly mid-off
O batsman
P silly mid-on
Q square leg
R umpire
S extra cover
T mid-off
U bowler
V umpire
W batsman
X mid-on
Y mid-wicket
Z long-off

bails

glove

stumps

pad

bat

crease

ball

innings [Wn3;C] **1** the period of time during which a team bats **2** (*fig*) a time when one is active, esp in a public position: *He's had his innings now; he must let the new chairman do the work.*
bowl [X9; IØ; (T1)] to throw (the ball) towards

the hitter (**batsman**) by swinging the arm above the head without bending the elbow
bowler [C] the person bowling
bat [C] the specially shaped wooden stick used for hitting the ball

batsman [C] the player who tries to hit the ball with the bat

field [I∅; T1] to catch or stop (a ball that has been hit)

fielder [C] any of the players fielding

over [C] (the period of) the act of bowling the ball at the batsman a particular number of times by one player in the other team from the wicket at one end: *In England there are six balls in an over, but in Australia there are eight.*

run [C] a point won by two batsmen running from one wicket to the other, passing each other on the way

four [C] four runs, usu gained by hitting the ball to the edge of the playing area

six [C] a hit that counts six runs, esp one that crosses the edge of the playing area before touching the ground: *He hit several sixes.*

century [C] 100 runs scored by one batsman

declare [I∅ (*at*)] to say that one's team will stop batting: *Their side declared at 234 (runs). Should we declare now?*

test match *also infml* **test** [C *often cap*] a cricket match played between teams representing different countries

K197 *nouns, etc* : **tennis**

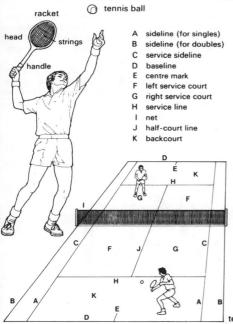

racket

○ tennis ball

head   strings

handle

A	sideline (for singles)
B	sideline (for doubles)
C	service sideline
D	baseline
E	centre mark
F	left service court
G	right service court
H	service line
I	net
J	half-court line
K	backcourt

tennis court

(tennis) racket, racquet [C] a light instrument consisting of a network of usu nylon stretched in a frame, with a handle, used for hitting the ball

serve 1 [I∅] to put the ball into play by hitting it: *She served. He serves well.* **2** [C] *not fml* an act of serving: *That was a good serve.*

service [U; C] the act of or occasion for serving: *Your service! The service was a let.*

let [C *usu sing*] (a service that must be taken again because of) the ball hitting the net: *Let!*

love [U] (in scoring) a score of nothing: *The score was 3 : 0 (three love).*

set [C] a group of six or more games, with the winner having at least two games more than the loser

delivery [U; C] ability to send the ball (with force): *Her delivery is pretty good. That was a good delivery!*

K198 *nouns, etc* : **golf**

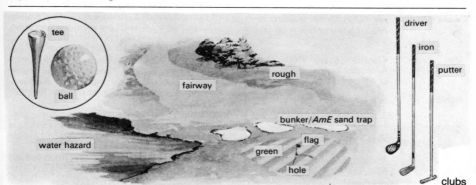

tee

driver

iron

putter

ball

rough

fairway

bunker/*AmE* sand trap

flag

water hazard

green

hole

clubs

golfer [C] a person who plays golf

golf club [C] **1** any one of the special kinds of sticks (**clubs**) used to hit the ball **2** an association organized so that its members can play golf, usu in a particular place: *He is a member of the local golf club.*

golf course [C] the large area, containing space for 9 or 18 fairways, green, and holes, in which a game of golf can be played

rough [(*the*) U] the uneven ground, usu with long grass, along the sides of fairways in a golf course: *He lost his ball in the rough.*

tee [C] a small heap of sand or a specially-shaped plastic or wooden object from which the ball is first driven at the beginning of play on each fairway

tee off [v adv IØ] to drive the ball from a tee: *They teed off.*

drive 1 [IØ] to hit the ball as far as possible from the tee **2** [C] an act of doing this: *That was a nice drive!*

slice 1 [C] a flight of the ball away from a course straight ahead and towards the side of the player's stronger hand **2** [T1; IØ] to hit (a ball) in a slice

hook 1 [C] a flight of a ball away from a course straight ahead and towards the side of a player's weaker hand **2** [T1; IØ] to hit (a ball) in a hook

putt 1 [T1; IØ] to strike (a ball) gently along the ground towards or into the hole **2** [T1; IØ *in comb*] to do this the stated number of times in reaching (the hole): *He three-putted the 17th hole.* **3** [C] an act of putting: *It took three putts before he got the ball into the hole/before he sank the ball.* **4** [C] the result of this: *That putt didn't go into the hole. His putt was too short.*

putter [C] **1** the club with which one putts **2** a person who putts

handicap [C] (in golf and other games) the amount by which a better player, animal, etc, is put at a disadvantage against others in competition: *What is his handicap? — He has a handicap of 4.*

par 1 [U] the number of strokes the average player should take to hit the ball into a hole or into all the holes: *Par for the 18th hole is 4. He did a par round* (= went round the course getting the average score). *He did the course in 4 under par, which was pretty good.* **2** [T1] to play the number of strokes for (a hole or all the holes) which is equal to par: *He parred the 18th hole.*

K199 *nouns, etc* : **horse riding**
[ALSO ⇒ A51]

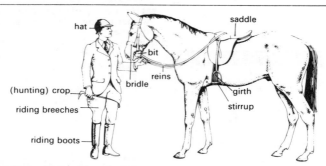

the movements and speeds of a horse
[C; IØ, T1]

walk (*slowest*)	He walked the horse across the field. The horsemen rode at a walk.
trot	The horse trotted away. The horsemen rode up (= nearer) at a trot.
canter	Several horses cantered past. They rode past at a fast canter.
gallop (*fastest*)	Gallop! They galloped past on their horses. They rode past at a gallop/at the gallop. He heard the sound of galloping horses.

riding, *also* **horse riding** [U] the skill or exercise of riding a horse: *Let's do some riding. Riding is his favourite sport. She is enjoying her riding lessons.*

rider [C] **1** someone who rides, esp a horse: *That is his horse, but who is the rider?* **2** [C9] someone who rides, esp a horse (with the stated degree of skill): *She's a good rider; she sits a horse well. I'm afraid he's no rider* (= he can't ride well).

horseman [C] someone who rides a horse generally, or on a particular occasion is riding a horse: *He is a good horseman. Several horsemen rode past.* **horsewoman** [*fem*]

show jumping [U] a riding competition judged on ability and (usu) speed in jumping a course of fences

jumper [C] a horse that is good at jumping

show jumper [C] a horse that is ridden in show-jumping

harness 1 [U; C *usu sing*] the leather bands held together by metal which are used to control a horse or fasten it to a cart **2** [T1] to put (esp a horse) in harness, esp for riding or pulling a vehicle: *He harnessed the horses to the cart.*

rein [C *often pl with sing meaning*] a long narrow band, usu of leather, by which a horse (other animal, or sometimes a child) is sometimes controlled and guided: *Don't hold the reins so tightly. Pull on the rein to stop the horse.* **draw rein** to go more slowly: *He didn't draw rein till he reached the river.* **give (free) rein to** to give freedom to (feelings or desires): *He gave free rein to his imagination.* **keep a tight rein on** to control firmly: *She kept a tight rein on the horse/(fig) on her feelings.* **take the reins** to become (or make oneself) the person driving a horse-drawn carriage or (*fig*) making the decisions

saddle 1 [C] a usu leather seat made to fit over the back of a horse, etc, for a rider to sit on **2** [T1] to put a saddle on: *Saddle the horses.* **saddle up** [v adv T1; I0] to get (a horse) ready: *Saddle up (your horses)!*

K200 *nouns, etc* : **horseracing, etc**

thoroughbred [C; Wa5;B] (an animal, esp a horse) descended from parents of one particular type with the (supposed) best qualities, esp a horse used for racing (**a racehorse**)

jockey [C] a person who rides in horse races, esp professionally

racecourse *also esp AmE* **racetrack** [C] a place where esp horses race; the whole area where horses race including the buildings nearby and the places from which people watch

races [*the* P] (an occasion of) horseracing: *He's at the races today.*

track [*the* R] *not fml* the racetrack, for horses or cars

turf [*the* R] **1** the racecourse for horses **2** horse-racing: *He is more interested in the turf than in working.*

paddock [C] the enclosure in which the horses are made ready for a race

starting gate [C] the line of boxes with small gates in which the horses and riders stand in a line, and which open at the same moment to start a race

straight [C] a straight part or place, esp on a racetrack

finishing post/line [C] the post or line at the last point in a race

flat racing [U] the sport of horseracing on flat ground with nothing to be jumped over

steeplechase 1 [C] a horse race in which the horses and riders must pass over various difficult jumps **2** [I0] to ride or run in a steeple-chase

point-to-point [C] a horse race across open country from one agreed place to another

K201 *nouns, etc* : **kinds of races in athletics**

[ALSO ⇒ M24]

race [C] **1** [(*against, between, with*)] a competition in speed and/or getting somewhere first: *They had a race and he lost the race. It was a ten-mile race. They won the boat race.* **2** *lit* an onward course as of time or life: *The old man's race of life was nearly run.* **3** (*fig*) a strong flow of water: *a tide-race* **a race against time** an effort to do something before a certain time [also ⇒ K101]

races [P] occasions in sports when people run in races against each other: *Did he win in the races?*

sprint 1 [I0; T1] to run (a short distance) as fast as possible: *He sprinted after the bus.* **2** [C] a short fast race: *He won the 100-metre sprint.*

marathon 1 [C; *the* R] a long race of many miles (or kilometres), esp at large sports occasions: *He ran in the marathon. He is a marathon runner.* **2** [C] (*fig*) any activity that tests one's power over a long time, etc: *They held a dancing marathon.* **3** [A] something very long: *He made a marathon speech of six hours.*

hurdles [U] a kind of running race in which one must also jump over fairly low wooden frames (**hurdles**): *She won the women's hurdles.*

relay 1 [C] *also* **relay race** a kind of running race in which a runner in a team passes a small stick (**a baton**) to the next runner in the team: *Our team won the relay. He's a good relay runner.* **2** [C] a fresh supply of people, horses, etc, for use in sending information or in going quickly from one place to another **3** [T1] to pass on (information, etc) in this way

dash 1 [L9; (I0)] to run quickly and suddenly: *The runners dashed past. I must dash (off) to catch my train. He suddenly dashed into the street. They've been dashing about all day.* **2** [C *usu sing*] a sudden quick run: *The prisoners made a dash for freedom.* **3** [C *usu sing*] a short race for runners: *He was in the 60-metre dash and came third.*

K202 *verbs & nouns, etc* : **jumping and throwing, etc, in athletics**

jump 1 [I0] to move suddenly and quickly away from where one has been, by using the legs: *He jumped up and down/over the water/into the water. He jumped ten feet. 'Don't jump!' they shouted to the man above them. She jumped to her feet and ran out of the room.* (*fig*) *He keeps jumping from one subject of conversation to another. Don't jump the gun* (= don't start running the race before the gun is fired; (*fig*) don't act too quickly before you are ready). **2** [T1] to jump over: *He jumped the stream.*

3 [I∅] (*fig*) (esp of money or a quantity) to rise suddenly: *The price of oil jumped sharply in 1973. The number of visitors jumped last year.* **4** [I∅] to make any quick sudden movement as a result of strong feeling: *His heart jumped for joy.* (*fig*) *The noise nearly made me jump right out of my skin!* **5** [T1] to attack suddenly: *They jumped me and ran off with all my money.* **6** [C] an act of jumping: *That was a good jump! She did a jump of two metres.* (*fig*) *The number of visitors took a jump last year.* **7** [C] something to be jumped: *The horse took the jump well. The horse fell at the water jump.*

high jump [C] a sport in which people jump over a bar which is raised higher and higher

long jump [C] a sport in which people jump as far as possible in distance along the ground: *He did well in the long jump. The standing long jump, when you can't take a run, is harder than the usual running long jump.*

vault 1 [T1; L9] to jump over (something) in one movement using the hands or a pole to gain more height or force: *He put his hand on the gate and vaulted it easily. He came to the gate and vaulted over. When he was young he could vault onto the back of a horse.* **2** [C] a jump made by vaulting: *He went over the gate in a single vault.*

pole vault [C; *the* R] a jump made with the help of a long pole: *He won the pole vault.* **pole-vault** [I∅] to jump in this way: *He's good at pole-vaulting/a good pole-vaulter.*

triple jump [*the* R; S] an athletics event in which people take off and land on one foot, then jump on one foot and land on the other, and finish with a jump onto both feet

leap 1 [I∅; T1] to jump with special force, very suddenly, etc: *He leaped up. She leapt (over) the wall.* (*fig*) *Prices just leapt last year. Her heart leapt when she saw him.* **2** [C] an act of leaping: *What a leap!*

hop 1 [I∅; T1] to jump on one foot or with both feet together: *This is a hopping race; let's see who can hop the fastest.* **2** [C] an act of hopping

skip 1 [I∅] to jump lightly or quickly, esp on one foot: *The girl was skipping over a rope.* **2** [C] an act of skipping: *She gave a quick skip. Her heart gave a skip when she saw him.*

clear [T1] to jump over or beyond (a usu stated thing): *He jumped and just cleared the bar/top of the wall. She cleared ten feet* (= jumped over or beyond ten feet).

put the shot to throw a heavy ball (**the shot**) with a forward movement of the hand from the shoulder **shot-putter** [C] a person who puts the shot **shot put** [*the* R] a competition or activity of doing this

throw the hammer to throw a heavy metal ball on the end of a wire as far as possible **throwing the hammer** the sport or competition of doing this

discus [C; *the* R] (the activity of throwing) a heavy plate of wood, metal, or stone: *Throwing the discus/The discus throw was an ancient Greek sport, and is included in athletics today.*

javelin [C; *the* R] (the activity of throwing) a light spear

K203 *verbs & nouns* : **swimming and other water sports**

[ALSO ⇒ M19]

swim 1 [I∅; T1; L9] (of persons and animals) to move a distance in the water: *Can you swim? He swam the 100 metres very well. She swam (across) the river.* **2** [C *usu sing*] an act or occasion of swimming: *Enjoy your swim! He went for a swim in the lake.* **swimmer** [C] a person who swims or is swimming

swimming [U] the sport and skill, etc, of swimming: *He went swimming in the river. Their swimming team won the races.*

crawl *also* **Australian crawl** [(*the*) S] a fast way of swimming while lying on one's stomach in the water, moving first one arm and then the other, and at the same time kicking the feet up and down

breaststroke [(*the*) S] a way of swimming in which the body is pushed forward by both arms before the face and a strong kicking movement of the legs rather like a frog [⇒ A94]

backstroke *also* **back crawl** [(*the*) S] a way of swimming on one's back

butterfly (stroke) [(*the*) S] a way of swimming in which both arms are lifted at the same time

dive 1 [I∅ (*in, off, from, into*)] to jump head first into water: *The boy ran to the side of the pool and dived in.* **2** [I∅ (*down, for*)] to go under the surface of the water: *They were diving for pearls.* **3** [I∅ (*down*)] (of a plane) to go down steeply and swiftly: *The plane dived sharply and then rose again.* **4** [L9] (on land) to move quickly, esp downwards, head first, or out of sight: *The rabbit dived into its hole. He got close to me and suddenly dived at/for my legs* **5** [L9] to move one's hand(s) quickly and suddenly deep into something, esp in order to get something out: *He dived into the bag and brought out two red apples.* **6** [L9 esp *in*] (*fig*) to enter quickly and suddenly into some matter or activity: *He had never studied French before, but he just dived in and started trying to speak it.* **7** [C] an act of diving: *She made a beautiful dive into the pool. When the shots sounded in the street we made a dive for the nearest doorway.*

diving board [C] a board fixed at one end, esp high off the ground, from which people dive into water

(swimming) pool [C] a large pool, indoors or outdoors, specially made for people to swim and play in: *He ran to the edge of the swimming pool and dived in at the deep end.*

deep end [C] the deep part of a swimming pool, esp deeper than a person's height

shallow end [C] the shallow part of a swimming pool

wade 1 [I∅] to move through water, snow, etc: *He waded (through the water) to get to us. The* children were wading in the sea. (*fig*) He waded slowly through the long, uninteresting book. **2** [T1] to cross by wading: *He waded the river.* **3** [S] an act of wading: *The children went for a wade.*

paddle 1 [I∅; T1] to put (the feet) or wade, esp in very shallow water or for pleasure: *The children went paddling in the sea. He paddled (his feet) in the warm water.* **2** [S] an act of paddling: *Let's go for a paddle in the sea.*

skin diving [U] the sport of underwater swimming with special apparatus **skin diver** [C] a person who goes skin diving

aqualung [C] an apparatus with air in a container to carry on one's back that helps one swim for a long time under water

surfing [U] the sport of riding waves that are coming towards the shore by standing or lying on a special board (a **surfboard**)

K204 *nouns & verbs* : **skating and skiing**

skateboarding

stick

skateboard

skiing

boot

ski

skating

runner

tobogganing

dog team

sledge

skate

(ice)skate [C] either of two special shoes (**skates**) fitted with a metal blade each, for moving fast on ice **(ice-)skate** [I∅] to move on ice skates: *Let's go ice-skating! She skates well.*

ski 1 [C] one of two long thin runners made of wood, plastic, or metal, worn on the feet for sliding over snow, esp down hills **2** [I∅; (T1)] to move (a distance) on skis: *She loves skiing. What are the skiing conditions like? He skied down the hillside. Can they manage to ski that distance?*

sledge 1 [C] *BrE* a vehicle made for sliding along snow or ice on two metal runners: *Small light sledges are used for going down slopes covered in snow.* **2** [C] *esp AmE* one of these made for carrying heavy loads across snow: *The sledge was pulled by dogs.* **3** [I∅] *BrE* to go or race down slopes on a sledge: *They went sledging a lot last winter.* **4** [I∅; T1] *esp AmE* to travel or carry (something) on a sledge

sled *esp AmE* **1** [C] a small sledge **2** [I∅] to go on a sled

sleigh [C] *old use & poet* a large sledge, esp one pulled by a horse or horses: *They went for a sleigh ride in the snow.*

toboggan [C] **1** a long light board curved up at the front, for carrying people over snow, esp down slopes for sport **2** [I∅] to go or race down slopes on a toboggan or (*esp BrE*) on a sledge: *He loves going tobogganing.*

roller skate [C] either of two special shoes (**skates**) that fit below one's usual shoes and have four small wheels, used esp by children: *The little boy wanted a pair of roller skates.* **roller-skate** [I∅] to move on these: *They went roller-skating.*

skateboard 1 [C] a short board with two small wheels at each end for standing or sitting on and riding **2** [I∅] to ride in this way

K205 *nouns* : **shooting at targets**

[ALSO ⇒ H245]

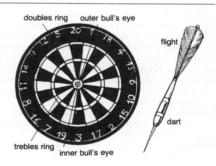

doubles ring   outer bull's eye

flight

dart

trebles ring   inner bull's eye

shooting [U] the act, sport, skill, etc, of using a gun, bow, etc: *They went shooting. They went shooting for pigeons/went pigeon shooting. He led the shooting party into the woods.*

shoot [C] an occasion, usu of a group, to shoot certain animals, birds, etc: *They held a pigeon shoot.*

aim [U] the act of aiming or pointing esp a gun, bow, or other object which one intends to fire or throw: *His aim with a gun isn't as good as his aim with a bow. Take aim! Fire!*

archery [U] the sport, skill, etc, of using a bow and arrows: *Archery is a very old sport. She took part in the archery competition.* **archer** [C] a person who shoots with a bow and arrow

darts [U] a game in which a small pointed object made of wood, plastic, etc (**a dart**) is thrown at a board marked with numbers (**a dartboard**): *He enjoys a game of darts at the pub. He's a good darts-player.*

target [C] **1** a special board at which one aims with a gun, bow, etc: *He hit the target every time. The shot missed the target.* **2** an animal, person, etc, at which someone aims and/or fires: *A moving target is difficult to hit.* **3** (*fig*) something which one can attack, complain about, etc: *The government was the target of his anger.* **4** (*fig*) something one wants to reach: *Our target for next year is a million pounds more business.*

bull's-eye *also infml* **bull** [C] the centre of a target, usu coloured black: *Bull's-eye! He hit the bull's-eye twice. He scored three bulls.*

inner [C] the ring in a target just round the bull's-eye: *She scored two bulls and an inner.*

outer [C] the ring round the outside of a target: *He scored no bulls, two inners, and several outers.*

K206 *verbs & nouns* : **fishing and angling**

[ALSO ⇒ A100]

fish 1 [I∅] to (try to) catch fish, either in smaller numbers in a river or lake while standing on the bank or in a small boat or in larger numbers in the sea from a larger boat, either as a sport or an occupation: *They were fishing for trout.* **2** [T1 (*out*)] to catch fish in (an area of water): *Can you fish this river? These waters have been fished out* (= so much that there are no fish left). **3** [I∅ (*for*)] (*fig*) *infml* to try to get, as if by fishing: *Stop fishing for compliments!* (= Stop trying to get me to say how nice you are)

fishing [U] the act, business, or sport of catching or trying to catch fish: *He has gone fishing. A fishing boat sailed into the harbour.*

fisherman [C] a person who fishes either for sport or (esp) as an occupation: *The fishermen were putting the fish in boxes.*

fishery [C] an area esp of a sea where a lot of fishing is done: *The boats were out in the North Sea fisheries.*

catch [C] the amount of fish caught, esp by fishermen at sea: *Did you get/have a good catch?—No; catches haven't been good lately.*

fishing rod *also* **rod and line** [C] a long rod, usu of wood, to which is fixed a strong thread (**a fishing line**) with a baited hook (**a fish hook**) on the end, used to catch fish, esp for sport

hook and line [C] a way of fishing usu as a sport, with or without a rod and using a line with a baited hook on it

net 1 [C] lengths of string, thread, etc, tied together to form squares and used esp to catch things, esp fish (**a fishing net**): *The fishermen dropped their nets into the sea.* **2** [T1] to catch in a net: *They netted a lot of fish/a good catch.*

angling [U] the sport of catching fish with a rod and line: *He has written a book about angling.*

angler [C] a person who fishes with a rod and line: *He's a keen angler.*

bait 1 [U] food or something which looks like food used to catch an animal or (esp) a fish esp when put on a hook: *What bait do you use?* **2** [T1] to put bait on: *He baited his hook, cast, and waited.*

cast 1 [I∅;(T1)] to send (one's line, hook, etc) out into the water by moving one's rod in a special quick action: *He cast beautifully.* **2** [C] an act of casting: *That was a nice cast.*

K207 *nouns, etc* : **mountaineering** [U]

mountaineering the skill, hobby, or sport of going up mountains, esp those which are difficult to go up: *He has been interested in mountaineering for years.* **mountaineer 1** [C] a person who is skilled in mountaineering **2** [I∅] to climb mountains

climbing the act of going up, esp mountains, esp as a sport, hobby, etc; *infml* mountaineering: *He started climbing as a boy and has climbed some of the highest mountains in the world.* **climber** [C] a person who climbs; *infml* a mountaineer

L

Space and time

The universe

L1 *nouns* : the universe and nature

universe [*the* R; (C)] everything that exists, esp the stars and space

cosmos [*the* R *sometimes cap*] *fml, poet & pomp* the universe

creation [*usu cap*] **1** [U] *esp poet* the whole universe **2** [*the* R] the story of the earth's origin esp as told in the Bible

space [U *often in comb*] what is outside earth's air and in which the sun, stars, etc, move: *They travelled through space to the moon in a spaceship.*

void [*the* R] *poet* space: *A ball of fire seemed to fall out of the void.*

nature [U *often cap*] **1** the way things are, esp plants and animals; the whole world, esp as something not used or changed by people: *The child loves everything to do with nature. Isn't Nature wonderful? It was so quiet that all Nature seemed to be asleep. He enjoys the beauties of nature. Some ancient peoples had nature gods/worshipped (the powers of) nature.* **2** also (*humor & with children*) **Mother Nature** the force which controls the world independently of people: *Cats are (Mother) Nature's way of limiting the number of mice. Growing crops in that place is a struggle against nature.*

L2 *nouns* : planets, suns, and stars

planet [C] a large body in space that moves round a star, esp round the sun: *The Earth is a planet. The planet Jupiter is very large.*

world **1** [C] *infml* a planet: *Nine worlds go round our sun.* **2** [*the* R] the planet earth: *He has been in most parts of the world.* **3** [*the* S *of*] a particular area, subject, or interest: *He has a book called 'The World of Sport'.*

sun **1** [*the* R] the great ball of burning gas which gives us light, heat, etc **2** [C] any other such ball

sunny [Wa1;B] warm and bright because of the sun: *a sunny day*; (*fig*) *a sunny smile*

star [C] a sun that is so far away that it seems just a point of light: *The night was clear and the sky was full of stars.*

moon **1** [*the* R] the body which moves round the earth once every 28 days, and can be seen shining palely in the sky at night: *It was a dark night; the moon was hidden behind the clouds.* **2** [S] this body as it appears at a particular time: *On the night of the attack, there was a moon that gave more help to the defenders than to the attacking army. Last night there was a full moon* (= with the whole front part lit up, when opposite the sun). **3** [C] a body that turns round a planet other than the earth: *Saturn has several moons.*

satellite **1** [C] a heavenly body moving round a larger one (a planet); a moon: *The moon is a satellite of the earth.* **2** [C; *by* U] a man-made object intended to move around the earth, moon, etc, for some purpose: *They sent up an unmanned satellite/a communications and weather satellite. The broadcast came from America by satellite and was heard at the same time in Europe.*

heavenly body [C] *esp old use, tech,* or *poet* a planet, star, satellite, etc

L3 *nouns* : constellations and galaxies, etc

constellation [C] a group of stars as seen from the earth: *Taurus and Orion are constellations.*

galaxy **1** [C] any one of the very large groups of stars which make up the universe **2** [*the* R *cap*] the large group of stars in which our own sun and its planets lie, as well as the constellations

Milky Way [*the* R] *infml* that part of the Galaxy seen by us from the earth as a whitish band in the night sky

solar system [*the* R; (C)] the nine planets and their moons, etc, together with the sun: *We may one day be able to go beyond our solar system; who knows?*

nebula [C] **1** a mass of gas and dust in space among the stars, appearing often as a bright cloud at night **2** a galaxy which has this appearance

nova [C] a star which suddenly becomes much brighter and then becomes gradually fainter

L4 *nouns* : **the planets and Zodiac** [R]

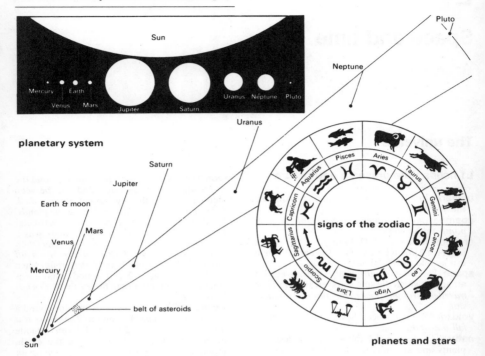

planetary system

belt of asteroids

signs of the zodiac

planets and stars

L5 *nouns* : **other objects in space** [C]

meteor 1 any of various small pieces of matter floating in space that form a short-lived line of light if they fall into the earth's air (**atmosphere**) **2** the line of light produced by this

meteorite a meteor that has landed on the earth without being totally burnt up

meteoroid 1 a small meteor that travels around the sun **2** a meteor considered without relation to the light it produces when entering the atmosphere

shooting star *infml* a meteor(ite) in the earth's air

planetoid a small planet [⇨ L2]

asteroid *also* **minor planet** one of many small planets between Mars and Jupiter

comet a heavenly body with a very bright head and long less bright tail that moves round the sun in orbit [⇨ L9]

L6 *adjectives, etc* : **relating to the universe, etc** [Wa5;B]

universal happening or found everywhere: *There is no language on earth that is completely universal.* **-ly** [adv]

cosmic relating to the universe or cosmos [⇨ L1] or to things happening in or coming from

space: *Cosmic rays* [⇨ L22] *travel great distances through space.*

planetary of or like a planet [⇨ L2]

worldwide [*also* adv] in or over all the world: *French cheeses are famous worldwide. His fame is worldwide. This book has worldwide sales.*

solar of or concerning the sun

stellar of or concerning the stars

lunar 1 of or concerning the moon **2** measured by the spinning of the moon: *A lunar month is the period between two new moons.* **3** made for use on or around the moon: *lunar vehicles*

galactic of or concerning a galaxy or (*cap*) the Galaxy [⇨ L3]

nebular of, related to, or like a nebula [⇨ L3]

L7 *nouns* : **astronomy and astrology** [U]

astronomy the scientific study of the sun, moon, stars, and other heavenly bodies

astronomic(al) [Wa5;B] **1** of, connected with, or like astronomy **2** (*fig*) very great: *The distance/price is astronomic.* **-(al)ly** [adv Wa4]

astronomer [C] a scientist who specializes in astronomy

astrology the art of understanding the (supposed) influence on events, character, and fate of the groupings and positions of the sun, moon, stars, and planets and of telling the future from them **astrological** [Wa5;B] of, connected with, or like astrology **-ly** [adv Wa4] **astrologer** [C] a person skilled in astrology

L8 nouns : the Zodiac

[⇨ PICTURE AT L4]

zodiac 1 [the R usu cap] an imaginary belt through space along which the sun, the moon, and the nearest heavenly bodies (**planets**) appear to travel, and which is divided into twelve equal parts (**signs**), each named after a group (**constellation**) of stars which were once in them **2** [C] a circular representation of this with pictures and names for each sign, esp as used by people (**astrologers**) who believe in the influence of the stars on one's character and fate

sign (of the Zodiac) [C] any of the twelve divisions of the year represented by groups of stars: *What sign were you born under?*

L9 nouns, etc : some astronomical terms

orbit 1 [C] **a** the path of one heavenly body round another: *the earth's orbit round the sun* **b** the path of a man-made object round the earth or another heavenly body **2** [C] (*fig*) the area within which one person or thing can have an effect upon others: *X is within Y's orbit.* **3** [Wv4;T1;IØ] to move in an orbit round (something): *How many times has Sputnik orbited the earth?*

gravity *also* **gravitation** [U] the natural force by which objects are attracted to each other, esp that by which a large mass pulls a smaller one to it: *Anything that is dropped falls towards the centre of the earth because of the pull of gravity.*

eclipse 1 [C] the disappearance, complete or in part, of the sun's light when the moon passes between it and the earth, or of the moon's light when the earth passes between it and the sun: *There will be an eclipse of the sun tomorrow.* **2** [C; U] (*fig*) the loss of fame, power, success, etc (*often in the phr* **in eclipse**): *Our political party suffered an eclipse at the last election when none of its representatives was elected to Parliament. She used to be a famous actress but she's now in eclipse; she never appears on the stage now.* **3** [T1 usu pass] (*fig*) to cover completely; make unimportant: *Our political party was eclipsed at the last election; no one was elected.* **partial eclipse** an eclipse which is not complete **total eclipse** an eclipse which is complete

L10 nouns : some geographical terms

[⇨PICTURE AT L12]

pole [C] either end of an imaginary straight line

(**axis**) around which a solid round mass turns, esp **a** (the lands around) the most northern and southern points on the surface of the earth or of another planet **b** the two points in the sky to the north and south around which stars seem to turn

axis [C] an imaginary straight line on which the earth or a planet turns

equator [the R often cap] an imaginary line (**line of latitude**) drawn round the world halfway between its most northern and southern points (**poles**)

hemisphere [C] a half of the earth, esp the northern or southern above and below the equator

tropic [C] one of the two imaginary lines (**lines of latitude**) drawn around the world at about 23½° north (**the tropic of Cancer**) and south (**the tropic of Capricorn**) of the equator

tropics [the P] the hot part of the world between the tropics of Cancer and Capricorn: *He lived in the tropics for years.*

zone [C] **1** one of the five divisions of the earth's surface according to temperature, marked by imaginary lines running round it from east to west: *Britain is in the northern temperate zone.* **2** an area or division marked off from others by particular qualities: *That is a danger zone; don't go there.*

L11 adjectives : some geographical terms

[ALSO ⇨ L63 HOT; L66 COLD]

polar [Wa5] of, near, like, or coming from lands near the North or South Pole (and therefore very cold)

equatorial [Wa5] of, concerning, near, or like the equator (and therefore very hot)

tropical 1 of, related to, concerning, or living in the tropics: *The tropical sun was too much for him.* **2** very hot: *We had almost tropical weather last summer.*

temperate 1 (of parts of the world) free from very high or very low temperatures: *The temperate areas of the world are found north or south of the tropics.* **2** (of persons) practising or showing self-control: *Try to be more temperate in your drinking.*

frigid 1 (of places) very cold; having a continuously low temperature: *The air on the mountain top was frigid. The parts of the world near the North and South Poles are called the frigid zones.* **2** (of persons) very unfriendly **3** (of a woman) having an unnatural dislike for sexual activity

torrid 1 (of places) very hot: *Most of the earth's torrid areas are found in the torrid zone between the tropics.* **2** (of feelings) strongly felt: *They had a torrid love affair.* **3** (of stories, etc) concerning or describing strong feelings, etc: *It was a torrid story of sex and violence.*

L12 *nouns* : **some terms relating to direction and position**

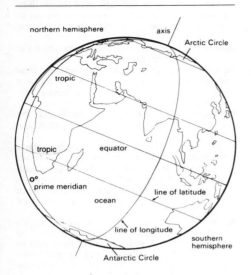

the globe

place on it may be stated or found: *What is the grid reference* [⇨ G91] *of the church?*

L13 *nouns, etc* : **compass directions**

the compass

direction [C; U] the point towards which a person or thing faces: *What direction was he going in? The house faces in a southerly direction* (= towards the south). *He has a good sense of direction* (= He can find his way easily from place to place).

point of the compass [C] a direction as marked on a compass [⇨ H122]

degree [C] a point of measurement of distance

bearing [C] the direction in which a place lies, a person travels, a line extends, etc (as measured in degrees): *He travelled on a bearing of 44 degrees west. Take a compass bearing on that building.* **bearings** [P] position in relation to direction: *The soldiers lost their bearings in the hills.*

latitude [U; S] the distance north or south of the equator measured in degrees: *The latitude of the ship is 20 degrees south.* **latitudes** [P] a district or area at a certain latitude: *High latitudes are those areas a long way north or south of the equator.*

meridian 1 [C] an imaginary line drawn from the top point of the earth (**the North Pole**) to the bottom round the edge of the earth, and used on maps to show position **2** [(*the*) R; (C)] *tech* the highest point, esp of a star: *The sun is at its meridian.* **3** [(*the*) R; (C)] *tech* midday, when the sun reaches its highest point

longitude [U; C] the position east or west of a meridian, usu measured, in degrees, from Greenwich: *Longitude 30 degrees west.*

grid [C] a system of numbered squares printed on a map formed from lines of latitude and longitude so that the exact position of any

north [*often cap*] **1** [(*the*) R] (the direction of) one of the four main points of the compass (**N**), which is on the left of a person facing the rising sun: *I'm lost—which direction is north? The house has a window facing the north. He stood near the north wall of the building.* **2** [*the* R; A] (of a wind) (coming from) this direction: *That's a cold north wind. The wind's in the north today.* **3** [*the* R] the part of a country which is further north than the rest

south [*often cap*] **1** [(*the*) R] (the direction of) one of the four main points of the compass (**S**), which is on the right of a person facing the rising sun **2** [*the* R; A] (of a wind) (coming from) this direction: *That's a warm south wind.* **3** [*the* R] the part of a country which is further south than the rest

east [*often cap*] **1** [(*the*) R] the direction in which the sun rises: *They say their prayers facing towards the east. The east window in the church is beautiful.* **2** [*the* R; A] (of a wind) (coming from) this direction: *That's a cold east wind.* **3** [*the* R; A] one of the four main points of the compass, which is on the right of a person facing north **4** [*the* R] the eastern part of the world, esp Asia **5** [*the* R] the part of a country which is further east than the rest

west [*often cap*] **1** [(*the*) R] one of the four main points of the compass which is on the left of a person facing north **2** [*the* R; A] (of a wind) (coming from) this direction **3** [*the* R] the western part of the world, esp Europe and the Americas **4** [*the* R] the part of a country which is further west than the rest

-ern [*suffix*] of or belonging to the stated direction: *northern, southern, eastern, western*

-erner [*suffix*] a person from the stated direction: *northerner*, etc

-erly [*suffix*] **1** [Wa2;B] of, towards, or in the stated direction: *northerly* **2** (of a wind) coming from the stated direction: *a westerly wind* **3** [C] the wind itself: *a westerly*

-ernmost [*suffix*] *fml* farthest in the stated direction: *easternmost*

orient [*the* R *often cap*] *esp fml or lit* Asia; the Far East **oriental 1** belongs to the orient **2** [C] a person from or in the orient

occident [*the* R *often cap*] *esp fml or lit* the area of the world most directly influenced by the ancient civilizations of Greece and Rome, usu thought of as 'the West'; esp Europe and the Americas **occidental 1** [B] belonging to the occident **2** [C] a person from or in the occident

L14 *adverbs* : **up north and down south** [Wa5]

up in or towards the north: *He's flying up to Glasgow from London. I'm going up to Scotland for a week. He went up north for a week.*
down in or towards the south: *He's flying down from Glasgow to London. I'll be down in Brighton next week. He went down south for a week.*

L15 *verbs* : **finding one's direction** [T1]

orientate *esp BrE*, **orient** *esp AmE* to give direction or guidance to: *I find it difficult to orientate myself in a strange place/* (*fig*) *to new people.* **dis-** [*neg*] *I feel disorientated; where do we go now?* **orientation** [C; U] the condition of knowing which direction is which **dis-** [*neg*]
reorientate *esp BrE*, **reorient** *esp AmE* to cause or help (someone) to find his or her direction again: *They reorientated themselves by using a map and a compass.*

Light and colour

L20 *nouns* : **light**

[ALSO ⇒ H119, H213]

light 1 [U *often in comb*] the natural force that is produced by or redirected from objects and other things, so that we see them: *sunlight; gaslight; firelight* **2** [C] something that produces such light and causes other things to be seen, such as a lamp **3** [U] a supply of light, esp in regard to its strength, quality, or kind: *powerful light; green light; poor light* **4** [U] *also* **daylight** the light of the sun or the time it lasts: *I must finish this painting while the light lasts.* **5** [C] something that will set something else, esp a cigarette, burning, such as a match or cigarette lighter **6** [C] a window, one of many pieces of glass in a window, or an opening in a roof or wall that allows light into a room **7** [U]

a supply of light that reaches a person or thing: *I cannot read while you're standing in my light. I am in my own light here; I need to face the window.* **8** [U] (*fig*) brightness, as in the eyes, showing happiness or excitement **9** [C] (*fig*) the bright part of a painting **10** [U] (*fig*) the condition of being or becoming seen or known or of being made known, as to the public (*esp in the phrs* **come/bring to light**): *The lost book came to light after a long search. The inquiry brought to light many unpleasant facts about the business company.* **11** [C] (*fig*) the way in which something or someone appears or is regarded: *The workers and the employers look at problems in quite a different light.* **12** [U] (*fig*) knowledge, understanding, or explanation: *He suddenly saw the light* (= understood). **light year** [C] *tech* the distance that light can travel in a year: *Some stars are thousands of light years from the earth. A light year is about six million million miles.*

highlight [C] **1** *tech* the area on a picture or photograph where most light appears to fall **2** (*fig*) an important detail which stands out from the rest: *The highlight of the evening was Mr Brown's speech. We'll show you film of the highlights of the competition, as there isn't time for the whole thing.*

L21 *nouns* : **darkness**

dark 1 [*the* U] the absence of light: *Can cats really see in the dark? Some children are afraid of the dark.* **2** [U] the time of day when there is no light (*esp in the phrs* **after dark; before dark**): *We don't go out after dark. Get home before dark.* **3** [U] a dark or deep colour: *the dark of her eyes* **in the dark 1** in secrecy: *business done in the dark* **2** without knowledge: *They kept the public in the dark about their agreement.*

darkness [U] the state or condition of having little or no light: *I couldn't see the road properly because of the darkness.*

gloom 1 [U] *esp emot* darkness **2** [U; C] a feeling of deep sadness (*often in the phr* **cast a gloom over**): *The news of defeat filled them all with gloom.*

shadow 1 [U; C *usu pl*] greater darkness where direct light, esp sunlight, is blocked off by something: *The sun came through the small window but most of the room stayed in shadow. He walked along in the shadows hoping no one would recognize him.* **2** [C] a dark shape made on a surface by something between it and direct light: *As the sun set, the shadows became longer. The tree cast* (= produced) *its shadow on the wall; its shadow fell on the wall.* **3** [C] a dark place having the effect of this: *The shadows under his eyes were caused by lack of sleep.* **4** [C] (*fig*) a form without substance or from which the real substance has gone: *After his illness he was only a shadow of his former self. She wore herself down to a shadow with* hard work and little food. **5** [C] (*fig*) a person or thing who follows another closely: *The dog was his master's shadow*. **6** [S] (*fig*) a very small bit: *He didn't have the shadow of an excuse. It is true beyond the shadow of a doubt.* **7** [C] (*fig*) the very strong power or influence of someone or something: *He had to live in the shadow of his famous father.* **8** [C] (*fig*) an unhappy or threatened feeling: *The accident cast* (= caused) *a shadow over the rest of our holiday.*

shade 1 [U] slight darkness or shelter from direct light, esp from sunlight outdoors, made by something blocking it: *He sat in the shade of a tree/wall. It was a hot day, 30 degrees in the shade. There was no shade to be found in the desert.* **2** [C *often in comb*] something that keeps out light or its full brightness: *a lampshade; a window shade; a green eyeshade* **3** [U;C *usu pl*] representation of shadow or darkness in a picture, painting, etc: *The artist used shade to good effect. It's a painting with beautiful lights and shades.*

L22 nouns : rays, gleams, and glimmers

ray [C9, esp *of*] **1** a narrow beam (of light), esp one of a group going out like a wheel from the same centre: *the sun's rays; A ray of moonlight came in through the curtains.* **2** (in science) a line (of the stated force): *take an X-ray photograph; kill with a death ray* **3** (*fig*) a very small sign (of hope or comfort): *There isn't a ray of hope left for us.*

beam [C] **1** a line of light shining out from some bright object **2** (*fig*) a bright look or smile : *'How lovely to see you!' she said, with a beam of welcome.*

flash [C] a sudden quick bright light: *He saw two flashes.*

burst [C] a sudden large amount (of light): *There was a burst of light as the bomb exploded.*

glow 1 [C] a light from something burning without flames or smoke: *The red glow in the sky above the factory. The oil-lamp gives a soft glow.* **2** [S] brightness of colour: *the glow of copper in the kitchen* **3** [S] (*fig*) the feeling and/or signs of warmth and colour in the body and face, as after exercise or because of good health: *There was a glow of health in her face. After drinking wine, his body felt a warm glow.* **4** [S] (*fig*) a strong feeling: *a glow of happiness/of anger*

gleam [C] **1** a shining light, esp one making objects bright: *They sat in the red gleam of the firelight.* **2** a sudden flash of light: *Gleams of sunshine came round the edges of the dark cloud.* **3** (*fig*) a sudden showing of a feeling or quality for a short time: *A gleam of interest came into his eye.*

glimmer [C] a faint unsteady light: *He saw the glimmer of a light.* (*fig*) *I haven't even a glimmer of an idea of what to do.*

shimmer [C; U] a soft trembling shining effect: *She liked the shimmer of glasses in the candlelight.*

shine [S; (U)] **1** brightness; shining quality: *The wooden surface had a beautiful shine. My shoes haven't got much shine left after that long walk.* **2** [*in comb*] the light of: *sunshine*

dazzle [S] brightness; a brightly shining whole: *The theatre was a dazzle of bright lights. He felt the dazzle of her smile.*

lustre *BrE,* **luster** *AmE, esp poet* **1** [U; S] (esp of surfaces, jewels, etc) the quality of being bright **2** [U] (*fig*) honour: *What he did adds lustre to the family name.*

L23 verbs : shining and lighting

shine 1 [I∅] to give off light; look bright: *It was a fine morning with the sun shining* (*down*). *The polished surface shone in the sun. Her eyes shone with laughter.* **2** [X9] to direct (a lamp, beam of light, etc): *The policeman shone his lamp along the dark passage.* **3** [Wv6;I∅](*fig*) to show up clearly as excellent: *He's a pretty good student, but sports are where he really shines/but he really shines at sports.*

shimmer [Wv4;I∅] to shine with a soft trembling light: *The water shimmered in the moonlight.*

gleam [I∅] **1** to give out a bright light: *The furniture gleamed after being polished.* **2** (of a feeling) to be expressed with a sudden light (in the eyes): *Amusement gleamed in his eyes.*

glimmer [I∅] to give a very faint unsteady light: *A faint light glimmered at the end of the passage.*

flash 1 [I∅] (of a light) to appear or exist for a moment: *The light flashed twice.* **2** [T1] to cause to do this: *He flashed the light in their faces.* **3** [L9] to move so as to cause a flash: *The car flashed past us.*

glow [I∅] **1** to give out heat and/or light without flames or smoke: *The iron bar was heated till it glowed. The cat's eyes glowed in the darkness.* **2** to show bright strong colours: *a garden full of glowing flowers* **3** to show redness and warmth in the face and the body esp after hard work or because of strong feelings: *I knew I had said something stupid, and my cheeks began to glow with shame. His face was glowing with the effort of running.*

beam 1 [L9] (of the sun or other shining objects) to send out light (and heat): *The sun beamed through the clouds.* **2** [L9] to smile brightly and happily: *The new father beamed with pleasure when he saw the baby for the first time.* **3** [T1] to express by smiling: *He beamed a cheerful welcome as he opened the door.*

dazzle [Wv3;T1] **1** to cause to be unable to see by throwing a strong light in the eyes: *The lights of the car dazzled me on the dark road.* **2** (*fig*) to cause wonder to: *The splendid room dazzled the young girl. She was dazzled by her sudden success.* **-ling** [Wa3;B] *a dazzling* *smile/white* **-lingly** [adv]: *dazzlingly beautiful*

light up [v adv] **1** [T1; I∅] to give light (to); make or become bright with light or colour: *The candles on the Christmas tree lit up the room. The street lit up when the lamps were turned on.* **2** [I∅] to cause (electric) lamps to begin shining, giving light: *When the sun sets, it's time to light up.* **3** [T1; I∅] (*fig*) to (cause to) become bright with pleasure or excitement: *Her face lit up when she saw he was coming.*

illuminate [T1] **1** to give light to: *They illuminated the square with bright lights.* **2** (*fig*) to make bright and clear: *'God illuminates my soul,' he said.* **3** to paint (esp old books) with gold and bright colours: *Some old books were beautifully illuminated with pictures painted around the first letter and down the sides of the page.* **illumination 1** [U] the act or state of illuminating or being illuminated **2** [C *usu pl*] pictures painted on the pages of old books: *Each illumination is a work of art.* **3** [U] the strength of light: *The illumination is too weak to show the detail of the painting.* **illuminations** [P] the lights used to make a town bright and colourful: *Some seaside towns have illuminations every year.*

radiate [T1] to give off (light, heat, etc): *The sun radiates light and heat.* (*fig*) *She radiated happiness.* **radiation** [U] **1** the act of sending out rays of heat, light, sound, etc **2** radioactivity **radioactive** [B] giving out energy in the form of rays which is harmful to living creatures **-ly** [adv] **radioactivity** [U] the condition of being radioactive

L24 *adjectives, etc* : **having light**

[ALSO ⇒ F270]

light [Wa1; B] having light; not dark; bright: *This is a nice light room.*

-lit [*comb form*] getting light from: *moonlit, sunlit, gaslit, etc*

bright [Wa1; B] **1** giving out or throwing back light very strongly; fully light; shining: *The sun is brighter than the moon. What a bright sunny day!* **2** (*fig*) famous; glorious: *one of the brightest moments in our country's history* **3** (*fig*) full of life, cheerful, happy, gay: *Her face was bright with happiness.* **4** (*fig*) showing hope or signs of future success: *You have a bright future ahead of you, my boy!* **-ly** [adv]

clear [Wa1; B] bright; free from anything that darkens; transparent: *The sky is clear now. What beautiful clear water.* **-ly** [adv]

sharp [Wa1; B] clear; easy to separate from other things: *The white house stood out in sharp detail against the dark hill behind.* **-ly** [adv]

brilliant [B] very bright, splendid, or showy in appearance: *The stars were brilliant in the clear night sky.* **-ly** [adv] **brilliance** [U] the state of being brilliant: *The brilliance of the light blinded him.*

luminous [B] giving light; bright **luminosity** [U] **1** *usu tech* the state or condition of being

luminous **2** the degree by which something is luminous

radiant 1 [B] sending out light or heat in all directions; shining: *the radiant sun* **2** [Wa5; A] *tech* sent out by radiation: *radiant heat* **3** [B (*with*)] (*fig*) (of a person or his appearance) showing love and happiness: *Her radiant face showed her happiness. She was radiant with joy.* **-ly** [adv] **radiance** [U] the state of being radiant (*defs* **1** & **3**): *The radiance blinded him.* (*fig*) *The radiance in her face showed her happiness.*

shiny [Wa1; B] (esp of a smooth surface) looking as if polished; bright: *She put powder on her nose to keep it from looking shiny. What a shiny new 10p coin!*

L25 *adjectives, etc* : **not having light** [B]

dark [Wa1] **1** partly or completely without light: *It's too dark to read now. In winter it gets dark here early.* **2** (*fig*) evil: *the dark powers that lead to war* **3** (*fig*) sad; expecting bad things to happen: *dark days ahead; Don't always look on the dark side of things.* **4** (*fig*) **a** secret; hidden: *He kept his plans dark.* **b** not easy to understand: *There is some dark meaning in his words.* **-ly** [adv]

gloomy [Wa1] **1** almost dark: *It was a gloomy day.* **2** (*fig*) having or giving little hope or cheerfulness: *Our future seems gloomy. She's feeling very gloomy.*

dull [Wa1] **1** (of colour or surfaces) not bright, strong, or sharp; not shining: *She wore a dress of some uninteresting dull colour. It was dull grey in colour.* **2** (of weather, the sky, etc) cloudy; grey; dark: *It's dull today; we shall have rain.*

dim [Wa1] not bright but not particularly dark: *The lighting in the room was rather dim.*

dismal 1 not bright, pleasant, or interesting: *What a dismal place this is!* **2** (*fig*) sad, unhappy, or causing unhappiness: *The news was really dismal.* **-ly** [adv]

shadowy [Wa2] **1** hard to see or know about clearly: *The face was shadowy; I did not know who it was. He is a shadowy and little-known historical figure.* **2** full of shade; in shadow: *He fell asleep in the shadowy depths of the forest.* **-iness** [U]

shady [Wa1] *not fml* covered and therefore not allowing too much light: *Let's sit under the tree; it's shadier there.*

faint [Wa2] **1** not having brightness, clearness, strength, etc: *The handwriting on the page was very faint. The colours became more faint/fainter as the sun set. She gave a faint cry.* **2** very small: *There is only a faint chance that he is still alive.* **-ly** [adv] **-ness** [U]

obscure 1 not easy to see, understand, etc: *The shapes of the buildings were obscure because of the distance/mist. His ideas seem very obscure to me.* **2** not famous: *He was the son of an* *obscure writer.* **3** [T1] to make dark and difficult to see, understand, etc: *He is trying to obscure the truth.* **4** [T1] to get between someone and something: *Don't obscure the light please.* **obscurity** [U]

vague [Wa2] not certain or definite, esp in talking, writing, etc: *She was very vague about her plans. He saw the vague shape of someone coming through the mist.* **-ly** [adv] **-ness** [U]

nebulous *esp fig* not clear; like a cloud: *I find most of his ideas pretty nebulous.* **-ly** [adv] **-ness, -losity** [U]

L26 verbs : **darkening and shading**

darken 1 [I0] to become or grow dark: *The sky darkened. (fig) His face darkened with anger when he heard the news.* **2** [T1] to make dark: *She drew the curtains and darkened the room. (fig) His death darkened our lives.*

dim 1 [I0] to lose light: *The sky slowly dimmed.* **2** [T1] to cause to lose light: *He dimmed the lamp.*

shade 1 [T1] to shelter from direct light or heat: *She shaded her eyes from the sun with her hand.* **2** [L9 (off), esp into] to change slowly or by slight degrees into something else: *This is a question where right and wrong shade into one another. The blue shaded off into grey.*

screen [T1] to shelter, hide, or lessen by blocking out light: *He screened the light with his hand.*

L27 nouns : **colour**

[ALSO ⇒ B50, 53; H93; I46]

colour *BrE,* **color** *AmE* **1** [U] the quality which allows the eyes to see the difference between (for example) a red flower and a blue flower when both are the same size and shape: *What colour is this paint?— It's red.* **2** [C; U] (a) substance used for giving colour to something; paint; dye: *The artist painted in water colours. How much colour should I use?*

pigment 1 a [U] dry coloured powder that is mixed with oil, water, etc, to make paint **b** [C] an example of this **2** [U] natural colouring matter of plants and animals, as in leaves, hair, skin, etc: *In old age, human hair often loses its pigment and becomes white.*

pigmentation [U] the spreading of colouring matter in parts of living things: *Some illnesses cause pigmentation of the skin.*

shade [C9] **1** a slightly different colour: *The walls were light blue and the door a deeper shade (of blue). They use cloth in various shades of pink.* **2** (fig) a slight (degree of) difference or variation: *There are several shades of opinion on this question. This word has several shades of meaning.*

tint [C] **1** *esp lit* a pale or delicate shade of a colour; slight degree of a colour: *There was a tint of red in the sky in the early evening.* **2** any

of various weak dyes for the hair **3** [*usu sing*] an act of giving the hair a special colour by tinting: *She paid £2 for a tint but she doesn't look any different.*

hue *esp poet* **1** [C] a colour: *The diamond shone with every hue under the sun.* **2** [U] a degree of brightness or colour: *The sky darkened in hue as night drew nearer.*

dye [C; U] a vegetable or chemical substance, usu liquid, used to colour things esp by dipping: *Have you a bright blue dye in the shop?*

spectrum [C] **1** *tech* a set of bands of light in the order of their wavelengths, into which a beam of light may be separated, as by a prism [⇒ H123] **2** *tech* a range of any of various kinds of waves: *a radio/sound spectrum* **3** (fig) an arrangement of unseparated members along a line; continuous range: *There was a wide spectrum of opinion(s) on this question.*

L28 verbs : **colouring**

colour *BrE,* **color** *AmE* **1** [T1; X(1), 7] to cause (something) to have colour or a different colour esp in painting, dyeing, etc: *The child is colouring the picture. He coloured the flower red and the sky blue. He coloured the flower (a beautiful shade of yellow).* **2** [T1] to give a special character to (a person, event, etc): *His story was coloured by his hatred of his mother. Personal feelings coloured his judgement.* **3** [I0] to take on or change colour: *The leaves have already started to colour; it will soon be winter.*

tint [Wv5;T1] to give a slight or delicate colour to (esp the hair): *He likes natural hair better than tinted. Can you tint it a little?*

discolour *BrE,* **-or** *AmE* [Wv5;I0; T1] to (cause to) change colour for the worse: *Sunlight had discoloured the red curtains. This material will discolour in hot water.*

shade [T1 (in)] to represent the effect of shade or shadow on (an object in a picture): *The shaded-in background added depth to the drawing. 'Shade it in here,' the teacher said.*

dye [T1; I0; X7; L7] to give or take (a stated) colour by means of dye: *She dyed the dress (red). Will this dress dye? The dress will dye red/dye very well. (fig) Sunset dyed the sky red.*

L29 nouns & adjectives : **the primary colours** [Wa1;U;C;B]

red	fresh blood
pink	healthy flesh
yellow	the yolk (yellow part) of a hen's egg
orange	the skin of the orange (a fruit)
blue	the clear cloudless sky during the day
violet	the petals of the violet (a flower)
purple	red and blue mixed together
green	fresh grass
brown	coffee mixed with milk; toasted bread

USES:
1 [C; U] (colour): *She liked the reds and yellows of the evening sky. Which of these pinks is darker? The brown in my paint box is too dark.* **2** [U] (clothes): *She wore blue. He was dressed in green.* **3** [B] (having that colour): *She wore a yellow dress. Let's paint the door green. Many types of roses are pink.*

L30 *nouns & adjectives* : **white and black** [Wa1;U;C;B]

white (of) a colour which is like that of a clean cloud in a sunny sky; (of) the colour of milk; (of) the colour which contains all the colours: *She wore white. He wore white trousers.*
black 1 (of) the colour of night; without light: *He wore a black hat. After her husband died she dressed in black.* **2** very dirty: *Your hands are black! Go and wash them.* **3** black paint or colouring: *She puts a lot of black round her eyes.*
grey *BrE*, **gray** *AmE* (of) a colour which is a mixture of white and black: *He wore a grey suit. The sky was grey/a dull grey.*

L31 *nouns & adjectives* **some secondary colours** [U; C; B]

crimson (of) a deep slightly purplish red colour
scarlet (of) a very bright red colour, often associated with marks of rank, office, etc: *The Queen's guards wear scarlet.*
vermilion bright reddish-orange
magenta (of) a dark purplish red colour
maroon (of) a very dark red-brown colour
purple [Wa1,3] **1** a dark colour made of a mixture of red and blue **2** [*the* U] formerly dark red or purple garments as worn only by people of very high rank **3** of the colour purple: *His hands were purple with cold. She became purple with anger* (= so angry that the blood rushed to her face and changed its colour).
aquamarine (of) the colour of the glass-like blue-green stone of the same name
turquoise (of) the bluish-green or greenish-blue colour of the mineral of the same name
indigo (of) a colour or dye of a dark blue-purple
amber (of) the colour of a yellowish-brown hard clear substance of the same name used for jewels, ornaments, etc
tan brown like leather
ochre *BrE*, **ocher** *AmE* the yellowish-brown colour of yellow earth
olive light green

L32 *nouns* : **the colours of metals** [U; C; B]

[ALSO ⇒ H67 METALS]

gold (like the metal) gold in colour
golden *esp poet & lit* like gold

silver (like the metal) silver in colour
silvery *esp apprec & lit* like silver
copper (like the metal) copper in colour
coppery more or less like copper
bronze like bronze in colour
leaden 1 of the colour of the metal lead; dull-grey **2** (*fig*) sad; heavy
steel like steel in colour
steely [Wa1] more or less like steel

L33 *adjectives* : **relating to colour** [B]

colourful *BrE*, **colorful** *AmE* **1** showily coloured; full of colour or colours; bright; gay: *She saw a bird with colourful wings.* **2** likely to excite the senses or imagination; rich in expressive variety or detail: *That was a colourful period of history. He has a colourful style of writing.*
coloured *BrE*, **colored** *AmE* [*esp in comb*] having the usu stated colour: *She wore a cream-coloured dress.*
variegated (esp of a flower or leaf) marked irregularly in spots, lines, masses, etc, of different colours
speckled coloured with small irregular marks, esp a large number on a surface: *The egg was speckled.*

L34 *adjectives* : **relating to colouring** [B]

dyed having been dyed: *She has dyed hair.*
stained having had a coloured liquid put on or into something
tinted having had a slight or delicate colour added
shaded (of drawings) having been given the effect of shade or shadow: *I like the shaded parts; they give depth to the drawing.*
discoloured *BrE*, **discolored** *AmE* having changed colour for the worse: *He had discoloured teeth, from smoking too much.*

L35 *adjectives* : **having little or no colour** [B]

colourless *BrE*, **colorless** *AmE* **1** without colour: *Water is colourless. It is a colourless liquid.* **2** weak in colour; pale: *He was colourless; we thought he was ill.* **3** (*fig*) dull; lacking variety, interest, character, excitement, etc: *He is one of the most colourless people I've ever met.* **-ly** [adv] **-ness** [U]
dull [Wa1] having colours that are or a colour that is not bright **dully** [adv] **-ness** [U]
drab [Wa1] **1** of a muddy yellowish brown or green colour **2** (*fig*) uninteresting; cheerless; dull: *They lead very drab lives.* **-ly** [adv] **-ness** [U]
faded having lost natural colour esp by being old or having been (left) in the light of the sun too

long: *The faded colours of the book had once been very bright. The colour was a faded blue.*

pale [Wa1] **1** not having much colouring matter; weak; not bright: (*fig*) *He is a pale copy of his brother.* **2** (of light) not bright: *the pale moonlight* **3** (of a person's face) having less than the usual amount of colour; rather white: *The illness makes the child look very pale.* **-ly** [adv] **-ness** [U]

pallid 1 (of coloured objects) unusually pale or lacking in deep colour: *a pallid sky* **2** (of the face, skin, etc) unusually or unhealthily pale: *He had a pallid look, as if he had been shut up without fresh air for a long time.* **-ly** [adv] **-ness** [U]

L36 *adjectives* : **having a lot of colour** [Wa1;B]

deep not affected by white: *The sky was deep blue.*

dark tending to have more black: *She wore a dark green dress; the dress was dark green.*

light having a lot of white: *His hair was light brown. She wore a light green dress.*

pale not having much black: *She wore a pale green dress.*

L37 *intensive adjectives* : **relating to colour** [B]

vivid 1 (of light or colour) bright and strong; producing a sharp sensation on the eye: *There was a vivid flash of lightning. She had vivid red hair.* **2** that produces or is able to produce sharp clear pictures in the mind; lifelike: *To the little boy's vivid imagination, the stick he held was a sword. The dream was so vivid that he felt himself to be awake. He gave a vivid description of what happened.* **3** (of a person's power of expression) having an effect on others) full of life and force: *The actor gave a vivid performance as the mad king.* **-ly** [adv] **-ness** [U]

livid 1 blue-grey, as of marks on the skin (**bruises**) after being hit **2** (of the face) very pale **3** *infml* very angry: *He was livid when we told him we'd lost his key.* **-ly** [adv] **-ness** [U]

lurid 1 unnaturally bright; (*deprec*) too strongly coloured: *What a lurid picture/sunset!* **2** (*fig*) shocking, esp because violent; unpleasant: *The papers gave lurid details of the murder.* **-ly** [adv] **-ness** [U]

L38 *verbs, etc* : **showing an increase of colour**

colour *BrE*, **color** *AmE* [IØ] to become red in the face; blush: *As soon as he started to argue he coloured quickly.*

blush 1 [Wv4;IØ (*at, for, with*)] to become red in

the face, from shame, because people are looking at one, etc: *She blushed when he asked what she was doing. He blushed at their praise.* **2** [IØ (*for*), 3] to be ashamed: *'When I see the prices that tourists are charged, I blush for my country,' he said. She blushed to admit that . . .* **3** [C] a case of blushing: *His words brought a blush to her face.* **spare one's blushes** *infml* to avoid making someone blush: *You shouldn't say all these nice things about me: spare my blushes!*

flush 1 [IØ;L7] (of a person, the skin, or the face) to turn red as a result of a (sudden) flow of blood to the skin: *She flushed when she couldn't answer his question. The boy flushed bright red with shame. The doctor said that the child looked flushed, and told her to stay in bed because she had a fever.* **2** [C] a flow of blood to the face **3** [S] the red appearance of the face as a result of this: *The sick boy had an unhealthy flush and breathed with difficulty.*

redden [IØ;T1] to become or make red
darken [IØ;T1] to become or make dark
crimson [IØ;T1] to become or make crimson

L39 *verbs* : **showing a decrease of colour**

lighten 1 [T1;IØ] to make or become brighter or less dark **2** [IØ] to brighten or light up with excitement, happiness, etc

pale 1 [T1;IØ] to make or become pale (*defs* **1**, **2**, and **3**): *Illness paled her cheek. His face paled at the sight of his enemy.* **2** [IØ (*before, beside*)] (*fig*) to seem less important, clever, beautiful, etc, when compared with: *All other anxieties paled beside the frightening fact of the fire coming close to the village.*

whiten [T1;IØ] to (cause to) become more white: *I must whiten my tennis shoes. The sky whitened as the sun rose.*

fade [IØ (*away*)] **1** to (cause to) lose colour, freshness, strength, etc: *The flowers faded when cut. The sun has faded the material. The illness caused his strength to fade away.* **2** (*fig*) to disappear or die gradually: *The shapes faded (away) into the night.*

Weather and temperature

L40 *nouns* : **weather, etc**

weather [U] the condition of wind, rain, sunshine, snow, etc, at a certain time or over a period of time: *What good weather/nice weather. We had a period of hot weather. What's the weather like today?* **weatherproof** [B] (esp of garments) which can keep out wind and rain: *This is a nice warm weatherproof* *coat.* **weatherbeaten** [B] **1** marked or damaged by the force of wind, sun, etc **2** (of a face or skin) browned by the wind and sun

(weather) forecast [C] a description of weather conditions as they are expected to be by those who study them (**meteorologists**): *What's tomorrow's weather forecast?*

climate [C] **1** the average weather conditions at a particular place over a period of years: *That island has a tropical climate.* **2** (*fig*) the general temper or opinions of a group of people or period of history: *I wouldn't have liked the (moral and political) climate of Britain before the First World War.*

clime [C9 *usu pl*] *poet* climate: *He often travelled in the warmer climes.*

temperature 1 [U;C] the amount of heat or cold in a place: *What was the temperature like this morning? The room had a temperature of 20°.* **2** [C] too much heat in the body: *The child has a temperature; send for the doctor.*

L41 *verbs* : **weather, etc**

acclimatize, -ise [T1; I∅ (*to*)] **1** cause (plants, animals, etc, or esp oneself) to become accustomed to the conditions of weather in a new part of the world: *It took them several months to acclimatize (themselves) to the hot weather.* **2** to cause (oneself or another) to become accustomed to new conditions and places

adjust [I∅ (*to*)] *not fml* to acclimatize oneself: *He hasn't adjusted (to the climate here) yet; it takes time.*

L42 *verbs* : **to change because of weather, time etc**

weather 1 [I∅] to be changed by the air and weather: *Rocks weather until they are worn away.* **2** [T1] to leave open to the air: *weathered wood; skin weathered by an outdoor life* **3** [T1] to pass safely through (a storm or difficulty): *Once the bad times were weathered, their life changed for the better.*

wear away [v adv T1; I∅] to (cause to) disappear slowly: *The wind has worn the rocks away. The illness wore away her strength.*

wear down [v adv] **1** [T1; I∅] to (cause to) be reduced bit by bit: *He finished the wood by rubbing until he wore the surface down/until the surface wore down.* (*fig*) *The illness wore her down.* **2** [T1] to reduce the force of: *We wore down their opposition after several hours' argument.*

erode 1 [T1 (*away*)] (of acids, water, wind, etc) to cut into; to wear or rub away: *The sea erodes the rocks.* (*fig*) *The King's power has been slowly eroded away.* **2** [I∅] to be or become worn away or rubbed away: *The coast is slowly eroding away.* **erosion** [U] the process of eroding or being eroded: *Soil erosion is bad in that part of the world.*

L43 *nouns* : **instruments, etc, relating to weather, etc**

barometer [C] **1** an instrument for measuring the pressure of the air in order to help to judge probable changes in the weather or one's height above sea level **2** (*fig*) something or someone that shows changes in public opinion **barometric** [Wa5;B] of or concerning barometers **-cally** [adv Wa4]

thermometer [C] an instrument for measuring the temperature of a place, person, etc

degree [C] a point of measurement of temperature: *Water freezes at 32 degrees Fahrenheit (32° F) or 0 degrees Centigrade (0° C). A healthy body temperature is 98.4 degrees Fahrenheit (98.4° F) in Britain, and 98.6 degrees Fahrenheit (98.6° F) in the USA.*

scale [C] **1** the line of marks which show how hot or cold something is **2** a system of arranging such marks: *The Fahrenheit and Centigrade scales are quite different.*

centigrade [*often cap*] **1** [R] a scale of temperature in which water freezes at 0° and boils at 100° **2** [Wa5;B;E] of, in or relating to this scale

Celsius [R] Centigrade

Fahrenheit 1 [R] a scale of temperature in which water freezes at 32° and boils at 212° **2** [Wa5;B;E] of, in or relating to this scale

freezing point 1 [R] the temperature (0° Centigrade) at which water becomes ice: *It's very cold today; the temperature has dropped to freezing point.* **2** [C] the temperature at which any particular liquid freezes: *The freezing point of alcohol is much lower than that of water.*

boiling point 1 [R] the temperature (100° Centigrade) at which water boils **2** [C] the temperature at which a liquid boils: *Water and oil have different boiling points.* **3** [R] (*fig*) the point at which high excitement, anger, etc, breaks into action: *Trouble in the city has reached boiling point.*

calorie [C] **1** a measure of heat; the amount of heat needed to heat one gramme of water by one degree Centigrade **2** a measure used when stating the amount of heat that a food will produce: *One slice of bread has 90 calories. You must count calories if you want to lose weight, because food with a lot of calories is fattening.* **calorific** [B] heat-producing: *This coal has a high calorific value.*

L44 *nouns* : **sky and air**

sky [(*the*) U; C *often pl with sing meaning*] the upper air; the space above the earth where clouds and the sun, moon, and stars appear: *The sky turned dark as the storm came near. There's a bit of blue sky between the clouds. We expect sunny skies for the next two days; the skies should remain sunny. The painting showed a bright blue sky. He lifted his hands to the skies in prayer.*

heavens [*the* P] *esp lit* the sky: *The heavens on a clear night are full of stars* [*also* ⇒ C325].

air 1 [U] the mixture of gases which surrounds the earth and which we breathe: *The fresh air made him feel hungry.* **2** [U] the sky or the space above the ground: *He jumped into the air.* **3** [U] the sky as something through which we fly: *Air travel is now very fast. I shall send the letter by air.* **4** [C] the general character or appearance of something; appearance of, or feeling caused by, a person or place: *He walked with an air of importance. There was an air of excitement at the meeting.*

atmosphere [C; U] **1** the mixture of gases that surround any heavenly body, esp the earth **2** the air, as in the sky or in an enclosed space: *The atmosphere in the room was hot and smoky.* **3** (*fig*) the feeling among a group or produced by the surroundings: *I like the happy atmosphere in that restaurant. There was a strange atmosphere in that house.* **atmospheric** [Wa5;B] of or concerning the earth's atmosphere **-ally** [adv Wa4]

vacuum [C] a space completely empty, esp of gas; a space from which air, gas, etc, has been removed

L45 nouns : **clouds, fog, steam, etc**

cloud 1 [C; U] (a variously-shaped weightless mass of) very small drops of water floating high in the air: *When there are black clouds you can tell it's going to rain. There's more cloud today than yesterday.* **2** [C] a variously-shaped weightless mass of dust, smoke, etc, which floats in the air: *Clouds of smoke rose above the bombed city.* **3** [C] a large number of things moving through the air as a mass: *a cloud of insects* **4** [C; U] (an area of) darkness in something otherwise transparent: *There was a cloud in the bottom of the beer.* **5** [C9] (*fig*) something that causes unhappiness or fear: *The sad news of her father's death was the only cloud in an otherwise happy year.* **cloudbank** [C] a thick mass of low cloud **cloudy** [Wa1;B] **1** full of clouds: *It was a cloudy day. The sky was cloudy.* **2** not clear or transparent: *cloudy beer/a cloudy mirror* **3** (*fig*) uncertain: *His memory has always been cloudy.* **-ily** [adv] **-iness** [U] **cloudless** [Wa5;B] without clouds; clear: *a cloudless sky/day*

fog 1 [U] very thick mist: *There was fog last night off the west coast. Yellow fog filled the streets and hid the daylight. A fog warning was broadcast on the radio.* **2** [C] a date or period of very thick mist: *We often have bad fogs on the south coast during winter.* **foggy** [Wa1;B] full of fog: *It was the foggiest night of the year.* **-ily** [adv] **-iness** [U]

vapour *BrE*, **vapor** *AmE* **1** [U; C] a gaslike form of a liquid (such as mist or steam) often caused by a sudden change of temperature: *A cloud is a mass of vapour in the sky. Strange vapours rose from the dark lake.* **2** [U9] *tech* the gas to

which the stated liquid or solid can be changed by the action of heat

steam 1 [U] water in the state of a gas produced by boiling **2** [A] using this under pressure to produce power or heat: *a steam engine* **3** [U] the mist formed when this begins to cool: *Steam formed on the insides of the kitchen windows.* **steamy** [Wa1;B] full of or like steam **-iness** [U]

mist 1 [C; U] (a period of or area with) cloudlike bodies made up of very small amounts of water floating in the air, near or reaching to the ground; thin fog: *The mountaintop was covered in mist.* **2** [U; (*the*) S] any condition in which small drops of water cause an uncertain view of anything, such as a glass surface when it has been breathed on, tears in the eyes, making it difficult to see: *She could hardly recognize her son through the mist of tears that filled her eyes.* **3** [(*the*) S] (*fig*) anything that darkens or clouds the mind, making understanding or good judgement difficult: *It was difficult to discover the truth through the mist of lies and half lies that filled his story.* **misty** [Wa1;B] of or like mist **-ily** [adv] **-iness** [U]

condensation [U] **1** small drops of liquid or solid substance formed by cooling; drops of liquid formed when steam cools: *There was condensation on the windows.* **2** *tech* the change from a gas to a liquid or sometimes to a solid

haze [S; U] **1** sort of light mist or smoke: *a haze of cigarette smoke* **2** (*fig*) feeling of confusion or uncertainty in the mind **hazy** [Wa1;B] [⇒ L72]

dew [U; C] the small drops of water which form on cold surfaces during the night: *The ground shone with dew in the early sunlight.* **dewy** [Wa1;B] of or like dew

L46 verbs : **clouds, fog, steam, etc**

cloud 1 [T1; I0 (*over*)] to (cause to) become covered with or as if with clouds: *The thick mist clouded the mountain tops. The sky's clouded over; I think it's going to rain.* **2** [T1] (*fig*) to make uncertain, unclear, confused, etc: *Age has clouded his memory. Drink clouded his thinking.* **3** [T1; I0 (*up*)] to (cause to) become less transparent or darker: *You'll cloud the beer if you shake the barrel. The wine clouded when he shook the bottle. The steam has clouded the windows up.*

fog [T1; I0 (*up*)] to (cause to) become difficult to see through because of a misty covering: *The steam has fogged (up) my glasses. My glasses are all fogged up.*

steam 1 [I0] to give off steam: *Their wet clothes began to steam in the warm room.* **2** [T1] to treat with steam: *She secretly steamed the letter open. This kind of fish tastes best if it is steamed.*

mist [T1 (*over, up*)] to cover with mist: *The railway carriage became so hot that air misted (up) the windows.*

haze [IØ;T1] to (cause to) become hazy [⇒ L72]

up [adv] (expressing completeness): *The windows misted up and we could not see out. This glass is all fogged up.*

ventilate [T1 *usu pass*] **1** to cause fresh air to get into and around (a place): *This room is well/badly ventilated.* **2** (*fig*) to state clearly and openly: *He angrily began to ventilate his opinions/feelings.* **ventilator** [C] an apparatus that ventilates a place **ventilation** [U] the act of ventilating; a system that ventilates

L47 *verbs* : **condensing and evaporating**

condense 1 [IØ] (of a gas) to become liquid, or sometimes solid, esp by becoming cooler: *The steam condensed and formed drops of water.* **2** [T1] to cause (a gas) to become liquid, or sometimes solid, esp by making cooler: *The drop in temperature condensed the steam to water.* **condensation** [U]

evaporate [IØ;T1] to (cause to) change into steam and disappear: *The sun will evaporate the water. The water has evaporated.* (*fig*) *My hopes are beginning to evaporate* (= disappear). **evaporation** [U]

vaporize, -ise [T1;IØ] to (cause to) change into vapour [⇒ L45]: *If you vaporize a liquid, other substances will be left behind. Water vaporizes when boiled.* **vaporization, -isation** [U]

atomize, -ise [T1] to break (a liquid) into a mist (= into many very small drops) by forcing it through a special instrument (**an atomizer**) and out through a very small hole, **atomization -isation** [U]

L48 *nouns* : **particular kinds of rain**

rain 1 [U] water falling in separate drops from the clouds; the fall of these drops: *The crops need rain. She went out in the rain without a coat. Come in out of the rain. Hail is frozen rain.* **2** [C9] a fall of the stated type: *A heavy rain began to fall.* **3** [S9 *of*] (*fig*) a thick fall of anything: *There was a rain of arrows/of questions.* **rainy** [Wa1;B] of or like rain

sleet [U] (partly) frozen rain; ice falling in fine bits

drizzle [U;S] a fine misty rain **drizzly** [Wa1;B] of or like drizzle

hail 1 [U] frozen rain drops which fall as little hard balls **2** [S9, esp *of*] (*fig*) a number of things which strike suddenly with violence causing pain or damage: *There was a hail of bullets/a hail of angry words.*

L49 *nouns* : **rain generally**

fall of rain [C] the amount or an occasion of rain falling: *There was a heavy fall of rain last night.*

rainfall [U;C] the amount of rain (snow, hail, etc) that falls in a particular place at or over a particular length of time: *The annual* (= yearly) *rainfall there is only 4 centimetres. We have had one of the heaviest rainfalls in years.*

shower [C] **1** a fall of rain or snow which does not last long: *Scattered showers are expected this afternoon. I went out and was caught in a shower.* **2** a fall of many small things or drops of liquid: *The bucket fell over, sending a shower of paint onto the men below the ladder.* **3** a quantity or rush of things coming at the same time: *They fired a shower of arrows. She got a shower of letters on her birthday.* **showery** [B] of or like showers: *What showery weather!*

rains [*the* P] the time of the year in tropical [⇒ L11] countries when a lot of rain falls: *The rains come in June in India.*

monsoon 1 [*the* R; (C)] **a** (the period or season of) heavy rains which fall in India and other countries near it from June to October: *If the monsoon is late again this year, many people and animals will die.* **b** *tech* a wind that blows from the Indian Ocean bringing these rains **2** [C] *infml* a very heavy fall of rain

cloudburst [C] a sudden very heavy fall of rain: *It wasn't just rain; it was a real cloudburst!*

downpour [C] a heavy fall of water, esp rain: *There was quite a downpour last night and we all got very wet.*

deluge [C] a great flood of water, esp as rain; a heavy rainstorm: *It was a real deluge and we got very wet!*

L50 *verbs* : **raining**

rain 1 [*it* IØ] (of rain) to fall: *It's raining. It began to rain (hard).* **2** [*it* T1] to drop (something) like rain: *They say it sometimes rains small fish.* **3** [X9;L9 (*on, upon*); esp *down*] to (cause to) fall like rain: *The bombs came raining down. Tears rained down her cheeks. Gifts rained* (*down*) *on the children. Their rich uncle rained* (*down*) *gifts upon the children.* **rain cats and dogs** to rain very heavily

drizzle [(*it*) IØ] to rain in very small drops or very lightly: *It's drizzling! It has started to drizzle.*

pour 1 [(*it*) IØ] to rain hard and steadily: *It's pouring this morning. What a pouring wet day!* **2** [IØ (*down*)] (of rain) to fall hard and steadily: *The rain is just pouring down.*

hail [(*it*) IØ] (of hail) to fall: *It's hailing. It hailed yesterday. It began to hail.*

sleet [(*it*) IØ] (of sleet) to fall: *It's sleeting.*

shower 1 [(*it*) IØ] to rain or pour down in showers: *It's started to shower; I'm sure to get wet. Nuts showered down when the tree was shaken.* **2** [D1 *with/on*] **a** to pour (on); scatter heavily (on): *They showered the married pair with rice.* **b** to give in large quantity: *They showered gifts on her/showered her with gifts.*

deluge [T1 *usu pass*] (*esp fig*) to cover with a great flood (as of rain): *We were deluged with letters.*

cascade [I0 (*down*)] to fall in or like a cascade [⇒ L96] or waterfall: *The water cascaded down.*

L51 *nouns* : **snow and ice**

snow [U] **1** water in the air which has frozen and falls to the ground in little soft white pieces (**flakes of snow, snowflakes**) **2** a mass of these on the ground: *The hills were covered with/in snow.* **snowy** [Wa1;B] having a lot of snow: *The weather has been snowy lately.* **-iness** [U]

fall of snow *also* **snowfall** the amount or an occasion of snow falling: *There was a heavy fall of snow last night.*

slush [U] **1** partly melted snow; watery snow **2** (*fig*) literature films, etc, concerned with silly love stories **slushy** [Wa1;B] of or like slush **-ily** [adv] **-iness** [U]

ice [U] water which has frozen to a solid: *The water turned to ice.* **icy** [Wa1;B] having a lot of ice; like ice: *icy weather* **icily** [adv] **iciness** [U]

frost 1 [U] weather at a temperature below the freezing point of water; frozen condition of the ground and or air: *Frost has killed several of our young plants. The radio has given a frost and icy roads warning for car drivers tomorrow.* **2** [C] a period or state of this: *There was a hard frost last night* (= a severe one). *Early frosts* (= ones near the season of autumn) *spoil the last of the flowers. The young shoots on the trees have been damaged by a late frost* (= one towards the end of spring). **3** [U] a white powdery substance formed on outside surfaces from very small drops of water when the temperature of the air is below freezing point: *The grass was covered with frost in the early morning.* **4** [*of* U] *tech* temperature below the freezing point of water: *There was 5 degrees of frost last night and the river's completely frozen.* **frosty** [Wa1;B] of or like frost **-tily** [adv] **-tiness** [U]

hoar frost *also* (*less common*) **hoar** [U] white frost, esp that seen on the grass after a cold night

L52 *verbs* : **snow and ice**

snow [(*it*) I0] (of snow) to fall: *It's snowing. It began to snow* (*hard*).

ice 1 [I0 *up, over*] to become covered with ice; to turn into ice: *The car has iced up; it won't move* **2** [T1] to make very cold by using ice.

frost 1 [T1; I0; (*over*)] to (cause to) become covered with frost: *The cold has frosted the windows. The fields have frosted over on this wintry morning.* **2** [Wv5;T1] (*fig*) to roughen the surface of a sheet of (glass) so that it is not possible to see through: *Frosted glass in windows and doors lets in less light than clear glass,* *but keeps a room private.* **3** [T1] to damage (esp a plant) with frost

L53 *nouns* : **small amounts of rain and snow** [C]

raindrop a small amount (**drop**) of rain: *There were raindrops on the car. Raindrops began to fall and it was soon raining heavily.*

snowflake a small piece of snow

L54 *nouns, etc* : **winds**

wind [U;C] strongly moving air: *There were high/strong/heavy winds last night. The rocks were shaped by sun, wind, and rain.* **windy** [Wa1;B] **1** of or like wind **2** with a lot of wind: *What a windy day! He stood on a windy hillside.* **windless** [Wa5;B] without wind: *The day was windless, without clouds moving. It was a windless day.* **windswept** [B] **1** (of a country) open to the wind where the soil can be blown off because there are no trees **2** (as if) blown into an untidy state: *She had a windswept appearance.* **windward 1** [Wa5;B; adv] into or against the direction of the wind: *The strong wind held us against the windward side of the wall.* **2** [U] the direction from which the wind is blowing: *The wind was so strong we could not sail to windward.*

prevailing wind [C] the common wind in a particular place, usu blowing from a particular direction: *The prevailing winds here at this time of year are westerly* (= coming from the west).

onshore wind [C] a wind blowing from the sea towards the land/shore

offshore wind [C] a wind blowing from the land/shore out to sea

breeze [C] a (usu light gentle) wind: *A slight breeze moved the leaves of the trees. A strong breeze got up* (= started to blow). **breezy** [Wa1;B] of or like a breeze **-zily** [adv]

gale [C] **1** a weather condition in which a strong wind blows: *The old tree was blown down in a gale.* **2** [*usu pl*] (*fig*) a sudden noise, esp laughter: *As the door opened gales of laughter came from inside.*

gust [C] **1** a sudden strong rush of air or of rain, smoke, etc, carried by wind: *A gust of wind blew the door shut. The wind blowing down the chimney sent gusts of smoke into the room.* **2** (*fig*) a short burst of feeling, esp anger: *In a gust of uncontrollable rage he broke the picture in pieces.* **gusty** [Wa1;B] of or like gusts **-tily** [adv]

blow [S] *naut or infml* a strong wind or windy storm: *We had a bit of a blow last night.* **blowy** [Wa1;B] windy

puff [C] a light quick movement of air: *A puff of wind blew the paper away. The wind came in sudden puffs and gusts.*

breath [C *usu sing*] *not fml* a movement (of air);

a very slight wind: *There's hardly a breath (of air/wind) this morning.*

L55 *nouns* : **storms** [C]

storm 1 [*often in comb*] rough weather conditions with wind, rain, and often flashes of light: *There was a storm/a thunderstorm/a snowstorm last night.* **2** [(*of*)] (*fig*) a sudden show of feeling: *She left in a storm of weeping.* **3** [(*of*)] (*fig*) a loud noise: *He heard a storm of cries.* **stormy** [Wa1;B] of or like storms; having a lot of storms **-ily** [adv] **-iness** [U]

blizzard a long severe snowstorm

hurricane a storm with a strong fast wind, esp as happens in the West Indies

whirlwind *also* **tornado**, *tech* **cyclone** a tall pipe-shaped body of rapidly circling air: *A whirlwind destroyed the towns on the coast.*

typhoon a very violent tropical storm in the Western Pacific

L56 *verbs* : **winds blowing**

blow 1 [(*it*) I∅] (esp of the wind, air, etc) to move, be active: *The wind is blowing hard. It's blowing hard tonight.* **2** [L9; X9 (I∅ (*in*); T1)] to (cause to) move (usu into the stated condition) by the force of a current of air: *The wind has blown my hat off. My papers are blowing about. I blew the dust off the book. The wind blew her hair. Her hair blew in the wind.* **blow back** [v adv I∅] to blow in the wrong direction: *If the gas blows back you must turn off the supply as it is dangerous.* **blow down** [v adv T1; I∅] to (cause to) fall by blowing: *The storm blew several trees down in the park.*

rage [Wv4; I∅] (of bad weather, pain, infectious diseases, etc) to be very violent: *The storm raged. She had a raging headache. The disease raged through the city for months.*

L57 *verbs* : **winds blowing less** [I∅]

lessen *also* **weaken**, **die down** [v adv] to become less (violent, etc): *The strong winds lessened in force. The storm is weakening.*

abate *fml* (of wind, storms, pain, etc) to lessen: *The storm abated on the third day.* **abatement** [U] the act or result of abating: *He belongs to the Noise Abatement Society; he thinks modern life is too noisy.*

L58 *nouns, etc* : **thunder and lightning**

thunder 1 [U] a loud noise in the clouds: *He could hear thunder over the hills.* **2** [U; C] any loud noise like this: *The thunder of the sea could be heard a long way inland.* **3** [I∅; (T1)] to produce (thunder or a noise like it): *The men thundered on the door to get in.* **thundery**

[B] of or like thunder; giving signs that thunder is likely: *What thundery weather!*

lightning 1 [U] a powerful flash of light in the sky passing from one cloud to another or to the earth, usu followed by thunder: *A great flash of lightning lit the night sky.* **2** [A] very quick, short, or sudden: *He made a lightning visit to the town.* **like lightning** very fast: *He ran like lightning.* **lightning conductor/rod** [C] a piece of metal, usu iron, fixed to a high building and joined by a thick wire to the ground to take the electricity of lightning into the ground so as to stop the lightning from setting fire, etc, to the building

thunderbolt [C] **1** a single strong flash of lightning esp when followed by thunder **2** (*fig*) a terrible surprise

thunderclap [C] a sudden loud noise of thunder

sheet lightning [U] lightning in the form of a sudden great flash

forked lightning [U] lightning that divides into many branches

thunder and lightning [U] thunder and lightning happening together

thunderstorm [C] a storm of thunder and lightning

L59 *adjectives* : **dry conditions** [B]

dry [Wa1] **1** not wet; not having water or liquid in any form on or below the surface: *The clothes are dry. The soil is too dry for planting.* **2** (of parts of the earth) emptied of water: *The well has gone dry. They walked along a dry riverbed.* **3** no longer liquid or sticky: *The paint on this door is not yet dry; be careful!* **4** no longer giving milk: *a dry cow* **5** using no liquid: *a dry method of doing it* **6** without tears or other liquid substances from the body: *dry weeping, a dry wound, a dry cough*; (*fig*) *After that sad story there wasn't a single dry eye left in the whole house!* **7** having or producing thirst: *I always feel dry in this hot weather doing this dry work in the sun.* (*fig*) *The plants look dry.* **8** (esp of bread) without butter or not fresh: *dry bread/cake* **9** without rain or wetness: *dry weather; dry heat*

arid (of land or a country) having so little rain that it is very dry and unproductive

L60 *adjectives, etc* : **not dry conditions** [B]

wet [Wa1] **1** containing or covered in liquid: *I can't go out till my hair's dry; it's still wet from being washed.* **2** rainy: *It's wet weather/a wet day. We can't go out; it's too wet.* **3** (*fig*) *infml deprec* (of a person) lacking in strength (of mind); too weak or unwilling to get things done: *Don't be so wet! Of course you can do it, if you only stop saying you can't!* **4** [*the* R] **a** rainy weather (*esp in the phr* **go out in/come in from the wet**): *I can't go out, because the coat I* *brought is too thin to protect me from the wet.* **b** wet material (esp after rain): *come and walk on the dry road, instead of going through the wet.*

moist [Wa1] **1** slightly wet: *The thick steam in the room had made the walls moist. The story was so sad that at the end my eyes were moist with tears.* **2** (of air, wind, etc) containing some water; damp: *The air became moister as we descended the hill towards the river bank.* **3** (esp of food) not unpleasantly dry: *This cake's nice and moist.*

dank [Wa1] unpleasantly wet and usu cold: *It is an unhealthy house with dank stone walls.* **-ness** [U]

damp 1 [Wa1] not as dry as (something) should be; slightly wetter than one would like **2** [U] wetness: *The damp in the air makes my old bones hurt.*

humid [Wa2] *fml & tech* (of air and weather) containing water; damp **humidity** [U] *fml & tech* the (amount of) water contained in the air: *It's difficult to work because of the humidity. The humidity has been measured and found higher than ever.* **humidify** [T1] to make humid

L61 *verbs* : drying

dry [I∅; T1] to (cause to) become dry: *Dry your wet hands. The wet clothes will soon dry in the sun.* **dry out** *also* **dry up** [v adv T1; I∅] to (cause to) become completely dry

desiccate [T1] *fml* to make completely dry: *The hot sun desiccated everything.* **desiccation** [U] the action of desiccating

dehydrate 1 [Wv5; T1] to dry; get all the water out from: *We dehydrate eggs to make egg powder.* **2** [I∅] to lose water from the body: *That sick man will dehydrate and die unless we get medical help.* **dehydration** [U] the action of dehydrating

shrivel [I∅; T1; (*up*)] to (cause to) dry out and become smaller by twisting into small folds: *The old lady had shrivelled hands. The plants were shrivelling (up) in the dry heat.*

L62 *verbs, etc* : not drying; becoming wet, etc

wet [T1] to cause to be wet: *Wet your finger and hold it up; the side that dries is the side the wind is blowing from.*

wet through [v adv T1] to wet completely: *The rain has wet me through. We're wet through!*

moisten [T1; I∅] to make or become slightly wet: *Some people moisten their fingers so as to count sheets of paper more easily. Her eyes moistened as she listened to the sad story.*

damp [T1] to make slightly wet: *Damp this cloth, please.*

dampen 1 [T1; I∅] to (cause to) become damp: *The rain hardly dampened the ground.* **2** [T1] (*fig*) to make (feelings) less happy: *Nothing can dampen my spirits on this glorious morning.*

soak 1 [I∅; T1; (*in*)] to (cause to) remain in a liquid esp to become soft or completely wet: *Leave the dirty clothes to soak. He likes to soak himself in a warm bath.* **2** [L9, esp *in, into, through*; T1 *usu pass*] (of a liquid) to enter (a solid) through the material of a surface: *The ink had soaked through the thin paper. The cloth was soaked with soapy water.* (*fig*) *The speaker waited for his remark to soak in.* **3** [T1 (*in*)] (*fig*) to keep (oneself) very busy with: *He soaked himself in the subject before daring to write about it.* **4** [X9, esp *out*] to remove by keeping or washing well in water: *The packet says this soap is the best at soaking out dirt.* **5** [C; *in* U] an act or state of soaking: *We want to give the dishes a good soak.*

drench [T1 (*to, with*)] to make (usu people, animals, or clothes) thoroughly wet: *I am drenched to the skin! I had no coat on when the rain started. I got a good drenching in the rain.*

drown 1 [T1] to cover completely with water, esp by a rise in the water level **2** [T1 (*with, in*)] to make thoroughly wet: *drowning the bananas with cream* **3** [I∅; T1] to (cause to) die from being under water for a long time: *The swimmer was found drowned.* **4** [T1 (*in*)] (*fig*) to cause (oneself) to become very active or deeply interested in something: *He drowned himself in work.* **5** [T1 (*out*)] to cause (a sound) not to be heard by making a loud noise: *His speech was drowned (out) by angry shouting.* **6** [T1 (*in*)] (*fig*) to drive out or under: *He drowned his sorrows in drink* (= alcohol).

duck [T1] to push (someone's body or head) down into water: *The older boys ducked the younger one in the river.* **ducking** [U; C] (an) act or result of ducking or being ducked

immerse [T1] **1** *fml & tech* to put deep under (water, etc) **2** to cause (oneself) to enter deeply into an activity: *I immersed myself in work.* **immersion** [U; C] the act or result of immersing or being immersed

L63 *adjectives* : hot, stuffy, etc [B]

[ALSO ⇨ L11]

hot [Wa1] **1** having a high temperature: *It's hot today. How hot is the water?* **2** (not usu of people) (*fig*) excitable: *He has a hot temper.* **3** (*fig*) clever and well informed: *He's very hot on politics.* **get hot** (in a game) to get near something hidden or to guess nearly right **not so hot** *infml* not very good; not as good as expected

warm [Wa1] **1** quite hot; pleasantly hot: *He drank the warm milk and sat beside the warm fire.* **2** able to keep in heat or keep out cold: *Wear your warmest clothes tonight.* **3** having or giving a feeling of heat: *We were warm from exercise. It was a warm climb.* **4** (*fig*) showing or marked by strong feeling, esp good feeling:

He is a warm supporter of the local team. They are all warm friends. **-ly** [adv]: *He spoke warmly about his friends in that town.* **5** (*fig*) marked by excitement or anger: *They had a warm argument.* **6** [F] (*fig*) *infml* (esp in children's games) near a hidden object, the right answer to a question, etc: *You're getting warm, warmer; no, now you're getting colder again.* **7** (*fig*) giving a pleasant feeling of cheerfulness or friendliness: *warm colours/a warm voice/a warm invitation*

blistering 1 raising blisters [⇒ B126] esp by great heat: *He was out too long in the blistering heat of the sun.* **2** (*fig*) very angry and intended to hurt: *blistering words/a blistering look/a blistering tongue* **-ly** [adv]

sweltering causing one to feel very hot and uncomfortable: *It's sweltering today.*

sultry [Wa1] **1** (of weather) hot, with a lack of air or air which is hard to breathe **2** (*fig*) (of a person) attractive, esp sexually

close [Wa1] **1** lacking fresh or freely moving air: *It's very close in here today.* **2** heavy: *This is the closest weather for a long time.*

stifling causing difficulty in breathing: *The air is stifling here; let's get out.*

stuffy [Wa1] (having air) which is not fresh: *This is a stuffy room/atmosphere. It's stuffy in here; open a window.*

L64 *nouns* : **hot, etc**

heat [U] **1** the quality or degree of being hot or cold: *What is the heat of the water in the swimming pool?* **2 a** hotness; warmth: *The heat from the fire dried their clothes.* **b** hot weather: *I can't walk about in this heat.* **3** (*fig*) a state of excitement: *She thought he had been rude and answered with some heat* (= angrily). *In the heat of the moment/argument/battle I lost my self-control.*

warmth [U] the state or quality of being warm: *He left the warmth of the fire. He was aware of the warmth of his feelings.*

warm *not fml* **1** [*the* S] a warm place, state, or condition: *Come into the warm, out of the cold.* **2** [S] the act or action of making oneself warm: *Come and have a warm by the fire.*

L65 *verbs* : **hot, etc**

heat [I∅;T1; (*up*)] to (cause to) become hot: *We'll heat some milk for the coffee. The water's heating for a bath.*

warm 1 [Wv4;T1;(I∅)] to cause to become warm: *They warmed their hands/themselves by the open fire. A hot drink warms on a cold day.* **2** [I∅] (of things rather than people) to become warm: *The water is warming in the pot over the fire.*

melt [I∅;T1] to (cause to) become liquid through heat: *The snow melted in the sun. They melted the metal.* (*fig*) *She melted when he said*

he loved her. (*fig*) *His kind words melted her anger.* **molten** [Wa5;B] (esp of metals, rock, etc) hot and melted

toast [T1] **1** to make hard and dry by heating: *She toasted the bread.* **2** to make warm by putting near a fire: *They toasted themselves by the fire.*

L66 *adjectives, etc* : **not hot**

[ALSO ⇒ L11]

cold [Wa1] **1** [B] having a low temperature: *It's a cold day. Ice cream is too cold for me; it hurts my teeth. The cold wind blew.* **2** [B] having a lower temperature than normal: *You've got cold hands today. It's a cold day for July, isn't it?* **3** [B] feeling no warmth: *I'm very cold today; I should have put a coat on. If you're cold try running and see if you get warmer. Old people feel cold as soon as autumn arrives.* **4** [F] (*fig*) *infml* (esp in children's games) still a long way from finding an object, the answer, etc: *You're getting colder; you'll never find it.* **-ness** [U] **cold snap** [C] a sudden short period of very cold weather

nippy [Wa1;B] *not fml* sharply cold: *It's a nippy winter morning.* **-iness** [U]

chilly [Wa1;B] **1** noticeably cold; cold enough to be uncomfortable: *It grew chilly when the fire went out. I feel chilly without a coat.* **2** (*fig*) unfriendly; discouraging; lacking warmth: *The king was given a chilly welcome when he arrived on the island.* **-iness** [U]

chill [Wa1;B] **1** *emot* cold: *That's a chill wind.* **2** (*fig*) unfriendly; discouraging: *The union leaders and employers had a chill meeting and reached no workable agreement.* **-ness** [U] **chilly** [adv]

freezing [Wa5] **1** [B] esp *infml* very cold: *It's freezing today! I'm freezing; let me near the fire.* **2** [R] the point where water freezes: *It must be five degrees below freezing today.*

icy [Wa1;B] (cold) like ice: *The weather's icy today, isn't it?* (*fig*) *He spoke in an icy voice.* **icily** [adv] **iciness** [U]

L67 *nouns* : **cold, etc**

cold [U] the absence of heat; low temperature; cold weather: *It's nice to put on a warm coat and go for a walk in the cold. Come in from the cold! Old people suffer from the cold in winter.*

chill [C *usu sing*] **1** a certain coldness: *There was a chill in the air this morning, wasn't there? I never go in the sea until the sun's taken the chill off the water.* **2** a discouraging feeling; a lowering of spirit: *The bad news put a chill into us all.*

freeze [C *usu sing*] **1** a period of very cold icy weather: *He slipped and broke his leg during the big freeze last winter.* **2** (*fig*) a fixing of prices or wages at a certain level: *The government is trying to put a freeze on wages. There was a price freeze last year.*

L68 adjectives : **not hot or cold**
[Wa1;B]

cool 1 not hot; pleasantly cold when one is hot or the weather is hot: *Have a cool drink. It was cooler under the trees.* **2** (*fig*) (of people) not very friendly: *She was rather cool towards us.* **-ly** [adv] **-ness** [U]
mild not as cold as one would expect; neither too warm nor too cold: *It's been a mild winter this year. That island has a mild climate.* **-ness** [U]

L69 verbs : **cold, etc**

cool [I0;T1] to (cause to) become less hot: *The hot water began to cool. Cool the drinks, please; put some ice in them.*
chill 1 [Wv5;I0;T1] to (cause to) become cold esp without freezing: *I want this wine to chill so I'll leave it in a cold place for an hour. This cold weather will chill you to the bone if you go out without a coat. We drank chilled beer.* **2** [I0;T1] *tech* **a** (of hot liquid metal) to harden on the surface through sudden cooling **b** to cause (metal) to harden like this **3** [Wv5;T1] to preserve (food) by keeping cold but not frozen: *chilled meat* **4** [Wv4;I0;T1] (*fig*) to (cause to) **a** have a feeling of cold as from fear: *Our hearts chilled when we heard the news. It was a chilling murder story.* **b** become discouraged or low in spirits: *Our spirits chilled when we saw our holiday hotel.*
freeze 1 [Wv4;5;T1;I0 (*up*); L7; X7] to (cause (water or another liquid) to) harden into ice as a result of great cold: *Water freezes at the temperature of 0 degrees Centigrade. The north wind has frozen the water in the garden. The lake has frozen up. The water has frozen solid.* **2** [Wv5;T1;I0;L7;X7] to (cause (esp a wet mixture or a machine) to) become solid at a very low temperature: *She slipped on the frozen mud. The cold has frozen the earth solid. The cold has frozen the lock on the car door.* **3** [Wv5T1;I0] to (cause (land, a solid surface, etc) to) become covered with ice and snow: *The roads are frozen in places. The frozen January countryside looked lifeless.* **4** [*it* I0] (of weather) to be at or below the temperature at which water becomes ice: *It's freezing tonight. It froze hard last night.* **5** [Wv4;I0] *infml* to be, feel, or become very cold: *It's freezing in this room; can't we have a fire? Aren't you freezing in that thin dress? The mountain climbers were lost in the snow, and nearly froze to death* (= died of cold). (*fig*) *His terrible stories made our blood freeze* (=made us cold with fear). **6** [T1] to make very cold, stiff, or without feeling: *He looks half frozen; he needs a hot drink. I was frozen stiff after sitting so long, and could hardly walk.* **7** [T1;I0] (*fig*) to (cause to) stop suddenly or become quite still or unable to show any feeling: *The race was so exciting to watch that it froze him to the spot. The teacher froze the noisy class with a single look. The*

child froze at the sight of the snake. She began to complain, but the words froze on her lips. A wild animal will sometimes freeze in its tracks when it smells an enemy. He seemed frozen with grief when his son died. **8** [Wv4,5;I0] (*fig*) to become unfriendly in manner: *She gave me a freezing look. After their quarrel, they sat in frozen silence.* **9** [Wv5;T1] to preserve (food) by means of very low temperatures: *Meat from New Zealand is frozen and brought to Britain in special ships. Frozen foods have taken the place of tinned foods in many homes.* **10** [L9] (of food) to be able to be preserved in this way: *Does this kind of fruit freeze well?* **11** [T1] (*fig*) to fix (prices or wages) officially at a given level for a certain length of time **12** [Wv5;T1] (*fig*) to prevent (business shares, bank accounts, etc) from being used, by government order
congeal [I0] to change from a liquid to a solid state, esp because of cold: *Blood congeals at low temperatures.*

L70 adjectives : **relating to good weather** [B]

fine [Wa1] clear and pleasant: *What a fine day it is today!* **-ness** [U]
fair [Wa1] quite clear and pleasant: *Do you think the weather will be fair for our journey?* **-ness** [U]
bright [Wa1] sunny, clear, and pleasant: *What a nice bright day!* **-ness** [U]
good not raining or cloudy: *We have had good weather generally this month. This is better weather than last July.* **-ness** [U]

L71 adjectives : **relating to bad weather** [B]

bad not clear and pleasant; raining, cloudy, etc: *We've had a lot of bad weather lately. This is the worst weather in years!* **-ness** [U]
foul [Wa1] very bad: *What a foul day it is!. This is the foulest day I can remember!* **-ness** [U]
rotten [Wa2] *esp emot* very bad: *The weather's been rotten all week!* **-ness** [U]
bleak [Wa1] **1** (of weather) cold and cheerless: *The weather in early December was bleak and unpleasant.* **2** (of places) without shelter from cold winds: *The old stone house stood on a bleak hillside struck by the full force of the east wind.* **3** (*fig*) (of future events) cold; cheerless; uninteresting; discouraging: *The future of this firm will be very bleak indeed if we keep losing money.* **-ly** [adv] **-ness** [U]

L72 adjectives : **relating to cloudy weather** [B]

overcast not sunny; very cloudy: *The morning was overcast and it rained in the afternoon.*

dull [Wa1] not sunny: *It was a dull November day.* **-ness** [U]
hazy [Wa1] **1** misty; rather cloudy: *The mountains were hazy in the distance.* **2** (*fig*) unclear; uncertain: *I'm rather hazy about the details of the arrangement. The details are rather hazy.* **-zily** [adv] **-ziness** [U]

Geography

L80 *nouns* : **geography**

geography [U] the study of the countries of the world and of the seas, rivers, towns, etc, on the earth's surface or any large part of it **geographic(al)** [Wa5;B] of or concerning geography **-(al)ly** [adv Wa4] **geographer** [C] a person skilled in the study of geography
topography [U] **1** the science of describing or representing the surface shapes of a particular place in detail, as on a map **2** the character of a particular place in detail, esp as regards shape or height **topographic(al)** [Wa5;B] of or concerning topography **-(al)ly** [adv Wa4] **topographer** [C] a person skilled in topography
features [P] the general appearance of land, sea, mountains, etc, on the earth, on maps, etc: *What are the main features of North Africa according to this map?*
contour [C] **1** [*often pl with sing meaning*] the shape of the outer limits of an area: *The contours of the British coast are very uneven.* (*fig infml*) *I like her contours.* **2** *also* **contour line** an imaginary line drawn on a map to show a particular height: *What height does this contour* (*line*) *represent?*

L81 *nouns* : **maps**

map [C] **1** a representation of the earth's surface, as if seen from above, showing the shape of countries, the position of towns, and the height of land, the rivers, etc **2** a plan of the stars in the sky **3** a representation showing the position or shape of anything (**put something**) **on the map** (to cause to be) considered important **off the map 1** (of a place) far away and unreachable **2** *infml* not in existence
chart [C] **1** a map, esp a detailed map of a sea area: *You'll need detailed charts if you want to sail across the Pacific Ocean.* **2** (a sheet of paper with) information written or drawn in the form of a table, picture, graph [⇒I45], etc, usu with the intention of making it easily understood: *If you look at the chart you can see that prices have fallen.*
cartography [U] the science or art of making maps **cartographic(al)** [Wa5;B] of, connected with, or like cartography **-(al)ly** [adv Wa4] **cartographer** [C] a person skilled in cartography

Ordnance Survey [*the* GU] an organization which makes detailed maps of Great Britain and Ireland

L82 *verbs* : **maps**

map [T1] to make a map of: *There are still many places which can never be fully mapped.*
chart [T1 (*out*)] **1** to make a map or chart; to show or record on a chart: *The scientist hoped to chart the sea area between France and Britain.* **2** (*fig*) *infml* to make a rough plan, in words or writing: *The union leader charted out his ideas for a new prices and incomes agreement, but they were poorly received.*

L83 *nouns* : **views and vistas**

view 1 [U] ability (esp of the person or thing stated) to see or be seen from a particular place; sight: *My view of the stage was blocked by the big hat of the woman sitting in front of me. The car turned the corner and was lost to our view/passed out of view* (= could not be seen any more). *The valley was hidden from view in the mist. When we reached the top of the mountain, we came in view of* (= were able to see) *a wide plain below. A wide plain came into view* (= was able to be seen). *He fell off his horse in full view of his friends* (= seen by all, and himself able to see all of them). *There was no shelter within view* (= that could be seen) *anywhere.* **2** [C (*of*)] **a** something seen from a particular place, esp a stretch of pleasant country: *One splendid mountain view followed another during our journey. There's no view from my bedroom window except of some factory chimneys.* **b** a picture or photograph of a piece of scenery, a building, etc: *This artist has painted views of the rocky west coast.* **3** [S (*of*)] a special chance to see or examine someone or something: *Have you had a close view of the princess? If we stand at this window, we'll get a better view* (*of the procession*).
scene [C] **1** a view of a place: *There is a beautiful scene from our hotel window. He is a painter of street scenes.* **2** a place where an event or action happens: *These objects were found at the scene of the crime. Hastings was the scene of a great battle.*
scenery [U] natural surroundings, esp in beautiful and open country: *This mountain scenery is just what I like.*
panorama [C (*of*)] **1** a complete view of a wide stretch of land: *From here we can see a fine panorama of the plains.* **2** a continuously changing view or scene: *They watched the panorama of the country from the train window.* **3** (*fig*) a thorough representation in words or pictures: *This book gives a panorama of life in England 400 years ago.* **panoramic** [B] of, concerning or like a panorama **-ally** [adv Wa4]

vista [C (*of*)] **1** a distant view, to which the eye is directed between narrow limits, such as rows of trees: *The trees and bushes in the garden were cleverly arranged so as to give many delightful vistas.* **2** (*fig*) a set of events stretching far into the future or back into the past, as seen in the imagination: *After her husband's death she saw her life as an endless vista of sadness.*

L84 *nouns* : land and islands

[ALSO ⇒ L112]

land 1 [U] the solid dry part of the earth's surface: *The storm blew fiercely over land and sea. Land travel and sea travel are both pleasant.* **2** [U9] a part of the earth's surface all of the same natural type: *forest land*; [*in comb*] *highland*; *lowland* **3** [C] *esp emot* a part of the earth's surface forming a political whole; country; nation: *There have been wars between these two lands. It is the land of my fathers; I hope to return there one day.* (*fig*) *He travelled to the land of the dead.* **4** [U] ground owned as property: *You are on my land. Land prices have risen quickly.* **5** [U] ground used for farming: *He works on the land; he is a land worker.* **6** [U] life in the country as opposed to that in towns and cities: *We must go back to the land.*
land mass [C] a very large area of land
continent 1 [C] any of the seven main unbroken land masses: *Africa is a continent; Greenland is not.* **2** [*the* R *cap*] Europe without the British Isles: *He's gone for a holiday on the Continent; France and Italy, I think.*
territory 1 [C] an area of land, esp under one government, usu foreign or of a special kind: *Oklahoma was once a territory but now it is a state of the United States of America.* **2** [C] the land where a (usu stated) person or animal lives: *Wolves have a territory into which other wolves do not usually go.* **3** [U] land: *These people want more territory to live in.* **territorial** [B] **1** of or concerning a territory **2** (of an animal) keeping and defending a territory
island [C] **1** a piece of land encircled by water **2** (*fig*) anything standing alone or apart from similar things: *No man is an island. This place is an island of pleasure among the sorrows of life.*
isle [C] *esp poet* an island
islet [C] a small island
atoll [C] a ring-shaped island, made of coral [⇒ A104], partly or completely enclosing an area of sea water (**lagoon** [⇒ L86])
archipelago [C] **1** a number of small islands grouped together **2** an area of sea containing such a group

L85 *nouns* : peninsulas and capes [C]

peninsula a piece of land almost completely surrounded by water but joined to a larger mass of land: *Italy is a peninsula.*

isthmus a narrow area of land with sea on each side, joined to a large land mass at each end
cape a mass of land going out from a larger mass into the sea: *The ship went round the cape/the Cape of Good Hope* (*in South Africa*).
headland *also* **point** an area of land running out from the coast to the sea
promontory *fml* a headland
spur a length of high ground coming out from a range of higher mountains

L86 *nouns* : large areas of water

sea 1 [*the* R; U *often pl with sing meaning*] the great body of salty water that covers much of the earth's surface; the water of the earth as opposed to the land: *Boats were sailing on the sea. Most of the earth is covered by sea. Sea water came into the boat. She enjoys sea travel. The sea seems quiet today. The boat sailed into quieter seas. He likes the warm sea(s) around the south of France.* **2** [C *often cap, esp in names*] a large body of water smaller than an ocean, as **a** part of the ocean: *the North Sea* (northeast of Britain) **b** a body of water (mostly) enclosed by land: *the Dead Sea; the Mediterranean Sea* **3** [S9, *esp of*] (*fig*) a large mass or quantity regarded as being like one of these: *The actor looked out from the stage into a sea of faces. She was sitting at her desk in a sea of papers.* **4** [*the* R; *to* U] the job of a sailor or member of a navy: *He went to sea at the age of 17. He went into business for himself after leaving the sea.* **5** [(*the*) R] the shore of the ocean; seaside (*often in names of towns in the phr* **-on-Sea**): *I spent the summer at the sea. It's a town with a beautiful position on the sea. He goes to Clacton-on-Sea every year.* **6** [C9 *often pl with sing meaning*] a disturbance on the surface of a body of water: *The ship ran into strong winds and heavy seas.* **at sea 1** during a ship's voyage on the sea: *The ship and its crew were lost at sea. He spent three months at sea.* **2** (*fig*) *infml* lost (in mind); not understanding: *I don't understand politics; I'm (all) at sea when people talk about the government.* **beyond the sea(s)** *lit & pomp* far away across the sea; in a distant country: *He sailed away to begin a new life beyond the seas.* **by sea** on a ship, or using ships: *He went by airplane/by air and sent his heavy boxes by ship/by sea.* **put (out) to sea** to go out into the sea on a boat: *From Southampton they put (out) to sea for a long voyage.* **high seas** [P] the seas of the world which do not belong to any particular country: *The ship sank while sailing the high seas.*
ocean 1 [(*the*) U] the great mass of salt water that covers most of the earth: *He went on an ocean voyage.* **2** [C *often cap as part of a name*] any of the great seas into which this mass is divided: *the Atlantic Ocean*
lake [C *often cap as part of a name*] a large body of water surrounded by land: *Lake Champlain*
loch [C *often cap as part of a name*] *ScotE* a lake:

They went out on the loch in a boat. Loch Lomond is a beautiful place.

mere [C] (*esp in names in N England*) a pool of water: *Windermere is in Cumbria.*

reservoir 1 [C] a place where liquid is stored, esp water for a city: *We often go sailing on the local reservoir.* **2** [C9, *esp of*] (*fig*) a large supply (of facts or knowledge): *This book is a reservoir of information about the English language.*

lagoon [C] a lake of sea water, partly or completely separated from the sea, as by banks of sand or rock

L87 *nouns* : **small areas of water** [C]

pond an area of still water smaller than a lake: *Most farms have a pond from which cattle can drink. There was a duck pond near the house.*

pool a (small) pond: *There were pools of water everywhere after the rain. They went swimming in the pool under the trees. He built a swimming pool in his garden.*

puddle a small amount of rainwater lying in a slight hollow in the ground: *There are a lot of puddles in the road after the rain.*

L88 *nouns* : **bays and straits** [C]

bay a wide opening in a coastline; a part of the sea or of a large lake enclosed in a curve of the land: *The ship sailed into the bay. Botany Bay is in Australia.*

gulf 1 a large deep stretch of sea partly enclosed by land: *Some people call that place the Persian Gulf, others the Arabian Gulf.* **2** a deep hollow in the earth's surface: *The ground trembled and suddenly a great gulf opened before us.* **3** (*fig*) a great area of division or difference, esp between opinions: *There is a wide gulf between the two sides and it is unlikely that they can ever be brought into agreement.*

arm (of the sea) a place where the sea comes some distance inland; a very deep narrow bay

fjord, fiord a narrow arm of the sea between cliffs or steep slopes, esp in Norway

sea loch *ScotE* an arm of the sea

strait [*often pl with sing meaning*] a narrow passage of water between (and esp) connecting two seas: *the Malay Straits*

channel 1 a narrow sea passage connecting two seas or oceans: *The English Channel separates England and France and connects the Atlantic Ocean and the North Sea.* **2** the deepest part of a river, harbour, or sea passage: *The current in the river's main channel is too swift for boats. Ships must follow the channel into the port.*

L89 *nouns* : **tides and currents**

tide [C] **1** the regular rise and fall of large areas of water, esp the seas, due to the pull of the moon and the sun: *There are two tides every day. At high tide the water is farthest up the beach [⇒L92] and at low tide it is farthest out.* **2** a current of water caused by this: *Strong tides make swimming dangerous.* **3** (*fig*) a movement, as of public opinion: *We must wait for a change in the tide before introducing this unpopular law.*

ebb [S] **1** [*the*] the flow of the sea away from the shore; the going out of the tide: *The tide is on the ebb.* **2** (*fig*) decay; failure; low state (*esp in the phr* **at a low ebb**): *Fred's courage seems to be at rather a low ebb; let's try to make him a bit more cheerful.*

flow *also* **flood** [*the* S] the flow of the sea towards the shore; the coming in of the tide: *The tide is on the flow.*

ebb tide [C] the tide as it ebbs (= goes out)

flood tide [C] the tide as it flows (= comes in)

current [C] a continuously moving mass of liquid or gas, esp one flowing through slower-moving liquid or gas: *The weak swimmer was swept away by the strong current and was drowned. A cold current flowing off the coast reduces temperatures in summer. The current is strongest in the middle of the river. He could feel the air currents.*

undercurrent [C] **1** a deep current, flowing below other currents, esp in a different direction **2** (*fig*) a hidden tendency in general feelings, opinions, etc: *There was an undercurrent of discontent.*

eddy [C] a circular movement of water, wind, dust, mist, smoke, etc: *The little paper boat was caught in an eddy and spun round and round in the water.*

course [C] the way or direction in which anything, esp water, moves: *The river took its course down from the hills to the sea. He followed the course of the river.* (*fig*) *In the course of time things got better.*

flood [C] **1** a (great) flow of water over land that is usu dry: *We had several bad floods this year.* **2** [(*of*)] (*fig*) a large amount: *We had a flood of letters today.*

spate [S9, *esp of*] **1** *esp BrE* a flood **2** (*fig*) a large number or amount, esp coming together in time: *There has been a spate of accidents on this road.* **in spate** full of rushing water: *The river was in (full) spate.*

L90 *verbs* : **tides and currents**

ebb [I0 (*away*)] **1** (of the sea) to flow away from the shore: *The tide is beginning to ebb.* **2** (*fig*) to grow less; become slowly lower and lower: *Fred's courage was beginning to ebb away, as he saw what a long distance he still had to climb*

flow [I0] (of the sea) to flow in towards the shore: *The tide is flowing strongly today.*

eddy [I0] to move round and round: *A little smoke eddied above the ashes of the fire.* (*fig*) *The crowd eddied about in the market-place.*

surge [IØ] (of water, etc) to move forward strongly: *The sea surged against the rocks.*

foam [Wv4;IØ (*up*)] to produce a large number of very small whitish-looking balls of air or gas (**bubbles**): *The liquid began to foam. The foaming waves struck the rocks.*

flood [IØ;T1] to flow over (a place that is usu dry): *The river is flooding. The sea flooded the town. We were flooded out* (= completely flooded). **flooding** [U] an occasion of water flowing or spreading where it does not usu go: *There was some bad flooding in the city last year.*

channel [T1 (*off*)] to cause to pass through or along a channel; send in a particular direction: *The water channelled its way through the earth.* (*fig*) *Some of the money has been channelled off for other purposes.*

funnel 1 [X9] to pass through or as if through a funnel [⇒ H153]: *He funnelled the oil into the bottle. The information is funnelled to a central point from many different places.* **2** [L9] (esp of something large or made up of many parts) to pass through a narrow space: *The large crowd funnelled out of the gates after the football match.* **3** [T1] to form into the shape of a funnel: *He funnelled his hands and whistled through them.*

L91 *nouns* : **waves**

wave [C *often pl*] a raised curving line of water on the surface esp of the sea, esp one of a number at even distances from each other: *The waves rose and fell.*

ripple 1 [C] a very small wave; a gentle waving movement: *There are ripples on a pool when the wind blows.* **2** [C] a wave-like mark: *The sea leaves ripples on the sand.* **3** [S9] a sound of or like gently running water: *I heard the ripple of the stream. There came a ripple of laughter from the crowd at the speaker's little joke.*

roller [C] a long heavy wave (on the coast): *He likes to swim among the Atlantic rollers.*

breaker [C] a large wave with a white top that rolls onto the shore

swell [S] one or more waves, esp when long and unbroken

tidal wave [C] **1** any very large, dangerous, and unusual sea wave **2** (*fig*) anything thought to be like this

foam [U] **1** a whitish mass of small balls of air or gas (**bubbles**) on the surface of a liquid or on skin: *The breaking waves were edged with foam. When the horse had finished the race its sides were wet with foam.* **2** any chemical substance in this form, such as one used in controlling dangerous fires

surf [U] the white foam formed by waves when they break on rocks, a shore, etc

surge [C] **1** the forward movement of esp water, esp in a wave: *the surge of the sea* **2** (*fig*) any strong movement like this: *feeling a surge of pity for someone*

L92 *nouns* : **coasts and shores**

coast 1 [C] the land next to the sea; seashore: *The ship was wrecked on the coast. There are dangerous rocks on Britain's western coast.* **2** [the R (*sometimes cap*)] an area bordering the sea: *Many old people go and live on the coast when they stop working. The town is on the South Coast.*

shore [C;U] the land along the edge of a large body of water: *The walked along the shore. She saw a boat about a mile from/off shore.* **on shore** on land; away from one's ship: *The sailors were warned not to get into trouble while they were on shore.*

line [C *usu in comb*] the line or edge of a coast, shore, etc: *The coastline of Western Scotland is very uneven.*

beach [C] **1** a shore of an ocean, sea, or lake, or the bank of a river covered by sand, smooth stones, or larger pieces of rock **2** a seashore area: *They were lying on the beach in the sun.*

sands [P] a stretch of sand: *He drove across the burning sands of the desert. The children were playing on the sands.*

shingle [U] small rough rounded pieces of stone lying in masses along a seashore: *It can be painful to walk on shingle with bare feet.*

L93 *nouns* : **rivers and streams** [C]

river a wide natural stream of water flowing between banks into a lake, into another wider stream, or into the sea: *They want to go swimming in the river/sailing on the river. They sailed down/up the river Amazon.* (*fig*) *Rivers of blood were spilt during the war.*

stream 1 a natural flow of water, usu smaller than a river: *He crossed the stream.* **2** anything flowing or moving on continuously: *a stream of people into and out of the house* **3** [*esp in comb*] (the direction of) a current of water: *They travelled upstream/downstream* (= against/ with the current).

torrent a very fast flow of liquid, esp water in rivers or as rain: *The mountain streams become torrents when the snow begins to melt. The rain was falling in torrents.* (*fig*) *She used a torrent of bad language to show what she thought of him.* **torrential** [B] of or like a torrent: *Torrential rains fell.* **-ly** [adv]

brook a small stream

burn *ScotE* a brook or stream

L94 *nouns* : **springs and tributaries** [C]

spring [*often pl*] a place where water comes naturally from the ground: *It is a town with mineral/hot springs. He drank from a clear mountain spring.*

source [(*of*)] **1** the place where a stream of water starts: *Where is the source of this river?*

2 (*fig*) a place from which something comes: *Can you find the source of the engine trouble?* **3** (*fig*) a person or thing that supplies information: *The reporter refused to name his sources.*

tributary [(*of*)] a stream or river that flows into a larger stream or river: *Are these streams tributaries of the Clyde?*

feeder *not fml* a tributary

L95 *nouns* : **river mouths** [C]

estuary the wide lower part or mouth of a river, which the sea enters at high tide: *They like to go sailing on the Thames estuary.*

mouth (river) an estuary: *The boat entered the mouth of a large river/a large river mouth.*

firth [*often cap esp in names*] *ScotE* an estuary or river mouth: *Edinburgh is near the Firth of Forth* (= of the river Forth). *Inverness is near the Moray Firth.*

delta a piece of low land shaped like a △ where a river branches out towards the sea: *The Nile Delta is in Egypt.*

L96 *nouns* : **falls and rapids**

waterfall [C] water falling straight down over rocks or an edge, sometimes from a great height **falls** [P *often cap in names*] a large broad waterfall: *He visited the Niagara Falls when he went to North America.*

cascade [C] **1** a steep high usu small waterfall, esp one part of a bigger waterfall **2** (*fig*) anything that is like this: *a cascade of flowers; a cascade of golden hair*

rapids [P] a part of a river where the water moves very fast over rocks **shoot the rapids** (of a boat) to pass quickly down this part of a river

L97 *nouns & verbs* : **fountains and sprays**

fountain [C] **1** [(*of*)] a flow of liquid, esp rising straight into the air **2** (an apparatus of pipes, sometimes hidden inside beautiful stone figures or bowls set in an ornamental lake or smaller piece of water in a garden, or other open space, producing) a stream of water that shoots straight up into the air **3** [(*of*)] (*fig*) the place where something begins or is supplied: *The ruler was respected by his people as the fountain of honour.* **4** *poet* a natural spring of water, rising out of the ground

jet 1 [C] a narrow stream of liquid, gas, etc, coming forcefully out of a small hole: *The firemen directed jets of water at the burning house.* **2** [C] a narrow opening from which this is forced out: *Put a match to the gas jet to light the gas.* **3** [IØ (*out*)] to come out as a jet

spray 1 [U] water in very small drops blown from the sea, a waterfall, etc **2** [U; C] (a can or other container holding) liquid to be sent

out in a spray under pressure: *He used a quick-drying spray paint. Did you bring along some insect spray? You can get this polish in a tube or in a spray.* **3** [T1 (*with*); IØ] to throw or force out liquid in small drops upon (a surface, person, field of crops, etc): *He sprayed the wall with paint. Our wheat needs spraying soon.*

spurt 1 [C] a short sudden strong increase in the flow of a liquid, in activity, speed, etc **2** [IØ (*out, up*)] to flow suddenly and strongly: *Blood spurted out of the cut in his arm.*

L98 *nouns* : **ditches and canals** [C]

ditch a long narrow not very deep V- or U-shaped passage cut into the ground, usu for water to flow through

trench 1 a long narrow hole cut in the ground; ditch **2** a deep ditch dug in the ground as a protection for soldiers: *My grandfather fought in the trenches in the First World War.*

channel 1 the bed of a stream of water: *When it rains water flows down this channel. We saw many dried rocky river channels as we crossed the desert.* **2** a passage for liquids: *There's a channel in the middle of the street to help water flow away when it rains. The rain water is caught in the channel and taken to the garden through pipes.* **3** [*often pl*] (*fig*) any course or way along which information travels or by which things are done: *He claims to have his own channels for finding out what is going on. Go through the official channels if you want the government to help.* **4** (*fig*) a way, course of direction of thought or action: *He needs a new channel for his activities.*

canal a waterway dug in the ground **a** to allow ships or boats to travel along it: *The Panama Canal joins two oceans.* **b** to bring water to or remove water from an area: *Canals have been built to take water to the desert.*

lock a stretch of water closed off by gates, esp on a canal, so that the level can be raised or lowered to move boats up or down a slope

L99 *nouns* : **banks**

bank [C] **1** land along the side of a river, lake, etc: *Shakespeare's theatre was on the bank of the Thames. They sat on the river bank. They live on the banks of the Nile.* **2** earth which is heaped up in a field or garden, often making a border or division: *In the southwest of England the little country roads often run between high banks.* **3** *also* **sandbank** sand under a shallow part of a sea: *The Dogger Bank in the North Sea can be dangerous for ships.* **4** a mass of snow, clouds, mud, etc: *The banks of dark cloud promised a heavy storm.* **5** a slope made at bends in a road or race-track, so that they are safer for cars to go round

-side [*comb form*] the land at the side of a river, lake, sea, etc: *riverside; lakeside; seaside*

embankment [C] a wide wall of stones or earth, which is built to keep a river from overflowing its banks, or to carry a road or railroad over low ground: *We must throw up an embankment to stop the river from flooding the town. The embankment has collapsed! We walked along the Thames Embankment.*

L100 nouns : dams and sluices [C]

dam a wall or bank built to keep back water: *The Aswan Dam helps to control the River Nile in Egypt.*

weir 1 a wall across a river, stopping the water above it **2** a wooden fence across a stream for catching fish

sluice a passage for water with an opening (a **sluice gate** or **sluice valve**) through which the flow can be controlled or stopped

L101 nouns : hills and mountains

| smaller & genl | hill |
| larger | mountain |

hill [C] a raised part of the earth's surface, not so high as a mountain and not usu so bare, rocky, etc: *There were several low/high hills near the town. The Aravalli Hills are in India.*

mountain 1 [C] a very large and high hill, esp of bare or snow-covered rock: *He looked down from the top of the mountain to the valley far below. He travelled along the mountain paths and met some mountain goats. The Rocky Mountains are in the United States.* **2** [C (of) often pl] a very large amount, mass, etc: *She has a mountain of dirty clothes to wash. Each morning the minister has to read mountains of papers and reports.*

mount [A (cap in place names)] a mountain: *Mount Olympus is in Greece.*

ben [C esp cap in place names] ScotE a mountain: *Ben Nevis is the highest mountain in Scotland.*

-side [comb form] the side of a mountain, hill: *mountainside; hillside*

slope [C] **1** a surface that slopes; a piece of ground going up or down: *He climbed the steep slope. They were on a ski slope/the lower slopes of the mountain.* **2** a degree of sloping; a measure of an angle from a level direction: *a slope of 30 degrees*

range [C9] a connected line (of mountains, hills, etc): *The Andes are a high mountain range. There are many ranges of hills in India.*

foothills [P] the lower parts of a mountain range, esp near a plain

L102 nouns : the highest parts of mountains and hills

top [comb form] the highest point of a mountain or hill: *mountaintop, hilltop*

peak [C] **1 a** a sharply pointed mountain top: *The (mountain) peaks are covered with snow all the year round.* **b** a whole mountain with a sharp top: *Here the high peaks begin to rise from the plain.* **2** a thing that curves to a point above a surface: *The wind blew the waves into great peaks.* **3** [C] the highest point, level, etc, esp of a varying amount, development, etc: *He brought the crowd to a peak of excitement. Sales have reached a new peak. This is a peak year for sales. The roads are full of traffic at peak hours.*

pinnacle [C] **1** a thin tall pointed rock or rocky mountain top **2** [(of) usu sing] the highest point or degree: *He was then at the pinnacle of his success.* **3** a pointed stone ornament like a small tower, built on a roof esp in old churches and castles

summit 1 [C (of)] the top, esp the highest point on the top of a mountain **2** [S9, esp of] (fig) the highest point, degree, etc: *He was at the summit of his powers.* **3** [A] (fig) the official position of heads of state: *a summit meeting* (= a meeting of leaders) **4** [C] (fig) a meeting between heads of state

L103 nouns : plateaus [C]

plateau 1 a large stretch of level land much higher than the land around it **2** (fig) a period of time during which the active development of something is not continued: *Business has now reached a plateau but we hope it will begin to increase again soon.*

tableland not fml a plateau

mesa esp AmE a plateau with steep sides, esp in the southwest of the USA

butte esp AmE a hill or small mesa rising above the flat country around it

L104 nouns : cliffs [C]

cliff a high very steep face of rock, ice, earth, etc: *He fell off a cliff into the sea. The White Cliffs of Dover are in Kent.* **cliff-face** the surface of a cliff: *He climbed up the cliff-face.*

crag a high steep rough rock or mass of rocks: *Salisbury Crags rise above the city of Edinburgh.*

escarpment 1 a long cliff on a mountainside **2** a steep slope just below the wall of a fort

precipice a steep or almost upright side of a high rock, mountain, or cliff

drop [usu sing] a fall: *There's a 100 ft. drop from these cliffs.*

abyss a great hole which appears to have no bottom: *He fell into an abyss.* (fig) *He was in an abyss of hopelessness after his wife left him.*

L105 *adjectives, etc* : **hills and mountains** [B]

hilly [Wa1] (of country or roads) full of hills
mountainous 1 full of or containing mountains: *Because of the mountainous nature of the country, the army couldn't advance quickly.* **2** (*fig*) very large or high: *mountainous debts; mountainous waves*
craggy [Wa1] full of or like crags
steep [Wa1] rising or falling quickly or at a large angle: *The hillside was very steep. It was too steep a hill to get up on a bicycle. There was a steep rise in prices/a steep drop in living standards.* **-ly** [adv] **-ness** [U]
precipitous 1 dangerously steep: *A precipitous path led up the mountain side.* **2** like (the edge of) a precipice; frighteningly high above the ground: *They looked down from the precipitous height of the church tower.* **-ly** [adv] **-ness** [U]
sheer [Wa1] **1** very steep; (almost) straight up and down without a break: *It was a sheer drop of a hundred feet to the sea, down a sheer cliff.* **2** [*also* adv] straight up or down: *The mountain rises sheer from the plain.*

L106 *nouns, etc* : **holes, fissures, caves, etc**

hole 1 [C] an opening or (esp deep) space in something solid: *He dug some holes in the garden and planted some bushes. There is a hole in the wall; we can get through it. I've a hole in my left sock.* **2** [C] (*fig*) *infml* a difficulty: *I'm in a hole; can you help me?* **3** [C] (*fig*) *infml* an uninteresting place: *What a hole that town is!* **4** [T1 *often pass*] to make a hole in: *The boat was holed by a large rock.* **5** [T1] to put in a hole: *The golfer [⇒K198] holed the ball from a distance of ten feet.*
hollow [C] a wide shallow hole, esp in a surface: *The hollow was full of trees but the higher ground was covered in grass. There were hollows under her eyes; she had not been sleeping well.*
socket [C] an opening, hollow place, or machine part that forms a holder or into which something fits: *His eyes nearly jumped from their sockets in surprise. Fit a candle/an electric light into a socket.*
crack [C] a narrow hole or opening; a line where something has broken but has not separated (much): *There were several cracks in the wall/rock.*
leak 1 [C] a crack or hole which allows a liquid or gas to flow in or out when it should not: *There's a leak in the water pipe; water is getting out.* **2** [C] liquid or gas flowing in or out in this way: *There was a gas leak and it caused a fire.* (*fig*) *There has been a leak of information.* **3** [I∅; T1] to (cause to) flow in or out through a leak: *The water leaked out/leaked from the pipe. The boat*

is leaking badly. (*fig*) *He leaked the news to his friends. News of the changes has leaked out.*
crevice [C] a narrow hole, crack, or opening, esp in rock: *He found a crevice in the rock and climbed down it.*
crevasse [C] a deep open crack, esp in thick ice: *The man fell into a crevasse.*
fissure [C] *tech* a deep and usu large crack in the ground, a mountain, etc
cave [C] a deep natural hollow place **a** underground, usu with an opening to the surface **b** in the side of a cliff or hill
cavern [C] a large deep cave
grotto [C] **1** a natural cave, esp of limestone, or an ornamental one made in a garden and ornamented with shells **2** a small cave-shaped shrine for religious worship
pothole [C] **1** a deep round hole in the surface of rock by which water enters and flows underground often through a cave **2** the cave itself
stalactite [C] a sharp downward-pointing part of a cave roof formed over a long time by mineral-containing water dropping from the roof
stalagmite [C] an upward-pointing part of a cave floor formed by drops from a stalactite and often joining it to form a solid pillar

L107 *nouns* : **valleys** [C]

valley 1 the land lying between two lines of hills or mountains often with a river running through it: *In the winter, the cattle are brought down from the mountains to the shelter of the valley.* **2** [C9 *usu sing*] the land through which the stated river or a great river system flows: *the Thames valley; the valley of the Ganges*
glen a narrow mountain valley, esp in Scotland or Ireland
gorge *also* **canyon** a deep narrow steep-sided valley usu with a river flowing through
ravine a deep narrow valley with steep sides
gully 1 a small narrow valley cut esp into a hillside by heavy rain **2** a deep ditch or other small waterway
defile a narrow passage, esp through mountains
gulch a narrow stony valley with steep sides formed by a rushing stream, esp in the western USA

L108 *nouns* : **plains, deserts, etc**

plain [C] a large stretch of flat land: *He is a farmer on the Great Plains of the USA.*
savanna(h) [C; U] an open flat stretch of grassy land in a warm and sometimes wet region
prairie [C; U] (esp in North America) a wide treeless grassy plain
range [C; U] land, esp prairie, where esp cattle can move about and eat the grass freely
moor [C] a wide, open, often raised area of land, covered with rough grass or low bushes that is not farmed because of its bad soil, and, in

Britain, is often used as a place where birds are kept safely, to be shot for sport at a certain season of the year

scrub [U] (land covered with) low trees and bushes

desert [C] a large area of land, esp if covered with sand, where no or few plants grow: *The north of Africa is mainly desert. The Sahara Desert is in North Africa. Mauretania is a desert country.*

oasis [C] an area in a desert which has water and where plants can grow

wilderness [U; C] land that has no signs of houses, roads, people, etc; a desert or other place far from where people usu live: *They lived in the wilderness/in a wilderness of stones, sea, and sky.*

L109 *nouns* : **marshes**

marsh [C; U] (a piece of) land that is all or partly wet, because of its low position

swamp [C; U] (an area of) soft wet land: *The land is no use for growing crops; it's mainly swamp.*

bog [C; U] *esp IrE* a swamp, esp one containing a great deal of decaying vegetable matter: *This path crosses five miles of bog/bogland.*

morass 1 [C] a stretch of low ground that is soft and wet to a great depth so that it is dangerous for walking **2** [S (*of*)] (*fig*) a difficult position or an evil state of living, from which it is almost impossible to free oneself: *How can he ever get out of this morass of trouble?*

quagmire [C] *esp emot & lit* a swamp or morass

quicksand [U] wet sand which pulls in any living things that try to cross it

L110 *nouns* : **woods and forests**

wood [C *often pl*] an area of land covered with trees: *They entered a wood. The woods are beautiful at that time of year.*

forest 1 [C; U] (a large area of land thickly covered with) trees and bushes, either growing wild or planted for some purpose: *A large part of central Africa is made up of thick forest. The forests of Canada produce wood for building. A forest is larger than a wood.* **2** [C (*of*) usu sing] (*fig*) a large number of upright objects close together: *When the teacher asked the boys an easy question, a forest of hands shot up.* **3** [C *sometimes cap as part of name*] *old use* a piece of land, with or without trees, where deer and other animals were and sometimes still are kept or hunted: *There are no trees in the deer forests of Scotland. Windsor Forest is in England.*

jungle 1 [C; U] a tropical forest too thick to walk through easily: *The jungle can be both beautiful and dangerous. He was studying jungle animals and birds.* (*fig*) *Without care, your garden will become a jungle.* (*fig*) *the jungle of business of*

the big city **2** [C] (*fig*) a disorderly mass of things that is hard to understand: *He could not understand the jungle of tax laws.*

L111 *nouns* : **small groups of trees, etc** [C]

thicket a thick growth of bushes and small trees: *The fox hid in the thicket where the dogs could not reach it.*

copse *also* **coppice** a wood of small trees or bushes

glade an open space without trees in a wood or forest

grove 1 a group of trees, planted or natural, sometimes (esp of fruit trees) in a garden: *an orange grove* **2** *old use* a group of trees forming a centre of worship

clump [(*of*)] a group of trees, bushes, plants, etc, growing together: *a clump of bushes*

clearing an area of land cleared of trees but surrounded by other trees: *We camped in a small clearing in the middle of the forest.*

L112 *nouns* : **general land terms** [C; U]

[ALSO ⇒ L84]

lowland	land or	plains
highland	country that	mountains
woodland	is (mainly)	woods
moorland		moors [⇒ L108]
scrubland		scrub [⇒ L108]
marshland		marsh [⇒ L109]
swampland		swamp [⇒ L109]
wetlands [P]		wet

L113 *nouns* : **sea level and eye level, etc**

sea level [R] the average height of the sea, used as a standard for measuring heights on land: *Mount Everest is 29,028 feet above sea level. Death Valley, California is 280 feet below sea level.*

waterline [C] *naut* the position which the water reaches along a ship's side

tidemark [C] **1** the mark left by the tide [⇒ L89] on a beach **2** (*fig*) anything like this

eye level [R] the height or level of one's eyes: *It was above eye level from where he was, so he had to look up at it.*

horizon 1 [(*the*) S] the limit of one's view across the surface of the earth, where the sky seems to meet the earth or sea **2** [C] (*fig*) the limit of one's thoughts (*esp in the phr* **broaden one's horizons**)

landmark [C] **1** an easily recognizable object,

such as a tall tree or building, by which one can tell one's position **2** (*fig*) something that marks an important point or change, as in a person's life or the development of knowledge **3** something marking the limits of a piece of land

L114 *adjectives, etc* : **relating to land and sea** [B]

terrestrial [Wa5] **1** of or related to the earth (rather than the moon, space, etc): *terrestrial life* **2** of, being, related to, or living on land (rather than in water): *the terrestrial parts of the earth's surface* **-ly** [adv]
continental 1 [Wa5] of or relating to a continent [⇨ L84] **2** [*cap*] belonging to Europe without the British Isles **3** [C] a person living on a continent, esp [*cap*] on the Continent of Europe
insular *fml* **1** [Wa5] of, concerning, or like an island: *Britain is an insular country.* **2** (*fig*) narrow (in mind); concerned with the interests of a small group, country, etc: *Because Britons have such different habits from other European countries some people say they are insular.*
peninsular of, relating to, or like a peninsula [⇨ L85]: *Wellington defeated Napoleon's armies in the Peninsular War* (= in the Iberian Peninsula).
marine [Wa5] **1** of, near, living in, found in, or obtained from the sea: *The rocks are covered by marine plants. Marine products come from sea animals and plants.* **2** of ships and their goods and trade at sea, esp concerning the navy
maritime [Wa5] relating to or connected with the sea: *Britain is a maritime country because it is an island and depends on ships. Maritime trade is important to Britain.*
oceanic [Wa5] of, concerning, or like an ocean [⇨ L86]
coastal [Wa5] of or related to the coast: *Ships should not enter shallow coastal waters.*
aquatic [Wa5] **1** living in or on water: *aquatic plants/animals* **2** happening in or on water: *Aquatic sports including swimming and rowing.*
tidal of, relating to, having, or like a tide or tides [⇨ L89]
amphibious able to live or move both on land and in water
cavernous 1 containing many caves or caverns: *The cavernous soft rocks of this area attract many scientists.* **2** very large and deep; being or suggesting a cavern **3** (of a sound) hollow-sounding
arboreal [Wa5] *tech* of, concerned with, or living in trees: *Monkeys are mainly arboreal animals.*
alpine 1 of or concerning any high mountain, esp the Alps **2** very high **3** (of plants) growing on parts of mountains that are too high for trees to grow on

L115 *nouns* : **natural disasters** [C]

earthquake *also infml* **quake** a violent shaking of part of the earth: *Earthquakes are common in Turkey and Iran; they are part of an earthquake zone* (= area).
volcano a hole in the surface of the earth out of which fire, smoke, and hot liquid rock (**lava**) come and which forms a mountain: *Mount Vesuvius in Italy is a volcano.* **volcanic** [B] of, concerning, or like a volcano: *These hills were formed by volcanic action.* **-ally** [adv Wa4]
crater 1 the usu large round hole at the top of a volcano **2** a hole made by a bomb, large shell, explosion or large object hitting a surface: *The surface of the moon is full of craters probably caused by falling meteorites* [⇨ L5].
avalanche 1 a large mass of snow and ice crashing down a mountainside: *The climbers were killed by/in an avalanche.* **2** [*usu sing*] (*fig*) a large quantity that has arrived suddenly: *She got an avalanche of letters. His own complaints started an avalanche of complaints from everybody in the hall.*
landslide a fall of a great amount of rock and earth from the side of a mountain, etc: *The climbers were killed by a landslide.* (*fig*) *The election was a landslide* (*victory*) *for our party.*
landslip a (usu smaller) landslide

Time generally

L130 *nouns* : **time and eternity**

time 1 [U] a continuous measurable condition from the past through the present and into the future: *The universe exists in space and time.* **2** [U] the passing of the days, months, and years, taken as a whole **3** [U9] a system of measuring this: *British Summer Time; European Central Time* **4** [(*the*) R] a particular point in the day stated in hours, minutes, seconds, etc: *What's the time? What time is it? What time is she coming?* **5** [U] an unlimited period in the future: *Time will heal your wounds. In time you'll forget. Only time will tell if you're right.*
eternity 1 [U] time without end; the state of time after death, which is said to be for ever: *Do you believe in eternity?* (*fig*) *This bomb will blow us all to eternity* (= kill us). **2** [C] a very long time which seems endless: *I was so anxious that every moment seemed an eternity.*

L131 *nouns, etc* : **history**

[ALSO ⇨ N17]

history 1 [U] the study of events in the past, such as those of a nation, arranged in order from the earlier to the later, esp that of the rulers and government of a country, social and trade conditions: *He studied the history of*

Rome. She has a lot of history books. **2** [U] the study of the development of anything: *There have been many changes in the history of the English language.* **3** [C] **a** a (written) account of history: *He wrote a short history of the last war.* **b** *old use* a historical play **4** [C] **a** any set of interesting events: *The village has no known history.* **b** a long story including details of many events: *She told me her life history.* **make history** to do or be concerned in something which will be recorded and remembered: *Great leaders make history.*

chronology 1 [U] the science which measures time and gives dates to events **2** [C] a list or table arranged according to the order of time: *The book is a chronology of man's history since the 10th Century.* **3** [C] the arrangement of events according to the order of time: *Do you agree with his chronology of events in the 13th century?*

genealogy 1 [U] (the study of) the history of members of a family from the past to the present **2** [C] an account of this for one particular family, esp when shown in a drawing with lines and names spreading like the branches of a tree **3** [U] the study of the development of any form of life or subject which changes through time, such as language **genealogical** [Wa5;B] of, connected with, or like genealogy **-ally** [adv Wa4]

family tree [C] *not fml* a genealogy (def 2): *He traced his family tree back to the 17th century.*

timetable 1 [C] a list showing the times of events, lessons, arrivals, departures, activities, etc: *Show me the class/railway timetable please.* **2** [T1] to give a time in a timetable for: *The meeting is timetabled for 3 pm.*

schedule 1 [C] *esp AmE* a timetable; list of events, activities, etc: *Has he made the examination schedule yet? Everything went according to schedule* (= happened as planned). **2** [T1] to put into a schedule: *The meeting is scheduled for 3 pm.*

anachronism 1 [C; U] the act, by mistake or intentionally, of placing something in the wrong period of time: *It was an anachronism to say that Julius Caesar looked at the clock.* **2** [C] a person or thing that is or appears to be in the wrong period of time: *Sailing boats are a pleasant anachronism in this age of fast travel.* **anachronistic** [B] not in the right or expected period of time: *'Sailing boats are anachronistic nowadays,' he said.* **-ally** [adv Wa4]

L132 *nouns* : **times, periods, and intervals**

time 1 [S9; U] a limited period as between two events, for the completion of an action, etc: *It will take you a long time to learn French properly. How much time will you need to think about my plan? Take more time and care over your work.* **2** [U9] the point at which something is expected to happen: *He died before his*

time (= too early in life). *The mother was nearing her time* (= the time she is expected to give birth). **3** [U9] the regular period of work of a worker: *I work full time, but my wife only works part time.* **4** [U] the rate of pay received for an hour's work: *I get time and a half for working on Saturdays and double time on Sundays.* **5** [U] free or spare time: *I have no time to deal with the matter today; I'm too busy. I doubt if he ever has time to watch television.*

while [S] a time, esp a short one: *Just wait for a while and then I'll help you.*

period [C] a stretch of time with a beginning and an end, but not always of measured length: *She worked for a period as a teacher. There were long periods when we had no news of him.*

spell [C (*of*)] *not usu fml* a length of time: *He did a spell of work in Australia. She likes to work for short spells over a long period; she says she gets more done that way.*

interval [C] a stretch of time between two events: *The interval between his visits was about a month. He came at intervals of about a month.*

cycle [C] a set of events happening in a certain order again and again: *Weather conditions often happen in cycles. There has been a cycle of too much work, then too little, then too much again.*

L133 *nouns* : **duration and transition**

duration [U] **1** continuance in time: *It was an illness of short duration.* **2** the time during which something exists or lasts, usu something non-material: *He will be in hospital for the duration of the school year.* **for the duration** for as long as something lasts: *We're in this business together for the duration.*

course [S (*of*)] (esp of time) onward movement: *In the course of time he became very famous. In the course of their talks they disagreed many times.*

passage [S (*of*)] *often fml* (of time) passing: *With the passage of time/of the years he became very rich.*

transition [C; U] (an example of) the act of changing or passing from one form, state, subject, or place to another over a period of time: *Our party supports a peaceful transition to rule by elected representatives of the people. The transition from childhood to manhood is often a difficult time for a young man. They were living in a period of transition.*

L134 *nouns* : **intervals and breaks**

interval [C] a stretch of time between two events esp in the middle of a play, concert, etc: *I like to eat ice cream in the interval. There was an interval of 20 minutes between the two parts of the concert.* **at intervals** (**of**) happening regularly after equal periods of time or appearing at equal distances (of): *twenty minute intervals; The seeds are planted at intervals of three inches/at three-inch intervals.*

intermission 1 [U] *fml* the act of pausing: *He worked 3 hours without intermission.* **2** [C] a pause before something re-starts, esp the time between two parts of a film

interlude [C] **1** a free period of time between activities: *Holidays are short interludes in a life of work.* **2 a** the time between parts of a play, concert, etc **b** a short play, talk, piece of music, etc, which are used to fill this time

break [C] *not fml* a pause for rest; period of time between activities: *There was a break in the concert. Let's have a coffee break.*

L135 *verbs* : **pausing, hesitating, and lapsing** [I0]

pause to make a pause; stop for a short time: *Why did you pause? Go on. He paused over the word as he did not know how to pronounce it.*

hesitate 1 [*also* I3] **a** to pause in or before an action: *Don't hesitate to go. He who hesitates is lost* (= loses his chance; will never succeed). **b** to be slow in deciding: *She hesitated over the choice between the two dresses. I'm hesitating about whether to go.* **2** (*as a polite form*) to be unwilling; find it unpleasant: *I hesitate to ask you, but will you lend me some money?*

lapse 1 [(*into*)] to sink, pass, or fall, slowly or by degrees: *He lapsed into silence.* **2** [(*from*)] to fail with regard to correct behaviour, belief, duty, etc **3** (of business agreements, titles, rights, etc) to come to an end, esp because of disuse, death, or failure to claim

L136 *nouns* : **pausing, hesitating, and lapsing**

pause [C (*in*)] a short but noticeable break (in activity or speech): *There was a pause in the conversation. The speaker had to make a pause, as he had forgotten what he was going to say. There was a pause in the game while the players had a drink.*

hesitation 1 [U] the act of hesitating: *Without hesitation, I would say. . . . I have no hesitation in saying. . . .* **2** [C] an example of this

lapse [C] **1** a gradual passing away, esp of time **2** a short period of time in the past **3** *law* the ending of a title, right, etc, owing to disuse, death, or failure to claim **4** a failure in correct behaviour, belief, duty, etc **5** a small fault or mistake, as one of memory, esp one that is quickly put right

L137 *nouns* : **moments and instants** [C]

moment a period of time so short that it may be considered as having no length; a point in time: *I had to think for a moment before I remembered his name. We had time for only a few moments' conversation. Wait a moment! He said he's written the book at odd moments* (= short periods of time when he had nothing else to do). *Eric's big moment in the play comes in the second act when he's alone and everyone's attention is fixed on him. She told her boy, 'It's very late; go to bed this moment!' I've only this moment* (= just) *remembered that I have to see the doctor this evening. The nation's at war; this is not the moment to quarrel among ourselves. Choose your moment well if you wish to ask your employer for higher wages.* **at any moment** very soon: *The train should arrive at any moment.* **at the last moment** only just in time; just before an activity starts: *He is never late for school, but he often comes in to the classroom at the last moment.* **not for a moment** at no time; not at all: *I wasn't for a moment deceived by his friendly words.* **the moment (that)** just as soon as; at exactly the time when: *We had not met for 20 years, but I recognized him the moment (that) I saw him. She knew he wasn't English the moment he began to speak.*

instant 1 a very short moment of time: *Not for an instant did I believe he had lied.* **2** (at) a point in time: *The instant I saw him I knew he was my brother.*

minute *infml* a very short space of time: *I'll be ready in a minute* (= very soon). *Are you ready yet?—No, but I won't be a minute.* (= I'll be ready very soon). *I'll wait a minute or two longer.*

tick *BrE infml* a moment: *I'll be with you in a tick.*

L138 *nouns* : **times and occasions**

[ALSO ⇒ N17]

time 1 [C *often pl*] a period or moment and the particular experience connected with it: *We had a good time at the party. The 1930s were hard times.* **2** [U *often in comb*] a particular point in the year, day, etc; the moment for a particular activity or event: *When it's time to go to bed I'll tell you. It's bedtime now! Springtime and summertime are very pleasant here.* **3** [C] the right occasion: *There is a time for everything.* **4** [R9] the particular moment at which something happens: *What time's opening/closing time here?* **5** [C] the period in which an action is completed, esp a race: *Her time was just under 4 minutes.*

occasion [C] *often fml* **1** a time when something happens: *On that occasion I was not at home.* **2** a proper time for something to happen: *A birthday is no occasion for tears.* **3** a special event or ceremony: *His wedding was a great occasion.* **4** an event that leads to other events; direct cause: *The occasion of the party was her return home.* **have (no) occasion to** to have (no) need or reason to: *I rarely have occasion to go* *there.* **on the occasion of** at the time of (a certain event) **rise to the occasion** to do well what has to be done at a given time **sense of occasion 1** a feeling for what is the right social behaviour at any particular event **2** an ability to recognize the special qualities that make any particular event different from or better than another

point [C] *not usu fml* the moment when something happens: *At that point he got up and left the room.*

L139 *adjectives* : **long and short**

long [Wa1] **1** [B] covering a great time: *He's taking a long time to get here.* **2** [B; E] covering a certain time: *How long is the speech? It's an hour long.* **3** [B] which seems to last more than is wished: *It was a long day, waiting for the news. They were the longest two days of my life.*

prolonged [B] continuing for a long time: *After prolonged argument they at last agreed what would be done.*

(quite) some [determiner] a certain amount of (time), usu quite long: *This work will take quite some time. He's been living there for some time now.*

short [Wa1;B] not long in time: *He took a very short time to get here. Is it a long speech or a short one?* **-ness** [U]

brief [Wa1;B] *fml* short, esp in time: *Life is brief. He had/took a brief look at the newspaper. She wrote him a brief letter of thanks. His letter was brief and to the point* (= it expressed exactly what he wanted to say, and no more). *It's a long letter, but* **in brief,** *he says 'No'.* **-ly** [adv] *He spoke briefly to them. Briefly, he said 'No'.* **brevity** [U] the state or condition of being brief: *The brevity of his speech surprised us; it only lasted three minutes.*

L140 *adjectives, etc* : **early, late, and punctual**

early 1 [Wa1;B;E] arriving, developing, happening, etc, before the usual, arranged, or expected time: *The train was ten minutes early.* **2** [Wa5;B] happening towards the beginning of the day, life, a period of time, etc: *She returned in the early morning.* **3** [Wa1;B] happening in the near future: *I hope for an early answer to my questions.* **4** [adv] before the usual, arranged, or expected time: *The bus arrived five minutes early.* **5** [adv] towards the beginning of a period: *The bush was planted early in the season.*

prior [Wa5;B (*to*)] *often fml* earlier; before a particular time: *I saw him prior to leaving. She can't see you at 11 o'clock; she has a prior engagement* (= a meeting agreed with someone else before you suggested this meeting).

late 1 [Wa1;B;E] arriving, developing, happening, etc, after the usual, arranged, or expected time: *The train was ten minutes late.* **2** [Wa5;B]

happening towards the end of the day, life a period, etc: *She returned in the late afternoon.* **3** [Wa5;A] happening a short time ago: *The late changes in the government surprised us all.* **4** [Wa1;A] just arrived; new; fresh: *Some late news of the war has just come in.* **5** [adv] after the usual, arranged, or expected time: *The bus arrived five minutes late.* **6** [adv] towards the end of a period: *The bush was planted late in the season.* **7** [adv] until or at a late time of the night: *They stayed up late.*

overdue [B;E] later than expected, arranged, etc: *Payment is overdue; we must be paid immediately. The train is ten minutes overdue.*

in (good) time before the time when something happens or must happen: *He came in good time to see her leave. Am I in time for the meeting?—Yes, you're in good time for it.*

punctual [B] not late; arriving, happening, doing something, etc, at the exact or agreed time: *She's never punctual in answering letters; she's always late. The cat makes a punctual appearance at mealtimes. We have a long journey tomorrow, so we want to make a punctual start.* **un-** [neg] **-ly** [adv]: *The train arrived punctually at ten o'clock.* **punctuality** [U] the state or condition of being punctual: *Our director demands punctuality; anyone who is late loses his job.*

on time at the right time; punctual: *The train arrived on time, so we didn't have to wait.*

prompt 1 [Wa1;B] (of an action) done or given quickly, at once, or at the right time: *He wrote a prompt answer to my letter. Prompt payment of bills helps the accounts in shops.* **2** [Wa5;B] (of a person) acting quickly and willingly when something has to be done: *This worker is always prompt in his duties.* **3** [adv] exactly (in regard to time): *The performance will start at 1 o'clock prompt.* **-ly** [adv] **-ness** [U]

timely [Wa2;B] *esp emot* happening at the right moment: *His arrival was timely. His arrival couldn't have been more timely; he helped them all to agree.*

L141 *combining forms* : **-time**

-time 1 when (something) happens: *nighttime* (= when it is night) **2** when one should have (something): *dinnertime:* (= the time for dinner)

day- when the sun is in the sky: *daytime; daylight*

night- when the sun is not in the sky: *nighttime; nightclothes*

life- when life goes on: *lifetime* (= the period of someone's life); *lifelong* (= lasting as long as one's life)

L142 *nouns, etc* : **past, present, and future**

past 1 [(*the*) S] the time earlier than now: *In the*

past I have had many jobs. **2** [*(the)* S] what happened in time (long) before now: *If only one could change the past, how different things might be.* **3** [S] **a** (of a country) history: *Our country has a glorious past.* **b** (of a person) life, actions, etc, before the present time, esp when these contain wrong-doing of some kind: *Stories were told that she was a woman with a past.* **4** [Wa5;A;E] (of time) earlier than the present: *I've not been feeling very well for the past few days.* **5** [Wa5;B] finished; ended: *Winter is past and spring has come.* **6** [Wa5;A] former: *She talked about her past successes. John Smith is a past president of our club.*

present [*(the)* R] time now: *We learn from the past, experience the present, and hope for the best in (the) future. At present he is in Canada. For the present I will do nothing, but next year things may be different.*

future 1 [*the* R; A] the time after the present; time yet to come: *The future is always unknown to us. You should save some money; it's wise to provide for the future. In future years, we shall remember this visit with pleasure. Keep this book for future use* (= to use at a later time). *Many people believe in a future life* (= another form of life after death). **2** [C] (expected, planned, arranged, etc, for) the life in front of a person; that which will happen to someone or something: *I wish you a very happy future. The future of this business company is uncertain, as it has very little money. That young man has a bright future before him as a painter* (= will become successful and famous). *This is my future wife* (= the woman whom I am going to marry). *We're leaving this town; our future home will be in London.* **3** [U] *infml* likelihood of success: *There's no future in trying to sell furs in a hot country.* **in future** *also* (*becoming rare*) **for the future** from now on: *In future, be more careful with your money.* **in the future** in time yet to come: *Who can tell what will happen in the future?* **in the distant future** at a very much later time: *Are you going to buy a house?—Not now; perhaps in the distant future.* **in the near future** *fml* soon   **in the not too distant future** not next week, but quite soon

L143 *nouns* : **times, periods, and ages**

time [C *often pl with sing meaning*] a particular length of time in history: *In Queen Victoria's time there were no aeroplanes. In ancient times this place was a forest. He is writing about the life and times of Henry VIII.*

days [P] *esp emot & lit* a particular time, esp in someone's life: *In his younger days he was a racing driver. They had nothing like this in the old days.* **the olden days** long ago: *Robin Hood lived in the olden days in Sherwood Forest.*

period [C] **1 a** a particular stretch of time in the development of a person, a civilization, the earth, an illness, etc: *The Victorian period of*

English history is the time when Victoria was queen. The time when Picasso painted pictures using a lot of blue colour is called his blue period. The Carboniferous Period was about 270,000,000 years ago. **b** the same stretch of time as stated or suggested before: *Lords and ladies of ancient times dressed in clothes of the period.* **2** a complete and repeated stretch of time fixed by the forces of nature: *The period taken by the earth to move round the sun is a year. The rainy period in India is from June to September.*

age [C] **1** [*usu sing, often cap*] a particular period in history: *The period in which man learned to make tools of iron is called the Iron Age. (infml) Oh, it happened ages ago* (= long ago)*!* **2** all the people living at a particular time: *This age doesn't know what it is to be really poor. (pomp) We shall plan for the ages to come.*

era [C] **1** a set of years which is counted from a particular point in time: *The Christian era is counted from the birth of Christ.* **2** a period of time in history named after an important event or development: *The era of space travel has begun.*

epoch [C] a period of historical time, or an age in the history of the Earth, during which events or developments of a stated kind happened: *The epoch of empires is past. The old queen's death seemed to end an epoch.*

L144 *adjectives* : **relating to time and history** [Wa5;B]

temporal 1 of or limited by time: *'When' and 'while' are temporal conjunctions.* **2** of or related to worldly affairs as opposed to religious affairs: *the temporal power of the church*
chronic (esp of diseases or illnesses) lasting a long time: *He suffers from chronic backache.* **-ally** [adv Wa4]
historical of or connected with history [⇒ L131]: *He writes historical plays. She is a member of the Historical Society.* **-ly** [adv Wa4]
chronological arranged according to the order of time: *The teacher gave the pupils a chronological list of events which in his opinion had caused the First World War.* **-ly** [adv Wa4]

L145 *adjectives* : **relating to times, moments, etc**

momentary [Wa5] **1** [B] lasting for a very short time: *Her feeling of fear was momentary; it soon passed. There was a momentary pause.* **2** [A] *fml and becoming rare* at every moment: *The escaped prisoner spent his days in momentary fear of being caught and sent back to prison.* **-rily** [adv]
contemporaneous [Wa5;B] (of two people or things) living or happening at the same time: *The two wars were contemporaneous, although*

they happened far away from each other. **-ly** [adv]

instantaneous [Wa5] happening at once: *In an accident of this type death is instantaneous; there is no time to suffer.* **-ly** [adv]

instant [Wa5;B] **1** to be done at once: *He wants an instant answer to all his questions! We try to provide an instant service.* **2** ready to be used: *They make instant coffee.* **3** *emot & emph* instantaneous: *The accident caused their instant deaths.* **-ly** [adv]

sudden [B] happening, done, etc, unexpectedly: *Her sudden death upset everybody.* **-ly** [adv] **all of a sudden** *infml* suddenly

immediate [B] done at once: *I want an immediate reply.* **-ly** [adv] **immediacy** [U] the nearness or urgent presence of something, which means it must be noticed and taken care of immediately: *The immediacy of the problem meant he had to drop everything and solve it. Television brings a new immediacy to world problems.*

urgent [B] needing to be done, seen, etc at once: *This matter is urgent; we must do it now.* **-ly** [adv] **-ency** [U] *fml: It is a matter of great urgency!*

L146 adjectives : **periodic and regular, etc**

periodic(al) [Wa5; B] happening repeatedly, usu at regular times: *The periodic movement of the moon round the earth takes 28 days. He suffered from periodic attacks of fever.* **-(al)ly** [adv Wa4]

regular [B] **1** happening often with the same length of time between the occasions: *He heard the regular noise (**tick**) of the clock.* **2** happening, coming, doing something, again and again at the same times each day, week, etc: *She has regular habits. Regular bowel movements are important to health. She is a regular customer in this shop. He has regular working hours.* **3** happening every time: *Regular attendance at church on Sundays is important for Christians.* **4** not varying: *The chairs were placed at regular distances. He drove at a regular speed.* **5** proper; according to rule or custom: *He knows a lot about the law but he's not a regular lawyer. Sign here, just to make things regular.* **6** *apprec* evenly shaped: *Her nose is very regular* **ir-** [neg] **-ly** [adv] **-ity** [U]

frequent [B] found or happening often; repeated many times; common: *Sudden rainstorms are frequent on the coast. The sick woman spoke slowly, with frequent pauses for breath. It is a frequent practice of his to go there.* **in-** [neg] **-ly** [adv] **-ncy** [U]

occasional [Wa5] [A; (B)] happening from time to time; not regular: *I do take occasional holidays but most of the time I work. We get the occasional visitor here.* **-ly** [adv] **2** [A] *fml or tech* written or intended for a special event, purpose, etc: *occasional poetry*

intermittent [B] happening from time to time, with pauses in between: *There was intermittent rain yesterday.* **-ly** [adv]

L147 adjectives : **historic, etc** [B]

historic **1** [Wa5] of the times whose history has been recorded: *They are arguing as to whether King Arthur was a real historic figure (= person) or whether he never existed at all.* **2** important in history: *This change in government is a historic event of our times.* **-ally** [adv Wa4]

epochal *fml & pomp* very historic; relating to a new epoch [⇒ L143]: *These are epochal events!*

epoch-making *esp emot & pomp* (esp of an event) very important; being or beginning an epoch: *The machinegun was an epoch-making invention.*

L148 verbs : **spending and passing time** [T1]

spend to use (time): *How does he spend his time now that the work is finished? She spent quite a lot of time doing that.*

pass to use (time), esp so that it should not seem so long: *She passed the time by picking flowers.*

while away [v adv] to pass (time) lazily: *He whiled away the time playing (on) the piano.*

L149 verbs : **time passing**

go by *also* **go on** [v adv I∅] (of time) to be used, move on: *As time went by she became more and more worried that something had happened to him.*

pass [I∅] to go by; be spent: *A year has passed since we last met.*

continue **1** [I∅; T1, 3, 4] to (cause to) go on happening: *The fighting continued for a week before the enemy were defeated. The government will continue to keep prices down. The priest continued praying.* **2** [I∅; T1] to (cause to) last or go forward: *The road continues in a straight line for 5 miles. The builders hope to continue the road right up to the border.* **3** [I∅ T1, 3, 4] to (cause to) start again after an interruption: *We stayed in Paris for a day and then continued south. After a short break the play continued. Will you continue gardening after dinner?* **4** [L9] to remain; stay: *This animal can continue in this state for a month. We continued in Cairo while he was in Alexandria.* **5** [X9 often pass; L9] to (cause to) stay in a particular job or office: *The king decided to continue Pitt as chief minister.*

last **1** [L9] to measure in length of time; go on; continue: *Nothing lasts for ever.* **2** [I∅] to remain of use, in good condition, or unweakened: *Her anger won't last.* **3** [D1 *no pass*; L1] to be enough for: *This food will last (them) (for) three days.*

endure [I0] *fml* **1** to last: *He is a great writer and his books will endure for ever.* **2** to remain alive and unweakened: *They had spent three days in the desert without water and could not endure much longer.*

persist 1 [I0 (*with*)] to continue firmly in spite of opposition or warning: *He persisted with his work.* **2** [I0] to continue to exist: *The bad weather will persist all over the country.*

persist in [v prep T4] to continue (doing something, esp that annoys someone else): *She persisted in singing although I asked her not to.*

prevail [I0 (*among, in*)] to (continue to) exist or be common: *Misty weather prevails in this part of the country. A belief in magic still prevails among many people.*

proceed 1 [I0 (*with*), 3] to begin and continue (some course of action): *Now that our plans are settled let us proceed. Tell us your name and then proceed with your story. As soon as he came in he proceeded to tell us all his troubles.* **2** [I0 (*with*)] *often fml* to continue (after stopping): *You needn't stop speaking when someone enters the courtroom; please proceed. Don't let me stop you; proceed with your work.* **3** [I0] *fml* to advance; move forward or move along a course: *After the ceremony at the railway station the minister and his guests proceeded to the palace. Do not proceed across a main road without first looking to the right and the left.*

L150 *adjectives* : **passing quickly** [Wa5]

passing [A] **1** not lasting very long: *She did not give the matter even a passing thought.* **2** quick; not thorough: *He had a passing look at the political news, then turned to the sports page.* **in passing** in the course of a statement (esp a statement about a different matter): *He was talking about his holiday in Spain, and he mentioned in passing that you were thinking of going there next year.*

fleeting [B] *esp lit* passing very quickly: *There was a fleeting look of surprise on his face when he heard the news. Enjoy the fleeting moments of happiness in life.* **-ly** [adv]

transient [B] **1** *also* **transitory** lasting for only a short time: *'Worldly wealth is transient; heavenly wealth lasts for ever,' said the priest. Everything in life is transitory.* **2** (of a person) staying only for a short time: *She is a transient guest at the hotel.*

L151 *adjectives, etc* : **temporary, etc**

temporary [Wa5; B] lasting only for a limited time: *Many students find temporary jobs during their summer holidays.* **-rily** [adv]: *I was temporarily delayed.* **-riness** [U]

short-term [Wa2; B] happening in, dealing with, or concerning a short period of time; in

or for the near future: *Our difficulties are only short-term, we hope.*

interim 1 [Wa5;A] (done) as a less complete part of something to be given in full later: *an interim measure; the interim report of the society* **2** [C] the time between two events: *In the interim they did nothing at all.*

provisional [Wa5; B] for the present time only with the strong probability of being changed: *After the war a provisional government was formed to control the country until they could hold elections.* **-ly** [adv]

transitional [Wa5;B] happening as one thing changes to another: *This trouble is purely transitional; it will stop when we have gone over completely to the new system.* **-ly** [adv]

L152 *adjectives* : **continuing, etc**

continuing [Wa5;A] going on: *We must have a continuing discussion on these matters till we form a plan of action.*

continual [B] *often deprec* happening all the time: *I hate these continual arguments; why can't you people agree sometimes?* **-ly** [adv]

continuous [B] continuing without interruption; unbroken: *The brain needs a continuous supply of blood. Life is more than a continuous game, you know. There is a continuous level plain between Ruritania and Flatland. The sign 'continuous performance' means that there is only a short pause between the end of one showing of the film and the beginning of the next.* **-ly** [adv]

constant [B] happening, present, or in use all the time: *We have constant hot water in the house. Her constant happiness is a constant surprise to me.* **-ly** [adv]: *She is constantly saying that; I wish she wouldn't!*

steady [Wa1;B] not stopping, changing or becoming irregular: *He is a very steady worker. She has a steady job at the factory.* **-ily** [adv]

ongoing [B] not likely to stop: *This is an ongoing business; I will be working on it for many years to come.*

nonstop [B; adv] **1** *not fml* without a pause or interruption: *The music played nonstop all night. They had nonstop music all night.* **2** (of a trip) without stopping before the end: *He flew nonstop from Delhi to New York.*

persistent [B] **1** continuing; not stopping, esp although expected to stop: *There was a persistent sound of running water, although he had turned all the taps off.* **2** (of a person) intending to continue with something: *She is a very persistent person and she'll get what she wants; she won't stop until she does.* **-ly** [adv] **persistence** [U] the state of being persistent

L153 *adjectives* : **permanent, etc**

[ALSO ⇒ L180, A12]

permanent [B] lasting or intended to last for a

long time or for ever: *The coat gives permanent protection against heavy rain. The dead artist's paintings are a permanent reminder of his great ability.* **im-** [neg] **-ly** [adv] **-nce** [U]

long-term [Wa2;B] happening in, dealing with or concerning a long period of time: *I hope that these difficulties won't be long-term ones.*

lasting [B] *esp emot* continuing for a long time: *We want a lasting peace.*

enduring [B] lasting: *He has enduring memories of her kindness to him.*

eternal [Wa5; B] going on for ever; without beginning or end: *Rome has been called the Eternal City. His religion promised him eternal life.* (*infml*) *I'm tired of your eternal complaints!* **-ly** [adv]

everlasting [Wa5; B] *emot* eternal: *His religion promises everlasting life.* (*infml*) *I'm tired of your everlasting complaints!*

perpetual [Wa5; B] **1** lasting for ever or for a long time: *the perpetual snows of the mountaintops* **2** *often deprec* **a** uninterrupted: *the perpetual noise of the machine* **b** happening often: *I'm tired of your perpetual complaints!* **-ly** [adv]

L154 nouns : **fate, etc**

[ALSO ⇨ N35]

fate 1 [R *often cap*] the (imaginary) cause beyond human control that decides events: *He expected to spend his life in Italy but fate had decided otherwise.* **2** [C] an end or result, esp death: *They met with a terrible fate/with various strange fates.* **as sure as fate** quite unavoidably: *Whenever I'm late as sure as fate I meet the President on the stairs!* **one's fate** one's future, considered to be already decided and outside one's control: *I wonder whether the examiners have decided our fate yet?*

destiny 1 [C] fate; that which must or has to happen: *It was the great man's destiny to lead his country to freedom. The two men's destinies were very different.* **2** [R *often cap*] that which seems to decide man's fate, thought of as a person or a force: *Destiny is sometimes cruel.*

predestination [U] **1** the belief that God has decided everything that will happen and that no human effort can change things **2** the belief that by God's wish some souls will be saved and go to heaven and others lost and go to hell [⇨ C325]

chance [U] the force that makes things happen seemingly without reason or cause: *I met him purely by chance. She didn't mean to go there; it was just chance. They had a chance meeting.*

doom [U] *esp poet* what must happen, usu seen as bad: *He met his doom in the battle. These people always talk about doom and disaster.*

L155 adjectives : **fate, etc** [Wa5]

fated [F3, 5c] caused or fixed by fate: *You and I were fated to meet. It was fated that we should meet.*

destined [B (*by, for*)] intended for some special purpose; fated; willed by God: *He was destined by his parents for life in the army. His work was destined never to succeed. I never thought I would marry her, but I suppose it was destined. When the destined meeting finally happened, everyone was surprised at the results.*

predestined [B (*to*), B3] fixed as if by fate: *He thought that whatever happened was predestined and nothing he did would change the result. She felt that she was predestined to lead her country to freedom. Such a foolish plan was predestined to failure.*

foredoomed [B (*to*)] *esp poet & emot* intended by (a bad) fate to reach a (usu bad) state or condition: *The business was foredoomed to failure.*

L156 verbs : **fate, etc**

predetermine 1 [T1; V3; *usu pass*] to fix unchangeably from the beginning: *The colour of a person's eyes and hair is predetermined by that of his parents.* **2** [T1] to calculate (the amount or cost of something not yet produced): *Owing to the possiblity of rises in prices and wages, it's not easy to predetermine the cost of producing this article in our factory.* **3** [X9; V3] to influence in advance: *Her voice, first heard over the telephone, predetermined me to like her.*

foreordain [Wv5;T1 (*to*), 5; V3: *usu pass*]*fml* to arrange or decide from the very beginning that or how something will happen or be done: *He was foreordained to succeed/to success.*

doom [Wv5;T1 (*to*); V3] *emot* to cause to experience or suffer something unavoidable and unpleasant, such as death or destruction: *From the start the plan was doomed (to failure/to fail). The prisoner is doomed (to die).*

condemn [Wv5;T1 (*to*); V3] *emot* to doom: *The plan was condemned to failure and he was condemned to die.* [also ⇨ G106]

L157 adjectives : **inevitable** [Wa5; B]

inevitable 1 which cannot be prevented from happening: *An argument was inevitable; they always argued.* **2** *infml* which always happens, or is present with someone or something else: *She was wearing her inevitable large hat.* **-bly** [adv Wa3] **-bility** [U]

inexorable whose actions or effects cannot be changed or prevented by one's efforts: *These are the inexorable facts. He was inexorable on that point.* **-bly** [adv Wa3] **-bility** [U]

inescapable which cannot be escaped from or avoided: *This is an inescapable fact. The result is inescapable.* **-bly** [adv Wa3]

ineluctable which cannot be escaped from (*esp in the phr* **an ineluctable fate**) **-bly** [adv Wa3]
unavoidable which cannot be avoided: *I'm afraid it's unavoidable; you must go/do it.* **-bly** [adv Wa3]: *He was unavoidably late for the meeting.*

L158 *verbs* : **foretelling things**

foretell [T1, 5, 6a; I0] to tell (what will happen in the future): *The magician foretold the man's death. He foretold that the man would die. Who can foretell (what will happen)?*
tell the future to foretell things: *Can she tell the future from cards or tea leaves?*
foresee [T1, 5, 6a] to form an idea or judgement about (what is going to happen in the future); expect: *He foresaw that his train would be delayed by bad weather. It's impossible to foresee whether she'll be well enough to come home from hospital next month. We should have foreseen this trouble months ago.*
see [T1] *esp poet* to foretell or foresee: *He saw the future in a dream.*
forecast [T1, 5, 6a] to say, esp with the help of some kind of knowledge (what is going to happen at some future time): *He is able to forecast the future. The teacher forecast that 15 of his pupils would pass the examination. Trying to forecast the weather is not easy.*
predict [T1, 5, 6a] to foretell (a future happening) as a result of knowledge, experience, reason, etc: *The weather scientists predicted a fine summer. She predicted that I would marry a doctor and I did/but I didn't.*
prophesy [T1, 5, 6a; I0] to give (a warning or statement about some future event, etc) esp as a result of an experience relating to God or a god: *He prophesied the end of the world.*
envisage, *AmE also* **envision** [T1, 4, 5, 6] to see in the mind as a future possibility (events, actions, etc): *Ford envisaged an important future for the motor car.*
visualize, -ise [T1 (*as*), 4, 6; V4] to form a picture of (something or someone) in the mind; to imagine: *Though he described the place carefully, I couldn't visualize it because it was so different from anything I'd known. Try to visualize sailing through the sky on a cloud. Can you visualize how he looked after we'd pulled him out of the river? Can you visualize what he looked like? I can't visualize him as chairman of the committee; I can't visualize him controlling a meeting.* **-zation, -sation** [U]
herald [T1 (*in*)] *esp poet* to be a sign of something coming: *The singing of the birds heralded (in) the new day.*

L159 *general nouns* : **foretelling things**

fortune-telling [U] the activities of a person, usu a woman, who is said to be able to tell people's fortunes (= their future good or bad luck) **tell one's fortune/fortunes** to do fortune telling: *Does she tell fortunes?— Yes; ask her to tell your fortune for you.* **fortune-teller** [C] a person who does fortune-telling/tells fortunes, esp for money [also ⇒ N35]
second sight [U] the supposed ability to see future or faraway things
forecasting [U] the activity of forecasting things: *I'm not good at forecasting.*
prophecy [U] the power of foreseeing and foretelling future events: *The old man had the gift of prophecy.*
prediction [U] the act of predicting: *Some people claim to have natural powers of prediction.*
precognition [U; C] *fml* knowledge of something that will happen in the future; esp as received in the form of a direct unexplainable message to the mind.
clairvoyance [U] *fml & tech* second sight; precognition **clairvoyant** [C; B] (a person who is) able to foresee things, etc
foresight [U] *usu apprec* the ability to imagine what will probably happen, allowing one to act to help or prevent matters; care or wise planning for the future: *With admirable foresight, she bought her house just before prices began to rise.*

L160 *particular nouns* : **foretelling things** [C, C5]

forecast a statement of future events, based on some kind of knowledge or judgement: *The weather forecast on the radio tonight tells of coming storms. The newspaper made a forecast that the government would only last for six months.*
prophecy a statement telling something that is to happen in the future: *Writers of the later parts of the Bible often speak of the prophecies of Isaiah. He made a prophecy that the boy would become a great national leader.* **prophet** a person who can make prophecies
prediction something that is predicted: *Scientists' predictions about the weather have often been proved wrong.*
foreboding [*also* U] a feeling of coming evil: *She thought of a lonely future with foreboding. She had a foreboding that she'd never see him again. I am glad my forebodings were wrong.*
omen [(*of*)] a sign that something is going to happen in the future: *a good/bad omen*

Beginning and ending

L170 *verbs* : **beginning things**
[ALSO ⇒ L179]

begin [T1, 3, 4; I0] to start; take the first step: *Are you sitting comfortably? Then I'll begin . . .*

He began by dancing/with a story/on another book/ at the beginning. She began the book/to write/writing. He began life as a poor man, but died rich. **to begin with** as the first reason: *We can't go. To begin with, it's too cold. Besides, we've no money.*

start 1 [I∅; T1, 3; *(off, out, for)*; L7] to begin (a course, journey, etc); set out (on): *It's a long trip; we'll have to start out/off early and start back for home in the afternoon. He started poor but quickly became rich. She started for the door before I could stop her. We're starting our trip next week. He started out to write an article, but it ended up as a book.* **2** [I∅; T1; *(up)*] to (cause to) come into being; begin: *How did the trouble start? It takes dry materials to start a fire. I'm no good at starting up conversations. The man who invented the car certainly started something!* **3** [I∅; T1, 3, 4; V4; *(with)*] to (cause to) go into (motion or activity); begin: *We start work at 8.30 every morning. It's started to rain/started raining. You should start saving money now. Give it a push to start it going. How shall we start the meeting? Let's start with business from last time. The clock keeps starting and stopping: what's wrong with it? I can't start the car/The car won't start. I think it's out of petrol. His father's money started him in business. We'll take turns, starting with you. What did you start to say? Where shall we start? What's a good starting point?* **4** [I∅ *(in, on)*] to begin doing a job or piece of work: *You're hired; when can you start? Will I have to start (in) on digging the garden tonight?* **5** [L9, esp *at, from*] to go from a particular point; have a beginning or lower limit: *Prices start at £5. The railway line starts from the coastal city. This history book starts at 1066.* **6** [T1] to begin using: *We've finished this bottle of wine; shall we start a new one? Start each page on the second line.* **start (all) over (again)** begin again as before or as at the first   **to start with** *also* **for a start** (used before the first in a list of facts, reasons, etc): *It won't work: to start with, it's a bad idea, and secondly it'll cost too much.* **start something** *infml* to make trouble; start a fight: *Are you trying to start something, friend?*

commence [I∅; T1, 3, 4] *fml or tech* to begin; start: *The battle commenced. Shouldn't we commence the attack? After the election the new government commenced to nationalize/nationalizing the banks.*

resume *fml* **1** [I∅; T1, 4] to begin again (something, or doing something) after a pause: *We resumed our journey after a short rest. We'll stop now and resume (working) at two o'clock.* **2** [T1] to take again: *He resumed his seat. When he got better he resumed his position as head of the firm.*

dawn [I∅] to (begin to) get light: *Day dawned.* (*fig*) *A new age began to dawn.*

L171 *formal verbs* : **beginning things**

launch [T1] **1** to send (a boat, esp one that has just been built) into the water **2** to send (a modern weapon or instrument) into the sky or space by means of scientific explosive apparatus **3** [*(at)*] to throw with great force: *He launched his spear at the lion's head.* **4** to cause (an activity, plan, way of life, etc) to begin

initiate [T1] to start (something) working: *He initiated a movement for a change in the law.*

inaugurate [T1 *usu pass*] **1** to introduce (someone) into a new place or job by holding a special ceremony **2** to start (a public affair) by a ceremony: *The new town plan was inaugurated by the Mayor at a special ceremony.* **3** to be the beginning of (esp an important period of time): *The introduction of free milk inaugurated a period of better health for children.*

institute [T1] to set up for the first time (a society, rules, action, etc): *to institute the office of chairman; to institute a criminal action*

instigate [T1] to start by one's action: *He instigated the five-year political plan.*

introduce [T1] **1** to bring in for the first time: *They introduced the idea that children could learn to read as babies. He says we have only £2 left, which introduces another difficulty.* **2** [*(to)*] to make known for the first time to each other or someone else, esp by telling two people each other's names: *I introduced them myself. I introduced John to Mary, two years before they were married. They introduced themselves.* **3** to produce the first part esp to suggest to explain something: *The first few notes introduce a new type of music.*

L172 *informal verbs* : **beginning things**

start up [v adv I∅; T1] to begin or start, esp in the very first stages: *The engine started up easily. He has just started up a new business.*

start off [v adv I∅; T1] to begin or start esp in movement, along a way, etc: *He started off happily but soon got tired. She started off (her talk) by telling them about life in India.*

set up [v adv T1] **1** to establish (an organization, business, etc): *Set up a committee to deal with the matter. A new government was set up after the war. He set up a school for young children/set up a bookshop.* **2** to prepare (an instrument, machine, etc) for use: *This difficult electrical wiring will take a day to set up.* **3** to produce; cause: *The decayed tooth has set up an infection in the jaw. The high winds set up some dangerous driving conditions.*

set out [v adv] **1** [I3] to begin a course of action: *He set out to paint the whole house but finished only the front part.* **2** [T1] *also* **set forth** to explain (facts, reasons, etc) in order, esp in writing: *The reasons for my decision are set out in my report.*

set off [v adv] **1** [I∅] *also* **set forth, set out** to begin a trip: *set off in search of the lost child; set off on a trip across Europe* **2** [T1] to cause (sudden activity): *The border attack set off a terrible war. The discovery of gold in California set off a rush to get there.*

set in [v adv IØ] (of natural forces, illnesses, etc) to start: *Winter set in early. Decay has set in; there is nothing we can do to stop it.*

bring in [v adv] **1** [T1] to introduce: *to bring in a bill (in Parliament); to bring in a new fashion* **2** [T1; V3] to ask to come to one's help: *We must bring in experienced people to advise.* **3** [T1; D1] to produce as profit or earnings: *The sale brought us in over £200. The boys are bringing in £40 a week.*

trigger off [v adv T1] *esp emot* to cause to start: *His words triggered off an argument. The fighting was triggered off by the attempt to murder the prince.*

break out [v adv IØ] (esp of diseases, trouble, etc) to start: *Cholera* [⇒ B143] *has broken out in the old part of the city. Her face broke out in a mass of spots.* **outbreak** [C] an act, occasion, or result of something breaking out: *an outbreak of cholera; a cholera outbreak; the outbreak of war*

burst into [v prep T1] *infml, emph & emot* to start, esp suddenly or quickly: *She burst into song* (= She started singing) *because she was so happy. When spring comes in that part of the world the trees just burst into life.*

L173 *verbs* : **ending things**

[ALSO ⇒ L181]

---

end [IØ; T1] to (cause to) stop happening, being done, etc: *The party ended at midnight. The war ended in 1945. He ended his letter with good wishes to the family.*

stop 1 [T1; IØ] to (cause to) end, esp suddenly, definitely, etc: *The rain stopped. We stopped the fight.* **2** [IØ] to pause: *I stopped at the first word I didn't recognize.* **3** [T1,4; IØ] to (cause to) cease moving or continuing an activity: *He put his hand out as a signal to the bus to stop. He put his hand out to stop the bus. We stopped working at teatime.* **4** [T1 (from); V4] to prevent: *I'm going; you can't stop me. You must stop her telling them. She must be stopped from telling them.* **5** [IØ] *infml* to stay, esp for a visit: *Are you stopping to tea? I'm not stopping.* **6** [T1 (up)] to block: *There's something inside stopping (up) the pipe. The pipe's stopped up.* **7** [T1] to hold back (the flow of blood) or the blood inside (a blood vessel): *Can't you stop the blood? Stop the wound with this material.*

halt [T1; IØ] *fml* to (cause to) stop: *Halt at the traffic lights. The train was halted by work on the line ahead.*

stall 1 [IØ] (esp of an engine) to stop running: *The engine stalled and the aeroplane crashed.* **2** [T1] to cause (an engine) to stop: *Don't stall the engine!*

finish 1 [IØ; T1, 4] to reach or bring to an end;

cause the end of (an activity): *What time does the concert finish? When do you finish your college course? I haven't finished reading that book yet.* **2** [Wv4; T1 (*off*)] to put the last touches or polish to (something that one has made): *I must finish (off) this dress I'm making. I'm just giving it the last finishing touches. This wood has not been finished; it is still rough.* **3** [T1 (*up, off*)] to eat or drink the rest of: *The cat will finish (up) the fish. Let's finish (off) the wine.* **4** [L9 (*up*)] to arrive or end (in the stated place or way): *We finished (up) in Paris. The party finished with a song. Let's have a last drink to finish up with.* **5** [T1] *infml* to take all the powers, hopes of success, etc, of (someone): *That race finished me. His wife's death has finished him.*

come to an end [IØ] to end, esp slowly: *The meeting came to an end at midnight.*

bring to an end [T1] to end, esp slowly: *Let's bring the meeting to an end soon; I want to go home.*

put an end to [T1] to end, esp with force: *You can't put an end to such an important matter in this way! He put an end to all further argument by telling them to be quiet.*

shut 1 [T1; IØ] to move into a covered, blocked, or folded-together position: *Shut the gate so that the dog can't get out. He shut his eyes and tried to sleep. The wood has swollen and the door won't shut. He shut the book and put it away.* **2** [X9] to keep or hold by closing: *He shut himself in his room to think. Shut out all wicked thoughts from your mind. She shut her skirt in the door and tore the edge.* **3** [T1; IØ] to stop operating: *In the evening the shops shut. The factory was shut in 1931.*

shut up [v adv] **1** [IØ; T1] to make (a place) safe before leaving, as a shop at the end of a business day: *Business was slow so he shut up (the shop) early for the day.* **2** [T1] to keep enclosed: *He shut himself up in his room.* **3** [T1] *infml* to make (someone) stop talking: *Can't you shut your friend up?* **4** [IØ *often imper*] *sl* to stop talking; be quiet: *Shut up! I'm trying to think. Will you please shut up!*

shut down [v adv] **1** [IØ] (as of a business or factory) to stop operating, esp for a long time or forever: *The whole company shuts down for three weeks' summer holiday. Since television was invented many cinemas have shut down.* **2** [T1] to cause to do this: *A strike has shut down several car factories.*

close 1 [T1; IØ] to (cause to) shut: *Close the windows and keep out the cold air. The door closed noiselessly.* **2** [T1; IØ] to (cause to) be not open to the public: *The street was closed to traffic on Saturdays. When does the shop close?* **3** [T1; IØ] to (cause to) stop operating: *The firm has decided to close its London branch.* **4** [T1] to bring to an end: *Close my account please. She closed her speech with a funny joke.* **5** [IØ; (T1)] to (cause to) come together: *His arms closed tightly round her.* **6** [T1; IØ] to (cause to) come together by making less space between: *The nurse closed the wound with stitches. The difference between rich and poor can never be closed. Close the crack with mud.*

close up [v adv I∅; T1] to close completely, but not necessarily for ever: *He closed up the shop and went home. Let's close up now. The wound has completely closed up.*

close down [v adv] **1** [T1; I∅] (of a business) to close forever: *The shop closed down. We must close the factory down, I'm afraid.* **2** [I∅] (of a radio or television station) to stop broadcasting for the night

cancel 1 [T1] to give up or call off (a planned activity, idea etc): *She cancelled her trip to New York as she felt ill. I hope the Queen doesn't cancel her visit to Australia this year.* **2** [T1; (I∅)] to declare that (something) is to be without effect: *She cancelled her order for a new car.* **3** [T1 (*out*)] to balance; equal: *The increase in strength of their navy is cancelled by that in our army.* **4** [T1] to cross out (writing) by drawing a line through it

cease [I∅; T1, 3, 4] *often fml* to (cause to) stop: *She cried for hours without ceasing. When will this quarrelling cease? The army ceased action. Cease firing! The old man ceased breathing/to breathe.*

desist [I∅ (*from*)] *fml* to do something no longer; cease: *I told him not to do it any more, and he desisted. You must desist from any further efforts to help him/from helping him.* (*law*) *So many people were against his activities that the judge ordered him to cease and desist.*

expire [I∅] to come to an end, usu after a particular length of time: *Our contract* [⇒ J137] *has expired; we must agree to new conditions of work.* **expiry** [U] the end of something which has expired: *What is the expiry date of your agreement?*

L174 *informal verbs* : **ending things** [v adv]

peter out [I∅] to come gradually to an end: *The coal in the mine finally petered out and they closed the mine. The money petered out.*

fizzle out [I∅] to come gradually to an end, esp in a sad or silly way: *His plans fizzled out; nobody thought they were any good anyway.*

dry up [I∅] to stop coming: *He used to get money from his family but the monthly payments have dried up.*

run out [I∅] (of supplies, etc) to come to an end: *His money ran out and he had to get work.*

give up [I∅; T1, 4] (of people) to stop (doing something): *He has given up smoking. I give up; I can't succeed!*

pack up 1 [I∅; T4] to finish (work): *When we've finished this pile of papers, let's pack up and go home. He packed up working and went home.* **2** [I∅] *esp BrE* (of a machine) to stop working: *It packed up on us yesterday.*

wear off [T1] to stop happening; disappear slowly: *The pain slowly wore off. The paint has*

worn off; *you'll need to paint the walls again. The effects of the drug began to wear off.*

wear out [I∅; T1] to (cause to) come to an end by long use: *His clothes have worn out. He has worn out his clothes.*

break down [v adv I∅] to stop working, happening, behaving, etc, properly: *The car broke down and he had to telephone for help. The talks between the two countries broke down and there was a danger of war. She suddenly broke down and started to cry.* **breakdown** [C] an act, occasion, or result of something breaking down: *The breakdown occurred on an empty road. There has been a breakdown in the talks.*

L175 *formal verbs* : **ending things**

terminate [T1; L9] to (cause to) come to an end, esp officially, definitely, suddenly, etc: *They have terminated the contract. The council meeting terminated at 2 o'clock. The railway line terminates here.* **termination 1** [C; U] (an example of) the act of terminating **2** [C] *tech* the last part or letter of a word

conclude [T1; I∅] to bring or come esp officially to an end: *He concluded (the meeting) by thanking everyone.*

finalize, -ise [T1] to finish (plans, arrangements, etc): *Everything has been finalized.*

abort [I∅; T1] *tech & often emot* to (cause to) come to an end early, violently, or wrongly: *The doctor aborted her baby. The plan was aborted before we could decide whether it would work or not.*

culminate in [v prep T1, (4); V4b] to reach the highest point, degree, or development in: *All his efforts culminated in failure. His many crimes culminated in him/his being sent to prison. The army's brave fighting culminated in total victory.*

complete [T1] to make complete; finish in the fullest possible form: *Have you completed the work yet?* **completion** [U] **1** the act of completing **2** the state of being completed

perfect [T1] to make perfect: *He slowly perfected the new apparatus until it did its work smoothly.* **perfection 1** [U] the act of making perfect **2** [U] the state of being perfect **3** [C] a perfect thing: *He has been talking about her perfections all week.*

L176 *verbs* : **coming to an end**

end up [v adv L1, 4, 7, 9] to finish in a particular place or way: *She ended up (by) dancing on the table* (= in the end she was dancing on the table). *He ended up (as) head of the firm. They ended up drunk. We may end up in China if we keep going.*

land up [v adv L9] *esp infml* to end up in a usu bad situation: *He landed up in hospital with a broken leg after the fight.*

finish up [v adv L9] to arrive or end in the stated

place or way: *We finished up in China. The party finished up with a fight/song. Let's have a drink to finish up with.*

prove [L (*to be*) 1, 7; X (*to be*) 1, 7] to show (oneself or itself) afterwards, in the course of time or experience, etc, to be of the quality stated: *On the long journey he proved himself to be an amusing companion. As it happened, my advice proved to be wrong. Perhaps this book will prove of some use to you in your study.*

turn out [v adv L (*to be*) 1, 7, 9] *not fml* to happen to be in the end: *He turned out to be a prince. How did everything turn out in the end?—Oh, it all turned out well.*

transpire [*it* I5] (of an event, secret, etc) to become gradually known: *It later transpired that the minister had tried to call an early election.*

L177 *verbs* : **putting off, delaying, and postponing**

put off [v adv] **1** [T1 (*till, until*)] to move to a later date: *If it rains the match must be put off. The meeting has been put off until next week. We've invited them to dinner, but we shall have to put it off because the baby's ill.* **2** [T1] to make excuses to (someone) in order to avoid a duty: *I'll pay you next week. —I won't be put off with a promise that you don't intend to keep.* **3** [T1] to arrange a meeting with (someone) again at a later time: *We've invited them to dinner, but we shall have to put them off because the baby's ill.* **4** [T1] (*fig*) **a** to discourage (someone): *The speaker was trying to make a serious point, but people kept putting him off by shouting.* **b** to cause dislike: *Those smelly animals put me off. His bad manners put me (right) off.*

delay 1 [T1, 4] to put off until later: *We decided to delay (going on) our holiday until next month.* **2** [T1] to stop for a time; cause to be late: *What delayed you so long?* **3** [I0] to move or act slowly, esp on purpose: *They're trying to delay until help arrives. Don't delay; act today!*

postpone [T1 (*until, to*)] *often fml* to delay; move to some later time: *We're postponing our holiday until August.*

suspend [Wv5;T1] **1** to put off for a period of time (esp the fulfilment of a decision): *They suspended the law/his punishment. He was given a suspended sentence* (= the punishment was not given unless there was more trouble). *Work was suspended (on the ship* (= on making the ship)). *His father suspended his money.* **2** [T1] to prevent from playing in a team, belonging to a group, etc for a time, usu because of bad behaviour or breaking rules: *He has been suspended from school.*

be off [v adv I0] to have been put off: *The meeting is off (till next week).*

hold back [v adv I0; T1] to (cause to) delay in

doing something: *He held back from doing it. Don't hold him back if he wants to go/to do it.*

hold up [v adv T1 *often pass*] to delay: *The building of the new road has been held up by bad weather.*

stall [I0] to avoid or delay giving a decision, answer, etc: *They are stalling (for time)*; they won't say 'yes' or 'no'.

retard [T1] *esp fml & tech* to make (someone or something) slow; delay; hold back: *If you stop the money, you will greatly retard our work.*

L178 *nouns* : **delaying and postponing**

delay 1 [U] the act of delaying or the state of being delayed: *Do it without (any) delay!* **2** [C] an example of being delayed: *There will be some delays on all roads because of heavy traffic this morning.* **3** [C] the time during which something or someone is delayed: *Delays of up to two hours were reported on all roads this morning.*

postponement 1 [U] the act of postponing: *There must be no postponement of the meeting!* **2** [C] an example of this: *I'm tired of all these postponements.*

suspension 1 [U] the act of suspending: *the suspension of the law angered many people.* **2** [C] an act of suspending or an occasion of being suspended: *There have been several suspensions lately at school, for bad behaviour.*

put-off [C] *infml* **1** an act of delaying something till later: *After several put-offs the match will be played today.* **2** a pretended reason for not doing something; excuse: *He says he's too busy to see you. That's just a put-off.*

holdup [C] a delay, as of traffic: *There have been a lot of holdups lately.*

retardation [U] the act of retarding or being retarded

L179 *nouns* : **beginnings**

[ALSO ⇒ L170, 1]

beginning [C] a start; starting point; origin: *She knows that subject from beginning to end.*

start [C] a beginning of activity or development; a condition, act, or place of starting: *The runners lined up at the start. The start of the film was quite exciting. It was love from the very start. Our plan is off to a good/poor start.*

commencement [U; C *usu sing*] *fml* the act of commencing: *When is the commencement of the performance?*

inception [C] *fml* beginning

origin [C; U] the state, condition, thing, etc, from which other things have come, developed, changed, etc: *What are the origins of life on earth? He is of French origin but he is now an American.*

source [C] **1** [(*of*)] a place from which something comes; a producing place or force: *We'll have to find a new source of income. Religious* faith can be a source of strength. I'll try to find the source of the engine trouble. **2** [usu pl] a person or thing that supplies information: *The reporter refused to name his sources. Sources close to the president say that. . . . The history book was written after careful study of the original sources* (= esp writings of the time).

resumption [C; U] *usu fml* an/the act of resuming: *The resumption of business after the holiday was not easy.*

launching [C] *fml* the act of launching

initiation [U; C] the/an act of initiating or being initiated

inauguration [U; C] the/an act of inaugurating or being inaugurated: *They all went to the inauguration of the new President.*

institution [U] the act of instituting or being instituted: *The institution of the new law was welcomed.*

instigation [U] the act of instigating or being instigated **at someone's instigation** by someone's act or request for action: *The plan has been changed at Mr Brown's instigation.*

introduction 1 [U] the act of introducing or being introduced **2** [C] the beginning part of anything, as of a piece of music **3** [C] a written or spoken explanation at the beginning of a book or speech **4** [C often pl] an occasion of telling people each other's names: *First let's make the introductions.*

L180 *adjectives* : **having no end** [Wa5;B]

[ALSO ⇒ L153, A12]

endless 1 never having an end: *The journey seemed endless. I'm tired of her endless complaints!* **-ly** [adv] **-ness** [U] **2** *tech* (of a belt, a chain, etc) circular; with the ends joined: *The machine drives an endless belt.*

unending *emot* endless; *I'm tired of these unending problems!*

incessant never stopping: *He is an incessant talker.* **-ly** [adv]: *He talks incessantly.*

ceaseless also **unceasing** *emot & poet:* incessant **-ly** [adv]

infinite 1 without limits or ends: *God's love is said to be infinite. He has an infinite love.* **2** *not fml* very large; as much as there is: *We have an infinite amount of time.* **-ly** [adv] **infinity** [U] **1** the state of being infinite **2** an infinite number or amount

L181 *nouns* : **ends**

[ALSO ⇒ L173–6]

end [C] **1** the point(s) where something stops, or beyond which it does not exist: *We talk about the ends of a rope/of a stick/of a box; the end of the road/of the railway. We live at this end of the village and the post office is at the other end.* **2** the furthest point from here: *They travelled to the ends of the earth* (= the furthest part, most difficult to reach). *He's down at the end of the garden.* **3** the latest point in time or in order: *the end of the year/of his life* **4** (*fig*) *euph* death: *His end was peaceful.* **come/draw to an end** (of something which goes on for some time) to finish: *The year was drawing to an end.* **in the end** at last: *He tried many times to pass the examination and in the end he succeeded.* **make an end of** *fml* to finish (esp something one is doing oneself): *Let us make an end of this foolish quarrel* **on end 1** (of time) continuously: *He sat there for hours on end.* **2** upright: *We had to stand the table on end to get it through the door.* **put an end to** to stop from happening any more: *They succeeded at last in putting an end to the war.*

stop [C] **1** the act of stopping or state of being stopped: *We made a stop on the way.* **2** a place on a road where buses or other public vehicles stop for passengers: *a bus stop* **3** a point or sign at which to stop: *There's a stop ahead.*

stoppage [C] **1** a blocked state which stops movement, as in a waste pipe or a pipe in the body **2** the state of being held back: *A stoppage of air is necessary to make certain consonant sounds.*

halt [C] **1** a stop or pause (*esp in the phr* **come to a halt**): *The car came to a halt just in time to prevent an accident.* **2** a small railway station: *a country halt*

finish [C] the last part (of something): *He was there at the finish, but not at the start.*

close [C] *often lit* the end, esp of an activity or of a period of time: *At the close of the party there were few guests who weren't drunk. She always prays at the close of the day.*

closedown [C] **1** *esp BrE* (of radio and television) the end of a period of broadcasting **2** (of a factory, business, etc) a general stopping of work: *A complete closedown over the holiday period would mean a great reduction in profits.*

terminus [C] the last stop on a bus line or the station at the end of a railway line

terminal [C] **1** a point at which connections can be made, where one thing stops and another starts **2** the bus station in the centre of a town for passengers going to or coming from an airport

termination [U; C] the act of terminating or ending: *When is the termination date of the agreement?*

conclusion [C] an act of concluding: *The conclusion of the work is in two months time.*

abortion [C] *often deprec* a plan or arrangement which breaks down before it can develop properly

culmination [C] the highest point: *The culmination of the doctor's life's work was his discovery of a cure for the common cold.*

cancellation 1 [U] the act of cancelling or of having been cancelled: *The cancellation of the order for planes led to the closure of the factory.* **2** [C] an example of this: *Because there have been two cancellations you can now come on the trip.*

L182 *adjectives, etc* : **first, etc** [Wa5]

first [determiner] being at the beginning: *He was the first person to land on the moon.* **-ly** [adv] [also ⇒ J5, 6]

initial [A] *fml* being (at) the beginning of a set: *The initial talks helped the later agreement.* **-ly** [adv]

prime [A] first in time, rank, or importance: *This is a matter of prime importance. He is Prime Minister of the country.*

primal *fml* **1** [B] first in importance: *a primal necessity* **2** belonging to, or as if belonging to, the earliest time in the world; original: *Its primal glories will never return.*

inaugural [A] *fml* **1** concerning an inauguration **2** serving to start something

introductory [B] which serves to introduce: *This is only an introductory meeting; we cannot really begin the work today.*

incipient [B] *fml & med* beginning: *incipient disease*

original [A] first; earliest: *the original settlers of a country*

L183 *adjectives, etc* : **early and premature**

early [Wa1;A] happening towards the beginning of something: *This is what they did in earlier times/in early China. From the earliest times people have lived in this valley.*

former [Wa5] *fml* **1** [A] of an earlier period: *Mr Heath, the former prime minister of Britain, spoke at the meeting.* **-ly** [adv Wa5] **2** [A; *the* (G)U] the first (of two people or things just spoken of): *If I were asked to choose between Spain and Italy for a holiday, I should choose the former (country)* (=Spain). *Of pigs and cows, the former* (=pigs) *are less valuable. Did he walk or swim?—The former seems more likely.*

erstwhile [Wa5;A] *esp fml & lit* former (def **1**): *They are erstwhile enemies, but now they are friends.*

previous [Wa5;A] happening, coming, or being earlier in time or order: *Have you had any previous experience or is this kind of work new to you? My previous employer has given me a letter to say that I am suitable for this job.* **-ly** [adv]

antecedent [Wa5;B (*to*)] *fml & tech* previous: *Tell us about the antecedent events/the events antecedent to the murder.*

premature [B] **1** developing, happening, ripening, or coming before the natural or proper time: *His premature death at the age of thirty-two is a great loss. Owing to the very hot weather, the crops are premature this year.* **2** [Wa5;*also* E] (of a human or animal baby, or a birth) born, or happening, after less than the usual period of time inside the mother's body: *a premature birth* **3** done too early or too soon;

hasty: *The general's decision to attack was premature. By his premature action he lost the battle.* **-ly** [adv]

forward [B] **1** *less common* early; having developed or progressed quicker than usual: *He is very well forward with his work now.* **2** *more common, sometimes deprec* (of children) more like an adult than a child: *He is very forward for his age. What a forward child she is?* **-ness** [U]

precocious [B] *sometimes deprec* (of esp a child) having grown up or developed earlier than usual; (*fml*) forward: *What a precocious child he is; he is only five and seems to know a lot about sex!* **-ly** [adv] **precocity** [U] the state of being precocious

L184 *adjectives* : **late and last-minute**

late [Wa1;B *usu compar & superl*] happening towards the end of something: *In early times they used horses but in later times they had cars. Later this year I'm going to Canada. What is the latest news? Is it a good car?—Well, it's their latest.*

latter [Wa5] *fml* **1** [A] nearer to the end; later: *The latter years of his life were peaceful.* **2** [A; *the* (G)U] the second (of two people or things just spoken of): *Of the pig and the cow, the latter is more valuable.*

subsequent [Wa5;B (*to*)] coming after something else, sometimes as a result of it: *We made plans for a visit but subsequent difficulties with the car prevented it. Subsequent to his visit came news of his illness.* **-ly** [adv]

last-minute [Wa5;A] happening when it is nearly too late: *They gave us some useful last-minute help.*

eleventh-hour [Wa5;A] happening at the very last moment, esp before something (usu undesirable) happens: *We had to make an eleventh-hour decision to stop the war.* **at the eleventh hour** at the last possible moment: *The war was stopped at the eleventh hour.*

L185 *adjectives, etc* : **last and final** [Wa5]

last 1 [A] coming after all others in order or time: *The last train leaves at ten o'clock.* **2** [A] being the only remaining: *It was his last year at college.* **3** [A] least suitable or likely: *He's the last person I thought would come!* **4** [A] nearest in time before the present: *That was the last time we met. We met last year and hope to meet again next year.* **5** [adv] after all others: *He came last in the race.* **6** [adv] on the occasion nearest in the past: *It was 1960 when we met last.* **7** [(*the*) (G)U] who/ which is/are last: *This is the last of the wine. These are the last of our friends.* **8** [*the* U] the latest moment; end: *He was faithful to the last.* **-ly** [adv] **at (long) last**

after a long time: *He came at last. At last he came.*

final 1 [A] last; coming in the end: *Z is the final letter in the alphabet. He had a final cup of tea before he left.* **2** [B] (of a decision, offer, etc) that cannot be changed: *I won't go and that's final! Is that your final offer?* **-ly** [adv]

finite [B] (of life, times, etc) having an end or limit: *All life is finite.*

terminal [B] **1** of or at the end or limit of something **2** of, being, related to, or for an illness that will cause death: *She is suffering from a terminal illness.* **-ly** [adv]

eventual [A] (of an event) happening at last as a result: *He did not live to see the eventual success of his efforts.* **-ly** [adv]

ultimate [A; (B)] **1** (the) last or farthest distant: *It is the ultimate point of land before the sea begins.* **2** considered as a foundation or base: *The sun is the ultimate store of power. The ultimate responsiblity lies with the president.* **3** greatest, after which no other can be considered: *He's done stupid things before, but to look for the escaping gas with a match really was the ultimate silliness.* **-ly** [adv]

Old, new, and young

L200 *adjectives, etc* : **old in time**

old 1 [Wa1;B; *the* (G)U] having lived or existed for a long time or long enough to show signs of age: *He sells old and new books. The old is sometimes more attractive than the new.* **2** [Wa1;B] having been in use for a long time or long enough to show signs of use: *old shoes; an old car* **3** [Wa5;A] (before nouns showing a relationship of equality) having continued in the relationship for a long time: *old and new friends; old enemies* **4** [Wa5;A] former: *What was her old name before she got married?* **5** [Wa5;A] known for a long time: *Not the same old story again. Good old John!* **6** [Wa5;A] (used for making a phrase stronger): *Come any old time. I can use any old thing.* **7** [Wa5;A] (of a language) of an early period in the history of the language: *Old English; Old Irish* **as old as the hills** very old

ancient 1 [B] in or of times long ago: *ancient Rome and Greece* **2** [B] having existed since a very early time: *ancient customs* **3** [C *usu cap*] a person, esp a Roman or Greek, who lived in times long ago **4** [C] *old use* an old man

prehistoric [Wa5;B] of or belonging to a time before recorded history: *prehistoric man; prehistoric burial grounds*

primeval *also* **primaeval** *BrE* [Wa5] **1** of the earliest period of the earth's existence: *The primeval oceans have all gone.* **2** very ancient; having existed a very long time: *primeval forests*

medieval *also* **mediaeval** *BrE* [Wa5] **1** of the Middle Ages, the period in history between about 1100 and 1500: *a medieval castle; medieval ideas* **2** *deprec not fml* very old or old-fashioned

L201 *special adjectives, etc* : **old in time** [B]

antique 1 being old and therefore valuable: *If this ring was antique and not modern the silver and workmanship would be of much better quality.* **2** of or connected with the ancient world, esp of Rome or Greece: *antique figures cut in stone*

antiquated old and not suited to present needs or conditions; not modern; old-fashioned

obsolete [Wa5] no longer used; out of date

obsolescent [Wa5;] becoming obsolete **obsolescence** [U] the state or condition of being obsolescent

outdated *also* **out-of-date** not generally used at a given date; not modern: *He uses outdated methods. His methods are really out-of-date.*

hoary [Wa1] **1** (of hair) grey or white **2** (of people) having grey or white hair **3** (*esp fig*) very old

old-fashioned (of a type that is) no longer common: *old-fashioned ideas; an old-fashioned house*

archaic (esp of language) belonging to the past; no longer used

prehistoric *deprec or humor* very old-fashioned; long used or known: *Is Simon's prehistoric car still working? His ideas on morals are really prehistoric.*

second-hand [Wa5] **1** already used by someone else and therefore considered old: *He bought a second-hand car.* **2** *also* **at second hand** [adv] indirectly: *She got the news second-hand.*

L202 *adjectives, etc* : **new**

new 1 [Wa1;B] having begun or been made only a short time ago or before: *a new government; new fashions; new wine* **2** [Wa5;B] not used by anyone before: *We sell new and used furniture. It's a used car, but good as new* (= as if it had never been used). **3** [Wa1;A] **a** being found or becoming known only now or recently in the past: *the discovery of a new star* **b** being in the stated position only a short time: *a new member of the club; the new nations of Africa; a college producing new teachers* **4** [Wa5;A] different from the earlier thing(s) done, known about, etc, or people known (about), for a longer time; (an)other: *Our teacher got a new job, so our class had to get a new teacher.* **5** [Wa5;A] (of things of the same kind in an ordered set) just beginning or to be begun, used, etc; fresh; (an)other: *a new day*

(= another day); *begin a new chapter in a book* **6** [Wa5;A;(B)] taken from the ground early in the season; first picked of a crop: *The new potatoes were small.* **-ly** [adv] **-ness** [U] **new to 1** just beginning to know about or do; still unfamiliar with: *The young lady was new to the job.* **2** unfamiliar to: *It's not a new idea but it's new to me; I hadn't heard it before.*

modern [B] **1** [Wa5] of the present time, or of the not far distant past; not ancient: *The modern history of Italy dates from 1860, when the country became united under one government. In this part of the city, you can see ancient and modern buildings next to each other.* **2** *often apprec* new and different from the past: *He has modern ideas in spite of his great age. The furniture he's just bought is very modern.* **3** [Wa5] (esp of a language) in use today; not ancient: *It's useful for a boy or girl to learn modern languages at school, such as French and German. The English spoken and written from about 1500 up to the present time is called Modern English.* **-ness, -ity** [U]

topical [B] happening and being talked about now: *His book is very topical at the moment.* **-ly** [adv Wa4]

current [Wa5;B] happening, being used, etc, now: *What are his current ideas on the subject?* **-ly** [adv]

contemporary 1 [Wa5;B] happening or existing at the same time as another or one another, esp now: *He is interested in contemporary politics.* **2** [C] a person living at the same time: *Tom and I are contemporaries; we were at school together.*

contemporaneous [Wa5;B (*with*)] *fml* originating, existing, or happening during the same period of time as another or each other: *The two events were contemporaneous.* **-ly** [adv]

present [Wa5;A] happening, existing, or working, etc, now: *Their present leaders are not very good.*

present-day [Wa5;A] modern; existing now: *Grandfather doesn't like present-day manners; he considers them careless.*

recent [B] having happened or come into existence only a short time ago: *recent history; a recent event; a recent copy of the newspaper* **-ly** [adv]

up-to-date [B] *usu not fml* modern; as new as anything in a given period: *We want our methods to be up-to-date. He uses up-to-date methods.*

up-to-the-minute [B] *not fml* very modern or recent: *He is full of up-to-the-minute information.*

L203 *special adjectives* : **new**

novel [B] new and interesting or special: *That's a novel idea!*

fresh [Wa1;B] **1** (esp of food, etc) newly prepared: *This bread is fresh; it's just made.* **-ly**

[adv] **2** (of air, etc) pure: *Breathe that lovely fresh air!* **-ness** [U]

original 1 [B] *often apprec* new; of a new type; unlike others of the same type: *an original idea/invention* **2** [B] *often apprec* able to be new or different from others in ideas or behaviour: *an original thinker* **3** [Wa5;A;(B)] not copied: *an original painting*

seminal [B] containing the seeds of later development; influencing others in a new way; original: *This is a seminal book.* **-ly** [adv]

pristine [Wa5;A;(B)] *fml or lit* **1** of the earliest time; unchanged from the first condition: *Nothing can bring back to these ruins the pristine beauty of the original building.* **2** pure; undamaged; fresh and clean: *When the snow began to melt, it lost its pristine whiteness.*

mint [Wa5;A] (of a coin or postage stamp) in perfect condition, as if new and unused: *a mint penny black stamp of Queen Victoria's time* **in mint condition** (of any objects which people collect for pleasure such as books, postage stamps, coins, etc) in perfect condition, as new and unused: *In that old bookshop, I was lucky enough to find an early copy of Byron's poems in mint condition.*

L204 *adjectives, etc* : **future, imminent, and impending** [Wa5]

future [(*the*) A] happening in or belonging to time still to come: *Who is the girl with Jim Smith?—Oh, that's the future Mrs Smith. If he doesn't change his methods his future difficulties will be great.*

forthcoming [B] planned for the near future: *He gave me a list of their forthcoming books.*

imminent [B] which is going to happen very soon: *His arrival is imminent. His thoughts were of the imminent death of his father. There's a storm imminent.* **-ly** [adv] **imminence** [U] the nearness of something which is going to happen: *The imminence of his death was seen by all.*

impending [B] *esp emot & lit* (esp of something unpleasant) about to happen: *The impending danger was too much for him; he ran away.*

prospective 1 [A] expected; probable; intended: *The prospective Member of Parliament for our town will be introduced to the local party tonight.* **2** [B] not yet in effect; coming into operation at some future time: *The agreement between the two companies is only prospective; it hasn't yet been signed.*

at hand about to happen: *'The end of the world is at hand!' he cried.*

nigh [F] *old use, lit, pomp & humor* at hand: *'The end of the world is nigh!' he cried*

L205 *nouns* : **age and antiquity**

age 1 [U; C] the period of time a thing has existed or a person has lived, esp if very long:

The bones showed signs of great age (= being very old). *Age changes everything.* **2** [C *often pl*] *infml* a long time: *It's been ages/an age since we met!*

antiquity [U] **1** the state of being very old; great age: *The nobleman was proud of his family's antiquity.* **2** the ancient world, esp of Rome or Greece: *The heroes of antiquity still live in our books.*

prehistory [U] (the study of) times before history [⇒ L131] was written: *He is interested in the prehistory of France.*

L206 *adjectives* : **young and junior**
[ALSO ⇒ C1–9]

young [Wa1;B] **1** in an early stage of life, growth, development, etc; recently born or begun: *a young girl/plant/country* **2** fresh and tasty: *young vegetables* **3** having only a little experience: *young in crime* **4** of, for, concerning or having the qualities of a young person **youngish** [B] more or less young

youthful [B] **1** *precise* characteristic of or having the qualities of youth **2** *loose* young

juvenile [B] **1** of, like, by, or for young people, no longer babies but not yet fully grown: *juvenile books; a juvenile court* **2** *deprec* young and foolish: *If I may say so, your arguments in favour of doing that are rather juvenile.*

adolescent [B] **1** relating to a boy or girl in the period between being a child and being a grown person **2** *deprec* not yet adult: *adolescent opinions*

teenage [Wa5;A] of or belonging to the ages 13–19: *He's 21, but he still has teenage ideas.*

junior [Wa5;F (*to*)] **a** a younger: *At 28 he was still junior to everyone else in the business.* **b** of lower rank: *He is junior to several men in the office, although he is older than they are.* **c** having done shorter service in an organization *He is junior to me; I was in the company long before he joined it.* **2** [B] **a** young: *He's too junior to try for that important job. She's the most junior person in the room.* **b** of low rank: *a group of junior army officers; a junior post in the government* **3** [Wa5; *the* A] youngest or least in rank or time of service: *The junior officer has the worst duties.*

L207 *adjectives, etc* : **mature and adult**
[ALSO ⇒ C1–9]

mature [Wa2;B] **1 a** fully grown and developed: *A monkey is mature at a few years old, but a human being is not mature till at least sixteen.* **b** typical of a fully developed mind, controlled feelings, etc; sensible: *You must not be jealous when your sister gets presents; you must learn to behave in a more mature way.* **2** (of cheese, wine, etc) ready to be eaten or drunk; ripe: *The wine will be kept in the barrels until it is mature.* **3** carefully decided, after a time of

thought: *a mature judgement* **im-**[neg] **-ly**[adv] **-ness,-ity** [U]

adult [B] relating to or for a fully-grown person or animal, esp a person over an age stated by law, usu 18 or 21: *He's an adult person now. It is a very adult film.*

grown-up [B] *not fml* adult; fully developed; no longer a child: *She has a grown-up daughter. His behaviour is very grown-up for his age* (= although he is young).

fully-grown *also* **full-grown** [Wa5;B] *esp emot* mature, adult: *Stop telling him what to do; he's a full-grown man now!*

ripe 1 [Wa1;B] (of fruit and crops) fully-grown and ready to be eaten: *He saw a field of ripe corn. Don't pick the apples, they're not very/not quite ripe yet.* **2** [Wa1;B] (of cheese or wine) old enough to be eaten or drunk **3** [Wa1;B] (of qualities) fully developed: *I must ask someone of riper judgement than myself what to do.* **4** [Wa5;F *for*] ready; fit: *The land is ripe for industrial development. She is not yet ripe for marriage.* **5** [F *in*] having grown to the possession (of): *He is a man ripe in experience.* **of ripe age** grown-up and experienced **of ripe(r) years** *euph or humor* no longer young **the time is ripe (for)** it is time; things are ready (for): *I won't tell her the news until the time is ripe (for it).*

seasoned [A; (B)] **1** (of wood, etc) made hard and fit for use: *Wood must be well seasoned before use* **2** (*fig*) (of people) made skilled, etc, by time, practice, and experience: *They are all seasoned men.*

veteran [Wa5] **1** [C (*of*) A] (a person) who has had experience in the stated form of activity, esp in war: *Grandfather is a veteran of the First and Second World Wars. They are veteran officers.* **2** [C; A] (a person) who has had long experience in some form of activity: *The minister is too much a veteran in the world of politics to care much about what his opponents say. At the age of twelve the boy was already a veteran traveller, having travelled all over the world with his father.* **3** [C; A] (a thing) that has grown old with long use: *Every year a race is held in England for veteran cars* (= those made before 1916). *This sewing machine is a real old veteran.*

senior 1 [Wa5;F (*to*)] **a** older: *At age 68 she was senior to everyone in the room.* **b** of higher rank: *His appointment as chairman makes him senior to several older men.* **c** having done longer service in an organization: *He is senior to me; he was in the company when I joined it.* **2** [B] **a** old: *He's too senior to try for a young man's job. He is the most senior person in the room.* **b** of high rank: *a meeting of the most senior army officers; a senior government position* **3** [Wa5; *the* A] oldest or highest in rank or time of service: *The senior officer was only a captain.*

middle-aged [B] of or belonging to the years between youth and old age: *a middle-aged man*

L208 *adjectives* : **old in years**

old 1 [Wa1;B;E] advanced in age; of age: *How old are you? You're old enough to dress yourself, child. He is as old as John. She is 16 years old. She is a 16-year-old girl.* **2** [Wa1;B; *the* P; *the* U] having lived for a long time or long enough to show signs of age: *The club is for both young and old people. The old and the young do not always understand each other.*

aged [B; *the* P] *often* very old: *He's very aged now; over 90 years old. He spoke to an aged woman. The sick and aged need help.*

elderly [B; *the* P] *often emph* (of a person) getting near old age: *an elderly man; My father is getting elderly now and can't walk very fast. These stairs are too steep to be convenient for the elderly.*

senile [B] *sometimes deprec* of or coming from old age; showing the weakness of body or esp of mind associated with old age

ancient [B] *often humor* very old

L209 *nouns* : **ages and birthdays**

age 1 [U;C] the period of time a person has lived or a thing has existed: *What is your age? He is ten years of age. At your age you should know better. When I was your age I was still at school. What ages are your children?* **2** [U] one of the periods of life: *When a man has reached forty he has reached middle age.* **3** [U] an advanced or old period of life: *His back was bent with age.* **4** [U; (C)] the particular time of life at which a person becomes able or not able to do something: *There are age limits for members of the society. People who are either under age or over age may not join.* **(become) of age** (to be or reach) the particular age, usu 18 or 21, when a person becomes responsible in law for his own actions, and is allowed to vote, get married, etc **aged** [Wa5;F9] *fml* being of the stated number of years: *My son is aged twelve (years).*

birthday [C] **1** the date on which someone was born **2** the day when this date falls: *Happy birthday to you. Let me wish you a happy birthday. Are you having a birthday party?*

date of birth *also* **birth date** [C] the date on which one was born: *What is your date of birth? His birth date was the 10th July 1950.*

L210 *nouns* : **times of life** [U]

youth 1 the period of being young, esp the period between being a child and being fully grown; early life **2** the appearance, health, etc, of someone who is young

adolescence the state of being or time when one is adolescent [⇒ L206] or becoming an adult

prime (of life) the time when one is at one's best:

He died in the prime of life, when he was 35 (years old). He died in his prime, in a car accident.

middle age the years between youth and old age: *He's nearly 60, but he still considers himself to be in middle age.*

old age the part of one's life when one is old

senility the weakness of mind or body associated with old age

seniority the state of being senior to (= older or in a place longer than) someone else, esp in an organization: *He has more seniority than me; he has been here twelve years and I have only been here six.*

L211 *verbs* : **growing, ageing, and maturing**

grow [I∅] to become older, bigger, etc: *That child is growing fast—Yes, he's growing to be a big boy; he has grown a lot in the last year. The tree grew tall.*

age [T1;I∅] **1** to (cause to) become old: *After his wife's death he aged quickly. The fear of what might happen aged him.* **2** to (cause to) become fitter for use with the passage of time; (cause to) have a fully-developed taste: *The wine aged well. We age the wine in the deepest part of the building for a long time.*

mature [I∅] to become fully grown and developed; become mature [⇒ L207]

ripen [I∅;T1] to make or become ripe: *The sun ripens the corn. The corn ripens in the sun.*

grow up [v adv I∅] to grow to become an adult: *He grew up in Liverpool.*

develop [T1;I∅: (*from* or *out of*)] to (cause to) grow, increase, or become larger or more complete: *to develop from a seed into a plant; to develop a business/one's mind. Different conditions develop different sides of a person's character. He has gradually developed a liking for that tropical fruit. A child develops rapidly between the ages of 13 and 16.*

evolve [I∅;T1] to (cause to) develop over a long time: *Most scientists think that humans evolved from animals like monkeys. His plan is a good one and has evolved over several years. They have evolved a new plan.* **evolution** [U] **1** the act of evolving **2** the evolving, esp of one kind of life into another, from simple early forms to much more complex later forms **evolutionary** [Wa5;B] of, concerning, or like evolution: *Evolutionary development has made us what we are.*

season 1 [Wv5;T1] to give long experience to: *a seasoned traveller/soldier* **2** [T1;I∅] **a** to make (wood) hard and fit for use by drying **b** (of wood) become hard and fit for use

date 1 [T1] to find out or show the date of: *I can't date that house exactly, but it must be very old. The unusual shape of this pot dates it at about AD 400.* **2** [T1] to write the date on: *Please date your letters to me from now on.* **3** [T1;I∅] to (cause to) seem no longer in fashion: *This type of music is beginning to date. Her clothes date her, I'm afraid.*

L212 nouns : **antiques and antiquities**

antique [C] **1** a piece of furniture, jewellery, etc, that is old and therefore rare and valuable **2** a work of art or some other thing from the ancient world, esp of Rome or Greece

antiquity [C *often pl*] a building, work of art, etc, remaining from ancient times: *We have visited several of the antiquities of Italy.*

original 1 [C] (usu of paintings) that from which copies can be made: *These paintings are copies; those are the originals.* **2** [*the* R] the language in which something was originally written (*esp in the phr* **in the original**): *They are studying English in order to read Shakespeare in the original.* **3** [C] *infml, sometimes humor or derog* a person whose behaviour, clothing, etc, are unusual

Periods of time and their measurement

L220 nouns : **day and night** [C; U]

day a period of light: *I can see by day, but not by night.* [also ⇨ L226]

night 1 a period of dark, when the sun cannot be seen: *The moon shines at night. Two nights ago I felt very ill. People get higher pay for night work/work done at night. Night began to fall* (= it started to get dark). *The enemy often attack by/at night.* **2** [C9, esp *of*] (*fig*) a period of experience without hope, knowledge, etc: *He went on through the night of doubt and sorrow.* [also ⇨ L224]

L221 nouns : **the beginning of the day**

dawn 1 [C; U] the time of day when light first appears; the first appearance of light in the sky before the sun rises: *They take the boat out every day at dawn. The dawns here in the mountains are beautiful.* **2** [*the* R (*of*)] (*fig*) the beginning or first appearance (of something not material): *the dawn of civilization/of history* **dawn is breaking** light is beginning to appear **at (the) break of dawn/day** when light is just beginning to appear **at the crack of dawn** at the very first light of day; very early in the morning: *We got up at the crack of dawn and went hunting.*

sunrise *also infml* **sun-up** [U; C] the time when the sun is seen to appear

first light [U] *esp poet* dawn: *We'll move at first light.*

break of day [(*the*) U] *also* **daybreak** [U] *often poet* dawn

L222 nouns : **morning**

morning 1 [C; (U)] the first part of the day, from the time when the sun rises, usually until the time when the midday meal is eaten: *What time did you wake up this morning? It was a beautiful morning, but it rained in the afternoon. He doesn't like to get up early in the morning. What are you doing tomorrow morning? One morning during our holiday, we visited an ancient castle. The doctor had a busy morning's work. She goes shopping on Tuesday and Friday mornings. I must go to the shops some time during the morning. I don't want to telephone him so late at night; can't it wait until morning? The people next door play their radio from morning till night.* **2** [A] of, in, or taking place in this part of the day: *a morning concert; the morning newspapers* **3** [C; (U)] the part of the day from midnight until midday: *He didn't get home until two o'clock in the morning.* **4** [S (*of*)] *lit, often apprec* the early part (of anything): *She's only twelve, still in the morning of her life.*

forenoon [*the* U] the time before midday; morning: *He went there in the forenoon.*

noon [U] the middle of the day; twelve o'clock in the daytime: *She left home at noon. Noon is the earliest time I can come.*

midday [U] noon: *He finishes work at midday on Saturdays. 'Mad dogs and Englishmen go out in the midday sun'*—(Noel Coward).

afternoon 1 [C; U] the period between midday and sunset: *I shall sleep in the afternoon. I shall have an afternoon sleep.* **2** [S (*of*)] *lit* a rather late period (as of time or life): *She spent the afternoon of her life in the South of France.*

L223 nouns : **evening**

evening [C; U] the end of the day and early part of the night, between the end of the day's work and time for bed: *It was a warm evening. By the time he gets home there won't be much evening left. What are you doing this/tomorrow evening? Where were you yesterday evening/(AmE) last evening? She works in the evening(s). (AmE also) She works evenings. He goes out on Sunday evening(s). She bought an evening newspaper.*

eve 1 [R9 *usu cap*] the night or the whole day before a religious feast or holiday (*esp in the phrs* **Christmas Eve, New Year's Eve**): *They went to a party on New Year's Eve.* **2** [S (*of*)] the time just before an important event: *He fell ill on the eve of the examination.*

sunset 1 [U] the time when the sun is seen to disappear as night begins: *They stopped at sunset.* **2** [C] how the sun looks at that time: *What a beautiful sunset.*

sundown [U] sunset: *They left at sundown.*

twilight [U] the time between light and dark, day and night: *She often sits in the garden at twilight.*

dusk [U] the time when daylight is fading; the darker part of twilight, esp at night: *The lights go on at dusk.*

L224 *nouns* : **times of the night**

night 1 [C] any of various parts of the dark period when the sun cannot be seen: *This evening is my night off* (= when I don't work). *She slept well all night. Where were you on the night of the 17th May?* **2** [C] an evening, considered as an occasion: *We saw the show on its first night* (= at its first performance, in the evening). *Saturday is our cinema night* (= We go to the cinema on Saturday evenings). *Tonight's our night out* (= We go out tonight).
hours of darkness [(*the*) P] *poet* night
midnight [U] 12 o'clock at night: *He never goes to bed before midnight. The clock struck midnight. The doctor received a midnight call.*
middle of the night [*the* R] the time between midnight and about three a.m.: *The doctor was called out in the middle of the night.*
small hours [*the* P] *esp poet* the hours soon after midnight (one, two, three o'clock)

L225 *nouns & adverbs* : **yesterday, today, and tomorrow**

yesterday 1 [U] the day before this one **2** [C] (*fig & poet*) time that is not long past **3** [adv] on the day before this one **4** [adv] only a short time ago: *I wasn't born yesterday* (= I'm not a fool).
today 1 [U] this present day: *Have you seen today's newspaper yet? Today's my birthday!* **2** [U] (*fig*) this present time, period, etc: *Young people of today have no manners.* **3** [adv] during or on the present day: *Are we going shopping today?* **4** [adv] (*fig*) during or at the present time: *We sell more cars abroad today than we've ever done before.*
this morning [R] the morning of today: *Is he coming this morning?*
tomorrow 1 [U] the day following today: *Tomorrow will be my birthday!* **2** [S; U] (*fig*) the future: *The world of tomorrow will be very different from the present time.* **3** [adv] during or on the day following today: *We've got some guests coming tomorrow so I'll have to tidy the house today. It rained yesterday and today so perhaps it will be sunny tomorrow.*
in the morning tomorrow morning, esp when said in the evening: *I haven't got what you want now, but I can get it for you in the morning.*
day before yesterday [*the* R] two days ago: *I was there the day before yesterday.*
day after tomorrow [*the* R] two days after today: *I'll be there the day after tomorrow.*
tonight 1 [U] the night of today: *Tonight is a very special occasion. Listen to tonight's news on the radio. I'm looking forward to tonight!* **2** [adv] on or during the night of today: *I've*

been really tired today so I think I'll go to bed early tonight. He's coming at nine o'clock tonight. Tonight we went to an Italian restaurant.
last night [R] the night of yesterday: *She came last night and left this morning.*
night before last [*the* R] two evenings or nights before today
this evening [R] the evening of today: *I'll go there this evening.*
yesterday evening [R] the evening of yesterday: *Yesterday evening we went to an Italian restaurant.*
tomorrow evening [R] the evening of tomorrow: *She is coming here tomorrow evening at eight.*

L226 *nouns* : **measuring time**

second 1 [C] one of the sixty parts into which a minute is divided: *You have twenty seconds in which to do the work.* **2** [S] *infml* a very short space of time: *I'll be ready in just a second.*
minute 1 [C] one of the sixty parts into which an hour is divided: *There are sixty seconds in a minute and sixty minutes in an hour. The train arrived at exactly four minutes past eight. It's only a few minutes' walk from here to the station* (= walk taking a very short time). **2** [S] *infml* a short space of time: *I'll be ready in a minute* (= very soon). *Are you ready yet?—No, but I won't be a minute* (= I'll be ready very soon).
the minute (**that**) as soon as: *Although we hadn't met for 25 years, I recognized him the minute (that) I saw him.*
hour [C] **1** the period of time, sixty minutes, of which twenty-four make a day **2** [*often pl*] a fixed point or period of time: *The hour has come for us to have a serious talk. My* (*working*) *hours have been changed.* **3** [*usu pl*] a certain period of time: *The hours I spent with you were the happiest of my life.* **4** [*the* R] a time of day when a new hour starts: *The clock struck the hour. He arrived on the hour.* **5** (*fig*) an important time: *In my hour of need* (= when I needed help) *no one helped me. Nothing can be done at this hour of the talks. His hour has come* (= something important, or death). **6** a distance which one can travel in an hour: *It's only an hour away.* **after hours** later than the usual times of work or business **out of hours** before or after the usual times **at all hours** (at any time) during the whole of a period of time: *The shop is open at all hours. They come home at all hours.* **zero hour** the time when something happens after a certain period of waiting has passed
half hour [*the* R] the point in time thirty minutes past an hour: *The clock struck* (*on*) *the half hour.*
half an hour [S] thirty minutes: *I'll come in half an hour/in half an hour's time.*
quarter of an hour [S] fifteen minutes: *I'll be there in about a quarter of an hour.*

quarter [C; *the* R] fifteen minutes before or after the hour: *The buses come on the quarter. It's (a) quarter past ten.*

three quarters of an hour [S] forty-five minutes: *Give me about three quarters of an hour to get there.*

day 1 [C] a period of 24 hours: *There are seven days in a week.* **2** [C *often cap*] a special date: *Christmas Day was a Wednesday this year.* **3** [*the* R; C9] a period of time: *In my day things were different. He's the man of the day.* **4** [C] a period of work: *She works an eight-hour day and a five-day week. She's paid by the day.* **5** [C9] a period of success or fame (*esp in the phr* **to have (had) one's day**): *He was a very good actor, but I'm afraid he's had his day now.* **6** [*the* R] a (period of) struggle or competition: *We've won/lost the day.* **7** [S] a point of time; occasion: *We must get together again some day. We have lost a hundred times, but one day we shall win!* **the other day** in the recent past: *I saw your friend Smith-Fortescue the other day.* **day and night** all the time: *He works day and night.* **day after day/day in, day out** continuously: *He works day in, day out.* **this day week/today week/a week today** *BrE* a week from today **from day to day/day by day** each day; as time goes on **from one day to the next** two days one after the other: *I never know her plans from one day to the next.* **to the day** exactly (in time): *We left Spain one year ago to the day* (= on this exact date last year). **call it a day** *infml* to finish working for the day; decide to stop work (*esp in the phr* **Let's call it a day**) **It's all in a day's work** it's all part of one's job **to this day** until now: *I haven't told him the whole story to this day!*

week [C] a period of seven days (and nights) esp from Sunday to Saturday: *He goes there twice a week. It's three weeks till Christmas. Take a week's holiday.* **Monday week** *also* **a week on Monday** a week after Monday, on the next Monday **a week last Monday/next/this Monday/on Monday** a week before or after: *It happened a week last Monday. How long ago did it happen? It will be a week on Thursday. He's arriving two weeks next Saturday.* **week in, week out** without change or rest **(working) week** the period of time over which one works as in a factory or office: *He works a forty-hour week. The five-day week is usual in most firms.*

fortnight [C] *esp BrE* a period of two weeks or 14 days: *He comes here once a fortnight/once every fortnight/once in every fortnight. She has gone on a fortnight's holiday.*

month [C] **1** *also* **calendar month** one of the twelve named divisions in the year: *August is often the hottest month of the year in England. February is a short month; in most years it has 28 days.* **2** a period of about four weeks, esp from a particular date to the same date about four weeks later: *The baby was born on 23 September, so he'll be exactly six months old tomorrow* (23 March). *He has a month's holiday each year, which he usually takes in July.*

quarter [C] three months of the year, esp for making payments: *I pay my rent by the quarter. He goes there once in every quarter.*

year [C] **1** a measure of time equal to about 365¼ days, which is the amount of time it takes for the earth to travel completely round the sun **2** *also* **calendar year** a period of 365 or 366 days divided into 12 months beginning on January 1st and ending on December 31st **3** a period of 365 days measured from any point: *I arrived here two years ago today.* **4** a period of a year or about a year in which something particular happens: *The school year is broken up with many holidays.* **year in, year out** happening regularly each year

decade [C] a period of ten years: *Prices have risen steadily during the past decade.*

century [C] **1** a period of a hundred years: *Many centuries have passed since that time.* **2** one of the hundred year periods counted forwards or backwards from the supposed year of Christ's birth: *We live in the 20th century.*

millenium 1 [C] a period of a thousand years **2** [*the* R *usu cap*] a future age in which all people will be happy, contented, and live in good conditions

L227 nouns, etc : clocks, etc

[ALSO ⇒ H118]

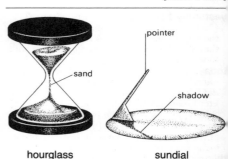

hourglass   sundial

clock [C] an instrument for measuring time: *There was a big clock at the top of the building. Is that clock right?—It's five minutes fast/slow.*

o'clock [adv] (used with the numbers from one to twelve in telling time) exactly (the hour stated) according to the clock: *What time is it? It's nine o'clock.*

USAGE In modern English, **o'clock** is used only in mentioning the exact hour, not the hour and a particular number of minutes: *nine o'clock* but *five past nine, half past nine,* etc.

sundial [C] an apparatus used esp in former times which shows the time according to where the shadow of the pointer falls when the sun shines on it

hourglass [C] a glass container made narrow in the middle so that the sand inside can run slowly from the top half to the bottom, taking one hour

metronome [C] an instrument with a moving arm that can be fixed to move from side to side a particular number of times per minute, and so give the speed at which a piece of music should be played

L228 *nouns, etc* : **parts of the clock, etc**

clock face,

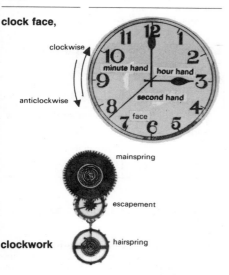

clockwork

tick 1 [*the* S (*of*)] the sound of a clock: *It was quiet; all I could hear was the tick of the clock.* **2** [I∅] (of clocks) to make this noise: *The clock stopped thicking/began to tick again.*
tick-tock 1 [S (*of*)] the sound made esp by a large clock **2** [I∅] (of clocks) to make this sound
stroke [C] the sound made by a clock on the hour: *After twelve strokes the sound died away. He arrived on the stroke of twelve* (= exactly at twelve).
chime 1 [C *usu pl*] the sound made by a set of bells: *Listen to the chimes of the church bells.* **2** [C] a musical sound like this: *The chime of the clock woke him up.* **3** [C *usu pl*] a set of bells, each having a different note, rung to produce a musical tune **4** [C] a musical instrument which makes a bell-like sound when struck **5** [I∅] (of clocks, bells, etc] to produce this sound
pendulum [C] **1** a weight hanging from a fixed point so as to swing freely **2** a rod with a weight at the bottom, used to control the working of a clock [⇒ PICTURE AT L229] **(the) swing of the pendulum** the change of public opinion from one idea to the opposite

L229 *nouns* : **kinds of clock** [C]

alarm (clock) a clock that can be set to make a

noise at any particular time to wake up sleepers: *What time shall I set the alarm (clock) for?*
grandfather clock a tall clock with a long wooden case and the face at the top

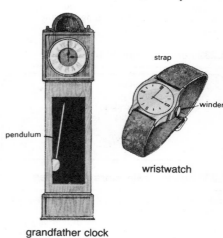

grandfather clock

watch a small clock that is worn on the wrist (**a wristwatch**) or carried in a pocket (**a pocket watch**): *My watch is slow/fast/correct.*

L230 *nouns* : **times on the clock**

the 12-hour clock	the 24-hour clock
1 am	0100 (hrs)
	(oh one hundred hours)
3 am	0300 hours
5.30 am	0530 hrs
7.15 am	0715 hrs
10 am	1000 hrs
	(ten hundred hours)
11.5 am	1105 hrs
	(eleven oh five hours)
12 noon	1200 hrs
	(twelve hundred hours)
1 pm	1300 hrs
	(thirteen hundred hours)
4 pm	1600 hrs
8 pm	2000 hrs
	(twenty hundred hours)
10 pm	2200 hrs
11.45 pm	2345 hrs
12 pm/midnight	2400 hrs

L231 *nouns* : **parts of a week** [C]

weekday 1 a day of the week, including Friday, not the weekend: *In Harlow there is one train timetable for weekdays, another for Saturdays, and another for Sundays.* **2** a day of the week, but not Sunday: *In Leeds there is one train timetable for weekdays and another for Sundays.*

weekend 1 Saturday and Sunday, esp when counted as a holiday **2** this period of time with the addition of Friday evening from the time of stopping work

L232 *nouns* : **days of the week**

Monday	Mon
Tuesday	Tues
Wednesday	Wed
Thursday	Thu
Friday	Fri
Saturday	Sat
Sunday	Sun

L233 *nouns* : **calendars and dates**

calendar [C] **1** a system of dividing the year into parts, etc: *The Christian and Muslim calendars are very different. A calendar month may have 31, 30, or in the case of February 28 days, and 29 in a leap year. A lunar month* (= the time it takes for the moon to circle the earth) *always has 28 days.* **2** a kind of sheet or book, often with pictures, which gives a list of the days and months of a particular year: *She bought a calendar for 1980/a 1980 calendar.* **Julian calendar** [*the* R] the calendar introduced by Julius Caesar in 46 BC and used esp in Europe until the Gregorian calendar began to be used instead **Gregorian calendar** [*the* R] the calendar generally used since 1582, when Pope Gregory XIII introduced it

date 1 [C] time shown by one or more of the following: the number of the day, the month, and the year (but not usu by month alone) **2** [C] a written or printed date: *This book has no date on it. The date on the coin is 1921.* **3** [U] a period of time in history (*esp in the phr* **of early/late date**): *This Greek dish is of very early date.*

AD [Latin *Anno Domini* 'the year of the Lord'] (the letters which mark the years of the Christian calendar): *1978 is actually 1978 AD.*

BC ['before Christ'] (the letters which mark the years before the supposed birth of Christ): *The city of Rome was founded* (= begun) *in the year 753 BC.*

AH ['after the Hegira' (= Mohammed's going from Mecca to Medina)] (the letters which mark the years of the Muslim or Islamic calendar)

leap year [C; U] (esp in the Gregorian calendar) every fourth year, containing one extra day (**February 29th**) to make 366 days, to bring the calendar into line with the true movement of the earth round the sun (= 365¼ days per year and not 365 exactly)

diary [C] **1** a daily record of esp the experiences, feelings, ideas, etc, of its writer **2** a book for

keeping such a record: *He wrote up the day's events in his diary.* **3** any record like this: *He writes a daily article in the local paper called 'One Man's Diary'.* **4** *also* **appointments book** a book arranged in calendar order with dates on its pages, in which appointments to meet people and other notes are kept: *Put these appointments and other times in the office diary, please.* **diarist** [C] an esp famous writer of diaries: *Samuel Pepys was a seventeenth-century English diarist.*

L234 *nouns* : **months of the year** [R]

January	Jan	July	Jul
February	Feb	August	Aug
March	Mar	September	Sep/Sept
April	Apr	October	Oct
May	May	November	Nov
June	Jun	December	Dec

L235 *adjectives & adverbs* : **daily, etc** [Wa5]

daily [B; adv] (happening, appearing, etc) once a day, or every day, or every day except Sunday and perhaps Saturday: *He goes there twice daily. The local daily newspaper is called The Daily News. He gets paid daily. He gets a daily wage.*

-ly [*suffix*] (*added to words like* **day, week,** *etc to* form an adjective or adverb) once every: *He makes monthly trips to London. He goes to London monthly. It's a weekly newspaper. She comes here fortnightly.*

L236 *combining form* : **mid-**

mid- (*with numbers, times, etc*) middle; in the middle of: *She's in her mid-twenties* (= is about 25 years old). *He starts his summer holiday in mid-July. It was a cold midwinter night.*

L237 *verbs* : **rising and setting** [H0]

rise 1 (of the sun, moon, or stars) to come up; appear above the horizon: *The sun rises in the east.* **2** to go up; get higher: *The river is rising after the rain. Smoke rose from the factory chimneys. Her voice rose higher and higher with excitement. New factories have risen on the edge of the town.* **3** *fml* to get out of bed; get up: *She rises before it is light.*

set (of the sun, moon, or stars) to go down; go below the horizon: *The sun sets in the west.*

L238 *nouns, etc* : **the seasons**

season [C; R] a period of time each year, as **a** spring, summer, autumn, or winter, marked by different weather and hours of daylight **b** marked by weather: *the cold season* **c** of (greater) activity of some kind: *the slow business season after Christmas; the London social season* **d** for some farming job: *the planting season* **e** of some animal activity: *the breeding season* **f** when a sport is played: *The football season begins next week.* **g** for hunting, fishing, etc: *During the season he goes shooting each week.* **h** around a holiday, esp Christmas: *Christmastime is called the season of good cheer.* **for a season** lit for a while; for a short time **in season 1** (of fresh foods) at the time of usual fitness for eating: *Fruit is cheapest in season.* **2** (esp of holiday business) at the busiest time of year: *Hotels cost more in season.* **3** (of animals) permitted to be hunted at that time

spring [U; C; (*the*) R] the season between winter and summer when things begin to grow again: *I like the trees in spring. She wore a new spring dress.*

summer 1 [U; C; (*the*) R] the season between spring and autumn when the sun is hot and there are many flowers: *in high summer* (= the warmest time); *a summer holiday; last summer; summer dresses* **2** [C] *esp old use & lit* a year of one's age: *He looked younger than his seventy summers.* **3** [*the* R] (*fig*) the best time (of a person's life, for a certain activity, etc): *That was the high summer of English literature.*

autumn, *AmE also* **fall** [U; C; (*the*) R] the season between summer and winter when leaves turn gold and fruits become ripe: (*fig*) *He has reached the autumn of his life.*

winter [U; C; (*the*) R] the season between autumn and spring when it is cold and most trees have lost their leaves: *I go on holiday in winter. She'll be home by winter. One winter we went to Switzerland. It was a very cold winter. Last winter we had a lot of snow. The last few winters have been very cold. He was wearing his winter clothes.*

-time [*comb form*] the time of the stated season: *In summertime we don't wear as many clothes as in wintertime.*

L239 *adjectives* : **the seasons** [B]

seasonal depending on the seasons, esp happening or active at a particular season: *He gets seasonal employment at a holiday camp. Selling heavy wool clothes is a seasonal business.* **-ly** [adv]

springlike like spring: *What lovely springlike weather for February!*

vernal *fml & lit* of, like, or appearing in the spring season: *the vernal woods*

summery like summer: *It's quite summery today, although it's only April.*

autumnal *often fml* like autumn: *the autumnal colours of the leaves*

wintry *also* **wintery** [Wa1] like winter, esp cold or snowy: *wintry clouds; a wintry scene*

L240 *nouns* : **special terms**

zenith 1 [*the* R] the point in the sky directly above a person on earth **2** [C *usu sing*] the highest point, as of hope or fortune: *Our spirits rose to their zenith after the victory.*

nadir 1 [*the* R] the point directly opposite the zenith **2** [C *usu sing*] the lowest point, as of hope or fortune: *After he lost the election, his spirits sank to their nadir.*

equinox [(*the*) C] one of the two times in the year (about March 21 and September 22) when all places in the world have day and night of equal length: *the vernal and autumnal equinoxes*

solstice [(*the*) C] either of the two times each year when the sun is farthest from the equator [⇨ L10]; the longest and the shortest days of the year: *The summer solstice is on June 22 and the winter solstice on December 22.*

phase [C] one of a fixed number of changes in the appearance of the moon or a body (**planet**) moving round the sun as seen from the earth at different times during their movement through space

L241 *adjectives* : **new and old** [Wa5;A]

new (of the moon) in its first phase: *It's a new moon tonight.*

old (of the moon) in its last phase

L242 *adjectives* : **relating to time** [Wa5;B]

diurnal 1 *fml or tech* of, related to, happening in, or active in the daytime rather than the nighttime: *the city's diurnal noises, a diurnal animal* **2** *poet & rare* taking a day's time or happening every day: *'Rolled round in earth's diurnal course/with rocks and stones and trees'* (Wordsworth). **-ly** [adv]

nocturnal *fml, tech, or poet* of, done, happening, or active at night: *a nocturnal visit; a nocturnal bird* **-ly** [adv]

annual 1 (of events) happening every year: *This show is an annual event here.* **2** (of plants) living for a year **-ly** [adv]

biennial 1 (of events) happening every two years: *A biennial art show was held in the city in 1970, 72, and 74.* **2** (of plants) living for two years and producing seed in the second year **-ly** [adv]: *It happens biennially.*

biannual (of events) happening twice in a year: *This is a biannual event, in February and September each year.* **-ly** [adv]

centennial (of events) happening every hundred years (*esp in the phr* **centennial anniversary**)

millenial (of events) **1** happening only once in a thousand years **2** relating to a period of a thousand years

L243 *nouns* : **anniversaries, etc** [C]

anniversary 1 a day which is an exact year or number of years after something has happened: *The anniversary of the day I first met you is next Friday. It's our wedding anniversary.* **2** a ceremony, feast, etc, held on this day

centenary *also esp AmE* **centennial** the day or year exactly a hundred years after a particular event: *In the USA July 4th 1876 was the centenary of the Declaration of Independence. They held their centenary celebrations here.*

Grammatical words and phrases relating to time

L250 *adverbs* : **the present moment**

now 1 at the present time: *I'm working now, but I'll see you later. Do it now, please, not tomorrow.* **2** *emph* (to get attention or in giving an order): *Now, sit down. Now listen to me. Now then, no more trouble!*

just now 1 at this moment: *We're having our dinner just now; come back later.* **2** a moment ago: *He telephoned just now; he wants money.*

at the moment at this moment or in this period of time: *I'm busy at the moment; come back later. At the moment he is in London, but he'll be back here next month.*

from now on from this time (into the future); starting now: *From now on I'll work harder.*

henceforth *also* **henceforward** *fml* from now on

L251 *adverbs* : **at a particular moment in the past**

then at that time in the past: *What were you doing in 1960?—Oh, I was still at school then.*

at that time *fml* then: *Was he working in 1960?—No, at that time he was still at school.*

some time ago quite a long time in the past: *I saw him some time ago in London, but haven't seen him since.*

once *esp lit & poet* some time ago: *He once knew her, but they are no longer friends. No one remembers that once-popular singer.*

at one time at a time in the past: *At one time he was the leader of the group, but his friend is the leader now.*

formerly *more fml* at one time (but not now):

Formerly France had a king, but not any more (= not now).

previously at an earlier time: *He is working in London now, but previously he was in New York. As I said previously, this is a new plan.*

L252 *adverbs* : **at a particular moment in the near future**

soon 1 [Wa5] before long; within a short time: *I shall move house soon. Soon after the party she felt ill. It soon became clear that. . . . They should be home very soon.* **2** [Wa1] quickly; early: *Please get this done as soon as possible; the sooner the better. I can't do it until after noon at the soonest. He got married as soon as he left university. How soon can you get here? I got there too soon; the shop wasn't open yet. Will Thursday be soon enough?* **3** [Wa1] (*in phrases expressing comparison*) readily; willingly: *I'd sooner die than marry him! Will you dance?—I'd just as soon not, if you don't mind.* **No sooner . . . than** When . . . at once: *No sooner had we sat down than we found it was time to go. No sooner said than done!* (= It'll be done/it has been done very fast) **sooner or later** at some time certainly; if not soon then later: *Sooner or later we must repair the roof.* **speak too soon** to assume [⇒ G8] a fact, result, etc, before it is certain: *I hope I'll get the job, but I mustn't speak too soon.*

in the near future *fml* quite soon: *He is planning to go to France in the near future.*

in a little while *usu infml* very soon: *I'm going out but I'll be back in a little while.*

shortly soon: *Mr Jones will be back shortly. He left shortly before you came in.*

L253 *adverbs* : **at some time in the future**

before (too) long before a lot of time passes; quite soon: *I can't do it now, but I'll do it before (too) long.*

by and by *infml* before long; at some future time: *He'll come back by and by.*

then at a particular time in the future: *I'm coming on Tuesday; I'll see you then.*

sometime at some time esp in the future but also in the past: *We'll meet again sometime soon, I hope. He met her sometime last year. The work will be finished sometime, but I don't know when.*

after some time after some time has passed: *After some time he met her again.*

at some future date *fml* sometime: *We can meet and deal with the matter at some suitable future date.*

eventually after a long time: *He eventually went home, but much later than he had hoped. What happened eventually?—Oh, they went to live in America.*

L254 *adverbs* : **at the end of some time**

at last after everything is finished or no more is expected: *At last the work was done and he could rest. She has come at last!*

at length *often fml* after a (very) long time: *At length he stopped reading, looked up and spoke to the waiting men.*

finally *emph* at last: *She has finally done what she promised to do. The letter finally came.*

in the end *often poet & emot* at last; finally: *They won in the end. In the end everyone was happy.*

L255 *adverbs* : **while something else is happening**

in the meantime in the time between (two events): *Go there and come back as soon as you can; in the meantime I'll go on with the work.*

meanwhile *also* **meantime** in the meantime: *He was in London for a week and meanwhile she went on with the work.*

at the same time when two or more things are happening: *He went to London and at the same time she went on with the work.*

simultaneously at exactly the same time: *They came into the room simultaneously, but through different doors.* **simultaneous** [Wa5;B] happening at the same time: *The two events were simultaneous.*

L256 *adverbs* : **up to a particular moment**

so far up to the present ·moment: *So far the weather has been good, but I think it is going to rain later today.*

up to now/then *usu not fml* up to this/that time: *Up to now the weather has been good. Up to then the weather was good, but. . . . I'm going to London next week but up to then I'll be here.*

up till now/then *more fml* up to now/then

up to this/that moment *fml* up to now/then

hitherto *very fml* (not used of the future) until this time: *Hitherto he has been able to do the work, but now he can't.*

yet 1 at this moment; now: *It is not time to go yet.* **2** at that moment; then: *It was not yet time to go.* **3** up to this moment; so far: *He hasn't done much yet.* **4** at this time as at earlier times; still: *He is yet a child.* **5** at a future time: *The plan may yet succeed.*

as yet up to this moment: *We have not succeeded as yet.*

by now/then (happening) before this/that time: *He left Edinburgh nine hours ago by car: he should be in London by now. By then he was in France.*

by this/that time *more fml* by now/then

already 1 by or before a stated or suggested

time: *He had already gone when I arrived.* **2** before: *I've been there already and don't want to go again.* **3** sooner than expected: *Have you eaten your food already? What a good boy you are!*

USAGE **already** takes the perfect tenses of the verb

L257 *adverbs* : **for all time and on all occasions**

always 1 at all times; at each time: *The sun always rises in the east. You are always beautiful. It is always a mess. The train is always on time. Do you sing in the bath?—Always!* **2** *esp emph* for ever: *I will love you always.* **3** *esp emph* again and again; with regularity; often: *You are always asking me for food.*

ever 1 at any time: *Nothing ever makes him angry. Do you ever go to concerts?—No, never/Yes, sometimes. If you're ever in Spain, come and see me. Have you ever been to Paris?—No, never./Yes (once). He hardly/scarcely ever (=almost never) goes out. She seldom (=not often) if ever wears trousers. If ever you want a drink, I'll give you one. I thought I'd better warn you, just in case David should ever mention it. It was the biggest room you ever saw.* **2** (after *as* or *than* in comparisons) at any time (before): *He drives his car as far as ever/faster than ever (before). It's more important than ever for you to eat properly.* **3** (after *as* and before the subject in comparisons, used for giving force to an expression): *I did it as fast as ever I could.* **4** (after *how, what, when, where, who, why,* used for giving force to a question): *What ever are you doing? How ever shall we get there?* **5** *old use or in comb* always: *The ever-increasing population of the city is causing difficulties.* **6** *AmE infml* (used for strengthening exclamations in the form of questions): *Is it ever big! Can he ever hit that ball!* **ever after** always after that: *They lived happily ever after* (end of a fairy story). **ever and anon** *poet* from time to time   **ever so/such** *infml, esp BrE* very: *It's ever so cold. She's ever such a nice girl.* **Yours ever** *also* **Ever yours** *infml* (used at the end of a letter above the signature)   **never ever** *infml* never: *I never ever do any washing.*

for always *esp emph* for all time: *He says that marriage is for always.*

forever, for ever *esp emph & poet* for all time: *'I'll love him forever!' she said.*

for good *emph* for all time: *She's leaving this place for good next week! She'll soon be gone for good.*

for good and all *infml emph* for all time

the whole time all the time that something is happening: *We enjoyed the party, but he sat there the whole time doing nothing and saying nothing.*

all along *not fml* for the whole time: *She said that she would do it but all along she planned to* *do something else. I thought all along that she wouldn't do it!*

never 1 not ever; not at any time: *I've never met him and I hope I never will meet him. He never gets up early in the morning. Never forget to lock the door at night. Never (before) have I met such a strange person.* **2** not (*esp in such phrs as* **never so much as** *and* **never do** *and in commands*): *Never fear!* (= don't worry). *He never so much as said 'Thanks'* (= didn't even thank me). *This dirty shirt will never do* (= isn't good enough to wear).* **never mind** *infml* **1** don't worry: *I forgot to bring your book—Never mind (about) that; I'll get it myself tomorrow.* **2** Don't pay any attention to what was just said: *Where's my book? Oh, never mind—I've found it.*

at no time *emph* never; on no occasion: *He says that he told me, but at no time did he say anything about it!*

L258 *adverbs* : **on some occasions only**

sometimes on some occasions: *He sometimes comes to see us, but not often. I think sometimes that she doesn't like him very much.*

occasionally *also* **(every) now and again, every so often, now and then, from time to time**; sometimes: *He occasionally comes to see us. He comes to see us from time to time. Every now and again he comes to see us. He comes here now and again. Now and then he comes to see us.*

once in a while occasionally but not often: *Once in a while he comes to see us.*

on and off *also* **off and on** *infml* occasionally: *I see him off and on. She goes there on and off.*

seldom not at all often: *He seldom eats breakfast. She goes there seldom, if ever. I see them very seldom now. She seldom, if ever, reads a book. He seldom or never reads.*

rarely seldom; almost never: *She rarely comes here now. He rarely reads a book.*

often 1 (at) many times: *How often do you go there?—Once a month. How often have you been there?—Twice. Often he doesn't know what he wants. He goes to London quite often.* **2** in many cases: *American girls are often very pretty.* **once too often** one time more than is allowed: *You've done that once too often and must be punished!*

frequently *more fml* (found or happening) often: *She frequently goes there.*

for a time/while for a certain length of time: *I'll work here for a time, then move on. He's been doing this for (quite) a while now; at least six months.*

for some time (now) for quite a long time: *She's been doing this work for some time; a year or more. For some time now he has been looking ill.*

L259 *conjunctions, adverbs, etc* : **when and while**

when 1 [adv] at what time?; how soon?: *When will they come? Do you know when they're coming?* **2** [adv] at which time: *At the time when we met he was living in Greece. It's the sort of day when you'd like to stay in bed.* **3**[conj] at (any time during) that time: *Come in when you've taken your coat off. She was beautiful when she was a girl. I jumped up when she called. When sleeping I never hear a thing.* **4** [conj] *genl (with present tense)* if: *No one can make a dress when they haven't learnt how.* **5** [conj] since: *I can't tell you anything when you won't listen.* **6** [conj] although: *She stopped trying when she might have succeeded next time.* **7** [conj] and then: *They arrive at six, when we all have dinner.* **8** [pron] what time: *Since when has that been so?* **9** [pron] which time: *I fell asleep at ten, before when I was reading for an hour.*

while [conj] **1** at the time when: *Don't talk while you're eating. He did not move while the music went on, but got up when it ended.* **2** although: *While I am willing to go, I would like it better if you went.* **3** on the other hand: *He likes coffee, while she likes tea.*

as [conj] **1** at the exact moment when: *She dropped the glass as she stood up.* **2** at the same moment as: *He saw her as they were both getting off the bus.*

all the time [conj] every moment when: *He sat quietly all the time she sang.*

the moment/instant/minute [conj] *not fml* at the exact time when: *She came the moment he asked her to. The instant I heard the news I came. He'll do it the minute he is free* (= has time).

as soon as [conj] at the first moment when: *As soon as I heard the news, I came. Do it as soon as you can, please.*

just as [conj] exactly at the time when: *He came in just as I was going out.*

every time [conj] at every time that (something happens): *John wins/loses every time we play.*

whenever 1 [conj] (not with perfect tense) when; at any time at all: *Come whenever you like.* **2** [conj] every time: *Whenever we see him we speak to him.* **3** [adv] at any time: *Whether they arrive tonight, tomorrow, or whenever, they'll be welcome.*

L260 *adverbs, prepositions, etc* : **before and after**

before 1 [adv] at an earlier time: *Haven't I seen you before?* **2** [prep] earlier in time than: *It happened before 1937. He got there before me.* **3** [conj] earlier than the time when: *He got there before I did.* **4**[conj] more willingly than: *He will die of hunger before he will steal.*

beforehand [adv] **1** in advance: *Please let me*

know your plans beforehand. **2** too early:
Don't be beforehand in making up your mind.
after 1 [adv] following in time or place; later: *We
arrived soon after. They were happy ever after.*
2 [prep] following in time or order; later than;
next: *We shall leave after breakfast. Soon after
the performance we went home. They will
return the day after tomorrow.* **3** [prep] following continuously: *Year after year went by without hearing of him. One joke after another came
pouring out of him.* **4** [prep] following in place
or order: *He entered the room after his father.
Your name comes after mine in the list.* **5** [prep]
as a result of; because of: *After the way he
treated me I shall never want to see him again.*
6 [prep] in spite of: *After all my care in packing
it the clock arrived broken. I gave him plenty of
directions but he got lost after all.* **7** [prep] in the
manner or style of: *It was a painting after the
great master.* **8** [prep] in accordance with: *You
are a man after my own heart; we think and act
alike in nearly all things.* **9** [conj] at a later time
than: *I found your coat after you had left the
house.*
ago [adv] back in time from now; in the past: *He
left ten minutes ago. It was a long while ago.
How long ago did he leave?*
(not) later than [prep, conj] (not) happening or
done after (a stated time): *Come not later than
eight o'clock. The work was finished later than
he had hoped.*
past [prep] after (a stated time): *It's half past
two now* (= 2.30 am or pm). *It was well past
midnight when he came home.*
to [prep] (in telling the time) before: *It's five
(minutes) to six* (= before six o'clock).

L261 *adverbs & conjunctions* : **many times**

as often as [conj] as many times as; each time
that: *As often as he does it, he fails.*
as often as not [adv] as many times one way as
the other; at least fifty per cent of the time:
They come here as often as not.
more often than not [adv] more times one way
than the other; more than fifty per cent of the
time: *More often than not he does help us.*

L262 *adverbs, etc* : **immediately**

immediately 1 [adv] at that exact moment: *I
came immediately after I'd eaten.* **2** [conj] as
soon as: *I came immediately I'd eaten.*
at once *emph* immediately: *He told them to do it
at once. Do it at once!*
at this/that very moment *emph* exactly now/
then: *I didn't expect him to come at this very
moment. He did it at that very moment.*
straight away/off *not usu fml* immediately: *He
did the work straight away.*
right away *not usu fml* immediately; without
delay: *Let's eat right away!*

instantly *emph & often fml* immediately; at
once: *He did it instantly.*
forthwith *esp older use & fml* immediately: *He
did it forthwith.*

L263 *adverbs* : **later**

later after a particular time: *I can't do it now, but
I'll do it later, perhaps tomorrow. Later, he
came back. He came back much later/a lot later.*
afterwards after a particular thing has happened or been done: *That was nothing in comparison with what happened afterwards! Afterwards he said he was sorry he did it.*
after the event *fml* later, after something (bad)
has happened: *I'm sorry.* —*It's easy to be sorry
after the event!*
later on *not usu fml* afterwards: *Later on he
came back to the house, when she had gone. I'll
do it later on; I can't do it now.*
after *infml* later; when something is finished:
Can I come and see you after?

L264 *prepositions, etc* : **till and until**

till [prep, conj] up to (a stated time): *I'll be here
till six o'clock, but not later/after. They waited
till he came. Don't go till I tell you to.*
until [prep, conj] more fml till: *I shall be here
until six o'clock, then I shall go. Wait until I tell
you to go. Until he comes, we cannot do anything.*
up to [prep] *infml & emph* till: *I'll be here up to
six, but not a minute more. He works up to
about eight in the evening every day.*
towards [prep] nearly at (a stated time):
*Towards the middle of the night he began to feel
tired and wanted to sleep. He left towards eight
o'clock.*

L265 *prepositions* : **during**

during 1 through the whole course of: *He swims
every day during the summer. They're open
from ten o'clock until six o'clock during the
week and on Saturdays from ten o'clock until
two o'clock.* **2** at some point in the course of:
*He came in during the night. Only two buses left
during the morning.*
inside *infml* before (a stated time) is finished:
I'll come inside half an hour.
within inside the limit of esp time; not beyond or
more than: *He'll arrive within an/the hour.*
at some time/point in *fml* at a particular time
within a longer time: *At some point in the
afternoon he telephoned her.*

L266 *adverbs & prepositions* : **through and almost**

through [prep] from the beginning to the end
of: *He worked (all) through the night.*

throughout [prep] *emph* through: *He worked throughout the night and the next day.*

for the whole of [prep] *fml* throughout: *Are you planning to work for the whole of the night?*

for [prep] during (a time); through the whole of: *He worked for five hours without a break* (= without stopping). *I'm staying here for two weeks.*

almost [adv] **1** just before: *It was almost midnight when he came home.* **2** just about, but not: *Last year she was very ill and almost died. Almost no one saw him there* (= Hardly anyone saw him there, but a few did).

about [adv] at almost or approximately (a stated time): *I'll come about ten o'clock.*

just about [adv] more or less at (a stated time): *He came at just about eight o'clock.*

near(ly) [adv] almost: *It was near(ly) ten o'clock when he left.*

more or less [adv] not exactly but nearly: *It's more or less time to leave. We got there more or less when we wanted to.*

roughly [adv] *infml* more or less: *Roughly when did he get there?*

approximately [adv] *fml* more or less: *She left at approximately eight o'clock. It takes approximately one week to do the work.*

close to/on [adv] *not fml* nearly: *It will be close on ten o'clock when we get there. Close to four hundred people came.*

L267 adverbs : again, and similar expressions

again once more; one more time; another time: *Please say that again. Do it again. Please come again. You must never do that again.*

over again once more; a second time: *Do it over again, please.*

again and again *also* **time and (time) again** *emph* very often: *She said it again and again until she could say it really well.*

over and over (again) *often deprec* again and again: *He kept singing the same song over and over again!*

on *emph* continuously; without stopping: *I won't go home yet; I'll work on/stay on a bit. He worked on through the night.*

on and on *very emph* continuously: *He talked on and on about his holiday till we were tired of it.*

away *often apprec* continuously: *That child plays away happily for hours. She worked away at it till she finished it successfully.*

repeatedly *fml & emph* often; again and again: *He repeatedly failed to pass the examination.*

L268 prepositions, etc : up to and including

up to and including [prep] from a first usu stated date to the end of (a second stated date): *He will be in London from April up to and including August 5th.*

inclusive [Wa5;E] including (a stated date): *He will be in London from Monday to Thursday inclusive.*

through [prep] *AmE* up to and including: *He will be in New York Monday through Thursday/April through August.*

L269 adjectives : on and off [Wa5;F]

on happening, working, etc: *The show is on from Monday to Saturday. He's on from 9 am to 5 pm.*

off not happening, working, etc: *The show is off; two of the actors are ill. He gets off (work) at 5 pm.*

L270 prepositions : for a period of time

for from the beginning to the end of (a stated time): *I'll be here for two weeks.*

over a period of *fml* for: *He has worked there over a period of years/ten years.*

L271 prepositions, etc : since and from a particular time

since 1 [prep] beginning at (a stated past time) and continuing to the present time or the time of speaking, writing, etc: *He has worked there since 1969, I've been here since January.* **2** [prep] during the period after (a stated past time): *I haven't seen her since March.* **3** [conj] after the past time when: *It's been years since I enjoyed myself so much as last night.* **4** [conj] continuously from the time when: *We've been friends since we met at school.* **ever since** *emph* since: *We've been friends ever since we were children.*

from [prep] beginning at (a stated time) and continuing (to some other stated time): *He worked there from 1962 to 1974.*

L272 prepositions : at, in, and on particular times

at (used with times, esp those on a clock, for meals, and certain important occasions, etc): *Come here at 6 pm. I'll meet you at 6. I told her about it at dinner last night. See you at Christmas!*

in 1 during (the stated period of months, years, etc): *I was in London in January/in 1974.* **2** during (certain events which go on for a long time: *He died in the war.*

on during (a day): *See you on Tuesday. On Monday I was in New York.*

L273 *verbs* : **helping verbs showing time**

[ALSO ⇨ G265 TENSES]

will 1 (to express the simple future tense): *The weather will be good tomorrow. He'll* (= He will) *come next week. If you study hard, you will pass the exam.* **2** to be willing to: *Will you come in now, please?* **3** (to express or answer a question or request): *Will you telephone me tomorrow?—Yes, I will/No, I will not/No, I won't.*

shall *esp Eng E* **1** (to express the simple future tense, with *I* and *we*): *We shall be going there soon. I shall do it next week.* **2** (for polite suggestion with *I* and *we*): *Shall I go or will you?* **3** *fml* (to express a strong promise, intention, or expectation): *It shall be done in exactly the way you want. That day shall come.* **4** *fml* (to express a command or what must be done): *This law shall have effect in Scotland.*

USAGE Where *shall* is used in the normal expression of the simple future tense, *will* can be used to express emphasis: *I certainly will come tomorrow!*

would 1 (past tense of **will**, esp as used in reported speech): *They said that the weather would be good the next day.* **2** (to express conditions, hopes, etc): *I would like to go, but I can't. If you helped her, she would be able to do it.*

should 1 (past tense of **shall**, esp as used in reported speech): *I knew if I kept trying I should succeed at last.* (*fml*) *He said he should return, and he did.* **2** (with *that*, after adjectives and such verbs as *intend, desire, demand, anxious*): *It's odd that you should mention his name. I was anxious that our plan should not fail.* **3** *esp Eng E* (used with *I* and *we* in conditional sentences with a past t, or about the past): *We should never have won without your help. I should stay out of trouble if I were you.* **4** (used in phrs like the following, to express humour or surprise): *As I left the house, who should come to meet me but my old friend Sam! At that point, what should happen but the car wouldn't start!*

be *not fml* (to express the future tense): *He is in London next week.*

be about to (to express an immediate future act): *I was about to leave when you came in, but I won't go now.*

be going to (to express a planned future): *He's going to go to New York next month. I was going to do it, but she did it first.*

have (to express perfect tenses): *I have been in France; have you* (*been there*)? *He hasn't seen her yet. She should have gone, but she hasn't.*

M

Movement, location, travel, and transport

Moving, coming, and going

M1 *verbs, etc* : **moving, coming, and going**

move 1 [T1; I∅] to (cause to) change place or bodily position: *The prisoner was tied so tightly that he couldn't move hand or foot. The child moved just as his father was taking a photograph of him. The baby hasn't moved since he was put to bed.* **2** [T1; I∅] to take or go from one place to another: *Please move your car; it's blocking my way out. The sick woman's bed was moved downstairs. He stood in the doorway, and wouldn't move out of my way. The talks have been moved from Paris to London.* **3** [I∅] to be in movement; go, walk, run, etc, esp in a particular way: *The guard blew his whistle and the train began to move. Have you ever seen a dancer move more gracefully?* **4** [X9; L9] to (cause to) change: *Attempts were made to move the talks from a consideration of principles to more practical ideas. The government's opinions on this matter haven't moved; they're still favourable.* **5** [I∅] *infml* to travel, run, etc, very fast: *That car was really moving; it must have been doing 90 miles an hour.* **6** [I∅] to change one's place of living or working: *Their present house is too small, so they've decided to move.* **7** [Wv4;T1] **a** to take (furniture and other articles) from one house, office, etc to another: *a moving van* **b** *infml* to take (a person's) furniture and other articles from one house, office, etc, to another: *We're being moved by Richardson and Company.* **8** [T1 (*to*)] to cause (a person) to have or show feelings, as of pity, sadness, anger, admiration, etc: *Her sad story moved all who heard it. The sick child's suffering moved his father to tears.* **9** [I∅ (*on*)] to take action (with regard to): *When will the government move on this important matter?* **10** [I∅] (of work, events, etc) to advance; go forward; get nearer to an end: *His business affairs aren't moving and his debts are increasing. Work on the new building is moving more quickly than was expected. Let's get things moving (= Let's take effective action).* **11** [T1; V3] to cause (a person) to act, change an opinion, etc: *This artist can paint only when the spirit moves him (= when he feels the desire to paint). Nothing will move him from his determination to marry that girl. I felt moved to speak.* **12** [L9, esp *among, in*] to lead one's life or pass one's time (esp with or among people of a certain class): *He hasn't moved much among educated people. She's a very wealthy woman and moves in the highest circles of society (= among people of high rank).* **13** [C] an act or result of moving, esp to do something: *He made no move to go.*

move about *also* **move around** [v adv] **1** [T1; I∅] to (cause to) move continually; fail to keep still: *Don't move about while I'm trying to take your photograph.* **2** [I∅] to change one's home, place of work, etc, continually

move along [v adv] **1** [I∅] to move further towards the front: *The people standing in the bus moved along, to make room for others.* **2** [T1; I∅] to move on (*def 2*)

move away [v adv I∅] to go to a new home in a different area: *Do the Simpsons still live here?—No, they've moved away.*

move in [v adv] **1** [I∅] to go to live in a new home: *We've bought the house, but we can't move in until next month.* **2** [I∅ (*on*)] to (prepare to) take control, attack, etc: *Our competitors have gone out of business, so now our company can move in. The police are moving in on the criminals hiding in the house.*

move off [v adv I∅] to leave; depart: *The guard blew his whistle and the train moved off. I think it's about time we were moving off (= we ought to leave now).*

move on [v adv] **1** [I∅ (*to*)] to change (to something new): *I think we've talked enough about that subject; let's move on.* **2** [T1; I∅] to (order to) go away to another place or position: *The man was drunk and was annoying people, so the policeman moved him on. 'Come on, sir, move on,' said the policeman. We're not welcome in this town; we must move on.*

move out [v adv I∅ (*of*)] to leave and cease to be or live in a place, home, etc: *They moved out last week.*

move over [v adv T1; I∅] to (cause to) change position in order to make room for someone or something else: *Move over and let your grandmother sit down.*

come 1 [I∅, 4] to move towards the speaker or a particular place: *Should I come now or later? Come here, you wicked boy; I'm going to punish you. Why don't you come when you know your dinner's ready? The little girl came running to her mother for sympathy.* **2** [I∅] to arrive where the speaker is or at a particular place: *Has Joyce come yet? I thought I heard* *her car. The train slowly came into the station.* **3** [I0] to arrive as expected or in the course of time: *Christmas comes once a year. Uncle's birthday's coming so we must remember to get him a present.* **4** [L9, esp *up to, down to*] to reach: *The water came (up) to my neck. Her hair came (down) to her knees. The water came through to/as far as my garden.* **5** [L9] to exist in a particular place: *In this list of goods the price comes next to the article.* **6** [Wv6;L9] to be (in a particular place in an ordered set): *Your family should always come before your job. My wife comes first, my children second.* **7** [I3] to happen: *How did Jean come to be invited to this party?* **8** [L9, esp *from, of*] to happen as a result of the stated cause: *Success in life does not come from being lazy. This accident came of your carelessness.* **9** [L7] to become: *The buttons on my coat came unfastened. The door came open.* **10** [L9] to be offered, produced, etc: *Shoes come in many shapes and sizes. Milk usually comes in bottles. Milk comes from cows.* **11** [L9] to move into view: *The sun came and went but mostly it was cloudy. Darkness came at 6 o'clock.*

go **1** [I0] to move away from the speaker or a particular place (usu so as to reach another): *I must go/be going. When does the train go? He went early.* **2** [L9] to travel or move: *We went by bus. It can go by post/in the post. The car's going too fast. We went to France for our holidays. His hand went to his gun.* **3** [Wv6;L9] to reach (as far as stated): *Which road goes to the station? The valley goes from east to west. The roots of the plant go deep.* **4** [I0] to start an action: *Get going* (= start) *on the work. I hope the water isn't cold when I jump in.—Here goes! The signal to begin a race is 'One, two, three, go!' or 'Ready, steady, go!'* **5** [I4] **a** to do (an activity): *to go walking/shopping/swimming* **b** [also I0 and] *infml* to do (something undesirable): *He went and told her the secret. You've gone and done it now! Don't go saying that.* **6** [I0] to be placed (esp usually): *The boxes (can) go on the shelf.* **7** [I0] (esp of machines) to work (properly): *This clock doesn't go. It goes by electricity.* **8** [L7] to become (by a natural change, or by changing on purpose): *She's going grey. Her hair's going grey. The milk went sour. He's gone blind/mad. This used to be a state school but it's gone independent. He went white with anger.* **9** [L7] to remain (in a certain state): *Her complaints went unnoticed. After his enemy's threats he went in fear of his life. Should a murderer go free/go unpunished? I usually go hatless. When the crops fail, the people go hungry.* **10** [I0 (*to, for*)] to be sold: *The clothes were going cheap. It went for so little. The house went to the one who made the highest offer. Any more offers?—Going to the man in the green hat. Going, going, gone!* **11** [L9, esp *in, on*] to be spent or used: *Half our money goes on food and clothes for the children. His time goes in watching television. My money goes a long way/doesn't go far* (= buys a

lot/buys little). **12** [I0] to cease or disappear: *Summer's going. Where's my pen? It's gone (off my desk).* **13** [*must, can, have to* I0] to be got rid of: *This car must go. We can't afford it any more.* **14** [Wv6;I0] to (have to) be accepted or acceptable: *What I say goes, so stop arguing. Anything goes* (= You can do as you like). *That goes for all of us* (= We all agree on this). *It goes without saying that his brother should help him.* **15** [I0] **a** to die or (sometimes) to become unconscious: *After George went she moved into a smaller house.* **b** to be damaged; to weaken or wear out: *My voice has gone because of my cold. These shoes are going.* **16** [L9] to happen (in a certain way): *The hours went slowly. How are things going? Do you think the result will go in our favour? The party went well. It will go hard with him* (= be difficult for him). **17** [I0] to lose one's usual powers of control (*in the phrs* **Let oneself go, far gone**): *He's pretty far gone* (as in illness, when overcome by feelings, or mad). **18** [L9] to make a movement: *When he shook hands he went like this.* **19** [Wv6;L9;(L5)] **a** to be stated, said, or sung in a certain way: *The story goes that he was murdered. This is how it goes— 'Mary had a little lamb'.* **b** to have or suit a certain tune: *It goes to a new tune. The tune goes something like this.* **20** [L9] to make (a sound): *The mirror went crack and fell off the wall.*

pass **1** [I0] to move or go forward; advance: *Because of the large crowd in the street the carriage was unable to pass.* **2** [T1;I0] **a** to reach and move beyond (a person or place): *I have been standing here for an hour but no one has passed (me).* **b** (of a car or motorist) to reach and move beyond (another car): *One should not pass at a bend in the road.* **3** [T1;I0] to get or go through, across, over, or between: *No one is allowed to pass the gates of the camp. The river is not deep enough here for a large ship to pass.* (*fig*) *Not a word about this matter will pass my lips.* **4** [X9;L9] to move, place, or be placed (in or for a short space of time): *We can pass a rope round this dead tree. A cloud passed across the sun.* (*fig*) *As he was drowning, all the events in his life seemed to pass before him. The policeman asked the people to pass along. The black cloud soon passed over.* **5** [D1 (*to*); T1] to give (esp by hand): *Please pass the bread; I can't quite reach it. He passed him the bread. He passed the bread to us.* **passable** [B] (of roads, etc) able to be travelled: *The snow has gone and the mountain roads are passable again.* **im-** [*neg*] **-bly** [adv Wa3]

get [L9] *genl & emph* to move; come or go: *Get on your way! He got out as quickly as he could.*

set [L9; V4] to start (oneself, someone or something) moving, coming, going, etc: *She set out (on the journey) yesterday. He set off down the road. He set the machine going.*

circle [T1; I0] to move in a circle (around): *The dog circled the sheep. There was an aeroplane circling in the sky above.*

circulate [I∅] to move around from place to place: *The traffic* (= all the vehicles) *in the city circulates fairly freely. A story is circulating about him among his friends; I don't know if it's true or not. Blood circulates in the body through our arteries and veins* [⇨ B36]. **circulation** [U] the act of circulating

approach 1 [T1; I∅] to move, come, or go near: *He approached slowly. He approached them slowly. Spring is approaching.* **2** [T1] to come or go to (someone) to talk about, suggest, ask for, etc something: *He approached me about this last week. Can you approach them on the matter for me?*

near [T1; I∅] *often lit* to come closer in distance or time (to); approach: *He got more nervous as the day neared. We could see the tall buildings as we neared New York.*

M2 *verbs, etc* : **(of a person or object) not moving**

[ALSO ⇨ L173]

stay 1 [I∅] not to move, go, come, etc: *You go; I'll stay here till you come back. She stayed where she was. My car stays in the garage most of the week. He stayed with her till she felt better.* **2** [L1, 7, 9] to continue to be (in an unchanged state): *I hope the soup will stay warm till they come. The room has stayed the same since he died; no one has changed anything.*

remain *usu fml* **1** [I∅] to stay; be left behind after others have gone or been removed: *When the others had gone, Mary remained and put back the furniture. Of the seven brothers only four now remain; the rest are dead.* **2** [L1, 7, 9] to continue to be (in an unchanged state): *Peter became a judge but John remained a fisherman. If you won't eat you'll just have to remain hungry! You can't let the room remain like this!* **remainder** [C; GC] what is left; the things or people, etc left when others are taken or go away: *Most people left and the remainder sat down to wait.*

stay put [I∅] *infml & emph* not to go, move, etc: *She stayed put where she was; she couldn't leave the house.*

stop [I∅] *usu not fml* to stay: *You go; I'll stop here till you come back.*

wait 1 [I∅] to stop or stay in a place without doing anything until someone arrives or something happens: *Wait here; don't go away. We'll wait until tomorrow; then, if you don't come, we'll go. They waited an hour but she didn't come. Have you been waiting long?* **2** [I∅ (*for*)] to be ready: *Your tea is waiting (for you): don't let it get cold.* **3** [T1] to take no action until the stated occasion (*esp in the phr* **wait one's turn**): *You must wait your turn to see the doctor.* **4** [S] an act of waiting: *I hope you haven't had a long wait.*

await [T1] *fml* **1** to wait for: *I am awaiting your reply.* **2** to be ready for: *A warm welcome awaits you.*

queue *BrE* **1** [C] a line of people, cars, etc, usu waiting to move on, or into somewhere; set of people waiting for something **2** [I∅ (*up, for*)] to form or join a line while waiting: *We had to queue for ages (for the bus).*

attend [T1] *fml* to be at; go regularly to: *What school does your son attend? They did not manage to attend the meeting.* **attendance 1** [U] the act of attendance: *Your attendance at the meeting is necessary.* **2** [C *usu sing*] number of people attending (a meeting, etc): *There was a large attendance at the meeting last night.* **3** [C] a note of the fact that someone has attended (a school, college, meeting, etc): *She had 180 attendances (at school) out of a possible 185.*

M3 *verbs* : **stopping (a person or object) from moving** [T1]

[ALSO ⇨ L173]

stop to cause to stay in one place after having been moving: *Stop the car; I want to get out.*

halt *emph* to stop: *Halt everything! They halted the train between stations.*

M4 *verbs* : **leaving and setting out**

leave 1 [T1; I∅ (*for*)] to go away (from): *He left the road and hit a tree. We must leave early. When shall we leave for the party?* **2** [T1; I∅] to cease to remain (in or with); stop working for (a business): *I am leaving England. He left his wife three months ago. She left (her job) to start her own business.* **3** [X1, 7, 9: *often pass*] to let stay; cause to be: *We left the work in the office. The window was left open. The book left me sad.* **4** [D1 (*for*); T1] to allow or cause to remain after going away: *The postman left a letter for us.* **5** [T1] to allow to remain untaken, unused, unchanged, uneaten, etc: *You've left your food.* **6** [T1] to allow to remain undone, perhaps until a later time: *Let's leave that for another day.* **7** [T1 (*with, to*), 4] to give into the care or charge of someone: *He left his cat with us. I'll leave it to you to buy the tickets. I'll leave buying the tickets to you.* **8** [T1] to have remaining after death: *He leaves a wife and two children.* **9** [D1 (*to*); T1] to give after the death of the giver: *I will leave this house to you. He left £40,000.*

go away [v adv I∅] not to stay: *Is he here?—No, he went away yesterday. They have gone away to France.*

go off [v adv I∅] to go away: *He has gone off somewhere; I don't know where. She went off with her friend's husband.*

depart [I∅ (*from*)] *fml* to leave (esp a place): *The royal train departed from the capital at 12 o'clock.*

depart from [v prep T1] to turn or move away from (something followed or done formerly): *I'd like to depart from the main subject of my* *speech for a few moments. His story departs from the truth.*

set out *also* **set off** [v adv I0] to start a journey: *He sets out early in the morning. They set out on their travels years ago and have never been seen again.*

start out *also* **start off** [v adv I0] to make a start (to a journey, work, etc): *He started off by planning everything carefully. What time did he start out?*

come out [v adv I0 (*of*)] to come from inside a place: *He came out (of the house) through a window.*

emerge [I0 (*from*)] *often fml & tech* **1** to come out: *A large animal emerged (from the water).* **2** (*fig*) to become known: *At last it has emerged that he stole the money.* **emergent** [Wa5;B] *usu tech* beginning to be seen, happen, etc **emergence** [U] the act of emerging

appear [I0 (*out of* or *from*)] to come into sight: *The men appeared out of the trees/from behind some trees. Where did he suddenly appear from?* **appearance** [U] the act of appearing: *Her appearance from behind a tree was unexpected.*

M5 *verbs* : arriving, reaching, and entering

arrive [I0] **1** to reach a place, esp the end of a journey: *We arrived home late. No letters arrived this morning.* **2** to happen; come: *At last our holidays arrived.* **3** (of a baby) to be born: *Her baby arrived during the night.* **4** to win success or a high place in society: *Now that his books were sold in every shop he felt that he had arrived.*

get in [v adv I0]*infml & genl* to arrive: *The train got in at 7 o'clock. He got in very late last night.*

come in [v adv I0] **1** to arrive as expected: *Has the train come in yet?* **2** (of the sea) to move towards the land: *The sea's coming in so don't stay on the sand too long.*

turn up [v adv I0] *not fml* to arrive or appear: *When do you think he'll arrive?—Oh, he'll turn up soon.*

reach 1 [T1] to arrive at; get to: *They reached London on Thursday. I reached the end of the book. The news only reached me yesterday.* **2** [L9;T1] (of things or places) to be big enough to touch; stretch out as far as: *The ladder won't quite reach (as far as) the window. The forest reaches for many kilometres. The garden reaches down to the lake.* **3** [D1;T1: (*down*)] to get or give by stretching out a hand or arm: *Reach down the child's cap from the hook.* **4** [I0;T1] to touch (something) by stretching out a hand or arm: *Can you reach that apple on the tree?—No, I'm not tall enough to reach (it).* **5** [L9] to stretch out a hand or arm for some purpose: *Reach across the table and pick up the book. The shopkeeper reached for a packet of tea. I reached up and put the parcel on top of the cupboard.* (*fig*) *He was reaching out*

towards a new idea. **6** [T1] to get a message to; to get in touch with (someone): *He can always be reached on the office telephone.* **as far as the eye can reach** to where the land meets the sky: *We can see nothing but houses as far as the eye can reach.*

get to [v prep T1] *not fml* **1** to move to: *Where did you get to after I left you in the shop?* **2** to reach: *Where have you got to in the book?* **3** to start: *to get to thinking about work*

descend (up)on [v prep T1] **1** to arrive suddenly at: *The whole family descended on us at Christmas.* **2** (of a group of people) to attack: *Thieves descended on the travellers.*

enter [I0;T1] *often fml* to come or go into (a room, house, etc): *He entered the house by a side door. When they entered, he departed.*

M6 *verbs* : letting in and out [T1]

let in [v adv] *infml* to allow (someone) to go or come in (to a house, etc): *He let them in by a side door. Please let us in; it's cold outside.*

admit *fml* to let in: *They were admitted into the house. Don't admit anyone who hasn't paid.*

let out [v adv] to allow (someone) to go or come out (of a house, etc): *Let me out! They let him out through a side door.*

usher in [v adv]*fml* to admit, esp in a welcoming ceremony: *They ushered in their guests. He ushered her in very politely.*

usher out [v adv] *fml* to let out, esp in a ceremonial way: *He ushered them out formally and with a great show of friendship and thanks.*

M7 *verbs* : welcoming and meeting

welcome [T1] **1** to greet (a person) when he or she in a new place: *The Queen welcomed him as soon as he got off the plane.* **2** to meet or be found by (a visitor) esp with pleasure: *They welcomed him with flowers. A warm fire welcomed him.*

greet *esp emot & emph* **1** [T1] to welcome with words or actions: *She greeted him with a loving kiss. He greeted us by shouting a friendly 'Hello'.* **2** [X9] to receive with an expression of feeling: *The speech was greeted by loud cheers. She greeted her birthday present with cries of delight.* **3** [T1] to come suddenly to the eyes, ears, etc: *Inside the room complete disorder greeted us. I awoke and was greeted by birdsong.*

meet 1 [T1] to be there at the arrival of: *I'll meet the 4 o'clock train. I'll meet you off the train. The taxi will meet the train/will meet you off the train.* **2** [I0] to gather together: *The whole school met to hear the speech.* **3** [T1;I0] to come together (with), by chance or arrangement: *We met unexpectedly. He met her for dinner.* **4** [I0] to come together or close: *The cars almost met head on* (= one front against the other) *but drew away and drove* *on.* **5** [T1; IØ] to get to know or be introduced (to) for the first time: *Come to the party and meet some interesting people. We met at Ann's party, didn't we, but I don't remember your name.* **6** [T1 (*with*)] to answer, esp in opposition: *His changes were met with cries of anger. Angry cries met his speech. We met his idea with interest.* **7** [T1] (*fig*) to pay: *Can you meet this amount?* **8** [T1] (*fig*) to satisfy: *Does this meet your needs?* **9** [T1; IØ] (*fig*) to touch (as if) naturally: *Their lips met (in a kiss). Her hand met his face in a violent blow.* **10** [T1] (*fig*) to find or experience: *I met a lot of difficulties in the work.*

meet up [v adv IØ (*with*)] *infml* to meet, esp not by a formal arrangement: *Let's meet up after the play. He met up with some very strange people there.*

meet with [v prep T1] to experience or find by chance: *I met with some difficulties when I tried to enter the country. They met with an accident on their way back.*

receive [T1] *fml* to welcome or greet (people when they come): *The Queen received them in the great hall.*

M8 *verbs* : **getting off, down, and out**

get off *infml & genl* **1** [v adv IØ] to come or go down: *He stopped the train/bus and got off.* **2** [v prep T1] to come or go down from: *He got off the train at Birmingham.*

get down [v adv IØ (*from*)] to come or go down, (esp from a horse) usu only for a short time: *He got down from his horse to help the wounded man.*

get out [v adv IØ (*of*)] to leave (a car, etc): *He opened the door of the car and got out.*

alight [IØ (*from*)] *fml* to get down from a car, bus, etc, esp at the end of a journey: *They alighted from the train soon after midday.*

descend [T1; IØ (*from*)] *often fml* to come, fall, or sink from a higher to a lower level; go down (along): *The sun descended behind the hills. She descended the stairs. The road climbs for miles and then descends. He descended from the train at Birmingham.* (*fig*) *I want to discuss all these points in descending order of importance.*

disembark [IØ; T1] to (cause to) get off a ship: *He disembarked at Southampton. They disembarked in mid-river into small boats. Can we disembark the goods here? The goods were disembarked in London.* **disembarkation** [U] the act or time of disembarking

sink [IØ] to go downwards: *The sun sank in the west. The ship sank (to the bottom of the sea). He sank behind a bush where no one could see him.* (*fig*) *Our spirits sank* (= We became unhappy). (*fig*) *The new idea took a long time to sink in (to his mind).* (*fig*) *She had a sinking* (= unpleasant) *feeling in her stomach.*

subside [IØ] **1** to fall or sink lower: *The land here is subsiding because of changes deep underneath. The river subsided when the heavy rains stopped.* **2** to become less: *The strong wind has subsided.* **subsidence** [U] the act or state of subsiding: *There is a lot of subsidence on this road; it was badly made.*

M9 *verbs* : **climbing and getting on**

climb **1** [IØ (*up*); T1] to go up, over or through, esp by using the hands and feet: *The old lady climbs up the stairs with difficulty. Do you think you can climb that tree? The cat's just climbed in through the window.* (*fig*) *He climbed the social ladder.* **2** [IØ (*up*); T1] to go up, over or down (esp mountains) as a sport: *Do you climb? Have you climbed any mountains this year?* **3** [IØ] to rise to a higher point; go higher: *It became hotter as the sun climbed in the sky. The plane climbed quickly.* **4** [IØ] to slope upwards: *The road climbed steeply.* **5** [IØ; T1] (esp of a plant) to grow upwards (on): *The rose tree has climbed right up the side of the house.* **6** [IØ *into* or *out of*] *infml* to get into or out of clothing usu with little or some effort: *The soldiers climbed into their uniforms at the sound of the warning bell.*

clamber [L9 (*about*), esp *over*] to climb, usu using both feet and hands and usu with difficulty or effort: *The child needed all his strength to clamber over the high wall. Stop clambering about over my new furniture.*

mount **1** [T1; IØ (*up*)] to get on (a horse, a bicycle, etc): *He mounted the bicycle and rode away. The soldiers stood beside their horses, waiting for the order to mount (up).* **2** [T1; IØ (*to*)] to go up; climb: *The old lady can mount the stairs only with difficulty. The climber mounted to the top of the steep cliff by cutting steps in the rock with his axe.* **3** [Wv5; T1 (*on*)] to provide (someone) with a horse or other animal, a bicycle, etc to ride on: *The prince mounted his guest on his best elephant. The soldiers were mounted on fine black horses. The mounted police.* **4** [T1 (*on*)] to put (someone) on horseback, on a bicycle, etc: *He lifted up his little son and mounted him on the donkey.* **5** [Wv4; IØ (*up*)] to rise in level or increase in amount: *The level of the water mounted until it reached my waist. The temperature mounted into the 90s. In spite of all his efforts, his debts continued to mount up. His fears for the safety of his daughter mounted as the days passed without news of her. The mounting cost of living has forced us to ask for higher wages.* **6** [T1] to fix on a support or in a surrounding substance; put in a position so as to be ready for use or to be shown: *He mounted the photograph on stiff paper and then framed it. The king's crown was of pure gold, in which precious jewels had been mounted. The dead insect was mounted on a card by means of a pin.* **7** [T1] to prepare or begin (an attack): *The opposing political party is getting ready to mount a powerful attack on the government.* **8** [T1] to prepare and produce (a play) for the stage: *It'll cost a great deal of money to mount this play.* **9** [T1] *tech* (of a male animal esp a large one) to get up on (a female animal) in order to breed

ascend *often fml* **1** [I∅] to go, come or move upwards or to a higher position: *The stairs ascended in a graceful curve. The aircraft ascended quickly.* **2** [T1] to climb; go up along: *He ascended the stairs. We ascended the hill.*

scale [T1] to climb, esp quickly on a high, difficult place: *They scaled the wall easily.* (*also poet & emot*) *The climbers scaled Mount Everest.*

get on *infml & genl* **1** [v adv I∅] to climb on to a train, animal, etc: *He got on at Birmingham. They brought him his horse and he got on.* **2** [v prep T1] to climb onto: *He got on the train at Birmingham. He got on his horse.*

board [T1; (I∅)] *fml & tech* to get onto (a train, ship, aeroplane, etc): *They boarded the plane at 1800 hours.*

embark 1 [I∅; T1 *usu pass*] to (cause to) get onto a ship: *They embarked at Southampton for New York. The soldiers were embarked quickly.* **2** [I∅ *on*] *fig esp poet & emot* to start: *They have embarked on a most interesting new plan.* **embarkation** [U] the act or time of embarking

M10 *nouns* : **movement and motion**

movement 1 [U] the act of moving or condition of being moved; activity: *Movement's painful when one's hurt one's back. There's little movement after sunset, in the streets of this quiet village. I enjoy a play that has plenty of movement. There hasn't been much movement this month in the cotton market* (= much buying or selling, or change in the price). **2** [C] a particular act of changing position or place: *He's very old and his movements are getting slower and slower. She heard a movement outside her bedroom door and got out of bed to see who was there.* **3** [GC] (*fig*) a group of people who make united efforts for a particular purpose: *The aim of the trade union movement was, and is, to obtain higher wages and better conditions for workers.* **4** [C] (*fig*) a general feeling, way of thinking, acting, etc, not directed by any particular person or group, towards something new, or away from something that exists: *Religious leaders are worried about the movement away from the churches, especially among young people. The old man thinks that the movement towards greater freedom for women has brought them too much freedom.*

motion 1 [U] the act, manner or state of moving: *The gentle rolling motion of the ship made me feel sleepy. The train was already in motion when he jumped on. Parts of the film were shown again in slow motion* (= making the movements appear slower than in real life). **2** [C] a single or particular movement or way of moving: *He made a motion with his hand, as if*

to tell me to keep back. The dancer's graceful motions pleased them. **put/set something in motion** to start something moving, being active, or working: *Pull this handle towards you to set this machine in motion. He warned the government that if it declared war, it would set in motion something that might spread to the rest of the world.*

mobility [U] the state or quality of being mobile [⇒ M14], able to move easily: *The younger player won the game, mainly because of his greater mobility. The army is in need of many more vehicles to increase its mobility.* **im-** [*neg*]

momentum 1 [U; C] *tech* the quantity of movement in a body, measured by multiplying its mass by the speed at which it moves: *As the rock rolled down the mountainside, it gathered momentum* (= moved faster and faster). **2** [U] (*fig*) the force gained by the movement or development of events: *The national struggle for independence is gaining momentum every day.*

impetus 1 [U] the force of something moving **2** [U; S] (*fig*) a push forward: *His speech gave (an) impetus to my ideas.*

inertia [U] **1** a property of matter by which an object tends to remain in motion or at rest: *The natural inertia of water makes it move more slowly than its container.* **2** (*fig*) slowness; lack of movement; laziness: *He had a feeling of inertia on that hot summer day.*

go *infml* **1** [C] an act of going or doing something: *Have a go at it; you might be able to do it. It's my go now.* **2** [U] power (to move or do things): *He is very good; he's full of go.*

step [C] **1** the act of putting one foot in front of the other in order to move along: *Take two steps forward and two steps back.* **2** the sound this makes: *I heard a step/footstep/footsteps on the stair.* **3 a** the distance between the feet when stepping: *The door is three steps away.* **b** a short distance: *It's just a step from my house to his.* **4** a flat edge, esp in a set of surfaces each above the other on which the foot is placed for climbing up and down; a stair, rung [⇒ D30] of a ladder, etc: *Mind the step outside the door. They climbed 154 steps.* **5** (*fig*) an act, esp in a set of actions, which should produce a certain result: *Our first step must be a change in working hours, then we must decide how to improve conditions.*

M11 *nouns* : **staying and stopping** [C]
[ALSO ⇒ L181]

stay (of persons) a period of staying in a place: *He enjoyed his stay in Athens.*

stop 1 an act of stopping: *The train made a stop at a station where it didn't usually stop.* **2** a place where a train, bus, etc can stop: *This is my stop* (= This is where I get off).

stopover a short stay between parts of a journey, as on a long plane journey

609

M13 MOVING

halt *often fml* **1** an act of halting **2** a place where something halts

M12 nouns : passages, arrivals, and departures

passage **1** [U (*of*)] the action of going across, by, over, through, etc in space: *The old bridge is not strong enough to allow the passage of heavy vehicles.* **2** [U (*of*)] (of time) course; onward flow: *the passage of the years; of time* **3** [U] the right or permission to go through or across something: *No single nation should control passage on the sea.* **4** [S; U (*from, to*)] (the cost of) a long journey by ship (or aircraft): *'A Passage to India' (E. M. Forster). He is too poor to afford the passage and he will have to work his passage by doing jobs on the ship.* **bird of passage** **1** a bird that regularly flies away to a distant country when the seasons change **2** (*fig*) a person who moves about from one place to another, and does not stay in one place for long

coming and going [U] *not fml* acts of moving about: *There has been a lot of coming and going between London and Paris lately; what's happening?*

departure [U; C] the action or an act of departing [⇒ M4]: *What is the departure time of the flight? Where do the departures depart from? The new system is a departure from our usual way of keeping records. The system is a new departure.* **take one's departure (from)** *fml* to leave: *It's getting late. I had better take my departure.*

arrival **1** [U; (C)] the act of arriving: *The arrival of the aircraft has been delayed. On (my) arrival home I was greeted by my parents.* **2** [C] a person who or thing that arrives or has arrived: *There were several new arrivals in the school. The new arrival was a large healthy baby boy.*

destination [C] a place which is set for the end of a journey or to which something is sent: *He reached his destination two hours late. The lovers kept their destination secret.*

entrance **1** [C; U] the act of entering: *The entrance of the two teams onto the football field was a great moment. The young actor made only two entrances (onto the stage). The police had to force an entrance into the house.* **2** [U] the right to enter: *a school entrance examination. the entrance money* (= money which must be paid) *to join a club* **3** [C] *genl* a gate, door, or other opening by which one enters: *the entrance to the railway station*

entry **1** [C (*into*)] the act of coming or going in; entrance: *Great Britain's entry into the war; to force an entry into a building* **2** [U] the right to enter: *You mustn't drive into a street with a 'No Entry' sign.* **3** [C] *esp AmE* a door, gate, or passage by which one enters: *Leave the boxes in the entry and we'll carry them up later.*

exit [C] **1** (often written over a door) a way out, esp from a theatre: *There's another exit at the back. The exit doors are opened at the end of the performance.* **2** an act of leaving, esp of an actor leaving the stage: *Make your exit through the door at the back of the stage.*
USAGE In America, the sign *(NO) EXIT* is much more common than in Britain, and the common British sign *WAY OUT* is not used.

welcome **1** [C] a greeting on arrival: *The Queen gave a welcome to the foreign visitors.* **2** [C] a show of kind acceptance: *They gave him the same welcome as they would to their own son.* **3** [C; (U)] a way of receiving or accepting: *They gave us a warm* (= kind) *welcome.*

greeting [C] **1** a form of words or an action used on meeting someone: *'Good morning,' I said, but she didn't return the greeting.* **2** the words used at the beginning of a letter: *They sent Mrs Brown a letter with the greeting 'Dear Sir'!*

greetings [P] good wishes, esp at special times: *Send them my Christmas greetings. Greetings and best wishes for the New Year.*

regards *also* **wishes** [P] an expression of friendly interest: *Give him my kindest regards when you see him. Best regards to everyone! She sends you her best wishes for your new job.*

reception **1** [C9] *fml* the act of receiving someone: *The reception he got was not friendly. He got an unfriendly reception.* **2** [C] *usu fml* an occasion at which people can meet an important person or persons: *He went to a special reception to meet the writer of the book.*

admission **1** [U] the allowing or being allowed to enter or join a school, club, building, etc: *Soon after his admission he became an officer of the society.* **2** [U] the money charged for entrance: *admission free* **3** [C] an act of allowing someone to enter or join: *How many admissions have been made to the hospital today? Go to the Admissions Office.*

admittance [U] *usu fml* the allowing or being allowed to enter; right of entry: *As the theatre was full I was unable to gain admittance.*

approach **1** [U] the act of approaching: *Their approach was slow.* **2** [C (*to*)] a way, road, etc to some place: *The approach to the house was beautiful. The approaches to the port of Southampton are always busy.* **3** [C] an act of coming or going to someone to talk about, suggest, ask for, etc something: *His approach was direct; he just came and asked for more money. They have made some approaches in the matter but we have not promised them anything.* **4** [C (*to*)] way of doing (something): *His approach to the question was very successful.*

M13 nouns : climbing, ascending, and descending

climb [C *usu sing*] **1** a journey upwards made by climbing; the act of climbing: *(fig) The minister's climb to power had taken twenty years.* **2** a place to be climbed; very steep slope; place where climbing is necessary: *There was a steep climb on the road out of town.*

ascent [U; C *usu sing*] *often fml* **1** the act of going, moving, climbing, or travelling up; act of rising; rise: *We made a successful ascent of the mountain. He made his first ascent in an aircraft.* (*fig*) *the ascent of man from his original state to modern civilization.* **2** a way up; upward slope, path, etc: *We pushed our bicycles up the ascent.*

ascension [U] *very fml* the act of going, coming, or moving upwards or to a higher position

descent [C; U] *often fml* the act or fact of going or coming down: *What is the angle of descent of this hill? The road makes a sharp descent just past the lake.* (*fig*) *His descent into a life of crime made his mother very unhappy.*

M14 *adjectives* : **moving**

mobile 1 [B] movable; able to move or be moved quickly and easily; not fixed in one position: *Many workmen aren't mobile; if they move to new employment they have difficulties in moving their families. She's much more mobile* (= able to move from place to place) *now that she's bought a car. mobile weapons* **2** [Wa5;A] contained and driven from place to place, in a vehicle: *a mobile shop; a mobile library* **3** [B] changing quickly, as of a person's face that quickly shows changes in his feelings or thoughts: *He has a mobile face, like an actor's.*

motive [Wa5;A] *usu tech* (of power, force, etc) causing movement: *The wind provides the motive power that turns this wheel.*

active [B] able to act, move, do things, etc: *He is very active for his age; he is 75 but gets around like someone much younger. She leads an active life, always doing things and meeting people.* **in-** [*neg*] **-ly** [adv]

busy [Wa1;B] (of places) full of movement and life: *The streets of London are always busy. Oxford Street in London is a busy place.* **-ily** [adv]

M15 *adjectives, etc*: **not moving**

immobile [B] unmoving: *The cars were immobile.* **immobility** [U] the state or condition of being immobile **immobilize** [T1] to cause to become immobile; stop from moving: *When its engine broke down, the car was immobilized for weeks. He tied him with ropes so that he was completely immobilized.*

motionless [B] without any movement; quite still: *The cat remained motionless, waiting for the mouse to come out of its hole. There wasn't the slightest wind to move the motionless flags.* **-ly** [adv]

static [B] not moving, or able or likely to move: *Some of our groups are static, others mobile. He leads a pretty static life now, but he used to travel a lot.* **-ally** [adv Wa4]

stationary [Wa5;B] **1** *often fml* (of vehicles, etc) not moving: *Do not alight* [⇒ M8] *from vehicles until they are stationary.* **2** for staying in one place; not intended to move or be moved: *These are stationary guns.*

still 1 [Wa5;F] *esp in commands* not moving: *Keep still while I tie your shoes. 'Sit still!' she told the child.* **2** [B] *esp lit & poet* not moving: *The still water of the river looked deep and dark.* **-ness** [U]

idle [Wa5;B] not working or moving: *The machines were lying idle.* **-ness** [U] **idly** [adv Wa3]: *He sat idly, doing nothing.*

M16 *adjectives, etc* : **moving quickly**
[ALSO ⇒ M33]

quick [Wa1;B] **1** moving or working at speed: *He's quick at his work. He's a quick worker. Be quick!* **2** soon finished: *She had a quick drink. He gave her a quick answer.* **-ly** [adv] **-ness** [U]

fast [Wa1] **1** [B] (of persons, animals, vehicles, etc) quick in moving, esp by nature: *That's a fast car. He's a fast runner/worker. Go faster!* **2** [adv] quickly: *He runs fast.*

swift [Wa1;B] *esp lit & poet* **1** fast: *He came to a swift-running river. She is a swift runner.* **2** ready or quick in action: *He gave them a swift reply.* **3** short or sudden: *She made a swift movement and was gone.* **-ly** [adv] **-ness** [U]

rapid [B] **1** quick-moving; fast: *It was a rapid journey. He is a rapid worker. The improvement was rapid. They asked questions in rapid succession.* **2** (of actions) done in a short time: *The school promised rapid results in the learning of languages.* **-ly** [adv] **-ity** [U]

speedy [Wa1;B] *infml* doing things or moving quickly: *That was speedy work. He's a speedy worker. They provide the speediest service in town.* **-ily** [adv]

fleet [Wa1;B] *lit & poet* quick in moving: *He is a fleet runner. He is fleet of foot* (= runs fast).

hasty [Wa1;B] **1** done in a hurry: *They had a hasty meal/ate a hasty meal. It was a hasty goodbye/a hasty decision.* **2 a** (of people or their acts) too quick in acting or deciding, esp with a bad result: *She's too hasty, if she would only think before speaking she wouldn't have so much trouble.* **b** quick to get angry: *You were too hasty in punishing her; she didn't mean to do wrong. He has a hasty temper.* **-ily** [adv] **-iness** [U]

hurried [B] done in haste: *Hurried work is not the best work.* **-ly** [adv] **-ness** [U]

rushed [F] *emph* hurried: *I feel really rushed; things are very busy at the moment. We're busy—just rushed off our feet!*

express [Wa5;A] *often tech* going or sent quickly: *He sent the letter by express post. She travelled by express train.*

M17 *adjectives* : **not moving quickly** [B]

slow [Wa1] **1** not moving or going on quickly;

having less than a usual or standard speed: *I like slow music. It was a slow poison. He caught the slow train to Birmingham.* **2** [(*in*); *also* B3] taking a long time or too long: *The government was slow in acting/slow to act. She's patient and slow to blame others.* **3** not good or quick in understanding; dull in mind: *He is a slow student.* **4** not very active; dull: *It has been a slow month for trading. Business is slow just now.* **5** (of a surface) not allowing quick movement: *slow muddy racing conditions* **-ly** [adv] **-ness** [U]

gentle [Wa1,3] slow and pleasant: *The horses moved at a gentle pace* (=slowly and pleasantly). **-tly** [adv Wa3] **-ness** [U]

sluggish slow-moving; not very active or quick: *a sluggish stream/car/engine; feeling rather sluggish in the heat of the day; a sluggish market with little trade being done* **-ly** [adv] **-ness** [U]

gradual happening slowly, esp step by step: *There was a gradual change in the weather.* **-ly** [adv]

M18 *nouns* : **speed**

[ALSO ⇒ M33]

speed [U; C] the quality or condition of moving fast; *The car was travelling at great speed. The speed of the car was 100 k.p.h.* (= kilometres per hour). *The two cars' speeds were the same.*

velocity **1** [C] *tech* speed in a certain direction; rate of movement: *There'll be strong winds tonight with velocities of 60 miles an hour and more.* **2** [S; U] **a** high speed (as of a moving vehicle): *The car came round the corner at such a velocity that the driver was unable to keep it on the road.* **b** *esp lit or fml* swiftness (as of events): *Effects followed upon his foolish action with frightening velocity.*

pace **1** [S] rate or speed in walking, marching or running or (*fig*) of development, advance of a plan, etc: *The old man can walk only at a very slow pace. The plans are being prepared at quite a good pace.* **2** [C] a single step in running or walking or the distance moved in one such step: *If you come one pace nearer, I will shoot you. The fence is ten paces from the house.* **3** [C usu sing] (esp of a horse) a manner or pattern of walking or running: *The natural paces of the horse are the walk, then the faster trot, and then the canter and gallop.* [⇒ K199] **keep pace with** to go forward at the same rate as: *This horse is too weak to keep pace with the others.* (*fig*) *You're thinking much too fast for me; I can't keep pace with you.* **set the pace** to fix the speed for others to copy: *If we let the fastest runner set the pace the others will be left behind.*

rate [C9] **1** [esp *of*] a speed, value, cost, etc measured by its relation to some other amount: *They travelled at the rate of 100 km an hour. He must pay at the rate of 10 per cent. The birth rate is the number of births compared to the number of the people.* **2** a (usu stated) speed: *He drove at a fearful rate.*

spurt [C] a sudden increase in speed: *In a quick spurt he passed the other runners.*

turn [C] the ability to increase speed (*esp in the phr* **turn of speed**): *He has a good turn of speed when he needs it.*

burst [C (*of*)] a strong increase esp of speed: *In a last burst he passed the others and won the race.*

M19 *verbs & nouns* : **particular ways of moving**

[ALSO ⇒ K101]

walk **1** [T1; I0] to (cause to) move on one's feet, at a speed which can be kept for a long time: *to walk to town; to walk a horse; to walk (for) 10 miles. He likes walking. Walking is healthy. I must walk the dog; he hasn't been out today.* **2** [T1] to pass over, through or along on foot: *to walk the roads; to walk a* **tightrope** (= a tightly stretched rope or wire high above the ground). **3** [T1] to follow for the purpose of measuring, examining, etc: *to walk (to) the border* **4** [L9] *lit* to follow a course of action or way of life: *to walk humbly in the sight of God* **5** [I0] (of a spirit) to move about in a form that can be seen: *Do the spirits of the dead walk at night?* **6** [T1] to cause to move by holding while going on foot: *to walk a bicycle* **7** [T1] to cause to move in a manner suggesting a walk: *Let's walk this ladder to the other side of the room.* **8** [X9; (T1)] to go on foot with (someone) to a particular place: *I walked her home.* **9** [C] an act or occasion of walking: *Let's go for a walk.* **10** [C] a way of walking: *His walk is just like his father's.*

step [L9] **1** to put one foot down in front of the other in order to move along **2** to walk: *Step outside, please. Step into the house while you're waiting.* **3** to put one's foot: *She stepped on a stone and twisted her ankle.* [⇒ B43]

run **1** [I0] to move on one's legs at a speed faster than walking: *'Don't try to run before you can walk' (saying). The children came running when she called them. The insect ran up my leg. They ran to help her. The child ran off to fetch his brother.* **2** [T1] to cover (a distance) in this way: *He ran a mile in four minutes.* **3** [T1] **a** to take part in (a race) in this way: *The children ran races in the park.* **b** to cause (an animal) to take part in a race: *We won't run this horse in any races this season.* (*fig*) *The Party is running three candidates* (=people trying to get elected) *in the next election.* **c** to cause (a race) to happen: *The bicycle race will be run in Holland next year.* **4** [X9; L9] **a** to cause (esp a ship or wheeled vehicle) to advance quickly: *I'll run the car into the car park.* **b** (esp of a ship or wheeled vehicle) to advance quickly: *The car ran down the hill. The train ran past the signal. The boat ran into port.* **5** [L9; X9] to (cause to) move quickly: *A thought ran through my mind. He ran his eyes over the list of figures.* **6** [I0; T1] **a** (of machines) to work; be in movement:

Don't touch the engine while it's running. **b** to cause (a machine) to work or be in movement: *I'll just run the engine for a minute.* **7** [L9; X9: (*by*, *on*)] **a** (of machines) to work (in a stated way or by a stated form of power): *The motor isn't running smoothly. This machine runs by electricity/runs off electricity.* (*fig*) *Is everything running well in your office?* **b** to cause (a machine) to work (in a stated way, or by a stated form of power): *Do you run the trains on oil or by steam power?* **8** [I0; T1] **a** (of public vehicles) to travel as arranged; go to and fro: *The trains don't run on Sundays/aren't running today. This bus runs between Manchester and Liverpool/from here to the Town Hall.* **b** to cause (a public vehicle) to travel in this way: *They're running a special train to the football match.* **9** [Nv4; L9] (of liquids, sand, etc) **a** to flow: *to wash in running water. The tears ran down his face. The water runs out of the pipe into the bucket.* (*fig*) *Your arguments run off her 'like water off a duck's back' (saying).* **b** to become by flowing: *The water ran cold/hot.* **10** [I0; L7] (of a container) **a** to pour out liquid: *Your nose is running. Is the tap still running?* **b** to reach (a state) by pouring out liquid: *The well has run dry.* **11** [T1; D1] **a** to cause (liquids, sand, etc) to flow, esp from a pipe: *Run the water till it gets hot.* **b** to fill (a bath) for (someone): *Please run me a nice hot bath.* **12** [Wv6; I0] to melt and spread by the action of heat or water: *The butter will run if you put it near the fire. I'm afraid the colours ran when I washed this shirt.* **13** [L9] to pass; stretch; continue: *There was a long passage running from end to end of the house. The road runs along the river bank/over the mountains/through a tunnel.* **14** [T1] to own and drive (a car): *He runs a pink Volksauto.* **15** [L9; X9] *not fml* **a** to take (somebody or something to somewhere) in a vehicle: *Can I run you home?* **b** to go quickly (to somewhere) esp in a vehicle: *Why not run over and see us one evening? I'll just run across to Mary's house and borrow some sugar.* **16** [T1 (*across*, *into*)] to bring (something) into a country unlawfully and secretly: *to run drugs/guns/arms (across the border/into a country).* **17** [C] an act or occasion of running: *The boys went for a run. Let's go for a run in the car.*

ride 1 [I0; T1] to travel along, controlling or sitting on (an animal, bicycle, etc): *Can you ride? Can you ride a horse/bicycle?* **2** [L9] (of a vehicle) to travel over a surface (in a stated manner): *This car rides smoothly.* **3** [C] an act or occasion of riding: *They went for a ride on their horses/bicycles. Let's go for a ride in the car/a car ride.*

hitchhike *also infml* **hitch** [I0] to go on a journey by being taken in other people's cars: *He hitchhiked/hitched across France.*

fly 1 [T1; I0] to (cause to) move through the air: *Birds can fly. The bird flew from tree to tree. The aeroplanes flew east. He flew the plane well. Can you fly (a plane)? Have you ever flown (in*

a plane)? **2** [I0] to pass quickly: *Time flew.* **3** [L9] to move quickly: *The car just flew along.*

sail 1 [L9; X9] **a** (of any ship) to travel on the water: *Watch the ships sail by.* **b** to command or direct (any ship) on the water: *The captain sailed his ship out to sea.* **2** [L9] (of people) to travel by ship: *We sailed across the Atlantic in five days.* **3** [I0] to begin a voyage: *We/Our ship sail(s) tomorrow (for New York).* **4** [T1] to move or travel on (water): *one of the first men/-ships to sail the Atlantic Ocean* **5** [L9] (*fig*) to move proudly, smoothly, or easily: *She sailed through the difficult examination with no mistakes. The birds sailed across the sky. He sailed into office with 98 per cent of the votes.* **6** [I0] to make short trips as a sport in a small boat with sails (*often in the phr* **go sailing**) **7** [C] an act or occasion of sailing: *They went for a sail on the river.*

swim 1 [I0] to move through water by moving limbs or a tail: *Some snakes can swim.* **2** [T1] to cross or complete (a distance) by swimming: *He swam the river. She can swim 100 metres.* **3** [I0 (*with*, *in*)] to be full of or covered with liquid: *Her eyes were swimming. The meat was swimming in fat.* **4** [I0] to cause one to feel dizzy [⇒ B111]; (seem to) spin round: *He was hot and tired and his head was swimming. The room seemed to swim in front of his tired eyes.* **5** [X9] to cause or help to swim: *She swam him across, holding his head up.* **6** [C] an act or occasion of swimming: *Let's go for a swim in the river.*

cross 1 [T1; (I0)] to go, pass, or reach across: *The soldiers took three days to cross the desert. The bridge crosses the river at its narrowest point. When the green light is on you're allowed to cross the road. 'Is it safe to cross?' asked the old lady.* **2** [I0] to lie or pass across each other: *I'll meet you at the place in the forest where the paths cross.* **3** [Wv5; T1] to put one of (a pair of things) above and across the other: *She sat on the floor with her legs crossed. He came in, sat down, and crossed his arms on his chest.* **4** [T1] (*fig*) to oppose (someone, his plans, wishes, etc): *She hates being crossed so don't argue with her.* **5** [T1] to draw a line across: *Remember to cross your 'ts' when you're writing.* **6** [Wv5; T1] to draw two lines across (a cheque) to show that it must be paid into a bank account: *I always send crossed cheques if I need to pay for something by post.* **7** [T1] to make a sign shaped like a cross on (oneself) as a religious act: *The old lady crossed herself as she left the church.* **8** [I0; T1] (of letters in the post, people travelling, etc) to meet and pass: *Your letter must have crossed mine in the post. We posted our letters on the same day so they crossed in the post.*

traverse [T1] *often lit & fml* to cross: *The road traverses a broad valley and then enters the hills. They traversed the valley on foot.*

file 1 [L9] to move in a line, one behind the other, in a particular direction: *The people filed in/out/past.* **2** [GC] a line of people, esp moving or standing one behind the other, or going in this way in one particular direction: *A file of soldiers passed.* **in single file** filing one at a time: *The soldiers passed in single file.*

roll 1 [I0; T1] to (cause to) move along by turning over and over: *The round stone began rolling down the hill. Roll the stones down the hill.* **2** [X9] to form by curling round and round: *He rolled the clay into a ball.* **3** [T1 *up*] to make into the shape of a tube in this way: *He rolled up the piece of paper.* **4** [T1 (*out*)] to make flat by rolling something rounded and heavy over it: *He rolled the grass. She rolled out the soft dough* (=material for making bread, cakes, etc). **5** [C] an act of rolling: *The dog had a roll on the grass.*

M20 *verbs & nouns* : **walking unevenly, unsteadily, etc**

limp 1 [I0] to walk unevenly usu because one leg has been hurt: *The wounded soldier limped badly/limped along the road.* **2** [S] an example of limping: *He walks with a limp.*

hobble [Wv3] **1** [I0] to walk in an awkward way, with difficulty: *I hurt my foot, but just managed to hobble along.* **2** [T1] to fasten together two legs (of a horse): *The horse has been hobbled so he can't run away.*

stagger 1 [I0] to have trouble standing or walking; move unsteadily on one's feet: *He was staggering along as if drunk. I was so tired I could hardly stagger to my feet.* **2** [T1] (*fig*) to cause to doubt or wonder; seem almost unbelievable to; shock: *That story staggers the imagination. I was staggered to hear such news.* **3** [C] an unsteady movement of a person having trouble walking or standing

lurch 1 [I0] to move with irregular sudden movements: *The wounded man lurched across the field.* **2** [C] a sudden movement forward or sideways: *The boat gave a lurch towards the rocks.*

tiptoe [I0] to walk on the toes: *He tiptoed towards the bedroom, trying not to be heard.* **on tiptoe** tiptoeing: *He went on tiptoe across the room.*

M21 *verbs & nouns* : **walking gently, etc**

amble 1 [L9] *infml* to walk at an easy gentle rate: *I ambled around the country roads for an hour.* **2** [I0] (of a horse) to move at an easy rate by lifting the two legs on one side and then the two on the other **3** [S] *infml* (a walk at) an easy gentle rate: *They came along at an amble.*

stroll 1 [L9] to walk, esp slowly, for pleasure **2** [S] an unhurried walk for pleasure: *He went for an evening stroll.*

saunter 1 [L9] to walk in an unhurried way: *I sauntered along the street with nothing to do.* **2** [S] *rare* a stroll

wander 1 [I0 (*about*)]; T1] to move about (an area) without a fixed course, aim, or purpose: *We love wandering (about) (the hills).* **2** [I0] (esp of streams, roads, etc) to follow a winding course: *The river wanders through some very beautiful country.* **3** [I0 (*off*)] (*fig*) to move away (from the main idea): *Don't wander off the point.* **4** [I0] (*fig*) (of people or thoughts) to be or become confused and unable to follow an ordinary conversation: *I'm afraid the old man's mind is wandering.*

M22 *verbs & nouns* : **walking strongly, etc**

[ALSO ⇒ C310–11]

stride 1 [L9] to walk with long steps or cross with one long step: *He strode out. He strode over the stream.* **2** [C] the act of making long steps: *In a few strides he crossed the room.*

strut [I0] to walk in a proud, strong way, esp with the chest out and trying to look important: *The male bird strutted in front of the female. The winner strutted forward to receive his prize.*

march 1 [I0] to walk with a regular, esp forceful step like a soldier: *They watched the soldiers marching. The army marched all night/20 miles. She was very angry and marched out of the shop.* (*fig*) *Time marches on.* **2** [X9] to force to walk (away): *The little boy behaved badly so she marched him up to bed. They caught the thief and marched him off (to the police station).* **3** [*the* U] the act of marching: *The soldiers went past at the march* (=marching). **4** [C] the distance covered while marching in a certain period of time: *It was a short/a day's march from the city to the camp. They made several night marches during army training.* **5** [S (*of*)] regular movement forward: *the march of time* **6** [C] a piece of music played in regular time, as of the movements in marching: *The band played a slow march followed by a quick march.* **line of march** *tech* the place or direction in which marchers move **on the march 1** moving forward: *The army were on the march at six o'clock.* **2** (*fig*) moving ahead and improving: *Science is on the march.*

pace 1 [L9] to walk with even steps: *The lion paced back and forward.* **2** [T1 (*out*)] to measure an area by this means: *He paced (out) the length of the hall.* **3** [T1] to set the speed (**pace**) for a walker, runner, etc by going in front of him or her: *He paced them for a kilometre.*

parade 1 [C] a march, esp as a way of showing how good soldiers are, marking an important occasion, etc **2** [I0 (*past*)] to march in a parade: *The soldiers paraded past the king.* **3** [T1] *often deprec* to make a show of: *She paraded her new jewels so that everyone could see them.*

procession [C] a line of people, vehicles, etc moving slowly forward behind each other, esp as part of a ceremony: *Who is in the procession today?*

M23 verbs & nouns : **walking long and far, etc**

hike 1 [I0] to travel about the country, or an area, on foot or without regular use of a vehicle **2** [C] a long walk in the country, such as one taken by a group of people for a whole day: *They came back tired (out) from their hike over the hills. (fig) That long hike up the hill has tired me out.* **3** [I0] to go on a hike

tramp 1 [L9] to walk with firm heavy steps. **2** [L9; T1] to walk through or over (a place): *I enjoy tramping through the hills on a sunny day. The children tramped the woods looking for berries.* **3** [L9; X9] also **trample** to press repeatedly with the feet: *Someone trampled on my toes on the bus. The farmer was very angry to find that his corn had been trampled down by the children.* **4** [C] a long walk: *They went for a tramp in the hills.*

stamp 1 [L9; T1] to push (one's foot) down heavily: *She stamped (her foot) in anger.* **2** [L9] to walk in this way: *He stamped angrily out of the house.* **3** [C] an act of stamping: *the stamp of a horse's foot*

stump [L9] to walk heavily and stiffly: *He was stumping about in his heavy shoes.*

trudge [L9] to walk with heavy steps, slowly and with effort: *The defeated soldiers trudged through the deep snow back towards Paris. He had to trudge (for) 20 miles to get home.*

ramble [Wv3] **1** [I0 (*about, through, among*)] to go on a long walk with no particular plan: *They rambled through the woods. We rambled about for hours in the old city.* **2** [I0 (about)] (*fig*) to talk or write in a disordered and wandering way: *The old lady began to ramble (about the days of her youth).* **3** [Wv4,6; I0] (of a plant) to grow loosely in all directions: *The wild roses rambled all over the fence.* **4** [C] a long walk with no particular plan: *They went for a ramble in the woods.*

trek 1 [L9] to make a long hard journey: *The settlers trekked across the desert to their new home.* **2** [C] such a journey: *The trek across the desert lasted many weeks.*

M24 verbs : **running and moving quickly, etc**

[ALSO ⇒ M33, K101]

race [I0, 3; X9] to (cause to) go very fast: *He came racing across the road. They raced to get help. We raced the sick woman to hospital. (fig) The holidays raced by. Her heart was racing (with fear).*

dash 1 [L9; (I0)] to run quickly and suddenly: *I must dash (off) to catch a train. He suddenly dashed into the street. They've been dashing about all day.* **2** [X9; L9] to (cause to) strike with great force: *The waves dashed the boat against the rocks. The waves dashed against the rocks.* **3** [X9; L9] to (cause to) break by being thrown with great force: *The glass bowl dashed to pieces against the stone floor.* **4** [T1] (*fig*) to destroy or ruin (hopes, spirits, etc): *The angry letter dashed my hopes that we could remain friends.*

career [L9] to move at great speed, usu dangerously: *The car careered past us and crashed into the wall.* **at full career** going as fast as possible: *The horse was running at full career when it fell and broke its leg.*

tear [L9] *infml* to move quickly: *The boy tore along on his bicycle. Cars tore past us.*

rip [L9] *infml* to go very fast: *The fast car ripped past us.*

belt [L9] *infml* to go or drive very fast: *He was just belting along in his car.*

pound [L9] to move quickly but heavily: *The great animals pounded towards him.*

zoom 1 [I0] (of an aircraft) to go quickly (esp upwards): *The plane zoomed up. (fig) The cost of living just zoomed.* **2** [L9] *infml* (of a driver or vehicle) to go quickly: *The car zoomed along the road. Jack went zooming past in his new car.*

zip [L9] to make the sound of something moving quickly and suddenly through the air or of cloth tearing: *The bullet zipped through the air.*

sweep 1 [T1; L9] to (cause to) move quickly: *The aeroplanes swept across the sky. The running water swept the leaves away.* **2** [L9] to extend over a large area in a curve: *The new road sweeps right round the old town.* **sweeping** [B] (*esp fig*) moving quickly and having a powerful effect: *He made sweeping changes in the law.*

M25 verbs & nouns : **running and moving lightly and quickly, etc**

scamper [L9] to run quickly and usu playfully: *The mouse scampered into its hole. Children were scampering about in the garden.*

scurry 1 [L9] to move in haste esp with short quick steps: *The mouse scurried into its hole when the cat appeared. She scurried about the house picking up her children's toys where they had left them.* **2** [S] a movement or esp sound of scurrying: *He heard the scurry of feet in the hall. There was a general scurry to leave the building at 5 o'clock.*

scuttle 1 [L9] to rush in short quick movements, esp to escape; scurry: *The children scuttled off/away when they saw the policeman.* **2** [S] an act of rushing away: *There was a general scuttle for shelter when the rain began to fall heavily.*

scramble 1 [L9] to move in a hurry, esp over a rough or steep surface: *Little animals scrambled away as we came near. I scrambled up the rock for a better look at the sea.* **2** [I3; L9, esp *for*] to struggle or compete with others eagerly or against difficulty: *The people were scrambling for shelter/scrambling to get out of the way. I had to scramble to find the money to pay.* **3** [S] an act of moving or climbing esp over a rough surface: *It's quite a scramble to get to the top of* *the hill.* **4** [S] an eager and disorderly struggle: *There is always a scramble for the best seats.*

dart 1 [L9] to move suddenly and quickly: *He darted out/towards the door. Insects were darting about before the storm.* **2** [X9] to send out suddenly and quickly: *The snake darted out its tongue. He darted an angry look at his enemy.* **3** [S] an act of darting: *He made a dart for the door.*

bolt 1 [I0] (esp of a horse) to run away suddenly, as in fear: *My horse bolted and threw me in the mud.* **2** [I0] *infml* (of a person) to hurry away: *The thief bolted when he saw the policeman.* **3** [T1 (*down*)] to swallow hastily: *He bolted (down) his breakfast.* **4** [S] an act of bolting: *The horse did a bolt.* **make a bolt for** to try to escape quickly by means of: *He made a bolt for the door/made a bolt for it* (= tried to run away).

M26 *verbs & nouns* : **crawling and creeping, etc**

crawl 1 [I0] to move slowly by drawing the body close to the ground or floor or on the hands and knees: *The baby crawled across the room. The wounded soldier crawled behind the wall for protection.* **2** [I0] to go very slowly: *The roads were very busy as the bus crawled home.* **3** [I0] to be completely covered by worms, insects or other such animals: *Don't eat that apple; it's crawling with worms. The child's hair was crawling so the teacher advised her to wash it thoroughly.* (*fig*) *After the explosion the town was crawling with police.* **4** [I0] (*fig*) to have an unpleasant sensation, as of worms, insects, etc, moving over one's skin: *The sight of snakes makes my flesh crawl. As it grew darker in the ruined church our flesh began to crawl with terror.* **5** [I0] (*fig*) *infml* to try and win the favour of someone of higher rank by being too nice to them, doing small jobs for them, etc: *She's not very clever, but she always gets good marks because she crawls to her teacher.* **6** [S] a very slow movement: *The traffic went at a crawl.*

creep 1 [I0] to move slowly and quietly with the body close to the ground: *The cat crept silently towards the mouse. The thief crept noiselessly along the passage. The policeman crept up on the criminal and seized him from behind.* **2** [L9] to move or advance slowly: *The sea crept slowly up the shore. The roads were very busy so we could only creep home. One hardly notices the way old age creeps up on one.* **3** [Wv4;I0] to grow along the ground or a surface: *Many grasses spread by creeping. It's a creeping plant.* **4** [I0] (*fig*) to have an unpleasant sensation, as of worms, insects, etc moving over one's skin: *Her flesh crept with fear.* **5** [C] *sl* an unpleasant person who tries to win the favour of a person of higher rank, esp by praising insincerely **6** [U] the slow movement of loose soil, rocks, etc: *soil creep*

wriggle 1 [I0] to twist from side to side either in one place or when moving along: *He wriggled uncomfortably on the hard chair. Worms wriggled across the wet path. The hole was full of wriggling snakes.* **2** [T1] *also* **wiggle** to move (a part of the body) in this way **3** [C] *also* **wiggle** a wriggling movement

slither [L9] to move in a slipping or twisting way like a snake: *The creature slithered down the tree.*

slide 1 [I0; T1] to (cause to) go smoothly over a surface: *He slid along the ice. He slid his glass across the table top.* **2** [L9] to pass smoothly or continuously; go slowly and unnoticed; slip: *She slid out of the room when no one was looking. He slid over/around the question without answering it. He just let things slide* (= gradually stopped taking care) *after his wife died.* **3** [C] a downward turn; a fall: *stop the slide in living standards* **4** [C] a slipping motion over a surface: *The car went into a slide on the ice.*

slip 1 [I0] to slide without wanting to: *She slipped on the wet stones and fell.* **2** [L9] to move quickly and quietly: *She slipped past us in the dark.* **3** [L9] to go without being seen, felt, noticed, etc: *She was happy and the time just slipped past.* **4** [I0] to fall, slide, etc from some usu stated place: *The greasy plate slipped from her fingers and broke on the floor.*

sidle [L9 (*up*)] to walk as if ready to turn and go the other way, esp secretively or nervously: *He sidled up to the stranger on the street and tried to sell him the stolen thing.*

sneak 1 [L9; X9] to (cause to) go quietly and secretly; go or take so as not to be seen: *They tried to sneak past the guard. He sneaked around to the back door. He tried to sneak his little brother into the theatre without paying.* **2** [T1] *sl* to steal secretly: *The boy was caught sneaking an apple from a shop.*

slink [L9] to move quietly and secretly, as if fearful or ashamed: *He slunk away into the night. The dog slunk (off) into its corner.*

M27 *verbs* : **loitering and lingering, etc**

loiter [I0] to move on or move about, stopping often: *The policemen saw someone loitering near the shop.*

linger [L9, esp *on*] **1** to wait for a time instead of going; delay going: *She should have gone out but lingered over her meal till it was too late. She lingered around the door telling the story of what had happened.* **2** to live on the point of death for some time, esp when suffering from a disease: *Better that she should have died peacefully than linger (on) for months.* **3** to be slow to disappear: *The pain lingered on for weeks. We don't need to get up early any more, but the habit lingers on.*

hang about *also* **hang around** [v adv;prep] *BrE infml* **1** [I0;T1] to wait or stay near or in (a place), often without purpose or activity: *She hung about for an hour, but he didn't come.* *'Young people today are always hanging about (the house) doing nothing,' he said angrily.* **2** [I0] to delay or move slowly: *Don't hang about; we've got a train to catch.* **3** [I0] also **hang on** to wait on purpose: *Hang on/about for a bit; I'll soon be ready.* **4** [T1] *deprec* to be friendly with: *I don't want my son hanging around (with) that nasty girl!*

mill about also **mill around** [v adv I0] to move without purpose in large numbers esp without going anywhere: *The crowd/the cattle were milling about in the streets.*

loll 1 [L9, esp *about, around*] to be in a lazy loose position: *She was lolling in a chair, with nothing to do.* **2** [T1; I0: (*out*)] to (allow to) hang down loosely: *His head lolled, as if he was falling asleep. The dog's tongue lolled out.*

lounge [L9, esp *about, around*] to be in a lazy, loose position or move in a lazy loose way: *He lounged about the house, doing nothing but getting in our way while we were working.*

M28 *verbs & nouns* : **flying in various ways**

[ALSO ⇒ M19 FLY]

soar [I0] *esp lit* **1** to fly; go fast or high (as) on wings; sail in the air: *The birds were soaring overhead.* **2** [Wv4] (*fig*) to go upward, esp far or fast: *They lived in times of soaring prices. The temperature soared to 80° on May 1.* **3** [Wv4] (*fig*) to go beyond what is ordinary or limiting: *'Let your spirit soar,' he said. She has a soaring imagination.* **4** [Wv4, 6] to be very high: *He looked at the soaring mountains/buildings. The cliffs soared 500 feet into the air.* **5** (of a motorless aircraft (**glider**) or the people in it) to go through the air

swoop 1 [I0 (*down*)] to descend sharply, esp in attack: *The plane swooped down on the town.* **2** [I0] to rush on someone to attack: *She waited outside the door and swooped on him when he came out.* **3** [C *usu sing*] a swooping action: *The police made their swoop at night and the robbers were caught.*

skim [T1] to move quickly over or lightly touching (a surface), esp when flying: *The plane flew so low that it just skimmed the water.*

flap 1 [I0; T1] to wave (something large and soft, like wings) slowly up and down or to and fro making a noise: *The large bird flapped its wings. She flapped a newspaper at the insect. She flapped at the insect with a newspaper.* **2** [I0] (of something large and soft, like wings) to move slowly up and down or to and fro, making a noise: *The sails flapped in the gentle wind. Her wet skirt flapped against her knees.* **3** [L9] (of a bird) to fly (slowly): *It flapped slowly off.* **4** [C] an act of flapping: *The big bird gave an angry flap of its wings.*

float [I0 (*down, along, past*)] to move slowly, noiselessly, and gently (through the air): *The clouds floated past them as they stood on the high mountain.*

glide 1 [L9] to move (noiselessly) in a smooth continuous manner, which seems easy and without effort: *The boat glided over the river. Fish were gliding about in the lake.* **2** [I0] to use a sort of plane (**glider**) which has no engine but follows movements of the air currents **3** [C] a gliding movement

hover [I0] **1** (of birds, certain aircraft, etc) to stay in the air in one place: *The hawk hovered over the mouse before catching it.* **2** (of people) to wait around one place: *They hovered behind the window trying to catch his attention.* (*fig*) *A question hovered on his lips.* (*fig*) *He's hovering between life and death.*

M29 *verbs, etc* : **driving and steering, etc**

drive 1 [T1; I0] to guide and control (a horse or vehicle): *He drove a horse/a cart/a car. She drives well. He/They drove to the station/in the park. He was driving when the accident happened.* **2** [T1] to take (someone) in a vehicle: *Can you drive me to the station?* **3** [T1] to direct force onto (a thing): *The engines drive the ship. An oil engine drives the pump. to drive a ball. to drive a nail* **4** [L9] (of a vehicle) to perform or go in the stated way: *This car drives easily.* **5** [C] an occasion of driving or being driven: *Let's go for a drive.*

motor [I0] *esp BrE becoming rare* to travel by car, esp by one that is privately owned; drive: *We spent all day by the sea and motored home in the evening.*

pilot 1 [X9] to help and guide: *He piloted the ship safely into harbour.* (*fig*) *He piloted the old lady through the crowd to her seat.* **2** [X9, esp *through*] to guide carefully to a successful result: *This politician has piloted several suggested laws through Parliament.* **3** [T1] to act as a pilot to (an aircraft or ship): *John pilots his own private aeroplane.*

steer 1 [X9; L9] to direct the course of (as a ship or vehicle): *They steered the boat into the wind/by the stars. He steered the car around the corner.* (*fig*) *She tried to steer the conversation towards her favourite subject.* **2** [X9; L9] to go in or hold to (a course); follow (a way): *The boat was steering (a course) for the harbour. We turned the car around and steered for home.* (*fig*) *I tried to steer a course between their approval and disapproval.* **3** [L9] (of a ship or vehicle) to allow being directed: *How does your car steer? Does it take the corners well?* **steer clear (of)** *not fml* to keep away from; avoid: *He steered clear of all the doubtful questions.*

guide [T1] **1** to control (the movements of): *I guided the car carefully into the garage.* (*fig*) *The government will guide the country through the difficulties ahead.* **2** to show (someone) the way by directing: *He guided the man through the streets to the railway station. He guided* *them around the Art Show. The light guided them back to harbour.* **3** [*usu pass*] to influence strongly: *Be guided by your feelings and tell her the truth before it's too late.*

navigate 1 [I0; T1] to direct the course of (a ship, aircraft, etc): *to navigate by the stars* (=using the positions of stars as a guide). *Is that big ship easy to navigate?* (*fig*) *Get in the car; I'll drive if you (hold the map and) navigate.* **2** [T1] to go by sea, air, etc from one side or end to the other (of a place): *He was the first man to navigate the Atlantic by air. The ship navigated the narrow sea passage safely.* (*fig*) *When you walk down, be careful how you navigate the stairs!* **navigation** [U] the skill or act of navigating ships, aeroplanes, etc **navigator** [C] a person skilled at navigating; a person given the work of navigating a vehicle

fly [T1; I0] to cause (an aeroplane) to go through the air: *He flew the plane to New York. Can you fly?*

cruise 1 [I0; T1] to sail in an unhurried way (across), searching for enemy ships or for pleasure: *British ships are cruising in the North Sea to protect our fishing boats.* **2** [Wv4; I0] (of a car, plane, etc) to move at a practical rather than high speed in order to make best use of petrol, oil, etc: *The car has a cruising speed of 60 miles an hour.* **3** [C] a sea voyage for pleasure: *They went on a cruise to the Greek islands.*

bus [I0; T1] to (cause to) go by bus: *They bussed to school. They bussed the children to school.*

ferry [I0; T1] to (cause to) move on or in a vehicle, esp a ferry, or to go to a place again and again as a ferry does: *They ferried him across the river in their little boat. All day the planes ferried the soldiers from the city to the mountains.*

M30 *verbs* : **going on a bicycle, etc**
[ALSO ⇒ M96]

cycle [L9; X9] to ride or travel on a bicycle: *He cycles every day. She cycled the distance easily.*
bicycle [I0] *esp formerly or AmE* to cycle: *They enjoy bicycling.*
pedal 1 [X9; L9] to move (a bicycle) along by pushing the pedals [⇒ M103] with the feet: *He pedalled the bicycle up the hill. I was just pedalling along.* **2** [T1] to work (a machine) by using pedals: *Pedalling a bicycle is very tiring work.* **3** [I0] to work the pedals of a machine: *His legs are too short to pedal.*

M31 *verbs* : **moving faster and slower**

accelerate *often fml* **1** [I0; T1] to (cause to) move faster **2** [T1] (*fig*) to cause to happen earlier: *Can you accelerate the workers' payment?* **acceleration** [U] the act of accelerating; the ability to accelerate: *The car's acceleration was very good.*

decelerate [I0; T1] *often fml* to (cause to) go slower: *We decelerated (the engine) long before we came to a stop.* **deceleration** [U] the act of decelerating; the ability to decelerate

speed 1 [L9; X9] to (cause to) go or pass quickly: *I saw a car speeding away. The time sped quickly by. They took action to speed the new law through Parliament.* **2** [I0] (*usu used in pres p*) to go or drive too fast; break the speed limit: *'Was I really speeding, officer?' she asked in surprise.*

speed up [v adv I0; T1] *not fml* to (cause to) go faster: *Can you speed things up a bit? The car began to speed up.*

slow [I0; T1: (*up, down*)] to (cause to) go at a slower speed: *The car slowed (down). Don't slow up now! Something is slowing up the work.* (*fig*) *You should slow down; you're working too hard.*

change *esp BrE*, **shift** *esp AmE* [I0 (*up, down; into, to*)] to cause the engine of a vehicle to be in a different (higher or lower) gear, usu to go faster or slower: *Change into second gear when you go up the hill. Change down before going up the hill, and then change up at the top.*
change gears *BrE*, **shift gears** *AmE* to make a change in speed and power by causing the engine of a vehicle to be in a different gear: *Change gear at the bottom of the hill.* (*fig*) *After beginning the speech seriously, he changed gear and told some jokes.*

M32 *verbs* : **coming to a stop, moving away, etc**

draw up [v adv I0] (of a vehicle) to get to a certain point and stop: *The car drew up and three men got out.*
draw out [v adv I0] to move faster out of esp a line of other vehicles (and begin to pass them): *The big car drew out suddenly.*
draw in [v adv I0] to arrive: *The train/car drew in.*
draw away [v adv I0 (*from*)] **1** to get further and further ahead: *Our boat is drawing away (from the others in the race).* **2** [*also* T1] to move away, usu quickly: *She drew (herself) away from him when he tried to kiss her.*
draw apart [v adv I0] to get further and further away (from each other): *The two boats/political parties are drawing apart.*
pull in [v adv] **1** [I0] (of a train) to arrive at a station **2** [I0] *also* **pull over** (of a vehicle or boat) to move to one side (and stop): *Let's pull in here by the river and rest.* **pull-in** [C] a place by the roadside where vehicles may stop and where drinks and light meals may be obtained
pull out [v adv] **1** [I0] (of a train) to leave a station **2** [T1; I0: (*of*)] to (cause to) leave (a place or time of trouble): *He saw that the firm was going to be ruined, so he pulled out.*
pull up [v adv] **1** [T1; I0] to (cause to) come to a stop: *The car pulled up outside the station.* **2** [I0

(to, with)] to come level (with another competitor in a race)

pull over [v adv T1; I0] to direct or move (one's vehicle) over to one side of the road: *The policeman drove just in front of me and gave me a sign to pull over.*

overtake 1 [T1; I0] to come up level (with) from behind (and perhaps pass): *A car overtook me although I was going very fast. Don't overtake on this road.* **2** [T1] (*fig*) (of something unpleasant) to reach suddenly and unexpectedly: *A strong wind/A sudden illness overtook him unexpectedly. We have been overtaken by events* (= new (and unpleasant) events have happened that have destroyed our plans).

overhaul [T1] to overtake (another vehicle) esp over a longer distance: *He left five minutes ago; we may be able to overhaul him if we drive fast.*

brake 1 [T1] *less common* to cause to slow or stop by (or as if by) a brake (= a means of stopping a vehicle): *He braked the car.* **2** [I0] *common* to use a brake: *He braked suddenly.*

M33 *verbs & nouns* : **hurrying and rushing**

[ALSO ⇒ M16, 18, 24]

hurry 1 [I0; T1] to (cause to) be quick in action, sometimes too quick: *Don't hurry; we're not late. He hurried across the road in front of a car. Don't hurry me.* **2** [X9] to send or bring quickly: *Doctors and nurses were hurried to the accident.* **3** [U] quick activity: *After all the hurry I was glad of a rest.* **4** [U] need for hurrying: *There's no hurry to return the book.* **in a hurry 1** too quickly: *You make mistakes if you do things in a hurry.* **2** eager: *You're never in a hurry to get up in the mornings.* **3** without difficulty: *I won't forget her kindness in a hurry.* **4** *infml* willingly: *I won't help her again in a hurry when she's been so ungrateful.* **in no hurry 1** willing to wait: *I'm in no hurry to go.* **2** not eager: *I'm in no hurry to go out in the rain.* **3** unwilling: *I'm in no hurry to help her after what she did.*

hasten *often fml* **1** [T1; I0] to (cause to) move or happen faster: *He hastened his steps. He hastened home.* **2** [I3] to be quick (to say) because the hearer may imagine something else has happened: *Let me hasten to tell you that your son is not badly hurt, although it was a serious accident.* **haste** [U] *often fml* hurry: *Why all this haste? In his haste (to do it) he forgot a lot of other things.*

rush 1 [I0] to hurry; act quickly: *There's plenty of time; we needn't rush.* **2** [L9; X9] to (cause to) move suddenly and hastily in the stated direction: *They rushed up the stairs/out into the street/towards their mother/all over the place. Doctors and medical supplies were rushed to the place of the accident.* **3** [T1] to do (a job) hastily and perhaps not carefully: *Let the butter melt slowly; you mustn't rush it.* **4** [T1 (into)] to force (someone) to act or decide hastily: *Let*

me think about it and don't rush me. I was rushed into buying these expensive boots. **5** [T1] to attack suddenly and all together: *Perhaps if we all rush him at once he'll drop his gun.* **6** [C] a sudden rapid hasty movement: *The cat made little rushes after the ball. There came a sudden rush of water out of the hole.* **7** [U] *not fml* (too much) haste: *We needn't leave yet; what's all the rush? We've got to paint the kitchen before tomorrow; it's a rush job.* **8** [U] great activity and excitement: *I hate shopping during the Christmas rush when everyone's buying presents.* **9** [S3, 9] a sudden great demand: *There's been a rush to see the new play/a rush for tickets for the football match.*

rush someone off his feet to make someone hurry too much or work too hard: *I've been rushed off my feet all day at the office and I'm tired.*

rush into [v prep T1] to go into (a state or condition) hastily and without enough thought (*in phrs like* **rush into marriage**): *Don't rush into it without thinking very carefully.*

shoot 1 [L9] to go fast or suddenly: *Blood shot out of the wound. He shot past me in his fast car.* **2** [Wv4; L9] (of pain) to move fast along a nerve: *Pain shot through his arm. It was not an ache but a shooting pain.* **3** [T1] to pass quickly by or along: *a car shooting traffic lights; a boat shooting the rapids* [⇒ L96] **4** [T1; I0] **a** to move (a sliding locking bar) across **b** (of such a bar) to move across: *He shot the bolt (of the door) so that nobody would get in.*

stampede 1 [C] a rush, esp of animals, esp when excited or frightened: *There was a stampede among the horses/frightened people when the fire started.* **2** [I0; T1] to (cause to) rush like this: *The horses stampeded. Don't stampede the horses!*

M34 *verbs & nouns* : **following, chasing, and hunting**

follow 1 [T1; I0] to come, arrive, go, or leave later (than); move behind in the same direction: *That dog's following us again; you can see it if you look behind you. The boy followed his father out. I'm sending the letter today; the packet will follow (later).* **2** [T1] to go in the same direction as; continue along: *The railway line follows the river for several miles. Follow the road until you come to the hotel.* **3** [T1] to go after in order to catch: *I think we're being followed.* **4** [T1] to go with; attend on: *The general was followed by a large number of army officers as he walked round the camp.* **5** [T1] to come next in order or on a list: *The number five follows the number four.* **6** [T1; I0] to happen or take place after (something): *May follows April. The storm was followed by a calm. We expect even greater successes to follow.* **7** [T1; I0] to come after in some position: *Queen Elizabeth II followed King George VI. He'll be a difficult man to follow; no one understands* *the work as he did.* **8** [T1] to carry on (a certain kind of work): *He follows the trade of baker. You must study hard if you intend to follow the law* (= be a lawyer). **9** [T1] to keep in sight; watch: *The cat followed every movement of the mouse. He followed her with his eyes* (= watched her movements closely). **10** [T1] to attend or listen to carefully: *He followed the speaker's words with the greatest attention.* **11** [T1] (*fig*) to take a keen interest in: *He follows all the cricket news. I follow Fulham* (= I'm a keen supporter of Fulham football team). **12** [T1] (*fig*) to accept and act by: *Why didn't you follow my advice? These orders must be followed at once. The village people will follow the customs of their grandfathers.* **13** [T1; I∅] (*fig*) to copy; take (something) as a guide: *He followed the example of his friend and went to the university. You'll spend lots on clothes if you always follow the fashion* (= dress in the latest manner). **14** [T1; I∅] (*fig*) to be or happen as a necessary effect or result (of): *Disease often follows war. Just because he's at the bottom of the class, it doesn't follow* (= you cannot reason from this) *that he has no brains; he may just be very lazy. As you're getting a better job, you'll be paid more.—No, that doesn't necessarily follow.* **as follows** as now to be told; as given in the list below: *The results are as follows: Philip Carter first, Sam Cohen second, Sandra Postlethwaite third.*

chase 1 [T1] to follow rapidly in order to catch: *The cat chased the mouse but could not catch it.* (*fig*) *Why do modern people chase material possessions* (= 'things' rather than values, etc)? **2** [X9] to drive away; cause to leave: *We must chase the enemy from our country. The old lady chased the thief out of the house. Did you chase that cat away?* **3** [L9, esp *about, around*] *infml* to rush; hurry: *Stop chasing about and sit down.* **4** [T1 (*down, up*)] to try to find: *The police are chasing information about this latest crime. The police have been trying to chase up the dead man's sister but they have no idea where she lives.* **5** [S] the act or occasion of chasing: *In the chase the policeman lost his dog. There was an exciting car chase after the thieves.* **6** [*the* R] *esp formerly* hunting: *He enjoys the excitement of the chase.*

pursue [T1] **1** to chase in order to catch, kill, or defeat: *The dogs pursued the fox across the fields. The police are pursuing an escaped prisoner.* **2** to follow closely; show continual attention to: *Wherever the travellers went in the Eastern city, they were pursued by beggars.* **3** (of something harmful) to follow and cause suffering to: *Bad luck pursued us all through the year.* **4** to make continual efforts to gain (something): *The poet has pursued fame all his life, but never experienced it.* **5** to continue (steadily) with; be busy with: *He is pursuing his studies at the university. The police are pursuing their enquiries into the murder. He could see he was losing the argument, so he said, 'I'd rather not pursue the matter.'* **pursuit** [U] **1** the

act of pursuing: *The police went in pursuit of the thieves. The pursuit of money is his main interest.* **2** the people and/or animals pursuing: *I think we have lost the pursuit here.*

go after [v prep T1] *not fml* to follow, chase, or pursue: *The dogs went after the fox.*

hunt 1 [T1; I∅] to go after in order to catch and kill (animals and birds) either for food or for sport **2** [T1; I∅] **a** to go after (foxes) on horseback with special dogs (**hounds**) **b** to do this in (an area) **c** to use (one's horse) for this: *to hunt one's horse* **3** [T1; I∅] to search (for): *The police are hunting the murderer. They hunted everywhere/high and low for her.* **4** [X9] to drive away: *You can't hunt the birds off the seeds; you'll have to trap them in cotton thread.* **5** [C *often in comb*] an act or occasion of hunting: *The hunt was on! The police have started a hunt for the woman's killer. She has taken part in many foxhunts there.* **6** [GC] the people (and animals) in a hunt: *The hunt passed through our wood.*

trail 1 [T1] to follow the trail [⇒ M131] of (a person, animal, etc): *The ground was soft and wet, so they were able to trail him to the house.* **2** [I∅] to pull or be pulled (along the ground, etc): *Her long dress trailed on the floor.*

M35 *verbs, etc:* **escaping, etc**

escape 1 [I∅ (*from, out of*)] (of a person) to reach freedom or safety: *He escaped from/out of the burning house. The prisoners have escaped!* **2** [I∅ (*from, out of*)] (of liquids or gases) to come out; find a way out: *They allow the water to escape. Some gas is escaping from the pipe.* **3** [I∅; T1, 4] (of a person) to avoid or keep free from (a stated evil): *He escaped death only by minutes. I hate him but I can't escape meeting him. He narrowly* (= only just) *escaped being drowned. Everyone else caught the disease but I escaped.* **4** [T1] (of an event, a fact, etc) to be unnoticed or forgotten by: *I'm afraid your name escapes me* (= I've forgotten it). *Nothing escaped his attention.* **5** [T1] (of a noise, words, etc) to be produced or made, usu unconsciously by (a person): *A whistle of surprise escaped him.* **6** [C; U: (*from, out of*)] (an example of) the act of escaping or fact of having escaped: *His successful escape from prison was in all the newspapers. The thief jumped into a car and made his escape. Escape from here is impossible. They made an escape attempt.* **7** [C (*of, from, out of*)] a case or the act of escaping by a liquid or gas: *There was an escape of gas (from the pipe).* **8** [S; U] something that frees one from unpleasant or dull reality: *She reads love stories as an escape.* **narrow escape** a case of only just avoiding (stated) evil: *That was a narrow escape all right, when our car turned over!*

flee [I∅; (T1)] *usu emot & lit* to escape (from) by hurrying away: *They all fled from the burning* *ship. (lit) 'I fled Him, down the arches of the years' (Francis Thompson).* **flee the country** to go abroad for safety

fly [IØ; (T1)] *usu imper & infin esp formerly & fml* to flee; escape: *Fly while you can! They told him to fly the country.*

get away [v adv IØ] *infml* to escape, flee: *The thief got away completely.* **getaway** [C] the act or occasion of getting away: *The thief made his getaway through a back window. The police found the getaway car (= the car used in the getaway) the next day.*

defect [IØ *(from, to)*] to desert a political party, group, or movement, esp in order to join an opposing one: *She defected (from our party to theirs).* **defection 1** [U] the act of defecting **2** [C] a case of defecting: *The leaders are becoming anxious about the growing number of defections from our party.*

elude [T1] **1** to escape from (somebody or something), esp by means of a trick: *The fox succeeded in eluding the hunters by running back in the opposite direction.* **2** (of a fact) to escape from the memory of (somebody): *I remember his face very well, but his name eludes me for the moment (= I can't remember it).*

decamp [IØ] **1** (esp of soldiers) to leave a place where one has camped **2** *infml & humor* to leave any place quickly (and usu in secret): *The police are about to discover us; we'd better decamp. The lodger has decamped without paying his bill.*

abscond [IØ *(with)*] *fml* to go away suddenly and secretly because one has done something wrong: *The director of the savings bank absconded with all the money in the bank. He absconded from the bank.*

break out [v adv IØ] *infml* to escape, esp from inside a large building, prison, group of guards, etc: *The prisoners broke out (of the prison).* **breakout** [C] an act or result of breaking out: *There has been a big prison breakout!*

M36 *nouns* : **things and persons chased, etc** [C]

quarry an animal or person that is hunted

fugitive a person escaping from the law, the police, danger, etc: *He's a fugitive from justice; he's trying to avoid being caught by the police.*

refugee a person who has had to leave his country for political reasons

defector a person who has defected

deserter a person who leaves his duty or his leader, esp one who leaves military service without permission [⇒ M38]

M37 *verbs, etc* : **avoiding and dodging**
[ALSO ⇒ K120 MISS]

avoid [T1, 4] **1** to escape: *He avoided punishment by running away. He avoided being*

punished. **2** to miss or keep away from, esp on purpose: *I avoided her by leaving by the back door. She avoided answering my questions.*

evade *fml* **1** [T1] to get out of the way of or escape from: *He evaded his enemy. The lion evaded the hunters.* **2** [T1, 4] *derog* to avoid (doing) (something one should do): *He tried to evade (paying) his taxes.* **3** [T1] *derog* to avoid answering (a question) properly: *Answer honestly and stop evading my questions!* **evasion 1** [U] the act of evading: *the fox's clever evasion of the dogs* **2** [C; U] an action or lack of action which evades: *George is in prison for tax evasion. It was a clear evasion of duty.* **3** [C] *derog* a statement which evades: *The minister's speech was full of evasions.* **evasive** [B] *derog* tending to evade: *He was very evasive about where he had been. Don't be so evasive; answer me honestly!* **-ly** [adv] **-ness** [U]

get (a)round [v prep T1, 4] *infml* to evade: *He somehow gets round paying a lot of tax; I don't know how. There's no getting round this difficulty.*

dodge 1 [IØ] to move suddenly aside: *I tried to hit him but he dodged.* **2** [T1] to avoid by so doing: *He dodged my blow.* **3** [T1] *infml* to avoid by a trick or in some dishonest way: *tax-dodging* **4** [C] an act of avoiding by a sudden movement of the body **5** [C] *infml* a clever way of avoiding something or of deceiving or tricking someone: *a tax dodge*

skip 1 [T1] to fail to attend or take part in (an activity); miss: *Let's skip the meeting/a meal.* **2** [IØ *(over)*; T1] to pass over or leave out (something in order); not do or deal with (the next thing): *She skipped (over) an uninteresting chapter of the book. Write your name at the top; then skip two lines and begin to write. Every time the record comes to that part of the music the needle skips.*

M38 *verbs, etc*: **leaving and deserting**

leave [T1 *(behind)*] to fail to take or bring, esp by accident: *I'm afraid I've left my books (behind) at home.*

desert 1 [Wv5;T1] to leave empty or leave completely and usu without intending to return: *the silent deserted streets of the city at night* **2** [T1] to leave at a difficult time or leave in a difficult position: *All my friends have deserted me! He deserted his wife and children.* *(fig) When he had to speak to her his courage suddenly deserted him.* **3** [IØ; T1] to leave (military service) without permission: *He deserted (the army) in Hong Kong.* **desertion 1** [U] the act of leaving one's duty, one's family, or military service without permission, esp if without the intention of returning: *He was shot for desertion in time of war.* **2** [C] an example of this: *There were several desertions from our ship in Hong Kong.*

abandon [T1] **1** to leave completely, never to return; desert: *The sailors abandoned the* *burning ship.* **2** to leave (a relation, or friend) in a thoughtless or cruel way: *He abandoned his wife and went away with all their money. This is a home for abandoned wives.* **3** to give up, esp without finishing, often to do something else: *The search was abandoned when night fell even though the child had not been found. The second plan was abandoned in favour of the first.* **4** [(*to*)] to give (oneself) up completely to a feeling, desire, etc: *He abandoned himself to grief. What abandoned behaviour!* **-ment** [U]

M39 *verbs & nouns* : **moving forward, etc**

advance 1 [I∅ (*on, upon* or *against*)] to move or come forward: *The soldiers advanced on the enemy. They advanced twenty miles.* **2** [I∅; T1: (*to*)] to (cause to) improve or move forward (in rank, interests, development, etc): *He worked so well that his employer soon advanced him.* **3** [T1] to bring forward to an earlier date or time: *The meeting has been advanced from next Tuesday to this Friday.* **4** [I∅] to move forward; develop; change: *A month has passed and the work has not advanced.* **5** [T1; I∅] *rare* to (cause to) increase; (cause to) rise: *Food prices have advanced rapidly this year. The firm advanced its prices.* **6** [S] forward movement: *There were so many people that our advance to the ticket office was slow. The enemy's advance was stopped. You cannot stop the advance of old age.* **7** [C] a development; improvement: *There have been great advances in space travel in the last 20 years.* **8** [A] going or coming before: *An advance party is a group (as of soldiers) that travels ahead of the main group. An advance copy is a copy of a book that comes out before the official date for sending out copies. An advance notice of a month is needed before you can do that.*
move forward [v adv I∅; T1] *infml* to advance: *The soldiers moved forward. The meeting has been moved forward from next Tuesday to this Friday. A month has gone by and the work hasn't moved forward at all.*
head [L9; X9: esp *for*] to move directly, esp over a longer distance: *Where were they heading?—The men were heading for the town when we met them.*
progress [I∅] **1** to advance: *The year is progressing. It will soon be autumn.* **2** to improve; develop (favourably): *She is progressing well after her operation.* **3** [U] advance; journey onward; forward movement in space: *The ship made slow progress through the rough sea. At midday the sun is at the highest point of its progress across the sky.* **4** [U] continual improvement or development: *Jane is still sick in hospital but she's making progress* (= is slowly getting better). *Civilization is considered to be the result of progress.* **5** [U] (natural) course; the state of continuing or

being done (*often in the phr* **in progress**): *During one's progress through life one has all kinds of experiences. The building of the school is now in progress.* **progression** [U; S] moving onwards: *Life is a progression; it never stops.* **progressive** [B] **1** moving forward or onward: *progressive changes* **2** *apprec* going on to new things: *progressive ideas/laws* **3** [Wa5] increasing by regular amounts: *progressive monthly payments* **-ly** [adv] **-ness** [U]

M40 *verbs & nouns* : **turning, twisting, and bending**

turn 1 [I∅; T1] to (cause to) go round: *The wheel was turning slowly. He turned the wheel. He made the wheel turn faster.* **2** [I∅; T1] to (cause to) change or move in a different direction: *The animal turned right round* (= turned to look in the opposite direction). *Turn left here, not right. He turned the car and drove away. She turned her face in my direction. He turned back and went home.* **3** [L7, 9; X7, 9] to (cause to) become different in a stated way: *He turned white with anger. His failures turned him against us. She has turned the old house into a lovely family home. The heavy rain turned the roads into rivers. The old woman used magic to turn the girl into a cat.* **4** [C] an act of turning: *Give the wheel a quick turn.* **turn on/off** [v adv T1] to cause (something like a tap, radio, etc) to work/not to work by turning (part of it): *He turned the tap/hose/water off.*
veer 1 [L9] (of a traveller, vehicle, or road) to turn or change direction: *The car was out of control and suddenly veered across the road. When you come to the rock, veer to the right and continue up the hill; don't follow the path that veers to the left.* **2** [L9] (of a person, or of opinion, talk, etc) to change from one intention, course, plan or opinion to another: *Her friends didn't think she was dependable, because she was always veering from one opinion to another. We were talking about food, and then suddenly the conversation veered round to stomach diseases.* **3** [T1; L9] *naut* to (cause (a ship) to) change course, esp away from the wind: *As they came nearer to the enemy the ships all veered to the west, to get a better position from which to attack.* **4** [I∅] *tech* (of the wind) to change direction, moving round the compass in the order North-East-South-West
twist 1 [T1] to turn quickly and forcefully: *Twist the handle to the right and the box will open.* **2** [L9] to move with a bending turning movement: *The dancer twisted sexily to the music. The snake twisted across the grass.* **3** [Wv5; T1] to hurt by pulling and turning sharply as in an accident: *I twisted my ankle* [⇒ B43] *when I fell downstairs. I had a twisted ankle.* **4** [I∅; T1] to (cause to) change shape by bending, curling, turning, etc: *His mouth twisted down at the corners as though he was going to cry. The child twisted the wire into the shape of a star. This*

wire twists too easily. **5** [T1 (*together*)] to wind (a number of threads, stems, etc) together: *She made a rope by twisting threads. The girls twisted the stems of the flowers together to make a crown for the winner of the games.* **6** [T1] to make (something) by doing this: *to twist a rope* **7** [X9, esp *round*] to wind (rope, cord, etc) around something: *She twisted her hair round her fingers to make it curl.* **8** [I0] to move in a winding course: *a stream twisting across the fields* **9** [X9, esp *off*) to pull or break off by turning and bending forcefully: *to twist an apple off a tree. The farmer twisted off a piece of bread to eat with his cheese.* **10** [T1] (*fig*) to change the true or intended meaning of (a statement, words, etc): *Stop twisting my words/ everything I say. They always twist the facts to suit their purpose.* **11** [C] an act or occasion of twisting: *Give the handle a twist; that will open the box.*

distort 1 [T1] to twist out of the true meaning: *Stop distorting what I've said. He gave a distorted account of what had happened.* **2** [T1] to twist out of a natural, usual, or original shape or condition: *His face was distorted by/with anger.* **3** [T1] (of a machine) to show, play, broadcast, etc improperly: *This radio distorts sound.* **distortion** [U; C] the act of distorting: *His distortion of the truth is terrible!*

pervert [T1] **1** to turn or twist one or something away from what is right, usual, etc: *He was a good boy but they perverted him. He was perverted by evil people.* **2** to use something for wrong purposes: *You are perverting justice by doing that!* **perversion** [U; C] an act of perverting; perverted behaviour of any kind

curve 1 [I0; T1] to (cause to) bend in the shape of a curve: *The road curved to the right. Heat the metal and curve it.* **2** [C] a line with a rounded shape; bend: *Make that line straight, not a curve. She has a beautiful body; plenty of curves.*

incline 1 [I0; T1] to (cause to) slope: *The road inclines at a steep angle. Incline the mirror at a better angle.* **2** [T1] to move downward: *to incline one's head (in greeting)* **3** [V3] to encourage (to feel, think, etc): *The news inclines me to change my mind.* **4** [I3; L9, esp *to, towards*] *fml* **a** to feel drawn to: *I incline to (take) the opposite point of view.* **b** to tend to; be likely to show (a quality): *He inclines to(-wards) tiredness in winter.*

bend 1 [T1; I0] to (cause to) be forced into or out of a curve or angle: *Bend the wire. Lead bends easily. (fig) He is very firm about it; I cannot bend him. He will not bend.* **2** [T1; L9] to (cause to) slope away from an upright position: *to bend over/down/forward/back. bend down with age. to bend down in worship* **3** [X9, esp *to*] to direct (one's efforts), as in aiming with a bow and arrow: *He bent his mind to the job.* **4** [C] the act or action of bending or the state of being bent **5** [C] something that is bent, as a curved part of a road or stream

lean 1 [I0] to be in a position that is not upright;

slope **2** [L9] to bend (from the waist): *He leaned forward/down/over to hear what she said.* **3** [L9] to support or rest oneself in a bent or sloping position **4** [X9] to rest (something) somewhere: *Lean it on/against the wall.* **5** [S (*of*)] the act or amount of leaning: *a lean of 90°*

stir 1 [T1] to move or turn, esp an instrument round in (a liquid, etc) esp in order to mix it or to mix something into it: *He stirred the soup.* **2** [X9] to put in by such a movement: *She stirred the sugar into the tea.* **3** [I0] to (begin to) move: *No one stirred in the house; everyone was asleep. He stirred in his sleep.* **4** [S] an act of stirring: *Give the soup a stir.*

M41 verbs, etc : **flowing**

flow 1 [I0] (of liquids, air, etc) to move along: *The river flows past his house. Water was flowing everywhere. (fig) When she started to write, her ideas began to flow.* **2** [C] an act or occasion of flowing: *The flow of water began to stop.*

discharge 1 [I0; T1] to send, pour, or let out (gas, liquid, etc): *The chimney discharges smoke. The River Rhine discharges (itself) into the North Sea.* **2** [U; C] an act of discharging; anything that is discharged: *The discharge of poison into the river killed all the fish.*

run [L9] (of rivers, water, etc) to flow, usu strongly: *Water was running down the walls. A river runs past his house.*

stream [L9] to flow strongly; move in or as a stream [⇒ L93]: *Water streamed across the floor. Tears streamed down her face. People streamed into the building.*

meander [L9; (I0)] **1** *esp lit* (of rivers and streams) to flow slowly, turning here and there: *meandering through the fields* **2** (of people or talk) to speak or move on in a slow, unthinking way: *He/his speech meandered on till we fell asleep.*

pour 1 [X9] to cause (a liquid) to flow esp from one thing in a higher position into another in a lower position: *He poured the wine into a glass. She poured the dirty water away/out.* **2** [L9] to move in large amounts or numbers: *The people poured past/along the street.*

spill 1 [T1; I0] to (cause to) pour out, as over the edge of a container, and be lost: *My hand slipped and spilt my drink* (= made my drink spill). *The bag broke and the flour spilt out.* **2** [L9, esp *over*] to spread or rush beyond limits: *The crowd spilled over from the church into the streets.* **3** [T1; I0] (*fig*) *infml* to let out or tell (secret information): *He threatened to spill (what he knew) to the police.* **4** [C] an act or amount of spilling: *clean up coffee spills*

drip 1 [I0] (of liquids) to fall in small drops: *Water dripped from the wet cloth.* **2** [C] a small drop of liquid falling in this way: *Drips fell from the trees.* **3** [S] the falling of liquid in this way: *There was a steady drip of water from the trees.* **4** [C] *tech* an apparatus for allowing drops of liquid to enter the body

dribble 1 [Wv3; IØ] (of liquids) to fall or run in a slow stream, esp from the mouth: *Water dribbled over the rocks.* **2** [Wv3; IØ; (T1)] to let (esp liquid in the mouth) flow out in drops: *He was dribbling all over his clothes.* **3** [C *usu sing*] liquid when it dribbles

trickle 1 [Wv3; L9] (of liquids, sand, etc) to flow or move slowly or in (quantities of) small drops, etc: *The water trickled down the wall. Sand trickled through his fingers. (fig) People trickled into the room.* **2** [S] a very small flow: *Only a trickle of water was left. (fig) There was a slow trickle of people all day.*

M42 *verbs & nouns* : **coasting and drifting**

coast [IØ] to (cause a vehicle to) keep moving without using continuous force: *The car coasted downhill with the engine off.*

drift 1 [IØ] to move or be carried slowly along, esp on water or in the air, esp in no particular direction: *The engine stopped and the boat began to drift. (fig) He is just drifting; he has no real aim in life.* **2** [IØ] (of snow) to move into large heaps: *The snow drifted against the house.* **3** [U] slow movement without any particular direction, plan, etc, esp on water or through the air; *(fig)* lack of purpose **4** [C] a large heap of esp snow or sand caused by the wind: *He was lost in a snowdrift. The drifts were two metres deep/high.*

M43 *verbs & nouns* : **bouncing and bobbing**

bounce 1 [IØ; T1] to (cause to) move, esp up, quickly, esp after striking something hard: *The ball bounced. He bounced the ball against/off the wall.* **2** [L9] to move suddenly in such a way: *She bounced in and told us the good news.* **3** [C] an act of bouncing **4** [U] *(fig)* life and strength: *He's young and full of bounce.*

bob 1 [IØ (*up, down*)] to move quickly, esp up and down: *Something was bobbing up and down in the water. The rabbit bobbed about as it ran and they couldn't catch it.* **2** [C] an act of bobbing

Putting and taking, pulling and pushing

M50 *verbs* : **putting and placing**

put 1 [X9] to move, set, place, lay, or fix (someone or something) in, on, or to a stated place: *Put the chair nearer the fire. He put some more wood on the fire. You put too much salt in this food. The police have put the thief in prison. She undressed the children and put them to*

bed. Put another button on this shirt (= sew it on). *He put a match to his cigarette* (= lit it). *Put that newspaper down while I'm talking to you!* **2** [X9] *tech* to turn, guide, or direct (a boat or horse) in a stated direction: *The captain put the ship back to port for repairs. He put his horse at the fence, but it refused to jump over.* **3** [X9] to push or send (with force): *He put his sword through his enemy's body. She put her pen through the mis-spelt word* (= crossed it out). **4** [X9] to make, place, set, or fix (something or someone) in connection with something else or an act of will or the mind: *It's time to put an end to the meeting* (= end it). *You won't succeed with the work unless you put your mind to it* (= study it). *Never put your trust in a stranger* (= don't trust a stranger). *I didn't break the window, but everyone has put the blame on me* (= blamed me). *I'll soon put a stop to that* (= stop it). *Whatever put such a strange idea into your head? His dirty clothes put his wife to shame* (= made her ashamed). *The prisoner was put to death* (= was killed). *He was put to the sword* (= killed with a sword). *The murderer will be put on trial. Your carelessness has put him in a temper. I may have been wrong, but put yourself in my place; what other action could I have taken?* **5** [X(7), 9] to cause to be (in a stated condition): *He put his books in order. You made a mistake; I'll put it right at once. He's put his knowledge of French to good use while he's been in France.* **6** [X9; (T1)] to ask (officially) for (something) to be considered: *The lawyer put several questions to the witness. (fml) I ask that the question be now put. The plan will be put before the director.* **7** [X9] to express (something) in words, esp in a particular and exact way: *She is—how shall I put it?—not exactly fat, but rather well-built for her age. His ideas were cleverly put. A lawyer must put his case quite clearly in court. I want to know how to put this in French. She was trying to put her feelings into words.* **8** [X9; (T1)] to write down; make (a written mark of some kind): *Put a cross opposite the spelling mistake. What shall I put at the end of the sentence? Put a question mark. I don't know what to put.* **9** [X9] to cause (a person or animal) to be busy; set to some kind of regular arrangement or work: *If I really put myself to it, I can finish this work today. Can we put the horse out for hire? Put all the boys to work.*

lay 1 [X9, esp *down*] to put, esp down on something: *Lay it down. Lay it on the table.* **2** [T1] to set in proper order or position: *This builder is able to lay bricks very quickly.* **3** [T1] to put knives, forks, etc on, ready for a meal (*esp in the phr* **lay the table**) **4** [T1] to cause to lie flat, settle, disappear, or cease to be active: *The rain quickly laid the dust. Her fears were soon laid (to rest).* **5** [T1; IØ] (of birds, insects, etc) to produce (an egg or eggs): *The hens aren't laying.* **6** [X9] to put into a condition, esp of ⌐weakness, helplessness, obedience, etc: *The country was laid in ruins.* **7** [X9] *(fig)* to make (a statement, claim, charge, etc) in a serious, official, or public way: *Your employer has laid a serious charge against you.* **8** [D1 *with/on*; T1 (*on*)] to spread or cover: *He wants to lay the floor with mats.*

set 1 [X9] to put (to stay) in a place: *Set a lamp on the table. The dish was set before the king. He set guards around the gate. The boat set us on the shore. He set pen to paper* (= began to write). *She set a match to the papers and watched them burn.* (*fig*) *They set him as leader over the group. His great height sets him apart* (= makes him clearly different) *from the others. He set duty before pleasure in his mind.* **2** [X7, 9] to make or cause to be in a stated condition: *He opened the cage and set the bird free. She set the mixed-up pages in order. Let's set the mistake right. He set the papers on fire/set fire to the papers.* **3** [T1] to fix or determine (a rule, time, standard, number, etc): *Let's set a date for the wedding. They set conditions for the agreement. He sets a high value on life. They set the price at £1000. He set (up) a new land speed record. You must set an example for others by good behaviour. Our fine products set the standard for the whole industry.* **4** [D1; T1; V3] to give (a piece of work) for (someone) to do: *Who set (the questions for) the examination? The teacher set the class various tasks. He then set them to write reports on what they'd done.* **5** [T1] to put into a position, esp into order for use: *He set the clock (by the time given on the radio). Set the camera for a long-distance shot. She set the table for dinner. The stage is set for the next part of the play. Set the heating control at 21 degrees. He set a trap for the mouse.* **6** [T1; I0] **a** to put (a broken bone or limb) into a fixed position for proper healing: *The doctor set my broken wrist.* **b** (of a broken bone or limb) to heal in a fixed position: *I mustn't use it until it has set completely.* **7** [T1] to fix firmly (a part of the body, esp regarded as showing one's intention, feelings, etc): *He set his jaw and refused to agree to anything I said. She's set her face against* (= she opposes) *her daughter's marriage. The child has set his heart on that toy; I wish I could buy it for him. I've set my mind on this plan and I don't want to give it up.*

fit 1 [Wv5;T1 (*up*)] to put (something, esp a piece of apparatus) in place: *The men fitted the telephone for her. The machines were fitted in/into position. This room has fitted carpets. Everything has been properly fitted up now.* **2** [I0; T1] (of clothes) to be put, worn, etc (by): *This suit fits/doesn't fit (me) well.*

fix [T1 (*up*)] to put into position, esp by fastening, using nails, etc: *The machines were fixed into the wall. Fix it up here.*

install [T1] *often tech* **1** to put in position ready for use: *Install the new machines here. They installed a modern bathroom in the old house.* **2** [*usu pass*] to put (someone) in a new position, place, etc esp at a special ceremony: *He was installed as president. They have just installed themselves in their new house.* **installation 1**

[U] the act of installing **2** [C] a ceremony of installing: *We were at the president's installation.* **3** [C] an example of this; something, esp a machine, factory, etc, which has been installed: *He is the head of the new army installation.*

rig up [v adv T1] *not fml* to put materials, equipment, etc together quickly, in order to make (something): *They rigged up a simple shelter against the storm.*

place 1 [X9] *often fml* to put or arrange in a certain position or condition: *Isn't that picture placed too high on the wall? Place the books on the shelf in order of the writers' names. You placed me in a very difficult position.* **2** [X9; (T1)] to find employment, a home, etc for: *He's quite highly placed in the government. Can you place these two homeless children?* **3** [T1] to pass to a person, firm, etc, that can perform the needed action: *I placed an order with them for 500 pairs of shoes. We shall lose money if we can't place these goods.* **4** [X9; (T1)] to make a judgment of the worth, social rank, etc of: *How high would you place her among the singers of this country?* **5** [T1] to remember fully all the details of, and where and when one last saw, heard, etc: *I've heard this music many times in the past, but at the moment I can't quite place it.* **6** [X9] to put (with certainty): *I place all my trust in you. The teacher places a great deal of importance on correct grammar.* **7** [T7, 9 *usu pass*] to state the position of (a runner) at the end of a race: *He was originally placed first, but after a complaint he was placed second.* **8** [X9] to put (money) for the purpose of earning interest: *His father placed £1000 in his account in the bank.*

clap [X9] *emph* to put, place, or send usu quickly and effectively: *She clapped her hands to her ears to keep the awful noise out. The guards clapped him in prison. He clapped the door shut.*

locate 1 [X9] *fml* to fix or set in a certain place: *He located his home in the country.* **2** [L9] *AmE* to settle (down) in a place **3** [T1] to find or learn the position of: *We have now located the missing equipment.*

situate [X9 *usu pass*] **1** *fml* to put in a particular place; locate: *The house was situated on a hill.* **2** (*fig*) *usu infml* to place among possibilities; to put in a condition: *How are you situated for money; do you have enough?*

position *often fml* **1** [X9; (T1)] to put in the proper position: *Please position the chairs for the committee meeting.* **2** [X9] to put in a (stated) position: *He positioned the cup carefully on the edge of the shelf.* **3** [T1] to find out the position of: *Can you position them?*

station [T1 *often pass*] *usu tech* to put in a place for a purpose: *The soldiers stationed themselves/were stationed in the centre of the town. She was stationed in Birmingham at the time.*

site [T1 *usu pass*] *usu tech* provide with a site (= position); locate: *The house was beautifully sited to catch the sunshine.*

pinpoint [T1] **1** to show the exact position of: *The two powerful beams of light pinpointed the man climbing up the wall of the building.* **2** (*fig*) to find or describe the exact nature or cause of: *Something is wrong with our plan but we haven't pinpointed the trouble yet.*

space [T1] to place (things) with a certain distance between each: *Space the boxes a metre apart (from each other). Are the words on the page properly spaced?*

perch **1** [L9, esp *on*, *upon*] (of a bird) to come to rest from flying: *The little bird perched on my finger.* **2** [X9; L9] to (cause to) go into or be in the stated position (esp unsafely, or on something narrow or high): *He perched a funny little hat on his head. She perched (herself) on a tall chair. He perched on the edge of the roof. A little village perched on the side of the mountain.*

M51 *verbs, etc* : carrying, taking, and bringing

carry **1** [T1] to have in one's arms, on one's back, etc while moving: *The monkey carried her babies on her back. The man carried a bag in one hand and a stick in the other. I can't carry you any further; you're too heavy.* **2** [T1] to act as the means by which (a person or thing) is moved from one place to another: *Zambian railways carry a lot of copper. Pipes carry oil across the desert. Telephone conversations are carried by wires.* **3** [T1] to bear the weight of (something) without moving: *This pillar carries the whole roof.* **4** [T1] *tech* to support with food: *This field can carry up to 10 cows.* **5** [T1] *infml* to keep or support with money, help, personal effort, etc: *Why should we carry you when you don't work hard? The two main actors carry the whole show. The company will carry you until your illness is better.* **6** [T1] to keep or hold (something) with one; wear: *Do you usually carry so much money around? In Britain police do not usually carry guns.* **7** [X9 no pass] to move or hold (oneself) in a certain way: *Jean carries herself very nicely and attracts all the men.* **8** [T1] to take from one person to another; spread: *Many serious diseases are carried by insects.* **9** [IØ] to be able to reach a certain distance; cover space: *She could never be a great singer because her voice does not carry!* **10** [T1] (of a shop) to have (goods) for sale: *This shop carries a very wide variety of clothes.* **11** [T1; IØ] (of a female) to be expecting (young or a child): *Our cow's carrying again.* **12** [T1] to contain: *The report carried a serious warning of future trouble. The king's letter carried a threat of the minister's dismissal.* **13** [X9] to increase, enlarge, or continue (someone or something) in space, time, or degree; take: *His ability carried him to the top of his profession. They're planning to carry the bridge across the river here.*

take **1** [D1 (*to*); T1] to carry from one place to another: *Don't forget to take your bag with you. We usually take the children to school in the car. This train will take you to London. I'm going to take this dress back to the shop because it doesn't fit properly. Take him another cup of tea.* **2** [T1] to use as a way of getting from one place to another: *My husband goes to work on the bus but takes the train coming home.*

bear [T1] *fml* to carry or take: *He bore the child on his back. In their hands they bore weapons.*

bring **1** [D1 (*to*); T1] to come with; come carrying (something) or leading (someone), etc: *Bring me the book. Bring the book with you when you come. Bring your friend to the party. Bring an answer. The prisoner was brought before the judge.* (*fig*) *The soldier's brave deeds brought him honour and glory.* (*fig*) *The beauty of the music brought tears to her eyes.* **2** [T1; V3] to cause or lead to: *Spring rains bring summer flowers. What brought you to do it? He could never bring himself to kill an animal or bird.* **3** [X9] to cause to reach a certain state: *Bring them in/out/back/together. He brought the gun into action. He brought the work to an end.* **4** [T1; V4] to cause to come: *Her cries brought the neighbours (running). Our sad letter brought many offers of help.*

fetch **1** to go and get and bring back: *Run and fetch the doctor! Please fetch me a clean handkerchief from my bedroom.* **2** (*fig*) to attract; cause to appear or come: *the story fetched the tears to my eyes.* **fetch and carry (for)** to do the small duties of a servant (for): *You can't expect me to fetch and carry for you all day!*

lift **1** [T1 (*up*)] to raise from one level and hold or move to another level: *Lift (up) the stone. The baby was lifted onto the bed.* **2** [T1 (*up*)] (*fig*) to raise to a higher level, condition, or quality **3** [IØ] (of moveable parts) to move or go upwards or outwards: *The top of this box won't lift.* **4** [T1 (*up*)] to raise or move upwards or to an upright position: *The dog lifted (up) its ears.* **5** [IØ] (esp of clouds, mist, etc) to move upwards, thin out, or disappear: *The low clouds began to lift.* **6** [T1] to bring to an end; remove: *The unpopular tax was soon lifted.* **7** [T1] (in some games) to cause (a ball) to rise **8** [T1] *infml* to steal (esp small articles) **9** [T1] to take and use (other people's ideas, writings, etc) as one's own without stating that one has done so **10** [T1] to dig up (root crops or plants) esp carefully **11** [T1] to make (the voice) loud, as in singing

shift **1** [IØ; T1] to change in position or direction; move from one place to another: *He shifted impatiently in his seat during the long speech. Fasten the load down to keep it from shifting at high speed. The wind shifted and blew the mist away. Don't try to shift the blame onto me! They've shifted their furniture all around.* **2** [C] a change in position or direction; an act or result of shifting: *There has been a shift in the wind/in political opinion.*

M52 *verbs* : **sending and transporting**

send 1 [D1 (*to*); T1; V3, 4] to cause to go or be taken to a place, in a direction, etc: *If you need money I'll send it/I'll send you some. You should send your shoes to be repaired. The explosion sent glass flying everywhere. If I can't bring the papers I'll have them sent to you.* **2** [X9; V3, 4] to cause, direct, order, etc (a person) to go: *He was a leader who seemed to be sent from God. He sent his army into battle. They sent their children to school in the town. The child was sent to buy some milk. The accident sent me looking for a new car.* **3** [X7, 9 esp *into*; V4] to cause to have a particular feeling or be in a particular state: *The news sent the family into great excitement. The victory sent our spirits rising. This noise will send me mad!* **4** [I0 (*for*), 3] to cause a message, request, or direction to go out; give a command, request, etc: *The king sent and had the man brought to him. The king sent for the man but he couldn't be found. He sent to tell us he couldn't come. Send for a doctor!* **5** [X9, esp *out*, *forth*] (of a natural object) to produce from itself: *The sun is sending out light all the time.* **6** [Wv6;T1] (*fig*) *infml* (esp of art or music) to be very pleasing and exciting to (someone): *Man, his playing really sends me!* **7** [D1 (*to*); T1, 5a] *lit* (esp of God) to give or provide: *Heaven send that we'll arrive safely! Heaven send us a safe journey!* **send word** to send a message: *He sent word that he'd be delayed.*

transfer 1 [T1; I0] to move from one place, job, person, thing, etc to another: *They transferred her from the London to New York branch after completion of her training. The office was transferred from Belfast to Dublin. This football player is hoping to transfer to another team soon.* **2** [T1; I0] to (cause to) move or change from one vehicle to another: *At London we transferred from the train to a bus. At the port the goods are transferred onto a ship.* **3** [T1] to move (a pattern, set of markings, etc) from one surface to another: *to transfer a pattern onto leather* **4** [T1] to give the ownership of (property) to another person: *The land was transferred to me by the king as a reward for my loyal service.*

transport [T1] **1** to carry (goods, people, etc) from one place to another: *to transport coal by train* **2** (in former times) to send a criminal to a distant land as a punishment: *The thief was transported to Australia.* **3** [*usu pass*] *fig & poet* to fill with delight, joy, or any strong feeling: *We were transported with joy when we heard the news.*

convey *often tech & fml* **1** [T1 (*from*, *to*)] to take or carry from one place to another: *Wires convey electricity from power stations to the user. We conveyed our goods to market in an old car.* **2** [T1, 5 (*to*)] to make (feelings, ideas, thoughts, etc) known: *Words convey meaning. I can't convey my feelings in words.*

deliver 1 [T1] to take and give to someone; hand over: *He delivered the goods to our office in Manchester. Postmen deliver letters.* **2** [I0] to take things to houses, offices, etc: *That big store will deliver if you want them to.* **delivery** [U;C] the act of delivering: *The delivery of letters is the business of post offices. We have two deliveries of letters a day.*

ship [T1] to send (things), esp in a ship: *He shipped the goods to Japan for us.*

dispatch, despatch [T1] **1** (to) to send off (to a place or for a stated purpose): *dispatch letters/ invitations; dispatch a boy to the shop to buy beer* **2** to finish quickly; get through (work, food, etc): *We soon dispatched the chocolate cake. They dispatched all their business in a day.*

M53 *verbs* : **taking, leading, and escorting** [T1]

[ALSO ⇒ M77]

---

take to help (someone) to a place by going there with him or her: *Take these people to a shop where they can get food.*

lead to take (someone) somewhere, esp over a longer distance or with some special authority: *He led them to the house. Lead us there! Can you lead us to safety?*

guide to show (someone) the way by leading esp because of special knowledge: *He guided the man through the streets to the railway station. He guided them round the Art Show.* (*fig*) *The light guided them into the harbour.*

conduct *fml* to take, lead, or guide: *He conducted them to his office.*

escort *polite* to go with (someone) as a guide: *May I escort you to your car?*

accompany 1 *sometimes fml* to go with (someone or something): *His wife accompanied him on his trip to London. I'll accompany you as far as the main road.* **2** [(*with*)] to do something or to happen while (something else) is being done or happening: *Music accompanied the film. He accompanied his talk with colour slides* [⇒ F270]. **accompaniment** [C] something that goes with something else: *Illness is often an accompaniment to eating poor food.*

M54 *verbs* : **sending and taking away**

---

send away *also* **send off** [v adv] **1** [T1] to send to another place: *He sent his son away to school in Germany. He sent the food away saying he was too old to eat it.* **2** [I0 (*for*), 3] to order (goods) to be sent by post: *I couldn't get this kind of lamp in town, so I sent away for it to a company in London.*

take away [v adv T1] to take to another place, esp because not wanted or needed: *Take these books away, please. I don't like it; take it away! They took the prisoner away.*

remove [T1 (*from*)] **1** to take away from a place; take off: *He removed a child from the class.*

Remove your hat. Remove your shoes in the mosque. **2** to get rid of; clean off: *Remove the mud from your shoes. Remove her fears.* **3** *fml* to dismiss: *That officer must be removed (from his position).* **removal** [U; C] the act or an example of removing: *His removal from London was a mistake.*

M55 *verbs* : **showing and directing** [X9]

[ALSO ⇨ M77]

show to go with and guide or direct (someone): *May I show you to your seat? Show the gentlemen in/out, please. Show him where to go.*

direct *fml* to show (someone) somewhere esp as a kind of command: *They directed him to his seat/where to go.*

usher *fml* to show or take (someone) somewhere esp ceremonially: *He was ushered in very politely. They ushered us to our seats.*

M56 *verbs & nouns* : **pulling**

pull 1 [T1; I∅] to take (something) along behind or after one while moving: *The horse was pulling a cart; it was pulling steadily.* **2** [T1; I∅; (X7)] to move (someone or something) to another place by holding and drawing along, sometimes with force: *Pull the mat in front of the fire.— I can't pull it; you're standing on it. He pulled his chair up to the table. The cupboard door is stuck and I can't pull it open.* **3** [T1; I∅ (*at*)] to take and move (someone or part of someone's body, garment, etc) roughly towards one, sometimes with the desire to hurt: *The child pulled (at) its mother's coat. The child pulled its mother by the coat. Don't pull the cat's tail! Don't pull the cat by the tail!* **4** [X9, esp *on, off*] to move (esp a (part of a) garment) to a different position with the hands: *He pulled his sock carefully over his swollen ankle. He pulled on his boots/pulled his boots on.* **5** [I∅] (of an apparatus) to move when taken or pressed towards one: *The handle pulls so easily that a child could open the door.* **6** [T1] to take or press towards one in order to cause an apparatus to work: *Aim the gun carefully before you pull the trigger* [⇨ H240]. **7** [T1] to stretch and sometimes damage, by using force: *He's pulled a muscle as a result of trying to lift the end of the piano. You've pulled this woollen garment out of its proper shape after washing it.* **8** [T1 (*out, up*)] to take up out of the earth: *She went into the garden to pull a few onions for dinner. Pull out these dead plants; pull them up.* **9** [C] *usu infml* an act of pulling: *Give it a good pull. Two more pulls and we've done it!* **10** [C; U] a strong attractive force: *The pull of the sun keeps the earth in its position.*

drag 1 [T1] to pull (a heavy thing) along: *The boy was dragging a great branch along. He*

dragged his foot as he walked. **2** [X9] to cause to come or go unwillingly: *Why must you drag me out to a concert on this cold night?* (*fig*) *There's no need to drag me into the quarrel.* **3** [I∅ (*on*)] to move along too slowly in space or time: *He dragged behind the others. The meeting dragged (on). The play dragged a bit in the third act.* **4** [I∅ (*along*)] to move along while touching the ground: *The end of her long dress dragged (along) in the dust.* **5** [C] something that is dragged along over a surface **6** [C; U] the or an act of dragging **7** [C (*on, upon*)] something or someone that makes it harder to advance towards a desired end: *They used to be good friends but now he feels she is a drag on him.*

haul 1 [T1; I∅] to pull hard: *He hauled the wood up the hill. They hauled in the fishing nets. They hauled away on the ropes.* **2** [C] an act of hauling **3** [C] the distance hauled: (*fig*) *It was a long haul home, carrying our bags up the hill.* **4** [C] **a** the amount of fish caught when fishing with a net: *a good haul* **b** (*fig*) the amount of something gained: *That money is quite a haul!*

heave 1 [I∅; X9] to pull and lift, esp forcefully towards oneself: *They heaved away at the heavy box. They heaved it up on the rope.* **2** [I∅] to rise and fall strongly and regularly: *His chest heaved after the race.* **3** [X9] *infml* to throw forcefully: *The children have just heaved a brick through my window.* **4** [C] an act of heaving: *Let's have a good heave and we'll move it!*

wrench 1 [X9] to pull hard with a twisting or turning movement: *He wrenched the bag from her hand.* **2** [T1] to twist and damage (a joint of the body): *to wrench one's ankle* **3** [C] an act or result of wrenching

tug 1 [I∅ (*at*); T1] to pull, esp hard and quickly: *Don't tug so hard! He tugged the wires out of the wall.* **2** [C] a quick hard pull: *Give it a good tug.*

draw [T1; L9] to pull steadily and continuously: *He drew the long rope up out of the water.*

tow 1 [T1] to pull (something) along by a rope, chain, etc: *One boat towed the other. He was towing another behind his own.* **2** [S] an act of towing: *My car has broken down; can I have a tow, please?* **towline** [C] a rope used for towing

M57 *verbs* : **pulling out**

pull out [v adv T1] to take (something) out with some force: *That tooth is decayed and should be pulled out. He pulled the cork out of the bottle.*

draw out [v adv T1] to pull out steadily: *He drew a paper out from underneath the books.*

extract [T1] *fml & tech* **1** to pull or take out, often with difficulty: *He extracted the tooth. Can you extract this piece of dirt from my eye?* (*fig*) *The police extracted the information from the criminal.* **2** to take out with a machine or instrument or by chemical means (a substance which is contained in another substance): *They* extracted gold from the rocks. Oil can be extracted from cottonseed.

withdraw 1 [T1 (*from*)] to take away or back: *He (with)drew five pounds from his bank account.* **2** [T1; I∅ (*from*)] to (cause to) move away or back: *The general withdrew the army. The army withdrew.* **3** [T1; I∅ (*from*)] to get or take (something) out; not take part (in): *He withdrew his horse from the race. He withdrew from the race.* **4** [T1] to make as if unsaid; to take back: *He withdrew the remark. I withdraw that point.* **5** [I∅] to move or turn oneself slightly out of a certain direction: *She withdrew against the wall as the car passed close by.*

M58 verbs & nouns : pushing

[ALSO ⇨ N154 FORCE, N334 PRESS]

push 1 [T1; I∅; X7] to use sudden or steady pressure in order to move (someone or something) forward, away from oneself, or to a different position: *He pushed me suddenly and I fell into the water. It's rather cold; please push the window up. He got off his bicycle and pushed it up the hill. Someone at the front was pulling and someone at the back was pushing. Don't push; wait your turn to get on the bus. Please push the door shut.* **2** [X9] **a** to make (one's way) by doing this: *He pushed his way to the front of the crowd.* **b** to cause (oneself) to move by doing this: *He pushed himself to the front of the crowd.* **3** [C] an act of pushing: *They gave the car a push to get it started. The door opened at a slight push.* **4** [U] *fig infml* active determination to succeed, esp by forcing oneself and one's wishes on others: *She's not very clever but she has plenty of push and has got herself a good job.* **5** [U] (*fig*) help or influence in someone's favour: *He got that job through push; his father is a friend of one of the directors of the firm.*
shove 1 [I∅; X9] to push, esp in a rough or careless way: *There was a lot of pushing and shoving to get on the bus. Help me shove this furniture aside.* (*fig*) *Don't try to shove all the work onto me!* **2** [L9, esp *over*] *infml* to move oneself: *Shove over, friend, and let me sit on the seat beside you.* **3** [C *usu sing*] *esp infml* a push, esp if forceful: *We gave the car a good shove and moved it out of the mud.*
thrust 1 [X9] to push forcefully and suddenly: *We thrust our way through the crowd. He thrust his hands into his pockets. The murderer thrust a knife in her back. The actress said she was perfectly happy until fame was thrust upon her.* **2** [I∅ (*at*)] to make a sudden forward stroke with a sword, knife, etc: *He thrust at me with his knife.* **3** [C] an act of thrusting; forceful forward push: *The general planned a thrust into enemy land. He made a thrust against the government in Parliament.* **4** [U] **a** the force directing an object, esp a plane, forward; forward-moving power of an engine **b** forceful pressure from one object onto another, as between the

stones in an arch: *If the thrust is not exactly right the arch will fall down.* **5** [C] a swift forward stroke with a knife, sword, etc
propel [T1] to move, drive, or push (steadily) forward: *One has to depend on the wind to propel a sailing boat. When the swimmer's arms became tired he propelled himself by kicking his feet up and down.* **propulsion** [U] the act or power of propelling anything
project 1 [Wv4; T1; I∅] to (cause to) stand out beyond an edge or surface: *Some creatures project their tongues to catch flies and other insects. At this point the land projects into the sea. His ears project noticeably; he has projecting ears.* **2** [T1] to (aim and) send through the air with force: *The tribesmen can project their spears with great skill.* **projection** 1 [U] the act or result of projecting **2** [C] anything that projects: *projections on a wall*
stick out [v adv I∅; T1] *infml* to project: *His ears stick out. She stuck out her tongue at them.*
protrude [Wv4; I∅] *tech, pomp & emph* to project strongly and often in an unsatisfactory way: *'His ears protrude too much,' she said.* **protrusion** 1 [U] the act of protruding **2** [C] anything that protrudes **protuberant** [B] protruding: *protuberant eyes* **protuberance** 1 [U] the state of being protuberant **2** [C] something protuberant
stuff 1 [X9, esp *into*] to push, esp as filling material: *Don't stuff anything else in, or the bag will burst.* **2** [T1 (*with*)] to fill: *to stuff a bag full; to stuff a shoe with newspaper;* (*fig*) *to stuff someone's head with nonsense* **3** [Wv5; T1] to fill the skin of (a dead animal), to make it look real: *a stuffed elephant*
stick [X9] **1** to push in (esp a pointed object): *She stuck some pins into the material.* **2** *infml* to put: *Stick it on the table.*

M59 verbs : throwing

throw 1 [D1 (*to*); T1; I∅] to send (something) through the air with a quick movement (as of the hand): *He threw the ball to me. He threw me the ball. She threw a stone into the water. He throws well.* **2** [T1 (*off*)] to cause to fall: *The horse threw its rider. The horse threw him off.* **3** [C] an act of throwing: *That was a good throw!*
cast *fml & tech* 1 [T1] to throw: *He cast the net into the river to catch fish.* **2** [C] an act of casting: *That was a good cast!*
fling 1 [D1; X7, 9; (T1)] to throw violently or with force: *Don't fling your clothes on the floor; hang them up. Every morning he flings the window open and breathes deeply. She flung her shoe at the cat.* **2** [X9] to move (part of oneself) quickly or violently: *She flung back her head proudly.* **3** [X9] to put suddenly, violently, or unexpectedly: *The military government flung its opponents into prison.* **4** [L9] to move oneself violently, esp in anger: *She flung around the room/from the house.*
chuck 1 [D1 (*to*); T1] *infml* to throw esp with a

short movement of the arms: *Chuck me the ball, please.* **2** [T1 (*in*, *up*)] *infml* to give up: *He's decided to chuck his old job (in). He's chucked in smoking again. He's decided to chuck his girl-friend.* **chuck (out)** to throw away: *Do you want to keep this book or should I chuck it out?* **chuck it (in)** stop it: *Chuck it or else I'll hit you! I wish you'd chuck it in.*

toss 1 [D1 (*to*); T1] *often infml* to throw, esp lightly, without great force: *He tossed me the ball. He tossed the ball to me. Toss it over here, please!* **2** [T1; I0] (of a coin) to throw up in the air to see which way it will fall: *Let's toss to see who goes first. I'll toss you for who goes first! He tossed and lost.* **3** [T1; I0: (*about*)] to move up and down, from side to side: *He couldn't sleep, and tossed and turned in bed all night. The ship tossed in/was tossed by the storm.* **4** [C] an act of tossing or tossing up; a quick movement: *The person who wins the toss starts the game. She gave an angry toss of her head when she heard what he had said about her.* **toss up** [v adv I0] to toss a coin to decide according to which side lands face upwards: *Let's toss up and see who goes first.* **toss-up** [C] an act of tossing up: *Who won the toss-up?* (*fig*) *It's a toss-up between them for the job* (= either of them could get the job).

scatter 1 [T1] to throw (usu many small things) here and there: *The wind scattered the pieces of paper. He scattered sand on the road.* **2** [T1] to send or drive, usu quickly, in different directions: *The soldiers scattered the people.* **3** [I0] (of things or persons) to go, usu quickly, in different directions: *The people scattered when the soldiers came.*

pelt [T1] to throw things at: *The people pelted him with fruit.*

sprinkle 1 [X9] to scatter in drops or small grains: *He sprinkled water on the grass/sand along the icy path.* **2** [T1 (*with*)] to scatter liquid, small bits, etc on or among something: *Sprinkle the path with sand.*

M60 *verbs* : **throwing things and sending things out**

[ALSO ⇒ D89]

throw away *also* **throw out** [v adv T1] to throw (something unwanted) out of a place: *Let's throw out all these old clothes.*

eject [T1 (*from*)] *fml & tech* to throw out with force: *The young men were making such a noise in the restaurant that the police came and ejected them.* **ejection** [U; C] the act of ejecting; an example of this

ejaculate [T1; I0] **1** *tech* to throw out suddenly and with force from the body (esp the male seed (**sperm**)) **2** *fml* to cry out or say suddenly and strongly: *Mary ejaculated loudly as the poisonous insect ran over her foot. 'Stop that!' he ejaculated.* **ejaculation** [U; C] the act or an example of ejaculating

emit [T1] *fml & tech* to send, give, throw, etc out

(esp noise, gas, etc): *The radio was emitting signals. The liquid emitted a terrible smell. The man emitted a shout of anger.* **emission** [U; C] the or an act of emitting: *the emission of smoke*

give off [v adv T1] *infml* to emit usu from the whole surface: *The steel sheets were giving off a lot of heat. The liquid gave off a terrible smell.*

M61 *nouns* : **extracting and withdrawing**

[ALSO ⇒ M57]

extract 1 [C; U *of*] a product obtained by extracting: *This is some kind of meat extract, isn't it?* **2** [C (*from*)] a passage of written or spoken matter that has been extracted: *She read me a few extracts from his letter.*

extraction 1 [U] the act of extracting: *The extraction of teeth can be painful.* **2** [C] an example of this: *Her teeth were so bad that she needed five extractions.*

withdrawal 1 [U] the act of withdrawing or state of being withdrawn: *The withdrawal of the army allowed the enemy into the city.* **2** [C] an example of this: *His withdrawals from the bank this month came to £800.*

M62 *verbs & nouns* : **sticking and wedging**

stick [I0] to remain in the same place; stop moving or working: *The door has stuck and I can't get out. The door's sticking and it's hard to pull it open.* [⇒ H11] **get stuck** *infml* to become unmovable: *The piece of wood got stuck between two stones.*

lodge 1 [L9] to be held or fixed firmly (in a place): *The piece of wood was lodged between two stones.* **2** [X9] to put or fix firmly: *He lodged the wood between two stones so that it would not move.*

wedge 1 [C] a piece of wood or metal shaped like a V, used esp to keep two things separate or firmly in position **2** [T1] to fix firmly with a wedge: *Wedge the door open/shut.* **3** [X9, esp *in*, *into*] to cause to be unable to move from a place: *The people sitting close to me wedged me in/into the corner.*

jam 1 [X9] to push forcefully and suddenly: *She jammed the top of the box down on my finger.* **2** [I0 (*up*)] **a** (of parts of machines) to get stuck **b** (of machines) to become unable to work because moving parts have got stuck: *Use the stairs while the lift is jammed.* **3** [T1] to crowd with people, cars, etc so that movement is difficult or impossible: *The crowds jammed the streets and no cars could pass.* **4** [X9; L9] to (cause to) be packed, pushed, or crushed tightly into a small space: *I can't jam another thing into this bag. Fifty boys were jammed into a very small classroom. The two pieces of wood always jam together unless I hold them apart. The bus was so full that I was jammed in and* couldn't move. **5** [T1] to block radio messages by using noise: *They tried to jam all enemy radio stations.* **6** [C] a tight mass of anything: *There was a great jam of people in the street. The traffic jams in London are famous.*

ram 1 [X9, esp *down*] to force into place with heavy pressure: *He rammed down the soil round the newly planted bush with his boots. She rammed some clothes into a small bag.* **2** [T1] to run into (something) very hard: *His car rammed mine.*

M63 *verbs* : closing, shutting, and sealing

[ALSO ⇒ D24, H133, L173]

close [T1; I∅] (of doors, etc) to make or become so that no person or thing can pass through: *Close the window. The window closed suddenly because of the strong wind. This door is hard to close* (= doesn't close easily). **closure** [C; U] (an example of) the act of closing: *There have been two factory closures in the past week. If we lose any more money we won't be able to avoid the firm's closure.*

shut [T1; I∅] *not fml* to close: *Shut the door! The door shut quietly behind him.*

seal [T1 (*up*)] *often fml* to close completely: *The entrance to the cave has been sealed; nothing can get in or out. They sealed up the entrance with great rocks.*

clog [T1; I∅: (*up*)] to (cause to) become blocked: *Don't clog your memory (up) with useless information. The river frequently clogs (up) with ships in the busy season so that the traffic can only move with difficulty.*

dam [T1 (*up*)] to keep (water, etc) back by means of a dam: *They dammed the river.* (*fig*) *He dammed up* [⇒ L100] *his feelings.*

M64 *verbs & nouns* : fastening and locking

[ALSO ⇒ D152, H38, N326]

fasten [T1; I∅] to (cause to) become tight or fixed in place: *She fastened the buttons of her coat. These buttons don't fasten properly. Fasten the gate firmly, please.* **fastening** [C *usu pl*] something that fastens things together or one thing to another: *The fastenings of the window are loose.* **fastener** [C] something that is made so as to fasten two things or parts of the same thing, esp in clothing, esp by being moved in some way: *She had a zip fastener* [⇒ D152] *on her dress.*

fix [T1] to make tight; fasten firmly or correctly in place: *He fixed the piece of wood to the wall. It is difficult to fix these pins in position; the cloth keeps moving.*

tie [T1; I∅: (*up*)] to fasten (with a rope, thread, wire, etc): *He tied the parcel with string. Tie (up) your shoes/your shoelaces* [⇒ D157]! *The*

knot wasn't properly tied. My dress ties at the back.

hitch [X9] to fasten by hooking a rope or metal part over another object: *He hitched the horse's rope over the pole. He hitched the horse to the pole. They hitched the wagons together. Another railway carriage has been hitched on.*

pin 1 [X9] to fasten or join with a pin: *Pin these pieces of cloth together. She pinned it to the inside of his pocket.* **2** [T1] to keep in one position: *The spear went through its body and pinned it to the ground. In the accident he was pinned under the car.*

bar [T1 *often pass*] **1** to close (a door etc) with a bar: *He barred the door.* **2** to make (a door, window, etc) safe by putting metal bars across it: *The windows are all barred; we can't get out.* **3** to stop (someone or something) going in a certain direction; block: *He stood in the door and barred my way. Nothing will bar him; he intends to become president some day. He has been barred from (taking part in) the meeting. Barring accidents* (= if there are no accidents), *we'll be there by ten o'clock.*

bolt [T1 *often pass*] to close (a door, etc) with a bolt: *He came in and bolted the door behind him.*

block [T1] **1** [*esp pass*; (*up*)] to make movement impossible on, through, etc: *You can't go; all the roads are blocked by/with snow. They blocked (up) the entrance to the cave with stones.* **2** (*fig*) to make impossible to happen: *They blocked the new law.* **blockage** also **block** [C] something which stops things from moving: *The blockage in the pipe stopped the water getting through.*

rope [T1] **1** to tie up with a rope [⇒ H46]: *He roped the two animals tightly together.* **2** to catch with a rope: *He roped the running animal round the neck.* **rope off** [v adv T1] to mark off with a rope: *The place where the horses must go has been roped off.*

knot 1 [C] a fastening of rope, thread, etc, made by twisting parts together, usu tightly: *He tied the pieces of string together with a tight knot. He made a knot in the rope. He tied the string in a knot, and I couldn't undo it.* **2** [T1; I∅] to tie in a knot or knots: *He knotted the rope. He knotted the ropes together. This rope doesn't knot as well as that one.*

lock 1 [T1; I∅: (*up*)] **a** to close (a door, place, etc) by turning a key in a lock [⇒ H133], etc: *He locked the door. He locked (the house) up for the night.* **b** (of a door, etc) to close and be fastened by a lock: *I heard the door lock behind me.* **2** [X9, esp *in*, *out*] to keep in or out of a place by locking a door etc: *He locked us out by mistake. Help, I'm locked in! She locked her jewels in the cupboard.*

M65 *verbs* : opening and unlocking

[ALSO ⇒ N273]

open [T1; I∅] to (cause to) become so that a

person or thing can pass through or out: *Open the window and let some air in/into the room. He opened the door. She opened her mouth to say something, but decided not to. This door doesn't open and shut properly. Open a tin of soup; I'm hungry.*

loosen [T1; IØ] to (cause to) become loose, free, not fastened, etc: *He loosened the neck of his shirt. They loosened the ropes round the animals. Loosen the rope a bit!*

unfasten [T1] to cause (clothes, gates, etc) to become loosened, opened, etc: *She unfastened her dress. Can you unfasten these knots?*

undo [T1] *infml* to loosen or unfasten: *He undid the knots in the string. Can you undo my dress at the back for me?*

untie [T1] to cause not to be tied: *Untie the prisoners; let them go free! He untied the ropes.*

unlock [T1] to cause not to be locked: *He unlocked the door but did not open it. If I had a key, I could unlock this box. (fig) How can we unlock all the secrets of nature?*

M66 adjectives & adverbs : **open and not open**

open 1 [B] (of doors, etc) allowing a person or thing to pass through: *The gate was open. They got in through an open window.* **2** [B] (of doors, boxes, etc) not having the door, top, etc closed or covered: *The box was open. They drove in an open car.* **3** [B] (of books) spread out: *The book was open at page 35. (fig) His life is an open book* (= he has no secrets). **4** [B] (fig) not yet decided, agreed, filled, etc: *This is an open question at the moment. The job is still open if you want it.* **5** [A; (F)] (fig) willing to think about new ideas: *He has an open mind in this matter.* **6** [Wa5;A] being outside houses, towns, etc: *He likes being out in the open air/the open countryside. The land was open and beautiful.* **7** [adv] in an open position: *He pushed the door open. The door stood (wide) open.*

closed *often fml* **1** [B] not open: *The door was closed. They talked about the matter behind closed doors* (= where no one could hear them). *Is the window open or closed?* **2** [F; (A)] (fig) finished: *The matter is closed; I don't want to talk about it any more.*

shut [F; (A); adv] *not fml* closed: *The door was shut. He pushed the door shut.*

M67 nouns : **openings** [C]

[ALSO L106]

opening 1 a space, esp in something which one expects to be solid, closed, etc: *He found an opening in the wall and climbed through (it).* **2** (fig) a good chance: *This new job is an opening for him, if he takes it.* **3** beginning: *At the opening of the meeting they were all very friendly, but not later.*

aperture *fml* **1** a hole, crack, or other narrow opening: *Light came in through an aperture in the wall.* **2** *tech* the opening in a camera, telescope, etc that admits light

gap an opening, esp a space which should be filled or closed: *Light came in through a gap between the curtains. He has a gap between his two front teeth. There are many gaps in our knowledge about how life began. The travellers passed through a gap in the mountains.*

Travel and visiting

M70 verbs : **visiting**

visit 1 [T1; IØ] to (go and) spend some time in (a place or, as a guest, someone's house): *While we're in Europe we ought to visit Belgium. Aunt Jane usually visits us for two or three weeks in the spring. Do you live in this town?—No, we're only visiting.* **2** [T1; IØ] to go to see (someone) or look at (a building or other place) for a short time: *This afternoon we're going to visit a friend in hospital. When we were in London we visited the Tower twice.* **3** [L9] *AmE* to stay: *Anyone who's visiting in Edinburgh ought to go and see the castle.* **4** [T1] to go to (a place) in order to make an official examination: *Schools have to be visited from time to time by education officers.* **5** [T1 *usu pass*] *lit* **a** to attack (a place): *20 years ago this area was visited by a terrible disease.* **b** to come into the mind of (someone): *Last night I was visited by a strange dream.*

call 1 [IØ (in)] to visit someone or a place, esp for a short time: *The doctor called while you were out. I'll call in and see you soon. He called in on them. He called in at their house on the way home.* **2** [T1; IØ] to telephone: *I'll call you when I get home.*

call on [v prep T1] to visit, esp for a short time or for business purposes: *I'll call on you tomorrow. Call on me any time you are in town.*

call back [v adv] **1** [IØ] to pay another visit: *The salesman will call back later.* **2** [T1; IØ] to return a telephone call (to): *I'll call (you) back.*

drop in also **pop in**, **look in** [v adv IØ (on) no pass] *infml* to visit (someone) without warning, informally: *He dropped in (on us) last night. Look in any time you're passing. Pop in whenever you can.*

drop by [v adv IØ] *infml* to visit someone informally: *He often drops by when he is in this part of the world.*

go/come and see [T1 *usu imper*] *not fml* to go/come to visit: *Go and see him when you are there. Come and see me soon.*

look up [v adv T1] *infml* to visit: *Look us up when you are in town; we'll be glad to see you.*

frequent [T1] *fml, pomp & humor* to go very often to; to visit frequently [⇒ L146]: *He frequents that place a lot.*

M71 *verbs* : **inviting and summoning people**

[ALSO ⇒ G117]

invite 1 [T1 (*to*)] to ask (somebody) to a social occasion: *We invited all our relatives. Why don't you invite me in (to the house)? I've been invited out* (= to a home or place outside one's own home)/*to dinner.* **2** [T1] to ask for, esp politely: *Questions were invited after the meeting.* **3** [T1; V3] to encourage or seem to cause (an action): *Some shops invite theft by making it easy to take goods.*

send for [v prep T1] to have someone go to tell another to come: *Send for John Smith; I want to talk to him. I was sent for and had to go.*

summon [T1] *fml* to order to come: *The king summoned his guards. He hasn't invited you; he has summoned you!*

M72 *verbs* : **Meeting people and things**

meet 1 [T1; I∅] to come together (with), by chance or arrangement: *We met in the street. I met her for dinner.* **2** [T1] to find or experience: *We met many difficulties in the work.* **3** [I∅] to come together or close: *The cars nearly met head-on* (= one front against the other) *at the dangerous corner.* **4** [T1; I∅] to get to know or to be introduced (to) for the first time: *We met some interesting people at Ann's party.* **5** [I∅] to join and fasten: *His trousers won't meet round his middle.* **6** [I∅] to gather together: *The whole school met to hear the speech.* **7** [T1; I∅] to touch (as if) naturally: *His lips met hers/Their lips met in a kiss.* **8** [T1 (*with*)] to answer, esp in opposition: *His speech was met with angry cries.* **9** [T1] to be there at the arrival of: *He met her off the train.* **There is more in (something) than meets the eye** it is not as simple as it looks

encounter [T1] *fml* **1** to meet or be faced by (something bad, esp a danger or a difficulty): *He encountered many difficulties. Tomorrow we will encounter the enemy.* **2** to meet unexpectedly: *He encountered a friend on the road.*

meet with [v prep T1] to meet or encounter something, usu bad: *He met with an accident on the way home.*

come across [v prep T1 *no pass*] not *fml* to meet or discover, esp by chance: *I came across an old friend in the park. I've just come across a beautiful poem in this book.*

bump into [v prep T1 *no pass*] *infml* to meet by chance: *I bumped into an old friend in town yesterday.*

chance (up)on also **happen (up)on, come (up)on** [v prep T1] *esp lit & poet* to meet, esp by chance

meet up with [v adv prep T1 *no pass*] to meet, esp in travelling or over a longer period: *On my trip to London I met up with some interesting people.*

pick up [v adv T1] *infml* to become friendly with (someone) after a short meeting: *You may be able to pick up a girl at the dance.* **pick-up** [C] *deprec* a person, esp a girl, picked up in this way

rendezvous [I∅] *tech* (esp of military movements) to meet by arrangement: *The two groups of men rendezvoused successfully.*

interview [T1] to meet (someone) and ask questions: *Have you interviewed anyone for the job yet? I was interviewed for a job last week. He went to London to be interviewed. The politician was interviewed on television.*

M73 *nouns* : **visiting and inviting**

visit [C (*to, from*)] an act or time of visiting: *He makes several business visits to America every year. During our visit to London we often went to the theatre. We've just had a visit from the police* (= the police have just visited us). **go on a visit** (to someone or something) to visit (someone or something), esp for a long stay: *In the summer we're going on a visit to relations in Scotland.* **pay a visit (to someone or something)/pay (someone or something) a visit** to visit (someone or something) usu for a short time and for a purpose: *I've had some pain recently; I must pay my doctor a visit.*

call [C] **1** a visit, esp if short or for business purposes: *The doctor's call lasted 10 minutes. How many calls have you made today and at what shops?* **2** also **(tele)phone call** an attempt to talk to someone on the telephone: *Were there any (phone) calls while I was out?*

invitation 1 [(*by*) U] the act of inviting: *The party is by invitation only.* **2** [C] an example of this; a card, letter, etc which serves to invite people: *Have you sent out the invitations yet? I've had an invitation to a wedding/a wedding invitation.*

summons [C] *fml* an order to come/go: *He received a summons from the king. She received several summonses but did not go.*

meeting 1 [C] the coming together of two or more people by chance or arrangement: *The meeting of the two men happened by chance. Our meeting in Tokyo was later than I expected.* **2** [C] a gathering of people, esp for a purpose **3** [(*the*) GC] the people in such a gathering: *Is this the opinion of the meeting?*

assembly [GC] *esp fml* a usu large meeting of people for a special purpose: *He spoke to the assembly/the General Assembly of the Church of Scotland.*

encounter [C] *sometimes fml* a sudden meeting (usu either unexpected or dangerous): *Did I ever tell you about my encounter with a lion?*

rendezvous [C] **1** an arrangement to meet at a certain time and place: *Let's make a rendezvous; where and when can we meet?* **2** the place (and time) chosen for meeting: *He was late for his rendezvous with Joan under the station clock. Under the station clock will be a suitable* *rendezvous.* **3** a popular place for people to meet: *This club is a rendezvous for writers.*

appointment 1 [*by* U] the agreement of a time and place for meeting: *He will only see you by appointment. The meeting was by appointment only.* **2** [C] a meeting at an agreed time and place: *I have several appointments today. She had an appointment with her/the doctor.*

interview [C] **1** a meeting where a person is asked questions by another or others, esp to decide whether he can take up a job or enter a university, etc **2 a** such a meeting between an important person and another or others who want to know about his actions, points of view, etc, sometimes broadcast on radio or television **b** an article written about this

date [C] *infml* an arrangement to meet someone, esp such an arrangement between a young man and woman: *He has a date tonight. I have a date with him tomorrow.*

session [C] a meeting, esp of a court of law, government, committee, etc, esp when people sit together formally and talk, decide about things, etc: *The morning session ends at 12 o'clock.*

sitting [C] **1** *less common* a session: *When does the sitting end?* **2** a time when a person can sit to eat, work, etc: *The meal will be served at two separate sittings. She finished all her work at one sitting. How many sittings are needed before the painting is finished?*

M74 *verbs* : **travelling**

travel [Wv3] **1** [IØ] to go from place to place, esp to a distant place; make a journey: *He travelled round the world for a year. Do you like travelling by plane? He's too ill to travel.* (*fig*) *His mind travelled over the events that had destroyed his country. We travelled a thousand miles on our first day.* **2** [L9] to go from place to place in order to sell and take orders for one's firm's goods: *My husband travels for a London firm.* **3** [L9] to pass, go, move, etc, as light, sound, etc: *Concorde travels faster than sound. At what speed does light travel?* (*fig*) *The news travelled fast.* **4** [T1] to go through or over: *The theatre groups travelled Europe from London to Athens.* **5** [IØ] *sl* to go very quickly: *We were really travelling when the police caught us.*

wander 1 [IØ (*about*); T1] to move about (an area) without a fixed course, aim or purpose: *We love wandering (about) (the hills).* **2** [IØ] (esp of rivers, roads, etc) to follow a winding course: *The river wanders through some very beautiful countryside.* **3** [IØ (*off*)] (*fig*) to move away (from the main idea): *Don't wander off the point!* **4** [IØ] (of people or thoughts) to be or become confused and unable to follow an ordinary conversation: *I'm afraid her mind is wandering a bit; she's very old.*

roam [IØ (*through, around*); T1] (of people) to wander with no very clear aim (through, around, etc): *The lovers roamed around/*

across/through/over the fields in search of wild berries. He spent his life in roaming. **to roam the world** to roam from place to place

tour [Wv4;L9, esp *round*; T1] to travel all over (a place): *We're touring (round) Italy for our holidays this year. They went on a touring holiday of Spain.*

rove [Wv4;IØ;T1] *esp poet* to wander; move continually (around): *He roved the seas in search of adventure. He has come home after years of roving. His eyes roved about the room. A roving band of robbers attacked them.*

journey [L9] *esp poet* to travel; to go on a journey or journeys: *She has journeyed all over the world. They journey from place to place.*

migrate [IØ (*from, to*)] **1** to move from one place to another; change one's place of living esp for a limited period: *Wealthy people often migrate in winter to warmer sunnier countries.* **2** (of birds and fish) to travel regularly from one part of the world to another, according to the seasons of the year

emigrate [IØ(*from, to*)] to leave one's own country in order to go and live in another: *If he can't earn his living here, he'll have to emigrate. He emigrated from England to Australia.*

immigrate [IØ] *rare* to come into a country to make one's life and home there: *He immigrated at the age of twenty and he's never left England since.*

commute [IØ (*between; from, to*)] to travel regularly a long distance between one's home and work (esp by train): *She commutes from Cambridge to London every day. Do you commute or do you live near your work? He commutes between Cambridge and London.*

be bound for [T1] to be going to; be about to go to: *The ship was bound for Singapore. Where are you bound for now?* **homeward bound** going home **outward bound** (esp of ships) going away from home, esp in Britain

M75 *nouns* : **travelling**

travel [U] the act of travelling: *Travel through tropical forests is dangerous and slow.*

travels [P] *esp infml & poet* acts of travelling: *Has he been on his travels again; where to this time? 'Travels with a Donkey' (Robert Louis Stevenson).*

voyage [C] a long journey esp by water: *Their voyage took them to many places. She went on a long sea voyage.*

wanderings [P] *esp infml & poet* movement from place to place or away from the proper or usual course or place, usu without any special purpose: *You must have seen a lot of strange things in your wanderings.*

tour 1 [C (*round*)] a journey during which several places of interest are visited: *They went on a tour round Europe.* **2** [C (*of, round*)] a brief trip to or through a place in order to see it: *He took us on a tour of the town. We went on a guided tour round the castle.* **3** [C9, esp *in*] a period of duty at a single place or job, esp abroad: *He did a five-year tour in Germany.* **4** [C; *on* U] a journey from place to place, as made by a company of actors in order to perform, by an important person to make official visits, by a sports team, etc: *The National Youth Theatre is on tour in the North at present. The Queen is making a tour of Canada next year. The England cricketers' tour of India has just begun.*

tourism [U] **1** the practice of travelling for pleasure, esp on one's holidays **2** the business of providing holidays, tours, hotels, etc for tourists: *Tourism is Spain's biggest industry.*

migration 1 [U] the act of migrating: *Scientists have studied the migration of fish from one part of the ocean to another.* **2** [C] a movement of many people, birds, etc in a body from one part of the world to another: *Wars always cause great migrations of people who have been taken prisoner or taken away to work.*

emigration [C; U] the act of emigrating: *They spent three months preparing for their emigration.*

immigration [U] the act of immigrating: *The immigration officer spoke to them.*

itinerary [C] *esp fml* a plan of a journey including places (to be) seen and visited: *What places are next on your itinerary?*

expedition [C] a (long) journey for a certain purpose: *He took part in a small expedition to photograph wild animals in Africa. They live in northern Scotland, so going to London is quite an expedition for them.*

journey [C] a trip of some distance, usu by land: *It's (a) three day journey on horseback/a long train journey from here to there. He's going on/making a long journey. I wished her a safe journey. 'Long Day's Journey into Night' (Eugene O'Neill).* (*fig*) *Life is a journey from birth to death.* **one's journey's end** *lit* **1** the end of any journey **2** the end of one's life **break one's journey** to interrupt one's journey: *He broke his journey from London to Rome at Paris.*

trip [C] *not fml* a journey, visit, or holiday to a particular place: *Where's John?—He's on a trip to India. We went for a day trip to France, to Calais.*

stage [C] a part of a journey: *They did the trip in three stages.*

passage [C] a journey or trip, esp by sea: *He enjoyed the passage out to India; it was a comfortable ship.*

crossing [C] a journey across the sea: *The worst part of the journey between London and Paris is the crossing.*

pilgrimage 1 [C; *on* U] a journey made by a pilgrim [⇒ M76] (*often in the phr* **go on (a) pilgrimage**): *Many Muslims go on pilgrimage to Mecca.* **2** [C] a journey made to visit a place for which one has a particular respectful interest: *Visitors to England often make a pilgrimage to Stratford-on-Avon where Shakespeare lived.*

sail 1 [S] a short trip, usu for pleasure, in a boat with sails [⇒ M157]: *Let's go for a sail this afternoon.* **2** [U; S] distance at sea measured by the time a ship would take to travel it: *The ship was still two days' sail from New York when its engine broke down.* **under sail** driven by sails and wind

caravan [C] a group of people travelling together, esp formerly, esp in desert countries with camels [⇒ A59]: *The camel caravan was going to Damascus. The caravan of men and animals began to move.*

M76 *nouns* : **people visiting and travelling** [C]

visitor [(*to*, *from*)] **1** a person who visits or is visiting (the stated or understood place or person): *The children don't like having to be specially polite to visitors. Visitors to the castle are asked not to take photographs. The castle gets lots of visitors from America.* **2** a bird which spends only part of the year in a country: *These birds are only summer visitors to Britain.*

caller a person who visits a place, esp for a short time or on business: *Have there been any callers while I was out?*

guest 1 a person who is in someone's home by invitation, for a short time, (as for a meal), or to stay (one or more nights): *He looks after his guests very well.* **2** a person who is invited out and paid for at a theatre, restaurant, etc (*in the phr* **someone's guest**): *They are coming to the concert as my guests.* **3** someone who is lodging in a hotel, or paying to stay in someone's home: *The hotel guests enjoyed their stay.* **4** [A] a person who is invited to perform, in a show or at a ceremony: *a guest artist* (= actor or singer); *a guest singer; a guest speaker*

host a person, usu a man, who receives and looks after guests in his home, a hotel, etc: *We were the hosts at the party. Our host told us lots of amusing stories.*

hostess 1 a woman host **2** the wife of a host: *Our host and hostess looked after us well.* **3** a woman whose work it is to look after travellers: *The hostesses were very pretty and good at their jobs.*

tourist 1 a person travelling for pleasure: *There is a cheap tourist hotel near the harbour. More tourists visit Spain for their holidays each year than any other country.* **2** a sportsman on tour [⇒M75, *def* 4]

traveller *BrE*, **traveler** *AmE* **1** a person who is travelling for any reason: *The train travellers arrived before the travellers on the bus.* **2** a person who has travelled a lot: *Richard Burton was a great 19th-century traveller.*

wayfarer *often poet* a traveller esp on foot: *Many wayfarers stop here to look at the church.*

wanderer a person who wanders, esp for pleasure or because he is lost

nomad 1 [*often pl*] a member of a tribe which travels about, esp to find grass for the animals:

the nomads of the desert **2** a person who wanders: *He walked across Europe for three months, but in the end he got tired of being a nomad.*

migrant a person, animal, or esp bird that migrates [⇨ M74] or is migrating: *Not all birds are migrants; some spend all their lives in one place. Migrant workers move from country to country in search of well-paid work.*

emigrant [(*from*, *to*)] a person leaving one country for another: *The ship carried hundreds of emigrants to the USA.*

émigré a person who leaves his own country, usu for political reasons, esp one who left France after the French Revolution or Russia after the Russian Revolution: *a Russian émigré; an émigré prince*

immigrant a person coming into a country from abroad to make his home there: *There are many immigrant workers in the city.*

passenger 1 a person going from one place to another in a public or private vehicle: *A passenger train is faster than a goods train.* **2** *BrE infml* a member of a team or other group who does not do his share of the work of the group

commuter a person who travels daily a long distance from home to work and back again: *Some London commuters spend a lot of each day travelling.*

voyager a person who travels by sea (esp where risks or difficulties may be met)

pilgrim a person who travels (esp a long way) to a holy place as an act of religious love and respect: *Christian pilgrims were travelling to Jerusalem.*

M77 *nouns* : **people guiding and taking** [C]

[ALSO ⇨ M53, 55]

guide 1 someone or something that shows the way, esp someone whose job is to show a place to tourists: *You need a guide to show you the city.* **2** *also* **guide book** a book which gives a description of a place for the use of visitors: *I bought a guide to the city of London.* **3** [*usu sing*] something which influences or controls a person's actions or behaviour: *It may not be a good thing to take your friend's experience as a guide.* **4** [(*to*)] a book which teaches the way to do something or gives the facts about something: *I'm reading 'A Guide to Wine-making'.*

escort 1 a person, often in ships or aircraft, who goes with another as a guide, helper, guard, or as an honour: *The prisoner travelled under police escort* (= with some policemen). *Your escorts are ready now, Mr President. He was given a naval escort.* **2** *esp fml* a man who takes a woman out for the evening: *Mary's escort arrived at 7 o'clock with a bunch of red roses.*

usher a person who leads others to their seats in a theatre, cinema, church, meeting, etc: *Please follow the usher.*

usherette a woman who does this, esp in a theatre or cinema

M78 *nouns* : **travel businesses** [C]

travel agency an agency or business, usu organized like a shop, which helps people get tickets for aeroplanes, trains, etc, go on trips, etc
travel agent one who works in or runs such a business

tourist agent/agency a travel agent/agency that helps arrange tours, holidays, etc

M79 *nouns* : **hotels, etc** [C]

[ALSO ⇨ D66, E121]

hotel a building offering rooms, meals, and other services to travellers: *Have you found us a good hotel?—Yes, The Royal Hotel. The hotel manager was very helpful.*

inn a hotel or place, esp outside a large town, where one can stay and/or drink alcohol, eat meals, etc: *He spent the night at an inn.*

guesthouse a private house where visitors may stay and have meals for payment: *She keeps a guesthouse in Fort William.*

bed and breakfast [C; U] *BrE* (a place that offers) a night's lodging and breakfast the following morning: *You can stay the night at a bed-and-breakfast (place).*

boardinghouse a private lodging house (not a hotel) that supplies meals

motel a hotel specially built for travelling motorists, made up of separate rooms or huts each with space for a car

hostel a building in which certain types of person can live and eat, as for students, young people working away from home, etc, often for a small payment **youth hostel** a hostel for esp younger people walking around the countryside on holiday, for which they pay small amounts of money

hostelry *old use & humor* an inn: *He drinks at our local hostelry.*

M80 *nouns* : **in hotels, etc**

reception [U] the office or department that receives visitors to a hotel or large organization: *Leave your key at reception. Ask the reception clerk.*

desk [S] *not fml* the reception of a hotel: *Leave your keys at the desk as you go out.*

lobby [C] the entrance hall of a hotel: *I'll meet you in the (hotel) lobby in five minutes.*

room [C] a room esp for sleeping in, in a hotel: *Can I have a room for the night, please?* **double room** a room for two people **single room** a room for one person

suite [C] a set of rooms esp in a large hotel: *He has a suite on the fifth floor.*

quarters [P] rooms, lodgings, etc esp for the night: *Let me show you to your quarters.*

M81 *nouns, etc* : **people in hotels, etc** [C]

receptionist (the job of) a person who receives people arriving in a hotel, visiting a doctor, etc
porter 1 a man in charge of the entrance to a hotel, school, hospital, etc **2** a person employed to carry travellers' bags at railway stations, airports, etc **3** a person employed to carry loads at markets
page 1 *also* **page boy** a boy servant in a hotel **2** [T1] to call (someone in a hotel) to reception, a telephone, etc: *Page Mr John Smith, please.*
doorman *esp AmE* a man at the door of a large hotel
commissionaire a doorman, esp in a special uniform, at the entrance of a large hotel: *The commissionaire will call a taxi for you, sir.*

M82 *verbs* : **in hotels, travelling, etc**

book [D1 (*for*); T1; I∅ (*up*)] to buy or arrange to have (tickets, rooms, etc) before the time when one uses them: *He has booked a room (for us). He has booked us a room in the hotel. Book (tickets) for me, please. Book now; there aren't many places left.*
reserve [T1] **1** to keep (for a special purpose): *reserve one's strength/some money; These seats are reserved for old and sick people.* **2** [*also* D1] *esp AmE* to book: *Reserve (me) a seat on the plane, please.*
hold [T1] to reserve (tickets, rooms, etc) for a length of time: *They will hold the rooms for us till Friday, but we must tell them by then whether we want them or not.*

M83 *nouns* : **in hotels, travelling, etc**

booking [C; U] act of booking, esp a seat: *All bookings must be made at least three weeks in advance. Booking well in advance is necessary. You can get tickets at the booking office.*
reservation [C; U] *esp AmE* a booking: *He made all the reservations for our holiday well in advance. Do you have room reservations, sir?*
ticket [C] a piece of paper or card or a small book allowing a person onto an aeroplane, bus, train, etc, into a theatre, cinema, etc: *Do you have all the tickets? You can get more tickets at the ticket office.*
seat [C] a place to sit in an aeroplane, bus, theatre, etc: *All the seats are taken/full/reserved/paid for.*
vacancy [C] an empty seat, room, etc: *There are no vacancies on the flight/in the hotel.*
place [C] *infml* a vacancy: *Are there any places left on Flight 241 to New York? Is that place taken, or can I have it?*

Vehicles and transport on land

M90 *nouns* : **transport**

transport, *AmE usu* **transportation** [U] **1** the act of transporting or condition of being transported [⇒ M51]. *The transport of goods by air costs a lot.* **2** a means or system of carrying people or goods from one place to another: *Moscow's public-transport system is very good. Many people prefer private transport in their cars to public transport on buses and trains.*
means of transportation [Wn3;C] a way of transporting or being transported: *What means of transportation do you have?—I go by car.*
traction [U] **1** the act of drawing or pulling a heavy load over a surface **2** the form or type of power used for this: *steam traction*
haulage [U] **1 a** the business of carrying goods by road: *road haulage* **b** the charge for this **2** the act of hauling
transit [(*in*) U] an act of moving or being moved over a distance: *The goods were lost in transit.*

M91 *nouns & adjectives* : **vehicles generally**

vehicle [C] **1** something in or on which people or goods can be carried from one place to another, esp **a** along roads, usually having wheels (such as a carriage, bicycle, car, cart, taxi, or bus) but sometimes made to slide over snow or ice: *At 5 o'clock the roads from the city are crowded with vehicles of all kinds.* **b** through space (*esp in the phr* **space vehicle**) **2** [(*for*)] (*fig*) something by means of which something else can be passed on or spread: *Impure drinking water can be a vehicle for disease. Television has become an important vehicle for spreading political ideas.* **3** [(*for*)] (*fig*) a means for showing off a person's abilities: *The writer wrote the big part in his play simply as a vehicle for the famous actress.*
vehicular [Wa5;B] of, concerning, having, or like a vehicle or vehicles: *vehicular transport*
conveyance [C] *fml & pomp* a vehicle that can take a person from one place to another: *That's a fine conveyance!*
horse-drawn [Wa5;B] (of vehicles) pulled or drawn by a horse or horses: *The city was once filled with horse-drawn transport, but now it is all powered vehicles.*
powered [Wa5;B *often in comb*] (of vehicles) supplied with or producing working force in a stated way or of a stated degree: *Powered transport is common everywhere in the world. It is a rather low-powered engine.*
tracked [Wa5;B] (of vehicles) running on continuous rolling tracks and not wheels: *Tanks* [⇒ H248] *are tracked vehicles.*
amphibious [Wa5;B] (of vehicles) able to move

both on land and in water: *Some kinds of tanks are amphibious.*

articulated [Wa5;B] (of vehicles) having parts joined in a way that allows easy movement: *An articulated vehicle is usually a large one in which the front part with the engine can be separated from the large carrying part and which can bend or turn easily where the two parts join.*

heavy goods vehicle [C] a large truck [⇒ M94] which carries large amounts of goods

M92 nouns : special, usu older, kinds of vehicles [C; by U]

cart 1 a usu two-wheeled wooden vehicle drawn by an animal, esp a horse and used for farming or for carrying goods **2** any of various types of small light wooden vehicles with two or four wheels and moved by hand **cart load** the amount a cart can carry

waggon *BrE*, **wagon** *AmE* a strong four-wheeled road vehicle, mainly for heavy loads, drawn by horses or oxen **waggon load** the amount a waggon can carry

dray a low strong four-wheeled cart without sides, used for carrying heavy loads

float any large usu flat vehicle, esp one carrying something to be seen in a procession

carriage 1 a wheeled vehicle, esp a private horse-drawn vehicle **2** a wheeled support for moving a heavy object, esp a gun: *gun carriages* **3** a movable part of a machine: *This printing machine has a carriage which holds and moves the paper.* **carriage and pair** a wheeled vehicle pulled by two horses

coach a large enclosed four-wheeled horse-drawn carriage, used esp in former times or in official ceremonies **coach load** the amount a coach can carry

stagecoach a coach which took people in stages on a long journey, the horses being changed at the end of each stage [⇒ M75]

buggy a light carriage pulled by one horse, made with two wheels in Britain and with four wheels in the USA

gig a small two-wheeled carriage drawn by one horse

trap a small two-wheeled cart pulled by one horse

chariot a two-wheeled horse-drawn seatless vehicle used in ancient times in battles and processions

M93 nouns : lighter motor vehicles, etc [C]

car 1 [*also by* U] a vehicle with three or usu four wheels and driven by a motor, esp one for carrying people: *The car has given man the freedom to travel when and where he wants. We came by car.* **2** any small vehicle in which people or goods are carried as part of a bal-

loon, airship, etc **car load** the amount a car can carry

motorcar *BrE fml* a car

motor *BrE becoming rare* a car

automobile [*also by* U] *esp AmE* a car

auto *esp AmE infml abbrev* a car

jeep [*also by* U] a type of small car suitable for travelling over rough ground

taxi [*also by* U] a car which may be hired by the public along with its driver, the price of a journey usu being calculated by a special machine (**taximeter**): *Let's take a taxi. Taxi!*

cab 1 [*also by* U] *esp AmE* a taxi: *Shall we walk or take a cab? Shall we walk or go by cab?* **2** [*also by* U] *formerly* a horse-drawn carriage for hire **3** the part of a bus, railway engine, etc in which the driver sits or stands

taxicab *fml* a taxi

saloon *BrE*, **sedan** *AmE* a car for four to seven passengers, with a roof, closed sides, and windows

estate (car), *also old use* **shooting brake** *BrE*, **station wagon** *AmE* a private motor vehicle which carries both people and goods, with folding or removable back seats and doors at the back which can be opened to put bags, cases, etc inside

sports car a fast usu smaller and lighter car with a top that folds back and down: *He took her out in his new red sports car.*

limousine a large car with the driver's seat separated from the back by a sheet of glass

M94 nouns : heavier motor vehicles [C; by U]

van a covered road vehicle for carrying goods and sometimes people: *a baker's van; a police van* **van load** the amount a van can carry

lorry a large motor vehicle for carrying big goods **lorry load** the amount a lorry can carry

truck 1 *esp AmE* a lorry **2** a fairly large vehicle with an open back, used for carrying goods **truck load** the amount a truck can carry

rig *AmE infml* a large truck

artic *BrE infml abbrev* an articulated [⇒ M91] lorry

tanker a heavy lorry with a large tank for carrying oil or other liquids

tractor a powerful motor vehicle with large wheels and thick tyres used for pulling farm machinery (**ploughs, drills,** etc) or other heavy objects

-tonner [*comb form*] a vehicle weighing a stated number of tons: *The lorry is a three-tonner.*

-wheeler [*comb form*] a vehicle with a certain number or type of wheels: *A three-wheeler is a car with three wheels.*

M95 nouns : buses, etc [C; by U]

bus a large passenger-carrying motor vehicle, esp one which carries the public on payment of small amounts: *He travels to work by bus. She ran to catch her bus. He missed both the buses and had to take a taxi.* **bus load** the amount a bus can carry

omnibus *fml & old use* a bus

coach *BrE* a bus used for long-distance travel or touring: *We went by coach.* **coach load** the amount a coach can carry

minibus a small bus

double-/single-decker (bus) a bus with two floors/one floor

M96 *nouns* : **bicycles and motorcycles, etc** [C; *by* U]

[ALSO ⇨ M103, O4]

bicycle a two-wheeled vehicle which one rides by pressing the feet on pedals [⇨ M103] which turn a chain wheel: *to ride a bicycle; to go/come by bicycle*

(pedal) cycle *more fml* a bicycle

(push) bike *infml* a bicycle

tricycle a three-wheeled vehicle, like a bicycle with one wheel at the front and two side by side at the back, esp for a child

trike *infml* a tricycle

motorcycle a large heavy vehicle like a bicycle, driven by an engine

motorbike 1 *infml BrE* a motorcycle **2** *AmE* a small light motorcycle

moped a bicycle which has a small engine, to help the rider esp when going uphill

scooter a small light vehicle like a motorcycle, in which the rider's legs are together in front of the seat and not one on either side as in a motorcycle

invalid carriage a usu three-wheeled vehicle like a tricycle, with or without a motor, for persons who cannot walk easily or at all

M97 *nouns* : **persons driving vehicles, etc** [C]

driver [*often in comb*] a person (skilled in) driving any vehicle such as a car, bus, train, etc: *He is a good driver. The bus driver drove well.*

chauffeur a person, usu in uniform, whose work it is to drive a car for someone else: *He has a big chauffeur-driven car.*

guard *BrE* a railway official in charge of a train

conductor 1 *BrE* a person who sells tickets on a bus, etc **2** *AmE* a guard on a train

conductress *BrE* a female conductor

coachman a person employed to drive a horse-drawn coach

motorist a person who drives and usu owns a car

charioteer the driver of a chariot

cyclist a person who rides and usu owns a bicycle

bicyclist *more fml* a cyclist

motorcyclist a person who rides and usu owns a motorcycle

road-user a person who uses a road in any way, but esp a motorist, cyclist, etc

pedestrian 1 a person walking (esp in a street or other place used by cars): *Pedestrians are said to cause many car accidents.* **2** [A] **a** *rare* connected with walking; done on foot: *a pedestrian tour round the town* **b** for pedestrians: *This is a pedestrian area; no cars are allowed here.*

M98 *nouns* : **smaller special vehicles, etc** [C]

barrow 1 a kind of table on two or four wheels which can be pushed about, on which goods are put to be sold in street markets **2** *infml* a wheelbarrow **3** a handcart

wheelbarrow a movable container with one wheel at the front, two handles at the back and a four-cornered part in which things can be carried, such as earth in a garden

wheelchair a chair with large wheels which can be turned by the sitter; a chair in which a person who cannot walk can be pushed from place to place

bath chair [*often cap B*] a wheelchair with a covering for the top and sometimes for the sides, in which sick people can be pulled or pushed from place to place

handcart a small cart which can be pushed or pulled by hand

pushcart a small cart pushed by hand, as used by a street trader selling fruit, for carrying shopping in a large store, etc

go-cart 1 a handcart **2** a small cart for a child to ride in **3** *also* **go-kart** a small low light vehicle with a motor used for racing

trolley a small cart with two or four wheels that is pushed by hand: *Bring in the tea trolley* (= the trolley with tea cups, etc on it).

pram *esp BrE* a four-wheeled carriage, pushed by hand, in which a baby can sleep or be taken about

perambulator *full name, fml & old use* a pram

(baby) buggy *AmE* a pram

pushchair *BrE*, **stroller** *AmE* a small usu folding chair on wheels for pushing a small child about

trailer a cart or wagon pulled along by a powered vehicle

M99 *nouns* : **vehicles for living in** [C]

[ALSO ⇨ D3]

caravan *BrE*, **trailer** *AmE* a vehicle that can be pulled by a car, which contains apparatus for cooking, beds for sleeping, etc and in which people can live, usu for holidays

caravanette *also* **motor caravan**, *also tdmk* **dormobile**, *BrE* **camper** *AmE* a van [⇨ M94] with seats and beds, usu for holidays

mobile home *genl* any kind of caravan, caravanette, etc

motor home *AmE* a large caravanette

M100 *nouns* : **parts of vehicles (outside)**

roof rack
boot/*AmE* trunk
rear window
rear light
roof
windscreen/*AmE* windshield
windscreen wiper
bonne:/*AmE* hood
wing/*AmE* fender
wing mirror /*AmE* rear-view mirror
headlight
door handle
tax disc
door
registration number
hubcap
tyre/*AmE* tire
numberplate /*AmE* license plate
bumper
sidelight
indicator light

M101 *nouns* : **parts of vehicles (inside)**

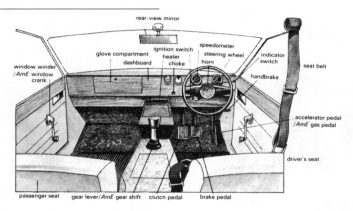

rear-view mirror
glove compartment
ignition switch
heater
speedometer
steering wheel
indicator switch
seat belt
dashboard
choke
horn
window winder /*AmE* window crank
handbrake
accelerator pedal /*AmE* gas pedal
driver's seat
passenger seat
gear lever/*AmE* gear shift
clutch pedal
brake pedal

M102 *nouns* : **the chassis and the (internal combustion) engine**

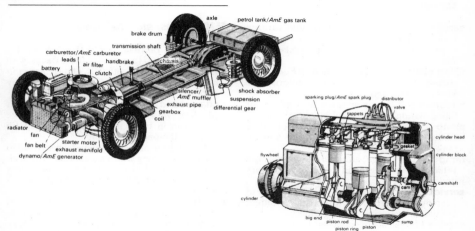

axle
petrol tank/*AmE* gas tank
brake drum
transmission shaft
carburettor/*AmE* carburetor
leads
handbrake
air filter
battery
clutch
chassis
silencer/ *AmE* muffler
shock absorber
exhaust pipe
suspension
gearbox
differential gear
coil
radiator
fan
starter motor
fan belt
exhaust manifold
dynamo/*AmE* generator

sparking plug/*AmE* spark plug
distributor
valve
tappets
cylinder head
gasket
cylinder block
flywheel
camshaft
cam
cylinder
big end
piston rod
piston ring
piston
sump

M103 *nouns* : **parts of a bicycle**
[ALSO ⇒ M96]

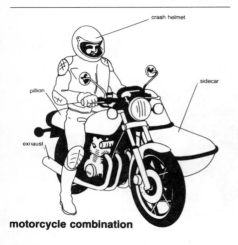

M104 *nouns* : **related to motorcycles**
[ALSO ⇒ M96]

motorcycle combination

M105 *nouns, etc* : **garages and servicing**

garage [C] a place where petrol is sold, cars are kept and repaired, etc: *I'm going to the garage to get some petrol. The garage owner wasn't there.*

filling station *also* **petrol station** *BrE*, *also* **gas station** *AmE* [C] a place where motorists [⇒ M97] can buy petrol

forecourt [C] the open space in a garage or filling station where petrol is sold

pump [C] the apparatus in a garage or filling station through which petrol can pass into the tank of a vehicle

ramp [C] (in a garage) an apparatus for raising a vehicle above the ground so that one can work underneath it

servicing *also* **maintenance** [U] the activity of keeping a vehicle in good running condition: *Do you do servicing at this garage?*

service 1 [C] an act of servicing: *Bring your car*

in for its 10,000-mile service next Tuesday. **2** [T1] to provide servicing for: *We'll service your car next Tuesday. Has your car been serviced recently?*

M106 *nouns* : **trams** [C]

tram *also* **tramcar** [*also by* U] a public vehicle, usu driven by electricity, that runs along rails set in the road

car [*also by* U] a carriage or vehicle for use on rails or a heavy wire (**a cable**)

streetcar [*also by* U] *AmE* a tram

trolley bus [*also by* U] a bus with a kind of pole at the top with a small wheel at the end (**a trolley**) that connects it to an electric wire so that it can run

cable car [*also by* U] a car that is pulled by a moving cable, for travelling up and down mountains

tramline *also* **tramway** the lines on which trams run

carrying cable the cable that carries a cable car

overhead wire the wire that provides electricity for trams, trolley buses, etc

M107 *nouns, etc* : **railways**

railway *BrE*, **railroad** *AmE* **1** [C; U] tracks for trains **2** [C; *by* U] a system of these tracks, with its engines, stations, officials, etc: *He got a job as a clerk on the railway. He works in a railway station.*

underground *also* **tube** *BrE*, *also* **subway** *AmE* [*the* R; C; *by* U] a railway system in which the trains run in tubes under the earth, esp (in Britain) the one in London

rail 1 [C; U] one of the pair of metal bars fixed to the ground, along which a train runs: *The accident was caused by some of the rails becoming bent in the heat.* **2** [A; *by* U] the railway: *rail travel; send it/travel by rail*

rails [P] railway track: *They laid* (= put down) *the rails quickly.* **jump the rails** (of a train) to leave the track suddenly (and dangerously)

line *also* **track** [C; U] (a) railway track, esp when used or ready for use and including the sleepers, ballast, etc: *There are some animals on the line/track.*

sleeper *BrE*, **(cross)tie** *AmE* [C] one of the large heavy pieces of wood, metal, etc used to support railway lines

ballast [U] **1** broken stones, etc placed under a railway line to make it firm and safe for trains **2** any heavy material used to make anything heavy, strong, or steady

permanent way [*the* R] *BrE* a railway track, sleepers, and ballast

gauge [C] the distance between the rails of a railway or between the wheels of a train, etc: *This track is standard gauge, not narrow gauge.*

tunnel [C] a hole, usu long, made in a hill, etc, through which a railway line can pass: *The train went into a tunnel.*

cutting [C] a passage cut through higher land so that a railway, road, etc can pass

siding [C] a short railway track connected to a main track, used for loading and unloading, for carriages not in use, etc

points [P] *BrE* a pair of short rails that can be moved to allow a train to cross over from one track to another

switch 1 [C] a set of points **2** [T1] to move (a train, etc) from one set of rails, line, position, etc to another

junction [C *sometimes cap*] a place where two or more railway lines meet, with points, signals, etc: *The train doesn't stop at Crewe Junction.*

signal [C] an apparatus with lights, red for stopping and green for moving, at the side of a railway line: *The signals were red, so the train stopped.*

signal box [C] a small building, esp at a junction, where signals are worked

gradient [C] a slope on a railway line

level crossing *BrE*, **grade crossing** *AmE* a place where a road crosses a railway, often with special gates to stop vehicles when a train is coming or passing

M108 *nouns* : **trains**

train [C; *by* U] a line of connected railway carriages drawn by an engine: *a goods/passenger train; Did you fly or come by train? Hurry or you'll miss the train!*

engine *also* **locomotive** [C] a machine which pulls trains

loco [C] *infml abbrev* a locomotive

express (train) [C] a fast train: *The 9.30 express to London leaves from platform 4.*

carriage *BrE*, **car** *AmE* [C] a railway passenger vehicle: *I'll be sitting in the third carriage from the engine.*

coach [C] *esp BrE* a railway passenger carriage, esp for day travel

(goods) waggon *also* **truck** [C] *BrE* an open railway vehicle for carrying goods

(freight) car [C] *AmE* a goods waggon

van [C] a covered railway carriage for carrying heavy goods and sometimes people: *luggage van*

guard's van [C] *BrE* the van often at the end of a train, in which the guard travels

trolley [C] a type of railway truck that can be pushed or driven by hand

rolling stock [U] everything on wheels that belongs to a railway, such as engines and carriages

dining car *also* **diner, restaurant car, buffet car** [C] a carriage on a train where meals are served

sleeping car *also* **sleeper** [C] a carriage on a train where people can sleep at night

M109 *nouns* : **places relating to railways, travel, etc** [C]

station *also* **depot** *AmE* a building, etc where passengers or goods are taken on and let off trains, buses, etc: *Can you tell me the way to the (railway) station? He was standing on the station platform. The bus station is in the centre of the town.*

terminus the end of a railway line or of a distance travelled by a bus, etc: *I'll meet you at the terminus.*

platform the raised level surface in a railway station alongside the rails, on which passengers can stand, etc when getting on and off trains

buffer one of a set of two large strong pieces of metal on hidden springs placed at the ends of railway lines and on railway engines, to lessen the force if an engine does not stop when it should, etc

waiting room a place where people can sit while waiting for a train, bus, or other service

left luggage (office) *BrE*, **baggage room** *AmE* the place in a station where passengers' cases, etc (**luggage, baggage**) can be left until they want them again

buffet a place in a station or on a train where one can get a meal, drink, etc

ticket office the place in a station, etc where one can buy a ticket for a train, bus, etc

timetable a large notice or a book which shows the times when trains, buses, etc arrive and depart

indicator a board in a station which shows the times when trains, buses, etc arrive and depart and where they do this

M110 *nouns* : **persons working on railways, etc** [C]

(engine) driver *BrE*, **engineer** *AmE* the driver of a train

guard *BrE*, **conductor** *AmE* the official in charge of a train

signalman the person in a signal box who changes the signals on a railway

porter a person employed to carry cases, etc (**luggage**) in railway stations, etc

stationmaster *also* **station manager** the official in charge of a railway station

M111 *verbs, etc* : **driving and travelling by car, etc**

[ALSO ⇒ M31]

change gear(s) *BrE*, **shift gear(s)** *AmE* [I∅] to move from one gear to another: *He changed gear badly.* **gear change/shift** [C] an act of changing gear

change up/down *also esp AmE* **shift up/down** [v adv I∅] to move from a lower to a higher/ higher to a lower gear

gears, etc [in U; Wa5;B]	position, etc
first, bottom **second** **third**	lowest
fourth/top	highest
reverse	going backwards
neutral	not in any gear

reverse [I∅; T1] to (cause to) go backwards: *The car reversed. He reversed the car into the garage. Do you know how to reverse (this car)?*

back [I∅; T1] *infml* to reverse: *The car backed into the garage. He backed the car out of the garage.*

dip [T1] to lower (the headlights of one's car, etc): *He dipped his lights as the other car came nearer.*

skid 1 [I∅] (of vehicles esp on roads) to slide sideways: *The car skidded across the icy road.* 2 [C] an act of skidding: *The car went into a bad skid on the icy road. You can see the skid marks* (= the marks of a skid) *on the road.*

fork [Wv6;I∅] (of roads, etc) to divide, esp into two: *The roads fork shortly; you should go left.* **fork left/right** (of a driver, car, etc) to take the stated direction: *Fork left at the inn.*

go straight on [I∅] to continue without turning left or right: *The road goes straight on for a mile, then bends. Go straight on; don't fork left or right.*

branch off [v adv I∅] to leave a road at some point, to go on another road: *Take the A1 to Doncaster, then branch off. He branched off at Doncaster.*

M112 *nouns & verbs* : **crashes and accidents**

crash 1 [I∅; T1] to (cause to) hit and damage (something), with force and a lot of noise: *The car crashed. The car crashed into the wall. He crashed his car (into a wall). The two cars crashed head on* (= hitting each other directly front to front as they moved). 2 [C] an act or occasion of crashing: *There was a car crash here last night. There have been a lot of crashes lately.*

collide [I∅ (*with*)] to crash together; to crash or knock (into something): *The two cars collided. He collided with me as he ran past. The train collided with a car at the level crossing* [⇒ M107].

collision [C; U] (an example of) the act of colliding: *Many people were killed in the collision between the bus and the car.* (*fig*) *A collision with Parliament could ruin the government's plans. The two trains are on a collision course* (= they will hit each other)!

derail [T1 *usu pass*] to cause (a train, etc) to go off its rails: *The train was derailed by the explosion and many people were killed.*

derailment [U; C] the act or an occasion of derailing

go off the rails *infml* to be derailed: *The train went off the rails and many people were killed.* (*fig*) *She has really gone off the rails; she has given up her job and has no money to live on!*

accident [C] a harmful and unexpected happening, esp a crash, collision, etc: *There have been a lot of road accidents in the town lately. Did you hear about the terrible rail accident, a derailment? He was killed in an accident in the factory. Factory accidents are quite common; people aren't always careful. It was an accident; he didn't mean to do it.*

Places

M120 *nouns* : **places and positions**

place 1 [C] a particular part of space or position in space: *This is the place where the accident happened. A person can't be in two places at once.* 2 [C] an empty space: *We must find a place on that wall for this new picture.* 3 [C *usu sing*] a position which one considers to be of value or importance: *Sports never had a place in his life.* 4 [C] a particular part of the earth's surface, stretch of land, town, etc: *They wandered from place to place. There's no place like home. Moscow is a very cold place in winter.* 5 [C] a particular spot or area on a surface: *There are several rough places on this table. She had a sore place on her hand.* 6 [C (*of*)] a room, building, or piece of land used for a particular stated purpose: *The town has many places of amusement such as theatres and cinemas. Is this your place of business?* 7 [C] a usual or proper position: *Put it back in its place. Which is your place at the table?* b a proper or suitable occasion or moment: *A public dinner isn't the place at which to talk about one's private affairs.* 8 [C] a person's position in a line of waiting people (**a queue**):

Will you keep my place while I go and get a cup of tea? **9** [C] (*fig*) **a** a particular part of a piece of writing: *This is the place in the story where the child dies.* **b** (*esp in the phr* **find/lose one's place**) the particular part (of a book, story, etc) that one is reading: *I put a piece of paper in the book to keep my place.* **10** [C *usu sing*] (*fig*) a position of respect or greatness: *The famous general is sure of a place in history.* **11** [C] a (numbered) position in the result of a competition, race, etc: *John took first place in the history examination.* **12** [C *usu sing*] any of the first three positions in the result of a horse race **13** [C *usu sing*] a position in employment, in a team, etc: *Mr Smith has offered young Tony a place in the bank. Do you think he's worth a place in the football team? He has won a place at the university.* **14** [C] a social position; rank: *He knows his place in society. This has been talked about in high places* (= by people of high rank and influence). **15** [S9] duty; what one has to do: *It's not your place to tell me what to do.* **16** [S9] one (numbered) point in an argument, explanation, etc: *In the first place I don't want to and in the second place I can't afford to.* **17** [C] a seat: *There were several empty places in church last Sunday.* **18** [S] *infml* a house; home: *They've bought a charming place in the country. Come over to our place.* **all over the place** *infml* **1** everywhere: *We searched all over the place.* **2** in disorder: *She's left her books spread all over the place.* **change places (with someone)** to exchange positions so that each goes where the other one was: *If we change places you'll be able to see better. Would you mind changing places with me, as I'm too hot here.* **lay/set a place for** to put the knives, forks, spoons, etc in position for (one person) at a meal table **put somebody in his place** to show somebody that one has a low opinion of him/her **take one's place 1** to go to one's special position for some activity: *Take your places for the next dance.* **2** to be considered as being: *This work will take its place among the most important paintings of this century.*

location [C (*of*)] *fml, tech, & pomp* a place where something happens: *Can you tell me the location of the college, please?* **on location** (of people making films) working at the place that the film is (supposed to be) about: *They are on location in Spain.*

locality [C] a (local) place; the place one is in: *Are there any good restaurants in the locality? They live in a nice locality. This is the locality where the accident took place.*

locale [C] **1** a place, esp where something particular happens or has happened: *They moved to a quieter locale.* **2** the place where a film, play, etc is supposed to happen: *The locale is northern England in the 1900s.*

locus [C] *tech* a place where esp a crime has happened: *This is the locus of the murder.*

position [C] **1** [*also in* U] a place where someone or something is (standing, put, etc): *The soldiers stayed in their positions on the hill. The*

chair wasn't in this position when I left the room. The chair is still in position; no one has moved it.* **2** [*also in* U] *also* (*fml*) **posture** a way of standing, sitting, etc: *Don't you find standing in this position uncomfortable? He sat in a cross-legged position on the floor.* **3** (*fig*) opinion: *He takes a different position from me in this matter.* **4** (*fig*) condition: *She's ill; she's in no position to go anywhere/to help you.*

situation 1 [C] a place, esp where something is or might be: *The house is in a beautiful situation. This is a good situation for a house.* **2** [S] (*fig*) condition: *The situation of the ship after the storm was very bad. I'm in no situation to help; I need help myself.*

site [C (*of*)] a place where something has happened, is happening, or will happen: *That is the site of the battle. This is the site for the new theatre. This is the new theatre site. The new theatre will be built on this site.*

lot [C] a piece of land: *There are some lots for sale; you could build a nice house on one of them.*

venue [C] **1** *usu fml* a meeting place arranged for some purpose or activity: *The venue of the big match is the football ground at Wembley.* **2** *law* the district where a law case is tried

spot [C *usu sing*] *infml* a place: *This is the spot where it happened. What a nice spot for a picnic* (= an outdoor meal)! *What a nice picnic spot!*

point [C] **1** a place in space or time, esp an exact position: *From that point in his travels he had begun his journey home. At some point during the trip she became ill.* **2** a piece of (high) land that stretches out into the sea, a lake, etc: *He stood on the Point, looking out to sea.*

haunt [C *usu pl*] *sometimes deprec* a place which a person, animal, etc often goes to, usu lives in, etc: *This inn is a haunt of thieves. He went back to the haunts of his childhood.*

whereabouts [P] a place where someone or something is, can be found, etc: *I don't know her whereabouts now. Her present whereabouts are not known.*

perch [C] **1** a branch, rod, etc, where a bird rests (often specially provided for the purpose): *The birds were using telephone wires as perches. There were two perches in the birdcage.* **2** (*fig*) a high position in which a person or building is placed: *From our perch up there on top of the cliff we can see the whole town.*

M121 nouns : space

space 1 [U] open or empty land, air, water, surfaces, etc: *There's plenty of space here to move about. He needs space in which to work. There isn't much space to work on that table.* **2** [U] the distance between one thing and another: *We need more space between the words on this page. There isn't much space for anyone to get between these cars; they're too close together.* **3** [C] such a distance: *The spaces between the words aren't wide enough. Leave a* *space; we can add the rest of the information later.*

room [U] space for something: *I need more room to move. Do you have enough room to yourself in the office? Make room, please; the doctor must get past! There's room in the car for one more person.*

stretch [C] a level area of land or water: *a pleasant stretch of country; a wide stretch of road*

expanse [C (*of*), *often pl with sing meaning*] a wide space (of the stated type): *He looked up at the starry expanse(s) of the sky.*

reach 1 [U (*of*)] the distance that one can reach: *Put the bottle within/beyond/out of (his) reach. I live within easy reach of the shops.* (*fig*) *beyond the reach of my imagination* **2** [S] the length of one's arm: *He has a longer reach than I have so he can climb better.* **3** [C] a straight stretch of water between two bends in a river: *He travelled to the upper reaches of the river.*

M122 *nouns* : **edges, boundaries, and borders**

edge 1 [C; *on* U] the narrowest part along the outside of something, esp of a cutting instrument or along the outside of a solid: *The edge of the knife was sharp. Can you stand a coin on edge?* **2** [C] (*sometimes fig*) the line or part along the last part of a piece of land, etc: *He stood on the edge of the cliff/on the cliff edge. She waited at the water's edge.* [⇒ M200]

limit [C] the farthest point to which something reaches; the point beyond which one cannot go: *These are the limits of our power; we can do no more. Is there a limit to what science can do?* **limitless** [Wa5;B] having no limits **within limits** to a certain extent: *Within limits, I agree with him.* **without limit(s)** to any extent: *Our help isn't without limits.* **off limits** (esp of places) not allowed: *That part of town is off limits to all soldiers.*

margin [C] **1** the white space at the top, bottom, and sides of a piece of paper on which written work has been or will be done: *The margins at the side of writing paper are sometimes drawn with a line. Don't write in the margin.* **2** (*fig*) anything like this; an edge or limit **3** the amount more than what is needed: *His plan included a time margin of two days in case anything went wrong.* **marginal** [B] of or like a margin (and therefore small or less important): *There has been only a marginal increase in sales.* **-ly** [adv]

threshold [C] **1** *now rare* a piece of wood or stone under the door of a house: *He stood on the threshold, waiting to go in.* **2** (*fig*) *now common* the place or time when something ends and something else begins: *She was on the threshold of a new life. The scientists were on the threshold of a great discovery.*

boundary [C] the edge or limit, esp of land inside a country: *Where are the boundaries of*

his land? He stopped the car on the boundary of the city/the city boundary. He marked the boundaries of the football field with white paint.

bounds [P] (*fig, esp lit & poet*) limits: *You must keep your hopes within reasonable bounds.* **out of bounds** outside the area allowed (to certain people): *The town is out of bounds to the pupils of the school/to the soldiers in the camp.* **in bounds** inside the area allowed: *Is the town in bounds to the soldiers?*

border [C] the edge or side(s) of anything but esp of the land belonging to two countries: *He waited for her at the border. They travelled along a border road. The guards at the border post would not let him through/in.* **border on** [v prep T1] to be on the border of: *Scotland borders on England.* (*fig*) *His ideas border on madness at times.* **borderline** [C] **1** *less common* the line which separates two countries **2** (*fig*) *more common* the line dividing two things: *His examination results were on the borderline (between passing and failing). His results were borderline. He got a borderline pass.*

frontier [C] **1** the limit or edge of the land of one country, where it meets land of another country: *They were shot trying to cross the frontier. Sweden has frontiers with Norway and Finland. A frontier guard stopped them.* **2** [*the* R; C] the border between settled and wild country, esp that in the USA in the past: *Areas near the frontier in America were rough and lawless in the old days.* **3** [C9, esp *of*, *often pl*] (*fig*) a border between the known and the unknown: *The frontiers of medical knowledge are being pushed farther outwards as time goes on.*

M123 *nouns* : **neighbourhoods and environments**

neighbourhood *BrE*, **-bor-** *AmE* **1** [C] a place where people live near each other: *This is a nice neighbourhood to live in. What are the neighbourhood shops like?* **2** [S] the area around a point or place: *They live in the neighbourhood of Birmingham.* (*fig*) *His price is, I think, in the neighbourhood of £10,000.*

vicinity **1** [U (*of*); C] the area very near to or around the stated place; neighbourhood: *Are there any shops in this vicinity?—No; the nearest is three miles away. In the vicinity of the station several taxis were standing.* **2** [U (*of, to*)] *fml* nearness: *Vicinity to a good school is important for parents of young children.* **in the vicinity of** *pomp* about: *His income is in the vicinity of £5,000 a year.*

environment **1** [C] all the surrounding conditions which influence growth and development: *Children need a happy home environment. My wife and I grew up in quite different environments.* **2** [*the* R] the natural conditions, such as air, water, and land, in which man lives: *They are passing new laws to prevent the pollution* (= spoiling and making dirty) *of the envi-*

ronment. **environmental** [Wa5;B] of or concerning the environment **-ly** [*adv*]

environs [P] *esp fml, lit & pomp* neighbourhood: *What fine environs they live in! I don't much like the city and its environs.*

surroundings [P] the place and conditions of life: *The surroundings a child grows up in may have an effect on his development. It's good to change one's surroundings occasionally.*

setting [C] **1** (*fig*) surroundings; environment: *The castle has a fine natural setting.* **2** a framework, etc in which an ornament is fixed or placed: *That is a beautiful setting for the pearls* [⇒ H65].

M124 *adverbs, etc* : **at home and abroad** [Wa5]

at home 1 in one's house, family, etc: *Is he at home tonight?—No, he's away; he's not at home.* (*fml*) *She is not at home to visitors* (= She does not want to see anyone). *How are things at home?* **2** in one's own country: *Matters at home are not going well.*

away from home not at home: *He's away from home at the moment; in London, I think.*

abroad in or to foreign places: *He is abroad on business at the moment. She went abroad twice last year. They live abroad.*

overseas [*also* A] (*used esp in Britain because it is an island*) abroad; from, to, in, etc places across the sea: *He has gone overseas. We get a lot of overseas visitors here. Our overseas trade is very important.*

M125 *nouns* : **roads and routes**

road [C; *by* U; *often in comb*] a prepared track or way along which wheeled vehicles can travel, usu between towns rather than within one: *It takes three hours by train and four by road* (= driving). *It's not really a road, only a path. He bought a road map of Western Europe. They were driving on the new road to Birmingham. There have been so many road accidents lately that you must teach the children about road safety.* **on the road 1** on a journey; travelling, esp for one's work **2** (of esp a theatrical company) giving a number of planned performances at different places: *Let's get the show on the road.* **rule(s) of the road** the agreement(s) as to which side vehicles or ships should take when meeting, passing, etc: *According to the rule of the road you must drive on the left in Britain.* **take to the road** to become a tramp (= a homeless poor person without work who walks from place to place)

way [(*the*) C (*to*)] a road or roads, etc esp that one can take to get from one place to another: *Can you tell me the way to Bristol Street, please? They live just across the way from here.*

-way [*comb form*] the surface, main part, direction, etc of a road, stretch of water, set of rails, etc: *Don't walk in the middle of the roadway.*

The railway runs near the highway [⇒ M127]. *The Thames is one of Britain's great waterways. Don't park in the driveway.*

lane [C] **1** *also* **country lane** a narrow road in the country: *They went along a country lane on their bicycles.* **2** a narrow street in a town, etc: *Go down that lane; it'll take you to North Street. He lives in Market Lane.* **3** a part of a road esp marked by lines, along which vehicles can move in one direction at certain speeds, etc: *Go in the outside lane. The road was wide and had four lanes, two each way.* **4** *also* **shipping lane** the usual route for ships to take from one place to another: *The ship did not follow the usual lanes.*

alley [C] *often deprec* a lane in a town, esp if dark and dirty: *The thief ran off down an alley.*

thoroughfare [C] a road or wide street that is open to other roads at both ends to allow vehicles and people through: *The street had a sign saying 'No Thoroughfare'; there was no way out at the other end. Oxford Street is a main London thoroughfare.*

route [C; *on* U] the way to go, esp over a longer distance and many roads: *What route are you taking from Edinburgh to London? He went there by a different route from us. They were on route to* (= going to) *Paris when I met them.*

pass [C (*over*, *through*)] a way over or through a line of mountains, esp a narrow passage higher than usual but lower than the tops of the mountains

M126 *nouns* : **special roads and streets in towns** [C *often cap*]

road an important, longer or wider way for vehicles, etc through a town, etc: *He lives in Cambridge Road. Be careful crossing the road.* **Rd** *abbrev* (part of the name of) a road in a town: *His address is 39 Forest Rd.*

street a less important, narrower or shorter road in a town, etc: *She lives in our street. Be careful crossing the street. Fleet Street is in London.* **St** *abbrev* (part of the name of) a street in a town: *Her address is 24 Cambridge St.*

avenue 1 a road or wide street in a town, or a road leading to a large house, esp if lined with trees: *What a fine tree-lined avenue.* **2** (*fig*) the way to some stated thing: *This is his avenue to success.* **Ave** *abbrev* (part of the name of) an avenue: *She lives at 12 Cedar Ave.*

drive 1 a small or short road leading to an esp larger house: *He parked his car in the drive.* **2** a street: *South Drive has many nice houses.* **Dr** *abbrev* (part of the name of) a drive: *Her address is 14 South Dr.*

walk 1 a place, esp a path or track that is well kept, where people can walk: *They went along the Cliff Walk.* **2** a street: *They live in a new house in Cedar Walk.*

terrace 1 a row of houses built together **2** a street with such terraces on each side: *They live in Orchard Terrace.* **Terr/Tce** *abbrev* (part of the name of) a terrace: *He lives at 14 Orchard Terr.*

way a street: *He lives at 19 Cedar Way.*

crescent a curved row of houses; a curved street: *They live in a beautiful 18th-century crescent in Bath. Her address is 14 Beech Crescent.* **Cres** *abbrev* (part of the name of) a crescent: *14 Beech Cres*

square [*esp in comb*] an open place in the shape of a square in a town, etc, usu with buildings round the sides: *The main city square was full of people. St Andrews Square is a beautiful old square in Edinburgh.* **Sq** *abbrev* (part of the name of) a square: *82 Green Sq*

place the name of some streets and squares in a town, etc: *She lives at No 4, Orchard Place.* **Pl** *abbrev* (part of the name of) a place: *4 Orchard Pl*

M127 *nouns*: **special roads and streets in the country** [C]

main road an important road from one town to another: *There has been a car crash on the main road. This is the main road to London. In winter it's better to keep to (= drive on) the main roads.*

trunk road a main road, esp as part of a system: *Britain has a lot of trunk roads running north–south.*

arterial road *fml & tech* a main or trunk road, running from a capital or important city to other cities as the arteries [⇒ B36] carry blood through the body

highway *esp BrE esp formerly* a main road; all main roads: *They travelled in peace on the King's Highway.*

high road *BrE formerly* a main road: (*fig*) *This is his high road to success.*

side road a smaller road leading to and from a main road: *He turned down a side road.*

feeder (road) a side road, esp as part of a system: *Feeder roads lead from the new town to the trunk road.*

back road a small unimportant road well away from any main road: *They got lost in a number of back roads that had no proper signposts (= signs to show where one can go).*

motor road a road that has been made esp for motor vehicles: *There is a good motor road on the island.*

M128 *nouns* : **special streets in towns**

high street *also* **main street** *AmE* [*the* R; A; (C)] the most important street, esp for businesses and shops, in a town: *I'll meet you in the high street, at the hotel at 2 o'clock. His shop is in the main street.*

main street [C] *genl* an important street in a town, etc: *London's main streets are always full of people.*

side street [C] a street, usu smaller, that leads

from a main street: *There are so many side streets in that town that I get lost (in them).*

back street [C] a small, unimportant street well away from any main street: *He grew up in the back streets of Glasgow.*

M129 *nouns* : **very large modern roads** [(*the*) C; A]

dual carriageway *BrE* a main road on which the traffic travelling in opposite directions is kept apart by a central band or separation of some sort

motorway *BrE*, **expressway**, **freeway** *AmE* a very wide road built esp for fast vehicles travelling long distances, and on which one is not usu allowed to stop

highway *AmE* a main road on which vehicles can travel fast: *He was killed in a crash on Highway 14.*

turnpike *AmE* an expressway or highway, esp if one pays to drive on it

M130 *nouns* : **no-entries and cul-de-sacs** [C]

no-entry a street which vehicles can enter at one end only: *You can't go through there; it's a no-entry. Can't you see the no-entry sign?*

one-way street a street in which vehicles can only travel one way; a no-entry: *This is a one-way street; you can't turn back.*

cul-de-sac a street with an opening at one end only: *They drove by mistake into a cul-de-sac. A high wall made the street a cul-de-sac.*

M131 *nouns* : **paths and tracks** [C]

path [*often in comb*] **1** a way across fields, through woods, over hills, etc for people and animals walking, etc: *He followed (= went along) a path through the trees. She climbed up the mountain path.* **2** (*fig*) the line along which something travels: *They marked the path of the plane on a map.* **3** (*fig*) a way to travel in life: *'Religions are just different paths to the same truth,' he said.*

track 1 a path made by people or animals moving along the same way all the time: *He walked along the track to the village. She climbed up the mountain track.* **2** the mark left by something as it moves: *The animal's tracks could be seen in the wet ground. The car left tracks in the mud. It was easy to follow his tracks.* **trackless** [Wa5;B] having no tracks or roads: *He was lost in the trackless hills.* **off the beaten track** away from (a place with) any tracks

trail 1 a rough path or track through wild country: *Keep to the trail; if you leave it, you'll get lost. She climbed up a lonely mountain trail.* **2** lines, marks, smells, etc left by an animal, person, thing, etc while moving: *The hunter* *followed the animal's trail. There was a trail of dirt across the kitchen floor.*

footpath a path, esp across fields, etc, for walking on: *There's a public footpath through the woods.*

pathway (the surface of) a path: *The pathway was rough and covered with stones.*

cart track a track made by carts and other such vehicles: *A cart track led to the farmhouse.*

M132 *nouns, etc* : **parts of roads, etc**

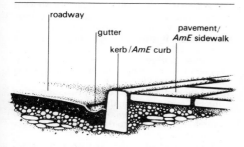

roadway
gutter
kerb/*AmE* curb
pavement/*AmE* sidewalk

pave [T1 *often pass*] to put flat stones, etc on (a road or other surface): *The road was paved with stones.*

paving stone *also* **flagstone** [C] a large flat stone used for paving paths, etc

pavement [C] **1** sidewalk *AmE* a paved surface or path at the side of a street for people to walk on **2** *AmE* the paved surface of a street

kerbstone [C] a raised stone separating the pavement from the road

cobble *also* **cobblestone** [C] a usu large rounded stone used esp formerly for paving streets **cobbled** [Wa5;B] paved with cobbles: *Parts of Edinburgh still have cobbled streets.*

tar [U] a thick black sticky substance, liquid when hot and hard when cold, used, esp with gravel, for making hard surfaces for roads, etc

gravel [U] small rough stones and sand, etc esp as **a** found in the bed of a river **b** used for putting surfaces on roads, paths, etc

chippings [P] gravel for or on roads: *Loose chippings covered the road.*

tarmac *also formerly & fml* **tarmacadam** [U] a mixture of tar and gravel used to make road surfaces, airport runways [⇒ M185], etc

pothole [C] a hole in a road, esp formed after a bad winter, too much rain, etc: *The road was full of potholes.*

gutter [C] a hollow along the side of a road, usu between the roadway and the kerb, along which dirty water can flow into drains [⇒ D42]: *He didn't like being pushed into the gutters by other people on the narrow pavement.* (*fig deprec*) *She did not want to talk to someone who had grown up in the gutter* (= to a person with no money, education, etc).

manhole [C] an opening, usu with a cover (**a manhole cover**) on or near a road, through which a man can enter a place where under-

ground pipes and such can be examined, repaired, etc

grating [C] a frame made of esp metal bars, to cover an opening esp over a drain in a roadway or gutter

verge [C] the edge or border (esp of a road, path, etc): *He drove his car onto the grass verge at the side of the road.* **on the verge of** (*fig*) very near to (the stated (change of) conditions or action): *She tried to hide her grief, but she was on the verge of tears. He was on the verge of speaking about the secret when he suddenly remembered his promise not to tell.*

roadside [C] the side of a road: *He sat at the roadside, waiting for his friend to come. They stopped at a roadside restaurant.*

M133 *nouns* : **lights on roads, etc** [C]

traffic light *also* **traffic signal** [*usu pl*] one of a set of coloured lights (red, amber/orange, green) used for controlling and directing traffic, esp where one road crosses another

zebra crossing (in Britain) a place on a busy street, painted with black and white lines to show that people have the right to walk across there and that car drivers must stop for them

Belisha beacon *also* **beacon** (in Britain) a flashing orange light on a black-and-white striped post that marks a zebra crossing

neon sign a brightly-coloured electrically-lit sign, usu advertising things for sale, hotels, etc, and containing a gas called neon

M134 *nouns, etc* : **bends and bumps, etc**

bend [C] a curve in a road, etc: *There are a lot of bad* (= very curved and therefore) *dangerous bends on this road. The driver took the bend too fast and crashed into a wall. Be careful; there's a sharp* (= very curved) *bend ahead.* **hairpin bend** [C] a bend that curves back like the letter U: *The mountain road was full of hairpin bends.*

corner 1 [C] the point where two streets or (sometimes) roads meet: *They were standing talking at the corner of the street/at the street corner/on the corner (of the street). The car went too fast round the blind corner* (= a corner where one cannot see what is coming the other way) *and hit another car.* **2** [I0] to turn a corner: *The car cornered too fast and went off the road.*

bump [C] a raised area in the surface of esp a road: *The car hit a bump.* **bumpy** [Wa1;B] full of bumps: *What a bumpy road/ride!*

gradient [C] *tech* the amount by which a road goes up or down: *They came to a hill with a gradient of 1 in 5* (= rising one metre in every five metres travelled).

M135 nouns, etc : **intersections and bypasses**

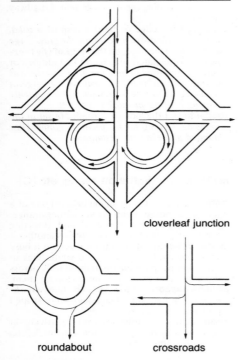

cloverleaf junction

roundabout   crossroads

intersection *also* **junction** [C] a place where two or more roads, etc meet: *The car slowed down at the junction/at the junction with the main road. Be careful at the intersection; there are a lot of accidents there.*

crossroads [Wn3;C] the place where two roads go across each other: *He stopped his car at the crossroads and studied the roadsigns.* (*fig*) *She says she has come to a crossroads in her life and must decide which way to go.*

crossing [C] **1** a place at which a road, river, etc, may be crossed: *The teacher warned the children that they should always cross the road at the crossing.* **2** a place where roads, lines, tracks, etc cross

roundabout *BrE* (**traffic**) **circle** *AmE* [C] an intersection where vehicles cannot go direct but must go round in all or part of a circle

cloverleaf (**junction**) [C] *esp AmE* an intersection of roads which resembles a leaf of the clover [⇒ A158] plant, allowing fast easy movement between two expressways: *At a cloverleaf one highway passes over the other, and both are joined by a system of curved feeder roads* [⇒ M127] *which let vehicles on and off the highways.*

bypass 1 [C] part of a main road that is built to go round a town, etc, instead of through it **2** [T1] to go round (a town, etc) on a bypass **3**

[T1] (*fig*) to go round (something): *He tries to bypass all the difficulties in life.*

M136 nouns, etc : **bridges and tunnels** [C]

bridge 1 [*often in comb*] a road or path that is built over a river, railway, or another road: *There's a footbridge over the river. Paris is famous for its many bridges over the Seine. The new Forth Road Bridge crosses the river Forth near the old Forth Railway Bridge, not far from Edinburgh.* **2** [T1] to put a bridge over (something): *They bridged the river with trees.*

suspension bridge a bridge hung from steel cables [⇒ H46] fixed to towers

cantilever bridge a bridge made of two cantilevers (= long armlike beams of metal) that meet in the middle

span 1 the distance between any two supporting objects, esp in the length of a bridge, etc: *the span of a bridge; a span of 80 metres* **2** [T1] to stretch from one side to the other: *Two bridges spanned the river.*

viaduct a long high bridge esp with many arches [⇒ D26] which carries a road or railway line across a valley

aqueduct a pipe, bridge, etc that carries a water supply, esp one that is built higher than the land around it, or that goes over a valley: *The Romans built many fine aqueducts which are still standing today.*

flyover *BrE*, **overpass** *AmE* a roadway that crosses above another roadway on a special bridge-like structure, esp on a motorway

subway *BrE* a path under a road or railway by which people can get from one side to the other

underpass a way under a road, either another road or (esp) a subway: *It's too dangerous to cross at the traffic lights; let's go by/under/through the underpass.*

tunnel an underground passage, way, road, etc, esp one dug under a mountain, hill, river, town, etc

Shipping

M150 nouns : **boats** [C]

a boat

| smaller & genl | boat |
| larger | ship |

boat [*also by* U; *often in comb*] a means of travelling on/across water: *He crossed the river in a small boat. He crossed the river by steamboat. He crossed to America by boat. The Queen Elizabeth II is a very big boat.*

ship [*also by* U; *often in comb*] **1** a large boat for carrying people or goods on the sea **2** *infml* any large vehicle, esp an aircraft or space vehicle

vessel *genl* a ship or (large) boat: *The Port of London is filled with vessels of all kinds. He owns a small fishing vessel; it's a motor vessel.*

craft [Wn3] a boat, esp of a small size; vessel

tub *infml & sometimes deprec* a boat: *You surely don't go to sea in an old tub like that!*

M151 *nouns* : **boats in general**

shipping [U] ships as a group: *A lot of the world's shipping passes through the English Channel.*

fleet [GC] **1** a (large) number of boats or ships, esp warships, sailing together or under one person's command: *A fleet of fishing boats left the harbour. He owns a fleet of 50 ships.* **2** a large number of any kind of vehicles: *a fleet of taxis/buses*

flotilla [C] a group of ships, esp of small warships

M152 *nouns* : **smaller kinds of boats** [C; *by* U]

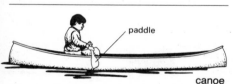

paddle

canoe

rowing boat *BrE*, **rowboat** *AmE* a small boat that is moved through the water by long poles with flat ends (**oars** [⇒ M168]): '*Rowing Boats for Hire*' (on a notice). *He crossed the river by rowing boat.*

canoe a long light narrow boat, pointed at both ends and moved by a flat piece of wood (**a paddle** [⇒ M168]) held in the hands: *We crossed the lake in a canoe/by canoe.*

dugout (canoe) a small light boat made by cutting out a deep hollow in a og or treetrunk

raft 1 a flat boat made of large rough pieces of wood: *They escaped from the wrecked ship on a raft.* **2** *also* **life raft** a flat rubber boat that can be filled with air, carried by aircraft and ships to save life **3** a flat floating framework used as a landing place for swimmers and for people with small boats **4** a number of tree trunks fastened together to be sent floating down the river

dinghy a small open boat used for pleasure or for taking people between a ship and the shore

skiff a small light boat for rowing or sailing by one person, esp if long and not very wide: *a racing skiff*

yacht a light sailing boat, esp one used for racing

motorboat a boat or small ship driven by an engine or electric motor, esp one made to travel fast

powerboat a powerful motorboat

launch a large usually motor-driven boat used for carrying people on rivers and lakes, in harbours, etc

tug *also* **tugboat** a small powerful boat used for guiding large ships into a port, up rivers, etc

landing craft a flat-bottomed boat that opens at one end, used for landing soldiers and army vehicles directly on enemy shores

ferry *also* **ferryboat 1** a boat of any size used to take people from one place to another and back, esp across a wide river or narrow sea: *Ferries cross the English Channel all the time. He caught the night ferry to France. You can cross the river by ferry.* **2** the place from which a ferry leaves: *I waited for him at the ferry.*

M153 *nouns* : **larger kinds of sailing boats** [C; *by* U]

sailing boat a boat with one or more masts and sails [⇒ M157]: *The sail of the sailing boat caught the wind and the boat began to move.*

sailing ship a ship with one or more masts and sails: *There were once many more sailing ships than today; most ships today are power-driven, not wind-driven.*

galley a ship which was rowed along by slaves, esp an ancient Greek or Roman warship, often having a sail

longship a kind of long narrow galley with one mast and a square sail once used in northern Europe: *the Viking longships*

galleon a large sailing ship, used formerly esp by the Spaniards

barque *esp BrE*, **bark** *esp AmE* **1** a sailing ship with three masts, having square sails on the first two and a three-cornered sail on the third **2** *often lit* any small sailing ship

brig a ship with two masts and large square sails on both of them

schooner a fast sailing ship with two or sometimes more masts and sails set lengthwise rather than across the ship

clipper a usu large long sailing ship with one or more special square sails (**lugsails**)

lugger a small ship with lugsails set in front and behind

M154 *nouns* : **powered ships** [C; *by* U]

steamship *also* **steamboat, steamer** a boat, usu large, powered by steam

(ocean) liner a large ship, esp a steamship, carrying esp a large number of passengers from one place to another or on a cruise [⇒ M29]

yacht a large boat used for pleasure, such as one kept by a rich person and usu with an engine

M155 *nouns* : **ships with special uses**
[C; *by* U]

cutter 1 a small fast boat belonging to a larger
ship, esp used for moving supplies or passengers to or from the land **2** a lightly-armed
government ship used for preventing smuggling [⇨ C230]

coaster a ship carrying goods along coasts but
not across great distances of water

trawler a fishing boat that uses a **trawl** (= a
strong net for catching fish just above the sea
bottom)

whaler a ship which (or a person in such a ship
who) hunts whales [⇨ A58]

tanker usu a large ship but also a road or rail
vehicle or a plane that is specially built to carry
large quantities of gas or liquid, esp oil

barge a usu large kind of boat with a flat bottom
and with an engine or to be pushed or pulled
through the water for carrying esp goods on or
across rivers, along coasts, etc

lighter a kind of barge used for taking goods
short distances from a large sea-going ship to
the shore or to another ship

M156 *nouns* : **merchant ships, etc**

merchant ship *also* **merchantman** [C; *by* U] a
ship used for carrying goods for trading

tramp steamer, tramp ship, tramp [C; *by* U] a
merchant ship that does not make regular trips
but takes goods to any port

merchant navy *also* **merchant marine** *AmE*,
also **mercantile marine** *BrE* [C] **1** those ships of
a nation which are used in trading: *a merchant
navy of 100 ships* **2** the people who work on
these ships: *Join the Merchant Navy!*

(shipping) line [C] a business that has merchant
ships and/or passenger ships travelling regularly from place to place

M157 *nouns* : **parts of ships**

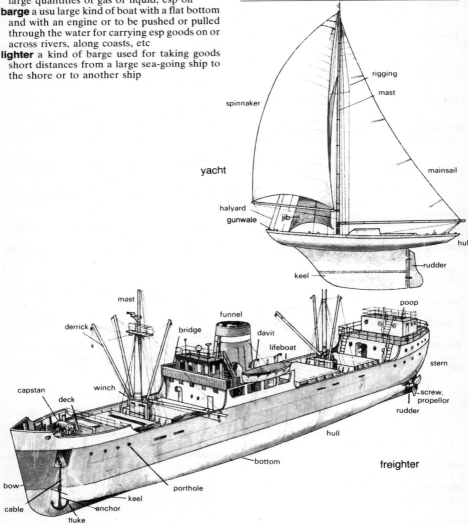

engine room [U] the part of a ship where the engines are

boiler room [C] the part of a ship containing the **boilers** (containers which are heated to change water into steam) used to drive certain kinds of ships' engines

fo'c'sle *also* **forecastle** [C] the front part of a ship where the sailors live

cabin [C] a room on a ship, esp with bunks (=beds) in it: *You are in Cabin 14, sir. Where is the captain's cabin?*

berth [C] a place on esp a ship but also a train where a person can sleep: *Have you got your berths on the ship yet?*

galley [C] a ship's kitchen

wheelhouse [C] the place on a small or older kind of ship where the captain stands at the **wheel** (see below)

crow's nest [C] a box or shelter near the top of a ship's mast from which a man can watch for danger, land, etc

gangway [C] an opening in the side of a ship and the movable board (the **gangplank**) used to make a bridge to the land or to another ship

companionway [C] the stairs leading from a deck to an area below

spar [C] a thick pole, esp used on a ship to support sails

rigging [U] all the ropes, sails, etc, with which a ship is fitted

halyard, halliard [C] a rope used to raise or lower a sail or flag

shrouds [P] any of the pairs of supporting ropes connecting a ship's masts to its sides

ratlines, ratlins [P] the set of short ropes forming a rope ladder for sailors to climb the shrouds of a ship

tiller [C] a long handle fastened to the top end of a small boat's rudder so that it can be turned easily

wheel [C] the wheel connected to the rudder of a ship by which its course is directed (*esp in the phrs* **be at/take the wheel**)

helm [C] the wheel or tiller of a ship; the place where the course of a ship is controlled (*esp in the phr* **at the helm**)

radar [U] a method of finding the position of solid objects by sending out radio waves and measuring any waves which are returned

sonar [U] a method of finding the position of solid objects underwater by sending out sound waves and measuring any waves which are returned

M158 *adverbs, nouns, etc* : **positions on ships, etc**

ahead forward; in front of a ship: *Full speed ahead! They saw another ship ahead.*

abaft behind; in the direction of the stern

windward towards the wind

leeward away from the wind

lee [*the* R; A] the side towards which the wind blows

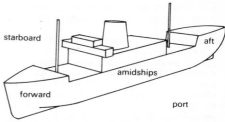

astern at, towards or behind the stern

ashore on(to) a shore: *The men went ashore.*

aboard on (esp a ship, plane, large vehicle, etc): *Is everyone aboard? They were all aboard ship last night.*

on deck on the deck; in the open air on a larger ship: *He was on deck.*

below not on deck: *He went below to his cabin* (=room).

afloat 1 floating: *The man was still afloat in the water.* **2** at sea; sailing: *She/It is one of the best ships afloat.*

overboard off a ship into the sea: *He fell overboard.*

aground (of a ship) on rocks, sand, etc: *The ship ran aground in a storm.*

M159 *nouns* : **harbours and yards**

harbour *BrE*, **harbor** *AmE* [C; (*into*, *in*) U] **1** an area of water which is sheltered from rougher waters such as those of the sea, so that ships are safe inside it: *We reached harbour at ten. Rio de Janeiro is a big natural harbour.* **2** (*fig*) a safe place

haven [C] **1** *rare & old use* a harbour **2** (*fig*) a place of calm and safety: *The child was safe in the haven of his mother's arms.*

port [C; (*into*, *in*) U; *often in comb*] **1** a town, city, or other place where there are harbours, etc and ships bring in and take away goods (and passengers): *Southampton is a famous port/a great seaport.* **2** a harbour

breakwater [C] any wall or structure that breaks the force of waves, esp at the entrance to a harbour

mole [C] a large wall-like structure esp of stone set up as a breakwater to (form) a harbour or to act as a road (as from the shore to an island)

M160 *nouns* : **quays and docks** [C]

quay an unmoving place where boats can land, often a stone-built area running out into a sea-harbour: *She was waiting at the quay as the ship came in/was waiting on the quayside.*

wharf a structure built on a shore, river bank, etc so that boats can come alongside to load and unload

dock 1 a wharf **2** the space or waterway between quays and wharves, etc esp in a port **3** anything like this **the docks** [P] wharves, quays, and their waterways all together **dockland** [U] an area of a city with docks in it **dockside** [C] the land beside a dock

pier 1 a bridgelike structure built out into the sea at which boats can stop and land their passengers or goods: *The ship is now loading at Pier Number 3.* **2** an ornamental bridgelike structure of wood, metal, etc built out into the sea at places where people go for holidays, with small buildings on it where people can eat and amuse themselves: *Have you been to the piers at Brighton and Blackpool? He liked Brighton Pier.*

jetty a quay, wharf, or pier esp if small: *The boat tied up at the jetty.*

dockyard a waterside area containing docks, quays, warehouses, etc, esp for building and repairing ships

navy yard *esp AmE* a government dockyard where warships etc are built, repaired, etc

shipyard a dockyard, esp for building ships

yard *infml* a dockyard or shipyard

dry dock [*also in* U] a structure able to hold a ship and then to be raised above the water or have the water removed so that the lower outside parts of the ship can be repaired etc: *The ship was in dry dock.*

slipway in a shipyard an area sloping down into the water, down which a newly built ship slides when ready for use

warehouse a building esp at the waterside where goods are stored **bonded warehouse** [C] a government place in which certain goods such as alcoholic drinks are kept until tax is paid on them

berth 1 the space provided for a ship beside a quay, in a harbour, etc: *Your berth is Berth 2 at Quay 14.* **2** the distance between a ship and the shore or another ship, etc

M161 *nouns* : **lighthouses, buoys, etc** [C]

lighthouse a tower or other structure, buildings, etc with a light to show ships that a place is dangerous

lightship a ship kept in a particular place with a light to show other ships that the place is dangerous

buoy 1 *also* **marker buoy** a floating object fastened to the bed of the sea to show ships where there are rocks, hidden dangers, etc **2** *also* **life buoy** any of several floating means of keeping a person who has fallen in the water from sinking

shallows [P] a shallow part of a sea, etc, esp if dangerous to ships: *Keep away from the shallows or you'll run aground* [⇒ M158].

shoal 1 a place where a sea, river, or other stretch of water is shallow **2** a sandbank

sandbank *also* **sandbar** a large mass or bar of sand formed in a sea or river and making the water shallow: *The boat went aground on a sandbank.*

bank *also* **bar** *infml* a sandbank or sandbar

M162 *nouns & verbs* : **crews**

crew 1 [GC] the person or people working on a ship, etc, esp the ordinary sailors: *What is the size of your crew?—We have a crew of 80. He is on the crew of that American ship. We went out in a boat yesterday; my wife was the captain and I was the crew. We need two more crew before the ship can leave port. Is he a member of our crew/one of our crew members? The captain, his officers and the crew all left the ship.* **2** [I0; T1 *usu pass*] to be the crew of (a ship, etc): *They crewed the ship well. The ship was crewed by women.*

complement [C] *tech* the full number of officers and other people needed for a ship: *We need two more officers and ten more crew to bring the ship to its full complement.*

man [T1] to serve as the crew of (a ship, big gun, etc): *They managed to man the ship although they weren't all sailors. Man the guns; we're being attacked! The ship was manned by women.*

M163 *nouns* : **sailors, etc** [C]

sailor a person who sails or works on a ship for money or pleasure: *He saw the whole world when he was a sailor in the Merchant Navy. She is an enthusiastic weekend sailor.*

seaman 1 an ordinary sailor, esp on a merchant ship [⇒ M156] or a warship **2** *apprec* a skilled or professional sailor **seamanship** [U] skill and knowledge in sailing, etc a ship

able-bodied seaman, able seaman, AB *abbrev* a trained ordinary sailor in a navy

deckhand a man or boy who is hired to do cleaning and other unskilled work on a ship, esp on the deck [⇒ M157]

hand *infml* a sailor: *All hands on deck!*

shipmate a person, usu a sailor, who works on the same ship: *He was one of my shipmates on the Hercules.*

stoker a person or machine that puts fuel [⇒ H80] into a furnace [⇒ H120]

boatman a man who looks after a small boat or who is skilled in sailing smaller boats

ferryman a man who looks after a ferry [⇒ M152]: *The ferryman took them across the river.*

docker *also* **longshoreman** *AmE* a man employed to load and unload ships, esp at docks [⇒ M160]

landlubber *infml* a person not used to the sea and ships

M164 *nouns* : **ship's officers, etc** [C]

captain [*also* A] (the title of) the person in command of a ship: *Where's the captain? Captain Jones commands this ship.*

skipper *infml* a captain: *Where's the skipper?*

master *fml* a captain: *Who's master of this ship?*

mate any of a number of officers having particular duties esp on a merchant ship [⇨ M156]

first mate *also* **first officer, chief mate, chief officer, mate** the officer next to captain esp on a merchant ship

second mate *also* **second officer** the officer next to the first mate

steward *also* **ship's steward** the officer on a passenger ship who looks after the needs of the passengers

purser the officer on an esp passenger ship who looks after its money matters and who keeps money, etc for its passengers

boatswain, bosun an officer on esp a merchant ship or warship in charge of the ship's general equipment

M165 *verbs* : **mooring and docking**

moor [T1;I∅] to fasten (a boat, ship, etc) to land, the bed of the sea, etc by means of a rope, chains, etc: *They moored just outside the harbour. The ship was moored just off the shore. Where can I moor?* **moorings** [P] **1** ropes and chains, etc used to moor a boat, ship, etc **2** a place where a boat, ship, etc can be moored

dock [I∅; T1] to (cause to) come into or remain in a dock [⇨ M160]: *The ship docked at Liverpool/was docked at Glasgow.*

berth [I∅; T1] to (cause to) come into a berth [⇨ M160]: *They berthed at Southampton. When the ship was safely berthed they went into the town.*

anchor 1 [T1] to fasten (a ship) to the sea bottom with an anchor [⇨ M157] **2** [I∅] to stop sailing: *We anchored off Newport.* **3** [T1;I∅] *(fig)* to (cause to) be fixed firmly: *My beliefs are firmly anchored in reality, I hope.* **anchorage** [C] a place near land where ships can anchor: *The entrance to the river is a good anchorage for ships.*

drop anchor [I∅] *not fml* to anchor a ship: *They dropped anchor just off the coast.*

tie up [v adv I∅; T1] *infml* to moor, dock, berth, etc: *Where will you tie up for the night? They tied up at Liverpool Docks.*

put in [v adv I∅ *(at)*] (of a ship) to come into (a harbour, etc): *They put in at Liverpool for fresh supplies.*

come/go alongside [v adv I∅] (of one ship) to come/go right up beside another ship: *They came/went alongside and asked to speak to the captain.*

M166 *verbs, etc* : **setting sail**

set sail [I∅ *(for)*] (of a ship, whether having sails or not) to leave a harbour, etc: *They set sail last night for Jamaica. The ship set sail two days late.*

sail 1 [I∅] to set sail: *The ship sailed last night. When are you sailing?* **2** [I∅] (of a boat, ship, etc) to move through the water: *Ships sail through the English Channel all year round*

(=all the time). **3** [T1] to cause (a boat, ship, etc) to move through the water: *He sailed the ship north.*

weigh anchor [I∅] *tech* to take up the anchor [⇨ M157] and leave: *The ship/They weighed anchor during the night and was/were gone by morning.*

cast off [v adv I∅] (of a boat or a person in a boat) to untie and move away from land: *We cast off tonight. Cast off!*

cruise [I∅] to make a sea journey, esp for pleasure: *They are cruising in the Caribbean at the moment.*

voyage [I∅] *esp old use* to go on a long journey by sea (**a voyage**): *They voyaged in a sailing ship to the China Seas.*

steam [L9] to move through water under the power of steam engines: *The warship steamed out of the harbour. The ships steamed past.*

row 1 [I∅; T1] to (cause a small boat) to move by using one or more oars: *They rowed the boat across the lake. He rowed upstream* (=up the river). **2** [S] a trip by this means: *Come for a row! It's a long row to Stavanger.*

paddle [I∅; T1] to (cause a small boat, etc to) move by using one or more paddles [⇨ M167]: *He paddled the boat across the river. They paddled downstream* (=down the river).

M167 *nouns* : **oars and paddles** [C]

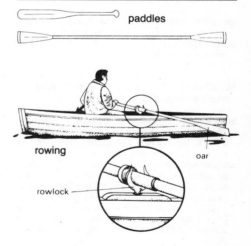

paddles

rowing

oar

rowlock

oar a long pole with a flat end used in small boats, esp rowing boats [⇨ M152], to push them through the water: *A rowing boat usually has two oars, one on each side.*

rowlock *BrE*, **oarlock** *AmE* a support esp on the side of a rowing boat to keep the oar in position

paddle a short oar with very broad rounded end at one or both ends, used for pushing canoes [⇨ M152], etc through the water

M168 *verbs* : **floating and sinking, etc**

float [IØ] to stay on or very near the surface of a liquid, esp water: *Some substances float, but others don't. Ships have a special shape which helps them float in the water. The great ship was like a floating building.*

submerge [IØ; T1] to (cause to) go under the surface of water, esp at a planned speed: *The submarine* [⇒ H249] *submerged slowly. (fig) Her happiness at seeing him submerged her former worries.*

dive [IØ] to submerge quickly: *The submarine dived when the planes approached.*

crash-dive [IØ] to dive very quickly: *The submarine crash-dived to escape the planes.*

capsize 1 [IØ] (esp of a boat or ship) to turn over: *The boat will capsize if you don't sit down.* **2** [T1] to turn (esp a boat or ship) over: *The large ship capsized the little boat. If you move suddenly in the boat you'll capsize us!*

overturn [IØ; T1] to (cause to) turn over: *The boat overturned but didn't sink. (fig) He overturned their plans and won after all.*

sink [IØ; T1] to (cause to) go under the surface of water and esp not to return to the surface again: *The ship sank. The big guns sank the ship. Help, we're sinking! Many ships have sunk on* (= because of hitting) *these rocks.*

go down *also* **go under** [v adv IØ] *emot* (of ships) to sink: *The warship went down with all hands* (= no sailors escaped). *The ship went under in a few minutes.*

go to the bottom *emot* to sink: *Many good ships went to the bottom during the war.*

surface [IØ] to come to the surface of water: *The submarine surfaced near the island.*

M169 *verbs & nouns* : **wrecking and marooning, etc**

wreck 1 [T1 *esp pass*] to destroy completely: *The ship was wrecked in a storm off Jamaica.* **2** [C] a ship lost at sea or (partly) destroyed on rocks etc: *The wreck sank in deep water.*

shipwreck *esp emot* **1** [T1 *usu pass*] to cause to suffer the wrecking of a ship: *They were shipwrecked in the Pacific. He was shipwrecked on a desert island* (= marooned, by being shipwrecked, on an island where no one lived). **2** [C; U] the occasion or result of being shipwrecked: *They suffered shipwreck in the Pacific.*

maroon [T1 *often pass*] **1** to put (someone) off a ship in a place where no one lives: *He was marooned on a desert island.* **2** to leave (one or more persons) alone, with no means of getting away: *They tried to cross the road in the wrong place and ended up marooned in the centre of the traffic.*

strand [T1 *usu pass*] to run (a ship) onto the shore: *The ship was stranded on the rocks. (fig) They were stranded in the mountains when their car broke down* (= stopped going).

shanghai [T1] **1** to make senseless by a blow or by drink and then put on a ship to serve as a sailor **2** [(*into*)] (*fig*) *infml* to trick or force into doing something unwillingly: *She shanghaied him into taking her mother to a film.*

pressgang 1 [GC] *formerly* a group of sailors under an officer which goes out to get men by force to work as sailors on their ship **2** [T1 *esp pass*] to force (someone) by this means to work as a sailor: *He was pressganged into the navy* [⇒ C290]. **3** [T1] (*fig*) to force: *Stop trying to pressgang me into doing things I don't want to do!*

Aircraft

M180 *nouns* : **aircraft and aviation**

aircraft [Wn3;C] any kind of flying machine in which a person or persons can travel: *He bought a book about aircraft. He's an aircraft engineer.*

aeroplane *BrE*, **airplane** *AmE* [C; *by* U] a flying machine, esp with wings and a tail and one or more propellers [⇒ M186]: *The aeroplanes flew overhead. The Mosquito was a twin-engined aeroplane* (= an aeroplane with two engines, one on each wing).

plane [C; *by* U] *infml* an aeroplane: *Can you fly this kind of plane? They went by plane.*

airliner [C; *by* U] a large passenger aeroplane

seaplane [C; *by* U] an aeroplane that can land on water

aero- [*comb form*] of the air, flying, or aeroplanes: *That factory makes aero-engines* (= engines for aeroplanes).

aerospace [U] **1** the atmosphere of the earth (= its **air**) and space beyond, considered together **2** (the making of) all aircraft, space vehicles, their parts, etc: *He works in the aerospace industry.*

aviation [U] **1** the act, skill, science, etc of flying aircraft: *Aviation is still quite a recent human activity.* **2** the making of aircraft: *The aviation industry is very important in the USA.* **3** the whole activity of flying aircraft: *He is in aviation/in the aviation business.*

M181 *nouns* : **jet aeroplanes** [C; *by* U]

jet (plane) a kind of aeroplane that is pushed through the air by one or more engines producing a flow of hot gas (**jet**): *They shot down two enemy jets. Jet planes were first built at the end of the Second World War.*

turbojet (a jet plane with) an engine which produces a very powerful jet

turboprop (an aeroplane with) a kind of jet engine combined with propellers [⇒ M186]

M182 *nouns, etc* : **balloons, etc** [C; *by* U]

balloon a large bag made of a light material such

airship

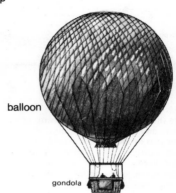

balloon

gondola

as silk or plastic filled with a gas lighter than air so as to rise and float above the ground and having a basket or similar container fixed below for passengers or scientific instruments

airship a kind of large balloon which can be moved under power through the air

glider 1 a plane without an engine **2** a person who uses such a plane

kite a frame of very light wood or metal covered with paper or cloth for flying in the air, often as a plaything, at the end of a long string

parachute 1 [C] an apparatus which looks like a large umbrella, fastened to persons or objects dropped from aircraft in order to make them faal slowly: *a parachute jump*. **2** [X9; L9] to (cause to) drop by means of a parachute

M183 *nouns* : **helicopters** [C; *by* U]

rotor

helicopter

helicopter a kind of aircraft which is made to fly by fast-turning metal blades (**rotors**) and which can land in a small space, take off without running along the ground and stay still in the air

chopper *esp AmE sl* a helicopter

M184 *nouns* : **spaceships** [C; *by* U]
[ALSO ⇒ H121, 251]

spaceship a vehicle for travel beyond the earth in space

spacecraft [Wn3] a space ship

rocket 1 a flying machine driven by burning gases from an engine (**rocket**) **2** *also* **rocketship** *older use* a space vehicle of this kind: *He wrote a book called 'Rocket to the Moon'.*

M185 *nouns* : **airports** [C]

airport an area of land with its buildings, open

spaces, etc where aircraft can land and take off, be kept, repaired, etc, esp for non-military purposes: *They left early for the airport, to fly to New York. Heathrow Airport is near London.*

airfield 1 a military airport: *The enemy attacked one of our airfields.* **2** a small airport **3** a piece of flat land on which aeroplanes can land and take off

airstrip a small airfield (*defs* **2** *and* **3**): *They only have a single airstrip where small planes can come in.*

aerodrome *esp older use* an airfield

runway 1 an airstrip **2** a long hard stretch of land, one of a number in an airport or airfield, on which aeroplanes can land and take off: *They are coming in to land on Runway 6.*

hangar a big building (**shed**) where planes are kept

control tower the tower in an airport or airfield from which aeroplanes are directed to land, take off, etc

departure lounge the large room, etc in an airport where passengers wait before boarding (= getting on to) their particular aeroplanes

M186 *nouns* : **parts of aircraft** [C]

airliner
tailplane
rudder
aileron
flap
fuselage
fin
cockpit
hatch
wing
nose
undercarriage

fuselage the main body of an aircraft, in which travellers and goods are carried

propeller two or more blades fixed to a central bar that is turned at high speed by an engine, used for driving a ship or aircraft

cabin the room at the front of an aircraft in which the pilot sits

joystick 1 a stick whose movement directs the movement of an aircraft **2** *infml* a stick whose movement controls the movement of any other machine

M187 *verbs* : **landing and taking off**

land [I0; T1] to (cause to) come down onto the ground again from the air: *The plane landed smoothly. He landed the plane in a field. When are we landing?*

crash-land 1 [I0] (of a plane) to crash in a controlled way so that as little damage as possible is done **2** [T1] to cause (a plane) to crash in this way: *The pilot crash-landed the plane after it had been struck by lightning.*

take off [v adv I0] (of an aeroplane, etc) to leave the ground: *When do we take off? They took off smoothly at 0800 hours.*

blast off [v adv I0] (of a rocket, etc) to leave the ground or a surface: *The rocketship blasted off from the surface of the moon.*

ground [T1 *usu pass*] to order (a pilot, aeroplane, etc) not to fly: *I've been grounded until the doctor says I can fly again. All aircraft are grounded due to bad weather.*

M188 *nouns* : **landing and taking off** [C]

landing an act of landing: *The plane made a smooth landing. The landing place was a field, not an airstrip* [⇒ M185].

crash landing an act of crash landing: *The pilot made a crash landing in some trees; none of the crew or passengers were hurt.*

takeoff an act or occasion of taking off: *When is the takeoff?—The takeoff time is 0800 hours. It was a smooth takeoff.*

flight a trip by an aeroplane, esp carrying passengers on a regular service: *When is your next flight to Rome? Would passengers for British Airways Flight 294 to Edinburgh please have their boarding passes* (=cards giving permission to go on a plane) *ready.*

blast-off [*also* U] an act or occasion of blasting off: *Blast-off is in 3 minutes.*

countdown the act of counting down to zero (=O) in preparing for blast-off: *The countdown has begun.*

M189 *nouns* : **people working on and with aeroplanes**

crew [GC] the persons helping to fly an aeroplane or aeroplanes: *The aircraft has a crew of four. Captain Anderson and his crew went aboard the plane.*

ground crew [GC] the persons at an airport, airfield, etc who help keep aircraft in good condition for flying

air crew [GC] the persons who fly aeroplanes

cabin staff [GC] the persons on a passenger aeroplane who look after the needs of the passengers

pilot [C] a person who flies an aeroplane or who is trained to fly one or more kind of aircraft: *Who is the pilot? He has his pilot's licence* (=he has been trained to fly).

copilot [C] the second pilot on an esp larger aeroplane on an esp longer flight

navigator [C] the person on a larger aeroplane who gives the pilot his or her position, knows where to go, etc

captain [C] the person in command of a larger aircraft, usu also the pilot

flier, flyer [C] *infml* a person flying an aircraft of any kind

aviator [C] *fml & old use* a flier

astronaut [C] a person who travels beyond the earth in space, or who has been trained to do so

cosmonaut [C] a Soviet astronaut

steward *also fem* **stewardess** a member of a passenger plane's cabin staff who looks after the passengers' needs, esp their food and drink

air hostess [C] *esp BrE* a stewardess

Location and direction

M200 *nouns* : **surfaces and edges** [C]
[ALSO ⇒ J46, M122]

surface 1 the outer part of something: *the earth's surface; the surface of the table; smooth/rough surfaces; A cube* [⇒ J44] *has six surfaces.* **2** the top of a body of liquid: *He swam (up) to the surface of the lake. A piece of wood floated on the surface of the water.* **3** (*esp fig*) that which can be seen (*esp in the phr* **on the surface**): *On the surface she was quite happy, but really/underneath she was sad.* **4** [Wa5] (of post) travelling by land and sea: *He sent the letter by surface mail, which took longer than air mail.*

edge 1 the narrowest part along the outside of a solid: *Can you stand a coin on its edge?* **2** a border: *He stood on the edge of the cliff/at the water's edge.*

rim the outside edge or border of esp a round or circular object: *the rim of a cup/wheel;* (*fig*) *the rim of the world*

brim 1 the outer edge of a cup, bowl, etc: *He filled the cup to the brim.* **2** the bottom part of a hat which turns outwards to give protection from sun or rain: *The cowboy's hat had a wide brim.*

brink (*esp fig*) the edge, esp of something high, dangerous, etc: *He stood on the brink of the cliff/of danger. The country is on the brink of war.*

crust a hard outer covering: *the earth's crust; a pie crust; a thin crust of ice*

M201 *nouns* : **higher and lower positions in objects, space, etc**

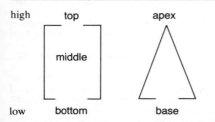

top 1 [C] the highest part: *He climbed to the top of the mountain. Start reading at the top of the page. The mountain tops were hidden in mist. We have a gate at the top of our stairs to stop the baby falling down/over.* **2** [C] the upper surface: *The top of his desk was covered with/in papers. The table top was dirty.* **3** [*the* R] (*fig*) the most important or worthiest part of anything: *He started life at the bottom and worked his way to the top.* **4** [C *usu pl*] (of a plant) the highest part(s), usu leaves: *Birds were flying through the treetops.* **5** [A] the highest one of

several: *Put the book on the top shelf. They live on the top floor.* **at the top of one's voice** as loudly as possible: *'Be quiet!' he shouted at the top of his voice.* **the top of the tree** *infml* the highest position in a profession: *He was a very successful lawyer and soon reached the top of the tree. Sir George is right at the top of the tree in the medical profession.* **at top speed** *not fml* very fast **on top of the world** *infml* very happy: *I feel on top of the world today!* **from top to toe** (of a person) completely: *She was dressed in green from top to toe.* **from top to bottom** (of a place or organization) all through; completely: *They had the house painted from top to bottom. He learnt the business from top to bottom.* **on (the) top (of) 1** over; above; resting on: *a glass of milk with cream on top* **2** in addition (to): *He lost his job and on top of that his wife left him.* **get on top of** to conquer or be too much for: *Things have been rather getting on top of me lately. I found the job difficult at first, but I soon got on top of it.*

tip [C] **1** the usu pointed end of something: *She burnt the tips of her fingers.* **2** a small piece or part serving as an end, cap, or point: *I only smoke cigarettes with tips.* **have (something) on the tip of one's tongue** to be about to remember (a name, word, etc): *It's on the tip of my tongue but I still can't remember your name.*

apex [C] *tech* the top or highest point of a triangle [⇒ J44], etc: (*fig*) *He was at the apex of his profession.*

middle 1 [C] the central part, point, or position: *He put the box in the middle of the table. He planted rose trees in the middle of the garden. This bill must be paid not later than the middle of the month. When they went to the theatre, he sat in the middle between his wife and daughter. A good story should have a beginning, a middle, and an end.* **2** [C] *infml* the waist or the part below the waist: *As a man grows old he often becomes fatter round the middle.* **3** [A] one equal in distance from either side: *He had the middle position.* **in the middle of something/doing something** in the course of or busy with something/doing something: *She was in the middle of cooking when the children came in. They were in the middle of a private conversation.*

centre *BrE*, **center** *AmE* [C] **1** *precise* the exact middle point of a circle, globe [⇒ H48], etc **2** *loose* middle: *She was standing in the centre of the room/group. She lives in the centre of the city/the city centre.*

core [C] **1** the harder centre part of some fruits **2** (*fig*) the central part of an idea, argument, etc: *Lack of money lay at the core of the trouble.*

heart [C] (*fig*) the central part of a matter or idea: *They tried to get to the heart of the matter.*

bottom 1 [C] the lowest part of anything: *He waited at the bottom of the hill. What word is that at the bottom of the page? The ship lay on the bottom of the sea/the sea bottom.* **2** [A] the lowest one of several: *Put the book on the bottom shelf. They live on the bottom floor.* **3**

[*the* R] (*fig*) the least important or worthy part: *She started at the bottom in her job and rose to the top position.*

base [C] the lowest part of (something) on which the other parts rest, are built, etc: *The statue has a base made (out) of stone/a stone base.*

M202 nouns : front, back, and sides

front 1 [*the* R (*of*)] the position directly before someone or something: *The teacher called the boy out to the front of the class. A pretty girl was walking past behind them, but the officer told the soldiers to look to the front.* **2** [*the* R (*of*); A] the surface or part facing forwards, outwards, or upwards: *The front of the cupboard is made of glass. The front of the postcard shows a picture of our hotel. This dress fastens at the front. He took a seat at the front/a front seat.* **3** [*the* R (*of*)] the most forward or important position: *The chief guest at the concert was led to a place at the front of the hall. He walked along to the front of the train.* (*fig*) *This new writer is rapidly coming to the front* (= becoming important). **4** [C] **a** the most important side of a building, containing the main entrance; the side of a building facing the street: *The front of the school faces south. Our house front is being repainted. In cities, shop fronts are often partly made of glass.* **b** a side of a large important building: *The west front of the church contains some fine old windows.* **5** [*the* R; (C)] a road, often built up and having a protecting wall, by the edge of the sea, esp in a town where people go for holidays: *The hotel is right on the sea front. The holidaymakers walked along the front to enjoy the air.* **6** [S9] the manner and appearance of a person: *Whatever his difficulties, he always presents a smiling front to the world. She was nervous meeting strangers, but she put on a bold front* (= acted as if she wasn't afraid) *and went to the party.* **7** [C] part of a garment covering the chest: *I've spilt soup down my front.* **8** [*the* R (*of*)] (of a book or newspaper) the beginning: *Write your name at the front of this dictionary.*

in front [adv] **1** ahead; in the position directly before someone or something: *The grandmother walked slowly, and the children ran on in front.* **2** in or at the part facing forwards: *This dress fastens in front.* **3** in the most forward or important position: *The driver sits in front and the passengers sit behind.* **in front of** [prep] **1** in the position directly before: *We couldn't read the notice on the board because several people were standing in front of it.* **2** in the presence of: *You shouldn't use such bad words in front of children.* **in the front of** in the most forward or important position: *He's sitting in the front of the car with the driver. In the front of the picture is the figure of a man.* **out front** *infml* in or amongst the people watching a theatrical or other performance: *My family are out front this*

evening, so I hope you give a good performance. **up front** *infml*, esp sport in the most forward position: *In football, the players who play up front get the most chances to score.*

face [C] the front of (something, esp if it is flat or like a person's face): *He climbed up the face of the building. The face of the clock/the clock face was dirty.*

back 1 [*the* R (*of*); A] the part of something or someone opposite the front: *The boy sat at the back of the class. She was at the back (of the car) when it happened. He took a seat at the back/a back seat.* **2** [*the* R; C] the surface or part facing backwards: *The back of the cupboard is made of wood. This dress fastens at the back.*

rear [*the* R (*of*); A] esp *fml* the back: *There is a garden at the rear of the house. He climbed in through a rear window. The rear wheel of the bicycle was bent.* **bring up the rear** to come last (as in a procession)

USAGE British speakers say **at the rear** for something that is behind outside: *a garden at the rear of the house* and **in the rear** for the back part of something: *Walk in the rear of the procession.* American speakers prefer **in the rear** for both

side 1 [*the* C (*of*)] a more or less upright surface of something, but not the top, bottom, front, or back: *There is a hole in the side of the box/the right side of the box/the right hand side of the box, but not the left/left hand/other side. She went in to the building by a door at the side/by a side door. She went in by the side (of the building), not the front.* **2** [C] any of the flat surfaces of something: *A square has four sides, but a circle has no sides. A cube has six sides/is a six-sided object.* **3** [C] either of the two surfaces of a piece of paper, cloth, etc: *The other side (of the sheet) is a different colour. Write on this side of the paper only.* **4** [C] one of the inside or outside surfaces of something: *Stand near/to that side of the room. The sides of the building were mainly of glass.* **5** [C (*of*)] an area thought of as relating to positions on the left or right of a point or line: *He was on this side (of the line) and I was on that side/the other side. Take whichever side you want. Stand to one side, please!* **6** [GC] (*fig*) part of a family: *He is German on his father's side. Her mother's side of the family aren't happy about her marriage.* **7** [C (*of*)] (*fig*) way of looking at life, a difficulty, etc: *There are many sides to this question and we must think carefully about it. Try to/and look on the bright* (= good) *side of things; everything isn't bad.* **on/from all sides** (from) everywhere: *Attacks came from all sides. On all sides there were difficulties.* **take sides** to support one group against another: *I won't take sides in this argument.*

sideways [adv;Wa5;B] **1** towards or from one side: *He moved sideways a little, to let her pass. She looked sideways at him.* **2** with one side first: *Bring the table through the door sideways.*

sidelong [Wa5;A;adv] to or from one side: *She*

gave him a sidelong look (= She looked at him without turning her head).

M203 *adverbs & prepositions, etc* : **about and around, etc**

about 1 [adv] *esp BrE* here and there; in all directions or places; on all sides: *The children were rushing about. Waste paper was lying about everywhere. They go about together most of the time. The visitors sat about on the floor.* **2** [adv F] *esp BrE* in the area; in a near place: *Is there anybody about?* **3** [adv] *esp BrE* from one place to another: *He has travelled about for years.* **4** [adv] *esp BrE* so as to face the opposite way: *The ship turned about and left the battle.* **5** [adv] *infml* in existence: *He's one of the best writers about at the moment.* **6** [adv F] *esp BrE* moving from place to place, as after getting out of bed; active (*esp in the phr* **up and about**): *Is he about yet? He may still be asleep.* **7** [adv] *infml* almost; nearly: *I'm about ready.* **8** [prep] *esp BrE* here and there in; in all directions or places of; on all sides of; around: *They walked about the streets. Books were lying about the room.* **9** [prep] *esp BrE* in the area of; near: *I lost my pen about here.* **10** [prep] with regard to; concerning: *Tell us about what happened. Do you have a book about the stars? He doesn't care about money. What about father? We can't just leave him here.* **11** [prep] on or near the body of: *There is a strange smell about him. I have no money about me.* **12** [prep] in the character of: *There is a sense of power about him.* **13** [prep] busy or concerned with: *Go to the market now and while you're about it buy yourself a pair of shoes.* **14** [prep] near in number: *There were about 20 people in the house.*

around 1 [adv] *esp AmE* about (*defs* 1, 2, 3, 4, 5): *The children were rushing around. Waste paper was lying around everywhere. The visitors sat around on the floor. Is there anybody around? He has travelled around for years. He turned around when he heard a noise behind him. He is up and around and it's only two days since his operation!* **2** [adv E] *esp AmE* in circular measurement; round: *The tree is five feet around.* **3** [adv] *infml* being in existence: *He is one of the finest writers around.* **4** [prep] on all sides of; all round; surrounding: *We sat around the table. He put a frame around the picture.* **5** [prep] *not fml* in some place near (to); in the area of: *He lives somewhere around London. Stay around the garden.* **6** [prep] from one place to another in; here and there in: *I travelled around the world for a few years.* **7** [prep] so as to have a centre or base in: *The society was built around a belief in God.* **8** [prep] so as to avoid or get past; round: *Let's go around the town, not through it.* (*fig*) *How can we get around the new taxes and keep some more money for ourselves?*

round 1 [adv] *esp BrE* with a circular move-ment or movements; spinning in or as if in a circle: *The earth turns round once in 24 hours. The wheels went round (and round).* (*fig*) *Your birthday will be/come round again soon.* **2** [adv] *esp BrE* in a circular position; surrounding a central point: *The field had a fence (all) round. The children gathered round to hear the story. Everybody round can hear the noise.* **3** [adv] *esp BrE* all over the place; in or into all parts; everywhere in an area: *Hand round the glasses. Send the invitations round. A strange story has been going round. Let's go into the palace and have a look round.* **4** [adv] *esp BrE* so as to face the other or stated way: *Turn the picture round to face the wall. He's got his hat on the wrong way round.* **5** [adv E] *esp BrE* in circular measurement: *The tree was five feet round.* **6** [adv] (of journeys) a not going the straightest way: *Walk/go/drive round by the cinema instead of coming straight home.* **b** to someone's home: *Come round and see me sometime! They invited us round for drinks.* **7** [prep] with a circular movement about (a central point): *The earth goes round the sun. Drake sailed (right/all)round the world and came back to England. They danced round (and round) the holy tree.* **8** [prep] in a circular position on all sides of (a central point): *Sit round the fire/round the table. Tie the belt round your waist.* **9** [prep] into all parts of; all over (a place): *Have a look round the shop. Let him show you round the castle.* **10** [prep] to or at the other side of, not going straight but changing direction: *He disappeared round the corner. She'll be coming round the mountain* (= not over or through the mountain). **11** [Wa1;B] circular: *Give me a round plate.* **12** [Wa1;B] shaped like a ball: *It was as round as an orange.* **13** [Wa1;B] (of parts of the body) fat and curved: *the child had round red cheeks.* **14** [Wa5;A] (of numbers) full; complete: *A round twenty people came.* **in round figures** (of numbers) not exactly, but to the nearest 10, 100, 1,000, etc without troubling about small amounts: *The car cost £9,778; that's £10,000 in round figures.* **-ness** [adv]

round (about) 1 [adv] in the neighbourhood: *He lives somewhere round (about).* **2** [prep] (with times, places, etc) more or less; about: *They arrived round (about) 5 o'clock. It'll cost somewhere round (about) £50.*

all over 1 [adv] in every part or place: *I feel hot all over. They went/looked all over but couldn't find him.* **2** [prep] in every part of: *We looked all over the house, but couldn't find the money. The news is all over (the) town that he is coming.*

everywhere [adv] in, at, or to every place: *I can't find it though I've looked everywhere. Pink elephants follow him everywhere he goes. We must clean the house; everywhere looks so dirty! I am working as hard as I can, but I can't do everything, or be everywhere at once* (= at the same time).

everyplace [adv] *AmE* everywhere

here and there from one place to another: *He ran about here and there, looking for his friends.*

around and about in many places: *She goes around and about, buying anything she wants.*

on [prep] **1** (for objects like fingers, sticks, etc) around: *He had a gold ring on the third finger of his left hand.* **2** about: *He wrote an interesting book on photography.*

concerning about (*def* 10): *I must write to him concerning his payment for last month's work.*

regarding *fml* about (*def* 10): *Regarding his wish to help us, I must say that . . .*

with regard to *also* **as regards** *more fml* regarding: *With regard to your request for more money, the committee wishes to state that . . .*

M204 adverbs, prepositions & adjectives : in, into, at, etc

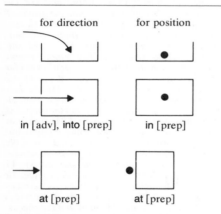

for direction   for position

in [adv], into [prep]   in [prep]

at [prep]   at [prep]

in 1 [adv] (so as to be) contained or surrounded; away from the open air, the outside, etc: *Open the bag and put the money in. Give him a cup of tea with sugar in. Let's go in there where it's warm.* **2** [adv] (so as to be) present (esp at home or under the roof of a building): *I'm afraid Mr Jones is out, but he'll be in/he'll come in again soon. Let's spend the evening in* (= at home) *watching television. I couldn't find that book in the library; it wasn't in. Someone had taken it out. 'Come in!'* (said when someone knocks at a door). *The train isn't in yet/will be in in five minutes.* **3** [adv] from a number of people, or from all directions to a central point: *Letters have been coming in/pouring in from everybody who heard the news on the radio. The crops were safely gathered in. Papers/Marks must be in by Monday.* **4** [adv] so as to be added or included where not formerly present: *The picture is almost finished; I can paint in the sky later. I very much like your play; could you write in a part for me?* **5** [adv] playing to score, ruling, etc: *Our side were in/went in to bat first. The Labour Party are in* (= elected) *at the moment.* **6** [adv] (so as to be)

fashionable: *Long skirts came in last year; they're in now.* **7** [adv] (of sea water) close to the coast; (so as to be) high: *The tide's* [⇨ L89] *coming in* (opposite = **going out**). *The tide is right in.* **8** [prep] (so as to be) contained by (something with depth, length, and height); within; inside: *She lives in this house. He keeps the money in a box. He sat in the car. They went swimming in the sea. It was wrapped in a cloth. He put the key in the lock. She was lying in bed* (compare *lying on the bed*, outside the covers). *I've got a sweet in my mouth.* (*not fml*) *He came in* (= into) *the room. Get in* (= into) *the car!* (*fig*) *I wonder what's in his mind?* **9** [prep] *infml* through in an inward direction: *He came in the door.* **10** [prep] surrounded by (an area); within and not beyond: *The cows were in the field. I saw my face in* (= framed by) *the mirror. There was a plant in the window* (= on a shelf just inside). *It was in the corner of the room* (compare *at the corner of the street*). *They live in the country. They were dancing in the streets. Everybody in the village/in New York/in India/in the world knows this. I saw it in the distance/in the sky/in the east. He was wounded in the stomach. They were walking in the forest. Please move; you're in my way.* (*fig*) *Everybody in the family/in the club knows her.* **11** [prep] surrounded by (material conditions): *in the rain; in the dark; in the sun; out in the open air* **12** [prep] attending; present at (certain sorts of place or establishment, named without 'the'): *He's in school/in prison/in church. The ship is in port/in harbour.* **13** [prep] (showing that something is included as part of): *I saw it in the newspapers. I read it in a book. There are 12 months in a year. In my opinion, he is a fool.* **14** [prep] (showing employment): *She's in business/in politics/in insurance/in the law. He took a university degree in history. He's in* (= works with, at) *plastics/building/furniture.* **15** [prep] wearing: *She was dressed in silk/in red/in a fur coat. He saw men in armour/in uniform.* **16** [prep] towards (a direction): *in this direction; in the wrong direction; in all directions at once* **17** [prep] using (a stated thing) to express oneself; with or by means of: *Write it in pencil/in ink/in French. Paint it in oils. It was printed in red. Say it in a few words/ in a loud voice. Put it in writing.* **18** [prep] (*with certain periods of time*) at some time during; at the time of: *in January; in Spring; in 1976; in the 18th century; in the (early) afternoon* (compare *on Monday afternoon*); *in the night* (compare *at night*); *in his youth; in the 1930s; in the First World War; in the past; in the middle of the summer* **19** [prep] (showing the way something is done or happens): *in public* (= publicly); *in secret* (= secretly); *in fun* **20** [prep] (*showing division and arrangement*) so as to be: *Pack them in 10s* (= 10 in each parcel)/*in rows/in groups/in the following order/in pairs. They stood in a circle. Cut it in two* (= into) *two pieces).* **21** [prep] (showing relation): *It was a slope of 1 in 3. He pays a tax of 40p in the £.* **22**

[prep] (showing quantity or number): *They came in large numbers. They arrived in (their) thousands.* **23** [prep] as to; when one considers (esp something that changes or can be compared): *She is weak in judgment/lacking in courage. This is better in every way than that. They're equal in distance. It is ten feet in length/in depth. There has been a change in society.* **24** [prep] having or so as to have (a condition):*in difficulties; in trouble; in danger; in good health; in ruins; in a hurry; in doubt; in a bad temper; in tears; to be/fall in love* **25** [prep] being a; as a; by way of: *What did you give him in return? She said nothing in reply.*

into [prep] **1** to the inside of: *They broke into the shop. He went down some steps into the garden. He's got to go into hospital. I put 10p into her hand.* **2** so as to be in: *He fell into the water. He got into a temper. She came into office* (= took on an official position). *It lasted well into this century. He's getting deeper into debt.* **3** so as to be: *He translated it into French. She joined them all into one company. He turned the prince into a rabbit. Divide it into five parts. She developed into a beautiful woman.* **4** *math* (used when dividing one number by another): *3 into 6 goes twice.* **5** *sl* keen on; interested in (a subject or belief): *He's given up photography now and he's into religion and modern music.*

home [adv] into position: *He pushed the piece of wood home* (= into its place). *She drove the nail home* (= fully into the wood) *with a hammer.*

at [prep] **1** (with something seen as a point in space): *He was at the door/at the shop/at the bus-stop/at the end of the road. He went to the door and stood at the door until I came. He lives in London, and our plane stopped at London (airport) on its way to New York. I met him at Paul's (home). I got it at the baker's (shop).* **2** (with a point in time): *at 10 o'clock; at Christmas; at the moment* **3** (with an intended aim, or object towards which a thing or action is directed): *After aiming (his gun) carefully at the bird, he missed it completely. He shot at the General (but missed).* (Compare *He shot the General (and killed him)). He threw the ball at me* (= intending to hit me). (Compare *He threw the ball to me* (= hoping that I would catch it)). *The dog bit at my leg (several times) (but missed).* (Compare *The dog bit me on the leg and I had to go to hospital). He ran at me with a knife (but never reached me).* (Compare *He ran to me and kissed me). He shouted at me (angrily).* (Compare *He shouted to me that I should be careful).* (*infml*) *I don't really play tennis very well, you know; I just play at tennis* (=for amusement). (*infml*) *I'm leaving you, dearest, because—how shall I put it?—you always seem to be talking at me rather than to me. 'Up and at them, boys!' shouted the general as we attacked.* (*fig*) *He looked at me. Who(m) did he look at?* (*fig*) *He smiled at me.* **4** (with words, actions, or ideas that are the cause of feeling or behaviour): *I was surprised/amused/pleased at* (=by) *his words. I was angry at his behaviour. I laughed at his foolishness* (and also: *I laughed at him). He smiled at my foolishness. I smiled at the thought of my future happiness.* **5** *AmE & ScotE* (with people and objects that are the cause of feeling or behaviour): *I was angry at* (= with)*John. I was pleased at* (= with) *John's present.* **6** (with the field or area about which a judgment is made): *He's good/clever/bad at organizing things. He's good/bad at games. She's getting on very well at her job.* **7** (before superlatives): *at best/at the best/at worst/at the worst/at the earliest/at the latest* **8** (used before certain nouns to express states, conditions, feelings, etc): *at work/at rest/at war/at school* **9** (with prices) for: *I bought 90 pencils at (a price or cost of) 10 cents each.* **10** (before the rate, degree, or position of something in a set or group): *at first; The temperature was at 90.* **11** (before ages): *at (the age of) 90* **12** (before speeds and rates): *at (a speed or rate of) 90 miles an hour; He left at a run.* **13** (before levels): *The water stopped rising at (a level of) 90 feet.* **14** (before distances): *at (a distance of) 90 miles* **at a/an 1** as a result of one; with or by means of one: *He reduced prices at a stroke. At a word from me she will come running.* **2** during one; in the course of one: *He ran up the stairs two at a time. They finished the drink at a sitting.* **at all 1** in any degree: *He doesn't smoke at all. He doesn't seem at all interested in my plan. If you feel at all ill come and see me without delay.* **2** ever: *Do you go there at all?* **not at all 1** (answering a question) No; Not a bit: *The place itself doesn't encourage you?—Not at all.* **2** (answering an apology) That's all right; It doesn't matter: *I'm sorry to trouble you.—Not at all.*

inside 1 [*the* R (*of*);A] the area that is in (something else); the part that is nearest to the centre, or that faces away from other people or from the open air: *Let's paint the inside of the house. This coat is fur on the inside and cloth on the outside. The inside of his left foot was painful. What are the inside measurements of the box?* **2** [*the* R] the side near the buildings when one is walking on the path beside a road: *Walk on the inside, away from the traffic.* **3** [A] (*fig*) the heart or centre of the action: *our inside man* (= someone who lets us know what's happening in a secret and/or important event); *the inside story* (= the details of something in the news esp as reported in the newspaper); *an inside job* (= theft done by somebody connected with the place, organization, etc which has been robbed) **4** [prep] on or to the inside of: *The girl was sitting inside the car. Just inside the walls of the city was a large building.* **5** [adv;Wa5;F] to or in the inside: *These chocolates have cream inside. The cream (which is) inside is very good. The children are playing inside because it's raining. He opened the box and looked inside.* **6** [adv;Wa5;F] *sl, esp BrE* in prison: *He's inside for murder. They put him inside for life.*

inside out [adv] in (or to) a form with the usual inside parts on the outside: *He put his socks on inside out.*

within 1 [prep] inside the limits of (esp time or distance); not beyond or more than: *They were within shouting distance.* (*fig*) *He kept within* (= did not break) *the law. Somebody within the organization told me.* **2** [prep] *esp old use & lit* inside (a place): *Within the walls of this house lies a secret.* **3** [adv] inside a place: '*This building to be sold. Enquire within*' (on a notice). (*lit & poet*) *A voice within* (= inside himself) *told him what to do.*

inward [Wa5;B] **1** (placed) on the inside: *Which side should be/go inward?—This is the inward side.* **2** moving towards the inside: *The inward movement from the doors crushed the people at the front of the room.* **3** of the mind or spirit: *He has an inward faith/happiness.* **-ly** [adv]: *He was outwardly happy but inwardly sad.*

inwards *also* **inward** *AmE* [adv] towards the inside: *The door slowly moved inwards.*

inner [Wa5;A] well inside; further in; inside some other thing: *The inner parts of the fruit taste better. He is a member of the club and of its special inner circle.*

inmost *also* **innermost** [Wa5;A;(F)] furthest in(side); (*fig*) most difficult to discover: *He was not allowed to visit the inmost part of the holy place. In her inmost heart she hoped he would return. She did not tell him her innermost feelings.*

interior 1 [Wa5;A] inside; indoors; farthest from the edge or outside (as of the inland areas of a country): *interior furnishings* **2** [C] *esp fml* the inside part of (something): *The interior of the building was empty. He travelled into the interior (of Africa).*

internal [Wa5;B] **1** of or in the inside, esp of the body: *The damage was internal; it was internal damage.* **2** not foreign: *internal trade* **-ly** [adv]: *The medicine is to be taken internally.*

M205 adverbs, prepositions & adjectives : out, from, etc

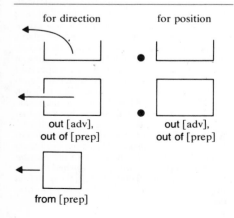

for direction	for position

out [adv], out of [prep] | out [adv], out of [prep]

from [prep]

out 1 [adv] away (from the inside); in or to the open air, the outside, etc: *Open the bag and take the money out. Pour out the tea. It's not in my pocket; it must have fallen out. He pulled my tooth out. Shut the door to keep the wind out. He put his tongue out.* **2** [adv] away (from home or from a building), so as to be absent: *I'm afraid Mr Jones is out/has gone out; he'll be back soon. Let's sleep out (in the garden). She stays out late at nights.* **3** [adv] away (from land, a town, one's own country): *He went out to Africa. They live right out in the country. The ship was a mile out at sea/was a day* (= a day's sail) *out from New York.* **4** [adv] to a number of people or in all directions: *He gave out all the tickets/spread out the cloth.* **5** [adv] completely; to the end; so as to be finished: *Clean out the room. I'm tired out. He'll be back before the month is out* (= is ended). **6** [adv] so as not to be there or not to exist: *Wash out the dirty marks. It can easily be rubbed out. You've left out an important word.* **7** [adv] in a loud voice; aloud: *Sing/Cry/Shout/Call out! Read out the names.* **8** [adv] **a** (of a player in a game such as cricket) so as to be no longer allowed to take part according to the rules: *Sussex were all out for 351. How's that?—Out!* (*fig*) *The Labour Party were then out* (= not in power; not ruling). **b** (of the ball in a game such as tennis) outside the line **9** [adv] so as to be clearly seen, shown, understood, etc: *Think/Plan it out properly. Find out the facts. The secret/The sun came out/is out. The black trees stood out against the snow. The new book came out last week.* **10** [adv] so as to be no longer fashionable: *Short skirts went out last year; they're out* (opposite **in**) *this year.* **11** [adv] (of a flower) so as to be fully open and ripe: *The roses are all coming out/are out now.* **12** [adv] *not fml* (after a superlative) ever; existing: *He's the stupidest man out.* **13** [adv] (of a fire or light) so as to be no longer lit: *Put the light out. Blow out the candle. The fire's gone out; it's been out for hours.* **14** [adv] away **a** from a surface: *I tore my stocking on a nail that was sticking out from that wooden box.* **b** from a set of things: *Pick out the best of the apples.* **15** [adv] so as to be no longer working because one is on strike [⇒ J238]: *The fishermen came out/are out in sympathy with the sailors. They will stop/stay/walk/be out (on strike).* **16** [Wa5;A] used for sending something away from one, to someone else: *Put the letter in the out tray.* **17** [Wa5;F] impossible: *I'm sorry, but that's completely out; it can't be done; it's really out of the question.* **18** [Wa5;F] (of a guess or sum, or the person responsible for it) incorrect: *He's badly out in his calculations. You would not be far out in thinking . . .* (= would not be very wrong if you thought . . .) **19** [prep] *not fml* (used for showing an outward movement) out of: *He went out the door.*

out of [prep] **1** from inside: *She walked out of the room. He is moving out of Orchard Gardens.* **2** from a state of: *He woke up out* *of a deep sleep.* **3** beyond the limits of: *The ship was now out of sight.* **4** from among: *Three out of four people choose Silver Box chocolates.* **5** in or into a state of loss or not having: *We're out of water!* **6** because of: *I came out of real interest, not just to have a good time!* **7** from or with (a material): *It's made out of wood.*

from [prep] **1** (*showing a starting point in place*) having left; beginning at (the): *The train starts from London. It goes from London northwards. It goes from London to the north. A cool wind blew from the sea. The boy was covered in mud from head to foot* (= all over). *She went from shop to shop trying to find what she wanted. These birds have come from over the sea.* **2** (*showing a starting point in rank, order, or position*) beginning with; beginning as: *Boys from the Third Class downwards usually take their examinations in the main hall of the school. He rose from office boy to director of the company in 15 years.* **3** (*showing a starting point in price or number*) starting at; at the lower limit of: *These coats are from ten pounds* (= the cheapest cost ten pounds). *There were from 60 to 80 people present.* **4** sent, given, supplied, produced, or provided by; originating in; out of: *I had a letter from her yesterday. Eggs are obtained from hens. Meat from New Zealand is sold in shops in Britain. The boy from the baker's has just called. A bright light shone from the room. He gets his good looks from his mother. Light comes from the sun. He claims to be descended from a race of kings. Where are you from?—I'm from Scotland* (= I'm Scottish). *Tell your brother from me that I want him to return my book. This music is from one of Mozart's operas.* **5** based on; using; out of: *Bread is made from flour. The plastic of which this dish was made, is made from chemicals. The shape of the car was developed from that of the horse carriage. I'm speaking from experience. She played the music from memory. All the characters in the book are drawn from real life.* **6** (*expressing the lessening or ceasing of an unwanted state*) instead of: *He needs a rest from work. This medicine may give you some relief from the pain in your head* (= it will help make the pain less). **7** (*showing the first of two states, where a complete change of condition is expressed*) out of; after being: *From being a thin weak boy, he became a healthy active soldier. Her behaviour is going from bad to worse. Translate this letter from English into French.* **8** (*expressing difference*) compared with; as being unlike: *He's different from his brother in character. I don't know anything about cars; I don't know one kind from another.* **9** (*showing a point of view*) using . . . as a position: *From the top of this hill you can see the sea. From a child's point of view, this book isn't interesting. It is a picture of a car seen from below. He was looking at me from over the top of a newspaper.* **10** (*in a state of separation*) with regard to: *His absence from class was soon noticed. It's hard for a child to be parted from its mother. He lives apart from his family.* **11** distant in regard to: *The village is five miles from the coast. It's only a few steps from here to the post office.* **12** out of; off; out of the reach of; out of the possession of: *She took the matches away from the child. Why did you move the books from the table? If you subtract 10 from 15, 5 remains/you get 5.* **13** (*in a state of protection, prevention, or separation*) with regard to: *She saved the child from the fire. A tree gave us shelter from the rain. They kept the bad news from the sick woman.* **14** because of; as a result of; through: *She suffered from heart disease. He wasn't ill; he stayed in bed from laziness. From no fault of their own, they lost all their money.* **15** judging by; considering: *From his appearance, you wouldn't think he was old. From the noise they were making, they might have been fighting.*

outside 1 [*the* R (*of*);A] the part of an object that is not inside; the part that is furthest from the centre, or that faces away towards other people or towards the open air: *Paint the outside of the house. This coat is fur on the inside and cloth on the outside. The outside of his left foot is painful.* **2** [Wa5;A] facing the outside: *He took off the outside covering/wrapping of the box. What are the outside measurements of the box?* **3** [Wa5;A] the open air: *Outside workers need warm clothes in winter.* **4** [Wa5;A] coming from or happening elsewhere: *We can't do it ourselves; we must get outside help. She only thinks of her house and babies and doesn't pay much attention to the outside world. She needs some outside interests and activities.* **5** [Wa5;A] (of a chance or possibility) slight; unlikely; distant: *She hasn't even an outside chance of winning.* **6** [Wa5;A] (of things that can be measured) greatest; most that can be allowed or accepted: *an outside figure of £100* **7** [prep] on or to the outside of: *People were waiting outside the door. There was a sign outside the cinema.* **8** [prep] beyond the limits of; not in: *He lives somewhere outside New York.* (*fig*) *It's quite outside my experience. People outside the organization don't understand it.* **9** [prep] more than (something that can be measured): *I'm afraid that's outside the figure I'd calculated on.* **10** [adv] to or on the outside: *Go and empty it outside. The children were playing outside in the street. It's quite dark outside; there's no moon. It looks big from outside.* **at the (very) outside** at the most; and not more: *I won't spend more than £100 at the outside.*

outward [Wa5;B] **1** (placed, seen, or happening) on the outside: *His outward appearance was clean.* **2** moving towards the outside: *The outward movement from inside the hall forced people into the streets.* **-ly** [adv]: *He was outwardly happy but inwardly sad.*

outwards [adv] towards the outside: *This door opens outwards.*

outer [Wa5;A] on the outside: *The outer hall*

leads to two inner halls. His outer garments (=clothes) *were dirty.*

outermost [Wa5;B] *esp lit* farthest from the inside, centre, etc: *The outermost parts of the city are the newest.*

open-air [Wa5;A] happening or being outside in the open, not under a roof: *They held an open-air meeting.*

outdoor [Wa5;A] happening outside a house, etc: *He plays a lot of outdoor games.* **outdoors** *also* **out-of-doors** [adv] outside a house, etc: *The children are playing outdoors somewhere.*

exterior 1 [Wa5;A;F *to*] outer; on or from the outside (esp of places); out of doors: *He climbed the exterior walls of the prison. The play begins with an exterior scene in a garden. The kitchen was exterior to the house.* **2** [C] *esp fml* the outside; the outer appearance or surface: *The exterior of the house was painted white. You mustn't judge people by their exteriors.*

external [Wa5;B] **1** on, of, or for the outside: *This medicine is for external use, not to drink. An external student studies outside the university. An external examination is organized by people outside one's own school.* **2** that can be seen but is not natural or real: *To all external appearances he was a quiet man, but he had a violent temper.* **3** foreign: *This newspaper doesn't pay enough attention to external affairs.* **-ly** [adv]

M206 *adverbs & adjectives, etc* : **here and not here**

here [adv] **1** [F] at, in, or to this place: *I live (right) here/two miles from here. Come here. It hurts here. He's here! I live near here. Here is where I want to stay. Come over* (=across to) *here. It's here (where) we met.* **2** *(often at the beginning of a sentence)* at this point of time: *I came to a difficulty and here I stopped.* **3** (used for introducing something or somebody, usu followed by the verb unless the subject is a pron): *Here comes John. Here he comes! Here's the book. Here is the news . . .* **4** [F] *infml (used after a noun)* being present; in this place: *This book here is the most useful. It's Professor Smith's secretary here* (=speaking on the telephone). **5** [interj] (used to call someone's attention): *Here! What are you doing?* **Here goes!** Now I'm starting this activity (esp something difficult): *I'll try to throw it to you—Ready?—Here goes!* **Here you are** Here's what you want: *Have you seen my book?—Here you are; it was on the table.* **Look here** *also* **See here** *emph* Now give attention to my warning: *See here, I can't allow this bad behaviour in my house.*

there [adv] **1** to, at, or in that place: *Do you often go there? He's hiding there, under the trees. I like living there. Go and stand over there* (compare *Come and stand over here*). **2** at that point of time: *I read to the bottom of the page and*

decided to stop there. **3** (used for drawing attention to someone or something, usu followed by the verb unless the subject is a pron): *There goes John. There he goes. There's the book. Hello there!* **4** *infml (usu used after a noun)* being present in that place: *I live in that house there.* **5** (used as the first word in a sentence or clause or as the second word in a question, as the subject of the verb, esp of *be*, *seem* and *appear*, when the real subject follows later): *There's a man at the door. Is there something/anything wrong? There's a hole in your trousers. There's been a car stolen. There's plenty to eat, isn't there? I don't want there to be any doubt about this. There's something (that) keeps making a funny noise. Is there any beer?—No, there isn't. There came a knock at the door.* **6** [interj] (used for comforting someone or for expressing victory, satisfaction, encouragement, sympathy, sadness, etc the meaning changing according to the setting (**context**) and the way it is expressed): *There! Do you feel better now? There, there; stop crying. There; I told you I was right! There; now I can have some peace. There; You've made me cry. But there! What can you expect for £5?* **get there** to succeed in reaching an aim: *You'll get there in the end if you work hard!* **There you are 1** here is what you wanted: *There you are! A nice cup of tea.* **2** I told you so: *There you are. I knew I was right.* **there and back** to a place and back again: *It's 4 hours there and back.* **there and then** *also* **then and there** at that time and place: *There and then he kissed her and asked her to marry him.* **There you go** *infml* you are doing again what you usually do: *There you go, talking about people behind their backs again.*

absent [Wa5] **1** [B *(from)*] not in or at a place: *Who is absent from the group? He was absent (from school) for two weeks. Who are the absent people?* **2** [A] not aware of what is happening: *He had an absent look on his face.* **-ly** [adv]: *He looked absently at the piece of paper.* **absence 1** [U *(from)*] the fact or state of not being in or at a place: *His absence from the meeting surprised us.* **2** [U] failure to be in or at a place when one should be: *Your absence was noticed.* **3** [C *(from)*] occasion or result of being absent: *His absences from work caused trouble. There were 140 absences from school today.* **4** [U] lack of something: *Cold is the absence of heat.* **absentee** [C *(from)*] a person who is absent esp from work: *How many absentees today?*

present [Wa5;B] in or at a place, esp that which is being spoken or written about: *How many of the group are present to-day? John Smith!—Present! (fml) Is she here?—No; she is not in the present group.* **presence** [U] the fact or state of being in or at a place: *His presence at the meeting was unusual.* **in one's presence** when one is there: *Don't talk about it in her presence; she'll be very angry.* **presence of mind** ability to think quickly: *Thanks to his presence of mind, we saved all the money.*

M207 *prepositions & adverbs* : **across, through, etc**

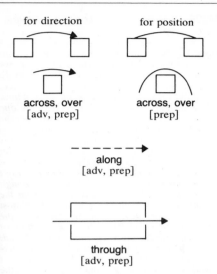

for direction　　　　for position

across, over　　　　across, over
[adv, prep]　　　　　　[prep]

along
[adv, prep]

through
[adv, prep]

across 1 [prep] from one side to the other of: *They built a bridge across the river.* **2** [adv; prep] to or on the opposite side (of): *Can you jump across? We swam across the river. We walked across the bridge. Now that we are across the bridge, we can sit down and rest. They live just across the road (from us).* **3** [prep] so as to cross: *The two lines cut across each other.*

over 1 [adv] across a distance or open space, either towards or away from the speaker: *They went over to the US. He's seen me! Look! He's coming over. He went over and collected the pictures. We must ask some people over for coffee.* **2** [adv] from one (person or group) to another: *Hand over that gun! He signed over the money to his son. He went over to (joined) the enemy.* **3** [adv] so as to be in each other's positions or be exchanged: *Let's change these two pictures over and hang this one up there.* **4** [adv] right through; completely from beginning to end: *He read/looked over the poems. You'd better think/talk it over carefully.* **5** [adv] (showing that something is repeated): *She's asked me several times over to buy her a fur coat.* **6** [adv] *AmE* again: *My sums were wrong and I had to do them over.* **7** [adv] remaining; not used when part has been taken: *Was there any money over? Leave some bread over for tomorrow. 3 into 7 goes twice and one over.* **8** [adv] so that another side is shown: *Turn the page over. The dogs were rolling over (and over) on the grass. 'Roll me over on my left side because my right side hurts me so' (song).* **9** [adv] up, out, and downwards across an edge: *The milk's boiling over! The gate's locked—Let's climb over.—Are you over yet?*

10 [adv] downwards to the side, from an upright position: *The big dog knocked the child over. He pushed me and I fell over.* **11** [adv] *esp AmE* during or beyond a certain period: *Don't leave now; Why not stay over till Monday?* **12** [adv] (*before an adjective or adverb*) too; more than is good: *Don't be over anxious about it. I'm not over keen on it. He didn't|do it over well* (= he did it badly). **13** [adv] so as to be covered and not seen: *Let's paint it over in green. Cover her over with a sheet.* **14** [prep] (so as to be) directly above; higher than, but not touching: *The lamp hung over/above the table* (compare *The lamp stood on the table*). *The doctor leaned over the body.* **15** [prep] (so as to be) completely or partly covering; resting on top of: *He spread his coat over the sleeping child. She kept her hand over the top of the bottle.* **16** [prep] to the other side of, esp by going up and then down again: *to jump over the wall/the ditch* (compare *across the ditch*, but not *across the wall*); *If we can't get over the mountain we must go round it.* **17** [prep] from side to side of: *There was a bridge over/across the river. The ball rolled over/across the grass. I read it over his shoulder. The car ran over a dog and killed it.* **18** [prep] on the far side of: *They live (just) over the street.* (*fig*) *We're over (past) the worst of our troubles now.* **19** [prep] down across the edge of: *He fell over a log/over the cliff.* **20** [prep] in or through many or all parts of: *They travelled (all) over Europe. The disease is spreading over the whole area. She poured water all over me.* **21** [prep] (showing command or control): *He ruled over a large kingdom. We have control over prices. The State has taken over the firm.* **22** [prep] higher in rank than; commanding: *I don't want anyone over me telling me what to do.* **23** [prep] more than (something that can be measured): *The temperature was over 30 degrees. He bought over 30 books and spent just over £50.* **24** [prep] during; in the course of (an event or period): *It was done over the last two years. They talked over lunch.* **25** [prep] till the end of; throughout (an event or period): *Are you staying in London over Christmas?* **26** [prep] (heard or said) by means of or using: *I heard it over the radio. I don't want to say it over the telephone.* **27** [prep] in connection with; on the subject of: *He has difficulties over his tax.* **28** [Wa5;F (*with*)] (of an event or period of time) finished; ended: *Let's do it now and get it over (with). That part of his job is over. It's all over with us now* (= we are ruined; we have nothing to hope for). **(all) over again** once more: *My sums were wrong and I had to do them all over again.* **and/or (a bit/a little) over** (of things that can be measured) and /or more; and /or upwards: *children of 14 and over (years); It cost £100 or a bit over.* **Over!** *also* **Over to you!** (*in radio signalling*) You speak now! **over and over (again)** repeatedly; again and again: *She's asked me over and over (again) to bring her a fur coat.* **over here** on or to this side: *Let's sit* *over here by this window.* **over there** on or to that side: *Let's sit over there by that window.* **over and above** as well as; besides: *He paid for the meal over and above the cost of the taxi.*

along 1 [prep] in the direction of the length of; towards the end of: *We walked along the road.* **2** [prep] in a line next to the length of: *Trees grew along the road. Bring it along here* (= along in this direction). **3** [adv] forward; on: *He asked us to move along.* **4** [adv (*with*)] with others or oneself: *I'll go along with you. You come along with me. Is he coming along too? I took my sister along (to the meeting).* **5** [adv] here or there; over; across: *I'll be along soon. Come along and visit us next week.* **all along** all the time: *I knew the truth all along.*

through 1 [prep] from one end or side to another, esp inside (something): *They made a hole through the wall. The main road passes through the town.* **2** [adv] from one end or side to another, esp inside something: *He opened the doors and went through to the hall. Please go through; he is waiting to see you.* **3** [Wa5;A;adv] going from one end or side to another, esp inside something: *This is the through train to London; it doesn't stop anywhere but goes straight through.* **4** [adv] (*fig*) not *fml* finished: *Are you through with your work now? I'm through with him; I never want to see him again!* **5** [adv; prep] completely; from beginning to end: *He read through the book/read the book through (from cover to cover). Please look through this work and see if it is properly done.* **6** [prep] by means of; from: *We heard about it through some friends.* **7** [prep] because of: *He became ill through being out all night in the rain.*

M208 *prepositions & adverbs* : **against**

against 1 [prep] so as to touch: *Put the boxes over there, against the wall.* **2** [prep] as a contrast [⇒ N192] with: *It is difficult to see anything against this bright light. The trees were black against the sky.* **3** forcefully towards, onto, etc: *The rain was beating against the windows. He hit his head against the wall.* **4** [prep; adv] in opposition (to): *He fought against them/against evil. She spoke against the new law. What he did was against the law and they sent him to prison. If I do this, it will be against my will* (= I won't want to do it). *In the voting there were ten for and three against. They are against war.* **5** [prep] to protect one from: *The doctor gave him an injection* [⇒ B174] *against the disease. Wear a warm coat against the cold.*

as against [prep] when compared with: *This job will give you £8,000 a year as against £6,000 in the other one; you must accept it!*

up against [prep] opposing; faced with: *In this fight he is up against one of the most dangerous enemies he has ever met.*

with [prep] against: *Stop fighting with him! He* *had a race with me and I won. We must be able to compete with foreign companies.*

M209 *adverbs, prepositions, adjectives, etc* : **near**

near 1 [adv; prep; Wa1;B (*to*)] (the word *to* may be used with *nearer* and *nearest*, but not usu with *near*) not being a long way from (a place, thing, etc) in distance, time, degree, quality, etc: *He's coming in the near future. Pick an apple from the nearest tree, the one nearest (to) the house. The building is near the station. How near is the station to here* (= from here)? *His opinion is very near my own; it's nearer (to) my own than any other. We had an attendance near 15,000 at the cricket match. It was a time (somewhere) near midnight. Don't go too near the edge of the cliff; just near enough to see over it. Was your answer very near the right one? She came near to tears* (= almost cried). *Call me again nearer (to) the time of the meeting.* **2** [Wa1;B] in a close relation or association: *All my near relatives live abroad.*

near- [*comb form*] **1** almost: *a near-perfect performance; music near-perfectly performed; a near-white colour* **2** something almost the stated thing: *a near-war* (= violence almost as bad as a war) **3** [Wa1;A] (of one of two things) **a** esp *BrE* left-hand: *Was it the nearside front wheel of the car or the offside wheel?* **b** closer: *Can we fish from the near bank of the river or must we cross over to the far bank?*

nearly [adv] just about but not: *Last year she was very ill and nearly died. It nearly happened.*

almost [adv] nearly: *Last year she was very ill and almost died. It almost happened.*

close [adv; Wa1;B (*together, to*)] near: *Stay close (together). They have a house close to the river. He is very close to the truth now.*

USAGE *near* and *close* are almost the same in meaning, but there are certain phrases in which each of these words is used before a particular noun and cannot be changed for the other. Notice *the near future; the near distance* (not **close**); *a close friend.*

alongside 1 [adv] close to and in line with the edge (of anything); along the side: *We brought our boat alongside.* **2** *also* **alongside of** [prep] side by side with: *We brought our boat alongside (of) the harbour wall.*

together [adv] **1** in or into one group, body, or place: *The people gathered together. John and Jean are living together but they have no plans to get married.* **2** in or into union: *Tie the ends together. Add these numbers together. Multiply 5 and 17 together. It's torn, but I'll stick it together again with paste.* **3** in or into relationship with one another: *We hope to bring the two enemies close enough together to make peace.* **4** at the same time: *We all shouted together. Why do all my troubles always come together?* **5** without interruption: *It rained for four days together.* **6** in agreement; combined:

We should all stand together to defend what we believe to be right. Together we carried the piano down the stairs. **7** considered as a whole; collectively: *He did more to win the war than the rest of us (put) together.* **8** into or in a condition of unity: *The argument does not hold together well.* **close/near together** [adv] near each other **together with** as well as; along with; in addition to: *He sent her some roses, together with a nice letter.*

with [prep] **1** in the presence of; beside; near, among, or including: *She is staying with a friend/living with her children. A man walked down the road with his dog. He acted with a Shakespeare company. The meal cost three pounds with wine. Mix the flour with some milk.* **2** having, possessing, or showing: *It was a book with a green cover/a child with a dirty face. The man with the big dog came in. She came in with a smile. They fought with courage.* **3** by means of: *He fought with a sword. She ate it with a spoon. I succeeded, with his advice. Cut it with the scissors.* **4** having as material or contents: *I filled it with sugar. It was covered with dirt. The cake was made with egg. It was a room crowded with people.* **5** in support of; in favour of: *He voted with the government. The whole country is with the prime minister. I agree with every word. You're either with me or against me.* **6** against: *Stop fighting with your brother! Have a race with me.* **7** in the same direction as: *He sailed with the wind. We were carried along with the crowd.* **8** at the same time (and rate) as: *With the dark nights comes the bad weather. Her hair became grey with the passing of the years. His earnings increased with his power.* **9** by comparison to: *to compare chalk with cheese; to match a coat with a skirt* **10** (separate) from: *She doesn't like to part with money. He broke with the past/his family.* **11** in spite of: *With all his advantages, he is still not a success. With the best will (= intention) in the world, I can't make her like me.* **12 a** because of: *She was singing with joy. The grass was wet with rain. His eyes were bright with excitement.* **b** because of having: *With three children we can't afford new furniture. With winter coming on, it's time to buy warm clothes. I can't go out with all these dishes to wash.* **13** in the care of: *Your secret is safe with me. Leave your little dog with me while you go on holiday. Can you trust him with a secret?* **14** concerning; in the case of: *What's wrong/the matter with you? Be careful with that glass. Be gentle with the baby. There's a difficulty with this new timetable.* **15** (joined) to: *Mix this with that.*

without [prep] *esp emph* not having; not with: *She came here without my knowledge* (= I didn't know that she had come here). *Don't go without us. He drove the car without taking proper care. She went out in the rain without a coat on.*

next to 1 [prep] *also old use* **next** in the closest place to: *the table next (to) the door; I don't like wool next to my skin. We live in the next-to-the-*

last house in the road. **2** [prep] closest in order, degree, etc to: *Next to riding, I like swimming best.* **3** [prep] *infml* in a position to know (about); in a close relation to: *I could never get next to him to find out what he was really like.* **4** [adv] *not fml* almost: *The speech said next to nothing. It's next to impossible to drive in this traffic.*

next 1 [Wa5;B;det] nearest; immediately following: *He doesn't live in this street but in the next one. Who is next? She will be the next (person) to go. He came one day and left the next. He is going there next week.* **2** [adv] after this or that: *What did she do next? When we next met him/met him next, he had lost all his money.*

next door [adv F (*to*)] in the next house: *She's the girl next door; she lives next door to me.* **next-door** [Wa5;A] *Our next-door neighbours are very friendly.*

beside [prep] very near or right next to: *Sit here beside me. Put the box there, beside the table.*

adjacent [Wa5;B (*to*)] (usu of land, rooms, etc but not people or numbers) *fml* next to (something) in position: *He has the adjacent room to mine/the room adjacent to mine.*

side by side the one beside the other: *They sat side by side.*

neighbouring *BrE*, **-bor-** *AmE* [Wa5;A] near one another: *We live in neighbouring houses. She lives in the neighbouring town, 15 or 16 kilometres away.*

surrounding [Wa5;A] around and nearby: *He lives somewhere in the surrounding area.*

handy [Wa1;B (*for*)] *not fml* nearby; ready for use: *Is there a telephone handy? This house is handier for the shops than that one.*

approximate [B] nearly correct but not exact: *The approximate number of boys in the school is 300. Please remember that the figure of 300 is only approximate.* **-ly** [adv] **approximate** [T1;L1] to bring or come near to: *Could you approximate the cost? The cost would approximate £5 million.* **approximate to** [v prep L1] to come near: *What was said approximated to the facts but still left a great deal out.* **approximation 1** [C (*to*, *of*)] a result, calculation, description, drawing, etc, that is not exact but is good enough: *300 is only an approximation of the right number.* **2** [U (*to*, *of*)] the state of being or getting near, as to a position, quality, or number

verge on *also* **verge upon** [v prep T1] to be close to: *Her plan verges on madness; we must not follow it.*

M210 adverbs & adjectives, etc : far

far 1 [adv; B (*from*); *from* U] (being) a long way (from a place, thing, etc) in distance, time, degree, quality, etc: *He didn't go far (from the house). Don't go too far. Is the shop far from here?—No; not far; it's quite near. He walked farther/further than we did, but she walked* *farthest/furthest of all. How much farther/ further is it to your house? How far is it to Edinburgh?—It's 150 kilometres farther/from here. He stood in the far corner of the room. They waited on the farther side of the hill. He went far further than he should have gone. He went far beyond what he should have done. She has far more money than you think. Have you come from far?* **2** [adv H] very much: *This book is far better/far more interesting than that one. She would far rather/far more interesting than that one. She would far rather/sooner go there than stay here.* (= She would much prefer going there to staying here). **as far as** to the degree that: *As far as I know, he is coming next week.* **far and away** *infml* very much: *This is far and away the best book I have read for a long time.* **far be it from me** *emph & pomp* I do not wish: *Far be it from me to tell you what to do with your money!* **by far** by a large amount: *This is by far the best news for a long time!* **a far cry from** very unlike: *His latest ideas are a far cry from what he used to say.* **few and far between** rare :'*Really good teachers are few and far between,' she said.* **so far so good** *infml* everything is good at the moment but will not necessarily stay that way: *Is the plan working?—So far so good.* **far and near** everywhere: *They travelled far and near.* **far and wide** in many far places: *He has travelled far and wide.*

far away *also* **far off** [adv; *from* U] a long way away: *Don't go too far away; I may need you. She comes from far away/far off.*

faraway *also* **far-off** [Wa5;A] distant, remote: *He heard the faraway sound of voices.* (*fig*) *She had a happy faraway look in her eyes; she was thinking of him.* (*poet*) *It happened in a far-off land.*

afar [adv] *lit, poet & old use* far away: *He heard the sound of voices coming from afar.*

distant *esp fml & tech* **1** [B; E] separate in space or time; far off/away: *This is a story of distant lands. He heard the distant sound of a bell. It may happen at some far distant time.* **2** [A] coming from or going to a distance: *It was a distant journey.* **3** [A] (of people) not closely related: *Those two boys don't look alike, but they are distant relations.* **-ly** [adv]: *They are distantly related.* **4** [B] not very close: *There is a distant relationship between those two ideas.* **5** [B] (*fig*) showing social distance or lack of personal warmth: *He is always very distant in manner towards me.* **-ly** [adv]: *He behaved very distantly towards her.* **distance** [U; C] the condition of being distant; the space between two places, things, times, qualities, etc: *Is it far?—No; it's no distance at all. What's the distance from Edinburgh to London? The distances between the towns are 20 and 25 kilometres.* (*fig*) *Socially he always keeps his distance from other people. Those mountains don't seem very high from a distance, but when you get near they are very big. I can see them in the distance* (=a long way away/off). *The distance in time between ancient Rome and modern New York is very great.*

remote [Wa2;B] **1** distant in space or time: *In the remote future it may happen.* **2** quiet and lonely; far from a city: *She lives in a remote village.* **3** widely separated (from); not close: *The connection between these two ideas is very remote. It is something remote from his experience.* **4** (of behaviour) not showing interest in others: *Her manner was polite but remote.* **5** (of a chance or possibility, esp with *-est*) slight: *I haven't the remotest idea what you mean.* **-ly** [adv] **-ness** [U]

extreme 1 [A] at the farthest point; at the very beginning or very end: *He died of extreme old age. They live in the extreme south of the country.* **2** [B] the greatest possible: *He died of extreme cold. The extreme cold killed him. The cold was extreme.* **3** [B] *Often derog* (of ideas, opinions, etc and those who hold them) going beyond the usual limits: *He has some very extreme political opinions. His ideas are pretty extreme.* **4** [C] something extreme, esp one of two opposite things: *That country has extremes of heat in summer and cold in winter. He used to be very fat; now he has gone to the other extreme and is very thin.* **extremely** [adv] very much: *I'm extremely pleased to see you.*

extremity [C *usu pl*] **1** farthest point: *The feet, hands and ears are the extremities of the body.* **2** cruel or violent punishments or ways of forcing someone to obey. *The people were subjected to the extremities of the dictatorship.*

M211 *prepositions & adverbs* : **between and among**

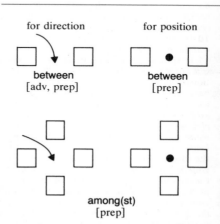

for direction   for position

between   between
[adv, prep]   [prep]

among(st)
[prep]

between 1 [prep] (of position or time): *He was standing between Mr A and Mr B. It happened between five and six o'clock. The house is between five and ten miles away.* **2** [prep] (showing connection): *It's a railway between two cities. There is a regular air service between the two cities. The marriage was between Mr A and Miss B. There's been a lot between us over the years, my dear.* **3** [prep] (showing division):

Divide it between the two children. You have a choice between two possibilities. What is the difference between this and that? There was a quarrel between the two families. **4** [prep] (showing the result of the shared activity of several people): *They all did the job between them. Between them they collected £50.* **5** [prep] taking together the total effect of (a set of things): *Between cooking, cleaning, washing, sewing, and writing, she was very busy.* **6** [adv] in or into a space or period of time that is between: *There's only the tree and the house; I can see nothing between.* **few and far between** *infml* rare; not often found: *Books as good as that are few and far between.*

among *also lit & fml* **amongst** [prep] **1** in the middle of; surrounded by: *I live among the mountains. I was among the crowd.* **2** in association with: *The minister was among those who spoke at the meeting.* **3** in the class of; one of: *This mountain is among the highest in the world. This is among the few books I really like.* **4** in shares to each of (usu three or more persons, etc): *Divide this cake among them.* **5** through the common action of: *They discussed the matter among themselves* (= together). *They made a lot of money among themselves.* USAGE **1** *between* (*def* **1**) must be followed by two things. It is right to say *between the two houses* or *between this house and the next.* It is common, but nonstandard, to say *between each house.* **2** some books say that *between* (*def* 1) should be followed by not more than two things and *among* by 3 or more: *Divide it between the two/among the three children.* But when we speak of definite position we always use between: *Ecuador lies between Colombia, Peru and the Pacific Ocean.*

He slept away the day. He slept the day away. **9** [Wa5;B] (of a sports match) played at the home place, sports field, etc of one's opponent: *It's an away match, not a home match.*

apart 1 [adv E; F] separate; away; distant: *The two buildings are three miles apart. We planted the trees wide apart. The house stands apart from the village. He kept himself apart from the other children.* **2** [adv] in or into pieces: *The pages of the book have come apart.* **3** [adv] independently; separately: *If I see the two boys apart I don't know which is which; I can't tell them apart/from each other/the one from the other.* **4** [adv] to or at one side, esp for a certain purpose: *He took me apart to have a private talk with me. He kept his best suit apart and wore it only on special occasions.* **5** [adv] not considering; aside: *A few little things apart, I am very pleased with the result. Joking apart, we really do need a bar.* **6** [Wa5;F] separate; unconnected; independent: *He is a man apart from all others.* **7** [F] holding very different opinions; divided: *They look alike but in ideas they are very far apart,* (*fig*) *worlds apart.* **apart from** [prep] without considering; except for; aside from: *Apart from him, everyone is happy.*

detached [B] **1** separate; not connected **2** (*fig*) (of a person or an opinion) not influenced by other people's opinions; not showing much personal feeling: *It is hard to take a truly detached look at one's own son.* **detachment** [U] **1** a condition of being detached **2** (*fig*) a condition of not showing any feelings or of not being influenced by others: *mental detachment*

asunder [adv] *esp lit* **1** apart from each other in position: *The war forced the parents and children asunder.* **2** into pieces: *The boat was torn asunder by the storm.*

M212 *adverbs & adjectives* : **away and apart**

away 1 [adv (*from*)] from this or that place; to or at another place: *Go away! He swam away from the ship. I hope to get away early in the morning. Turn your eyes away. I shall be away three weeks. He went away across the mountains. He is away, is he?—Yes; he's in Greece.* **2** [adv] in another place, esp in a place that is enclosed or locked: *I have put the gun away.* **3** [adv] at a distance: *Stand away from that hole. He lives three miles away. He wasn't very far away when it happened.* **4** [adv] so as to remove or separate: *He cut away a dead branch. He cut a diseased part away.* **5** [adv] to an end; to nothing: *The sounds died away. The water boiled away.* **6** [adv] out of one's possession, control, use, etc: *He gave everything away. He signed away his rights/he signed his rights away.* **7** [adv (*at*)] often *apprec* all the time; continuously: *He worked away (all the time). He cut away at the thick branch. She sings away happily for hours.* **8** [adv] so as to pass (a period of time) completely as stated:

M213 *adverbs, etc* : **back and aside**

back [adv]

back 1 [adv] towards or at the back [⇨ M202]: *She tied her hair back. Sit well back or you won't be able to fasten your seat belt.* **2** [adv] away from the front, the speaker, etc: *Stand back! The house stood a little way back from the road.* **3** [adv] where or how (one or something) was before: *Put the book back (on the shelf) when you've finished it. You can borrow my car but please bring it (straight) back. Back in Nigeria (where I was born), we used to play a lot of tennis. She came back to fetch the basket which she'd left behind. The car broke down and we had to walk all the way back (home). Let me know when you're back/when you get back.* (*fig*) *Nobody wants him back as President.* **4** [adv] *not fml* ago; in the past: *We met him three years back. We met right back in the* *days when we were students.* **5** [adv] in return or reply: *Telephone me back when you know the answer. If you don't use the ticket, perhaps you'd get the money back. If the dog bites you, will you bite it back?* **6** [adv] towards the beginning (esp of a book): *You will find it six pages further back.* **7** [adv] so as to be delayed or made slower: *The child's bad health has kept/held him back at school.* **8** [adv] (of a clock) so as to show an earlier time: *He put the clock back an hour.* **9** [Wa5;A] (of money) owed from an earlier time: *He is owed £100 back pay.* **10** [Wa5;A] at the back: *He left by the back door/back yard. She works in the back room.*

backwards [adv] in the opposite from the usual way, esp of moving: *He slowly began to walk backwards. The car went backwards into the wall. You're doing the work backwards; you should start at the other end!*

back to front (esp of clothes) with the back part at the front: *He had his shirt on back to front.*

in reverse (esp of vehicles) backwards: *The car was moving in reverse.*

aside 1 [adv] to or towards the side: *She stepped aside to let him pass.* (*fig*) *The old leader stepped aside to allow an able young woman to be elected.* **2** [adv] out of the way; away (esp for a limited time): *He put his work aside. If you will keep that book aside for a few minutes I will go and get the money for it. He put aside his work.* **3** [adv] away from one's thoughts; not being considered: *Joking aside, we really must do something.* **4** [C] words spoken by an actor to those watching the play, and not intended to be heard by the other characters **5** [C] a remark in a low voice not intended to be heard by everyone present **6** [C] a remark or story told during a speech but which has no part in the speech: *Most of his speech was uninteresting, but luckily he made many amusing asides.*

M214 *prepositions & adverbs* : **to and towards**

to 1 [prep] in a direction towards: *He was on the road to London. She stood up and walked to the window. He pointed to the moon. She threw the ball to me* (= for me to catch. Compare *She threw the stone at me* = to hurt me). **2** [prep] in the direction of; so as to have reached: *We're hoping to go to Greece for our holidays this year. Do you walk to work or go by bus? The criminal was sent to prison for five years.* **3** [prep] as far as: *The water came to our necks. The temperature rose to 40 degrees.* **4** [prep] towards; reaching the state of: *The politician lost many friends in rising to power. He usually works hard but has a tendency to laziness. She sang the baby to sleep.* **5** [prep] as far as the state of: *The man was kicked to death by the wild horse. The coat was torn to pieces. Wait until the lights change to green.* **6** [prep] in

a touching position with: *The two lovers danced cheek to cheek. The paper stuck firmly to the wall.* **7** [prep] facing or in front of: *They stood face to face/back to back. I was sitting with my back to the engine.* **8** [prep] as far as; until and including: *Count (from 10) to 20. I read the book from beginning to end. They stayed from Friday night to/till Sunday morning. It's ten miles (from there) to London. I'm wet to the skin. They were killed to a man/to the last man* (= they were all killed). **9** [prep] for the attention or possession of: *Have you told all your news to him? Did you give your information to the police? I want a present to give to my wife. This is a letter to Mary from George.* **10** [prep] for; of: *Have you got the key to this lock? It's a job as secretary to a doctor.* **11** [prep] in relation with; in comparison with: *I know he's successful but he's nothing to what he could have been. The result of the match was 5 points to 3. The railway line runs parallel to the road. This wine is second to none* (= is the best). **12** [prep] along with: *We sang the song to a new tune today.* **13** [prep] forming; making up; being in degree or amount: *There are 100 pence to every pound. You can get goods equal to £50; I'll pay.* **14** [prep] in accordance with: *Your dress isn't really to my liking. They make suits to order. You will hear of something to your advantage.* **15** [prep] (with words about addition) as well as; and: *Add 2 to 4. In addition to John, there are the girls.* **16** [prep] in honour of: *Let's drink to the health of our respected foreign guests. They built a temple to their god.* **17** [prep] with the aim or purpose of: *A passing motorist came to our help.* **18** [prep] for the possession of: *The prince has no right to the title. There are three claimants to the crown.* **19** [prep] in the position of: *Scotland is to the north of England.* **20** [prep] per: *This car does 30 miles to the gallon.* **21** [prep] (of time) before: *It's five (minutes) to four.—No; it's only ten to four. How long is it to/till dinner?* **22** [prep] (*with* **know** *in pass*) by: *He is well known to the police. Is she known to you?* **23** [prep] so as to cause (esp a feeling): *He broke it, (greatly) to my annoyance. To my great surprise, we won!* **24** [prep] as far as concerns: *To me this seemed silly. It looked to him like a rabbit. The book was of great interest to many people. They're not married, to my knowledge.* **25** [prep] in connection with: *What's your answer to that? In obedience to your wishes.... She's always kind to animals. This'll do a lot of good to your chest.* **26** [prep] (*between two numbers*) **a** between (a number) and (a number): *It lay in ten to twelve feet of water. She's 40 to 45.* **b** compared with: *It's 100 to 1 he'll lose* (= 100 times as likely). **27** [adv] into consciousness: *John didn't come to for half an hour after he'd fallen and hit his head. I always take a long time coming to in the morning. They brought her to by pouring cold water on her.* **28** [adv] into a shut position: *The wind blew the door to.* **29** (used before a verb to show it is the infinitive, but not before *can, could, may, might, will, would, shall, should, must, ought to*; sometimes left out when the verb is understood. Note the following patterns: **a** (after verbs): [I3] *He lived to be 90.* [T3] *It wants to be fed.* [V3] (usu with reported commands) *He told them to shoot* (= He said 'Shoot!'). *He told them (not) to.* [L (*to be*) 1] *He seems (to be) a fool.* [L (*to be*) 7] *It proved (to be) possible.* [X (*to be*) 1] *They supposed her (to be) their daughter.* [X (*to be*) 7] *They wished him (to be) dead.* **b** (after *how, where, who, whom, whose, which, when, what,* or *whether*): [D6b] *Tell me where to go.* [T6b] *He knows what to do. I don't know how to. She wondered whether or not to/whether to or not.* **c** (after nouns): [C3] *They made an attempt to land.* [P3] *She has the qualifications to drive.* [U3] *She had some reason to leave. He got the urge to clear up.* **d** (after adjectives): [B3] *It's an easy thing to do.* [F3] *I'm glad/sorry/happy to say . . .* **e** (when speaking about the verb, as in grammar): *'To find' takes a direct object. To wear boots would be safest. It would be safest (for you) to wear boots. What they really ought to have done was to refuse.* **f** (when speaking of purpose) in order to: *They left early to catch the train. I want some scissors to cut my nails (with).* **g** (in the patterns *used, ought, going* + *to*): *I was going to make a very stupid remark.* **h** (in the pattern *too X to Y, X enough to Y*): *He's too fat to dance. It's cold enough to snow.* **i** (in the pattern *to X* = *if I can*): *To be honest, I don't know anything about it. To put it another way, do you like him? To begin with, let's . . .* **j** (in phrs like **in order to, so as to**) **k** (in the pattern *There is* + noun + *to*): *There's lots to do. There were plenty of things to eat. There's Bob to consider* (= he must be considered).

towards *also esp old use* **toward** [prep] **1** in the direction of: *The road runs towards the south. The house faces towards the hills.* (*fig*) *I can't feel angry towards him; I like him too much.* **2** (*fig*) in order to get: *They are working towards peace. They are moving towards an agreement.*

forward 1 [adv] to the front: *He moved forward to meet them. 'Forward!' cried the general, and led his men in the attack.* **2** [Wa5;A] at the front: *The general went to see the soldiers in the forward positions.*

forth [adv] *esp old use & fml* forward; out: *They went forth to fight for their king and country. The machine sent forth loud noises.*

up [adv] to or towards esp the speaker: *He came up and spoke to us. The boy ran up and told us what happened.*

M215 *adverbs* : **from place to place**

from place to place from one place, position, etc to another: *He goes from place to place, trying to sell his goods.*

to and fro *esp lit* from one place to another,

again and again: *He went busily to and fro, trying to sell his goods.*

backwards and forwards 1 from a back or further position to a front or nearer position, again and again: *The animal kept running backwards and forwards, trying to get out.* **2** from one side to the other: *The pendulum* [⇒ L228] *of the clock moved backwards and forwards.*

back and forth *esp lit* backwards and forwards

M216 *adverbs & prepositions* : **on and upon**

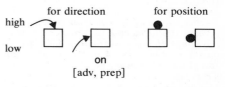

high
for direction   for position
low
on
[adv, prep]

on 1 [adv] continuously, instead of stopping: *He worked on (and on) all night.* **2** [adv] further: *If you walk on you'll come to the church.* **3** [adv] forwards: *If any letters come while you're away, shall I send them on (to you)?* **4** [adv] in or with a state of being connected or in place: *with his coat on; He had nothing* (= no clothes) *on. Keep the lid on.* **5** [adv] with the stated part forward: *The two cars crashed head on.* **6** [adv] (esp of electrical apparatus) connected to the electrical supply; lit; in use: *The light/the gas is on. Is the radio on?* (*fig*) *Her songs really turn me on.* **7** [adv] (of something that has been arranged) happening or going to happen: *Breakfast is on now. There's a new film on at the cinema, but it's coming off on Sunday. Is the party tomorrow still on? I've got nothing on tonight, so let's go out.* **8** [adv] (of an actor, dancer, etc in a theatre) actually performing: *You're on in two minutes!* **9** [prep] (so as to be) touching (a surface) **a** *also fml* **upon**: *There was something on the table/the wall. She had a ring on her finger. He jumped on/upon the horse. She wrote on the paper. They live on an island. He got a blow on the head.* **b** (*fig*): *It's all on page 23 of the book.* **10** [prep] *also fml* **upon** supported by, hanging from, or fastened to: *He jumped on one foot. The ball is on a string. The flag was on a pole. The wheels weren't on my car.* **11** [prep] *also fml* **upon** to; towards; in the direction of: *They marched on Rome. Make an attack on the enemy. She was on my right. The sun shines on us.* **12** [prep] *also fml* **upon a** very near: *The town was (right) on the river/the border.* **b** along (esp a long or flat surface): *Trees were on both sides of the street.* (*fig*) *I was on my way to college.* **13** [prep] *also fml* **upon** (before the *-ing* form of verbs) on the occasion of or directly after: *On thinking about the idea, I decided against it.* **14** [prep] *also fml* **upon** about: *It's a book on India. It was a poem* called 'On the Morning of Christmas Day'. **15** [prep] (*before certain means of travelling, esp large vehicles*) by means of or in: **a** *on foot/ horseback* **b** *also fml* **upon** *on a ship*; *on the 9 o'clock train* (compare *in a car; by ship; by train*) **16** [prep] by means of: **a** *They live on potatoes. A car runs on petrol.* **b** (*with certain machines or processes*): *I heard it on the radio. Speak on the telephone.* **c** *He cut his foot on a piece of glass.* **17** [prep] *also fml* **upon** because of; as a result of; through: *He promised on his honour to do it. Act only on your lawyer's advice.* **18** [prep] with the support of (money): *Try to live on your own income. He went round the world on the money his aunt gave him.* **19** [prep] in a state of: **a** (*before a noun or* **the**) *on fire; on sale; on holiday; on the cheap* (= cheaply); *on offer, on purpose* (compare *by accident*) **b** *also fml* **upon** (*before expressions of travelling*): *He went on a journey. I'd better be on my way now* (= I'd better be go now). **20** [prep] *also fml* **upon** as a member of: *I serve on a committee.* **21** [prep] working for; belonging to: *She's on the Times newspaper. Which side was he on in the game?* **22** [prep] *also fml* **upon** (after expressions of money or effort): *a tax on income* **23** [prep] *also fml* **upon** (*between repeated words meaning unpleasant things*) added to; after: *They suffered defeat on defeat, loss on loss.* **24** [prep] *infml* (*before personal prons*) with: *Have you got any money on you?* **25** [prep] (*often with alcoholic drinks*) with . . . paying: *Have a drink on me. Have another on me!*

USAGE *A book on rabbits* is a more scientific book than one *about rabbits*, which might be a children's story.

onwards *also esp AmE & fml* **onward** [adv] forward in space or time: *They travelled onwards. 'Onward, Christian soldiers' used to be sung often in churches.*

onto *also* **on to** [prep] to a position or point on: *He jumped onto the horse.*

M217 adverbs, prepositions, etc : **off**

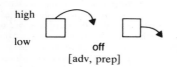

high

low

off
[adv, prep]

off 1 [adv] **a** from or no longer in a place or position; away: *He went off yesterday. Get off at the next stop, Keep off! Send him off! Off you go! 'Off'! he shouted. Goodbye, I'm off now.* **b** aside; to one side or away, esp from a main road, etc: *He turned off into a side road. You turn off here.* **2** [adv] in or into a state of being disconnected or removed; away: *The lid blew off. The handle came off. He came in with his shoes off.* **3** [adv E] to or at a (stated) distance away in time or space; away: *It was two miles*

off. *The end of the work is still several years off.* **4** [adv] so as to separate: *The soldiers blocked the area off. They cut his ear off.* **5** [adv] to, into, or resulting in a state of nonexistence, completion or discontinuance: *They killed the animals off. I'll finish the business off now.* **6** [adv] away or free from regular work: *Take some time off for lunch. He had Monday off.* **7** [adv] (of food) no longer good to eat or drink: *Milk goes off very quickly in the hot weather.* **8** [Wa5;F] (of dishes in a restaurant) no longer being served: *I'm afraid the lamb's off; can I get you anything else?* **9** [F] (of behaviour) not what one has a right to expect; rather unkind, dishonest, etc: *I thought it was a bit off, not even answering my letter!* **10** [Wa5;F] (of something that has been arranged) not going to happen after all: *I'm afraid the party's off because my wife's ill.* **11** [adv] (of the runners in a race) started: *They're off!* **12** [Wa5;F] (of electrical apparatus) not connected to the electrical supply: *Turn the light off. Is the radio off?* (*fig*) *Loud music really turns me off.* **13** [prep] not on; away from (a surface that is touched or rested on): *Get off my foot! Keep off the grass. He jumped off the horse. She fell off her bicycle.* **14** [prep] from (something that supports or holds up): *Take the curtains off their hooks. They ate off golden plates.* **15** [prep] away from, as when subtracting: *Cut a piece off the cake. Take £5 off the price.* **16** [prep] to or at a (stated) distance away from something, in space or time: *The ship was blown off (her/its) course.* (*fig*) *He went (right) off the subject.* (*fig*) *We are a long way off understanding this yet.* **17** [prep] (esp of a road) turning off (a larger one): *It's a narrow street off the High Street.* **18** [prep] in the sea near: *The ship sank (a mile) off Land's End. They were sailing off the coast of France.* **19** [prep] (of a person) **a** no longer keen on or fond of: *I've gone/I'm right off love stories for some reason. He's off his food.* **b** no longer taking (esp medicine): *Bill's off drugs now.*

M218 adverbs, prepositions, etc : below, beneath, and under

below 1 [adv] in a lower place; on a lower level: *He came up from below. He waited down below. He looked down at the valley below.* **2** [adv] *esp lit* on earth: *My words fly up; my thoughts remain below. Words without thoughts never to heaven go* (Shakespeare, *Hamlet*). **3** [adv] *old euph* in or to hell: *He had so offended me that I wished him below.* **4** [adv] on or to a lower deck (= floor) of a ship: *The captain told the sailors to go below.* **5** [adv] in, to, or at a lower rank or number **6** [adv] lower on the same page or on a following page: *See p. 85 below.* **7** [adv] under the surface of the water **8** [Wa5;E] written or mentioned lower on the same page or on a following page: *The information below was provided by my good* *friend Captain Smith-Fortescue.* **9** [prep] lower in amount, rank, etc than: *below $5; below the age of 17; below the average income; below a general in rank*

beneath *fml* **1** [adv] in or to a lower position; below: *the sky above, the earth beneath* **2** [adv] directly under; underneath: *up from beneath* **3** [prep] *esp lit* in or to a lower position; directly under or at the foot of: *everything beneath the moon; a village beneath the hills* **4** [prep] (*fig*) not suitable to the rank of; unworthy of: *Such behaviour is beneath you. That remark is beneath my notice.*

under **1** [adv] in or to a lower place: *The ship went under* (**sank**). (*fig*) *His business went under* (**failed**). **2** [prep] in or to a lower place than; below: *The box is under the table.* (*fig*) *She is struggling under difficulties.* **3** [prep] less than; *under £5; a temperature (of) under 30°/of 30° and under* **4** [prep] lower in rank than; serving: *They work under a kind leader/ under his kind leadership.* **5** [prep] beneath the surface or covering of: *You can hardly see her face under all that hair.* **6** [prep] during the rule of: *Spain under Franco* **7** [prep] during; in the state or act of: *under discussion; under renewal* **8** [prep] (of land) bearing (a crop): *Many parts of Asia are kept under rice.* **9** [prep] in the class of: (*often in the phr* **under the heading of**): *In this book, you'll find 'tiger' under 'cats'.* **10** [prep] (*fig*) having (often a mistaken idea): *You were under the mistaken impression* [⇒ G9] *that . . . He goes under the name of Smith.* **11** [prep] in; during; because of: *Under present conditions no change is possible.* **under age** too young in law, esp for drinking alcohol, entering certain public places alone, driving a car, etc. **under cover (of)** hidden or sheltered (by): *under cover of darkness* **under way** starting out; beginning to move

underneath [prep; adv] *esp fml* fully under (something): *The child was hiding underneath the table. He lifted the cloth and went underneath.*

M219 *prepositions, adverbs, etc* : **above and over**

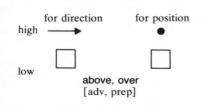

for direction   for position

high

low

above, over
[adv, prep]

above **1** [prep] higher than: *Buildings rose above our heads. We flew above the clouds.* **2** [prep] (*fig*) more than: *She values safety above excitement.* **3** [prep] (*fig*) higher in rank or power than: *The captain of a ship is above a seaman.* **4** [prep] (*fig*) higher in quality than;

not having (bad thoughts, plans, etc or doing bad acts): *He wouldn't steal; he's above that. He's above stealing.* **5** [prep] (*fig*) out of reach of (because too great, good, etc): *His behaviour is above praise.* **6** [prep] (*fig*) too good, proud, etc for: *She was above asking for money. He's not above doing what is necessary.* **7** [adv] in or to a higher place: *The clouds above began to get thicker. The office is just above. A cry from above warned me of the danger.* **8** [adv] on an earlier page or higher on the same page: *For an explanation of this point see above. Consider the facts mentioned above.* **9** [adv] more: *How many people were at the meeting?—20 or above.* **10** [adv] higher, esp in rank: *It was an army meeting for captains and above.* **11** [adv] *euph* in or to heaven: *He was called above* (= he died). **12** [Wa5;B;E; *the* GU] *fml* mentioned on an earlier page or higher on the same page: *For an explanation see the above sentence. See the sentence above. The above is the most important fact. The above are the most important facts. I met the above (person) in June of last year.* **above-mentioned** [*the* GU; Wa5;A] *fml & pomp* (the person or thing) mentioned above: *Does the above-mentioned work here?* **above all** most important of all: 'This above all—to thine own self be true' (Hamlet). **above oneself** **1** having too much trust in one's own cleverness **2** very excited **over and above** in addition; as well: *Over and above everything else, you'll need money.*

over **1** [prep] being or having been put higher than (someone or something): *The bed had a light over it. The trees over us kept the hot sun off us.* **2** [prep] lying on or covering: *Put a cloth over the food.* **3** [prep] across (esp in a higher place): *Some planes flew over us.* **4** [prep] across and down: *She fell over the edge of the cliff into the sea.* **5** [prep] on the far side of: *We are over the wall now; let's go.* (*fig*) *She is over the worst of her troubles.* **6** [prep] on or through many or all parts of: *He has been all over the world.* **7** [prep] throughout or during: *I got to know him well over the years.* **8** [prep] in command or control of: *They set him over us to make us work better. What king ruled over us at that time?* **9** [prep] above in rank: *A captain is over a sergeant* [⇒ C297]. **10** [prep] by means of: *We got the news on/over the radio.* **11** [prep] in connection with: *The two men fought over the one woman. He has difficulties over paying his taxes.* **12** [prep] more than: *The heat was over 30 degrees. He has over 200 books here. It costs over £5,000.* **13** [prep] till the end of: *Are you staying here over Christmas?* **14** [adv] up, out, and downwards across an edge: *The milk's boiling over! The gate's locked; let's climb over—are you over yet?* **15** [adv] downwards to the side, from an upright position: *The big dog knocked the child over. He pushed me and I fell over.* **16** [adv] so that another side is shown: *Turn the page over. The dogs rolled over (and over) on the grass.*

o'er [adv; prep] *lit & old use* over: *They went o'er the hill and far away.*

overhead 1 [adv] right above one/one's head; in the sky directly above: *Several planes flew overhead. I can hear people walking overhead* (= in the room above). *The electric wires are carried overhead on high structures called pylons.* **2** [Wa5;A] passing overhead; not touching the ground: *overhead wires*

overland [adv;Wa5;B] going all the way to a place by land: *They travelled overland from France to India. They took the overland route* (= way) *to India.*

M220 *prepositions, adverbs, etc* : **after and behind**

after 1 [prep] following in place or order: *He entered the room after his father. Your name comes after mine in the list.* **2** [prep] behind: *Shut the door after you.* **3** [prep] in spite of: *After all my care in packing it the clock arrived broken.* **4** [prep] in the manner or style of: *It was a painting after the great master.* **5** [prep] in accordance with: *You are a man after my own heart; we think and act alike in nearly all things.* **6** [prep] in search of (esp in order to punish); with a desire for: *The policeman ran after the thief. They are after me. They're going after gold. Money and power are what he's after. He's probably after you* (= with sexual intentions); *not that I blame him.* **7** [prep] concerning; about: *Somebody asked after you today.* **8** [prep] with the name of: *The boy was named after his uncle.* **9** [Wa5;A] in the back part, esp of a boat: *the after deck* [⇒ M157]

behind 1 [prep] at the back of; in a place, state, or time formerly held by: *We stayed (close) behind the advancing army.* (*fig*) *What do you think was the intention behind writing the play?* **2** [prep] to or at the back, or further side or part, of: *We ran behind the house. She stood behind a tree. I ran out from behind it.* **3** [prep] lower than (as in rank); below: *We were three points behind the team in first place.* **4** [prep] in support of, in favour of: *We're (right) behind you all the way!* **5** [adv] back; at the back; where (someone or something) was before: *He stayed behind. If he can't go faster leave him behind. If he can't go faster leave him behind.* **6** [adv] backwards; towards the back: *to go behind* **7** [adv (*with, in*)] (*fig*) late; slow: *I'm afraid I'm a lot behind in/with my work. She was never behind in offering advice.* **behind the times** old-fashioned; out of date: *I'm sorry to say so, my dear, but your clothes are a bit behind the times.* **behind the scenes** in secret: *We don't seem to be doing anything, but there's a lot going on behind the scenes.* **behind someone's back** *infml* unknown to the person concerned: *She says nasty things about you behind your back!*

back of *also* **in back of** [prep] *AmE infml* behind: *He hid in back of the house.* (*fig*) *What's back of his strange behaviour?*

M221 *prepositions, adverbs, etc* : **in front, before, and ahead**

in front [adv] in a position to the front (of someone, something): *I'll go in front; you come after.*

in front of [prep] in a position to the front of (someone, something): *He was standing in front of me when it happened.*

before 1 [prep] *esp lit* in front of: *She stood before him. A wide valley lay before the travellers.* (*fig*) *What is the case before the court? Your life is still before you.* **2** [prep] (*fig*) in a higher or more important position than: *He put quality before quantity.* **3** [adv] *becoming rare* in advance; ahead: *We sent the servant on before (with our bags).*

ahead [adv] well in front or before (someone or something): *Wait here; I'll go ahead and see if everything is all right.* (*fig*) *Go ahead; tell us what happened* (= Begin to tell us now).

ahead of [prep] well in front of or before: *He went on ahead of us to see if everything was all right.* (*fig*) *She is ahead of all the other girls in her class in English.* (*fig*) *He is ahead of his time in his work.*

foremost [Wa5;B] **1** being the most easily seen, etc because well in front: *Who is the foremost person in the group over there?—That's my father.* **2** (*fig*) most important; best: *She is the foremost lawyer in town.*

M222 *prepositions, adverbs, etc* : **through and via**

through, *also AmE infml* **thru 1** [prep] in at one side, end, or surface of (something) and out at the other: *He went through a door. Water flows through this pipe. The scientist looked through a telescope* [⇒ H123] *at the stars. I can't get my needle through this thick cloth. He pushed his way through the crowd to the door. We couldn't see through the mist. Is it quicker to drive round the town or straight through the middle?* **2** [prep] by way of: *The murderer must have climbed in through the open window.* **3** [prep] by means of: *I got this book through the library. It was through John that they found out.* **4** [prep] as a result of; because of: *The soldier ran away through fear. The war was lost through bad organization.* **5** [prep] from the beginning to the end of: *I don't think the old man will live through the night. I read right through the article but found it uninteresting. She nursed him through his illness.* **6** [prep] over the surface of or within the limits of: *We travelled through France and Belgium on our holidays.* **7** [prep] among or between the parts or single members of: *The monkeys swung through the trees. We walked through the flowers.* (*fig*) *I searched through my papers.* **8** [prep] having finished, or so as to finish, successfully: *Did you get through your examination?* **9** [prep] without stopping for: *He drove* *through a red light.* **10** [prep] against and in spite of (a noise): *I could hear his voice through the crashing of the bombs.* **11** [adv] in at one side, end or surface, and out at the other: *I can't get this needle through; the cloth's too thick. The soldiers wouldn't let us through.* **12** [adv *(to)*] all the way; along the whole distance: *Does this train go right through to London?* **13** [adv] in every part; thoroughly: *I got wet through in the rain.* **14** [adv] from the beginning to the end; to completion: *Have you read the letter through?* **15** [adv] to a favourable or successful state: *How did you do in your examinations?—I got through with good marks.* **16** [adv] in a state of being connected to a person or place by telephone: *Can you put me through to Mr Jones?—You're through now.* **17** [A] allowing a free or continuous journey: *This is a through road. Is this a through train or do I have to change?* **18** [F *(with)*] finished; done: *I'm not through just yet; I should be finished in an hour.* **19** [F *(with)*] finished; no longer effective: *As far as racing is concerned your illness means you're through.* **20** [F *(with)*] *infml* having no further relationship: *Jane and I are through. I'm through with men/alcohol/you!* **go through with** to do or continue (something) in spite of difficulties **see (something) through** to continue with (something) until the end **through and through** completely; in every way: *He's an Englishman through and through.*

throughout 1 [prep] in, to, through, or during every part of: *It rained throughout the night. The disease spread throughout the country. Throughout the 16th century there were wars.* **2** [adv] *(usu in end position)* right through; in every part; in, to, through or during every part: *The house is painted throughout. The prince remained loyal to the king throughout.*

via [prep] **1** travelling or sent through (a place) on the way: *We flew to Athens via Paris and Rome.* **2** *(fig)* by means of; using: *I've read this French play via an English translation. I sent a message to Mary via her sister.*

by [prep] *less common* via: *Go by London and Paris; it's quicker.*

M223 *prepositions & adverbs* : **past and beyond**

in direction and position

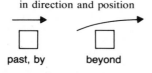

past, by   beyond

past 1 [prep] farther or at a greater distance than: *The hospital is about a mile past the school.* **2** [prep] up to and then continuing (to pass): *The boys rushed past us. I was walking past the school with my friend when it hap-*

pened. **3** [prep] *emph* beyond the possibility of: *This writer's books are past my understanding. The sick man's condition is past all hope.* **4** [adv] to and beyond a point in space or time: *Children came running past. Days went past without any news.*

beyond 1 [prep] at a (very) great distance farther than (a place); well past: *The houses lie just/well beyond the village.* *(fig)* *He is beyond help now; he is dying.* *(fig)* *Her scientific work is quite beyond me/my understanding.* **2** [adv] *less common* farther or well past a place: *This wall is as far as we can go; don't go beyond.*

by [prep; adv] *less common* past: *He drove by us in his car. A bird flew by.*

M224 *prepositions, adverbs, adjectives, etc* : **up**

up 1 [prep] to or in a higher or rising position along; to the far end of: *He climbed up the hill/the stairs/the ladder. His office is up the stairs. They live just up the road.* **2** [prep] against the direction of the current: *to go/be up (the) river; sailing up the Seine* **3** [prep] *BrE nonstandard* to; up to: *I'm going up the West End tonight.* **4** [adv] towards or into a higher position; from below to a higher place: *Can you lift that box up onto the shelf for me? The boy climbed up to a higher branch on the tree. It gets hot quickly when the sun comes up. The level of the river has gone up several feet. Up you come!* **5** [adv] above; at or in a higher position: *The plane was flying 30,000 feet up. What's going on up there?* **6** [adv] to, into, or in a sitting or standing position: *He got up from his chair. Please sit up straight. Stand up when the teacher comes in! I don't want to stand (up) for a whole hour. Up (with you), you lazy girl!* **7** [adv] from or off a surface: *Please pick that plate up (off the table).* **8** [adv] to the surface from below it: *He swam a long way under water and then came up for air. The miners crowded up out of the mine. The drowned girl was washed up on the shore.* **9** [adv] from or away from the floor, the ground, the ground floor, or the bottom: *The sleeping dog jumped up when it saw its master. She's gone up to her bedroom. Up (with you), you lazy girl!* **10** [adv] so as to be completely finished: *The money's all used up. Finish up the cake. The party ended up with a song. He won't eat up his vegetables.* **11** [adv] so as to be all in small pieces: *Cut up the meat. Tear up the newspaper.* **12** [adv] out of the stomach through the mouth, when vomiting (= being sick): *I'm afraid he's brought his dinner up*

again. **13** [adv] in or towards the north: *He's flying up to Glasgow from London. I'll be up in Scotland all the week.* **14** [adv] *BrE* to or in a city or place of importance (esp London, Oxford, or Cambridge) from or compared with one supposed to be of less importance: *We usually go (from the country) up to London for a week every Christmas. When is John going up to Oxford?* **15** [adv] **a** to or towards a point away from the speaker, esp a point at a higher level: *Will you walk up to the shop with me? I'll meet you up in the market in an hour.* **b** towards and as far as the speaker: *He came right up (to me) and asked my name.* **16** [adv] (*with verbs of fixing or fastening*) firmly; tightly; so as to be closed, covered, or joined: *She tied up the parcel. He locked up the house. Button up your coat. Nail up the door so they can't open it.* **17** [adv] (showing or making an increase or higher level of price, quantity, or quality): *I'm afraid the price of food is going up (and up). Production has gone up this year.* **18** [adv] to a state of greater activity, force, strength, power, etc: *The fire was burning up brightly. Please turn the radio up* (= louder) *a bit. Keep your spirits up!* **19** [adv] so as to be together: *Please add up/count up these figures. They collected up the fallen apples. She mixed flour and sugar up in a bowl.* **20** [adv] to or in a higher or better condition: *That family has certainly come up in the world* (= socially). **21** [adv] so as to be in a raised position: *Roll your trouser legs up. He turned up his collar to keep his neck dry.* **22** [adv] *emph* more loudly: *Speak up!* **23** [adv] (so as to be) on top: *The box was the right/ wrong way/side up.* **24** [Wa5;F] in a raised position; so as to be in place or be seen: *high up in the mountains; right up in the sky; He hung the picture up (on the wall). The flag's up* (= on the pole). *Hands up (if you know the answer)! There's a notice up (on the board) about it. The new house hasn't been up* (= built) *long.* **25** [Wa5;F] above the horizon: *The sun is up.* **26** [Wa5;F] out of bed: *It's very early in the morning and no one is up yet. She's not very ill; she'll be up in a day or two. We stay up late on Saturday nights.* **27** [Wa5;A;E] directed or going up: *He took the up train (to London).* **28** [F] at a higher level: *Sales are up. The temperature is up 10 degrees today. The wind's up a lot since last night.* **29** [Wa5;F] finished; ended: *Time's up! My holiday will be up in three days. It's all up with him now; nothing can save him from prison.* **30** [Wa5;F] *lit* prepared to fight: *The whole country was up, ready to drive out the enemy.* **31** [Wa5;F] (of a road) being repaired; with a broken surface: *'Road Up' (sign)* **32** [Wa5;F] (in horse racing) riding: *Here comes the Queen's horse, with Lester Piggott up!* **33** [Wa5;F] *not fml* accused of an offence; in court: *He was up before the judge again. She was had up for stealing.* **34** [T1] *infml* to raise; increase: *They upped the price of petrol.* **35** [Wv6;I0 (and)] *infml* (used for adding force to the account of a surprising

action) to get or jump up (and): *He upped and left. I upped and told him what I thought of him!* **up and down 1** higher and lower: *to jump up and down* **2** backwards and forwards: *to walk up and down (in a room)* **Up (with)** We want or approve of: *Up the workers!*

up to [prep] towards, esp higher or nearer to: *He climbed up to the top of the hill. She came up to me and asked me my name.*

upward [Wa5;B] going higher: *He made an upward movement with his arm. The growth of the plant was sideways rather than upward.*

upwards also esp *AmE* **upward** [adv] to a higher place or position: *They climbed upwards (to the top of the mountain). Look upwards!* **upwards of** more than: *There were upwards of 100 people at the meeting.*

upper [Wa5;A] higher, usu of two things: *He had blood on his upper lip.*

uppermost [Wa5;B] (*esp fig*) highest; receiving the most attention: *Which matter is uppermost in your mind at the moment?—My uppermost thought is to win the game.*

upside down [adv] with the usual position changed so that the top is underneath and the bottom above: *The plane turned over and flew upside down.* **upside-down** [Wa5;A]: *He was working in an almost upside-down position.*

M225 prepositions & adverbs, etc : down

high

low

down

down 1 [prep] to or in a lower or descending position: *He ran down the hill. He looked down the barrel of the gun. She came down the stairs/ down the road.* **2** [prep] to or in the direction of the current of: *to go/be down the river* **3** [prep] (fig) from an earlier point in time to (a later one): *We can't look ahead down the years and know what the future will bring.* **4** [prep] *BrE nonstandard* to; down to: *I'm just going down the shops.* **5** [adv] towards or into a lower position; from above to a lower place: *Can you lift that box down from the shelf for me? The boy climbed down to a lower branch on the tree. It gets cold quickly when the sun goes down now. The man bent down to kiss the child.* **6** [adv] to or into a sitting or lying position: *Please sit down. You may feel better if you go and lie down.* **7** [adv] to or onto a surface: *Please put that cup down (on the table).* **8** [adv] to or towards the floor, the ground, the ground floor, or the bottom: *Put your bags down anywhere. He was knocked down by a car. The telephone wires were blown down by the storm. Go down and see what the noise is. Down, dog!*

(fig) *Our team went down (to defeat), fighting hard.* **9** [adv] into the body by swallowing: *Can't you get the medicine down?* **10** [adv] in or towards the south: *He's flying down to London from Glasgow. Then he intends to take the train from London down to Brighton.* **11** [adv] *BrE* from a city or place of importance (esp London, Oxford, or Cambridge) to one supposed to be of less importance: *We usually go (from London) down to Bath for a week every summer. When is John coming down from Oxford?* **12** [adv] to or towards a point away from the speaker, esp a point at a lower level: *Will you walk down to the shop with me? I'll meet you down in the market in an hour.* **13** [adv] (*with verbs of fixing or fastening*) firmly; tightly; safely: *Have you stuck down the back of the envelope? Is the floor covering nailed down firmly?* **14** [adv] on paper; in writing: *Did you write/copy/mark/put down the telephone number?—I have it down somewhere. Put me down (on the list) for 25 pence for Anne's wedding present. I think I am down (on the list) to introduce the main speaker at the meeting.* **15** [adv] (of that part of a sum of money to be paid at once): *You can buy this car for £30 down and £5 a week for 3 years. Can you put down £4?* **16** [adv] (showing or making a decrease or lower level of price, quantity, or quality): *I'm glad to see that the price of food is going down. Production has gone down this year. Let's mark down* (= reduce) *the prices. We must hold our spending down.* **17** [adv] at or in a low position or place of less importance: *What's that down there in the corner? 'How are we going to keep them down on the farm after they've seen Paris?'* (song) **18** [adv] to the moment of catching, getting, or discovering: *The men rode/hunted the lion down. The police ran the thief down.* **19** [adv] to a state of less activity, force, strength, power, etc: *Let the fire burn down. Can you quieten the children down? Please turn the radio down* (= lower) *a bit.* **20** [adv] to or in a lower or worse condition: *The cruel rulers had kept the people down for many years. That family has certainly come down in the world* (= socially). **21** [adv] from an earlier or past time: *This old idea has appeared and reappeared in various places down through the ages. These jewels have been passed down in our family from mother to daughter for 300 years.* **22** [adv] until thicker,

thinner, different, smaller, lower, weaker, or powdery: *Boil it down. Water this drink down. The heels of his shoes had worn down. He got his report down to only 3 pages. He crushed grains of corn down into a powder to make flour.* **23** [Wa5;F] in a low position, esp lying on the ground: *The fighter is down! The telephone wires are down!* **24** [Wa5;F] below the horizon: *The sun went down.* **25** [Wa5;F] downstairs: *It's very early in the morning, and no one is down yet.* **26** [Wa5;A;E] directed or going down: *He took the down train (from London).* **27** [F] being at a lower level: *The water is down. Sales are down.* **28** [Wa5;F *with*] in bed (with an illness): *He's down with a cold.* **29** [Wa5;F] being in a state of reduced or low activity: *The fire is down.* **30** [F] (*fig*) sad; in low spirits: *I feel down today. Don't let bad news get you down.* **31** [Wa5;F] behind an opponent (by): *She was down (by) 15–40 in the 3rd game, but went on to win the match.* **32** [Wa5;F] *esp AmE infml*; finished; done: *8 down and 2 to go.* **33** [adv] into silence: *The crowd shouted the speaker down.* **34** [adv] until clean: *I washed the car down/rubbed the horse down.* **down with** I/We don't want: *Down with the minister! Down with the laws that have kept us slaves!* **down to** to and including a lower degree or position in a set: *Everyone works, from the president down to the boy who sweeps the floors. I have only read down to the middle of the page. You do from 'A' down to 'L' and I'll do from 'M' down to 'Z'.* **down to the ground** *infml* perfectly; completely: *That suits me down to the ground.* **down on** *infml* having a low opinion of or dislike for: *Don't be down on him.* **have a down on someone** *infml* to have a low opinion of, or feel dislike for, someone **hit/kick someone when he's down** *infml* to take an unfair advantage of someone **down for** entered on the list for (a race, school, etc): *The baby is already down for a famous school.*

downward [Wa5;B] towards or in a lower place or condition: *A downward movement of prices/of the head;* (fig) *the downward path to ruin*

downwards also esp *AmE* **downward** [adv] **1** from a higher to a lower place or condition **2** towards the ground or floor: *He lay on the floor face downwards.* **3** from an earlier time: *downwards through the years*

N

General and abstract terms

Being, becoming, and happening

N1 *verbs* : **being and existing**

[ALSO ⇒ A1]

be 1 [I∅] to exist, happen, etc: *'To be or not to be, that is the question.' Can this really be?* **2** [L1, 3, 4, 5a, 6a, 6b, 7, 8, 9; (I∅)] (acts as a connecting verb): *I am here now and you are there. They are alone in the house; no one else is with them. Isn't it good? Yes, it is. The food is cooked; it is cooked food. The work is now all done. What is this thing? It's a kind of gun.* **3** [I4] (forms the continuous tenses of verbs): *I'm going now. You were saying something when I stopped you. Have they been asking a lot of questions? When will you be having dinner?* **4** [I4, 8] (forms the passive voice of verbs): *Smoking is not permitted. He was told about it yesterday. The house was being painted. She has been invited to the party.*

exist [I∅] to live or be real: *Do fairies exist? The Roman Empire existed for several centuries. Even if you don't want to believe it, the fact exists. A plant cannot exist without water.*

prevail [I∅] *fml* to be common, usual: *These ideas prevail throughout the whole country.*

N2 *verbs* : **seeming and appearing to be**

seem [Wv6] **1** [I3; (*it*) L (*to be*) 1, 7, 9] to give the idea or effect of being: *She always seems (to be) sad. I seem to have caught a cold. There seems (to be) every hope that business will get better. Things are not always what they seem. You must do whatever seems right to you.* **2** [*it* I5a, b, 6a (*as if*)] *often fml* to appear to be true: *It seems (as if) there will be an election soon. So it seems. It would seem (= it seems) there is no way out of our difficulty. I agree it seems not.*

appear [Wv6] **1** *often fml* [I3; (*it*) L (*to be*) 1, 7, 9] to seem: *He appears to want to leave. You appear well this morning. He appears to be your friend but I doubt if he is. It appears (to be) a true story. It appears true that she will win* (= That she will win appears true). **2** [*it* I5a, b, 6a (*as if*)] to seem true: *It appears (that) she will win* (= It appears as if she will win). *Will she win?—So it appears.—It appears so.—So it would appear.*

purport *usu fml* **1** [T3] to claim (doubtfully); have an (intended) appearance of being: *The letters, which purported to be signed by the general, were a trick of the enemy.* **2** [T1, 5] to mean or be a probable sign of (something important): *The increasing strength of the opposition party may purport the fall of the government.*

strike 1 [T1] *not fml* to seem: *He strikes me as a difficult person* (= He seems to me to be a difficult person). **2** to come suddenly to the mind of: *It struck me that we ought to make a new plan.*

look as if *also* **look like** *usu infml* to seem to be (going to): *It looks as if he will come. He looks like coming.*

loom [L9, esp. UP] **1** to be seen, but not clearly, and therefore appearing large and dangerous: *The trees loomed (up) against the lights of the house.* **2** to become suddenly large and frightening: *The thought that he would soon have no money loomed (up) before him.*

N3 *nouns* : **states and conditions**

being [U] *often fml & lit* **1** the fact that someone or something is: *What is the real nature of being?* **2** how someone or something is, feels etc: *She felt happy to the (very) depths of her being. The news shook him to the (very) roots of his being.*

existence [U] the fact that someone or something exists: *He doesn't believe in the existence of God. Several new countries came into existence in 1918.*

state [C] the way in which something or someone exists: *Different substances exist in different natural states. The noun 'redness' describes the state of being 'red'. He is in a good state of health/mind at the moment.*

condition 1 [C (*of*)] a state of being or existence: *They got used to the condition of weightlessness in space.* **2** [U; C *usu sing*] a degree of fitness, readiness for use, health, etc: *The house is in (a) good condition outside but inside its condition is poor. The child was found in a bad condition, not having eaten for many days.*

conditions [P] the way things are: *What are conditions like in that country now? Living conditions in the house were not good.*

quality [C] something that a person, thing, idea, etc has which makes him, her, or it different, special, interesting, etc: *One quality of wood is that it burns/can burn. He has many good qualities, but his best quality is his kindness.*

consistency [C; U] quality, esp the amount by which an esp thick liquid or a soft material is the same throughout: *The thick liquid had a smooth consistency.*

characteristic [C (*of*)] a special and easily recognized quality of someone or something: *One of the main characteristics of British politics is the importance of class divisions. A useful characteristic of the cat is its ability to see in the dark.*

attribute [C] *esp fml* a particular quality, condition, sign, feeling, etc which someone or something has: *Kindness is one of his many fine attributes. Hard work is a necessary attribute in a businessman if he wishes to be a success. Speech is a human attribute not found in other living things.*

feature [C9] an important quality in or part of something: *There are several features in this plan which I don't like.*

trait [C] a special feature, esp as a natural part of something, someone's nature, etc: *One of his best traits is kindness. She inherited this trait from her mother* (= Her mother had this trait and now she has it too).

N4 *nouns* : appearances

[ALSO ⇨ N352]

appearance [U; C *usu sing*] the way something or someone appears to the eye: *Her appearance was neat and tidy. In appearance he was tall and strong.*

semblance [S9, esp *of*] *fml* an appearance; outward form or seeming likeness: *There was a pile of papers all over the desk with no semblance of order.*

look [(*the*) S] *infml* appearance: *He has the look of someone who can do these things well.*

N5 *nouns* : essence, nature, and character

essence 1 [U (*of*)] the central or most important quality of a thing, which makes it what it is; inner nature of a thing, by which it can be recognized or put into a class: *The essence of his religious teaching is love for all men. Honesty is the essence of John's character. He's the essence of honesty* (= is very honest). **2** [C; U] the most important part of a drug, food, etc, which remains after taking away the unimportant part: *essence of roses; meat essence* **in essence** *fml* in its/one's nature; essentially: *Lions are in essence lazy.* **of the essence** *fml* & *pomp* very important: *We must hurry. Time is of the essence.*

nature [U; C] **1** the qualities which make some-

one or something different from others: *What is the nature of the new chemical? It's not in her nature to do anything rude; she's polite by nature* (= she has a polite nature). **2** (*usu with* to + *verb*) one of those qualities: *It's his nature to be generous. It's only human nature to like money* (= everyone likes money).

character 1 [C; U: (*of*)] how something is; nature: *What is the exact character of the work? The whole character of the city has (been) changed.* **2** [C; U] how a person is, feels, thinks, behaves, etc: *That man has an evil character. Her character is very good; I've known her for years.* **3** [U] *apprec* good, strong qualities in a person: *She is a woman of character. What character he showed when he did that noble act!*

kind [U] *usu fml* basic nature: *They are different in size, but not in kind. A difference in degree can become a difference in kind. This work is of the same kind as that. The two things are of a kind* (= the same).

personality 1 [U; C] the whole nature or character of a particular person: *He has a weak personality. Forceful personality is needed for this job. Children have personalities that are not fully developed.* **2** [U; C] the state of existing as a particular person: *Can a man who has lost his mind and gone mad be said to have a personality?* **3** [U] unusual, strong, exciting character: *People with a great deal of personality often have admiring friends and bitter enemies.*

N6 *nouns* : kinds and types

kind 1 [C] a group the members of which all have certain qualities: *There are people of many different kinds here. It is the only one of its kind. Haven't you got any other kind/type/sort?* **2** [C *of*] a group which is part of a larger group: *There are many different kinds of people here. She doesn't want that kind of work. He had a kind of feeling that he'd never had before.* (*infml*) *I don't like that kind of a book/those kind of books.* (**be**) **someone's kind** (to be) of the same kind as someone: *How can they be lovers when she's not his kind at all?* **a kind of** *infml* an unusual kind of; weak or unclear kind of: *He had a kind of feeling that he would get a letter from his daughter today.* (*nonstandard*) *a kind of a feeling* **kind of** *infml* fairly; rather; more or less but not completely: *He is kind of clever. He kind of smiled at me.*

sort 1 [C (*of*)] kind: *It's a cheap sort of paper. That's just the sort of thing I want. People of all sorts come here* (= all sorts of people come here): *I don't like books of that sort/(infml) those sort of books.* **2** [C9 *usu sing*] *infml* person: *That was nice of her; she's not such a bad sort after all.* **a sort of** *infml* a weak, unclear, or unusual kind of: *I had a sort of feeling you'd say that.* (nonstandard) *a sort of a feeling* **of sorts/a sort** of a poor or doubtful kind: *It's a painting of sorts, but hard to describe. It was wine of a* *sort, but I couldn't drink it.* **it takes all sorts (to make a world)** any society consists of people who vary greatly in their habits, characters, opinions, etc: *He has a long beard and wears flowers in his hair!—Well, it takes all sorts.*

type *more fml* [C] **1** a particular kind, class, or group; group or class of people or things very like each other and different from those outside the group or class: *This is a new type of dictionary* (= a dictionary of a new type). *What type of plant is this? There are many types of large flesh-eating animal. It is a seedless type of orange. This type of wine is only made in France.* **2** a person or thing considered an example of such a group or class: *He is a fine type of politician. Abraham Lincoln is the type of politician who rises to power from humble origins.* **true to type** showing the nature, behaviour, or appearance expected of the group to which a person or thing belongs: *When that sort of person cheats at cards, I am not at all surprised: they're just acting true to type.*

class [C] *fml & tech* a division of people, animals or things for any purpose, but esp according to behaviour or rank: *There is a class of people who think like that. There are various classes of fish. Nouns and verbs are classes of words.* [⇒ C150, 1]

form [C (*of*)] a kind or type of thing, idea, etc, esp according to shape or plan: *There are many forms of life on earth. What form of help do you need?–Money?*

nature [S] *fml* kind: *They were ceremonies of a very solemn nature.*

N7 *nouns* : **examples and specimens**

example [C] **1** something taken from a number of things of the same kind, which shows the usual quality of the rest or shows a general rule: *Her rudeness was a typical example of her usual bad manners. Our teacher gave us some examples of how the word is used.* **2** [(*to*)] *apprec* a person, or his behaviour, that is worthy of being copied: *Mary's courage is an example to us all. Mary is a wonderful example of courage.* **3** [(*to*)] a piece of behaviour that may be copied by other people (*often in the phrs* **set/follow a good/bad example**): *He arrived at the office early, to set an example/a good example to the others. I'm afraid the boy is going to follow his father's bad example.* **4** a warning: *I'm going to send you to prison for three weeks and let this be an example to you!* **for example** here is one of the things or people just spoken of: *A lot of people here, for example John, prefer coffee. Mary's lazy; yesterday for example she stayed in bed all day.*

instance [C (*of*)] an example or occasion (of something): *Let me give you some instances of what I mean.* **for instance** for example (esp in order to show a special example): *You can't depend on her; for instance, she arrived late for*

that important meeting yesterday. **in the first instance** first of all; as a beginning; at the beginning

specimen **1** [C] a single typical thing or example: *It is a good specimen of 15th-century advertising. He's still a fine specimen of health. These animals are good specimens of their kind.* **2** [C] one or a piece of something for being shown, tested, etc: *They gathered rock and plant specimens. The doctor wanted a specimen of his blood.* **3** [C9] *infml & deprec* a person unusual in some way: *She's a strange specimen, isn't she?*

sample [C] **1** a small part representing the whole; typical small quantity, thing, event, etc: *The nurse took a sample of my blood/a blood sample. I'd like to see some samples of your work. They took a sample of a hundred people for their test of public opinion.* **2** a small trial amount of a product given away free: *He gave away some free samples/sample bottles of a new kind of cooking oil.*

ideal [C] **1** a perfect example: *This is the ideal we all have in mind but never reach.* **2** [*often pl*] a belief in (perfect) standards: *He has very high ideals. She was full of youthful ideals then; not now.* **idealism** [U] **1** belief in ideals: *youthful idealism* **2** the belief that ideas are the only real things **idealist** [C] **1** a person with ideals **2** one who believes in idealism (def **2**) **idealistic** [B] having ideals; believing in idealism **-ally** [adv] **idealize, -ise** [T1; IØ] to see (something or things generally) as perfect or better than it is/they are: *He idealizes; he doesn't see life as it really is.* **idealization, -isation 1** [U] the act of idealizing **2** [C] an example of this; something idealized; something made as a perfect example

quintessence [*the* S *of*] *esp fml & lit* the perfect example: *She is the quintessence of kindness.*

N8 *verbs* : **typifying and embodying** [T1]

typify 1 to represent in a typical manner (as by an image, form, model, or likeness): *In this book we have tried to typify the main classes of verbs.* **2** [Wv6] to be a typical mark or sign of: *The book showed the care that typifies all his work.* **3** [Wv6] to serve as a typical example of: *Abraham Lincoln typifies the politician who rises from humble origins to a position of power and influence.*

instance to give as an example or instance: *When they asked him for an example, he instanced her actions last summer.*

exemplify 1 to give an example of: *The teacher exemplified the use of the word.* **2** to be an example of: *This exemplifies what I mean.*

represent 1 (esp of a painting) to show; be a picture of: *This painting represents a storm at sea. The tall stone figure represented Victory.* **2** to be a sign of; stand for: *The red lines on the map represent railways.* **3** [*usu pass*] (of a member of a group) to be present as an example of (that group): *'a soup in which 20 kinds of vegetables were represented'* (Hawthorne) **4** *fml* to act the part of: *He represented Brutus in the school play.*

express [also T6a (*how*)] to show (a fact, feeling opinion, etc) in words or in some other way: *The prices are expressed in both dollars and pounds. I can't express how grateful I am/ what I mean.*

realize, -ise to carry out; make real (a hope or purpose): *She realized her intention of becoming an actress.*

embody 1 (of words, writings, etc) to express: *Words embody thought. The letter embodied all his ideas. Our laws embody our way of life.* **2** (of things) to contain or include: *The new car embodies many improvements.*

incarnate 1 [*usu pass*] to put (an idea, spirit, etc) into bodily form: *According to the Christian religion, God was incarnated in Jesus Christ.* **2** *old use* to embody

N9 nouns : representing and embodying

representation [U;C] the act or condition of representing or being represented; something that represents: *'No taxation without representation' means that if people pay taxes they should be represented in Parliament. This painting is a representation of a storm at sea.*

realization, -isation 1 [*the*+U *of*] becoming real (as of a hope or purpose): *This is the realization of my hopes; it is a great day for me.* **2** [C] something made real: *In English there are many realizations in sound of the letter 'r'.*

embodiment [C] someone or something in which something is embodied (esp in the phr **the embodiment of**): *His enemies called him the embodiment of evil. To them he is an embodiment of evil.*

incarnation 1 [U] the state of being incarnate **2** [C] a form having a body: *They believe he is an incarnation of their god.* **3** [C] a perfect or full example: *She is the incarnation of all good things.*

N10 adjectives : typical and characteristic [B (of)]

typical 1 combining and showing the main signs of a particular kind, group, or class: *It was a typical British summer/a typical 18th century church.* **2** showing the usual behaviour or manner: *It was typical of him to be so rude.* **un-** [*neg*] **typically** [adv] **1** in a typical manner: *typically American* **2** on a typical occasion: *Typically, he would come in late and then say he was sorry.* **3** in a typical case or example; if true to type: *They were*

large vessels made of clay, typically having long curved necks.

characteristic [also B5] typical; representing a person's or thing's usual character: *It was characteristic of her to be rude to you. It is characteristic that such a political movement should favour violence.* **un-** [*neg*] **-ally** [adv Wa4]

representative typical; being an example (of what others are like): *This is a representative collection of ancient Greek art. Are your opinions representative of those of the other students?* **un-** [*neg*] **-ly** [adv]

N11 nouns : truth and fact

truth 1 [U] the state of being true: *'Truth is important; don't tell lies.' he told his son.* **2** [*the* U] what is (believed to be) true: *Tell (me) the truth! The truth is often painful. Is there any truth in his story?—Yes, some truth/No, no truth at all. He says that his religion is the truth and ours is not.* **3** [C] a thing that is (believed to be) true: *Let me tell you a few truths about your friend!* **to tell the truth** to be honest about something: *Well, to tell the truth, I don't like them.* **in (all) truth** *fml* to tell the truth: *In truth, I must admit I don't like them very much.*

reality 1 [U] the quality or state of being real; real existence: *She believed in the reality of fairies.* **2** [C] something real: *Her dream of marrying Frederick became a reality.* **3** [U] everything that is real: *Don't try to escape from reality.* **in reality** in spite of what was thought: *In reality, he helped them; he was not trying to make life difficult for them at all!*

fact 1 [C, C5] something that has actual existence or an event that has actually happened or is happening: *Scientists attempt to find reasons for facts. Certain facts have become known about the materials on the moon. It is a fact that I am writing this sentence. The fact that I am writing this sentence is not surprising; it is my job.* **2** [C] information regarded as being true and as having reality: *The story of the fire is not an accepted fact.* **3** [U] what is known to be true: *This is fact, not fiction; it happened!* **as a matter of fact, in (actual) fact, in point of fact** really; actually: *Officially he is in charge but in actual fact his secretary does all the work. He doesn't mind. In point of fact he's very pleased. He finished it yesterday, as a matter of fact.*

actuality 1 [U] the state of being real; existence **2** [U; C *usu pl*] something that is real; fact: *He looks poor but in actuality he has plenty of money. You have to accept the actualities of life.*

N12 nouns : fiction and fantasy

fiction 1 [U] things which are not true: *Give me facts, please, not fiction!* **2** [C] an idea, system, etc which is (perhaps) useful for some purposes but which does not really exist in fact:

The Equator [⇒ L10] *doesn't really exist, but it is a convenient fiction.*

imagination [C *often with poss*] the workings of one's mind to form a picture or idea, esp mistakenly: *These difficulties are all in your imagination.*

fantasy [C; U] something very strange, usu in the imagination or a dream: *Her mind is full of fantasies about what will happen to her if she goes abroad. It's all fantasy; nothing like that happened to him.*

fallacy [C; U] a belief, argument, idea, etc that is untrue: *It is a complete fallacy to suppose that the sun goes round the earth.*

N13 *adjectives* : **true and real**

true [Wa1] **1** [B] correct in fact: *His story is true; I was there and I saw what happened.* **un-** [*neg*] **2** [A] exact: *This is a true copy of the letter.* **truly** [adv]: *He is a truly great man.*

real [Wa5;B] actually existing; true, not false: *Is your ring brass or real gold? What was the real reason for your absence? The real amount was only £5.* **-ly** [adv]: *I really do want you to come. Can he really help us?* **realism** [U] **1** the showing (in books, films, etc) of life as it really is **2** the state of mind that deals with life as it really is **realist** [C] a person who believes in being realistic [⇒N230] and accepts the way life really is

factual [B] based on fact; giving the facts; true: *He gave a factual account of what happened.* **-ly** [adv]

actual [Wa5;A] existing as a real fact: *The actual amount of money was not known although they knew it was large.* **-ly** [adv] *Can he actually help us?* **in actual fact** in reality; in actuality; actually

concrete [Wa5;B] real; being part of things as they can be seen, touched, etc and not as ideas, general rules, etc: *Animals and stones are concrete, but our names for them are not.* **-ness** [U]

apparent [A; (B)] seeming to be something, esp true or real, but not (necessarily) so: *He was our apparent friend, but he actually did not help us. His friendship was more apparent than real.* **-ly** [adv]: *Apparently he went there last week. Did he go?—Apparently.*

virtual [Wa5;A] being more or less something in fact, although not in name: *She is the virtual ruler of the country, although he is the king.* **-ly** [adv]

N14 *adjectives* : **not true or real** [B]
[ALSO ⇒ I13]

false [Wa1] *esp poet & emph* not true or correct: *What she says is false; it is a lie!* **-ly** [adv] **-ness, -sity** [U]

fallacious of, like, or caused by a fallacy; *fml* false: *Her argument is completely fallacious.* **-ly** [adv] **-ness** [U]

nonexistent [Wa5] having no existence, except perhaps in someone's imagination: *The things she fears are nonexistent.*

fictitious [Wa5] belonging to fiction [⇒ N12] and not fact; not happening in real life: *These people were fictitious; they never lived.* **-ly** [adv]

imaginary not real, but produced from pictures in someone's mind: *All the characters in this book are imaginary. My daughter has an imaginary friend.*

fabulous [Wa5] belonging to some fantasy and not to real life: *He told us stories about the fabulous things that happened to him when he was abroad.* **-ly** [adv]

fanciful *often deprec* **1** showing imagination rather than reason and experience: *a fanciful poet* **2** unreal; imaginary: *What a lot of fanciful talk!* **3** odd in appearance, esp in being highly ornamented: *fanciful designs* **-ly** [adv]

N15 *verbs* : **becoming and growing**
[ALSO ⇒ N92 DEVELOP]

become [L1, 7, 8] to come to be: *He became king. The weather became warmer. The news became known at 10 o'clock. It became necessary for us to go.*

get [L (*to be*) 1, 7, 8] *infml* to become: *The weather got warmer. I'm getting cold sitting here. The cat got trapped in the tree. You're getting to be a bad influence on my children.*

grow [L7] to become, esp slowly: *The weather grew warmer. I began to grow cold, sitting doing nothing.*

fall [L7, 9] to become, esp quickly or suddenly: *He fell ill and died. She fell silent.*

N16 *verbs* : **happening and taking place**

happen 1 [I0 (*to*)] (of events) to be, continue, etc: *What happened?—Nothing happened. A funny thing happened to me last night. It happened so quickly (that) I didn't know what to do. Be careful; don't let anything happen to that child.* **2** [Wv6; *it* I5] to be true (as if) by chance: *It (so) happened that I saw him yesterday.* **3** [Wv6;I3] to have the good or bad luck: *You don't happen to have any money with you, do you? I happened to see him yesterday.*

take place [I0] *genl* to happen, esp in a particular place or at a particular time: *The meeting took place at 10 o'clock as planned. Where did all these things take place?*

occur *usu fml* **1** [I0] (esp of unplanned events) to happen; take place: *A serious accident occurred yesterday.* **2** [L9; (I0): *often neg*] (esp of something not alive) to exist: *That sound doesn't occur in his language.*

arise [I0] to come into being or into notice; happen; appear: *Problems will arise as we do the work. A strong wind arose and blew our boat on to the rocks.*

turn up [v adv IØ] *not fml* to happen: *He hopes something will turn up to help him in his present difficulties.*

crop up [v adv IØ] *not fml* to arise, happen, or appear unexpectedly: *Some difficulties have cropped up at work so I'll be late coming home tonight. When did that word first crop up in English? The matter cropped up in the course of our conversation.*

come up [v adv IØ] *not fml* to happen, esp suddenly and unexpectedly: *Something new has just come up and I must go and attend to it immediately.*

coincide [IØ *(with)*] **1** (of two or more things, esp events) to happen at the same time: *My holiday coincides with yours. Our holidays coincide.* **2** to be in agreement: *Their ideas on this matter seem to coincide.*

chance [Wv6;I3; *it* I5] *esp lit* to take place by chance; happen by accident: *She chanced to be in the park when I was there. If it should chance to rain we'll take a taxi home. It chanced that a doctor was in the room when the woman became ill.*

come to pass [IØ, 5] *old use, lit & fml* to happen: *And so it came to pass that he met the king.*

ensue [Wv4; IØ *(from)*] *esp fml* to happen as a result: *Trouble ensued from his silly actions* (=His silly actions caused trouble).

go on [v adv IØ] *infml* to happen, esp over a length of time: *What has been going on here? This has been going on for at least a year.*

become of [v prep T1] to happen to, esp as time passes: *Whatever became of John after he left here? I haven't seen him for years.*

N17 *nouns* : **happenings and events**

happening [C] **1** something which happens: *When did these happenings take place?* **2** *esp AmE* an unprepared performance or other event to get people's attention

occurrence [C] a happening: *That was a strange occurrence.* **of . . . occurrence** *fml* frequent to the degree stated: *It was an event of rare occurrence.*

event [C] a happening, usu an important one: *What were the chief events of 1979?* **at all events** in spite of everything; in any case: *She had a terrible accident, but at all events she wasn't killed.* **in either event** whichever happens: *I don't know whether I'm going by car or by train, but in either event I'll need money.* **in that event** if that happens: *It may rain.—In that event, we won't go.* **in the event of (something)** if (something) happens: *He asked his sister to look after his children in the event of his death.* **in the natural/normal course of events** in the way things ordinarily happen: *Aren't you a bit worried? In the natural course of events your daughter should have been married by now.* **(quite) an event** an important and unusual happening: *Meeting you was an event in her life.* **in any event** whatever may happen (in the future): *I'll probably see you tomorrow, but in any event I'll telephone.* **in the event** *esp BrE* as it happened; when it actually happened: *We were afraid he would be nervous on stage, but in the event he performed beautifully.*

phenomenon [C] **1** a fact or event in nature or society as it appears or is experienced by the senses, esp one that is unusual and/or of scientific interest (*often in the phr* **natural phenomenon**): *Scientists study the phenomena of nature. Snow in Egypt is an almost unknown phenomenon. Unmarried mothers should not be regarded simply as a social phenomenon.* **2** a very unusual person, thing, event, etc: *A child who can play the piano at the age of two would be called a phenomenon.* [⇨F239 PRODIGY]

incident [C] **1** an event, esp one in a story: *That was one of the strangest incidents in my life.* **2** an event involving violence, such as fighting or explosions: *There were incidents between the soldiers of the two armies even though the war had ended. At a recent incident two bombs exploded.* **incidental** [C; B *(to)*] **1** (something) happening or appearing as an occasional part of something important which spreads over a period of time: *That scene is quite incidental to the play as a whole. Fish is an incidental in our meals, rather than a regular thing.* **2** (something) unimportant: *That's an incidental; the real point of the story is this.* an **incidental matter incidentals** [P] additional things which one needs or which appear to be necessary after the day-by-day things have been done, bought, etc: *I had to buy soap, a toothbrush, and a few other incidentals for the journey. There were the ironing, hanging the curtains, and a few more incidentals like that to do.* **incidentally** [adv] (used to add something interesting to what was said before, either on that or another subject): *I must go now. Incidentally, if you want that book I'll bring it next time.*

contingency [C] *usu fml* an unexpected event or incident: *In such a contingency* (=if such a thing happens), *telephone me immediately.*

adventure 1 [C] an unusual or exciting event or set of events: *For a child of 10 it is quite an adventure to go away from home for some weeks. He had many adventures when he lived in the mountains studying wild animals.* **2** [U] exciting and interesting happenings: *She has led a life of adventure.* **adventurous** [B] liking or containing adventures: *He is an adventurous child. It was an adventurous holiday.* **un-** [*neg*] **-ly** [adv] **-ness** [U] **adventurer** [C] **1** a person who looks for adventure **2** *deprec* a person who lives by deceiving others **adventuress** [C] *deprec* a woman adventurer (esp def **2**)

affair [C] an event or set of events, esp where some part is a mystery: *It was a strange affair and no one knows exactly what happened. We must try to get to the bottom of* (=find out about) *this affair. 'The Mysterious Affair at Styles'* (Agatha Christie)

coincidence [C; (by) U] a happening at the same time of two or more events, esp when not planned, expected, or probable: *What a coincidence, meeting you here! These things often happen by coincidence. She doesn't believe in coincidences; she thinks everything is planned.* **coincidental** [B] of, concerning, like, or happening as a coincidence **-ly** [adv]

N18 nouns : situations and circumstances

situation [C] **1** a position or condition at the moment: *He made some remarks on the political situation. I'm in a difficult situation and I don't know what to do.* **2** a position in certain surroundings: *The defence of Britain is helped by its island situation.*
state of affairs [S] *often emot* a situation (def **1**): *What a terrible state of affairs! What can we do in a state of affairs like this?*
circumstance [C] a fact, detail, condition, or event concerned with and usu influencing another event, person, or course of action: *Weather is a circumstance we must take into account when choosing where to go for our holidays. When it's a question of life or death, money isn't an important circumstance. You haven't mentioned one circumstance that might account for his behaviour. The circumstances suggest a sexual crime. The police want to consider each circumstance in turn.*
circumstances [P] **1** the state of affairs, esp the sum of all conditions, facts, or events which are beyond one's control: *The circumstances forced me to accept a very low price when I sold the house.* **in/under no circumstances** never; regardless of events: *Under no circumstances will there be wage control while I head the government.* **in/under the circumstances** because of the conditions; because things are as they are: *I wanted to leave quickly but under the circumstances (my uncle had just died) I decided to stay another night.* **2** the state of a person's material affairs, esp with regard to the amount of money he has: *What are his circumstances? He seems to be in easy circumstances since he had his pay increase. The family lived in reduced circumstances after they lost their property.*
things [P] *infml* circumstances: *I'm afraid that as things are at the moment, I can't help you. Hullo, John. How are things (with you)?*

N19 nouns : accidents and disasters [C]

[ALSO ⇒ M112]

accident something, esp something unpleasant, undesirable, or damaging that happens unexpectedly or by chance: *He was killed in a car accident. I had an accident in the kitchen and broke all the glasses.* **by accident of** by the

chance, luck, or fortune of: *By accident of birth he was rich.* **accidental** [B] happening as an accident; not intended: *What happened was accidental; he didn't mean to do it.* **-ly** [adv]: *She was accidentally hurt by a piece of glass from the broken window.*
disaster [also U] (a) sudden great misfortune: *The loss of the ship was a disaster. The election results will bring political disaster.* **disastrous** [B] of or like a disaster; terrible: *His accident had a disastrous effect on the family. The farmers suffered a disastrous loss of crops, animals, and money because of the bad weather.* **-ly** [adv]
catastrophe a terrible disaster: *The loss of all those ships was a catastrophe.* **catastrophic** [B] of or like a catastrophe: *The terrible weather caused catastrophic damage.* **-ally** [adv Wa4]
cataclysm a terrible disaster, esp in nature: *The floods were a cataclysm from which the local people never recovered.* **cataclysmic** [B] of or like a cataclysm **-ally** [adv Wa4]
holocaust the loss of many lives, esp by burning: *The factory fire turned into a holocaust when the wind changed direction.*

N20 nouns : emergencies and trouble

[ALSO ⇒ F91]

emergency [C] an unexpected and dangerous happening, situation, or threat: *Ring the bell in an emergency. They went out through the emergency exit. They lived on emergency rations.*
crisis [C] **1** a turning point in the course of anything; uncertain time or state of affairs; moment of great danger or difficulty: *That country has many governmental/political crises. We must bring things to a crisis if we want a decision to be made.* **2** the turning point in a serious illness, at which there is a sudden change for better or worse: *As soon as he reaches the crisis we'll know if he's going to live or die.* [⇒ N45]
trouble [U] *infml* any emergency, crisis, etc: *We had some trouble in the city last night, but it's all right now.*
jam also **spot** [C usu sing] *infml* an emergency, usu for one person: *I'm in a (bit of a) jam; can you help me? She's in a spot and needs help.*

Possibility, chance, and necessity

N30 adjectives & nouns : possible and probable

[ALSO ⇒ N313]

possible 1 [B] that can exist, happen, or be done: *There are only two possible causes of* *this. It isn't possible to divide a 5-inch stick into 3 parts each 2 inches long. I'll do everything possible to help you. I'll do every possible thing I can. I'll help you if possible* (=if it is possible). *Be as kind to her as possible.* **2** [B] that may or may not be, happen, or be expected: *It is possible but not probable that I shall go there next week. There will be a possible change in the weather tomorrow.* **3** [B] acceptable; suitable: *one of many possible answers; A new dress would be a possible gift for Mary's birthday.* **4** [*the* U] that which can be or can be done: *Politics has been called the art of the possible. Let's not talk about wild plans, but concern ourselves only with the possible.* **5** [C] a person who or thing that might be suitable: *He is a possible for the cricket team.* **im-** [*neg*]: *It is impossible for us to go.* **-bly** [adv] **possibility** [U;C] that which is possible: *It is beyond possibility that he can come! What are the possibilities; could he win?* **im-** [*neg*]

feasible [B] possible in some particular way: *According to some scientists, it is feasible to travel to the stars. That's a feasible plan!* **-bly** [adv] **-ibility** [U]

probable 1 [B] that may be expected to happen; that has a good chance of being true; likely: *It's possible that it will rain if the wind changes but with such a cloudless sky it doesn't seem probable. It's probable that he won't return to England because he's been offered a good job in Scotland.* **2** [C] a probable choice, winner, etc: *Before Saturday's football team is chosen there will be a match between the probables and the possibles.* **im-** [*neg*] **-bly** [adv] **probability 1** [U (*of*); U5] the degree of being probable: *What is the probability of life/that there is life on other worlds?* **2** [C] a probable event or result: *War became a probability.* **im-** [*neg*]

likely [Wa2] **1** [F, F3, 5] probable; expected: *Are we likely to arrive in time? Is it likely that he'll arrive so late?—No, it's not very likely. It seems likely that they're out.* **2** [B] suitable to give results: *This is a likely plan! He's the most likely of the people who've asked for the job.* **3** [adv] probably (*esp in the phrs* **very likely, most likely**) *They'll very likely come by car. As likely as not* (= probably) *they'll come by car. They'll quite likely do that.* **likelihood** [U] the condition of being likely; something likely: *Is there any likelihood of him/his coming?—No, no likelihood at all.*

apt [Wa2;F3] having the nature to do or probability of doing something; likely: *This kind of shoe is apt to slip on wet ground.* **-ness** [U]

N31 *adverbs & modals* : **possible**

perhaps [adv Wa5] **1** it may be; possibly: *Perhaps I am wrong, but I think he is 41 years old.* **2** (in making polite requests): *Perhaps you would be good enough to read this* (= Would you be . . . ?)

maybe [adv Wa5] *not fml* perhaps: *Will they*

come?—Maybe not. Maybe I'm wrong, but I think he'll do it.

may [I0, 2] **1** to be in some degree likely to: *He may come or he may not. This news is so strange that you may not believe it. Wherever you may go you may find examples of his evil doings. Why hasn't he come?—He may have been hurt* (= we still don't know whether he has or not). **2** to have permission to; be allowed to: *May I leave this with you? May I come in?—Yes, you may. She may have visitors in hospital, but they mayn't stay for more than a few minutes. I may say I find your questions rather rude* (= it is my opinion that they are rude). **3** (usu with the subject following the v) I/We hope very much that: *May there never be another world war!* **4** *also* **might** although . . . do/does: *You may think you're very clever, but that doesn't give you the right to order me about* (= although you think you're clever, that doesn't . . .) **5** (in clauses) **a** (expressing purpose) can: *Sit here, so that I may see your face more clearly.* **b** (with words expressing hope, wish, or fear) will: *The doctor fears that she may not live much longer.* **may well** to be very likely to: *His appearance has changed so much that you may well not recognize him. The team may well have won the football match, but I don't know because I wasn't there.* **may/might (just) as well** to have no strong reason not to: *There's nothing to do, so I may as well go to bed.*

might [I0, 2] **1 a** to be in some small degree likely to: *He might come or he might not. This news is so strange that you might not believe it.* **b** to have been in some degree likely to: *Did you see how that car nearly hit me? I might have been killed* (= but I wasn't). **2** *polite* (in questions) to have permission to; be allowed to: *Might I come in?—Yes, you may.* **3** (in clauses) **a** (expressing purpose) could: *I wrote down his telephone number, so that I might remember it.* **b** (with words expressing hope, wish, or fear) would: *The prisoner had hopes that he might be set free.* **4** (suggesting that a person should do something, behave in a certain way, etc) should: *You might at least say thank you when someone helps you.* **5** could have been expected to (*in the phr* **might have** + *past p*): *You might have known she'd refuse. I might have known he'd do something silly; he's been acting strangely all week.* **6** (in reported speech) may (defs **1, 2, 3, 5**): *He told us that he might come, but he might not. He asked whether he might leave it with him. He said he feared that she might not live much longer.* (*fml*) *He said I might go if I wished.* **7** may (def **4**): *You might think you're very clever, but that doesn't give you the right to order me about.* **might well** to be likely to: *We lost the football match, but we might well have won if one of our players hadn't been hurt.* **might (just) as well** may (just) as well: *No one will eat this food; it might just as well be thrown away.* **8** becoming rare past t of **may**: *In former times the king* might do nothing without asking the permission of parliament (= was not allowed to do anything). **9** pomp or humor (in questions) do/does: *And what might this mean* (= what does this mean)? *Who might you be* (= who are you)?

can [I∅, 2] **1** to know how to: *I can swim well. I couldn't/wasn't able to do that new job; it was too difficult. Can you sing?—Of course I can.* **2** to be able to: *I can see you easily from here. This man could heal all diseases. Let's go where we can practise our religion freely. I'll see what can be done. She has everything that money can buy. It can be expressed in different words. This car can hold six people comfortably.* **3** to be allowed to (by rules): *You can't pick the ball up in football. 'I can and I will dismiss the government,' said the angry king.* **4** to allow oneself to: *You can hardly blame him for doing that. I can't take your coat without paying you for it.* **5** to have permission to; may: *The teacher said we could go to the shops for sweets. (infml) Can we go to the shops for sweets, please, Miss?* **6** (used for expressions of surprise in question form): *What(ever) can it possibly be?* **7** to have to; must: *If you don't be quiet you can leave the room.* **8** (expressing doubt about a possibility) may; might: *What can the police want with me; I've done nothing wrong. Can he still be alive after all these years?* **9** (with verbs expressing actions of the five senses and of the mind): *I can see you easily from here. I couldn't understand him when he spoke very fast.* **10** (with requests) will: *Can you hold on a minute, please?*

could [I∅, 2] **1** past t of **can**: *I can't sing now, but I could when I was young. I couldn't get the tickets yesterday* (Compare: *Luckily, I was able to get the tickets yesterday*). **2** (used instead of **can** in reported speech): *I can't go. He said he couldn't go.* **3** (used, often with **if**, to say that something would or might be possible): *I could come tomorrow (if you like).* (Compare: *I can come tomorrow*, which shows more desire to come). *You could earn more if you could work a little harder. The car won't start!—Couldn't you try pushing it? This could be your only chance to go.* **4** (with requests) would (*more polite than* **can**): *Could you please hold on a minute?* **5** (suggesting that a person should do something, behave in a certain way, etc) should; ought to (have): *You could at least have met me at the station, couldn't you?* **6** (in clauses expressing purpose) might; would be able to: *I wrote down his telephone number so that I could remember it.*

N32 modals : **probable**

should [I∅, 2] **1** (expressing what is likely) will probably: *The effect of the tax should be felt in higher prices. We needn't get ready yet; the guests shouldn't come for another hour.* **2** (used for expressing what is possible but not likely, in

conditional sentences about the future): *I don't think it will happen, but if it should, what shall we do?* (fml) *Should you be interested* (= If you should be interested), *I have a book on the subject you might like to see.*

ought [I∅, 3] will probably; can be naturally expected (to do something): *Prices ought to come down soon. You ought to be hungry by now. The car ought to go all right now. What are you doing here? You ought to be in Bristol!*

will [I∅, 2] **1** may likely (be); is probably: *The person you mentioned will be the father of the boy of the same name, is that right? This will be just what she wants.* **2** is/are proved or expected (to): *These things will happen. Oil will float on water. If people study, they will learn* (= If people study, they learn). **3** is/are suited to; has/have the power to: *This car will hold six people comfortably.*

would [I∅, 2] (past of **will** & expressing less certainty, more politeness, etc): *The person you mentioned would be the father, is that right? That would be in 1976, I think. If people studied, they would learn (but they don't).*

N33 adjectives : **certain and sure**

certain 1 [B] established beyond all doubt or question; known: *There's no certain cure for this illness. What will happen is not yet certain.* **un-** [neg] **2** [F] having no doubt: *I'm certain she saw me yesterday. He was too certain of her love to be deceived by such talk.* **un-** [neg] **3** [B; F3, 5] sure to happen: *It's almost certain that the government will lose the next election. It is certain death to go there!* **4** [F3, 5a] (of people) sure: *Be certain to tell him, please. She's certain to do well at that job.* **make certain a** to enquire: *Make certain (that) you know what time the train goes.* **b** to do something in order to be sure (of getting something): *We went to the theatre early and made certain we all got seats/ made certain of getting seats.* **5**[f] rare clever; practised; unfailing: *His ear for music was certain.* **certainly** [adv] **1** without doubt: *He's certainly the best king we've ever had!* **2** (as a polite or strong way of answering a question) yes; of course: *Will you help me?—Certainly I will.* **certainly not** (as a strong way of answering): of course not: *Will you lend me your comb?—Certainly not.* **certainty 1** [U] the state of being certain; freedom from doubt: *I can't say with certainty what my plans are.* **2** [C] a clearly established fact: *It's a certainty that the government will win the next election. It is a certainty that this horse will win the race. Are there any certainties in life?*

sure [Wa1] **1** [F] having no doubt: *I think so, but I'm not sure.* **2** [F3] certain (to happen): *He is sure to come. It's sure to rain.* **3** [B] certain in effect; to be trusted: *One thing is sure; he can't have gone far. He made a sure step out of the mud.* **un-** [neg] **make sure of something/that a** to find our for certain: *Make sure of the time*

688

b to arrange: *Make sure that you get here.* **c** esp *old use* to believe as certain: *He made sure it was true.* **surely** [adv] **1** as expected; certainly: *She'll surely win!* **2** [Wa5] (suggesting hope that something will happen): *Surely he can do it. Surely you don't expect me to do it?* **3** [Wa5] *esp AmE* certainly (def **2**): *Will you do it?—Surely.* **sure of** certain of having, being right about, etc: *Are you sure of these things?* **sure of oneself** confident in life: *She seems very sure of herself, but she isn't really.* **to be sure** it must be accepted (that): *To be sure, some people may disagree but that doesn't mean I'm wrong.* **ensure** [T1, 5] to make sure or certain: *His help ensured our success/ensured that we were successful.*

confident [B; F (*of*, 5a)] sure (esp of one's own or someone's abilities, good intentions, etc): *She was confident (that) she would win. He had a confident look on his face.* **confidence** [U] sure belief: *I have the fullest confidence in him. His confidence (in himself) will help him do well.* **diffident** [B (*about*)] not confident: *She is very diffident about her abilities.* **diffidence** [U] lack of confidence

definite [B] **1** having very clear limits: *He set definite standards for his students.* **2** without any uncertainty or unclearness: *We demand a definite answer.* **3** unquestionable; undoubted: *That book of his will be a definite success.* **4** having or showing firmness of opinion and willingness to act quickly: *They are very definite people.* **in-** [*neg*] **-ly** [adv]

positive [B] very definite; sure: *Are you positive about what happened?—Yes, quite positive.* **-ly** [adv]

express [Wa5;A] **1** (of a command, wish, etc) clearly stated: *It was her express wish that you should have her jewels after her death.* **2** (of an intention or purpose) special; clearly understood: *I came here with the express purpose of seeing you.* **3** (of a likeness) exact: *Everything the child does is an express copy of her elder sister's behaviour.*

conclusive [B] allowing a decision to be made; final and clear: *He gave us conclusive proof that she murdered the man.* **in-** [*neg*] **-ly** [adv] **-ness** [U]

flat [Wa5:B] complete; firm; with no more argument (*esp in the phr* **a flat refusal**): *I'm not coming and that's flat. He gave us a flat refusal to help.* **-ly** [adv]: *He flatly refused to help.*

decided [B] definite; clear: *There has been a decided improvement in his health/the weather.* **-ly** [adv]: *His health has decidedly improved.*

N34 modals : certain and sure

bound [F3] quite certain (to do something): *He's bound to come if we ask him. It isn't bound to happen just because you want it to. You're bound to lose your money if you do that.*

must [I2] to be, do, etc, very probably or certainly: *You must know the reason. You must*

live near my friend, if you live in New Street. I must look funny in this hat! There must be some more tea in the pot. I think they must have left early.

N35 nouns : luck, fortune, and misfortune

[ALSO ⇒ L154]

luck [U] **1** that which happens, either good or bad, to a person in the course of events by, or as if by, chance: *Luck was with us and we won easily. What luck did you have in your search? I can't find any work here so I'll try my luck in the city. I've had bad luck all week.* **2** success as a result of chance: *I wish you luck. I have had no luck today. What luck I met you!* **be down on one's luck** to have bad luck, esp to be without money: *He's down on his luck; we should help him.* **be in/out of luck** to have/not have good fortune: *You're in luck; we have what you want! I'm quite out of luck today.* **for luck** to bring good fortune: *I am giving you this ring for luck.* **worse luck** unfortunately: *He reached the food before I did, worse luck.*

chance [U] the way in which things happen seemingly without any cause: *Leave it to chance* (=Don't plan; just wait and see what happens). *I met him by chance.*

fortune 1 [U] chance, esp as an important influence on one's life; luck; fate: *It's never been his fortune to travel far from home. The car broke down on a lonely road, but by good fortune another car came along and its driver offered to help. She had the good fortune to be free from illness all her life.* **2** [C *often pl*] whatever comes by chance, good or bad; that which will happen to a person in the future: *Through all his changing fortunes he never lost courage. The fortunes of war bring death to many, while others escape unharmed. That old woman tells fortunes* (=claims to tell about a person's future by examining his hand, studying a pack of cards, a glass ball, etc). *I had my fortune told last week.* **3** [U] success; good luck: *Fortune smiled on him* (=everything went well for him). *Fortune favours the brave* (=brave people often succeed).

misfortune 1 [U] bad luck, often of a serious nature: *His failure in business was due not to misfortune, but to his own mistakes.* **2** [C] a very unfortunate accident or event: *She believed that the greatest of her misfortunes was that she'd never had any children.*

mercy [C *usu sing*] *not fml* a fortunate happening: *It's a mercy we didn't know of her illness till afterwards, as we would have been so worried.*

N36 nouns : opportunities and chances

opportunity [C (*for*, *of*), C3; U] a favourable moment or occasion (for doing something):

What a wonderful opportunity! He had several good opportunities to go, but he never took them. (fml) May I take this opportunity to thank you all for coming? (fig) Opportunity knocks (at the door) only once.

chance 1 [C (*of*), C3] *not fml* an opportunity: *Can I have a chance to try? Give me another chance, please. She had the chance to go, but she decided not to.* **2** [C; U: (*of*, 5)] possibility or probability: *What chance is there that she will come? Is there any chance that he can do it?—No; no chance (at all).*

prospect 1 [U9, esp *of*] a reasonable hope or possibility: *There is no prospect of more money at the moment.* **2** [U9; S9] something expected or probable: *He doesn't like the prospect of leaving this town.* **prospects** [P] chances (of success): *What are his prospects in his new work?*

advantage [C; U] something which makes or may make someone or some other thing better, happier, luckier, etc than others, than before, etc: *Are there any special advantages to/for us if we follow your plan? There is no advantage in doing that. I may get some advantage if I go.* **dis-** [*neg*]: *Poor eyesight is a disadvantage in life.* **advantageous** [B] *fml* causing an advantage: *It will be more advantageous to you if you go now.* **dis-** [*neg*] **-ly** [adv] **have an advantage over** to have a better chance of doing or getting something than: *He had an advantage over us; he had more money.* **take advantage of** to make good use of: *You should take advantage of the low prices and buy now.*

turn *also* **shot** [C] a chance (to do something), esp after others have done it: *It's my turn now! Can I have a turn?*

go [C] *esp BrE infml* a chance (to do something): *Can I have a go now, please? Is it my go now?*

N37 adjectives : lucky and random

lucky [Wa1;B] having, resulting from, or bringing good luck: *He's a lucky man! It was lucky for me that I saw you when I did.* **-ily** [adv]: *Luckily I saw him just when I needed him.*

fortunate [B] having or bringing good fortune; lucky: *She's fortunate enough to have very good health. He's fortunate in having a good wife. It was fortunate for her that she met the doctor just when she needed him. He's fortunate in business* (= all his affairs succeed). *She won the tennis game by a fortunate stroke that put the ball just inside the line.* **un-** [*neg*] **-ly** [adv]: *Fortunately for me he was at home when I needed him. Fortunately she found the money she had lost.*

auspicious [B] *fml* **1** of good fortune; lucky: *This is an auspicious day for us!* **2** giving, promising, or showing signs of future success: *The opening of the railway was an auspicious event since it brought wealth to the town.* **in-** [*neg*] **-ly** [adv]

opportune [B] fortunate, because happening at the right time: *Your coming here was really opportune! He waited for a more opportune moment to speak to her.* **in-** [*neg*] **-ly** [adv]

random [A] unplanned; happening by chance [⇒ N35]: *Don't ask random questions. They used random numbers, not numbers in a particular order.* **-ly** [adv] **-ness** [U] **at random** by chance; in no special order: *He spoke to people at random.*

haphazard [B] **1** *emot & emph* random **2** *deprec* without organization: *He works in a very haphazard way.* **-ly** [adv]

chance [Wa5;A] happening quite accidentally: *We had a chance meeting about a month ago.*

N38 nouns : dangers and threats

[ALSO ⇒ F135]

danger 1 [U] the possibility of harm or loss: *The sign says 'Danger: Falling Rocks'. This is a place where children can play without danger. The man's life had been in danger, but now he was out of danger. He is in (great, real, etc) danger of losing all his money if he continues to buy useless objects.* **2** [C] a case or cause of danger: *What are the dangers of smoking? This building is a danger to the public; it could fall down any time.*

risk *esp emot* **1** [S; U: (*of*, 5)] a danger (of); something that may have a (stated) bad result: *There's some/a great/no/not much risk (of fire). There's a certain risk that he may find out the truth.* **2** [C] a danger: *Fishermen face a lot of risks in their daily lives.* **3** [C9] (in insurance and insurance contracts) **a** a (stated) danger: *fire risk/war risk* **b** someone or something that is a (stated) danger to the insurance company: *I'm afraid she's a poor risk for life insurance; her health is so bad.* **at one's own risk** agreeing to bear any loss or danger: *'Anyone swimming in this lake does so at his own risk'* (notice). **at owner's risk** (of things kept for other people) with the owner agreeing to bear any loss or damage: *We send these goods at owner's risk.* **at risk** *fml* in danger: *The disease is spreading, and all children under 5 are at risk.* **at the risk of a** with danger of: *He saved my life at the risk of losing his own. At the risk of seeming rude, I must say . . .* **b** also **at risk to** with danger to: *He saved my life at the risk of his own/at (great) risk to his own.* **run/take risks/a risk** to do dangerous things; take chances/a chance: *You have to take a lot of risks in my job. You're running a big risk in trusting him. We'll just have to take the risk that George may come home.* **run/take the risk of doing something** to do (something dangerous): *I don't want to run the risk of meeting George.*

peril *esp poet* **1** [U] (great) danger: *She faced terrible peril in the forest that night. They went in peril of their lives from wild animals. The city is in peril!* **2** [C] a (great) danger: *He feared the perils of the sea.*

jeopardy [U] *esp fml, lit & pomp* danger (*esp in the phr* **in jeopardy**): *His foolish behaviour may put his whole future in jeopardy. He faced great jeopardy in the city.*

hazard [C; (U)] danger: *Life is full of hazards. Ice on the roads is a hazard to drivers in cold countries in wintertime.*

N39 *verbs* : **dangers and threats**

endanger [T1] to cause danger to: *You will endanger your health if you work so hard.*

risk *esp emot* **1** [T1] to place in danger: *You will risk your health if you work so hard. He is always risking his money at cards! He risked his own life to save mine.* **2** [T1, 4] to take the chance of: *He risks failure doing that. She risked losing her money at cards. He risked his parents' anger by marrying her.*

imperil [T1] *esp poet* to put (something or someone) in danger: *She imperilled his life.*

jeopardize, -ise [T1] *esp fml, lit & pomp* to endanger: *His foolish behaviour may jeopardize his whole future.*

hazard [T1] *esp poet & emot* to endanger: *He hazarded his life to save the child.*

chance [T1, 4; (V4)] to take a chance with; risk: *You shouldn't chance all your money at once. I'll chance another game of cards if you will. Let's chance getting wet and walk home.* **chance it** *infml* to take a chance of success, though failure is possible; take a risk: *She only had five minutes to get to the station but she wanted a book so she chanced it and went into a shop. I don't know if we can get it but let's chance it.*

threaten [I0; T1] (of danger, etc) to seem to be about to happen (to): *If danger threatens, call me. Trouble was threatening the city.*

N40 *adjectives* : **dangerous** [B]

dangerous able or likely to cause danger: *He is a dangerous person; keep away from him. It's dangerous to smoke.* **-ly** [adv]

risky [Wa2] *esp emot & not fml* (esp of actions) dangerous: *Robbing banks is risky as well as wrong.* **riskily** [adv]

perilous *esp emot, poet & lit* dangerous; risky. **-ly** [adv]

hazardous *esp poet & emot* dangerous: *They went on a hazardous journey in small boats down the River Zaire.* **-ly** [adv]

chancy [Wa1] *infml* dangerous; risky: *That's a chancy business and I'm not doing it!*

dicey [Wa1] *sl* risky and uncertain: *Don't mention it to him, it's too dicey; he might be angry.*

N41 *adjectives* : **threatening** [B]

threatening suggesting a threat or danger: *He behaved/spoke in a threatening way to her.* **-ly** [adv]: *He behaved threateningly.*

forbidding having a fierce, unfriendly, or dangerous look: *Because she has a forbidding manner she's slow in making friends. The travellers' way was blocked by a forbidding range of mountains.* **-ly** [adv]

fateful *esp lit* (of a day, event, or decision) important (esp in a bad way) for the future: *I remember that fateful night when I met her.* **-ly** [adv]

ominous being an omen [⇒L160], esp of something bad: *Ominous black clouds filled the sky.* **-ly** [adv]: *He spoke ominously about the future.*

ill-omened *esp lit & poet* bringing bad luck: *I don't want to see that ill-omened place again!*

N42 *verbs* : **being important** [*usu nonassertive*]

matter [(it) I0 (to)] to be important: *It doesn't matter if I miss my train, because there's another later. I don't think anybody matters to her apart from herself. It doesn't matter to me whether they come or not. 'Nothing matters now,' he said sadly.*

signify [I0 (to)] *fml or emph* to matter: *It doesn't signify to him whether you come or go. 'Nothing signifies since he died,' she said sadly.*

weigh [L9, esp *with*] *esp emot or emph* to matter: *Does it weigh with you at all what she does?—No; it doesn't weigh much with me.*

N43 *adjectives* : **important** [B]

important 1 which matters a lot: *It's important to find out what he is doing. It's important that you know about this.* **2** (of people) powerful; having influence: *He is an important man in the church.* **un-** [*neg*] **importance** [U] (the reason for) being important: *The importance of washing one's hands is to prevent infection.*

significant *esp fml* important and full of meaning: *These are very significant points which we must consider carefully.* **in-** [*neg*] **-ly** [adv] **significance** [U; S] *esp fml* importance: *Is there any significance in what he said?—No; no significance at all. I find it of some significance that she did not come.*

weighty [Wa1] having or seeming to have importance: *He made a weighty speech to the party.* **-iness** [U]

serious 1 of an important kind; needing or having great skill or thought: *This subject has never been paid any serious attention. He is a serious artist and this is a serious piece of art. Let's have a serious talk about your future.* **2** not (to be) easily or lightly dealt with; not slight: *Serious damage was done by the storm. Serious crime is increasing in the city.* **3** not joking or funny; (intended) to be considered as sincere: *Let's go for a walk.—In this storm? Are you serious? You can't be serious! After a few jokes his speech turned serious.* **4** (esp of a person's manner or character) thoughtful; solemn; not gay or light-hearted: *You look very serious today; is anything wrong?* **-ly** [adv] **-ness** [U]: *I must tell you in all seriousness to be more careful with your money.*

grave [Wa1] **1** important and needing attention, and (often) worrying: *This is grave news. The sick man's condition is grave. He has grave responsibilities.* **2** serious or solemn in manner: *His face was grave as he told them about the accident. He is as grave as a judge, I've never seen him laugh.* **-ly** [adv] *She is gravely ill.* **-ness** [U]: *The graveness of his face worried her.* **gravity** [U] *fml* graveness: *He spoke with great gravity.*

solemn 1 (esp of persons) serious and not smiling: *He looked at her with a solemn expression.* **2** (esp of ceremonies, etc) done in a serious way: *Burial of the dead is usually a solemn ceremony.* **-ly** [adv] **-ness** [U] **solemnity 1** [U] *fml* solemness **2** [C *usu pl*] a solemn ceremony

sober [Wa2] quiet, serious, or morally good: *He leads a sober life. She looked at him with a sober expression.* **-ly** [adv] **-ness** [U] **sobriety** [U] *fml* soberness **in-** [*neg*]

intent [(*on*)] doing things with great seriousness: *He had an intent look on his face. She was intent on her work and heard nothing.* **-ly** [adv] **-ness** [U]

basic most important; on which everything depends; from which everything else develops: *These points are basic; without them, the plan cannot work.* **-ally** [adv]

fundamental *fml* basic: *These are fundamental questions; we must think about them. They want to make fundamental changes in the law.* **fundamentals** [P] the basic parts of or facts about something: *He does not understand the fundamentals of modern scientific work.*

N44 *adjectives & nouns* : **necessary and essential**

necessary [B] **1** [(*to, for*)] that must be had or obtained; needed: *Food is necessary for life. This is the power necessary to a government. He made the necessary changes. It's necessary for him to go. It's necessary that he (should) do it.* **2** [Wa5] that must be; that cannot be different or avoided; determined or fixed by the nature of things: *Death is the necessary end of life.* **un-** [*neg*] **-arily** [adv] **necessary evil** *fml* something bad or unpleasant which, however, produces good results that could not be obtained in any other way: *I don't like work, but it's a necessary evil.* **necessity 1** [C *esp pl*] something that one must have, esp in order to live: *Where do they get the necessities of life?* **2** [U] great need: *This is a matter of necessity; it must be done.* **3** [U] lack of food, money, etc: *The family is in a state of real necessity.*

essential [B] **1** [(*to, for*)] *esp emph* necessary: *We can live without clothes, but food and drink are essential to life/for the preservation of life.* **2** forming the central part of: *Her most essen-*

tial quality is kindness. **3** [C *often pl*] something which is essential: *Food is one of the essentials of life.* **in-, non-** [*neg*] **-ly** [adv]

vital 1 [B (*to, for*)] very necessary (for some purpose expressed or suggested); of the greatest importance: *If you're to avoid being discovered, it's vital that you should hide immediately. This point is vital to my argument. Your support is vital for the success of my plan. I believe you're hiding one of the vital facts; without a knowledge of that, I can't help you.* **2** [B] full of life and force; *Their leader's vital and cheerful manner filled his men with courage.* **3** [Wa5;A] necessary for life (in order to stay alive): *The dead girl's body had lost all its vital heat. He was lucky that the bullet hadn't entered a vital organ* (= any organ, such as the heart, etc, without which life cannot continue). **-ly** [adv]

key [Wa5;A] very important; that is necessary for success: *He is a very important man with a key position in the company. He is a key man in the company. We are in danger because the enemy hold all our key towns.*

indispensable [B (*to*)] completely necessary; without which or whom nothing can be done: *Books are indispensable things in our way of life. He is indispensable to our work; we cannot do it without him.*

must [C, *usu sing*] *not fml* something necessary; something that a person should see, hear, do, etc: *Don't miss seeing that film; it's a must.*

N45 *adjectives* : **very important or necessary, etc** [B]

acute very serious and needing immediate action: *The problem is now acute and you must do something!* **-ly** [adv] **-ness** [U]

pressing 1 demanding or needing attention, action, etc now: *Pressing business matters prevented him from taking a holiday.* **2** asking for something and urging it strongly: *My friends gave me a pressing invitation. They were so pressing that I couldn't refuse them.*

urgent badly needing attention, action, etc now: *He received an urgent telephone call to go home. It's urgent; come quick!* **urgency** [U] the state of being urgent: *In a matter of urgency telephone me immediately.*

crucial [(*to, for*)] very necessary; of deciding importance: *He came at a crucial moment/at a crucial point in the talks. The answer to this question is crucial for the future of the human race.* **-ly** [adv]

imperative *usu fml* very necessary; urgent; which must be done: *It's imperative to drink in hot weather if you don't want to be ill.*

critical 1 of, related to, or being the deciding moment (**crisis** [⇒N20]) in the course of anything: *He reached a critical stage of the fever. It was a critical point in the fighting. This is of critical importance! It was a critical time in our history.* **2** very serious or dangerous: *He* was suffering from a critical illness. His condition is reported as being critical. **3** necessary: *Courage, honesty, and firmness are critical qualities that no politician should lack.* **4** [Wa5] tech (in science) of, being, or related to a fixed value as of pressure, temperature, etc at which a substance changes suddenly: *Critical pressure is the smallest amount of pressure that can make a gas at critical temperature liquid. Critical temperature is the temperature above which a gas cannot become liquid even if the pressure changes.* **-ly** [adv] *critically ill*

drastic having a strong or serious effect: *The doctors took drastic action to stop the disease from spreading. If you don't help him, he may do something drastic to get the money!* **-ally** [adv Wa4]

N46 *adjectives* : **not very important** [B]

trivial of little worth or importance: *It was a trivial offence. Why do you get angry over such trivial matters? He is rather a trivial young man.* **-ly** [adv] **triviality** [C] something trivial: *She only talks about the trivialities of life.*

trifling of slight importance; of little value: *It was a trifling matter/sum of money; forget it.* **-ly** [adv]

petty *usu deprec* not important: '*Don't ask me to think about such petty matters!' he said angrily.* **-tiness** [U]

mere [Wa5;A] no more or better than and therefore not important: *She is a mere child; she doesn't understand.* **-ly** [adv Wa5]: *He is merely here to help; nothing more.*

General, usual, unusual, etc

N50 *adjectives* : **absolute and general**

absolute [Wa5;B] **1** not depending on or measured by comparison with other things: *Is there such a thing as absolute truth?* **2** without any conditions: *I have made you an absolute promise that I will help you.* **3** not allowing any doubt; completely certain: *The police have absolute proof that he was the murderer.* **-ly** [adv]

overall [Wa5;A;E] **1** including everything: *What are the overall measurements of the room? The fish measured 5 feet 3 inches overall.* **2** [adv] on the whole; generally: *Overall, prices are still rising.*

general 1 [A; (B)] not detailed; describing the main thing(s) only: *Give me a general idea of the work. The school's general timetable does not include German, but a special timetable will be made for you.* **2** [Wa5:A;(B)] not limited to one thing, place, etc: *There is a general increase in crops during good weather.*

N51 *adverbials* : **generally**

generally [adv] for most things, in most places, at most times, for most people, etc: *Well, generally, I agree, but not on this point. He generally goes there on Wednesdays. Generally speaking/Speaking generally, I agree.*

in general *also* **as a whole** generally; under most conditions; in most cases: *People in general/as a whole don't do things like that.*

all in all *also* **by and large** *also* **on the whole** when (something is) considered fully: *Well, all in all, I think he's right. By and large, your idea is a good one. On the whole, he is a good worker.*

altogether [Wa5] **1** considering all things; on the whole: *It was raining, but altogether it was a good trip.* **2** completely; thoroughly: *It is not altogether bad. This is an altogether different state of affairs. It was altogether the best trip of my life!* **3** everyone or everything included: *Twenty-one people were there altogether, counting us.*

in all with everything or everyone included: *Twenty-one people were there in all.*

for the most part with most things understood or most people considered: *I think that for the most part he's right. People for the most part agreed with him.*

N52 *adjectives* : **relative and conditional** [B]

relative 1 [Wa5] compared to each other or to something else: *What are the relative costs of building in stone and in brick? After his troubles, he's now living in relative comfort. His good health is only relative; he's better than he was, but not well yet. Is truth absolute [⇒ N50], or relative?* **2** [*to*] *fml* connected (with); on the subject (of): *What are the facts relative to this question?* **-ly** [adv] **-tivity** [U]

dependent [(*up*)*on*] depending on certain things happening: *Well, this is all dependent on whether he says 'yes' or 'no'.*

conditional [(*up*)*on*] depending upon certain conditions and therefore not absolute or necessarily always so: *His agreement is conditional on your help. These things are conditional; they depend on many other things.* **-ly** [adv]

contingent [(*up*)*on*] *fml* dependent; conditional: *The payment of the money is contingent upon your good behaviour.*

N53 *adjectives* : **general and common**

general [B] concerning or happening to everyone or in most places: *These difficulties are general among people of his age; everyone has them. The price of food is a matter of general anxiety. The general opinion is that he is a good chairman. She is a general favourite. At* *first only a few people wanted to go, but now interest has become general.* **-ly** [adv]

common [B] happening or found everywhere or in many places: *These birds are very common here. It is quite common for people to do things like that.* **un-** [*neg*] **-ly** [adv]

prevalent [B *(among, in)*] *usu fml* existing commonly, generally, or widely (in some place or at some time): *The habit of travelling by aeroplane is becoming more prevalent each year. Eye diseases are prevalent in some tropical countries.* **-ly** [adv] **-lence** [U]

prevailing [Wa5;A] **1** (of a wind) that blows over an area most of the time: *The prevailing winds on this coast are from the west and often bring rain.* **2** most common or general (in some place or at some time): *He wore his hair in the prevailing fashion.*

widespread [B] found, placed, etc in many places: *Such ideas are very widespread.*

sweeping [B] general; not particular and lacking in useful details or enough thought and care: *Her sweeping statements about life show that she is still very young.*

N54 *adjectives* : **particular and specific**

particular **1** [Wa5;A] worthy of notice; special; unusual: *I'm in a particular hurry today. There was nothing in the letter of particular importance.* **2** [Wa5;A;(B)] single and different from others; of a certain sort: *I don't like this particular hat, but the others are quite nice.* **3** [B *(about, over)*] **a** careful and exact: *Give me a full and particular description of what happened.* **b** showing (too) much care or interest in small matters: *He is very particular about having his breakfast at exactly 8 o'clock.* **c** hard to please: *He is very particular about his food.* **in particular** especially: *I noticed his eyes in particular, because they were very large.* **-ly** [⇒ ʃ..]

local [B] belonging to a particular place: *These difficulties are not just local, they are widespread* [⇒ N53]. *He is one of the local men, not a visitor.* **-ly** [adv]

individual [Wa5;A] **1** (often with *each*) single; particular; separate: *Each individual leaf on the tree is different.* **2** suitable for each person or thing alone: *Individual attention must be paid to every fault in the material.* **3** (of manner, style, ways of doing things) particular to the person, thing, etc concerned and different from others: *She has her own individual style of doing things, and an individual walk/way of walking.* **-ly** [adv]

specific **1** [B] detailed and exact; clear in meaning; careful in explanation: *Be specific in your examination answers. He gave us a specific statement of the case.* **2** [Wa5;A] particular; certain; fixed, determined, or named: *He uses a specific tool for each job.* **-ally** [adv]

N55 *adjectives* : **special and unique** [B]

special **1** [Wa5] of a particular kind: *Do you have a special reason for the request? There is a special train to Liverpool for the football match. This is a special case deserving special treatment.* **2** particularly great or fine: *Tonight is a special occasion, and we have something very special for dinner. He is a special friend of mine. There was no special difficulty.* **-ly** [adv]

rare [Wa1] **1** unusual; uncommon: *This is a rare event. She collects rare books. It's very rare for him to be late.* **-ly** [adv] **-ness** [U] **2** *infml esp ScotE* unusually good: *The party was rare fun.* **3** (esp of air) thin; light: *He found the rare air of the mountains difficult to breathe.* **rare old** *infml esp BrE* unusually good, strong, etc: *She was having a rare old time at the party, wasn't she?*

unique **1** [Wa5] being a single one of its type **2** *infml* unusual: *I am in a rather unique position, as my job is different from anyone else's.* **-ly** [adv] **-ness** [U]

N56 *adjectives* : **usual and habitual**

usual [B] that is expected; that happens most of the time: *We will meet at the usual time. We paid the usual amount. Is it usual to have milk with meals?—Wine would be more usual.* **-ly** [adv] **as usual** as is common or has happened before: *As usual, he arrived last.*

normal [B] according to what is expected: *Normal working hours are from 9 to 5. The normal order of words is subject—verb. What are normal temperatures during November? It's perfectly normal to get angry with your mother sometimes. Rainfall has been about/below normal this July.* **2** (of a person) developing in the expected way; without any disorder in mind or body: *He is a normal child in every way.* **-ly** [adv]

habitual [Wa5] **1** [A] happening all the time: *She gave her habitual greeting.* **2** [A;(B)] (done) by habit: *He's a habitual liar. His lying is habitual.* **-ly** [adv]: *He is habitually late.*

customary [B] established by or according to custom; usual; habitual: *He sat in his customary place on the bus going to work. It is customary to give people gifts on their birthday.*

N57 *adjectives, etc* : **standard and average**

standard **1** [B] of the usual kind; not rare or special: *These nails come in three standard sizes. On this car, a three-litre engine is standard. We have a standard way of acting in these cases.* **2** [A] generally recognized as excellent, correct, or acceptable: *It's one of the standard books on the subject. This is the standard spelling/pronunciation.* **non-** [*neg*]: *That kind of English is non-standard.*

stock [Wa5;A] **1** commonly used, esp without meaning: *stock phrases* **2** kept in stock [⇒ J157], esp because of a standard or average type: *stock sizes*

regular 1 [B] **a** happening often with the same length of time between the occasions: *the regular tick* (=noise) *of the clock* **b** happening, coming, doing something, again and again at the same times each day, week, etc: *He has very regular habits. She is a regular customer here. They work regular hours.* **c** happening every time: *regular attendance at church* **d** not varying: *The chairs were placed (at) regular distances apart. Drive at a regular speed.* **ir-** [*neg*] **-ly** [adv] **-ity** [U; C] **2** [B] proper; according to rule or custom: *He knows a lot about the law but he's not a regular lawyer. Sign here, just to make things regular.* **3** [B] *apprec* evenly shaped: *Her nose is very regular.* **4** [Wa5;A] *infml* complete; thorough: *His wife is a regular slave; she always has to bring him tea in bed.* **5** [Wa5; B] *esp AmE* ordinary: *Do you want the regular size or this big one?*

routine 1 [B] (esp of work) ordinary and regular: *routine activities* **2** [U] a regular way of doing things: *one's usual daily routine*

average [Wa5;B] neither more nor less in any way, better or worse, too much or too little, too good or too bad, etc: *He is an average man; there's nothing special about him. She had average success in life. His height is average.* **-ness** [U]

N58 *adjectives* : **ordinary, familiar, and common**

ordinary [B] **1** not unusual; common: *He says he's just an ordinary man, living in an ordinary house, with ordinary hopes and fears.* **2** if nothing unusual happens: *In the ordinary way, he is back by five.*

familiar 1 [B (*to*)] of or like what one knows in ordinary life; generally known, seen, or experienced: *It was a familiar sight.* **un-** [*neg*] **2** [F *with*] having a thorough knowledge (of): *I am familiar with that book/tool. It is a story with which everyone is familiar.* **un-** [*neg*] **3** [B] without tight control; informal; easy: *He wrote in a familiar style.* **4** [B] too friendly for the occasion: *The man's unpleasant familiar behaviour angered the girl.*

everyday [Wa5;A] belonging to ordinary life: *She just talks about everyday matters, nothing interesting.*

commonplace [B] *sometimes deprec* found everywhere or in most places, and therefore not interesting or special: *Such events are commonplace here. She has a rather commonplace face, don't you think?*

common-or-garden [A] *infml* ordinary and well-known and therefore not very interesting: *We just have the usual common-or-garden furniture here. It's just another common-or-garden matter, nothing big.*

plain [Wa1;B] having no unusual, special, or very interesting qualities: *He sat down to a meal of very plain food.*

humdrum [B] too ordinary; without variety or change: *She says she leads a humdrum existence here, never doing anything interesting.*

N59 *adjectives* : **easy**

easy [Wa1:B, B3] **1** not causing trouble, hardship, etc: *This is an easy book to read. John is easy to please* (= it is not difficult to please him). *He is an easy man to get to know. He is easy to get to know.* **2** comfortable and without worry or anxiety: *He has stopped working now and leads a very easy life.* **-ily** [adv] **easy on the ear/eye** *infml* nice to listen to/look at: *My new secretary can't spell, but she's certainly easy on the eye.* **by easy stages** (on a journey) only short distances at a time: *We came home by easy stages, stopping several nights on the way.*

simple [Wa1,3;B,B3] *esp infml* easy: *I'll explain (it) in simple language. She says that doing these calculations is simple/that these calculations are simple. It's simple; look, I'll show you how!* **-ply** [adv] **-ness** [U] **-plicity** [U; C]

straightforward [B] **1** expressed or understood in a direct way, without difficulties: *This is a straightforward calculation.* **2** honest; without hidden meanings: *He gave her a straightforward answer.* **-ly** [adv] **-ness** [U]

N60 *adjectives* : **not easy** [B]

difficult 1 [*also* B3] not easy; hard to do, make, understand, etc: *English is difficult/a difficult language to learn. This poem is difficult to understand. It was very difficult to put the tent up because of the wind.* **2** (of people) unfriendly and always quarrelling; not easily pleased: *She is a difficult child. Don't be so difficult!* **difficulty 1** [U] the quality of being difficult; trouble: *She had difficulty (in) understanding him. He spoke with difficulty. She did it without much/any difficulty.* **2** [C *often pl*] something difficult; a trouble: *I'm in a bit of a difficulty at the moment. Stop raising difficulties; the plan will work!*

hard [Wa1] **1** [*also* B3] difficult (to do or understand): *There were some hard questions on the examination paper. It's hard to know what he's really thinking.* **2** full of difficulty and trouble: *It's a hard life! He gave me a hard time* (= hurt me in body or mind, as in having teeth pulled out or being questioned closely). **3** [(*on*)] (of people, punishments, etc) not gentle (to); showing no kindness (to): *You're a hard woman. She was very hard on me* (= unkind to me). **4 a** forceful: *Give him a hard push!* **b** needing or using force of body or mind: *This is hard work.* **5** unpleasant to the senses, esp because too bright or too loud: *Her hard voice could be heard across the room. She paints her face with hard colours.* **-ness** [U] **be hard on** to wear (something) out easily or quickly: *Children are very hard on their shoes.* **do (something) the hard way** to learn by experience, not by teaching; to act alone and with difficulty **play hard to get** to pretend lack of interest in something/someone so that the person concerned will persuade one **take (some/a few) hard knocks** to have difficulties **take a hard look (at)** to examine in order to make improvements to some old thing, plan, etc **drive a hard bargain** to be firm in making an agreement most profitable to oneself

stiff [Wa1] *usu not fml* **1** difficult to do: *This is a stiff job!* **2** too much to accept; unusual in degree: *It's a bit stiff to expect us to go out again at this time of night! The cost is stiff.* **-ness** [U]

tough [Wa1] *usu infml* difficult: *This is a tough calculation.* **-ness** [U]

arduous *esp lit, fml & pomp* needing much effort; difficult: *It was an arduous climb. He does not enjoy arduous work.* **-ly** [adv]

awkward causing difficulty: *The piece of wood was an awkward shape and he couldn't cut it properly. That's an awkward question; I'm not sure how to answer it. That's an awkward time; I don't know if I am free to come then. It's a bit awkward for me to come at that time. This is an awkward part of the work; do it carefully.* **-ly** [adv] **-ness** [U]

N61 *adjectives* : **simple and elementary** [B]

simple [Wa1,3] having only a few parts and therefore not difficult to understand or needing much care, etc: *Many forms of life are very simple. His system for doing this is much simpler than theirs, and easier to use.* **-ply** [adv] **-ness** [U] **-plicity** [U;C]

primitive **1** simple; roughly made or done; not greatly developed or improved: *Small seashells have sometimes been used as a primitive kind of money.* **2** *deprec* old-fashioned and inconvenient: *Life in this village is too primitive for me; if you want any water you have to pump it up from a well.* **3** of or belonging to the earliest stage of development, esp of life or of man: *Primitive man made himself primitive tools from sharp stones and animal bones. What was the primitive form of that language?* **-ly** [adv] **-ness** [U]

early [Wa1] belonging to the first and therefore simplest stages of anything: *This is an early example of his art. Early man lived a primitive life.*

elementary **1** *esp fml* (of a question) simple and easy to answer **2** concerned with the beginnings, esp of education and study: *He finished his elementary education at the age of 11. These are elementary exercises for the piano.*

N62 *adjectives* : **not simple and elementary** [B]

complex having many esp different parts (and therefore difficult to understand): *This is a complex machine; take care with it. These ideas are complex; I must study them carefully.* **complexity** **1** [U] the state of being complex: *I was surprised by the complexity of the matter.* **2** [C] anything complex: *I don't understand all these complexities.*

complicated *usu deprec* (too) complex: *What a complicated machine; I can't possibly use it! Don't ask me such complicated questions!*

elaborate full of detail; carefully worked out and with a large number of parts: *It is an elaborate machine. The curtains had an elaborate pattern of flowers. She gave us an elaborate description of her new house.* **-ly** [adv]

intricate containing many detailed parts which make it difficult to understand: *It is an intricate idea and would need a lot of intricate work.* **-ly** [adv] **intricacy** **1** [U] the state of being intricate **2** [C *often pl*] anything intricate: *He doesn't understand the intricacies of the subject.*

involved **1** having related parts which are difficult to understand; complicated: *The reasons are very involved, but the fact is that I can't buy the house after all.* **2** (of people) closely concerned in relationships and activities with others, esp in a personal or sexual relationship: *He's not a very involved person; he seems to have no interests and no friends. He's deeply involved and feels he must marry her because everyone expects it.*

sophisticated **1** complicated; complex: *sophisticated machinery/arguments* **2** having or showing a knowledge of social life and behaviour: *The child is quite sophisticated for his age. She wears very sophisticated clothes.* **sophistication** **1** [U] the state of being sophisticated **2** [C] an example of this

advanced **1** far on in development: *He is spending a year in advanced studies.* **2** modern in ideas, way of living, etc: *Most people find her advanced ideas difficult to accept.*

fancy [Wa1] *infml deprec* too complicated; unusual: *I'm tired of all his fancy ideas; I wish he would forget them.*

N63 *verbs* : **generalizing, specifying, etc**

generalize, -ise [T1;I∅] to make (things) as general as possible; to talk generally (about): *He generalizes too much.* **generalization, -isation** [U;C] the or an act, result, etc of generalizing

particularize, -ise [T1;I∅] to give the details of (something) one by one: *There were various causes, which I need not particularize now.* **particularization, -isation** [U;C] the or an act, result, etc of particularizing

localize [T1] to make or keep something local: *The doctors tried to localize the disease.* **localization, -isation** [U] the act, result, *etc* of localizing

specify [T1, 6a, b] to be specific [⇒N54] about; to give exact details of (something): *Can you specify exactly what you need?* **specification** [U; C] the act, result, etc of specifying; something specified

normalize, -ise [I∅; T1] **1** to (cause to) be normal; (of relations between countries) to come back to a normal or friendly state: *The enemies were slow to normalize their relations after the war.* **normalization, -isation** [U] the act of normalizing

standardize, -ise [Wv5; T1] to make (something, or a number of things) standard: *English spelling was standardized many years ago.* **standardization, -isation** [U] the act of standardizing

regulate [T1] **1** to fix or control; bring order or method to: *He tried to regulate his habits. Can you regulate the pressure of the tyres? They are a well-regulated family.* **2** to make (a machine, esp a clock or watch) work correctly: *Your watch is always slow; it needs to be regulated.* **regulation** [U] the act of regulating

regularize, -ise [T1] to make lawful and official (a state of affairs that has already gone on for some time): *They had been living together for years and at last regularized the position and got married.* **regularization, -isation** [U] the act of regularizing

simplify [T1; I∅] to make (something) simple or simpler: *We must simplify the work; it is too difficult at the moment.* **simplification 1** [U] the act of simplifying **2** [C] an example or result of this **3** [C] anything simplified

complicate [T1] *often deprec* to make (too) complex: *Don't complicate life for me!* **complication 1** [U] the state of being complicated; the action of making something complicated **2** [C *often pl*] anything complicated: *Why must there always be complications; why can't things be simple?*

elaborate [I∅ (*on*); T1] to add more detail to (something): *Just tell us the facts and don't elaborate (on them).* **elaboration** [U] **1** the action of making something elaborate **2** fuller description of something: *Your idea needs elaboration.*

N64 *verbs & adjectives* : **accustoming, familiarizing, etc**

accustom [T1 (*to*)] to make used to: *He had to accustom himself to the cold weather of his new country. I am accustomed to sleeping out of doors.*

familiarize with, -ise [v prep D1] to inform about; cause to know well: *He familiarized himself with the town. I'd like to familiarize you with what is happening here.*

acquaint with [v prep D1] to make (someone) familiar with (something): *Let me acquaint you with the facts. I have acquainted myself with the subject.* **be acquainted (with) 1** *often fml* to have knowledge of: *I am acquainted with the facts already.* **2** to know socially: *We are acquainted; we met at a party last year.*

be familiar with *often fml* to know (well) (how to do, use, etc): *Are you familiar with this work/machine?*

be used to to be familiar with; to have a lot of experience of: *He is used to these things/to looking after himself.*

be accustomed to *fml* to be used to: *He is, I assure you, fully accustomed to such things/ quite accustomed to caring for himself.*

get used/accustomed to *usu not fml* to become used/accustomed to: *You must try to get used to the work. He got accustomed to looking after himself.*

N65 *verbs & nouns* : **limiting, restricting, and controlling**

limit 1 [T1 (*to*)] to keep below or at a certain point: *We must limit our spending. We must limit ourselves to an hour/to one cake each.* **2** [C *often in comb*] the point below or at which something must or should be kept: *This is the limit of our spending; we mustn't spend any more. Is there a speed limit on this road?—Yes; 40 mph.* **3** [*the* R] *infml* something or someone that causes anger, cannot be accepted, etc: *Oh, he is the limit; what an annoying child!* **limitation 1** [U] the act of limiting: *They were talking about the limitation of dangerous weapons.* **2** [C] anything which limits: *His bad eyesight is a limitation; there are certain things he can't do because of it. Aren't there any limitations on his spending money?*

restrict [T1 (*to*)] to keep within limits; keep (to a certain limit): *He restricted himself to (smoking) two cigarettes a day. These laws are intended to restrict the sale of alcohol. The trees restrict the view from this house.* **restriction 1** [U] the act of restricting: *They talked about the restriction of the money supply, so that people could not spend so much.* **2** [C *often pl*] anything which restricts: *Are there any restrictions here on what we can do?* **restrictive** [B] (for the purpose of) restricting: *Their government is very restrictive about money leaving the country.*

control 1 [T1] to limit esp by using the law or force: *It is necessary to control the numbers of people coming to these cities; there are too many people there already.* **2** [U (*over*)] the power or ability to control: *He has control over the whole factory. She has no control over her children at all. The car went out of control (= no one could drive it properly) and hit a wall.* **controls** [P] **1** the apparatus for controlling, driving, etc a vehicle, machine, etc: *She sat at the controls (of the plane).* **2** [(*on*)] laws, restrictions, etc: *The government has placed/imposed controls on money going out of the country*

check 1 [T1] *esp emot* to stop or hold back: *The doctors worked hard to check (the spread of) the dangerous disease.* **2** [C (*on*)] an act of stopping, limiting, or controlling: *We must keep a (close) check on the way he spends our money. The new medicine acted as a check on the (spread of) disease.*

curb 1 [T1] *esp emot* to limit or control: *I wish he would curb his temper* (=try not to be so angry). **2** [C] a thing which curbs something: *They have put/placed a curb on how much money we can spend.*

moderate [Wv4;T1] to limit (something) so as to be less violent, strong, powerful, unacceptable, etc: *Try to moderate your anger/demands/desires.* **moderation** [U] the act of moderating

temper [T1] to moderate or make softer, more pleasant, etc: *She tempered her demands and he was able to accept most of them.*

restrain [T1] *often fml* to prevent or stop (someone from doing something), esp forcefully: *If you try to go, you will be restrained. Restrain yourself; you are getting so angry.* **restraint 1** [U] the condition of restraining or being restrained: *He showed no restraint in what he did.* **2** [C] something that restrains: *If you change this law, you will take away all the restraints on thieves.*

stunt [Wv5;T1] to stop (something or someone) in growth: *If a child smokes cigarettes, it can stunt his growth. The valley was full of stunted trees.*

N66 *verbs & nouns* : **modifying, qualifying, etc**

[ALSO ⇒ 120]

modify [T1] **1** to change (something, such as a plan, an opinion, a condition, or the form or quality of something) esp slightly: *These plans must be modified if they're to be used successfully. Nothing you say in his favour will make me modify my bad opinion of him.* **2** to make (something, such as a claim or condition) less hard to accept or bear: *The two governments will never reach an agreement unless one or the other modifies its demands.* **modification 1** [U] the act of modifying: *These plans need modification.* **2** [C] an example or result of modifying: *With the new modifications the car is better than ever.*

qualify [T1] to limit (esp the meaning of something stated): *Qualify that statement; it's too strong. Adjectives qualify nouns.* **qualification 1** [U] the act of qualifying: *Your remark needs qualification; it is too strong.* **2** [C] an example or result of qualifying: *He has made some qualifications to what he said.*

amend 1 [T1;I0] *lit* to (cause to) become better; improve: *You should try to amend your way of living.* **2** [T1] to make changes in the words of (a rule or law): *They amended the law to meet modern needs.* **amendment 1** [U] the act of

amending: *This law badly needs amendment.* **2** [C] an example or result of this: *The new amendments to the law were badly needed.*

N67 *adjectives* : **special and remarkable**

special [B] not usual or ordinary: *I have a special difficulty; can I tell you about it?* **-ly** [adv]

especial [A] *fml, emph & old use* special: *We have an especial need of help at this time.* **-ly** [adv]

extraordinary 1 [B] very special, strange, etc: *What an extraordinary hat!* **2** [B] more than what is ordinary: *She was a girl of extraordinary beauty.* **3** [Wa5;A] (of arrangements) as well as the ordinary one(s): *The committee meets regularly on Fridays, but there will be an extraordinary meeting next Wednesday.* **-rily** [adv]

signal [A] *lit, fml & pomp* very special and usu good: *It is a signal honour to have you visit us!* **-ly** [adv]

remarkable [B (for)] worth speaking of; unusual: *a most remarkable sunset; She is remarkable for her sweet temper.* **-bly** [adv]

N68 *adjectives* : **strange and peculiar**

strange [Wa1] **1** [B] hard to accept or understand; surprising: *It's strange you've never met him. What a strange idea!* **2** [B] not known or experienced before: *The street he stood in was strange to him. He stood in a strange street.* **3** [F *to*] not experienced (in) or accustomed to: *She is strange to her new duties, but she'll soon learn.* **4** [A] *old use* foreign: *He was a traveller in a strange country.*

odd 1 [Wa1;B] strange; unusual: *He is rather an odd person* **2** [Wa5;A] not part of a pair or set: *Whose is this odd shoe?* **3** [Wa5;A] not regular; occasional: *He does odd jobs in his odd moments.* (*esp BrE*) *Life would be very dull without the odd adventure now and then.* **-ly** [adv] **-ness** [U]

peculiar 1 [B] strange; unusual (esp in a troubling or displeasing way): *What a peculiar thing to say. This food has a peculiar taste.* **2** [B] rather mad: *He was always rather peculiar, and now he's become quite mad.* **3** [F] *infml* rather ill: *I'm feeling rather peculiar; I think I'll go and lie down.* **4** [B] *esp old use* special; particular: *I think you'll find this letter of peculiar interest.* **5** [F *to*] *fml* belonging only (to a particular person, place, time, etc): *It is a way of speaking peculiar to people in this part of the country.* **-ly** [adv]

queer [Wa1;B] **1** *not fml* strange: *What a queer story! It's queer, but I'm sure he knew all about what happened.* **2** *infml* not well: *I'm feeling queer; I think I'll go home.* **3** *infml* mad (*esp in the phr* **queer in the head**): *He has been a bit* queer for years. There are a lot of queer people there. **-ly** [adv] **-ness** [U]

funny [Wa1;B] not fml strange; unexpected; hard to explain: What can that funny noise be? It's a funny thing, but I put the book here five minutes ago and now I can't find it. He's a funny sort of person; I don't understand him at all. **-nily** [adv]: Funnily enough, I knew what he meant although he didn't speak English.

curious [B] strange and interesting: It is a curious fact that he has plenty of money but never works. How curious of her to do that! What a curious thing to do! **-ly** [adv] **-ness** [U]

suspicious [B] **1** having or causing one to suspect [⇒G96] that someone or something is not right, safe, etc; doubtful or strange: He looks very suspicious to me, standing there outside the house in the dark. **2** [(of, about)] feeling suspicion, doubt, etc because something is strange, etc: I'm suspicious of her; what does she want? **-ly** [adv]: He's behaving very suspiciously.

fishy [Wa1;B] sl suspicious; strange; peculiar: This is a fishy business; I don't like it! **-shily** [adv] **-shiness** [U]

quaint [Wa1;B] interesting and pleasing because strange, unusual, or old: What a quaint old building! **-ly** [adv] **-ness** [U]

N69 adjectives : **very strange and unnatural**

weird [Wa1;B] **1** strange; unnatural: She watched all the weird happenings in a film about the dead coming to life. **2** infml unusual and not sensible or acceptable: She has some weird ideas. **-ly** [adv] **-ness** [U]

eerie [Wa2;B] causing fear because strange: It's eerie to walk through a dark forest at night. **-rily** [adv] **-riness** [U]

uncanny [Wa2;B] mysterious; not natural or usual: It seemed uncanny to hear her voice from the other side of the world. **-nily** [adv] **-niness** [U]

fantastic [B] very strange: The painter drew fantastic shapes. What fantastic ideas he has! **-ally** [adv; Wa4]

eccentric [B] (of a person or his behaviour) peculiar; unusual; rather strange: If you go to the palace in tennis shoes, they will think you are eccentric. **-ally** [adv; Wa4]

idiosyncratic [B] (of something about, or done by, one person) very peculiar and unusual: His behaviour has been very idiosyncratic lately. **-ally** [adv; Wa4]

monstrous [B] like a monster [⇒ N71]; very unusual, esp in a frightening way; frighteningly large or bad: What a monstrous creature! It's monstrous to expect us to do this! **-ly** [adv]

freak [Wa5;A] (esp of things) unnatural; very unusual: The country's been having freak weather; it's been very hot during the winter.

freakish [B] (esp of persons) unusual; unreasonable; strange: Her behaviour's

becoming so freakish that I wonder whether she isn't mad. **-ly** [adv]

deviant [B] different from an accepted standard; moving away from the usual: Deviant children need help. Deviant behaviour may be against the law.

N70 nouns : **special and strange**

speciality, also esp AmE **specialty** [C] **1** a special field of work or study: Her speciality is ancient Greek poetry. **2** [(of)] a particularly fine or best product: Fish baked in pastry is the specialty of this restaurant.

oddity [C] something odd: That kind of flower is certainly an oddity in this country.

peculiarity 1 [U] the quality of being peculiar: Peculiarity of dress may make people laugh at you. **2** [C] something which is peculiar: Bad driving is said to be a peculiarity of women. We have got used to his peculiarities of behaviour.

curiosity [C] someone or something curious: Her strange way of dressing made her a bit of a curiosity. The little old town is full of curiosities.

eccentricity 1 [U (of)] the quality of being eccentric: They laughed at the eccentricity of the mad queen's behaviour. **2** [C] an example of eccentric behaviour: They laughed at the mad queen's eccentricities.

idiosyncrasy [C] **1** a peculiarity of one person: Liking wild flowers in his garden is his personal idiosyncrasy. **2** infml a peculiar act: One of their idiosyncrasies was when they camped out in the garden.

N71 nouns : **persons and things which are very strange and unnatural** [C]

freak 1 a living creature of unnatural form: One of the new lambs is a freak; it was born with two tails. At the circus there's a freak with 8 fingers on each hand; you have to pay to see him. **2** infml a person with rather strange habits or ideas **3** a peculiar happening: By some strange freak, a little snow fell in Egypt a few years ago. **4** a sudden strange wish or change of mind: Her idea of having a garden with nothing but blue flowers in it was a freak of fancy. **5** [C9] sl a person who takes a special interest in the stated thing: He is a film freak.

monster 1 an animal, plant, or thing of unusually great size or strange form: That dog's a real monster; I've never seen such a big one. Some modern aircraft are monsters compared with those of 50 years ago. **2** a creature, imaginary or real, that is unnatural in shape, size, or qualities, and usu with an appearance so ugly as to be frightening: He read about sea monsters. She dreamt that terrible monsters with flaming eyes and sharp teeth were chasing her through the wood. **3** [(of)] derog a person whose evil qualities or actions are such as to raise strong feelings of dislike, hatred, fear, etc: *The judge told the murderer that he was a monster, not fit to be called a human being. History tells us of rulers in ancient times who were monsters of cruelty.* **4** [A] unusually large (in size or number): *Have you ever seen such monster vegetables as those growing here? The police were quite unable to control the monster crowds.*

monstrosity *emot* a terrible monster; something very deviant [⇒ N69]; something very ugly or silly: *His plan is a monstrosity! She bought a monstrosity of a hat.*

deviant a person or thing that is different or moves away from an accepted standard: *Sexual deviants often have difficulties with the law. 'The Hope of the Deviant' is the title of a book.*

mutant a living thing which has a quality not the same as any of its parents' qualities but produced by a change in the material of all its cells (**a mutation**)

pervert a person whose sexual behaviour is different from (what is considered) natural

N72 *nouns* : **unusual beings** [C]

giant 1 a man who is much bigger than is usual **2** (in fairy stories) a very big, strong creature in the form of a man, but often unfriendly to human beings and very cruel and stupid **3** a person of great ability: *Shakespeare is a giant among writers.*

titan *esp poet* a giant, esp if very powerful

dwarf 1 a person, animal or plant of much less than the usual size: *Their second son is a dwarf. She has several dwarf rose bushes.* **2** any of various small imaginary manlike creatures in fairy stories: *She likes the story of Snow White and the Seven Dwarfs.*

pygmy, pigmy 1 a member of a race of very short people **2** any person or animal of much less than usual height **3** a person of no importance, esp with regard to skill or brain power: *He considers himself a great singer, but he's a pygmy when compared with real musicians.*

Size, importance, and availability

N80 *nouns* : **size and quantity**

[ALSO ⇒ J65]

size 1 [U] the largeness or smallness (of something): *What size is the box? What size (of) shoes do you take (= wear)? It is not a matter of weight; it's a question of size.* **2** [C] an example or measurement of this: *What sizes of shoes do you have in the shop? He wears a size 8 shoe.*

quantity [U;C] *esp fml* (a statement of) how much (of something) is there, is wanted, etc: *This is a question of quantity, not quality. What quantity of salt do you need? They gave him large quantities of food.*

amount [C] *not usu fml* **1** a quantity: *Large amounts of money were spent on the bridge.* **2** total quantity or sum: *He could only pay half the amount he owed.*

handful 1 [C (*of*)] an amount that can be held in one hand: *He gave them each a handful of money.* **2** [C (*of*)] a small number or amount: *They have only a handful of people to help them.* **3** [C] a large amount: *When he was ill his hair came out in handfuls. He threw whole handfuls of money in the air!* **4** [S] *infml* something that causes a lot of difficulties: *Having four small children in the house is quite a handful!*

volume [U;C] *esp tech* an amount produced esp by some kind of (industrial) activity: *The volume of passenger travel on the railways is increasing. Great volumes of smoke came out of the hole.*

mass 1 [C] a quantity or heap of matter: *The ship cut its way slowly through masses of ice.* **2** [C] a large number (of persons or things): *His story is a mass of lies. Her garden is a mass of flowers.*

bulk 1 [U] *emph* size, shape, mass, or quantity: *Great bulk does not always mean great weight.* **2** [C *usu sing*] an unusually large, fat, or shapeless body: *The elephant lowered its great bulk by kneeling.* **3** [*the* R (*of*)] the main or greater part: *The bulk of the work has already been done.*

fit [S9] the size, shape, etc by which something fits or does not fit: *These shoes are a good fit; I'll buy them.*

N81 *adjectives* : **big**

big [Wa1] **1** [B] of more than average size, weight, force, importance, etc: *How big is it? No bigger than a pin. It's a big elephant/a big mouse. That child is big for his age. The big question is what to do next. He is a big-boned person. Don't cry; you're a big boy/girl now. The big moment has come at last!* **2** [A] (esp of people) doing a great deal of some activity: *He is a big eater/a big spender.* **3** [F; (B)] *esp AmE sl* very popular: *Frank Sinatra is very big in Las Vegas.* **-ness** [U]

large [Wa1;B] **1** more than usual in size, number, or amount: *He was a large man.* **2** having much room or space: *How large the room is!* **-ness** [U]

great 1 [Wa1;A;(B)] large in amount or degree: *Take great care. It was a great loss to us all. He has a great deal too much money/power. We have great hopes for her future.* **2** [Wa5;A] (often before another adj of size) big: *That great (big) tree takes away all the light.* **3** [Wa1;A] *often apprec* (of people) unusually active of the type: *She is a great talker and he is a great listener.* **4** [Wa1;B] *usu apprec* of excellent quality or ability: *He likes reading about the great men of the past. He was a great king/artist.* **5** [Wa1;A] *apprec* important: *This is a great occasion!* **6** [Wa1;B;Wa5 *as interj*] *infml* splendid; very enjoyable: *What a great idea! I've got the use of a car.—Great!* **7** [Wa5;A] (used in names to mark something important of its type): *The Great Wall of China; the Great Fire of London (1666).* **-ness** [U]

grand 1 [Wa1;B] (large and) splendid in appearance: *There's a grand view of the mountains.* **2** [Wa1;B] (of people) important or (esp) thinking oneself so: *The king's court was full of nobles and grand ladies. She's too grand to talk to us.* **3** [Wa1;B] *infml* very pleasant; delightful: *That was a grand party.* **4** [Wa5;A] complete (*esp in the phr* **the grand total**) **5** [Wa5;A] (used in certain titles): *the Grand Duchy of Lancaster*

N82 *adjectives* : **very big** [B]

vast [Wa1] very large and wide; great in size or amount; spreading a great distance: *The vast plains of this country spread for hundreds of miles. He is very valuable to his employer because of his vast experience in the business. The group of actors was brought from New York to London at vast expense.* **-ly** [adv] **-ness** [U]

huge [Wa1] **1** very big in size: *He lived in a huge house.* **2** *infml* very big in the mind's view: *The party was a huge success.* **-ly** [adv] **-ness** [U]

immense *usu apprec* very large: *There has been an immense improvement in his health.* **-ly** [adv] **-sity** [U;C] great size: *They were lost in the immensity/immensities of space.*

enormous very large indeed: *It was an enormous house/meal/amount of money. There is an enormous difference between the two countries.* **-ly** [adv] **-ness** [U] **-mity** [U9]

colossal very large in size or quantity: *It was a colossal building/a colossal rate of interest.* **-ly** [adv]

gigantic unusually large in amount or size: *He made gigantic efforts to save them.* **-ally** [adv Wa4]

titanic very large and strong: *The titanic forces of the earth can be seen when volcanoes erupt* (= explode into activity). **-ally** [adv Wa4]

terrific *infml* **1** very great in size or degree: *He drove at a terrific speed.* **2** very good; enjoyable; admirable: *It was a terrific play/book/party.* **-ally** [adv Wa4]

prodigious wonderful esp because of size, amount, or quality; very great: *He never forgets anything; his memory is prodigious. He made a prodigious effort.* **-ly** [adv]

gargantuan *esp lit* very big: *He ate a gargantuan meal.*

N83 *adjectives* : **very big in special ways**

gross [Wa1;B] unpleasantly large and fat, etc: *In his old age he became gross through/from over-eating* (= eating too much). **-ly** [adv] **-ness** [U]

massive [B] **1** of great size; strong and heavy **2** (esp of the head) large and solid-seeming **3** (of qualities and actions) great; powerful: *We must make massive efforts to improve things. The government has massive support from the people.* **-ly** [adv] **-ness** [U]

voluminous [B] **1** (of containers) very large; able to hold a lot: *She had a voluminous shopping bag.* **2** (of a (part of a) garment) very loose and full; using much cloth: *She wore a voluminous skirt.* **3** *often deprec* producing or containing much writing: *He is a voluminous writer and has produced a voluminous report.* **-ly** [adv]

bulky [Wa2;B] **1** having bulk [⇒ N80] esp if large of its kind or rather fat: *The elephant is a bulky animal.* **2** having great size or mass in comparison with weight: *He was wearing some kind of a bulky woollen garment to keep warm.*

large-scale [Wa5;B] happening in large quantities to many people over a wide area, etc: *There has been a large-scale change in what people eat in that country in the last ten years.*

king-size [Wa5;A] *not fml* (esp of things being sold) very large: *He bought a king-size box of chocolates for her.*

big-time [Wa5;B] *not fml* relating to the top rank (esp in sport or the amusement business): *Don't worry; you're big-time now.*

mammoth [Wa5;A] *esp emot & emph* of large size: *It was a mammoth performance, with hundreds of actors: It needs a mammoth effort to move that heavy table.*

giant [Wa5;A] *not fml & often apprec* (of) large size: *They have built a giant factory just outside the town.*

astronomic(al) [Wa5;B] *emph* very large; too large to count: *They are asking really astronomic prices for these things now. The distance is astronomic; don't ask me how far!* **-ally** [adv Wa4]

N84 *adjectives* : **quite big, etc**

substantial [B] **1** big enough to be satisfactory: *He gave us substantial help. It was a substantial supply of food.* **2** considerable; important: *He wants to make substantial changes.* **3** solid; strongly made: *It is a substantial desk.* **4** concerning the important part or meaning: *The substantial truth of his report is hidden by his untidy methods of presenting his ideas.* **-ly** [adv]: *He helped them substantially.*

sizeable, sizable [B] quite large: *She bought a sizeable house outside Birmingham. It's a sizeable garden; he can grow all the vegetables he needs in it.*

considerable [B] *esp euph* (quite) large: *His father left him a considerable amount of money.* **-bly** [adv Wa3]: *He helped them considerably.*

fair [Wa5;A] *not fml* (quite) large: *How far is it to the town?—Oh, it's a fair distance. Is it big?—Yes, it's a fair size.* **-ly** [adv]: *Is it big?—Yes, it's fairly big.*

N85 *adjectives, etc* : **not big**

small 1 [Wa1;B] little in size, weight, force, importance, etc; not large: *He was a small man, only five feet tall. It's a book written for small children. The girl is small for her age. There was only a small number of people there. It's the smallest shoe size in the shop. The space is big enough only for the smallest of cars.* **2** [Wa5;A] doing only a limited amount of business or activity: *He is a small businessman* (= owns a small business). *There are many small farmers in the area.* **3** [A] (*esp with nouns marked* [U]) very little; slight: *They had small hope of success. She took small interest in politics.* **-ness** [U] **4** [adv] in a small manner: *He writes so small I can't read it.* **in a small way** modestly; not grandly: *He was in business in a small way at home.*

little 1 [Wa1;A; (B)] small: *There was a little door in the wall. Two little insects were on the glass.* **2** [Wa5;A] short: *I saw her a little while ago.* **3** [B] young: *My little girl* (= daughter) *is too little to ride a bicycle.* **4** [Wa1;B] not important: *He often forgets the little people who voted him into power.* **5** [adv] to only a small degree: *It is a little known fact that.* . . . **6** [adv] *esp poet & pomp* (with verbs of feeling and knowing) not at all: *They little thought that the truth would be discovered. He little cares/Little does he care whether we live or die!* **7** [adv] rarely (*esp in the phr* **very little**): *I go there very little now.* [⇒ N97]

N86 *adjectives, etc* : **very small**

tiny [Wa1;B] very small indeed: *There's a tiny insect on your hand; look! This is the tiniest car I've ever seen.* **-iness** [U]

wee [Wa1;B] *esp ScotE often affec* (very) small: *He's just a wee boy; he's only five.*

teeny *also* **teeny-weeny** *also* **teensy-weensy** [Wa1;B] *infml* (used esp when speaking to children) very small: *Would you like a teeny bit more to eat?*

minute [Wa2;B] **1** very small, in size or degree: *His writing's so minute that it's difficult to read.* **2** giving attention to the smallest points; very careful and exact: *The teacher wrote a minute report on the pupil's work and behaviour.* **-ly** [adv] **-ness** [U]

miniature 1 [Wa5;A] (of something copied or represented) very small: *The child was playing on the floor with his collection of miniature farm animals.* **2** [C (*of*)] a very small copy or representation of anything **in miniature** very like the stated thing or person, but much smaller: *That little boy is his father in miniature.*

minuscule [Wa5;B] very small indeed: *What minuscule handwriting!*

infinitesimal [Wa5;B] very small indeed **-ly** [adv]: *Atoms are infinitesimally small.*

microscopic [Wa5;B] *often infml* very small: *It's impossible to read his microscopic handwriting.* **-ally** [adv Wa4]

N87 *adjectives* : **small in special ways** [Wa5]

small-scale [B] happening in small quantities to few people over a limited area, etc: *He runs a small-scale business locally.*

small-time [B] *not fml, often deprec* relating to the lowest rank (esp in sport or the amusement business): *'I'm tired of small-time acting!' she said.*

pygmy, pigmy [A] *often tech, humor, or deprec* very small: *They have pigmy elephants in that country. Don't expect his pygmy brain to understand these scientific matters.*

dwarf [A] *sometimes tech* small, less than the usual size: *There is a dwarf apple tree in the garden.*

N88 *adjectives* : **neither big nor small** [Wa5]

average [B] not specially big or small: *He is of average height. His height is average.*

medium [A] *often tech* of middle size, amount, quality, value, etc; not great or small: *The room is of medium size. He bought a medium-priced car.*

middling [B] *not fml* that is between large and small in size, degree, etc; that is neither good nor bad in quality, kind, etc: *The house is large, but the rooms are only of middling size. His last book had a middling success. She enjoyed her holiday, though the weather was only middling.*

N89 *adjectives* : **big, esp in importance**

major [Wa5;A] greater when compared with others in size, number, or importance: *The car needs major repairs. The play is a major success. There has been a major improvement in his work.*

main [Wa5;A] first in importance or size: *This is a busy main road. Our main meal is in the evening. Note down the main points of the speech. Soldiers guarded the main gates. The main body of walkers got separated from the ones at the back.* **-ly** [adv]: *There were mainly women in the room. He's mainly interested in money.*

principal [Wa5;A] *often fml* main; most important; of highest rank: *The Nile is one of the principal rivers of Africa. The principal need of this village is a pure water supply.* **-ly** [adv Wa4]: *They are principally concerned with making more money.*

chief [Wa5;A] *not fml* main; principal: *Their chief aim is to make more money. Our chief hope is to help people.* **-ly** [adv]: *He's chiefly interested in sex.*

senior 1 [B (*to*)] (esp of people) more important: *He is the senior officer; let's ask him.* **2** [C] a person who is older, or of higher rank, etc (than another): *He is my senior by three years/ in the office.*

superior 1 [Wa5;A] *fml & tech* higher in position **2** [Wa5;B (*to*)] (of people and things) of greater importance, quality, or value, etc: *I want to speak to your superior officer. This is a superior cloth; it's much better than the others.* **3** [C] a person who is higher in position (than another): *He is my superior and I must do what he says.* **superiority** [U] the state of being superior: *The superiority of these goods to the others is easy to see.*

N90 adjectives : small, esp in importance [*usu* Wa5]

minor [B] less when compared with others, in size, number, or importance: *The car needs a few minor repairs. He has written one or two minor books. There have only been minor improvements in his work.*

lesser [A] not so great in worth, degree, size, etc; smaller: *To go there is the lesser evil/lesser of two evils; to stay here would be worse.*

subsidiary [B (*to*)] of second importance to the main company, plan, work, etc: *They have a subsidiary factory in the south.*

dependent [B (*on*)] that depends on: *Success is dependent on the results of this examination. Have you any dependent children?*

subordinate [B (*to*)] of a lower rank or position: *a subordinate worker. Your wishes are subordinate to the company's aims.*

junior 1 [B (*to*)] (esp of people) less important: *He spoke to a junior official and got no real help.* **2** [C] a person who is younger or of lower rank etc (than another): *He is my junior by three years/in the office.*

inferior [B (*to*)] **1** *fml & tech* lower in position **2** (of people and things) not good or less good in importance, quality, or value: *inferior work; His work is inferior to mine. He's so clever, he makes me feel inferior.* **inferiority** [U] the condition of being or feeling inferior: *inferiority to others; a sense of one's inferiority.*

negligible [B] very small; too small to be worth bothering about: *It is a negligible amount of money.* **-bly** [adv]

N91 adjectives & nouns : **maximum, minimum, and optimum**

maximum [C (*of*); A] the largest number, amount, etc: *What's the maximum distance you've ever walked? Today we reached the maximum temperature this year. He smokes a maximum of ten cigarettes a day. The lamp will give you the maximum of light. The sound has reached its maximum* (= its loudest).

maximal [Wa5;B] as great as possible: *The plant reaches maximal size in two months.* **-ly** [adv]

minimum [C (*of*); A] the least, or the smallest possible, quantity, number, or degree: *This price is his minimum; he refuses to lower it further. He couldn't avoid losing some money in his business, but he kept his losses to a minimum. The minimum pass mark in this examination is 40 out of 100. He couldn't join the police, because he was below the minimum height allowed by the rules.*

minimal [Wa5;B] of the smallest possible amount, degree, or size: *Fortunately, the storm only did minimal damage to the farmer's crops. Her clothing was minimal.* **-ly** [adv]

optimum [C; A] best or most favourable: *The optimum rainfall for growing rubber is about 100 inches a year. The optimum is 100 inches a year.*

optimal [Wa5;B] relating to the best: *The optimal rainfall is about 100 inches a year. 100 inches is optimal.* **-ly** [adv]

N92 verbs : **growing and getting bigger**

[ALSO ⇒ N15]

grow [I0; T1] to (cause to) get bigger: *The plant began to grow (larger and larger). Can you grow any plants here?—No, very little grows here. The little plant grew into a tree. He has grown into a man. As the weeks went on his troubles grew.*

sprout [I0; T1] to (cause to) begin to grow: *The seeds began to sprout. The young tree sprouted leaves.* (*fig infml*) *That boy is really sprouting!* (*fig*) *The idea sprouted quickly. He began to sprout ideas.*

develop 1 [T1; I0: (*from, into*)] to (cause to) grow, increase, or become larger or more complete: *It has developed from a seed into a plant. That engine develops a lot of heat. Different conditions develop different sides of a person's character. He has gradually developed a liking for that fruit. A child develops rapidly between the ages of 13 and 16.* **2** [T1] to study or think out fully; present fully: *I'd like to develop this idea a little more fully before I go on to my next point.* **3** [T1] to bring out the possibilities of (esp land or natural substances): *We must develop all the natural substances in our country which can make us rich. Look at all that empty land just waiting to be* *developed!* **4** [T1; I∅] to (cause to) begin to be seen, become active, or show signs of: *Trouble is developing among the sailors. He seems to be developing an illness.*

spread 1 [T1; I∅: (*out*)] to stretch or extend in space or time: *He stood up and spread* (*out*) *his arms. His visits to Canada were spread* (*out*) *over five years.* **2** [D1 *with/on*] to put (a covering) on (a surface): *She spread butter on the bread.* **3** [I∅] to extend to cover a larger area: *In the last hundred years the city has spread greatly. The water spread slowly across the ground.*

swell [Wv5 **swollen**] **1** [I∅ (*up*)] to increase in fullness and roundness: *Her ankle swelled after the fall.* **2** [T1] to increase the size or amount of: *He took a job to swell his pocket/funds* (=money). **3** [T1; I∅] (*fig*) to fill: *Her heart swelled with pride. Pride swelled her heart.* **4** [T1 (*out*)] to fill, giving a round shape: *The cat's stomach was swelled with milk/swollen with milk.*

inflate [Wa5;T1] **1** to cause to swell with gas, air, etc: *He inflated the plastic ball.* **2** (*fig*) to feel greater, more important, etc than necessary, desirable, etc: *They are inflated with their own power.*

blow up [v adv T1] *infml* to inflate (def **1**): *He blew up the plastic ball. Blow the bicycle tyres up.*

increase [T1; I∅] *often fml* to make or become larger in amount or number: *The population of this town has increased. I increased the amount of water to be added during cooking.*

wax *rare* **1** [I∅] to grow: *The moon waxes at this time of the month.* **2** [L7] *old use* (of a person) to become (*usu in the phr* **wax merry/happy,** etc): *He waxed merry as he drank.*

expand 1 [I∅; T1: (*by, into*)] to (cause to) grow larger: *Iron expands when it is heated. He breathed deeply and expanded his chest. The narrow path expanded into a wide road. You should expand this short story by 50 pages.* **2** [I∅] (of a person) to become more friendly and willing to talk: *This quiet young man expands only when he is among friends.*

prolong [T1] to make longer: *Some people have tried to find a means of prolonging life.* **prolongation** [U; C] the action or result of prolonging

extend 1 [L9] (of space, land or time) to reach, stretch, or continue: *The Roman Empire extended to/as far as the Atlantic Ocean. The hot weather extended into October.* **2** [T1] to make longer or greater, esp so as to reach a desired point: *He wants to extend his garden/extend the railway to the next town. The US has greatly extended its influence in world affairs.* **3** [T1] to stretch out to the limit (a part of one's body): *a bird with its wings extended; He refused to take the hand extended in friendship.* **4** [D1 (*to*); T1] *fml* to give or offer (help, friendship, etc) to (someone): *She extended a warm welcome to him. She extended him a warm welcome. Government help will be*

extended where it is needed. The bank will extend you credit (= the right to borrow money). **5** [T1 *usu pass*] to cause to use all possible power: *The horse won the race easily without being fully extended.*

enlarge [I∅; T1] to (cause to) grow larger or wider: *This photograph probably won't enlarge well. They built three new rooms to enlarge the school.* (*fig*) *Travel enlarges the mind.*

magnify [T1] to make (something) appear larger than in reality: *Cells of the body must be magnified several times before they can be seen.* (*fig*) *There is no need to magnify your difficulties. He is an official of low rank, though he magnifies his own importance.*

multiply 1 [T1; I∅] to increase: *to multiply one's chances of success; Our chances multiplied.* **2** [I∅] to breed: *When animals have more food, they generally multiply faster.*

amplify 1 [T1] to make larger or greater **2** [T1] to increase the strength of (something, esp sound coming through electrical instruments) **3** [T1; I∅ (*on, upon*)] to explain in greater detail: *He amplified on his remarks with drawings and figures.*

maximize, -ise [T1] to make as large as possible to increase to the maximum [⇒ N91]: *We must maximize our profits next year.*

add to [v prep T1, 6] to increase by adding one thing to another: *Can you add to what you have paid? Your carelessness adds to our problems.*

augment [T1; (I∅)] *usu fml & tech* to make or become bigger, more valuable, better, etc: *He augments his earnings by growing his own food.*

supplement [T1 (*by, with*)] *fml* to add to: *She supplements her diet/rations* (= food) *with eggs and fruit from the farm. He supplemented his income by working in the evenings.* **supplementary** [Wa5;B] in the nature or for the purposes of a supplement; added; extra

swamp [T1 *often pass* (*with*)] to give too much of (something): *We were swamped with letters from people wanting work. They swamped us with work; there was more than we could do.*

exceed [T1] to be greater or do more than: *His ability exceeds hers. The driver was exceeding the speed limit in the town and the police took his name and address.* **exceedingly** [adv] *esp fml* very much: *I'm exceedingly pleased to meet you. It was exceedingly good of you to come!*

dwarf [T1] to make (something) seem small: *That new building is so big that it dwarfs all the others.*

N93 nouns : **growing and getting bigger**

growth 1 [U] the act of growing: *The garden looks good; there's been plenty of growth this* *year. The growth of real democracy is slow.* **2** [C *usu sing*] an act or result of growing: *He has a good growth of hair.*

development 1 [U] the act of developing: *'The development of our country is a matter of the first importance,' he said.* **2** [C] an example of this; something new: *What developments have there been in the matter since I left?—No fresh developments.*

spread [C *usu sing*] the amount by which something spreads: *The spread of civilization has been slow.*

expansion [U] the act of expanding: *People have known about the expansion of iron due to heat for a long time. This road needs expansion.*

inflation [U] the act of inflating

extension 1 [U] the act of extending: *They hope for the extension of the road to reach their village.* **2** [C] an example or result of this; anything extended: *He built an extension onto his house. We need an extension of time to pay the money back.*

extent [U] the amount by which something extends or is extended: *Do you know the extent of the damage to the house? To what extent* (= by how much) *have they changed the law?*

extensive [B] having a great extent: *They have made extensive changes in the law.* **-ly** [adv] **-ness** [U]

addition 1 [U] the act of adding, esp of adding numbers together **2** [C] something added: *A newly born child is often called an addition to the family.*

enlargement 1 [U] the act of enlarging **2** [C] an example of this; anything enlarged

increase [C; U] more of anything: *We need increases in money. There has been an increase in the amount of water in the lake. Crime there is on the increase* (= increasing).

increment [C] *fml* an increase, esp in money paid for work done: *He got an increment of £50.*

magnification 1 [U] the act of magnifying **2** [C] an example of this; anything magnified; *tech* the amount by which anything is or can be magnified

multiplication *usu fml* [U] the act or result of multiplying: *The multiplication in the number of rabbits in Australia worried the farmers.*

amplification *usu fml* [U] the act or result of amplifying: *Your remarks will need some amplification by means of drawings or photographs.*

augmentation *usu fml* **1** [U] the act of increasing or of being increased in size or amount **2** [C] that which is added to something; an increase: *He received an augmentation of £2,000 a year.*

supplement [C] **1** an additional amount of something: *She has been ill and must have supplements to her ordinary food.* **2** an additional written part, at the end of a book, or as a separate part of a newspaper, magazine, etc: *The big Sunday papers have colour supplements, often called the Sunday supplements.*

N94 *verbs* : **growing and getting smaller**

lessen [I∅; T1] to become or make less: *The noise lessened. Lessen the noise, please!*

grow less [v adv I∅] to become less: *The noise slowly grew less.*

diminish [I∅; T1] to (cause to) become or seem smaller: *His illness diminished his strength. That country's money is diminishing in value. The power of the Crown has increased, is increasing and ought to be diminished* (from a speech in Parliament, 1780).

dwindle [I∅ (*away*)] *often emot* to become smaller and smaller or less and less, usu slowly: *The number of people helping us dwindled steadily until there were only four left.*

decrease [T1; I∅] to (cause to) become less in size, number, strength, amount, or quality: *Our sales are decreasing. I shall have to decrease your wages.*

decline [I∅] **1** to move from a better to a worse position: *His power/health/influence has begun to decline now that he is old. The old man declined rapidly and soon died. That old lady wants to spend her declining years by the sea. Rome reached a position of great power and then slowly declined. 'Standards of quality are declining everywhere,' he said.* **2** *fml or lit* to slope or move downwards: *About 2 miles east, the land begins to decline towards the river. The sun was declining in the west.*

wane *rare* [Wv4; I∅ (*away*)] to grow gradually less until becoming nothing: *The moon waned.* (*fig*) *Their hopes waned* (*away*).

shrink 1 [I∅; T1] to (cause to) become smaller, as from the effect of heat or water: *Washing wool in hot water will shrink it/make it shrink. Meat shrinks by losing some of its fat in cooking. The value of money shrinks faster in some countries than others.* **2** [L9] to move back and away: *Fearing a beating; the dog shrank into a corner.* **shrunken** [B] having shrunk: *His face looked shrunken from lack of food and sleep.*

deflate [T1] **1** to let air, gas, etc out of: *He deflated the tyres of the car.* **2** (*fig*) to make (someone) feel smaller, less important, etc than necessary, desirable, etc: *She really deflated him with her nasty remarks about his clothes.*

let down [v adv T1] *infml* to deflate (def **1**): *Someone let down my bicycle tyres!*

reduce 1 [T1; (I∅)] *often fml* to (cause to) become smaller or less: *He reduced the amount of money they could spend. Her weight needs reducing.* **2** [X9] to cause to do, feel, etc (a stated thing): *He reduced her to tears. Her words reduced him to angry silence.*

minimize, -ise [T1] to make as small as possible; reduce to the minimum [⇒ N91]: *He hopes to minimize the amount of work he does.*

condense [Wv5; T1] to make (esp books, etc) smaller, esp by reducing the number of words: *This is a condensed version of the book; it's* *only half as long as the original book. He condensed his speech to half its original length.*

contract [I0; T1] to (cause to) become smaller, esp in mass: *Metals contract when they lose heat. The animal contracted its body.* **contraction 1** [U] the act of contracting **2** [C] the shortened form of something, esp a word or phrase **3** [C] an act of contracting

telescope 1 [I0; T1] to (cause to) become shorter by crushing, as in a violent accident: *The two buses telescoped together killing all the passengers. The railway carriage was telescoped in the accident but luckily there were no passengers inside.* **2** [I0] to become shorter by one part sliding over another: *This instrument will telescope small enough to fit into this box.*

cut down [v adv I0 (*on*)] *esp infml & emot* to reduce: *We must cut down on our spending.*

N95 *nouns* : **growing and getting smaller**

diminution *fml* **1** [U] an act of diminishing **2** [C *usu sing*] an example of this: *The new law caused a diminution in the power of the Church.*

decrease [U; C] an act or result of decreasing: *Crime is on the decrease in that city. We need a great decrease in the number of deaths on the roads.*

decline [C *usu sing*] a period or amount of declining, esp as something or someone gets near the end: *Edward Gibbon wrote 'The Decline and Fall of the Roman Empire'. There is a sharp decline in interest in sports in our town. She went into a decline and soon died.* **on the decline** declining: *In our town interest in sports is on the decline.*

shrinkage 1 [U] the act of shrinking: *This kind of cloth isn't affected by shrinkage when washed.* **2** [C] (*esp fig*) an example of this: *There has been a shrinkage in the numbers of people going there.*

deflation [U] the act of deflating

reduction 1 [U] the act of reducing: *The reduction in the numbers of people working in the factory has caused difficulties.* **2** [C] an example or result of this: *They made reductions in the number of people working in the factory.*

condensation 1 [U] the act of condensing: *The condensation of a book like that is difficult.* **2** [C] an example or result of condensing: *I read a condensation of the book.*

N96 *determiners & adverbials, etc* : **much, many, etc**

much 1 [det] (*usu in neg sentences and questions*) great in quantity, amount, degree: *I haven't got much interest in cooking. I don't have very much time.* **2** [det] (in all types of sentences, expressing amount): *How much time have we got? I have too much work to do.* **3** [adv Wa5] (*usu in neg sentences and questions*)

a often: *I don't read much because I don't have the time.* **b** to a great degree: *I don't like that idea much.* (*esp fml*) *I'm much surprised to hear that. Much to my surprise/displeasure she forgot our meeting* (= surprising/displeasing me greatly by that). **4** [adv Wa5] (in all types of sentences in the phrs **how much? too much, very much,** expressing amount): *How much do you like him?—I like him very much. I've been walking too much in the hot sun.* **5** [adv Wa5] (*with compar & superl*) by a large amount: *It was much worse than I thought.* **6** [adv Wa5] by a large degree: *She is much the quickest worker.* **7** [adv Wa5] nearly: *In most ways she is much the same as usual. Today was much like yesterday.* **8** [adv Wa5] **much more/less** and even more/less so: *I can hardly bear to walk, much less run.* **9** [pron] (*esp in neg sentences or questions*) a large quantity, amount, etc: *Some was lost, but much was saved. We haven't seen much of you* (= you haven't visited us) *recently. Much of the work is already finished. I borrowed the book but I haven't read very much (of it) yet.* **not much good at** not very good at: *He's not much good at games.* **not up to much** not very good or well: *The film's not up to much, although the actors are good. I don't feel up to much after my cold.* **not much of a** not a very good: *It's not much of a day for a walk* (= bad weather). **as much again** twice the amount: *I got £10 but he got as much again!* **I thought as much** I expected that (esp something bad): *So they found out he's been cheating. I thought as much.* **as much as one can do** the most possible **without so much as** not doing or saying even so little as: *She went off without so much as telling me.* **this/that much** the particular amount or words: *I'll say this much, he's a good worker* (*although I don't like him personally*). **too much for** having too many difficulties; too hard for: *Climbing the smallest hill is too much for her since her illness.* **as much as** the amount that: *When you cook meat, there's never as much as when you bought it.*

more 1 [adv Wa5 (*than*)] (used for forming the compar of most adjectives and adverbs that have more than two syllables, and of many that have only two): *His illness was more serious than the doctor first thought. I asked him if he could explain the matter more simply. The first question is more difficult than the second.* **2** [adv Wa5 (*than*)] to or in a greater degree; for a longer space of time: *He'll never be a good games player if he doesn't practise more. He seems to care more for his dogs than for his children. Surprisingly, her face had more the appearance of anger than pleasure.* **3** [adv] again (*in the phrs* **any more, once more, no more**): *The old man stays in his village now; he doesn't travel any more* (= any longer). *The teacher said he'd repeat the question once more. The ship sank below the waves, and was seen no more* (= no longer, never again). **4** [U] a greater amount, quantity, part, etc (*esp in the phrs* **more than, even more**): *As he grows older,* he spends *more* of his time in bed. He owns *more* of this land than any other member of his family. He already owns half the land; now he wants even *more*. I've got *more* than you. **5** [U] an additional amount, quantity, part, etc: *I've given you all you asked for; what more d'you want? Have you had enough to eat, or would you like some more?—Yes; give me some more of that cake. If you stay at that hotel, you'll have to pay a little more. He'd like to know more about the young man his daughter wishes to marry. Tell me more!* (= I'm interested in what you say) **6** [pron] a greater number of people or things (*esp in the phrs* **more than, even more**): *Many people support the government, but more are against it. How many rooms are there in this house?—More than in mine.* **7** [det] a greater number or amount of: *There are more cars on the road in summer than in winter.* **and what is more** also and more importantly, seriously, etc: *You've come late for school and what's more you've lost your books.* **more and more** to or in a degree that continues to increase; increasingly: *As time went on, he found it more and more difficult to support his family.* **more than a little** *pomp or fml* very: *If you tell your father what you've done, he'll be more than a little angry.* **no more** neither: *He can't afford a new car, and no more can I.* **no more . . . than** in no greater degree . . . than: *He's no more fit to be a minister than a schoolboy would be.* **the more . . ., the more/less** to the degree that . . . , to an equal/less degree: *The more angry he became, the more she laughed at him. The more difficult the questions are, the less likely I am to be able to answer them.* **more than meets the eye** additional things which make the matter less simple than it appears: *There's more in her refusal than meets the eye; I think she's trying to hide something.* **see more of someone** to meet someone again, or more often: *He liked the girl and thought he'd like to see more of her.* **the more . . ., the more/less** by the amount that . . . , by a greater/less amount: *The more he gives his children, the more they want. The more I see of him, the less I like him.*

most 1 [(*the*) det] greatest in number, quantity, or degree: *The money should be shared among those who have (the) most need of it. The youngest of his children takes (the) most interest in his lessons. The storm did most damage to the houses on the edge of the cliff.* (= those houses were damaged more than others). *Which is most—10, 20, or 30?* **2** [det] nearly all: *He's visited most countries in Europe. Most English words form their plural by adding s.* **3** [adv Wa5] (forming the superl of adjectives and adverbs with more than one syllable): *Which do you think is the most comfortable hotel in this town? All the questions were difficult, but which did you think was most difficult?* **4** [adv Wa5] in the greatest or highest degree; more than anything else: *What people most like about the doctor is his kindness. I like all kinds of books, but most of all I like books about history. You can help me most by preparing the vegetables for dinner.* **5** [adv Wa5] (used for giving force) **a** (to an adjective) very: *He thanked his host for a most enjoyable party. It's most dangerous to play with explosives.* **b** (to an adverb) quite; very: *Whatever happens, I shall most certainly attend the meeting. He'll most probably sell the house and go and live with his daughter.* **6** [adv Wa5] *esp infml AmE* almost: *He plays cards most every evening. Most everyone in this small town possesses a car.* **7** [*the* R] the greatest amount: *We tried to stop the house burning down, but the most we could do was to save some of the pictures and furniture.* **8** [pron] the greatest number, quantity, part, etc; nearly all: *Most of the children in this school come from poor homes. Most of his time is spent travelling. A few people were killed in the fire, but most were saved.* **at (the) most/at the very most** not more than (the stated amount): *She's at most 25 years old. It'll take an hour, at the very most, to drive home.* **for the most part** nearly completely; mainly; in almost all cases or respects: *Summers in the south of France are for the most part dry and sunny. I agree for the most part with what you say.* **make the most of** to get the best use or greatest gain from: *Make the most of your free time; don't waste it in sleep. He doesn't do well because he doesn't make the most of his ability. Make the most of your appearance/yourself, and people will find you attractive.*

many 1 [det] a great number of: *How many letters are there in the alphabet? Were there many people at the play? You have too many books on that shelf. There are so many that I can't choose.* (*fml*) *Many people would like to take holidays abroad. He ate three cakes in as many seconds* (= one a second). **2** [pron] a great number: *Take more apples; I don't want many for myself. How many are there? He ate three and said he could eat as many again* (= three more). **3** [P *of*] a great number: *Not many of us will pass the examination. Many of us will live to see great changes.* **a good/great many** *infml* a large number: **many a man, hour, etc** many men, hours, etc **one, two, three, etc too many** one (etc) more than is needed **many's the time, day, etc that** there have been many times, days, etc **one too many for (somebody)** clever enough to beat **the many** (only compared to **the few**) the large numbers of people who possess little

a lot *genl & infml* **1** much: *I like it a lot.* **2** (*used with* of) a large number: *A lot of people come here.*

a number of some; many: *He knows a number of people here.*

numerous [B] *fml* being very many: *I spoke to him about it on numerous occasions* (= often).

majority [(*the*) GC (*of*)] the greater number (of persons, things, etc); more than half: *The majority (of the people) want/wants peace.*

very [Wa5] **1** [adv] (used to make a statement

stronger or to emphasize an adjective): *It is very hot today. He drives very fast. She's very pretty, isn't she? He is looking very much better now. It is his very own car.* **2** [A] this (person, thing, etc) and no other: *You are the very person I wanted to meet. The very idea of doing it angered him.* **3** [A] (used to emphasize a noun): *It happened at the very beginning/end of the meeting.*

indeed [adv Wa5] **1** (used after **very** + adjective to make the meaning even stronger): *The crowds were very large indeed.* **2** often derog (used to show surprise and interest): *Did he, indeed?*

N97 *determiners & adverbials* : **not much, many etc**

little [det; pron; U] (of mass nouns) not much; not enough: *The little I have is not worth giving. I have very little (money, food, etc) left. I understood little of what he said. She has so little time to enjoy herself. I had little difficulty in finding the house* (=I found it easily). **little by little** gradually

a little 1 a small amount, but at least some: *She had a few eggs and a little milk left. Give me a little of that wine. Would you like some more cake?—Just a little, thank you. I had a little difficulty in finding the house* (=it wasn't so easy to find the house). *She speaks a little French; not much. Does she speak any French?—A little.* **2** a short time: *He came back after a little. Can't you stay a little longer? In a little over 10 years life in that city was very different. Let's walk for a little.* **3** *also infml* **a little bit** to some degree; rather: *I was a little annoyed. It's a little bit silly, isn't it!*

few [det; pron; Wa1;GU] not many; not enough: *Few people came. How few?—Very few indeed. I have very few (chocolates) left. Few of the children were tired. There are so few that I can't give you one/any. She has so few chances to enjoy herself. There were no fewer than a hundred cars there* (=There were 100, or more, cars there.) *Which of you has the fewest mistakes? There were too few machines for the work. We are many and they are few. For the last few years he has been abroad.* **few and far between** rare; not happening often: *Holidays are few and far between.* **the few** (compared to **the many**) the small number of people with special needs or desires: *Only the few are likely to enjoy this music.*

a few a small number, but at least some: *She had a few eggs and a little milk. There are only a very few left. I'm keeping a few for him. Let's invite a few friends to come with us. Here are a few more chocolates. Can you stay for a few days longer?* **quite a few**, *also emph* **a good few** several; more than a few: *Quite a few of us are worried. You'll have to wait a good few weeks for more!*

less [((than)] (*comp of* **little**) not as much: *I have some bread, but he has less. There is less time*

than I thought. She wanted to do more for you; she certainly couldn't do less (than she did). (ironical) He couldn't possibly have done less than he did (=He did almost nothing).

least (*superl of* **little**) **1** the smallest in size, amount, degree, measure, etc: *He has the least money of us all. He was the least surprised of us all.* **2** slightest: *He's not the least bit worried.* **3** [*the* U] the smallest thing, amount, degree, etc: *Giving him food was the least we could do.* **at least** if nothing else: *The food wasn't good, but at least it was cheap.* **at (the) least** not less than: *It costs at least 5 pounds. At the least, it costs 5 pounds.* **least of all** especially not: *I don't want anyone to come, least of all him!*

minority [GC *usu sing*] **1** the smaller number (of persons, things, etc); less than half: *A minority of the people want/wants war.* **2** a group of people, things, etc that is smaller than others: *Black people are a minority in the United States.*

N98 *determiners & pronouns* : **some and any**

a [det] (**an** *before a vowel sound*) **1** one in particular: *He bought a bottle of wine.* **2** any one (of a number): *We need a new house; this one is too small for us now that we have children.* **3** *genl* one: *Can I have a piece of cake/a pound of butter, please?* **4** for each (one): *It costs 10p a pound* (=for each pound). **5** (with someone's name) one whom I have not met before: *There is a Mr Jones to see you, sir.* **6** (with someone's name) someone of the same kind as: *What is the chance of a second Einstein?*

some 1 [det] a certain amount or number of: *Have some (more) wine. He bought some cakes. Some people came to see her. He had to wait some time before he came. Would you like some (more) bread?—Yes, I'll have some/a little more, thanks.* **2** [det] quite a large amount of: *He has been waiting here (for) some time.* **3** [det] *infml* a very good: *I really enjoyed myself; that was some party!* **4** [det] *infml* a very bad: *Some party that was; I didn't enjoy myself at all!* **5** [det] not known or important (*esp in the phr* **some . . . or other**): *I read it in some book or other. Some fellow told me; I can't remember who/his name.* **6** [pron (*of*)] a number or amount: *Some of the men came. She gave some of the meat to the cat. Can I have some, please?*

several 1 [det] more than two but fewer than many: *I know several people named Green. I make several visits each year to London.* **2** [Wa5;A] *esp old use and fml* (with plural nouns) of the stated people or things; separate; respective: *They stated their several opinions one at a time. They shook hands and went their several ways.* **3** [Wa5;A] *lit* various; different: *The walls were built at several times by different people.* **4** [pron] a few but not many; some: *Several of the apples are bad and several more have worm holes.*

any 1 [det] one or some of whatever kind; every: *Any child would know that. Ask any man you meet. Come any time you want (to).* **2** [det; pron (*of*)] one or more others; one or more among: *Have you any (other) books besides these? Do you want any of these?—Yes; I'd like some. Have you any bread?—Yes; a little./Yes; plenty.*

N99 adverbs, etc : **scarcely, hardly, and only** [Wa5]

only 1 [adv] and nothing more; and no one else: *Only five minutes more, please! Ladies only* (notice). *Only ladies can come in here. He only sits and looks out of the window. It was something known only to us. He saw only five men. Only five of the men did he see. It is made from fresh fruit only. Not only he but the whole family went. I saw him only yesterday (= and no longer ago). Only a doctor can do that.* **2** [conj] but, esp **a** (before limiting conditions): *You may go, only come back early.* **b** (before unfortunate events): *He wants to go, only he can't.* **c** *also BrE* **only that** (before the reason why something will probably not happen): *I'd do it with pleasure, only I'm too lazy. He'd succeed, only he's rather lazy.* **if only** (expressing a strong wish to desire): *If only she would come! If she would only come!*

only too very: *I'm only too happy to come. It was only too true, I'm afraid.*

only just 1 almost not: *I've only just enough money. They only just caught the train. He was only just able to walk.* **2** just a moment before: *They've only just (now) arrived! We'd only just got home when he called.*

just [adv] **1** *not fml* only: *He's just a boy; he can't do all that work. She just stood there, saying nothing.* **2** almost not; to the amount needed, but not more than: *The falling tree just missed the house. I need just another hour to finish the work.* **3** almost (at once); very soon: *He was just leaving when you came. We left just after they did. She was just about to write to them.* **4** a short time ago: *He has just arrived from London. She was just arrived from London.* **5** *not fml* exactly: *Tell me just what you did, no more. This book is just right for him.* **6** without a doubt: *The trip was just wonderful!*

hardly [adv] **1** almost not; with difficulty: *I could hardly wait to hear the news. I could hardly speak for laughing.* **2** only just; not really: *I hardly know the people I work with. I've hardly finished; I can't come out.* **3** not at all; not really: *I can hardly ask him directly for more money. This is hardly the time for buying new clothes; I've only got just enough money for food. You can hardly blame me if you didn't like the place, as you were the one who begged me to take you there. It's hardly fair to punish the child when she didn't know she was doing wrong.* **4** (in time) only just: *We'd hardly arrived before we had to go back.* **5** almost not: *I hardly ever go out these days (= never).*

You've hardly eaten anything. You've eaten hardly anything (= nothing). Hardly anybody likes him, because he's so rude (= nobody).

scarcely [adv] *often fml* **1** almost not: *She spoke scarcely a word of English. I really couldn't lend him £10; I scarcely know him!* **2** *esp pomp* (almost) certainly not: *Did you go in a taxi? —Scarcely that; I hadn't any money even for a bus. You could scarcely have found a better person for the job than Miss Winkle.*

barely [adv] *emph* hardly; just and no more: *He was barely able to walk.*

N100 adverbials : **too, also, besides, etc** [adv Wa5]

too 1 [(*for*, 3)] (before adjectives and adverbs) more than enough; to a higher degree than is necessary or good: *You're going (much) too fast; slow down! This dress is (a bit) too small (= not big enough) for me; I'll have to get a bigger one. If the coffee's too hot, leave it to get cool. There's been (far) too little rain lately and the crops are dying through lack of water. It's too soon (for us) to tell whether you'll be found guilty or not. It's too hot a day to work. He's too much of a coward (= too cowardly) to fight.* **2** (not at the beginning of a clause) in addition; as well: *I can dance and sing too. I can dance; I can sing too.* (compare: *I can't dance; I can't sing either*). *When I told her I'd been to Paris too! (= as well as London, Rome, etc) she was very jealous. Have you been to Paris too? (= as well as me) It snowed yesterday; in July too!* **3** *infml esp AmE* indeed; so: *I won't do it—You will too!* **only too** very: *I'm only too pleased to be able to help you.*

as well (not at the beginning of a clause) *not fml* too: *He's going and I'm going as well.*

as well as in addition to (being): *He was kind as well as sensible. As well as walking he likes fishing and shooting.*

also *more fml* **1** as well; too: *Were you at the film? I was also there.* **2** in addition: *As well as seeing the film I also went for a meal.* **not only X but (also)** both X and Y: *It was not only colourful but (also) noisy.*

additionally *fml* as one more (person, thing); too: *Additionally, we want you to come. He said, additionally, that you should come.*

in addition (to) *fml* additionally: *In addition, we want you to come. You are to come in addition to the others.*

moreover *often fml & emph* in addition (to that which has been stated); also: *The price is too high, and moreover, the house isn't in a suitable position.*

besides 1 in addition; also: *I don't want to go, (and) besides I'm tired. This car belongs to Smith, and he has two others besides. I don't like those blue socks; what have you got besides?* **2** [prep] in addition to: *There were three others present at the meeting besides us.*

by the way (introducing a new subject or one

that has not been mentioned earlier) as something more: *By the way, what do you think of her new dress?*

incidentally (used to add something interesting to what was said before, either on that or another subject); by the way: *I must go now; incidentally, if you want that book I'll bring it next time.*

furthermore *fml & emph* (used to introduce additional matter into an argument) also; in addition: *The house isn't big enough for us and furthermore, it's too far from the town.*

over and above *usu emph* in addition to: *Over and above this, we need more time.*

even 1 (used just before the surprising part of a statement, to add to its strength) which is more than might be expected: *Even John doesn't go out in the summer* (so certainly nobody else does). *John doesn't go out even in the summer* (so certainly not in the winter). *John doesn't even go out in the summer* (so he certainly won't go swimming). *He passed me in the street and he never even spoke to me* (= he didn't even speak to me). **2** (used for adding force to an expression) indeed; (and) one might almost say: *He looked happy, even gay.* (*infml*) *He looked happy, gay even.* **3** (used before a comparative) still; yet: *It was cold yesterday, but it's even colder today. He finished his work even more quickly than usual.* **even as** just at the same moment as: *He fell even as I stretched out my hand to help him.* **even if/though** though: *Even if you don't like wine* (= though you may not like wine), *try a glass of this!*—(compare *If you like wine, try a glass of this!*) **even now/so/then** in spite of what has/had happened; though that is true: *I (have) explained everything, but even now/then she doesn't/didn't understand. It's raining; even so, I think we should go.*

N101 *determiners, etc* : **both, each, either, etc**

both 1 [det] being two: *Both his eyes were hurt in the accident. She learned to use both hands equally well.* **2** [pron] the one as well as the other: *Both of us are coming. Both of his eyes were hurt. We are both well. John and Mary have both won prizes. John and Mary both have won prizes. Why not use both? Why not do both?* **both . . . and . . .** not only but also . . . *She spoke with both kindness and understanding. He both speaks and writes Swahili. She is well known both for her kindness and for her understanding.*

every [det] all, but esp one by one: *He talked to every person at the meeting. Every person spoke to him. She used to come every day but now she only comes once a week. Drink some of this medicine every three hours* (= let three hours pass before you take any more).

each 1 [det] every one separately: **a** (esp before a singular [C] noun): *She cut the cake into*

pieces and gave one to each (*good*) child. Each (*good*) child gets one piece of cake. Each one of the (*good*) children. **b** (after esp plural nouns, pronouns): (*The boys*) *John, Peter and Bill each say they came first in the race. They each live in a big city; one in London and the other in New York. They each want to do something different.* **2** [pron] both or all (of two or more) separately: *She cuts the cake into pieces and gives one to each of the (good) children. John and Mary never agree; each wants to do something different. He tells each of us only what we have to know.* **3** [adv Wa5] for or to every one: *The tickets are £1 each.*

else [adv Wa5] (after question words, some pronouns and adverbs) **1** besides; in addition: *I've said I'm sorry. What else can I say?* (= What more). *Who else* (= which other person) *did you see? Where else did he go? Does anybody else want to look at this book? I don't know the answer. You must ask somebody else. There isn't much else I can do to help you. This is someone else's bicycle, not mine.* **2** in/at a different place, time, or way; apart from that mentioned: *I can't come on Tuesday. When else can we meet? Everybody else but me has gone to the party.* **or else 1** or otherwise; or if not: *He must pay £100 or else go to prison. The book must be here, or else you've lost it.* **2** (used alone for expressing a threat): *Do what I tell you or else!*

either 1 [det] one or the other of two: *He's lived in London and Manchester but he doesn't like either city very much. I've cut the cake in two; you can have either half.* **2** [det] one and the other of two; each: *He sat in the car with a policeman on either side of him.* **3** [pron] one or the other of two: *He has lived in London and Manchester, but he doesn't like either (of them). Either of these two dictionaries is/are useful.* **4** [conj] (used before the first of two or more choices which are expressed by like noun phrases, verb phrases, etc, separated by **or**): *It's either a boy or girl. He must either sing a song or tell a funny story. Choose either red (or) black or green. You either love him or hate him.* **5** [adv] (used with neg expressions) also: *I haven't read this book, and my brother hasn't either* (= both haven't read it). *I can't swim!—I can't either!* (= I, too, am unable to swim). *Didn't he recognize you either? They're not going down but they're not going up either; they're sort of steady.*

or [conj] **1** (used between two or more choices after **either**): *The water is either too hot or too cold, never just right!* **2** (used for a choice like this but without **either**): *You can go or stay; decide now. They can come on Monday or Tuesday or Friday, but not on Wednesday or Thursday.* **3** (used to show a result) otherwise; if not: *You must work or go hungry.* **4** that is; which means: *He believes in democracy or the rule of the people, by the people, and for the people.*

either-or an unavoidable choice between only

two possibilities: *You may both be right in what you say; it's not a simple either-or. We fight, or we don't; it's an either-or decision.*

neither 1 [det; pron] not one and not the other of two: *Which of the books did you like?—Neither (of them); they were both dull! Neither road out of town is good, but this one is better than the other. Two books that are neither of them very good* (= neither is good). *(They) neither of them wanted to go.* **2** [conj] (used before the 1st of two or more choices which are expressed by like noun phrases, verb phrases, etc, separated by **nor**) not either: *They went neither by day nor by night* (= never). *He neither ate, drank, nor smoked; he liked neither the meal nor the cigarettes.* **3** [adv] (used after an expression or sentence with **no, not, never,** etc) nor; no more; also not: *I can't swim—Neither can I! (infml) Me neither!* (= I can't either).

nor [conj] **1** (used between the two or more choices after **neither**): *It's just warm, neither cold nor hot.* **2** (used before the 2nd, 3rd, etc choices after **not**) and/or not: *The job cannot be done by you nor (by) me, nor (by) anyone else.* **3** (used at the beginning of an expression just before a verb) and also . . . not: *I don't want to go; nor will I* (= and I won't). *We have many enemies; nor can we be sure of all our friends/(BrE also) and nor can we be sure of our friends. The meal didn't cost much nor was it very good/(BrE also) and nor was it very good.*

USAGE *BrE* uses *and* and *but* before *nor* (def **3**). *AmE* does not. Both *BrE* and *AmE* can use *and* and *but* before *neither*: *. . . but/and neither was it very good.*

neutral 1 [B] not taking or belonging to either side in a war, argument, etc: *He wants to stay neutral in their quarrel.* **2** [B] not strong: *She likes neutral colours, not bright reds and blues.* **3** [C] a person or country that is neutral: *We were neutrals in that war.* **neutrality** [U] state or condition of being neutral: *The USA's neutrality in the Second World War ended when she was attacked.* **neutralize, -ise** [T1] to make neutral; to take away the special effects of: *neutralizing an area of land/a poison* **neutralization, -isation** [U] the act or result of neutralizing

otherwise 1 [conj] or else; if not: *Go now; otherwise you won't get there tonight. Do it now; otherwise, don't do it at all.* **2** [adv Wa5] in other ways: *She's not very clever, but otherwise she's a nice girl.* **3** [adv Wa5] *usu fml* in another way: *He asked to see you but I said he couldn't; you were otherwise engaged* (= busy with someone or something else) *at the time.*

each other *also* **one another** [pron] (not subject of a clause) each of two or more does something to the other(s): *Susan and Robert kissed each other* (= Susan kissed Robert and Robert kissed Susan). *They give presents only to each other, not to me. John and Peter wear each other's shirts.*

USAGE Some people like to say *each other* about two people or things, and *one another* about more than two, but this is not a strict rule

mutual [Wa5;B] **1** equally shared by each one: *They have mutual interests and a mutual love of flowers. I saw our mutual friends, the Smiths.* **2** equally so, one towards the other: *They are mutual enemies.* **-ly** [adv]

rest [*the* GU (*of*)] what is left; the ones that still remain: *We'll eat some of the butter and keep the rest (of it) for breakfast. He's only got one shirt, because all the rest (of them) are being washed. John's English and the rest of us are Welsh.*

N102 *adjectives, etc* : **enough and sufficient**

enough 1 [A; E: (*for*, 3)] as much of (a quantity) or as many of (a plural) as may be necessary: *The child doesn't drink enough milk. We have enough seats for everyone. She has enough money/money enough to buy a car.* **2** [adv Wa5 (*for*, 3)] to the necessary amount or degree: *It's warm enough (to swim). He didn't run fast enough (to catch the train). The child has been punished enough. Is he old enough for the army? I was foolish enough to believe his lies* (= I believed them). **3** [adv Wa5] not very but only rather: *She cooks well enough and she would cook very well indeed if she took more trouble.* **4** [pron] a quantity or number which satisfies need: *I have enough to do. Not enough is known about this subject. I've had enough* (= too much) *of your rudeness!* **oddly/curiously/strangely enough** although this is old/curious/strange: *He's lived in France for years, but strangely enough he can't speak a word of French.* **sure enough** *infml* as expected: *He said he would come, and sure enough he came.* **fair enough** *infml* all right; satisfactory and reasonable: *You can eat the ones I don't want.—That's fair enough!* **enough and to spare** more than is necessary: *You may pick some apples from our tree; we have enough and to spare.* **more than enough** more than is necessary; too much: *Don't give him any more cake; he's had more than enough.* **enough of a fool** foolish enough: *He's enough of a fool to do it!* **enough of a man** manly enough: *Are you enough of a man for this dangerous job?*

USAGE **1** *Enough* can come before or after a plural or a [U] noun (*enough money/people, money/people enough*) but must come after a singular [C] noun (*fool enough*). **2** *Enough + that* (*He's old enough that he can do it*) is quite common, particularly in *AmE*, but teachers and examiners do not like it. **3** *Sufficient* has the same meaning as *enough* (defs 1, 4) but is more formal. It is more often used for degree (*sufficient reason*) while *enough* is used for quantity. *Sufficiently* has the same meaning as *enough.*

sufficient [Wa5;B (*for*), 3] *often fml* enough: *There is sufficient food for everybody. We have sufficient to feed everybody.* **in-** [*neg*] **-ly** [adv] **sufficiency** [U] *often fml* **1** the state of being or having enough **2** [S (*of*)] a supply which satisfies: *We have a sufficiency of coal.* **in-** [*neg*]

adequate [B] **1** [(*for*)] enough for the purpose: *We took adequate food for the short holiday.* **2** only just enough: *We had adequate food but none to waste.* **3** [(*to*)] having the necessary ability or qualities: *I hope you will prove adequate to the job.* **4** [Wa5] only just good enough: *The performance was adequate, though hardly exciting.* **in-** [*neg*] **-ly** [adv] **-quacy** [U]

N103 adverbs & adjectives : **plenty and plentiful**

plenty [adv Wa5] *not fml* quite (in the phr **plenty . . . enough**): *There's no need to add any more—it's plenty big enough already.*

plentiful [B] existing in quantities or numbers that are (more than) enough: *Fruit is plentiful this year. The camp has a plentiful supply of food.* **-ly** [adv]

abundant [B] more than enough: *There are abundant supplies of firewood in the forest.* **-ly** [adv]

ample [Wa2;B] **1** (usu before nouns of types [U] or [P]) enough or more than is necessary: *We have ample money for the journey.* **2** with plenty of space; large: *There is room for an ample garden.* **-ply** [adv]

bountiful [B] *esp lit* freely given; plentiful: *The king gave them bountiful gifts.* **-ly** [adv]

generous [B] more or bigger than usual: *She gave him a generous helping* (= amount) *of food.* **-ly** [adv]: *He gave generously to help the poor.*

lavish [B] **1** very free, generous, or wasteful in giving or using: *He is a lavish spender. She was lavish with her help and lavish of her time.* **2** given or spent in great quantity: *He gave her lavish praise.* **-ly** [adv]

excessive [B] too much; too great: *The prices at this hotel are excessive. She takes an excessive interest in clothes.* **-ly** [adv]

N104 nouns, etc : **plenty**

plenty **1** [pron] a large amount or number, esp as much as or more than is needed or wanted: *Do you need any more money?—No, we have plenty. We have £100 and that's plenty. Plenty of chairs are needed for the meeting. Plenty of space is needed too. If you want some chairs, there are plenty in here. She gave the boys plenty to eat. Be sure to arrive in plenty of time* (= early enough). **2** [U] the state of having a large supply esp of the needs of life: *Those were years of plenty when everyone had enough to eat.*

abundance [S (*of*); U] *usu fml* a great quantity; plenty: *At the feast there was food and drink in abundance. There was an abundance of corn last year.*

bounty **1** [U] *esp lit* generosity: *a rich lady famous for her bounty to the poor* **2** [C] something that is given generously **3** [C] a prize given by a government for some special act: *There is a bounty of £10 for every dangerous animal killed.*

excess **1** [S; U: 9 esp *of, over*] the fact of exceeding, or an amount by which something exceeds (the stated amount): *This excess of losses over profits will ruin the business.* **2** [S; U: 9 esp *of, over*] *deprec* something more than is reasonable; more than the reasonable degree or amount: *He eats to excess. He praised the book to excess.* **3** [A] additional; more than is usual, allowed, etc: *You'll have to pay excess postal charges on this letter. Excess profits tax is paid to the government by companies that make very high profits.* **in excess of** more than: *He advised his son never to spend in excess of his income.*

N105 adjectives, etc : **not plentiful** [Wa1]

short **1** [B *of*] not having enough: *We're short of water at the moment.* **2** [F] *infml* not having enough money: *Can you lend me £5? I'm a bit short at the moment.* **3** [E] less than the right number or amount: *We're two people short for the job.*

scarce **1** [B] not much or many compared with what is wanted; hard to find; not plentiful: *Good fruit is scarce just now and costs a lot.* (*infml*) *Pretty girls are scarce in this town.* **2** [adv] hardly; scarcely: *I could scarce believe my eyes.* [⇒ N99]

rare [B] not common; not easy to find; very scarce: *Animals are rare in that place. That's a rare animal.* **-ly** [adv] **-ness** [U]

N106 nouns : **not plenty**

[ALSO ⇒ F8]

shortage [C; U] a lack of things: *There is a shortage of good building wood. Those were times of general shortage.*

scarcity [U; C] a state of being scarce; lack: *Those were times of scarcity* (*of money*). *We have scarcities of all kinds of necessary goods.*

rarity **1** [U] the quality of being rare **2** [C *usu sing*] something uncommon: *Women who bake their own bread are becoming a rarity.*

dearth [S *of*] *esp lit & emot* a lack or shortage: *There has been a dearth of good new ideas lately.*

N107 *verb forms* : **having or not having enough**

be enough [I∅ (*for*)] to be what is needed: *This food is enough for our needs.*

suffice [I∅ (*for*)]*fml & old use* to be enough: *An hour should suffice (for the journey). The food did not suffice for them. Suffice it to say that . . .* (= I will say only that . . .)

be short of [v adv prep T1] not to have enough of: *We are (rather) short of money at the moment.*

be out of [v adv prep T1] to have none of: *We are (quite) out of paper at the moment but are hoping to get some next week.*

be without [v prep T1] *esp fml* not to have: *They are without water at the moment.*

do without [v prep, v adv T1, 4; I∅] to live or continue in spite of lacking (something or someone): *It is bad to do without sleep. The director cannot do without a secretary. If there's no sugar you will have to do without. Mr Jones is not here; you must do without speaking to him.*

N108 *adjectives* : **moderate and fair** [B]

moderate 1 [Wa5] of middle degree, power, or rate; neither large nor small, high nor low, fast nor slow, etc: *It's a large house, but the garden is of moderate size. At the time of the accident, the train was travelling at a moderate speed. The wind will be light to moderate.* **2** (done or kept) within sensible limits: *He's a moderate drinker; he only drinks one or two beers a day. The workers' demands are moderate; they're asking for only a small increase in their wages.* **3** [Wa5] *often euph* of average or less than average quality or amount: *The teacher thinks that this pupil has only moderate ability.* **moderation** [U] the condition of being moderate (def **2**): *She shows moderation in everything he does. What she did showed (a) lack of moderation.* **-ly** [adv]

modest 1 a not large in quantity, size, value, etc: *Please accept this modest gift; it's all I can afford. He stayed at a small modest hotel.* **b** not having or showing a desire for much or too much: *The servant girl was very modest in her demands and asked for only a small increase in wages.* **2** *apprec* avoiding or not showing anything that is improper or impure: *She is a quiet modest girl. The old lady said that young women should wear more modest dresses* (= that don't leave so much of their bodies uncovered). **im-** [*neg*] **3** *apprec* having or expressing a lower opinion than is probably deserved, of one's ability, knowledge, skill, successes, etc: *The young actress is very modest about her success; she says it's due as much to good luck as to her own abilities. After the war, the general wrote a very modest book about the part he'd played in winning it.* **-ly** [adv] **-y** [U]

fair [Wa1] **1** not too much or too little (for a

purpose); just right: *He was fair in the amount of money he gave to each of them.* **un-** [*neg*] **2** neither too good nor too bad: *His examination results were fair, not wonderful.* **-ly** [adv]: *It's a fairly interesting book; nothing wonderful.*

reasonable 1 (esp of prices) fair; not too much: *They charged a reasonable price.* **2** (of a person or his behaviour) sensible: *He is a reasonable man. It was a perfectly reasonable thing to do.* **un-** [*neg*] **-bly** [adv]

N109 *adjectives, etc* : **available**

available [B] **1** able to be got, obtained, used, etc: *There is water available at the hut. I'm sorry, sir, those shoes are not available in your size. Are there any available cars I can use?* **2** able to be visited or seen; not busy: *The doctor is (not) available now. He is available to see you now.* **un-** [*neg*] **availability** [U] the state or condition of being available: *I'm not sure about the availability of this medicine; I'll telephone and check.*

ready [Wa1; F, F3] available; able to be reached, used, etc: *Are your men ready to work? Keep your gun ready in case of trouble.*

in stock available in a shop, store, etc: *Do you have these books in stock?—No, sir, they aren't in stock at present.*

to hand *fml* available for collection, use, etc: *Sir, the books you ordered are now to hand.*

N110 *adjectives, etc* : **spare and extra** [Wa5]

spare [B] beyond what is needed or used: *Do you have any spare money? What do you do in/with your spare time* (= when not working)? *These pieces are spare; I don't need them.*

extra 1 [A; adv] beyond what is usual or necessary: *We need extra money. She bought an extra loaf of bread. He had to work extra hard to get more money.* **2** [E; F] as well as the regular charge: *Dinner costs £3 and the wine is extra. They charge extra for wine, £3 extra.* **3** [C] something or someone extra: *We have all the most important things; we don't need any extras.*

additional [B] more than at first: *The meal costs £3 and there is an additional 20p for service. We need some additional help; we can't do it alone.* **-ly** [adv]

surplus [B; S] (an amount) additional to what is needed or used, esp of money: *After paying the rent they were left with no surplus for food. They sold the surplus goods.*

superfluous [B] more than is necessary or wanted: *This bread is superfluous; we already have as much as we can eat.* **-ly** [adv] **-fluity** [U]

Doing things

N120 *verbs* : **doing and acting**

do **1** [T1] (with actions and non-material things): *I want you to do some repairs for me. He does science at school. The car can do 80 miles an hour. I shan't do anything for you. There's nothing more to do/to be done. Look at what a little hard work can do! What are you doing?* **2** [T1] (with action nouns ending in *-ing*): *He does (the) cooking and she does (the) washing. It's teaching that he does.* **3** [T1] *infml* (with places) to visit and see everything interesting in: *They did Oxford in three days.* **4** [T1; L7,9; D1] (with certain particular non-material expressions): *I did my best (to help him). I used to do business with him. Those who do good will find peace. This medicine will do you good. I hope you will do better in future. You did right (in telling me). He had only done his duty, after all. That won't do (you) any harm. I have some work to do. I hope you will do me the honour of paying me a visit. Will you do me a kindness? Hard work does wonders. Let her do her worst; I'm not afraid! You did wrong in agreeing to the plan.* **5** (with people and non-material things) to give or provide with: **a** [D1 (*to*); T1]: *Your fine behaviour does you honour. That picture of her doesn't do her justice.* **b** [D1 (*for*); T1] *Do me a favour.* **6** [L9] to behave; act: *When in Rome, do as the Romans do. Do as you're told! You did well in coming to see me quickly.* **7** [T1 *no pass*] *esp BrE* (with people) to serve by means of action with things: *The hairdresser will do you next. They did me very well at that hotel (with their good food and clean rooms).* **8** [T1] (with things) to arrange: *She did her hair, and then did the flowers.* **9** [T1] (with things) to clean: *He did his teeth and she did the room after doing the dishes.* **10** [T1] *esp BrE* (with people) to cheat; have: *I'm afraid he's done you on that sale, my friend! You've been done!* **11** [T1] (with people) to perform as or copy the manner of: *Olivier did 'Othello' last night. He does Harold Wilson very well.* **12** [T1 *no pass*] *esp BrE* (with people) to be enough for: *Will £5 do you?* **13** [T1] (with things) to cook: *They do fish very well in that restaurant.* **14** [D1 (*for*); T1] (with things) to prepare: *Do (us) a report on that book. He did a complete suit in only 3 days!* **15** [IØ (*for*)] (usu in the infinitive) to be suitable: *That won't do. How would this do? It does not do to work too much. This little bed will do for our youngest daughter. Will £5 do? How will £5 do?* **16** [L9] to advance towards a desired state: *The sick man is doing well under his doctor's care. After the birth, mother and child are doing well/nicely. He did well in business during the war and became rich. Our firm is doing well. They did poorly on/in the examination.* **17** [IØ] (in the *-ing*

form) happening: *What's doing at your place tonight? There's nothing doing in this town at night.* **18** [I2 *neg*] (a helping verb, as in): *Don't go. Don't be silly! (esp BrE) Don't let's go. (nonstandard AmE) Let's don't go.* **19** [I2] *emph* (a helping verb, as in): *He never comes.—You're wrong; he does come! Go, yes, do go! Be seated; please do be seated.* **20** [IØ] (in place of another verb, as in): *He likes it, and so does she. He doesn't like it, and neither does she.* **21** [IØ] (in place of another verb, as in): *He looks hungry.—So he does!* **22** [IØ] (in place of another verb, as in): **a** *fml Have you visited her?—Yes; I have done so (many times).* **b** *(BrE) Have you visited her?—Yes; I have done. Will you come for the weekend?—Yes; I may do.* **23** [IØ] (in place of another verb, as in): *Did he come?—Yes; he did.* **24** [IØ] (in place of another verb, as in): **a** *He likes it doesn't he?* **b** *He likes it, doesn't he!* **c** *(esp BrE) He likes it, does he?* **25** [IØ] (in place of another verb, as in): *He knows English better than he did. He rose early as he had always done.* **26** [T1] (in place of another verb, as in): *What he does is (to) teach. What John did to his suit was (to) ruin it.* **27** [T1] in place of another verb, as in: *What are you doing?—(I'm) cooking. What have you done?* **28** [IØ] *emph* (as in): *That will do! That's enough! That will do! It's perfect as it is. That will do! I order you to stop before it's too late.* **What . . . doing** (often expressing disapproval) why?: *What is that book doing on the floor? What is that child doing up so late at night? He should be in bed! What is that very poor woman doing buying an expensive fur coat?* **be up and doing** *infml* to be active: *He's up and doing by 5 o'clock in the morning!* **How do you do?** *polite* (a form of words used when introduced to someone; in later meetings, say 'How are you?')* **How are you doing?** *infml, esp AmE* an informal greeting to a friend **What do you do (for a living)?** What is your work? **do it yourself** *infml* the idea of doing repairs and building things oneself, instead of paying workmen: *She's very interested in do it yourself. She's a great do-it-yourself-er.* **do one's (own) thing** *sl* to do what is personally satisfying, even though others may disapprove **nothing doing** *sl* no: *Will you lend me £5?—Nothing doing.* **do or die** *fml* to succeed or die; do everything possible to succeed: *Now is the moment to do or die!* **That does it! Now you've done it!** (expressions showing that enough, or too much has been done): *That does it; it's perfect. That does it! I refuse to work with you any more!*

act [IØ] **1** to do something (to stop something happening, to help someone, etc): *Act now before it is too late. We must act at once. If you had acted in time, this would not have happened. He acted on the advice (= He did what she advised).* **2** [L9] to behave: *She has been acting very strangely lately.* **3** [L9] to do some work: *He acted as chairman at the meeting. I can't go; will you act for me/act on my behalf,* *please?* **4** [L9] (of chemicals, etc) to have an effect on: *Water acts on iron and makes it rust.*

transact [T1] *fml* to do, engage in, or carry on (as a piece of business): *Have you transacted all your business yet?* **transaction 1** [U] the act of transacting **2** [C] an example of this

be up to [v adv prep T1] *infml, often deprec* to be doing: *What is he up to now? What funny* (= strange) *business is he up to? Those children must be up to something bad; they're too quiet!*

be at [v prep T1] *infml* to be doing, working, etc: *What are you at now? He is at his old game of telling lies* (= He is telling lies again).

tackle [T1] *infml* to begin or try to do something, esp forcefully: *He tackled the job as quickly as possible.*

N121 *verbs* : **reacting and responding** [IØ]

react 1 [(*to*)] to act in reply; to behave differently as a result: *When the sun comes out the flowers react by opening wide. How did he react to your suggestion?* **2** [(*with*)] *tech* (of a substance) to change when mixed with another

respond 1 [(*by, to, with*)] to act in return: *He responded* (*to my suggestion*) *with a laugh/by laughing.* **2** [(*to*); *also* T5a] *esp fml* to answer: *I offered him a drink but he didn't respond* (*to my offer*). '*I can't marry you,*' *she responded sadly.* **responsive** [B (*to*)] acting in return; easily persuaded: *She wasn't very responsive to our request for money.* **un-** [*neg*] **-ly** [adv] **-ness** [U]

N122 *verbs, etc* : **repeating and doing again**

repeat 1 [T1, 5] to do again: *I'm afraid he has repeated his mistake.* **2** [T1, 6a] to say (something heard or learnt): *repeat a poem; Don't repeat what I told you.* **3** [IØ] *infml* (of food that one has eaten) to be tasted afterwards in the mouth: *I find that onions repeat.* **not bear repeating** (of words) to be too bad to say again: *I won't tell you what he said when the bomb went off—it doesn't bear repeating!* **repeat a course/a year** (in education) to remain in the same class for a further year **repeat an order** (in business) to supply the same article again **repeat oneself** to say or be the same thing again and again: *I love listening to Freddie's stories—he never repeats himself. History seems to be repeating itself.*

re-do [T1] to do again: *Re-do the bathroom* (= paint it again) *in pink.*

echo 1 [C; (U)] the return of sound when it strikes a surface: *There is a good echo in this big room. The echoes of their shouts came back from the hillsides.* **2** [C] (*fig*) any repeating of anything that suggests an echo: *His words were an echo of his mother's.* **3** [IØ; T1] (to cause to) come back as an echo: *The hills echoed with the shouts of the men.* **4** [T1] (*fig*) to repeat: *He*

echoes her opinions; he has no thoughts of his own. Stop echoing my ideas!

practise *also* **practice** *AmE* **1** [T1, 4; IØ] to perform (an action) repeatedly or do (esp a musical exercise) regularly in order to gain skill: *She's been practising the same tune on the piano for nearly an hour. You mustn't practise the drums while the baby is sleeping. They're practising singing the new song. You'll never learn to ride a bicycle unless you practise.* **2** [T1] to train (a person or animal) by repeated exercises: *She practised the child in telling the time.* **3** [Wv4; T1] to act in accordance with (the ideas of one's religion or other firm belief): *Do most Christians practise their religion? a practising Jew* **4** [T1] *fml* to (force oneself to) show or use (some necessary quality in behaviour): *In dealing with sick old people nurses must practise great patience.* **5** [T1] *fml* to make a habit or practice of: *Our income has decreased and now we have to practise economy* (= have to avoid spending money). **6** [T1] to perform (something needing special knowledge) according to rule: *Some people practise magic, or calling up the spirits of the dead.* **7** [Wv4; IØ (*as*); T1] to do (the work of) or work regularly as (a doctor, lawyer, etc): *He's passed his law examinations and is now practising* (*as a lawyer*). *One brother practises medicine and the other practises law. a practising doctor* **8** [T1 (*on, upon*)] to make unfair use of (a trick) for one's own advantage: *That shopkeeper practised a deception on me.* **practitioner** [C] **1** a person who practises a skill or art **2** a person who works in a profession esp a doctor or lawyer: *medical practitioners*

N123 *verbs* : **functioning and performing**
[ALSO ⇒ I103, N134]

function [IØ] *often fml* (esp of a thing) to be in action; work: *The machine won't function properly unless you oil it well. Death happens when the brain ceases to function.*

behave 1 [L9] to act in a certain way: *He behaved well/badly at the meeting. I'm not sure how they will behave when they meet.* **2** [IØ; T1] to keep (oneself) in a polite or acceptable manner: *The car behaved itself* (= went well, although it might have broken down).

perform [IØ; T1] to do (something) fully: *The doctor performed all his duties carefully. She performed well last night.*

discharge [T1] *fml* to perform (a duty or promise): *The nurse discharged her duties with loving care.*

N124 *adjectives* : **active and functional**

active [B] able to act, function, etc; working well: *He is still active although he is very old now. Please don't expect active help from us; we* *can't do much. She takes an active part in the work of the club. The volcano is still active* (=might still give out fire etc). **in-** [*neg*] **-ly** [adv]

functional [B] **1** made for or concerned with practical use without ornamentation: *Some people don't like the look of functional modern chairs, made on functional principles, even though they're comfortable. A hospital should be planned as a functional building.* **2** [Wa5] made for or having a special purpose: *The workman's been taught to use that one particular machine; such functional training doesn't fit him for any other kind of work.* **3** [Wa5] *med* (of a disease or disorder) having an effect only on the working of an organ, not on the organ itself **-ly** [adv]

working [Wa5;A] **1** able to work, move, etc: *They made a working model* (= small copy) *of the machine before they tried to build it.* **2** useful for work: *She was wearing her working clothes. How many working days do we have next week?*

dynamic [B] **1** [Wa5] *tech* of or relating to force or power that produces movement **2** *often apprec* (of people, ideas, etc) full of or producing power and activity: *He is a dynamic person. It was a dynamic period in history.* **-ally** [adv Wa4]

vigorous [B] **1** forceful; strong; healthily active: *As a cricketer he's vigorous rather than skilful.* **2** using or needing forcefulness and strength: *The politician made a vigorous speech in defence of the government. He did some vigorous exercises.* **3** (of a plant) healthy; growing strongly **-ly** [adv]

N125 *adjectives* : **passive and inert** [B]

passive being acted on but doing nothing in return: *She is very passive; things happen but they don't seem to affect her.* **-ly** [adv]: *He listened passively to what they said.*

inert 1 [Wa5] lacking the power to move: *inert matter* **2** [Wa5] without active chemical properties: *inert gases* **3** (of people) slow to act; lazy

extinct 1 (esp of animals, plants, etc) no longer found alive as a type: *Dinosaurs* [⇒ A94] *are extinct animals. Many kinds of animals are in danger of becoming extinct.* **2** no longer active: *Arthur's Seat in Edinburgh is an extinct volcano* [⇒ L115]. **extinction** [U] the state of being extinct

dormant inactive, esp not actively growing or producing typical effects: *dormant seeds; dormant animals asleep for the winter; a dormant disease/volcano;* (*fig*) *Many people disliked the plan, but opposition remained dormant because nobody could think of a better one.*

ornamental *often derog* perhaps beautiful, but not really necessary: *In her new book there are several passages that are only ornamental.* **-ly** [adv]

N126 *adjectives, etc* : **latent and potential**

latent [B] existing but not yet noticeable or active or fully developed **-ly** [adv]

potential 1 [Wa5;B] existing in possibility; not at present active or developed, but able to become so: *Every seed is a potential plant. He is seen as a potential leader of our political party.* **-ly** [adv] **2** [U] the potential ability to do something: *He is still young but he has great potential/the potential to win.* **potentiality** [U;C] (a) power or quality that is potential: *This is a country of great potentiality/potentialities.*

N127 *nouns* : **acts, actions, etc**

act [C] *often fml & pomp* something which has been done, could be done, etc: *Murder is a terrible act. From his acts he seems to be a fool. If you did that it would be an act of great kindness.*

action [C; U] *genl* something which is done: *We need action, not words! His actions suggest that he is a fool. The machine works with an up-and-down action.* **in-** [*neg* U]

activity 1 [U] the state of being active: *Activity is better than doing nothing. There was very little activity in the city last night.* **in-** [*neg*] **2** [C] something that one does: *Climbing mountains is one of his many activities.*

function [C] a special duty (of a person) or purpose (of a thing): *The function of a chairman is to lead and control meetings. The brain performs a very important function; it controls the nervous system of the body. The function of an adjective is to describe or add to the meaning of a noun.*

behaviour *BrE*, **behavior** *AmE* [U] general way of acting or functioning: *The behaviour of these animals is very interesting.*

performance [U] the action of performing: *Good performance sells a car* (= If a car performs well, it can be sold easily). *The policeman died in the performance of his duty.*

vigour *BrE*, **vigor** *AmE* [U] forcefulness; strength shown in power of action in body or mind: *He began his work with vigour and soon cut the tree up into logs. In his speech, he attacked his opponents with great vigour.*

reaction 1 [C (*to*)] a case of reacting: *What was your reaction to the news?* **2** [S; U] (a) change back to a former condition: *For a time everybody admired the new actor, but then (a) reaction set in and they got tired of him.* **3** [U] the quality of being reactionary [⇒ C113]: *His efforts were defeated by the forces of reaction.* **4** [C; U] (in science) **a** (a) force exercised by a body in reply to another force: *Action and reaction are equal and opposite* (Newton). **b** (a) change caused in a chemical substance by the action of another

response [U; C] the act of responding: *They*

gave no response to our offer. Our invitation met with no response.

repetition 1 [C; U] the action or an act of re-peating: *The performance improved with each repetition. Let there be no repetition of this behaviour!* **2** [U] the exercise of repeating words **repetitive** [B] tending to repeat or be repeated: *He is a bit repetitive; he tells you the same things again and again.* **-ly** [adv] **-ness** [U]

practice 1 [U; C] (a) (regularly) repeated per-formance or exercise in order to gain skill in some art, game, etc: *It takes a great deal of practice to be really good at this sport. Every English lesson starts with pronunciation prac-tice. We have 3 choir* [⇒ K43] *practices a week. In training for the race he goes for a practice run each morning. He used to be good at cricket but now he's out of practice* (= unable to perform with skill because of lack of practice). **2** [U] actual use or performance as compared with the idea, intention, rules, etc, on which the action is based: *It's claimed that this tin-opener is a very good invention, but in practice it's not easy to use. We've made our plans and now we must put them into practice.* **3** [U] experience; knowledge of a skill as gained by this: *Have you had any practice in nursing the sick? The student teachers are now doing their teaching practice.* **4** [U] a standard course of action that is accepted as correct or desirable: *It is the practice in English law to consider a person as not guilty until he has been proved guilty. You may not do it in your country but if you come to mine you'll find it's quite common practice here.* **5** [C *usu sing*] *often fml* a firmly fixed custom or regular habit: *It's not the usual prac-tice for shops to stay open after 6 p.m. Driving fast along a winding road is a dangerous prac-tice. I'll lend you the money this time, but I don't intend to make a practice of it. Tribal practices often have the force of law.* **6** [C *usu pl*] *often deprec* an act that is often repeated esp sec-retly, in a fixed manner or with ceremony: *The Christian church had a great struggle to stop magical practices among its people.* **7** [U] regu-lar work of a doctor or lawyer: *Is Doctor Jones still in practice here?* **8** [C] **a** the business of a doctor or lawyer, esp as having a money value because of his trusted connection with the people he serves: *How many lawyers' practices are there in the town? Doctor Jones has sold his practice.* **b** the place where this business is done: *Where was his practice?–In the High Street.* **c** the kind or number of people using his services: *Did he have a large practice? No, it was a small but wealthy practice.* **sharp practice** *derog* behaviour or a trick in business or work that is dishonest but not quite unlawful

deed [C; *in* U] *esp pomp, lit & old use* something done on purpose: *Deeds are more important than words. He is an honourable man in word and in deed.*

doings *infml* **1** [P] things that are done, things that happen, or social activities: *There are a lot of doings at the Smiths' house tonight.*

2 [Wn3; C] *BrE* any small thing, esp the name of which one forgets or does not know: *Put the doings on the table.*

work [U] something done, esp often or for money: *What work are you doing today? Have you finished your work/that work yet?* [⇒ I101]

workings [P] *not fml* the way in which some-thing works or acts: *What a strange idea; the workings of his mind are unlike anyone else's.*

goings-on [P] *infml, usu deprec* activities, usu of an undesirable kind: *There was shouting and loud music and all sorts of goings-on I can't describe!*

N128 *verbs* : **managing and coping**

manage 1 [I∅; T1, 3] (often with **can, could**) to (be able to perform a difficult movement or action): *It's heavy, but I can manage* (*to carry*) *it. She can't manage alone on the stairs. She managed the stairs alone/without help.* **2** [I∅] to succeed in living esp on a small amount of money: *We have very little, but we manage.* **3** [T1] *infml, often polite* (with **can, could**) to take (for a special use): *I can't manage another mouthful. I could manage another holiday soon, I'm so tired. I couldn't manage two weeks holiday this year, only one. I can't manage Tuesday—make the meeting Wednesday.*

cope [I∅ (*with*)] to deal successfully with some-thing: *She felt unable to cope with* (*driving in*) *heavy traffic after her accident.* (*esp BrE*) *After her nervous illness she lost the ability to cope.*

make do [I∅ (*with*)] *infml* to use (something) even though it may not be enough or perfect: *We haven't got meat so we'll have to make do with bread.*

get by [v adv I∅] **1** [(*on*)] to continue to live: *She can't get by on such a small income.* **2** to be good enough, but not very good: *Your work will get by, but try to improve it.*

fare [(*it*) L9] **1** to manage; get on; progress; succeed: *How did you fare in the exam? I think I fared well/badly.* **2** *esp lit* to turn out; happen: *It fared ill with them.*

N129 *verbs* : **doing well and looking up, etc** [I∅]

do well to manage well: *He is doing* (*very*) *well now.*

get better to become better: *The weather is getting better now. She was ill but now she's getting better.*

come on [v adv] *infml* **1** to become better: *She was ill but she's coming on* (*well*) *now.* **2** to be developing: *How is your work coming on now?*

look up [v adv] *infml* to become better: *Things are looking up now; business is good.*

N130 verbs : succeeding, etc

[ALSO ⇒ N164]

succeed 1 [I∅ (*in*)] to gain a purpose or reach an aim: *He succeeded in preventing her from leaving. She succeeded the second time she took the examination.* **2** [I∅] to do well, esp in gaining position or popularity in life: *He is the type of person who succeeds anywhere. to succeed in life* **3** [T1] to follow after: *A silence succeeded his words.*

come off [v adv I∅] *infml* to succeed: *The sale came off and he made a lot of money.*

improve 1 [T1] to use well and/or to make better: *I want to improve my abilities. I'll improve the shape of the handle so it's easier for you to use.* **2** [I∅] to get better: *His health's improving. He's improving in health.*

pick up [v adv] *infml* **1** [I∅] to improve, esp in health: *Mother is picking up again after her operation. Trade is picking up, I hear.* **2** [T1] to make (someone) feel better: *I need a holiday to pick me up.*

better oneself [I∅] *esp old use* to make oneself better; do better in life: *He has bettered himself by studying hard.*

prosper [I∅] *esp fml & lit* **1** to succeed in life: *He has begun to prosper.* **2** (of business, etc) to get much better: *His business is prospering.*

excel [Wv6;L9] to do or be better than others: *She excelled (over everyone else) in the examinations.*

N131 verbs : accomplishing and achieving [T1]

accomplish (*often in the phrs* **accomplish something/nothing/a great deal,** etc) to succeed in doing; finish successfully; perform: *We tried to arrange a peace but accomplished nothing. Has he accomplished anything by all these years of work?*

achieve 1 to finish successfully (esp something, anything, nothing): *He will never achieve anything unless he works harder.* **2** to get as the result of action; gain (something non-material): *He hopes to achieve all his aims by the end of the year. He achieved fame with his last book.*

fulfil *also* **fulfill** *AmE* **1** [*usu pass*] to make or prove to be true; cause to happen as foretold or appointed: *The old belief that the world would come to an end after 1,000 years was not fulfilled.* **2** to make true; carry out (something wished for or planned, such as hopes, prayers, desires, etc): *At last his hopes have been fulfilled; his first son has been born. If he's lazy, he'll never fulfil his ambition of being/to be a doctor.* **3** to develop and express the abilities, qualities, character, etc, of (oneself); fully: *She succeeded in fulfilling herself both as an actress and as a mother.* **4** to supply or satisfy (a need, demand, purpose): *The demand for new cars is so great that it can't be fulfilled for several*

months. **5** to keep or carry out faithfully (a promise, agreement, etc): *If you make a promise you should fulfil it. The builder hasn't fulfilled his contract to finish the house by September.* **6** to carry out (an order, command, conditions, etc); obey: *The doctor's instructions must be fulfilled exactly; the sick man's life depends on it.* **7** to do or perform (a duty, office, etc): *A nurse has many duties to fulfil in caring for the sick. A chimney fulfils the function* [⇒ N127] *of taking away smoke.*

attain to succeed in arriving at, esp after effort; reach: *He attained the position of minister. His skill had attained perfection before he died. How can we attain such wealth?*

N132 verbs : passing and failing [T1]

pass 1 [*also* I∅] to be successful in (an examination, test, etc): *Did she pass? He passed all his tests.* **2** to let (someone) pass (an examination, test, etc): *They passed him. He was passed as fit by the doctor.*

fail 1 [*also* I∅] not to pass: *Did she fail? He failed most of the tests.* **2** to say, etc that (someone) has failed: *They failed him. He was failed by the doctor.*

N133 nouns : success and failure

success 1 [U] the act of succeeding in something: *Success at last! The book is finished!* **2** [U] a good result: *Our efforts met with success.* **3** [C] a person or thing that succeeds or has succeeded: *Although he has no money he has clever children and that makes him a success. His book has come out/his play has been performed and it's a success.* **4** [U9] *esp old use* a result: *What success?* **successful** [B] showing success: *He is a successful writer.* **un-** [*neg*] **-ly** [*adv*]

improvement [U;C] (a sign of) improving or being improved: *There's been an improvement in your work this year. Several improvements were made to our office, and it's much more comfortable now.*

accomplishment [C] a skill, ability, etc accomplished after esp years of effort: *Her fine piano-playing is her greatest accomplishment. What are his accomplishments in his subject?*

achievement 1 [U] the successful finishing or gaining of something: *Can one be happy without a feeling of achievement in life?* **2** [C] something successfully finished or gained esp through skill and hard work: *He was proud of his daughter's achievements.*

fulfilment *also* **fulfillment** *AmE* **1** [U; (C)] satisfaction after successful effort: *When the teacher heard that all his students had passed their examination well, he felt a sense of fulfilment.* **2** [U] the act of fulfilling or condition of being fulfilled: *The help that we give her depends on her fulfilment of her promise to* *work harder. After many years, his plans have come to fulfilment.*

attainment 1 [U] the act of attaining: *His attainment of the position of minister after all these years surprised everybody.* **2** [C] a skill, ability, etc got after much effort; an accomplishment: *Singing Welsh songs is one of his many attainments.*

prosperity [U] success in life or business: *This little town shows all the signs of prosperity. He owes his prosperity to hard work* (= He worked hard and therefore he has prospered).

pass [C] **1** a success in an examination, etc: *Did he pass?—Yes, he got a good pass.* **2** a person who has passed in an examination, etc: *There were 15 passes.*

fail [C] *not fml* a lack of success in an examination, etc: *He passed two subjects but got a fail in the third.*

failure 1 [U] lack of success: *Failure in business has made him very unhappy. She fears failure and so she won't even try.* **2** [C] a person who has failed: *She thinks she is a failure in life/in everything she does. There were 15 passes and 2 failures in the test.*

N134 *verbs* : **executing and implementing things**

[ALSO ⇒ N123]

execute [T1] **1** to carry out; perform or do completely (an order, plan or piece of work): *The plan was good, but it was badly executed. The soldier executed the captain's orders.* **2** *law* to carry out the orders in (a will [⇒ C123]): *He asked his brother to execute his will.* **3** *law* to make effective in law (an important written paper) by having it signed, witnessed, etc **4** to perform (music, dance steps, etc) **execution** [U (*of*)] the act of executing: *The soldier failed in the execution of his duties.*

implement [T1] to start (something) working; to put to practical use: *He tried to implement his ideas too quickly and people wouldn't accept them.* **implementation** [U] the act of implementing: *He succeeded in the implementation of his ideas.*

N135 *verbs* : **undertaking and taking on, etc**

undertake 1 [T1] to take up (a position); to start on (work): *He undertook responsibility for the changes. He undertook the leadership of the team.* **2** [T3, 5] to promise or agree: *He undertook to improve the working arrangements.*

take on [v adv T1] to be responsible for doing: *He agreed to take on the new job. I can't take on any more work at the moment.*

agree to do [T1] to say that one will do (something): *He agreed to do the job.* **agreement 1** [U] the act of agreeing: *Their agreement about the matter surprised me.* **2** [C] an

example or occasion of this: *We have come to an agreement about doing the job.* **3** [C] a piece of paper which shows what people agree to do and which each person signs: *Have you seen/signed the agreement yet?*

accept [T1] *more fml* to agree to do: *Will you accept the job?* **acceptance 1** [U; C] the act of accepting: *His acceptance of the job pleased us.* **2** [C] an example or occasion of this: *We offered 20 places in the school and so far we have had 18 acceptances.*

assume [T1] to take as one's duty, responsibility, etc: *The new government assumed power last week. She assumed office as chief minister. I must assume responsibility for the work now that he is dead.* **assumption** [U (*of*)] the act of assuming: *Her assumption of office takes place next week.*

N136 *verbs* : **refusing and rejecting**

[ALSO ⇒ G127, 8]

refuse [I0; T1, 3; D1] not (to accept or do or give): *He asked her to marry him but she refused (to marry him). She refused his offer. She refused him even a kiss.*

reject [T1] to refuse strongly; not accept: *He rejected their offer of a job/their help.*

N137 *verbs* : **avoiding, etc**

avoid [T1, 4] **1** to miss or keep away from, esp on purpose: *I avoided her by leaving by the back door. She avoided answering my questions.* **2** to escape: *I avoided punishment by running away. I avoided being punished.* **avoidance** [U] the act of avoiding

evade 1 [T1] to get out of the way of or escape from: *He evaded his enemy. The lion evaded the hunters. Why does Mary keep evading me?* **2** [T1, 4] *derog* to avoid (doing) (something one should do): *He tried to evade (paying) his taxes.* **3** [T1] *derog* to avoid answering (a question) properly: *Answer honestly and stop evading my questions!* **evasion 1** [U] the act of evading **2** [C] an example of this

shirk [T1, 4; I0] to avoid (unpleasant work) because of laziness, lack of determination, etc: *We mustn't shirk our cleaning job/doing our cleaning. Is that boy still shirking? Tell him to get on with the job!* **shirker** [C] a person who shirks (work, etc)

dodge 1 [I0] to move suddenly aside: *I tried to hit him but he dodged.* **2** [T1] to avoid by so doing: *He dodged my blow.* **3** [T1] *infml* to avoid by a trick or in some dishonest way: *tax-dodging* **dodger** [C] a person who dodges (paying taxes, etc)

wriggle out of [v adv prep T1, 4] to avoid (a difficulty) by clever trickery, by pretending, etc: *You know you're to blame, so don't try to wriggle out of it.*

N138 *verbs & nouns* : **trying**

try 1 [T1, 4] to test by use and experience to find the quality, worth, desirability, effect, etc: *Have you tried this new soap? Have you tried this hotel? We tried growing our own vegetables but soon found it was harder than we'd imagined. Try a new method. Try your luck and you might win. I tried baking this cake but didn't like the result.* **2** [IØ; T3, (T1)] to attempt: *I don't think I can do it but I'll try. I've tried again and again but I still can't do it. You should try to make more of an effort with your appearance. He tried to stand on his head but couldn't. Try harder next time. I tried to get you a room at this hotel but it was full. Try Mrs Jones; she might lend you £1.* **3** [T4] to attempt and do; experience: *I tried standing on my head but it gave me a headache. Try doing more exercises; you'll soon lose weight.* **4** [T1] to attempt to open (a door, window, etc): *I think the door's locked but I'll try it just in case.* **try and (do)** *not fml* (not used in verb forms with **tried** or **trying**), to try to (do): *You must try and come to the party. I always try and help her* (compare *I'm always trying to help her*). *I'll try and telephone you.* **5** [C] *infml* an act of trying: *Come on; give it a try. We made several tries but failed every time.*

attempt 1 [Wa5; T1,3,4] *esp fml* to make an effort at; try: *He attempted the examination but failed. I attempted to speak but was told to be quiet. I attempted walking until I collapsed and fell over. He was found guilty of attempted murder even though the other man did not die.* **2** [C, C3] an act of attempting: *His attempts to help us failed. She made no attempt to stop him.*

endeavour *BrE*, **endeavor** *AmE usu fml, lit & pomp* **1** [I3] to try: *He endeavoured to climb the mountain.* **2** [C; U] an attempt: *All his great endeavours succeeded at last.*

strive *esp lit & pomp* **1** [L9, esp *for/against*; I3] to struggle hard (to get or conquer): *He strove for recognition as an artist/to be recognized as an artist. He strives against his illness.* **2** [IØ (*with*)] *old use* to fight

sample [T1] to try (something, esp food) to learn what it is like: *Sample this. He sampled it and didn't like it.*

N139 *verbs & nouns* : **helping**

help 1 [T1; IØ; V3] **a** to do part of an activity (for someone); to be of use to (someone in doing something): *Could you help me up the stairs? The shock helped him (to) walk. Your sympathy helps a lot. Can I help?* **b** to make better: *Crying won't help (you).* **2** [T1,4; V4] to avoid; prevent; change; have control over (only in the phrs **can/can't/couldn't help**): *I couldn't help crying. I can't help my big feet. She can't help herself, she doesn't mean to be so rude.* **it can't be helped** These things happen, so we must accept it. *You've broken it now; it*

can't be helped. **I can't help it** It's not my fault; I can't stop it, etc: *Why are you crying?—I just can't help it. Well you can't help it if she ran away across the road; it was just an accident.* **no more than one can help** as little as is possible or necessary: *He never does more work than he can help.* **3** [U] the act of helping: *You're not much help to me just sitting there. You gave me a lot of help; thank you.* **4** [C] something which helps: *You're a good help to me. The new fire is a good help in this cold weather.* **5** [C] a person who does some of someone else's work: *A help comes in twice a week to clean the house.* **Help! a** Please bring help, I'm in danger. **b** Oh, dear!

assist [T1; IØ; (*in*); V3] *esp fml* to help, support, or aid: *She assisted him in building the house. Good glasses will assist you to read. I have no money left; can you assist me?* **assistance** [U] the act of assisting: *Could you give us some assistance with this work? Can I be of (any) assistance in any way? Thank you for your kind assistance.* **assistant** [C] a person who assists another esp more important person: *She got one of her assistants to do the work.*

aid 1 [T1 (*with, in*); V3] *usu fml* to give support to; help: *Who aided him with money? I aided him to find some water/in finding some water.* **2** [U] the act of aiding: *We need all the aid we can get.* **3** [C] something that aids in some usu stated way: *He wears a hearing aid* (=something that helps him hear better).

support 1 [T1] to bear the weight of, esp preventing from falling: *You support the bottom while I lift the top. He supported her on his arm.* **2** [T1] **a** to provide money for (a person) to live on: *He supports a family. He supports his old mother.* **b** to help, with sympathy or practical advice, money, food, etc: *She supported him in his trouble.* **3** [T1] to approve of and encourage: *You must support the new political party. She supports birth control. I will support him if he suggests a change in the committee.* **4** [T1] to be in favour of: *The results support my original idea.* **5** [T1] (with **can/cannot**) to bear: *I can support so much bad behaviour and no more.* **6** [T1] to be loyal to, esp by attending performances: *They support Chelsea (football team). They support the local playhouse.* **7** [U] the act of supporting: *We need more support if we are going to win the election.* **8** [C] an example of this; something or someone that supports: *He was a great support to us all in our time of need. These wooden supports help to hold up the old building.*

benefit 1 [T1] to help by doing something good, useful, etc: *His work did not benefit him; he got no money for it.* **2** [IØ (*by, from*)] to gain; help oneself: *How will I benefit if I go? No one benefited from the news.* **3** [U; C] advantage, help, or profit: *What benefit do we get if we do that? There's no real benefit for me if I go. He got all the benefits; we got all the hard work. This medicine will be of real benefit to you; take it.*

pander to [v prep T1] *emot often deprec* to give

too much help and encouragement to (someone, or to certain feelings, ideas, etc): *She just panders to him/to his every desire. 'Films often pander to people's need to see blood and violence,' he said angrily.*

auxiliary 1 [C] a person who helps others in the work they do: *These auxiliaries have made our work much easier. She is an auxiliary teacher.* **2** [Wa5;B] used in helping: *The auxiliary fire service helps our full-time firemen when there are very big fires in the city.*

N140 *verbs* : not helping [T1]
[ALSO ⇒ L173 STOP]

hinder [(*from*)] **1** to stop (someone from doing something): *You're hindering me in my work by talking all the time. You're hindering me from working.* **2** to prevent (an activity from being done): *You're hindering my work.* **hindrance** [C] something or someone that hinders: *Helping him is a hindrance to my own work. Some people think that children are important; others, that they are just hindrances.*

thwart *esp emot* to oppose successfully: *I was thwarted in my plans by the weather. Uncle hates being/to be thwarted. His illness has thwarted his hopes of winning the competition.*

impede *often fml* to get in the way of; to make something difficult to do: *Poverty impedes education. Having no car impedes his movements.* **impediment** [C] something which impedes something else: *He has a speech impediment, and can't say 's' properly. There is no impediment to their marriage.*

prevent [(*from*); *also* V4] **1** to keep (something) from happening or existing: *These rules are intended to prevent accidents. What can we do to prevent this disease spreading?* **2** to stop or hold back (someone or something): *I intend to go and nothing you can do can prevent me. I couldn't prevent him from spending the money.* **prevention** [U] the act of preventing something or someone: *The prevention of disease is more important than trying to cure it later.* **preventive** *also* **preventative** [B] concerning or for the purpose of preventing: *preventive medicine*

hamper to cause difficulty in movement or activity to: *The sun hampered my movements.* (*fig*) *I was hampered by my poor knowledge of French.*

keep [(*from*)] to delay or hinder: *What kept you from doing it/coming? You're late; what kept you?*

Causing

N150 *verbs* : making and causing
[ALSO ⇒ I1]

make 1 [D1 (*for*); T1] to produce by work or action: *She made a cake. I'll make myself/you a* cup of coffee. The children are making a lot of noise. Cheese is made from milk.* **2** [X1, 7; V8] to put into a certain state, position, etc: *Too much food made him ill. The king married her and made her his queen. He made himself heard across the room. He made his ideas known/made known what he felt.* **3** [T1] to earn, gain, or win (money or success): *He makes a lot (of money) in his job. He makes a living* (= earns enough to live). *I hope you make a success of your work.* **4** [V2; V3 *pass*] to cause (a person to do something/a thing to happen): *The pain made him cry out. She was made to wait for over an hour. Some people say stepping on a worm makes it rain.* **5** [V2; V3 *pass*; X1, 7] to represent as being, doing, happening, etc; to cause to appear as: *In the film the battle is made to take place in the winter. This photograph makes her (look) very young.* **6** [T1; X1, (*to be*) 7, 9)] to calculate (and get as a result): *He added up the figures and made a different answer from the one I got. I make it nearly three years since I saw him. What time do you make it? Is that the right time? I make it later. He made the speed to be over the limit.* **7** [L1] to add up to; to come to (an amount) as a result: *Two and two make four.* **8** [L1] to be counted as (first, second, etc): *This makes our third party this month. That makes four who want to go.* **9** [L1; D1] to have the qualities of (esp something good): *No one could have made him a better wife. This story makes good reading. The hall would make a good theatre.* **10** [T1] *infml* to travel (a distance) or at (a speed): *The train was making seventy miles an hour. He made a few more yards before he fell to the ground.* **11** [T1] to arrive at or on: *We made the station in time to catch the train. We just made the train* (= almost missed it). *We finally made the party.* **12** [T1 (*of*); X1] to form (into or from): *Experience has made him a man. The navy has made a man of him.* **13** [X9, esp *into, out of*] to change or produce (to or from): *Working in the kitchen made the boy into a good cook/a good cook out of the boy. We made the material into a skirt/a skirt out of the material.* **14** [T1] to establish (a law) **15** [D1 (*to*); T1] to give (a suggestion of payment or a gift): *I'll make you an offer of a hundred pounds. Let me make you a present of it.* **16** [T3] *fml, also* **to make as if** to be about to: *He made (as if) to speak, but I stopped him.* **17** [T1] *infml* to give the particular qualities of: *It's the bright paint which really makes the room.* **18** [T1] (used with a noun instead of a verb alone): *He made a promise/no answer* (= He promised/did not answer). *They were making a search of the room. We made an early start. She made a good choice. He's made his decision. An important discovery has been made.* **make believe** to pretend: *The children are making believe that they're princes and princesses.* [⇒ K173] **make it 1** to succeed **2** to arrive in time

cause [T1; V3; D1 (*to, for*)] to lead to; be the cause of: *What caused his illness? His foolish-*

ness caused me to lose my temper. I wish you wouldn't cause me such worry. I think you like causing trouble for people. Why do you cause me to do what I dislike doing most; is it to punish me?

get 1 [V4] to bring (something) to a start: *I'll get the car going.* **2** [V3] to cause to do: *I got him to help (me) when I moved the furniture. I can't get the car to start.* **3** [X7] to bring (into a certain state): *I'll get the children ready for school. I can't get the car started.* **4** [X9] to put or move into a place: *I can't get it through the door. Get that cat out of the house before your mother sees it! We must get him home.* **5** [T3] to succeed in (doing) (often with future meaning): *When you get to know him you find he's quite different from how you imagined. If I get to see him I'll ask him about it.*

get . . . done to have (something) done: *I'll get this work done by tomorrow afternoon.*

engineer [T1] to arrange or cause by clever, esp secret planning: *He had powerful enemies who engineered his ruin.*

N151 *verbs* : **causing things to happen in special ways**

arouse [T1] to cause (something or someone) to do something or be active, often forcefully: *Her anger was aroused by his silly actions. That book aroused my interest in fishing.*

stir [T1] *esp lit* to cause, arouse: *That book has stirred my interest in fishing.* **stir up** [v adv T1] *emph* to arouse: *He is always trying to stir up trouble here.*

precipitate [T1 *(into)*] *usu fml* to cause (something) to happen or (someone) to do something more quickly than expected, desired, etc: *The killing of the king precipitated the war. His action precipitated them into the war.*

prompt 1 [T1; V3] to cause or urge (someone) to do something: *He's never acted so foolishly before; what could have prompted him? Hunger prompted him to steal.* **2** [T1] to be the cause of (a thought, action or feeling): *The sight of the ships prompted thoughts of his distant home.*

provoke [T1] to cause, esp forcefully: *If you do that you will provoke trouble. His silly actions provoked laughter.*

provoke into [v prep D1; V4b] to cause or force (someone) into (an action or doing something): *Her rudeness provoked me into striking her.*

incite [T1 *(to)*; V3] to encourage or cause (someone) to take (a strong action) or to have (a strong feeling): *His remarks incited me to anger. The army was incited to rebellion* [⇒ C135] *He incited them to rise up against their leaders.* **incitement 1** [U] the act of inciting **2** [C] something which incites: *His words were an incitement to rebellion.*

render 1 [X7] to cause to be: *His fatness renders him unable to touch his toes.* **2** [D1 *(to)*; T1] *fml* to give (help): *You have rendered me a service.* **render an account** to send an account of money that is owed **render thanks** to thank someone, esp God: *Let us render thanks (to God) for what we have received.*

induce 1 [T1 *often pass*] **a** to cause to begin (*only in the phr* **induce labour**) by using medical drugs: *Labour* [⇒ B181] *has been induced.* **b** *infml* to cause (a baby) to be born, or (a mother) to give birth, by medical means: *The baby was induced by drugs given to the mother, so that it could be born more quickly. She wanted to give birth naturally, but she had to be induced.* **2** [T1] to produce (an effect): *Too much food induces sleepiness.* **3** [V3] to lead (someone) into an act often by persuasion: *I was induced to come against my will. What induced her to come uninvited?*

involve [Wv6;T1, 4] to make necessary: *Being a soldier can involve getting killed.*

N152 *nouns* : **causes and reasons**

[ALSO ⇒ G18]

cause 1 [C] something which produces an effect; a person, thing, or event that makes something happen: *A cigarette was the cause of the fire. What was the cause of the last war? Her stupidity is the cause of all her trouble.* **2** [U] reason: *Don't complain without cause. There's no cause for you to leave; I still love you. There's more cause for you to go to mother's than stay here. Is there sufficient cause for you to sell this house?* **3** [C] a principle or movement strongly defended or supported: *His cause was the freedom of his people: for this he would die if necessary.* **4** [C] *law* the reason for action in a court of law; a matter over which a person goes to law **make common cause (with)** to take action together for a particular purpose: *The government and the opposition made common cause to win the war.* **causal** [Wa5;B] *tech* **1** of or showing the relationship of cause and effect **2** being a cause: *a causal force* **3** (in grammar) expressing a cause: *a causal phrase* **-ly** [adv] **-ity** [U]: *the laws of causality*

reason 1 [C *(for)*, C3, 5a,c, 6a *why*; U3] the cause of an event; the explanation or excuse for an action: *The reason for the flood was all that heavy rain. I have many reasons to fear him. The reason that/why he died was lack of medical care. There is/We have reason to believe that he was murdered.* **2** [C *(for)*, C3, 5a] what makes one decide on an action; the cause of an intention: *What is your reason for wanting to enter the country?*

N153 *nouns* : **results and effects**

result 1 [C] what happens because of something else: *The war was the result of their desire for more land. What results did you get from your tests?—The results show that he was right.* **2** [I0] to happen as a result: *If the police leave, disorder will result. Disorder resulted from his actions.* **result in** [v prep T1] to come to (something) as a result: *Their desire for more land resulted in a war.*

effect [U; C: (*on, upon*)] **1** a special or particular result: *Life is all cause and effect. The effects of the illness were bad. Unfortunately, our efforts had no effect.* **2** a result produced on the mind: *Her new red dress produced quite an effect on everyone. Don't look at the details, consider the general effect. He only said it for effect. I heard some wonderful sound effects on the radio last night.* **to . . . effect** with . . . general meaning: *He called me a fool, or words to that effect. He has made a declaration to the effect that all fighting must cease at once. I have already told him the information, and written a letter to the same effect.* **into effect** into (esp lawful) operation: *A new system of taxation will come/go/be brought/be put into effect next May.* **in effect 1** in (esp lawful) operation: *The old system of taxation will remain in effect until next May.* **2** for all practical purposes; it is more or less true to say: *Her brother is king, but she is, in effect, the real ruler of Ruritania.* **take effect 1** to come into (esp lawful) operation: *The new system of taxation will take effect next May.* **2** to begin to produce results: *The medicine quickly took effect.* **give effect to** to carry out: *He gave effect to his dead brother's wishes.*

issue [C] *rare* a result: *He is hoping for a good issue to this matter.*

consequence 1 [C *usu pl*] something that follows from an action or condition; result: *Before you do anything you should always consider the consequences.* **2** [U] *fml* importance: *Is it of much consequence to you that the government has lost the election? He's a man of little consequence (to anyone).* **in consequence (of)** *fml* as a result (of): *In consequence of your bad work I am forced to dismiss you.* **consequent** [Wa5;A;F *on*] being what follows or is caused by something else: *All right, you want us to stop work for a month, but will you pay the consequent costs if we are forced to do the work next year and not now? His success was consequent on his hard work.*

end result [C] the last result of all: *What was the end result of all the arguing and discussing?*

end product [C] *tech* something which is produced as the result of a number of operations: *Our raw material is wood and our end product is paper.*

aftereffect [C *often pl*] an effect which happens later than expected or usual: *This illness may have some aftereffects when he is much older.*

side effect [C *often pl*] an effect in addition to the effect wanted: *This medicine will help you but it has certain other side effects which may cause you a little trouble.*

by-product [C] **1** something formed in addition to the main product: *Silver is often obtained as a by-product when separating lead from rock.* **2** an additional result sometimes unexpected

or unintended: *Unemployment can be a by-product of higher taxes.*

spin-off [C; (U)] *not fml* a result which is unexpected and in addition to the expected results of an action, etc: *Was there any profitable spin-off to all this scientific work?*

aftermath [C *usu sing*] the result or period following a bad event such as an accident, storm, war, etc: *Life was much harder in the aftermath of the war.*

N154 *verbs* : **causing action**
[ALSO ⇒ M58 PUSH, N334 PRESS]

force 1 [T1; V3] to use force to cause (someone) to do something: *She didn't want to go, so he forced her (to go). Don't try to force me to do it/into doing it! (fig) The heavy rain forced us to stay at home.* **2** [T1; X7] to open by force: *He forced the door (open).*

compel [T1; V3: *often pass*] *esp fml* to force: *He was compelled to do it against his will (= although he did not want to). The rain compelled us to stay indoors. Don't feel compelled to come if you don't want to. Threats will never compel my obedience! (fig) His cleverness and skill compel our admiration.*

impel [T1 (*into*); V3] (*usu fig*) (of ideas, feelings, etc) to push or force (someone) forward: *Hunger impelled me to finish my work quickly.*

oblige 1 [V3 *usu pass*] to make (someone) feel it necessary (to do something): *Your bad behaviour obliges me to dismiss you. I feel obliged to say 'No'.* **2** [T1] *polite* to do (someone) a favour: *Could you oblige me by opening the window? Could you oblige me with a match?* (= please give me a match). **(I'm) much obliged (to you)** *polite* (I'm) very grateful (to you)

coerce [T1] **1** [(*into*)] to make (an unwilling person or group of people) do something by using force, threats of punishment, etc: *The government coerced the unions into accepting the pay limit by threatening to call an election.* **2** [*often pass*] to keep (a person, group of people, or activity) under control by using force, threats of punishment, etc; repress: *The working people have been coerced by their employers for too long!* **3** [*often pass*] to gain acceptance for (a course of action) by force or the threat of force: *Our agreement to the plan was coerced; we were not free to say no to it!*

pressurize, -ise 1 [T1 (*into*); V3] to (try to) make (someone) do something by means of forcible persuasion or influence: *Certain groups are pressurizing the minister to free the prisoners. They have pressurized him into freeing the prisoners.* **2** [Wv5;T1] to control the air pressure inside (a (part of a) high-flying aeroplane, etc) so that the pressure does not become much lower than that on earth: *a pressurized cabin*

pressure [T1 (*into*); V3] to pressurize

bully [T1 (*into*); V3] to force in a nasty way,

often with the intention of getting someone to do something: *He was always bullying smaller boys (into doing things).*

subject to [v prep D1 *often pass*] to cause to experience esp by force: *The people were subjected to foreign rule. They were subjected to a very difficult examination.* **subjection** [U] the state of being subjected to something

subordinate [T1 (*to*)] to cause (something) to be less important than some other thing: *He subordinated his personal needs to his political interests.* **subordination** [U] the act of subordinating

push 1 [T1 (*into*); V3] to force (someone) to do something by continued urging: *I'm not pushing you; if you don't want this job, don't take it. She has such a weak will that she can be pushed into anything. My friends are all pushing me to enter politics.* 2 [T1; I0] to force (someone or something) on the notice of others, as a means of success: *They aren't really pushing their business enough and are losing money on it; they ought to push their goods more. She isn't a good actress, but she pushes herself as much as she can.* (*esp AmE*) *When my son had a cold, the doctor said, 'Push liquids; make him drink a lot'.* 3 [T1 (*for*)] to hurry or trouble (someone) by continual urging: *If you push a worker too hard, he may make mistakes. He keeps pushing me for payment of the debt.* 4 [T1; (I0)] (*fig*) *infml* to sell (unlawful drugs) by acting as a connection between the suppliers and the people who need to, or can be persuaded to, buy

oust [T1 (*from*)] (of a living being) to force (a living being) out (of): *Tigers have almost ousted lions from India. He hopes to oust the president in the next elections/oust them from power.*

N155 *nouns* : **causing action**
[ALSO ⇒ B92, N235]

force [U] strength, power, etc used to make someone do something, something happen, etc: *He used force to get what he wanted. They used force to open the locked door.*

compulsion *fml* 1 [U] force or influence that makes a person do something (*often in the phr* **under compulsion**): *The governor had to use compulsion to make the people pay taxes. I will pay nothing under compulsion.* 2 [C, C3] a strong usu unreasonable desire that is difficult to control: *Her compulsion to drink soon made her ill. Drinking is a compulsion with her.*

coercion [U] 1 the act of coercing or of being coerced: *You can't get me to be quiet by coercion!* 2 government by force: *Coercion isn't the best way of ruling an empire; a ruler must win his people's love.*

pressure 1 [U (*of*)] the action of pressing with force or weight: *Food is broken up in the mouth by the pressure of the teeth.* 2 [U; C] the strength of this force: *He asked the garage*

worker to test the air pressure in his tyres. These air containers will burst at high pressures. It was a pressure of 4 kilos to the square inch.* 3 [U] discomfort caused by a sensation of pressing: *The sick man complained of a feeling of pressure in his chest.* 4 [U; C] *also fml* **atmospheric pressure** the (force of the) weight of the air: *Low pressure often brings rain.* 5 [C; U: (*of*)] trouble that causes anxiety and difficulty: *He faced the pressure of family anxieties. The combined pressures of high taxation and high wages are ruining this shoe factory.* 6 [U] forcible influence (used for obtaining a desired action) (*esp in the phrs* **bring pressure (to bear) on someone (to do something)**): *They put pressure on him. The police brought pressure to bear on him to say what they wanted.* 7 [U (*of*)] high rate of speed and activity: *We are working at high pressure to get the report ready for tomorrow's meeting. Villagers are unaccustomed to the pressure of modern city life.*

inducement [U; C, C3] encouragement; something, esp money, which persuades one to act: *He offered me an inducement. The promise of a holiday at the seaside is no great inducement to study hard, when I don't like the seaside anyway.*

friction [U] 1 the rubbing of one thing against another: *Friction produces heat.* 2 (*fig*) argument, disagreement, etc: *There was quite a lot of friction at the meeting.*

cogency [U] the power to prove or produce belief; quality of being cogent: *The cogency of the priest's arguments made me believe in God.*

N156 *adjectives* : **causing action** [B]

forceful having or using force, pressure, etc: *He's very forceful in getting what he wants.* **-ly** [adv] **-ness** [U]

forcible done by or using force: *The police made a forcible entry into the locked house.* **-bly** [adv]

compulsive resulting from compulsion; too strong to stop or prevent: *He is a compulsive eater; he eats all the time.* **-ly** [adv]: *She smokes compulsively.*

compelling that compels; strong: *Did he have a compelling reason for going?* **-ly** [adv]

coercive for the purpose of coercing or intended to coerce: *They used coercive measures against us/on him.* **-ly** [adv]

cogent having the power to produce or produce belief; forceful in argument; convincing: *I have cogent reasons for voting for the workers' party.*

N157 *verbs* : **persuading, etc**
[ALSO ⇒ G87]

persuade [T1; V3] to get someone to do something by giving reasons: *I tried to persuade her (to join the club).*

724

dissuade [T1 (*from*)] to prevent from doing something by giving reasons: *I tried to dissuade her (from joining the club).*

urge [T1; V3] to try hard to make someone (do something); persuade strongly: *I urged her to go. He needs no urging; he'll do it willingly.*

coax 1 [T1 (*into/out of*)] to make (someone) do what one wants by very pleasant behaviour and words: *She coaxed him into going/out of his bad temper.* **2** [X9] to get (something one wants) by persuading someone: *He coaxed a promise out of her.* **-ingly** [adv]

wheedle *emot, emph & sometimes deprec* to coax **1** [T1 (*into/out of*)]: *She wheedled him into going/out of his bad temper.* **2** [X9]: *He wheedled a promise out of her.* **-lingly** [adv]

N158 *verbs* : **making necessary, requiring, etc**

[ALSO ⇨ F7]

necessitate [Wv6;T1,4] *fml* to make necessary: *Your remarks may necessitate my thinking about the question again. A smaller car is necessitated by the high price of petrol.*

need [Wv6;T1] to find or make necessary: *We need more men. This suggestion needs careful thought. He gave us some much-needed help.*

demand [T1] *fml* to need urgently: *This work demands your attention without delay!*

require [Wv5] **1** [T1, 4, 5c] *esp fml* to need: *This suggestion requires careful thought. The floor requires washing. His health requires that he (should) go to bed early. I'm looking for the required ladder.* **2** [T1 (*of*), 5c; V3] *fml* to demand; order, expecting obedience: *All passengers are required to show their tickets. Do you require anything of me? He passed the required examinations to become a doctor. He requires that they (should) work all night.*

N159 *modals* : **making necessary**

must [Wv2;I0,2] **1** to find it necessary to; be or feel required to: *I must leave at six. I said I must leave but I stayed. The teacher says they mustn't talk during lessons. Old people used to say children must be seen and not heard. Must I drink this soup? I must admit I don't like her.* **2** to be necessary: *The house must be clean if there are guests.*

ought [Wv2,6;I0,3] *usu fml* to feel strongly required to: *I ought to leave at six. The teacher says they ought not to/oughtn't to talk during lessons.*

have (got) [Wv2;I3] *genl & often infml* to be forced; must: *Do you have to go now? I've got to go. I'll have to telephone later. I have (got) to go at six.*

be [Wv1,6;I3] *usu emph & often fml* must; be required: *You are to leave at six, and not later! He was to come but he didn't.*

need [Wv2,6;I0,2,3] *often less fml* must: *I really do need to go now; if I don't, I'll miss my train.* (as neg of **must**) *You don't need to/needn't go now if you don't want to.*

N160 *verbs* : **helping or not helping actively**

[ALSO ⇨ G119]

promote [T1] **1** to help actively in forming or arranging (a business, concert, play, etc): *Who is promoting this boxing match? The three brothers are promoting a company to make aircraft.* **2** to bring (goods) to public notice in order to increase (sales): *The company are promoting their new sort of toothbrush on television. It seems to promote the sales of this product.* **promotion 1** [U] the act of promoting **2** [C] an act or occasion of promoting

encourage [Wv4;T1(*in*);V3] to give courage or hope (to someone); urge (someone) on to fresh efforts: *She gave him an encouraging smile. He encouraged me in my work. They encourage the children to paint pictures.* **encouragement 1** [U] the act of encouraging or being encouraged: *He needs some encouragement; help him. What she said was no encouragement at all!* **2** [C] something that encourages: *It's an encouragement for him to get this help.*

discourage 1 [Wv4,5;T1] to take away courage and spirit from: *It discourages me/It's very discouraging that every time I try to ride a bicycle I fall off. It makes me feel very discouraged.* **2** [T1, 4] to try to prevent (an action) esp by showing disfavour; put difficulties in the way of: *I discourage the use of tobacco. We discourage smoking in the school.* **3** [T1 (*from*)] to try to prevent (someone) from doing something esp by showing disfavour: *His mother discouraged him from joining the navy, saying that it was a hard life, but he refused to be discouraged.* **discouragement 1** [U] the act of discouraging or being discouraged: *His discouragement showed on his face.* **2** [C] something that discourages: *I'm going on with the work no matter what discouragements happen.*

N161 *verbs* : **starting things**

[ALSO ⇨ L170 START]

set up [v adv T1] **1** to do all the necessary things to start (a business, etc): *He set up the whole plan. She set up the business all by herself* (= no one helped her). **2** to do all the necessary things to start (someone) (in a business, etc): *He set his son up in business.*

establish [Wv5;T1] *often fml* **1** to set up: *They established a shop/school/business/new state.* **2** [(*as, in*)] to place (oneself or another) in a (stated) firm or good position: *He established his son in business. He established himself as the most powerful minister in the new government. He holds an established position in the* company. How can you marry before you've established yourself? **3** [also T5a, 6a] to find out or make certain of (a fact, answer, etc): *He tried to establish the truth of the story. The police can't establish whether the woman was murdered or not. It is an established fact that ...* **4** to make (a rule): *We've established a rule in this club that everyone buys his own drinks.* **5** to cause people to believe in or recognize (a claim, fact, etc): *She established her fame as an actress. He established his claim to be king. It was an old-established custom. That is a long-established custom here.* **establishment 1** [U] the act of establishing: *The successful establishment of the new businesses in the city pleased everybody.* **2** [C] something established: *That company is one of the great business establishments in our country.*

found [T1] to do the first things necessary to start (a city, society, movement, etc): *Romulus is supposed to have founded the city of Rome. The club was founded in 1844.*

base 1 [T1] [*on*] to build or set up and develop (other things, esp arguments, plans, stories, etc) on (something): *He based his argument on the need to grow more food. The book is based on fact/on something that really happened.* **2** [X9, *usu pass*, esp *in*] to give (oneself) a home or base [⇒ J227] for travelling: *He is based in London. He is London-based, but works for a Chicago-based company.*

N162 verbs : looking after things [v prep T1, 4]

look after to do all the necessary things to help, care for, etc (someone or something): *She looks after her old mother very well. I'll look after you; don't worry. Could you look after the shop while I'm away, please?*

attend to to do all the necessary things so that (something) is all right: *Yes, I'll attend to the matter myself in the morning. Please attend to this immediately.* **attention** [U] the act of attending, listening, etc to someone or something: *Please give your attention to this matter as soon as you can. The teacher wanted the whole class's attention. Pay attention, please!* **attentive** [B (*to*)] giving attention to someone or something; listening carefully: *You must be more attentive to your teacher/at school. He was very attentive to her needs.* **in-** [*neg*] **-ly** [adv]

see to to attend to; take care of: *See to it that you don't make this mistake next time. You ought to have your eyes seen to by a doctor. If I see to getting the car out, will you see to closing the windows?*

N163 verbs, etc : getting things done

get ... done *emph* to do: *I'll get that job done as soon as possible.*

manage to do to be able to do: *I hope I can manage to do the job soon.*

fix [T1] *not fml* to get (something) done, esp for someone else or because it is not working well, etc: *Don't worry; I'll fix it/everything for you. He fixed it so that we could go tomorrow.*

decide 1 [I0; T1, 3, 5, 6a, b; V3] to (cause to) come to an opinion (about): *She decided to help him. They decided to go. What have you decided (about this/in this matter)?* **2** [T1] to cause to be decided: *His words decided the matter (for us). The matter hasn't been decided yet.* **decided** [B] having formed an opinion; made a decision: *She was quite decided in the matter; she would go and no one would stop her.* **decision 1** [U] the ability to decide things, esp quickly: *He lacks decision. They acted with decision.* **2** [C] an act or result of deciding: *We talked for a long time but couldn't come to a decision/take a decision. I hope you've made/taken the right decision. She doesn't like making his decisions for him.* **decisive** [B] deciding easily and forcefully; causing something to be done, finished, won, etc: *He is very decisive in business. The battle was decisive; they won the war.* **in-** [*neg*] **-ly** [adv] **-ness** [U]

settle [Wv3] **1** [T1, 5, 6a, b] to decide on; fix; make the last arrangements about: *We still haven't settled the date of our holiday/when we'll take our holiday. We've settled that we'll go to Wales, but we haven't settled how to get there. I'll be glad when it's all settled.* **2** [T1; L9 (*with*)] to end (an argument, esp in law); to bring (a matter) to an agreement: *They settled their quarrel in a friendly way. The contract was settled after long talks. The two companies settled their disagreement out of court (= without bringing it to court formally). On his unpaid taxes, he settled with the government for 50p in the £.* **3** [T1] to pay (a bill or money claimed): *Will this £5 settle what I owe? The insurance company settled the claim quickly and for the full amount of the claim.* **settle one's affairs** to put all one's business matters into order, esp for the last time: *He settled his affairs before joining the army in 1940.* **That settles it** *infml* That has decided the matter: *The car won't start.—That settles it; we can't go out tonight.* **settlement 1** [U] the act of settling or being settled: *Settlement of the matter has been delayed for years.* **2** [C *usu sing*] an example or result of this: *They have been talking for weeks; have they reached a settlement yet?—No; no settlement has been reached.* **3** [(*in*) U (*of*)] payment: *Leave the bill with me for settlement. He gave us £300 in settlement of the debt (= money owed).*

resolve 1 [L9, esp *on*; T3, 5, 6b] to decide: *He resolved on/against going out. She must resolve to work harder/that she will work harder. Have you resolved where to go next?* **2** [L9, esp *on*; T3, 5] (of a committee or public body) to decide: *The committee resolved on/against appointing a new secretary. Parliament has resolved that ...* **3** [T1] to settle or clear up (a difficulty): *The matter was resolved by making George sleep on the floor.* **4** [U] *esp lit* strong determination: *He acted with resolve to win back what he had lost.* **resolution** [C, C3, 5c] an act of resolving something: *He made a resolution to work harder. The committee passed a resolution that the work would be done.*

determine 1 [T3] to decide strongly, forcefully: *He determined to work harder.* **2** [T1, 6a, b] to cause something to be decided: *How can you determine the amount of money needed if you don't know all the costs? The money we have will determine how long we can stay there. The exact amount is difficult to determine.* **determination** [U] **1** strength in deciding to do something: *He worked with great determination; he would win! She lacks determination; she won't do well in this work.* **2** *fml & less common* the act of determining (something): *The determination of the exact amount of money needed is not easy.* **determined** [B] having firmly decided: *He is determined to go; no one will stop him.*

make up one's mind *common & not fml* to decide: *He made up his mind to do it. She made up her mind that she would win. Have you made up your mind how to do it yet?*

N164 *verbs* : **making things better** [T1]
[ALSO ⇒ N130]

improve 1 to use well and/or to make better: *I want to improve my abilities. I'll improve the shape of the handle so it's easier for you to use.* **2** [Wv5] to increase the value of (land or property) as by farming, building, etc: *Improved property is worth more.*

better to do better than: *Can you better his price for the house* (= Can you offer a better price)? *He can easily better their work.*

ameliorate *fml* to make (conditions, etc) better: *'We must try to ameliorate the housing conditions of the people,' said the politician.* **amelioration** [U]

enhance to add to (the value, beauty, etc of something): *Her green dress enhanced (the colour of) her red hair. If you have a good garden it will enhance the value of your house.* **enhancement** [U] the act of enhancing; the condition of being enhanced

N165 *verbs* : **controlling things**

control [T1] to have the power to move, lead, change, etc (someone or something) or not to do so: *He completely controls their lives/what they do. Please try to control your feelings.*

direct [T1] to control (work, people working, etc): *He directed the whole job; without him we couldn't have done it.*

superintend [T1] to be in control of (esp a group of people working): *He superintended*

all their work personally. **superintendent** [C] a person who superintends

supervise [T1; I0] to watch (a person, group, etc) to make sure that something, esp work, is properly done: *Who is supervising these men?* **supervisor** [C] a person who supervises

effect [T1] *fml & old use* to cause, produce, or have as a result: *I will effect my purpose; no one shall stop me! Unfortunately, the new medicine could not effect a cure.*

affect [T1] **1** to have an effect [⇒ N153] on, esp in a bad way: *His work has affected his health; he isn't well. Will our future here be affected by his decision?* **2** to cause feelings of sorrow, anger, love, etc in: *She was deeply affected by the news of his death.* **3** (of a disease) to attack: *The disease is affecting his lungs now.*

influence [T1] to affect, esp strongly: *One's health influences one's behaviour. Don't let me influence your decision.*

guide [T1 *usu pass*] to influence, esp strongly or in a certain way: *Be guided by your feelings and tell her the truth before it's too late.*

govern [T1] **1** to control or guide (actions and feelings): *The need for money governs all his plans. Don't let bad temper govern your decision. I hope you will be governed by my advice.* **2** [*often pass*] to decide the nature of: *The rise and fall of the sea is governed by the movements of the moon.*

harness [T1 *often pass*] to bring (something, esp a kind of power) under control for a useful purpose: *In the modern world mountain rivers have been harnessed to provide electricity. Mankind harnessed the atom for peaceful and for military purposes.*

manipulate [T1] **1** to handle or control (esp a machine) usually skilfully: *He manipulated the controls.* **2** to use (someone) for one's own purpose by skilfully controlling and influencing, often in an unfair or dishonest manner: *They would not have accepted his suggestion if he hadn't manipulated them into agreeing.*

manoeuvre *BrE*, **maneuver** *AmE* [T1] to move or manipulate esp from one position or place to another, esp as part of a plan or with skill: *He slowly manoeuvred the large box into its position against the wall. The enemy were manoeuvred out of their good position on the hill. He manoeuvred me into selling the car when I didn't want to!*

preside [Wv4; I0(*over*)] (esp of leaders at meetings, etc) to control or be in charge: *Who will preside at the committee meeting? Our chairman won't be here, so Mr Smith will preside. The presiding officer told us the results of the election.*

chair [T1; I0] *not fml* to preside over: *Who is chairing (the meeting) tonight?*

N166 *nouns* : **controlling things**

control 1 [(*in*) U (*over*)] the act of controlling; ability to control: *Who is in control here? She* *has control over everyone there.* **2** [C *usu pl*] something which controls: *The government has placed controls on people taking money out of the country; you can only take so much and no more.*

direction [(*under*) U] the act or occasion of directing: *The work will be done under his direction and no one else's.*

guidance [(*under*) U] the act of guiding; the condition of being guided: *They will work under our guidance. With some guidance from us, their work will improve.*

influence 1 [U;C: (*over*, *with*)] **a** power to affect or get results from someone without asking or doing anything: *He has a strange influence over the girl. My influence with her is not very strong. Her influence made me a better person.* **b** a person with this power: *He's an influence for good in the club.* **2** [C (*on*)] an action of power; effect: *Wages have an influence on prices. The stars' influence on men has yet to be proved.* **3** [U] the power to get good results, which important men have by using their wealth, position, etc: *He is a man of influence. He tried to use his influence to get a job.* **under the influence of** in the power of; easily affected by (people, things): *He's under the influence of drugs/unsuitable friends.* **a good/bad influence** an influence which has (the power to produce) a good/bad effect: *He has a good influence on us. He's a bad influence.*

manipulation 1 [U] the act of manipulating or condition of being manipulated: *Some people can put back a misplaced joint, like the shoulder, by careful manipulation.* **2** [C] an example of this: *By his various manipulations he has managed to become rich.*

N167 *verbs* : **running and managing things**

run 1 [T1] to control; be in charge of and cause to work (an organization or system): *Who's running this country? to run a hotel/a youth club; We're running a new system of payment. I don't want to run your life for you!* **2** [L9, esp *for*] to have official force (during a period of time): *The insurance has only another month to run.*

manage 1 [T1] to control (esp a business): *He manages the family business. She has managed the company for many years and manages it very well.* **2** [I0;T1, 3] to be able (to do something); succeed (in doing something):*Can you do it without help?—Yes, I can manage/I'll manage all right. They managed it/to do it. She somehow managed to get the big box into the house.* **3** [T1] to deal with or guide, esp by using skill: *She manages the money very well. She knows how to manage him when he's angry.*

maintain [T1] **1** to continue to have, do, etc as before: *He took the lead and maintained it till the end of the race. The soldiers maintained the*

attack until they took the town. If he maintains his efforts, he will succeed. **2** to support with money: *He is too poor to maintain his family. He maintains two homes.* **3** to keep in existence: *It isn't easy to maintain life in the desert/ to maintain one's health/to maintain order in the streets.* **4** to keep in good condition, by making repairs to and taking care of: *He maintains the house/car/railway line.*

organize [T1;I0] **1** to form (parts) into a whole; bring into working order: *He was the first to organize the work in this way.* **2** to keep in working order: *We want you to organize the everyday work of the factory. Is he good at organizing?* [⇒ N194]

N168 *verbs* : **controlling things completely**

master [T1] **1** to gain control over: *The horse tried to run away, but he succeeded in mastering it.* **2** to gain as a skill: *He never mastered the art of public speaking. I am not too old to master a new language.*

dominate 1 [T1;I0 (*over*)] to have or exercise controlling influence or power (over): *Her desire to dominate (other people) has caused trouble in her family. Her desire to do her duty dominates over everything else.* **2** [T1;L9] to have the most important place or position (in): *Sports and not learning, seem to dominate (in) that school. French wines no longer dominate the wine trade of the U.S.A. American wines are now widely sold there.* **3** [T1] to rise or to be higher than; provide a view from a height above: *The church dominated the whole town.*

domineer [I0 (*over*)] *usu derog* to show a desire to control others, usu without any consideration of their feelings or wishes: *I wouldn't work for someone who tries to domineer (over everyone) as Mrs Smith does.*

N169 *adjectives* : **controlling things** [B]

effective 1 having a noticeable or desired effect; producing the desired result: *He made an effective speech. His efforts to improve the school have been very effective. She is the most effective ruler that Ruritania has ever had.* **2** [Wa5] actual; real; able to work, serve, or take part: *The club is large, but its effective membership is only 23. What is the effective strength of our army? Her brother is king, but she is the effective ruler of Ruritania.* **in-** [*neg*] **-ly** [adv]

effectual *fml* (of actions but not of the people who do them) producing the complete effect intended; effective: *He took effectual action against unemployment.* **in-** [*neg*] **-ly** [adv] **-ness** [U]

efficient working well and without waste: *That efficient worker gets all her work done in less time than anyone else. Our efficient new* machines are much cheaper to run. **in-** [neg] **-ly** [adv]

influential having influence: *It was an influential decision and he is an influential man.* **-ly** [adv]

masterly showing great skill: *It was a masterly speech.*

masterful having or showing an ability or wish to control others: *He spoke in a masterful manner.* **-ly** [adv] **-ness** [U]

dominant 1 dominating: *My sister had a very dominant nature; we all did what she wanted. The Town Hall was built on a dominant hill where everyone could see it.* **2** (of paired body parts) being stronger than the other: *The right hand is dominant in most people.* **3** [Wa5] *tech* (of groups of qualities passed on from parent to child) being the quality that actually appears in the child when more than one are passed on: *Brown eyes are dominant in that family.* **-ly** [adv]

domineering *usu derog* having or showing a strong tendency to domineer: *Her brother was so domineering that she never had a chance of pleasing herself. He has a domineering manner.* **-ly** [adv]

N170 *nouns* : **controlling and managing things**

running [(*the*) U *of*] the way in which something is run: *Who looks after the running of the factory?*

management 1 [U (*of*)] the act of managing, esp a business or money: *The college runs courses in management/management courses.* **2** [U] skill in dealing with something or someone: *He didn't do very well in the test, but he got the job; more by luck than management.* **3** [GC] the people who are in charge of a firm, industry, etc, considered as one body: *The workers are having talks with the management.*

maintenance [U] the act of maintaining (defs **2**, **3** & **4**): *Who looks after the maintenance of these machines?*

organization 1 [U] the act of organizing or being organized: *'This factory needs proper organization,' he said.* **2** [C] something organized esp a business: *Which organization does he work for?*

mastery [U (*over, of*)] the condition of having mastered or being able to master someone or something; control: *He has complete mastery over the horses. Her mastery of French is excellent; she speaks it like a French person.*

domination [U (*over, of*)] the act of dominating (*esp def* **1** & **2**); the power to dominate: *Her desire for domination over the others caused trouble in the family. That nation once wanted world domination* (= to dominate the world).

dominance [U] the state or condition of being dominant: *The dominance of some animals over others is part of nature.*

effectiveness [U] the state or condition of being effective: *The effectiveness of his speech*

surprised me; I didn't expect it to be so useful. **in-** [neg]

efficiency [U] the state or condition of being efficient: *He was pleased by the efficiency of the new workers/machines.* **in-** [neg]

Resemblance, difference, and change

N180 *verbs* : **being like and looking like** [T1]

be like [v prep] to be of the same or nearly the same kind (in some way) as (someone or something else): *He is very like his father. This box is quite like that one.*

look like [v prep] to be like to the eye: *He looks very like his father. This coat looks just like that one, but it isn't the same material.*

resemble [(*in*)] *often fml & esp of persons* to look or be like: *She resembles her sister in appearance but not in character. He greatly resembles his father.*

take after [v prep; Wv6] to look or behave like (a relative): *Mary really takes after her mother; she has the same eyes, nose, and hair and even stands in the same way.*

N181 *adjectives, etc* : **like and same**

like 1 [prep] (more or less) the same as: *Is his house like this one?—Yes, just like it. This town looks (a bit/little) like the other one. All the towns look (a lot) like each other.* **2** [prep] in the same way as: *Stop acting like a child!* (*fig*) *She ran like the wind.* **3** [prep] what one could expect from: *It was (just) like her to do a nasty thing like that! Isn't it just like a man to forget what day it is today!* **4** [prep] (with **feel**) ready for: *I feel like (going for) a walk; anybody coming with me?* **5** [prep] (with **look** and **-ing** form) as if about to: *She looks like winning the race.* **6** [prep] (*esp in the phr* **it looks like**) to seem probable: *It looks like a good time for a change. It looks like snow.* **7** [F] the same in many ways: *He and his brother are very like.* **8** [Wa5;A] with the same qualities: *Like thinking produces like ideas.* **9** [prep] with the same qualities as: *He was more like a son to me than my own son.*

USAGE **like** is also used by some people as a conj, in *Do it like I do* and *She looks like she'll win the race.* Many people prefer **as** and **as if** in such sentences: *Do it as I do it*, and *She looks as if she'll win the race.*

alike 1 [F] being (almost) the same in appearance, quality, character, etc; like one another: *The two brothers are very much alike. You two are more alike than I thought.* **2** [adv] in (almost) the same way; equally: *She treats all her children alike.*

same [pron Wa5;B;(*as*)] (used with **the**, **this**, **that**, etc) (being) this or that one or kind and not any other: *Did you two go to the same school?—Yes; he went to the same school as I did*/(*infml*) *as me. He left in the morning, but he returned the same day, in the evening. When I asked her, she said the same* (*as he had said*). *What did she say?—The same. This book is* (*just*) *the same as that one, isn't it?—Yes; both books are the same. Your brother did well at school; I hope you will do the same. Do you agree* (*with me*)?—*Yes; I feel the same* (*as you* (*do*)). (*emph*) *That same painting was stolen before* (=Someone once stole that painting and now it has been stolen again). **be all the same**, **to come/amount to the same thing** to make no difference: *Can I go?—Go or stay; it's all the same to me.*/*It all amounts to the same thing as far as I am concerned.* **just the same** *infml* in the same way: *He treats all his children just the same.* **one and the same** exactly the same: *The two men were one and the same* (=It was the same man; you only thought there were two). **as** [conj] in the way or manner that: *Do as I say!*

similar [B] **1** [(*to*)] like or alike; of the same kind; partly or almost the same: *He likes bread, cake, and other similar foods. We have similar opinions; my opinions are similar to his.* **2** [Wa5] *tech* exactly the same in shape but not size: *Similar triangles have equal angles.* **dis-** [*neg*] **-ly** [adv]

identical [Wa5;B (*to*, *with*)] *fml* exactly the same (as): *This book is identical to that one, isn't it?—Yes; the books are identical.* **-ly** [adv Wa4]

uniform [Wa5;B] **1** with every part the same; even; regular: *The dress is a uniform colour.* **2** the same in every way: *The dresses were of uniform value.*

equal [Wa5] **1** [B (*in*, *to*)] (of two or more) the same in size, number, value, rank, etc: *Cut the cake into six equal pieces. Women demand equal pay for equal work* (=equal to men). *Mary is quite equal to Bill in brains. They both fought with equal bravery. Which of these shall I buy? The prices are equal.* **2** [F *to*] (of a person) having enough strength, ability, etc (for): *Bill is quite equal to* (*the job of*) *running the office.* **un-** [*neg*] **equal to the occasion** able to meet or deal with whatever happens: *Mary won't be frightened to meet the Queen. I'm sure she'll be perfectly equal to the occasion.* **on equal terms** (meeting or speaking) as equals; without difference of rank: *They're both generals, so they can talk to each other on equal terms.*

even [Wa5;B] equal: *The two boxers were an even match* (=had equal strength and ability). *We are even now; you did something bad to me and I have paid you back* (=done something bad to you in return). *I'll get even with him one day!* **un-** [*neg*] **-ly** [adv]: *They were evenly matched.*

level [Wa5;B] equal; having the same success,

ability, etc; making the same progress: *The two girls are* (*just*) *about level in mathematics. They were level in the race till the last few metres, then he went ahead to win.*

comparable [B (*with*, *to*)] *fml* **1** that can be compared: *Both of these coats are comparable in size. Churchill is comparable to Wellington in his greatness.* **2** worthy of comparison: *Our house is not comparable with yours; ours is small, while yours is a palace.* **in-** [*neg*] **-bly** [adv]

complementary [(*to*)] serving to complete; supplying what is lacking or needed by another or each other for completion: *In the 18th century many British politicians favoured friendship with Prussia because they thought that the Prussian army was complementary to the British navy. Irish farming and British industry are complementary. Each provides what the other needs.*

such [det; pron] **1** *often fml* (often with **as**) of the same kind, quality, or degree: *Such men as these are dangerous.* (=Men like these are dangerous). *Such a man is dangerous. No such person exists. All such books are interesting* (=All books like that are interesting). *He has read many such books. Are you going to Paris?—No such luck! He is going to Paris or some such place. Such people* (*as they are*) *can help you a lot.* **2** *often emph* so much: *He is such a helpful person. I've never seen such a book as this before!* **3** *usu fml* of the kind already mentioned: *Is that what you want?—Yes; such is my wish.* **4** (after **as**) because of being: *I am the club secretary and as such I can help you.* **4** (often with **as**) *fml* the person(s) or thing(s) mentioned: *Such as you see is all we have. Take such as you need.* **5** that, these, or those: *Such is my hope!* **suchlike** *infml* of that kind: *She likes tennis and suchlike games.* **such-and-such** any one of a number: *If I ask such-and-such a person, what will he say?* **such as it is** not of a specially good kind or quality: *This is my work, such as it is.* **such as to** *fml* of a kind so as to cause something: *His bad behaviour was such as to anger everyone.* **such that** *fml* of such a kind: *His bad behaviour was such that he angered everyone.* **such . . . that** so (something) that: *His idea was such a good one that we all agreed to use it.* **as such** in that form or kind: *He is a good man and is known as such to everybody. It is not an agreement as such, but will serve as one.*

N182 *adjectives, etc* : **not like**

different [Wa5] **1** [B (*from*, *than*, *to*)] not of the same kind: *Mary and Jane are quite different. Mary is different from*/*than*/*to Jane. She's different than Jane is. He's a different man from what he was over 10 years ago.* **2** [A (*from*, *than*, *to*)] separate; other: *John and Peter belong to different age groups. This is a different car from the one I drove yesterday.* **3** [A] (*with* *pl*) various; several that are not the same: *We make this dress in (three/a lot of) different colours.* **4**[B] *trade & infml* unusual; special: *Buy Sloppo, the soap that is different!* **-ly** [adv]

USAGE **different(ly) from** is correct in both *BrE* and *AmE*. Some *BrE* speakers now say **different to**: *He is different to me*, and some *AmE* speakers say **different than**: *He is different than I am*, but teachers and examiners do not really like either of these. **Indifferent** can only be followed by to: *I am indifferent to this person* (= He or she is not important to me).

unlike [prep] not like: *This book is quite unlike anything I've ever read before.*

unalike [F] not like (one another): *They are brothers but they are quite unalike.*

dissimilar [B] unlike; not similar: *The two brothers are quite dissimilar.*

distinct [B] **1** [(*from*)] different; separate: *Those two ideas are quite distinct. They wanted to form a new and completely distinct political party.* **2** clearly seen, heard, understood, etc; plain; unmistakable: *There was a distinct smell of burning. There has been a distinct change in people's style of life.* **-ly** [adv]: *Speak more distinctly.*

distinctive [B] clearly marking a person or thing as different from others: *Each rank in the army has a distinctive sign to wear.* **-ly** [adv]: *He writes very distinctively, don't you think?*

diverse [B] different; various: *He has many diverse interests.* **-ly** [adv]

several [Wa5;A] *fml* different; various: *The people left the house and went their several ways.*

respective [Wa5;A] of or for each one; particular and separate: *My husband and I are going to visit our respective mothers.* **-ly** [adv] **irrespective of** [prep] without regard to: *They send information every week, irrespective of whether it is useful or not.*

N183 *adjectives* : **opposite** [Wa5]

opposite 1 [B (*to*)] as different as possible: *He went in the opposite direction from us. (fig) He is very interested in the opposite sex. His political position is opposite to ours.* **2** [F; E: (*to*)] facing: *Who lives in the house opposite? He sat opposite, doing nothing.*

contrary [B (*to*)] of the other kind; completely different: *I don't agree; I hold a contrary opinion/an opinion contrary to yours.* **contrary to** [prep] in opposition to: *Contrary to all advice the king dismissed the government and ordered elections.*

reverse [A; (B (*to*))] opposite in position; back: *The reverse side of the cloth is a different colour.* **in (the) reverse order** from the end to the beginning: *It would be silly to begin at Z and write the dictionary in reverse order.*

converse *tech* opposite or contrary in direction

N184 *adjectives* : **different and varied**

different [B] not the same; not like: *This is not what I want; I want a different one. These dresses are quite different from those, aren't they? He has all sorts of different things.* **-ly** [adv]

differential [Wa5;B] of, showing, or depending on a difference: *The government has differential taxes for different kinds of people.*

varied [B] **1** of different kinds: *Different people have the most varied ideas about what is important in life; some value fame, others money or freedom.* **2** not staying the same; changing: *He leads/has a varied life. Going through Britain by car you see the most varied country; the scenes change every hour.*

various 1 [A; (F)] different from each other; of (many) different kinds: *Of all the various ways of cooking an egg, I like boiling best. When he left university, he found it hard to choose between the various offers of work that were made to him. His abilities were very great and very various. Your reasons for not wanting to meet Smith may be many and various, but you must still meet him.* **2** [Wa5; A] several; a number of: *I have various letters to write. Various people among those present thought they'd heard the aircraft.* **-ly** [adv]

assorted [B] **1** of various types mixed together: *I took her a bag of assorted fruits.* **2** (*in comb*) suited by nature or character; matched: *That husband and wife are a well-assorted pair.*

divers [Wa5;A] *old use* many different: *Divers persons were present, of all stations in life.*

perverse [B] **1** (of people, actions, etc) purposely continuing in what is wrong or unreasonable: *Not even the most perverse person would fail to agree that this is wrong.* **2** (of people or events) unreasonably opposed to the wishes of (other) people; awkward and annoying: *We all wanted to go tomorrow, but she had to be perverse and choose to go today. There has been a perverse change in the weather.* **3** (of behaviour) different or turned away from what is right or reasonable: *He has a perverse habit of feeling sorry for evil people.* **-ly** [adv] **-ness, -sity 1** [U] the quality or state of being perverse **2** [C] a perverse act

N185 *adjectives, etc* : **others and alternatives**

other [det; pron] **1** (with *the, one's, both, all, every*) the remaining (one or ones) of a set; what is/are left as well as that/those mentioned: *He was holding the wheel of the car with one hand and waving with the other (one). She's cleverer than (any of) the others/than the other girls in her class. Why are you alone? Where are all the others/the five other boys/the other five boys/the rest? These trousers are wet; I'll change into my others/my other ones* (= I have only two pairs). **2** (with *than*) additional (person or thing); more as well: *You can't go by car, but there are plenty of other ways of getting there. John and some other boys went swimming* (compare *John and some girls*). *Some of them are red; others are brown* (compare *the others are brown* = all the rest). *I'm not going to pay £50 for that; not until I've seen a few others. You'll have to use this chair; there's no other (than this).* **3** (with *than*) not the same; not this, not oneself, not one's own, etc: *He enjoys spending other people's money* (= not his own). *Others may laugh at her but I think she's sweet. I'm busy now; come some other day. He isn't here for the beer—he came for quite other reasons (than that).* **each other** one another: *Paul and Charles bit each other* (= Paul bit Charles and Charles bit Paul). **every other 1** all the others; all that remain **2** every 2nd: *They go to the US every other year; they went in 1974 and 1976 and they're going again in 1978.* **one after the other/after another** not together, but first one, then the next, etc: *They were walking down the narrow path one after the other.* **some . . . or other/or another** (showing that one is not certain): *He said something or other about it. We'll do it some time or (an)other.* **the other day/evening/night** (on) a recent day/evening/night: *I saw him (only) the other day* (and not longer ago). **the other end/side** the far or opposite of two ends/sides from this one: *There was a voice at the other end of the telephone. They live on the other side of London (from me).* **this, that, and the other** *infml* all sorts of things: *We were sitting in the sun talking of this, that, and the other.*

USAGE **other** is not used after **an**; the word is then **another**. Compare *Show me another/ some others/some more. Would you like another/any others/any more?* But we can say *I have only one other sister besides her.*

other than [prep] **1** except: *There's nobody here other than me. Have we anything to drink other than milk?* **2** not; anything but: *She can hardly be other than grateful.* **3** otherwise than; in any other way than: *You can't get there other than by swimming.*

another 1 [det] being one more of the same kind: *Have another piece of cake. Have another one.* **2** [det] different from the first or other: *Look at the difficulty another way.* **3** [det] some other; later: *I'm in a hurry; I'll see you another time.* **4** [pron] one more of the same sort; an additional one: *Your egg is bad; have another. She has taken another of my books. He was a great runner; we shall never see such another.* **5** [pron] a person other than oneself: *Is it brave to die for another?* **6** [pron] a different one: *They went from one shop to another.* **one another** each other: *They love one another.*

alternate [Wa5;B] **1** (of two things) happening by turns; first one and then the other: *We had a week of alternate rain and sunshine.* **2** every second: *He works on alternate days, not every*

day. **3** (esp of leaves on a stem) found first on one side of the stem and then on the other: *That plant has alternate leaves.* **-ly** [adv] **alternate** [IØ] to do something in turn: *They alternate in coming; he comes one week and she comes the next. They alternate between going there and coming here. He alternates the one machine with the other.* **alternation** [U] the act of alternating

alternative 1 [Wa5;A] (of two things) that may be used, had, done, etc; instead of another; other: *We returned by the alternative road.* **2** [C] *precise* something, esp a course of action, that may be taken or had instead of one other: *The alternative to being taken prisoner was to die fighting. We had to fight; there was no (other) alternative.* **3** [C] *precise* a choice between two or more courses or things: *You have the alternative of fighting or being taken prisoner.* **4** [C (*to*)] *loose* one of two or more courses, ideas, things, etc: *There are several alternatives to your plan.* **-ly** [adv]

N186 *nouns* : likeness and resemblance

likeness 1 [U (*between*)] the condition of someone or something being like another: *She couldn't see any likeness between the children.* **2** [C *usu sing*] an example of this: *That picture is a good likeness.*

resemblance [C;U: (*between*)] (a) likeness: *There's a strong resemblance between him and her, isn't there?—I don't see the resemblance!*

sameness [U (*of*)] **1** the state of being the same; very close likeness or identity: *I mistook one book for the other because of the sameness of their covers.* **2** *usu* unpleasant lack of variety; monotony: *Don't you ever get tired of the sameness of the work in this office?*

identity 1 [U] sameness; exact likeness: *There's no doubt about the identity of the two signatures.* **2** [U; C] who or what a particular person or thing is: *Please prove your identity. What was the identity of the man who spoke to him?*

uniformity [U] the state of having every part etc the same: *I didn't like the uniformity of all the buildings and houses in the town; it was very uninteresting.*

conformity [U] action or behaviour that is in agreement with established rules, customs, etc: *Conformity to society's customs is advisable if you want a happy life.* **in conformity (with)** in agreement with: *She always tries to dress in conformity with the latest fashions. That was not in conformity with the law. Your ideas and your practices are not in conformity.*

similarity 1 [U] the quality of being alike or like something else; resemblance: *How much similarity is there between the two religions?* **2** [C] a point of likeness: *Their differences are more noticeable than their similarities.*

correspondence [U; C *usu sing*] part by part agreement or likeness: *There isn't much* correspondence between what happens in science and in religion. There is a close correspondence between the way they do this in France and in Britain. French methods have a close correspondence with British methods.

equality [U] the state or condition of being equal: *Modern countries generally try to give their people equality before the law* (= to make everyone equal in law). *He is working for equality between men and women.* **in-**[*neg*]

N187 *nouns* : **difference and distinction**

difference 1 [C (*between*)] a way of being unlike: *There are several important differences between cricket and football.* **2** [S; U: (*between, in, of, to*)] (an) amount of unlikeness: *The difference between 5 and 11 is 6. What's the difference in temperature between the day and the night?—Oh, there's a difference of 30 degrees. Flowers make no/a/a lot of/some/all the difference to a room. It doesn't make much/any/the least difference to me what you do/whether you go or stay.* **3** [C *often pl*] a slight disagreement: *We have our little differences but we're good friends.* **split the difference** to agree on an amount halfway between: *You say £10 and I say £12 so let's split the difference and call it £11.*

differential *tech* [C] **1** a difference in payments, etc, usu shown as a percentage (= part of a hundred), between different kinds of workers: *The more highly-trained workers think that the differentials are not as large as they should be.* **2** *maths* a very small difference between two values in a scale

distinction 1 [C; U; (*between*)] a special or particular difference: *Can you make/draw a distinction between these two ideas?—No; there is no distinction between them. He was kind to everyone, without distinction of rank or wealth.* **2** [S; U] the quality of being unusual, esp of being unusually good in mind or spirit; worth: *He is a writer of true distinction. She has a natural distinction of manner.*

N188 *nouns* : **opposites, etc**

opposite [C; *the* U: (*of*)] a person or thing that is as different as possible (from another): *Black and white are opposites. You are nice; he is just the opposite.*

converse [*the* U (*of*)] *tech* something that is the opposite esp turned around in order (of something else): *'Cold in winter and hot in summer' is the converse of 'hot in summer and cold in winter.'*

obverse [*the* U] **1** *tech* the front side of a coin or coinlike object (**medal**) **2** [(*of*)] *fml* the side (of something), part, or thing that is most noticeable or intended to be shown

reverse [*the* U (*of*)] something that is directly

opposite in position or order to: *CBA is the reverse of ABC.*

corollary [C] *fml* **1** something that naturally follows from something else; result: *The corollary of your argument is that wages must be kept high even if that means mass unemployment.* **2** a statement that follows, without needing further proof, from another statement for which proof exists

contrary [*the* U (*of*)] a thing or action that is quite different in kind (from another): *His action is the contrary of what he said he would do.* **on the contrary** (used for expressing strong opposition to what has just been said) not at all: *I believe you like your job.—On the contrary, I hate it!* **to the contrary** to the opposite effect: *Unless you hear (something)to the contrary, I'll meet you here at 7 o'clock. I know she's unhappy, (despite) all her arguments to the contrary.*

N189 *nouns* : **variety and diversity**

variety 1 [U] the state of varying [⇨ I16]; difference of condition or quality: *She didn't like the work, because it lacked variety; she was doing the same things all the time.* **2** [S (*of*)] a group or collection containing different sorts of the same thing or people: *Everyone arrived late at the party, for a variety of reasons. In the streets of a city like London you see a great variety of people, all classes and colours. This shop sells many different dresses at different prices. Yes, there's quite a variety.* **3** [C] a type which is different from others in a group to which it belongs: *An eager gardener is always looking for new varieties of plants.*

assortment [C] a group or quantity of mixed things or of various examples of the same type of thing; mixture: *This tin contains an assortment of sweets.*

diversity [S; U: (*of*)] the condition of being different or having differences; variety: *Mary has a great diversity of interests; she likes sports, travel, photography, and making radio sets.*

N190 *verbs* : **being different** [I0]

differ 1 [(*from, in, as to*)] to be unlike: *Nylon and silk differ. Nylon differs from silk in/as to origin and cost. Nylon differs from silk in being a man-made material and in being cheaper.* **2** [(*with*), (*about, on, over*)] (of people) to have an unlike or opposite opinion; disagree: *My husband and I often differ but we're quite happy together. He differed with his brother about/on/over a political question.* **agree to differ** to stop trying to persuade each other: *I think you're wrong, but let's agree to differ.* **I beg to differ** *euph* I disagree with you

contrast [(*with*)] to show a difference when looked at together: *Your actions contrast* *unfavourably with your principles. Your actions and your principles contrast unfavourably.*

deviate [(*from*)] to be different or move away (from an accepted standard of behaviour, or from a correct or straight path): *Don't deviate from the rules.* (fig) *Don't deviate from the subject we've been talking about. He always deviates when I try to keep him talking about it.* **deviation 1** [U] the act of deviating **2** [C] an example of this; something which deviates or has deviated

diverge [(*from*)] to go out in different directions: *After university their lives diverged and they did not meet again for 50 years. I'm afraid our opinions diverge (from each other) (from a common starting point).* **divergent** [B] diverging or likely to diverge: *We have divergent opinions on this subject, I'm afraid.* **divergence 1** [U] the act of diverging **2** [U] the state of being divergent

N191 *verbs* : making things the same, different, etc

equal [Wv6;T1] to be equal to; be as good as: *She equals him in ability. You will never be able to equal his success.*

equate [T1 (*with*)] to consider or make (two or more things or people) equal: *You can't equate his poems and/with his plays. It's impossible to equate the two (of them).*

parallel [T1] **1** to equal; match [⇒ N226]: *No one has parelleled her success in sport.* **2** to be or go (**run**) parallel to: *The road parallels the river.* **unparalleled** [Wa5;B] having no parallel; having nothing the same kind anywhere: *Her work is quite unparalleled.*

rival [T1] to be equal to: *He is very good; he rivals the best in his sport/subject. Her work is quite unrivalled* (= No one can do better or as well).

compare [T1 (*to, with*)] **1** to examine or judge (one thing) against another in order to show the points of likeness or difference: *If you compare Marx's work with Hegel's you'll find many differences. If you compare both of our cars you'll find them very much alike.* **2** to liken; show the likeness or relationship of (one thing) and another: *It's impossible to compare Buckingham Palace and my little house.*

liken [T1 *usu pass* (*to*)] *esp old use, fml & lit* to compare: *The heart can be likened to a pump.*

contrast [T1] to compare (two things or people or one thing or a person with another) so that differences are made clear: *In this book the writer contrasts good with/and evil. It's interesting to contrast the relationship of church and state in France and Britain.*

oppose [T1 (*to*)] to contrast (one thing) with another: *If we oppose 'love' and 'like', as well as 'love' and 'hate', we can understand 'love' better.*

N192 *nouns & adjectives* : making things the same, different, etc

comparison 1 [U] the act of comparing people, things, etc: *The comparison of different religions is very interesting. By comparison (with the other man), he is perfect.* **2** [C] an example, occasion, or result of this: *Let's make a comparison between them.* **3** [U] likeness (*esp in the phr* **no comparison**): *There is no comparison between them; they are not alike at all.*

comparative [Wa5;A;(B)] for the purpose of comparison: *They made a comparative study of the two kinds of plants. Comparative religion is a study which compares the world's religions.* **-ly** [adv]: *This work is comparatively easy* (= It is easy compared with that other work).

analogy 1 [C (*to, with, between*)] a degree of likeness or sameness (to or with something, or between two things): *There is an analogy between the way water moves in waves and the way light travels.* **2** [U] the act of explaining by comparing with another thing that has a certain likeness: *He argued by analogy that if a bird moves its wings so should an aircraft.* **3** [C] the state in which two things are alike in many ways: *He considered the analogy of a bird and an aircraft.* **4** [U] (in the study of languages) the way in which the form of a word is changed or decided because of another word that is like it

analogical [Wa5;B] of, concerning, like, or for the purpose of making an analogy **-ly** [adv]

analogue, analog [C] something that is similar in one or more ways to some other thing

analogous [B (*to*)] having a degree of likeness or sameness (to or with something, or between two things): *Waves of water and the way light travels are analogous.* **-ly** [adv]

contrast 1 [U] the act of contrasting people, things, etc: *Contrast can help make something more interesting, by placing it beside something quite different. He doesn't work hard but by contrast with her, he is a hard worker!* **2** [C] an example of this: *India is a land of contrasts, of rich and poor, old and new.*

contrastive [Wa5;B] for the purpose of contrast: *They made a contrastive study of the two languages, to show how different they are.* **-ly** [adv]

equation 1 [U] the act of equating: *The equation of these two things is not right; they are not equal.* **2** [C] an example of this: *He makes easy equations of/between things that are not equal.*

N193 *verbs* : identifying and distinguishing

identify [T1] **1** to prove or show what (a particular person or thing) is: *Identify yourself, please; who are you? I identified myself to them by showing them my papers. I identified the coat at once; it was my brother's. I identified the criminal. I couldn't identify his face. How do you identify phrasal verbs* [⇒ G271]? **2** to show or feel to be exactly the same: *He identifies the two tastes; for him they aren't different.*

identification [U] **1** the act of identifying or state of being identified **2 a** (in Britain and the USA) papers esp with a photograph and/or signature which prove that one is the person one says one is, often for purposes of payment by cheque [⇨J82] **b** (in some countries) a card which must be carried all the time and shown to policemen to prove that one is a citizen of that country: *May I have the money?—First, let me see your identification/let me have some identification/do you have any means of identification on you?*

distinguish 1 [T1] to recognize by some mark or typical sign: *I can distinguish them by their uniform.* **2** [Wv6;T1] to hear or see clearly: *I can distinguish objects at a great distance.* **3** [T1 (*from*); I∅ (*between*)] to make or recognize differences: *I can distinguish (between) those two objects/ideas. I can distinguish (between) right and wrong. I can distinguish right from wrong.* **4** [Wv6;T1] to set apart or mark as different: *Elephants are distinguished by their long noses* (**trunks**). **5** [T1] to make unusually good: *He distinguished himself by his performance in the examination.*

differentiate 1 [T1 (*from*); I∅ (*between*)] to see or express a difference (between): *I can't differentiate (between) these two flowers. Can you differentiate this kind of rose from the others? It's unfair of her to differentiate between her two children like that.* **2** [T1 (*from*)] (of a quality) to make different by the presence: *What is it that differentiates these two substances? Its strange way of making a nest differentiates this bird from others.* **differentiation** [U; C] the act, result, etc of differentiating

N194 *verbs & nouns* : **sorting and classifying**

sort [T1 (*out*)] to separate things of one sort or kind from things of another sort; to put in groups, etc: *Sort these letters into those going abroad and those with local addresses. She tried to sort out the papers.* (*fig*) *I'll leave you to sort these matters out* (= to find a solution, answer, etc).

arrange [T1] to set in a good or pleasing order: *She arranged the flowers well. He arranged his clothes before meeting her. He arranged the table for dinner.* **arrange for** [v prep T1; V3: (*with*)] to take action to cause or get: *I've arranged (with my firm) for a taxi (to pick us up at 10 o'clock).* **arrangement 1** [U] the act of putting into or of being put into order: *The arrangement of the flowers only took a few minutes. The Japanese are interested in the art of flower arrangement.* **2** [C] something that has been put in order: *There were some beautiful arrangements at the flower show. What a beautiful flower arrangement!* **3** [C (*about, for, with,* 3)] something arranged, planned, or

agreed in a particular way: *I have an arrangement with my bank by which they let me use their money before I have been paid. We could make an arrangement to meet at 10 o'clock. I have made my arrangements and can't change them now.*

classify [T1] **1** to arrange or place (animals, plants, books, etc) into classes [⇨N6]; divide according to class: *Librarians spend a lot of time classifying books.* **2** to mark or declare (information) secret officially **classification 1** [U] the act of classifying or being classified **2** [C] an example or result of this; the group into which something is classified

class [T1 (*as*)] to consider or place (someone or something) as part of a system: *She classed him as one of the best players of the game in the country.*

grade 1 [Wv5;T1] to separate into levels: *The potatoes are graded according to size and quality.* **2** [C; A] a level into which persons or things are classified or organized, esp according to ability, size, etc: *What grade did he get in the examination?—Top grade. These are Grade 3 eggs.*

organize, -ise [T1 (*into*); V3] to form (parts) into a whole, persons into a group, etc: *Can he organize these people into a political party?* **-ization, -isation** [U; C] [⇨N167, 170]

system [C] **1** a number of things arranged to make one working whole: *The solar system consists of the sun and nine planets* (= worlds) *around it.* **2** the way in which things are arranged to work; a work plan: *His new system for providing information works well.* **3** a set of thoughts, ideas, etc which belong together: *There are many different systems of thought in the world.* **systematic** [B] following, like a system; well-organized: *She has a very systematic way of doing things.* **un-** [*neg*] **-ally** [adv Wa4] **systemic** [Wa5;B] *tech* belonging to or showing a system: *systemic grammar*

systematize, -ise [T1] to arrange in a system or by a set method: *We must systematize our working arrangements or nothing will ever get done.* **-ization, -isation** [U; C]

codify [T1] to classify (esp laws) into a single system or code [⇨ C181]: *Hammurabi codified the laws of ancient Babylon.* **codification 1** [U] the act of codifying **2** [C] an example or result of this

rank [L9; X9] come or put in a certain class or rank [⇨ C150]: *Tokyo ranks as the world's largest city. Where do you rank Wordsworth as a poet?*

order 1 [U] the way in which things are arranged: *What order did you do the work in? He wrote down the names in alphabetical order, beginning with A and ending with Z.* **2** [U] a state in which everything is arranged properly: *Everything in the house is in order.* **3** [T1 usu pass] to arrange in order: *The work was all properly ordered, just as he wanted it.*

list 1 [C] a number of things written down or printed, etc in a particular order for a particular purpose: *He made a list of the things he needed.* **2** [T1] to make a list of: *He listed the things he wanted.*

dispose [T1] *fml & old use* to put things into an arrangement or position: *The general disposed his men for the battle.* **disposition** [U] *fml* the way in which things are arranged in position: *The disposition of the furniture in the room did not please her.*

Rightness, fairness, purpose, use, and strength

N210 *adjectives* : **suitable, right, and proper**

suitable [B] fit for a purpose; convenient: *She is the most suitable person for the job. What time is suitable for us to meet?* **un-** [*neg*] **-bly** [adv Wa3] **suitability** [U] the state of being suitable: *I'm not sure of his suitability for the job.*

right [Wa5;B] most suitable; best for a particular purpose: *Are we going in the right direction? Is this the right thing to do?* **-ly** [adv] **-ness** [(*the*) U]: *I believe in the rightness of what she's doing.* **right enough** *not fml* **a** satisfactory: *The bed was right enough but the food was nasty.* **b** *also* **sure enough** as was expected: *I told him to come, and right enough he arrived the next morning.* **Right you are!** *also* **Right oh!** *sl* Yes; I will; I agree: *Shut the window, please.—Right you are!*

proper 1 [Wa5;A] right; suitable; correct: *The child is too ill to be nursed at home; she needs proper medical attention at a hospital. Is Tony making proper use of his time at work, or does he waste it in doing nothing?* **2** [Wa5;A] correct (for a purpose): *These pages aren't in their proper order; page 22 comes after page 26. You don't know the proper way to hold a hammer.* **3** [B] respectable; paying great attention to what is considered correct in society (*sometimes in the phr* **prim and proper**): *I don't consider that short dress is proper for going to church in. His mother had trained him to be a very proper young man.* **4** [Wa5;A] *apprec* fine; splendid; admirable; good-looking: *You've made a proper job of that* (= have done it well). *He's a proper man* (= one whom women are willing to like). **5** [Wa5;A] *often deprec, esp BrE* thorough; complete: *I've come out without the key of the house—You're a proper fool! He gave his disobedient son a proper beating.* **6** [Wa5;A] *infml* real; actual: *The little boy wanted a proper dog as a pet; he didn't want a toy dog.* **7** [F *to*] *fml* belonging only or especially to; natural to: *The princess had the manners proper to a person of high birth.* **8** [Wa5;E] itself; in its actual most limited meaning not including additional things: *Many people call themselves Londoners though they live in areas that aren't part of the city proper.* **im-** [*neg*] (defs 1, 2, 3) **-ly** [adv]

appropriate [B (*for, to*)] correct or suitable: *His bright clothes were not appropriate for a funeral.* **in-** [*neg*] **-ly** [adv]

fit [Wa1;B (*for*)] (of people) suitable: *He isn't really fit for this job; he doesn't have the right training.* **un-** [*neg*]

fitting [B] *esp emot or emph* (of things, words, actions, etc) suitable; proper: *It isn't fitting for you to dress like that today! He gave them a fitting reply to their request.* **-ly** [adv]

apt [Wa2;B] exactly suitable or fitting: *That was a very apt remark; it fitted the occasion beautifully.* **-ly** [adv]: *That was aptly put* (= said). **-ness** [U]

relevant [B] **1** connected with the subject; suitable to what is happening, etc: *I know he's rich but it's not relevant to what we are doing.* **2** [(*to*)] connected (with): *The man's colour isn't relevant to whether he's a good lawyer or not.* **ir-** [*neg*] **-ly** [adv] **relevance** [U] the condition of being relevant: *What is the relevance of your argument to the matter we are discussing?* **ir-** [*neg*]

apposite [B (*to, for*)] *fml* exactly suitable to the present moment, condition, etc: *His apposite remarks caused people to think him wise. Her remarks were apposite to the occasion.* **-ly** [adv] **-ness** [U]

N211 *adjectives* : **valid and sound**

valid [B] **1** (of a reason, argument, etc) having a strong firm base; able to be defended: *If you can't give me a valid reason for breaking your promise, I shan't trust you again.* **2** *law* written or done in a proper manner so that a court of law would agree with it: *The agreement is not valid, because one of the people who signed it is not lawfully old enough to do so.* **3** [Wa5] having value; that can be used lawfully for a stated period or in certain conditions: *The train ticket is valid for three months. The old British coin worth 2 shillings and 6 pence is no longer valid.* **in-** [*neg*] **-ly** [adv]

worthy 1 [Wa1;B (*of*); B3] deserving: *She is worthy of our help/dislike. He is a worthy winner. They are not worthy to be chosen.* **2** [Wa1;B] *esp old use* to be admired, respected, etc: *He is a worthy man.* **3** [*comb form*] **a** deserving: *blameworthy; praiseworthy* **b** suitable for (use on/in, etc): *roadworthy; airworthy* **c** fit to be given/used as: *creditworthy; newsworthy* **-ily** [adv] **-iness** [U]

sound [Wa1;B] **1** *esp emot* valid; dependable; trustworthy: *He is a sound man; he is just right for the job.* **2** in good condition: *The house is sound; buy it.* **un-** [*neg*] **-ness** [U]

all right, *sometimes* **alright** [Wa5] **1** [F] valid, sound, etc enough: *He's all right.* **2** [adv] satisfactorily: *He'll do the job all right.*

okay, OK [Wa5] *infml* **1** [F; (B)] *infml* all right: *She seems okay now.* **2** [adv] all right; satisfactorily: *That car goes okay now.* **3** [adv] all right; agreed; yes **a** (asking for agreement, esp to a suggestion): *Let's go there, okay?* **b** (expressing agreement): *Shall we go there?—Okay.* **c** (giving permission): *Can I use your car?—Okay.*

N212 *adjectives* : **correct and precise**

correct [B] having the right nature or quality; being the right answer; (of something) as it should be: *He was quite correct about what would happen. Your reply is correct.* **in-** [*neg*] **-ly** [adv] **-ness** [U]

exact 1 [Wa5;A] (esp of things that can be measured) correct and without mistakes: *The exact time is three minutes and thirty-five seconds past two. Tell me his exact words.* **2** [B] marked by thorough consideration or careful measurement of small details of fact: *His memory is very exact; he never makes mistakes. He is a very exact watchmaker who will do a good job.* **in-** [*neg*] **-ly** [adv] **-ness** [U] **the exact same** *nonstandard* exactly the same X; the very same X: *That's the exact same man who was here last night!*

precise [B] **1** exact in form, detail, measurements, time, etc: *He made some very precise calculations. The precise words I used were 'I may not come', not 'I must not come'. At the precise moment that I put my foot on the step the bus started.* **2** particularly; exact: *You're the precise person I was hoping to meet; I need your advice at once.* **3** sharply clear: *My new television set gives precise pictures. A lawyer needs a precise mind.* **4** (too) careful and correct in regard to the smallest details: *A scientist must be precise in making tests. She is a very precise old lady with precise manners.* **im-** [*neg*] **-ly** [adv] **-ness** [U]

accurate [B] **1** careful and exact: *The hunter took accurate aim. This is an accurate statement of what happened. She is an accurate worker.* **2** free of mistakes; exactly correct: *This is an accurate copy.* **in-** [*neg*] **-ly** [adv] **accuracy** [U] the quality of being accurate: *Most people admire accuracy in work.* **inaccuracy** [U; C]

N213 *adjectives* : **opportune** [B]

opportune 1 (of times) right for a purpose: *This is an opportune moment to speak.* **2** coming at the right time: *He made an opportune remark.* **in-** [*neg*] **-ly** [adv]

psychological *infml* exactly right in relation to someone's feelings, needs, etc: *You spoke at the psychological moment, just when you should have.* **-ly** [adv Wa4]

N214 *adjectives* : **pure**

[ALSO ⇨ D179]

pure 1 [Wa1;B] unmixed with any other substance: *The metal is pure silver. Is this garment* made of pure wool or of wool mixed with nylon?* **2** [Wa1;B] clean; free from dirt, dust, bacteria [⇨ A37] or any harmful matter: *The air by the sea is pure and healthy. This is very pure drinking water.* **3** [Wa1;B] of unmixed race: *He bought a pure Arab horse. There's very little pure blood in any nation now.* **4** [Wa1;B] free from evil; without sexual thoughts or experience: *She was still a pure young girl, pure in thought and deed.* **5** [Wa1;B] (of colour or sound) clear; unmixed with other colours or sounds: *It was a sunny day with a cloudless sky of the purest blue.* **6** [Wa1;B] (of a musical note) of exactly the correct highness or lowness: *The voices of the young boys singing in church were high and pure.* **7** [Wa5;A] *infml* complete; thorough; only: *By pure chance he found the rare book he needed in a little shop.* **8** [Wa5;A] (of an art or branch of study) considered only for its own nature as a skill or exercise of the mind, separate from any use that might be made of it: *pure science* **9** [Wa1;B] *fml* (of a thing) clean according to the rules of religious ceremony **im-** [*neg*] **-ly** [adv] **-ness** [U] **purity** [U] the state of being pure **impurity 1** [U] the state of being impure **2** [C] something impure: *They removed the impurities from the water.* **pure and simple** *infml* thorough; and nothing else: *What you did was carelessness pure and simple!*

perfect [*usu* Wa5] **1** [B] of the very best possible kind, degree, or standard: *The weather during our holiday was perfect. What a perfect rose! He committed the perfect crime* (= one in which the criminal is never discovered). **2** [B] agreeing in every way with an example accepted as correct: *He's only been studying for a year, but already his English is almost perfect.* **3** [B] complete, with nothing missing, spoilt, etc: *She still has a perfect set of teeth.* **4** [B (*for*)] suitable and satisfying in every way: *This big house is perfect for our large family. He'd be perfect for the job. He is the perfect man for the job!* **5** [A] *often infml* complete; thorough: *She is a perfect stranger to us. It's perfect nonsense to say you're 200 years old!* **6** [B] skilled to the highest degree; thoroughly and completely trained (*esp in the phr* **Practice makes perfect**) **im-** [*neg*] **-ly** [adv] **-ness** [U]

ideal [Wa5;B] **1** perfect, because the best one can think of: *This is an ideal place for a holiday.* **2** expressing possible perfection which is unlikely to exist in the real world: *He had an ideal view of how nations should be governed.* **-ly** [adv]

flawless *also* **faultless** [Wa5;B] perfect; with no flaw [⇨ N217] or fault: *It was a flawless argument.* **-ly** [adv] **-ness** [U]

spotless [Wa5;B] pure; very clean; having no spots or marks of dirt **-ly** [adv] **-ness** [U]

immaculate [Wa5;B] *esp fml* pure; flawless; faultless; spotless **-ly** [adv] **-lacy** [U]

absolute [Wa5;B] perfect: *He is a man of absolute honesty. You must have absolute trust in me.* **-ly** [adv] *I trust her absolutely.*

chaste [Wa1;B] **1** pure in word, thought, and deed, esp being without sexual activity: *The priest was chaste in mind and body.* **2** *apprec* simple; not too ornamented: *He wrote in a pure, chaste style.* **chastity** [U] the state of being sexually pure: *Chastity in thought, word, and deed is a good thing. 'Defend your chastity if you want to stay morally pure,' the priest said.*

N215 verbs : putting and making things right

[ALSO ⇒ I18]

right [T1] to put (something) right again: *The cat righted itself during the fall and landed on its feet. I hope your troubles will soon right themselves/soon be righted.*

put right *also* **set right** [T1b] **1** to put into the correct position: *Put the picture right. Put the clock right* (= made the hands show the right time). **2** to cure: *A week by the sea will soon put you right again.* **3** *also* **put straight** to give correct information to (someone who has a wrong opinion) often rather sharply: *He thought it was Thursday, but I soon put him right/straight.*

get right [T1b] **1** to make no mistakes in (something, esp a calculation or performance): *Come on; try to get it right!* **2** *also* **get straight** to be correctly informed about (something): *Have you got it right/straight now?*

rectify [T1] **1** *fml* to put right: *Please rectify the mistakes in my bill.* **2** [Wv5] *tech* to make pure: *He used rectified alcohol.* **rectification** [U] the act of rectifying or being rectified

correct [T1] **1** to make right: *Correct my spelling if it's wrong.* **2** to improve by punishing: *His father used to correct his bad behaviour by sending him to bed without anything to eat.* **correction 1** [U] the act of correcting or being corrected **2** [C] an example of this

validate [T1] to make valid: *In order to validate the agreement between yourself and your employer, you must both sign it.* **in-** [neg] **validation** [U] the act of validating or being validated

purify [T1] to make pure: *They purified the water by removing the dirt from it.* **purification** [U] the act or result of purifying

purge 1 [D1 *from/of*; T1] *esp poet & emot* to make clean and free from (evil or impure things) *'We must purge ourselves of our evil ways', he said.* **2** [D1 *from/of*; T1] to get rid of (waste matter) from (the body) by using a strong medicine **3** [D1 *from/of*; T1] to remove (people) from (a group), esp forcefully: *They purged the party of those who did not agree with him.* **4** [C] an act of purging: *They had a purge in the party.* **5** [C] medicine for purging

refine [Wv5;T1 *usu pass*] **1** to make (something, esp sugar, oil, metal, etc) pure by taking other things out: *refined sugar* **2** to make (someone, something) more pleasing socially: *a refined voice* **refinement** [U] **1** the act of refining **2** the

state of being refined: *a person of great refinement*

N216 adjectives : not right [B]

[ALSO ⇒ F65]

wrong [Wa2] **1** not correct: *This sum is wrong. No, you're wrong; she didn't say that. The clock's wrong; it's later than the time it shows.* **2** evil; against moral standards: *Telling lies is wrong/It's wrong to tell lies.* **3** not suitable: *This is the wrong time to make a visit.* **-ly** [adv] **-ness** [U]

faulty [Wa1] imperfect; having faults; not looking right or working properly: *The radio is faulty; it needs to be repaired. He has a faulty understanding of French history.* **-tily** [adv]

flawed *tech or emot* imperfect: *This diamond is flawed. His character seems good but is flawed by a habit of telling lies.*

defective 1 lacking something necessary; faulty: *He sold us defective machinery.* **2** *tech* lacking one or more of the usual grammatical forms: *'Must' and 'can' are defective verbs with no -ing forms.* **3** (of a person) well below the average in body or esp in mind: *The child is defective, I'm afraid.* **-ly** [adv] **-ness** [U]

deficient [(*in*)] having none or not enough of; lacking in: *The food here is deficient in iron. He is deficient in skill and can't do the job.*

anomalous *esp fml & tech* different in some (unsatisfactory) way from what is normal or usual: *His illness is an anomalous condition of the heart.* **-ly** [adv]

N217 nouns : faults and flaws

fault 1 [C] something wrong, esp in how something works or someone behaves; wrong quality: *There's a fault in this building; it isn't safe. He has several faults, but telling lies isn't one of them. The main fault in his work is careless spelling.* **2** [S] responsibility for something wrong or bad that has been done: *It's my fault; I caused all the trouble. It happened through no fault of hers. She was not at fault; don't blame her.*

flaw [C] a small sign of damage, such as a mark or crack, that makes an object not perfect: *There was a flaw in the plate.* (*fig*) *There are several flaws in this contract.*

defect [C] something lacking or imperfect; a fault: *The machine is unsafe because of the defects in it. He suffers from a hearing defect.*

deficiency 1 [U] the quality or state of being deficient: **2** [C] a case of this; a lack: *The deficiencies in this plan are very clear and it can't possibly succeed.*

shortcoming [C] *often euph* a fault, usu not too bad: *'We all have our little shortcomings', she said.*

drawback [C (*to, of*)] *esp emot* a difficulty or disadvantage; something that can cause trouble: *The only drawback to/of the plan is that it costs too much.*

failing [C] *esp euph or emot* something which makes someone or something else imperfect: *I'm afraid one of his failings is telling lies.*

bug [C] *sl* a fault: *We have had a number of bugs in the machine, but it's working well now.*

N218 *nouns* : **difficulties, problems, and anomalies**

difficulty 1 [U] the state or quality of being hard to do or understand; trouble: *I'm having a little difficulty doing this work; can you help me? Did you have any difficulty finding him?—No; no difficulty at all./No; I found him without difficulty. She did it, but with difficulty.* **2** [C]an example of this; something that causes trouble: *I'm in difficulties over this work; I can't finish in time. He was working under difficulties; it wasn't easy.*

problem [C] **1** a (serious) difficulty that needs attention and thought; a difficult situation: *I've left my money at home.—That's no problem; I can lend you what you need. The unemployment problem in this area is getting worse. It's a problem to know what to do with him when he leaves school; he doesn't seem fit for any kind of job. The car won't start; I don't know whether the problem is in the engine or in the electrical system.* **2** [*usu sing*]*infml* a person who causes (some special) difficulty: *As a dinner guest Celia is a problem; there are many kinds of food she doesn't eat.*

snag [C] *esp BrE, not fml* a hidden or unexpected difficulty: *There's been a snag. Our plans have hit a snag and we can't go on until it is dealt with.*

hitch [C] *not fml* a difficulty which delays something for some time: *There was a slight hitch in his plans. A technical hitch prevented the lights from working. The meeting went off without a hitch.*

anomaly [C] *esp fml & tech* **1** an unusual irregularity: *The anomaly of his position is that he is very famous but still doesn't make much money.* **2** a person who, or thing that, is different from the usual type

N219 *nouns & verbs* : **mistakes**

mistake 1 [C] a wrong thought, act, etc; anything done, said, believed, etc due to wrong thinking or understanding, lack of knowledge or skill, etc: *The teacher found several spelling mistakes in the pupils' written answers. 'You've made too many mistakes', he said; 'you'll have to do the exercise again'. There must be some mistake in this bill; please add up the figures again.* **2** [T1 (*for*); T6a] to make a mistake about (someone or something): *I mistook her for her sister* (= I thought she was her sister).

Don't mistake what he said; he will do it if it is necessary. They completely mistook his reasons for doing it. **and no mistake** *infml* (used for giving force to an expression) without the slightest doubt: *That apple's a big one and no mistake.* **by mistake** as a result of being careless, forgetful, etc: *The nurse gave the child the wrong medicine by mistake. She put salt into her cup of tea by mistake.* **make no mistake** do not have the slightest doubt; be quite sure: *If you don't improve your behaviour, you'll be punished; make no mistake about it.* **there's no mistake about it** it is quite certain; there can be no doubt about it: *There's no mistake about it, he's the biggest fool I've met.*

error *often fml* **1** [C] a mistake; something done wrongly or an example of bad behaviour: *The bank made an error in my account. It wasn't all Jane's fault when she left Bill; there were errors on both sides.* **2** [U] the state of being wrong in behaviour or beliefs: *The accident was caused by human error. I did it in error* (= by mistake). *A mistake in the map led the traveller into error.*

err [I∅] *esp lit & old use* to make a mistake; do something wrong: *He erred in coming here; he should have gone.*

slip [C] a slight mistake: *'Too' was a slip of the pen; I meant to write 'to'.* **slip up** [v adv I∅ (*over*)]*infml* to make a mistake: *He slipped up over their names* (= He was wrong about their names; he made a mistake about them).

lapse 1 [C] a small fault or mistake, as one of memory, esp one that is quickly put right: *It was just a lapse of judgment; it won't happen again.* **2** [C] a failure in correct behaviour, belief, duty, etc **3** [I∅ (*into*)] to return (to something usu bad that was done earlier): *He has lapsed once again into his old drinking habits.*

discrepancy [C; U; (*between*)] difference; lack of agreement (between stories, amounts, etc): *There is a good deal of discrepancy/There are many discrepancies between his description of the battle and yours. You paid £5 and the bill says £3; how do you explain the discrepancy?*

oversight [C; U] (an) unintended failure to notice or do something: *I meant to do it; the mistake was the result of (an) oversight.*

boob *sl* **1** [C] an esp foolish mistake: *I think I've made a boob.* **2** [I∅] to make an esp foolish mistake: *He has boobed again.*

N220 *verbs* : **proving things**

prove 1 [T1, 5a, 6a] to show to be true; to show that someone did something: *Can you prove that there is life on other worlds? He was able to prove his theory by producing plenty of evidence. You did it, didn't you?—Prove it!* **2** [T1] to show to be good, useful, bad, useless, etc: *Time proved his ability and wisdom.*

substantiate [T1]*fml* to prove, esp by producing evidence of truth: *Can you substantiate what you have just said against him?*

N221 *nouns* : **proving things**

proof 1 [U;C: (5, *of*)] (a) way of showing that something is true: *I believe what you say; I don't want any proof. I wouldn't demand proof of identity from a friend. Have you any proof that you weren't there at 9 o'clock last night? Blood on a person's hands isn't always a proof that he's been fighting. He says he isn't guilty but we shall need proof of that.* **2** [U] the action of being shown to be true or a fact: *Is life on other worlds capable of proof?* **3** [C] a test or trial to find out whether someone or something has a (necessary) quality, standard of strength, etc (*often in the phr* **put to the proof**): *A soldier's courage is put to the proof in battle. This material will stand any proof* (= pass any test) *of the hardness claimed for it by its makers.* **4** [C] *math* a test made of the correctness of a calculation [⇒ J34] **5** [C] *geom* the reasoning that shows a statement (**theorem**) to be true

evidence [U (*of, for*), U5] **1** (esp in science or law) words which prove a statement, support a belief, or make a matter more clear: *Several witnesses gave evidence about it.* **2** objects which do this: *When the police arrived he had already destroyed the evidence* (= papers, films, etc) *that showed he was guilty.* **evidence(s) of/that** signs or proof of/that: *There are evidences that somebody has been living here.* **bear/show evidence of** to show signs or proof of: *The child bears evidence of having been badly treated.* **in evidence** able to be seen and noticed: *Mrs Jones was much in evidence* (= very noticeable) *at the party. Mr Jones was nowhere in evidence* (= could not be found).

substantiation [U] *fml* the action of substantiating; evidence: *What you have said needs substantiation.*

data [P; U] facts, information, esp of a particular kind obtained in a particular way and kept in a particular place or system: *The data that you want for the study of local diseases are/is ready for examination. We don't have enough data to make a decision. The data is/are not sufficient.*

N222 *adjectives* : **clear and evident** [B; F5]

clear *also* **plain** [Wa1] easy to see, understand, etc, esp as being true, untrue, etc: *It is clear that he stole the money. It's plain that they are unhappy.* **-ly** [adv] **clarify** [I0; T1] to (cause to) become clearer and more easily understood: *When will the government clarify its position on equal pay for women?* **clarification 1** [U] the act of clarifying **2** [C] an example of this

evident *often fml* plain, esp to the senses; clear because of evidence: *It's evident that you've been drinking. Her evident unhappiness made us unhappy.* **-ly** [adv]

obvious easy to see or understand; clear; which must be recognized: *It's obvious that a boy isn't strong enough to lift an elephant.* **-ly** [adv]

apparent *fml* obvious: *It is apparent that he can't be trusted.*

N223 *adjectives* : **fair and just** [B]

fair [Wa1] giving each person what he or she should have: *Be fair; that money is mine, not yours. It isn't fair; I should get that money, not him.* **un-** [*neg*] **-ly** [adv]: *The money was fairly divided among them.*

just 1 fair; in accordance with what is right and true: *He is a very just man and it is a just law. To be just to him, he's always worked hard* (*even though he is unpleasant*). **2** well-deserved: *You have received a just reward/punishment.* **3** proper; fitting: *The payment is just. It's just that you should be rewarded for your work.* **4** exact: *We must have a just balance between the two of them.* **un-** [*neg*] **-ly** [adv]: *He was justly punished.* **-ness** [U]

equitable *fml* fair and just: *We must make an equitable division of the money.* **in-** [*neg*] **-bly** [adv]

balanced having or showing fairness: *He gave a balanced judgment.*

even-handed *often emot* fair and equal; equally balanced: *Justice should be even-handed.* **-ly** [adv] **-ness** [U]

N224 *nouns* : **fairness and justice** [U]

fairness the quality of being fair: *He is well-known for his fairness.* **un-** [*neg*]

justice 1 the quality of being just; rightness; fairness: *He claimed—with justice, I might add—that he had not received his fair share. I hope you will receive justice. In justice to him, he has done a lot of good work in the past* (*even though he is unpleasant*). **2** correctness: *The justice of these remarks was clear to everyone.* **3** the action or power of the law: *We must bring these criminals to justice.* **do justice to someone/do someone justice** to treat someone in a fair way; show the true value of: *To do him justice, he's done some good work* (even if he is unpleasant). *Your new hat doesn't really do you justice.*

equity 1 *fml* the quality of being equitable: *They shared the work of the house with perfect equity.* **2** *tech* (esp in the law systems of English-speaking countries) the principle of justice which may be used to correct a law, when that law would cause hardship in special cases

N225 *nouns* : **balance and harmony**

balance [U] **1** the state in which someone or something stays in position and does not fall over or down: *He managed to keep his balance as he walked along the top of the narrow wall, then just at the end he lost his balance and fell.* **2** the state in which two or more things are equal in weight, position, power, etc: *In a pair of scales* [⇒ H127] *the two pans will be in perfect balance when the same weight is in each.* (*fig*) *If one large country becomes too strong it upsets the balance of power in the world.* **off balance** ready to fall: *He was thrown off balance when she ran into him.* **on balance** when everything is considered: *I think that, on balance, he is a useful man.*

harmony 1 [U; (S)] a state of agreement (in feelings, ideas, etc); peacefulness: *My cat and dog never fight; they live together in perfect harmony. After their quarrel a new harmony was felt between them.* **2** [U; (C)] the pleasant effect made by parts being combined into a whole: *The harmony of sea and sky made a beautiful picture.* **harmonious** [B] in a state of harmony: *There is a harmonious relationship between the two countries.* **-ly** [adv] **-ness** [U]

unison [U] **1** the singing of the same note by everybody at the same time (*esp in the phr* **in unison**) **2** (*fig*) perfect agreement (*esp in the phr* **in unison**): *We are all in unison about it.*

accord *fml, euph & pomp* **1** [U] harmony, esp between nations **2** [C *usu sing*] an agreement for peace and friendly relations between nations

accordance [U] *fml* agreement; harmony (*esp in the phr* **in accordance with**): *In accordance with your wishes the money has been sent to Switzerland. What he did is quite in accordance with the law.*

concord 1 [U] friendly relationship; harmony; complete peace and agreement: *The two tribes had lived in concord for many centuries.* **2** [C] *tech* an agreement, esp a treaty, establishing peace and friendly relations: *Both sides willingly signed the concord which ended the disagreement between them.*

discord [C; U] **1** (a case of) disagreement between people: *A good deal of discord/various discords have arisen in the university over this question.* **2** (esp in music) (a) lack of agreement heard when sounds are made or notes played which do not sound well together: *His music has too much discord in it. He played some ugly discords on the piano.* **discordant** [B] full of or showing discord **-ly** [adv]

N226 *verbs* : **balance and harmony**

[ALSO ⇒ N330]

balance 1 [T1; I∅] to (cause to) be steady, to (cause to) keep a position and not fall over or down: *He balanced (himself) on top of the narrow wall. Can you balance on your hands?* **2** [T1; I∅] to (cause to) be of equal weight, importance, or influence to (something/each other): *The weight here balances the weight there. The two weights balance (perfectly).*

poise [X9 *usu pass*] to place in such a way as to balance, be steady, etc; to hold (something) esp raised in a usu stated position: *The stone was poised in his hand, ready to be thrown.*

poised [Wa5;F3,9] ready (to do something): *He was poised to go.*

harmonize, -ise [T1; I∅ (*with*)] to (cause to) become harmonious or in agreement, balance, etc: *Conditions must be harmonized between our two countries. Her clothes harmonize well with the colours in the room.*

accord [I∅ (*with*)] to harmonize; have the same meaning (as): *The two stories don't accord. Your story doesn't accord with his.*

align [T1; I∅] to come, bring, form, make, or arrange into a line or suitable position: *The soldiers were aligned ready for battle. Are these walls properly aligned?* **alignment 1** [U] the act of aligning: *We must get the walls in (to) proper alignment.* **2** [C] an example of this

match 1 [T1 (*in, for*)] **a** to be equal to (a person in a quality): *You can't match him in knowledge of wild plants/his knowledge of wild plants.* **b** to find an equal for: *This hotel can't be matched for good service and food.* **2** [I∅; T1] to be like or suitable for use with (something else): *The curtains don't match the paint. The hat and shoes don't match.* **3** [T1] to find something like or suitable for: *I need some yellow wool like this; can you match it, please?*

correspond [I∅ (*with, to*)] to harmonize or match: *Her story of what happened does not correspond exactly with/to his. The house corresponded closely to what he wanted.* **correspondence** *usu fml* **1** [U] the condition of corresponding: *What correspondence is there between the two sets of information?* **2** [C] an example or occasion of this: *The correspondences are interesting; the two sets of information are very alike.*

N227 *verbs* : **justifying and explaining**

justify [T1 (*to*), 4] **1** to give a good reason for: *How can you justify your behaviour? 'to justify the ways of God to man'* (Milton) **2** to be a good reason for: *Nothing can justify such behaviour. What can justify doing it?* **justification** [U;C] (a) (good) reason for doing something: *There is no justification for what he did.*

account for [v prep] **1** [T1, 4, 6a: (*to*)] to give an explanation or reason for: *He could not account for his foolish mistake. It is difficult to account for the absence of policemen at the meeting. All the men* (= soldiers) *are present and accounted for, sir.* **2** [T1, 6a; (*to*)] to give a statement showing how money or goods left in one's care have been dealt with: *He has to account to the chairman for all the money he spends.* **3** [T1] *infml* to kill, shoot, or catch: *I think I accounted for three of the attackers.*

answer for [v prep T1] to give reasons why (something esp unsatisfactory) is so; be responsible for the state of (something): *He must answer for the loss of the money.*

explain [T1, 6a] to give or be the reason for; account for: *Can you explain your stupid*

behaviour? That explains why he's not here.
explain oneself 1 to make one's meaning clear: *I don't understand what you're talking about. Would you explain yourself a little?* **2** to give reasons for one's behaviour: *Late again, Smith? I hope you can explain yourself.* [also ⇒ G81, 2]
rationalize, -ise [I∅; T1] to find reasons for (one's own unreasonable behaviour or opinions): *He tried to rationalize his fears. Stop rationalizing; that's not the real reason for what you did.* **rationalization, -isation** [U; C] the or an act or result of rationalizing; an example of this

N228 *nouns* : uses, purposes, and ambitions

[ALSO ⇒ I29]

use 1 [U] the act of using or state of being used [⇒ I26]: *His use of English is improving.* **2** [U] the ability or right to use something: *He is old but he has the full use of his mind and body. She was given the use of the library.* **3** [C; U] the purpose or reason for using something: *What use does this tool have/serve? This book has a use as an ornament.* **4** [U] the usefulness or advantage given by something: *Is this book any use? What's the use of worrying?* **5** [U] custom; habit; practice: *There is no law, but we accept that local use has the force of law.* **have no use for (esp a person)** to think of no value; to dislike **in use** being used **of use** *esp fml* useful: *This machine will be of (great) use to us.* **out of use** no longer used: *That type of machine is out of use. That expression has gone out of use.* **make use of** to use well; take advantage of: *Can you make use of these books?*
utility 1 [U (*of*)] the degree of usefulness **2** [C *often pl*] any useful service for the public, such as supplies of water to the home, the bus service, etc
validity [U (*of*)] the state or condition of being valid [⇒ N211]: *You don't know enough about the subject to question the validity of my statements.*
worthwhileness [U (*of*)] the state or condition of being worthwhile [⇒ N230], worth doing: *I do not question the worthwhileness of her work; she does very useful work.*
purpose 1 [C] use; effect; result: *Don't waste your money; put it to some good purpose.* **2** [U] steady determination in following an aim: *It's no use deciding to become a doctor if you lack purpose in setting yourself to the necessary studies; you must have a sense of purpose.* **3** [C] an intention or plan; reason for an action: *Did you come to London for the purpose of seeing your family, or for business purposes? The purpose of his life seems to be to enjoy himself.* **a play with a purpose** intended to express the writer's political beliefs, not just to be amusing **answer/fulfil/serve one's/the purpose(s)** to be or do all that is needed: *I haven't got a pen here,*

but a pencil will answer the same purpose. **on purpose 1** intentionally; not by accident: *I'm sorry I stepped on your toe; it was an accident.—It wasn't. You did it on purpose.* **2** with a particular stated intention: *I came here on purpose to see you.* **to little/no/some/much/good purpose** with little/no/some/much/good result or effect: *You acted to good purpose when you bought that car; it was both good and cheap.* **to the purpose** useful; connected with what is being considered or what is needed: *His remarks about gardening were hardly to the purpose in an argument about farming.*
design [U] purpose; purposeful planning: *Do you think the house was burnt down by accident or by design?*
end [C] *esp lit & poet* purpose: *What is his end in life; why does he work so hard? When we say 'the end justifies the means' we suggest that any way of getting what you want is all right; that is not necessarily true.*
ambition 1 [U; C] strong desire for success, power, riches, etc: *That politician is full of ambition; one of his ambitions is to become a minister.* **2** [C] that which is desired in this way: *That big house on the hill is his ambition.*
ambitious 1 [B, B3] having a strong desire for success, power, riches, etc: *He is an ambitious man. He is ambitious to succeed in politics.* **2** [B] showing or demanding a strong desire for success, great effort, great skill, etc: *It's an ambitious attempt; I hope it succeeds.* **un-** [neg] **-ly** [adv] **-ness** [U]
aim [C] the desired result of one's efforts; purpose; intention; ambition: *What is your aim in working so hard? He told me about his aims in life.*
goal [C] *esp lit* aim; ambition: *His goal in life is to become a great politician/writer/singer.*
point [U] *usu not fml & often emph & emot* the use or purpose: *What's the point of doing that? There's no point in going there today; no one will be there.*

N229 *adjectives* : useful and sensible [B]

useful 1 effective in use: *That is a useful idea. Money is always useful.* **2** able to help: *He's a useful person to have around.* **-ly** [adv] **-ness** [U] **outlive/outlast its (one's) usefulness** to continue to be present when old and no longer effective in the proper way
helpful able or willing to help or be useful: *She's a very helpful (kind of) person. Try to be more helpful to people. That's a helpful idea.* **-ly** [adv] **-ness** [U]
handy [Wa1] **1** useful and simple to use: *This is a handy little box.* **2** clever in using the hands: *She's handy with her needle.* **3** *infml* nearby: *The shops are quite handy.* **-iness** [U] **come in handy** to be useful from time to time: *These tools should come in handy some day; let's keep them.*

sensible reasonable; having or showing good sense: *a sensible person/choice* **-bly** [adv]

profitable 1 useful; resulting in advantage: *She spent a profitable day cleaning the house thoroughly.* **2** resulting in money gain: *He has a profitable business selling television and radio sets. attempts to make the business more profitable.* **-bly** [adv] **-ability** [U]

N230 *adjectives* : **practical and purposeful** [B]

practical 1 useful in helping to do something: *That's a very practical idea; let's make use of it immediately. She's a very practical person; she's good at cooking and gardening as well as teaching. Come on; try to be more practical and less theoretical* [⇒ G9; I71]! **2** concerned with the way in which things are actually done: *It's a good idea but there may be practical difficulties in doing it.* **im-** [neg] **-ly** [adv Wa4]

pragmatic doing things in the way that seems best at the time or in the particular place, and not necessarily following any general idea about how to do things: *She is a pragmatic person and does things quickly without waiting to discuss how to do them.* **-ally** [adv Wa4]

realistic 1 (of persons) practical because understanding how things are: *Let's have a realistic discussion of our difficulties.* **2** (of things) true to life: *He paints very realistic pictures.* **-ally** [adv Wa4]

down-to-earth *emph* practical; true to life: *Talking won't help, we need down-to-earth action to save us. He spoke in a very down-to-earth way.*

matter-of-fact *not fml* concerned with facts, not imagination; practical, not fanciful: *'Now let's find out what really happened,' he said in his matter-of-fact way.*

utilitarian concerned with practical use; not made for or interested in forms, thoughts, etc: *This equipment is utilitarian, not a work of art.*

empirical (of people or methods) guided only by practical experience rather than by scientific ideas out of books: *They learnt the boiling-point of water by the empirical method; they boiled some and then measured the temperature.* **-ly** [adv; Wa4]

worthwhile *esp emot* worth doing; worth the trouble taken: *She has a very worthwhile job. Her interest makes our efforts worthwhile.*

purposeful 1 directed towards a (special) purpose: *All the cook's actions as she prepared the meal were purposeful; she had no time to waste.* **2** full of or expressing determination: *He's a purposeful young man who knows what he wants to do in life, and will probably succeed in doing it.* **-ly** [adv]

N231 *adjectives* : **not useful, purposeful, etc**

useless [B] **1** not of any use: *A coat is useless in a hot country.* **2** not giving hope of success: *Weeping is useless; action may have some results.* **3** *infml* not able to do anything properly: *You're useless! You've done it wrong again!* **-ly** [adv] **-ness** [U]

purposeless [B] having no purpose or meaning: *Though she's rich she doesn't lead* (= live) *a purposeless existence; she works hard helping the poor and sick.*

aimless [B] having no aim: *He leads a very aimless life/existence; he never does anything worthwhile.* **-ly** [adv] **-ness** [U]

pointless [B] *esp emph & emot* having no point: *Going there is pointless; it won't help anybody!* **-ly** [adv] **-ness** [U]

vain [Wa5;A] *esp lit & emot* without result; useless: *After a number of vain attempts to climb the mountain we were forced to return to camp.* **-ly** [adv]: *He tried vainly to do it.*

futile [B] *often deprec* **1** (of an action) having no effect; unsuccessful; useless: *All his attempts to unlock the door were futile, because he was using the wrong key. Don't waste time by asking futile questions.* **2** (of a person) worthless; of no importance; lacking ability to succeed: *That futile young man does nothing but waste money.* **futility 1** [U] the condition of being futile **2** [C] something futile

dud *not fml* **1** [Wa5;B] of no use; not able to work (properly): *These matches are dud; they won't light.* **2** [C] a person or thing that is of little use: *He's a dud; he can't help you.*

N232 *adjectives* : **ready and prepared**

ready [Wa1] **1** [F (*for*), F3] prepared and fit (for use): *Is breakfast ready? The letters are ready for the post/ready to be signed. I'm not ready yet. Where are my shoes?* **un-** [neg] **2** [F3] (of a person) willing (to do something): *She's always ready to help.* **3** [A] (of thoughts or their expressions) quick: *She has a ready tongue* (= can talk well). *He is a man of ready wit.* **4** [F] within reach: *He slept with his sword ready.* **-ily** [adv] **-iness** [U] **make ready** to prepare oneself: *They made ready for the attack.*

prepared 1 [Wa5;B] got ready in advance: *The chairman read out a prepared statement* (which he had written before the meeting). **2** [F3] willing: *I'm not prepared to listen to all your weak excuses.*

N233 *adjectives* : **strong and powerful** [B]

[ALSO ⇒ B91]

strong [Wa1] **1** having (a degree of) power, esp of the body: *She is not very strong after her illness. How strong is he?* **2** powerful against harm; not easily broken, spoilt, moved or changed: *He wore strong shoes. She has strong beliefs. He held the door back with his strong arm. The support of the minister puts him in a* *strong position in the election.* **3** [E] of a certain number: *Our club is a hundred strong* (= has 100 people in it). **4** violent: *There was a strong wind last night.* **5** powerful or effective: *His was a strong argument. There is a strong smell of cats.* **6** unacceptable: *It's a bit strong to punish them for such a small thing.* **7** (esp of drinks) having a lot of the material which gives taste: *The tea is too strong. Mix my drink strong* (= not with much water). **-ly** [adv]

intense strong (in quality or feeling): *The cold was intense. She felt intense sorrow at/over what had happened.* **-ly** [adv]

dynamic *often apprec* (of people, ideas, etc) full of or producing power and activity: *She is a very dynamic worker. His dynamic ideas helped all of us.* **-ally** [adv; Wa4]

potent 1 (of medicines, drugs, drinks, etc) having a strong and/or rapid effect on the body or mind: *This wine is too potent for me; it makes me feel unsteady.* **2** *fml* (of arguments, reasoning, etc) strongly effective; causing one to agree **3** (of a male) sexually active **4** *lit or fml* having great power, esp politically **-ly** [adv]

powerful 1 very strong; full of force: *He is a very powerful swimmer; he has powerful arms and legs. The horse had a powerful kick. It was a powerful army.* **2** of great ability; easily producing ideas: *The great scientist had a powerful brain. Her imagination is too powerful.* **3** strong or great in degree: *Onions have a powerful smell. Electric current is often powerful enough to kill. He wears powerful glasses.* **4** having a strong effect: *The minister made a powerful political speech. This wine is very powerful.* **5** having much control and influence: *Powerful nations sometimes try to frighten weaker ones.* **6** having or using great working or electrical power: *It is a powerful car with a powerful engine.* **-ly** [adv] **-ness** [U]

mighty [Wa1] *esp old use & lit* powerful; strong: *He was a mighty man and could lift whole trees.* **-tily** [adv] **-tiness** [U]

arbitrary 1 of power that is uncontrolled and used without considering the wishes of others: *The arbitrary decisions of the factory owners caused anger among the workers.* **2** *often deprec* decided by or based on personal opinion or chance rather than reason: *I didn't know anything about any of the books so my choice was quite arbitrary. Arbitrary statements have little value.* **-trarily** [adv] **-trariness** [U]

N234 *adjectives* : **strong in special ways** [B]

sturdy [Wa1] **1** strong and firm, esp in body: *The little boy was running on his sturdy legs. That's a sturdy table.* **2** determined in action: *They kept up a sturdy opposition to the plan.* **-ily** [adv] **-iness** [U]

robust 1 having or showing very good health: *a robust young man.* **2** *euph & not derog* (of

jokes, conversation, etc) rather rude; not suited to polite society **-ly** [adv] **-ness** [U]

tough [Wa1] **1** strong; not easily weakened; able to suffer uncomfortable conditions: *Only tough breeds of sheep can live in the mountains. He is a tough fighter.* **2** not easily cut, worn or broken: *This material is as tough as leather. This is very tough cloth.* **3** difficult to cut or eat: *What tough meat this is!* **4** difficult to do; not easy; demanding: *That was a tough lesson/job. We have a tough struggle in front of us.* **5** unyielding; hard: *The government has threatened to get tough with people who try to avoid paying taxes.* **6** rough; violent; disorderly: *They are tough criminals.* **7** *infml* too bad; unfortunate: *Tough luck! It really is tough that it had to happen to you of all people.* **as tough as old boots 1** very tough: *This meat's as tough as old boots.* **2** very strong: *He's never lost a day's work through illness. He's as tough as old boots.* **3** unable to feel pity, sympathy, etc: *Our teacher's as tough as old boots so we never expect sympathy from her.*

stout [Wa1] **1** strong; thick; too solid to break: *He cut a stout stick to help him walk. He wore stout walking shoes.* **2** *often lit & pomp* brave; determined: *She is a stout supporter of the team. He put up a stout defence against them.*

stalwart *esp lit* **1** [B] strong, brave and loyal: *He is a stalwart supporter of the king.* **2** [C] a stalwart person: *He is one of our stalwarts.*

N235 *nouns* : **strength and energy**
[ALSO ⇒ B92, H80, N155]

strength 1 [U] the quality of being strong, or degree of being strong: *He can lift heavy weights because of his strength. What is the strength of this material? She has great strength of character.* **2** [U] something providing strength or power: *His personal knowledge is the strength of his argument.* **3** [U] force, esp measured in numbers: *They came in strength to see the fight. They were four men below strength. They need more guns to bring the army up to (full) strength.* **4** [C usu pl] a strong quality: *What are his strengths and weaknesses?* **on the strength of 1** because of: *I bought it on the strength of his advice.* **2** in the likelihood of: *I baked a cake on the strength of their coming.*

intensity [U] **1** the quality of being intense **2** an appearance showing strong feeling: *I was surprised by the intensity of her face as she looked at him.*

dynamism [U] **1** (in a person) the quality of being dynamic: *Harry is bursting with dynamism.* **2** *tech* a system of thought that explains everything in the world as the result of natural forces acting upon each other

potency [U] the quality or state of being potent; power: *He has lost his sexual potency. Medicines not stored away from the air will lose their potency.*

power [U] **1** strength and force, esp of armies, machines, etc: *They have great power over our lives.* **2** ability; authority: *It isn't (with)in my power to help them.*

energy 1 [U] (of people) the quality of being full of life and action; power and ability to do a lot of work: *Young people usually have more energy than the old.* **2** [C *often pl with same meaning*] the power which one can use in working: *You must apply/devote all your energies to this job* (=to concentrate your energy on it).

might [U] *esp old use & lit* power; strength: *He was a man of great might. The Greeks faced the whole might of the Persian Empire.*

N236 adjectives : not strong and powerful [B]

[ALSO ⇒ B93]

weak [Wa1] **1** not strong enough to work or last properly **a** (of parts of objects): *A weak wall like that can't hold up this house.* **b** (of organs of the body): *He has a weak heart.* **2** not strong in character: *He is too weak to defend his rights.* **3** not as well as usual in body esp after illness: *His legs felt weak. My head was weak after drinking the wine.* **4** containing mainly water: *I don't like weak tea.* **5** not reaching a good standard: *His work is rather weak.* **-ly** [adv] **-ness** [U]

fragile 1 easily broken or damaged: *This old glass dish is very fragile; it's in a very fragile condition.* **2** easily destroyed; not likely to last: *Their happiness was very fragile.* **3 a** slight in body or weak in health: *The old lady looks very fragile.* **b** *usu humor* not in a good condition of health and spirits; weak: *'I'm feeling rather fragile this morning', he said; 'I must have drunk too much (alcohol) last night'.* **fragility** [U] the condition of being fragile

frail [Wa1] weak, esp because old and/or ill: *His health is frail. Her arms looked very frail and she couldn't lift the box.* **-ty** [U] **frailty** [U] the condition of being frail

feeble [Wa1, 3] **1** very weak: *His body grew feebler as the illness got worse.* **2** very unsatisfactory: *What a feeble story; do you expect me to believe it?* **-bly** [adv] **[-ness** [U]

puny [Wa1] *usu deprec* small and weak; poorly developed: *She was a puny child, with puny little arms and legs, the result of lack of proper food. Puny man looks out at the universe.*

rickety weak in the joints and likely to break: *He was pushing a rickety old cart.*

impotent 1 having no power: *'Your army is impotent against mine!' he laughed.* **2** [Wa5] (of a male) sexually inactive **-ly** [adv]: *They watched impotently while he took the money.*

N237 verbs & nouns : strengthening and concentrating

strengthen 1 [I∅] to gain strength: *His body* slowly strengthened. **2** [T1] to make strong or stronger: *He strengthened the city walls.*

intensify [I∅; T1] to become or to make more intense, stronger, more effective,etc: *The sound intensified. He intensified his demands for more money.*

intensification 1 [U] the act of intensifying **2** [C] an example or amount of this

shore up [v adv T1] to strengthen or give support to (something weak or in danger of falling); strengthen; keep from failing or falling: *The government took action to shore up farm prices. His foolish plans are shored up with even weaker arguments.*

reinforce [T1] to strengthen by adding materials: *She reinforced the coat by sewing pieces of leather on the elbows.* *(fig)* *He will reinforce the argument with facts.*

reinforcement [U] the act of strengthening by adding materials: *Her reinforcement of the coat was a success.*

concentrate 1 [L9; X9] to (cause to) come together in or around one place: *Industrial development is being concentrated in the south of the country. The crowds concentrated in the centre of the town near the royal palace.* **2** [T1] *tech* to strengthen by reducing the per cent of water in a solution (=a mixture of some substance and water) **3** [I∅; T1; *(on, upon)*] to keep or direct (all one's thoughts, efforts, attention, etc): *I'm never able to concentrate so early in the morning. Unless you concentrate more on your work you'll be dismissed! She concentrated all her efforts upon succeeding at work.*

concentration 1 [U] the act of concentrating or being concentrated: *The concentration of industry in the south of the country angered the people in the north. His concentration is very good; when he is working he never hears anything else.* **2** [C *usu sing*] an act of bringing people, forces, etc together: *There has been a concentration of enemy forces near the river.*

focus 1 [*in, out of* U; C] the point where lines of light meet; the point at which the eye can see or an apparatus, etc can show a picture clearly: *The group of people was not in focus/was out of focus, so the photograph was not clear.* **2** [*(the)* U *(of)*] *(fig)* the part of great interest or activity: *The older part of the city was the focus of the trouble.* **3** [T1] **a** to bring to a focus: *The piece of glass focused the sunbeams on the paper, which began to smoke.* *(fig)* *He focused his mind on his work.* **b** to arrange (the glass in an apparatus) so as to obtain a clear picture: *You must focus the camera before you try to take a picture.* **c** to make (a picture) clear by doing this: *Did you enjoy the cinema?—No, the film wasn't properly focused.* **4** [I∅ *on*] to be focused on: *The camera focused on the horse.* **5** [I∅] *infml* to think clearly: *I'm tired; I just can't focus at all.*

exert [T1] to use (strength, skill, etc): *She couldn't open the door, even by exerting all her strength. My wife's been exerting a lot of pres-*

sure on me to change my job. *Lord Rosendale has exerted all his influence to help you.* **exert oneself** to make an effort: *He never exerts himself to help anyone.*

exertion 1 [U] the act of exerting: *A certain amount of bodily exertion is needed to keep people healthy.* **2** [C] an example of this; effort: *His exertions were useless; the door wouldn't open.*

N238 *verbs* : **not strengthening; making weak**

weaken 1 [T1; I0] to (cause to) be weak in form, material or health: *Pulling down the next door house weakened our wall. The illness weakened her heart. This illness weakens the sufferer. She weakened as the illness grew worse.* **2** [I0] to become less determined: *She asked so many times that in the end we weakened and let her go.*

enfeeble [T1 *often pass*] to make (someone) weak: *He was enfeebled by his long illness.*

dilute [T1 (*with*)] to make (a liquid) weaker or thinner (by mixing another liquid with it): *He diluted the paint with oil. The water will dilute the wine.* (*fig*) *The strength of the army was diluted by the use of untrained men.* **dilution** [U] the act of diluting or the state of being diluted

water down [v adv; T1 *often pass*] **1** to weaken (a liquid) by adding water: *Waiter, this soup/beer/drink has been watered down!* **2** (*fig*) to weaken the effect of (something): *His political statement has been watered down so as not to offend anyone.*

sap [T1] *esp emot* to make weak: *That long illness has sapped his strength/his will to live.*

N239 *verbs & modals* : **strength and ability**

be able [I3] to have the power, skill, knowledge, money, time, etc necessary (to do something): *Is he able to go?—No; he isn't able to.—No; he can't. As I had plenty of time/money, I was able to help her more. I am better/more able to help her now than I was last year.* **enable** [V3] to make it possible for (someone) (to do something): *The money enabled him to go for a much-needed holiday.* **enablement** [U]

can [Wv2; I0,2] **1** *genl* be able to: *Is he able to do it?—Yes; he can.— (fml) No; he cannot.— (infml) No; he can't. He can do it and so can I. I thought I could* (= would be able to) *do it, and I can!* **2** be allowed to; *not fml* may: *Can I go now, please?—Yes; you can.* **3** be (able to) by nature: *She can be very unfriendly sometimes when she feels like it.*

could [Wv2; I0,2] **1** *past of* **can** def **1**: *He could do it then, but he can't do it now. Could she go?—No; she couldn't.* **2** *polite* be allowed to; *less fml* might: *Could I go now, please?—Yes;*

you may. **3** *past of* **can** def **3**: *She could be very unfriendly sometimes when she felt like it.*

Fullness, heaviness, thickness, stiffness, roughness, etc

N250 *adjectives* : **full**

full 1 [Wa2;B (*of*)] (of a container) filled with liquid, powder, etc, as near to the top as is convenient in practice: *They brought us out a pot full of steaming coffee. Do you want a full cup of tea, or half a cup? You haven't drunk any of your tea; your cup's still full. Why does grandmother always give you the fullest glass of orange drink? It's rude to speak with your mouth full* (= while you are eating). *This bag of flour is only half full* (= contains half the amount that it can hold). (*fig*) *My heart's too full for words* (= my feelings are too deep for me to express them). *Don't fill my cup too full.* **2** [Wa5;A;F (*of, with, up*)] (of a container) filled to the top; holding as much as possible: *You can't put any more liquid into a full bottle. After the storm, the holes in the road were full of rainwater. The bath's full up; someone forgot to turn off the water. The drawer was full up with old clothes.* (*fig*) *When he heard of his son's wonderful success, his cup was full* (= he was contented; he had everything he could wish for). **3** [Wa2;A;F (*up*)] (of a space) containing as many people, objects, etc, as possible; crowded: *The train's full* (*up*); *there are no seats left at all. I don't like travelling on a full train. As this page is now full, I can't write any more. The doctor has a very full day before him.* (= he has work to do all the time). **4** [F *of*] containing or having plenty (of): *The field was full of sheep feeding on the new grass. This work's full of mistakes; I've never seen work more full of mistakes. Her eyes were full of tears. Every time they meet us, they're full of complaints about something.* **5** [Wa1;A;F (*up*)] *infml* well fed, often to the point of discomfort; satisfied: *I can't eat any more; I'm full up. You ought not to go swimming on a full stomach.* **6** [Wa1;B] complete; whole: *The full truth of the matter can never be told. He's been working here for a full year. Please write down your full name and address. She's never enjoyed a full measure of happiness* (= as much happiness as she deserved). *This medical book is very full on* (= deals very thoroughly with) *the subject of children's diseases, but less full on how to prevent them. She rose to her full height* (= stood up very straight and proudly). *My foot caught in the step, and I fell full length* (= flat on the ground). *He was lying full length on the bed* (= stretched out). *He has led a full life* (= has had every kind of experience); *his life has been full. The tennis player gave the ball* the full treatment (= hit it as hard as possible. **7** [Wa5;A] the highest or greatest possible: *He drove the car at full speed through the town. Only a very good student can obtain full marks in such a difficult examination. Up on the hill, the full force of the wind can be felt. The hunting dogs were in full cry after the fox. The horsemen were riding over the plain at full gallop* (= as fast as they could). **8** [F *of*] **a** having the mind and attention fixed only (on); thinking and talking of nothing else (except): *Some people are too full of their own troubles to care about the difficulties of others. She's always full of herself. She's always full of her own importance. He's full of his coming journey to America.* **b** overflowing (with a feeling, quality, etc): *The children were full of excitement at the thought of their holiday.* **9** [Wa1;B] (of a part of a garment) wide; flowing; fitting loosely: *This coat doesn't fit you well; it's too full in front. This dress has a full skirt.* **10** [Wa1;B] (of a shape, a body or its parts) **a** *often apprec* round; rounded; fleshy: *Her face was full when she was younger; now it's much thinner. The woman had full round breasts. The moon's full tonight.* **b** *euph* fat: *This shop sells dresses for the fuller figure.* **11** [Wa1;A] *apprec* (of colour, smell, sound, taste or substance) deep, rich and powerful: *He likes wine with a full body* (= having strength or substance). *This fruit hasn't got a really full flavour; it needs more sun on it.* **12** [Wa1;F *of*] *lit* having had one's share and more: *He died in 1900, full of years and honours* (= after a long life in which he was greatly honoured) **13** [Wa5;A] possessing all the rights or qualities of the stated position: *Only full members of the club are allowed to vote at meetings.* **14** [adv] very; quite (in the phr **full well**): *They knew full well that he wouldn't keep his promise.* **15** [H] straight; directly: *The ball struck him full on the chest. The sun shone full on her face.* **fully** [adv] **1** [Wa5] quite; at least: *It's fully an hour since he left.* **2** completely; altogether; thoroughly: *I don't fully understand his reasons for leaving. Is she fully satisfied with the present arrangement? She is a fully trained nurse.*

full up [Wa5;F] *not fml* completely full or filled: *The bus is full up; let's go.*

loaded [B] filled, esp with things: *The car is loaded; it's a fully loaded car, full of books, clothes and so on. He carried a loaded gun.*

laden *esp tech* **1** [B (*with*)] heavily loaded: *It was a heavily laden ship. The bushes were laden with fruit.* **2** [F *with*] (*fig*) deeply troubled: *He was laden with sorrow.*

packed [B] (of a room, building, etc) crowded; full of people: *The hall was packed for the meeting last night. The speaker addressed a packed hall.*

crowded [B] **1** completely full; filled with a crowd: *They got onto a crowded bus, after walking in the crowded streets.* **2** uncomfortably close together: *The passengers were crowded on the bus.*

occupied [Wa5;B] (of rooms, etc) full; being used: *That room is occupied; let's use this one.*

N251 adjectives : complete

[ALSO ⇒ N50]

complete 1 [B] with nothing missing or left out; fully finished: *The work is now complete; we can have a holiday.* **in-** [*neg*] **2** [B] all of: *He read the complete book.* **3** [A] very great: *It was a complete surprise to me to learn what she did. This is complete nonsense; I can't understand any of it!* **-ly** [adv] **-ness** [U]

absolute [B] **1** *emph* complete: *He is a man of absolute honesty. You must have absolute trust in me.* **2** having complete power: *An absolute ruler can do just as he pleases.* **-ly** [adv] **-ness** [U]

total [Wa5;B] *emph* full, complete: *The work was a total success/failure. The man is a total stranger to me!* **-ly** [adv]: *What he said is totally untrue!*

entire [Wa5;A] *often fml* complete: *He was there the entire morning. She bought an entire set of Shakespeare's plays. I am in entire agreement with you.* **-ly** [adv] **-ty** [U]

thorough 1 [B] complete in every way: *They made a thorough search of the house.* **2** [Wa5;A] being fully or completely (the stated thing): *He is a thorough fool! The play was a thorough success.* **3** [B] careful with regard to detail: *She is a thorough worker.* **-ly** [adv]: *After a hard day's work I feel thoroughly tired.*

utter [Wa5;A] *emot & emph* complete: *He is an utter fool and talks such (utter) nonsense* (= things which do not make sense)*! -ly* [adv]: *She must have been utterly mad to have done that!*

exhaustive [B] *often fml* thorough; dealing completely with a subject: *She will make an exhaustive study of it. He made exhaustive inquiries about her.* **-ly** [adv] **-ness** [U]

radical [B] (of changes) thorough and complete: *He made some radical improvements in the work.* **-ly** [adv; Wa4]

sweeping [B] **1** including many things: *They have sweeping plans for change.* **2** not careful or correct in detail; too general: *What a sweeping statement to make!*

thoroughgoing [B] very thorough; complete in every way: *He is a thoroughgoing fool! The changes were really thoroughgoing.*

far-reaching [B] having effects on many things; sweeping: *They made far-reaching changes in the laws.*

outright 1 [Wa5;A] complete: *We won an outright victory.* **2** [adv] completely: *He's been paying for that house for years; now he owns it outright.* **3** [adv] completely and clearly: *She won outright.* **4** [adv] completely and without delay: *be killed outright* **5** [adv] (completely and) openly: *Tell him outright just what you think.*

N252 *determiners, etc* : **all**

[ALSO ⇒ J14]

all 1 [determiner] (shows the complete amount or quantity of, or the whole of an uncountable noun): *Not all food is good to eat. We worked hard all year.* **2** [determiner] (includes every similar or separate part of a group of countable nouns): *All children want presents on their birthdays. Please answer all questions on this list.* **3** [determiner] the greatest possible amount of: *The doctor came with all speed.* **4** [determiner] every; any: *We have lost all hope. He is a good musician beyond all doubt.* **5** [determiner] (being influenced or controlled by or as if by the stated characteristic, quality, or body organ): *I am listening carefully; I'm all ears. I can't play the piano today; I feel awkward and am all thumbs.* **6** [predeterminer] the complete amount or quantity of; the whole of: *He ate all his food. He ate it all. We walked all the way. We worked hard all last year. All that I have I will give.* **7** [predeterminer] every member or separate part of; everyone of: *All his children are girls. All questions must be answered. You must answer them all. They must all be answered.* **8** [predeterminer] every member or separate part taken together: *All the angles of a square are equal.* **9** [adv; H] altogether; completely; wholly: *The table was all covered with papers. I am all in favour of your suggestion. She sat all alone.* **10** [adv] to a very great degree; so much; much: (in the phr **all the**): *If we get help the work will get finished all the sooner. You will feel all the better for talking about it.* **11** [adv] for each side: *The score at the football match was three all; neither side won.* **12** [pron] everybody, everything, or everyone: *All of the food. All of the boys. All enjoyed themselves. We all had fun. He gave all he had. The laws apply to all. I have done it all. The doctor did all he could for the sick man. I brought all of them.* **13** [U] *rare* everything one possesses or considers valuable: *She gave her all for the good of the political party.* **14** [*comb form*] consisting or made only of (as in **all-wool**): *This is an all-wool dress.* **15** [*comb form*] of, for, or concerning the whole of: *It was an all-England football team.* **of all people** *infml* surprisingly; out of all the people who might be expected to be present, to be able to help, to be suitable, etc: *He knows I dislike him and yet he asked me, of all people, to help him. To see George, of all people, in the Ritz Hotel!* **all along** *infml* all the time: *I knew that all along.* **all but** almost; nearly: *I am all but ready.* (**not**) **all there** *infml* (not) having a good quick mind **all the same** *infml* even so; anyway: *You say the bridge is safe; I shall take care all the same.* **all the same to** *infml* not making any difference or causing any worry to: *If it's all the same to you; I'll turn the radio off. It's all the same to me whether you stay or go.* **all told** making the total; altogether: *There were 60 people at the party all told.* **all up (with)** *infml* at an end; ruined: *It's all up with him now his business has failed.* **all in all** *infml* considering everything; on the whole, generally: *All in all we had a good time.* **and all** *infml* and everything or everybody: *All the fish may be eaten, head, tail, bones and all.* **(not) at all** (not) in any way: *I do not agree with you at all. Do you feel ill at all? Do you feel at all ill?* **for all** in spite of: *They could not open the box for all their efforts.* **for all one knows, cares, etc** *infml* as far as one knows, cares, etc: *For all I know he may well be innocent, but I really don't care.* **in all** making the total; altogether: *There were 60 people at the party in all.* **it was all one could do (not) to** *infml* it was very difficult (not) to: *It was all I could do not to laugh at his serious speech. It was all I could do not to cry.* **not at all** (an expression used in reply to an expression of thanks): *Thank you, it was very kind of you.—Not at all.* **not so/as good, cold, fast, etc as all that** *infml* not so very good, cold, fast, etc **once (and) for all** for the last time; finally: *Once and for all I must ask you to be quiet.*

whole 1 [Wa5;B] not divided into any parts: *He wanted the whole cake for himself.* **-ness** [U] **2** [Wa5;A] not less than all of: *Let's go there for the whole week. He told us the whole truth.* **3** [C *usu sing (of)*] the complete amount, thing, etc; all: *They walked over the whole of that area. He wants the whole of the cake for himself. We can't treat the group as a whole, but must pay attention to each member.* **wholly** [adv] fully: *I am wholly in agreement with you. It's a wholly new experience for us.* **as a whole, on the whole** generally: *The country as a whole is peaceful. On the whole I like his plan.*

lot [*the* GU (*of*)] *infml* all: *Did you do all the work/read all the books?—Yes; I did/read the lot.—Yes; the lot.* (*usu deprec*) *He told the lot of them to go; he didn't want to see them again.*

N253 *adjectives* : **full-scale and wholesale**

full-scale [Wa5] **1** [B] (of a model, drawing, copy, etc) of the same size as the object represented: *He made a full-scale model of an elephant, but he couldn't get it out of the room.* **2** [A] large; making use of all known facts, information, etc: *He's writing a full-scale history of 19th-century France.* **3** [A] (of an activity) of not less than the usual kind; not shortened, lessened, etc in any way; total: *The quarrel between the two countries nearly developed into a full-scale war.*

whole-hearted [B] with all one's ability, interest, etc: *You have my whole-hearted attention.*

wholesale [B] in too large, unlimited numbers: *They made a wholesale rush from the burning cinema. They gave us presents wholesale.*

N254 adjectives, etc : not full

empty 1 [Wa5;B] containing nothing: *He wanted an empty cup.* **2** [Wa5;B] (of a house or building) with nobody in it; in which nobody is living: *There are 3 empty houses in our street. You mustn't go out and leave the house empty.* **3** [Wa1;B(*of*)] not having the contents which are usually there: *He drove through the empty streets. He drove through streets empty of traffic.* **4** [Wa5;B(*of*)] *derog* (of words, talk, etc) without sense or purpose; meaningless, unreal: *She made him empty promises. Her words were empty of meaning.* **-ily** [adv] **-iness** [U]

vacant [Wa5;B] **1** empty; not filled with anything: *He bought a vacant piece of land.* **2** (of a house, room or seat) not being used or lived in: *The house has been vacant for several months, so you might be able to buy it.* **3** (of a position in employment) not at present filled: *I'm looking for work; are there any positions vacant in your firm? The part of a newspaper in which jobs are advertised is often called 'situations vacant'.* **4 a** (of the mind) not thinking; empty **b** showing lack of active or serious thought: *She had a vacant look on her face.* **c** foolish; senseless: *The madman gave a vacant laugh.* **-ly** [adv] **-ncy** [U]

vacuous [B] **1** foolish, esp in showing no sign of ideas, thought or feeling: *When he wasn't thinking of something important his face often had a vacuous expression.* **2** without purpose; meaningless: *He talked about the vacuous life of many rich people.* **-ly** [adv]

void 1 [Wa1;F *of*] empty (of); without; lacking: *That part of the town is completely void of interest for visitors.* **2** [Wa5;B] *esp law* (of any kind of official agreement) having no value or effect from the beginning: *An agreement signed by a child, to repay borrowed money, is void.* **3** [Wa5;B] *lit* completely empty: *The desert stretching away before the traveller seemed frighteningly void.*

blank 1 [Wa5;B] without writing, print or other marks: *Use a blank page or a blank sheet of paper. Please write your name in the blank space at the top of the page.* **2** [Wa1:B] expressionless, without understanding, without interest: *I tried to explain but he just gave me a blank look. He looked blank. Every day seemed blank and meaningless.* **3** [C] an empty space: *Fill in the blanks in this printed card.* (*fig*) *When I tried to remember her name my mind was a complete blank.* **4** [C] a piece of paper with spaces for putting in information: *When you have completed the blank send it back to me.* **-ly** [adv] **-ness** [U]

N255 adjectives & combining forms : not complete

partial [Wa5;B] not complete: *The play was only a partial success.* **-ly** [adv]

half-, *tech* **semi-** [*comb form*] **1** being half [⇒ J14]: *The work is half-finished. A semicircle is half a circle.* **2** partial: *He was only half-conscious/semiconscious at the time.*

part- [*comb form*] being part of: *He made a part-payment of £1,000 for the car. The work is now part-complete.*

N256 verbs : filling things

fill [IØ;T1: (*up, in, with*)] to (cause to) become full: *The hole filled with water. Water filled the hole. He filled the bottle with water. They filled up/in the hole with small stones. The room filled with people* (= A lot of people came/went into the room). *People filled the room. She filled the house with her friends.* **filling** [C; U] anything that fills something else: *I need a new filling in this tooth.*

load 1 [T1; IØ: (*up*)] to put a full amount on or in (something): *Load the car. Have you finished loading up?* **2** [T1 (*into, onto*)] to place a full amount of: *Load the books into the back of the car.*

pack 1 [Wv5;D1(*for*);T1;IØ] to put (things, esp one's belongings) into cases, boxes, etc) for travelling or storing: *Let's pack some food and go out for the day. She made him a packed lunch. You can pack some of your clothes in my case if you like. She packed her husband some eggs for his dinner. We leave tomorrow but I haven't begun to pack yet.* **2** [Wv5;X9;L9: esp *down, in, together*] to fit, crush, or push into a space: *If you pack those things down we can get a little more in the box. The railwaymen were packing the people into the train like animals. The moment the door was opened, people began to pack into the hall. It was a packed hall.* **3** [X9; IØ] to settle or be driven closely together or into a mass: *The wind packed the snow against the side of the house. The sea is very dangerous when the ice begins to pack in this way.* **4** [L9] to be suitable for easy putting into cases, boxes, etc: *These bottles pack easily, but the others do not, because of their shape.* **5** [T1] to prepare and put (food) into tins or other containers for preserving or selling in shops: *They intend to build a factory here for packing the fruit that grows in the district.* **6** [T1] to cover, fill, or surround closely with a protective material: *These pipes should be packed, to prevent water from getting out. Pack some paper round the dishes in the box so that they will not break.*

crowd 1 [Wv5;T1] to fill by pressing together in: *In the week before the holidays shoppers crowded all the stores. His desk was crowded with books.* **2** [L9; X9] to press tightly: *Guests crowded into the dining room. People crowded round the scene of the accident. As soon as the doors were open people crowded into the theatre. The travellers crowded onto the train. He crowded more books onto the shelf.* **3** [T1] *sl* to put pressure on: *to crowd a debtor for pay-*

ment **crowd out** [v adv: T1b *usu pass*] to refuse entrance because of lack of space: *Your article was crowded out of the magazine; I'm sorry. So many people attended the meeting that many of us were crowded out.*

occupy 1 [T1] to fill (a certain position, space or time): *She occupies an important position in the government. His books occupy a lot of space.* **2** [T1] to be in (a certain place) during a particular period of time: *He occupied a house/a bed/a railway carriage.* **3** [T1] to hold (an enemy's country, town, etc) **4** [T1] to take and hold possession of **5** [X9] to cause to spend time (doing something): *He occupied himself in/with collecting stamps.*

plug [T1 (*up*)] to fill a hole by putting a plug or other thing in it: *He plugged the hole (up) with a cloth.*

N257 *verbs* : **filling forms, etc** [T1]

fill in *esp BrE*, **fill out** *esp AmE* [v adv] to write what is necessary on esp an official form (= sheet of paper): *He filled in/out the form. She filled in her name and address. When you've filled out the form, give it to me.*

fill up [v adv] to write everything that is necessary on (a form): *Fill up these forms, please.*

complete [Wv5] *fml* to fill in, out or up (a form, etc): *Complete these papers, please. Send the completed form to us.*

N258 *verbs* : **emptying things**

empty 1 [T1] to make empty: *They emptied the bottle* (= drank all that was in it). **2** [I0 (*into*)] (of a place, a container, etc) to send or move its contents somewhere else: *The room emptied very quickly. The River Nile empties* (=*flows*) *into the Mediterranean Sea.* **3** [T1 (*out, into, onto*)] to put or move (the contents of a container) somewhere else: *He emptied out all his pockets onto the table. You can empty the rest of the water into this bowl.*

unload 1 [T1; I0] to take from (a vehicle, ship, etc) things which have been put (= **loaded**) into it, making it empty: *Unload the car! Let's unload now.* **2** [T1] to take (things from a usu stated vehicle, ship, etc): *They unloaded the books from the car.* **3** [I0] (of vehicles, ships, etc) to have things taken out: *The ship was unloading.*

discharge [I0; T1] *tech* **1** (of a ship, etc) to unload: *Has the ship discharged (its cargo) yet?* **2** to unload (a ship, etc): *It will take two days to discharge this ship.*

unpack [T1; I0] to take things (from a box, case, etc) things which have been put (= **packed**) in it: *He unpacked his bags. Let's unpack now.*

drain 1 [T1; I0: (*away, off, out*)] to (cause to) flow off gradually or completely: *Drain all the water out. The water drained (off/away).* (*fig*) *money draining away in silly spending.* **2** [T1 (*off, of*); I0 (*of*)] to (cause to) become gradu-

ally dry or empty: *Let the wet glasses drain before you put them away. She was so afraid (angry) that her face (was)drained of blood and she was white with fear/anger.* (*fig*) *War drains a nation of youth and wealth.* **3** [T1] to carry away the surface water of: *They want to drain the land to make crops grow better on it. The river drains the valley.* **4** [T1 (*off*)] to empty by drinking the contents of: *He drained (off) the glass of beer.* **5** [T1 (*of*)] to make weak and tired by using up the forces of body, mind or feelings: *After that noisy argument I feel completely drained (of feeling).* **drain dry** to drain until dry; drain completely: *Let the wet glasses drain dry before you put them away. Drain the glasses dry. I feel drained dry (of feeling).*

N259 *adjectives* : **heavy** [B]

heavy [Wa1] **1** of a certain weight esp that which makes it difficult to carry, move or lift: *The bag is too heavy for me.* **2** of unusual force or amount: *heavy rain; a heavy blow; heavy fighting; a heavy punishment.* **3 a** serious, esp if uninteresting: *This book is heavy reading.* **b** (esp of periods of time) full of hard work: *I've had a heavy day. It's a heavy timetable.* **4** (*fig*) sad: *a heavy heart; heavy news.* **5 a** feeling difficulty or slowness in moving; waking, etc: *My head is heavy. She's a heavy sleeper.* **b** difficult to do or move in: *This is heavy work.* **6** (of food) rather solid and bad for the stomach **7** (of weather) **a** still without wind, dark, etc **b** (at sea) stormy with big waves **-ily** [adv] **-iness** [U]

burdensome *esp lit & emot* heavy and difficult to carry: *He lifted the burdensome load.* (*fig*) *Life can be burdensome sometimes.*

weighted [Wa5; *usu* F (*towards*, *against*)] giving advantage: *The examinations are weighted in favour of the people who have read the right books. The competition was weighted against the younger children.*

weighty [Wa1] *esp lit* heavy: *That's a weighty box; what's in it?* **-ily** [adv] **-iness** [U]

ponderous 1 slow and awkward because of size and weight: *The fat woman's movements were ponderous.* **2** *derog* dull and solemn; lacking lightness or gaiety: *He is a writer with a very ponderous style.* **3** sometimes *deprec* large and heavy: *An elephant has a ponderous body.* **-ly** [adv]

heavyweight [Wa5; *also* C] (someone or something that is) rather large (and serious), esp a written work, speech, or idea: *He's a heavyweight boxer/a political heavyweight. That's a heavyweight book!*

N260 *adjectives* : **not heavy** [B]

light [Wa1] **1** of a certain weight that makes it easy to carry, move or lift: *That bag is nice and light; what is it made of? The box is very light; is there anything in it?* **2** of little force or amount:

light rain; a light blow; light fighting; a light punishment **3 a** not (too) serious: *This book is the kind of light reading I like.* **b** (esp of periods of time) without hard work: *I've had quite a light day today. My timetable is light this year.* **4** (*fig*) happy: *Her heart was light and she sang as she went along.* **5 a** feeling that it is easy to move, wake, etc; moving quickly: *He is light on his feet. She is a very light sleeper.* **b** easy to do or move in: *This is light work.* **6** (of food) not too solid and good for the stomach **-ly** [adv] **-ness** [U]

lightweight [Wa5; *also* C] (someone or something that is) smaller (and not serious), esp a person, written work, speech or idea: *He is a lightweight boxer/a political lightweight. His ideas are pretty lightweight.*

airy [Wa1] **1** *derog* having little substance; empty: *Nothing results from his airy plans and promises.* **2** of, like or in the air **3** (*fig*) light-hearted; gay; happy; careless: *She had a light airy manner.* **-ily** [adv] **-iness** [U]

N261 *adjectives* : **thick**

[ALSO ⇒ N307]

thick [Wa1] **1** [B] **a** having a large distance between opposite surfaces; not thin: *thick bread; a thick board* **b** (of a round object) wide in relation to length: *thick wire* **2** [E] measuring in depth, width or from side to side: *It is a board two inches thick/five centimetres thick.* **3** [B] (of liquid) not watery; not flowing easily; heavy: *thick soup* **4** [B] difficult to see through; dense: *thick mist* **5** [B] (esp of an accent) very noticeable **6** [F *with*] (esp of the air) full of: *The air was thick with smoke.* **7** [B] (of a voice) not clear in sound: *His voice sounded thick because of his cold.* **8** [B] closely packed; made of many objects set close together: *The flowers grew thickest near the wall.* **9** [B] *infml* (of a person) stupid **10** [B] *sl* beyond what is reasonable or satisfactory: *Your demands really are too thick.* **11** [B (*with*)] *infml* very friendly: *Jean and John seem very thick (with each other).* **12** [adv] so as to be thick; thickly: *The dust lay thick on the furniture.* **-ly** [adv] **-ness** [U] **lay it on thick** *infml* to praise, thank, etc, someone too much

dense [Wa1;B] **1** (having parts that are) closely packed or crowded together: *a dense crowd/ forest; dense trees* **2** difficult to see through: *a dense mist.* **3** (*fig*) difficult to understand because packed with ideas: *dense writing* **4** (*fig*) stupid; difficult to reach with ideas: *a dense mind; a dense boy* **-ly** [adv] **-ness, -sity** [U]

viscous [B] *esp tech* (of a liquid) thick and sticky; that does not flow easily **-ly** [adv]

N262 *adjectives* : **not thick** [B]

thin [Wa1] **1 a** having a smaller distance between opposite surface; not thick: *a thin board; thin ice; thin paper* **b** (of a round object) narrow in relation to length: *thin wire* **2** (of a liquid) flowing easily; weak: *This beer's too thin to enjoy. The disease left him with thin blood.* **3** not closely packed; made of few objects widely separated: *Your hair's getting very thin.* **4** easy to see through; not dense: *The air on top of the mountain was very thin.* **5** (esp of a sound or note) lacking in strength: *thin high notes* **6** (*fig*) lacking force or strength; poor: *The teacher said my excuse was too thin to believe.* **7** [adv] so as to be thin: *Spread the butter thin.* **-ly** [adv] **-ness** [U]

watery **1** containing (too much) water and therefore thin: *watery soup* **2** full of water **3** very pale in colour

N263 *verbs* : **relating to heaviness, thickness, etc** [T1]

[ALSO ⇒ J60]

burden (*with*) *often pass* to weigh heavily on: *He was burdened with a heavy load.* (*fig*) *She is burdened with troubles.*

lighten [*also* I0] to (cause to) become light: *He lightened the load by taking something off.* (*fig*) *His troubles have lightened a little.*

thicken [*also* I0] **1** to (cause to) become thick or thicker: *I always thicken my soups by adding flour. This sauce won't thicken.* **2** to (cause to) become more confused and difficult to understand: *The plot thickened.*

condense [*also* I0] *esp tech & fml* **1** to (cause to) become thicker or more dense **2** to change from a gas to a liquid: *The steam condensed into water.* **condensation** [U] [*also* ⇒ L45]

thin [*also* I0] **1** to (cause to) become thin: *We should wait until the mist thins before driving on. He thinned the wine by adding water.* **2** [(*out*)] **a** to move (esp young plants) further apart from one another to allow free growth; **b** (of trees, etc) to appear or be less close together: *The woods thinned out near the lake.*

N264 *adjectives* : **hard, stiff, etc**

hard [Wa1] **1** [B] which cannot easily be broken or pressed down or bent: *The ice is as hard as a rock. The snow was frozen hard.* **2** [B] **a** forceful: *She gave him a hard push.* **b** needing or using force: *This is hard work.* **3** [B] full of difficulty and trouble: *They had a hard life. He gave me a hard time.* **4** [B (*on*)] (of people, punishments, etc) not gentle (to); showing no kindness (to): *You're a hard woman. She was very hard on me* (= unkind to me). **5** [A] based on or looking for facts; firm: *This difficulty demands a lot of hard thinking. She gave him a hard searching look.* **6** [B] unpleasant to the senses, esp because too bright or too loud: *Her hard voice could be heard across the room. She paints her face with hard colours.* **-ness** [U] **7** [adv] **a** in a hard way; with great effort: *He tries*

hard to understand, but it's too difficult for him. Look hard at this picture. Think hard and work hard. **b** strongly; heavily; in large amounts over a period of time: *I was breathing hard as I stopped running. It's raining harder than ever.*
be hard on to wear (something) out easily or quickly: *Children are very hard on their shoes.*
do (something) the hard way to learn by experience, not by teaching; act alone and with difficulty **hard at it** working with all one's force in some activity **be hard hit (by)** to suffer loss because of (some event): *He was hard hit when prices went up, because he had no hope of a wage rise.* **be hard done by** to be unfairly treated: *I was very hard done by in receiving less money than anybody else after I had worked twice as hard.* **(it) come(s) hard to** to be (an action) difficult to do: *It comes hard to live on a small amount of money when you've been rich.* **(it) go(es) hard with** to be (an experience) difficult to accept: *It goes hard with him to be alone so often.* **die hard** (of habits) to be lost with difficulty: *Old habits die hard.* **take (it) hard** to suffer deeply: *She failed her examination, and she's taking it very hard.* **be hard put (to it)** to (do something) to have great difficulty (in doing something): *I was hard put to it to keep the house warm when the heating was turned off.*
stiff [Wa1] **1** [B] not easily bent: *What stiff paper! Shoes are often stiff when they're new.* **2** [B] not easily moved, turned, etc: *Beat the eggs until stiff.* **3** [B] formal; not friendly: *a stiff smile. The guest felt a bit stiff surrounded by people he didn't know, but after a few drinks he became quite gay.* **4** [B] painful when moved: *I feel stiff after my long walk. His stiff aching muscles felt better after a hot bath.* **5** [F] *infml* too much to accept; unusual in degree: *It's a bit stiff to expect us to go out again at this time of night. The cost is stiff.* **-ly** [adv] **-ness** [U]
rigid [B] **1** *esp tech* stiff; not easy to bend: *The tent was supported on a rigid framework.* **2** (of a person or his character or opinions) firm; fixed; not easy to change: *He's very rigid in his ideas on marriage. He knows the rigid discipline of army life.* **-ly** [adv] **-ness** [U]
firm [Wa1;B] strong, solid and hard; not moving easily: *Some soft foods become firm when cold. Is the ice on the lake firm enough to walk on?* **-ly** [adv] **-ness** [U]
tough [Wa1;B] difficult to break, eat, cut, etc: *This meat is very tough. Use a tougher cloth; this one is too easily torn.* **-ness** [U]
crisp [Wa1;B] **1** hard; dry; easily broken: *crisp pastry* **2** firm; fresh: *a crisp apple; crisp vegetables* **3** newly made or prepared; fresh: *He gave me a crisp pound note. His shirt was crisp and clean.* **4** (*fig*) (of hair) tightly curled: *She wore jewels in her beautiful crisp hair.* **5** (*fig*) (of style, manners, etc) quick; showing no doubts or slowness; clear: *a quick crisp reply; a crisp manner of speaking* **6** (*fig*) (of the air, weather, etc) cold; dry; refreshing: *a crisp winter day; the crisp autumn wind* **7** [IØ;T1] to

(cause to) become crisp (**1, 2**) esp by cooking or heating: *If you cook this pastry at a high temperature it should crisp nicely.*

N265 *adjectives* : **hard in special ways** [B]

harsh [Wa1] **1** unpleasant in causing pain to the senses: *It was a harsh light (too strong for the eyes). They were harsh colours. He had a harsh voice. This cloth is harsh to the touch* (= rough). **2** (of people, punishments, etc) showing cruelty or lack of kindness: *The punishment was too harsh.* **-ly** [adv] **-ness** [U]
severe [Wa2] **1** not kind or gentle in treatment; not allowing failure or change to rules, standards, etc; stern; strict: *He is a severe judge of other people. She had a severe look on her face. These are very severe military rules.* **2** very harmful or painful; serious or uncomfortable: *It is the severest winter for 10 years. He faces severe difficulties/penalties.* **3** needing effort; difficult: *It is a severe test of ability/a severe competition.* **4** plain; without ornament; austere: *He liked the severe beauty of the simple church building. Her hair was tied straight back in a severe way.* **5** expressing a strongly unfavourable judgment; very critical: *The Times certainly didn't like the new film; their remarks were very severe.* **-ly** [adv] **-ness** [U]
strict [Wa1] **1** severe, esp in rules of behaviour: *This is a strict rule. They are very strict with their children.* **2** exact: *He gave us a strict interpretation of the facts.* **-ly** [adv] **-ness** [U]
rigorous 1 severe; painful: *He did not enjoy the rigorous hardships of the journey.* **2** careful and exact: *He made a rigorous study of the plants in the area.* **-ly** [adv] **-ness** [U]
disciplined having discipline [⇒ N267]; severe in training; controlled: *His army is a very disciplined force; it is highly disciplined.*
stern [Wa1] **1** very firm or hard towards others' behaviour: *She is a stern teacher.* **2** difficult or hard to bear: *What stern punishment!* **3** showing firmness esp with disapproval: *He gave the child a stern look.* **-ly** [adv] **-ness** [U]
austere 1 lacking comfort; hard: *We led an austere life in the mountains.* **2** lacking the ability to enjoy life; self-controlled; serious: *He is an austere person with an austere manner.* **3** without ornament; plain: *It was an austere style of painting.* **-ly** [adv] **-ness** [U]

N266 *nouns* : **kinds of hardness**

severity 1 [U] the state or quality of being severe: *He treated them with severity. The severity of his punishment was undeserved.* **2** [C *usu pl*] a severe act or condition: *He has known all the severities of army life.*
rigour *BrE*, **rigor** *AmE* [U] **1** hardness; lack of mercy: *He deserves to be punished with the full rigour of the law.* **2** [the U9 *often pl* with the

same meaning] severe conditions: *He will suffer all the rigour(s) of winter/of army life.* **3** [U] (of a subject of study) exactness that demands clear thinking: *We need the rigour of scientific proof.*

rigidity [U] the quality of being rigid: *He knows the rigidity of the framework/of her opinions.*

discipline 1 [U] training of the mind and body to produce obedience and self-control: *school/military discipline* **2** [U] control gained as a result of this training: *There's no discipline among those soldiers. The teacher can't keep discipline in her classroom.* **3** [U] punishment: *That child needs discipline; give me my stick.* **4** [C] a method of training: *Learning poetry is a good discipline for the memory.* **5** [C] a branch of learning studied at a university: *You're no good at history, so you'd better choose one of the other disciplines.*

austerity 1 [U] the quality of being austere **2** [C *usu pl*] an austere act, practice, or manner: *We practised various austerities to make our money last longer.* **3** [U] a way of life that does not cost much, esp one forced on a country in time of war: *It was a period of austerity.*

N267 adjectives : not hard [B]

soft [Wa1] **1** not firm against pressure; giving in to the touch; changeable in shape; not hard or stiff: *This is a nice soft chair/bed. His foot sank slightly into the soft ground. The book had a soft* (= paper) *cover. He shaped the clay while it was soft.* **2** less hard than average: *Lead is one of the softer metals.* **3** smooth and delicate to the touch: *What lovely soft skin you have! This is the softest finest wool.* **4** restful and pleasant to the senses, esp the eyes: *The restaurant had soft lights and played soft music. It was a soft summer evening. She had beautiful soft brown eyes.* **5** quiet; not making much noise; not loud: *Her whisper was so soft I could hardly hear it.* **6** not violent; gentle: *Soft winds came from the south. She felt a soft touch on her shoulder.* **7** not angry or excited; making calm: *He gave a soft answer to the angry questions.* **8** *not fml* not showing or needing hard work; easy: *This is a soft life! He has a soft job with few duties and good pay.* **9** weak in condition of the body: *I'm afraid my office job is letting me get soft. 'Children these days are too soft!' he said.* **10** *not fml* easily persuaded; easy to make agree or do what one wishes: *You must think I'm soft if you think I'll let you do that!* **-ly** [adv] **-ness** [U]

gentle [Wa1,3] not violent; soft in movement: *a gentle wind; a gentle slope* (= not steep). **2** kind and ready to help others: *She's a very gentle person, who never loses her temper.* **-tly** [adv] **-tleness** [U]

tender [Wa2] **1** not hard or tough: *Cook the meat a long time so that it's really tender.* **2** delicate; too easily crushed; needing careful handling: *tender flowers.* **3 a** easily hurt; sensi-

tive; delicate: *After riding such a long way on a bicycle his bottom was very tender.* **b** painful; sore: *a tender tooth.* **4** young; inexperienced: *a child of tender years.* **5** gentle and loving; sympathetic; kind: *He has a tender heart. The woman gave her child a tender look.* **6** that might offend or hurt people: *One should always avoid tender subjects of conversation at parties.* **-ly** [adv] **-ness** [U]

delicate 1 finely made; delightful: *a delicate piece of silk, a delicate pattern, delicate food and wine.* **2** finely made; needing careful handling; easily broken or hurt: *The body is a delicate machine. Treat this delicate glass carefully.* **3** needing careful treatment or tact [⇒ G39]; likely to go wrong at any moment: *a delicate affair/position/subject.* **4** easily made ill; easily yielding to illness: *He is a delicate child, in delicate health.* **5** very pleasing but perhaps not easy to recognize, taste, smell, see, etc: *delicate tastes/smells/colours.* **6** sensitive: *He has a delicate ear and a delicate sense of touch. That delicate instrument can record even very slight changes.* **7** sensitive to bad manners in oneself or in others: *Some delicate people don't like to offend; others don't like to be offended. She has delicate feelings.* **-ly** [adv] **-ness** [U]

mild [Wa1] gentle, soft: *What lovely mild weather! He has a very mild manner with children but is much harder on adults.* **-ly** [adv] **-ness** [U]

limp [Wa1] lacking strength or stiffness: *The book had limp covers* (= with a soft cloth cover rather than hard protective back). *The heat was too much for her; she went limp and fell to the ground.* **-ly** [adv] **-ness** [U]

N268 adjectives : not stiff [B]

flexible 1 that can bend or be bent easily: *This piece of metal is very flexible.* **2** (*fig*) that can change or be changed to be suitable for new needs, changed conditions, etc: *The government must be flexible in its handling of this dangerous state of affairs.* **in-** [*neg*] **-bly** [adv] **-bility** [U]

supple [Wa1,3] **1** bending or moving easily, esp in the joints of the body: *She has a supple body.* **2** (*fig*) quick in thinking, changing one's ideas, values, etc

pliable 1 easily bent without breaking: *Baskets are often made of pliable stems.* **2** (*fig*) able and willing to change or to accept new ways and ideas: *It's necessary to be pliable in a changing world.*

pliant 1 pliable: *The wires were pliant and easily bent into the shapes he wanted.* **2** (*fig*) easily influenced; yielding to the wishes or commands of others: *She has a pliant nature and will agree to do as the rest of us wish.* **-ly** [adv] **-ancy** [U]

plastic [Wa5] **1** easy made, bent, formed into different shapes: *Clay is a plastic material.* **2** [Wa5;A] concerned with changing the shape of something: *The plastic arts turn materials into the special shapes desired by the artists.* **-ticity** [U]

elastic 1 (of material such as rubber) which springs back into the original or natural shape after being stretched: *She wore an elastic swimsuit.* (*fig*) *Lions move with elastic grace.* **2** not stiff or fixed; able to be changed to fit all cases: *The club has elastic rules. With his elastic character he will soon be cheerful again.* **in-** [neg]

yielding 1 able to bend; not stiff or fixed **2** likely to agree with or give in to others: *He has a yielding character and will soon change his mind.*

springy [Wa1] coming back easily to the original shape: *It was a springy old wood floor.* **-ily** [adv] **-iness** [U]

N269 *verbs & nouns* : **bending, stretching, and slanting**

[ALSO ⇒ N295]

bend 1 [T1;I0] to (cause to) be forced into or out of a curve or angle: *He bent the wire. The wire bent easily.* (*fig*) *He is very firm about it: I cannot bend him. He will not bend.* **2** [X9] (*fig*) to direct (one's efforts) to: *He bent his mind to the job.* **bent on** determined to do: *He is bent on becoming a doctor/going to India.*

stretch 1 [T1] to (cause to) become wider or longer: *You must stretch these new shoes by wearing them. My wool coat stretched when I washed it.* **2** [T1] to cause to reach full length or width: *Try to stretch the rope between these two poles.* (*fig*) *You are stretching my patience to the limit. This is a job which stretches one/one's powers.* **3** [L9] to spread out: *The waters of the sea stretched round them as far as the eye could see.* **4** [I0] to be elastic: *Rubber bands stretch.* **5** [T1] to cause to go beyond a limit (of rule or time): *Let's stretch the rules and leave work early. He stretched the lesson for five minutes.* **6** [L9] to last: *His visits stretched over three months.* **7** [T1;I0] (*out*) to straighten (the limbs or body) to full length: *She got out of bed and stretched. He stretched his arms above his head. The cat stretched out in front of the fire.* **8** [C *usu sing*] an act of stretching: *He gave the rubber a good stretch* (= he stretched it well). **stretch one's legs** to have a walk, esp after sitting for a time **stretch a point,** *also infml* **stretch it a bit** to make a rule, remark, etc mean what one wants it to: *We'll stretch a point and let the baby travel free, though you should have bought him a ticket. Is that true? Aren't you stretching it a bit?*

yield [I0] to bend, break, etc, because of a strong force: *The table is beginning to yield under that heavy weight.*

give [I0] *infml* to yield: *The table began to give under his weight.*

spring 1 [L9;T1] to move or work suddenly, esp as if moving under force, jumping hard, etc:

The cat sprang on the bird. He sprang out of bed when he saw what time it was. He sprang the trap and caught the animal. (*fig*) *They are always springing surprises on us.* **2** [C] an act of springing: *The cat's sudden spring caught the bird by surprise.* **3** [C] something, esp a piece of metal, that springs back into position after being pushed, pulled, bent, etc: *The car has good springs. The bed has springs.* **4** [U] the power to spring back: *That piece of wood has little spring in it.* (*fig*) *He was unhappy, and lost the spring in his step* (= in the way he walked).

flex [T1] to bend repeatedly before use so as to make smooth and loose in movement; to bend and move (one of one's limbs, muscles, etc), so as to stretch and loosen esp in preparation for work: *The gardeners flexed their muscles and began to dig.*

slope 1 [Wv4;T1: (*up, down*)] to (cause to) be at an angle from lower to higher: *The road sloped steeply down. He sloped the roof steeply so that rain water would run off. The house had a sloping roof.* **2** [C] a surface, line, etc that slopes: *They walked up the slope. He stood on the slopes of the mountains and looked down. The surface was at a slope; it wasn't flat.* **3** [U] the amount by which a surface, line, etc slopes: *The roof should have plenty of slope, so that rain water can run off.*

slant 1 [Wa4,5;I0;T1] to (cause to) be at an angle from straight up and down or across; (cause to) slope: *a slanting roof; The roof line slants upwards from left to right.* **2** [T1 *usu pass*] (*fig*) to express (facts, a report, etc) in a way favourable to a particular opinion: *The news of the meeting was slanted to make it seem that an agreement was reached.* **3** [S] a slanting position: *The wall seemed to be built at a slant.*

incline *fml* **1** [I0; T1] *esp tech* to (cause to) slope: *The road inclines at a steep angle. Incline the mirror at a better angle.* **2** [T1] to move downward: *He inclined his head in greeting.* **incline** [C] a slope: *The vehicle began to roll down the incline.* **inclination 1** [U] the act of inclining or state of being inclined: *The inclination of the mirror was 15°* (= 15 degrees). **2** [C] an act or degree of inclining: *She greeted us with a slight inclination of the head. The mirror was at an inclination of 15°.*

crook 1 [T1;I0] to (cause to) bend: *She crooked her arm to make carrying the parcel easier. The river crooks to the right just below the bridge.* **2** [C] a bend or curve: *a crook in the river; She carried the parcel in the crook of her arm.* **crooked** [B] not straight; twisted; bent: *You've hung that picture on the wall crooked; try to straighten it. His fingers are crooked because he hurt his hand in an accident.*

N270 *adjectives* : **tight** [Wa1;B]

tight 1 fitting closely and not easy to put on, take off, move, loosen, open, etc: *These trousers are too tight; I can hardly get them on. The top of* *the bottle was tight; he couldn't get it off.* **2** stretched: *Is the rope tight?—Yes; it's tight enough.* **-ly** [adv] **-ness** [U]

taut tightly drawn; stretched as tight as possible: *Pull the string taut! The rope was taut.* **-ly** [adv] **-ness** [U]

N271 adjectives : not tight [Wa1;B]

slack 1 (of a rope, wire, etc) not pulled tight **2** not firm; weak; loose: *slack laws/control* **3** not properly careful or quick: *be slack in doing one's duty* **4** not busy or active: *Winter is the slack season at most hotels. Business is slack just now.* **-ly** [adv] **-ness** [U]

loose 1 not firmly fixed; not tight; not strong: *This pole is coming loose and will soon fall over.* **2** (of clothes) not fitting tightly, esp because too big **3** made of parts that are not tight together: *a loose weave/soil* **4** not bound together, as with string or in a box: *I bought these sweets loose.* **5** not fastened, tied up, shut up, etc; free from control: *The animals broke loose and left the field. The dog is too dangerous to be left loose. I have one loose hand but the other is tied.* **6** not exact: *That word has many loose meanings. He is a loose thinker.* **7** *deprec* having many sexual adventures: *She is a loose woman.* **8** *deprec* not well controlled: *She has a loose tongue and will tell everybody.* **9** careless, awkward, or inexact: *Loose play lost them the match.* **10** (of the bowels) not able to control the waste matter inside **11** not given a fixed purpose: *loose money.* **at a loose end** having nothing to do **cut loose** to break away from a group of condition: *After the quarrel he cut loose from his family and went abroad.*

N272 verbs : relating to hardness, tightness, etc [I0; T1: (up)]

harden to (cause to) become hard: *The snow hardened into ice.* (*fig*) *His face hardened with anger when he heard the bad news.*

stiffen to (cause to) become stiff: *He stiffened when someone came up behind him.*

firm to (cause to) become firm: *The ground was soft after the rain but now it has firmed up.*

soften to (cause to) become soft: *They softened the substance by heating it.*

tighten to (cause to) become tight: *He tightened the ropes.* (*fig*) *Her face tightened with fear.*

tauten to (cause to) become taut: *The rope tautened.*

clench to close tightly: *She clenched her teeth. Her teeth clenched.*

N273 verbs : relating to slackness

slacken [I0; T1: (off, up)] to (cause to) become slack: *They slackened (off) the ropes.* (*fig*) *The rain slackened off* (=grew less). (*fig*) *You should slacken up; you're working too hard.*

loosen [I0; T1: (off, up)] to (cause to) become loose: *The rope slowly loosened itself as the boat moved back and forward. He tried to loosen up (his body) by doing exercises.*

loose [T1] *rare* **1** to let loose; untie; make free **2** to free from control: *The wine loosed his tongue.*

N274 adjectives : even, smooth, and steady [B]

even [Wa2] **1** (of surfaces) having no point or part higher or lower than any other: *The wood is nice and even.* **2** (of qualities, etc) being the same everywhere: *The temperature of all the rooms is even/an even 20°.* **un-** [neg] **-ly** [adv]: *All the rooms are heated evenly.* **-ness** [U]

smooth [Wa1] **1** having an even surface without sharply raised or lowered places, points, lumps, etc; not rough: *The sea looked calm and smooth. It's a smooth road. The car's tyres were worn smooth. She has a lovely smooth skin.* (*fig*) *They tried to make the way smooth to reaching an agreement.* **2** even in movement without sudden changes or breaks: *He brought the car to a smooth stop. It's a calm day; we should have a smooth crossing to France. They are very smooth dancers.* **3** (of a liquid mixture) without lumps; evenly thick: *Beat until smooth.* **4** (of a taste) not bitter or sour; pleasant in the mouth: *a smooth pipe tobacco.* **5** (*fig*) *often deprec* very or too pleasant, polite, or untroubled in manner; avoiding or not showing difficulties: *What smooth manners he has! Distrust a very smooth salesman. It was a smooth argument, but he didn't accept it.* **-ly** [adv] **-ness** [U]

consistent always acting, behaving, thinking, etc in the same way; not changing easily: *He is a very consistent person; he doesn't change his opinions much. Try to be more consistent in what you do.* **in-** [neg] **-ly** [adv] **consistence, consistency** [U]

steady [Wa1] **1** firm; sure in position or movement; not shaking: *Hold that candle steady. It was a delicate job needing a steady hand/steady nerves. It isn't the steadiest of tables, so don't sit on it!* **2** moving or developing evenly; not wildly varying: *He kept up a steady speed. We need steady growth in industry. A steady east wind blew.* **3** not changing: *He has a steady income/job. Share prices closed steady* (=at the same prices as yesterday). **4** dependable; of good habits; not silly; serious: *She needs to marry someone steady.* **un-** [neg] **-ily** [adv] **-iness** [U]

stable [Wa2] firmly fixed; not easily moved or changed; very steady: *That country doesn't have a stable government. Their marriage is stable.* **un-** [neg] **stability** [U] the state of being stable: *The stability of their government/marriage is not as certain as it once was.* **in-** [neg]

stolid (of persons) steady; showing no excitement when strong feelings might be expected **-ly** [adv] **-ness** [U]

N275 *adjectives* : **not smooth and steady** [B]

rough [Wa1] **1** having an uneven surface; not smooth: *The cat had a rough tongue. It was a dog with a rough coat. The rough road made the cart shake.* **2** (of weather, the sea or a sea journey) stormy and violent; not calm: *There were rough winds and it was a very rough crossing to France.* **3** *not always derog* (of people or behaviour) not gentle, tender, or polite; using force; (typical of someone) strong and simple: *He has a certain rough humour. This car has had a lot of rough treatment. They play rough games; it's a rough school. Play nicely and don't be rough!* **4** (of food and living conditions) not delicate; simple; suitable only for strong people: *It was a rough but plentiful dinner with a rough country wine. Life was rough out in the Wild West when I was a boy.* **5** (of plans, calculations, etc) not (yet) in detail; unpolished; not in the finished form: *It's just a rough drawing/a first rough attempt/a very rough translation.* **6** [Wa5;A] (of paper) for making the first attempts at drawing or writing something: *Try it on a bit of rough paper.* **7** (of sounds) not gentle or tuneful: *He has a rough voice.* **8** *infml* unfortunate and hard to bear: *She has had a very rough time. What rough luck!* **-ly** [adv] **-ness** [U] **rough on** *infml* unfortunate for (someone): *It's a bit rough on him, losing his toe!* **rough and ready**, *also* **rough-and-ready** simple and without comfort; rough: *The living conditions were a bit rough and ready, as there were no beds.*

coarse [Wa1] **1** (esp of cloth, substances, etc) very rough esp to touch: *Jute is a strong coarse cloth.* **2** having large pieces: *This sugar is pretty coarse. Some kinds of sand are coarser than others.* **3** (*fig*) *usu deprec* not polite, esp in speech: *What coarse manners he has!* **-ly** [adv] **-ness** [U]

crude [Wa1] **1** in a raw or natural state; unprepared; untreated: *He sells crude oil/crude rubber. We must examine the crude facts closely before we can understand their meaning.* **2** showing or lacking grace, education, or delicacy of feeling: *What crude behaviour/crude people!* **3** not skilfully made, done or finished: *It was just a crude shelter in the forest. Don't use such crude methods. They made a crude attempt to kill the King.* **-ly** [adv] **-ness** [U]

bumpy [Wa1] **1** with many lumps: *It was a bumpy road and we had a bumpy ride.* **2** *infml* with parts that are high (or good) and parts that are low (or bad): *We've had rather a bumpy time (of it) since the war.* **3** (of music, poetry, etc) with uneven time: *bumpy dance music* **-ily** [adv] **-iness** [U]

rugged [Wa2] **1** rough and uneven; not regular in form: *The countryside was rugged and mountainous. The man had a rugged face.* **2** strong; able to accept difficulties: *He is a pretty rugged person.*

jagged rough and sharp: *He cut his hand on a jagged piece of glass. It was a land of jagged mountains.*

serrated jagged, like the teeth of a saw [⇒ H142]: *The piece of metal had a serrated edge.*

N276 *verbs* : **smoothing and steadying, etc**

steady [T1;I0] to make or become steady, settled, regular or less changing: *He started to fall, then steadied himself. He needs a wife to steady him. A cup of tea will steady your nerves. Share prices steadied in weak trading.*

stabilize, -ise [T1;I0] *esp tech* to (cause to) become firm, steady or unchanging: *The ship stabilized so as to move more smoothly on the water. After this rise, prices may begin to stabilize.* **-ization, -isation** [U]

even out [v adv: I0;T1] to (cause to) become level or equal: *Prices should even out. We must even things out. Even out the differences between the parties.*

even up [v adv: T1] to make (something, or two things) equal: *If you two sit at the other table, that will even up the groups. I'll pay for the taxi, to even things up.*

smooth [T1] **1** [(*out, down*)] to make smooth(er): *She smoothed out a tablecloth. He smoothed down the boards before painting. They tried to smooth the way for an agreement.* **2** [(*away*)] to remove (roughness) from a surface: *It's a face cream that claims to smooth away wrinkles in the skin.*

roughen [I0;T1] to (cause to) become rough: *The cold wind roughened her skin.*

coarsen [I0;T1] to (cause to) become coarse

N277 *adjectives* : **comfortable and convenient** [B]

comfortable pleasant to be, live, sit, move, etc in or on; taking away pain, worry, etc: *She has a very comfortable home. He sat in the most comfortable chair. This is a nice comfortable car to travel in. He was still in pain but had quite a comfortable night.* **un-** [*neg*] **-bly** [adv]

convenient that is not difficult to do; not causing difficulty: *Come at the time that is most convenient to you. I find it convenient to live just outside the town.* **in-** [*neg*] **-ly** [adv] **-nce** [U;C]: *I don't want to be an inconvenience to anyone.*

Actions and positions

N290 *verbs* : **standing and sitting**

stand **1** [I0] to be upright on the feet without moving: *He stood near the door. Who is that person standing over there?* **2** [T1] to cause to be upright: *Stand the wood in that corner. He stood the child on a chair.* **3** [L9] to be: *Every man there stood over six feet tall. (fig) As things stand, we can't win the war. Their profit for the year stands at £100,000.* **4** [L9] to be in or have a position: *The house stood near the river. Where do these books go?—They stand on that shelf.* **5** [I∅] (fig) not to change: *Can I go?—No; I said you couldn't go, and my decision still stands.* **6** [L9] to go in a stated direction and stand: *He stood back in order to see better. Stand out of my way! Stand aside! He stood by, waiting to help if needed. They were sitting, but when he came in they stood up* (= got out of their chairs; rose to their feet).

sit 1 [L9] to rest in a position with the upper body upright and supported at the bottom of the back, as on a chair or other seat: *They all sat keeping warm by the fire. If you can't find a seat you'll have to sit on the floor. He sat at his desk working.* **2** [L9; X9: esp *down*] to (cause to) go into this position; (cause to) take a seat: *Sit down, please; sit in that chair there. She sat the baby (down) on the grass.* **3** [I∅] (of an animal) to be on or go into a position with the tail end of the body resting on a surface **4** [L9] to have a position in an official body: *He sits on several committees.* **5** [I∅] (of a body) to have one or more meetings: *The court sat until all the arguments for both sides had been heard.* **6** [I∅] to lie; rest; have a place (and not move): *He left the papers sitting on the desk. The books were sitting unread on the shelf. The village sat on the side of a hill. The coat doesn't sit well* (= fits badly) *on you.* **7** [I∅ (*for*)] to have one's picture painted or photographed; pose: *Please sit for a photograph/sit for your portrait.* **8** [T1] *BrE* to take (a written examination): *She will sit her A-levels next year.* **9** [T1] to keep one's seat on (a horse) **10** [I∅] (of a hen) to cover eggs to bring young birds to life: *Don't go near the hens while they're sitting.*

squat [I∅] to sit on a surface with legs drawn fully up or under the body, esp balancing on the front of the feet

kneel [I∅ (*on, down*)] to go down or remain on the knee(s): *She went into the church, knelt (down) and began to pray. I saw her kneeling on the floor of the church.*

N291 *verbs, etc* : **rising and getting up**

rise 1 [I∅] to go up; get higher: *The river is rising after the rain. Smoke rose from the factory chimneys. Her voice rose higher and higher with excitement. New factories have risen on the edge of the town.* **2** [I∅] *fml* to get out of bed; get up: *She rises before it is light.* **3** [I∅ (*up*)] to stand up from lying, kneeling, or sitting: *He rose from his knees. She rose to greet her guests. I cannot rise because of my broken leg.* **4** [I∅] *fml* (of a group of people) to end a meeting: *We/The court will now rise for dinner.* **5** [I∅] (fig) (of price, amount, temperature, etc) to

increase, get higher: *Tea/The price of tea has risen by 5 pence/has risen to 30 pence.* **6** [Wv4;I∅] (fig) (of land) to slope upward: *The road rises steeply from the village.* **7** [Wv6;L9] (fig) (esp of a river) to begin: *The River Rhine rises in Switzerland. The quarrel rose from/out of a misunderstanding.* **8** [Wv6;L9] to show above the surroundings: *Trees rose over the roof-tops. A high mountain rises between the two valleys.* **9** [I∅] to come up to the surface of a liquid: *The fish are rising; perhaps we'll catch one.* **10** [L9 esp *from, to*] (fig) to move up in rank: *I hope to rise in my profession. He rose from the rank of captain to the rank of general.* **11** [I∅] (of uncooked bread) to swell: *The bread won't rise properly.* **12** [I∅] (fig) (of feelings) to become more cheerful: *My spirits rose when I saw the result.* **13** [I∅] (fig) (of wind or storms) to get stronger **14** [C *usu sing & often in comb*] an act, occasion or result of rising, becoming more: *There has been a sharp rise in the temperature today. The rise in the number of road accidents worries us. What a beautiful sunrise!*

get up [v adv T1; I∅] *not fml* **1** to (cause to) rise from bed in the morning **2** to (cause to) leave one's bed after illness **3** to rise from a seat, floor, etc: *She got up from her seat. The child fell down and then got up again.*

arise [I∅] **1** *fml, old use & poet* to get up, as from sitting or lying; stand up: *'I will arise and go now, and go to Innisfree'* (W. B. Yeats) **2** *rare* to move or go upwards: *We watched the smoke arise from the houses.* **3** (fig) to come into being or into notice; happen; appear: *Problems will arise as we do the work. A strong wind arose and blew our boat on to the rocks.*

pick oneself up *infml* to get up, esp after falling: *After he fell off his horse, he picked himself up and said that he wasn't hurt.*

rear [I∅] (esp of an animal like a horse) to rise up on the back legs: *His horse reared.*

N292 *verbs & nouns* : **falling, etc**

fall 1 [I∅] to descend or go down freely, as by weight or loss of balance: *The clock fell off the shelf. It fell three feet. He fell into the lake.* **2** [I∅ (*over, down*)] to come down from a standing position, esp suddenly: *He fell to his knees and begged forgiveness. Five trees fell over in the storm. She slipped and fell (down).* **3** [I∅ (*on*)] (fig) to come or happen, as if by descending: *Night fell quickly. A silence fell on the room. His eyes fell on the body. A light fell on the wall. Christmas falls on a Friday this year.* **4** [I∅] to become lower in level, degree or quality: *The temperature fell 4°* (= became 4 degrees lower). *Their voices fell to a whisper.* **5** [L7, 9] (fig) to pass into a new state or condition; become: *He fell asleep/fell in love. The book was old and soon fell apart.* **6** [L9] to hang loosely: *Her hair falls over her shoulders/down her back.* **7** [I∅] (fig) **a** to be defeated or captured: *The city fell (to the enemy).* **b** to lose office or a high position: *The government has fallen.* **8** [L9] to slope in a downward direction: *The land falls towards the river/away from the farm.* **9** [L9] to drop down wounded or dead, esp to die in battle: *A prayer was said in memory of those who fell in the war/the fallen. Six tigers fell to the hunter's gun.* **10** [I0] (of the face) to take on a look of sadness, disappointment, shame, etc esp suddenly: *Her face fell when I told her the news.* **11** [C] an act, occasion or result of falling: *He hurt himself in a fall from his horse. There was a fall of snow last night. (fig) There has been a fall in sales/in the price of oil.* **fall flat** to fail to produce the desired effect or result: *His jokes fell flat and amused nobody.* **fall short** to fail to reach a desired result, standard, etc: *We hoped to build 100 houses this year but we have fallen short (of our aim).*

trip 1 [I0; T1 (*over, up*)] to (cause to) catch one's foot and lose one's balance: *The child ran, tripped and fell down. The fisherman tripped over a root and fell into the river. The mat tripped me up and I fell flat on my face. The boy put his leg out to trip the girl.* **2** [I0; T1; (*up*)] to (cause to) make a mistake as in a statement or behaviour: *If you hadn't tripped over the spelling of 'their' and 'they're' you'd have got full marks. This lawyer always tries to trip witnesses up by asking confusing questions.* **3** [T1 (*up*)] to catch or trip in a mistake: *The lawyer tripped the witness with a clever question.* **4** [L9] to move or dance with quick light steps: *The little girl tripped down the path.* **5** [T1] to start or set free (a switch, spring, etc): *A thief climbing in through the window tripped the wire and set the bells ringing.*

collapse 1 [I0; (T1)] to (cause to) fall down or inwards suddenly: *The roof collapsed during the storm. The weight of snow collapsed the roof.* **2** [I0; T1] **a** (of an object) to fold into a shape that takes up less space: *This table collapses, so I can store it easily when I'm not using it.* **b** to cause (an object) to fold into a shape that takes up less space: *Collapse the table and put it away, please.* **3** [I0; T1] *med* **a** (of a lung or blood vessel) to fall into a flattened mass: *We must take him to hospital at once; his right lung seems to have collapsed and he can't breathe.* **b** to cause (a lung or blood vessel) to fall into a flattened mass: *The doctors had to collapse her right lung to save her life.* **4** [I0] to fall helpless or unconscious: *This man has collapsed; call for the doctor!* **5** [I0] (*fig*) to fail suddenly and completely: *All opposition to the government has collapsed. The empire collapsed in 1918.* **6** [U] the state of collapsing or having collapsed: *The collapse of the new building surprised everyone. (fig) I have just heard about the collapse of his business/all his plans. He was in a state of collapse after he heard the bad news.* **7** [S] an act or occasion of collapsing: *He suffered a collapse and died.*

N293 verbs, etc : raising and lowering

raise [T1] **1** to push or move upward: *Raise the window. Raise the lid of the box. He raised his hat. They tried to raise the wrecked ship from the bottom of the sea.* **2** to move (a part of the body) upward, often as a sign: *She raised her finger to her lips as a sign for silence. The boy raised his hand to show that he could answer the teacher's question.* **3** to set in an upright position: *He raised the fallen child to its feet.* **4** to cause to rise: *The wind raised the fallen leaves from the ground.* **5** [(*to*)] to make higher in amount, degree, size, etc: *They want to raise the rent/your pay/the standard of English.* **6** to collect together: *They hope to raise an army/raise enough money for a holiday.* **7** *esp AmE* to produce, cause to grow or increase and look after (living things): *Let's raise a family/raise horses/raise wheat.* **8** to bring up and talk about (a subject): *There's an important point I want to raise.* **9** *fml* to build (something high and noticeable): *He raised a monument to his dear father.* **10** to make (a noise): *The men raised a cheer/a shout.* **11** to cause people to make (a noise): *He told a funny story so as to raise a laugh.* **12** to cause people to have (feelings): *His long absence raised doubts/fears about his safety.* **13** to cause to end (an official rule forbidding something): *Raise the embargo* (= order forbidding movement of ships or trade). **14** to bring back to life (a dead person): *Jesus was said to raise people from the dead.* **15** to make a higher bid (= statement of what one expects to win) than (a player in a game of cards): *I'll raise you!*

lift 1 [T1] *less fml* to raise, esp of heavier things or separate objects: *I can't lift it; it's too heavy to lift. He lifted the child up. Lift it onto the table.* **2** [I0] to rise up: *After the clouds lifted we could see the mountains. When the mist lifted I could see for miles.* **3** [T1; I0] *esp BrE infml* to steal: *He was caught lifting (things).* **4** [T1] *not fml* to take (something from some other place) and use as one's own: *Did you lift this bit (of your story) from a book, or is it your own work?* **lifter** [C *in comb*] a person who lifts: *He is a weight-lifter* (= he lifts heavy objects for sport). *She is a shoplifter* (= she steals things from shops).

hoist [T1] to raise up by force, esp when using ropes on board ship: *He hoisted it over his shoulder. The sailors hoisted the flag. They hoisted sail. The goods were hoisted aboard.*

lower 1 [T1; I0] to move or let down in height: *He lowered the box into the big hole.* **2** [T1; I0] to make or become smaller in amount, price, degree, strength, etc: *Lower the price/your voice.* **3** [T1; V3] to bring (someone, esp oneself) down in rank, worth, or opinion, as by doing something unworthy: *By stealing from his father he has lowered himself for ever. I wouldn't lower myself to speak to him.*

let down [v adv; T1] *infml* to lower (def **1**): *They let him slowly down into the water/hole.*

N294 *verbs, etc* : **dropping**

drop 1 [I∅ (*down*)] to fall, esp suddenly or straight: *The shot bird dropped like a stone. The bomb dropped on their house.* **2** [T1] to allow to fall: *She dropped the book on the floor. They dropped bombs on the city.* **3** [I∅] (of wind, temperature, etc) to fall; become less: *The temperature has dropped 2 degrees. The wind is dropping now.* **4** [T1] (*fig*) *esp emph* to stop doing, meeting, etc, esp suddenly: *He has dropped smoking. She wants to drop history from her course. He dropped all his old friends when he became famous.* **5** [C *usu sing*] a distance or movement straight down: *It's a long drop from the top of the building to the street. It was a drop of 100 feet. There was a sudden drop in the temperature.*

let ... fall *not fml* to drop, esp by not doing anything else: *He let the cup fall on the floor; I don't know why; he could have caught it all right.* (*fig*) *She let it fall* (= told us informally) *that he was coming soon.*

let go *not fml* to stop holding and therefore to drop: *He let go the cup and it got broken.*

dip 1 [I∅; T1] to (cause to) drop slightly, perhaps just for a moment: *Grain prices dipped yesterday. The sun dipped below the western sea. You should dip the car's headlights* (= lights at the front) *when you meet another car at night. The soldier dipped the flag as he passed the Queen.* **2** [T1 (*in, into*)] to put (something) in/into a liquid for a moment and then take out: *dip one's hand into the water* **3** [T1] to put (an animal) quickly into a chemical liquid that kills insects: *dip the sheep* **4** [T1] to put (a garment) into a liquid (**dye**) to change the colour **5** [C] an act or occasion of dipping: *There was a dip in grain prices yesterday.* **6** [C *often in comb*] the liquid into which animals or garments are dipped: *sheepdip; blue dip*

N295 *verbs & nouns* : **bending and leaning**

[ALSO ⇒ N269]

bend 1 [L9; (T1)] to (cause to) move or slope (all or part of one's body, a body, etc) away from an upright position: *She bent over to look at the stones. He was bent (down) with age.* **2** [C] an act of bending, esp part of the body

bow [I∅] **1** to bend the upper part of the body forward, esp as a sign of greeting, respect or worship: *He bowed and asked us to enter the house.* **2** [C] an act of bowing: *He gave/made a low bow and asked us to enter the house.* **bowed** [F (*with*)] *esp lit* bent: *He was bowed with age/illness/troubles. His back was bowed (with hard work).*

buckle 1 [I∅] (*esp of metal*) to bend under a weight: *This steel won't buckle; it's too strong.* **2** [C *usu sing*] a result of buckling: *That piece of metal has a bad buckle in it.*

warp 1 [T1; I∅] (*esp of wood*) to (cause to) become bent or twisted out of the natural shape: *The sun warped the wood. The wood warped in the sun.* (*fig*) *His evil life has warped his character; he has a warped mind.* **2** [C *usu sing*] a twist or bend: *This wood has a bad warp in it.*

lean 1 [I∅] to be in a position that is not upright; slope: *The wall was leaning slightly.* **2** [L9] to bend (from the waist): *He leaned forward/down/over to hear what she said.* **3** [L9] (*against, on*) to support or rest oneself in a bent or sloping position: *He leaned against the table. Lean on me till you feel better.* **4** [X9] to rest (something) somewhere: *Lean it on/against the wall.* **lean over backwards (to)** to make every possible effort (to): *He leaned over backwards to help them.*

tilt 1 [Wv4; T1; I∅] to (cause to) slope as by raising one end: *Tilt the barrel to make sure it's empty! With each wave the sinking ship tilted over further. The table tilted and all the plates slid on to the floor.* **2** [U; S] angle of tilting: *The house seemed to be built at a tilt. The tilt of his hat made him look funny.*

duck [I∅; T1] to bend, esp down, quickly to avoid being hit by something, seen by someone, etc: *He ducked his head/ducked behind a low wall.*

bank [I∅; T1] to (cause to) bend, turn or incline sideways while turning: *The plane banked sharply before landing/to avoid hitting the building. We thought he was going to hit the building, but he banked the plane at the last moment.*

N296 *verbs & nouns* : **shaking and swinging**

shake 1 [I∅; T1; X7] to (cause to) move quickly up and down and to and fro: *She was shaking with laughter/anger/fear. The wet dog shook himself. He shook his hands free from the rope around them. The medicine is to be shaken before use. The angry crowd shook their fists* (= closed hands) *at the police.* **2** [X9] to put or remove by this kind of motion: *He shook salt on his food. She shook the sand out of her shoes.* **3** [I∅; T1] to take and hold (someone's right hand) in one's own for a moment, sometimes moving it up and down, as a sign of greeting, goodbye, agreement, or pleasure (*esp in the phr* **shake hands** (**with someone**)): *The two men shook hands (with each other)/shook each other's hands/shook each other by the hand.* (*infml*) *If you agree, let's shake (on it).* **4** [T1 (*off*)] *not fml* to get rid of; free oneself from, escape from: *If you can shake your friend (off) I'd like to speak to you alone. The thief ran fast and shook off the policeman running after him.* **5** [T1 (*up*) *often pass*] to trouble the mind or feelings of; upset: *She was badly shaken (up) by the accident/by the bad news.* **6** [T1] to make less certain;

weaken: *He has a faith in God which he says nothing can shake.* **7** [C] an act of shaking: *Give it a shake.* **shake one's head** to move one's head from side to side to answer 'no' or show disapproval

swing 1 [T1: I∅] to (cause to) move backwards and forwards or round and round, from a fixed point once or regularly: *The mirror swung round. They were swinging their arms.* **2** [I∅] to ride on a swing (= a seat with ropes, hanging from a support) **3** [T1] to wave (something) around in the air, esp as a weapon: *He swung his stick, hitting his enemy a crushing blow.* **4** [I∅ (*for*)] *infml* to be hanged to death, as a punishment: *He'll swing (for that/it/his crime).* **5** [L9] to turn quickly: *He swung away from the rest and went home alone.* **6** [L9] to change greatly, once or regularly: *She swung from happiness to tears. The value of the pound swung downwards.* **7** [X9; L9] **a** to move (oneself) while hanging from a fixed point: *They were swinging on the gate.* **b** to move (oneself) forward from one fixed point to another, by a movement through the air: *They swung over the wall. They swung themselves down from the top of the car.* **8** [C] an act of swinging **in full swing** fully active: *The work was in full swing when we arrived.*

sway 1 [T1: I∅] to (cause to) swing from side to side: *She swayed the baby's cradle* (= bed) *with her foot until the baby went to sleep. The dancers swayed to the music.* **2** [X9; L9] to (cause to) swing to one side: *The weight of the passengers swayed the car to the right. The ship was swaying over.* **3** [T1] (*fig*) to influence: *When choosing a job don't be swayed by false promises of future high earnings. Don't let him sway you* (*from your decision*). **4** [S] a swaying movement

reel 1 [L9] to walk unsteadily as if drunk: *He came reeling up the street.* **2** [I∅ (*back*)] to step away suddenly and unsteadily, as after a blow or shock: *When she hit him he reeled (back) and almost fell.* **3** [I∅] to be shaken in the mind: *Numbers always make my head reel.* **4** [I∅] to seem to go round and round: *The room reeled before my eyes.*

N297 *verbs & nouns* : **turning and twisting**

turn 1 [I∅; T1] to (cause to) move round a fixed point: *The wheel turned slowly. Turn the hands of the clock until they point to 9 o'clock.* **2** [I∅; T1] to (cause to) move round or partly round: *He turned the key in the lock. The handle turned and the door began to open.* **3** [T1] to do or perform by moving round a fixed point: *She turned a neat circle on the ice.* **4** [I∅ (*over*)] to roll from side to side or backwards and forwards: *My husband turned in bed all night; he couldn't sleep because of the heat. The ship pitched and turned in the rough sea.* **5** [I∅; T1] to (cause to) change direction: *He*

turned the car into a narrow street. The car turned into the hotel entrance. The ball turned sharply when it hit the ground. **6** [T1] to go round: *The car turned the corner.* **7** [L9] to direct oneself in a particular direction: *Turn right here and left at the end of the street. The little girl turned round and ran to her father. She turned away and wept.* **8** [I∅ (*round*)] to bend round; look round: *He turned and waved.* **9** [X9] to point, set or direct in a particular direction: *The police turned their guns on the marching workers.* **10** [X9; L9] **a** to cause (one's attention, interest, mind, etc) to be directed towards or away from something: *He turned his thoughts to home.* **b** (of one's attention, interest, mind, etc) to be directed towards or away from something: *His attention turned to the pretty young girl.* **11** [T1] to hurt (one's ankle [⇒ B43]) by twisting: *She turned her ankle falling downstairs.* **12** [T1; I∅] to (cause to) feel uneasy, sick, etc: *Fatty food turns my stomach. My stomach turns at the sight of blood.* **13** [Wv5, 6; T1] to become; reach; pass (a certain age, time, amount, etc): *a man turned 40. It's just turned 3 o'clock* (= is just after 3 o'clock). **14** [T1] to get by buying or selling; gain: *He turned a small profit.* **15** [T1] to plough (the soil, field, etc): *Has this field been turned this year?* **16** [Wv5; T1] to form or express gracefully: *That's a nicely-turned phrase.* **17** [X9 esp *away, out*] to cause to go; send; drive: *She turned him out from her door. Her father would turn her out if he knew she took drugs.* **18** [X9] to throw into disorder or confusion: *The robbers had turned the room upside down.* **19** [T1; I∅] to (cause to) change position so that the bottom becomes the top, the hidden side uncovered, the inner side the outer, etc: *He turned the page. The page won't turn; it seems to be stuck. He turned the meat over in the pan.* **20** [C] an act of turning; single movement completely round a fixed point: *One turn of the key and the door should open.* **21** [C] a change of direction: *a turn in the road/river* **22** [*the* R (*of*)] a point of change in time: *at the turn of the century* **23** [S] a movement or development in direction: *The conversation took an interesting turn. The sick man took a turn for the worse last night. That's an unusual turn of events* (= thing to happen). **24** [S] a particular style, habit, tendency: *He's got an artistic turn so he's going to art college.* **25** [C9] a deed or action with the stated effect: *He did me a good turn but she has done me several bad turns.*

rotate 1 [I∅] to move round a centre: *The earth rotates on its axis* (= a supposed line through the centre on which it turns). **2** [T1] to change from one state to another in regular order: *He rotates his men from one place to another.* **rotation** [U] the act of rotating movement round a centre; regular change **in rotation** one thing or person regularly after another **rotary** [Wa5; B] turning like a wheel: *rotary action*

twirl 1 [I∅; T1] to (cause to) turn round and

round quickly: *The secretary twirled the pencil round in her fingers.* **2** [I∅; T1] to (cause to) curl: *His hair twirled right round his ears. She twirled his hair round her fingers.* **3** [C] an act of twirling: *He gave the stick a twirl.*

whirl 1 [X9; I∅] to (cause to) move round and round very fast: *The dancers whirled. It was picked up by the wind and whirled into the air.* **2** [X9; L9] to (cause to) move away in a hurry: *The car whirled them off to the wedding. The days whirled past.* **3** [I∅] (*fig*) to give the feeling of turning very fast: *His senses were whirling. Her thoughts whirled in her terror.* **4** [S] The act or sensation of whirling (esp in the phr **in a whirl**): *My head's in a whirl: I must sit down and think.* **5** [S] (*fig*) a very fast movement: *What a whirl of activity!*

revolve 1 [I∅] *fml & tech* to turn, esp in a circle: *The wheel slowly revolved on its axis* (= centre point). *The earth revolves round the sun.* **2** [T1] (*fig*) to think about: *He revolved the matter in his head/mind.* **revolution 1** [U] movement in a circle: *He described the revolution of the earth round the sun.* **2** [C] *also infml* **rev** an example of this: (*tech*) *The wheel described a full revolution* (=turned once on its axis). *The wheel was turning at 50 revolutions a minute/per minute.*

spin 1 [I∅; T1] to (cause to) revolve very quickly: *The dancer spun on his toes. He spun the wheel* (*hard*). **2** [L9] to move in this way: *The ball spun along the ground.* **3** [U; S] the turning movement: *Spin can cause round or pointed objects to move as they turn. He gave the ball a spin.*

round [T1] to go all the way along (something that has a turn or bend in it): *The car rounded the corner smoothly.*

wind 1 [I∅; T1] to (cause to) move by turning here and there: *The river wound through the valley. They wound their way through the forest; there was no straight road to follow.* **2** [X9] **a** to put (something, esp a string, etc) round something else: *She wound the thread round the stick/the cloth round her finger.* **b** to move in this way: *He wound the rope onto the pole. She wound the thread off the reel* (=special short stick for holding wound thread). **3** [T1 (*up*)] (of springs in clocks, etc) to turn tighter and tighter: *He wound* (*up*) *his watch. This clock needs winding/needs to be wound only once a week.*

twist 1 [T1 (*together*)] to wind (a number of threads, stems, etc) together: *He made a rope by twisting threads together. The girls twisted the stems of the flowers together to make a crown for the winner of the games.* **2** [T1] to make (something) by doing this: *He tried to twist a rope out of threads.* **3** [T1] to wind, (rope, hair, etc) around something: *She twisted her hair round her fingers to make it curl.* **4** [I∅] to move in a winding course: *There was a stream twisting across the fields.* **5** [T1] to turn, esp forcefully: *Twist the handle to the right and the box will open.* **6** [L9] to move with a bending, turning movement: *The dancer twisted*

sexily to the music. *The snake twisted across the grass.* **7** [Wv5; T1] to hurt by pulling and turning sharply as in an accident: *I twisted my ankle when I fell downstairs.* **8** [I∅; T1] to (cause to) change shape by bending, curling, turning, etc: *His mouth twisted down at the corners as though he was going to cry. The child twisted the wire into the shape of a star. This wire twists too easily.* **9** [X9, esp *off*] to pull or break off by turning and bending forcefully: *He twisted an apple off the tree. The farmer twisted off a piece of bread to eat with his cheese.* **10** [T1] to change the true or intended meaning of (a statement, words, etc): *The police twisted my words to make me look guilty. They always twist the facts to suit their purpose.* **11** [C] an act of twisting: *I'll give your arm a twist if you don't behave.* **12** [C; (U)] anything such as thread, rope, etc made by twisting two or more lengths together: *It takes a lot of skill to make bread into twists. In his hand he held a twist of wool. a twist of tobacco* (= a roll of tobacco leaves twisted together). **13** [C9] (*fig*) a particular tendency of mind or character: *a criminal twist* **14** [C] a turn: *a road with a lot of twists in it* **15** [C] an unexpected change or development: *a peculiar twist of history*

twiddle [T1] to turn without special purpose or in small ways continuously: *Stop twiddling the knobs* [⇨ H115] *of the radio!* **twiddle one's thumbs** (*esp fig*) to do nothing (except move one thumb round the other when the hands are together)

coil 1 [T1; I∅; (*up*)] to wind or twist (something like a rope) into a spiral (= a number of circles one above the other); to curl round and round: *He coiled* (*up*) *the rope. The snake coiled up and then began to uncoil.* **2** [C] anything like this, esp a length of rope or wire wound in a spiral

curl 1 [I∅; T1; (*up*)] to twist, wind, grow, etc in small tight coils; to bend more or less out of straight: *Her hair curls naturally. The smoke curled up from the fire. The burnt paper had curled* (*up*) *at the edges. The cat curled* (*itself*) *up in a warm place.* (*fig*) *He curled his lip with dislike.* **2** [C] something which curls, esp hair: *She has natural curls. A curl of smoke rose from the fire.* **curly** [Wa1; B] having curls: *Her hair is naturally curly.*

loop 1 [T1] to form, bend, twist or tie into a loop; to put loops in: *He looped the rope into coils.* **2** [T1] to move by means of loops: *The curtains were looped back so that we could look out of the window.* **3** [I∅] to make a loop while moving: *The plane looped several times.*

divert [T1] **1** to cause to turn aside or from one use or direction to another: *They diverted the river to supply water somewhere else. The police diverted traffic from one street to another.* **2** [(*from*)] to turn (a person or a person's attention) away from something; with good or bad result: *A pleasant walk diverted him* (*from his work*) *and he returned to it with a clear mind. A loud noise diverted my attention* (*from cook-*

ing) *and everything was burnt.* **diversion 1** [U] a turning aside from a course, activity or use: *the diversion of a river to supply water somewhere else; the diversion of someone's attention.* **2** [C] something that turns someone's attention away from something else that one does not wish to be noticed: *I claim that your last argument was a diversion to make us forget the main point. That attack was really a diversion to draw the enemy's fire from our main army. We created a diversion.*

N298 *verbs & nouns* : **shaking and vibrating**

shake 1 [I0; T1; X7] to (cause to) move quickly up and down and to and fro: *The house shook when the bomb exploded. The explosion shook the house.* **2** [X9] to put or remove by this kind of motion: *He shook salt on his food. She shook the sand out of her shoes.*

tremble 1 [Wv3,4; I0] to shake uncontrollably as from fear, cold, excitement, etc: *The children trembled with fear when they saw the policeman. As he spoke about the dead king his voice began to tremble and tears came to his eyes.* **2** [Wv3,4; L9 (*for*)]; I3] to feel fear or anxiety; be worried: *The fishermen's wives trembled for their husbands' safety. I tremble to think what's going to happen.* **3** [C] an act of trembling: *There was a tremble in his voice as he told us the bad news.* **in fear and trembling** very much afraid: *The criminals waited in fear and trembling for the judge's decision.*

shiver 1 [I0] to shake, esp (of people) from cold or fear; tremble: *I stood shivering in the wind. Our enemies must be shivering in their shoes* (= very afraid). **2** [C] an act of shivering: *He gave a shiver of fear.*

quiver 1 [Wv4; I0 (*with, at*)] to tremble a little: *I quivered (with pleasure/fear) at the sound.* **2** [T1] (of an animal) to move a delicate part of the body: *The rabbit quivered its nose. The insect quivered its wings.* **3** [C *usu sing*] an act of quivering

quake [I0 (*at, with*)] to shake; tremble esp forcefully: *I quake with fear at the thought!*

shudder 1 [I0 (*at*)]; I3] to shake uncontrollably for a moment, as from fear, cold, or strong dislike; tremble: *She shuddered at the sight of the dead body. I shudder to think what would happen if you slipped and fell.* **2** [C] an act of shuddering: *She turned aside from the sight with a shudder.*

beat 1 [I0; T1] to (cause to) move regularly, esp up and down: *The bird's wings began to beat. The bird beat its wings. His heart stopped beating and he died.* **2** [(*the*) S (*of*)] the act, noise, etc of beating: *He could hear the beat of birds' wings.* [*also* ⇒ B36]

throb 1 [I0] *emph* (of the heart) to beat: *His heart throbbed with excitement.* **2** [I0] to beat strongly; work regularly, esp like the heart: *The ship's engines began to throb. Her head*

was throbbing with pain. **3** [(*the*) S (*of*)] the act of throbbing: *They heard the throb of a ship's engine/of distant drums.*

vibrate [I0] **1** to move from side to side or up and down very quickly and continuously: *The ship's engines caused the whole ship to vibrate.* **2** to make a throbbing sound: *His words vibrated with anger.* **vibration** [U; C] the action or state of vibrating **vibrant** [B] **1** *less common* vibrating, esp so as to produce sound **2** *more common* (*fig*) full of life and therefore interesting, exciting, etc: *vibrant music*

pulse [I0] to beat or move regularly like a pulse [⇒ B36]; *poet* to throb: *His blood was pulsing strongly.*

pulsate [I0] *tech* to beat strongly; to become larger then smaller regularly: *The mass of jelly seemed to pulsate with life.* **pulsation** [U] the act of pulsating: *the pulsation of the heart*

N299 *verbs* : **shaking one's head and nodding**

shake one's head to move the head from side to side to answer 'no' or show disapproval: *He shook his head angrily when I asked him if he was coming.*

shake of the head an act of shaking one's head: *He answered with a shake of the head.*

nod 1 [I0; T1] to bend (one's head) forward and down, esp to show agreement or give a greeting or sign: *She nodded (her head) when she passed me in the street. The president nodded and everyone sat down around the table. He nodded as if to say yes.* **2** [T1] to show in this way: *They nodded their agreement.* **3** [I0] to bend downward or forward: *The flowers were nodding in the wind.* **4** [C] an act of nodding: *When I asked him if he would do it, he gave a friendly nod.*

N300 *verbs & nouns* : **waving and wielding**

wave 1 [I0; T1] to (cause to) move from side to side or up and down: *The flags waved in the wind. The soldiers waved their flags.* **2** [I0] to move the hand in this way, as a signal, greeting, etc: *Wave to your father.* **3** [T1; (D1 (*to*)] to express in this way: *They waved us goodbye* (= waved goodbye to us). **4** [X9] to signal or direct in this way: *The policeman waved the cars on/waved the people back.* **5** [C] an act of waving the hand: *She greeted us with a friendly wave.*

wield [T1] to control the action of: *He wields a lot of power.* (*old use & lit*) *He wielded his sword well.*

brandish [T1] to wave (esp a weapon) about: *The soldier brandished his sword.* (*fig*) *She brandished a newspaper at me and said, 'Have you read this?'*

wag 1 [T1; I∅] **a** (of people and other living creatures) to shake (esp a movable body part) quickly from side to side: *The dog wagged its tail with pleasure. She wagged her finger at me and said, 'Don't come home so late again.'* **b** (of such a body part) to shake from side to side: *The dog's tail wagged.* **2** [C *usu sing*]: *The dog greeted him with a wag of its tail.*

waggle *not fml* **1** [T1; I∅] to wag frequently from side to side: *The dog waggled it tail. The dog's tail waggled. He waggled a piece of paper in his hands.* **2** [C] an act of waggling: *The dog gave a waggle of its tail.*

N301 *verbs* : **hanging, etc**

hang 1 [T1] to fix (something) at the top so that the lower part is free: *Let's hang the curtains. Hang your coat (up) on the hook. She's hanging the washing out.* **2** [L9] to be in such a position: *The curtains hang well. Her hair hangs down to her knees.* **3** [T1 *usu pass*] to show (a set of paintings) publicly: *His pictures were hung at an important gallery.* **4** [T1] **a** to fix (wallpaper) on a wall **b** to fix (a door) in position on hinges [⇒ H134]

suspend 1 [X9 (*from*)] to hang from above: *He suspended the rope from a tree. He was caught on a branch as he fell and was suspended above the ground.* **2** [T1 *pass*] to hold still in liquid or air: *The sun broke over the trees and dust could be seen suspended in the beam of light.* **suspension** [U; A] the act of suspending: *The bridge is built on the principle of suspension; it is a suspension bridge.*

dangle 1 [I∅] to hang loosely: *His keys were dangling from a chain.* **2** [T1; I∅] to (cause to) swing loosely: *He dangled the keys on his chain.* **3** [X9, esp *in front of* or *before*] (*fig*) to try to attract someone by promising or describing: *He dangled the pleasures of Paris in front of her to get her to work for him.* **keep someone dangling** (*fig*) *infml* to keep someone waiting and not knowing what the result will be: *She likes to keep her lovers dangling. Don't keep me dangling; tell me if I passed the test.*

N302 *adjectives* : **upright, etc** [B]
[ALSO ⇒ J42]

upright 1 standing straight up: *She stood upright.* **2** (*fig*) honest, fair, responsible, etc: *He is an upright citizen.* **-ly** [adv] **-ness** [U]

vertical [Wa5] **1** (of an object) standing upright: *Telegraph poles must be set in the ground so that they are vertical.* **2** (of a line or surface) forming an angle of 90 degrees with the level ground, or with a straight line in a figure: *For a car that went over the edge of the road, there was a vertical fall to the sea below.* **3** pointing or moving directly upwards or downwards: *A vertical takeoff aircraft is one that can rise straight from the ground, without first running along for some distance.* **-ly** [adv Wa4]

erect upright; standing straight up on end, not leaning over or lying down: *Hold your head erect.* **-ly** [adv] **-ness** [U]

N303 *adjectives* : **slanting, etc** [B]
[ALSO ⇒ J42, N269]

slanting, slanted [Wa5] being at an angle from straight up and down or across; sloping: *The house had a slanting/slanted roof.*

oblique [Wa5] **1** in a sideways direction; sloping: *an oblique line* **2** (*fig*) indirect: *an oblique suggestion* **-ly** [adv] **-ness** [U]

N304 *adjectives* : **flat, etc** [B]
[ALSO ⇒ J42]

flat [Wa1] **1** (of surfaces) having no raised or higher parts: *The surface of most tables is flat. The land is flatter near the sea; it is hilly here.* **2** (of certain drinks) old and having no gas: *The beer was flat.* **-ness** [U]

level *esp tech* flat: *Football fields should be level. Football should be played on level ground.* **-ness** [U]

prone [Wa5] (esp of persons) lying flat and face down: *He lay prone on the ground. He lay in a prone position.*

prostrate 1 [Wa5] lying in a flat position or stretched out flat, with the face to the ground: *She fell forward and lay in a prostrate position until she was helped up.* **2** (of a nation, country, etc) conquered and powerless **3** in a state of such bodily weakness that one can hardly move: *They were all prostrate from the terrible heat.* **4** [(*with*)] having lost all strength, courage, and ability to act, as a result of some experience: *She was prostrate with grief.* **-tion** [U]

N305 *adjectives* : **high, tall, etc** [Wa1]
[ALSO ⇒ J63, 64]

high [B] **1** (not usu of people) reaching some distance above ground, esp a large distance: *That's a very high wall/building. How high is it? Is it higher than that one?* **2** at a point above the ground, esp a long way above: *How high is he on the mountain now? These books are too high (up) for me; I can't reach them. The plane was high in the sky.* **3** (*fig*) important: *He has a high office in the government.* **4** (*fig*) showing greatness: *He is a man of high principles.* **-ly** [adv]: *She praised him highly* (= greatly).

tall [B] (esp of people) having a greater than average height: *He's the tallest man I've ever seen. That's a tall building/a tall tree!* **-ness** [U]

deep 1 [B] going far downward: *It was a very deep well.* **2** [B] going well inward from an outer surface: *The wound is deep; it's a deep* *wound.* **3** [B] not near the surface of the body: *deep organs of the body* **4** [B] going well back from a front surface: *That's a deep cupboard!* **5** [B] going far from the side towards the centre: *The cloth had deep borders of bright red.* **6** [B] (in cricket) near the outer limits of the playing area: *It was a hit to deep right field.* **7** [E] going a stated amount in an understood direction, usu downward or backward: *The shelf was 30 inches deep. The cars were parked three deep.* **8** [B] difficult to understand: *He understands the deep scientific principles of the thing.* **9** [B] *BrE* (of people) difficult to get to know well: *She is rather a deep person.* **10** [A] mysterious and strange: *It was a deep dark secret.* **11** [F] towards the centre and far from the entrances: *They lived in a house deep in the forest.* **12** [F] distant in time or space: *They lived deep in the Middle Ages.* **13** [B] well below the level of the conscious mind: *She has a deep disorder of the character.* **14** [B *esp in comb*] covered, enclosed or filled to a stated degree: *He was ankle-deep in mud.* **15** [B] seriously bad or damaging: *He is in deep debt.* **16** [B] *apprec* having or showing a fine ability to understand things thoroughly: *She has a deep mind and is a deep thinker.* **17** [B] strong; difficult to change: *She was in a deep sleep. He has a deep influence over her.* **18** [B] (of a sound or of breath) low; coming from far down in the chest **19** [adv] to a deep position: *He drove the knife in deep/deep into her body.* **-ly** [adv]: *She loved him deeply.*

N306 *adjectives & adverbs* : **not high, tall, etc** [Wa1]

short [B] not tall; less than the usual height: *He is tall but his brother is much shorter. The grass is very short.—Yes; it has just been cut short.* **-ness** [U]

low 1 [B] not measuring much from the base to the top; not high: *a low wall* **2** [B] being not far above the ground, floor, base or bottom: *a low shelf. That comes low on the list of jobs to be done.* **3** [B] being or lying below the general level of height: *a low bridge; low ground. The river is getting low and will soon dry up.* **4** [B] being near or at the bottom or lowest point: *His money was at a low point.* **5** [F] on the ground, as after a blow, or dead: *I laid him low with my gun.* **6** [F] lacking in strength or energy; weak: *He is low with an illness.* **7** [F] *also* **low-spirited** lacking spirit; unhappy: *He felt low and unable to laugh.* **8** [B] small in size; degree, amount, worth, etc: *a low figure* **9** [A] having only a small amount of a particular substance, quality, etc: *low-fat milk* **10** [A] regarding something as of little worth; unfavourable: *I have a low opinion of that book.* **11** [B] near the bottom in position or rank: *He was a man of low birth.* **12** [B] not worthy, respectable, good, etc: *low behaviour; low language* **13** [B] cheap: *a low price* **14** [B]

for a slow or slowest speed: *Use a low gear when driving slowly.* **15** [F] hidden; unnoticed (*esp in the phr* **lie low**): *We lay low until the police had gone.* **16** [B] not greatly developed; simple: *low plant life* **17** [B] (of a musical note) deep **18** [B] not loud; soft: *a low voice* **19** [adv] in or to a low position, point, degree, manner, etc: *shoot low* **20** [adv] near the ground, floor, base, etc; not high **21** [adv] (in music) in or with deep notes **22** [adv] quietly; softly: *speak low*

shallow [B] **1** not deep; not far from top to bottom: *It was a shallow river/dish. They were playing at the shallow end of a swimming pool.* **2** (*fig*) lacking deep or serious thinking: *He is a shallow thinker whose opinions aren't worth much.* **3** (of breathing) not taking much air into the lungs **-ly** [adv] **-ness** [U]

N307 *adjectives* : **wide, etc** [Wa1;B]
[ALSO ⇒ J63, 64]

wide 1 large from side to side or edge to edge: *This skirt is too wide. The river is much wider here than further north.* **2** covering a large space or range of things: *People came from over a wide area. He has wide interests.* **-ly** [adv] **-ness** [U]

broad *esp emot, lit, poet* **1** wide: *That man has broad shoulders.* **2** stretching out far and wide: *The countryside has many broad fields.* **3** (*fig*) not limited; generous in thoughts: *He has a broad mind in these matters; he is broad-minded.* **-ly** [adv]: *Broadly speaking, I agree with you.*

long covering a great distance in space or time: *It is a long way from here to that place, longer than you think. He has been waiting here a long time, longer than he expected.*

thick 1 (esp of materials) being large from one side to the other: *This piece of wood is thicker than that piece.* **2** (of liquids) moving slowly; not easy to pour: *The soup is thick today; it was thinner yesterday.* **-ly** [adv] **-ness** [U]

N308 *adjectives* : **not wide, etc** [Wa1;B]

narrow 1 small from one side to the other, esp in comparison with length or with what is usual: *It is a narrow river. String is narrower than rope. The gate is too narrow for a car; we'll have to walk through.* **2** limited; small: *The price went up and down within narrow limits. The secret is known only to a narrow group of people. in the narrow meaning of the word; His way of looking at the world is very narrow and misses a lot of life's variety and colour.* **3** (*fig*) almost enough or not successful: *He won by a narrow majority. She had a narrow escape.* **4** *fml* careful and thorough: *He made a narrow examination of the facts.* **-ly** [adv] **-ness** [U]

thin (of a round object) narrow in relation to

length: *She used a very thin thread.* **-ly** [adv] **-ness** [U]

fine 1 very thin, small, etc: *This is very fine thread; I must be careful not to break it. A fine rain began to fall. He cut the pencil to a fine point.* **2** [adv] to become fine: *He cut the pencil very fine.* **-ly** [adv] **-ness** [U] **cut it fine** (*fig*) *infml* to leave very little time to do something: *He cut it very fine and nearly missed his train.*

N309 *verbs* : relating to height, width, etc

flatten [IØ;T1 (*out, down*)] to (cause to) become flat: *He flattened* (*out*) *the rounded piece of clay. The storm flattened* (*down*) *the corn. The land is hilly here, but it flattens out nearer the sea.*

level [IØ;T1; (*out, off*)] to (cause to) become level: *They levelled the buildings* (= knocked them down and so made the area level). *Level out this field; we want to play games on it. The amount of work is levelling off now* (= becoming more normal).

prostrate [T1] **1** [*also* IØ] to put (someone, esp oneself, or something) in a prostrate [⇒ N304] position: *The worshippers prostrated* (*themselves*) *before the image of their god.* **2** [Wv4; *usu pass*] to cause to be prostrate: *It was a prostrating illness. She was prostrated by the death of her husband.* **prostration** [U]

heighten [T1; IØ] (*esp fig*) to (cause to) become high or higher or greater: *Adding red to the picture heightened its warlike effect.*

deepen [T1; IØ] to (cause to) become deep or deeper: *'The mystery deepens, my friends,' said Sherlock Holmes. We'll have to deepen the well if we want more water.*

shorten [T1; IØ] to (cause to) become short or shorter: *The days shorten in Britain as the winter comes on. Can you shorten this dress for me?*

lower 1 [T1; IØ] to make or become smaller in amount, price, degree, strength, etc: *Lower the price/your voice.* **2** [T1; IØ] to move or let down in height: *Lower your aim before you shoot.* **3** [T1] (*fig*) to bring (someone, esp oneself) down in rank, worth or opinion, as by doing something unworthy: *By stealing from his father he has lowered himself for ever.*

widen [T1; IØ] (to cause to) become wide or wider: *The road widened. They widened the road near the village.*

broaden [T1; IØ] to (cause to) become broad or broader: *His smile broadened. Can you broaden the bands of colour?*

lengthen [T1; IØ] to (cause to) become long or longer: *He lengthened the rope by tying another piece to it.*

narrow 1 [IØ; T1] to (cause to) decrease in width: *The river narrows* (*down*) *at this point. In the bright sunlight she had to narrow her eyes* (= partly close them). **2** [T1 (*down*)] to reduce

in size; limit: *Let's narrow* (*down*) *what we mean by 'justice'. The new law will narrow his power.*

take in [v adv; T1] to make the width of (a dress, etc) less: *She took the dress in* (*by*) *several centimetres. This dress needs taking in/to be taken in a bit.*

pare 1 [T1 (*down*)] to cut away the thin outer covering, edge or skin of (something) usu with a sharp knife: *to pare one's fingernails; to pare an apple before eating it; to pare a stick down to make it fit into a hole* **2** [X9, esp *away, off*] to cut away (the thin outer covering, edge or skin of something) usu with a sharp knife: *It isn't necessary to pare the peel off before you eat that fruit.*

N310 *verbs, etc* : lying

lie 1 [L9, esp *down*] (of a person) to be in a flat resting position, as on the ground or a bed **2** [Wv6;L9, esp *down*] to put the body into such a position **3** [L7,9] to be or remain in a flat position on a surface: *the book that is lying on the table* **4** [L9] to be in a described place, position or direction: *The town lies to the east of us. Our home lies north.* (*fig*) *The truth lies somewhere between the statements of the two men.* **5** [L9] to be, remain, or be kept in a described condition or position: *The man lay in prison for seven years.* **6** [L9] to have an unpleasant effect on; cause continual anxiety, discomfort, etc: *The problem lay heavily on his mind. A curse has always lain over that family.* **7** [L9] to be the responsibility; be: *The decision lies with you. It lies in the judge's power to punish criminals.* **8** [L7,9] to remain unused, unwanted, unknown, etc **9** [L7,9] (of a dead body) to be buried **10** [IØ] (of a point or claim in a law court) to be successfully arguable or proved **11** [L9] *old use* to stay, as with friends or at a hotel

sprawl 1 [X9 *usu pass*; L9, (*out*)] to stretch out (oneself or limbs) awkwardly in lying or sitting: *He found her sprawled out in a comfortable chair asleep.* **2** [Wv4;L9 (*out*)] to spread ungracefully: *the city sprawls for miles in each direction. It was a great sprawling city.* **3** [S] a sprawling position **4** [S] an irregular spreading mass or group: *a sprawl of buildings.*

lounge 1 [IØ] to stand or sit in a leaning lazy manner: *She was lounging in a large chair. He lounged against the wall.* **2** [(*around, about*); X9, esp *away*] to pass (time) in a lazy manner, doing nothing: *He enjoys lounging about /lounging his time away.*

N311 *verbs* : tending and inclining

tend 1 [L9] to move or develop one's course in a certain direction: *Our course tended to the north. Interest rates are tending upwards.* **2** [T3; L9, esp *towards*] to do or go as a natural likelihood: *Janet tends to get very angry if you annoy her. Joan always tended towards politics at school so no one was surprised when she said she wanted to be a politician.*

incline 1 [V3] to encourage (to feel, think, etc): *The news inclines me to change my mind. I feel inclined to change my mind.* **2** [I3; L9, esp *to*] to feel drawn: *I incline to take the opposite point of view. I incline to the opposite point of view.* **3** [L9, esp *to*] *fml* to tend; be likely to show (a quality): *I incline to(wards) tiredness in winter.*

N312 *adjectives* : **prone, liable, and inclined**

[ALSO ⇒ N30 LIKELY]

prone 1 [F *to*; F3] having the probability of (usu something undesirable): *One is more prone to make mistakes when one is tired. Old people are prone to loss of memory/to losing their memory/to lose their memory. He is prone to colds, especially in winter.* **2** [*in comb*] having a tendency to have (usu something undesirable): *Mary is always falling over; she's accident-prone. He is trouble-prone; he's always getting into trouble.*

liable 1 [F *to*] often getting: *She is liable to bad colds.* **2** [F3] by nature likely to, esp from habit or tendency: *He's liable to shout when angry.*

inclined [F3] **1** encouraged; feeling a wish to: *I'm inclined to help. The news makes me inclined to change my mind.* (*polite*) *I'm inclined to disagree.* **2** likely; leading to: *He's inclined to help anybody who asks him. I'm inclined to get tired easily.*

N313 *nouns* : **tendencies and habits**

tendency 1 [C, C3] a natural likelihood of developing, acting, or moving in a particular way: *She's always had a tendency to be fat. Recently, business has shown a tendency to improve.* **2** [C (*towards*)] a special natural skill or cleverness: *He has artistic tendencies. Her tendency had always been towards history so we were surprised when she failed her examination in it.*

inclination 1 [U; C (*to, towards*, 3) often *pl*] what one likes, liking; wish for: *You always follow your own inclinations instead of thinking of our feelings. I've no inclination towards life as a doctor/no inclination to be a doctor. In life you follow necessity, not inclinations.* **2** [C3] *fml* a tendency: *She has an inclination to get fat.*

bias [C; U] tendency or inclination, often of an undesirable kind: *He has a strong bias towards telling lies.* [*also* ⇒ F12, 13]

leaning [C *often pl with same meaning*] *esp lit* tendency, bias: *He has leanings towards crime.*

propensity [C (*for, to*), C3] *fml* a natural tendency of the mind or character towards a particular (usu undesirable) kind of behaviour:

That dog has biting propensities. She has a propensity for complaining/a propensity to sudden anger. A propensity to spend money as soon as you get it won't help you to become rich.

proclivity [C (*to, towards*), C3] *fml & pomp* inclination

bent [S (*for*)] a natural liking or tendency towards: *He has a bent for working with engines.*

habit [U; C (*of*)] (an example of) customary behaviour: *He smokes out of habit/by habit, not for pleasure. I have the habit of smoking. She has many bad habits.*

N314 *modals* : **tendencies and habits**

can be to have a habit of being: *He can be annoying at times, if you let him, but usually he's very helpful.*

could be (*past t of* **can be**): *He could be annoying at times, if you let him, but usually he was very helpful.*

will to be inclined to: *He will sit there for hours sometimes, doing nothing at all.*

would (*past t of* **will**): *He would sit there for hours sometimes, doing nothing at all.*

Cutting, joining, breaking, and destroying

N320 *verbs* : **cutting and carving**

[ALSO ⇒ B130]

cut 1 [T1; I∅] to make a narrow opening in (something) with a sharp edge or instrument, accidentally or on purpose: *Don't cut your fingers on the broken glass. This knife won't cut; perhaps it needs sharpening. You'll need a strong pair of scissors to cut through that thick cloth. I cut my face shaving this morning.* **2** [T1 (*up*)] to divide (something) by separating with a sharp edge or instrument: *The boys cut the cake in two and ate half each. After they'd killed the woman the murderers cut up her body and burned it. Cut the ropes and set me free.* **3** [T1] to make (something) by using a sharp instrument: *The hunters cut their way through the forest with axes. Did you follow the pattern exactly when cutting (out) the pieces of cloth for a suit? To prepare the ground for planting, cut a deep trench and fill with fine soil. He cut a hole in the piece of wood.* **4** [I∅] to be able to be separated, divided or marked as with a sharp instrument: *A freshly baked cake doesn't cut easily. This material seems to have cut very nicely.* **5** [X9, esp *away, off, out*] to separate (something) from the main part of something with a sharp instrument; remove with a sharp instrument: *The murderer's head was cut off with an axe. She cut the advertisement out of the* *newspaper so that she wouldn't forget it. Cut the dead wood away from the trees.* **6** [D1 (*for*); (T1)] to separate (a part of something) for (someone): *The old lady cut the priest a piece of cake.* **7** [T1] to shorten or improve with a sharp instrument (*note the phrs* **cut short/long**): *Your finger nails need cutting. Are you going to have your hair cut short? It's time the grass was cut; it's getting very long. 'With his tail cut short and his ears cut long, Oh where can my little dog be?'* (old song). **8** [T1] to grow (a tooth): *Our baby's just cutting her first teeth so she needs some medicine to reduce the pain.* **9** [T1 (*off*)] to interrupt (a supply of gas, electricity, etc): *The water was cut (off) for two hours yesterday while the road was being repaired. Our electricity was cut off because we didn't pay the bill.* **10** [T1 (*out*)] to remove (parts (of)): *All the scenes showing sex or violence were cut from the film before it was shown on television.* **11** [Wv4;T1;L9] to hurt the feelings of (someone): *His cruel remark cut me deeply. It was a cutting remark.* **12** [T1] *infml* to be absent on purpose from (a class, school, etc): *I felt tired this morning so I stayed in bed and cut school.* **13** [X9, esp *down*] to cause (a tree) to fall; bring down (a tree) with an axe, saw, etc: *Lots of trees are cut for wood every year. We must not let them cut down such fine trees just to build a road!* **14** [T1] to gather in (corn, wheat, etc) **15** [L9] to change direction suddenly: *The player ran for the ball but suddenly cut to the left to get a better position.* **16** [I0;T1] to divide (a pile of playing cards) in two before dealing **17** [T1] to cross: *The line AC is cut by line PQ at point Z.* **18** [T1] to make (a ball) spin by striking: *The player confused his opponent by cutting the ball to the right.* **19** [I0] to stop photographing a scene when making a film: *'Cut!' shouted the director.* **20** [T1 (*back*)] to make (esp a public service) smaller, less frequent, etc: *Where I live they're cutting (back) rail services, postal deliveries and school meals.* **21** [T1] to walk across rather than round (a corner): *A path had been worn in the grass where people had cut the corner.* **22** [T1] to make (a record): *When did this singer cut his first record?* **23** [X9] to set (someone or something) free or loose by cutting a rope, metal, etc: *I was trapped under the twisted wreck of the crushed car for an hour before the firemen cut me free. I cut myself loose with my knife.* **24** [T1] to make less: *Your story is too long; it needs cutting. If we cut prices, perhaps we can increase sales.* **25** [C] an act or result of cutting: *Broken glass can cause cuts. There's a knife cut* (= a cut caused by a knife) *in this piece of cloth.* **26** [S] the way in which something has been cut: *I like the cut of that dress.* **27** [C *esp in comb*] an act of stopping esp the flow of gas, electricity, etc: *We have had several power cuts lately; one cut lasted 10 hours.* **cutting** [C] **1** a piece cut off a plant to be planted in another place: *Can I have some cuttings from these plants for my garden?* **2** a piece cut out of a

newspaper: *He has a book full of newspaper cuttings about his films.*

hew 1 [X9;L9] to cut (into) by striking blows with an axe or weapon: *They hewed the door to pieces. They hewed at the door/hewed away.* **2** [T1 (*down*)] to cut down by blows: *to hew (down) trees* **3** [T1] to cut (something) from a large mass and shape by blows: *Miners hew coal. They hewed it out of the rock. They hewed their way through the forest.* **4** [T1 (*out*)] (*fig*) to cause to exist or develop by the use of one's efforts: *He hewed out an important position for himself in the company.*

hack 1 [X9;L9] to cut (up), esp roughly or in uneven pieces: *He hacked the tree down. He hacked away all night. They hacked their way through the trees.* **2** [C *usu sing*] a rough cutting movement or blow: *He made a hack at the log.* **3** [C] a cut from a kick or blow esp in a game

slice 1 [Wv5;T1 (*up*)] to cut (up) into thin wide flat pieces: *He sliced the bread. She sliced up the meat.* **2** [D1 (*for*); T1; (*off*)] to cut off in slices: *Slice me off a piece of meat. Slice off a piece of meat for me.* **3** [C] such a thin wide flat piece: *Have another slice of meat.*

chop 1 [T1 (*off, up, down*)] to cut esp into pieces by striking again and again with a knife, axe, etc: *She chopped (up) the vegetables to make soup. He was in the garden chopping wood for the fire. They chopped the branches off (the tree). Chop that tree down. They chopped their way through the thick bushes.* **2** [C] an act of chopping: *He cut the piece of wood in two with one chop of the axe.* **3** [C] a downward movement of the open or closed hand: *He killed the man with a chop across the neck.*

carve 1 [D1 (*for*); T1; I0; (*in from, out of/into*)] to cut (usu wood or stone) in order to make (a special shape) for (someone or something): *He carved the stone into the figure of a man. The artist carved her an interesting ornament from the piece of wood. She carved the wood. What did she carve for you? Does she carve? This artist carves in gold.* **2** [T1 (*on, in*)] to cut (a shape) into something: *The lovers carved their names on the tree.* **3** [I0;T1] to cut (meat) into pieces or slices: *It's your turn to carve the meat. Who's going to carve?* **4** [D1 (*for*); T1; (*out*)] to make by hard work: *He carved out a name for himself. He carved himself a nice position in the business. Our father carved out our position in society, not you!*

whittle [T1 (*down, away*)] to cut (wood) to a smaller size by taking off small thin pieces: *He was whittling a piece of wood/whittling down a piece of wood.* (*fig*) *Lack of sleep whittled his strength away.*

chisel [T1 (*out*)] to cut or shape with the tool called a chisel [⇒ H140]: *He chiselled the piece of wood into the shape of a head.*

segment [T1] *usu tech* to cut or divide into parts or segments [⇒ H32, J46]: *Where should we segment these words?* **segmentation** [U]

prune 1 [T1 (*back*)] to cut off or shorten some of the branches of (a tree or bush) in order to improve the shape, growth, flowering, etc: *The trees need to be pruned. She was pruning back the roses* (= cutting off the rosebushes' branches to a point near the main stem). **2** [T1 (*away, back; from, of, off*)] to remove (branches, stems, etc) in this way: *We should prune away these weak diseased stems from the bush.* **3** [T1 (*away, down; from, of, off*)] to take out anything useless from (something); lessen in amount by careful choice: *You should prune the speech down; it's too long. We can't afford to spend so much on this building; we must prune the costs.*

trim [T1] to cut little pieces off (something) here and there to make it look better, neater, etc: *She trimmed his hair/beard. The bushes need trimming.*

N321 *verbs* : **severing and disconnecting**

sever [T1; I∅] **1** to break or (be) cut up, esp into two parts: *She used scissors to sever the threads. The rope severed under the heavy weight. The two countries have severed their relations* (= ceased to deal officially with each other). **2** [(*from*)] to (cause to) go apart, esp with force; separate: *The handle of the cup severed when it hit the floor. The island is severed from the mainland by 50 miles of water.*

shear **1** [T1] to cut off (esp wool) from esp sheep: *He sheared the sheep. His hair is so long it needs shearing, not cutting!* **2** [T1] *esp lit* to cut off (hair) or hair from: *He looked strange with his closely shorn head.* **3** [I∅; T1; (*off*)] *tech* **a** (esp of thin rods, pins, etc) to break in two under a sideways or twisting force **b** to cause (esp a thin rod, pin, etc) to break in this way **be shorn of** to lose by the action of another: *The king was shorn of his power by his nobles.*

disconnect [T1] **1** [(*from*)] to undo the connection of (material things): *disconnect the telephone; disconnect a water pipe from the main supply* **2** to break the telephone connection between (two people): *I think we've been disconnected. Will you ring that number again, please?*

N322 *verbs & nouns* : **separating and dividing**

separate **1** [T1; I∅] to (cause to) be apart or separate [⇒ M212]: *Separate the longer ones from the shorter ones. The outside parts have begun to separate from the inside parts.* **2** [T1] to keep apart: *The policeman separated the two fighters.* **3** [I∅] to move apart: *They were happily married when I last saw them in 1970, but now they have separated.* **separation** **1** [U] the state of being separated or the act of separating: *Separation of the two groups is necessary; if not, they will kill each other.* **2** [C *usu sing*] an

example or result of this: *After a separation of three years they are living together again as husband and wife.*

part [T1; I∅] **1** *esp fml, lit & emot* to separate, esp into two groups, parts, positions, places, etc; to (cause to) be apart: *The soldiers parted as the king's men approached. 'We must part you now,' he said sadly to the mother and child. They were parted by the war. We were parted as children and did not meet again for 20 years.* (*fig*) *I don't agree with you; we must part* (*company*) *on that point* (= we must disagree). **2 a** (of the hair) to separate into two **b** to separate (one's hair): *He parts his hair in the middle/on the left.* **parting** **1** [U] the act or occasion of parting: *Their parting was very sad. The parting of the crowd allowed the king's men to pass through.* **2** [C] a separation of the hair into two parts: *He has a middle parting. Her parting is on the right.* **3** [A] on leaving: *His parting orders were for them to continue the fight.*

divide **1** [T1; I∅ (*into*)] to (cause to) become two or more: *Does this table divide?—Yes; it divides into two separate parts. This class is too large; we shall have to divide it. Divide this line into 20 equal parts.* **2** [T1 (*from*)] to be that which separates (two things) or comes between (two parts of one thing): *The new road will divide the farm. A low brick wall divides our garden from/and our neighbour's garden.* **3** [T1 (*between*)] to use (different amounts of the same thing) for different purposes: *He divides his time between reading and writing.* **4** [T1 (*by* or *from*)] to separate into groups according to some system: *Divide the books according to subject/by subject. Divide the younger children and/from the older children. Divide them by age.* **5** [T1 (*up, between, among* or *with*)] to separate and give out or share: *This fruit is for all of you so divide it equally. Divide the cake* (*up*) *between/among you. Divide the cake with your sister.* **6** [T1] to be an important cause of disagreement between; to separate into opposing groups: *I hope this disagreement does not divide us. Opinions are divided on the question.* **7** [T1; I∅] to (cause to) vote by separating into one group for and one group against: *Parliament divided on the question and the Government won narrowly. The opposition tried to divide Parliament again soon afterwards.* **division** **1** [U] the act, occasion or result of dividing or being divided: *Division of the work is necessary; one person cannot do it all. The division of the money among them was fairly done. The division of the children into groups was according to age.* **2** [C] a result of dividing; one part into which something is divided: *Was that a fair division of the work/money? He runs the sales division of the company.* **3** [C] a dividing line, etc: *The wall serves as a division between the land of the two families. In England divisions between social classes are still clearly marked.* **4** [C] a separation into two groups for voting purposes: *There was a division in Parliament on the mat-*

ter, and our party won the vote. **divisive** [B] causing divisions: *These plans are divisive; they will divide the country into opposing groups.*

split 1 [IØ; T1; (*up*)] *not fml* to divide into parts, groups, etc: *After the class the students split up. They split the class into three groups. Let's split up the money now.* **2** [C] *not fml* a division: *His ideas have caused a split in the group; some like them, some don't.* **3** [C] a long narrow break, cut or tear: *There's a split in this piece of wood/down the back of her coat.*

break down [v adv; T1] *infml* to divide, split, etc: *The scientists tried to break down the substance into its parts. The weather slowly breaks down rocks into soil.*

sunder [T1] *fml & lit* to separate or break into two parts: *Their friendship was sundered by the news.*

disengage [IØ; T1] to (cause to) separate or detach (a person, oneself or a thing from some other person or thing): *The two armies disengaged. The driver of the vehicle disengaged the gear.* **disengagement** [U]

detach [T1; (IØ)] to unfasten and take away; to separate (one thing from another): *He detached all the tops from the bottles.* **detachment** [U]

partition [T1] to divide, esp a country: *British India was partitioned into India and Pakistan.* **partition off** [v adv; T1] to divide (one part of a place) off from another by using a partition [⇒ D22]: *He partitioned off a corner of the big room.*

branch [IØ] to divide into branches like parts of a tree: *The road branched and he went left.*

N323 *verbs & nouns* : **cutting off and isolating** [T1]

cut off [v adv] **1** [*also* D1 (*for*)] to separate by cutting: *She cut off a small piece of cake and gave it to me.* **2** to disconnect: *We were cut off in the middle of our telephone conversation.* **3** [(*from*)] to block off or surround so that further movement out or in is impossible: *The enemy cut off all the supplies from the advancing army. When the city was cut off, everyone knew that total defeat was certain.* **4** to take from (a person) the right to have one's property when one is dead: *If you marry that girl I'll cut you off completely/without a penny!*

isolate [*often pass*] **1** to cause to be alone or separated from others: *His illness isolated him from other people. Several families have been isolated by the lack of buses.* **2** to keep apart (from other people) so that a disease will not be spread: *He has been isolated until we know whether he has caught the disease.* **3** to separate one substance from others so that it can be examined alone: *They have isolated the virus* [⇒ A37] *in its pure form.* **isolation** [U] the act, occasion or result of isolating or being isolated: *This is a dangerous disease; isolation of all the people who have been close to the dead*

man is necessary. All the people must be kept in isolation until it is clear that they don't have the disease. He lived on a small island, in isolation from modern life.

insulate 1 to use a material as or act as a protection against unseen forces passing through another: *Many houses could be warmer if they were insulated so that heat is not lost. My flat is sound-proof because some material in the walls insulates it from the next one. Always insulate the wires which carry an electric current.* **2** [(*from*)] (*fig*) to protect (a person) from ordinary experiences: *Don't insulate your mother from everyday difficulties even if she is old.* **insulation** [U] **1** the act or result of insulating or being insulated: *These electric wires need insulation.* **2** the materials used for this: *This thick cloth is a good insulation against the cold.* **insulator** [C] a substance, material, apparatus, etc that insulates, esp an electrical apparatus for supporting wires

N324 *verbs & nouns* : **piercing and probing**

pierce [T1] **1** [*also* IØ] (to use something sharp or pointed in order) to go into or through (something): *The needle pierced her finger. He pierced the rubber ball with a knife. Arrows and spears are weapons that pierce.* **2** to make (a hole) using a pointed instrument: *This bird pierces holes in trees with its beak* [⇒ A122]. **3** to force or make (a way) into or through (something): *We pierced our way through the thick forest.* (*fig*) *He couldn't pierce her unfriendly manner.* **4** (of light, sound, pain, etc) to be suddenly seen, heard or felt in or through (someone or something): *A cry of fear pierced the silence. The cold pierced him to the bone. No light has ever pierced down here.*

prick 1 [T1 (*with*, *on*)] to make a very small hole or holes in the skin or surface of (something or oneself) with a sharp-pointed object: *When she was sewing she pricked her finger and made it bleed. A bee pricks the skin with its sting. She pricked herself on a needle.* **2** [T1 (*off*, *out*, *in*)] to make (a small hole or other mark) in a surface by using a pointed tool: *Prick a few holes in the centre of the pastry. He pricked out a circle in the metal.* **3** [T1; IØ] to (cause to) feel a sensation of light sharp pain on the skin: *The leaves of this plant prick if you touch them. My skin pricks sometimes if I get too hot. The pepper in the food pricked the back of his throat.* (*fig*) *Her conscience pricked her.* **4** [C] a small mark or hole made by pricking: *There were pricks at the top of the papers where they had been pinned together.* **5** [C *usu sing*] an act of pricking: *He burst it with a slight prick of the needle.* **6** [C] a small sharp pain: *He felt a sharp prick when he stepped on an upturned nail.* (*fig*) *She felt the pricks of conscience* (= discomfort of the mind after wrongdoing).

penetrate 1 [IØ (*into*, *through*); T1] to enter,

pass, cut or force a way into or through (something): *The knife penetrated his stomach. This nail will not penetrate. Rain has penetrated right through this coat. No noise penetrated the room.* **2** [I∅] (of sound) to be easily heard at a distance: *You can hear him all over the building; he doesn't know how his voice penetrates.* **3** [T1] to see into or through: *My eyes could not penetrate the darkness.* **4** [T1] to understand: *It was a long time before scientists could penetrate the mystery of the atom.* **5** [Wv5 (*with*); T1] to fill: *The whole country is penetrated with discontent.* **6** [I∅] *infml* to come to be understood: *I heard what you said but it didn't penetrate.* **7** [T1] to come to understand the truth behind (something false) (*esp in the phr* **penetrate someone's disguise**) [⇒ F208, N356] **penetration** [U] the act or result of penetrating or being penetrated: *He was killed by penetration of the stomach by a sharp instrument, probably a knife.*

puncture 1 [T1 *often pass*] to make a hole in (something, esp a tyre) esp so that the air inside gets out: *My bicycle tyre is punctured.* **2** [C] such a hole: *I've got a puncture in my tyre.*

N325 *verbs* : joining and linking
[ALSO ⇒ J17]

join [T1; I∅; (*together, up, with*)] **1** to (cause to) come together; to (cause to) become one or nearly one thing: *The two rivers joined. Three roads join (together) near here. He joined (up) the two pieces of wood together with nails. He joined one piece of wood to the other with nails. The priest joined the man and woman in marriage. They joined the two islands with a bridge.* **2** to become one (of); to enter: *He joined us at the restaurant. Won't you join (our club)? Please join with us in this work. They joined together to do the work.*

connect [T1; I∅; (*together, up, with, to, by*)] *esp fml & tech* to join; to fix together: *Connect these wires together. He connected (up) the wires. You must connect this wire with/up to that one. This road connects with the other at Newtown. He picked up the telephone and asked to be connected with London. She has been connected with our company (=She has worked with us) for many years. He is connected to our family by marriage. The two families are connected by marriage. The towns are connected by good road and rail services.* **disconnect** [T1 (*from*)] *usu tech* to separate (one thing from another): *He disconnected the wires/our telephone.*

attach 1 [T1 (*to*)] to join or fix (one thing to another): *He attached the rope to his boat. The house has a garage attached to it.* (*fml*) *Attached you will find* (=You will find attached) *a copy of his letter to us.* (*fig*) *They attached themselves to the politician because they hoped he would become president one day.* (*fig*) *Do you attach much importance to what*

she says?—*Yes; I attach a lot of importance to her words.* **2** [L9, esp *to*] (*fig*) to be put; come: *We know it was his fault; no blame attaches to you.* **3** [T1 *usu pass*] to send on duty for a limited time: *He was attached to the special group in Greece for two months.*

combine [I∅; T1; (*with, into*)] to (cause to) come together; join or mix: *The two groups combined to do the work. They combined the two groups into one. She combined a visit to Scotland with a trip to London.*

affix [T1 (*to*)] *often fml* to attach, stick or fasten (one thing to another thing): *He affixed the stamp to the letter. When '-ness' is affixed to an adjective it forms a noun.* **affixation** [U]

unite 1 [T1; I∅] *esp emph* to join together into one: *They united the two pipes. The two colours mixed and united.* **2** [I∅ (*in*); I3] to act together for a purpose: *They united (in their attempts) to form a club.* **3** [T1] to join in marriage: *They were united by the local priest.* **4** [I∅] to join in an agreement: *The countries united for trading purposes.*

unify [T1] **1** to make all the same: *Let's unify the systems.* **2** to make (parts) into one (whole): *They tried to unify the nations/to unify the country.*

integrate [T1] **1** to make (something) complete from a number of parts: *The group is now fully integrated and working well.* **2** to bring (something or someone) into a group from a position outside it: *She has been fully integrated into the group.* **integration** [U]

link 1 [T1 (*together*)] to join or connect: *The road links all the new towns. I can't link him with those people; I don't think he knows them at all.* **2** [I∅ (*together, up*)] to be joined: *The pieces link together.*

coalesce [I∅] to grow together or unite so as to form one group, body, mass, etc **coalescence** [U]

amalgamate 1 [I∅] (of businesses) to join or unite **2** [T1] to join (businesses) into one: *The two companies (were) amalgamated.* **amalgamation 1** [U] the act or result of amalgamating **2** [C] an example of this

band together [v adv; I∅] to come together; unite: *They banded together to form a new political party.*

N326 *verbs* : tying and tethering
[ALSO ⇒ D152, M64]

tie 1 [T1 (*together, up*)] to join the ends of (pieces of thread, rope, etc) together: *He tied the ropes (together) in a knot that would be difficult to untie again.* **2** [I∅ (*together*)] to be fastened together: *How do these things tie (together)?* **3** [T1 (*down*)] (*fig*) to be kept busy by: *His work ties him down a lot; he doesn't get a holiday very often.* **4** [T1 *up*] (*fig*) to agree: *They want to tie up the agreement/tie the matter up as soon as possible.*

bind 1 [T1 (*up*)] *esp lit, fml & emph* to tie: *Bind*

the prisoner with rope. Bind the prisoner's arms. (fig) He stood there, bound by the magic of her voice. **2** [X9] to put by tying: *Bind the prisoner to his chair with rope. Bind the prisoner's arms together. He bound a cloth round his head.* **3** [T1 (**up**)] to tie together: *She bound (up) her hair.* **4** [T1 (*up*)] to put bandages [⇒ B175] on or round: *She bound (up) his wounds.* **5** [T1] to fasten together and enclose in a cover: *They bound the book.* **6** [T1] to strengthen or ornament with a band of material: *The edges of the floor mat are coming undone because they have not been bound properly.* **7** [T1;I∅] to (cause to) stick together: *The cold weather has bound the earth so hard that planting is difficult. This type of soil binds (hard) (easily) in cold weather.* **8** [I∅;(T1)] to make it hard for (someone) to move the bowels: *Eggs are considered a binding food.* **9** [T1] to cause to obey esp by a law or a solemn promise: *I am bound by my promise. I have bound myself by an agreement. It was a binding agreement.* **10** [T1 (*together*)] *esp emot* to unite: *Many things bind us (together).* **11** [I∅] to have a uniting, limiting or controlling effect: *These promises and agreements are binding.* **12** [V3] to make or declare it necessary for (someone) to do something: *They bound me to remain silent. I bound myself to pay back the debt I owed.*

bond [Wv5;T1 *usu pass*] to fix or join (esp the surfaces of materials) securely together, esp with heat, glue [⇒ H9], etc: *Are the sheets properly bonded?*

fuse **1** [T1;I∅; (*together*)] to join or become joined by melting: *Copper and zinc are fused to make brass. The aircraft came down in flames and the heat fused most of the parts together into a solid mass.* **2** [T1 (*together*)] to unite; make into one: *The two small political parties were fused into a powerful group by one powerful leader.* **3** [T1;I∅] to (cause (metal) to) melt in great heat: *Lead will fuse at a lower temperature than some other metals.*

yoke [T1 (*together*)] to join with or as if with a yoke: *Yoke the oxen together. Yoke the oxen to the load. (fig) They are yoked in marriage.*

tether [Wv5;T1] to fasten (an animal) with a tether: *The rider tethered his horse to a fence. The cows were tethered in the middle of a field.*

N327 *nouns* : **relating to joining, tying, etc**

junction **1** [U] *fml* the act, occasion or result of joining or being joined: *They hope to effect a junction* (= meet or cause things to meet) *soon.* **2** [C] an example of this; a place where things (esp roads, railways, etc) meet: *London is a junction of many roads and also of many influences.*

conjunction [C9;U] *fml & pomp* a junction, esp a coming together of events: '*This is a very*

unusual conjunction of sad happenings,' he said when he heard the bad news.

adjunct [C (*to*)] *usu tech* something added or joined to some other thing that is larger or more important, in order to change it (in some useful way)

connection **1** [U] the act, occasion or result of connecting or being connected: *We are waiting for the connection of our new telephone.* **2** [C] an example of this: *Is there any connection between what you said last month and what he has now done?—No; no connection at all.—Yes; there's a close connection (between the two).* **3** [C] a thing which connects; a place where things connect: *The apparatus has several connections by which it can be fixed to the larger machine. I can't see any connection between these wires; is there one?* **4** [C] a vehicle, ship, plan, etc which comes at a particular time just after another, so that passengers can go from one to the other: *His train was late so he missed his connection to Paris.* **5** [C *usu pl*] someone one knows in business, etc: *He has good connections in Birmingham.* **in connection with** *fml* about: *He wrote to me in connection with the new houses we are building.*

connexion *esp BrE now rare* connection

relation, *also* **relationship** [U;C] connection, esp of cause and effect [⇒ N152]: *What is the relation between wages and prices in that industry?* **bear no/little/some relation to** to match not at all/not much/partly, in number, amount or size: *The actual cost bears no relation to what we thought it was going to be.* **in/with relation to** *fml* concerning; with regard to (used in business letters): *What are the prices like, in relation to costs?*

attachment **1** [U] the act, occasion or result of attaching or being attached: *The attachment of the rope to the boat was easy.* **2** [C] something (which can be) attached, esp something smaller to something larger for a special purpose: *He has a lot of attachments to his camera for taking pictures under special conditions.*

combination **1** [U] the act of combining or result of being combined **2** [C] an example of this; a group of persons or things combined for some purpose: *A combination of several mistakes led to the terrible plane crash.*

combine [C] *not fml* a group of people who have combined for a particular purpose, esp in business, politics, etc: *a local business combine*

unity **1** [U;C] the state of being one complete whole or condition of being united: *a new unity between different branches of the church; unity of colour in a picture* **2** [U] agreement of aims and interests: *The argument spoilt their former unity.* **3** [U] *tech* the number one

unification [U] **1** the act or result of unifying (any groups): *the unification of a country* **2** the state of being unified

union **1** [U] the act of joining or state of being joined into one **2** [C] (*often cap*) a group of countries or states joined together: *The Presi-*

dent gave his speech on the state of the Union. **3** [U] a state of agreement and unity: *They lived in unspoilt union.* **4** [C; U] (unity in) marriage: *joined in perfect union; a union blessed by children* **5** [C] (esp in names and titles) a club or society: *to join the students' union*

fusion 1 [U] the act, occasion or result of fusing: *The fusion of copper and zinc makes brass.* **2** [C *usu sing*] an example of this; an act of joining, uniting, etc: *There has been a fusion of political interests; several parties have suddenly joined together.*

join [C] the place where two things, esp pieces of material, are joined or held together usu by some other means: *Can you see the join (between the pieces of wood)?—No; I wouldn't have known there was a join if you hadn't told me.*

link [C] **1** something or someone that serves to connect or unite other things or persons: *That one mountain road is their only link with other places. He is the link between the two groups. Although they live here now, they still have many links with the country in which they were born.* **2** one ring in a chain [⇒ H46]: *One of the links is broken.* (*fig*) *There is a missing link in the chain of evidence* [⇒ N221]. **linkup** [C] a point of joining or connection: *a road linkup; a television linkup between American and Europe*

tie [C] *esp emot* something that holds or keeps people together: *There are many ties of friendship between the two countries. Family ties were always strong even though the different family members lived far apart. There are ties of blood* (= is a blood relationship) *between the two families.*

bond 1 [C] *esp emot* something that joins or unites people; a tie: *There are strong bonds of friendship between them. A bond of affection unites them. Common experiences form a bond between us.* **2** [S] a join, esp if strong and made by heat, glue [⇒ H9], etc: *They pressed the two surfaces together to get a good, firm bond.* **3** [C *usu sing*] **a** an agreement esp in law that one or more persons or groups must keep **b** the paper on which such an agreement is written or printed

yoke 1 [C] a wooden bar used for joining two animals, esp oxen together in order to pull heavy loads, farm vehicles, etc **2** [Wn2;C] two animals joined together by such a bar: *six yoke(s) of oxen* **3** [C] a frame fitted across a person's shoulders for carrying two equal loads **4** [C] that part of a garment from which the rest hangs, as the part of a dress around the shoulders or the part of a skirt around the waist **5** [*the* R (*of*)] (*fig*) power, control, etc: *They were brought under the yoke of the king.* **6** [C (*of*) *usu sing*] (*fig*) something that binds people or things together: *the yoke of marriage*

tether [C] a rope or chain to which an animal is tied so that it is free to move within a limited area **at the end of one's tether** unable to suffer something any longer

N328 *verbs, etc* : **relating and associating**

relate [T1] to see, show, have, or be a connection to or between (esp words, ideas, difficulties, etc): *I can't relate those two ideas. Does this matter relate to what he did last year?*

connect [T1 (*with*)] (of words, ideas, etc) to bring together, esp for a particular reason, esp in the mind: *I always connect the colour blue with being sad because the 'blues' are a sad kind of music.*

associate 1 [T1 (*with, together*)] to see a close relationship or connection between (two things): *I always associate him and her/him with her (in my mind). I always associate them together. Many people associate happiness with having money.* **2** [T1 : I∅ (*with*)] to connect (esp oneself) esp in business, social life, etc: *I don't really want to be associated/to associate (myself) with them any more; I don't like their ideas.* **association 1** [U] the act, occasion or result of associating or being associated: *I want no further association with them.* **2** [C] an example of this: *Her English improved because of a long association with British and American people. What associations does the colour blue have for you?*

N329 *verbs & nouns* : **affiliating and incorporating**

affiliate [Wv5;T1;I∅ (*with, to*)] to join or connect officially or socially: *I think we should affiliate with the society from the next town. He affiliated himself to the society. The vote agreed that we should affiliate. All the affiliated organizations are in favour of the plan.* **affiliation 1** [U] the act of affiliating or being affiliated **2** [C] an example or result of this

incorporate [T1 (*into* or *with*)] to make (something) a part of a group; to include: *They incorporated this new idea into their plans. The new plan incorporates the old one. They incorporated the new plans with the old.* **incorporation 1** [U] the act of incorporating or being incorporated **2** [C] an example or result of this

N330 *verbs & nouns* : **correlating and interrelating**

[ALSO ⇒ N226]

correlate [I∅;T1; (*with*)] to (show to) have a close shared relationship or causal [⇒ N152] connection: *It is impossible to correlate the new discoveries with what we knew already so we must completely change our previous opinions on the subject. This doesn't correlate with what we know already. Can science and religion be correlated? The doctors correlated alcoholism and/with severe brain disease.* **correlation 1** [U] the act of correlating: *The two sets of figures* need correlation. *What is the correlation between temperatures and the growth of plant life here?* **2** [C *usu sing*] an example of this: *There is a close correlation between the two sets of figures.*

interrelate [I∅; T1 *usu pass* (*with*)] to connect (to each other or with something else) in a way that makes one depend on the other: *Wages and prices interrelate/are interrelated.* **interrelation,** *also* **interrelationship 1** [U] an act of interrelating **2** [C] an example of this

N331 *verbs, etc* : **tearing and pulling to pieces**

tear 1 [Wv5; T1] to pull apart or into pieces by force, esp so as to leave irregular edges: *Why did you tear the cloth when I'd advised you to cut it with scissors? How did you tear your coat? The boy tore the flesh of his legs climbing up a tree. The untidy girl tore the paper into little pieces and threw it across the room. I've only got an old torn dress to wear so I can't go to the dance.* **2** [X9] to make by doing this: *The girl tore a hole in her dress climbing over the wall.* **3** [X9 (*away, off, out, up*)] to remove by force: *The nasty child tore some of the pages out of his brother's book. The strong wind tore the flag off the pole. Our roof was torn off in the storm. The foreigners seized our country, tore the mineral wealth out of our ground and treated us like slaves.* (*fig*) *The unhappy children were torn from their parents.* **4** [I∅] to become torn: *This material tears easily so be careful when you wear it.* **5** [T1 (*apart*) *usu pass*] to divide by the pull of opposing forces; destroy the peace of: *a country torn apart by war; a heart torn by sadness; The prince was torn by loyalty to his family and his love for the girl.* **6** [L9] *infml* to move excitedly with great speed: *The excited children tore noisily down the street.* **7** [C] the result of something being torn: *There's a tear in my coat.*

rip 1 [T1] to pull and/or tear forcefully: *He ripped the cloth into small pieces.* **2** [X9] to put or pull in this way: *She ripped the paper off the box.* **3** [I∅] to be torn: *Her skirt ripped when it was caught on a nail.* **4** [C] an example or result of this: *There's a rip in her skirt.*

rend 1 [T1 (*apart*)] *lit & emph* to divide by force; split: *She wept and rent her garments. The quarrel rent the family* (*apart/in two*). *A terrible cry rent the air.* **2** [X9 (*from, off*)] to pull violently: *The cruel soldiers were rending babies from their mothers' arms.*

pull apart [v adv T1] to separate or tear to pieces by force: *He pulled the two fighting men apart. The large animal pulled the smaller one apart with its great arms.*

N332 *verbs, etc* : **coming and falling to pieces**

come apart [v adv I∅] to come to pieces: *The apparatus came apart when he touched it and all the pieces fell to the floor.*

fall apart [v adv I∅] to fall to pieces; to fall in pieces to the floor, etc: *The plane fell apart and crashed to the ground.*

disintegrate [I∅; T1] *fml & tech* to (cause to) come apart (as if) into small pieces: *The ancient walls were disintegrated by time and weather. Is society beginning to disintegrate?* **disintegration** [U]

N333 *verbs* : **breaking**

break 1 [T1; I∅] to (cause to) separate into parts with suddenness or violence, but not by cutting or tearing: *He broke a window/a leg. The rope broke when they were climbing. The window broke into pieces.* **2** [X9; L9] to (cause to) become separated from the main part with suddenness or violence, but not by cutting or tearing: *He broke a branch off a tree. A large piece of ice broke away from the main mass.* **3** [T1; I∅] to (cause to) become unusable by damage to one or more parts: *He broke his wristwatch by dropping it. This machine is broken and must be repaired.* **4** [L7; X7] to (cause to) become suddenly or violently: *The prisoner broke free/loose. The box broke open when it fell. They broke the door down.* **5** [T1] to cut into: *to break the skin; to break the soil* **6** [T1] to disobey, not help; not act in accordance with: *to break the law/a promise* **7** [L9] to force a way (into, out of, or through): *He broke into the shop and stole £100.* **8** [T1] to bring forcefully under control: *to break a horse; to break a child's spirit* **9** [T1] to do better than: *to break a record in sports* **10** [C] the result of breaking or being broken: *There's a break in the fence and the animals got out through it.* **breakage 1** [U] the act or result of breaking: *We lost a lot of bottles through breakage.* **2** [C] an example of this: *There have been too many breakages lately. All breakages must be paid for.*

smash 1 [I∅; T1] to (cause to) break into pieces violently: *The dish smashed on the floor; the fall had smashed it.* **2** [T1; I∅] to go, drive, throw or hit forcefully, as against something solid; crash: *He smashed his foot through the thin door. They smashed their way out of the building. The car smashed into a tree.* **3** [T1; I∅; (*up*)] to (cause to) be destroyed or ruined; wreck: *He smashed (up) his car. They smashed the enemy's defences. He lost all his money when his company smashed* (*up*). **4** [C] a powerful blow: *It was a smash that sent his opponent to the floor.* **5** [C] a breaking into pieces; crash: *He heard the smash of glasses breaking on the floor.* **6** [C] (*fig*) a failure of a business

shatter 1 [T1; I∅] to break suddenly into small pieces; smash: *A stone shattered the window; the glass shattered.* **2** [T1; I∅] to damage badly; ruin; wreck: *The long illness shattered his* health. Bad examination results shattered her hopes of university. **3** [Wv4,5;T1] infml to shock; have a strong effect on the feelings of: It was a shattering performance. There was a shattered look on his face. **4** [C] a shattering: He heard the shatter of breaking windows.

blast **1** [IØ; X9] to break up (esp rock) by explosions: The road is closed because of blasting. They are trying to blast away the face of this rock. **2** [T1] to strike with explosives: The warships blasted the port until all the boats were sunk. **3** [T1] lit to cause to dry up and die esp by great heat, cold or lightning: Every green thing had turned brown, blasted by the icy breath of winter. **4** [T1] fml to kill; destroy: His future was blasted by having been in prison. **5** [T1; IØ] euph damn [⇒ G112, 13]: Blast you! Get off my foot! You can't take my own car away from me, blast it all! Blast! **6** [C] an unexpected quick strong movement of wind or air: the icy blast(s) of the north wind **7** [C; U] An explosion or the very powerful rush of air caused by an explosion: During the bombing many people were killed or wounded by the blast. **8** [C] the very loud usu unpleasant sound of a wind instrument: He blew several loud blasts on his horn. **(at) full blast** (of work, activity, etc) fully: He was working (at) full blast in order to complete the order before the holidays.

split **1** [T1; IØ] to break or cut into parts esp along a length: He split the piece of wood with an axe. This wood splits easily. Her coat split down the back. **2** [C] an act or result of splitting: There's a split in the wood/the back of your coat.

crack **1** [IØ; T1] to (cause to) make a sudden explosive sound: The guns cracked. When the slaves began to weaken their master would crack his whip threateningly. The whip cracked threateningly. **2** [Wv5;IØ;T1] to (cause to) break without dividing into separate parts; split: Don't pour hot water into the glass or it will crack. The labourer cracked the rocks with a heavy hammer. You've cracked the window but luckily you've not broken it. I don't like drinking from cracked cups. **3** [IØ;T1 (open)] to (cause to) break open: The plant will not grow until the seed has cracked open. This nut's shell is very strong. I can't crack it. Although the criminals used explosives they were unable to crack the safe. **4** [IØ;T1] to (cause to) change suddenly or sharply in direction, level, loudness, etc: His voice cracked with strong feeling as he spoke about his dead brother at the funeral. **5** [IØ (up)] to fail as a result of difficulties from inside or outside; lose control or effectiveness: Pressure of work caused John to crack up. **6** [T1] to strike with a sudden blow: The teacher cracked the disobedient pupil's fingers with his ruler. **7** [T1; IØ (against)] to (cause to) strike with a sudden blow: The boy fell and cracked his head against the wall. His head cracked against the wall. **8** [T1] (fig) to discover the secret of: The police cracked the case and caught the criminals. Have you been able to

crack the code (= secret writing) used by the enemy? **9** [T1] (fig) infml to open (a bottle) for drinking: We cracked five bottles of wine last night so you can imagine how drunk we were. **10** [T1; IØ] to (cause to) reduce to separate pieces: This is a cracking plant where oil is cracked. **11** [C] a loud long explosive sound: They heard a crack of thunder/cracks of thunder. **12** [(the) S] a sudden (repeated) explosive sound: The crack of the guns could be heard. **13** [C] a narrow space or opening: The door was opened just a crack. I could see a narrow crack of light between the curtains. **14** [C] a line of division caused by splitting; very narrow thin mark or opening caused by breaking, but not into separate parts: The cup had a crack in it so I refused to drink from it. There was a crack in the window. **15** [C] a sudden sharp blow: She gave him a crack on the head for disobedience. **16** [C] infml an attempt: This is her first crack at writing a book. I had a crack but failed. **17** [C] also **wisecrack** a clever quick forceful joke, reply, or remark

splinter **1** [IØ; T1] to break into small needle-like pieces: The blow splintered the glass. The glass splintered. **2** [IØ (off)] to separate from a larger organization: The dissatisfied groups splintered off. **3** [C] a small needle-like piece broken off something: He needed protection from steel splinters thrown off by the machine. She got a splinter in her finger. **4** [A] (of a group) that has separated from a larger body: It is a religious splinter group/a splinter organization.

snap **1** [IØ] to break suddenly in two pieces: The piece of wood snapped (in two). The rope snapped and he fell. **2** [IØ] to make a short sharp sound, like a piece of wood breaking **3** [C usu sing] (the sound of) a snapping action: He heard the snap of pieces of wood.

N334 verbs & nouns : **pressing, rubbing, and crushing**

[ALSO ⇒ D176 CRUMPLE, M58 PUSH, N154 FORCE]

press **1** [T1] to push steadily or strongly against: He pressed the soft clay into a flat shape. Her finger pressed the button and the machine started (working/moving). (fig) The enemy soldiers pressed the attack (= kept on attacking). (fig) The enemy pressed us hard. **2** [L9] to push or move with force: They pressed closer. The people pressed past the guards and attacked the building. **3** [T1] to push, esp from opposite sides: He pressed her hand (hard). He pressed her to him (= against his body). **4** [IØ] (fig) to need action or attention: His work presses heavily on him. This is pressing business; it must be done now. **5** [IØ on] to hurry; keep moving: The tired travellers pressed on in the hope of finding an inn before night fell (= began). **6** [T1; IØ for] to urge or ask strongly, forcefully: I don't want to press you, but I must get my money back soon. The people *were pressing for changes in the law.* **7** [T1 (*out*)] to make by pressing: *They pressed the shapes out by means of a machine.* **8** [C usu sing] an act of pressing: *He gave her hand a hard press.* **9** [C] a machine for pressing: *a wine press*

compress 1 [T1] to press together esp to get (something) into a smaller space: *This machine compresses air.* **2** to put into fewer words; condense or summarize: *He managed to compress everything into ten pages.* **compression** [U]

depress [T1] **1** *fml* to press down: *Depress this button in case of fire.* **2** to cause to sink to a lower level or position: *Does mass unemployment depress wages?* **depression 1** [U; C] an act of pressing down or the state of being pressed down **2** [C] a part of a surface lower than the other parts: *The rain collected in several depressions on the ground.* **3** [C] an area where the pressure of the air is low in the centre and higher towards the outside: *A depression usually brings bad weather.*

rub 1 [IØ] to move (one thing) against another, esp while pressing: *He rubbed his hands together. The metal is rubbing when the wheel turns. Rub some oil on your skin.* **2** [IØ] (of surfaces) to slide in this way esp so as to wear or cause pain: *The metal rubs against the wood when the wheel turns.* **3** [X9] to remove by this means: *He rubbed the oil off with a cloth. Rub out those words; they are not needed.* **4** [C usu sing] an act of rubbing: *Give your arms a good rub.*

crush 1 [T1] to press with great force so as to break, hurt or destroy the natural shape or conditions: *Don't crush this box; there are flowers inside! The tree fell on top of the car and crushed it. If that rock had fallen on us it would have crushed us to death. For centuries the weight of the sea crushed the decaying bones of sea animals and turned them into chalk.* **2** [T1] to break into a powder by pressure: *This machine crushes wheat grain to make flour.* **3** [IØ T1] to press tightly: *The people crushed through the gates as soon as they were opened. We can't crush any more people onto this train; it's too full already.* **4** [Wv4;T1] to destroy completely, esp by using force: *Ten years of marriage had not crushed his spirit. The military government has successfully crushed all opposition. It was a crushing defeat/a crushing reply.* **5** [T1; IØ] to crumple [⇒ D176]: *Don't crush my dress!* **6** [S] uncomfortable pressure caused by a great crowd of people: *There was such a crush on the train that I could hardly breathe.* **7** [C usu sing] *infml* a social gathering attended by an uncomfortably great number of people

squeeze 1 [T1, X7] to push hard from all sides or opposite sides: *He squeezed her hand. She squeezed the orange. She squeezed the orange dry* (= squeezed all the liquid out of it). **2** [T1 often pass] to get caught tightly and painfully: *He squeezed his fingers in the door/got his*

fingers squeezed in the door when she closed it too suddenly. **3** [X9] to get, move or force by squeezing: *He squeezed the toothpaste out of its tube. The bus was full of people, but they managed to squeeze (their way) onto it. She squeezed past.* **4** [IØ] to be squeezed: *Oranges squeeze quite easily.* **5** [C usu sing] an act of squeezing: *He gave her a squeeze. Give the orange another squeeze.*

squash 1 [Wv5;T1;IØ] to force or be forced into a flat shape; crush: *I sat on my hat and squashed it. Some of the berries at the bottom have been squashed. A squashed orange lay on the floor.* **2** [X9; L9] to push or fit into a small space: *May I squash in next to you? Will you be able to squash all your furniture into such a small house?* **3** [T1] (*fig*) to force into silence or inactivity: *She was/felt squashed by the unkind remark.* **4** [S] a large number esp of persons close together: *The squash in the doorway was terrible.* **5** [S] a sound of squashing: *The fruit landed with a squash.*

N335 *verbs & nouns* : **hitting, striking, bashing, and bruising**

hit 1 [T1] *genl* to bring something against (something else) forcefully: *He hit the other man (hard) with a stone/his hand. Don't hit me again! The car hit a wall.* **2** [T1] to cause to suffer: *The bad news hit him hard. The men were hard hit by the loss of their jobs.* **3** [C] an act of hitting, esp by throwing, dropping, etc something: *The plane dropped a bomb, making a direct hit on the house.*

strike 1 [T1] *esp emph, lit or emot* to hit: *'He struck me!' she cried. He struck the other man hard on the face. He struck him a blow on the face.* **2** [T1] to make something by using force: *He struck a match and lit the fire.* (*fig*) *We must strike a balance* (= find a middle point) *between the two ideas. They struck a bargain* (= agreed) *about the price of the house.* **3** [IØ; T1] (of clocks) to make a striking sound: *The clock struck (four).* **4** [IØ] to attack: *The enemy struck at night.* **5** [C] an attack: *The enemy made a night strike.*

knock 1 [IØ; T1] to strike a blow (on), esp making a noise at the same time: *He knocked on the door. She knocked her head against the wall.* **2** [X9] to cause to move, fall, etc by striking: *He knocked the girl off her bicycle. The car knocked the old man down.* **3** [C] an act or noise of knocking: *He heard a knock on/at the door. He got a bad knock from a car.*

kick 1 [T1; IØ] to hit (someone or something) with the foot: *He kicked the boy/ball (hard). Don't kick! He kicked the ball away.* **2** [IØ] to move the feet forcefully: *The child was pulled away, kicking and shouting.* **3** [IØ] to move back forcefully: *That gun kicks when you fire it.* **4** [C] an act of kicking: *He gave the ball a (hard) kick. That gun has quite a kick.*

bash 1 [T1 (*in* or *up*)] *usu infml* to hit hard, so as to crush, break, or hurt in some way: *He bashed his finger (with a hammer). He bashed the door in and entered the room. If you speak to me like that I'll bash your face in! I bashed up my car and it's a total loss.* **2** [S] *usu infml* a hard or fierce blow: *He gave him a bash on the nose.*

have a bash (at) *BrE sl* to make an attempt (at): *I've never rowed a boat before but I don't mind having a bash (at it).*

bruise 1 [Wv5;T1] to cause one or more discoloured spots on: *She fell and bruised her knee. He had a bruised knee.* **2** [I0] to show one or more such spots: *Her skin/The skin of soft fruit bruises easily.* **3** [C] a discoloured place where the skin of a human, animal, or fruit has been injured by a blow but not broken

blemish 1 [T1] to spoil the beauty or perfection of: *Her beautiful face was blemished by the marks of an old wound.* (*fig*) *His character had been blemished by suggestions of dishonesty.* **2** [C] a mark which blemishes; (*fig*) *esp poet* a fault: *She has no blemishes of any kind.*

N336 *verbs & nouns* : **bursting, etc**

burst 1 [T1;I0] to (cause to) break suddenly, esp by pressure from within: *The bottle/tyre burst. He burst a blood vessel* [⇒ B36]. *She burst the chains that held her.* (*fig*) *The storm burst and we all got wet.* (*fig*) *My heart will burst (with grief/joy).* **2** [X9;L9] to (cause to) come into a stated condition suddenly, often with force: *She burst free (from the chains). She burst out of the chains. She burst through the door into the room. In spring the young flowers burst open. The police burst open the door.* **3** [I0 (*with*), 3] (*in the* **-ing** *form*) to be filled to breaking point (with a substance or usu pleasant feeling): *That bag is bursting (with potatoes). I am bursting with joy. He is bursting to tell you the news.* **4** [C] a sudden outbreak or effort, noise, light, etc: *There was a burst of laughter/of speech. He heard several bomb bursts.*

explode 1 [Wv5;I0;T1] **a** (esp of a bomb or other explosive) to blow up or burst: *an unexploded bomb* **b** to cause (esp a bomb or other explosive) to blow up or burst: *The soldiers exploded a bomb under the bridge.* **2** [I0 (*in, with*)] (of a person) to show sudden violent feeling: *explode with/in anger. If I have to wait much longer I shall explode.* **3** [I0] (of a feeling) to burst out suddenly: *His anger exploded.* **4** [Wv5;T1 *often pass*] to destroy (a belief): *The idea that the earth goes round the sun was exploded long ago. It is an exploded belief.* **explosion** [C] **1** (a loud noise caused by) an act of exploding: *When she lit the gas there was a loud explosion. The explosion of an atomic* [⇒ H8] *bomb destroyed a whole city.* **2** a sudden bursting out (of the stated feeling or its expression): *He could hear explosions of loud laughter.* **3** (*fig*) a sudden increase (*esp in the phr* **the population explosion**) **explosive 1**

[B] able or likely to explode: *These substances are highly explosive.* **2** [C] an explosive substance

erupt [I0] (of a mountain with fire inside it (**volcano**)) to pour out fire: *Mount Vesuvius hasn't erupted for a good many years.* (*fig*) *He erupted with anger.* **eruption** [C;U] **1** (an example of) the action of erupting: *The volcano was in a state of eruption.* (*fig*) *There were several eruptions* (= outbreaks) *of infectious disease.* **2** (the sudden appearance of) an unhealthy spot or area on the skin

go off [v adv I0] *not fml* to explode: *The bomb went off, killing four people.*

blow up [v adv T1;I0] *not fml* to (cause to) explode; to destroy or damage in this way: *The enemy soldiers blew up the bridge to stop our trains crossing. The bridge suddenly blew up; the soldiers had planted* (= put) *a bomb under it.*

N337 *verbs & nouns* : **hurting and harming**

[ALSO ⇒ B122, 129]

hurt 1 [I0;T1] to give pain or cause injury to (a person, animal, etc): *She accidentally cut her finger with a knife and it hurts. He hurt his arm when he fell. The child was more afraid than hurt. Did she hurt herself when she fell? My shoes are tight and they hurt like mad* (= hurt a lot). **2** [T1;I0] to cause (someone) to feel upset: *His angry words hurt (her). I felt hurt when you didn't come to see me.* **3** [it I0] *not fml* cause trouble: *It won't hurt if we wait a few days before answering his letter.* **4** [U] *esp old use* a cause of pain or trouble: *Did he suffer any hurt? I meant her no hurt. It was a real hurt to his feelings.*

spoil [T1] **1** to cause to be in a bad condition; to make worse or less satisfactory (than before): *He spoiled his painting by putting too much red paint on it. She has spoilt her work by being careless. Bad weather will spoil our holiday.* **2** [Wv5] to do too much for (esp a child); to be too kind and gentle to: *You'll spoil that child if you give him everything he wants as soon as he starts crying. They have only one child and they really spoil her. What a spoilt child!*

damage 1 [Wv5;T1] to break, spoil or cause loss of value to (things) without destroying: *He damaged my car with a stone. The bus was badly damaged when it hit the wall. Sea water damaged the ship's goods. His angry words damaged their marriage. Her chances of winning the game were damaged by some bad moves at the beginning. People won't buy damaged goods at the same price as undamaged goods.* **2** [U] the result of damaging or being damaged; loss: *The fire caused a lot of damage (to the buildings). The storm did great damage to the farms. Who will pay for all this damage?* **damages** [P] *law* money asked for or given to someone because of damage, trouble caused, etc

harm *esp emot* **1** [T1] to hurt, spoil or damage: *Smoking a lot of cigarettes can harm and even kill over a long period of time. Did he harm the child?—No; she wasn't harmed/she's unharmed. There was a fire in our street but our house wasn't harmed. Come on; getting up early won't harm you!* **2** [U] a condition which harms: *The storm did a lot of harm. Keep the child out of harm's way* (= away from harm). *He didn't mean any harm* (= he didn't intend to harm anyone). *There's no harm in going to see him, is there? There's no harm in trying; let's do it.*

mar [T1] *esp emph & emot* to spoil: *Age cannot mar her beauty. The noise marred the peace of the night.*

impair [T1] *fml* to spoil or weaken: *Too much study impaired his abilities.* **-ment** [U]

adulterate [T1] to make (something, esp food) less good or pure by adding some other thing: *He adulterated the good oil with cheaper stuff, but sold the mixture at the same high price.* **adulteration 1** [U] the act or result of adulteration: *'This adulteration of our food must stop,' he said.* **2** [C usu sing] an example of this

wrong 1 [T1] to do something wrong or bad to (someone): *He greatly wronged her by what he did.* **2** [U] wrong things done: *He did her wrong. The wrong he did her was great.* **3** [C] a wrong thing done: *These wrongs have gone on too long; they must end!*

slight [T1] to treat (someone) rudely as if unimportant or not very good, useful etc: *When he talked about their work, he slighted her several times. She felt slighted by what he said.*

N338 *verbs* : **destroying**

[ALSO ⇒ A8, 13 KILL; I14 DEMOLISH]

destroy 1 [T1; (I∅)] to tear down or apart; ruin; put an end to the existence or effectiveness of (something): *The enemy destroyed the city. The storm has destroyed my crops. He seems to like nothing but hating and destroying.* (*fig*) *You have destroyed my life and all my hopes.* **2** [T1] *euph* to kill (esp an animal): *The dog is mad and ought to be destroyed.* **destruction** [U] **1** the act of destroying or state of being destroyed: *They watched the destruction of the forest by fire. The army left the enemy town in (a state of) complete destruction.* **2** that which destroys: *Pride was her destruction, for it caused the loss of all her friends.* **destructive** [B] **1** causing destruction: *What a destructive storm!* **2** wanting or tending to destroy: *He's very good at making destructive arguments against things, but he never offers any ideas of his own.* **-ly** [adv] **-ness** [U]

wreck 1 [Wv6;T1] to cause (esp a ship or vehicle) to be destroyed: *The ship was wrecked on the rocks.* **2** [T1] *esp emot* to destroy: *The weather has completely wrecked our plans.* **3** [C] something that has been wrecked: *The car*

was a wreck. [*also* ⇒ M170] **wreckage** [U] material from something that has been wrecked: *The road was covered with wreckage from the explosion in the building.*

ruin 1 [Wv5;T1] to destroy or spoil (completely): *The rain will ruin the crops. An explosion ruined this building. It was an ancient ruined city.* **2** [Wv5;T1 *usu pass*] to cause total loss of money to: *I was ruined by that law case; I'm a ruined man!* **3** [U] the state of being ruined: *He was faced with complete ruin. The castle fell into ruin* (= became ruined). **4** [C] something ruined: *The castle is now a ruin. He walked among the ruins of ancient Rome. The city was in ruins after the war.* **ruinous** [B] causing ruin; being a ruin **-ly** [adv]: *We found the house ruinously expensive* (= it cost too much and ruined us).

obliterate [T1] to remove all signs of; destroy: *The village was obliterated.* **obliteration** [U]

eradicate [T1] to destroy completely and put an end to (something bad): *These diseases must be eradicated.* **eradication** [U]

sack 1 [T1] (esp of an army in former times) to destroy buildings, take things of value, and usu harm or kill people in (a conquered place, esp a city) **2** [(*the*) S] the action of sacking a city: *the sack of Troy; put the city to the sack* (= sack it)

annihilate [T1] to destroy completely: *The army annihilated the enemy.* (*fig*) *His argument was annihilated.* **annihilation** [U] **1** complete destruction, esp of armies, enemies, etc **2** the destruction of body and soul

wipe out [v adv T1 *usu pass*] *esp emot* to destroy completely: *The village was wiped out in the fighting. The soldiers were wiped out to a man* (= all killed).

root out [v adv] **1** [T1] to get rid of completely; destroy (something bad): *This disease could easily be rooted out.* **2** [D1 (*for*); T1] to find by searching: *I'll try and root you out something dry to wear.*

stamp out [v adv T1] to put out, stop, or destroy: *He stamped out the fire with his foot.* (*fig*) *Doctors are trying to stamp this disease out completely.*

N339 *verbs* : **undermining and disrupting**

[ALSO ⇒ C133]

undermine [T1] **1** to wear away the earth beneath, removing support: *The house is unsafe since the foundations were undermined by floods.* **2** to weaken or destroy by stages: *Her continued unkindness undermined his belief in her gentleness. If you always say she is wrong you'll undermine her confidence. Illness undermined his strength.*

disrupt [T1] to bring or throw into disorder: *to disrupt a public meeting by continual shouting. An accident has disrupted railway services into and out of the city.* **disruption 1** [U] the act, occasion or result of disrupting **2** [C] an example of this

N340 *verbs* : **getting worse**

deteriorate [IØ] to become worse: *Her work was once very good but lately it has deteriorated badly.* **deterioration** [U]
worsen [IØ; (T1)] to (cause to) get worse: *Conditions in the city worsened as the disease spread. The rain has worsened our difficulties.*

Showing, hiding, finding, saving, and similar words

N350 *verbs, etc* : **showing and indicating**

show 1 [T1, 5; D1] to let (something or someone) be seen; to cause (something or someone) to be seen: *He showed me the book. He showed the book to me. She showed that she wasn't happy by leaving the room. That short dress shows a lot of leg!* (*fig*) *He showed great courage in coming here tonight.* **2** [D; T: (1, 6a, b)] (*fig*) to make clear: *Please show me what I did wrong/where I went wrong.* **3** [D1 (*to*); T1] (*fig*) to give: *Show him some kindness. She showed a lot of kindness to him.* **4** [IØ (*on, in*)] to be seen: *Her anger showed (on her face/in her actions). Does the dirty mark still show on my shirt?* **show itself** to be easily seen: *His anger showed itself clearly.* **show oneself** *esp deprec* to be present: *Do you think he will dare (to) show himself at the meeting after what he said?* **show one's face** *deprec* to let oneself be seen: *I don't dare show my face there again after what I did!*
point 1 [IØ; T1] to (raise a hand, finger, stick, etc to) show the position or direction of (something or someone): *He pointed to the house. She raised her hand to point the way. He pointed towards the men and said, 'It was those men who did it.' He just stood there, pointing and saying nothing.* **2** [IØ; T1: (*at, towards*)] to direct or be directed: *He pointed the gun straight at her. The gun pointed towards them. The big guns pointed out across the valley.*
indicate *often fml* **1** [T1] to point to: *I asked him where my sister was and he indicated the shop opposite. The signpost indicates the direction of London from here.* **2** [T1, 5a] to make or be a sign (for): *He indicated that I could leave. His answer indicated that I could leave. In many writing systems a circle indicates the sun.* **3** [T5a, b] to make clear: *I indicated that his help was not welcome.* **4** [T1 *often pass*] to show a need for; suggest: *The change in his illness indicates the use of stronger drugs. His argument is weak; a lot of re-thinking is indicated.* **5** [T1; IØ] to show (the direction in which one is

turning in a vehicle) by making signs with the hand or flashing the special coloured lights on the sides of a car at front and back: *He's indicating left. I wish he'd indicate (clearly). Do taxis in London ever indicate?*
point out [v adv T1, 5a] *not fml* to show or make clear: *He pointed out the house I was asking for. She pointed out that his help was not welcome.*

N351 *verbs* : **showing and demonstrating, etc**

show [T1] to show in public: *When do you intend to show the dog?*
show off [v adv] **1** [IØ] *usu deprec* to behave so as to try to get admiration for oneself, one's abilities, etc: *Stop showing off!* **2** [T1] to allow to be seen as something fine or beautiful: *She loves showing off her new clothes. That dress shows her figure off very well.*
demonstrate 1 [T1, 5, 6a, b] to show clearly: *Please demonstrate how the machine works.* **2** [T1, 5] to prove or make clear, esp by reasoning or giving many examples: *She demonstrated that 2 and 2 are 4.* **3** [T1] to show the value or use of, esp to a possible buyer: *Let me demonstrate our wonderful new machine to you, sir.* **4** [IØ] to arrange or take part in a public show of strong feeling or opinion, often with marching, big signs, etc: *The students demonstrated in favour of better teaching.*
demonstrative [B] **1** [Wa5] for the purpose of demonstrating something: *'This' is a demonstrative pronoun.* **2** showing feelings openly: *He isn't a demonstrative person.* **un-** [*neg*] **-ly** [*adv*]: *She welcomed him demonstratively, with a kiss.* **demonstration** [U;C] the act of demonstrating: *She went to a cookery demonstration.*
exhibit 1 [IØ; T1] to show in public, as for sale, or in a competition (objects, sometimes of an understood type): *Let's exhibit the paintings/ flowers/new cars. He is a young painter who has not yet exhibited (his work).* **2** [T1] to show other people that one possesses (a feeling, quality, etc): *They began to exhibit signs of fear/guilt.*
display [T1] *esp fml & pomp* to show: *He wants to display fruit in the shop/to display the national flag in his window/to display his true feelings.*
feature 1 [IØ (*in*)] to be seen, found, etc (in something else, esp of a person in a film, story, etc): *She features in the new film called 'Strange Love'. These present difficulties featured largely in the chief minister's speech yesterday.* **2** [T1] to have (someone or something) in a film, story, etc: *The new film features that great actor Henry Smith.*

N352 *nouns* : **showing and indicating**

show 1 [C] an act of showing: *They voted by a show of hands* (= each one voted by raising his or her hand). 2 [S] *often deprec* such an act, esp if done too much or without good intentions: *He made a great show of friendliness towards us.*

showing 1 [C] an act of putting on view: *a showing of new fashions* **2** [S] a record of success or quality; performance: *a good/poor showing by the local team* **3** [*on* S] a statement or understanding of a state of affairs: *On any showing it'll be an interesting election. On the government's own showing they won't win by very many votes.*

indication 1 [U] the action of indicating: *Please give me some indication of what to do.* **2** [C *often pl* (*of*, 5)] a sign or suggestion: *There are clear indications that the weather is changing. He gave an indication that our help might be needed.*

appearance [C; (*in*) U] what shows or is seen: *His appearance was rather unsatisfactory; he looked tired and dirty. The young man had the appearance of being older than he was/ of being unhappy. Don't judge by appearances, because appearances can be deceptive* (= things are not always the way they appear to be). *In appearance he was fair-haired, blue-eyed and about 30 years old. She had a slightly foreign appearance.*

N353 *nouns* : **showing and demonstrating**

show 1 [C *esp in comb*] a collection of things that are shown esp to the public esp as part of a competition: *They went to the flower show. Is the horse show at the showground* (= field, etc where shows are held)? **2** [S] the way in which things are shown: *The flowers made a fine show!* **3** [C *esp in comb*] a kind of public entertainment [*also* ⇒ K73]: *There's a film show on tonight; are you coming? Some television shows are better than others.*

exhibition [C] **1** a public show of objects: *an international trade exhibition* **2** [(*of*)] an act of exhibiting [⇒ N351]: *What an exhibition of bad temper!* **make an exhibition of oneself** to behave foolishly in public: *Get up off the floor and stop making such an exhibition of yourself!* **on exhibition** being shown publicly: *Some of the children's paintings are now on exhibition at the school.*

exhibit [C] **1** something that is exhibited, esp in a museum **2** something brought into a law court to prove the truth: *Exhibit A was a knife which, the police said, belonged to the prisoner.* **3** *AmE* an exhibition

exposition 1 [C] an international exhibition of the products of industry **2** [C; U] (an act of) explaining and making clear: *a full exposition of his political beliefs; The beginning of the book is mostly exposition, telling us who the characters are.*

display 1 [C; (U)] the act or action of displaying [⇒ N351]: *We saw a display of great skill.* **2** [C]

a collection of things displayed: *a display of fruit; to put things in a display case* **on display** being shown publicly

demonstration 1 [U; C, C5] the act of demonstrating: *the demonstration of a machine. The demonstration that you are wrong will not be difficult, my dear sir.* **2** [C] *also infml* **demo** a public show of strong feeling or opinion, often with marching, big signs, etc: *a demonstration against the war*

N354 *verbs* : **revealing and exposing**
[ALSO ⇒ F210]

reveal 1 [T1] to allow to be seen: *The dress reveals part of her stomach. The curtains opened, to reveal a darkened stage.* **2** [T1 (*as*), 5; X (*to be*) 1, 7] to make known (to be): *She suddenly revealed (the fact) that she was not married. These letters reveal him as/reveal him to be an honest man.*

expose [T1] **1** [Wv5; (*to*)] to uncover, so as to leave without protection: *She exposed her skin to the sun. The soldiers were warned to remain hidden and not to expose themselves.* (*fig*) *Her youth and beauty will expose her to many dangers. The house is in an exposed position, on top of a high hill.* **2** to leave (a baby) to die of cold and hunger out of doors: *The ancient Greeks are said to have exposed their unwanted babies.* **3** [(*to*)] to make known (a secretly guilty person or action): *I threatened to expose him/the plan (to the police).* **4** to place in view: *He exposed his goods for sale in the market.* **5** to uncover (a film) to the light, when taking a photograph: *This film has already been exposed.* **expose (oneself or another) to** to make (oneself or another) suffer: *His fatness exposes him to a lot of joking at the office.*

show up [v adv T1; I∅] to (cause to) be easily seen: *The cracks in the wall only show up when the light shines on them.*

N355 *nouns* : **revealing and exposing**

revelation 1 [U (*of*)] the making known (of something secret) **2** [C; *the* C5] a (surprising) fact that is made known: *We listened to her strange revelations about her past. The revelation that the world is round surprised them. This is quite a revelation to me; I had no idea that you were a priest.*

exposure 1 [U] the state of being exposed to the weather: *He nearly died of exposure on the cold mountain.* **2** [C; U *to*] (a case of) being exposed (to a stated influence): *much exposure to danger; a short exposure to sunlight* **3** [C; U (*of*)] a case of exposing or the experience of being exposed: *I threatened him with public exposure. There were repeated exposures in the newspapers of the Government's mistakes.* **4** [C] the amount of film that must be exposed to take one photograph: *I have three* *exposures left on this film.* **5** [C] the length of time that a film must be exposed to take a photograph: *You'd better give it an exposure of 1/100 of a second. These two pictures were taken with different exposures.* **6** [U] the act of exposing **7** [S9] the direction in which a room or house faces: *My bedroom has a southern exposure.*

N356 *verbs* : **hiding and covering up**
[ALSO ⇒ F208]

hide 1 [Wv5; T1] to put or keep out of sight; to make or keep secret: *I hid the broken plate behind the table. You're hiding some important facts. Don't hide your feelings; say what you think. The sun was hidden by/behind the clouds. His words had a hidden meaning.* **2** [I0 (*from*)] to place oneself or be placed so as not to be seen: *I'll hide behind the door.* (*fig*) *Where's that book hiding? He is hiding from the police. Quick, hide! The sun was hidden by/behind the clouds.* **3** *also esp AmE* **blind** [C] a place where a person can watch wild animals, birds, etc without being seen by them **in hiding** hiding oneself: *The criminals were in hiding from the police. He has been in hiding for months.*

conceal [Wv5; T1 (*from*), 4] *esp fml* to hide; to keep from being seen or known: *It is wrong for a man to conceal things from his wife. Trees concealed the entrance to the park. There is a concealed entrance here. He concealed having been there. Conceal yourself, quickly!* **concealment** [U] **1** the act of concealing: *Concealment of stolen property is a crime punishable by imprisonment.* **2** the state or condition of being concealed: *The criminals stayed in concealment until the police had passed.*

disguise 1 [T1 (*as*)] to change the usual appearance, etc of, so as to hide the truth: *She disguised herself as a man, but she couldn't disguise her voice. The secret door was disguised as a mirror.* **2** [T1] to hide (the real state of things): *He disguised his fear by looking angry/under an angry expression. There's no disguising the fact/it is impossible to disguise the fact that business is bad.*

cover [T1] to place one thing over or in front of (another) so as to hide or protect in this way: *She covered the money with a cloth so that he couldn't see it.*

cover up [v adv T1] *not fml* to cover or hide as fully as possible, esp so as to keep hidden: *Cover up your legs and keep them warm. They tried to cover up their mistakes.* **cover-up** [C] an act of covering up: *We don't want another cover-up; tell us the truth!*

secrete [T1] *fml & pomp* to hide or keep in a secret place: *They have secreted the papers somewhere in the house.* **secretion** [U] the act of secreting

obscure [T1] to make less clear, harder to understand, see, find, etc: *The view of the town*

was obscured by smoke. He hopes to obscure the facts by telling lies.

N357 *verbs* : **finding and discovering**

find 1 [T1] to get or get back (something or someone that has been lost, hidden, unknown, not expected, etc): *I lost my knife but I've found it again. Did you manage to find the book that you'd lost? She found some money in the pocket of an old coat. Oil has been found in large quantities off the coast of Scotland. We must find an answer to this problem. He was found dead in his garden.* **2** [T1, 5] to know or learn by finding, looking, studying, etc: *How do you find her?—I have always found her to be honest and helpful. The next day we found that he had gone with all the money. I'm sorry; I find that I can't help you* (= I thought I could, but now I can't). **3** [Wv6; X7, 9] *law* to decide someone to be: *She was found guilty of murder* (= It was agreed in a court of law that she murdered someone). **4** [T1] to come to naturally: *Water always finds its own level.* **5** [X9 *usu pass*] to know that (something) exists or happens: *Lions are found in Africa. He can be found in that restaurant most evenings.*

discover 1 [T1, 5, 6; V3] to learn (a fact or the answer to a question): *We soon discovered the truth. Did you ever discover who sent you the flowers? We never discovered how to open the box. Scientists have discovered that this disease is carried by rats.* **2** [T1] to find (something existing but not known before, often a place or a scientific fact): *Columbus is said to have discovered America in 1492. Oil has been discovered under the North Sea. I discovered a fly in my coffee.*

track down [v adv T1] to find (someone or something) by hunting or searching: *The police tracked him down.*

trace [T1] **1** to follow the course or line of (something or someone): *The soldiers traced the river down to the sea. The criminal was traced to London.* **2** [(*back*)] to find the origins of by finding proof of by going back in time: *His family can trace its history back to the 10th century. The whole false story was traced back to an opposition politician.* **3** to follow the course, development or history of: *He tried to trace the beginning of the labour movement.* **4** to find or discover by looking in many places, etc: *I can't trace the letter you sent me.*

N358 *verbs* : **finding out**

find out [v adv] **1** [T1, 5, 6a, b; I0] to find or learn by asking, studying, talking to people, searching, etc: *How did you find out his name? They soon found out that he was lying. I don't know but I'll try to find out. Where is my book?—Find out!* **2** [T1] to discover that (someone) is not honest: *He was stealing their money, but they soon found him out.*

get at [v prep T1] *infml* to manage to find out: *I'm afraid we just can't get at the information; no one will help us.*

determine [T1, 6a, b] *fml* to find out exactly: *The police wanted to determine all the facts/ what exactly happened. We're only trying to determine the truth.* **determination** [U] the action of finding out: *The determination of all the facts is not easy.*

detect [T1] *esp fml & tech* to find out: *We have been able to detect some improvement as a result of the medicine. I seemed to detect some anger in his voice. The soldiers detected a bomb in the building.* **detection** [U] the act of detecting: *The detection of crime is the business of the police.* **detector** [C] an apparatus for detecting something: *a lie detector; a metal detector*

N359 *verbs* : **seeking and searching**

seek 1 [T1 (*out*); I∅ (*after, for*)] *usu fml, old use or lit* to make a search (for); look (for); try to find or get (something): *'Seek and you shall find' (the Bible). He sought shelter from the rain/sought out his friend in the crowd. She will seek (after) the truth in the matter/seek public office* (= an official position). *He was seeking among his untidy papers for the right one.* 2 [T1] *fml* (to go) to ask for: *You should seek advice from your lawyer on this matter.* 3 [T3] *esp lit* to try; make an attempt: *They sought to punish him for his crime but he escaped.* 4 [T1] to move naturally towards: *Water seeks its own level. The compass pointer always seeks the north.* **not far to seek** easily seen or understood: *The reason for his failure was not far to seek; he was ill during the examination.* **seeker** [C] a person who seeks something or someone: *He says he is a seeker after truth.*

search [I∅ (*through, into*); T1 (*for, after*)] to look at, through, into, etc or examine (a place) carefully and thoroughly to try to find something: *They searched the woods for the lost child. He searched (through) his pockets for a cigarette. She searched her Bible for a word of comfort. (fig) He had spent his life searching after fame. The police searched the thief but found no weapon on him. The scientists were searching for a cure for the common cold. I've searched my conscience* (= tried to find fault with myself) *and I still think I did the right thing.* **search me!** *infml* I don't know!: *What's the time?—Search me: I haven't got a watch.* **searcher** [C] a person who searches **search party** [C] a group which is searching for someone or something

hunt [T1; I∅] 1 to go after (animals and birds) in order to catch and kill them, either for food or sport 2 to search (for): *The police are hunting the murderer. They hunted everywhere/high and low.* **hunter** [C] a person who hunts esp animals

stalk 1 [T1] to hunt (esp a wild animal) by moving slowly and quietly nearer without

being seen: *The lion stalked the deer.* 2 [S] such a hunt or hunting action: *He was on a stalk.* **stalker** [C] a person who stalks or is stalking

poach [I∅; T1] to hunt or steal (esp birds, small animals, etc) on someone else's land: *He has been poaching on her land for years, poaching mainly fish and rabbits.* **poacher** [C] a person who poaches

prey on/upon [v prep T1] to hunt and eat: *Cats prey on mice.*

track [T1] to follow the track of (an animal, aircraft, ship, person, etc): *We tracked the rabbit to its hole. Some special scientific instruments are used for tracking planes.* **tracker** [C] a person who tracks esp animals

scout 1 [I∅; T1] to go through (a place) ahead of others to get information: *He used to scout for the army. They scouted the hills for enemy positions.* 2 [C] a person who does this: *He was a scout for the army/an army scout.*

comb [T1] *not fml* to search thoroughly: *The police combed the hills for the murderer.*

rifle [T1] to search thoroughly and without care, esp so as to steal anything of value from (a place, container, etc): *She rifled the cupboards for everything of any value.*

bag [T1] 1 to catch and esp put in a bag, esp after hunting and killing: *He bagged several rabbits.* 2 *infml* to kill: *He bagged an elephant.*

N360 *verbs* : **investigating and examining**

investigate [T1] to examine thoroughly the reasons for, the character of, etc: *to investigate the crime. He has been investigated and found blameless.* **investigator** [C] a person who investigates

probe [I∅ (*into*); T1] 1 to search with a long thin metal instrument: *The doctor probed gently inside the man's ear; he probed without finding anything wrong. He probed the mud with a stick, looking for the ring he had dropped.* 2 to examine (something) thoroughly; search into: *She tried to probe my mind and discover what I was thinking. Stop probing! We intend to probe into this matter until we're satisfied there's been no deception.*

explore [T1] 1 to travel into or through (a place) for the purpose of discovery: *He explored Central Africa.* 2 to examine carefully (esp a subject or question), in order to learn more: *Let's explore the various ways of saving money/explore all the possibilities.* **explorer** [C] a person who explores, esp places which are unknown or not well known: *Livingstone and Stanley were famous 19th-century African explorers* (= They explored Africa).

examine [T1] 1 to look at (a person or thing) closely, in order to find out something: *The doctor examined her carefully. My bags were examined when I entered the country. The employer examined the workers' complaints.* 2 [(*in* or *on*)] to ask (a person) questions, in order to measure knowledge or find out something, as in a school or a court of law: *The teacher examined the children on/in English literature*. **need (one's) head examined** to seem foolish or slightly mad: *If she wants to go swimming in this weather she needs her head examined!* **examiner** [C] a person who examines something or esp someone: *His examiners listened to his answers*.

check [T1] to look at or examine in order to see that/if something is all right: *I've added all the numbers; would you please check them/check my addition, please? He checked the list of names to see that no one had been left out*.

inspect [T1] *fml* (esp of an official examining, checking, etc) to look carefully at, esp to see if everything is as it should be: *He inspected the child's hands to see if they were clean. They inspected the work of the school*. **inspector** [C *often in comb*] a person, esp an official, who inspects something or someone: *The school inspector was pleased with the school's work*.

check up [v adv I∅ (*on*); T1] to make inquiries (about): *When is the train leaving?—I don't know; I'll go and check up. He went to check up the times of the trains*.

check on [v prep T1, 6a, b] to make inquiries about the activities of or facts about (something or someone): *They tried to check on her past life. Stop checking on me/on where I go and what I do!*

check over [v adv T1] to examine or look carefully at (as a machine): *He checked over the car's engine before they left*.

scrutinize, -ise [T1] *fml & emph* to examine closely: *This report should be scrutinized and any mistakes reported to me*.

vet [T1] *not fml* to inspect (a plan, etc) before giving esp official approval: *His plan needs careful vetting; vet it thoroughly*.

research [Wv5;T1] to do research on; study the history and general information on: *She has researched the subject well. This is a well-researched book*.

N361 *nouns* : **finding, discovering, etc**

find 1 [S] *esp apprec* something or someone found: *Getting that book was a real find; I've been looking for it for months! My new secretary is very good; quite a find, in fact*. **2** [C] an act of finding: *They were looking for oil and made several exciting finds off the Scottish coast*.

findings [P] an opinion, decision, etc, esp of a judge, etc, after studying the facts or evidence [⇒ N221], etc: *What were his findings in the matter? The committee's findings are not available to the public*.

discovery 1 [*the* U5, 9 esp *of*] the event of discovering: *The discovery of oil on their land made the family rich. She was shocked at the discovery that he was a thief*. **2** [C] a case of discovering something: *They made an impor-*

tant scientific discovery. **3** [C] something discovered: *A collector of rare insects will show us some of his latest discoveries*.

trace [C] **1** a mark or sign showing the former presence or passage of some person, vehicle or event: *We could find no trace of an ancient ruin. Did the police find any trace of the murderer? We've lost all trace of our daughter* (= we no longer know where she is). **2** a very small amount of something: *There are traces of poison in the dead man's blood*.

search [C; *in* U] an act of searching: *They made a long search for the lost child. He went in search of a doctor for his sick wife. The birds were flying south in search of winter sun. The police search discovered no illegal drugs on the ship. He made a search of the public records*.

hunt [C *often in comb*] **1** an act of hunting: *a long hunt through the countryside*; *a bear hunt*; *an elephant hunt* **2** a fox-hunt; the people who regularly hunt foxes together; the area they hunt **3** a search: *Our hunt for a house is at last at an end*.

investigation 1 [U] the act of investigating or being investigated **2** [C] an examination of facts to find reasons, causes, etc

exploration [C; U] an act or the action of exploring: *He went on a journey of exploration into China. They made a full exploration of all the reasons for and against closing the railway*.

examination 1 [C (*in* or *on*)] a spoken or written test of knowledge: *She will enter for/sit (for)/take/pass/fail a public examination. Our teacher set us a stiff examination in English. The school is holding the examinations this week*. **2** [C; U] (an act of) examining: *The doctor carried out the medical examination. You will have to undergo* (= have) *a medical examination. The metal looked like gold, but on closer/further examination was found to be brass*. **3** [C; U] (an act of) questioning someone in a court of law: *The examination of all the witnesses took a week*. **under examination** being examined; not yet decided: *The matter of whether to increase the size of the navy is still under examination*.

exam [C] *infml* an examination: *Did she pass all her exams? His exam results were good*.

probe [C] **1** a long thin metal instrument, usu with a rounded end, used by doctors to search the inside of a wound, a hole in a tooth, etc **2** an instrument of a like shape, used to feel inside a hollow or a deep place **3** *also* **space probe** **a** an apparatus sent into the sky to examine conditions in outer space **b** an act of sending such an apparatus into the sky **4** (esp in newspapers) a careful and thorough inquiry or examination: *A newspaper probe into hospital conditions has led the public to ask for improvements*. **5** an act of probing

check [C *usu sing*] an act of checking, of looking at (something or someone) to see if everything is all right: *I've added the numbers; please do a check on them to see if the addition is correct*.

He made a careful check of all the names on the list, so that no one would be left out.

checkup [C] *not fml* an esp short or quick examination, inspection or check: *Do a quick checkup on his work; I'm not satisfied with it. She went to the doctor for a checkup.*

inspection 1 [U] the act of inspecting or being inspected: *On inspection the work was found to be unsatisfactory.* **2** [C] an act, occasion or result of inspection: *He made an inspection of the school. The inspection showed that the work had been done well.*

scrutiny [U;(C)] (a) close study or look; (a) careful and thorough examination: *The table looked old, but (a) closer scrutiny showed it to be a modern product. Under the man's steady scrutiny the girl began to feel uncomfortable.*

research [U;C] careful examination of a subject in order to find out new facts about it or a new way of describing, understanding, using, etc it: *His work is mainly (in) research. He is engaged in research work. His researches are nearly finished now.*

N362 *verbs* : **losing and misplacing**

lose 1 [D1;T1] to cause or come to have (something or someone) no longer: *I've lost my book/job. He lost his life in the war. Carelessness lost her the job.* **2** [T1] to be too late for: *He stayed and talked so much that he lost his train.* **3** [T1] to be unable to see, hear, etc: *I lost (sight of) him in the mist. She didn't speak very loudly, so we lost a lot of what she said.*

misplace [T1] *often pass* **1** to put in an unsuitable or wrong place or position: *Among all this old furniture that modern chair looks misplaced. Some of the pages in that book are misplaced; page 42 comes before page 36.* **2** [Wv5] to have (good feelings) for an undeserving person or thing: *She treated the beggar with misplaced kindness; he was neither grateful nor deserving. Your trust in that man is misplaced; he'll deceive you if he gets the chance. He has a misplaced faith in his own abilities.* **3** to mislay: *I've misplaced my glasses again.*

mislay [Wv5;T1] to put (something) in a place and forget where; lose (something) in this way often only for a short time: *I wonder where I put the letter; I've mislaid it somewhere. He's always mislaying his keys; he never remembers where he's put them. He found the mislaid keys.*

N363 *verbs* : **saving and rescuing**

save 1 [T1 (*from*)] to rescue from danger; make safe: *Help! Save me! 'God save the King!' He saved his friend from falling. The dog saved his life.* **2** [I0 (*up, for*)] to keep and add to an amount of money for later use: *Children should learn to save. We're saving (up) for a new car.* **3** [D1;T1 (*for*)] to keep and not spend or use, as for a special purpose or use

later: *It'll save me 50p if I buy the large size box. He saved his strength for an effort in the last minute of the race. It will save time if we drive the car instead of walking.* **4** [D1;T1, 4; (*esp BrE*) X4] to make unnecessary (for (someone)): *Will you go to the shop for me? It'll save (me) a trip; It'll save (me) going into town. A brush with a long handle will save you from having to bend down so far to clean the floor. It's a labour-saving instrument.*

save on [v prep D1;T1] to save and not use so much, esp by spending or costing less money: *We're saving on petrol by walking everywhere we can. Living near the shops saves us lots of money on petrol.*

keep [T1] to look after; have in a safe place: *Keep my money and books till I come back. He kept the child out of harm's way (=safe) until she came back.*

preserve [T1 (*from, against*)] to keep (someone or something) safe, healthy, in good condition, free from danger, change, outside influences, etc: *He tried to preserve the child from danger. They tried to preserve their customs against the effects of the modern world. It's a fine old house; it should be preserved. 'To preserve your freedom you must fight!' he said.*

conserve [T1] to use (a supply) carefully without waste; preserve: *We must conserve our forests if we are to ensure a future supply of wood. Try to conserve some of your strength for the last part of the fight.*

husband [T1] *usu fml* to save carefully or make the best use of: *The soldiers husbanded their strength and their food, waiting for the enemy to attack.*

rescue [T1 (*from*)] to save (from harm or danger); set free: *He rescued a man from drowning/a cat from a high tree/his stamp collection from the burning house.*

salvage [T1] *tech* to save (esp goods, ships, etc) from being destroyed or for some kind of use after being damaged: *They salvaged the ship from the bottom of the sea. Can you salvage anything from the fire?*

N364 *verbs* : **keeping back and reserving** [T1]

keep back [v adv (*from*)] to refuse to give or tell: *He kept the money back for himself. You are keeping something back; you must tell me! They kept the information back from him.*

reserve *esp fml* to keep back, esp for later or one's own special use: *I reserve my right to be silent; I don't have to answer your questions. She reserved the best wine for her own family. Reserve your strength for later; you'll need it.*

withhold [(*from*)] *esp fml, tech & pomp* to refuse to give: *They said that he was deliberately withholding information from the police (=that he chose to do so). Please don't withhold anything; tell me everything!*

N365 *verbs* : **guarding and keeping safe**

[ALSO ⇒ C225]

keep safe [T1 (*from*)] to keep (someone or something) in a safe place or condition, away from danger, etc: *Keep the child safe till I come back. He kept the city safe from enemy attack.*

guard 1 [T1 (*against*)] to keep (someone or something) safe, esp by being there to watch: *Guard the town well. He guarded the family against every danger.* **2** [I0 *against*] to do something to stop something happening: *He tried to guard against every possible danger. She put on warm clothes to guard against the cold.*

protect [T1] **1** [(*against* or *from*)] to keep safe (from harm, loss, etc) esp by guarding or covering: *The hard shell of a nut protects the seed inside it. A line of forts was built along the border to protect the country against attack. He raised his arms to protect his face from the blow.* **2** [(*against* or *from*)] to protect from being dangerous by separating, covering, etc: *These electric wires are protected by a rubber covering.* **3** to help (one's country, industry or the sale of goods produced in one's own country) by taxing foreign goods of the same kind and so making them dear to buy **4** [(*against*)] to guard (someone or something) against possible future loss, damage, etc by means of insurance: *We are protected against loss of our travelling bags.* **protective** [B] serving to protect: *The men fighting the fire wore protective clothing.* **-ly** [adv] **-ness** [U]

secure 1 [D1 (*for*); T1] to get esp as the result of effort: *He's lucky to have secured himself such a good job. She secured a nurse for her sick husband.* **2** [T1 (*from*, *against*)] to make safe: *The officer in charge secured the camp against attack.* **3** [T1] to hold or close tightly: *They secured the windows when the storm began to blow.*

keep [T1] (esp in sport, *esp in the phr* **keep goal**) to guard: *He keeps goal* (= guards the goal [⇒ K121]) *for our football team.*

shield [T1 (*from*)] to protect or hide from harm or danger: *She lied to the police to shield her guilty friend. He raised an arm to shield himself from the blow.*

ward off [v adv T1] to keep (something dangerous or harmful) away, usu forcefully: *She warded off the man's blow with her arm.*

N366 *nouns* : **losing, saving, etc**

loss 1 [U] the act or fact of losing possession: *His loss of blood was serious.* **2** [U] the harm, pain, damage, etc caused by losing something: *He was unable to hide his great loss.* **3** [S] failure to keep or use: *The vehicle developed a loss of power.* **4** [U] failure to win or obtain **5** [C] a person, thing or amount that is lost: *The army suffered heavy losses in the battle.*

rescue [C] an act of rescuing: *There have been 3 rescues of climbers lost on the mountains this Christmas. A rescue team are trying to reach the trapped miners.* **come/go to someone's rescue** to come/go and help someone: *She couldn't do her Latin exercise, but her father came to her rescue.*

safety [U] the condition of being safe; freedom from danger, harm, or risk: *When birds learn to fly they leave the safety of the nest. The safety of the ship is the captain's responsibility. Let's try to stay together in a group; there's safety in numbers.*

salvage [U] **1** esp large goods and objects saved from damage: *Have you any salvage for sale?* **2** the act of saving goods, a ship, etc from damage or for some kind of use after being wholly or partly destroyed: *The salvage of the ship was difficult work.* **3** money paid for such work: *How much is the salvage on that ship?*

save [C] *not fml, esp in sport* an act of saving: *The goalkeeper's* [⇒ K191] *saves stopped the other team from winning.*

preservation [U] **1** [(*of*)] the act or action of preserving: *New medical knowledge has helped in the preservation of life and health.* **2** the state of being or remaining in (a stated) condition after a long time: *The old building is in a good state of preservation except for the wooden floors.*

preserve [C] **1** *rare* a reserve for animals **2** [*often pl with sing meaning*] something one considers to be specially one's own: *He says that we should write about something different; we are on his preserves if we write about this.* **poach/trespass on someone's preserves 1** *old use* to hunt animals on another person's land **2** (*fig*) to take a share in activities, interests, etc considered to be someone else's special subject, etc

conservation [U] **1** the act of conserving; preservation **2** the controlled use of a limited supply to prevent waste or loss: *Most people have come to accept the need for conservation if we are to ensure a supply of minerals, food, forests, etc for the future.* **conservationist** [C] an active supporter of conservation (def **2**) **conservation of energy** [(*the*) U] *tech* the scientific principle that the total amount of energy within the universe can never vary **conservation of mass/matter** [(*the*) U] *tech* the scientific principle that the total mass within the universe can never vary

reservation 1 [U] the act of reserving esp information from people, or things for later use: *His reservation of the money for his own use was a criminal act.* **2** [C] a piece of land set apart for North American Indians to live on: *The Sioux returned to their reservation. He left the reservation to work in the city.*

reserve [C *usu in comb*] a place set apart esp for animals (= game): *He works on an African game reserve/nature reserve.*

salvation 1 [U] *esp fml* preservation from loss, ruin, or failure: *You're in trouble; your salva-*

tion depends on quick action. I can't help; you'll have to work out your own salvation. **2** [C *usu sing*] something that saves; a cause or means of saving: *'God is our salvation,' said the priest.* (*humor*) *That cup of tea was my salvation; now I feel much better!*

protection 1 [U] the action of protecting or state of being protected: *The prisoner was taken from the prison to court under police protection. Such a thin coat gives little protection against the cold.* **2** [S] a person who or thing that protects: *Shoes are a protection for the feet. God is our protection and our strength.* **3** [U] the condition of having an agreement with an insurance [⇨ J159] company to save oneself from having to pay for accidents, loss, etc: *I crashed my car yesterday; I'm glad I'd got protection.*

guard 1 [(*on*) U (*against*)] a state of being watchful and protective against danger, trouble, etc; readiness to meet danger, trouble, etc: *Be on guard/on your guard against them! Keep guard all night; they may attack at any time.* **2** [C (*against*); *often in comb*] something which guards: *Having life insurance is a guard against difficulties for one's family if one dies. Put the (fire) guard in front of the fire; we don't want pieces of hot wood falling out.*

watch 1 [S (*on*)] an act of watching for danger, guarding something, etc: *The police kept a watch on that house for two weeks. Keep watch on him!* **2** [*the* GU] *esp formerly* a group of men who guard people and property at night: *the city watch*

security 1 [U] the state of being secure: *'What security my religion gives me!' she said.* **2** [C] something which protects or makes secure: *My savings are my security against hardship.* **3** [U] property of value promised to a lender in case repayment is not made or other conditions are not met: *He offered his house as security for his large debt.* **4** [U] protection against lawbreaking, violence, enemy acts, escape from prison, etc: *For security reasons* (= reasons of security) *the passengers have to be searched. Tight security was in force during the President's visit. It's a maximum/minimum security prison. The security forces* (= police and army) *were unable to keep order in the streets. The factory employs a security guard at night.* **5** [C *usu pl*] a paper

(esp a bond or piece of stock [⇨ J113, 14]) giving the owner the right to some property: *He trades in government securities.*

care [U] **1** protection: *She left the child in the care of a friend.* **2** close, serious attention to work, trouble, etc: *She worked slowly and with great care. Take care not to make any more mistakes.* **careful** [B] taking or showing care: *He is a very careful driver.* **-ness** [U] **-ly** [adv]: *Drive carefully.* **careless** [B] not taking or showing (enough) care: *He is a careless driver.* **-ness** [U] **-ly** [adv]: *He drives very carelessly.*

N367 *adjectives* : **safe**

safe [Wa1] **1** [F (*from*)] out of danger [⇨ N38]; not threatened by harm; not able to be hurt; protected: *Come inside where you'll be safe from the storm. Your money will be safe in the bank.* **2** [F] not hurt; unharmed: *They came through the storm safe and sound* (= safe). **3** [B (*for*)] not allowing danger or injury: *Is this a safe place to swim? Keep these papers in a safe place. Is it safe to go out at night here? Leave your money with me; it'll be in safe hands.* **4** [B] not likely to cause risk or disagreement: *It's safe to say* (*it seems a safe bet that*) *crime will continue at a high rate this year.* **5** [B] (of a seat in Parliament) certain to be won in an election by a particular party: *It was once a safe seat for Labour, but might go either way at the next election.* **on the safe side** *not fml* taking no risks; being more careful than may be necessary: *Let's be on the safe side and take more money than we think we'll need.* **play it safe** *infml* to take no risks: *It's warm now, but I'll play it safe and take some heavy clothes on the trip too.* **as safe as houses** *infml* very safe from risk: *Your money will be as safe as houses in that company.* **un-** [*neg*] **-ly** [adv] **-ness** [U]

secure [Wa2;B] **1** [(*from, against*)] *often fml* safe; protected against danger or risk: *a building secure from/against attack* **2** closed firm or tight enough for safety: *Make the windows secure before leaving the house.* **3** having no doubt, fear, or anxiety: *She feels secure here.* **4** sure to be won, or not to be lost; certain: *a secure job; His place in history is now secure.* **in-** [*neg*] **-ly** [adv]

Index

A

a /ə; *strong* eɪ/, **an** /ən;
strong æn/
  det N98

AB /ˌeɪˈbiː/
  n M163

abaft /əˈbɑːft/
  adv M158

abandon /əˈbændən/
  v D90, M38

abandonment
/əˈbændənmənt/
  n D91

abate /əˈbeɪt/
  v L57

abatement /əˈbeɪtmənt/
  n L57

abbess /ˈæbɪs, ˈæbes/
  n C347

abbey /ˈæbi/
  n C350

abbot /ˈæbət/
  n C347

abbreviate /əˈbriːvieɪt/
  v G161

abbreviation
/əˌbriːviˈeɪʃən/
  n general G161
    writing G274

abdomen /ˈæbdəmən,
æbˈdəʊ-/
  n B34

abdominal /æbˈdɒmɪnəl||
-ˈdɑ-/
  adj B34

abduct /æbˈdʌkt, ab-/
  v C232

abduction /æbˈdʌkʃən,
əb-/
  n C232

abductor /æbˈdʌktər/
  n C232

abhor /əbˈhɔːʳ, æb-/
  v F32

abhorrence /əbˈhɒrəns/
  n F33

abhorrent /əbˈhɒrənt||
-hɔr-/
  adj F34

ability /əˈbɪlɪti/
  n G43

able /ˈeɪbəl/
  adj G42, N239

able-bodied seaman
  n M163

able seaman /ˌ··ˈ··/
  n C298

ablution(s) /əˈbluːʃənz/
  n D172

aboard /əˈbɔːd|| əˈbord/
  adv M158

abort /əˈbɔːt||-ˈɔrt/
  v B180, L175

abortion
/əˈbɔːʃən||əˈbɔr-/
  n B180, L181

abortionist /əˈbɔːʃənɪst||
əˈbɔr-/
  n B180

about /əˈbaʊt/
  adv, prep
    time L266
    space M203
    be about to L278

above /əˈbʌv/
  adv, prep M219

aboveboard /əˌbʌvˈbɔːd,
əˈbʌvbɔːd|| əˈbʌvbord/
  adj F192

abridge /əˈbrɪdʒ/
  v G161

abridgment
/əˈbrɪdʒmənt/
  n G161

abroad /əˈbrɔːd/
  n, adv M124

abscess /ˈæbses/
  n B127

abscond /əbˈskɒnd, æb-||
æbˈskɑnd/
  v M35

absence /ˈæbsəns/
  n M206

absent /ˈæbsənt/
  adj M206

absentee /ˌæbsənˈtiː/
  n M206

absent-minded /ˌ··ˈ···/
  adj G46

absolute /ˈæbsəluːt/
  adj N50, 214, 251

absorb /əbˈsɔːb,
əbˈzɔːb||-ɔrb/
  v take in E5
    interest K10

absorbent /əbˈsɔːbənt,
-ˈzɔː-||-ɔr-/
  adj E5

absorbing /əbˈsɔːbɪŋ,
-ˈzɔː-||-ɔr-/
  adj F225

absorption /əbˈsɔːpʃən,
-ˈzɔː-||-ɔr-/
  n E5

abstract /əbˈstrækt, æb-/
  remove *v* H24

abstract /ˈæbstrækt/
  adj G7
  n G161

abstract noun /ˈ··, ·ˈ/

n G270

absurd /əbˈsɜːd|| -ɜrd/
  adj G46

absurdity /əbˈsɜːdɪti,
-ˈzɜː-|| -ɜr-/
  n G47

abundance /əˈbʌndəns/
  n N104

abundant /əˈbʌndənt/
  adj N103

abuse /əˈbjuːz/
  v speech F148
    action I26

abuse /əˈbjuːs/
  n speech F149
    action I27

abusive /əˈbjuːsɪv/
  adj F150

abysmal /əˈbɪzməl/
  adj F58

abyss /əˈbɪs/
  n L104

academic /ˌækəˈdemɪk/
  n I134
  adj I148

academy /əˈkædəmi/
  n I131, 133

accelerate /əkˈseləreɪt/
  v M31

acceleration
/əkˌseləˈreɪʃən/
  n M31

accelerator
/əkˈseləreɪtəʳ/
  n M101 (picture)

accent /ˈæksənt||
ˈæksent/
  n G230, 232

accent /əkˈsent|| ˈæksent/
  v G231

accentuate /əkˈsentʃueɪt/
  v G231

accentuation
/əkˌsentʃuˈeɪʃən/
  n G232

accept /əkˈsept/
  v agree G14, 125,
    N133
    take G108

acceptance /əkˈseptəns/
  n taking G109
    agreeing G126, N135

access /ˈækses/
  n D24

accessory /əkˈsesəri/
  n D154

accident /ˈæksɪdənt/
  n M112, N19

accidental /ˌæksɪˈdentl/
  adj N19

acclimatize /əˈklaɪmətaɪz/

v L41

accommodate
/əˈkɒmədeɪt|| əˈkɑ-/
  v D61

accommodation
/əˌkɒməˈdeɪʃən|| əˌkɑ-/
  n D66

accompaniment
/əˈkʌmpənimənt/
  n music K35
    general M53

accompanist
/əˈkʌmpənɪst/
  n K39

accompany /əˈkʌmpəni/
  v music K32
    general M53

accomplice /əˈkʌmplɪs||
əˈkɑm-, əˈkʌm-/
  n C42

accomplish /əˈkʌmplɪʃ||
əˈkɑm-, əˈkʌm-/
  v N131

accomplished
/əˈkʌmplɪʃt|| əˈkɑm-,
əˈkʌm-/
  adj G42

accomplishment
/əˈkʌmplɪʃmənt||
əˈkɑm-, əˈkʌm-/
  n skill G43
    finishing N133

accord /əˈkɔːd|| -ɔrd/
  give *v* D101
  agreement *n* N225
  agree *v* N226

accordance /əˈkɔːdəns||
-ɔr-/
  n N225

accordingly /əˈkɔːdɪŋli||
-ɔr-/
  adv G286

according to /əˈkɔːdɪŋ
tə, -tʊ|| -ɔr-/
  prep G90

account /əˈkaʊnt/
  n story G82, 157
    money J105, 222
    on account of G288

accountable
/əˈkaʊntəbəl/
  adj C209

accountancy
/əˈkaʊntənsi/
  n J222

accountant /əˈkaʊntənt/
  n J232

account for /·ˈ·‿·/
  v G81, N227

accuracy /ˈækjərəsi/
  n N212

accurate /ˈækjərət/
adj N212
accusation
/ˌækjuˈzeɪʃən‖ -kjə-/
n in law C204
general G107
accuse /əˈkjuːz/
v in law C203
general G106
accused /əˈkjuːzd/
n C207
accustom /əˈkʌstəm/
v N64
be accustomed to N64
ace /eɪs/
n K131 (picture)
ache /eɪk/
n B121
v B122
achieve /əˈtʃiːv/
v N131
achievement
/əˈtʃiːvmənt/
n N133
aching /ˈeɪkɪŋ/
adj B123
achingly /ˈeɪkɪŋli/
adv B123
acid /ˈæsɪd/
adj F283
n H73
acidity /əˈsɪdɪti/
n taste F283
general H73
acknowledge
/əkˈnɒlɪdʒ‖ -ˈnɑ-/
v G108
acknowledgment
/əkˈnɒlɪdʒmənt‖ -ˈnɑ-/
n G109
acne /ˈækni/
n B148
acorn /ˈeɪkɔːn‖ -ɔrn,
-ərn/
n A153
acoustic guitar
/əˈkuːstɪk ɡɪˈtɑː/
n K46 (picture)
acquaintance
/əˈkweɪntəns/
n C40
acquaintanceship
/əˈkweɪntənsʃɪp/
n C40
acquaint with /əˈkweɪnt
wɪð/
v N64
acquiesce /ˌækwiˈes/
v G125
acquiescence
/ˌækwiˈesəns/
n G126
acquiescent
/ˌækwiˈesənt/
adj G125
acquire /əˈkwaɪə/
v gain D83
learn G32
buy J130
acquired /·ˈ·ˈ/
adj I12
acquisition
/ˌækwɪˈzɪʃən/

n general D83
buying J134
acquit /əˈkwɪt/
v C211
acquittal /əˈkwɪtl/
n C211
acre /ˈeɪkə/
n J68
acrid /ˈækrɪd/
adj F279
acrobat /ˈækrəbæt/
n K88
acrobatic /ˌækrəˈbætɪk/
adj K88
acronym /ˈækrənɪm/
n G274
across /əˈkrɒs‖ əˈkrɔs/
adv, prep measuring
J63
general M207
act /ækt/
government *n* C181
behave *v* F10
entertainment *n* K73
play *v* K79
in a play *n* K80
general *v* N120
general *n* N127
acting /ˈæktɪŋ/
n K71
action /ˈækʃən/
n law C204
war C270, 276
general F11, N127
industrial action J238
active /ˈæktɪv/
adj energetic B95,
I105, M14
in grammar G266
functional N124
activity /ækˈtɪvɪti/
n K6, N127
actor /ˈæktə/
n K82
actress /ˈæktrɪs/
n K82
actual /ˈæktʃuəl/
adj N13
actuality /ˌæktʃuˈælɪti/
n N11
acute /əˈkjuːt/
adj of an illness B123
clever G37
serious N45
acute (accent)
n G151
acute angle
n J43 (picture)
A D /eɪ diː/
n L233
ad /æd/
n G214
adage /ˈædɪdʒ/
n G236
adam's apple /ˌædəmz
ˈæpəl/
n B10 (picture), B21
adapt /əˈdæpt/
v general I16
music K33
adaptation
/ˌædəpˈteɪʃən/
n I17

adapter /əˈdæptə/
n H210
add /æd/
v J31
adder /ˈædə/
n A90
addict /ˈædɪkt/
n E81
addiction /əˈdɪkʃən/
n E81
addictive /əˈdɪktɪv/
adj E81
addition /əˈdɪʃən/
n counting J35
general N93
in addition to N100
additional /əˈdɪʃənəl/
adj N100
additionally /əˈdɪʃənli/
adv N100
additive /ˈædɪtɪv/
adj J35
address /əˈdres/
speaking *v* G64
speaking *v* G65
place *n* G191
place *v* G192
form of address G233
add to
v N92
adenoids /ˈædɪnɔɪdz,
ˈædən-/
n B10 (picture)
adequacy /ˈædɪkwəsi/
n N102
adequate /ˈædɪkwɪt/
adj F54, N102
adhere /ədˈhɪə/
v H11
adherent /ədˈhɪərənt/
n C331
adhesive /ədˈhiːsɪv/
adj, n H12
adjacent /əˈdʒeɪsənt/
adj M209
adjectival /ˌædʒɪkˈtaɪvəl/
adj G260
adjective /ˈædʒɪktɪv/
n G260
adjudicate /əˈdʒuːdɪkeɪt/
v K111
adjudication
/əˌdʒuːdɪˈkeɪʃən/
n K111
adjudicator
/əˌdʒuːdɪˈkeɪtə/
n K111
adjunct /ˈædʒʌŋkt/
n N327
adjust /əˈdʒʌst/
v I20, L41
adjustment
/əˈdʒʌstmənt/
n I17, 21
administer
/ədˈmɪnɪstə/
v rule C99
give D100
administration
/ədˌmɪnɪˈstreɪʃən/
n C100
administrative
/ədˈmɪnɪstrətɪv‖

-streɪtɪv/
adj C100
administrator
/ədˈmɪnɪstreɪtə/
n C101
admirable /ˈædmərəbəl/
adj F142
admiral /ˈædmərəl/
n C298
admiration
/ˌædməˈreɪʃən/
n F141
admire /ədˈmaɪə/
v F140
admirer /ədˈmaɪərə/
n F140
admission /ədˈmɪʃən/
n confession C109
entrance M12
admit /ədˈmɪt/ **-tt-**
v confess G108
let in M6
admittance /ədˈmɪtəns/
n M12
admonish /ədˈmɒnɪʃ‖
-ˈmɑ-/
v G123
admonishment
/ədˈmɒnɪʃmənt‖ -ˈmɑ-/
n G124
admonition
/ˌædməˈnɪʃən/
n G124
adolescence
/ˌædəˈlesəns/
n C9, L210
adolescent /ˌædəˈlesənt/
n C9
adj C9, L206
adopt /əˈdɒpt‖ əˈdɑpt/
v child C14
general C108
adoption /əˈdɒpʃən‖
əˈdɑp-/
n child C14
general G109
adorable /əˈdɔːrəbəl‖
əˈdor-/
adj F24
adoration /ˌædəˈreɪʃən/
n F22
adore /əˈdɔːr‖ əˈdor/
v religion C332
general F20
adoring /əˈdɔːrɪŋ‖
əˈdor-/
adj F23
adorn /əˈdɔːn‖ -ɔrn/
v D111
adornment /əˈdɔːnmənt‖
-ɔr/
n D111
adult /ˈædʌlt, əˈdʌlt/
n, adj C9, L207
adult education
n I133
adulterate /əˈdʌltəreɪt/
v N337
adulteration
/əˌdʌltəˈreɪʃən/
n N337
adulterer /əˈdʌltərə/
n C30

arbitrate /'ɑ:bɪ̩treɪt|| 'ɑr-/
   v G12
arbitration
   /,ɑ:bɪ̩'treɪʃən|| 'ɑr-/
   n G13
arbitrator /'ɑ:bɪ̩treɪtəʳ/
   n G12
arboreal /ɑ:bɔ:rɪəl||
   ɑr'bo-/
   adj L114
arc /ɑ:k|| ɑrk/
   n J46, J44 (table)
arcade /ɑ:'keɪd|| ɑr-/
   n D27
arch /ɑ:tʃ|| ɑrtʃ/
   n of the foot B44
      (picture)
      general D26
      of a shoe D157
archaeological
   /,ɑ:kɪə'lɒdʒɪkəl||
   ,ɑrkɪə'lɑ-/
   adj I77
archaeologist
   /,ɑki'ɒlədʒɪ̩st|| ,ɑrki'ɑ-/
   n I77
archaeology
   /,ɑ:ki'ɒlədʒi|| ,ɑrki'ɑ-/
   n I77
archaic /ɑ:'keɪ-ɪk/
   adj G274, L201
archaism /ɑ:'keɪ-ɪzəm,
   'ɑ:keɪ-|| 'ɑrki-/
   n G274
archangel /'ɑ:keɪndʒəl||
   ɑrk-/
   n C323
archbishop /,ɑ:tʃ'bɪʃəp||
   ,ɑrtʃ-/
   n C347
arched /ɑ:tʃt|| ɑrtʃt/
   adj D26
archer /ɑ:tʃəʳ|| 'ɑr-/
   n K205
archery /'ɑ:tʃəri|| 'ɑr-/
   n K205
archipelago
   /,ɑ:kɪ̩'peləgəʊ|| ,ɑr-/
   -goes or -gos
   n L84
architect /'ɑ:kɪ̩tekt|| 'ɑr-/
   n D2
architectural
   /,ɑ:kɪ̩'tektʃərəl|| ɑr-/
   adj D2
architecture
   /'ɑ:kɪ̩təktʃəʳ|| 'ɑr-/
   n D2
archway /'ɑ:tʃweɪ|| ɑrtʃ-/
   n D26
Arctic Circle /'ɑ:ktɪk||
   'ɑr-/
   n L12 (picture)
ardent /'ɑ:dənt|| ɑr-/
   adj F226
ardour BrE, **ardor** AmE
   /'ɑ:dəʳ|| 'ɑr-/
   n F228
arduous /'ɑ:djʊəs||
   'ɑrdʒʊəs/
   adj N60
area /'eərɪə/
   n J65

arena /ə'ri:nə/
   n K118
arguable /'ɑ:gjʊəbəl||
   'ɑr-/
   adj G83
argue /'ɑ:gju:|| 'ɑr-/
   v quarrel C45, F106
      discuss G83
argument /'ɑ:gjʊmənt||
   'ɑrgjə-/
   n quarrel C45, F107
      discussion G84
argumentative
   /,ɑ:gjʊ'mentətɪv||
   ,ɑrgjə-/
   adj C45, F108
arid /'ærɪ̩d/
   adj E135, L59
Aries /'eəri:z, 'æri-i:z/
   n L4 (picture)
arise /ə'raɪz/ **arose**
   /ə'rəʊz/, **arisen** /ə'rɪzən/
   v happen N16
      rise N291
aristocracy
   /,ærɪ̩'stɒkrəsi|| -'stɑ-/
   n C153
aristocrat /'ærɪ̩stəkræt,
   ə'rɪ-|| ə'rɪ/
   n C157
aristocratic
   /,ærɪ̩stə'krætɪk, ə,rɪ-||
   ə,rɪ-/
   adj C157
arithmetic /ə'rɪθmətɪk/
   n J30
arithmetical
   /,ærɪθ'metɪkəl/
   adj J30
arm /ɑ:m|| ɑrm/
   of the body n B10, 41
   with weapons v C308
   of the sea n L88
armada /ɑ:'mɑ:də|| ɑr-/
   n C294
armament /ɑ:məmənt||
   'ɑr-/
   n C309, H230
armchair /ɑ:mtʃeəʳ,
   ,ɑ:m'tʃeəʳ|| 'ɑrm-,
   ,ɑrm-/
   n D113
armed forces /,· '·· /
   n C290
armed services /,· '··· /
   n C290
armistice /'ɑ:mɪ̩stɪ̩s||
   'ɑrm-/
   n C284
armour BrE, **armor**
   AmE /'ɑ:məʳ|| 'ɑr-/
   n C305, H248
armoured car /,·· '· /
   n H248
armpit /'ɑ:m,pɪt|| 'ɑrm-/
   n B10 (picture), B41
arms /ɑ:mz|| ɑrmz/
   n C309, H230
army /'ɑ:mi|| 'ɑr-/
   n C290
aroma /ə'rəʊmə/
   n F278
aromatic /,ærə'mætɪk/

adj F279
around /ə'raʊnd/
   adv, prep M203
   around and about
   M203
arouse /ə'raʊz/
   v N151
arrange /ə'reɪndʒ/
   v music K33
      general N194
   arrange for
   v N194
arrangement
   /ə'reɪndʒmənt/
   n music K22, 35
      general N194
arrears /ə'rɪəz|| -ɪrz/
   n J102
arrest /ə'rest/
   v, n C226
   house arrest C252
arrival /ə'raɪvəl/
   n M12
arrive /ə'raɪv/
   v M5
arrogance /'ærəgəns/
   n F144
arrogant /'ærəgənt/
   adj F143
arrow /'ærəʊ/
   n H234
arrowhead /'ærəʊhed/
   n H234
arrow slit /'·· ,· /
   n D9 (picture)
arse /ɑ:s|| ɑrs/
   n B33
arsenal /'ɑ:sənəl|| 'ɑr-/
   n H230
arsenic /'ɑ:sənɪk|| 'ɑr-/
   n H73
arson /'ɑ:sən|| 'ɑr-/
   n C237
arsonist /'ɑ:sənɪst|| 'ɑr-/
   n C237
art /ɑ:t|| ɑrt/
   n I40, 41
artefact /'ɑ:tɪ̩fækt|| 'ɑr-/
   n H111
arterial /ɑ:'tɪərɪəl|| ɑr-/
   adj blood B36
      road M127
artery /'ɑ:təri|| 'ɑr-/
   n B36 picture at B36
art form /'· ,· /
   n I40
artful /'ɑ:tfəl|| 'ɑr-/
   adj F197
art gallery /'· ,··· /
   n I59
arthritic /ɑ:'θrɪtɪk|| ɑr-/
   adj, n B145
arthritis /ɑ:'θraɪtɪ̩s|| ɑr-/
   n B145
artic /'ɑ:tɪk/
   n M94
artichoke /'ɑ:tɪ̩tʃəʊk||
   'ɑr-/
   n A151
article /'ɑ:tɪkəl|| 'ɑr-/
   n story G159
      in grammar G272
      general H30

articulacy /ɑ:'tɪkjʊləsi||
   ɑr-/
   n G241
articulate /ɑ:'tɪkjʊleɪt||
   ɑr'tɪkjə-/
   v G231
articulate /ɑ:'tɪkjʊlɪ̩t||
   ɑr'tɪkjə-/
   adj G240
articulated vehicle
   /·,···· '··· /
   n M91
articulation
   /ɑ:,tɪkjʊ'leɪʃən||
   ɑr,tɪkjə-/
   n G232
artifact /'ɑ:tɪ̩fækt|| 'ɑr-/
   n H111
artifice /'ɑ:tɪ̩fɪ̩s|| 'ɑr-/
   n F207
artificial /,ɑ:tɪ̩'fɪʃəl||
   ,ɑr-/
   adj I12
artillery /ɑ:'tɪləri|| ɑr-/
   n C305
artilleryman
   /ɑ:'tɪlərimən|| ɑr-/
   n C306
artisan /,ɑ:tɪ̩'zæn||
   'ɑrtɪ̩zən/
   n I72
artist /'ɑ:tɪ̩st|| 'ɑr-/
   n painter I51
      performer K39
artiste /ɑ:'ti:st|| ɑr-/
   n K39
artistic /ɑ:'tɪstɪk|| ɑr-/
   adj I52
artistry /'ɑ:tɪ̩stri|| 'ɑr-/
   n I54
artless /'ɑ:tləs|| 'ɑr-/
   adj F196
artwork /'ɑ:t,wɜ:k||
   'ɑrt,wɜrk/
   n G178
arty /'ɑ:ti|| 'ɑrti/
   adj I52
arty-crafty /,ɑ:ti'krɑ:fti||
   ,ɑrti'kræfti/
   n I52
as /əz; strong æz/
   because conj G289
   general adv, conj L259,
      N181
as against
   prep M208
ascend /ə'send/
   v M9
ascension /ə'senʃən/
   n M13
ascent /ə'sent/
   n M13
ascetic /ə'setɪk/
   n, adj C345
asceticism /ə'setɪ̩sɪzəm/
   n C345
ascribe to /ə'skraɪb/
   v G14
ascription /ə'skrɪpʃən/
   n G14
ash /æʃ/
   n tree A155
      dust E85, H84

· /, **bed-sit** /, · ' · /
  n D7
bedspread/cover
  /'bedspred/
  n D115
bedstead /'bedsted/
  n D115
bedtime story /'bedtaɪm,
  stɔ:ri‖ ˌstori/
  n K174
bedwetting /'bedˌwetɪŋ/
  n B147
bee /bi:/
  n A110
beech /bi:tʃ/
  n A155
beef /bi:f/
  n E32
  v G102
beefburger /'bi:fbɜ:gəʳ‖
  -ɜr-/
  n E37
beehive /'bi:haɪv/
  n E140
beer /bɪəʳ/
  n E66
beet /bi:t/
  n A151
beetle /'bi:tl/
  n A110
beetroot /'bi:tru:t/
  n plant A151
  food E30
before /bɪ'fɔ:ʳ‖ bɪ'for/
  adv time L260
  space M221
  before (too) long
  L253
beforehand /bɪ'fɔ:hænd‖
  -fɔr-/
  adv L260
befriend /bɪ'frend/
  v C44
beg /beg/ -gg-
  v G100
beggar /'begəʳ/
  n C170
  v J119
beggary /'begəri/
  n J121
begin /bɪ'gɪn/ **began**
  /bɪ'gæn/, **begun**
  /bɪ'gʌn/
  v L170
beginner /bɪ'gɪnəʳ/
  n I136
beginning /bɪ'gɪnɪŋ/
  n L179
behave /bɪ'heɪv/
  v F10, N123
behaviour BrE, **behavior**
  AmE /bɪ'heɪvɪəʳ/
  n F11, N127
behead /bɪ'hed/
  v C258
behind /bɪ'haɪnd/
  n B33
  adv, prep M220
behold /bɪ'həʊld/ **beheld**
  /bɪ'held/
  v F263
beholden /bɪ'həʊldn/
  adj F78

being /'bi:ɪŋ/
  n A30, N3
belch /beltʃ/
  v, n B117
belfry /'belfri/
  n C349
belief /bɪ'li:f/
  n C320, 321, G14
believable /bɪ'li:vəbəl/
  adj G15
believe /bɪ'li:v/
  v C332, G14
believer /bɪ'li:vəʳ/
  n C333
belisha beacon /bəˌli:ʃə
  'bi:kən/
  n M133
bell /bel/
  n of a door D24
  H124 (picture), K45
  (picture)
bellicose /'belɪkəʊs/
  adj C273
belligerent /bɪ'lɪdʒərənt/
  adj C273
  n C301
bellow /'beləʊ/
  v G129
  n G130
bellows /'beləʊz/ **bellows**
  n H158
belly /'beli/
  n A51 (picture), B34,
  E34 (picture)
belly button /' · · , · · /
  n B34
belong /bɪ'lɒŋ‖ bɪ'lɔŋ/
  v D80
belongings /bɪ'lɒŋɪŋz‖
  bɪ'lɔŋ-/
  n D82
belong to
  v D80
beloved /bɪ'lʌvd/
  adj, n F24
below /bɪ'ləʊ/
  adv, prep M158, 218
belt /belt/
  general n D152, H44,
  241
  clothing v D153
  move v M24
ben /ben/
  n L101
bench /bentʃ/
  n in law C200
  general D113
bend /bend/ **bent** /bent/
  v M40, 269, 295
bend
  n M40, 134, N269, 295
beneath /bɪ'ni:θ/
  adv. prep M218
benefactor /'benɪˌfæktəʳ/
  fem **benefactress** /-trəs/
  n C214
beneficence
  /bɪ'nefɪsəns/
  n F170
beneficent /bɪ'nefɪsənt/
  adj F170
beneficial /ˌbenɪ'fɪʃəl/
  adj F170

beneficiary /ˌbenɪ'fɪʃəri‖
  -fɪʃieri/
  n C214
benefit /'benɪfɪt/
  v, n N139
benevolence
  /bɪ'nevələns/
  n F170
benevolent /bɪ'nevələnt/
  adj F170
benign /bɪ'naɪn/
  adj F170
bent /bent/
  n N313
benzene /'benzi:n,
  ben'zi:n/
  n H82
benzine /'benzi:n,
  ben'zi:n/
  n H82
bequeath /bɪ'kwi:ð,
  bɪ'kwi:θ/
  v C212
bequest /bɪ'kwest/
  n C213
bereave /bɪ'ri:v/
  bereaved or **bereft**
  /bɪ'reft/
  v C50
bereaved /bɪ'ri:vd/
  adj C52
bereavement
  /bɪ'ri:vmənt/
  n C50
beret /'bereɪ‖ bə'reɪ/
  n D146
berry /'beri/
  n A134
berserk /bɜ:'sɜ:k, bə-‖
  bər'sɜrk, 'bərsɜrk/
  adj G52
berth /bɜ:θ‖ bɜrθ/
  bed n M157
  ships n M160
  ships v M165
beseech /bɪ'si:ʃ/
  besought /bɪ'sɔ:t/ or
  beseeched
  v G100
beside /bɪ'saɪd/
  prep M209
besides /bɪ'saɪdz/
  adv N100
besiege /bɪ'si:dʒ/
  v C275
besought /bɪ'sɔ:t/
  p tense of **beseech**
best /best/
  adj superl of **good**
bestial /'bi:stɪəl/
  adj A31
best man /, · ' · /
  n C33
bestseller /ˌbest'seləʳ/
  n G168
bet /bet/ **bet** or **betted**;
  pres p **betting**
  v K122
bet
  n K122
betray /bɪ'treɪ/
  v C137, F203
betrayal /bɪ'treɪəl/

  n C138, F204
betrothal /bɪ'trəʊðəl/
  adj C29
betrothed /bɪ'trəʊðd,
  bɪ'trəʊθt/
  adj C28
  n C31
better /'betəʳ/
  adj comp of **good** B110
  v N164
better oneself
  v N130
betters /'betəz‖ -ərz/
  n C155
between /bɪ'twi:n/
  adv, prep M211
beverage /'bevərɪdʒ/
  n E2, 60
beware /bɪ'weəʳ/
  v G123
beyond /bɪ'jɒnd‖
  bɪ'jɑnd/
  adv, prep M223
biannual /ˌbaɪ'ænjʊəl/
  adj L242
bias /'baɪəs/ -s- or -ss-
  v F13
bias
  n F3, 12, N313
Bible /'baɪbəl/
  n C337
biblical /'bɪblɪkəl/
  adj C337
bibliographical
  /ˌbɪblɪə'græfɪkəl/
  adj G163
bibliography
  /'bɪbli'ɒgrəfi‖ -'ɑg-/
  n G163
biceps /'baɪseps/
  n B10 (picture)
bicker /'bɪkəʳ/
  v F106
bicycle /'baɪsɪkəl/
  v M30
  n M96
bicycle pump /' · · · , · /
  n H114 (picture)
bicyclist /'baɪsɪklɪst/
  n M97
bid /bɪd/
  n J183
bidet /'bi:deɪ‖ bɪ'det (Fr
  bɪdɛ)/
  n D40
biennial /baɪ'enɪəl/
  adj L242
big /bɪg/ -gg-
  adj N81
bigamist /'bɪgəmɪst/
  n C30
bigamous /'bɪgəməs/
  adj C30
bigamy /'bɪgəmi/
  n C30
big-time /' · · · /
  adj N83
big toe /, · ' · /
  n B44 (picture)
big top /, · ' · /
  n K89
bike /baɪk/
  n M96

804

n D97

cm
abbrev J67

cms
abbrev J67

coach /kəʊtʃ/
teach *v* G33
trainer *n* I134
vehicle *n* M92, 95,
M108

coaching /ˈkəʊtʃɪŋ/
n G35

coachman /ˈkəʊtʃmən/
-**men** /mən/
n M97

coal /kəʊl/
v H77
n H81, 84

coalesce /ˌkəʊəˈles/
v N325

coal gas /ˈ·ˌ·/
n H82

coalscuttle /ˈkəʊlˌskʌtl/
n D36

coarse /kɔːs‖ kɔrs/
adj C168, N275

coarsen /ˈkɔːsən‖ ˈkɔr-/
v N276

coast /kəʊst/
n L92
v M42

coastal /ˈkəʊstl/
adj L114

coaster /ˈkəʊstəʳ/
n M155

coat /kəʊt/
clothing *n* D142
covering *n* H93
cover *v* H95

coax /kəʊks/
v G87, N157

cob /kɒb‖ kab/
n A134, 152

cobble /ˈkɒbəl‖ ˈka-/
n M132

cobbled /ˈkɒbəld‖ˈka-/
adj M132

cobbler /ˈkɒbləʳ‖ˈka-/
n D163

cobblestone
/ˈkɒbəlstəʊn‖ˈka-/
n M132

cobra /ˈkɒbrə, ˈkəʊ-‖
ˈkəʊ-/
n A90

coca cola /ˌkəʊkə
ˈkəʊlə/
n E61

coccyx /ˈkɒksɪks‖ ˈkak-/
coccyxes or **coccyges**
/kɒkˈsaɪdʒiːz‖ ˈkaksɪ̯-/
n B11 (picture)

cock /kɒk‖ kak/
n bird A70
penis B40

cockatoo /ˌkɒkəˈtuː‖
ˈkakətuː/ **-toos**
n A75

cockerel /ˈkɒkərəl/
n A70

cockle /ˈkɒkəl/
n A103

cockpit /ˈkɒkˌpɪt‖ ˈkak-/

n M186 (picture)

cockroach /ˈkɒk-rəʊtʃ‖
ˈkak-/
n A110

cocktail /ˈkɒkteɪl‖ ˈkak-/
n E67

cocoa /ˈkəʊkəʊ/
n E62

coconut /ˈkəʊkənʌt/
n A153

cod /kɒd‖ kad/
n A100

code /kəʊd/
in law *n* C181
writing *n*, *v* G147

codification
/ˌkəʊdɪ̯fɪ̯ˈkeɪʃən/
n N194

codify /ˈkəʊdɪ̯faɪ/
v N194

coeducation
/ˌkəʊedʒʊˈkeɪʃən‖
-dʒə-/
adj I131

coerce /kəʊˈɜːs‖ -ˈɜrs/
v N154

coercion /kəʊˈɜːʃən‖
-ˈɜrʒən/
n N155

coercive /kəʊˈɜːsɪv‖
-ˈɜr-/
adj N156

coffee /ˈkɒfi‖ ˈkɔfi, ˈkafi/
n E17, 62

coffee pot /ˈ··ˌ·/
n H173

coffee table /ˈ··ˌ··/
n D112

coffin /ˈkɒfɪ̯n‖ ˈkɔ-/
n C56

cogency /ˈkəʊdʒənsi/
n N155

cogent /ˈkəʊdʒənt/
adj N156

cognition /kɒɡˈnɪʃən‖
kag-/
n G1

cognitive /ˈkɒɡnɪ̯tɪv‖
ˈkag-/
adj G7

cognizance /ˈkɒɡnɪ̯zəns‖
ˈkag-/
n G34

cognizant /ˈkɒɡnɪ̯zənt‖
ˈkag-/
adj G36

co-habit /ˌkəʊˈhæbɪ̯t/
v C27

co-habitation
/ˌkəʊˌhæbɪ̯ˈteɪʃən/
n C27

cohere /kəʊˈhɪəʳ/
v H11

coherence /kəʊˈhɪərəns/
n G41, 241

coherent /kəʊˈhɪərənt/
adj G7, 40, 240

cohesion /kəʊˈhiːʒən/
n H11

cohesive /kəʊˈhiːsɪv/
adj H11

coil /kɔɪl/
contraceptive *n* B181

electrical *n* H212
general *v*, *n* N297

coin /kɔɪn/
v I1
n I81

coinage /ˈkɔɪnɪdʒ/
n money J81
words G234

coincide /ˌkəʊɪ̯nˈsaɪd/
v N16

coincidence
/kəʊˈɪnsɪ̯dəns/
n N17

coincidental
/kəʊˌɪnsɪ̯ˈdentl/
adj N17

coition /kəʊˈɪʃən/
n A16

coitus /ˈkɔɪtəs, *med*
ˈkəʊɪ̯təs/
n A16

coke /kəʊk/
n drink E61
coal H81

cola /ˈkəʊlə/
n E61

cold /kəʊld/
illness *n* B140
unfriendly *adj* C47
cool *adj* E60, L66
cool *n* L67

cold snap /ˈ··/
n L66

collaborate /kəˈlæbəreɪt/
v C137

collaborator
/kəˈlæbəreɪtəʳ/
n C139

collapse /kəˈlæps/
v, *n* N292

collar /ˈkɒləʳ‖ ˈka-/
n D161
v D98

collar-bone /ˈ··ˌ·/
n B11 (picture)

colleague /ˈkɒliːɡ‖ ˈka-/
n C42

collect /kəˈlekt/
v H26

collection /kəˈlekʃən/
n H26

collective /kəˈlektɪv/
adj, *n* H26

collective noun
/·ˌ··ˈ·/
n G270

collector /kəˈlektəʳ/
n H26

college /ˈkɒlɪdʒ‖ ˈka-/
n I133

collide /kəˈlaɪd/
v M112

collie /ˈkɒli‖ ˈkali/
n A54

collier /ˈkɒliəʳ/
n I115

colliery /ˈkɒljəri‖ ˈkal-/
n I113

collision /kəˈlɪʒən/
n M112

collocate /ˈkɒləkeɪt‖
ˈka-/
v G231

collocation
/ˌkɒləˈkeɪʃən‖ ˌka-/
n G232, 235

colloquial /kəˈləʊkwɪəl/
adj G238

colloquialism
/kəˈləʊkwɪəlɪzəm/
n G235

colon /ˈkəʊlən/
n in the body B35
(picture)
punctuation G151

colonial /kəˈləʊnɪəl/
adj C93
n C94

colonialism
/kəˈləʊnɪəlɪzəm/
n C111

colonialist
/kəˈləʊnɪəlɪ̯st/
n, *adj* C113

colonist /ˈkɒlənɪ̯st‖ ˈka-/
n C92

colonization
/ˌkɒlənaɪˈzeɪʃən‖·
ˌkalənɪ̯-/
n C92

colonize /ˈkɒlənaɪz‖
ˈka-/
v C92

colonnade /ˌkɒləˈneɪd‖
ˌka-/
n D27

colonnaded
/kɒləˈneɪdɪd‖ kal-/
adj D27

colony /ˈkɒləni‖ ˈka-/
n of animals A40
area C81, 92

colossal /kəˈlɒsəl‖
kəˈla-/
adj good F53
large N82

colour *BrE*, **color** *AmE*
/ˈkʌləʳ/
n B50, I46, L27
v L28, 38

coloured *BrE*, **colored**
AmE /ˈkʌləd‖ -ərd/
adj L33, B50

colourful *BrE*, **colorful**
AmE /ˈkʌləfəl‖ -ər-/
adj L33

colourless *BrE*, **colorless**
AmE /ˈkʌlələs‖ -ər/
adj L35

colt /kəʊlt/
n A51

column /ˈkɒləm‖ ˈka-/
n line C293, I159
building D26

columnist /ˈkɒləmɪ̯st,
-ləmnɪ̯st‖ ˈka-/
n G204

coma /ˈkəʊmə/ **comas** or
comae /ˈkəʊmiː/
n B146

comatose /ˈkəʊmətəʊs/
adj B146

comb /kəʊm/
of birds *n* A70
(picture), 121
for hair *v* D175

808

complicate
/'kɒmplɪ�068keɪt|| 'kɑm-/
v N63
complicated
/'kɒmplɪ̰keɪtɪ̰d|| 'kɑm-/
adj N62
complication
/kɒmplɪ̰'keɪʃən|| ,kɑm-/
n N63
compliment
/'kɒmplɪ̰mənt|| 'kɑm-/
v G70
n G71
component
/kəm'pəʊnənt/
n, adj H4
compose /kəm'pəʊz/
v G141, 142, K33,
G173
be composed of H21
composer /kəm'pəʊzəʳ/
n G172, K39
composite /'kɒmpəzɪ̰t||
kɑm'pɑ-/
adj H3
n H6
composition
/,kɒmpə'zɪʃən|| ,kɑm-/
n G158, H2, K22
compositor
/kəm'pɒzɪ̰təʳ|| -'pɑ-/
n G176
compound /'kɒmpaʊnd||
'kɑm-/
in grammar adj, n
G274
not simple adj H3
substance n H6
compound /kəm'paʊnd/
v I23
compound interest
/, · · ' · · /
n J112
comprehend
/,kɒmprɪhend|| ,kɑm-/
v G31
comprehensible
/,kɒmprɪ'hensəbəl||
'kɑm-/
adj G40
comprehension
/,kɒmprɪ'henʃən||
,kɑm-/
n G34, 41
comprehensive
/,kɒmprɪ'hensɪv||
,kɑm-/
adj general H20
school I131
compress /kəm'pres/
v N334
comprise /kəm'praɪz/
v H21, H22
compulsion
/kəm'pʌlʃən/
n N155
compulsive /kəm'pʌlsɪv/
adj N156
compulsory
/kəm'pʌlsəri/
adj C191
computation
/,kɒmpjuː'teɪʃən||

,kɑmpjə-/
n J35
compute /kəm'pjuːt/
v J34
computer /kəm'pjuːtəʳ/
n J34
comrade /'kɒmrɪ̰d,
-reɪd|| 'kɑmræd/
n C42
con /kɒn|| kɑn/ -nn-
v C234
con
n C233
concave /,kɒn'keɪv˜,
kən-|| ,kɑn'keɪv˜, kən-/
adj J45
conceal /kən'siːl/
v F208, N356
concealed /kən'siːld/
adj F195
concealment
/kən'siːlmənt/
n F208, N356
concede /kən'siːd/
n G108
conceit /kən'siːt/
n F144
conceited /kən'siːtɪ̰d/
adj F143
conceive /kənsiː'v/
v of living things A18
imagine G8
concentrate
/'kɒnsəntreɪt|| 'kɑn-/
v N237
concentration
/,kɒnsən'treɪʃən|| ,kɑn-/
n N237
concept /'kɒnsept||
'kɑn-/
n G9
conception /kən'sepʃən/
n beginning A18
imagination G9
conceptual
/kən'septʃuəl/
adj G7
concern /kən'sɜːn|| -ɜrn/
v F25
n F25, 90
concerned /kən'sɜːnd||
-ɜr-/
adj F87, 92
concerning /kən'sɜːnɪŋ||
-ɜr-/
prep M203
concert /'kɒnsət||
'kɑnsərt/
n K34
concerto /kən'tʃɜːteʊ||
-'tʃɜrtəʊ/
n K35
concession /kən'seʃən/
n G109
conclude /kən'kluːd/
v decide G10
end L175
conclusion /kən'kluːʒən/
n decision G11
end L181
conclusive /kən'kluːsɪv/
adj N33
concord /'kɒŋkɔːd||

'kɑŋkɔrd/
n N225
concrete /'kɒŋkriːt||
kɑn'kriːt/
n H66
adj N13
concubine
/'kɒŋkjubaɪn|| 'kɑŋ-/
n C35
concur /kən'kɜːʳ/
v G125
concurrence
/kən'kʌrəns|| -'kɜr-/
n G126
condemn /kən'dem/
v blame G106
to doom L156
condemnation
/,kɒndəm'neɪʃən,
-dem-|| ,kɑn-/
n G107
condensation
/,kɒnden'seɪʃən, -dən||
,kɑn-/
n water L45, 47
reduction N95
condense /kən'dens/
v of gasses L47
reduce N94
thicken N263
condiment /'kɒndɪ̰mənt||
'kɑn-/
n E49
condition /kən'dɪʃən/
n health B113
general N3
on condition that
G288
conditional /kən'dɪʃənəl/
in grammar n, adj
G267
general adj N52
condolence
/kən'dəʊləns/
n F175
condom /'kɒndəm||
'kɑn-, 'kʌn-/
n B181
condor /'kɒndɔːʳ||
'kɑndər, -dɔr/
n A78
conduct /kən'dʌkt/
v of electricity H203
guide M53
conduct /'kɒndʌkt,
-dəkt|| 'kɑn-/
n F11
conductance
/kən'dʌktəns/
n H204
conduction /kən'dʌkʃən/
n H204
conductor /kən'dʌktəʳ/
n substance H203
person K42, M97,
110
conductress
/kən'dʌktrɪ̰s/
n M97
cone /kəʊn/
n plant A130 (picture),
A134
shape J44 (picture)

confectionery
/kən'fekʃənəri/
n E53
confederacy
/kən'fedərəsi/
adj C91
confederate
/kən'fedərɪ̰t/
n C42, 94
adj C93
confederation
/kən,fedə'reɪʃən/
n C91
confer /kən'fɜːʳ/ -rr-
v give D101
talk G62
conference /'kɒnfərəns||
'kɑn-/
n G65
confess /kən'fes/
v G108
confession /kən'feʃən/
n G109
confide /kən'faɪd/
v G63
confidence /'kɒnfɪ̰dəns||
'kɑn-/
n N33
confidence trick
/' · · · . . /
n C233
confidence trickster
/' · · · , . . /
n C235
confident /'kɒnfɪ̰dənt||
'kɑn-/
adj N33
confidential
/,kɒnfɪ̰'denʃəl/
adj F195
confine /kən'faɪn/
v C251
confinement
/kən'faɪnmənt/
n C252
confirm /kən'fɜːm|| -ɜrm/
v C125
confirmation
/,kɒnfə'meɪʃən||
,kɑnfər-/
n G126
conflict /'kɒnflɪkt|| 'kɑn-/
n C270, 271
conflict /kən'flɪkt/
v F106
conform /kən'fɔːm||
-ɔrm/
v F10
conformist /kən'fɔːmɪ̰st||
-ɔr-/
n C165
conformity /kən'fɔːmɪ̰ti||
-ɔr-/
n F10, N186
confound /kən'faʊnd/
v F88
confront /kən'frʌnt/
v C277
confrontation
/,kɒnfrən'teɪʃən|| ,kɑn-/
n C270, 271
Confucian /kən'fjuːʃən/
adj C328

814

dam /dæm/
  n C12, L100
  v M63
damage /'dæmɪdʒ/
  v, n N337
dame /deɪm/
  n C5
damn /dæm/
  v G112, 114
  n, adj, interj G113
damp /dæmp/
  adj L60
  v L62
dampen /'dæmpən/
  v L62
dance /da:ns|| dæns/
  n K20, 26
  v K32
danceband
  /'da:ns,bænd|| 'dæns-/
  n K37
dancer /'da:nsə'|| 'dæn-/
  n K39
dancing /'da:nsɪŋ|| 'dæn-/
  n K20
dancing girl /'···, ·/
  n K39
dandelion /'dændɨlaɪən/
  n A158
dandruff /'dændrəf, -drʌf/
  n B51
danger /'deɪndʒə'/
  n N38
dangerous /'deɪndʒərəs/
  adj N40
dangle /'dæŋgəl/
  v N301
dank /dæŋk/
  adj L60
dare /deə'/
  pres t neg contr **daren't**
  v F135
daredevil /'deədevəl|| 'deər-/
  n F133
daring /'deərɪŋ/
  adj F129
  n F132
dark /da:k|| da:rk/
  adj B53, L25, 36
  n B53, L21
  in the dark L21
darken /'da:kən|| da:rkən/
  v L26, 38
darkness /'da:knɨs/
  n L21
darkroom /'da:kru:m, -rʊm|| 'da:rk-/
  n K59
darling /'da:lɪŋ|| 'da:r-/
  n, adj F24
darn /da:n|| da:rn/
  v I19
  n I21
dart /da:t|| da:rt/
  moving *v, n* M25
  in sport *n* K205
dartboard /'da:tbɔ:d|| 'da:rtbord/
  n K206 (picture)

darts /da:ts|| da:rts/
  n K205
dash /dæʃ/
  punctuation *n* G151
  in athletics *v, n* K201
  general *v* M24
dashboard /'dæʃbɔ:d|| -bord/
  n H115, M101
  (picture)
data /'deɪtə, 'da:tə/
  n G194, N221
date /deɪt/
  fruit *n* A150
  meet *v* C20
  person *n* C21
  time *n* L211
  time *n* L233
  meeting *n* M73
date of birth /,···'·/
  n L209
daughter /'dɔ:tə'/
  n C12
dawn /dɔ:n/
  v L170
  n L221
dawn on
  v G31
day /deɪ/
  n L141, 143, 220, 226
daydream /'deɪdri:m/
  n, v B85
daylight /'deɪlaɪt/
  n L20
day off /, · '· /
  n L231
day shift /'· , · /
  n I112
daze /deɪz/
  n B85
dazed /deɪzd/
  adj B85
dazzle /'dæzəl/
  n L22
  v L23
deacon /'di:kən/ *fem*
  deaconess /-kənɨs, -kə'nes/
  n C347
dead /ded/
  adj A3
deaden /'dedn/
  v B162
deadly /'dedli/
  adj A11
deaf /def/
  adj B133
deafen /'defən/
  v B133
deal /di:l/ **dealt** /delt/
  v K130
deal
  n business J137
  in cards K130
dealer /'di:lə'/
  n J188
deal in
  v J153
dean /di:n/
  n I134
dear /dɪə'/
  loved *adj, n* F24
  costly *adj* J196

dear departed /, ···'··· /
  n C52
dearth /dɜ:θ|| dɜrθ/
  n N106
death /deθ/
  n A4
deathly /'deθli/
  adj A11
death's head /'··, · /
  n B11
debatable /dɪ'beɪtəbəl/
  adj G83
debate /dɪ'beɪt/
  v G83
  n G84
debit /'debɨt/
  v J109
  n J110
debit side /'···· /
  n J110
débris /'debri:, 'deɪ-|| də'bri:, deɪ-/
  n H14
debt /det/
  n J102
debtor /'detə'/
  n J103
deca- /'dekə-/
  prefix J67
decade /'dekeɪd, de'keɪd/
  n L226
decamp /dɪ'kæmp/
  v M35
decapitate /dɪ'kæpɨteɪt/
  v C258
decapitation /dɪ,kæpɨ'teɪʃən/
  n C258
decay /dɪ'keɪ/
  v A2
  n A4
deceased /dɪ'si:st/
  adj, n C51
deceit /dɪ'si:t/
  n C234, F204
deceitful /dɪ'si:tfəl/
  adj F191, 205
deceive /dɪ'si:v/
  v C234, F203
decelerate /,di:'seləreɪt/
  v M31
deceleration /,di:selə'reɪʃən/
  n M31
December /dɪ'sembə'/
  n L234
decency /'di:sənsi/
  n F202
decent /'di:sənt/
  adj F54, 198
deception /dɪ'sepʃən/
  n C234, F204
deceptive /dɪ'septɪv/
  adj C234
deci- /'desɨ/
  prefix J67
decide /dɪ'saɪd/
  v N163
decided /dɪ'saɪdɨd/
  adj N33, 163
deciduous /dɪ'sɪdʒuəs/
  adj A135

decimal /'desɨməl/
  adj, n J3
decimal fraction /,···'··/
  n J3
decimal point /,···'·/
  n J3
decipher /dɪ'saɪfə'/
  v G147
decision /dɪ'sɪʒən/
  n N163
decisive /dɪ'saɪsɪv/
  adj N163
deck /dek/
  n of cards K130
  of boats M157
  (picture)
deckhand /'dekhænd/
  n M163
declaration /,deklə'reɪʃən/
  n G73
declarative /dɨ'klærətɪv/
  adj G267
declare /dɪ'kleə'/
  v general G72
  in cricket K196
decline /dɪ'klaɪn/
  refuse *v* G127
  go down *v* N94
  going down *n* N95
decode /,di:'kəʊd/
  v G147
decompose /,di:kəm'pəʊz/
  v A2
decomposition /,di:kɒmpə'zɪʃən|| -kɑm-/
  n A4
decorate /'dekəreɪt/
  v D111
decoration /,dekə'reɪʃən/
  n D111
decrease /dɪ'kri:s/
  v N94
decrease /'di:kri:s/
  n N95
decree /dɪ'kri:/
  n C180
  v C183
decrepit /dɪ'krepɨt/
  adj B134
decry /dɪ'kraɪ/
  v F148
deduce /dɪ'dju:s|| dɪ'du:s/
  v G10
deduct /dɪ'dʌkt/
  v J109
deduction /dɪ'dʌkʃən/
  n G11, J163
deed /di:d/
  n N127
deep /di:p/
  adj measurement J63
  colour L36
  general N305
deepen /'di:pən/
  v N309
deep end /'·, ·/
  n K203

diaphanous
/daɪˈæfənəs/
adj F270

diaphragm /ˈdaɪəfræm/
n B181

diarist /ˈdaɪərɪ̥st/
n G162

diarrhoea *BrE*, **diarrhea**
AmE /ˌdaɪəˈrɪə/
n B147

diary /ˈdaɪəri/
n G162

dice /daɪs/ **dice**
n K133

dice
v K133

dicey /ˈdaɪsi/
adj N40

dictate /dɪkˈteɪt‖ ˈdɪkteɪt/
v G115, J236

dictates /ˈdɪkteɪts/
n G116

dictation /dɪkˈteɪʃən/
n G116, J236

dictator /dɪkˈteɪtəʳ‖
ˈdɪkteɪtər/
n C102

dictatorial
/ˌdɪktəˈtɔːrɪəl‖ -ˈtor-/
adj C102

dictatorship
/dɪkˈteɪtəʃɪp‖ -teɪtər-/
n C95

diction /ˈdɪkʃən/
n G232

dictionary /ˈdɪkʃənəri‖
-neri/
n G165

dictum /ˈdɪktəm/ **-ta** /-tə/
or **-tums**
n G236

die /daɪ/ **died**, *pres p*
dying /ˈdaɪ-ɪŋ/
v A2

die
n K133

die down
v L57

diesel (oil) /ˈdiːzəl/
n H82

diet /ˈdaɪət/
v B103, E10
n E1

differ /ˈdɪfəʳ/
v N190

difference /ˈdɪfərəns/
n N187

different /ˈdɪfərənt/
adj N182, 184

differential /ˌdɪfəˈrenʃəl‖/
in engines *n* M102
(picture)
general *adj* N184
general *n* N187

differentiate
/ˌdɪfəˈrenʃieɪt/
v N193

differentiation
/ˌdɪfərenʃiˈeɪʃən/
n N193

difficult /ˈdɪfɪkəlt/
adj not friendly C47
hard N60

difficulty /ˈdɪfɪkəlti/
n N60, 218

diffidence /ˈdɪfɪ̥dəns/
n N33

diffident /ˈdɪfɪ̥dənt/
adj N33

dig /dɪg/ **dug** /dʌg/,
pres p **digging**
n I113

dig
n I114

digest /ˈdaɪdʒest/
n G161

digest /daɪˈdʒest, dɪ̥-/
v E5

digestible /dɪˈdʒestɪ̥bəl/
adj E108

digestion /daɪˈdʒestʃən,
dɪ̥-/
n E5

digestive /daɪˈdʒestɪv,
dɪ̥-/
adj E5

digger /ˈdɪgəʳ/
n I114

diggings /ˈdɪgɪŋz/
n I113

dig in
v eat E4
dig I114

digit /ˈdɪdʒɪ̥t/
n J2

digital /ˈdɪdʒɪ̥tl/
adj J2

dignified /ˈdɪgnɪ̥faɪd/
adj C171

dignity /ˈdɪgnɪ̥ti/
n C171

digraph /ˈdaɪgrɑːf‖
-græf/
n G273

digs /dɪgz/
n D66

dig up /ˌ·ˈ·/
v C53

dike /daɪk/
n D22

diligence /ˈdɪlɪ̥dʒəns/
n I101

diligent /ˈdɪlɪ̥dʒənt/
adj I104

dilute /daɪˈluːt/
v N238

dilution /daɪˈluːʃən/
n N238

dim /dɪm/
adj L25
v L26

dime /daɪm/
n J85

dimension /daɪˈmenʃən,
dɪ̥-/
n J61

diminish /dɪ̥ˈmɪnɪʃ/
v N94

diminution
/ˌdɪmɪ̥ˈnjuːʃən‖ -ˈnuː-/
n N95

din /dɪn/
n F273

dine /daɪn/
v E15

diner /ˈdaɪnəʳ/
n restaurant E15,
M108
person E15

dinghy /ˈdɪŋgi/
n M152

dingo /ˈdɪŋgəʊ/ **-goes**
n A54

dining car /ˈ··· ˌ·/
n M108

diningroom
/ˈdaɪnɪŋˌruːm, -rʊm/
n D37, 112

dinner /ˈdɪnəʳ/
n E13, 14

dinosaur /ˈdaɪnəsɔːʳ/
n A94

diocesan /daɪˈɒsɪ̥sən‖
-ˈɑ-/
adj C348

diocese /ˈdaɪəsɪ̥s/
n C348

dip /dɪp/ **-pp-**
v M111, N294

dip
n N294

diphtheria /dɪfˈθɪərɪə,
dɪp-/
n B143

diphthong /ˈdɪfθɒŋ,
ˈdɪp-‖ -θɔŋ/
n G273

diploma /dɪ̥ˈpləʊmə/
n I141

diplomacy /dɪ̥ˈpləʊməsi/
n C105, G39

diplomat /ˈdɪpləmæt/
n C107

diplomatic /dɪpləˈmætɪkˊ/
adj C105, G39

diplomatic corps
/ˌ···ˈ·/
n C105

dipstick /ˈdɪpˌstɪk/
n M102 (picture)

direct /dɪ̥ˈrekt, daɪ-/
honest *adj* F194
order *v* G115, K79,
N165
in grammar *adj* G269
straight *adj* J45
show *v* M55

direct current (D.C.)
/·, ·ˈ··/
n H202

direction /dɪ̥ˈrekʃən,
daɪ-/
n compass L12
guidance N166

directions /dɪ̥ˈrekʃənz/
n G116

directive /dɪ̥ˈrektɪv, daɪ-/
n G116

director /dɪ̥ˈrektəʳ, daɪ-/
n I135, J231, K83

directory /daɪˈrektəri,
dɪ̥-/
n G165

dirt /dɜːt‖ dɜrt/
n D182, H64

dirty /ˈdɜːti‖ ˈdɜr-/
adj D180
v D181

disability /ˌdɪsəˈbɪlɪ̥ti/

n B113

disable /dɪsˈeɪbəl/
v B129

disablement
/dɪsˈeɪbəlmənt/
n B129

disagree /ˌdɪsəˈgriː/
v F106, G127

disagreement
/ˌdɪsəˈgriːmənt/
n F107, G128

disappoint /ˌdɪsəˈpɔɪnt/
v F157

disappointment
/ˌdɪsəˈpɔɪntmənt/
n F158

disarm /dɪsˈɑːm‖ -ˈɑrm/
v C308

disarmament
/dɪsˈɑːməmənt‖ -ˈɑr-/
n C308

disaster /dɪˈzɑːstəʳ‖
dɪˈzæ-/
n N19

disastrous /dɪˈzɑːstrəs‖
dɪˈzæ-/
adj N19

disband /dɪsˈbænd/
v J212

disc /dɪsk/
n general J44
record K50

discard /dɪsˈkɑːd‖ -ɑrd/
v H15

discharge /dɪsˈtʃɑːdʒ‖
-ɑr-/
v releasing C211, J212,
M41, N258
electricity H203
fire H245
perform N123

discharge /dɪsˈtʃɑːdʒ,
ˈdɪstʃɑːdʒ‖ -ɑr-/
n C211, H202, J212,
M41

disciple /dɪˈsaɪpəl/
n I136

disciplinarian
/ˌdɪsɪ̥plɪˈneərɪən/
n G33

disciplinary /ˈdɪsɪplɪnəri,
dɪsɪ̥ˈplɪ-‖ ˈdɪsɪ̥plɪneri/
adj G33

discipline /ˈdɪsɪ̥plɪn/
train *v* G33
subject *n* I139
rigour *n* N266

disciplined /ˈdɪsɪ̥plɪnd/
adj N265

discolour *BrE*, **discolor**
AmE /dɪsˈkʌləʳ/
v L28

discoloured *BrE*,
discolored *AmE*
/dɪsˈkʌləd‖ -lərd/
adj L34

disconnect
/ˌdɪskəˈnekt/
v N321

discontented
/ˌdɪskənˈtentɪ̥d/
adj F81

discord /ˈdɪskɔːd‖

dumb /dʌm/
n B133
adj G45
dumbfound /dʌm'faʊnd/
v F237
dumpy /'dʌmpi/
adj B105
dung /dʌŋ/
n B66, E136
dungarees /,dʌŋgə'ri:z/
n D160
dungeon /'dʌndʒən/
n C150
duration /djʊ'reɪʃən‖
dʊ-/
n L133
during /'djʊərɪŋ‖'dʊ-/
adv L265
dusk /dʌsk/
n L223
dust /dʌst/
v D177
n H63
dustbin /'dʌst,bin/
n H176
dust pan /'dʌstpæn/
n H156 (picture)
dusty /'dʌsti/
adj H63
Dutch cap /,·'·/
n B181
dutiful /'dju:tɪfəl‖ 'du:-/
adj F63
duty /'dju:ti‖ 'du:ti/
n morality F63
tax J160
duty officer /'··,···/
n C300
dwarf /dwɔ:f‖ dwɔrf/
n N72, 87
v N92
dwell /dwel/ **dwelt**
/dwelt/ *or* **dwelled**
v D60
dweller /'dwelər/
n D60
dwelling /'dwelɪŋ/
n D65
dwelling-place /'··,·/
n D65
dwindle /'dwɪndl/
v N94
dye /daɪ/ **dyes, dyed,**
dyeing
v H95, L28
dye
n H93, L27
dyed /daɪd/
adj L34
dying /'daɪ·ɪŋ/
adj A3
dyke /daɪk/
n D22
dynamic /daɪ'næmɪk/
adj N124, 233
dynamism
/'daɪnəmɪzəm/
n N235
dynamo /'daɪnəməʊ/
n H114
dynastic /dɪ'næstɪk‖
daɪ-/
adj C98

dynasty /'dɪnəsti‖ 'daɪ-/
adj C98
dysentery /'dɪsəntəri‖
-teri/
n B147
dyspepsia /dɪs'pepsɪə,
-'pepʃə/
n B150
dyspeptic /dɪ'speptɪk/
adj B150

E

each /i:tʃ/
det, pron, adv N101
eager /'i:gər/
adj F226
eagerness /'i:gənɪs‖
'i:gər-/
n F228
eagle /'i:gəl/
n A78
ear /ɪər/
n on a body A51
(picture),
54 (picture), A120,
B10 (picture), B23
of corn A152
early /'ɜ:li‖ 'ɜrli/
adv, adj L140, 183,
N61
earn /ɜ:n‖ ɜrn/
v D83, J218
earnings /'ɜ:nɪŋz‖ 'ɜr-/
n J219
ear-ring /'ɪə,rɪŋ/
n D159
earshot /'ɪəʃɒt‖ 'ɪərʃɑt/
n F273
earth /ɜ:θ‖ ɜrθ/
n soil H63
electricity H205
planet L4 (picture)
earthly /'ɜ:θli‖ 'ɜrθli/
adj C339
earthquake /'ɜ:θkweɪk‖
'ɜrθ-/
n L115
earthworm /'ɜ:θwɜ:m‖
'ɜrθwɜrm/
n A113
earwig /'ɪə,wɪg‖ 'ɪər-/
n A110
ease /i:z/
n F222, G43
v B162, F223
easel /'i:zəl/
n I47
east /i:st/
n L13
easy /'i:zi/
adj relaxed B89
simple N59
easy terms /,··'·/
n J148
eat /i:t/ **ate** /et, eɪt‖ eɪt/,
eaten /'i:tn/
v E3
eatable /'i:təbəl/
adj E108

eatables /'i:təbəlz/
n E1
eater /i:tər/
n E3
eating-house /'··,·/
n E120
eating-place /'··,·/
n E120
eats /i:ts/
n E1
eat up
v E3
ebb /eb/
n L89
v L90
ebb tide /'··/
n L89
eccentric /ɪk'sentrɪk/
adj N69
eccentricity
/,eksen'trɪsɪ̥ti, -sən-/
n N70
ecclesiastic
/ɪ,kli:zi'æstɪk/
n C344
ecclesiastical
/ɪ,kli:zi'æstɪkəl/
adj C338
echo /'ekəʊ/ **-oes**
n N122
echo, *3rd p sing pres t*
echoes
v N122
eclipse /ɪ'klɪps/
n, v L9
economic /,ekə'nɒmɪk,
i:-‖ -'nɑ-/
adj J126
economical
/,ekə'nɒmɪkəl, i:-‖
-'nɑ-/
adj J126, 198
economics /,ekə'nɒmɪks,
,i:-‖ -'nɑ-/
n J141
economize /ɪ'kɒnəmaɪz‖
ɪ'kɑ-/
v J127
economy /ɪ'kɒnəmi‖
ɪ'kɑ-/
n J123, 126, 141
ecumenical
/,i:kjʊ'menɪkəl‖ ,ekjə-/
adj C338
ecumenism
/i:'kju:mɪ̥nɪzəm‖ ek-/
n C338
eddy /'edi/
n L89
v L90
edge /edʒ/
n of a blade H145
limit M122
position M200
edible /'edəbəl/
adj E108
edifice /'edɪ̥fɪ̥s/
n D3
edit /'edɪ̥t/
v G142
edition /ɪ'dɪʃən/
n G180
editor /'edɪ̥tər/

n G172
editorial /,edɪ̥'tɔ:rɪəl‖
-'tor-/
n G159
educable /'edjʊkəbəl‖
'edʒə-/
adj I148
educate /'edjʊkeɪt‖
'edʒə-/
v G33
educated /'edjʊkeɪtɪ̥d‖
'edʒə-/
adj G36
education /,edjʊ'keɪʃən‖
,edʒə-/
n G35
educational
/,edjʊ'keɪʃənəl‖ ,edʒə-/
adj I148
educationalist
/,edjʊ'keɪʃənəlɪ̥st‖
,edʒe-/
n I148
educative /'edjʊkətɪv‖
'edʒə-/
adj I148
educator /'edjʊkeɪtər‖
'edʒə-/
n I148
eel /i:l/
n A100
eerie /'ɪəri/
adj N69
effect /ɪ'fekt/
n N153
v N165
effective /ɪ'fektɪv/
adj N169
effectiveness
/ɪ'fektɪvnɪ̥s/
n N170
effectual /ɪ'fektʊəl/
adj N169
efficiency /ɪ'fɪʃənsi/
n N170
efficient /ɪ'fɪʃənt/
adj N169
effluent /'efluənt/
n H14
effort /'efət‖ 'efərt/
n I101
effortless /'efətləs‖
'efərt-/
adj I101
egalitarian
/ɪ'gælɪ̥'teərɪən/
n, adj C154
egalitarianism
/ɪ,gælɪ̥'teərɪənɪzm/
n C154
egg /eg/
n in life A19, 111
as food E31
egg plant /'egplɑ:nt‖
'egplænt/
n plant A151
food E30
eh /eɪ/
interj G293
eiderdown /'aɪdədaʊn‖
-dər-/
n D115
eight /eɪt/

n J4
eighth note /'···/
  n K28
eighty /'eɪti/
  n J4
either /'aɪðə'|| 'iː-/
  det conj pron adv N101
either-or
  N101
ejaculate /ɪ'dʒækjʊleɪt||
  -kjə-/
  v M60
ejaculation
  /ɪˌdʒækjʊ'leɪʃən|| -kjə-/
  n M60
eject /ɪ'dʒekt/
  v M60
ejection /ɪ'dʒekʃən/
  n M60
elaborate /ɪ'læbərət/
  adj N62
elaborate /ɪ'læbəreɪt/
  v N63
elaboration
  /ɪˌlæbə'reɪʃən/
  n N63
elastic /ɪ'læstɪk/
  n H89
  adj N268
elbow /'elbəʊ/
  n B10 (picture), B41
elder /'eldə'/
  n general C9
  in a church C344
elderberry /'eldəbəri||
  'eldər,beri/
  n A154
elderly /'eldəli|| 'eldərli/
  adj L208
elect /ɪ'lekt/
  v C115
election /ɪ'lekʃən/
  n C117
electioneer /ɪˌlekʃə'nɪə'/
  v C115
elector /ɪ'lektə'|| -tər,
  -tɔr/
  n C117
electoral /ɪ'lektərəl/
  adj C117
electoral roll /·ˌ···'·/
  electoral register
  /·ˌ···'···/
  n C118
electorate /ɪ'lektərɪt/
  n C118
electric /ɪ'lektrɪk/
  adj H201
electrical /ɪ'lektrɪkəl/
  adj H201
electric chair /·ˌ···'·/
  n C260
electric drill /·ˌ···'·/
  n H146 (picture)
electric guitar /·ˌ···'·/
  n K46
electricity /ɪˌlek'trɪsɪti/
  n H83, 200
electric razor /·ˌ···'··/
  n H140 (picture)
electron /ɪ'lektrɒn||
  -trɑn/
  n H5

electronic /ɪˌlek'trɒnɪk||
  -'trɑ-/
  adj H201
electronics
  /ɪˌlek'trɒnɪks|| -trɑ-/
  n H200
elegance /'elɪgəns/
  n F40
elegant /'elɪgənt/
  adj F39
elegy /'elɪdʒi/
  n G170
element /'elɪmənt/
  n H4
elemental /ˌelɪ'mentl/
  adj H8
elementary /ˌelɪ'mentəri/
  adj N61
elements /'elɪmənts/
  n I75
elephant /'elɪfənt/
  n A59
elevator /'elɪveɪtə'/
  n D30, H117
eleven /ɪ'levən/
  n J4
eleventh hour /·ˌ···'·/
  adj L184
eliminate /ɪ'lɪmɪneɪt/
  v kill A8
  in sport K104
elimination
  /ɪˌlɪmɪ'neɪʃən/
  n A9
élite /eɪ'liːt, ɪ-/
  n C153
  adj C303
elk /elk/
  n A57
elm /elm/
  n A155
elocution /ˌelə'kjuːʃən/
  n G232
eloquent /'eləkwənt/
  adj G67
else /els/
  adv N101
elude /ɪ'luːd/
  v M35
elusive /ɪ'luːsɪv/
  adj M35
emaciated /ɪ'meɪʃieɪtɪd/
  adj B101
emaciation
  /ɪˌmeɪsi'eɪʃən/
  n B101
emancipate
  /ɪ'mænsɪpeɪt/
  v C165
emancipation
  /ɪˌmænsɪ'peɪʃən/
  n C165
emasculate
  /ɪ'mæskjʊleɪt|| -skjə-/
  v A18
embalm /ɪm'bɑːm/
  v C53
embankment
  /ɪm'bæŋkmənt/
  n L99
embargo /ɪm'bɑːgəʊ||
  -ɑr-/ -goes
  n C197

embark /ɪm'bɑːk|| -ɑrk/
  v M9
embarkation
  /ˌembɑː'keɪʃən|| -ɑr-/
  n M9
embarrass /ɪm'bærəs/
  v F151
embarrassing
  /ɪm'bærəsɪŋ/
  adj F153
embarrassment
  /ɪm'bærəsmənt/
  n F152
embassy /'embəsi/
  n C108
embattled /ɪm'bætld/
  adj C273
ember /'embə'/
  n H84
embezzle /ɪm'bezəl/
  v C234
embezzlement
  /ɪm'bezəlmənt/
  n C233
embezzler /ɪm'bezlə'/
  n C235
emblem /'embləm/
  n H130
embodiment
  /ɪm'bɒdɪmənt|| ɪm'bɑ-/
  n N9
embody /ɪm'bɒdi||
  ɪm'bɑdi/
  v N8
embrace /ɪm'breɪs/
  v, n C22
embroider /ɪm'brɔɪdə'/
  v I57
embroidery /ɪm'brɔɪdəri/
  n I57
embryo /'embriəʊ/ -os
  n A19
embryonic /ˌembri'ɒnɪk||
  -'ɑnɪk/
  adj A19
emerald /'emərəld/
  n H65
emerge /ɪ'mɜːdʒ|| -ɜr-/
  v M4
emergence /ɪ'mɜːdʒəns||
  -ɜr-/
  n M4
emergency /ɪ'mɜːdʒənsi||
  -ɜr-/
  n N20
emergent /ɪ'mɜːdʒənt||
  -ɜr-/
  adj M4
emigrant /'emɪgrənt/
  n M76
emigrate /'emɪgreɪt/
  v M74
emigration
  /ˌemɪ'greɪʃən/
  n M75
émigré /'emɪgreɪ/
  n M76
emissary /'emɪsəri||
  -seri/
  n C107
emission /ɪ'mɪʃən/
  n M60
emit /ɪ'mɪt/ -tt-

v M60
emotion /ɪ'məʊʃən/
  n F2
emotional /ɪ'məʊʃənəl/
  adj F4
emotive /ɪ'məʊtɪv/
  adj F4
emperor /'empərə'/
  n C96
emphasis /'emfəsɪs/ -ses
  /siːz/
  n general G78
  in language G232
emphasize /'emfəsaɪz/
  v general G77
  in language G231
emphatic /ɪm'fætɪk/
  in verb tenses n G265
  general adj G232
empire /'empaɪə'/
  n C92
empirical /ɪm'pɪrɪkəl/
  adj N230
employ /ɪm'plɔɪ/
  v I26, J211
employee /ɪm'plɔɪ-iː,
  ˌemplɔɪ'iː/
  n J229
employer /ɪm'plɔɪə'/
  n J228
employment
  /ɪm'plɔɪmənt/
  n I27, J211
empress /'emprɪs/
  n C96
empty /'empti/
  adj N254
  v N258
enable /ɪ'neɪbəl/
  v N239
enact /ɪ'nækt/
  v C184
enactment /ɪ'næktmənt/
  n C184
encamp /ɪn'kæmp/
  v D62
encampment
  /ɪn'kæmpmənt/
  n D68
encash /ɪn'kæʃ/
  v J108
enchant /ɪn'tʃɑːnt||
  ɪn'tʃænt/
  v F26
enchanting /ɪn'tʃɑːntɪŋ||
  ɪn'tʃæn-/
  adj F29
enchantment
  /ɪn'tʃɑːntmənt||
  ɪn'tʃænt-/
  n F28
encircle /ɪn'sɜːkəl||
  -ɜr-/
  v H25
encirclement
  /ɪn'sɜːkəlmənt|| -ɜr-/
  n H25
enclose /ɪn'kləʊz/
  v H25
enclosure /ɪn'kləʊʒə'/
  n H25
encode /ɪn'kəʊd/
  v G147

freakish /'fri:kɪʃ/
adj N69
freckle /'frekəl/
n B53
freckled /'frekəld/
adj B53
free /fri:/ **freed**
v C165
free
adj C165, J198
freedom /'fri:dəm/
n C165
freedom fighter
/'··, ··/
n C136
free enterprise /, · '····/
n J142
free kick /· ' · /
n K192
freeway /'fri:weɪ/
n M129
freeze /fri:z/ **froze**
/frəʊz/, **frozen**
/'frəʊzən/
of food *v* E106
freeze
n L67
freezer /'fri:zər/
n H133
freezing /'fri:zɪŋ/
adj L66
freezing compartment
/'···, ··/
n H133
freezing point /'···/
n L43
freight /freɪt/
n, v J157
freight car /'···/
n M108
French dressing /, · '···/
n E50
French fried potato
/, · · · '··/
n E48
French fry /, · '·/
n E48
French horn /· ' · /
n K45
French letter /· '···/
n B181
frenzied /'frenzid/
adj F226
frenzy /'frenzi/
n F228
frequent /'fri:kwənt/
adj L146
frequent /fri'kwent‖
fri'kwent, 'fri:kwənt/
v M70
frequently /'fri:kwəntli/
adv L258
fresco /'freskəʊ/
n I45
fresh /'freʃ/
adj new E108, L203
rude F155
freshen /'freʃən/
v D177
freshness /'freʃn̩s/
F156
fret /fret/
n K45 (picture)

friar /'fraɪər/
n C345
friction /'frɪkʃən/
n N155
Friday /'fraɪdi/
n L232
fridge /frɪdʒ/
n H133
friend /frend/
n C40, 42
be friends with C44
friendly /'frendli/
adj C46
friendship /'frendʃɪp/
n C40
frigate /'frɪgɪt/
n H249
fright /fraɪt/
n F120
frighten /'fraɪtn/
v F122
frightened /'fraɪtnd/
adj F121, 125
frightening
adj F123
frightful /'fraɪtfəl/
adj F61, 124
frigid /'frɪdʒɪd/
adj L11
fritter /'frɪtər/
n E46
frock /frɒk‖ frak/
n D139
frog /frɒg‖ frag, frɔg/
n A94
frogspawn /'frɒgspɔ:n‖
'frag-, 'frɔg-/
n A94
from /frəm; *strong* frɒm‖
frəm; *strong* frʌm,
fram/
prep as a result G289
with numbers J37
for time L271
general M205
front /frʌnt/
n in war C272
in general M202
in front (of) M221
front door /, · ' · /
n D24
frontier /'frʌntɪər‖
frʌn'tɪər/
n M122
frontline /ˌfrʌnt'laɪn⁻/
n C272
front room /· '·/
n D37
frost /frɒst‖ frɔst/
n L51
v L52
frosty /'frɒsti‖ 'frɔsti/
adj L51
frown /fraʊn/
v F242
n F243
fruit /fru:t/
n A130, 134, 150
fruitful /'fru:tfəl/
adj E135
fruit juice /'···/
n E61
fruity /'fru:ti/

adj A134
frustrate /frʌ'streɪt‖
'frʌstreɪt/
v F230
frustrating /frʌ'streɪtɪŋ/
adj F231
frustration
/frʌ'streɪʃən/
n F232
fry /fraɪ/
v E100
fuck /fʌk/
v C24
fuel /fjʊəl‖ fju:əl/ -**ll**-
BrE, -**l**- *AmE*
v H77
fuel
n H80
fugitive /'fju:dʒɪtɪv/
n M36
fulcrum /'fʊlkrəm, 'fʌl-/
-**crums** *or* -**cra** /krə/
n H150
fulfil, fulfill *AmE* /fʊl'fɪl/
v N131
fulfilment, fulfillment
AmE /fʊl'fɪlmənt/
n N133
full /fʊl/
adj N250
fullback /'fʊlbæk/
n K193 (picture)
full-bodied /· ' ··⁻/
adj B104
full-grown /· ' ·⁻/
adj L207
full-scale /ˌfʊl'skeɪl⁻/
adj N253
full stop /· ' · /
n G151
full-time /· ' ·⁻/
adj J224
n K192
full-up /· ' ·⁻/
adj N250
fully-grown /· · ' ·⁻/
adj L207
fumes /fju:mz/
n H84
fun /fʌn/
n K2
function /'fʌŋkʃən/
work *v* I28, N123
working *n* I29, N127
value *n* J40
party *n* K2
functional /'fʌŋkʃənəl/
adj N124
fund /fʌnd/
n J80, 115
v J80
fundamental
/ˌfʌndə'mentl/
adj, n N43
funds /fʌndz/
n J80
funeral /'fju:nərəl/
n, adj C54
(funeral) courtege
/'····, ·/
n C55
funeral director
/'····, ··/

n C55
funfair /'fʌnfeər/
n K72
fungus /'fʌŋgəs/ -**gi**
/dʒaɪ, gaɪ/ *or* -**guses**
n A140
funnel /'fʌnəl/ -**ll**- *BrE,*
-**l**- *AmE*
v L90
funnel
n tool H153 (picture)
chimney M157
(picture)
funny /'fʌni/
adj amusing K3
peculiar N68
unwell B111
fur /fɜ:ʳ/
n A126, H88
fur coat /· ' · /
n D143
furious /'fjʊəriəs/
adj F104
furlong /'fɜ:lɒŋ‖ 'fɜːlɔŋ/
n J66
furlough /'fɜ:ləʊ‖ 'fɜr-/
n J240
furnace /'fɜ:nɪs‖ 'fɜr-/
n H120
furnish /'fɜ:nɪʃ‖ 'fɜr-/
v D111
furnishings /'fɜ:nɪʃɪŋz‖
'fɜr-/
n D110
furniture /'fɜ:nɪtʃəʳ‖ 'fɜr-/
n D110
furrow /'fʌrəʊ‖ 'fɜr-/
n E142
furry /'fɜ:ri/
adj A126
further /'fɜ:ðəʳ‖ 'fɜr-/
comp of **far**
furthermore
/ˌfɜ:ðə'mɔ:ʳ‖
'fɜrðərmɔr/
adv G286, N100
furthest /'fɜ:ðɪst‖ 'fɜr-/
superl of **far**
furtive /'fɜ:tɪv‖ 'fɜr-/
adj F193
fury /'fjʊəri/
n F103
fuse /fju:z/
in electricity *n* H208
in electricity *v* H209
join *v* N326
fusebox /'fju:zbɒks‖
-baks/
n H208
fuselage /'fju:zəlɑ:ʒ‖
-səlɑʒ/
n M186
fuse wire /'· · /
n H208
fusilier /ˌfju:zə'lɪəʳ/
n C307
fusillade /ˌfju:zɪ'leɪd‖
-s̩-/
n H243
fusion /'fju:ʒən/
n 327
futile /'fju:taɪl‖ -tl/
adj N231

geology /dʒiˈɒlədʒi‖ -ɑlə-/
n I75

geometric
/ˌdʒɪəˈmetrɪk/
adj J30

geometry /dʒɪˈɒmᵻtri‖ -ˈɑm-/
n J30

germ /dʒɜːm‖ dʒɜrm/
n A19, 37

German measles
/ˌ·· '··/
n B143

germinate /ˈdʒɜːmᵻneɪt‖ ˈdʒɜr-/
v A18

gerund /ˈdʒerənd/
n G270

gesticulate
/dʒeˈstɪkjʊleɪt‖ -kjə-/
v G197

gesticulation
/dʒeˌstɪkjʊˈleɪʃən‖ -kjə-/
n G197

gesture /ˈdʒestʃəʳ/
n G196
v G197

get /get/ **got** /gɒt‖ gɑt/,
got *or* **gotten** *AmE*
/ˈgɒtn‖ ˈgɑtn/, *pres p*
getting
v receive D83, G32,
217, J218
understand G31
make J36
buy J130
move M1
become N15
arrange N150

get acquainted
v C44

get (a)round
v M37

get at
v imply G88
find out N358

get away /ˈgetəweɪ/
v D89, M35

getaway /ˈgetəweɪ/
n M35

get back
v D86
get one's own back
F185

get better
v B163, N129

get by
v N128

get done
v N150, 163

get down
v swallow E4
write G143
descend M8

get hot
adj L63

get in
v put H23
collect J154
arrive M5

get off
v release C211
remove D133
descend M8

get on
v dress D133
ascend M9

get out
v remove D89, H24
produce G174, H24
leave M8

get ready
v D177, I22

get rid of
v D89, 90, H15

get right
v N215

get round
v G87

get straight
v N215

get stuck
v M62

get to
v M5

get-together /'· ···/
n K2

get to know
v C44

get up
v N291

getup /ˈgetʌp/
n D132

get weaving
v I57

get well
v B163

ghastly /ˈgɑːstli‖ ˈgæstli/
adj F38, 61

ghee, ghi /giː/
n E40

ghetto /ˈgetəʊ/ **-tos**
n C81

ghost /gəʊst/
n C324

ghostly /ˈgəʊstli/
adj C324

giant /ˈdʒaɪənt/
n N72
adj N83

gibbon /ˈgɪbən/
n A50

giblets /ˈdʒɪblᵻts/
n E35

gift /gɪft/
n present D102
skill G43

gifted /ˈgɪftᵻd/
adj G42

gig /gɪg/
n M92

gigantic /dʒaɪˈgæntɪk/
adj N82

giggle /ˈgɪgəl/
n F240
v F241

gigot /ˈdʒɪgət/
n E34 (picture)

gill /gɪl/
n of a fish A100
(picture), A122
measure J66

gin /dʒɪn/
n E65, K132

ginger /ˈdʒɪndʒəʳ/
n B53

ginger ale, ginger beer
/ˌ·· '·'···/
n E61

gin rummy /ˌ· ··/
n K132

gipsy /ˈdʒɪpsi/
n C170

giraffe /dʒᵻˈrɑːf‖ -ˈræf/
n A59

girder /ˈgɜːdəʳ‖ ˈgɜr-/
n H40

girdle /ˈgɜːdl‖ ˈgɜr-/
n D149

girl /gɜːl‖ gɜrl/
n C2, 5, 161

girlfriend /ˈgɜːlfrend‖ ˈgɜrl-/
n C21

giro /ˈdʒaɪərəʊ/
n J104

gist /dʒɪst/
n H36

give /gɪv/ **gave** /geɪv/,
given /ˈgɪvən/
v pass to D99
provide G100
pay J132
stretch N269

give in
v C282

give odds
v K123

give off
v M60

give out
v D104

give up
v surrender C282
stop D92, J214
despair F6
finish L174

glad /glæd/ **-dd-**
adj F70

gladden /ˈglædn/
v F76

glade /gleɪd/
n L111

glance /glɑːns‖ glæns/
v F263
n F265

gland /glænd/
n B4

glandular /ˈglændjʊləʳ‖ -dʒə-/
adj B4

glass /glɑːs‖ glæs/
n for enlarging H123
cup H172

glasses /ˈglɑːsᵻz‖ glæs-/
n H123 (picture)

glassful /ˈglɑːsfʊl‖ ˈglæs-/
n H172

glasshouse /ˈglɑːshaʊs‖ glæs-/
n D54

gleam /gliːm/
n L22
v L23

glen /glen/
n L107

glide /glaɪd/
v, n M28

glider /ˈglaɪdəʳ/
n M182

glimmer /ˈglɪməʳ/
n L22
v L23

glimpse /glɪmps/
v F263
n F265

global /ˈgləʊbəl/
adj H48

globe /gləʊb/
n H48

globular /ˈglɒbjʊləʳ‖ ˈglɑbjə-/
adj H48

gloom /gluːm/
n L21

gloomy /ˈgluːmi/
adj L25

glorification
/ˌglɔːrᵻfᵻˈkeɪʃən‖ ˌglo-/
n F141

glorify /ˈglɔːrᵻfaɪ‖ ˈglo-/
v F141

glorious /ˈglɔːrɪəs‖ ˈglo-/
adj F53, 141

glory /ˈglɔːri‖ ˈglori-/
n, v F141

-glot /glɒt‖ glat/
comb form G239

glottis /ˈglɒtᵻs‖ ˈglɑ-/
n B36 (picture)

glove /glʌv/
n D155, K196 (picture)

glove puppet
/'· ,··/
n K90

glow /gləʊ/
n L22
v L23

glue /gluː/ **glued**, *pres p*
gluing *or* **glueing**
v H10

glue
n H9

gluey /ˈgluːi/
adj H12

gnaw /nɔː/
v E6

gnome /nəʊm/
n C357

go /gəʊ/ **went** /went/,
gone /gɒn‖ gɑn/; *pres p*
going
v work I103
move M1

go, goes
n M10, 36

go after
v M34

goal /gəʊl/
n in sport K121, 191
(picture)
aim N228, K193

goalpost /ˈgəʊlpəʊst/
n K193 (picture)

goat /gəʊt/
n A56 (picture)

go away
v M4

haemorrhoids
/'hemərɔɪdz/
n B147

haft /hɑːft‖ hæft/
n H42, 145

haggis /'hægɪs‖ -gises or gis
n E37

haggle /'hægəl/
v J145

hail /heɪl/
n L48
v L50

hair /heə ʳ/
n A126, B10 (picture), B51 picture)

hairbrush /'heəbrʌʃ‖ 'heər-/
n D178

haircut /'heəkʌt‖ 'heər-/
n D183

haired /heəd‖ heərd/
comb form B51

hairdo /'heəduː‖ 'heər--dos
n D183

hairdresser
/'heə,dresə ʳ‖ 'heər-/
n D186

hairnet /'heənet‖ 'heər-/
n D184

hairpiece /'heəpiːs‖ 'heər-/
n D184

hairpin /'heə,pɪn/
n object D159
bend M134

hairspring /'heə,sprɪŋ‖ 'heər-/
n L228 (picture)

hair stylist /' · · · /
n D186

hairy /'heəri/
adj A126, B51

half /hɑːf‖ hæf/ **halves**
hɑːvz‖ hævz/
adj, n J14

half- /hɑːf/
comb form
in the family C18
general N255

half a crown /, · · ' · ˉ/ **half crown** /, · ' · / **half crowns**
n J83

half a dozen /, · · ' · · ˉ/ **half dozen** /, · ' · / **half dozens**
n J16

half an hour /, · · ' · ˉ/
n L226

halfback /'hɑː,fbæk‖ 'hæf-/
n K194

half-day /· · /
n J240

half-holiday /, · ' · · · /
n J240

half-hour /· ' · /
n L226

half note /' · · /
n K28

halfpenny /'heɪpni/
halfpennies or **halfpence**
n J83

half time /hɑːf'taɪm ˉ/
n K192

half-track /'hɑː,ftræk/
n H248

halfway line /' · · , · /
n K193

half-wit /' · · /
n G48

halibut /'hælɪbət/
n A100

hall /hɔːl/
n D29, 33

halliard /'hæljəd‖ -ərd/
n M157

hallo /hə'ləʊ, he-, hæ--los
interj G291

hall of residence
/, · · ' · · · /
n D33

hallucinate /hə'luːsɪneɪt/
v B85

hallucination
/hə,luːsɪ'neɪʃən/
n B85

halt /hɔːlt/
v L173
n L181, M3, 11

halve /hɑːv‖ hæv/
v J15

halyard /'hæljəd‖ -ərd/
n M157

ham /hæm/
n food E32, 34 (picture)
actor K82

hamburger
/'hæmbɜːgə ʳ‖ -ɜr-/
n E37

hamlet /'hæmlɪt/
n C80

hammer /'hæmə ʳ/
general n, v H144 (picture)
in athletics n K202

hammock /'hæmək/
n D116

hamper /'hæmpə ʳ/
n N140

hand /hænd/
n of the body n B42 (picture)
give v D100
meat n E34 (picture)
person n I112, M163
of cards n K130
of a clock n L228
to hand N109
at hand L204

handbag /'hændbæg/
n D154

handbill /'hændbɪl/
n H130

handbook /'hændbʊk/
n G162

handcart /'hændkɑːt‖ -ɑrt/
n M98

hand down
v C212

hand drill /' · · /
n H146 (picture)

handful /'hændfʊl/
n N80

handgun /'hændgʌn/
n H237

handicap /'hændɪkæp/
n general B113
in golf K198

handicapped
/'hændɪkæpt/
adj B113

handicraft /'hændɪkrɑːft‖ -kræft/
n I41

handiwork /'hændɪwɜːk‖ -ɜrk/
n I41

handkerchief
/'hæŋkətʃɪf‖ -kər-/
n C154

handle /'hændl/
touch v F260
of a knife n H145
deal v J153

hand-me-downs /' · · · /
n D130

hand out
v D104

handout /'hændaʊt/
n D104

hand over
v D100

handsome /'hænsəm/
adj F39

handwriting
/'hænd,raɪtɪŋ/
n G145

handwritten /,hænd'rɪtnˉ/
adj G146

handy /'hændi/
adj, adv near M209
useful N229

hang /hæŋ/ **hung** /hʌŋ/
v general N301

hang, hanged
v kill C258

hang about
v M27

hangar /'hæŋə ʳ/
n M185

hang around
v M27

hanging /'hæŋɪŋ/
n C258

hangings /'hæŋɪŋz/
n D120

hangman /'hæŋmən-men /mən/
n C259

hang on
v M27

hang onto
v D93

hankie /'hæŋki/
n D154

ha'penny /'heɪpni/
n J83

haphazard /,hæp'hæzədˉ‖ -ərd/
adj N37

happen /'hæpən/
v N16

happening /'hæpənɪŋ/

n N17

happen (up)on
v M72

happiness /'hæpɪnɪs/
n F74

happy /'hæpi/
adj F70

harbour, BrE **harbor**
AmE /'hɑːbə ʳ‖ 'hɑr-/
n M159

hard /hɑːd‖ hɑrd/
adj difficult N60
stiff N264

hardback /'hɑːdbæk‖ 'hɑrd-/
n G164

hardboard /'hɑːdbɔːd‖ 'hɑrdbɔrd/
n H71

hard currency /, · ' · · · /
n J89

hard drug /· ' · /
n E80

harden /'hɑːdn‖ 'hɑrdn/
v N272

hard labour BrE, **-labor**
AmE /, · ' · · /
n C256

hardly /'hɑːdli‖ 'hɑrdli/
adv N99

hard of hearing /, · · ' · · ˉ/
adj B133

hard palate /, · ' · /
n B26

hardware /'hɑːdweə ʳ‖ 'hɑrd-/
n J195

hardware store /' · · , · /
n J195

hardwood /'hɑːdwʊd‖ 'hɑrd-/
n H71

hard-working /, · ' · · ˉ/
adj I104

hare /heə ʳ/
n A60

harem /'heərəm, hɑː'riːm‖ 'hærəm/
n C30

harlot /'hɑːlət‖ 'hɑr-/
n C36

harm /hɑːm‖ hɑrm/
v, n N337

harmonica /hɑː'mɒnɪkə‖ hɑr'mɑ-/
n K45 (picture)

harmonious
/hɑː'məʊnɪəs‖ hɑr-/
adj N225

harmonize /'hɑːmənaɪz‖ 'hɑr-/
v music K25
general N226

harmonium
/hɑː'məʊnɪəm‖ hɑr-/
n K48 (picture)

harmony /'hɑːməni‖ 'hɑr-/
n music K25
general N225

harness /'hɑːnɪs‖ 'hɑr-/
of animals n, v K199
to control v N165

harp /hɑːp|| hɑrp/
  n K46 (picture)
harpist /'hɑːpɪ̯st|| hɑrp-/
  n K46
harpsichord
  /'hɑːpsɪkɔːd||
  'hɑrpsɪkɔrd/
  n K48 (picture)
harsh /hɑːʃ|| hɑrʃ/
  adj N265
harvest /'hɑːvɪ̯st|| 'hɑr-/
  n E133
  v E138
harvester /'hɑːvɪ̯stəʳ||
  'hɑr-/
  n E139
hashish, hash /'hæʃiːʃ,
  -ɪʃ/
  n E86
haste /heɪst/
  n M33
hasten /'heɪstən/
  v M33
hasty /'heɪsti/
  adj. M16
hat /hæt/
  n D146, F33
  v F32
hatch /hætʃ/
  lay *v* A5
  arrange *v* C137
  cover *n* D35
hatchet /'hætʃɪ̯t/
  n H143 (picture)
hate /heɪt/
  n F33
  v F32
hateful /'heɪtfəl/
  adj F34
hatred /'heɪtrɪ̯d/
  n F33
haul /hɔːl/
  v, n M56
haulage /'hɔːlɪdʒ/
  n M90
haunt /hɔːnt/
  v F209
  n M120
have /v, əv, həv; *strong*
  hæv/ **had** /d, əd, həd;
  strong hæd/ *3rd pers*
  sing pres t **has** /s, z, əz,
  həz; *strong* hæz/, *pres t*
  neg contr **haven't**
  /'hævənt/, *3rd pers sing*
  pres t neg contr **hasn't**
  /'hæzənt/, *past t neg*
  contr **hadn't** /'hædənt/
  v in sex C24
  possess D81, J135
  eat E3
  in verb tenses L273
  modal N159
have in
  v H17
haven /'heɪvən/
  n M159
have on
  v D133
have out
  v discuss G83
  remove H24
haversack /'hævəsæk||

-ər-/
  n H184
hawk /hɔːk/
  n A78
hawser /'hɔːzəʳ/
  n H46
hawthorn /'hɔːθɔːn||
  ɔrn/
  n A157
hay /heɪ/
  n E141
hay fever /' ··· /
  n B149
haystack /'heɪstæk/
  n E141
hazard /'hæzəd|| -ərd/
  n N38
  v N39
hazardous /'hæzədəs||
  -zər-/
  adj N40
haze /heɪz/
  n L45
  v L46
hazelnut /'heɪzəlnʌt/
  n A153
hazy /'heɪzi/
  adj L72
he /i, hi; *strong* hiː/
  pron G280 (table)
head /hed/
  of the body *n* A51, 53
  (pictures), A120, B10
  (picture), B20, E34
  (pictures)
  person *n* C101, 160,
  I135
  of a tool *n* H145
  in football *v* K192
  move *v* M39
headache /'hedeɪk/
  n B151
headboard /'hedbɔːd||
  -bɔrd/
  n D115 (picture)
header /'hedəʳ/
  n K192
headgear /'hedgɪəʳ/
  n D146
headlamp /'hedlæmp/
  n M100 (picture)
headland /'hedlənd/
  n L85
headlight /'hedlaɪt/
  n M100
headline /'hedlaɪn/
  n G159
headmaster
  /,hed'mɑːstəʳ||
  'hed,mæstər/
  n I135
headmistress
  /,hed'mɪstrɪ̯s||
  'hed,mɪstrɪ̯s/
  n I135
headquarters
  /'hed,kwɔːtəz,
  ,hed'kwɔːtəz|| -ɔrtərz/
  n J227
headscarf /'hedskɑːf||
  -ɑrf/
  n D146
headstone /'hedstəʊn/

n C59
head teacher /,·'··ʳ/
  n I135
heal /hiːl/
  v B161
healer /'hiːləʳ/
  n B166
healing /'hiːlɪŋ/
  n B165
health /helθ/
  n B112
healthful /'helθfəl/
  adj B110
healthy /'helθi/
  adj B110
heap /hiːp/
  n H34
  v H35
hear /hɪəʳ/ **heard** /hɜːd||
  hɜrd/
  v in law C206
  general F272
hearing /'hɪərɪŋ/
  n in law C205
  general F273
hearse /hɜːs|| hɜrs/
  n C55
heart /hɑːt|| hɑrt/
  n general B36 (picture),
  E32
  in cards K131
  (picture)
  centre M201
heart attack /'···/
  n B144
(heart)beat /'hɑːtbiːt||
  'hɑrt-/
  n B36
heartbroken
  /'hɑːt,brəʊkən|| 'hɑrt-/
  adj F86
heartburn /'hɑːtbɜːn||
  'hɑrtbɜrn/
  n B150
heart disease /'···/
  n B144
heart failure /'··,··/
  n B144
hearth /hɑːθ|| hɑrθ/
  n D36
hearthrug /'hɑːθrʌg||
  'hɑr-/
  n D118
heartless /'hɑːtlɪ̯s||
  hɑrtlɪ̯s/
  adj F179
heat /hiːt/
  in sport *n* K103
  temperature *n* L64
  temperature *v* L65
heater /'hiːtəʳ/
  n H120, M101
  (picture)
heath /hiːθ/
  n A139
heathen /'hiːðən/
  n, adj C339
heather /'heðəʳ/
  n A139
heave /hiːv/
  v, n M56
heaven /'hevən/
  n C325

heavenly /'hevənli/
  adj C325, 338
heavenly body /,···'··/
  n L2
heavens /'hevənz/
  n L44, C325
heavy /'hevi/
  adj N259
heavy goods vehicle
  /,···'···/
  n M91
heavy industry
  /,··'···/
heavy petting
  /,hevi'petɪŋ/
  n C23
heavyweight /'heviweɪt/
  adj, n N259
Hebrew /'hiːbruː/
  adj C328
hectare /'hektɑːʳ, -teəʳ||
  -teər/
  n J67 (table)
hecto- /'hektəʊ/
  comb form J67
hedge /hedʒ/
  n E142
hedgehog /'hedʒhɒg||
  -hɑg/
  n A61
heel /hiːl/
  n of foot B10, 44
  (pictures)
  of shoe D157
hefty /'hefti/
  adj B105
he-goat /'··/
  n A56
heifer /'hefəʳ/
  n A52
height /haɪt/
  n J64
heighten /'haɪtn/
  v N309
heir /eəʳ/
  n C214
heiress /eərɪ̯s/
  n C214
heirloom /'eəluːm|| 'eər-/
  n C213
helicopter /'helɪ̯kɒptəʳ||
  -kɑp-/
  n M183 (picture)
helium /'hiːlɪəm/
  n H74
hell /hel/
  n C325
hellish /'helɪʃ/
  adj C325
hello /hə'ləʊ, he-/
  interj G291
helm /helm/
  n M157
helmet /'helmɪ̯t/
  n D146
helmeted /'helmɪ̯tɪ̯d/
  adj D146
help /help/
  v, n N139
helpful /'helpfəl/
  adj F170, N229
helping /'helpɪŋ/
  n E16

informal /ɪnˈfɔːməl‖ -ɔr-/
adj C172

information
/ˌɪnfəˈmeɪʃən‖ -ər-/
n G194

infuriate /ɪnˈfjʊəriˌeɪt/
v F102

infuriated /ɪnˈfjʊəriˌeɪtɪd/
adj F104

infuriating /ɪnˈfjʊəriˌeɪtɪŋ/
adj F105

ingenious /ɪnˈdʒiːnɪəs/
adj G37

ingenuity /ˌɪndʒɪ̥ˈnjuːˌtɪ‖
-ˈnuː-/
n G39

ingot /ˈɪŋɡət/
n H38

ingredient /ɪnˈgriːdɪənt/
n in cooking E113
in general H4

inhabit /ɪnˈhæbɪ̥t/
v D60

inhabitable
/ɪnˈhæbɪtəbəl/
adj D60

inhabitant /ɪnˈhæbɪ̥tənt/
n D63

inhalation /ˌɪnhəˈleɪʃən/
n B37

inhale /ɪnˈheɪl/
v B37

inherent /ɪnˈherənt/
adj A7

inherit /ɪnˈherɪ̥t/
v C212

inheritance /ɪnˈherɪ̥təns/
n C213

inheritor /ɪnˈherɪ̥tə ʳ/
n C214

inimical /ɪˈnɪmɪkəl/
adj C47

initial /ɪˈnɪʃəl/ -ll- *BrE*,
-l- *AmE*
v G148

initial
n G148
adj L182

initiate /ɪˈnɪʃɪeɪt/
v C334, L171

initiation /ɪˌnɪʃɪˈeɪʃən/
n L179

inject /ɪnˈdʒekt/
v B174

injection /ɪnˈdʒekʃən/
n B174

injunction /ɪnˈdʒʌŋkʃən/
n C204

injure /ˈɪndʒə ʳ/
v B129

injury /ˈɪndʒəri/
n B129

injustice /ɪnˈdʒʌstɪ̥s/
n C187

ink /ɪŋk/
n H93
v H95

in-law /ˈ···/
n C18

in memoriam
/ɪn mɪ̥ˈmɔːrɪəm‖
-ˈmor-/
n C59

inmost /ˈɪnməʊst/
adj M204

inn /ɪn/
n M79

innards /ˈɪnədz‖ -ər-/
n B35

innate /ɪˈneɪt/
adj A7

inner /ˈɪnə ʳ/
n K205
adj M204

innermost /ˈɪnəməʊst‖
-nər-/
adj M204

innings /ˈɪnɪŋz/ **innings**
n K196

innocent /ˈɪnəsənt/
adj C209, F196

innuendo /ˌɪnjuˈendəʊ/
-*does* or -*dos*
n G89

inoculate /ɪˈnɒkjʊleɪt‖
ɪˈnɑkjə-/
v B174

inoculation /ɪˌnɒkjʊˈleɪʃən‖
ɪˈnɑkjə-/
n B174

input /ˈɪnpʊt/
n H202

inquire /ɪnˈkwaɪə ʳ/
v G92

inquiring /ɪnˈkwaɪərɪŋ/
adj F227

inquiry /ɪnˈkwaɪəri‖
ɪnˈkwaɪəri, ɪŋˈkwəri/
n G95

inquisitive /ɪnˈkwɪzɪ̥tɪv/
adj F227

inquisitiveness
/ɪnˈkwɪzɪ̥tɪvnɪ̥s/
adj F229

insane /ɪnˈseɪn/
adj G52

insanity /ɪnˈsænɪ̥ti/
n G53

inscribe /ɪnˈskraɪb/
v G141

inscription /ɪnˈskrɪpʃən/
n G147

insect /ˈɪnsekt/
n A32

insert /ɪnˈsɜːt‖ -ɜrt/
v H23

insertion /ɪnˈsɜːʃən‖ -ɜr-/
n H23

inside /ɪnˈsaɪd ʳ/
time *prep* L265
place *n, adj, prep, adv*
M204

inside out /ˌ···ˈ··/
adv M204

insides /ɪnˈsaɪdz ʳ/
n B35

insight /ˈɪnsaɪt/
n G9

insincere /ˌɪnsɪnˈsɪə ʳ/
adj F193

insinuate /ɪnˈsɪnjʊeɪt/
v G88

insinuation
/ɪŋˌsɪnjʊˈeɪʃən/
n G89

insipid /ɪnˈsɪpɪ̥d/

adj E111, F282

insist /ɪnˈsɪst/
v G77

insistence /ɪnˈsɪstəns/
n G78

insolence /ˈɪnsələns/
n F156

insolent /ˈɪnsələnt/
adj F155

insolvency /ɪnˈsɒlvənsi‖
-ˈsɑl-/
n J120

insolvent /ɪnˈsɒlvənt‖
-sɑl-/
adj J120

insomnia /ɪnˈsɒmnɪə‖
-sɑm-/
n B149

inspect /ɪnˈspekt/
v C310, N360

inspection /ɪnˈspekʃən/
n C311, N361

inspector /ɪnˈspektə ʳ/
n N360

install /ɪnˈstɔːl/
v M50

installation
/ˌɪnstəˈleɪʃən/
n M50

instalment /ɪnˈstɔːlmənt/
n G163, J150

instance
n N7
v N8

instant /ˈɪnstənt/
n L137
adj L145

instantaneous
/ˌɪnstənˈteɪnɪəs/
adj L145

instantly /ˈɪnstəntli/
adv L262

instead /ɪnˈsted/
adv, prep D88

instead of /ˈ···/
prep D88

instep /ˈɪnstep/
n of a foot B44
(picture)
of a shoe D157

instigate /ˈɪnstɪ̥geɪt/
v L171

instigation /ˌɪnstɪ̥ˈgeɪʃən/
n L179

instinct /ˈɪnstɪŋkt/
n F2

instinctive /ɪnˈstɪŋktɪv/
adj F4

institute /ˈɪnstɪ̥tjuːt‖
-tuːt/
v L171

institution
/ˌɪnstɪ̥ˈtjuːʃən‖ -ˈtuː-/
n C75, 183, L179

instruct /ɪnˈstrʌkt/
v G33, 115

instruction /ɪnˈstrʌkʃən/
n G35, 116

instructional
/ɪnˈstrʌkʃənəl/
adj I148

instructive /ɪnˈstrʌktɪv/
adj I148

instructor /ɪnˈstrʌktə ʳ/
n I134

instrument /ˈɪnstrəmənt/
n H111

instrumentalist
/ˌɪnstrəˈmentəlɪ̥st/
n K39

insular /ˈɪnsjʊlə ʳ‖
ˈɪnsələr/
adj L114

insulate /ˈɪnsjʊleɪt‖
ˈɪnsə-, ˈɪnʃə-/
v N323

insulation /ˌɪnsjʊˈleɪʃən‖
ˌɪnsə-/
n N323

insulator /ˈɪnsjʊleɪtə ʳ‖
ˈɪnsə-/
n N323

insult /ɪnˈsʌlt/
v F148

insult /ˈɪnsʌlt/
n F149

insulting /ɪnˈsʌltɪŋ/
adj F150

insurance /ɪnˈʃʊərəns/
n J159

insurance policy
/ˈ···ˌ···/
n J159

insure /ɪnˈʃʊə ʳ/
v J158

insurgency
/ɪnˈsɜːdʒənsi‖ -ˈsɜr-/
n C135

insurgent /ɪnˈsɜːdʒənt‖
-sɜr-/
n C136

insurrection
/ˌɪnsəˈrekʃən/
n C135

integer /ˈɪntɪdʒə ʳ/
n J2

integral /ˈɪntɪ̥grəl/
adj J2

integrate /ˈɪntɪ̥greɪt/
v N325

integrity /ɪnˈtegrɪ̥ti/
n F200

intellect /ˈɪntɪ̥lekt/
n G1

intellectual
/ˌɪntɪ̥ˈlektʃʊəl/
adj, n G7

intelligence
/ɪnˈtelɪ̥dʒəns/
n G39

intelligent /ɪnˈtelɪ̥dʒənt/
adj G37

intelligible
/ɪnˈtelɪ̥dʒəbəl/
adj G40

intend /ɪnˈtend/
v G16

intense /ɪnˈtens/
adj N233

intensification
/ɪnˌtensɪ̥fɪˈkeɪʃən/
n N237

intensifier
/ɪnˈtensɪ̥faɪə ʳ/
n G272

intensify /ɪnˈtensɪ̥faɪ/

lucky /'lʌki/
adj N37
ludo /'lu:dəʊ/
n K135
luggage /'lʌgɪdʒ/
n H185, M109
lugger /'lʌgə'/
n M153
lugsail /'lʌgseɪl/
n M153
lumbago /lʌm'beɪgəʊ/
n B145
lumber /'lʌmbə'/
n junk H13
wood H70
lumberjack
/'lʌmbədʒæk|| -ər-/
n H70
lumberman
/'lʌmbəmən||
-bər-/ -**men** /mən/
n H70
luminosity
/,lu:mɪ'nɒsɪti|| -'nɑ-/
n L24
luminous /'lu:mɪnəs/
adj L24
lump /lʌmp/
n H31
lump together
v H35
lunacy /'lu:nəsi/
n G53
lunar /'lu:nə'/
adj L6
lunatic /'lu:nətɪk/
adj G52
n G54
lunch /lʌntʃ/
n E14
v E15
luncheon /'lʌntʃən/
n E14
lung /lʌŋ/
n B36 (picture), B37
lurch /lɜ:tʃ|| lɜrtʃ/
v, n M20
lurid /'lʊərɪd, 'ljʊərɪd||
'lʊərɪd/
adj L37
lurk /lɜ:k|| lɜrk/
v F209
luscious /'lʌʃəs/
adj E110
lust /lʌst/
n F8
lust after/for
v F6
lustre, luster /'lʌstə'/
n L22
Lutheran /'lu:θərən/
n, adj C330
luxury /'lʌkʃəri/
n J117, 134
-ly /li/
suffix L235
lynx /lɪŋks/
n A53
lyric /'lɪrɪk/
n G170
adj G171
lyrical /'lɪrɪkəl/
adj G171

lyrics /'lɪrɪks/
n K23

M

ma /mɑ:/
n C13
MA /,em'eɪ/
n I143
machine /mə'ʃi:n/
n H112
machinery /mə'ʃi:nəri/
n H113
machine gun /·'···/
n H239
machinist /mə'ʃi:nɪst/
n I72
mackerel /'mækərəl/
n A100
mad /mæd/
adj F104, G52
madam /'mædəm/
n C5, 37
madden /'mædn/
v F102
maddening /'mædənɪŋ/
adj F105
madman /'mædmən/
-**men** /mən/
n G54
madness /'mædnɪs/
n G53
maestro /'maɪstrəʊ/ -**tros**
or -**tri** /tri:/
n K85
mag /mæg/
n G201
magazine /,mægə'zi:n||
'mægəzi:n/
n book G201
for weapons H230
of a gun H237
(picture)
magenta /mə'dʒentə/
n, adj L31
magic /'mædʒɪk/
n C354
adj C355
magical /'mædʒɪkəl/
adj C355
magician /mə'dʒɪʃən/
n C356
magistrate
/'mædʒɪstreɪt/
n C202
magnanimous
/mæg'nænɪməs/
adj F173
magnet /'mægnɪt/
n H122
magnetic /mæg'netɪk/
adj H201
magnetism
/'mægnɪtɪzəm/
n H200
magnification
/,mægnɪfɪ'keɪʃən/
n N93
magnificent
/mæg'nɪfɪsənt/

adj F53
magnify /'mægnɪfaɪ/
v N92
magpie /'mægpaɪ/
n A74
mahogany /mə'hɒgəni||
mə'hɑ-/
n H72
Mahomet /mə'hɒmɪt||
-hɑ-/
n C327
Mahummad /mə'hʌmɪd/
n C327
maid /meɪd/
n C7
maiden /'meɪdn/
n C7
maidservant
/'meɪdsɜ:vənt|| -ɜr-/
n C161
mail /meɪl/
n G191
v G192
mailbag /'meɪlbæg/
n G193
mailbox /'meɪlbɒks||
-bɑks/
n G193
mailman /'meɪlmən,
-mæn/ -**men** /mən/
n G193
maim /maɪm/
v B129
main /meɪn/
adj N89
main course /,·'·/
n E17
main office /,·'···/
n J227
main road /,·'·/
n M127
mains /meɪnz/
n D42
mainspring /'meɪnsprɪŋ/
n L228 (picture)
main street /,·'·/
n M128
maintain /meɪn'teɪn,
mən-/
v C185, D94, J125,
N167
maintenance
/'meɪntənəns/
n C185, D95, J123,
M105, N170
maize /meɪz/
n A152
majestic /mə'dʒestɪk/
adj C171
majesty /'mædʒɪsti/
adj C98
major /'meɪdʒə'/
person *n* C297 (table)
in music *n* K30
big *adj* N89
majority /mə'dʒɒrɪti||
mə'dʒɔ-/
n C117, N96
major key /,··'·/
n K30
make /meɪk/ **made**
/meɪd/
v in sex C24

general E101, I1,
N150
calculate J36
earn J218
make
n I2
make away with
v A10
make-believe /'meɪk
bɪ,li:v/
n K173
make believe
v K173
make do
v N128
make friends with
v C44
make game of
(someone)
v K6
make love
v C24
makeup /'meɪkʌp/
n D185
make up
v the face D185
form H22
make use of
v J26
male /meɪl/
adj, n A14
male nurse /,·'·'/
n B166
male prostitute /,·'···/
n C36
malice /'mælɪs/
n F178
malicious /mə'lɪʃəs/
adj F177
mallet /'mælɪt/
n H144 (picture), K190
malnutrition
/,mælnjʊ'trɪʃən|| -nʊ-/
n E5
malt /mɔ:lt/
n E65
mam /mæm/
n C13 (table)
mama /mɑ:mɑ:/
n C13 (table)
mamba /'mæmbə||
'mɑmbə, 'mæmbə/
n A90
mammal /'mæməl/
n A32
mammalian
/mæ'meɪlɪən/
adj A32
mammoth /'mæməθ/
n A59
adj N83
mammy /'mæmi/
n C13 (table)
man /mæn/ **men** /mən/
n general A50, C2, 161
in board games K137
man, -nn-
v M162
manage /'mænɪdʒ/
v N128, 163
control N167
management
/'mænɪdʒmənt/

n D186

massive /ˈmæsɪv/
adj N83

mass media /ˌ·ˈ···/
n G208

mass noun /ˌ·ˈ·/
n G270

mast /mɑːst‖ mæst/
n H42, M157 (picture)

master /ˈmɑːstəʳ‖ ˈmæ-/
n C6, 160, I51, 117,
134, 147, M164
v C280, N168

masterful /ˈmɑːstəfəl‖
ˈmæstər-/
adj N169

masterly /ˈmɑːstəli‖
ˈmæstərli/
adj N169, I147

master of ceremonies
/ˌ···ˈ····/
n K85

master's degree /ˈ···ˌ·/
n I142

mastery /ˈmɑːstəri‖
ˈmæ-/
n N170

masticate /ˈmæstɪkeɪt/
v E6

mastication
/ˈmæstɪkeɪʃən/
n E6

mastiff /ˈmæstɪf/
n A54

masturbate /ˈmæstəbeɪt‖
-ər-/
v C26

masturbation
/ˌmæstəˈbeɪʃən‖ -ər-/
n C26

mat /mæt/
n D118, K140

match /mætʃ/
for fire *n* H120
game *n* K102
equal *v* N226

matchbox /ˈmætʃbɒks‖
-bɑks/
n H120

mate /meɪt/
v A15
n C40, 42, M164

material /məˈtɪəriəl/
information *n* G160
substance *n* H1
substantial *adj* H8
cloth *n* H85

maternal /məˈtɜːnəl‖
-ɜr-/
adj C12

maternity /məˈtɜːnɪti‖
-ɜr-/
adj C12

matey /ˈmeɪti/
adj C46

mathematical
/ˌmæθɪˈmætɪkəl/
adj J30

mathematician
/ˌmæθɪməˈtɪʃən/
n J30

mathematics
/ˌmæθɪˈmætɪks/

n J30

maths *BrE*, **math** *AmE*
/mæθ(s)/
n J30

mating /ˈmeɪtɪŋ/
n A16

matrimonial
/ˌmætrɪˈməʊniəl/
adj C29

matrimony /ˈmætrɪməni‖
-məʊni/
n C29

matron /ˈmeɪtrən/
n B166, C32

matron of honour
/ˌ···ˈ··/
n C33

matter /ˈmætəʳ/
subject *n* G243
substance *n* H1
be important *v* N42

matter-of-fact /ˌmætər
əvˈfækt/
adj N230

mattress /ˈmætrɪs/
n D115

mature /məˈtʃʊəʳ/
adj L207
v L211

maul /mɔːl/
v B129

mausoleum
/ˌmɔːsəˈliəm/
n C57

maxim /ˈmæksɪm/
n G236

maximal /ˈmæksɪməl/
adj N91

maximize /ˈmæksɪmaɪz/
v N92

maximum /ˈmæksɪməm/
maxima /ˈmæksɪmə/ *or*
-mums
adj N91

May /meɪ/
n L234

May, *neg contr* **mayn't**
modal N31

maybe /ˈmeɪbi/
adv N31

mayonnaise /ˌmeɪəˈneɪz‖
ˈmeɪəneɪz/
n E50

mayor /meəʳ‖ ˈmeɪəʳ/
n C101

mayoress /ˈmeərɪs‖
ˈmeɪərɪs/
n C101

M.B. /ˌemˈbiː/
n I143

M.C., MC /ˌemˈsiː/
n K85

M.D. /ˌemˈdiː/
n I143

me /mi; *strong* miː/
pron G280 (table)

mead /miːd/
n E67

meal /miːl/
n food E13
flour E43

mean /miːn/ **meant**
/ment/

v intend G16
signify G199

mean
nasty *adj* F177
ungenerous *adj* F180
average *n* J39

meander /miˈændəʳ/
v M41

meaning /ˈmiːnɪŋ/
n G200, 237

means /miːnz/ **means**
n I42

meantime /ˈmiːntaɪm/
adv L255

meanwhile /ˈmiːnwaɪl‖
adv L255

measles /ˈmiːzəlz/
n B143

measure /ˈmeʒəʳ/
v J60
n J61

measurement
/ˈmeʒəmənt‖ -ər-/
n J61

meat /miːt/
n B4, E31

mechanic /mɪˈkænɪk/
n I72

mechanical /mɪˈkænɪkəl/
adj I73

mechanics /mɪˈkænɪks/
n I75

mechanism
/ˈmekənɪzəm/
n H113

MEd /ˌemˈed/
n I143

medal /ˈmedl/
n K110

medallist *BrE*, **medalist**
AmE /ˈmedəlɪst/
n K110

media /ˈmiːdiə/
n G208

median /ˈmiːdiən/
n J39

mediaeval, medieval
/ˌmediˈiːvəl‖ ˌmiː-/
adj L200

medical /ˈmedɪkəl/
adj B170, I71
n B178

medical practitioner
/ˌ···ˈ···/
n B166

medicated /ˈmedɪkeɪtɪd/
adj B170

medication
/ˌmedɪˈkeɪʃən/
n B171

medicinal /mɪˈdɪsənəl/
adj B170

medicine /ˈmedsən‖
ˈmedɪsən/
n B168, 171

medicine cabinet/chest
/ˈ···ˌ···/
n D40

medicine man /ˈ···ˌ·/
n C356

mediocre /ˌmiːdiˈəʊkəʳ/
adj F54

meditate /ˈmedɪteɪt/

v C333, G4

meditation
/ˌmedɪˈteɪʃən/
n C333, G5

medium /ˈmiːdiəm/ **-dia**
/diə/ *or* **-diums**
method *n* G208, I42
average *n, adj* J39, N88

medium, mediums
n person C343

medium wave /ˈ···ˌ·/
n G210

meet /miːt/ **met** /met/
v M7, 72

meeting /ˈmiːtɪŋ/
n M73

meet up
v M7

meet up with
v C44, M72

meet with
v M72

mega- /ˈmegə/
comb form J67

melodic /mɪˈlɒdɪk‖
mɪˈlɑ-/
adj K22

melodious /mɪˈləʊdiəs/
adj K22

melodrama
/ˈmelədrɑːmə/
n K71

melodramatic
/ˌmelədrəˈmætɪk/
adj K77

melody /ˈmelədi/
n K22

melt /melt/
v L65

member /ˈmembəʳ/
n J229

Member (of Parliament)
/ˌ···ˈ···/
n C119

membership
/ˈmembəʃɪp‖ -ər-/
n C75

membrane /ˈmembreɪn/
n B4

memoirs /ˈmemwɑːz‖
-ɑrz/
n G167

memorial /mɪˈmɔːriəl‖
mɪˈmor-/
n C59

memorize /ˈmeməraɪz/
v G32

memory /ˈmeməri/
n G21

men /men/
soldiers *n* C300

mend /mend/
v I19
n I21

menial /ˈmiːniəl/
n C161
adj I104

menopause /ˈmenəpɔːz/
n A16

menstrual /ˈmenstruəl/
adj A16

menstruate /ˈmenstrueɪt/
v A16

menstruation
/ˌmenstrʊ'eɪʃən/
n A16
mensuration
/ˌmenʃə'reɪʃən||
-sə'reɪ-/
n J61
mental /'mentl/
adj G7
mentality /men'tælɨti/
n G1
mention /'menʃən/
v G90
n G91
menu /'menjuː/
n E16
meow /mi'aʊ/
v A43
mercantile marine
/ˌmɜːkəntaɪl mə'riːn||
mɜrkəntiːl, -taɪl-/
n M156
mercenary /'mɜːsənəri||
'mɜrsəneri/
n C301
adj F180
merchandise
/'mɜːtʃəndaɪz, -daɪs||
'mɜr-/
n J157
merchant /'mɜːtʃənt||
/mɜr-/
n J139
merchantman
/'mɜːtʃəntmən|| 'mɜr-/
-men /mən/
n M156
merchant marine
/ˌ···'·ˑ/
n M156
merchant navy /ˌ··'··-ˑ/
n M156
merchant ship /'····/
n M156
merciful /'mɜːsɪfəl||
'mɜr-/
adj F174
merciless /'mɜːsɪləs||
'mɜr-/
adj F179
mercury /'mɜːkjʊri||
'mɜrkjəri/
n H68
Mercury /'mɜːkjʊri||
'mɜrkjəri/
n L4 (picture)
mercy /'mɜːsi|| 'mɜrsi/
n F175, N35
mere /mɪəʳ/
n L86
adj N46
merge /mɜːdʒ|| mɜrdʒ/
v I23
merger /'mɜːdʒəʳ||
'mɜr-/
n I23
meridian /mə'rɪdɪən/
n L12
merit /'merɨt/
v D83
n K12
meritorious
/ˌmerɨ'tɔːrɪəs|| -'tor-/

merry /'meri/
adj F71
merry-go-round
/ˈ··· , ·/
n K171
mesa /'meɪsə/
n L103
mesmerism
/'mezmərɪzəm/
n B86
mesmerize /'mezməraɪz/
v B86
mess /mes/
v D181
n D182
mess about
v F101
message /'mesɪdʒ/
n G195
messenger
/'mesəndʒəʳ/
n G198
messiah /mɨ'saɪəʳ/
n C343
messianic /ˌmesi'ænɨk/
adj C343
metacarpals
/ˌmetə'kɑːpəlz|| -ɑr-/
n B11 (picture)
metal /'metl/
n H67
metallic /mɨ'tælɨk/
adj H67
metalwork /'metlwɜːk||
-ɜrk/
n I116
metalworker
/'metlwɜːkəʳ|| -ɜrk-/
n I116
metamorphic
/ˌmetə'mɔːfɪk|| -'mor-/
adj H61
metaphor /'metəfəʳ/
n G244
metaphoric(al)
/ˌmetə'fɑrɪk(əl)|| -'fɔ-,
-'fɑ-/
adj G246
metatarsal bones
/ˌmetə'tɑːsəl bəʊnz||
-ɑr-/
n B11 (picture)
meteor /'miːtɪəʳ/
n L5
meteoroid /'miːtɪərɔɪd/
n L5
meteorite /'miːtɪəraɪt/
n L5
meteorological
/ˌmiːtɪərə'lɒdʒɪkəl||
-'lɑ-/
adj I75
meteorologist
/ˌmiːtɪə'rɒlədʒɨst||
-'rɑ-/
n I75
meteorology
/ˌmiːtɪə'rɒlədʒi|| -'rɑ-/
n I75
meter /'miːtəʳ/
n H115
methane /'miːθeɪn|| 'me-/

n H74
method /'meθəd/
n I42
methodical /mɨ'θɒdɪkəl||
mɨ'θɑ-/
adj I42
Methodism
/'meθədɪzəm/
n C330
Methodist /'meθədɨst/
n, *adj* C330
metonymic
/ˌmetə'nɪmɨk/
adj G246
metonymy /mɨ'tɒnɨmi||
-tɑn-/
n G244
metre *BrE*, **meter** *AmE*
/'miːtəʳ/
n J67
metric /'metrɨk/
adj J62
metronome
/'metrənəʊm/
n L227
metropolis /mɨ'trɒpəlɨs||
mɨ'trɑ-/
n C82
metropolitan
/ˌmetrə'pɒlɨtn||-'pɑ-/
adj C85
mew /mjuː/
v A43
miaow /mi'aʊ/
v A43
mice /maɪs/
n A60
microbe /'maɪkrəʊb/
n A37
microphone
/'maɪkrəfəʊn/
n K55
microscope
/'maɪkrəskəʊp/
n H123
microscopic
/ˌmaɪkrə'skɒpɨk||
-'skɑ-/
adj H123, N86
mid- /mɪd/
comb form L236
midday /ˌmɪd'deɪˈ||
'mɪd,deɪ/
n L222
middle /'mɪdl/
n M201
middle age /ˌ··'·ˑ/
n L210
middle-aged /ˌ··'·ˑ/
adj L207
middle class /'··'·ˑ/
n C152
middle finger /ˌ··'··-ˑ/
n B42 (picture)
middle-of-the-road
/ˌmɪdl əv ðə 'rəʊd-/
n C112
middling /'mɪdəlɪŋ/
adj F54, N88
midnight /'mɪdnaɪt/
n L224
mid-off /ˌ·'·/
n K196 (picture)

mid-on /ˌ·'·/
n K196 (picture)
midriff /'mɪdrɨf/
n B34
midshipman
/'mɪdʃɪpmən/ -**men**
/mən/
n C300
mid-wicket /ˌ·'···/
n K196 (picture)
midwife /'mɪdwaɪf/
-**wives** /waɪvz/
n B166
midwifery /'mɪd,wɪfəri||
-,waɪfəri/
n B168
might /maɪt/
neg contr **mightn't**
v N31
might
n N235
mighty /'maɪti/
adj N233
migraine /'miːgreɪn,
'maɪ-|| 'maɪ-/
n B151
migrant /'maɪgrənt/
n M76
migrate /maɪ'greɪt||
'maɪgreɪt/
v M74
migration /maɪ'greɪʃən/
n M75
mike /maɪk/
n K55
mild /maɪld/
n E66
adj L68, N267
mildew /'mɪldjuː|| -duː/
n A140
mile /maɪl/
n J66, 68
mileage /'maɪlɪdʒ/
n J68
militancy /'mɪlɨtənsi/
n C273
militant /'mɪlɨtənt/
adj C273
n C301
military /'mɪlɨtəri||
-teri/
adj C291
military policeman
/'····'··ˑ/
n C306
milk /mɪlk/
n E41
v E42
Milky Way /ˌ··'·ˑ/
n L3
mill /mɪl/
n I108, 109
mill about/around
v M27
millenial /mɨ'lenɪəl/
adj L242
millenium /mɨ'lenɪəm/
-**nia** /nɪə/
n L226
miller /'mɪləʳ/
n I109
millet /'mɪlɨt/
n A152

n C13 (table)
monarch /'mɒnək||
'mɑnərk, -ɑrk/
n C96
monarchic(al)
/məˈnɑːkɪk(əl)||
məˈnɑr-/
adj C93
monarchist /'mɒnəkɪ̯st||
'mɑnər-/
n C94
monarchy /'mɒnəki||
'mɑnərki/
adj C90
monastic /məˈnæstɪk/
adj C351
monasticism
/məˈnæstɪ̯sɪzəm/
n C351
monastery /'mɒnəstri||
'mɑnəsteri/
n C351
Monday /'mʌndi/
n L232
money /'mʌni/
n J80
moneylender
/'mʌni,lendə'/
n J103
money order /'···,··/
n J82
mongrel /'mʌŋgrəl||
'mɑŋ-, 'mʌŋ-/
n A35, 54
monk /mʌŋk/
n C345
monkey /'mʌŋki/
n A50
monkey nuts /'··,·/
n A153
monkey wrench /'··,·/
n H149 (picture)
monkish /'mʌŋkɪʃ/
adj C345
mono /'mɒnəʊ|| 'mɑ-/
adj K54
monogamous
/məˈnɒgəməs|| məˈnɑ-/
adj C30
monogamy /məˈnɒgəmi||
məˈnɑ-/
n C30
monoglot /'mɒnəglɒt,
-nəʊ-|| 'mɑnəglɑt/
adj G239
monologue *BrE*,
monolog *AmE*
/'mɒnəlɒg|| 'mɑnəlɔg,
-lɑg/
n G66
monophonic
/,mɒnəˈfɒnɪk||
,mɑnəˈfɑ-/
adj K54
monophthong
/'mɒnəfθɒŋ||
'mɑnəfθɔŋ/
n G273
monopolize
/məˈnɒpəlaɪz|| məˈnɑ-/
v J138
monopoly /məˈnɒpəli||
məˈnɑ-/

n business J138
game K135
monosyllabic
/,mɒnəsɪˈlæbɪk|| ,mɑ-/
adj G273
monotonous
/məˈnɒtənəs|| məˈnɑ-/
adj F231
monsoon /mɒnˈsuːn||
mɑn-/
n L49
monster /'mɒnstə'||
'mɑn-/
n N71
monstrosity
/mɒnˈstrɒsɪ̯ti||
mɑnˈstrɑ-/
n N71
monstrous /'mɒnstrəs||
'mɑn-/
adj N69
month /mʌnθ/
n L226
monthly /'mʌnθli/
n G202
monument
/'mɒnjʊmənt|| 'mɑnjə-/
n C59
mood /muːd/
n general F2
in grammar G261
moody /'muːdi/
adj F4
moon /muːn/
n L2, L4 (picture)
moor /mʊə'/
n L108
v M165
moorings /'mʊərɪŋz/
n M165
moorland /'mʊələnd||
'mʊər-/
n L112
moose /muːs/ **moose**
n A57
mop /mɒp|| mɑp/
n H156 (picture)
v H157
moped /'məʊped/
n M96
moral /'mɒrəl|| 'mɔ-/
adj F65
morale /məˈrɑːl|| məˈræl/
n F2
morality /məˈrælɪ̯ti/
n F63
morals /'mɒrəlz|| 'mɔ-/
n F63
morass /məˈræs/
n L109
morbid /'mɔːbɪ̯d|| 'mɔr-/
adj B111, G52
morbidity /mɔːˈbɪdɪ̯ti||
mɔr-/
n G52
more /mɔː'|| mor/
det etc N96
more or less /,··'·'/
adv L266
moreover /mɔːˈrəʊvə'||
mo-/
adv N100
morgue /mɔːg|| mɔrg/

n C58
morning /'mɔːnɪŋ||
'mɔr-/
n L222
moron /'mɔːrɒn||
'mɔrɑn/
n G48
moronic /məˈrɒnɪk||
məˈrɑ-/
adj G48
morphia /'mɔːfɪə||
'mɔr-/
n E87
morphine /'mɔːfiːn||
'mɔr-/
n E87
mortal /'mɔːtl|| 'mɔrtl/
adj A11, C52
mortality /mɔːˈtælɪ̯ti||
mɔr-/
n A4
mortar /'mɔːtə'|| 'mɔr-/
n substance H66
weapon H239
mortgage /'mɔːgɪdʒ||
'mɔr-/
n, v C215
mortician /mɔːˈtɪʃən||
mɔr-/
n C55
mortuary /'mɔːtʃʊəri||
'mɔrtʃʊeri/
n C58
Moslem /'mɒzlɪ̯m||
'mɑz-/
adj C328
n C329
mosque /mɒsk|| mɑsk/
n C351
mosquito /məˈskiːtəʊ/
-toes
n A110
moss /mɒs|| mɔs/
n A140
most /məʊst/
det etc N96
motel /məʊˈtel/
n M79
moth /mɒθ|| mɔθ/
n A110
mother /'mʌðə'/
general *n* C12
general *v* C14
in religion *n* C346
motherhood /'mʌðəhʊd|
-ər-/
adj C12
motherly /'mʌðəli| -ər-/
adj C12
(mother of) pearl
/,···'·'/
n H65
motif /məʊˈtiːf/
n I6
motion /'məʊʃən/
n M10
motionless /'məʊʃənləs/
adj M15
motivate /'məʊtɪ̯veɪt/
v G18
motivation
/,məʊtɪ̯ˈveɪʃən/
n G18

motive /'məʊtɪv/
n G18
adj M14
motor /'məʊtə'/
engine *n* H113
drive *v* M29
car *n* M93
motorbike /'məʊtəbaɪk||
-tər-/
n M96
motorboat /'məʊtəbəʊt||
-tər-/
n M152
motorcar /'məʊtəkɑː'||
-tər-/
n M93
motor caravan
/'məʊtəkærəvæn/
n M99
motorcycle
/'məʊtə,saɪkəl|| -tər-/
n M96
motorcyclist
/'məʊtə,saɪklɪ̯st|| -tər-/
n M97
motor home /'···/
n M99
motorist /'məʊtərɪ̯st/
n M97
motor road /'···/
n M127
motorway /'məʊtəweɪ||
-tər-/
n M129
motto /'mɒtəʊ|| 'mɑ-/
-tos *BrE*, **-tos** or **-toes**
AmE
n G236
mould /məʊld/
growth *n* A140
shape *v* I5
shaping *n* I6
mouldy /'məʊldi/
adj E108
moult /məʊlt/
v H15
mound /maʊnd/
n H34
mount /maʊnt/
n L101
v M9
mountain /'maʊntɪ̯n/
n L101
mountaineer
/,maʊntɪ̯ˈnɪə'/
n, v K207
mountaineering
/,maʊntɪ̯ˈnɪərɪŋ/
n K207
mountainous
/'maʊntɪ̯nəs/
adj L105
mourn /mɔːn|| morn/
v C50, F84
mourner /'mɔːnə'||
'mor-/
n C55
mournful /'mɔːnfəl||
'morn-/
adj F86
mourning /'mɔːnɪŋ||
'mor-/
n C55

orchestral /ɔː'kestrəl||
ɔr-/
adj K37
orchestra pit /' ··· , · /
n K91
orchid /'ɔːkɪ̰d|| 'ɔr-/
n A158
ordain /ɔː'deɪn|| ɔr-/
v C334
order /'ɔːdəʳ|| ɔr-/
n C182, 188, G116,
J82, 156, N194
v C183, G115, J154
orderly /'ɔːdəli|| 'ɔrdərli/
n B166, C306
adj D179
orderly officer
/' ··· , ··· /
n C300
ordinal number /, ··· ' ··· /
n J1
ordinance /'ɔːdɪ̰nəns||
ɔrdənəns/
n C180
ordinary /ɔ:dənri||
'ɔrdəneri/
adj N58
ordination /,ɔ:dɪ̰'neɪʃən||
,ɔr-/
n C334
ordnance /'ɔ:dnəns||
'ɔr-/
n C305
Ordnance Survey
/, ··· ' ··.ˉ/
n L81
ore /ɔ: ˈ|| ɔr/
n H67
organ /'ɔ:gən|| 'ɔr-/
n of the body B4
in music K48
(picture)
organic /ɔ:'gænɪk|| ɔr-/
adj B2
organism /'ɔ:gənɪzəm||
'ɔr-/
n A30
organist /'ɔ:gənɪst|| 'ɔr-/
n K48
organization
/,ɔ:gənaɪ'zeɪʃən||
,ɔrgənə-/
n N170
organize /'ɔ:gənaɪz||
'ɔr-/
v N167, 194
orgasm /'ɔ:gæzəm/
n C23
orient /'ɔ:rɪənt, 'ɒr-|| 'o-/
n L13
v L15
oriental /,ɔ:ri-entl, ,ɒ-||
,o-/
adj, n L13
orientate /'ɔ:rɪənteɪt,
'ɒ-|| 'o-/
n L15
orientation
/,ɔ:rɪən'teɪʃən, ,ɒ-||,o-/
n L15
origin /'ɒrɪ̰dʒɪ̰n|| 'ɔ-, 'ɑ-/
n L179
original /ə'rɪdʒɪ̰nəl,

-dʒənəl/
adj L182, 203
n L212
original sin /·, ··· ' · /
n C341
ornament /'ɔ:nəmənt||
'ɔr-/
n D111
ornament /'ɔ:nəment||
'ɔr-/
v D111
ornamental
/,ɔ:nə'mentəl|| ,ɔr-/
adj N125
ornamentation
/,ɔ:nəmən'teɪʃən|| ,ɔr-/
n D111
orphan /'ɔ:fən|| 'ɔr-/
n C3
orphanage /'ɔ:fənɪdʒ||
'ɔr-/
n C3
orphaned /'ɔ:fənd|| 'ɔr-/
v C52
orthodox /'ɔ:θədɒks||
'ɔrθədɑks/
adj general C166
in religion C330
Orthodox Church
/, ··· ' · /
n C330
orthodoxy /'ɔ:θədɒksi||
'ɔrθədɑksi/
n C166
ostracism /'ɒstrəsɪzəm||
'ɑs-/
n C196
ostracize /'ɒstrəsaɪz||
'ɑ-/
v C195
ostrich /'ɒstrɪtʃ|| 'ɔ-, 'ɑ-/
n A76 (picture)
other /'ʌðəʳ/
pron, det N185
each other N101
otherwise /'ʌðəwaɪz||
'ʌðər-/
conj, adv N101
ouch /aʊtʃ/
interj G293
ought /ɔ:t/ *pres t neg*
contr **oughtn't** /'ɔ:tənt/
modal N32, 159
ounce /aʊns/
n J66 (table)
our(s) /aʊəz|| aʊərz/
pron G281 (table)
ourselves /aʊə'selvz||
aʊər-/
pron G282 (table)
oust /aʊst/
v N154
out /aʊt/
prep M205
adv M205, N107
outbreak /'aʊtbreɪk/
n B137, L172
outbuilding /'aʊt,bɪldɪŋ/
n D54, E140
outdated /,aʊt'deɪtɪ̰dˉ/
adj L201
outdoor /,aʊt'dɔ:ˈ||
-'dɔr/

adj D24, K116, M205
outer /'aʊtəʳ/
n K205
adj M205
outermost /'aʊtəməʊst||
-ər-/
adj M205
outfit /'aʊt,fɪt/
n, v D131
outhouse /'aʊthaʊs/
-houses /,haʊzɪ̰z/
n D54, E140 (picture)
outlaw /'aʊtlɔ:/
v C195
n C228
outlay /'aʊtleɪ/
n J122
outline /'aʊtlaɪn/
v I43
n I45
out-of-date
/,aʊt əv 'deɪtˉ/
adj L201
out-of-doors
/,aʊt əv 'dɔ:zˉ|| 'dɔrz/
adj M205, D4
outpatient /'aʊt,peɪʃənt/
n B167
outpatients
(department)
/' ···· , · /
n B179
output /'aʊtpʊt/
n of electricity H202
in production I2
outright /aʊt'raɪt/
adj, adv N251
outside /aʊt'saɪd,
'aʊtsaɪd/
prep M205
outstanding
/aʊt'stændɪŋ/
adj owed J101
excellent G24
out-tray /'aʊt,treɪ/
n J235
outvote /,aʊt'vəʊt/
v C115
outward bound
/'aʊtwəd baʊnd|| -ərd-/
adj M74
outward(s) /'aʊtwəd(z)||
-ərd(z)/
adj, adv M205
ova /'əʊvə/
pl of **ovum** *n* A19
ovary /'əʊvəri/
n A131
oven /'ʌvən/
n H120
over /'əʊvəʳ/
n K196
adv, prep M207, 219
overall /,əʊvər'ɔ:lˉ/
adj N50
overalls /'əʊvərɔ:lz/
n D160
overboard /'əʊvəbɔ:d||
'əʊvərbord/
adv M158
overcast /,əʊvə'kɑ:stˉ||
,əʊvər'kæstˉ/
adj L72

overcoat /'əʊvəkəʊt||
-vər-/
n D143
overcome /,əʊvə'kʌm||
-vər-/ **-came** /ˈkeɪm/,
-come /ˈkʌm/
v C280
overdo /,əʊvə'du:|| -vər-/
-did /dɪd/, **-done** /ˈdʌn/
v B90
overdraft /'əʊvədrɑ:ft||
'əʊvərdræft/
n J102
overdraw /,əʊvə'drɔ:||
-vər-/ **-drew** /ˈdru:/,
-drawn /ˈdrɔ:n/
v J108
overdue /,əʊvə'dju:ˉ||
,əʊvər'du:ˉ/
adj owed J101
general L140
overestimate
/,əʊvər'estɪ̰meɪt/
v J143
overhaul /,əʊvə'hɔ:l||
-vər-/
repair *v* I20
repairing *n* I21
pass *v* M32
overhead /,əʊvə'hedˉ||
-vər-/
adv, adj M219
overhead wire /, ··· ' · /
n M106
overjoyed /,əʊvə'dʒɔɪdˉ||
-vər-/
adj F72
overland /,əʊvə'lændˉ||
-vər-/
adv, adj M219
overload /,əʊvə'ləʊd||
-vər-/ **-loaded** *or* **-laden**
/ˈleɪdən/
v H209
overload /'əʊvələʊd||
-vər-/
n H210
overlook /,əʊvə'lʊk||
-vər-/
v G20
overpass /'əʊvəpɑ:s||
'əʊvərpæs/
n M136
overrate /,əʊvə'reɪt/
v J143
overrun /,əʊvə'rʌn/ **-ran**
/ˈraen/, **-run** /ˈrʌn/
v C275
overseas /,əʊvə'si:zˉ||
-vər-/
adv, adj M124
overseer /'əʊvəsɪəʳ||
-vər-/
n I117
oversight /'əʊvəsaɪt||
-vər-/
n N219
overstate /,əʊvə'steɪt||
-vər-/
v G79
overstatement
/,əʊvə'steɪtmənt|| -vər-/
n G80

n A20
program /'prəʊgræm/
-mm- *or* -m-
v J34
program
n G212
programme /'prəʊgræm/
-mm-
v J34
programme
v G212
progress /'prə'gres/
v M39
progress /'prəʊgres||
'prɑ-/
n M39
progression /prə'greʃən/
n M39
progressive /prə'gresɪv/
in acting *v* K79
in grammar *adj, n*
  G265
general *adj* M39
prohibit /prə'hɪb̜ɪt||
prəʊ-/
v C195
prohibition
/ˌprəʊhɪ'bɪʃən/
n C196
prohibitive /prə'hɪb̜ɪtɪv||
prəʊ-/
adj J197
project /'prɒdʒekt||
'prɑ-/
n G17, I140
project /prə'dʒekt/
v in films K59
general M52
projected /prə'dektɪ̜d/
adj K59
projectile /prə'dʒektaɪl/
n H251
projection /prə'dʒekʃən/
n in photography K59
general M52
projectionist
/prə'dʒekʃən̜ɪst/
n K59
projector /prə'dʒektər/
n K59
proletarian
/ˌprəʊlɪ̜'teərɪən/
n, adj C153
proletariat
/ˌprəʊlɪ̜'teərɪət/
n C153
prologue *BrE*, **prolog**
AmE /'prəʊlɒg|| -lɔg,
-lɑg/
n G163
prolong /prə'lɒŋ|| -'lɔŋ/
v N92
prolongation
/ˌprəʊlɒŋ'geɪʃən|| -lɔŋ-/
n N92
prolonged /prə'lɒŋd||
-'lɔŋd/
n L139
prominence
/'prɒmɪ̜nəns|| 'prɑ-/
n F268
prominent /'prɒmɪ̜nənt||
'prɑ-/
adj F268

promise /'prɒmɪ̜s|| 'prɑ-/
n G110
v G111
promising /'prɒmɪ̜sɪŋ||
'prɑ-/
adj F142, G111
promontory
/'prɒməntəri||
'prɑməntori/
n L85
promote /prə'məʊt/
v advance J215
support N160
promotion /prə'məʊʃən/
n N160
v J215
prompt /prɒmpt||
prɑmpt/
in acting *v* K79
in grammar *n* K81
in time *adj* L140
cause *v* N151
prone /prəʊn/
adj flat N304
likely N312
prong /prɒŋ|| prɔŋ/
n H154
pronoun /'prəʊnaʊn/
n G272, 280, 281
pronounce /prə'naʊns/
v G61, 72, 231
pronouncement
/prə'naʊnsmənt/
n G73
pronunciation
/prə'nʌnsi'eɪʃən/
n G232
proof /pruːf/
n N221
prop /prɒp|| prɑp/
n H40
propel /prə'pel/ -ll-
v M52
propeller /prə'pelər/
n M157 (picture)
propensity /prə'pensɪ̜ti/
n N313
proper /'prɒpər|| 'prɑ-/
adj N210
proper noun /ˌ·· '·/
n G270
propertied /'prɒpətid||
'prɑpər-/
adj D82
property /'prɒpəti||
'prɑpərti/
n D82
prophecy /'prɒfɪ̜si||
'prɑ-/
n L159, 160
prophesy /'prɒfɪ̜saɪ||
'prɑ-/
v L158
prophet /'prɒfɪ̜t|| 'prɑ-/
n C343, L160
proportion /prə'pɔːʃən||
-'pɔr-/
n J40
proportional
/prə'pɔːʃənəl|| -'pɔr-/
adj J40
proportionate
/prə'pɔːʃən̜ɪt|| -'pɔr-/

adj J40
proposal /prə'pəʊzəl/
n in marrying C27
general G89
propose /prə'pəʊz/
v in marrying C27
general G88, E71
proposition
/ˌprɒpə'zɪʃən|| ˌprɑ-/
n G89
proprietor /prə'praɪətər/
n D82
propulsion /prə'pʌlʃən/
n M52
prose /prəʊz/
n G166
prosecute /'prɒsɪkjuːt||
'prɑ-/
v C206
prosecution
/ˌprɒsɪ'kjuːʃən|| ˌprɑ-/
n C207
proselyte /'prɒsɪ̜laɪt||
'prɑ-/
n C331
proselytism
/'prɒsɪ̜lətɪzəm/
n C331
proselytize /'prɒsələtaɪz||
'prɑ-/
v C340
prospect /'prɒspekt||
'prɑ-/
n N36
prospect /prə'spekt||
'prɑspekt/
v I114
prospector /prə'spektər||
'prɑspektər/
n I114
prospective /prə'spektɪv/
adj L204
prosper /'prɒspər|| 'prɑ-/
v N130
prosperity /prɒ'sperɪ̜ti||
prɑ-/
n J117, N133
prosperous /'prɒspərəs||
'prɑ-/
adj J116
prostitute /'prɒstɪ̜tjuːt||
'prɑstɪ̜tuːt/
n C36
prostitution
/ˌprɒstɪ̜'tjuːʃən||
ˌprɑstɪ̜'tuːʃən/
n C36
prostrate /'prɒstreɪt||
'prɑ-/
adj N304
prostrate /prɒ'streɪt||
'prɑstreɪt/
v N309
protect /prə'tekt/
v C225, N365
protection /prə'tekʃən/
n N366
protective /prə'tektɪv/
adj N365
protectorate
/prə'tektərɪ̜t/
n C92
protest /prə'test/

v C130
protest /'prəʊtest/
adj C131
Protestant
/'prɒtɪ̜stənt|| 'prɑ-
n C330
adj C330
Protestantism
/'prɒtɪ̜stəntɪzəm|| 'prɑ-/
n C330
protocol /'prəʊtəkɒl||
-kɔl/
n C105
protractor /prə'træktər||
prəʊ-/
n H151 (picture)
protrude /prə'truːd||
'prəʊ-/
v M52
protrusion /prə'truːʒən||
prəʊ-/
n M52
protuberance
/prə'tjuːbərəns||
prəʊ'tuː-/
n M52
protuberant
/prə'tjuːbərənt||
prəʊ'tuː-/
adj M52
proud /praʊd/
adj F142, 143
prove /pruːv/ *v* **proved**
/pruːvd/, **proved** *or esp*
AmE **proven** /'pruːvən/
v happen L176
show N220
proverb /'prɒvɜːb||
'prɑvɜrb/
n G236
proverbial /prə'vɜːbɪəl||
-ɜr-/
adj G236
provide /prə'vaɪd/
v D100
province /'prɒvɪ̜ns||
'prɑ-/
n C79
provincial /prə'vɪnʃəl/
n C83
adj C85
provincialism
/prə'vɪnʃəlɪzm/
n C38
provisional /prə'vɪʒənəl/
adj L151
provisions /prə'vɪʒənz/
n E1
provocation
/ˌprɒvə'keɪʃən|| ˌprɑ-/
n F103
provocative
/prə'vɒkətɪv|| -'vɑ-/
adj F105
provoke /prə'vəʊk/
v upset F100
cause N151
provoke into
v N151
provost /'prɒvəst||
'prəʊ-, 'prɑ-/
n C101
prow /praʊ/

n H243
riddance /ˈrɪdəns/
v D91
riddle /ˈrɪdl/
n K175
ride /raɪd/ **rode** /rəʊd/,
ridden /ˈrɪdn/
v K101, M19
rider /ˈraɪdəʳ/
n K199
ridicule /ˈrɪdɪkjuːl/
v F244
n F245
ridiculous /rɪˈdɪkjʊləs||
kjə-/
adj F245
riding /ˈraɪdɪŋ/
n K199
rid of /rɪd/ **rid of** *or*
ridded of, rid of, *pres p*
ridding of
v D89
get rid of D89, H15
rifle /ˈraɪfəl/
n H238 (picture)
v N359
rig /rɪg/
equipment *n* H110
vehicle *n* M94
rigging /ˈrɪgɪŋ/
n M157
right /raɪt/
in politics *adj* C112
good *n* F64
good *adj* F65
in boxing *n* K144
suitable *adj* N210
correct *v* N215
right angle /ˈ··, ·· ·/
n J43
right angled /ˈ··, ·· ·/
adj J43
right away /, ·· ˈ· ·/
adv L262
rights /raɪts/
n G179
right wing /, raɪtˈwɪŋ ̄/
adj, n C112
rigid /ˈrɪdʒɪd/
adj N264
rigidity /rɪˈdʒɪdɪti/
n N266
rigorous /ˈrɪgərəs/
adj N265
rigour *BrE*, **rigor** *AmE*
/ˈrɪgəʳ/
n N266
rig up, -gg-
v M50
rim /rɪm/
n M200
rime /raɪm/
n G166, 169
rind /raɪnd/
n A134
ring /rɪŋ/ **rang** /ræŋ/,
rung /rʌŋ/
v bell F276
telephone G217
ring
n on a finger D159
bell F276
circle H49

area K89
ring finger /ˈ··, ·· ·/
n B42
ringleader /ˈrɪŋ, liːdəʳ/
n C139
ringmaster /ˈrɪŋ, mɑːstəʳ||
-, mæ-/
n K85
ring up
v G217
rink /rɪŋk/
n K117
rinse /rɪns/
v D170, 183
n D171
riot /ˈraɪət/
n C131
v C134
riotous /ˈraɪətəs/
adj C134
RIP /, ɑː raɪˈpiː/
n C59
rip /rɪp/ **-pp-**
v move M24
tear N331
rip
n N331
ripe /raɪp/
adj L207
ripen /ˈraɪpən/
v L211
ripple /ˈrɪpəl/
n, v L91
rise /raɪz/ **rose** /rəʊz/,
risen /ˈrɪzən/
rebel *v* C134
increase *v* J90
come up *v* L237
get up *v* N291
rise
n increase J91, 220
getting up N291
rising /ˈraɪzɪŋ/
n C135
risk /rɪsk/
v F135, N39
n N38
risky /ˈrɪski/
adj N40
rissole /ˈrɪsəʊl/
n E37
ritual /ˈrɪtʊəl/
n, adj C335
rival /ˈraɪvəl/
n K106
v N191
rivalry /ˈraɪvəlri/
n K106
river /ˈrɪvəʳ/
n L93
rivet /ˈrɪvɪt/
n, v H148
roach /rəʊtʃ/
n A100 (picture)
road /rəʊd/
n M125, 126
roadside /ˈrəʊdsaɪd/
n M132
road-user /ˈ· ·· ·/
n M97
roadway /ˈrəʊdweɪ/
n M132 (picture)
roam /rəʊm/

v M74
roar /rɔːʳ|| rɔr/
v, n F276
roast /rəʊst/
n E36,100
v E100
rob /rɒb|| rɑb/ **-bb-**
v C232
robber /ˈrɒbəʳ|| ˈrɑ-/
n C231
robbery /ˈrɒbəri|| ˈrɑ-/
n C230
robe /rəʊb/
n D139, 150
v D153
robin /ˈrɒbɪn|| ˈrɑ-/
n A74 (picture)
robot /ˈrəʊbɒt|| -bɑt,
-bət/
n H112
robust /rəˈbʌst,
ˈrəʊbʌst/
adj B91, N234
rock /rɒk|| rɑk/
n stone H60
music K26, 36
rocket /ˈrɒkɪt|| ˈrɑ-/
n H121, 251, M184
rocketship /ˈrɒkɪtʃɪp||
-ˈrɑ-/
n M184
rocking chair /ˈrɒkɪŋ
tʃeəʳ|| ˈrɑ-/
n D113
rock 'n' roll /, rɒk ən
ˈrəʊl|| , rɑk-/
n K26
rod /rɒd|| rɑd/
n general H42
for fishing K206
rodent /ˈrəʊdənt/
n A32
roe deer /ˈrəʊ, dɪəʳ/
n A57
role /rəʊl/
n K84
roll /rəʊl/
list *n* C118
bread *n* E44, 50
tube *n* H41
of cloth *n* H47
moving *v, n* M19
roller /ˈrəʊləʳ/
n L91
roller skate /ˈ·· , · /
n, v K204
rolling stock /ˈrəʊlɪŋ
, stɒk|| stɑk/
n M108
roman /ˈrəʊmən/
n, adj G149
Roman Catholic
/, ·· ˈ· ·· ̄/
n, adj C330
Roman Catholicism
/, ·· · ˈ· ·· /
n C330
Roman nose /ˈ· ·· ·/
n B25 (picture)
roof /ruːf/
of the mouth *n* B26
of a house *n* D20
general *n, v* D21

of a car *n* M100
(picture)
roofrack /ˈruː fræk/
n M100 (picture)
rook /rʊk/
n bird A78
in chess K138
rookery /ˈrʊkəri/
n A78
rookie /ˈrʊki/
n C302
room /ruːm, rʊm/
n of a house D33, M80
space M121
rooster /ˈruːstəʳ/
n A70 (table)
root /ruːt/
of a plant *n* A130
in language *n* G274
in maths *n* J38
root out
v N338
rope /rəʊp/
n H46
v M64
rope off
v M64
rose /rəʊz/
n A158
rosé /ˈrəʊzeɪ|| rəʊˈzeɪ /
n E69
rot /rɒt|| rɑt/ **-tt-**
v A2
rot
n A4
rotary /ˈrəʊtəri/
adj N297
rotate /rəʊˈteɪt|| ˈrəʊteɪt/
v N297
rotation /rəʊˈteɪʃən/
n N297
rotor /ˈrəʊtəʳ/
n M183 (picture)
rotten /ˈrɒtn|| ˈrɑtn/
adj A2, E111, F57,
L71
rotund /rəʊˈtʌnd/
adj B100
rough /rʌf/
n K198
adj N275
roughage /ˈrʌfɪdʒ/
n E1
roughen /ˈrʌfən/
v N276
roughly /ˈrʌfli/
adv L266
roulette /ruːˈlet/
n K134
round /raʊnd/
of drinks *n* E71
bullet *n* H242
shape *adj* J45
in sport *n* K103
around *adv, prep* M203
turn *v* N297
roundabout
/ˈraʊndəbaʊt/
circuitous *adj* J45
for playing *n* K171
on road *n* M135
rounded /ˈraʊndɪd/
adj J45

rounders /'raʊndəz‖
  -ərz/
  n K190
round up
  v H26
roundup /'raʊndʌp/
  n G161, H26
rout /raʊt/
  v C280
  n C283
route /ruːt‖ raʊt/
  n M125
routine /ruː'tiːnʲ/
  in entertaining n K73
  general n, adj N57
rove /rəʊv/
  v M74
row /raʊ/
  v C45, F106
  n C45, F107
row /rəʊ/
  line n J41, K92
  a boat v, n M166
rowboat /'rəʊˌbəʊt/
  n M152
rowing boat /'·· ˌ·/
  n M152
rowlock /'rɒlək‖ 'rɑ-/
  n M167
royal /'rɔɪəl/
  n C96
  adj C97
royalist /'rɔɪəlɪst/
  n C94
royalty /'rɔɪəlti/
  n person C98
  money G179
rub /rʌb/ -bb-
  v, n N334
rub
  n N334
rubber /'rʌbər/
  n eraser G152 (picture)
  substance H70
rubber sheath /ˌ·· '·/
  n B181
rubbish /'rʌbɪʃ/
  n H13
rubble /'rʌbəl/
  n H14
rub in
  v G77
rub out
  v G144
ruby /'ruːbi/
  n H65
rucksack /'rʌksæk/
  n H184
rudder /'rʌdər/
  n M157 (picture)
rude /ruːd/
  adj C168, F155
rudeness /'ruːdnəs/
  n F156
rue /ruː/
  v F85
rueful /'ruːfəl/
  adj F86
ruffian /'rʌfiən/
  n C169
rug /rʌg/
  n D118
rugby ball /'·· ·/

n K193 (picture)
rugby (football) /'rʌgbi/
  n K190
Rugby League /ˌ·· '·/
  n K190
Rugby Union /ˌ·· '··/
  n K190
rugged /'rʌgɪd/
  adj N275
rugger /'rʌgər/
  n K190
ruin /'ruːɪn/
  v, n N338
ruinous /'ruːɪnəs/
  adj N338
rule /ruːl/
  governing v C99
  governing n C100
  principle n C180
  decide v C183
  instrument n H151
    (picture)
ruler /'ruːlər/
  n person C96
  instrument H151
    (picture)
ruling /'ruːlɪŋ/
  n C182
ruling class /ˌ·· '·/
  n C152
rum /rʌm/
  n E65
rummy /'rʌmi/
  n K132
rumour BrE, rumor
  AmE /'ruːmər/
  n, v G194
rump /rʌmp/
  n bottom B33
  meat E34 (picture)
run /rʌn/ ran /ræn/, run
  /rʌn/, pres p running
  control v C99, N167
  in elections v C116
  work v I103
  in sport v K101
  score n K121, 196
  move v M19
  flow v M41
run down
  v F148
rundown /rʌn'daʊnʲ/
  adj B111
rung /rʌŋ/
  n D30
runner /'rʌnər/
  n G198
runner up /ˌ·· '·/
  runners up or runner
  ups
  n K109
running /'rʌnɪŋ/
  n N170
run out
  v J155, L174
runway /'rʌnweɪ/
  n M185
rural /'rʊərəl/
  adj C85
rush /rʌʃ/
  v, n M33
rushed /rʌʃt/
  adj M16

rush into
  v M33
rust /rʌst/
  n, v H69
rustle /'rʌsəl/
  v C232
rut /rʌt/
  n E142
ruthless /'ruːθləs/
  adj F179
rye /raɪ/
  n plant A152
  drink E65

S

sabotage /'sæbətɑːʒ/
  n C138
saboteur /ˌsæbə'tɜːʳ/
  n C139
sabre BrE, saber AmE
  /'seɪbər/
  n H231
sack /sæk/
  container n H183
  from a job v J212
  destroying n, v N338
sackful /'sækfʊl/
  n H183
sacrament /'sækrəmənt/
  n C335
sacred /'seɪkrɪd/
  adj C338
sacrifice /'sækrɪˌfaɪs/
  n C335
sacrificial /ˌsækrɪ'fɪʃəl/
  adj C335
sacrilege /'sækrɪlɪdʒ/
  n C336
sacrilegious
  /ˌsækrɪ'lɪdʒəs/
  adj C336
sad /sæd/
  adj F80
sadden /'sædn/
  v F84
saddle /'sædl/
  meat n E34 (picture)
  of an animal n A54
    (picture)
  on a horse n, v K199
  on a bicycle n M103
    (picture)
saddle up
  v K199
safe /seɪf/
  n J104
  adj D367
safety /'seɪfti/
  n general N366
  in baseball K194
safety pin /'·· ˌ·/
  n H126 (picture)
safety razor /'·· ˌ··/
  n H140 (picture)
Sagittarius
  /ˌsædʒ'teəriəs/
  n L4 (picture)
sail /seɪl/
  travel v M19, 166

journey n M75
  part of a boat n M157
    (picture)
sailing boat/ship /'·· ˌ· /
  n M153
sailor /'seɪlər/
  n C295, M163
saint /seɪnt/
  n C343
sainthood /'seɪnthʊd/
  n C343
saintly /'seɪntli/
  adj C343
sake /seɪk/
  n G289
salad /'sæləd/
  n E50
salad dressing /'·· ˌ·· /
  n E50
salary /'sæləri/
  n J219
sale /seɪl/
  n J134, 183
sales clerk /'seɪlzklɑːk‖
  -klɜrk/
  n J189
salesgirl /'seɪlzgɜːl‖ -ɜrl/
  n J189
saleslady /'seɪlzˌleɪdi/
  n J189
salesman /'seɪlzmən/
  -men /mən/
  n J140, 189
sales representative
  /'·· ˌ·· ··· /
  n J140
saleswoman
  /'seɪlzˌwʊmən/ -women
  /-mən/
  n J140, 189
saliva /sə'laɪvə/
  n B60
salivary /sə'laɪvəri‖
  'sælɪveri/
  adj B60
salivary gland /·'·· ·ˌ· /
  n B35 (picture)
salivate /'sælɪveɪt/
  v B61
salivation /ˌsælɪ'veɪʃən/
  n B61
sallow /'sæləʊ/
  n B53
salmon /'sæmən/ salmon
  n fish A100 (picture)
  meat E32
salon /'sælɒn‖ sə'lɑn/
  n D37
saloon /sə'luːn/
  n for drinks E121
  car M93
saloon bar /·'· ˌ· /
  n E121
saloon keeper /·'· ˌ·· /
  n E124
salt /sɔːlt/
  in food n E49
  in food v E105, 106
  taste adj F283
  substance n H73
salty /'sɔːlti/
  adj E49, F283
salubrious /sə'luːbrɪəs/

adj B110
salute /sə'lu:t/
  v C310
  n C311
saluting base /·'··· ‚ ·/
  n C312
salvage /'sælvɪdʒ/
  material *n* H13
  rescuing *v* N363
  rescuing *n* N366
salvation /sæl'veɪʃən/
  n in religion C341
  general N366
salvo /'sælvəʊ/ -**vos** *or*
-**voes**
  n H243
same /seɪm/
  adj N181
sameness /'seɪmnɪs/
  n N186
sample /'sɑ:mpəl‖ 'sæm-/
  n N7
  v N138
sanctification
/‚sæŋktɪfɪ'keɪʃən/
  n C342
sanctify /'sæŋktɪfaɪ/
  v C342
sanction /'sæŋkʃən/
  v C192
  n C194
sanctions /'sæŋkʃənz/
  n C197
sanctuary /'sæŋktʃʊəri‖
-tʃueri/
  n C351
sand /sænd/
  n H63
sandal /'sændl/
  n D156
sandbank /'sændbæŋk/
  n L99, M161
sand bar /'···/
  n M161
sands /sændz/
  n L92
sandstone /'sændstəʊn/
  n H62
sandwich /'sænwɪdʒ/
  n E50
sandy /'sændi/
  adj H63
sane /seɪn/
  adj G50
sanitary /'sænɪtəri‖ -teri/
  adj B177
sanitation /‚sænɪ'teɪʃən/
  n B177
sanity /'sænɪti/
  n G51
sap /sæp/ -**pp**-
  v N238
sap
  n A133
sapling /'sæplɪŋ/
  n A132
sapper /'sæpə'/
  n C306
sapphire /'sæfaɪə'/
  n H65
sarcasm /'sɑ:kæzəm‖
'sɑr-/
  n G245

sarcastic /sɑ:'kæstɪk‖
sɑr-/
  adj G246
sardine /sɑ:'di:n‖ sɑr-/
  n A100
Satan /'seɪtn/
  n C326
Satanic /sə'tænɪk/
  adj C326
satchel /'sætʃəl/
  n H184
satellite /'sætɪlaɪt/
  n L2
satin /'sætɪn/
  n H87
satire /'sætaɪə'/
  n G245
satirical /sə'tɪrɪkəl/
  adj G246
satirize /'sætɪraɪz/
  v G247
satisfaction
/‚sætɪs'fækʃən/
  n F75
satisfactory
/‚sætɪs'fæktəri/
  adj F54
satisfied /'sætɪsfaɪd/
  adj F73
satisfy /'sætɪsfaɪ/
  v F76
Saturday /'sætədi‖ -ər-/
  n L232
Saturn /'sætən‖ -ərn/
  n L4 (picture)
satyr /'sætə'/
  n C357
sauce /sɔ:s/
  n E39
saucepan /'sɔ:spæn/
  n H174
saucer /'sɔ:sə'/
  n H172
saucerful /'sɔ:səfʊl/
  n H172
saunter /'sɔ:ntə'/
  v, *n* M21
sausage /'sɒsɪdʒ‖ 'sɔ:-/
  n E37
sausage meat /'··· ‚ ·/
  n E37
sausage roll /‚ ··'·/
  n E37
savage /'sævɪdʒ/
  n C169
  adj F110
savagery /'sævɪdʒəri/
  n F109
savanna(h) /sə'vænə/
  n L108
save /seɪv/
  in religion *v* C340
  money *v* J106
  rescue *v* N363
  rescuing *n* N366
save on
  v N363
save up
  v J106
savings /'seɪvɪŋz/
  n J113
savings account
/'··· ‚ ·/

n J105
saviour *BrE*, **savior**
AmE /'seɪvɪə'/
  n C343
savour *BrE*, **savor** *AmE*
/'seɪvə'/
  v F280
  n F281
savoury *BrE*, **savory**
AmE /'seɪvəri/
  n E17
  adj F282, 283
saw /sɔ:/ **sawed, sawn**
/sɔ:n/ *esp BrE or* **sawed**
esp AmE
  v H142
saw
  n H142 (picture)
say /seɪ/ **said** /sed/, *3rd*
pers pres t **says** /sez/
  v G60, 115
say ... again
  v G76
saying /'seɪ-ɪŋ/
  n G236
scab /skæb/
  n B128
scabbard /'skæbəd‖
-ərd/
  n H231
scabies /'skeɪbiz/
  n B148
scaffold /'skæfəld,
-fəʊld/
  n C260
scaffolding /'skæfəldɪŋ/
  n H116
scale /skeɪl/
  skin *n* A126
  range *n* H115, L43
  for weighing *n* H125
  in music *n* K29
  climb *v* M9
scalene /'skeɪli:n/
  adj J45
scalp /skælp/
  n B20
scalpel /'skælpəl/
  n B176 (picture)
scamper /'skæmpə'/
  v M25
scan /skæn/ -**nn**-
  v F263, G140
scan
  n F265
scapular /'skæpjʊlə‖
-pjələ/
  n B11 (picture)
scar /skɑ:r/ -**rr**-
  n, *v* B128
scarce /skeəs‖ skeərs/
  adj N105
scarcely /'skeəsli‖ -ər-/
  adv N99
scarcity /'skeəsɪti‖ -ər-/
  n N106
scare /skeə'/
  n F120
  v F122
scared /skeəd‖ skeərd/
  adj F125
scarf /skɑ:f‖ skɑrf/ **scarfs**
or **scarves** /skɑ:vz‖

skɑrvz/
  n D151
scarlet /'skɑ:lɪt‖ -ɑr-/
  n L31
scarlet fever /‚ ··'··· /
  n B143
scary /'skeəri/
  adj F123, 125
scatter /'skætə'/
  v M59
scatter-brained
/'skætəbreɪnd‖ -ər-/
  adj G46
scavenger /'skævɪndʒə'/
  n A39
scenario /sɪ'nɑ:riəʊ‖
-'næ-, -'ne-/ -**rios**
  n K81
scene /si:n/
  n in a play K80
  general L83
scenery /'si:nəri/
  n in a theatre K91
  general L83
scent /sent/
  v F277
  n F278
scented /'sentɪd/
  adj F279
sceptic /'skeptɪk/
  n G95
sceptical /'skeptɪkəl/
  adj G95
scepticism
/'skeptɪsɪzəm/
  n G95
schedule /'ʃedju:l‖
'skedʒʊl, -dʒəl/
  n, *v* L131
scholar /'skɒlə'‖ 'skɑ-/
  n I136, 147
scholarship /'skɒləʃɪp‖
'skɑlər-/
  n money I136
  knowledge I147
scholastic /skə'læstɪk/
  adj I136, 147
school /sku:l/
  of fish *n* A40
  train *v* G33
  place *n* I131, 133
schoolboy /'sku:lbɔɪ/
  n I136
schoolchild /'sku:ltʃaɪld/
  n I136
schoolgirl /'sku:lgɜ:l‖
'ɜrl/
  n I136
schoolmaster
/'sku:l‚mɑ:stə'‖ -‚mæ-/
  n I134
schoolmistress
/'sku:l‚mɪstrɪs/
  n I134
schooner /'sku:nə'/
  n M153
science /'saɪəns/
  n I70
scientific /‚saɪən'tɪfɪk/
  adj I73
scientist /'saɪəntɪst/
  n I72
scissors /'sɪzəz‖ -ərz/

scoff /skɒf|| skɔf, skɑf/
laugh v F244
laughing n F245
eat v E4

scone /skɒn, skəʊn||
skəʊn, skɑn/
n E44

scooter /ˈskuːtəʳ/
n M96

scope /skəʊp/
n D107

scorch /skɔːtʃ|| -ɔr-/
n H75
v H76

score /skɔːʳ|| skor/
to have sex v C24
number n J16
in music n K27
in sport v K104
in sport n K121

Scorpio /ˈskɔːpiəʊ||
-ɔr-/
n L4 (picture)

Scorpion /ˈskɔːpɪən||
-ɔr-/ʼ
n A112 (picture)

Scotch /skɒtʃ|| skɑtʃ/
n E65

scour /skaʊəʳ/
v D170
n D171

scourer /ˈskaʊərəʳ/
n D178

scout /skaʊt/
v, n N359

scowl /skaʊl/
v F242
n F243

scrabble /ˈskræbəl/
n K135

scrag /skræg/
n E34 (picture)

scramble /ˈskræmbəl/
cooking v E100
moving v, n M25

scrap /skræp/ -pp-
v H15

scrap
n waste H13
piece H33

scratch /skrætʃ/
v, n B130

scrawl /skrɔːl/
v G141
n G145

scream /skriːm/
v G129
n G130

screech /skriːtʃ/
v G129
n G130

screed /skriːd/
n G145

screen /skriːn/
in photography n, v K59
in cinema n K70
cover v L26

screw /skruː/
in sex v C24
general n, v H148
(picture)

of boats n M157
(picture)

screwdriver
/ˈskruːˌdraɪvəʳ/
n H149 (picture)

screwnail /ˈskruːneɪl/
n H148

scribble /ˈskrɪbəl/
v G141
n G145

scribble down
v G143

scribbler /ˈskrɪbələʳ/
n G172

scribe /skraɪb/
n G172

script /skrɪpt/
n writing G145, 147, 162
for a play K81

scripted /ˈskrɪptɪd/
adj G162

scriptural /ˈskrɪptʃərəl/
adj C336

scripture /ˈskrɪptʃəʳ/
n C336

scriptwriter
/ˈskrɪptˌraɪtəʳ/
n G172, K83

scroll /skrəʊl/
n G162

scrotum /ˈskrəʊtəm/ -ta
/tə/ or -tums
n B40

scrub /skrʌb/ -bb-
v D170

scrub
n wash D171
land L108

scrubbing brush /ˈ··ˌ·/
n D178

scrubland /ˈskrʌblənd,
-ˌlænd/
n L112

scruff /skrʌf/
n B21

scrum /skrʌm/
n K193

scrum half /ˌskrʌmˈhɑːf||
-ˈhæf/
n K193

scruple /ˈskruːpəl/
n F63

scrupulous
/ˈskruːpjʊləs|| -pjə-/
adj F63

scrutinize /ˈskruːtɪ̥naɪz/
v N360

scrutiny /ˈskruːtɪ̥ni/
n N361

scullery /ˈskʌləri/
n D38

sculpt /skʌlpt/
v I49

sculptor /ˈskʌlptəʳ/ fem
sculptress /-trɪ̥s/
n I51

sculptural /ˈskʌlptʃərəl/
adj I48

sculpture /ˈskʌlptʃəʳ/
n I48
v I49

scurry /ˈskʌri/

v, n M25

scuttle /ˈskʌtl/
container n D36
moving v, n M25

scythe /saɪð/
n H154
v H155

sea /siː/
n L86

seabird /ˈsiːbɜːd|| -bɜrd/
n A72

seagull /ˈsiːgʌl/
n A72 (picture)

seal /siːl/
animal n A58
stamp n H127
stamp v H128
close v M63

sea-level /ˈsiːˌlevəl/
n L113

sea lion /ˈ··ˌ··/
n A58

sea loch /ˈ··ˌ·/
n L88

seam /siːm/
layer H32, 67
in sewing I58

seaman /ˈsiːmən/ -men
/mən/
n C295, 298, M163

seaplane /ˈsiːpleɪn/
n M180

search /sɜːtʃ|| sɜrtʃ/
v N359
n N361

searcher /ˈsɜːtʃəʳ|| ˈsɜr-/
n N359

search party /ˈ··ˌ··/
n N359

seasickness /ˈsiːˌsɪkni̥s/
n B120

season /ˈsiːzən/
of food v E105
through time v L211
time n L238

seasonal /ˈsiːzənəl/
adj L239

seasoned /ˈsiːzənd/
adj L207

seasoning /ˈsiːzənɪŋ/
n E49

seat /siːt/
bottom n B33
chair n, v D113
place n M83
in a vehicle n M101
(picture)

seating /ˈsiːtɪŋ/
n D113

sea urchin /ˈ··ˌ··/
n A104

seaweed /ˈsiːwiːd/
n A140

second /ˈsekənd/
not first adj, n J6
in music n K42
in time n L226
of gears n, adj M111
(table)

second /sɪˈkɒnd||
sɪˈkɑnd/
v J215

secondary /ˈsekəndəri||

-deri/
adj J7

secondment
/sɪˈkɒndmənt|| -ɑn-/
n J215

secondary modern
school /ˌ···ˈ···/
n I131

secondary school
/ˈ···ˌ·/
n I131

second hand /ˌ··ˈ·/
n L228

secondhand
/ˌsekəndˈhænd/
adj, adv L201

second in command
/ˌ···ˈ·/
n C300

second mate /ˌ··ˈ·/
n M164

secondment
/sɪˈkɒndmənt|| sɪˈkɑnd-/
n J215

second officer /ˌ··ˈ···/
n M164

seconds /ˈsekəndz/
n E16

second sight /ˌ··ˈ·/
n L159

secret /ˈsiːkrɪ̥t/
adj F195
n F207

secretariat
/ˌsekrəˈteəriət/
n C104

secretary /ˈsekretəri||
-teri/
n in government C101
in an office J232

secrete /sɪˈkriːt/
v produce I1
hide N356

secretion /sɪˈkriːʃən/
n producing I1
hiding N356

secretive /ˈsiːkrɪ̥tɪv,
sɪˈkriːtɪv/
adj F193

sect /sekt/
n C321

sectarian /sekˈteəriən/
adj C338

section /ˈsekʃən/
n in army C292
general H32
in maths J41

sectional /ˈsekʃənəl/
adj H32

sector /ˈsektəʳ/
n J44 (picture)

secular /ˈsekjʊləʳ|| -kjə-/
adj C339

secure /sɪˈkjʊəʳ/
v N365
adj N367

security /sɪˈkjʊərɪ̥ti/
n in banking J114
general N366

sedan /sɪˈdæn/
n M93

sedation /sɪˈdeɪʃən/
n B173

sedative /'sedətɪv/
n B173
sediment /'sedɪmənt/
n H14, 63
sedimentary
/ˌsedɪ'mentəri/
adj H61, 63
sedition /sɪ'dɪʃən/
n C131
seditious /sɪ'dɪʃəs/
adj C131
seduce /sɪ'dju:s/
v C24
seduction /sɪ'dʌkʃən/
n C24
seductive /sɪ'dʌktɪv/
adj C25
see /si:/ **saw** /sɔ:/, **seen**
/si:n/
with the eye *v* F263
consider *v* G12
understand *v* G31
foresee *v* L158
see
n C348
seed /si:d/
n A19, 134
v E137
seedbox /'si:dbɒks||
-bɑks/
n A131
seedling /'si:dlɪŋ/
n A132
seek /si:k/ **sought** /sɔ:t/
v N359
seeker /'si:kər/
n N359
seem /si:m/
v N2
seer /'sɪər/
n C343
seesaw /'si:sɔ:/
n, *v* K171
see to
v N162
see-through /'si: θru:/
adj F270
segment /'segmənt/
n of fruit A150
speech G273
general H32
of a circle J44
(picture), J46
segment /seg'ment/
v N320
segmental /seg'mentl/
adj H32
seize /si:z/
v take C281
hold D96, 98
seize upon
v D96
seizure /'si:ʒər/
n illness B144
seizing C281, D97
seldom /'seldəm/
adv L258
select /sɪ'lekt/
general *v*, *adj* D84
best *adj* F52
selection /sɪ'lekʃən/
n D84
selective /sɪ'lektɪv/

adj D84
selector /sɪ'lektər/
n D84
self /self/ **selves** /selvz/
pron G282
self assurance /ˌ··'···/
n G86
self-determination /ˌself
dɪˌtɜː'neɪʃən|| -tɜr-/
n C95
self-government
/ˌself 'gʌvəmənt/
n C95
selfish /'selfɪʃ/
adj F57, 180
selfless /'selfləs/
adj F56
self-service
/ˌself'sɜːvɪs' || -ɜr-/
n J180
sell /sel/ **sold** /səuld/
v J130
sell off
v J184
sell out
v J203, J155
sellout /'selaut/
n F204
semantic /sɪ'mæntɪk/
adj G238
semanticist
/sɪ'mæntɪsɪst/
n G287
semantics /sɪ'mæntɪks/
n G237
semblance /'sembləns/
n N4
semen /'si:mən/
n A19
semester /sɪ'mestər/
n I138
semi /'semi/
n D6
semi- /'semɪ/
comb form N255
semi-breve /'semɪbri:v/
n K28
semi-circle /'semɪˌsɜːkəl||
-ɜr-/
n J44 (picture)
semi-colon
/ˌsemɪ'kəulən||
'semɪˌkəulən/
n G151
semi-conscious /'···/
adj B80
semi-detached (house)
/ˌsemɪdɪ'tætʃt/
adj, *n* D6
seminal /'semɪnəl/
adj of semen A19
of ideas L203
seminar /'semɪnɑ:r/
n I137
semi-quaver
/'semɪˌkweɪvər/
n K28
senate /'senɪt/
n C103
senator /'senətər/
n C103
senatorial /ˌsenə'tɔ:rɪəl||
-'to-/

adj C103
send /send/ **sent** /sent/
v post G192
general M52
send away
v M54
send back
v D86
send for
v M71
send off
v M54
send out
v G217
send word
v M52
senile
adj B134, L208
senility /sɪ'nɪlɪti/
n L210, B134
senior /'si:nɪər/
older *adj* L207
major *adj*, *n* N89
seniority /ˌsi:ni'ɒrɪti||
-'ɔ-, -'ɑ-/
n L210
sensation /sen'seɪʃən/
n F2, 228
sensational
/sen'seɪʃənəl/
adj wonderful F53, 225
of the senses F261
sense /sens/
feel *v* F1, 260
thought *n* G39
meaning *n* G200, 237
senses /'sensɪz/
n F261
sensibility /ˌsensə'bɪlɪti/
n F234
sensible /'sensəbəl/
adj N229
sensitive /'sensɪtɪv/
adj F234
sensitivity /ˌsensɪ'tɪvɪti/
n F234
sensitize /'sensɪtaɪz/
v F234
sensory /'sensəri/
adj F262
sensual /'senʃuəl/
adj F262
sensuous /'senʃuəs/
adj F262
sentence /'sentəns/
in law *v* C210
in law *n* C256
in language *n* G235
sentiment /'sentɪmənt/
n F2
sentimental
/ˌsentɪ'mentl/
adj F4
sentinel /'sentɪnəl/
n C223
sentry /'sentri/
n C223
sepal /'sepl/
n A131 (picture)
separate /'sepəreɪt/
v N322
separated /'sepəreɪtɪd/
adj C28

separation /ˌsepə'reɪʃən/
n N322
September /sep'tembər/
n L234
sepulchre *BrE*,
sepulcher *AmE*
/'sepəlkər/
n C57
serene /sɪ'ri:n/
adj F221
serenity /sɪ'renɪti/
n F222
serf /sɜːf|| sɜrf/
n C163
sergeant /sɑ:dʒənt||
'sɑr-/
n C220, 297 (tables)
serial /'sɪərɪəl/
n G168
serial number
n J1
series /'sɪəri:z/ **series**
n in stories G168
in maths J40
serious /'sɪərɪəs/
adj N43
sermon /'sɜːmən|| 'sɜr-/
n C335
serpent /'sɜːpənt|| 'sɜr-/
n A90
serpentine /'sɜːpəntaɪn||
sɜr-/
adj A90
serrated /sɪ'reɪtɪd, se-/
adj N275
serum /'sɪərəm/ **-rums** *or*
-ra /rə/
n B174
servant /'sɜːvənt|| 'sɜr-/
n C161
serve /sɜːv|| sɜrv/
in prison *v* C263
in working *v* D108
of meals *v* E15
general *v* I28
in tennis *v* K197
service /'sɜːvɪs|| 'sɜr-/
in religion *n* C335
general *n* D108
in tennis *n* K197
of cars *n*, *v* M105
service industry
/'··, ···/
n I100
serviceman /'sɜːvɪsmən||
'sɜr-/ **-men** /mən/
n C295
servicing /'sɜːvɪsɪŋ||
'sɜr-/
n M105
servile /'sɜːvaɪl|| 'sɜrvəl,
-vaɪl/
adj C164
servility /sɜː'vɪlɪti|| sɜr-/
n C164
serving /'sɜːvɪŋ|| 'sɜr-/
n E16
servitor /'sɜːvɪtər|| 'sɜr-/
n C161
servitude /'sɜːvɪtju:d||
'sɜrvɪtu:d/
n C164
session /'seʃən/

n I138, M73
set /set/ **set**, *pres p*
setting
   v mend B161
      print G173
      go down L237
      move M1
      prepare M50
set
   n group C74, J40
      on stage K91
      in tennis K197
setback /'setbæk/
   n C283
set down
   v G143
set fire to
   v H77
set forth
   v L172
set free
   v C165
set in
   v L172
set off
   v begin L172
      leave M4
set out
   v begin L172
      leave M4
set right
   v I18, N215
set sail
   v M166
settee /se'ti:/
   n D114
setter /'setə'/
   n A54
setting /'setɪŋ/
   n G242, M123
settle /'setl/
      live in *v* D61, 62
      chair *n* D114
      decide *v* N163
settled /'setld/
   adj D62
settle down
   v D62
settle for
   v J145
settle in(to)
   v D62
settlement /'setlmənt/
   n town C80
      decision N163
settler /'setlə'/
   n D63
set up
   v in printing G173
      establish L172
      start N161
seven /'sevən/
   n J4
seventy /'sevənti/
   n J4
sever /'sevə'/
   v N321
several /'sevərəl/
   det N98
   adj N182
severe /sɪ'vɪə'/
   adj B123, N265
severity /sɪ'verɪti/

n N266
sew /səʊ/ **sewed**, **sewn**
   /səʊn/
   v I57
sewage /'sju:ɪdʒ, 'su:-||
   'su:-/
   n D42
sewer /'sju:ə', 'su:ə'||
   'su:ər/
   n D42
sewerage /'sju:ərɪdʒ,
   'su:-|| 'su:-/
   n D42
sex /seks/
   n A14, 16, C23
   v A16, C23
sextant /'sekstənt/
   n H151
sexual /'sekʃʊəl, -sjʊəl||
   'sekʃʊəl/
   adj A14
sexual intercourse
   /ˌ··· '··· /
   n A16, C23
sexuality /ˌsekʃʊ'ælɪti,
   -sjʊ-|| ˌsekʃʊ-/
   n A14
sexy /'seksi/
   adj C25
shack /ʃæk/
   n D4
shade /ʃeɪd/
      ghost *n* C324
      on a lamp *n* H214
      darkness *n* L21
      darken *v* L26, 28
      colour *v* L27
shaded /'ʃeɪdɪd/
   adj L34
shadow /'ʃædəʊ/
   n L21, L227 (picture)
shadowy /'ʃædəʊi/
   adj L25
shady /'ʃeɪdi/
   adj L25
shaft /ʃɑ:ft|| ʃæft/
   n general H42, 145
      in a mine I114
shaggy /'ʃægi/
   adj A126
   n B53
shake /ʃeɪk/ **shook** /ʃʊk/,
   shaken /'ʃeɪkən/
   v, *n* general N296, 298
      of the head N299
shall /ʃəl/ *neg contr*
   shan't /ʃɑ:nt|| ʃænt/
   modal L273
shallow /'ʃæləʊ/
   adj N306
shallow end /'··· /
   n K203
shallows /'ʃæləʊz/
   n M161
sham /ʃæm/
   n I10
   adj I13
shame /ʃeɪm/
      pity *n* F82
      dishonour *v* F151
      dishonour *n* F152
shamefaced
   /ˌʃeɪm'feɪst'/

adj F153
shameful /'ʃeɪmfəl/
   adj F153
shameless /'ʃeɪmləs/
   adj F154
shampoo /ʃæm'pu:/
   -pooed, *pres p* **-pooing**,
   3rd pers sing pres t
   -poos
   v D170
shampoo, **-poos**
   n D171, 183
shandy /'ʃændi/
   n E66
shanghai /ʃæŋ'haɪ/
   v M169
shank /ʃæŋk/
   n of a horse A51
      (picture)
      of lamb E34 (picture)
shanty /'ʃænti/
   n D4
shanty town /'ʃæntitaʊn/
   n C81 D4
shape /ʃeɪp/
   v I5
   n I6
shapely /'ʃeɪpli/
   adj F39
share /ʃeə'/
      give *v* D104
      part *n* D105, H37
      in commerce *n* J114
shareholder
   /'ʃeə,həʊldə'|| 'ʃeər-/
   n J114, 230
share out
   v D104
shareout /'ʃeəraʊt/
   n D104
shark /ʃɑ:k|| ʃɑrk/
   n A101 (picture)
sharp /ʃɑ:p|| ʃɑrp/
      of pain *adj* B123
      of tools *adj* H159
      in music *n* K31
      clear *adj* L24
sharpen /'ʃɑ:pən|| 'ʃɑr-/
   v H159
sharpener
   /'ʃɑ:pənə', 'ʃɑ:pnə'||
   'ʃɑr-/
   n H159
shatter /'ʃætə'/
   v, *n* N333
shattered /'ʃætəd|| -tərd/
   adj B97
shave /ʃeɪv/
   n D172
   v D173
shaver /'ʃeɪvə'/
   n D178
shawl /ʃɔ:l/
   n D143
she /ʃi; strong ʃi:/
   pron G280
sheaf /ʃiːf/
   sheaves /ʃi:vz/
   n in farming E142
      (picture)
      general H182
shear /ʃɪə'/ **sheared**,
   sheared *or* **shorn** /ʃɔ:n||

ʃorn/
   v N321
shears /ʃɪəz|| ʃɪərz/
   n H141
sheath /ʃi:θ/ **sheaths**
   /ʃiːðz/
   n contraceptive B181
      cover H140
      container H178
sheathe /ʃiːð/
   v H187
sheath knife /'·ˌ·/
   n H140
shed /ʃed/ **shed**, *pres p*
   shedding
   v H15
shed
   n D54
sheep /ʃi:p/ **sheep**
   n A56
sheepdog /'ʃi:pdɒg||
   -dɔg/
   n A54
sheepman /'ʃi:pmən,
   -ˌmæn/ **-men** /mən/
   n E143
sheer /ʃɪə'/
   adj L105
sheet /ʃi:t/
   n for a bed D115
      of paper G153
      of metal H43
sheet lightning
   /ˌ·'·· ˌ·ˌ··/
   n L58
she-goat /'ʃi:ˌgəʊt/
   n A56
sheikh /ʃeɪk|| ʃi:k/
   n C96
sheikhdom /'ʃeɪkdəm||
   'ʃi:k-/
   adj C90
shelf /ʃelf/ **shelves** /ʃelvz/
   n J190
shell /ʃel/
      covering *n* A126, 134,
         153, 154, G102
      shoot *v* C279, H245
      bullet *n* H242
shellfish /'ʃel,fɪʃ/ **shellfish**
   n A32
shelter /'ʃeltə'/
   n, *v* D67
shepherd /'ʃepəd|| -ərd/
   n E143
sheriff /'ʃerɪf/
   n C202, 222
sherry /'ʃeri/
   n E68
shield /ʃi:ld/
   n H232 (picture),
      M100
   v N365
shift /ʃɪft/
      clothing *n* D149
      in working *n* I112
      sending *v*, *n* M52
      of gears *n*, *v* M31, 111
shift gears
   v M32
shift up/down
   v M111
shilling /'ʃɪlɪŋ/

six /sɪks/
n number J4
in cricket K196
sixpence /ˈsɪkspəns/
n J83
sixteenth note
n K28
sixty /sɪksti/
n J4
size /saɪz/
n N80
sizeable, sizable
/ˈsaɪzəbəl/
adj N84
skate /skeɪt/ **skate** *or* **skates**
n A100 (picture)
skate /skeɪt/ **skate** *or* **skates**
n fish A100
skate
n, *v* on ice K204
skateboard /ˈskeɪtˌbɔːd|| -bɔrd/
n K204
skateboarding
/ˈskeɪtˌbɔːdɪŋ|| -bɔrd-/
n K204 (picture)
skating /ˈskeɪtɪŋ/
n K204 (picture)
skeletal /ˈskelɪ̣tl/
adj B11
skeleton /ˈskelɪ̣tn/
n B11 (picture)
skeptic /ˈskeptɪk/
n G95
skeptical /ˈskeptɪkəl/
adj G95
skepticism
/ˈskeptɪ̣sɪzəm/
n G95
sketch /sketʃ/
writing *n* G159
draw *v* I43
picture *n* I45
play *n* K76
sketchbook /ˈsketʃbʊk/
n I47
sketching /ˈsketʃɪŋ/
n I44
sketchpad /ˈsketʃpæd/
n I47
ski /skiː/ **skis**
n K204
ski, skied /skiːd/, *pres p* **skiing**
v K204
skid /skɪd/ **-dd-**
v M111
skid
v M111
skiff /skɪf/
n M152
skiing /ski-ɪŋ/
n K204 (picture)
skilful *BrE*, **skillful** *AmE*
/ˈskɪlfəl/
adj G42
skill /skɪl/
n G43
skilled /skɪld/
adj in general G42
of a worker I112
skim /skɪm/ **-mm-**
v read G140
fly M28
skim(med) milk /ˌ· ˈ· /
n E41
skin /skɪn/ **-nn-**
v E102, H88
skin
n A126, B50, H88
skin and bones /ˌ· · ˈ· /
adj B101
skin diving /ˈ· ˌ· · /
n K203
skin-diver /ˈskɪnˌdaɪvəʳ/
n K203
skinny /ˈskɪni/
adj B101
skip /skɪp/ **-pp-**
v K202, M37
skip
n K202
skipper /ˈskɪpəʳ/
n M164
skirmish /ˈskɜːmɪʃ|| -ɜr-/
n C276
skirt /skɜːt|| skɜrt/
n D141
skirting-board /ˈskɜːtɪŋ ˌbɔːd|| ˌbɔrd/
n D34 (picture)
skull /skʌl/
n B11 (picture)
sky /skaɪ/
n L44
sky-scraper /ˈskaɪ ˌskreɪpəʳ/
n D8
slab /slæb/
n H43
slack /slæk/
adj N271
slacken /ˈslækən/
v N273
slacks /slæks/
n D140
slander /ˈslɑːndəʳ|| ˈslæn-/
v, *n* C236
slanderous /ˈslɑːndərəs|| ˈslæn-/
adj C236
slang /slæŋ/
n G230
slangy /ˈslæŋi/
adj G230
slant /slɑːnt|| slænt/
aspect *n* G243
bend *v*, *n* N269
slanted /ˈslæntɪ̣d/
adj N303
slanting /ˈslɑhntɪŋ/
adj N303
slapstick /ˈslæpˌstɪk/
n K75
slash /slæʃ/
cut *n*, *v* B130
punctuation mark *n* G151
slate /sleɪt/
n, *v* D21
slaughter /ˈslɔːtəʳ/
v A8
n A13
slave /sleɪv/
n C163
v I102
slavery /ˈsleɪvəri/
n C164
slay /sleɪ/ **slew** /sluː/, **slain** /sleɪn/
v A8
sled /sled/ **-dd-**
v K204
sled
n K204
sledge /sledʒ/
n, *v* K204 (picture)
sleep /sliːp/ **slept** /slept/
v B82
sleep
n B83
sleep around
v C24
sleeper /ˈsliːpəʳ/
n wood H39, M107
train M108
sleeping /ˈsliːpɪŋ/
adj B81
sleeping car /ˈ· · ˌ· /
n M108
sleep with
v C24
sleepy /ˈsliːpi/
adj B81
sleet /sliːt/
n L48
v L50
sleeve /sliːv/
n D161
sleigh /sleɪ/
n K204
slender /ˈslendər/
adj B101
slice /slaɪs/
piece *n* E33, 45, H31, N320
in golf *n*, *v* K198
cut *v* N320
slide /slaɪd/ **slid** /slɪd/
v M26
slide
n picture F270
apparatus K171
general M26
slight /slaɪt/
adj B101
v N337
slim /slɪm/ **-mm-**
adj B101
v B103
slim down
v B103
slime /slaɪm/
n H63
slimy /slaɪmi/
adj H63
sling /slɪŋ/ **slung** /slʌŋ/
n in medicine B175 (picture)
weapon H236
of a rifle H241
slingshot /ˈslɪŋʃɒt|| -ʃɑt/
n H236 (picture)
slink /slɪŋk/ **slunk** /slʌŋ/
v M26
slip /slɪp/ **-pp-**
v M26
slip
n clothing D149
mistake N219
in cricket K196
slipover /ˈslɪpˌəʊvəʳ/
n D144
slipper /ˈslɪpəʳ/
n D156
slip up
v N219
slipway /ˈslɪpweɪ/
n M160
slither /ˈslɪðəʳ/
v M26
slogan /ˈsləʊgən/
n H130
sloop /sluːp/
n H249
slope /sləʊp/
n L101, N269
slot /slɒt|| slɑt/
n H148
slow /sləʊ/
general *adj* G45, M17
general *v* M31
slow down (strike)
/ˈ· · ˌ· /
n J238
sludge /slʌdʒ/
n H14
slug /slʌg/
n worm A113
bullet H242
sluggish /ˈslʌgɪʃ/
adj M17
sluice /sluːs/
n L100
slum /slʌm/
n C81
slush /slʌʃ/
n L51
slushy /slʌʃi/
adj L51
sly /slaɪ/
adj F197
small intestine
n picture at B35
small /smɔːl/
adj N85
small arms /ˈ· · || ˌ· ˈ· /
n H230
small change /ˌ· ˈ· /
n J81
smallholder
/ˈsmɔːlˌhəʊldəʳ/
n E143
smallholding
/ˈsmɔːlˌhəʊldɪŋ/
n E131
small hours /ˈ· · /
n L224
small intestine /ˌ· · ˈ· · /
n B35 (picture)
small of the back
/ˌ· · · ˈ· /
n B32
smallpox
n B143
small-scale /ˌsmɔːl ˈskeɪl⁻/
n N87
small time /ˈ· ˌ· /

n N87

smart /smɑː t‖ smɑrt/
  adj tidy D179
  clever G37

smarten up
  v D177

smash /smæʃ/
  v, n N333

smashing /'smæʃɪŋ/
  adj F51

smell /smel/ **smelled** *or*
  smelt /smelt/
  v F277
  n F278

smelling salts /'··· ,·/
  n B173

smelly /'smeli/
  adj F279

smile /smaɪl/
  n F240
  v F241

smith /smɪθ/
  n H158

smithy /'smɪði‖ -θi, ði/
  n H158

smock /smɒk‖ smak/
  n D160

smoke /sməʊk/
  tobacco *n* E83
  tobacco *v* E88
  preserve *v* E106
  general *v* H76
  general *n* H84

smoker /'sməʊkə'/
  n E88

smokeless /'sməʊkl̦s/
  n H84

smoky /'sməʊki/
  adj H84

smooth /smuːð/
  adj N274
  v N276

smudge /smʌdʒ/
  n, v H64

smuggle /'smʌgəl/
  v C232

smuggler /'smʌglə'/
  n C231

smuggling /'smʌglɪŋ/
  n C230

smut /smʌt/
  n H64

smutty /'smʌti/
  n H64

snack /snæk/
  n E13

snack bar /'· ,·/
  n E120

snag /snæg/
  n N218

snail /sneɪl/
  n A113

snake /sneɪk/
  n A90

snakes-and-ladders
  /, sneɪks ən 'lædəz‖
  -dɑrz/
  n K135

snap /snæp/ -**pp**-
  v photograph K59
  break N333

snap
  n photograph K59

card game K132
break K333

snap shot /'·· ·/
  n K59

snare /sneə'/
  v F206
  n F207

snarl /snɑː l‖ snɑrl/
  v F242
  n F243

snatch /snætʃ/
  v D96, M26

snatch at
  v D96

sneak /sniː k/
  v M26

sneaky /'sniː ki/
  adj F197

sneer /snɪ ə'/
  v F244
  n F245

sneeze /sniː z/
  v, n B117

snicker /'snɪ kə'/
  v, n A43

sniff /snɪ f/
  v B117, F277
  n B117, F278

sniffle /'snɪ fəl/
  v B117

snipe /snaɪ p/
  n A77
  v H252

sniper /'snaɪ pə'/
  n H252

snob /snɒb‖ snab/
  n C159

snobbery /'snɒbəri‖
  'snab-/
  n F144

snobbish /'snɒbɪʃ‖
  'sna-/
  adj C159

snooker /'snuː kə'‖ 'snu-/
  n K141

snore /snɔː'‖ snor/
  v, n B117

snort /snɔː t‖ snɔrt/
  v, n A43, B117

snot /snɒt‖ snat/
  n B60

snotty /'snɒti‖ 'snati/
  adj B60

snotty-nosed /'····/
  adj B60

snout /snaʊt/
  n A122

snow /snəʊ/
  n L51
  v L52

snowdrop /'snəʊdrɒp‖
  -drɑp/
  n A158

snowfall /'snəʊfɔː l/
  n L51

snowflake /'snəʊfleɪ k/
  n L53

snowy /'snəʊi/
  adj L51

snub /snʌb/ -**bb**-
  v F148

snub
  n F149

snub nose /, ·'·/
  n B25 (picture)

snug /snʌg/
  adj F221

snuggle /'snʌgəl/
  v C22

so /səʊ/
  conj G286

soak /səʊk/
  v, n L62

soap /səʊp/
  n H91

soap powder /'·· ,··/
  n H91

soapy /'səʊpi/
  adj H91

soar /sɔː'‖ sor/
  v M28

sob /sɒb‖ sab/ -**bb**-
  v F248

sob
  n F248

sober /'səʊbə'/
  not drunk *adj* E72
  solemn *adj* N43

sober up
  v E72

sobriety /sə'braɪ əti/
  n N43

soccer /'sɒkə'‖ 'sa-/
  n K190

sociable /'səʊʃəbəl/
  adj C46

social /'səʊʃəl/
  general *adj* C85
  science *adj* I71
  party *n* K2

social climber /, ··'··'/
  n C159

social democracy
  /, ··· '···/
  n C111

social democrat
  /'·· '···/
  n C113

socialism /'səʊʃəlɪ zəm/
  adj C111

socialist /'səʊʃəlɪst/
  adj C113

social sciences
  /, ··'···‖ '·· ,···/
  n I76

society /sə'saɪ ̦ti/
  n C72, 73, 75

sociological
  /, səʊsɪ ə'lɒdʒɪ kəl,
  , səʊʃɪ ə-‖ -'lɑ-/
  adj I76

sociologist
  /, səʊsi'ɒlədʒ̦st, , səʊʃi-‖
  -'al-/
  n I76

sociology /, səʊsi'ɒlədʒi,
  , səʊʃi-‖ -'alə-/
  n I76

sock /sɒk‖ sak/
  stocking *n* D158
  punch *n, v* K144

socket /'sɒk̦t‖ 'sa-/
  electric H210
  hole L106

soda /'səʊdə/
  n drink E61

substance H73

sodium /'səʊdɪ əm/
  n H73

sofa /'səʊfə/
  n D114

soft /sɒft‖ sɔft/
  adj N267

soft drink /, ·'·/
  n E60

soft drug /, ·'·/
  n E80

soften /'sɒfən‖ 'sɔ-/
  v N272

soft furnishings /, ·'···/
  n D110

soft goods /'··/
  n J195

soft palate /, ·'···/
  n B26

softwood /'sɒftwʊd‖
  'sɔft-/
  n H71

soil /sɔɪl/
  v D181
  n H63

soiled /sɔɪld/
  adj D180

solace /'sɒl̦s‖ 'sa-/
  n F175
  v F176

solar /'səʊlə'/
  adj L6

solar system /'·· ,··/
  n L3

soldier /'səʊldʒə'/
  n C295

soldierly /'səʊldʒəli‖
  -ərli/
  adj C295

sole /səʊl/
  fish *n* A100
  of foot *n* B44 (picture)
  of shoe *n* D157
  only *adj* J11

solemn /'sɒləm‖ 'sa-/
  adj N43

solemnity /sə'lemn̦ti/
  n N43

solemnize /'sɒləmnaɪ z‖
  'sa-/
  v C334

solfa /, sɒl'fɑː ‖ , səʊl-/
  n K29

solicit /sə'lɪ șt/
  v G100

solicitor /sə'lɪ ștə'/
  n C201

solid /'sɒl̦d‖ 'sa-/
  n H7
  adj H8

solidification
  /sə'lɪ d̦fɪ̦'keɪ ʃən/
  n H8

solidify /sə'lɪ d̦faɪ /
  v H8

solidity /sə'lɪ d̦ti/
  n H8

solidus /'sɒl̦dəs‖ 'sa-/
  -**di** /-daɪ /
  n G151

solitary /'sɒl̦təri‖
  'sal̦teri/
  adj C48

U